DICTIONARY OF PALI PROPER NAMES

DICTIONARY
OF
PALI PROPER NAMES

G. P. MALALASEKERA

IN TWO VOLUMES
VOLUME ONE
A - Dh

ISBN : 978-93-5324-395-1 (Set)

ISBN : 978-93-5324-396-8 Vol. 1 (HB)

First Published, London, 1937-38

Published, 2020

Published by

Facsimile Publisher
12 Pragati Market
Ashok Vihar, Ph-2
Delhi-110052
E-mail: books@facsimilepublisher.com

Printed at: G. Print Process, Delhi.

Dictionary of Pali Proper Names

Author: G. P. Malalasekera

INDIAN TEXTS SERIES

DICTIONARY
OF
PĀLI PROPER NAMES

BY

G. P. MALALASEKERA, M.A., PH.D.(LOND.)
HEAD OF THE DEPARTMENT OF INDO-ARYAN STUDIES AT
THE CEYLON UNIVERSITY COLLEGE

VOL. I.

A — DH

LONDON
JOHN MURRAY, ALBEMARLE STREET, W. 1
PUBLISHED FOR THE GOVERNMENT OF INDIA
1937

TO

MY TEACHER AND FAR MORE THAN TEACHER

CAROLINE A. F. RHYS DAVIDS

IN REVERENT AFFECTION AND INTENSE GRATITUDE

"*Paṭipādesi me maggaṃ tava ñāṇena, cakkhumā.*"

GENERAL NOTE

ONE of my abiding memories of the days in the Nineties, when work under and with Rhys Davids became an essential part of my married life, was the foreground-presence of three interleaved volumes. These were Robert H. Childers's Pāli Dictionary (a copy bequeathed by him to my husband) and the Pāli Text Society's *Journal* for 1888, almost monopolized by an Index of Pāli Names by the Swiss scholar Edward Müller-Hess. Daily those interleaved pages were becoming ever more filled, to say nothing of marginal additions, so keenly did Rhys Davids record as soon as it appeared the New—or shall I say, the Newly-risen from the Once-had-been.

Even then the question of loyal collaborators in the new Dictionary and that of raising funds to print it were exercising energy and patience. The Names Dictionary, as less yet otherwise important, he consigned to a list of desirable publications worthy to be included in the programme of the Indian Texts Series, a subvention which he had persuaded Lord Curzon, at a Calcutta interview, to make. In that list, to give prior place to the works of other men, he gave it a place so low down that its publication could not come within his lifetime. Others would garner and arrange what he had reaped.

I did not find the assigning of this an easy task. For a scholar in the best sense the work was not creative enough. For the analytical scholar its range was too scattered in space and time. And the scholar is a hopeful animal who will accept work he has neither time nor serious intention to take up without delay. Meanwhile I had to nurse impatience and wait.

Then a keen and gifted student, once my pupil, consented to fill the breach. With Dr. Malalasekera, to undertake is to will to begin work there and then. And now, working as men-of-will work, in the leisure intervals of an educational appointment, with yet another large task on his shoulders—the *Mahāvaṃsa-Ṭīkā*, published in 1935—unbaffled by a temporary breakdown through over-work, he has come as editor of the Names Dictionary to see land ahead.

He has naturally not rested content with the materials collected by Rhys Davids. That collecting came to an end with the end of an earth life in 1922. Since that date the Pāli Text Society has published 28 volumes of first editions of texts, and some 14 annotated translations. And this is to say nothing of other contributions made elsewise, referring to names associated with Buddhist history. Nor is there yet an end to all that. For yet a few years the collecting of addenda will be necessary. None the less the hour for the book's appearance is come, and I am happy to have been yet here to say so.

C. A. F. RHYS DAVIDS.

PREFACE

Dr. Stede, the illustrious editor of the Pāli Text Society's Pāli-English Dictionary, having said, in his Afterword to that great work: "It will be worth the trouble to explore more thoroughly that range of civilisation which lies enshrined in the Pāli Canon," added in a footnote, "In connection with this I may point out that one of the greatest needs of Pāli scholarship is a Dictionary of Names . . . the Name Dictionary will be an indispensable supplement to the Word Dictionary." That was in 1925, when I was yet a student at the School of Oriental Studies, with the privilege of having Dr. Stede as one of my teachers.

Somewhere in 1930 when, in the course of a letter to Dr. Stede, I casually inquired what progress had been made with the Names Dictionary, which (after the death of Rhys Davids), I knew he was keen to edit, he wrote back to say that owing to circumstances beyond the control of those most concerned, nothing further had been done since 1925, and that he had abandoned the idea of doing the work himself because he was far from being well and was very busy with his teaching at the School. He also indicated that there was much difficulty in getting someone else suitable to undertake the task. Thereupon I wrote to Mrs. Rhys Davids, as President of the Pāli Text Society, offering my services in the compilation of the Names Dictionary, if I could be of any possible use. She replied very promptly and most encouragingly. The publication of the Names Dictionary, she said, was not in the hands of the P.T.S.; the work was to be included in the Indian Text Series, issued under the ægis of the India Office in Whitehall. Now that her husband, by whom the Dictionary had been originally prepared, was no more, the choice of an Editor ultimately lay with the authorities of the India Office, though the P.T.S. would naturally have a large say in the matter. She would certainly recommend to the Council of India that the compilation be given over in my charge.

There followed the usual inevitable delays, and it was not till July, 1931, that the India Office, in consultation with the Government of India, accepted Mrs. Rhys Davids' recommendation and asked me to undertake the work. Meanwhile Mrs. Rhys Davids had, with remarkable but characteristic generosity, sent me, of her own accord, her husband's copy of the P.T.S. *Journal* for 1888, containing Edward Müller's "Index of Pāli Proper Names," interleaved with numerous additional references entered by Rhys Davids himself. I was, however, at the time deeply engrossed with my critical edition of the Mahāvaṃsa Ṭīkā (since published by the P.T.S.) for the Ceylon Government, and was therefore not able to devote much attention to the Names Dictionary till 1933.

The original suggestion was that I should limit my "sources to the Tripiṭaka, the fifth century Commentaries on the Pāli Canon, a few post-Piṭakan works, published by the P.T.S., separately or in Journals, and the Milindapañha." I was "not to compile a Lexicon, but to follow in general the method adopted by Müller in *J.P.T.S.*, 1888, giving, only in the case of the more important names, short translations from a few specified references, the material to go into one not very bulky volume." Mrs. Rhys Davids was confident that the work could be finished in a year. I took advantage of a visit I paid to Europe in 1932 to discuss these matters with Mrs. Rhys. Davids, Dr. Stede, Professor Turner, Dr. Barnett, Dr. Sylvan Lévi and other eminent Orientalists, and with the authorities of the India Office. As a result of these discussions the original scheme was considerably modified, and I was enabled to give myself greater freedom in the selection of sources and in following my own preferences in the treatment of the materials.

When I came to examine the materials at my disposal I found that I had undertaken a truly stupendous task. Müller's plan, in general, was to give a name and a description of it, followed by a series of references—*e.g.*, "*Yasa*, son of Kākaṇḍaka; took a principal part at the Council of Vesāli, C. xii. 1, 1 *et seq.*, 2. 1 *et seq.*; Smp. 293, 312; Dpv. v. 23; Mah. 15-19, 42." In his bibliography he indicated that he had indexed the Vinaya Piṭaka, the Majjhima, Aṅguttara and Saṃyutta Nikāyas, the Mahāparinibbāṇa and Sāmaññaphaḷa Suttas of the Dīgha Nikāya, the Sutta Nipāta, the Thera- and Therī-gāthā, Udāna, Buddhavaṃsa, Cariyāpiṭaka, Dhammapada (text only), the Jātaka, Puggalapaññatti, the Mahāvaṃsa and Dīpavaṃsa and the Milindapañha, and, of the Commentaries, the first volume of the Sumaṅgala-Vilāsinī, the portion of the Samantapāsādikā quoted in Vol. III. of Oldenberg's Vinaya, and a few extracts from the Paramatthadīpanī on the Udāna and Thera- and Therī-gāthā. I soon discovered, however, that except in the case of the Vinaya Piṭaka and the Dīpavaṃsa there were numerous and serious omissions.

Rhys Davids, in his interleaved copy of Müller's Index, had inserted a very large number of fresh names and numerous additional references in the case of names already included by Müller. This lightened my task considerably, but not to the extent I should have desired. For it is a well-known fact that a scholar's collectanea, however carefully prepared, can be used, if at all, by another only after a great deal of trouble and with extreme caution. Everyone has his peculiar intentions and his peculiar methods in the handling and arrangement of scientific materials. I found, for instance, that I could not verify numerous references because of the absence of a "key" to some of Rhys Davids' abbreviations. Of the Indexes to the volumes published by the P.T.S. only those of the Aṅguttara, Saṃyutta and Majjhima Nikāyas and the Sutta Nipāta Commentary were found to be at all adequate, but even in these cases I soon discovered that if I relied solely on the passages referred to in the Indexes, without knowing what went before in the context and what followed, I should miss a great deal of valuable information and run grave risk of inaccuracy. As a result of these considerations, I decided that the only safe course to adopt would be to go through the books myself and make my own indexes and notes. And this I did, except in the case of the Vinaya Piṭaka, where I found Müller's Index unimpeachable. As regards the Commentaries, the indexes both of the P.T.S. volumes and those issued in the Simon Hewavitarne Bequest Series were quite unsatisfactory. It will be seen, therefore, that I hold myself entirely responsible for the accuracy (or otherwise) of the references contained in this Dictionary.

The work in its present form includes, besides other materials, information obtained from the whole of the Tipiṭaka and all the Commentaries thereon. It was my intention, at first, to index the Ṭīkās as well, but after reading through several of them I decided that the additional material to be gleaned from them would not be sufficient recompense for the trouble and inevitable delay involved. There was also the difficulty of obtaining satisfactorily uniform editions of the Ṭīkās, in spite of the great attention apparently devoted to these texts in Burma. Among non-Canonical works, I have included, besides the Milindapañha, the Mahāvaṃsa, Dīpavaṃsa, Mahābodhivaṃsa, Sāsanavaṃsa, Gandhavaṃsa, and the Sāsanavaṃsadīpa. I have also included the Cūlavaṃsa, chiefly in order to complete the information contained in the Mahāvaṃsa, and the Mahāvaṃsa Ṭīkā, because it contains valuable data regarding names occurring in the Mahāvaṃsa. It was suggested, while the work had made considerable progress, that I should not forget the many short volumes in P.T.S. *Journals—e.g.*, the Jinacarita, Dāṭhāvaṃsa, etc. References to some of them are already given in the main body of the Dictionary, while others will be given in the Appendix, at the end of the second Volume. I have attempted to give the names of all Suttas and Jātakas and of Pāli works of any literary importance written in India, Burma and Ceylon, prior to about 1700 A.C. With regard to these works it was not my intention to do more than merely mention their names; for further details concerning them reference should be made to Bode's *Pāli Literature of Burma* and my *Pali Literature of Ceylon,* both published by the R.A.S. in their Prize Publication Fund Series. In some cases doubts arose in my own mind as to the exact category of "names."[1] Where such doubt existed, I included the name in the Dictionary. It will be seen that I have also included a few articles on what, strictly speaking, are Common and not Proper Names—*e.g.*, Asura, Cakkavatti Deva, Buddha (in addition to Gotama), Mahāpurisa, Māra, etc. My only excuse is that detailed information on these topics is not available elsewhere without reference to numerous texts.

In order that this Dictionary might be completed within reasonable limits, both of time and space, I have deliberately avoided mention of Buddhist Sanskrit Texts, except to give very occasional references to the Mahāvastu, Divyāvadāna, Jātakamālā and the Avadānaśataka, where I felt that such references would be useful. The great mass of information to be found in Buddhist Sanskrit Texts would supply more than ample material for at least one other volume of this nature. For the same reason I have refrained from any special effort to refer, for purposes of this Dictionary, to articles in various books and journals, published in Europe and India, dealing with matters discussed herein. I have satisfied myself with only such references as had already come under my notice in the course of my studies, one way or another.

Two books, that reached me after I had more or less finished the work of indexing, proved of great use; the first, *A Dictionary of Buddhist Proper Names, especially in India*, by Professor C. Akanuma of Nagoya, Japan; and the second, *The Geography of Early Buddhism*, by Dr. B. C. Law of Calcutta. Professor Akanuma's work is, unfortunately for me, in Japanese, and my ignorance of that language prevented my making full use of it, but many of the references are given in Roman script and helped me to check my own indexes. Dr. Law's book was of more immediate benefit to me. I wish to acknowledge my indebtedness to both these authors.

It now remains for me to express my gratitude to some of those that helped in various ways to bring this work to its close. First and foremost is my teacher, Mrs. Rhys Davids, but for whose active sympathy, forceful assistance and kindly guidance in all its stages this Dictionary could never have been undertaken, much less completed. Throughout its progress I have been impelled by the desire to offer it to her, with deep humility, as a token of my great *gurubhakti*. It is a matter of intense satisfaction to me that this ambition has been fulfilled.

To the Secretary of State for India in Council I am exceedingly grateful for the honour he has done me in allowing me the privilege of continuing the work originally entrusted to a scholar of the unique distinction of the late Professor Rhys Davids. I trust I have, in some small measure at least, succeeded in justifying the confidence he thought fit to place in me.

[1] *Re* Pāli proper names see Rhys Davids in *Dialogues*, i. 193 f.

I should like also to add my gratitude to Mr. W. T. Ottewill, O.B.E., Superintendent of Records at the India Office, for his unfailing courtesy and kindness.

To my friends and erstwhile students at the Ceylon University College, Mr. K. C. Fernando, Mr. D. E. Hettiaracchi, Mr. M. A. Perera, Mr. J. V. Fonseka, Mr. N. D. Wijesekera and Dr. O. H. de A. Wijesekera, I am indebted for their willing assistance in looking up some of the references in Buddhaghosa's Commentaries. To the Rev. A. P. Buddhadatta, whom I have had occasion to consult more than once, I am grateful for the benefit of his erudition.

Finally, to Alice de Zoete Elliot—she dislikes appellations—I owe more than I can hope to repay. When I told her about the Dictionary, she most cheerfully volunteered to revise the whole of my manuscript articles and to type them for the printer—in itself a stupendous task. This undertaking she has most scrupulously and assiduously fulfilled, in spite of great inconvenience, trouble and discomfort, making many sacrifices in order to help me. My friendship with her—which began when we were fellow-students at the School of Oriental Studies and soon ripened into deep affection—and with her versatile husband, Dr. Elliot, has been among the greatest joys and blessings of my life. It is not too much to say that the completion of this task within so short a time as four years would never have been possible but for her great assistance and heartening support.

For all deficiencies in this Dictionary—I am profoundly conscious of them —and for all errors of omission and commission I sincerely apologise. It has meant very strenuous work for nearly four years without a break of any sort, work undertaken in addition to the duties which devolved upon me as a full-time teacher in charge of a department of studies at the Ceylon University College. In these circumstances it was inevitable that the following pages should contain numerous imperfections. The fact that printing has been going on all the time the Dictionary was in progress has also been a great drawback to its uniformity in various features. If I had been allowed ten years within which to complete the work, I might, perhaps, have made a better job of it, but everybody intimately concerned with the undertaking was anxious that it should be finished with the least possible delay. I only hope that my efforts will in some slight degree help in the exploration of that wonderful culture and civilisation which lie enshrined in Pāli tradition.

The second and final volume of the Dictionary will be issued in the course of this year. *Subham astu.*

G. P. MALALASEKERA.

January 1937.

P.T.S. means published by the Pali Text Society.

SHB. means published in the Simon Hewavitarne Bequest Series (Colombo).

A.=Aṅguttara Nikāya, 6 vols. (P.T.S.).

AA.=Manorathapūraṇī, Aṅguttara Commentary, 2 vols. (S.H.B.).

Abhs.=Abhidhammatthasaṅgaha (P.T.S. Journal, 1884).

Anāgat.=Anāgatavaṃsa (P.T.S. Journal, 1886).

Ap.=Apadāna [illegible]

[illegible]

Dial.=Dialogues of the Buddha [illegible]

Dpv.=Dīpavaṃsa [illegible]

Dvy.=Divyāvadāna [illegible]

Ep. Zey.=Epigraphia Zeylanica [illegible]

ERE.=Encyclopaedia [illegible]

LIST OF ABBREVIATIONS

P.T.S. means published by the Pāli Text Society.
SHB. means published in the Simon Hewavitarne Bequest Series (Colombo).
A=Aṅguttara Nikāya, 5 vols. (P.T.S.).
AA.=Manorathapūraṇī, Aṅguttara Commentary, 2 vols. (S.H.B.).
AbhS.=Abhidhammatthasaṅgaha (P.T.S. *Journal*, 1884).
Anāgat.=Anāgatavaṃsa (P.T.S. *Journal*, 1886).
Ap.=Apadāna, 2 vols. (P.T.S.).
ApA.=Apadāna Commentary (S.H.B.).
AvŚ.=Avadāna Śataka, ed. Speyer (Bibl. Buddhica).
Barua: History of Pre-Buddhist Indian Philosophy (Calcutta).
Beal: Romantic Legend of the Buddha (Kegan Paul).
Beal: Buddhist Records of the Western World (Kegan Paul).
Bode: The Pāli Literature of Burma (R.A.S.).
Brethren=Psalms of the Brethren, by Mrs. Rhys Davids (P.T.S.).
Bu.=Buddhavaṃsa (P.T.S.).
BuA.=Buddhavaṃsa Commentary (S.H.B.).
CAGI.=Cunningham's Anct. Geography of India, ed. Majumdar (Calcutta).
CNid.=Culla-Niddesa (P.T.S.).
Codrington: Short History of Ceylon.
Compendium=Compendium of Philosophy (P.T.S.).
Cv.=Cūlavaṃsa, ed. Geiger, 2 vols. (P.T.S.).
Cv. *Trs.*=Cūlavaṃsa, translated by Geiger, 2 vols. (P.T.S.).
Cyp.=Cariyāpiṭaka (P.T.S.).
CypA.=Cariyāpiṭaka Commentary (S.H.B.).
D.=Dīgha Nikāya, 3 vols. (P.T.S.).
DA.=Sumaṅgala Vilāsinī, 3 vols. (P.T.S.).
Dāṭh.=Dāṭhāvaṃsa (P.T.S. *Journal*, 1884).
DhA.=Dhammapadaṭṭhakathā, 5 vols. (P.T.S.).
DhS.=Dhammasaṅgani (P.T.S.).
DhSA.=Atthasālinī (P.T.S.).
Dial.=Dialogues of the Buddha, 3 vols. (Oxford).
Dpv.=Dīpavaṃsa, ed. Oldenberg (Williams and Norgate).
Dvy.=Divyāvadāna, ed. Cowell and Neill (Cambridge).
Ep. Zey.=Epigraphia Zeylanica (Oxford).
ERE.=Encyclopædia of Religion and Ethics.

Giles: Travels of Fa Hsien (Cambridge).
GS.=Gradual Sayings, 5 vols. (P.T.S.).
Gv.=Gandhavaṃsa (P.T.S. *Journal*, 1886).
I.H.Q.=Indian Historical Quarterly (Calcutta).
Ind. An.=Indian Antiquary.
Itv.=Itivuttaka (P.T.S.).
ItvA.=Itivuttaka Commentary (P.T.S.).
J.=Jātaka, ed. Fausboll, 5 vols.
JA.=Journal Asiatique.
J.P.T.S.=Journal of the Pāli Text Society.
J.R.A.S.=Journal of the Royal Asiatic Society.
KhpA.=Khuddakapāṭha Commentary (P.T.S.).
KS.=Kindred Sayings, 5 vols. (P.T.S.).
Kvu.=Kathāvatthu (P.T.S.).
Lal.=Lalita Vistara, ed. S. Lefmann.
Law: Kṣatriya Clans in Buddhist India.
Law: Geography of Early Buddhism.
M.=Majjhima Nikāya, 3 vols. (P.T.S.).
MA.=Papañca Sūdanī, Majjhima Commentary, 2 vols. (Aluvihāra Series, Colombo).
Mbv.=Mahābodhivaṃsa (P.T.S.).
Mhv.=Mahāvaṃsa, ed. Geiger (P.T.S.).
Mhv. *Trs.*=Mahāvaṃsa Translation, by Geiger (P.T.S.).
Mil.=Milindapañha, ed. Treckner (Williams and Norgate).
MNid.=Mahā Niddesa, 2 vols. (P.T.S.).
MNidA.=Mahā Niddesa Commentary (S.H.B.).
MṬ.=Mahāvaṃsa Ṭīkā (P.T.S.).
Mtu.=Mahāvastu, ed. Senart, 3 vols.
Netti.=Nettippakaraṇa (P.T.S.).
NidA. See MNidA.
NPD.=P.T.S. Pali-English Dictionary.
PHAI.=Political History of Anct. India, by Chaudhuri, 2nd. ed. (Calcutta).
P.L.C.=The Pali Literature of Ceylon, by Malalasekera (R.A.S.).
PS.=Paṭisambhidāmagga, 2 vols. (P.T.S.).
PSA.=Paṭisambhidāmagga Commentary (S.H.B.).
Pug.=Puggalapaññatti (P.T.S.).
Pv.=Petavatthu (P.T.S.).
PvA.=Petavatthu Commentary (P.T.S.).
Rockhill: Life of the Buddha (Kegan Paul).
S.=Saṃyutta Nikāya, 5 vols. (P.T.S.).
SA.=Sāratthappakāsinī, Saṃyutta Commentary.
SadS.=Saddhammasaṅgaha (P.T.S. *Journal*, 1890).

Sās.=Sāsanavaṃsa (P.T.S.).
Sisters=Psalms of the Sisters, by Mrs. Rhys Davids (P.T.S.).
Sp.=Samantapāsādikā, 4 vols. (P.T.S.).
SN.=Sutta Nipāta (P.T.S.).
SNA.=Sutta Nipāta Commentary, 2 vols. (P.T.S.).
Svd.=Sāsanavaṃsadīpa, by Vimalasāra Thera (Colombo, 1929).
Thag.=Theragāthā (P.T.S.).
ThagA.=Theragāthā Commentary, 2 vols. (S.H.B.).
Thig.=Therīgāthā (P.T.S.).
ThigA=Therīgāthā Commentary (P.T.S.).
Thomas: The Life of Buddha (Kegan Paul).
Ud.=Udāna (P.T.S.).
UdA.=Udāna Commentary (P.T.S.).
VibhA.=Sammoha-Vinodanī, Vibhaṅga Commentary (P.T.S.).
Vin.=Vinaya Piṭaka, 5 vols., ed. Oldenberg (Williams and Norgate).
Vsm.=Visuddhimagga, 2 vols. (P.T.S.).
VT.=Vinaya Texts, trs. by Rhys Davids and Oldenberg, 3 vols. (Sacred Books of the East).
Vv.=Vimānavatthu (P.T.S.).
VvA.=Vimānavatthu Commentary (P.T.S.).
ZDMG.=Zeitschrift der Deutschen Morgenländischen Gesellschaft.

NOTE ON THE USE OF THE DICTIONARY

An effort has been made to avoid repetition as far as possible. Generally speaking, the information appearing under any particular word should not, therefore, be regarded as complete until reference has also been made to the words given in that article in **Clarendon type.** Reference should likewise be made to the Appendix given at the end of Volume II.

The arrangement of words is purely alphabetical—*i.e.*, according to the Pāli alphabet. Cerebral ḷ follows dental l. There is great discrepancy in the texts regarding the use of cerebrals, especially ḷ and ṇ. Thus, a word not appearing in its place under the cerebral letter may be found under the corresponding dental and *vice versa.*

There has been a certain amount of unavoidable confusion in the arrangement of words beginning with the Pāli equivalent for the prefix meaning "junior," as opposed to **Mahā.** Reference should be made under all three heads, **Cūla, Cūḷa** and **Culla,** before the search for a word is abandoned.

There is also lack of uniformity in the texts regarding the use of the prefix **Mahā.** Sometimes it is an integral part of the word, sometimes merely an honorific. It is necessary, therefore, to look—*e.g.*, under both **Saṅgharakkhita** and **Mahā°**—before the list of possible Saṅgharakkhita's is exhausted.

Potential trouble also lurks with regard to the hyphen. Generally speaking, the names of Jātakas and Suttas are given without a hyphen—*e.g.*, **Kapi Jataka, Kavi Sutta**—and these words follow the usual order. Thus **Kapi Sutta** is given before **Kapiṭṭha** and **Kavi Sutta** before **Kaviṭṭha-vana.** Where a word is hyphened, either because it is a true compound or merely for convenience, it is regarded as a single word. The presence or absence of a hyphen affects the order, and a certain amount of circumspection is, therefore, requested in looking for compound names, or those that appear to be so.

The regnal years given for the rulers of Ceylon are taken from the chronological table in Geiger's Translation of the *Cūlavaṃsa*, Vol. II., pp. ix-xv, and should be regarded as only provisional. A.C. = After Christ.

DICTIONARY OF PĀLI PROPER NAMES

Akataññu Jātaka (No. 90).—A merchant is befriended by a colleague in another country but refuses to return the service. The servants of the latter thereupon take revenge. The story is related to **Anāthapiṇḍika,** who experiences similar ingratitude at the hands of a fellow-merchant.[1]

[1] J. i. 377-9.

1. **Akataññatā Sutta.**—One who is of bad conduct in deed, word and thought, and is ungrateful; is born in purgatory.[1]

[1] A. ii. 226.

2. **Akataññatā Sutta.**—Same as above.[1]

[1] A. ii. 229.

Akatti.—See **Akitti.**

Akaniṭṭhā devā.—A class of devas, living in the highest of the five **Suddhāvasā** (Pure Mansions).[1] In the *Mahāpadāna Sutta*[2] the Buddha mentions that he visited their abode and conversed with beings who were born there as a result of the holy lives they had lived under various Buddhas. In the *Sakkapañha Sutta*[3] Sakka speaks of them as the highest devas, and expresses his satisfaction that he, too, will be born among them in his last life. Buddhaghosa says they are so called because of their supremacy in virtue and in happiness, and because there are no juniors among them (*sabbeh'eva saguṇehi ca bhavasampattiyā ca jeṭṭhā n'atth'ettha kaniṭṭhāti akaniṭṭhā*).[4] In the Visuddhimagga (p. 634) their world is spoken of as a Brahmaloka where Anāgāmis are born and enter complete Nibbāna (p. 710).[5] The duration of life among these devas is 16,000 Kalpas.[6] Sometimes Anāgāmis are born among the Avihā devas and finish their existence, in a subsequent birth, among the Akaniṭṭhās. These are called "*uddhaṃsotā.*"[7] The Akaniṭṭha-bhavana is the upper limit of the

[1] D. iii. 237.
[2] D. ii. 52 f.
[3] *Ibid.*, 286.
[4] DA. ii. 480. VbhA. 521 [*āyunā ca paññaya ca Akaniṭṭhā jeṭṭhakā sabba-devehi panītatarā devā* (=DA. iii. 739)].
[5] Also ItA. 40; DA. iii. 740.
[6] Kvu. 207.
[7] DhA. iii. 289 f.; see also S. v. 201.

rūpāvacara-bhūmi[8]; it is also spoken of as the highest point of the universe, Avīci being the lowest. Thus the quarrel among the **Kosambī** monks spread even up to the Akaniṭṭhā devā,[9] as did the shouts of the assembly at the severing of the branch of the Bodhi tree.[10]

[8] Ps. i. 84. [9] J. iii. 487. [10] Mbv. 150-1; see also Mil. 284.

Akarabhaṇḍa.—A village in Ceylon dedicated by King **Kittisirirājasīha** to the Tooth-relic.[1]

[1] Cv. c. 23.

Akalaṅka.—A Coḷa officer who fought against the Siṇhalese army of **Parakkamabāhu I.** during the latter's invasion of the Paṇḍu kingdom.[1]

[1] Cv. lxxvii. 17, 55, 80, 90.

Akālarāvi Jātaka (No. 119).—A cock belonging to a school of young brahmins had its neck wrung because it crowed in and out of season. A monk, who is inconsiderately noisy, is the cause of the story being told.[1] In the Dhammapada Commentary[2] the name of the story is given as *Akālarāvikukkuṭa-Jātaka*, and is related of the thera **Padhānikatissa,** who is stated to have been the cock of the Jātaka story.

[1] J. i. 435-6. [2] iii. 142 f.

Akitti (*v.l.* **Akatti**).—The Bodhisatta in one of his births. He was a brahmin magnate of Benares, who, after giving away all his wealth in charity, retired to the forest with his sister, **Yasavatī.** When gifts were brought to him as homage to his holiness, he sought obscurity, and, leaving his sister, dwelt in **Kāradīpa,** then known as **Ahidīpa,** eating the leaves of a Kāra-tree sprinkled with water. By virtue of his asceticism Sakka's throne was heated, and **Sakka** (**Anuruddha** in a previous birth), having tested him, and being satisfied that worldly attainments were not his aim, granted him various boons, including one that Sakka should not visit him any more and disturb his asceticism![1] His story is given in the Cariyāpiṭaka (p. 1), to illustrate *dānaparamitā.* In the *Nimi Jātaka*[2] he is mentioned in a list of eleven sages, who, by their holy lives, passed the Peta world to be born in Brahma's heaven. In the Jātaka-mālā[3] his name occurs as **Agastya,** but he should not be confused with the Vedic sage of that name.[4] Perhaps he belonged to the **Kassapagotta,** because, in the conversation related in the Jātaka story, Sakka addresses him as "Kassapa."[5]

[1] J. iv. 236 f.

[2] J. vi. 99, the others being the seven brothers **Yāmahanu, Somayāga, Manojava, Samudda, Māgha, Bharata** and **Kālikarakkhiya**; and **Aṅgīrasa, Kassapa** and **Kisavaccha.** See also KhA. 127 f.

[3] No. 7.

[4] See Vedic Index *s.v.*

[5] J. iv. 240-1.

Akitti Jātaka (No. 480).—See *s.v.* **Akitti.** It was related at Jetavana, of a generous donor who lived at Sāvatthi. This man invited the Buddha, and during seven days gave many gifts to him and to the monks. On the last day he presented the company of arahants with all necessaries. The Buddha praised the man's generosity and told him how wise men of old shared their possessions with others, even when they themselves had nothing to eat but kāra-leaves and water.[1]

[1] J. iv. 236 ff.

Akitti-tittha.—The ford by which **Akitti** crossed the river after he left Benāres.[1]

[1] J. iv. 237.

Akitti-dvāra.—The gate through which **Akitti** left the city.

[1] J. iv. 237.

Akusala Sutta.—The man who is sinful in action of body, speech and mind is born in purgatory.[1]

[1] A. i. 292.

Akusaladhamma Sutta.—On the unprofitable and profitable states.[1]

[1] S. v. 18.

Akusalamūla Sutta.—On the three roots of demerit: greed, malice and delusion.[1]

[1] A. i. 201; *cf.* M. i. 47, 489.

Akodha-avihiṃsā Sutta.—On mildness and kindness, the verses being put into the mouth of Sakka.[1]

[1] S. i. 240.

Akodhana Sutta.—See **Accaya-akodhana Sutta.**

Akkantasaññaka Thera.—An arahant. In a previous birth he gave his ragged garment to the Buddha **Tissa.** Once he was born as a king named **Sunanda.**[1]

[1] Ap. i. 211 f.

Akkamaniya Vagga.—The third section of the Ekanipāta of the Anguttara Nikāya.[1]

[1] A. i. 5-6.

Akkamaniya Sutta.—The uncultivated mind is an intractable thing and conduces to great loss; the cultivated mind has the opposite qualities.[1]

[1] A. i. 5 f.

Akkosa Vagga.—The fifth section of the Dasaka Nipāta of the Anguttara Nikāya.[1]

[1] A. v. 77-91.

1. **Akkosa Sutta.**—Preached to **Akkosaka-Bhāradvāja** to the effect that insults hurled at those who revile not come back to the reviler, just as gifts of hospitality not accepted by the guests are left behind with the host.[1]

[1] S. i. 161 f.

2. **Akkosa Sutta.**—On the five evil results that attend a monk guilty of reviling others.[1]

[1] A. iii. 252.

Akkosaka-Bhāradvāja.—A brahmin of **Rājagaha** who—incensed that his eldest brother, a member of the Bhāradvāja clan and, probably its head,[1] had been converted by the Buddha—visits the Buddha and insults him. Later he is himself converted and becomes an arahant.[2] The soubriquet of Akkosaka was given him by the Saṇgītikārā to distinguish him as the author of a lampoon of 500 verses against the Buddha.[3] **Asurindaka-Bhāradvāja** was his younger brother[4]; he had two others, **Sundarī Bhāradvajā** and **Bilaṅgika-Bhāradvāja,** who also became converts and, later, arahants.[5]

[1] KS. i. 201, n. 4; see also *s.v.* **Dhānañjānī.**
[2] S. i. 161 f.; MA i. 808.
[3] SA. i. 177.
[4] *Ibid.*, i. 178.
[5] DhA. iv. 163.

Akkosaka-Bhāradvāja Vatthu.—The story of **Akosaka-Bhāradvāja** given above.[1]

[1] DhA. iv. 161 f.

Akkosaka Vagga.—The twenty-second section of the Pāñcakanipāta of the Aṅguttara Nikāya.[1]

[1] A. iii. 252-6.

Akkhakkhāyika.—A famine in the mountain-region of **Koṭṭa** in Ceylon, during the reign of **Duṭṭhagāmiṇi.** The king sold his earrings and procured a meal for five *khīṇāsava* theras.[1] The famine was so called because nuts called *akkha* (*Terminalia Bellerica*) were eaten, which at other times were used as dice. In the Aṭṭhakathā, quoted by the Mahāvaṃsa Ṭīkā,[2] the famine is called **Pāsānachātaka.**

[1] Mhv. xxxii. 29-30.
[2] p. 593.

Akkhakhaṇḍa.—A section of the *Vidhurajātaka* which deals with events leading up to the surrendering of **Vidhura** by the king, when the latter lost his wager with **Puṇṇaka.**[1]

[1] J. vi. 286.

Akkhaṇa Sutta.—On the eight inopportune occasions for the living of the higher life.[1]

[1] A. iv. 225 f.

1. **Akkhanti Sutta.**—The five evil results of the want of forbearance.[1]

[1] A. iii. 254.

2. **Akkhanti Sutta.**—The same as above with slight variations in detail.

[1] A. iii. 255.

Akkhama Sutta.—The qualities which an elephant used by the king should have and similar qualities that should be possessed by a monk.[1]

[1] A. iii. 157 f.

Akkhara-Kosa.—See **Ekakkhara Kosa.**

Akkharamālā.—A short treatise in Pāli stanzas on the Pāli and Siṃhalese alphabets, by **Nāgasena,** a Ceylon scholar of the eighteenth century.[1]

[1] P.L.C., 285.

Akkharavisodhanī.—A late Pāli work written in Burma.[1]

[1] Sās. 154.

Akkhipūjā.—A festival held by **Asoka** in honour of the Buddha when **Māhakāla** created for him a figure of the Buddha. The festival lasted for seven days.[1] The Mahāvaṃsa Ṭīkā explains it by saying that the king fasted for seven days, standing gazing at the figure with unwinking eyes. But even at the time of the Ṭīkā there seems to have been uncertainty regarding the meaning of the word.[2]

[1] Mhv. v. 94. [2] See MṬ. 209 f.

Akhilā.—Chief woman disciple of **Sikhī**[1]; the Commentary calls her **Makhilā.**[2]

[1] Bu. xxi. 21. [2] BuA. 204; also J. i. 41.

Agati Sutta.—Three discourses on *agati* and *gati*—here defined as wrong action done under the influence of desire, hate or delusion—and its opposite, right action.[1]

[1] A. ii. 18 f.

Agada.—Cakkavatti, sixteen times in succession; **Subāhu** Thera in a previous birth.[1]

[1] ThagA. i. 124.

Agahya Sutta.—Devas and men delight in objects, sounds, etc., but, through the instability of these, they live in sorrow.[1]

[1] S. iv. 126 f.

1. **Agārava Sutta.**—On the five qualities that make a monk rebellious and unamenable to discipline.[1]

[1] A. iii. 7 f.

2. **Agārava Sutta.**—A monk who is rebellious will never lead the higher life nor attain in the end to peace of mind.[1]

[1] A. iii. 14 f.

3. **Agārava Sutta.**—The rebellious monk will never live according to the dhamma, nor thereby ultimately win insight.[1]

[1] A. iii. 15 f.

Agāriya Vimāna.—A palace in the Tāvatiṃsa world, occupied by a couple who, as humans in Rājagaha, had done many deeds of piety.

[1] Vv. vi.; VvA. 286-7.

Aggañña Sutta.—Twenty-seventh of the Dīgha Nikāya.[1] It is a kind of Buddhist book of Genesis, dealing, among other things, with the evolution of the world, of man and of society. The pretensions of the brahmins to be the legitimate heirs of Brahmā are examined and rejected; righteousness is declared to be above lineage.[2] It was preached to **Vāseṭṭha** and **Bhāradvāja** at the **Pubbārāma.**

The larger portion of this sutta (from the beginning of the genesis part to the election of the first king) is found in the Mahāvastu.[3]

[1] D. iii. 80 f.
[2] For a summary of the sutta see Dial. i. 105 f. *Cf. Madhura Sutta.*
[3] i. 338-48.

Aggadhanuggahapaṇḍita.—See **Cūḷa Dh°.**

Aggadhamma Sutta.—On the six qualities requisite for the attainment of arahantship, which is the highest state (*aggadhamma*).[1]

[1] A. iii. 433-4.

Aggapaṇḍita.—A native of Burma and author of the **Lokuppattipakaraṇa,** written at Pagan in the thirteenth century.[1] The Piṭakatthamain calls the work **Lokuppattipakāsanī.**[2] The Sāsanavaṃsa[3] speaks of three monks by the name of Aggapaṇḍita: **MahāAggapaṇḍita** (evidently our author), **DutiyaAggapaṇḍita** (his saddhivihārika), and **TatiyaAggapaṇḍita** (his nephew), all of **Arimaddanapura** and all famed for their learning.

[1] Gv. 64, 67. [2] Bode, 16, n. 3. [3] 74.

Aggappasāda Sutta.—Mentioned in the Visuddhimagga[1] in reference to the epithet "anuttara" as applicable to the Buddha.

[1] i. 207; also Sp. i. 120 and KhA. 19. The sutta has not been traced. It has been suggested (Vm. i. 207, n. 2), that it is the same as the *Gārava Sutta.* I think it probably refers to A. ii. 34, the section on the *aggappasādā.* (See Appendix.)

Aggapīṭhaka-pāsāda.—A building in the inner city of **Anurādhapura.** It is said that when **Iḷanāga** entered the city in splendour, after the festival at the Tissa-tank, his chariot was drawn by his former enemies, the **Lambakaṇṇas,** who were yoked to the chariot, and that the line thus made extended from the tank to the Aggapīṭhaka-pāsāda.[1]

[1] MṬ. 646.

Aggapupphiya Thera.—One of the arahants. In a previous birth he had offered flowers, from the top of a tree, to **Sikhī,** hence the name. In a later birth he was a cakkavati named **Amita.**[1]

[1] Ap. i. 229.

1. **Aggabodhi.**—Son of **Bhayasīva,** of the Moriya clan. He became the viceroy of **Mahānāga.**[1]

[1] Cv. xli. 70, 93.

2. **Aggabodhi I.**—King of Ceylon (A.D. 568-601), **Mahānāga's** nephew. For an account of his reign see Cv. xlii. 1-39. He is sometimes identified with Bhayasīva's son.[1]

[1] See Geiger, Cv., trans. i. 64, n. 1.

3. **Aggabodhi II.**—King of Ceylon (A.D. 601-11). Nephew of Aggabodhi I. Also called **Khuddaggabodhi** or **Khuddarāja.**[1]

[1] Cv. xlii. 38 f.

4. **Aggabodhi III.**—King of Ceylon (A.D. 628 and 641), son of **Silāmeghavaṇṇa**; also called **Sirisaṅghabodhi.** He had to flee from the throne several times.[1]

[1] Cv. xliv. 83-144.

5. **Aggabodhi.**—Cousin of **Dāṭhopatissa II.** (A.D. 650-58), under whom he was Yuvarāja, ruling **Dakkhiṇadesa.**[1]

[1] Cv. xlv. 23.

6. **Aggabodhi.**—Son of **Mahātissa,** claiming descent from **Okkāka** and **Saṇghasivā.** He was independent ruler of Rohaṇa.[1]

[1] Cv. xlv. 38-48.

7. **Aggabodhi IV.**—King of Ceylon; also called **Sirisaṅghabodhi**; he reigned between A.D. 626 and 641 and died of an incurable disease.[1]

[1] Cv. xlvi. 1-38.

8. **Aggabodhi V.**—King of Ceylon (A.D. 711-17), probably the eldest son of **Mānavamma.**[1]

[1] Cv. xlviii. 1 and lvii. 25; see Geiger, Cv. trans. i. 108 n. and 195, n. 2.

9. **Aggabodhi VI.**—King of Ceylon (A.D. 727-66), son of **Kassapa,** brother of Mahinda I., and, at one time, ruler of **Pācīnadesa.**[1] He became king under the name **Silāmegha.**[2]

[1] Cv. xlviii. 32.
[2] *Ibid.*, vv. 42, 60, 61, 76, 90; see Geiger, Cv. trans. i. 114, n. 2.

10. **Aggabodhi VII.**—King of Ceylon (A.D. 766-72), son of **Mahinda I.** He was first ruler of **Dakkhiṇadesa** and, later, joint king with Aggabodhi VI. He married **Saṅghā,** daughter of the latter, and became king on his death.[1]

[1] Cv. xlviii. 39, 60, 61, 68, 80.

11. **Aggabodhi.**—Maternal cousin of **Saṅghā,** wife of Aggabodhi VII. When Saṅghā, estranged from her husband, joined the nuns at her father's suggestion, he ran away with her, but was later caught, and the family became reconciled.[1]

[1] Cv. xlviii. 50, 60-1.

12. **Aggabodhi VIII.**—King of Ceylon (A.D. 801-12), probably brother of **Mahinda III.**[1]

[1] Cv. xlix. 43-64; see also Cv. trans. i. 126 n.

13. **Aggabodhi IX.**—King of Ceylon (A.D. 828-31), son of **Dappula II.**[1]

[1] Cv. xlix. 83-92.

14. **Aggabodhi,** a minister of Sena III., and ruler of Malaya. He built the **Nāgasāla-pariveṇa.**[1]

[1] Cv. liii. 36.

Aggabodhipadhānaghara.—A building erected by **Aggabodhi IV.** for the use of the thera **Dāṭhāsiva.** Several villages were made over for its maintenance.[1]

[1] Cv. xlvi. 11 ff.

Aggabodhipariveṇa.—A building belonging to the **Jetavanārāma** of Anurādhapura and erected by **Potthasāta,** general of Aggabodhi IV.[1]

[1] Cv. xlvi. 23.

Aggaḷapura.—A city where **Revata** went on his way from **Soreyya** to **Sahajāti,** prior to the Council of Vesāli.[1]

[1] Vin. ii. 300.

Aggavatī Parisā Sutta.—On the three kinds of companies: the distinguished, the discordant and the harmonious.[1]

[1] A. i. 242-4.

Aggavaṃsa.—Thera of Pagan. He wrote a Pāli grammar, the **Saddanīti,** in 1154.[1] He was tutor to King Narapatisithu of Pagan.[2] The Gandha-Vaṃsa calls him a native of Jambudīpa,[3] but his name occurs among the famous residents in the retired monastery of the northern plateau above Pagan, the cradle of Pāli-Burmese literature.[4]

[1] Gv. 63; SvD. v. 1238; Sās. 74.
[2] Bode, 16.
[3] p. 67.
[4] Forchhammer Report, p. 2; Jardine Prize Essay, p. 34.

Aggasāvaka Vatthu.—The chronicle of **Sāriputta** and **Moggallāna.**[1]

[1] DhA. i. 83-114.

Aggāni Sutta.—The four perfections: of virtue, concentration, wisdom and release.[1]

[1] A. ii. 79; see *GS.* ii. 88, n. 2.

Aggāḷava Cetiya.—The chief shrine at **Āḷavī**[1] (hence probably the name), originally a pagan place of worship, but later converted into a Buddhist vihāra. The Buddha stopped here on many occasions during his

[1] SnA. i. 344; SA i. 207.

wanderings, and this was the scene of several Vinaya rules, *e.g.* against monks digging the ground[2] and cutting trees,[3] using unfiltered water for building purposes,[4] sleeping in the company of novices,[5] giving new buildings in hand.[6] The **Chabbaggiyā** are censured here for a *nissaggiya* offence.[7] The *Vaṅgīsa Sutta* was preached there to **Vaṅgīsa,** on the occasion of the death of his preceptor, **Nigrodhakappa.**[8] In the early years of Vaṅgīsa's novitiate he stayed at the shrine with his preceptor, and disaffection arose within him twice, once because of women, the second time because of his tutor's solitary habits,[9] and later, again, through pride in his own powers of improvisation (*paṭibhāna*).[10] Here, again, the Buddha utters the praises of **Hatthaka Āḷavaka,** who visits him with a large following, whose fealty has been won (according to Hatthaka) by observing the four characteristics of sympathy (*saṅgahavatthūni*) learnt from the Buddha.[11]

Many lay-women and nuns flocked there by day to hear the Buddha preach, but none were there when he preached in the evenings.[12] It was here that the *Maṇikaṇṭha Jātaka* was related,[13] also the *Brahmadatta Jātaka,*[14] and the *Aṭṭhisena Jātaka,*[15] all in connection with the rules for building cells. See also *s.v.* **Āḷavī.**

[2] Vin. iv. 32.
[3] *Ibid.*, 34.
[4] *Ibid.*, 48.
[5] *Ibid.*, 16.
[6] Vin. ii. 172 f.
[7] Vin. iii. 224;
[8] Sn. 59 f.
[9] S. i. 185-6.
[10] *Ibid.*, 187.
[11] A. iv. 216-20.
[12] J. i. 160.
[13] J. ii. 282.
[14] J. iii. 78.
[15] *Ibid.*, 351.

1. **Aggi Sutta.**—A number of monks go to the **Paribbājakārāma** at **Sāvatthi,** and have a courteous discussion with the Paribbājakas, who claim that their teaching is the same as the Buddha's. The monks are unable to refute their claim and seek the Buddha's advice. He tells them that the *bojjhaṅgas* form the distinctive feature of the Dhamma and that the Paribbājakas, if questioned about them, would not be able to answer.[1]

[1] S. v. 112.

2. **Aggi Sutta.**—On the seven kinds of fires.[1]

[1] A. iv. 41.

Aggika Jātaka (No. 129).—The story of a jackal, who, when his hair is singed by a forest fire, pretends to be a saint of the name of **Bhāradvāja** and eats the rats that trust him.[1]

[1] J. i. 461 f.

1. **Aggika-Bhāradvāja.**—A brahmin of **Sāvatthi,** of the Bhāradvāja clan. The Buddha, while on his rounds, sees him tending the fire and preparing oblations, and stands for alms in front of his house. The brahmin abuses him, calling him *muṇḍaka* and *vasala.* Thereupon the Buddha preaches to him the *Vasala Sutta* (or, as it is sometimes called, the Aggika Bhāradvāja Sutta), and wins him over to the faith.[1] The sobriquet Aggika was given to him because he was a tender of the sacred fire.[2]

[1] Sn. 21-5. [2] SnA. i. 174 f.

2. **Aggika-Bhāradvāja.**—A brahmin of **Rājagaha,** evidently different from the above, also a fire-tender. He prepares a meal for sacrifice, and when the Buddha, out of compassion for him, appears before his house for alms, he says the meal is meant only for one who has the "threefold lore" (the three Vedas). The Buddha gives the brahmin another interpretation of the "threefold lore"; (see **Aggika Sutta** below). The brahmin, thereupon, becomes a convert, enters the Order, and, in due course, attains arahantship.[1]

[1] S. i. 166 f.; SA. i. 179.

3. **Aggika-Bhāradvāja.**—The name assumed by the jackal in the *Aggika Jātaka* (*q.v.*).

Aggika-Bhāradvāja Sutta.—Another name for the Vasala Sutta.

Aggika Sutta.—Preached by the Buddha to **Aggika-Bhāradvāja** (2). The brahmin exalts the knowledge of the three Vedas. The Buddha tells him that a mere babbling of Vedic runes does not make a brahmin of a man who is defiled within and is deceitful. He should have a knowledge of former lives, of other worlds and of the higher lore (*abhiññā*) that gives cessation of birth. Aggika-Bhāradvāja offers the Buddha the prepared meal as a fee for his teaching, but the Buddha rejects it because "the Buddhas do not accept wages." The brahmin should, if he so desire, extend his hospitality to him for his holiness, and not for his ability to chant verses.[1]

[1] S. i. 166-7.

Aggikkhandopama Sutta.—Preached by the Buddha while touring in **Kosala** with a large concourse of monks, the sight of a blazing fire being made the occasion for the discourse. It were better for a man to seek shelter in, embrace and lie down upon the raging flames than to live in the guise of a monk and accept the alms of the faithful while being guilty of evil conduct.[1] It is said that while the sutta was being preached sixty monks vomited hot blood, sixty left the Order in diffidence and sixty others became arahants.[2] The Commentary adds that the Buddha foresaw this result, and that later many of the monks, hearing of the discourse and fearing dire consequences for themselves, returned to the lay-life in such large numbers that the Order became rapidly depleted.

It was to counteract this result that the **Cūlaccharāsaṅghāta Sutta** was preached.[3] This sutta is mentioned as an example of a sermon based on some immediate experience, in this case, a fire.[4] It was preached by **Mahinda** in Ceylon, in the **Nandana** pleasaunce, on the day the **Mahāmeghavana** was gifted to the Saṅgha[5]; and also by **Yonaka Dhammarakhita,** in **Aparantaka.**[6]

The vomiting of hot blood, mentioned here, is made the subject of a dilemma in the Milinda.[7]

1 A. iv. 128 f.
2 *Ibid.*, 135.
3 AA. i. 38-40.
4 MA. i. 14; also AA. i. 32, 267.
5 Mhv. xv. 176; Mbv. 133.
6 Mhv. xii. 34; Mbv. 114.
7 p. 164.

1. **Aggidatta.**—Chaplain to the King of Kosala, first to **Mahākosala,** and then to his son **Pasenadi.** Later he renounced the world and, with a large band of followers, wandered about Aṅga, Magadha and Kururaṭṭha, teaching a cult of nature-worship. The Buddha, seeing his *upanissaya*, sent **Moggallāna** to convert him. Moggallāna went to Aggidatta's hermitage, but being refused shelter there, vanquished, by a display of *iddhi*-power, a nāgarāja, **Ahicchatta,** who lived in the neighbourhood, and occupied the nāga's abode. While Aggidatta and his followers stand awestruck at this event, the Buddha appears, and realising that the Buddha is even greater than Moggallāna, they pay homage to him. The Buddha preaches to them on the error of their ways. At the end of the discourse they become arahants.[1]

1 DhA. iii. 241-7.

2. **Aggidatta.**—A brahmin of **Benares** and father of the Bodhisatta, when the latter was born as **Somadatta.** The old man lived by ploughing, and one of his oxen having died, he decided, on the advice of his son, to ask the king for an ox. Somadatta, with great patience, trained him in all the formalities to be gone through in an appearance at court, but at the crucial moment when Aggidatta was making his petition to the king, he used the word "take" where he meant to use "give." Somadatta's

presence of mind saved the situation.[1] In the *Somadatta Jātaka* the name Aggidatta does not appear. In the present age he was the thera **Lāludāyī.**

[1] DhA. iii. 124-5. [2] J. ii. 164 f.

3. **Aggidatta.**—A brahmin of **Khemavatī,** father of the Buddha **Kakusandha.** His wife was named **Visākhā.**[1]

[1] D. ii. 7; Bv. xxiii. 14; J. i. 42.

4. **Aggidatta.**—See Gahvaratīriya.

1. **Aggideva.**—Fifth son of **Devagabbhā** and **Upsāgara,**[1] and one of the ten brothers who were famed as the **Andhaveṇhudāsaputtā.**

[1] J. iv. 81 f.; PvA. 93 and 111.

2. **Aggideva.**—See Aggibhagavā.

3. **Aggideva.**—A cakkavatti who lived eleven kalpas ago; a previous birth of **Pāpanivāriya** Thera.[1]

[1] Ap. i. 213.

Agginibbāpaka (*v.l.* Agginibbāpana), a cakkavatti of eighty-six kalpas ago; a previous birth of **Māṇava** Thera,[1] also called (in the Apadāna[2]) **Sammukhāthavika.**

[1] ThagA. i. 162 f. [2] i. 158-9.

Aggibrahmā.—Nephew of **Asoka** and husband of **Saṅghamittā.** He entered the Order on the same day as **Tissakumāra,** Asoka's brother.[1]

[1] Mhv. v. 169; Sp. i. 51; Mbv. 102.

Aggi-Bhagavā.—A deity (probably identical with the Vedic **Agni**), worship of whom brought, as reward, birth in the Brahma-world. On the day a son is born, a fire (*jātaggi*) is kindled; when the son comes of age and wishes to renounce household life, this fire is taken to the forest and homage is paid to Aggi-Bhagavā.[1]

In the *Naṅguṭṭha Jātaka*[2] the Bodhisatta, having received an ox as a gift, wishes to offer the flesh to Aggi-Bhagavā, but thinking that the deity will not relish a saltless meal, he goes away in search of salt. He returns to find that the ox has been eaten by hunters, only the tail, one leg and the skin being left. "If thou, Aggi-Bhagavā, hast not the power to look after thine own, how canst thou guard me?" So saying,

[1] J. i. 285. [2] *Ibid.*, 494-5.

he quenches the fire with water and becomes an anchorite. In the verses of this context Aggi is addressed as **Jātaveda.**

In the *Santhava Jātaka*,[3] too, the Bodhisatta is a votary of the deity. Once when he makes an offering of milk mixed with ghee the flames blaze forth and burn his hut, and thereupon he loses faith. In this story Aggi-Bhagavā seems to be identified with **Mahā Brahmā.**[4]

In the exegesis to the *Bhuridatta Jātaka*,[5] the deity is spoken of as **Aggideva,** and mention is made of an enquiry made of learned brahmins by a king, **Mujalinda,** as to the way to heaven. In answer he is told that Aggideva is the brāhmaṇadevatā *par excellence*, and that he should be offered fresh ghee. See also **Jātaveda.**

[3] J. ii. 43-5. [4] See also KS. i. 209, n. 4. [5] J. vi. 202.

Aggimāla (*v.l.* **Aggimālī**).—A mythological sea which stands like a blazing bonfire and is filled with gold.[1] It is one of the seas crossed by the merchants mentioned in the *Suppāraka Jātaka.*

[1] J. iv. 139-40.

Aggimittā.—One of the nuns who accompanied **Saṅghamittā** to Ceylon.[1]

[1] Dpv. xv. 78; xviii. 11.

Aggimukha.—A species of snake; bodies bitten by them grow hot.[1]

[1] DhsA. 300; Vsm. 368.

Aggivacchagotta Sutta (*v.l.* **Aggivaccha Sutta**).—Preached at **Jetavana** to the wanderer **Vacchagotta** on the danger and futility of theorising about the world, life, etc.[1] The sutta is evidently so called because the simile of a fire is used. A blazing fire is visible, but, once extinguished, none can say whither it has disappeared.

[1] M. i. 483 ff.

Aggivaḍḍhamānaka.—A tank made by King **Vasabha** of Ceylon[1] (*v.l.* **Abhi°**).

[1] Mhv. xxxv. 95.

Aggivessa.—One of the guards of King **Eḷeyya.**[1] Is this a gotta name ? (See below.)

[1] A. ii. 181.

Aggivessana.—Probably the name of a brahmin clan, the Agniveśyāyanas, and the Kṣatriyas who were so styled, took the name from their brahmin purohitas.[1] The name is used by the Buddha in addressing

[1] Further Dialogues, i. 162 n.

Saccaka Nigaṇṭhāputta,[2] and also **Dīghanakha Paribbājaka.**[3] In the *Dantabhūmi Sutta*[4] the novice **Aciravata** is thus addressed by Prince **Jayasena,** who visits him, and also by the Buddha.

[2] M. i. 229 f.; 237 f. [3] *Ibid.*, 497 f. [4] M. iii. 128 f.

Aggisama.—The thera Pupphathūpiya was born sixteen times in succession as cakkavatti and ruled under this name.[1]

[1] Ap. i. 156.

Aggisāma.—See **Abhisāma.**

Aggisikha.—The name borne by the thera **Gatasaññaka** when in previous births he was cakkavatti three times in succession.[1]

[1] Ap. i. 127.

Aggismiṃ Sutta.—The five evil qualities of fire.[1]

[1] A. iii. 256.

Aghamūla Sutta.—On the root of pain.[1]

[1] S. iii. 32.

Aṅkura.—Tenth son of **Devagabbhā** and **Upsāgara,**[1] and one of the **Andhakaveṇhudāsaputtā** (*q.v.*). Aṅkura gave his share of the kingdom, won by the dāsaputtā, to his sister **Añjanā,** and started in trade.[1] The Petavatthu[2] contains an account of Aṅkura's later career. Once he took a caravan of a thousand carts from **Dvāravatī** to **Kamboja,** led by himself and a brahmin colleague. On the way their water supply fails, but they are befriended by a yakkha of great power, who, in his previous life, had been one of Aṅkura's trusted and loyal servants. Annoyed by the suggestion of the brahmin that instead of proceeding to Kamboja they should entice the yakkha back with them to Dvāravatī, the yakkha appears before them in person, and in answer to Aṅkura's questions, tells him that he had been a tailor in **Bheruva,** where lived the generous **Asayha.** When suppliants came in search of Asayha's house, the tailor showed them the way. Impressed by the story, Aṅkura returns forthwith to Dvāravatī, and spends the rest of his life, 60,000 years,[3] in acts of unparalleled munificence.[4] He is reborn in Tāvatiṃsa.

In the assembly of the devas who gather to listen to the Buddha's preaching of the Abhidhamma, Aṅkura occupies a place in the back row,[5]

[1] J. iv. 81 f.

[2] Pv. 23 ff.; PvA. 111 ff.

[3] 10,000 says DhA. (*loc infra*); Sp. i. 245.

[4] There were as many as 3,000 cooks to supply food in his alms-halls and 60,000 youths to cut firewood.

[5] 12 leagues away (DhA. iii. 219); 10 leagues away (Pv. 28, v. 65.)

while **Indaka,** who had given but one spoonful of rice to **Anuruddha** Thera, sits quite close to the Buddha. The Buddha notices this and remarks that Indaka had been lucky in finding a worthy donee; the recipients of Aṅkura's gifts had not been distinguished for their holiness. Gifts should, therefore, be given discriminately. At the end of this discourse Aṅkura becomes a sotāpanna.[6]

[6] DhA. iii. 222; *ibid.*, iv. 82. See also Lüders, ZDMG. 58, 700.

Aṅkura Vatthu.—The story of **Aṅkura.**[1]

[1] DhA. iv. 80-2.

AṅkurapetaVatthu.—See **Aṅkura.** According to MA. (i. 225) and DA. (i. 178), in this story the word *brahmacariya* is used to mean *veyyāvacca* (service).

Aṅkolaka Thera.—An arahant. In a previous birth he had offered an aṅkola-flower to **Siddatha** Buddha. Once, thirty-six kalpas ago, he was a cakkavatti named **Devagajjita.**[1]

[1] Ap. i. 199.

Aṇkolaka-pupphiya Thera.—An arahant. In a previous birth he had made an offering of an aṅkola-flower to the Buddha **Paduma.**[1] In the ThagA.[2] the Apadāna verses are attributed to the thera **Anūpama,** with wnom he is probably to be identified.

[1] Ap. i. 287. [2] i. 335-6.

1. **Aṅga.** (See also **Aṅgā.**)—One of the stock list of the sixteen Powers or Great Countries (*Mahājanapadā*), mentioned in the Piṭakas.[1] It was to the east of Magadha, from which it was separated by the River **Campā,** and had as its capital city **Campā,** near the modern Bhagalpur.[2] Other cities mentioned are **Bhaddiya**[3] and **Assapura.**[4]

The country is generally referred to by the name of its people, the Aṅgā, though occasionally[5] the name **Aṅgaraṭṭha** is used. In the Buddha's time it was subject to Magadha,[6] whose king **Bimbisāra** was,

[1] *E.g.*, A. i. 213; iv. 252, 256, 260. The countries mentioned are Aṅga, Magadha, Kāsi, Kosala, Vajjī, Mallā, Cetī, Vaṃsā, Kuru, Pañcāla, Macchā, Surāsena, Assaka, Avantī, Gandhāra, and Kamboja. Other similar lists occur elsewhere, *e.g.* D. ii. 200 (where ten countries are mentioned); see also Mtu. i. 34 and i. 198; and Lal. 24 (22).

[2] Cunningham, pp. 546-7.

[3] DA. i. 279; DhA. i. 384.

[4] M. i. 271.

[5] *E.g.*, DhA. i. 384.

[6] ThagA. i. 548.

we are told, held in esteem also by the people of Aṅga,[7] and the people of the two countries evidently used to pay frequent visits to each other.[8]

We never hear of its having regained its former independence, and traditions of war between the two countries are mentioned.[9]

In the Buddha's time the **Aṅgarājā** was just a wealthy nobleman, and he is mentioned merely as having granted a pension to a brahmin.[10]

The people of Aṅga and Magadha are generally mentioned together, so we may gather that by the Buddha's time they had become one people. They provide **Uruvela-Kassapa** with offerings for his great sacrifice.[11] It was their custom to offer an annual sacrifice to **Mahā-Brahmā** in the hope of gaining reward a hundred thousand fold. On one occasion **Sakka** appears in person and goes with them to the Buddha so that they may not waste their energies in futile sacrifices.[12]

Several discourses were preached in the Aṅga country, among them being the *Soṇadaṇḍa Sutta* and the two *Assapura Suttas* (Mahā° and Cūla°).

The *Mahāgovinda Sutta* seems to indicate that once, in the past, **Dhataraṭṭha** was king of Aṅga. But this, perhaps, refers to another country.[13] **Soṇa Koḷivisa,** before he entered the Order, was a squire (*paddhagu*) of Aṅga.[14]

[7] MA. i. 394.
[8] J. ii. 211.
[9] *E.g.*, J. iv. 454; J. v. 316; J. vi. 271.
[10] M. ii. 163.
[11] Vin. i. 27.
[12] SA. i. 269-70.
[13] Dial. ii. 270 n.; see also *The Rāmāyana* i. 8, 9, 17, 25.
[14] Thag. v. 632.

2. **Aṅga.**—King. Chief lay supporter of **Sumana** Buddha[1]; the Buddhavaṃsa mentions **Varuṇa** and **Saraṇa** as Sumana's *aggupaṭṭhākā* and **Udena** as *upaṭṭhāka*.

[1] BuA. 130.
[2] Bu. v. 28.

3. **Aṅga.**—A king of Benares on whose feet hair grew. He inquired of the brahmins the way to heaven, and was told to retire to the forest and tend the sacred fire. He went to Himavā with many cows and women and did as he was counselled. The milk and ghee left over from his sacrifices were thrown away, and from them arose many minor rivers, the Ganges itself, and even the sea.

Later he became Indra's companion.[1]

[1] J. vi. 203.

4. **Aṅga.**—King of the Aṅga country, between whom and King **Magadha** there was constant war, with varying fortunes. In the end, Magadha, with the help of the Nāga king **Campeyya,** seized Aṅga and slew him.[1]

[1] J. iv. 453.

5. **Aṅga.**—One of the Pacceka Buddhas mentioned in the list in the Apadāna Commentary.[1]

[1] ApA. i. 107.

1. **Aṅga Sutta.**—The five powers of woman: beauty, wealth, kin, sons and virtue.[1]

[1] S. iv. 247.

2. **Aṅga Sutta.**—Systematic attention as potent factor for the seven limbs of wisdom (bojjhaṅgā).[1]

[1] S. v. 101.

3. **Aṅga Sutta.**—Friendship with the virtuous as potent factor for the *bojjhaṅgas.*[1]

[1] S. v. 102.

4. **Aṅga Sutta.**—The four limbs of sotāpatti: consorting with the good, hearing the good dhamma, mindful attention and practice according to the dhamma.[1]

[1] S. v. 404.

Aṅgagāma.—A tank built by **Parakkamabāhu I.**[1]

[1] Cv. lxxix. 37.

Aṅgaka.—Given as an example of a name, Aṅgaka-mānavo.[1]

[1] DA. i. 36.

Aṅgaṇika-Bhāradvāja.—Son of a very rich brahmin in **Ukkaṭṭhā,** near the Himālaya. Having learnt all the arts and sciences, he left the world and practised penance for the purpose of obtaining immortality. He met the Buddha in the course of his wanderings and, having entered the Order, in due course acquired sixfold *abhiññā.*

Later he lived in a forest near the village of **Kuṇḍiya** of the **Kurus,** and the verses ascribed to him in the Theragāthā[1] were spoken at **Uggārāma,** near by, to some brahmin acquaintances who had come from **Uttarāpatha.**

In a previous birth he had met **Sikhī** Buddha and paid homage to him.

[1] vv. 219-21; ThagA. i. 339-41.

Aṅgati.—King of **Videha;** he ruled at **Mithilā.** His chief queen bore him a daughter **Rujā,** all his other 16,000 wives being barren.

His ministers were **Vijaya, Sunāma** and **Alāta.**

He questions an ascetic, **Guṇa,** as to the various moral duties, and following his advice, devotes himself solely to pleasure. Rujā, however, is virtuous and tries to deliver him from his heretical beliefs, but it is not till the Bodhisatta—who had been born as the MahāBrahmā **Nārada** —comes down to earth in the guise of an ascetic, and frightens the king with descriptions of the various hells, that Aṅgati is convinced of the error of his ways.

He was a former incarnation of **Uruvela Kassapa.**[1]

[1] J. vi. 220-55.

Aṅganakola.—A village in South Ceylon, the residence of **Ambapāsāna-vāsī-Cittagutta.**[1]

[1] MṬ. 552.

Aṅganasālaka.—A village given by **Aggabodhi II.** to the **Abhaya-(giri-)vihara.**[1]

[1] Cv. xlii. 63.

Aṅgamu.—A place in Ceylon identified with the modern Ambagamuva.[1] The **Senāpati Deva** once encamped there.[2]

[1] Geiger Cv. trans. i. 298, n. 3. [2] Cv. lxx. 130.

Aṅgarājā.—The chieftain of Aṅga in the Buddha's time. See **Aṅga.**

Aṅgā.—Chieftains of Aṅga, so called, according to the Dīgha Nikāya Commentary,[1] because of the beauty of their limbs. Their name was customarily (*rūḷhi-vasena*) used to denote their country.

[1] i. 279.

1. **Aṅgāni Sutta.**—The five qualities of exertion (*padhāna*).[1]

[1] A. iii. 65.

2. **Aṅgāni Sutta.**—On the five qualities which a monk should have and the five which he should discard to complete his duties in the religion and attain its highest eminence.[1]

[1] A. v. 16-17.

Aṅgārapabbata.—A blazing mountain of white hot coal, one of the tortures of the **Mahāniraya.**[1]

[1] Kvu. 597.

Aṅgika Sutta.—On the development of the fivefold Ariyan Samādhi.[1]

[1] A. iii. 25-9.

1. **Aṅgirasa** (*v.l.* **Aṅgīrasa**).—A name applied to the Buddha several times in the Piṭakas.[1] In the Commentaries three etymologies are given: Buddhaghosa says that "it means emitting rays of various hues from the body," and that the word is therefore applicable to all Buddhas alike.[2] Dhammapāla adds that it signifies being possessed of attainments such as virtue, and also that according to some, Aṅgirasa was a personal name given by the Buddha's father in addition to Siddhatha.[3] It is, however, well-known that, according to Vedic tradition, the Gautamas belong to the Aṅgīrasa tribe[4]; the word, as applied to the Buddha, therefore, is probably a patronymic, in which case we have another example of a Kṣatriya tribe laying claim to a brahmin gotra.[5]

[1] *E.g.*, Vin i. 25; D. iii. 196; S. i. 196; A. iii. 239; Thag. v. 536; J. i. 116.

[2] DA. iii. 963.

[3] ThagA. i. 503. It is worth noting that in AA. i. 381 Siddatha is referred to as Aṅgīrasa Kumāra.

[4] See *Vedic Index s.v.* **Gotama.**

[5] See Thomas: *Life and Legend of the Bhuddha*, p. 22-3.

2. **Aṅgirasa.**—Another name (*Aṅgirasa gahapati*) for **Asayha.**[1]

[1] Pv. p. 25, vv. 23 and 27 ff.; also PvA. 124.

3. **Aṅgirasa.**—One of the ten ancient seers who conducted great sacrifices and were versed in Vedic lore.[1] The same ten are also mentioned as being composers and reciters of the Vedas.[2]

[1] The others being Aṭṭhaka, Vāmaka, Vāmadeva, Vessāmitta, Yamataggi, Bhāradvāja, Vāseṭṭha, Kassapa and Bhagu. The list occurs in several places, *e.g.* Vin i. 245; A. iii. 224; M. ii. 169, 200.

[2] D. i. 238.

4. **Aṅgirasa.**—A celebrated physician.[1] Rhys Davids suggests that the connection of the name Aṅgirasa with the physician is due to the charms against disease to be found in the Atharva Veda.[2]

[1] Mil. 272.

[2] Mil. trans. ii. 109, n. 3.

5. **Aṅgirasa.**—A king, mentioned among the descendants of **Mahāsammata.**[1]

[1] Mhv. ii. 4; and Dpv. iii. 6.

6. **Aṅgirasa.**—An ascetic. The name occurs in a list of eleven ascetics who, because of their holy lives, passed the Peta world and were born in Brahma's heaven.[1]

[1] J. vi. 99. For the others see **Akitti.**

7. **Aṅgirasa.**—An ascetic, **Aṅgīrasa Gotama,** who was killed by the thousand-armed **Ajjuna.** The ascetic disturbed the animals when

Ajjuna was waiting to hunt, and the king, in anger, shot at him with a poisoned arrow.[1] This Aṅgīrasa is probably to be identified with one of the foregoing.

[1] J. v. 135, 144 and 145; DA. i. 266.

Aṅgīrasī.—A term of affection (Radiant One) used by **Pañcasikha** in addressing **Suriyavaccasā**.[1]

The Commentary[2] explains that she was so called because her limbs shone (*aṅge rasmiyo assāti Aṅgīrasī.*)

[1] D. ii. 265.

[2] DA. iii. 701.

Aṅguttara Nikāya.—The fourth division of the Sutta Piṭaka, consisting of eleven nipātas (sections) and 9,557 suttas.[1] The suttas are arranged in numbered lists, probably as aids to memory. Thus we find set out in order first the units, then the pairs, the trios etc., up to groups of eleven. This method of arrangement has evidently influenced the subject matter as well, for we seldom see any reasoned arguments. The lists are often curtly given and curtly explained.[2]

At the first Council **Anuruddha** was asked to be the custodian of this Nikāya of 120 bhānavāras and to read it to his pupils.[3]

When the Buddha's religion fades away, the first portion of the Sutta Piṭaka to disappear will be the Aṅguttara Nikāya from the eleventh section to the first, and in that order.[4]

It was also sometimes called **Ekuttara.**[5] The Aṅguttara Nikāya quotes the Parāyana, which is evidence of its late compilation.[6]

The Commentary to the Aṅguttara Nikāya is called **Manorathapūraṇī.**

[1] A. v. 361; DA. i. 23; Gv. 56.

[2] See also Hardy's remarks, A. v. introd. p. vii.

[3] DA. i. 15; Mbv. 94.

[4] MA. 881.

[5] Mil. 392. It is worthy of note that the Ekottarāgama Sūtra of the Chinese is unlike the Anguttara Nikāya (A. i. introd. ix., n. 4).

[6] i. 133 and 134; ii. 45. For other quotations in and from the Aṅguttara Nikāya see A. v., introd. p. ix., nn. 3 and 4.

Aṅguttaraṭṭhakathā.—Quoted in the exegesis to the Jātaka.[1]

[1] J. i. 131.

Aṅguttara-ṭīkā.—By **Candagomi,** evidently an author of Ceylon.[1]

[1] Svd. v. 1201.

Aṅguttaranavaṭikā.—By **Sāriputta,** author also of **Sāratthadīpanī**—Vinaya-ṭīkā (*q.v.*).[1]

[1] Gv. 71.

Aṅguttarāpa.—A country north of the river **Mahī,** evidently a part of Aṅga on the other side of that river (*Aṅgā eva so janapado ; Gaṅgāya [Mahāmahīgaṅgāya] pana yā uttarena āpo, tāsam avidūrattā Uttarāpāti vuccati*).[1]

It was here, in the village **Āpaṇa,** that the Buddha was staying when the **Jaṭila Keṇiya** came to see him; here also was preached the *Sela Sutta.*[2] From **Bhaddiya** (in Aṅga),[3] the Buddha went to Aṅguttārapa and thence to Āpaṇa.[4]

The country was probably rich because we find as many as 1,250 monks accompanying the Buddha on his tour.[5]

Other suttas preached here are the *Poṭaliya,*[6] and the *Laṭukikopama.*[7]

Āpana seems to have been the chief township, because it is always mentioned in connection with Aṅguttarāpa.

[1] SnA. ii. 437.
[2] Sn. 102 f.
[3] DhA. i. 384.
[4] Vin. i. 243-5; DhA. iii. 363.
[5] Sn. 102 f.
[6] M. i. 359.
[7] *Ibid.*, 447.

Aṅgulimāla (Aṅgulimālaka).—A robber who was converted by the Buddha in the twentieth year of his ministry, and who, later, became an arahant.[1] He was the son of the brahmin **Bhaggava,** chaplain to the king of Kosala, his mother being **Mantānī.** He was born under the thieves' constellation, and on the night of his birth all the armour in the town shone, including that belonging to the king. Because this omen did no harm to anyone the babe was named **Ahiṃsaka.**[2]

At Takkasilā he became a favourite at the teacher's house, but his jealous fellow-students poisoned his teacher's mind, and the latter, bent on his destruction, asked as his honorarium a thousand human right-hand fingers. Thereupon Ahiṃsaka waylaid travellers in the **Jālinī** forest in Kosala and killed them, taking a finger from each. The finger-bones thus obtained he made into a garland to hang round his neck, hence the name Aṅgulimāla.

As a result of his deeds whole villages were deserted, and the king ordered a detachment of men to seize the bandit, whose name nobody knew. But Aṅgulimāla's mother, guessing the truth, started off to warn him. By now he lacked but one finger to complete his thousand, and seeing his mother coming he determined to kill her. But the Buddha, seeing his *upanissaya*, went himself to the wood, travelling thirty yojanas,[3] and intercepted Aṅgulimāla on his way to slay his

[1] His story appears both in the Majjhima Cy., 743 ff., and in the Thag. Cy., ii. 57 ff. The two accounts differ in certain details; I have summarised the two versions.

[2] The Thag. Cy. says he was first called **Hiṃsaka** and then **Ahiṃsaka.** See also *Ps. of the Brethren*, 323, n. 3.

[3] DA. i. 240; J. iv. 180.

mother. Aṅgulimāla was converted by the Buddha's power and received the "*ehi bhikkhu pabbajjā*"[4] while the populace were yelling at the king's palace for the robber's life. Later, the Buddha presented him before King **Pasenadi** when the latter came to Jetavana, and Pasenādi, filled with wonder, offered to provide the monk with all requisites. Aṅgulimāla, however, had taken on the dhutaṅgas and refused the king's offer.

When he entered Sāvatthi for alms, he was attacked by the mob, but on the admonition of the Buddha, endured their wrath as penance for his former misdeeds.

According to the Dhammapadaṭṭhakathā[5] he appears to have died soon after he joined the Order.

There is a story of how he eased a woman's labour pains by an act of truth. The words he used in this *saccakiriyā* (*yato ahaṃ sabbaññutabuddhassa ariyassa ariyāya jātiyā jāto*) have come to be regarded as a *paritta* to ward off all dangers and constitute the **Aṅgulimāla Paritta.** The water that washed the stone on which he sat in the woman's house came to be regarded as a panacea.[6]

In the *Aṅgulimāla Sutta* he is addressed by Pasenādi as **Gagga Mantāṇiputta,** his father being a Gagga. The story is evidently a popular one and occurs also in the Avadāna Šataka (No. 27).

At the Kosala king's *Asadisadāna*, an untamed elephant, none other being available, was used to bear the parasol over Aṅgulimāla. The elephant remained perfectly still—such was Aṅgulimāla's power.[7]

The conversion of Aṅgulimāla is often referred to as a most compassionate and wonderful act of the Buddha's, *e.g.* in the *Sutasoma Jātaka*,[8] which was preached concerning him. The story of Aṅgulimāla is quoted as that of a man in whose case a beneficent kamma arose and destroyed former evil kamma.[9]

It was on his account that the rule not to ordain a captured robber was enacted.[10]

For his identification with **Kalmāsapāda** see *J.P.T.S.*, 1909, pp. 240 ff.

[4] Thag. 868-70.
[5] iii. 169.
[6] M. ii. 103-4; MA. 747 f.
[7] DhA. iii. 185; also DA. ii. 654.
[8] J. v. 456 f.; see also J. iv. 180; SnA. ii. 440; DhA. i. 124.
[9] AA. i. 369.
[10] Vin. i. 74.

Aṅgulimāla Paritta.—See above; referred to also in the Milindapañha (p. 151) in a list of Parittas.

Aṅgulimāla-piṭaka.—Given in a list of heretical works.[1]

[1] SA. ii. 150; Sp. iv. 742.

Aṅgulimāla Sutta.—Contains the story of the bandit's conversion and the bliss of his deliverance.[1]

[1] M. ii. 97 ff.

Acarin Sutta.—The Buddha, as he walked about, sought the satisfaction, the misery and the escape that come from the earth element. He found these and discovered that they exist also in the other three elements.[1]

[1] S. ii. 171.

1. **Acala.**—Thera. One of the eminent monks present at the foundation of the **Mahā Thūpa.**[1]

[1] MṬ. 526.

2. **Acala.**—Assistant to the architect of the **Mahā Thūpa.**[1]

[1] MṬ. 535.

Acala Cetiya.—The name given to the spot at the entrance to **Saṅkassa,** where the Buddha first placed his right foot on his descent from Tāvatiṃsa.[1]

[1] DhA. iii. 227 (but see Appendix).

Acintita Sutta.—The four unthinkables: the Buddhas, their musings, world-speculation and the point of action.[1]

[1] A. ii. 80.

Aciravata.—A novice who had a conversation with Prince **Jayasena** on the life of the bhikkhu. Aciravata repeats this conversation to the Buddha who thereupon preaches the *Dantabhūmi Sutta.*[1] The novice is throughout addressed as **Aggivessana.**

[1] M. iii. 128 ff.

1. **Aciravatī.**—A river, the modern Rāpti in Oudh; one of the **Pañcamahānadī,**[1] the five great rivers flowing from the Himālaya eastwards (*pācīnaninnā*[2]) into the sea. During the hot season it ran dry, leaving a bed of sand.[3] It flowed through Kosala, and at Savatthi an *udumbara* grove grew on its banks; it could be seen from the terrace of **Pasenadi's** palace.[4] To the south of it was **Manasākaṭa,** and on its southern bank was a mango grove where the Buddha sometimes resided.[5] The

[1] Vin. ii. 237.
[2] S. v. 39, etc.
[3] A. iv. 101.
[4] Vin. iv. 111-12; SnA. i. 19.
[5] D. i. 235-6.

Tevijja Sutta was preached here, and the Aciravatī is used in a simile to prove the futility of sacrifices and prayers: it is of no use standing on one bank of the river and calling to the other bank to come over.

In the river were many bathing places, in some of which courtesans bathed naked; the bhikkhunis did likewise until a rule was passed prohibiting it.[6] The **Chabbaggiya** nuns, however, continued to do so even afterwards.[7]

The river was crossed in rafts[8]; it sometimes became so full[9] that disastrous floods occurred, in one of which **Viḍūḍabha** and his army were swept into the sea.[10]

In sheltered spots monks and brahmins used to bathe,[11] and once **Sāriputta** himself bathed there.[12] The **Sattarasa-vaggiya** monks frequented the river for water-sports.[13]

Once the Buddha was told that the **Pañcavaggiya** monks were in the habit of seizing the cows that crossed the river.[14]

The elder **Sīvalī** stopped on the banks of the Aciravatī while on his way to the Himālaya with five hundred monks.[15] In the time of **Kassapa** Buddha the river flowed round Sāvatthi and, at the eastern fort, flowed into a wide and deep lake on which separate bathing places were made for the king, the people, the Buddha and the Order respectively.[16]

The people on the banks were in the habit of casting nets for fish.[17] Near the river was **Daṇḍakappa,** a Kosalan village, and while staying there **Ānanda** bathed in the river with many other monks.[18]

Two occasions are mentioned on which monks hit in the eye swans flying over the river.[19] It was here that **Paṭācārā's** child was drowned.[20]

Kapila was born here as a golden fish as a result of his evil deeds.[21] In the Avadāna Šataka[22] the name is given as **Ajiravatī,** and according to I Tsing (p. 156) means the river of the Aji (dragon).

6 Vin i. 293; iv. 278.
7 Vin. iv. 259. f.
8 Vin. iii. 63.
9 D. i. 244-5; M. iii. 117; J. iv. 167.
10 DhA. i. 360.
11 Vin. iv. 161.
12 AA. i. 315.
13 Vin. iv. 111-12.
14 Vin. i. 191.
15 AA. i. 139.
16 MA. i. 371.
17 UdA. 366.
18 A. iii. 402.
19 J. i. 418 and ii. 366. See also DhA. iv. 5 and 8 f.
20 DhA. ii. 264.
21 *Ibid.*, iv. 41; see also *Kapila S.*
22 i. 63; also ii. 60.

2. **Aciravatī.**—A canal which ran westwards from the **Mahāvālukagaṅgā** in Ceylon; from it flowed four other canals eastwards: the **Sataruddhā, Nibbindā, Dhavalā** and **Sīdā.**[1]

1 Cv. lxxix. 51-3.

1. **Acela-Kassapa.**—A naked ascetic. He visited the Buddha at **Ujuññā** in the **Kaṇṇa-katthala** deer-park and asked him if it were true that he disparaged all penance and reviled ascetics. Their conversation is recorded in the *Kassapa-Sīhanāda Sutta.*[1] After the usual four months' probation, he joined the Order and in due course became an arahant.[2] In the Majjhima Nikāya[3] we are told that he was an old friend of **Bakkula** Thera, and that after a conversation with him obtained his ordination (under him).

See also **Acela-Kassapa** (3).

[1] D. i. 161 ff.
[2] *Ibid.*, 177; but according to DA. (i. 363) he was ordained forthwith.
[3] M. iii. 124 ff.; also AA. i. 171.

2. **Acela-Kassapa.**—An old family friend of **Cittagapahati.** Having been for thirty years a paribbājaka, he admits to Citta that he had thereby obtained no particular excellence of knowledge. Citta tells him of his own attainments and Kassapa expresses a desire to enter the Order. He is duly ordained, and shortly afterwards becomes an arahant.[1]

[1] S. iv. 300 ff.

3. **Acela-Kassapa.**—The Kassapa mentioned in the *Acela Sutta,*[1] probably to be identified with Acela-Kassapa (1), though the stories of their conversions are different.

[1] S. ii. 18 f.; see also SA. ii. 26 f.

1. **Acela Sutta.**—Contains a series of questions asked of the Buddha by a paribbājaka named **Acela-Kassapa,** probably Acela-Kassapa (3).[1]

[1] S. ii. 18 f. (See Appendix.)

2. **Acela Sutta.**—Contains the story of the conversion of **Acela-Kassapa** (2).

Acelaka Vagga.—Fifth of the Pācittiya of the Vinaya Piṭaka.[1]

[1] Vin. iii. 195 ff.; *ibid.*, v. 19-21.

Accaya (akodhana) Sutta.—Speaks of two kinds of fools—the one who does not see his offence as such, and the other who does not accept a right ruling.[1]

[1] S. i. 239.

Accāyika Sutta.—The urgent duties of a farmer and of a monk.[1]

[1] A. i. 239-40.

Accima.—King. One of the descendants of **Mahāsammata.**[1] He had twenty-eight sons and grandsons, of immeasurably long life, who reigned in **Kusāvatī, Rājagaha** and **Mithilā.**

[1] Dpv. iii. 8; Mtu. ii. 5 ff.; see also Mtu. i. 348. MṬ. 126.

Accimukhī.—A nāga princess, daughter of **Dhataraṭṭha,** the nāga king. She was half-sister to the Bodhisatta **Bhūridatta** and helped his brother **Sudassana** to rescue the Bodhisatta from the clutches of the snake-charmer **Ālambāna.** She could shoot flames from her mouth and spit the deadliest poison. The story is related in the *Bhūridatta Jātaka.*[1]

In the present age she was the bkikkhunī **Uppalavaṇṇā**[2] (*v.l.* **Accimukhī**).

[1] J. vi. 157 ff. [2] *Ibid.*, 219.

1. **Accuta.**—A treasurer who, in **Kakusandha's** time, built a saṅghārāma of golden bricks on the spot where, later, **Anāthapiṇḍika** built the **Jetavanārāma.**[1] He was the chief lay disciple of Kakusandha and was a Mahāsāla-seṭṭhi.[2]

[1] J. i. 94; ApA. i. 82. [2] DA. ii. 424; see also Bv. xxiii. 22.

2. **Accuta.**—A Pacceka Buddha, mentioned in a list of Pacceka Buddhas.[1]

[1] M. iii. 70; ApA. i. 106-7.

3. **Accuta.**—A hermit, black-toothed and with matted hair, who lived in the **Vaṅka** forest near **Vaṅkagiri.** He directed **Jūjaka** to **Vessantara's** dwelling in the forest.[1] He was a previous incarnation of **Sāriputta.**[2]

[1] J. vi. 532. [2] *Ibid.*, 593.

Accutagāmabyāmaka.—One of the Pacceka Buddhas in a nominal list.[1]

[1] M. iii. 70. ApA. i. 107.

Accutagāmī.—One of **Vijaya's** companions in colonising Ceylon. He founded a settlement at **Ujjenī.**[1] The Mahāvaṃsa[2] mentions the founding of Ujjeni, but does not give Accutagāmī's name.

[1] Dpv. ix. 32, 36. [2] vii. 45.

Accutadevā.—A class of devas mentioned among those assembled on the occasion of the preaching of the *Maha-Samaya Sutta.*[1]

[1] D. ii. 260.

Accutavarṇadanta.—One of **Ekarāja's** elephants.[1]

[1] J. vi. 135. But see Jāt. trans. vi. 72.

Accenti Sutta.—The hours pass away, be heedful therefore.[1]

[1] S. i. 3.

Acchagallaka (or **Acchagiri**).—A vihāra built by King **Sūratissa** to the east of **Anurādhapura** and near **Dahegallaka.**[1] According to the Mahāvaṃsa Ṭīka,[2] **Devānampiyatissa** had also built an **Acchavihāra** to the south of the city, and in order that one might be distinguished from the other, Sūratissa's work was called **Purimāyacchagallaka.** It was there that **Vaṭṭāgamaṇi Abhaya** held a festival in honour of the Buddha with the help of the thera **Mahātissa** of **Kuppikkala.**[3]

[1] Mhv. xxi. 60. [2] MṬ. 424. [3] Mhv. xxxiii. 67-8.

Acchagiri.—See **Acchagallaka.**

Accharā Sutta.—Connected with a monk, who, through over-exertion, died as he leaned against the terrace-post. His life-work unfinished, he is born in Tāvatiṃsa leaning against a door-post. Accosted by the nymphs with song and music, he thinks he is yet a monk till they bring a cheval-glass and reveal to him his figure. In disappointment he seeks the Master, who preaches to him.[1]

[1] S. i. 33; SA. i. 67 f.

1. **Acchariya Sutta.**—The Buddha teaches the marvellous and the path thereto.[1]

[1] S. iv. 371.

2. **Acchariya Sutta.**—The four marvels that are manifested in connection with the birth of a Tathāgata.[1]

[1] A. ii. 130-1; *cf.* D. ii. 13, 15; M. iii. 118.

Acchariyabbhuta (or **Acchariyadhamma**) **Sutta.**—The wonders attendant on the nativity of a being destined to become a Buddha, described from the time of his leaving the Tusita heaven. Ānanda gives them in detail with the Buddha listening and giving his approval.[1]

[1] M. iii. 118 ff.

Ajakaraṇī.—The river on whose banks was the **Loṇagiri** (or **Lena°**) vihāra where lived the Thera **Sabbaka (Sappaka).**[1] Here also, in a

[1] Thag. 307 ff.

cave, dwelt the Thera **Bhūta.**[2] This river was probably a branch of the **Aciravatī.**[3]

[2] *Ibid.*, 518 f.; ThagA. i. 493 f.

[3] *Brethren*, 187, n. 2.

Ajakalāpaka.—A yakkha who tried to frighten the Buddha, but who, later, became his disciple.[1] When he returned from a certain yakkha-assembly he found the Buddha seated on his couch, as had already been told to him in the assembly by **Satāgira** and **Hemavata** (*q.v.*). In anger he tried in various ways to cast out the Buddha, but failed in his efforts and ended by becoming his disciple.[2]

Two explanations are given of his name: *aje kalāpetvā bandhanena aja-koṭṭhāsena saddhiṃ baliṃ paṭicchati, no aññathā . . . kecipana ajake viya satte lāpetīti, Ajaka-lāpako ti*[3] (those bringing him sacrifices bleat like goats).

[1] Ud. 4-5.

[2] UdA. 63 ff. For a note on this passage see *J.P.T.S.* 1886, 94 ff.

[3] UdA. 64.

Ajakalāpaka-cetiya.—A shrine at **Pāvā** at which sacrifices were offered to **Ajakalāpaka.**[1]

[1] Ud. 4.

Ajagara.—A peta who lived in **Gijjhakūṭa.** He was seen there by **Mogallāna,** but not by Moggallāna's companion **Lakkhaṇa** Thera. Later, in answer to a question by Lakkhaṇa Thera, the Buddha revealed the peta's past. He had been a bandit in **Kassapa** Buddha's time, and having been unintentionally offended by the treasurer **Sumaṅgala,** who had built a Gandhakuṭi for Kassapa, he sought to take revenge on him and to make him angry by committing various heinous crimes against him. But the latter showed no wrath, and once, after having given alms to the Buddha, he gave over the merit, so gained, to the bandit. He thereupon repented, but his evil kamma was too great for him to be able to win any special attainment.[1]

[1] DhA. iii. 60 ff.

Ajapāla.—Son of the chaplain of King **Esukārī** (*q.v.*). He renounced the world with his three elder brothers. He was **Anuruddha** in the present age.[1]

He was given the name **Ajapāla** because he grew up among the goat-herds.

[1] J. iv. 476 ff.

Ajacca.—One of the disciples mentioned in the *Sīlavīmaṃsana Jātaka* as having tried to win their teacher's daughter and failed.[1]

[1] J. iii. 19.

Ajajjara Sutta.—See **Ajara Sutta.**

Ajapāla-nigrodha.—A banyan tree which is famous in Buddhist literature. It was in **Uruvelā,** on the banks of the **Nerañjarā,** near the Bodhi tree, and a week after the Enlightenment the Buddha went there and spent a week cross-legged at the foot of the tree. There he met the **Huhuṅkajātika** brahmin.[1] Two weeks later he went there again from the **Rājāyatana**[2] (*q.v.*). It was then that the Brahmā **Sahampati** appeared to him and persuaded him to preach the doctrine, in spite of the difficulty of the task.[3] This was immediately after the meal offered by **Tapassu** and **Bhalluka,** so says the Majjhimā Aṭṭhakathā.[4] When the Buddha wishes to have someone as his teacher, Sahampati appears again and suggests to him that the Dhamma be considered his teacher.[5]

By Ajapāla-nigrodha it was, too, that, immediately after the Enlightenment, Māra tried to persuade the Buddha to die at once.[6] Several other conversations held here with Māra are recorded in the Saṃyutta.[7]

Here, also, the Buddha spent some time before the Enlightenment,[8] and it was here that **Sujātā** offered him a meal of milk-rice.[9]

Here, in the fifth week after the Enlightenment, Māra's daughters tried to tempt the Buddha.[10]

Several etymologies are suggested for the name: (*a*) in its shadow goatherds (*ajapālā*) rest; (*b*) old brahmins, incapable of reciting the Vedas, live here in dwellings protected by walls and ramparts (this derivation being as follows: *na japantī ti = ajapā, mantānaṃ anajjhāyakā = ajapā, ālenti arīyanti nivāsaṃ etthāti = Ajapālo ti*); (*c*) it shelters the goats that seek its shade at midday.[11] The northern Buddhists say that the tree was planted by a shepherd boy, during the Bodhisatta's six years' penance, to shelter him.[12]

The *Brahmā Sutta*[13] and the *Magga Sutta,*[14] both on the four satipaṭṭhānā, and another *Brahmā Sutta*[15] on the five *indriyāni,* were preached

[1] Vin. i. 2-3.
[2] *Ibid.*, 4.
[3] *Ibid.*, 5-7; in the eighth week after the Enlightenment, says Buddhaghosa, SA. i. 152.
[4] i. 385; J. i. 81.
[5] A ii. 20 f.; S. i. 138 f.
[6] D. ii. 112.
[7] S. i. 103 f.
[8] D. ii. 267.
[9] J. i. 16, 69.
[10] *Ibid.*, 78, 469.
[11] UdA. 51.
[12] Beal, *Romantic Legend of the Buddha*, 192, 238; Mtu. iii. 302.
[13] S. v. 167.
[14] *Ibid.*, 185.
[15] *Ibid.*, 232 f.

concerning thoughts that occurred to the Buddha on various occasions at the foot of this tree, when he sat there soon after the Enlightenment. On all these occasions Brahmā Sahampati appeared to him and confirmed his thoughts. Several old brahmins, advanced in years, visited the Buddha during this period and questioned him as to whether it were true that he did not pay respect to age. To them he preached the four *Thera-karaṇā dhammā.*[16]

[16] A. ii. 22.

Ajara Sutta.—The Buddha teaches the undecaying and the path thereto[1] (*v.l.* **Ajajjara**).

[1] S. iv. 369; Vm. i. 294.

Ajarasā Sutta.—Preached to a deva in praise of wisdom.[1]

[1] S. i. 36.

Ajātasattu.—Son of **Bimbisāra,** King of Magadha, and therefore half-brother to **Abhayarājakumāra.** He succeeded his father to the throne. His mother was a daughter of **Mahākosala,**[1] and he married **Vajirā, Pasenadi's** daughter,[2] by whom he had a son **Udāyibhadda.**[3]

Ajātasattu grew up to be a noble and handsome youth. **Devadatta** was, at this time, looking for ways and means of taking revenge on the Buddha, and seeing in the prince a very desirable weapon, he exerted all his strength to win him to his side. Ajātasattu was greatly impressed by Devadatta's powers of *iddhi* and became his devoted follower.[4] He built for him a monastery at Gayāsīsa and waited upon him morning and evening carrying food for him, sometimes as much as five hundred cartloads in five hundred cooking pans.[5]

Devadatta incited him to seize the throne, killing his father if necessary. When Bimbisāra learnt of the prince's intentions he abdicated in his favour. But Devadatta was not satisfied till Bimbisāra, who was one of the Buddha's foremost supporters, was killed.[6]

Ajātasattu helped Devadatta in several of the latter's attempts to kill the Buddha.[7] Later he was filled with remorse for these past misdeeds as he confesses himself[8]; but evidently, for very shame, he refrained

[1] J. iii. 121.

[2] J. iv. 343.

[3] D. i. 50.

[4] Vin ii. 185; J. i. 185-6.

[5] S. ii. 242.

[6] DA. i. 135-7. According to the *Saṅkicca Jātaka* (J. v. 262 ff.) he had killed his father in previous births too.

[7] See *s.v.* Devadatta. In the *Sañjīva Jātaka* (J. i. 510 f.) we are told that in past lives he had associated with the sinful and once lost his life as a result.

[8] D. i. 85.

from visiting the Buddha till he was won over by the persuasions of his physician **Jīvaka Komārabhacca.** And when in the end he did go to the Buddha, it was in great fear and trembling; so nervous was he that he imagined conspirators in the very silence surrounding the Buddha where he dwelt in the monsatery, in Jīvaka's Mango grove at Rājagaha.[9] It was on the occasion of this visit that the *Sāmaññaphala Sutta* was preached. The king admits that he had been to various teachers before, but had failed to find satisfaction in their teachings. It is noteworthy that the Buddha greets the king cordially on his arrival and makes no mention whatever of the king's impiety. Instead, when Ajātasattu expresess his repentance at the end of the discourse, the Buddha accepts his confession and lets him off almost too lightly. But after the king had departed the Buddha tells the monks how the king's misdeeds had wrought his undoing both in this world and the next, for if he had not been guilty of them, the Eye of Truth (Sotāpattimagga, says the Commentary) would have been opened for him on the occasion of this sermon.[10] Henceforth the king became a loyal adherent of the Buddha's faith, though, as far as we know, he never waited again either upon the Buddha or upon any member of the Order for the discussion of ethical matters.[11] He was so full of love and respect for the Buddha that when he heard of Upaka Maṇḍikāputta having spoken rather impolitely to the Buddha, he at once flew into a rage.[12]

Sakka said of him that among the *puthujjanas* he was most possessed of piety.[13] When the Buddha died, in the eighth year of Ajātasattu's reign,[14] the latter's ministers decided not to tell him the news at once, in case he should die of a broken heart. On the pretext of warding off the evil effects of a dream, they placed him in a vat filled with the four kinds of sweet (*catumadhura*) and broke the sad news gently to him. He immediately fainted, and it was not till they put him in two other vats and repeated the tidings that he realised their implication.[15] He forthwith gave himself up to great lamentation and despair, "like a madman," calling to mind the Buddha's various virtues and visiting various places associated in his mind with the Buddha. Later he sent

[9] D. i. 49-50; J. v. 262-9. An illustration of this visit is the subject of one of the bas-reliefs on the Barhut Tope (Cunningham, Pl. xvi., fig. 36, and p. 135).

[10] D. i. 85-6. It is said that from the day of his father's death he could not sleep on account of terrifying dreams, particularly after he had heard of Devadatta's dire fate (J. i. 508). He slept after his visit to the Buddha (DA. i. 238).

[11] But see DA. i. 238, where we are told "*tiṇṇaṃ ratanānaṃ mahāsakkāraṃ akāsi.*"

[12] A. ii. 182.

[13] DA. ii. 610.

[14] Mhv. ii. 32.

[15] DA. ii. 605-6.

messengers to claim his share of the Buddha's relics, and when he obtained them he prolonged the rites held in their honour till the arahants had to seek Sakka's aid to make the king take the relics away to Rājagaha, where he erected over them a stone thūpa.[16] Two months afterwards, when the first Council was held, he gave the undertaking his royal patronage and assisted the monks who took part in it with all his power.[17]

Several incidents connected with Ajātasattu's reign are mentioned in the books. Bimbisāra had married a sister of Pasenadi, and when he was killed she died of grief. The revenue of a Kāsī village had been given to her by her father, Mahākosala, as part of her dowry, but after Bimbisāra's murder, Pasenadi refused to continue it. Thereupon Ajātasattu declared war on his uncle.[18] At first he was victorious in three battles, but, later, he was defeated by Pasenadi, who followed the military advice of an old monk, the Elder **Dhanuggahatissa**; Ajātasattu was taken captive with his army. On giving an undertaking not to resort to violence again, he was released, and to seal the friendship, Pasenadi gave him his daughter **Vajirā** as wife, and the revenue of the disputed village was gifted to her as bath-money.[19]

Ajātasattu evidently took his reverses very unsportingly. (See the *Haritamāta Jātaka*, J. ii. 237 f.)

Later, when through the treachery of Pasenadi's minister, **Dīgha Kārāyana,** his son **Viḍūḍabha** usurped the throne, Pasenadi, finding himself deserted, went towards Rājagaha to seek Ajātasutta's help, but on the way he died of exposure and Ajātasattu gave him burial.[20]

About a year before the Buddha's death, Ajātasattu sent his chief minister and confidant, the brahmin **Vassakāra,** to the Buddha to intimate to him his desire to make war on the **Vajjians** and to find out what prediction the Buddha would make regarding his chances of victory. The Buddha informed the brahmin that the Vajjians practised the seven conditions of welfare which they had learnt from him, and that they were therefore invincible.[21] The Saṃyutta Nikāya mentions the Buddha as saying that the time would come when the Vajjians would relinquish their strenuous mode of living and that then would come

[16] DA. ii. 610.

[17] Sp. i. 10-11; DA. i. 8-9.

[18] Before this, uncle and nephew seem to have been on very friendly terms. Once Ajātasattu sent Pasenadi a wonderful piece of foreign fabric, sixteen cubits long and eight broad, mounted on a pole to serve as a canopy. This Pasenadi gave to Ananda (M. ii. 116).

[19] S. i. 82-5; J. ii. 403-4; Avš. 54-7; J. iv. 343 f.; DhA. iii. 259.

[20] See *s.v.* Pasenadi.

[21] D. ii. 72 f.

Ajātasattu's chance.[22] This chance came about three years later, for by the treachery of Vassakāra, he succeeded in sowing dissension among the leading families of Vesāli. Having thus weakened them, he swooped down upon the place with an overwhelming force and completely destroyed it.[23] Rumours are mentioned of King **Caṇḍappajjota** making preparations for a war on Ajātasattu to avenge the death of his friend Bimbisāra, but no mention is made of actual fighting.[24]

Of the end of Ajātasattu's reign the books mention very little except that he was killed by his son Udaya or Udāyībhadda,[25] who had been born on the day that Bimbisāra died as a result of his tortures.[26]

We are told that Ajātasattu had feared that his son might kill him and had therefore secretly hoped that Udaya would become a monk.[27]

Ajātasattu's reign lasted thirty-two years.[28] It was he who built the fortress of **Pālātiputta** (*s.v.*), which later became the capital of Magadha.

We do not know what Ajātasattu's real name was.[29] The title **Vedehiputta** which always accompanies his name probably means "son of the Videha lady." At the time of Buddhaghosa there seems to have been much confusion about the meaning of this word. According to Buddhaghosa[30] Vedehi means "wise." There seems to have been another explanation which Buddhaghosa rejects—that Ajātasattu was the son of the Videha queen. Videhi was probably the maiden, family, or tribal (not personal) name of his mother. According to a Tibetan authority her personal name was **Vāsavī**, and she was called Videhi because she was from Videha.[31] (See also *s.v.* **Vedehikā.**)

Two explanations are given of the epithet Ajātasattu. According to Buddhaghosa he was so called because the soothsayers predicted his enmity to his father even before his birth, and a story is told of how his mother, at the time of his conception, had a longing to drink blood from Bimbisāra's right hand. The longing was satisfied, but when the queen heard the soothsayer's prediction, she tried, in many ways, to bring about a miscarriage.[32] In this she was prevented by the king. Later

[22] S. ii. 268. According to the Jainas, Ajātasattu fought with **Ceḍaga,** king of Vesāli, for the possession of an extraordinary elephant (Hoernle on *Ājīvaka* in ERE i.).

[23] For details see *s.v.* **Licchavi.**

[24] M. iii. 7; MA. ii. 853; see also *Buddhist India*, p. 13.

[25] Mhv. iv. 1.

[26] DA. i. 137.

[27] DA. i. 153.

[28] Mhv. ii. 31; but see Geiger's Introd. to Mhv. trans. xi ff.; also Samaddar: *Glories of Magadha*, 17, n. 3; also Vincent Smith: *Early History of India*, pp. 26 ff.

[29] By the Jains he is called **Kuṇika** or **Koṇika,** which again is probably a nickname (Dial. ii. 79, n. 1).

[30] DA. i. 139.

[31] Rockhill, p. 63. In the Pāli books she is often referred to as **Kosaladevī** *q.v.*

[32] DA. i. 133 ff.; J. iii. 121-2; the park where she tried to bring about the miscarriage was called **Maddakucchi** (SA. i. 61).

both parents grew to be very fond of him. There is a story of the prince, holding his father's finger, visiting **Jotika's** marvellous palace and thinking that his father was a fool for not taking Jotika's wealth. When he became king he acquired Jotika's palace.[33]

To show Bimbisāra's love for the babe, an incident is mentioned of how once, when the prince was yelling with pain because of a boil on his finger, the nurses took him to the king who was then holding court. To soothe the child, the king put the offending finger in his mouth, where the boil burst. Unable to spit the pus out the king swallowed it.[34] The other explanation is that also found in the Upaniṣads,[35] and this is probably the correct one. It says that the word means "he against whom there has arisen no foe."

According to the Dīgha Commentary,[36] Ajātasattu was born in the Lohakumbhiya niraya after his death. He will suffer there for 60,000 years, and later will reach nibbāna as a Pacceka Buddha named **Viditavisesa** (*v.l.* **Vijitāvī**). Ajātasattu's crime of parricide is often given as an example of an upacchedaka-kamma which has the power of destroying the effect of meritorious deeds.[37] He is also mentioned as the worst kind of parricide.[38]

Ajātasattu seems to have been held in hatred by the Nigaṇṭhas. The reason is probably that given in the Dhammapada Commentary,[39] where it is said that when **Moggallāna** had been killed by thieves, spies were sent out by the king to discover the murderers. When arrested, the murderers confessed that they had been incited by the Nigaṇṭhas. The king thereupon buried five hundred Nigaṇṭhas waist-deep in pits dug in the palace court and had their heads ploughed off.

[33] DhA. iv. 211 and 222 f. As a boy he used to visit the Buddha with his father (DA. i. 152).
[34] DA i. 138.
[35] Dial. ii. 78 f.
[36] i. 237-8.
[37] *E.g.*, AA. i. 369.
[38] *E.g.*, AA. i. 335.
[39] iii. 66 f.

1. **Ajita.**—A monk. He devoted his time to explaining the Pāṭimokkha rules to the monks. At the time of the Second Council he was a monk of ten years' standing and was appointed to assign seats to the Theras.[1]

[1] Vin. ii. 305.

2. **Ajita.**—A paribbājaka who visited the Buddha, and at whose instigation the Buddha preached to the Bhikkhus on the difference between *dhamma* and *adhamma*.[1]

[1] A. v. 229 ff.

3. **Ajita.**—A brahmin, the Bodhisatta in the time of **Sobhita** Buddha.[1]

[1] J. i. 35.

4. **Ajita.**—General of the **Licchavis** and follower of the Buddha. Immediately after his death he was born in Tāvatiṃsa; he visited the Buddha to refute a statement made about him by the naked ascetic **Pāṭikaputta** to the effect that he had been born in the Mahāniraya as a result of having followed the teaching of the Buddha.[1]

[1] D. iii. 15-16; DA. iii. 825.

5. **Ajita-mānava.**—One of the disciples of **Bāvarī** who visited the Buddha at the request of their teacher. He was the first to question the Buddha, and the questions asked by him form the **Ajitamānavapucchā** of the Parāyana Vagga of the Sutta Nipāta.[1] At the end of the conversation he became arahant with a thousand followers and entered the Order.[2] He was the son of a Brahmin of Sāvatthi, price-assessor (*aggāsaniya*) to the King of Kosala.[3]

According to the Aṅguttara Commentary[4] he was the nephew of Bāvarī, and the latter particularly asked him to come back to him with news of the interview with the Buddha.[5]

In a previous birth he offered a kapittha-fruit to Vipassī Buddha. He is probably to be identified with the **Kapittha-phaladāyaka** Thera of the Apadāna.[6] A verse attributed to Ajita-mānava is found in the Theragāthā.[7] The Ajita-pucchā are referred to in the Saṃyutta,[8] where they are expounded by the Buddha to Sāriputta.

[1] Sn. 197 f.
[2] SnA. 587, but see ThagA. (*infra*), where he is said to have become an arahant later.
[3] ThagA. i. 73 f.
[4] i. 184.
[5] ThagA. *loc cit.*
[6] Ap. ii. 449.
[7] v. 20.
[8] ii. 47 f.

6. **Ajita.**—Thera,[1] probably to be identified with Ajita (5), but the story of his past differs completely from that of Ajita-mānava given in the Thag. Commentary. In the time of the Buddha Padumuttara he lit a lamp in front of the Enlightened One. As a result of this he enjoyed happiness in heaven for 60,000 kappas, and when he was born from Tusita in this Buddha-age there was a great light on the day of his birth. He is stated to have been a disciple of Bāvarī,[2] but he heard of the Buddha while in Himavā. Later he became an arahant.

[1] Ap. i. 335 ff.
[2] *Ibid.*, 337, 28.

7. **Ajita.**—The lay name of **Metteya** Buddha in his last birth, when he will attain Enlightenment.[1]

[1] Anāgata-Vaṃsa, pp. 43, 45, 56.

8. **Ajita.**—A Pacceka-Buddha who lived ninety-one kappas ago. **Dāsaka** Thera, in a previous birth, gave him mangoes to eat[1] (*v.l.* **Ajina**).

[1] ThagA. i. 68.

9. **Ajita.**—A brahmin, a previous birth of **Citapūjaka** Thera; he offered flowers to **Sikhī** Buddha.[1]

[1] Ap. i. 243.

Ajita Sutta.—Preached by the Bhuddha to **Ajita** the Paribbājaka on the difference between *dhamma* and *adhamma*.[1]

[1] A. v. 229 ff.

Ajitakesakambala (Ajitakesakambalī).—Head of one of the six heretical sects mentioned in the Piṭakas as being contemporaneous with the Buddha. He is described as a Titthaka (heretical teacher), leader of a large following, virtuous and held in esteem by the people.[1]

According to the *Sāmaññaphala Sutta*,[2] where **Ajātasattu** describes a visit paid to Ajita, he taught the doctrine of "cutting off," *i.e.* annihilation at death. He was a nihilist who believed in neither good nor evil. The answer Ajita gave to Ajātasattu is given elsewhere[3] as being the view of a typical sophist. His name is often introduced into the stereotyped list of the six teachers even where the views they are alleged to have expressed do not conicide with those attributed to Ajita in the Sāmaññaphala Sutta.[4] He was called Kesakambali because he wore a blanket of human hair, which is described as being the most miserable garment. It was cold in cold weather, hot in the hot, evil-smelling and uncouth.[5]

According to the *Mahābodhi Jātaka* the Buddha had already refuted Ajita's view in previous births.[6] Ajita was evidently much older in years than the Buddha, for we find **Pasenadi,** in the early years of his friendship with the Buddha, telling him that he was a young novice compared with Ajita.[7]

[1] S. i. 68.

[2] D. i. 55. In Tibetan sources he is stated to have taught that all beings must dwell in Saṃsāra for 84,000 mahākalpas before they come to an end; nothing can prevent that. Rockhill: 103-4.

[3] *E.g.*, S. iii. 207; M. i. 515.

[4] *E.g.*, S. iv. 398, where he is represented as talking about the rebirths of his adherents—he who denied rebirth. In A. i. 286 he seems to have been confused with **Makkhali Gosāla.**

[5] DA. i. 144; MA. i. 422-3.

[6] J. v. 246.

[7] S. i. 68.

In the Milinda-pañha the king says that he had visited a teacher named Ajitakesakambala. This cannot possibly refer to our Ajita; the reference is probably to a teacher belonging to the same school of thought.[8] References to ascetics wearing hair garments are found in several passages of the Pāli canon.[9]

[8] "There is neither fruit nor result of good or evil karma," p. 4. His views are given on p. 25 without mention being made of his name. But see note 2 to the Mil. trans., p. 8.

[9] D. i. 167; M. i. 77, 238; A. i. 240; for a discussion of Ajita's views see Barua: *PreBuddhistic Indian Philosophy*, pp. 287 ff.

Ajitañjaya.—King of **Ketumatī.** He was a previous birth of **Todeyya** Thera, *q.v.*

Ajitapucchā or **Ajitapañhā.**—Second sutta of the Parāyanavagga of the Sutta Nipāta. See **Ajita-(mānava).**

Ajitaraṭṭha (*v.l.* **Addika-** or **Addila-raṭṭha**).—The country in which the seṭṭhi **Ghosita** was born, in a previous life, as a poor man named **Kotūhalaka.**[1]

[1] DA. i. 317; DhA. i. 169 f.

Ajina.—Thera. He belonged to a poor brahmin family of Sāvatthi, and was so called because at birth he was wrapped in an antelope skin. He saw the presentation of Jetavana and, impressed by the majesty of the Buddha, joined the Order and later became an arahant. But because of past misdeeds he remained unhonoured and unknown, and on this account was despised by worldly novices.[1] He is evidently to be identified with **Ghatamaṇḍadāyaka** Thera of the Apadāna.[2] In a previous birth he gave butter as medicine to the Pacceka Buddha, **Sucintita.**

[1] Thag. 129-30; ThagA. i. 250 f.

[2] ii. 436.

Ajinadāyaka.—A thera who later became arahant. He gave a piece of antelope skin to **Sikhī** Buddha. Five kappas ago he was a cakkavatti, **Sudāyaka.**[1]

[1] Ap. i. 213-14.

Ajīvaka, given as a possible name.[1]

[1] J. i. 403.

Ajeḷaka-Sutta.—Many are those who do not abstain from accepting goats and sheep.[1]

[1] S. v. 472.

Ajjuka.—A monk of Vesālī. In settling a dispute regarding the estate of his lay-supporter, he was accused of partisanship by one of the parties concerned and was reported to **Ānanda.** The case went up before **Upāli,** who decided in favour of Ajjuka,[1] and was commended by the Buddha for this decision.[2]

[1] Vin.iii.66-7. [2] ThagA.i.370; AA.i.172.

1. **Ajjuna.**—Thera. Son of a councillor of Sāvatthi. In his youth he first joined the Order of the Nigaṇṭhas; being dissatisfied, he was won over by the Buddha's Twin-miracle and, entering the Order, reached arahantship.[1] He is evidently to be identified with **Sālapupphadāyaka** Thera of the Apadāna.[2] In **Vipassī** Buddha's time he was born as a lion and gave the Buddha a flowering branch of a sāla-tree.

[1] Thag. v. 88; ThagA.i.186. [2] i.169.

2. **Ajjuna.**—A Pacceka Buddha, who lived ninety-one kappas ago. **Panasaphaladāyaka** Thera (*q.v.*) gave him a ripe jackfruit.[1]

[1] Ap.i.297.

3. **Ajjuna.**—A Pacceka Buddha who lived ninety-four kappas ago. **Ajelaphaladāyaka** Thera gave him an *ajela*-fruit.[1]

[1] Ap.ii.446.

4. **Ajjuna.**—The seventh son of **Devagabbhā** and **Upasāgara**; one of the **Andhakaveṇhuputtā**[1] (*q.v.*).

[1] J.iv.81; Pv.93.

5. **Ajjuna.**—King of the **Kekakā,** and a great archer. He annoyed the sage **Gotama** and was destroyed in spite of his bulk and his thousand arms.[1] In the *Sarabhaṅga Jātaka* he is mentioned as having sinned against **Aṅgīrasa.**[2] He is identified with **Arjuna,** called **Kārtavīraya** of the *Kathāsaritsāgara,*[3] and in the Uttarakaṇḍa of the Rāmāyana.[4]

He used to offer sacrifices to the gods.[5]

[1] J.v.267.
[2] J.v.135; also DA.i.266.
[3] ii.639.
[4] Sarga 32.
[5] J.vi.201.

6. **Ajjuna.**—The eldest of the five sons of King **Pāṇḍu,** all of whom were married to **Kaṇhā.** On discovering her liason with a hunch-backed slave and her treachery towards themselves, they gave her up

and retired to Himavā.[1] Ajjuna was a previous birth of the bird-king **Kuṇāla.**[2]

[1] J. v. 425 f. [2] *Ibid.*, 427.

Ajjunapupphiya Thera, probably identical with **Sambhūta** Thera (*q.v.*).

Ajjuhattha-pabbata.—See **Ambahaṭṭha-pabbata.**

Ajjhohāra.—One of the six huge mythical fishes of the Great Ocean. It was five hundred yojanas in length and lived on the fungi that grow on rocks.[1]

[1] J. v. 462.

Añcanavana.—See **Añjanavana.**

Añjana.—The Sākyan, son of **Devadaha,** and father of **Mahāmāyā** and **Mahāpajāpatī,** wives of **Suddhodana.** His wife was **Sulakkhaṇā.**[1] According to the Mahāvaṃsa,[2] he was the son of Devadahasakka and had a sister **Kaccānā;** his queen was **Yasodharā.** In addition to the daughters mentioned above he had two sons, **Daṇḍapāṇi** and the Sākiyan **Suppabuddha.** See also *s.v.* **Suppabuddha.**

[1] Ap. ii. 538, v. 115; see also ThigA. 152. [2] ii. 17 ff.

Añjanadevī.—Daughter of **Devagabbhā** and **Upasāgara.** When her ten younger brothers, the **Andhakaveṇhuputtā,** had conquered all Jambudīpa and were living at **Dvāravatī,** they divided the kingdom into ten, forgetting their sister. **Aṅkura,** however, gave her his share and went into business. Later when all the members of her family, except Aṅkura, perished, she escaped destruction.[1]

[1] J. iv. 80, 84, 88, 89; PvA. 111-12.

Añjana-pabbata.—One of the six peaks of the **Himālaya** from which rose the five great rivers and round which were the seven lakes.[1]

Pabbata, one of the seven chief pupils of the Bodhisatta **Jotipāla,** had his hermitage there.[2]

[1] J. v. 415. [2] *Ibid.*, 133.

Añjana-vana (*v.l.* **Añcana-vana**).—A garden at **Sāketa.** In it was a Deer-park where the Buddha used to stay. On one such occasion **Kakudha** came to see him,[1] and also the paribbājaka **Kuṇḍaliya**[2] who

[1] S. i. 54. [2] S. v. 73.

lived near by. Here were preached the *Sāketa Sutta*,[3] the *Sāketa Jātaka*[4] and the *Jarā Sutta*.

When **Ānanda** was staying there a nun of the Jaṭila persuasion visited him and questioned him on the use of samādhi.[5]

The Thera **Jambugāmiyaputta**[6] dwelt there while yet a novice. Once the Buddha was staying at Añjanavana with a large company of monks and some of the monks slept on the sandbanks of the river **Sarabhū** near by. During the night floods rose and the Thera **Gavampati** controlled the water by his mystic powers.[7]

The elder **Bhūta**[8] stayed in Añjana-vana while visiting his relatives in Sāketa, and the Thera **Añjanavaniya** spent the rainy season there on a couch.[9] There **Sujātā** met the Buddha, and having listened to his discourse became an arahant.[10]

In ancient times the king of Kosala used to hunt in this garden, thus it was that the deer **Nandiya** met him.[11]

The garden was so-called because it was thickly covered with *añjana*-creepers that bore collyrium-coloured flowers. Others say that añjana s the name of a spreading tree.[12]

3 *Ibid.*, 219.
4 J. i. 308; DhA. iii. 317 ff.; SnA. 531.
5 A. iv. 427-8.
6 ThagA. i. 86; SnA. 531.
7 *Ibid.*, i. 104; Thag. v. 38.
8 ThagA. i. 494.
9 *Ibid.*, i. 127.
10 Thig. vv. 145-50.
11 J. iii. 270 f.
12 ThagA. i. 128; SA. iii. 195.

Añjanavaniya Thera.—Son of a rājā in Vesālī, in the Vajjian territory. At that time Vesāli was faced by the threefold terror of drought, disease and demons. The Buddha quelled the panic by preaching the *Ratana Sutta*. In the great concourse of listeners was the rājā's son who thereupon left the world. He dwelt in the Añjana-vana, and in the rainy season, having procured an old couch, he put it on four stones and covered it all round with grass, leaving an open space to serve as door; there he spent his time meditating till he became an arahant.[1]

In a previous birth he was a garland-maker, named **Sudassana,** and gave flowers to **Padumuttara** Buddha. He was sixteen times born as a king, named **Devuttara.**

He is evidently identical with **Muṭṭhipupphiya** of the Apadāna.[2]

1 Thag. v. 55; ThagA. i. 127 f.
2 i. 142.

Añjanavasabha.—The state elephant of **Dhanañjaya,** king of the Kurus. It was credited with the power of bringing rain; the brahmins of **Dantapura** in Kaliṅga, therefore, begged for it during a severe drought.

But the elephant was of no avail, the rain did not come, and so it was returned to Dhanañjaya.[1]

[1] J. ii. 368 f.; DhA. iv. 88 f.

Añjalī.—One of the nuns who accompanied **Saṅghamittā** to Ceylon.[1]

[1] Dīp. xviii. 24.

Añjasa.—A king of two kappas ago, father of **Sunanda,** a previous birth of **Upāli.**[1]

[1] Ap. i. 45, v. 111; ThagA. i. 367.

Añña Sutta.—On the results of developing the four satipaṭṭhānā.[1]

[1] S. v. 181.

"Aññaṃjīvāṃ aññaṃsarīraṃ" Sutta.—That the body is one thing and the soul another is the view held by some people.[1]

[1] S. iii. 215.

Aññaṇā Sutta.—Five of the same name recording conversations with the paribbājaka **Vacchagotta** regarding the results of ignorance.[1]

[1] S. iii. 257-9.

1. **Aññatara Sutta.**—On the chain of causation.[1]

[1] S. ii. 75-6.

2. **Aññatara Sutta.**—Few are born among men because beings do not see the four Ariyan truths.[1]

[1] S. v. 465.

Aññatara-Brahma Sutta.—A certain Brahmā thought no recluse or brahmin could come to his world. The Buddha, **Mogallāna, Mahākassapa, Mahākappina** and **Anuruddha** all appeared there and refuted his views.[1]

[1] S. i. 144 f.

Aññatara-Bhikkhu Sutta.—Two of this name containing questions on the holy life and the destruction of the āsavā.[1]

[1] S. v. 7-8.

Aññatara° Vatthu.—Several stories given in the Dhammapada Commentary are designated only by such titles as Aññatara-itthi vatthu, Aññatara-kuṭumbika vatthu, etc. For reference to such stories see DhA. Index (Vol. v.).

Aññatitthiya Bhānavāra. Ends the sixteenth chapter of the second khandhaka of the Mahāvagga.[1]

[1] Vin. i. 115.

Aññatitthiya Vagga.—Several discourses on the views of other teachers.[1]

[1] S. v. 27 f.

Aññatitthiya Sutta.—Describes a visit of **Sāriputta** to some heretical teachers in Rājagaha and the discussions that ensued. **Ānanda** reports the incident to the Buddha, who approves and explains the questions further.[1]

[1] S. ii. 32 f.

Aññāta-Koṇḍañña (*v.l.* **Aññā-Koṇḍañña**) **Thera.**—He was the son of a very wealthy brahmin family of **Doṇavatthu** near Kapilavatthu and was born before the Buddha. He came to be called by his family name Koṇḍañña. He was learned in the three Vedas, excelling in the science of physiognomy. When the Buddha was born he was among the eight brahmins[1] sent for to prognosticate, and though he was yet quite a novice he declared definitely that the babe would be a Buddha. Thereafter he lived awaiting the Bodhisatta's renunciation. After this happened he left the world with four others, and the five later became known as the **Pañcavaggiyā.**[2] When, after the Enlightenment, the Buddha visited them at Isipatana and preached the *Dhammacakkappavattana Sutta*, Koṇḍañña and eighteen crores of brahmas won the Fruit of the First Path. As he was the first among humans to realise the Dhamma the Buddha praised him saying "*aññāsi vata bho Koṇḍañño*" twice; hence he came to be known as Aññata Koṇḍañña.[3] Five days later when the *Anattalakkhaṇa Sutta* was preached be became arahant.[4] He was the first to be ordained with the formula "*ehi, bhikkhu*" and the first to receive higher ordination. Later, at Jetavana, amidst a large concourse of monks, the Buddha declared him to be the best of those who first comprehended the Dhamma.[5] He was also declared to be pre-

[1] The others being **Rāma, Dhaja, Lakkhaṇa, Manti, Bhoja, Suyāma** and **Sudatta.** In the Milinda (236), where the eight names are given, Koṇḍañña appears as Yañña.

[2] J. i. 65 f.; AA. i. 78-84; ThagA. ii, 1 ff.

[3] Vin. i. 12; UdA. 324, 371; Mtu iii. 333. It is interesting to note that in the Burmese MSS. the name appears as Aññāsi-K°. The Cy. explains Aññāta-K° by "*paṭivedha* K°." In the ThagA. he is called Aññā-K°. Mrs. Rhys Davids suggests that Aññā was his personal name (*Gotama the Man*, p. 102).

[4] Vin. i. 13-14.

[5] AA. i. 84.

eminent among disciples of long-standing (*rattaññūnaṃ*[6]). In the assembly of monks he sat behind the two chief disciples. Finding that his presence near the Buddha was becoming inconvenient to himself and others,[7] he obtained the Buddha's permission to go and live on the banks of the **Mandākinī** in the **Chaddanta-vana,** where he stayed for twelve years, only returning at the end of that period to obtain the Buddha's leave for his parinibbāna. The elephants in the forest took it in turns to bring him his food and to look after him. Having bidden farewell to the Buddha, he returned to Chaddanta-vana, where he passed away.[8] We are told[9] that all Himavā wept at his death. The obsequies were elaborately performed by eight thousand elephants with the deva **Nāgadatta** at their head. All the devas from the lowest to the highest brahma world took part in the ceremony, each deva contributing a piece of sandalwood. Five hundred monks, led by **Anuruddha,** were present. The relics were taken to Veluvana and handed over to the Buddha, who with his own hand deposited them in a silver cetiya which appeared from the earth. Buddhaghosa states that the cetiya existed even in his time.[10]

Several verses attributed to Koṇḍañña are given in the Theragāthā, admonishing fellow celibates to lead the higher life, because everything is impermanent, bound to ill and void of soul.[11]

On one occasion he preached to **Sakka** at the latter's own request; Sakka expressed himself as greatly pleased because the sermon was worthy even of the Buddha.[12]

Vaṅgīsa once extolled his virtues in the presence of the Buddha.[13]

In Padumuttara's time Koṇḍañña had been a rich householder, and, seeing one of the monks given preference in seniority, he wished for a similar rank for himself in the future. Towards this end he did many acts of piety, one of them being to build a golden chamber over the Buddha's relics. In Vipassī's time was a householder, **Mahākāla,** and gave to the Buddha the first-fruits of his field in nine stages of their produce.[14]

According to the Apadanā,[15] he offered the first meal to Padumuttara after his Enlightenment.

Puṇṇa Mantānīputta was his nephew and was ordained by him.[16]

6 A. i. 23.

7 For his reasons see AA. i. 84; SA. i. 216.

8 SA. i. 218; AA. i. 84.

9 SA. i. 219.

10 *Ibid.*

11 Thag. 674-88.

12 Thag. v. 673; ThagA. ii. 3.

13 S. i. 193.

14 ThagA. ii. 1; DhA. i. 80.

15 i. 48 f.; *The Divy* (430) mentions another previous birth of Koṇḍañña.

16 ThagA. i. 37.

Aññatitthiya Sutta.—The answers that should be given to followers of other faiths if they should question about lust, malice and delusion.[1]

[1] A. i. 199-201.

Aṭaṭa.—One of the **Avīci** hells appearing in a list of names of purgatories.[1] Buddhaghosa[2] says these are not names of separate hells, but only periods of time in **Avīci** apportioned to each entrant by the working of Kamma.

[1] S. i. 150; Sn. 126.

[2] SA. i. 170; SnA. 476.

Aṭṭakaraṇa Sutta.—See **Attha°**.

1. **Aṭṭhaka.**—A celebrated sage, composer and reciter of sacred runes, mentioned together with nine others,[1] as the ancient ṛṣis of the brahmins. They abstained from food at unseasonable times. They were the first teachers of the **Tevijja** brahmins[2] and great sacrifices were conducted by them.[3]

Various teachings are attributed to them, *e.g.* that they recognised five kinds of brahmins—brahmasama, devasama, mariyāda, sambhinnamariyāda, and brāhmaṇacaṇḍāla.[4] These sages did not claim to have discerned and realised the five qualities—truth, austerities, chastity, study and munificence—specified by the brahmins for the attainment of merit and the achievement of what is right,[5] though their followers behaved as if they did. Nor did they claim that they personally saw and knew that "here alone resides the truth and everything else is vain."[6] In the Vimānavatthu Commentary it is said that the Buddha had realised those things of which these sages thought and for which they wished.[7] (*Brahmacintitan ti brahmehi Aṭṭhakādīhi cintitam, pañcacakkhunā diṭṭhaṃ.*)

It is said that Aṭṭhaka and the other seers had the divine eye and had incorporated the teachings of **Kassapa** Buddha into their own scriptures. Thus (at that time) the three Vedas were in conformity with the Dhamma. But later the brahmins went back on these teachings.[8]

Aṭṭhaka is generally identified with Aṣṭaka mentioned as the author of Ṛg-veda x. 104, unless the name be taken as a corrupt reading under which some representation of **Atri** may lurk.[9]

[1] **Vāmaka, Vāmadeva, Vessāmitta, Yamataggi, Aṅgīrasa, Bhāradvāja, Vāseṭṭha** and **Bhagu.** Vin i. 245; D. i. 104; DA. i. 273.

[2] D. i. 238.

[3] A. iv. 61.

[4] A. iii. 224 ff.

[5] M. ii. 199-200.

[6] M. ii. 169.

[7] p. 265.

[8] DA i. 273.

[9] VT. ii. 130, n. 2.

2. **Aṭṭhaka.**—King. Mentioned in a list of kings who in times past had been unable to get beyond the domain of sense in spite of making great gifts and holding great sacrifices.[1]

[1] J. vi. 99.

3. **Aṭṭhaka.**—King. Mentioned in a list of former kings who had followed righteousness and who, by waiting diligently on ascetics and recluses, had gone to Sakka's heaven.[1]

[1] J. vi. 251.

4. **Aṭṭhaka.**—King. When **Daṇḍaka**, having sinned against **Kisavaccha,** was destroyed with his realm, three of the subordinate lords within his kingdom—**Kaliṅga, Aṭṭhaka** and **Bhīmaratha**—went to consult the Bodhisatta **Sarabhaṅga** on the fate of Daṇḍaka and his fellow-sinners. Their doubts were set at rest, and at the end of Sarabhaṅga's discourse they became free of their sensuality (*kāmarāga.*)[1] **Sakka** himself was present at the interview and asked questions of Sarabhaṅga.

[1] J. v. 135-49.

5. **Aṭṭhaka.**—Pacceka Buddha. Mentioned in a nominal list.[1]

[1] M. iii. 70; Ap. i. 107.

Aṭṭhakanagara.—A city, from which came the householder **Dasama** who, while on a visit to **Pāṭaliputta** on business, went to see Ānanda at **Beluvagāma** and questioned him.[1] The conversation is recorded in the *Aṭṭhaka-nāgara Sutta.*

[1] M. i. 349 f.; A. v. 342-7.

Aṭṭhaka-nāgara Sutta.—Gives an account of questions asked by Dasama of Aṭṭhakanagara of Ānanda while the latter was in Beluvagāma. It deals with the eleven portals leading to Nibbāna by which one may save oneself.[1]

[1] M. i. 349 f.; A. v. 342-7.

Aṭṭhaka-Vagga.—The fourth division of the Sutta Nipāta. It consists of sixteen suttas, all of which are explained in the Mahā Niddesa. It may also have been the name of divisions of other books, because we are told that once **Soṇa** Thera intoned before the Buddha all the verses of the Books of the Eights (**Aṭṭhaka-vaggikāni**).[1]

[1] Vin. i. 196-7. The DhA. (iv. 101-2) says he recited the 16 portions of the Aṭṭhakavagga.

Nandamātā Upāsikā was once reciting the Aṭṭhakavagga and the Parāyanavagga on the roof of her house, and **Vessavana,** while on the way with his followers to see the Buddha, listened to her recital.[2] According to this tradition, the Aṭṭhakavagga was already being recited in the Buddha's own time.

In Sanskrit the title was known as *Artha-varga* and was so understood by the Chinese translators. No one has explained what the title means nor has interpreted the second sutta (*Guhaṭṭhaka*) except as "The eight verses on the cave," and similarly with the three following suttas: *Duṭṭhaṭṭhaka, Suddhaṭṭha* and *Paramaṭṭhaka*, each of eight verses. The fact that it is commented on separately in the *Mahā Niddesa* and was translated into Chinese makes it appear probable that it was once a separate work.[3]

[2] SnA. i. 370; but see A. iv. 63, where only the Parāyana is mentioned.
[3] See Thomas, *op. cit.*, 274.

Aṭṭhaka Sutta.—Two of the same name. They deal with the methods of mastering the feelings, of bringing about their cessation and of the six ways of calming them.[1]

[1] S. iv. 221 f.

Aṭṭhakathā-Therā.—Mentioned in the Dīgha Commentary[1] as being capable of solving the doubts that arose in the mind of **Mahā Sīvali** Thera of the village hermitage.

[1] iii. 728.

Aṭṭhakathācariyā.—Composers (?) of the Commentaries. They lived prior to Buddhaghosa, because he refers to them.[1]

[1] *E.g.*, AA. i. 273.

1. **Aṭṭhaṅgika Sutta.**—Things that flow together and coalesce do so because they contain a common element (*dhātu*) which makes possible such confluence, *e.g.* right views accord with right views by virtue of their common quality.[1]

[1] S. ii. 168.

2. **Aṭṭhaṅgika Sutta.**—On the unworthy man, the still more unworthy man and the worthy man.[1]

[1] A. ii. 220 f.

Aṭṭhaṅgika-magga Sutta.—The Āriyan eightfold path, called the path that goes to the uncompounded (*asaṅkhata*).[1]

[1] S. iv. 367.

Aṭṭhapuggala Sutta.—Two suttas on the eight persons who are worthy of homage and of gifts.[1]

[1] A. iv. 292, 293.

Aṭṭhama.—Pacceka Buddha, one of the names given in a list of such.[1]

[1] M. iii. 70; ApA. i. 106.

Aṭṭhasata Sutta (°Pariyāya).—Method of describing the 108 feelings—thirty-six each of the past, present and future.[1]

[1] S. iv. 231.

Aṭṭhasadda Jātaka.—Preached at Jetavana. **Pasenadi,** having heard one night a cry uttered by four inhabitants of hell, sought the advice of the Buddha.[1] The Buddha tells him of a former king of Benāres who, when seated on his bed at midnight, heard eight unusual sounds which frightened him till they were shown by the Bodhisatta to be quite natural.[2]

[1] The story is given in full in the *Lohakumbhi Jātaka*; J. iii. 43 f. [2] J. iii. 428-34.

Aṭṭhasahassa.—A district of **Rohaṇa** in Ceylon[1] to the east of the modern **Valaveganga.**[2]

[1] Cv. lxi. 24; lxxv. 154. [2] See Geiger, Cv. trans., i. 227, n. 4.

Aṭṭhāna Jātaka.—On the untrustworthiness and treacherousness of women. A young merchant, **Mahādhana,** patronised a courtesan, giving her a thousand pieces daily. One day, having no time to fetch the money, he went empty handed and was cast out. Thereupon, in disgust, he became an ascetic.[1]

The story is related to a monk who wished to leave the Order on account of a woman.

[1] J. iii. 474 ff.

Aṭṭhāna Vagga.—A group of the "impossibilities"; examples of such are the simultaneous existence of two Buddhas, or the following of a good result from an evil deed.[1]

[1] A. i. 26-30.

Aṭṭhānaparikappa Sutta.—Mentioned in the *Atthasālinī*[1]; it evidently refers to Aṅguttara i. 222. The sutta states that it were easier for the four great elements to change their characteristics than for an Ariyan

[1] p. 336.

disciple possessed with unvarying faith in the Buddha, the Dhamma and the Saṅgha, to be born in purgatory among lower animals or in the *peta*-world.

Aṭṭhika Sutta.—A group of suttas dealing with the benefits occurring from meditating on skeletons.[1]

[1] S. v. 129 ff.

Aṭṭhipesī Sutta.—Preached about a *peta*, a mere skeleton, seen near **Gijjhakūṭa** by **Moggollāna** and **Lakkhaṇa.** He had been a cattle-butcher in Rājagaha.[1]

[1] S. ii. 254.

Aṭṭhisena.—The Bodhisatta. He came of a brahmin family of Benares, studied at Takkasilā and later became a *religieux*. He lived in the royal garden at the king's request, but would never ask the king for anything even when pressed to do so.[1]

[1] J. iii. 352 f.

Aṭṭhisena Jātaka (No. 403).—The story of **Aṭṭhisena** as given above. Some monks in **Ālavī** were begging everywhere for materials and aid to build houses for themselves. People were annoyed by their solicitations and avoided them. When **Mahākassapa** came to Ālavī people ran away from him thinking he too was one of the monks. On enquiry he learnt the reason and told it to the Buddha, who was then at the **Aggālava-cetiya.** The Buddha rebuked the monks, saying that formerly samaṇas and recluses, even though offered their choice by kings, never asked for alms, holding that begging from others was neither agreeable nor pleasant. The *Maṇikaṇṭha Jātaka*[1] was also preached on the same occasion.

[1] J. ii. 282 ff.

Aṭṭhissara.—The name under which **Devadatta,** having suffered for five parts of a kappa in purgatory, will become Pacceka Buddha.[1]

[1] DhA. i. 125; Mil. 111.

Aḍḍha Vagga.—Third section of the Pañcaka Nipāta of the Jātaka Commentary.[1]

[1] J. iii. 211-227.

Aḍḍha Sutta (2).—That Ariyan disciple is wealthy who possesses four things: unwavering loyalty to the Buddha, the Dhamma and the Saṅgha, and virtues held in esteem by the Ariyans.[1]

[1] S. v. 402.

Aḍḍhakāsī Therī.—In Kassapa Buddha's time she had been a nun well established in the precepts. But she reviled an arahant therī by calling her a prostitute, and for this she was born in purgatory. In the present age she was the daughter of a rich and distinguished citizen of Benares but, because of her former evil speech, became a prostitute in Rājagaha. Having heard the Buddha preach, she entered the Order of the bhikkhunis. Wishing to obtain the higher ordination from the Buddha, she set out for Sāvatthi, but was waylaid and stopped by libertines. So she sent a man to ask the Buddha's advice and he permitted her to be ordained by a messenger.[1] Her case established a precedent.[2] Later she attained arahantship.

It has been suggested[3] that her name "half Kāsī" might mean that she charged five hundred pieces from her patrons. For, according to Buddhaghosa, Kāsī means one thousand, and anything worth one thousand is called *kāsiya*.

Another explanation is, however, given by Dhammapāla.[4] The revenue which accrued to the king for one day from Kāsī was a thousand. Aḍḍhakāsī's patrons had to give a like sum to spend a night with her. This is referred to in one of the verses attributed to her in the Therīgāthā.[5] For this reason she was called Kāsī. But later, many men, not being able to afford a thousand, would pay half the amount and spend the day with her. As a result she became known as Aḍḍhakāsī.

1 Thig. vv. 25-6; ThigA. 30 ff.; Vin. ii. 277; Ap. ii. 610-11.
2 Sp. i. 242.
3 VT. iii. 360, n. 3; and VT. ii. 195-6, n. 3.
4 ThigA. 32.
5 v. 25.

Aḍḍhacandiya Thera.—An arahant. In a previous birth he gave Tissa Buddha a bouquet of flowers in the shape of a crescent moon. He was once a king named **Devapa.**[1]

1 Ap. i. 231.

Aḍḍhacelaka Thera.—In a previous birth he gave half a garment to Tissa Buddha. He was thirty-two times king, under the names of **Samanta** and **Odana.** He became an arahant.[1]

1 Ap. i. 134.

Aḍḍhabhūta Sutta.—Preached in the **Kalandakanivāpa** at Veḷuvana. Everything is afflicted: eye, objects, eye-consciousness, etc. (*v.l.* **Andhabhūta**[1]).

1 S. iv. 20-1.

Aḍḍhamāsaka.—King. He was a poor man of Benares. He saved a halfpenny (*aḍḍha-māsaka*) and hid it in a brick wall. When the festvial came round, wishing to take pårt in the fun with his wife, who had also saved a halfpenny, he travelled six leagues in the hot sun to fetch his savings from the hiding-place. King **Udaya** saw him as he passed by the palace singing, and having discovered his mission, gave him half of his kingdom. The man chose the half in which his halfpenny lay concealed. He later became an ascetic. His story is given in the *Gaṅgamāla Jātaka*.[1] He was **Ānanda** in the present age.[2]

[1] J. iii. 449 ff.; iv. 174.

[2] *Ibid.*, iii. 454.

Aṇimaṇḍavya.—See **Maṇḍavya.**

Aṇḍabhariġāmakūṭaka Sutta.—Story of a village cheat, born as a peta. His secret organs (*aṇḍa*) were huge in size. He was among the petas seen by Mahāmoggallāna on his way to Rājagaha from Gijjhakūṭa, in company with the Elder Lakkhaṇa. He had been a corrupt judge in Rājagaha and had taken bribes and given unjust judgments.[1]

[1] S. ii. 258.

[2] SA. ii. 162.

Aṇḍabhūta Jātaka (No. 62).—On the innate wickedness of woman. A girl is bred from infancy among women only, never seeing any man but her husband, the king's chaplain. The latter had embarked on the enterprise of so bringing up the girl, in order to defeat the king at dice, because the king was in the habit of winning by a declaration of truth to the effect that all women were treacherous; the chaplain wanted to find an exception in order to falsify the declaration. For a time the experiment succeeds, but later, as a result of the king's scheming, the girl starts an intrigue with a flower-seller as lover and is discovered.[1] The Jātaka is so called because the woman in the story was guarded from the time she lay in her mother's womb as a fœtus (*aṇḍabhūta*).

The story was related concerning a monk who was worried by his passions.

[1] J. i. 289 ff.

Atappā-devā.—A class of devas whose company mortals long for.[1] They belong to the **Suddhāvāsā.**[2] According to Buddhaghosa[3] they are so called because they torment no one (*na kañci sattaṃ tapenti*). They are *anāgāmīs*.[4]

[1] M. i. 289; iii. 103.

[2] D. ii. 52; D. iii. 237.

[3] DA. ii. 480; VibhA. 521.

[4] ItA. 40.

Atarandā-mahābhodikkhandha.—A village in **Rohaṇa** where the forces of **Dhamilādhikāri** destroyed the rebels.[1]

[1] Cv. lxxv. 97.

Aticāri Sutta.—That an adulteress is born in purgatory.[1]

[1] S. iv. 242.

Atitti Sutta.—There is no satiety in sleep, in drinking liquor and in sexual intercourse.[1]

[1] A. i. 261.

Atideva.—The Bodhisatta born as a brahmin in the time of Revata Buddha. Having heard the Buddha preach he gave him his upper garment.[1] He belonged to **Rammavatī.**[2]

[1] J. i. 35; Bu. vi. 10; Mbv. 10. [2] BuA. 134.

Atinivāsa Sutta.—The five evil results of long dwelling (*atinivāsa*).[1]

[1] A. iii. 258.

Atipaṇḍita.—The Bodhisatta was once born as the son of a merchant-family in Benares and was named **Paṇḍita.** He entered into partnership with another man, named Atipaṇḍita, who tried to deceive him but in vain.[1]

[1] J. i. 405 f.

1. **Atimuttaka.**—A cemetery near **Benares,** where robbers used to deposit their stolen goods. Two ascetics, **Maṇḍavya** and **Dīpāyana,** lived there.[1]

[1] J. iv. 28 f.

2. **Atimuttaka.**—A novice, nephew of **Saṅkicca.** On his way to his parents to obtain, at Saṅkicca's behest, permission for the higher ordination, he was attacked by thieves; he was set free on promising not to mention their whereabouts. Later, he saw his parents take the same road, but refrained from warning them on account of his promise. The thieves, marvelling at his integrity, wished to be ordained under him. He took them to Saṅkicca and later on to the Buddha.[1]

In Atthadassi's time he was a rich householder and held great almsgivings for the monks after the Buddha's death.[2]

He is mentioned as one who shone in the assembly of relatives.[3]

His name is often spelt **Adhimuttaka.**

[1] DhA. ii. 252-3; SA. i. 44-5; but see ThagA. ii. 11 f., where his encounter with the thieves is mentioned as having taken place *after* he became arahant. The rest of the story also is different.

[2] Ap. i. 88.

[3] SA. i. 45.

Atimuttaka-sāmanera Vatthu.—See **Atimuttaka** (2).

Atimbara.—Minister of **Duṭṭhagāmaṇi.**[1]

[1] SdS. 77.

Atītānāgatapaccuppanna Suttas.—Three in number. Seeing that the *saṅkhāras* are (1) impermanent, (2) ill, and (3) without the self, the Ariyan disciple cares not for what is past, is not in love with the present and seeks dispassion for the future.[1]

[1] S. iii. 19-20.

Atītena Sutta.—Seeing that the eye, ear, etc., of the past are impermanent, the Ariyan disciple should cease desiring them.[1]

[1] S. iv. 151.

1. **Atula.**—An upāsaka of Sāvatthi. He went with five hundred others to listen to **Revata,** who, however, being fond of solitude, would not preach to him. In anger he went to **Sāriputta** who, on hearing his grievances, discoursed at length on the Abhidhamma. Annoyed thereat he repaired to **Ānanda,** to whom he told the story. Ānanda preached them a very short sermon, and the upāsakas in despair sought the Buddha. The Buddha pointed out to them that they had been too hasty in their condemnation. At the end of the discourse Atula and his companions gained the First Fruit of the Path.[1]

[1] DhA. iii. 325-9.

2. **Atula.**—A nāga king. The Bodhisatta in the time of **Sumana** Buddha. He had music played before the Buddha and gave him a pair of robes.[1]

[1] J. i. 34; Bu. v. 15 f.; Mbv. 10.

3. **Atula.**—A nāga king. The Bodhisatta in **Vipassi** Buddha's time. He offered the Buddha a golden seat embossed with jewels.[1]

[1] J. i. 41; Mbv. 11; Bu. xx. 10 f.

4. **Atula.**—A celebrated physician of old, mentioned in a list with six others.[1]

[1] Mil. 272.

5. **Atula.**—Son of **Sikhī,** who later became Sikhī Buddha. His mother was **Sabbakāmā.**[1]

[1] Bu. xxi. 17; DA. ii. 422.

Atulamba.—The mango tree produced by the juggler **Bhaṇḍu-kaṇṇa** to make Prince **Mahāpanāda** laugh. The mango is known as **Vessavaṇa's** mango and it is impossible to approach it.[1]

[1] J. iv. 324; see also ii. 397.

Atulya.—King. A previous birth of **Āsanatthavika** Thera. Twenty-seven kappas ago he was king seven times under this name.[1]

[1] Ap. i. 255.

1. **Atta Sutta.**—Self-possession is the forerunner of the Eightfold Path.[1]

[1] S. v. 36.

2. **Atta Sutta.**—The self-possessed monk develops the Eightfold Path.[1]

[1] S. v. 37.

Attakāra Sutta.—On individuality and non-individuality; preached in answer to a brahmin's questions.[1]

[1] A. iii. 337 f.

Attānuvāda Sutta.—On the four kinds of fears: fear of self-reproach, of others' reproach, of punishment, and of woeful state.[1]

[1] A. ii. 121 f.

Attadaṇḍa Sutta.—The fifteenth sutta of the Aṭṭhakavagga of the Sutta Nipāta.[1] It was preached by the Buddha when he went to settle the quarrel between the Sākiyans and the Koliyans. It was the last to be preached on that occasion. At the end of the discourse their quarrels ceased and five hundred Sākiyan and five hundred Koliyan youths entered the Order by way of *ehibhikkhupabbajjā*.[2] The sutta deals with various aspects of self-control and a description of one who might be called a *muni*.

[1] Sn. 182 f.

[2] SnA. 566-9; J. v. 413-4.

Attantāpa Sutta.—On the self-tormentor who practices various austerities, and the tormentor of others—butcher, fisherman, etc.—and those who, like some kings, torment both themselves and others.[1]

[1] A. ii. 203 ff.

Attadattha Thera.—When the Buddha announced that he would pass away in four months, many *puthujjana*-monks, out of affection for him, stayed near him, not knowing what to do. But Atthadattha, determined to realise the aim of his pabbajjā in the Buddha's lifetime, dwelt apart, in earnest striving. His action was reported to the Buddha who, on learning what his purpose was, greatly praised him and held him up as an example to the others. At the end of the Buddha's sermon the thera became an arahant.[1]

[1] DhA. iii. 158-64.

Attahita Sutta.—Three suttas on the four kinds of people in the world: bent on their own profit; on another's profit; on the profit of both; on the profit of neither.[1]

[1] A. ii. 97 ff.

Attadīpa Vagga.—Of the Saṃyutta Nikāya,[1] contains ten suttas on the nature of the body and the self.

[1] S. iii. 42 ff.

Attadīpa Sutta.—Monks should be refuges unto themselves, the Dhamma should be their refuge. They should seek for the very source of things in the impermanence of the five *Khandhas.*[1]

[1] S. iv. 42 f.

Attāḷhidhātusena Vihāra.—A monastery built by King **Dhātusena.**[1]

[1] Cv. xxxviii. 49.

Atthakaraṇa Sutta.—**Pasenadi** tells the Buddha how, when he was sitting in the judgment-hall (*atthakaraṇa*), eminent nobles and brahmins and burgesses deliberately told lies because of their worldly desires and he was disgusted. The Buddha tells him that their action in doing so will be a source of ill to them for a long time[1] (*v.l.* **Aṭṭa**°).

[1] S. i. 74 f.

Atthakāma Vagga.—The fifth section of Eka Nipāta of the Jātakaṭṭhakathā.[1]

[1] J. i. 234-61.

Atthakula Sutta.—The reasons why certain families, having attained great possessions, fail to last long.[1]

[1] A. ii. 249 f.

1. **Atthadassī.**—The fourteenth of the twenty-four Buddhas. He was born in **Sobhana** in the **Sucindhanu** pleasaunce, his parents being **Sāgara** and **Sudassanā.**[1] He was so called because at his birth people recovered

[1] Bu. xv.; BuA. 178 ff.

long-buried treasures. His wife was **Visākhā** and his son **Sena** (**Sela** according to the Buddhavaṃsa Commentary). He lived for 10,000 years as a householder in three palaces—**Amaragiri, Suragiri** and **Girivāhana.** He left home on a horse called **Sudassana.** His penance lasted eight months, and his meal of milk-rice was given by a nāga woman, **Sucindharā.** A nāga, **Dhammaruci,** gave him the grass which he spread at the foot of the campaka tree, where he reached Enlightenment. His first sermon was preached in the **Anomā**-park near Anoma. His chief disciples were **Santa,** the king's son, and **Upasanta,** son of the chaplain of **Sucandaka.** His chief women disciples were **Dhammā** and **Sudhammā. Abhaya** was his attendant, and his patrons were **Nakula** and **Nisabha** among the laymen, and **Makilā** and **Sunandā** among the lay-women. The Bodhisatta was a jaṭila, **Susīma** of Campaka, and he offered the Buddha a canopy of flowers brought from the deva-world. Atthadassī died at the age of 100,000 years at Anomārāma in Anupama and his relics were scattered in various places. He appeared in the Maṇḍakappa, in the company of two others, Piyadassī and Dhammadassī.[2]

[2] J. i. 39.

2. **Atthadassī.**—A thera in Ceylon who, in company with two others, **Buddhamitta** and **Buddhadeva,** asked that the Jātakaṭṭhakathā be written.[1] He was probably an incumbent of the Mahāvihāra in Anurādhapura.[2]

[1] J. i. 1; Gv. 68. [2] See *Pāli Lit. of Ceylon*, 125.

3. **Atthadassī.**—One of the mythological kings of **Kapilavatthu.**[1]

[1] Dīp. iii. 41.

4. **Atthadassī.**—A thera in Ceylon, supposed by some to be the author of the **Bhesajjamañjūsā** and to have been the head of the **Pañca-mūla-pariveṇa.**[1]

[1] *Pāli Lit. of Ceylon*, 215.

Atthavasa Vagga.—The seventeenth chapter of the Duka Nipāta of the Aṅguttara Nikāya.[1] It deals with the aims behind the Buddha's injunctions to monks with regard to the practice of *samatha* and *vipassanā*, to be employed as remedies against lust, etc.

[1] A. i. 98-100.

1. **Atthavyākhyāna.**—By **Cūlabuddha** Thera of Ceylon; a book on grammar or exegesis.[1]

[1] Sās. 34; Bode: *Pāli Lit. of Burma*, 28.

2. **Atthavyākhyāna.**—By **Culla-Vajira** (of Ceylon).[1]

[1] Gv. 60.

3. **Atthavyākhyāna.**—By **Culla-Vimalabuddhi;** written, says the Gandhavaṃsa, independently, according to his own convictions.[1]

[1] Gv. 70.

Atthasandassaka Thera.—An arahant. In Padumuttara's time he was a brahmin named **Nārada.** Seeing the Buddha going along, attended by his monks, he uttered the Buddha's praises in three stanzas. 130 kappas ago he was born as a king named **Sukhitta.**[1] He is probably identical with **Nāgita** Thera.

[1] Ap. i. 168.

Atthasālinī (Aṭṭhasālinī).—Buddhaghosa's commentary on the Dhammasaṅganippakaraṇa of the Abhidhamma Piṭaka. It was originally written in India,[1] but was probably revised in Ceylon as it mentions[2] the Samantapāsādikā, also various Aṭṭhakathās and the Visuddhimagga.

[1] Mhv. xxxvi. 225; Sās. 31. [2] pp. 97-8.

Atthassadvāra Jātaka (No. 84).—The Bodhisatta was once born as a very wealthy seṭṭhi in Benares. He had a son who, when only seven years old, showed great intelligence and anxiety for his own spiritual welfare. One day the boy asked his father which were the paths leading to welfare and on being told them he followed their teaching.

The story was told in reference to a similar child, the son of a wealthy seṭṭhi of Sāvatthi. The father, not being able to answer the boy's questions, took him to the Buddha at Jetavana.[1]

[1] J. i. 366-7.

"Atthinukhopariyāya" Sutta.—Is there a method by following which a monk could affirm that he has won insight? "Yes," answers the Buddha; a monk beholding an object or hearing a sound, etc., recognises it with the eye of wisdom and of reason, whether it produces in him lust, etc., or not. This method leads to insight apart from belief, hearsay, etc.[1]

[1] S. i. 138.

Atthirāga Sutta.—All existence is the result of attachment to the four kinds of food: *kabaliṅkāra* (solid food), *phassa* (contact), *manòsañcetanā* (will), and *viññāṇa* (consciousness). This is explained with various similes.[1]

[1] S. ii. 101-4.

Attho Sutta.—See **Virocana-asurinda Sutta.**

Athabbana (Āthabbana).—A branch of knowledge, dabbling in which is forbidden to monks.[1] When spoken in conjunction with the three Vedas, it is mentioned as a fourth branch of Veda with *itihāsa* as the fifth.[2] It is explained as *āthabbaṇika-manta-payoga* (the trade of the wonder-worker[3]).

[1] Sn. vs. 927. [2] DA. i. 247. [3] SnA. ii. 564.

Athalayunnāḍa.—A district in S. India.[1]

[1] Cv. lxxvi. 261.

Athalayūru-naḍāḷvāra.—A Damila chieftain.[1]

[1] Cv. lxxvi. 140, 260; lxxvii. 27.

Adanta Vagga.—The fourth chapter of the Eka Nipāta of the Aṅguttara Nikāya.[1] It consists of ten suttas on the untamed mind.

[1] A. i. 6 f.

Adaḷidda Sutta.—The rich man is he who possesses the seven *bojjhaṅgā.*[1]

[1] S. v. 100.

Adassanā Sutta (five).—Diverse opinions arise in the world because of the failure to see the five *saṅkhārā* their nature, etc.[1]

[1] S. iii. 260.

Aditi.—Mother of the sun, who is called **Ādicca,** which is explained as *Aditiyā putto.*[1]

[1] DA. iii. 963.

Adinna Sutta.—Few are they that abstain from taking what is not given.[1]

[1] S. v. 469.

Adinnapubbaka.—A brahmin of Sāvatthi, father of **Maṭṭakuṇḍalī,** so called because he never gave anything to anyone. When, later, Maṭṭakuṇḍali, having been born in heaven, visits him and persuades him to take refuge with the Buddha, he invites the Buddha with his monks to a meal at his house. At the conclusion of the meal Maṭṭakuṇḍalī appears again and Adinnapubbaka, after listening to the Buddha's preaching, attains the First Fruit of the Path.[1]

[1] DhA. i. 25-30; VvA. 322 f.

Addilaraṭṭha.—A kingdom where once lived a poor man named **Kotūhaḷaka,** who, in the present age, became **Ghosita-seṭṭhi.** Food being very scarce in the country, Kotūhaḷaka and his family left it.[1]

[1] DA. i. 317; MA. i. 539.

Adīnasattu.—See **Alīnasattu.**

Adukkhamasukhī Sutta.—A group of twenty-six suttantas, dealing with various heresies regarding the soul.[1]

[1] S. iii. 220-2.

Addha Vagga.—The seventh chapter of the Devatā Saṃyutta of the Saṃyutta Nikāya.[1] The Saṃyutta Commentary[2] calls it **Anvavagga.**

[1] S. i. 39-41. [2] SA. i. 75. See also KS. i. 54, n. 4.

Addhariyā-brāhmaṇā.—The word occurs in a list of brahmin teachers in the *Tevijja Sutta.*[1] They teach a state of union with Brahmā. These are evidently Adhvaryu brahmins.

[1] D. i. 237.

Addhuvasīla.—A youth who stole ornaments to win the daughter of his teacher. He failed in his quest. The story is given in the *Sīlavīmaṃsana Jātaka.*[1]

[1] J. iii. 18-20.

Adhanapālī.—Given as an example of a name.[1]

[1] J. i. 403.

Adhamma.—A Kāmāvacara god, **Devadatta,** in a previous birth. He appeared to men on fast days and admonished them to lead evil lives. Once he met **Dhamma** (the Bodhisatta), and the two had a discussion in mid-air, at the end of which Adhamma plunged headlong into hell.[1]

His vehicle was called **Adhammayāna.**

[1] J. iv. 100-3.

Adhamma Vagga.—The tenth chapter of the Eka Nipāta of the Aṅguttara Nikāya.[1] It consists of forty-two suttas, dealing chiefly with the harm that arises from monks describing what is not Dhamma as Dhamma and *vice versâ.*

[1] A. i. 16-19.

Adhamma Sutta.—Three suttas describing *dhamma* and *adhamma* and their different qualities.[1] In the last **Ānanda** explains in detail what the Buddha taught to the monks in brief.

[1] A. v. 222 ff.

Adhammavādī.—A monk who lived soon after the death of Kassapa Buddha. Having been guilty of various offences, he was charged by his colleague **Dhammavādī**; he persuaded certain *vinayadhara* monks to give an *ex parte* judgment in his favour.[1] The two monks who were chiefly responsible for this judgment were later known as **Hemavata** and **Sātāgira.**[1]

[1] SnA. i. 195-7.

Adhammika Sutta.—The evils resulting from the unrighteousness of kings and the benefits of their righteousness.[1]

[1] A. ii. 74 f.

Adharaṭṭeri.—A district in S. India.[1]

[1] Cv. lxxvii. 69.

Adhikakkā.—A ford, evidently a well-known bathing-ghat, where pilgrims used to bathe in order to obtain purification from their sins. It is mentioned in a list of rivers and ghats.[1]

[1] M. i. 39.

Adhikaraṇa Vagga.—The second chapter of the Duka Nipāta of the Aṅguttara Nikāya. It consists of ten suttas on the value of self-examination in disputes and several other topics, such as the reasons for being born in heaven and in purgatory, abstention from immorality, the holiness of the letter of the Dhamma, etc.[1]

[1] A. i. 52-8.

Adhikaraṇasamatha Vagga.—One of the divisions of the Suttavibhaṅga on the procedure for settling disputes.

Adhicitta Sutta.—The qualities necessary for the monk developing higher consciousness.[1]

[1] A. ii. 256 f. It is quoted in the Vibhaṅga Commentary, 229 f.

Adhicchattiya Thera.—An arahant. In a previous birth he placed a parasol on the thūpa containing the relics of **Atthadassī** Buddha.[1] He is evidently identical with **Sāmidatta**[2] (*v.l.* **Chattādhichattiya**).

[1] Ap. i. 170. [2] ThagA. i. 189.

Adhigama Sutta.—On the qualities requisite for acquiring good states and for fostering them.[1]

[1] A. iii. 431 f.

1. **Adhimutta.**—A brahmin of Sāvatthi. Dissatisfied with brahmin learning, he looked for salvation elsewhere, and hearing the Buddha preach at the presentation of Jetavana, entered the Order, becoming an arahant in due course.[1] A verse addressed by him to some corpulent monks is found in the Theragāthā.[2]

In Padumuttara's time he was a learned brahmin and became an ascetic. Later he met the Buddha, offered him a bark-robe and uttered his praises in song. He is probably identical with **Sabbakittika** of the Apadāna.[3]

[1] ThagA. i. 224. [2] v. 114. [3] i. 323-4.

2. **Adhimutta.**—See **Atimuttaka** (2).

Adhimutti Sutta.—Preached to **Ānanda** on the ten powers of a Tathāgata.[1]

[1] A. v. 36 f.

Adhokuraṅgāma.—A village in the district of **Āḷisāra** in North Ceylon; a fortification there of **Gajabāhu** was captured by **Parakkamabāhu I.**[1]

[1] Cv. lxx. 171.

Adhogaṅgā.—See **Gaṅgā.**

Adhopupphiya Thera.—An arahant. In a previous birth he was a hermit of great power in Himavā and offered flowers to **Abhibhū,** the chief disciple of **Sikhī** Buddha. Soon afterwards he was eaten up by a boa-constrictor.[1]

[1] Ap. i. 128-9.

Anaṅgana Jātaka.—Mentioned in the Aṅguttara Commentary,[1] among the Jātakas revealed by the Buddha at **Saṅkassa** in answer to the questions asked by **Sāriputta.** No story of this name is found in the Jātaka Commentary, but the verse quoted in the Aṅguttara Commentary is found in the *Jhānasodhana Jātaka*,[2] for which evidently this was another name. An *Anaṅgana Vatthu* is mentioned in the Samantapāsādikā,[3] but the reference is not clear, and probably refers to *Anaṅgana Sutta* (*infra*).

[1] i. 74. [2] J. i. 473 f. [3] i. 158.

Anaṅgana Sutta.—A record of a conversation between **Sāriputta** and **Moggallāna** on the nature of blemishes (*aṅganāni*) and on the benefits of recognising and removing them.[1]

[1] M. i. 24 ff.

Anataṃ Sutta.—See **Anta.**

Anaṇaka Sutta.—The four kinds of bliss possible to a householder: a bliss of ownership, of wealth, of debtlessness and of blamelessness.[1]

[1] A. ii. 69 f.

Anaticārī Sutta.—A woman who is no adulteress will be born in heaven.[1]

[1] S. iv. 244.

1. **Anatta Sutta.**—Preached to **Rādha** at Sāvatthi in answer to his question " What is not-self ?"[1]

[1] S. iii. 196.

2 and 3. **Anatta Suttas.**—The occasion is the same. That which is without a self must be put away.[1]

[1] S. iii. 199 and 201.

4. **Anatta Sutta.**—The idea of "not-self," when cultivated, conduces to great profit.[1]

[1] S. v. 133.

Anattaniya Sutta.—For that which does not belong to the self, desire must be put away.[1]

[1] S. iii. 78.

Anattalakhaṇa Vatthu.—The story of five hundred monks. The Buddha, knowing their past, advises them to reflect on the " selfishness " of the khandhas.[1] These monks had devoted themselves to meditation on this topic for 20,000 years in the dispensation of Kassapa Buddha.

[1] DhA. iii. 406-7.

Anattalakhaṇa Sutta.—Preached five days after the *Dhammacakkapavattana Sutta* to the **Pañcavaggiya** monks, all of whom became arahants at the conclusion of the sermon.[1] No self is to be found in any of the five khandhas, all of which are impermanent and subject to woe. The

[1] Vin. i. 13-14; J. i. 82; iv. 180; Dpv. i. 34; MA. i. 390; AA. i. 57, 84.

sutta does not deal with the question as to whether the self exists or not; it only shows that the khandhas are not the self.

In the Saṃyutta Nikāya[2] the discourse is called the **Pañca Sutta,** the five referred to being the **Pañcavaggiyā** who listened to it.

[2] iii. 66 f.

1. **Anattā Sutta.**—All the khandhas are without the self. The Āriyan disciple feels revulsion towards them realising that, for him, there is no hereafter.[1]

[1] S. iii. 21.

2. **Anattā Sutta.**—Same as above.[1]

[1] S. iii. 77.

3. **Anattā Sutta.**—All objects of the senses (sights, sounds, etc.), both external (*bāhira*) and personal (*ajjhatta*), are void of a self.[1]

[1] S. iv. 2, 4, 6.

4. **Anattā Sutta.**—Everything is void of self.[1]

[1] S. iv. 28.

Anattena Sutta.—Lust and desire for that which is without a self should be put away.[1]

[1] S. iii. 178.

Anatthatāya Sutta.—Negligence (*pamāda*) conduces to great loss.[1]

[1] A. i. 16.

Anatthapucchakabrāhmaṇa Vatthu.—Story of a brahmin who asked the Buddha whether he knew only of that which was good or did he know evil as well ? The Buddha set his doubts at rest.[1]

[1] DhA. ii. 227-9.

Ananutappiya Sutta.—Preached by **Sāriputta** on how a monk should deport himself so as to have no occasion for repentance.[1]

[1] A. iii. 294 f.

Ananusociya Jātaka (No. 328).—The Bodhisatta was born as a rich brahmin in Benares. After his education at Takkasilā his parents wished him to marry. After much persuasion he agreed to do so, if they could find a woman like a golden image which he would make. Emissaries were sent out and they found a girl of sixteen, **Samillabhāsinī,** in the Kāsi kingdom.

She did not wish to marry either, but yielded to her parent's wishes. Though the two young people were married they lived in celibacy and when their parents died they gave away their immense wealth and became ascetics. Samillabhāsini died of dysentery caused by unsatisfactory meals. The Bodhisatta coming back from his begging-rounds found her dead on a bench, but proceeded to eat his meal much to the surprise of the onlookers. On being questioned, "Why should I weep?" he said "that which has the quality of dissolution is dissolved."

The story was related in reference to a landowner who, when his wife died, gave himself up to despair. The Buddha, seeing his *upanissaya*, went out to meet him and told him the story, whereupon he obtained the First Fruit of the Path.[1]

[1] J.iii.92-7.

Ananussuta Sutta.—The five-fold power of a Tathāgata.[1]

[1] A.iii.9 f.

Ananta.—The serpent king referred to under **Anantapokkharaṇi,** but not elsewhere mentioned in the old books. He is also called **Anantabhoga.** For details see Hopkins' *Epic Mythology* (pp. 23-4).

Anantakāya.—An attendant of King **Milinda** who was sent by the king to escort **Nāgasena** from the monastery to Sāgala. On his way he questioned the Elder about the soul and we are told that the latter talked to him from the Abhidhamma to such effect that Anantakāya became a convert.[1] He is probably to be identified with **Antiochus,** attendant of Menander.[2]

[1] Mil.30-1. [2] Milinda Questions, I. xix., xlii.

Anantajāli.—King. A previous birth of **Bhājanadāyaka** fifty-three kappas ago[1] (*v.l.* **Antarajāli**).

[1] Ap. i. 218.

Anantajina.—An epithet of the Buddha. When **Upaka,** the ājīvika, saw the Buddha, and heard of his attainments, Anantajina was one of the names he used in uttering the Buddha's praises.[1] Later, when having quarrelled with his wife **Cāpā,** he sought the Buddha at Sāvatthi, it was "Anantajina" he asked for.[2]

[1] ThagA. i. 220. [2] *Ibid.*, 222; SnA. i. 260; MA. i. 389.

Anantapokkharaṇī.—A pond constructed by **Parakkamabāhu I.** in **Pulatthipura.** The steps surrounding the pond were laid like the coils of the serpent-king **Ananta.**[1]

[1] Cv. lxxiii. 120.

Anantarapeyyāla.—One of the sections of the Vidhura Jātaka.[1]

[1] J. vi. 304.

Anantarabhaṇḍaka-tittha.—A ford in the **Mahāvāluka-gaṅgā** in Ceylon.[1]

[1] Cv. lxxii. 16.

Anantavā Sutta.—On the world as being unlimited.[1]

[1] S. iii. 215.

1. **Anabhirati Jātaka** (No. 65).—Women cannot be regarded as private property. They are common to all; they extend universal hospitality.

The Bodhisatta was once a famous teacher of Benares. A pupil of his, finding his wife unfaithful, was so affected by the discovery that he kept away from classes. When asked why, he told his teacher the whole story; the latter consoled him by telling him that all women were unfaithful.

The story was told to an upāsaka who came to visit the Buddha. Once, on discovering his wife's faithlessness, he had words with her and kept away from the vihāra.[1]

[1] J. i. 301-2; see also DhA. iii. 348 ff., where the details given are slightly different.

2. **Anabhirati Jātaka** (No. 185).—Told to a young brahmin of Sāvatthi who knew the three vedas by heart. When he married his mind became darkened. He visited the Buddha, who talked to him pleasantly and discovered in the course of conversation that his memory had grown weak. The same thing had happened to him in the past, said the Buddha. Serenity of mind is essential for good memory.[1]

[1] J. ii. 99-101.

Anabhirati Sutta.—The idea of distaste for all the world, if cultivated, is fruitful.[1]

[1] S. v. 132.

Anabhirati-bhikkhu Vatthu.—The story of a discontented monk. When the monk was away engaged in study, his father fell sick and died before his son could be summoned to see him. The father, on his death-bed, left with his other, younger son, a hundred pieces, to be given to the monk. At first the monk refused to accept the money, but later he felt a desire to take it and to return to the lay life. Indecision made him ill and he was taken before the Buddha. The latter, by getting him to enumerate the things which he could buy with the money, made it clear to him that the amount of his inheritance would be very little, and that no amount of wealth could ever be sufficient to gratify one's needs, relating the *Mandhātā Jātaka* to illustrate the truth of his words.[1]

[1] DhA. iii. 238-45.

Anabhisamaya Sutta.—Preached to the wanderer **Vacchagotta.** Diverse opinions arise in the world through not seeing the nature of the body, etc.[1]

[1] S. iii. 260.

Anamatagga Saṃyutta.—The fifteenth section of the Saṃyutta Nikāya. It contains a collection of sayings on the incalculable beginning of Saṃsāra.[1] After the Third Council, the Thera **Rakkhita,** who went to **Vanavāsa,** preached the Anamatagga Saṃyutta there and converted 60,000 persons.[2] On the fourth day of **Mahinda's** visit to Ceylon he preached this Saṃyutta in the Nandanavana in Anurādhapura.[3] The **Pātheyyaka** monks became arahants after listening to the Buddha preaching the **Anamataggāni.**[4]

[1] S. ii. 178 ff.
[2] Mhv. xii. 32 f.
[3] *Ibid.*, xv. 186; Sp. i. 81; Mbv. 114.
[4] DhA. ii. 32.

Anāgata Sutta.—The five kinds of anticipatory fears that should make a forest-ḍwelling monk zealous and active.[1]

[1] A. iii. 100 f.

Anāgatavaṃsa.—A poem on the story of **Metteyya,** the future Buddha, by an elder named **Kassapa,**[1] an inhabitant of the Coḷa country.[2] The poem is probably based on an older work.[3] A ṭīkā exists, written by an **Upatissa,** possibly the author of the Mahābodhivaṃsa. The introductory verses of the poem state that the story was preached by the Buddha at Sāriputta's request. For the text see *J.P.T.S.*, 1886, pp. 32 ff.

[1] Gv. 61.
[2] Svd. v. 1204.
[3] P.L.C., 160 f.

Anāgāmī Sutta.—The six qualities necessary for the third Fruit of the Path.[1]

[1] A. iii. 421.

Anāgāmi-thera Vatthu.—Story of a monk who became anāgāmi; when asked by his pupils, however, he did not say anything regarding his attainment. After death he was born in the **Suddhāvāsā.** His pupils, grieving for him in their ignorance, were enlightened by the Buddha.[1]

[1] DhA. iii. 288-9.

Anātha.—A Pacceka Buddha of thirty-one kappas ago. **Uddālapupphiya** Thera, in a previous birth, offered him an *uddāla*-flower.[1]

[1] Ap. i. 288.

Anāthapiṇḍika.—A banker (*seṭṭhi*) of **Sāvatthi** who became famous because of his unparalleled generosity to the Buddha. His first meeting with the Buddha was during the first year after the Enlightenment, in **Rājagaha,**[1] whither Anāthapiṇḍika had come on business. His wife was the sister of the seṭṭhi of Rājagaha, and when he arrived he found the seṭṭhi preparing a meal for the Buddha and his monks on so splendid a scale that he thought that a wedding was in progress or that the king had been invited. On learning the truth he became eager to visit the Buddha, and did so very early the next morning.[2] He was so excited by the thought of the visit that he got up three times during the night. When, at last, he started for **Sītavana,** the road was quite dark, but a friendly yakkha, **Sīvaka,** sped him on with words of encouragement. By force of his piety the darkness vanished.

The Buddha was staying in the Sītavana, and when Anāthapiṇḍika reached there spirits opened the door for him. He found the Buddha walking up and down, meditating in the cool air of the early dawn. The Buddha greeted him and talked to him on various aspects of his teaching. Anāthapiṇḍika was immediately converted and became a Sotāpanna. He invited the Buddha to a meal the next day, providing everything himself, although the seṭṭhi, the Mayor of Rājagaha and King **Bimbisāra,** asked to be allowed to help. After the meal, which he served to the Buddha with his own hand, he invited the Buddha to spend the rainy season at Sāvatthi, and the Buddha accepted, saying "the Tathāgatas, O householder, take pleasure in solitude." "I understand, O Blessed One, I understand," was the reply.

When Anāthapiṇḍika had finished his business at Rājagaha he set out towards Sāvatthi, giving orders along the way to his friends and ac-

[1] The story is given in Vin. ii. 154 ff;. SA. i. 240 ff., etc.
[2] Vin. ii. 155-6.

quaintances[3] to prepare dwellings, parks, rest-houses and gifts all along the road to Sāvatthi in preparation for the Buddha's visit. Understanding the request implied in the Buddha's words when he accepted the invitation, Anāthapiṇḍika looked out for a quiet spot near Sāvatthi where the Buddha and the monks might dwell, and his eye fell on the park of **Jetakumāra.** He bought the park at great expense and erected therein the famous **Jetavanārāma.**[4] As a result of this and of his numerous other benefactions in the cause of the Sāsana, Anāthapiṇḍika came to be recognised as the chief of alms-givers.[5]

Anāthapiṇḍika's personal name was **Sudatta,** but he was always called Anāthapiṇḍika[6] (feeder of the destitute) because of his munificence; he was, however, very pleased when the Buddha addressed him by his own name.[7] He spent eighteen crores on the purchase of Jetavana and a like sum on the construction of the vihāra; another eighteen crores were spent in the festival of dedication. He fed one hundred monks in his house daily in addition to meals provided for guests, people of the village, invalids, etc. Five hundred seats were always ready in his house for any guests who might come.[8]

Anāthapiṇḍika's father was the seṭṭhi **Sumana**[9].

Anāthapiṇḍika married a lady called **Puññalakkhaṇā**[10]; he had a son **Kāla** and three daughters, **Mahā-Subaddhā, Cūla-Subaddhā** and **Sumanā.** Mention is also made of a daughter-in law, **Sujātā** by name, daughter of **Dhanañjaya** and the youngest sister of **Visākhā.** She was very haughty and ill-treated the servants.[11]

The son, in spite of his father's efforts, showed no piety until he was finally bribed to go to the vihāra and listen to the Buddha's preaching.[12] The daughters, on the other hand, were most dutiful and helped their father in ministering to the monks. The two elder ones attained to the First Fruit of the Path, married, and went to live with the families of their husbands. Sumanā obtained the Second Fruit of the Path, but remained unmarried. Overwhelmed with disappointment because of

[3] He had many friends and acquaintances and he was *ādeyyavaco* (his word was held to be of weight), *loc. cit.*, p. 158. But see J. i. 92, where it is said that Anāthapiṇḍika bore all the expenses of these preparations. Vihāras were built costing 1,000 pieces each, a yojana apart from each other.

[4] *q.v.* for details.

[5] A. i. 25.

[6] AA. i. 208; MA. i. 50.

[7] Vin. ii. 156.

[8] AA. i. 208-9. He fed 1,000 monks daily says DhA. i. 128; but see J. iii. 119, where a monk, who had come from far away and had missed the meal hour, had to starve.

[9] AA. *loc. cit.*

[10] J. ii. 410; J. iii. 435. She was the sister of the seṭṭhi of Rājagaha. SA. i 240.

[11] J. ii. 347.

[12] See *s.v.* Kāla.

her failure in finding a husband, she refused to eat and died; she was reborn in Tusita.[13]

The *Bhadraghaṭa Jātaka*[14] tells us of a nephew of Anāthapiṇḍika who squandered his inheritance of forty crores. His uncle gave him first one thousand and then another five hundred with which to trade. This also he squandered. Anāthapiṇḍika then gave him two garments. On applying for further help the man was taken by the neck and pushed out of doors. A little later he was found dead by a side wall.

The books also mention a girl, **Puṇṇā,** who was a slave in Anāthapiṇḍika's household. On one occasion when the Buddha was starting on one of his periodical tours from Jetavana, the king, Anāthapiṇḍika, and other eminent patrons failed to stop him; Puṇṇā, however, succeeded, and in recognition of this service Anāthapiṇḍika adopted her as his daughter.[15] On uposatha days his whole household kept the fast; on all occasions they kept the *pañcasīla* inviolate (J. iii. 257).

A story is told of one of his labourers who had forgotten the day and gone to work; but remembering later, he insisted on keeping the fast and died of starvation. He was reborn as a deva.[16]

Anāthapiṇḍika had a business village in Kāsi and the superintendent of the village had orders to feed any monks who came there.[17] One of his servants bore the inauspicious name of **Kālakaṇṇi** (curse); he and the banker had been playmates as children, and Kālakaṇṇi, having fallen on evil days, entered the banker's service. The latter's friends protested against his having a man with so unfortunate a name in his household, but he refused to listen to them. One day when Anāthapiṇḍika was away from home on business, burglars came to rob his house, but Kālakaṇṇi with great presence of mind drove them away.[18]

A similar story is related of another friend of his who was also in his service.[19]

All his servants, however, were not so intelligent. A slave woman of his, seeing that a fly had settled on her mother, hit her with a pestle in order to drive it away, and killed her.[20]

A slave girl of his borrowed an ornament from his wife and went with her companions to the pleasure garden. There she became friendly with a man who evidently desired to rob her of her ornaments. On discovering his intentions, she pushed him into a well and killed him with a stone.[21]

[13] DhA. i. 128 f.
[14] J. ii. 431.
[15] MA. i. 347-8.
[16] MA. i. 540-1.
[17] Vin. iv. 162 f.
[18] J. i. 364 f.
[19] *Ibid.*, 441.
[20] *Ibid.*, 248 f.
[21] J. iii. 435.

The story of Anāthapiṇḍika's cowherd, **Nanda,** is given elsewhere (*s.v.* Nanda).

All the banker's friends were not virtuous; one of them kept a tavern.[22]

As a result of Anāthapiṇḍika's selfless generosity he was gradually reduced to poverty. But he continued his gifts even when he had only bird-seed and sour gruel. The devatā who dwelt over his gate appeared before him one night and warned him of his approaching penury; it is said that every time the Buddha or his monks came to the house she had to leave her abode over the gate and that this was inconvenient to her and caused her to be jealous. Anāthapiṇḍika paid no attention to her warnings and asked her to leave the house. She left with her children, but could find no other lodging and sought counsel from various gods, including Sakka. Sakka advised her to recover for Anāthapiṇḍika the eighteen crores that debtors owed him, another eighteen that lay in the bottom of the sea, and yet eighteen more lying unclaimed. She did so and was readmitted.[23]

Anāthapiṇḍika went regularly to see the Buddha twice a day, sometimes with many friends,[24] and always taking with him alms for the young novices. But we are told that he never asked a question of the Buddha lest he should weary him. He did not wish the Buddha to feel obliged to preach to him in return for his munificence.[25] But the Buddha of his own accord preached to him on various occasions; several such sermons are mentioned in the Aṅguttara Nikāya: on the importance of having a well-guarded mind like a well-protected gable in a house[26]; on the benefits the recipient of food obtains (life, beauty, happiness, strength); on the four obliagtions that make up the pious householder's path of duty (*gihisāmikiccāni*[27]—waiting on the Order with robes, food, lodgings, medical requirements); on the four conditions of success that are hard to win (wealth gotten by lawful means, good report, longevity, happy rebirth); on the four kinds of happiness which a householder should seek (ownership, wealth, debtlessness, blamelessness).[28] Then again, on the five kinds of enjoyment which result from wealth rightfully obtained (enjoyment—experienced by oneself and by one's friends and relations, security in times of need, ability to pay taxes and to spend on one's religion, the giving of alms to bring about a happy rebirth[29]);

[22] J. i. 251.

[23] DhA. iii. 10 ff.; J. i. 227 ff.

[24] J. i. 95 ff.; he went three times says J. i. 226.

[25] DhA. i. 3.

[26] A. i. 261 f.

[27] Referred to also in S. v. 387, where Anāthapiṇḍika expresses his satisfaction that he had never failed in these obligations.

[28] These various tetrads are given in A. ii. 64 ff.

[29] A. iii. 45-6.

the five things which are very desirable but difficult to obtain (long life, beauty, happiness, glory, good condition of rebirth[30]); the five sinful acts that justify a man's being called wicked (hurting of life, etc.[31]); the inadvisability of being satisfied with providing requisites for monks without asking oneself if one also experiences the joy that is born of ease of mind (evidently a gentle warning to Anāthapiṇḍika[32]).

The Buddha preached the *Velāma Sutta* to encourage Anāthapiṇḍika when he had been reduced to poverty and felt disappointed that he could no longer provide luxuries for the monks.[33] On another occasion the Buddha tells Anāthapiṇḍika that the Sotāpanna is a happy man because he is free from various fears: fear of being born in hell, among beasts, in the realm of Peta or in some other unhappy state; he is assured of reaching Enlightenment.[34]

Elsewhere the Buddha tells Anāthapiṇḍika that it is not every rich man who knows how to indulge in the pleasures of sense legitimately and profitably.[35]

There is, however, at least one sutta preached as a result of a question put by Anāthapiṇḍika himself regarding gifts and those who are worthy to receive them[36]; and we also find him consulting the Buddha regarding the marriage of his daughter, **Cūla Subhaddā**.[37]

Anāthapiṇḍika died before the Buddha. As he lay grievously ill he sent a special message to **Sāriputta** asking him to come (again, probably, because he did not want to trouble the Buddha). Sāriputta went with **Ānanda** and preached to him the *Anāthapiṇḍikovāda Sutta*.[38] His pains left him as he concentrated his mind on the virtuous life he had led and the many acts of piety he had done. Later he fed the Elders with food from his own cooking-pot, but quite soon afterwards he died and was born in the Tusita heaven. That same night he visited the Buddha at Jetavana and uttered a song of praise of Jetavana and of Sāriputta who lived there, admonishing others to follow the Buddha's teaching.

In heaven he will live as long as Visākhā and Sakka.[39] Various incidents connected with Anāthapiṇḍika are to be found in the Jātakas. On one occasion his services were requisitioned to hold an inquiry on a bhikkhunī who had become pregnant.[40]

Once when the Buddha went on tour from Jetavana, Anāthapiṇḍika

[30] A. iii. 47-8.
[31] *Ibid.*, 204.
[32] *Ibid.*, 206-7.
[33] A. iv. 392 ff.
[34] *Ibid.*, 405 f., also S. v. 387 f.
[35] A. v. 177 ff.
[36] A. i. 62-3.
[37] DhA. iii. 466.
[38] M. iii. 258 f.; see also S. v. 380-7, which contain accounts of incidents connected with this visit.
[39] DA. iii. 740.
[40] J. i. 148.

was perturbed because there was no one left for him to worship; at the Buddha's suggestion, an offshoot from the Bodhi tree at Gayā was planted at the entrance to Jetavana (J. iv. 229).

Once a brahmin, hearing of Anāthapiṇḍika's luck, comes to him in order to find out where this luck lay so that he may obtain it. The brahmin discovers that it lay in the comb of a white cock belonging to Anāthapiṇḍika; he asks for the cock and it is given to him, but the luck flies away elsewhere, settling first in a pillow, then in a jewel, a club, and, finally, in the head of Anāthapiṇḍika's wife. The brahmin's desire is thus frustrated.[41]

On two occasions he was waylaid by rogues. Once they tried to make him drink drugged toddy. He was at first shocked by their impertinence, but, later, wishing to reform them, frightened them away.[42]

On the other occasion, the robbers lay in wait for him as he returned from one of his villages; by hurrying back he escaped them.[43]

Whenever Anāthapiṇḍika visited the Buddha, he was in the habit of relating to the Buddha various things which had come under his notice, and the Buddha would relate to him stories from the past containing similar incidents. Among the Jātakas so preached are: *Apaṇṇaka*, *Khadiraṅgāra*, *Rohiṇī*, *Vāruṇī*, *Puṇṇapāti*, *Kālakaṇṇi*, *Akataññū*, *Verī*, *Kusaṇāli*, *Siri*, *Bhadraghaṭa*, *Visayha*, *Hiri*, *Sirikālakaṇṇī* and *Sulasā*.[44]

Anāthapiṇḍika was not only a shrewd business man but also a keen debater. The Aṅguttara Nikāya[45] records a visit he paid to the Paribbājakas when he could think of nothing better to do. A lively debate ensues regarding their views and the views of the Buddha as expounded by Anāthapiṇḍika. The latter silences his opponents. When the incident is reported to the Buddha, he speaks in high praise of Anāthapiṇḍika and expresses his admiration of the way in which he handled the discussion.

During the time of Padumattara Buddha Anāthapiṇḍika had been a householder of Haṃsavatī. One day he heard the Buddha speak of a lay-disciple of his as being the chief of alms-givers. The householder resolved to be so designated himself in some future life and did many good deeds to that end. His wish was fulfilled in this present life. Anāthapiṇḍika is sometimes referred to as **Mahā Anāthapiṇḍika** to distinguish him from **Cūla Anāthapiṇḍika.**

41 J. ii. 410 f.
42 J. i. 268.
43 *Ibid.*, 413.
44 For details see under the respective names.
45 A. v. 185-9.

Anāthapiṇḍika Vagga.—The second chapter of the Devaputta Saṃyutta of the Saṃyutta Nikāya contains a series of verses spoken before the Buddha on various occasions by devas, the last of them being **Anāthapiṇḍika** (reborn in the deva world).[1]

[1] S. i. 51 ff.

1. **Anāthapiṇḍika Sutta.**—Similar to the *Anāthapiṇḍikovāda Sutta* (*infra*), but the greater part of this discourse is taken up with the words of consolation, courage and suggestion addressed by **Sāriputta** to the banker, and we are told that his pains were allayed. No mention is made of the advice not to cling to matters mundane, nor of the death of the banker almost immediately afterwards. Instead, it is stated that Sāriputta and Ānanda were given a meal from the banker's own cooking-pot and that they went away after thanking him. Ānanda reports to the Buddha the news of their visit, and the Buddha praises Sāriputta for his wisdom.[1]

[1] S. v. 380-5.

2. **Anāthapiṇḍika Sutta.**—The same as the above, but **Ānanda** is given as the admonisher and **Anāthapiṇḍika** is made to claim that he had not violated a single one of the obligations binding on a householder (*gihi-sāmīcakāni sikkhāpadāni*).[1]

[1] S. v. 385-7.

3. **Anāthapiṇḍika Sutta.**—Records a visit paid by **Anāthapiṇḍika** to the Buddha, who tells him of the five kinds of guilty dread (*pañca-bhayāni verāni*) which are allayed in the Ariyan disciple, and of the four limbs of the Stream-winner (*sotāpattiyaṅgāni*).[1]

[1] S. v. 387-9.

Anāthapiṇḍika-putta-Kāla Vatthu.—Story of the conversion of Anāthapiṇḍika's son **Kāla** (*q.v.*).[1]

[1] DhA. iii. 189-92.

Anāthapiṇḍikovāda Sutta.—Addressed by **Sāriputta** to **Anāthapiṇḍika** when he lay on his deathbed. It was an exhortation to him not to cling to mundane things. It is said that at the end of the sermon the banker wept aloud, never before having heard such a homily. Soon after, he died and was born as a deva, in which form he came to Jetavana and paid homage to the Buddha.[1]

In this sutta Sāriputta says that such sermons were not vouchsafed to the white-robed laity but reserved for the duly-ordained,[2] a statement sometimes quoted as evidence of an esoteric doctrine in Buddhism.

[1] M. iii. 258-63. [2] *Ibid.*, 261.

Anāthapiṇḍika makes a request that such suttas should also be preached to laymen because there are young men whose eyes are but slightly dimmed.

Anāthapiṇḍika-Seṭṭhi Vatthu.—Story of the goddess, guardian of Anāthapiṇḍika's gate.[1]

[1] DhA. iii. 9 ff.; for details see **Anāthapiṇḍika.**

Anāthapiṇḍikassārāma.—See **Jetavana.**

Anālaya Sutta.—The Buddha teaches the destruction of attachment and the path leading thereto.[1]

[1] S. iv. 372.

Anāsava.—A Pacceka Buddha found in a list of Pacceka Buddhas. He lived in **Isigili.**[1]

[1] M. iii. 70; Ap. i. 107.

Anāsava Sutta.—The Buddha teaches that which is free from āsavas and the way thereto.[1]

[1] S. iv. 369.

Anikadatta.—See **Anikaratta.**

Anikaratta.—Ruler of **Vāraṇavatī.** He came to **Mantāvatī** as a suitor for the hand of **Sumedhā,** but did not succeed in his quest, as Sumedhā became a bhikkhunī after having converted Anikaratta and his retinue[1] (*v.l.* **Anikadatta**).

[1] Thig. v. 462-515; ThigA. 272f.; Ap. ii. 512.

1. **Anicca Vagga.**—The second chapter of the Khanda Samyutta.[1]

[1] S. iii. 21-5.

2. **Anicca Vagga.**—The first chapter of the Saḷāyatana Samyutta.[1]

[1] S. iv. 1-6.

3. **Anicca Vagga.**—The fifth chapter of the same.[1]

[1] S. iv. 28-30.

1. **Anicca Sutta** (see also **Yadanicca Sutta**). Preached at Sāvatthi; all khandhas are impermanent.[1]

[1] S. iii. 21.

2. **Anicca Sutta.**—Preached at Sāvatthi, in reply to a monk's question.[1]

[1] S. iii. 21.

3. **Anicca Sutta.**—At Sāvatthi, preached in reply to **Rādha's** questions.[1]

[1] S. iii. 195.

4. **Anicca Sutta.**—Same as (3); desire for what is impermanent should be repelled.[1]

[1] S. iii. 199.

5. **Anicca Sutta.**—Same as (4).[1]

[1] S. iii. 200.

6. **Anicca Sutta.**—All the external senses are impermanent.[1]

[1] S. iv. 1-2.

7. **Anicca Sutta.**—The same. Personal senses, past, present and future, are impermanent.[1]

[1] S. iv. 3-4.

8. **Anicca Sutta.**—On the impermanence of external sense-perceptions.[1]

[1] S. iv. 5.

9. **Anicca Sutta.**—All is impermanent.[1]

[1] S. iv. 28.

10. **Anicca Sutta.**—All feeling, pleasant, painful and neutral is impermanent.[1]

[1] S. iv. 214.

11. **Anicca Sutta.**—The idea of impermanence, if cultivated, is beneficial.[1]

[1] S. v. 132.

1. **Aniccatā Sutta.**—The disciple who realises the impermanence of all khandhas has no rebirth.[1]

[1] S. iii. 44-5.

2. **Aniccatā** (or **Saññā**) **Sutta.**—The idea of impermanence, if cultivated, destroys sensual lust, lust for rebirth, ignorance and conceit.[1]

[1] S. iii. 155-7.

Aniccadhamma Sutta.—Desire for that whose nature is impermanent should be destroyed.[1]

[1] S. iii. 199.

Aniccā Sutta.—On the seven kinds of persons who are worthy of homage and of gifts.[1]

[1] A. iv. 13-14.

1. **Anitthigandhakumāra.**—The Bodhisatta, born as the son of a king of Benares. He hated the sight of women until he was seduced by a dancing-girl. He was banished from home together with the girl, and they lived in a forest-hut, where the girl tempted an ascetic and robbed him of his mystic power. The Bodhisatta, realising this, gave up the woman, and himself became an ascetic. The story is told in the *Cullapalobhana-Jātaka.*[1]

[1] J. ii. 329-31.

2. **Anitthigandhakumāra.**—Similar to the above, the story being called the *Mahāpalobhana-Jātaka.*[1]

[1] J. iv. 469-73.

3. **Anitthigandhakumāra.**—Another **Anitthigandha,** of **Sāvatthi.** He refused to marry unless a woman could be found rivalling in beauty an image which he had made. Envoys were sent out and, in **Sāgala,** they discovered a sixteen-year-old girl to answer to the desired qualifications. The marriage was arranged, but the girl, being very delicate, died on the way to the bridegroom's house. On learning the news of her death he was sorely grieved and gave himself up to despair. The Buddha, seeing his capabilities, visited his home and preached to him. At the end of the sermon he became a Stream-enterer.

The story in which this account is given is called *Anitthigandhakumāra Vatthu.*[1]

[1] DhA. iii. 281-4. Compare with this the story of the ***Kusa Jātaka.***

4. **Anitthigandhakumāra.**—A Pacceka Buddha. He was the son of the King of Benares. In a previous birth he had been a monk for 20,000 years, during the dispensation of Kassapa Buddha. His story is very similar to that of No. 3 above, the wife chosen being the daughter of **Maddava,** King of **Sāgala.** When the princess died, on her way to be married, the prince gave himself up to contemplation and became a Pacceka Buddha.[1] A stanza attributed to him is included in the *Khaggavisāna Sutta.*[2]

[1] SnA. 67 ff.; ApA. i. 126-7. [2] Sn. p. 6, v. 36.

Anitthigandhakumāra Vatthu.—See **Anitthigandhakumāra** (3).

Anidassana Sutta.—The invisible and the path leading thereto.[1]

[1] S. iv. 370.

Animitta Sutta.—Preached by **Moggallāna**; it records an occasion when he experienced unconditioned rapture of the heart (*animittacetosamādhi*).[1]

[1] S. iv. 268.

Animisa-cetiya.—The shrine built on the spot where the Buddha spent a week after the Enlightenment, gazing unwinking at the seat at the foot of the Bodhi tree, the seat of his great victory. It was to the north of the Bodhi tree.[1]

[1] J. i. 77.

Aniyata.—The third division of the Pārājikā of the Sutta Vibhanga.[1]

[1] Vin. iii. 187-94.

Aniruddha.—See **Anuruddha.**

Anivatta Brahmadatta.—A king of Benares; so called because he never left a thing half done. One day on his way to the park he saw a forest fire which made him wish to burn all his defilements. Later, he saw men catching fish; one large fish broke through the net and escaped. Wishing to escape himself, he left the world and later became a Pacceka Buddha.[1]

A stanza attributed to him is included in the *Khaggavisāna Sutta.*[2]

[1] SnA. i. 114-15; ApA. i. 159-60. [2] Sn. v. 62.

Anissukī Sutta.—A woman who is faithful, modest, scrupulous, not wrathful and rich in wisdom, will be reborn in a happy condition.[1]

[1] S. iv. 244.

Anīgha.—A Pacceka Buddha; occurs in a list of Pacceka Buddhas.[1]

[1] M. iii. 70; ApA. i. 107.

1. **Anīkaṅga.**—Son of **Vikkamabāhu II.** He was killed by **Vīradeva.**[1]

[1] Cv. lxi. 40.

2. **Anīkaṅga.**—Known as the Mahādipāda. In 1209 he killed the reigning Prince, **Dhammāsoka,** and reigned in Pulatthinagara for seventeen days. He was slain by **Vikkantacamūnakka.**[1]

[1] Cv. lxxx. 43.

Anītika Sutta and **Anītikadhamma Sutta.**—On the state that is free from ill and the path thereto.[1]

[1] S. iv. 371.

Anukampaka Sutta.—The five ways in which a resident monk shows his sympathy for his lay supporters.[1]

[1] A. iii. 263 f.

Anukevaṭṭa.—A brahmin, clever in stratagem. He was used by **Mahosadha** to defeat **Cūlaṇi-Brahmadatta** when the latter laid siege to **Videha.** Anukevaṭṭa pretended to be a traitor to his own people, and having won Brahmadatta's confidence, persuaded him to raise the siege and go back.[1]

[1] J. vi. 406-9.

Anugāra.—An eminent wandering ascetic. He is mentioned as living in the **Paribbājakārāma** in the **Moranivāpa** in Veḷuvana near Rājagaha. He was probably one of the company who was with **Sakuludāyi** when the Buddha came to visit the latter.[1]

[1] M. ii. 1.

Anuggaha Sutta.—Right belief is endowed with five advantages.[1]

[1] A. iii. 20-1.

Anujīvisamiddha.—A Damila chief, ally of **Kulasekhara.**[1]

[1] Cv. lxxvii. 33.

Anujjā (*v.l.* **Anojā**).—Wife of **Vidhurapaṇḍita.** She had a thousand sons whom she summoned to bid farewell to Vidhura when he went away with **Puṇṇaka.**[1] She is depicted as a brave woman.

[1] J. vi. 290.

Anutīracārī.—An otter who had a dispute with another otter, **Gambhīracārī,** about a fish. They appealed to a jackal, **Māyāvī,** and lost in the bargain, the jackal claiming the middle of the fish as the price of his arbitration, leaving only the head and the tail for the otters.[1]

[1] J. iii. 333 f.; DhA. iii. 141-2.

Anuttariya Vagga.—The third chapter of the Chakka Nipāta of the Anguttara Nikāya.[1]

[1] A. iii. 309-29.

Anuttarasaṅgāmavijaya (Dhammapariyāya).—One of the names by which the **Bahudhātuka Sutta** is known.[1]

[1] M. iii. 68.

1. **Anuttāriya Sutta.**—The six unsurpassables.[1]

[1] A. iii. 284.

2. **Anuttāriya Sutta.**—A detailed explanation of the above.[1]

[1] A. iii. 325 f.

Anudhamma Sutta.—The bhikkhu, who conforms to the Dhamma, should live in disgust for the body, feeling, etc.[1]

[1] S. iii. 40-1.

Anupada Vagga.—The second section of the Uparipaññāsa of the Majjhima Nikāya.[1]

[1] M. iii. 25 ff.

Anupada Sutta.—Preached at Sāvatthi in Jetavana in praise of **Sariputta's** learning and understanding. It is really a description of the perfect disciple who has risen to mastery and perfection in noble virtue, noble concentration, noble perception and noble deliverance. It contains psychological introspective analyses which are expanded in the Dhammasaṅgani.[1]

[1] M. iii. 25 ff.

Anupanāhī Sutta.—The woman who is not wrathful will be born in a happy condition.[1]

[1] S. iv. 244.

1. **Anupama.**—City where **Vessabhū** Buddha was born.[1] The Buddhavaṁsa,[2] however, gives the name of the city as **Anomā.**

[1] BuA. 205, 206. [2] xxii. v. 18.

2. **Anupama.**—Pleasaunce in Anupama where **Vessabhū** was born and where, after Enlightenment, he performed the twin-miracle.[1]

[1] BuA. 206.

3. **Anupama.**—Son of **Phussa** Buddha.[1] The Buddhavaṃsa[2] gives his name as **Ānanda.**

[1] BuA. 193, 194. [2] xix. 16.

4. **Anupama.**—Son of **Siddhattha** Buddha.[1]

[1] Bu. xvii. 15.

5. **Anupama.**—City where, in Anomārāma, **Atthadassī** Buddha died.[1]

[1] BuA. 181.

6. **Anupama.**—A brahmin village in the time of **Anomadassī** Buddha.[1]

[1] BuA. 142.

7. **Anupama.**—An ājīvaka who gave grass to **Sumana** Buddha for his seat.[1]

[1] BuA. 125.

8. **Anupama.**—Son of **Sumana** Buddha.[1]

[1] Bu. v. 23.

9. **Anupama.**—A banker, father of **Anupamā** (1).[1]

[1] BuA. 122.

10. **Anupama.**—A banker, father of **Anupamā** (2).[1]

[1] BuA. 125.

1. **Anupamā.**—Daughter of the banker **Anupama** (9), of the village of the same name. She gave a meal of milk-rice to **Anomadassī** Buddha just before his Enlightenment.[1]

[1] BuA. 142.

2. **Anupamā.**—Daughter of the banker Anupama (10), of the village **Anoma.** She gave a meal of milk-rice to **Sumana** Buddha just prior to his Enlightenment.[1]

[1] BuA. 125.

3. **Anupamā.**—See **Māgandiyā.**

Anupalakkhaṇā Sutta.—Diverse views are the result of want of discrimination.[1]

[1] S. iii. 261.

Anupādāya Sutta.—The holy life is lived with final emancipation, free from grasping, as its aim.[1]

[1] S. v. 29.

Anupiya (Anupiyā).—A township in the **Malla** country to the east of **Kapilavatthu.** In the mango grove there (the **Anupiya-ambavana**) the Buddha, having arrived from **Anomā** and having ordained himself, spent the first week after his renunciation, before going to **Rājagaha,** thirty leagues away.[1] He went there again after his return from Kapilavatthu, whither he had gone to see his relations, and large numbers of Sākiyan princes joined the Order, including Bhaddiya, Anuruddha, Ānanda, Bhagu, Kimbila, Devadatta and their barber, Upāli.[2]

It was during this stay that the Buddha preached the *Sukhavihāri Jātaka.*[3] From Anupiya the Buddha went to Kosambī.[4] Near Anupiya was the pleasaunce where the paribbājaka of the **Bhaggava-gotta** lived. The Buddha visited him once while staying at Anupiya and it was then that he preached the *Pāṭika Sutta.*[5]

Anupiya was the birthplace of **Dabba Mallaputta.**[6]

Once when **Soṇa Poṭiriyaputta** was meditating the Buddha sent forth a ray of glory from the mango grove to encourage him.[7]

The mango grove belonged to the **Malla-rājās;** they built a vihāra therein for the Buddha's residence.[8]

The name is sometimes spelt Anopiya and Anūpiya.[9] See also *s.v.* **Anomā.**

1 J. i. 65-6.
2 Vin. ii. 180 f.; AA. i. 108; DhA. i. 133; iv. 127.
3 J. i. 140.
4 Vin. ii. 184.
5 D. iii. 1 ff.
6 ThagA. i. 41; the Ap., however, says Kusinārā (ii. 473).
7 ThagA. i. 316.
8 UdA. 161; DA. iii. 816.
9 J. i. 140.

Anupubba.—Seṭṭhi of Sāvatthi. He was so called because he engaged himself in a series of good works, each being of greater merit than the last, with the object of freeing himself from suffering. In the end he entered the Order, but finding the rules too numerous and irksome, he wished to return to the lay-life. His colleagues took him to the Buddha, who asked him to observe one rule only—guarding his mind; he agreed and became a Stream-enterer.[1]

1 DhA. i. 297-300.

Anubuddha Sutta.—Preached at **Bhaṇḍagāma,** on the importance of understanding.[1]

1 A. ii. 1 f.

Anumāna Sutta.—Preached by **Mahāmoggallāna** in the **Bhesakalāvana** at Suṃsumāragiri in the Bhagga country. It deals with the admonishing of monks and with self-examination. It is of interest to note that there is no reference to the Buddha throughout the discourse.[1] Buddhaghosa says that this discourse was known to the Porāṇā as the **Bhikkhu-pātimokkha,** and adds that this self-examination should take place three times each day.[2] The description of the evil-minded monk given in the sutta is often quoted.[3]

[1] M. i. 95-100. [2] MA. i. 294. [3] *E.g.*, Sp. iii. 612.

Anumānapañha.—One of the most famous chapters of the *Milinda Pañha.*[1] It deals with the problem of inferring the existence of the Buddha from facts known about him and connected with him. It also includes a description of the City of Righteousness—*Dhammanagara*—the Buddhist Utopia, and gives an excellent idea of city life at the time the chapter was written.

[1] 329-47.

Anura.—A general of the **Vaṅga** king's army, maternal cousin of **Sīhabāhu,** father of **Vijaya.** When Sīhabāhu left the lion's den with his mother and sister they came across Anura who was ruling the border country. Later Anura married Sīhabāhu's mother.[1]

[1] Mv. vi. 16-20; MṬ. 246.

Anurāja.—Son of **Sunanda,** King of **Surabhi,** at the time of Maṅgala Buddha. He visited the Buddha in the company of his father, and, having listened to his preaching, became an arahant.[1]

[1] BuA. 119-20.

1. **Anurādha.**—An Elder. Once when he was staying in a forest hut in the Mahāvana in Vesāli, near to where the Buddha was, certain wandering ascetics came to him and asked him whether or not a Tathāgata exists after death; dissatisfied with his answer they called him "fool" and went away. Thereupon Anurādha sought advice from the Buddha, who asked him "How, inasmuch as it cannot be said of a Tathāgata even in this very life that he really exists, can anything be said regarding him after death ?"[1]

[1] S. iii. 116-19; the same story is repeated, with slight expansions, in S. iv. 380-6.

2. **Anurādha.**—One of those that accompanied **Vijaya** to Ceylon. He later became one of his ministers and founded **Anurādhagāma.**[1]

[1] Mhv. vii. 43.

3. **Anurādha.**—A Sākiya prince, brother of **Bhaddakaccānā**; a great-uncle of **Paṇḍukabhaya.** He founded a settlement at **Anurādhagāma** and constructed a tank, to the south of which he erected a house for himself. Later he handed this over to Paṇḍukābhaya.[1]

[1] Mhv. vii. 43-4.

Anurādhagāma.—The name given to the settlement founded by the two Anurādhas. It was near the **Kadamba-nadī.**[1] The capital, **Anurādhapura,** was later founded near it.

[1] Mhv. ix. 9; x. 76.

Anurādhapura.—The capital of Ceylon for nearly fifteen centuries. It was built on the site of settlements started by the two **Anurādhas** on the bank of the Kadamba river, and was founded under the constellation Anurādha, hence the name.[1] **Paṇḍukābhaya** (394-307 B.C.) was the founder of the city, to which he removed the capital from Upatissagāma,[2] and there it remained up to the time of Aggabodhi IV. (A.D. 626-41). After a short period it became once more the capital, and continued to be so until the royal residence was removed elsewhere.[3] It was finally deserted in the eleventh century.

Paṇḍukābhaya beautified the city with the artificial lakes Jayavāpi and Abhayavāpi. It was round the last-named lake that the king laid out the city, including four suburbs, a cemetery, special villages for huntsmen and scavengers, temples to various pagan deities and residences for the engineer and other officials. Abodes were also provided for devotees of various sects, such as the Jainas, the Ajīvakas, wandering monks and brahmins. There were also hospitals and lying-in homes. Guardians of the city (*Nagaraguttikā*) were appointed, one for the day and another for the night.[4]

Paṇḍukābhaya's son and successor, **Muṭasiva,** laid out the beautiful **Mahāmegha Park** with fruit and flowering trees[5]; this was to the south of the city; between it and the southern wall of the city was another park called **Nandana** or **Jotivana.**[6]

In the reign of Piyatissa, who succeeded Muṭasiva (when Buddhism had been introduced into the land), the king, together with his nobles

[1] MṬ. 293; Mhv. x. 76; this tradition seems to have been forgotten later, for in the Mbv. (116) there is a suggestion that the city was so called because it was the dwelling of satisfied people (*anurodhijana*); or is this mere alliteration ?

[2] Mhv. x. 75-7.

[3] See Cv. xlvi. 34, where the new capital, **Pulatthinagara,** is first mentioned as a royal residence.

[4] For a full description see Mhv. x. 80-102.

[5] Mhv. xi. 2.

[6] Mhv. xv. 2, 11.

and people, erected many noble edifices in support of the new religion. Ten of the most noted were in Anurādhapura,[7] and the Mahāmeghavana, which was given over to the Buddhist Saṅgha, henceforth became the centre of Buddhism in the island. In this park was also planted, by Piyatissa, the branch of the Sacred Bodhi Tree which came from Gayā.[8]

Soon afterwards the city was taken by the Tamils but was recaptured by **Duṭṭhagāmaṇi** (101-77 B.C.), the hero of the Mahāvaṃsa. Many chapters of the chronicle are devoted to descriptions of the numerous buildings erected by him in Anurādhapura for the glorification of the national faith,[9] chief among them being the **Maricavatti-vihāra,** the **Lohapāsāda** and the **Mahā Thūpa.**

A few years later the Tamils once more overcame the city and held it till **Vaṭṭagāmaṇi** (29-17 B.C.) drove them off. In his reign was built the mighty **Abhayagiri Thūpa** and the vihāra attached to it.[10]

The subsequent history of the city is a record of how succeeding kings repaired, added to, or beautified, these various monuments and the steps they took for their preservation. The only later monument of real importance is the **Jetavanārāma** built by King **Mahāsena**[11] (A.D. 334-61).

About this time the fame of Anurādhapura as the chief centre of Buddhist culture attracted many visitors from abroad in search of learning. The most famous of these was the great commentator **Buddhaghosa.**[12] It was also during this period that **Dhātusena** (A.D. 460-78) reorganised the water supply of the city and built the **Kālavāpi.**[13]

From this time onward the country suffered from a series of dynastic intrigues and civil wars, each party appealing to the Tamils of South India for help and protection. As a result, the district round Anurādhapura was overrun by Tamil freebooters and became impossible to defend; the seat of government was therefore removed to **Pulatthipura** about the beginning of the ninth century, where it continued, except for a brief interval to the eleventh century. Finally, about A.D. 1300, at a date not exactly known, the whole district was abandoned, having become a kind of no-man's land; it then rapidly relapsed into jungle. For quite a long time, however, and even after Pulatthipura became the state capital, Anurādhapura was regarded as a centre of religious activity, and its monuments were restored from time to time.[14]

[7] For list see Mhv. xx. 17 ff.

[8] For details see Mhv. xviii. and xix.

[9] Mhv. xxvi.-xxxii.

[10] Mhv. xxxiii. 80-3.

[11] Mhv. xxxvii. 33 f.

[12] *Ibid.*, 215 ff.; also Fa Hien.

[13] *Ibid.*, xxxviii. 42.

[14] Mhv. lxxvi. 106-20; lxxviii. 96 f.; lxxxviii. 80 f.

Various scraps of information regarding Anurādhapura and its inhabitants are found scattered in the commentaries.[15]

It was famous throughout Jambudīpa for its virtuous monks, and men came from there to visit them.[16]

The city wall, which existed at the time the Mahāvaṃsa was written, had been built by King **Vasabha**[17], and was, according to the Ṭikā,[18] eighteen cubits in height.

[15] *E.g.*, that it had two *indakhīlas* (Sp. iii. 299); its main street ran from Thūpārāma, where the chief entrance to the city lay (UdA. 238; DA. ii. 573).

[16] *E.g.*, the brahmin who came from Pātaliputta to see **Mahānāga** Thera (AA. i. 384).

[17] Mhv. xxxv. 97,

[18] p. 654.

Anurārāma.—A monastery to the north of **Mahāgāma** in South Ceylon, built by King **Vasabha,** who also bestowed on it one thousand *karīsa* of land in the village of **Heḷigāma.**[1]

In **Vohāratissa's** time the Thera **Mahātissa** lived there.[2]

King Vasabha also built an uposatha hall for the vihāra.[3]

[1] Mhv. xxxv. 83; MṬ. 652. [2] Mhv. xxxvi. 30. [3] *Ibid.*, 37.

1. **Anuruddha Thera.**—First cousin of the Buddha and one of his most eminent disciples. He was the son of the Sākyan **Amitodana** and brother of **Mahānāma.** When members of other Sākyan families had joined the Order of their distinguished kinsman, Mahānāma was grieved that none had gone forth from his own. He therefore suggested to his brother that one of them should leave household life. Anuruddha was at first reluctant to agree, for he had been reared most delicately and luxuriously, dwelling in a different house for each season, surrounded by dancers and mimes. But on hearing from Mahānāma of the endless round of household cares he agreed to go. He could not, however, get his mother's consent until he persuaded his cousin **Bhaddiya** to go with him. Together they went with Ānanda, Bhagu, Kimbila, Devadatta and their barber Upāli, to the Blessed One at the **Anupiya** Mango Grove and were ordained. Before the rainy season was over Anuruddha acquired the *dibbacakkhu*,[1] and he was later ranked foremost among those who had obtained this attainment.[2]

He then received from **Sāriputta,** as topic of meditation, the eight thoughts of a great man.[3] He went into the **Pācīnavaṃsadāya** in the Ceṭi country to practise these. He mastered seven, but could not learn the eighth. The Buddha, being aware of this, visited him and taught

[1] Vin. ii. 180-3; Mtu. iii. 177 f.

[2] A. i. 23.

[3] The list is given in A. iv. 228 ff. Another conversation he had with Sāriputta before becoming an arahant is reported in A. i. 281-2.

it to him. Thereupon Anuruddha developed insight and realised arahantship in the highest grade.[4]

Anuruddha appears in the suttas as an affectionate and loyal comrade-bhikkhu, full of affection to his kinsman, the Buddha, who returned his love. In the assembly he stood near the Buddha.[5] When the Buddha, disgusted with the quarrels of the Kosambī monks, went away to seek more congenial surroundings, it was to Pācīnavaṃsadāya that he repaired, where were Anuruddha, **Nandiya** and **Kimbila.** The *Upakkilesa Sutta* (M. iii. 153 f.), on the sweets of concord and freedom from blemish, seems to have been preached specially to Anuruddha on that occasion, for we are told at the end that he was pleased to have heard it, no mention being made of the other two. And again in the *Naḷakapāna Sutta* (M. i. 462 ff.), though a large number of distinguished monks are present, it is to Anuruddha that the Buddha directly addresses his questions, and it is Anuruddha who answers on behalf of them all. See also the *Cūḷa-* and the *Mahā-Gosiṅga* Suttas.

Anuruddha was present when the Buddha died at Kusinārā, and knew the exact moment of his death; the verse he uttered on that occasion is thoughtful and shows philosophic calm, in contrast, for example, with that of Ānanda.[6] Anuruddha was foremost in consoling the monks and admonishing them as to their future course of action. It was Anuruddha again that the **Mallas** of Kusinārā consulted regarding the Buddha's last obsequies.[7] Later, at the First Council, he played a prominent part and was entrusted with the custody of the Aṅguttara Nikāya.[8]

In one of the verses ascribed to Anuruddha in the Theragātha[9] it is said that for twenty-five years he did not sleep at all, and that for the last thirty years of his life he slept only during the last watch of the night. The same source[10] mentions an occasion where a goddess, **Jālinī,**[11] who had been his wife in a previous birth, seeing him grown old and grey with meditation, seeks to tempt him with the joys of heaven, but he tells her he has no need of such things, having attained to freedom from rebirth.

His death took place in **Veḷuvagāma** in the Vajji country, in the shade of a bamboo thicket.[12]

[4] A. iv. *loc. cit.*; AA. 108-9; Thag. 901.

[5] Bu. v. 60.

[6] D. ii. 156-7. On this see Oldenberg, *Nachrichten der Wissenschaften zu Göttingen*, 1902, pp. 168 f.; and Przyluski-JA. mai-juin, 1918, pp. 485 ff.

[7] D. ii. 160 f.

[8] DA. i. 15.

[9] 904; ThagA. ii. 72.

[10] Thag. 908; also S. i. 200.

[11] ThagA. ii. 73; this story is given in detail in SA. i. 225-6.

[12] Thag. 919. See also *Psalms of the Brethren*, p. 331, n. 1. I cannot trace the reference to Hatthigāma.

In Padumuttara Buddha's time he had been a rich householder. Hearing one of the monks declared best among possessors of the celestial eye, he wished for a similar honour for himself in the future. He did acts of great merit towards that end, including the holding of a great feast of light in front of the Buddha's tomb. In Kassapa Buddha's age he was born in Benares; one day he placed bowls filled with clarified butter all round the Buddha's tomb and lighted them, himself walking round the tomb all night, bearing on his head a lighted bowl.

Later he was reborn in a poor family in Benares and was named **Annabhāra** (lit. "food-bearer"). One day, while working for his master, the banker **Sumana,** he gave his meal to a Pacceka Buddha, **Upariṭṭha.** The banker, having heard from the deity of his parasol of Annabhāra's pious deed, rewarded him and set him up in trade. The king, being pleased with him, gave him a site for a house, the ground of which, when dug, yielded much buried treasure. On account of this great accretion of wealth he was given the rank of **Dhanaseṭṭhi.**[13]

According to the Dhammapada Commentary (i. 113), as a result of his gift to the Pacceka Buddha, Anuruddha never lacked anything he desired—such had been the wish he expressed. A charming story is related in this connection. Once when playing at ball with his friends he was beaten and had to pay with sweets. His mother sent him the sweets, but he lost over and over again until no more sweets were to be had. His mother sent word to that effect, but he did not know the meaning of the words "there isn't." When his mother, to make him understand, sent him an empty bowl, the guardian deity of the city filled it with celestial cakes, so that he should not be disappointed. Thereafter, whenever Anuruddha sent for cakes, his mother would send him an empty vessel, which became filled on the way[14] !

The Apadāna[15] mentions another incident of his past. Once, in Sumedha Buddha's time, Anuruddha, having seen the Buddha meditating alone at the foot of a tree, set up lights round him and kept them burning for seven days. As a result he reigned for thirty kappas as king of the gods, and was king of men twenty-eight times. He could see a distance of a league both by day and night.

On various occasions Anuruddha had discussions with the Buddha, and he was consulted by disciples, both monks and laymen, on points of doctrine and practice. In the Anuruddha Sutta[16] he goes with **Abhiya Kaccāna** and two others to a meal at the house of **Pañcakaṅga,** the king's carpenter. At the end of the meal the carpenter asks him the

[13] ThagA. ii. 65 ff.; Thag. 910; DhA. iv. 120 ff.

[14] See also DhA. iv. 124 ff.

[15] i. 35.

[16] M. iii. 144 f.

difference between that deliverance of the heart (*cetovimutti*) that is boundless (*appamāṇa*) and that which is vast (*mahaggata*). The discussion leads on to an account of the four states of rebirth among the brilliant gods (**Ābhā**), and in reply to the questions of **Abhiya Kaccāna**, Anuruddha proceeds to explain their nature. At the end of the discourse we find Anuruddha acknowledging that he himself had lived among these gods.

In the Saṃyutta Nikāya[17] he is mentioned as questioning the Buddha about women, how they come to be born in happy states and how in woeful purgatory. A similar inquiry is mentioned in the Aṅguttara Nikāya. Anuruddha had been visited by some **Manāpakāyikā** devas, who had played and sung to him and shown their power of changing their complexions at will. He comes to the Buddha and asks how women could be born among these devās.[18]

We find him[19] being asked by Sāriputta and Moggallāna about the *sekha* and *asekha* and about super-knowledge (*abhiññā*). In dealing with this passage the Commentary[20] states that Anuruddha used to rise early, and that after ablutions he sat in his cell, calling up a thousand kappas of the past and the future. With his clairvoyant eye he knew the thousandfold universe and all its workings.

The *Anuruddha Saṃyutta*[21] gives an account of a series of questions asked by Moggallanā on the *satipaṭṭhānā*, their extent, etc. Anuruddha evidently laid great emphasis on the cultivation of the *satipaṭṭhānā*, for we find mention of them occurring over and over again in his discourses. He attributes all his powers to their development, and admonishes his hearers to practise them.[22] Once he lay grievously ill in the Andhavana in Sāvatthi, but the pain made no impression on his mind, because, he says, his mind was well grounded in the *satipaṭṭhānā*.[23] Apart from his teaching of the *satipaṭṭhānā*, he does not seem to have found fame as a teacher. He was of a retiring disposition and never interfered in any of the monks' quarrels.

Mention is often made of Anuruddha's *iddhi*-powers. Thus, he was one of those who went to the Brahma-world to curb the pride of the Brahmā who had thought that no ascetic could reach his world.[24] The mother of the yakkha **Piyaṅkara**, while wandering in search of food,

17 S. iv. 240-5.

18 A. iv. 262 ff.

19 S. v. 174-6, also 299 f.

20 SA. iii. 183.

21 S. v. 294.

22 *Ibid.*, 299-306. He himself considered the dibbacakkhu as the highest attainment. Thus in the Mahāgosiṅga Sutta (M. i. 213) he declares it to be more worthy than knowledge of the doctrine, meditation, forest-life, discourse on the abhidhamma or self-mastery.

23 S. v. 302, but see DhA. iv. 129, where he suffered from wind in the stomach.

24 S. i. 145. The others being **Moggallāna, Mahākassapa** and **Mahākappina.**

heard him at night reciting some verses from the Dhammapada and stood spellbound listening.[25]

His iddhi, however, does not seem to have enabled him to prevent his fellow-dweller **Abhiñjika** from talking too much,[26] nor his other fellow-dweller **Bāhiya** from attempting to create dissension in the Order.[27] Among the Vajjians he seems to have been held particularly in esteem, together with Nandiya and Kimbila. A yakkha named **Dīgha** tells the Buddha how the Vajjians are envied by the inhabitants of the deva and brahma worlds on account of the presence of these distinguished monks in their country.[28]

In numerous Jātakas Anuruddha is identified with personalities occurring in the *Atītavatthu*. In several cases he is mentioned as having been **Sakka,** the *deus ex machina* of the story in question.[29] Elsewhere he is identified with different personalities: he was **Pabbata** in the *Indriya* (iii. 469) and in the *Sarabhanga* (v. 151); the king in the *Candakinnara* (iv. 288); one of the seven brothers in the *Bhisa* (iv. 314); the dove in the *Pañcūposatha* (iv. 332); **Ajapāla** in the Hatthipāla (iv. 491); **Sucirata** in the *Sambhava* (v. 67); **Pañcasikha** in the *Sudhābhojana* (v. 412) and the charioteer in the *Kurudhamma* (ii. 381).

Anuruddha's name occurs in several of the legends of the Dhammapada Commentary apart from those already mentioned. In the story of **Cūḷasubhaddā** it is stated that after the Buddha had visited **Ugganagara** at Cūḷasubhaddā's request and enjoyed her hospitality, Anuruddha was asked to stay behind at Ugganagara for her benefit and that of the new converts.[30] When the Buddha spent a rainy season in Tāvatiṃsa preaching the Abhidhamma, it was Anuruddha who kept the people on earth informed of his doings.[31]

In the Sumanasāmanera Vatthu[32] we are told how Anuruddha, having himself attained salvation, sought for his friend and benefactor of a past birth, **Sumana-seṭṭhi.** Sumana-seṭṭhi had been born near the Vindhyā forest as **Cūḷasumana,** son of Anuruddha's acquaintance **Mahāmuṇḍa,** and Anuruddha ordained him at the age of seven. The lad became arahant in the tonsure-hall.

According to the Peta Vatthu,[33] it was by virtue of a spoonful of food

[25] S. i. 209; SA. i. 237-8.

[26] S. ii. 203-4.

[27] A. ii. 239.

[28] In the Cūlagosiṅga Sutta, M. i. 210.

[29] Thus in the Maṇicora (J. ii. 125); Guttila (ii. 257); Ayakūṭa (iii. 147); Mahāsūka (iii. 494); Cullasūka (iii. 496); Kaṇha (iv. 14); Akitti (iv. 242); Sādhīna (iv. 360); Siri (iv. 412); Mahāsutasoma (v. 511); Sāma (vi. 95); Nimi (vi. 129); Mahāsumagga (vi. 329); Vessantara (vi. 593).

[30] DhA. iii. 471.

[31] *Ibid.*, 218 f.; SnA. (ii. 570), states that the Buddha went to Tāvatiṃsa at Anuruddha's request.

[32] DhA. iv. 120 ff.

[33] Pv., p. 27, vv. 58-60

given by him to Anuruddha that **Indaka** entered Tāvatiṃsa, and the same gift enabled him to surpass in glory **Aṅkura,** who had spent all his wealth in practising generosity.

Anuruddha had a sister, **Rohiṇī,** who suffered from a skin disease and, therefore, remained indoors; she would not see the Elder when he visited her relations. But he insisted on seeing her and persuaded her to sell her ornaments and build a resting hall for the Buddha and his monks. She later became a Stream-enterer and was reborn as Sakka's consort.[34]

In Mahāyāna books Anuruddha's name appears as **Aniruddha.** In the Lalitavistara he is mentioned as wearing the Bodhisatta's ornaments when the latter renounced the world. He is sometimes spoken of as a son of Dronodana.[35] According to the Dulva, it was Anuruddha who, finding Ānanda still *asekha*, got him turned out of the First Council until he became an arahant.[36]

[34] DhA. iii. 295 f.

[35] Thus, *e.g.*, Mtu i. 75; iii. 117. See Beal, *Records of Western World*, ii. 38 n. for meaning of Anuruddha.

[36] *Rockhill*, p. 151.

2. **Anuruddha.**—A Pacceka Buddha, to whom **Nanda** Thera in a previous birth offered a canopy of lotus flowers.[1]

[1] Ap. ii. 350.

3. **Anuruddha** (or **Anuruddhaka**).—One of the parricide kings of **Magadha.** He killed his father **Udayabhaddaka** and was himself slain by his son **Muṇḍa.**[1]

[1] Mhv. iv. 2-3; Mbv., p. 96; but see DA. i. 153, where Anuruddha is given as **Mahāmuṇḍa's** son and **Nāgadāsa's** father. In the Divyāvadāna (p. 359) Anuruddha's name does not appear at all in the list of Bimbisāra's successors.

4. **Anuruddha.**—Personal attendant of **Piyadassī** Buddha. It was in reply to his question that the Buddha revealed the future attainments of **Nigrodha** Thera[1] and of **Tissa** Thera.[2]

[1] ThagA. i. 75; Ap. i. 431.

[2] ThagA. i. 273.

5. **Anuruddha.**—Personal attendant of **Koṇḍañña** Buddha.[1]

[1] Bu. iii. 30; J. i. 30.

6. **Anuruddha.**—Author of the Abhidhammattha-saṅgaha, Paramattha-vinicchaya, Nāmarūpapariccheda and, perhaps, of the Anuruddha Sataka.[1] He was an incumbent of the **Mūlasoma** Vihāra and probably lived in the eleventh or twelfth century.[2]

[1] Gv. 61, 67; SdS. 64; Sās. 69.

[2] For details see P.L.C., *s.v.*

7. **Anuruddha.**—Teacher of **Mahāsumma** Thera. He once offered to the Saṅgha a bowl filled with ghee. The incident is mentioned in a discussion as to whether a bowl, that had been bought for a particular monk, could be used by the community of monks.[1] This bowl had been bought for the Elder, but it was used by the community and was, therefore, *kappiya*.

[1] Sp. iii. 698-9.

8. **Anuruddha.**—King of Rāmañña. He helped **Vijayabāhu I.** of Ceylon to re-establish the Order in Ceylon.[1] He is also called **Anorata** (*q.v.*).

[1] Cv. lx. 5-7; see, however, Geiger, Cv. trans. i. 214, n. 4.

1. **Anuruddha Sutta.**—Preached by Anuruddha Thera to **Pañcakaṅga,** the king's carpenter, at Sāvatthi, on the conclusion of a meal given by him to the Elder and three others. It explains the two kinds of emancipation of mind, the "boundless" and the "vast," and the results of developing them, which produce birth among the Brilliant Gods. **Abhiya-Kaccāna,** who was evidently one of Anuruddha's companions on this occasion, asks him the reason for the difference in degree of the brilliance of the gods; he is answered to his satisfaction.[1]

[1] M. iii. 144-52.

2. **Anuruddha Sutta.**—Records the incident of **Jālini's** visit to Anuruddha Thera, and her unsuccessful efforts to tempt him with the joys of heaven.[1]

[1] S. i. 200.

3. **Anuruddha Sutta.**—The Buddha explains to Anuruddha, in answer to his questions, why beings are born as women.[1]

[1] A. i. 281.

4. **Anuruddha Sutta.**—Two Suttas on how **Sāriputta** admonished **Anuruddha** to give up boasting about his attainments and concentrate on *amata-dhātu*, and how Anuruddha following the advice became an arahant.[1]

[1] A. i. 281-3.

5. **Anuruddha Sutta.**—On the eight thoughts of a great being (*mahā-purisa vitakka*).

Anuruddha had acquired seven of them and the Buddha paid him a special visit to teach him the eighth, which brought him arahantship. Later the Buddha repeated the sermon to the monks.[1]

[1] A. iv. 228 ff.

6. **Anuruddha Sutta.**—The Buddha explains to **Anuruddha** how women may be born among the *Manāpakāyikadevā.*[1]

[1] A. iv. 262 ff.

Anuruddha Saṃyutta.—The fifty-second section of the Saṃyutta Nikāya. It forms the eighth section of the Mahāvagga, and contains accounts of incidents connected with **Anuruddha,** his meditations in the Jetavana on the *satipaṭṭhāna* and the benefits of their development, his admonition to the monks on the banks of the **Sutana** River, his conversations with **Sāriputta** and **Moggallāna** in Sāketa and in the Ambapāli Grove, his sermon in the **Saḷalāgāra,** his illness while staying in **Andhavana,** and his accounts of how he came by his psychical powers, etc.[1]

[1] S. v. 294 ff.

1. **Anula.**—A Thera, incumbent of the **Koṭipabbatamahāvihāra** in Ceylon. He evidently possessed the celestial eye and, seeing how **Sumanā,** wife of **Lakuṇṭaka-atimbara,** had once been a pig, he expressed marvel that such things should happen. She heard his exclamation, and having learnt from him the story of that past life, she herself got the power of seeing her past lives.[1]

[1] DhA. iv. 50-1.

2. **Anula.**—See **Mahā Anula.**

Anulatissapabbata.—A vihāra in **Gaṅgārāji** in East Ceylon, built by **Kaniṭṭhatissa.**[1]

[1] Mhv. xxxvi. 15.

1. **Anulā.**—Daughter of **Muṭasiva,** King of Ceylon, and wife of **Mahānāga,** who was brother and sub-king to **Devānampiya-Tissa.** With five hundred other women she heard **Mahinda** preach the Petavatthu, the Vimānavatthu and the Sacca Saṃyutta, and together with the others became a Stream-enterer.[1] Later, hearing the sermon preached by Mahinda in the Mahāmeghavana, she, with others, became a Sakadāgāmī, and expressed to the king their wish to receive ordination. It was to enable these to be ordained that **Saṅghamittā** was sent for.[2] Until the arrival of Saṅghamittā, Anulā and her companions observed the ten precepts and lived in the **Upāsikā Vihāra.**[3] After her ordination Anulā became an arahant[4] and was the first woman arahant in Ceylon.

[1] Mhv. xiv. 56-7; Dpv. xi. 8; xii. 82.

[2] Mhv. xv. 18-19; Sp. i. 90 ff.; Dpv. xv. 73 ff.

[3] Mhv. xviii. 9-12. The Ṭīkā (p. 388) says they took on the *ekāsanikaṅga* vow as well; see also Mbv. pp. 121, 144, 167.

[4] Mhv. xix. 65; xvi. 41.

2. **Anulā.**—Widow of **Khallāṭanāga,** King of Ceylon, and later wife of **Vaṭṭagāmaṇi.**[1] When Vaṭṭagāmani had to flee from his enemies, she was the only one of his wives whom he took with him, because she was with child.[2] Later, when they were hiding in Malaya, under the protection of **Tanasiva,** Anulā quarrelled with the wife of Tanasiva and, as a result, Vaṭṭagāmani killed him.[3]

[1] Mhv. xxxiii. 35, 36. [2] *Ibid.*, 45. [3] *Ibid.*, 62 ff.

3. **Anulā.**—Wife of **Coranāga** and Queen of Ceylon for four months (in A.D. 12-16). She was a lewd woman and killed her husband that she might marry **Mahācūḷa's** son, **Tissa.** She soon got tired of him and poisoned him. Then, in succession, she had as husbands **Siva,** a palace guard; **Vaṭuka,** a Tamil carpenter; **Tissa,** a woodcarrier; the **Damiḷa Niliya,** a palace priest—all of whom she removed by poisoning. The last one she killed because she wished to live indiscriminately with thirty-two palace guards.

In the end she was killed by **Kuṭakaṇṇatissa.**[1]

[1] Mhv. xxxiv. 16-34; Dpv. xix. 50 ff.

4. **Anulā.**—The chief woman-disciple of **Kassapa** Buddha.[1]

[1] Bu. xxv. 40; J. i. 43.

5. **Anulā.**—Daughter of **Cūḷaseṭṭhi** of Benares. She lived with her husband in **Andhakavinda,** and after her father's death she fed brahmins in his name, but this pious act was of no benefit to him.[1]

[1] PvA. 105 ff.

6. **Anulā.**—One of the chief women-supporters of **Mangala** Buddha.[1]

[1] Bu. iv. 25.

Anulepadāyaka Thera.—An arahant. In **Atthadassī's** time he supplied plaster to a monk for carrying out some repairs to a building.[1]

[1] Ap. i. 251.

Anulomadāyaka Thera.—An arahant. He built a railing round **Anomadassī's** Bodhi tree and the Buddha expressed delight with it. As a result, in a later birth he became a king named **Sabbagghana** (*v.l.* **Sabboghana**).[1] He is evidently to be identified with **Mettaji** Thera.[2]

[1] Ap. i. 173. [2] ThagA. i. 194.

Anuvattanā Sutta.—Like a cakkavatti's eldest son, who, because of five qualities, administers the kingdom like his father, so does **Sāriputta** administer the Kingdom of Righteousness founded by the Buddha.[1]

[1] A. iii. 148-9.

Anuvindakā.—Name of a people, mentioned with hosts of others, as seeking and finding hospitality in the house of **Jatukaṇṇika,** when, in a previous birth, he was a banker in **Haṃsavatī.**[1]

[1] Ap. ii. 359.

Anusaṃsāvaka Thera.—An arahant. In a past birth he gave a spoonful of rice to the Buddha **Vipassī.**[1]

[1] Ap. i. 247.

1. **Anusaya Sutta.**—Preached to **Rāhula** in reply to a question asked by him as to how insidious tendencies (*anusayā*) could be got rid of.[1]

[1] S. ii. 252; see Rahūla Sutta (2).

2. **Anusaya Sutta.**—The holy life is lived for the uprooting of the *anusayā.*[1]

[1] S. v. 28.

3. **Anusaya Sutta.**—The five faculties (*indriyāni*), when cultivated, conduce to uprooting of *anusayā.*[1]

[1] S. v. 236.

4. **Anusaya Sutta.**—Concentration on breathing conduces to destruction of *anusayā.*[1]

[1] S. v. 340.

Anusayā Sutta.—On how the *anusayā* can be uprooted.[1]

[1] S. iv. 32.

Anusāsikā.—The name of the greedy bird in the *Anusāsika Jātaka.*[1]

[1] J. i. 429.

Anusāsika Jātaka (No. 115).—Preached at Jetavana regarding a gluttonous sister, who sought alms in quarters unvisited by other sisters. In order to keep these areas for herself she warned others of dangers lurking there. One day, while begging for alms, her leg was broken by a ram, and her secret discovered. The story of the past is of a greedy bird, which, after cunningly warning others against the dangers of the road in which she found food, is herself crushed to death by a carriage on that same road. The sister is identified with the bird.[1]

[1] J. i. 428-30.

1. **Anusissa.**—An ascetic. He was the chief student of the Bodhisatta **Sarabhaṅga,** who lived with him. He is identified with **Ānanda.**[1]

[1] J. iii. 463, 469.

2. **Anusissa.**—Probably the same as **Anusissa** (1). An ascetic and student of the Bodhisatta **Jotipāla,** who, in the latter part of the story, is identified with **Sarabhaṅga,** without any explanation being given. When various kings, together with Sakka, visited Sarabhaṅga to consult him on their doubts, it was Anusissa who, at the request of his brother-ascetics, introduced them to the Bodhisatta. Here, too, he is identified with **Ānanda.**[1]

[1] J. v. 133-40; 151.

Anusota Sutta.—On four classes of persons: those who go with the stream and those who go against it; those who stand fast and those who have crossed over.[1]

[1] A. ii. 5 f.

1. **Anussati Sutta.**—The six topics of recollectedness.[1]

[1] A. iii. 284.

2. **Anussati Sutta.**—A detailed explanation of the above.[1]

[1] A. iii. 312 ff.

Anūna.—The name used by the yakkha **Puṇṇaka** to hide from **Dhanañjaya** his real name, lest he should be mistaken for a slave. The word has the same meaning as Puṇṇaka.[1]

[1] J. vi. 273-4.

Anūpama Thera.—He belonged to a wealthy family of Kosala and obtained his name ("Peerless") because of his beauty. When he came of age, urged by the workings of his *upanissayakamma* (efficient cause), he left the world and dwelt in the forest, practising insight. For some time his mind wandered, but later he put forth great effort and became an arahant.[1]

Thirty-seven kappas ago he had offered flowers to a Pacceka Buddha named **Paduma.**[2] He is evidently to be identified with **Aṅkolapupphiya** Thera of the Apadāna.[3]

[1] Thag. vv. 213-14. [2] ThagA. i. 334-6. [3] i. 287.

Anūpiya.—See **Anupiya.**

Anekavaṇṇa.—A devaputta in Tāvatiṃsa, who, because of his good deeds, excelled even Sakka in majesty. When he appeared in the streets of Tāvatiṃsa, Sakka fled in shame.[1]

The Vimānavatthu[2] gives his past story which he revealed to **Moggallāna.** He had been a monk under **Sumedha** Buddha, but later, feeling disheartened, left the Order. When the Buddha died he was seized with repentance for having lost his opportunity, and paid homage to the Buddha's shrine and observed the precepts.

[1] DhA. i. 426-7.
[2] pp. 74-5; VvA. 318 ff.

Anekavaṇṇavimāna.—The abode of **Anekavaṇṇa-devaputta.**[1]

[1] Vv. 74-5.

Anejakā.—A class of devas mentioned as having been present on the occasion of the preaching of the *Mahā-Samaya Sutta.*[1]

[1] D. ii. 160.

1. **Anojā.**—Wife of **Mahākappina,** while he was king, before he entered the Order. She had been his wife in former births as well and had helped him in his good works. In this age she was of equal birth with Mahākappina and became his chief consort. She was so called because her complexion was the colour of *anoja*-flowers.

When Kappina made his renunciation, she and her companions followed him in chariots, crossing rivers by an act of truth (*saccakiriyā*), saying "the Buddha could not have arisen only for the benefit of men, but for that of women as well."

When she saw the Buddha and heard him preach, she and her companions became Stream-enterers. She was ordained by **Uppalavaṇṇā.**[1] In the Visuddhimagga it is said that Mahākappina was present when she heard the Buddha preach, but the Buddha contrived to make him invisible. When she asked whether the king was there, the Buddha's reply was "Would you rather seek the king or the self?" "The self" was the answer.[2]

[1] AA. i. pp. 176 ff.; SA. ii., pp. 178 ff.
[2] p. 393. The conversation on the "self" seems to have been borrowed from Vin. i. 23.

2. **Anojā.**—See **Anujjā.**

1. **Anotatta.**—One of the seven great lakes of Himavā.[1] It is surrounded by five mountain peaks, **Sudassanakūṭa, Citrakūṭa, Kāḷakūṭa, Gandhamādana** and **Kelāsa.** Sudassanakūṭa is concave, shaped like

[1] The others being **Kaṇṇamuṇḍa, Rathakāra, Chaddanta, Kuṇāla, Mandākinī** and **Sīhappapāta.**

a crow's beak and overshadows the whole lake, which is hidden also by the other peaks. The lake is 150 leagues long, 50 leagues wide and 50 leagues deep. All the rains that fall on the five peaks and all the rivers that rise in them flow into the lake. The light of the sun and of the moon never falls directly on the water but only in reflection. This means that the water is always cool, hence the name. Many bathing places are found therein free from fish and tortoises, with crystal clear waters, where Buddhas, Pacceka Buddhas and arahants bathe, and whither devas and yakkhas come for sport. Four channels open out of the lake in the direction of the four quarters: **Sīhamukha, Hatthimukha, Assamukha** and **Usabhamukha.** Lions abound on the banks of the Sīhamukha; elephants, horses and cattle respectively on the others. Four rivers flow from these channels; the eastward river encircles the lake three times, waters the non-human regions of Himavā and enters the ocean. The rivers that flow north and westward flow in those directions through regions inhabited by non-humans and also enter the ocean. The southward river, like the eastward, flows three times round the lake and then straight south over a rocky channel for sixty leagues and then down a precipice, forming a cascade six miles in width. For sixty leagues the water dashes through the air on to a rock named **Tiyaggala,** whereon by the force of the impact of the waters the **Tiyaggala-pokkharaṇi** has been formed, fifty leagues deep. From this lake the waters run through a rocky chasm for sixty leagues, then underground for sixty leagues to an oblique mountain, **Vijjha,** where the stream divides into five, like the fingers of the hand. The part of this river which encircles the original lake Anotatta is called **Āvaṭṭagaṅgā**; the sixty leagues of stream which run over the rocky channel, **Kaṅhagaṅgā**; the sixty leagues of waterfall in the air, **Ākāsagaṅgā;** the sixty leagues flowing out of the **Tiyaggala-pokkharaṇī** and through the rocky gorge is called **Bahalagaṅgā,** and the river underground, **Ummaggagaṅgā.** The five streams into which the river is divided after leaving the oblique mountain Vijjha are called **Gaṅgā, Yamunā, Aciravatī, Sarabhū** and **Mahī.**[2]

A wind called **Siñcanakavāta** (sprinkling wind) takes water from the Anotatta lake and sprinkles the **Gandhamādana** mountain with it.[3] The lake is one of the last to dry up at the end of the world.[4] To be bathed in the waters of the lake is to be thoroughly cleansed. Thus the Buddha's mother, on the day of her conception, dreamt that she had been taken to the lake and had bathed there. This was interpreted to mean that she would give birth to a holy son.[5]

[2] SnA. ii. 407; 437-9; MA. ii. 585 f.; AA. ii. 759-60.

[3] SnA. i. 66.

[4] A. iv. 101.

[5] MA. ii. 918.

During periods when the world does not possess a Buddha, the Pacceka Buddhas, who dwell in Gandhamādana, come amongst men and wash their faces in the lake before starting on their aerial journey for Isipatana[6] or elsewhere.[7] The Buddha would often go to Anotatta for his ablutions and proceed from there to **Uttarakuru** for alms, returning to the lake to have his meal and spend the hot part of the day on its banks.[8]

Examples are given of other holy men doing the same.[9]

There are many bathing-places in the lake; those for the Buddhas, Pacceka Buddhas, monks, ascetics, the Four Regent gods and other inhabitants of the deva-worlds, and for the goddesses, were all separate from each other. In the bathing-place of the goddesses there once arose a dispute between **Kālakaṇṇī** and **Sirī** as to which should bathe first.[10] Other instances are given of goddesses bathing in the lake and resting on the banks of the **Manosilātala** next to it.[11]

It was considered the summit of *iddhi*-power to be able to obtain water from Anotatta. Thus, when the Buddha wished to make known the great powers of **Sumana-Sāmanera,** he expressed a desire to have water fetched from the lake in which to wash his feet; no one was willing or able to fetch it except the novice Sumana.[12] And **Soṇa,** to show his *iddhi* to the 101 kings who escorted his brother **Nanda** to his hermitage, brought water from Anotatta for them and for their retinue.[13] To provide water from the lake for the personal use of some eminent person is considered one of the best ways of showing him esteem. Thus, when a friendship was established between the king of the swans, **Javahaṃsa,** and the king of Benares, the former brought the famous water from Anotatta to the king for his ablutions.[14] **Paṇṇaka,** the Nāga king of Anotatta, promised to supply water to Sumana-Sāmanera as amends for his earlier discourtesy[15]; and **Nanda,** when he wished to ask his brother's forgiveness for disobedience, thought it a good way of showing his repentance to bring him water from the lake.[16] This water had curative powers; **Anuruddha's** abdominal affliction was cured by its use.[17] To be able to use water from Anotatta daily was a great luxury and a sign of real prosperity. Gods brought to Asoka eight pingo-loads of lake water in sixteen pots for his use.[18] **Vessavaṇa** employed yakkhiṇis to

6 MA. i. 386.

7 *E.g.*, J. iii. 319, iv. 368.

8 *E.g.*, before his visit to Uruvelakassapa (Vin. i. 28); and again during the three months he spent in Tāvatiṃsa (DhA. iii. 222); see also J. i. 80.

9 *E.g.*, Mātaṅgapaṇḍita, J. iv. 379; see also DhA. ii. 211.

10 J. iii. 257 ff.

11 *E.g.*, J. v. 392.

12 DhA. iv. 134 ff.

13 J. v. 320-1.

14 J. iv. 213.

15 DhA. iv. 134. Also ThagA. 457, where the story is given in detail.

16 J. v. 314.

17 DhA. iv. 129.

18 Sp. i. 42; Mhv. v. 24; 84; xi. 30.

fetch water for him in turn, each turn lasting for four to five months. It was exhausting work and some of them died before their term of service was over.[19]

Regular assemblies of the devas and yakkhas were held on the banks of Anotatta, at which contests of skill took place.[20] Sometimes the Buddha would go there with a company of monks and preach or make proclamations.[21] Monks would often dwell there in meditation and come when summoned.[22]

A *mahā-kappa* is measured by reckoning the amount of time that would be required to empty the Anotatta lake, by dipping into it a blade of *kusa*-grass, and shaking out from it one drop of water once in every hundred years.[23]

Just as the water of Anotatta, having ultimately entered the ocean through the Ganges, would never turn back, so the Bodhisatta, in his last birth, would never turn back from his purpose of becoming Buddha for the sake of becoming a cakkavatti.[24]

The Divyāvadāna speaks of a class of devas who dwelt near Anotatta, whom it calls **Anavatapta-kāyikādevatā.**[25]

19 DhA. i. 40.
20 *E.g.*, among the daughters of Vessavaṇa, demonstrating their ability to dance (VvA. 131-2).
21 *E.g.*, Ap. i. 299.
22 Dvy. 399.
23 PvA. 254.
24 Mil. 286-7.
25 p. 153.

2. **Anotatta.**—One of the tanks built by **Parakkamabāhu I.** of Ceylon. A canal called the **Bhagīrathī** flowed from it.[1]

1 Cv. lxxxix. 49.

Anottappamūlakā-tīni Sutta.—Through an element (*dhātuso*) beings meet together, the indiscreet with the indiscreet, the untaught with the untaught, the unwise with the unwise and *vice versa.*[1]

1 S. ii. 163.

Anottāpī Sutta.—Records a conversation between **Mahākassapa** and **Sāriputta** in Isipatana. A man without ardour (*anātāpī*) and without care (*anottāpī*) is incapable of Enlightenment and Nibbāna.[1]

1 S. ii. 195 f.

Anodhi Suttā.—Three suttas on the development of unlimited reflection of *anicca, dukkha* and *anattā.*[1]

1 A. iii. 443 f.

Anopama.—Birthplace of the **Vessabhū** Buddha and capital of his father, King **Suppatīta.**[1]

[1] D.ii.7; but Bu. xxii.18 gives it as **Anoma.** The BuA. (p. 205) calls it **Anūpama.**

1. **Anopamā.**—Daughter of the Treasurer **Majjha** of Sāketa. She was so called ("Peerless") because of her beauty. When she grew up, all sorts of eminent men sought her hand with rich gifts, but she was unwilling to marry. She heard the Buddha preach and, meditating on his sermon, attained the Third Fruit of the Path. Later she entered the Order, and on the seventh day thereafter became an arahant.[1]

[1] Thig. vv. 151-6; ThigA. 138 f.

2. **Anopamā.**—See **Māgandiyā.**

1. **Anoma.**—Birth-city of **Vessabhū** (see **Anopama**).

2. **Anoma.**—A mountain near **Himavā.**[1]

[1] Ap. ii. 345.

3. **Anoma.**—A pleasaunce in **Khema** where **Tissa** Buddha was born.[1]

[1] BuA. 188.

4. **Anoma.**—An ascetic of great power, who lived in the time of **Piyadassī** Buddha. He gave a jewelled chain to the Buddha and offered him a meal of fruit. In the present age he became **Hemaka** Thera.[1]

[1] Ap. ii. 351-4.

5. **Anoma.**—A king of Jambudīpa, fifty kappas ago; a previous birth of **Bakkula** Thera.[1]

[1] Ap. i. 329.

6. **Anoma.**—A township in the time of **Sumana** Buddha; the residence of **Anupamā,** who offered the Buddha a meal of milk-rice.[1]

[1] BuA. 125.

7. **Anoma.**—One of the two chief disciples of **Anomadassī** Buddha.[1] He preached to **Sarada-tāpasa** on the occasion when the latter made up his mind to become an *aggasāvaka* himself.

[1] J. i. 36; BuA. 145; DhA. i. 88 ff. The Bu (viii. 22) calls him **Asoka.**

8. **Anoma.**—The personal attendant of **Sobhita** Buddha.[1]

[1] J. i. 35; BuA. 140; The Bu. (vii. 21) calls him **Anuma.**

9. **Anoma.**—An *ājīvaka* who gave grass to **Anomadassī** for his seat.[1]

[1] BuA. 142.

10. **Anoma.**—The city in whose park **Atthadassī** preached his first sermon.[1]

[1] Bu. xv. 18.

11. **Anoma.**—The birth-city of **Piyadassī** Buddha, and capital of King **Sudinna.**[1]

[1] J. i. 39. According to the Bu. (xiv. 15) it was called Sudhañña.

1. **Anomadassī.**—The seventh Buddha. He was born in the park **Sunanda** in Candavatī, his parents being **Yasavā** and **Yasodharā.** He lived in three palaces: **Siri, Upasiri** and **Vaḍḍha.**[1] His wife was **Sirimā** and his son **Upavāna.** He renounced household life at the age of 10,000 years, leaving home in a palanquin, and practised austerities for ten months. A maiden, **Anupamā,** gave him a meal of milk-rice before his Enlightenment, and the ājīvaka, **Anoma,** provided him with grass for his seat, his Bodhi being an *ajjuna* tree.

His first sermon was preached in the park **Sudassana** in **Subhavatī.** The Twin-Miracle was performed at **Osadhī** at the foot of an *asana* tree. **Nisabha** and **Asoka** (*v.*l. **Anoma**) were chief among his monks, and **Sundarī** and **Sumanā** among his nuns. Among laymen, **Nandivaḍḍha** and **Sirivaḍḍha** were his foremost supporters, and among laywomen, **Uppalā** and **Padumā.**

King **Dhammaka** was his royal patron; his constant attendant was **Varuṇa.** He lived to be 100,000 years old and died at **Dhammārāma.**

He held three assemblies at which were present 800,000, 700,000 and 600,000 respectively.

The Bodhisatta was a powerful yakkha-chief and entertained the Buddha and his following.[2]

It was a sermon preached by Nisabha and Anoma, the chief disciples of this Buddha, that made **Sarada-tāpasa (Sāriputta** in his last birth) wish to become an *aggasāvaka* himself. Later, **Sirivaḍḍha (Moggallāna),** at Sarada's suggestion, entertained the Buddha and wished for the post of second disciple under **Gotama.**[3]

Bakkula Thera was an ascetic in Anomadassī's day. The Buddha once suffered from an abdominal affliction and it was this ascetic who cured him.[4]

It is said that at Anomadassī's birth seven kinds of jewels rained down

[1] **Sirivaḍḍha,** according to BuA.

[2] Bu. x.; BuA. 141-6.

[3] DhA. i. 88-94.

[4] AA. i. 169; Mil. 216.

from the sky and that this was the reason for his name. From the time of his conception the aura of his body spread round him to a distance of eighty hands.[5]

[5] BuA. 141.

2. **Anomadassī.**—An ascetic who gave grass for his seat to **Sikhī** Buddha.[1]

[1] BuA. 201.

3. **Anomadassī.**—A Saṅgharāja of Ceylon, at whose request the *Hatthavanagalla-Vihāra-Vaṃsa* was written.[1] He was the author of a Sinhalese work on astrology, the *Daivajña-kāma-dhenu*, and he is generally identified with the Elder for whom, according to the Cūlavaṃsa,[2] **Patirājadeva,** minister to Parakkamabāhu II., built in **Hatthavanaggalla,** following the king's orders, a temple of three storeys and a lofty pinnacle.

[1] D'Alwis' edition, p. 7, n. 6.

[2] lxxxviii. vv. 37-9; see also P.L.C., 219.

4. **Anomadassī.**—An Elder of Ceylon, at whose request a pupil of **Ānanda Vanaratana** wrote a commentary called *Sāratthasamuccaya* on four Bhānavāras of the Tipiṭaka.[1]

[1] P.L.C., 227. The work has now been published in the Simon Hewavitarana Bequest Series (Colombo), vol. xxvii. For a discussion on this Anomadassī see the Introduction, p. x-xi.

Anomasatta.—An epithet of the Buddha.[1]

[1] UdA. 304; KhA. 170.

1. **Anomā.**—A river thirty leagues to the east of **Kapilavatthu,** where **Gotama** went after leaving home.[1] It was eight *usabhas* in breadth, but **Kanthaka** cleared it in one leap. It was here that Gotama cut off his hair and beard and put on the orange garments of the ascetics, brought to him by the Brahmā **Ghaṭikāra.**

On its banks was the mango grove of **Anupiya.**[2] Three kingdoms lay between it and Kapilavatthu.[3] From the river to **Rājagaha** was a distance of thirty leagues, which Gotama took seven days to walk.[4] It took him a whole night to ride from Kapilavatthu to Anomā.[5]

[1] According to the *Lalita Vistara*, the river was only six yojanas from the city, and Cunningham accepts this (p. 485 ff.).

[2] J. i. 64 f.; SnA. 382.

[3] BuA. 5. The countries of the Sākiyans, Koliyans and Mallas; see *Expositor* i. 43 n., where Kapilavatthu, Devadaha and Koliya are mentioned as the three kingdoms.

[4] J. i. 65; SnA. 382.

[5] VvA. 314.

The name seems to have meant "Glorious," or "not Slight."[6]

Cunningham[7] identifies the river with the modern Aumi. He states his belief that the word means "inferior," to distinguish it from other and larger rivers in the neighbourhood, and that the original name in Pāli was Omā. According to him the confusion in names arose from a misunderstanding of **Channa's** reply. It is difficult to accept this suggestion because evidently, according to the tradition quoted in the Jātaka commentary and elsewhere, the name of the river was taken as a good augury for the accomplishment of Gotama's desires.

Thomas,[8] on the other hand, suggests that Anomā did not necessarily really exist. There was possibly an actual locality to the east of Kapilavatthu traditionally associated with Gotama's flight. It was probably near Anupiya of the Malla country, and the names given to it, such as **Anomā, Anomiya, Anuvaniya, Anumaniya,** were corruptions of Anupiya in the popular dialects of the neighbourhood.[9]

[6] See J. i. 65, where Gotama asks Channa the name of the river and Channa replies "It is Anoma (glorious)." "Good," says Gotama, "my renunciation shall also be *anomā*." The Burmese name is Anauma (Bigandet. p. 41).

[7] p. 486 ff.; in the Sutta Nipāta (vv. 153, 177) and again in the Saṃyutta (i. 33) the Buddha is spoken of as Anomanāma. Buddhaghosa (SA. i. 67) explains this as meaning having no "defect," endowed with perfection (*sabbaguṇasamannāgatattā avekalla-nāmaṃ; paripūranāmaṃ*).

[8] *Loc cit.*, p. 61 and n. 1.

[9] The Mahāvastu does not mention a river; it only mentions a town, **Anomiya,** twelve leagues from Kapilavatthu. The names **Anuvaineya** and **Maneya** occur in the Lalitavistara.

2. **Anomā.**—Mother of **Nārada** Buddha.[1]

[1] Bu. x. 18; J. i. 37.

1. **Anomārāma.**—A pleasaunce in **Anupama. Atthadassī** Buddha died there.[1]

[1] Bu. xv. 26.

2. **Anomārāma.**—A pleasaunce in the city of **Kañcanavelu. Siddattha** Buddha died there.[1]

[1] Bu. xvii. 24; BuA. 188.

Anomiya Sutta.—Contains verses in praise of the Buddha who is called the Peerless (*Anomanāma*).[1] The verses are found also in the Sutta Nipāta.[2]

[1] S. i. 33.

[2] Sn., p. 177.

Anorata.—The name by which **Anuruddha** (Anawrata), King of Burma (**Ramañña**), is generally known. He was a religious reformer and was helped in his task by a Talaing monk, **Arahanta.**[1]

[1] Bode: *Pāli Lit. of Burma*, pp. 11-13.

Anta Jātaka (No. 295).—Preached at Veḷuvana regarding **Devadatta** and **Kokālika,** who were going about singing each other's praises in order to obtain followers. The story of the past is of a jackal who was eating the carcase of a bull. A crow, seeing him, flattered him, hoping to get some of the flesh. The jackal and the crow were Devadatta and Kokālika respectively.[1]

[1] J. ii. 440-1.

Anta Vagga.—The first chapter of the Uparipaññāsaka of the Khanda Saṃyutta of the Saṃyutta Nikāya.[1]

[1] S. iii. 157 ff.

Anta Sutta.—The Buddha teaches the end, as well as the way thereto.[1] See also *Antā Sutta.*

[1] S. iv. 373.

Antaka.—See **Māra.**

Antaramegiri.—A monastery built by King **Dhātusena.**[1]

[1] Cv. xxxviii. 48.

Antaravaḍḍhamāna.—A mountain in Ceylon. A story connected with it is given in the Saṃyutta Commentary.[1] A farmer, who had taken the precepts from **Piṅgala Buddharakkhita** of **Ambariyavihāra,** lost a bull while ploughing. In looking for it he came to this mountain, where he was seized by a large snake. He was strongly tempted to kill the snake, but honouring his vows, he refrained. The snake left him. *v.l.* **Uttaravad°.**

[1] SA. ii. 112-13; DhsA. 103.

Antaraviṭṭhi.—One of the villages given by **Vijayabāhu I.** to the **Lābhavāsī** monks. It was situated in Rājaraṭṭha not far from Pulatthipura,[1] probably between that town and Koṭṭhasāra. It is mentioned in an account of battles which apparently took place in the neighbourhood of Pulatthipura.[2]

[1] Cv. lx. 68.
[2] *Ibid.*, lxi. 46; lxx. 322; see also Cv. trans. i. 221, n. 4, and 229, n. 2.

Antarapeyyāla.—A section of the Nidāna Saṃyutta containing twelve suttas with abridged contents.[1]

[1] S. ii. 130 ff.

Antarasobbha.—A locality in Ceylon. It was here that **Duṭṭhagāmaṇi** subdued the Damila chief **Mahākoṭṭha.**[1]

Later, King **Manāvamma** built the **Devavihāra** at Antarasobbha.[2] The Majjhima Nikāya Commentary[3] mentions that **Maliyadeva** preached the *Mahāsaḷāyatanika Sutta* here, and that on that occasion sixty monks became arahants.

[1] Mhv. xxv. 11. [2] Cv. lviii. 4; [3] ii. 1024.

Antarāgaṅga.—A monastery in Ceylon to which **Jeṭṭhatissa III.** gave the village of **Cullamātika.**[1]

[1] Cv. xliv. 100.

Antalikkhacara.—A king who reigned thirty-two kappas ago; **Ākāsukkhipiya** Thera in a previous birth.[1]

[1] Ap. i. 230.

Antavā Sutta.—The origin of the view that the world is limited.[1]

[1] S. iii. 214.

Antā Sutta.—The four separate divisions: *Sakkāya*, its arising, ceasing, and the way thereto.[1]

[1] S. iii. 157-8.

Antureḷi.—One of the villages given by King **Aggabodhi IV.** for the maintenance of the **Padhāna-ghara,** which he built for the Thera **Dāṭhāsiva.**[1]

[1] Cv. xlvi. 13.

Antevāsī Sutta.—A monk dwells at ease without a pupil or a teacher, the pupil or co-resident (*antevāsī*) being the name given to evil and unprofitable states of mind which arise in him and abide in him through the senses. Such states are also called "teacher" (*ācariya*) because they beset and master him.[1]

[1] S. iv. 136-8.

Andu.—A village near Pulatthipura.[1]

[1] Cv. lix. 5.

Andha Sutta.—On the three classes of persons: the blind, the one-eyed, and the two-eyed.[1]

[1] A. iii. 128 f.

Andhā.—Mentioned in the Samantapāsādikā,[1] together with the Damiḷas, as being non-Ariyan (*milakkha*); the name is probably the same as **Andhaka(ā)** (*q.v.*).

[1] i. 255; see also VibhA. 387-8, where the Andhaka-language is mentioned. In Buddhaghosa's time the Vedas were taught in the Andha language also (MA. i. 113).

Andhakaraṭṭha.—See **Andhakā** (1).

Andhakavinda.—A village in the Magadha country, three *gāvuta* from **Rājagaha.** Between it and Rājagaha is the river **Sappinī,** which rises in the Gijjhakūṭa.[1] Once the Buddha went from Benares to Andhakavinda with 1,250 monks, and many people followed them carrying cartloads of provisions that they might feed them in turn. There were so many awaiting their turn that a certain brahmin (referred to as **Andhakavindabrāhmaṇa**) had to wait two months for his to come round. At the end of two months, finding that his own affairs were going to ruin and that there was no likelihood of his turn coming soon, the brahmin went to the provision-room to see what deficiency he could possibly supply. Seeing there neither rice, milk, nor honey-lumps, he approached Ānanda, and having, through him, obtained the Buddha's permission, the brahmin prepared a meal of milk-rice and honey-lumps for the Buddha and the monks. At the conclusion of the meal the Buddha spoke of the tenfold good qualities of milk-rice.[2]

During the same visit of the Buddha, a newly converted minister of the district prepared meat dishes for the fraternity, but being disappointed that the monks, who had had a meal of solid milk-rice earlier, could not eat large quantities of his dishes, he was rather rude to them. Later he expressed remorse, and the Buddha assured him that heaven would be his inheritance.[3] It was on the way back from Andhakavinda to Rājagaha that the Buddha met **Belaṭṭha Kaccāna.**[4]

Once when the Buddha was staying at Andhakavinda the Brahmā **Sahampati** came and lighted the place with his effulgent beauty till

[1] Vin. i. 109; Vin. Texts i. 254, n. 2.

[2] Vin. i. 220 f.; it was this praise uttered by the Buddha that made **Visākhā** ask him, as a favour, that she should be allowed to supply milk-rice to the monks throughout her life (*ibid.*, 293); see also UdA. 112.

[3] Vin. i. 222 f. This was the occasion for the rule that monks who have been invited to a meal in one place should not accept milk-rice somewhere else earlier in the same day.

[4] Vin. i. 224 f.

late at night; then he sought the Buddha and sang before him verses of exhortation meant for the monks, urging them to lead the holy life.[5]

Here, too, the Buddha mentioned to Ānanda the necessity of admonishing and encouraging new members of the Order with regard to five things: good conduct, control of the faculties of sense, abstinence from too much talking, love of solitude and the cultivation of right views.[6]

Once in Andhakavinda the Buddha suffered from disease of the wind. Ānanda was asked to obtain gruel for the complaint. The wife of the village physician supplied the gruel with great devotion, and as a result was born in Tāvatiṃsa, where her abode was known as the **Kañjikādāyika-vimāna.**[7] Another lay devotee built a Gandhakuṭi for the Buddha at Andhakavinda, and personally looked after the Buddha while he was there. This upāsaka was also, as a result, born in Tāvatiṃsa in a golden vimāna.[8]

Cūḷaseṭṭhi's daughter, **Anulā,** lived in Andhakavinda after her marriage and it was there that she gave alms on behalf of her dead father.[9]

[5] S. i. 154.
[6] A. iii. 138-9; referred to in Sp. iv. 789.
[7] VvA. 185-6.
[8] *Ibid.*, 302-3.
[9] PvA. 105-9.

Andhakavinda Brāhmaṇa.—See under **Andhakavinda.** His story is given as an illustration of how followers of the Buddha would often pursue him with manifold gifts.[1]

[1] *E.g.*, UdA. 112.

Andhakavinda Vagga.—The twelfth section of the Pañcaka Nipāta of the Aṅguttara Nikāya.[1]

[1] A. iii. 136-42.

1. **Andhakavinda Sutta.**[1]—Records the incident of **Sahampati** visiting the Buddha in **Andhakavinda** (*q.v.*).

[1] S. i. 154.

2. **Andhakavinda Sutta.**—Preached at **Andhakavinda** to **Ānanda** on five things regarding which new entrants to the Order should be admonished.[1]

[1] A. iii. 138 f.

Andhakaveṇhu.—Husband of **Nandagopā,** serving-woman of **Devagabbhā.**

The ten sons of Devagabbhā by **Upasāgara** were brought up as the children of Nandagopā and Andhakaveṇhu and later became known as **Andhakaveṇhudāsaputtā**[1] (*q.v.*).

[1] J. iv. 79-81.

Andhakaveṇhu-(dāsa)-puttā. Ten brothers, sons of **Devagabbhā** and **Upasāgara.**

As it had been foretold at Devagabbhā's birth that one of her sons would destroy the lineage of **Kaṃsa,** each time a son was born to her, fearing lest he be put to death, she sent him secretly to her serving-woman, **Nandagopā;** the latter had married **Andhakaveṇhu** and, by good fortune, daughters were born to her at the same time as sons to Devagabbhā; these daughters she sent to Devagabbhā in exchange for the latter's sons.

The ten sons were named **Vāsudeva, Baladeva, Candadeva, Suriyadeva, Aggideva, Varuṇadeva, Ajjuna, Pajjuna, Ghatapaṇḍita** and **Aṅkura.**[2] They had also a sister, **Añjanadevī.** When they grew up they became highway robbers, seizing even a present sent to their uncle, King Kaṃsa. Thus they became notorious as the Andakaveṇhudāsaputtā. The king, having learnt of their true descent, devised various plans for their destruction. Two famous wrestlers, **Cānura** and **Muṭṭhika,** were engaged to have a public wrestling match with them. The brothers accepted the challenge and looted several shops for clothes, perfumes, etc., to be used for the occasion. Baladeva killed both the wrestlers. In his death-throes Muṭṭhika uttered a prayer to be born as a yakkha; his wish was fulfilled and he was born as such in the **Kāḷamattiya** forest. When the king's men attempted to seize the brothers, Vāsudeva threw a wheel which cut off the heads of both the king and his brother the viceroy, **Upakaṃsa.**

The populace, terrified, begged the brothers to be their guardians. Thereupon they assumed the sovereignty of **Asitañjana.** From there they set out to conquer the whole of Jambudīpa, starting with **Ayojjhā** (whose king, Kāḷasena, they took prisoner) and **Dvāravatī,** which they captured with the help of **Kaṇhadīpāyana.**

They made Dvāravatī their capital and divided their kingdom into ten shares, forgetting their sister, **Añjanadevī.** When they discovered their mistake, Aṅkura gave her his share and took to trade.[3]

In course of time the brothers had many sons and daughters, the average human age at that time being 20,000 years. Later their sons annoyed the sage Kaṇhadīpāyana by dressing up a lad as a woman and asking him what child she would bring forth. "A knot of acacia wood," he answered, "with which will be destroyed the line of Vāsudeva."

[2] Cowell sees in this story the kernel of a nature-myth (Jātaka, trans. iv. 51 n.); *cf.* with this the Kṛṣṇa legend in the Harivamsa; see also Wilson's *Viṣṇu Purāṇa* (Hall's Ed.), v. 147 f.; and the article on Kṛṣṇa in Hopkins' *Epic Mythology*, pp. 214 f.

[3] Ankura's later history is found in PvA. 111 ff. See *s.v.* **Aṅkura.**

They laughed at the sage and kicked him. On the seventh day the lad voided from his belly a knot of acacia wood which they burnt, casting the ashes into the river. From those ashes, which stuck near the city gate, an *Eraka*-plant sprang up. One day, while disporting themselves in the water, the kings, with their families and followers, started a sham quarrel and plucked leaves from the *Eraka*-plant to use as clubs. The leaves turned into weapons in their hands, and they were all killed except Vāsudeva, Baladeva, Añjanadevī, and their chaplain, all of whom fled in a chariot. Thus were the words of the sage fulfilled.

In their flight they reached the Kāḷamattiya forest in which Muṭṭhika had been born as a yakkha. When Muṭṭhika saw Baladeva he assumed the shape of a wrestler and challenged him to a fight. Baladeva accepted the challenge and "was gobbled up like a radish-bulb."

Vāsudeva proceeded on his way with the others and at night lay in a bush for shelter. A huntsman, mistaking him for a pig, speared him; when Vāsudeva heard that the huntsman's name was **Jarā** (Old Age) he reconciled himself to death. Thus they all perished except Añjanadevī,[4] of whose later history nothing is mentioned.

In the *Kumbha Jātaka*[5] it is suggested that the Andhakaveṇhus were destroyed as a result of indulging in drink. This story was evidently well known to tradition as it is so often referred to.[6]

[4] J. iv. 79 ff.
[5] J. v. p. 18.
[6] *E.g.*, in the *Saṅkicca Jāt.* (v. 267) and in Vv., p. 58.

1. **Andhakā.**—Mentioned in a list of tribes that came to pay homage to **Jatukannika** Thera when he was born as a banker in Haṃsavatī.[1]

The **Andhakaraṭṭha** was on the banks of the **Godhāvarī** and near where **Bāvarī** lived. **Assaka** and **Aḷaka,** mentioned in the Vatthugāthā of the Parāyanavagga,[2] are described in the Sutta Nipāta Commentary as Andhaka kings.[3] In the Aitareya Brāhmaṇa[4] the Andhakas are mentioned together with the Pulindas, etc., as an outcast tribe. They again appear associated in the time of Asoka.[5] The Mahābhārata[6] places the Pulindas, the Andhas and the Sabaras in the Dakṣiṇapatha.

[1] Ap. ii. 359.
[2] Sn. 977.
[3] SnA. ii. 581; Vincent Smith places them originally in Eastern India between the Kṛṣṇa and Gōdāvarī rivers (*Z.D.M.G.* 56, 657 ff.); see also Burgess: *Arch. Reports on W. India*, ii. 132 and iii. 54. Cunningham: 603-607.
[4] vii. 18.
[5] Vincent Smith: *Z.D.M.G.* 56, 652 f.
[6] xii. 207, 42.

2. **Andhakā.**—An important group of monks that seceded from the **Theravāda.** They included as minor sects **Pubbaseliyas, Aparaseliyas,**

Rājagirikas and **Siddhatthikas.**[1] They were still powerful in Buddhaghosa's time.[2] The Andhakas are not mentioned as a special sect either in the Mahāvaṃsa or in the Dīpavaṃsa, though in the Mahāvaṃsa the sects spoken of above as offshoots of the Andhakas (Rājagiriyā, Siddhatthikā, Pubba- and Apara-seliyā) are given.[3] There were various doctrines held by all the Andhakas either in common with other sects or alone, and various other doctrines held only by some of the minor groups of Andhakas.[4]

1 *Points of Controversy*, p. 104 (extract from Kathāvatthu Cy.).

2 *Ibid.*, xxxiv.

3 Mhv. v. 12 f.; also the Mbv. 97. For a very valuable account of the different schools and their relation to each other, see *Points of Controversy*, pp. xxxv-xlv. About the Andhakas see particularly pp. xliii. ff.

4 For a summary of these see *Points of Controversy*, pp. xx-xxiv.

Andhakāra.—A village in Ceylon, one of the villages given by **Aggabodhi IV.** for the maintenance of the *Padhāna-ghara* built by the king for the Thera **Dāṭhāsiva.**[1]

1 Cv. xlvi. 12.

Andhakāra Vagga.—The second section of the Pācittiya in the Bhikkhunīvibhaṅga.[1]

1 Vin. iv. 268-71.

Andhakāra Sutta.—The ignorance of Ill, its arising, etc., is greater and more fearsome than the darkness of interstellar space (*lokantārika*).

1 S. v. 454-5.

Andhaṭṭhakathā.—One of the Commentaries used by Buddhaghosa.[1] It was handed down at *Kāñcipura* (Conjevaraṃ) in South India.

1 Sp. iv. 747.

Andhanāraka.—One of the villages given by **Aggabodhi IV.** for the maintenance of the *Padhāna-ghara* built for the Elder **Dāṭhāsiva.**[1]

1 Cv. xlvi. 13.

Andhapura.—A city in the **Seriva** country, on the bank of the river **Telavāha.** It was whilst doing business as a hawker here that the Bodhisatta, born as Seriva, crossed the wishes of another hawker, who in the present age was **Devadatta.** This was the beginning of Devadatta's enmity towards the Buddha.[1]

1 J. i. 111, 113.

Andhabhūta Sutta.—See **Aḍḍhabhūta Sutta.**

Andhavana.—A grove to the south of **Sāvatthi,** one *gāvuta* away from the city. It was well guarded and monks and nuns used to resort there in search of solitude. During the time of Kassapa Buddha, thieves waylaid an *anāgāmī upāsaka* in this forest; his name was **Sorata,**[1] and he had been touring Jambudīpa collecting money for the Buddha's cetiya. They gouged out his eyes and killed him. Thereupon the robbers all lost their sight and wandered about the forest blind; hence the name of the forest ("Blind," usually, but wrongly, translated "Dark"). It had retained its name during two Buddha-periods.[2]

There was a Meditation Hall (*padhāna-ghara*) built there for the use of contemplative monks and nuns.[3] Stories are told of those, particularly the nuns, who were tempted by **Māra** in the Andhavana.[4]

Once when **Anuruddha** was staying there he became seriously sick.[5] It was here that the Buddha preached to **Rāhula** the discourse (*Cūla-Rāhulovāda*) which made him an arahant.[6]

Among others who lived here from time to time are mentioned the Elders **Khema, Soma,**[7] and **Sāriputta**[8], the last-mentioned experiencing a special kind of *samādhi* (where he realised that *bhavanirodha* was *nibbāna*).

The Theragātha Commentary[9] records a discussion here between Sāriputta and **Puṇṇa** regarding purification (*visuddhikamma*). The *Vammikā Sutta*[10] was the result of questions put by an anāgami Brahmā, his erstwhile colleague, to **Kumāra-kassapa,** while he was in Andhavana.

Once bandits laid an ambush for **Pasenadi** as he went through the forest to pay his respects to the Buddha, attended by a small escort, as was sometimes his wont. He was warned in time and had the wood surrounded, capturing and impaling or crucifying the bandits on either side of the road through the wood. We are told that though the Buddha knew of this, he did not chide the king because he had certain reasons for not doing so.[11]

The Therī **Upalavaṇṇā** was raped in a hut in the forest by a young

[1] **Yasodhara,** according to the Samyutta Cy.

[2] The story is given in MA. i. 336 ff. and SA. i. 148.

[3] MA. i. 338.

[4] *E.g.*, **Āḷavikā, Somā, Kisāgotamī, Vijayā, Uppalavaṇṇā, Cālā, Upacālā, Sisūpacālā, Selā, Vajirā**; J. i. 128 ff. and ThigA. 64, 66, 163.

[5] S. v. 302.

[6] S. iv. 105-7; AA. i. 145.

[7] A. iii. 358.

[8] *Ibid.*, v. 9.

[9] i. 39.

[10] M. i. 143 ff.

[11] See SA. i. 131-2. Mrs. Rhys Davids doubts the authenticity of this story; KS. i. 127 n.

brahmin named **Ānanda,** and it is said that from that time nuns did not live in Andhavana.[12]

The Pārājikā[13] contains stories of monks who committed offences in the forest with shepherdesses and others, and also of some monks who ate the flesh of a cow which had been left behind, partly eaten, by cattle thieves.[14] It was here that Uppalavaṇṇā obtained the piece of cow's flesh which she asked **Udāyi** to offer to the Buddha, giving Udāyi her inner robe as " wages " for the job.[15]

The **Pārichattakavimāna**[16] was the abode which fell to the lot of a woman who having plucked an asoka-flower, while getting firewood in Andhavana, offered it to the Buddha.

The rule forbidding monks to enter a village clad only in their waist cloth and nether garment was made with reference to a monk whose robe had been stolen by thieves in Andhavana.[17]

[12] DhA. ii. 49, 52.
[13] Vin. iii. 28 ff.
[14] *Ibid.*, 64.
[15] The story is told in Vin. iii. 208-9.
[16] VvA. 172 ff.
[17] Vin. i. 298.

1. **Anna Sutta.**—All creatures desire food, so food should be given in charity.[1]

[1] S. i. 32.

2. **Anna Sutta.**[1]

[1] A. ii. 86 f.; but see GS. ii. 96, n. 1.

1. **Annabhāra.**—A well-known *paribbājaka* who lived in the Paribbājakārāma on the banks of the River **Sappinī** near Rājagaha. He is mentioned as staying with the well-known paribbājakas, **Varadhara** and **Sakuludāyi.** The Buddha visits them and talks about the four factors of Dhamma (*dhammapadāni*) which are held in esteem by everyone: not-coveting, not-malice, right-mindfulness, right-concentration.[1]

On another occasion they discuss the " brahmin truth." The Buddha visits them and tells them what he considers to be the brahmin truths (*brāhmaṇasaccāni*): that no creatures are to be harmed; all sense-delights are impermanent, painful and changing; all becomings are impermanent, etc.; a brahmin is one who has no part in or attachment to anything any more.[2]

[1] A. ii. 29-31.
[2] *Ibid.*, 176-7.

2. **Annabhāra.**—A former birth of **Anuruddha** Thera. His story is given in the account of the Elder.

1. **Annasaṃsāvaka Thera.**—An arahant. Four kappas ago he had given a meal to **Siddattha** Buddha.[1]

[1] Ap. i. 78.

2. **Annasaṃsāvaka.**—A second thera of the same name whose story is identical with the above and who is very probably the same person.[1]

[1] Ap. i. 261.

Anva Vagga.—See **Addha Vagga.**

Apagata Sutta.—Records a conversation between the Buddha and **Rāhula** in Jetavana. The Buddha explains how the mind is freed from notions of " I " and " mine."[1]

[1] S. ii. 253; see **Rāhula Sutta** (3).

Apacara.—A king of the first kappa. He was the son of **Cara** and reigned in **Sotthivatī-nagara** in the **Cetiya** country. He was one of the ancestors of the Sākiya race. He belonged to the race of **Mahāsammata** and was possessed of four *iddhi*-powers: walking on air, being guarded by four devas, diffusing the fragrance of sandalwood from his body and the fragrance of the lotus from his mouth.

When he was prince he had promised to appoint as his family priest his fellow-student **Kosakalamba,** brother of the royal chaplain **Kapila,** when he should become king. But when Apacara came to the throne, Kapila obtained the post for his own son and became an ascetic. When the king realised what had happened he offered to get the post back for Kosakalamba by means of a lie. The latter protested, because lies had hitherto been unknown in the world; but the king persisted in his desire even in spite of Kapila's warning, and seven times in succession uttered a lie to the effect that the post of chaplain belonged by right of seniority to Kosakambala and not to Kapila's son. At the first lie he lost his *iddhi*-powers and fell to earth, and with each succeeding lie he fell deeper and deeper into the earth until the flames of Avīci seized him. He was the world's first liar.

He had five sons, who sought Kapila's protection, and leaving the city founded five cities, which were called **Hatthipura, Assapura, Sīhapura, Uttarapañcāla** and **Daddarapura,** because of certain tokens connected with them.[1] According to the Sutta Nipāta Commentary (ii. 352) **Makhādeva** was his son. The king was a previous birth of **Devadatta.**[2]

[1] For details see under those names.

[2] The story is related in the *Cetiya Jātaka* (J. iii. 454-61; see also Mhv. ii. 2; DA. i. 258 f.; Dpv. iii. 5).

v.l. **Upacara, Upavara** and **Uparuvara.** The Milinda (p. 202) calls him **Suraparicara.**

Apaccakkhakamma Suttā.—Five discourses in which the Buddha explains to **Vacchagotta** how diverse opinions arise through want of clearness about the facts of body, feeling, perception, activities and consciousness.[1]

[1] S. iii. 262.

Apaccupalakkhaṇā Sutta.—Same as the above, only substituting "through not discriminating" for "through want of clearness."[1]

[1] S. iii. 261.

Apaccupekkhanā Sutta.—Same as the above, but substituting "through not looking into" for "through not discriminating."[1]

[1] S. iii. 262.

Apaṇṇaka Jātaka (No. 1).—Preached at Jetavana to **Anāthapiṇḍika** and his five hundred friends, who were followers of other schools. They had gone with the banker to hear the Buddha preach and became converts. But when the Buddha left Sāvatthi and went to Rājagaha they reverted to their old faiths, coming back to the Buddha when he returned to Sāvatthi.

The story of the past is of two merchants who travel with caravans across a desert. One, beguiled by goblins, throws away his drinking water and is devoured with all his people and cattle. The other completes his journey safely, not putting faith in the goblins. The moral is that the followers of false teachers are led astray. The foolish merchant was **Devadatta.**[1] This Jātaka will be among the last to be forgotten when the Dhamma disappears from the world at the end of the Kāliyuga.[2]

[1] J. i. 95 ff. [2] AA. i. 51.

1. **Apaṇṇaka Vagga.**—The eighth chapter of the Catukka Nipāta of the Aṅguttara Nikāya. It consists of ten suttas on various topics, including an extract from the *Mahāparinibbāna* Sutta and a sutta containing reasons why women are excluded from public assemblies and serious business.[1]

[1] A. ii. 76-83.

2. **Apaṇṇaka Vagga.**—The first section of the Ekanipāta of the Jātakaṭṭhakatthā.[1]

[1] J. i. 95-142.

1. **Apaṇṇaka Sutta.**—Preached to a gathering of brahmins in **Sālā.** On informing the Buddha that they had no favourite teacher in whom they had confidence, they were told that they should embrace and fulfil the Sound Doctrine (*apaṇṇaka-dhamma*), and the Buddha proceeded to explain it. In the course of this elucidation reference is made to the teachings of several other schools of thought, particularly those of the Jainas and the Ājīvakas, including the six Environments of life (*abhijāti*).[1]

The sutta concludes with the arahant-ideal as the height to be attained by the being who tortures neither himself nor others, and who is given to torturing neither himself nor others, but lives here and now beyond all appetites, blissful and perfected.[2]

[1] For a discussion of some of these see Further Dial. i. 293, n. 1.

[2] M. i. 400-13. For a derivation of the name see Weber: *Ind. Str.* iii. 150, and Kuhn: *Beitr.*, where the word is derived from *a-praśna-ka*. Buddhaghosa defines it as *aviruddha advejjhagāmi ekasaṅgāhiko* (MA. ii. 630).

2. **Apaṇṇaka Sutta.**—As sure as the cast of a true die (*apaṇṇakamaṇi*) are the results of failures or successes of *sīla*, etc.[1]

[1] A. i. 270.

Apaṇṇakatā Sutta.—On the three qualities which make a monk proficient in following the sure course (*apaṇṇakapaṭipadā*): guarding the senses, moderation in eating and wakefulness.[1]

[1] A. i. 113 f.

Apadāna.—The thirteenth division of the Khuddakanikāya. It is a Buddhist *Vitæ Sanctorum* and contains 547[1] biographies of monks and forty biographies of nuns, all mentioned as having lived in the time of the Buddha. In addition to these, there are two introductory chapters, the *Buddhāpadāna* and the *Paccekabuddhāpadāna*, dealing with the Buddha and the Pacceka Buddhas respectively. It is worth noting that the Buddhāpadāna contains no account of the Buddha's life, either as Gotama or earlier, as Bodhisatta (see, however, *s.v.* **Pubbakammapiloti**). Nor does the Paccekabuddhāpadāna contain any life-histories. The stanzas are what might be more appropriately described as *udāna*, and appear in the *Khaggavisāna Sutta* of the Sutta Nipāta.[2]

[1] The Cy. gives details of eleven more theras not found in the text: **Yasa, Nadīkassapa, Gayākassapa, Kimbila, Vajjiputta, Uttara, Apara-Uttara, Bhaddaji, Sivika, Upavāna** and **Raṭṭhapāla.**

[2] Cp. the *Mahāpadāna Sutta* (D. ii. 1 ff.), where the word Apadāna is used as meaning the legend or life-story of a Buddha or a Great One—in this case the seven Buddhas. Or does Mahāpadāna mean the Great Story, *i.e.* the story of the Dhamma and its bearers and promulgation : cp. the title of the Mahāvastu (Dial. ii. 3).

Most of the stories are found in the Paramatthadīpanī, the Commentary to the Thera- and Therī-gāthā, extracted from the Apadāna with the introductory words, "*tena vuttaṃ Apadāne.*" But in numerous instances the names under which the verses appear in the Paramatthadīpanī differ from those subjoined to the verses in the Apadāna. In several cases it is a matter of the Commentary giving a name while the Apadāna gives only a title.[3] Sometimes the stories are duplicated in the Apadāna itself, the same story occurring in two places with a very slight alteration in words, even the name of the person spoken of being the same. Most often no reason can be assigned for this, except, perhaps, careless editing.[4]

The Apadāna is regarded as one of the very latest books in the Canon, one reason for this view being that while later books like the Buddhavaṃsa mention only twenty-four Buddhas previous to Gotama, the Apadāna contains the names of thirty-five. It is very probable that the different legends in the collection are of different dates.[5]

According to the Sumaṅgala Vilāsinī,[6] the **Dīghabhānakas,** who included the Khuddaka Nikāya in the Abhidhammapiṭaka, did not recognise the Apadāna. The **Majjhimabhānakas** included it in the Khuddaka Nikāya, which they regarded as belonging to the Suttapiṭaka.

There is a Commentary to the Apadāna called the **Visuddhajanavilāsinī.**

[3] *E.g.*, **Usabha Thera** (ThagA. i. 320), called **Kosumbaphaliya** (Ap. ii. 449); and **Isidinna** (ThagA. i. 312), called (Ap. ii. 415) **Sumanavījaniya.**

[4] *E.g.*, Annasaṃsāvaka i Ap. i. 78 and again i. 261; see also the Introduction to the P.T.S. Edition.

[5] On these and other matters connected with the Apadāna, see Rhys Davids' article in ERE. and Muller's *Les Apadānas du Sud* (Congress of Orientalists, Leyden, 1895).

[6] i. 15. See also Przyluski: *La Légende de l'Empereur Açoka*, pp. viii f., 214.

Apadāniya Thera.—An arahant. Ninety-two kappas ago he had eulogised the life history (*apadānaṃ kittayissaṃ*) of the Buddha.[1]

[1] Ap. i. 241.

Apadika.—A river. **Vasabha** Thera, in a previous birth as the jaṭila **Nārada,** erected on its banks a cetiya in memory of the Buddha[1] (*v.l.* **Aparika**).

[1] ThagA. i. 258; Ap. ii. 437.

Apanthaka.—Given as a personal name in a passage where it is stated that names are mere designators, they signify nothing. Thus "Panthakas" (Guides) too lose their way, so do "Apanthakas."[1]

[1] J. i. 403.

Aparagotama.—See **Gotama** (3).

Aparagoyāna.—One of the four great continents into which the earth is divided. It is to the west of **Sineru** and is seven thousand yojanas in extent. It is surrounded by five hundred islands.[1] According to the Aṅguttara Nikāya,[2] each *cakkavāḷa* (world-system) has an Aparagoyāna. It is inhabited by men,[3] but they have no houses and sleep on the ground.[4] In the centre of the continent is a *Kadamba* tree, whose trunk is fifteen yojanas in girth and whose trunk and arms are fifty yojanas in length. This tree stands for a whole kappa.[5] When the sun rises in Jambudīpa, it is the middle watch of the night in Aparagoyāna; sunset in Aparagoyāna is midnight in Jambudīpa, and sunrise is noon in Jambudīpa, sunset in Pubbavideha and midnight in Uttarakuru.[6]

A *cakkavatti*-king first conquers Pubbavideha in the east and Jambudīpa in the south, and then sets out to win Aparagoyāna in the west and Uttarakuru in the north.[7] Thus King **Mandhātā,** having conquered Jambudīpa, journeys on with his retinue to Aparagoyāna and conquers it straight away.[8]

Puṇṇaka, in his play with **Dhanañjaya,** staked a jewel, by gazing into which the continent of Aparagoyāna could be seen.[9]

In this context the name given is **Goyāniya.**[10]

Some of the inhabitants came with Mandhātā from Aparagoyāna to Jambudīpa and settled down there. The country they colonised was called **Aparanta.**[11]

[1] SnA. ii. 443.
[2] i. 227; v. 59.
[3] KhA. 123.
[4] ThagA. ii. 187-8.
[5] DhsA. 298; AA. i. 264; Vm. 206.
[6] DA. iii. 868.
[7] Mbv. 73-4; BuA. 113.
[8] Dvy. 215.
[9] J. vi. 278; so also in the necklace mentioned in the *Hārapradāna Jāt.* (Mtu. ii. 68).
[10] So also in the Mahāvastu: **Aparagodānika, °godāniya** (ii. 159, 378, etc.). In the Dulva it is called **Aparagaudani** (Rockhill, 84).
[11] DA. ii. 482; MA. i. 484.

Aparaṇṇa.—A vulture who lived in **Gijjhapabbata.** He had a son **Migālopa,** strong and mighty, able to fly higher than his fellows. In spite of his father's warning, he flew too high and was dashed to pieces by the **Verambha** winds.

The Bodhisatta is identified with Aparaṇṇa.[1]

[1] J. iii. 255-6.

Aparantaka (Aparanta).—One of the countries to which **Asoka** sent missionaries after the Third Council. The leader of the mission was

Yonaka Dhammarakkhita.[1] He preached to the people the *Aggikkhandopamā Sutta* and 37,000 people embraced the new faith, a thousand men and even more women entering the Order.[2] The country comprises the territory of Northern Gujarāt, Kāthiāwar, Kachch and Sindh.[3] Probably Buddhism was known in Aparānta during the time of the Buddha himself.[4]

It is said that when **Mandhātā** brought all the four continents under his sway people from the three other continents came over to Jambudīpa and lived there. When the king died they found themselves unable to get back, and begged his minister to allow them to start settlements in Jambudīpa itself. He agreed, and the settlement of those who had come from Aparagoyāna was for that reason called Aparanta[5] (*v.l.* **Aparantaka**).

[1] Mhv. xii. 5; Dpv. viii. 7.

[2] Mhv. xii. 34-6; Sp. i. 67.

[3] Fleet *J.R.A.S.* 1910, p. 427; Bhandarkar in his *Early History of Dekkan* puts it in North Konkan (p. 23); see also Burgess: *Arch. Reports* ii. 131. According to Hsouien Thsang, the country seems to comprise Sindh, Western Rājaputāna, Cutch, Gujarat and a portion of the adjoining coast on the lower bank of the Narmadā. Cunningham · *Anct. Geog. of India*, notes, p. 690; and Law: *Early Geography* 56 ff.

[4] Dutt: *Early Hist. of Bsm.* p. 190; Dvy., pp. 45 ff.; but the reference is to **Sunāparanta.**

[5] DA ii. 482; MA. i. 184.

Aparantā.—Mentioned in a list of tribes.[1]

[1] Ap. ii. 359.

Aparaseliyā.—A sub-sect of the **Andhakā.** Their beliefs seem to have been similar to those of the **Pubbaseliyā.**[1] Their centre was **Dhanakaṭaka,** in the Andhaka country, somewhere near Kāñcipura and Amarāvati on the S.E. coast of India.[2] According to one tradition they were connected with the **Cetiyavādins.**[3]

[1] KvuA. quoted in *Points of Controversy,* pp. 5 and 104. See also Dpv. v. 54; Mhv. v. 12: Mbv. 97. For their beliefs see de la Vallée Poussin: *J.R.A.S.*, April, 1910, pp. 413 ff.

[2] *Points of Controversy,* xliii; see also Watters *On Yuan Chwang,* ii. 214 ff.

[3] For a discussion of this see *Points of Controversy,* xliii-iv.

1. **Aparājita.**—One of the Pacceka Buddhas mentioned in the *Isigili Sutta.*[1]

[1] M. iii. 70; also ApA. i. 107 and MA. ii. 890.

2. **Aparājita.**—A *cakkavatti* who lived seven kappas ago, an earlier birth of **Avyādhika** Thera.[1]

[1] Ap. i. 215.

3. **Aparājita.**—A householder of **Bandhumatī.** When his elder brother, **Sena,** left the world and became an arahant under **Vipassī** Buddha, Aparājita sought his advice as to how he could use his wealth to perform some act of great merit. He was asked to build a *Gandhakuṭi* for the Buddha, which he did, using all manner of precious metals and stones and surrounding it with various kinds of luxury, such as perfumed water. The chamber was on three occasions filled knee-deep with jewels to be taken by anyone who came to hear the Buddha preach. At the opening of the Gandhakuṭi, Aparājita entertained 6,800,000 monks for nine months. In this age he was born as the banker **Jotika.** In an earlier birth he had given sugar-cane to a Pacceka Buddha.[1]

[1] DhA. iv. 199-207.

4. **Aparājita.**—Nephew of the foregoing. He asked his uncle to let him have a share in the building of the *Gandhakuṭi*, but was refused. So he built an elephant stable next to it.

In the present age he was the banker **Meṇḍaka.**[1]

[1] DhA. iv. 203.

Aparādiṭṭhi Sutta.—A certain Brahmā thought that no recluse or brahmin could come to his world. To refute his views, the Buddha went there and sat in the air above the Brahmā, flames radiating from his body. The Buddha was followed by **Moggallāna, Mahākassapa, Mahākappina** and **Anuruddha.** The Brahmā was at first agitated by their presence, but later he was delighted on learning from Moggallāna, who was questioned by an attendant Brahmā, that there were many more disciples of the Buddha who could do as he and the others had done, and that they were holy men.[1]

[1] S. i. 144-6.

Aparika.—See **Apadika.**

Aparihāni Sutta.—There are seven things that decline not, viz., the seven *bojjhangas*.[1]

[1] S. v. 85; see also *ibid.*, 94.

1. **Aparihāniya Sutta.**—On the six things that lead away from ruin.[1]

[1] A. iii. 310; *cf.* A. iii. 329-30.

2. **Aparihāniya Sutta.**—A devatā visits the Buddha at Jetavana and mentions six things which lead away from ruin. The Buddha makes that a topic for a sermon to the monks.[1]

[1] A. iii. 330 f.

Apalāla.—A nāga king, converted by the Buddha. He is mentioned together with **Āravāla, Dhanapāla** and **Pārileyyaka.** The name appears in passages where the Buddha's powers are discussed.[1] "Was not the Buddha honoured even by beasts such as Āravāla, etc.?"

The story of the conversion of Apalāla does not, as far as I can discover, occur in the canonical books. In the Samantapāsādikā[2] the story of the conversion of Apalāla (*Apalāladamana*) is given among the stories not included in the Three Councils (*saṅgīti*), but that it was known quite early in Ceylon is evidenced by the fact that, among the scenes from the Buddha's life represented in the relic-chamber of the **Mahā-Thūpa,** the conversion of Apalāla is mentioned.[3] The Divyāvadāna[4] makes reference to the story, and states that the nāga was converted shortly before the Buddha's death. Hiouen Thsang gives the story in detail.[5] During Kassapa Buddha's time, Apalāla had been a powerful man called **Gaṅgi.** By means of his charms he subdued the dragons that attacked the country, and the people, in gratitude, agreed to give him tribute. Later some of them forgot their promise and he, in wrath, became a dragon after his death.

The Buddha Gotama visited him and preached to him. He was converted, but, for his sustenance, he was allowed to have one gathering of the crops every twelve years. It is for this reason that the White River (**Śubhavastu**) overflows every twelfth year. The story is found in the Sūtralaṅkāra and other Mahāyāna books.[6]

[1] *E.g.*, BuA. 29.
[2] iv. 742.
[3] Mhv. xxx. 84.
[4] pp. 348, 385.
[5] Beal: *Records of the Western World* i. 122; also Legge: *Fa Hien's Travels*, p. 29 n.
[6] See Nariman: *Sanskrit Buddhism*, pp. 194, 274.

Apalāladamana.—See **Apalāla.**

Apalokita.—See **Apalokina.**

Apalokina Sutta.—The Buddha teaches the undecaying and the path that leads thereto[1] (*v.l.* **Apalokita**).

[1] S. iv. 370. On the name see KS. iv. 262, n. 2.

Apassena.—A *cakkavatti* who lived six kappas ago; a previous birth of **Ārakkhadāyaka** Thera.[1]

[1] Ap. i. 215.

Apāyimha Vagga.—The ninth section of the Ekanipāta of the Jātaka.[1]

[1] J. i. 360-79.

1. **Apāra Sutta.**—The seven *bojjhaṅgā*, if cultivated, conduce to no more going to the hither or further shore.[1]

[1] S. v. 81. On the name see KS. v. 225, n. 3.

2. **Apāra Sutta.**—The same as above, regarding the four bases of psychical power (*iddipādā*).[1]

[1] S. v. 254.

Apāsādika Sutta.—Two discourses on the evils of being unamiable.[1]

[1] A. iii. 255-6.

Apilāpiya.—A *cakkavatti* of eighty-six kappas ago; a former birth of **Tikaṇḍipupphiya** Thera.[1]

[1] Ap. i. 202.

Aputtaka.—A wealthy burgess of Sāvatthi who died intestate. In the Saṃyutta Nikāya[1] we find **Pasenadi,** King of Kosala, visiting the Buddha at noonday and telling him that he had just finished having the banker's wealth removed to the royal coffers, " eight millions of gold to say nothing of silver." And yet Aputtaka ate nothing except sour husk-gruel left over from the previous day and wore only hempen garments.

In the next Sutta of the same Nikāya[2] the Buddha is reported as revealing the banker's past. In a former birth he had given alms to a Pacceka Buddha, **Tagarasikhī,** but later he repented and wished that he had given the food to slaves and workmen.

He had, in the same birth, slain the only son of his brother for the sake of his fortune.

As a result of the alms he was born seven times in the deva-worlds and seven times as a rich man of Sāvatthi. His repentance made him inclined to deny himself enjoyment of sense-desires. Owing to the murder of his nephew in his previous birth, he was childless in this, and he died intestate. After this life he was born in Mahāroruva purgatory.[3]

[1] i. 89-91.

[2] i. 91-3.

[3] The *Mayhaka Jāt.* (J. iii. 299 f.), contains the whole story of the banker's past and present, giving many graphic details not found in the Saṃyutta account, but it does not mention the seven births in heaven or in Sāvatthi. It adds that the king's men took seven days and nights to remove the treasure. Aputtaka is there referred to not as Aputtaka but as **Āgantuka** (Strange). See also DhA. iv. 76-80.

1. **Aputtaka Sutta.**—Contains the earlier part of the story of **Aputtaka** as given above, and the moral to be drawn therefrom: namely, that the

mean man, who acquires wealth, pleases neither himself nor others, but is like a lake of delicious waters lying in a savage region. On the other hand, the rich man who is generous is like a lake near a village.[1]

[1] S. i. 89-91.

2. **Aputtaka Sutta.**—Contains an account of **Aputtaka's** past, as related above; the wealth that a man stores here has to be left behind for others; hence let him make a good store for life elsewhere by using this wealth well.[1]

[1] S. i. 91-3.

Aputtaseṭṭhi Vatthu.—The story of Aputtaka given above.[1]

[1] DhA. iv. 76-80.

Appaṃ-supati Sutta.—The five kinds of persons who sleep but little.[1]

[1] A. iii. 156.

Appakā (or **Virata**) **Vagga.**—The eighth chapter of the Sacca Saṃyutta of the Saṃyutta Nikāya.[1]

[1] S. v. 468-70.

Appacintī.—A fish who lived in the Ganges with his brothers **Bahucintī** and **Mitacintī.** He and Bahucintī were caught in a fisherman's net and were rescued by Mitacintī.[1]

[1] The story is told in the *Mitacintī Jāt.* (i. 427-8).

Appaṭivāni Sutta.—By him who knows not birth and becoming, grasping, craving, feeling, contact, etc., there must be no turning back in the search for knowledge.[1]

[1] S. ii. 132.

Appaṭividitā Sutta.—Spoken by a deva; a Buddha has arisen, now is the time for those who have not perceived the truth to do so.[1]

[1] S. i. 4.

Appaṭivedhā Sutta.—Preached to **Vacchagotta.** Divers opinions arise in the world through want of perception of the nature of the body, etc.[1]

[1] S. iii. 261.

Appamatta Sutta.—See **Asamatta.**

Appamattaka Vagga.—The nineteenth chapter of the Eka Nipāta of the Aṅguttara Nikāya. In the spiritual world, by analogy with Nature, only a few are selected out of many who will be lost.[1]

[1] A. i. 35-8.

Appamateyya Sutta.—See **Matteyya.**

Appamāṇasubhā.—A class of devas of the **Rūpaloka** belonging to the plane of third jhāna.[1] Their life-term is thirty-two æons (*kappas*).[2] Beings are born there who are possessed of faith, virtue, learning, munificence and wisdom.[3]

[1] Abhs. p. 21.
[2] *Ibid.*, 23; see also Kvu. 207; VibhA. 520.
[3] M. iii. 102.

Appamāṇābhā.—A class of devas of the **Rūpaloka,** belonging to the plane of second jhāna.[1] Their life-term is four kappas.[2] Beings are born there who have absorbed the idea of boundless brilliancy,[3] or who are possessed of faith, virtue, learning, munificence and wisdom.[4]

[1] Abhs., p. 21.
[2] *Ibid.*, 23; see also Kvu. 207; VibhA. 520.
[3] M. iii. 147.
[4] *Ibid.*, 102.

1. **Appamāda Vagga.**—The second chapter of the Dhammapada.

2. **Appamāda Vagga.**—In the fifth division of the Saṃyutta Nikāya (Mahāvagga) several chapters are found called Appamādavagga. Thus the fifth of the Magga Saṃyutta,[1] the tenth and the fifteenth of the Bojjhaṅga,[2] the seventh of the Satipaṭṭhāna,[3] the ninth and the fourteenth of the Indriya,[4] the second of the Sammappadhāna,[5] the second and the seventh of the Bala,[6] the fifth of the Iddhipāda[7] and the second of the Jhāna.[8]

[1] S. v. 41-5.
[2] 135. 138.
[3] 191.
[4] 240, 242.
[5] 245.
[6] 250, 252.
[7] 291.
[8] 308.

1. **Appamāda Sutta** (2).—Preached to **Pasenadi.** Diligence is the one quality that acquires and keeps welfare both in this life and in the next; just as the elephant's foot is chief among all feet, so is diligence the best of qualities.[1]

[1] S. i. 86, 87.

2. **Appamāda Sutta.**—Diligence must be practised by those who know not the nature of birth, becoming, etc.[1]

[1] S. ii. 132.

3. **Appamāda Sutta** (2).—Digilence is the harbinger of the arising of the Ariyan Eightfold Way.[1]

[1] S. v. 30, 32.

4. **Appamāda Sutta** (2).—Diligence is most useful for the arising of the Ariyan Eightfold Way[1]; there is no other single condition like it for the arising and perfection of the Way.[2]

[1] S. v. 33. [2] *Ibid.*, 35, 36, 37.

5. **Appamāda Sutta.**—On four occasions on which earnestness should be applied.[1]

[1] A. ii. 119 f.

6. **Appamāda Sutta.**—Preached in answer to a brahmin's question. Earnestness is a quality which, if developed, brings success both in this world and in the next.[1]

[1] A. iii. 364.

7. **Appamāda Sutta.**—Same as **Aparihāniya Sutta** (2), with the addition of *samādhigāravatā.*[1]

[1] A. iv. 27 f.

8. **Appamāda Sutta.**—Earnestness is the best and highest of all qualities.[1]

[1] A. v. 21 f.

Appamādovāda.—The name given to the stanzas in the Dhammapada (Nos. 21-23) on heedfulness.[1]

[1] J. v. 66.

Appameyya Sutta.—Of three classes of persons, the arahant is the immeasurable (*appameyya*).[1]

[1] A. i. 266.

1. **Appassuta Sutta.**—A woman who has small knowledge is born in purgatory.[1]

[1] S. iv. 242.

2. **Appassuta Sutta.**—Four classes of persons, some of small learning and some of wide learning.[1]

[1] A. ii. 6 f.

Appiyā.—See **Suppiyā.**

Appihā.—A Sāmanera who lived in the **Suvaṇṇakuṭi** in **Dakkhiṇagiri vihāra.** On the day after his ordination his mother had prepared seats and alms for eight monks, and, by the power of *iddhi*, these were made to suffice for 68,000 monks. The story is told in order to show the power of *iddhi* in connection with the **Mahā Thūpa** ceremonies[1] (*v.l.* **Ambasuppiya).**

[1] MṬ. 552.

Apheggusāra.—A treatise, of about the fourteenth century, on Abhidhamma topics, written by a scholar of Haṃsavatī in Burma.[1]

[1] Bode: *op. cit.*, 36 and n. 2; Sās. 48.

Apheggusāradīpanī.—A book composed at Haṃsavatī, probably by **Mahāsuvaṇṇadīpa,** teacher of Queen **Sīvalī.** In Nevill's MS. Catalogue in the British Museum it is described as an *anuṭīkā* dealing with matter in the **Abhidhammatthavibhāvanī.**[1]

[1] Bode: *op. cit.* 36, n. 2.

Ababa Niraya.—A name given not to a special purgatory but to a period of time in **Avīci.** One term of Ababa is equal to four hundred of Abbuda; an Abbuda being reckoned as the time taken to remove twenty Kosalan Khāris (equal to a cartload) of *tila*-seeds, taking one seed at the end of each century.[1]

[1] Sn. p. 126; S. i. 152; SA. i. 170; see also KS. i. 190, n. 1 and 2. SnA. (ii. 477) gives an Abbuda as equal to 100,000 *ninnahutas*; AA. ii. 853.

1. **Abbuda.**—A period of suffering in Avīci. For details see **Ababa.**

2. **Abbuda.**—A king of long ago; a former birth of **Niggaṇṭhipupphiya** Thera.[1]

[1] Ap. i. 263.

Abbha Sutta.—Thunder clouds arise sometimes because the **Abbhāvalāhaka** devas wish to give joy to their bodies.[1]

[1] S. iii. 256.

Abbhañjanadāyaka Thera.—An arahant. In a previous birth he had given ointment to the Buddha **Koṇḍañña.** As a result, fifteen kappas ago he was born as a *cakkavatti*, **Cirappa.**[1]

[1] Ap. i. 236.

Abbhantara Jātaka (No. 281).—The Sister **Bimbādevī** had suffered from flatulence, and was cured with mango-juice and sugar which **Sāriputta** had obtained from the king of Kosala, at **Rāhula's** request. The king, having heard of Bimbādevī's affliction, ordered that she should be continually supplied with mango-syrup. On being told of the incident, the Buddha revealed this story of the past to show that it was not the first time that Sāriputta had obtained mango-syrup for Bimbādevī.

The *atītavatthu* is about the chief queen of a king of Benares. Sakka, becoming nervous on account of the austerities of an ascetic, wishes to destroy him, and arouses in the queen a desire for a " Midmost Mango " (*Abbhantara-Amba*). After prolonged search—during which the ascetic and his companions are driven from the royal park because they are reported to have eaten the mangoes there—a favourite parrot of the palace is commissioned to find the Midmost Mango. He goes to Himavā, and learns from the parrots of the seventh mountain range that the mango grows on a tree which belongs to **Vessavana** and which is most strictly guarded. He goes stealthily by night to the tree, but is caught by the guardian goblins, who decide to kill him. He tells them that he is delighted to die in the performance of his duty, and thereby wins their respect. Following their counsel, he seeks the assistance of an ascetic, **Jotirasa,** living in a hut called **Kañcanapatti,** to whom Vessavaṇa sends a daily offering of four mangoes. The ascetic gives the parrot two mangoes, one for himself and one for the queen.[1]

Ānanda was the parrot and Sāriputta Jotirasa.

[1] J. ii. 392-400.

Abbhantara Vagga.—The fourth division of the Ṭikā Nipāta of the Jātakaṭṭhakathā.[1]

[1] J. ii. 392-430.

Abbhavalāhakā.—One of the Cloud-group of devas. They are embodied in the thunder clouds (cumulus clouds), and when they wish to revel and delight themselves, thunder clouds make their appearance in the sky.[1]

[1] S. iii. 256.

Abbhahattha.—See **Ambahattha.**

Abbhasa.—Eleven kappas ago there were thirty-five kings of the name of Abbhasa, all former births of **Nīta** Thera[1] (*v.l.* **Ambaraṃsa**).

[1] ThagA. i. 182.

Abbhāhata Sutta.—The world is persecuted by death, age, decay and craving.[1]

[1] S. i. 40. The verses appear also in the story of **Sirimaṇḍa** Thera (Thag. v. 448).

Abbhuta Sutta.—The Buddha preaches the marvellous and the path leading thereto.[1]

[1] S. iv. 371.

Abbhutadhamma.—Name given to one of the nine divisions (*aṅga*) of the Dhamma.[1] Buddhaghosa (DA. i. 24) defines it as including all the passages treating of wonders, *e.g.* the four marvellous things described in the *Mahāparinibbāna Sutta.*[2]

[1] Vin. iii. 8; M. i. 133; A. ii. 103; Pug. 43; Mil. 344, etc. [2] D. ii. 145.

1. **Abbhutadhamma Sutta.**—On the marvel that when a Tathāgata preaches the Dhamma, folk give up their usual predispositions and listen to it.[1]

[1] A. ii. 131 f.

2. **Abbhutadhamma Sutta.**—See Appendix.

Abbhokāsa Sutta.—The five kinds of those who seek solitude.[1]

[1] A. iii. 220.

1. **Abhabba Sutta.**—Various events and the conditions requisite for their presence.[1]

[1] A. v. 144 f.

2. **Abhabba Sutta.**—The ten conditions essential for arahantship.[1]

[1] A. v. 209.

1. **Abhaya Thera.**—An arahant. He was a brahmin of Sāvatthi who, having heard the Buddha preach, entered the Order. One day, while going to the village for alms, he was disturbed in mind by an attractively dressed woman, but he recollected himself and developed insight.[1]

In a former birth he had met **Sumedha** Buddha in the forest and had offered him a wreath of *salala*-flowers. Nineteen kappas ago he was born sixteen times as king, his name being **Nimmita.** He is probably to be identified with the Thera **Vaṭaṃsakiya** of the Apadāna.[2]

[1] Thag. v. 98; ThagA. i. 201-2. [2] i. 174.

2. **Abhaya.**—Commonly called **Abhayarājakumāra.** He was the son of King **Bimbisāra** and of **Padumavatī,** the *belle* of Ujjeni. When the

boy was seven years old, his mother sent him to the king and he grew up with the boys of the court. He first came under the influence of the **Nigaṇṭha Nātaputta,** who taught him a dilemma to set the "Samaṇa Gotama." In the Buddha's reply, the prince recognised the defeat of the Nigaṇṭha and the supreme Enlightenment of the Exalted One, whose disciple he then became. Later, when the king died, Abhaya was disturbed in mind, and entered the Order. On the occasion of the preaching of the *Tālacchiggalūpama Sutta,*[1] he became a Stream-enterer and afterwards attained arahantship.[2] The *Abhayarājakumāra Sutta*[3] contains the dilemma episode. It also mentions that at the time the prince had a little son of whom he was evidently very fond.

In the Saṃyutta Nikāya[4] he is stated as having visited the Buddha at Gijjhakūṭa and discussed with him the views of **Pūraṇa Kassapa.** The Buddha teaches him about the seven bojjhaṅgas.

In the Vinaya,[5] Abhaya is mentioned as having discovered **Jīvaka Komārabhacca** lying on a dung-heap (cast there by the orders of his mother, the courtesan **Sālāvatī),** and having brought him up.

The Aṅguttara Commentary,[6] on the other hand, says that Abhaya was Jīvaka's natural father.

As a reward for quelling a disturbance on the frontier, Abhaya was given a skilled nautch girl by his father, Bimbisāra. For seven days he enjoyed her company to the exclusion of all else, but on the seventh day she died. Disconsolate, he sought comfort from the Buddha, who assuaged his grief.[7]

The Apadāna[8] gives the story of his past. He had been a brahmin of Haṃsavatī, skilled in the Vedas; having heard the Buddha **Padumuttara** preach, he was converted and joined the Order, where he spent his time singing the greatness of the Buddha.

The Theragāthā Commentary[9] quotes, in his story, some verses in the Apadāna, which in the Apadāna itself are ascribed to a Thera **Ketakapupphiya.** They state that he offered a *ketaka*-flower to the Buddha **Vipassī.** Perhaps Ketakapupphiya was the title of another thera, whose real name was Abhaya, and hence the stories were confused.[10]

See also **Abhaya** (3).

1 Probably the same as S. v. 455 and M. iii. 169.

2 Thag. 26; ThagA. i. 83-4 also ThigA. 39. In ThagA. his mother's name does not appear.

3 M. i. 392 ff.

4 S. v. 126-8.

5 i. 269.

6 i. 216.

7 DhA. iii. 166-67; *cf.* the story of **Santati.**

8 ii. 502-4.

9 i. 83-4.

10 ii. 449-50.

3. **Abhaya.**—A Licchavi of **Vesāli** generally,[1] but wrongly, identified with **Abhayarājakumāra.** On one occasion he comes with another Licchavi, **Paṇḍita Kumāraka,** to **Ānanda** in the Kūṭāgārasālā in Vesāli, and discusses with him certain views held by **Nigaṇṭha Nātaputta**. Ānanda teaches him the Buddha's three Ways of purification.[2] On another occasion he visits the Buddha, again at Vesāli, with the Licchavi **Sāḷha;** the latter asks the Buddha's views on purity of morals and self-mortification. The Buddha tells him of the Ariyan Way and explains its implications by various similes.[3] We are not told that either of them became converts on this occasion.

[1] *E.g.*, GS. i. 200, n. 2; ii. 211, n. 2; KS. v. 107, n. 2.

[2] For details see A. i. 220-2.

[3] See A. ii. 202-4.

4. **Abhaya.**—A Thera. He and **Tissadatta** Thera are mentioned together, in several Commentaries[1] as examples of persons worthy of being associated with, because of their possession of ready attention (*upaṭṭhita-sati*). This perhaps refers to **Abhaya** (1) or, more probably, to one of the three **Abhayas** mentioned with their titles in the Dīgha Commentary on the Mahāparinibbāna Sutta[2] in its exegesis on the word *upaṭṭhita-sati.*

[1] DA. iii. 786; MA. i. 234; AA. i. 273; VibhA. 275.

[2] DA. ii. 530: **Mahāgatimba-Abhaya, Dīghabhānaka-Abhaya** and **Tipiṭaka-Culābhaya** (*q.v.*).

5. **Abhaya.**—King of Ceylon (then known as **Ojadīpa**) in the time of **Kakusandha** Buddha. His capital was **Abhayanagara.**[1]

[1] Sp. i. 86; Mhv. xv. 59.

6. **Abhaya.**—King of Ceylon (414-394 B.C.). He was the eldest son of **Paṇḍuvāsudeva** and reigned in **Upatissagāma.** Later, when the usurper **Paṇḍukābhaya** came to the throne, he killed all his other nine uncles, sparing only Abhaya, because the latter had befriended both him and his mother, **Ummādacittā.**[1] Abhaya was made *Nagaraguttika* (Guardian of the City), administering the government by night; he was the first holder of that office.[2]

[1] It was he who prevented Cittā from being killed at birth, Mhv. ix. 3.

[2] Mhv. ix. 3, 9; x. 52, 80, 105.

7. **Abhaya.**—Personal attendant of **Atthadassī** Buddha.[1]

[1] Bu. xv. 19.

9

8. **Abhaya.**—Eldest son of King **Muṭasiva** of Ceylon. He renounced the succession in favour of his younger brother, Tissa, who later became known as **Devānampiyatissa.**[1]

[1] MṬ. 302.

9. **Abhaya.**—Father of **Khañjadeva.**[1]

[1] Mhv. xxiii. 78.

10. **Abhaya.**—A monk, chief of the ascetics who dwelt in the **Pañcaparivenamūla** monastery. He was sent by King **Kittisirimegha** (*q.v.*) to fetch the king's son.[1]

[1] Cv. lxvii. 61.

11. **Abhaya.**—Author of the *Mahāṭīkā* on **Saddatthabhedacintā.**[1] He was a native of Pagan, and is also credited with the authorship of the **Sambhandhacintā-ṭīkā.**[2]

[1] Gv. 63. [2] Bode, *op. cit.*, 22, and n. 8.

12. **Abhaya.**—A brigand, commonly called **Cora-Abhaya** (*q.v.*).

13. **Abhaya (Abhayupassaya).**—A nunnery built by King **Mahāsena.**[1]

[1] Mhv. xxxvii. 43.

14. **Abhaya.**—Nephew of **Khallāṭanāga.**[1]

[1] MṬ. 444.

For others named Abhaya see under their titles, *e.g.* **Mahāgatimba, Dīghabhānaka, Meghavaṇṇa,** etc.

Abhaya Sutta.—On what fearlessness means.[1]

[1] A. iv. 455.

Abhayagallaka.—A vihāra in Ceylon built by King **Mahācūḷi-Mahātissa.**[1]

[1] Mhv. xxxiv. 8.

Abhayagiri.—A celebrated monastic establishment on the north side of **Anurādhapura,** consisting of a vihāra and a mighty thūpa. Only the thūpa now stands. It was built by King **Vaṭṭagāmaṇi Abhaya** on the site of the ancient **Titthārāma,** 217 years, 10 months and 10 days after the founding of the Mahāvihāra.[1] Tradition states that when the king was fleeing from the Tamils he passed the Titthārāma on his way, and the **Nigaṇṭha Giri,** who then lived there, made insulting remarks about him. The king vowed, if he were returned to the throne, to build a vihāra on that spot[2]; he fulfilled his vow, and the name of the vihāra was a combination of his own name and of that of the Nigaṇṭha. The monastery was given in charge of the Thera **Mahātissa** of **Kuppikala** and of two other monks, Kuppikala having befriended the king in his misfortunes.

The vihāra advanced rapidly in wealth and in power, but quite soon the monks seceded from the Mahāvihāra fraternity because, according to the Mahāvaṃsa,[3] an incumbent of the Mahāvihāra, **Mahātissa** by name, was expelled from the monastery for frequenting lay families. His disciple, **Bahalamassutissa,** went in anger to Abhayagiri and formed a separate faction.

A Sinhalese chronicle, the Nikāya Saṅgraha,[4] states that these dissentients were soon after joined by a body of **Vajjiputtaka** monks from the **Pallārāma** in India, under the leadership of a teacher called **Dhammaruci,** and the sect which they together founded in Ceylon became known as the **Dhammaruci Nikāya,** with headquarters in Abhayagiri.

For quite a long while the two fraternities, that of the Mahāvihāra and that of the Abhayagiri, seem to have lived in amity, alike enjoying the munificence of patrons.[5] Thus, **Gajabāhukagāmaṇi** raised the height of **Abhayuttara-thūpa** (as the thūpa at Abhayagiri seems to have been called) and made the **Gāmaṇitissa-tank** to be used for the cultivation of land for the maintenance of the vihāra[6]; **Kaniṭṭhatissa** built a splendid structure in the same vihāra for the Thera **Mahānāga;** it was called the **Ratanapāsāda.**[7]

But in the reign of **Vohārakatissa,** the Abhayagiri monks openly adopted the heretical **Vaitulya Piṭaka.**[8] An inquiry was held by the king with the help of his minister **Kapila,** the heretical books were burnt and the monks of Abhayagiri disgraced.[9]

Soon afterwards, however, the heretics won over the king **Mahāsena** to their side and destroyed the establishment of the Mahāvihāra, carrying away all the materials to Abhayagiri.[10] Later, Mahāsena repented of his ways, burnt the books of the Abhayagiri monks and transferred his

[1] Mhv. xxxiii. 78-83.
[2] *Ibid.*, 43-4.
[3] *Ibid.*, 95 ff.
[4] pp. 11, 12; also P.L.C. 42.
[5] *Ibid.*, 52 f.; Mhv. xxxv. 20, 57, 119-22; xxxvi. 7-14.
[6] *Ibid.*, xxxv. 119-22.
[7] xxxvi. 7, 8.
[8] Of the Mahāyānists (see Mhv. trans. 259, n. 2).
[9] Mhv. xxxvi. 40-1.
[10] P.L.C. 53; Mhv. xxxvii. 10-16.

patronage to the Mahāvihāra. But the Abhayagiri fraternity must soon have recovered its prestige, for we find Mahāsena's successor, **Sirimeghavaṇṇa,** planting a bodhi tree (called **Tissavasabha**)[11] in Abhayagiri and surrounding it with a stone terrace.[12] A few years later both **Mahānāma** (409-31) and his queen became active supporters of **Abhayagiri.**[13] **Dhātusena** is stated to have enlarged the **Abhayuttara-vihāra,**[14] and **Silākāla** is credited with several benefactions to the vihāra and its bodhi tree[15]; **Mahānāga** gave the weaver's village of **Jambela** to the **Uttaravihāra**[16]; **Aggabodhi I.** built a bathing-tank there,[17] while his successor, **Aggabodhi II.,** built the **Dāṭhāggabodhi** house, so called after himself and his queen.[18]

In the monastery at Abhayagiri there seems to have been a stone image of the Buddha, referred to under various names, **Silāsaṃbuddha, Kālasela, Kālasatthā, Silāsatthā** and **Silāmayamuninda.**[19] It was evidently held peculiarly sacred. **Buddhadāsa** placed a *nāgamaṇi* in its eye[20]; this was soon lost, and we find Dhātusena replacing it, adorning and decorating the statue in various ways.[21] Silāmeghavaṇṇa had it restored and redecorated and made provision for its maintenance.[22] The same king, we are told, attempted to carry out a reform of the Abhayagiri monks, but this attempt ultimately brought disaster on him.[23] **Jeṭṭhatissa** gave to the vihāra the village of **Mahādāragiri.**[24] Dāthopatissa built the **Kappūra-pariveṇa** attached to the vihāra, and also a monastery **Tiputthulla,** encroaching on the precincts of the Mahāvihāra, notwithstanding the protests of the monks belonging to the latter.[25] **Aggabodhi VII.** added the **Sabhattudesabhoga,**[26] and **Mahinda II.** the **Mahālekha-pariveṇa** as well as the many-storeyed **Ratanapāsāda** with its costly ornamentation.[27]

Sena I. built the **Vīraṅkurārāma** and gave it to the **Mahāsaṅghikas,**[28] while his consort, **Saṅghā,** erected a dwelling house, **Mahindasena,**[29] and his courtier, **Uttara,** yet another dwelling house, called **Uttarasena,** for the maintenance of which he provided. Two other courtiers, **Vajira** and

11 Cv. trans. i. 9, n. 3.

12 Cv. xxxvii. 91.

13 *Ibid.*, 212.

14 *Ibid.*, xxxviii. 61.

15 *Ibid.*, xli. 31-2.

16 Another name for Abhayagiri; see Cv. trans. i. 8, n. 2; 61, n. 6.

17 Cv. xlii. 28.

18 *Ibid.*, 63-5.

19 Cv. xxxix. 7; xxxviii. 65; 61-2; see also vv. 51, 77, 87. There was also in Abhayagiri another image called the **Abhiseka** (*q.v.*).

20 Cv. xxxvii. 123.

21 For details see Cv. xxxviii. 62 ff.

22 *Ibid.*, xliv. 68.

23 *Ibid.*, 75 ff.

24 *Ibid.*, 96.

25 *Ibid.*, xlv. 29 ff.

26 *Ibid.*, xlviii. 64.

27 *Ibid.*, 135-40; see also Geiger's trans. 123, n. 2.

28 Cv. l. 68-9.

29 *Ibid.*, 79.

Rakkhasa, built two dwelling houses, called respectively **Vajirasenaka** and **Rakkhasa.**[30]

In the reign of **Sena II.** the **Paṃsukulika** monks, who till then had evidently lived in Abhayagiri,[31] separated and formed special groups. **Saṅghā,** queen of **Udaya II.,** erected and endowed the building known as the **Saṅghasenapabbata.**[32] **Kassapa IV.** built a pāsāda bearing his name and assigned to it a village,[33] while his successor, **Kassapa V.,** erected the **Bhaṇḍikā-pariveṇa** and the **Silāmeghapabbata,** endowing each with a village.[34]

Sena III. spent 40,000 *kahāpanas* for a stone paving round the cetiya. The Abhayagiri monks befriended both **Vijayabāhu I.** (then known as **Kitti**) and his brother, and out of gratitude Vijayabāhu built the **Uttaramūla-pariveṇa,** which was probably attached to the vihāra itself.[35]

In the reign of **Parakkamabāhu I.,** when that monarch had established himself on the throne, it is said that he tried to reform the monks of the Abhayagiri, but he found the task hopeless.[36] He found that the Abhayagiri-thūpa had been destroyed by the vandalism of the Tamils, and he had it restored to a height of 160 cubits.[37] When Anurādhapura was finally abandoned, Abhayagiri fell into ruin and decay, the monastery being completely destroyed.

It is clear that even at the outset there was considerable rivalry between the monks of Abhayagiri and those of the Mahāvihāra. The rivalry seems originally to have been mainly personal, but it later developed into differences in doctrinal opinion. Of the exact nature of these latter we have no information, owing, chiefly, to the book-burnings carried out by pious kings in the excess of their zeal for the purity of the Faith. For the same reason we are unable to ascertain what part, if any, the Abhayagiri fraternity played in literary activity. It has been suggested, however, that both the **Jātakaṭṭhakathā**[38] and the **Sahassavatthuppakaraṇa,**[39] another compilation of tales, were the work of the Abhayagiri monks.

Fa-Hsien evidently spent the two years of his stay in Ceylon with the Abhayagiri fraternity because the books he took away with him were those of the unorthodox schools. According to him, there were, at this time, 5,000 monks in Abhayagiri.[40]

In the chronicles Abhayagiri is referred to under several names: **Abhayuttara, Abhayavihāra, Abhayācala** and **Uttaravihāra.**

30 *Ibid.*, 83.
31 Cv. trans. i. 108, n. 1.
32 Cv. li. 86-7.
33 *Ibid.*, lii. 13; Cv. trs. i. 162, n. 4.
34 Cv. lii. 58-9.
35 Cv. lvii. 18, 23.
36 *Ibid.*, lxxviii. 21 ff.
37 *Ibid.*, 98.
38 P.L.C. 124, 125.
39 *Ibid.*, 128.
40 Fa Hsien's Travels, 67 ff.

Abhayagirikā.—The monks of the **Abhayagiri-vihāra.**[1]

[1] Mhv. xxxiii. 97-8.

Abhayaṅkara.—One of the royal elephants of King **Vasavatti** of Benāres.[1]

[1] J. vi. 135.

Abhayanagara.—The capital of King **Abhaya** (5), King of Ceylon, when the island was known as **Ojadīpa.** It lay to the east of the **Kadamba** river.[1]

[1] Mhv. xv. 58-9.

Abhayanāga.—Younger brother of King **Vohārikatissa.** With the help of his uncle **Subhadeva** he conspired against the king and, obtaining the assistance of the Damiḷas, he overthrew and killed him. Abhayanāga reigned for eight years (A.D. 291-9).[1]

[1] Mhv. xxvi. 42-53.

Abhayattherī.—See **Abhayā.**

Abhayamātā.—A Therī. She was a courtesan named **Padumavatī,** the *belle* of **Ujjenī.** King **Bimbisāra,** having heard of her beauty, expressed to his *purohita* a wish to see her. The *purohita,* by the power of his spells, enlisted the assistance of a yakkha, **Kumbhīra,** who took the king to Ujjenī. She bore to the king a son, **Abhayarājakumāra,** who later joined the Order and became an arahant. It was on his account that Padumavatī came to be called Abhayamātā. She heard Abhayarājakumāra preach and leaving the world herself became an arahant.[1] Two verses attributed to her are found in the Therīgāthā.[2] In the time of the Buddha **Tissa,** seeing him going round for alms, with glad heart she gave him a spoonful of food. As a result, she was thirty-six times queen among the gods and was chief queen of fifty *cakkavattis.*[3] She is evidently identical with **Kaṭacchubhikkhadāyikā** of the Apadāna.[4]

[1] ThigA. 31-2.
[2] 33, 34.
[3] ThigA. 32.
[4] ii. 516-7.

Abhayarājakumāra Sutta.—It contains the episode of Prince **Abhaya** (*q.v.*) visiting the Buddha at Rājagaha and setting him the questions suggested by **Nigaṇṭha Nātaputta :** Would a Tathāgatha say anything unpleasant or disagreeable to others ? If he did, how would he differ from ordinary men ? If he did not, how was it that the Buddha spoke of **Devadatta** as a reprobate, a child of perdition, etc.—words which angered and upset Devadatta ?

The Buddha answered that the question needed qualification and, noticing that the prince was nursing his little boy, who lay in his lap, asked him what he would do if a pebble or a stick got into his mouth. "I should pull it out even if the blood flowed." "Just so would a Buddha state unpleasant truths in due season if necessary and profitable."

At the end of the discourse Abhaya accepts the Buddha as his Teacher.[1]

[1] M. i. 391 ff.

Abhayarāja-pariveṇa.—A building erected by King **Vijayabāhu IV.** in connection with the **Vanaggāmapāsāda Vihāra.** He built it in order that he might give the merits arising therefrom to his father, **Parakkamabāhu II.** It was richly endowed.[1]

[1] Cv. lxxxviii. 51-2; Cv. trans. ii. 186, n. 4.

Abhayavāpi.—A tank in **Anurādhapura** built by King **Paṇḍukābhaya.**[1] At its lower end was the settlement of the yakkha **Cittarāja.**[2] In the hot weather it ran dry, and on one occasion **Devānampiyatissa** used its mud for building a temporary structure in which to deposit the relics brought from Jambudīpa.[3] The hall which **Duṭṭhagāmaṇi** built round the **Maricavaṭṭi** Vihāra extended into a part of the Abhaya tank.[4] In the reign of **Bhātikābhaya** water was taken from the tank, by means of machines, up to the top of the **Mahā Thūpa,** for the sprinkling of the flowers offered there.[5] The tank is generally identified with the modern Basavakkulam.[6]

[1] Mhv. x. 88.
[2] *Ibid.*, 84.
[3] *Ibid.*, xvii. 35.
[4] *Ibid.*, xxvi. 20.
[5] *Ibid.*, xxxiv. 45.
[6] Geiger, Mhv. trans. 74, n. 3.

Abhaya-Vihāra.—Another name for **Abhayagiri Vihāra.**

Abhayasamāna Sutta.—Preached to **Jāṇussoni** on those who have no fear when death comes to them.[1]

[1] A. ii. 173 f.

Abhayā.—A Therī. She belonged to a family in **Ujjeni** and was the playmate of **Abhayamātā** (Padumavatī). When the latter joined the Order, Abhayā, too, left the world. As she was meditating in **Sītavana,**

the Buddha sent forth a ray of glory to encourage and help her; she thereupon became an arahant.[1] Two verses are attributed to her in the Therīgāthā.[2]

In the time of **Sikhī** Buddha she was born in a noble family and became the chief queen of the Buddha's father, **Aruṇavā.** One day she offered to the Buddha some lotuses which the king had given her. As a result, in later births her body was the colour of the lotus and bore the perfume of the lotus.

Seventy times she reigned as queen of heaven and she was chief queen of sixty-three *cakkavattis*.[3] She is evidently to be identified with **Sattuppalamālikā** of the Apadāna.[4]

[1] ThigA. 33-4.
[2] 35, 46.
[3] ThigA. *loc. cit.*
[4] ii. 517-18.

Abhayācala.—Another name for **Abhayagiri.**

Abhayuttara.—A name for **Abhayagiri.**

Abhayupassaya.—A nunnery; see **Abhaya** (13).

Abhayūvara.—The name of the eighth *bhānavāra* (portion for recitation) of the first Khandhaka of the Mahāvagga of the Vinaya Piṭaka.

Abhayebalākapāsāna.—A locality in **Anurādhapura,** one of the spots included in the Sīmā marked out by **Devānampiyatissa.**[1] It was on the **Abhayavāpi.**[2]

[1] Mhv. xv. 13; see Appendix B of Geiger's text.
[2] Mbv. 135.

Abhijāna Sutta.—See **Parijāna.**

Abhiñjika Thera.—A fellow-dweller of **Anuruddha.** On one occasion when the Buddha asks **Mahā Kassapa** to preach to the monks, the latter reports that it is impossible to talk to them because monks like **Bhaṇḍa,** colleague of **Ānanda,** and Abhiñjika, were engaged in wordy warfare. The Buddha sends for them and admonishes them. Having heard his discourse, they express regret for their behaviour and promise to cultivate self-restraint in the future[1] (*v.l.* **Abhijika, Ābhiñjika).**

[1] S. ii. 204-5.

Abhiññā Vagga.—The twenty-sixth section of the Catukka Nipāta of the Aṅguttara Nikāya. It consists of ten suttas.[1]

[1] A. ii. 246-53.

1. **Abhiññā Sutta.**—On higher knowledge and its applications.[1]

[1] A. ii. 246 f.

2. **Abhiññā Sutta.**—A group of suttas on qualities that could be obtained by an understanding of *rāga* (lust).[1]

[1] A. iii. 277.

Abhiññāpariññeyya Sutta.—Everything should be known and comprehended as impermanent, woeful, void of self.[1]

[1] S. iv. 29.

Abhiññeyya Sutta.—Same as above.

Abhiṇha Jātaka (No. 27).—The story of a dog and an elephant who grew up to be great friends and became indispensable to each other. The dog used to amuse himself by swinging backwards and forwards on the elephant's trunk. One day the merchant sold the dog. The elephant went off his food and would not be consoled till the dog was brought back.

The story was told in reference to two monks of Sāvatthi who were very intimate with one another and spent all their time together.[1]

[1] J. i. 189 f.

Abhidhamma Piṭaka.—The third division of the Piṭakas. It consists of seven books: the **Dhammasaṅgaṇi, Vibhaṅga, Kathāvatthu, Puggalapaññati, Dhātukathā, Yamaka** and **Paṭṭhāna,** all designated by the name of **Pakaraṇa.** Only in the Chronicles and the Commentaries is the word used as the title of a third Piṭaka.[1] In the Canon itself[2] the word means "special dhamma," *i.e.* the Doctrine pure and simple (without admixture of literary treatment or personalities, etc.), and is sometimes coupled with the word *abhivinaya.*[3] It has been suggested[4] that, as the word *abhidhamma* standing alone is not found either in the Sutta Nipāta, the Saṃyutta, or the Aṅguttara, and only once or twice in the Dīgha and Majjhima, it probably came into use only towards the end of the period in which the four great Nikāyas grew up.[5]

The **Mahāsaṅghikas** refused to include the Abhidhamma in the Piṭakas at all, as they did not regard it as the word of the Buddha.[6]

[1] See the discussion of this in DA. i. 15, 18 f.

[2] *E.g.*, Vin. i. 64; iii. 144; iv. 344.

[3] *E.g.*, D. iii. 267; M. i. 272.

[4] New Pāli Dict. *s.v.*

[5] See Dial. iii. 199 on a possible origin of the Adhidhamma.

[6] Dpv. v. 32-8.

According to the **Dīghabhānakas** the Abhidhamma Piṭaka also included the whole of the Khuddaka Nikāya except the Cariyāpiṭaka, Apadāna and Buddhavaṃsa.[7]

According to another division, the five Nikāyas are not divisions of the Dhamma but of the whole Canon, and in the fifth are included both the Vinaya and the Abhidhamma.[8]

There is a legend recorded by Buddhaghosa that the Abhidhamma was first preached by the Buddha in Tāvatiṃsa at the foot of the Pāricchataka tree, when he was seated on Sakka's throne, during his visit to his mother in Tāvatiṃsa. Later it was taught by him to Sāriputta on the banks of the Anotatta Lake, whither Sāriputta had gone to minister to the Buddha during the latter's visit to Tāvatiṃsa.[9]

The legend further relates that after the Enlightenment the Buddha spent the fourth week in the **Ratanaghara,** revolving in his mind the intricate doctrines of the Abhidhamma in all their details.[10]

According to the Cullavagga version of the Councils[11] the Abhidhamma Piṭaka was not rehearsed at either Council.

The fact that the Abhidhamma is not mentioned in the suttas and that only Dhamma and Vinaya are usually referred to, only proves that at one time the Abhidhamma did not form a separate Piṭaka. As a matter of fact, it is not held even by the commentators to be the word of the Buddha in the same sense as the suttas. One section of it, the Kathāvatthu,[12] was taught only at the Third Council.

As far as we know, the seven books of the Abhidhamma are peculiar to the Theravādins, though there is evidence that other schools, chiefly the Vaibhāṣikas (Sarvāstivādins) and the Sautrāntikas, held the Abhidhamma books sacred.[13]

As far as the contents of the Abhidhamma are concerned, they do not form a systematic philosophy, but are a special treatment of the Dhamma as found in the Sutta-Piṭaka. Most of the matter is psychological and logical; the fundamental doctrines mentioned or discussed are those already propounded in the suttas and, therefore, taken for granted.[14] Apart from the Commentaries on the seven books, an exegetical work on the whole Piṭaka, called the **Abhidhamma Mūlaṭīkā,** was written by **Ānanda Vanaratanatissa** of the **Vanavāsī** school in Ceylon.

The ṭīkā was evidently based on Buddhaghosa's Commentaries, but

[7] DA. i. 15.

[8] *Ibid.*, 23.

[9] VibhA. p. 1; AA. i. 71, etc.

[10] J. i. 78.

[11] Chaps. xi. and xii: but see DA. i. 15 *contra.*

[12] But see **Kathāvatthu.**

[13] See Tāranātha: *Geschichte des Buddhismus* (56) 156 (296).

[14] For a discussion of the contents see article on *Abhidhamma* in ERE.

Ānanda occasionally dissents from Buddhaghosa. The work was written at the request of an Elder, **Buddhamitta,** and was revised by **Mahā Kassapa** of Pulatthipura.

An *Anuṭīkā* was written by **Culla Dhammapāla.**[15]

[15] Gv. 60, 69. For details see P.L.C., pp. 210-12. The Gv. (72) also mentions **Abhidhammagaṇḍhi,** probably a glossary.

Abhidhammattha-vikāsinī.—A ṭīkā on **Buddhadatta's Abhidhammāvatāra** written by **Sumaṅgala.**[1]

[1] Gv. 62; Svd. v. 1227.

Abhidhammattha-saṅgaha. — A compendium of the Abhidhamma written by **Anuruddha,** incumbent of the **Mūlasoma Vihāra.**[1] A *ṭīkā* called the *Porāṇa Ṭīkā* exists, written by **Navavimalabuddhi** of Ceylon.[2]

Other explanatory works on the Abhidhammattha-saṅgaha are those by **Sumaṅgala** and **Chappaṭa,** the **Sīhalavyākhyāna** by **Candagomi,** the *Anuṭīkā* by **Vepullabuddhi,** two *Navānuṭīkā,* one by **Ariyavaṃsa** and the second by an unknown author, and a *Vivaraṇa.*[3]

[1] For details see P.L.C. 168-72.

[2] *Compendium of Philosophy,* Preface ix.

[3] See Sās. 69. 71; Svd. 1202, 1223; Gv. 64, 65, 75.

Abhidhammapaṇṇarasaṭṭhāna. — Written by **Nava(Culla-)Vimalabuddhi,** explaining some passages of the Abhidhamma.[1]

[1] Gv. 64, 74; Bode, *op. cit.*, 27-8.

Abhidhammavibhānavā.—A *ṭīkā* on the **Abhidhammatthasaṅgaha** by **Sumaṅgala,** pupil of Sāriputta (Navavimalabuddhi).[1] It is the most famous of the exegetical works on the Abhidhammatthasaṅgaha.[2]

[1] Gv. p. 62; Svd. 1227.

[2] *Compendium of Philosophy,* Preface ix.

Abhidhammāvatāra.—An Abhidhamma treatise by **Buddhadatta** of Uragapura. The book was written in India in the Coḷa country. It is an introduction to the study of the Abhidhamma, and there is much similarity between it and the Visuddhimagga, though Buddhadatta's diction is less involved and ambiguous than that of Buddhaghosa; his vocabulary is extraordinarily rich and his style more graphic.

The work is mostly in verse with, here and there, a prose commentary supplied by the author himself.[1]

Two *ṭīkās* on it exist, one by **Vācissara Mahāsāmi** of the Mahāvihara and the other by **Sumaṅgala,** pupil of Sāriputta.[2]

[1] Gv. 69; see P.L.C. 107-8 for details.

[2] Sās. 34.

Abhidhānappadīpikā.—A Pāli Dictionary written in the twelfth century by **Moggallāna** Thera of Ceylon, following the style and the method of the Sanskrit Amarakoṣa. It is in three parts, dealing with "celestial, terrestrial and miscellaneous objects," and each part is subdivided into several sections, which are not all mutually exclusive. The whole book is a dictionary of synonyms, all the names given to one particular thing being grouped together and put into verse for the purpose of memorisation.

A *Saṃvaṇṇanā* was written by a Burmese Officer-of-State under King **Kittisīhasūra** (A.D. 1351), and there exists a Burmese translation of the eighteenth century. In Ceylon itself a *sanna* (paraphrase) and a *ṭīkā* have been written, the sanna being the older and by far the more valuable work.[1]

[1] Gv. 62, 63; Svd. v. 1253; Sad. 65; see also P.L.C. 187-9; Bode, *op. cit.*, 67.

Abhinandana Sutta.—He who takes delight in any or all of the five khandhas takes delight in suffering; he who does not is released therefrom.[1]

[1] S. iii. 31.

Abhinandamāna Sutta.—One who is enamoured of body, etc., becomes Māra's bondsman; by not being enamoured one becomes free.[1]

[1] S. iii. 75.

Abhinandena Sutta (2).—By taking delight in the eye, ear, etc., one takes delight in Ill; by not so doing one is released from Ill. Similarly with regard to sights, sounds, etc.[1]

[1] S. iv. 13.

Abhinivesa Sutta.—Bondage of and dependence upon the fetters arise as a result of clinging to the five khandhas.[1]

[1] S. iii. 186.

1. **Abhinīhāra Sutta.**—Of those who engage in meditation, some are possessed of both skill in concentration and power of resolve, others are otherwise.[1]

[1] S. iii. 267.

2. **Abhinīhāra Sutta.**—Same as above, but "range of concentration" is substituted for "concentration."[1]

[1] S. iii. 276.

Abhibhuyya Sutta.—A woman possessed of the five powers (beauty, wealth, kin, sons and virtue) continues to get the better of her husband.[1]

[1] S. iv. 246.

1. **Abhibhū.**—Chief disciple of **Sikhī** Buddha.[1] In the *Aruṇavatī Sutta* it is said that he went with Sikhī to a Brahma-world and, at the Buddha's request, preached a sermon to the accompaniment of great magical powers. He proved that by using just such speech as if he were preaching to a gathering of monks, he could, standing in the Brahma-world, make his voice heard by its thousand realms.[2] The verses spoken on this occasion are, in the Theragāthā, ascribed to **Abhibhūta.**[3]

In the Aṅguttara Nikāya[4] we find Ānanda asking the Buddha how far Abhibhū's powers bore relation to those of a Buddha, and the Buddha replying that Abhibhū was a mere disciple, and proceeding to describe the immeasurable powers of the Tathāgatas.

Abhibhū was a brahmin because we find him so addressed in the Aruṇavatī Sutta referred to above, but in the Buddhavaṃsa Commentary[5] he is spoken of as a *rājaputta.*

In the Paṭisambhidhāmagga Commentary[6] his story is given as an example of *vikubbana-iddhi* whereby a person could make himself seen in many places at the same time. We are told that he developed *nīla-kasiṇa,* to attract to himself the attention of the world systems.

The Thera **Adhopupphiya** had been a hermit in Himavā during the time of Sikhī Buddha and had offered flowers to Abhibhū.[7]

[1] D. ii. 9; J. i. 41; Bu. xxi. 20.
[2] S. i. 154 f.
[3] v. 1147-8.
[4] i. 226 f.; AA. i. 436 f.
[5] p. 202.
[6] 488 f.
[7] Ap. i. 128-9.

2. **Abhibhū.**—A class of devas belonging to the Arūpa-plane.[1] They live in the same plane as the **Vehapphalā.** In the *Mūlapariyāya Sutta* the word is used to denote all the **Asaññasattādevā.** Buddhaghosa explains the word by saying *abhibhavī ti Abhibhū; kiṃ abhibhavī ti? cattāro khandhe, arūpino.* They are beautiful and long-lived, and are therefore considered to be eternal and identical with Brahmā.[2] In the *Brahma-nimantanika Sutta*[3] the Buddha claims to be Abhibhū (= the conqueror).

[1] M. i. 1. [2] MA. i. 30. [3] M. i. 329.

3. **Abhibhū.**—The name of a Bodhisatta who obtained *vivaraṇa* under **Gotama.** He will become the sixth Buddha after Gotama.[1]

[1] Anāgata Vaṃsa, p. 37.

1. **Abhibhū Sutta.**—On the immeasurableness of a Buddha's powers.[1]

[1] A. i. 226 f.; also called the **Sīhanāda Sutta** in the Commentary.

2. **Abhibhū Sutta.**—On the eight stages or stations of mastery over the senses (*abhibhāyaphanāni*).[1]

[1] A. iv. 305 f.

Abhibhūta.—A Thera. He was born in the Rājā's family in **Veṭṭha** (*v.l.* **Veṭṭhipura**) and succeeded to his father's estate. When the Buddha came to the city during a tour, Abhibhūta heard him and invited him for a meal; he later entered the Order and became an arahant. Three verses ascribed to Abhibhūta occur in the Theragāthā, uttered, it is said, when his kinsmen and retainers came to him lamenting that he had left them without a leader.[1] The second of these verses is elsewhere[2] attributed to **Abhibhū,** chief disciple of Sikhī Buddha. But in the Milindapañha,[3] Nāgasena ascribes the second verse to the Buddha, and in the *Mahāparinibbāna Sutta*[4] the third verse also is ascribed to him. The second verse is also assigned to the Buddha in the Divyāvadāna,[5] but elsewhere in the same book[6] it is said to have been uttered by devas.

In a former birth Abhibhūta had been a householder in the time of **Vessabhū** Buddha and became a believer in the Faith, to which he was led by his friends. When the Buddha died, the populace gathered together to obtain relics, but Abhibhūta, having quenched the pyre with fragrant water, was first able to take those which he desired.[7]

He is evidently to be identified with **Citakanibbāpaka** Thera of the Apadāna.[8]

[1] Thag. vv. 255-7; ThagA. i. 372 f.
[2] S. i. 156.
[3] 245.
[4] D. ii. 121.
[5] p. 200.
[6] p. 569.
[7] ThagA. i. 372.
[8] ii. 408.

Abhimārapayojanā.—Name given to the conspiracy into which **Devadatta** and **Ajātasattu** entered, to have archers shoot at the Buddha and so kill him.[1]

[1] J. i. 142; vi. 130 f.; DA. i. 154.

Abhiya Kaccāna.—See **Sabhiya Kaccāna.**

Abhirādhana.—A friend of **Sambhuta Sītavaniya.** He went with Sambhuta, **Bhūmija** and **Jeyyasena** to hear the Buddha preach.[1]

[1] ThagA. i. 47.

Abhirāmā.—One of the three palaces occupied, as a layman, by **Nārada** Buddha.[1]

[1] Bu. x. 19.

Abhirūpā-Nandā Therī.—She was born in Kapilavatthu as the daughter of the chief of the Sākiyan **Khemaka** and was named Nandā. Owing to her great beauty and charm she became known as Abhirūpā-Nandā.

On the day appointed for her to select her husband, the Sākiyan youth, on whom her choice was to have fallen, died,[1] and her parents made her leave the world against her will. Even after she had entered the Order she avoided going into the Buddha's presence, being infatuated with her own beauty and fearing the Master's rebuke. In order to induce her to come to him, the Buddha directed **Mahā Pajāpati** to see that all the nuns came for instruction. When Nandā's turn came she sent another in her place. The Buddha refused to recognise the substitute, and Nandā was compelled to go herself. As she listened to the Buddha preaching, he, by his magic power, conjured up a beautiful woman and showed her becoming aged and fading, causing anguish to arise in Nandā's heart. At the opportune moment, the Buddha drove home the truth of the impermanence of beauty. Meditating on this topic, she later became an arahant.[2]

The two verses preached to her by the Buddha, which she made the subject of her meditations, are given in the Therīgāthā.[3]

In the time of Vipassī Buddha, Nandā had been the daughter of a wealthy burgess in the Buddha's native town of Bandhumatī. Having heard the Buddha preach she became his pious follower, and, at his death, made an offering of a golden umbrella decked with jewels to the shrine built over his ashes.[4]

The verses quoted in the Therīgāthā Commentary, as having been taken from the Apadāna, really belong to **Mettā,** and are found in the Apadāna (ii. 515) ascribed to **Ekapiṇḍadāyikā.** The correct verses are found in the Apadāna under the name of Abhirūpā Nandā, and agree with the story given in the text of the Therīgāthā Commentary.

[1] The Apadāna account (ii. 609) does not mention the suitor's death, but states that many sought her hand and caused great trouble, to avoid which her parents made her join the Order.

[2] ThigA. 81 f.; SnA. i. 241-2.

[3] vv. 19, 20.

[4] Ap. ii. 608.

Abhivaddhamānaka.—See **Aggivaddhamānaka.**

1. **Abhisaṇḍa Sutta** (3).—Unvarying loyalty to the Buddha, to the Dhamma, to the Saṅgha and possession of virtues dear to the Ariyan—these are the four floods of merit that bring happiness.[1]

[1] S. v. 391-2.

2. **Abhisaṇḍa** or **Sayhaka Sutta** (3).—Same as above; the measure of merit that accrues as a result of these four floods is incalculable, like the waters of the ocean.[1]

In the second and third suttas of both these groups the fourth quality is given in (*a*) as possession of a heart free from stinginess, delighting in self-surrender; in (*b*) as possession of insight into the rise and fall of things, insight that is Ariyan.

[1] S. v. 399-402.

3. **Abhisanda Sutta.**—The five yields of merit (*puññabhisandā*) which accrue to a monk because of concentration of mind in various activities.[1]

[1] A. iii. 51 f.

4. **Abhisanda Sutta.**—The eight yields of merit that a monk can obtain by practising various qualities.[1]

[1] A. iv. 245 f.

Abhisamaya Kathā.—The third chapter of the Paññāvagga of the Paṭisambhidāmagga.[1]

[1] ii. 215 ff.

Abhisamaya Vagga.—The sixth chapter of the Sacca Saṃyutta of the Saṃyutta Nikāya.[1]

[1] V. 459 ff.

Abhisamaya Saṃyutta.—The thirteenth Saṃyutta, forming the second section of the Nidāna Vagga of the Saṃyutta Nikāya.[1]

[1] ii. 133 ff.

Abhisambodhialaṅkāra.—A Pāli poem in one hundred stanzas written by **Saranaṅkara Saṅgharāja** of Ceylon in the eighteenth century. It treats of the life of the Buddha from the time of his birth as Sumedha, during the régime of Dīpaṅkara, to his last birth as Siddhattha.[1]

[1] P.L.C. 281.

Abhisambuddha-gāthā.—The name given to the stanzas which illustrate and summarise the Jātaka stories, when such stanzas are mentioned as having been spoken by the Buddha himself, either after the Enlightenment or before it, while he was yet a Bodhisatta.[1]

[1] See Buddhist Birth Stories, Introd.

Abhisammata.—A king of sixty-three kappas ago; a previous birth of **Pāṭalipupphiya** Thera.[1]

Ap. i. 123.

Abhisammataka.—A yakkha chieftain. **Upavāna** Thera, who at the time of Padumuttara Buddha had been a very poor man, set up his *uttarāsaṅga* as a banner on the shrine erected over the relics of the Buddha. Abhisammataka had been appointed by the devas as guardian of the offerings at the shrine, and he went round the shrine three times carrying the banner, while he himself remained invisible.[1]

[1] ThagA. i. 308; Ap. i. 72.

Abhisāma.—A king of fifteen kappas ago; a previous birth of **Udakāsanadāyaka** Thera.[1]

[1] Ap. i. 218.

Abhiseka.—The name of a statue of the Buddha in the **Abhayagiri-vihāra.** King **Dhātusena** had a golden ornament made for it,[1] and in the time of Kassapa I., a senāpati, named **Migāra,** built a house for it.[2] Migāra also instituted a dedication festival for "Abhiseka Buddha."[3]

[1] Cv. xxxviii. 67.
[2] *Ibid.*, xxxix. 6.
[3] *Ibid.*, 40; see also Geiger's trans, i. 35, n. 7; 36, n. 2.

Amaccharī Sutta.—A woman should not be stingy and she should be wise.[1]

[1] S. iv. 244.

Amata.—The Lake of Immortality, in searching for which **Bhaddasāla** met the Buddha **Nārada.**[1]

[1] BuA. 154.

Amata Vagga.—The fifth chapter of the Satipaṭṭhāna Saṃyutta of the Saṃyutta Nikāya.[1]

[1] S. v. 184-90.

1. **Amata Sutta.**—The Buddha teaches the Deathless and the path thereto.[1]

[1] S. iv. 370.

2. **Amata Sutta.**—Dwell with mind well established in the four *Satipatthānā*, but let not that be to you the Deathless, *i.e.* do not confuse the means with the end.[1]

[1] S. v. 184; also KS. v. 161, n. 1.

3. **Amata Sutta.**—On the nature of deathlessness.[1]

[1] A. iv. 455.

Amatadundubhi.—One of the names under which the *Bahudhātuka Sutta* is known.[1] Like soldiers in the field of battle, so the disciples in the path, developing insight after the method of this sutta, raise aloft the standard of Arahantship—hence the name.[2]

[1] M. iii. 67. [2] MA. ii. 888.

Amadha.—See **Damatha.**

1. **Amara.**—See **Amaravatī.**

2. **Amara.**—A city in the time of **Siddhattha** Buddha. The Buddha, being there, made his way to the pleasaunce (**Amaruyyāna**) of the city, leaving his footprints to show his path. The two chiefs of the city, **Sambahula** and **Sumitta,** brothers, seeing the footmarks, went themselves to the pleasaunce, and having listened to the Buddha's preaching became arahants.[1]

[1] BuA. 186.

1. **Amaragiri.**—One of the three palaces occupied by **Atthadassī** Buddha during his lay life.[1]

[1] Bu. xv. 15.

2. **Amaragiri.**—A monastery in Ceylon, in which lived the Elder **Vanaratana.** In the time of **Bhuvanekabāhu IV.** it seems to have been the home of the orthodox monks.[1]

[1] P.L.C. 240.

Amarapura.—A city of Burma, founded by King Bodōpayā.[1] The Elder **Nāṇābhivaṃsa** lived there and was head of the group of monks known as the Amarapura sect. These monks, later, took to Ceylon a number of Pāli texts, these being either of Burmese authorship or else better known to the Burmese fraternity than to the Siṇhalese.[2]

Bode, p. 74; Sās. 130. [2] Bode, p. 78.

1. **Amaravatī.**—Also called **Amara.** A city in the time of **Dīpaṅkara** Buddha. **Sumedha** was born there in a very rich family and renounced the world after having given his wealth away.[1] According to the Mahābodhivaṃsa[2] the city was so called because it was inhabited by men like gods.

[1] Bu. ii. 6; J. i. 6; DhA. i. 68, etc. [2] p. 2.

2. **Amaravatī.**—A city in the time of **Koṇḍañña** Buddha eighteen leagues in extent. It was in the **Devavana,** near the city, that Koṇḍañña preached his first sermon[1] (*v.l.* **Arundhavatī).**

[1] BuA. 108-9.

3. **Amaravatī.**—The city of **Sakka,** king of the gods.[1]

[1] Sp. i. 49; Cv. lxxx. 5; it is described in the Mahābhārata iii. 1714 ff.; see also Hopkins, *Epic Mythology,* 140 f.

Amarā (Amarādevī).—Wife of **Mahosadha.** She was the daughter of a merchant who had fallen on evil days. Mahosadha, while seeking for a wife, met her as she was taking a meal to her father and entered into conversation with her. He asked her various questions and she answered in riddles. Mahosadha went to her father's house and plied his trade as a tailor, taking the opportunity of observing the girl's behaviour. He tested her temper and her character in various ways, and being satisfied that she was altogether desirable, he married her with the approval of Queen **Udumbarā.** She became popular with everybody and was of great assistance to her husband in frustrating the attempts of his enemies to work him harm.[1]

In the present age Amarā was the beautiful **Bimbādevī.**[2]

In the Milinda[3] the king mentions the story of Amarādevī having been left behind in the village while her husband was away on a journey, and of her resisting a temptation to be unfaithful to him. " If that be true, how," asks the king, " could you justify the Buddha's statement[4] that 'all women will go wrong, failing others, even with a cripple '? " Nāgasena explains this by saying that Amarā did not sin because she had neither real secrecy nor opportunity nor the right-wooer !

[1] J. iv. 364-72, 392; the story appears also in Mtu. ii. 83.

[2] J. vi. 478.

[3] pp. 205 ff.

[4] Incidentally, these words do not really belong to the Buddha. They appear in the *Kuṇāla Jātaka* (J. v. 435), which is a specimen of Indian folk-lore and not of Buddhist belief.

Amarādevī-pañha.—The name given to the riddle in which Amarā tells **Mahosadha** the way to her house: " *Yena sattu bilaṅgā ca dviguṇapalāso* *ca pupphito, yenādāmi tena vadāmi yena nādāmi na tena vadāmi esa maggo yavamajjhakassa etam channapatham vijānāhīti."*

The scholiast explains it thus: entering the village you will see a cake shop and then a gruel shop; further on an ebony tree in flower, take a path to the right.

This riddle referred to in J. i. 425 as the Amarādevipañha, is, however, called **Channapathapañha** in the *Ummagga Jātaka* itself, where it actually occurs in the story.[1]

[1] J. vi. 365-6.

Amarinda.—Name given to **Sakka,** king of the gods.[1]

[1] *E.g.*, ThigA. 151, 112.

Amita.—A king of twenty-five kappas ago; a previous birth of **Aggapupphiya** Thera[1] (*v.l.* **Amitobhava, Amitogata**).

[1] Ap. i. 229.

Amitañjala.—A king of fourteen kappas ago; a previous birth of **Sālapupphiya** Thera[1] (*v.l.* **Asitañjala**).

[1] Ap. i. 219.

1. **Amitā.**—One of the two chief women disciples of **Padumuttara** Buddha.[1]

[1] Bu. xi. 25; J. i. 37; SA. ii. 68; DA. ii. 489.

2. **Amitā.**—One of the two daughters of **Sīhahanu** (the other being **Pamitā**) and therefore a sister of **Suddhodana,** the Buddha's father. She married **Suppabuddha** the Sākyan and had two children, **Bhaddakaccānā** and **Devadatta.** She was a grand-daughter of **Devadahasakka.**[1]

She is the paternal aunt of the Buddha, referred to as being the mother of **Tissa** Thera[2] (*v.l.* **Amatā**).

[1] Mhv. ii. 16-22; see Rockhill, p. 13, where her son is called **Kalyānavardhana.**

[2] ThagA. i. 105; MA. i. 289.

Amitābha.—A king of twenty-five kappas ago; a previous birth of **Ekasaññaka** Thera.[1]

[1] Ap. i. 210.

Amitodana.—Son of **Sīhahanu** and **Kaccānā** (daughter of **Devadahasakka**) and brother of **Suddhodhana.**[1] He was the father of **Mahānāma** and **Anuruddha.**[2] Elsewhere[3] **Ānanda** is also called a son of Amitodana.

[1] Mhv. ii. 20; SnA. i. 357. [2] DhA. iv. 124. [3] DA. ii. 492; AA. i. 162.

In Sanskrit sources[4] he is spoken of as Amṛtodana and the father of **Devadatta.** Mention is also made of another son of his, the **Sakka Paṇḍu,** who escaped the slaughter of the Sākyans by **Viḍūḍabha.**[5]

[4] *E.g.,* Rockhill, p. 13, and Bigandet i. 13; see also Mtu. i. 352
[5] Mhv. viii. 18, 19.

Amitobhava.—See **Amita.**

Amitta.—See **Somamitta.**

Amittaka.—See **Amittabhā.**

Amittatāpana.—A king of seventeen kappas ago; a previous life of **Paviṭṭha** Thera,[1] probably to be identified with **Ekadaṃsaniya** of the Apadāna.[2]

[1] ThagA. i. 185. [2] i. 168.

Amittatāpanā.—The young wife of the brahmin **Jūjaka** of Kāliṅga. She had been given away by her parents in payment of a debt. Being mocked at by the friends she met at the watering-place, she insisted on being provided with servants. It was in order to meet with her wishes that Jūjuka went to **Vessantara** to beg for the latter's children to be used as slaves.[1]

In the present Buddha-age, Amittatāpana was **Ciñcamāṇavikā.**[2]

[1] J. vi. 521-4. [2] *Ibid.*, 593.

Amittabhā.—A king of twenty-five kappas ago; a former life of **Bhojanadāyaka** Thera[1] (*v.l.* **Amittaka**).

[1] Ap. i. 253.

Amoraphaliya Thera.—An arahant. Ninety-one kappas ago he gave an *amora*-fruit to **Vipassī** Buddha.[1] The verses ascribed to him in the Apadāna are, in the Theragāthā Commentary, attributed to two monks, **Isidatta**[2] and **Gotama**[3] (*v.l.* **Amodaphaliya**).

[1] Ap. ii. 447. [2] ThagA. i. 238. [3] *Ibid.*, i. 256.

1. **Amba Jātaka** (No. 124).—During a very severe drought a hermit, living in the Himālaya at the head of five hundred ascetics, provided water for the animals, using the hollowed trunk of a tree as trough. In gratitude the animals brought him various fruits, enough for himself

and his five hundred companions. The story is related regarding a brother who was very zealous in his duties, doing everything well and wholeheartedly. Because of his great goodness the people fed regularly every day five hundred of the Brethren.

[1] J. i. 449-51.

2. **Amba Jātaka** (No. 474).—The story of a brahmin youth who learnt a charm from a wise Caṇḍāla. The charm had the power of making lovely and fragrant mangoes grow out of season. The youth exhibited his skill before the king, but when asked the name of his teacher he lied and said he had been taught in Takkasilā. Immediately the charm escaped his memory and all his power deserted him. At the king's suggestion he went back to the teacher to ask his forgiveness and to learn the charm anew, but the teacher would have none of him and the youth wandered away into the forest and died there.

The story is told in reference to **Devadatta** who had repudiated the Buddha as his teacher and as a result was born in Avīci.[1]

The youth was a former birth of Devadatta.

[1] J. iv. 200-7.

Amba Sutta.—The four kinds of mangoes (ripe, etc.) and four corresponding classes of monks.[1]

[1] A. ii. 106 f.

1. **Ambagāma.**—A village in Ceylon near **Pulatthipura** identified with the modern Ambagamuva. A battle was fought there between the forces of **Gajabāhu** and **Parakkamabāhu I.**[1] **Parakkambāhu II.** built a bridge, thirty-four cubits in length, over the **Khajjotanadī** at Ambagāma.[2]

[1] Cv. lxx. 321. [2] *Ibid.*, lxxxvi. 23.

2. **Ambagāma.**—One of the villages near **Vesāli** visited by the Buddha on his last tour.[1] It was between Bhaṇḍagāma and Bhoganagara, on the road from Vesāli to Kusinārā. This was evidently the road which led from Vesāli northwards to the Malla Country, for other villages in the vicinity of Ambagāma were Hatthigāma and Jambugāma.

It is noteworthy that **Anupiya,** although in the Malla country, is not mentioned in the list of these villages. Thomas[2] thinks that this is because the route to Kusinārā passed to the east of Anupiya.

[1] D. ii. 123. [2] *Op. cit.*, 148, n. 1.

Ambaṅganaṭṭhāna.—The spot where **Devānampiyatissa** gave a mango to **Mahinda.** The Elder ate the mango and had the stone planted in the ground. Immediately a tree grew from it and the earth trembled. The Elder declared that the spot would become a place of assembly for the Saṅgha of Ceylon and would be called Ambaṅgana.[1]

[1] Sp. i. 101.

Ambacora Jātaka (No. 344).—The story of a wicked ascetic who built for himself a hut in a mango orchard on the river bank near Benares and ate the ripe mangoes as they fell. In order to frighten him Sakka made the orchard appear as if it had been plundered by thieves. The ascetic, coming back from his begging-round and seeing what had happened, charged the four daughters of a merchant who had just entered the garden with having stolen the mangoes. They denied the charge and swore dreadful oaths to support their statement. Thereupon he let them go.

The story was told about an Elder who had entered the Order in his old age and who, instead of practising his duties, looked after mangoes. Thieves stole his manoges, and he charged with the theft the four daughters of a rich merchant who happened to visit the park. They swore oaths to prove that they were not guilty and were released.[1]

[1] J. iii. 137-9.

1. **Ambaṭṭha** (usually called **Ambaṭṭha-mānava**). A brahmin youth of the Ambaṭṭha clan who lived with his teacher, **Pokkharasādi,** at **Ukkaṭṭhā.** He was learned in the three Vedas and the correlated branches of knowledge, including the Lokāyata, as recorded in the *Ambaṭṭha Sutta.*[1] Once, at the request of his teacher, he visited the Buddha in the **Icchānaṅkala** wood and seems to have opened his conversation by reviling the Sākyans and calling them menials. It appears that Ambaṭṭha had once gone on some business of Pokkharasādi's to Kapilavatthu, to the Mote Hall of the Sākyans, and had been insulted there.[2]

Asked by the Buddha to what family he belonged, Ambaṭṭha replied that he came of the **Kaṇhāyana-gotta;** thereupon the Buddha traced the family back to its ancestor, who had been the offspring of a slave girl of **Okkāka,** named **Disā.** The child had been able to talk as soon as he was born and, because of this devilish trait, had been called **Kaṇha** (devil), hence the family name.[3] Ambaṭṭha makes no remonstrance against this genealogy and, under pressure, accepts it as true. This gives the Buddha an opportunity of preaching on the futility of feeling vanity regarding one's caste and on the worth of morality and conduct.[3]

[1] D. i. 87 ff. [2] *Ibid.*, 91.

[3] **Kaṇha** later became a mighty seer and married **Maddarūpī,** daughter of **Okkāka** (D. i. 96-7).

At the end of the discourse the Buddha walked up and down outside his chamber so that Ambaṭṭha might see on his body the thirty-two signs of a great man. Ambaṭṭha goes back to Pokkharasādi and reports the whole interview. Pokkharasādi is greatly incensed, abuses Ambaṭṭha and kicks him. Later Pokkharasādi goes himself to the Buddha and invites him for a meal. At the end of the meal the Buddha instructs him in his Doctrine and is accepted as the Teacher both of Pokkharasādi himself and of his followers and dependants at Ukkaṭṭhā. Pokkarasādi himself becomes a *Sotāpanna*.[4]

We are not told that Ambaṭṭha became a follower of the Buddha. Buddhaghosa says[5] that the Buddha knew that Ambaṭṭha would not profit by his discourse in his present life (*iminā attabhāvena magga-pātubhāvo natthi*), and that therefore a sermon with the idea of converting him would only have meant spending unnecessary time. Ambaṭṭha himself only visited the Buddha on account of his interest in physiognomy. According to Buddhaghosa the idea of the Buddha in preaching the Ambaṭṭha Sutta at such length was that it might be repeated to Pokkharasādi.

It is conjectured that the Ambaṭṭha, who is identified with **Kāvinda,** one of the counsellors of King **Vedeha,** in the *Ummagga Jātaka*,[6] probably refers to the Ambaṭṭha of this sutta.

[4] DA. i. 278. [5] DA. i. 274. [6] J. vi. 478.

2. **Ambaṭṭha.**—A king of old, at whose court **Rāhulamātā** in one of her former lives had been a handmaid. In that life she had given alms to a holy man and, as a result, became in her next birth consort of the King of Benares.[1]

[1] J. iii. 413-14.

Ambaṭṭhakola.—A district in Ceylon near the modern Kurunegala, fifty-five miles from Anurādhapura. When **Duṭṭhagāmaṇi** planned to build the **Mahā Thūpa** silver appeared near a cave in this district by the power of the devas and was discovered by a merchant who reported the find to the king; the king himself came to gather the silver for the thūpa.[1]

Later, **Amaṇḍagāmaṇi Abhaya** built the **Rajatalena Vihāra** here.[2] It was in this district, in the neighbourhood of the **Kuṭhāri Vihāra,** that **Moggallāna** defeated his brother the parricide **Kassapa I.**[3]

According to the Mahāvaṃsa Ṭīkā it was in Ambaṭṭhakola that King **Mahācūlī Mahātissa** worked in **Soṇṇagiri** in a sugar mill to earn money for an alms-giving[4] (*v.l.* **Ambaṭṭhakolalena**).

[1] Mhv. xxviii. 20-35; MṬ. 512.
[2] Mhv. xxxv. 4, 5.
[3] Cv. xxxix. 21 ff.
[4] MṬ. 624; Mhv. xxxiv. 4 f.

Ambaṭṭha-gotta.—The clan to which **Ambaṭṭha-mānava** belonged. The **Kaṇhāyana-gotta** was probably one of its chief sections, or, perhaps, the family of its original ancestors. In the Buddha's time the clan was evidently considered very aristocratic, at least by its own members, for they looked down upon even the Sākyans as scourings from their kinsmen's feet, though the Sakyans themselves seem to have laughed at the pretensions of the Ambaṭṭhas.[1] Nor were the Ambaṭṭhas brahmins by birth; some of them were farmers and traders and some even sold their daughters for gold.[2]

The Ambaṭṭhas were of an old stock and were well known. Besides the Ambaṭṭha-mānava mentioned above, another Ambaṭṭha, called **Sūra,** is spoken of in the Piṭakas.[3]

[1] See **Ambattha-mānava** above.

[2] J. iv. 363; they were called brahmins by courtesy *vohāravasena* (*ibid.*, 366). According to the *Mānavadhammaśāstra,* they were not sprung from Kṣatriya father and a slave (presumably Śūdra) mother, as given in the *Ambaṭṭha Sutta,* but from a brahmin father and a Vaiśya mother.

[3] *E.g.*, A. i. 26; iii. 451

Ambaṭṭha-vijjā.—The charm learnt by **Kaṇha,** ancestor of the Kaṇhāyanas, from the ascetics of Dakkhiṇajanapada. The charm had the power of disarming those who tried to attack its possessor. With the aid of this charm Kaṇha won **Maddarūpī,** daughter of Okkāka.[1]

[1] D. i. 96; DA. i. 265.

Ambaṭṭha Sutta.—Preached at **Icchānaṅkala** when **Ambaṭṭha-mānava** visited the Buddha.[1]

Reference is made to the Commentary on this sutta where a detailed explanation is given of the term *cārikā.*[2] It is regarded, together with the *Soṇadaṇḍa* and *Kūṭadanta* Suttas, as one of the chief discussions which the Buddha had with his opponents.[3] The eight kinds of *vijjā* are detailed therein.[4]

[1] D. i. 87 ff.

[2] AA. i. 407.

[3] MA. ii. 697.

[4] Sp. i. 116; ii. 495.

Ambaṭṭhaja.—Seventy kappas ago there were fourteen kings of this name, all former lives of **Ambadāyaka** Thera.[1]

[1] Ap. i. 117.

Ambatittha.—A village in the **Cetiya** country near **Bhaddavatikā.** When the Buddha was on tour near there he was repeatedly warned by the cowherds not to go to Ambatittha as in the Jaṭila's hermitage in the village dwelt a mighty Nāga. While the Buddha was yet in Bhadda vatikā the Elder **Sāgata** went to the Jaṭila's hermitage and took up his abode near the fireplace. The Nāga showed his resentment, but Sāgata was able to overcome him by means of his *iddhi*-powers. Later Sāgata visited the Buddha at Bhaddavatikā and went with him to Kosambī. The fame of the Elder's victory over the Nāga had preceded him and the inhabitants of Kosambī were lavish in their hospitality to him. He drank wine in their houses and had to be carried to see the Buddha. The latter made this the occasion for declaring the drinking of intoxicants to be a *pācittiya*-offence.[1]

[1] Vin. iv. 108-10; AA. i. 178.

1. **Ambatitthaka.**—A Tamil stronghold surrounded by a river and a moat; it was captured by **Duṭṭhagāmaṇi** after a siege of four months.[1] The crafty Damiḷa **Titthamba** lived there, and it is said that, in the end, he was conquered by a conspiracy in which Duṭṭhagāmaṇi offered to allow him to marry Duṭṭhagāmaṇi's mother.[2] Near here was a ford across the **Mahāvāluka-gaṅgā.**

[1] Mhv. xxv. 7-9. [2] MṬ. 473 f.

2. **Ambatitthaka.**—A Jaṭila living at **Ambatittha** (1).

Ambatthala.—A little tableland immediately below the **Silākūṭa** of the **Missaka** Mountain in Ceylon. It was near here that **Mahinda** and his companions alighted after their aerial journey from Jambudīpa.[1] There King **Mahādāṭhika-Mahānāga** built the **Ambatthala Thūpa,** risking his own life in order to make the building secure. He made a cover for the whole thūpa and, at its dedication, held the great **Giribhaṇḍapūjā.**[2] **Kaṇiṭṭhatissaka** built a monastery attached to the thūpa,[3] which **Goṭhābhaya** renovated.[4]

The vihāra was rebuilt or enlarged by **Dhātusena.** He intended to give it into the charge of the Theravādins, but ultimately gave it to the Dhammarucikas at the latters' request.[5] **Sirimeghavaṇṇa** had a life-size golden image of Mahinda placed in the Ambatthala Cetiya.[6]

It is said that the place was so called after the riddle of the mango tree (Mhv. xiv. 17 ff.) with which Mahinda put Devānampiyatissa's discernment to the test. Even now mango trees are planted near the ceitya in memory of the event.[7]

Other names for the place are **Cetiyambatthala**[8] and **Therambatthalaka.**[9]

[1] Mhv. xiii. 20.
[2] *Ibid.*, xxiv. 68-81.
[3] *Ibid.*, xxxvi. 9.
[4] *Ibid.*, 106.
[5] Cv. xxxviii. 76.
[6] *Ibid.*, xxxvii. 69.
[7] Cv. trans. i. 4, n. 5.
[8] Cv. xxxvii. 69.
[9] Mhv. xxxvi. 106.

Ambadāyaka Thera.—An Arahant. He had been a monkey in the time of **Anomadassī** Buddha and, having seen the Buddha in Himavā, offered him a mango fruit. As a result of this he enjoyed happiness in deva worlds for fifty-seven kappas and was fourteen times king under the name of **Ambaṭṭhaja.**[1]

[1] Ap. i. 116-17.

Ambadugga.—A tank in Ceylon, built by **Kuṭakaṇṇatissa.**[1]

[1] Mhv. xxxiv. 33.

Ambapālī (Ambapālikā),—A courtesan of **Vesālī.** She is said to have come spontaneously into being at Vesāli in the gardens of the king. The gardener found her at the foot of a mango tree—hence her name—and brought her to the city. She grew up so full of beauty and of grace that many young princes vied with each other for the honour of her hand. Finally, in order to end their strife, they appointed her courtesan. Later she became a devout follower of the Buddha, and building a vihāra in her own garden, gave it to him and the Order. This was during the Buddha's last visit to Vesāli shortly before his death. It is said that when Ambapālī heard of the Buddha's visit to **Koṭigāma** near Vesāli she and her retinue drove out of the city in magnificent chariots to meet him, and, after hearing a discourse, invited him and the monks to a meal the next day. The Buddha accepted this invitation and had, as a result, to refuse that of the Licchavis of Vesāli.[1]

It was after this meal that Ambapālī gave over her park, the **Ambapālivana,** to the Buddha and the Order. The Buddha accepted the gift and stayed there some time before going on to **Beluva.**[2]

Ambapālī had a son, **Vimala-Kondañña,** who was an eminent Elder. Having heard him preach one day, she renounced the world and, working for insight by studying the law of impermanence as illustrated in her own ageing body, she attained arahantship.[3]

Nineteen verses ascribed to her are found in the Therīgāthā.[4]

In the time of **Sikhī** Buddha she had entered the Order. While yet

[1] While returning from her visit to the Buddha, Ambapālī was so elated at the idea of having the Buddha to a meal the next day, that she refused to make way for the Licchavi princes who were on their way to the Buddha. She refused to give up her invitation for anything in the world. The DA. says that just before Ambapālī's visit to him, the Buddha admonished the monks to be steadfast and mindful, lest they should lose their heads about her (DA. ii. 545).

[2] Vin. i. 231-3; D. ii. 95-8; the two accounts vary in details, *e.g.* in the Dīgha version the Buddha was already in Ambapālivana, and not in Koṭigāma, when the courtesan visited him.

[3] ThigA. 206-7.

[4] 252-70.

a novice, she took part in a procession of bhikkhunis, and was doing homage at a shrine when an arahant therī in front of her hastily spat in the court of the shrine. Seeing the spittle and not knowing who had committed the fault, she said in reproof, "What prostitute has been spitting here?" It was owing to this remark that she was born as a courtesan in her last birth.[5]

The Apadāna (quoted also in ThigA.) gives some more details about her. She had been a daughter of a Khattiya family in the time of **Phussa** Buddha and had done many good deeds in order to be beautiful in later births. As a result of the abuse of the nun (referred to above) she had been born in hell and later had, for ten thousand lives, been a courtesan. In **Kassapa** Buddha's time she had practised celibacy.[6]

It is said that she charged fifty kahāpanas a night from her patrons and that Vesāli became very prosperous through her. It was this that prompted **Bimbisāra** to get a courtesan for his own city of Rājagaha.[7]

Among Ambapālī's patrons was Bimbisāra, and he was the father of her son Vimala-Koṇḍañña.[8]

In the Theragāthā[9] there are two verses which, according to tradition, were spoken by **Ānanda** in admonition of monks who lost their heads at the sight of Ambapālī. Whether this was before or after she joined the Order we are not told.

[5] ThigA. 206-7.
[6] Ap. ii. 613 ff.; ThigA. 213 f.
[7] Vin. i. 268.
[8] ThagA. i. 146.
[9] vv. 1020-21; ThagA. ii. 129.

Ambapāli Vagga.—The first chapter of the Satipaṭṭhāna Saṃyutta in the Mahāvagga of the Saṃyutta Nikāya.[1]

[1] S. v. 141-8.

1. **Ambapāli Sutta.**—Preached at **Ambapālivana.** The four *satipaṭṭhānā* form the sole way that leads to the purification of beings, and to the realisation of Nibbāna, etc.[1]

[1] S. v. 140.

2. **Ambapāli Sutta.**—A conversation between **Anuruddha** and **Sāriputta** in **Ambapālivana.** Sāriputta asks the reason of Anuruddha's serenity and beauty of complexion. It is due to the practice of the four *satipaṭṭhānā*, says Anuruddha; he himself spends all his time in the practice of them, and so generally do all arahants.[1]

S. v. 301.

Ambapālivana.—The grove presented by **Ambapālī** to the Buddha and the Order. It was in Vesāli and was given to the Buddha during his last tour in that town, at the conclusion of the meal to which Ampabālī had invited him.[1] But both the Buddha and the monks seem to have stayed there previously during their visits to Vesāli.[2] The Buddha is stated to have preached three suttas in the grove, two of them being on the value of the *satipatthānā*.[3] In the third sutta[4] he dwells on the impermanence of all *saṅkhāras* and proceeds to describe the process by which the whole world will ultimately be destroyed by seven suns arising in the world and drying everything up. In this sutta appears also the story of the teacher **Sunetta,** who, even after becoming the Great Brahmā, is yet subject to old age and death.

The Saṃyutta also records a conversation that took place between Anuruddha and Sāriputta during a stay in Ambapālivana.[5]

The grove was planted with mangoes and was so called because it belonged to Ambapālī.[6]

[1] Vin. i. 231-3.

[2] Thus according to D. ii. 94 the Buddha was already in the grove before Ambapālī visited him; see also S. v. 301, which must refer to an incident before the Buddha's last tour, because Sāriputta was still alive.

[3] S. v. 141 ff.

[4] A. iv. 100-6.

[5] S. v. 301.

[6] DA. ii. 545.

Ambapāsāna.—A monastery in the village of **Aṅganakola** in South Ceylon, where lived the Elder **Cittagutta.**[1]

[1] MṬ. 552.

1. **Ambapiṇḍiya Thera.**—An arahant. He had been a Dānava named **Romasa** and had given a cluster of mangoes to **Vipassī** Buddha.[1]

[1] Ap. i. 247.

2. **Ambapiṇḍiya.**—An arahant. He had been an elephant in the time of **Siddattha** Buddha. Having seen the Buddha in the forest, the elephant gave him a bunch of mangoes. As a result he was born in Tusita.[1]

[1] Ap. i. 395.

Ambamāla Vihāra.—A monastery in Rohaṇa built by **Dappula I.**[1]

[1] Cv. xlv. 55.

Ambayāgadāyaka Thera.—An arahant. Ninety-one kappas ago, going to the forest in pursuit of his trade, he met the Buddha and gave him an offering of mangoes[1] (*v.l.* **Appa**°).

[1] Ap. i. 221.

Ambayāgu(yāga ?)-dāyaka Thera.—An arahant. Ninety-four kappas ago he had met a Pacceka Buddha named **Sataraṃsī,** when the latter had just awakened from *samādhi,* and had given him a broth (?) made of mangoes.[1]

[1] Ap. i. 284.

Ambaraṃsa.—See **Abbhasa.**

Ambara-Ambaravatī.—The double name of a city in **Uttarakuru.**[1]

[1] D. iii. 201; DA. iii. 966.

Ambariya Vihara.—A monastery in Ceylon, the residence of **Piṅgala-Buddharakkhita** Thera. It was near **Antaravaḍḍhamāna-pabbata.**[1] It was also the residence of **Piṇḍapātika-Tissa** Thera.[2]

[1] SA. ii. 113; MA. i. 165; DhsA. 103.

[2] AA. i. 277.

Ambala.—Probably the name of a tower in the Jetavana monastery. The *Sunakha Jātaka* was preached there about a dog who lived in its resting-hall.[1]

[1] J. ii. 246.

Ambalaṭṭhikā.—A royal park on the road between Rājagaha and Nālandā. It contained a royal rest-house (*rājāgāraka*) in which the Buddha and members of the Order used to stay in the course of their journeyings. It was on one such occasion that the *Brahmajāla Sutta* was preached.[1] Buddhaghosa[2] says that it was a shady and well-watered park, so called because of a mango sapling which stood by the gateway. It was surrounded and well guarded by a rampart, and its rest-house was adorned with paintings for the king's amusement.

It was one of the spots in which the Buddha rested during his last tour, and we are told that while there he discoursed to a large number of monks.[3] But the most famous of the Buddha's sermons in Ambalaṭṭhikā seems to have been the *Rāhulovāda Sutta* named *Ambalaṭṭhika-Rāhulovāda Sutta,* because of its having been preached in the park.[4] From the context it appears as though Ambalaṭṭhikā was within walking distance from the **Kalandakanivāpa** in Rājagaha.[5]

[1] Vin ii. 287; D. i. 1.

[2] DA. i. 41-2.

[3] D. ii. 81; he remained there one night (UdA. 408).

[4] M. i. 414 ff.

[5] But see below (4) for a more probable explanation.

2. **Ambalaṭṭhikā.**—A park in the brahmin village **Khānumata.** The Buddha went there during one of his tours through **Magadha.** On this

occasion was preached the *Kūṭadanta Sutta.*[1] Buddhaghosa[2] says the park was like the pleasaunce of the same name between Rājagaha and Nālandā.

[1] D. i. 127.

[2] DA. i. 294.

3. **Ambalaṭṭhikā.**—There was a place of this name to the east of the **Lohapāsāda** in Anurādhapura. Once when the **Dīghabhānaka** Theras recited the *Brahmajāla Sutta* there, the earth trembled from the water upwards.[1]

On another occasion King **Vasabha** heard the Dīghabhānakas reciting the *Mahāsudassana Sutta,* and thinking that they were discussing what they had eaten and drunk, he approached closer to listen; when he discovered the truth he applauded the monks.[2]

The place referred to here was probably not a park, but a building which formed part of the Lohapāsāda. In the Mahāvaṃsa account[3] of the building of the Lohapāsāda we are told that the plans were copied from the gem-palace of the goddess **Bīraṇī.** The central part of the palace was called the **Ambalaṭṭhikapāsāda.** "It was visible from every side, bright, with pennons hung out."

Duṭṭhagāmaṇi probably included a similar central part in the Lohapāsāda.[4]

[1] DA. i. 131.

[2] *Ibid.*, ii. 635.

[3] Mhv. xxvii. 11-20.

[4] This view is strengthened by No. 4 below.

4. **Ambalaṭṭhikā.**—According to Buddhaghosa,[1] the Ambalaṭṭhikā, in which the *Rāhulovāda Sutta* of that name was preached, was not a pleasaunce, but a *pāsāda,* a kind of meditation hall (*padhānaghara-saṅkhepa*) built in the outskirts of **Veluvanavihāra** for the use of those who desired solitude. It is said that **Rāhula** spent most of his time there, from the day of his ordination as a seven-year-old boy.

[1] MA. ii. 635.

Ambalaṭṭhika-Rāhulovāda Sutta.—Preached by the Buddha at **Ambalaṭṭhikā** (near Veluvana) to **Rāhula.** It deals with falsehood. Like a minute drop of water is the recluseship of those who shrink not from deliberate lying, it is thrown away, upset; it is empty and void. There is nothing evil they will not do, they run every risk, like an elephant who guards not his trunk. One should practise constant reflection, thereby abandoning all things conducive to woe, either to oneself or to others, and develop self-control and purity.[1] Rāhula was evidently yet very

[1] M. i. 414-20.

young at the time of this sermon, for we find the Buddha making use of frequent similes, and pointing them out to him.[2]

The Commentary says that it was preached because very young novices might be tempted to say things both proper and improper; they were likely to imagine things. This sutta is to warn Rāhula against the use of lies.[3]

The Ambalaṭṭhika-Rāhulovāda Sutta is among the portions of scripture mentioned in the Bhābrā Edict of Asoka as being essentially worthy of study by all monks[4] (*v.l.* **Ambalaṭṭhiya**°).

[2] According to the Cy., he was at the time only 7 years old (MA. ii. 636).

[3] MA. ii. 635 f.; AA. i. 145; ii. 547.

[4] See Mookerji: *Asoka*, p. 119.

Ambalala.—A locality in Rohana, near the **Kaṇṭakavana,** where the forces of **Parakkamabāhu I.,** under **Rakkha,** were victorious in battle.[1]

[1] Cv. lxxiv. 58.

1. **Ambavana.**—A *padhānaghara* in Ceylon, built by **Kassapa III.**[1]

[1] Cv. xlviii. 25.

2. **Ambavana.**—A district in Ceylon, near the village of **Khīravāpi.** It was not far from Pulatthinagara. The name is preserved in that of the Ambangaṅga which flows through the valley of Matale.[1]

[1] Cv. lxvi. 85; lxix. 9; lxx. 98, 191-6. See also Cv. trans. i. 260, n. 1.

See also under **Anupiya, Kakuttha, Jīvaka, Cunda, Todeyya, Pāvārika** and **Vedaññā** for other localities designated as **Ambavana** and connected with these names.

Ambavāpi.—A tank at **Būkakalla** in Ceylon. It was given over to the **Māṭambiya-padhānaghara** by the Damila, **Potthakuṭṭha.**[1]

[1] Cv. xlvi. 19-20.

Ambavāsavāpi.—One of the tanks restored by **Parakkamabāhu I.** before his great war.[1]

[1] Cv. lxviii. 43. For identification see Cv. trans. i. 280, n. 5.

Ambasakkhara.—One of the Licchavi chieftains of Vesāli during the Buddha's time. He was a nihilist by persuasion.

Once while going through the city he saw a beautiful woman. Wishing to possess her, he commandeered her husband's services and one day ordered him to bring mud and lotuses from a pond three leagues away, his life to be the penalty if he did not return the same evening. Meanwhile Ambasakkhara ordered the guards to shut the city gates earlier than usual. The woman's husband returned to the city before nightfall, but finding the gates shut, he asked a thief, who was impaled just outside, to bear witness to his having arrived before sunset.

The thief's uncle had been a pious merchant in Vesāli, but had been beheaded for alleged implication in his nephew's theft. He had been reborn as a *peta*, and because of his good deeds he possessed various powers. By reason, however, of having once hidden, in jest, the clothes of a friend who was bathing in the river, he was born naked. Every night he came to see his nephew and encouraged him to go on living, in spite of his impalement, because the *peta* knew that suffering in hell awaited the thief after death.

When the man with the lotuses asked the thief's assistance in proving his innocence, he was advised to await the *peta's* arrival that night and to get his counsel. This the man did, and when, the next day, he was summoned before Ambasakkhara, he cited the *peta* as witness for his defence. Ambasakkhara agreed to test the truth of the story, and in the night he saw the *peta* and learnt all that had happened. Greatly marvelling, he offered to help the *peta* in getting rid of his nudity. He was asked to seek the holy Elder **Kappitaka** who lived in **Kapinaccanā** in the Vajji country and give him robes in the *peta's* name. This was done, and the *peta* immediately appeared before them clad in heavenly robes. From that time Ambasakkhara was converted to the Faith, and after having listened to a sermon by Kappitaka became a *Sotāpanna.* The impaled thief was set free and was cured by the royal physician; he later attained to the state of an arahant.[1]

[1] Pv. 45-57; PvA. 215-44.

Ambasakkharapeta Vatthu.—The story of **Ambasakkhara** and the *peta*, as given above. The Elder **Kappitaka** related the story to the Buddha, and the Buddha made it an occasion for a discourse to the assembled multitude.[1]

[1] PvA. 243-4.

Ambasaṇḍā.—A brahmin village in Magadha to the east of Rājagaha. To the north of the village was the **Vediyaka** mountain, in which was the **Indasālaguhā,** where the *Sakkapañha Sutta* was preached. On the occasion of the preaching, as Sakka with his retinue came to visit the Buddha, the village was bathed in radiance.[1]

The name arose from the fact that the village lay in the vicinity of many mango groves.[2]

[1] D. ii. 263 f.

[2] DA. iii. 697.

Ambasāmanera.—Name of **Silākāla.** When he was a novice in the Order, at **Bodhimaṇḍa Vihāra,** he fulfilled his duties to the community with zeal and skill. Once he presented a mango-fruit to the Saṅgha, and the monks, being pleased, gave him this name.[1]

[1] Cv. xxxix. 48 ff.

Ambasuppiya.—See **Appihā.**

Ambahattha.—A hill in **Sunāparanta** where the Elder **Puṇṇa** stayed for some time after his arrival in that country. His younger brother lived near there in the merchants' village and gave him alms[1] (*v.l.* **Ajjuhattha, Abbhahattha**).

[1] MA. ii. 1015; SA. iii. 15.

Ambāṭaka Thera.—An arahant. Fourteen kappas ago he had given a mango to a Buddha.[1]

He is probably identical with **Rājadatta** Thera.[2]

[1] Ap. ii. 394.
[2] ThagA. i. 403.

Ambāṭakavana.—A grove at **Macchikāsaṇḍa,** belonging to **Cittagahapati.** Being pleased with the Elder **Mahānāma** of Macchikāsaṇḍa, Citta invited him to a meal, and after listening to his discourse, gave the grove to the Order. At the dedication of the gift the earth trembled. Later he built a splendid monastery there, the **Ambāṭakārāma,** for the use of monks from all parts.[1] It became the residence of large numbers of monks, and discussions often took place there between Cittagahapati and the resident bhikkhus.[2]

Among eminent Elders who visited the place were **Isidatta** of Avanti (who answered Citta's questions regarding the reason for the existence of various views in the world),[3] **Mahaka** (who, by his magic powers, produced rain and thunderstorms and later showed a special miracle to Citta),[4] **Kāmabhū** (who discoursed to Citta on various topics),[5] and **Godatta.**[6] The Elder **Lakuṇṭaka Bhaddiya** also lived there, in solitude, wrapt in meditation.[7]

Behind Ambaṭaka was **Migapathaka,** which was Citta's tributary village[8] (*v.l.* **Ambāḷavana**).

[1] AA. i. 209; DhA. ii. 74.
[2] S. iv. 281-97.
[3] *Ibid.*, 283-8.
[4] *Ibid.*, 288-91.
[5] *Ibid.*, 291-5.
[6] *Ibid.*, 295-7.
[7] Thag. v. 466.
[8] SA. iii. 93.

Ambāṭakiya Thera.—An arahant. Thirty-one kappas ago he had met the Buddha **Vessabhū** in the mountains and given him a mango.[1]

[1] Ap. ii. 399.

Ambālavāpi.—A tank restored by **Parakkamabāhu I.**[1] A canal known as **Tambapaṇṇi** flowed from the tank northwards.[2]

[1] Cv. lxviii. 46. [2] *Ibid.*, lxxix. 50.

Ambāḷavana.—See **Ambāṭaka.**

Ambila-janapada.—A district in Ceylon. In it was the **Rajatalena.**[1]

[1] MṬ. 400.

Ambilapassava.—A village in Ceylon, near **Kurunda,** the residence of **Mahāsiva.**[1] **Aggabodhi I.** built a vihāra there and gave the village for its maintenance. The vihāra and the village were dedicated to the ascetics of the Theravāda fraternity.[2]

[1] Near Mannar, Cv. trans. i. 66, n. 6. [2] Cv. xlii. 17.

Ambilayāgu.—A village in Ceylon. It was the residence of **Dāṭhānāma,** father of **Dhātusena.**[1]

[1] Cv. xxxviii. 15.

Ambilahāra Vihāra.—A monastery in Ceylon. On one occasion the Thera **Tipitaka-Culla Nāga** preached there the *Mahā Saḷāyatanika Sutta.* The audience of men was one gāvuta in extent, and that of gods a league. At the end of the sermon a thousand monks became arahants.[1]

[1] MA. ii. 1025.

Ambilāpika.—A village given by **Jeṭṭhatissa III.** for the supply of food to **Kassapagirivihāra.**[1]

[1] Cv. xliv. 98.

Ambillapadara.—A village given by **Aggabodhi III.** to the **Cetiyapabbata** monastery.[1]

[1] Cv. xliv. 122.

Ambuṭṭhi.—A tank built by **Upatissa II.**[1]

[1] Cv. xxxvii. 185.

Ambuyyāna.—A monastery in Ceylon. **Udaya I.** (or **Dappula**) built in it the dwelling-house **Dappulapabbata.**[1] It was finished later by **Sena I.**[2]

[1] Cv. xlix. 30; trs. i. 126 n. 1. According to Cv. l. 80, it was built not by the king but by **Mahādeva.**

[2] Cv. l. 80.

Ayakūṭa Jātaka (No. 347).—The Bodhisatta was once born in Benares and became its king. At that time people were in the habit of sacrificing animals to the gods in order to win their favour, but the Bodhisatta proclaimed that no living creature should be slain. Being enraged at the loss of their food, the *yakkhas* sent one of their number to the Bodhisatta. He came to the Bodhisatta's bed at night meaning to strike him a deadly blow. Thereupon Sakka's throne grew hot, and learning the cause, Sakka himself came and stood guard over the Bodhisatta. The latter saw the yakkha standing over him ready to strike but powerless, and only learnt later, to his great encouragement, that Sakka had been there to protect him.[1]

The reason for the telling of the story is given in the *Mahākaṇha Jātaka*.

[1] J.iii. 145-7.

Ayoguḷa Sutta.—Ānanda asks the Buddha if the Buddha can, by psychic powers, reach the Brahma world in his mind-made body as well as in his physical body. The Buddha says he can, and proceeds to explain how by concentrating body in mind and mind in body the body becomes radiant and plastic. Like an iron ball heated throughout the day, or a tuft of cotton seed on a ball of thistledown, wafted lightly on the wind, so the body, at such time, rises from the ground into the air and takes on manifold forms of magic power.[1]

[1] S. v. 282-4.

Ayoghara.—The Bodhisatta was once born as the son of the king of Benares. Both the earlier children of the Queen Consort had been eaten up by a she-goblin. For the third child, therefore, an iron house (*ayoghara*) was built, and in this the Bodhisatta was born, hence his name, **Ayoghara.** Meanwhile the she-goblin had died, but yet the Bodhisatta grew up in the iron house. When he was sixteen his father, wishing to give him the kingdom, had him taken in ceremonial procession round the city. Wondering at all that he saw, he asked why he had been denied the sight of all these things before. When told the reason, he reflected that all life was a prison, that though he had escaped the goblin, there still remained old age and death. Accordingly, at the end of the procession, he announced his intention of renouncing the world. His parents and many others being converted to his views, they followed him into the forest, where a special hermitage was built for them by **Vissakamma** under Sakka's orders.[1]

[1] J. iv. 490-99.

Ayoghara Jātaka (No. 510).—The story of Prince **Ayoghara** as given above.

The story was told regarding the Buddha's Renunciation.

In the Jātakamālā the name appears as Ayogṛha.[1]

[1] Jārakamālā, No. 32.

1. **Ayojjhā.**—A city of the Ganges.[1] Two visits of the Buddha to this city are recorded in the Canon; on one accasion he preached the *Phena Sutta*[2] and on the other the *Dārukkhandha Sutta.*[3] In both these references the city is said to be on the Ganges; the town usually called Ayojjhā (**Ayodhya**) is certainly not on this river. The records, therefore, go back either to a confused or an unintelligent tradition,[4] or may possibly refer to another settlement made by colonists from the original Ayojjhā. It is worthy of note that in the Dārukkhandha Sutta some of the MSS. read Kosambī for Ayojjhā. But even Kosambī (*q.v.*) was on the Jumnā and not on the Ganges.

During the Buddhist period, Ayojjhā on the Sarayū was the capital of Dakkhiṇa Kosala, the *janapada* roughly corresponding to modern Oudh. This, the Ayodhyā of the Rāmāyana, is about a mile from the modern Fyzabad. In the Jātaka Commentary[5] there is a mention of Ayojjhā, which here evidently refers to the city of the Sanskrit epics. It is called the capital of King **Kālasena.** It was besieged by the **Andhaveṇhuputtā,** who breached the wall and took the king prisoner. Having thus subjugated the city, they went to Dvāravatī.

The Dīpavaṃsa[6] mentions **Ayujjhanagara** as the capital of King **Arindama** and of fifty-five of his descendants.

According to Buddhaghosa,[7] the people of Ayujjhanagara built for the Buddha a vihāra in a spot surrounded by forest near a curve of the river.

Once a warrior named **Jagatipāla,** of the race of Rāma, came to Ceylon from Ayojjhā, and having slain **Vikkampaṇḍu,** the heir-apparent to the throne, ruled in Rohaṇa for five years.[8]

[1] But see below in this article.
[2] S. iii. 140 ff.
[3] S. iv. 179 f.
[4] See Thomas: *op. cit.*, 15; *cf.* Sāketa.
[5] J. iv. 82.
[6] iii. 15.
[7] SA. ii. 233-4.
[8] Cv. lvi. 13 ff.

2. **Ayojjhā.**—Capital of Siam. From there **Vijayarājasīha,** King of Ceylon, obtained monks for his own country.[1] A few years later his successor, **Kittisirirājasīha,** sent an embassy there for the same purpose.

The King of Siam showed the embassy every mark of favour and granted them the monks. The monks, who came from Ayojjhā to Ceylon, re-established the ordination of monks in the Island.[2]

[1] Cv. xcviii. 91 f.
[2] *Ibid.*, c. 60-139; see also *J.R.A.S.* (*Ceylon Branch*), 1903, No. 54, pp. 17 ff.

1. **Ayoniso** (or **Vitakkita**) **Sutta.**—A certain monk staying in a forest tract in Kosala was occupied with evil and wrongful thoughts. The *deva* of the forest, desiring his welfare, drew near and admonished him to give up his muddled ways and fix his thoughts on the Buddha, the Dhamma and the Saṅgha.[1]

[1] S. i. 203.

2. **Ayoniso Sutta.**—In one who practices unsystematic attention, sensual desires arise afresh and grow; similarly malevolence, sloth and torpor. In him the *satipaṭṭhānā* fade away. The reverse happens in the case of the man who practises systematic attention.[1]

[1] S. v. 84.

Ayya-Uttiya(°**ika**). Brother of **Tissa,** king of **Kalyāṇī.** He was the queen's lover and, being discovered, fled from the capital and lived in a district which was later named after him. He sent a letter to the queen by a man disguised as a monk, but the ruse was discovered.[1] For the rest of the story see *s.v.* **Kalyāṇi-Tissa.**

[1] Mhv. xxii. 13 ff.; MṬ. 307.

Ayyakā Sutta.—**Pasenadī's** grandmother died at the age of 120. He had been very fond of her, and would have done anything to have kept her. He was so grieved at her death that he came to the Buddha for consolation. The Buddha tells him that all creatures have to die.[1]

[1] S. i. 96 ff.

Ayyakā-kālaka.—The Bodhisatta was once born as a bull as black as jet. While still a young calf he was given by his owners to an old woman, who reared him like a son; hence his name ("Grannie's Blackie"). The village lads used to ride on him for play. Once he saw a merchant trying to get his five hundred carts across a ford; the merchant's bulls were not strong enough for the task, and seeing the Bodhisatta the merchant tried to make use of his services. The Bodhisatta agreed only after he had been promised a thousand. The task completed, the merchant tried to cheat him, paying only half the promised amount. But the bull would not let him go till all the money had been paid. The earnings so obtained he took to the old woman, who was greatly pleased.[1]

[1] J. i. 194-6.

Ayyamitta Thera.—An Elder who lived in **Kassakalena.** In his begging village was an *upāsikā* who looked after him like her own son. One day the Elder, while on his begging rounds, heard her giving orders to her daughter regarding his food. He realised that the woman was undergoing great privations in order to provide him with luxuries, and feeling that he was unworthy of such attention, went back to Kassakalena and sat down on his couch, determined not to rise till he had become an arahant. During the night his object was achieved and the *deva* in the cave uttered his praise in song. The following morning he went as usual for his alms and the *upāsikā* knew that he had realised his quest.[1]

He is also called **Mahāmitta.**

[1] DA. iii. 790-1. [2] VbhA. 279.

Araka.—The Bodhisatta, born as a brahmin teacher. His story is told in the *Araka Jātaka*. He is referred to also in the *Dhammaddhaja Jātaka*,[1] where the Bodhisatta relates how, as Araka, he had developed thoughts of lovingkindness and practised the *brahmavihārā* for seven years and then was born in the Brahma-world.

His name appears again in the Aṅguttara Nikāya[2] in a list of teachers, and we are told that among Araka's pupils those who followed his teachings were born in the Brahma-world, while the others were born in various purgatories. In the Aṅguttara context no special mention is made of his having taught the *brahmavihāras*.

[1] J. ii. 195. [2] A. iv. 136-8.

Araka Jātaka (No. 169).—The Bodhisatta was once born in a brahmin's family and was named **Araka;** when he grew up he embraced the religious life and lived in the Himālaya as a teacher with a large following. He taught his pupils the value of the four *brahmavihāras*. After his death he was born in the Brahma-world and remained there for seven æons.

The story was told to the monks at Jetavana in reference to the *Metta Sutta*.[1]

[1] J. ii. 60-2.

Araka Sutta.—The teachings of **Araka** (*q.v.*).[1]

[1] A. iv. 136 ff.

Araja.—One of the palaces occupied by **Dhammadassī** before he became the Buddha.[1]

[1] Bu. xvi. 14.

Arañjaragiri.—A chain of mountains in **Majjhimadesa.** Not far away from it was a very populous town on a river. In this river many men bathed, and along its banks sat beautiful courtesans tempting them. It was one of these courtesans that tempted the sage **Nārada.**[1]

Arañjagiri was one of the places passed by **Vessantara** and his family on their way from their home to **Vaṅkagiri.** From the city of Jetuttara to Suvaṇṇagiritāla was five leagues and it was five leagues more to Kontimāra; thence to Arañjaragiri was five and again five to Dunniviṭṭha.[2] This was the road followed by banished men[3] (*v.l.* **Arañjara°**).

[1] J.iii.463. [2] *Ibid.*, vi.514. [3] *Ibid.*, 493.

Arañña.—Four great Araññas are often mentioned in literature.[1] They had once been the sites of very populous and prosperous kingdoms, but had later been destroyed by the gods because of offences committed by their kings against holy men. The four Mahā Araññas are: **Daṇḍaka°, Kāliṅga°, Mejjha°,** and **Mātaṅga°.** Details of these are found under each respective name.

[1] *E.g.*, M.i.378.

Arañña Jātaka (No. 348).—The Bodhisatta was once born in a brahmin family. He learned all the arts in Takkasilā, but when his wife died he went with his son to be an ascetic in the Himālaya. One day a girl came to the hermitage, fleeing from brigands, and corrupted the virtue of the youth. But when she tried to induce him to go away with her, he wished to consult his father. The father warned him against leaving the hermitage and taught him the way to mystic meditation.[1] The reason for telling the story is given in the *Culla-Nāradakassapa Jātaka.*

[1] J.iii.147-9.

1. **Arañña Vagga.**—The third section of the Tika Nipāta of the Jātakaṭṭhathā.[1]

[1] J.ii.354 ff.

2. **Arañña Vagga.**—The nineteenth section of the Pañcaka Nipāta of the Aṅguttara Nikāya. It consists of ten suttas, describing ten classes of men, each excelling in a special kind of asceticism, and in each class one is named as being the best among five who devote themselves to the same life, though from different motives.[1]

[1] A.iii.219-21.

1. **Arañña Sutta.**—Spoken before the Buddha by a forest-dwelling spirit who had been impressed by the simple life of the brethren in the

woods. The Buddha tells him the reason for their serenity and their beauty of complexion.[1]

[1] S. i. 5.

2. **Arañña Sutta.**—On the kind of monk who should seek the forest.[1]

[1] A. ii. 252.

3. **Arañña Sutta.**—On the advantages of developing *ānāpānasati*.[1]

[1] A. iii. 121.

4. **Arañña Sutta.**—On the qualities a monk should have to benefit by living in forest hermitages.[1]

[1] A. iii. 135 f.

Araññakuṭikā.—Mention is made of several forest hermitages in the Buddha's time. There was one, for instance, near Rājagaha, where Mahā Moggallāna[1] used to spend his time and also Mahā Kassapa.[2] Evidently other monks of the Order dwelt there from time to time, *e.g.* the novice **Aciravata.**[3] There was one hermitage near **Dīghambalika**[4] and another near Himavā,[5] where the Buddha sometimes went.

[1] J. iii. 33. [2] *Ibid.*, 71. [3] M. iii. 128. [4] DhA. ii. 235. [5] *Ibid.*, ii. 31, 129.

Araññavāsī Nikāya.—A group of monks in Ceylon who seem to have spent most of their time in solitary spots engaged in meditation. They owed allegiance to the Mahāvihāra. They are first heard of in the sixth century when, in the reign of Aggabodhi II., the King of Kalinga came over to Ceylon and joined the Order under the famous Elder **Jotipāla.** This fraternity seems to have been closely associated with the Buddhists of Kāliṅga. Among famous scholars belonging to it were: **Ānanda Vanaratanatissa, Vedeha, Coḷa Buddhappiya, Culla Dhammapāla, Medhaṅkara,** his pupil **Ānanda** and **Siddhattha.**

The Araññavāsins were specially esteemed by **Parākkammabāhu** of **Dambadeniya.**[1]

[1] For details about them see P.L.C. 210-13, 226, 229.

Araññasatta.—A king of twenty kappas ago; a previous birth of **Nimittasaññaka** Thera[1] (*v.l.* **Araññamanna; Araññasanta**).

[1] Ap. i. 261.

Araṇañjaha.—See **Aruṇañjaha.**

Araṇadīpiya Thera.—An arahant. Ninety-four kappas ago he had been a *deva*, and coming back to earth had, with great devotion, lighted five lamps for the use of others. As a result, fifty-five kappas ago he was born as a king, **Samantacakkhu**[1] (*v.l.* **Apaṇṇad°**, **Araṇṇad°**).

[1] Ap. i. 231.

Araṇavibhaṅga Sutta.—The 139th Sutta of the Majjhima Nikāya. It was preached at Jetavana and contains a statement and an exposition of the middle path of peace between the two extremes of pleasures of sense —low, ignoble and unprofitable—and self-mortification, also painful and unprofitable. The path is the Noble Eightfold Path: in preaching the doctrine the preacher should neither appreciate nor depreciate it, he should teach the truth in abstract terms of general principle. He should not be a tale-teller nor confront anyone with improper remarks; he should speak slowly and not hurriedly; he should neither affect provincialisms in speech nor depart from recognised parlance.

At the end of the discourse a young man, **Subhūti,** is praised because he walked where calm dwelt.[1]

[1] M. iii. 230-7; MA. ii. 977-8.

Araṇā Sutta.—On the Undefiled. Preached in answer to a *deva's* questions as to who are undefiled and fit to receive homage from everyone. Monks, says the Buddha, are so worthy.[1]

[1] S. i. 44-5.

Araṇi Sutta.—There are five indriyas: those of ease, discomfort, happiness, unhappiness and indifference. Just as from the rubbing together of two sticks warmth and heat are produced, so, from their separation, warmth and heat, thus born, are quenched; similarly from contact, experienced as agreeable, arises the faculty of ease (*sukhindriya*), etc.[1]

[1] S. v. 211-13.

1. **Araṇemi.**—A brahmin teacher of a past age, given in a list of six teachers, who were *purohitas*.[1] They practised *ahiṃsā* and, abstaining from flesh, got rid of their lusts. As a result, they were born in the Brahmaloka. They had many disciples.

[1] A. iii. 373. The others being **Sunetta, Mūgapakkha, Kuddālaka, Hatthipāla** and **Jotipāla.** In A. iv. 135 f. a seventh name is added, **Araka**; see also Divy, 632.

2. **Araṇemi.**—Tibetan sources mention a king, **Araṇemi Brahmadatta** of Sāvatthi, who was father of **Pasenadi.** He was exiled from his kingdom and lived in Campā.[1] But see **Mahākosala.**

[1] Rockhill, pp. 16, 70.

1. **Arati Sutta.**—Once when **Vaṅgīsa** was in Āḷavī he noticed that his teacher, **Nigrodha Kappa,** never left his cell after his return from the alms-round. Disaffection arose in Vaṅgisa's heart and he was troubled by thoughts of lust. He composed several verses by way of self-admonition and uttered them to himself. These form the Arati Sutta.[1]

[1] S. i. 186-7.

2. **Arati Sutta.**—Three evil states and the means of removing them.[1]

[1] A. iii. 448.

Aratī.—One of the three daughters of **Māra,** the others being **Taṇhā** and **Ragā.**[1] Seeing their father disconsolate after his repeated attempts to foil Gotama's quest for Enlightenment, they offered to tempt the Buddha with their wiles. This was in the fifth week after the Enlightenment. With Māra's approval, they came to the Buddha in various forms and in various guises, as he sat at the foot of the **Ajapala** banyan tree, and danced and sang before him. In the end the Buddha told them that he was beyond temptation by the pleasures of the senses and they went back to their father.[2]

In the Saṃyutta account, they are said to have asked the Buddha questions regarding himself and his teachings. Aratī's question was how a man who had already crossed the five floods could cross the sixth.[3]

[1] In the *Buddha-Carita* (xiii.), their names are **Ratī, Prītī** and **Tṛṣṇā**; in the Lal. (353), **Rati, Aratī** and **Tṛṣṇā.**

[2] S. i. 124-7; J. i. 78-80, 469; DhA. i. 201 f., iii. 196, 199; SN. v. 835.

[3] For explanation see KS. i. 158, n. 3.

Arammā.—A tribe mentioned in a list of tribes.[1]

[1] Ap. ii. 359.

Aravacchā.—One of the rivers crossed by **Kappina** on his way from his kingdom of **Kukkuṭavatī** to see the Buddha at Sāvatthi. The river was one league deep and two leagues wide. No boat was available, but the king and his retinue crossed it on horseback by meditating on the Three Jewels and the supreme power of the Buddha.[1] Later Kappina's queen did likewise.[2]

[1] DhA. ii. 119-20.

[2] *Ibid.*, 124.

Aravāḷa.—A Nāga king, who lived in the **Aravāḷadaha** in Kasmīra-Gandhāra. He had been in the habit of destroying the crops of the people by causing hail-storms. When **Majjhantika** Thera was sent by Moggaliputtatissa's Council to convert Kasmīra-Gandhāra, the thera went to Aravāladaha and standing in the air above it showed himself to the Nāgas. Hearing of this the nāga king came out and tried to frighten the Elder with various terrors. When all his attempts had failed he acknowledged defeat and the thera preached to him. He and his 84,000 followers were established in the Refuge and the Five Precepts[1] (*v.l.* **Āravāḷa**).

[1] Sp. i. 65; Mhv. xii. 9-20.

Aravāḷadaha.—The lake in which **Aravāḷa** lived.

1. **Arahaṃ Sutta.**—Would an arahant by speaking of "I" and "mine" show thereby proneness to notions of self or soul? The Buddha says "No." He would thereby only conform to common usage in such matters.[1] Buddhaghosa says that the question was asked by a forest *devatā* who had heard forest-dwelling arahants talk thus. She was worried by the question as to whether they had any "*māna*" at all.[2]

[1] S. i. 14-15. [2] SA. i. 41.

2. **Arahaṃ Sutta.**—An arahant is one who has really seen the arising, ending, etc., of the five grasping groups (*upādānakkhandhā*).[1]

[1] S. iii. 161.

3. **Arahaṃ Sutta.**—That noble disciple is released by perfect insight (*sammadaññā*) who has really seen the satisfaction in, the misery of, the escape from, the five *indriyas*.[1]

[1] S. v. 194.

4. **Arahaṃ Sutta.**—The monk who has really seen the arising, the perishing, etc., as above.[1]

[1] S. v. 194.

5. **Arahaṃ** (or **Buddha**) **Sutta.**—It is by the cultivation of the four *iddhipādā* that the Tathāgata is called Arahant or Fully Enlightened One.[1]

[1] S. v. 257.

6. **Arahaṃ Sutta.**—Arahants, fully enlightened ones, have full understanding of the four Ariyan truths as they really are.[1]

[1] S. v. 433.

7. **Arahaṃ Sutta.**—Six qualities requisite for arahantship.[1]

[1] A. iii. 421.

1. **Arahatta Vagga.**—The eighth section of the Chakka Nipāta of the Aṅguttara Nikāya. It deals with the six qualities for realising arahantship and for living in complete peace.[1]

[1] A. iii. 429-34.

2. **Arahatta Vagga.**—The seventh chapter of the Khandha Saṃyutta of the Saṃyutta Nikāya.[1]

[1] S. iii. 73-81.

1. **Arahatta Sutta.**—Records a conversation between the Paribbājaka **Jambukhādaka** and **Sāriputta.** "What is arahantship?" "The destruction of lust, hatred and illusion." "And the path thereto?" "The Noble Eightfold Path."[1]

[1] S. iv. 252.

2. **Arahatta Sutta.**—Six qualities requisite for arahantship.[1]

[1] A. iii. 430.

Arahanta.—A Talaing monk, the preceptor and advisor of **Anuruddhā.** King of Burma. He made far-reaching reforms in the Burmese Saṅgha of his day.[1]

[1] Bode, *op. cit.*, 12-13.

1. **Arahanta Vagga.**—The first chapter of the Brāhmaṇa Saṃyutta of the Saṃyutta Nikāya.[1]

[1] S. i. 160-72.

2. **Arahanta Vagga.**—The seventh section of the Dhammapada.

Arahanta Sutta (2).—Of all the forms of becoming, the arahants have the best in all the worlds. They attain this by right insight with regard to the *saṅkhāras.*[1]

[1] S. iii. 82-4.

1. **Arahā Sutta.**—Preached at Sāvatthi to **Rādha.** A monk who sees, in their true nature, the coming to pass and the passing away, the satisfaction of, misery in, and escape from, the five groups of grasping, is called an arahant.[1]

[1] S. iii. 193.

2. **Arahā Sutta.**—Same as above, the six sense-faculties being substituted for the five groups of grasping.[1]

[1] S. v. 205.

3. **Arahā Sutta.**—Same as above, the five *indriyas* (controlling faculties) being substituted for groups of grasping.[1]

[1] S. v. 208.

Arikāri.—A monastery in Ceylon. It is not recorded by whom it was first built. **Udaya I.** found it in a dilapidated condition and had it repaired. He also built there a house for the distribution of food and added a *pāsāda.*[1]

[1] Cv. xlix. 32.

1. **Ariṭṭha.**—A monk. He had been subjected by the Saṅgha to the *ukkhepanīyakamma* for refusal to renounce a sinful doctrine, namely, that the states of mind declared by the Buddha to be stumbling-blocks are not such at all for him who indulges in them.

Ariṭṭha left the Order and would not come back until the *ukkhepanīyakamma* was revoked.[1]

He was a vulture-trainer (*gaddhabādhiputta*).[2]

His case is cited as that of a *pācittaya*-offence because he refused to give up a wrong doctrine even after the monks had three times requested him to do so.[3]

In spite of the *ukkhepanīyakamma* the **Chabbaggiya** monks kept company with Ariṭṭha, thereby committing a *pācittaya*-offence.[4] We find the Buddha rebuking the nun **Thullanandā** for associating with Ariṭṭha after the *ukkhepanīyakamma.*[5]

In was Ariṭṭha's heresy that led to the preaching of the *Alagaddūpama Sutta.*[6] In the Saṃyutta Nikāya,[7] Ariṭṭha is mentioned as having said to the Buddha that he practised concentration in breathing and as having described how he did it. The Buddha, thereupon, instructs him as to how such concentration can be done perfectly and in every detail. In the Samanatapāsādikā Ariṭṭha is mentioned in a list of enemies of the *Sāsana.*[8]

[1] Vin. ii. 25-8.
[2] See note in VT. ii. 377.
[3] Vin. iv. 135.
[4] *Ibid.*, 137.
[5] *Ibid.*, 218.
[6] M. i. 130 ff.
[7] S. v. 314-15.
[8] Sp. iv. 874.

2. **Ariṭṭha.**—An *upāsaka* mentioned in the Aṅguttara Nikāya[1] in a list of householders and *upāsakas* who had seen and realised immortality and

[1] iii. 451.

were possessed of unwavering faith in the Buddha, the Dhamma and the Saṅgha. They practised Ariyan conduct and had won wisdom and liberty.

3. **Ariṭṭha.**—A Pacceka Buddha, mentioned in a list of Pacceka Buddhas.[1]

[1] M. iii. 69; ApA. i. 106; also Netti, 143.

4. **Ariṭṭha.**—Nephew of **Devānampiyatissa.** See **Mahā Ariṭṭha.**

5. **Ariṭṭha.**—Son of the Nāga king, **Dhataraṭṭha.** See **Kāṇāriṭṭha.**

6. **Ariṭṭha.**—A messenger of **Vessavaṇa,** employed by him to take his proclamations and publish them.[1]

[1] D. iii. 201.

Ariṭṭha Sutta.—Records a conversation—already referred to (*s.v.* **Ariṭṭha** 1)—between Ariṭṭha and the Buddha regarding concentration on breathing. The Buddha asks the monks whether they practise such concentration. Ariṭṭha says that he himself does and proceeds to explain his method. The Buddha, while not condemning it, explains to him how concentration could be made perfect in every detail.[1]

[1] S. v. 314-15.

Ariṭṭhakā.—A class of *devas* who were present at the preaching of the *Mahāsamaya Sutta.* They were like azure flowers in hue (*ummāpupphanibhāsino*).[1]

[1] D. ii. 260. Buddhaghosa, however, explains "ummāpupphanibhāsina" as being the name of another class of *devas* (DA. ii. 690).

Ariṭṭhajanaka.—Son of King **Mahājanaka,** whom he succeeded as King of **Mithilā.** His brother was **Polajanaka,** the viceroy, who later killed him and captured his kingdom. Ariṭṭhajanaka's son was the Prince **Mahājanaka,** who was the Bodhisatta.[1]

[1] J. vi. 30-42.

Ariṭṭha-ṭhapita-ghara.—See **Sirivaḍḍhaghara.**

Ariṭṭhapabbata.—A mountain in Ceylon half-way between Anurādhapura and Pulatthipuva. It is identified with modern Riṭigala, and is near the modern Habarane in the North-Central Province.[1] **Paṇḍukābhaya** lived there for seven years, awaiting an opportunity to make war on his uncles, and it was near there that he ultimately defeated them.[2] At the foot of the mountain, **Sūratissa** built the **Makulaka Vihāra.**[3] **Lañjatissa** built a vihāra on the mountain and called it **Ariṭṭha Vihāra.**[4]

Jeṭṭhatissa occupied the mountain before his fight with **Aggabodhi III.**, and it was there that he organised his forces.[5]

Sena I. built a monastery on the mountain for the use of the **Paṃsukulikas** and endowed it with large revenues.[6]

At the present day the place is extremely rich in ruins.[7]

1 Mhv. trans. 72, n. 3.
2 Mhv. x. 63-72.
3 *Ibid.*, xxi. 6.
4 *Ibid.*, xxxiii. 27.
5 Cv. xliv. 86.
6 *Ibid.*, l. 63.
7 See Hocart: *Memoirs of the Arch. Survey of Ceylon* i. 44.

Ariṭṭhapura.—A city in the kingdom of **Sivi,** over which King **Sivi** reigned.[1] It was also the birthplace of **Ummadantī.**[2] It lay on the road from Mithilā to Pañcāla.[3]

1 J. iv. 401. 2 *Ibid.*, v. 212. 3 *Ibid.*, vi. 419.

Ariṭṭha Vihāra.—The monastery built by **Lañjakatissa** in **Ariṭṭhapabbata.**[1]

1 Mhv. xxxiii. 27; Mhv. trans. 230, n. 6.

Arindama.—The Bodhisatta, born as King of Benares and son of the Magadha King of Rājagaha. During the time of **Sikhī** Buddha he held a great almsgiving for the Buddha and his monks; he presented to the Order a fully caparisoned elephant which he redeemed by giving suitable gifts to the height of an elephant.[1] He had as friend the chaplain's son, **Soṇaka.** They both studied in Takkasilā and at the conclusion of their studies they travelled about in search of experience. In the course of their travels Arindama was elected to succeed the King of Benares who had died childless, and Soṇaka became a Pacceka Buddha. Forty years later Arindama wished to see Soṇaka, but no one could tell him his whereabouts in spite of the offer of a large reward. Ten years later Soṇaka saw the king through the good offices of a lad of seven, who belonged to the harem and had learnt a song composed by the king expressing his desire to meet Soṇaka. At the meeting, however, the king failed to recognise him. Soṇaka, not revealing his identity, spoke to the king about the joys of renunciation, and disappeared through the

1 J. i. 41; Bu. xxi. 9.

air. The king, moved by his words, decided to give up the throne and to follow the ascetic life. He appointed his eldest son **Dīghāvu** king in his stead, handed over to him all his possessions, and developing supernatural faculties was born in the Brahma world.[2]

Arindama is mentioned together with **Mahājanaka** as an example of a king who renounced a mighty kingdom to lead a hermit's life.[3] The story also appears in the Mahāvastu,[4] but the details given differ from those of the Jātaka version. There Arindama is spoken of as the King of Mithilā.

In both accounts Dīghāvu's mother, the king's chief queen, is spoken of as having died before the king's renunciation.

According to the Buddhavaṃsa Commentary,[5] Arindama's capital was **Paribhuttanagara.** (*v.l.* **Arindamaka.**)

[2] J. v. 247-61.
[3] *Ibid.*, iii. 489.
[4] iii. 449 ff.
[5] BuA. 203.

2. **Arindama.**—King in the time of **Sumana** Buddha. A great dispute had arisen at this time regarding *nirodha* and all the inhabitants of many thousand world systems were divided into two camps. In order to settle their doubts, the disputants, with Arindama at their head, sought the Buddha. The Buddha sat on Mount **Yugandhara** while Arindama, with his ninety thousand crores of followers, sat on a golden rock, which by the power of his merit had sprung from the earth near **Saṅkassa.** The Buddha preached to them, and at the end of the sermon they all became arahants.[1]

[1] BuA. 128-9.

3. **Arindama.**—King of **Uttara.** When **Revata** Buddha visited his city the king went to see him, accompanied by three crores of people. The next day a great almsgiving was held for the Buddha and the monks, and also a festival of light covering a space of three leagues. The Buddha preached to the assembly, and one thousand crores of people realised the Truth.[1]

[1] Bu. vi. 4; BuA. 133.

4. **Arindama.**—A king of forty-one kappas ago; a former birth of **Sannidhāpaka** Thera.[1]

[1] Ap. i. 97.

5. **Arindama.**—King of **Haṃsavatī.** When the king, through carelessness, had lost his wealth, his *seṭṭhi* (**Jatukaṇṇika** in a former birth) made good the loss by giving him the seven kinds of jewels.[1]

Ap. ii. 360.

6. **Arindama.**—The name given to the **Cakkavatti's** *cakkaratana* because it brings all his enemies into subjection.[1]

[1] Mbv. 72.

Arimaddana.—The name given in the Pāli chronicles to the city of Pagan in Burma (**Rāmañña**).[1] During the time of **Parakkamabāhu I.** of Ceylon, the King of Arimaddana quarrelled with him, ill-treated his envoys, and seized by force a princess sent from Ceylon to Kamboja. Parakkama sent a punitive expedition under the **Damiḷādhikāri Ādicca,** who reduced the country to subjection.[2]

Later **Vijayabāhu II.** of Ceylon entered into friendly negotiations with the ruler of Arimaddana, and wrote him a letter in the Māgadha language composed by himiself. As a result, a friendly treaty was made between them which also resulted in closer contact between the monks of the two countries.[3]

According to some authorities, quoted by Minayeff,[4] the city was full of learned women. The Gandhavaṃsa[5] mentions a list of twenty-three teachers who wrote their works in Arimaddana. From this context it appears that Arimaddana was known also as **Pukkāma** (*Pukkāmasaṅkhāte Arimaddananagare*). This is supported by evidence from elsewhere.[6] It was a minister in Arimaddana who wrote the **Nyāsappadīpaṭīkā.**[7] Arimaddana was also the city of birth of the Thera **Chapaṭa.**[8]

[1] Bode: *op. cit.*, 14.
[2] Cv. lxxvi. 10-75.
[3] *Ibid.*, lxxx. 6-8.
[4] *Récherches sur Bouddhisme*, p. 70.
[5] p. 67.
[6] Forchhammer: *Jardine Prize Essay*, pp. 29, 32. *Ind. Ant.* 1893, p. 17
[7] Svd. v. 1240.
[8] *Ibid.*, 1247.

Arimaddavijayagāma.—A village and a tank. The **Somavatī** canal was built by Parakkamabāhu I. to connect the Arimaddavijayagāma with the **Kaddūravaḍḍhamāna** tank.[1]

[1] Cv. lxxix. 56.

Arimanda.—A city in which the Bodhisatta was born as the Khattiya **Vijatāvī** in the time of the Buddha **Phussa.**[1]

[1] BuA. 194.

1. **Ariya.**—A country and people in South India. **Palandīpa** was one of its divisions. It once had a king named **Vīradeva** who led an expedition against **Jayabāhu I.** of Ceylon.[1]

It was also the name of a dynasty, the Aryan dynasty of the Pāṇḍya (**Paṇḍu**) in South India.[2]

[1] Cv. lxi. 36 f.
[2] *Ibid.*, lxiii. 15; see also Cv. trans. i. 239, n. 1.

2. **Ariya.**—A fisherman of a settlement near the north gate of Sāvatthi. The Buddha, seeing his *upanissaya* for *sotāpatti*, passed with the congregation of monks close by the spot where he was fishing and stopped not far from him. Then the Buddha proceeded to ask the monks their names, and noticing that the fisherman himself expected to be questioned, he asked him his. On learning that it was Ariya, the Buddha suggested to him that he was unworthy of the name, because a real Ariya never injured any living thing. At the end of the discourse the fisherman became a *sotāpanna*.[1]

[1] DhA. iii. 396-8.

3. **Ariya.**—A Pacceka Buddha mentioned in the list of the *Isigili Sutta*.[1]

[1] M. iii. 70; also ApA. i. 107.

1. **Ariya Sutta.**—The seven *bojjhaṅgas*, if cultivated, lead to the Ariyan qualities which conduce to salvation (*ariyāniyyānikā*).[1]

[1] S. v. 82.

2. **Ariya Sutta.**—The four *satipaṭṭhānas*, if cultivated, lead to the utter destruction of ill.[1]

[1] S. v. 166.

Ariyakoṭi.—A monastery (probably in Ceylon), the residence of **Mahā Datta** Thera.[1]

[1] MA. i. 131.

Ariyapariyesanā Sutta.—Preached in Sāvatthi in the hermitage of the brahmin **Rammaka.** Some monks expressed to Ānanda their desire to hear a discourse from the Buddha, as it was so long since they had heard one. He advised them to go to the hermitage of Rammaka where their wishes might be fulfilled. The noontide of that same day Ānanda spent with the Buddha at the **Pubbārāma** in the Migāramātupāsāda and in the evening, after the Buddha had bathed in the **Pubbakoṭṭhaka,** Ānanda suggested to him that he might go to Rammaka's hermitage. The Buddha assenting, they went together. The Buddha, finding the monks engaged in discussing the Doctrine, waited till their discussion was over. Having inquired the topic thereof, he praised them and proceeded to tell them of the two quests in the world—the noble and the ignoble. He described how he, too, before his Enlightenment, had followed the quest, apprenticing himself to various teachers, such as

Āḷāva-Kālāma and **Uddaka Rāmaputta,** and how, on discovering that they could not give him what he sought, he went to Uruvelā and there found the consummate peace of Nibbāna.[1] The Sutta then proceeds to give an account of the Buddha's first reluctance to preach, of Sahampati's intervention, of the meeting with the Ājīvaka Upaka and the first sermon preached to the Pañcavaggiyas. Finally the sutta expounds the pleasures of the senses, the dangers therefrom and the freedom and confidence which ensue when one has overcome desire.[2]

In the Commentary[3] the sutta is called **Pāsarāsi,** evidently because of the simile found at the end of the discourse where the pleasures of the senses are compared to baited traps.

The Atthasālinī quotes it.[4]

[1] This biographical account is also found in the *Mahā-Saccaka, Bodhirājakumāra* and *Saṅgārava Suttas.* It is in part repeated in the Vinaya and the Dīgha Nikāya.

[2] M. i. 160-75.

[3] MA. i. 369 ff.

[4] p. 35.

Ariyabālisika Vatthu.—The story of the fisherman **Ariya** given above, **Ariya** 2.

1. **Ariyamagga Vagga.**—The fifteenth chapter of the Dasaka Nipāta of the Aṅguttara Nikāya.[1] It consists of ten suttas on right views and wrong views and their train of consequences.

[1] A. v. 244-7.

2. **Ariyamagga Vagga.**—The nineteenth chapter of the Dasaka Nipāta of the Aṅguttara Nikāya.[1] It consists of ten suttas on the ten transgressions and the abstinence therefrom.

[1] A. v. 278-81.

Ariyamagga Sutta.—The Ariyan way consists of deeds neither dark nor bright with results neither dark nor bright.[1]

[1] A. ii. 235 f.

Ariyamuni.—One of the monks who were sent to Ceylon by the King of **Ayojjhā,** at the request of **Kittisirirājasīha,** to re-establish the upasampadā Ordination in Ceylon. He is mentioned as second in order to **Upāli,** the leader of the delegation of Siamese monks.[1]

[1] Cv. c. 95; also Cv. trans. ii. 282, n. 2.

1. **Ariyavaṃsa.**—A compilation, probably of the life-histories of men eminent in the Buddhist Order, made in Ceylon and read aloud publicly for the edification of the people. The reading of the Ariyavaṃsa seems once to have been a regular feature of gatherings in the Buddhist vihāras on feast days. King **Vohāraka-Tissa** made endowments for the giving of alms throughout Ceylon on the occasions when the Ariyavaṃsa was read.[1]

A sutta called *Ariyavaṃsa Sutta* is mentioned in the Commentaries[2] as an example of a discourse preached by the Buddha on his own initiative (*attajjhāsaya*). This perhaps refers to the sermon on the four Ariyavaṃsā in the Aṅguttara Nikāya.[3] See also **Mahā-Ariyavaṃsa.**

[1] Mhv. xxxvi. 38; Mhv. trans. 258, n. 6. [2] DA. i. 50; MA. i. 14. [3] A. ii. 27.

2. **Ariyavaṃsa.**—A celebrated teacher and author of the fifteenth century. He came from Pagan and was a member of the **Chapaṭa** sect. He was a pupil of the famous Ye-din ("water-carrier") of Sagaing,[1] and with great zeal and enthusiasm learnt the *Abhidhammattha-vibhāvanī* from his teacher. Later, Ariyavaṃsa wrote a commentary on this work and called it the **Maṇisāramañjūsā.** A charming anecdote is related of how he read the work to his colleagues and readily accepted their corrections with gratitude.

Among his other works are the **Maṇidīpa,** a ṭīkā on the Atthasālinī, a grammatical treatise, the **Gandhābharaṇa,** and a study of the Jātakas called the **Jātakavisodhana.**

Ariyavaṃsa spent only a part of his life at Sagaing and afterwards taught at Ava, where the king was sometimes among his listeners. He was among the first of Burmese *litterateurs* to write a metaphysical work in the vernacular—an Anuṭīkā on the Abhidhamma.[2] The Gandha-Vaṃsa[3] attributes to him another work, the **Mahānissara** (Mahānissaya ?), but no mention is made of it in the Sāsanavaṃsa.

[1] For an account of him see Bode, *op. cit.*, 41 f. [2] Sās. p. 41 ff. [3] 64-5.

Ariyavaṃsālaṅkāra.—A book written by **Ñāṇābhisāsanadhaja Mahādhammarājaguru** Thera of Burma, author of the **Peṭakālaṅkāra** and other books.[1]

[1] Sās. 134.

Ariyavasā Sutta.—The ten dwellings of Ariyans, past, present and future.[1]

[1] A. v. 29.

1. **Ariyasāvaka Sutta.**—Preached at Sāvatthi. The well-taught Ariyan disciple does not wonder as to the cause and effect of things, he knows

that it really is the arising and the passing away of the world. His is the knowledge of the trained man; he is possessed of the insight of revulsion, he stands knocking at the door of the deathless.[1]

[1] S. ii. 77.

2. **Ariyasāvaka Sutta.**—Same as above, with a very slight variation in the final paragraph, in the wording, not in the sense.[1]

[1] S. ii. 79.

Ariyā Sutta.—The four *iddhipādas*, if cultivated, conduce to the utter destruction of Ill. They are *ariyaniyyānikā.*[1]

[1] S. v. 255.

Ariyākari.—A monastery in Rohaṇa in South Ceylon. **Dappula** gave it to the village of **Mālavatthu** and built therein an image house. He also had a valuable *uṇṇaloma* and a *hemapaṭṭa* made for the image there.[1]

[1] Cv. xlv. 60-1.

Ariyālaṅkāra.—There were four theras of this name in Burma, all famous for their Pāli scholarship. The first (Ariyālaṅkāra of Ava) excelled in *dhātupaccayavibhāga, i.e.* was an accomplished grammarian.[1] His pupil, Ariyālaṅkāra the younger, is credited with exegetical works on the Atthasālinī, the Saṅkhepavaṇṇanā, the Abhidhammatthavibhāvanī and the Vibhaṅga. He also wrote a Pāli ṭīkā called the **Sāratthavikāsinī** on the Kaccāyanabheda, and he made in Burmese what amounted to a revised edition of Kaccāyana's grammar.[2]

The two others do not seem to have written any works which have been preserved.

[1] Sās. p. 106-12.
[2] *Ibid.*, 110-11; Bode, *op. cit.*, 52-3.

Aruka Sutta.—On the man whose mind is like an open sore, as opposed to one who is lightning-minded or diamond-minded.[1]

[1] A. i. 123 f.

1. **Aruṇa.**—A khattiya, father of **Sikhī** Buddha and husband of **Pabhāvatī.**[1] Aruṇa's chief queen became the Therī **Abhayā** in the present age.[2] Another of his wives became, in her last life, the Therī **Somā,**[3] who is perhaps to be identified with **Uppaladāyikā** of the Apadāna.[4] In the Saṃyutta Nikāya[5] he is called **Aruṇavā.**

[1] Bu. xxi. 15; J. i. 41; AA. i. 436.
[2] ThigA. 41.
[3] ThigA. 66.
[4] Ap. ii. 601 f.
[5] S. i. 155.

2. **Aruṇa.**—The Assaka[1] king of **Potali** in the **Assaka** country. The Kāliṅga king of that time, longing for a fight, but finding no one willing to accept his challenge, at last devised a plan. He sent his four beautiful daughters, in a covered carriage and with an armed escort to the various cities in the neighbourhood, proclaiming that any king, who took them as wives, would have to fight their father. No one was found willing to take the risk till they came to Potali in the Assaka country. Even the Assaka king at first merely sent them a present by way of courtesy, but his minister, **Nandisena,** fertile in expedients, urged the king to marry them, saying that he himself would undertake to face the consequences. The Kāliṅga king at once set out with his army. On his way to Potali, he came across the Bodhisatta, who was leading the ascetic life and, without revealing his identity, consulted him regarding his chances of success in the fight. The Bodhisatta promised that he would see Sakka about it the next day and, having done so, informed the king that the Kāliṅga forces would win. Nandisena heard of this prophecy but, nothing daunted, he gathered together the Assaka forces and all their allies; then, by a well-planned manœuvre, he managed to have the tutelary deity of Kāliṅga (who was fighting for the Kāliṅga king) killed by Assaka. Thereupon the Kāliṅga king was routed and fled. The Bodhisatta, finding that his prophecy had turned out false, sought Sakka in his distress; Sakka consoled him thus: "Hast thou never heard that even the gods favour the bold hero of intrepid resolve, who never yields ?"

Later, at the suggestion of Nandisena, the Assaka king demanded of Kāliṅga's ruler dowry for his four daughters, and the Kāliṅga king acceded to his request.[2]

[1] In the main story the king's name is given as **Assaka,** but the scholiast says his real name was **Aruṇa.**

[2] The story is told in the *Kāliṅga Jātaka* (J. iii. 3 ff.).

3. **Aruṇa.**—The pleasaunce near **Anupama** where the Buddha **Vessabhū** first preached to his chief disciples, **Soṇa** and **Uttara.**[1]

[1] Bu. xxii. 22, BuA. 205.

4. **Aruṇa.**—The name of the lotus that grows in the Nāga world. It was one of **Uppalavaṇṇā's** wishes to have a body of the colour of the Aruṇa-lotus.[1]

[1] Ap. ii. 554 (v. 39).

5. **Aruṇa.**—A class of devas present at the preaching of the *Mahā-Samaya Sutta.* They were of diverse hue, of wondrous gifts, mighty powers, comely and with splendid following.[1]

[1] D. ii. 260.

Aruṇaka.—Thirty-six kappas ago there were seven kings of the name of Aruṇaka, all previous births of the Thera **Vatthadāyaka.**[1]

[1] Ap. i. 116.

Aruṇañjaha.—Seventy kappas ago there were sixteen kings of the name of Aruṇañjaha. They were all past births of **Asokapūjaka** Thera.[1]

[1] Ap. i. 199.

Aruṇapāla.—A king of thirty-five kappas ago, a former birth of **Kanikārapupphiya** Thera (who is evidently identical with **Ujjaya**[1]). In the *Theragāthā* Commentary[2] he is called **Aruṇabala.**

[1] Ap. i. 203. [2] i. 119.

Aruṇapura.—A city in the time of the Buddha **Sikhī. Ambapālī** was born there in a brahmin family.[1] It is probably identical with **Aruṇavatī** (*q.v.*).

[1] Ap. ii. 613; ThigA. i. 213.

Aruṇabala.—See **Aruṇapāla.**

1. **Aruṇavatī.**—The city and the country of King **Aruṇavā,** and the birthplace of **Sikhī** Buddha.[1] It was from there that Sikhī and **Abhibhū** went to the Brahma-world to preach to Brahmā and his attendants.[2] At that time **Salalapupphiya** Thera was a confectioner in Aruṇavatī.[3] See also **Aruṇapura.**

[1] Bu. xxi. 15. [2] S. i. 155 f. [3] Ap. i. 218.

2. **Aruṇavatī.**—A vihāra in the village of **Iṭṭhakāvatī** in Magadha. **Sāriputta** once lived there.[1]

[1] PvA. 67.

Aruṇavatī Sutta.—Records the incident of the visit of **Abhibhū** to the Brahma-world.[1] Abhibhū chose as his theme action and energy, and the verses he uttered on that occasion, beginning "*Ārabhatha, nikkhamatha, yuñjatha buddhasāsane*" are often quoted.

Buddhaghosa[2] says that Abhibhū chose this theme out of all the doctrines to be found in the Tipiṭaka because he knew that the subject would commend itself to all his hearers, human and non-human.

Milakkhatissa Thera of Ceylon, hearing a novice in Pācīnapabbata recite the Aruṇavatī Sutta, listened to the stanzas, and feeling that they had been preached to encourage zealous monks like himself, he exerted

[1] S. i. 154 f., etc.; see *s.v.* Abhibhū (1). [2] SA. i. 172-3.

himself and became an anāgāmī. Soon afterwards he became an arahant.[3]

The sutta is said to have been preached by the Buddha on the full-moon day of *Jeṭṭhamāsa*.[4]

[3] AA. i. 21-2. [4] *Ibid.*, i. 436.

Aruṇavā.—See **Aruṇa** (1).

Arundhavatī.—See **Amaravatī** (2).

Aruppala.—One of the villages given by **Kittisirirājasīha** for the maintenance of the **Gaṅgārāma Vihāra.**[1]

[1] Cv. c. 212.

Alakadeva.—A thera who accompanied **Majjhima** to Himavā.[1] He converted one of the five districts there and ordained 100,000 monks.[2] The Dīpavaṃsa[3] gives his name as **Mūlakadeva.**

[1] Sp. i. 68. [2] Mbv. 115. [3] viii. 10.

Alakā.—The town of the god Kubera,[1] evidently another name for **Āḷakamandā.**

[1] Cv. lxxiv. 207; lxxx. 5.

Alakkhī.—The goddess of Ill-luck. She delights in men of evil deeds.[1]

[1] J. v. 112-14.

Alaṅkāranissaya.—A scholiast on **Saṅgharakkhita's** *Subodhālaṅkāra*, written by a Burmese monk in A.D. 1880.[1]

[1] Bode, *op. cit.*, 95.

Alagakkonāra.—An eminent prince of Ceylon in the time of **Vikkamabāhu IV.** He was of the **Giri** family and lived in **Peraddoṇī** (modern Perādeniya). The *Cūḷavaṃsa* does not recount much of him, save that he was full of virtue and piety and that he did many good deeds, such as the advancement of the Order; also that he was the founder of **Jayavaḍḍhanakoṭṭa,** which soon after became the capital of Ceylon.[1] The Sinhalese chronicles, however,[2] tell us a good deal about him, the most important fact being that he succeeded in breaking the power of the Jaffna king which was then at its height. Formerly it was believed that Alagakkonāra later became king under the name of **Bhuvanekabāhu V.,** but now that opinion has been given up.[3]

[1] Cv. xci. 3-9.
[2] See Cv. Trs. ii. 212, n. 4.
[3] *Ibid.*, 213, n. 4, and the references given there.

Alagaddūpama Sutta.—Preached at Jetavana to **Ariṭṭha** concerning his heresy. Ariṭṭha held that according to the Doctrine, as he understood it, the states of mind, *e.g.* pleasures of sense, declared by the Buddha to be stumbling-blocks, are not such at all to the man who indulges in them. The Buddha questioned Ariṭṭha regarding this, and when Ariṭṭha acknowledged that such was his view, the Buddha rebuked him as having not even a spark of illumination regarding the Dhamma and the Vinaya.

Foolish persons, who have learned the Doctrine by heart but fail to study its import, quite miss the real meaning of their memorising and find no joy in it, using it solely as a means of stricture on others or of bandying verbal quotations; they are like a man who, finding a serpent, seizes it by its tail or coils and gets bitten, meeting thereby death or deadly hurt. But those, who comprehend all that the Doctrine embodies, resemble a man who pins a serpent securely down with a forked stick and grasps it firmly by its neck.

This sutta also contains the parable of the raft. The Doctrine is like a raft to be used in crossing the flood and then to be abandoned. Even good things must eventually be discarded, therefore, how much more bad things?

The last part of the sutta contains questions, chiefly on the mastery of self, asked by various monks, which the Buddha proceeds to explain.[1]

The sutta is quoted by Buddhaghosa[2] as an example of a discourse of which the meaning is illustrated by a variety of similes (*atthena upamaṃ parivāretvā*). (*v.l.* **Alagadda Sutta.**)

[1] M. i. 130 ff.; MA. i. 321 ff. [2] MA. i. 136.

Alambusā.—The nymph sent by **Sakka** to tempt the sage **Isisiṅga,** as related in the *Alambusā Jātaka*. In the present age she was the wife of the monk with reference to whom the Alambusā Jātaka was related.[1] Her name appears in the *Vimānavatthu*[2] in a list of nymphs who minister with song and dance to Sakka and his queens.

[1] J. v. 152-61. [2] p. 16, v. 10. See also CSB. 29, Pl. 15.

Alambusa Jātaka (No. 523).—**Isisiṅga,** son of the Bodhisatta and of a doe, who had drunk water into which the Bodhisatta's semen had fallen, lived the ascetic life like his father. He had been warned by his father about the wiles of women, and lived in the forest practising the most severe austerities. By virtue of the power of these austerities, Sakka's abode trembled, and Sakka, fearing his rivalry, sent down a beautiful celestial nymph, **Alambusā,** to tempt him and despoil him of his virtue.

This she succeded in doing, and for three years he lay unconscious in her embrace. At last, realising what had happened, he forthwith forsook sensual desire, and developing mystic meditation, attained to jhāna. Alambusā pleaded for forgiveness, which was readily granted. The story was related in reference to the temptation of a monk by the wife he had had during his lay life.[1]

In the *Dīgha Nikāya* Commentary[2] the name of the ascetic is given as **Migasiṅgi,** and the story is quoted as an instance of a wrong explanation of the cessation of consciousness.

[1] J. v. 152-61. See also the *Naḷinikā J.* (v. 193 f.) where Isisiṅga is tempted by **Naḷinikā.**

[2] ii. 370; see also Sp. i. 214. Cp. the story of Ṛṣyaśṛṅga in the Rāmāyana (i. 9). The story is found in the Bharhut Tope (see Cunningham, CSB. 29, Pl. 15).

Alasaka.—The name of a disease, of which **Korakhattiya** died.[1] Rhys Davids translates it as "epilepsy" and suggests that its name is a negative of *lasikā*, the synovial fluid.[2]

[1] D. iii. 7.

[2] *Dial.* iii. 12, n. 2.

Alasandā.—A city in the land of the **Yonas.** There was a large Buddhist community there and it is said, in the *Mahāvaṃsa*,[1] that on the occasion of the foundation of the Mahā Thūpa by Duṭṭhagāmaṇi, the thera **Yonaka Mahā Dhammarakkhita** came to **Anurādhapura** from Alasandā with 30,000 monks.

In the *Milindapañha*[2] Alasandā is mentioned in a list of places, among which are China, Benares and Gandhāra. Elsewhere in the same book,[3] King Milinda is mentioned as saying that he was born in a village named **Kalasi** in Alasandā, but he speaks of Alasandā as an island. It was about two hundred leagues from **Sāgala.**

It is generally accepted[4] that Alasandā was the name of an island in the Indus in the territory of Baktria. Geiger[5] thinks that it is probably to be identified with the town founded by the Macedonian king in the country of Paropanisadae near Kabul.

In the Apadāna[6] the Alasandakā are mentioned in a list of tribes.

[1] xxix. 40.

[2] p. 327.

[3] 82, 83.

[4] *E.g.*, in *Questions of King Milinda*, i., p. xxiii (see also CHI., p. 550).

[5] Mhv. trs. 194, n. 3.

[6] i. 359.

Alāta.—A minister and general of **Aṅgati,** King of **Videha.** He is described as wise, smiling, a father of sons and full of experience. When Aṅgati consulted his ministers as to ways and means of finding diversion for himself and his subjects, Alāta's counsel was that they should set out to battle with a countless host of men. The suggestion of another minister, **Vijaya,** was that the king should visit some *samaṇa* or brahmin, and this idea it was that won the king's approval. Thereupon Alāta persuaded Aṅgati to visit the Ājīvika **Guṇa** of the Kassapa family, who evidently enjoyed Alāta's patronage. When Guṇa preached his doctrine that good and evil actions were alike fruitless, he was supported by Alāta, who stated that in a previous birth he had been **Piṅgala,** a cow-killing huntsman in Benares, and that he had committed many sins for which, however, he had never suffered any evil consequences.

Later, Aṅgati's daughter **Rujā** explains that Alāta's present prosperity is the result of certain past acts of righteousness and that time will eventually bring him suffering on account of his evil deeds. Alāta himself, she says, is not aware of this because he can remember only one previous birth, while she herself can recall seven.[1]

Alāta was a previous birth of **Devadatta.**[2]

In the text he is sometimes[3] also called **Alātaka,** perhaps for the purposes of metre.

[1] See the *Mahā Nārada-Kassapa Jātaka* (J. vi. 222 ff.).

[2] *Ibid.*, 255.

[3] *E.g.*, pp. 221, 230.

Alīnacitta.—King of Benares; one of the lives of the Bodhisatta. He was so-called ("Win-heart") because he was born to win the hearts of the people. He was consecrated king at the age of seven. His story is related in the *Alīnacitta Jātaka*.

Alīnacitta Jātaka (No. 156).—Story of the Bodhisatta, when he was born as **Alīnacitta,** King of Benares.

An elephant, while walking in the forest, trod on a splinter of acacia wood left there by carpenters while felling forest trees for wood for buildings in Benares. In great pain he came to the carpenters and lay down before them. They removed the splinter and owing to their treatment the wound healed. The elephant, in gratitude, spent the rest of his life working for them, and, before his death, he enlisted his son, white in colour, magnificent and high-bred, in their service. One day a half-dry cake of the young one's dung was carried into the river by the flood,[1] and, floating down, stuck near the bathing place of the king's elephants in Benares. The royal elephants, scenting the noble animal, refused to enter the water and fled. Having discovered the reason for their behaviour, the king decided to obtain the animal for himself, and going up-stream in a raft, he saw the carpenters and the white elephant working for them. The merchants agreed to give him

[1] We are told that noble animals never dung or stale in water.

to the king, but the elephant refused to move till the carpenters were adequately compensated. The animal was taken in procession to the city and with his help the king became supreme ruler over India.

In course of time the Queen Consort bore a son to the king, but the king died before his birth. The Kosala king thereupon laid siege to Benares, but desisted from attack for seven days, astrologers having predicted that at the end of that time the child would be born. The men of Benares had agreed to surrender unless the baby proved to be a boy. After seven days the queen bore a son named **Alīnacitta,** and the inhabitants of Benares gave battle to the Kosala king. The queen, being told that they were in danger of defeat, dressed the baby and took him to the elephant for protection. The elephant had been kept in ignorance of the king's death, lest he himself should die of a broken heart. But, on hearing the news, he sallied forth into battle and soon brought back the Kosala king as captive.

Alīnacitta became, in due course, king over the whole of Jambudīpa.[2]

This story and that of the *Saṃvara Jātaka* were both related in connection with a monk who had become faint-hearted. For details see *s.v.* **Saṃvara.** The elephant of the Jātaka was the faint-hearted monk and the father-elephant was **Sāriputta.**

This Jātaka also was related by the Buddha, with reference to the Elder **Rādha** whom Sāriputta had taken under his special spiritual protection and guidance, in gratitude for a ladleful of food that Rādha, as layman, had once given him. The Buddha pointed out that this was not the first time that Sāriputta had shown his gratitude.[3]

[2] J. ii. 17-23. [3] DhA. ii. 106.

Alīnasattu.—The Bodhisatta, born as son of **Jayaddisa** (*q.v.*), King of **Uttarapañcāla** in **Kampilla.** When the boy grew up, fully instructed in all the arts, his father made him Viceroy. Later, Jayaddisa's life having become forfeit to the man-eating ogre (*porisāda*), Alīnasattu volunteered to offer himself in his father's place. The ogre, impressed by the prince's fearlessness and by the readiness with which he carried out his offer, refused to eat him and absolved him from his undertaking. Alīnasattu preached to him the five moral laws and, having discovered that the ogre was really a human being, offered him the throne, which, however, the latter would not accept.[1]

In lists of births in which the Bodhisatta is mentioned as having practised *sīlapāramitā*, the Alīnasattu Jātaka is mentioned[2] (*v.l.* **Adīnasattu, Alīnasatta, Ālīnasatta**).

[1] J. v. 22 ff. [2] *E.g.*, J. i. 45.

Alomā (Aloṇā ?).—A poor woman of Benares. She saw the Buddha going on his begging round, and having nothing else to offer, gave him, with very pious heart, some dried flesh, old and saltless. She thought constantly of her gift, and after death was born in a vimāna in Tāvatiṃsa, where **Moggallāna** came across her and heard from her her story[1] (*v.l.* **Ālomā**).

[1] Vv. 39; VvA. 184.

1. **Aḷaka.**—A country on the banks of the **Godhāvarī** River. It was at a spot between the territories of the Aḷaka and the Assaka kings that **Bāvarī** lived.[1] To the north of Aḷaka was **Patiṭṭhāna.**[2]

[1] Sn. 977. [2] Sn. 1011.

2. **Aḷaka.**—An Andhaka king of the Aḷaka country.[1] See **Aḷaka** (1).

[1] SnA. ii. 580-1.

Aḷakhiya-rāyara.—One of the Tamil generals who fought on the side of **Kulasekhara** against **Parakkama-bāhu I.**[1]

[1] Cv. lxxvi. 145.

Aḷagvānagiri.—A locality in South India, captured by the forces of **Parakkama-bāhu I.**[1]

[1] Cv. lxxvii. 12.

Aḷajanapada.—A district which the thera **Isidatta** visited on his return journey from a pilgrimage to the **Mahā-Vihāra.** The children of Aḷajanapada collected some fruit-rinds, which had been left behind by the fruit-gatherers, and gave them to Isidatta and his companion, **Mahāsoṇa.** It is said that this was the only meal they had for a week.[1]

[1] VibhA. 447.

Aḷattūru.—Name of two Damiḷa chiefs in the army of **Kulasekhara.** They took part in various battles and were eventually conquered by the forces of **Parakkamabāhu I.**[1]

[1] Cv. lxxvi. 140, 184, 214, 217, 220, 305.

Aḷandanāgarājamahesī.—The name occurs in the *Samantapāsādikā*,[1] in a discussion as to what is and what is not, *kappiya* for the monks. Monks should not accept or use a pond or any such thing, unless it has been properly gifted to them. But if the real owners of the pond, etc., or their heirs, or, if no heirs exist, the chief of the district, having dis-

[1] iii. 680.

covered that the pond was being used by monks, were to give it to the monks, then the gift becomes *kappiya*, "as in the case of the bucket of water taken by the monk of **Cittalapabbata** and **Alandanāgarājamahesī**"—evidently meaning that the water was later given to the monk by the *mahesī*, thereby making it *kappiya*.

Aḷāra.—A landowner of **Mithilā,** described also as **Videha** and **Videhiputta,** an inhabitant of the Videha country.[1] While journeying on business, in a carriage, attended by five hundred waggons, he saw the Nāga king, **Saṅkhapāla,** being ill-treated by lewd men who had captured him and, feeling sorry for the Nāga, Aḷāra gave gifts to the men and their wives and thus obtained his release. Saṅkhapāla, thereupon, invited Aḷāra to the Nāga kingdom where, for a whole year, Aḷāra lived in all splendour. Later, realising that the Nāga's wonderful possessions were the fruit of good deeds done in the past, he became an ascetic in Himavā and afterwards took up his abode in the king's park in Benares. The king, seeing him on his begging-rounds, was pleased with his deportment and invited him to the palace. There, at the king's request, he told him the story of his encounter with Saṅkhapāla and his subsequent life and exhorted the king to do acts of piety.

Later he was born in the Brahma-world.[2]

Aḷāra was a previous birth of **Sāriputta.**[3] (*v.l.* **Āḷāra.**)

[1] J. v. 166, 167. [2] See the Saṅkhapala J. (v. 161 ff.). [3] *Ibid.*, 177.

Aḷāra Kālāma.—See **Āḷāra Kālāma.**

1. **Allakappa.**—A country near **Magadha.** When the **Bulis** of Allakappa heard of the Buddha's death, they sent messengers to the Mallas asking for a portion of the relics, claiming that they too, like the Buddha, were *khattiyas*. Having obtained them, they later built a thūpa over them.[1] Allakappa seems to have had a republican form of government, but its importance was not very great. According to the Dhammapada Commentary,[2] Allakappa was ten leagues in extent and its king was on intimate terms of friendship with the King of **Veṭhadīpaka.** They spent a great deal of their time together, so that the two countries must have been near each other.

[1] D. ii. 166-7; Bv. xxviii. 2. [2] DhA. i. 161.

2. **Allakappa.**—The King of **Allakappa** and friend of King **Veṭhadīpaka.** They both renounced their kingdoms and became ascetics in the Himālaya. At first they lived in the same hermitage, but later separated and lived apart, meeting once a fortnight, on fast-days.

Veṭhadīpaka died and was born a mighty king of devas. Soon after, when visiting Allakappa, he learned that the latter's asceticism was being disturbed by wild elephants. Veṭhadīpaka gave him a lute with which to charm them, and spells whereby he might influence them. The lute had three strings; at the plucking of the first, the elephants ran away at once, of the second they ran away but looked back at each step, but when the third was plucked, the leader of the herd came and offered the player his back on which to sit.

Some time later, Allakappa met the Queen of **Parantapa,** King of **Kosambi,** with her son **Udena,** who had been born in the forest, the queen having been carried thither by a large bird of prey. Allakappa took them to the hermitage and looked after them, in ignorance of their high estate. He later lived with the queen as his wife. One day he perceived, by the occultation of Parantapa's star, that the king was dead; he told this to the queen who then confessed her identity and that of Udena, the legitimate heir to the throne. Allakappa gave to Udena the magic lute and taught him the spells that by their power he might gain his heritage. See *s.v.* Udena.

Avakaṇṇaka.—Given in the *Pācittiya* rules[1] as an example of a low name (*hīnanāma*).

[1] Vin. iv. 6 ff.

1. **Avaṭaphaliya Thera.**—An arahant. In a previous birth, ninety-four kappas ago, he gave an *avaṭa* (tāla ?) fruit to the Pacceka Buddha **Sataraṃsī.**[1] He is probably identical with **Sambula Kaccāyana.**[2]

[1] Ap. ii. 409. [2] ThagA. i. 314.

2. **Avaṭaphaliya Thera.**—His story is similar to that of (1) except that the name of the Pacceka Buddha seems to have been **Sahassaraṃsī** (or is this an epithet ?).[1] He is probably to be identified with **Meḷajina** Thera.[2]

[1] Ap. ii. 445. [2] ThagA. i. 252.

Avaṇṭaphaladāyaka Thera.—An arahant. Ninety-four kappas ago he had given a fruit without a stalk (*avaṇṭa*) to a Pacceka Buddha named **Sataraṃsi.**[1]

[1] Ap. i. 294.

1. **Avanti.**—One of the four great monarchies in the time of the Buddha, the other three being **Magadha, Kosala** and **Vaṃsa** (or **Vatsa**). Avanti

is also mentioned among the sixteen great janapadas.[1] Its capital was **Ujjenī** (*q.v.*). But according to another account,[2] **Māhissati** is mentioned as having been, at least for some time, the capital of Avanti. It is quite likely that ancient Avanti was divided into two parts, the northern part having its capital at Ujjenī and the southern part (also called **Avanti Dakkhiṇāpatha**) at Māhissati (Māhiśmatī).[3] This theory is supported by the fact that in the Mahābhārata,[4] Avanti and Māhiśmatī are referred to as two different countries.

In the Buddha's time, the King of Avanti was **Pajjota,** a man of violent temper,[5] and therefore known as **Caṇḍa Pajjota.** He wished to conquer the neighbouring kingdom of **Kosambī,** of which **Udena** was king, but his plans did not work out as he had anticipated. Instead, his daughter **Vāsuladattā** became Udena's wife and the two countries continued to be on friendly terms.[6]

The kingdom of **Assaka** is invariably mentioned in connection with Avanti. Even in the Buddha's life-time, Avanti became a centre of Buddhism. Among eminent monks and nuns who were either born or resided there, are to be found **Mahā Kaccāna, Nanda Kumāraputta, Soṇa Kuṭikaṇṇa, Dhammapāla, Abhayarājakumāra, Isidatta** and **Isidāsī.**

It is said that when Pajjota heard of the Buddha's advent to the world, he sent his chaplain's son, **Kaccāna,** with seven others, to invite him to Avanti.

Having listened to the Buddha's teaching, the messengers became arahants, and when Kaccāna conveyed to the Buddha the king's invitation to Avanti, he was asked by the Buddha to return and represent him. Kaccāna returned to Avanti and converted Pajjota to the faith of the Buddha.[7] Henceforward Mahā Kaccāna seems to have spent a good deal of his time in Avanti, dwelling in the city of **Kuraraghara** in the **Papāta Pabbata.**[8]

The religion thus introduced, however, does not seem to have spread to any extent until much later; for we find Mahā Kaccāna experiencing great difficulty in collecting ten monks, in order that Soṇa Kuṭikaṇṇa might receive the higher Ordination; in fact it was not until three years had elapsed that he succeeded.[9] Later, when Soṇa Kuṭikaṇṇa visited the Buddha at Sāvatthi, he conveyed to the Buddha Mahā Kaccāna's request that special rules might be laid down for the convenience of the

[1] A.i.213; iv.252, 256, 260.

[2] D.ii.235.

[3] Bhandarkar: *Carmichael Lectures* (1918), p. 54.

[4] ii.31, 10.

[5] Vin.i.277.

[6] The romantic story of this marriage is given in DhA. i. 191 ff. For a summary see *s.v.* **Vāsuladattā.**

[7] ThagA. i. 485.

[8] S. iii.9. 12; iv. 115-16; A. v. 46; also UdA. 307.

[9] Vin. i. 195.

monks of Avanti Dakkhiṇāpatha and of other border countries.[10] The Buddha agreed, and among the rules so laid down were the following: (1) The higher Ordination could be given with only four monks and a Vinayadhara. (2) Monks are allowed the use of shoes with thick linings (because in Avanti the soil is black on the surface, rough and trampled by cattle). (3) Monks are enjoined to bathe frequently (the men of Avanti attaching great importance to bathing). (4) Sheepskins, goat-skins, etc., could be used as coverlets. (5) Robes could be accepted on behalf of a monk who has left the district, and the ten days' rule with regard to such a gift will not begin until the robes have actually reached the monk's hands[11] (this, evidently, because of difficulty of access).

By the time of the Vesāli Council, however, Avanti had become one of the important centres of the orthodox school, for we find **Yasa Kākaṇḍakaputta** sending messengers to Avanti to call representatives to the Council, and we are told that eighty-eight arahants obeyed the summons.[12]

Among other localities in Avanti (besides those mentioned above) were **Ghanaselapabbata, Makkarakaṭa** and **Veḷugāma,** and, in Jaina works, we find mention also of **Sudarśanapura.**[13]

Even in the Buddha's day there were rumours of the King of Avanti making preparations to attack Magadha, but we are not told that he ever did so.[14] Subsequently, however, before the time of Candagupta, Avanti became incorporated with Magadha. Before **Asoka** became King of Magadha he was the Magadha Viceroy of Avanti and ruled in Ujjeni, and it was in Ujjeni that **Mahinda** and **Saṅghamittā** were born and grew up.[15] But the country seems to have retained its name at least as late as the second century A.D., as may be seen from Rudradāman's Inscription at Junagaḍh.[16]

Avanti is now identified with the country north of the Vindhaya Mountains and north-east of Bombay, roughly corresponding to modern Mālwa, Nimār and adjoining parts of the Central Provinces.[17]

In the *Milindapañha*[18] Avanti is mentioned as one of the three maṇḍalas or great divisions of Jambudīpa, the other two being **Pācīna** and **Dakkhiṇāpatha.**

According to a late tradition recorded in the Buddhavaṃsa,[19] the Buddha's mat (*nisīdana*) and rug were deposited, after his death, in Avanti.

It has sometimes been suggested that Avanti was the home of modern

[10] *Ibid.*, 197-8.

[11] *Cp.* the first *nissaggiya* rule (Vin. iii. 195-6).

[12] Vin. ii. 298-9.

[13] Law: *Kṣatriya Tribes*, p. 148.

[14] *E.g.*, M. iii. 7.

[15] Mhv. xiii. 8 ff.

[16] *Buddhist India*, p. 28.

[17] Law: *Geography of Early Buddhism*. p. 22.

[18] Trs. ii. 250, n. 1.

[19] Bu. xxviii. 10.

Pāli.[20] It has further been suggested that the Avanti school of monks—founded by Mahā Kaccāna, who was considered the greatest analytical exponent of the Buddha's time—living in comparative isolation (as seen above) on account of difficulty of access,[21] and laying special stress on *dhutavāda* practices[22]—developed branches of knowledge dealing mainly with grammar and doctrinal interpretation by ways of exegetical analysis. The Pāli grammar ascribed to Kaccāyana and the *Netti-ppakaraṇa* were both works of this school.[23]

Avanti was one of the parts into which the earth was divided by King **Renu,** with the help of his Great Steward, **Mahā-Govinda.** The King of Avanti at the time was **Vessabhū** and his capital Māhissati.[24]

[20] *E.g.*, in *Bud. India*, pp. 153-4.

[21] **Avanti,** however, lay on the road taken by **Bāvarī's** ten disciples on their way from **Patiṭṭhāna** to **Sāvatthi.**

[22] Vin. ii. 299.

[23] For a discussion of this see PLC. 181 ff.

[24] D. ii. 235-6.

2. **Avanti.**—King of Ujjeni in a past age. During his reign the Bodhisatta was born, under the name of **Citta,** in a Caṇḍāla village outside Ujjeni. His story is related in the *Citta-Sambhūta Jātaka.*[1]

[1] J. iv. 390 ff.

Avantiputta.—King of **Madhurā.** His mother was the sister of **Pajjota,** King of **Avanti,** hence the name Avantiputta.[1] He once went in royal state to visit **Mahā Kaccāna** who was staying in the **Gundā** Grove in Madhurā. Their discussion is recorded in the *Madhura Sutta.*[2] It is said that after the interview Avantiputta became a follower of the Buddha's teaching.

[1] MA. ii. 738.

[2] M. ii. 83-90.

Avandiya.—A Damiḷa chief who fought on the side of **Kulasekhara** against **Parakkamabāhu I.**[1]

[1] Cv. lxxvi. 146.

Avaruddhaka.—A yakkha. Having served **Vessavaṇa** for twelve years, he received, as his reward, permission to take the boy, who later became known as **Āyuvaddhana.** On the day destined for the boy's death, Avaruddhaka, coming to claim his possession, found the Buddha and his disciples there, reciting texts and taking other measures to avert his death. Avaruddhaka had to step back twelve leagues to make room for his superiors and had eventually to go away without getting the boy.[1]

[1] DhA. ii. 237-8.

Avaroja.—A householder in the time of **Vipassī** Buddha; he had a nephew who was also called Avaroja after his uncle. When the uncle undertook to build a *gandhakuṭi* for the Buddha, the nephew wished to have a share in the work, but this the uncle would not allow. The former thereupon proceeded to erect a **Kuñjarasālā** (Elephant Hall), on the site opposite the *gandhakuṭi,* adorned with the seven kinds of precious minerals. In the centre of the Kuñjarasālā was a jewelled pavilion beneath which was a Preacher's Seat. At the foot of the seat were set four golden rams, of which there were two more under the foot-rest and six round the pavilion. At the festival of dedication, Avaroja invited the Buddha with sixty-eight thousand monks, giving alms to suffice for four months and various gifts to monks and novices.

This Avaroja, the nephew, became **Meṇḍaka,** the famous seṭṭhi of Benares, in the present age.[1]

A story similar to that of the two Avarojas is told of **Aparājita,** uncle and nephew of the same name, who also were householders in the time of **Vipassī** Buddha. We are told that this nephew also became Meṇḍaka Seṭṭhi in his last birth.[2] We have here, evidently, a confusion of legends.

[1] DhA. iii. 364 ff. [2] *Ibid.*, iv. 202-3.

Avavādakā.—A Licchavi girl. Her father was a Nigaṇṭha who had come to Vesāli to hold discussions and had there met a Nigaṇṭhī whom he married. Avavādakā had three sitsers, **Saccā, Lolā** and **Paṭācārā** and one brother **Saccaka.** The children learnt from their parents one thousand theses for discussion, and on the death of the parents the sisters became Paribbājakas. In the course of their wanderings, whenever they entered a city, they would set up at the city-gate a jambu-twig, as a challenge to anyone who might wish to hold a philosophic discussion with them. In Sāvatthi, **Sāriputta** accepted the challenge, and at the end of the discussion he converted them. They later became arahants. The story of their past is given in the *Culla Kāliṅga Jātaka.*[1]

[1] J. iii. 1 ff.

Avāriya Jātaka (No. 376).—Once, when the Bodhisatta was an ascetic, at the invitation of the King of Benares, he dwelt in the royal garden, admonishing the king on the virtues of righteousness and compassion. Being pleased with him, the king wished to present him with a village of which the revenue was a thousand, but the ascetic declined the gift. For twelve years the ascetic lived in the park; then, desiring a change, he went away, and in the course of his wanderings, arrived at a ferry on the Ganges, where lived a foolish ferryman named **Avāriyapitā.** He took the Bodhisatta across, on the latter's promising to tell him how to increase his wealth, his welfare and his virtue. On reaching the other side, the Bodhisatta advised the ferryman on the desirability of getting his fare before crossing if he wished to increase his wealth; he then proceeded to recite to him the stanzas on the virtue of compassion, which, for twelve years, he had daily recited to the king. Incensed at feeling that he had been cheated out of his money, the ferryman started striking the ascetic; his wife, coming along with his food, tried to stop him. Thereupon he struck her, upsetting the food and causing her womb to miscarry. He was brought before the king and punished.

Good advice is wasted on fools, like fine gold on beasts.

The story was told regarding a foolish ferryman of **Aciravatī.** When a certain monk came to him one evening to be taken across the river, the ferryman was annoyed and steered so badly that he wet the monk's robes and delayed him. The two ferrymen were the same.[1]

[1] J. iii.228-32.

Avāriya Vagga.—The first division of the *Chakka Nipāta* of the *Jātakaṭṭhakathā.*[1]

[1] J.iii.228-74.

Avāriyapitā.—The ferryman of the *Avāriya Jātaka.*

Avāriyā.—Daughter of **Avāriyapitā.**[1]

[1] J. iii. 230.

Avikakkā (*v.l.* for **Adhikakkā**).

1. **Avijjā Vagga.**—The thirteenth chapter of the *Khandha Saṃyutta.*[1]

[1] S.iii.170-7.

2. **Avijjā Vagga.**—The sixth chapter of the *Saḷāyatana Saṃyutta.*[1]

[1] S.iv.30-5.

3. **Avijjā Vagga.**—The first chapter of the *Magga Saṃyutta.*[1]

[1] S.v.1-12.

1. **Avijjā Sutta.**—The ignorance of *puthujjanas* consists in not knowing the nature, the arising, the ceasing and the path thereto, of the five khandhas.[1]

[1] S.iii.162.

2. **Avijjā Sutta.**—In him who knows and sees the eye, objects, etc., as impermanent, ignorance vanishes and knowledge arises.[1]

[1] S. iv. 30.

3. **Avijjā Sutta.**—When ignorance is abandoned, knowledge springs up. This state is reached by knowing, by seeing the eye, etc., as impermanent.[1]

[1] S. iv. 49-50.

4. **Avijjā Sutta.**—When it is realised that nothing should be adhered to, that all phenomena are changeable and become otherwise, ignorance disappears and knowledge arises.[1]

[1] S. iv. 50.

5. **Avijjā Sutta.**—The ninth sutta of the *Sāmaṇḍaka Saṃyutta.*[1]

[1] S. iv. 261-2.

6. **Avijjā Sutta.**—When ignorance leads the way, wrong views arise, wrong aims, etc.; the reverse happens with knowledge.[1]

[1] S. v. 1.

7. **Avijjā Sutta.**—Ignorance is ignorance about Ill, its arising, its ceasing and the way thereto.[1]

[1] S. v. 429.

Avijjāpaccaya Sutta.—Two suttas. Conditioned by ignorance, activities (*saṅkhārā*) come to pass, and so on for each factor of the *Paticcasamuppāda.*[1]

[1] S. ii. 60-3.

1. **Avitakka Sutta.**—**Ānanda,** seeing **Sāriputta,** remarks on his calm demeanour and his translucent colour and asks him how they came about. Sāriputta explains that he had spent the day in the second jhāna, in single-pointedness of mind, apart from thought applied and sustained (*avitakka avicāra*).[1]

[1] S. iii. 236.

2. **Avitakka Sutta.**—**Moggallāna** tells the monks how he had obtained the second jhāna with the assistance of the Buddha.[1]

[1] S. iv. 263.

Avidūre Nidāna.—The story of **Gotama** the Buddha, from the time of his leaving the Tusita heaven until the attainment of his Enlightenment at the foot of the Bodhi-tree, is called Avidūre Nidāna.[1] The whole of the story agrees word for word with the account given in the **Madhuratthavilāsinī**, Buddhaghosa's Commentary on the Buddhavaṃsa; possibly they were both drawn from the same source.[2]

[1] J. i. 2; 47-77.

[2] PLC. 125-6.

Avihā.—A class of devas. Their world ranks among the five foremost of the *rūpa*-worlds, the **Suddhāvāsā.**[1] Anāgāmīs are born in Avihā and there attain arahantship.[2] Mention is made of seven persons who became arahants immediately after being born in the Avihā world: **Upaka, Palagaṇḍa, Pukkusāti, Bhaddiya, Kuṇḍadeva, Bāhudanti** and **Piṅgiya.**[3] The name Avihā means "not falling from prosperity" (*attano sampattiyā na hāyantīti Avihā*).[4] The duration of life in Avihā is one thousand kappas.[5] *Uddhaṃsotas* start their career from Avihā and end in **Akaniṭṭhā.**[6]

The Buddha once visited Avihā.[7]

[1] D. ii. 52; iii. 237; M. iii. 103.

[2] ItA. 40.

[3] MA. ii. 999.

[4] VibhA. 521; DA. ii. 480.

[5] DA. iii. 740.

[6] PsA. 319; DhA. iii. 289-90.

[7] D. ii. 50-1.

Avihiṃsā Sutta.—See **Akodha Sutta.**

Avīci.—One of the eight great purgatories (*mahāniraya*).[1] It is ten thousand leagues in extent and forms part of a *cakkavāḷa*.[2]

The *Milindapañha* (p. 5), however, places it outside the sphere of the earth. Spence Hardy[3] mentions a tradition which says that Avīci is seven hundred miles directly under the Bodhi Tree at Gayā. In later books, *e.g.* the Dhammapada Commentary, it is represented as being under the earth, for we are told that the earth opened wide to allow the flames of Avīci to escape and to drag down sinners into its bowels.[4] It seems to have been specially designed for those who had committed very grievous crimes, among whom are **Devadatta; Cunda,** the pork butcher; **Ānanda,** who raped his cousin the Therī **Uppalavaṇṇā;** the ascetic **Jambuka,** who in a previous birth had insulted an arahant; the murderer of the Pacceka Buddha **Sunetta; Sīvalī,** who in a former birth had blockaded a city for seven years; **Suppabuddha,** who insulted the Buddha; **Mallikā,** because of her misbehaviour with a dog (she was only there seven days); **Ciñcā-Māṇavikā,** because she falsely accused the Buddha; and **Kapila,** brother of **Sodhana,** for reviling pious monks.[5]

[1] J. v. 266.

[2] SnA. ii. 443.

[3] *Manual of Buddhism*, p. 26.

[4] *E.g.*, DhA. i. 127, 147; iii. 181.

[5] For details and references see under these names; see also Mil. 357.

According to Buddhaghosa, Avīci is often called Mahā Niraya.[6] Descriptions of it are to be found in several places in the four Nikāyas.[7] It is a quadrangular space, one hundred leagues each way, four-doored, walled all round and above with steel and with floor of incandescent molten steel.

The *Dhammapadaṭṭhakathā* gives a description of the tortures that await the entrant to Avīci. When, for instance, Devadatta entered there, his body became one hundred leagues in height, his head, as far as the outer ear, entered into an iron skull; his feet sank up to the ankles in iron, an iron stake as thick as the trunk of a palmyra tree came from the west wall, pierced the small of his back and, penetrating his breast, entered the east wall. Other similar stakes came from the south and from the north and transfixed him.[8]

The fire of Avīci is so powerful that it destroys the eyes of anyone looking at it from a distance of one hundred leagues.[9] It would destroy in a moment a rock as large as a gabled house, yet beings born there remain undestroyed, as though reposing in their mother's womb.[10]

Beings born in Avīci suffer for periods of varying lengths; thus, Mallikā, Pasenadi's queen, remained only for seven days,[11] while Devadatta is destined to pass there 100,000 kappas.[12] The Sutta Nipāta[13] gives the names of various specified periods of suffering, which, according to Buddhaghosa,[14] are to be spent in Avīci; they are **Abbuda, Nirabbuda, Ababa, Ahaha, Aṭaṭa, Kumuda, Sogandhika, Uppalaka, Puṇḍarīka,** and **Paduma,** taken in a geometrical progression of twenty (*i.e.* twenty Abbudas = one Nirabbuda, etc.).

Another mode of suffering in Avīci is described as **Sarājita.**[15]

It is noteworthy that the word Avīci occurs only once in the four Nikāyas—namely, in a passage in the *Cakkavatti-Sīhanāda Sutta* of the *Dīgha Nikāya*[16]—but in this context there is no indication that the name refers to a purgatory. The word is not found in a list of purgatories given in the *Sutta Nipāta*[17] and in the *Saṃyutta.*[18] It is, however, found in a poem in the *Itivuttaka* (No. 89) which recurs both in the *Vinaya*[19] and in the *Dhammasaṅgaṇi,*[20] and there it is specifically called a *niraya.*

In the *Dīgha* passage mentioned above, the reference to Avīci is in connection with a tremendous growth of population which will occur in Jambudīpa in a future age. Houses will be so close that a cock could fly from any one to the next, and one would think it Avīci (*avīci maññe*).

6 AA. i. 376.
7 *E.g.*, M. iii. 183; A. i. 141-2.
8 DhA. i. 148.
9 A. i. 142.
10 DhA. i. 127; Mil. 67.
11 DhA. iii. 121.
12 *Ibid.*, i. 148.
13 p. 126.
14 SnA. i. 476.
15 SA. iii. 100.
16 D. iii. 75; repeated in A. i. 159.
17 pp. 126-31.
18 i. 152.
19 ii. 203.
20 Section 1280.

Rhys Davids suggests[21] that the word (which he translates as Waveless Deep) might have been originally used to denote density of population. Buddhaghosa[22] explains it as "*nirantara-pūrita*" perhaps in the sense that it is filled with fire. In the Visuddhimagga[23] the word appears to be a synonym for *jarā* (disintegration) and is used in connection with the disintegration of earth, water, mountains, sun, moon, etc.

Avīci is often referred to as the lowest point of the universe.[24] The chief suffering endured there is that of heat.[25]

[21] Dial. iii. 73, n. 1.
[22] DA. iii. 855.
[23] ii. 449.
[24] Thus, *e.g.*, Vsm. ii. 390, 486; Mbv. 57.
[25] MNidA., p. 8.

Avela.—One of the palaces used by the Buddha **Revata** in his last lay-life.[1]

[1] Bu. vi. 17.

Avyākata Vagga.—The fourth chapter of the *Sattaka Nipāta* of the *Aṅguttara Nikāya*.[1] It contains ten suttas on various subjects such as the seven states of man (*purisagati*), *anupādā parinibbāna*, the knowledge Brahmas possess regarding *sa-upādisesa-* and *anupādisesa-nibbāna*, imparted to them by Moggallāna, the reason why the Dhamma will not last long, the seven kinds of wives who are like murderers, etc.

[1] A. iv. 67-98.

Avyākata Saṃyutta.—The forty-fourth section of the Saṃyutta Nikāya.[1]

[1] S. iv. 374-403.

Avyādhika Thera.—An arahant. In a previous birth he built an *aggisālā* for **Vipassī** Buddha and a hospital and hot baths for the sick. Later, seven kappas ago, he was a king named **Aparājita.**[1]

[1] Ap. i. 215.

Avyāpajjha Sutta.—The Buddha teaches the harmless and the path thereto.[1]

[1] S. iv. 371.

Asaṅkiya Jātaka (No. 76).—The Bodhisatta was born as a brahmin in Benares and became an ascetic. In the course of his wanderings he once travelled with a merchant caravan. The caravan halted for the night, but while the merchants slept, the ascetic spent his time pacing up and down. Robbers, coming to plunder the caravan, were prevented from so doing by the watchfulness of the ascetic. The next day the merchants, discovering what had happened, asked him if he had felt no fear at the sight of the robbers. "The sight of robbers causes what is known as fear only to the rich. I am penniless, why should I be afraid?" he answered.

After death he was born in the Brahma world.

The story was told to an *upāsaka* of Sāvatthi who had likewise prevented a caravan from being robbed. "In guarding himself a man guards others; in guarding others he guards himself."[1]

[1] J. i. 332-4.

Asaṅkhata Saṃyutta.—Also called **Nibbāna Saṃyutta.** The forty-third section of the *Saṃyutta Nikāya.*[1]

[1] S. iv. 359-73.

Asaṅkhata Suttas.—A group of suttas describing the way to the uncompounded (*asaṇkhata*).[1]

[1] S. iv. 362 ff.

Asaññataparikkhāra-bhikkhu Vatthu.—The story of a monk who failed to keep his requisites in order. Exposed to rain, sun and white ants, they soon went to pieces. His conduct was reported to the Buddha, but when questioned about it, he did not show much concern, saying it was a mere trifle. The Buddha showed him the folly of his conduct and laid down a rule that no monk should fail to remove a bed which he had spread in the open air.[1]

[1] DhA. iii. 15-16.

Asaññasattā.—Inhabitants of the fifth of the nine abodes of beings (*sattāvāsā*). These beings are unconscious and experience nothing.[1] As soon as an idea occurs to them they fall from their state.[2] Brahmin ascetics, having practised continual meditation and attained to the fourth jhāna, seeing the disadvantages attached to thinking, try to do away with it altogether. Dying in this condition, they are reborn among the Asaññasattā, having form only, but neither sensations, ideas, predispositions nor consciousness. They last only as long as their power of jhāna; then an idea occurs to them and they die straightaway.[3]

The **Andhakas** held that these devas were really only sometimes conscious, which belief the **Theravādins** rejected as being absurd.[4]

The Elder **Sobhita** was once born among the Asaññasattā and could remember that existence. These devas are long-lived.[5]

[1] A. iv. 401. [2] D. i. 28. [3] DA. i. 118. [4] Kvu. 262. [5] ThagA. i. 291.

Asatthārāma.—The place where the Buddha **Piyadassī** died.[1]

[1] Bu. xiv. 27.

1. **Asadisa.**—The Bodhisatta born as the son of **Brahmadatta,** King of Benares. **Brahmadatta** was also the name of Asadisa's brother. When the father died, the kingdom was offered to Asadisa, but he refused it and handed it over to his brother. Finding that his presence in the city was causing anxiety to the latter, he left Benares and entered into the service of another king, as archer. He attained great fame by his wonderful feats of archery. Once he brought down a mango with the downward shot of an arrow, which, in its upward flight, reached the realm of the **Cātummahārājikā,** whence it was turned back by another arrow, which, having accomplished its purpose, rose to Tavatiṃsa.

Later, on hearing that seven kings had beleaguered his brother's kingdom, Asadisa shot an arrow, bearing a message, into the dish from which the kings were eating, and they all fled.

He soon afterwards became an ascetic and at his death was born in the Brahma world.[1]

[1] J. ii. 86-92.

2. **Asadisa.**—A brahmin village, the residence of **Sunettā** who gave milk rice to the Buddha **Siddhattha.**[1]

[1] BuA. 185.

Asadisa Jātaka (No. 181).—The story of the prince **Asadisa.** It was told in reference to the Great Renunciation to show that in former lives also the Bodhisatta had renounced a royal state.[1] The latter part of the story is given in the *Mahāvastu* and is called the *Śarakṣepana Jātaka.*[2] The story is figured in the Bharhut Stūpa[3] and in the Sanchi Tope.[4] King **Kittisiri** of Ceylon wrote a beautiful poem in Sinhalese based on this Jātaka.[5]

[1] J. ii. 86-92.
[2] Mtu. ii. 82-3.
[3] Cunningham, p. 70, and Plate xxvii. 13.
[4] Fergusson, *Tree and Serpent Worship,* p. 181, Plate xxxvi.
[5] Cv. Supplement 101, vs. 13.

Asadisa Vagga.—The fourth section of the *Duka Nipāta* of the *Jātakaṭṭhakathā.*[1]

[1] J. ii. 86-113.

Asadisadāna.—The celebrated almsgiving which **Pasenadi,** under the guidance and inspiration of **Mallikā,** held, in order to outdo his citizens in their generosity to the Buddha and the Order. The almsgiving was attended with unparalleled splendour, khattiya maidens fanning monks while elephants held white parasols over them and golden boats filled with perfumes and flowers were placed in the gay pavilion where the monks were fed. Four gifts of priceless value were given to the Buddha, a white parasol, a couch whereon to rest, a stand and a footstool. These gifts were never after equalled by those of anyone else, each Buddha receiving these gifts only once in his lifetime.[1]

The *Āditta*, the *Dasabrāhmaṇa* and the *Sivi Jātakas* were all preached in reference to the Asadisadāna.

[1] DA.ii.653-4; DhA.iii.183-6.

Asadisadāna Vatthu.—The story of the **Asadisadāna** and its sequel, the story of **Pasenadi's** two ministers **Kāḷa** and **Juṇha.**[1]

[1] See *s.v.* **Kāḷa.**

Asaddha Sutta.—Like joins with (literally "flows together with") like, unbelievers with unbelievers, the lazy with the lazy, etc.[1]

[1] S.ii.159.

Asaddhamūlakāpañca Sutta.—The same in its main features as the **Asaddha Sutta.**[1]

[1] S.ii.160-1.

Asanabodhiya Thera.—An arahant. In **Tissa** Buddha's time he planted the *Asana*-tree, which was the Buddha's Bodhi-tree, and tended it for five years. The Buddha was very pleased with him and foretold for him a glorious future. For thirty kappas he dwelt among the devas; seventy-seven kappas ago he was a cakkavatti named **Daṇḍasena,** and one kappa later he was seven times king under the name of **Samantanemi.** Twenty-five kappas ago he was a khattiya, **Puṇṇaka** by name.[1]

[1] Ap.i.110-11.

Asani Sutta.—What is the falling of a thunderbolt compared with the danger for a learner (*sekha*) arising from gains, favours and flattery ?[1]

The Commentary explains that a thunderbolt destroys one life-span only, while gains, etc., bring a man to infinitely prolonged misery.[2]

[1] S.ii.229. [2] SA.ii.154.

Asandhimittā.—Chief queen of **Dhammāsoka.** He gave for her use one of the eight loads of water brought for him from **Anotatta.**[1] She was a faithful follower of the Buddha's teaching and died in the thirtieth year of Asoka's reign.[2] When preparations were being made to take the branch of the Bodhi-tree to Ceylon, she offered to the tree all kinds of ornaments and various sweet-scented flowers.[3]

[1] Mhv. v. 85; two says Sp. (i. 42). [2] Mhv. xx. 2. [3] Mbv. 152.

Having learnt from the monks that the voice of the karavīka bird was like that of the Buddha, she had a karavīka given her by the king, and listened to his song. Thrilled with joy at the thought of the sweetness of the Buddha's voice, she attained to the First Fruit of the Path.[4]

She was called Asandhimittā because the joints in her limbs were visible only when she bent or stretched them.[5]

In a previous birth, when Asoka was born as a honey merchant and gave honey to the Pacceka Buddha, she was the maid who pointed out the honey-store to the Pacceka Buddha. She had then wished that she might become the queen consort of the King of Jambudīpa and be possessed of a lovely form with invisible joints.[6]

[4] DA.ii.453; MA.ii.771. [5] MṬ. 136. [6] Mhv. v. 59-60.

1. **Asappurisa Sutta.**—The man who has wrong view, wrong aim, etc., is called " unworthy " (*asappurisa*); he who has the opposite qualities is " worthy."[1]

[1] S. v. 19.

2. **Asappurisa Sutta.**—The same as the first, with the addition of " the still more unworthy," possessed also of wrong knowledge and wrong liberation, and " the still more worthy " having the opposite qualities.[1]

[1] S. v. 20.

1. **Asama.**—The chief disciple of **Sobhita Buddha.**[1] He was the Buddha's step-brother, and it was to him and to his brother **Sunetta** that the Buddha preached his first sermon.[2]

[1] Bu. vii. 21; J. i. 35. [2] BuA. 137.

2. **Asama.**—Father of **Paduma** Buddha and King of **Campā.**[1]

[1] Bu. ix. 9; BuA. 146.

3. **Asama.**—Chief lay-supporter of **Paduma** Buddha[1]; probably the same as his father. See **Asama** (2).

[1] Bu. ix. 23.

4. **Asama.**—A devaputta who once visited the Buddha at Veluvana, in the company of **Sahali, Nivika, Ākoṭaka, Veṭambari** and **Māṇava-Gāmiya.** They were disciples of different teachers and, standing before the Buddha, each uttered the praises of his own teacher. Asama eulogised **Pūraṇa-Kassapa.**[1] Perhaps Asama is the name of a class; See **Asamā** (1).

[1] S. i. 65.

Asamatta Sutta.—Association with the worthy, listening to the Dhamma, systematic reflection and living according to the precepts of the Dhamma—these things, if cultivated, lead to infinite insight.[1]

This sutta should probably be called **Appamatta;** the text gives both names.

[1] S. v. 412.

Asamapekkhanā Sutta.—By not seeing the nature of body, etc., diverse opinions arise in the world. Preached at Sāvatthi to the Paribbājaka **Vacchagotta.**[1]

[1] S. iii. 261.

1. **Asamā.**—A class of devas, present at the preaching of the **Mahā Samaya** Sutta. They are mentioned together with the **Yama** twins.[1]

[1] D. ii. 259.

2. **Asamā.**—Mother of **Paduma** Buddha and wife of King **Asama.**[1]

[1] Bu. ix. 16; J. i. 36.

3. **Asamā.**—Chief woman-disciple of **Padumuttara** Buddha.[1]

[1] Bu. xi. 25; DA. ii. 489; J. i. 37.

Asamāhita Sutta.—Like joins with like, *e.g.* the unconcentrated with the unconcentrated, because of some fundamental quality (*dhātu*) common to both.[1]

[1] S. ii. 166.

Asampadāna Jātaka (No. 131).—The Bodhisatta was born in Rājagaha and became known as **Saṅkhaseṭṭhi,** worth eighty crores. He had a friend, **Piliyaseṭṭhi,** in Benares, equally wealthy. Piliya having lost all his wealth, sought the assistance of Saṅkha, who gave him one-half of all his possessions. Later, Saṅkha, himself becoming bankrupt, went with his wife to Benares to seek help from Piliya; the latter, however, dismissed him with half a quartern of pollard. On the way back Saṅkha was recognised by an erstwhile servant of his whom he had given to Piliya. This servant befriended Saṅkha and his wife, and with the help of his companions, brought to the king's notice Piliya's ingratitude. The king, having tried the case, wished to give all Piliya's wealth to Saṅkha, but at the latter's request restored to him only what he had, in days of prosperity, given to Piliya.

The story is related in reference to **Devadatta's** ingratitude.[1]

[1] J. i. 465-9.

Asampadāna Vagga.—The fourteenth section of the *Eka Nipāta* of the *Jātakaṭṭhakathā*.[1]

[1] J.i. 465-86.

Asayha.—A rich seṭṭhi of **Bheruva.** He gave generously to holy men and to the needy. After death he was born in Tāvatiṃsa. A former servant of **Aṅkura,** who had settled down as a tailor in Bheruva, used to show the way to those who sought the house of Asayha, and was, therefore, reborn as a powerful yakkha.[1] In the *Peta-Vatthu* stanzas Asayha is once spoken of as **Aṅgirasa.**[2]

[1] PvA. 112.

[2] p. 25, v. 23.

Asallakkhaṇā Sutta.—Preached to the Paribbājaka **Vacchagotta.** Through want of discernment of the nature of the body, etc., diverse opinions arise in the world.[1]

[1] S.iii. 261.

Asātamanta Jātaka (No. 61).—The Bodhisatta was once a famous teacher in **Takkasilā.** A young brahmin of Benares came to study under him and, after completing his course, went back home. His mother, however, was anxious that he should renounce the world and tend **Aggibhagavā** in the forest. She accordingly sent him back to the Teacher that he might learn the "Asātamanta" (Dolour Text). The Teacher had a mother aged 120 years, on whom he himself waited. When the youth came back to learn the Asātamanta, he was asked to look after the old woman. She, falling in love with him, hatched a plot to kill her son.

The Bodhisatta, having been told of this plot, made a wooden figure and placed it in his bed. The mother, thinking to kill her son, struck it with an axe, and discovering that she had been betrayed, fell down dead. The youth, having thus learnt the Asātamanta, returned to his parents and became a hermit. **Kāpilānī** was the mother in the story, **Mahā Kassapa** the father and **Ānanda** the pupil.

This story, together with the **Ummadantī Jātaka,** was related to a passion-tossed monk to warn him of the evil nature of women.[1]

[1] J. i. 285-9.

Asātarūpa Jātaka (No. 100).—Once the Bodhisatta was King of Benares. The Kosala king waged war on him, slew him and bore off his queen to make her his own wife. The king's son escaped through a sewer and later came back with a large army to give battle. His mother, hearing of his doings, suggested that he should blockade the city instead.

This he did, and the blockade was so close that on the seventh day the people cut off the head of the king and brought it to the prince.

It was this prince who became **Sīvalī** in the present age; the blockade was the reason for his remaining seven years in his mother's womb, and for her being seven days in bringing him forth. His mother was **Suppavāsā,** daughter of the **Koliya** king.

The story was related by the Buddha to explain to the monks the reason for Suppavāsā's long pregnancy.[1]

[1] J. i. 407-10. This Jātaka appears, with variations in detail, in DhA. ii. 198 ff.

Asiggāha Silākāla.—See **Silākāla.**

1. **Asita.**—Often called the Buddhist Simeon, though the comparison is not quite correct. He was a sage and the chaplain of **Sīhahanu,** father of **Suddhodana.** He was the teacher of the Suddhodana, and later his chaplain. He came morning and evening to see the king, Suddhodana, who showed him as great respect as he had while yet his pupil; this, we are told, is a characteristic of Sākya kings. With the king's leave, Asita renounced the world and lived in the king's pleasaunce. In due course he developed various *iddhi* powers. Thenceforward he would often spend the day in the *deva* worlds. Once, while in Tāvatiṃsa, he saw the whole city decked with splendour and the gods engaged in great rejoicing. On inquiry he learnt that **Siddhattha Gotama,** destined to become the Buddha, had been born. Immediately he went to Suddhodana's home and asked to see the babe. From the auspicious marks on its body he knew that it would become the Enlightened One and was greatly overjoyed, but realising that he himself would, by then, be born in an *Arūpa* world and would not therefore be able to hear the Buddha preach, he wept and was sad. Having reassured the king regarding the babe's future, Asita sought his sister's son, **Nalaka,** and ordained him that he might be ready to benefit by the Buddha's teaching when the time came. Later Asita was born in the Arūpa world.[1]

According to Buddhaghosa,[2] Asita was so-called because of his dark complexion. He also had a second name, **Kaṇha Devala.**[3] Other names for him were **Kaṇha Siri,**[4] **Siri Kaṇha**[5] and **Kāḷa Devala.**[6]

He is evidently to be distinguished from **Asita Devala** (*q.v.*), also called **Kāḷa Devala.**

The *Lalita Vistara* has two versions of Asita's prophecy, one in prose and one in verse, which, in their chief details, differ but slightly from

[1] Sn., pp. 131-36; SnA. ii. 483 ff.; J. i. 54 f.

[2] SnA. ii. 483.

[3] *Ibid.*, 487.

[4] Sn. v. 689.

[5] SnA. 487.

[6] J. i. 54.

the Pāli version. In the former his nephew is called **Naradatta,** and Asita himself is represented as being a great sage dwelling in the Himālaya but unknown to Suddhodana.

Here is evidently a confusion of his story with that of Asita Devala.

In the Mahāvastu version[7] he is spoken of as the son of a brahmin of **Ujjeni,** and he lives in a hermitage in the Vindhyā mountains. It is noteworthy that in the Jātaka version he is called, not an *isi*, but a *tāpasa*, an ascetic practising austerities. And there we are told that when the king brought the boy, the future Buddha, and prepared to make him do reverence to the ascetic, the babe's feet turned up and placed themselves on the ascetic's head. For there is no one fit to be reverenced by a Bodhisatta, and had they put the babe's head at the feet of the ascetic, the ascetic's head would have split into seven pieces.

The *tāpasa* could see forty kappas into the past and forty kappas into the future.[8]

[7] ii. 30 f.
[8] J. i. 54-5. See *Thomas, op. cit.,* pp. 38 ff., on the growth of the Asita legend.

2. **Asita.**—A Pacceka Buddha, mentioned in a list of Pacceka Buddhas.[1]

[1] M. iii. 70; ApA. i. 107.

3. **Asita.**—A garland-maker in the time of **Sikhī** Buddha. While taking a garland to the palace, he saw the Buddha and offered it to him. As a result, twenty-five kappas ago he became a king named **Dvebhāra.** In the present age he was known as **Sukatāveḷiya** Thera.[1]

[1] Ap. i. 217.

1. **Asita Devala.**—A sage (*isi*). His story is given in the *Assalāyana Sutta.*[1] Once there were seven brahmin sages living in thatched cabins in the wilds. They conceived the view that the brahmins are the highest class of men and that they alone are the legitimate sons of Brahmā. Hearing of this, Asita Devala appeared before their hermitage in orange attire, with stout sandals and staff, and shouted for them. The brahmins cursed him with the intention of shrivelling him into a cinder, but the more they cursed the more comely and handsome grew Asita. Feeling that their austerities were evidently fruitless, they questioned Asita who urged them to discard their delusion. Having learnt his identity, they saluted him and wished to be instructed; Asita examined and cross-questioned them about their pretensions regarding

[1] M. ii. 154 ff.

their lineage and they could find no answer. They thereupon followed his advice and renounced their claims to superiority.

Buddhaghosa says that Asita Devala was the Bodhisatta.[3]

[3] MA.ii.785.

2. **Asita Devala.**—More commonly called **Kāḷa Devala,** probably identical with (1) above, and mentioned in the *Indriya Jātaka.*[1] He was one of the seven chief disciples of the Bodhisatta **Sarabhaṅga** and lived with many thousand sages in **Avanti Dakkhiṇāpatha.** He had a younger brother **Nārada,** also an ascetic, who lived in **Arañjara.** When Nārada became enamoured of a courtesan on the river-bank near Arañjara, Kāḷa Devala flew to him, and in due course brought **Sālissara, Meṇḍissara** and **Pabbatissara** to admonish him. When they, too, failed in their efforts to convert Nārada, Kāḷa Devala brought the master of all sages, Sarabhaṅga, who with their help persuaded Nārada to give up his love.

In this present age Kāḷa Devala became **Mahā Kaccāna.**[2]

[1] J. iii. 463 ff. [2] *Ibid.*, 469.

Asitañjana.—A city in the **Kaṃsa** district in **Uttarāpatha** and capital of King **Mahākaṃsa** and the **Andhakaveṇhudāsaputtā.**[1] It was also the birthplace of the two merchants **Tapassu** and **Bhalluka.**[2]

[1] J. iv. 79; PvA. 111. [2] AA. i. 207.

Asitañjala.—See **Amitañjala.**

Asitābhū.—Wife of Prince **Brahmadatta.** Her story is given in the *Asitābhū Jātaka.*

Asitābhu Jātaka (No. 234).—The Bodhisatta was once a holy ascetic living in the Himālaya. At that time the king of Benares, growing jealous of his son Prince **Brahmadatta,** banished both him and his wife, **Asitābhū.** They went to the Himālaya and lived in a hut of leaves. One day the prince, becoming enamoured of a Candakinnarī, followed her, forsaking his wife. Asitābhū went to the Bodhisatta and, having developed various superhuman powers, returned to her hut. Brahmadatta, having failed in his quest, returned to the hut where he found his wife poised in mid-air uttering songs of joy over her new-found freedom. When she left, he lived in solitude till, at his father's death, he succeeded to the throne.

The story was told in reference to a young girl, the daughter of a servitor of the two chief disciples. She was married, but finding her husband neglectful of her, visited the two Chief Disciples. Under their instruction she attained the First Fruit of the Path and embraced the religious life, ultimately becoming an arahant.

She was Asitābhū in the previous birth.[1]

The story is referred to in the Vibhaṅga Commentary[2] in connection with a King of Benares who, having gone into the forest with his queen to eat roast flesh, fell in love with a kinnarī and deserted his wife. When he returned to his queen he found her flying through the air away from him, having developed *iddhi* powers. A tree-sprite then uttered a stanza, citing the example of Asitābhū.

[1] J. ii. 229 ff. [2] p. 470 f.

Asipattavana.—One of the tortures of purgatory. In the distance the grove appears as a mango grove, and when the inhabitants of purgatory enter, wishing to eat the mangoes, leaves which are sharp like swords fall on them, cutting off their limbs.[1]

[1] Sn. v. 673; SnA., ii. 481.

Asibandhakaputta.—A *gāmaṇi* (headman). He came to the Buddha in the **Pārileyyaka** Mango Grove in Nālandā and asked him various questions, recorded in the *Saṃyutta Nikāya.*[1] One of these related to the custom among the **Pacchābhūmaka** (Westlander) brahmins (where, perhaps, he himself belonged) of lifting a man up when dead and carrying him out, calling him by name to speed him heavenward. Surely the Buddha who is an arahant, etc., could make the whole world go to heaven thus if he chose. To this the Buddha answers no, and explains, by various similes, that only a man's kamma can determine where he will be reborn. On another occasion, the Buddha tells him, in answer to a question, that the Buddha teaches the Dhamma in full only to certain disciples and not to others; just as a farmer sowing seed selects, first the best field, then the moderate, and lastly, the field with the worst soil.

Asibandhakaputta tells the Buddha that, according to Nigaṇṭha Nātaputta,[2] as a man habitually lives so goes he forth to his destiny. The Buddha points out the absurdity of this view and tells him that all Tathāgatas lay down definite rules for the guidance of their followers, so that they may attain development.

It is recorded[3] that once, when Nālandā was stricken with famine, Asibandhaka visited Nigaṇṭha Nātaputta, who asks him to go and defeat the Buddha in debate. Asibandhaka is at first reluctant, but his teacher propounds to him a dilemma to put to the Buddha, and he agrees to go. Is it true that the Buddha extols compassion to clansmen ? Why, then,

[1] iv. 312 ff. [2] He is described as a *Nigaṇṭha-Sāvaka* (S. iv. 317).
[3] *Ibid.*, 322 ff.

does the Buddha ask for alms in a place stricken with famine? The Buddha's answer is that there are eight ways of injuring clansmen, and that begging for alms is not one of them. And Asibandhakaputta, pleased with the answer, declares himself to be a follower of the Buddha.

Asibandhakaputta's conversation with the Buddha, in which the Buddha tells him that only a man's kamma can determine the state of his rebirth, is quoted in the *Nettippakaraṇa*.[4]

[4] pp. 45-47.

Asilakkhaṇa Jātaka (No. 126).—In Benares was a brahmin who could tell, by smelling them, whether swords were lucky or not. One day, while testing a sword, he sneezed and cut off the tip of his nose. The king had a false tip made and fastened to his nose so that no one could tell the difference.

The king had a daughter and an adopted nephew, who, when they grew up, fell deeply in love with each other. They wished to marry, but the king, having other plans, kept them apart. The prince bribed an old woman to get his beloved for him. The old woman reported to the king that his daughter was under the influence of witchcraft and that the only way of curing her was to take her to the cemetery under armed escort, where she must be laid on a bed under which was a corpse, and there she must be bathed for the purpose of exorcism.

The prince was to impersonate the corpse, being provided with pepper in order that he might sneeze at the right moment; the guard were warned that if the exorcism succeeded, the dead body would sneeze, rise up and kill the first thing it could lay hold of. The plot succeeded, the guard taking to their heels when the prince sneezed. The two lovers were married and were forgiven by the king. Later, they became king and queen.

One day the sword-testing brahmin was standing in the sun when the false tip of his nose melted and fell off. He stood hanging his head for very shame. "Never mind," laughed the king, "sneezing is bad for some, but good for others. A sneeze lost you your nose, but a sneeze won for me both my throne and my queen."

The story was related in reference to a brahmin of the kingdom of Kosala who tested swords by smelling them. He accepted bribes and passed the swords only of those who had won his favour. One day an exasperated dealer put pepper on his sword so that when the brahmin smelt it he sneezed, slitting his nose. The monks were once talking about him when the Buddha entered and told them the story of the past.

The two brahmins were one and the same man in different births.[1]

[1] J. i. 455-8.

Asisūkarika Sutta.—Records the incident of **Moggallāna** seeing a Peta while on the way, with **Lakkhaṇa,** from Gijjhakūṭa to Rājagaha. The Peta travelled through the air which was bristling with sword blades. The swords kept rising and falling directly on his body, while he uttered cries of pain.[1]

[1] S. ii. 257.

Asīti Nipāta.—The twenty-first section of the *Jātakaṭṭhakathā.*[1]

[1] J. v. 333-511.

1. **Asubha Sutta.**—There are four modes of progress with reference to a monk who lives contemplating the unloveliness of the body, the repulsiveness of food, etc. His attainment, however, may be sluggish if his five indriyas (of faith, energy, etc.) are dull.[1]

[1] A. ii. 150 f.

2. **Asubha Sutta.**—The idea of the foul, if cultivated, leads to great profit.[1]

[1] S. v. 132.

Asubhakammika Tissa Thera.—Referred to in the *Majjhima* Commentary[1] as an example of a monk in whom lustful desires ceased because he dwelt on the Impurities and associated only with worthy friends. He was an arahant.

[1] MA. i. 228; J. iii. 534; see also MṬ. 401.

Asura.—In Pāli Literature the Asuras are classed among the inferior deities together with the *supaṇṇas, gandhabbas, yakkhas,*[1] *garuḷas* and *nāgas.*[2] Rebirth as an Asura is considered as one of the four unhappy rebirths or evil states (*apāyā*), the others being *niraya, tiracchānayoni* and *pettivisaya.*[3] The fight between the Devas and the Asuras is mentioned even in the oldest books of the Tipiṭaka and is described in identical words in several passages.[4] A chief or king of the Asuras is often referred to as **Asurinda,**[5] several Asuras being credited with the rôle of leader, most commonly, however, **Vepacitti**[6] and **Rāhu.**[7] Besides these we find

[1] DA. i. 51.

[2] Mil. 117.

[3] *E.g.*, It. 93; J. vi. 595; J. v. 186; Pv. iv. 11.

[4] *E.g.*, D. ii. 285; S. i. 222; iv. 201 ff.; v. 447; M. i. 253; A. iv. 432; also S. i. 216 ff.

[5] **Sakka** was also called **Asurinda** and **Asurādhipa**; see, *e.g.*, J. i. 66 (*Asurindena paviṭṭhadevanagaram viya*) and J. v. 245, where we are told that from the time he conquered the Asuras he was called Asurādhipa.

[6] *E.g.*, S. i. 222; iv. 201 ff.; J. i. 205

[7] A. ii. 17, 53; iii. 243.

Pahārāda[8] (*v.l.* **Mahābhadda**), **Sambara**[9], **Verocana**,[10] **Bali**,[11] **Sucitti**[12] and **Namucī**.[13]

The Asuras are spoken of as dwelling in the ocean after having been conquered by **Vajira-hattha** (Indra[14]) and are called **Vāsava's** brethren, of wondrous powers and of great glory. They were present at the preaching of the *Mahā Samaya Sutta*.[15] Buddhaghosa[16] says that they were all descendants of an Asura maiden named **Sujātā**.

There were evidently several classes of Asuras, and two are mentioned in the Piṭakas, the **Kālakañjakas** and the **Dānaveghasas**. The Dānaveghasas carried bows in their hands.[17] The Kālakañjakas were of fearsome shape,[18] and were considered the lowest among the Asuras.[19]

Once the Asuras dwelt in Tāvatiṃsa together with the devas. When **Magha Māṇavaka** was born as Sakka, he did not relish the idea of sharing a kingdom with others, and having made the Asuras drunken, he had them hurled by their feet on to the steeps of **Sineru**. There they tumbled into what came to be known as the **Asurabhanava**, on the lowest level of Sineru, equal in extent to Tāvatiṃsa. Here grew the **Cittapātali** tree, and when it blossomed the Asuras knew they were no longer in the deva-world. Wishing to regain their kingdom, they climbed Sineru, "like ants going up a pillar." When the alarm was given, Sakka went out to give battle to them in the ocean, but being worsted in the fight, he fled in his **Vejayantaratha**. Fearing that his chariot hurt the young Garuḷas, he had it turned back. The Asuras, thinking that Sakka had obtained reinforcements, turned and fled right into the Asurabhavana. Sakka went back to his city and in that moment of victory, the **Vejayantapāsāda** sprang up from the ground. To prevent the Asuras from coming back again, Sakka set up as guard in five places Nāgas, Garuḷas, Kumbhaṇḍas, Yakkhas and the Four Great Kings. Everywhere were images of Indra bearing the thunderbolt in his hand.[20]

The Asuras are sometimes called **Pubbadevā**[21] and their kingdom is 10,000 leagues in extent.[22]

8 A. iv. 197, 200.

9 S. i. 227.

10 S. i. 225; probably another name for **Rāhu** (see DA. ii. 689).

11 D. ii. 259.

12 *Ibid.*

13 *Ibid.*

14 Elsewhere (J. v. 139) called **Asurappamaddana**.

15 See DA. ii. 689.

16 This cannot be the **Sujātā, Vepacitti's** daughter, whom Sakka married (J. i. 205-6). See also **Dānavā**.

17 See *s.v.*

18 D. ii. 259.

19 D. iii. 7; see also *s.v.* **Kālañkajaka** and **Vepacitti**.

20 J. i. 202-4; DhA. i. 272-80; the same story, differing slightly in details, is found in SnA. 484-5. There it is said that when Sakka was born among them, the Asuras received him with great cordiality; see also the various incidents of the Asura war mentioned in the *Saṃyutta Nikāya* I. 216 ff.

21 SnA. 484.

22 *Ibid.*, 485; elsewhere, in the same page, it is given as 100,000 leagues.

In Buddhaghosa's time, the bygone lustre of the word Asura (as equivalent to Ahura) seems to have faded. His explanation[23] of the name is interesting. When Sakka was born with his followers in the Asura-world (which later became Tāvatiṃsa) the Asuras prepared a drink called *gaṇḍapāna*. Sakka warned his companions not to drink it, but the Asuras became drunk and were thrown down Sineru. Halfway down they regained consciousness and made a vow never to drink intoxicants (*surā*) again; hence their name Asura.

The Aṅguttara Commentary[24] defines Asura as *bībhaccha*, awful, vile. They had a drum called **Āḷambara** (*q.v.*), made of a crab's claw. They left it behind in their flight from Sakka, and since then Sakka has the use of it.[25]

[23] SA.i.260. [24] ii.526. [25] J.ii.344.

Asura Vagga.—The tenth chapter of the *Catukka Nipāta* of the *Aṅguttara Nikāya*. It consists of ten suttas containing the classification of four kinds of individuals to be found in the world, with more or less detailed descriptions of them.[1]

[1] A.ii.91-101.

Asura Sutta.—The first of the *Asura Vagga*. Four individuals exist in the world: the *asura* (*a*) with a retinue of *asuras*, (*b*) with a retinue of *devas*; the *deva* (*a*) with a retinue of *devas*, (*b*) with a retinue of *asuras*. The first is himself immoral, as is his company, and so on correspondingly with the others.[1]

[1] A.ii.91.

Asurinda (Asurindaka) Sutta.—Recounts an interview between the Buddha and **Asurinda Bhāradvāja** in Veluvana. When Asurinda heard that **Bhāradvāja** (probably the chief of the clan) had entered the Order, he was greatly vexed, and going up to the Buddha he abused him. The Buddha remaining silent, Asurinda thought that he acknowledged defeat. But the Buddha enlightened him, saying that the worse of the two is he who, when reviled, reviles back; he who does not so revile wins a twofold victory: he seeks the good both of himself and of the other.[1]

[1] S.i.163 f.; SA.i.178.

Asurindaka Bhāradvāja.—One of the **Bhāradvājas.** His interview with the Buddha is described above, in the *Asurinda Sutta*. He was the third of the Bhāradvāja brothers, all of whom eventually became followers of the Buddha.[1] "The name (demon-chief) is so pagan for a brahmin"

[1] MA.ii.808.

says Mrs. Rhys Davids,[2] and "the Buddha's reply so suggestive of Sakka's (in *Saṃyutta* i. 221) that a bifurcated or transferred legend seems fairly plausible."

[2] KS. i. 203, n. 2.

Asela.—Son of **Muṭasiva,** and youngest brother of **Devānampiyatissa.** When the two Damiḷas, **Sena** and **Guttaka,** conquered **Sūratissa** and captured the throne, Asela defeated them and reigned in Anurādhapura for ten years (155-145 B.C.).[1] He was ultimately conquered by **Eḷāra.**[2]

Asela was one of nine brothers, the others being **Abhaya, Devānampiyatissa, Uttiya, Mahāsīva, Mahānāga, Mattābhaya, Sūratissa** and **Kīra.**[3]

He built a cetiya in the **Asokamālaka.**[4]

[1] Mhv. xxi. 11; Cv. lxxxii. 20; Epy. Zeyl. iii., Introd., p. 5, n. 1.
[2] Mhv. xxi. 13.
[3] MṬ. 303.
[4] *Ibid.*, 253.

1. **Asoka.**—King of Magadha. He was the son of **Bindusāra.** Bindusāra had sixteen wives who bore him 101 sons. The Pāli Chronicles (*Dīpavaṃsa* and *Mahāvaṃsa*)[1] mention only three of the sons, viz. **Sumana** (**Susīma** according to the northern legends) the eldest, **Asoka,** and **Tissa** (uterine brother of Asoka) the youngest. The *Mahāvaṃsa Ṭīka*[2] gives the name of his mother as **Dhammā** and calls her Aggamahesī (Bindusāra's chief queen); she belonged to the **Moriyavaṃsa.** The preceptor of Dhammā's family was an Ājīvaka called **Janasāna.**[3]

In his youth Asoka was appointed Governor of **Avanti** with his capital at **Ujjeni.**[4] When Bindusāra lay on his death-bed, Asoka left Ujjeni and came to **Pāṭaliputta** where he made himself master of the city and possessor of the throne. He is stated in the *Mahāvaṃsa*[5] to have killed all his brothers except Tissa that he might accomplish his purpose, and to have been called **Caṇḍāsoka** on account of this outrage.[6] It is impossible to say how much truth there is in this account of the accession. Asoka's Rock Edicts seem to indicate that he had numerous brothers, sisters and relations alive at the time they were written in Pāṭaliputta

[1] The chief Pāli sources of information regarding Asoka are *Dīpavaṃsa* (chaps. i., v., vi., vii., xi., etc.), *Mahāvaṃsa* (v., xi., xx., etc.), *Samantapāsādikā* (pp. 35 ff.). Other sources are the Divyāvadāna *passim,* and the *Avadānaśataka* ii. 200 ff. For an exhaustive discussion of the sources and their contents see Prszlyski, *La Légende de l'Empereur Asoka.*

[2] p. 125; Mbv. 98. In the northern tradition (*e.g., Aśokāvadānamālā*) she is called **Subhadrāngī,** daughter of a brahmin of Campā.

[3] Which probably explains Asoka's earlier patronage of the Ājīvakas.

[4] The Divy. says he was in **Takkasilā** with headquarters in **Uttarāpatha,** where he superseded Susīma and quelled a rebellion.

[5] v. 20; Mbv. 98.

[6] Mhv. v. 189.

and other towns.[7] His brother Tissa he appointed as his *uparāja*,[8] but Tissa (*q.v.*) became a religious devotee attaining arahantship. The *Theragāthā* Commentary[9] refers to another younger brother of Asoka, **Vītāsoka,** who also became an arahant.

Asoka had several wives. His first wife was the daughter of a merchant of **Vedisagiri,** whom he met when stopping at the merchant's house on his way to Ujjeni.[10] Her name was **Devī,** also called **Vedisa-Mahādevī,** and she was a Sākyan, descended from a Sākyan family who migrated to Vedisa to escape from **Viḍūḍabha.**[11] Of Devī were born a son **Mahinda,** and a daughter **Saṅghamittā,** who became the wife of **Aggibrahmā** and mother of **Sumana.** Devī evidently did not follow Asoka to Pāṭaliputta, for his *aggamahesī* there was **Asandhamittā.**[12] Asandhamittā died in the thirtieth year of Asoka's reign, and four years later he raised **Tissarakkhā** to the rank of queen.[13]

According to Mahāvaṃsa,[14] Asoka's accession was 218 years after the Buddha's death and his coronation was four years later. The chronicles[15] contain various stories of his miraculous powers. His command spread a yojana into the air and a yojana under the earth. The devas supplied him daily with water from the Anotatta Lake and with other luxuries from elsewhere. Yakkhas, Nāgas and even mice and karavīka birds ministered to his comfort, and thoughtful animals came and died outside his kitchen in order to provide him with food.

At first Asoka maintained the alms instituted by his father, but soon, being disappointed in the recipients, he began looking out for holy men. It was then that he saw from his window, his nephew, the young novice **Nigrodha.** Owing to their friendship in a past birth,[16] Asoka was at once drawn to him and invited him into the palace. Nigrodha preached to him the *Appamādavagga* and the king was greatly pleased. He ceased his benefactions to other religious orders and transferred his patronage to Nigrodha and members of the Buddhist Order. His wealth, which, according to the *Samantapāsādikā* (i. 52), amounted to 500,000 pieces

[7] See Mookherji, *Asoka*, pp. 3-6.

[8] Mhv. v. 33.

[9] i. 295 f. The northern works give quite a different account of his brothers. See Mookherji, p. 6.

[10] Mhv. xiii. 8 ff.

[11] Mbv., pp. 98, 116.

[12] Mhv. v. 85.

[13] *Ibid.*, xx. 1-3. The Allahabad Pillar Inscription mentions another queen, **Kāruvākī,** mother of **Tīvara.** The Divy. (chap. xxvii.) gives another, **Padmāvatī,** **Kunāla**'s mother. Besides the children mentioned above, names of others are given: **Jalauka, Cārumatī** (Mookherji, p. 9).

[14] v. 21, 22.

[15] *Ibid.*, 22 ff.

[16] Asoka, Devanampiyatissa and Nigrodha had been brothers, traders in honey, and they gave honey to a Pacceka Buddha. Asandhamittā had been the maiden who showed the honey-shop to the Pacceka Buddha. The story is given in Mhv. v. 49 ff.

daily, he now spent in doing acts of piety—giving 100,000 to Nigrodha to be used in any manner he wished, a like sum for the offering of perfumes and flowers at the Buddha's shrines, 100,000 for the preaching of the Dhamma, 100,000 for the provision of comforts for members of the Order, and the remainder for medicines for the sick. To Nigrodha, in addition to other gifts, he sent sets of robes three times each day, placing them on the back of an elephant, adorned by festoons of flowers. Nigrodha gave these robes to other monks.[17]

Having learnt from **Moggaliputta-Tissa** that there were 84,000 sections of the Dhamma, he built in various towns an equal number of vihāras, and in Pāṭaliputta he erected the **Asokārāma.** With the aid of the Nāga king **Mahākāla,** he created a life-size figure of the Buddha, to which he made great offerings.

His two children, Mahinda and Saṅghamittā, aged respectively twenty and eighteen, he ordained under Moggaliputta-Tissa and **Dhammapālā,** in the sixth year of his reign.[18] This raised him from a *paccadāyaka* to a *sāsanadāyādin.*

In order to purge the Order of undesirable monks and heretical doctrines, Moggaliputta-Tissa held the Third Council under the king's patronage. It is said that the pious monks refused to hold the uposatha with those they considered unworthy. The king, desirous of bringing about unity in the Saṅgha, sent a minister to restore amity, but the minister, misunderstanding his orders, beheaded many holy monks, being at last stopped by the king's brother Tissa, who was then a monk.[19]

At the conclusion of the Council, held in the seventeenth year of his reign,[20] Asoka sent forth theras to propagate the Buddha's religion: **Majjhantika** to **Kasmīra** and **Gandhāra, Mahādeva** to **Mahisamaṇḍala, Rakkhita** to **Vanavāsa, Yona Dhammarakkhita** to **Aparantaka, Mahārakkhita** to **Yona, Majjhima** to the **Himālaya** country and **Soṇa** and **Uttara** to **Suvaṇṇabhūmi ; Mahinda** with **Iṭṭhiya, Uttiya, Sambala** and **Bhaddasāla** he sent to Lankā.[21] In the eighteenth year of his reign he sent to Lankā, at Devanampiyatissa's request, Saṅghamittā, with a branch of the great Bodhi Tree at **Buddhagayā.**[22] A little earlier he had sent by his grandson Sumana, some relics of the Buddha and the Buddha's alms-bowl to be deposited in the thūpas of Lankā.[23]

[17] MA. ii. 931.

[18] *Ibid.*, v. 197, 209.

[19] *Ibid.*, vs. 240 ff.

[20] *Ibid.*, 280; in the northern texts Moggaliputta-Tissa's name is given as **Upagupta.** It was for this Council that the Kathāvatthu (*q.v.*) was written.

[21] *Ibid.*, xii. 1-8. For particulars of these missions and identification of the places mentioned, see under the different names; this list appears also in the *Samantapāsādikā*, where further interesting details are given. For a discussion on them see Mookherji, pp. 33 ff.

[22] Mhv. xx. 1.

[23] *Ibid.*, xvii. 10 ff.

Asoka reigned for thirty-seven years.[24] In his later life he came to be called **Dhammāsoka** on account of his pious deeds.[25] The *Dīpavaṃsa* gives his name in several places as **Piyadassī**.[26]

The Chronicles state that Asoka and Devanampiya Tissa of Ceylon had been friends—though they had never seen each other—even before Mahinda's mission to Ceylon. Tissa had sent him, as a friendly gesture, various gifts, and Asoka had returned the courtesy. He sent an embassy of his chosen ministers, bearing gifts marvellous in splendour, that Tissa might go through a second coronation ceremony, and the messengers were directed to give this special message to the king: "I have taken refuge in the Buddha, Dhamma and Saṅgha and declared myself a follower of the religion of the Sākyaputta. Seek then, even thou, oh best of men, converting thy mind with believing heart, refuge in these best of gems."[27]

The *Milindapañha*[28] mentions an encounter of Asoka with a courtesan of Pāṭaliputta, **Bindumatī**, who, in order to show the king the power of an Act of Truth, made the waters of the Ganges to flow back. According to the *Petavatthu Aṭṭhakathā*[29] there was a king of **Suraṭṭha**, called **Piṅgala**, who used to visit Asoka in order to give him counsel. Perhaps he was an old friend or tutor of the king.

Asoka is called a *dīpacakkavatti* as opposed to *padesarājās* like Bimbisāra and **Pasenadi**.[30]

[24] *Ibid.*, xx. 6. [25] *Ibid.*, v. 189.

[26] *E.g.*, vi. 1, 2, 25. The title Devānampiya used by Asoka in his inscriptions was also used by Tissa, Asoka's contemporary in Ceylon, and by Asoka's grandson **Dasaratha** (Nāgarjunī Hill Cave Inscription). It was used also by other kings in Ceylon: **Vaṅkanāsika Tissa**, **Gajabāhukagāminī** and **Mahallaka-Nāga** (Ep. Zeyl. i. 60. f).

[27] Mhv. xi. 18-36.

[28] p. 121.

[29] 244 ff.

[30] Sp. ii. 309.

2. **Asoka.**—See **Kālāsoka.**

3. **Asoka.**—See **Vitāsoka.**

4. **Asoka.**—A brahmin in the time of **Kassapa** Buddha. He provided eight meals daily for the monks and entrusted the distribution of them to his serving-woman **Bīraṇī** (*q.v.*).[1]

[1] Mhv. xxvii. 11.

5. **Asoka.**—Attendant to **Vipassī** Buddha.[1] He was once ill and was cured by a doctor who, in this age, was **Tikicchaka (Tekicchakānī)** Thera.[2]

[1] J. i. 41; Bu. xx. 28. [2] Ap. i. 190; ThagA. i. 442.

6. **Asoka.**—The chief disciple of the future Buddha **Metteyya.**[1] According to the *Mahāvaṃsa*[2] he should be identified with **Duṭṭhagāmaṇī.**

[1] Anāgatavaṃsa. v. 97. [2] xxxii. 81.

7. **Asoka.**—A monk of **Ñātikā.** Once when the Buddha was staying at **Ñātikā** in the **Giñjakāvasatha,** Ānanda mentions to the Buddha that Asoka Thera had died, and asks where he had gone. The Buddha tells him that Asoka was an arahant and had realised Nibbāna.[1]

[1] S.i.358.

8. **Asoka.**—See **Anoma** (7).

9. **Asoka.**—A mountain near **Himavā.** There, in the time of **Sumedha** Buddha, **Vissakamma** built a hermitage.[1]

[1] Ap.ii.342.

Asokapūjaka Thera.—An arahant. Ninety-four kappas ago he was the king's park-keeper in **Tivarā** and offered an Asoka flower to the Buddha **Paduma.** Seventy kappas ago he became king sixteen times under the name **Aruṇañjaha.**[1]

[1] Ap.i.199.

Asokamālaka.—One of the spots in the **Mahāsāgara** garden, north of the **Nāgamālaka,** where the Buddha **Kassapa** preached to the assembled populace on his visit to Ceylon. Four thousand people were converted.[1] Later King **Asela** erected a cetiya there.[2]

[1] Mhv. xv. 153 ff. [2] MṬ. 253.

Asokamālā.—The wife of Prince **Sāli.** She was a *caṇḍāla* woman of exceedingly great beauty, and the prince married her, thus renouncing his right to the throne.[1] The two had been husband and wife, named **Tissa** and **Nagā,** in a previous existence and had lived in **Muṇḍagaṅgā** in Ceylon. One day the husband received a pig from a hunter in payment of some smith's work he had done. Having prepared the animal for food, he expressed the wish that eight holy monks might come to accept alms from him. His wife joining him in this wish, they decorated the house, prepared eight seats, strewed the village path with sand and awaited the guests. **Dhammadinna** Thera of **Piyaṅgudīpa,** having divined the man's wish, came to the village with seven colleagues. After they had eaten, they gave thanks and went away. The man was born as

Mhv. xxiii. 2-4.

Sāli the son of **Duṭṭhagāmaṇi,** but his wife was born as a *caṇḍāla* as punishment for an offence in another existence. She had been the youngest of seven daughters of a carpenter and was one day scolded by her mother for untidiness. In anger she used to her mother the same abusive terms as had been hurled at her. This undutiful behaviour caused her to be born as the daughter of a *caṇḍāla.*[2]

[2] MṬ. 606 f.

1. **Asokā.**—A nun of **Ñātikā.** When **Ānanda** announces her death to the Buddha at **Ñātikā** in the Giñjakāvasatha, and inquires where she had been born, the Buddha says that she had been reborn spontaneously in the **Suddhāvāsā,** there to pass away, destined never to return.[1]

[1] S. v. 358.

2. **Asokā.**—One of the two chief women disciples of **Maṅgala** Buddha.[1]

[1] Bu. iv. 24; J. i. 34.

Asokārāma.—A monastery in **Pāṭaliputta,** built by **Asoka** and finished in three years. It was there that the king's brother **Tissa** was ordained. When the monks had refused for seven years to hold the uposatha ceremony, Asoka sent his minister to summon them to the Asokārāma. There the misguided minister beheaded several theras who refused to obey his orders. It was there that **Moggaliputta Tissa** held the Third Council and made a compilation of the Dhamma.[1]

Asoka used to feed 60,000 monks daily at the Asokārāma.

On the day of the foundation of the **Mahā Thūpa** in Anurādhapura, sixty thousand monks under **Mittiṇṇa** came from Asokārāma.[2] There, too, lived **Dhammarakkhita,** the teacher of **Nāgasena.**[3]

Indagutta Thera was appointed by the king to superintend the building of the vihāra.[4]

It was from Asokārāma that **Mahinda** set out on his mission to Ceylon.[5]

[1] Mhv. v. 80, 163, 174, 236, 276.
[2] *Ibid.*, xxix. 36.
[3] Mil. 16-18.
[4] Sp. i. 48-9.
[5] *Ibid.*, 69.

Assa Sutta.—Once **Assa,** the "Jockey" (*assāroha*) of **Rājagaha** came to the Buddha to ask if it were true that a horse-trainer, if he exerted himself in the performance of his duties, would be born among the **Sarañjita** devas? The Buddha tells him that such a view is a perverted one and that its result is rebirth either in purgatory or as an animal. Assa expresses his consternation and declares himself thenceforth a follower of the Buddha.[1]

[1] S. iv. 310.

1. **Assaka.**—A king mentioned in the *Nimi Jātaka*, in a list of kings, such as **Dudīpa, Sāgara, Sela,** etc., who, in spite of all their great sacrifices, were not able to go beyond the Peta-world.[1]

[1] J. vi. 99.

2. **Assaka.**—King of **Potali** in the kingdom of **Kāsi.** His queen consort **Ubbarī** was very dear to him, and when she died he was plunged into grief. He put her corpse in a coffin, placed it under his bed and lay thereon, starving for seven days. The Bodhisatta was then an ascetic in the Himālaya, and just at this time he visited Potali. There, in the royal park, the king came to see him because he was told that the ascetic would show him Ubbarī. The Bodhisatta showed him Ubbari now reborn as a dung-worm in the park, because, being intoxicated with her own beauty, she had done no good deeds. Seeing the king incredulous, the ascetic made her speak, and she declared that she cared much more for the dung-worm, who was now her mate, than for Assaka who had been her husband in her previous life. Assaka went back to the palace, had the body disposed of, married another queen and lived righteously.[1]

[1] J. ii. 155-8.

3. **Assaka.**—King of **Potanagara** in the **Assaka** country, soon after the Buddha's death. He was the father of **Sujāta** and had two wives. He bequeathed his kingdom to the son of the younger wife.[1]

See also **Aruṇa** (2).

[1] VvA. 259-60.

4. **Assaka.**—The country of Assaka is one of the sixteen *Mahājanapadas* mentioned in the *Aṅguttara Nikāya.*[1] It does not, however, occur in the list of twelve countries given in the *Janavasabha Sutta.*[2] The Assakas are said to have had settlements on the **Godāvarī,** and **Bāvarī's** hermitage[3] was in their territory, in close proximity to the Aḷaka or Muḷaka (the district round Paithan).[4]

The country is mentioned with Avanti[5] in the same way as Aṅga with Magadha, and its position in the list between Sūrasena and Avanti makes it probable that when the list was drawn up, its position was immediately to the north-west of Avanti. It is probable, in that case, that the Godāvarī settlement, in the **Dakkhiṇāpatha,** was a later colony.

In the *Assaka Jātaka*[6] mention is made of a king Assaka whose realm was in the kingdom of **Kāsi.** It is significant, in this connection, that the

[1] A. i. 213; iv. 252, 256, 260.

[2] *qv.*

[3] Sn. v. 977.

[4] Law, *Early Geography*, 21.

[5] J. v. 317.

[6] *Ibid.*, ii. 155.

capital of Assaka, variously called **Potana**[7] or **Potali**,[8] is not mentioned in the reference to the Godāvarī.

According to the *Culla Kāliṅga Jātaka*,[9] at one time the King of Assaka (**Aruṇa**) accepted the challenge of King **Kāliṅga** of **Dantapura** to war, and defeated him. Later Assaka married Kāliṅga's daughter and the relations between the two countries were amicable. In the Hāthigumphā Inscription of Khāravela it is related that Khāravela, regardless of King Sātakarṇī, sent a large army to the west (*pachime disam*) to strike terror into Assaka (or Asika) nagara. Law[10] thinks that the Assaka of the Culla Kāliṅga Jātaka, the Asikanagara of the Hāthigumphā Inscription and the Assaka of the Sutta Nipāta are one and the same place. This would probably be correct if Potana and Potali were regarded as two different cities, capitals of two different settlements having the same name.

Sanskrit authors speak of both Aśmakā and Aśvakā. It is not possible to say whether these represent two distinct tribes or whether they are variant names for the same people. Asaṅga mentions Aśmaka in his *Sūtrālaṅkāra* as a territory on the basin of the Indus. This would make it identical with the Assakenus of Greek writers, that is to the east of the Sarasvati, about twenty-five miles from the sea on the Swat valley. Pāṇini mentions the Aśmakas.[11] The *Mārkaṇḍeya Purāṇa* and the *Bṛhat Saṃhitā* place Assaka to the north-west. The Assaka capital, Potana, it has been suggested, is the Paudanya of the Mahābhārata.[12] In the Commentary to Kauṭilya's Arthaśāsta, Bhaṭṭasvāmi identifies Aśmaka with Mahārāṣṭra.[13]

Soon after the Buddha's death, a King Assaka was the ruler of Potali, and he and his son **Sūjata** were converted by **Mahā Kaccānā**.[14]

In the time of King Reṇu, the Assaka king of Potana was **Brahmadatta**.[15]

In the Buddha's time the Assaka king is described as an **Andhakarājā**. He took a thousand for the plot of land sold for Bāvarī's hermitage.[16]

7 *E.g.*, D.ii.235; J.iii.3.
8 *E.g.*, J.ii.155.
9 *Ibid.*, iii.3-5.
10 *Op. cit.*, p. 21.
11 iv.173.
12 i.77, 47.
13 Law, *op. cit.*, 22.
14 VvA. 259-67.
15 D.ii.236.
16 SnA.ii.581.

Assaka Jātaka (No. 207).—The story of King **Assaka** (2). It was related to a monk who was distracted by the recollection of a former wife. He was Assaka in the previous birth.[1]

1 J.ii.158.

Assakaṇṇa.—One of the mountains round **Sineru.**[1] It is higher than **Vinataka,** and between these two flows the **Sīdantara Samudda.**[2]

[1] SnA. ii. 443; Sp. i. 119. [2] J. vi. 125.

Assagutta Thera.—A dweller in the **Vattaniya** hermitage. **Nāgasena's** teacher sent him to Assagutta to spend the rainy season with him. There was an old woman, a devout follower of the Faith, who had for thirty years or more looked after Assagutta; it was while preaching to her that Nāgasena became a Sotāpanna.[1]

When Nāgasena had completed his course, Assagutta sent him on to Pāṭaliputta to **Dhammarakkhita.**[2] It was Assagutta who interceded with Sakka to persuade **Mahāsena** to leave the deva-world and be born in the world of men as Nagasena. He was evidently the leader of the Saṅgha at the time, for it was he who summoned an assembly at **Yugandhara** to discuss the danger caused by Milinda's controversies.[3] In the Commentaries[4] he is quoted as an example of a *kalyānamitta,* full of compassion, association with whom leads to the destruction of ill-will.

[1] She, too, became a sotāpanna (Mil. 16).
[2] *Ibid.*
[3] *Ibid.*, 6.
[4] DA. ii. 779; AA. i. 28; VibhA. 272.

1. **Assaji Thera.**—The fifth of the **Pañcavaggiya** monks. When the Buddha preached the *Dhammacakkappavattana Sutta,* he was the last in whom dawned the eye of Truth, and the Buddha had to discourse to him and to **Mahānāma** while their three colleagues went for alms.[1] He became an arahant, together with the others, at the preaching of the *Anattalakkhaṇa Sutta.*[2] He was responsible for the conversion of **Sāriputta** and **Moggallāna.** Sāriputta, in the course of his wanderings in search of Eternal Truth, saw Assaji begging for alms in Rājagaha, and being pleased with his demeanour, followed him till he had finished his round. Finding a suitable opportunity, Sāriputta asked Assaji about his teacher and the doctrines he followed. Assaji was at first reluctant to preach to him, because, as he said, he was but young in the Order. But Sāriputta urged him to say what he knew, and the stanza which Assaji uttered then, has, ever since, been famous, as representing the keynote of the Buddha's teaching:

> " *ye dhammā hetuppabhavā tesaṃ hetuṃ Tathāgato āha*
> *tesañ ca yo nirodho, evaṃvādī Mahāsamaṇo.*"

[1] Vin. i. 13. He became a *sotāpanna* on the fourth day of the quarter (AA. i. 84).
[2] Vin. i. 14; J. i. 82.

Sāriputta immediately understood and hurried to give the glad tidings to Moggallāna that he had succeeded in his quest.[3]

Sāriputta held Assaji in the highest veneration, and we are told that from the day of this first meeting, in whatever quarter he heard that Assaji was staying, in that direction he would extend his clasped hands in an attitude of reverent supplication, and in that direction he would turn his head when he lay down to sleep.[4]

One day when Assaji was going about in Vesāli for alms, the Nigaṇṭha **Saccaka,** who was wandering about in search of disputants to conquer, saw him, and questioned him regarding the Buddha's teaching because he was a well-known disciple (*ñātaññatara-sāvaka*). Assaji gave him a summary of the doctrine contained in the Anattalakkhaṇa Sutta. Feeling sure that he could refute these views attributed to the Buddha, Saccaka went with a large concourse of **Licchavis** to the Buddha and questioned him. This was the occasion for the preaching of the *Cūla-Saccaka Sutta.*[5] The Commentary[6] tells us that Assaji decided on this method of exposition because he did not wish to leave Saccaka any loophole for contentious questioning. The *Saṃyutta Nikāya*[7] records a visit paid by the Buddha to Assaji as he lay grievously sick in **Kassapārāma** near Rājagaha. He tells the Buddha that he cannot enter into jhāna because of his difficulty in breathing and that he cannot win balance of mind. The Buddha encourages him and asks him to dwell on thoughts of impermanence and non-self.

[3] Vin. i. 30 ff.; the incident is related in the DhA (i. 75 ff.) with slight variations as to detail.

[4] DhA. iv. 150-1.

[5] M. i. 227 ff.

[6] MA. i. 452.

[7] S. iii. 124 ff.

2. **Assaji.**—One of the leaders of the **Assaji-Punabbasukā** (*q.v.*), the other being **Punabbasu.** He was one of the **Chabbaggiyā,** the others being **Mettiya, Bhummajaka, Paṇḍuka** and **Lohitaka.**[1]

[1] J. ii. 387; MA. ii. 668.

Assaji Sutta.—Records the incident, mentioned above, of the Buddha's visit to Assaji (1).[1]

[1] S. iii. 124-6.

Assaji-Punabbasukā.—The followers of **Assaji** and **Punabbasu.** They lived in **Kiṭāgiri,** between Sāvatthi and Āḷavi, and were guilty of various evil pract es. They used to grow flowers, make wreaths and garlands, and send them to girls and women of respectable families and also to slave girls, to lie with such women, and disregard the precepts regarding the eating of food at the wrong time, using perfumes, visiting shows, singing and playing games of various sorts.[1] Their abandoned ways of life won popularity for them, and virtuous monks, who did not belong to their group, were not welcomed by the people of the neighbourhood.

The Buddha heard of their nefarious doings from a monk who had been sojourning in the district, and having convened a meeting of the Saṅgha, sent **Sāriputta** and **Moggallāna,** together with a number of other monks, (for the recalcitrants were passionate and violent), to carry out the *Pabbājaniyakamma* (Act of Banishment) against them. The deputation of the Saṅgha went to Kīṭāgiri and made an order that the Assaji-Punabbasukā should no longer dwell there, but the latter, instead of obeying the injunction, abused the monks, accusing them of partiality, and not only departed from Kīṭāgiri, but also left the Order. When the matter was reported to the Buddha he had the *Pabbājaniyakamma* revoked (" because it had served no purpose ").[2]

In the *Dhammapada* Commentary[3] we are told that Assaji and Punabbasu had originally been disciples of Sāriputta and Moggallāna, and that when the two Aggasāvakas admonished them and their followers on the wickedness of their conduct, some of them reformed themselves and a few retired to the householder's life.

The Assaji-Punabbasukas seem to have had a special dislike for Sāriputta and Moggallāna. Once the Buddha, on his way somewhere from Sāvatthi, accompanied by Sāriputta, Moggallāna and five hundred others, sent word to the Assaji-Punabbasukas to prepare sleeping places for them. They sent answer that the Buddha was very welcome, but not Sāriputta and Moggallāna, because " they were men of sinful desires and influenced by such desires."[4]

But elsewhere[5] even the Buddha is represented as having been lightly regarded by them. When it was reported to them that the Buddha lived on only one meal a day and found that it made him well and healthy, their reply was that they themselves ate in the evening and the early morning and at noon and outside prescribed hours, and that they found this quite agreeable and saw no reason for changing their mode of life. It is true, however, that even on this occasion when the Buddha sent for them, they came dutifully and listened patiently to his admonition on the necessity of implicit obedience to a teacher in whom they had faith, and we are told that they were " even gladdened in their hearts " after hearing the Buddha. There is, however, no evidence that they reformed after hearing him.

[1] They violated eighteen precepts (Sp. iii. 625).

[2] Vin. ii. 9-13, 14, 15.

[3] ii. 109.

[4] Vin. ii. 171.

[5] Kīṭāgiri Sutta (M. i. 473 ff.).

In the Commentaries[6] the Assaji-Punabbasukā are mentioned as an example of those who paid no heed to precepts great or small, which they had undertaken to observe.

The *Samantapāsādikā*[7] mentions that Kiṭāgiri was chosen by them as residence because it was watered by both monsoons, produced three crops, and had suitable sites for buildings.

They were five hundred in number.

[6] *E.g.*, DA. ii. 525. [7] iii. 614.

Assaji-Punabbasuka-Vatthu.—The story of the visit of the Aggasāvakas to the **Assaji-Punabbasukā,** mentioned above.[1]

[1] DhA. ii. 108-10.

Assatara.—A tribe of Nāgas present at the preaching of the *Mahāsamaya Sutta.*[1] Buddhaghosa[2] says they lived at the foot of **Sineru** and were so powerful that they could resist even the **Supaṇṇas.**[2]

They were among the Nāgas assembled by **Dhataraṭṭha** to help him in winning **Samuddajā.**[3] They are always mentioned with the **Kambala** Nāgas.

[1] D. ii. 259. [2] DA. ii. 688. [3] J. vi. 165.

Assapāla.—The second son of King **Esukārī's** chaplain. He was born in the world of men at Sakka's request. His father had him brought up among the keepers of horses (*assapālā*) so that he might not wish to renounce the world. His brothers were **Hatthipāla, Gopāla** and **Ajapāla.** He followed Hatthipāla into the ascetic life and lived on the banks of the Ganges.[1]

He was Sāriputta in the present age.[2]

[1] J. iv. 476 ff. [2] *Ibid.*, 491.

Assapura.—A city in the kingdom of **Aṅga.** It was here that the *Mahā Assapura* and *Cūla Assapura* Suttas were preached by the Buddha.[1]

According to the *Cetiya Jātaka*, Assapura was built by the second of the five sons of King **Upacara** of **Ceti,** on the spot where he saw a pure white horse. It lay to the south of **Sotthivatī,** Upacara's capital.[2]

[1] M. i. 271 ff.; *ibid.*, 281 ff.; MA. i. 483. [2] J. iii. 460.

Assapura Suttas.—See **Mahā Assapura** and **Cūla Assapura.**

1. **Assamaṇḍala.**—A ford on the **Mahāvāḷukagaṅgā** in Ceylon.[1] Geiger refers to a legend which connects this with **Kacchakatittha,** in which case it should be near the Mahāgantoṭa, east of Polonnaruva.[2]

[1] Cv. lxxii. 27. [2] Cv. *Trs.* ii. 321, n. 5.

2. **Assamaṇḍala.**—One of the spots included in the area marked off by **Devānampiyatissa** for the Sīmā of the **Mahāvihāra.**[1]

[1] Mv. xv. 15 in Appendix B to Geiger's Edition.

Assamukha.—One of the four rivers that flow out of the **Anotatta** Lake. Many horses are found on its banks.[1]

[1] SnA. ii. 438; UdA. 301.

Assalāyana.—A young brahmin, sixteen years old, of **Sāvatthi,** very learned in the Vedas and allied subjects. Five hundred brahmins staying in the city asked him to hold a discussion with the Buddha and refute his views. He agreed only after repeated requests, because, he said, Gotama was a thinker with views of his own and, therefore, difficult to defeat in controversy. He visits the Buddha and asks what he has to say concerning the claims of the brahmins to be the only superior class, the legitimate sons of Brahmā. The Buddha points out to him that such pretensions are baseless, and that virtue, which alone leads to purity, can be cultivated by any of the four classes. Assalāyana sits silent and upset at the end of the discourse, but when the Buddha relates to him a story of the past where **Asita Devala** had defeated brahmins who held these same views, Assalāyana feels relieved and expresses his admiration of the Buddha's exposition. He declares himself a follower of the Buddha.[1] Buddhaghosa[2] tells us further that Assalāyana became a devoted follower of the faith and built a cetiya in his own residence for worship, and that all his descendants, down to Buddhaghosa's day, built similar cetiyas in their houses.

Assalāyana is probably to be identified with the father of **Mahākoṭṭhita,** (*q.v.*), his wife being **Candavatī.** There is, however, one difficulty connected with this theory: Mahākoṭṭhita says that he was won over to the faith after hearing the same sermon of the Buddha as converted his father (*yadā me pitaraṃ Buddho vinayī sabbasuddhiyā*).[3] It is unlikely, if the identification be correct, that this refers to the *Assalāyana Sutta,* because at the time of that Sutta, Assalāyana was only sixteen years old; but there exists no record of any other sutta preached to Assalāyana, dealing with "*sabbasuddhi.*"

[1] M. ii. 147 ff. [2] MA. ii. 785. [3] ThagA. i. 31; Ap. ii. 480.

Assalāyana's name occurs in a list of eminent brahmins found in the *Sutta-Nipāta* Commentary.[4]

[4] i. 372.

Assalāyana Sutta.—Records the conversation between the Buddha and **Assalāyana** when the latter went to visit him.[1]

[1] M. ii. 147 ff.

Assārāma.—The place of death of **Sikhī** Buddha.[1] The *Buddhavaṃsa*[2] calls it **Dussārāma.**

[1] BuA. 204. [2] Bu. xxi. 28.

Assāroha.—Probably a nickname for the horse-trainer whose visit to the Buddha is recorded in the **Assa Sutta.** He is described as a *gāmaṇi* (head man of a village).[1]

[1] S. iv. 310.

Assāsa Sutta.—A conversation between **Sāriputta** and the Paribbājaka **Jambukhādaka** as to what constitutes comfort (*assāsa*) and how it might be won.[1]

[1] S. iv. 254.

Assu Sutta.—Preached at **Sāvatthi.** The tears shed by a person faring in Saṃsāra, as a result of various sorrows, are greater in quantity than the waters of the four oceans. One should therefore feel repulsion for all things of this world.[1]

[1] S. ii. 179-80.

Assutavata Sutta.—The untaught might well be repelled by the body, seeing its decay, but not by the mind or consciousness, which is like a monkey letting go of one thing only to grasp another. The well-taught disciple is repelled not only by the body but by all the *khandhas* and wishes to be free from them.[1]

[1] S. iv. 94.

Assutavā Sutta.—From the adjusted friction of two sticks fire is born; if there is no friction there is no fire. Similarly, from contact feeling is born: if contact ceases feeling ceases. The well-taught disciple knows this and attains freedom.[1]

[1] S. iv. 95.

Ahaha.—One of the purgatories mentioned in the *Sutta-Nipāta* list.[1] It is the name given to a period of suffering in **Avīci** and is equivalent in duration to twenty **Ababā.**[2]

[1] p. 126. [2] SnA. ii. 476; S. i. 152.

Ahiṃsaka.—The earlier name of **Aṅgulimāla** (*q.v.*).

Ahiṃsaka Sutta.—Records the interview between the Buddha and **Ahiṃsaka Bhāradvāja.**[1]

[1] S. i. 164.

Ahiṃsaka Bhāradvāja.—One of the Bhāradvāja brothers. He came to the Buddha at Sāvatthi and the Buddha suggested to him the desirability of living up to his name by practising *ahiṃsā*. It is said that later he became an arahant.[1] Buddhaghosa[2] is uncertain as to the reason for the name which he says was given to him by the Recensionists. He suggests that he was so called, either because his actual name was such, or because of the nature of the discussion between him and the Buddha.

[1] S. i. 164. [2] SA. i. 179.

Ahiguṇḍika Jātaka (No. 365.)—The story of a snake-charmer in Benares who had also a tame monkey. Once, during a festival, he left the monkey with a corn-factor (the Bodhisatta) and set out to earn money by making sport with the snake. The monkey was well looked after by the Bodhisatta. Seven days later the snake-charmer returned drunk and ill-treated the monkey. When the man was asleep the monkey escaped and refused to come back in spite of his former owner's fine words.

The story was told with reference to a novice who was ordained by a distinguished Elder. The Elder ill-treated the lad who, in exasperation, left the Order. The Elder persuaded him to return, but when this had happened twice again, the lad refused to come back.[1] The novice is identified with the monkey of the story.

[1] J. iii. 197-9.

Ahicchatta.—A king of the Nāgas. He lived in the heap of sand which was made by **Aggidatta** (*q.v.*) and his followers, who had made a vow to bring from somewhere a jar of sand and empty it at an agreed spot whenever a sinful thought occurred to them. When **Moggallāna** visited Aggidatta and asked him for a lodging, Aggidatta refused to give him one, but Moggallāna, in spite of his protests, occupied the sandhill. Moggallāna overcame the power of the Nāga king by his iddhi-power, and when Aggidatta and his followers visited him the next morning, they found Ahicchatta standing with his hood over Moggallāna's head as protection for him from the sun.[1]

[1] DhA. iii. 241 ff.

Ahidīpa.—The old name for **Kāradīpa,** near **Nāgadīpa. Akitti** spent some time there.[1]

[1] J. iv. 238.

Ahinda Sutta.—For self-protection one should practise amity for the four royal families of snakes: **Virūpakkha, Erāpatha, Chabyāputta** and **Kaṇhā-gotamaka.** It was preached when a monk was bitten by a snake at Sāvatthi.[1]

[1] A. ii. 72. *Cp.* Vin. ii. 109; SA. ii. 144.

Ahipāraka.—Commander-in-chief and friend and counsellor of **Sivi,** King of **Ariṭṭhapura.**—They had been to **Takkasilā** together and were friends from boyhood. Ahipāraka's wife was **Ummadantī** of ravishing beauty. Their story is given in the *Ummadantī Jātaka.*[1] In the present age he was **Sāriputta.**[2]

[1] J. v. 209 ff. [2] *Ibid.*, 227.

Ahipeta.—Seen by **Moggallāna** as he came from Gijjhakūta to Rājagaha in the company of **Lakkhaṇa.** He revealed the peta's story in the presence of the Buddha. In the long past men had erected a bower of leaves and grass on the banks of the river near Benares for a Pacceka Buddha. Here residents from the city would visit him morning and evening with offerings. On the way they had to pass a field, which in their many journeyings they trampled and damaged. The farmer tried in vain to prevent them. One day, in exasperation, when the Pacceka Buddha was away, the farmer burnt his bower, destroying everything in it. When he confessed his guilt the followers of the Pacceka Buddha beat him to death. He suffered in Avīci till the earth was elevated one league, and was thereafter born a peta, twenty-five leagues in length, his body enveloped in flames.[1]

[1] DhA. ii. 64 ff.; see also S. ii. 254.

1. **Ahirika Sutta.**—A man who is void of faith, virtue and shame is destined to be born in hell.[1]

[1] A. ii. 227.

2. **Ahirika Sutta.**—The man who is shameless destroys his welfare, the man who has shame works his weal.[1]

[1] A. ii. 229.

"Ahirikamūlakā cattāro" Sutta.—Four suttas based on the fact that like coalesces with like, the shameless with the shameless, etc.[1]

[1] S. ii. 162 f.

Ahogaṅgā.—A mountain in North India, on the Upper Ganges. There, for some time, lived the thera **Sambhūta Sāṇavāsī,** and it was there that **Yasa Kākaṇḍaputta** saw him. The meeting of arahants to discuss what measures should be taken against the **Vesālī** monks was also held there, and at the meeting were present monks from the Western country and from **Avanti-Dakkhiṇāpatha.**[1] **Moggaliputta** lived in Ahogaṅgā all alone for seven years, prior to the Third Council for which he was awaiting the right time.[2] The Mahāvaṃsa describes it as being "further up the Ganges" (*uddhaṃ Gaṅgāya*).

Moggaliputta Tissa came from Ahogaṅgā to **Pāṭaliputta** on a raft.[3]

[1] Vin. ii. 298-9.

[2] Mhv. v. 233; see also Vin. Texts, ii. 146, n. 1. (The Mbv., p. 106, says *upari Gaṅgāya*; see also Sp. i. 57).

[3] Sp. i. 57.

Ā

Ākaṅkha Vagga.—The eighth chapter of the *Dasaka Nipāta* of the *Aṅguttara Nikāya*. It consists of ten suttas on such subjects as the "thornless" life, the obstacles to desired things, **Migasālā's** questions on the future life of individuals, the likeness of a bad monk to a crow, the qualities of the Nigaṇṭhas, etc.[1]

[1] A. v. 131-51.

1. **Ākaṅkheyya Sutta.**—The sixth sutta of the *Majjhima Nikāya*, preached at **Jetavana.** A monk must conform to the sīla, the pāṭimokha and the sikkhāpadas, whatever be his yearnings, whether to be beloved of his fellows, to be given robes etc., to gain the four jhānas, to make an end of dukkha or to be possessed of such powers as *dibbacakkhu*, etc.[1] This sutta is often mentioned[2] as an example of a discourse preached by the Buddha of his own accord (*attano ajjhāsayen'eva*).

[1] M. i. 33-6.

[2] *E.g.*, DA. i. 50; MA. i. 13.

2. **Ākaṅkkheyya Sutta.**—Preached to the monks at **Jetavana** on the ambitions that should stir a monk's heart.[1]

[1] A. v. 131-3.

1. **Ākāsa Sutta.**—A conversation between **Sāriputta** and **Ānanda** at **Sāvatthi** on the attainment of and dwelling in the sphere of the infinity of space.[1] The full title of the Sutta should be **Ākāsānañcāyatana.**

[1] S. iii. 237.

2. **Ākāsa Sutta.**—Just as divers winds blow in the sky, in different directions—hot, cool, dustless, etc.—so in the body arise divers feelings.[1]

[1] S. iv. 218.

3. **Ākāsa Sutta.**—**Moggallāna** tells the monks how he won the power of dwelling in the realm of infinite space (*ākāsānañcāyatana*).[1]

[1] S. iv. 266.

4. **Ākāsa Sutta.**—Just as divers winds blow in the sky, so when a monk cultivates the Noble Eightfold Path, the *satipaṭṭhānas*, the *sammappadhānas*, the *iddhipādas*, the *indriyas*, the *balas* and the *bojjhaṅgas* reach fulfilment.[1]

[1] S. v. 49.

1. **Ākāsagaṅgā.**—The river that flows southward from the **Anotatta** Lake receives, in its different stages, various names. That part of it which flows sixty leagues through the air is called **Ākāsagaṅgā.**[1] The Buddha's discourse on various topics (*pakiṇṇakakathā*) is like the downward flow of the Ākāsagaṅgā[2]; so also is the eloquence of clever preachers.[3]

The fine clay to be found in the area (thirty yojanas in extent) over which the Ākāsagaṅgā falls to earth, is called, on account of its fineness, " butter clay " (*navanīta-mattikā*). This clay was brought by arahant sāmaṇeras to be spread over the foundation of the **Mahā Thūpa** in Anurādhapura.[4] The spot where it is found is called **Tintasīsakola.**[5]

[1] SnA. ii. 439; MA. 586, etc.
[2] AA. i. 94; DhA. iii. 360.
[3] *E.g.*, DhA. iv. 18; J. ii. 65.
[4] Mhv. xxix. 5 f.
[5] MṬ. 515.

2. **Ākāsagaṅgā.**—A vast channel built by **Parakkamabāhu I.** to bring water from the **Kāragaṅgā** to the **Parakkamasamudda.**[1]

[1] Cv. lxxix. 25.

Ākāsagotta.—A physician of **Rājagaha** who lanced the fistula of a monk. Meeting the Buddha, he told him of the lancing, trying to make fun of it. The Buddha, having made inquiries, declared the performance of such an operation a *thullaccaya* offence.[1]

[1] Vin. i. 215-16.

Ākāsacetiya.—A cetiya in **Rohaṇa** in South Ceylon, not far from **Cittalapabbata Vihāra,** so named because it is situated on the summit of a rock. It is not known when and by whom it was built. King **Kākavaṇṇa-Tissa** fixed to it stone slabs, to make it easier of ascent.[1]

There were probably two cetiyas of the same name, one being in Rohaṇa and the other to the east of Anurādhapura. It is the latter which is mentioned in the thirty-third chapter of the Mahāvaṃsa.[2]

Vaṭṭagāmaṇi, going up with his queen to the Ākāsacetiya, saw his minister, **Kapisīsa,** who had just come down from the cetiya, where he had been sweeping the courtyard, sitting by the road: because he did not fling himself down before the king, the latter slew him in anger.

This Ākāsacetiya was near **Acchagalla Vihāra,** which, according to the *Mahāvaṃsa Ṭīkā,*[3] was to the east of Anurādhapura.

It may be that Ākāsacetiya was a common name for any vihāra built on the summit of a rock, for the Commentaries[4] speak also of an Ākāsacetiya at **Sumanagiri** (**Sumanakūṭa**) at which the Tamil general **Dīghajantu** offered a red silken robe.

[1] Mhv. xxii. 26.
[2] Vers. 68-9.
[3] MṬ. 302.
[4] AA. i. 375; MA. ii. 955.

Ākāsānañcāyatanūpagādevā.—A class of devas born in the Realm of Infinite Space (*ākāsānañcāyatana*[1]). They belong to the Arūpa world and their life term is twenty thousand kappas.[2] Their mind arises and ceases moment by moment.[3] In the description of the *Arūpāvacara-bhūmi,* these devas represent the lowest limit, the highest being the **Nevasaññānāsaññā.**[4]

[1] M. iii. 103.
[2] A. i. 267; AbhS., p. 23.
[3] Kvu. i. 207-8.
[4] Ps. i. 84.

Ākāsukkhipiya Thera.—An arahant. In a previous birth he had offered a lotus flower to the Buddha **Siddhattha** and had thrown another up into the sky above him. Thirty-two kappas ago he was a king named **Antalikkhacara.**[1]

[1] Ap. i. 230.

1. **Ākiñcañña Sutta.**—A conversation between **Sāriputta** and **Ānanda** on the sphere of Nothingness (**ākiñcaññāyatana**).[1]

[1] S. iii. 237.

2. **Ākiñcañña Sutta.**—**Moggallāna** tells the monks how he entered on and dwelt in the realm of Nothingness.[1]

[1] S. iv. 267.

Ākiñcāyatanūpagādevā.—A class of devas born in the *Ākiñcāyatana*, the third Arūpa world.[1] Their life term is sixty thousand kappas.[2]

[1] M. iii. 103. [2] AbhS. 23.

Ākoṭaka.—A deva who visited the Buddha at **Veḷuvana** accompanied by **Asama, Sahali, Niṅka, Veṭambari** and **Māṇava-Gāmiya.** Ākoṭaka spoke before the Buddha in praise of various teachers of other schools: **Pakuddha-Kātiyāna** (*sic.*), **Nigaṇṭha, Makkhali** and **Pūraṇa.** Veṭambari made rejoinder to Ākoṭaka, speaking disparagingly of the teachers he had mentioned.[1]

[1] S. i. 65.

Āgantuka.—A banker of **Sāvatthi.** He was rich, but he neither enjoyed his wealth himself nor gave it to others; he ate rice-dust with sour gruel, wore coarse clothes and went about in an old chariot with a parasol of leaves over his head. After death he was born in **Roruva-niraya.** He died heirless and it took seven days and seven nights for the king's men to remove his wealth to the royal treasury.

In reply to a question of **Pasenadi,** the Buddha revealed why Āgantuka had been a miser: in a past birth, while going to the king's court, he had met the Pacceka Buddha **Tagarasikhī** begging for alms and had ordered his servant to give the food prepared for himself (Āgantuka) to the Pacceka Buddha. On his way back, seeing the Pacceka Buddha returning with the excellent food from the merchant's house in his alms-bowl, he wished he had distributed it among his own servants instead, as they would have done some work in return.[1]

The reason for Āgantuka being heirless is related in the *Mayhaka Jātaka.*

[1] J. iii. 299-300.

Āgantuka Sutta.—Like to a guest-house into which come folk from all quarters to take up their residence, a monk, who develops the Noble Eightfold Path, realises those states (the five *upādānakkhandhā*) that should be realised, abandons those (*avijjā and bhavataṇhā*) that should be abandoned and cultivates *samatha* and *vipassanā*.[1]

[1] S. v. 51-2.

Āgāra Sutta.—Like a guest-house to dwell in which come folk from all quarters, noblemen and brahmins, commoners and serfs, so, in the body, divers feelings arise, pleasant, painful and neutral, carnal (*sāmisa*) and non-carnal.[1]

[1] S. iv. 219.

Āghāta Vagga.—The seventeenth chapter of the *Pañcaka Nipāta* of the *Aṅguttara Nikāya*. It contains ten suttas on various topics, including a dispute between **Sāriputta** and **Udāyi**.[1]

[1] A. iii. 185-202.

1. **Āghāta Sutta.**—On nine things which cause enmity to be born.[1]

[1] A. iv. 408.

2. **Āghāta Sutta.**—On the nine ways of getting rid of feelings of enmity.[1]

[1] A. iv. 408-9.

1. **Āghātavinaya Sutta.**—The five ways of repressing ill-will: by producing *mettā*, *karuṇā* and *upekkhā*, by getting rid of forgetfulness and by reflecting on the power of kamma[1].

[1] A. iii. 185-6.

2. **Āghātavinaya Sutta.**—A sermon by **Sāriputta** to the monks on the way in which ill-will arises in men, and the methods by which it may be overcome. These methods are illustrated by various similes.[1]

[1] A. iii. 186-90.

Ācāmadāyikā.—A family in **Rājagaha** was afflicted with plague and all its members died except one woman. She broke through a wall[1] and went and lived in the backyard of another house. The inmates of the house, having compassion on her, gave her the remnants of their food. One day, **Mahā Kassapa,** rising after seven days and nights from *nirodha-samāpatti*, knowing that he could be of use to the poor woman, appeared before her asking for alms. Having nothing but rice-water to give him,

[1] That being the customary method of avoiding infection.

she asked him to go elsewhere, but the Elder showed his desire to accept her gift and refused alms offered to him by **Sakka** and by the inmates of the house behind which the woman lived. With great joy she gave him the rice-water, and the Elder then told her that three births earlier she had been his mother. That same night she died and was born in a *vimāna* among the **Nimmānaratī** gods. Her story forms the basis of the *Ācāma-dāyikā-Vimāna Vatthu.*[2]

[2] Vv. p. 17; VvA. 99 ff.

Ācāraviṭṭhigāma.—A village three leagues to the north-east of **Anurādhapura.** When **Duṭṭhagāmaṇī** was seeking for materials for the building of the **Mahā Thūpa,** nuggets of gold, from a span to a finger's breadth in size, appeared in the village.[1]

[1] Mhv. xxviii. 13-15.

Ājañña Jātaka (No. 24.)—Once, when **Brahmadatta** was ruling in Benares, seven kings laid siege to the city. A warrior sent by Brahmadatta harnessed two horses (brothers) and, sallying forth from the city, overcame six camps and captured six kings. Just then the elder horse (who was the Bodhisatta) was wounded. The charioteer unfastened the horse's armour as he lay on his side, and started to arm another horse. The Bodhisatta addressed the charioteer and said that as an Ājañña horse he must fight on. The charioteer set him on his feet again and, with his help, captured the seventh camp and its king.

The Bodhisatta, having counselled the victorious king to show mercy to his captives, died, and his body was burnt with all honours.

The story was told to a monk who had given up striving.[1]

[1] J. i. 181-2.

1. **Ājañña Sutta.**—Like a king's thoroughbred horse possessed of beauty, strength, speed and good proportions, a monk worthy of offerings should have beauty (of life), strength (of character), speed (of insight) and good proportions (of necessaries).[1]

[1] A. ii. 250-1.

2. **Ājañña Sutta.**—Same as above, but speed of insight in a monk is depicted as ability to enter into the four jhānas.[1]

[1] A. ii. 251-2.

3. **Ājañña Sutta.**—On eight qualities that a horse should possess in order to be worthy of being used by the king, and on eight similar qualities essential in the ideal monk.[1]

[1] A. iv. 188 ff.

1. **Ājāni Sutta.**—The five qualities of a thoroughbred horse in the service of the king and the similar qualities of a good monk.[1]

[1] A. iii. 248.

2. **Ājāni Sutta.**—Three suttas giving six similar qualities.[1]

[1] A. iii. 282-4.

Ājānīya Sutta.—Three discourses identical, in the main, with the **Ājañña Sutta** (1), but the fourth quality (good proportions) is omitted. The suttas differ from one another in the definition of " speed " in the case of the monk.[1]

[1] A. i. 244.

Ājīvaka Sutta.—A conversation between **Ānanda** and a householder, a follower of the **Ājīvakas.** The householder questions Ānanda as to whose doctrine is well taught, who are the rightly conducted and who are the welfarers in the world. Ānanda tells him the characteristics which are helpful in arriving at a decision on these questions, without praising one's own creed or decrying another's. The man expresses great satisfaction.[1]

[1] A. i. 217 ff.

Ājīvakā.—A class of naked ascetics (see, *e.g.*, Vin. i. 291), followers of **Makkhali Gosāla,** regarded, from the Buddhist point of view, as the worst of sophists. Numerous references to the Ājīvakas are to be found in the Piṭakas, only a few of them being at all complimentary. Thus in the *Mahā Saccaka Sutta*[1] they are spoken of as going about naked, flouting life's decencies and licking their hands after meals. But they never incurred the guilt of obeying another man's command, of accepting food specially prepared for them, of accepting food from people while eating, from a pregnant woman, or nursing mother, or from gleanings in time of famine; they would never eat where a dog was already at hand, or where hungry flies were congregated. They never touched flesh, fish or intoxicants, and they had a rigid scale of food rationing. It is mentioned that they did not always find it possible to adhere to this rigid code of conduct.

[1] M. i. 238; see also S. i. 66, where a *deva* praises Gosāla as a man who had attained to perfect self-control by fasting and austere practices. He had abandoned speech and wordy strife with any person, was equable, a speaker of truth, a doer of no evil. That the life of the Ājīvakas was austere may be gleaned from their condemnation of monks carrying parasols (Vin. ii. 130).

It is stated in the *Tevijja Vacchagotta Sutta*[2] that far from any Ājīvaka having put an end to sorrow, the Buddha could recall only one Ājīvaka during ninety-nine kappas who had even gone to heaven, and that one too had preached a doctrine of *kamma* and the after-consequences of actions. Elsewhere[3] they are spoken of as children of a childless mother. They extol themselves and disparage others and yet they have produced only three shining lights: **Nanda Vaccha, Kisa Saṅkicca** and **Makkhali Gosāla.** A fourth leader, **Paṇḍuputta,** of wagon-building stock, is mentioned in the *Anaṅgana Sutta*[4]; there is also the well-known **Upaka** (*q.v.*).

There is no doubt that the Ājīvakas were highly esteemed and had large followings of disciples.[5] They had eminent followers such as high court officials,[6] and that, for centuries at least, they retained an important position, is shown by their being thrice mentioned in the Asoka Edicts as receiving royal gifts.[7]

The doctrines held by the Ājīvakas are mentioned in several places, but the best known account is in the *Sāmaññaphala Sutta* where they are attributed to Makkhali Gosāla by name.[8] He maintained that there is no cause or reason for either depravity or purity among beings. There is no such thing as intrinsic strength, or energy or human might or endeavour. All creatures, all beings, everything that has life, all are devoid of power, strength and energy; all are under the compulsion of the individual nature to which they are linked by destiny; it is solely by virtue of their birth in the six environments (*chaḷabhijātiyo*) that they experience their pleasure or pain. The universe is divided into various classes of beings, of occupations and methods of production. There are eighty-four hundred thousand periods during which both fools and wise alike, wandering in transmigration, shall at last make an end of pain. The pleasures and pain, measured out as it were with a measure, cannot be altered in the course of transmigration; there can be neither increase nor decrease thereof, neither excess nor deficiency.

The fundamental point in their teaching seems, therefore, to have been "*saṃsāra-suddhi,*" purification through transmigration, which probably meant that all beings, all lives, all existent things, all living substances attain and must attain, perfection in course of time.

According to Buddhaghosa,[9] in the classification of the Ājīvakas, "all beings" (*sattā*) meant all kinds of animals, camels, cows, asses, etc.; "all lives" (*pāṇā*) comprised all sensitive things and sentient creatures divided into those with one sense (*ekendriya*), those with two senses and so forth;

[2] M. i. 483. [3] M. i. 524. [4] M. i. 31.

[5] See, *e.g.*, **Pasenadi's** evidence in S. i. 68, apart from **Ajātasattu's** visit mentioned in the *Sāmaññaphala Sutta*; also S. iv. 398.

[6] Vin. ii. 165; iv. 71.

[7] Hultsch: *Asoka Inscriptions*, see Index.

[8] D. i. 53-4. See also M. i. 516 f.

[9] DA. i. 161.

"all existent things" (*bhūtā*) denoted all living beings divided into generic types—viz., those produced from an egg, or born from the womb, or sprung from moisture, or propagated from seed; and "all living substances" (*jīvā*) denoted rice, barley, wheat, etc.

The division of men into six classes (*chaḷabhijātiyo*) is noteworthy. Buddhaghosa describes these as being *kaṇha, nīla, lohita, halidda, sukka* and *paramasukka*. This closely resembles the curious Jaina doctrine of the six Leśyas.[10] In the Aṅguttara Nikāya[11] a similar doctrine is attributed to **Pūraṇa Kassapa.**

Gosāla's theory[12] of the divisions of the universe into fourteen hundred thousand principle states of birth—(*pamukhayoniyo*) and into various methods of regeneration—viz., seven kinds of animate (*saññigabbhā*) production, *i.e.* by means of separate sexes; seven of inanimate (*asaññigabbhā*), such as rice, barley, etc.; seven of production by grafting (*nigaṇṭhigabbhā*), propagating by joints, such as sugar cane, etc.—seems to show that the Ājīvakas believed in infinite gradations of existence, in the infinity of time, and also in the recurrent cycles of existence. Each individual has external existence, if not individually, at least in type. In the world as a whole everything comes about by necessity. Fate (*nigati*) regulates everything, all things being unalterably fixed. Just as a ball of string when cast forth spreads out just as far as, and no farther than it can unwind, so every being lives, acts, enjoys and ultimately ends, in the manner in which it is destined (*sandhavitvā, saṃsaritvā dukkhassantaṃ karissanti*). The peculiar nature (*bhāva*)[13] of each being depends on the class or species or type to which it belongs.

Among the views of the *Puthusamaṇas* (other teachers), the Buddha regarded the doctrine of the Ājīvakas as the least desirable. It denied action (*kiriya*), endeavour (*viriya*), and result of action (*kamma*), and was therefore despicable (*paṭikhitto*).[14] The Buddha knew of no other single person fraught with such danger and sorrow to all devas and men as was Makkhali; like a fish-trap set at a river mouth, Makkhali was born into the world to be a man-trap for the distress and destruction of men.[15]

According to Buddhaghosa,[16] **Pūraṇa,** by propounding a theory of the passivity of soul, denied action; **Ajita,** by his theory of annihilation, denied

[10] Given, *e.g.*, in the *Uttarādhyāyana Sūtra* (Jacobi's *Jaina Sūtras* ii. 213). This seems to involve a conception of mind which is originally colourless by nature. The different colours (*nīla*, etc.) are due to different habits or actions. The supreme spiritual effort consists in restoring mind to its original purity. *Cp.* with this the Buddha's teaching in A. iii. 384 ff. and M. i. 36.

[11] iii. 383-4.

[12] D. i. 54; see also S. iii. 211.

[13] DA. i. 161.

[14] A. i. 286.

[15] A. i. 33.

[16] DA. i. 166.

retribution, whereas **Makkhali**, by his doctrine of fate, denied both action and its result.

It has been suggested[17] that Makkhali Gosāla's doctrine of the eight developmental stages of man (*aṭṭha purisabhūmi*) was a physical antecedent of the Buddha's doctrine of the eight higher spiritual ranks (*aṭṭha purisapuggalā*). Buddhaghosa[18] gives the eight stages as follows: *manda*, *khiḍḍā*, *vīmaṃsana*, *ujugata*, *sekha*, *samaṇa*, *jina* and *panna*.

The first stage extends from the first day of birth to the seventh. In the second stage those who have come from evil states cry constantly, those from happy conditions smile, remembering their past lives. The third stage is marked by the infant beginning to walk with the help of others. The time of his being able to walk alone is the *ujugata-bhūmi*. The period of study is *sekha-bhūmi*, of leaving household life, *samaṇa-bhūmi*; the period of knowledge (*vijānana*), of constant association with teachers, is the *jina-bhūmi* and the last stage when the jina remains silent (pannaka), is called the *paṇnaka-bhūmi*. This seems to indicate a development of the mental and spiritual faculties, side by side with physical growth, an interaction of body and mind.

There seems to have been a great deal of confusion, even at the time of the compilation of the Nikāyas, as to what were the specific beliefs of the Ājīvakas. Thus in the *Mahāli Sutta* of the *Saṃyutta Nikāya*[19] some of Gosāla's views (*natthi hetu, natthi paccayo sattānam saṅkilesāya*) are attributed to Pūraṇa Kassapa. The Aṅguttara Nikāya in one place[20] apparently confounds Makkhali Gosāla with Ajita Kesakambala, while elsewhere[21] Pūraṇa Kassapa's views regarding the chaḷabhijāti are represented as being those of Makkhali.

There was a group of Ājīvakas behind Jetavana. The monks saw the Ājīvakas perform various austerities, such as squatting on their heels, swinging in the air like bats, scorching themselves with five fires, and they asked the Buddha whether these austerities were of any use. "None whatever," answered the Buddha, and then proceeded to relate the *Naṅguṭṭha Jātaka*.[22]

The Ājīvakas used to be consulted regarding auspicious days, dreams, omens, etc.[23]

There was a settlement of Ājīvakas in **Anurādhapura**, and **Paṇḍukābhaya** built a residence for them.[24]

[17] *E.g.* Barua: *Pre-Buddhistic Indian Philosophy*, p. 314.

[18] DA. i. 162; see also Hoernle's *Uvāsaga-Dasāo*, ii. p. 24, where *paṇṇaka* is given for *panna*. cp. J. iv. 496-7 (*manda-dasaka*, *khiḍḍā-dasaka*, *aṇṇa-dasaka*, etc.).

[19] iii. 69.

[20] i. 286.

[21] iii. 383-4.

[22] J. i. 493 f.

[23] See, *e.g.*, J. i. 287 and MṬ. 190.

[24] Mhv. x. 102.

Thomas,[25] following Hoernle, thinks that the term (Ājīvaka) was probably a name given by opponents, meaning one who followed the ascetic life for the sake of a livelihood. Hence we cannot infer that the name which was found as late as the thirteenth century always refers to the followers of Makkhali Gosāla. This point is certainly worth investigating.

[25] *Op. cit.*, p. 130. But see DhA. i. 309, where the different kinds of religieux are distinguished as *acelaka*, *ājīvaka*, *nigaṇṭha* and *tāpasa*. For a detailed account of the Ājīvakas see Hoernle's Article in *ERA.* and Barua's paper in the *Calcutta University Journal of the Dept. of Letters*, vol. ii.

Āṭānāṭā.—A city in **Uttarakuru**, mentioned with **Kusināṭā**, **Parakusināṭā** and **Nāṭāpuriyā**.[1]

[1] D. iii. 200.

Āṭānāṭiya Sutta.—The thirty-second sutta of the *Dīgha Nikāya*, preached at the **Gijjhakūṭa**.[1]

The Four Great Kings having set a guard over the four quarters, visited the Buddha. Having saluted him and sat down with hosts of other yakkhas, **Vessavaṇa** told the Buddha that the yakkhas did not, for the most part, believe in the Buddha for the reason that they did not find it pleasant or agreeable to abstain from the things which he declared to be evil—such as the taking of life, theft, etc. And in order that the Buddha's disciples, haunting lonely and remote parts of the forest where the yakkhas dwelt, might find protection from them, Vessavaṇa suggested that the Buddha might learn the Āṭānāṭiya word-rune (*rakkha*). The Buddha agreeing, Vessavana proceeded to recite it.

It opens with a salutation to the seven Buddhas, beginning with **Vipassī.** The remainder contains a list of the gods and other superhuman beings, the Four Great Kings heading the list; these last are described at some length; forty-one other gods are mentioned as a kind of appendix or afterthought, all mentioned one after another with no attempt at group division and without any details, in what are, apparently, mnemonic doggerels.

A part of the *Mahāsamaya Sutta* (sections 10-20) looks very much like an improved and enlarged edition of this list of bare names.

The Buddha learnt the word-rune and taught it to the monks.

The Āṭānāṭiya Sutta is now regarded as a *Paritta*, and its influence pervades a hundred million world systems.[2] In Ceylon, for instance, it is recited with great fervour at the conclusion of the Paritta ceremonies, particularly in times of illness, in order to ward off evil spirits.

It is included in the list of Parittas found in the *Milinda-pañha.*[3]

[1] D. iii. 194 ff. [2] VibhA. 430.
[3] p. 151; on the importance of this sutta in the history of India, see Rhys Davids, *Buddhist India*, pp. 219-37.

Āṇañjasappāya Sutta.—Preached to the monks, with **Ānanda** at their head, by the Buddha at **Kammassadhamma** in the Kuru country. It deals with real Permanence (*āṇañjasappāya*) and with the various ways of meditating on impassibility and the attainments and true release. True deathlessness is only the heart's deliverance (*anupādā cittassa vimokkho*), and there are several stages of the paths that lead to it.[1] Buddhaghosa[2] says that this sutta described the arahantship of the *Sukkhavipassakā*. Arahantship is mentioned in nine different connections in the sutta, which is therefore praised as being well taught (*sukathitaṃ*).

[1] M. ii. 261 ff. [2] MA. ii. 851.

Āṇi Sutta.—Like the **Ānaka** drum of the **Dasārahas,** in which the drumhead vanished, leaving only the framework of pegs, even so is it with the Suttantas of the Tathāgata which are deep in meaning. They lie neglected and forgotten while men will turn their attention to the Suttantas of poets and the utterances of disciples, full of words; these they will learn and master instead of the Buddha's own teachings.[1]

[1] S. ii. 266-7.

Āṇimaṇḍavya.—See **Aṇimandavya.**

1. **Ātappa Sutta.**—By him who sees not and knows not decay, death, etc., as they really are, energy must be shown.[1]

[1] S. ii. 132.

2. **Ātappa Sutta.**—On the occasions on which ardent energy (*ātappa*) should be exerted.[1]

[1] A. i. 153.

Ātuma Thera.—The son of a seṭṭhi in **Sāvatthi.** When he grew up his mother proposed to find him a wife, but on account of his *upanissaya,* he left the world and was ordained. His mother tried to entice him back but he declared his great determination and, developing insight, became an arahant.[1]

In **Vipassī's** time he had been a householder and had made offering to Vipassī of perfumed water and fragrant powder.

Thirty-one kappas ago he was a king named **Sugandha**. Ātuma is probably identical with **Gandhodakiya** Thera of the Apadāna.[2]

[1] Thag. v. 72; ThagA. i. 160f. [2] Ap. i. 157-8.

Ātumā.—A town that lay between **Kusinārā** and **Sāvatthi.** Once the Buddha, with a large company of bhikkhus, visited the town. At that time there dwelt in it a monk who had been ordained late in life (a *buḍḍhapabbajita*, identified by Buddhaghosa[1] with the *buḍḍhapabbajita* **Subhadda**) and had formerly been a barber. He had two sons, handsome, elegant and well versed in the barber's art. When the monk heard of the Buddha's coming, he sent his sons from house to house to collect salt and oil and rice and meal. The young men, using all their powers of persuasion, collected a large quantity of each of these things, and when the Buddha arrived in Ātumā and went to stay in the **Bhūsāgāra,** they made ready rice-gruel and offered it to him. The Buddha, however, would not accept it as the monk, who had had the food collected, had been guilty of an unlawful act in that one monk had begged for others.

It was on this occasion that it was declared to be a *dukkaṭa* offence for a monk, who had formerly been a barber, to carry about with him a barber's equipment.[2]

In the *Mahā Parinibbāna Sutta*[3] the Buddha tells **Pukkusa** of another occasion on which he was staying in the Bhūsāgāra in Ātumā. There was a thunderstorm and two peasants (brothers) and four oxen were struck by lightning. A large number of people having gathered at the place, one of them asked the Buddha if he were aware of the accident. But the Buddha had been in a state of concentration and had neither seen nor heard anything of it. Such was the state of calm of his mind.

[1] DA. ii. 599. [2] Vin. i. 249-50. [3] D. ii. 131-2.

Ādāsamaṇḍapa.—One of the numerous buildings erected by **Parakkamabāhu I.** in the **Dīpuyyāna** in **Pulatthipura.** It was so called because its walls were made of mirrors.[1]

[1] Cv. lxxiii. 119.

Ādāsamukha.—The Bodhisatta born as the King of Benares. He was the son of **Janasandha** (also called **Dasaratha**), and because his face was resplendent with beauty like a well-polished golden mirror, he was called Ādāsamukha. His father died when he was seven years old, and the courtiers tested the boy in various ways before crowning him king.

Reports of his wisdom soon spread abroad and once, when an old servant of his father's (**Gāmaṇi Caṇḍa**) was being brought to the court to answer various charges, fourteen problems were entrusted to him by different inhabitants of the kingdom to be placed before the king for solution. The king solved them all and ruled righteously. The story is given in the *Gāmaṇi Caṇḍa Jātaka.*[1]

[1] J. ii. 297-310.

Ādicca.—Another name for **Suriya,** the Sun.[1] Buddhaghosa explains the name as meaning **Aditi's** son (*Aditiyā putto*). Ādicca was also the gotta-name of the Sākyans who were called the **Ādiccā.**[2] Buddhaghosa[3] gives it as a gotta-name of the Khattiyas, together with **Koṇḍañña-gotta.**

See also below, *s.v.* **Ādiccabandhu.**

[1] D. iii. 196. [2] Sn. v. 423. [3] VibhA. 466.

Ādicca Damilādhikāri.—A distinguished official of public accounts, one of the ministers of **Parrakamabāhu I.** He asked for and was given the leadership of the successful expedition against **Rāmañña.**[1] He appears to have died soon after the campaign.[2]

[1] Cv. lxxvi., vers. 39, 63-4; for details see under Parakkamabāhu I.
[2] See Cv. *Trs.* ii. p. 69, n. 3.

Ādicca Sutta.—Just as dawn is the harbinger of the arising of the sun, so is friendship with the good (*kalyānamittatā*) the harbinger of the arising of the seven bojjhaṅgas.[1]

[1] S. v. 101; *cp.* S. v. 29.

1. **Ādiccabandhu.**—An often-used epithet of the Buddha.[1] The *Vimanavatthu* Commentary[2] says that **Ādicca** (the Sun) belonged to the **Gotamagotta,** as did also the Buddha, hence his epithet Ādiccabandhu; other explanations are given in the same context: the Buddha is born in the same *ariyā jāti* and is the descendant of the Sun (*taṃ paṭicca tassa ariyāya jātiya jātattā*), or the Sun is the Buddha's kinsman because the Sun is the Buddha's *orasaputta* (breast-born son) inasmuch as the Sun is the Buddha's disciple. It is in this sense that in the *Saṃyutta Nikāya*[3] the Buddha speaks of the sun as "*mama pajā,*" which Buddhaghosa[4] explains as meaning disciple and spiritual son.

Ādicca is described as *tapataṃ mukhaṃ* (chief of heat-producing things).[5]

[1] *E.g.*, D. iii. 197; Sn. v. 1128; Thag. 26, 158, 417, etc.
[2] p. 116.
[3] S. i. 57.
[4] SA. i. 86.
[5] MA. ii. 783.

2. **Ādiccabandhu.**—A Pacceka Buddha who was instrumental in enabling the author (son of the King of Benares) of the twentieth verse of the *Khaggavisāna Sutta* to become a Pacceka Buddha. Ādiccabandhu saw that the young prince, who had renounced the world and was living in his father's park near the city, did not, on account of the visits of his parents and others, have sufficient peace of mind to develop his power of meditation.

He, therefore, visited the prince and persuaded him to go into the forest by showing him how real *pabbajitas* lived. The first two lines of the *Sutta Nipāta* verse (No. 54) were uttered by Ādiccabandhu.[1]

[1] Sn. v. 54; SnA. i. 104-5; see also ApA. i. 105, 152.

Ādiccupaṭṭhāna Jātaka. (No. 175).—The story of a monkey who used to visit the hermitage of some ascetics whose leader was the Bodhisatta ; when they were away in the village, he upset everything he could lay hands on, and did much damage generally. When the ascetics were about to return from the village to the hermitage after the rainy season, the people brought them various foods, and the monkey, thinking to get some for himself, stood outside their hut worshipping the sun. The people, impressed by the monkey's holy demeanour, started praising his virtues, whereupon the Bodhisatta revealed to them his true character.[1]

The story was related concerning a rogue.

[1] J. ii. 72-3.

Āditta Jātaka (No. 424).—Once the Bodhisatta was born as **Bharata,** King of **Roruva,** in the country of **Sovīra.** He was very righteous and much beloved, and his chief queen, **Samuddavijayā,** was wise and full of knowledge.

The king, wishing to give alms to Pacceka Buddhas instead of to others far less holy, consulted the queen, and acting on her advice, made proclamation to his people that they should keep the precepts. He himself observed all holy days and gave great gifts in charity. One day he offered flowers to the eastern quarter, and making obeisance, wished that any Pacceka Buddha in that quarter might come to accept his alms. His wish not being fulfilled, he repeated, on the following days, the same ceremony to the other quarters till, on the fourth day, seven Pacceka Buddhas came to him from the north where they lived in **Nandamūlapabbhāra.** The king and queen fed them for seven days and gave them robes and all the other requisites of an ascetic. The Pacceka Buddhas departed one by one, each expressing his thanks in a stanza and exhorting the king and queen to lead pure lives.

The story was related in reference to **Pasenadi's Asadisadāna,** to show that wise men of old also gave gifts to holy men, with discretion.[1]

This is evidently the story referred to as the *Sucira Jātaka* in the introduction to the *Dasa Brāhmaṇa Jātaka*[2] and again as the *Sovīra Jātaka* in the introductory story of the *Sivi Jātaka.*[3]

[1] J. iii. 469-74. [2] J. iv. 360. [3] *Ibid.*, 401.

Āditta Vagga.—The fifth chapter of the *Devatā Saṃyutta* of the *Saṃyutta Nikāya.*[1]

[1] S. i. 31-6.

1. **Āditta Sutta.**—Spoken before the Buddha at **Jetavana** by a deva who visited him. Like a man who rescues what he can from his burning house, let the wise man enjoy his possessions and give them away with discernment. Thus will he attain to happiness hereafter.[1]

[1] S. i. 31.

2. **Āditta Sutta.**—All the *khandhas* are on fire. Seeing this, the Ariyan disciple feels revulsion from them and, through knowledge, attains to freedom.[1]

[1] S. iii. 71.

3. **Āditta Sutta.**[1]—Same as the **Ādittapariyāya Sutta.** (See below.)

[1] S. iv. 19.

Ādittapariyāya Sutta.—The name given to the discourse preached by the Buddha at **Gayāsīsa** in Gayā, after his conversion of the **Tebhātikajaṭilā** (**Uruvela Kassapa, Nadī Kassapa** and **Gayā Kassapa**).

Everything is burning: the eye, the eye-consciousness (*cakkhuviññāna*), and the contact of the eye with objects (*cakkhu-samphassa*), and the sensations that arise thereform. It is the same with the other senses: they are aflame with lust, anger, ignorance and the anxieties of birth, decay, death, etc.; knowing this, the follower of the Noble Eightfold Path feels revulsion towards them and divests himself of passion for them and ultimately attains supreme freedom.

At the end of the discourse the thousand monks, erstwhile *jaṭilas*, who had been listening, became arahants.[1]

It is said that the Ādittapariyāya was preached on the **Piṭṭhipāsāna** at Gayāsīsa.[2] This is the third recorded address of the Buddha. It is also called the **Āditta Sutta.** (See **Āditta Sutta** 3).

[1] Vin. i. 34-5; J. i. 82; iv. 180. [2] AA. i. 166; ThagA. i. 435.

" Ādittena " Sutta.—It were a good thing if the sense organs were seared with a red-hot iron, for then there would be no grasping of marks or details of objects cognizable by the senses. It were a good thing to be asleep, for then the mind would not be applied to evil ends. But it were better to ponder on the impermanence of the sense organs, their sensations, the consciousness and the contacts connected with them and all that has to do with the mind, because that pondering would produce repulsion and dispassion, freedom and realisation of freedom.[1]

[1] S. iv. 168 f.

Ādipādakajambu.—A locality in Ceylon where the **Ādipāda Vikkamabāhu** defeated **Mānābharaṇa** and his brothers.[1]

[1] Cv. lxi. 15.

Ādipādapunnāgakhaṇḍa.—A locality in **Rohaṇa** in the south of Ceylon. It was in the district of **Guttasāla.** Here an encounter took place between the forces of **Parakkamabāhu I.** and those of the rebels in Rohaṇa.[1]

[1] Cv. lxxv. 14.

Ādimalaya.—One of the generals of **Vijayabāhu I.** He openly rebelled against the king and came with his troops to the village of **Andu,** near **Pulatthipura.** The king went out against him and destroyed him.[1]

[1] Cv. lix. 4-6.

Ādiya Sutta.—Preached at **Jetavana** to **Anāthapiṇḍika** on the five uses (**ādiyā**) of possessions legitimately obtained: one enjoys them oneself; entertains with them one's friends and relations; uses them in times of need; employs them in the discharge of one's duties to the king, to religion, to one's relations, both living and dead; and in doing good deeds which will bring happiness in future lives.[1]

[1] A. iii. 45 f.

Ādhāradāyaka Thera.—An arahant. He gave a stool (**ādhāraka**) to **Sikhī** Buddha. Twenty-seven kappas ago he became king four times under the name of **Samantavaruṇa.**[1]

[1] Ap. i. 207.

Ādhipateyya Sutta.—The three "mandates" which should guide a monk: the self, the world, the Dhamma.[1]

[1] A. i. 147 f.; on the significance of the sutta see Mrs. Rhys Davids, *J.R.A.S.*, April 1933, pp. 329 ff.

Ānaka (*v.l.* **Āṇaka**).—A *mutiṅga* (kettle-drum) belonging to the **Dasārahas.** As it grew old and began to split, they fixed in another peg, and this process was continued, until, at last, the original drumhead vanished, leaving only the framework of pegs.[1] The origin of the drum is related in the *Kakkaṭa Jātaka*. When the Golden Crab, there mentioned, was trampled to death by the elephants, his two claws broke away from his body and lay apart in the **Kulīradaha,** where he lived. During the floods the water flowed from the Ganges into this lake, running back again when the floods subsided. The two claws were thus carried into the Ganges. One of them reached the sea, and the **Asuras,** picking it up, made thereof the drum named **Āḷambara.** The other was picked up by the Ten Royal Brothers (evidently the Dasārahas mentioned above) while playing in the river, and they made of it the little drum Ānaka.[2]

In the *Saṃyutta* Commentary[3] it is said that the drum was like molten wax in colour, because the crab's claw had been dried by wind and sun. The sound of the drum was heard for twelve leagues, and it was, therefore, used only on festive occasions. On hearing it, the people assembled hurriedly, in various conveyances, decked with splendour. It was called Ānaka because it brought the people together as if summoning them (*mahājanaṃ pakkositvā viya ānetī ti Ānako*). Later, when the original drumhead had vanished, it could hardly be heard even inside a hall.

The Ānaka drum is used as a simile in the **Āṇi Sutta.**[4]

[1] S. ii. 266.

[2] J. ii. 344; the Jātaka is quoted in SA. ii. 167-8, with several variations in detail.

[3] ii. 167-8.

[4] S. ii. 266-7; see also KS. ii. 178, n. 4.

Ānañcāyatana Sutta.—On the three infinite spheres: infinite space, infinite consciousness, and sphere of nothingness.[1]

[1] A. i. 267.

Anañjasappāya Sutta.—See **Āṇañjasappāya Sutta.**

1. **Ānanda.**—One of the principal disciples of the Buddha. He was a first cousin of the Buddha and was deeply attached to him.

He came to earth from **Tusita** and was born on the same day as the Bodhisatta, his father being **Amitodana** the Sākyan, brother of **Suddhodana.**[1] **Mahānāma** and **Anuruddha** (*q.v.*) were therefore his brothers (or probably step-brothers).

Ānanda entered the Order in the second year of the Buddha's ministry, together with other Sākyan princes, such as **Bhaddiya, Anuruddha, Bhagu,**

[1] According to the Mtu. (iii. 176), Ānanda was the son of **Śuklodana** and the brother of **Devadatta** and **Upadhāna.** His mother was **Mṛgī.**

Kimbila and **Devadatta,** and was ordained by the Buddha himself,[2] his *upajjhāya* being **Belaṭṭhasīsa.**[3] Soon after, he heard a discourse by **Puṇṇa Mantāniputta** and became a *Sotāpanna.*[4]

During the first twenty years after the Enlightenment, the Buddha did not have the same personal attendants all the time. From time to time various monks looked after him, among them being **Nāgasamāla, Nāgita, Upavāna, Sunakkhatta,** the novice **Cunda, Sāgata, Rādha** and **Meghiya.** We are told that the Buddha was not particularly pleased with any of them. At the end of twenty years, at an assembly of the monks, the Buddha declared that he was advanced in years and desired to have somebody as his permanent body-servant, one who would respect his wishes in every way.[5]

All the great disciples offered their serviecs, but were rejected by the Buddha. Ānanda alone was left; he sat in silence. When asked why he did not offer himself, his reply was that the Buddha knew best whom to choose. When the Buddha signified that he desired to have Ānanda, the latter agreed to accept the post on certain conditions. The Buddha was never to give him any choice food or garment[6] gotten by him, nor appoint for him a separate "fragrant cell" (residence), nor include him in the invitations accepted by the Buddha. For, he said, if the Buddha did any of these things, some would say that Ānanda's services to the Buddha were done in order to get clothes, good fare and lodging and be included in the invitations. Further he was to be allowed to accept invitations on behalf of the Buddha; to bring to the Buddha those who came to see him from afar; to place before the Buddha all his perplexities, and the Buddha was to repeat to him any doctrine taught in his absence. If these concessions were not granted, he said, some would ask where was the advantage of such service. Only if these privileges were allowed him would people trust him and realise that the Buddha had real regard for him. The Buddha agreed to the conditions.

Thenceforth, for twenty-five years,[7] Ānanda waited upon the Buddha, following him like a shadow, bringing him water and toothpick, washing

[2] Vin. ii. 182.

[3] ThāgA. i. 68; also DA. ii. 418 ff.; Vin. i. 202; iv. 86.

[4] In S. iii. 105 Ānanda acknowledges his indebtedness to **Puṇṇa** and gives an account of Puṇṇa's sermon to him.

[5] The Buddha says that sometimes his attendants would not obey him, and on certain occasions had dropped his bowl and robe and gone away, leaving him.

[6] Ānanda did, however, accept one of the two robes given by *Pukkusa* the Mallan to the Buddha (D. ii. 133); Buddhaghosa explains this by saying that Ānanda's period of service had now come to an end, and also he wished to be free from the accusation that even after having served the Buddha for twenty-five years, the Buddha had never made him any gift. It is further stated that Ānanda offered the robe to the Buddha later (DA. ii. 570).

[7] Thag. v. 1039.

his feet, accompanying him everywhere, sweeping his cell and so forth. By day he was always at hand, forestalling the Master's slightest wish; at night, stout staff and large torch in hand, he would go nine times round the Buddha's Gandha-kuṭi in order to keep awake, in case he were needed, and also to prevent the Buddha's sleep from being disturbed.[8]

Many examples are given of Ānanda's solicitude for the Buddha, particularly during the Buddha's last days, as related in the *Mahā Parinibbāna Sutta.* Ānanda was the Buddha's equal in age (having been born on the same day), and it is touching to read of this old and most devoted attendant ministering to his eminent cousin, fetching him water, bathing him, rubbing his body, preparing his bed, and receiving last instructions from him on various matters of importance. It is said that when the Buddha was ill, Ānanda became sympathetically sick.[9] He was aware of every change that occurred in the Buddha's body.[10]

Once, when acting on the instructions of **Devadatta,** the royal mahouts let loose **Nālāgiri,** maddened with drink, on the Buddha's path, so that he might trample the Buddha to death, Ānanda, seeing the animal rushing towards them, immediately took his stand in front of the Buddha. Three times the Buddha forbade him to do so, but Ānanda, usually most obedient, refused to move, and it is said that the Buddha, by his *iddhi*-power, made the earth roll back in order to get Ānanda out of the elephant's path.[11] Sometimes, the extreme zealousness of Ānanda drew on him the Buddha's rebuke—*e.g.*, when he prepared *tekaṭuka* gruel (gruel with three kinds of pungent substances) for the Buddha when he was suffering from wind in the stomach. The gruel was prepared from food kept indoors and was cooked by Ānanda himself, indoors; this was against the rules, but Ānanda knew that the gruel would cure the Buddha.[12]

Ānanda was most efficient in the performance of the numerous duties attached to his post. Whenever the Buddha wished to summon the monks or to send a message to anyone, it was to Ānanda that he entrusted the task.[13]

[8] The account here given is summarised from AA. i. 159 ff. and from ThagA. ii. 121 ff. On the boons see J. iv. 96, where Ānanda had asked for boons in the past too. The Tibetan sources give a different and interesting version of Ānanda's entry into the Order. See Rockhill. *Life of the Buddha,* 57-8.

[9] D. ii. 99.

[10] *E.g.*, the brightening of his features after **Janavasabha's** visit (D. ii. 204); and the fading of his complexion just before death, which was apparent when the Buddha put on the robe given by **Pukkusa** (*ibid.*, 133).

[11] J. v. 335-6; it was in this connection that the *Cūḷahaṃsa Jātaka* was preached to show that Ānanda had, in previous births also, renounced his life to save that of the Buddha; see also DhA. i. 119. The *Cullavagga* account of the Nālāgiri incident makes no mention of Ānanda's past (Vin. ii. 195).

[12] Vin. i. 210-11.

[13] See, *e.g.*, D. ii. 199; 147; Vin. i. 80; M. i. 456.

He reported to the Buddha any news which he heard and thought interesting.[14] Laymen and laywomen, wishing to give alms to the Buddha and the monks, would often consult him in their difficulties, and he would always advise them.[15] When the monks came to him expressing their desire to hear the Buddha preach, he did his best to grant their wish.[16] Sometimes when Ānanda felt that an interview with the Buddha would be of use to certain people, he would contrive that the Buddha should talk to them and solve their doubts; thus, for instance, he arranged an interview for the **Nigaṇṭha Saccaka**[17] and the brahmins **Saṅgārava** and **Rammaka.**[18] Similarly he took **Samiddhi** to the Buddha when he found that Samiddhi had wrongly represented the Buddha's views.[19] When he discovered that **Kimbila** and a large number of other monks would greatly benefit if the Buddha would preach to them on *ānāpānasati*, he requested the Buddha that he should do so.[20]

Again, when at Vesāli, as a result of the Buddha's talks to the monks on *asubha*, a large number of them, feeling shame and loathing for their bodies, committed suicide, Ānanda suggested to the Buddha that he might teach the monks some method by which they might obtain insight (*aññā*).[21]

In order that people might still worship the Buddha when he was away on tour, Ānanda planted the **Ānanda-Bodhi** (*q.v.*).

Ānanda was, however, careful that people should not weary the Buddha unnecessarily. Even when he told the Buddha about the suicide of the monks (mentioned above), he was careful to wait till the Buddha had finished his fortnight's solitude, because he had given orders that he should not be disturbed.

When **Subhadda** wanted to see the Buddha as he lay on his death-bed, Ānanda refused to let him in until expressly asked to do so by the Master.[22] That same day when the **Mallas** of **Kusinārā** came with their families to pay their last respects to the Buddha, Ānanda arranged them in groups, and introduced each group so that the ceremony might be gone through without delay.[23]

[14] *E.g.*, the death of **Nigaṇṭha Nātaputta**, of which he learnt from **Cunda Samaṇuddesa** (D. iii. 118; M. ii. 244); also Devadatta's conspiracy to harm the Buddha (Vin. ii. 198).

[15] *E.g.*, the **Andhakavinda Brāhmaṇa** (Vin. i. 220-1); **Roja** the **Malla** (*ibid.*, 248); see also *ibid.*, 238 f.

[16] *E.g.*, when the Buddha retired into the **Pārileyya** forest (S. iii. 95; DhA. i. 50 f.).

[17] M. i. 237.

[18] S. i. 163; M. i. 161.

[19] M. iii. 208.

[20] S. v. 323. Ānanda's requests were, however, not always granted. Once, for instance, though he asked the Buddha three times to recite the Pāṭimokkha, the Buddha refused to do so until an offending monk had been removed (Vin. ii. 236 f.).

[21] S. v. 320 f.

[22] D. ii. 149.

[23] *Ibid.*, 148.

He often saved the Buddha from unpleasantness by preventing too pious admirers from trying to persuade the Buddha to do what was against his scruples.[24]

Among Ānanda's duties was the task of going round to put away anything which might have been forgotten by anyone in the congregation after hearing the Buddha preach.[25]

Ānanda was often consulted by colleagues on their various difficulties. Thus we find **Vaṅgīsa**[26] confiding to him his restlessness at the sight of women and asking for his advice. Among others who came to him with questions on various doctrinal matters were **Kāmabhū,**[27] **Udāyī,**[28] **Channa,**[29] and **Bhadda.**[30] Nor were these consultations confined to his fellow-monks, for we find the brahmins **Ghosita**[31] and **Uṇṇābha,**[32] the **Licchavis Abhaya** and **Paṇḍitakumāraka,**[33] the paribbājakas **Channa**[34] and **Kokanuda,**[35] the *upāsikā* **Migasālā,**[36] a householder of **Kosambī**[37] and **Pasenadi Kosala,**[38] all coming to him for enlightenment and instruction. Sometimes the monks, having heard a brief sermon from the Buddha, would seek out Ānanda to obtain from him a more detailed exposition, for he had the reputation of being able to expound the Dhamma.[39]

It is said that the Buddha would often deliberately shorten his discourse to the monks so that they might be tempted to have it further explained by Ānanda. They would then return to the Buddha and report to him Ānanda's exposition, which would give him an opportunity of praising Ānanda's erudition.[40] In the *Sekha Sutta*[41] we are told that after the Buddha had preached to the Sākyans of **Kapilavatthu** till late at night, he asked Ānanda to continue the discourse while he himself rested. Ānanda did so, and when the Buddha awoke after his sleep, he commended Ānanda on his ability. On another occasion, the Buddha asks Ānanda to address the monks on the wonders attendant on a Buddha's birth, and the **Acchari-**

[24] *E.g.*, **Bodhirājakumāra,** when he asked the Buddha to walk over the carpets in his mansion, **Kokanada** (Vin. ii. 128; M. ii. 94).

[25] DhA. i. 410.

[26] S. i. 188; Thag. vers. 1223-6.

[27] S. iv. 165-6.

[28] S. v. 166-8; A. iv. 449.

[29] S. iii. 133-4.

[30] S. v. 171-3; ThagA. i. 474; he could not, however, be of use to his fellow-celibate Bhaṇḍu (*q.v.*).

[31] S. iv. 113.

[32] S. v. 272.

[33] A. i. 220.

[34] A. i. 215.

[35] A. v. 196.

[36] A. iii. 347, and again A. v. 137.

[37] A. i. 217.

[38] M. ii. 112. It was on this occasion that Pasenadi presented Ānanda with a valuable piece of foreign material which had been sent to him by **Ajātasattu.**

[39] A. v. 225; S. iv. 93.

[40] MA. i. 81; for such praise see, *e.g.*, A. v. 229. It is said that once when a certain landowner asked the Buddha how he could show honour to the Dhamma, the Buddha told him to show honour to Ānanda if he wished to honour the Dhamma (J. iv. 369).

[41] M. i. 353 ff.

yabbhuta-Dhamma Sutta is the result. The Buddha is mentioned as listening with approval.[42]

Sometimes Ānanda would suggest to the Buddha a simile to be used in his discourse, *e.g.* the *Dhammayāna* simile[43]; or by a simile suggest a name to be given to a discourse, *e.g.* the *Madhupiṇḍika Sutta*[44]; or again, particularly wishing to remember a certain Sutta, he would ask the Buddha to give it a name, *e.g.* the *Bahudhātuka Sutta.*[45]

Several instances occur of Ānanda preaching to the monks of his own accord[46] and also to the laity.[47] The *Sandaka Sutta* records a visit paid by Ānanda with his followers to the paribbājaka **Sandaka,** and describes how he won Sandaka over by a discourse. Sometimes, as in the case of the *Bhaddekaratta Sutta,*[48] Ānanda would repeat to the assembly of monks a sermon which he had previously heard the Buddha preach. Ānanda took the fullest advantage of the permission granted to him by the Buddha of asking him any question he desired. He had a very inquiring mind; if the Buddha smiled he would ask the reason (M. ii. 45, 50, 74; A. iii. 214 f.; J. iii. 405; iv. 7).

Or if he remained silent, Ānanda had to be told the reason (S. iv. 400). He knew that the Buddha did nothing without definite cause; when **Upavāna,** who stood fanning the Buddha, was asked to move away, Ānanda wished to know the reason, and was told that Upavāna prevented various spirits from seeing the Buddha (D. ii. 139). The Buddha was always willing to answer Ānanda's questions to his satisfaction. Sometimes, as in the case of his question regarding the dead citizens of **Ñātikā** (D. ii. 91 ff.),[49] a long discourse would result.[50]

Most often his consultations with the Buddha were on matters of doctrine or were connected with it—*e.g.*, on *nirodha* (S. iii. 24); *loka* (S. iv. 53); *suñña* (S. iv. 54; M. iii. 104-24); *vedanā* (S. iv. 219-21); *iddhi* (S. v. 282-4; 286); *ānāpānasati* (S. v. 328-34); *bhava*, etc. (A. i. 223 f.); on the *chaḷabhijāti* of Pūraṇa Kassapa (*q.v.*); the aims and purposes of *sīla* (A. v. 1 f., repeated in v. 311 f.); the possibilities of *samādhi* (A. v. 7 f., repeated in v. 318 and in A. i. 132 f.); on *saṅghabheda* (A. v. 75 ff.); the qualities requisite to be a counsellor of monks (A. iv. 279 ff.); the power of carrying possessed by a Buddha's voice (A. i. 226 f.); the conditions necessary for a monk's happi-

[42] M. iii. 119 ff.

[43] S. v. 5.

[44] M. i. 114; cp. **Upavāna** suggesting the name for the *Pāsādika Sutta* (D. iii. 141).

[45] M. iii. 67.

[46] *E.g.*, A. ii. 156 f.; v. 6.

[47] *E.g.*, A. ii. 194.

[48] M. iii. 189 f.

[49] In this case the discourse concluded with a description of the Dhammādāsa (Mirror of Truth) to be used for all time; see also S. v. 356-60.

[50] The *Pabbajjā Sutta* (Sn. 72 ff.), was preached because of Ānanda's request that the Buddha should give an account of his renunciation (SnA. ii. 381); see also *Pubbayogāvacara Sutta* (SnA. i. 47).

ness (A. iii. 132 f.); the different ways of mastering the elements (M. iii. 62 f.); the birthplace of "noble men" (DhA. iii. 248); and the manner in which previous Buddhas kept the Fast-day (DhA. iii. 246). To these should be added the conversations on numerous topics recorded in the *Mahāparinibbāna Sutta*. Some of these questions—*e.g.*, about earthquakes (D. ii. 107 ff.; A. iv. 312 ff.) and the different kinds of spirits present at the death of the Buddha (D. ii. 139 f.)—seem to have been put into Ānanda's mouth in order that they might be used as pegs on which to hang beliefs connected with them which were current among later-day Buddhists.

Not all the Suttas addressed to Ānanda are, however, the result of his questions. Sometimes he would repeat to the Buddha conversations he had had with others and talks he had overheard, and the Buddha would expound in detail the topics occurring therein.

Thus, for instance, a conversation with Pasenadi Kosala on *Kalyānamittatā* is repeated and the Buddha explains its importance (S. i. 87-9; v. 2-3); Ānanda tells the Buddha about his visit to the **Paribbajakārāma** in **Kosambi** and what he there heard about a bhikkhu being called *niddasa* after twelve years of celibacy. The Buddha thereupon expounds the seven *niddasavatthu* (A. iv. 37 ff.). The account conveyed by Ānanda of **Udāyī** preaching to a large crowd leads to an exposition of the difficulties of addressing large assemblies and the qualities needed to please them (A. iii. 184). A conversation between Udāyī and the carpenter **Pañcakaṅga** on feelings is overheard by Ānanda and reported to the Buddha, who gives a detailed explanation of his views on the subject (S. iv. 222 f.; M. i. 397 f.). The same thing happens when Ānanda mentions to the Buddha talks he had heard between **Sāriputta** and the Pāribbājakas (S. ii. 35-7) and between the same Elder and **Bhūmiya** (S. ii. 39-41). Sometimes—as in the case of the upāsikā **Migasālā** (A. iii. 347; v. 137)—Ānanda would answer questions put to him as best he could, and seek the Buddha's advice and corrections of his interpretation of the Doctrine.

When the monks asked Ānanda whether the Buddha's predictions regarding the results of Devadatta's crimes were based on actual knowledge, he furnished them with no answer at all until he had consulted the Buddha (A. iii. 402). Similarly, when **Tapussa** questions him as to why household life is not attractive to laymen, Ānanda takes him straight away to the Buddha, who is spending his siesta in the **Mahāvana** in **Uruvelakappa** (A. iv. 438 f.). Once Ānanda fancies that he knows all about causation, and tells the Buddha how glad he is that he should understand this difficult subject. The Buddha points out to him that he really knows very little about it and preaches to him the *Mahānidāna Sutta* (D. ii. 55 ff.; S. ii. 92-3).

When Ānanda realises that the Buddha will die in a short while, with childlike simplicity, he requests the Buddha to make a last pronouncement regarding the Order (D. ii. 98 ff.; S. v. 152-4).

On several occasions it is news that Ānanda brings to the Buddha—*e.g.*, about the death of the Nigaṇṭha Nātaputta, and about Devadatta's plots, already mentioned—which provoke the Buddha to preach to him: **Phagguna** has died, and at his death his senses seemed very clear; so they would, says the Buddha, and proceeds to speak of the advantages of listening to the Dhamma in due season (A. iii. 381 f.). Or again, **Girimānanda** is ill and would the Buddha go and see him? The Buddha suggests that Ānanda should go and tell Girimānanda about the ten kinds of **saññā** (*aniccasaññā*, etc.), and the patient will recover (A. v. 108 f.). Ānanda desires to retire into solitude and develop zeal and energy; would the Buddha tell him on which topics to meditate? And the Buddha preaches to him the doctrine of impermanence (S. iii. 187; iv. 54-5).

The Buddha, however, often preached to Ānanda without any such provocation on various topics—*e.g.*, on the nature of the *saṅkhāra* (S. iii. 37-40); on the impossibility of the monk without faith attaining eminence in the *sāsana* (A. v. 152 ff.); on the power the Buddha has of knowing which doctrines would appeal to different people and of preaching accordingly (A. v. 36 f.); on immorality and its consequences (A. i. 50 f.); on the admonitions that should be addressed to new entrants to the Order (A. iii. 138 f.); on the advice which should be given to friends by those desiring their welfare (A. i. 222).

The various topics on which the Buddha discoursed to Ānanda as recorded in the *Mahā Parinibbāna Sutta*, have already been referred to. Some of them—*e.g.*, on the eight assemblies, the eight positions of mastery, the eight stages of deliverance (D. ii. 112)—seem to be stereotyped later additions. On the other hand, with regard to the accounts of the honours to be paid to a Buddha's dead body, the places of pilgrimage for the pious, and various other similar subjects, it is impossible to say how far they are authentic. In a few instances the remarks addressed to Ānanda seem to be meant for others, to be heard by them or to be conveyed to them—*e.g.*, in the dispute between **Udāyī** and **Sāriputta,** when they both seek the Buddha for him to settle the differences in opinion between them (A. iii. 192 ff.); or, again, when the recalcitrant Udāyī fails to answer the Buddha's question on subjects of reflection (*anussatiṭṭhāna*), and Ānanda gives an answer which the Buddha approves (A. iii. 322 ff.). A question asked by Ānanda as to whether there are any scents which spread even against the wind, results in the well-known sermon about the fame of the holy man being wafted everywhere (A. i. 222 f.; DhA. i. 420 ff.). Once or twice Ānanda intervenes in a discussion between the Buddha and another, either to ask a question or to suggest a simile which he feels could help the Buddha in establishing his point—*e.g.*, in the interviews of **Uttiya Paribbājaka** (A. v. 194), of the brahmin **Saṅgārava** (A. i. 169), and again of **Viḍūḍabha,** son of Pasenadi (M. ii. 130).

In the *Mahā Māluṅkyā Sutta* (M. i. 433), it is Ānanda's intervention which evokes the discourse on the Five Fetters. Similarly he intervenes in a discussion between the Buddha and **Pārāsariya's** pupil, **Uttara,** and persuades the Buddha to preach the *Indriyabhāvanā Sutta* on the cultivation of the Faculties (M. iii. 298 ff.).

Buddhaghosa gives a list of the discourses which bring out the eminence and skill of Ānanda; they are the *Sekha, Bāhitiya, Āneñjasappāya, Gopaka-Moggallāna, Bahudhātuka, Cūlasuññata, Mahāsuññata, Acchariyabbhuta, Bhaddekaratta, Mahānidāna, Mahāparinibbāna, Subha* and *Cūḷaniyaloka-dhātu.* (For particulars of these see under the respective names.) The books give accounts of several conversations between Ānanda and his eminent colleagues, such as Sāriputta.[51] He seems to have felt happy in their company and did not hesitate to take to them his difficulties; thus we find him asking Sāriputta why only certain beings in this world reach *parinibbāna* (A. ii. 167); on another occasion he asks Sāriputta about the possibilities of *samādhi* (A. v. 8). On the other hand, at least twice (A. iii. 201 f.; 361 f.), when Ānanda asks his questions of Sāriputta, the latter suggests that Ānanda himself should find the answer, and having heard it, Sāriputta praises him highly and extols his abilities.

Ānanda's special friends seem to have been Sāriputta, Moggallāna, Mahā Kassapa, Anuruddha and Kaṅkhā Revata.[52] He was the *Saṅgha-navaka* among them all, yet they held him in high esteem.[53] Ānanda and Sariputta were very special friends. It is said that Sāriputta loved Ānanda because the latter did for the Buddha what Sāriputta would wish to have done himself, and Ānanda respected Sāriputta because he was the Buddha's chief disciple. Young men who were ordained by either of them would be sent to the other to learn under him. They shared between them any good thing given to them. Once Ānanda was presented by a brahmin with a costly robe; immediately he wished to give it to Sāriputta, but as the latter was away at the time, he obtained the Buddha's permission to keep it for him till his return.[54]

The *Saṃyutta Nikāya*[55] contains an eulogy on Sāriputta by Ānanda,

[51] See also his conversation with **Musīla,** and **Saviṭṭha** and **Nārada** at Kosambī in the **Ghositārāma** (S. ii. 113 f.).

[52] *E.g.*, M. i. 212 f.

[53] MA. i. 436.

[54] Vin. i. 289; Sp. iii. 636-7; MA. i. 436.

[55] i. 63-4.

where the latter speaks of his comprehensive and manifold wisdom, joyous and swift, of his rampant energy and readiness to accept advice. When he hears of Sāriputta's death from Cunda the Samaṇuddesa, he goes to the Buddha with Cunda (not wishing to break the news himself) and they take with them Sāriputta's bowl and outer robe, Cunda carrying the ashes, and there Ānanda confesses to the Buddha that when he heard the news he felt as thought his body were drugged, his senses confused and his mind become a blank.[56] The Commentary adds[57] that Ānanda was trembling "like a cock escaping from the mouth of a cat."

That **Mahā Kassapa** was fond of Ānanda, we may gather from the fact that it was he who contrived to have him elected on the First Council, and when Mahā Kassapa heard of Ānanda's attainment of arahantship, it was he who led the applause.[58] Ānanda held him in the highest veneration, and on one occasion refused to take part in an *upasampadā* ordination because he would have to pronounce Kassapa's name and did not consider this respectful towards the Elder.[59] In their conversations, Kassapa addresses Ānanda as "*āvuso*," Ānanda addresses Kassapa as "*bhante*." There is an interview recorded between them in which Kassapa roundly abuses Ānanda, calling him "corn-trampler" and "despoiler of families," and he ends by up saying "this boy does not know his own measure." Ānanda had been touring **Dakkhiṇagiri** with a large company of monks, mostly youths, and the latter had not brought much credit upon themselves. When Kassapa sees Ānanda on his return to Rājagaha, he puts on him the whole blame for the youths' want of training. Ānanda winces at being called "boy"; "my head is growing grey hairs, your reverence, yet I am not vexed that you should call me 'boy' even at this time of day." **Thullanandā** heard of this incident and showed great annoyance. "How dare Mahā Kassapa," she says, "who was once a heretical teacher, chide the sage Ānanda, calling him 'boy'?" Mahā Kassapa complains to Ānanda of Thullanandā's behaviour; probably, though we are not told so, Ānanda apologised to him on her behalf.[60]

On another occasion, Ānanda, after a great deal of persuasion, took Kassapa to a settlement of the nuns. There Kassapa preached to them, but the nun **Thullatissā** was not pleased and gave vent publicly to her displeasure. "How does Kassapa think it fit to preach the doctrine in the presence of the learned sage Ānanda? It is as if the needle-pedlar were to deem he could sell a needle to the needle-maker." Kassapa is incensed at these words, but Ānanda appeases him by acknowledging that he (Kassapa) is in every way his superior and asks him to

56 S. v. 161; Thag. vers. 1034-5.
57 SA. i. 180.
58 DA. i. 11.
59 Vin. i. 92.
60 S. ii. 217 ff.

pardon Tissā. "Be indulgent, your reverence," says he, "women are foolish."[61]

In this passage Ānanda is spoken of as **Vedehamuni**. The Commentary[62] explains it by *paṇḍitamuni*, and says further, *paṇḍito hi ñāṇasaṅkhātena vedena īhati sabbakiccāni karoti, tasmā vedeho ti vuccati ; vedeho ca so muni cā ti vedehamuni.*[63]

It was perhaps Ānanda's championship of the women's cause which made him popular with the nuns and earned for him a reputation rivalling, as was mentioned above, even that of Mahā Kassapa. When **Pajāpatī Gotamī,** with a number of Sākyan women, undaunted by the Buddha's refusal of their request at Kapilavatthu, followed him into Vesāli and there beseeched his consent for women to enter the Order, the Buddha would not change his mind.

Ānanda found the women dejected and weeping, with swollen feet, standing outside the **Kūṭāgārasālā.** Having learnt what had happened, he asked the Buddha to grant their request. Three times he asked and three times the Buddha refused. Then he changed his tactics. He inquired of the Buddha if women were at all capable of attaining the Fruits of the Path. The answer was in the affirmative, and Ānanda pushed home the advantage thus gained. In the end the Buddha allowed women to enter the Order subject to certain conditions. They expressed their great gratitude to Ānanda.[64] In this connection, the Buddha is reported as having said[65] that had Ānanda not persuaded him to give his consent to the admission of women to the Order, the Sāsana would have lasted a thousand years, but now it would last only five hundred.

This championing of the women's cause was also one of the charges brought against Ānanda by his colleagues at the end of the First Council. (See below.)

Perhaps it was this solicitude for their privileges that prompted him to ask the Buddha one day why it was that women did not sit in public

[61] S. ii. 215 ff.; the Tibetans say that when Kassapa died, Ajātasattu was very grieved because he had not been able to see the monk's body. Ānanda took the king to the mountain where it had been buried and showed it to him (Rockhill, *op. cit.*. p. 162 and n. 2).

[62] SA. ii. 132.

[63] Compare with this the derivation of **Vedehiputta** in connection with Ajātasattu. See also *s.v.* **Vedehikā.** The Mtu. (iii. 176-7) says that when the Buddha went away from home Ānanda wished to join him, but his mother was unwilling. because his brother. Devadatta, had already gone away. Ānanda therefore went to the Videha country and became a muni. Is this another explanation of the term Vedehamuni ?

[64] Vin. ii. 253 ff. Ānanda is again found as intermediary for Pajāpatī Gotamī in M. iii. 253 f.

[65] Vin. ii. 256.

assemblies (*e.g.* courts of justice), or embark on business, or reap the full fruit of their actions.[66]

That Ānanda was in the habit of preaching frequently to the nuns is evident from the incidents quoted above and also from other passages.[67] He seems also to have been in charge of the arrangements for sending preachers regularly to the nuns. A passage in the *Saṃyutta* Commentary[68] seems to indicate that Ānanda was a popular preacher among laywomen as well.

They would stand round him when he preached, fanning him and asking him questions on the Dhamma. When he went to Kosambī to impose the higher penalty on **Channa,** the women of King **Udena's** harem, hearing of his presence in the park, came to him and listened to his preaching. So impressed were they that they gave him five hundred robes.[69] It was on this occasion that Ānanda convinced Udena of the conscientiousness with which the Sākyaputta monks used everything which was given to them, wasting nothing. The king, pleased with Ānanda, gave him another five hundred robes, all of which he distributed among the community.

A similar story is related of the women of Pasenadi's palace and their gift to Ānanda. The king was at first angry, but afterwards gave Ānanda one thousand robes.[70]

The *Dhammapada* Commentary[71] says that once Pasenadi asked the Buddha to go regularly to the palace with five hundred monks and preach the Law to his queens **Mallikā** and **Vāsabhakhattiyā** and to the other women in the palace. When the Buddha said that it was impossible for him to go regularly to one place he was asked to send a monk, and the duty was assigned to Ānanda. He therefore went to the palace at stated times and instructed the queens. Mallikā was found to be a good student, but not so Vāsabhakhattiyā.

The *Jātaka* Commentary[72] says that the women of the palace were themselves asked which of the eighty chief disciples they would have as their preacher and they unanimously chose Ānanda. For an incident connected with Ānanda's visits to the palace see the *Mahāsāra Jātaka* and also *s.v.* **Pasenadi.**

According to the *Aṅguttara* Commentary[73] Ānanda was beautiful to look at.

Ānanda's services seem often to have been sought for consoling the sick. Thus we find **Anāthapiṇḍika** sending for him when he lay ill (M. iii.

[66] A. ii. 82. See also GS. ii. 92, n. 2, on the interpretation of the last word.

[67] *E.g.*, S. v. 154 ff.; Thag. v. 1020; ThagA. ii. 129.

[68] i. 210.

[69] Vin. ii. 290.

[70] J. ii. 24 ff.

[71] i. 382 ff.

[72] i. 382.

[73] ii. 533.

258), and also **Sirivaḍḍha** (S. v. 176 f.) and **Mānadinna** (*ibid.*, 177 f.). He is elsewhere mentioned as helping the Buddha to wait on a sick monk.[74]

We are told that when the Buddha had his afternoon siesta, Ānanda would spend his time in waiting upon the sick and talking to them.[75] Ānanda was never too busy to show gratitude to his friends. When a certain crow-keeper's family, members of which had been of special service to him, had been destroyed by a pestilence, leaving only two very young boys, he obtained the Buddha's special permission to ordain them and look after them, though they were under the requisite age.[76]

When Ānanda discovered that his friend Roja and Malla had no real faith in the Buddha, he was greatly grieved and interceded on his special behalf with the Buddha that he should make Roja a believer. Later he obtained the Buddha's permission for Roja to offer a meal of potherbs.[77] In another place we find Roja presenting Ānanda with a linen cloth.[78] According to the *Jātakaṭṭhakathā*[79] Roja once tried to persuade Ānanda to go back to the lay-life.

His sympathy is also shown in the story of the woman who asked to have a share in the Vihāra built by **Visākhā.** She brought a costly carpet, but could find no place in which to put it; it looked so poor beside the other furnishings. Ānanda helped her in her disappointment.[80]

Once in Jetavana, in an assembly of monks, the Buddha spoke the praises of Ānanda, and ranked him the foremost bhikkhu in five respects: erudition, good behaviour (*gatimantānaṃ*, power of walking, according to Dhammapāla), retentive memory, resoluteness and personal attention.[81] Again, shortly before the Buddha's death, he speaks affectionately of Ānanda[82]; Ānanda knew the right time to bring visitors to the Tathāgata; he had four exceptional qualities, in that whoever came to see him, monks or nuns, laymen or laywomen, they were all filled with joy on beholding him[83]; when he preached to them they listened with rapture and delight, which never tired.[84]

Another proof of the Buddha's esteem for Ānanda is the incident of his asking Ānanda to design a robe for the monks to be in pattern like a field in Magadha (Vin. i. 287).

[74] Vin. i. 302.

[75] Sp. iii. 651.

[76] Vin. i. 79; to a young monk who used to wait on him and do various services for him, Ānanda gave five hundred robes presented to him by Pasenadi; the monk distributed them to his colleagues.

[77] Vin. i. 247-9.

[78] *Ibid.*, i. 296.

[79] ii. 231.

[80] DhA. i. 415 f.

[81] A. i. 24 f.

[82] D. ii. 144-5; A. ii. 132; A. v. 229; SA. ii. 94 f.

[83] He was called Ānanda because he brought joy to his kinsmen (ThagA. ii. 123).

[84] But see the story of **Atula** (DhA. iii. 327), who is not satisfied with Ānanda's preaching.

In spite of Ānanda having been the constant companion of the Buddha —probably because of that very fact—it was not until after the Buddha's parinibbāna that Ānanda was able to realise Arahantship.[85] Though he was not an arahant he had the paṭisambhidā, being among the few who possessed this qualification while yet learners (Sekhā).[86] When it was decided by Mahā Kassapa and others that a Convocation should be held to systematise the Buddha's teachings, five hundred monks were chosen as delegates, among them, Ānanda. He was, however, the only non-arahant (*sekha*) among them, and he had been enjoined by his colleagues to put forth great effort and repair this disqualification. At length, when the convocation assembled, a vacant seat had to be left for him. It had not been until late the previous night that, after a final supreme effort, he had attained the goal.[87]

It is said that he won sixfold *abhiññā* when he was just lying down to sleep, his head hardly on the pillow, his feet hardly off the ground. He is therefore described as having become an arahant in none of the four postures. When he appeared in the convocation, Mahā Kassapa welcomed him warmly and shouted three times for joy.[88] In the convocation, Ānanda was appointed to answer Mahā Kassapa's questions, and to co-operate with him in rehearsing the Dhamma (as opposed to the Vinaya).

Ānanda came to be known as **Dhammabhaṇḍāgārika,** owing to his skill in remembering the word of the Buddha; it is said that he could remember everything spoken by the Buddha, from one to sixty thousand words in the right order. and without missing one single syllable.[89]

In the first four Nikāyas of the *Sutta Piṭaka*, every sutta begins with the words "Thus have I heard," the "I" referring to Ānanda. It is not stated that Ānanda was present at the preaching by the Buddha of every sutta, though he was present at most; others, the Buddha repeated to him afterwards, in accordance with the conditions under which he had become the Buddha's attendant.

We are told that Ānanda had learnt eighty-two thousand *dhammā*

[85] Buddhaghosa gives a long account of Ānanda's struggle for final emancipation (DA. i. 9 ff.); see also Vin. ii. 286.

[86] VibhA. 388.

[87] He had been occupied in consoling the laity after the Buddha's death and had had no time for practising meditation. In the end it was a *devatā* in the woodland grove in Kosala, where he was staying, who pointed out the urgency of the matter (S. i. 199-200); but see **ThagA.** i. 237. where the credit for this is given to a **Vajjiputta** thera.

[88] According to the **Majjhimabhāṇakā,** says Buddhaghosa, Ānanda appeared on his seat while the others looked on, having come through the earth; according to others he came through the air. According to ThagA. ii. 130, it was a Brahmā of the **Suddhāvāsa** who announced Ānanda's attainment of arahantship to his colleagues at the Convocation.

[89] **ThagA.** ii. 134.

(topics) from the Buddha himself and two thousand from his colleagues.[90] He had also a reputation for fast talking; where an ordinary man could speak one word Ānanda could speak eight; the Buddha could speak sixteen words for each one word of Ānanda.[91] Ānanda could remember anything he had once heard up to fifteen thousand stanzas of sixty thousand lines.[92]

Ānanda lived to be very old[93]; a hymn of praise sung at his death is included at the end of the stanzas attributed to him in the *Theragāthā*.[94]

That the Buddha's death was a great blow to him is shown by the stanzas he uttered immediately after the event.[95] Three months earlier he had heard for the first time that death of the Buddha was near at hand and had besought him to live longer. The reply attributed to the Buddha is a curious one, namely, that on several previous occasions, at Rājagaha and at Vesālī,[96] he had mentioned to Ānanda that he could, if he so desired, live for a whole *kappa*, and had hinted that Ānanda should, if he felt so inclined, request him to prolong his life. Ānanda, however, having failed to take the hint on these occasions, the opportunity was now past, and the Buddha must die; the fault was entirely Ānanda's.[97] It was when Ānanda was temporarily absent from the Buddha's side that the Buddha had assured **Māra** that he would die in three months.[98]

As the end approached, the Buddha noticed that Ānanda was not by his side; on enquiry he learnt that Ānanda was outside, weeping and filled with despair at the thought that the Master would soon be no more, and that he (Ānanda) would have to work out his perfection unaided. The Buddha sent for him and consoled him by pointing out that whatever is born must, by its very nature, be dissolved. Three times he said, " For a long time, Ānanda, you have been very near to me by acts of love, kind and good, never varying, beyond all measure," and he exhorted him to be earnest in effort, for he would soon realise emancipation.[99]

Once, earlier, when Udāyī had teased Ānanda for not having benefited from his close association with the personality of the Master, the Buddha had defended Ānanda, saying, " Say not so, Udāyī; should he die without attaining perfect freedom from passion, by virtue of his piety, he would seven times win rule over the devas and seven times be King of Jambudīpa. Howbeit, in this very life shall Ānanda attain to Nibbāna."[100]

[90] Thag. v. 1024.

[91] MA. i. 283.

[92] MA. i. 501.

[93] One hundred and twenty years, says DhA. ii. 99; he is bracketed with **Bakkula,** as having lived to a great age (AA. ii. 596).

[94] Vers. 1047-9.

[95] D. ii. 157.

[96] See, *e.g.*, D. 102 f.

[97] *Ibid.*, 114-18.

[98] *Ibid.*, 105-6.

[99] *Ibid.*, 144. It was on this occasion that the *Palāsa Jātaka* was preached (J. iii. 23 ff.).

[100] A. i. 228.

Ānanda did his best to persuade the Buddha to die in one of the great cities, such as Rājagaha or Sāvatthi, and not in Kusinārā, the little wattle-and-daub town (as he called it) in the middle of the jungle. He was not satisfied until the Buddha had revealed to him the past history of Kusinārā, how it had once been **Kusāvatī,** the royal capital of the mighty **Mahā Sudassana.**[101]

Just before the Buddha died, Ānanda was commissioned to inform the Mallas of the impending event, and after the Buddha's death, Anuruddha entrusted him, with the help of the Mallas of Kusināra, with all the arrangements for the funeral.[102] Ānanda had earlier[103] learnt from the Buddha how the remains of a Tathāgata should be treated, and now he was to benefit by the instruction.

At the end of the First Council, the duty of handing down unimpaired the Dīgha Nikāya through his disciples was entrusted to Ānanda.[104] He was also charged with the duty of conveying to **Channa** the news that the higher penalty (*brahmadaṇḍa*) had been inflicted on him by the Saṅgha. Ānanda had been deputed by the Buddha himself to carry out this, his last administrative act,[105] but Ānanda, not wishing to undertake the responsibility alone (knowing that Channa had a reputation for roughness), was granted a number of companions, with whom he visited Channa. The latter expressed repentance and was pardoned.[106] Perhaps it was because both the Buddha and Ānanda's colleagues knew of his power to settle disputes that he was chosen for this delicate task.[107]

Ānanda's popularity, however, did not save him from the recriminations of his fellows for some of his actions, which, in their eyes, constituted offences. Thus he was charged[108] with: (1) having failed to find out from the Buddha which were the lesser and minor precepts which the Saṅgha were allowed to revoke if they thought fit[109]; (2) with having stepped on the Buddha's rainy-season garment when sewing it; (3) with having allowed the Buddha's body to be first saluted by women[110]; (4) with having omitted to ask the Buddha to live on for the space of a kappa[111]; and (5) with having exerted himself to procure the admission of women into the Order.[112]

Ānanda's reply was that he himself saw no fault in any of these acts, but that he would confess them as faults out of faith in his colleagues.

101 D. ii. 146.

102 *Ibid.*, 158, ff.

103 *Ibid.*, 141 f.

104 DA. i. 15.

105 D. ii. 154.

106 Vin. ii. 290-2.

107 See S. ii. 235 f., where the Buddha classes him with Sāriputta and Moggallāna for his ability to settle disputes among the monks.

108 Vin. ii. 288-9.

109 See D. ii. 154.

110 Not mentioned elsewhere, but see Rockhill, *op. cit.*, p. 154.

111 D. ii. 115.

112 Vin. ii. 253.

On another occasion he was found fault with (1) for having gone into the village to beg for alms, clothed in his waist-cloth and nether garment[113]; (2) for having worn light garments which were blown about by the wind.[114]

The last years of his life, Ānanda seems to have spent in teaching and preaching and in encouraging his younger colleagues. Among those who held discussions with him after the Buddha's passing away are mentioned **Dasama** of the **Aṭṭhakanagara,**[115] **Gopaka Moggallāna**[116] and **Subha Todeyyaputta.**[117]

The Pāli Canon makes no mention of Ānanda's death. Fa Hsien,[118] however, relates what was probably an old tradition. When Ānanda was on his way from Magadha to Vesāli, there to die, Ajātasattu heard that he was coming, and, with his retinue, followed him up to the Rohiṇī River. The chiefs of Vesāli also heard the news and went out to meet him, and both parties reached the river banks. Ānanda, not wishing to incur the displeasure of either party, entered into the state of *tejokasiṇa* in the middle of the river and his body went up in flames. His remains were divided into two portions, one for each party, and they built *cetiyas* for their enshrinement.[119]

In the time of **Padumuttara** Buddha Ānanda had been the son of **Ānanda,** King of **Haṃsavatī,** and was therefore a step-brother of Padumuttara. His name was **Sumana.** King Ānanda allowed no one but himself to wait on the Buddha. Prince Sumana having quelled an insurrection of the frontier provinces, the king offered him a boon as reward, and he asked to be allowed to entertain the Buddha and his monks for three months. With great reluctance the king agreed, provided the Buddha's consent was obtained. When Sumana went to the vihāra to obtain this, he was greatly impressed by the loyalty and devotion of the Buddha's personal attendant, the monk **Sumana,** and by his *iddhi*-powers. Having learnt from the Buddha that these were the result of good deeds, he himself determined to lead a pious life. For the Buddha's residence Prince Sumana bought a pleasaunce named **Sobhana** from a householder of that same name and built therein a monastery costing one hundred thousand. On the way from the capital to Sobhana Park he built vihāras, at distances of a league from each other. When all preparations were completed, the Buddha went to Sobhana with one hundred thousand monks, stopping at each vihāra on the way. At the festival of dedication of the Sobhana Vihāra, Sumana expressed a wish to become a personal attendant of a future Buddha, just as Sumana was of

113 Vin. i. 298.

114 *Ibid.*, ii. 136.

115 M. i. 349 f.

116 *Ibid.*, iii. 7; Thag., ver. 1024.

117 D. i. 204 ff.

118 Giles trans. 44. The story also occurs in DhA. ii. 99 ff., with several variations in detail.

119 See also Rockhill, *op. cit.*, 165 f.

Padumuttara. Towards this end he did many good deeds. In the time of **Kassapa** Buddha he gave his upper garment to a monk for him to carry his begging-bowl in it. Later he was born in heaven and again as King of Benares. He built for eight Pacceka Buddhas eight monasteries in his royal park[120] and for ten thousand years he looked after them. The Apadāna mentions[121] that he became ruler of heaven thirty-four times and king of men fifty-eight times.

Ānanda's name occurs in innumerable Jātakas; he is identified with **Suriyakumāra** in the *Devadhamma Jātaka* (i. 133), **Cullalohita** in the *Muṇika* (i. 198), **Pajjuna** in the *Maccha* (i. 332), **Kālakaṇṇi** in the *Kāla-kaṇṇi* (i. 365), **Rādha** in the *Rādha* (i. 496), **Poṭṭhapāda** in the *Rādha II.* (ii. 134), **Cullanandiya** in the *Cullanandiya* (i. 202), **Gāmaṇicaṇḍa** in the *Gāmaṇicaṇḍa* (ii. 310), **Cullalohita** in the *Sālūka* (ii. 420), **Dabbasena** in the *Ekarāja* (iii. 15), **Poṭṭhapāda** in the *Kalābu* (iii. 100), **Bārāṇasīseṭṭhi** in the *Pūtha* (iii. 121), **Vedehatāpasa** in the *Gandhāra* (iii. 369), **Sumaṅgala** in the *Sumaṅgala* (iii. 444), **Anusissa** in the *Indriya* (iii. 469), **Maṇḍavya** in the *Kaṇhadīpāyana* (iv. 37), **Pottika** in the *Nigrodha* (iv. 43), **Pañca-sikha** in the *Biḷārakosiya* (iv. 69), **Rohineyya** in the *Ghata* (iv. 69), **Yu-dhiṭṭhila** in the *Yuvañjaya* (iv. 123), **Bharata** in the *Dasaratha* (iv. 130), **Mātali** in the *Kaṇha* (iv. 186), the *Sudhābhojana* (v. 412), the *Nimi* (vi. 129), and the *Kulāvaka* (i. 206), **Kāliṅga** in the *Kāliṅgabodhi* (iv. 236), **Vissakamma** in the *Suruci* (iv. 325), **Sambhūtapaṇḍita** in the *Sambhūta* (iv. 401), **Cittamiga** in the *Rohantamiga* (iv. 423), **Sumukha** in the *Haṃsa* (iv. 430), **Anusissa** in the *Sarabhaṅga* (v. 151), **Somadatta** in the *Cullasutasoma* (v. 192), **Sunanda** the charioteer in the *Ummadantī* (v. 227), the younger brother of **Kusa** in the *Kusa* (v. 312), **Nanda** in the *Soṇa-Nanda* (v. 332), **Sumukha** in the *Cūlahaṃsa* (v. 334), and the *Mahāhaṃsa* (v. 382), the brahmin **Nanda** in the *Mahā Sutasoma* (v. 511), **Somadatta** in the *Bhūridatta* (vi. 219). He was also the barber in the *Makhādeva* (i. 139), the *antevāsika* in the *Asātamanta* (i. 289), the bandit-leader in the *Takka* (i. 299), the brahmin in the *Sārambha* (i. 375), the *Sattubhasta* (iii. 351), the *Palāsa* (iii. 25), the *Juṇha* (iv. 100), and the *Sālikedāra* (iv. 282); the tree-sprite in the *Kusanāḷi* (i. 443), the elephant trainer in the *Sumedha* (i. 446), the younger brother of the Bodhisatta in the *Maṇikaṇṭha* (ii. 286), the marauder in the *Seyya* (ii. 403), the inhabitant of a frontier village in the *Mahā Assārohaka* (iii. 13), the attendant in the *Saṅkha* (iv. 22), one of the seven brothers in the *Bhisa* (iv. 314), the physician **Sīvaka** in the *Sivi* (iv. 412), and the arrow-maker in the *Mahā-Janaka* (vi. 68).

Several times he was born as an animal. Thus he was a parrot in the

[120] ThagA. ii. 121 ff.

[121] i. 52 f.

Saccaṅkira (i. 327), the *Abbhantara* (ii. 400) and the *Mahā-ummagga* (vi. 478), a jackal in the *Guṇa* (ii. 30), the father-goose in the *Vinīlaka* (ii. 40), the tortoise in the *Kacchapa* (ii. 81), the iguana in the *Cullapaduma* (ii. 121), the otter in the *Sasa* (iii. 56), the younger swan in the *Neru* (iii. 248), the crab in the *Suvaṇṇakakkaṭaka* (iii. 298), the wise nāga in the *Mahāpaduma* (iv. 196), the tawny dog in the *Mahābodhi* (v. 246) and the vulture king in the *Kuṇāla* (v. 456).

He was many times king: in the *Nigrodhamiga* (i. 153), the *Kukkura* (i. 178), the *Bhojājānīya* (i. 181), the *Ājañña* (i. 182), the *Tittha* (i. 185), the *Mahilāmukha* (i. 188), the *Mudulakkhaṇa* (i. 306), the *Kuddāla* (i. 315), the *Mahāsupina* (i. 345), the *Attisa* (i. 354), the *Mahāsāra* (i. 387), the *Sālittaka* (i. 420), the *Bandhanamokkha* (i. 440), the *Ekapaṇṇa* (i. 508), the *Gagga* (ii. 17), the *Suhanu* (ii. 32), the *Mora* (ii. 38), the *Susīma* (ii. 50), the *Gijjha* (ii. 52), the *Kalyāṇadhamma* (ii. 65), the *Kalāyamuṭṭhi* (ii. 76), the *Saṅgāmāvacara* (ii. 95), the *Vālodaka* (ii. 97), the *Giridanta* (ii. 99), the *Pabbatūpatthara* (ii. 127), the *Puṇṇanadī* (ii. 175), the *Kacchapa* (ii. 178), the *Kosiya* (ii. 209), the *Guttila* (ii. 257), the *Saṅkappa* (ii. 277), the *Kuṇḍaka-Kucchi-Sindhava* (ii. 291) the *Siri* (ii. 415), the *Nānacchanda* (ii. 429), the *Supatta* (ii. 436), the *Chavaka* (iii. 30), the *Sayha* (iii. 33), the *Brahmadatta* (iii. 81), the *Rājovāda* (iii. 112), the *Kesava* (iii. 145), the *Sussoṇḍi* (iii. 190), the *Avāriya* (iii. 232), the *Nandiyamiga* (iii. 274), the *Dhajaviheṭha* (iii. 307), the *Kukku* (iii. 321), the *Sutanu* (iii. 330), the *Aṭṭhisena* (iii. 355), the *Mahākapi* (iii. 375), the *Dalhadhamma* (iii. 388), the *Susīma* (iii. 397), the *Aṭṭhasadda* (iii. 434), the *Aṭṭhāna* (iii. 478), the *Cullabodhi* (iv. 27), the *Mātiposaka* (iv. 95), the *Bhaddasāla* (iv. 157), the *Mittāmitta* (iv. 199), the *Amba* (iv. 207), the *Javahaṃsa* (iv. 218), the *Dūta* (iv. 228), the *Rurumiga* (ii. 263), the *Sarabhamiga* (ii. 275), the *Uddālaka* (iv. 304), the *Dasabrāhmaṇa* (iv. 368), the *Bhikkhāparampara* (iv. 374), the *Sattigumba* (iv. 437), the *Kumbha* (v. 20), the *Tesakuṇa* (v. 125) and the *Sāma* (vi. 95).

He was King of Benares in the *Kāka* (i. 486), the *Tacasāra* (iii. 206) and the *Saṅkhapāla* (v. 177); King **Mallika** in the *Rājovāda* (ii. 5), the Kosala King in the *Maṇikuṇḍala* (iii. 155), King **Vaṅka** in the *Ghata* (iii. 170), the **Kosavya** King in the *Dhūmakāri* (iii. 402), King **Aḍḍhamāsaka** in the *Gaṅgamāla* (iii. 454), and King **Dhanañjaya** in the *Sambhava* (v. 67), and the *Vidhurapaṇḍita* (vi. 329).

In the *Mahā Nāradakassapa Jātaka*[122] Ānanda was born as **Rujā**, daughter of King **Aṅgati.**

The *Dhammapada* Commentary[123] states that once when Ānanda was a blacksmith he sinned with the wife of another man. As a result, he

[122] J. vi. 255.

[123] i. 327.

suffered in hell for a long time and was born for fourteen existences as some one's wife, and it was seven existences more before the results of his evil deed were exhausted.

There seems to be some confusion as to the time at which Ānanda entered the Order. In the Canonical account[124] he became a monk in the second year of the Buddha's ministry. In the verses attributed to him in the *Theragātha*,[125] however, he says that he has been for twenty-five years a learner (*sekha*). It is concluded from this that Ānanda must have joined the Order only in the twentieth year after the Enlightenment and the whole story of his having been ordained at the same time as Devadatta is discredited.[126] The verses occur in a lament by Ānanda that his master is dead and that he is yet a learner. The twenty-five years which Ānanda mentions probably refer to the period during which he had been the Buddha's personal attendant and not to his whole career as a monk. During that period, "though he was but a learner, no thoughts of evil arose in him," the implication being that his close connection with the Buddha and his devotion to him gave no room for such. He, nevertheless, laments that he could not become an *asekha* while the Buddha was yet alive. If this interpretation be accepted—and I see no reason why it should not be—there is no discrepancy in the accounts of Ānanda's ordination.

[124] *E.g.*, Vin. ii. 182.
[125] Vers. 1039 ff.
[126] See. *e.g.*, Thomas *op. cit.*, 123. See also Rhys Davids' article on Devadatta in ERE.

2. **Ānanda.**—A Khattiya king of **Haṃsavati,** father of **Padumuttara** Buddha.[1] He had, by another wife, a daughter **Nandā,** who became the therī **Pakulā** in the present age.[2] Once, with twenty of his ministers and twenty thousand of his subjects, he appeared before Padumuttara Buddha at **Mithilā** and, having received the "*ehi-bhikkhu-pabbajjā,*" they became arahants.[3] The Buddha went back with them to Haṃsavatī where he preached the *Buddhavaṃsa.*[4]

One of Ānanda's sons was the prince **Sumana,** step-brother to Padumuttara, who became Ānanda, the personal attendant of **Gotama Buddha.**[5]

[1] J. i. 37; Bu. xii. 19.
[2] ThigA. 91.
[3] MA. ii. 722; DA. ii. 488.
[4] BuA. 160.
[5] ThagA. ii. 122.

3. **Ānanda.**—Step-brother of **Maṅgala** Buddha. He came to Maṅgala Buddha with ninety crores of followers; having heard the Buddha's preaching, they all became arahants.[1]

[1] J. i. 30.

4. **Ānanda.**—Son of **Tissa** Buddha, his mother being **Subhaddā.**[1]

[1] Bu. xviii. 18.

5. **Ānanda.**—Son of **Phussa** Buddha, his mother being **Kisāgotamī.**[1] The *Buddhavaṃsa* Commentary,[2] however, gives his name as **Anupama.**

[1] Bu. xix. 16. [2] p. 192.

6. **Ānanda.**—A Pacceka Buddha of ninety-one kappas ago. The thera **Citakapūjaka,** in a previous birth, came down from the deva-loka and cremated the Pacceka Buddha's body with due honour.[1] According to the *Majjhima Nikāya* and its Commentary,[2] there were four Pacceka Buddhas of this name.

[1] Ap. i. 227. [2] M. iii. 70; MA. ii. 890.

7. **Ānanda.**—A king of vultures. He dwelt with ten thousand vultures in **Gijjhakūṭa** and came to hear **Kuṇāla** preach. At the end of Kuṇāla's sermon Ānanda, too, discoursed in the same strain, dwelling on the evil qualities of women " keeping to facts within his knowledge."[1] He lived in the **Kuṇāladaha** with **Nārada, Devala, Puṇṇamukha,** the cuckoo, and **Kuṇāla.**[2] In the present age the vulture-king was Ānanda Thera, the Buddha's attendant.[3]

[1] J. v. 424, 447-50. [2] SnA. i. 359. [3] J. v. 456.

8. **Ānanda.**—A king of fishes, appointed by the fishes themselves to rule over them.[1] He was one of the six monsters of the deep. He lived on one side of the ocean and all the fishes came to him morning and evening to pay their respects. He lived on rock-slime (*sevāla*) till one day he swallowed, by mistake, a fish. Liking the taste very much, he found out what it was, and from that day he ate fish, unknown to his subjects. Seeing their numbers diminish, they began to grow inquisitive, and one day one of their wise ones hid in the lobe of Ānanda's ear and discovered him eating the fish which straggled behind. When this was reported to the other fish, they fled in terror and hid themselves. Ānanda, desirous of eating them, searched everywhere; believing that they lay inside a mountain, he encircled it with his body. Seeing his own tail on the other side of the mountain and believing it to be a fish trying to escape, he crunched it in a rage. The tail was fifty leagues long and he suffered excruciating pain. Attracted by the smell of blood, the fish collected round and ate him bit by bit. His skeleton was as big as a mountain, and holy ascetics, flying through the air and seeing it below

[1] J. i. 207; ii. 352.

them, told men about it and the story became famous throughout Jambudīpa. **Kāḷahatthi** is reported as relating this story to the king in the *Mahā Sutasoma Jātaka.*[2] Ānanda is referred to as an example of great deceitfulness.[3]

[2] J. v. 462-4. [3] MA. i. 138.

9. **Ānanda.**—A yakkha to whom a shrine, called the **Ānanda Cetiya,** was dedicated. The Cetiya was in **Bhoganagara** and was later converted into a Buddhist Vihāra.[1] There the Buddha stayed during his ḷast sojourn, and mention is made of a sermon he preached there to the monks on the Four Great Authorities (*cattāro mahāpadesā*).[2] From there he went to **Pāvā.**

[1] AA. ii. 550. [2] D. ii. 123-6; A. ii. 167.

10. **Ānanda.**—A banker of **Sāvatthi.** He had eighty crores of money, but was a great miser. He had a son, **Mūlasiri,** and once a fortnight he would gather his kinsfolk together and, in their presence, admonish his son as to the desirability of amassing wealth, always increasing it, giving none away. When the banker died he was born in a Caṇḍāla family outside the city gates. The king appointed Mūlasiri banker in his place.

From the time of Ānanda's conception among the Caṇḍālas, misfortune dogged their footsteps. Knowing that a Jonah had come among them, they caused a search to be made and, as a result of their investigations, they sent the pregnant mother away. When the child was born he was a monstrosity with his organs all out of place. When old enough, he was given a potsherd and told to beg his living. One day he came to the house in which he had lived in his former life, and though he managed to enter it, he was discovered and thrown out by the servants. The Buddha happened to be passing by, and sending for Mūlasiri, he told him that the beggar had been his father. Being convinced by certain proofs, Mūlasiri believed and took refuge in the Buddha.[1] It is said that eighty-four thousand beings attained deathlessness on the occasion of the Buddha preaching to Mūlasiri about his father Ānanda.[2]

[1] DhA. ii. 25-8; the story is referred to in the *Milindapañha* (p. 350).
[2] AA. i. 57.

11. **Ānanda.**—Author of the *Mūlaṭikā* on Buddhaghosa's Commentaries on the Abhidhamma.[1] He was originally a native of India, but came over to Ceylon and became head of the **Vanavāsi** fraternity in the Island. He probably lived about the eighth or ninth century A.D. and

[1] Gv. 60, 69; Sās. 69.

wrote the Mūlaṭikā at the request of a monk named **Buddhamitta.** He is probably identical with **Ānanda,** teacher of **Culla Dhammapāla** (see below).[2] He was also known as **Vanaratana Tissa** from his connection with the Vanavāsi school.

[2] P.L.C. 202 f.; 216 f.

12. **Ānanda.**—Teacher of **Culla Dhammapāla,** author of the *Saccasaṅkhepa.*[1] The *Saddhamma Saṅghala*[2] says that Ānanda was the author of the *Saccasaṅkhepa.* See also above (**Ānanda** 11).

[1] *q.v.* [2] ix.

13. **Ānanda.**—Teacher of **Buddhappiya,** author of the *Rūpasiddhi.* He was a native of Ceylon, for Buddhapiya refers to him as "*Tambapaṇṇiddhaja.*" He too belonged to the **Vanavāsī** sect and wrote a Siṇhalese interverbal translation to **Piyadassi's** *Pada-Sādhana* and another to the *Khudda-Sikkhā.* He was a disciple of **Udumbaragiri Medhaṅkara,** pupil of **Sāriputta,** and he probably lived in the time of **Vijayabāhu III.**[1]

He was the teacher of **Videha,** author of the *Samantakūṭavaṇṇanā.*[2] See also **Buddhavaṃsa Vanaratana Ānanda.**

[1] P.L.C. [illegible]1. [2] *Ibid.*, 220.

14. **Ānanda.**—Author of the *Saddhammopāyana,* also called **Abhayagiri-Kavicakravarti Ānanda** and probably belonging to the same period as **Ānanda** (13). His friend and companion, for whom his book was written, was **Buddhasoma.** An Ānanda, probably a later writer, is also the author of a Siṇhalese Commentary on the Saddhammopāyana.[1]

[1] P.L.C. 212.

15. **Ānanda.**—Companion of **Chapaṭa** and co-founder of the **Sīhala-Saṅgha** of Burma.[1] He was later cut off from the community for trying to send to his kinsfolk an elephant presented to him by King **Narapati.** His companions suggested that the animal should be let loose in the forest, in accordance with the Buddha's teaching regarding kindness to animals. Ānanda's reply was that the Buddha had also preached kindness to kinsfolk.[2] He died in 1246.[3]

[1] Sās. 65.
[2] Bode: *op. cit.*, 24.
[3] Forchammer: *Jardine Prize Essay,* p. 35.

16. **Ānanda.**—Of **Haṃsavatī.** Author of the *Madhusāratthadīpanī,* a *ṭīkā* on the Abhidhamma.[1]

[1] Sās. 48; but see Bode: *op. cit.*, 47-8.

17. **Ānanda.**—Called **Māṇava,** in order to distinguish him from others. He was a brahmin youth, maternal cousin of the therī **Uppalavaṇṇā,** with whom he had been in love when she was a laywoman. One day when Upalavaṇṇā returned from her alms-rounds to her hut in **Andhavana,** where she was living at the time, Ānandamāṇava, who was hiding under her bed, jumped up and seized her. In spite of her protestations and admonitions, he overcame her resistance by force and, having worked his will of her, went away. As if unable to endure his wickedness, the earth burst asunder and he was swallowed up in **Avīci.**[1]

In order that such assaults should not be repeated, **Pasenadi Kosala** erected, at the Buddha's suggestion, a residence for the nuns within the city gates, and henceforth they lived only within the precincts of the city.[2]

[1] DhA. ii. 49-50. [2] *Ibid.*, 51 f.

Ānanda Vagga.—The eighth chapter of the *Ṭika Nipāta* of the *Aṅguttara Nikāya.* It consists of ten suttas, the last of which contains a prophecy regarding **Ānanda.**[1]

[1] A. i. 215-28.

1. **Ānanda Sutta.**—Preached by **Ānanda** to **Vaṅgīsa.** Once as they were going together for alms to Sāvatthi, Vaṅgīsa confessed that he was disaffected. Ānanda advised him on how to overcome the disaffection by proper cultivation of the senses.[1]

[1] S. i. 188.

2. **Ānanda Sutta.**—Once **Ānanda** was living in a forest tract in the **Kosala** country and was much occupied in talking to the laity who came to see him. A deva of the forest, desiring his welfare, came up to him and suggested that he might stop his constant babbling and meditate instead.[1] According to Buddhaghosa,[2] this was soon after the Buddha's death, shortly before Ānanda became arahant. People, knowing of his close attendance on the Master, were ever asking for details about the Parinibbāna and when they mourned he had to admonish them. He used to wander about, taking with him the Buddha's begging bowl and robe. In the *Theragāthā*[3] the same admonition is put into the mouth of a **Vajjiputta** monk.

[1] S. i. 199. [2] SA. i. 225. [3] ver. 119; ThagA. i. 237.

3. **Ānanda Sutta.**—Preached by the Buddha to **Ānanda,** who asked how *nirodha* could be obtained. By the cessation of the five *khandhas,* answered the Buddha.[1]

[1] S. iii. 24-5.

4. **Ānanda Sutta.**—A conversation between the Buddha and **Ānanda,** at *Jetavana.* Ānanda is asked in what things one discerns the arising (*uppāda*), passing away (*vaya*), and constant change (*aññathatta*). The answer is "in the five khandhas." The Buddha praises Ānanda for his answer.[1]

[1] S. iii. 37-8.

5. **Ānanda Sutta.**—Same as above, except that the discernment is not only with regard to the present, but also to the past and the future.[1]

[1] S. iii. 38-9.

6. **Ānanda Sutta.**—**Ānanda** tells the monks in **Jetavana** how when he and his colleagues were novices, **Puṇṇa Mantāniputta** was very helpful to them and instructed them as to how the conceit of self (*asmimāna*) arose and how it could be overcome. Having heard him, Ānanda says he fully understood the Dhamma.[1]

[1] S. iii. 105-6.

7. **Ānanda Sutta.**—Preached at **Jetavana. Ānanda** asks the Buddha about psychic power (*iddhi*), its basis and cultivation, and the practice thereof. The Buddha enlightens him.[1]

[1] S. v. 285-6.

8. **Ānanda Sutta.**—Same as above, with the addition of *Ānanda's* declaration that the monks consider the Buddha as their guide, etc.[1]

[1] S. v. 286.

9. **Ānanda Sutta.**—Preached at **Jetavana. Ānanda** is instructed as to how concentration on breathing (*ānāpānasati*) leads to the four *satipaṭṭhānas* and how these, in turn, bring to completion the seven *bojjhaṅgas.* These last lead to complete knowledge and release (*vijjā-vimutti*). The methods of their development are explained in detail.[1]

[1] S. v. 328-33.

10. **Ānanda Sutta.**—Same as above, the only difference being the same as between 7 and 8.

11. **Ānanda Sutta.**—Records a visit paid to **Ānanda** at **Jetavana** by **Sāriputta,** who was also staying there. Sāriputta tells Ānanda that *sotāpannas* are those that have no disloyalty to the Buddha, the Dhamma and the Saṅgha. They have no such immorality as is possessed by the uneducated *putthujjanas.*[1]

[1] S. v. 362-4.

12. **Ānanda Sutta.**—Preached at the **Ghositārāma** in **Kosambi.** **Ānanda** asks the Buddha how monks could enjoy ease (*phāsuvihāra*) and the Buddha tells him.[1]

[1] A. iii. 132-4.

13. **Ānanda Sutta.**—A conversation between **Ānanda** and **Mahā Koṭṭhita** with regard to what happens after the passionless, remainderless ending of the six spheres of contact.[1]

[1] A. ii. 162. The P.T.S. text puts this under *Koṭṭhita Sutta*, but both the Commentary and the Uddāna at the end of the Vagga treat it as a separate sutta.

14. **Ānanda Sutta.**—**Ānanda** goes to **Sāriputta** and asks him how far a monk could learn the Dhamma, remember it, reflect upon it and teach it to others. Sāriputta suggests that Ānanda should answer the question himself, which Ānanda does. At the end of the discourse Sāriputta utters an eulogy on Ānanda and calls him the pattern of the true monk.[1]

[1] A. iii. 361-2.

15. **Ānanda Sutta.**—Preached by the Buddha in reply to **Ānanda's** question as to how notions of "I" and "mine" and the tendency to vain conceit could be completely destroyed.[1] This sutta refers to the *Puṇṇaka-pañha* of the *Parāyaṇa*.

[1] A. i. 132 f.

16. **Ānanda Sutta.**—A conversation between **Ānanda** and **Udāyī** on the wonders of a Tathāgata's attainment and the nature of perception. In the course of the dialogue Ānanda mentions a visit paid to him by a nun who was a follower of the Jaṭilas, and her questions on *samādhi*.[1]

[1] A. iv. 426.

17. **Ānanda Sutta.**—A discourse given to the monks by **Ānanda** on the good man and the wicked man.[1]

[1] A. v. 6 f.

18. **Ānanda Sutta.**—On the ten qualities that a monk should possess if he would benefit by the practice of the Buddha's teachings.[1]

[1] A. v. 152 ff.

Ānanda or **Atthatta Sutta.**—The paribbājaka **Vacchagotta** visits the Buddha and asks him if there is a self. The Buddha makes no reply even when the question is repeated, and Vacchagotta goes away. The Buddha, later, explains to **Ānanda**, in reply to his inquiry, that he remained silent because whatever answer he gave to Vacchagotta's question, it would be capable of being misunderstood and misinterpreted.[1]

[1] S. iv. 400-1.

Ānandakumāra.—A shipwright, who, with three hundred others, was sent by **Mahosadha** to the Upper Ganges to secure timber wherewith to build three hundred ships in preparation for Mahosadha's visit to the capital of **Pañcāla** in order to erect buildings for King **Vedeha.**[1]

[1] J. vi. 427.

Ānandabodhi.—The bodhi-tree planted by **Ānanda** at the entrance to **Jetavana.** The people of **Sāvatthi,** led by **Anāthapiṇḍika**, suggested to Ānanda that some place should be provided where they might offer flowers and perfumes in the name of the Buddha, when the Buddha was away on his periodical tours. After consultation with the Buddha, Ānanda obtained, with **Moggallāna's** assistance, a fruit from the bodhi-tree at **Gayā,** and had it planted at the gateway of Jetavana in the presence of a large and distinguished gathering, including **Pasenadi Kosala** and **Visākhā.** The seed was planted by Anāthapiṇḍika in a golden jar filled with fragrant earth. Immediately a sapling sprang up, fifty cubits tall, with five branches, each fifty cubits long. The king poured round the tree perfumed water from eight hundred jars of gold and silver. In order to consecrate the new tree, the Buddha, at Ānanda's request, sat under it for one night, in the rapture of *samāpatti*. Because the tree was planted by Ānanda, it became known as Ānandabodhi.[1] Pilgrims who came to the Buddha at Jetavana were in the habit of paying respect to the Ānandabodhi.[2] The *Paduma Jātaka* and the *Kāliṅgabodhi Jātaka* were both preached in reference to this bodhi-tree.

[1] J. iv. 228-30. [2] J. ii. 321.

Ānanda-bhaddekaratta Sutta.—Preached at **Jetavana. Ānanda** discourses to the assembled monks on the nature of the True Saint (*Bhaddekaratta*). The Buddha appears on the scene and on being told of Ānanda's discourse, asks him how exactly he had proceeded. Ānanda repeats to him the *Bhaddekaratta Sutta* (*q.v.*), which he had previously learnt from the Buddha. The Buddha recites it himself from beginning to end and praises Ānanda for his skill.[1]

[1] M. iii. 189-91.

Ānandamānava.—See **Ānanda** (17).

Ānandā.—One of the five daughters of the chief queen of the king of the third **Okkāka** dynasty.[1] The *Mahāvaṃsa Ṭīkā*[2] says that Okkāka was the youngest of the sixteen kings of the **Mahāsammata** dynasty and makes no mention of three Okkāka dynasties.

The name of Okkāka's chief queen was **Hatthā** (*v.l.* **Bhattā**).

[1] DA. i. 258: SnA. i. 352. [2] p. 84.

"Ānandena" Sutta. The Buddha is asked by **Ānanda** to tell him of a doctrine which would make him more ardent and intent. The Buddha teaches him the doctrine of impermanence.[1]

[1] S. iii. 187-8.

Ānāpāna Kathā.—The third section of the *Mahāvagga* of the *Paṭisambhidāmagga*.[1]

[1] Ps. i. 162 ff.

Ānāpāna Vagga.—The seventh chapter of the *Bojjhaṅga Saṃyutta* of the *Saṃyutta Nikāya*.[1]

[1] S. v. 129-32.

Ānāpāna Saṃyutta.—The fifty-fourth section of the *Saṃyutta Nikāya*.[1]

[1] S. v. 311-41.

Ānāpāna Sutta.—The idea of in-breathing and out-breathing, if cultivated and developed, leads to much profit.[1]

[1] S. v. 132.

Ānāpānasati Sutta.—Preached at **Sāvatthi** on **Komudī,** the full-moon day of the fourth month. The monks had gathered together to see the Buddha and eminent disciples had been busy instructing their pupils in the various attainments.[1] Seing them thus assembled, the Buddha was pleased with their demeanour and described how in the confraternity of monks were to be found men of various degrees of attainment. Some of them practised the cultivation of mindfulness by breathing exercises and the Buddha proceeded to explain how it was done. Such mindfulness leads to the development of the four *satipaṭṭhānas*, and these, in turn, to the seven *bojjhaṅgas*. Through them one attains deliverance through understanding.[2]

[1] The Commentary says the Buddha had not gone on tour as usual because he wanted to give the monks opportunity of developing their attainments. (MA. ii. 895-6.)

[2] M. iii. 78-88.

1. **Ānisaṃsa Vagga.**—The tenth chapter of the *Chakka Nipāta* of the *Aṅguttara Nikāya.* It consists of eleven suttas on various subjects.[1]

[1] A. iii. 441-5.

2. **Ānisaṃsa Vagga.**—The first chapter of the *Dasaka Nipāta* of the *Aṅguttara Nikāya,* consisting of ten suttas.[1]

[1] A. v. 1-14.

Ānisaṃsa Sutta.—On the six advantages of realising the first fruit of the Path (*Sotāpattiphala*).[1]

[1] A. iii. 441.

Āpaṇa.—A city in the **Aṅguttarāpa** country (probably its capital). The Buddha once visited the city with 1,250 monks and the whole company was entertained by the **Jaṭila Keṇiya.**[1] From Āpaṇa the Buddha went on to **Kusinārā.**[2] In the *Saṃyutta Nikāya,*[3] Āpaṇa is spoken of as a township of the **Aṅgas** (*Aṅgānaṃ nigamo*) and the Buddha is mentioned as having stayed there with **Sāriputta.** Several suttas were preached at Āpaṇa, among them the *Poṭaliya Sutta* (regarding **Poṭaliya**),[4] the *Laṭukikopama Sutta* (to **Udāyi**),[5] the *Sela Sutta* (regarding **Sela**)[6] and the *Saddha or Āpaṇa Sutta.*[7] Āpaṇa was a brahmin village and was the home of the Elder **Sela.**[8] On the occasion of the Buddha's visit to Āpaṇa, during which he converted Sela and Keṇiya, he seems to have stayed at Āpaṇa for over a week and ordained three hundred monks in the company of Sela.[9]

According to Buddhaghosa,[10] the village was called Āpaṇa because it had twenty thousand bazaars (*āpaṇā*) and was therefore distinguished for its shops (*āpaṇānaṃ ussannattā*). Near the village, on the banks of the river **Mahī,** was the woodland where the Buddha stayed during his visits.

[1] Vin. i. 245 ff.
[2] *Ibid.,* 247.
[3] v. 225.
[4] M. i. 359 ff.
[5] M. i. 447 ff.
[6] M. ii. 146 ff; Sn. pp. 102 ff.
[7] S. v. 225-7.
[8] ThagA. ii. 47.
[9] Sn., p. 112.
[10] MA. ii. 586.

Āpaṇa Sutta.—See **Saddha Sutta.**

Āpatti.—A section of the *Vinaya Piṭaka,* the fourth chapter of the *Parivāra.*[1]

[1] Vin. v. 91 ff.

Āpatti Vagga.—The twenty-fifth chapter of the *Catukka Nipāta* of the *Aṅguttara Nikāya*, containing ten suttas on various subjects.[1]

[1] A. ii. 239-46.

1. **Āpatti Sutta.**—**Ānanda** informs the Buddha at **Ghositārāma** in **Kosambī**, that **Bāhiya's** efforts to bring about dissension in the Order had not been suppressed because **Anuruddha**, being Bāhiya's colleague, did not want to interfere. The Buddha tells him that they should not depend on **Anuruddha** for interference in disputes, for he was by temperament unfitted for such action. He then proceeds to discourse to Ānanda on the four probable reasons for a monk being desirous of creating dissension.[1]

[1] A. ii. 239 f.

2. **Āpatti Sutta.**—Deals with the four kinds of fears produced by transgressions, involving either being taken in the act and punished or having to confess guilt and receive punishment.[1]

[1] A. ii. 240-3.

Āpā.—A class of deities who were present at the preaching of the *Mahāsamaya Sutta.*[1]

Buddhaghosa[2] says they were born as devas because of their having practised *āpokasiṇa* in previous lives.

[1] D. ii. 259. [2] DA. ii. 689.

Āpāna.—One of the **Vanni** chiefs of Ceylon, brought into subjection by **Bhuvanekabāhu I.**[1]

[1] Cv. xc. 33.

Āpāyika Vagga.—The twelfth chapter of the *Tika Nipāta* of the *Aṅguttara Nikāya.*[1] It contains ten suttas on various topics.

[1] A. i. 265-73.

Āpāyika Sutta.—On three persons who are doomed to purgatory.[1]

[1] A. i. 265.

Ābhassara.—A Brahma-world where live radiant devas from whose bodies rays of light are emitted, like lightning. It belongs to the **Rūpaloka** and is in the plane of second *jhāna.*[1] The devas living there subsist on joy (*pītibhakkha*).[2] Their span of life is two kappas and there is no guarantee

[1] Abhs. v. 3; Compendium 138, n. 4. [2] S. i. 114; DhA. iii. 258; J. vi. 55.

that a person who has been born there may not later be reborn in an unhappy condition.[3] From time to time these devas utter shouts of joy saying "*aho sukhaṃ, aho sukhaṃ.*" This sound is the best of sounds. These devas are completely enveloped in ease (*sukhena abhisaññā parisaññā*).[4] Their world forms the third station of consciousness (*viññāṇaṭṭhiti*), they are of uniform body, but their perceptions are diverse (*ekattakāyā nānattasaññino*).[5] During the periods of the development of the world many beings are born in the Ābhassara realm and they are then called the highest of the devas, yet even they change their condition.[6] In lists of devas[7] they are given below the **Appamāṇābhā** and above the **Subhā.**

Bodhisattas are sometimes born in the Ābhassara world,[8] but they are never born in Arūpa worlds even when they have developed *Arūpajhānas*. **Baka Brahmā** was born in Ābhassara after having passed through **Vehapphala** and **Subhakiṇṇa,** and it was then that he conceived the belief that he was eternal.

The Buddha visited him and convinced him of the error of his belief.[9] When the universe is dissolved after the lapse of a long epoch and is again evolved, beings are mostly born in the Ābhassara world. When, sooner or later, the world begins to re-evolve (*vivaṭṭati*), the **Brahmavimāna** appears, but it is empty. Then some being or other, either because he has finished his life there or because his merit is exhausted, leaves the Ābhassara world and is reborn in the Brahmavimāna. Others follow his example, and it is then that the first to be reborn in the Brahma-world thinks of himself as Brahmā, the eternal, etc.[10]

When inhabitants of the Ābhassara-world are reborn as humans, their existence continues to be like that which they had in the brahma-world itself. As time goes on, however, they lose their qualities and develop the characteristics, both physical and mental, of human beings.[11] Buddhaghosa[12] says that their birth on earth is *opapātika* (by spontaneous regeneration) and they are mind-born (*manomaya*).

On the occasions when the world is destroyed by fire, the fire spread up to the Ābhassara-world; when by water, the water rises to the **Subhakiṇṇa**; when by wind, the wind reaches to the **Vehapphala.**[13]

According to Buddhaghosa,[14] the Ābhassaras are so called because radiance spreads from their bodies in all directions, like flames from a

[3] A. ii. 127; but see Abhs. v. 6, where their life-span is given as eight kappas.

[4] A. iii. 202; D. iii. 219.

[5] A. iv. 40, 401; D. ii. 69; D. iii. 253.

[6] A. v. 60.

[7] *E.g.*, M. i. 289.

[8] AA. i. 73; J. i. 406, 473; M. i. 329; MA. i. 553; SA. i. 162.

[9] J. iii. 359.

[10] D. iii. 29.

[11] For details see D. iii. 84 ff., PsA. 253.

[12] DA. iii. 865.

[13] CypA. 9.

[14] MA. i. 29; VibhA. 520; *cp.* DA. ii. 510.

torch (*daṇḍadīpikāya acci viya etesaṃ sarīrato ābhā chijjitvā chijjitvā patantī viya sarati visaratī ti Ābhassarā*).

Ābhā.—A generic name for devas distinguished for their brilliance, such as the **Parittābhā** and the **Appamāṇābhā**.[1]

[1] M. iii. 102; MA. ii. 902.

Ābhā Vagga.—The fifteenth chapter of the *Catukka Nipāta* of the *Aṅguttara Nikāya*. It consists of ten suttas on such subjects as the four splendours, the four due seasons, the four sins and virtues of speech and the four choicest parts (*sāras*).[1]

[1] A. ii. 139-41.

Ābhā Sutta.—There are four radiances: that of the moon, the sun, of fire, and of wisdom, the last being the chief.[1]

[1] A. ii. 139.

Āmakadhañña-peyyāla.—The ninth chapter of the *Sacca Saṃyutta* of the *Saṃyutta Nikāya*. It contains a list of the gifts which Āriyan monks abstain from accepting.[1]

[1] S. v. 470-3.

Āmagandha.—A brahmin. Before the appearance of the Buddha in the world, Āmagandha became an ascetic and lived in the region of the Himālaya with five hundred pupils. They ate neither fish nor flesh. Every year they came down from their hermitage in search of salt and vinegar, and the inhabitants of a village near by received them with great honour and showed them every hospitality for four months.

Then one day the Buddha, with his monks, visited the same village, and the people having listened to his preaching became his followers. That year when Āmagandha and his disciples went as usual to the village, the householders did not show towards them the same enthusiasm as heretofore. The brahmin, enquiring what had happened, was full of excitement on hearing that the Buddha had been born, and wished to know if he ate "*āmagandha*," by which he meant fish or flesh. He was greatly disappointed on learning that the Buddha did not forbid the eating of *āmagandha*, but, desiring to hear about it from the Buddha himself, he sought him at Jetavana. The Buddha told him that *āmagandha* was not really fish or flesh, but that it referred to evil actions, and that he who wished to avoid it should abstain from evil deeds of every kind. The same question had been put to the Buddha **Kassapa** by an ascetic named **Tissa**, who later became his chief disciple. In giving an account of the conversation between Kassapa Buddha and Tissa, the Buddha preached to Āmagandha the **Āmagandha Sutta.** The brahmin and his followers entered the Order and in a few days became arahants.[1]

[1] Sn., pp. 42-5; SnA. i. 278 ff.

Āmagandha Sutta.—The conversation between the Buddha and the brahmin **Āmagandha** mentioned above.[1] According to Buddhaghosa[2] this was merely a reproduction of the conversation of the Buddha **Kassapa** with the ascetic **Tissa,** who later became his chief disciple.

The sutta is particularly interesting as being one of the few passages in which sayings of the previous Buddhas are recorded. The Buddha's view is put forward as being identical with that which had been enunciated long ago, with the intended implication that it was a self-evident proposition accepted by all the wise.

[1] Sn. 42 ff. [2] SnA. i. 280 ff.

Āmaṇḍagāmaṇī Abhaya.—Son of **Mahādāṭhika** and King of Ceylon for nine years and eight months. His younger brother, by whom he was ultimately slain, was **Kanirajānu-Tissa,** and he had two children, a son **Cūḷābhaya** and a daughter **Sīvalī. Iḷanāga** was his nephew.

Āmaṇḍagāmaṇī heightened the cone of the **Mahā Thūpa** and made additions to the **Lohapāsāda** and the **Thūpārāma.** He also built the **Rajatalena Vihāra** and the **Mahāgāmeṇḍi** tank to the south of **Anurādhapura,** which latter he gave for the use of the **Dakkhiṇavihāra.** He enacted an order that there should be no slaughter of animals in Ceylon and had gourds planted everywhere. To the whole brotherhood of monks in the island he once gave robes and alms-bowls filled with *kumbhaṇḍaka* fruits (pumpkins) and thereafter he was known by the name of Āmaṇḍagāmaṇī.[1]

His brother Kaṇirajānu-Tissa, having killed him, succeeded to the throne.[2] Āmaṇḍagāmaṇī is also referred to as **Āmaṇḍa** and **Amaṇḍiya.**

[1] *Āmaṇḍa* is evidently a synonym of *Kumbhaṇḍaka.*
[2] Mhv. xxxv. 1-10; MṬ. 640.

Āmaṇḍaphaladāyaka Thera.—An arahant. In a previous birth, while carrying a pingo laden with fruit, he saw the Buddha **Padumuttara** and offered him an *āmaṇḍa* fruit (pumpkin ?). In the present age he became an arahant.[1]

[1] Ap. ii. 459.

Āmalakīvana.—A grove at **Cātumā.** The Buddha once stayed there, and it was on that occasion that the *Cātuma Sutta* was preached.[1]

[1] M. i. 456.

Āmalacetiya.—A thūpa in Ceylon. It is not known who built it. **Aggabodhi I.** erected a parasol over it.[1]

[1] Cv. xlii. 62.

Āmisakiñcikkha Sutta.—One of the suttas in a group of eight, dealing with people who will not lie for the sake of gain—and, in this case, for the sake of anything worldly whatsoever.[1]

[1] S. ii. 234.

1. **Āyatana Sutta.**—Once when the Buddha was staying in the Kūṭāgārasālā in **Vesāli,** he preached to the monks a sermon on the six spheres of contact (*saḷāyatana*). The monks listened with rapt attention until **Māra,** making a terrible din, disturbed their peace of mind. The Buddha admonished the monks not to be led away by Māra, and the latter, discomfited, disappeared.[1]

[1] S. i. 112.

2. **Āyatana Sutta.**—The four Āriyan truths are concerned with the six personal spheres of sense. Effort should be made to realise this.[1]

[1] S. v. 426.

Āyasmanta.—A general of King **Sāhasamalla.** Āyasmanta deposed the king and installed **Kalyāṇavatī,** chief queen of **Kittinissaṅka,** on the throne of Ceylon. It was he who really administered the government, the queen's power being only nominal. The *Cūlavaṃsa* calls him a man of almost unsurpassable courage, a descendant of the **Khandhāvara** family. He slew the **Adhikārin Deva** and had a vihāra erected at **Valliggāma.** He also built a *pariveṇa* called after him **Sarājakulavaḍḍhana** (this evidently being one of his honorific titles) and gave land and other possessions for its maintenance. He had a text-book of law compiled for the use of administrators.

He was slain by the **Mahādipāda Anīkaṅga.**[1]

[1] Cv. lxxx. 33-44. For further details see Geiger Cv. *Trs.* ii. 130, n. 2.

Āyāgadāyaka Thera.—An arahant. In a previous birth he worshipped with gladsome heart the thūpa of **Sikhī** Buddha and gave carpenters money to build an *āyāga*.[1] As a result he was born in deva worlds and could bring even the devas into subjection. He could produce rain at will.[2]

[1] A long almshall, says ApA. [2] Ap. i. 89-90.

1. **Āyācana Vagga.**—The twelfth chapter of the *Duka Nipāta* of the *Aṅguttara Nikāya*. It contains eleven suttas on different topics.[1]

[1] A. i. 89-91.

2. **Āyācana Vagga.**—The third chapter of the *Rādha Saṃyutta* of the *Saṃyutta Nikāya*.[1]

[1] S. iii. 198-200.

1. **Āyācana Sutta.**—The good monk, if he would perfectly aspire, should wish to be like **Sāriputta** and **Moggallāna**; the nun to be like **Khemā** and **Uppalavaṇṇā**; the householder like **Citta** and **Hatthaka**; the house-mistress like **Khujjuttarā** and **Veḷukaṇṭakī**, the mother of **Nanda.**[1]

[1] A. ii. 164.

2. **Āyācana Sutta.**—Contains the story of the reluctance felt by the Buddha, while meditating at **Uruvelā,** in the eighth week after the Enlightenment, to preach his doctrine to the world, feeling that it would not appeal to the human temperament; and of the appearance before him, of the **Brahmā Sahampatī,** who had read his thoughts and who entreated him to overcome this reluctance. He assured the Buddha that there were in the world many who would comprehend the Dhamma if they heard it. The Buddha saw that this assurance was justified and agreed to set forth as a teacher.[1]

The sutta appears verbatim in the *Vinaya*[2] and almost verbatim in the *Dīgha Nikāya*,[3] as an episode in the life of each of the Buddhas mentioned there, but with two variants; the Brahmā repeats his request three times and the stanzas in which the request is made, as given in the *Saṃyutta*, are omitted.

[1] S. i. 136 ff. [2] i. 4 ff. [3] ii. 36 ff.

Āyācitabhatta Jātaka (No. 19).—Once the squire of a certain village, in the **Kāsi** country, promised the deity of a banyan tree a sacrifice should his enterprise succeed. When he came back from his journey he slew a number of creatures and took them to the tree. The deity of the tree appeared and admonished the squire, saying that no one could attain deliverance by means of slaughter.

The story was related in answer to a question by some monks, who had noticed that many people when going on a business journey would slay living creatures and offer them to various deities in order that their ventures might be successful. The monks wished to know if such sacrifices were of any good.[1]

The Jātaka is also known as the *Pāṇavadha Jātaka.*[2]

[1] J. i. 169. [2] Feer: JA. 1876, p. 516.

1. **Āyu Sutta.**—Preached at the **Kalandakanivāpa** in **Rājagaha.** The Buddha tells the monks that human life is very brief and has its sequel elsewhere. Therefore good must be done and the holy life must be lived. **Māra** approaches the Buddha and suggests that men should take no heed of death, but should enjoy life like a babe replete with milk. The Buddha points out to him the error of such a view.[1]

[1] S. i. 108.

2. **Āyu Sutta.**—Preached at the same place, on another occasion. **Māra** utters the same sentiment and the Buddha refutes his views. Māra retires vanquished.[1]

[1] S. i. 108-9.

Āyupāla.—A thera who lived in the **Saṅkheyya Pariveṇa** near **Sāgala.** King **Milinda's** royal astrologer informed the Elder that the king wished to see him, and the king, having obtained his permission, visited him at the Pariveṇa, attended by five hundred **Yonakas.** The king discussed with the Elder the aim of those who became monks, and Āyupāla was unable to meet the king's arguments.[1]

[1] Mil. 19 f.

Āyupālā (Āyupālī).—An arahant therī, preceptor of **Saṅghamittā.**[1]

[1] Mhv. v. 208; Sp. i. 51.

Āyuvaḍḍhana Kumāra.—Two brahmins of **Dīghalambika** became ascetics and practised austerities for forty-eight years. Then one of them returned to the world and having procured cattle and money, married and begot a son whom he called **Dīghāyu.** Later, when his former companion came to the city, the householder visited him with his wife and child. When they made obeisance to him, the ascetic said, "Long life to you" to the man and his wife, but not to the child. When questioned, the ascetic told them that their son had but seven days to live, and suggested that they should visit the Buddha and ask him if there were any means of averting the child's fate. They did so and the Buddha, who was then staying at the **Araññakuṭikā** in **Dīghalambika,** told them to erect a pavilion outside the door of their house. This they did, and in the pavilion the monks recited the *Paritta* continuously for seven days with the child seated before them on a bench. On the seventh day the Buddha himself came and hosts of devas gathered round him. The yakkha **Avaruddhaka,** who had been granted the boon of eating Dīghāyu, appeared to claim him at the time appointed for his death, but on account of the presence of the devas, he could not come near the boy. The Buddha recited the *Paritta* all night long, and when the seventh day had passed Avaruddhaka could no longer claim the child. The Buddha declared that the boy would live for one hundred and twenty years and he was renamed **Āyuvaḍḍhana.** When he grew up he became the leader of five hundred lay disciples.[1]

[1] DhA. ii. 235 ff.

Āyussa Sutta.—Two in number, on the five conditions (such as excessive eating), which do not bestow long life, and on the five conditions which do.[1]

[1] A. iii. 145.

Āyūra. Minister of **Maddava,** king of **Benares.** When Maddava was grieved at the loss of his wife, Āyūra and his colleague **Pukkusa** helped the king's counsellor **Senaka** to quench the king's sorrow. The story is told in the *Dasaṇṇaka Jātaka*[1].

In the present age Āyūra became **Moggallāna.**[2]

[1] J. iii. 337 ff. [2] *Ibid.*, 341.

Ārakkha Sutta.—Earnest care should be exerted to guard one's thoughts from running riot among passionate things, from being malicious, from being deluded and from following the path laid down by various recluses (false teachers ?).[1]

[1] A. ii. 120.

1. **Ārakkhadāyaka Thera.**—An arahant. In a previous birth he built a railing (*vedi*) round the thūpa of the Buddha **Siddhattha** and made provision for its protection. Six kappas ago he was a king named **Apassena.**[1]

[1] Ap. i. 214-15.

2. **Ārakkhadāyaka Thera.** An arahant. He put a fence round the thūpa of the Buddha **Dhammadinna** and arranged for its protection. This act resulted in his becoming an arahant in the present age.[1]

[1] Ap. i. 253.

Ārañjara.—See **Arañjara.**

Ārabhati Sutta.—There are five kinds of people in the world. Those who commit faults and repent, etc.[1]

[1] A. iii. 165-7.

Ārabbhavatthu Sutta.—On the eight occasions in which exertion should be applied.[1]

[1] A. iv. 334 f.

1. **Ārammaṇa Sutta.**—Some who practise meditation are skilled in concentration, but not in the object of concentration (*ārammaṇa*), some *vice versa*, some are skilled in both, some in neither.[1]

[1] S. iii. 266.

2. **Ārammaṇa Sutta.**—Some are skilled in the object of concentration but not in the range of it, etc. (*As before.*)[1]

[1] S. iii. 275.

Āravāḷa.—See **Aravāḷa.**

Āramā Vagga.—The sixth division of the *Pācittiya* of the *Bhikkhunī Vibhaṅga.*[1]

[1] Vin. iv. 306-17.

Ārāma Sutta.—See **Sāriputta-Koṭṭhita** Sutta.

Ārāmadaṇḍa.—A brahmin. Once when **Mahā Kaccāna** was staying at **Varaṇā** on the banks of the **Kaddamadaha,** Ārāmadaṇḍa came to see him and asked him why nobles quarrelled with nobles, brahmins with brahmins, and householders with householders. "Because of their bondage and servitude to sensual lusts," answered Mahā Kaccāna; and for the same reason recluses quarrelled with recluses. "Is there anybody in the world who has passed beyond this bondage?" "Yes," said Mahā Kaccāna, "in **Sāvatthi** lives the Exalted One," and he proceeded to describe the Buddha's virtues. Ārāmadaṇḍa stood up with clasped hands and, turning in the direction of Sāvatthi, he uttered his adoration of the Buddha. Thenceforward he became a disciple of Mahā Kaccāna.[1]

[1] A. i. 65-7.

Ārāmadāyaka Thera.—An arahant. In a past life he planted a garden with shady trees for the Buddha **Siddhattha,** and gave the Buddha the fruits and flowers that grew there. Thirty-seven kappas ago he was born seven times as king, by name **Mudusītala.**[1]

[1] Ap. i. 251.

1. **Ārāmadūsaka Jātaka** (No. 46).—Once in Benares there was a festival and all the townsfolk assembled to keep holiday. The king's gardener, wishing to join in the festivities, approached the king of the monkeys who lived in the royal garden and, pointing out to him all the benefits the monkeys had derived from their residence there, asked him if he would get the monkeys to water the trees in the gardener's absence. The monkey-king agreed and, when the man had gone, distributed the water-skins and water-pots among the monkeys. In order that the water should not be wasted, he gave instructions to the monkeys that they should pull out the trees by the roots and give plenty of water to those plants whose roots went deep and little to those with small roots. A wise man, happening to see this being done, and reflecting how with every desire to do good, the foolish only succeed in doing harm, rebuked the monkey-king.

The story was told by the Buddha while staying in a hamlet in **Kosala.** The squire of the village invited the Buddha and his monks to a meal and at the conclusion of the meal gave them leave to stroll about in the grounds. In their walk the monks came across a bare patch of land and learnt from the the gardener that it was caused by a lad who had been asked to water the plants there and who, before watering them had pulled them out to see how they grew. This was reported to the Buddha, who related the story of the past.[1]

[1] J. i. 249-51. The story is sculptured in the Bharhut Stūpa. See Cunningham, Pl. xlv. 5.

2. **Ārāmadūsaka Jātaka** (No. 268).—Same as the above except that the monkeys are asked to water the garden for seven days, and the conversation between the wise man (in this case a young man of good family belonging to Benares) and the monkey-king is different.

The story is told in reference to a lad in **Dakkhiṇāgiri** and not in **Kosala** as above.[1]

[1] J. ii. 345-7.

Ārāmassa.—A village in Ceylon, given by **King Udaya I.** for the maintenance of a *Loharūpa* (bronze statue) of the Buddha.[1]

[1] Cv. xlix. 17.

Ārāmikagāma.—The name given to the village in which lived the five hundred park-keepers who were given by **Bimbisāra** to the Elder **Pilindavaccha.** It was near **Rājagaha** and was also called **Pilindagāma.** Pilindavaccha depended for his alms on the residents of this village.[1]

[1] Vin. i. 207-8; iii. 249.

Āriyakkhattayodhā.—The mercenary soldiers employed in Ceylon. Their chief was a general called **Ṭhakuraka.** When the Senāpati **Mitta** obtained possession of the throne, he sought to win the favour of these soldiers by giving them money. This they refused to accept and Ṭhakuraka, going up to Mitta as he sat on the throne, cut off his head. On being questioned, he said that he had done the deed at the command of the lawful king, **Bhuvanekabāhu I.,** who had become a refugee. The Āriya soldiers then joined forces with the Sīhala army and restored Bhuvanekabāhu to the throne.[1]

Geiger[2] thinks that these mercenaries must have come from South India. The name of their general, Ṭhakuraka, however, seems to indicate that they were Rajputs.

[1] Cv. xc. 16-30.

[2] Cv. *Trs.* ii. 202, n. 3.

Āriyacakkavatti.—A Damiḷa general who came with a large army from the **Paṇḍu** kingdom and landed in Ceylon during the famine in the reign of **Bhuvanekabāhu I.** We are told that though he was no "Āriya" he was a dignitary of great power. He laid waste the kingdom and entered the capital **Subhagiri.** There he seized the Tooth Relic and the costly treasures which were kept with it and took them back to King **Kulasekhara**[1].

[1] Cv. xc. 43-7. Kulasekhara reigned 1268-1308. His general Āriyacakkavatti is mentioned in a South Indian Inscription (No. 110, in the *Annual Report of Epigraphy, Southern Circle, Madras,* 1903).

Ārohanta.—One of the chief ministers at **Sāvatthi.** He joined the Order of monks and his wife became a nun. They had their meals together and she waited on him, fetching him water and fanning him. He forbade her to wait on him as it was improper and, angered by his words, she poured the water over his head and struck him with the fan. For this she was rebuked by the Buddha.[1]

[1] Vin. iv. 263.

1. **Ālamba.**—Probably the name of a divine musician, one of a large number who wait on **Sakka** and on his wives.[1] Dhammapāla[2] quotes this view and objects to it, saying that the name is not that of a musician but of a musical instrument. The opinion that the name denotes a celestial musician seems, however, to be the right one.[3]

[1] Vv., pp. 16, 47.
[2] VvA. 96.
[3] For a discussion see Hardy: *Vimānavatthu Commentary* (P.T.S. Ed.), 372-3.

2. **Ālamba.**—See **Ālambāyana.**

Ālambagāma.—A tank in Ceylon built by **Jeṭṭhatissa.**[1]

[1] Mhv. xxxvi. 131.

Ālambanadāyaka Thera.—An arahant. In a past birth he gave an ālambana (prop ?) to the Buddha Atthadassī. Sixty kappas ago he was born three times as king under the name of **Ekāpassita.**[1]

[1] Ap. i. 213.

Ālambāyana.—Originally the name of a spell taught to an ascetic by a Garuḍa king who had unwittingly torn up by its roots a banyan tree which grew at the end of the ascetic's walk. The ascetic taught it to a poor brahmin of Benares who had gone into the forest to escape his creditors and who ministered to the ascetic. The brahmin became known as Ālambāyana after he learnt the spell. Having learnt it he left the forest and was walking along the banks of the **Yamunā**, when he came across a host of Nāgas, sitting, after their sports, round the Nāga gem which grants all desires. The Nāgas, hearing the man repeat the charm, fled in terror, believing him to be the Garuḍa, and he took possession of their jewel. Soon after, Ālambāyana met an outcast brahmin with his son, **Somadatta**, and on their agreeing to show him the Nāga King, **Bhūridatta**, he gave them the jewel. With the help of his spell Ālambāyana tamed Bhūridatta and went about giving exhibitions of the Nāga's skill. Bhūridatta was finally rescued by his brother **Sudassana** and his sister **Accimukhī**. In the contest of skill which Ālambāyana had with Sudassana, Accimukhī (*q.v.*) assumed the form of a frog and let drip three drops of poison on her brother's hand, and these were allowed to fall into a hole specially prepared and filled with cow-dung. A flame burst out and Ālambāyana was smitten with the heat. His skin changed colour and he became a white leper.

The story is told in the *Bhūridatta Jātaka.*[1]

The name Ālambāyana appears also as **Ālambāna** and as **Ālamba.**

[1] J. vi. 179-97.

Alindaka.—Probably the name of a monastery in Ceylon where lived the thera **Mahā Phussadeva** (*q.v.*).[1]

[1] SA.iii. 154; VibhA. 352.

Āluvadāyaka Thera.—An arahant. Thirty-one kappas ago he gave an *āluva* (fruit ?) to the Pacceka Buddha **Sudassana,** near Himavā.[1]

[1] Ap. i. 237.

Āloka Sutta.—There are four lights: of the moon, the sun, of fire and of wisdom, the light of wisdom being the chief.[1]

[1] A. ii. 139.

Ālokalena.—A cave in the cleft of a mighty primeval landslide, not far from the modern Matale in Ceylon. According to tradition it was here that the Buddhist scriptures were first reduced to writing in Ceylon under the patronage of a chieftain of King **Vaṭṭagāmaṇi.** The Burmese believe that Buddhaghosa's *Aṭṭhakathās* were also written in this spot.[1] In the eighteenth century King **Vijayarājasīha** built images of the Buddha in the rock cave.[2]

[1] Mhv. xxiii. 100 f. See PLC. 43 f.

[2] Cv. xcviii. 65.

Āḷakamandā.—A city of the gods, mighty, prosperous and full of devas.[1] It was one of the chief cities of **Uttarakuru,** and a royal residence of **Kuvera.**[2] It is probably another name for **Alakā.** The name is used as a simile to describe cities of great wealth.[3] In the *Culla Vagga*[4] the word is used as an adjective (*vihārā āḷakamandā honti*) to mean crowded with people, and Buddhaghosa explains it by saying "*āḷakamandā ti ekaṅganā manussābhikiṇṇā.*"

[1] D. ii. 147, 170; Mil. 2.

[2] D. iii. 201; Cv. xxxix. 5.

[3] *E.g.*, Cv. xxxvii. 106; lxxxi. 3; MṬ. 411; BuA. 55.

[4] Vin. ii. 152.

Āḷambara.—The drum of the **Asuras** made from the claw of the crab of **Kulīradaha.** (For the story see *s.v.* **Āṇaka.**) When the Asuras were defeated in battle they left the drum in their flight and **Sakka** took possession of it. Its sound resembled a peal of thunder and for that reason, probably, came to be called **Āḷambara-megha.**[1]

[1] J. ii. 344.

Āḷava Sutta.—Records the conversation between the Buddha and **Ālavaka Yakkha** (*q.v.*) at **Āḷavī.**[1]

[1] S. i. 213-15.

1. **Āḷavaka.**—The king of **Āḷavi**. He was in the habit of holding a hunt once in seven days to keep his army in trim. One day when he was hunting, the quarry escaped from where the king lay in wait and, according to custom, it became the king's duty to capture it. He, therefore, followed the animal for three leagues, killed it and, having cut it in half, carried it in a pingo. On his way back he happened to pass under the banyan tree which was the abode of the Yakkha **Āḷavaka.** The Yakkha had been granted a boon by the Yakkha-king, which allowed him to eat anybody who came within the shadow of the tree. Accordingly, he seized the king, but later released him on obtaining his promise that he would provide him at regular intervals with a human being and a bowl of food.[1] For the rest of the story see **Āḷavaka Yakkha.**

[1] SnA. i. 217 ff.

2. **Āḷavaka.**—The yakkha referred to above. King **Āḷavaka**, with the help of the Mayor of the town (*Nagaraguttika*) and his ministers, was able to keep his promise for some time, by sending criminals to the Yakkha. The Yakkha's power was such that at the sight of him men's bodies became as soft as butter. Soon there were no criminals left, and each household was forced to contribute one child for sacrifice to the Yakkha. Then women, about to bring forth children, began to leave the king's capital. Twelve years passed in this manner and the only child left was the king's own son, **Āḷavaka Kumāra.** When the king learnt this, he ordered the child to be dressed in all splendour and taken to the Yakkha. The Buddha, with his Eye of Compassion, saw what was going to happen and went to the Yakkha's abode.

Āḷavaka was away at a meeting of the Yakkhas in Himavā. His doorkeeper **Gadrabha** admitted the Buddha, after warning him of the Yakkha's unmannerly nature. The Buddha went in and sat down on Āḷavaka's throne while Gadrabha went to Himavā to announce to his master the Buddha's arrival. While the Buddha was there, preaching to Āḷavaka's women-folk, the Yakkhas **Sātāgira** and **Hemavata,** passing through the air on their way to the assembly in Himavā, being made aware of the Buddha's presence by their inability to fly over him, descended to Āḷavaka's palace and made obeisance to the Buddha before resuming their journey.

When Āḷavaka heard from Gadrabha and from Sātāgira and Hemavata of the Buddha's visit, he was greatly incensed and uttering aloud his name, he hurried to his abode. There with all the various supernatural powers he could command he tried to dislodge the Buddha from his seat, but without success, even his special weapon, the **Dussāvudha** being of no avail against the Buddha. Then, approaching the Buddha, Āḷavaka asked him to leave his house, which the Buddha did. He then summoned the Buddha back and he came. Three times this happened and three times the Buddha obeyed, judging compliance to be the best way of softening his wrath, but the fourth time the Buddha refused to return. Thereupon Āḷavaka expressed his desire to ask questions of the Buddha, hoping thereby to fatigue him. The Buddha agreed, and when he had answered all the questions to Āḷavaka's satisfaction, the latter became a Sotāpanna.[1]

At dawn of day, King Āḷavaka's men brought the young prince, Āḷavaka-Kumāra to the Yakkha, as sacrifice. Hearing the Yakkha's shouts of joy at the close of the Buddha's sermon, they greatly marvelled. When they announced to Āḷavaka that they had brought their offering, and handed him the child, he was much ashamed because of the Buddha's presence. Āḷavaka gave the child to the Buddha, who blessed him and gave him back to the king's messengers. The boy, having passed from the Yakkha's hands to those of the Buddha, and from there to the king's men, thereafter became known as **Hatthaka Āḷavaka.**[2]

When the king and the citizens heard that the Yakkha had become a follower of the Buddha, they built for him a special abode near that of **Vessavaṇa** and provided him with endless gifts of flowers, perfumes, etc., for his use.[3] Āḷavaka's abode was thirty leagues from **Sāvatthi,** and the Buddha covered the whole journey in one day.[4] The abode was near a banyan tree and on the ground (*bhummaṭṭhaṃ,*) well protected with walls, etc., and covered on the top by a metal net, it was like a cart enclosed on all sides. It was three leagues in extent, and over it lay the road to Himavā by air.[5] Ascetics, having seen the glittering palace, often called to find out what it was. Āḷavaka would ask them questions regarding their faith, and when they could not answer he would assume a subtle form and, entering their hearts, would drive them mad.[6]

Āḷavaka shouted his name before starting from Himavā to vanquish the Buddha. He stood with his left foot on **Manosilātala** and his right on **Kelāsakūṭa.** His shout was heard throughout Jambudīpa and was one of the four shouts, mentioned in tradition, as having travelled so far.[7] Āḷavaka had a special weapon, the **Dussāvudha**, comparable to Sakka's **Vajirāvudha,** Vessavaṇa's **Gadāvudha** and Yama's **Nayanāvudha.** It

[1] SnA. i. 239.

[2] *Ibid.*, 239-40.

[3] The story of Āḷavaka, of which the above is a summary, is given in full in SnA. i. 217-40 and in SA. i. 244-59. It is also given in brief in AA. i. 211-12 and with some difference in detail.

[4] SnA. i. 220.

[5] *Ibid.*, 222.

[6] *Ibid.*, 228.

[7] *Ibid.*, 223; for the others see *s.v.* **Puṇṇaka, Vissakamma** and **Kusā.**

had the power, if it were thrown into the sky, of stopping rain for twelve years and if cast on the earth of destroying all trees and crops for a like period. If hurled into the sea it would dry up all the water, and it could shatter Sineru into pieces. It was made of cloth and is described as a vatthāvudha, and it was worn as a part of the Yakkha's upper garment (*uttariya*).

There are three salient features in the story of Āḷavaka which link it closely to the large circle of stories grouped by Professor Watanabe[8] under the title of *Kalmāsapāda* stories: (1) The man-eating Yakkha; (2) the captured king saving himself by a promise to provide the Yakkha with offerings, and the sanctity of that promise; and (3) the conversion of the Yakkha.

The conversion of Āḷavaka is considered one of the chief incidents of the Buddha's life.[9]

Āḷavaka's name appears in the *Atānāṭiya Sutta*, among the Yakkhas to whom followers of the Buddha should appeal for protection in time of need.[10] (See also **Āḷavaka Sutta.**)

[8] *J.P.T.S.* 1909-10, pp. 240 ff.
[9] *E.g.*, J. iv. 180; vi. 329; Mhv. xxx. 84.
[10] D. iii. 205.

1. **Āḷavaka Sutta.**—Records the eight questions asked of the Buddha by **Āḷavaka Yakkha** and the answers given by the Buddha. It is said[1] that Āḷavaka's parents had learnt the questions and their answers from **Kassapa** Buddha and had taught them to Āḷavaka in his youth; but he could not remember them and, in order that they might be preserved, he had them written on a gold leaf with red paint, and this he stored away in his palace. When the Buddha answered the questions he found that the answers were exactly the same as those given by Kassapa.[2]

The sutta appears both in *Sutta Nipāta*[3] and in the *Saṃyutta Nikāya*.[4] The Āḷavaka Sutta is also included in the collection of *Parittas*.

[1] SnA. i. 228.
[2] *Ibid.*, 231.
[3] pp. 31-3.
[4] i. 213 ff.

2. **Āḷavaka Sutta.**—A conversation between the Buddha and **Hatthaka Āḷavaka** in which the Buddha states that he is among those who enjoy real happiness.[1]

[1] A. i. 136 f.

Āḷavaka-gajjita.—Mentioned in a list of works considered by Buddhaghosa to be heretical.[1]

[1] SA. ii. 150; Sp. iv. 742.

Āḷavaka-pucchā.—A name for the questions asked by Āḷavaka of the Buddha and mentioned in the *Āḷavaka Sutta* (*q.v.*). When the Sāsana gradually falls into abeyance, questions such as these and the questions in the *Sabhiya-pucchā*, will remain in the memories of men, but they will not suffice to keep the religion alive.[1]

[1] VibhA. 432.

Āḷavakā (*v.l.* **Āḷavikā**).—A name given to the monks of **Āḷavī.** Buddhaghosa[1] says that all children born in Āḷavī were called Āḷavakā. The **Āḷavakā-bhikkhū** are mentioned several times in the *Vinaya*[2] in connection with offences relating to *navakamma* (repairing and reconstruction of buildings), and rules are laid down by the Buddha restricting these monks in their activities. Once when one of the monks was cutting down a tree which was the abode of a devatā, the sprite was sorely tempted to kill him, but restraining her wrath she sought the Buddha and complained to him. The Buddha praised her forbearance and preached the *Uraga Sutta.*[3]

In the introductory story of the *Maṇikaṇṭha Jātaka*[4] it is stated that the importunities of these monks so annoyed the residents of Āḷavī that they fled at the approach of any yellow-robed monk.

[1] Sp. iii. 561.
[2] ii. 172 ff.; iii. 85; iv. 34-5.
[3] SnA. i. 4-5.
[4] J. ii. 282-3.

Āḷavandapperumāla.—A Damiḷa general defeated by **Parakkamabāhu I.**[1] He belonged to the immediate retinue of King **Kulasekhara.** In the battle of **Pātapa** he was wounded and fled, but his enemies succeeded in slaying the horse on which he rode.[2] He is perhaps to be identified with **Āḷavanda** who was slain by Parakkamabāhu in the village of **Vaḍali.**[3]

[1] Cv. lxxvi. 128. [2] *Ibid.*, 223, 232. [3] *Ibid.*, 134.

Āḷavi-Gotama.—A thera, who, according to Buddhaghosa,[1] attained arahantship through faith. He is mentioned in the *Sutta Nipāta*[2] in a verse spoken by the Buddha to **Piṅgiya** when the Buddha appeared in a ray of light at **Bāvarī's** hermitage.

[1] SnA. ii. 606. [2] vers. 1146.

1. **Āḷavikā.**—See **Āḷavakā.**

2. **Āḷavikā.**—A nun. See **Selā.**

Āḷavikā Sutta.—Contains the conversation between **Āḷavikā (Selā)** and Marā which ended in the latter's discomfiture.[1]

[1] S. i. 128 f.

Āḷavī.—A town thirty yojanas from **Sāvatthi**[1] and probably twelve from Benares.[2] It lay between Sāvatthi and **Rājagaha.**[3] The Buddha, on several occasions, stayed at Āḷavī at the **Aggāḷava** shrine (*q.v.*) which was near the town. In the sixteenth year after the Enlightenment, the Buddha spent the whole of the rainy season at Āḷavī and preached the doctrine to 84,000 listeners.[4] The King of Āḷavī was known as **Āḷavaka** and the inhabitants as **Āḷavakā.** The town later became famous as the residence of **Āḷavaka Yakkha** and of **Hatthaka Āḷavaka.** The therī, **Selā** was born in Āḷavī and was therefore known as **Āḷavikā.**[5] There was evidently a large community of monks at Āḷavī, some of whom seem to have chiefly occupied themselves with building vihāras for themselves.[6]

Once, while at Sāvatthi, the Buddha saw a poor farmer of Āḷavī, ready for conversion and decided to go and preach in that town. The farmer's ox had strayed away, and he looked for it for quite a long while before finding it; he knew that the Buddha was in Āḷavi and decided that he still had time to visit the Buddha, and he set off without taking any food. Meanwhile at Āḷavī the Buddha and his monks had been served with a meal by the people, but the Buddha waited until the farmer came before returning thanks. On the farmer's arrival the Buddha ordered that some food should be given him, and when the man was comforted and his mind was ready the Buddha preached a sermon, at the end of which the man became a Sotāpanna.[7]

On another occasion the Buddha came all the way from **Jetavana** to Āḷavī for the sake of a weaver's daughter.[8]

Āḷavī has been identified by Cunningham and Hoernle with Newal or Nawal in the Urao district in the United Provinces, and by Nandalal Dey, with Aviwa, twenty-seven miles north-east of Etwah.[9]

Mrs. Rhys Davids states that Āḷavī was on the bank of the Ganges,[10] probably basing her view on the declaration of Āḷavaka in the *Sutta Nipāta*[11] that he would throw the Buddha "pāra-Gaṅgāya" (over to

[1] SnA. i. 220.

[2] See Watters: ii. 61; Fa Hsein, 60, 62.

[3] The Buddha goes from **Sāvatthi** to **Kiṭāgiri,** thence to **Āḷavi,** and finally, to **Rājagaha.** (Vin. ii. 170-5.)

[4] BuA. 3.

[5] ThigA. 62-3.

[6] See *s.v.*, Aḷavakā.

[7] DhA. iii. 262-3.

[8] For the story see DhA. iii. 170 f.

[9] Law: *Geog. of. Early Buddhism*, p. 24.

[10] *Ps. of the Brethren*, 408.

[11] p. 32.

the other side of the Ganges) unless his questions were answered. I believe that here "pāra-Gaṅgāya" is merely a rhetorical expression and has no geographical significance.

Āḷāra.—See **Aḷāra.**

Āḷāra Kālāma.—One of the two teachers to whom **Gotama,** after his renunciation, first attached himself,[1] the other being **Uddaka Rāmaputta.** In the *Ariyapariyesāna Sutta*[2] the Buddha describes his visit to Āḷāra. Gotama quickly mastered his doctrine and was able to repeat it by heart; but feeling sure that Āḷāra not only knew the doctrine but had realised it, he approached him and questioned him about it. Āḷāra then proclaimed the *Ākiñcaññāyatana*, and Gotama, putting forth energy and concentration greater than Āḷāra's, made himself master of that state. Āḷāra recognised his pupil's eminence and treated him as an equal, but Gotama, not having succeeded in his quest, took leave of Āḷāra to go elsewhere.[3] When, after having practised austerities for six years, the Buddha attained Enlightenment and granted **Sahampati's** request to preach the doctrine, it was of Āḷāra he thought first as being the fittest to hear the teaching. But Āḷāra had died seven days earlier.[4]

The books mention little else about Āḷāra. The *Mahā Parinibbāna Sutta*[5] mentions a Mallian, **Pukkusa,** who says he had been Āḷāra's disciple, but who, when he hears the Buddha's sermon, confesses faith in the Buddha. Pukkusa describes Āḷāra to the Buddha as one who practised great concentration. Once Āḷāra was sitting in the open air and neither saw nor heard five hundred passing carts though he was awake and conscious.

As already stated above, the aim of Āḷāra's practices is stated to have been the attainment of Akiñcaññāyatana, the stage of nothingness. Whether this statement is handed down with any real knowledge of the facts of his teaching, it is not now possible to say. Aśvaghoṣa, in his *Buddhacarita*,[6] puts into the mouth of Ārāḍa or Āḷāra, a brief account of his philosophy. It has some resemblance—though this is slight—to the Sāṅkhya philosophy, but in Āḷāra's teaching some of the salient characteristics of the Sāṅkhya system are absent. In reply to Gotama's questions about the religious life and the obtaining of final release,

[1] In the *Milindapañha* (p. 236) Āḷāra is mentioned as Gotama's fourth teacher. The ThigA. (p. 2) says he went to Bhaggava before going to Āḷāra. The Mtu. (ii. 117 f.) and the Lal. (330 f.), give quite different accounts.

[2] M. i. 163-5; also 240 ff.; ii. 94 ff. 212 ff.

[3] VibhA. 432.

[4] Vin. i. 7.

[5] D. ii. 130; Vsm. 330.

[6] xii. 17 ff.

Āḷāra describes a system of spiritual development which is identical with the methods of the Buddhist monk up to the last attainment but one. The monk reaches the four jhānas and then attains successively to the states of space, infinity and nothingness. The last three stages are described in the terms of the first three of the four Attainments.[7]

According to Buddhaghosa,[8] **Bharaṇḍu Kālāma** was a disciple of Āḷāra at the same time as Gotama and is therefore described as the Buddha's *purāṇa-sabrahmacārī.*[9] Buddhaghosa further tells us[10] that in Āḷāra Kālāma, Āḷāra was his personal name. He was so called because he was *dīgha-piṅgala* (long and tawny).

[7] For a discussion on this see Thomas, *op. cit.*, p. 229-30; see also MA. ii. 881; VibhA. 432.

[8] AA. i. 458.

[9] A. i. 277.

[10] DA. ii. 569.

Āḷāhanapariveṇa.—One of the religious buildings constructed in **Pulatthipura** by **Parakkamabāhu I.** Attached to it was a splendid *pāsāda* for the thera **Sāriputta.**[1]

Geiger[2] identifies this with the group of buildings lying outside the city, now popularly, but wrongly, called the **Jetavanārāma.**

[1] Cv. lxxviii. 48-9.

[2] Cv. *Trs.* ii. 107, n. 2.

Āḷigāma.—A stronghold in the **Āḷisāra** district on the banks of the modern Ambaṅgaṅga. Here **Parakkamabāhu's** forces fought a decisive battle with those of **Gajabāhu.**[1]

[1] Cv. lxx. 113 ff., and Geiger's note thereon in the Cv. *Trs.* i. 296, n. 4.

1. **Āḷisāra.**—A district in Ceylon, now Elahera in the Matale district, north-east of Nālanda on the Ambaṅgaṅga. Once the whole district was given over by **Vijayabāhu**[1] for the support of the monks of **Pulatthipura.**[1] Later the district was the scene of several fights between the forces of **Gajabāhu** and **Parakkamabāhu I**. The conquest of Āḷisāra enabled Parakkamabāhu to capture Pulatthipura.

[1] Cv. lx. 14, and Geiger's note thereon in the Cv. *Trs.* i. 215, n. 6.

2. **Āḷisarā.**—A canal in Ceylon, probably leading from the Ambaṅgaṅga. King **Vasabha** gave a share of the water of the canal to the **Mucela-Vihāra** in **Tissavaḍḍhamānaka.**[1]

[1] Mhv. xxxv. 84.

1. **Āvaṭṭagaṅgā.**—The name given to the river which, flowing from the southern channel of **Anotatta** (*q.v.*), circles the lake three times before becoming the **Kaṇhagaṅgā.**[1]

[1] SnA. ii. 439, etc.

2. **Āvaṭṭagaṅgā.**—A canal which branched off to the south from the **Anotattavāpi** made by **Parakkamabāhu I.**,[1] evidently called after (1).

[1] Cv. lxxix. 50.

Āvaraṇa Sutta.—There are five things that overwhelm the mind and weaken the insight: *kāmacchanda, vyāpāda, thīnamiddha, uddhaccakukkucca* and *vicikicchā.*[1]

[1] A. iii. 63-4.

Āvaraṇatā Sutta.—Six conditions which make it impossible, even if he hear the dhamma, for a man to enter on the Path (*niyāmaṃ okkamituṃ*) which consists of good deeds: killing father, mother or arahant, willingly causing physical hurt to the Buddha, bringing dissension among the monks, being foolish, half-witted, deaf and dumb.[1]

[1] A. iii. 436-7.

Āvaraṇa-nīvaraṇa Sutta.—(Also called **Nīvaraṇāvaraṇa**). The five things, as above, which overwhelm the mind and weaken the insight and the seven *bojjhaṅgas* which counteract them and conduce to the attainment of emancipation through knowledge.[1]

[1] S. v. 94-6.

Āvantikā.—The name given to monks of **Avanti** who helped **Yasa Kākaṇḍakaputta** to overcome the heresy of the **Vajjiputtakas.**[1]

[1] Mhv. iv. 19 ff.

Āvāsika Vagga.—The twenty-fourth chapter of the *Pañcaka Nipāta* of the *Aṅguttara Nikāya.* It consists of ten suttas dealing with the qualities of a resident monk which make him worthy of honour and agreeable, or otherwise.[1]

[1] A. iii. 261-7.

Āveṇika Sutta.—There are five special (*āveṇika*) woes which a woman has to undergo as distinct from a man: at a tender age she goes to her husband's family, leaving her relations; she is subject to menses; to pregnancy; to labour at child-birth; and she has to wait upon a man.[1]

[1] S. iv. 239.

Āveyya.—A king of fifty-nine kappas ago, a former birth of **Samādapaka** Thera.[1] *v.l.* **Āvekkheyya.**

[1] Ap. i. 185.

Āvopupphiya Thera.—An arahant. He heard **Sikhī** Buddha preach and, being pleased with the sermon, threw a heap of flowers into the sky, above the Buddha, as an offering to him. Twenty kappas ago he became a king under the name of **Sumedha.**[1]

[1] Ap. i. 112.

Āsaṅka Jātaka (No. 380).—Once the Bodhisatta was an ascetic in the Himālaya. At that time a being of great merit left Tāvatiṃsa and was born as a girl in the midst of a lotus in a pool near the Bodhisatta's hermitage. The Bodhisatta, noticing some peculiarity in the growth of the lotus, swam to it and recovered the girl, whom he brought up as his daughter, giving her the name of **Āsaṅkā. Sakka,** coming to visit him, saw the girl, and, inquiring what he could do for her comfort, he provided her with a crystal palace and divine food and raiment. She spent her time waiting on the Bodhisatta. The King of Benares, having heard of her great beauty, came to the forest with a large following and asked for her hand. The Bodhisatta agreed, on condition that the king would tell him her name. The king spent a whole year trying to guess it and, having failed, was returning home in despair, when the girl, looking out of her window, told him of the creeper **Āsāvatī,** for whose fruits gods wait for one thousand years. She thus encouraged him to try again. Another year passed and she again raised hopes in the disappointed king by relating to him the story of a crane whose hopes Sakka had fulfilled. At the end of the third year the king, disgusted by his failure, started to go home, but again the girl engaged him in conversation, and in the course of their talk the girl's name was mentioned. When the king was told that the word had occurred in his talk, he returned to the Bodhisatta and told it to him. The Bodhisatta then gave Āsaṅkā in marriage to the king.[1] See also the **Indriya Jātaka.**

[1] J. iii. 248-54.

Āsaṅkā.—The adopted daughter of the Bodhisatta in the *Āsaṅka Jātaka*. She was so called because she came to him when he crossed the water owing to his doubt (*āsaṅkā*) as to what was in the lotus.[1]

[1] J. iii. 250.

Āsanatthavika Thera.—An arahant. In a previous birth, while wandering about in the forest, having lost his way, he came across the cetiya named **Uttama,** of **Sikhī** Buddha. Calling to mind the Buddha's good qualities, he uttered his praises and paid him homage at the altar in the cetiya. Twenty-seven kappas ago he was king seven times under the name of **Atulya.**[1]

[1] Ap. i. 255.

Āsanupaṭṭhāyaka Thera.—An arahant. 118 kappas ago, in a previous birth, he had provided a seat (*sīhāsana*) for the Buddha **Atthadassī** and had waited upon him. 107 kappas ago he was a king named **Sannibbāpakakhattiya.**[1] He is probably identical with **Ramaṇīyakuṭika** Thera.[2]

[1] Ap. i. 144. [2] ThagA. i. 132 ff.

1. **Āsava Sutta.**—On the six qualities which make a monk worthy of honour and offerings, due to destruction of the āsavas, and also on the methods which lead to such destruction.[1]

[1] A. iii. 387-94.

2. **Āsava Sutta.**—Ten things that conduce to the destruction of the *āsavas*: the eight factors of the Noble Eightfold Path, in addition to *sammāñāṇa* and *sammāvimutti.*[1]

[1] A. v. 237.

1. **Āsavakkhaya Sutta.**—Five things, if practised, lead to the destruction of the *āsavas*: reflection on what is loathsome, the thought of disgust with regard to food, revulsion from all things, the perception of impermanence in all composite things and the thought of death.[1]

[1] A. iii. 83.

2. **Āsavakkhaya Sutta.**—The holy life is lived for the destruction of the *āsavas.*[1]

[1] S. v. 28.

3. **Āsavakkhaya Sutta.**—The five *indriyas* of *saddhā*, etc., if cultivated, lead to the destruction of the *āsavas.*[1]

[1] S. v. 236.

4. **Āsavakkhaya Sutta.**—Intent concentration on in-breathing and out-breathing conduces to the destruction of the *āsavas.*[1]

[1] S. v. 340.

5. **Āsavakkhaya Sutta.**—In him who knows ill, etc., the *āsavas* are destroyed.[1]

[1] S. v. 434.

Āsavānaṃ-khaya Sutta.—By cultivating the five indriyas (*saddhā*, etc.) a monk in this very life realises the liberation by insight which is without the *āsavas*.[1]

[1] S. v. 203.

Āsā.—Daughter of **Sakka.** Once when **Nārada** was on his way to **Kañcanaguhā** where he dwelt and which stood at the head of **Manosilātala**, he carried in his hand a **Pāricchattaka** flower, and the four daughters of Sakka—**Āsā, Saddhā, Siri** and **Hirī**—who were in Manosilātala, resting from their sports in **Anotatta**, on seeing him, asked him for the flower. He said he would give it to the one among them whom they chose to be their queen. He himself was asked to choose the queen, but he referred them to Sakka who, in his turn, sent them to the ascetic **Macchariya-Kosiya** in the Himālaya. Sakka sent in advance a cup of ambrosia to the ascetic and told his daughters that the one among them, with whom Kosiya should share his ambrosia, would be deemed the best. When they appeared before Kosiya he asked their names, and chose Hirī for the honour of sharing his meal. In rejecting Āsā, Kosiya said, " They tell me that whoever pleases you, to him, by accomplishing the fruition of hope, you grant life, whosoever pleases you not, to him you grant it not. In this case success does not come to him through you, but you bring about his destruction." He spoke in like terms to the other two.

The story occurs in the Sudhābhojana Jātaka.[1]

[1] J. v. 392 ff.

Āsā Vagga.—The eleventh chapter of the *Eka Nipāta* of the *Aṅguttara Nikāya*.[1] It contains twelve suttas on various topics.

[1] A. i. 86-8.

Āsāvatī.—A creeper which grows in the **Cittalatāvana** in **Tāvatiṃsa.** In its fruit a divine drink is hidden, and they who drink of it once are intoxicated for four months and lie on a divine couch. It bears fruit only once in a thousand years, and the gods wait patiently for that period for a drink of the fruit.[1]

[1] J. iii. 250-1; Ap. i. 41.

Āsiṃsa Vagga.—The sixth section of the *Eka Nipāta* of the *Jātakaṭṭhakathā*.[1]

[1] J. i. 261-84.

Āsīvisa Vagga.—The nineteenth chapter of the *Saḷāyatana Saṃyutta* of the *Saṃyutta Nikāya*.[1]

[1] J. iv. 172-204.

1. **Āsīvisa Sutta.**—Preached at Sāvatthi. Man has to tend four snakes of fierce heat and fearful venom—the four *mahābhūtas*; he is constantly followed by five murderous foes—the five *upādānakkhandhā*; he is pursued by a murderous housebreaker with uplifted sword—passionate desire (*nandirāga*); while trying to escape them, he wanders into an empty village, where everything is empty—the sixfold personal sense sphere (*ajjhattikāyatana*), and into it come village-plunderers—the sixfold external sense-spheres (*bāhirāyatana*.) Fleeing from there he comes to a broad sheet of water beset with danger on the hither side; the further side is secure from fear, but there is no boat and no bridge—the fivefold flood (*ogha*), the hither shore being *sakkāya* and the further shore *nibbāna*.[1]

[1] S. iv. 172-5.

2. **Āsīvisa Sutta.**—There are four kinds of snakes in the world: the venemous but not fierce, the fierce but not venemous, the one that is both and the one that is neither. Similarly there are four kinds of persons: the one quick to get angry but with short-lived anger, the one slow to get angry but with lasting anger, etc.[1]

[1] A. ii. 110-11.

Āsīvisopama Sutta.—Probably refers to **Āsīvisa Sutta** (1), but may be (2). It was preached by the thera **Majjhantika** to the Nāga-king **Aravāḷa** and the people of **Kasmīra** and **Gandhāra.** Eighty thousand of the listeners accepted the new religion and one hundred thousand were ordained after the sermon.[1] It was also preached by **Mahinda** in Ceylon in the **Nandanavana** at **Anurādhapura** on the third day after his entry into the city. Thirty thousand people were converted.[2]

[1] Sp. i. 66; Mhv. xii. 26. [2] *Ibid.*, xv. 178-9; Sp. i. 80; Mbv. 133.

Āseva Sutta.—If, just for the duration of a finger snap, a monk indulges a thought of good-will, such a one is verily a monk.[1]

[1] A. i. 10.

Āsevitabba Sutta.—On the characteristics of the person who should be followed.[1]

[1] A. i. 124 f.

1. **Āhāra Sutta.**—Preached at Jetavana on the four sustenances (*āhārā*) that maintain beings by bringing them to birth and keeping them after

birth; also the cause of these sustenances and the method of their cessation.[1]

[1] S. ii. 11-12.

2. **Āhāra Sutta.**—A group of suttas dealing with the food of the *nīvaraṇas* and of the *bojjhaṅgas*, and with the condition that follows on the absence of their food.[1]

[1] S. v. 102-7.

Āhuneyya Vagga.—The first chapter of the *Chakka Nipāta* of the *Aṅguttara Nikāya*. It consists of ten suttas.[1]

[1] A. iii. 279-88.

1. **Āhuneyya Sutta.**—Preached at Jetavana. The six reasons connected with the control of the senses by virtue of which a monk becomes worthy of homage and of gifts.[1]

[1] A. iii. 279.

2. **Āhuneyya Sutta.**—Six other qualities connected with the *abhiññā* which make a monk so worthy.[1]

[1] A. iii. 280-1.

3. **Āhuneyya Suttā.**—Two suttas giving eight qualities that make a monk worthy of homage, etc.[1]

[1] A. iv. 290 f.

4. **Āhuneyya Sutta.**—On nine persons worthy of homage: those who have attained the four Fruits of the Path, those four who are on the way thereto and the *Gotrabhū* (one who has entered the lineage of the Āriyan).[1]

[1] A. iv. 373.

5. **Āhuneyya Sutta.**—On ten persons described differently from the above, worthy of homage, etc.[1]

[1] A. v. 23.

I.

Iṅgirisi.—The Pāli name for the English.[1]

[1] *E.g.*, Cv. ci. 29.

Icchā Sutta.—Wishes it is which hold the world prisoner; by subjugating them, liberty is gained.[1]

[1] S. i. 40.

Icchānaṅgala.—A brahmin village in the **Kosala** country. It was while staying in the woodland thicket (*vanasaṇḍa*) there that the Buddha preached the *Ambaṭṭha Sutta.*[1] From this sutta, the village would seem to have been near **Pokkharasādi's** domain of **Ukkaṭṭhā.** It was the residence of "Mahāsāḷa" brahmins. The *Sutta Nipāta*[2] (which spells the name as **Icchānaṅkala**) mentions several eminent brahmins who lived there, among them **Caṅkī, Tārukkha, Pokkarasāti, Jānussoṇi** and **Todeyya.** There were also two learned youths, **Vāseṭṭha** and **Bharadvāja** at Icchānaṅkala, who, finding it impossible to bring their discussion to a conclusion, sought the Buddha, then staying in the village. Their interview with the Buddha is recorded in the *Vāseṭṭha Sutta.*[3] Buddhaghosa[4] says that learned brahmins of Kosala, deeply versed in the Vedas, were in the habit of meeting together from time time[5] at Icchānaṅgala in order to recite the Vedas and discuss their interpretation.[6]

According to the *Saṃyutta Nikāya,*[7] the Buddha once stayed for three months in the jungle thicket at Icchānaṅgala, in almost complete solitude, visited only by a single monk who brought him his food. But from the *Aṅguttara Nikāya,*[8] it would appear that the Buddha was not left to enjoy the solitude which he desired, for we are told that the residents of Icchānaṅgala, having heard of the Buddha's visit, came to him in large numbers and created a disturbance by their shouts. The Buddha had to send **Nāgita,** who was then his personal attendant, to curb the enthusiasm of his admirers.

[1] D. i. 87. [2] p. 115.
[3] *Ibid.*, 115 ff.; M. ii. 146 ff.
[4] SnA. ii. 462.
[5] Once in six months (MA. ii. 796).
[6] These brahmins met at Ukkaṭṭhā, under Pokkharasāti, when they wished to cleanse their caste (*jātisodhanatthaṃ*), and at Icchānaṅkala in order to revise their Vedic hymns (*mante sodhetukāmā*), MA. ii. 796.
[7] v. 325.
[8] iii. 30 f.; *cf.* iii. 341 and iv. 340 ff.

Icchānaṅgala Sutta.—Preached to the monks at **Icchānaṅgala** at the end of the three months' solitude referred to above. Should anyone ask the monks how the Buddha spent his time during the rainy season, they should reply that he spent it in intense concentration on in-breathing and out-breathing. A life spent by anyone in such concentration would be a life spent according to the Āriyan way and would lead to the destruction of the *āsavas*.[1]

[1] S. v. 325 f.

Icchānaṅgalaka.—An upāsaka of **Icchānaṅgala.** He was a devoted disciple of the Buddha and had been in the habit of visiting him often.[1] Once he visited the Buddha at **Jetavana** after a long interval, and on being asked why he had been absent so long, he replied that he had been kept busy by various duties. Thereupon the Buddha sang the joy of the life free from ties.[2]

[1] UdA. 115. [2] Ud., p. 13.

Iṭṭiya.—See **Iṭṭhiya.**

Iṭṭhakāvatī.—A village in **Magadha,** mentioned, together with **Dīgharājī,** as the residence of the **Saṃsāramocaka** heretics. Near by was the **Āruṇavatīvihāra,** where **Sāriputta** once stayed with a company of monks. The village had retained its name for five hundred years.[1]

The *Petavatthu*[2] contains the story of a woman of **Iṭṭhakāvatī** who was born as a *peta*.

[1] PvA. 67. [2] pp. 12-13.

1. **Iṭṭhā Sutta.**—Preached to **Anāthapiṇḍika** on five things in the world which are very desirable but are difficult to attain—longevity, beauty, happiness, fame, happy rebirth—and on the means of obtaining them.[1]

[1] A. iii. 47-9.

2. **Iṭṭhā Sutta.**—The ten desirable things in the world, the obstacles to their attainment and the methods of procuring them.[1]

[1] A. v. 135 f.

Iṭṭhiya.—One of the monks who accompanied **Mahinda** on his visit to Ceylon.[1] King **Sirimeghavaṇṇa** had an image of Iṭṭhiya made and placed beside that of Mahinda and his companions in the vihāra which he built in the south-eastern corner of his palace. He inaugurated a year's festival in honour of these images[2] (*v.l.* **Iṭṭiya, Iddhiya**).

[1] Mhv. xii. 7; Dpv. xii. 12; Sp. i. 71; Mbv. 116; DhsA. 32.
[2] Cv. xxxvii. vv. 87 ff.

Iḍagaḷissara.—A village in South India where **Kulasekhara** had an encampment in his fight with the Siṃhalese forces.[1]

[1] Cv. lxxvi. 149.

Iṇa Sutta.—Deals at length with the disadvantages, both material and moral, of poverty and consequent indebtedness.[1]

[1] A. iii. 351-4.

Itivuttaka.—The fourth book of the *Khuddaka Nikāya*, containing 110 suttas, each of which begins with the words: *vuttaṃ h'etaṃ Bhagavatā*. According to Dhammapāla,[1] the suttas were preached from time to time by the Buddha to **Khujjuttarā** at **Kosambī.** She then repeated them to the five hundred women of **Udena's** palace, chief of whom was **Sāmāvatī.** In order to emphasise to her audience the fact that she was reporting the Buddha's words and not her own, she prefaced each sutta with the phrase quoted above. There was no need to describe any special circumstances in which the suttas were preached, because they were familiar to Khujjuttarā's audience.

At the Rājagaha Council, **Ānanda** repeated the suttas to the Assembly and they were gathered into this collection.

Itivuttaka is also the name given to one of the nine divisions (*aṅga*) into which the Buddha's preaching is divided and it is defined as follows: *vuttaṃ h'etaṃ Bhagavatā ti ādinayappavattā dasuttarasataṃ suttantā Itivuttakam ti veditabbaṃ.*[2]

In the scholiast of the *Kummāsapiṇḍa Jātaka,*[3] the Itivuttaka is mentioned in the plural (*Itivuttakesu*) and a sutta is quoted from it, extolling the virtues of generosity. Perhaps, the *Itivuttaka* was compiled as a result of a critical study of the authentic teachings of the Buddha, considered in a certain light and made for a specific purpose.

[1] ItA. 24 ff. [2] DA. i. 24. [3] J. iii. 409 (l. 21).

Itthi Vagga.—The seventh section of the *Eka Nipāta* of the *Jātakaṭṭhakathā.*[1]

[1] J. i. 285-315.

1. **Iddhi Sutta.**—**Anuruddha** tells the monks that by cultivating the four *satipaṭṭhānas,* he enjoys psychic power in many ways, such as multiplying himself. He can reach even to the Brahma world.[1]

[1] S. v. 303.

2. **Iddhi Sutta.**—Same as above, but the psychic power is that of the divine power of hearing all things, far and near.[1]

[1] S. v. 304.

Iddhikathā.—The second division of the *Paññāvagga* of the *Paṭisambhidāmagga.*[1]

[1] Ps. ii. 205-15.

Iddhipāda Vagga.—The ninth chapter of the *Navaka Nipāta* of the *Aṅguttara Nikāya.*[1] It consists of ten suttas dealing with the cultivation of the four *iddhipādas.*

[1] A. iv. 463-4.

1. **Iddhipāda Sutta.**—The cultivation of the four *iddhipādas* and of exertion (*ussoḷhi*) brings insight (*aññā*) in this life, or the Third Fruit of the Path.[1]

[1] A. iii. 81-2.

2. **Iddhipāda Sutta.**—The Buddha, even as Bodhisatta, before the Enlightenment, developed the four *iddhipādas* and exertion, and as a result enjoyed great psychic power.[1]

[1] A. iii. 82-3.

3. **Iddhipāda Sutta.**—The four *iddhipādas* form the path leading to the Uncompounded (*asaṅkhata*).[1]

[1] S. iv. 360.

4. **Iddhipāda Sutta.**—The path mentioned above should be practised, accompanied by concentration and effort, compounded with desire, energy, idea and investigation.[1]

[1] S. iv. 365.

Iddhipāda Saṃyutta.—The fifty-first division of the *Saṃyutta Nikāya,*[1] consisting of eight chapters. It is the seventh section of the *Mahāvagga.*

[1] S. v. 254-93.

Iddhiya.—See **Iṭṭhiya.**

Iddhivaḍḍhana.—One of the palaces, occupied during his lay-life by **Sumana** Buddha.[1]

[1] BuA. 125; Bu. v. 22 gives other names for his palaces.

Idhalokika Sutta.—Two suttas preached by the Buddha to **Visākhā** at the **Migāramātupāsāda.** To achieve victory in this world a woman should have four qualities: she should efficiently discharge her duties as housewife, should win the esteem of her servants and the affection of her husband and should look after his wealth. For victory in the next world, she should be possessed of faith, virtue, generosity and wisdom.[1]

[1] A. iv. 269 ff.

Inandapada.—A Damiḷa chieftain whom **Kulasekhara** enlisted as his ally. He was a troop leader in **Uccaṅkuṭṭha.**[1]

[1] Cv. lxxvii. 74 ff.

1. **Inda.**—Given in the *Āṭānāṭiya Sutta* as the name of the ninety-one sons of **Dhataraṭṭha,** king of the **Gandhabbas.** They are represented as being of great strength and followers of the Buddha.[1]

The name is also given as that of the ninety-one sons of **Virūḷha,** king of the **Kumbhaṇḍas**[2]; of **Virūpakkha,** king of the **Nāgas**[3]; and of **Kuvera,** king of the **Yakkhas.**[4] Further on in the same sutta, Inda is mentioned with **Soma, Varuṇa** and others as a Yakkha, to whom appeal should be made by disciples of the Buddha when needing protection.[5] In the *Mahā Samaya Sutta,*[6] also, Inda is mentioned as the name of the Sons of the Regent Gods of the Four Quarters.

[1] D. iii. 197.
[2] *Ibid.*, 198.
[3] p. 199.
[4] p. 202.
[5] p. 204.
[6] D. ii. 257 f.

2. **Inda.**—The Pāli equivalent of the Vedic Indra. He is referred to only very seldom in the *Nikāyas.* In one such passage[1] he is mentioned with **Soma, Varuṇa, Isāna, Pajāpati, Brahmā, Mahiddi** and **Yāma,** as a god whom brahmins invoke and pray to, for union with Brahmā after death. In another place,[2] he is described as being seated in the company of **Pajāpati** and other gods in the Assembly Hall, named **Sudhammā.** Two of his companions, having listened to the admonition of **Gopaka,** became disciples of the Buddha and, as a result, far surpassed in glory Inda and his other companion devas. In the same context, **Vāsava,** ruler of the gods, identified with **Sakka,** is addressed by Gopaka as "**Indra.**"

By the time of the compilation of the *Nikāyas*, the hold of the Vedic god Indra on the mind of the people seems to have become greatly

[1] D. i. 244-5.
[2] *Ibid.*, ii. 274; in M. i. 140; J. v. 411 and vi. 568, he is mentioned with Brahmā and Pajāpati; in J. iv. 568, 571 is a list in which Inda appears with Brahmā, Pajāpati, Soma, Yama and Vessavaṇa.

weakened and Indra has been merged in **Sakka,** although, strictly speaking, Indra and Sakka are quite different conceptions. (See *s.v.* **Sakka.**)

In the later literature, however, particularly in the *Jātakaṭṭhakathā*, Indra's name occurs frequently, but always as identified or identifiable with Sakka. In one place at least[3] the scholiast says, "*Sakko ti Indo.*"

In the *Ayakūṭa Jātaka*,[4] for example, Indra is called king of the gods (*devārājā*) in one verse, and in the next he is identified with **Maghavā,** husband of **Sujā,** and described as "*devānaṃ indo.*" Indra is most revered of the gods.[5] He is free from old age and death, and is, therefore, the happiest type of king,[6] a condition that could be attained by sacrifice.[7] Alone he conquered the **Asuras.**[8] He is spoken of as the lord of victors (*jayataṃ pati*),[9] and he is the embodiment of the greatest valour.[10]

Sometimes he visits the earth in disguise.[11] He is also represented as punishing people guilty of heinous crimes; with his thunderbolt he smites them.[12]

The scene of his pleasures is in the **Nandana** pleasaunce,[13] and his is the ideal enjoyment of pleasure, surrounded by friends[14] and by adoring wives.[15] The gods of **Tāvatiṃsa** are called **Inda-purohitā,** because, with Inda as their chief, they seek to promote the welfare of gods and men.[16] Inda is called **Tidivapuravara** and **Suravaratara.**[17] His capital is **Masakkasāra.**[18]

In the sacrifice the *palāsayaṭṭhi* (*Butea* shoot), used by the sacrificing priest, is described as Indra's right hand.[19]

Indra's gotta, or clan, is the **Kosiya**[20]; he is called **Vatrabhū** in reference to his victory over **Vatra** (Skt. Vṛtra),[21] and mention is made of his thunderbolt, the **Indavajira**[22]; thus he is called Vajirahattha.[23] The sound of Indra's thunderbolt striking its victim, surpasses all other sounds by its intensity, its volume and its fearfulness[24]; no obstruc-

[3] J. v. 115.
[4] J. iii. 146.
[5] Sn. vs. 316.
[6] *Ibid.*, 515.
[7] *Ibid.*, 517.
[8] J. iv. 347; he is therefore called **Asurinda** and **Asurādhipa**; see *s.v.* **Asura.**
[9] J. v. 322.
[10] Mhv. xxx. 10.
[11] J. v. 33.
[12] DhA. iv. 105.
[13] J. v. 158.
[14] J. v. 506; Sn. v. 679.
[15] J. vi. 240.
[16] J. vi, 127; the Tāvatiṃsa gods are also described as being **Sa-Indakā** (*ibid.*, 568).
[17] D. iii. 176.
[18] J. vi. 271; but see **Amarāvatī.**
[19] J. vi. 212.
[20] *Ibid.*, 501.
[21] J. v. 153.
[22] J. i. 354.
[23] D. ii. 259; DA. ii. 689.
[24] UdA. 67.

tion can stop the progress of Indra's Vajira and it never misses its mark; it is *avirajjhanaka.*[25]

After his victory over the Asuras, images of him were made (**Indapaṭimā**) and placed round **Cittakūṭa** to frighten the Asuras away, in case they attempted to retrieve their lost honour.[26]

To be born into the company of Indra (*Indasahavyatā*) is considered very fortunate.[27]

A species of coral red insect (*kimi*), noticeable after rain, are called *Indagopakā*. The reason for this name is not clear.[28]

The *Udāna Commentary*[29] seems to give **Viḍojā** as an epithet of Indra; but this is probably a wrong reading, the correct one being, as in some MSS., "*Visamucchājapaṃ japanti.*"

Inda was a special protector of cows, and when men began to kill these creatures he visited his wrath on them.[30]

[25] VibhA. 333.
[26] J. vi. 125-6; see also J. i. 203-4; DhA. i. 280.
[27] *E.g.*, J. v. 411.
[28] See *Brethren*, p. 18 n., and *N.P.D.s.v.*
[29] p. 75, n. 12.
[30] Sn. v. 310.

1. **Indaka.**—A yakkha who lived in **Indakūṭa,** near **Rājagaha.** When the Buddha was staying at Indakūṭa, the yakkha questioned him as to how the soul finds its material counterpart. The Buddha, in reply, described how the embryo evolved into its final shape by the laws of physical growth and not by a soul's fiat.[1]

Buddhaghosa[2] says that the yakkha was an animist (*puggalavādin*).

[1] S. i. 206.
[2] SA. i. 231.

2. **Indaka.**—A deva. He had been a youth who gave a spoonful of food to **Anuruddha**. In consequence he was born in **Tāvatiṃsa** as a deva of great power and majesty. When the Buddha went to Tāvatiṃsa to preach the *Abhidhamma*, in the assembly of the gods who gathered there, those of lesser powers had to yield place to their superiors. Thus **Aṅkura** (*q.v.*), who, at the start, was very near the Buddha, found himself twelve leagues away. But not so Indaka; the power of his merit was very great and no deva was mighty enough to displace him; he had been lucky in the recipient of his gift. Aṅkura's generosity, much more lavish than Indaka's, had been bestowed on men who were not holy. Such was the explanation the Buddha gave in the assembly of the gods, on seeing the discrepancy between the positions of the two devas, Indaka surpassing the other in ten qualities.[1]

[1] Pv. pp. 27 f.; PvA. 136-8; DhA. iii. 219-20; 80-1.

In one place, in the *Petavatthu*,[2] Indaka is called a yakkha, but the *Commentary*[3] says it means *deva-putta*. He is, therefore, different from **Indaka** (1).

[2] p. 28, v. 69. [3] p. 139.

Indaka Sutta.—Contains the question asked by **Indaka** and the Buddha's reply.[1]

[1] S. i. 206.

Indakūṭa.—A peak near **Rājagaha,** the abode of the yakkha **Indaka.** The Buddha once lived there.[1]

[1] S. i. 206.

Indakhīla Sutta.—Like a tuft of cotton-wool or a ball of thistledown, wafted by every wind, are recluses and brahmins who do not understand, as they really are, the facts of Ill; like an *indakhīla*, unshakable, unquakable, are those who do so understand.[1]

[1] S. v. 443-5.

1. **Indagutta.**—A thera. He superintended the construction of the **Mahāthūpa** at Anurādhapura.[1] **Duṭṭhagāmaṇī** consulted him with regard to all details and appointed him *kammādhiṭṭhāyaka* from the commencement of the work.[2] He had great psychic powers, and at the festival of the dedication of the Thūpa he created a parasol of copper, as great as the universe, to ward off any harm that might befall those taking part in the celebrations.[3] He was at the side of the king throughout the festival,[4] and, by virtue of his power, all the inhabitants of Ceylon, who wished to worship the relics at the Mahāthūpa, were enabled to go to Anuradhapura the moment the wish to do so entered their hearts, and to return the same day.[5]

This Indagutta is probably to be identified with the thera Indagutta, the head of a great pariveṇa in **Rajāgaha,** who came to Ceylon with eighty thousand monks to be present at the foundation-ceremony of the Mahāthūpa.[6]

[1] Mhv. xxxviii. 98: Dpv. xix. 5, 6, 8.
[2] MṬ. 550 f.
[3] Mhv. xxxi. 85.
[4] *Ibid.*, 105.
[5] *Ibid.*, 115.
[6] *Ibid.*, xxix. 30.

2. **Indagutta.**—The thera appointed by the monks of **Pāṭaliputta** to superintend the work of building the eighty-four thousand vihāras undertaken by **Asoka.** The thera, by his power, made it possible for the dedication festivals of all the vihāras to be performed on the same day.[1]

[1] Mhv. v. 174; Sp. i. 49.

Indadvāra.—One of the fourteen gates of **Pulatthipura** built by **Parakkamabāhu I.**[1]

[1] Cv. lxxiii. 160.

Indapatta (Indapattana, Indapaṭṭha).—A town in the **Kuru** country. In the *Kurudhamma Jātaka,*[1] **Dhanañjaya Koravya** (*q.v.*), is mentioned as its king and as the owner of **Añjanavasabha,** the elephant of wondrous power. The town was seven leagues in extent[2] and there was a road that ran straight from Indapatta to Bārāṇasī.[3] In times past, Indapatta was considered one of the three chief cities of Jambudīpa, the others being **Uttarapañcāla** and **Kekaka.**[4] According to a verse found at the end of the *Buddhavaṃsa,*[5] the Buddha's razor and needle were enshrined at Indapaṭṭa.

The modern Delhi stands on the site of Indapatta.

[1] J. ii. 365 f.; also J. iii. 400; iv. 361; v. 457; vi. 255; Cyp. i. 3, v. 1.
[2] J. v. 57; 484.
[3] *Ibid.*, 59.
[4] J. ii. 213, 214.
[5] Bu. xxviii. 11.

Indavarī.—Chief among the lay-women who supported **Nārada** Buddha.[1]

[1] Bu. x. 25.

Indasama.—A king of thirteen kappas ago; a previous birth of **Setuccha** Thera,[1] also called **Khajjakadāyaka.**[2]

[1] ThagA. i. 207.
[2] Ap. i. 182.

Indasamānagotta.—A hermit who lived, with a large number of other anchorites, in the Himālaya. He had a young elephant which he had reared; being headstrong and rough in speech, he would not listen to the warning of his teacher, the Bodhisatta, that it was dangerous to have such a pet. Once while the hermits were away the elephant was seized with a frenzy, and when his master returned it killed him.[1]

[1] J. ii. 41-3. Perhaps the man's name was **Kosiya,** because we are told (J. vi. 501) that **Inda** was of the **Kosiyagotta. Kātiyāna,** who was a brahmin of the Kosiyagotta (ThagA. i. 450), is addressed in a verse (416) of the *Theragāthā* as **Indasagotta.**

Indasamānagotta Jātaka.—The story of **Indasamānagotta,** given above. It was told in reference to an unruly monk, who is identified with the hermit of the Jātaka.[1]

For details see the *Gijjha Jātaka.*

[1] J. ii. 41 ff.

Indasālaka.—A cave, the size of a bed in a monk's cell, near **Vallipāsāṇa Vihāra.** It was the residence of **Mahā-Nāgasena** Thera. When he was ill, eight thousand arahants and the inhabitants of the two deva worlds, led by **Sakka,** came to look after him. They all found room in the cave.[1]

[1] MṬ. 552.

Indasālaguhā.—A cave on the **Vediya** mountain, to the north of **Ambasaṇḍā,** which was a brahmin village, east of **Rājagaha.** Once, when the Buddha was staying there, **Sakka** visited him and asked him the questions recorded in the *Sakkapañha Sutta.*[1]

Buddhaghosa[2] says that the cave lay between two overhanging rocks, with a large *sāla*-tree at the entrance. The village community had added walls with doors and windows and had ornamented it with polished plaster scroll-work and garlands and had presented it to the Buddha. In Fa Hsien's time,[3] it was still inhabited and he describes it as being one yojana north-east of **Nālandā.** Hiouen Thsang,[4] however, found it deserted. Both pilgrims noticed marks on the rock; according to Fa Hsien they were the answers to Sakka's questions written by the Buddha with his finger, while Hiouen Thsang says that both questions and answers were written on the stone.

The cave is identified with one about two miles to the south-west of the modern village of Giriyek.[5]

It is said that on the occasion of the preaching of the *Sakkapañha Sutta*, eight hundred million devas realised the Truth.[6]

[1] D. ii. 263. [2] DA. iii. 697.
[3] Giles, 48 f.
[4] He calls it *Indraka-saila-gūhā* (Beal ii. 180-1).
[5] CAGI. 539 ff.; Stein, *Ind. Antiq.* 1901, p. 54.
[6] Mil. 349.

Indranagarī.—The capital of **Indra,**[1] evidently another name for **Amarāvatī.**

[1] Cv. lxxxviii. 121.

Indriya Jātaka (No. 423).—Once an ascetic named **Nārada,** younger brother of **Kāḷadevala,** became a disciple of the Bodhisatta **Jotipāla** (also called in the story **Sarabhaṅga),** and lived in the mountainous country of **Arañjara.** Near Nārada's hermitage was a river, on the banks of which courtesans used to sit, tempting men. Nārada saw one of these courtesans, and becoming enamoured of her, forsook his meditations and pined away for lack of food. Kāḷadevala, being aware of this, tried to wean him from his desires. Nārada, however, refused to be comforted, even when his colleagues, **Sālissara, Meṇḍissara** and **Pabbatissara** admonished him. In the end Sarabhaṅga himself was summoned and Nārada, having listened to the words of his Master, was persuaded to give up his passion.

The story was told in reference to a backsliding monk. He went about for alms with his teachers and instructors but, being their junior, he received very little attention. Dissatisfied with his food and treatment, he sought his wife of former days. She provided him with every comfort and gradually tempted him with the desire to become a householder again. When the monk's fellow-celibates discovered his wish, they took him to the Buddha who preached to him this Jātaka, showing that in a past life, too, he had been sorely tempted by the same woman. Nārada was identified with the backsliding monk and the courtesan with the wife of his lay-days.[1]

The Buddha is stated on this occasion to have preached also the *Kaṇḍiṇa Jātaka,*[2] the *Rādha Jātaka,*[3] the *Ruhaka Jātaka,*[4] the *Kaṇavera Jātaka,*[5] the *Asaṅka Jātaka*[6] and the *Alambusā Jātaka.*[7]

The *Indriya Jātaka* is also referred to in the *Kāmavilāpa Jātaka,*[8] but the connection between the two stories is not clear; perhaps the reference is to another story of the same name.

1 J. iii. 461-9.
2 J. i. 153 ff.
3 *Ibid.*, 495 ff.
4 J. ii. 113 ff.
5 J. iii. 58 ff.
6 *Ibid.*, 248 ff.
7 J. v. 152 ff.
8 J. ii. 443 ff.

1. **Indriya Sutta.**—The monk possessed of six qualities—the five indriyas (*saddhā*, etc.), and the freedom of mind brought about by the destruction of the *āsavas*—is worthy of offerings, etc.[1]

1 A. iii. 281.

2. **Indriya Sutta.**—Where control of the faculties of sense (*indriya*) is not found, morality ceases to exist and, in consequence, concentration, insight into and knowledge of reality as it is, detachment and the feeling of revulsion, insight into liberation—these also cease to exist. When such control is present all the other qualities are also present.[1]

1 A. iii. 360.

3. **Indriya Sutta.**—If a monk, observing the rise and fall in the faculties of sense, is repelled by them and lusts not for them, the knowledge arises in him that he is free and that for him there is no hereafter. Thus would he be perfect in faculty.[1]

1 S. iv. 140.

4. **Indriya Sutta.**—The five *indriyas* (*saddhā*, etc.), are called the Path that goes to the Uncompounded (*asaṅkhata*).[1]

[1] S. iv. 361.

5. **Indriya Sutta.**—The five indriyas (*saddhā*, etc.), when practised with singleness of heart, dispassion, and cessation that conduces to abandonment, form the Path leading to the Uncompounded.[1]

[1] S. iv. 365.

6. **Indriya Sutta.**—**Anuruddha** tells his colleagues that by cultivating the four *satipaṭṭhānas*, he knows, as they really are, the nature of the minds of other beings, of other persons (*indriyaparopariyatti*).[1]

[1] S. v. 305.

Indriyakathā.—The fourth division of the *Mahāvagga* of the *Paṭisambhidāmagga*.[1]

[1] ii., pp. 1-35.

Indriyagocara Sutta.—Mentioned in the *Atthasālinī*,[1] Buddhaghosa's Commentary on the *Dhammasaṅgani*. The quotation given from it is: "*ekaṃ mahābhūtaṃ upādāya pāsādo paṭhavidhātuyā tīhi mahābhūtehi susaṅgahito āpodhātuyā ca tejodhātuyā ca vāyodhātuyā ca.*" The sutta has, so far, not been traced elsewhere.

[1] pp. 307-8.

Indriyabhāvanā Sutta.—Preached at **Kajaṅgalā** in the **Mukheluvana.** When a young brahmin, **Uttara,** pupil of **Pārāsariya,** visits the Buddha, the Buddha asks him what was the teaching of Pārāsariya on the development of the indriyas. It is that a man should neither see forms with his eyes, nor hear words with his ears, says Uttara. Whereupon the Buddha retorts that in that case the deaf and the blind have reached development. When Uttara sits silent and discomfited, **Ānanda** intervenes and begs the Buddha to expound his teaching on the subject. The Buddha agrees and preaches this sutta, with a variety of similes.[1]

In the *Theragāthā Commentary*[2] we are told that the thera Pārāpariya (probably identical with Pārāsariya mentioned above) was taught the *Indriyabhāvana Sutta* by the Buddha. He learnt it by heart, and pondering over its meaning, attained insight. The *Theragāthā*[3] gives a summary of the musings of Pārāpariya which lead to his attainment.

[1] M. iii. 298-302. [2] ii. 17. [3] vv. 726 ff.

The only connection between the Sutta and this summary is identity of subject, not identity of treatment. Perhaps Pārāpariya's musings were only prompted by the sutta and were independent of its actual words.

Indriyāni Sutta.—There are four *indriyas*: *saddhā, viriya, sati* and *samādhi.*[1]

[1] A.ii.141.

Irandatī.—A Nāga maiden, daughter of the Nāga King, **Varuṇa.** When she learned that her mother, **Vimalā,** longed for the heart of **Vidhura,** she determined to get for herself a husband who would satisfy her mother's craving. So she went to the Himālaya and having spread a bed of fragrant flowers, lay thereon and sang. **Vessavaṇa's** nephew, a yakkha, **Puṇṇaka,** heard her and offered himself as her husband. She took him to her father who agreed to give him Irandatī, if he could bring Vidhura's heart. When Puṇṇaka fulfilled this condition, as described in the *Vidhura-paṇḍita Jātaka*, Irandatī became his wife.[1]

[1] J. vi. 263-327.

Ilaṅkiya.—A Damiḷa chieftain of South India, conquered by **Parakkamabāhu I.**[1] Later, Ilaṅkiya became the ally of Parakkamabāhu, who gave him earrings and other ornaments as a mark of royal favour, also conferring on him the coveted title of **Rājavesibhujaṅga-Silāmegha.**[2]

[1] Cv. lxxvi. 98. [2] *Ibid.*, 191-2; on the title see Geiger, Cv. *Trs.* ii. 10, n. 3.

Ilaṅga.—See **Sena Ilaṅga** and **Rakkhaka Ilaṅga.**

Illisa.—A seṭṭhi of **Rājagaha.**[1] He was lame and hunch-backed and also had a squint. He was an infidel and a miser, never giving away any of his wealth nor enjoying it himself.

For seven generations his ancestors had been generous, but **Illīsa** burnt down the almonry and drove away the poor from his house.

Once, at the sight of a yokel drinking, with a piece of dried fish as a relish, Illīsa was sorely tempted to drink himself. For a long time he fought the temptation, but he sickened with longing, and having sent a slave with a single penny to the tavern, he got some toddy; he ordered the slave to put the jar of spirits in a thicket by the riverside so that he might drink unseen.

[1] At the opening ot the story the king of Benares is mentioned, but it is to Rājagaha that Sakka comes (see p. 350), so Rājagaha was evidently Illīsa's residence.

Meanwhile Illīsa's father, who had been born as **Sakka,** having learnt, as a result of investigations, that his son had become a miser, came down to earth to wean him from his folly. Assuming in every detail the form of Illīsa, he entered the king's palace and offered all the wealth of Illīsa to the king. On the offer being refused, he went to Illīsa's house and gave orders to the servants to throw open all the treasure chambers and give the wealth to the poor. The servants took the disguised Sakka to be Illīsa himself, and Illīsa's wife, believing her husband's sudden generosity to be due to his drunkenness, acquiesced in the instructions.

Among those who profited by this unexpected good fortune was a countryman who had been Illīsa's carriage-driver. Filling the carriage with seven things of value, he set out along the road, passing by the thicket wherein Illīsa lay drinking. The man was singing Illīsa's praises, and at mention of his name Illīsa came out, and seeing the man going away with his belongings tried to stop him. But the man, not recognising him, knocked him down and went on his way. Illīsa hurried home but was turned out of his house by the porters, and at length he sought the king. The king, having heard his story, made enquiries and discovered the existence of two Illīsas, alike in every respect, down to the minutest detail, even to a wart on the head.

Not even Illīsa's wife and children, not even his barber, could distinguish him from the second Illīsa.

Bereft of all hope, Illīsa swoons, Sakka reveals himself and tells Illīsa that the wealth is really his and not Illīsa's, the latter not having earned it. He urges Illīsa to do good and practise generosity, or he would die, smitten by Indra's thunderbolt.

Illīsa, taking heed of the warning, becomes a virtuous man.[2]

[2] J. i. 349 ff.

Illīsa Jātaka (No. 78).—The story of **Illīsa** as given above. The Jātaka was related in reference to the conversion by **Moggallāna** of the banker **Maccharikosiya** (*q.v.*) of **Sakkhara.** Illīsa of the past is identified with Macchariyakosiya.[1] The story is given as an example of *iddhi* by means of which Moggallāna made a little thing increase manyfold.[2]

[1] J. i. 345 ff. [2] Vsm. ii. 403.

Iḷanāga.—King of Ceylon (A.D. 93-102). He was the nephew of King **Āmaṇḍagāmaṇi Abhaya**. Āmaṇḍa was succeeded by his son **Cūḷābhaya** and he by his younger sister **Sīvalī.** After Sīvalī had reigned for four months, Iḷanāga dethroned her and became king himself. In the first year of his reign he incurred the displeasure of the powerful **Lambakaṇṇas** and was deprived of his throne and taken captive. It is said that the king was rescued from prison by his state elephant and that he escaped to **Rohaṇa.** Three years later he gave battle to the Lambakaṇṇas at **Kapallakkhaṇḍa** and massacred most of them. He had the noses and toes of the rest cut off as punishment.

He was succeeded by his son **Candamukha Siva.** To his state elephant, who had helped him, he gave the tract of land called **Hatthibhoga.**

During his exile in Rohaṇa, Iḷanāga built two tanks, the **Tissa** and the **Dūra,** and restored the **Nāgamahāvihāra,** which he gave to **Mahāpaduma,** thera of **Tulādhāra,** who had preached to him the *Kapi Jātaka*. He also gave land for its maintenance.[1]

[1] Mhv. xxxv. 14-45; Dpv. xxi. 41 f.

Isayo Araññakā (or **Gandha**) **Sutta.**—Long ago, many seers of virtuous conduct lived in leaf huts in a wild forest.[1] One day, **Sakka** and **Vepacitti** visited them. Vepacitti entered the hermitage by the principal gate, keeping his shoes on and his sword by his side, thereby insulting the seers and committing sin. Sakka, on the other hand, went in by the usual entrance, doffing his shoes and sword; with his canopy folded up, he stood to leeward of the seers, rendering them homage with clasped hands. The seers, addressing Sakka, asked him if he did not feel disgust at their smell, inasmuch as they were humans and he a god. Sakka answered that the scent of virtuous men is lovely, like unto a wreath of varied blossoms.[2]

[1] According to Buddhaghosa, they lived in the Himālaya (SA. i. 265); Vepacitti and Sakka were father- and son-in-law; sometimes they quarrelled, sometimes, as here, they were friends.

[2] S. i. 226.

Isayo Samuddakā (or **Sambara**) **Sutta.**—Long ago, many virtuous seers lived in huts on the seashore. At that time there was a war between the gods and the Asuras. The seers considered the gods righteous but feared harm from the Asuras. They went, therefore, to **Sambara,** lord of the Asuras, and asked him for a pledge of safety; he refused, saying that the seers were followers of **Sakka.** The seers thereupon cursed him to suffer everlasting terror. It is said that that same night Sambara woke up thrice, seized with fright.[1]

Buddhaghosa[2] adds that as a result of this curse, Sambara's mind became deranged and he came to be called **Vepacitti** (crazy-nerve).

[1] S. i. 227-8.

[2] SA. i. 266.

Isigaṇa.—Perhaps the name of a Pacceka Buddha, whom the Bodhisatta once reviled. The reading is, however, very uncertain.[1]

[1] Ap. i. 299; see footnote.

Isigili.—One of the five mountains round **Rājagaha** and one of the beauty-spots of the city.[1] There was, on one side of it, a black stone called the **Kālasilā.** This was a favourite haunt of the Buddha and the members of the Order.[2] It was also the scene of the suicide of **Godhika** and **Vakkali**[3] and of the murder of **Moggallāna** by the brigands.[4]

In the *Cūḷa Dukkhakkhaṇḍa Sutta* it is said that a large number of Nigaṇṭhas lived at Kālasilā, never sitting down, undergoing paroxysms of acute pain and agony, following the teachings of **Nigaṇṭha Nātaputta.** The Buddha questioned them as to their practises and preached to them the above-mentioned Sutta, which he afterwards repeated to **Mahānāma.**[5]

Once when the Buddha was dwelling at Kālasilā, he sang the praises of Rājagaha, giving Ānanda a chance, if he so desired, of asking him to live on for a *kappa*; but Ānanda did not take his opportunity.[6]

The books refer to several other visits of the Buddha to **Isigilapassa.** During one of these visits he heard **Vaṅgīsa's** high eulogy of **Moggallāna.**[7]

In the *Isigili Sutta*[8] the Buddha is represented as saying that while the other mountains round Rājagaha—**Vebhāra, Paṇḍava, Vepulla** and **Gijjhakūṭa**—had changed their old names, Isigili retained its former name and designation.

Five hundred Pacceka Buddhas once resided in Isigili for a long time; they could be seen entering the mountain, but once entered, there was no more sign of them. Men, observing this, said that the mountain swallowed up the sages and so it came by its name of Isigili (*Isī gilatī ti =Isigili*).

Buddhaghosa[9] adds that when the Pacceka Buddhas returned from their begging rounds, the rock would open like a folding door to admit them. Within the rock they had made for themselves cloisters, dwelling-houses, etc.

[1] D. ii. 116.
[2] See *e.g.*, Vin. ii. 76, where Dabba Mallaputta is asked by monks to provide for them accommodation there; see also Vin. iii. 41.
[3] S. i. 121; iii. 121 f.
[4] J. v. 125 f; DhA. iii. 65.
[5] M. i. 91 ff.
[6] D. iii. 116.
[7] S. i. 194; Thag. vv. 1249 ff.
[8] M. iii. 68-71.
[9] MA. ii. 889.

Isigili Sutta.—The 116th Sutta of the Majjhima Nikāya.[1] Preached to the monks at Isigili. It explains how **Isigili** came by its name, and gives a list of the Pacceka Buddhas who once dwelt there.

[1] M. iii. 68 ff.

Isiṇḍā.—A tribe mentioned in a list of various tribes.[1]

[1] Ap. ii. 359.

1. **Isidatta.**—A thera. He was the son of a caravan guide at **Vaḍḍhagāma** (*v.l.* **Veḷugāma**) in **Avanti.** By correspondence he became the unseen friend of **Citta-gahapati** of **Macchikāsaṇḍa.** The latter once sent him a letter regarding the excellences of the Buddha, and Isidatta, being pleased with the account given of the Buddha's religion, entered the Order under **Mahā-kaccāna** and in due course became an arahant. Later, with Mahākaccāna's leave, he visited the Buddha in the **Majjhimadesa** and was warmly received by him.[1] A verse uttered by Isidatta, in response to the Buddha's enquiry regarding his welfare, is recorded in the *Therāgāthā.*[2]

Isidatta had been a householder in the time of **Vipassī** Buddha and once, having seen the Buddha walking along the street and being pleased with his demeanour, he gave him an *āmoda*-fruit.[3] He is, probably, identical with **Amodapaliya** of the *Apadāna.*[4]

According to the *Samyutta Nikāya,*[5] Isidatta was once staying with a number of senior monks at Macchikāsaṇḍa in the **Ambāṭaka** grove. Citta-gahapati invited the monks to a meal. On this occasion Citta asked a question regarding the Buddha's teaching on the diversity of the elements. The chief Elder, being unable to answer, remained silent. Isidatta, though the most junior of the whole company, obtained the chief Elder's permission, and answered the question to the satisfaction of Citta. Citta likewise asked questions regarding various views, such as the infinity of the world, etc. At the end of the discourse, Citta discovered, by accident, that the Elder who had preached to him was none other than his unseen friend, Isidatta. Delighted with the discovery, he invited Isidatta to spend his time at Macchikāsaṇḍa, promising to provide him with all requisites. But that same day Isidatta left Macchikasaṇḍa and never returned.[6]

[1] ThagA. i. 238.
[2] v. 120.
[3] ThagA. *loc. cit.*
[4] ii. 447.
[5] iv. 283-8, also AA. i. 210.
[6] Because, says Buddhaghosa (AA. i. 210), he did not wish to stay after having been recognised.

2. **Isidatta.**—An equerry or chamberlain (*thapati*) of **Pasenadi,** King of Kosala. Isidatta is always mentioned with **Purāṇa.** Their duty was to look after the ladies of the king's harem when these went riding the elephant into the park. This often brought them into close contact with the ladies, and they confessed to the Buddha that it was difficult not to have evil thoughts regarding them.

Isidatta and Purāṇa were once at **Sādhuka**[1] on some business. They heard that the Buddha was having a robe made before starting on his rounds and they waited for an opportunity to talk to him. When the opportunity came they followed the Buddha and told him how glad they always were when he was near them and how sad when he was away on tour. The Buddha preaches to them the glory of the homeless life and urges them to put forth energy. He speaks very appreciatively of their loyalty to him and to his religion and congratulates them on the possession of virtuous qualities, such as sharing all their goods with holy men, a rare quality.[2]

According to the *Saṃyutta Commentary,*[3] Isidatta was a *Sakadāgāmī* and Purāṇa a *Sotāpanna.*

In the *Dhammacetiya Sutta,*[4] Pasenadi tells the Buddha how impressed he is by the reverence Isidatta and Purāṇa show for the Buddha and his teachings. "They are my carriage-builders," says the king, "and they depend on me for their livelihood and all their honours, yet these men do not serve me as whole-heartedly as they do the Lord."

Once the king spent the night in a cramped little house. Isidatta and Purāṇa, who were with him, having spent the best part of the night in discussing the Doctrine, lay down to rest with their heads in the direction in which they thought the Buddha to be, and their feet towards the king!

Isidatta was the uncle of the woman-disciple **Migasālā,** whose father was Purāṇa.

Purāṇa is described as a *brahmacāri,* but not Isidatta, yet, after death, they were both born in **Tusita.** Migasālā asks Ānanda how it was that people of different characters could have the same rebirth.[5]

Isidatta is mentioned by the Buddha among those who had the six qualities that brought realisation of immortality—unwavering loyalty to the Buddha, the Dhamma and the Saṅgha, Āriyan virtue, wisdom and liberation.[6]

The *Anāgata Vaṃsa*[7] says that when the future Buddha **Metteyya** leaves the household life, eighty-four thousand others, led by Isidatta and Purāṇa, will accompany him.

[1] Their own property, according to Buddhaghosa (SA.i.215).

[2] S. v. 348-52; Netti. 134 f.

[3] i. 215.

[4] M. ii. 123 f.

[5] A. iii. 348 f.; v. 138 f., 143 f. From MA. ii. 756, it would appear as if Isidatta was the brahmacāri. The word cannot here mean "celibate," for Purāṇa must have had a wife because Migasāla calls him her father (*pitā*).

[6] A. iii. 451.

[7] v. 58.

3. **Isidatta.**—King of Soreyya. **Anomadassī** Buddha preached to him and to eighty thousand of his followers. They all became arahants.[1]

[1] BuA. 143-4.

4. **Isidatta.**—One of the three leaders of the monks in Ceylon during the time that **Brāhmaṇatissa-cora** laid waste the land. The other two were **Cūḷasiva** and **Mahāsoṇa.** For the story connected with them see *s.v.* **Mahāsoṇa.**

1. **Isidatta Sutta.**—Records the questions of **Citta-gahapati** and the answers given by **Isidatta** Thera on the diversity of the elements.[1]

[1] S. iv. 283-5.

2. **Isidatta Sutta.**—The same, on the various views that arise in the world. Isidatta answers that they are all due to *sakkāyadiṭṭhi*; he then proceeds, in reply to further questions, to explain how *sakkāyadiṭṭhi* arises and how its absence is brought about.[1]

[1] S. iv. 286-8.

Isidāsa.—A thera. He had a brother, also a monk, named **Isibhatta.** Having spent the rainy season in **Sāvatthi,** they went to take up their abode in a certain village. The people there gave them food and robes, but they refused to accept their share of these, because, according to the rule, the robes are the property of the Saṅgha until the Kaṭhina-ceremony has been performed. The story is mentioned in connection with accepting robes elsewhere than in the spot where the rainy season has been spent.[1]

[1] Vin. i. 299.

Isidāsī Therī.—She was the daughter of a good and wealthy merchant of **Ujjenī.** Having come of age, she was given in marriage to the son of a merchant in **Sāketa.**

For one month she lived with him as a devoted wife; then because of her past kamma, her husband became estranged from her, and turned her out of the house. She was married again with the same result, and a third time to a friar. Isidāsī's father persuaded him to give up the pilgrim's life; he dwelt with his wife only for a fortnight and refused to stay with her any more. Isidāsī then met the therī **Jinadattā,** whom she entertained to a meal at her house. Under Jinadattā, Isidāsī joined the Order and became an arahant.

The *Therīgāthā*,[1] which contains forty-seven verses ascribed to her, describes not only her present life, but also her past lives. She had been a worker in gold in **Erakaccha** and had committed adultery in that life. As a result she was born in hell for a long time, and, in subse-

[1] vv. 400-47.

quent births became an ape, a goat, an ox, a hermaphrodite slave and a carter's daughter. In this last birth she was sold to a merchant in payment of her father's debts. When she was sixteen, the merchant's son, **Giridāsa,** fell in love with her and married her. He had already one wife, and the new one caused dissension between her and her husband. Therefore it was that in this life she was hated by her husbands. This account of her sojourn in saṃsāra was related by Isidāsī in response to a request by one of her fellow-nuns, **Bodhī.**[2]

Mrs. Rhys Davids thinks[3] that Isidāsī's verses in the *Therīgāthā* suggest late literary craft and bear the impress of late literary creation. The scene is Pāṭaliputta, and not any of the usual towns mentioned in the Canon, and the name of Isidāsī's sponsor—Jindattā—is, she says, significant. Perhaps there are traces here of Jainistic influence.

In the *Dīpavaṃsa*[4] Isidāsī (**Isidāsikā**) is mentioned in a list of eminent therīs who were leaders of the Order of bhikkhunīs.

² ThigA. 260 ff. ³ *Sisters*, Introd. pp. xxii f. ⁴ xviii. 9.

Isidinna.—A thera. He was the son of a seṭṭhi in **Sunāparanta.** He witnessed the miracle of the Buddha's acceptance of the **Candana-mālā,**[1] and, having heard the Buddha preach, he became a *Sotāpanna.* While still living the life of a householder, a compassionate spirit urged him to give it up. He entered the Order and soon after became an arahant.[2]

The *Theragāthā*[3] contains two verses which he uttered in confessing *aññā.* They were the same as were spoken to him by his friendly spirit.

In the time of **Vipassī** Buddha, he was a householder and did homage to the Buddha's Bodhi-tree with a fan made of *sumana*-flowers.[4] He is probably identical with **Sumanavījaniya** of the *Apadāna.*[5]

¹ Probably the **Candanamālaka** (*q.v.*).
² ThagA. i. 312-3.
³ vv. 187-8.
⁴ ThagA. 312 f.
⁵ Ap. ii. 415.

1. **Isipatana.**—An open space near Benares, the site of the famous **Migadāya** or Deer Park. It was eighteen leagues from **Uruvelā,** and when **Gotama** gave up his austere penances his friends, the **Pañcavaggiya** monks, left him and went to Isipatana.[1] After his Enlightenment the Buddha, leaving Uruvelā, joined them in Isipatana, and it was there that he preached his first sermon, the *Dhammacakkappavattana Sutta,* on the full-moon day of **Āsāḷha.**[2] There, also, the Buddha spent his first rainy season.[3]

¹ J. i. 68.

² Vin. i. 10 f.; on this occasion 80 *koṭis* of Brahmas and innumerable gods attained the comprehension of the Truth (Mil. 30); (130 *koṭis* says Mil. 350). The Lal. (528) gives details of the stages of this journey. The Buddha, having no money with which to pay the ferryman, crossed the Ganges through the air. When Bimbisāra heard of this, he abolished the toll for ascetics.

³ BuA., p. 3.

All the Buddhas preach their first sermon at the Migadāya in Isipatana; it is one of the four *avijahitaṭṭhānāni* (unchanging spots), the others being the *bodhi-pallaṅka*, the spot at the gate of **Saṅkassa,** where the Buddha first touches the earth on his return from **Tāvatiṃsa,** and the site of the bed in the **Gandhakuṭi** in **Jetavana.**[4]

Isipatana is mentioned by the Buddha as one of the four places of pilgrimage which his devout followers should visit.[5]

Isipatana was so-called because sages, on their way through the air (from the Himalayas), alight here or start from here on their aerial flight (*isayo ettha nipatanti uppatanti cāti-Isipatanaṃ*).

The Migadāya was so-called because deer were allowed to roam about there unmolested.

Pacceka Buddhas, having spent seven days in contemplation in the **Gandhamādana,** bathe in the **Anotatta** Lake and come to the habitations of men through the air, in search of alms. They descend to earth at Isipatana.[6]

Sometimes the Pacceka Buddhas come to Isipatana from **Nandamūlaka-pabbhāra.**[7]

Several other incidents connected with the Buddha, besides the preaching of the first sermon, are mentioned as having taken place in Isipatana. Here it was that one day at dawn **Yasa** came to the Buddha and became an arahant.[8] It was at Isipatana, too, that the rule was passed prohibiting the use of sandals made of talipot leaves.[9] On another occasion when the Buddha was staying at Isipatana, having gone there from Rājagaha, he instituted rules forbidding the use of certain kinds of flesh, including human flesh.[10] Twice, while the Buddha was at Isipatana, **Māra** visited him but had to go away discomfited.[11]

Besides the *Dhammacakkappavattana Sutta* mentioned above, several other suttas were preached by the Buddha while staying at Isipatana, among them the *Pañca Sutta* (S. iii. 66 f.), the *Rathakāra* or *Pacetana Sutta* (A. i. 110 f.), the two *Pāsa Suttas* (S. i. 105 f.), the *Samaya Sutta* (A. iii. 320 ff.), the *Kaṭuviya Sutta* (A. i. 279 f.), a discourse on the *Metteyyapañha* of the *Parāyana* (A. iii. 399 f.), and the *Dhammadinna Sutta* (S. v. 406 f.), preached to the distinguished layman **Dhammadinna,** who came to see the Buddha.

Some of the most eminent members of the Saṅgha seem to have resided at Isipatana from time to time; among recorded conversations at

[4] BuA. 247; DA. ii. 424.

[5] D. ii. 141.

[6] MA. i. 387; AA. i. 347 adds that sages also held the *uposatha* at Isipatana.

[7] MA. ii. 1019; PsA. 437-8.

[8] Vin. i. 15 f.

[9] *Ibid.*, i. 189.

[10] *Ibid.*, i. 216 ff.; the rule regarding human flesh was necessary because Suppiyā made broth out of her own flesh for a sick monk.

[11] S. i. 105 f.

Isipatana are several between **Sāriputta** and **Mahākoṭṭhita**,[12] and one between Mahākoṭṭhita and **Citta-Hatthisāriputta**.[13]

Mention is made, too, of a discourse in which several monks staying at Isipatana tried to help **Channa** in his difficulties.[14]

According to the *Mahāvaṃsa*, there was a large community of monks at Isipatana in the second century B.C. For, we are told that at the foundation ceremony of the **Mahā Thūpa** in Anurādhapura, twelve thousand monks were present from Isipatana led by the Elder **Dhammasena**.[15]

Hiouen Thsang[16] found, at Isipatana, fifteen hundred monks studying the Hīnayāna. In the enclosure of the Saṅghārāma was a vihāra about two hundred feet high, strongly built, its roof surmounted by a golden figure of the mango. In the centre of the vihāra was a life-size statue of the Buddha turning the wheel of the Law. To the south-west were the remains of a stone stūpa built by Asoka.[17] In front of it was a stone pillar to mark the spot where the Buddha preached his first sermon. Near by was another stūpa on the site where the Pañcavaggiyas spent their time in meditation before the Buddha's arrival, and another where five hundred Pacceka Buddhas entered Nibbāna. Close to it was another building where the future Buddha **Metteyya** received assurance of his becoming a Buddha.

Hiouen Thsang quotes the *Nigrodhamiga Jātaka*[18] to account for the origin of the Migadāya. According to him the Deer Park was the forest gifted by the king of Benares of the Jātaka, where the deer might wander unmolested.

According to the *Udapāna Jātaka*,[19] there was a very ancient well near Isipatana which, in the Buddha's time, was used by the monks living there.

In past ages Isipatana sometimes retained its own name,[20] but more often it was known by different names.[21] Thus in **Vipassī's** time it was known as **Khema-uyyāna.** It is the custom for all Buddhas to go through the air to Isipatana to preach their first sermon. Gotama, however, walked all the way, eighteen leagues, because he knew that

[12] S.ii.112.f; iii.167 f.; iv.162 f.: 384 ff.

[13] A. iii. 392 f.

[14] S. iii. 132 f.

[15] Mhv. xxix. 31.

[16] Beal: *Records of the Western World*, ii. 45 ff.

[17] The *Divy.* (389-94) mentions Asoka as intimating to Upagupta his desire to visit the places connected with the Buddha's activities, and to erect *thūpas* there. Thus he visited Lumbinī, Bodhimūla, Isipatana, Migadāya and Kusinagara; this is confirmed by Asoka's lithic records, *e.g. Rock Edict*, viii.

[18] J. i. 145 ff.

[19] J. ii. 354 ff.

[20] *E.g.*, in the time of Phussa Buddha (Bu. xix. 18), Dhammadassī (BuA. 182) and Kassapa (BuA. 218). Kassapa was born there (*ibid.*, 217).

[21] For these names see under those of the different Buddhas.

by so doing he would meet **Upaka,** the Ājīvaka, to whom he could be of service.[22]

Isipatana is identified with the modern Saranath, six miles from Benares. Cunningham[23] found the Migadāya represented by a fine wood, covering an area of about half a mile, extending from the great tomb of Dhammek on the north to the Chaukundi mound on the south.

[22] DA. ii. 471. [23] Arch. Reports, i. p. 107.

2. **Isipatana.**—A monastery built by **Parakkamabāhu I.** in the suburb **Rājavesibhujaṅga,** of **Pulatthipura.**[1]

[1] Cv. lxxviii. 79; but see lxxiii. 151-5 and Cv. Trs. ii. 18, n. 3.

Isibhatta Thera.—Brother of **Isidāsa** (*q.v.*).

Isibhūmaṅgaṇa.—A spot in **Anurādhapura** where half the relics of **Mahinda** were buried by King **Uttiya.**[1] The *Dīpavaṃsa*[2] calls it **Isibhūmi.**

[1] Mhv. xx. 46. [2] xvii. 109.

Isimuggadāyaka.—A Thera. He gave *isimugga* mixed with honey to **Padumuttara** Buddha and 108,000 monks. As a result, forty-four kappas ago he was born thirty-eight times as king, his name being **Mahisamanta.**[1]

[1] Ap. i. 193-4.

Isisinga.—A hermit, the son of the Bodhisatta and a doe. His story is related in the *Alambusā Jātaka* and in the *Naḷinikā Jātaka* (*q.v.*).

Issatta Sutta.—**Pasenadi** questions the Buddha as to how gifts should be given and the Buddha's answer is that they should be bestowed where the heart is pleased to give. The further question is asked as to whom, when given, does a gift bear much fruit. To the virtuous, irrespective of class, says the Buddha, and he instances the case of a youth skilled in war as opposed to one who is untrained and unskilled, no matter what his social status. The Buddha proceeds to describe the qualities which are possessed by the virtuous man.[1]

The Commentary[2] describes this interview as a public one, taking place before a large audience, among whom are teachers of rival schools, "scratching the ground with their feet." Their fame had suffered owing to the popularity of the Buddha and they had represented him as exhorting the people to give only to himself and to his followers. Pasenadi here gives the Buddha opportunity to vindicate himself.

[1] S. i. 98 f. [2] SA. i. 129 f.

Issara Sutta.—One of the Suttas in the *Devatā Saṃyutta.* Questions are asked as to what makes for lordship among men, what is the supreme commodity, etc., and the answer is that power of command it is which brings lordship and that women are the supreme commodity, etc.[1]

[1] S. i. 43.

Issarasamaṇārāma (Issarasamaṇavihāra, Issarasamaṇaka).—One of the monasteries at **Anurādhapura.** It was built by **Devānampiyatissa** on the spot where the prince **Ariṭṭha** dwelt with his five hundred followers after having received their ordination from **Mahinda.**[1] The building of this monastery was the seventh of the great tasks performed by Devānampiyatissa.[2]

One of the eight saplings from the Bodhi-tree at Anurādhapura was planted at Issarasamaṇārāma.[3]

Candamukha Siva built a tank near **Maṇikāragāmaka** and gave it for the use of the vihāra,[4] while **Vasabha** built in the monastery an uposatha-hall[5] and **Vohāraka Tissa** constructed a wall round it.[6] **Kassapa I.** restored the buildings and enlarged the grounds. He also bought villages which he presented to the monastery for its maintenance. He had two daughters, **Bodhī** and **Uppalavaṇṇā,** and he gave their names and his own to the vihāra. When the king wished to hand over the vihāra to the Theravāda monks they refused to accept it, fearing the reproach of the people that it was the work of a parricide. Then the king dedicated it to the image of the Buddha and the monks accepted it saying that it belonged to their Master.[7]

According to the *Mahāvaṃsa Ṭīkā,*[8] the vihāra was also called **Kassapagiri,** probably after its restoration by Kassapa I., mentioned above.[9] See also *s.v.* **Kassapagiri.**

It had originally been called Issarasamaṇa because of its association with the five hundred noblemen (*issaradārakā*) who joined the Order with Ariṭṭha.[10] The *Ṭīkā* adds[11] that **Sāliya,** son of **Duṭṭhagāmaṇi,** enlarged the vihāra out of the tribute brought to him by the men of his tributary villages to the south of Anurādhapura. He used to observe the *uposatha* on fast days at the vihāra and spend the day in the *Mahindaguhā* there.

In the *Samantapāsādikā*[12] the vihāra is called **Issaraṇimmāna.**

[1] Mhv. xx. 14; xix. 66.
[2] *Ibid.,* xx. 20.
[3] *Ibid.,* xix. 61; Mbv. 162.
[4] Mhv. xxxv. 47.
[5] *Ibid.,* 87.
[6] *Ibid.,* xxxvi. 36.
[7] Cv. xxxix. 10-14; see also 9 below.
[8] pp. 407 and 652.
[9] See also Cv. Trs. i. 43, n. 7, and Ep. Zeyl. i. 31 ff., where the *vihāra* is called "Isurameṇu-Bo-Upulvan-Kasubgiri" in an inscription of Mahinda IV.
[10] MṬ. 416.
[11] 607.
[12] i. 100.

Issariya.—A Damiḷa general whom **Duṭṭhagāmaṇi** subdued at **Hāḷakola.**[1]

[1] Mhv. xxv. 11.

Issā Sutta.—The nun who is possessed of five qualities, including envy, goes to hell without any doubt.[1]

[1] A. iii. 140.

Issāpakata-itthi Vatthu.—The story of a woman who, finding that her husband had relations with a female servant, bound the servant hand and foot, cut off her nose and locked her up in a secret chamber. In order to hide the deed from her husband, she took him to the monastery to hear the Buddha preach. Some relatives of hers came to the house and discovering what had happened, released the servant. She went to the monastery where her mistress was listening to the Buddha's sermon and proclaimed aloud the wrong done to her. The Buddha, thereupon, pointed out the folly of doing evil in the hope that it would not be found out. We are told that both the woman and her husband became *Sotāpanna* at the end of the sermon. The servant was set free.[1]

[1] DhA. iii. 486-7.

Issukī Sutta.—A woman who is faithless, shameless, unscrupulous, envious and of weak wisdom is reborn in purgatory.[1]

[1] S. iv. 241.

Ī.

Īsadhara.—One of the seven ranges of mountains round **Sineru.** It is the abode of deva kings and of devas and yakkhas.[1] It is higher than **Karavīka,** and between these two is a **Sīdantara-samudda**; next to **Īsadhara** and higher than it is **Yugandhara,** and between them is another **Sīdantara-samudda.**[2]

The *Mahāvastu*[3] calls it Iśāndhara (suggesting its probable etymology).

[1] SnA. ii. 443; Sp. i. 119; Dvy. 217. [2] J. vi. 125. [3] ii. 300.

Īsādantā.—A class of elephants mentioned with **Hemavatas** and others.[1] They have trunks like the poles of a carriage, slightly curved.[2]

[1] Vv. xx. 9. [2] VvA. 104.

Īsāna.—One of the chief devas. In the *Tevijja Sutta*[1] he is mentioned with **Indra, Soma, Varuṇa, Pajāpati** and **Brahmā,** as being invoked by the brahmins.

He was in the battle of the devas against the asuras and led a section of the deva host. Indra tells the devas that if, during the struggle, they felt faint-hearted, they should look at the crest of his own banner or at that of Pajāpati, Varuṇa or Īsāna, and their fear would disappear.[2]

In the assembly of the gods, Īsāna gets the fourth seat next to Varuṇa. He is in beauty and longevity equal to Indra.[3]

Īśāna is an older name for Rudra (Śiva).[4] The conception of him had so far changed by the time of Buddhaghosa that in Buddhaghosa's accounts he is given a seat near Sakka and inferior to his. Perhaps he was one of the thirty-three gods of **Tāvatiṃsa.**[5]

[1] D. i. 244.
[2] S. i. 219.
[3] SA. i. 262.
[4] Böthlinck and Roth: *Worterbuch.*
[5] KS. i. 281, n. 4.

U.

Ukkaṃsamāla.—A learned monk of Ava. He was well versed in literature and wrote two books dealing with the Pāli language, the *Vaṇṇabodhana* and the *Likhananaya.*[1]

[1] Sās., p. 120.

Ukkaṃsika.—A king of **Rāmañña,** a great patron of learning.[1]

[1] For details about him see Bode, *op. cit.*, 50, 52.

Ukkacelā.—See **Ukkā°**.

Ukkaṭṭhā.—A town in Kosala, near the Himālaya. It has been given, free from all taxes (as *brahmadeyya*), to **Pokkharasātī** by the king of Kosala, in recognition of the former's skill. It was thickly populated and had much grassland, woodland and corn.[1] The **Icchānaṅgala** wood was in the neighbourhood, and when the Buddha was staying in the wood **Pokkharasātī** first sent his pupil **Ambaṭṭha** and then went himself to visit the Buddha.[2]

There was a road which connected Ukkaṭṭhā with **Setavyā**[3] and with **Vesāli.**[4]

[1] D. i. 87; DA. i. 245.
[2] See the *Ambaṭṭha Sutta.*
[3] A. ii. 37. Chatta goes from Setavyā to Ukaṭṭhā to learn under Pokkharasāti (VvA. 229).
[4] J. ii. 259.

It was in the **Subhagavana** at Ukkaṭṭhā that the *Mūlapariyāya Sutta*[5] was preached and the *Mūlapariyāya Jātaka*[6] was related in connection with it. Ukkaṭṭhā was the residence of **Aṅganika-Bhāradvāja.**[7]

Buddhaghosa[8] explains that the city was so called because it was built by the light of torches (*ukkā*) at night, in order that it might be completed within the auspicious time.

In the *Brahmanimantika Sutta,*[9] the Buddha says that it was while he was residing at Subhagavana that be became aware of the erroneous views of **Baka-brahma** and went to the Brahma-world to teach Baka the truth. The *Divyāvadāna* calls the city Ukkatā.[10]

[5] M.i. 1 ff.
[6] J.ii. 259 ff.
[7] ThagA. 339.
[8] MA.i.9 ; AA.ii.504.
[9] M.i.326; but see S.i.142; J.iii.359.
[10] p. 621.

Ukkaṇṭhita-aññatarabhikkhussa Vatthu.—The name given in the *Dhammapada Commentary*[1] to the story of **Anupubba** (*q.v.*).

[1] i. 297-300.

Ukkanagara.—A vihāra (presumably in Ceylon). It was the residence of the thera **Mahāvyaggha** and seven hundred others.[1]

[1] Mhv. xxxii. 54.

Ukkalā.—A district (*janapada*) in the region identified with modern Orissa.[1] The merchants **Tapassu** and **Bhalluka** were on the way from Ukkalā, when a certain deva, an erstwhile relative of theirs, advised them to visit the Buddha at **Rājāyatanamūla,** near Uruvelā, and to offer food to him, which they did.[2] They were on the way to **Majjhimadesa.**[3] According to the *Theragāthā Commentary*[4] there were caravan-drivers of a city called **Pokkharavatī** (probably a town in Ukkalā). Their destination was evidently **Rājagaha,** for we find them visiting the Buddha there after the first sermon and hearing him preach.

The men of Ukkalā, together with those of Vassa and Bhañña, are represented as being deniers of cause and effect, deniers of reality (*ahetuvādā, akiriyavādā, natthikavādā*).[5]

The *Mahāvastu*[6] places Ukkalā in the **Uttarāpatha** and mentions Adhiṣṭhāna as the place from which Tapussa and Bhalluka hailed.

The *Mahābhārata*[7] mentions the Ukkalas several times in lists of tribes (*v.l.* Okkalā).

[1] CAG., p. 733.
[2] Vin.i.4.
[3] J.i.80.
[4] i.48 f.
[5] A.ii.31; S.iii.72; M.iii.78; Kvu. 60; AA.ii.497; see also KS.iii.63, and GS.ii.34, n.3.
[6] iii.303.
[7] *E.g.*, in Bhīsmapārvan ix. 365; Droṇa iv. 122.

Ukkācelā.—A village in the **Vajji** country, on the banks of the Ganges, on the road from **Rājagaha** to **Vesāli** and near the latter.[1] Once while **Sāriputta** was staying there, the Paribbājaka **Sāmaṇḍaka** visited him and talked to him about Nibbāna.[2] Some time later, after the death of Sāriputta and Moggallāna within a fortnight of each other, the Buddha came to Ukkacelā on his way to Vesāli and at a gathering of the monks uttered high praise of the two chief disciples and spoke of the loss the Order had sustained by their death.[3]

The *Cūlagopālaka Sutta* was also preached at Ukkacelā.[4]

Buddhaghosa[5] says that when the city was being built, on the day its site was marked out, fish came ashore at night from the river, and men, noticing them, made torches (*ukkā*) out of rags (*celā*), dipped them in oil, and by their light caught the fish. On account of this incident the city was called Ukkācelā (*v.l.* **Ukkacelā, Ukkāvelā**).

1 UdA. 322. 2 S. iv. 261-2. 3 *Ibid.*, v. 163 f. 4 M. i. 225. 5 MA. i. 447.

Ukkācelā Sutta.—The incident mentioned above, of the Buddha praising his two chief disciples, after their death.[1]

1 S. v. 163.

Ukkāsatika Thera.—An arahant. Ninety-four kappas ago he had seen the Pacceka Buddha **Kosika,** in Himavā, engaged in meditation, and for seven days he had one hundred torches kept lighted near the Buddha. On the eighth day he gave alms to the Pacceka Buddha. As a result he was born in **Tusita,** and from his body rays of light issued, spreading one hundred leagues. Fifty-five kappas ago he reigned as king of Jambudīpa, with his capital in **Sobhana,** built by **Vissakamma** himself, entirely of gold.[1]

1 Ap. ii. 414-15.

Ukkoṭana Sutta.—Few are those that refrain from accepting bribes to prevent justice, from cheating and from crooked ways; numerous those that do not so refrain.[1]

1 S. v. 473.

Ukkhā Sutta.—It would be better to cultivate thoughts of love (*mettā*) at morning, noon and eventide, than to give a morning gift of one hundred *ukkhās*[1] and the same at noon and in the evening.[2]

1 The Commentary explains *ukkhā* as being a large pot with a large mouth (*mahā-mukha-ukkhalī*); SA. ii. 164.

2 S. ii. 264.

Ukkhittapadumiya Thera.—An arahant. In the time of **Padumuttara** Buddha he had been a garland-maker of **Haṃsavatī.** Once while he was picking lotuses in a pond, the Buddha appeared before him with numerous disciples. The garland-maker picked a lotus and threw it up into the air, wishing it to remain above the Buddha's head; by the Buddha's power it did thus remain. As a result, the garland-maker was reborn in Tāvatiṃsa in a palace named **Satapatta.** A thousand times he was king of the devas and five hundred times king of men.[1]

[1] Ap. i. 275 f.

Ukkhepakaṭa-Vaccha Thera.—He was the son of a brahmin of the **Vaccha** family. Having heard the Buddha preach, he entered the Order and dwelt in a village settlement in **Kosala.** He learnt the doctrine from the various monks who came there from time to time, but it was not until he learnt from **Sāriputta** that he was able to distinguish between *Sutta, Vinaya* and *Abhidhamma.* He thus became versed in the Three *Piṭakas* even before the First Council.[1] He practised meditation and soon attained arahantship.[2] Later he became a teacher of the doctrine.

According to Dhammapāla,[3] the soubriquet **Ukkhepakaṭa** was given to him because he was able to teach and recite passages from the three Piṭakas "casting them in their proper setting, according as they belonged to each Piṭaka." The title was meant to emphasise his eminent repertory of orally-learnt doctrine.

He had been a householder in the time of the Buddha **Siddhattha** and had helped a guild who built a hall for the Buddha by giving them a pillar for the building.

Fifty-five kappas ago he was a king named **Yasodhara** and twenty-one kappas ago another king named **Udena.** His seven-storied palaces were all built on one pillar. He is probably to be identified with **Ekatthambhika** Thera of the **Apadāna.**[4]

[1] On this see *Brethren*, p. 66. n. 1.
[2] Thag. v. 65; ThagA. i. 147 f.
[3] ThagA. i. 149.
[4] i. 56-7.

1. **Ugga.**—A banker in the time of **Konāgamana** Buddha; he was one of the Buddha's chief lay-supporters and built for him a residence, half a league in extent, on the site of the later **Jetavana.**[1]

[1] J. i. 94; Bu. xxiv. 24.

2. **Ugga.**—The chief minister of **Pasenadi,** king of Kosala.[1] He once visited the Buddha and told him how he rivalled in power and wealth the seṭṭhi **Migāra,** grandson of **Rohaṇa.** He was worth one hundred

[1] AA.ii.697.

thousand in gold alone, to say nothing of silver. The Buddha tells him that all this wealth could easily be lost in various ways, not so the seven kinds of Āriyan wealth (*saddhā*, *sīla*, etc.).[2]

[2] A. iv. 6-7.

3. **Ugga.**—One of those that formed the retinue of the rājā **Eḷeyya.** He was a follower of **Uddaka-Rāmaputta,** whom the king too held in veneration.[1]

[1] A. ii. 180.

4. **Ugga.**—A householder of **Hatthigāma(ka)** of the **Vajji** country. Among householders he was declared by the Buddha to be the best of those who waited on the Order (*saṅghupaṭṭhākānaṃ*).[1] On his father's death he was appointed to the post of seṭṭhi. Once when the Buddha went to Hatthigāma during a tour and was staying in the **Nāgavanuyyāna** there, Ugga came to the pleasaunce, with dancers, at the conclusion of a drinking-feast of seven days' duration. At the sight of the Buddha he was seized with great shame and his intoxication vanished. The Buddha preached to him and he became an *anāgāmī*. Thereupon he dismissed his dancers and devoted himself to looking after members of the Saṅgha. Devas visited him at night and told him of the attainments of various monks, suggesting that he should choose only the eminent ones as the recipients of his gifts. But what he gave, he gave to all with equal delight.[2]

The Buddha once stated that Ugga was possessed of eight special and wonderful qualities. One of the monks, hearing the Buddha's statement, went to Ugga and asked him what these qualities were. Ugga replied that he was not aware of what the Buddha had in mind and proceeded to explain eight wonderful things that had happened to him, viz.: (1) As soon as he saw the Buddha, his state of drunkenness vanished and he made obeisance to the Buddha, who talked to him on various topics, such as *dāna*, *sīla*, etc. (2) When the Buddha saw that Ugga's mind was ready, he preached to him the Four Truths, which he understood and realised. (3) He had had four young and beautiful wives; when he took the vow of celibacy, he made ample provision for them; for one of them he obtained the husband of her choice, because she so desired, and this he did with no tinge of jealousy. (4) All his immense wealth he shared with men of good and lovely conduct. (5) On whatever monk he waited, he did it with whole-heartedness; to the monk's preaching he listened earnestly; if the monk did not preach, Ugga

[1] A. i. 26. [2] AA. i. 214-5.

himself taught him the doctrine. (6) Devas told him of the different attainments of various monks, but he gave to all alike, without distinction. (7) He felt no pride that he should hold converse with devas. (8) He did not worry about death because the Buddha had assured him that he would never more return to this world.

The monk reports this conversation to the Buddha and the Buddha tells him that these were the very qualities he had in mind when praising Ugga.[3]

The *Saṃyutta Nikāya*[4] records a visit paid to the Buddha by Ugga, at Hatthigāmaka. He asked the Buddha why it was that some beings attained full freedom in this very life, while others did not. Because of grasping, says the Buddha.

Ugga had been a householder in the time of **Padumuttara** Buddha. He once heard the Buddha preach and declare, at the end of his sermon, one of his lay disciples to be the best of those who waited on the Order. He wished for himself a similar attainment and did many good deeds towards that end.[5] *v.l.* **Uggata.**

[3] A iv. 212-6. [4] S. iv. 109 f. [5] AA. i. 214.

5. **Ugga.**—A householder of **Vesāli,** declared by the Buddha to be the best of those who gave agreeable gifts (*manāpadāyakānaṃ*).[1]

His original name is not known. He came to be called Ugga-seṭṭhi, because he was tall in body, lofty in morals and of striking personality. The very first time he saw the Buddha, he became a *sotāpanna* and later an *anāgāmī*. When he was old, the thought came to him one day, while he was alone, " I will give to the Buddha whatever I consider most attractive to myself and I have heard from him that such a giver obtains his wishes. I wish the Buddha would come to my house now." The Buddha, reading his thoughts, appeared before his door with a following of monks. He received them with great respect and, having given them a meal, announced to the Buddha his intention of providing him and the monks with whatever they found agreeable.[2]

While staying at the **Kūṭāgārasālā** in Vesāli, the Buddha once declared to the monks that Ugga was possessed of eight marvellous qualities. The rest of the story is very similar to that of **Ugga** of **Hatthigāmāka,** given above. This Ugga states as the first wonderful thing which happened to him, the faith he found in the Buddha at their very first meeting; three and four are the same; the fifth is that whatever monk he waits on, he does it whole-heartedly; the sixth, that if the monk

[1] A. i. 26; in SA. iii. 26 he is wrongly described as *aggo panītadāyakānam*—the title of **Mahānāma.**

[2] AA. i. 213-4.

preaches he would listen with attention, if the monk does not preach, Ugga would teach to him the doctrine; the seventh is the same; the eighth that he has got rid of all the *orambhāgiya-saṃyojanas* mentioned by the Buddha. The conversation is reported to the Buddha who agrees that Ugga does possess the qualities mentioned.[3]

The *Saṃyutta Nikāya*[4] repeats under Ugga of Vesāli the same discussion with the Buddha as was given in connection with Ugga of Hatthigāma, regarding the reason why some beings do not attain complete freedom in this very life. This is perhaps due to uncertainty on the part of the compilers as to which Ugga took part in the original discussion.

A sutta in the *Aṅguttara Nikāya*[5] gives a list of things of which Ugga himself was fond. We are told that he offered these things to the Buddha. The list includes rice-cakes made in the shape of Sāla-blossoms, the flesh of sucking pig and Kāsi robes. These and other things were given not only to the Buddha, but, according to the Commentary,[6] also to five hundred monks. The Sutta goes on to say that Ugga died soon after and was born among the **Manomayadevā.** He visited the Buddha from the deva-world and stated that he had achieved his goal (of reaching arahantship).

He is included in a list of householders who possessed six special qualities: unwavering loyalty to the Buddha, the Dhamma and the Saṅgha, Āriyan conduct, insight and liberation.[7]

His desire to become chief of those who give agreeable things was first conceived in the time of **Padumuttara** Buddha, when he was a householder in Haṃsavatī; he heard the Buddha describe one of his disciples as being a giver of such gifts.[8]

[3] A. iv. 208-12.
[4] S. iv. 109 f.
[5] A.iii. 49-51.
[6] AA. ii. 602.
[7] A. iv. 451.
[8] AA. i. 213.

6. **Ugga.**—A thera. He was the son of a banker in **Ugga,** in the Kosala country. When the Buddha was staying in the **Bhaddārāma** there, Ugga heard him preach and entered the Order. Soon afterwards he became an arahant.[1]

He had been a householder in the time of **Sikhī** Buddha and offered him a *ketaka*-flower. As a result, he was born twelve times as king. He is probably to be identified with **Sudassana** Thera of the *Apadāna.*[2]

[1] Thag. v. 80; ThagA. i. 174-5.
[2] i. 164-5.

7. **Ugga.**—A banker of the city of **Ugga ;** he was a friend of **Anāthapiṇḍika** and, according to some accounts, his son married Anāthapiṇḍika's

daughter, **Cūḷa Subhaddā.** He and his family had been followers of the Nigaṇṭhas, but they later became followers of the Buddha through the intervention of Subhaddā. For the story see *s.v.* **Cūḷa Subhaddā.** See also **Kāḷaka** (1).

8. **Ugga.**—A township (*nigama*) in **Kosala.** The Buddha stayed there at the **Bhaddārāma.**[1] The town was the residence of the banker **Ugga,** and was once a stronghold of the Nigaṇṭhas; after the conversion of Ugga's family, through **Cūḷa Subhaddā's** intervention, the people became faithful followers of the Buddha and for some time **Anuruddha** lived there, at the Buddha's special bidding, to preach to the new converts.[2] Probably the **Uggārāma,** mentioned in the story of **Aṅganika Bhāradvāja,**[3] was also in Ugga, in which case it was near the village of **Kuṇḍiya** of the Kuru country.

[1] ThagA. i. 174.

[2] DhA. iii. 465-9; according to ThagA. i. 65 **Mahā Subhaddā** also lived in Ugga, in a family of unbelievers.

[3] ThagA. i. 339; *Brethren*, 157, n. 4.

1. **Ugga Sutta.**—Records the conversation between the Buddha and **Ugga** (2) (*q.v.*), minister of King **Pasenadi.**[1]

[1] A. iv. 6-7.

2. **Ugga Sutta.**—Deals with the eight wonderful qualities of **Ugga** of Vesālī.[1] See **Ugga** (5).

[1] A iv. 208-12.

3. **Ugga Sutta.**—Deals with the eight wonderful qualities of **Ugga** of **Hatthigāmaka.**[1] See **Ugga** (4).

[1] A. iv. 212-6.

1. **Uggata.**—See **Ugga** (4).

2. **Uggata.**—A khattiya of the city of **Sumaṅgala,** father of **Sujāta** Buddha.[1]

[1] J. i. 38; Bu. xiii. 20.

3. **Uggata.**—The Kāliṅga king who, with **Bhīmaratha,** king of **Sañjayantī,** and **Aṭṭhaka,** king of **Hastināpura,** sought the Bodhisatta **Sarabhaṅga** to learn from him where the kings **Kalābu, Nālikīra, Ajjuna** and **Daṇḍakī** had been born after the destruction of themselves and their kingdoms as a result of their ill-treatment of holy men.[1]

[1] J. v. 135 ff.

Their story is given in the *Sarabhaṅga Jātaka* (*q.v.*).

The scholiast of the Jātaka[2] takes Uggata to be not the name of the Kāliṅga king but a descriptive epithet, and explains it by saying *cando viya suriyo viya ca pākaṭo paññāto.*

The *Mahāvastu*,[3] however, definitely mentions Ugga as the name of the king, in the same way as Bhīmaratha and Aṣṭhamaka (Aṭṭhaka), and gives the capitals of the two latter as Sañjayantī and Hastināpura respectively.

[2] *Ibid.*, 137. [3] iii. 364 f.

4. **Uggata.**—King during the time of **Sobhita** Buddha. He built a vihāra named **Surinda** at **Sunandavatī** and another named **Dhammagaṇārāma** at **Mekhalā** and dedicated them to the Buddha and the Order. At the festival of dedication of the former one hundred crores became arahants and at that of the latter, ninety crores.[1]

[1] Bu. vii. 9 f.; BuA. 139.

5. **Uggata.**—Twenty-nine kappas ago there were sixteen kings of the name of Uggata, all previous incarnations of the Thera **Citakapūjaka.**[1]

[1] Ap. i. 151.

6. **Uggata.**—King of one thousand and fifty-one kappas ago; a previous life of **Dhajadāyaka** Thera.[1]

[1] Ap. i. 109.

7. **Uggata.**—Fourteen kappas ago there were four kings named Uggata, previous births of **Parappasādaka**[1] or **Bhūta**[2] Thera.

[1] Ap. i. 114. [2] ThagA. i. 494.

Uggatasarīra.—A Mahāsāḷa brahmin, so called because he was tall in person and eminent in wealth.[1] Having made preparations for a great sacrifice, in which numerous animals were to be slaughtered, he visited the Buddha at Jetavana to consult him as to the efficacy of the sacrifice. Three times he told the Buddha that he had heard that the laying down (*ādhāna*) of the fire and the setting up (*ussāpana*) of the sacrificial post bore great fruit. Three times the Buddha agreed that it was so, and Uggatasarīra was about to conclude that the Buddha approved of his sacrifice, when **Ānanda** intervened and suggested that the Buddha should be asked to explain his meaning and to give his advice as to the efficacy of the sacrifice. The Buddha thereupon declared that there were

[1] AA. ii. 714.

three fires to be cast off: *rāga*, *dosa* and *moha*; and three fires that should be honoured: *āhuneyyaggi*, *gahapataggi* and *dakkhiṇeyyaggi*. The *āhuneyyaggi* was represented by the parents; the *gahapata*, by wife, children, servants and retainers; the *dakkhiṇeyya*, by holy men and recluses.

At the end of the discourse, Uggatasarīra became a convert to the Buddha's faith and set free the animals destined for the sacrifice.[2]

[2] A. iv. 41-6.

Ugganagara.—See **Ugga** (8).

Uggarinda.—One of the chief lay supporters of **Nārada** Buddha.[1]

[1] Bu. x. 25.

1. **Uggasena.**—King of Benares. The Nāga king, **Campeyya,** was brought before him by a brahmin snake-charmer for a performance, but when the king learnt from the Nāga's sister, **Sumanā,** what had happened, he caused the Nāga to be set free. Later, Campeyya took him to the Nāga-world and shewed him every honour. Uggasena's subjects were allowed to bring back from the Nāga-world whatever they desired.[1]

The story is told in the *Campeyya Jātaka* (*q.v.*).

In the present age Uggasena became **Sāriputta.**[2]

[1] J. v. 458 ff.; Mtu. ii. 177 ff. [2] J. v. 468.

2. **Uggasena.**—Son of a banker of **Rājagaha.** He fell in love with a very skilful acrobat, married her and followed her about with her troupe. When he discovered that she despised him for his lack of skill as an acrobat, he learnt the art and became a clever tumbler. The Buddha knew that Uggasena was ready for conversion and entering Rājagaha while Uggasena was displaying his skill before a large crowd of people, withdrew their attention from his skilful feats. Seeing Uggasena's disappointment, the Buddha sent **Moggallāna** to ask him to continue his performance, and while Uggasena was displaying his skill by various tricks, the Buddha preached to him, and Uggasena became an arahant, even as he stood poised on the tip of a pole, and later became a monk. His wife also left the world soon after and attained arahantship.

In the time of **Kassapa** Buddha they were husband and wife. On their way to the shrine of the Buddha where they worked as labourers, they saw an Elder and gave him part of the food they had with them and expressed the desire that they should, one day, like him, realise the Truth. The Elder, looking into the future, saw that their wish would be fulfilled and smiled. The wife, seeing him smile, said to her husband that the Elder must be an actor, and the husband agreed. Because of this remark they became actors in this life, but through their pious gift they attained arahantship.[1]

[1] DhA. iv. 59-65; also *ibid.*, 159.

3. **Uggasena.**—King, husband of Queen **Dinnā** (*q.v.*)

Uggasena-Nanda.—King of **Magadha,** one of the nine **Nanda** kings.[1]

[1] Mbv. 98.

Uggasena Vatthu.—The story of **Uggasena** of Rājagaha (**Uggasena** 2).[1]

[1] DhA. iv. 59-65; *ibid.*, 159.

Uggaha Meṇḍakanattā.—The grandson of the banker **Meṇḍaka;** he lived in **Bhaddiya.** Once when the Buddha was staying in the **Jātiyāvana** at Bhaddiya, Uggaha invited him and three monks to a meal at his house. At the conclusion of the meal, he asked the Buddha to speak a few words of advice to his daughters who were about to be married.[1] The Buddha preached to them the **Uggaha Sutta.**[2]

[1] The Commentary says that their nuptials were already in progress at the time of the Buddha's visit (AA. ii. 597).

[2] A. iii. 36 ff.

Uggaha Sutta.—Preached at **Bhaddiya** to the daughters of **Uggaha Meṇḍakanattā** just before their marriage. A wife should rise betimes before her husband, and sleep after him; she should respect his wishes, give him pleasure and be of sweet speech. His parents and elders and all those whom he holds in esteem, should she reverence and honour; she should be skilful in all the duties of the household; she should look after the servants in the house and supervise their duties, provide them with all necessaries and be kind and helpful to them; she should safeguard her husband's interests and look after his wealth; she should be of virtuous conduct in every way.[1]

[1] A. iii. 36 ff.

Uggārāma.—A pleasaunce, probably near the village **Kuṇḍiya** of the Kurus. **Aṅgaṇika Bhāradvāja** is said to have visited it once.[1] See also **Ugga** (8).

[1] ThagA. i. 339.

Uggāhamāna-Samaṇa-Maṇḍikāputta.—A Paribbājaka. Once when he was staying near Sāvatthi in Mallikā's pleasaunce at the **Samayappavādaka** hall, the carpenter (ṭhapati), **Pañcakaṅga,** on his way to see the Buddha, visited him and had a conversation with him, which conversation Pañcakaṅga later reported to the Buddha.[1] The details are given in the *Samaṇa-Maṇḍikā Sutta.*

According to Buddhaghosa,[2] the Paribbājaka's original name was **Sumana,** but he was called Uggāhamāna because he had the ability to learn a few things (because he was always learning things ?).

Chalmers[3] suggests that perhaps his mother's name was originally Sumanā and that it was altered to *Samaṇā,* just as there is the further tendency to read *muṇḍikā* for the second part, in order to make her name mean "shaveling recluse" on familiar Pāli analogy.

[1] M. ii. 22 f. [2] MA. ii. 710.
[3] Further Dialogues ii. 12 n.

Ugghaṭitaññu Sutta.—Some people in the world are quick withal and learn by taking hints; others learn when full details are given; some have to be led on by instruction; others just learn the text but do not understand it.[1]

[1] A. ii. 135.

Uccaṅkuṭṭha.—A locality in South India; it was the residence of many famous troop-leaders, whom **Kulasekhara** won over to his side in his fight against **Parakkamabāhu I.**[1]

[1] Cv. lxxvii. 78.

Ucchaṅga Jātaka (No. 67).—Three men who were ploughing on the outskirts of a forest were mistaken for bandits and taken before the king. While they were being tried a woman came to the palace and with loud lamentations begged for "wherewith to be covered." The king ordered a shift to be given to her but she refused, saying that that was not what she meant. The king's servants came back and reported that what the woman wanted was a husband. When the king had her summoned and questioned, she admitted that it was so. Being pleased with the woman, the king asked in what relationship the three prisoners stood to her. She answered that one was her husband, one her brother and one her son. When the king asked which of the three she wished to have released, she chose the brother, because, she said, the two others were replaceable. Well pleased with her, the king released all three.

The story was related in reference to a woman in a village in Kosala who obtained, from the king of Kosala, the release of three men in similar circumstances and in the same way.[1]

[1] J. i. 306-8.

Uccatalaṅka.—The residence of **Mahānāga** Thera[1] (*v.l.* **Uccavālika, Uccavālaṅka**).

[1] VibhA. 489.

Ucchaṅgapupphiya Thera.—An arahant. In the time of **Vipassī** Buddha he was a garland-maker of **Bandhumatī.** He saw the Buddha walking along the street with a large following of monks, and taking a flower from his lap he offered it to the Buddha.[1]

[1] Ap. ii. 374-5.

Uccaṅgamāya.—A Pacceka Buddha found in a list of Pacceka Buddhas.[1]

[1] M. iii. 70; ApA. i. 107.

Ucchiṭṭhabhatta Jātaka (No. 212).—In a village near Kāsī, a brahmin's wicked wife received her lover when her husband was away. She prepared a meal for her lover and while he ate she stood at the door watching for her husband. The brahmin appearing before he was expected, the lover was bundled into the store-room. The woman put some hot rice over the food left unfinished by her lover and gave the plate to her husband. When asked why the rice was hot on the top and cold at the bottom, she remained silent. The Bodhisatta, who had been born as a poor acrobat, had been at the door of the house waiting for alms and had seen all that had happened. He informed the brahmin of his wife's conduct and both wife and lover received a sound beating.

The story was told to a monk who hankered after his wife. The Buddha related the story in order to show him that in a past birth this same wife had made him eat the leavings of her paramour.[1]

[1] J. ii. 167 ff.

Ucchu.—The name given to one of the stories of the *Petavatthu.* The *peta* referred to had been a resident near **Veḷuvana.** Once he was going along the road eating a sugar cane and carrying a bundle of sugar canes. Behind him came another man of good conduct, with a child. The child, seeing the sugar cane, begged for some of it with great lamentations. The good man wishing to console the child, walked up to the sugar cane-eater and tried to make friends. His efforts were, however, unsuccessful, and when he begged for a piece of sugar cane for the child, the man sulkily threw him a bit from the end of the sugar cane. This man, after his death, was born as a *peta*. Around him was a forest of sugar canes, but whenever he attempted to eat any of them he got badly bruised and wounded. One day **Moggallāna** saw him, and having discovered his antecedents told him about his past profitless life. He made the *peta* get for him a piece of sugar cane, which he offered to the Buddha and the monks. As a result of this, the *peta* was reborn in **Tāvatiṃsa.**[1]

[1] Pv., pp. 61 f.; PvA. 257 ff.

Ucchukhaṇḍika.—A thera. He was a gate-keeper in Bandhumatī during the time of Vipassī Buddha and once gave to the Buddha a cut of sugar cane.[1] He is probably identical with **Kosiya** Thera.[2]

[1] Ap. ii. 393. [2] ThagA. i. 431 f.

1. **Ucchu-vimāna,** also called **Ucchudāyikā-vimāna.** A girl, who belonged to a pious family in Rājagaha, used to give to holy men half of anything she received. She was given in marriage to a family of unbelievers. One day she saw **Moggallāna** going about for alms, and having invited him to her house she gave him a piece of sugar cane which had been set aside for her mother-in-law, whose approval of the gift she hoped to win. But when the mother-in-law heard of what had happened in her absence, she flew into a rage and struck the girl with a stool. The girl died immediately and was born in **Tāvatiṃsa.**

Later she visited Moggallāna and revealed her identity.

Her palace came to be called **Ucchudāyikā-vimāna.**[1]

[1] Vv. 24 f.; VvA. 124 ff.

2. **Ucchu-vimāna.**—The story is the same as the above except that the mother in-law struck the girl with a clod of earth.[1]

[1] Vv. 44 f.; VvA. 203 ff.

Ujita.—A caravan-driver, who, with his friend **Ojita,** gave the first meal to **Sikhī** Buddha after his Enlightenment.[1]

[1] ThagA. i. 48.

Ujuññā (Ujjuññā).—A district and a town in **Kosala.** Once when the Buddha was staying at the Deer Park in **Kaṇṇakatthala** in the neighbourhood of the city, **Pasenadi,** who happened to be at Ujuññā on business, visited the Buddha. On this occasion was preached the *Kaṇṇakatthala Sutta*.[1]

It was here too that Nigaṇṭha **Kassapa** came to see the Buddha. This visit is recorded in the *Kassapa Sīhanāda Sutta*.[2]

[1] M. ii. 125 ff.; MA. ii. 757. [2] D. i. 161 ff.

1. **Ujjaya, Ujjāya.**—A Pacceka Buddha, mentioned in the list in the *Isigili Sutta*.[1]

[1] M. iii. 70.

2. **Ujjaya.**—A thera. He was the son of a Sotthiya-brahmin of **Rājagaha,** and became proficient in the three Vedas. Dissatisfied with the teaching of the Vedas, he went to the Buddha and heard him preach at Veḷuvana. Later he entered the Order and retired into the forest, having learnt a subject for meditation. Soon after he became an arahant.

In a past life he had offered a *kaṇikāra*-flower to the Buddha.

Thirty-five kappas ago he was a king named **Aruṇabala.**[1]

He is probably identical with **Kaṇikārapupphiya** of the *Apadāna*.[2]

[1] Thag. v. 67; ThagA. i. 118 f. [2] Ap. i. 203.

3. **Ujjaya.**—A brahmin. He once went to the Buddha and asked him if he thought well of sacrifices. The Buddha replied that he was opposed to sacrifices which involved the slaughter of animals, but sacrifices not necessitating butchery, such as, for instance, a long-established charity, an oblation for the welfare of the family, had his approval.[1]

The same *Nikāya*[2] records another visit of Ujjaya wherein he tells the Buddha that he wishes to observe a period of retreat (*upavāsa*), and asks for a teaching which will bring welfare both in this world and in the next. See below **Ujjaya Sutta** 2.

[1] A. ii. 42. [2] A. iv. 285 f.

1. **Ujjaya Sutta.**—Records the questions asked by the brahmin **Ujjaya** regarding sacrifice, and the Buddha's answer.[1] See above **Ujjaya** 3.

[1] A. ii. 42.

2. **Ujjaya Sutta.**—**Ujjaya's** request to the Buddha (referred to above under **Ujjaya** 3) for a teaching which would bring him welfare in both worlds and the Buddha's reply thereto, detailing four qualities which would bring prosperity in this world—the accomplishments of exertion (*uṭṭhānasampādā*), and of protection (*ārakkhasampadā*), friendship with the good (*kalyānamittatā*), and regular living (*samajīvitā*)—and four

others for bringing happiness in the next—viz., the four *sampadā* (accomplishments) of *sīla* (morality), *citta* (concentration and meditation), *cāga* (generosity), and *paññā* (higher wisdom).[1]

[1] A. iv. 285-9.

Ujjuhāna.—A hill thickly covered with jungle and abounding in streams which get overfull during the rains and make living on the hill uncomfortable.

According to others, Ujjuhāna is the name of a bird, capable of bearing cold and rain with comfort.[1]

[1] Thag. 597; ThagA. i. 536.

Ujjenī.—The capital of **Avanti** (*q.v.*). In the Buddha's time, **Caṇḍa-Pajjota**[1] was king of Ujjenī and there was friendly intercourse between that city and **Magadha,** whose king was **Seniya Bimbisāra.**[2]

There was an old trade-route from Ujjenī to Benares and the merchants of the two cities showed healthy rivalry not only in trade, but also in matters of culture.[3]

It was while going with a caravan to Ujjenī, that **Soṇa Kuṭikaṇṇa** met the Peta, whose words made him decide to renounce household life.[4]

The road taken by **Bāvarī's** disciples ran through Ujjenī.[5]

Ujjenī was also the birthplace of **Mahā Kaccāna,**[6] of **Isidāsī,**[7] of **Abhaya**[8] and of the courtesan **Padumavatī,** mother of Abhayā.[9]

Before succeeding to his father's throne at **Pāṭaliputta, Asoka** reigned for several years as Viceroy at Ujjenī, and it was during this period that **Mahinda** and **Saṅghamittā** were born.[10]

Mahinda spent six months in **Dakkhiṇagiri Vihāra** in Ujjenī, prior to his visit to Ceylon.[11]

From the same vihāra forty thousand monks were present, under the leadership of **Mahā Saṅgharakkhita,** at the foundation of the **Mahā Thūpa** in Anurādhapura.[12]

The Jātakas[13] speak of Ujjenī as having been the capital of Avanti

[1] Vin. i. 276; DhA. i. 192.

[2] After Bimbisāra's death, however, Pajjota seems to have contemplated a war against Ajātasathu. See M. iii. 7.

[3] See, *e.g.*, J. ii. 248 ff., where the merchants of Benares compare their musician Guttila with Mūsila, the chief fiddler of Ujjenī.

[4] UdA. 307 f.

[5] Sn. v. 1011.

[6] ThagA. i. 483.

[7] Thig. v. 405.

[8] ThagA. 41.

[9] ThigA. 39.

[10] Mhv. xiii. 10 ff.; Mbv. 99; Sp. i. 70.

[11] Mhv. xiii. 5.

[12] *Ibid.*, xxix. 35.

[13] *E.g.*, in J. iv. 390, where Avanti Mahārāja rules in Ujjenī as capital of Avanti.

from very ancient times. But in the *Mahāgovinda Sutta*,[14] **Māhissatī** is mentioned as the capital of Avanti. Perhaps Māhissatī lost its importance later and gave place to Ujjenī, for we find Māhissatī mentioned just before Ujjenī among the places passed by Bāvarī's pupils on their way to Sāvatthi.[15]

Ujjenī is identical with the Greek Ozenē, about 77° E. and 23° N.[16]

[14] D. ii. 235. [15] Sn. v. 1011. [16] *Bud. India*, p. 40; see also CAGI. 560, and Beal (ii. 270) for Hiouen Thsang's description of it.

2. **Ujjenī.**—A city in Ceylon, founded by **Vijaya's** minister **Accutagāmī.**[1]

[1] Dpv. ix. 36; Mhv. vii. 45.

3. **Ujjenī.**—A township (*nigama*), the residence of the banker's daughter **Rucinandā,** who gave a meal of milk-rice to **Padumuttara** Buddha just before his Enlightenment.[1]

[1] BuA. 158.

Ujjenika.—Name given to the inhabitants of **Ujjenī.**[1] **Pajjota** is called **Ujjenika (Ujjenaka) rājā.**[2]

[1] Mil. 331. [2] MA. ii. 738.

Ujjhaggika Vagga.—The second division of the *Sekhiyā* of the *Vinaya Piṭaka.*[1]

[1] Vin. iv. 187-8.

Ujjhānasaññikā.—The name given to a group of devas who once visited the Buddha at Jetavana late at night. They charged the Buddha with inconsistency, but later, begging his forgiveness, they were pardoned by him.[1] Buddhaghosa[2] says that they did not belong to any separate deva-world but were given this name by the Theras of the Council on account of their captious remarks. They had heard the Buddha praise his monks for self-denying practices while he himself wore raiment of silk, fine cloth or linen, ate food worthy of a rājā, dwelt in a Fragrant Cell like unto a deva-mansion and used good medicines.

[1] S. i. 23-5. [2] SA. i. 50 f.

Ujjhānasaññino Sutta.—Records the visit of the **Ujjhānasaññikā** devas to the Buddha.[1]

[1] S. i. 23-5.

Ujjhānasaññī.—A thera. He was so called because he went about finding fault with the monks. He was reported to the Buddha, who thereupon delivered a sermon blaming action such as his.[1]

[1] DhA. iii. 376-7.

Uṭṭhāna Sutta.—The Buddha was once staying in the upper storey of the **Migāramātupāsāda** when he heard the new entrants to the Order, in the cells below, making a great uproar, talking about the food they had eaten, and other such worldly topics. The Buddha desired **Moggallāna** to come and, when he appeared, the Buddha asked him to frighten the monks by a display of *iddhi*-power.

By his psychic power Moggallāna caused the whole building to rock to and fro like a ship, and when the monks, in terror, sought the Buddha's protection, he explained to them that Moggallāna gave them the fright as a lesson to them to lead active and energetic lives, for death lays hold of the slothful.

The monks having listened to the Buddha's sermon, concentrated their minds on it, and soon after became arahants.[1]

[1] Sn. vv. 331-4; SnA. i, 336 f; *cf.* S. v. 269. ff.

Uḍḍita Sutta.—Preached in answer to a question by one of the devas. The world is all strung up by cords of craving and is escorted by decay.[1]

[1] S. i. 40.

Uṇṇalomaghara.—A building belonging to the **Rājāyatanadhātuvihāra** in **Nāgadīpa.** It was erected by **Aggabodhi II.**[1]

[1] Cv. xlii. 62.

Uṇṇābha.—A brahmin. He once visited the Buddha at **Sāvatthi** and asked him whether the five sense-faculties (*indriyāni*), which were of different scope and range, had any common ground of resort (*paṭisaraṇa*). The Buddha replies that the mind is their common resort and, in answer to further questions, explains that there is nothing beyond Nibbāna; that the holy life has Nibbāna for its ending.

When the brahmin, greatly pleased with the Buddha's teaching, goes away, the Buddha tells the monks that Uṇṇābha has become an *anāgāmī* and would, therefore, after death, no longer return to this world.[1]

The same *Nikāya*[2] records a visit of Uṇṇābha to **Ānanda** at **Kosambī.** He asks Ānanda what is the aim of holy life and, on being

[1] S. v. 217 f. [2] *Ibid.*, 272 f.

told that it is the abandoning of desire by means of jhāna, suggests that it would be a task without end. But Ānanda, by means of an illustration, explains how the task does come to an end, and Uṇṇābha expresses great satisfaction with the answer. Perhaps this refers to another brahmin of the same name.

Uṇṇābha Sutta.—The conversation between the Buddha and **Uṇṇābha** referred to above.[1]

[1] S. v.

Uṇṇanābhi.—A spider, as big as a chariot wheel, which lived in a cave in Mount **Cittakūṭa.** During the rains the geese who lived on the mountain entered his cave for shelter. Every month the spider would make a web, each thread of which was as thick as a cow's halter, at the entrance of the cave. At the end of the rains a young goose, who had been given two portions of food to make him strong would break the web and the geese would fly away. Once the rains lasted five months and the geese, having no food, were forced to eat their eggs and then their young. When the time came for them to fly away, none of them were strong enough to break the web and the spider sucked the blood of them all. That was the end of the **Dhataraṭṭha** geese.[1]

[1] J. v. 469-70.

Uṇha Sutta.—When the **Uṇhavalāhaka-devā** wish to revel their bodies, the weather becomes hot, according to their desire.[1]

[1] S. iii. 251.

Uṇhanagara.—A village, the birthplace of **Hatthadāṭha** (*q.v.*).[1]

[1] Cv. xlvi. 45.

Uṇhavalāhakā.—A class of devas who live in the **Cātummahārājika** world.[1] When they wish for heat to revel their bodies, the weather becomes hot. (See **Uṇha Sutta** above.)

[1] NidA. 108; VibhA. 519.

Utuḷhipupphiya Thera.—An arahant. He made a garland of *utuḷhi*-flowers and offered it to a bodhi-tree. This was at the beginning of this kappa.[1]

[1] Ap. ii. 398.

Utta.—A thera. He and his friend **Dhanuggahatissa** lived in a hut near the **Jetavana** vihāra. One night, couriers of **Pasenadi,** seeking for counsel as to how to win the war against **Ajātasattu,** overheard a conversation between these two Elders, and acting upon the suggestion contained therein, Pasenadi became victorious.[1]

For the story see (*s.v.*) **Danuggahatissa.**

[1] J. ii. 403-4.

2. **Utta.** See **Datta (Mantidatta).**

1. **Uttama.**—Author of the *Bālāvatāra-ṭīkā* and the *Liṅgatthavivaraṇa-ṭīkā*. He was a native of Pagan.[1]

[1] Gv. 63, 73; see also Bode, *op. cit.*, 22 and n. 1.

2. **Uttama.**—The name given to a cetiya connected with **Sikhī** Buddha. **Āsanatthavika** Thera, in a previous birth, came across this cetiya while wandering in the forest and did obeisance to it.[1]

[1] Ap. i. 255.

3. **Uttama.**—A general of **Māṇābharaṇa.** He was defeated at **Vacāvāṭaka** by **Rakkha.**[1]

[1] Cv. lxx. 295.

Uttamadevī Vihāra.—A monastery to the east of **Anurādhapura.**[1]

[1] UdA. 158; MA. i. 471.

1. **Uttamā.**—A therī. She was born in a banker's family in Sāvatthi and, having heard **Paṭācārā** preach, entered the Order. She could not attain the climax of her insight, till Paṭācārā, seeing the state of her mind, gave her admonition. Uttamā thereupon became an arahant.[1]

According to the *Apadāna* (quoted in *ThigA.*) she joined the Order at the age of seven and attained arahantship within a fortnight.

In the time of **Vipassī** Buddha she had been a slave-girl in a house in **Bandhumatī.** At that time King **Bandhumā** (Vipassī's father) kept fast-days, gave alms and attended sermons, and the people followed his pious example. The slave-girl joined in these pious acts, and on account of her thoroughness in the observance of fast-days, she was, after death, reborn in **Tāvatiṃsa.** She became the chief queen of the king of the devas sixty-four times, and she was a Cakkavatti's wife in sixty-three births.

She is evidently identical with **Ekūposathikā** of the *Apadāna.*[2]

[1] Thig. vv. 42-4; ThigA. 46 ff. [2] Ap. ii. 522 f.

2. **Uttamā.**—A therī. She was the daughter of an eminent brahmin of **Kosala.** Having heard the Buddha preach during one of his tours, she left the world and soon won arahantship. She, too, had been a slave-girl in **Bandhumatī** in **Vipassī's** time. One day, seeing an arahant seeking alms, she gladly offered him cakes.[1]

She is probably identical with **Modakadāyikā** of the *Apadāna.*[2]

[1] Thig. vv. 45-7; ThigA. 49 f.

[2] ii. 524 f.

1. **Uttara.**—A thera. He was the son of an eminent brahmin of **Rājagaha.**[1] He became proficient in Vedic lore and renowned for his breeding, beauty, wisdom and virtue. The king's minister, **Vassakāra,** seeing his attainments, desired to marry him to his daughter; but Uttara, with his heart set on release, declined, and learnt the Doctrine under **Sāriputta.** Later he entered the Order and waited on Sāriputta.

One day Sāriputta fell ill and Uttara set out early to find a physician. On the way he set down his bowl by a lake and went down to wash his mouth. A certain thief, pursued by the police, dropped his stolen jewels into the novice's bowl and fled. Uttara was brought before Vassakāra who, to satisfy his grudge, ordered him to be impaled. The Buddha, seeing the ripeness of his insight, went to him and placing a gentle hand, "like a shower of crimson gold," on Uttara's head, spoke to him and encouraged him to reflection. Transported with joy and rapture at the Master's touch, he attained sixfold *abhiññā* and became arahant. Rising from the stake, he stood in mid-air and his wound was healed. Addressing his fellow-celibates, he told them how, when he realised the evils of rebirth, he forgot the lesser evil of present pain.[2]

In the time of **Sumedha** Buddha, he had been a Vijjādhara. Once, while flying through the air, he saw the Buddha at the foot of a tree in the forest and, being glad, offered him three *kaṇikāra* flowers.

By the Buddha's power, the flowers stood above him forming a canopy. The Vijjādhara was later born in Tāvatiṃsa, where his palace was known as **Kaṇikāra.**

He was king of the gods one hundred and five times, and king of men one hundred and three times.

According to the *Apadāna* (quoted in *ThagA.*), he became an arahant at the age of seven. This does not agree with the rest of the story and is probably due to a confusion with some other Uttara.

Uttara is probably to be identified with **Tiṇikaṇikārapupphiya** of the Apadāna.[3]

[1] Of Sāvatthi, according to the *Apadāna.*

[2] Thag. vv. 121-2; ThagA. i. 240 ff.

[3] Ap. ii. 441 ff.

2. **Uttara.**—A thera. He was the son of a brahmin of **Sāketa.** While on some business at **Sāvatthi,** he saw the Twin Miracle and, when the Buddha preached the *Kālakārāma Sutta* at Sāketa, he entered the Order. He accompanied the Buddha to Rājagaha and there became an arahant.[1]

During the time of **Siddhattha** Buddha he had been a householder and became a believer in the Buddha. When the Buddha died, he called together his relations and together they paid great honour to the relics.

He is evidently identical with **Dhātupūjaka** of the *Apadāna.*[2]

It is probably this thera who is mentioned in the *Uttara Sutta*[3] (*q.v.*).

[1] Thag. vv. 161-2; ThagA. i. 283 f. [2] ii. 425. [3] A. iv. 162 ff.

3. **Uttara.**—A devaputta who visits the Buddha at the **Añjanavana** in **Sāketa.** He utters a stanza, and the Buddha, in another stanza, amplifies what he has said.[1]

[1] S. i. 54.

4. **Uttara.**—A thera. At the time of the Vajjian heresy, he was the attendant of the Elder **Revata** and had been twenty years in the Order. The **Vajjians** of **Vesāli** went to him and, after much persuasion, succeeded in getting him to accept one robe from them. In return for this he agreed to say before the Saṅgha that the **Pācīnaka** bhikkhus held the true Doctrine and that the **Pātheyyaka** monks did not. Thereafter Uttara went to Revata, but Revata, on hearing what he had done, instantly dismissed him from attendance upon him. When the Vesālī monks were informed of the occurrence, they took the *nissaya* from Uttara and became his pupils.[1]

[1] Vin. ii. 302-3; Mhv. iv. 30.

5. **Uttara.**—An arahant. He, with **Soṇa,** was sent by **Asoka,** at the conclusion of the Third Council, to convert **Suvaṇṇabhūmi.** They overcame the female demon and her followers, who had been in the habit of coming out of the sea to eat the king's sons, and they then recited the *Brahmajāla Sutta.* Sixty thousand people became converts, five hundred noblemen became monks and fifteen hundred women of good family were ordained as nuns.

Thenceforth all princes born in the royal household were called **Soṇuttara.**[1]

[1] Mhv. iv. 6; 44-54; Sp. i. 68 f.; Mbv. 115; The *Dīpavaṃsa* speaks of **Soṇuttara** as one person (viii. 10).

6. **Uttara.**—A brahmin youth (**Uttara-māṇava**), pupil of **Pārāsariya.** He once visited the Buddha at **Kajaṅgalā** in the **Mukheluvana** and the Buddha preached to him the *Indriya-bhāvanā Sutta.*[1]

Perhaps it is this same māṇava that is mentioned in the *Pāyāsi Sutta.* When **Pāyāsi Rājañña** was converted by **Kumāra Kassapa,** he instituted almsgiving to all and sundry, but the gifts he gave consisted of such things as gruel and scraps of food and coarse robes. Uttara, who was one of his retainers, spoke sarcastically of Pāyāsi's generosity, and on being challenged by Pāyāsi to show what should be done, Uttara gave gladly and with his own hands excellent foods and garments. As a result, after death, while Pāyāsi was born only in the empty **Serisakavimāna** of the **Cātummahārājika** world, Uttara was born in Tāvatiṃsa.[2]

[1] M. iii. 298 ff.

[2] D. ii. 354-7; see also VvA. 297 f. where the details are slightly different.

7. **Uttara.**—A youth of **Kosambī,** son of a minister of King **Udena.** When his father died, the youth was appointed by the king to carry out certain works in the city which his father had left unfinished.

One day, while on his way to the forest to fell timber, he saw **Mahā Kaccāna** and, being pleased with the thera's demeanour, went and worshipped him. The thera preached to him, and the youth invited him and his companions to a meal in his house. At the conclusion of the meal Uttara followed Mahā Kaccāna to the vihāra and asked him to have his meals always at his house. He later became a Sotāpanna and built a vihāra. He persuaded most of his relations to join in his good deeds, but his mother refused to help and abused the monks. As a result she was born in the peta-world.[1] (See **Uttaramātā.**)

[1] PvA. 140 ff.

8. **Uttara.**—A brahmin youth. When **Erakapatta,** king of the Nāgas, offered his daughter's hand to anyone who could answer his questions—hoping thereby to hear of a Buddha's appearance in the world—Uttara was among those who aspired to win her. The Buddha, wishing for the welfare of many beings, met Uttara on his way to the Nāga court and taught him the proper answers to the questions. At the end of the lesson, Uttara became a Sotāpanna. When he repeated the answers before the Nāga maiden, Erakapatta was greatly delighted and accompanied him to the Buddha, who preached to him and to the assembled multitude.[1]

DhA. iii. 230 ff.

9. **Uttara.**—A pupil of **Brahmāyu.** He was sent by his teacher from **Mithilā** to **Videha,** to find out if the Buddha bore the marks of the Superman. Having made sure of the presence of all the thirty-two marks on the Buddha's person, he dogged the Buddha's footsteps for seven months, in order to observe his carriage in his every posture. At the end of that period, he returned to Brahmāyu and reported what he had seen.[1] Buddhaghosa[2] says that Uttara became known as **Buddhavīmaṃsaka-māṇava** on account of his close watch over the Buddha.

[1] M. ii. 134 ff; SnA. i. 37.
[2] MA. ii. 765.

10. **Uttara.**—A youth, evidently a personal attendant of **Pasenadi.** The Buddha taught him a stanza to be recited whenever the king sat down to a meal. The stanza spoke of the merits of moderation in eating.[1]

[1] DhA. iv. 17; but see S. i. 81-2 for a different version of what is evidently the same incident. There the youth is called **Sudassana.**

11. **Uttara.**—A royal prince to whom **Konāgamana** Buddha preached at **Surindavatī** on the full-moon day of Māgha. He later became the Buddha's *aggasāvaka.*[1]

[1] Bu. xxiv. 22; BuA. 215; J. i. 43.

12. **Uttara.**—Younger brother of **Vessabhū** Buddha. The Buddha preached his first sermon to **Uttara** and **Soṇa** at the **Aruṇa** pleasaunce near **Anupama.** Later Uttara became the Buddha's *aggasāvaka.*[1]

[1] Bu. xxii. 23; BuA. 205; J. i. 42; D. ii. 4.

13. **Uttara.**—Son of **Kakusandha** Buddha in his last birth.[1]

[1] Bu. xxiii. 17.

14. **Uttara.**—The name of the Bodhisatta in the time of **Sumedha** Buddha. He spent eighty crores in giving alms to the Buddha and the monks and later joined the Order.[1]

[1] J. i. 37-8; Bu. xii. 11.

15. **Uttara.**—A khattiya, father of **Maṅgala** Buddha.[1]

[1] Bu. iv. 22; J. i. 34.

16. **Uttara.**—Son of **Padumuttara** Buddha in his last birth.[1] He was the Bodhisatta.[2]

[1] Bu. xi. 21.
[2] SA. ii. 67; DA. ii. 488; but see J. i. 37 and Bu. xi. 11, where the Bodhisatta's name is given as the **Jaṭila Raṭṭhika.**

17. **Uttara.**—Nephew of King **Khallaṭanāga** of Ceylon. He conspired with his brothers to kill the king, and when the plot was discovered committed suicide by jumping on to a pyre.[1]

[1] MṬ. 612.

18. **Uttara.**—A banker, a very rich man of **Sāvatthi.** He had a son, designated as **Uttara-seṭṭhi-putta,** whose story is given in the **Vaṭṭaka Jātaka**[1] (*q.v.*).

[1] J. i. 432 ff.

19. **Uttara.**—The city in which **Maṅgala** Buddha was born.[1]

[1] Bu. iv. 22; J. i. 34.

20. **Uttara.**—The city of King **Arindama. Revata** Buddha preached there to the king and the assembled multitude.[1]

[1] BuA. 133.

21. **Uttara.**—A township (*nigama*), near which **Revata** Buddha spent seven days, wrapt in meditation. At the conclusion of his meditation, the Buddha preached to the assembled multitude on the virtues of *nirodhasamāpatti.*[1]

[1] BuA. 133-4. This may be the same as No. 20.

22. **Uttara.**—One of the palaces occupied by **Paduma** Buddha before his Renunciation.[1]

[1] Bu. ix. 17.

23. **Uttara.**—A township of the **Koliyans.** Once, when the Buddha was staying there, he was visited by the headman **Pāṭaliya.**[1] *v.l.* **Uttaraka.**

[1] S. iv. 340.

24. **Uttara.**—A nunnery built by King **Mahāsena.**[1]

[1] Mhv. xxxvii. 43.

25. **Uttara.**—A general of **Moggallāna I.**[1]

[1] Cv. xxxix. 58.

26. **Uttara.**—A padhānagara built by **Uttara** (25).

27. **Uttara.**—A minister of **Sena I.** He built in the **Abhayuttara Vihāra** a dwelling-house called **Uttarasena.**[1]

[1] Cv. l. 83.

28. **Uttara.**—A thera who, with sixty thousand others, came from the **Vattaniya** hermitage in the **Vindhyā** forest to be present at the foundation ceremony of the **Mahā Thūpa** in Anurādhapura.[1]

[1] Mhv. xxix. 40; Dpv. xix. 6.

29. **Uttara.**—A banker of **Uttaragāma,** father of **Uttarā** (13).[1]

[1] BuA. 116.

30. **Uttara.**—An ājīvaka who offered eight handfuls of grass to **Maṅgala** Buddha for his seat.[1]

[1] BuA. 116.

1. **Uttara Sutta.**—The conversation between **Uttara** devaputta (**Uttara** 3) and the Buddha. One's life is short, says the devaputta ; one should, therefore, gather merit, in order to gain bliss. Rather, answers the Buddha, reject the bait of all the worlds and aspire after final Peace.[1]

[1] S. i. 54.

2. **Uttara Sutta.**—Preached to the monks by **Uttara** Thera (**Uttara** 6) at Mount **Saṅkheyya** at **Dhavajālikā** in **Mahisavatthu.** From time to time we should reflect on our own misfortunes as well as on those of others, and likewise on our successes. **Vessavaṇa** heard this sutta being preached as he was journeying from north to south on some business. He went to **Tāvatiṃsa,** where he informed **Sakka** of what he had heard Uttara say. Sakka, thereupon, appeared before Uttara and asked him whether his sermon was based on his own illumination (*paṭibhāna*), or on what he had heard from the Buddha. Uttara's reply was that his words were garnered from the Doctrine of the Buddha just as a man takes a handful of grain from a heap of grain. Sakka then repeated the whole sermon on the same subject, which he had heard the Buddha preach to the monks at **Gijjhakūṭa** in Rājagaha.[1]

[1] A. iv. 162-6.

Uttarakā.—A village of the **Bumus.** The Buddha once stayed there and **Sunakkhatta** was in his company. At that time **Korakkhattiya** was also staying there.[1]

[1] D. iii. 6.

Uttarakumāra.—The Bodhisatta. See **Uttara** (16).

1. **Uttarakuru.**—A country often mentioned in the Nikāyas and in later literature as a mythical region. A detailed description of it is given in the *Āṭānāṭiya Sutta.*[1] The men who live there own no property nor have they wives of their own; they do not have to work for their living. The corn ripens by itself and sweet-scented rice is found boiling on hot oven-stoves. The inhabitants go about riding on cows, on men and women, on maids and youths. Their king rides on an elephant, on a horse, on celestial cars and in state palanquins. Their cities are built in the air, and among those mentioned are **Āṭānāṭā, Kusināṭā, Nāṭapuriyā, Parakusināṭā, Kapīvanta, Janogha, Navanavatiya, Ambara-Ambaravatiya** and **Āḷakamandā,** the last being the chief city.

The king of Uttarakuru is **Kuvera,** also called **Vessavaṇa,** because the name of his citadel (? *rājadhāni*) is **Visāṇa.** His proclamations are made known by **Tatolā, Tattalā, Tatotalā, Ojasi, Tejasi, Tetojasi, Sūra, Rāja, Ariṭṭha** and **Nemi.** Mention is also made of a lake named **Dharaṇī** and a hall named **Bhagalavatī** where the **Yakkhas,** as the inhabitants of **Uttarakuru** are called, hold their assemblies.

The country is always spoken of as being to the north of **Jambudīpa.** It is eight thousand leagues in extent and is surrounded by the sea.[2] Sometimes[3] it is spoken of as one of the four **Mahādīpā**—the others being **Aparagoyāna, Pubbavideha** and **Jambudīpa**—each being surrounded by five hundred minor islands. These four make up a **Cakkavāḷa,** with Mount Meru in their midst, a flat-world system. A cakkavattī's rule extends over all these four continents[4] and his chief queen comes either from the race of King **Madda** or from Uttarakuru; in the latter case she appears before him of her own accord, urged on by her good fortune.[5]

The trees in Uttarakuru bear perpetual fruit and foliage, and it also possesses a *Kapparukkha* which lasts for a whole kappa.[6] There are no houses in Uttarakuru, the inhabitants sleep on the earth and are called, therefore, *bhūmisayā.*[7]

The men of Uttarakuru surpass even the gods of **Tāvatiṃsa** in four things: they have no greed (*amamā*),[8] no private property (*apariggahā*), they have a definte term of life (*niyatāyukā*)[9] and they possess great

[1] D. iii. 199 ff.; here Uttarakuru is spoken of as a city (*pura*); see also Uttarakuru in Hopkins: *Epic Mythology,* especially p. 186.

[2] DA. ii. 623; BuA. 113.

[3] *E.g.,* A. i. 227; v. 59; SnA. ii. 443.

[4] D. ii. 173; DA. ii. 623.

[5] DA. ii. 626; KhA. 173.

[6] AA. i. 264; MA. ii. 948.

[7] ThagA. ii. 187-8.

[8] The people of Uttarakuru are *acchandikā* (VibhA. 461).

[9] One thousand years, after which they are born in heaven, says Buddhaghosa (AA. ii. 806).

elegance (*visesabhuno*). They are, however, inferior to the men of Jambudīpa in courage, mindfulness and in the religious life.[10]

Several instances are given of the Buddha having gone to Uttarakuru for alms. Having obtained his food there, he would go to the **Anotatta** lake, bathe in its waters and, after the meal, spend the afternoon on its banks.[11] The power of going to Uttarakuru for alms is not restricted to the Buddha; Pacceka Buddhas and various ascetics are mentioned as having visited Uttarakuru on their begging rounds.[12] It is considered a mark of great *iddhi*-power to be able to do this.[13]

Jotika's wife was a woman of Uttarakuru; she was brought to Jotika by the gods. She brought with her a single pint pot of rice and three crystals. The rice-pot was never exhausted; whenever a meal was desired, the rice was put in a boiler and the boiler set over the crystals; the heat of the crystals went out as soon as the rice was cooked. The same thing happened with curries.[14] Food never ran short in Uttarakuru; once when there was a famine in **Verañjā** and the Buddha and his monks were finding it difficult to get alms, we find **Moggallāna** suggesting that they should go to Uttarakuru for alms.[15] The clothes worn by the inhabitants resembled divine robes.[16]

It was natural for the men of Uttarakuru not to transgress virtue, they had *pakati-sīla*.[17]

Uttarakuru is probably identical with the Kuru country mentioned in the Ṛg-Veda.[18]

[10] A. iv. 396; Kvu. 99.
[11] See, *e.g.*, Vin. i. 27-8; DhsA. 16; DhA. iii. 222.
[12] See, *e.g.*, J. v. 316; vi. 100; MA. i. 340; SnA. ii. 420.
[13] *E.g.*, **Rohita** (SA. i. 93); also Mil. 84.
[14] DhA. iv. 209 ff.
[15] Vin. iii. 7.
[16] See, *e.g.*, PvA. 76.
[17] Vsm. i. 15.
[18] See *Vedic Index* (*s.v.*)

2. **Uttarakuru.**—A garden laid out by **Parakkamabāhu I.**[1]

[1] Cv. lxxix. 11.

Uttarakurukā.—The inhabitants of **Uttarakuru.**[1]

[1] A. iv. 396.

Uttaragāma.—A village in Ceylon, the residence of **Piṅgala-Buddharakkhita** Thera. There were one hundred families living there and the Elder had, at some time or other, entered into *samāpatti* at the door of each of their houses, while waiting for alms.[1]

[1] MA. ii. 978.

Uttaracūḷabhājaniya.—Mentioned in the **Vibhaṅga** Commentary.[1]

[1] p. 308.

Uttarajīva.—A monk of Pagan, who came to the **Mahāvihāra** in Ceylon in A.D. 1154. He was accompanied by **Chapaṭa** and brought with him a copy of the *Saddanīti* which had just been written by **Aggavaṃsa.**[1]

[1] P.L.C. 185.

Uttaratissārāma.—A monastery in Ceylon, built by **Tissa,** minister of **Vaṭṭagāmaṇi.** It was dedicated to the thera **Mahātissa** of **Kambugalla**[1] (**Kapikkala** ?).

[1] Mhv. xxxiii. 92; MṬ. 622.

Uttaradesa.—A province of Ceylon, probably to the north of **Anurādhapura.** It was often occupied by the Tamils, and its chiefs refused to acknowledge allegiance to the Siṇhalese kings. Its people had to be subdued from time to time by the Siṇhalese kings, in order to establish the peace of the land and the security of the throne.[1]

The district formed a convenient landing-place for invaders coming to Ceylon from India, where they might complete their preparations.[2] It is sometimes called **Uttararaṭṭha.**[3]

[1] See, *e.g.*, Cv. xliv. 71; xlvii. 3, 54; xlviii. 83-4, 95, 112.

[2] *E.g.*, Cv. l. 14.

[3] *E.g.*, Cv. lxx. 92.

Uttaradhātusena-vihāra.—Built by King **Dhātusena.**[1]

[1] Cv. xxxviii. 48.

Uttarapañcāla.—A city. When **Apacara (Upacara),** king of **Ceti,** was swallowed up by the fires of Avīci, because of his falsehood, his five sons came to the brahmin **Kapila** and sought his protection. He advised them to build new cities. The city built by the fourth son was called Uttarapañcāla. It was founded in the north of Ceti, on the spot where the prince saw a wheel-frame (*cakkapañjara*) entirely made of jewels.[1] According to the scholiast to the *Kāmanīta Jātaka,*[2] however, and also according to the *Kumbhakāra Jātaka,*[3] Pañcāla or Uttarapañcāla is the name of a country (*raṭṭha*) whose capital was **Kampilla,** while in the *Brahmadatta Jātaka,*[4] Uttarapañcāla is given as the name of the city

[1] J. iii. 461.

[2] J. ii. 214.

[3] J. iii. 379 ff.

[4] iii. 79; also in the scholiast of the *Citta-Sambhūta Jātaka* (iv. 396). Pañcāla was also the name of the king of Uttarapañcāla in the *Sattigumba Jātaka* (iv. 430), the *Jayaddisa Jātaka* (v. 21), and the *Gaṇḍatindu Jātaka* (v. 98). In all these Uttarapañcāla is spoken of as a city in Kampilla. In the *Mahā Ummagga Jātaka* (vi. 391 ff.), **Cuḷani Brahmadatta** is the king of Uttarapañcāla.

and Kampilla as that of the country and we are told that a king Pañcāla reigned there.

In the *Somanassa Jātaka*,[5] mention is made of a city named Uttarapañcāla in the Kuru country, with **Reṇu** as its king. Whether the reference is to a different city it is not possible to say. See also **Pañcāla.**

[5] J. iv. 444.

Uttarapāla.—A thera. He was the son of a brahmin in **Sāvatthi.** When he had attained to years of discretion he saw the Twin Miracle and entered the Order. One day, amid desultory recollection, he was beset by sensual desires, but after a violent mental struggle, he arrested his evil thoughts and attained arahantship.

In the time of **Vipassī** Buddha, he had made a bridge for the Buddha to cross.[1]

He is evidently identical with **Setudāyaka** of the *Apadāna.*[2]

[1] Thag. 252-4; ThagA. i. 371 f.

[2] ii. 408.

1. **Uttaramadhurā.**—See *s.v.* **Madhurā.**

2. **Uttaramadhurā.**—The pleasaunce in which **Maṅgala** Buddha was born.[1]

[1] BuA. 115.

1. **Uttaramātā.**—Mother of **Uttara,** who was a son of **Udena's** minister. (See **Uttara** 7.) She was miserly, and when her son gave alms she abused him, and spoke disparagingly of the holy men who accepted his gifts. On one occasion, however, she approved of a gift of a tuft of peacock's feathers at the festival of dedication of a vihāra. After death she was born as a peta. Because of her approval of the gift of peacock's feathers she had lovely hair, but when she stepped into the river to drink water, all the water turned into blood.[1] For fifty-five years she wandered, famished and thirsty, till one day, seeing the Elder **Kaṅkhā-Revata** spending the day on the banks of the Ganges, she approached him, covering her nudity with her hair, and begged him for a drink. The Elder, having learnt from her her story, gave food and drink and clothes to the monks on her behalf and she obtained release from her suffering and enjoyed great bliss.[2]

According to the *Visuddhimagga*,[3] Uttaramātā was able to go through the sky because of the psychic power inborn in her as a result of Kamma. This probably refers to another woman. (See below 2.)

[1] She had told her son that his gifts would turn into blood in his next birth.

[2] Pv. 28 f.; PvA. 140 ff.

[3] ii. 382.

2. **Uttaramātā.**—A yakkhiṇī, mother of **Punabbasu** and **Uttarā.** Once as she passed **Jetavana** at sunset looking for food, with her daughter on her hip and holding her son by his finger, she saw the assembly, intently listening to the Buddha's sermon. She, too, hoping to get some benefit, listened quietly and with great earnestness, hushing her children to quietness. The Buddha preached in such a manner that both she and her son could understand, and at the end of the sermon they both became *Sotāpannā.* She immediately got rid of her sad yakkha-state and obtained heavenly bliss, and took up her residence in a tree near the Buddha's Fragrant Chamber.

Little Uttarā was too young to realise the Truth.[1]

[1] S. i. 210; SA. i. 238-40; DA. ii. 509 f.

Uttaramūla Nikāya.—One of the fraternities of monks in Ceylon, an off-shoot of the **Abhayagiri** sect. Their headquarters were probably at the **Uttaroḷa** Vihāra, built by King **Mānavamma,** and given to the monks of the Abhayagiri Vihāra, for having consented to take into the Order his elder brother, in spite of the fact that he had lost one eye as the result of some yoga practices. The first chief of Uttaroḷa was the king's brother himself and he was in charge of six hundred monks. He was granted great honours and privileges together with five classes of servants to minister to him. He was also appointed to supervise the guardians of the Tooth Relic.[1] From a Tamil inscription of Mānavamma we find that he kept up his patronage of the Uttaramūla Nikāya, and it is recorded that he gave over the custodianship of the Tooth Relic to a monk of this fraternity, named **Moggallāna.**[2]

Anuruddha, author of the *Anuruddha Śataka* and the *Abhidhammattha-Saṅgaha*, describes himself in the colophon to the former work as an " Upasthavira " of the Uttaramūla Nikāya.

In later years this Nikāya produced many an illustrious star in Celyon's literary firmament, among them the grammarian **Moggallāna, Vilgammūla,** Mahā Thera and **Śrī Rāhula.**[3]

[1] Cv. lvii. 7-11, and 16-26; also Geiger's *Trs.* i. 194, n. 2 and 3.

[2] Epi. Zey., vol. ii., pt. vi., pp. 250 ff.

[3] For details about them see P.L.C., *passim.*

Uttara-rāja-putta.—Mentioned in the *Samantapāsādikā*[1] as having sent to the Elder **Mahāpaduma** a shrine made of gold, which the Elder refused to accept, as it was not permissible for him to do so.

[1] Sp. iii. 544.

Uttaravaḍḍhamāna.—See **Antaravaḍḍhamāna.**

Uttaravinicchaya.—A commentary on the *Vinaya Piṭaka*, written by **Buddhadatta** as a supplement to his own **Vinayavinicchaya.** In manuscripts the two works are usually found together. It was dedicated by the author to one of his pupils **Saṅkhapāla. Vācissara** wrote a *ṭīkā* on it.[1]

[1] Gv. 59, 62. The work has been published by the P.T.S. (1928).

Uttara-Vihāra.—Another name for the **Abhayagiri-Vihāra** (*q.v.*). The inhabitants of the Uttaravihāra seem to have kept a chronicle, in the same way as did the dwellers of the **Mahā-Vihāra.** This is often referred to in the *Mahāvaṃsa Ṭīkā*, as the *Uttara-Vihāra-aṭṭhakathā* and the *Uttara-Vihāra-Mahāvaṃsa.* Judging from the quotations from this work given in the *Mahāvaṃsa Ṭīkā*, the Uttara-Vihāra chronicle seems to have differed from the tradition of the Mahā-Vihāra more in detail than in general construction. It is not possible to say whether it contained exegetical matter on the Pāli Canon besides matters of historical interest.[1]

[1] For a detailed account of the work see Geiger. *The Dīpavaṃsa and the Mahāvaṃsa*, pp. 50 ff.: also my edition of the *Mahāvaṃsa Ṭīkā.*

Uttarasena.—A dwelling-house in the **Abhayuttara-vihāra (Abhayagiri)** built by **Uttara,** a minister of **Sena I.** He provided it with all the necessaries.[1]

[1] Cv. l. 83.

Uttarahimavanta.—See **Himavā.**

1. **Uttarā.**—A therī. She was born in **Kapilavatthu** in a Sākyan family. She became a lady of the Bodhisatta's court and later renounced the world with **Pajāpatī Gotamī.** When she was developing insight, the Buddha appeared before her to encourage her and she became an arahant.[1]

[1] Thig. v. 15; ThigA. 21 f.

2. **Uttarā.**—She was the daughter of a clansman's family in Sāvatthi. Having heard **Paṭācārā** preach, she entered the Order and became an arahant.

The *Therīgāthā* contains seven verses uttered by her after becoming an arahant, the result of her determination not to leave the sitting posture till she had won emancipation. Later she repeated these verses to Paṭācārā.[1]

[1] Thig. vv. 175-81; ThigA. 161-2.

3. **Uttarā.**—In the *Theragāthā* two verses[1] are attributed to **Ānanda,** as having been spoken by him in admonition to an *upāsikā* named Uttarā, who was filled with the idea of her own beauty. Some say, however, that these verses were spoken in admonition to those who lost their heads at the sight of **Ambapālī.**[2]

[1] Thag. vv. 1020-1. [2] ThagA. ii. 129.

4. **Uttarā Nandamātā.**—Chief of the lay-women disciples who waited on the Buddha.[1] In the *Aṅguttara Nikāya,*[2] she is described as the best of women disciples in meditative power (*jhāyīnaṃ*), but this may refer to another Uttarā. She is again mentioned[3] in a list of eminent lay-women disciples, who observed the fast (*uposatha*) of the eight precepts.

According to the *Aṅguttara Commentary,*[4] she was the daughter of **Puṇṇasīha (Puṇṇaka)** (*q.v.*), a servitor of **Sumana-seṭṭhi** of Rājagaha. Later, when Puṇṇasīha was made *dhana-seṭṭhi* because of the immense wealth he gained by virtue of a meal given to **Sāriputta,** he held an almsgiving for the Buddha and his monks for seven days. On the seventh day, at the end of the Buddha's sermon of thanksgiving, Puṇṇasīha, his wife and daughter, all became Sotāpannā.

When Sumana-seṭṭhi asked for Uttarā's hand for his son, his request was refused because Sumana's family did not belong to the Buddha's faith. Puṇṇa sent word to Sumana that Uttarā was the Buddha's disciple and daily offered flowers to the Buddha, costing a kahāpaṇa. Later, however, when Sumana promised that Uttarā should be given flowers worth two kahāpaṇas, Puṇṇa agreed and Uttarā was married. After several unsuccessful attempts to obtain her husband's permission to keep the fast, as she had done in her parents' house, she got from her father fifteen thousand kahāpaṇas and with these she purchased the services of a prostitute named **Sirimā,** to look after her husband for a fortnight, and with his consent she entered on a fortnight's *uposatha.* On the last day of the fast, while Uttarā was busy perparing alms for the Buddha, her husband, walking along with Sirimā, saw her working hard and smiled, thinking what a fool she was not to enjoy her wealth. Uttarā, seeing him, smiled at the thought of his folly in not making proper use of his wealth. Sirimā, thinking that husband and wife were smiling at each other, regardless of her presence, flew into a fury and, seizing a pot of boiling oil, threw it at Uttarā's head. But Uttarā was at that time full of compassion for Sirimā, and the oil, therefore, did not hurt

[1] Bu. xxvi. 20.
[2] i. 26.
[3] A. iv. 347; AA. ii. 791.
[4] i. 240 ff.

her at all. Sirimā, realising her grievous folly, begged forgiveness of Uttarā, who took her to the Buddha and related the whole story, asking that he should forgive her. The Buddha preached to Sirimā and she became a Sotāpanna.

The *Vimānavatthu Commentary*[5] and the *Dhammapada Commentary*[6] give the above story with several variations in detail. According to these versions, at the end of the Buddha's sermon to Sirimā, Uttarā became a Sakadāgāmī and her husband and father-in-law Sotāpannas.

After death Uttarā was born in **Tāvatiṃsa** in a vimāna. **Moggallāna** saw her in one of his visits to Tāvatiṃsa and, having learnt her story, repeated it to the Buddha.

It is curious that Nanda is not mentioned in either account. It has been suggested[7] that Uttarā Nandamātā may be identical with **Veḷukaṇṭakī-Nanda-mātā**, but I do not think that the identification is justified. Uttarā's story is given in the *Visuddhimagga*[8] to prove that fire cannot burn the body of a person who lives in love, and again,[9] as an instance of psychic power being diffused by concentration.

[5] pp. 631 ff.; Vv. 11 f.
[6] iii. 302 ff.; see also iii. 104.
[7] *E.g.*, *Brethren* 41, n. 1.
[8] p. 313.
[9] p. 380-1; also Ps. ii. 212; PsA. 497.

5. **Uttarā.**—Wife of **Puṇṇasīha** (**Puṇṇaka**) and mother of **Uttarā** (4).[1] For her story see **Puṇṇasīha.**

[1] VvA. 63; DhA. iii. 302.

6. **Uttarā.**—Daughter of **Nandaka,** general of **Piṅgala,** king of **Suraṭṭha.**[1] For her story see *s.v.* **Nandaka.**

[1] PvA. 241 f.

7. **Uttarā.**—A little yakkhinī, sister of **Punabbasu.** For her story see **Uttaramātā** (2).

8. **Uttarā.**—Mother of **Maṅgala** Buddha.[1]

[1] Bu. iv. 18; J. i. 34.

9. **Uttarā.**—A brahmin lady, mother of **Konāgamana** Buddha, and also his *Aggasāvikā.*[1]

[1] J. i. 43; D. ii. 7; Bu. xxiv. 17, 23.

10. **Uttarā.**—*Aggasāvikā* of **Nārada** Buddha.[1]

[1] J. i. 37; Bu. x. 24.

11. **Uttarā.**—Wife of **Paduma** Buddha in his last lay life.[1]

[1] Bu. ix. 18.

12. **Uttarā.**—One of the chief women supporters of **Vipassī** Buddha.[1]

[1] Bu. xx. 30.

13. **Uttarā.**—Daughter of the banker **Uttara.** She gave a meal of milk-rice to **Maṅgala** Buddha just before his Enlightenment.[1]

[1] BuA. 116.

Uttarāpa.—The name given to the region to the north of the river **Mahī.**[1] See also **Aṅguttarāpa.**

[1] SnA. ii. 437.

Uttarāpatha.—The northern division of **Jambudīpa.** Its boundaries are nowhere explicitly stated in Pāli literature. It has been suggested[1] that Uttarāpatha was originally the name of a great trade-route, the nothern high road which extended from **Sāvatthi** to **Takkasilā** in **Gandhāra,** and that it lent its name—as did the **Dakkhiṇāpatha**—to the region through which it passed. If this be so, the name would include practically the whole of Northern India, from **Aṅga** in the east to **Gandhāra** in the north-west, and from the **Himālaya** in the north to the **Vindhyā** in the south.[2] The chief divisions included in this territory are mentioned in the Pāli literature as **Kasmīra-Gandhāra** and **Kamboja.** This region was famous from very early times for its horses and horse-dealers,[3] and horses were brought down for sale from there to such cities as Benares.[4]

In Uttarāpatha was **Kaṃsabhoga,** where, in the city of **Asitañjana,** King **Mahākaṃsa** reigned.[5] The *Divyāvadana*[6] mentions another city, Utpalavatī.

According to the *Mahāvastu,*[7] **Ukkala,** the residence of Tapassu and **Bhalluka,** was in Uttarāpatha, as well as Takṣaśilā, the famous university.[8]

There was regular trade between Sāvatthi and Uttarāpatha.[9]

Aṅganika Bhāradvāja had friends in Uttarāpatha.[10]

[1] See Law, *Early Geog. of Bsm.,* pp. 48 ff.

[2] According to the brahmanical tradition, as recorded in the *Kāvyamīmāmsā* (p. 93), the Uttarāpatha is to the west of Prithudaka (Pehoa, about fourteen miles west of Thāneswar).

[3] See, *e.g.,* Vin. iii. 6; Sp. i. 175.

[4] J. ii. 287.

[5] J. iv. 79.

[6] p. 470.

[7] iii. 303.

[8] Mtu. ii. 166.

[9] PvA. 100.

[10] ThagA. i. 339.

Uttarāpathaka.—A resident of **Uttarāpatha.**[1]

[1] J. ii. 31; Vin. iii. 6.

1. **Uttarārāma.**—An image-house constructed by **Parakkamabāhu I.** to the north of **Pulatthipurā.** It was hewn out of the actual rock and had three grottoes, made by expert craftsmen—the Vijjādhara grotto, the grotto with the image in sitting posture and the grotto with the recumbent image.[1]

[1] Cv. lxxviii. 74 ff.; for a description of it see Cv. *Trs.* ii., 111, n. 2; Bell: *Arch. Survey of Ceylon for* 1907, pp. 7 ff.

2. **Uttarārāma.**—The monastery where **Maṅgala** Buddha held his second Great Assembly (*Sannipāta*) in the presence of his kinsmen.[1]

[1] BuA. 120.

Uttarāla.—A tank repaired by **Parakkamabāhu I.**[1]

[1] Cv. lxviii. 47.

Uttarāḷha.—A dwelling-house (*pariveṇa*) which probably belonged to the **Abhayagiri-vihāra.** In it **Sena I.,** while he was yet *Mahādipāda*, built cells which bore his name.[1] **Sena II.** built a *pāsāda* there.[2]

[1] Cv. l. 77. [2] *Ibid.*, li. 75; see also Cv. *Trs.* i. 145, n. 2.

Uttari (-manussadhamma) Sutta.—There are six things without getting rid of which it is impossible to obtain qualities of a transcendental nature (*uttarimanussadhammā*), to say nothing of Āriyan insight and wisdom. Those things are forgetfulness, want of discrimination, lack of control of the senses, intemperance in eating, deceitfulness and prattle.[1]

[1] A. iii. 430.

Uttarikā.—A diminutive form of **Uttarā** used by **Uttaramātā** (*q.v.*), the yakkhiṇī, in addressing her daughter.[1]

[1] S. i. 210.

Uttarī.—A nun. She continued going on her rounds for alms until she reached the age of one hundred and twenty. One day, when returning from her round, she met a monk in the street and gave him all she had in her bowl. On the second and third days she did likewise. On the fourth day, as she was going her round, she met the Buddha in a very crowded spot. She stepped back and, while doing so, she trod on the skirt of her robe which had slipped down. Unable to keep her feet, she fell down. The Buddha came up and spoke to her. She became a Sotāpanna.[1]

[1] DhA. iii. 110-11.

Uttareyyadāyaka Thera.—An arahant. In **Padumuttara's** time he was a learned brahmin of **Haṃsavatī.** One day, when going to bathe with his pupils, he saw the Buddha and gave him his upper garment (*uttarīya*). The garment remained in the sky, forming a canopy over the Buddha and his monks. As a result, for thirty thousand kappas, Uttareyyadāyaka was born in the deva-worlds, and fifty times he became king of the gods. On thirty-six occasions he was king of men. Everywhere he went a canopy of fine material appeared over him and he obtained all he wished for.[1]

[1] Ap. i. 272-3.

Uttaromūla, Uttaroḷa.—See **Uttaramūla.**

Uttika.—See **Uttiya.**

Uttiṇṇa Thera.—He came from **Kasmīra,** at the head of 280,000 monks, to be present at the foundation-ceremony of the **Mahā Thūpa** in Anurādhapura.[1]

[1] Mhv. xxix. 37.

1. Uttiya, Uttika.—He was the son of a brahmin of **Sāvatthi.** When he came of age, he left the world, seeking " the Deathless," and became a Paribbājaka. One day, on his travels, he came to the place where the Buddha was preaching and entered the Order, but because of the impurity of his morals he could not win his goal. Seeing other bhikkhus who had achieved their object, he asked the Buddha for a lesson in brief. The Buddha gave him a short lesson, which he used for his meditations. During these meditations he fell ill, but in his anxiety he put forth every effort and became an arahant.[1]

In the time of **Siddhattha** Buddha he was a crocodile in the river **Candabhāgā.** One day, seeing the Buddha's desire to cross to the other bank, the crocodile offered him its back to sit on and took him across.

Seven times he was king of the devas, and three times ruler of men.[2]

This Uttiya is evidently identical with the thera of the same name mentioned in the *Saṃyutta Nikāya.* In one sutta[3] the Buddha explains to him, in answer to his question, the character of the five sensual elements and the necessity for their abandonment. Elsewhere[4] he is represented as asking the Buddha for a lesson in brief, which the Buddha gives him. Dwelling in solitude, he meditates on this and becomes an arahant.

[1] Thag. v. 30; ThagA. i. 89 f.

[2] Ap. i. 79-80.

[3] S. v. 22.

[4] *Ibid.*, 166.

Perhaps he is also identical with **Uttiya Paribbājaka,** who is represented in the *Aṅguttara Nikāya*[5] as asking the Buddha various questions on the duration of the world, etc., and as being helped by **Ānanda** to understand the real import of the Buddha's answers.

[5] A. v. 193 ff.

2. **Uttiya Thera.**—He was one of four companions—the others being **Godhika, Subāhu** and **Valliya**—who were born at **Pāvā** as the sons of four **Malla-rājās.** They were great friends, and once went together on some embassy to **Kapilavatthu.** There they saw the Buddha's Twin Miracle, and, entering the Order, they soon became arahants. When they went to **Rājagaha, Bimbisāra** invited them to spend the rainy season there and built for each of them a hut, carelessly omitting, however, to have the huts roofed. So the theras dwelt in the huts unsheltered. For a long time there was no rain and the king, wondering thereat, remembered his neglect and had the huts thatched, plastered and painted. He then held a dedication festival and gave alms to the Order. The Elders went inside the huts and entered into a meditation of love. Forthwith the sky darkened in the west and rains fell.

In the time of **Siddhattha** Buddha the four were householders and friends; one of them gave to the Buddha a ladleful of food, another fell prostrate before the Buddha and worshipped him, the third gave him a handful of flowers, while the fourth paid him homage with *sumana*-flowers.

In **Kassapa's** time, too, they were friends and entered the Order together.[1]

[1] Thag. vv. 51-4; ThagA. i. 123-6.

3. **Uttiya Thera.**—He was a Sākyan of **Kapilavatthu.** When the Buddha visited his kinsmen and showed them his power, Uttiya was converted and entered the Order. One day, while begging in the village, he heard a woman singing and his mind was disturbed. Checking himself, he entered the vihāra much agitated and spent the siesta, seated, striving with such earnestness that he won arahantship.[1]

In the time of **Sumedha** Buddha he was a householder and gave to the Buddha a bed, complete with canopy and rug.

Twenty kappas ago he was three times king under the name of **Suvaṇṇābha.**

He is probably identical with **Pallaṅkadāyaka** of the **Apadāna.**[2]

[1] Thag. v. 99; ThagA. i. 202-3.

[2] Ap. i. 175.

4. **Uttiya.**—In the *Kathāvatthu*[1] mention is made of a householder Uttiya, together with **Yasa-Kulaputta** and **Setu-mānava,** as having attained arahantship while living amid the circumstances of a layman's life.

[1] i. 268.

5. **Uttiya.**—One of the theras who accompanied **Mahinda** on his mission to Ceylon.[1] King **Sirimeghavaṇṇa** had an image of Uttiya made and placed in the image house which he built at the south-eastern corner of his palace.[2]

[1] Mhv. xii. 8; Dpv. xii. 12; Sp. i. 70; Mbv. 116. [2] Cv. xxxvii. 87.

6. **Uttiya.**—King of Ceylon for ten years[1] (207-197 B.C.). He was the fourth son of **Muṭasīva** and succeeded **Devānampiyatissa.** In the eighth year of his reign died **Mahinda,**[2] and in the ninth, **Saṅghamittā.**[3] He held great celebrations in honour of these two illustrious dead and built thūpas in various places over their ashes. The *Mahāvaṃsa Ṭīkā*[4] adds that Uttiya built a cetiya at the **Somanassamālaka.**

[1] Dpv. xii. 75; Mhv. xx. 57.
[2] *Ibid.*, 33.
[3] *Ibid.*, 49.
[4] p. 253.

7. **Uttiya.**—One of the seven warriors of King **Vaṭṭagāmaṇī.** He built the **Dakkhiṇa-vihāra** to the south of **Anurādhapura.**[1]

[1] Mhv. xxxiii. 88.

8. **Uttiya.**—See **Ayya-Uttiya.**

1. **Uttiya** or **Uttika Sutta.**—**Uttiya** Thera visits the Buddha and asks him for an explanation of the five sensual elements (*kāmaguṇā*) mentioned by him. The Buddha explains them, and declares that they should be abandoned in order that the Noble Eightfold Path might be cultivated.[1]

[1] S. v. 22.

2. **Uttiya** or **Uttika Sutta.**—**Uttiya** asks the Buddha for a teaching in brief, on which he might meditate while dwelling in solitude. The Buddha tells him that he must purify " the rudiments in good states " (*ādim eva visodhehi kusalesu dhammesu*), and proceeds to mention the four satipaṭṭhānas. As a result of developing the latter Uttiya became an arahant.[1]

[1] S. v. 166.

3. **Uttiya** or **Uttika Sutta.**—The **Paribbājaka Uttiya** visits the Buddha and asks him his views regarding the eternity of the world, the end of

the world, the identity of body and soul, and the continuation of the existence of the Tathāgata after death. The Buddha replies that he teaches nothing about such things, but that the object of his teaching is to enable beings to realise emancipation. Thereupon Uttiya asks the Buddha whether the world is led to follow that teaching. The Buddha remains silent. **Ānanda,** wishing to prevent any misunderstanding on the part of Uttiya, explains that there is no "leading," but that the Buddha knows that all those who escape from the world do so along a certain path, just as the gate-keeper of a well-guarded town knows that whoever enters that town must, inevitably, use the one entrance.[1]

[1] A. v. 193-5.

Udaka.—See **Uraga.**

Udakagāma.—A village in Ceylon given by King **Kittisirirājasīha** for the maintenance of the **Gaṅgārāma-vihāra.**[1]

[1] Cv. c. 213.

1. **Udakadāyaka Thera.**—An arahant. In a former birth he saw the Buddha **Siddattha** having his meal and brought him a pot of water. Sixty-one kappas ago he became a king named **Vimala.**[1] He is probably identical with **Sānu Thera.**[2]

[1] Ap. i. 205. [2] ThagA. i. 115.

2. **Udayadāyaka Thera.**—An arahant. In a previous birth he filled a vessel of water for **Padumuttara** Buddha. As a result, he could find water in any spot he wished.[1] His *Apadāna*-verses are found in the *Theragāthā Commentary* under the names of two theras: **Mahā Gavaccha**[2] and **Gaṅgātīriya.**[3]

[1] Ap. ii. 437. i. 57. [3] i. 249.

Udakadāyikā Therī.—An arahant. In a previous birth she was a water-carrier and maintained her children on her wages. Having nothing else to give, she regularly provided water in a bath for others. As a result, she was born in heaven and was fifty times queen of the deva-king and twenty times queen of kings on earth. She could produce rain at will, and her body knew neither heat nor dirt.[1]

[1] Ap. ii. 521-2.

Udakapabbata.—A mountain in the region of **Himavā.**[1]

[1] J. v. 38; Ap. ii. 434.

Udakapūjaka Thera.—An arahant. In a previous birth he saw **Padumuttara** Buddha journeying through the air and wished to offer him some water. He, therefore, threw some water into the air, which the Buddha, out of compassion, stopped to receive.

Sixty-five kappas ago Udakapūjaka became king three times under the name of **Sahassarāja.**[1]

He is probably identical with **Kuṭivihāriya Thera.**[2]

[1] Ap. i. 142-3. [2] ThagA. i. 129.

Udakarahada Suttā (2).—There are four kinds of sheets of water: (1) Flat (*uttāna*) but deep in appearance (*obhāsa*); (2) deep but flat in appearance; (3) flat and flat in appearance; (4) deep and deep in appearance. So, also, there are four classes of people: handsome in appearance but shallow in mind; not handsome in appearance but deep in knowledge; neither handsome nor wise; both handsome and wise.[1]

[1] A. ii. 105-6.

Udakavana.—The name of King **Udena's** park at **Kosambī** on the river. It was a favourite spot of **Piṇḍola-Bhāradvāja,** who often spent the day there. On one occasion when he was there, Udena came with the women of the palace to the pleasaunce to enjoy himself. When the king fell asleep the women wandered about the park and, seeing Piṇḍola, they went up to him and he preached to them. The king, on waking, was enraged to find the women absent and, on learning the cause, went to Piṇḍola and questioned him. Piṇḍola, knowing that the king had no wish to learn, sat silent. The king, in great anger, threatened to cast a net of red ants on the Elder, but before he could carry out his threat, Pīṇḍola vanished through the air.[1]

[1] SnA. ii. 514 f.; SA. iii. 27 f.

Udakāsanadāyaka Thera.—An arahant. Thirty-one kappas ago he had been an ascetic, and at the door of his hermitage he placed a bench for travellers and provided water for them. Fifteen kappas ago he was a king named **Abhisāma.**[1]

[1] Ap. i. 218.

Udakāsecana.—Thirty-three kappas ago there were eight kings of this name, all previous births of **Bodhisaññaka** (**°siñcaka**) **Thera.**[1]

[1] Ap. i. 131.

Udakūpama Sutta.—There are seven kinds of people in the world who are like objects that fall into wells: Some having sunk into the water remain there; others continue sinking and rising; some having risen once will not sink again; others having risen will look round, etc. Similarly, some having fallen into sin never escape therefrom, others are prone to weakness but often check themselves, etc.[1]

[1] A. iv. 11-13.

Udaṅgana.—See **Uraga.**

Udañcani Jātaka (No. 106).—The Bodhisatta and his son lived in a hermitage. One evening when the Bodhisatta came back with fruits to the hermitage, he found that his son had neither brought in food and wood nor lit the fire. When questioned by his father, he answered that during the latter's absence a woman had tempted him, and was waiting outside for him to go with her, if he could obtain his father's consent. The Bodhisatta, seeing that his son was greatly enamoured of the woman, gave his consent, adding that if ever he wished to come back he would be welcome. The young man went away with the woman, but after some time, realising that he had to slave to satisfy her needs, he ran away from her and returned to his father.[1]

For the circumstances relating to the telling of the story, see the **Culla-Nārada-Kassapa Jātaka.**

[1] J. i. 416-7.

Udapānadāyaka Thera.—An arahant. Ninety-one kappas ago he had built a well for **Vipassī** Buddha and offered it to him.[1]

[1] Ap. i. 188.

Udapānadūsaka Jātaka (No. 271).—In times gone by, the Bodhisatta, having embraced the religious life, dwelt with a body of followers at **Isipatana.** A jackal was in the habit of fouling the well from which the ascetics obtained their water. One day the ascetics caught the jackal and led him before the Bodhisatta. When questioned, the jackal said that he merely obeyed the " law " of his race, which was to foul the place where they had drunk.

The Bodhisatta warned him not to repeat the offence.

The story was related concerning the fouling of the water at Isipatana by a jackal. When this fouling was reported to the Buddha, he said it was caused by the jackal which had been guilty of the same offence in the *Jātaka*-story.[1]

[1] J. ii. 354 ff.

1. **Udaya.**—A brahmin of **Sāvatthi.** One day the Buddha came to his house and he filled the Buddha's bowl with the food prepared for his own

use. Three days in succession the Buddha came, and Udaya, feeling annoyed, said to the Buddha: "A pertinacious and greedy man is the Samaṇa Gotama that he comes again and again." The Buddha pointed out to him how, again and again, the furrow has to be sown to ensure a continuous supply of food, how over and over again the dairy-folk draw milk, and how again and again birth and death come to the slow-witted. At the end of the sermon both Udaya and his household became followers of the Buddha.[1]

[1] S.i.173f.; SA.i.199-200.

2. **Udaya.**—A brahmin, pupil of **Bāvarī.** When his turn came to question the Buddha, he asked him to explain emancipation through higher knowledge and the destruction of *avijjā*. Because Udaya had already attained to the fourth *jhāna*, the Buddha gave his explanation in the terms of *jhāna*. At the end of the sermon Udaya realised the Truth.[1]

[1] Sn. 1006, 1105-11; SnA.ii. 599-600.

3. **Udaya** (or **Udayana**).—A prince of **Haṃsavatī.** It was to him and to **Brahmadeva,** that **Tissa** Buddha preached his first sermon in the Deer Park at **Yasavatī.** He later became one of the two chief disciples of Tissa Buddha.[1]

[1] Bu. xviii.21; J.i.40; BuA.189.

4. **Udaya.**—The Bodhisatta born as king of Benares. In his previous birth he had been a servant of **Suciparivāra** (*q.v.*). On fast days it was the custom in Suciparivāra's house for everyone, even down to the cowherds, to observe the *uposatha*, but this servant, being new to the place, was not aware of this. He went to work early in the morning and returned late in the evening. When he discovered that all the others were keeping the fast he refused to touch any food and, as a result, died the same night. Just before death he saw the king of Benares passing in procession with great splendour, and felt a desire for royalty. He was therefore born as the son of the king of Benares and was named Udaya. In due course he became king, and one day, having seen **Aḍḍhamāsaka** (*q.v.*) and learnt his story, he gave him half his kingdom. Later, when Aḍḍhamāsaka confessed to him the evil idea that had passed through his mind of killing the king in order to gain the whole kingdom, Udaya, realising the wickedness of desire, renounced the kingdom and became an ascetic in the **Himālaya.** When leaving the throne he uttered a stanza containing a riddle which was ultimately solved by **Gaṅgamāla** (*q.v.*).[1]

[1] J. iii. 444 ff.

5. **Udaya.**—King of Ceylon, Udaya I. (A.C. 792-797), also called **Dappula.** He was the son of **Mahinda II.** and his wife was the clever **Senā.** He had several children, among them **Devā,** who was given in marriage to **Mahinda,** son of the **Ādipāda Dāṭhāsiva** of Rohana.[1]

[1] For details of his reign see Cv. xlix. 1 ff.; also Cv. *Trs.* i. 126, n. 1.

6. **Udaya.**—A brother of **Sena I.** and his Ādipāda. During the king's absence from the capital, he married **Nālā,** daughter of his maternal uncle, and took her to **Pulatthinagara,** but the king forgave him and later, when his elder brother **Mahinda** died, made him Mahādipāda, sending him as ruler of the Southern Province. Soon after, however, Udaya fell ill and died.[1] According to an inscription, he had a son who, under **Kassapa IV.,** became Mahālekhaka.[2]

[1] Cv. l. 6, 8, 44, 45.
[2] See Cv. *Trs.* i. 138, n. 3 and 142, n. 1.

7. **Udaya.**—Son of **Kittaggabodhi,** ruler of **Rohaṇa** in the time of **Sena I.**[1]

[1] Cv. l. 56.

8. **Udaya.**—King of Ceylon, Udaya II. (A.C. 885-896), a younger brother of **Sena II.** and afterwards his *yuvarāja.*[1] He succeeded Sena II. and reigned eleven years. During his reign the province of **Rohaṇa** was brought once more under the rule of the king.

[1] Cv. li. 63, 90 ff.; Cv. *Trs.* i. 156, n. 4.

9. **Udaya.**—King of Ceylon, Udaya III. (A.C. 934-937). He was the son of **Mahinda,** a younger brother of **Sena II.,** and his mother was **Kittī** or **Kittā.** He was first *yuvarāja of* **Dappula IV.** and later succeeded him as king.[1]

[1] Cv. liii. 4, 13 ff.; Cv. *Trs.* i. 172, n. 5 and 174, n. 6.

10. **Udaya.**—King of Ceylon, Udaya IV. (A.C. 945-953). He was a friend of **Sena III.** (perhaps his younger brother[1]) and was his *yuvarāja.* On Sena's death, Udaya succeeded him and reigned for eight years. During his reign the **Coḷas** invaded Ceylon, but were repulsed.[2] Among his religious activities was the erection of the **Maṇipāsāda,** which, however, he could not complete.[3]

[1] See *Ep. Zey.* ii. 59.
[2] Cv. liii. 28, 39 ff.; also Cv. *Trs.* i. 177, n. 2.
[3] Cv. liv. 48.

11. **Udaya.**—Younger brother and *yuvarāja* of **Sena V.** In Sena's quarrel with his mother, Udaya took the side of the latter.[1]

[1] Cv. liv. 58, 63.

12. **Udaya.**—Senāpati of **Sena V.** He was appointed by the king while the real Senāpati was away in the border country. When the latter heard of the appointment, he marched against the king and defeated his forces. Sena was forced to come to terms with the Senāpati and banish Udaya from the country.[1]

[1] Cv. liv. 61, 68.

13. **Udaya.**—See also **Udāyī-bhadda.**

Udaya Jātaka (No. 458).—The story of **Udayabhadda** and **Udayabhaddā** (*q.v.*). The story was related in reference to a back-sliding monk; the details are given in the **Kusa Jātaka.** The Udaya Jātaka also bears certain resemblances to the **Ananusociya Jātaka.**

1. **Udaya Sutta.**—The conversation between the Buddha and the brahmin **Udaya** (see **Udaya** 1).[1]

[1] S. i. 173 f.

2. **Udaya Sutta.**—See **Udaya(-māṇava)-pucchā.**

Udaya(-māṇava)-pucchā or **Udaya-pañhā.**—The questions asked of the Buddha by **Udaya-māṇava,** pupil of **Bāvarī** (see **Udaya** 2), and the Buddha's replies thereto.[1] They deal with the attainment of *samāpatti.*[2]

[1] Sn. vv. 1105-11; SnA. ii. 599-600.

[2] AA. i. 363.

Udayaggabodhi.—A *pariveṇa* built by **Aggabodhi VIII.** and named after himself and his father (**Udaya I.**).[1]

[1] Cv. xlix. 45; see also *Ep. Zey.* i. 216, 221, 227.

Udayana.—See **Udaya** (3).

1. **Udayabhadda.**—The Bodhisatta, born as king of Benares. He was so called ("Welcome") because he was born to his parents as a result of their prayers. He had a step-sister, **Udayabhaddā.** When his parents wished him to marry, he refused, but in the end, yielding to their entreaties, he made a woman's image in gold and desired them to find a wife who resembled it. Udayabhaddā alone could rival the image, so she was wedded to Udayabhadda. They lived together in chastity and, in due course, when Udayabhadda died, the princess became queen. The king was born as Sakka, and honouring a promise he had made to the princess to return and announce to her the place of his birth, he visited her as soon as he remembered her, and, before

revealing himself, tested her in various ways. Being satisfied with her conduct, he instructed her and went away. The princess, renouncing the kingdom, became a recluse. Later she was born in **Tāvatiṁsa** as the Bodhisatta's handmaiden.[1]

[1] J. iv. 104 ff.

2. **Udayabhadda.**—See **Udāyibhadda.**

Udayabhaddā.—Step-sister and wife of **Udayabhadda** (*q.v.*). In the verses she is also called **Udayā.**

Udayā.—See **Udayabhaddā.**

Udāna.—A short collection of eighty stories, in eight *vaggas*, containing solemn utterances of the Buddha, made on special occasions. The *Udāna* proper, comprising the Buddha's utterances, is mostly in verse, in ordinary metres (Śloka, Triṣṭubh, Jagatī), seldom in prose.[1] Each *Udāna* is accompanied by a prose account of the circumstances in which it was uttered. The book forms the third division of the *Khuddakanikāya.*[2] *Udāna* is also the name of a portion of the *Piṭakas* in their arrangement according to matter (*aṅga*). Thus divided, into this category fall eighty-two suttas, containing verses uttered in a state of joy.[3]

The prose-and-verse stories of the *Udāna* seem to have formed the model for the *Dhammapada Commentary.*[4] The *Udāna* is also the source of twelve stories of the same Commentary and contains parallels for three others. About one-third of the *Udāna* is embodied in these stories.[5]

[1] *E.g.*, iii. 10; viii. 1, 3, 4.

[2] DA. i. 17; but see p. 15, where it is the seventh.

[3] DA. i. 23-4; see also UdA. pp. 2-3.

[4] See *Bud. Legends*, i. 28.

[5] See, *ibid.*, i. 47-8, for details.

Udāyi-thera-Vatthu.—See **Lāḷudāyi.**

Udāyibhadda (Udāyibhaddaka).—Son of **Ajātasattu.** When Ajātasattu, after the death of his father, paid his first visit to the Buddha and saw the Buddha seated amidst the monks in a scene of perfect calm and silence, his first thought was: "Would that my son, Udāyibhadda, might have such calm as this."[1] Buddhaghosa[2] explains this thought by saying that Ajātasattu feared that his son might follow his own example and kill him as he had killed his own father. His fears were justified, for he was killed by his son Udāyibhadda, who reigned

[1] D. i. 50.

[2] DA. i. 153.

for sixteen years. The latter, in his turn, was killed by his son **Anuruddhaka.**[3] It was in Udāyibhadda's eighth year that **Vijaya,** king of Ceylon, died, and in his fifteenth year that **Paṇḍuvasudeva** came to the throne.[4] The **Dīpavaṃsa**[5] calls him **Udaya** and the *Mahābodhivaṃsa*,[6] **Udayabhadda.** See also *s.v.* **Kālāsoka.**

[3] Mhv. iv. 1 ff. According to *Dvy.* (369) his son was **Muṇḍa.**

[4] Sp. i. 72.

[5] iv. 38; v. 97; xi. 8.

[6] p. 96.

1. **Udāyī Thera,** also called **Mahā Udāyi** (and **Paṇḍita Udāyī**), to distinguish him from others.—He was the son of a brahmin of **Kapilavatthu.** He saw the power and majesty of the Buddha when the latter visited his kinsmen and, entering the Order, in due course became an arahant. When the Buddha preached the *Nāgopama Sutta*,[1] on the occasion when **Seta,** King **Pasenadi's** elephant, was publicly admired, Udāyī was stirred to enthusiasm by thoughts of the Buddha and uttered sixteen verses, extolling the virtues of the Buddha, comparing him to a great and wondrous elephant.[2] Once when Udāyī was staying at **Kāmaṇḍā,** in **Todeyya's** mango-grove, he converted a pupil of a brahmin of the **Verahaccāni** clan and, as a result, was invited by Verahaccāni herself to her house. It was only on his third visit to Verahaccāni that Udāyī preached to her and she thereupon became a follower of the Faith.[3] The *Saṃyutta Nikāya*[4] also records a conversation between Udāyī and **Ānanda,** when Udāyī asks if it is possible to describe the consciousness, too, as being without the self. On another occasion[5] Udāyī has a discussion with **Pañcakaṅga** on *vedanā.* Ānanda overhears their conversation and reports it to the Buddha, who says that Udāyī's explanation is true, though not accepted by Pañcakaṅga. Elsewhere[6] Udāyī is mentioned as asking the Buddha to instruct him on the *bojjhaṅgas*, and once, at **Desaka (Setaka ?)** in the **Sumbha** country, he tells the Buddha how he cultivated the *bojjhaṅgas* and thereby attained to final emancipation.[7]

He is rebuked by the Buddha for his sarcastic remark to Ānanda, that Ānanda had failed to benefit by his close association with the Master. The Buddha assures him that Ānanda will, in that very life, become an arahant.[8]

[1] See A. iii. 344 f.

[2] Thag. vv. 689-704; ThagA. ii. 7 f.; Udāyī's verses are repeated in the *Aṅguttara* (iii. 346-7) but the Commentary (ii. 669) attributes them to **Kāludāyī.**

[3] S. iv. 121-4.

[4] iv. 166 f.; another discussion with Ānanda is mentioned in A. iv. 426 f.

[5] M. i. 396 ff.; S. iv. 223-4; the Commentary (SA. iii. 86 and MA. ii. 629) here describes Udāyī as "Paṇḍita."

[6] S. v. 86 ff. [7] *Ibid.*, 89. [8] A. i. 228.

Udāyī was evidently a clever and attractive preacher, for he is mentioned as having addressed large crowds, a task demanding great powers, as the Buddha himself says when this news of Udāyī is reported to him.[9] According to Buddhaghosa,[10] it is this same Udāyī (Mahā Udāyī) who, having listened to the **Sampasādaniya** Sutta, is beside himself with joy at the contemplation of the wonderful qualities as set forth in that Sutta, and marvels that the Buddha does not go about proclaiming them. Buddhaghosa[11] seems to identify him also with the Udāyī to whom the **Laṭukikopama** Sutta[12] was preached.

[9] A. iii. 184.
[10] DA. iii. 903.
[11] MA. i. 526.
[12] M. i. 447 ff.

2. **Udāyī.**—A thera. It was once his turn to recite the *Pāṭimokkha* before the Saṅgha, but because he had a crow's voice (*kākasaraka*), he had to obtain permission to make a special effort so that his recitation might be audible to the others.[1] It is, perhaps, this same monk who is mentioned in the *Vinaya* as having been guilty of numerous *Saṅghādisesa* offences.[2] He is censured again and again and various penalties are inflicted on him, nevertheless he repeats his offences.[3] In the *Nissaggiya*[4] a story is told of a nun, a former mistress of Udāyī, who conceived a child through touching a garment worn by him. Once when **Uppalavaṇṇā** asked him to take some meat to the Buddha, he demanded her inner robe as his fee.[5] He seems to have been very fond of the company of women and they returned his liking.[6] There was evidently a strain of cruelty in him, for we are told of his shooting crows and spitting them with their heads cut off.[7] He is described as being fat.[8]

He is perhaps to be identified with **Lāḷudāyī** (*q.v.*).

[1] Vin. i. 115.
[2] *Ibid.*, iii. 110 f., 119 f., 127 f., 137 f., 135 ff.
[3] *Ibid.*, ii. 38 ff.
[4] *Ibid.*, iii. 205 f.
[5] *Ibid.*, 208.
[6] See, *e.g.*, Vin. iv. 20, 61, 68.
[7] *Ibid.*, iv. 124.
[8] *Ibid.*, iv. 171.

3. **Udāyī.**—A brahmin. He visited the Buddha at Sāvatthi and asked if the Buddha ever praised sacrifice. The Buddha's answer was that he did not commend sacrifices which involved butchery, but praised those which were innocent of any killing.[1]

[1] A. ii. 43 f.

4. **Udāyī.**—See also under **Kāḷudāyī, Lāḷudāyī** and **Sakuludāyī.** As they are all, from time to time, referred to as Udāyī it is not always possible to ascertain which is meant. The Commentary is not an infallible guide.

1. **Udāyī Sutta.**—A conversation between **Ānanda** and **Udāyī** in the **Ghositārāma** at Kosambī. Ānanda explains how the Buddha has proved that not only the body but even consciousness is without self.[1]

[1] S. iv. 166 f.

2. **Udāyī Sutta.**—**Udāyī** visits the Buddha at **Desaka** (?) in the **Sumbha** country and describes how he had realised *nibbāna* by developing the *bojjhaṅgas*.[1]

[1] S. v. 89 f.

3. **Udāyī Sutta.**—**Ānanda** reports to the Buddha that **Udāyī** preached to a very large following of laymen. The Buddha says that this is not an easy thing to do; he who preaches to a large audience must see (1) that his talk has a logical reference, (2) that it has reasoning (*pariyāya*), (3) that it is inspired by kindness (*dayā*), (4) that it is not for worldly gain, (5) that it causes pain to no one.[1]

[1] A. iii. 184.

4. **Udāyī Sutta.**—The Buddha asks **Udāyī** (**Lāḷudāyī** according to the Commentary) as to what are the topics of recollection. Three times he asks the question, but Udāyī sits silent. The Buddha then says he knew Udāyī was a fool, and puts the question to Ānanda, who explains five such topics connected with the *jhānas*.[1]

[1] A. iii. 322-5.

1. **Udumbara.**—A thera of **Makuva,** author of a *ṭīkā* on the *Peṭakopadesa*.[1]

[1] Gv. 75, 65.

2. **Udumbara.**—A village. **Revata** went there from **Kaṇṇakujja** and stopped there before proceeding to **Aggalapura** and **Sahajāti.** Thither the Elders followed him to ask his opinion on the Vajjian heresy.[1]

[1] Vin. ii. 299.

Udumbara Jātaka (No. 298).—The story of two monkeys. One, small and red-faced, lived in a rock cave. During heavy rains, the other, a large and black-faced monkey, saw him, and wishing to have the shelter for himself, sent him away, on the pretext that outside in the forest there was plenty of food to be had. The small monkey was taken in by the trick, and when he came back he found the other monkey, with his family, installed in the cave.

The story was told in reference to a monk who lived comfortably in a village hermitage and was ousted from there by another monk whom he had welcomed as a guest.[1]

[1] J. ii. 444-6.

Udumbaragiri.—See **Dhūmarakkha.**

Udumbara-devī.—Wife of **Piṅguttara.** She was the daughter of a teacher in **Takkasilā** and was given to Piṅguttara because he was the eldest pupil. But he was unhappy with her, and on the way to his home, when she climbed up a fig (*udumbara*) tree to pluck fruits for herself, he put thorns round the tree and ran away, leaving her. The king, coming along, saw her and married her. She was called Udumbara-devī because of the circumstances in which she was found. When the king suspected her of infidelity to him, **Mahosadha** saved her from ignominy, and she became thereafter his best friend and helped him in all his doings, treating him, with the king's permission, as her younger brother. When the king planned to kill Mahosadha, Udumbara-devī warned him in time and enabled him to evade the treachery of his enemies at court.[1]

In the present age she was **Diṭṭhamaṅgalikā.**[2]

[1] J. vi. 348, 352, 355, 363, 368, 384.

[2] *Ibid.*, 478.

Udumbaraphaladāyaka Thera.—An arahant. In the time of **Vipassī** Buddha he was a householder. Meeting the Buddha walking along the bank of the river **Vinatā,** he plucked some figs and gave them to him.[1]

He is probably identical with **Paccaya Thera.**[2]

[1] Ap. i. 295.

[2] See ThagA. i. 341.

Udumbarika-Sīhanāda Sutta.—Preached at the **Udumbarikā-paribbājakārāma. Sandhāna,** on his way to see the Buddha, stopped at the paribbājakārāma because it was yet too early for his interview, and started talking to the paribbājaka **Nigrodha.** Nigrodha spoke disparagingly of the Buddha's love of solitude. Seeing the Buddha walking along the banks of the **Sumāgadhā,** Nigrodha invited him to his hermitage and asked him various questions. The Buddha turned the discussion on to the merits and demerits of self-mortification and ended up by declaring the purpose of his own teaching. Though Nigrodha expresses great admiration for the Buddha's exposition, he and his disciples do not become followers of the Buddha.[1] Buddhaghosa says,[2] however, that this sutta will stand them in good stead in the future.

[1] D. iii. 36 ff.

[2] DA. iii. 844.

Udumbarikā.—A queen (*devī*) who built the **Udumbarikā Paribbājakārāma** near **Rājagaha.**[1] Close to the *ārāma* was the lotus-pond **Sumāgadhā** and a feeding ground for peacocks (**Moranivāpa**).[2] It was here that the **Udumbarikā Sīhanāda Sutta** was preached.

[1] D. iii. 36; DA. iii. 832.

[2] D. iii. 39.

1. **Udena.**—King of **Kosambī.** He was the son of **Parantapa.** His mother, when pregnant with him, was carried off by a monster-bird and deposited on a tree near the residence of **Allakappa.** The child was born in a storm (*utu* ?)—hence the name. Allakappa, having discovered the mother and child, took them under his protection. One day, when Udena was grown up, Allakappa saw by the conjunction of the planets that Parantapa had died. When he announced the news, Udena's mother revealed to him her identity. Allakappa taught Udena the various charms he knew for taming elephants and sent him to Kosambī, with a large following of elephants, to claim the kingdom. Some time after he became king, Udena appointed **Ghosaka** as his treasurer, and one day, having seen Ghosaka's adopted daughter, **Sāmāvatī,** going to the river to bathe, sent for her and married her. Later he married, in very romantic circumstances, **Vāsuladattā,** daughter of **Caṇḍa Pajjota,** king of **Ujjeni.**[1] Udena had another wife, **Māgandiyā** (*q.v.*), who took advantage of her new position to wreak vengeance on the Buddha for having once slighted her. When Sāmāvatī was converted to the Buddha's faith by her handmaiden **Khujjuttarā,** Māgandiyā tried to poison the king's mind against her, but the attempt was frustrated, though Sāmāvatī very nearly lost her life at the king's hand. When Udena realised how grievously he had wronged her, he promised to grant her a boon, and, as the result of her choice, the Buddha sent **Ānanda** with five hundred monks to the palace every day, to preach to the women of the court. Udena himself does not seem to have been interested in religion. Once when he discovered that the women of the court had given five hundred costly robes to Ānanda, he was annoyed, but when in answer to his questions Ānanda explained to him that nothing given to members of the Order was wasted, he was pleased and himself made a similar offering of robes to Ānanda.[2] His encounter in his park the **Udakavana** (*q.v.*) with **Piṇḍola Bhāradvāja,** in somewhat similar circumstances, did not, however, end so happily. Udena's women had

[1] The *Dhammapadaṭṭhakathā* (i. 161 ff.) contains a whole story-cycle of Udena from which these details, except where otherwise stated, are taken. For details of other persons mentioned in the article and their encounters with Udena, see under their respective names.

[2] Mentioned also in Vin. ii. 291. The incident took place after the Buddha's death.

given Piṇḍola their robes, and when the king questioned Piṇḍola as to the appropriateness of the gift, he remained silent. Udena threatened to have him bitten by red ants, but Piṇḍola vanished through the air.[3] Later[4] we find him visiting Piṇḍola again on friendly terms and receiving information as to how young members of the Order succeeded in curbing their passions in spite of their youth. In this context Udena calls himself a follower of the Buddha.

Udena had a son named **Bodhi,**[5] among whose activities the building of a palace, called **Kokanada,** is specially recorded. It is clear from the incident of the presentation of robes to Ānanda, referred to above, as well as by a definite statement to that effect contained in the *Petavatthu Commentary,*[6] that Udena survived the Buddha; but whether his son Bodhi succeeded him or not is not known.

Among Udena's possessions mention is made of his bow, requiring one thousand men to string it,[7] and of his elephant **Bhaddavatikā.**[8]

Udena is sometimes referred to as **Vaṃsarājā** (king of the **Vaṃsas**),[9] the Vaṃsas or the Vacchas being the inhabitants of Kosambī. In the *Udāna Commentary*[10] he is called **Vajjirājā.** The *Milinda-pañha*[11] tells a story of a woman called **Gopāla-mātā,** who became a queen of Udena. She was the daughter of peasant-folk, and, being poor, she sold her hair for eight pennies, with which she gave a meal to **Mahā Kaccāna** and his seven companions. That very day she became Udena's queen.

[3] SnA. ii. 514-5; SA. iii. 27; in a previous birth too, as **Maṇḍavya,** Udena had been guilty of abusing holy men (see the **Mātaṅga Jātaka,** J. iv. 375 ff.).

[4] S. iv. 110 f.

[5] J. iii. 157.

[6] p. 140.

[7] DhA. i. 216.

[8] J. iv. 384.

[9] *E.g.,* J. iv. 375; the *Dvy.* (*e.g.,* 528) calls him **Vatsarājā.**

[10] p. 382.

[11] p. 291.

2. **Udena.**—A thera. He once stayed, after the Buddha's death, in the **Khemiyambavana** near Benares. There the brahmin **Ghoṭamukha** visited him. Their conversation is recorded in the **Ghoṭamukha Sutta** (*q.v.*). At the end of Udena's sermon, the brahmin offered to share with him the daily allowance he received from the **Aṅga** king. This offer was refused, and at Udena's suggestion Ghoṭamukha built an assembly-hall for monks at **Pāṭaliputta ;** this assembly-hall was named after him.[1]

See also **Udena** (9).

[1] M. ii. 157 ff.

3. **Udena.**—An upāsaka of **Kosala.** He built a vihāra for the Order, and he invited monks for its dedication, which took place during the

Vassa. It being against the rules to go on a journey before the *Vassa*, the monks asked him to postpone the dedication. This annoyed him. When the matter was referred to the Buddha, he altered the rule so that a journey lasting not more than seven days could be undertaken during the *Vassa*.[1]

[1] Vin. i. 139.

4. **Udena Thera.**—The personal attendant of **Sumana** Buddha.[1]

[1] Bu. v. 24; J. i. 34.

5. **Udena.**—A king. He joined the Order under **Koṇḍañña** Buddha, with ninety crores of followers, all of whom became arahants.[1]

[1] BuA. 111.

6. **Udena.**—A yakkha. See **Udena Cetiya.**

7. **Udena.**—A king, father of **Siddhattha** Buddha;[1] also called **Jayasena.**[2]

[1] Bu. xvii. 13.

[2] BuA. 187.

8. **Udena.**—A king, a former birth of **Ukkhepakata-vaccha Thera,**[1] called in the *Apadāna*,[2] **Ekatthambhika.**

[1] ThagA. i. 148.

[2] i. 56.

9. **Udena Thera.**—An arahant, probably identical with **Udena** (2). During the time of **Padumuttara** Buddha he was a hermit, with eighty-four thousand others, living in a hermitage near **Paduma-pabbata** in the Himālaya. Having heard the Buddha's praises from a yakkha, he visited Padumuttara, offered him a lotus flower and spoke verses in praise of him.[1]

[1] Ap. ii. 362 ff.

Udena Cetiya.—A shrine of pre-Buddhistic worship, to the east of **Vesālī.** It is mentioned with other shrines at Vesālī—**Gotamaka, Sārandada, Sattamba, Cāpāla** and **Bahuputta**—all of which are described as beautiful spots.[1] Rhys Davids conjectures that these were probably trees or barrows.[2] The *Dhammapada Commentary*[3] describes the Udena and the Gotamaka shrines as "*rukkhacetiyas*" to which men pay homage in order to have their wishes fulfilled. The *Dīgha Commentary*[4]

[1] D. ii. 102; S. v. 260; A. iv. 309; see also D. iii. 9.

[2] Dial. ii. 110, n. 1, but see Law: *Geography of Early Buddhism*. 74 ff.

[3] iii. 246.

[4] ii. 554; AA. ii. 784; UdA. 323.

says that in the Buddha's time a vihāra had been erected on the spot where this shrine stood and that this vihāra had previously been dedicated to the yakkha **Udena.**

Udena Vatthu.—The story cycle of King **Udena,** in many respects the most interesting of all the stories of the *Dhammapada Commentary.*[1] It consists of six stories of diverse origin and character, dealing with the fortunes of the king, his three queen-consorts and his treasurer. Only two of the stories are really concerned with Udena, the rest being introduced by familiar literary devices. Versions of each of the six stories occur in the writings of Buddhaghosa, indicating that they go back to a common source. Parallels to one or more stories are also to be found in the *Divyāvadāna,* the *Kathāsaritsāgara* and other Sanskrit collections and in the Tibetan Kandjur.[2]

[1] DhA. i. 161-231.
[2] For an analysis of the cycle and its parallels see Burlinghame, *Bud. Legends,* i., pp. 51 and 62 ff.

Udda Jātaka.—See **Uddālaka Jātaka.**

Uddaka.—See **Uddaka-Rāmaputta.**

Uddaka Sutta.—Preached by the Buddha. He states therein how **Uddaka-Rāmaputta,** unjustifiably, claims to have mastered all learning and all ill, and explains what such learning and mastery really are.[1]

[1] S. v. 83 f.

Uddaka-Rāmaputta.—One of the teachers under whom **Gotama,** after leaving the world and before he became the Buddha, received instruction.[1] Uddaka taught him the doctrine which had been realised and proclaimed by his father **Rāma,** which was the attainment of the state of "neither-consciousness-nor-unconsciousness" (corresponding to the fourth Jhāna). When Gotama had mastered this, Uddaka made him more than his own equal by setting him over the whole company of his disciples as their teacher. But Gotama, finding this doctrine unsatisfactory, abandoned it.[2] The Buddha evidently had a high regard for Uddaka-Rāmaputta, for after the Enlightenment, when looking for someone to whom the Dhamma might be preached, and who was capable of realising its import at once, his thoughts turned to Uddaka, but Uddaka was already dead.[3]

In the **Vassakāra Sutta** of the *Aṅguttara Nikāya*[4] it is mentioned that

[1] J. i. 66, 81.
[2] M. i. 165 ff., 240 ff.; DhA. i. 70-1.
[3] Vin. i. 7.
[4] ii. 180.

King **Eleyya,** together with his bodyguard, **Yamaka, Moggalla** and others, were followers of Rāmaputta and that they held him in great esteem. In the *Saṃyutta Nikāya*[5] the Buddha says that Uddaka claimed to be " versed in lore and to have conquered everything, digging out the root of Ill," though he had no justification for such a claim.

Again, in the **Pāsādika Sutta,**[6] the Buddha tells **Cunda** that when Uddaka said " seeing, he seeth not," he had in mind a man who saw the blade of a sharpened razor but not its edge—a low, pagan thing to speak about.

In the Sanskrit books Uddaka-Rāmaputta is called Udraka.[7]

[5] iv. 83 f.
[6] D. iii. 126-7.
[7] Mtu. ii. 119-20; *Dvy.* 392; Lal. 306 f.

Uddālaka.—Son of the Bodhisatta (then chaplain of the king of Benares) and a slave-girl, whom he first met in the royal park. The boy was so called because he was conceived under an *uddāla*-tree. When grown up he went to **Takkasilā** and later became leader of a large company of ascetics. In the course of their travels he and his followers came to Benares, where they received great favours from the people. Attracted by his reputation, the king once visited him with the royal chaplain. On that occasion Uddālaka arranged that he and his followers should feign to be very holy men given up to various austerities. The chaplain, seeing through their dishonesty and discovering the identity of Uddālaka, persuaded him to leave his asceticism and become chaplain under him.[1]

[1] J. iv. 298-304.

Uddālaka Jātaka (No. 487).—The story of **Uddālaka** given above. It was related in reference to a monk who led a deceitful life. The monk is identified with Uddālaka.[1] On the same occasion were preached the **Makkaṭa, Kuhaka** and **Setaketu Jātakas.**

[1] J. iii. 232. The Jātaka is depicted in the *Bhārhūt* Tope (see Cunningham, Plate XLVI.).

Uddāladāyaka Thera.—An arahant. In a previous birth, thirty-one kappas ago, he saw a Pacceka Buddha **Kakudha,** near a river, and gave him an *uddālaka* flower.[1]

[1] Ap. i. 225.

Uddālapupphiya Thera.—An arahant. Thirty-one kappas ago he gave an *uddāla* flower to a Pacceka Buddha, **Anātha,** on the bank of the Ganges.[1]

[1] Ap. i. 288.

Uddesavibhaṅga Sutta.—The Buddha utters the brief statement that a monk should always so guard his mind that it may not be externally diffused nor internally set. The monks repeat this statement to **Mahā Kaccāna,** who gives a detailed exposition thereof. When the Buddha is told of Kaccāna's explanation, he praises his erudition.[1]

[1] M.iii.223 ff.

Uddhakandaraka.—A vihāra in South Ceylon, founded by **Mahānāga,** brother of Devānampiyatissa.[1]

[1] Mhv. xxii. 9.

Uddhakuraṅgāma.—A village and a fortification in the district of **Āḷisāra.** It was captured by **Parakkamabāhu's** general, **Māyāgeha.**[1]

[1] Cv. lxx. 171.

Uddha-gaṅgā.—See **Gaṅgā.**

1. **Uddhagāma.**—A district (?) in Ceylon. It contained the village of **Vasabha,** which was given to the **Jetavana** Vihāra by **Mahānāga.**[1]

[1] Cv. xli. 97.

2. **Uddhagāma.**—A village in **Rohaṇa.** The forces of **Parakkamabāhu I.** carried on a campaign there for three months.[1]

[1] Cv. lxxiv. 92.

Uddhacūlābhaya.—Nephew of **Devānampiyatissa.** He restored the **Mahiyaṅgana-thūpa** and made it thirty cubits high.[1]

[1] Mhv. i. 40.

Uddhacca Sutta.—Conceit, want of restraint and of diligence, should all be destroyed by calm (*samatha*), restraint and earnestness.[1]

[1] A. iii. 449.

Uddhanadvāra.—A village in **Rohaṇa.** There the Ādipāda **Vikkamabāhu** gained a victory.[1] It was in the region called **Aṭṭhasahassa,** and **Sirivallabha,** who reigned over this district, made Uddhanadvāra his capital. The village formed one of the centres of battle in the campaign of **Parakkamabāhu I.**[2]

[1] Cv. lxi. 16, 25.

[2] Cv. lxxiv. 86, 113; lxxv. 182. For its identification see Cv. *Trs.* i. 29, n. 4.

Uddhambhāgiya Sutta.—The Noble Eightfold Way should be cultivated in order to destroy the five " upward " fetters—lust of form and of the formless, conceit, excitement and nescience.[1]

[1] S. v. 61 f.

Uddharaṭṭha.—See **Pañcuddharaṭṭha.**

Uddhavāpi.—A village and a tank. The **Māragiri Nigrodha** (*q.v.*) was stationed there.[1]

[1] Cv. lxxii. 164, 174.

Uddhumātaka Sutta.—The idea of an inflated corpse, if developed, conduces to peace from bondage.[1]

[1] S. v. 131.

Unnama.—A Damiḷa chief whom **Duṭṭhagāmaṇi** defeated in his campaign.' He was a nephew of **Tamba** and his stronghold was also called Unnama.[1]

[1] Mhv. xxv. 14, 15; MṬ. 474.

Unnavalli.—A vihāra to which **Aggabodhi I.** gave the village of **Ratana.**[1]

[1] Cv. xlii. 18.

1. **Upaka.**—An Ājīvaka whom the Buddha met on his way between **Gayā** and the Bodhi Tree, after he set out from **Isipatana** for the preaching of the First Sermon. Upaka questioned the Buddha on his attainments, and when the Buddha told him what he had accomplished he asked the Buddha if he were "**Anantajina.**" When the Buddha acknowledged it, Upaka shook his head saying, " It may be so, friend," and went along by another road.[1] It is said[2] that the Buddha walked all the way from the Bodhi Tree to Isipatana—instead of flying through the air, as is the custom of Buddhas—because he wished to meet Upaka.

After this meeting Upaka went to the **Vaṅkahāra** country and there, having fallen desperately in love with **Cāpā** (*q.v.*), the daughter of a huntsman who looked after him, starved for seven days and in the end persuaded the huntsman to give her to him in marriage. For a living, Upaka hawked about the flesh brought by the huntsman. In due course Cāpā bore him a son, **Subhadda.** When the baby cried, Cāpā sang to him saying, " Upaka's son, ascetic's son, game-dealer's boy, don't cry," thus mocking her husband. In exasperation he told her of

[1] J. i. 81; Vin. i. 8; M. i. 170-1; DhA. iv. 71-2.

[2] DA. ii. 471.

his friend Anantajina, but she did not stop teasing him. One day, in spite of her attempts to keep him, he left her and went to the Buddha at **Sāvatthi.** The Buddha, seeing him coming, gave orders that anyone asking for Anantajina should be brought to him. Having learnt from Upaka his story, the Buddha had him admitted to the Order. As a result of his meditation, Upaka became an *anāgāmi* and was reborn in the **Avihā** heaven.[3] The *Saṃyutta Nikāya*[4] records a visit paid to the Buddha by Upaka and six other beings born in Avihā. According to the *Majjhima Commentary*,[5] Upaka became an arahant as soon as he was born in Avihā.

In the *Therīgāthā* he is also called **Kāla**[6] and his birth-place is given as **Nāla,** a village near the Bodhi Tree, where he is said to have been living with his wife at the time he left her.[7]

Later, Cāpā, too, left the world and became an arahant therī.

The *Divyāvadana*[8] calls Upaka **Upagaṇa.**

The enumeration of the Buddha's virtues which was made to Upaka is not regarded as a real *dhammadesanā* because it took place before the preaching of the first sermon. It produced only a *vāsanā-bhāgiya* result, not *sekha-* or *ribaddha-bhāgiya.*[9]

The words of the Buddha's speech to Upaka are often quoted.[10]

[3] ThigA. 220 ff.; MA. i. 388 f. Upaka's story is also given in SnA. i. 258 ff., with several variations in detail.

[4] i. 35, 60.

[5] i. 389.

[6] v. 309. This may have been a term of affection used because of his dark colour.

[7] ThigA. 225.

[8] p. 393.

[9] UdA. 54.

[10] *E.g.*, Kvu. 289.

2. **Upaka Maṇḍikāputta.**—He once visited the Buddha at **Gijjhakūṭa** and stated before him his view that whoever starts abusive talk of another, without being able to make good his case, is blameworthy. The Buddha agrees and says that Upaka himself has been guilty of this offence.[1] Upaka protests against being caught in a big noose of words, like a fish caught as soon as he pops up his head. The Buddha explains that it is necessary for him to teach with endless variations of words and similes. Upaka is pleased with the Buddha's talk and reports the conversation to **Ajātasattu.** The king shows his anger at the man's presumption in having remonstrated with the Buddha,[2] and the Commentary adds that he had him seized by the neck and cast out.

Buddhaghosa[3] says that Upaka went to visit the Buddha in order to find out whether the Buddha would blame him for being a supporter

[1] The Commentary (AA. ii. 554) explains that Upaka was a supporter of Devadatta.

[2] A. ii. 181 f.

[3] AA. ii. 554-5.

of **Devadatta.** According to others, he came to abuse the Buddha because he had heard that the Buddha had consigned Devadatta to hell.

He was apparently of low caste, and Ajātasattu addresses him as "salt-worker's boy" (*loṇakārakadāraka*).[4]

[4] A.ii.182.

Upaka Sutta.—Records the visit paid to the Buddha by **Upaka Maṇḍakāputta** (*q.v.*).[1]

[1] A.ii.181 f.

Upakaṃsa.—Son of **Mahākaṃsa,** king of **Asitañjana** and brother of **Kaṃsa.** When Kaṃsa became king, Upakaṃsa was his viceroy. Upakaṃsa was killed by a disc thrown by **Vāsudeva,** son of **Devagabbhā.**[1]

[1] J.iv.79-82.

Upakañcana.—A brahmin, brother of the Bodhisatta **Mahākañcana.** Their story is related in the **Bhisa Jātaka** (*q.v.*).[1]

[1] J.iv.305 ff.

1. **Upakārī.**—A city of the **Pañcālas.**[1] Here was the entrance to the tunnel through which King **Vedeha** escaped to **Mithilā,** as related in the **Mahā Ummagga Jātaka** (*q.v.*).

[1] J.vi.448, 450, 458, 459.

2. **Upakārī.**—A city where **Sumedha** Buddha preached to a large concourse of people.[1]

[1] BuA.165.

1. **Upakāḷa.**—A Pacceka Buddha mentioned in a list of Pacceka Buddhas.[1]

[1] M.iii.70; ApA.i.107.

2. **Upakāḷa.**—A *niraya,* also the name of the tortures in the same *niraya.*[1]

[1] J.vi.248.

Upacara.—See **Apacara.**

1. **Upakkilesa Sutta.**—Preached at **Pācīnavaṃsadāya** to **Anuruddha, Nandiya** and **Kimbila.** It was at the time of the quarrel of the **Kosambī** monks; the Buddha, in search of quietness, goes to **Bālakaloṇaka,** preaches there to **Bhagu** and proceeds to Pācīnavaṃsadāya, where he

tells his cousins how they should develop meditation, getting rid of all obstacles.[1]

[1] M.iii.152 ff. The verses of the sutta are also found in the Vinaya version (i. 34 ff.). Some of the verses are included in the *Dhammapada* (vv. 328-30) and in the **Khaggavisāna Sutta** of the Sutta Nipāta (vv. 11, 12).

2. **Upakkilesa Sutta.**—Gold ore must be purified from all its dross before it can be used for making ornaments, etc.; similarly, the mind must be freed from its impurities—the five *nīvaraṇas*—before it can be used for acquiring the higher knowledge.[1]

[1] A. iii. 16-19.

3. **Upakkilesa Sutta.**—Four things prevent the sun and the moon from shining with their full brilliance—clouds, mist, smoke and dust and Rāhu. Similarly four things diminish the holiness of ascetics and recluses—intoxicants, sex, money and wrong livelihood.[1]

[1] A. ii. 53 f.

Upacāla.—Son of **Upacālā** and nephew of **Sāriputta** and **Khadiravaniya-Revata.** He was ordained by Revata.[1] He is mentioned in the *Aṅguttara Nikāya*[2] in a list of very eminent disciples, together with **Cāla, Kakkaṭa, Kalimbha, Nikaṭa** and **Kaṭissaha.** They lived in the **Kūṭāgārasālā** in Vesāli, but when the **Licchavis** went there to visit the Buddha, they moved to the **Gosiṅgasālavana** in search of quiet.

[1] Thag. v, 43; ThagA. i. 110.

[2] v. 133.

1. **Upacālā.**—Sister of **Sāriputta** (his other sisters being **Cālā, Sisūpacālā**) and mother of Upacāla. When Sāriputta left the world to join the Order of monks, his three sisters followed his example and became nuns. It is said that when Upacālā was taking her siesta in **Andhavana, Māra** tried to arouse in her sensual desires, but she vanquished him and became an arahant. Her conversation with Māra is recorded in the *Therīgāthā.*[1]

[1] vv. 189-95; ThigA. 165 f. The *Saṃyutta* (i. 133 f.) mentions the temptation of all three sisters by Māra and their conquest of him. But in this account, Upacālā's verses are put into Cālā's mouth, Sisūpacālā's are ascribed to Upacālā and Cālā's to Sisūpacālā.

2. **Upacālā.**—The chief of the women disciples of **Phussa** Buddha.[1] See also **Upasālā.**

[1] J. i. 41; Bu. xix. 20.

3. **Upacālā.**—Chief of the women supporters of **Sumana** Buddha.[1]

[1] Bu. v. 28.

Upacālā Sutta.—The story of Māra's unsuccessful attempt to cause the therī **Upacālā** to sin.[1]

[1] S. i. 133.

Upajotiya.—One of the door-keepers summoned by **Maṇḍavya** to turn **Mātaṅga** out of his house.[1]

[1] J. iv. 382.

Upajjhā Sutta.—A monk goes to his teacher and confesses to him the difficulty he experiences in living the celibate life profitably. The teacher takes him to the Buddha, who suggests to him a different way of conduct. The monk acts according to the Buddha's advice and becomes an arahant. On being informed of this, the Buddha makes it a topic for a sermon.[1]

[1] A. iii. 69-71.

Upajjhāya.—A gatekeeper of **Maṇḍavya,** summoned by him to drive out **Mātaṅga.**[1]

[1] J. iv. 382.

Upajjhāyavatta-bhāṇavāra.—The thirtieth chapter of the first Khandaka of the *Mahāvagga.*

1. **Upaṭṭhāna Sutta.**—The Buddha asks **Ānanda** if he considers that every kind of moral practice produces like results. Ānanda says they do not, and proceeds to explain his point of view. The Buddha agrees with him, and when Ānanda has gone away, tells the monks that though Ānanda is yet a learner (*sekha*), it would not be easy to find his equal in insight.[1]

[1] A. i. 225.

2. **Upaṭṭhāna Sutta.**—Five qualities which make an invalid difficult for anyone to look after, and the absence of which makes him a good patient.[1]

[1] A. iii. 143-4.

3. **Upaṭṭhāna Sutta.**—On five qualities requisite for an attendant on the sick.[1]

[1] A. iii. 144-5.

4. **Upaṭṭhāna Sutta.**—Record of a conversation between a deva and a monk who dwelt in a forest tract in **Kosala.** During his siesta the monk would often fall asleep, and the deva, wishing his welfare and desiring to agitate him, draws near and asks him not to give himself up to somnolent habits. The monk replies to the effect that once a man has obtained insight by the suppression of desire and lust, there is no need to plague himself with unnecessary exertions.[1]

According to the Commentary,[2] the monk was an arahant. He had far to go to procure food, and when he came back, tired out, he would bathe and rest.

[1] S. i. 197 f. [2] SA. i. 232.

Upaṭṭhāyaka Thera.—An arahant. In a previous birth he provided **Siddhattha** Buddha with a personal attendant (*upaṭṭhāka*). Fifty-seven kappas ago he was born as a king, named **Balasena.**[1]

[1] Ap. i. 241.

Upaḍḍha Sutta.—Preached at the Sākyan township of **Sakkara. Ānanda** mentions to the Buddha his view that half the holy life consists in friendship with the good. The Buddha says that it is not the half but the whole of the holy life, and proceeds to explain.[1] In the *Kosala Saṃyutta*[2] we find the Buddha relating this incident to **Pasenadi.**

[1] S. v. 2. [2] S. i. 87.

Upaḍḍhadussadāyaka Thera.—An arahant. In the time of **Padumuttara** Buddha, he had been a labourer, and seeing a monk, named **Sujāta,** looking for rags for a robe, he gave him half the garment he wore. As a result he became king of the gods thirty-three times and king of men seventy-seven times.[1]

[1] Ap. ii. 436 f.

Upatapassī Thera.—Author of the **Vuttamālā.** He was incumbent of the **Gatārā Pariveṇa** and was the nephew of **Sarasigāmamūla Mahāsāmi.**[1]

[1] P.L.C. 253 f.

1. **Upatissa.**—The personal name of **Sāriputta** (*q.v.*).

2. **Upatissa.**—Purohita to **Vijaya,** king of Ceylon. He founded a settlement at **Upatissagāma.**[1]

[1] Mhv. vii. 44; Dpv. ix. 32, 36.

3. **Upatissa I.**—King of Ceylon. He reigned for forty-two years between A.C. 362 and 409. He was the eldest son of **Buddhadāsa.** He was of very kindly disposition and lived a simple life, eating of the food served in the **Mahāpāli** alms-hall. It is said that once, when the roof of his palace started leaking at night, he lay all night in the wet, being loth to disturb any of the servants. During a period of drought and famine, he organised a religious festival, causing rain to fall. He built the **Rajuppala, Gijjhakūṭa, Pokkharapāsaya, Valāhassa, Ambuṭṭhi** and **Goṇḍigāma** tanks and the **Khaṇḍarāja Vihāra,** besides hospitals and almshouses for women in travail, the blind and the sick. He was murdered by his queen-consort, who had an intrigue with his younger brother, **Mahānāma.**[1]

[1] For an account of Upatissa's reign see Cv. i. 37, 179 ff.

4. **Upatissa II.**—King of Ceylon. He was the husband of the sister of **Moggallāna I.** and was his general. He killed **Sīva I.** and became king, his reign lasting only one year and a half (A.C. 522-24). He had a son **Kassapa,** called **Girikassapa** by virtue of his prowess, and a daughter who married **Silākāla. Silākāla** became a rebel and seized Upatissa's kingdom.[1] Upatissa belonged to the **Lambakaṇṇa** clan, and in Siṇhalese writings is called Lämäṇi-upatissa.[2]

[1] For an account of Upatissa see Cv. xli. 5 f. [2] Cv. *Trs.* i. 52, n. 1.

5. **Upatissa.**—Son of **Silākāla** and brother of **Dāṭhāpabhuti** and **Moggallāna II.** He was a good-looking young man and was his father's favourite. He was killed by **Dāṭhāpabhuti.**[1]

[1] Cv. xli. 33 ff.

6. **Upatissa Thera.**—Called **Pāsāṇadīpavāsī Upatissa.** He appears to have written a Commentary on the *Mahāvaṃsa,* which the author of the *Mahāvaṃsa Ṭīkā* used for his own work, sometimes criticising its comments.[1]

[1] See, *e.g.*, MṬ. 47.

7. **Upatissa.**—Thera of **Tambapaṇṇidīpa** (Ceylon), perhaps to be identified with No. 6 above. He and his colleague, **Phussadeva,** are often mentioned as being expert exponents of the *Vinaya.* Upatissa had two pupils, **Mahāpaduma** and **Māhāsumma,** who became very famous as *vinayadharā.* Mahāpaduma "read" through the Vinaya eighteen

times with his teacher, and Mahāsumma nine times.[1] Buddhaghosa evidently regarded with great respect the explanations of various Vinaya questions as given by Upatissa, for he often quotes him.[2]

[1] Sp. i. 263 f. [2] See, *e.g.*, Sp. ii. 456; iii. 624, 714; iv. 890.

8. **Upatissa.**—**Sāriputta's** father and chieftain of **Nāḷaka** or **Upatissagāma** (*q.v.*). His proper name was **Vaṅganta** (*q.v.*), Upatissa being, evidently, his clan name.[1]

[1] SnA. i. 326.

9. **Upatissa Thera.**—Author of the Pāli *Mahābodhi-vaṃsa.* He lived in Ceylon, probably in the tenth century.[1]

[1] For details see P.L.C. 156 ff.

10. **Upatissa Thera.**—He wrote a commentary on **Kassapa's** *Anāgatavaṃsa.*[1]

[1] Gv. p. 72.

11. **Upatissa.**—A Pacceka Buddha, found in a nominal list.[1] The name is also found in the *Apadāna.*[2]

[1] M. iii. 69. [2] i. 280; ii. 454.

12. **Upatissa Thera.**—Sometimes called **Arahā Upatissa,** author of the *Vimuttimagga.*[1] He probably lived about the first century B.C.[2]

[1] P.L.C. 86. [2] *J.P.T.S.* 1919, pp. 69 ff.; see also NidA. (P.T.S.); introd. vi f.

13. **Upatissa Thera.**—Author of the *Saddhammappajjotikā*, the commentary on the *Mahā Niddesa*, written at the request of **Deva Thera.**[1]

His residence was on the western side of the **Mahā Cetiya** within the precincts of the **Mahāvihāra** in Anurādhapura, and it was built by a minister, **Kittissena.**

Some MSS. give the author's name as **Upasena.** For his age, see *s.v.* **Saddhammappajjotikā.**

[1] NidA. ii. 108.

Upatissa Sutta.—Preached by **Sāriputta.** He tells the monks that there is nothing in the whole world, a change in which would cause him sorrow. Not even a change regarding the Buddha, he emphasises, in answer to a question by **Ānanda.**[1]

[1] S. ii. 274 f.

1. **Upatissagāma.**—A brahmin village near **Rājagaha.** It was the birthplace of **Sāriputta.**[1] Its real name was **Nāḷaka** (*q.v.*), but it was called Upatissagāma, evidently because its chieftains belonged to the Upatissa clan. It is probable that Sāriputta's father, who was head of the village (*gāmasāmi*), was also called **Upatissa.**[2]

[1] ThagA. ii. 93; DhA. i. 73.
[2] See SnA. i. 326.

2. **Upatissagāma** (sometimes called **Upatissanagara**).—The settlement founded by **Vijaya's** chaplain, **Upatissa,** on the banks of the **Gambhīra-nadī,** about seven miles to the north of **Anurādhapura.**[1] It was the seat of government till Anurādhapura became the capital.[2] Soon after **Mahinda's** arrival in Ceylon many young men joined the Order, and among them there were five hundred from Upatissagāma.[3]

[1] Mhv. vii. 44; Mhv. *Trs.* 58, n. 4; Dpv. ix. 36; x. 5.
[2] See, *e.g.*, Mhv. viii. 4; x. 48.
[3] *Ibid.*, xvii. 60.

Upatissā.—One of the two chief women-disciples of **Koṇḍañña** Buddha.[1]

[1] Bu. iii. 31; J. i. 30.

Upadduta Sutta.—Everything in the world is oppressed.[1]

[1] S. iv. 29.

Upadhi.—A Pacceka Buddha, whose name occurs in a list of names.[1]

[1] ApA. i. 107.

Upananda.—A thera. He belonged to the Sākyan clan. Several incidents connected with him are mentioned in the *Vinaya.* Once he promised to spend the rainy season with **Pasenadi Kosala,** but on his way there he saw two lodgings where robes were plentiful and so kept *Vassa* in those lodgings instead. Pasenadi was greatly annoyed and when, in due course, the matter reached the ears of the Buddha, Upananda was rebuked and a set of rules was passed regarding promises made about the rainy season.[1] On another occasion Upananda spent the rainy season at **Sāvatthi,** but when the time came for the monks to gather together and divide the robes that had been given to them, he went from village to village, taking his share of the robes from everywhere. The Buddha sent for him and rebuked him in the presence of the Order, but the rebuke had evidently no effect, for we find him again spending the *Vassa* alone in two residences, with the idea of obtaining many robes. The Buddha, however, ordered that only one portion should be

[1] Vin. i. 153.

given to him.[2] His greediness was not confined to robes. Once he was invited to a meal by an official, a follower of the Ājīvakas. He went late, and finding no room left for him, made a junior monk get up and give him his seat. There was a great uproar, but Upananda had his way.[3] Elsewhere he is accused of having appropriated two lodgings for himself at the same time, one at Sāvatthi and the other somewhere in the country. He was evidently unpopular among the monks, because on this occasion we find him spoken of as "a maker of strife, quarrelsome, a maker of disputes, given to idle talk, a raiser of legal questions."[4] Upananda was fond of money, for we find in the *Vinaya*[5] a statement to the effect that "on the occasion of the matter of Upananda the Sākyan, the Buddha distinctly laid down a precept by which gold and silver were forbidden." Upananda had been given his meals regularly by a certain family. Once a dish of meat was prepared for him, but a little boy in the house started to cry for the meat, and it was given to him. Upananda insisted that a *kahāpana* should be paid to him in lieu of the meat.[6] Upananda was once asked to preach to those that came to Jetavana. Among the visitors was a banker, and when the banker expressed the desire to give something to Upananda to show his appreciation of the sermon, Upananda wished to have the robe that the man wore. The banker was embarrassed, and promised to go home at once and fetch him another robe, even better than the one he had on. But Upananda was adamant, till, in despair, the man gave him his robe and went away. Again, when Upananda heard that a certain man wished to offer him a robe, he went to the man and told him what kind of robe he wanted, and said he would accept no other.[7] A story is also told of a Paribbājaka exchanging his own garment for one belonging to Upananda, which was of rich colour. Two other Paribbājakas told him that he had lost in the bargain, so he wished to cry off the deal, but Upananda positively refused.[8] He did not, however, always come off best in a bargain. Once he gave a robe to a colleague, on condition that the latter should join him in his tours. The condition was agreed to, but later, when the recipient monk heard that the Buddha was going on tour, he preferred to join the Buddha's company. The robe was not returned to Upananda, who had to be reported to the Buddha for the violent language he used to the defaulter.[9] Upananda is mentioned as quarrelling with the **Chabbaggiya** monks[10] and, at another time, as going his alms-rounds with a colleague with whom he quarrelled when

[2] Vin. i. 300.
[3] *Ibid.*, ii. 165.
[4] *Ibid.*, 168. [5] *Ibid.*, 297.
[6] *Ibid.*, iii. 236 f.
[7] *Ibid.*, 215.
[8] *Ibid.*, 240 f.
[9] *Ibid.*, 254 f.
[10] *Ibid.*, iv. 30.

the rounds were over, refusing to give him any of the food obtained. The unfortunate monk had to starve because it was then too late to go out begging again.[11] We are not told whether Upananda deliberately set out to have a quarrel in order that he might keep all the food himself!

Nor were all Upananda's misdemeanours confined to greed for possessions. We are told that once a complaint was made to the Buddha that Upanandada had gone to the house of an acquaintance and had sat down in the bedroom of the woman of the house, talking to her. The husband ordered food to be brought to Upananda, and when that was done, asked him to leave. But the woman wished him to stay and he refused to go away.[12] On two other occasions he is mentioned as visiting the houses of his acquaintances and being found by the husbands, seated alone with their wives.[13]

With most laymen, however, he was evidently popular. Mention is made of a meal where the donor kept all the other monks waiting for quite a long while, till Upananda should arrive, after his visits to various households.[14] And, again, of food being sent to the monastery with express instructions that the other monks should eat only after Upananda had done so.[15]

Episodes regarding Upananda's misdeeds are not confined to the *Vinaya*. In the **Dabbhapuppha** Jātaka[16] we are told that he was in the habit of preaching contentment to others. When they, touched by his preaching, cast away their good robes, etc., Upananda collected them for himself. Once he cheated two brethren of a costly blanket. When the matter was brought to the Buddha's notice, this Jātaka was related to show how in previous births, too, he had plundered other people's goods. He had been a jackal called **Māyāvī**, and had cheated two other jackals of a *rohita*-fish they had caught. Again, in the **Samudda** Jātaka,[17] he is described as a great eater and drinker; he would not be satisfied even with cart-loads of provisions. The Jātaka tells of how he once was born as a water-crow and tried to prevent the fish from drinking the sea-water lest he should not have enough for himself. Buddhaghosa calls him a *lolajātika,* held in contempt by his eighty thousand fellow Sākyans who joined the Order.[18] Elsewhere he is referred to as a well-known example of one who never practised what he preached and, therefore, did not benefit by his cleverness.[19]

[11] Vin. iv. 92 f.

[12] *Ibid.*, 94.

[13] *Ibid.*, 95-7; see also 121, 127 and 168, for other offences committed by him.

[14] *Ibid.*, 98.

[15] *Ibid.*, 99.

[16] J. iii. 332 ff.; see also DhA. iii. 139 ff.

[17] J. ii. 441 f.

[18] Sp. iii. 665.

[19] *E.g.*, AA. i. 92; MA. i. 348; Vsm. i. 81.

Upananda had under him two novices, **Kaṇḍaka** and **Mahaka,** who seem to have resembled their teacher in being undesirables. They were found guilty of an unnatural offence, and the Buddha ordered that no one should ordain them.[20]

[20] Vin. i. 79. This order seems to have been rescinded later (see Vin. i. 83).

2. **Upananda.**—A king of fifty-seven kappas ago; a previous birth of **Tindukadāyaka** Thera.[1]

[1] Ap. i. 201.

3. **Upananda.**—Four Pacceka Buddhas, mentioned in the **Isigili Sutta.**[1]

[1] M. iii. 70.

4. **Upananda.**—Commander-in-chief of the **Magadha** kingdom. He was present at the conversation, recorded in the **Gopaka-Moggallāna Sutta,** between **Ānanda** and **Vassakāra.**[1]

[1] M. iii. 13.

Upananda-Sākyaputta-Thera-Vatthu.—A group of stories concerning the greediness and rapacity of **Upananda Sākyaputta.**[1]

[1] DhA. iii. 139 ff.; *cf.* J. iii. 332 ff.

Upanāhī Sutta.—Preached in answer to the questions of **Anuruddha.** The five qualities, including grudging, which lead a woman to be reborn in purgatory.[1]

[1] S. iv. 241.

1. **Upanisā Sutta.**—On causal association.[1]

[1] S. ii. 29 f.

2. **Upanisā Sutta.**—On how, to the wicked man, the possibilities of all high attainments are destroyed, not so to the man who is righteous.[1]

[1] A. v. 313 f.

3. **Upanisā Sutta.**—The same as 2, but the Sutta is ascribed to **Sāriputta.**[1]

[1] A. v. 315 f.

Upanisinna Vagga.—The fourth chapter of the *Rādha Saṃyutta* of the *Saṃyutta Nikāya.*[1]

[1] S. iii. 200 ff.

Upanita.—A Pacceka Buddha, mentioned in the **Isigili Sutta.**[1]

[1] M.iii.70.

Upanemi.—A Pacceka Buddha, mentioned in nominal lists.[1]

[1] M.iii.70; ApA.i.107.

Upaneyya Sutta.—A deva visits the Buddha at **Jetavana** and utters a stanza in which he says that life is short, and one should accumulate merit in order to obtain bliss. The Buddha replies that all who fear death should aspire to the final peace.[1]

[1] S.i.2.

Upamañña.—The family (*gotta*) to which **Pokkharasāti** belonged. He was, therefore, called **Opamañña.**[1]

[1] M.ii.200; MA.ii.804.

Upaya Sutta (wrongly called **Upāya**).—Attachment (*upaya*) is bondage, aloofness is freedom. With the abandonment of lust, lust's foothold is cut off and, thereby, rebirth, etc., is destroyed.[1]

[1] S.iii.53.

Upayanti Sutta.—When the ocean rises with the tide, the rivers, their tributaries, the mountain lakes and tarns, all rise as a result. Likewise rising ignorance makes, in turn, becoming, birth and decay and death to rise and increase.[1]

[1] S.ii.118 f.

Uparāmā.—One of the two chief women disciples of **Paduma** Buddha.[1] The *Buddhavaṃsa*, however, gives their names as **Rādhā** and **Surādhā**.

[1] J.i.36.

Uparigaṅgā.—See **Gaṅgā.**

Upariṭṭha.—A Pacceka Buddha.[1] In a previous life, when **Anuruddha** was born as **Annabhāra,** he offered alms to the Pacceka Buddha and made various wishes which were fulfilled in later births.[2] Upariṭṭha had spent seven days in meditation on **Gandhamādana,** and when he appeared before Annabhāra, the latter ran home to his wife, fetched the food which had been prepared for themselves and gave it to Upariṭṭha. Upariṭṭha ate the meal seated on Annabhāra's garment, which was spread on the ground for him.[3]

[1] M.iii.69; ApA.i.106.
[2] DhA.i.113 f.
[3] AA. i. 105; Thag. 910; ThagA. ii. 66.

Uparimaṇḍakamāla.—A vihāra (?) in Ceylon, the residence of **Mahārakkhita** Thera (*q.v.*).[1]

[1] J. vi. 30.

Uparimaṇḍalaka-malaya.—A vihāra (?) in Ceylon, the residence of **Mahāsaṅgharakkhita** Thera.[1]

[1] J. iv. 490.

Uparuci.—A king of thirty-eight kappas ago; a previous birth of **Sucintita** Thera.[1]

[1] Ap. i. 134.

1. **Uparevata.**—A sāmaṇera, son of **Padumuttara** Buddha. It was the sight of this novice which made **Rāhula,** then born as the Nāga-king **Saṅkha,** wish to become a Buddha's son.[1] According to the *Buddhavaṃsa*,[2] however, Padumuttara's son was called **Uttara.** Uparevata, though very young in years (*taruṇalalitadāraka*), was possessed of great *iddhi*-powers and the Nāga-king was greatly impressed by him.[3]

[1] SnA. i. 340; MA. ii. 722.
[2] xi. 21.
[3] AA. i. 142 f. Here the nāga king is called **Paṭhavindhara.**

2. **Uparevata.**—Nephew of **Sāriputta.** When Sāriputta went to **Nālaka** on his last visit, in order to die there, Uparevata saw him outside the village, seated under a banyan tree. He was asked to announce Sāriputta's arrival to the latter's mother, and to make preparations for accommodating Sāriputta's five hundred followers.[1]

[1] DA. ii. 551; SA. iii. 175.

Upavatta (Upavattana).—The *sāla*-grove of the **Mallas** of **Kusināra,** on the further side of the **Hiraññavatī.** This was the last resting-place of the Buddha on his last tour, and here he passed away, lying on a bed placed between two *sāla* trees.[1] Here **Subhadda** visited the Buddha in the earlier part of the last night of his life, was converted and gained admission into the Order, afterwards winning arahantship.[2] It was here, too, that the Buddha asked the monks if they had any doubts they wished to hear solved regarding the Buddha, the Dhamma and the Saṅgha, *magga* and *paṭipadā*, or any questions they wished to ask,[3] and here he gave his last admonition to the monks.[4] Ānanda tried to persuade him to die in a place of greater importance, and the Buddha,

[1] D. ii. 137 ff.; Dpv. xv. 70.
[2] See also DhA. iii. 377.
[3] A. ii. 79.
[4] S. i. 157; see also Ud. 37 f.

in order to disabuse his mind, preached to him the **Mahā Sudassana Sutta.**[5]

Buddhaghosa says[6] that the road to the *sāla*-grove from the Hiraññavatī led from the further bank of the river, like the road from the **Kadambanadī** to the **Thūpārāma** in Anurādhapura which led through the **Rājamātu-vihāra.** The row of *sāla*-trees stretched from south to east and then continued to the north ("like the chief street in Anurādhapura"). Hence the name Upavattana. The grove was to the south-west of Kusināra.[7]

[5] D. ii. 169 f. [6] DA. ii. 572 f. [7] UdA. 238.

1. **Upavāṇa.**—A thera. He belonged to a very rich brahmin family of **Sāvatthi,** and having seen the Buddha's majesty at the dedication of **Jetavana,** he entered the Order and became an arahant with sixfold *aññā*. For some time, before **Ānanda** was appointed *upaṭṭhāka*, Upavāna waited on the Buddha. Once when the Buddha was attacked by cramp, Upavāṇa, with the help of his lay-friend **Devahita,** obtained hot water and suitable medicines, with which the ailment was healed; the Buddha, thereupon, expressed his gratitude.[1]

When the Buddha lay on his death-bed at **Kusinārā,** Upavāṇa was by his side fanning him; the Buddha, seeing that he obstructed the vision of the devas who had come to pay their last homage to the Teacher, asked Upavāṇa to move away.[2]

Two occasions are mentioned on which Upavāṇa consulted the Buddha on matters of doctrine, once regarding the arising of suffering[3] and once on the immediate and practical use of the Dhamma (*sandiṭṭhikadhamma*).[4] There is also recorded a visit of Upavāṇa to **Sāriputta** when they were both staying in the **Ghositārāma** at Kosambī. Sāriputta asks him about the *bojjhaṅgas* as being conducive to a happy life and Upavāṇa explains.[5] On another occasion Upavāṇa is the enquirer, and he asks Sāriputta about the "end-maker" (*antakara*); Sāriputta explains that the "end-maker" is the one who knows and sees things as they really are.[6]

When an unpleasant interview took place between Sāriputta and **Lāludāyī** (*q.v.*) and no one was found to support Sāriputta, the matter is reported to the Buddha, who declares that **Ānanda** should have taken Sāriputta's side. Soon afterwards Ānanda seeks Upavāṇa and tells him that he was too timid to interfere, and if the Buddha referred to the

[1] ThagA. i. 308 ff.; this ailment does not seem to be mentioned in Milinda 134 f. where several others are given. This incident is given at greater length in S. i. 174 f.; see also DhA. iv. 232 f.

[2] D. ii. 138 f.

[3] S. ii. 41-2.

[4] *Ibid.*, iv. 41.

[5] *Ibid.*, v. 76.

[6] A. ii. 163.

matter again, would Upavāṇa undertake to answer? In the evening the Buddha engages Upavāṇa in conversation and asks him to explain the five qualities which make a monk esteemed and loved by his colleagues. At the end of the discourse the Buddha applauds Upavāṇa.[7]

In **Padumuttara's** time Upavāṇa had been a poor man. Seeing people making great offerings at the Buddha's Thūpa, he was much touched, and having washed his upper garment, he hung it as a flag over the Thūpa. A yakkha named **Abhisammataka,** who was the guardian of the cetiya, took the flag three times round the cetiya, he himself remaining invisible.

A monk whom the man consulted after this miracle foretold that for thirty thousand kappas he would be in the deva-worlds and that he would be deva-king eighty times. One thousand times he was *Cakkavatti.* In his last life his wealth was eighty crores. When he was *Cakkavatti,* his banner was held aloft, three leagues in height.[8]

[7] A.iii.195 f. [8] Ap.i.70 ff.

2. **Upavāṇa.**—Son of **Anomadassī** Buddha.[1]

[1] Bu.viii.19.

1. **Upavāṇa Sutta.**—The conversation referred to above, between **Upavāṇa** and **Sāriputta,** on the *antakara.*[1]

[1] A.ii.163 f.

2. **Upavāṇa Sutta.**—The Buddha explains to **Upavāṇa** the arising of sorrow (*dukkha-samuppāda*).[1]

[1] S.ii.41 f.

3. **Upavāṇa Sutta.**—The Buddha explains, in answer to a question of **Upavāṇa,** how the Dhamma is immediate in its results (*sandiṭṭhika*).[1]

[1] S.iv.41 f.

4. **Upavāṇa Sutta.**—The conversation referred to above, between **Sāriputta** and **Upavāṇa,** where the latter explains how the *bojjhaṅgas* conduce to a happy life.[1]

[1] S.v.76 f.

Upavāla.—See **Uvāḷa.**

1. **Upasanta.**—One of the two chief disciples of **Atthadassī** Buddha.[1] He was the son of the chaplain of **Sucandaka** and the friend of **Santa.**

[1] Bu.xv.19; J.i.39.

Santa and Upasanta visited the Buddha and for seven days entertained the Buddha and his monks. The two entered the Order with ninety-eight thousand followers.[2]

[2] BuA. 179 f.

2. **Upasanta.**—A Pacceka Buddha to whom the thera **Vajjita,** in a previous birth thirty-one kappas ago, gave a *campaka*-flower.[1]

[1] ThagA. i. 336; Ap. i. 288.

3. **Upasanta (Upasantaka, Upasaññaka).**—The body-servant of **Vessabhū** Buddha.[1] He was the king of **Nārivāhana** city and was converted by the Buddha, taking over with him a large following.[2]

[1] D. ii. 6; Bu. xxii. 23; J. i. 42. [2] BuA. 206.

Upasama Sutta.—The Buddha explains to a monk, in answer to a question, how one may become perfect in the *indriyas*.[1]

[1] S. v. 202. For the title see KS. v. 178, n. 3.

Upasamā Therī.—She was born in a Sākyan family in **Kapilavatthu** and became a lady of the Bodhisatta's court. Later, in the company of **Pajāpatī Gotamī,** she renounced the world and entered the Order. One day, while she was meditating, the Buddha sent forth a ray of glory and admonished her. She, thereupon, developed insight and became an arahant.[1]

[1] Thig. v. 10; ThigA. 12 f.

Upasampadā Vagga.—The sixteenth chapter of the *Pañcaka Nipāta* of the *Aṅguttara Nikāya*. The suttas of this chapter deal with the qualities requisite for a monk who wishes to receive the *upasampadā*, to give *nissaya*, to institute a novice, to become an official in the Order, etc.[1]

[1] A. iii. 271-8.

Upasampadā Sutta.—On the qualities which a monk should possess in order to admit others to the Order.[1]

[1] A. v. 72.

Upasāgara.—Son of **Mahāsāgra,** who was the king of **Uttaramadhurā.** Upasāgara's elder brother was **Sāgara,** and when their father died, Upasāgara became his brother's viceroy. Having been suspected of an intrigue in the king's zenana, he fled to the court of **Upakaṃsa** in

Asitañjano. There he fell in love with **Devagabbhā,** and when she was with child he married her and they lived in **Govaḍḍhamāna.** Their children were the notorious **Andhakaveṇhu-dāsaputtā.**

Upasāla.—Younger brother of **Paduma** Buddha and, later, one of his two chief disciples.[1]

[1] Bu. ix. 21; BuA. 147; J. i. 36.

Upasālā.—According to the *Buddhavaṃsa Commentary*,[1] **Sālā** and **Upasālā** were the two chief women disciples of **Phussa** Buddha. The *Buddhavaṃsa*,[2] however, calls them **Cālā** and **Upacālā.**

[1] 194.

[2] xix. 20.

Upasāḷha.—A wealthy brahmin of **Rājagaha.** He lived near the monastery, but was an unbeliever and had nothing to do with the Buddha or his monks. He had a wise and intelligent son. When Upasāḷha was old, he told his son that, after death, he wished to be burnt in a cemetery unpolluted by any outcast. Being asked by the son to point out such a spot, he took him to **Gijjhakūṭa** and shewed him a place. As they were descending the hill, the Buddha, perceiving their *upanissaya*, waited for them at the foot, and when they met he asked where they had been. Having heard their story, he related the **Upasāḷha Jātaka,** shewing that in the past, too, Upasāḷha had been fastidious about cemeteries. At the conclusion of the discourse, both father and son were established in the First Fruit of the Path.[1]

[1] J. ii. 54 ff.

Upasāḷha Jātaka (No. 166).—Preached to **Upasāḷha.** The story of the past is that of a brahmin **Upasāḷhaka** (identified with Upasāḷha). He instructed his son that after death he should be burnt in a cemetery unpolluted by the presence of outcasts. While descending **Gijjhakūṭa,** having ascended the mountain in order to find such a spot, they met the Bodhisatta, who was a holy ascetic, possessed of various attainments and mystic powers. When the Bodhisatta had heard their story, he revealed to them that on that very same spot Upasāḷha had been burnt fourteen thousand times, and preached to them the way of deathlessness.[1]

The Upasāḷhaka Jātaka was preached by the Buddha to the novice **Vanavāsī-Tissa** when the Buddha visited him in his forest solitude.[2]

[1] J. ii. 54 ff.

[2] DhA. ii. 99.

1. **Upasiri.**—One of the palaces occupied by **Anomadassī** Buddha in his last lay-life.[1]

Bu. viii. 18.

2. **Upasiri.**—A palace similarly occupied by **Sujāta** Buddha.[1]

[1] Bu. xiii. 21.

Upasīdarī.—A Pacceka Buddha, mentioned in the **Isigili Sutta.**[1]

[1] M. iii. 70.

Upasīva.—One of the disciples of **Bāvarī.**[1] The questions he asked the Buddha, when he visited him in the company of his colleagues, are recorded in the **Upasīva-māṇava-pucchā.**[2] Upasīva joined the Order and became an arahant. According to the *Apadāna,*[3] in the time of **Padumuttara** he had been an ascetic in a mountain named **Anoma,** near Himavā. Once the Buddha visited his hermitage and the ascetic spread a seat for him with grass and flowers and gave him fruit to eat. He also gave the Buddha a quantity of fragrant aloe-wood. As a result, he was born in heaven for thirty thousand kappas and was seventy-one times king of the devas. The *Apadāna*-account makes no mention of Bāvarī.

[1] Sn. v. 1007. [2] *Ibid.*, vv. 1069-76. [3] ii. 345 ff.

Upasīva-māṇava-pucchā.—The sixth sutta of the **Pārāyanavagga.** It contains the questions asked of the Buddha by **Upasīva** and the answers thereto.[1] One of Upasīva's questions was as to how the floods (*ogha*) may be crossed. We are told that he was an *ākiñcaññāyatanalābhī.*[2]

[1] Sn. vv. 1069-76. [2] SnA. ii. 593 f.; see also *Culla-Niddesa*, p. 101.

Upasumbha.—An image of the Buddha placed in the **Bahumaṅgala-cetiya** at **Anurādhapura.** King **Dhātusena** had a diadem of rays made for the statue.[1]

[1] Cv. xxxviii. 66.

Upaseṇā.—One of the chief women supporters of **Tissa** Buddha.[1]

[1] Bu. xviii. 23.

Upaseṇī.—Daughter of **Vasavatti,** king of **Pupphavatī** and sister of **Candakumāra.** She narrowly escaped death when the king, on the advice of his chaplain, wished to offer human sacrifices. The story is told in the **Kaṇḍahāla Jātaka.**[1]

[1] J. vi. 134.

1. **Upasena Thera.**—Maternal uncle of **Vijitasena** Thera and brother of **Sena.** He was an elephant-trainer, and having heard the Buddha preach, he entered the Order and, in due course, became an arahant. He ordained Vijitasena.[1] According to the *Mahāvastu,*[2] Sāriputta was converted to Buddhism not by **Assaji,** as recorded in the *Piṭakas,* but by an Elder named Upasena, who is, perhaps, to be identified with the Upasena. The *Mahāvastu* also mentions[3] an Upasena who was nephew to the **Tebhātika Jaṭilas.** When the Tebhātikas accepted the Buddha as their teacher, they cast the garments, etc., which they had used as ascetics, into the Nerañjarā, on the banks of which was Upasena's hermitage. When Upasena saw the robes, etc., he knew that something must have happened to his uncles. He went at once to see them and, having heard the good tidings of their new-found bliss became a monk himself. It is not stated whether this Upasena is identical with the Elder of the same name mentioned above as the teacher of Sāriputta.

[1] ThagA. i. 424. [2] iii. 60 ff. [3] *Ibid.*, 431 f.

2. **Upasena Vaṅgantaputta.**—He was born in **Nāḷaka** as the son of **Rūpasārī,** the brahminee, his father being **Vaṅganta.** He was the younger brother of **Sāriputta.**[1] When he came of age, he learnt the three Vedas, and, having heard the Buddha preach, entered the Order. When his ordination was but one year old, he ordained another bhikkhu, to increase the number of holy ones, and went with him to wait upon the Buddha. The Buddha roundly rebuked him for this hasty procedure,[2] and Upasena, wishing to earn the Master's praise on account of the very cause of this rebuke, practised insight and became an arahant. Thereafter he adopted various *dhutaṅgas* and persuaded others to do likewise. In a short time he had a large retinue, each member of which was charming in his way, and the Buddha declared Upasena to be the best of those who were altogether charming (*samantapāsādikānaṃ*).[3] Buddhaghosa says[4] that Upasena was famed as a very clever preacher (*paṭhavighuṭṭhadhammakathika*), and many joined him because of his eloquence. He visited the Buddha when the Buddha had enjoined on himself a period of solitude for a fortnight; the monks had agreed that anyone who went to see the Buddha would be guilty of a *pācittiya* offence, but the Buddha, desiring to talk to him, asked one of Upasena's followers if he liked

[1] UdA. 266; DhA. ii. 188.

[2] Vin. i. 59; Sp. i. 194; J. ii. 449.

[3] A. i. 24.

[4] AA. i. 152; also Mil. 360, where more details are given of how Upasena admitted monks into the Order and of the conditions imposed on them; for a slightly different version see Vin. iii. 230 ff.; it is said there that after Upasena's visit, the Buddha allowed monks who practised *dhutaṅgas,* to visit him even during his periods of retreat. See also Sp. iii. 685 f.

rag-robes. " No, Sir, but I wear them out of regard for my teacher," was the reply.

In the *Theragātha*[5] are found several verses ascribed to Upasena as having been spoken by him in answer to a question by his *saddhivihārika*, regarding what was to be done during the dissensions of the **Kosambī** monks. The *Milinda-pañha*[6] contains several other verses attributed to Upasena similar in their trend of ideas and admonitions. The *Udāna* states[7] that once when he was taking his siesta he reviewed the happiness he enjoyed and the glories of the life he led under the guidance of the Buddha. The Buddha, noticing this, proclaimed his approval.

One day, while Upasena was sitting after his meal in the shadow of the **Sappasoṇḍika-pabbhāra,** fanned by the gentle breeze, mending his outer robe, two young snakes were sporting in the tendrils overhanging the cave. One fell on his shoulder and bit him, and the venom spread rapidly throughout his body; he called to **Sāriputta** and other monks who were near, and requested that he might be taken outside on a couch, there to die. This was done, and his body " was scattered there and then like a handful of chaff."[8]

Upasena had been, in **Padumuttara's** day, a householder of **Haṃsavatī.** One day he heard the Buddha declare one of his monks to be the best of those who were altogether charming, and wished for a similar declaration regarding himself by some future Buddha. Towards this end he did many deeds of piety.[9] The *Apadāna*[10] mentions that he gave a meal to Padumuttara and eight monks, and at the meal placed over the Buddha's head a parasol made of *kaṇikāra*-flowers. As a result, he was thirty times king of the devas and twenty-one times cakkavatti.

Upasena is given, together with **Yasa Kākaṇḍakaputta,** as an example of one who observed the *Vinaya* precepts thoroughly, without imposing any new rules or agreements.[11]

[5] vv. 577-86; the first verse is quoted in the Milinda (371) and also the fifth (395).
[6] pp. 393, 394.
[7] p. 45 f.; UdA. 266 ff.
[8] S. iv. 40 f.; SA. iii. 10.
[9] ThagA. i. 525.
[10] i. 62. The verses quoted from the Apadāna in the ThagA. are slightly different.
[11] DA. ii. 525.

3. **Upasena Thera.**—Mentioned in the *Gandhavaṃsa*[1] as the author of the *Saddhammappajjotikā*, the commentary on the *Mahā Niddesa*. But see **Upatissa** (13).

[1] 61, 66; also Svd. 1197.

4. **Upasena.**—Son of **Sujāta** Buddha.[1]

[1] Bu. xiii. 22.

Upasena Sutta.—Records the incident of the death of **Upasena Vaṅgantaputta** from a snake-bite. Summoned by him, **Sāriputta** looked at him and said that he noticed no change at all in Upasena, either in his body or in his faculties. Upasena answered that that was because he had long before quelled all lurking tendencies of " I " and " mine."[1]

[1] S. iv. 40 f.

Upasoṇā.—One of the two chief women disciples of **Sumana** Buddha.[1]

[1] Bu. v. 27; J. i. 24.

Upassaṭṭha Sutta.—Everything is oppressed: eye, ear, etc.[1]

[1] S. iv. 29.

Upassaya Sutta.—**Ānanda,** with great difficulty, persuades **Mahā Kassapa** to accompany him to a settlement of nuns. Mahā Kassapa goes and preaches to them, but **Thulla-Tissā,** not being pleased with the sermon, upbraids Mahā Kassapa for what she calls his impertinence in preaching when Ānanda is present. " How does the needle-pedlar deem he could sell a needle to the needle-maker ?" Kassapa is upset, and Ānanda asks for forgiveness in the nun's name, for women, he says, are foolish, and one must be indulgent to them. Kassapa reminds the audience that it was he himself and not Ānanda who was declared by the Buddha to be the Buddha's equal in the attainment of the *jhānas.*[1]

[1] S. ii. 214.

Upassayadāyaka-vimāna.—The abode of a pious man who was born in **Tāvatiṃsa** as a result of having given a night's shelter to a holy monk. The *vimāna* was of gold and was twelve *yojanas* in height.[1]

[1] Vv. 64; VvA. 291 f.

Upassuti Sutta.—Once when the Buddha was staying in the Giñjakāvasatha in Nāṭikā, he meditated in solitude and uttered a teaching setting forth how, from the objects and the senses, arise consciousness and contact and, ultimately, the whole body of Ill. A certain monk overheard this, and when the Buddha saw him, he asked the monk to learn the discourse by heart and bear it in mind, because it would lead to the righteous life.[1]

[1] S. iv. 90 f.

Upāgatabhāsaniya Thera.—An arahant. In the time of **Vipassī** Buddha he was a Rakkhasa in a lake in Himavā. Once the Buddha visited this sprite who paid homage to him.[1]

[1] Ap. i. 233.

1. **Upādāna Sutta.**—Enjoyment brings about craving, grasping, becoming, birth, etc., and, in turn, the whole mass of Ill.

It is like a fire with many loads of faggots, constantly supplied with fuel.[1]

[1] S. ii. 84 f.

2. **Upādāna Sutta.**—On grasping and the things that make for it.[1]

[1] S. iii. 167.

3. **Upādāna Sutta.**—The Buddha teaches the things that make for grasping and the fetters arising therefrom.[1]

[1] S. iv. 89.

4. **Upādāna Sutta.**—On grasping and the things that encourage it.[1]

[1] S. iv. 108.

5. **Upādāna Sutta.**—**Jambukhādaka** asks **Sāriputta** what grasping is. Sāriputta says there are four kinds: grasping after sensuality, opinion, rule and ritual and theory of self.[1]

[1] S. iv. 258.

Upādāna-parivaṭṭa Sutta.—On the five khandhas as grasping and the series of four truths in regard to each khandha—*i.e.*, the khandha itself, its arising, its cessation and the way thereto. He who fully understands these is fully liberated.[1]

[1] S. iii. 58 ff.

Upādāna-paritassanā Sutta.—Two discourses on how grasping and worry arise and how they can be got rid of.[1]

[1] S. iii. 15-18.

Upādāya Sutta.—Personal weal and woe are dependent on the eye, ear, etc. But these are impermanent, woeful, of a nature to change. Therefore should one not lust for them.[1]

[1] S. iv. 85 f.

Upādiyamāna Sutta.—When asked by a certain monk to give a topic for reflection, the Buddha tells him that if a man clings, he is Māra's bondsman. If he cling not, he is free. The Buddha asks the monk what he understands by this and is pleased with the explanation. The monk meditates on this and becomes an arahant.[1]

[1] S. iii. 73 f.

Upāya Sutta.—See **Upaya Sutta.**

1. **Upāli Thera.**—One of the most eminent of the Buddha's immediate disciples. He belonged to a barber's family in **Kapilavatthu** and entered the service of the **Sākyan** princes. When **Anuruddha** and his cousins left the world and sought ordination from the Buddha at **Anupiyā** Grove, Upāli accompanied them. They gave him all their valuable ornaments, but, on further consideration, he refused to accept them and wished to become a monk with them. The reason given for his refusal is that he knew the Sākyans were hot-headed, and feared that the kinsmen of the princes might suspect him of having murdered the young men for the sake of their belongings.

At the request of the Sākyan youths, the Buddha ordained Upāli before them all, so that their pride might be humbled.[1] Upāli's *upajjhāya* was **Kappitaka.**[2] When Upāli went to the Buddha for an exercise for meditation, he asked that he might be allowed to dwell in the forest. But the Buddha would not agree, for if Upāli went into the forest he would learn only meditation, while, if he remained amongst men, he would have knowledge both of meditation and of the word of the Dhamma. Upāli accepted the Buddha's advice and, practising insight, in due course won arahantship. The Buddha himself taught Upāli the whole of the *Vinaya Piṭaka.*[3]

In the assembly of the Saṅgha, the Buddha declared him to be the most proficient of those who were learned in the *Vinaya* (*vinayadharānaṃ*).[4] He is often spoken of as having reached the pinnacle of the *Vinaya*, or as being its chief repository (*Vinaye agganikkhitto*),[5] and three particular cases—those of **Ajjuka,**[6] the **Bhārukacchaka** monk[7] and **Kumāra-Kassapa**[8]—are frequently mentioned in this connection as instances where Upāli's decisions on *Vinaya* rules earned the special commendation of the Buddhा. In the Rājagaha Council, Upāli took a leading part, deciding all the questions relative to the *Vinaya*, in the same way as Ānanda decided questions regarding the Dhamma.[9]

In accordance with this tradition, ascribing to Upāli especial authority regarding the rules of the Order, various instances are given of Upāli

[1] Vin. ii. 182; DhA. i. 116 f.; see also Bu. i. 61; but see BuA. 44; the Tibetan sources give a slightly different version (see Rockhill, *op. cit.*, pp. 55-6); according to the *Mahāvastu* (iii. 179), Upāli was the Buddha's barber, too.

[2] Vin. iv. 308.

[3] ThagA. i. 360 f., 370; AA. i. 172.

[4] A. i. 24; see also Vin. iv. 142, where the Buddha is mentioned as speaking Upāli's praises.

[5] *E.g.*, Dpv. iv. 3, 5; v. 7, 9.

[6] Vin. iii. 66 f.

[7] *Ibid.*, 39.

[8] AA. i. 158; MA. i. 336; J. i. 148; DhA. iii. 145.

[9] Vin. ii. 286 f.; DA. i. 11 f.; Mhv. iii. 30.

questioning the Buddha about the *Vinaya* regulations. Thus we find him consulting the Buddha as to the legality or otherwise of a complete congregation performing, in the absence of an accused monk, an act at which his presence is required.[10] Again, he wishes to know if, in a matter which has caused altercations and schisms among members of the Order, the Saṅgha declares re-establishment of concord without thorough investigation, could such a declaration be lawful ?[11] When a monk intends to take upon himself the conduct of any matter that has to be decided, under what conditions should he do so ? What qualities should a monk possess in himself before he takes upon himself to warn others ?[12] In what case can there be an interruption of the probationary period of a monk who has been placed on probation ?[13]

A whole list of questions asked by Upāli and answers given by the Buddha on matters pertaining to the *Vinaya* rules is found in the chapter called *Upāli-Pañcaka* in the *Parivāra.*[14]

It is not possible to determine which of these and other questions were actually asked by Upāli, and which were ascribed to him on account of his traditional reputation.

It is said[15] that even in the Buddha's lifetime monks considered it a great privilege to learn the *Vinaya* under Upāli. The monks seem to have regarded Upāli as their particular friend, to whom they could go in their difficulties. Thus, when certain monks had been deprived by thieves of their clothes, it is Upāli's protection that they seek.[16]

The canon contains but few records of any discourses connected with Upāli, apart from his questions on the *Vinaya*. In the *Aṅguttara Nikāya*[17] he is mentioned as asking the Buddha for a brief sermon, the Buddha telling him that if there were anything that did not conduce to revulsion and detachment, Upāli could be sure that such things did not form part of the Buddha's teaching. There is a record of another sermon[18] which the Buddha is stated to have preached when Upāli expressed the desire to retire into the solitude of the forest. The Buddha tells him that forest-life is not for the man who has not mastered his mind or attained to tranquillity.

For other sermons see *s.v.* **Upāli Sutta** and **Ubbāhika Sutta.**

Three verses are ascribed to Upāli in the *Theragāthā*[19] where he ad-

[10] Vin. i. 325 f.

[11] *Ibid.*, i. 358 f.

[12] *Ibid.*, ii. 248 ff.

[13] *Ibid.*, ii. 33 f.

[14] *Ibid.*, v. 180-206; see also the *Upālivagga* of the *Aṅguttara Nikāya* (v. 70 ff.).

[15] *E.g.*, Vin. iv. 142; Sp. iv. 876.

[16] Vin. iii. 212; see also the story of **Ramaṇīyavihārī** (ThagA. i. 116).

[17] A. iv. 143 f.

[18] A. v. 201 ff.

[19] vv. 249-51; but see *Gotama the Man*, p. 215; another verse ascribed to Upāli, but so far not traced elsewhere, is found in the *Milinda* (p. 108).

monishes the brethren to seek noble friends of unfaltering character, to learn the monks' code of discipline and to dwell in solitude.

In the time of **Padumuttara,** Upāli was a very rich brahmin named **Sujāta.** When the Buddha came to his father's city in order to preach to him the Dhamma, Sujāta saw him, and in the assembly he noticed an ascetic named **Sunanda,** holding over the Buddha for seven days a canopy of flowers. The Buddha declared that Sunanda would, in the time of Gotama Buddha, become famous as the Elder **Puṇṇa Mantānīputta.** Sujāta, too, wished to see the future Buddha Gotama, and having heard Padumuttara praise the monk **Pāṭika** as chief of the Vinayadharas, he wished to hear, regarding himself, a similar declaration from Gotama. With this end in view he did many deeds of merit. chief of which was the erection of a monastery named **Sobhana,** for the Buddha and his monks, at an expense of one hundred thousand.

As a result he was born in heaven for thirty thousand kappas and was one thousand times king of the devas. One thousand times, too, he was cakkavatti.

Two kappas ago there was a Khattiya named **Añjasa,** and Upāli was born as his son **Sunanda.** One day he went to the park riding an elephant named **Sirika**, and met, on the way, the Pacceka Buddha **Devala**, whom he insulted in various ways. Sunanda was, thereupon, seized with a sensation of great heat in his body, and it was not till he went with a large following to the Pacceka Buddha and asked his pardon that the sensation left him. It is said that if the Buddha had not forgiven him, the whole country would have been destroyed. This insult paid to the Pacceka Buddha was the cause of Upāli having been born as a barber in his last birth.[20]

Buddhaghosa[21] says that while the Buddha was yet alive Upāli drew up certain instructions according to which future Vinayadharas should interpret *Vinaya* rules, and that, in conjunction with others, he compiled explanatory notes on matters connected with the *Vinaya*.

In direct pupillary succession to Upāli as head of the Vinayadharas was **Dāsaka,** whom Upāli had first met at the **Valikārāma,** where Upāli was staying.[22] Upāli taught him the whole of the *Vinaya*.

Upāli's death was in the sixth year of **Udāyibhadda's** reign.[23]

[20] Ap. i. 37 ff.
[21] Sp. i. 272, 283.
[22] Mhv. v. 107.
[23] Dpv. v. 7 ff.

2. **Upāli.**—A lad of **Rājagaha.** His parents, wishing him to live a life of ease, did not have him instructed in any of the usual means of livelihood, lest he should be inconvenienced while learning them. After

much consideration, they decided to have him ordained. He joined the Order with sixteen other companions equally young, and it is said that they rose at dawn and started shouting for food. This was the reason for the rule that no one under twenty years of age should receive the *upasampadā* ordination.[1]

[1] Vin. i. 77 f.

3. **Upāli Thera.**—The *Apadāna*[1] contains the story of a thera named **Upāli,** who is to be distinguished from the eminent disciple of that name, though the *Apadāna* verses obviously point to a confusion of the legends of the two. The *Apadāna Commentary* distinguishes this monk as "**Bhāgiṇeyya Upāli,**" and states that he was a nephew of the Venerable **Upāli.** He was born in **Kapilavatthu** and was ordained by his uncle, who later became an arahant.

Bhāgiṇeyya Upāli had been a householder in the time of **Padumuttara.** Later he left the world and became an ascetic in Himavā. There he met the Buddha and the monks, and uttered their praises in song. As a result he was eighteen times king of the devas and twenty-five times king of men.

[1] i. 91 f.

4. **Upāli.**—Distinguished as **Upāli-Gahapati.** He lived at **Nālandā** and was a follower of **Nigaṇṭha Nātaputta.** He was present when **Dīgha-Tapassī** reported to Nātaputta an account of his visit to the Buddha in the **Pāvārika** Mango-grove. Upāli undertook to go himself to the Buddha and refute his views, in spite of the protestations of Dīgha-Tapassī. At the end of his discussion with the Buddha, which is recorded in the **Upāli Sutta,** Upāli is converted and invites the Buddha to a meal. Although the Buddha enjoins upon Upāli that his benefactions to the Nigaṇṭhas should not cease because of his conversion, Upāli gives instructions that no Nigaṇṭha be admitted to his presence, but that if they need food it shall be given to them. Hearing a rumour of his conversion, first Tapassī, and later Nātaputta himself, go to Upāli's house, where they learn the truth. When Nātaputta is finally convinced that Upāli has become a follower of the Buddha, hot blood gushes from his mouth.[1] According to Buddhaghosa,[2] Nātaputta had to be carried on a litter to **Pāvā,** where he died shortly after.

Upāli became a *sotāpanna.*[3]

He is mentioned, with **Ānanda, Citta-gahapati, Dhammika-upāsaka** and **Khujjuttarā,** as one who had acquired the four *Paṭisambhidā* while being yet a learner (*sekha*).[4]

[1] M. i. 371 ff.
[2] MA. ii. 621, 830.
[3] MA. ii. 620.
[4] Vsm. ii. 442; VibhA. 388.

5. **Upāli Thera.**—Head of the chapter of monks sent from Siam, at the request of **Kittisirirājasīha,** to re-establish the *Upasampadā* ordination in Ceylon. He was held in great esteem by the king of Ceylon and often preached to him. Upāli died in Ceylon of an incurable disease of the nose, and his funeral obsequies were held with great solemnity.[1]

[1] Cv. c. 71, 94, 117, 127, 142.

Upāli Gāthā.—The stanzas in which **Upāli-Gahapati** uttered the Buddha's praises when **Nātaputta** asked him what kind of man was his new-found teacher.[1] These verses are often quoted; they contain one hundred epithets as applied to the Buddha.[2]

[1] M. i. 386 f. [2] Sp. i. 257.

Upāli Vagga.—The fourth chapter of the *Dasaka Nipāta* of the *Aṅguttara Nikāya.* It contains records of various discussions between **Upāli** (1) and the Buddha and two between **Ānanda** and the Buddha, regarding matters connected with the *Vinaya.*[1]

[1] A. v. 70-7.

1. **Upāli Sutta.**—Records the events that lead to the conversation of **Upāli-Gahapati** (*q.v.*). The Buddha is asked, first by **Dīgha-Tapassī** and then by Upāli, as to which of the three kinds of deeds—of body, speech and mind—are the most criminal. Those of mind, says the Buddha; those of body, say the followers of **Nātaputta.** By various illustrations the Buddha convinces Upāli that his contentions are wrong. The sutta concludes with a series of verses (the **Upali Gāthā**) in which Upāli sings the Buddha's praises.[1]

[1] M. i. 371 ff.

2. **Upāli Sutta.**—**Upāli** Thera visits the Buddha and asks him for what purpose the various precepts have been laid down for disciples and why the *pāṭimokkha* has been recited ? For ten purposes, says the Buddha, and proceeds to enumerate them. Similarly, ten reasons are given which justify the suspension of the *pāṭimokkha.*[1]

[1] A. v. 70 f.

3. **Upāli Sutta.**—**Upāli** (1) visits the Buddha and expresses a desire to retire to the solitude of the forest. Such a step is not desirable for those who have not attained to tranquillity of mind, says the Buddha, and explains his meaning by various similes. A full-grown elephant

could disport himself in a deep lake according to his fancy, not so a hare or a cat. The sutta goes on to describe how, as a result of the arising of a Tathāgatā in the world, a householder would listen to the Dhamma, renounce the world, give up all evil practices and gradually attain to full development of the four *jhānas*. Upāli is advised to live among the monks and not go into the forest.[1]

[1] A. v. 201 ff.

Upāli-pañcaka.—One of the chapters of the *Parivāra*, containing various questions asked by **Upāli** (1) regarding *Vinaya* rules and the Buddha's explanations of the same.[1]

[1] Vin. v. 180-206.

Upāli-pucchā-bhānavāra.—The sixth chapter of the ninth *Khandhaka* of the *Mahāvagga*.[1]

[1] Vin. i. 322-8.

1. **Upāsaka Vagga.**—The second chapter of the *Brāhmaṇa Saṃyutta*.[1]

[1] S. i. 172 ff.

2. **Upāsaka Vagga.**—The eighteenth chapter of the *Pañcaka Nipāta* of the *Aṅguttara Nikāya*; on various matters, chiefly connected with laymen.[1]

[1] A. iii. 203-18.

3. **Upāsaka Vagga.**—The tenth chapter of the *Dasaka Nipāta* of the *Aṅguttara Nikāya*.[1]

[1] A. v. 176-206.

Upāsabha.—Name of a Pacceka Buddha.[1]

[1] M. iii. 69; MA. ii. 890; ApA. i. 106.

Upāsikā Vihāra.—A nunnery in **Anurādhapura**, built by **Devānampiyatissa,** for the accommodation of **Anulā** and her followers, pending the arrival of **Saṅghamittā.**[1] Later, Saṅghamittā took up her residence there and it was enlarged by the addition of twelve buildings, three of which gained peculiar sanctity because in these were set up the mast, the rudder and the helm of the ship that had brought the Bodhi-tree to Ceylon, and these buildings were called, respectively, the **Kūpayaṭṭhithapita-ghara,** the **Piyaṭhapita-ghara** and the **Arittaṭhapita-ghara** Even when other sects arose, these twelve buildings were occupied by the **Hatthāḷhaka** (or orthodox) nuns.[2]

[1] Mhv. xviii. 12.

[2] *Ibid.*, xix. 68 ff.; the *Ṭīkā* (p. 408) says the houses were originally called **Cūlagaṇāgāra, Mahāgaṇāgāra** and **Sirivaḍḍhāgāra.**

Upāhana Jātaka (No. 231).—Once the Bodhisatta was an elephant-trainer and taught his art to a young man of Kāsi. The latter wished to take service under the king, but would not accept any fee less than that paid to his teacher. A contest of skill was arranged to settle the point. The night before the contest the Bodhisatta taught an elephant to do all things awry, going back when told to go forward, etc. At the time of the contest the pupil could not match this in any way and was defeated and stoned to death by the onlookers. The Bodhisatta thereupon declared that a low-bred churl was like an ill-made shoe (*upāhana*).

The story was told concerning the base ingratitude of **Devadatta.**[1]

[1] J. ii. 221 ff.

Upāhana Vagga.—The ninth section of the *Duka Nipāta* of the *Jātakaṭṭhakathā.*[1]

[1] J. ii. 221-42.

Upekkhaka Sutta.—**Moggallāna** tells the monks how he entered in and abode in the fourth *jhāna.*[1]

[1] S. iv. 265 f.

1. **Upekhā Sutta.**—**Ānanda** says that **Sāriputta's** senses are clean and his face translucent. How has he spent the day ? Sāriputta answers that he has been in the fourth *jhāna*, wherein is neither pleasure nor pain but pure equanimity.[1]

[1] S. iii. 237.

2. **Upekhā Sutta.**—The idea of equanimity, if cultivated, conduces to great gain.[1]

[1] S. v. 131.

1. **Uposatha.**—King, son of **Varakalyāṇa** and an ancestor of the Sākyan tribe. His son was **Mandhātā.**[1] He was one of the kings at the beginning of the *kappa.*[2] In the *Dīgha Commentary*[3] he is given as the son of **Varamandhātā** and the father of **Cara.** In the northern texts he is called **Uposadha.**[4]

[1] Dpv. iii. 4.
[2] J. ii. 311; iii. 454.
[3] DA. i. 258.
[4] Mtu. i. 348; Divy. 210.

2. **Uposatha.**—The name of the Elephant-Treasure of the Cakkavatti **Mahāsudassana.** He was "all white, sevenfold firm (*sattappatiṭṭha*), wonderful in power, flying through the sky."[1] In the *Lalita Vistara* his name is given as **Bodhi.**

[1] D. ii. 174; M. iii. 173 f.

Uposatha is also the name of a tribe of elephants, the ninth in a series of ten tribes, of ascending importance.[3] It is said that a cakkavatti's elephant belongs either to the **Chaddanta** tribe or to the Uposatha. If a Chaddanta elephant comes to a cakkavatti, it is the youngest of the tribe that comes, if an Uposatha elephant, then it will be the foremost.[4] When the cakkavatti dies, the elephant goes back to his fellows.[5] The strength of an Uposatha elephant is equal to that of one thousand million men.[6] In the *Milindapañha*,[7] the king of the Uposatha elephants is described as being gentle and handsome, eight cubits in height and nine in girth and length, shewing signs of rut in three places on his body, all white, sevenfold-firm. Just as this elephant could never be put into a cowpen or covered with a saucer, so could no one keep as slaves the children of **Vessantara.**

[3] DA.ii. 573; UdA. 403.
[4] DA. ii. 624; J. iv. 232, 234; KhA. 172.
[5] DA.ii. 635.
[6] BuA. 37.
[7] p. 282.

3. **Uposatha.**—Known as **Uposatha-kumāra.** The eldest of the ninety-nine brothers of **Saṃvara,** king of Benares. When Saṃvara ascended the throne, his brothers protested and laid siege to his city; but Uposatha, having discovered by means of questions put to Saṃvara, that he was in character by far the best suited for kingship, persuaded the others to renounce their claims to the throne. Uposatha is identified with **Sāriputta.**[1]

[1] J. iv. 133 ff.

Uposatha Vagga.—The fifth chapter of the *Aṭṭhaka Nipāta* of the *Aṅguttara Nikāya*, containing suttas on the *uposatha*, among other things.[1]

[1] A. iv. 248-73.

1. **Uposatha Suttā.**—Suttas dealing with questions asked by monks of the Buddha as to why certain Nāgas (egg-born, womb-born, moisture-born and born without parents) should keep the fast day, divesting themselves of their Nāga forms! The Buddha replies that they do so because they wish to be born in happy states.[1]

[1] S. iii. 241 f.

2. **Uposatha Sutta.**—One *uposatha*-day, the Buddha, surrounded by the company of monks, was seated in the **Migāramātu-pāsāda,** in **Sāvatthi.** Looking round and finding them seated in silence, he spoke

their praises, saying how some of them had won access to the devas, some to Brahmā, others to the Imperturbable (*ānejja*), and yet others to the Āriyan state.[1]

[1] A. ii. 183 f.

3. **Uposatha Sutta.**—One *uposatha*-night, during the first watch, **Ānanda** approaches the Buddha and asks him to recite the *Pāṭimokkha*. Three times he asks, but the Buddha remains silent, and at last says that the assembly is impure. **Mahāmoggallāna,** who is present, looks round, and seeing there a monk given up to wicked ways, asks him to leave. On his refusing to do so, Moggallāna takes him by the hand and leads him away. Thereupon the Buddha proceeds to explain how, just as the sea is full of eight kinds of marvels, so is the Dhamma.[1]

[1] A. iv. 204 ff.

4. **Uposatha** (*v.l.* **Uposathaṅga**) **Sutta.**—**Visākhā,** having taken the uposatha vows, visits the Buddha at noontide in the **Migāramātu-pāsāda.** The Buddha explains to her that there are various ways of observing the sabbath; these he describes as the herdsman's sabbath, the sabbath of the naked ascetics and the sabbath of the Āriyans.[1]

[1] A. i. 206 f.

Uposathakhaṇḍa.—The second section of the **Bhūridatta Jātaka.**[1]

[1] J. vi. 168-70.

Uposathakhandhaka.—The second chapter of the *Mahāvagga* of the *Vinaya Piṭaka.*[1]

[1] Vin. i. 101-36.

Uposathakkhandha Sutta.—One of the discourses occurring in the *Uposathakhandha*. It is quoted in the *Atthasālinī* as authority that might be used by any opponent to prove that an immoral act of speech also arises in the mind-door. The *Commentary* proceeds to explain how this argument could be refuted.[1]

[1] DhsA. 92 f.

Uposatha-vinicchaya.—A *Vinaya* treatise, written in Burma.[1]

[1] Bode, *op. cit.*, 44.

Uposatha-vimāna.—See **Uposathā.**

Uposathā.—A pious lay-devotee of **Sāketa.** She did many deeds of merit, and was born in **Tāvatiṃsa,** her abode being known as the **Uposatha-vimāna.** It is said that she was known in Sāketa as **Uposathā,** because of the life she led. She expresses to **Moggallāna** her remorse that she should have desired to be born in **Nandana-vana,** instead of listening to the Buddha's teaching and putting an end to all birth.[1]

[1] Vv. 20 f.; VvA. 115 f.

"Uppajjanti" Sutta.—On the power of earnestness (*appamāda*).

[1] A. i. 11.

Uppaṭi Vagga.—See **Sukhindriya Vagga.**

Uppaṭika Sutta.—On the five controlling faculties (*indriyāni*)—of discomfort, of unhappiness, of ease, of happiness and of indifference—and on how they are conditioned and how they cease to be.[1] According to the *Commentary,*[2] the title of this sutta should be **Uppaṭipāṭika Sutta** (the sutta which deals with reference to what has gone before).

[1] S. v. 213 f. [2] SA. iii. 192.

Uppatha Sutta.—Questions asked by a *deva* and the Buddha's answers to them. Lust is the road that leads astray, life perishes both night and day, women are they that stain celibacy, the higher life cleanses without bathing.[1]

[1] S. i. 38.

Uppanna (or **Uppāda**) **Sutta.**—Two suttas which state that the seven *bojjhaṅgas* do not arise without the manifestation of a Tathāgata.[1]

[1] S. v. 77.

1. **Uppala.**—A Pacceka Buddha mentioned in the **Isigili Sutta.**[1]

[1] M. iii. 70.

2. **Uppala.**—One of the yakkhas who guarded **Jotiya's** palace. He had two thousand followers.[1]

[1] DhA. iv. 209.

3. **Uppala.**—Father of the warrior **Ummāda-Phussadeva.**[1]

[1] Mhv. xxiii. 82.

4. **Uppala (Uppalaka).**—A Niraya.[1] Buddhaghosa[2] says, however, that it is not a special hell, but the name of a period of suffering in hell.

[1] S. i. 152; Sn. p. 126. [2] SnA. ii. 476 f.; see also A. v. 173.

5. **Uppala.**—One of the treasure-troves that rose up from the earth on the day of the Bodhisatta's birth. It was three *gāvutas* in extent.[1]

[1] DA. i. 284.

Uppaladāyikā Therī.—Thirty-one kappas ago she was the wife of the Khattiya **Aruṇa** of **Aruṇavatī.** One day, being filled with anguish that she had not done any good deed which would bring her a happy condition of rebirth, she begged her husband for a holy recluse on whom she could wait. Her wish was granted, and she gave to the recluse a bowl of excellent food and perfume, the whole covered with a large robe. As a result, she was born in **Tāvatiṃsa** and became for a thousand times the consort of the king of the *devas.* Her body was always of the hue of the lotus and she had all womanly beauty. In her last birth she was born in a Sākyan family and joined the Bodhisatta's court at the head of a thousand women. Later, she left the world and became an arahant, seven days after joining the Order.[1] A set of verses in which she sang the praises of the Buddha, appear at the end of the *Apadāna* account. She is perhaps to be identified with **Somā** Therī.

[1] Ap. ii. 601-3.

Uppalavaṇṇa.—The god to whom **Sakka** entrusted the guardianship of **Laṅkā** and its people. He met **Vijaya** and his followers when they landed in Ceylon and sprinkled water on them and wound a sacred thread about their hands for protection.[1] The god is generally identified with **Viṣṇu,** though there is evidence to show that, at least in later mythology, the two gods were distinct. Somewhere about A.D. 790, a shrine was erected to **Uppalavaṇṇa** in **Devanagara** (modern Dondra) in South Ceylon. This shrine was later plundered by the Portuguese. King **Vīrabāhu** offered there a sacrifice of victory[2] and **Parakkamabāhu II.** rebuilt the shrine.

[1] Mhv. vii. 5.

[2] Cv. lxxxiii. 49; see also Cv. *Trs.* ii. 152, n. 3.

1. **Uppalavaṇṇā Therī.**—One of the two chief women disciples of the Buddha. She was born in **Sāvatthi** as the daughter of a banker, and she received the name of Uppalavaṇṇā because her skin was the colour of the heart of the blue lotus. When she was come of age, kings and commoners from the whole of India sent messengers to her father, asking for her hand. He, not wishing to offend any of them, suggested that Uppalavaṇṇā should leave the world. Because of her *upanissaya,* she very willingly agreed and was ordained a nun. Soon it came to her turn to perform certain services in the *uposatha*-hall. Lighting

the lamp, she swept the room. Taking the flame of the lamp as her visible object, she developed *tejokasiṇa* and, attaining to *jhāna*, became an arahant possessed of the four special attainments (*paṭisambhidā*). She became particularly versed in the mystic potency of transformation (*iddhivikubbana*). When the Buddha arrived at the **Gaṇḍamba**-tree to perform the Twin Miracle, Uppalavaṇṇā offered to perform certain miracles herself, if the Buddha would give his consent, but this he refused.[1] Later, at **Jetavana,** in the assembly of the Saṅgha, he declared her to be the chief of the women possessed of *iddhi*-power.[2] The *Therīgāthā*[3] contains several verses attributed to her.

Three of them had been uttered in anguish by a mother who had been unwittingly living as her daughter's rival with the man who later became the monk **Gaṅgātīriya** (*q.v.*). Uppalavaṇṇā repeated them to help her to reflect on the harm and vileness of sensual desires. Two others are utterances of joy on the distinctions she had won and another records a miracle she performed before the Buddha, with his consent. The rest contain a conversation[4] between Uppalavaṇṇā and Māra, wherein she tells him that she has passed completely beyond his power.

The books give several episodes connected with Uppalavaṇṇā. Once a young man named **Ānanda,** who was her cousin and had been in love with her during her lay-life, hid himself in her hut in **Andhavana** and, in spite of her protestations, deprived her of her chastity. It is said that he was swallowed up by the fires of Avīci. From that time onwards, nuns were forbidden to live in Andhavana.[5] It is said[6] that this incident gave rise to the question whether even arahants enjoyed the pleasures of love and wished to gratify their passions. Why should they not? For they are not trees nor ant-hills, but living creatures with moist flesh. The Buddha most emphatically declared that thoughts of lust never entered the hearts of the saints. On another occasion, Uppalavaṇṇā came across, in Andhavana, some meat left behind, obviously for her, by some kind-hearted thief; having cooked the meat, she took it to the Buddha at Veluvaṇa. Finding him away on his alms-rounds, she left the meat with **Udāyī,** who was looking after the vihāra, to be given to the Buddha, but Udāyi insisted on Uppalavaṇṇā giving him her inner robe as a reward for his services.[7]

According to the *Dhammapada Commentary,*[8] the miracle which Uppalavaṇṇā volunteered to perform at the Gaṇḍamba-tree, was the assumption

[1] ThigA. 190, 195.

[2] A. i. 25.

[3] vv. 234-5.

[4] A conversation, more or less identical with the foregoing, is recorded in S. i. 131 f.

[5] DhA. ii. 49 f.; the incident is referred to in Vin. iii. 35.

[6] *E.g.*, DhA. iv. 166 f.

[7] Vin. iii. 208 f.

[8] iii. 211.

of the form of a cakkavatti, with a retinue extending for thirty-six leagues and the paying of homage to the Buddha, with all the cakkavatti's followers, in the presence of the multitude.

Mention is made of a pupil of Uppalavaṇṇā who followed the Buddha for seven years, learning the *Vinaya*.[9]

The Buddha declares that **Khemā** and Uppalavaṇṇā are the measure of his women disciples, and that the believing nun, if she would aspire perfectly, should aspire to be like them.[10]

In **Padumuttara's** time Uppalavaṇṇā saw a woman disciple who was declared to be the best of those possessed of supernormal power, and wished for herself a similar rank in the dispensation of a future Buddha. In the time of **Kassapa,** she was one of the seven daughters of **Kikī,** king of Benares, and having done many good deeds, was born in heaven. Later, she was born in the world of men and had to work for her own living. One day she gave to a Pacceka Buddha, who had just risen from *samādhi*, a meal of fried rice in his bowl and covered it with a beautiful lotus; the meal had been prepared for herself. The lotus she afterwards took back but again replaced it, asking the Pacceka Buddha's forgiveness. She expressed a wish that she should beget as many sons as there were grains of rice in her gift, and that lotuses should spring up under her feet as she walked. In her next birth she was born in a lotus. An ascetic adopted her as his daughter, but when she grew up, the king of Benares, hearing of her beauty, asked the ascetic for her hand and made her his chief queen, under the name of **Padumavatī.** The king's other wives were jealous of her beauty, and when the king was away, quelling a rising of the border tribes, they concealed in caskets the five hundred sons, chief of whom was the prince **Mahāpaduma** (*q.v.*), that were born to Padumavatī, and told the king that Padumavatī was a non-human and had given birth to a log of wood. Padumavatī was sent away in disgrace, but later, through the instrumentality of **Sakka,** the trick was exposed, and Padumavatī regained all her former power and glory. (Her temporary downfall was due to her having withdrawn her gift of a lotus to the Pacceka Buddha.) Later, when Mahāpaduma and his brothers became Pacceka Buddhas, Padumavatī died of a broken heart and was born in a village outside **Rājagaha.** There some of the Pacceka Buddhas who had been her sons discovered her, and they all came to a meal at her house. At the conclusion of the meal she offered them blue lotuses, and expressed the wish that her complexion should be like the matrix of the blue lotus.[11]

9 Vin. ii. 261.

10 A. i. 88; ii. 164; S. ii. 236.

11 This account is a summary of the *Therīgāthā Commentary*, pp. 182 ff.; AA. i. 188 ff.; but see also DhA. ii. 48 f.

The *Apadāna*[12] account of the past lives of Uppakavaṇṇā differs from the above in several details. According to this account, in **Padumuttara's** time she was a Nāga maiden named **Vimalā** and was impressed by the *iddhi*-powers displayed by a nun, hence her wish for similar powers. The *Apadāna* also mentions Uppalavaṇṇā's birth as the daughter of a banker of Benares, in the time of **Vipassī.** She gave great alms to the Buddha and the monks and made offerings of lotuses. She was the second daughter of Kikī and her name was **Samaṇaguttā.** In her next birth she became the ravishing daughter of **Tirīṭavaccha** of **Ariṭṭhapura.** In her last birth she became an arahant within a fortnight of her ordination.

Uppalavaṇṇā's name occurs several times in the *Jātakas.* In the **Kharādiya Jātaka**[13] she was a deer, the sister of the Bodhisatta; in the **Tipallatthamiga Jātaka**[14] she was the mother of **Rāhula,** then born as a stag. She is identified with the old woman, the foster-mother of **Ayyakāḷaka,**[15] with the queen **Mudulakkhaṇā,**[16] the brahminee in the **Sārambha,**[17] the courtesan in the **Kurudhamma,**[18] the brahmin's daughter (and sister of Rāhula) in the **Dhonasākha,**[19] **Siridevī** in the **Sirikālakaṇṇi,**[20] the goddess in the **Bhisapuppha,**[21] **Manoja's** sister in the **Manoja,**[22] the ascetic's daughter in the **Kumbhakāra,**[23] the deity in the **Jāgarajā,**[24] in the **Saṅkha,**[25] and in the **Kiñchanda,**[26] the sister in the **Bhisa,**[27] **Sutanā** in the **Rohantamiga,**[28] the younger sister in the **Jayaddisa,**[29] **Kuṇḍalinī** in the **Tesakuṇa,**[30] **Ummadantī** in the **Ummadantī,**[31] **Hiridevatā** in the **Sudhābhojana,**[32] the goddess of the parasol in the **Mūgapakkha,**[33] the ocean spirit in the **Mahājanaka,**[34] the goddess in the **Sāma,**[35] **Selā** in the **Khaṇḍahāla,**[36] **Accimukhī** in the **Bhūridatta,**[37] **Bherī** in the **Mahā-ummagga**[38] and **Kaṇhajinā** in the **Vessantara.**[39]

It was Uppalavaṇṇā who ordained **Anojā** and her companions, by the express wish of the Buddha.[40]

[12] ii. 551. But vv. 1-15 quoted in the ThigA. differ from those in the *Apadāna,* and agree with the ThigA. account.
[13] J. i. 160.
[14] *Ibid.*, 164.
[15] *Ibid.*, 196.
[16] *Ibid.*, 306.
[17] *Ibid.*, 375.
[18] J. ii. 381.
[19] J. iii. 168.
[20] *Ibid.*, 264.
[21] *Ibid.*, 310.
[22] *Ibid.*, 324.
[23] *Ibid.*, 383.
[24] *Ibid.*, 405.
[25] J. iv. 22.
[26] J. v. 11.
[27] J. iv. 314.
[28] *Ibid.*, 423.
[29] J. v. 36.
[30] *Ibid.*, 125.
[31] *Ibid.*, 227.
[32] *Ibid.*, 412.
[33] J. vi. 29.
[34] *Ibid.*, 68.
[35] *Ibid.*, 95.
[36] *Ibid.*, 157.
[37] *Ibid.*, 219.
[38] *Ibid.*, 478.
[39] *Ibid.*, 593.
[40] AA. i. 178.

2. **Uppalavaṇṇā.**—One of the two daughters of **Kassapa I.** of Ceylon, the other being **Bodhī.** The king built a vihāra and called it by his own name together with those of his daughters.[1]

[1] Cv. xxxix. 11; see also Cv. *Trs.* i. 43, n. 7.

Uppalavaṇṇā Sutta.—Records a conversation between **Uppalavaṇṇā** and **Māra.**[1] The ideas are the same as those contained in the verses found in the *Therīgāthā*[2] but the wording is somewhat different.

[1] S. i. 131 f. [2] vv. 230-5.

Uppalavāpī.—A village in Ceylon where king **Kuṭakaṇṇa** spent some time. There he invited the thera **Cūḷasudhamma** and made him live at the **Mālārāma** Vihāra.[1]

[1] VibhA. 452.

Uppalā.—One of the chief women supporters of **Anomadassī** Buddha.[1]

[1] Bu. viii. 24.

Uppātasanti.—A Pāli work written by an unknown thera of Laos in the sixteenth century. It seems to have dealt with rites or charms for averting evil omens or public calamities.[1]

[1] Bode, *op. cit.*, 47, and n. 5.

1. **Uppāda Sutta.**—See **Uppanna Sutta.**

2. **Uppāda Sutta.**—The arising of the four elements is the uprising of suffering, their ceasing is its cessation.[1]

[1] S. ii. 175.

3. **Uppāda Sutta.**—Same as No. 2, but with the substitution of the five *khandhas* for the four elements.[1]

[1] S. iii. 31 f.

Uppāda Saṃyutta.—The twenty-sixth section of the *Saṃyutta Nikāya.*[1]

[1] S. iii. 228-31.

1. **Uppāde Sutta** (2).—The eight conditions—right views, etc.—come into being only on the arising of a Tathāgata.[1]

[1] S. v. 14.

2. **Uppāde Sutta.**—The five controlling faculties (*indriyāni*) of *saddhā*, *sati*, etc., arise only upon the manifestation of a Tathāgata.[1]

[1] S. v. 235.

Uppādetabba Sutta.—On six states which a person holding right views will never reach.[1]

[1] A. iii. 438.

" **Uppādena Sutta** " (2).—The uprising of the six sense objects—forms, sounds, etc.—is the uprising of Ill, the persisting of disease, the manifestation of decay and death. The cessation of the former leads to the disappearance of the latter.[1]

[1] S. iv. 14.

1. **Ubbarī.**—A princess. In the time of **Kakusandha** she was a hen. Having heard a monk repeat a formula of meditation, she was born as a royal princess and named **Ubbarī.** Seeing a heap of maggots in the privy, she meditated thereon and entered the first *jhāna* and was born in the Brahma-world. In the time of **Gotama** Buddha she was reborn as a sow in **Rājagaha,** and the Buddha, seeing her, smiled and related her past to **Ānanda.** Later she was born in the royal household in **Suvaṇṇabhūmi,** then, in succession, in a horse-dealer's house in **Suppāraka** and in a mariner's household in **Kāvīra.** Then she was reborn in a nobleman's house in **Anurādhapura,** and again in the village of **Bokkanta** in South Ceylon, as the daughter of a householder named **Sumana.** She was called **Sumanā,** after her father. When her father moved to the village of **Mahāmuni** in **Dīghavāpi, Lakuṇṭaka Atimbara,** prime minister of **Duṭṭhagāmaṇi,** met her and married her, and she went to live in **Mahāpunna.**

Having recollected her past births from some words uttered by the Elder **Anula** of **Koṭipabbata,** she joined the Order of **Pañcabalaka** nuns. At **Tissamahārāma** she heard the *Mahā Satipaṭṭhāna Sutta* and became a *Sotāpanna*. Later, having heard the *Āsīvisopama Sutta* in **Kallaka-Mahāvihāra,** she attained arahantship. On the day of her death she related her story, first to the nuns and then in the assembly, in the presence of the Elder **Mahā Tissa** of **Maṇḍalārāma.**[1]

[1] DhA. iv. 46 ff.

2. **Ubbarī.**—The wife of **Cūḷanī Brahmadatta,** king of **Kapila** in the **Pañcāla** kingdom. She was a daughter of a poor woman in the village, and the king met her while on his wanderings disguised as a tailor,

which disguise he assumed in order to find out news of the people for himself. She was given the name Ubbarī on the day of her marriage, and Cūḷanī made her his chief queen. When the king died, she went to the cemetery day after day, lamenting for her dead husband and refusing to be comforted. One day the Bodhisatta, who was an ascetic in Himavā, noticed her with his divine eye and appeared before her. Having heard her story, he pointed out to her that eighty-six thousand kings of Pañcāla, all bearing the name of Cūḷanī Brahmadatta, had been burnt in that very spot and that she had been the queen of them all. Thereupon, Ubbarī abandoned her grief and renounced the world. She developed thoughts of loving-kindness and in due course was reborn in the Brahma-world.[1]

She is probably to be identified with the queen of Cūḷanī Brahmadatta, king of Pañcāla, mentioned in the **Mahā-Ummagga Jātaka,**[2] in which case her original name was **Nandā-devī.** According to the scholiast,[3] Ubbarī is not a proper name but means any women of the court (*orodha*).

[1] Pv. 32; PvA. 160-8. [2] J. vi. 473, 475. [3] *Ibid.*, 473.

3. **Ubbarī.**—Queen Consort of **Assaka,** king of **Potali** in the Kāsi kingdom. She was extremely beautiful and, when she died, the king had her body embalmed and placed in a coffin which was put under his bed. She, however, was born as a dung-worm because she had been intoxicated by her own beauty. The story is related in the **Assaka Jātaka.**[1]

[1] J. ii. 155 ff.

4. **Ubbarī.**—Wife of the Prince **Brahmadatta,** mentioned in the **Dhonasākha Jātaka.**[1] On his deathbed the king thinks of her longingly and speaks of her as being of swarthy hue.

[1] J. iii. 161.

Ubbarī-peta-Vatthu.—The story of **Ubbarī** (2).

Ubbarī Vagga.—The second chapter of the *Petavatthu.*[1]

[1] Pv. 32 ff.

Ubbāha Sutta.—Preached to **Upāli** (1) on the ten qualities requisite in a monk who serves on a committee, appointed for the purpose of taking a referendum in matters of discipline.[1]

[1] A. v. 71 f.

Ubbirī Therī.—She was born in the family of a very rich burgess of **Sāvatthi** and was married to the king of **Kosala** (probably **Pasenadi**). After a few years a daughter was born to her, whom she named **Jīvā** (*v.l.* **Jīvantī**). The king was so pleased with the child that he had Ubbirī anointed as queen. But the girl died soon afterwards, and Ubbirī, distracted, went daily to the charnel-field. One day, as she sat lamenting on the bank of the **Aciravatī,** the Buddha appeared before her in a ray of glory. Having listened to her story, the Master pointed out to her that in that same burial-ground, eighty-four thousand of her daughters, all named Jīvā, had been burnt. Pondering on the Master's words, she developed insight and became an arahant.

When she was a young girl in **Haṃsavatī** in the time of **Padumuttara** Buddha, she was one day left alone in the house. Seeing an arahant begging for alms, she invited him in and gave him food. As a result she was born in **Tāvatiṃsa.** Eighty times she reigned as queen in heaven and seventy times as queen among men.[1]

No mention is made in the *Therīgāthā Commentary* of her having joined the Order, but the *Apadāna*[2] states that she did so.

[1] Thig. vv. 51-2; ThigA. 53 ff. [2] ii. 525 f.

Ubbhaṭaka.—A mote-hall built by the **Mallas** of **Pāvā.** When it was finished they invited the Buddha to be its first occupant. The Buddha went with the monks and spent the night in the hall. It was on this occasion that **Sāriputta** recited the **Saṅgīti Sutta.**[1]

Buddhaghosa[2] says that the hall was so-called ("Thrown-aloft-er"), because of its great height.

[1] D. iii. 207 ff. [2] DA. iii. 971.

Ubbhida.—A *khattiya* of sixty thousand kappas ago; a former birth of **Mahā Kassapa.**[1] *v.l.* **Ubbiddha, Uddiya.**

[1] Ap. i. 34.

Ubhaka.—One of the ten sons of **Kāḷāsoka** and, later, king of Magadha.[1] *v.l.* **Ubhata, Usabha.**

[1] Mbv. 98.

Ubhatobhaṭṭha Jātaka (No. 139).—Once in a village of line-fishermen one of the men took his tackle and went with his little son to fish. A snag caught hold of his line, but the man, thinking it was a big fish, sent his son home to ask his mother to pick a quarrel with the neighbours in order to keep them occupied lest they should claim a share of his catch. When the boy had gone, the fisherman went into the water to drag the fish, but he struck against the snag and was blinded in both eyes. Moreover a robber stole his clothes from the bank and his wife was taken before the village chief and fined and beaten for quarrelling. The Bodhisatta who was a Tree-deva saw all this happen and drew a moral from it. The story was told in reference to **Devadatta,** who is identified with the fisherman, all his enterprises having come to grief.[1]

[1] J. i. 482-4.

Ubhatovibhaṅga.—A collective term, comprehending the *Bhikkhu-vibhaṅga* and the *Bhikkhuṇī-vibhaṅga* of the *Vinaya Piṭaka.* It consists of sixty-four *bhāṇavāras.*[1]

In the ninefold division of the Buddha's teachings—*sutta, geyya,* etc.—the *Ubhato-vibhaṅga* falls into the category of *sutta.*[2] Sometimes the word seems to be used as *varia lectio* for *Ubhato-vinaya.*[3]

[1] DA. i. 13; Sp. i. 15.
[2] DA. i. 23; Gv. 57.
[3] *E.g.,* Vin. ii. 287; see also Dpv. vii. 43.

Ubho Sutta (*v.l.* **Ubhatobhāga**). On the twofold emancipation.[1]

[1] A. iv. 453.

1. **Ummagga Jātaka.**—See **Mahā-Ummagga Jātaka.**

2. **Ummagga Jātaka.**—The *Samantapāsādikā*[1] mentions a work called the **Gūḷha-Ummagga** in a list of heretical works which pass off as the word of the Buddha, but which are the teachings of unbelievers.

[1] iv. 742.

Ummagga Sutta.—A certain monk approaches the Buddha and asks various questions: "By what is the world led? By what is it drawn along? Under the sway of what that has arisen, does it go?" The Buddha praises the questioner: "Happy is your approach" (*bhaddako te ummaggo*) and says that the answer to his question is "thought." "Of what sort is the man widely learned who knows the Dhamma?" "He who understands the meaning and text of the Dhamma and is set on living in accordance with it." Similarly, the man of great wisdom is he who thinks for the profit both of himself and of the whole world.[1]

[1] A. ii. 177 f. (On the title of the sutta and the meaning of the word *ummagga* see GS. ii. 184, n. 5.)

Ummagga-gaṅgā.—A name given to a part of the river which flows from the east of **Anotatta,** before it ultimately divides into the five great rivers, **Gaṅgā, Yamunā,** etc. The Ummagga-Gaṅgā is the continuation of the **Bahala-Gaṅgā** and flows for sixty leagues under the earth, till it reaches the rock named **Vijjha.**[1]

[1] SnA. ii. 439; AA. ii. 760; UdA. 302.

Ummadantī.—The daughter of the banker **Tirīṭavaccha** of **Ariṭṭhapura.** When she came of age, she was so beautiful that all who saw her lost control of themselves. At her father's request, **Sivi,** the king of the country (who was the Bodhisatta) sent fortune-tellers to examine her, with a view to making her his wife, but the brahmins, on seeing her, were so intoxicated with passion that Ummadantī had them driven out of the house. They returned and told the king that she was a witch, and she was, therefore, given in marriage to **Ahipāraka,** son of the commander-in-chief. Ummadantī bore the king a grudge for having refused her hand, and one feast day, when the king passed under her window, she threw flowers at him to attract his attention. From the moment that the king saw Ummadantī, he was beside himself with longing for her and lay on his couch raving about her. When Ahipāraka heard what had happened he offered his wife to the king, but Sivi was too righteous to hear of accepting the gift, and by a supreme effort of will he overcame his infatuation.

In a former birth Ummadantī was born in a poor family of Benares, and on a certain festal day having seen some holy women clad in robes dyed scarlet with safflower she asked her parents for a similar robe. Realising that they were too poor to afford the gift, she worked for a long time for another family, and they finally gave her a robe. When she was about to don it, after a bath in the river, she saw a disciple of Kassapa Buddha standing without any proper clothes, his robes having been stolen from the river bank. She first gave him half her garment, then, seeing how radiant he looked in it, she gave him also the other half and uttered a prayer that in a further existence she should surpass all other women in looks and be of maddening beauty.

She is identified with the Therī **Uppalavaṇṇā.**[1]

The story is related in the **Ummadantī Jātaka.**[2]

[1] See also ThigA. 192, v. 28, quoted from the Apadāna. [2] J. v. 209 ff.

Ummadantī Jātaka (No. 527).—The story of **Ummadantī,** as given above. The story was related in connection with a backsliding brother who, having seen a very beautiful woman as he was going his alms-rounds in **Sāvatthi,** gave himself up to despair and had to be led to the Buddha for admonition.[1] The story is also found, with certain slight variations, in the *Jātakamālā* under the title of *Ummādayantī Jātaka.*[2]

The tale of a maiden who made all who saw her mad, and of the love-smitten monarch who preferred walking in the right path and even meeting death itself to indulging in passion, is found also in the *Kathāsaritsāgara.*[3]

[1] J. v. 209 ff.
[2] No. xiii.
[3] *E.g.*, in the 15th, 23rd and 91st *taraṅga*.

Ummāda-Cittā.—Mother of **Paṇḍukābhaya,** king of Ceylon. She was the daughter of **Bhaddakaccānā** and **Paṇḍuvāsudeva,** and when she was born the brahmins foretold that her son would kill all his uncles. Her brothers, therefore, resolved to kill her, but she was saved by her eldest brother **Abhaya.** She was put in a chamber built on a single pillar, with an entrance through the king's bedroom. But **Dīghagāmaṇī** fell in love with her and visited her at night with the help of a hook-ladder. Later, when with child, she was given to him in marriage.[1]

She was given the name of Ummāda-Cittā because the mere sight of her beauty drove men mad.[2]

[1] Mhv. ix. 1 ff.; Dpv. x. 4.
[2] Mhv. ix. 5.

Ummāda-Phussadeva.—See **Phussadeva.**

Ummāpupphā.—A class of devas present at the preaching of the **Mahāsamaya Sutta.**[1] They are so-called because their bodies were azure in colour, like *ummā*-flowers.[2]

[1] D. ii. 260.
[2] DA. ii. 690; see also *ibid.*, 562; MA. ii. 706.

1. **Ummāpupphiya Thera.**—An arahant. In a past birth when a festival was being held in honour of the *thūpa* erected over the relics of **Siddhattha** Buddha, he placed an *ummā*-flower on the *thūpa.* Nine kappas ago he became king eighty-five times under the name of **Somadeva.**[1]

He is probably identical with **Cakkhupāla** Thera.[2]

[1] Ap. i. 172.
[2] See ThagA. i. 196.

2. **Ummāpupphiya Thera.**—An arahant. In a past birth he saw the Buddha **Siddhattha** wrapt in *samādhi* and offered him, in homage, azure (*ummā-*) flowers, which formed a canopy above the Buddha's

head. Later, Ummāpupphiya was born in **Tusita.** Fifty-five kappas ago he was a king called **Samantacchadana.**[1]

[1] Ap. i. 258.

Ummi Sutta.—Four perils have to be faced by those who go down into the water: waves, sharks, whirlpools and sea-monsters. Like perils await those who go from the household life to homelessness.[1]

[1] A. ii. 123 ff. This sutta is included as part of the *Cātuma Sutta* (M. i. 460 f.).

Uyyānadvāra.—A gate in **Pulatthipura,** built by **Parakkamabāhu I.**[1]

[1] Cv. lxxiii. 162.

Uraga.—A mountain near **Himavā.** In a previous birth, **Gosāla** Thera saw there a rag-robe hanging, to which he paid homage[1] (*v.l.* **Udaka** and **Udaṅgana**).

[1] ThagA. i. 79; Ap. ii. 434.

1. **Uraga Jātaka** (No. 154).—King **Brahmadatta** of Benares once held a festival to which came the inhabitants of many worlds. A Nāga in the crowd, not noticing that the person beside him was a Garuḍa, laid a hand on his shoulder; discovering his mistake, he was frightened to death and ran away, pursued by the Garuḍa. The Nāga, coming to a river, where an ascetic, who was the Bodhisatta, was bathing, took refuge in the ascetic's bark-garment. The Garuḍa, though able to see the Nāga, would not attack him out of respect for the ascetic. The latter took both of them to his hermitage and made them friendly towards each other by preaching the blessings of loving-kindness.

The story was related in reference to two soldiers who were in the habit of quarrelling whenever they met. Not even the king could reconcile them. The Buddha visited them at their homes and, having made them both sotāpannas, took them to see each other. Thenceforth they were great friends, and people marvelled at the Buddha's power.[1]

The **Nakula Jātaka** was also preached in this connection.

[1] J. ii. 12-14.

2. **Uraga Jātaka** (No. 354).—The Bodhisatta was once a brahmin in Benares. His household consisted of himself, his wife, a son, a daughter, a daughter-in-law and a female slave. They lived happily together, and on the Bodhisatta's advice kept their thoughts constantly fixed on the inevitableness of death. One day, while burning some rubbish in the field, the son was bitten by a snake and died. The father laid

his body under a tree, and having sent word to his house that all the others should come with perfumes and flowers, when bringing his meal, he went on with his work. After the meal they made a funeral pyre and burnt the body, but not one of them wept a single tear. By virtue of their piety, **Sakka's** throne was heated and he appeared to them in disguise. He questioned them separately as to whether their lack of any show of grief for the dead meant that they did not love him. Being convinced that their composure was due to their practice of the thought of death, he revealed his identity, and filled their house with the seven kinds of treasures. The story was related to a landowner of **Sāvatthi** who, when his son died, gave himself up to despair. The Buddha visited him and consoled him.[1]

This story is referred to in the *Dhammapada Commentary.*[2]

[1] J.iii.162 ff.

[2] DhA.iii.277.

1. **Uraga Vagga.**—The first chapter of the **Sutta Nipāta.** It consists of twelve suttas.[1]

[1] Sn. 1 ff.

2. **Uraga Vagga.**—The first section of the *Peta-Vatthu.* The last story in the section is called **Uraga Peta-Vatthu.**[1]

[1] Pv., p. 11.

Uraga Sutta.—The first sutta of the *Sutta Nipāta.* It was preached at the **Aggāḷava Cetiya** in **Āḷavī.** The Āḷavaka monks cut down trees to build new houses for themselves, and one of them in felling a tree which was the abode of a tree-sprite hurt her child's hand. Though sorely tempted to kill the monk on the spot, the sprite checked herself and made complaint to the Buddha, who asked her to occupy another tree.[1] The first stanza of the sutta was preached to the devatā. The *Sutta-Nipāta Commentary*[2] gives the occasions on which the other stanzas were preached. Buddhaghosa[3] says that the devatā mentioned above took up her residence in **Jetavana,** on a spot indicated to her by the Buddha, and had, therefore, the privilege of listening to the Buddha's sermons at close quarters, even when there were great assemblies of the devas present and less powerful devas, like herself, had generally to yield place to the more powerful. She could not be dislodged from the place appointed to her by the Buddha.

[1] SnA.i.3 f.; the story is also given in Vin.iv.34 and in DhA.iii.229 f.

[2] SnA.i.15 ff.

[3] Sp.iv.761.

Uragapura.—The residence of **Buddhadatta** (*q.v.*), author of the *Jinālaṅkāra* and several other books. Uragapura was probably in Southern India on the banks of the Kāveri.[1]

[1] P.L.C. 106 f.

Uracchadā.—One of the nine daughters of King **Kikī.** She was born with the semblance of a necklet upon her neck and shoulders, as though drawn by a painter, hence her name, Uracchadā. When sixteen years old she heard Kassapa Buddha preach, and became a *sotāpanna*. That same day she attained arahantship, entered the Order and passed into Nibbāna.[1]

In the time of Vipassī, both Uracchadā and Queen **Māyā** (mother of Gotama Buddha) were born as the daughters of King **Bandhumā.** One day the king received a present of a golden wreath, worth a thousand, and a box of precious sandalwood. He gave the sandalwood to the elder daughter and the wreath to the younger. The two girls, wishing to present their gifts to the Buddha, obtained the king's consent. The elder princess powdered the sandalwood and filled a golden box with it. The younger had the wreath made into a necklet and placed it in a golden casket. They then went to the Buddha, and the elder reverently sprinkled his body with sandalwood and scattered it in his cell with the prayer, " May I, in time to come, be the mother of a Buddha like you." The younger reverently placed the necklet on the Buddha and prayed, " Until I attain arahantship, may this ornament never part from my body."[2]

According to the *Vimānavatthu Commentary*,[3] Uracchadā's name was **Uracchadamālā** and her teacher was a brahmin named **Gopāla,** who was also present when the Buddha preached to Uracchadamālā. But he did not acquire any special attainments.

[1] J. vi. 481. [2] *Ibid.*, 480. [3] pp. 270 f.

Urucetiya.—See **Mahāthūpa.**

Urudhammarakkhita.—A thera who came from the **Ghositārāma** in Kosambī, with thirty thousand monks, to be present at the foundation ceremony of the **Mahāthūpa.**[1]

[1] Mhv. xxix. 34.

Urubuddharakkhita.—An Elder who was present at the foundation ceremony of the **Mahāthūpa.** He came from the **Mahāvana** in Vesāli, with eighteen thousand monks.[1]

[1] Mhv. xxix. 33.

Urusaṅgharakkhita.—An Elder who came with forty thousand monks from the **Dakkhiṇāgiri** in Ujjeni, to be present at the **Mahāthūpa** foundation ceremony.[1]

[1] Mhv. xxix. 35.

1. **Uruvela Sutta.**—Preached at **Jetavana.** The Buddha tells the monks how, when he was at **Uruvelā**, under the **Ajapāla** tree, he realised that there was no one in the world worthy to be his teacher. So he decided to obey and serve the Dhamma. **Sahampati** appeared and told him that such had been the custom of previous Buddhas also.[1]

[1] A. ii. 20 f.

2. **Uruvela Sutta.**—The Buddha tells the monks how a number of brahmins had visited him at **Uruvelā** and asked him if it were true that he did not reverence old men ? He taught them how it was not old age which deserved reverence, but the qualities which men possessed, and he set forth those qualities.[1]

[1] A. ii. 22 f.

Uruvelakappa.—A township of the **Mallas** in the Malla country. Once when the Buddha was staying there, **Bhadragaka,** the headman of the town, visited him, and the Buddha preached to him a sermon on the arising and the cessation of Ill.[1] It was perhaps on the same occasion that the Buddha was visited by the headman **Rāsiya,** and he seems to have talked to him on various topics connected with the doctrine.[2] Record is also made of a sermon preached by the Buddha at Uruvelakappa and addressed to the monks regarding the importance of insight (*ariyañāna*).[3]

Once when the Buddha was staying at Uruvelakappa, he informed **Ānanda** that he wished to spend the day alone in the **Mahāvana,** and he went there and sat down at the foot of a tree. Meanwhile the householder **Tapassu** arrived and told Ānanda that he could not understand how young men in the prime of life found any attraction in renouncing the world. Ānanda took Tapassu to the Buddha, who set his doubts at rest.[4]

[1] S. iv. 327 f.
[2] *Ibid.*, 330 ff.
[3] *Ibid.*, v. 228 f.
[4] A. iv. 438 ff.

Uruvela-Kassapa.—One of three brothers, the **Tebhātika-Jaṭilas,** living at **Uruvelā.** He lived on the banks of the **Nerañjarā** with five hundred disciples. Further down the river lived his brothers **Nadī-Kassapa** with three hundred disciples and **Gayā-Kassapa** with two hundred. The Buddha visited Uruvela-Kassapa and took lodging for the night where the sacred fire was kept, in spite of Kassapa's warning that the spot was inhabited by a fierce Nāga. The Buddha, by his magical powers, overcame, first this Nāga and then another, both of whom vomited fire and smoke. Kassapa being pleased with this exhibition of *iddhi*-power, undertook to provide the Buddha with his daily food. Meanwhile the Buddha stayed in a grove near by, waiting for the time when Kassapa should be ready for conversion. Here he was visited by the Four Regent Gods, **Sakka, Brahmā** and others. The Buddha spent the whole rainy season there, performing, in all, three thousand five hundred miracles of various kinds, reading the thoughts of Kassapa, splitting firewood for the ascetics' sacrifices, heating stoves for them to use after bathing in the cold weather, etc. Still Kassapa persisted in the thought, "The great ascetic is of great magic power, but he is not an arahant like me." Finally the Buddha decided to startle him by declaring that he was not an arahant, neither did the way he followed lead to arahantship. Thereupon Kassapa owned defeat and reverently asked for ordination. The Buddha asked him to consult with his pupils, and they cut off their hair and threw it with their sacrificial utensils into the river and were all ordained. Nadī-Kassapa and Gayā-Kassapa came to inquire what had happened, and they, too, were ordained with their pupils. At Gayāsīsa the Buddha preached to them the Fire Sermon (**Āditta-pariyāya**), and they all attained arahantship.

From Gayāsīsa the Buddha went to Rājagaha with the Kassapas and their pupils, and in the presence of **Bimbisāra** and the assembled populace Uruvela-Kassapa declared his allegiance to the Buddha.[1]

Later, in the assembly of monks, Uruvela-Kassapa was declared to be the chief of those who had large followings (*aggaṃ mahāparisānaṃ*).[2] Six verses attributed to him are found in the *Theragāthā*,[3] wherein he reviews his achievement and relates how he was won over by the Buddha.

In the time of **Padumuttara** Buddha he was a householder, and having seen the Buddha declare a monk[4] to be the best of them with large followings, wished for himself to be so honoured in a future life, and did many works of merit towards that end.

Later, he was born in the family of **Phussa** Buddha as his younger step-brother, his father being **Mahinda.**[5] He had two other brothers. The three quelled a frontier disturbance and, as a reward, obtained the

[1] This story of the conversion of the Kassapas is given in Vin. i. 24 ff. and in AA. i. 165 f.; also in ThagA. i. 434 ff.

[2] A. i. 25.

[3] vv. 375-80.

[4] **Sīhaghosa** was his name (Ap. ii. 481).

[5] According to Bu. xix. 14, Phussa's father was **Jayasena.**

right to entertain the Buddha for three months. They appointed three of their ministers to make all the arrangements and they themselves observed the ten precepts. The three ministers so appointed were, in this age, **Bimbisāra, Visākha** and **Raṭṭhapāla.**

Having sojourned among gods and men, the three brothers, in their last birth, were born in a brahmin family, the name of which was **Kassapa.** They learnt the three Vedas and left the household life.[6]

According to the **Mahā-Nārada-Kassapa Jātaka,**[7] Uruvela-Kassapa was once born as **Aṅgati,** king of **Mithilā** in the Videha country. He listened to the teachings of a false teacher called **Guṇa** and gave himself up to pleasure, till he was saved by his wise daughter **Rujā,** with the help of the Brahmā **Nārada,** who was the Bodhisatta.

Uruvela-Kassapa was so called partly to distinguish him from other Kassapas and partly because he was ordained at Uruvelā. At first he had one thousand followers, and after he was ordained by the Buddha all his followers stayed with him and each of them ordained a great number of others, so that their company became very numerous.[8]

The scene of the conversion of Uruvela-Kassapa is sculptured in Sanchi. According to Tibetan sources, Kassapa was one hundred and twenty years old at the time of his conversion.[9] Hiouen Thsang found a stūpa erected on the spot where the Buddha converted Kassapa.[10]

Belaṭṭhasīsa was a disciple of Uruvela-Kassapa and joined his teacher when the latter was converted.[11] **Senaka** Thera was Kassapa's sister's son.[12] **Vacchapāla** was among those who joined the Order, after having seen Kassapa pay homage to the Buddha at Rājagaha.[13]

[6] AA. i. 165 f.; DhA. i. 83 ff.; Ap. ii. 481 ff.
[7] J. vi. 220 ff.; Ap. ii. 483.
[8] AA. i. 166.
[9] Rockhill, *op. cit.*, 40.
[10] Beal, *Bud. Records*, ii. 130.
[11] ThagA. i. 67.
[12] *Ibid.*, 388.
[13] *Ibid.*, 159.

Uruvelapaṭṭana.—See **Uruvelā** (2).

Uruvela-pāṭihāriya-bhāṇavāra.—The twenty-first chapter of the first *Khandhaka* of the *Mahāvagga* in the *Vinaya Piṭaka.*

Uruveḷa.—One of the chief lay supporters of Sumedha Buddha.[1]

[1] Bu. xii. 25.

Uruvelamaṇḍala.—A district in **Rohaṇa,** in South Ceylon, where the ministers **Bhūta, Rakkha** and **Kitti** obtained a decisive victory over their enemies. This battle enabled them to get possession of the Buddha's

Bowl and the Tooth Relic.[1] Geiger thinks that the place was near the modern Monarāgala.[2]

[1] Cv. lxxiv. 125-6. [2] Cv. *Trs.* ii. 33, n. 1.

Uruvela-vihāra.—A vihāra in Ceylon, restored by **Vijayabāhu I.**[1] It may have been in the city called **Devanagara.**[2]

[1] Mhv. lx. 59. [2] Cv. *Trs.* i. 220, n. 2.

1. **Uruvelā.**—A locality on the banks of the **Nerañjarā,** in the neighbourhood of the Bodhi-tree at Buddhagayā. Here, after leaving **Āḷāra** and **Uddaka,** the Bodhisatta practised during six years the most severe penances. His companions were the **Pañcavaggiya**-monks, who, however, left him when he relaxed the severity of his austerities.[1] The place chosen by the Bodhisatta for his penances was called **Senā-nigama.**[2] The *Jātaka* version[3] contains additional particulars. It relates that once the Bodhisatta fainted under his austerities, and the news was conveyed to his father that he was dead. **Suddhodana,** however, refused to believe this, remembering the prophecy of **Kāḷadevala.** When the Bodhisatta decided to take ordinary food again, it was given to him by a girl, **Sujātā,**[4] daughter of **Senānī** of the township of Senānī. In the neighbourhood of Uruvelā were also the **Ajapāla** Banyan-tree, the **Mucalinda**-tree and the **Rājāyatana**-tree, where the Buddha spent some time after his Enlightenment, and where various shrines, such as the **Animisa-cetiya,** the **Ratanacaṅkama-cetiya** and the **Ratanaghara** later came into existence.[5] From Uruvelā the Buddha went to **Isipatana,** but after he had made sixty-one arahants and sent them out on tour to preach the Doctrine, he returned to Uruvelā, to the **Kappāsikavanasaṇḍa** and converted the **Bhaddavaggiyā.**[6] At Uruvelā dwelt also the **Tebhātika-Jaṭilas: Uruvela-Kassapa, Nadī-Kassapa** and **Gayā-Kassapa,** who all became followers of the Buddha.[7]

According to the Ceylon Chronicles,[8] it was while spending the rainy season at Uruvelā, waiting for the time when the Kassapa brothers should be ripe for conversion, that the Buddha, on the full-moon day of Phussa, in the ninth month after the Enlightenment, paid his first visit to Ceylon.

Mention is made of several temptations of the Buddha while he dwelt at Uruvelā, apart from the supreme contest with Māra, under the Bodhi-

[1] M. i. 166. [2] On this name see *s.v.*
[3] J. i. 67 f. [4] For details see **Sujātā.**
[5] For the incidents connected with these various places see *s.v.*
[6] Vin. i. 23 f.; DhA. i. 72.
[7] Vin. i. 25.
[8] *E.g.*, Mhv. i. 17 ff.; Dpv. i. 35, 38, 81.

tree. Once Māra came to him in the darkness of the night in the guise of a terrifying elephant, trying to frighten him. On another dark night when the rain was falling drop by drop, Māra came to the Buddha and assumed various wondrous shapes, beautiful and ugly. Another time Māra tried to fill the Buddha's mind with doubt as to whether he had really broken away from all fetters and won complete Enlightenment.[9] Seven years after the Buddha's Renunciation, Māra made one more attempt to make the Buddha discontented with his lonely lot and it was then, when Māra had gone away discomfited, that Māra's three daughters, **Taṇhā, Ratī** and **Ragā,** made a final effort to draw the Buddha away from his purpose.[10] It was at Uruvelā, too, that the Buddha had misgivings in his own mind as to the usefulness of preaching the Doctrine which he had realised, to a world blinded by passions and prejudices. The Brahmā **Sahampatī** thereupon entreated the Buddha not to give way to such diffidence.[11] It is recorded that either on this very occasion or quite soon after, the thought arose in the Buddha's mind that the sole method of winning Nibbāna was to cultivate the four *satipaṭṭhānas* and that Sahampatī visited the Blessed One and confirmed his view.[12] A different version occurs elsewhere,[13] where the thought which arose in the Buddha's mind referred to the five controlling faculties (*saddhindriya*, etc.), and Brahmā tells the Buddha that in the time of Kassapa he had been a monk named **Sahaka** and that then he had practised these five faculties.

The name Uruvelā is explained as meaning a great sandbank (*mahā velā, mahanto vālikarāsi*). A story is told which furnishes an alternative explanation: Before the Buddha's appearance in the world, ten thousand ascetics lived in this locality, and they decided among themselves that if any evil thought arose in the mind of any one of them, he should carry a basket of sand to a certain spot. The sand so collected eventually formed a great bank.[14] In the *Divyāvadāna*,[15] the place is called Uruvilvā. The *Mahāvastu*[16] mentions four villages as being in Uruvelā: Praskandaka, Balākalpa, Ujjaṅgala and Jaṅgala.

[9] S. i. 103 ff.
[10] *Ibid.*, 124 f.
[11] *Ibid.*, 136 ff.; Vin. i. 4 f.
[12] S. v. 167; and again, 185.
[13] *Ibid.*, 232.
[14] AA. ii. 476; UdA. 26; MA. i. 376; MT. 84.
[15] p. 202.
[16] ii. 207.

2. **Uruvelā.**—A township in Ceylon, founded by one of the ministers of **Vijaya.**[1] According to a different tradition,[2] it was founded by a brother of **Bhaddakaccānā,** called Uruvela. Uruvelā was evidently a

[1] Dpv. ix. 35; Mhv. vii. 45.
[2] *Ibid.*, ix. 9; perhaps this refers to another settlement.

port as well, because we are told that when **Duṭṭhagāmaṇī** decided to build the **Mahā-Thūpa,** six wagonloads of pearls as large as myrobalan fruit, mixed with coral, appeared on dry land at the **Uruvela-paṭṭana.**[3] Near Uruvelā was the **Vallī-vihāra**, built by **Subha.**[4]

Geiger[5] thinks that Uruvelā was near the mouth of the modern Kalā Oya, five yojanas—*i.e.* about forty miles—to the west of **Anurādhapura.**

[3] *Ibid.*, xxviii. 36. [4] *Ibid.*, xxxv. 58. [5] Mhv. *Trs.* 189, n. 2.

3. **Uruvelā.**—A village to which Queen **Sugalā** (*q.v.*) fled, taking the sacred relics, the Alms Bowl and the Tooth Relic.[1] It is identified with Etimole about five or six miles south-east of Monorāgala.[2] It is perhaps to be identified with **Uruvelamaṇḍapa.**

[1] Cv. lxxiv. 88. [2] Cv. *Trs.* ii. 29, n. 4.

Uruveḷā.—One of the two chief women disciples of **Kassapa** Buddha.[1]

[1] J. i. 43; Bu. xxv. 40.

Uladāgāma.—A village in **Rohaṇa** where a battle took place between the forces of **Parakkamabāhu I.** and the rebels.[1]

[1] Cv. lxxv. 18.

Ulūka Jātaka (No. 270).—Once the birds wanted to select a king because all the other animals had kings. It was proposed to make the owl king, but when the vote came to be taken, a crow stood up and objected, saying: " If this is how he looks when he is being consecrated king, how will he look when he is angry ?" The owl gave him chase and the birds chose a goose instead. Here began the eternal enmity of the owl and the crow. The story was told by the Buddha when it was reported to him that the owls near **Jetavana** were killing numerous crows nightly.[1]

[1] J. ii. 351-4.

Uḷāra-vimāna.—The daughter of a family in **Rājagaha,** which waited upon **Mahamoggallāna ;** was very generous and always gave away in alms the half of anything which she possessed. She was given in marriage to the son of a family of unbelievers. One day, seeing Moggallāna begging for alms, she invited him and gave him some cakes which had been put away by her mother-in-law. When the latter heard of it she was greatly enraged, and struck the girl with a pestle.

The girl died and was born in **Tāvatiṃsa,** her palace being called the **Uḷāravimāna.** Later, Moggallāna visited her there.[1]

[1] Vv. p. 24; VvA. 120.

Uḷuṅkasaddaka.—The nickname of a young novice who lived with **Mahākassapa** and who later burnt down the Elder's hut in **Rājagaha.** His story is related in the **Kuṭidūsaka Jātaka** (*q.v.*).[1]

[1] J. iii. 71 ff.

Uḷumpa.—A township of the Sākyans. The Buddha once stayed there and was visited by **Pasenadi,** king of Kosala, who felt remorse for the murder of his general **Bandhula.** The king went alone inside the Gandhakuṭi, laying aside the symbols of royalty which he left with his minister **Dīgha-Kārāyana.** When the king came out, he found that all his followers had gone, leaving behind only one horse and a serving-woman. On learning that **Viḍūḍabha** had been made king, Pasenadi left for Rājagaha, to seek the help of Ajātasattu, and died outside the city-gates.[1]

[1] J. iv. 151 f.; DhA. i. 356.

Ullapanagāma.—A village where there was a bridge of thirty cubits, built over the **Mahāvālukagaṅgā** by **Devappatirāja,**[1] The village is identified with the modern Ulapane, four miles from Gampola.[2]

[1] Cv. lxxxvi. 23. [2] Cv. *Trs.* ii. 173, n. 3.

Ullabhakolakaṇṇikā. Evidently a village in Ceylon. A woman of this village, having learnt that the Thera **Dīghabhāṇaka-Abhaya** was reciting the *Ariyavaṃsa-paṭipāda,* went all the way to hear him, a distance of five leagues, nursing her baby the while. She arrived at the vihāra and, having laid the baby down, listened to two preachers. Earlier in the day, when Abhaya Thera, having finished a portion of the sermon, was about to take some refreshment, she censured him, saying that he should have refreshed himself earlier. The thera agreed and finished the sermon and, at the last word, the woman became a sotāpanna.[1]

[1] AA. i. 386.

Uvāḷa Thera.—He was examined by the Saṅgha in connection with an offence he had committed. He first denied it, then confessed it, then denied it again, and made countercharges and spoke lies, knowing them to be such. The Buddha requested the monks to carry out the *tassa-pāpiyyasikā-kamma* against him[1] (*v.l.* **Upavāla**).

[1] Vin. ii. 85 f.; where the details of procedure are also given.

1. **Usabha Thera.**—An arahant. He was born of a wealthy family in Kosala and entered the Order, when the Buddha accepted **Jetavana.** Finishing his novitiate, he dwelt amidst the mountains. Going out one day from his cave after the rains, he saw the loveliness of the woods and mountains and reflected, "These trees and creepers, though unconscious, yet by the season's fulfilment, have won full growth. Why should not I, who have obtained suitable season, win growth by good qualities ?" Pondering thus, he strove and obtained insight.[1]

In the time of **Sikhī** Buddha, he was a devaputta and offered flowers to the Buddha, which remained as a canopy over the Buddha's head for seven days. Ten kappas ago he was a king named **Jutindhara.** He is evidently to be identified with **Mandāravapūjaka** of the *Apadāna.*[2]

[1] Thag. v. 110; ThagA. i. 217 f. [2] Ap. i. 178.

2. **Usabha.**—He was born of a Sakyan family in **Kapilavatthu.** When the Buddha visited his family, Usabha saw his power and wisdom and entered the Order. But he fulfilled no religious duties, passing the day in society and the night in sleep. One night he dreamt that he shaved, put on a crimson cloak, and, sitting on a elephant, entered the town for alms. There, seeing the people gathered together, he dismounted, full of shame. Filled with anguish at the thought of his own muddleheadedness, he strove after insight and became an arahant.[1]

In the time of **Sikhī** Buddha he was a householder and gave to the Buddha a *kosamba*-fruit. He is evidently identical with **Kosambaphaliya** of the *Apadāna.*[2]

[1] Thag. 197-8; ThagA. i. 319 f. [2] Ap. ii. 449.

3. **Usabha.**—A Pacceka Buddha, mentioned in the *Isigili Sutta.*[1]

[1] M. iii. 70.

4. **Usabha.**—A seṭṭhi of **Kālacampā,** father of **Soṇa Koḷvisa.**[1]

[1] AA. i. 131; ThagA. i. 544.

Usabhakkhandha.—Son of Dīpaṅkara.[1] See also **Samavattakkhandha.**

[1] Bu. ii. 209; Mbv. 4.

Usabhamukha.—One of the four channels leading out of the **Anotatta** lake. The river which flows out of this channel is called **Usabhamukhanadī,** and cattle are abundant on its banks.[1]

[1] SnA. ii. 438; UdA. 301.

1. **Usabhavatī.**—A city where, in the pleasaunce near by, **Paduma** Buddha spent a rainy season. The citizens gave a special *kaṭhina*-robe to his chief disciple, **Sāla.**[1] According to the *Buddhavaṃsa Commentary,*[2] **Piyadassī** Buddha preached his first sermon in the same pleasaunce, but the *Buddhavaṃsa*[3] gives its name as **Ussāvana.**

[1] BuA. 148. [2] p. 173. [3] xiv. 119.

2. **Usabhavatī.**—The city in which the Buddha **Vessabhū** died, at the **Khemārāma.**[1]

[1] BuA. 209.

Usinnara.—See **Usīnara.**

Usīnara.—King of Benares in the time of **Kassapa** Buddha. His story is related in the **Mahā-Kaṇha Jātaka.**[1] He is mentioned in a list of kings who, although they gave great gifts, could not get beyond the domain of sense.[2] He is, however, elsewhere[3] mentioned as having been born in **Sakka's** heaven as a result of waiting diligently on brahmins and recluses.

[1] J. iv. 181 ff. [2] J. vi. 99. [3] *Ibid.*, 251.

Usīraddhaja.—A mountain range forming the northern boundary of **Majjhimadesa.**[1]

[1] Vin. i. 197; DA. i. 173; J. i. 49; KhA. 133; MA, i. 397, etc.

Usukāraṇiya Sutta.—Describes one of the *petas* of **Gijjhakūṭa,** seen by **Moggallāna,** while in the company of **Lakkhaṇa.** The peta had been a judge in **Rājagaha** and had been cruel to criminals. The peta's body bristled with arrows.[1]

[1] S. ii. 257.

Ussada.—A Niraya. It resembled a city with four gates and a wall. **Mittavindaka,** arriving at Ussaka in his wanderings, saw there a man supporting a wheel as sharp as a razor, which to Mittavindaka appeared like a lotus-flower. Mittavindaka took it from him, and realising then what it was, tried to escape, but was unsuccessful. This was the suffering undergone by those who had smitten their mothers. **Sakka,** during a visit to Ussaka, saw Mittavindaka, but could do nothing for him.[1]

[1] J. iv. 3 f.; iii. 206 f.

Ussada was considered a place of great suffering,[2] and also a place where those who, having promised a gift fail to give it, are born.[3] Once the Bodhisatta was born in Ussada, for cruelty during his reign as king of Benares, and he suffered for eighty thousand years.[4] Beings born there have their tongues pierced with glowing hooks and are dragged about on a floor of heated metal.[5]

In the scholiast to the **Matakabhatta Jātaka**[6] reference is made to sixteen Ussada-nirayā.

Revatī (*q.v.*) was once cast into Ussada-niraya.[7]

[2] *E.g.*, J. iv. 493.
[3] *Ibid.*, 405.
[4] J. vi. 2.
[5] *Ibid.*, 112.
[6] J. i. 168.
[7] VvA. 223.

Ussānaviṭṭhi.—A village in Ceylon, given by King **Udaya I.** for the maintenance of the *pāsāda* in the **Pucchārāma-vihāra.** It was a poor village, but the king made it rich.[1]

[1] Cv. xlix. 28.

Ussiliya-Tissa Thera.—He was a resident of the **Abhayagiri-vihāra.** When the monks of this vihāra tried to introduce the **Vaitulya** heresy, he refused to be associated with them and went, with a few others, to **Dakkhiṇagiri-vihāra.** There they formed the **Sāgaliya** sect under a monk named **Sāgala.**[1]

[1] P.L.C. 56.

Ussoḷhi Sutta.—Exertion (*ussoḷhi*) must be made by those who see not decay and death as they really are.[1]

[1] S. ii. 132.

Ū

Ūcena.—A district in South India, from which soldiers came to oppose the forces of the general **Laṅkāpura.** He subdued them.[1]

[1] Cv. lxxvi. 247, 260.

Ūmi Sutta.—See **Ummi Sutta.**

Ūriyeri.—A locality in South India. In it was a fortress which was besieged by **Laṅkāpura** and **Jagadvijaya.**[1]

[1] Cv. lxxvii. 58, 62.

Ūvaraṭṭha.—See **Hūvaraṭṭha.**

Ūhā-nadī.—A river in the **Himālaya,** evidently difficult of access.[1]

[1] Mil. 70.

E

Eka Sutta.—Neither beauty, nor wealth, nor kin, nor sons, nor virtue, can avail a woman who is mastered by a man with the power of authority.[1]

[1] S. iv. 246.

Ekakkharakosa.—A well-known Pāli vocabulary, composed in the sixteenth century by **Saddhammakitti,** pupil of **Ariyavaṃsa.**[1] It is evidently based on similar Sanskrit works. There exists also a *ṭīkā* to the work.

[1] Bode, *op. cit.*, 45.

Ekacakkhu.—A city of **Jambudīpa,** where reigned **Kambalavasana** (or **Kambalavasabha**) and his descendants, thirty-two in number, also **Brahmadeva** and his descendants, fifteen in number.[1]

[1] Dpv. iii. 19, 24.

Ekacampakapupphiya Thera.—An arahant. Thirty-one kappas ago he had given a *campaka*-flower to the Pacceka Buddha, **Upasanta.**[1] He is probably identical with **Vajjita** Thera.[2]

[1] Ap. i. 288. [2] ThagA. i. 336 f

Ekacāriya Thera.—An arahant. One hundred thousand kappas ago, when in Tāvatiṃsa, he heard sounds of great excitement because a Buddha had been born in the world. He visited the Buddha on his death-bed and offered a *mandārava*-flower. Sixty thousand kappas ago he was three times king under the name of **Mahāmallajana.**[1]

[1] Ap. i. 196.

1. **Ekacintita.**—Sixteen kappas ago there were eighteen kings of this name. They were previous births of **Sumaṅgala** Thera.[1]

[1] Ap. i. 148; ThagA. i. 111.

2. **Ekacintita Thera.**—An arahant. When in the deva-world, his term of life having come to an end, he was filled with anxiety as to where he should seek rebirth. A disciple of **Padumuttara,** named **Sumana,** seeing his plight, advised him to seek refuge in the Buddha. He followed the advice and escaped sorrow.[1]

[1] Ap. i. 194 f.

Ekachattiya Thera.—An arahant. In the time of **Atthadassī** he was an ascetic with a large following, living on the banks of the **Candabhāgā.** He visited the Buddha with his followers and held a white parasol over the Buddha's head. Seventy-seven kappas ago he lived in the deva-world as king of the devas. He was king of men one thousand times.[1]

[1] Ap. ii. 367 ff.

Ekajjha.—A king of fifty-seven kappas ago; a previous birth of **Phaladāyaka** Thera.[1]

[1] Ap. i. 239.

1. **Ekañjalika Thera.**—An arahant. Ninety-one kappas ago he saw **Vipassī** Buddha and paid homage to him with clasped hands.[1]

[1] Ap. i. 80.

2. **Ekañjalika.**—A king of fourteen kappas ago, a previous birth of **Ekañjaliya** Thera.[1]

[1] Ap. i. 236.

1. **Ekañjaliya Thera.**—An arahant. Ninety-two kappas ago he provided a place of residence for the Buddha **Tissa** in an *udumbara*-grove and spread for him a carpet of flowers and paid homage to him with clasped hands. Once he was a king, called **Ekañjalika.**[1]

[1] Ap. i. 236.

2. **Ekañjaliya Thera.**—An arahant. Ninety-four kappas ago he saw the Pacceka Buddha **Romasa,** on the banks of a river and, being pleased with his radiant appearance, paid homage to him with clasped hands.[1]

[1] Ap. i. 281.

Ekatthambha-pāsāda.—One of the buildings erected by **Parakkamabāhu I.** It rose sheer from the ground and was crowned with a *maṅkara* (dolphin). In it was a golden chamber on a golden column, resembling a cave, for the use of the king.[1]

[1] Cv. lxxiii. 92 ff; see also Cv. *Trs.* ii. 11, n. 4.

Ekadaṃsaniya Thera.—An arahant. In the time of **Atthadassī** Buddha, he was named **Nārada-Kesava.** He heard the Buddha preach and, gladdened by the sermon, did him homage. Seventeen kappas ago he became a king under the name of **Amittatāpana** (*v.l.* **Amittavāsana** ?).[1]

He is probably identical with **Paviṭṭha** Thera.[2]

[1] Ap. i. 168 f.

[2] ThagA. i. 185.

1. **Ekadīpiya Thera.**—An arahant. Ninety-four kappas ago he kept a lamp lighted all night near the thūpa built over the relics of **Siddhattha** Buddha. For seventy-seven kappas he was in heaven and was thirty-one times king of the devas. Twenty-eight times he was king among men. His body shone like the sun, and he could see a distance of one hundred leagues. His palace in heaven was called **Ekadīpī.** He entered the Order at the age of four (?) and in a fortnight became an arahant.[1]

[1] Ap. ii. 373.

2. **Ekadīpiya Thera.**—An arahant. In the past he had lighted a lamp before the *salaḷa*-bodhi of the Buddha **Padumuttara.** Sixteen thousand kappas ago he was four times king under the name of **Candābha.**[1]

[1] Ap. i. 189.

Ekadīpī.—The abode of **Ekadīpiya** when he was born in the deva-world. There were always one hundred thousand lights burning in Ekadīpī.[1]

[1] Ap. ii. 373.

Ekadvāra.—A vihāra built by King **Subha** to the east of **Anurādhapura,** at the foot of the **Ekadvārika-pabbata.**[1]

[1] Mhv. xxxv. 58; MṬ. 648.

Ekadvārika. See **Ekadvāra.**

Ekadussadāyaka Thera.—An arahant. In the time of **Padumuttara** Buddha he was a grass-cutter of **Haṃsavatī** and gave to the Buddha his only upper garment. As a result he reigned in heaven thirty-six times and was king of men thirty-three times. He had the power of obtaining garments at will wherever he happened to be.[1]

[1] Ap. ii. 379 f.

1. **Ekadhamma Vagga.**—The sixteenth chapter of the *Eka-nipāta* of the *Aṅguttara Nikāya.* It contains ten suttas, in which ten subjects of reflection (*anussati*) are mentioned as being conducive to inner emancipation.[1]

[1] A. i. 30.

2. **Ekadhamma Vagga.**—The first chapter of the *Ānāpānā Saṃyutta* of the *Saṃyutta Nikāya.*[1]

[1] S. v. 311-41.

Ekadhamma-peyyāla.—Two groups of suttas in which various things are mentioned singly, each of them being given as a condition most useful for the arising of the Ariyan Eightfold Way.[1]

[1] S. v. 32 ff.

1. **Ekadhamma Sutta.**—There is no other single condition which, when developed, is conducive to the abandonment of bonds as much as the seven *bojjhaṅgas.*[1]

[1] S. v. 88.

2. **Ekadhamma Sutta.**—There is one condition which, if cultivated, yields great fruit, viz., the concentration on in-breathing and out-breathing. The sutta also describes the method of its practice.[1]

[1] S. v. 311 f.

1. **Ekadhammasavaṇiya Thera.**—He was the son of a banker in **Setavyā** and he went to see the Buddha who was visiting the town and staying in the **Siṃsapā**-wood. The Buddha preached to him on the impermanence of all component things and at the end of the sermon he became an arahant. He received his name because he won insight by hearing the Dhamma only once.

In the time of **Padumuttara** Buddha he was a tree-sprite and, coming across some monks who had lost their way, he looked after them, gave them food and directed them to their destination. After the death of **Kassapa** Buddha, he was born as the son of **Suyāma** and great-grandson of **Kikī** and became king of Benares under the name of **Kikī Brahmadatta.** Not finding anyone capable of preaching the Doctrine to him, he left his throne in disgust and started on his way to **Himavā.** As he went along the road, **Sakka** appeared before him and quoted to him some lines on the impermanence of all things. Satisfied therewith, the king returned to his capital.[1]

The Apadāna verses regarding this thera quoted in the *Theragāthā Commentary* are, in the *Apadāna* itself,[2] attributed to an Elder named **Maggasaññaka,** with whom he is evidently to be identified. Five kappas ago he became king twelve times under the name of **Sacakkhu.** *v.l.* **Ekadhammika.**

[1] Thag. v. 67; ThagA. i. 151 f. [2] i. 152 f.

2. **Ekadhammasavaṇiya Thera.**—An arahant. In the time of **Padumuttara** he was a Jaṭila of great power. Once when journeying through the air he found his progress suddenly stopped and, on investigation, discovered that below him, on the ground, the Buddha was preaching.

He listened to the sermon, which dealt with impermanence, and, returning to his hermitage, meditated on this topic. Later he was born in Tāvatiṃsa. Fifty-one times he reigned as king of heaven for thirty thousand kappas and twenty-one times he was king of men. In this last life he heard a monk in his father's house preaching a sermon in reference to the impermanence of all component things. At the end of the sermon he remembered his former attainments and, seated there, reached arahantship. He was only seven years old at the time.[1]

[1] Ap. ii. 385.

Ekadhammika.—See **Ekadhammasavaṇīya** (1).

Ekadhītu Sutta.—A devout lay-sister should admonish her only daughter to be like **Khujjuttarā** or **Veḷukaṇṭakiyā Nandamātā,** or, if she goes to homelessness, like **Khemā** and **Uppalavaṇṇā.**[1]

[1] S. ii. 236.

Ekanāḷā.—A brahmin village near **Dakkhiṇagiri,** to the south of **Rājagaha.** Once, during the eleventh year of his ministry, the Buddha visited the village and preached to **Kāsī-Bhāradvāja** the sutta which bears his name and which converted him to the faith.[1] Near the village was the **Dakkhiṇagiri-vihāra.**[2]

[1] Sn. pp. 12 ff.; SnA. i. 136; S. i. 172 ff. [2] SA. i. 188.

Ekanāḷika.—A famine that broke out in Ceylon during the time of King **Kuñcanāga.** The people were reduced to very little food, but the king maintained, without interruption, a great alms-giving (*mahāpeḷā*) appointed for five hundred monks.[1]

[1] Mhv. xxxvi. 20.

Ekantaka Sutta.—See **Janapada** and **Sedaka Sutta.**

Ekantadukkhī and **Ekantasukhī Suttā.**—Two suttas dealing with the respective views that after death the self is sheer suffering and that it is sheer bliss.[1]

[1] S. iii. 219 f.

Ekapaññita.—See **Ekaphusita.**

Ekapaṇṇa Jātaka (No. 149).—The Bodhisatta was once a brahmin ascetic of great iddhi-power and dwelt in the Himālaya. One day he entered Benares and took up his residence in the royal park. The king, pleased with his demeanour, invited him into the palace and asked him to spend the rainy season in the park. The king had an ill-natured son, named **Duṭṭhakumāra,** and despairing of ever being able to reform him, handed him over, as a last resort, to the ascetic. One day, when the ascetic was walking about in the garden with the prince, he asked him to taste the leaf of a young *Nimba*-plant. The prince did so, but at once spat it out, because of its intense bitterness. "If such bitterness should reside in the baby-tree, how will it be when it grows up ?" said the Bodhisatta, and thereupon drew a moral with regard to the prince's own conduct. The prince benefited by the lesson, and thenceforth changed his nature.

The story was told in reference to a Licchavi-Kumāra called **Duṭṭha.**[1]

[1] J. i. 504-8.

Ekapattadāyaka Thera.—An arahant. In the past, ninety-one kappas ago, he was a potter of **Haṃsavatī,** and once gave a well-made bowl of clay to the Buddha. As a result, he always had his food in gold and silver bowls.[1] He is probably identical with **Mahācunda** Thera.[2]

[1] Ap. ii. 444. [2] See ThagA. i. 262.

Ekapada Jātaka (No. 238).—Once the Bodhisatta was born as a rich merchant in Benares. One day his son, sitting on his lap, asked him for one word which comprehended all things. The Bodhisatta said it was "skill" (*dakkhayya*). The story was told in reference to a lad in Sāvatthi who asked his father "the *Dvārapañha*" (question regarding the entrance to the Path). The father, not being able to answer the boy, brought him to the Buddha.[1]

[1] J. ii. 236 f.

Ekapadumiya Thera.—An arahant. In the time of **Padumuttara** Buddha he was a king of swans, and seeing the Buddha near the lake where he lived, picked a lotus flower and held it in his beak above the Buddha.[1]

[1] Ap. i. 276 f.

Ekapiṇḍadāyikā Therī.—An arahant. Ninety-one kappas ago she was the wife of King **Bandhumā,** of **Bandhumatī.** Wishing to do some good-deed to ensure for herself a happy rebirth, she asked the king for his sanction, and fed a nun and gave her various gifts. Later she was born thirty times in Tāvatiṃsa as queen of the gods. She was the wife of twenty kings among men.[1] She is probably identical with **Mettā** Therī.[2]

[1] Ap. ii. 515 f. [2] ThigA. 36 f.

Ekapuggala Vagga.—The thirteenth chapter of the *Eka Nipāta* of the *Aṅguttara Nikāya.* It consists of seven suttas, six on the Tathāgata and one on **Sāriputta.**[1]

[1] A. i. 22 f.

Ekapuggala Sutta.—A group of suttas on the uniqueness of the Tathāgata.[1] The sutta is quoted in the *Kathāvatthu*[2] and the *Milindapañha.*[3]

[1] A. i. 22 f. [2] i. 65. [3] p. 242.

1. **Ekapuṇḍarīka.**—A paribbājakārāma, the residence of **Vacchagotta.**[1] It was near the **Kūṭāgārasālā** in the **Mahāvana** of **Vesāli.** The Buddha went there to see Vacchagotta, and it was on this occasion that the **Tevijja-Vacchagotta Sutta** was preached.[1] Buddhaghosa says[2] that the place was so called because in it grew a solitary White Mango Tree (*setambarukkha*).

[1] M. i. 481 f. [2] MA. ii. 673.

2. **Ekapuṇḍarīka.**—An elephant belonging to **Pasenadi.** It was while riding on this elephant that the king met **Ānanda.** The king followed the Elder to the monastery, and their conversation is recorded in the **Bāhitika Sutta.**[1]

Over the elephant's ribs there was a white spot (*paṇḍaraṭṭhāna*), the size of a palmyra-fruit, hence his name.[2]

[1] M. ii. 112 f. [2] MA. ii. 752.

3. **Ekapuṇḍarīka Thera.**—An arahant. Ninety-four kappas ago he met the Pacceka Buddha, **Romasa,** and gave him a lotus-flower as an offering of homage.[1]

[1] Ap. i. 238.

Ekaputtika-Brahmadatta.—King of Benares. He had only one son, of whom he was extremely fond. One day when the king was enjoying himself in the royal park, the boy was suddenly taken ill and died at once. Lest the king should die of a broken heart, the ministers did not tell him for two days. The king thereupon reflected on the nature of death and developing insight became a Pacceka Buddha. His verse is included in the **Khaggavisāna Sutta.**[1]

[1] Sn. v. 41; SnA. i. 85 f.; ApA. i. 138.

Ekapupphiya Thera.—An arahant. Ninety-one kappas ago he was a Pisāca at the southern gate of the city (**Bandhumatī** ?), and seeing the Buddha, offered him a single flower.[1]

[1] Ap. i. 240.

Ekaphusita.—A king of twenty-six kappas ago, a previous birth of **Saccasaññaka** Thera.[1] *v.l.* **Ekapaññita.**

[1] Ap. i. 209.

Ekabala.—A kingdom in Jambudīpa, whose king was **Saṅkhapāla.** Once the king raised a large army and **Mahosadha's** spies brought him news of it; thereupon Mahosadha sent his parrot to find out what it was all about.[1]

[1] J. vi. 390.

Ekabījī Sutta.—On the five controlling powers (*indriyāni*)—faith, energy, mindfulness, concentration, and insight—and the results that follow from cultivating these to a greater or lesser degree.[1]

The text calls this Sutta **Ekābhiññā Sutta,** but without authority.[2]

[1] S. v. 204. [2] See KS. v. 180, n. 1.

Ekabbohārā.—One of the divisions of the **Mahāsaṅghikas.**[1] They were so called because they held that "all the doctrines are understood by a unique and immediate wisdom, for all the doctrines of the Buddha are comprehended by the intellect."[2] They held, among other things, that the Tathāgathas were not subject to worldly laws, that the Dhammacakkas of all Tathāgathas did not agree; the Bodhisatta did not pass through the successive stages of embryonic development; that he is born at will among inferior beings for the salvation of mankind; with our wisdom the four truths are perfectly understood; he who has perfectly acquired right restraint has cast off all *yoga* (attachment).[3]

[1] Dpv. v. 40; Mhv. v. 4. [2] Rockhill, *op. cit.*, 183. [3] *Ibid.*, 187 f.

Ekamandāriya Thera.—An arahant. Ninety-one kappas ago he was a youth in Tāvatiṃsa and, seeing the Buddha **Vipassī** in samādhi, brought a *mandārava*-flower and held it above the Buddha's head for seven days.[1]

[1] Ap. i. 286.

1. **Ekarāja.**—King of Benares. He was the Bodhisatta. A minister, whom he expelled on the ground of misconduct in the royal harem, took service under **Dabbasena,** king of Kosala, and incited him to make war on Ekarāja. The latter was captured while sitting on the dais in the midst of his councillors and hanged head downwards by a cord from the lintel of a door. In this position Ekarāja cultivated thoughts of loving-kindness towards his enemy and attained a stage of complete absorption in mystic meditation. His bonds burst and he sat cross-

legged in mid air. Dabbasena was, meanwhile, seized with a burning pain in his body and, on the advice of his courtiers, had Ekarāja released, whereupon the pains disappeared. Realising Ekarāja's holiness, Dabbasena restored the kingdom to him and asked his forgiveness.[1]

In the **Ekarāja Jātaka,** reference is made to the **Mahāsīlava Jātaka** (*q.v.*) for details regarding the expulsion of the minister for misconduct and of the subsequent events. But there the king is called **Sīlava** and not Ekarāja. The two stories contain certain similarities but the details vary very much. See also the **Seyya Jātaka,** where the king is called **Kaṃsa,** and compare it with the **Ghata Jātaka.** The Ekarāja Jātaka is given as an example of a birth in which the Bodhisatta practised *mettā* to perfection.[2] The story of Ekarāja is the last in the *Cariyā-Piṭaka.*[3] According to the *Cāriyā Piṭaka Commentary,*[4] Ekarāja was a title given to the king on account of his great power, in which case his real name might have been Sīlava, as mentioned above. The scholiast on the Ekarāja Jātaka,[5] however, says that Ekarāja was the king's personal name.

1 J. iii. 13-15.
2 *E.g.*, BuA. 51; Mbv. 11.
3 No. xiv.
4 p. 205.
5 J. iii. 14.

2. **Ekarāja.**—King of **Pupphavatī** (Benares). He was the son of **Vasavatti** and the father of **Candakumāra.** For his story see the **Kaṇḍahāla Jātaka.**[1] He belonged to the **Koṇḍaññagotta.**[2]

1 J. vi. 131 ff.
2 *Ibid.*, 137.

Ekarāja Jātaka (No. 303).—The story of **Ekarāja** (*q.v.* 1). For the circumstances relating to the story see **Seyyaṃsa Jātaka.**

Ekavajjaka-Brahmadatta.—A king. He was extremely obliging, and would grant an interview to any who desired it, no matter what the circumstances. He always allowed the person interviewing him to do so unattended, and thence came to be known as **Ekavajjaka** ("going alone"). Once, two of his ministers quarrelled because they wanted to rule over the same district. The king, realising the evil effects of greed, developed insight and became a Pacceka Buddha. His verse is included in the **Khaggavisāṇa** Sutta.[1]

1 Sn. v. 40; SnA. i. 84 f.

Ekavandiya Thera.—An arahant. Thirty-one kappas ago he saw the Buddha **Vessabhū** and, with devout heart, worshipped him. Twenty-four kappas ago he was a king named **Vigatānanda.**[1]

1 Ap. i. 217.

1. **Ekavihāriya Thera.**—An arahant. In the time of **Kassapa** Buddha he entered the Order and dwelt in solitude. In this life, too, he was fond of dwelling alone.[1]

[1] Ap. ii. 390 f.

2. **Ekavihāriya.**—A monk greatly famed for his love of solitude. When they told the Buddha of him, the Buddha sang his praises in the midst of the assembly.[1]

[1] DhA. iii. 471 f.

3. **Ekavihāriya.**—See **Tissakumāra,** brother of Asoka.

Ekasaṅkhiya Thera.—An arahant. In the past, when a festival was being held in honour of **Vipassī's** Bodhi-tree, he blew a conch-shell for a whole day as homage to the Buddha. Seventy-one kappas ago he became a king named **Sudassana.**[1]

[1] Ap. ii. 391.

1. **Ekasaññaka Thera.**—An arahant. In the past he gave a meal to a monk named **Khaṇḍa,** a disciple of **Vessabhū** Buddha. Forty kappas ago he was a king named **Varuṇa.**[1] The *Apadāna Commentary* says he was given the name Ekasaññaka because in his last life he remembered his gift to Khaṇḍa.

[1] Ap. i. 121.

2. **Ekasaññaka Thera.**—An arahant. Thirty-one kappas ago he saw a rag-robe hanging in the forest, and gladdened by the sight worshipped it. Twenty-five kappas ago he was a king named **Amitābha.**[1]

[1] Ap. i. 210 f.

Ekasāṭaka.—A very poor brahmin who lived in the time of **Vipassī** Buddha. He was so called because he and his wife had, between them, only one upper garment, worn by whichever of them happened to be going out. The Buddha was in the habit of preaching every seven years. On one such occasion the brahmin listened to the Buddha's sermon, and being greatly pleased, wishing to make an offering, he gave the Buddha his upper garment after a hard mental struggle as to whether he could afford the gift. Having made the gift, he shouted with joy saying, "I have won." The king of the city, **Bandhumā,** having heard the shout and learnt the reason, gave to the brahmin various rich gifts, including the *sabbaṭṭhaka*,[1] all of which the latter presented to the Buddha, keeping, at the king's special request, a single pair of garments for himself and his wife. The king later made Ekasāṭaka his chaplain.[2]

Ekasāṭaka is given in the *Aṅguttara Commentary*[3] as a previous birth of the Elder **Mahā Kassapa.** The *Dhammapada Commentary*[4] mentions another brahmin, **Culla-Ekasāṭaka** by name. He is, however, stated as having lived in the time of Gotama Buddha, although the story related is, in most respects, identical with that given above, except that the king in the story of Culla-Ekasāṭaka is **Pasenadi,** king of Kosala. No mention is made of the brahmin being created *purohita.* Moreover, this brahmin received as gift only the *sabbacatukka* (groups of four) and not the *sabaṭṭhaka.* More important still, Culla Ekasāṭaka is identified with **Mahā Ekasāṭaka,** the latter being mentioned as having lived in the time of **Vipassī** Buddha. Here we evidently have a confusion of legends.

The story of Ekasāṭaka is related in the *Milindapañha*,[5] as one of seven cases in which an act of devotion received its reward in this very life.

[1] The *sabbaṭṭhaka* seems to have been a gift of various things in groups of eight: eight elephants, eight horses, eight thousand pieces of money, etc. (DhA. iii. 3); but see Mil. *Trs.* ii. 147, n. 1, where it is spoken of as an office.

[2] AA. i. 92 ff.; also ThagA. ii. 136.

[3] *loc. cit.*

[4] DhA. iii. 1 ff.

[5] pp. 115, 291.

Ekasālā.—A brahmin village in the **Kosala** kingdom. The Buddha once stayed there, and when a large congregation of the laity were listening to him, **Māra,** thinking to darken their intelligence, suggested to him that he should not teach others. The Buddha refuted the suggestion of Māra, who retired discomfited.[1]

[1] S. i. 111.

Ekassara.—A king of ninety-four kappas ago; a previous birth of **Kisalayapūjaka** Thera.[1]

[1] Ap. i. 200.

Ekāpassita.—Sixty-two kappas ago there were three kings of this name, all previous births of **Ālambanadāyaka** Thera.[1]

[1] Ap. i. 213.

Ekābhiñña Sutta.—See **Ekabījī.**

1. **Ekāsanadāyaka Thera.**—An arahant. In the time of **Padumuttara** Buddha he was an ascetic named **Nārada-Kassapa,** living near the

mountain **Kosika.** Once he saw the Buddha walking through the forest, and having provided him with a seat, spoke words in praise of him. The Buddha preached to him a short sermon. Fifty times **Ekāsanadāyaka** became king of the gods and eighty times he ruled over men. Wherever he wished he could find a seat, even in the forest or in a river.[1]

[1] Ap. ii. 381 f.

2. **Ekāsanadāyaka.**—A Thera. In the time of **Padumuttara,** he, with his wife, left the deva-world, and coming amongst men waited upon a monk named **Devala.**[1]

[1] Ap. i. 226.

Ekāsanadāyikā Therī.—An arahant. She is evidently identical with **Ubbirī** Therī (*q.v.* for her story of the past).

Ekāsanika Sutta.—On the five classes of monks who practise the *ekāsanikaṅga.*[1]

[1] A. iii. 220.

Ekāhavāpi.—One of the tanks built by **Parakkamabāhu I.**[1]

[1] Cv. lxxix. 28.

Ekuttara.—See **Aṅguttara.**

Ekuddāna (Ekuddāniya) Thera.—An arahant. He was the son of a wealthy brahmin of Sāvatthi, and being convinced of the Buddha's majesty, as seen at the presentation of the Jetavana, he entered the Order. He dwelt in the forest fulfilling his novitiate, and once came to the Buddha to learn of him. The Buddha, seeing **Sāriputta** near him wrapt in contemplation, uttered a stanza, that to the monk of lofty thoughts and heedful, sorrow comes not.[1] The monk learnt this stanza, and returning to the forest, ever and anon reflected on it. He thus came to be called Ekuddāniya. One day he obtained insight and became an arahant. Later, when **Ānanda** asked him to preach a sermon, it was this stanza that he took as his text.

We are told that in the time of **Atthadassī** Buddha he was a chief of the yakkhas, and when the Buddha died he went about lamenting that he had not made use of his opportunities. A disciple of the Buddha, named **Sāgara,** meeting him, advised him to make offering to the Buddha's thūpa. In **Kassapa's** time he was a householder, and heard the Buddha

[1] See *Dhammapada,* 259.

utter the stanza mentioned above. He entered the Order, and for twenty thousand years practised meditation, repeating the stanza, but gained no attainment.[2]

It is said[3] that on fast-days Ekuddāna, alone in the forest, sounded the call for the deities of the forest to attend the preaching of the Law, and uttered his stanza, whereupon the deities made loud applause. One fast-day two monks, versed in the Tipiṭaka, visited Ekuddāna with a retinue of five hundred each. Seeing them, Ekuddāna's heart was glad and he said: "Today we will listen to the Law." On being asked for an explanation, he described how, when the Dhamma was expounded, the forest grove was filled with the applause of devas. Thereupon one of the Elders recited the Dhamma and the other expounded it, but there was no sound. In order to dispel their doubts, Ekuddāna took his seat and pronounced his one stanza. The sound of the plaudits of the devas filled the forest. The Elders were greatly offended at the conduct of the devas and complained to the Buddha. The Buddha explained to them that the important thing was not the amount of knowledge but the quality of the understanding.

It it noteworthy that the verse, attributed above to Ekuddāniya, occurs in the *Vinaya*[4] as having been constantly used by **Cūlapanthaka.** Whenever it was his turn to preach to the nuns at Sāvatthi they expected no effective lesson, since he always repeated the same stanza, namely, that which is above attributed to Ekuddāniya. The thera, hearing of their remarks, forthwith gives an exhibition of his iddhi-power and of his knowledge of the Dhamma, thereby winning their tribute of admiration.

[2] ThagA. i. 153 f.; Thag. v. 68. [3] DhA, iii. 384 f. [4] Vin. iv. 54.

Ekūposathikā Therī.—Arahant. In the past she was a slave-girl, a water-carrier in the city of **Bandhumatī.** Seeing the King **Bandhumā** keeping the fast, she took the precepts herself and kept them well. Sixty-four times she became the queen of rulers in heaven, and was sixty-three times queen among men. Her complexion was always of a golden hue. In her last life she left the world at the age of seven, and attained arahantship within eight months.[1] She is probably identical with **Uttamā** Therī.[2]

[1] Ap. ii. 522 f. [2] See ThigA. 46 ff.

Ekūnavīsatipañha. The section of the **Mahā-Ummagga Jātaka** which deals with the nineteen questions solved by **Mahosadha** when the other wise men of the court had failed to unravel them.[1]

[1] J. vi. 334-45.

Ejā Sutta.—Two suttas on the evils of passion (*ejā*) and the ways of getting rid of it.[1]

[1] S. iv. 64-6.

Eṇikūla.—See **Eṇī.** The scholiast to the *Jātaka*[1] explains the name in the following way: "*Eṇiyā nāma nadiyā kūle.*"

[1] J. iii. 361.

Eṇijaṅgha Sutta.—One of the suttas in the *Devatā-Saṃyutta*. A deva asks the Buddha how it is possible to wander indifferent to the calls of sense, limbed like the antelope (*eṇi*) or the lion. The Buddha answers, by getting rid of the desires of sense.[1]

[1] S. i. 16.

Eṇiphassā.—A name, either of some kind of musical instrument or, more probably, of a class of celestial musicians who waited on **Sakka** and his queens.[1]

[1] Vv. xviii. 11; l. 26; VvA. 94, 211; for explanation see 372.

Eṇī.—A river. According to the **Bakabrahma Jātaka** (*q.v.*), one of **Baka's** good deeds which brought him rebirth in the Brahma-world was that of having set free the inhabitants of a village on the banks of the Eṇī (*Eṇikūle*), when the village was raided. Baka was then an ascetic named **Kesava** and the Bodhisatta was his disciple **Kappa.**[1]

[1] S. i. 143; J. iii. 361; SA. i. 163.

Etadagga Vagga.—The fourteenth chapter of the *Eka Nipāta* of the *Aṅguttara Nikāya*. It contains the names of the Buddha's disciples, men and women, each distinguished by some special qualification.[1]

[1] A. i. 23-6.

"Etaṃ-mama" Sutta.—On how the view arises: "This is mine, this am I."[1]

[1] S. iii. 181.

Eraka Thera.—An arahant. He was the son of an eminent family of Sāvatthi. He had many advantages over others, among them beauty and charm. His parents married him to a suitable wife but, because it was his last life, he sought the Buddha. After hearing the Buddha preach he left the world, but for several days he was overcome by evil thoughts. The Buddha thereupon admonished him in a verse, and Eraka gained arahantship.[1]

In the time of **Siddhattha** Buddha he was a householder. One day he saw the Buddha and, having nothing to give, cleaned the road along which the Buddha walked and stood looking at him with clasped hands. Fifty-seven kappas ago he was a king named **Suppabuddha.**

He is probably identical with **Maggadāyaka** Thera of the *Apadāna*.[2]

[1] Thag. v. 93; ThagA. i. 192 f.; for the name see *Brethren*, p. 86, n. 2.
[2] Ap. i. 173.

Erakaccha.—A city in the country of the **Dasaṇṇas.** It was the residence of the banker **Dhanapālaka.**[1] **Isidāsī** was once reborn there as a wealthy craftsman, a worker in gold.[2]

[1] Pv. 20; PvA. 99 ff. [2] Thig. 435; see also *Buddhist India*, p. 40.

Erakapatta.—A Nāga king. In the time of **Kassapa** Buddha he was a monk. One day, while in a boat, he grasped an *eraka*-leaf, and through his failing to let go, the leaf was broken off. Though he practised meditation for twenty thousand years in the forest, at the moment of his death he thought of the lapse with great remorse and was reborn in the Nāga-world as large as a dug-out canoe, much to his grief and despair. When a daughter was born to him he taught her a song and, once a fortnight, he appeared with her on the surface of the Ganges, where she danced on his hood and sang the song. She was offered in marriage to anyone who could sing a reply to her song. Erakapatta hoped thereby to become aware of it when a Buddha should appear in the world. Many suitors came, and an interval between two Buddhas passed and still no one was successful. At last a young brahmin, **Uttara** (*q.v.*), well-schooled for the task by the Buddha, appeared before the Nāga-maiden and answered all her questions. (Uttara himself became a *sotāpanna* when he finished learning his lesson from the Buddha.) Erakapatta at once knew that a Buddha had come, and asked Uttara to take him to the Teacher. At the sight of the Buddha, Erakapatta was seized with great sorrow on account of his condition, but the Buddha preached to him and consoled him. It is said that the Nāga king would have attained the Fruit of Conversion had it not been for his animal nature.[1]

[1] DhA. iii. 230-6.

Erakāvilla.—A village in **Rohaṇa** in Ceylon where King **Mahāsena** built a vihāra after destroying a temple of the unbelievers.[1]

[1] Mhv. xxxvii. 41; MṬ. 685.

Eraṇḍagalla.—A tank built by **Vijayabāhu I.**[1]

[1] Cv. lx. 49.

Erāpatha.—A royal family of Nāgas, mentioned together with **Virūpakkhas, Chabbyāputtas,** and **Kaṇhagotamakas,** all of them described as "Nāgarājakulāni."[1] For their own protection, monks are advised to fill their hearts with amity for these four classes of Nāgas.[2]

[1] J. ii. 145.

[2] A. ii. 72; Vin. ii. 109 f.

1. **Erāvaṇa.**—**Sakka's** elephant. He was once the elephant of the king of Magadha, who gave him to **Māgha** and his companions to help them in their good works on earth. As a result, when Magha and the others were reborn in **Tāvatiṃsa,** Erāvaṇa was born there himself and became their companion. Ordinarily he was a deva like the others, because there are no animals in the deva-world, but when they went to the park to play, Erāvaṇa assumed the form of an elephant, one hundred and fifty leagues in size. For the thirty-three devas Erāvaṇa erected thirty-three heads (*kumbha*), each two or three quarters of a league in girth. Each head had seven tusks, each fifty leagues long, each tusk bore seven lotus plants, each plant seven flowers, each flower seven leaves, and on each leaf danced seven nymphs (**Padumaccharā**). For Sakka himself there was a special head, **Sudassana,** thirty leagues around, above it a canopy of twelve leagues all of precious stones. In the centre was a jewelled couch one league long, on which Sakka reclined in state.[1]

In the **Dhammika Sutta**[2] Erāvaṇa is mentioned among the devas who visited the Buddha to pay him homage. He is also mentioned among the Nāgas present at the preaching of the **Mahāsamaya Sutta.**[3] It is emphasised in several places[4] that Erāvaṇa is a devaputta and a Nāga only by birth (*jātiyā*). The *Jātakas*[5] mention Sakka as riding Erāvaṇa, particularly when making comparisons between kings parading on the backs of elephants.[6] Erāvaṇa is one of the chief features of Tāvatiṃsa.[7]

[1] DhA. i. 273 f.; also SnA. i. 368 f. (where there are a few slight variations).

[2] Sn. v. 379.

[3] D. ii. 258; perhaps here a king of snakes is meant, because he is mentioned with others who are avowedly snakes.

[4] *E.g.*, MA. i. 472; DA. ii. 688; also VvA. 15 and Kvu. ii. 599.

[5] J. v. 137.

[6] *E.g.*, *Ibid.*, iii. 392.

[7] *Ibid.*, vi. 278.

2. **Erāvaṇa.**—The name of the elephant belonging to **Candakumāra** (*q.v.*).[1]

[1] J. vi. 147.

Erāhuḷu.—A locality in Ceylon, near which an engagement took place between the forces of **Parakkamabahu I.** and his foes.[1] It is identified with the present district Eravur, north-west of Batticaloa.[2]

[1] Cv. lxxiv. 91. [2] Cv. *Trs.* ii. 30, n. 3.

Erukkaṭṭa (Erukkhāvūra).—A village in South India, occupied by **Kulasekhara** in his fight with the Sinhalese forces under **Laṅkāpura.**[1]

[1] Cv. lxxvi. 149, 167.

Eḷakamāra.—King of Benares. The king of **Kosala** invaded his father's kingdom and, having killed the king, took away the queen, who was pregnant. When the child was born he was cast into the cemetery lest he should be slain by the Kosala king. The boy was discovered by a goatherd and brought up as his son, but from the day of the boy's arrival in the goatherd's home, the latter's animals began to die off. He was therefore named Eḷakamāra ("Goat's Bane"). The goatherd, thereupon, put him into a pot and cast him into the river, where he was picked up by a low-caste mender of old rubbish and adopted as his son. When he grew up the boy went to the palace with his father, and there the princess **Kuraṅgavī,** of great beauty, fell in love with him. The servants discovered them guilty of illicit relations and reported them to the king. When the lad was about to be put to death for his misdemeanour, the queen, possessed by the spirit of Eḷakamāra's dead father, who had been born as his guardian angel, confessed that he was no mere outcaste, but the son of the king of Benares. The Kosala king restored to Eḷakamāra his father's inheritance and married him to Kuraṅgavī. **Chalaṅgakumāra** was given to him as his teacher, and was later appointed commander-in-chief.

Kuraṅgavī misbehaved with Chalaṅgakumāra as well as with his servant, **Dhanantevāsī.**[1]

The story of Eḷakamāra was one of the stories mentioned by **Kuṇāla** in his famous sermon on the frailty of women.[2]

[1] J. v. 430 ff. [2] *Ibid.*, 424.

Eḷāra.—King of **Anurādhapura** (145-101 B.C.) He was a native of Coḷa, and having come to Ceylon, overpowered the reigning king, **Asela,** and captured the throne. The *Mahāvaṃsa* says[1] that he ruled with "even justice towards friend and foe," and many stories are related showing his love of fairness and his kindness. Although an unbeliever, he paid the greatest respect to Buddhism, and he is credited with having persuaded the gods, by his determination, to send rain over his kingdom

[1] xxi. 14 f.

only at convenient times. Eḷāra had a general named **Mitta**[2]; the chief of his forces was **Dīghajantu,** while his royal elephant was called **Mahāpabbata.** In the great battle between Eḷāra's forces and the Sinhalese soldiers under **Duṭṭhagāmaṇī,** Eḷāra was slain in single contest with the latter. In recognition of the dead king's chivalry, great honours were paid to him at his funeral and a monument was erected over his ashes. For many generations all music was stopped while passing the monument as a mark of respect to the honoured dead.[3]

According to the *Mahāvaṃsa Ṭīkā,*[4] a shrine was erected on the spot where Eḷāra's ashes were buried, and it was called the **Eḷārapaṭimāghara.** It was to the south of Anurādhapura, beyond the potters' village.

[2] *Ibid.*, xxiii. 4. [3] *Ibid.*, xxv. 54-74; Dpv. xviii. 49 ff. [4] p. 349.

Eḷeyya.—A rājā, probably of **Magadha.** He was a devout follower of **Uddaka-Rāmaputta.** In his retinue were **Yamaka, Moggalla, Ugga, Nāvindaki, Gandhabba,** and **Aggivessa,** all of whom were also followers of the same teacher.[1]

[1] A. ii. 180 f.

Esanā Sutta.—A group of suttas on the three kinds of longing (*esanā*): the longing for sensual delights, for becoming, for the holy life. These are spoken of in relation to the Noble Eightfold Path.[1] The same is repeated for (1) the seven *bojjhaṅgas,*[2] (2) the four *satipaṭṭhānas,*[3] (3) the *indriyas,*[4] (4) the five *balas,*[5] (5) the *iddhipādas,*[6] and (6) the *jhānas.*[7]

[1] S. v. 54 f.
[2] *Ibid.*, 136.
[3] 191.
[4] 240, 242.
[5] 250, 252.
[6] 291.
[7] 309.

Esikā.—A country in **Jambudīpa. Paṇṇakata** was a city of Esikā, and in it was born one of the women described in the **Caturitthivimāna** (*q.v.*).[1]

[1] Vv. 42; VvA. 195.

1. **Esukārī.**—A brahmin who visits the Buddha at Jetavana and asks him various questions on castes and their distinctions, from the point of view of their functions. The Buddha replies that birth's invidious bar has been laid down by the brahmins, without consulting anybody else; all four castes alike can live the good life, which is the true service, and follow the Dhamma, which is the true wealth. At the end of the discourse Esukārī declares himself to be a follower of the Buddha.[1]

[1] M. ii. 177 ff.

2. **Esukārī.**—King of Benares. He and his chaplain were great friends; neither of them had any sons. They agreed that if either of them should have a son the possessions of both should be given to him. By the intercession of a tree-sprite the chaplain had four sons—**Hatthipāla, Assapāla, Gopāla,** and **Ajapāla.** But when they grew up, one after the other, they renounced the world, and were later joined by the chaplain and the king, with all their retinues.

Esukārī was a previous birth of **Suddhodana.**

The story is related in the **Hatthipāla Jātaka.**[1]

[1] J. iv. 473 ff.

Esukārī Sutta.—Records the conversation between the brahmin **Esukārī** (*q.v.*) and the Buddha.[1]

[1] M. ii. 177 ff.

"Eso me attā" Sutta.—On the view "this is the self, it is permanent," etc.[1]

[1] S. iii. 182.

O

Okāsalokasūdanī.—A work by an anonymous author, mentioned in the *Gandhavaṃsa.*[1] It seems to have also been called **Okāsaloka.**[2]

[1] p. 62. [2] p. 72.

Okilini-Sapattaṅgārakokiri Sutta.—The story of a peta mentioned in the *Lakkhaṇa Saṃyutta.* She was seen going through the air, parched and sooty, uttering cries of distress. **Moggallāna** declares[1] that she had once been the head queen of a king of **Kaliṅga.** One day, seeing the king show fondness for a dancer who was massaging him, she was moved with jealousy and scattered a brazier of coals over the woman's head.

[1] S. ii. 260; SA. ii. 163.

Okkantika Saṃyutta.—The twenty-fifth division of the *Saṃyutta Nikāya,* and the fourth section of the *Khandha Vagga.*[1]

[1] S. iii. 225-8.

Okkalā.—The people of **Okkalajanapada**[1]; mentioned also in the *Apadāna*[2] in a list of tribes.

See **Ukkalā.**

[1] MA. ii. 894. [2] ii. 359.

1. **Okkāka.**—A king, ancestor of the **Sākyas** and the **Kolians.** In the **Ambaṭṭha Sutta**[1] it is stated that Okkāka, being fond of his queen and wishing to transfer the kingdom to her son, banished from the kingdom the elder princes by another wife. These princes were named **Okkāmukha, Karakaṇḍa, Hatthinika,** and **Sinipura.**[2] They lived on the slopes of the Himālaya and, consorting with their sisters and their descendants, formed the Sākyan race. The legend, thus briefly given, is enlarged on with great detail in the Commentaries. According to Buddhaghosa, there are three dynasties with a king named Okkāka at the head of each, all of them lineal descendants of the primeval king, **Mahāsammata,** and in the line of succession of **Makādeva.**

The Okkāka of the third dynasty had five queens—**Bhattā, Cittā, Jantū, Jālinī** and **Visākhā**—each with five hundred female attendants. The eldest queen had four sons—mentioned above—and five daughters—**Piyā, Suppiyā, Ānandā, Vijitā** and **Vijitasenā.**[3]

When Bhattā died, after the birth of these nine children, the king married another young and beautiful princess and made her the chief queen. Her son was **Jantu,** and being pleased with him, the king promised her a boon. She claimed the kingdom for her son, and this was the reason for the exile of the elder children.[4] The *Mahāvaṃsa*[5] mentions among Okkāka's descendants, **Nipuṇa, Candimā, Candamukha, Sivisañjaya, Vessantara, Jāli, Sīhavāhana** and **Sīhassara.** The last named had eighty-four thousand descendants, the last of whom was **Jayasena.** His son **Sīhahanu** was the grandfather of the Buddha. The *Dīpavaṃsa*[6] list resembles this very closely.

Okkāka had a slave-girl called **Disā,** who gave birth to a black baby named, accordingly, **Kaṇha.** He was the ancestor of the **Kaṇhāyanas,** of which race the **Ambaṭṭha**-clan was an offshoot. Later, Kaṇha became a mighty sage and, by his magic power, won in marriage **Maddarūpī,** another daughter of Okkāka.[7]

According to the **Brāhmaṇadhammika Sutta,**[8] it was during the time of Okkāka that the brahmins started their practice of slaughtering animals for sacrifice. Till then there had been only three diseases in the world—desire, hunger and old age ; but from this time onwards the enraged devas afflicted humans with various kinds of suffering.

[1] D. i. 92.

[2] The *Mahāvastu* (which confuses Ikṣvāku with his ancestor Sujāta) mentions five sons of Ikṣvāku: Opura, Ulkāmukha, Karaṇḍaka, Hastikaśīrsa and Nipura (i. 348). See also Rockhill, p. 9 ff.

[3] The Mtu. calls them Śuddhā, Vimalā, Vijitā, Jālā and Jālī.

[4] DA. i. 258 f.; SnA. i. 352 f.

[5] ii. 12-16.

[6] iii. 41-5.

[7] D. i. 93, 96.

[8] Sn. p. 52 ff.; AA. ii. 737.

It is said[9] that the name Okkāka was given to the king because when he spoke light issued from his mouth like a torch (*kathanakāle ukkā viya mukhato pabhā niccharati*).

Although the Sanskritised form of the Pāli name is Ikṣavāku, it is unlikely that Okkāka is identical with the famous Ikṣavāku of the *Purāṇas*, the immediate son of Manu, son of the Sun. The Pāli is evidently more primitive, as is shown by the form Okkāmukha, and the name Ikṣavāku looks like a deliberate attempt at accommodation to the Purānic account.[10]

According to the *Mahāvastu*, Ikṣavāku was the king of the Kosalas and his capital was **Sāketa**—*i.e.* Ayodhyā. See also *s.v.* **Sākya.**

The *Cūlavaṃsa* mentions among Okkāka's descendants, **Mahātissa, Sagara** and **Sāhasamalla** (*q.v.*).

[9] DA. i. 258. [10] For discussion see Thomas, *op. cit.*, p. 6.

2. **Okkāka.**—King of **Kusāvatī** in the **Malla** country. He had sixteen thousand wives, the chief of whom was **Sīlavatī.** As a result of her consorting with Sakka, two sons were born, **Kusa** and **Jayampati.** The story is related in the **Kusa Jātaka.**[1]

[1] J. v. 278 ff.

Okkāmukha.—King of **Kapilavatthu.** He was an ancestor of the Sākyans and the eldest son of **Okkāka** (*q.v.*) and his queen **Bhattā** (or **Hatthā**).

Ogadha or **Saṭayha Sutta.**—An Ariyan disciple who is possessed of unwavering loyalty to the Buddha, the Dhamma and the Saṅgha, is bound to win, in time, to the bliss in which the holy life is steeped (*ogadha*).[1]

[1] S. v. 343 f. For the name see KS. v. 298, n. 1.

Ogāḷha or **Kulagharaṇī Sutta.**—A certain monk living in a forest tract in Kosala was held in very high esteem (*ajjhogāḷhappatto*) by a certain family. A deva of the forest, wishing to urge him to greater effort, went to the monk in the guise of the housewife (*kulagharaṇī*) of the family, and asked him why it was that people spent their time in endless talk. Was he not disturbed by it? The monk answered that a recluse should not be disturbed by other people's talk.[1] The *Commentary*[2] explains that the monk was already an arahant, but the devatā did not know it and could not therefore understand why he spent his

[1] S. i. 201. [2] SA. i. 227.

time in visiting householders, hence her question wishing to make him live in solitude.

Ogha Vagga.—Several chapters in the *Saṃyutta Nikāya* are called by this name; thus, in the *Magga Saṃyutta* (S. v. 59), the *Bojjhaṅga* (v. 136, 139), the *Satipaṭṭhāna* (v. 191), the *Indriya* (v. 241, 242), the *Sammappadhāna* (v. 247), the *Bala* (v. 251, 253), the *Iddhipāda* (v. 292) and the *Jhāna* (v. 309).

1. **Ogha Sutta.**—A deva visits the Buddha at Jetavana and asks him how he crossed the "Flood." "Unstayed and unstriving," answers the Buddha. The deva is puzzled by the answer, until it is explained to him that a wrong support of footing and misdirected effort are as fatal as drowning straight away. The deva expresses his adoration of the Buddha.[1] The *Commentary*[2] adds that the deva was conceited, thinking he knew all about the saintship of a Buddha, hence the enigmatic reply, in order to puzzle him (*v.l.* **Oghataraṇa Sutta**).

[1] S. i. 1. [2] SA. i. 14.

2. **Ogha Sutta.**—**Sāriputta** explains to **Jambukhādaka** the four floods: of sensual desire, of becoming, of wrong views, of ignorance.[1]

[1] S. iv. 257 f.

3. **Ogha Sutta.**—**Sāriputta** explains the four floods to **Sāmaṇḍaka.**[1]

[1] S. iv. 261 f.

4. **Ogha Sutta.**—The Buddha instructs the monks on the four floods.[1]

[1] S. v. 59.

Oghātaka.—A poor brahmin of **Kosala,** father of **Muttā** Therī.[1]

[1] ThigA. 14.

Ojadīpa.—The name given to Ceylon in the time of **Kakusandha** Buddha. Its capital was **Abhayanagara** and its king **Abhaya.** The Buddha visited Ojadīpa and occupied the **Mahātittha** garden.[1] Its mountain was **Devakūṭa,** the modern **Piḷayakūṭa.**[2]

[1] Mhv. xv. 57 ff.; Dpv. i. 73; ix. 20; xvii. 5, 16, 23; xv. 35-8; Sp. i. 83.
[2] Mbv. 126.

Ojasī.—Servant of **Kuvera.** He takes Kuvera's messages and makes them known in **Uttarakuru.**[1]

[1] D. iii. 201; DA. iii. 967.

Ojita.—One of the two merchants, the other being **Ujita,** leaders of caravans, who gave the first meal to **Sikhī** Buddha after his Enlightenment.[1] They correspond to **Tapassu** and **Bhallika** in the account of **Gotama** Buddha.

[1] ThagA. i. 48.

Oṭṭabhāsā.—One of the eighteen languages prevalent in the world, none of which are suited for the proclamation of the Dhamma.[1]

[1] VibhA. 388.

Oṭṭhaddha.—One of the **Licchavis.** His personal name (*mūla-nāma*) was **Mahāli,** but he was called Oṭṭhaddha because he had a hare-lip (*aḍḍhoṭṭhatāya*).[1] He went to visit the Buddha at the **Kūṭāgārasālā** in Vesalī, at a time when the Buddha had given orders that no one should be allowed to see him; but through the intervention of the novice **Sīha,** Oṭṭhaddha was admitted to the Buddha's presence with a large retinue of followers, all splendidly adorned in various ways, though it is stated that earlier in the day they had taken the *uposatha*-vows. The conversation that took place between Oṭṭhaddha and the Buddha is recorded in the **Mahāli Sutta.**[2] Buddhaghosa calls Oṭṭhaddha a rājā.

[1] DA. i. 310. [2] D. i. 150 ff.

Oḍḍaka.—A name of a tribe, occurring in a list of tribes.[1]

[1] Ap. ii. 358.

Oṇata Sutta.—On four classes of people in the world: the low and low, the high and high, the high and low, and the low and high.[1] The *Commentary* explains that each person is such and such but may, or will, become such and such.

[1] A. ii. 86; also found at Pug. 52 and Pug. 7.

Otturāmallaka.—The chieftain of **Dhanumaṇḍala** who was brought under subjection by the general **Rakkha.**[1]

[1] Cv. lxx. 17, 18, 28.

Odakā Sutta.—Numerous are those that are born in water compared with those born on land. This is on account of their ignorance of the four Ariyan truths.[1]

[1] S. v. 467.

Odātagayhā.—A class of eminent devas (described as *pāmokkhā*), among those present at the preaching of the **Mahāsamaya Sutta.**[1]

[1] D. ii. 260.

Odumbaragāma.—A tank built by **Parakkamabāhu I.**[1]

[1] Cv. lxviii. 48.

Odumbaraṅgana.—A village given by **Jeṭṭhatissa III.** to the Padhānaghara at the **Mahānāga** Vihāra.[1]

[1] Cv. xliv. 97.

1. **Opamañña.**—One of the names of **Pokkharasāti.**[1] He was so called because the name of his family (*gotta*) was **Upamañña.**[2]

[1] M. ii. 200. [2] MA. ii. 804.

2. **Opamañña.**—A Gandhabba chieftain, who was among those present at the preaching of the **Mahāsamaya Sutta.**[1] He is mentioned in the **Āṭānātiya Sutta,**[2] in a list of eminent yakkha generals.

[1] D. ii. 258. [2] *Ibid.*, iii. 204.

Opamma Saṃyutta.—The twentieth section of the *Saṃyutta Nikāya*, so called because it is rich in parables (*opamma*).[1]

[1] S. ii. 262 ff.

Oparakkhī.—One of the four wives of **Candakumāra** (*q.v.*).[1]

[1] J. vi. 148.

Opavuyha Thera.—An arahant. In the past he offered an *ājāniya*-horse to the Buddha **Padumuttara,** but the Buddha's chief disciple, **Devala,** informed him that the Buddha could not accept the gift. Thereupon he gave other suitable gifts to the value of the horse. Twenty-eight times he was king of all Jambudīpa. Thirty-four kappas ago he was a cakkavatti of great power.[1]

[1] Ap. i. 106 f.

Opasāda.—A brahmin village in **Kosala,** the residence of **Caṅkī,** who lived in royal fief granted to him by **Pasenadi.** To the north of the village was a forest of *sāla*-trees where oblations were offered to various deities. The Buddha once stayed here in the course of his wanderings.[1]

[1] M. ii. 164.

Obhāsa Sutta.—Of the four brilliances—those of the sun, the moon, fire, and wisdom—the brilliance of wisdom is the chief.[1]

[1] A. ii. 139 f.

1. **Orambhāgiya Sutta.**—The five fetters concerned with the lower stages of existence: *sakkāyadiṭṭhi, vicikicchā,* etc. They could be destroyed by developing the Noble Eightfold Way.[1]

[1] S. v. 61.

2. **Orambhāgiya Sutta.**—The five lower fetters could be destroyed by practising the four *satipaṭṭhānas.*[1]

[1] A. iv. 459.

Orima Sutta.—On the hither and the further shores—*e.g.*, false belief (*micchādiṭṭhi*)—is the hither shore and its opposite (*sammādiṭṭhi*), the further shore.[1]

[1] A. v. 233.

Ovāda Vagga.—The third section of the *Pācittiya* rules in the *Suttavibhaṅga.*[1]

[1] Vin. iv. 49-69; also v. 16-18.

Ovāda Sutta.—The Buddha explains to **Ānanda,** in answer to a question, the eight qualities necessary in a monk in order for him to be appointed spiritual adviser to his fellows.[1]

[1] A. iv. 279 f.

Orittiyūrutombama.—A locality in South India.[1]

[1] Cv. lxxvi. 299.

Olandā.—The name given in the *Cūlavaṃsa* to the Dutch in Ceylon.[1]

[1] See Cv. Index.

Osadha.—See **Mahosadha.**

1. **Osadhī.**—The morning star, used in describing typical whiteness (*odātā, odātavaṇṇā,* etc.),[1] and also great brightness and purity (*parisuddha-Osadhītārakā viya*).[2] Buddhaghosa[3] says that it is so called because, when it appears in the sky, people gather medicines and drink them by its sign. (*Sukkā tārakā tassā udayato paṭṭhāya tena saññāṇena osadhāni gaṇhanti pi pivanti pi : tasmā Osadhī tārakā ti vuccati.*)

The *Itivuttaka Commentary*[4] gives another explanation: that it contains bright rays of light, and that it gives efficacy to various medicines (*ussannā pabhā etāya dhīyati osadhīnaṃ vā anubalappadāyikattā Osadhī*).

[1] D. ii. 111.

[2] It. 20; MA. ii. 638, 772; also Vsm. ii. 412.

[3] MA. ii. 714.

[4] ItA. 72.

It is also used in similes to typify constancy, like the star Osadhī, which, in all seasons, keeps to the same path and never deviates therefrom (*sabbautusu attano gamanavīthiṃ vijahitvā aññāya vīthiyā na gacchati sakavīthiyā va gacchati*).[5]

[5] BuA. 89.

2. **Osadhī.**—The city at the gates of which **Anomadassī** Buddha performed the Twin-Miracle[1] and, therefore, a former name of **Saṅkassa** (*q.v.*).

[1] BuA. 143.

K

1. **Kaṃsa.**—Another name, according to the scholiast,[1] for **Brahmadatta,** king of Benares and father of **Samuddajā.**

[1] J. vi. 198 (25).

2. **Kaṃsa.**—King of Benares, and called **Bārāṇasiggaha** because he was ruler of Benares. According to the **Seyya Jātaka,**[1] he was the king who was seized by the monarch of Kosala, owing to the treachery of a disloyal courtier, and who was later set free on account of his great piety. In the **Ekarāja Jātaka,** which purports to relate the same story, and again in the **Mahāsīlava Jātaka,** the king is referred to by other names. We probably have here a confusion of legends due to an effort to make three similar stories into one and the same.

It is probably this same Kaṃsa Bārāṇasiggaha who is referred to in the **Tesakuṇa Jātaka,** by the owl **Vessantara.**[2] There the scholiast explains Bārāṇasiggaha as *catūhi saṅgahavatthūhi Bārāṇasiṃ gahetvā vattanto.*

[1] J. ii. 403. [2] J. v. 112.

3. **Kaṃsa.**—Son of **Mahākaṃsa** and brother of **Upakaṃsa** and **Devagabbhā.** Later he became king of **Asitañjana** in **Kaṃsabhoga** in the **Uttarāpatha.** He was killed by **Vasudeva,** one of the **Andhakaveṇhudāsaputtā.**[1]

[1] J. iv. 79 f.

Kaṃsabhoga.—A division of **Uttarāpatha,** its capital being **Asitañjana,** where **Mahākaṃsa** and his successors ruled.[1]

[1] J. iv. 79; PvA. 111.

Kaṃsavaṃsa.—The race of **Mahākaṃsa**; this race was destroyed by the sons of **Devagabbhā.**[1]

[1] J. iv. 79.

Kakacūpama Sutta.—The twenty-first sutta of the *Majjhima Nikāya*, preached to **Moliya-Phagguna,** who was reported to the Buddha for frequenting the society of nuns and losing his temper when reproached therefor. A monk should not give way to anger even though he be sawn limb from limb with a two-handed saw (*ubhatodaṇḍakena kakacena*). The name of the sutta was given by the Buddha himself.[1]

The sutta contains the story of the lady of Sāvatthi, called **Videhikā,** who had a reputation for gentleness until tested by her servant girl and found wanting. The saw is only one of numerous similes which occur in the discourse. It is quoted in the **Mahāhatthipadopama Sutta,**[2] and is elsewhere[3] given as an example of a sutta preached on account of someone's lack of patience.

[1] M. i. 122 ff. [2] *Ibid.*, 189. [3] *E.g.*, DA. i. 123.

Kakaṇṭaka Jātaka.—The same as the Kakaṇṭaka-Pañha (*q.v.*).

Kakaṇṭaka Pañha.—The story, mentioned in the **Mahāummaga Jātaka,**[1] of the chameleon to whom the king gave one halfpenny's worth of meat a day for having shown him deference. One fast-day there was no meat to be had, and the man who supplied it tied the money round the chameleon's neck. The next time the animal saw the king it refused to salute him, because it felt itself to be his equal on account of the wealth round its neck.

[1] J. vi. 346 f.

Kakaṇṭaka Vagga.—The fifteenth chapter of the *Ekanipāta* of the *Jātakaṭṭhakathā.*[1]

[1] J. i. 487-511.

Kakuṭṭhā (Kakutthā, Kukuṭṭhā). A river near **Kusinārā** in which the Buddha bathed and from which he drank water before entering Kusinārā for his *parinibbāna.* On its bank was a mango-grove where the Buddha rested awhile on a robe spread for him by **Cundaka**; there he reassured Cunda, telling him that no blame attached to him for having provided the Buddha with the meal which was to be his last.[1] It is said[2] that when the Buddha bathed in the river, its banks and all the fishes it contained became golden.

[1] D. ii. 129, 134 f.; Ud. viii. 5; UdA. 402 f. [2] DA. ii. 571.

1. **Kakudha** (*v.l.* **Kakkaṭa**).—A lay disciple of the Buddha who dwelt at **Nādikā.** When the Buddha arrived at Nādikā on his last journey, **Ānanda** asked him what had happened to Kakudha, who was already dead. The Buddha replied that Kakudha had found birth in the highest heavens, there to pass away entirely.[1]

[1] D. ii. 92.

2. **Kakudha.**—A deva. He visited the Buddha at the **Añjanavana** in **Sāketa,** and asked him whether he experienced feelings of pleasure and sorrow. The Buddha replied that he had overcome such feelings and was utterly free, whereupon Kakudha uttered his praises.[1] The *Commentary*[2] says that this Kakudha was a Brahmā and that he was an attendant of **Moggallāna,** thus identifying him with Kakudha (3 below). He lived with the thera in his youth, died in a Jhāna-trance and was reborn in the Brahma-world.

[1] S. i. 54 f. [2] SA. i. 89.

3. **Kakudha.**—Probably identical with **Kakudha** (2). He was an inhabitant of **Koḷiya** and was an attendant of **Moggallāna.** Having died, he was reborn among the mind-born (*Manomaya*) devas and his form was so great that it was as extensive as " two of three common rice-fields in a Magadha village, and yet so constituted that he was in the way neither of himself nor of others." Becoming aware of **Devadatta's** plans for obtaining possession of the leadership of the Saṅgha, Kakudha reported the news to Moggallāna, who passed it on to the Buddha. The Buddha asked Moggallāna to keep the matter secret. Moggallāna informed the Buddha that he knew from experience that Kakudha's predictions proved true.[1]

[1] Vin. ii. 185 f.

4. **Kakudha.**—A Pacceka Buddha of thirty-one kappas ago, to whom **Uddāladāyaka** Thera, in a previous birth, gave a flower.[1]

[1] Ap. i. 225.

5. **Kakudha.**—A bird in the time of **Padumuttara** Buddha and a previous birth of **Malitavambha** Thera. The bird gave the Buddha a lotus[1]. *v.l.* **Kukkuṭṭha.**

[1] ThagA. i. 211; Ap. i. 180.

6. **Kakudha Kaccāna.**—See **Pakudha Kaccāna.**

7. **Kakudha.**—A little pond in **Mahāmeghavana** between the site of the **Mahā-Thūpa** and the **Thūpārāma.** The Mahā-Thūpa was at the upper end of the pond, and the spot had been consecrated by the visit of the four Buddhas of the present kappa.[1] **Lañjatissa** appears to have filled up the pond at great expense, the land around having become water-logged.[2] The bund (*pāli*) of the pond formed part of the *Sīmā* at **Anurādhapura.**[3]

[1] Mhv. xv. 53 ff. [2] *Ibid.*, xxxiii. 23 f; MṬ. 611. [3] Mbv. 135 f.

Kakudha Vagga.—The tenth chapter of the *Pañcaka Nipāta* of the *Aṅguttara Nikāya.*[1]

[1] A. iii. 118-26.

1. **Kakudha Sutta.**—Records the visit of the deva **Kakudha Koḷiyaputta** to **Moggallāna,** bringing him news of **Devadatta's** intention to destroy the Order. The sutta also contains a description of the five kinds of teachers who are impure in their conduct, their mode of livelihood, their preaching of the Dhamma, their system of exposition and their insight, and who yet are protected by their disciples because of love of gain.[1]

[1] A. iii. 122 ff.

2. **Kakudha Sutta.**—Records the visit of the devaputta **Kakudha** to the Buddha at the **Añjanavana** in **Sāketa.** See **Kakudha** (2).

Kakusandha.—The twenty-second of the twenty-four Buddhas and the first of the five Buddhas of the present **Bhaddakappa.** He was the son of the brahmin **Aggidatta,** chaplain of **Khemaṅkara,** king of **Khemavatī,** and **Visākhā.** He was born in the Khema pleasaunce, and lived for four thousand years in the household in three palaces—**Ruci, Suruci** and **Vaḍḍhana** (or **Rativaḍḍhana**). His wife was **Virocamānā** (or **Rocaṇī**), and he had a son, **Uttara.** He left the world riding in a chariot, and practised austerities for only eight months. Before his Enlightenment, he was given a meal of milk-rice by the daughter of the brahmin **Vajirindha** of the village **Sucirindha,** and grass for his seat by the yavapālaka **Subhadda.** His bodhi was a *Sirīsa*-tree, and his first sermon was preached to eighty-four thousand monks in the park near the city of **Makila.** He performed the Twin-Miracle under a *Sāla*-tree at the gates of **Kaṇṇakujja.** Among his converts was a fierce yakkha named **Naradeva.** He held only one assembly of his monks.• Kakusandha's body was forty cubits in height, and he died at the age of forty thousand years in the Khema pleasaunce. The thūpa erected over his relics was one league high.

The Bodhisatta was at that time a king named **Khema.** The Buddha's chief disciples were **Vidhura** and **Sañjīva** among monks, and **Sāmā** and **Campā** among nuns. His personal attendant was **Buddhija. Accuta** and **Samana, Nandā** and **Sunandā** were his most eminent lay-supporters.[1] Kakusandha kept the fast-day (*uposatha*) every year.[2] In Kakusandha's time a Māra, named **Dūsī** (a previous birth of **Moggallāna**), gave a great deal of trouble to the Buddha and his followers, trying greatly the Buddha's patience.[3] The *Saṃyutta Nikāya*[4] mentions that during the time of Kakusandha, the Mount **Vepulla** of Rājagaha was named **Pācīnavaṃsa** and the inhabitants were called **Tivarā.**

The monastery built by Accuta on the site where, in the present age, **Anāthapiṇḍika** erected the **Jetavanārāma,** was half a league in extent, and the ground was bought by golden kacchapas sufficient in number to cover it.[5]

According to the Ceylonese chronicles,[6] Kakusandha paid a visit to Ceylon. The island was then known as **Ojadīpa** and its capital was **Abhayanagara,** where reigned King **Abhaya.** The **Mahāmeghavana** was called **Mahātittha.** The Buddha came, with forty thousand disciples, to rid the island of a pestilence caused by yakkhas and stood on the **Devakūṭa** mountain from where, by virtue of his own desire, all inhabitants of the country could see him. The Buddha and his disciples were invited to a meal by the king, and after the meal the Mahātittha garden was presented to the Order; there the Buddha sat, in meditation, in order to consecrate various spots connected with the religion. At the Buddha's wish, the nun **Rucānandā** brought to the island a branch of the sacred bodhi-tree. The Buddha gave to the people his own drinking-vessel as an object of worship, and returned to Jambudīpa, leaving behind his disciples **Mahādeva** and **Rucānandā** to look after the spiritual welfare of the new converts to the faith.

In Buddhist Sanskrit texts the name of the Buddha is given as **Krakucchanda.**[7]

[1] D. ii. 7; Bu. xxiii.; J. i. 42; BuA. 209 ff.

[2] DhA. iii. 236.

[3] M. i. 333 ff.; Thag. 1187.

[4] ii. 190 f.

[5] J. i. 94.

[6] Dpv. ii. 66; xv. 25, 34; xvii. 9, 16, etc.; Mhv. xv. 57-90

[7] See especially Divy. 254, 418 f.; Mtu. iii. 247, 330.

2. **Kakusandha Thera.**—Author of the Sinhalese *Dhātuvaṃsa*, probably a translation from the Pāli. He is generally assigned to the fifteenth century.[1]

[1] P.L.C. 255.

Kakusandha Sutta.—To **Kakusandha**, as to the Buddha before he was enlightened, came thoughts of the suffering in the world and of how it could be stopped.[1]

[1] S. ii. 9.

1. **Kakkaṭa.**—An eminent monk mentioned, with **Cāla, Upacāla, Kalimbha, Nikaṭa** and **Kaṭissaha,** as staying with the Buddha at the **Kūṭāgārasālā** in Vesāli. When the **Licchavis** started coming there to pay their respects to the Buddha, the monks, desiring solitude, went into the woodlands near by, such as the **Gosiṅgasālavana.**[1]

[1] A. v. 133 f.

2. **Kakkaṭa.**—A lay disciple of **Nādikā (Ñatikā)** mentioned with several others.[1] He is evidently identical with **Kakudha** (1).

[1] S. v. 138.

Kakkaṭa Jātaka (No. 267).—Once a golden crab as large as a threshing-floor lived in **Kulīradaha** in the Himālaya, catching and eating the elephants who went into the lake to drink. In terror they left the district. The Bodhisatta, being born among the elephants, took leave of his father, and went back into the lake with his friends. The Bodhisatta, being the last to leave the water, was caught by the crab's claws; hearing his cries of pain, all the other elephants ran away except his mate, whom he entreated not to leave him.

Realising her duty, the she-elephant spoke to the crab words of coaxing and of flattery; the crab, fascinated by the sound of a female voice, let go his hold. Whereupon the Bodhisatta trampled him to death. From the two claws of the crab were later made the **Ānaka** and the **Āḷambara** drums (*q.v.*).

The story was related in reference to the wife of a landowner of Sāvatthi. Husband and wife were on their way to collect some debts when they were waylaid by robbers. The robber chief, wishing to possess the wife for her beauty, planned to kill the husband. The wife expressed her determination to commit suicide if her husband were killed, and they were both released. The she-elephant of the Jātaka was the landowner's wife.[1]

This Jātaka is illustrated in the Barhut Stupa.[2]

The Kakkaṭa Jātaka is mentioned[3] among those preached by the Buddha giving instances where **Ānanda** offered his life for that of the Bodhisatta. The reference is evidently to the **Suvaṇṇakakkaṭa Jātaka** (*q.v.*).

[1] J. ii. 341-5. [2] Cunningham; Bharhut plate xxv. 2. [3] DhA. i. 119.

The story is also found in the *Saṃyutta Commentary*,[4] but there the Bodhisatta's life is saved not by his mate but by his mother.

[4] SA. ii. 167.

Kakkaṭarasadāyaka-vimāna Vatthu.—The story of a farmer in **Magadhakhetta,** who gave a meal consisting of broth made of crab to a monk suffering from earache, and cured him. The farmer was born after death in a palace in Tāvatiṃsa. At the entrance to the palace was the figure of a ten-clawed crab, finished in gold.[1]

[1] Vv. 54; VvA. 243 ff.

Kakkara Jātaka (No. 209).—The story of a wise bird who, seeing a farmer trying to catch him, avoided him till the farmer was quite exasperated. In the end the farmer camouflaged himself like a tree, but the bird laughed in his face.

The story was related in reference to a monk, a fellow-celibate of **Sāriputta.** This monk was very careful about his body, and earned the reputation of a dandy. The bird is identified with the monk.[1] This story bears some resemblance to the second *Śakuntaka Jātaka* in the *Mahāvastu*, particularly to the latter part of it.[2] *v.l.* **Kukkura.**

[1] J. ii. 161 f

[2] Mtu. ii. 250.

Kakkarapatta.—A township of the **Koḷiyans.** It was while the Buddha was staying there that the Koliyan **Dīghajānu** came to see him.[1]

[1] A. iv. 281.

Kakkāru Jātaka (No. 326).—Once a great festival was held in Benares, attended by both humans and non-humans. Among the latter were four gods from Tāvatiṃsa, wearing wreaths of *kakkāru*-flowers, the fragrance of which filled the town. When men wondered at the fragrance, the gods shewed themselves and their wreaths. Men asked for these flowers, but the gods explained that they could only be worn by those possessed of certain virtues. The king's chaplain, hoping to deceive the gods, claimed possession of these virtues. The wreath was put on his head and the gods disappeared. The chaplain was seized with great pain in his head, but on trying to remove the wreath he found it impossible to do so. When he had suffered for seven days, the king, hoping to save his life, held another similar festival at which the gods were again present. The chaplain confessed his guilt and obtained relief. The story was told in reference to the vomiting of blood by **Devadatta** when his disciples left him.[1] *v.l.* **Kakkaru, Takkaru.**

[1] J. iii. 86-90.

Kakkārupupphiya Thera.—An arahant. Ninety-two kappas ago he was a deva in the Yāma-world and, approaching the Pacceka Buddha **Gotama,** offered him a *kakkāru*-flower.[1] *v.l.* **Kekkāru°.**

[1] Ap. i. 286.

Kakkārupūjaka Thera.—An arahant. Thirty-one kappas ago he was a deva and offered a *kakkāru*-flower to the Buddha **Sikhī.** Nine kappas ago he was a king named **Sattuttama.**[1] He is evidently identical with **Jenta** Thera.[2]

[1] Ap. i. 177.

[2] ThagA. i. 219.

Kakkoḷa.—A district in South India which supplied soldiers to **Kulasekhara.**[1]

[1] Cv. lxxvii. 2.

Kakkhalaviṭṭhi.—A village given by **Jeṭṭhatissa III.** for the maintenance of the **Veḷuvana-vihāra** (near Anurādhapura).[1]

[1] Cv. xliv. 99.

Kakkhaḷa.—A nickname given to **Jeṭṭhatissa I.** When certain of his ministers shewed reluctance to accompany his father's funeral procession, he finally persuaded them; but when they were assembled he had the gates shut on them, put them to death, and had their bodies empaled on stakes round his father's pyre. Hence his name.[1]

[1] Mhv. xxxvi. 118-22.

Kaṅkhā-Revata Thera.—He belonged to a very wealthy family in Sāvatthi. One day, after his midday meal, he went with others to hear the Buddha preach and, accepting the word of the Buddha, he entered the Order.[1] He attained arahantship by way of practising jhāna, and so proficient in jhāna did he become that the Buddha declared him chief of the monks who practised it.[2] Before he became an arahant he was greatly troubled in mind as to what was permissible for him to use and what was not (*akappiyā muggā, na kappanti muggā paribhuñjitum*, etc.). This characteristic of his became well known, hence his name.[3]

In the time of **Padumuttara** he was a brahmin of **Haṃsavatī,** well versed in the Vedas. One day, while listening to the Buddha's preaching, he heard him declare a monk in the assembly as chief among those who practised *jhāna*, and himself wished for the same honour under a

[1] According to the *Apadāna* (ii. 491), he heard the Buddha preach at Kapilavatthu.

[2] A. i. 24; Ud. v. 7; AA. i. 129 f.; Thag. 3; ThagA. 33 f.

[3] UdA. 314.

future Buddha.[4] He is often mentioned in company with other very eminent disciples—*e.g.*, **Anuruddha, Nandiya, Kimbila, Kuṇḍadhāna** and **Ānanda**—at the preaching of the **Naḷakapāna Sutta.**[5] The **Mahāgosiṅga Sutta**[6] records a discussion between **Moggallāna, Mahā Kassapa, Anuruddha, Revata** and **Ānanda,** and there we find Revata praising, as the highest type of monk, one who delights in meditation and has his habitation in the abodes of solitude.

Kaṅkhā-Revata appears to have survived the Buddha.

In the **Uttaramātu-peta Vatthu,**[7] **Uttara's** mother having been born as a peta, and having wandered about for fifty-five years without water, came upon Revata enjoying the siesta on the banks of the Ganges and begged him for succour. Having learnt her story, Revata gave various gifts to the Saṅgha in her name, and so brought her happiness.

[4] Ap. ii. 419 f.
[5] M. i. 462.
[6] *Ibid.*, 212 ff.
[7] PvA. 141 ff.

Kaṅkhāvitaraṇī. A commentary, also called **Mātikaṭṭhakathā,** by **Buddhaghosa** on the *Pātimokkha* of the *Vinaya Piṭaka.* The colophon also contains a summary, a kind of *uddāna*, of the contents. It is stated that the work was written at the request of a thera named **Soṇa,** and Buddhaghosa declares most emphatically that there is not even a single word in the book which is not in conformity with the Canon or the Commentaries of the **Mahāvihāra.**[1] The *Gandhavaṃsa*[2] mentions a *ṭīkā* on the Kaṅkhāvitaraṇī named **Vinayatthamañjūsā,** written by **Buddhanāga** at the request of **Sumedha.**

[1] p. 204 (ed. *Hewavitarane Bequest Series*); Gv. 59, 69.
[2] 61 f., 71; also Svd. 1212.

Kaṅkheyya Sutta.—The Sākyan **Mahānāma** visits **Lomasavaṅgīsa** at the **Nigrodhārāma** in Kapilavatthu and asks him if the learner's way of life is the same as that of a Tathāgata. No, says the Elder; a learner strives to abandon the five hindrances (*nīvaraṇa*); the arahants have already completely destroyed them.[1]

[1] S. v. 327 f.

Kaṅgakoṇḍakalappa.—A Damiḷa chief, ally of **Kulasekhara.**[1]

[1] Cv. lxxvii. 75.

Kaṅgakoṇḍapperayara.—A Damiḷa chief, subdued by **Parakkamabāhu I.**[1]

[1] Cv. lxxvi. 179.

Kaṅgakoṇḍāna.—A fortress in South India.[1]

[1] Cv. lxxvi. 183.

Kaṅgayara.—A Damiḷa chief, ally of **Kulasekhara**; he was vanquished by **Laṅkāpura,** general of Parakkamabāhu I.[1]

[1] Cv. lxxvi. 140, 260, 316; lxxvii. 15.

Kacaṅgala.—See **Kajangala.**

Kaccāna.—See **Mahā-Kaccāna, Pakudha-Kaccāna, Pubba-Kaccāna, Sambula-Kaccāna, Sabhiya-Kaccāna,** etc. See also **Kaccāyana.**

Kaccāna or **Kaccāyana** is the name of a family, the **Kaccānagotta.**[1]—A monk named Kaccānagotta is mentioned in the *Saṃyutta Nikāya*[2] as visiting the Buddha at Sāvatthi and questioning him on right view. The Buddha's discourse on this occasion is referred to by **Ānanda** in a conversation with **Channa.**[3] See also **Kātiyānī.**

Kañcana-māṇava belonged to the Kaccānagotta.[4]

The **Kaccānagotta** is mentioned among the higher castes, together with **Moggallāna** and **Vāsiṭṭha.**[5]

[1] AA. i. 116, 410.
[2] S. ii. 16 ff.
[3] S. iii. 134.
[4] AA. i. 116, 410.
[5] Vin. iv. 6.

Kaccāna Peyyāla.—Mentioned in the *Aṅguttara Commentary*[1] together with the **Madhupiṇḍika Sutta** and the **Pārāyaṇa Sutta** as an exposition of **Mahā Kaccāna,** in consequence of which the Buddha declared the Elder to be chief among those who could explain in detail what had been stated briefly. The reference is probably to the **Kaccāna Sutta.**

[1] AA. i. 118.

Kaccāna Sutta.—A discourse to the monks by **Mahā Kaccāna** on the six topics of recollection—the Buddha, Dhamma and Saṅgha, one's own virtues, generosity and the devas.[1] It is quoted in the *Visuddhimagga,*[2] where it is stated that to speak of casual happenings as a mere arising is to contradict both the **Padesavihāra Sutta** and the **Kaccāna Sutta.** See also **Kaccāna Peyyāla.**

[1] A. iii. 314 ff.
[2] p. 519.

1. **Kaccānā.**—A Sākyan princess, daughter of **Devadahasakka** of **Devadaha** and sister of **Añjanasakka.** She married **Sīhahanu** and had

five sons and two daughters: **Suddhodana, Dhotodana, Sakkodana, Sukkodana, Amitodana, Amitā** and **Pamitā.**[1]

[1] Mhv. ii. 17-20.

2. **Kaccānā.**—See **Bhaddakaccānā.**

Kaccāni Jātaka (No. 417).—A young man devoted himself, after his father's death, entirely to his mother, till the latter, much against his will, brought him a wife. The wife plotted to estrange mother and son, and the old woman had to leave the house. The wife, having given birth to a son, went about saying that if the mother-in-law had been with her such a blessing would have been impossible. When the old woman heard of this, she felt that such things could only be said because Right (*Dhamma*) was dead and, going into the cemetery, she started to perform a sacrifice in memory of the dead Right. **Sakka's** throne becoming heated, he came down and, hearing her story, reconciled the old woman with her son and daughter-in-law by means of his great power. In the stanza spoken by Sakka, the old woman is addressed as **Kaccāni** and **Kātiyānī.** The scholiast explains that she belonged to the **Kaccānagotta.**

The story was related to a young man of Sāvatthi who looked after his aged mother till his wife came: then the wife undertook to tend her and for some time did her duties well. Later, she grew jealous of her husband's love for his mother, and contrived by various means to make the son angry with the old woman. Finally, she asked her husband to choose between herself and his mother. The young man, without hesitation, stood up for his mother, and the wife, realising her folly, mended her ways.[1]

[1] J. iii. 422-8.

Kaccāni Vagga.—The first section of the *Aṭṭhaka Nipāta* of the *Jātakaṭṭakathā.*[1]

[1] J. iii. 422-28.

1. **Kaccānī.**—The old woman whose story is related in the story of the past in the **Kaccāni Jātaka.**

2. **Kaccānī.**—See also **Kātiyānī.**

Kaccāyana Thera.—Author of the *Kaccāyanavyākaraṇa* (*q.v.*), the oldest of the Pāli grammars extant. Orthodox tradition identifies him with **Mahā Kaccāna.** He was probably a South Indian and belonged to the Avanti school founded by Mahā Kaccāna.[1] He was, perhaps, also the author of the *Nettippakaraṇa* (*q.v.*). Kaccāyana probably belongs to the fifth or sixth century A.D.

The *Gandhavaṃsa*[2] ascribes to Kaccāyana the authorship of the *Kaccāyanagandha*, *Mahāniruttigandha*, *Cūḷaniruttigandha*, *Peṭakopadesagandha*, *Nettigandha* and *Vaṇṇanītigandha*.

[1] P.L.C. 179 ff.; Gv. 66; Svd. 1233 f. [2] p. 59.

2. **Kaccāyana Thera.**—An arahant. He was a disciple of **Padumuttara** Buddha, and was declared by him to be chief among those who could expound in detail what the Buddha stated in brief. It was this declaration made in the presence of **Mahā Kaccāna,** which made the latter, in that birth an ascetic in Himavā, wish for a like proficiency for himself under a future Buddha.[1]

[1] Ap. ii. 464; ThagA. i. 484.

3. **Kaccāyana.**—In the **Vidhurapaṇḍita Jātaka,** the yakkha **Puṇṇaka** calls himself and is addressed as **Kaccāyana,**[1] **Kaccāna**[2] and **Kātiyāna.**[3] The scholiast seems to offer no explanation.

[1] J. vi. 273. [2] *Ibid.*, 283, 286, 301, 327. [2] *Ibid.*, 299, 306, 308.

4. **Kaccāyana.**—See also *s.v.* **Kaccāna.**

Kaccāyanagandha.—One of the six books ascribed to **Mahā Kaccāyana**[1]; it probably refers to the **Kaccāyanavyākaraṇa.**

[1] Gv. 59.

Kaccāyanabheda.—Also called **Kaccāyanabhedadīpikā.** A treatise on Kaccāyana's grammar, written by **Mahāyasa** of Thatōn, probably about the fourteenth century. A *ṭikā* on it, called the **Sāratthavikāsinī,** was written by **Ariyālaṅkāra.**[1]

[1] Svd. 1250; Bode, *op. cit.*, 36 f., but see Gv. 74, where the author is called Dhammānanda.

Kaccāyanayoga.—A name given to the aphorisms in **Kaccāyanavyākaraṇa** (*q.v.*).[1]

[1] Bode, *op. cit.*, p. 21.

Kaccāyanavaṇṇanā.—A commentary on Kaccāyana's grammar by a thera of Ceylon, named **Vijitāvī.**[1] It deals with the sections on *Sandhikappa.*[2]

[1] Svd. 1242. [2] Bode, 46.

Kaccāyana-vyākaraṇa.—A treatise on Pāli grammar by **Kaccāyana.** The treatise is in eight divisions, each division comprising *suttas* or rules, expressed with great brevity; *vutti* or supplements, to render the suttas intelligible; *payoga* or grammatical analyses, with examples, and *nyāsa* or scholia, explanatory notes of the principal grammatical forms in the shape of questions and answers. The nyāsa often exists as a separate book, called the *Mukhamattadīpanī.* Orthodox tradition ascribes the whole work to **Mahā Kaccāna,** but another tradition, recorded in the **Kaccāyanabheda,** states that the aphorisms are by **Kaccāyana,** the vutti by **Saṅghānandī,** the illustrations by **Brahmadatta** and the nyāsa by **Vimalabuddhi**—all perhaps belonging to the same school of Avanti (see above, *s.v.* **Kaccāna**).

Kaccāyana's work shows clearly the influence of Sanskrit grammar, chiefly the *Kātantra.* Many later works were written about the Kaccāyana (as it is called) or were based on it, the chief among them being the **Rūpasiddhi,** the **Kaccāyanabheda,** the **Kaccāyanasāra** and the **Kaccāyanavaṇṇanā** (*q.v.*).[1]

[1] For details see P.L.C. 179 ff.; Bode, 21.

Kaccāyanasāra.—A resumé of the *Kaccāyanavyākarana* by **Mahāyasa,**[1] probably of the fourteenth century. It contains quotations from such treatises as the *Bālavatāra, Rūpasiddhi, Cūlanirutti* and *Sambandhacintā.* One *ṭikā* on it was written by Mahāyasa himself, and another, called the *Sammohavināsinī,* by **Saddhammavilāsa.**[2]

[1] But see Bode, 36, n. 3, and Gv. 74.

[2] Bode, 37.

Kacchaka-(Kaccha-)tittha.—A ford in the **Mahāvāḷuka-gaṅgā,** near the **Dhūmarakkha** mountain. It was here that **Paṇḍukābhaya** captured the Yakkhiṇī **Cetiyā.**[1] This was a strategic point in the wars with the Tamils, and we find **Kākavaṇṇatissa** entrusting its protection to his son **Dīghābhaya.**[2] It is probable that, some time afterwards, the place fell into the hands of the Tamils, for we find Duṭṭhagāmaṇī mentioned as having captured it from the Tamil general **Kapisīsa.**[3] According to the *Mahāvaṃsa Ṭīkā*[4] the place was nine leagues from Anurādhapura, but **Nimila** journeyed there and back in one day.

The *Aṅguttara Commentary*[5] mentions that a man named **Mahāvācakāla** was once born there as a crocodile, a fathom in length, for having cast doubts on the efficacy of the Buddha's religion. Once he swallowed

[1] Mhv. x. 59.

[2] *Ibid.*, xxiii. 17.

[3] *Ibid.*, xxv. 12.

[4] 322, 366.

[5] i. 367.

sixty carts with the bulls attached to them, the carts being filled with stone.

The ford is now identified with Mahāgantoṭa, the spot where the Ambaṅgaṅga and the Mahaveligaṅga meet.[6] The Ambaṅgaṅga was probably called Kacchakanadī, and at the spot where it met the Mahaveligaṅga, King **Subha** built the **Nandigāmaka-vihāra.**[7] See also **Assamaṇḍala.**

[6] Geiger, Mhv. *Trs.*, 72, n. 2.

[7] See Mhv. xxxv. 58, and MṬ. 472; on this passage see also Geiger's *Trs.*, p. 250, n. 2; MṬ. 472.

Kacchakadaha.—A lake, evidently near the **Kāḷavallimaṇḍapa.** The thera **Mahānāga** of Kāḷavallimaṇḍapa filled his mouth with water from the lake before entering the village for alms, thus ensuring that his meditations should not be interrupted by needless conversation.[1]

[1] VibhA. 352.

1. **Kacchapa Jātaka** (No. 178).—The story of a tortoise who would not leave the lake where he lived even though all the other tortoises, knowing there would be a drought, swam in time to the neighbouring river. When the drought came, he buried himself in a hole. There he was dug up by the Bodhisatta who was digging for clay, having been born as a potter. The tortoise's shell was cracked by the potter's spade and he died, having uttered two verses on the folly of clinging too much to things. The Bodhisatta took his body to the village and preached to the villagers.

The story was told to a young man of Sāvatthi who, when the plague broke out in his house, listened to his parents' advice and escaped through a hole in the wall. When the danger was past he returned and rescued the treasure hoarded in the house and, one day, visited the Buddha with many gifts.

Ānanda is identified with the tortoise of the story.[1]

[1] J. ii. 79-81.

2. **Kacchapa Jātaka** (No. 215).—The story of a tortoise who became friendly with two geese living in the **Cittakūṭa** mountain. One day the geese invited the tortoise to their abode, and when he agreed they made him hold a stick between his teeth, and seizing the two ends flew away with him. The children of the village, seeing them, started shouting, and the tortoise, being of a talkative nature, opened his mouth to reprimand them and fell near the palace of the king of Benares, crushing himself to death. The Bodhisatta, who was the king's minister, seized

the opportunity for admonishing his master, who was an inveterate talker, on the virtues of silence.

The tortoise is identified with **Kokālika,** in reference to whom the story was related.[1] For details see the **Mahātakkāri Jātaka.**

[1] J. ii. 175-8; repeated also in DhA. iv. 91 f.

3. **Kacchapa Jātaka** (No. 273).—The story of how a monkey insulted a tortoise by introducing his private parts into the tortoise as the latter lay basking in the sun with his mouth open. The tortoise caught hold of the monkey and refused to release him. The monkey went for help, and the Bodhisatta, who was an ascetic in a hermitage near by, saw the monkey carrying the tortoise. The Bodhisatta persuaded the tortoise to release the monkey.

The story was related in reference to the quarrelsome ministers of the king of **Kosala.**[1]

[1] J. ii. 359-61.

Kacchapagiri.—Another name, according to the *Mahāvaṃsa Ṭīkā*[1] for the **Issarasamaṇavihāra.** It is perhaps a variation of **Kassapagiri** (*q.v.*).

[1] MṬ. 652.

Kacchavāla.—A monastery built for the **Paṃsukalikas** by **Vajira,** general of **Dappula II.**[1]

[1] Cv. xlix. 80.

Kajaṅgala (Kajaṅgalā).—A township which formed the eastern boundary of the **Majjhimadesa.** Beyond it was **Mahāsālā.**[1] In the Buddha's time it was a prosperous place where provisions could easily be obtained (*dabbasambhārasulabhā*).[2] Once when the Buddha was staying in the **Veḷuvana** at Kajaṅgala, the lay followers there heard a sermon from the Buddha and went to the nun **Kajaṅgalā** to have it explained in detail.[3] On another occasion the Buddha stayed in the **Mukheluvana** and was visited there by **Uttara,** the disciple of **Pārāsariya.** Their conversation is recorded in the **Indriyabhāvanā Sutta.**[4] In the *Milindapañha,*[5] Kajaṅgala is described as a brahmin village and is given as the place of **Nāgasena's** birth. In the **Kapota Jātaka** mention is made of Kajaṅgala, and the scholiast[6] explains that it may be the same as Benares. According to the scholiast of the **Bhisa Jātaka,**[7] the tree-spirit mentioned

[1] Vin. i. 197; DA. i. 173; MA. i. 316, etc.; AA. i. 55, etc.; J. i. 49; Mbv. 12.
[2] J. iv. 310.
[3] A. v. 54 f.
[4] M. iii. 298 ff.
[5] p. 10.
[6] J. iii. 226-7.
[7] J. iv. 311.

in that story was the chief resident monk in an old monastery in Kajaṅgala, which monastery he repaired with difficulty during the time of **Kassapa** Buddha.

Kajaṅgala is identified with the Kie-chu-hoh-khi-lo of Hiouen Thsang, which he describes as a district about two thousand *li* in circumference.[8] It may also be identical with the town Puṇḍavardhana mentioned in the *Divyāvadāna*.[9] The *Avadānaśataka*[10] calls it Kacaṅgalā.

[8] Beal, *Bud. Records*, ii. 193, and n.; see also Cunningham, A.G.I. 723.

[9] p. 21 f.

[10] ii. 41.

Kajaṅgalā.—A nun who lived in **Kajaṅgala.** Once when the Buddha was residing in the **Veḷuvana** there, the inhabitants of the village went to her and asked her to explain in detail what the Buddha had taught them in brief. This she did, and when the matter was reported to the Buddha, he praised her very highly.[1] The exposition given by her is quoted in the *Khuddakapāṭha Commentary*.[2] Her story is given in detail in the *Avadānaśataka*.[3]

[1] A. v. 54 ff.

[2] pp. 80, 83, 85.

[3] ii. 41 ff.

1. **Kañcana.**—One of the three palaces used by **Sumedha** Buddha in his last lay life.[1] The *Commentary*[2] calls it **Koñca.**

[1] Bu. xii. 19.

[2] BuA. 163.

2. **Kañcana.**—See **Kañcanaveḷa.**

3. **Kañcana.**—See **Mahā Kañcana** and **Upakañcana.**

4. **Kañcana.**—See **Kañcanamāṇava.**

Kañcanakkhandha Jātaka (No. 56).—The Bodhisatta was once born as a farmer and, while ploughing his field, came upon a nugget of gold, four cubits long and as thick as a man's thigh, which had been buried by a merchant in bygone days. Finding it impossible to remove the gold as a whole, he cut it into four and carried it home easily. The story was related in reference to a monk who wished to leave the Order because he was frightened by all the rules his teachers asked him to learn and obey. The Buddha gave him three rules—to guard voice, body and mind—and the monk won arahantship. Even a heavy burden becomes light if carried piece by piece.[1]

[1] J. i. 276-8.

Kañcanagiri.—See **Kañcanapabbata.**

Kañcanaguhā.—A cave in the region of the Himālaya, according to one description,[1] in the face of the **Cittakūṭapabbata.** This cave was the abode of the Bodhisatta when he was born as a lion, as described in the **Virocana Jātaka,**[2] and again in the **Sigāla Jātaka.**[3] Near by was the **Rajatapabbata.** This cave was also the dwelling-place of the geese mentioned in the **Kacchapa Jātaka,**[4] and in the cave grew the **Abbhantaramba,**[5] the property of **Vessavaṇa.** In the scholiast to the **Hatthipāla Jātaka,**[6] the Kañcanagūha is mentioned as the abode of the spider **Unnābhi** and the ninety-six thousand geese who took shelter in it, waiting for the rains to clear. Near the cave was the **Chaddantadaha** and the Buddha, when he was born as the elephant **Chaddanta,** made the cave his headquarters.[7] In this context the cave is described as being in the **Suvaṇṇapabbata** (probably another name for Kañcanapabbata) to the west of the Chaddanta lake, and is said to be twelve leagues in extent. There lived the elephant king with eight thousand companions. **Nandatāpasa** once lived for seven days at the entrance to the cave, going to **Uttarakuru** for his food.[8]

The **Pākahaṃsas** of great power also lived in the cave,[9] once as many in number as ninety thousand.[10]

In the **Sudhābhojana Jātaka,**[11] the cave is stated to have been on the top of **Manosilātala.**

The Kañcanagūha is mentioned in literature as the dwelling-place of maned lions (*kesarasīhā*).[12]

[1] J. ii. 176; but see J. v. 357, where it is said to be near Cittakūta.
[2] J. i. 491 f.
[3] J. ii. 6.
[4] *Ibid.*, 176.
[5] *Ibid.*, 396.
[6] J. iv. 484.
[7] J. v. 37 f.
[8] *Ibid.*, 316, 392.
[9] *Ibid.*, 357, 368.
[10] *Ibid.*, 381.
[11] *Ibid.*, 392.
[12] *E.g.*, UdA. 71, 105.

Kañcanadevī.—Daughter of the king of Benares and sister of the Bodhisatta, **Mahākañcana.** With her brothers she renounced the world and lived in a hermitage after her parents' death. Her story is told in the **Bhisa Jātaka.**[1] She was a previous birth of **Uppalavaṇṇā.**[2]

[1] J. iv. 305 ff.
[2] *Ibid.*, 314.

Kañcanapatti.—The hut in the **Kañcanapabbata,** where lived the ascetic **Jotirasa,** friend of **Vessavaṇa.**[1]

[1] J. ii. 399.

1. **Kañcanapabbata.**—A mountain in Himavā.[1] It was near **Kañcanaguhā,** and on it grew the **Abbhantaramba** of **Vessavaṇa.** On the mountain,

[1] J. ii. 396 ff.

in a hut, lived the ascetic **Jotirasa,** tending the sacred fire. The mountain formed one of the salient features of the Himālaya region.[2] It is in the northern quarter of Himavā, and from its slopes flows the **Sīdānadī.**[3] In the **Nimi Jātaka**[4] mention is made of two Kañcanapabbatā between which the Sīdānadī flows. The mountain is sometimes referred to as **Kañcanagiri**[5] and sometimes as **Suvaṇṇapabbata.**[6] The Buddha **Sumana** held his second assembly of disciples on the Kañcanapabbata, when ninety thousand crores of people were present.[7]

[2] J. v. 415.
[3] J. vi. 101.
[4] *Ibid.*, 100.
[5] *E.g.*, UdA. 411.
[6] J. vi. 100.
[7] J. i. 34.

2. **Kañcanapabbata.**—See **Kanakapabbata.**

Kañcanamālā.—Probably the name of **Sakka's** white parasol. It was five leagues in circumference.[1]

[1] J. v. 386.

Kañcanamāṇava. The name given to **Mahā Kaccāna** by his parents, **Kaccāna** being the family name. He was called Kañcana because his body was of a golden colour.[1]

[1] ThagA. 483; AA. i. 116.

Kañcanavana.—A pleasaunce near **Ujjeni,** where **Mahā Kaccāna** lived on his return to Ujjeni after his ordination.[1]

[1] AA. i. 118.

Kañcanaveḷa.—Son of **Piyadassī** Buddha, his mother being **Vimalā.**[1] The *Buddhavaṃsa Commentary*[2] calls him **Kañcana.**

[1] Bu. xiv. 17.
[2] p. 172.

Kañcanaveḷu.—The city in which **Siddattha** Buddha died, in the park **Anoma.**[1]

[1] BuA. 188.

Kañcamba.—A Damiḷa chieftain who fought against **Laṅkāpura.**[1]

[1] Cv. lxxvii. 17.

Kañcīpura.—See **Kāñcipura.**

Kaṭakandhakāra.—A monastery or a village where lived the thera **Phussadeva,** mentioned in the scholiast to the **Hatthipāla Jātaka**[1] and

[1] J. iv. 490.

in the **Mūgapakkha Jātaka.**[2] Perhaps this residence was identical with the Kaṭandhakāra mentioned in the *Cūlavaṃsa.*[3] **Kassapa II.** paid much respect to an Elder of unknown name who lived there. It is said that the king had the sacred texts written down with a short summary in honour of this Elder. Geiger thinks[4] that the Padhānaghara called **Mahallarāja,** which had been erected by **Aggabodhi III.,** brother of Kassapa II., in company with the Yuvarāja **Māna,** was attached to the Kaṭandhakāra monastery.

2 J. vi. 30; see also Vsm. i. 228. 3 Cv. xlv. 3. 4 Cv. *Trs.* i. 89, n. 4.

Kaṭagāma.—A village in which the Ādipāda **Vikkamabāhu** defeated **Jayabāhu** and his brothers.[1]

1 Cv. lxi. 16.

Kaṭacchubhikkhadāyikā Therī.—An arahant. Ninety-two kappas ago she gave a ladleful of food to the Buddha **Tissa.** As a result, she was thirty-six times chief queen of the king of heaven and wife of fifty kings of men.[1] She is evidently to be identified with **Abhayamātā.**[2]

1 Ap. ii. 516 f. 2 ThigA. 39 f.

Kaṭattha.—One of the yakkhas who guarded **Jotika's** palace. He was at the sixth gate and had six thousand yakkhas with him.[1]

1 DhA. iv. 209.

Kaṭadorāvāda (?).—A village in **Rohaṇa** in South Ceylon.[1] It may be the same as **Kaṇṭakadvāravāta.**[2]

1 Cv. lxxiv. 164. 2 Geiger, Cv. *Trs.* ii. 36, n. 3.

Kaṭandhakāra.—See **Kaṭakandhakāra.**

Kaṭamorakatissa (Kaṭamorakatissaka).—One of the monks whom **Devadatta** incited to join him in stirring up discord among the Saṅgha, the others being **Kokālika, Khaṇḍadevīputta** and **Samuddadatta.**[1] Kaṭamorakatissa was held in high esteem by **Thullānandā,** for we are told that one day, on arriving at a house where she was a constant visitor, and on being told that several of the Buddha's eminent disciples, such as **Sāriputta, Moggallāna, Mahā Kaccāna,** had also been invited, as they happened to be at Veḷuvana near by, she expressed great disappointment that these had been invited, when such most eminent disciples (*mahānāgā*) as Devadatta, Kaṭamorakatissa, etc., were available.[2]

1 Vin. ii. 196; iii. 171. 2 *Ibid.*, iv. 66.

On another occasion, wishing to ordain a nun who was going through a probationary course, she summoned the monks, but seeing a great quantity of food and wishing to let only her favourites enjoy it, she dismissed the monks on a false pretext, keeping with her only Devadatta, Kaṭamorakatissa and their colleagues.[3]

Kaṭamorakatissaka was one of the monks about whom dissatisfaction was expressed to the Buddha, by the two Pacceka-brahmā, **Subrahmā** and **Suddhāvāsa.**[4]

[3] Vin. iv. 335. [4] S. i. 148.

Kaṭāhaka.—The son of a female slave of the Bodhisatta when he was a rich treasurer in Benares. For his story, see the **Kaṭāhaka Jātaka.**

Kaṭāhaka Jātaka (No. 125).—Once when the Bodhisatta was a rich treasurer in Benares a son was born to him. A female slave in the house gave birth to a son on the same day. The boys grew up together, the slave's son being called **Kaṭāhaka.** Kaṭāhaka acquired various arts in the company of his master. When he grew up he was appointed as the Treasurer's private secretary. One day he visited a merchant on the frontier, carrying a letter purporting to be from the Treasurer (in which he was stated to be the son of the latter), asking for the hand of the merchant's daughter in marriage. The merchant was overjoyed, and the marriage took place. Kaṭāhaka gave himself great airs and spoke contemptuously of everything "provincial." The Treasurer, discovering what had happened, decided to visit the merchant, but Kaṭāhaka went to meet him on the way, and paying him all the honour due from a slave, begged him not to expose him. Meanwhile, he had misled his wife's relations into the belief that the homage, paid by him to the Treasurer, was but the regard due from a son to his father. He was not like the sons of other parents, but knew what was due to his father. The Bodhisatta, being pleased, did not expose the slave, but on learning from Kaṭāhaka's wife that Kaṭāhaka always complained of his food, he taught her a stanza which contained the threat—not intelligible to her, though clear to Kaṭāhaka—that if Kaṭāhaka continued to make a nuisance of himself, the Treasurer would return and expose him. Thenceforth Kaṭāhaka held his peace.

The story was related in reference to a monk who used to boast of his high lineage and the wealth of his family until his pretensions were exposed.[1]

According to the *Dhammapada Commentary,*[2] the story was told in

[1] J. i. 451 ff. [2] DhA. iii. 357 ff.

reference to a monk named **Tissa** who would complain, no matter what attentions were paid to him.

Kaṭiyāgāma.—A village in Ceylon where **Gajabāhu's** officers slew large numbers of his enemies.[1]

Cv. lxx. 67.

Kaṭivāpi.—One of the tanks repaired by **Parakkamabāhu I.**[1]

[1] Cv. lxxix. 34.

Kaṭissabha.—A lay disciple of the Buddha at **Nādikā,** one of those, who, after their death, were declared by the Buddha, in answer to a question by **Ānanda,** to have destroyed the five *orambhāgiya* fetters and to have become inheritors of the highest heaven, thence never to return.[1] *v.l.* **Kaṭissaha.**

[1] D. ii. 92; S. v. 358 f.

1. **Kaṭissaha Thera.**—An arahant. He was one of those who were staying with the Buddha at the **Kūṭāgārasālā** in Vesāli. When the **Licchavis** began to visit the Buddha in large numbers, they left the monastery and retired to places of solitude, such as **Gosiṅgasālavana.**[1]

[1] A. v. 133.

2. **Kaṭissaha.**—One of the chief supporters of **Dhammadassī** Buddha.[1]

[1] Bu. xvi. 20.

Kaṭunnarū.—A tank in South Ceylon repaired by **Vijayabāhu I.**[1] and again by **Parakkamabāhu I.,** before his ascent to the throne.[2]

[1] Cv. lx. 48. [2] *Ibid.*, lxviii. 46.

Kaṭuvandu.—A locality near **Anurādhapura.**[1]

[1] Cv. lxxii. 188.

Kaṭuviya Sutta.—Once when the Buddha was going about for alms near the fig-tree at the cattle tethering in the neighbourhood of **Isipatana,** he saw a monk, whose delight was in the empty outer joys of sense, and admonished him, saying that flies will settle on and attack him who is corrupt and reeks with the stench of carrion. Hearing this, the monk was greatly stirred. Later the Buddha repeated the admonition to the assembled monks and explained that greed was corruption, malice the stench of carrion and evil ways of thought the flies.[1]

[1] A. i. 280 f.

Kaṭṭha Sutta.—On the five evil results of not using a toothbrush, and the five advantages of using one.[1]

[1] A. iii. 250.

Kaṭṭhakā.—A class of devas present at the **Mahāsamaya.**[1] *v.l.* **Kaṭhakā.**

[1] D. ii. 261.

Kaṭṭhantanagara.—A town near the **Kāṇavāpi** tank. It was here that King **Sena II.** had the dam of the tank repaired.[1]

[1] Cv. li. 73.

1. **Kaṭṭhavāhana.**—A king. A previous birth of **Bāvarī.** Kaṭṭhavāhana had been a very clever carpenter of Benares, having under him sixteen thousand and sixteen assistants. They paid periodical visits to the Himālaya forests, felled trees, and having prepared the timber which was suitable for building purposes, brought it down the Ganges and erected houses for the king and for the people. Growing tired of this work, these carpenters made flying machines of light wood, and going northwards from Benares to Himavā, established by conquest a kingdom, the chief carpenter becoming the king. He came to be called Kaṭṭhavāhana, the capital was named **Kaṭṭhavāhananagara** and the country **Kaṭṭhavāhanaraṭṭha.** The king was righteous and the people very happy and the country prospered greatly. Later Kaṭṭhavāhana and the king of Benares became sincere friends, and free trade, exempt from all taxes, was established between the two countries. The kings sent each other very costly and magnificent gifts. Once Kaṭṭhavāhana sent to the king of Benares eight priceless rugs in eight caskets of lacquered ivory, each rug being sixteen cubits long and eight cubits wide and of unsurpassed splendour. The Benares king, wondering how he could adequately return the courtesy, decided to let his friend learn the great news of the appearance in the world of the Buddha (**Kassapa**), the Dhamma and the Saṅgha. This message was written on a gold leaf and the leaf enclosed in many caskets, one inside the other, the innermost casket being made of the seven kinds of jewels and the outermost of costly wood. The caskets were placed on a splendid palanquin and sent on the back of a royal elephant, accompanied by all the insignia of royalty. All along the route the honours due to a king were paid to the casket, and Kaṭṭhavāhana himself escorted the elephant from the frontiers of his kingdom to the capital. When Kaṭṭhavāhana discovered the message, he was overjoyed, and sent his nephew with sixteen of his ministers and sixteen thousand followers to investigate

the matter and convey his greetings to the Buddha. The envoys arrived at Benares only after the Buddha's death, but hearing from the Buddha's disciples of the Doctrine he had proclaimed to the world, the ministers and their followers entered the Order, while Kaṭṭhavāhana's nephew was sent back to report the news to the king, taking with him the Buddha's water-pot, a branch of the Bodhi tree and a monk versed in the Doctrine. The king, having learnt the Doctrine, engaged in various works of piety till his death, after which he was born among the **Kāmāvacara** devas.[1]

[1] SnA. ii. 575 ff.

2. **Kaṭṭhavāhana.**—King of Benares. He was the Bodhisatta, son of **Brahmadatta,** king of Benares, and of a faggot-gatherer, whom the king met in a grove, singing as she picked up the sticks. His story is related in the **Kaṭṭhahāri Jātaka.**[1]

[1] J. i. 133 ff.; DhA. i. 349; J. iv. 148.

3. **Kaṭṭhavāhana.**—A king. He had been a master builder and built for **Bodhirājakumāra,** a palace called **Kokanadā,** unrivalled in its splendour. In order to prevent the building of a similar palace for anyone else, the prince decided to make away with the master builder at the conclusion of his work, and confided his plan to his friend **Sañjikāputta.** The latter, being most distressed at this suggestion of wanton cruelty, warned the builder who, procuring seasoned timber with sap well dried, under pretence that it was needed for the palace, shut himself up and fashioned a wooden Garuḍa-bird, large enough to hold himself and his family. When his preparations were complete, the builder with his family mounted the bird and rode away through the air to the Himālaya, where he founded a kingdom and became known as King Kaṭṭhavāhana.[1]

The story of the building of the palace is mentioned in the introduction to the **Dhonasākha Jātaka,**[2] but there we are told that the prince put out the builder's eyes, and no mention is made of the wooden bird and the subsequent story.

[1] DhA. iii. 135 f. [2] J. iii. 157.

Kaṭṭhavāhananagara.—The city of king **Kaṭṭhavāhana** (1).[1] It was one whole day's journey from Benares and twenty yojanas from Sāvatthi.[2]

[1] SnA. ii. 576. [2] *Ibid.*, 579.

Kaṭṭhahāra Sutta.—Some pupils of a **Bhāradvāja** brahmin, faggot-gatherers (*kaṭṭhahārakā*), came across the Buddha engaged in meditation in a forest in Kosala and informed their teacher of it. He went to the Buddha and questioned him as to his purpose in dwelling in the forest. The brahmin expressed himself as being pleased with the information.[1]

[1] S. i. 180.

Kaṭṭhahāra-Bhāradvāja.—See **Kaṭṭhahāra Sutta.**

Kaṭṭhahāri Jātaka (No. 7).—**Brahmadatta,** king of Benares, while wandering about in a grove, seeking for fruits and flowers, came upon a woman merrily singing as she gathered sticks. He became intimate with her, and the Bodhisatta was conceived then and there. The king gave the woman his signet ring, with instructions that if the child was a boy, he should be brought to the court with the ring. When the Bodhisatta grew up his playmates nicknamed him "No-father." Feeling ashamed, he asked his mother about it and, on hearing the truth, insisted on being taken to the king. When confronted with the child, the king was too shy to acknowledge his parentage, and the mother, having no witness, threw the child into the air with the prayer that he should remain there if her words were true. The boy, sitting cross-legged in the air, requested the king to adopt him, which request was accepted, his mother being made queen consort. On his father's death he became king under the name of **Kaṭṭhavāhana.**

The story was told to **Pasenadi** on his refusal to recognise the claim to the throne of **Viḍūḍabha** (*q.v.*), his son by **Vāsabha-Khattiyā.**[1]

Perhaps the story has some connection with that of Duṣyanta and Śakuntalā, as given in the *Mahābhārata* and later amplified by Kālidāsa in his drama.

[1] J. i. 133 ff.; iv. 148; DhA. i. 349.

Kaṭṭhahāla-pariveṇa.—A monastic residence in or near **Anurādhapura.** A monk from **Piyaṅgalla,** who was asked to participate in the building of the **Mahā Thūpa,** stayed in the pariveṇa during his visit to Anurādhapura.[1]

[1] Mhv. xxx. 34.

1. **Kaṭhina Vagga.**—The first section of the *Mahāvibhaṅga* of the *Parivārapāthā.*[1]

[1] Vin. v. 1-10.

2. **Kaṭhina Vagga.**—The first section of the *Nissagiya.*[1]

[1] Vin. iii. 195-223.

Kaṭhinakkhandha.—The seventh chapter of the *Mahāvagga* of the *Vinaya Piṭaka.*[1]

[1] Vin. i. 253-67.

Kaḍakuḍḍa.—A general of **Gajabāhu,** captured by the Senāpati **Deva** and sent to **Parakkamabāhu I.**[1] Later he seems to have been appointed general by Parakkamabāhu himself and given the title of **Laṅkāpura,** for we find him fighting on the side of the king and being entrusted with important campaigns.[2]

[1] Cv. lxx. 143. [2] *Ibid.*, lxxii. 39, 222, 272; lxxv. 181.

Kaḍiliya.—A Damila chief who was defeated by the forces of **Parakkamabāhu I.** at **Kuṇḍayaṅkoṭṭa.**[1]

[1] Cv. lxxvi. 177.

Kaṇakāgamana.—See **Koṇāgamana.**

Kaṇavera Jātaka (No. 318).—Once the Bodhisatta was born as a robber in a village in Kāsī and became notorious for his banditry. When the people complained of him to the king, the latter had him arrested by the governor of the province and condemned to death. While being led to execution with a wreath of red *kaṇavera*-flowers on his head, he was seen by **Sāmā,** the chief courtesan of the city, and she immediately fell in love with him for his comely and striking appearance. Sāmā, sending word to the governor that the robber was her brother, persuaded him, by means of a bribe of one thousand pieces of money, to set him free and send him to her for a little while. Then, using all her guile, she substituted for the robber a youth who was enamoured of her and who had happened to visit her that day. This youth was killed in the place of the robber, who was brought to Sāmā, and she showered on him all her favours. Fearing that when Sāmā grew tired of him she might betray him, the robber went with her one day into the park and, on the pretence of embracing her, squeezed her till she swooned, then taking all her ornaments, made good his escape. Sāmā, all unsuspecting, imagined him to have run away from fear of having killed her by his too violent embraces, and she used all her ingenuity in searching for him, such as bribing some wandering minstrels to sing, wherever they went, a set of stanzas declaring that she was still alive and loved none but him, her lover. One day the robber heard the stanzas and learned from the minstrels that Sāmā still longed for him, but he refused to return, sending her word that he doubted her constancy. In despair, Sāmā returned to her former means of livelihood.[1]

[1] J. iii. 58-63.

The occasion for the telling of this story is given in the **Indriya Jātaka.** The story is referred to in the **Sulasā Jātaka**[2] and in the scholiast to the **Kuṇāla Jātaka.**[3]

[2] J. iii. 436. [3] J. v. 446.

Kaṇaverapupphiya Thera.—An arahant. Ninety-four kappas ago he was a king named **Gopaka** (?), and seeing the Buddha **Siddhattha,** accompanied by his monks, walking in the city, the king, from his balcony, scattered *kaṇavera*-flowers over them. Eighty-seven kappas ago he became king four times.[1] He is probably identical with **Bandhura Thera.**[2]

[1] Ap. i. 182. [2] ThagA. i. 208.

Kaṇikāracchadaniya Thera.—An arahant. He once met the Buddha **Vessabhū** enjoying his siesta in the forest, and being pleased with his appearance, made a canopy of *kaṇikāra*-flowers over the Buddha's head. Twenty kappas ago he became king eight times under the name of **Soṇṇābha.**[1]

[1] Ap. i. 183.

Kaṇikārapupphiya Thera.—An arahant. Ninety-two kappas ago he saw the Buddha **Tissa** and offered him a *kaṇikāra*-flower. Thirty-five kappas ago he was a king named **Aruṇapāla** (*v.l.* **Aruṇabala**).[1] He is probably identical with **Ujjaya** Thera.[2]

[1] Ap. i. 203. [2] ThagA. i. 118 f.

Kaṇikāra-Vimāna.—A palace in **Tāvatiṃsa,** sixty leagues high and thirty broad, which **Uttara** Thera occupied as a result of having, in a previous birth, offered a *kaṇikāra*-flower to **Sumedha** Buddha.[1]

[1] ThagA. i. 241.

Kaṇikārapadhānaghara.—A meditation-hall in **Khaṇḍacela Vihāra,** where lived **Padhāniya** Thera.[1]

[1] MA. i. 65.

Kaṇikāravālikasamudda Vihāra.—The residence of the Thera **Sāketa-Tissa,** during a whole rainy season.[1]

[1] AA. i. 44.

Kaṇirajānu Tissa.—King of Ceylon (A.D. 89-92). He slew his elder brother **Āmaṇḍagāmaṇi Abhaya** and occupied the throne. He once gave judgment in a lawsuit concerning the *uposatha*-house in the **Cetiyagiri vihāra,** and sixty monks who were found guilty of treason against him were captured by his orders and flung into a cave called **Kaṇira.** Hence, probably, his name.[1]

[1] Mhv. xxxv. 9 ff.; MṬ. 640; Dpv. xx. 38.

Kaṇira-pabbhāra.—A cave, probably in the side of the **Cetiyagiri,** into which King **Kaṇirajānu Tissa** ordered sixty monks to be flung, they having been found guilty of high treason.[1]

[1] Mhv. xxxv. 11.

Kaṇṭaka (*v.l.* **Kaṇḍaka**).—A novice ordained by **Upananda.** Kaṇṭaka committed an offence with another novice, **Mahaka.** When this became known, a rule was passed that no monk should ordain two novices[1]; this rule was, however, later rescinded.[2] Elsewhere,[3] Kaṇṭaka is mentioned as being expelled from the Order for having had sexual intercourse with a nun, **Kaṇṭakā** by name. According to the *Pacittiya*,[4] Kaṇṭaka held the same false views as **Ariṭṭha** (*q.v.*), and for that reason he was expelled from the Saṅgha. The **Chabbaggiya** monks, however, received him into their ranks and gave him every encouragement. In the *Samantapāsādikā*[5] Kaṇṭakasāmanera is mentioned with Ariṭṭha and the Vajjiputtakas, as having been an enemy of the Buddha's religion.

[1] Vin. i. 79.
[2] *Ibid.*, 83.
[3] *Ibid.*, 85.
[4] *Ibid.*, 138 f.
[5] iv. 874.

Kaṇṭaka Sutta.—When the Buddha was staying at the **Kuṭāgārasālā** in Vesāli, the **Licchavis,** with their retinues, came to visit him in large numbers and created a great uproar. Some of the Buddha's eminent disciples who were with the Buddha, such as **Cāla, Upacāla, Kakkaṭa, Kaḷimbha, Nikaṭa** and **Kaṭissaha,** therefore, retired into various woodland solitudes, such as **Gosiṅgasālāvana,** which were close by. The Buddha praised them, saying that noise was an obstruction to meditation, and preached this sutta on the ten kinds of obstruction.[1]

[1] A. v. 133-5.

Kaṇṭakacetiya.—A cetiya on **Cetiyapabbata.** Here **Kāḷa-Buddharakkhita** Thera (*q.v.*) preached the **Kāḷakārāma Sutta.**[1]

See also **Katthaka** and **Kantaka.**

[1] MA. i. 469 f.

Kaṇṭakadvāravāta.—A village in **Rohaṇa** where the forces of **Parakkamabāhu I.** inflicted a severe defeat on their enemies.[1] It is identified with the modern Kaṭupelella.[2]

[1] Cv. lxxiv. 85. [2] Cv. *Trs.* ii. 29, n. 3.

Kaṇṭakapeṭaka.—A district on the frontier of the **Dakkhiṇadesa** of Ceylon, probably to the east or north-east of Matale.[1]

[1] Cv. lxix. 10; Cv. *Trs.* 283, n. 2.

Kaṇṭakavana.—A locality in **Rohaṇa** where the general **Rakkha** built a stronghold and attacked the enemy forces.[1]

[1] Cv. lxxiv. 56.

Kaṇṭakā (*v.l.* **Kaṇḍakā**).—A nun who was guilty of unchastity with the novice **Kaṇṭaka** (*q.v.*).[1]

[1] Vin. i. 85.

Kaṇṭakī Suttā.—A group of three suttas. **Sāriputta** and **Moggallāna** go to **Anuruddha** and ask him various questions. Anuruddha says that the four *satipaṭṭhānas* should be attained both by the *sekha* and the *asekha* (the learner and the adept), and declares that he himself came to understand the thousandfold world-system by developing these four.[1]

[1] S. v. 298 f.

Kaṇṭakīvana.—A grove near **Sāketa.** The conversation which took place there between **Sāriputta** and **Moggāllāna** is recorded in the **Padesa Sutta.**[1] A discussion which took place there on another occasion between these two and Anuruddha, is given in the **Kaṇṭakī Sutta.**[2] The grove was evidently also called **Tikaṇṭakī**[3] and the *Commentary* describes it as *mahā-karamadda-vana*, *karamadda* being a shrub (*carissa carandas*). The Buddha also stayed in this grove, and a sermon preached by him to the monks is recorded in the **Ṭikaṇṭakī Sutta.**[4]

[1] S. v. 174 f.
[2] *Ibid.*, 298 f.
[3] *q.v.*
[4] A. v. 169.

Kaṇṭhaka.—See **Kanthaka.**

Kaṇṭhapiṭṭhi.—An important village, among those given by **Aggabodhi IX.** to a number of small vihāras in order that the monks of these vihāras could obtain rice-gruel without going, as formerly, to the **Mahāvihāra.**[1]

[1] Cv. xlix. 89.

Kaṇḍaka.—See **Kaṇṭaka.**

Kaṇḍakā.—See **Kaṇṭakā.**

Kaṇḍakī.—See **Kaṇṭakī.**

Kaṇḍadevamālava.—A Damiḷa chief who fought against **Parakkamabāhu's** general **Laṅkāpura,** and was defeated at **Muṇḍikkāra.** Later, when Kaṇḍadevamālava owned allegiance to Parakkamabāhu, **Laṅkāpura** restored Muṇḍikkāra to him and appointed him chief of the two districts of **Maṅgala.**[1]

[1] Cv. lxxvi. 187, 208, 210.

Kaṇḍanagara.—A locality in Ceylon; to the north of it was the **Girinelavāhanaka Vihāra,** built by **Sūratissa.**[1]

[1] Mhv. xxi. 6.

Kaṇḍamba.—A Damiḷa chief, ally of **Kulasekhara.**[1]

[1] Cv. lxxvii. 55, 80, 90.

Kaṇḍaraggisāma.—A celebrated physician, mentioned in a list of such.[1]

[1] Mil. 272.

Kaṇḍarāyana.—A brahmin. He visited **Mahā Kaccāna** at the **Gundavana** near **Madhurā** and accused him of not paying due respect to elderly brahmins, but when Mahā Kaccāna preached to him he expressed delight and offered himself as the Thera's disciple.[1] *v.l.* **Kuṇḍarāyana.**

[1] A. i. 67 f.

Kaṇḍari.—King of Benares; his story is given in the **Kaṇḍari Jātaka** (*q.v.*).

Kaṇḍari Jātaka (No. 341).—**Kaṇḍari,** a king of Benares, was very handsome; each day he received one thousand boxes of perfume for his use, and his food was cooked with scented wood. His wife, **Kiṇṇarā,** was very beautiful; his chaplain was **Pañcālacaṇḍa.** One day, Kiṇṇarā, on looking out, saw a loathsome cripple in the shade of a *jambu*-tree near her window, and conceived a passion for the man. Thereafter she would wait for the king to fall asleep and would then, nightly, visit the cripple, taking him dainty foods and having her pleasure with him. One day the king, returning from a procession, saw the misshapen creature, and asked the chaplain if such a man could ever win the love of a woman. The cripple, hearing the question, proudly boasted of his intimacy with the queen. At the chaplain's suggestion the king watched the queen's movements that same night, and saw the cripple abuse her and strike her for being late in coming. The blow fell on her ear breaking off her ear ornament, which the king picked up.

The next day he ordered the queen to appear before him in all her ornaments, and having proved that he knew of her infidelity, handed her over to the chaplain to be executed. Pañcālacaṇḍa, pitying the woman, begged that she should be pardoned, because in being unchaste she had but obeyed the instincts common to all women. To prove his contention, Pañcālacaṇḍa took the king with him and, in disguise, they wandered through Jambudīpa, testing the virtue of various women, including that of a young bride who was being taken to her husband's house. Convinced that all women were alike, the king spared Kiṇṇarā's life, but drove her out of the palace together with the cripple, and caused the *jambu*-tree to be cut down.

The story was among those related by the bird **Kuṇāla** to his friend **Puṇṇamukha,** testifying to the unfaithfulness of women. Kuṇāla is identified with Pañcālacaṇḍa.[1]

[1] J. v. 437-40; J. iii. 132.

Kaṇḍina Jātaka (No. 13).—A mountain stag fell in love with a doe who had gone into the forest from the village during the time of the ripening of the corn. When the time came for the doe to return to the village, the stag, in his love, accompanied her. The people of the village, knowing of the deers' return, lay in ambush for them. The doe, seeing a huntsman, sent the stag on ahead, and he was killed and eaten. The doe escaped. The Bodhisatta, who was a forest-deva, seeing the incident, preached to the other forest-dwellers on the three infamies: it is infamy to cause another's death; infamous is the land ruled by a woman: infamous are the men who yield themselves to women's dominance.[1]

The circumstances in which the story was related are given in the **Indriya Jātaka.**

[1] J. i. 153-6.

Kaṇḍiyūru.—A Damiḷa chieftain and ally of **Kulasekhera.**[1]

[1] Cv. lxxvi. 140.

1. **Kaṇḍula.**—The state-elephant of **Duṭṭhagāmiṇi.** He was of the **Chaddanta** race, and was left by his mother and discovered by a fisherman, **Kaṇḍula,** after whom he was named.[1]

[1] Mhv. xxii. 62 f.

He grew up to be of great strength. When Duṭṭhagāmiṇī's father died, his younger son, **Tissa,** took possession of the queen-mother and of Kaṇḍula, the state-elephant, and fled, but in the battle between the brothers, Kaṇḍula shook himself free from Tissa and went over to Duṭṭhagāmiṇī, whom he served to the end of his life. Kaṇḍula took a prominent part in the campaign against the Damiḷas, distinguishing himself particularly in the siege of **Vijitapura.**[2] In the single combat between **Eḷāra** and Duṭṭhagāmiṇī. Kaṇḍula attacked Eḷāra's elephant, Mahāpabbata, and disabled him.[3] It is said that once the warrior **Nandhimitta** seized Kaṇḍula by his tusks and forced him on to his haunches, and Kaṇḍula nursed a grudge against him until Nandhimitta rescued him from being crushed under a gate-tower which fell on him during his attack on Vijitapura.[4]

[2] Mhv., xxiv. 15, 89.
[3] Mhv., xxv. 5-83.
[4] *Ibid.*, 22, 39 f.; see also Dpv. xviii. 53; Mbv. 133.

2. **Kaṇḍula.**—The fisherman who found the elephant **Kaṇḍula** and reported the matter to the king.[1]

[1] Mhv. xxii. 62 f.

Kaṇḍuveṭṭi.—A Damiḷa chief and vassal prince of South India, ally of **Kulasekhera.**[1]

[1] Cv. lxxvii. 79.

Kaṇḍuveṭhi.—A city in India, the capital of **Narasīha;** perhaps a variant reading of **Kaṇḍuvetti.**[1] Hultszch[2] says that both names are synonyms with Kādavarū, a designation of the Pallava kings.

[1] Cv. xlvii. 7.
[2] *J.R.A.S.* 1913, p. 527.

Kaṇṇakatthala.—A deer-park in **Ujuññā.** There the Buddha sometimes stayed; he was once visited there by **Acela Kassapa,** to whom he preached the **Kassapasīhanāda Sutta,**[1] and again by **Pasenadi,** king of Kosala; to him he preached the **Kaṇṇakatthala Sutta.**[2]

[1] D. i. 161.
[2] M. ii. 125.

Kaṇṇakatthala Sutta.—**Pasenadi** visits the Buddha at the Deer Park in **Kaṇṇakatthala** and conveys to him the greetings of his two queens **Somā** and **Sakulā.** He then enquired of the Buddha if it were true that, according to him, no recluse or brahmin could claim absolute knowledge and insight. The Buddha explains that his teaching is that no one can know and see everything at one and the same time. The king proceeds to ask whether there is any distinction of caste in the matter of deliverance and whether there are any gods. **Viḍūḍabha** and **Ānanda** join in the discussion, and then **Sañjaya Ākāsagotta,** charged with having spread a wrong interpretation of the Buddha's teaching, is announced and lays the blame on Viḍūḍabha. The arrival of the king's chariot puts an end to the dispute.[1]

[1] M. ii. 125 ff.

Kaṇṇakujja.—A district in **Jambudīpa**; it is mentioned in a list of places passed by the Buddha on his way from **Verañjā** to **Bārāṇasī,** across the Ganges, the route passing through **Verañjā, Soreyya, Saṅkassa, Kaṇṇakujja, Payāgatittha,** here crossing the river to Benares.[1] It may have been the very road followed by **Revata** when going from **Saṅkassa** to **Sahajāti,** this road passing through **Kaṇṇakujja, Udumbara,** and **Aggalapura.**[2]

In the *Dīpavaṃsa*[3] the city is called **Kaṇṇagoccha,** and is said to have been the capital of nine kings of the **Mahāsammata** race, the last king being **Naradeva.**

According to Hiouen Thsang, the distance from Saṅkassa to Kaṇṇakujja was two hundred *li*, or thirty-three miles, in a north-west direction. Fa Hsien gives the distance as forty-nine miles.[4]

According to the *Buddhavaṃsa Commentary,*[5] it was at Kaṇṇakujja that **Phussa** Buddha first preached to his two chief disciples. Again,[6] it was at the gates of Kaṇṇakujja that the Buddha **Kakusandha** showed the *Twin Miracle.*

[1] Vin. iii. 11. [2] Vin. ii. 299.
[3] iii. 26; MṬ. (82) calls it Kaṇṇagotta.
[4] *Buddhist Records*, p. 205; Giles, p. 47. For a descriptive account see CAGI. 433 ff.; see also Mtu. ii. 442 f.; 459 f.; 485 and iii. 16, 34.
[5] p. 193.
[6] BuA. 210.

Kaṇṇagoccha, Kaṇṇagotta.—See **Kaṇṇakujja.**

Kaṇṇapeṇṇā.—A river in the **Mahiṃsaka** country, running out of Lake **Saṅkhapāla.** At the bend of the river and near its source was the mountain **Candaka,** near which the king of Magadha lived in a hut of leaves, and where he was visited by the Nāga **Saṅkhapāla.**[1] The river must have formed a lake at this bend, the lake being referred to as **Kaṇṇpeṇṇā-daha.**[2]

[1] J. v. 162 f. [2] *Ibid.*, 168.

Kaṇṇamuṇḍa, Kaṇṇamuṇḍaka.—One of the seven great lakes of **Himavā.**[1] Its waters never grew hot.[2] Once a mango from a tree growing on the banks of this lake came into the possession of King **Dadhivāhana,** and from its stone grew a tree which bore very sweet fruit.[3]

[1] A. iv. 101; DA. i. 164; J. v. 415; AA. ii. 759; MA. ii. 692, etc.
[2] SnA. ii. 407.
[3] J. ii. 104.

Kaṇṇāṭa.—The name given in the *Cūḷavaṃsa* to the Kanarese of South India. They are often mentioned as mercenary soldiers in Ceylon.[1]

[1] *E.g.*, Cv. lv. 12; lx. 24, 26; lxx. 230.

Kaṇṇāvaḍḍhamāna.—A mountain in Ceylon, the residence of the Nāga-king, father of **Cūḷodara** and brother-in-law of **Mahodara.**[1]

[1] Mhv. i. 49; but see my edition of the *Mahāvaṃsa-Ṭīkā*, where I take the name of the mountain to be Vaḍḍhamāna.

Kaṇṇikāragalla.—A tank in Ceylon, restored by **Gajabāhu.**[1]

[1] Cv. lxviii. 45.

1. **Kaṇha.**—A name for **Māra** (*q.v.*).[1]

[1] *E.g.*, Sn. v. 355; M. i. 377; D. ii. 262; Thag. v. 1189.

2. **Kaṇha.**—The name of the Bodhisatta; he was born in a brahmin family and later became a sage. He is also called **Kaṇha-tāpasa,** and is mentioned among those the memory of whose lives caused the Buddha to smile.[1] See **Kaṇha Jātaka** (2).

[1] DhsA. 294, 426.

3. **Kaṇha.**—Another name of **Vāsudeva**[1]; the scholiast explains that he belonged to the **Kaṇhāyanagotta** (*q.v.*).

[1] J. iv. 84, 86; vi. 421; PvA. 94 ff.

4. **Kaṇha.**—Son of **Disā,** a slave girl of **Okkāka.** He was called Kaṇha because he was black and, like a devil (*kaṇha*), spoke as soon as he was born. He was the ancestor of the **Kaṇhāyanagotta.**[1] Later he went into the Dekkhan and, having learnt mystic verses, became a mighty seer. Coming back to Okkāka, Kaṇha demanded the hand of the king's daughter **Maddarūpī.** At first the request was indignantly refused, but when Kaṇha displayed his supernatural powers he gained the princess.[2]

[1] D. i. 93.
[2] *Ibid.*, 96 f.; DA. i. 266.

5. **Kaṇha.**—A Pacceka Buddha, mentioned in the *Isigili Sutta.*[1]

[1] M. iii. 71.

6. **Kaṇha.**—A dog. See **Mahā-Kaṇha.**

7. **Kaṇha.**—See **Kaṇhadīpāyana.**

1. **Kaṇha Jātaka** (No. 29).—The story of **Ayya-kāḷaka** (*q.v.*). The story was related by the Buddha to the monks, who expressed great wonder at the miracles performed by him at **Saṅkassa.** It was not only in his last birth that he performed wonders.

The old woman in the story is identified with **Uppalavaṇṇā.**[1]

The story is also given in the *Aṅguttara Commentary,*[2] with a few additional details. The *Dhammapada Commentary*[3] refers to it as the **Kaṇhausabha Jātaka.**

[1] J. i. 193 ff. [2] i. 415. [3] iii. 213.

2. **Kaṇha Jātaka** (No. 440).—The story of **Kaṇha-tāpasa.** He was the only son of a brahmin in Benares and inherited great wealth; he was educated at **Takkasilā.** When his parents died he gave away all his wealth and retired to the Himālaya, where he practised rigid asceticism, never entering a village, eating the produce of only one tree, and living not even in a hut. He acquired great mystic powers, and **Sakka's** throne was heated by his virtue. Sakka visited him and, having tested him and asked him various questions, granted him six boons. The ascetic chose only such things as pertained to the life of renunciation. Sakka decreed that the tree under which the ascetic lived should bear fruit perennially.

The Sakka of the story was **Anuruddha.** It is said that the acetic was called Kaṇha on account of his dark complexion.

The story was related to **Ānanda** in explanation of the Buddha's smile as he was passing a certain spot in the **Nigrodhārāma** in Kapilavatthu; it was the spot where the ascetic Kaṇha practised his meditations.[1]

[1] J. iv. 6 ff.

Kaṇhausabha Jātaka.—See **Kaṇha Jātaka** (1).

Kaṇhagaṅgā.—The name of one part of the river which flows from **Anotatta.** This part is sixty leagues long and flows over a rocky bed.[1]

[1] SnA. ii. 439; AA. ii. 760; UdA. 302; MA. ii. 586, etc.

Kaṇhagundāvana.—See **Gundāvana.**

Kaṇhadāsa.—The donor of the vihāra in **Kāveripaṭṭana,** where lived **Buddhadatta,** author of *Madhuratthavilāsinī*, the commentary on the *Buddhavaṃsa.*[1]

[1] BuA. 249.

Kaṇhadinna Thera.—An arahant. He belonged to a brahmin family in **Rājagaha.** Having heard **Sāriputta** preach, he entered the Order and became an arahant. In the past he met the Buddha **Sobhita** and offered him a *punnāga*-flower.[1]

He is evidently the same as Kaṇhadinna, son of **Bhāradvāja** Thera (*q.v.*[2]), and is probably identical with **Giripunnāgiya** of the *Apadāna.*[3]

[1] Thag. v. 179; ThagA. i. 304. [2] ThagA. i. 303. [3] ii. 416.

1. **Kaṇhadīpāyana.**—An ascetic of great power. When the **Andhakaveṇhudāsaputtā** found themselves unable to capture **Dvāravatī,** because the city rose into the air when attacked, they sought the ascetic's help. He told them that an ass wandered round the city and brayed at the sight of an enemy, when the city immediately rose up into the sky. The Andhakaveṇhus sought the ass and begged for his help. Acting on the ass's advice, they tied eight great iron posts to the gates, thus preventing the city from rising. In this way they captured it.[1]

Later, their sons, wishing to test Kaṇhadipānyana's powers of clairvoyance, played a practical joke on him. They tied a pillow to the belly of a young lad, and dressing him up as a woman, took him to the ascetic and asked when the baby would be born. The ascetic replied that on the seventh day the person before him would give birth to a knot of acacia wood which would destroy the race of **Vāsudeva.** The youths thereupon fell on him and killed him, but his prophecy came true.[2] This ascetic is evidently not the one mentioned in the Jātaka bearing his name, for there he is identified with the Bodhisatta, while in the story given above the Bodhisatta was the ascetic's contemporary and was called **Ghaṭapaṇḍita** (*q.v.*).

The immolation of Kaṇhadīpāyana and its consequences are often referred to.[3]

[1] J. iv. 83. [2] *Ibid.*, 87. [3] *E.g.*, J. v. 114; 267, 273.

2. **Kaṇhadīpāyana.**—An ascetic; his story is given in the **Kaṇhadīpāyana Jātaka.**

Kaṇhadīpāyana Jātaka (No. 444).—During the reign of **Kosambika** in **Kosambī,** two brahmins, **Dīpāyana** and **Maṇḍavya,** gave away their vast wealth and lived for fifty years as ascetics in **Himavā.** After that, while on a pilgrimage to Benares, they were entertained by a householder who was also named **Maṇḍavya.** Dīpāyana journeyed on while the ascetic Maṇḍavya remained in a cemetery near Benares. There some robbers left some stolen goods outside his hut, and Maṇḍavya, being charged before the king, was impaled, but by virtue of his great powers he continued to live. Dīpāyana came to see his friend, and finding him thus and learning that he bore no ill-will towards anyone, took up his abode under his impaled body. Gouts of gore fell from Maṇḍavya's wound on to Dīpāyana's golden body and there dried, forming black spots; so he came to be called **Kaṇha-Dīpāyana.** When the king heard of this, he had Maṇḍavya released with a piece of the stake still inside him, on account of which he came to be called **Āṇi-Maṇḍavya.** Dīpāyana returned to the householder Maṇḍavya, whose son **Yaññadatta** he helped to heal by an Act of Truth, the child having been bitten by a snake while playing ball. The lad's parents then performed acts of Truth. In this declaration of Truth it was disclosed that Dīpāyana had no desire for the ascetic life, that the father did not believe in the fruits of generosity, and that the mother had no love for her husband. They thereupon admonished each other and agreed to mend their ways.

The Maṇḍavya of the story was **Ānanda,** his wife **Visākhā,** the son **Rāhula,** Āṇi-Maṇḍavya **Sāriputta** and Kaṇha-Dīpāyana the Bodhisatta.[1]

The occasion for the story is the same as that for the **Kusa Jātaka** (*q.v.*).

In one verse Kaṇha-Dīpāyana is addressed merely as Kaṇha.[2]

The story is also given in the *Cariyāpiṭaka.*[3]

[1] J. iv. 27 ff. [2] *Ibid.*, p. 33. [3] p. 99 f.

Kaṇhadevala.—Another name for **Asita.**[1]

[1] SnA. ii. 487.

Kaṇhanadī.—Another name for **Kāḷanadī,** the river forming the boundary of **Rohaṇa.**[1]

[1] Cv. liii. 20; Cv. *Trs.* i. 173, n. 5.

Kaṇhapakka Vagga.—The first chapter of the *Mātugāma Saṃyutta.*[1]

[1] S. iv. 238-43.

Kaṇhamitta.—The real name of the thera **Valliya** (*q.v.*) of **Vesālī.** *v.l.* **Gaṇḍimitta.**

Kaṇhavāṭa.—A locality in **Rohaṇa.**[1]

[1] Cv. lxxv. 174.

Kaṇhasiri.—Another name for **Asita.**[1]

[1] Sn. v. 689.

1. **Kaṇhā.**—Daughter of the king of **Kosala.** Before she was born, **Brahmadatta,** king of Benares, killed her father and carried off her mother. When the child was born, Brahmadatta adopted her as his own daughter; she is, therefore, called *dvepitikā* (=having two fathers). The king promised to grant her a boon, and she held a *svayaṃvara*, at which she chose as her husbands all the five sons of King **Paṇḍu ; Ajjuna, Bhīma, Nakula, Yuddhiṭṭhila,** and **Sahadeva.**[1]

By her strong passions she won the love of them all. Not satisfied with them, she also made love to a hump-backed slave who was in her service. One day, when she was sick, all her husbands were gathered round her, and she made signs to each of them to show that she loved him best. Ajjuna, however, was suspicious, and by questioning the hump-back, learnt the truth. The five brothers left her and retired to the Himālaya, where they became ascetics. The story was related by **Kuṇāla,** who is identified with Ajjuna.[2]

[1] According to the Mahābhārata, Draupadī, daughter of the Pañcāla king, was the wife of these five princes.

[2] J. v. 424, 426 f.

2. **Kaṇhā.**—See **Kaṇhājinā.**

Kaṇhāgotamakā, Kaṇhāgotamikā.—A royal family of **Nāgas.**[1]

[1] A. ii. 72; J. ii. 145.

Kaṇhājinā.—Daughter of **Vessantara** and **Maddī.** She was so called because, at birth, she was laid on a black skin.[1] When Vessantara retired to the forest, his wife and children accompanied him to **Vaṅkagiri.** Later, both Kaṇhājinā and her brother **Jāli** were given to **Jūjaka** as slaves and were ill-treated by him. For sixty leagues they travelled with him, led and guarded by the gods, till they came to the court of their grandfather **Sañjaya,** king of **Sivi,** and there they were released, Kaṇhājinā's price being one hundred elephants, one hundred male and female slaves, etc. The children afterwards rejoined their parents and lived happily at the court.[2]

[1] J. vi. 487.

[2] *Ibid.*, 513 ff.

Kaṇhājinā is identified with **Uppalavaṇṇā**.[3] In the verses she is sometimes called **Kaṇhā**.[4]

Vessantara's gift of his children is considered the greatest of his gifts.[5]

[3] J.vi. 593.

[4] *E.g.*, 546, 548, 553.

[5] *E.g.*, *Milinda*, 117, 275, 284; Cyp. p. 80; DhA. i. 406; AA. i. 64.

Kaṇhayāna.—The name of the family to which belonged **Vāsudeva**[1] and **Ambaṭṭha**.[2] The family was descended from a sage named **Kaṇha.** (See **Kaṇha** (4).)

[1] J. iv. 84; vi. 421.

[2] D. i. 93.

Kataka.—A village in Ceylon granted by **Aggabodhi IV.** for the maintenance of the *padhanāghara*, which he built for the Elder **Dāṭhāsiva.**[1]

[1] Cv. xlvi. 12.

" Kati chinde " Sutta.—Preached in answer to a deva's question as to how many bonds an arahant should cut. Five, says the Buddha.[1]

[1] S. i. 3.

Kattala.—A village in South India belonging to **Toṇḍamāna.**[1]

[1] Cv. lxxvii. 51.

Kattikapabbata.—A village in **Rohaṇa** given by **Dappula I.** to the **Tissavihāra.**[1]

[1] Cv. xlv. 59.

Kattikā.—Name of a constellation and also of a month (October to November), during which the full moon is near the constellation of Pleiades (*kattikā*). It is the last month of the rainy season.[1] The fulmoon day of the month was observed as a festival and great rejoicings were held, particularly at night.[2]

[1] See, *e.g.*, *Netti*. 143. For details see N.P.D. *s.v.*

[2] *E.g.*, J. i. 433; 499, 508.

Katthaka Cetiya.—A structure built by the queen consort of **Udaya I.**[1] Can this be identical with **Kaṇṭaka Cetiya** (*q.v.*) ?[2] The *Sumaṅgalavilāsinī*[3] mentions a **Katthakasāla-pariveṇa** (*v.l.* **Kanthakasāla, Kandarasālā**), the abode of a monk named **Mahāsaṭṭhivassa** (*q.v.*) who lived in the time of King **Vasabha.** Kanthakasāla (? Katthakasāla)-pariveṇa was also the residence of a young novice who won the esteem of **Tissa,** a minister of King **Saddhā-Tissā.**[4]

[1] Cv. xlix. 23.

[2] See also Cv. *Trs.* i. 129, n. 3.

[3] DA. i. 291.

[4] AA. i. 262.

Katthakasāla.—See **Katthaka Cetiya.**

Katthī Sutta.—Preached to the monks at **Sahajāti** by **Mahā-Cunda.** It deals with ten qualities of which a monk should rid himself if he is to increase and prosper in the *dhammavinaya.*[1]

[1] A. v. 157 ff.

1. **Kathā Sutta.**—A monk should not indulge in childish talk—*e.g.*, about kings, robbers, ministers, etc.—but should speak only of Ill and things connected therewith.[1]

[1] S. v. 419 f.

2. **Kathā Sutta.**—On the five qualities which help a monk who practises *ānāpānasati* to attain to the immovable state (*akuppaṃ*). These qualities include conversation which enlarges the mind.[1]

[1] A. iii. 120 f.

Kathāvatthu.—The fifth of the seven books of the *Abhidhamma Piṭaka.*[1] It seems to have been compiled when the contents of at least the *Dhammasaṅganī*, the *Vibhaṅga* and *Paṭṭhāna* were already accepted as orthodox. Tradition ascribes its compilation to **Moggaliputta-Tissa** at the end of the Third Council, held under Asoka's patronage, at **Pāṭaliputta.**[2] It was rejected by some on the ground that it was set forth two hundred and eighteen years after the Buddha's death, and was hence only a disciple's utterance; but the Commentaries take the view that the *mātikā*, the principles taught therein, were laid down by the Teacher himself, and that the whole work should be regarded as the utterance of the Buddha, just as the **Madhu-piṇḍika Sutta,** preached really by **Mahā-Kaccāna,** is considered as the Buddha's teaching. The book consists of twenty-three chapters, and is a collection of discussions (*kathā*) and refutations of the heretical views of various sects on matters connected with theology and philosophy. The Buddha's authority is accepted as final.[3]

It has sometimes been suggested[4] that Asoka's Rock Edict IX. has been influenced by the Kathāvatthu. The therī **Khemā,** chief of the Buddha's women disciples, describes herself as being "Kathāvatthu-visāradā,"[5] thus strengthening the theory that the Kathāvatthu was known already in the Buddha's time.

The *Udāna Commentary*[6] refers to a *Kathāvatthupakaraṇa-Ṭīkā* for details of certain points raised.

[1] Sometimes called the third, *e.g.*, in Mbv. 94.

[2] Mhv. v. 278; Dpv. vii. 41, 56-8.

[3] See the very valuable Preface to the *Points of Controversy*, by Mrs. Rhys Davids, vii ff. See also Rhys Davids on "Questions discussed in the Kathāvatthu," *J.R.A.S.* 1892.

[4] *E.g.*, *J.R.A.S.* 1915, 805 ff.

[5] ThigA. 135.

[6] UdA. 94.

1. **Kathavatthu Suttā.**—A group of seven suttas on the topics of discourse—past, future, and present—and the qualities which show whether a person is competent or incompetent to discuss. The profit of talk is the release of the mind from grasping.[1]

[1] A. i. 197 f.; *cf.* D. iii. 220 (*Kathāvatthūni*).

2. **Kathāvatthu Sutta.**—Monks should not indulge in idle talk, as of kings, robbers, great ministers, etc. There are, for monks, ten suitable topics of conversation, such as contentment, virtue, energy, wisdom, etc.[1]

[1] A. v. 128 f.

Kathāvivaraṇa.—A book mentioned in the *Gandhavaṃsa.*[1]

[1] p. 65.

Kathika Sutta.—The true preacher is one who preaches revulsion from the body, its fading away and its cessation.[1]

[1] S. iii. 163.

1. **Kadamba, Kadambaka.**—The river that flows past **Anurādhapura,** on the eastern side, now called the Malvatu Oya.[1] Near the river was the **Nivatta-cetiya.**[2] The river ford, the **Gaṅgalatittha,**[3] formed the beginning of the boundary line of the *sīmā* of the **Mahāvihāra,** and this line also ended at the river bank.[4] The road from Anurādhapura to **Cetiyagiri** lay aross the Kadamba-nadī, and pious kings, such as **Mahā-Dāṭhika-Mahā-Nāga,** spread carpets from the river up to the mountain so that pilgrims could wash their feet in the river and approach the mountain shrines with clean feet.[5]

The road from the Kadamba river to Thūpārāma passed through the **Rājamātudvāra.**[6] **Moggallāna II.** dammed up the river among the mountains and thus formed three tanks, the **Pattapāsāṇavāpi,** the **Dhanavāpi,** and the **Garītara,**[7] and **Udaya II.** built a weir for the overflow of the river.[8]

In the time of **Kakusandha** Buddha, the capital of Ceylon, **Abhaya-nagara,** lay to the east of **Kadambanadī.**[9]

See also **Kalamba.**

[1] Mhv. vii. 43; and *Trs.* 58, n. 3.
[2] Mhv. xv. 10.
[3] MṬ. 361.
[4] Mhv. xv. 191.
[5] *Ibid.*, xxxiv. 78.
[6] SA. i. 173.
[7] Cv. xli. 61.
[8] *Ibid.*, li. 130.
[9] Mhv. xv. 59; Dpv. xv. 39; xvii. 12; see also Mbv. 120, 134 f.

2. **Kadamba.**—A mountain near **Himavā.** Seven Pacceka Buddhas once lived there.[1]

[1] Ap. ii. 382.

Kadambagona.—A vihāra built by **Aggabodhi V.** in **Mahāthala,** and probably presented to the **Paṃsukūlins.**[1]

[1] Cv. xlviii. 3; Cv. *Trs.* i. 110, n. 1.

1. **Kadambapupphiya Thera.**—An arahant. Ninety-four kappas ago he saw seven Pacceka Buddhas on a mountain named **Kukkuṭa,** near Himavā, and honoured them with *kadamba*-flowers. Ninety-two kappas ago he became king seven times, under the name of **Phulla** (*v.l.* **Puppha**[1]). He is probably identical with **Saṅgharakkhita** Thera.[2]

[1] Ap. i. 178.
[2] ThagA. i. 216.

2. **Kadambapupphiya Thera.**—An arahant. Ninety-one kappas ago he saw the Buddha **Vipassī** pass by his house and offered him a *kadamba*-flower.[1]

[1] Ap. i. 287.

Kadaligāma.—A village to the north of **Samantakūṭa** and on the road which led to it from the north. It is situated on a small river which joins the Maskeli river and ultimately flows into the Kelani river. **Vijayabāhu I.** built rest-houses at the village for the use of pilgrims coming to Samantakūṭa.[1]

Kadalī is to be identified with the modern Kehelgamuva.[2]

Perhaps the **Kadalisenagāma,** where **Devappatirāja** built a bridge of one hundred staves, may be the same village, but this is questionable.[3] This is more likely to be the modern Kehellenāva.[4]

[1] Cv. lx. 66.
[2] Cv. *Trs.* i. 221, n. 3.
[3] Cv. lxxxvi. 41.
[4] Cv. *Trs.* ii. 174, n. 3.

Kadalīnivātaka.—A locality in Ceylon situated on the road from **Dakkhiṇadesa** (more exactly **Mahāgalla**) to **Anurādhapura.**[1] A battle took place there between King **Saṅghatissa** and King **Moggallāna** (afterwards Moggallāna III.).[2] A later battle was fought there between **Aggabodhi VI.** and Prince **Aggabodhi** of **Dakkhiṇadesa.**[3]

[1] Cv. *Trs.* i. 114 n. 3; i. 74, n. 2.
[2] Cv. xliv. 6.
[3] *Ibid.*, xlviii. 50.

Kadalīpattagāma.—A village in **Rohaṇa** near the ford called **Nīlavalā,** and close to the modern Mātara.[1]

[1] Cv. lxxv. 49; Cv. *Trs.* ii. 48, n. 2.

Kadalīpupphiya.—See **Kandalīpupphiya.**

Kadalīphaladāyaka Thera.—An arahant. Thirty-one kappas ago he saw a Buddha and gave him a banana fruit.[1] He is probably identical with **Cūlaka** Thera.[2]

[1] Ap. i. 297. [2] ThagA. i. 334.

Kadalīvāta.—One of the Vanni kings of Ceylon, head of the mercenary soldiers who were driven out of Ceylon by **Bhuvanekabāhu I.**[1]

[1] Cv. xc. 33.

Kaddamadaha.—A lake, on the bank of which was **Vāraṇā,** where **Mahā-Kaccāna** once stayed, and where he was visited by the brahmin **Ārāmadaṇḍa.**[1]

[1] A. i. 65.

Kaddūragāma.—A village near **Ālisāra**; the village entrenchment was captured by **Māyāgeha,** general of **Parakkamabāhu I.**[1]

[1] Cv. lxx. 105.

Kaddūravaḍḍhamāna.—A tank in Ceylon. It was joined up to the **Giritālaka** tank by the **Kāverī** canal, and to the **Arimaddavijayaggāma** tank by the **Somavatī** canal. It formed part of the irrigation schemes of **Parakkamabāhu I.**[1]

[1] Cv. lxxix. 55 f.

Kanakadattā.—A nun, disciple of **Koṇāgamana,** who brought a branch of the Buddha's *udumbara*-bodhi to Ceylon. She, with her following, was left behind by the Buddha.[1] *v.l.* **Kantakānandā** and **Kandanandā.**

[1] Dpv. xvii. 17.

Kanakapabbata.—A mountain near **Saṅkassa.** There King **Arindama** questioned the Buddha **Sumaṅgala** about *nirodha,* and eighty crores of beings realised the Truth. The mountain came into existence as a result of Arindama's good fortune.[1] *v.l.* **Kañcanapabbata.**

[1] Bu. v. 13; BuA. 129.

Kanakamuni.—See **Koṇāgamana.**

Kanakāgamana.—See **Koṇāgamana.**

Kanasiya.—A Damila chief, conquered by **Laṅkāpura** at **Tirivekambama.**[1]

[1] Cv. lxxvi. 238.

Kanāda.—A teacher of philosophy, mentioned with **Kapila,** as teaching that the soul was limitless (*na antavā*).[1]

[1] UdA. 339.

Kaniṭṭha-Tissa, Kaniṭṭha-Tissaka.—King of Ceylon (227-245 A.D.). He was the younger brother of **Bhātika-Tissa.** He built the **Ratanapāsāda** at **Abhayagiri** for **Mahānāga** of **Bhūtārāma,** and he also built at Abhayagiri a wall, a great pariveṇa, and the **Maṇisoma-vihāra.** He built a cetiya at **Ambatthala,** restored the temple at **Nāgadīpa,** and made the **Kukkuṭagiri** cells. Among his other works were fourteen pāsādas at the **Mahāvihāra,** a road to the **Dakkhiṇavihāra,** the **Bhūtārāma-vihāra,** the **Rāmagoṇaka,** the **Nandatissa** monastery, the **Anulatissa-pabbata-vihāra,** the **Niyelatissārāma,** the **Pīlapiṭṭhi-vihāra,** and the **Rājamahā-vihāra.**

He had two sons, **Khujjanāga** and **Kuñcanāga** (*q.v.*).[1]

[1] Mhv. xxxvi. 6 ff.

Kantaka-cetiya.—A building on the **Cetiyapabbata.** Near it were many rock cells, sixty-eight of which were built by **Devānampiya-Tissa.**[1] Can this be the same as Kaṇṭaka-cetiya (*q.v.*)? See also **Katthaka.**

[1] Mhv. xvi. 12.

Kantakānandā.—See **Kanakadattā.**

Kanthaka (*v.l.* **Kaṇṭhaka**).—The horse on which **Gotama** left his father's palace, accompanied by his attendant **Channa.** It is said that when Kanthaka was saddled for the journey, he realised the importance of the hour and neighed loudly for joy, but the gods muffled the sound of his neighing as also that of his footsteps as he galloped through the streets; ordinarily the sound of his neighing and galloping could be heard throughout **Kapilavatthu.** He was eighteen cubits long from neck to tail and proportionately broad, quite white in colour, like a clean conch-shell.

In this journey of Gotama, Channa held on to Kanthaka's tail. The horse had the strength, had it been necessary, to clear the ramparts of the city, eighteen hands high, at one bound, with the prince and Channa on his back. Just outside Kapilavatthu the prince stopped the horse, in order to take a last look at the city. A cetiya was later erected on this spot and called **Kanthakanivatta-cetiya.** The horse travelled thirty leagues between midnight and the following morning, as far as the river **Anomā.** It is said that Kanthaka could travel round the whole *cakkavāla* in one night. With one leap the horse cleared the river, which was eight fathoms wide. On arriving on the opposite bank, the Bodhisatta gave orders that Kanthaka should be taken back to Kapilavatthu, but Kanthaka kept looking back at his master, and when the Bodhisatta disappeared from view the horse died of a broken heart, and was reborn in **Tāvatiṃsa** under the name of **Kanthaka-devaputta.**[1]

Kanthaka was born on the same day as the Bodhisatta.[2] In heaven he had a magnificent palace of *veḷuriya* gems, which **Moggallāna** visited on one of his tours in Tāvatiṃsa.[3]

[1] J. i. 62-5; Mtu. ii. 159 f., 165, 189, 190; VibhA. 34, etc.; Buddhacarita, v. 3, 68; vi. 53 ff.

[2] J. i. 54; BuA. 106, 234, etc.

[3] Vv. 73 f.; VvA. 311-18; see also DhA. i. 70; iii. 195.

Kanthakanivatta-cetiya.—See **Kanthaka.**

Kanthakasāla-pariveṇa.—See *s.v.* **Katthaka.**

Kandagalaka.—A bird, a former birth of **Devadatta.** See the **Kandagalaka Jātaka.**

Kandagalaka Jātaka (No. 210).—The Bodihsatta was once a woodpecker named **Khadiravaniya,** and he had a friend named **Kandagalaka.** One day Khadiravaniya took Kandagalaka with him into the acacia wood (*khadiravana*) and gave him insects from the acacia trees. As Kandagalaka ate them, pride rose in his heart and, feeling he could get food without his friend's assistance, he told him so. In spite of the warning of Khadiravaniya, Kandagalaka pecked at an acacia trunk, broke his beak, and fell down dead.

The story was related in connection with **Devadatta's** attempts to imitate the Buddha, these attempts ending in his own ruin. Kandagalaka is identified with Devadatta.[1]

[1] J. ii. 162-4.

Kandanandā.—See **Kanakadattā.**

Kandara Vihāra.—A monastery in Ceylon, built by **Thūlanātha,** younger son of **Saddhātissa.**[1] According to the *Mahāvaṃsa Ṭīkā,*[2] the vihāra was in **Rohaṇa.**

[1] Mhv. xxxiii. 15. [2] p. 442.

Kandaraka.—A wandering ascetic who visited the Buddha at **Campā.** See **Kandaraka Sutta.** Buddhaghosa[1] describes him as a *channaparibbājaka* (a clothed ascetic).

[1] MA. ii. 565.

Kandaraka Sutta.—Once, when the Buddha was at **Campā,** on the banks of Lake **Gaggarā,** he was visited by **Pessa,** the elephant trainer's son, and **Kandaraka,** the Wanderer. Pessa saluted the Buddha and sat down, while Kandaraka, after his salutation, remained standing. Surveying the assembly of monks gathered round the Buddha and observing their great silence, Kandaraka expressed his admiration of the Buddha's training. The Buddha explained that all Buddhas school their disciples in the four *satipaṭṭhānas.* Pessa stated that it was far more difficult to train men than animals. The Buddha agreed and enumerated the four kinds of people in the world: those who torment themselves, torment others, torment both themselves and others, and, lastly, those who torment neither, dwelling beyond appetites, in bliss and holiness. Pessa stated that he respected only the fourth class, and having given his reasons went away. The Buddha expressed his regret that Pessa could not wait to hear the differences between these four kinds of people; and at the request of the monks the Buddha proceeded to describe them.[1]

[1] M. i. 339 ff.

Kandaramasuka.—See **Kaḷāramaṭṭhuka.**

Kandarasāla.—See **Katthaka.**

Kandalīpupphiya Thera.—An arahant. Ninety-four kappas ago he was a farmer on the banks of the **Sindhū,** and seeing the Buddha **Siddhattha** wrapt in meditation, offered him seven *kandalī*-flowers and paid him homage.[1] *v.l.* **Kadalī.**

[1] Ap. i. 257.

Kannamuṇḍa, Kannakatthala.—See **Kaṇṇamuṇḍa,** etc.

Kapallakkhaṇḍa.—A locality in Ceylon on the field of **Haṅkārapiṭṭhi.** Here was fought a fierce battle between **Iḷanāga** and the **Lambakaṇṇas,** in which the latter were slain in large numbers.[1]

[1] Mhv. xxxv. 34.

Kapallapūva.—A cave near the gateway of **Jetavana,** into which **Macchariyakosiya** (*q.v.*) and his wife threw away the cakes which were left over after they had fed the Buddha and five hundred monks. From this act the spot took its name Kapallapūva (Crock-cake).[1]

[1] J. i. 348; DhA. i. 373.

Kapālanāga.—A vihāra built by **Dāṭhā,** wife of **Aggabodhi II.**[1]

[1] Cv. xlii. 65.

1. **Kapi Jātaka** (No. 250).—Once when the Bodhisatta was living the ascetic life in the Himālaya, his wife having died, a monkey came in the rainy weather to the hermitage clad in an anchorite's robe which he had found in the forest. The Bodhisatta recognised the monkey and drove him away.

The story was told in reference to a hypocritical brother.[1]

[1] J. ii. 268 ff.

2. **Kapi Jātaka** (No. 404).—Once the Bodhisatta and **Devadatta** were both born as monkeys. One day a mischievous monkey took his seat on the arch which was over the gateway to the park and, when the king's chaplain passed under the arch, he let excrement fall on his head, and, on the chaplain looking up, even into his mouth. The chaplain swore vengeance on the monkeys, and the Bodhisatta, hearing of it, counselled them to seek residence elsewhere. His advice was followed by all except the monkey, who was Devadatta, and a few of his followers. Some time after, the king's elephants were burnt through a fire breaking out in their stalls. A goat had eaten some rice put out to dry and was beaten with a torch; his hair caught fire and the fire spread to the stalls. The chaplain, seizing his opportunity, told the elephant-doctors that the best remedy for burns was monkey-fat, and five hundred monkeys in the royal gardens were slain by archers for the sake of their fat.

The story was told in reference to Devadatta being swallowed up by the earth.[1]

[1] J. iii. 355 f.; *cp.* **Kāka Jātaka.**

3. **Kapi Jātaka.**—See the **Mahā-kapi Jātaka.**

Kapiṭṭha.—A village near **Cittalapabbata-vihāra,** the residence of **Phussadeva**[1] (*v.l.* **Gaviṭa**).

[1] Mhv. xxiii. 82.

Kapiṭṭhaphaladāyaka Thera.—An arahant. Ninety-one kappas ago he saw the Buddha **Vipassī** walking along the street and, pleased with his demeanour, offered him a *kapiṭṭha*-fruit.[1] He is probably identical with either **Nisabha**[2] or **Ajita.**[3]

[1] Ap. ii. 449. [2] ThagA. i. 318. [3] *Ibid.*, i. 73.

Kapiṭṭhavana.—A park on the banks of the **Godhāvarī** and the residence of **Bāvarī.**[1] According to Buddhaghosa[2] it was an island (*antaradīpa*) in the fork of the river, and was three leagues in extent. It lay between the kingdoms of **Assaka** and **Aḷaka,** and was purchased from these two kings for two thousand pieces. The kings gave another two leagues to Bāvarī as a gift. The park had been the residence of holy men of old, such as **Sarabhaṅga**[3] and **Sālissara,**[4] and it was called Kapiṭṭhavana from being covered with *kapiṭṭha*-trees (elephant apple)—*v.l.* **Kaviṭṭhavana, Kapiṭṭhakavana.**

[1] ThagA. i. 73.
[2] SnA. ii. 581.
[3] J. v. 132.
[4] J. iii. 463; see also Mtu. iii. 363.

Kapinaccanā.—A locality, probably near **Vesāli,** where lived the thera **Kappitaka,** teacher of **Upāli.**[1] It was so called because monkeys and men used to dance there.[2] Kapinaccanā may have been a name for the cemetery near Vesāli where Kappitaka (*q.v.*) lived.[3]

[1] Pv. 50. [2] PvA. 231. [3] Vin. iv. 308.

1. **Kapila.**—Father of **Pippali-māṇava,** who is better known as **Mahā-Kassapa.**[1]

[1] ThagA. ii. 142; but see ThigA., p. 73, verses 56, 57.

2. **Kapila.**—A brahmin, the Bodhisatta born as the chaplain of **Upacara,** king of **Cetiya.** The king had promised the post of chaplain to his friend **Korakalamba,** Kapila's younger brother, and when reminded of his promise, undertook to recover it from Kapila's son who had been given the appointment at Kapila's request. The king, in spite of Kapila's warning, attempted to fulfil his promise by lying, and, as a result, he was swallowed up in **Avīci.** The king's five sons thereupon sought Kapila's protection, and at his advice they left Ceti and founded

five cities: **Hatthipura, Assapura, Sihapura, Uttarapañcāla,** and **Dadda-rapura.**[1]

Kapila is sometimes called **Kapilatāpasa**[2] and **Kapila-isi.**[3] His encounter with the Cetiya king is evidently a famous legend, and is often referred to.[4]

[1] J. iii. 454 ff.
[2] J. v. 273.
[3] *Ibid.*, 267.
[4] *E.g.*, in the *Saṅkicca Jātaka* (J. v. 267).

3. **Kapila.**—A brahmin, the Bodhisatta. When the sons of **Okkāka** went into voluntary exile and were looking for a spot on which to found a city, they came upon Kapila in his hermitage in Himavā by the side of a lake. He was versed in the science of *Bhūmicāla*, and was, therefore, acquainted with the qualities associated with various sites. He knew that any city built on the site of his hermitage would become the capital of Jambudīpa and that its inhabitants would be invincible. He therefore advised them to found a settlement there. They followed his advice and named the settlement **Kapilavatthu** after him (*q.v.*). A hermitage was built near it for the use of Kapila.[1]

[1] DA. i. 259 f.; MṬ. 132 f.; SnA. ii. 353; see also Mtu. i. 348 ff.

4. **Kapila.**—A monk. He was the younger brother of **Sodhana,** his mother being **Sādhinī** and his sister **Tāpanā.** The whole family entered the Order of **Kassapa** Buddha; Sodhana learnt meditation and became an arahant. Kapila learnt the three Piṭakas and, intoxicated with his learning, disagreed with everybody, right or wrong. He would heed no admonition, and followed a life of evil conduct in which he was followed by his mother and sister. One day, when Kapila was reciting the *Pāṭimokkha*, none of the other monks gave the responses, and in anger he declared that there was neither *Dhamma* nor *Vinaya*. Thus he put obstacles in the way of religion, and was reborn in **Avīci.** Later he was born in **Aciravatī** as a fish, **Kapilamaccha.** Some fishermen, having caught him, took him to the king of **Kosala.** At the fish was of golden hue, the king took him to the Buddha, desiring an explanation of his colour. When the fish opened his mouth the whole of **Jetavana** stank. The Buddha questioned the fish and made him confess his sins. Struck with remorse, the fish died and was reborn once more in hell.[1]

[1] DhA. iv. 37 ff.; SnA. ii. 305 f.; SA. ii. 152; see also UdA. 179 f.; ThagA. i. 356.

5. **Kapila.**—A sinful monk who lived in a village near **Kosambī.** He was the friend of **Paṇḍaka** (*q.v.*).[1]

[1] Vin. iii. 67.

6. **Kapila.**—The *Majjhima Commentary*[1] has a reference to a monk named Kapila, who, because of his greed for possessions, is described as having been reborn with a flaming *saṅghāṭi*-robe (*saṅghāṭī pi ādittā hoti*). This probably refers to a monk mentioned in the *Pārājikā*,[2] who was reborn as a peta and who could be seen going through the air with his robe aflame.

[1] i. 75. [2] Vin. iii. 107.

7. **Kapila.**—A city, called **Kapilanagara,** capital of **Pañcālaraṭṭha.** This city once had **Cūḷani-Brahmadatta** as its king.[1] Perhaps it is this city that is mentioned in the *Dīpavaṃsa*[2] as having been the capital of **Abhītatta** (*v.l.* **Ajitajina**) and his eighty-four thousand descendants.

[1] PvA. 161; Netti. 142. [2] iii. 17; MṬ. 127.

8. **Kapila.**—A brahmin of **Sāgala,** in the **Madda** Country, father of **Bhaddā-kapilānī.** Kapila's wife was **Sucīmatī.**[1] The word Kapilāni is probably derived from his name.

[1] ThigA. 73; Ap. ii. 583.

9. **Kapila.**—A great physician, mentioned in a list of eminent physicians of old.[1]

[1] Mil. 272.

10. **Kapila.**—A minister of King **Vohārika-Tissa.** He was appointed by the king to suppress the **Vetulya** doctrine and hold the heretics in check.[1]

[1] Mhv. xxxvi. 41; Dpv. xxii. 44.

11. **Kapila.**—An ancient teacher of philosophy, mentioned together with **Kanāda** as having taught that the soul was limitless (*na antavā*).[1] He is probably identical with the founder of the Sāṅkhya system.

[1] UdA. 339; see also Śvetaśvatara Upaniṣad v. 2, and Rāmāyana i. 40.

12. **Kapila.**—An ancient seer, probably of Ceylon, in whose honour **Parakkamabāhu I.** built the **Kapila-vihāra** near **Pulatthipura,** with many-storied buildings, frescoes, and other ornamentations.[1]

[1] Cv. lxxviii. 92 ff.

Kapila Sutta.—Preached by the Buddha to the people assembled to hear his explanation of the golden colour of the fish, **Kapila-maccha** (see Kapila (4)[1]). The *Sutta Nipāta* calls it **Dhammacariya Sutta** (*q.v.*).

[1] SnA. i. 305 f.; DhA. iv. 42; UdA. 180; ThagA. i. 356.

Kapila-nagara.—See **Kapila** (6).

Kapilapura.—See **Kapilavatthu.**

Kapila-maccha.—See **Kapila** (4).

Kapila-maccha Vatthu.—The story of **Kapila-maccha.**[1]

[1] DhA. iv. 37 ff.

Kapilavatthu.—A city near the Himālaya, capital of the **Sākyans** (*q.v.*). It was founded by the sons of **Okkāka,** on the site of the hermitage of the sage **Kapila**—see Kapila (3).[1] Near the city was the **Lumbinīvana** (*q.v.*) where the Buddha was born, and which became one of the four places of pilgrimage for the Buddhists. Close to Kapilavatthu flowed the river **Rohiṇī,** which formed the boundary between the kingdoms of the Sakyans and the **Koliyans.**[2] In the sixth century B.C. Kapilavatthu was the centre of a republic, at the head of which was **Suddhodana.** The administration and judicial business of the city and all other matters of importance were discussed and decided in the **Santhāgārasālā.**[3] It was here that **Viḍūḍabha** was received by the Sakyans.[4] The walls of the city were eighteen cubits high.[5] From Kapilavatthu to the river **Anomā,** along the road taken by Gotama, when he left his home, was a distance of thirty yojanas.[6] The city was sixty leagues from **Rājagaha,** and the Buddha took two months covering this distance when he visited his ancestral home, in the first year after his Enlightenment. On this journey the Buddha was accompanied by twenty thousand monks, and **Kāludāyī** went on ahead as harbinger. The Buddha and his company ilved in the **Nigrodhārāma** near the city and, in the midst of his kinsmen, as he did at the foot of the **Gaṇḍamba,** the Buddha performed the **Yamakapāṭihāriya** to convince them of his powers.[7]

On this occasion he preached the **Vessantara Jātaka.** The next day the Buddha went begging in the city to the great horror of his father, who, on being explained that such was the custom of all Buddhas, became a *sotāpanna* and invited the Buddha and his monks to the palace. After the meal the Buddha preached to the women of the palace who, with the

[1] J. i. 15, 49, 50, 54, 64, etc.; see also Divy 548, and Buddhacarita I. v. 2.

[2] DhA. iii. 254.

[3] D. i. 91; J. iv. 145.

[4] J. iv. 146 f.

[5] J. i. 63; according to Mtu. (ii. 75) it had seven walls.

[6] J. i. 64.

[7] J. i. 87 ff.; this journey to Kapilavatthu was one of the scenes depicted in the relic-chamber of the *Mahā-Thūpa* (Mhv. xxx. 81).

exception of **Rāhulamātā,** had all come to hear him. At the end of the sermon, Suddhodana became a *sakadāgāmī* and **Mahā-Pajāpatī** a *sotāpanna.* The Buddha visited Rāhulamātā in her dwelling and preached to her the **Candakinnara Jātaka.** The next day **Nanda** was ordained, and seven days later **Rāhula.**[8] As a result of the latter's ordination, a rule was passed by the Buddha, at Suddhodana's request, that no one should be ordained without the sanction of his parents, if they were alive. On the eighth day was preached the **Mahādhammapāla Jātaka,** and the king became an *anāgāmī.* The Buddha returned soon after to Rājagaha, stopping on the way at **Anupiyā,** where the conversions of **Ānanda, Devadatta, Bhagu, Anuruddha,** and **Kimbila** took place. During the visit to Kapilavatthu, eighty thousand Sakyans from eighty thousand families had joined the Buddhist Order.[9] According to the *Buddhavaṃsa Commentary,*[10] it was during this visit that, at the request of **Sāriputta,** the Buddha preached the **Buddhavaṃsa.** It is not possible to ascertain how many visits in all were paid by the Buddha to his native city, but it may be gathered from various references that he went there several times; two visits, in addition to the first already mentioned, were considered particularly memorable. On one of these he arrived in Kapilavatthu to prevent the Sakyans and the Koliyans, both his kinsmen, from fighting each other over the question of their sharing the water of the Rohiṇī; he appeared before them as they were preparing to slay each other, and convinced them of the futility of their wrath. On this occasion were preached the following Jātakas: the **Phandana,** the **Daddabha,** the **Laṭukika,** the **Rukkhadhamma,** and the **Vaṭṭaka**—also the **Attadaṇḍa Sutta.** Delighted by the intervention of the Buddha, the two tribes each gave him two hundred and fifty youths to enter his Order and, with these, he went on his alms rounds alternately to Kapilavatthu and to the capital of the Koliyans.[11] On this occasion he seems to have resided, not at the Nigrodhārāma, but in the **Mahāvana.**

The second visit of note was that paid by the Buddha when Viḍūḍabha (*q.v*), chagrined by the insult of the Sakyas, invaded Kapilavatthu in order to take his revenge. Three times Viḍūḍabha came with his forces, and three times he found the Buddha seated on the outskirts of Kapilavatthu, under a tree which gave him scarcely any shade; near by was a shady banyan-tree, in Viḍūḍabha's realm; on being invited by Viḍūḍabha to partake of its shade, the Buddha replied, " Let be, O king; the shade of my kindred keeps me cool." Thus three times Viḍūḍabha had to

[8] Also Vin. i. 82.
[9] Vin. ii. 180; DhA. i. 112; iv. 124, etc.
[10] BuA. 4; Bu. p. 5 f.
[11] J. v. 412 ff.; the Sammodamāna Jātaka also seems to have been preached in reference to this quarrel (J. i. 208).

retire, his purpose unaccomplished; but the fourth time the Buddha, seeing the fate of the Sakyans, did not interfere.[12]

The Buddha certainly paid other visits besides these to Kapilavatthu. On one such visit he preached the **Kaṇha Jātaka.**[13] Various Sākyans went to see him both at the Nigrodhārāma and at the Mahāvana, among them being **Māhānāma,**[14] **Nandiya,**[15] **Vappa,**[16] and perhaps **Sārakāṇi.**[17]

During one visit the Buddha was entrusted with the consecration of a new mote-hall, built by the Sakyans; he preached far into the night in the new building, and, when weary, asked Moggallāna to carry on while he slept. We are told that the Sakyans decorated the town with lights for a yojana round, and stopped all noise while the Buddha was in the mote-hall.[18] On this occasion was preached the **Sekha Sutta.**[19]

The books record a visit paid by the **Brahmā Sahampati** to the Buddha in the Mahāvana at Kapilavatthu. (This appears, from the context, to have been quite close to the Nigrodhārāma.)

The Buddha, worried by the noisy behaviour of some monks who had recently been admitted into the Order, was wondering how he could impress on them the nature of their calling. Sahampati visited him and, being thus encouraged, the Buddha returned to Nigrodhārāma and there performed a miracle before the monks; seeing them impressed, he talked to them on the holy life.[20]

A curious incident is related in connection with a visit paid by the Buddha to Kapilavatthu, when he went there after his rounds among the Kosalans. Mahānāma was asked to find a place of lodging for the night; he searched all through the town without success, and at length the Buddha was compelled to spend the night in the hermitage of **Bharaṇḍu,** the Kālāman.[21] On another occasion we hear of the Buddha convalescing at Kapilavatthu after an illness.[22]

Not all the Sakyans of Kapilavatthu believed in their kinsman's great powers, even after the Buddha's performance of various miracles. We find, for instance, **Daṇḍapāṇī** meeting the Buddha in the Mahāvana and, leaning on his staff, questioning him as to his tenets and his gospel. We are told that in answer to the Buddha's explanations, Daṇḍapāṇī shook his head, waggled his tongue, and went away, still leaning on his staff, his brow puckered into three wrinkles.[23] Others were more con-

12 J. iv. 152.
13 J. iv. 6 ff.
14 S. v. 369 f.; A. iii. 284 f.; iv. 220 f.; v. 320 f.
15 S. v. 403 f.; 397 f.; A. v. 334 f.
16 A. ii. 196; M. i. 91.
17 S. v. 372.
18 MA. ii. 575.
19 M. i. 353 ff.
20 S. iii. 91 f.; Ud. 25.
21 A. i. 276 f.
22 A. i. 219.
23 M. i. 108 f.; this was the occasion for the preaching of the Madhupiṇḍika Sutta.

vinced and patronised the Order—*e.g.*, **Kāla-Khemaka** and **Ghaṭāya,** who built cells for monks in the Nigrodhārāma.[24]

It is said that the Buddha ordained ten thousand householders of Kapilavatthu with the "*ehi-bhikkhu-pabbajā.*"[25]

Mahānāma (*q.v.*) was the Buddha's most frequent visitor; to him was preached the **Cūladukkhakkhandha Sutta.**[26]

The **Dakkhiṇāvibhaṅga Sutta** was preached as the result of a visit to the Buddha by **Mahāpajāpatī-Gotamī.** Apart from those already mentioned, another Sākyan lady lived in Kapilavatthu, **Kāligodhā** by name, and she was the only kinsman, with the exception of the Buddha's father and wife, to be specially visited by the Buddha.[27]

The inhabitants of Kapilavatthu are called **Kapilavatthavā.**[28]

From Kapilavatthu lay a direct road to **Vesālī,**[29] and through Kapilavatthu passed the road taken by **Bāvarī's** disciples from **Aḷaka** to **Sāvatthi.**[30]

From the Mahāvana, outside Kapilavatthu, the forest extended up to the Himālaya, and on the other side of the city it reached as far as the sea.[31]

It is significant that, in spite of the accounts given of the greatness of Kapilavatthu, it was not mentioned by Ānanda among the great cities, in one of which, in his opinion, the Buddha could more fittingly have died than in Kusinārā.[32] After the Buddha's death, a portion of the relics was claimed by the Sakyans of Kapilavatthu, and a shrine to hold them was erected in the city.[33] Here was deposited the rug (*paccattharaṇa*) used by the Buddha.[34]

In the northern books the city was called Kapilavastu, Kapilapura, and Kapilāvhayapura.[35] According to the Dulva,[36] the city was on the banks of the **Bhagīrathī.**

The identification of Kapilavatthu is not yet beyond the realm of conjecture. Hiouen Thsang[37] visited the city and found it like a wilderness. The Asoka inscriptions of the Lumbinī pillar and the Niglīva pillar are helpful in determining the site. Some identify the modern village of Piprāwā—famous for the vases found there—with Kapilavatthu.[38] Others, including Rhys Davids, say there were two cities,

[24] M. iii. 109. As a result of noticing these cells, the Buddha preached the Mahāsuññata Sutta.

[25] Sp. i. 241.

[26] M. i. 91 f.

[27] S. v. 396.

[28] *E.g.*, S. iv. 182.

[29] Vin. ii. 253.

[30] Sn. p. 194.

[31] MA. i. 449; UdA. 184; Sp. ii. 393.

[32] D. ii. 146.

[33] *Ibid.*, 167; Bu. xxviii. 2.

[34] Bu. xxviii. 8.

[35] *E.g.*, Lal. p. 243, 28; The *Buddhacarita* (I. v. 2) calls it Kapilasyavastu.

[36] Rockhill, p. 11.

[37] Beal ii., p. 13 f.

[38] *E.g.*, Fleet, *J.R.A.S.* 1906, p. 180; CAGI. 711 f.

one ancient and the other modern, founded after Viḍūḍabha's conquest, and the ancient one they call Tilaura Kot. But the theory of two Kapilavatthus is rejected by some scholars.[39]

[39] *J.R.A.S.* 1906, pp. 453, 553. See also the article by Mukherji on Kapilavastu in ERE.

Kapila-vihāra.—See **Kapila** 12.

1. **Kapisīsa.**—A Tamil general subdued by **Duṭṭhagāmaṇī** at **Kacchatittha** after a siege of four months.[1] *v.l.* **Kavisīsa.**

[1] Mhv. xxv. 12.

2. **Kapisīsa.**—A minister of King **Vaṭṭhagāmaṇī.** One day when the king, accompanied by his queen, was going up the steps of the **Ākāsacetiya** at **Acchagallavihāra,** he saw the minister, who had come down after the sweeping of the cetiya, sitting by the roadside. Because Kapisīsa failed to prostrate himself before the king, the latter slew him.[1]

[1] Mhv. xxxiii. 68 f.

Kapīvantā.—A city to the north of **Uttarakuru.**[1]

[1] D. iii. 201.

Kapulpelanda.—See **Kabupelanda.**

1. **Kapota Jātaka** (No. 42).—Once the Bodhisatta was born as a pigeon and lived in a straw basket hung in the kitchen of the seṭṭhi of Benares. A crow, sniffing the savour of the food being cooked in the kitchen and longing to taste it, struck up a friendship with the pigeon in order to gain admission. In the evening, having searched for his food in the pigeon's company, he accompanied him home, and the seṭṭhi's cook, on seeing him, provided a basket for him. One day, seeing some fish being prepared, the crow feigned illness and stayed behind in his basket, in spite of the warnings of the pigeon, who suspected his real reason. The cook caught the crow stealing a piece of fish and, in order to punish him, plucked his feathers and soused him in a pickle of ginger and salt and cumin mixed with sour butter-milk. The pigeon, on his return, found him in this state and, having learnt his story, flew away, not wishing to live there any more. The crow died and was flung on the dustheap.

The story was related in reference to a greedy monk who was identified with the crow.[1]

[1] J. i. 241 ff.

2. **Kapota Jātaka** (No. 375).—The same as above, except for a few details. When the theft was discovered, the cook made a mixture of moist ginger and white mustard, pounded with a rotten date, and after wounding the crow with a potsherd, rubbed the stuff into the wound and fastened the potsherd round its neck.[1]

[1] J. iii. 224 ff.

Kapotakandara.—A grotto, probably near **Rājagaha,** where, later, a vihāra, called the **Kapotakondara-vihāra,** was built. The grotto was at one time the residence of a large number of pigeons (*kapotā*), hence the name.[1] On one occasion **Sāriputta,** having recently shaved his head, was seated there wrapt in *samādhi,* and a yakkha, passing overhead with his friend to an assembly of yakkhas, yielded, despite the warning of his friend, to the temptation to give a knock on the monk's shining head. The yakkha immediately fell down and was swallowed up in the fires of hell. Sāriputta had but a slight headache after the blow, which was, it is said, heavy enough to crush an elephant.[2]

According to the *Visuddhimagga,*[3] Sāriputta entered into a trance at the very moment the blow was dealt him.

[1] UdA. 244. [2] Ud. 39 f.; Thag. vs. 998 f.; PsA. 494. [3] p. 380.

1. **Kappa.**—One of **Bāvarī's** disciples. The questions he asked of the Buddha are recorded in the **Kappamānavapucchā** (*q.v.*). He became an arahant.[1]

[1] Sn. vv. 1007, 1092-5; SnA. ii. 597.

2. **Kappa Thera.**—An arahant. He was the son of a provincial governor in **Magadha** and was addicted to self-indulgence. The Buddha, seeing him in his net of wisdom, visited him and admonished him, speaking to him of the filthy nature of the body, illustrating his sermon with a wealth of simile and metaphor. Kappa was greatly impressed and joined the Order. He became an arahant, as his head was being shaved. In the time of the Buddha **Siddhattha** he was a rich householder, and offered at the Buddha's shrine a *kapparukkha* containing objects of great value. Wherever he was born celestial trees grew outside his door. Seven kappas ago he was eight times king under the name of **Sucela.**[1] He is probably identical with **Kapparukkhiya** of the *Apadāna.*[2]

[1] Thag. 567-76; ThagA. i. 521 ff. [2] Ap. i. 91.

3. **Kappa.**—In the *Saṃyutta Nikāya*[1] two suttas are connected with a monk called Kappa, who is probably identical with Kappa (2). In both suttas he asks the Buddha how it is possible to cultivate knowledge and thought so as to be free from thoughts of " I " and " mine " with regard to the body. The same questions, receiving the same answers, are elsewhere attributed to **Rāhula.**[2]

[1] S. iii. 169 f. [2] S. ii. 253 f.

4. **Kappa.**—A young brahmin (**Kappakumāra**) who was the Bodhisatta. He later became a sage and the disciple and friend of **Kesava.** For his story see the **Kesava Jātaka.**[1] The story is also referred to in the **Bakabrahma Jātaka,**[2] and mentioned in the *Saṃyutta Nikāya,*[3] where **Bakabrahmā** is identified with Kappa's teacher, **Kesava.** *v.l.* **Kappaka.**

[1] J. iii. 142 ff. [2] *Ibid.*, 361; DhA. i. 342 f. [3] S. i. 144; SA. i. 164; MA. i. 555.

5. **Kappa.**—See **Nigrodha-Kappa.**

1. **Kappa Sutta.**—Two suttas where **Kappa Thera**—see Kappa (3)—asks the Buddha how it is possible to get rid of thoughts of " I " and " mine," and to have conceit regarding the body utterly destroyed.[1]

[1] S. iii. 169 f.; see also S. ii. 253 f.

2. **Kappa Sutta.**—On the four incalculable periods of the æon (*kappa*): when it rolls up, stands still, rolls out, and remains in that condition.[1]

[1] A. ii. 142; *cf.* D. i. 14; 109; Mil. 232.

Kappaka.—See **Kappa** (4).

Kappakagāma (Kappukagāma).—A vihāra in Ceylon, the residence of the thera **Deva.** It was from him that King **Vohārika-Tissa** heard the Doctrine and, as a mark of favour, the king restored five buildings belonging to the Kappakagāma monastery.[1]

[1] Mhv. xxxvi. 29.

Kappakandara (*v.l.* **Kappukandara**).—A village, river, and monastery, all of the same name. The village was the birthplace of **Bharaṇa,** one of **Duṭṭhagāmaṇi's** generals.[1] On the river was a ford called **Javamāla,** crossed by Duṭṭhagāmaṇi while fleeing from his brother **Tissa.**[2] According to this context, the river must have been in **Rohaṇa,** and Geiger[3]

[1] Mhv. xxiii. 64. [2] *Ibid.*, xxiv. 22. [3] Mhv. *Trs.* 165, n. 5.

thinks that it is probably identical with the modern Kumbukkan-Oya. The *Mahāvaṃsa Ṭīkā*[4] says that Malayamahādeva came to Kappakandara **Piyaṅgudīpa** to receive alms from Duṭṭhagāmaṇī.

[4] p. 593.

Kappagallaka.—A village in **Rohaṇa** where **Mahinda V.** founded a town which, for some time, was the seat of his government.[1]

[1] Cv. lv. 11.

Kappaṭa.—A merchant of Benares, the Bodhisatta. He was a potter and owned a donkey who carried loads of pots and could travel seven leagues a day. Once Kappaṭa took the donkey to **Takkasilā,** where the latter became so enamoured of a female donkey that he refused to go home until the merchant promised to find him a mate equally beautiful. On reaching home the merchant offered to fulfil his promise, but refused to supply any extra food for the animal's mate or for the foals if any were born. This opened the donkey's eyes, and he renounced his desire for a mate. The donkey is identified with **Nanda,** and the female donkey with **Janapadakalyāṇī Nandā.**[1]

[1] DhA. i. 103 f.

Kappaṭakura Thera.—An arahant. He belonged to a poor family of **Sāvatthi,** where he went about in rags, pan in hand, seeking for rice grains (*kura*), hence his name (" Rags and Rice "). Later he sold grass for a living. One day, having heard a monk preach, he entered the Order, leaving his rags in a certain place; seven times disaffection grew within him, and each time he took up his rags and put them on. When the Buddha heard of this he admonished the monk severely, and the latter, greatly disturbed, developed insight and became an arahant.

In the time of **Vipassī** Buddha he was a householder, and offered the Buddha a few *ketakī*-flowers on the banks of the river **Vinatā.**[1] He is probably identical with **Ketakapupphiya** of the *Apadāna.*[2]

[1] Thag. 199 f.: ThagA. i. 320 ff. [2] Ap. ii. 449.

Kapparukkhiya Thera.—An arahant. Ninety-four kappas ago he placed a *kappa-rukkha* made of cloth of various colours in front of the *thūpa* of the Buddha **Siddhattha.** Seven kappas ago he was king eight times under the name of **Sucela.**[1] He is probably identical with **Kappa Thera.**[2]

[1] Ap. i. 90 f. [2] ThagA. i. 521 f.

Kappāyana.—A name of **Nigrodha-Kappa**[1]; given out of respect for him, says the *Commentary.*[2]

[1] Sn. v. 354. [2] SnA. i. 350.

Kappāsagāma.—A village in Ceylon. There **Kittī,** queen consort of **Mahinda IV.,** built a bathing tank for the monks.[1]

[1] Cv. liv. 51.

Kappāsika (Kappāsiya)-Vanasaṇḍa.—A grove near **Uruvelā.** There the **Bhaddavaggiyā** (*q.v.*) came across the Buddha while seeking for a woman who had run away with certain of their belongings. The Buddha preached to them and they entered the Order, obtaining various Fruits of the Path, from the first to the third.[1]

[1] Vin. i. 23 f.; J. i. 82; DhA. i. 72; Dpv. i. 34; AA. i. 57, 84; ThigA. 3.

Kappiñcimpekula.—A Damiḷa chieftain, ally of **Kulasekhara.**[1]

[1] Cv. lxxvii. 79.

Kappitaka Thera.—He was *upajjhāya* to **Upāli,** and once lived in a cemetery near **Vesālī.** In the cemetery the **Chabbaggiya**-nuns buried the ashes of one of their leaders and erected a thūpa near Kappitaka's cell. The Elder, disturbed by the sound of their lamentations, broke the thūpa and scattered the materials. The nuns, greatly angered, plotted to kill him, but he was warned by Upāli, and lay hidden elsewhere until the nuns had destroyed his cell and gone away under the impression that he was dead. The nuns blamed Upāli for upsetting their arrangements.[1] According to the *Petavatthu* and its *Commentary,*[2] Kappitaka lived in **Kapinaccāna** (near Vesāli), and there the Licchavi **Ambasakkhara** offered him alms on behalf of a *peta.* He was evidently at one time a Jaṭila, with a large following of Jaṭilas, for he is described as "*jaṭilasahassassa abbhantaro thero.*"[3]

[1] Vin. iv. 308. [2] Pv. 50; PvA. 229 ff. [3] Sp. iv. 937; PvA. 230.

Kappina.—See **Mahā-Kappina.**

1. **Kappina Sutta.**—**Mahā-Kappina** visits the Buddha who, seeing him from afar, tells the monks that Mahā-Kappina is highly gifted and of wondrous power, a gifted preacher and radiant; one of those who had gained the object of renunciation. The Buddha proceeds to say how

one, clothed in wisdom and virtue, is best among beings, and how the Noble One is best of shining objects in that he shines always.[1] The verses of this sutta are also quoted elsewhere.[2]

[1] S. ii. 284. [2] *E.g.*, D. iii. 98; Dh. vs. 387.

2. **Kappina Sutta.**—The Buddha sees **Mahā-Kappina** sitting cross-legged, with body erect, and mindful. He points him out to the monks, telling them that he can sit thus without shaking or wavering of his body because he has developed concentration on breathing.[1]

[1] S. v. 315 f.

Kappuka°.—See **Kappaka°**.

Kappūra-pariveṇa.—A building in the **Abhayagiri-vihāra**, erected by **Dāṭhopatissa II.**[1] Later, **Aggabodhi II.** built a *pāsāda* there,[2] and **Sena I.** erected a *pariccheda* (probably rows of single cells).[3] (See also **Kappūra-mūlāyatana**).

[1] Cv. xlv. 29. [2] *Ibid.*, xlvi. 21. [3] *Ibid.*, l. 77.

Kappūramūlāyatana.—This probably refers to the **Kappūra-pariveṇa Yasodharā**, daughter of **Vijayabāhu I.**, built there a large and beautiful image house.[2]

[1] Geiger: Cv. *Trs.* i. 222, n. 7. [2] Cv. lx. 83.

Kabupelanda.—A village and monastery in Ceylon. In the monastery once lived a *sāmaṇera*, possessed of great iddhi powers, who, not heeding the advice of his teacher, fell in love with a weaver's daughter and, as a result, lost all his powers. Later, the woman lost her sight through a blow from him, and he was reduced to abject poverty. The sāmaṇera's teacher had warned him of just this, but the warning was of no avail.[1] *v.l.* **Kammupelanda, Kampupelanda, Kapupelanda.** See also **Kupuveṇa.**

[1] VibhA. 294 f.; but see MA. ii. 699 f., where the names are spelt differently.

Kampilla (**Kampillaka, Kampilliya**).—A city in **Uttarapañcāla,** and probably its capital. **Dummukha** was once its king.[1] Sometimes[2] Kampilla is spoken of as being a kingdom, of which Uttarapañcāla was a city.

Once **Alīnasatta** is spoken of as Kampilla because he was the king of the city of the same name.[3]

[1] J. iii. 379; J. ii. 214; also Mtu. i. 283. [2] *E.g.*, J. iii. 79; iv. 396; v. 21; vi. 391; 464.
[3] J. v. 34; see also Rāmāyana i. 34.

Kambala.—A tribe of Nāgas. They were present at the *Mahāsamaya*,[1] and are mentioned with the **Assataras** as living at the foot of **Sineru.**[2]

[1] D. ii. 258. [2] J. vi. 165.

Kambaladāyaka-Tissa.—A name given to the monk who was later known as **Vanavāsī-Tissa** (*q.v.*). Though only seven years old, he was of great merit, and when he saw monks suffering from the cold he undertook to find them blankets. One thousand monks went to **Sāvatthi** with him, and in a very short while he obtained for them more than the requisite number of blankets. Thenceforth he was called by the name of **Kambaladāyaka.**[1]

[1] DhA. ii. 89 f.

Kambugallaka.—See **Hambugallaka.**

Kamboja (Kambojaka).—One of the sixteen **Mahājanapadas** which, with **Gandhāra,** belonged, not to the **Majjhimadesa** but, evidently, to the **Uttarāpatha.**[1] It is often mentioned as the famous birthplace of horses (*assānaṃ āyatanaṃ*).[2] In the **Kuṇāla Jātaka**[3] we are told that the Kambojas caught their horses by means of moss (*jalajāta*), and the scholiast[4] explains at length how this was done. They sprinkled the moss with honey and left it in the horses' drinking place; from there, by means of honey sprinkled on the grass, the horses were led to an enclosure.

In the **Assalāyana Sutta**[5] it is stated that in **Yoṇa** and in Kamboja, and also in the neighbouring countries, there were, in the Buddha's time, only two classes of people, masters and slaves, and that a master could become a slave or *vice versa*. The Commentary[6] explains that a brahmin would go there with his wife for purposes of trade and would die there. His wife would then be compelled to work for her living and her children would become slaves.

The Jātakas[7] would lead us to believe that the people of Kamboja had lost their original customs and had become barbarous. Elsewhere[8] Kamboja is mentioned as a place not visited by women of other countries. The country was evidently on one of the great caravan routes, and there was a road direct from **Dvāraka** to Kamboja.[9]

[1] A. i. 213; iv. 252, 256, 260.

[2] *E.g.*, DA. i. 124; AA. i. 399; Vsm. 332; also J. iv. 464.

[3] J. v. 445.

[4] *Ibid.* 446.

[5] M. ii. 149.

[6] MA. ii. 784.

[7] *E.g.*, J. vi. 208, 210; see also Manu. x. 44.

[8] A. ii. 82; on the reading of this passage, however, see GS. ii. 92, n. 2. The Commentary (AA. ii. 523) distinctly supports the reading Kamboja.

[9] Pv. p. 23.

According to Asoka's Rock Edict, No. XIII. (Shābhāzgarhi Text), Kamboja was among the countries visited by Asoka's missionaries. The country referred to is probably on the banks of the Kabul river.[10]

In later literature[11] Kamboja is the name given to Western Siam.

[10] Mookerji: Asoka, 168, n. 1. [11] *E.g.*, Cv. lxxvi. 21, 55.

Kamma Vagga.—The twenty-fourth chapter of the *Catukka Nipāta* of the *Aṅguttara Nikāya*. It contains ten suttas on various kinds of deeds, the four classes of ascetics and the blessings of a good man.[1] The Commentary calls it **Magga-vagga.**

[1] A. ii. 230-9.

1. **Kamma Sutta.**—Blameworthy action of body, speech and mind, and wrong views, bring about much demerit.[1]

[1] A. ii. 252.

2. **Kamma Sutta.**—Seven qualities which lead monks away from ruin (*aparihāniyā dhammā*): abstention from delight in (1) worldly activity, (2) disputation, (3) sleep, (4) society, (3) evil desires, (6) evil friends, (7) being easily satisfied with regard to attainments.[1]

[1] A. iv. 22.

3. **Kamma Sutta.**—Preached at **Gijjhakūṭa.** The Buddha sees **Sāriputta** walking with several other eminent monks, including **Moggallāna, Mahā Kassapa, Anuruddha, Puṇṇa Mantāṇiputta, Upāli, Ānanda,** and **Devadatta,** and praises each for some particular quality. He ends this discourse by saying that beings of similar disposition come together.[1]

[1] S. ii. 155.

4. **Kamma Sutta.**—On action—new and old—the ceasing of action and the way leading to such cessation, which is the Noble Eightfold Path.[1]

[1] S. iv. 132.

Kammakathā.—The seventh chapter of the *Mahāvagga* of the **Paṭisambhidāmagga.**[1]

[1] Ps. ii. 78-80.

Kammakāraṇa Vagga.—A group of ten suttas, forming the first section of the Duka Nipāta, on various subjects, such as faults and their punishment, worldly and spiritual striving, the two things (fear and shame) which guard the world, etc.[1]

[1] A. ii. 47 ff.

Kammakkhandha.—The first section of the *Cullavagga* of the *Vinaya Piṭaka.*[1]

[1] Vin. ii. 1-28.

Kammapatha Vagga.—The third chapter of the *Dhātu Saṃyutta.*[1]

[1] S. ii. 111 f.

Kammavibhaṅga Sutta.—See **Cūla°** and **Mahā°.**

Kammavācā.—A compilation of the rules and the ritual regarding admission into the Saṅgha.[1]

[1] Bode: *op. cit.*, 6 f.

Kammassadhamma.—See **Kammāsadamma.**

Kammahārattaka.—General of King **Khallāṭanāga.** He led a revolution against the king and killed him in the capital. The king's brother **Vaṭṭagāmaṇi,** however, killed the general and took over the government.[1]

[1] Mhv. xxxiii. 33; see also MṬ. 612.

Kammāragāma.—A village in **Rohaṇa,** identified with modern Kamburugamuva. It was one of the places passed by the **Kañcukināyaka** of **Parakkamabāhu I.** in his victorious progress.[1]

[1] Cv. lxxv. 47; Cv. *Trs.* ii. 48, n. 2.

Kammāradeva.—A locality in **Anurādhapura,** included in the *sīmā* marked out by **Devānampiya-Tissa.** On its left was the cemetery for the lower castes.[1]

[1] Mbv. 135; also Mhv. xv. 13 (see Geiger's edition, p. 332).

Kammāsa.—See **Kammāsapada.**

Kammāsadamma, Kammāsadhamma (*v.l.* **Kammassa°**).—A township of the **Kurūs.** The Buddha, during the course of his wanderings, stayed there several times; the exact place of his residence is, however, mentioned only once, namely the fire-hut of a brahmin of the **Bhāradvāja-gotta,** where a grass mat was spread for him by the brahmin. It was on this occasion, according to the **Māgandiya Sutta,**[1] that, after a long discussion, **Māgandiya** was converted. Several important discourses were preached at Kammāsadamma, among them being the **Mahānidāna Sutta,**[2] the

[1] M. i. 501.

[2] D. ii. 55; S. ii. 92.

Mahāsatipaṭṭhāna Sutta,[3] and the **Ānañjasappāya Sutta.**[4] The *Saṃyutta Nikāya*[5] contains a discourse on handling experiences by way of casual relations, and the *Aṅguttara*[6] a discourse on the ten noble states (*ariyavāsā*), both preached at Kammāsadhamma. Buddhaghosa[7] says that the people there were full of wisdom and their food was nutritious; it was therefore a compliment to their intellectual calibre that the Buddha should have preached these suttas to them.

Even in Buddhaghosa's day the name of the township had two different spellings, and two etymologies are suggested for the names.[8] The place was called Kammāsadamma because it was here that the man-eating ogre, **Kammāsapāda** (*q.v.*) was tamed and civilised by the Bodhisatta. (*Kammāso ettha damito ti, Kammāsadammaṃ-Kammāso ti Kammāsapādo porisādo vuccati.*) The spelling Kammāsadhamma is explained on the ground that the people of the Kuru country had a code of honour called the **Kuruvattadhamma**; it was here that Kammāsa (already referred to) was converted and made to accept this code, hence the name of the township. (*Kururaṭṭhavāsīnaṃ kira kuruvattadhammo, tasmiṃ Kammāso jāto, tasmā taṃ ṭhānaṃ "Kammāso ettha dhamme jāto" ti Kammāsadhammaṃ ti vuccati.*)

According to the Jātakas, there are two places of the same name, called **Cūḷakammāsadamma** and **Mahākammāsadamma** respectively, to distinguish one from the other. Mahākammāsadamma, which was evidently the original place, was founded on the spot where the porisāda of the **Mahāsutasoma Jātaka** was tamed,[9] while Cūḷakammāsadamma was the name given to the place where **Jayaddisa** showed his prowess by his spiritual victory over the ogre in the **Jayaddisa Jātaka.**[10]

In the Divyāvadāna,[11] the place is called Kammāsadamya. It was the residence of the nuns **Nanduttarā** and **Mittākālikā.**[12]

[3] D. ii. 290; M. i. 55.
[4] M. ii. 26.
[5] ii. 107 f.
[6] v. 29 f.
[7] SA. ii. 89.
[8] DA. ii. 483.
[9] J. v. 411.
[10] J. v. 35 f.
[11] pp. 515 f.
[12] ThigA. 87, 89.

Kammāsapāda.—The name given to the *porisāda* (cannibal) in the **Mahāsutasoma Jātaka** (*q.v.*). Before becoming man-eater he was the king of Benares, and was later weaned from his evil habit by the Bodhisatta **Sutasoma.** He is identified with **Aṅgulimāla.**[1]

Buddhaghosa[2] explains the name ("Spot-foot") as being given because of a wound he once received, which healed, leaving a scar like a piece of well-grained timber (*cittadārusadiso*). This refers to the flight

[1] J. v. pp. 503 f., 511.
[2] DA. ii. 483.

of the *porisāda* from his pursuers, when he trod on an accacia stake (*khānu*) which pierced his foot.[3]

According to Buddhaghosa,[4] the cannibal in the **Jayaddisa Jātaka** was also called Kammāsa or Kammāsapāda. The place where the *porisāda* was tamed was called **Kammāsadamma** (*q.v.*).

[3] J. v. 472.

[4] DA. ii. 483. See also Watanabe's article, "The Story of Kalmāsapāda and its Evolution in Indian Literature." *J.P.T.S.* 1909, pp. 236 ff.

Kammupelanda.—See **Kabupelanda.**

Kayanibbinda Jātaka.—See **Kāyavicchinda.**

Kayavikkaya Sutta.—Few are they who abstain from buying and selling, more numerous they who do not.[1]

[1] S. v. 473.

1. **Karakaṇḍa, Karakaṇḍaka.**—Son of the head of the third **Okkāka** dynasty and of his queen **Hatthā.**[1] He is also called **Karaṇḍaka.**[2]

[1] SnA. ii. 352; DA. i. 258; Mtu. i. 348.

[2] Mtu. i. 352.

2. **Karakaṇḍa.**—See **Karaṇḍu.**

Karajakāya Vagga.—The twenty-first chapter of the *Dasaka Nipāta* of the *Aṅguttara Nikāya.* It contains suttas on ten conditions which lead beings to hell, the ten conditions which give a lay-woman confidence in her house, etc.[1]

[1] A. v. 283-303.

Karaṇīyametta Sutta.—See **Metta Sutta.**

Karaṇīyavimāna.—A certain layman of **Sāvatthi** bathed in the **Aciravatī,** and on his return, seeing the Buddha, invited him to a meal. The Buddha accepted and was waited on with great devotion. As a result the layman was born in **Tāvatiṃsa,** in a palace which came to be called **Karaṇīyavimāna.** A further story is told similar to the above, except that the person fed is a monk and not the Buddha.[1]

[1] Vv. 55; VvA. 248 f.

1. **Karaṇḍaka.**—A hermitage (*assamapada*) near the Himālaya. The Bodhisatta, when born as an elephant as related in the **Mātiposaka**

Jātaka (*q.v.*), returned to Karaṇḍaka after the death of his mother. The hermitage was the residence of five hundred ascetics, and the king, out of regard for the Bodhisatta, looked after them.[1]

[1] J. iv. 95.

2. **Karaṇḍaka.**—See **Karakaṇḍa.**

3. **Karaṇḍaka.**—See **Karaṇḍu.**

Karaṇḍaka Jātaka.—See **Samugga Jātaka.**

Karaṇḍu (*v.l.* **Karakaṇḍa, Karaṇḍaka, Karakaṇḍaka**). King of **Dantapura** in the **Kāliṅga** kingdom. One day in his park he ate mangoes from a tree laden with fruit; his retinue doing likewise, the tree was soon stripped bare. Returning home, the king noticed the state of the tree and compared it with another tree which, having no fruit, was spared such ravages. Reflecting on this topic, he became a Pacceka Buddha and went to the **Nandamūla-pabbhāra** with three others—**Naggaji, Nimi,** and **Dummukha.** The story of these four is given in the **Kumbhakāra Jātaka.**[1]

[1] J. iii. 376 ff.

Karatiya.—A yakkha, mentioned in the **Āṭānāṭiya Sutta** as being one of the chief yakkhas who should be invoked by followers of the Buddha when they need protection.[1]

[1] D. iii. 204.

Karamba.—A Damiḷa chief, ally of **Kulasekhara.**[1]

[1] Cv. lxxvi. 139.

Karambiya.—A seaport. Thither came a man, saved from a wreck, without any clothes, who set up as a naked ascetic and became known by the name of Karambiya (*v.l.* **Karambhiya**). Among his followers was a Nāga-king, **Paṇḍara,** and also a Garuḍa-king. At the latter's request, he persuaded Paṇḍara to tell him how the Nāgas escaped destruction by the Garuḍas, and later he divulged the secret to the Garuḍa-king. The ascetic's treachery was discovered, and when he swore his innocence his head split in seven and he was dragged to **Avīci.** The story is given in the **Paṇḍara Jātaka,**[1] and is referred to in the *Milindapañha.*[2]

[1] J. v. 75 ff. [2] p. 201.

Karavāḷagiri.—A locality in Ceylon where once **Parakkamabāhu I.** set up his camp.[1]

[1] Cv. lxxii. 134.

Karaviṭṭhavilatta.—A tank in Ceylon. It was restored by **Parakkamabāhu I.**[1]

[1] Cv. lxviii. 48.

Karavīka.—One of the seven mountains surrounding **Sineru.**[1] Between Karavīka and **Īsādhara** lay a **Sīdantarasamudda.**[2]

[1] SnA. ii. 443; Sp. i. 119; Vsm. 206; DhsA. 298.

[2] J. vi. 125; see also Mtu. ii. 300, where it is called Khadiraka, and Divy. 217, 450.

Karindaka.—A mountain, headquarters of **Dāṭhāpabhuti** in his fight against **Moggallāna.**[1]

[1] Cv. xli. 45.

Karinda-nadī.—A river in South Ceylon. Near its source was the **Paṇjalipabbata.**[1]

[1] Mhv. xxiii. 14; also Mhv. *Trs.* 221, n. 1.

Karuṇā Sutta.—The idea of *karuṇā* (pity), if cultivated, is very fruitful.[1]

[1] S. v. 131.

Karumbūḷatta, Kurummaḷatta.—A Damiḷa chief, ally of **Kulasekhara.** He was subdued by **Laṅkāpura.**[1]

[1] Cv. lxxvi. 139, 216.

Karumhā.—A class of spirits, present at the *Mahāsamaya.*[1]

[1] D. ii. 260.

Karerikuṭikā.—One of the four principal buildings of **Jetavana,** the others being **Kosambakuṭi, Gandhakuṭi,** and **Salaḷaghara,** each being erected at a cost of one hundred thousand. Karerikuṭikā was built by **Anāthapiṇḍika** and was raised on pillars. A *maṇḍapa* of Kareri (*varuṇa*) trees stood at the entrance to the kuṭikā, hence its name.[1] Here was preached the **Mahāpadāna Sutta.**[2]

[1] DA. ii. 407. The Bharhut bas-relief, however, makes of it a one-roomed cottage (Dial. ii. 4, n. 1). SnA. (ii. 403) has **Candanamālā** for Salaḷaghara.

[2] D. ii. 1 ff.

Karerimaṇḍalamālā.—A pavilion near the **Karerikuṭikā,** evidently a hall with a thatched roof supported by wooden pillars, but with no walls.[1] Buddhaghosa calls it a *nisīdanasālā* (sitting-hall). Between this hall and the Gandhakuṭi was the **Karerimaṇḍapa.** Probably the term Karerimaṇḍalamālā was used to denote all the grounds within the Gandhakuṭi, the Karerikuṭikā and this hall (*Gandhakuṭi pi Karerikuṭikā pi sālā pi Karerimaṇḍalamālo ti vuccati*).[2] Dhammapāla, however, says that only the maṇḍapa and the sālā were called Karerimaṇḍalamālā. He explains maṇḍalamālā thus: *tiṇapaṇṇacchadanaṃ anovassakaṃ maṇḍalamālo; atimuttakādi latāmaṇḍapo ti apare.*[3] The monks seem to have been in the habit of sitting out here and talking on various topics at the close of the day. One such topic is recorded in the *Udāna*,[4] for discussing which the monks drew on themselves the Buddha's stern rebuke.

[1] D. ii. 1; Dial. ii. 5, n. 2.
[2] DA. ii. 407.
[3] UdA. 203.
[4] Ud., p. 30 f.

Karoṭi.—A class of spirits, associated with the Nāgas and forming one of the five defences of the Devas against the Asuras. The Jātaka scholiast says that Karoṭi is a name for the **Supaṇṇas** (a species of Garuḍa), and that they were so called because of their food and drink which were called Karoṭi (*tesaṃ karoṭi nāma pānabhojanaṃ*).[1]

[1] J. i. 204; *cp.* Karoṭapānayah, given as the name of a class of Yakṣas (Mtu. i. 30, 394); also Dvy. 218.

"Karoto" Sutta.—Discussion of the view that there is neither merit nor demerit in any kind of action whatsoever, whether good or bad.[1] The reference is evidently to the heresy of **Pūraṇa Kassapa.**[2]

[1] S. iii. 208.
[2] *Cp.* D. i. 52.

Kalakacchagāma.—A village in Ceylon, near **Kalyāṇī.** At the **Nāgamahāvihāra** there the thera **Maliyadeva** preached the **Cha-chakka Sutta;** sixty monks heard it and became arahants.[1]

[1] MA. ii. 1025.

Kalaṇḍuka.—A servant of the Treasurer of Benares (Bārāṇasī-seṭṭhi). See **Kalaṇḍuka Jātaka.**

Kalaṇḍuka Jātaka (No. 127).—**Kalaṇḍuka** was the servant of the Treasurer of Benares. He ran away, and with the help of a forged letter, just as did **Kaṭāhaka** (*q.v.*), married the daughter of a border merchant.

The Treasurer sent a parrot to seek for him. The parrot saw him hawking and spitting out milk at his wife's head in order to assert his power, and, wishing to teach him a lesson, threatened to expose him. The Treasurer, hearing from the parrot of Kalaṇḍuka's whereabouts, had him brought back and reduced again to slavedom.[1]

[1] J. i. 458.

Kalandakagāma.—A village near **Vesālī**; it was the birthplace of **Sudinna.**[1] Buddhaghosa[2] says the name was given because of the squirrels who lived there.

[1] Vin. iii. 11. [2] Sp. i. 202.

Kalandakanivāpa.—A woodland in **Veḷuvana.** Here food (*nivāpa*) was regularly placed for the squirrels. It is said that once a certain rājā went there for a pincic and, having over-drunk, fell asleep. His retinue, seeing him sleeping, wandered away, looking for flowers and fruits. A snake, attracted by the smell of liquor, approached the king from a neighbouring tree-trunk, and would have bitten him had not a tree-sprite, assuming the form of a squirrel, awakened him by her chirping. In gratitude the rājā gave orders that thenceforth the squirrels in that locality should be fed regularly.[1] Kalandakanivāpa was evidently a favourite resort of the Buddha and his monks.

See *s.v.* **Veḷuvana.**

[1] UdA. 60; SnA. ii. 419. According to some, it was the gift of a merchant named Kalandaka (Beal: *Romantic Legend*, p. 315); Thibetan sources identify the rājā with Bimbisāra and say that the snake was a reincarnation of the owner whose land the king had confiscated. According to these same sources the name is Kalantaka and is described as the name of a bird (Rockhill: *op. cit.*, p. 43).

Kalandakaputta.—See **Sudinna. Kalanda** or **Kalandaka** was the name, not of his father, but of his village.[1]

[1] Sp. i. 202.

Kalandagāma.—A brahmin village in Ceylon, where King **Mahāsena** built a vihāra on the site of an old Hindu temple.[1]

[1] Mhv. xxxvii. 41.

Kalanda-Vihāra.—A vihāra built in **Kālāyana-Kaṇṇikā** in **Rohaṇa,** by King **Mahādāṭhika-Mahānāga.**[1] **Aggabodhi VII.** is also credited with having built a **Kalanda-vihāra,**[2] but he may have only renovated an already existing one. Near the vihāra was **Brāhmaṇagāma.**[3]

[1] Mhv. xxxiv. 89; MṬ. 635. [2] Cv. xlviii. 70. [3] MṬ. 685.

Kalamba (*v.l.* **Kaḷamba**).—A river near **Anurādhapura,** probably identical with **Kadamba**[1] (*q.v.*). The river was to the east of **Anurādhapura.**[2]

[1] Sp. ii. 474. [2] MA. ii. 653.

Kalambaka-Vihāra.—A monastery built by King **Saddhātissa.**[1]

[1] Mhv. xxxiii. 8.

Kalambatittha-Vihāra.—A vihāra in Ceylon. In it once lived fifty monks who agreed on the full-moon day of Āsāḷha not to talk to each other until they became arahants. Their goal was reached within a month.[1] This vihāra is very probably identical with **Galambatittha** (*q.v.*).

[1] DA. i. 190; SA. iii. 155; SnA. i. 57; VibhA. 353; MA. i. 209 f.

Kalambadāyaka Thera.—An arahant. Ninety-four kappas ago he met a Pacceka Buddha named **Romasa** and gave him a radish (*kalamba*).[1]

[1] Ap. ii. 393.

Kalalahallika.—A village and tank near **Āḷisāra.** There was a fortification there. The tank was restored by **Parakkamabāhu I.**[1]

[1] Cv. lxviii. 48; lxx. 73, 163; also Cv. *Trs.* i. 301, n. 1.

Kalasigāma.—The birthplace of **Milinda** in the Island of **Alasandā** (or Alexandria) in the Indus.[1] Rhys Davids[2] thinks that the name is identical with that of the Greek settlement Karisi.

[1] Mil. 83. [2] *Milinda Questions*, i., p. xxiii.

Kalahanagara.—A village built on the spot where **Paṇḍukābhaya** defeated the soldiers sent by the father of **Suvaṇṇapālī** to rescue her.[1]

[1] Mhv. x. 42; see also Mhv. *Trs.* 71, n. 1, for its identification.

Kalahayināḍu.—A district in South India.[1]

[1] Cv. lxxvi. 261.

Kalahavivāda Sutta.—One of the six suttas preached at the *Mahāsamaya* (*q.v.*) held in the Mahāvana near Kapilavatthu. It deals with the origin of contentions and disputes. Disputes arise about objects which one holds dear; such affection is the result of desire, etc. It forms the eleventh sutta of the *Aṭṭhakavagga* of the *Sutta Nipāta.*[1]

It is said that the discourse was specially meant for those in the Assembly, whose temperament was malicious (*dosacaritānaṃ*).[2] We are told that **Mahā-Pajāpatī** heard the sutta and renounced the world.[3]

[1] Sn. vv. 862 ff.; SnA. 361, 551 ff. [2] MNidA. 222. [3] ThigA. 3, 141.

Kalābu.—King of **Kāsī.** He tortured the ascetic **Khantivādī** who was the Bodhisatta. He was therefore swallowed up in **Avīci.** He was a previous incarnation of **Devadatta.** The story is given in the **Khantivādī Jātaka.**[1]

[1] J. iii. 39 ff.; he is often referred to, *e.g.*, J. v. 135. 143 ff.

Kalāyamuṭṭhi Jātaka (No. 176).—**Brahmadatta,** king of Benares, once started off during the rainy season to quell a border rising. He stopped on the way, while his men steamed peas and put them into troughs for the horses to eat. A monkey came down from a tree hard by, filled his mouth and hands with peas, went back to his tree and started eating. One pea fell down, and he, letting all the other peas fall, clambered down to seek for the lost one. The Bodhisatta, who was the king's counsellor, pointed out to the king how fools of little wit spend a pound to win a penny. On hearing this the king went back to Benares.

The story was told to **Pasenadi,** who was going on a similar expedition during the rains, and on the way visited the Buddha at **Jetavana.** The king in the story is identified with **Ānanda.**[1]

[1] J. ii. 74 ff.

Kalāra Sutta.—**Kalārakhattiya** tells **Sāriputta** of **Moliya-Phagguna's** secession. Sāriputta says that Moliya-Phagguna did not find satisfaction in the Dhamma, and assures Kalāra that he himself has no doubts whatever either about the past or about the future. Kalāra reports this conversation to the Buddha, who sends for Sāriputta and asks him a series of questions. The Buddha praises his answers, but Sāriputta confesses to his colleagues later that he felt nervous over the first question, but when the Buddha accepted his answer to that he recovered his confidence.[1]

[1] S. ii. 50 ff.

Kalārakkhattiya.—A monk. He visits **Sāriputta** and tells him of **Moliya-Phagguna's** secession from the Order. The account of the incident is included in the **Kalāra Sutta** (*q.v.*).

Kalārakhattiya Vagga.—The fourth chapter of the *Nidāna Saṃyutta.*[1]

[1] S. ii. 47-68.

Kalikāla.—A Damiḷa chieftain, conquered by **Laṅkāpura.**[1]

[1] Cv. lxxvi. 214 f.

Kalikāla-sāhicca-sabbaññupaṇḍita.—A honorific (" all-knowing scholar of the Dark Age ") given to **Parakkamabāhu II.** on account of his vast erudition.[1]

[1] Cv. lxxxii. 3.

Kaliṅga.—See **Kāliṅga.**

Kaliṅgara Sutta.—Preached at the **Kūṭāgārasālā** in **Vesālī.** As long as the **Licchavīs** sleep on straw (*kaliṅgara*) so long will they be able to protect themselves from their enemy, **Ajātasattu ;** when they begin to sleep on soft couches they will suffer defeat. Thus it is also with monks and Māra.[1]

[1] S. ii. 267 f.

Kalimbha Thera (Kalimma).—One of the monks who lived in the **Kūṭāgārasālā** in **Vesālī.** Finding that the peace of the **Mahāvana** was being disturbed by the **Licchavīs** who came to see the Buddha, he, with the other monks, went to **Gosiṅgasālavana.**[1]

[1] A. v. 133 f.

Kalyāṇa (Kalyāṇaka).—A king of the **Mahāsammata** race. He was the son of **Vararoja** and one of the ancestors of the Sākyans. His son was **Varakalyāṇa.**[1]

[1] DA. i. 258; SnA. i. 352; J. ii. 311; iii. 454; Mhv. ii. 2; Dpv. iii. 4; Mtu. i. 348.

Kalyāṇadhamma Jātaka (No. 171).—The Bodhisatta was once a rich merchant in Benares. One day, when he had gone to pay his respects to the king, his mother-in-law visited his wife. The former was deaf, and on asking her daughter if they were happy, and receiving the reply that the husband was a very good man, like a hermit, she heard only the word " hermit," and she raised a great uproar thinking that her son-in-law had turned hermit. The news spread like wildfire, and as the merchant was on his way home he was told by someone that all the members of his household were weeping because he had become a hermit. Thinking that auspicious words should not be trifled with, the merchant went to the king, took his leave, and became an ascetic in the Himālaya.

The story was told in reference to a merchant of **Sāvatthi** to whom the same thing happened when he went to pay his respects to the Buddha.[1]

The story is also given in the *Jātakamālā*, where it is called the *Śreṣṭhi Jātaka.*[2]

[1] J. ii. 63-5. [2] No. 20.

Kalyāṇadhamma Vagga.—The third chapter of the *Duka Nipāta* of the *Jātaka*.[1]

[1] J. ii. 63-86.

Kalyāṇi-Tissa.—A king of **Kalyāṇī,** father of **Vihāramahādevī** (*q.v.*).[1] He was great-grandson of **Muṭasīva** and grandson of **Uttiya.** His younger brother was called **Ayya-Uttiya.**[2]

[1] Mhv. xxii. 12 ff. [2] MṬ. 431.

Kalyāṇamitta Vagga.—The eighth chpater of the *Eka Nipāta* of the *Aṅguttara Nikāya*.[1]

[1] A. i. 14 f.

1. **Kālyaṇamitta Sutta.**—Just as the dawn is the harbinger of the rising sun, so is friendship with the good the forerunner of the Noble Eightfold Way.[1]

[1] S. v. 29.

2. **Kalyāṇamitta Sutta.**—Friendship with the good is the most useful condition for the arising of the Noble Eightfold Way.[1]

[1] S. v. 31.

3. **Kalyāṇamitta Sutta.**—There is no better means of perfecting the Noble Eightfold Way than friendship with the good.[1]

[1] S. v. 32.

Kalyāṇavatī.—The first queen-consort of **Kittinissaṅka.** After the death of **Sāhasamalla** she carried on the government of Ceylon for six months (according to some six years, 1202-1208 A.C.) with the help of her general, **Āyasmanta.** She built a vihāra called the **Kalyāṇavatī-vihāra** in the village of **Paṇṇasālaka.**[1]

[1] Cv. lxxx. 34 ff.; also Cv. *Trs.* ii. 130, n. 3.

Kalyaṇigāma.—A village, probably in or near **Kalyāṇī**; it was the residence of **Mahātissa Thera.**[1]

[1] SnA. i. 6.

Kalyāṇi-cetiya.—The cetiya built on the spot where the Buddha preached to **Maṇiakkhika** and his followers.[1] According to tradition it enshrined the throne on which the Buddha sat, and has been a place of pilgrimage from that day to this.[2] **Vohārika-Tissa** erected a parasol on the cetiya.[3] (See also **Kalyāṇi-vihāra.**)

[1] Mhv. i. 75 f. [2] See, *e.g.*, VibhA. 295; MA. ii. 701. [3] Mhv. xxxvi. 34.

Kalyāṇi-(Kalyāṇika)-vihāra.—A monastery attached to the **Kalyāṇi-cetiya.** It was from the earliest times the residence of eminent monks, such as **Dhammagutta** (the Earth-shaker) and his five hundred colleagues[1] and of **Godattatthera.**[2] Here a thera, called **Piṇḍapātiya,** once recited the **Brahmajāla Sutta,** and the earth trembled as he finished his recital.[3] Near the vihāra was the village of **Kāḷadīghavāpigāma,** where monks who lived in the monastery went for alms.[4]

King **Kaṇiṭṭha-Tissa** built in this monastery an uposatha-hall.[5] **Vijayabāhu III.** restored the vihāra, which had been damaged by the Damiḷas, and reconstructed the cetiya, crowning it with a golden finial. He also built a gate-tower on the eastern side.[6]

In the fourteenth century **Alagakkonāra** seems to have bestowed great patronage on the monastery, and to have done many things for its improvement.[7]

Even in the fifteenth century the monastery was evidently considered one of the chief centres of the Saṅgha in Ceylon, for we find that the monks, sent by **Dhammaceti** from Rāmañña to Ceylon, received their ordination in the sīmā of Kalyāṇi-vihāra, and that on their return they consecrated a sīmā in Pegu known as the **Kalyāṇi-sīmā.**[8]

1 Mhv. xxxii. 51. 2 MA. i. 100.
3 DA. i. 131.
4 SnA. i. 70; AA. i. 13.
5 Mhv. xxxvi. 17.
6 Cv. lxxxi. 59 f.
7 See *Ceylon Antiquary and Literary Register* i. 152; ii. 149, 182.
8 Bode, *op. cit.*, 38.

Kalyāṇippakaraṇa.—A record of the famous **Kalyāṇī** inscriptions set up near Pegu by **Dhammaceti,** giving details of the consecration of the **Kalyāṇisīmā** in Pegu by the monks who received their ordination at the **Kalyāṇi-vihāra** in Ceylon.[1]

1 Bode, 23, 38 f.; P.L.C. 257 f.

Kalyāṇī.—The name of a river and of the district near its mouth in Ceylon. The Buddha visited the Kalyāṇī country in the eighth year after the Enlightenment, in company with five hundred monks, on the second day after the full-moon of **Vesākha** and, seated on the spot where the **Kalyāṇi-cetiya** was later built, he preached to the Nāgas and their king **Maṇiakkhika,** at whose invitation he had come.[1] Once a king reigned in Kalyāṇī named **Kalyaṇi-Tissa,** who had a daughter **Vihāramahādevī** (*q.v.*). According to the legends connected with her, Kalyāṇī was at one time

1 Sp. i. 89; Mhv. i. 63, 75 ff.; Dpv. ii, 42, 53; J. ii. 128.

much further from the sea than it is now. The sea swallowed up several leagues of land.[2] King **Yaṭṭhāla-Tissa** built a five-storied pāsāda in the town, which was later restored by **Parakkamabāhu II.**[3]

The Kalyāṇī district formed the fighting base of several campaigns.[4]

[2] Mhv. xxii. 12 ff. [3] Cv. lxxxv. 64. [4] *E.g.*, Cv. lxi. 35, 39; lxxii. 151.

Kalyāṇī Sutta.—No beautiful woman (*janapadakalyāṇī*) can persistently possess the heart of a man who is fond of gain, favours, and flattery.[1]

[1] S. ii. 235.

Kallaka-vihāra.—A monastery in Ceylon, near **Bhokkantagāma.** There **Sumanā,** wife of **Lakuṇṭaka Atimbara,** heard the preaching of the **Āsīvisopama Sutta** and became an arahant.[1]

[1] DhA. iv. 51.

Kallakaveḷāra.—A Damiḷa chief, brother of **Toṇḍamāna's** wife. He was slain by **Laṅkāpura.**[1]

[1] Cv. lxxvii. 40, 50.

Kallakālena.—A monastery in Ceylon, built by **Saddhātissa.**[1]

[1] Mhv. xxxiii. 7.

Kallagāma.—A village in Ceylon. In the village was the **Maṇḍālārāmaka-vihāra** (*q.v.*).[1]

[1] AA. i. 22, 52.

Kallara.—A district in South India.[1]

[1] Cv. lxxvi. 246, 259.

Kallavā Sutta.—Of those who meditate some are clever in concentration but are not fully expert in meditation, some are the reverse, some have neither quality, while others have both.[1]

[1] S. iii. 265.

Kallavāla, Kallavālamutta.—A village in **Magadha. Mahā-Moggallāna** lived there immediately after his ordination, and on the seventh day, while meditating there, he became an arahant, being admonished by the Buddha, who warned him against sloth.[1]

[1] A. iv. 85; ThagA. ii. 94; DhA. i. 79; AA. i. 91.

Kallita Sutta.—A man may be skilled in ease in concentration, but not in the range thereof, nor in resolve, zeal, perseverance, or profit.[1]

[1] S. iii. 275.

Kāḷārajanaka.—King of **Mithilā.** He was the son of **Nimi** and belonged to the **Makhādeva** dynasty. Whereas other kings of his race left the household at the approach of old age, he broke the tradition by not doing so. He was the last king of this dynasty. His son was called **Samaṅkara.**[1] **Kaḷārajanaka** was so called because he had long, projecting teeth.[2]

[1] M. ii. 82; DA. iii. 851; Mhv. ii. 11; Dpv. iii. 37; but see J. vi. 129, where he, too, is said to have renounced the world and brought the family to an end.

[2] MA. ii. 738.

Kaḷāramatthuka.—A naked ascetic of **Vesālī,** held in high repute by the **Vajjians.** He had taken seven vows: to wear no garments, to be chaste, to maintain himself only by spirituous drinks and flesh, eating no rice or gruel, never to go beyond the **Udena** shrine, the **Gotamaka** shrine, the **Sattamba** shrine, and the **Bahuputta** shrine. **Sunakkhatta** once visited him and asked him questions, but Kaḷāramatthuka would not listen, and showed resentment at being interrogated. When Sunakkhatta reported this to the Buddha, the Buddha predicted that the ascetic would, before long, wear garments, be married, eat rice and gruel, go beyond the limits he had until now observed, and fall in fame. And so it came to pass.[1] *v.l.* **Kandaramasuka, Kalāra, Kaḷāra-maṭṭhaka.**

[1] D. iii. 9 ff.

1. **Kavi Sutta.**—Contains a question asked by a deva about poets, and the Buddha's reply thereto.[1]

[1] S. i. 38.

2. **Kavi Sutta.**—On the four kinds of poets: the imaginative (*cintā-kavi*), the traditional (*suta-kavi*), the didactic (*attha-kavi*), and the extempore (*paṭibhāna*).[1]

[1] A. ii. 230.

Kaviṭṭhavana.—See **Kapiṭṭhavana.**

Kavisīsa.—See **Kapisīsa.**

Kasagāma.—A village in Ceylon, given to the **Moraparivena** by **Dāṭhopatissa II.**[1]

[1] Cv. xlv. 28

Kasālla.—A tank in South Ceylon repaired by **Parakkamabāhu I.**[1] A fortress of this name is also mentioned, where **Gokaṇṇa** was defeated.[2]

[1] Cv. lxviii. 48. [2] *Ibid.*, lxx. 72.

Kasiṇa Sutta.—The ten spheres of *kasiṇa* (*kasiṇāyatanāni*)—*e.g.*, *paṭhavi*, *āpo*, *tejo*, etc.[1]

[1] A. v. 46.

Kasī Sutta.—See **Kasī-Bhāradvāja.**

Kasī-Bhāradvāja.—A brahmin of the **Bhāradvāja** clan, living at **Ekanāḷā**, in **Dakkhiṇāgiri.** The Buddha visited him in the eleventh year after the Enlightenment.[1] The brahmin was so called on account of his profession of agriculture. On the day of his festive sowing (*maṅgalavappa*), the Buddha visited him alone (having seen his *upanissaya* for arahantship), and stood near the place where food was being distributed to a very large number of people engaged in the festival. The brahmin, seeing the Buddha begging for alms, suggests that the Buddha should work for his living—plough and sow just as he does.[2] The Buddha answers that he, too, is a farmer, and explains his meaning to the bewildered brahmin, who, greatly pleased, offers him a large bowl filled with milk-rice. The Buddha refuses the gift on the plea that Buddhas never accept wages for their sermons. At the Buddha's own suggestion the food is cast into the river because no one is capable of digesting food once offered to a Tathāgata.[3] When the rice touches the water it crackles and smokes and the brahmin, greatly marvelling, falls at the Buddha's feet and professes himself henceforth the Buddha's follower. Soon after, he enters the Order, and in due course becomes an arahant.[4]

[1] Thomas, *op. cit.*, p. 117.

[2] The Sūtrālaṅkāra says the brahmin threw water on the Buddha in order to drive him away (Sylvain Lévy, JA. 1908, xii. 99).

[3] The food had become too rich because the gods had added *ojā* to it. (See also Mil. 231.)

[4] Sn. 12 ff.; SnA. 131 ff.; the Saṃyutta does not mention his arahantship (S. i. 171 ff.), though the Commentary does so (SA. i. 188 ff.).

Kasī Bhāradvāja Sutta.—The Buddhist Parable of the Sower, forming the fourth sutta of the Uraga Vagga of the *Sutta Nipāta.*[1] It contains the story of the Buddha's visit to **Kasī-Bhāradvāja** given above. The Buddha tells him that in his work as a Teacher are to be found all the elements of a farmer's duties: faith is the seed, insight the plough, mindfulness the

[1] Pp. 12 ff.; also found in the *Saṃyutta* (i. 171 ff.) under the name of **Kasī-Sutta** and included in the *Paritta.*

ploughshare and goad, energy the burden-bearing team. The harvest produced by the sowing is *nibbāna* and the food *ambrosia*, free from suffering and sorrow.

Kasmīra.—A district in Northern India, the modern Kashmir. In the Pāli texts it is always mentioned with **Gandhāra** and probably once formed part of that kingdom.[1] At the end of the Third Council, **Moggaliputta** sent the thera **Majjhantika** to propagate the religion in Kasmīra-Gandhāra. Majjhantika quelled the power of the Nāga-king **Aravāḷa** (*q.v.*), who was a menace to the inhabitants, and converted him to the faith, while the yakkha **Paṇḍaka** and his wife **Hāritā**, with their five hundred sons, became *sotāpannas*. The thera preached the **Āsīvisūpama Sutta** to the assembled multitude and won eighty thousand converts, while one hundred thousand persons entered the Order. We are told that from that time onwards the yellow robe was held in great esteem in Kasmīra.[2] There was evidently a large community of monks at Kasmīra, till long after the coming of Majjhantika, for we are told that two hundred and eighty thousand monks, led by **Uttiṇṇa,** came from Kasmīra to **Anurādhapura** on the occasion of the foundation ceremony of the **Mahā Thūpa.**[3]

In Hiouien Thsang's time Kasmīra seems to have been an independent kingdom whose king was given to serpent-worship while his queen was a follower of the Buddha. Near the capital was a stūpa which enshrined a tooth of the Buddha. This tooth was soon after taken away by Harṣavardhana of Kanoj.[4]

Sāgala is mentioned as being twelve leagues from Kasmīra.[5]

[1] See also PHAI., p. 93. The Jātakas mention the countries separately as comprising two kingdoms ruled by a single king (*e.g.*, J. iii. 364, 378).

[2] Mhv. xii. 3, 9 ff.; Dpv. viii. 4; Sp. i. 64 ff.; see also Beal, *op. cit.*, i. 134, n. 39.

[3] Mhv. xxix. 37.

[4] CAGI. 104 ff.; Beal, i. 116 f., etc.

[5] Mil. 82.

Kassaka Sutta.—Once the Buddha was at **Sāvatthi** preaching to the monks on nibbāna. **Māra** appears in the guise of a peasant, dishevelled, wearing hempen garments, with a mighty plough on his shoulder, and asks the Buddha if he has seen his oxen. The Buddha declares, unequivocally, that he has no eyes for things owned; having escaped completely from worldly desires, possessions and ownership, his mind furnishes no gateway for Māra.[1]

[1] S. i. 114.

Kassakagiri.—See **Kassapagiri.**

Kassakalena.—A cave (probably in Ceylon), which was the residence of the Elder **Mahāmitta** (*q.v.*).[1]

[1] VibhA. 279 f.; SA. iii. 136 f.

1. **Kassapa.**—Also called **Kassapa Dasabala** to distinguish him from other Kassapas. The twenty-fourth Buddha, the third of the present æon (the **Bhaddakappa**) and one of the seven Buddhas mentioned in the Canon.[1] He was born in Benares, in the Deer Park at **Isipatana,** of brahmin parents, **Brahmadatta** and **Dhanavatī,** belonging to the **Kassapagotta.** For two thousand years he lived in the household, in three different palaces, **Haṃsa, Yasa** and **Sirinanda.**[2] He had as chief wife **Sunandā,** by whom he begot a son, **Vijitasena.** Kassapa left the world, travelling in his palace (*pāsāda*), and practised austerities for only seven days. Just before his Enlightenment his wife gave him a meal of milk-rice, and a *yavapāla* named **Soma** gave him grass for his seat. His bodhi was a banyan-tree, and he preached his first sermon at Isipatana to a crore of monks who had renounced the world in his company. He performed the Twin-Miracle at the foot of an *asana*-tree outside **Sundaranagara.** He held only one assembly of his disciples; among his most famous conversions was that of a yakkha, **Naradeva** (*q.v.*). His chief disciples were **Tissa** and **Bhāradvāja** among monks, and **Anulā** and **Uruvelā** among nuns, his constant attendant being **Sabbamitta.** Among his patrons, the most eminent were **Sumaṅgala** and **Ghaṭīkāra, Vijitasenā** and **Bhaddā.** His body was twenty cubits high, and, after having lived for twenty thousand years, he died in the **Setavya** pleasaunce at **Setavyā** in Kāsī. Over his relics was raised a thūpa one league in height, each brick of which was worth one crore. It is said[3] that there was a great difference of opinion as to what should be the size of the thūpa and of what material it should be constructed; when these points were finally settled and the work of building had started, the citizens found they had not enough money to complete it. Then an *anāgāmī* devotee, named **Sorata,** went all over Jambudīpa, enlisting the help of the people for the building of the thūpa. He sent the money as he received it, and on hearing that the work was completed, he set out to go and worship the thūpa; but he was seized by robbers and killed in the forest, which later came to be known as the **Andhavana** (*q.v.*).

Upavāna, in a previous birth, became the guardian deity of the cetiya, hence his great majesty in his last life.[4]

Among the thirty-seven goddesses noticed by **Guttila,** when he visited

[1] D. ii. 7.

[2] The BuA. (217) calls the first two palaces Haṃsavā and Yasavā.

[3] MA. i. 336 ff.

[4] DA. ii. 580; for another story of the building of the shrine see DhA. iii. 29.

heaven, was one who had offered a scented five-spray at the cetiya.[5] So did **Alāta** offer *āneja*-flowers and obtain a happy rebirth.[6]

The cause of **Mahā-Kaccāna's** golden complexion was his gift of a golden brick to the building of Kassapa's shrine.[7]

At the same cetiya, **Anuruddha,** who was then a householder in Benares, offered butter and molasses in bowls of brass, which were placed without any interval around the cetiya.[8]

Among those who attained arahantship under Kassapa is mentioned **Gavesī**, who, with his five hundred followers, strove always to excel themselves until they attained their goal.[9]

Mahākappina, then a clansman, built, for Kassapa's monks, a pariveṇa with one thousand cells.[10]

Bakkula's admirable health and great longevity were due to the fact that he had given the first fruits of his harvest to Kassapa's monks.[11]

During the time of Kassapa Buddha, the Bodhisatta was a brahmin youth named **Jotipāla** who, afterwards, coming under the influence of **Ghaṭīkāra,** became a monk.[12] This Ghaṭīkāra was later born in the Brahma-world and visited **Gotama,** after his Enlightenment. Gotama then reminded him of this past friendship, which Ghaṭīkāra seemed too modest to mention.[13]

The *Majjhima Nikāya*[14] gives details of the earnestness with which Ghaṭīkāra worked for Jotipāla's conversion when Kassapa was living at **Vehaliṅga.** The same sutta bears evidence of the great regard Kassapa had for Ghaṭīkāra.

The king of Benares at the time of Kassapa was **Kikī** (*q.v.*), and the four gateways of Kassapa's cetiya were built, one by Kikī, one by his son **Paṭhavindhara,** one by his ministers led by his general, and the last by his subjects with the treasurer at their head.[15]

It is said that the Buddha's chief disciple, Tissa, was born on the same day as Kassapa and that they were friends from birth. Tissa left the world earlier and became an ascetic. When he visited the Buddha after his Enlightenment, he was greatly grieved to learn that the Buddha ate meat (*āmagandha*), and the Buddha preached to him the *Āmagandha Sutta* (*q.v.*), by which he was converted.[16]

The Ceylon Chronicles[17] mention a visit paid by Kassapa to Ceylon in

5 J. ii. 256.
6 J. vi. 227.
7 AA. i. 116.
8 AA. i. 105.
9 A. iii. 214 ff.
10 AA. i. 175.
11 MA. iii. 932.
12 Bu. xxv.; BuA. 217 ff.; D. ii. 7; J. i. 43, 94; D. iii. 196; Mtu. i. 303 ff., 319.
13 S. i. 34 f.
14 M. ii. 45 f.
15 SnA. i. 194.
16 *Ibid.*, 280 ff.
17 Mhv. xv. 128 ff.; Sp. i. 87; Dpv. xv. 55 ff.; Mbv. 129.

order to stop a war between King **Jayanta** and his younger brother. The island was then known as **Maṇḍadīpa,** with **Visāla** as capital. The Buddha came with twenty thousand disciples and stood on **Subhakūṭa,** and the armies seeing him stopped the fight. In gratitude, Jayanta presented to the Buddha the **Mahāsāgara** garden, in which was afterwards planted a branch of the Bodhi-tree brought over by **Sudhammā,** in accordance with the Buddha's wish. The Buddha preached at the **Asokamālaka,** the **Sudassanamālaka** and the **Somanassamālaka,** and gave his rain-cloak as a relic to the new converts, for whose spiritual guidance he left behind his disciples **Sabbananda** and **Sudhammā** and their followers. In Kassapa's time Mt. **Vepulla** at **Rājagaha** was known as **Supassa** and its inhabitants as the **Suppiyas.**[18]

But many other places had the same names in the time of Kassapa as they had in the present age—*e.g.*, **Videha,**[19] **Sāvatthi,**[20] **Kimbila**[21] and **Bārāṇasī.**[22]

Besides the *Āmagandha Sutta* mentioned above, various other teachings are mentioned as having been first promulgated by Kassapa and handed on down to the time of Gotama and retaught by him. Such, for instance, are the questions (*pucchā*) of **Āḷavaka** and **Sabhiya** (*q.v.*) and the stanzas taught to **Sutasoma** by the brahmin **Nanda** of **Takkasilā.**[23] The **Mittavinda Jātaka** (No. 104) is mentioned as belonging to the days of Kassapa Buddha.[24]

Mention is also made of doctrines which had been taught by Kassapa but forgotten later, and Gotama is asked by those who had heard faint echoes of them to revive them.[25] A sermon attributed to Kassapa, when he once visited Benares with twenty thousand monks, is included in the story of **Paṇḍita-Sāmaṇera.**[26] It was on this occasion that Kassapa accepted alms from the beggar **Mahāduggata** in preference to those offered by the king and the nobles.

Kassapa held the uposatha only once in six months.[27]

Between the times of Kassapa and Gotama the surface of the earth grew enough to cover **Sūkarakata-leṇa.**[28]

The records of Chinese pilgrims contain numerous references to places connected with Kassapa. Hiouien Thsang speaks of a stūpa containing the relics of the whole body of the Buddha, to the north of the town, near Śrāvasti, where, according to him, Kassapa was born.[29] Mention is also

18 S. ii. 192.
19 J. vi. 122.
20 *Ibid.*, 123.
21 *Ibid.*, 121.
22 *Ibid.*, 120.
23 J. v. 476 f.; 483.
24 J. i. 413.
25 *E.g.*, MA. i. 107, 528; AA. i. 423.
26 DhA. ii. 127 ff.
27 *Ibid.* iii. 236.
28 MA. ii. 677.
29 Beal, *op. cit.*, ii. 13.

made of a footprint of Kassapa.[30] Stories of Kassapa are also found in the *Divyāvadāna.*[31] The *Dhammapada Commentary*[32] contains a story, which seems to indicate that, near the village of **Todeyya,** there was a shrine thought to be that of Kassapa and held in high honour by the inhabitants of the village. After the disappearance of Kassapa's Sāsana, a class of monks called **Setavattha-samaṇavaṃsa** (" white-robed recluses ") tried to resuscitate it, but without success.[33]

[30] *Ibid.* i., Introd. ciii.
[31] *E.g.*, pp. 22 f.; 344 f.; 346 f.; see also Mtu., *e.g.*, i. 59, 303 f.
[32] iii. 250 f.
[33] VibhA. 432.

2. **Kassapa Thera.**—The son of an **Udicca-brahmin** of **Sāvatthi,** who died when Kassapa was still young. Having heard the Buddha preach at **Jetavana,** he entered the First Fruit of the Path and, with his mother's leave, became a monk. Some time later, wishing to accompany the Buddha on a tour after the rains, he went to bid his mother farewell, and her admonition to him on that occasion helped him to win insight and become an arahant.[1]

In the time of **Padumuttara** Buddha he had been a brahmin versed in the Vedas. One day, seeing the Buddha and wishing to pay homage, he cast a handful of *sumana*-flowers into the air over the Buddha's head, and the flowers formed a canopy in the sky. In later births he was twenty-five times king, under the name of **Ciṇṇamāla** (*v.l.* **Cittamāla**).[2]

He is probably identical with **Sereyyaka Thera** of the *Apadāna.*[3]

[1] Thag. v. 82. [2] ThagA. i. 177 f. [3] i. 155.

3. **Kassapa.**—A devaputta. He visited the Buddha late one night at **Jetavana** and uttered several stanzas, admonishing monks to train themselves in their tasks, laying particular stress on the cultivation of Jhāna.[1]

Buddhaghosa[2] says that Kassapa had heard the Buddha preach the *Abhidhamma* in **Tāvatiṃsa.** Having heard only a portion of the doctrine and not being sure of the admonition given by the Buddha to the monks regarding the practice of Jhānavibhaṅga, Kassapa thought he could supply the omission. The Buddha, knowing his capabilities, allowed him to give his views, and expressed his approval at the end of Kassapa's speech.

[1] S. i. 46. [2] SA. i. 82.

4. **Kassapa.**—A sage (*isi*); one of the famous sages of yore, of whom ten are several times mentioned in the books[1] as having been brahmin

[1] *E.g.*, D. i. 104, 238; M. ii. 169, 200; A. iii. 224; iv. 61; J. vi. 99.

sages, who composed and promulgated the mantras and whose compositions are chanted and repeated and rehearsed by the brahmins of the present day. For details see *s.v.* **Aṭṭhaka.**

5. **Kassapa** (called **Kassapa-māṇava**).—The Bodhisatta in the time of **Piyadassī** Buddha. He was a brahmin versed in the Vedas, and having heard the Buddha preach, built a monastery costing one thousand crores.[1]

[1] J. i. 38; Bu. xiv. 9 f.; BuA. 176.

6. **Kassapa.**—Another name for **Akitti** (*q.v.*).[1]

[1] J. iv. 240, 241; see also *Jātakamālā* vii. 13.

7. **Kassapa.**—A brahmin ascetic, the Bodhisatta, father of **Nārada,** whose story is given in the **Cūla-Nārada Jātaka** (*q.v.*).[1]

[1] J. iv. 221 f.

8. **Kassapa.**—A brahmin ascetic, father of the Bodhisatta in the story of the **Kassapamandiya Jātaka.**[1]

[1] J. iii. 38.

9. **Kassapa.**—A great sage, the Bodhisatta, father of **Isisiṅga.**[1] The scholiast explains that Kassapa was the *gotta* or family name.

[1] J. v. 157, 159.

10. **Kassapa.**—An ascetic, also called **Nārada,** who lived in a hermitage near Mt. **Kosika** in Himavā. He saw the Buddha **Padumuttara** in the forest, invited him into the hermitage, provided a seat and asked for words of advice. He was a former birth of **Ekāsanadāyaka** Thera.[1]

[1] Ap. ii. 381.

11. **Kassapa.**—A seṭṭhi, probably of **Rājagaha,** who built the **Kassapakārāma,** named after him.[1]

[1] SA. ii. 230.

12. **Kassapa.**—Son of **Dhātusena** by a morganatic marriage. He slew his father and became king of Ceylon as **Kassapa I.** (478-96 A.C.). Fearing the revenge of his brother **Moggallāna,** he erected the fortress at **Sīhagiri** and dwelt there. Later, repenting of his patricide, he did many meritorious deeds by way of amends,[1] chief of which was the restoration of the **Issarasamaṇārāma,** to which he added buildings named after his daughters,

[1] For details see Cv. xxxix. 8 ff.

Bodhi and **Uppalavaṇṇā.** In a fight with his brother's forces his army fled in disorder, and Kassapa cut his throat with a dagger.[2]

[2] *Ibid.*, xxxviii. 80 ff.; xxxix. 1 ff.

13. **Kassapa.**—Son of **Upatissa III.** of Ceylon. He had sixteen companions as brave as himself and, with their help, several times repulsed the attacks of **Silākāla,** when the latter revolted against the king. He became known as **Girikassapa** on account of his prowess. In the last campaign Silākāla was victorious, and Kassapa, with his parents and his loyal followers, fled to **Merukandara,** but they lost their way and were surrounded by Silākāla. When the royal elephant fell Kassapa cut his own throat.[1]

[1] Cv. xli. 8-25.

14. **Kassapa.**—Younger brother of **Aggabodhi III.**; he was made viceroy when **Māna** was killed.[1] When Aggabodhi had recovered the kingdom from the usurper **Dāṭhopatissa,** which he did only after various reverses in his fortunes, Kassapa abused his influence and plundered various sacred edifices to provide for his army.[2] On Aggabodhi's death in exile in **Rohaṇa,** Kassapa defeated Dāṭhopatissa, who claimed the throne, and became king in his place (**Kassapa II.** 641-50). He did not, however, wear a crown, the regalia having probably been stolen. As king he repented of his former misdeeds and did various acts of merit.[3] He paid special honour to **Mahādhammakathī** Thera of **Nāgasālā** and to the Thera of **Kaṭandhakāra.**

His children all being young at the time of his death, he entrusted the government to his sister's son, **Māna.**[4] According to the chronicles, **Mānavamma** was the son of Kassapa.[5] He also had a son named **Mana.**[6]

[1] Cv. xliv. 123 f.
[2] *Ibid.*, 137 ff.
[3] For details see Cv. xliv. 147 ff.; xlv. 1 ff.
[4] *Ibid.*, 8.
[5] *Ibid.*, xlvii. 2.
[6] *Ibid.*, lvii. 4.

15. **Kassapa (Kassapa III.,** 717-24 A.C.).—A younger brother of **Aggabodhi V.** (?); Kassapa's younger brother was **Mahinda I.**[1] and his son **Aggabodhi.**[2]

[1] Cv. xlviii. 20-26.
[2] *Ibid.*, 32.

16. **Kassapa.**—One of the three younger brothers of **Sena I.,** the others being **Mahinda** and **Udaya.**[1] Kassapa was appointed Ādipāda and fought valiantly against the forces of the **Paṇḍu** king, who was then invading Ceylon, but, finding his efforts of no avail, he fled to **Koṇḍivāta.**[2] He was

[1] Cv. l. 6.
[2] *Ibid.*, vv. 25 ff.

later killed at **Pulatthipura** by the orders of the Paṇḍu king.[3] He had four sons, the eldest of which was named **Sena.**[4]

[3] *Ibid.*, vv. 46. [4] *Ibid.*, vv. 47.

17. **Kassapa.**—Son of **Kittaggabodhi,** ruler of **Rohaṇa.** When his eldest brother was murdered by his paternal aunt, Kassapa fled to the court of King **Sena I.,** but, later, with Sena's help, he won his father's inheritance.[1] He was probably killed by the Adipāda **Kittaggabodhi.**[2]

[1] Cv. l. 54 ff. [2] *Ibid.*, li. 96; and Cv. *Trs.* i. 157, n. 2.

18. **Kassapa.**—Younger brother of **Sena II.** and **Udaya II.** He was Mahādipāda or Yuvarāja under Udaya,[1] and later became king as **Kassapa IV.** (896-913 A.C.).[2] His daughter **Senā** married **Kassapa V.**[3]

[1] Cv. li. 91. [2] *Ibid.*, lii. 1 ff. [1] *Ibid.*, li. 93.

19. **Kassapa.**—Son of **Sena II.** The king gave him a special share of his own revenues and a share of the extraordinary revenues of the island.[1] Two wives of his are mentioned: **Saṅghā** and **Senā.**[2] He became Yuvarāja under **Kassapa IV.** and ruled over **Dakkhiṇadesa,**[3] and, at the death of the king, he became ruler of Ceylon as **Kassapa V.** (probably 913-23 A.C.).[4] He is sometimes referred to as the son of the twice-consecrated queen (*dvayābhisekajāta*), his mother being Saṅghā, daughter of **Kittaggabodhi** (1) and **Devā.** In inscriptions Kassapa is referred to as **Abhaya-Silāmeghavaṇṇa.**[5] He was evidently a learned man, and a Sinhalese Commentary to the *Dhammapadaṭṭhakathā* is attributed to him.[6] He had one wife, **Vajirā,**[7] a second, **Devā,**[8] and a third, **Rājinī.**[9] He had a son, **Siddhattha,** who died young, and another, who was given the title of **Sakkasenāpati.** The latter led an expedition to help the **Paṇḍu** king against the King of **Coḷa,** but he died of plague in Coḷa.[10]

[1] Cv. li. 18, 20.
[2] *Ibid.*, 18, 92.
[3] *Ibid.*, lii. 1.
[4] *Ibid.*, 37 ff.
[5] Cv. *Trs.* i. 165, n. 3.
[6] Edited by D. B. Jayatilaka, Colombo (1933).
[7] Cv. lii. 62. [8] *Ibid.*, 64.
[9] *Ibid.*, 67.
[10] *Ibid.*, 72-8.

20. **Kassapa.**—Son of **Sena V.**[1]

[1] Cv. liv. 69.

21. **Kassapa.**—Son of **Mahinda V.**[1] When Mahinda was captured and taken away by the **Coḷas,** the people took charge of the young Kassapa and

[1] Cv. lv. 10.

brought him up. When the boy was twelve years old the Coḷa king sent an army over to Ceylon to seize him; but this plan was frustrated by the official **Kitti,** of **Makkhakudrūsa,** and the minister **Buddha,** of **Māragallaka.**[2] Kassapa ascended the throne as **Vikkamabāhu,** but refused to be crowned until he should have conquered the **Damiḷas** in his kingdom. While preparations were afoot towards this end, he died of a *vātaroga*. He reigned twelve years (1029-1041 A.C.).[3] He is perhaps to be identified with the prince Kassapa who married **Lokitā,** cousin of Mahinda V., and by whom he had two sons, **Moggallāna** and **Loka.**[4]

[2] *Ibid.*, 24-9. [3] Cv. lvi. 1-6; Cv. *Trs.* i. 190, n. 3. [4] Cv. lvii. 28 f.; Cv. *Trs.* i. 195, n. 3.

22. **Kassapa.**—Chief of the **Kesadhātus** (*q.v.*). For some time he carried on the government at **Rohaṇa,** where he defeated the **Damiḷas.** He refused to own allegiance to **Kitti** (afterwards **Vijayabāhu I.**), and after six months of rule in **Khadiraṅgaṇi,** full of resentment that his services against the Damiḷas had not been recognised, he marched against Kitti and was slain in a battle near **Kājaragāma.**[1]

[1] Cv. lvii. 65-75.

23. **Kassapa.**—A prince of **Jambudīpa** who, during the reign of **Parakkamabāhu I.** of Ceylon, sent costly gifts to the king of **Rāmañña;** the Rāmañña king forbade the envoys to land and insulted them. This is mentioned as one of the acts which led Parakkamabāhu to send an expedition against Rāmañña.[1]

[1] Cv. lxxvi. 28 f.

24. **Kassapa Thera.**—According to the *Gandhavaṃsa*[1] he was the author of the **Anāgatavaṃsa** and also of the **Mohavicchedanī,** the **Vimaticchedanī** and the **Buddhavaṃsa.** This Buddhavaṃsa is evidently not the canonical work of the same name. The *Sāsanavaṃsadīpa*[2] says that a Kassapa, an inhabitant of Coḷa, was the author of a **Vimativinodanī.** The *Sāsanavaṃsa*[3] calls this a *Vinayaṭīkā* and the author an inhabitant of the Damiḷa country. The Mohavicchedanī is there described as a *lakkhaṇagandha* (a treatise on grammar ?) and is ascribed to another Kassapa.

[1] p. 61. [2] Verse 1204 (see also 1221). [3] p. 33; see also P.L.C. 160.

25. **Kassapa.**—A Kassapa Thera is mentioned in the *Sāsanavaṃsa*[1] as having been among those responsible for the establishment of the religion in **Yoṇakaraṭṭha.** He was an inhabitant of **Majjhimadesa.**

[1] p. 50.

26. The *Sāsanavaṃsa*[1] mentions a **Kassapa** Thera of **Arimaddana,** in the time of King **Narapati.** While on tour he reached a country called **Pollaṅka,** where the people grew very fond of him and where he became known as **Pollaṅka** Thera. Some time later he was crossing to Ceylon and the vessel in which he was refused to move. Lots were drawn, as it was necessary to discover who aboard the vessel was the sinner. The lot fell repeatedly on Kassapa, because, in a former life, he had harassed a dog in the water. He was accordingly thrown overboard, but was rescued by **Sakka,** in the form of a crocodile. The thera reached **Yakkhadīpa** (*q.v.*) and there, as a result of practising compassion, the blind yakkhas gained their sight. Kassapa went later to **Sīhaladīpa,** whence he returned home with relics and seeds of the Bodhi-tree and models of the **Mahācetiya** and **Lohapāsāda.**

[1] p. 71.

27. **Kassapa.**—The name is sometimes used as a shortened form of **Kassapagotta** (*q.v.*).[1] **Nārada-tāpasa** is also once addressed as Kassapa.[2]

[1] *E.g.*, J. vi. 224, 225, etc., in reference to the Ājīvaka Guṇa. [2] J. vi. 58.

28. **Kassapa.**—See also **Acela Kassapa, Uruvela°, Kumāra°, Gayā°, Dasabala°, Nadī°, Nārada°, Pūraṇa°, Mahā°** and **Lomasa°.** Kassapa was evidently a well-known *gotta* name[1] and people born in a family bearing that name were often addressed as Kassapa—*e.g.*, **Uruvela-Kassapa**[2] and, again, **Nāgita Thera.**[3]

[1] See, *e.g.*, MA. i. 584. [2] Thus at AA. i. 165. [3] D. i. 151.

Kassapa Saṃyutta.—The sixteenth section of the **Saṃyutta Nikāya.**[1] It contains various suttas connected with **Mahā-Kassapa** (*q.v.* for details). Mahā-Kassapa's verses in the *Theragāthā* reflect the sentiments contained in these suttas. The discussion on the *lokiya*-aspect of the *sammappadhānā*, as given in the *Kassapa Saṃyutta*, is referred to in the commentaries.[2]

[1] S. ii. 192-225. [2] *E.g.*, VibhA. 291.

1. **Kassapa Sutta.**—Two suttas containing an account of the visit paid to the Buddha by **Kassapa,** the devaputta (*q.v.*).[1]

[1] S. i. 46 f.

2. **Kassapa Sutta.**—Contains the thoughts that came to **Kassapa** Buddha, before his Enlightenment, on the nature of becoming, of cessation, etc.[1] The same thoughts are also attributed to the other Buddhas, from **Vipassī** downwards. For details see **Gotama Sutta.**

[1] S. ii. 9; *cf.* D. ii. 30 f.

Kassapakārāma (Kassapārāma).—A monastery in **Rājagaha,** probably near **Veḷuvana.** It was here that **Assaji** stayed during his last illness, when the Buddha visited him to comfort him.[1] The monastery was built by a banker called **Kassapa.**[2]

[1] S. iii. 125. [2] SA. ii. 230.

Kassapagiri.—A monastery in Ceylon. **Jeṭṭhatissa III.** gave the village of **Ambilāpika** for the supply of food to the monks of Kassapagiri,[1] and **Kassapa III.** showed this monastery his special favour.[2]

The monastery probably formed part of what—in an inscription of **Mahinda IV.** found at **Vessagiri**—is called the "Isuramenu-Bo-Upulvan-Kasubgiri-Vihāra." It would appear that **Kassapa I.** founded a great monastic establishment out of the Vessagiri and **Issarasamaṇa** Vihāras and that this enlarged monastery was named after his two daughters **Bodhī** and **Uppalavaṇṇā** and also after Kassapa himself. This establishment was evidently referred to briefly as Kassapagiri.[3]

The name **Kacchapa giri** (*q.v.*) found in the Mahāvaṃsa Ṭīkā[4] is apparently a wrong reading for Kassapagiri, in which case the identification is important, for here we have "*Issarasamaṇasaṅkhāte Kacchapagirivihāre.*" See also **Kassapavihāra.**

[1] Cv. xliv. 98.
[2] *Ibid.*, xlviii. 24.
[3] See Ep. Zey. i. 31 ff.; i. 216; and Cv. *Trs.* i. 43, n. 7.
[4] p. 652; see also 407, which has **Kassapagiri.**

1. **Kassapagotta.**—Apparently the general name given to those belonging to the family of **Kassapas.** Thus the Ājīvaka **Guṇa** is addressed as **Kassapagotta**[1] and again as **Kassapa.**[2] See also **Kassapa** (28).

[1] J. vi. 222. [2] *Ibid.*, 224, 229, 235.

2. **Kassapagotta.**—A monk living in **Vāsabhagāma** in the **Kāsi** kingdom. He was in the habit of showing extreme hospitality to the monks who came there from other parts. Once some monks who visited him enjoyed his hospitality and stayed on. After some time, feeling that they had outstayed their welcome, Kassapagotta grew tired of looking after them and was blamed by them for his neglect. He therefore went to **Campā,** where he laid his case before the Buddha, who declared that no blame attached to him.[1]

[1] Vin. i. 312 ff.

3. **Kassapagotta.**—A monk living in **Paṅkadhā** in the **Kosala** country. He heard the Buddha preach a sermon, but was not satisfied with it and kept on thinking: "This recluse" (meaning the Buddha) "is much too

scrupulous" (*adhisallikhat'evāyam*). Later, he was filled with remorse and, having sought the Buddha at **Rājagaha,** begged forgiveness for his thoughtlessness.

The Buddha praised him for having seen his transgression, and for his confession thereof and determination to practise self-restraint.[1]

[1] A. i. 236 f.

4. **Kassapagotta.**—A monk, perhaps to be identified with one of the foregoing. He was once staying in a forest tract in **Kosala** and, seeing a trapper pursuing deer, intervened and protested against the man's earning his living by such cruel means. The trapper was too preoccupied with his quarry to pay much attention to what was said. A deva of the forest drew near the monk and instructed him not to waste his time in preaching to a man who heard but did not understand what was being said. Kassapa was agitated and, according to the Commentary, gave himself up to much striving and became an arahant.[1]

[1] S. i. 198 f.; SA. i. 223.

5. **Kassapagotta.**—One of the monks who accompanied the thera **Majjhima** on his journey to the country of the Himālaya for the purpose of converting it to Buddhism.[1] In a relic-urn, found in Tope No. 2 of Sāñchi group, were the ashes of this monk, where he is described as "Hemavatācariya."[2]

[1] Dpv. viii. 10; Sp. i. 68; Mbv. 115; MṬ. 317. [2] Cunningham: *Bhilsā Topes,* 287.

Kassapagotta or **Cheta Sutta.**—Relates the story of the attempt made by **Kassapagotta** (4) to convert a huntsman.[1]

[1] S. i. 198 f.

Kassapapāsāda.—A building attached to the **Abhayagiri-vihāra** and erected by **Kassapa IV.** A village was made over for its maintenance.[1] It is identified with the "Kasub-vad-mahapahā" mentioned in an inscription of **Mahinda IV.** in the **Jetavanārāma.**[2]

[1] Cv. lii. 13. [2] Ep. Zey. i. 216.

Kassapamandiya Jātaka (No. 312).—Once the Bodhisatta, on the death of his mother, gave away all the wealth in the house and, together with his father and younger brother, lived as an ascetic in the Himālaya. During the rains the three came down to the haunts of men and at the end of the rainy season returned to the hermitage. The Bodhisatta went on ahead to prepare the hermitage, leaving the father and the younger brother to follow. The lad, finding the father's progress very slow, tried to hurry him, much to the latter's annoyance. The two quarrelled, and thus were so late that the Bodhisatta came to look for them. On hearing what had happened, he told the father, who is called **Kassapa**, that the old should have patience with the young.

The story was told in reference to a nobleman of **Sāvatthi,** who became a monk and who, on his mother's death, was joined by his father and younger brother. All three went to a village retreat to fetch robes, and things happened as in the past. As a result, it was not till the next day that they could pay their respects to the Buddha, who, hearing what had occurred, related the Jātaka.[1]

[1] J. iii. 36-9.

Kassaparājaka.—A monastery begun by a young prince, called **Kassapa,** in the time of King **Dappula** and finished by **Sena I.**[1] An inscription[2] mentions that a "Kasubraja-vehara" (probably the same as the above), was restored by **Kassapa V.**

[1] Cv. l. 81. [2] Ep. Zey. i. 42 ff.

Kassapa-vihāra.—A monastery to which **Dāṭhopatissa II.** gave the village of **Senāmagāma.**[1] This monastery is probably to be identified with **Kassapagiri-vihāra.**

[1] Cv. xlv. 27.

Kassapasīhanāda Sutta.—The eighth sutta of the *Dīgha Nikāya.* It consists of a dialogue between the Buddha and **Acela-Kassapa** on self-mortification, and contains an account of some of the practices prevalent among the **Ājīvakas.** The Buddha claims that the insight and self-control and self-mastery of the arahant are much harder of attainment than the merely physical practices of the ascetics, which are far more evident to the vulgar. The Buddha states that self-mortification is an actual hindrance to spiritual development, for it turns a man's mind from more essential matters.

It is said that at the conclusion of the Sutta, Kassapa entered the Order and, in due course, became an arahant.[1]

[1] D. i. 161-77.

Kassapasena.—A monastery built by the Senāpati of **Kassapa IV.** It was given to the **Sāgalikas.**[1] It was restored by **Kassapa V.**[2]

[1] Cv. lii. 17. [2] Ep. Zey. ii. 40.

Kassapiyā, Kassapikā.—A division of the **Sabbatthivādī** sect. The **Saṅkantikas** were an offshoot of the **Kassapiyā.**[1] The *Kathāvatthu Commentary*[2] states that the Kassapiyā held that the past survives, as presently existing, in part.

[1] Mhv. v. 9; Dpv. v. 48; Mbv. 96. [2] *Points of Controversy*, p. 101.

Kassipiṭṭhika-vihāra.—A monastery in Ceylon, built by King **Dhātusena.**[1]

[1] Cv. xxxviii. 49.

Kāka.—Slave of King **Caṇḍa-Pajjota.** His father was non-human, and he himself could travel sixty leagues a day. When Pajjota discovered that **Jīvaka** had fled, after administering to him some medicine containing ghee, he sent Kāka to overtake Jīvaka and bring him back, giving Kāka strict injunctions not to eat anything offered by Jīvaka. Kāka came upon the physician at **Kosambī** having his breakfast. Jīvaka invited him to eat, but he refused. In the end, however, he consented to eat half a myrobalan, which he thought would be harmless, but into which Jīvaka had introduced some drug hidden in his finger nail. Kāka purged violently and was very alarmed. Jīvaka told him that all he desired was for him to be slightly delayed and left him, after having handed over to him the elephant **Bhaddavatikā,** which he had used in his flight.[1]

[1] Vin. i. 277 f.; DhA. i. 196.

1. **Kāka Jātaka** (No. 140).—The Bodhisatta was once born as a crow. One day a crow dropped filth on the king's chaplain as he was returning from the bath arrayed in all his splendour. He thereupon conceived hatred against all crows. Soon after that a woman slave, watching some rice spread out in the sun to dry, was angered by a goat who, as soon as she fell asleep, started to eat the rice. In exasperation she fetched a torch and struck the goat's shaggy back, which caught fire. To ease its pain, the goat ran into the hayshed near the king's elephant-stalls and rolled in the hay. In the conflagration that ensued many of the elephants were badly burnt, and when the chaplain was consulted, remembering his anger against crows, he said that the cure for burns was crows' fat. Crows were accordingly being mercilessly slaughtered; the Bodhisatta, hearing of this. sought the king and explained to him the chaplain's motive. Crows had no fat, he said, because their life is passed in ceaseless dread. The king, being greatly pleased with the Bodhisatta's act, granted immunity to all living beings, showing particular favour towards crows.

The circumstances which led to the recital of the story are described in the **Bhaddasāla Jātaka** (*q.v.*). The king in the story was **Ānanda.**

2. **Kāka Jātaka** (No. 146).—Once a crow came with his mate to the seashore and ate freely of the remnants of a sacrifice which had been offered by men to the Nāgas and drank freely of the strong drink which he found. Both crows became drunk, and, while trying to swim in the surf, the hen-crow was washed into the sea and eaten by a fish. Hearing the husband's lamentations, many crows gathered together and started to empty the ocean, working away until ready to drop from weariness. Seeing their plight, the Bodhisatta, who was then a sea-sprite, caused a bogey to appear from the sea, frightening them away.

The story was told in reference to a number of monks who had joined the Order in their old age. They went for alms to their former wives' and children's houses, and gathering together at the house of the wife of one of them (she being particularly beautiful), placed together what each had received and ate it with sauces and curries prepared by the beautiful wife. The woman died, and the aged monks, returning to the monastery, wept aloud for their benefactress, the giver of sauces. The matter was reported to the Buddha, who identified the crows of the past with the foolish monks.[1]

According to the *Dhammapada Commentary*,[2] the name of the woman was **Madhurapācikā.**

[1] J. i. 497-9. [2] iii. 422.

2. **Kāka Jātaka** (No. 395).—The Bodhisatta was once a pigeon and lived in a net basket in the kitchen of a Benares merchant. A greedy crow, becoming intimate with him, came to live there. The cook discovered the crow trying to steal some food, and, pulling out his feathers, sprinkled him with flour, hung a chowrie round his neck and flung him into the basket.

The story closely resembles those of the **Kapota Jātaka** and the **Lola Jātaka** (*q.v.*), and is related in reference to a greedy monk.[1]

The Kapota Jātaka[2] makes reference to a Kāka Jātaka of the **Navanipāta.** There is no such story in the Ninth Book; perhaps it is a wrong reading for the **Cakkavāka Jātaka** (No. 434), where the story is also related with reference to a greedy monk.

[1] J. iii. 314-16; see also Cunningham: Bharhut Stūpa, xlv. Pl. 7. [2] J. i. 241.

Kāka Sutta.—The wicked monk is like a crow in that he possesses the same ten qualities: offensiveness, recklessness, shamelessness, excessive greed, cruelty, gruesomeness, want of strength, "earthyness" (? *oravitā*), bewilderment and meanness.[1]

[1] A. v. 149; see also G.S. v. 101.

Kākaṇḍaka.—A brahmin, father of Yasa Thera, the latter being generally referred to as **Yasa Kākaṇḍakaputta** (*q.v.*).[1]

[1] Mhv. iv. 12, 49, 57, etc.; Dpv. v. 23; Mbv. 96.

Kākadīpa.—An island to the east of Ceylon. A part of the expeditionary force sent by **Parakkamabāhu I.** to **Rāmañña** landed on this island, captured some of the inhabitants and brought them to Ceylon, where they were presented to the king.[1] Kākadīpa may have been the name of one of the Andaman Islands.

[1] Cv. lxxvi. 57.

Kākaneru.—One of the highest mountains in the world; mentioned together with **Mālāgiri, Himavā, Gijjha, Sudassana** and **Nisabha.**[1]

[1] J. vi. 204, 212.

Kākanda, Kākandī.—The commentaries speak of Kākanda as a sage of yore and mention him in the company of **Savattha** and **Kusumba.** His residence later came to be called Kākandī.[1]

[1] SnA. i. 300; *cp.* KhA. 110; UdA. 55.

Kākannāḍu.—A district in South India subdued by the forces of **Parakkamabāhu I.**[1]

[1] Cv. lxxvi. 262.

Kākavaṇṇa-Tissa (Kākavaṇṇa).—A king of the **Rohaṇa**-dynasty in Ceylon. He was the great-grandson of **Mahānāga,** brother of **Devānampiya-Tissa,** and his father was **Goṭhābhaya.**[1] His capital was at **Mahāgāma.** He had as wife, **Devī** (better known as **Vihāradevī**), daughter of **Tissa,** king of **Kalyāṇi,** who had been cast into the sea to expiate her father's crimes.[2] Their children were **Duṭṭhagāmaṇi Abhaya** and **Saddhā-Tissa.** Kākavaṇṇa-Tissa gathered round him all the foremost Sinhalese warriors of the time so that they should be available for Gāmaṇi, when the time came for his campaign against the Damiḷas.[3]

But at the start Kākavaṇṇa-Tissa was very reluctant to allow his son to make preparations for such a campaign,[4] so much so that, in exasperation, the young prince once sent his father some female ornaments to indicate that the king was no man.[5] Kākavaṇṇa-Tissa was very pious, and is said to have built sixty-four vihāras, sixty-four years being also the length of his reign.[6] Among the religious edifices built by him

[1] Mhv. xv. 170 f.; Mbv. 132.
[2] Mhv. xxii. 20 ff.
[3] *Ibid.*, xxiii. 2.
[4] *Ibid.*, xxii. 82 f.
[5] *Ibid.*, xxiv. 4.
[6] *Ibid.*, xxiv. 12; see also AA. i. 279.

were the **Tissamahārāma,** the **Cittalapabbatavihāra**[7] and the **Mahānuggala Cetiya.** He was cremated at Tissamahārāma.[8] He evidently received his name on account of his dark colour. The *Dīpavaṃsa*[9] speaks of Kākavaṇṇa-Tissa's daughters as having been proficient in the history of the Religion (*saddhammavaṃsakovidā*).

[7] Mhv. xxii. 23.
[8] xxiv. 8, 13.
[9] Dpv. xviii. 20; were their names **Mahilā** and **Samantā** ?; see also xix. 21 f.

Kākavaliya, Kākavalliya.—One of the five bankers (*seṭṭhi*) of limitless wealth in **Bimbisāra's** kingdom, the others being **Jotiya, Jaṭila, Meṇḍaka,** and **Puṇṇaka.**[1] He was once very poor, and **Mahā-Kassapa,** having spent seven days in *samādhi*, stood at his door, wishing to do him a favour. Kākavaliya's wife saw the Elder and poured into his bowl the saltless sour gruel she had cooked for her husband. The Elder took it and put it into the hands of the Buddha, who resolved that it should suffice for the large assembly of monks. On the seventh day after that, Kākavaliya was appointed *seṭṭhi*.[2] He is quoted as an example of one who was able to give gifts which bore fruit in this very existence, because his gift contained the four purities: lawful acquisition, greatness of volition, virtue in the recipient and consummate virtue in the giver.[3]

[1] DhA. i. 385; AA. i. 220. [2] Vsm. ii. 403. [3] DhsA. 161 f.; see also AA. i. 48, 364.

Kākātī.—Chief queen of the Bodhisatta, in one of his births as king of Benares. See **Kākātī Jātaka.**

Kākātī Jātaka (No. 327).—**Kākātī** was the chief queen of the King of Benares (the Bodhisatta). A certain Garuḍa king came disguised as a man and played at dice with the king. Having fallen in love with Kākātī, the Garuḍa carried her off to his abode by the Simbalī-Lake and there lived with her. The king, missing his queen, sent his physician, **Naṭakuvera,** to look for her. The physician hid himself in the Garuḍa's plumage and thus reached the palace where Kākātī was. There he enjoyed her favour and returned to Benares in the Garuḍa's wing. While the Garuḍa and the king were playing at dice, Naṭakuvera sang a song telling of his experiences with Kākātī. The Garuḍa, realising what had happened, brought the queen back to Benares.

The story was related by the Buddha to a monk who was discontented on account of a woman. The monk is identified with Naṭakuvera.[1]

The story is among those related by the bird **Kuṇāla,** in the **Kuṇāla Jātaka.** There[2] we learn that the Garuḍa's name was **Venateyya,** who is identified with Kuṇāla.

The Kākātī Jātaka very closely resembles the **Sussondī Jātaka.**[3]

[1] J. iii. 90-2. [2] J. v. 428. [3] J. iii. 187 ff.

Kākālaya.—A village in Ceylon where there was a Damiḷa stronghold captured by **Parakkamabāhu II.**[1]

[1] Cv. lxxxiii. 12.

Kākola.—A hell; beings born there are dragged about by flocks of ravens, vultures and hawks, and eaten alive.[1]

[1] J. vi. 247.

Kācaragāma, Kājaragāma, Kāṭaragāma.—A village in South Ceylon, on the **Maṇigaṅgā** (Mänik-gaṅga), about ten miles to the north of Tissamahārāma, on the old road from **Mahāgāma** to **Guttasāla.** It was evidently an important centre even in the time of **Devānampiya-Tissa,** because we find that the nobles of Kājaragāma are mentioned among those taking part in the festival of the Bodhi-Tree when it was brought over by **Saṅghamittā.**[1] In the village was planted one of the eight saplings produced from the Bodhi-Tree.[2] A vihāra was erected in Kācaragāma by **Aggabodhi,** ruler of **Rohaṇa,**[3] among the occupants of which is mentioned **Milakkha-Tissa** Thera.[4] The place was of strategic importance, and was sometimes used as the seat of the government in Rohaṇa.[5] The village is now chiefly famous for the celebrated shrine of Skanda.

[1] Mhv. xix. 54.
[2] *Ibid.*, 62; Mbv. 161 f.; Sp. i. 100.
[3] Cv. xlv. 45.
[4] AA. i. 22.
[5] *E.g.*, by **Loka** (Cv. lvii. 2), by **Kassapa,** the **Kesadhātu** (*ibid.*, 66 ff.); see also Cv. lviii. 6.

Kāñcipura (*v.l.* **Kāñcipura**).—A city in Southern India on the Coromandel coast, capital of the Pallavas, and one of the seven sacred towns of India; it is the modern Conjevaram. It was once the centre of Buddhism in South India and was one of the places of pilgrimage visited by Hiouien Thsang. He mentions that during his stay there three hundred monks came to Kāñcipura from Ceylon, fleeing from the political disturbances in that country.[1] In Pāli Literature the locality is noteworthy as the birthplace of the Commentator **Dhammapāla** and perhaps also of **Anuruddha,** author of the **Abhidhammattha-Saṅgaha.**[2] Some identify Kāñcipura with Satiyaputta of Asoka's Rock Edict II.[3]

[1] Beal, *op. cit.*, ii. 228 f.; CAGI. 627.
[2] P.L.C. 113, 169.
[3] *E.g.*, *J.R.A.S.*, 1918, 541 f.; see also Bhandarkar, *Anct. Hist. of Deccan* pp. 47, 52.

Kāṇagāma.—A village and tank in **Rohaṇa.** There **Aggabodhi** of Rohaṇa built three hospitals for the blind and the sick and a large image-house in the **Paṭimā-vihāra.**[1] **Parakkamabāhu I.** repaired the tank.[2]

[1] Cv. xlv. 43.
[2] *Ibid.*, lxxix. 35.

Kāṇatālavana-tittha.—A ford in the **Mahāvāluka-gaṅgā,** a point of strategic importance.[1]

[1] Cv. lxxii. 19.

Kāṇapaddāvuda.—A locality in Ceylon. There a she-bear attacked **Parakkamabāhu I.** (then the Ādipāda), but was killed by him.[1]

[1] Cv. lxvii. 40.

Kāṇamātā.—A pious lay woman of **Sāvatthi,** mother of **Kāṇā** (*q.v.*).

Kāṇamūla.—A locality in Ceylon, near the **Kālavāpi.**[1]

[1] Cv. lxxii. 183.

Kāṇavāpi.—A tank near the **Cetiyagiri,** given by **Sena I.** for the use of the monks there.[1] **Sena II.** built a dam across it at **Kaṭṭhantanagara,**[2] and both **Vijayabāhu I.**[3] and **Parakkamabāhu I.**[4] restored it.

[1] Cv. l. 72.
[2] *Ibid.*, li. 73.
[3] *Ibid.*, lx. 50.
[4] *Ibid.*, lxxix. 34.

Kāṇā.—Daughter of **Kāṇamātā.** After she married she visited her mother, and one day, while she was there, her husband sent for her. Her mother, not wishing her to return empty-handed, asked her to wait till she had made some cakes. When the cakes were ready, a monk came to the door and Kāṇā gave him some. Four other monks came, and the cakes were finished. Four times Kāṇā's husband sent for her and four times the same thing happened. So, in anger, the husband took another wife. Kāṇā, learning this, was so greatly annoyed that she reviled and abused every monk she saw until no monk dared go into her street. The Buddha, hearing of this, visited Kāṇā's mother, and having finished his meal there, sent for Kāṇā, argued with her, and convinced her that the monks were not to blame inasmuch as they had only taken what was given them. At the end of the Buddha's discourse Kāṇā became a sotāpanna. The king saw the Buddha returning from Kāṇā's home and, on learning what had happened, sent for her, adopted her as his daughter, and arranged for her marriage with a rich nobleman. Thenceforward Kāṇā's generosity to the monks became proverbial.[1]

It was on Kāṇā's account that the **Babbu Jātaka** (*q.v.*)[2] was preached. Kāṇā is identified with the mouse of the story.

[1] Vin. iv. 78 f.; DhA. ii. 149 ff.; the *Samantapāsādikā* (iv. 819) gives a somewhat different account; there, when Kāṇā's husband heard that the Buddha had been to see her, he sent for her and she returned.

[2] J. i. 477 f.

She was called Kāṇā because she was so beautiful that those who saw her became blind with passion for her (*ye ye taṃ passanti, te te rāgena kāṇā honti*).[3]

Both Kāṇā and her mother are mentioned among those who kept the eightfold fast.[4]

[3] Sp. *loc. cit.*

[4] A. iv. 349; AA. ii. 791.

Kāṇāriṭṭha.—One of the four sons of the Nāga-king **Dhataraṭṭha** and his queen **Samuddajā,** the others being **Sudassana, Bhūridatta** and **Subhaga.** When Kāṇāriṭṭha heard that his mother was a human, wishing to test her one day while drinking her milk, he assumed a serpent's form and struck her foot with his tail. Samuddajā threw him on to the ground with a shriek and accidentally struck his eye with her nail, thereby blinding him. Henceforth he, whose name had been Ariṭṭha, was known as Kāṇāriṭṭha.[1] When, after Bhūridatta's disappearance (see **Bhūridatta Jātaka**) from the Nāga-world, his brothers set out to search for him, Kāṇāriṭṭha was sent to the world of the gods, for he was so cruel by nature that they knew that if he went to the world of men he would destroy it by fire.[2] When, after his search, he returned to the Nāga-world, he was appointed door-keeper of Bhūridatta's sick-room; there, seeing Subhaga dragging a brahmin roughly into the Nāga-world, he prevented him from ill-treating the man and told him of the greatness of all brahmins, illustrating his words with various stories.[3] It is said that in his immediately preceding birth, he had been a brahmin, well-versed in sacrificial lore. Bhūridatta heard (from his bed) Ariṭṭha's undue praise of brahmins and refuted his statements.[4]

Kāṇāriṭṭha is identified with **Sunakkhatta.**[5]

[1] J. vi. 168.

[2] *Ibid.*, 190.

[3] *Ibid.*, 197; for details see pp. 200 ff.

[4] *Ibid.*, 205 ff.

[5] *Ibid.*, 219.

1. **Kātiyāna.**—A name by which the yakkha **Puṇṇaka** (*q.v.*) is addressed.[1] It is a variant of **Kaccāna.**[2]

[1] J. vi. 299, 306, 308.

[2] *Ibid.*, 283, 286, 301, 327.

2. **Kātiyāna.**—The name of a *gotta*, probably a variant of **Kaccāyana, Kaccāna** (*q.v.*).

3. **Kātiyāna Thera.**—The son of a brahmin of the **Kosiya-gotta** in **Sāvatthi,** he was called Kātiyāna after his mother's family. When his friend **Sāmaññakāni** joined the Order, he followed his example and exerted himself in meditation, sleeping but little. One night, overcome by sleep,

he fell on the terrace where he was pacing to and fro, and the Buddha, seeing him, went himself to help him and urged him not to give up his efforts but to concentrate and contemplate. Aided by this admonition, Kātiyāna soon became an arahant. The Buddha's sermon is included in the *Theragāthā*.[1]

From the story of Sāmaññakāni, given in the Theragāthā Commentary,[2] it would appear that Kātiyāna was, for some time, a *paribbājaka*. He was destitute, having, since the appearance of the Buddha, lost all his support from the laity. He therefore sought Sāmaññakāni and asked his advice, which he followed by joining the Order.

[1] Thag. vv. 411-16; ThagA. i. 450 f. [2] i, p. 99 f.

4. **Kātiyāna.**—See **Pakudha.**

1. **Kātiyānī** (*v.l.* **Kaccānī**).—A lay devotee, declared by the Buddha to be most eminent among women for unwavering loyalty (*aveccappasāda*).[1]

She resolved to win this eminence in the time of **Padumuttara** Buddha. In this age she was born in the city of **Kuraraghara** and she had a devoted friend called **Kāḷī.** One day she went with Kāḷī to hear the thera **Soṇa Kuṭikaṇṇa** preach to his mother, and while she was there thieves entered her house. The servant girl, who was sent to fetch oil for lighting the lamps, brought news of the presence of the thieves, but Kātiyānī refused to leave until the thera's sermon should be finished. The leader of the thieves, who had watched the incident, was so pleased with her that he gave orders that all the goods stolen from her house should be restored. At the end of the sermon Kātiyānī became a sotāpanna. The next day the thieves came and asked her forgiveness. She took them to the Elder, who ordained them, and there they all became arahants.[2]

[1] A. i. 26. [2] AA. i. 245 f.

2. **Kātiyānī.**—See **Kaccānī Jātaka.**

Kāpaṭhika (*v.l.* **Kāpaṭika**).—A young brahmin, sixteen years old, well versed in the Vedas, and with his head shaven. He was "of good stock, well informed, a good speaker and a scholar of ability." He visited the Buddha at **Opasāda,** where he interrupted a conversation which the Buddha was holding with some aged brahmins; they rebuked him for interrupting his elders, but **Caṅkī** (*q.v.*), who happened to arrive at that moment, interceded on his behalf. The Buddha, knowing that Kāpaṭhika had questions to ask of him, gave him an opportunity for so doing, and there followed a discussion on various points, detailed in the **Cankī Sutta.** At the end of the discussion the youth declared himself a disciple of the Buddha.[1] In the Sutta the Buddha addresses Kāpaṭhika as **Bhāradvāja,** perhaps because he belonged to that gotta.

[1] M. ii. 168 ff.

Kāpi.—Son of **Kotūhalaka** and his wife **Kāḷī.** When his parents fled from **Ajitaraṭṭha** to **Kosambī** from fear of the plague, they, being starved, found it very difficult to carry the child. Seven times the father tried to abandon the child, but the mother prevented him.[1]

[1] DhA. i. 169 f.

Kāpilānī.—See **Bhaddā Kāpilānī.**

Kāma Jātaka (No. 467).—**Brahmadatta,** king of Benares, had two sons. When he died the elder refused the crown and retired into a frontier village. The people there, discovering his identity, offered to pay their taxes to him instead of to the king, and the king, at his request, agreed. As his power increased, the prince became more covetous and demanded the kingdom, which the younger brother gladly renounced. But the elder's greed was insatiable, and **Sakka,** to teach him a lesson, came in the guise of a young man and offered to capture for him three cities. The king made up his mind to accept the offer; but then the young man could not be found, and the king fell ill of greed. The Bodhisatta, just returned from Takkasilā, heard of this, and having obtained the king's leave to treat him, cured him of this disease by showing him the futility of his wishes. Thereafter the king became a righteous ruler.[1]

The story was told in reference to the brahmin to whom the **Kāma Sutta** was preached. The **Kāmanīta Jātaka** was also preached in this connection.

[1] J. iv. 167 ff.

1. **Kāma Sutta.**—The first of the **Aṭṭhakavagga** of the **Sutta Nipāta.** The Buddha, seeing a brahmin felling trees on the banks of the **Aciravatī** and preparing a field for corn, spoke to him. He spoke again to the brahmin on several other occasions, when the latter was engaged in various operations in the field. The brahmin, pleased by the Buddha's courtesy, resolved to invite him to a meal when the harvest should be gathered. But the day before the reaping of the corn heavy rains fell, the river was flooded and the corn all washed away. The Buddha had foreseen that this would happen and visited the brahmin to console him. It was on this last occasion that this sutta was preached. At the end of the sermon the

brahmin became a sotāpanna.[1] In the **Kāmanīta Jātaka** he is referred to as **Kāmanīta-brāhmaṇa.**[2]

[1] Sn. vv. 766-71; SnA. ii. 511 ff.; J. iv. 167 f.; *cp.* DhA. iii. 284 f.; see also MNid. i. 1 ff.
[2] J. ii. 212.

2. **Kāma Sutta.**—Contains questions asked by a deva and the Buddha's answers thereto. A man should not become a slave or surrender himself as prey to others and speech should always be gentle.[1]

[1] S. i. 44.

3. **Kāma** or **Kāmaguṇa Sutta.**—On the five kinds of pleasures of the senses.[1]

[1] A. iv. 458; S. v. 60.

Kāmaṇḍā.—A village in which was the mango-grove of **Todeyya** (*q.v.*). **Udāyī** once stayed there and was visited by a resident pupil of the brahmin lady of the **Verahaccāni** clan.[1]

[1] S. iv. 121 f.

Kāmada.—A devaputta who visited the Buddha and told him that the path of the Ariyan disciples was hard to follow and their goal hard to win. The Buddha pointed out to him that the difficult thing had been and was being accomplished.[1]

The Commentary[2] explains that Kāmada had been a *yogāvacara* on earth, but had died before he could attain to any Fruits of the Path and that here he laments his disappointment.

[1] S. i. 48. [2] SA. i. 83.

Kāmada Sutta.—Contains the account of **Kāmada's** visit to the Buddha.[1] It is quoted in the *Nettippakaraṇa.*[2]

[1] S. i. 48. [2] p. 148.

Kāmanīta.—The name by which the brahmin, mentioned in connection with the **Kāma Jātaka,** the **Kāma Sutta** and the **Kāmanīta Jātaka,** is referred to.[1]

[1] J. ii. 212.

Kāmanīta Jātaka (No. 228).—The king of Benares had two sons; the elder became king, but was full of greed for wealth. The rest of the story resembles that of the **Kāma Jātaka**; the three cities which **Sakka** proposes to win for the king are given as **Uttarapañcāla, Indapatta** and **Kekaka.**

In this case the physician who cures the king is Sakka himself, who is identified with the Bodhisatta.[1] The story was related in the same circumstances as the **Kāma Jātaka.**

[1] J. ii. 212-16.

Kāmabhū.—A monk, evidently held in high esteem by his colleagues. He is mentioned as staying in **Kosambī,** in **Ghosita** Park, and as asking **Ānanda** certain questions, recorded in the **Kāmabhū Sutta** (1).[1] Two other suttas bearing the same name record visits paid to Kāmabhū by **Cittagahapati** at **Ambāṭakavana** in **Macchikāsaṇḍa.**[2]

[1] S. iv. 165. [2] *Ibid.*, 291, 293.

1. **Kāmabhū Sutta.**—**Kāmabhū** visits **Ānanda** at **Ghositārāma** in **Kosambī** and asks him whether the senses are the bonds of objects or objects the bonds of senses. Ānanda answers that neither is true; the bond is the desire and lust that arise owing to the senses and the objects with which they come in contact. The Buddha, for instance, is free from such bondage.[1]

The same question is asked of **Sāriputta** by **Koṭṭhita,** who receives the same reply.[2]

[1] S. iv. 165. [2] *Ibid.*, 162 f.

2. **Kāmabhū Sutta.**—**Cittagahapati** visits **Kāmabhū** at **Ambāṭakavana** in **Macchikāsaṇḍa** and is asked to solve a riddle:

Nelaṅgo setapacchādo ekāro vattatī ratho
Anīghaṃ passa āyantaṃ chinnasotaṃ abandhanaṃ.

Citta explains this as referring to the Arahant and points out the significance of each term.[1] In the *Udāna*[2] the words of the riddle are mentioned as having been used by the Buddha in reference to **Lakuṇṭaka-Bhaddiya.**

[1] S. iv. 291 f. [2] p. 76; UdA. 370 f.; *cf.* DhsA. 398.

3. **Kāmabhū Sutta.**—Records another visit of **Citta** to **Kāmabhū.** Citta asks a series of questions about the activities of the body, speech and mind and their cessation. Kāmabhū explains them to Citta's satisfaction.[1]

[1] S. iv. 293.

Kāmabhogī Sutta.—Preached at **Jetavana** to **Anāthapiṇḍika** on the ten classes of wealthy men (*kāmabhogī*), so far as they deserve praise or blame. Some of them obtain their wealth by evil means, enjoy it in evil ways, and do not share it with others; others are different in different degrees.[1]

[1] A. v. 176-82.

Kāmavilāpa Jātaka (No. 297).—The story is similar to that of the **Puppharatta Jātaka** (*q.v.*). As the man stood impaled he looked up, and seeing a crow flying through the air, hailed him and sent a message to his wife, informing her where his possessions lay concealed and asking her to enjoy them.[1] In the introduction to the Jātaka it is said that the *paccuppannavatthu* is given in the Puppharatta Jātaka and the *atītavatthu* in the **Indriya Jātaka.** There seems to be an error here, for the first story of the Indriya Jātaka[2] (unless another story is meant) bears no resemblance to the Kāmavilāpa Jātaka.

[1] J. ii. 443 f.; *cp.* Nos. 34 and 216. [2] J. iii. 461 ff.

Kāmaseṭṭha.—One of the greater yakkhas who should be invoked if any follower of the Buddha be molested by an evil spirit.[1] In the **Mahāsamaya Sutta**[2] he is mentioned among the vassals of the Four Great Kings—versed in craft, hoodwinking wizards, clever in feigning.

[1] D. iii. 204. [2] D. ii. 258.

Kāmānākkoṭṭa.—A fortress in South India, which was occupied by the Damiḷa chiefs **Paṇḍimaṇḍala, Vīragaṅga** and **Kaṅgakoṇḍa.**[1]

[1] Cv. lxxvi. 180.

Kāmboja.—See **Kamboja.**

1. **Kāya Sutta.**—Mindfulness relating to the body is the path to the Uncompounded (*asaṅkhata*). This the Buddha has taught his disciples.[1]

[1] S. iv. 359.

2. **Kāya Sutta.**—Just as the body is sustained by material food so are the five hindrances maintained by their own foods. The sutta explains what these foods are.[1]

[1] S. v. 64 f.

3. **Kāya Sutta.**—Same as above, but in reference to the seven *bojjhaṅgas*.[1]

[1] S. v. 65 f.

4. **Kāya Sutta.**—There are certain things that should be got rid of by action, others by speech, yet others by mind. The sutta explains what these things are and how to get rid of them.[1]

[1] A. v. 39 f.

Kāyagatāsati Sutta.—Preached at **Jetavana,** on how to cultivate mindfulness of body so that it may produce abundant fruit and the ten blessings that result therefrom.[1] This sutta, like the **Ānāpāṇa,** is really only a sectional presentation of the **Satipaṭṭhāna Sutta.** For the special nature of this sutta see the *Vibhaṅga Commentary* (p. 226).

[1] M. iii. 88 ff.

Kāyagalla.—See **Kāsagalla.**

Kāyaduccarita Sutta.—On the five evil results of wickedness in bodily action.[1]

[1] A. iii. 267.

Kāyavicchandanaka Sutta.—Another name for the **Vijaya Sutta** of the **Sutta Nipāta.**[1]

[1] SnA. i. 241.

Kāyavicchinda Jātaka (No. 293).—The Bodhisatta was once a brahmin of Benares and fell sick of jaundice. The physicians failed to cure him, and his family were in despair. He resolved that if he recovered he would embrace the religious life; soon afterwards he was cured, became an ascetic and cultivated the *abhiññā* and the *samāpatti.*

The story was told in reference to a man in **Sāvatthi** who had a like experience. He entered the Order and became an arahant.[1] *v.l.* **Kaya-nibbinda.**

[1] J. ii. 436-8.

Kāyaviratigāthā.—A beautiful Pāli poem, of two hundred and seventy-four verses, on the subjection of sensuality, written in Ceylon, probably in the seventeenth century. A *ṭīkā* on the poem is ascribed to a monk of **Pakudhanagara** (Pegu ?).[1]

The work is in two sections, the first describing the formation of the body, its foulness and its worthlessness, and the second dealing with the mind and the advantages of developing the same regardless of the body. There is a Sinhalese translation probably by the author himself.[2]

[1] Gv. 65, 75; Bode, *op. cit.*, 44, n. 7. [2] P.L.C. 285.

1. **Kāyasakkhi Sutta.**—**Saviṭṭha** and **Mahā-Koṭṭhita** once visit **Sāriputta.** Sāriputta asks them: Which is the most excellent—one who has testified to the truth with body, one who has won view, or one released by faith ? Saviṭṭha prefers the one released by faith, Mahā-Koṭṭhita the one who has testified to the truth with body, while Sāriputta's preference is for the one who has won view, for in him insight is most developed.

Together they go to the Buddha and put the case before him; the Buddha tells them that it is not an easy matter to decide.[1]

[1] A. i. 118 f.

2. **Kāyasakkhi Sutta.**—A description of the *kāyasakkhī*—one who has attained and experienced the four *jhānas*.[1]

[1] A. iv. 451 f.

Kāyasatti.—A Thera, incumbent of the **Vijayabāhu-pariveṇa.** King **Parakkamabāhu IV.** built for him a two-storeyed pāsāda of great splendour and gave him the village of **Sālaggāma.**[1]

[1] Cv. xc. 91 f.

Kārakapupphamañjarī.—A work on Pāli grammar, written by **Attaragama Baṇḍāra Rājaguru** in the eighteenth century, dealing with *kāraka* or case-relations—*i.e.*, syntax.[1]

[1] P.L.C. 283.

Kāragaṅgā.—A river in Ceylon. It was dammed between the hills with a great barrier by **Parakkamabāhu I.**, and its waters were conveyed by a canal, the **Ākāsagaṅgā,** to form the **Parakkamasamudda** (*q.v.*).[1] Another canal, the **Godāvarī,** is mentioned as branching off from the Kāragaṅgā and flowing into the Parakkamasāgara.[2]

[1] Cv. lxxix. 24. [2] *Ibid.*, v. 57.

Kāraṇapālī.—A brahmin employed as superintendent of works by the **Licchavis** of **Vesāli.** One morning early he saw **Piṅgiyānī** evidently returning from somewhere, and on inquiry learnt that he had been to see the Buddha. Kāraṇapālī asked him what he thought of the Buddha, and Piṅgiyānī sang his praises, illustrating his meaning with various figures of speech. Convinced by Piṅgiyānī's earnestness, Kāraṇapālī knelt on the ground and expressed his homage to the Buddha.[1]

The Commentary[2] says that the man's name was **Pāla** (or **Pālī**), and he was called Karaṇapālī because he supervised the business of various chieftains' families.

[1] A. iii. 236 ff. [2] AA. ii. 636.

Kāraṇapālī Sutta.—Records the meeting mentioned above of **Kāraṇapālī** with **Piṅgiyānī.**[1]

[1] A. iii. 236-9.

Kāraṇḍava Sutta.—Once, while the Buddha was at **Campā** on the banks of the **Gaggarā** Lake, a monk, charged by his colleagues with an offence, reviled them; the Buddha, hearing of it, insisted that the man should be expelled, lest the rest of the community should suffer by his presence. He illustrated his argument with various similes, among them that of the owner of a barley-field who, seeing among his corn a diseased plant (*yava-kāraṇḍava*) which failed to ripen, would uproot it and throw it away lest the other plants should be affected.[1]

[1] A. iv. 168-72.

Kāraṇḍiya (Kāraṇḍika).—A brahmin student, the Bodhisatta. His story is given in the **Kāraṇḍiya Jātaka.**

Kāraṇḍiya Jātaka (No. 356).—Once the Bodhisatta was a brahmin youth named **Kāraṇḍiya,** in Benares. He became the chief pupil of a world-famed teacher in **Takkasilā,** who was in the habit of preaching the moral law to whomever he met regardless of their fitness to receive it. One day Kāraṇḍiya was sent with his colleagues by his teacher to accept some cakes offered by the inhabitants of a village and to bring the teacher's share. On the way back Kāraṇḍiya saw a cave and started throwing stones into it. Told of this by the other boys, the teacher questioned Kāraṇḍiya, who replied that it was his ambition to make the whole world level. If his teacher thought he could make the whole world moral, why should he himself not make it level ? The teacher understood and accepted the lesson.

The story was told in reference to **Sāriputta** who preached to all who came to him, including even hunters and fishermen. They listened to him with respect, but failed to follow his teaching. On the remonstrances of his colleagues Sāriputta was offended, and the matter came to the Buddha's knowledge. Sāriputta is identified with the teacher of old.[1]

[1] J. iii. 170-4.

Kāradīpa.—An island in the **Damiḷa** country, near **Nāgadīpa.** Its original name was **Ahidīpa. Akitti** took up his residence there and lived on the leaves and fruits of the *kāra*-tree which grew there. On account of this the island came by its new name.[1]

[1] J. iv. 238.

Kāranvī.—A wood in which the Elder **Cittaka** sojourned for some time.[1] The Commentary suggests[2] that kāraṃ is the name of a tree and that from this tree the wood was named. *v.l.* **Kārambhiya.**

[1] Thag. v. 22. [2] ThagA. i. 78.

Kārapiṭṭhi.—A village in Ceylon. **Moggallāna III.** built there the **Mogallāna-vihāra.**[1]

[1] Cv. xliv. 50.

1. **Kārambhiya.**—See **Kāranvī.**

2. **Kārambhiya.**—See **Karambiya.**

Kāraliyagiri.—A monastery in Ceylon, the residence of a thera named **Nāga,** who taught the monks the *Dhātukathā* after having given up the study of the scriptures for eighteen years.[1]

[1] Vsm. i. 96.

Kārāyaṇa.—See **Dīgha-kārāyaṇa.**

Kārikā.—A grammatical work in Pāli, written by the Elder **Dhamma-senāpati** at the **Ānanda-vihāra** in Pagan. A *ṭīkā* on the work is ascribed to the same author.[1]

[1] Gv. p. 63, 73; Bode, *op. cit.*, 16 and n. 1.

Kārusā.—Mentioned with the **Bhaggas** in a list of tribes.[1]

[1] Ap. ii. 359.

1. **Kāla Sutta.**—There are four seasons: one for hearing the Dhamma, one for discussing it, one for attaining calm, and the last for attaining insight.[1]

[1] A. ii. 140.

2. **Kāla Sutta.**—The above explained with an illustration.[1]

[1] A. ii. 140.

3. **Kāla Sutta.**—There are five gifts which, if given, are seasonable: gifts to a guest, a traveller, a sick person, one in scarcity, and first fruits to a holy man.[1]

[1] A. iii. 41.

1. **Kāḷa.**—Son of **Anāthapiṇḍika.**—As he showed no signs of piety his father, feeling very distressed, made a solemn promise to give him a thousand if he kept the fast-day. Kāḷa won the money, and the next day he was promised a thousand if he would listen to the Buddha preaching and learn a single verse of the Dhamma. He listened to the Buddha's sermon, but by the will of the Buddha he could not keep in mind a single verse until the sermon came to an end. He then became a sotāpanna

and accompanied the Buddha and the monks to his father's house. There, when in the presence of them all Anāthapiṇḍika gave Kāḷa the money, he refused to accept it, and the Buddha explained what had happened.[1]

[1] DhA. iii. 189 ff.

2. **Kāḷa.**—An Elder. A certain woman ministered to him as though he were her son, but when she expressed her desire to see the Buddha, Kāḷa tried to dissuade her from doing so. One day she visited the Buddha without telling Kāḷa of her intention, and when he learnt where she had gone he hurried to the Buddha and tried to prevent him from preaching to her, in case she should stop caring for him.[1]

[1] DhA. iii. 155 f.

3. **Kāḷa.**—Minister of **Pasenadi.** He was grieved when the king spent his fortune in giving alms to the Buddha and his monks at the **Asadisadāna**; the Buddha, knowing his thoughts, spoke but a single stanza by way of thankoffering at the end of the *dāna* lest Kāḷa's head should split in seven pieces in anger. When the king learnt, on inquiry, why the Buddha had so acted, he dismissed Kāḷa from his service.[1]

[1] DA. ii. 654 f.; DhA. iii. 186-8; also ii. 89.

4. **Kāḷa.**—An Elder of **Kosala.** He joined the Order in his old age and lived in the forest with his friend **Juṇha.** Once the question arose between them as to which part of the month was cold, and being unable to decide the question, they sought the Buddha, who preached to them the **Māluta Jātaka** (*q.v.*).[1]

[1] J. i. 165.

5. **Kāḷa.**—The name given by his wife to the **Ājīvaka Upaka**[1] because he was dark in complexion.[2]

[1] ThigA. i. 223. [2] *Ibid.*, 226.

6. **Kāḷa.**—King of the Nāgas; see **Mahākāḷa.**

7. **Kāḷa.**—A young stag, son of the Bodhisatta; a previous birth of **Devadatta.** The story is given in the **Lakkhaṇa Jātaka.**[1]

[1] J. i. 142 f.

8. **Kāḷa.**—See **Kāḷahatthi.**

9. **Kāḷa.**—One of the Nirayas.[1]

[1] J. vi. 248.

10. **Kāḷa.**—A Pacceka Buddha, mentioned in a list of Pacceka Buddhas.[1]

[1] M. iii. 70; ApA. i. 107.

11. **Kāḷa.**—Brother of **Pasenadi,** king of **Kosala.**[1]

[1] Dvy. 153.

12. **Kāḷa.**—See also **Cullakāḷa, Mahā-Kāḷa** and **Kāḷudāyi.**

*1. **Kāḷaka.**—A seṭṭhi of **Sāketa.** His son was the husband of **Cūḷa-Subhaddā** (*q.v.*) and therefore son-in-law of **Anāthapiṇḍika.** Kāḷaka was a follower of the **Nigaṇṭhas.** When the Buddha visited Sāketa, at the request of Cūḷa-Subhaddā, Kāḷaka listened to his sermon and became a sotāpanna. He gave his park, the **Kāḷakārāma,** to the Buddha, and built a vihāra there after removing, by force, the Nigaṇṭhas, who were in possession.[1]

[1] AA. ii. 482 f.; but see DhA. iii. 465 f., where the seṭṭhi's name is given as **Ugga** of **Uggapura**; see also Dvy. 402, where the name of the city is **Puṇḍavardhana** and that of Anāthapiṇḍika's daughter **Sumāgadhā.**

2. **Kāḷaka.** Senāpati of King **Yasapāṇi** of Benares, a previous birth of **Devadatta.** The story is given in the **Dhammaddhaja Jātaka.**[1]

[1] J. ii. 186 ff.

3. **Kāḷaka.**—See **Ayya-Kāḷaka.**

4. **Kāḷaka.**—See A. v. 164, Sutta No. lxxxvii. Is Kāḷaka here a proper name or a generic name (Kāḷaka-bhikkhu) meaning a wicked monk ? I am inclined to take it as the latter. See **Kāḷaka(-bhikkhu) Sutta.**

Kāḷaka Sutta.—Preached by the Buddha at **Kāḷakārāma** in **Sāketa** when he visited the city at the request of **Cūḷa-Subhaddā.**[1]

The Tathāgata knows and comprehends whatsoever is seen, heard, comprised, attained, searched into, etc., in the whole world, but he is not subject to it.[2]

This sutta is sometimes referred to as the **Kāḷakārāma Sutta.**[3] It is said that at the conclusion of the Kāḷakārāma Sutta the earth trembled, as though bearing witness to the Buddha's statement.[4]

[1] AA. ii. 482 f.
[2] A. ii. 24 f.
[3] *E.g.*, ThagA. i. 284.
[4] DA. i. 130-1.

* In the documents compounds of Kāla- are spelt sometimes as Kāḷa-, sometimes as Kāla-. I have adopted the former throughout as being more convenient.

It was this sutta which helped **Mahārakkhita** to convert the country of the **Yoṇakas.**[5] The sutta was also preached by **Kāḷa Buddharakkhita** at the **Cetiyapabbata** to a concourse of people, among whom King **Tissa** (probably **Saddhā-Tissa**) was also present.[6]

[5] Sp. i. 67; Mhv. xii. 39; Mbv. 114; Dpv. viii. 9. [6] MA. i. 470.

Kāḷaka(-bhikkhu) Sutta.—A discourse delivered by the Buddha (*Kāḷakaṃ bhikkhuṃ ārabbha*—see Kāḷaka 4). It deals with ten dispositions which if present in a monk prevent his being loved or respected, and from being apt to meditate or to lead an ascetic and lonely life, and with the ten opposite dispositions.[1]

[1] A. v. 164 ff. On the name see A. v. 176, n. 7; also GS. v. 110, n. 1.

Kāḷakagāma.—A village in Ceylon in which was the **Maṇḍalārāma,** the residence of the Elder **Mahāsoṇa** (*q.v.*).[1]

[1] VibhA. 448.

Kāḷakañjakā.—A class of **Asuras** (*q.v.*). They were present at the **Mahā Samaya,** and are spoken of as being of a fearsome shape.[1] They are the very lowest of the Asura groups, and the Buddha warns **Sunakkhatta** that **Korakkhattiya** will, after his death from epilepsy, be born among them; and it did so happen.[2] Bodhisattas are never born among the Kāḷakañjakas.[3] Sometimes,[4] when Asuras are mentioned, the Commentaries explain the word as meaning the Kāḷakañjakas. Beings born among them suffer from excessive thirst, which they are unable to quench even by immersing themselves in the Ganges.[5] The Kāḷakañjakas resemble the petas in shape, sex-life, diet and length of life, and they intermarry with them.[6]

[1] D. ii. 259; also DA. iii. 789, 820.
[2] D. iii. 7 f.; J. i. 389.
[3] J. i. 44; BuA. 224.
[4] *E.g.*, J. v. 187; PvA. 272.
[5] For a story of one of them see VibhA. 5.
[6] Kvu. 360.

1. **Kāḷakaṇṇī.**—A friend of **Anāthapiṇḍika.** They had made mud-pies together and had gone to the same school. Later, Kāḷakaṇṇī fell on evil days and sought the protection of his friend, who appointed him to look after his business. Anāthapiṇḍika's friends and acquaintances remonstrated against the employment of a man with so inauspicious a name, but Anāthapiṇḍika heeded them not. One day, when Anāthapiṇḍika was away, a gang of robbers tried to enter his house, but Kāḷakaṇṇī, with great presence of mind, asked the few remaining servants to beat drums all over the house, thereby giving the impression that the house was fully occupied. The robbers fled leaving their weapons, and Kāḷakaṇṇī was

greatly praised. When Anāthapiṇḍika reported the matter to the Buddha, the Buddha related the **Kāḷakaṇṇī Jātaka,** containing a similar story of the past.[1]

[1] J. i. 364 f.

2. **Kāḷakaṇṇī.**—The name of the treasurer's friend in the story of the past, as given in the **Kāḷakaṇṇī Jātaka** (*q.v.*).

3. **Kāḷakaṇṇī.**—Daughter of **Virūpakkha.** She had a dispute with **Sirī,** daughter of **Dhataraṭṭha,** as to their order of precedence in bathing in **Anotatta.** The story is given in the **Siri-Kāḷakaṇṇi Jātaka.**[1] In the story she is also addressed as **Kāḷī.**[2] In another place she is referred to as **Alakkhī.**[3]

[1] J. iii. 257 ff. [2] *Ibid.*, 261. [3] J. iv. 378.

Kāḷakaṇṇī Jātaka (No. 83).—The story of a seṭṭhi of Benares who had a friend named **Kāḷakaṇṇī.** The rest of the story resembles that given above, about **Kāḷakaṇṇī,** friend of **Anāthapiṇḍika.**[1] In the same connection was preached the **Kusanāḷi Jātaka.**[2] There the Kāḷakaṇṇī Jātaka is referred to as **Kāḷakaṇṇī Vatthu.**

[1] J. i. 364 f. [2] *Ibid.*, 441 f.

Kāḷakārāma.—The park presented to the Buddha by **Kāḷaka,** and the monastery he built therein for the Buddha. The Buddha stayed there on his visit to **Sāketa** at **Cūḷa-Subhaddā's** request.[1]

[1] A. ii. 24; AA. ii. 482.

Kāḷakārāma Sutta.—See **Kāḷaka Sutta.**

Kāḷakūṭa.—One of the five mountain ranges surrounding **Anotatta.** It has the colour of *añjana* (collyrium).[1]

[1] SnA. ii. 437; UdA. 300; AA. ii. 759; MA. ii. 585.

Kāḷakhemaka.—A Sakyan. His name was **Khemaka,** but as he was dark he was called Kāḷakhemaka. He built a monastery in **Nigrodhārāma,** near **Kapilavatthu,** and once, during robe-making time, many monks lived there. On this occasion the Buddha preached the **Mahā-Suññatā Sutta.**[1]

[1] M. iii. 109; MA. ii. 906.

Kāḷagallaka.—A village in Ceylon, probably near modern Kurunegala. An elephant-stable was there, from which **Bhuvanekabāhu I.** took an elephant.[1]

[1] Cv. xc. 9.

Kāḷagāma.—A village in Ceylon. A minister of this village is given as an example of a man who committed suicide in remorse (*vippaṭisārī*).[1]

[1] SnA. i. 30.

Kāḷagiri.—See **Kāḷapabbata.**

Kāḷagiribhaṇḍa.—A district in Ceylon. The forces of **Parakkamabāhu I.** fought there twenty battles before it could be brought under subjection.[1] It is identified with the modern Kalugalboḍa-raṭa.[2]

[1] Cv. lxxii. 62.
[2] Cv. *Trs.* i. 325, n. 1.

Kāḷacampā.—A city in **Aṅga**; it was sixty leagues from **Mithilā,** with which it was connected by a cart-road.[1] To Kāḷacampā came sages from the Himālaya to procure salt and sour condiments.[2] There lived **Puṇṇaka's** relations.[3] **Varuṇa,** the Nāga king, tells **Vidhūra** that he (Varuṇa) and his wife were once inhabitants of Kāḷacampā.[4] Kāḷacampā is probably another name for **Campā** (*q.v.*); in fact, the name Campā is used more than once in reference to Kāḷacampā.[5] According to the *Aṅguttara Commentary,*[6] **Soṇa Koḷivisa** was born in Kāḷacampā; the *Theragāthā Commentary,*[7] however, speaks of his birthplace as Campā.

[1] J. vi. 31 f.
[2] *Ibid.*, 256.
[3] *Ibid.*, 274.
[4] *Ibid.*, 317.
[5] *E.g.*, J. vi. 32.
[6] AA. i. 131.
[7] ThagA. i. 544.

Kāḷatittha.—A locality in **Rohaṇa.** There **Vikkamapandu** had his seat of government.[1] It is identified with the modern Kalutara, at the mouth of the Kaḷuganga.

[1] Cv. lvi. 12.

Kāḷadīghagāma.—A village in Ceylon, evidently near **Kaḷyāṇi Vihāra,** for the monks of the vihāra are spoken of as visiting the village for alms. A girl of the village once met a young monk who went there, and fell in love so deeply that she died of her longing for him; when the monk realised what he had missed by not being aware of her love, he, too, died of a broken heart.[1]

[1] SnA. i. 70; ApA. i. 128; the story is slightly different in AA. i. 13 f.

Kāḷadīghavāpi.—A lake, evidently in Ceylon. **Cūḷapiṇḍapātika-Tissa** saw an elephant's corpse floating in the lake and made it his subject of meditation for arahantship.[1]

[1] Vsm. i. 191.

Kāḷadīghāvika.—A *padhānaghara* built by **Hatthadāṭha.**[1]

[1] Cv. xlvi. 46.

1. **Kāḷadeva.**—Thera, incumbent of **Vajagaragiri-vihāra.** He is mentioned as having known the exact passage of time without the help of an "hour-glass" (*yāmayantanāḷika*).[1]

[1] MA. i. 100 f.

2. **Kāḷadeva.**—A soothsayer who prophesied for King **Paṇḍuvāsudeva** the arrival of a wife from India.[1]

[1] MṬ. 272.

1. **Kāḷadevala.**—A sage; see **Asita-Devala** (2).

2. **Kāḷadevala.**—An ascetic, friend and counsellor of **Suddhodana.**[1] See **Asita** (1). He was a frequent visitor at the palace, and the Buddha's mother always took the precepts from him until she conceived the Buddha.[2]

[1] J. i. 54, 67, 88; vi. 479. [2] MA. ii. 922.

Kāḷanadī.—A river in Ceylon, the present Kaluganga. **Devapatirāja** built over the river a bridge of eighty-six cubits and laid out a garden of cocopalms from the river to **Bhīmatittha-vihāra.**[1]

[1] Cv. xlvi. 40, 44.

Kāḷanāga.—See **Mahā-Kāḷa.**

Kāḷanāgara.—The family to which the general **Parakkama** belonged.[1]

[1] Cv. lxxx. 49.

Kāḷapabbata.—A mountain range in Himavā, sixty leagues in height. Here **Irandatī** sang her song, hearing which **Puṇṇaka,** on his way to a meeting of the yakkhas, plighted his troth to her. After Puṇṇaka had won **Vidhura,** he took him to Kāḷapabbata, and there tried by various means to kill him. His attempts failed, and Vidhura, learning the motive for his act, preached to him, seated on the top of the mountain, and converted him.[1] In some places the mountain is called **Kāḷagiri.**[2]

[1] J. vi. 255, 264, 302 ff., 309, 326.
[2] *E.g.*, *ibid.*, 302, 304, 309, 326; see also Mtu. ii. 300.

Kāḷapāsāṇa.—A tank in Ceylon; one of sixteen tanks built by King **Mahāsena.**[1]

[1] Mhv. xxxvii. 49.

Kāḷapāsāṇa(-pāsāda)-pariveṇa. A building attached to the **Tissārāma** in the **Nandanavana** in **Anurādhapura,** erected for the use of **Mahinda. Devānampiyatissa** was anxious that there should be no delay in erecting the building, and therefore had the necessary bricks dried with torches for the sake of speed. The building was dark in colour, hence its name.[1] There was once a pond near the gate of the pariveṇa, called **Marutta.**[2]

[1] Mhv. xv. 203 f.; MṬ. 363. [2] MṬ. 344 f.

Kāḷapilla.—A locality in **Rohaṇa** in Ceylon. There the troops of **Parakkamabāhu I.** defeated those of **Gajabāhu.**[1]

[1] Cv. lxx. 325.

Kāḷabāhu.—A monkey, a previous birth of **Devadatta.** See the **Kāḷabāhu Jātaka.**[1]

[1] J. iii. 97 ff.

Kāḷabāhu Jātaka (No. 329).—Once the Bodhisatta was a parrot named **Rādha** and his brother was **Poṭṭhapāda.** They were captured by a fowler and brought to the court of **Dhanañjaya,** king of Benares, where they were paid great attention. Later, a monkey, **Kāḷabāhu,** was added to the collection of animals, and the people in the palace lost interest in the parrots, much to the annoyance of Poṭṭhapāda. Soon, however, the children became frightened of the monkey's tricks and he was sent away, just as Rādha had prophesied to his brother.

Ānanda was Poṭṭhapāda, and **Devadatta,** Kāḷabāhu.

The story was told in reference to Devadatta's attempt to kill the Buddha by letting loose **Nālāgiri.**[1]

[1] J. iii. 97 ff.

Kāḷa-Buddharakkhita.—A Thera of Ceylon, an arahant. He belonged to a minister's family and was born in a village near **Dakkhiṇagiri-vihāra.** When he came of age, he entered the Order, learned the whole of the Tipiṭaka, and, on going with a large concourse to see his teacher, was asked to give up his following and go into solitude to practise meditation. He went to the **Vātakasitapabbata-vihāra,** practised meditation and became an arahant. While living in the **Cetiyapabbata-vihāra,** he was once worshipping at the **Kaṇṭaka-cetiya** and was seated at the foot of a *Kālatimabara* tree.[1] One of the monks asked him a question on the **Kāḷakārāma Sutta** and the Elder preached a sermon based on the sutta. King **Tissa** (probably **Saddhā-Tissa**), who was in the vicinity, came to listen to the sermon,

[1] Legend says on the night of the new moon, thus completing the circle of Kāḷas!

which lasted throughout the night; the king remained standing the whole time. Greatly pleased, the king, at the end of the sermon, offered the sovereignty of Ceylon to the monk.

It is said that the Elder had been the Nigaṇṭha **Mahā-Saccaka** in the time of the Buddha, and that the Buddha had preached to him the **Mahā-Saccaka** Sutta, not because he could understand it then, but because the Buddha knew that it would help him to rise to eminence in this last life as Kāḷa-Buddharakkhita.[2]

[2] MA. i. 469 f.

Kāḷa-bhikkhu Sutta.—See **Kāḷaka(-bhikkhu) Sutta.**

Kāḷamattika.—A tank given by **Jeṭṭhatissa** for the use of the **Cetiya-pabbata-vihāra.**[1]

[1] Mhv. xxxvi. 130.

Kāḷamattiya, Kāḷamattika.—A forest. **Muṭṭhika,** after his death, was born as a goblin in this forest, and when **Baladeva** reached the spot during his flight, Muṭṭhika challenged him to a wrestling match and ate him up " like a radish-bulb."[1]

[1] J. iv. 82, 88.

Kāḷamahī.—A branch of the river **Mahā-Mahī,** which it later rejoins.[1]

[1] SnA. i. 27.

Kāḷavalli.—A tank repaired by **Parakkamabāhu I.**[1]

[1] Cv. lxxix. 36.

Kāḷavallimaṇḍapa.—A vihāra in Ceylon, the residence of the Elder **Mahānāga.**[1] It was near the village **Nakulanagara**[2] and was situated in **Rohaṇa.**[3]

[1] DA. i. 190, 191; SnA. i. 56; VbhA. 352, 353; J. iv. 490; MṬ. 606.

[2] DhsA. 339.

[3] AA. i. 384.

Kāḷavilaṅgika.—See **Mahā Kassapa.**

1. **Kāḷavela.**—A monastery in Ceylon, the residence of **Mahā-Moliya-deva** Thera[1] (*q.v.*).

[1] J. vi. 30.

2. **Kāḷavela.**—A servant of **Dīghagāmaṇi.**. He refused to promise the brothers of **Ummādacittā** that he would kill her if she gave birth to a boy, and so he was killed by them and reborn as a yakkha.[1] Later he saved the life of this boy, **Paṇḍukābhaya,** who was being carried in a basket,[2] and when Paṇḍukābhaya came to the throne, he founded a settlement for Kāḷadeva to the east of **Anurādhapura.**[3] It is said that on feast days the yakkha appeared in visible form in company with Paṇḍukābhaya.[4] **Mahāsena** afterwards built a thūpa on the site of Kāḷavela's shrine.[5]

[1] Mhv. ix. 22 f.
[2] *Ibid.*, x. 4.
[3] *Ibid.*, vs. 84.
[4] *Ibid.*, vs. 104.
[5] Mhv. xxxvii. 44.

1. **Kāḷasilā.**—The black rock by the side of **Isigili** (*Isigilipasse*). It was there that **Moggallāna** was murdered[1] and that **Godhika**[2] and **Vakkali**[3] committed suicide. It was a lonely spot, and we are told that when monks came from afar to **Rājagaha** they would ask **Dabba Mallaputta** to find them lodgings there because they wished to see evidence of Dabba's *iddhi*-powers.[4] The Buddha is mentioned[5] as having stayed at **Kāḷasilā** with a great company of monks. On one such occasion the Buddha is said to have given **Ānanda** an opportunity of asking him to continue to live for a whole æon. But Ānanda failed to do so.[6] The Buddha is elsewhere[7] described as residing at Kāḷasilā with five hundred monks, all of whom were arahants. Moggallāna discovered their powers, and thus earned the praise of **Vaṅgīsa.**

The *Saṃyutta Commentary*[8] speaks of a **Kāḷasilāvihāra.** In the **Cūḷadukkhakkhandha Sutta,**[9] it is said that Kāḷasilā was also the residence of some Nigaṇṭhas, followers of **Nāthaputta.**

[1] J. v. 125 f.; DhA. iii. 65 f.; ApA. i. 206.
[2] S. i. 120 f.; DhA. i. 431 f.
[3] S. iii. 124.
[4] Vin. ii. 76; iii. 159.
[5] S. i. 194.
[6] D. ii. 116.
[7] ThagA. ii. 209.
[8] SA. ii. 229.
[9] M. i. 92.

2. **Kāḷasilā.**—See **Kāḷasela.**

Kāḷasutta.—One of the principal hells.[1] Beings born there are placed on a floor of heated iron, marked with a black thread made red hot, and then cut into pieces along the markings.[2]

[1] J. v. 266, 267, 268.
[2] *Ibid.*, 270.

Kāḷasumana.—Thera. One of those responsible for preserving the *Vinaya* in Ceylon after the death of **Mahinda.**[1]

[1] Vin. v. 3; Sp. i. 104.

1. **Kāḷasena.**—King of **Ayojjhā.** The **Andhakaveṇhuputtā** besieged his city and took the king prisoner.[1]

[1] J. iv. 82.

2. **Kāḷasena.**—One of the leaders of the Yakkhas in Ceylon. He was ruler of the Yakkha-city of **Sirīsavatthu.** He married **Polamittā,** and it was at the wedding-feast of these two that **Vijaya** attacked the city with **Kuveni's** help and destroyed the Yakkhas.[1] *v.l.* **Mahākāḷasena.**

[1] Mhv. vii. 32 ff. MṬ. 259.

Kālasela.—A statue of the Buddha. See **Silāsambuddha.**

Kāḷahatthi.—Commander-in-chief of the Porisāda, the man-eating king, mentioned in the **Sutasoma Jātaka.** When Kāḷahatthi discovered the king's wickedness, he persuaded him to leave the city, and gave over the sovereignty to the king's son. Some time later, when Sutasoma had cured Porisāda of his cannibalistic tendencies, Kāḷahatthi agreed to restore him to the throne.[1]

Kāḷahatthi is identified with **Sāriputta.**[2] In several places[3] he is addressed as **Kāḷa.**

[1] J. v. 460-70; 508 ff. [2] *Ibid.*, 511. [3] *E.g.*, *ibid.*, 461, 465, 468.

Kāḷāgiri.—See **Kāḷapabbata.**

Kāḷāgiri-khaṇḍa.—That section of the **Vidhurapaṇḍita Jātaka** which ends with the bringing of **Vidhura** by **Puṇṇaka** to the realm of the Nāgas.[1]

[1] J. vi. 314.

1. **Kāḷāma.**—See **Āḷāra-Kāḷāma.**

2. **Kāḷāma.**—The name, probably, of a gotta or family. Mention is made of a *nigama* belonging to them in **Kosala,** which was called **Kesaputta.** The sermon preached by the Buddha on his visit to Kesaputta is justly famous.[1] The Kāḷāmas were Khattiyas.[2] Among members of this family specially mentioned by name are **Bharaṇḍu-Kāḷāma,** who was once a co-disciple of the Bodhisatta, and **Āḷāra-Kāḷāma,** the teacher of **Gotama** before his Enlightenment.[3]

[1] A. i. 188 ff. [2] AA. i. 418. [3] See *s.v.*

Kāḷāyanakaṇṇika.—A locality in **Rohaṇa.** There **Mahādāṭhika Mahānāga** built two vihāras, **Maṇināgapabbata** and **Kalanda.**[1]

[1] Mhv. xxxiv. 89; MṬ. 637.

Kāḷāvaka.—The tribe of ordinary elephants, each one of which possesses the strength of ten men.[1]

[1] MA. i. 263; UdA. 403; VibhA. 397; BuA. 37, etc.

Kāḷāsoka.—Son of **Susunāga** and king of Magadha for twenty-eight years. The tenth year of his reign completed one hundred years from the date of the Buddha's death. During the reign of Kāḷāsoka the **Vajjian** heresy appeared among the Saṅgha, and at first the king took the side of the Vajjians. Later, his sister **Nandā** persuaded him to transfer his patronage to the orthodox monks, and a convocation was held, with his support, at the **Vālikārāma** in **Vesāli,** at which the Vajjians were proved in the wrong.[1] Kāḷāsoka had ten sons, who carried on the government after him for twenty-two years.[2] He and Paṇḍukābhaya were contemporary kings for many years.[3]

There is great difference of opinion as to the identity of Kāḷāsoka. Some hold that he is the same as Kākavaṇṇa of the Purāṇas and Udāyin of the Jaina traditions, and that these names are merely other appellations of Udayabhadda of the Pāli sources. Kāḷāsoka is credited with having removed the capital of Magadha from **Rājagaha** to **Pāṭaliputta.**[4]

[1] Mhv. iv. 7, 8, 9, 31, 38, 39, 42, 63; Dpv. iv. 44, 52; v. 25, 80, 99; Sp i. 33.

[2] Mhv. v. 14.

[3] Sp. i. 72.

[4] The whole question of Kāḷāsoka is discussed by Geiger in his Introd. to the Mhv. *Trs.* xliii. f.

Kāli.—A tank in Ceylon, built by King **Vasabha.**[1] It was among those repaired by **Parakkamabāhu I.**[2]

[1] Mhv. xxxv. 95.

[2] Cv. lxviii. 45.

Kāli Sutta.—The Buddha, while staying at the **Nigrodhārāma,** visits his kinswoman **Kāḷigodhā** of **Kapilavatthu,** and tells her of the four qualities to be found in the *sotāpanna*—unwavering loyalty to the Buddha, the Dhamma and the Saṅgha, freedom from all taint of stinginess, delight in self-surrender and in the dispensing of charitable gifts. Kāḷigodhā states that she possesses all these qualities.[1]

[1] S. v. 396.

Kālikarakkhiya.—An ancient sage mentioned in a list of sages, together with **Samudda, Bharata, Aṅgīrasa, Kassapa, Kisavaccha** and **Akitti.**[1]

[1] J. vi. 99.

Kālikā.—See **Kāḷī** (9).

Kāḷigotamī.—See **Gotamī** (1).

Kāḷigodhā.—A Sākyan lady. She is declared to be a *sotāpanna*, and a conversation between her and the Buddha, who visited her while staying at the **Nigrodhārāma** in **Kapilavatthu,** is recorded in the **Kāli Sutta**[1] (*q.v.*). In the sutta she is addressed as **Godhā**; she may have belonged to the same family as **Godha** (*q.v.*). She was the mother of **Bhaddiya** Thera, declared to be the best of the monks of aristocratic birth.[2]

The *Aṅguttara Commentary*[3] states that her name was Godhā, and that she was called Kāḷi because of her dark colour. She was the most senior of the Sākyan ladies of the time. **Dhammapāla** speaks of her as *āgataphalā, viññātasāsanā.*[4]

[1] S. v. 396.
[2] Thag. v. 864; A. i. 23; ThagA. ii. 55.
[3] AA. i. 109.
[4] UdA. 161.

1. **Kāliṅga, Kaliṅga.**—An inhabitant of **Ñātika.** While staying in Ñātika, at the **Giñjakāvasatha,** the Buddha tells **Ānanda** that Kāliṅga was reborn after death in the **Suddhavāsā,** and that there he would attain to *nibbāna.*[1]

[1] D. ii. 92; S. v. 358 f.

2. **Kāliṅga.**—A country: the **Kāliṅgaraṭṭha.** It is one of the seven political divisions mentioned in the time of the mythical king **Reṇu** and is given first in the list, its capital being **Dantapura** and its king **Sattabhū.**[1] It is not, however, included in the list of sixteen Janapadas appearing in the *AṅguttaraNikāya*,[2] but is found in the extended list of the *Niddesa*.[3] A later tradition[4] states that after the Buddha's death, a Tooth was taken from among his relics and placed at Kāliṅga, where it was worshipped. From Kāliṅga the Tooth was brought to Ceylon, in the time of King **Sirimeghavaṇṇa,** by **Hemamālā,** daughter of **Guhasīva,** king of Kāliṅga, and her husband **Dantakumāra,** a prince of the **Ujjeni** royal family. In Ceylon the Tooth became the "Palladium" of the Sinhalese kings.[5]

The Jātakas contain various references to Kāliṅga. There was once a great drought in Dantapura, and the king, acting on the advice of his ministers, sent brahmins to the king of Kuru to beg the loan of his state elephant, **Añjanavasabha,** credited with the power of producing rain. On this occasion, however, the elephant failed and the Kāliṅga

[1] D. ii. 235 f.; see also Mtu. iii. 208; the Mtu. also mentions a king Uggata of Dantapura (iii. 364 f.).
[2] A. i. 213, etc.
[3] CNid. ii. 37.
[4] Bu. xxviii. 6.
[5] Cv. xxxvii. 92; see also Cv. *Trs.* i. 7, n. 4; the *Dāṭhādhātuvaṃsa* gives details (*J.P.T.S.* 1884, pp. 108 ff.).

king, hearing of the virtues practised by the king and people of Dantapura, offered them himself, upon which rain fell.[6] Another king of Kāliṅga was a contemporary of **Aruṇa,** the Assaka king of **Poṭali.** The Kāliṅga king, in his eagerness for a fight, picked a quarrel with Aruṇa, but was worsted in battle, and had to surrender his four daughters with their dowries to Aruṇa.[7]

The **Kāliṅgabodhi Jātaka** (*q.v.*) relates the story of another ruler of Kāliṅga while, according to the **Sarabhaṅga Jātaka** (*q.v.*), a certain king of Kāliṅga[8] went with two other kings, **Aṭṭhaka** and **Bhīmaratta,** to ask **Sarabhaṅga** questions referring to the fate of **Daṇḍakī.** There they heard the sage preach, and all three kings became ascetics. Another king of Kāliṅga was **Nāḷikīra** (*q.v.*), who, having ill-treated a holy man, was swallowed up in the **Sunakha-niraya,** while his country was laid waste by the gods and turned into a wilderness (**Kāliṅgārañña**).[9] In the **Kumbhakāra Jātaka**[10] the Kāliṅga king's name is **Karaṇḍu.**

From early times there seems to have been political intercourse between the peoples of Kāliṅga and **Vaṅga; Susīmā,** grandmother of **Vijaya,** founder of the Sinhalese race, was a Kāliṅga princess, married to the king of Vaṅga.[11] Friendly relations between Ceylon and Kāliṅga were evidently of long standing, for we find in the reign of **Aggabodhi II.** (601-11 A.C.) the king of Kāliṅga, together with his queen and his minister, coming over to Ceylon intent on leading the life of a recluse and joining the Order under **Jotipāla.** Aggabodhi and his queen treated them with great honour.[12] Later, the queen consort of **Mahinda IV.** came from Kāliṅga, and **Vijayabāhu I.** married a Kāliṅga princess, **Tilokasundarī.**[13] We are told that scions of the Kāliṅga dynasty had many times attained to the sovereignty of Ceylon and that there were many ties of relationship between the royal families of the two countries.[14] But it was **Māgha,** an offspring of the Kāliṅga kings, who did incomparable damage to Ceylon and to its religion and literature.[15]

According to the inscriptions, **Asoka,** in the thirteenth year of his reign, conquered Kāliṅga, and this was the turning-point in his career, causing him to abhor war.[16] Among the retinue sent by him to accom-

[6] See the Kurudhamma Jātaka (J. ii. 367 ff.), also DhA. iv. 88 f. A similar story is related in the Vessantara Jātaka (vi. 487), where the Kāliṅga brahmins ask for and obtain Vessantara's white elephant that he may stay the drought in Kāliṅga.

[7] J. iii. 3 f.

[8] J. v. 135 f.

[9] The Kāliṅga-arañña is referred to in the Upāli Sutta (M. i. 378); the story is related in J. v. 144 and, in greater detail, in MA. ii. 602 ff.

[10] J. iii. 376.

[11] Mhv. vi. 1; Dpv. ix. 2 ff.

[12] Cv. xlii. 44 ff.

[13] *Ibid.*, lix. 30.

[14] *Ibid.*, lxiii. 7. 12 f.

[15] *Ibid.*, lxxx. 58 ff.

[16] Mookerji: Asoka, pp. 16, 37, 214.

pany the branch of the Sacred Bodhi Tree on its journey to Ceylon, were eight families of Kāliṅga.[17]

Asoka's brother **Tissa,** later known as **Ekavihāriya,** spent his retirement in the Kāliṅga country with his instructor **Dhammarakkhita,** and there Asoka built for him the **Bhojakagiri-vihāra.**[18]

According to the **Vessantara Jātaka,**[19] the brahmin village **Dunniviṭṭha,** residence of **Jūjaka,** was in Kāliṅga.

Kāliṅga is generally identified with the modern Orissa.[20]

17 Sp. i. 96.

18 ThagA. i. 506.

19 J. vi. 521.

20 CAGI. 590 ff.; Law: *Early Geography*, 64; see also Bhandarkar: *Anct. Hist. of Deccan*, p. 12.

3. **Kāliṅga.**—Various kings of Kāliṅga are mentioned either as Kāliṅgarājā or simply as Kāliṅga. For these see Kāliṅga (2). We also hear of **Culla Kāliṅga** and **Mahā Kāliṅga.** Culla Kāliṅga is sometimes called **Kāliṅga-kumāra.**[1]

1 J. iv. 230.

4. **Kāliṅga.**—Son of **Culla-Kāliṅga.** See the **Kāliṅgabodhi Jātaka.**

5. **Kāliṅga.**—A Damiḷa chief, ally of **Kulasekhara.**[1] He was a brother of the wife of **Toṇḍamāna.**[2]

1 Cv. lxxvi. 174, 214, 217, 222.

2 *Ibid.*, lxxvii. 40.

6. **Kāliṅga.**—Another Damiḷa chief, conquered by **Bhuvenakabāhu I.**[1]

1 Cv. xc. 32.

7. **Kāliṅga.**—See **Kāliṅga-bhāradvāja.**

Kāliṅgabodhi Jātaka (No. 479).—The Kāliṅga king of **Dantapura** had two sons, **Mahā Kāliṅga** and **Culla Kāliṅga.** Soothsayers foretold that the younger would be an ascetic, but that his son would be a cakkavatti. Knowing of this prophecy, Culla Kāliṅga became so arrogant that Mahā Kāliṅga, on coming to the throne, ordered his arrest. But Culla Kāliṅga fled to Himavā and lived there as an ascetic. Near his hermitage lived the king and queen of **Madda** who had fled with their daughter from their city of **Sāgala.** Soothsayers had predicted that the princess's son would be a cakkavatti, and all the kings of Jambudīpa sought her hand. Her parents, not wishing to incur the enmity of any of the kings, fled with her from the city. One day a wreath of mango-flowers which the princess dropped into the river was picked up by Culla Kāliṅga, who thereupon went in search of her. With her parents' consent he married her, and to these two was born a son whom they called **Kāliṅga.** When the stars revealed that Mahā Kāliṅga had died, Kāliṅga was sent to Dantapura, to a courtier who had been an ally of Culla Kāliṅga. The prince's identity having been duly established, he was crowned king, and his chaplain, **Kāliṅga-bhāradvāja,** taught him the duties of a cakkavatti. On the fifteenth day after his coronation, the tokens of a cakkavatti king appeared before him.[1] One day while riding through the air with his retinue, he came to the Bodhi-tree under which Buddhas attain Enlightenment, and though he prodded his elephant until it died the animal found it impossible to fly over the spot. The royal chaplain investigated matters and reported his finding to the king who, having learnt from the chaplain of a Buddha's virtues, paid great honour to the tree for seven days. See also **Samaṇakolañña.**

Kāliṅga is identified with **Ānanda** and Kāliṅga-bhāradvāja with the Bodhisatta.

The story was related in reference to the Bodhi-tree planted, at Ānanda's suggestion, by **Anāthapiṇḍika,** at the entrance to Jetavana, in order that people might worship it while the Buddha was away on tour. As soon as a seedling was planted from the great Bodhi-tree at **Gayā,** it grew into a tree fifty cubits high, and the Buddha consecrated it by spending one night under it, wrapt in meditation.[2]

The **Kāliṅgabodhi Jātaka** is found also in the **Mahābodhi-vaṃsa**[3]; there it is given in much greater detail and differs in minor details from the Jātaka version, containing, among other things, a long description of dibba-cakkhu and the seven gems of a cakkavatti.

[1] For details see J. iv. 232. [2] J. iv. 228-36. [3] Mbv. 62 ff.

Kāliṅga-bhāradvāja.—The chaplain of King **Kāliṅga.** See the **Kāliṅgabodhi Jātaka.** He was the Bodhisatta, and is sometimes called **Kāliṅgabrāhmaṇa.**[1]

[1] *E.g.*, J. iv. 235.

Kāliṅgārañña.—See **Kāliṅga** (2).

Kālindī.—A channel in the irrigation system of **Parakkamabāhu I.,** flowing southward from the **Maṇihīra** tank.[1]

[1] Cv. lxxix. 54.

1. **Kāḷī.**—See **Kāḷakaṇṇī** (3).

2. **Kāḷī.**—Called **Kururagharikā,** described among laywomen as the best of those who believe even from hearsay (*anussavappasannānaṃ*).[1] She was the mother of **Soṇa Kuṭikaṇṇa,** and her husband belonged to **Kururaghara** in **Avantī.** When with child, she came to her parents in **Rājagaha,** and there, while enjoying the cool breeze on the balcony above her roof (*sīhapañjare*), she overheard the conversation which took place between **Sātāgira** and **Hemavata** on the excellences of the Buddha and of his teaching; as she listened, faith in the Buddha grew in her and she became a *sotāpanna.* That same night Soṇa was born. Later, Kāḷī returned to Kururughara and there waited on **Mahā Kaccāna.** When Soṇa entered the Order under Kaccāna and visited the Buddha, she gave him a costly rug to be spread in the Buddha's chamber. When Soṇa returned home after this visit, Kāḷī asked him to preach to her in the same way as he had earlier preached to the Buddha, earning the applause of the Buddha himself and of the devas of the ten thousand worlds.

Kāḷī was considered most senior among the women who became *sotāpannas* (*sabbamātugāmānaṃ antare paṭhamakasotāpannā sabbajeṭṭhikā*).[2] She was the constant companion and staunch friend of **Kātiyānī.**[3] Kāḷī's wish to attain to the eminence which she reached in this life was made in the time of Padumuttara Buddha when she heard a laywoman declared pre-eminent among those who had begotten faith by hearsay.[4]

A conversation between her and Mahā Kaccāna is related in the **Kāḷī Sutta** (*q.v.*).

[1] A. i. 26.
[2] AA. i. 133 ff.; SnA. i. 208 f.
[3] AA. i. 245.
[4] *Ibid.*, 247.

3. **Kāḷī.**—Maidservant of **Videhikā** of **Sāvatthi.** Videhikā was reputed to be gentle and meek, but Kāḷī, who was a bright girl and a good worker, thought she would test her mistress. One day she rose late and, on being reproved, spoke very lightly of her fault. Finding that Videhikā lost her temper, Kāḷī repeated her offence several times, until one day her mistress struck her with a lynch-pin, drawing blood from her head. Kāḷī ran out and roused the neighbourhood with her shrieks. Videhikā's reputation for meekness was no more. The story is related in the **Kakacūpama Sutta.**[1]

[1] M. i. 125 f.

4. **Kāḷī.**—A **Māra**-woman, sister of **Dūsī** (*q.v.*) and mother of the Māra of the present age (**Vasavatti** ?).[1]

[1] M. i. 333.

5. **Kāḷī.**—A crematrix (*chavadāhikā*) of **Sāvatthi.** Seeing **Mahākāḷa** meditating in the cemetery, she cut off from a recently cremated body its thighs and arms, and making of them a sort of milk bowl, placed it near where the Thera sat.[1]

[1] Thag. 151; ThagA. i. 271; more details are given in DhA. (i. 57 ff.).

6. **Kāḷī.**—A Yakkhiṇī. A householder, having a barren wife, married another woman, a friend of the former. Every time a child was conceived, the first wife brought about a miscarriage; at last the second wife died through a miscarriage and, on her deathbed, vowed to take her revenge. After several births, in which each, alternately, devoured the children of the other, the second wife became an ogress named **Kāḷī** and the first wife was born in a good family. Twice the ogress ate the latter's children; on the third occasion **Kāḷī** was occupied in **Vessavaṇa's** service and the child was left unhurt. On his naming day the parents took him to Jetavana, and there, as the mother was giving suck to her child, while her husband bathed in the monastery pool, she saw the ogress and, being terrified, dashed into the monastery where the Buddha was preaching. The guardian deity, **Sumana,** prevented Kāḷī's entrance, but the Buddha, having heard the story, sent for Kāḷī and preached to her, whereupon she became a *sotāpanna.* The Buddha persuaded the two women to become friends, and Kāḷī lived in the house of the other; but being uncomfortable there and at various other lodgings provided for her, she ultimately lived outside the village. There her aid was invoked for the protection of the crops, and eight ticket-foods (*salākabhatta*) were established in her honour.[1]

[1] DhA. i. 37 ff.

7. **Kāḷī.**—Wife of **Kotūhalaka** (*q.v.*) and mother of **Kāpi.**[1] When Kotūhalaka was born as **Ghosaka,** she became his wife after having saved his life.[2] See **Ghosaka.**

[1] DhA. i. 169. [2] *Ibid.*, 181.

8. **Kāḷī.**—A maidservant of the seṭṭhi of **Kosambī.** She it was who secured **Ghosaka** (*q.v.*) for the seṭṭhi, and when the seṭṭhi wished to get rid of him, the task was entrusted to her. Seven times she tried to have him killed, but all her attempts failed.[1] Later **Kāḷī** confessed her share in the seṭṭhi's crime, and seems to have been forgiven by both Ghosaka and his wife.[2]

[1] DhA. i. 174 ff. [2] *Ibid.*, 186 f.

9. **Kāḷī.**—A courtesan of Benares, sister of **Tuṇḍila.** She earned one thousand a day. Tuṇḍila was a debauchee, and so wasted her money that she refused to give him any more and had him cast out. A merchant's son, visiting Kāḷī, found Tuṇḍila in despair and gave him his own clothes. When the latter left the courtesan's house the next day, the clothes with which he had been provided according to custom were taken away, and he had to walk the streets naked.

The story is included in the **Takkāriya Jātaka.**[1] In the stanzas of the Jātaka Kāḷī is also called **Kāḷikā.**

[1] J. iv. 248 ff.

Kāḷī Sutta.—**Kāḷī Kururaghara** visits **Mahā-Kaccāna** and asks him for a detailed exposition of one of the stanzas in the **Kumāripañhas.**[1] Mahā-Kaccāna explains, and his explanation deals with the ten *kasiṇas.*[2]

[1] The stanza occurs at S. i. 126.

[2] A. v. 46 f.

Kāḷudāyī Thera.—Son of one of **Suddhodana's** ministers at **Kapilavatthu ;** he was born on the same day as the Buddha and grew up as his playfellow. After Gotama left the world, Suddhodana made Kāḷudāyī one of his most trusted counsellors. When the king heard of his son's Enlightenment he sent several of his ministers with large retinues to bring the Buddha to Kapilavatthu, but they all became arahants as soon as they heard the Buddha's preaching and then forgot their mission. In the end the king sent Kāḷudāyī, on the understanding that he should first be allowed to join the Order.[1] He went to the Buddha and, having listened to him, himself became an arahant. When the rains fell, covering the earth with the glory of leaves and flowers, Kāḷudāyī felt that it was time for the Buddha to visit his kinsmen, and gave him their invitation, singing the season's beauties in a series of verses. The Buddha took sixty days in covering the sixty leagues from Rājagaha to Kapilavatthu, and each day Kāḷudāyī went by air to the king's palace to tell him of the progress made in the journey and to bring back to the Buddha from the palace a bowl full of excellent food. By the time the Buddha reached his home his kinsmen were already full of faith in him. Because Kāḷudāyī accomplished this feat, he was declared pre-eminent among those who gladdened the clans (*kulappasādakānaṃ aggo*[2]).

It is said that he was called Udāyī because he was born on a day on which the citizens were full of joy (*udaggacittadivase jātattā*), and called Kāḷa because of his slightly dark colour.[3]

[1] According to Mtu. iii. 233, he was accompanied by Channa in this mission.

[2] A. i. 25; Thag. 527-36; J. i. 54, 86 f.; AA. i. 107, 117; ThagA. i. 497 ff.; UdA. 168; DA. ii. 425.

[3] AA. i. 167; ThagA. i. 498.

According to the *Apadāna*,[4] Kāḷudāyī had been the son of a minister of **Haṃsavatī** during the time of **Padumuttara** Buddha, and having heard the Buddha utter the praises of a monk skilled in converting families, had wished for the same eminence.

The *Aṅguttara Nikāya*[5] records a conversation between Udāyī (who, according to Buddhaghosa,[6] is to be identified with Kāḷudāyī) and **Ānanda.** Udāyī asks Ānanda to explain in detail a question which is recorded in the *Saṃyutta Nikāya*[7] as having been asked of the Buddha by **Pañcālacaṇḍa-devaputta** (see **Pañcāla Sutta**).

The *Dhammapada Commentary*[8] refers to an assembly at which Kāḷudāyī was present, his body of golden hue, sitting near **Pasenadi,** at sunset, with the moon rising in the eastern sky. Ānanda looks at them and declares how the Buddha suffuses them all with his glory.

Kāḷudāyī is identified with **Sakka** in the **Bhisa Jātaka.**[9]

[4] ii. 500 f.; see also Ap. i. 86 f., where another set of verses is attributed to Kāḷudāyī.
[5] A. iv. 449 f.
[6] AA. ii. 815.
[7] S. i. 48.
[8] iv. 143.
[9] J. iv. 314.

Kālussa.—A village given by **Udaya I.** to the **Nīlārāma.**[1]

[1] Cv. xlix. 16.

Kāḷūpakāḷa.—The name of the warders in charge of a hell bearing the same name. They smite their victims with arrows and spears.[1]

[1] J. vi. 248.

Kālūla.—A monastery in Ceylon. **Aggabodhi VIII.** gave a village for its maintenance.[1]

[1] Cv. xlix. 47.

Kāvinda.—One of the legal ministers (*dhammānusāsaka*) of King **Vedeha** of **Mithilā.**[1] On the fast-day of the dark fortnight a Yakkha named **Naradeva** took possession of him and he barked like a mad dog. His son, knowing this, shut him up indoors on these occasions.[2] When the king discovered this, Kāvinda was cast into prison and ordered to be flogged for plotting against **Mahosadha,** but at the latter's request he was pardoned.[3]

In the present age he was **Ambaṭṭha.**[4]

[1] J. vi. 330 ff.
[2] *Ibid.*, 383.
[3] *Ibid.*, 389.
[4] *Ibid.*, 478.

Kāvīra.—A seaport in the Damiḷa country. **Akitti** lived in a park near by.[1] **Sumanā,** wife of **Lakuṇṭaka Atimbara,** was once born in Kāvīra in a mariner's family.[2]

[1] J. iv. 238. [2] DhA. iv. 50.

Kāveri.—A channel flowing from the **Giritaḷāka** tank to **Kaddūravaḍḍhamāna.** This channel formed part of the irrigation system of **Parakkamabāhu I.**[1]

[1] Cv. lxxix. 55.

Kāsagalla.—A monastery which was repaired by **Vijayabāhu I.**[1] *v.l.* **Kāyagalla.**

[1] Cv. lx. 61.

Kāsapabbata.—A mountain in Ceylon, once the headquarters of **Paṇḍukābhaya.**[1] It lay on the way from **Vijitapura** to **Anurādhapura. Duṭṭhagāmaṇī** encamped there and constructed a tank near by.[2]

[1] Mhv. x. 27. [2] *Ibid.*, xxv. 50; see also Mhv. *Trs.* 70 n.

Kāsaya.—Inhabitant of **Kāsi.**[1] *Cf.* **Kāsiyo.**

[1] J. ii. 402.

Kāsāva Jātaka (No. 221).—A poor man of Benares, having entered into a contract with ivory workers to supply elephants' tusks, went into the forest clad in a Pacceka Buddha's yellow robe, and standing in the path of the elephants, slew the last one of the herd each day. The Bodhisatta, being the leader of the elephants, on discovering what was happening, threatened to kill the man; but receiving his promise never to visit the forest again, he let him go free on account of his robe.

A trader, coming to Rājagaha on business, contributed a magnificent yellow robe to an almsgiving organised by the townspeople. There was some dispute as to whether **Sāriputta** or **Devadatta** should receive the robe; but the majority favouring Devadatta, he cut the robe into strips and wore it in great style. When the matter was reported to the Buddha, he related the above Jātaka story, in which Devadatta is identified with the huntsman.[1]

[1] J. ii. 196 ff.

Kāsāva Vagga.—The eighth section of the Duka Nipāta of the *Jātaka Commentary.*[1]

[1] J. ii. 196-221.

1. **Kāsi** (**Kāsika**).—One of the sixteen **Mahājanapadas**,[1] its capital being **Bārāṇasī** (*q.v.*). At the time of the Buddha, it had been absorbed into the kingdom of **Kosala**, and **Pasenadi** was king of both countries.[2] The **Mahāvagga**,[3] however, mentions a **Kāsika-rājā** (king of Kāsi ?) who sent a robe to **Jīvaka**. Buddhaghosa[4] says that this was a brother of Pasenadi and son of the same father. He was probably a sub-king of Pasenadi. Pasenadi's father, **Mahākosala**, on giving his daughter in marriage to **Bimbisāra**, allotted her a village of Kāsi (**Kāsigāma**, *q.v.*) as bath money.[5] Even at this time, however, the memory of Kāsi as an independent kingdom seems to have been still fresh in men's minds. It is very frequently mentioned as such in the Jātakas and elsewhere. Kāsi was once ruled by the **Bhāratas**, one of whom, **Dhataraṭṭha**, was its king in the time of **Reṇu**.[6] There seem to have been frequent wars between the countries of Kāsi and Kosala, victory belonging now to one, now to the other. In one such war, **Dīghīti** (*q.v.*), the Kosala king, was defeated by the king of Kāsi, but Dīghīti's son Dīghāvu won back the kingdom.[7] In another war the Kāsi king, **Mahāsīlava**, was taken captive by the ruler of Kosala, but his kingdom was later restored to him.[8]

The traditional name of the king of Kāsi from time immemorial was evidently **Brahmadatta** (*q.v.*), and references to kings of that name abound in the Jātakas. Sometimes the king is referred to merely as Kāsi-rājā. Among other kings of Kāsi mentioned are **Kikī**[9] and **Kalābu**.[10]

The extent of the Kāsi kingdom is given as three hundred leagues.[11]

The capital of Kāsi is generally given as **Bārāṇasī**, but it is said that when **Asoka** was king of Kāsi his capital was in **Potali**,[12] and another king, **Udaya-bhadda**, had his seat of government in **Surundha**.[13] It is possible that these cities did not form part of the regular kingdom of Kāsi, but became annexed to it during the reigns of some of the more powerful kings.

Kāsi was evidently a great centre of trade and a most populous and prosperous country. Frequent mention is made of caravans leaving Kāsi to travel for trade. One highway went through Kāsi to Rājagaha[14] and another to Sāvatthi.[15] Kāsi was famed for her silks, and Kāsi-robes were most highly esteemed as gifts, each robe being valued at

[1] A. i. 213, etc.
[2] D. i. 288; M. ii. 111.
[3] Vin. i. 281.
[4] See Vinaya Texts ii. 195, n. 2.
[5] J. iv. 342; J. ii. 403; SA. i. 110, 120 f., etc.
[6] D. ii. 235 f.
[7] Vin. i. 334; J. iii. 487; DhA. i. 46.
[8] J. i. 262, etc.; see also i. 409; UdA. 123.
[9] M. ii. 49.
[10] J. iii. 39.
[11] J. v. 41; also iii. 304, 391.
[12] J. iii. 155.
[13] J. iv. 104 ff.
[14] Vin. i. 212.
[15] *Ibid.*, ii. 10; Mhv. v. 114.

one hundred thousand.[16] Mention is also made of the perfumes of Kāsi (*Kāsi-vilepana*[17] and *Kāsi-candana*[18]).

Besides those already referred to, other names of places mentioned in literature as belonging to Kāsi, are **Vāsabhagāma, Macchikāsaṇḍa** (the kammantagāma of **Anāthapiṇḍika**), **Kiṭāgiri** and **Dhammapālagāma** (*q.v.*). Kāsi and Kosala are frequently mentioned together.[19]

[16] See, *e.g.*, J. vi. 151, 450; (see also **Aḍḍhakāsi**).
[17] J. i. 355.
[18] A. iii. 391; UdA. 332.
[19] *E.g.*, A. v. 59.

2. **Kāsi,** or **Kāsika.**—A city, the birthplace of **Phussa** Buddha.[1] There he preached the *Buddhavaṃsa*.[2] The city is probably to be identified with Benares, which is sometimes referred to as Kāsipura.[3] It is also called Kāsipurī.[4]

[1] Bu. xix. 14; J. i. 41.
[2] BuA. 193.
[3] *E.g.*, DhA. i. 71; J. v. 54; vi. 165; M. i. 171; DhsA. 35; Cv. xli. 37.
[4] PvA. 19.

Kāsika.—A city. Sixty-five kappas ago the Thera **Bodhighariya** lived there as cakkavatti. The city was built by **Vissakamma** and was ten leagues in length and eight in width. It was built entirely of precious metals. The king's palace was called **Maṅgala.**[1]

[1] Ap. ii. 401.

Kāsika.—The name of a tribe; probably the inhabitants of **Kāsi.**[1]

[1] Ap. ii. 359.

Kāsikhaṇḍa.—A district in Ceylon; in it was the **Mahādevarattakurara-vihāra.**[1]

[1] Cv. xli. 101.

Kāsigāma, Kāsinigama.—Probably the actual name of the village in Kāsi which was given by **Mahākosala** to his daughter when she married **Bimbisāra.** The village produced a revenue of one hundred thousand, and was given to the queen for her bath and perfume money. After Bimbisāra's death, **Pasenadi** withdrew the gift from **Ajātasattu,** which act was the cause of a war between the two. Later, when Pasenadi's daughter **Vajirā** was married to Ajātasattu, the village was given back as part of her dowry.[1]

[1] J. ii. 403; iv. 342; S. i. 82 ff.; SA. i. 110, 120 f.; AA. ii. 833; DhA. iii. 259.

Kāsipura.—See **Kāsi** (2).

Kāsiyo.—The inhabitants of **Kāsi.**[1]

[1] J. v. 377, etc.

Kāsumāriphalakadāyaka Thera.—An arahant. Thirty-one kappas ago he gave a *kāsumāri*-fruit to the Buddha.[1] He is probably to be identified with **Sīvaka Sāmaṇera.**[2]

[1] Ap. i. 294. [2] ThagA. i. 61.

Kāsumāriphaliya Thera.—An arahant. The verses attributed to him are the same as those of **Kāsumāriphaladāyaka.** He is probably to be identified with **Jotidāsa Thera.**[1]

[1] Ap. ii. 445.

Kāsmīra.—See **Kasmīra.**

Kāhallivāpi.—A tank restored by **Parakkamabāhu I.**[1]

[1] Cv. lxxix. 37.

Kiṃsīla Sutta.—Preached by the Buddha in reply to a question put by **Sāriputta** beginning with the word *kiṃsīla.* Sāriputta visited the Buddha, taking with him a young man, son of a friend of his father. The youth had joined the Order under Sāriputta renouncing his immense wealth, but he could gain no attainment. Sāriputta desired him to hear an exposition by the Buddha, hence his question.[1]

One who aspires to the highest good should not be envious, obstinate, or careless, but diligent in his training, cultivating self-restraint and chastity, intent in the *dhamma*, making the *dhamma* his first and last concern.[2]

This sutta is the ninth of the *Culla Vagga* of the *Sutta Nipāta,* and derives its name from the first word (*kiṃsilo*) in Sāriputta's question.

[1] SnA. i. 331. [2] Sn. pp. 56 f.

Kiṃsukapupphiya Thera.—An arahant. Thirty-one kappas ago he had offered a *kiṃsuka*-flower to the Buddha.[1] In the *Theragāthā Commentary* his verses are attributed to two different theras: **Jambugāmiya**[2] and **Somamitta.**[3]

[1] Ap. ii. 435. [2] ThagA. i. 86 f. [3] *Ibid.*, 268.

Kiṃsukapūjaka Thera.—An arahant. Ninety-four kappas ago he had offered a *kiṃsuka*-flower to the Buddha **Siddhattha.**[1]

[1] Ap. i. 283.

Kiṃsukavatthu.—A village in **Rohaṇa.** Here the forces of **Rakkha** and **Bhūta** fought a fierce battle against their enemies.[1]

[1] Cv. lxxiv. 75 f.

Kiṃsukā Sutta.—A monk asks a fellow-monk as to when a monk's insight is said to be fully purified. When he really understands the arising and the passing away of the six-fold sense sphere answers the other. Not being satisfied, the first monk asks others who, in turn, declare in similar terms of the five *upādānakkhandhas*, the four *mahābhūtas*, etc. Finally he asks the Buddha, who says that the answers of the monks were like those of men who, on being asked what the *kiṃsuka* (Judas) tree was like, describe it, not as it really is, but as each one of them happens to have seen it. The Buddha explains the monk's question by means of the parable of a city, strongly guarded, having six gates and a watchful warden of the gates, receiving messengers from various quarters.[1] *Cf.* **Kiṃsukopama Jātaka.**

[1] S. iv. 191 ff.

Kiṃsukopama Jātaka (No. 248).—Four monks came to the Buddha and asked him for a topic of meditation. He gave them various topics and they, having retired to various places, all became arahants: one by understanding the six-fold sphere, the second the five *khandhas*, the third the four *mahābhūtas*, and the fourth the eighteen *dhātu*. They returned and related to the Buddha each the particular excellence attained by him, and one of them asked the Buddha how all these methods could lead to Nibbāna. The Buddha related a story of the past where four sons of **Brahmadatta,** king of Benares, having asked their charioteer to show them a *kiṃsuka*-tree, are shown the tree at four different times: when the buds were just sprouting, when the leaves were green, at the time of blossoming, and at the time of fruit-bearing.

When asked to describe the tree, the first likened it to a burnt stump, the second to a banyan tree, the third to a piece of meat, and the fourth to an acacia. The matter was referred to the king, who solved the difficulty.

The king was the Bodhisatta.[1]

[1] J. ii. 265 f.

Kiṃsukopama Sutta.—Mentioned in the **Kiṃsukopama Jātaka**[1]; evidently the same as the **Kiṃsukā Sutta.**

[1] J. ii. 265.

Kikī.—King of Benares at the time of the Buddha **Kassapa.** When the Buddha arrived in Benares, the king, having listened to his sermon, entertained the Buddha and his monks at the palace. When the Bhudda was asked to spend the rainy season there he refused, as he had already accepted the invitation of **Ghaṭīkāra** of **Vehaliṅga.** Kikī was at first hurt by the refusal, but when the Buddha described Ghaṭīkāra's virtues, the king was pleased and sent five hundred cartloads of provisions to Ghaṭīkāra who, however, curtly refused the gift.[1]

One of Kikī's daughters was **Uracchadā,** who attained arahantship at the age of sixteen. He had seven other daughters—**Samaṇī, Samaṇā, Guttā, Bhikkhudāsikā, Dhammā, Sudhammā** and **Saṅghadāsī**—who, in this Buddha-age became respectively **Khemā, Uppalavaṇṇā, Paṭācārā, Gotamā, Dhammadinnā, Mahāmāyā** and **Visākhā.**[2] He had also a son, **Paṭhavindhara** (**Puthuvindhara**), who succeeded him to the throne.[3] During the life of the Buddha Kassapa Kikī waited on him with many kinds of gifts,[4] and at his death built one of the four gates outside the Buddha's cetiya. The gate was a league in width.[5] According to the *Aṅguttara Commentary,*[6] Kikī was the *aggupaṭṭhāka* of Kassapa.

In the Sanskrit books he is called Kṛkī, and is mentioned as owning a palace called Kokanada.[7]

[1] D. ii. 7; M. ii. 49 ff.

[2] J. iv. 481; in the Ap. (ii. 561 f.) the names are Samaṇī, Samaṇaguttā, Bhikkhuṇī, Bhikkhadāyikā, Dhammā, etc., and they are mentioned as having lived celibate lives; see also *s.v.* Sattamba; both the Apadāna and the ThigA. (17, 103 f.) omit the name of Mahāmāyā from this list and have, instead, the name of Bhaddā Kuṇḍalakesā, identifying her with Bhikkhadāyikā. The Mtu. (i. 303 f.) mentions another daughter Mālinī Kisāgotamī.

[3] ThagA. i. 151.

[4] SnA. i. 281, 283.

[5] *Ibid.*, 194.

[6] AA. i. 420.

[7] *E.g.*, Mtu. i. 325; Divy. 22 f.; Avadānaś i. 338, etc.

Kikī-Brahmadatta.—Son of **Suyāma** and great grandson of King **Kikī**; see **Ekadhamma-Savaṇiya Thera** (1).

Kikumāra.—The name of a tribe mentioned in the *Apadāna.*[1]

[1] Ap. ii. 359.

Kiṅkinikapupphiya Thera.—An arahant. Ninety-one kappas ago, in the time of Buddha **Vipassī,** he saw the Buddha bathing and offered him *kiṅkinika*-flowers. Seventy-seven kappas ago he was a king named **Bhīmaratha.**[1] He is probably identical with **Sirivaḍḍha Thera.**[2]

[1] Ap. i. 204.

[2] ThagA. i. 107.

Kiccārattarayara.—A Damiḷa chief of **Coḷa,** an ally of **Nigaḷadha.**[1]

[1] Cv. lxxvii. 17.

Kiñcikkha Sutta.—See **Āmisakiñcikkha Sutta.**

Kiñchanda Jātaka (No. 511).—A chaplain of the king of Benares, who took bribes and gave false judgments, is reborn to a state of suffering all day, but as a result of having given a mango fruit to a woman who was keeping the fast, he enjoys great glory throughout the night in a charming mango-grove. His king, who had become an ascetic, eats a mango which had been carried by the river from this grove, and wishes for some more. He is transported by a river nymph (**Uppalavaṇṇā** of this age) to the mango-grove, where he hears from his erstwhile chaplain the story of his alternate bliss and misery. The Buddha related the story to some of his lay disciples who were keeping the fast.[1] The king is identified with the Bodhisatta.

[1] J. v. 1 ff.

Kiñjaka.—See **Giñjaka.**

Kiñjakesara (*v.l.* **Kiñcakesara**).—Sixty-eight kappas ago there were four kings of this name, all previous births of **Bimbijāliya Thera.**[1]

[1] Ap. i. 225.

Kiṭāgiri (*v.l.* **Kiṭāgiri**).—A village of the **Kāsis,** on the road from **Kāsi** to **Sāvatthi.** It was the headquarters of the followers of **Assaji** and **Punabbasu,** who lived there, behaving in a shameless and wicked manner. A certain monk, on his way to Jetavana, passed through the place and was asked by a pious layman to complain to the Buddha of their ill-behaviour. On hearing of it, the Buddha sent **Sāriputta** and **Moggallāna** to proclaim on them an act of banishment.[1] Some time after, when the Buddha visited the place with a large company of monks, including Sāriputta and Moggallāna, the **Assajipunabbasukā,** were asked to provide lodgings for the visitors. They agreed to do so for the Buddha, but would have nothing to do with Sāriputta and Moggallāna.[2]

According to Buddhaghosa,[3] Kiṭāgiri was the name of a *nigama* (township). In the *Samantapāsādikā*[4] it is called a *janapada,* favoured by adequate rain and fruitful crops, and therefore chosen by the Assaji-Punabbasukas.

[1] J. ii. 387; Vin. ii. 9 f.; iii. 179 f.; DhA. ii. 108 f.

[2] Vin. ii. 171.

[3] MA. ii. 668.

[4] iii. 613 f.

Kiṭāgiri Sutta.—Preached at **Kiṭāgiri** to the **Assajipunabbasukā,** who were reported to the Buddha as having ridiculed the idea that they should themselves have only one meal a day because the Buddha and his devoted disciples did so. The Buddha sent for them and impressed on them that all his teachings were based on experience and knowledge and should therefore be followed by them. Chaffering such as their's was not seemly in the seeker after truth.[1]

[1] M. i. 473 ff.

Kiṭṭakaṇḍaka.—A tank restored by **Gajabāhu.**[1]

[1] Cv. lxviii. 45.

Kiṇṇarā (*v.l.* **Kinnarā**).—Wife of **Kaṇḍari,** king of Benares. See **Kaṇḍarī Jataka.**

Kitava.—King of Benares. His son became known in this Buddha-age as **Kuṇḍinagariya Thera.**[1] From the *Petavatthu*[2] Kitava would appear to be the king, not of Benares but of **Rājagaha (Giribbaja).**

[1] PvA. 177 f., 263 f. [2] iv. 7.

Kitavāsa.—King of Benares. A son was born to him who was named **Duṭṭhakumāra,** and who, according to the fortune-tellers, would die for lack of water. In order to falsify the prophecy, the king guarded his son closely, made numerous tanks near the city, and saw that vessels of water were placed wherever possible. One day, while returning from the park, the prince saw a Pacceka Buddha, and being angry that obeisance should be paid to the Buddha instead of to himself, he took the Buddha's bowl and dashed it on the ground. The prince's body burst into flames, but all the water around having dried up, they could not be quenched and he was swallowed up in hell. When Kitavāsa heard of this he was greatly grieved, but on reflection he realised that his grief sprang from affection, and thenceforth resolved to fix his love on nothing.

Kitavāsa is identified with **Chattapāṇi** of the **Dhammaddhaja Jātaka,** Chattapāṇi himself being a former birth of **Sāriputta.**[1]

The story of Kitavāsa's son bears close resemblance to that of Kitava's son (see **Kuṇḍinagariya Thera**). Perhaps Kitava and Kitavāsa are identical.

[1] J. ii. 194 ff.

1. **Kittaggabodhi.**—Nephew of **Dappula II.** He married **Devā,** King Dappula's daughter, and leaving his brother, who was also called Dappula,

with the king, went to **Rohaṇa,** and having subdued that country, became king there.[1] He had four sons—**Mahinda, Kassapa, Sena** and **Udaya**—and three daughters—**Saṅghā, Tissā** and **Kitti.**[2]

[1] Cv. xlix. 71. [2] *Ibid.*, l. 50 ff.

2. **Kittaggabodhi.**—Ādipāda and son of **Mahinda,** uparāja to **Sena II.** and **Kitti.** He rebelled against **Udaya II.** and fled to **Rohaṇa,** whose ruler he killed. He was taken captive by Prince **Mahinda,** son of **Kassapa,** the yuvarāja of **Udaya II.,** with the help of the general **Vajiragga,** in Malaya, and was probably killed by the latter at **Guttasāla.**[1]

[1] Cv. li. 94 ff.

Kittaggabodhipabbata.—A tank restored by **Vijayabāhu I.**[1]

[1] Cv. lx. 49.

Kittā.—See **Kitti** (12).

1. **Kitti.**—A court official of **Kassapa Vikkamabāhu,** son of **Mahinda V.** He lived in **Makkhakudrūsa,** and when the **Coḷas** pillaged **Rohaṇa,** he, with the help of the minister **Buddha** of Māragallaka, defeated them and drove them to **Pulatthipura.** When the king offered him a boon, he desired that the portion of his revenues appropriated by the monks should be remitted.[1]

[1] Cv. lv. 26 ff.

2. **Kitti.**—Commander-in-chief of **Kassapa Vikkamabāhu.** When the king died he seized the throne and reigned for eight days, till he was killed by **Mahālāna-Kitti.**[1]

[1] Cv. lvi. 7 f.

3. **Kitti.**—The name of **Vijayabāhu I.** before he became king.[1]

[1] Cv. lvii. 3, 46, 49.

4. **Kitti.**—Commander-in-chief of **Vikkamabāhu.** He was slain by **Vīradeva.**[1]

[1] Cv. lxi. 41.

5. **Kitti Laṅkādhinātha.**—A general of **Parakkamabāhu I.** His son was **Laṅkāpura.** They both took part in the great fight against **Gajabāhu.** In recognition of his services he was given the office of **Laṅkādhikari**; he was earlier known as the **Saṅkhanāyaka.** He helped in liberating Gajabāhu from the power of **Mānābharaṇa,** and later defeated the forces

of Gajabāhu when they attacked Parakkamabāhu.[1] Kitti took part in the campaigns of Parakkamabāhu against his foes, these latter being defeated at the **Yakkhasūkara** ford and at **Billagāma.** Later, as a result of disregarding the king's instructions, Kitti fell into the enemy's hands at **Surulla.**[2] He was, however, pardoned and sent to **Dīghavāpi,** where he helped in winning for Parakkamabāhu the Sacred Bowl and the Tooth Relic.[3]

[1] Cv. lxx. 205, 215-20, 278, 300, 316. [2] *Ibid.*, lxxii. 21, 122, 138.
[3] *Ibid.*, lxxiv. 90, 110, 119, 136 ff.

6. **Kitti.**—Another general of **Parakkamabāhu I.**; one of the two **Daṇḍanāyakabhātaro** (*q.v.*), the other being **Saṅkhadhātu.** Kitti was granted the rank of **Nagaragalla.**[1]

[1] Cv. lxx. 280; lxxii. 162.

7. **Kitti Ādipotthakī.**—A minister of **Parakkamabāhu I.** He was first stationed at the **Assamaṇḍala** ford and later at **Maṅgalabegāma.** Afterwards he was sent to Anurādhapura against **Mahinda** and to Kyānagāma against **Mānābharaṇa.**[1] He seems to have been known also as **Bhaṇḍārapotthakī**[2] and **Jīvitapotthakī.**[3]

[1] Cv. lxxii. 27, 160, 207. [2] *Ibid.*, lxxii. 82. [3] *Ibid.*, lxxiv. 90.

8. **Kitti Laṅkāpura.**—A general of **Parakkamabāhu I.** and son of **Kitti Laṅkādhinātha.**[1] During the king's campaign against his enemies, Kitti was posted at **Balapāsaṇa.**[2]

[1] Cv. lxx. 218. [2] *Ibid.*, lxxiv. 178.

9. **Kitti Nagaragiri.**—A general of **Parakkamabāhu I.** He was one of the generals in charge of the Sinhalese expedition to **Rāmañña** and led the attack against the port of **Kusumi.**[1]

[1] Cv. lxxvi. 60.

10. **Kitti Kesadhātu.**—A general of **Parakkamabāhu I.** He was one of the leaders of the Sinhalese army which fought against the Damiḷas.[1] He may be identical with **Kitti** (9).

[1] Cv. lxxvi. 255, 269.

11. **Kitti Senāpati.**—General of **Līlāvatī.** He deposed **Coḍagaṅga,** placed Līlāvatī on the throne, and carried on the government for three years (1197-1200).[1] He was a patron of learning.[2]

[1] Cv. lxxx. 30. [2] P.L.C. 207.

12. **Kitti** (*v.l.* **Kittā**).—Daughter of **Kittaggabodhi,** ruler of **Rohaṇa,** and wife of **Mahinda,** uparāja of **Sena I.**[1] Her brothers were **Kassapa, Sena** and **Udaya.** She had one daughter and four sons, one of whom was the Ādipāda of Kittaggabodhi.[2]

[1] Cv. l. 50, 60. [2] *Ibid.*, li. 16, 94.

13. **Kitti.**—Queen of **Mahinda IV.** She built a pariveṇa to the west of the **Thūpārāma,** and had baths built there and in **Kappāsagāma** and **Cīvaracetiya.** She dedicated a golden banner twelve cubits long to the **Mahā Thūpa.**[1]

[1] Cv. liv. 50 ff.

Kittigāma.—A village in Ceylon, near **Koṭapabbata.** It was the birthplace of **Theraputtābhaya,** one of **Duṭṭhagāmaṇi's** chief warriors.[1]

[1] Mhv. xxiii. 55.

Kittinissaṅka, also known as **Nissaṅka Malla,** king of Ceylon (1187-1196 A.C.). He was uparāja of **Vijayabāhu II.,** and became king after the murder of **Mahinda VI.** Among his acts of piety were the building of a stone temple for the Tooth Relic at **Pulatthipura** and the embellishment of the famous rock-temple at **Jambukola-vihāra.** His son was **Vīrabāhu.**[1]

[1] For other details see Cv. lxxx. 30 ff.; also Cv. *Trs.* ii. 127, n. 1 and 2.

Kittinissaṅka-vihāra.—A monastery built by **Kittinissaṅka** and adorned with one hundred pāsādas. He made endowments for its maintenance.[1]

[1] Cv. lxxx. 21.

Kittirājavālukagāma.—A village in **Rohaṇa.** A battle was fought there during the campaigns of **Parakkamabāhu I.**[1]

[1] Cv. lxxv. 17.

1. **Kittisirimegha.**—Son of **Moggallāna II.** and king of Ceylon from 556 A.C. The length of his reign is uncertain; he was slain by **Mahānāga.**[1] **Rūpavatī,** queen of **Parakkamabāhu I.,** was probably a lineal descendant of this king.[2]

[1] Cv. xli. 65-92; see also Cv. *Trs.* i. 61, n. 2. [2] Cv. lxxiii. 136, 142.

2. **Kittisirimegha.**—Son of **Mittā,** sister of **Vijayabāhu I.** and of a Paṇḍu king (**Paṇḍurājā**). **Mānābharaṇa** and **Sirivallabha** were his brothers, and he married Vijayabāhu's daughter, **Lokanāthā.**[1] After

[1] Cv. lix. 42, 44.

Vijayabāhu's death, Kittisirimegha ruled over the province of **Dvādasasahassaka** at **Mahānāgahula** with Mittā and **Jayabāhu I.**[2] After the death of Mānābharaṇa, Kittisirimegha took over also his province of Rohaṇa.[3] When **Gajabāhu** succeeded **Vikkamabāhu II.** Kittisirimegha fought against him, but was defeated by the king's officer **Gokaṇṇa,** and retired to his own province, where he was later joined by **Parakkamabāhu** at **Saṅkhanāyakatthalī.**[4] Parakkama stayed with him, being adopted as his son, and his *upanayana* was held under Kittisirimegha's orders at **Baddalatthalī.**[5] When, however, Parakkama escaped from the prince's protection, he sent an army to capture him, but without success.[6] Later, Parakkama himself went to see Kittisirimegha in the company of his mother **Ratnāvalī,** and Kittisirimegha gave orders to his followers to regard the prince as their master. He himself died soon after.[7]

[2] *Ibid.*, lxi. 22-7.
[3] *Ibid.*, lxiii. 2.
[4] *Ibid.*, lxiii. 20, 34, 43.
[5] *Ibid.*, lxiv. 18, 25, 36.
[6] *Ibid.*, lxvi. 57 ff.
[7] *Ibid.*, lxvii. 16, 55, 60, 83, 87.

3. **Kittisirimegha.**—Son of **Mānābharaṇa** by his second queen **Pabhāvatī.** His grandfather was **Sirivallabha.**[1] His father, on his deathbed, repented of the harm he had done to the Buddha's religion and asked his son to do reparation by joining **Parakkamabāhu I.** The latter, on hearing this, sent for Kittisirimegha and made him a member of his court.[2]

[1] Cv. lxiv. 24.
[2] *Ibid.*, lxxii. 303, 311.

Kittisirirājasīha.—King of Ceylon (1767-1782 A.C.).[1]

[1] For details of his reign see Cv. xcix. and c.

Kittisīhasūra.—An important officer of state in Burma who, in 1531, wrote a *Saṃvaṇṇanā* on the **Abhidhānappadīpikā.**[1]

[1] Bode: *op. cit.*, p. 67.

Kittisena.—Son and successor of **Kumāradhātusena.** He reigned only for nine months and was killed by his mother's brother, **Sīva.**[1]

[1] Cv. xli. 4.

Kinti Sutta.—Preached at **Baliharaṇa** in **Kusinārā.** The Buddha tells the monks that they should school themselves in the higher lore taught by him, such as the *satipaṭṭhāna, iddhipāda,* etc., and lays down rules on the treatment of monks who dispute about the meaning and letter of the Doctrine and of those who are guilty of transgressions. The sutta derives its name from the first words (*kinti*) uttered by the Buddha in beginning the sermon.[1]

[1] M. ii. 238 ff.

Kindada Sutta.—Records part of a conversation between a deva and the Buddha at **Jetavana.** The deva asks what one should give in order to obtain certain results, such as strength, beauty, etc.—the Buddha explains.[1]

[1] S. i. 32.

Kinnara Jātaka = Bhattāṭiya Jātaka.—Found on the Bhīlsa Tope under this name, evidently to distinguish it from the **Candakinnara Jātaka.**[1]

[1] See Cunningham: Bhilsa Tope, Pl. 27.

Kinnarā.—See **Kiṇṇarā.**

Kinnughaṇḍu.—One of the great Yakkhas, mentioned in the *Āṭānāṭiya Sutta*, to be invoked when disciples of the Buddha are worried by evil spirits.[1] He is one of the vassals of the Four Regent Gods.[2]

[1] D. iii. 204.
[2] D. ii. 258.

Kipillikā.—See **Kimikāla.**

Kimattha Sutta.—When Paribbājakas, holding other views, should ask why members of the Buddha's Order live the holy life, the reply should be "for the full understanding of *dukkha.*" They should also be told of the way to such understanding.[1]

[1] S. v. 6.

1. **Kimatthi Sutta.**—The first part is identical with **Kimattha Sutta.** If further questioned as to what is *dukkha*, monks should answer, "eye is *dukkha*, rūpa objects are *dukkha*, eye-contact, etc."[1]

[1] S. iv. 138.

2. **Kimatthi Sutta.**—A discussion between **Sāriputta** and **Jambukhādaka** at **Nālaka.** "What is the purpose of the good life?" "The comprehension of Ill." "Is there a way thereto?" "Yes, the Noble Eightfold Way."[1]

[1] S. iv. 253.

3. **Kimatthi Sutta.**—See also **Sāmaṇḍaka Saṃyutta.**

1. **Kimatthiya Sutta.**—On the purpose of good actions, how good conduct gradually rears a summit of righteousness, from *avippaṭisāratā* to *vimuttiñāṇadassana*. The sutta is a conversation between the Buddha and **Ānanda.**[1]

[1] A. v. 1 f.

2. **Kimatthiya Sutta.**—Same as above.[1]

[1] A. v. 311 f.

Kimikālā.—A river near **Jantugāma. Meghiya** Thera was attracted by a mango-grove on its banks and asked the Buddha's permission to meditate there. Twice the Buddha refused; the third time he gave his permission. Meghiya went, but soon returned, finding that he could not concentrate his mind there. The river was evidently in the neighbourhood of **Cālikā.**[1] According to the *Udāna Commentary*,[2] it was so called because it abounded in black worms (*kāḷakimīnam bahulatāya*). *v.l.* **Kipillikā.**

[1] A. iv. 354 f.; ThagA. i. 149; Ud. iv. 1.

[2] UdA. 217.

Kimila, Kimilā.—See **Kimbila, Kimbilā.**

Kimpakka Jātaka (No. 85).—The Bodhisatta was once the leader of a caravan. During a journey through a forest he gave orders to his men not to eat any fruit without his leave. Seeing the fruit of a *kimpakka*-tree, which in appearance and flavour resembled a mango, some of the men ate of the fruit and died in spite of efforts to save them.

The story was related to a monk who was stirred to lust by the sight of a beautifully dressed woman in **Sāvatthi.** Lusts of the senses are like the fruit of the kimpakka-tree, sweet and attractive in the hour of enjoyment, but leading later to death.[1]

[1] J. i. 367 f.

1. **Kimbila, Kimila, Kimmila.**—Thera. A Sākyan of **Kapilavatthu.** He was converted with **Bhaddiya** and four other Sākyan nobles at **Anupiyā,** shortly after the Buddha's visit to Kapilavatthu.[1] The *Theragāthā Commentary*[2] says that while at Anupiyā the Buddha, in order to arouse Kimbila, conjured up a beautiful woman in her prime and then showed her to him passing into old age. Greatly agitated, Kimbila sought the Buddha, heard the Doctrine and, having entered the Order, in due course

[1] Vin. ii. 182; DhA. i. 112 f.

[2] ThagA. i. 235 f.; Thag. 118, 155 f., According to DhA. (i. 117) Kimbila became an arahant soon after ordination together with Bhagu; see also J. i. 140 and AA. i. 108.

won arahantship. Kimbila seems to have maintained throughout his early friendship with **Anuruddha,** dwelling with him and **Nandiya,** now in this wood or park, now in that. The Buddha visited them at **Pācīnavaṃsadāya** when he was going away, disgusted with the recalcitrant monks of **Kosambī.**[3] They were in the **Gosiṅgasālavana** when the Buddha preached to them the **Cūla-Gosiṅga Sutta,** at the conclusion of which, **Dīgha Parajana Yakkha** sang the praises of all three.[4] Their number was increased by the presence of **Bhagu, Kuṇḍadhāna, Revata** and **Ānanda,** on the occasion when the Buddha preached the **Naḷakapāna** Sutta in the **Palāsavana** at **Naḷakapāna.**[5]

In three different places in the *Aṅguttara Nikāya*[6] record is made of a conversation between Kimbila and the Buddha, when Kimbila asks how the Dhamma could be made to endure long after the Buddha's death and what were the causes which might bring about its early disappearance. The conversation took place in the **Veḷuvana (Niceluvaṇa ?)** in Kimbilā. According to the *Aṅguttara Commentary,*[7] however, it would appear that the Kimbila mentioned here was not Kimbila the Sākyan but another. We are told that this Kimbila was a *seṭṭhiputta* of Kimbilā. He joined the Order and acquired the power of knowing his previous births. He recollected how he had been a monk at the time when Kassapa Buddha's religion was falling into decay, and seeing how the Faith was neglected by its followers, he made a stairway up a cliff and lived there as a recluse. It was this memory of his previous life which prompted Kimbila's question.

Elsewhere[8] the Buddha is reported as questioning Kimbila at the same spot on the question of breathing. Kimbila remains silent though the question is put three times. Ānanda intervenes and suggests that the Buddha should himself furnish the answer so that the monks may learn it and profit thereby.

In the time of **Kakusandha** Buddha, Kimbila had been a householder; after the Buddha's death he erected a pavilion of salala-garlands round his cetiya.[9] He is probably to be identified with **Salalamaṇḍapiya** Thera of the *Apadāna.*[10]

The *Dhammapada Commentary*[11] mentions a story which shows how delicately nurtured Kimbila was. One day, in a discussion with his friends, Anuruddha and Bhaddiya, as to where rice came from, Kimbila remarked that it came from the granary (*koṭṭhe*).

[3] Vin. i. 350; J. iii. 489; see also Upakkilesa Sutta (M. iii. 155 ff.) and ThagA. i. 275 f.

[4] M. i. 205 ff.

[5] *Ibid.*, i. 462 ff.

[6] A. iii. 247; 339; iv. 84.

[7] AA. ii. 642.

[8] S. v. 322 f.

[9] ThagA. i. 235.

[10] Ap. i. 333.

[11] DhA. i. 115; iv. 126.

2. **Kimbila.**—A seṭṭhiputta of Kimbilā who later became a monk. See **Kimbila** (1).

Kimbila Vagga.—The twenty-first section of the **Pañcaka Nipāta** of the *Aṅguttara Nikāya.* It contains ten suttas of which the Kimbila Sutta is the first.[1]

[1] A. iii. 247-51.

Kimbila Sutta.—Records the conversation which took place at **Veḷuvana (Niceḷuvana ?)** in **Kimbilā** between **Kimbila** (*q.v.*) and the Buddha, regarding the continuance of the Doctrine after the Buddha's death.[1]

[1] A. iii. 247, 339; iv. 84.

Kimbilā.—A town on the banks of the Ganges. It was in a *veḷuvana*[1] there the Buddha stayed and where the **Kimbila** and **Kimbilā** Suttas were preached.[2] According to the *Aṅguttara Commentary,*[3] it was the birthplace of the seṭṭhiputta **Kimbila (Kimbila** 2). The city existed in the time of Kassapa Buddha and was the residence of the woman who later became **Kaṇṇamuṇḍapetī.**[4] Among the palaces seen by **Nimi** when he visited heaven was that of a deva who had been a very pious man of Kimbilā.[5] Another such pious person of the same city was **Rohaka** with his wife **Bhadditthikā.**[6]

[1] More probably a *niceḷuvana*; the *Aṅguttara Commentary* (ii. 642) explains it as a *Mucalindavana.*

[2] A. iii. 247, etc.; S. iv. 181 f.; v. 322.

[3] AA. ii. 642.

[4] Pv. 12; PvA. 151.

[5] J. vi. 121.

[6] Vv. xxii. 4; VvA. 109.

Kimbilā Sutta.—Preached at **Kimbilā.** The Buddha asks **Kimbilā** (*q.v.*) a question on the practice of breathing, and when he fails to reply **Ānanda** requests the Buddha to teach the answer to the monks. The sutta deals with the method of breathing and the results thereof.[1]

[1] S. v. 322 f.

Kirapatika.—A household of **Vesalī,** a pious follower of the Buddha. Once when the Buddha was staying in Vesalī a poor man, wishing to give alms to him and to the monks, asked Kirapatika for money to provide the alms; Kirapatika gladly gave him much money and the Buddha and the monks were invited. But the monks, having heard of the man's poverty, had a full meal earlier, so that when the man served them with the food he had prepared they could eat but very little. The man was greatly offended and the Buddha, hearing of it, made an order to the monks prohibiting such conduct.[1]

Buddhaghosa[2] says that the householder's name was **Kira,** but that he was called Kirapatika on account of his great influence. He gave his workmen regular and generous wages.

[1] Vin. iv. 75 f. [2] Sp. iv. 817.

Kirāṭi.—A locality in Ceylon, near **Āḷisāra.** There **Māyāgeha** once captured a fortification.[1]

Kirāṭi may be the name of a tiny river.[2]

[1] Cv. lxx. 165. [2] See Cv. *Trs.* i. 301, n. 1.

Kirāta.—Probably the name given to a tribe of jungle men. Their language is classed with those of the **Oṭṭas,** the **Andhakas,** the **Yonakas** and the **Damiḷas,** as a language of the **Milakkhas** (non-Aryans).[1]

[1] *E.g.*, DA. i. 176; VibhA. 388; see also Zimmer: Altind. Leben 34.

Kirāvāpi.—A tank restored by **Parakkamabāhu I.**[1]; the modern Kiraveva.[2]

[1] Cv. lxviii. 47. [2] Cv. *Trs.* i. 280, n. 5.

Kirindagāma.—A village in **Rohaṇa.**[1]

[1] Cv. lxxiv. 97; for its identification see Cv. *Trs.* ii. 30, n. 5.

Kiriya Sutta.—The three ways (*dāna, sīla, bhāvanā*) of acquiring merit, considered in the eight different results produced according as the one or the other is practised, in small measure or great.[1]

[1] A. iv. 241 f.

Kilañjadāyaka Thera.—An arahant. Ninety-four kappas ago he was a worker in reeds in **Tivarā** and gave a mat of rushes to be offered to the Buddha **Siddhattha.** Seventy-seven kappas ago he was a king named **Jutindhara** (*v.l.* **Jalandhara**).[1]

[1] Ap. i. 219.

Kilesa Saṃyutta.—The twenty-seventh division of the *Saṃyutta Nikāya.*[1]

[1] S. iii. 232-4.

1. **Kilesa Sutta.**—The five kinds of alloy which are used with gold—iron, copper, tin, lead and silver—and the similar five corruptions of

the heart—sensual desire, malevolence, sloth and torpor, excitement and worry, doubt and wavering.[1]

[1] S. v. 92 f.

2. **Kilesa Sutta.**—The seven *bojjhaṅgas* lead to liberation by knowledge.[1]

[1] S. v. 93.

Kilesamāra.—See **Māra.**

Kilesiya Sutta.—In the Commentary to the **Rathavinīta Sutta**[1] mention is made of a Kilesiya Sutta in which the Buddha preached **Bhagu** Thera the virtues of solitude. I have not been able to trace a sutta of this name. The *Theragāthā Commentary*[2] says that the Buddha visited Bhagu at **Bālakaloṇakagāma** after his attainment of arahantship to congratulate him on his solitude (*ekavihāraṃ anumodituṃ*). The *Saṃyutta Commentary*[3] goes further and says that the Buddha visited him on the way from Kosambī to Pācīnavaṃsadāya, and that during this visit the Buddha preached to him the advantages of solitude (*ekacāravāse ānisaṃsaṃ*) for the whole day after the midday meal and the whole night (*sakalapacchābhattañ c'eva tiyāmarattiñ ca*). The Vinaya passage,[4] however, which records this visit does not make mention of any such special sermon, but merely says that the Buddha inquired after Bhagu's health and wellbeing. *v.l.* **Saṅkilesiya Sutta.**

[1] MA. i. 361.
[2] ThagA. i. 380.
[3] SA. ii. 222.
[4] Vin. i. 350.

Kisalayapūjaka Thera.—An arahant. Ninety-four kappas ago he was born in **Dvāravatī.** One day, seeing the Buddha **Siddhattha** going through the air with his attendant monks, he threw up into the sky, as an offering, an asoka shoot covered with buds. Twenty-seven kappas ago he was a king named **Ekassara.**[1]

[1] Ap. i. 200.

Kisa-Vaccha (also called **Vaccha Kisa**[1]).—A hermit (*isi*), the chief disciple of **Sarabhaṅga.** Desiring solitude, he lived in the park of King **Daṇḍakī,** near **Kumbhavatī** in **Kaliṅga.** A certain courtesan of the city walking about in the park, having lost the king's favour, saw Kisa-Vaccha, and considering the sight an ill-omen, she spat on him and threw her tooth stick at his head. That same day she received again the patronage of the king and decided that it was as a result of spitting on the hermit. Later,

[1] J. v. 150, 267.

when the purohita lost his office, she advised him to do as she had done, and by coincidence he, too, was restored. Some time after, the king going to quell a border rising, was advised to spit on the ascetic and throw his tooth stick at him; in this way he would find good luck. The king followed this advice, all his soldiers doing likewise. The king's general, a supporter of Kisa-Vaccha, bathed the holy man, and on being told that the Gods would destroy the kingdom unless apology were made, urged the king to apologise. The king was, however, unwilling, and the whole tract of Kaliṅga, sixty leagues in extent, was turned into a waste; only three people escaped unhurt—Kisa-Vaccha, the king's general, and **Matuposaka Rāma.** Kisa-Vaccha himself was taken in a palanquin to Sarabhaṅga by two of Sarabhaṅga's pupils.[2] The story was evidently well known in India and is often referred to.[3]

Kisa-Vaccha is mentioned in a list of eleven sages.[4] He is identified with **Kolita (Moggallāna).**[5]

[2] J. iii. 463, 469; v. 133-6; MA. ii. 599 ff.

[3] *E.g.*, J. v. 267; DA. i. 266.

[4] *E.g.*, J. vi. 99.

[5] J. v. 151.

Kisasaṅkicca.—A naked ascetic (*acelaka*), contemporary with the Buddha and evidently a well-known head of a school; mentioned in company with **Nanda Vaccha** and **Makkhali Gosāla.**[1] Kisasaṅkicca is spoken of as one of the three shining lights of the **Ājīvakas**[2] and is classified among the *paramasukkhābhijātas* in the *chaḷabhjāti* of the Ājīvakas (*q.v.*).[3] Buddhaghosa[4] says that Kisa was his personal name and Saṅkicca that of his gotta.

[1] *E.g.*, M. i. 238.

[2] *Ibid.*, 524.

[3] A. iii. 384; DA. i. 162.

[4] MA. i. 463.

1. **Kisāgotamī Therī.**—An arahant. She was declared chief among women disciples with respect to the wearing of coarse robes (*lūkhacīvaradharāṇaṃ*).[1] She came from a poor family in **Sāvatthi.**[2] Gotamī was her name—she was called Kisā because of her thinness. She was married into a rich family, by whom she was disdainfully treated[3]; but as soon as she bore a son she was shown respect. The boy, however, died when just old enough to run about; his mother, distraught with grief, fearful

[1] A. i. 25; the DhA (iv. 156) contains a story of the Buddha speaking to Sakka the praises of Kisāgotamī.

[2] Of a seṭṭhikula, which had fallen on evil days, says the Apadāna (p. 565, vs. 19).

[3] Except by her husband says the Apadāna (*loc. cit.* 20). The DhA. (ii. 270 ff.) account, however, makes no mention of her ill treatment; on the contrary, it leads us to expect that she should have been greatly esteemed because, prior to her arrival, her father-in-law's wealth, forty crores in amount, had all turned into charcoal. When she touched the charcoal it once more became gold. This account is found also in SA. i. 149.

lest the dead child should be taken from her, went about with him on her hip, seeking medicine to revive his life. People laughed at her, until one wise man, realizing her condition, directed her to the Buddha. The Buddha asked her to bring him a mustard seed from a house where no one had yet died. In the course of her search for the impossible her frenzy left her, and having grasped the truth, she laid the child in the charnel field, and returning to the Master begged admission to the Order. She became a *sotāpanna*, and soon after, when her insight was developed, the Buddha appeared before her in a blaze of radiance and, listening to his words, she became an arahant.[4]

In the verses ascribed to her in the *Therīgāthā*,[5] she incorporates the story of **Paṭācārā** in her own psalm, as though to utter more fully the pageant and tragedy inherent in woman's lot, whereof her own sorrow was but a phase.

In the time of **Padumuttara** Buddha she was a householder's daughter in **Haṃsavatī,** and having heard the Buddha assign to a bhikkhunī the foremost rank among wearers of coarse robes, she vowed that one day the same rank should be her's.

In the time of **Kassapa** Buddha she was the fifth daughter of **Kikī** and her name was **Dhammā.** Then she entered the Order and lived a celibate life.[6] She is identified with the lizard in the **Tittira Jātaka.**[7]

The *Saṃyutta Nikāya*[8] records a visit paid to her by **Māra** as she sat resting in **Andhavana.** He was forced to retire discomfited.

[4] ThigA. 174 ff.; Ap. ii. 564 f.; DhA. i. 270 ff.; AA. i. 205.

[5] vv. 213-23.

[6] Ap. ii. 564 f.; ThigA. 190 f.

[7] J. iii. 543.

[8] i. 129 f.

2. **Kisāgotamī.**—A Khattiya-maiden of **Kapilavatthu.** She saw from her balcony **Siddhattha Gotama** returning in his chariot to his palace on receipt of the news that a son had been born to him. Gotamī was gladdened by the sight of him, and gave vent to her exultation in the famous "nibbuta-pada" (*nibuttā nūna sā mātā*, etc.).

Gotama was pleased by the mention of the word *nibbuta*, which to him meant deliverance, and as a mark of his gratitude sent her the necklace of pearls which he wore, worth one hundred thousand. She accepted it gladly as a token of his love.[1] She is sometimes[2] spoken of as a cousin of Gotama, his father's brother's daughter (*pitucchādhītā*).

[1] J. i. 60 f.; BuA. 232 f.

[2] *E.g.*, DhA. i. 70; DhSA. 34. A parallel has been drawn between this story and that of Luke xi. 27.

3. **Kisāgotamī.**—Wife of the Buddha **Phussa** in his last lay life. Their son was **Ānanda.**[1]

[1] Bu. xix. 16.

4. **Kisāgotamī.**—One of the chief women supporters of the Buddha **Tissa.**[1]

[1] Bu. xviii. 23.

1. **Kisāgotamī Vatthu.**—See **Kisāgotamī** (2).[1]

[1] DhA. i. 70 f.

2. **Kisāgotamī Vatthu.**—The story of **Kisāgotamī** (1). The introductory part gives an account of her marriage.[1]

[1] DhA. ii. 270 ff.

3. **Kisāgotamī Vatthu.**—The story of **Kisāgotamī** (1) becoming a *sotāpanna.*[1]

[1] DhA. iii. 432 f.

4. **Kisāgotamī Vatthu.**—The Buddha praises **Kisāgotamī** (1) in presence of **Sakka.**[1]

[1] DhA. iv. 156 f.

Kihimbila.—One of the villages given by **Aggabodhi IV.** for the maintenance of **Dāṭhāsiva's** *padhānughara.*[1]

[1] Cv. xlvi. 12.

Kiṭāgiri.—See **Kiṭāgiri.**

Kiḷakoṭṭa.—A locality in South India where **Laṅkāpura** fought with the Damiḷas.[1]

[1] Cv. lxxvi. 297.

Kiḷaṇakhaṇḍa.—The section of the **Bhūridatta Jātaka** which deals with the capture of **Bhūridatta** and the preparations for an exhibition of his dancing powers.[1]

[1] J. vi. 186.

1. **Kiḷamaṅgala.**—A district in South India which **Laṅkāpura** subdued and gave over to **Māḷava.**[1] Its chieftain (*nāḍālvāra*) was **Kulasekhara's** ally.[2] It was one of the two divisions of **Maṅgala,** the other being called **Melamaṅgala.**

[1] Cv. lxxvi. 209-11. [2] *Ibid.,* lxxvii. 80.

2. **Kiḷamaṅgala.**—A Damiḷa chieftain, ally of **Kulasekhara.**[1]

[1] Cv. lxxvii. 80.

Kiḷākāra.—One of the gardens laid out by **Parakkamabāhu I.**[1] There was a sluice of the **Parakkamasamudda** at the end of the garden, and from this sluice branched off the **Salaḷavatī** canal.[2]

[1] Cv. lxxix. 12. [2] *Ibid.*, 43.

Kiḷāmaṇḍapa.—A building in **Parakkamabāhu's Dīpuyyāna.** There the king used to amuse himself with "connoisseurs of the merry mood."[1]

[1] Cv. lxxiii. 117.

Kiḷenilaya.—A town in South India on the borders of **Madhurā.**[1]

[1] Cv. lxxvii. 83.

Kukuṭṭhā.—A river; see **Kakuṭṭhā.**

Kukku Jātaka (No. 396).—Contains several parables which the Bodhisatta, as counsellor to **Brahmadatta,** king of Benares, employed for the king's instruction. Like the peak of a roof which falls unless tightly held by the rafters, is a king who must be supported by his subjects who have been won over by his righteousness. As a citron must be eaten without its peel, so must taxes be gathered without violence. Like the lotus, unstained by the water in which it grows, is the virtuous man untainted by the world.

The king is identified with **Ānanda.**[1] The occasion for the story is given in the **Tesakuṇa Jātaka.**

[1] J. iii. 317 ff.

Kukku Vagga.—The first section of the *Satta Nipāta* of the *Jātaka Commentary.*[1]

[1] J. iii. 317-63.

1. **Kukkuṭa.**—One of three bankers of **Kosambī,** the others being **Ghosaka** and **Pāvāriya.** Having heard from some ascetics, whom they had entertained, of the appearance of the Buddha, they went with these ascetics to **Sāvatthi,** each carrying offerings in five hundred carts. Having heard the Buddha preach, they became *sotāpannas.* They gave alms to the Buddha for a fortnight, and then, with his permission, returned to Kosambī. They built monasteries in their gardens for the use of the Buddha and his monks, that built by Kukkuṭa being called the **Kukkuṭārāma.** The Buddha stayed one day at a time in each monastery, and on that day accepted the hospitality of its founder.[1]

[1] DA. i. 318 f.; DhA. i. 203 ff.; AA. i. 234 f.; PsA. 414.

It is said[2] that the bankers built a monastery for each league on the road between Sāvatthi and Kosambī for the use of the Buddha during his journeys.

[2] MA. i. 540 f.

2. **Kukkuṭa.**—A frontier town near **Himavā**; the capital of a kingdom three hundred leagues in extent, where **Mahā Kappina** once ruled. There were three rivers to cross on the way from Kukkuṭa to Sāvatthi.[1] See also **Kukkuṭavatī.**

[1] ThagA. i. 507 f.; Ap. ii. 469.

3. **Kukkuṭa.**—A rock near **Himavā.** Seven Pacceka Buddhas once lived there.[1]

[1] ThagA. i. 216; Ap. i. 178.

1. **Kukkuṭa Jātaka** (No. 383).—The story of a cat who tried to deceive a cock—with the idea of eating him—by offering to become his wife. Her efforts failed. The cock was the Bodhisatta.

The story was told to a monk who was tempted by the sight of a woman.[1]

This Jātaka is illustrated in the Bharhut Stūpa.[2]

[1] J. iii. 265 f.

[2] Cunningham: Pl. xlvii. 5.

2. **Kukkuṭa Jātaka** (No. 448).—The Bodhisatta was once the chief of a large flock of fowls. A falcon, by means of engaging speech, tried to become friendly with him in order to eat him, but his attempts failed. There could be no friendship between fowl and falcon, said the Bodhisatta. The story was related in reference to **Dedavatta's** attempts to kill the Buddha.[1] *v.l.* **Kukkuha.**

[1] J. iv. 55 ff.

Kukkuṭagiri-pariveṇa.—A row of cells built by **Kaniṭṭhatissa** after he had demolished the boundaries of the **Mahāvihāra.**[1] They were later restored by **Mahāsena.**[2] The place is also referred to as the **Kukkuṭārāma.**[3] See also Appendix.

[1] Mhv. xxxvi. 10.

[2] *Ibid.*, xxxvii. 15; MṬ. 678.

[3] *E.g.*, Mhv. xxxvii. 15.

Kukkuṭamitta.—A hunter. The daughter of a rich man in **Rājagaha** looks out of her window on the seventh storey and seeing the hunter pass through the street, falls in love with him. Learning from her slave that he is leaving the city the next day, she leaves her home secretly, joins Kukkuṭamitta on the road and elopes with him. Seven sons are born to them who, in course of time, marry and set up households of their own. One day, perceiving that the whole family is ripe for conversion, the Buddha goes to the place where Kukkuṭamitta's nets are spread, leaves there his footprint and sits down under a tree. The hunter, having caught nothing, suspects that someone has set the animals free and on seeing the Buddha draws his bow. By the Buddha's power he is rooted to the spot, and likewise his sons who come with their wives to seek him. Kukkuṭamitta's wife also comes, and seeing what has happened exclaims in riddling phrase: "Do not kill my father." (It transpires that she had become a *sotāpanna* while yet a girl.) The family ask pardon of the Buddha, and all become *sotāpannas*. When the monks hear of this, they complain that Kukkuṭamitta's wife, though a *sotāpanna*, had all this while assisted her husband to take life. The Buddha assures them that such is not the case. A man may take poison in his hand, but if there be no wound there no harm comes to him.

In a previous existence, a county treasurer bid against a city treasurer for the principal share in the building of a shrine for the relics of **Kassapa Buddha.** When the city treasurer bid more than the county treasurer possessed, the latter offered to devote himself to the service of the shrine, together with his wife, his seven sons and their wives. Kukkuṭamitta was the county treasurer.[1]

[1] DhA. iii. 24-31.

Kukkuṭaṇḍakhādikā Vatthu.—A girl eats the eggs of a hen, the hen conceives a grudge against her and is reborn as a cat, who eats the eggs of the hen, who is the girl reborn. For five hundred births they thus return hatred for hatred. Finally the girl is reborn in **Sāvatthi** as a woman, and the hen as an ogress. The ogress eats two of the woman's children, and is about to eat the third when the woman seeks refuge in the monastery. The Buddha admonished them to return good for evil and they become friends.[1]

[1] DhA. iii. 449 f.; cp. the story of **Kāḷī** (6).

Kukkuṭavatī.—According to some accounts the city, where **Mahā Kappina** ruled before he became a monk, is called, not **Kukkuṭa** (*q.v.*), but Kukkuṭavatī. Perhaps the former was the name of the county and the latter that of its capital. From here to **Sāvatthi** was a distance of one hundred and twenty leagues, and there was a trade route between the two cities which merchants travelled on foot (*jaṅghavāṇijā*), and also a route from the **Majjhimadesa.** Three rivers had to be crossed on the way: the **Aravacchā,** the **Nīlavāhanā** and the **Candabhāgā.**[1]

[1] DhA. ii. 116 ff.; a less detailed account is given in SA. ii. 177 f. and AA. i. 175 f.

Kukkuṭasūkara Sutta.—Few abstain from accepting fowls and swine, many do not.[1]

[1] S. v. 472.

1. **Kukkuṭārāmā.**—A monastery in Kosambī, built by the seṭṭhi **Kukkuṭa** (*q.v.*).[1]

[1] DA. i. 318, etc.

2. **Kukkuṭārāma.**—A pleasaunce in **Pāṭaliputta.** It was evidently the residence of monks from very early times, probably, for some time, of the Buddha himself. The *Mahāvagga*[1] mentions the names of several theras who lived there: **Nīlavāsi, Sāṇavāsi, Gopaka, Bhagu, Phalikasandana.** The *Saṃyutta Nikāya*[2] records several discussions which took place there between **Ānanda** and **Bhadda.** It may have been a favourite resort of Ānanda, for we find the householder **Dasama** of **Aṭṭhakanagara** going there to enquire as to his whereabouts.[3] It was also (probably at a later date) the residence of **Nārada** who converted King **Muṇḍa,**[4] and afterwards of **Soṇaka,** the *upajjhāya* of **Siggava,** and of **Caṇḍavajji,** the teacher **Mogaliputta-Tissa.**[5] Buddhaghosa[6] mentions that the Kukkuṭārāma was made by **Kukkuṭa Seṭṭhi,** but gives no further particulars. Here there is probably some confusion with the ārāma of the same name at **Kosambī.** Hiouen Thsang[7] says that the Kukkuṭārāma was to the south-east of the old city of Pāṭaliputta and was built by **Asoka** when he first became a convert to the Buddha's religion. "It was a sort of first-fruit and a pattern of majestic construction." Only the foundation of the building was left at the time of Hiouen Thsang's visit. It is probable that this account refers to the **Asokārāma** which Asoka built as the first of his Buddhist structures, and that the Asokārāma was constructed on the site of the old Kukkuṭārāma. It is significant that the Pāli books, in recording Asoka's doings, make no mention of a Kukkuṭārāma existing in his time, though the Sanskrit texts, the *Divyāvadāna,*[8] for instance, makes frequent reference to it. If the conjecture made above, namely that the Asokārāma replaced the Kukkuṭārāma, be correct, it may have been that the place was known by both names in Asoka's time.

[1] Vin. i. 300.
[2] S. v. 15 f.; 171 f.
[3] A. v. 342; M. i. 349.
[4] A. iii. 57 f.
[5] Mhv. v. 122.
[6] MA. ii. 571; AA. ii. 866.
[7] Beal: *op. cit.* ii, 95.
[8] *E.g.*, pp. 381 f., 430 ff.; see also Smith: Asoka, 183, 193 f.

3. **Kukkuṭārāma.**—See **Kukkuṭagiri-pariveṇa.**

Kukkuṭārāma Suttā.—Three suttas which contain discussions between **Ānanda** and **Bhadda,** at the **Kukkuṭārāma** in **Pāṭaliputta,** regarding the righteous life.[1]

[1] S. v. 15 f.

Kukkuṭika.—See **Gokulika.**

Kukkuṭṭha.—See **Kakudha** (5).

Kukkuṭṭhā.—See **Kakuṭṭhā.**

Kukkura.—A rock near **Himavā.** The Buddha **Vipassī** once visited it, and **Pupphathūpiya** lived there in a previous birth.[1]

[1] Ap. i 158.

1. **Kukkura Jātaka** (No 22).—Because his carriage straps, left in the rain, are gnawed by his own dogs, the king of Benares orders all dogs except his own to be killed indiscriminately. The Bodhisatta, who is the leader of the pack of dogs in the cemetery, visits the king, points out to him his iniquity, and reveals the truth by causing an emetic to be administered to the king's dogs. Having convinced the king, the Bodhisatta teaches him the ten stanzas of Righteousness found in the **Tesakuṇa Jātaka** (*dhammañ cara mahārāja*, etc.).[1] Great are the benefactions made to dogs thereafter. The Bodhisatta's teaching lasted for ten thousand years under the name of **Kukkurovāda.**

The king is identified with Ānanda.[2] The occasion for the story is given in the **Bhaddasāla Jātaka.**

[1] J. v. 123. [2] J. i. 175 ff.

2. **Kukkura Jātaka.**—See **Kakkara.**

Kukkuravatika Sutta.—Preached at **Haliddavasana** to **Puṇṇa,** follower of the Bovine Vow (living like an ox), and to **Acelaka Seniya,** follower of the Canine Vow. In answer to their persistent questions, the Buddha says that the further state of both is either purgatory or rebirth as an animal (among cattle and dogs respectively). He then proceeds to describe the four kinds of actions: (1) Dark, with dark outcome; (2) bright, with bright outcome; (3) both dark and bright with similar outcome; and

(4) neither dark nor bright with corresponding outcome. Both Puṇṇa and Seniya take refuge in the Buddha, Seniya later becoming an arahant.[1]

[1] M. i. 387 ff.

Kukkurovāda.—See **Kukkura Jātaka** (1).

Kukkuḷa.—One of the nirayas. King **Daṇḍaki** was born there because of his heinous crime.[1] **Sarabhaṅga** spoke of him as suffering there, sunk in a mass of glowing coals (*kukkuḷa*) one hundred leagues deep; huge glowing sparks fall on him and enter his body through nine sores.[2] Beside this niraya are the **Gūthaniraya** and the **Simbalivana.**[3]

[1] J. v. 114, 143; ItvA. 195. [2] J. v. 144. [3] M. iii. 185.

Kukkuḷa Vagga.—The fourteenth chapter of the **Khandha Saṃyutta.**[1]

[1] S. iii. 177-80.

Kukkuḷa Sutta.—The Ariyan disciple feels aversion from body, feeling, etc., because he knows that they are a mass of glowing embers.[1]

[1] S. iii. 177.

Kukkuha.—See **Kukkuṭa** (2).

Kujjatissa Thera.—An arahant. He lived in **Maṅgana** in Ceylon, and was mentioned by the Saṅgha to King **Saddhātissa** as being worthy of his special worship. The king travelled five leagues to see him, but the thera, lest the king should invite him to the palace, lay down on a bed at the time of the king's arrival and started scratching letters on the floor. The king decided that the thera was not an arahant and went away. When he was blamed for having displeased so pious a king, the thera undertook to make amends. He requested that, after his death, he should be placed in a covered palanquin containing also a second bed. This was done and the palanquin travelled by air to **Anurādhapura,** performing many miracles, applauded by the people. In Anurādhapura it circled round the **Thūpārāma** and the **Silācetiya** and, when it reached the **Lohapāsāda,** the thera **Mahāvyaggha** entered the palanquin, lay down on the spare bed and entered nibbāna. The king made offerings of flowers and perfumes to the palanquin and it descended to earth, for such had been Kujjatissa's desire. The bodies were burnt and thūpas were erected over the relics.[1]

[1] AA. i. 384 f. He is probably identical with **Khuddaka-Tissa** (*q.v.*).

Kuñcanāga, Kuñjanāga.—Son of **Kaniṭṭhatissa** and king of Ceylon (246-8 A.C.) He slew his elder brother **Khujjanāga.** During his reign occurred the **Ekanāḷika** famine, but the king maintained his benefactions uninterrupted. He was deposed by **Sirināga.**[1]

[1] Mhv. xxxvi. 19 ff.; Dpv. xxii. 33.

1. **Kuñjara.**—Devānampiyatissa's elephant, tied to the plough which marked the *sīmā* of the **Mahāvihāra.**[1]

[1] Dpv. xiv. 28; Mbv. 134; see also Mhv., p. 331.

2. **Kuñjara.**—One of the chief lay patrons of **Revata Buddha.**[1]

[1] Bu. vi. 23.

Kuñjarahīnaka.—A monastery built by **Lañjatissa.**[1]

[1] Mhv. xxxiii. 27.

Kuṭakaṇṇatissa (Kuṭikaṇṇatissa).—Second son of **Mahācūḷi** and king of Ceylon (16-38 A.C.). He had entered the Order through fear of the infamous **Anulā,** but later he led an army against her and slew her. He founded the **Peḷagāma-vihāra,** built the **Vaṇṇaka** canal, and laid out the **Padumassara** park. He founded, for his mother, a nunnery called the **Dantageha.** He had also constructed a wall, seven cubits high, round **Anurādhapura. Bhātikābhaya** was his son and successor.[1] The *Dīpavaṃsa*[2] appears to call him **Kuṭikaṇṇa-Abhaya,** and speaks of him as a very devoted supporter of the nuns.

Kuṭakaṇṇa had a horse of the Ājānīya race called **Guḷavaṇṇa.**[3]

Two theras are mentioned in the *Vibhaṅga Commentary*[4] as having been held in special esteem by the king—**Cūlasudhamma Thera** of **Girigāmakaṇṇa** and **Tipiṭaka-Cūlanāga Thera.**

[1] Mhv. xxxiv. 28 ff.

[2] Dpv. xviii. 37; but see xx. 31, where he is called **Tissa** and his son **Nāga.**

[3] SA. i. 27; MA. ii. 654.

[4] VibhA. 452.

1. **Kuṭajapupphiya Thera.**—An Arahant. Ninety-two kappas ago he offered a *kuṭaja*-flower to **Phussa Buddha.** Seventeen kappas ago he was king three times under the name of **Pupphita.**[1]

[1] Ap. i. 191.

2. **Kuṭajapupphiya Thera.**—Thirty-one kappas ago, while travelling through the air, he saw the Pacceka Buddha **Sudassana** at **Cāvala** near

Himavā, and offered him a kuṭaja flower.[1] He is probably identical either with **Hārita**[2] or **Candana Thera.**[3]

[1] Ap. ii. 451. [2] ThagA. i. 88. [3] *Ibid.*, i. 395 f.

Kuṭidāyaka Thera.—An arahant. Ninety-one kappas ago he made a hut for a Buddha. Thirty-eight kappas ago he was king sixteen times under the name of **Sabbattha-abhivassī.**[1]

[1] Ap. i. 229.

Kuṭidūsaka Jātaka (No. 321).—A *siṅgila*-bird, seeing a monkey shivering in the rain, suggested to him that he should build a nest. The monkey, in envy, destroyed the bird's nest.

The story was told in reference to a novice **Uluṅkasaddaka,** who had burnt down **Mahā-Kassapa's** hut in a forest near **Rājagaha.** At that time Mahā Kassapa had two novices, one serviceable and helpful and the other ill-behaved. Whatever was done by his comrade the latter would pretend that he himself had done it. One day, in exasperation, the good novice heated water for the Elder's bath and then hid it in a back room, leaving only a little in the boiler. When the other novice saw the steam rising he informed the Elder that his bath was ready. When asked where was the water, he let a ladle down into the almost empty boiler and the ladle rattled. When the story became known he was nick-named Uluṅkasaddaka (" Rattle-ladle ").

Being found fault with on this and several other occasions, he bore the Elder a grudge, and one day, having set fire to the Elder's hut, he ran away. Later he was born first as a *peta* and then in **Avīci.** This incident was reported to the Buddha by monks who came from Rājagaha.

The monkey of the Jātaka is identified with the wicked novice.[1]

[1] J. iii. 71 ff.

Kuṭidūsaka Vagga.—The third chapter of the *Catukka Nipāta* of the *Jātaka Commentary.*[1]

[1] J. iii. 71-102.

Kuṭidhūpaka Thera.—An arahant. In a past birth he looked after the cell of **Siddhattha** Buddha and burnt incense in it from time to time.[1]

[1] Ap. i. 223 f.

1. **Kuṭivihārī Thera.**—An arahant. He was the son of a nobleman in the **Vajji** country, and having heard the Buddha preach the **Ratana Sutta** he left the world. One day, while striving after insight, he was

caught in the rain and sought shelter in a woodman's hut. As soon as he sat down there on a mat he became an arahant. The Buddha, having heard by virtue of his divine ear the conversation between the monk and the watchman, uttered verses of approbation. The monk was so called because he obtained insight in a hut.

In the past he had given cool water to **Padumuttara** Buddha.[1]

He is probably identical with **Udakapūjaka Thera** of the *Apadāna.*[2]

[1] Thag. v. 56; ThagA. i. 129 f. [2] Ap. i. 142 f.

2. **Kuṭivihārī Thera.**—An arahant. His story is similar to the above. He pursued his meditations in a very old hut and had thoughts of building another ; but a spirit, seeking his welfare, pointed out to him in words which, though simple, carried a profound meaning, that a new hut would mean new pain. Thus urged on, Kuṭivihāri became an arahant.

In the past he gave a fan of split reeds to **Padumuttara** Buddha.[1] He is probably identical with **Naḷamāliya Thera** of the *Apadāna.*[2]

[1] Thag. v. 57; ThagA. i. 130 f. [2] Ap. i. 143 f.

Kuṭumbariya.—A monastery in **Rohaṇa.** A novice living there was in the habit of getting two ladles of rice at the house of a **Lambakaṇṇa** in the district. It was a time of scarcity, and one day, seeing a guest in the house, he took only one ladleful. The Lambakaṇṇa was greatly pleased, and when he reported the matter to his friends and acquaintances, they gave the novice sixty meals in perpetuity.[1]

[1] AA. ii. 262.

Kuṭumbiyaṅgana.—A village in Ceylon in the district of **Giri.** It was the birthplace of **Veḷusumana.**[1] *v.l.* **Kumbiyaṅgana.**

[1] Mhv. xxiii. 68.

1. **Kuṭumbiyaputta-Tissa Thera.**—He once went to **Jetavana** with twenty-nine of his friends from **Sāvatthi** to make offerings to the Buddha. Having heard the Buddha's preaching, they all became monks. After five years' residence with their teachers, they wished to retire into solitude and obtained from the Buddha topics for their meditations. While on the way to the forest, Kuṭumbiyaputta-Tissa weakened in his determination and turned back. When the rains were over, the others, having won arahantship, returned and reported their various attainments to the Buddha. Kuṭumbiyaputta heard the Buddha praise them, and made up his mind to follow their example and so to go back with them the next day to the forest. That same night, however, filled with a

yearning not to delay in beginning his austerities, he slept in an upright posture; but in the middle of the night he fell down and broke his thigh-bone. This accident delayed the departure of the other monks, and the Buddha, hearing of it, blamed Tissa for his unesasonable zeal and related the **Varaṇa Jātaka,** showing how, in the past too, he had behaved similarly.[1]

The Commentaries[2] lead us to believe that Kuṭumbiyaputta did ultimately attain arahantship, for he is mentioned several times with **Pītimalla** and others as an example of one who put forth great exertion while suffering severe pain, in order to win his goal.

[1] J. i. 316 f.
[2] *E.g.*, SA. ii. 216; AA. i. 29; see also *s.v.* **Padhānakammika-Tissa.**

2. **Kuṭumbiyaputta-Tissa.**—An arahant. He lived in **Piyaṅgudīpa. Duṭṭhagāmaṇi,** fleeing from the battle at **Cūḷaṅganiyapiṭṭhi,** wished to give a share of his food to a monk before sitting down to eat. When the meal-time was announced, the thera **Gotama,** hearing it with his divine ear, sent Kuṭumbiyaputta to receive the share set apart for the brotherhood.[1] It transpired later that the food so received was divided by Kuṭumbiyaputta among twelve thousand monks in Piyangudīpa.[2]

[1] Mhv. xxiv. 22 ff.; xxxii. 31 f. [2] *Ibid.*, xxxii. 55; MṬ. 598.

Kuṭeṇḍu.—A vassal of the **Cātummahārājikas,** present at the preaching of the **Mahā Samaya Sutta.**[1]

[1] D. ii. 258.

Kuṭelitissamahāvihāra.—A monastery in Ceylon. It was once the residence of a Sāmaṇera of great *iddhi*-power who later lost all these powers as a result of falling in love with a weaver's daughter of **Kabupelanda.**[1] It may perhaps be the same as the **Kūṭāli-vihāra** (*q.v.*).

[1] VibhA. 293; but see MA. ii. 700.

Kuṭṭapiṭi.—A large village given by **Kittisirirājasīha** for the maintenance of the sacred Footprint in **Samanakūṭa.**[1]

[1] Cv. c. 225.

Kuṭṭhuka.—The general of **Sena II.** He built the *pariveṇa,* which was called **Senasenāpati.**[1] See also **Potthakuṭṭha.**

[1] Cv. li. 88.

Kuṭhārasabhā.—Some sort of council chamber, probably attached to the Court in Ceylon. **Kittisirimegha** is mentioned as employing the services of the head of the sabhā to fetch the prince **Parakkamabāhu** from his retreat.[1]

[1] Cv. lxvi. 61.

Kuṭhārivihāra.—A monastery in **Ambaṭṭhakola** used by **Moggallāna I.** as his headquarters in his campaign against **Kassapa I.**[1]

[1] Cv. xxxix. 21.

Kuḍḍadhāna.—See **Kuṇḍadhāna.**

Kuṇappunallura.—A market town in South India in the district of **Vīragaṅga.**[1]

[1] Cv. lxxvi. 131.

1. **Kuṇāla.**—One of the seven great lakes in the region of the **Himālaya.** The Buddha once visited it with a large concourse of Sākyan youths who had joined the Order, and on that occasion he preached the **Kuṇāla Jātaka** (*q.v.*).[1] The sun's rays never reached the waters of the lake, which were therefore never warm.[2] According to Buddhaghosa,[3] the Kuṇāla Jātaka was actually preached on the banks of the Kuṇāladaha.

[1] J. v. 415; MA. ii. 692, 1021; AA. ii. 759, etc.

[2] SnA. ii. 407.

[3] *Ibid.*, i. 358; DA. ii. 675.

2. **Kuṇāla.**—The Bodhisatta, born as the king of the Citrakokilas. He lived in a beautiful forest in the **Himālaya,** attended by three thousand five hundred hen birds. He was carried about on a stick by two birds while in front, behind, above and below flew his vast retinue, guarding him from all harm and providing for all his needs. He distrusted and despised all womankind, and his stories of their wiles, as related by him to his friend **Puṇṇamukha,** are given in the **Kuṇāla Jātaka** (*q.v.*).

Kuṇāla Jātaka (No. 536). **Kuṇāla,** king of the Citrakokilas, though well served by his hen birds, always despised them and found fault with them. The king of the Phussakokilas, **Puṇṇamukha,** on the other hand, always sang the praises of his escort. One day the two kings met, and Puṇṇamukha asked Kuṇāla why he was not more gracious to his ladies. "Because I know too much about women," was the answer; but Puṇṇamakha was not in a mood to discuss the matter any more. Later, Puṇṇamukha fell ill, and his hen birds deserted him and came to Kuṇāla. He drove them away, ministered to Puṇṇamukha, and cheered him. Some time after, Kuṇāla, seated on the **Manosilātala** in Himavā,[1] started to tell

[1] According to Buddhaghosa (D. ii. 675), this was on the banks of the Kuṇāladaha (*q.v.*).

his friend of the wickedness of women. Hearing of this, many inhabitants of numerous worlds came to listen to him, among them **Ānanda,** king of the vultures, and the ascetic **Nārada.** Many were the instances given by Kuṇāla to illustrate the deceitfulness, ingratitude and immorality of women—among them the stories of **Kaṇhā, Saccatapāvī, Kākātī, Kuraṅgavī,** Brahmadatta's mother who sinned with **Pañcālacaṇḍa,** the queen **Kiṇṇarā, Pañcapāpā** and **Piṅgiyānī.** Kuṇāla's diatribe was followed by Ānanda's, and his by Nārada's, each claiming to speak from facts within their knowledge. In the stories related by Kuṇāla, the bird-king is identified with one of the characters concerned in each story, so that he was able to speak with authority. Thus he was **Ajjuna,** one of Kaṇha's husbands; the goldsmith in the story of Saccatapāvī; the Garuḍa in Kākātī's tale; **Chalaṅgakumāra,** who misconducted himself with Kuraṅgavī; Pañcālacaṇḍa, lover of Brahmadatta's mother; the chaplain, also called Pañcālacaṇḍa, who saved Kiṇṇarā from her husband's wrath; **Baka,** one time husband of Pañcapāpā; and Brahmadatta, husband of Piṅgiyānī.

Puṇṇamukha is identified with **Udāyī,** the vulture-king with **Ānanda** and Nārada with **Sāriputta.**

The preaching of the Kuṇāla Jātaka was followed by that of the **Mahāsamaya Sutta.**

This Jātaka was related in order to destroy the discontent that rose in the hearts of the Sākyan youths, kinsmen of the Buddha, who, having entered the Order, were troubled by the thought of the wives they had left behind. The Buddha therefore took them to the Himālaya, showed them the magnificent beauty of the region, particularly the miraculous splendours of the Kuṇāladaha, and there preached to them. At the end of the Jātaka they all became arahants. We are told[2] that that very day they became arahants. See also the **Cūḷa Kuṇāla Jātaka.**

[2] J. v. 412-56; also DA. ii. 674 ff.; AA. i. 173. For particulars of the names mentioned in this article see *s.v.*

Kuṇālā.—The name of a river (*mahānadī*) which flows out of the Kuṇāladaha. It dries up when, at the end of the kappa, the fourth sun rises.[1]

[1] A. iv. 101.

Kuṇhāna.—See **Kuṇḍadhāna.**

Kuṇḍa.—A yakkha who once inhabited a forest, called **Kuṇḍadhāna**[1] after him.

[1] UdA. 122.

Kuṇḍakakucchisindhava Jātaka (No. 254).—A householder was lodging in a poor old woman's house on the road from Benares to **Uttarāpatha.** During his stay there his thoroughbred mare foaled, and the foal was given to the woman at her request, in part payment of her charges. She brought up the foal as though he were her own child. Some time after, the Bodhisatta, who was then a householder, happened to pass the same way and discovered the thoroughbred's presence by the behaviour of his own horses. The woman agreed to part with the foal to him for a large price on condition that he should be provided with all manner of luxuries. The Bodhisatta kept his word, and when the king came to inspect his horses, made the foal, who knew his own worth, exhibit his marvellous powers. The king installed him as his state horse, and thereafter the lordship of all India passed into the king's hands.

The story was told in reference to **Sāriputta.** Once, when the Buddha was returning to **Sāvatthi** after a tour, the citizens decided to celebrate his arrival by each one taking on himself the task of feeding a certain number of monks in the Buddha's retinue. A poor old woman wished to feed a monk, but all the monks were already allotted, only Sāriputta remaining. She invited him to her house, and he accepted her invitation. When it became known that Sāriputta was to feed with her, the king and all the rich citizens of Sāvatthi sent her food and garments and money to help in her entertainment of the Elder. As a result, through the kindness of Sāriputta, she became rich in a single day.

Sāriputta is identified with the thoroughbred of the Jātaka.[1]

This is evidently the same story as that which, in the *Dhammapada Commentary,*[2] is called the **Kuṇḍakasindhavapotaka Jātaka.** But there the story is related, not in reference to Sāriputta, but to the Buddha himself, because he accepted a cake of rice-husks from the slave-woman **Puṇṇā** (*q.v.*). This is probably due to some confusion with two or more stories of similar import. See also **Kuṇḍakapūva Jātaka.**

[1] J. ii. 286 ff. [2] iii. 325.

Kuṇḍaka-kumāra.—The lay name of the ascetic **Khantivādī** (*q.v.*).[1]

[1] J. iii. 39.

Kuṇḍakapūva Jātaka (No. 109).—The Bodhisatta was once a tree-sprite in a castor-oil tree and received worship and offerings from many people. Among them was a very poor man who, having nothing else to offer at the tree, took a cake made of husk powder. But when he saw the other rich offerings, he felt that the sprite would never accept so humble a gift and wished to eat the cake himself. The tree-sprite appeared, took the offering, and revealed to the man that heaps of treasure lay buried under the tree. The man informed the king of this, and the king, in return, appointed him royal treasurer.

The story was told in reference to a poor man of **Sāvatthi**. Once the people of a whole street in that town pooled their resources in order to entertain the Buddha and his monks to a meal of rice-gruel and cakes. The poor man, unable to afford anything else, made a bran-cake and by sheer determination put it in the alms-bowl of the Buddha himself. When it became known that the Buddha had accepted it, people of all classes crowded round the man offering him wealth if he would share with them the merit he had gained. After consulting with the Buddha, the man accepted the offers, and the gifts he received amounted to nine crores. That same evening the king appointed him treasurer.[1]

[1] J. i. 422 f.

Kuṇḍakasindhavapotaka Jātaka.—See **Kuṇḍakakucchisindhava Jātaka.**

Kuṇḍadhāna Thera.—An arahant. He was proclaimed the first among those who received food tickets (*salāka*).[1] He came of a brahmin family of **Sāvatthi** and his name was **Dhāna**. He knew the Vedas by heart, and when advanced in years, heard the Buddha preach and joined the Order. From that day, however, in all his movements the form of a young woman followed him wherever he went, though he himself could not see the figure. This caused great merriment and evoked many sarcastic remarks, which he could not understand. When he went for alms women would put into his bowl two portions of food, saying, "One is for your Reverence and the other for your friend, the young lady, your companion." In the monastery the novices and young monks would point at him and say: "Look, our venerable one has become a *koṇḍa*" (gallant ?). From this he became known as **Koṇḍa-** or **Kuṇḍadhāna.** Driven to distraction by this teasing, he became abusive and was reported to the Buddha, who bade him be patient as he was only being pursued by the remnant of an evil kamma. **Pasenadi,** king of Kosala, hearing of Kuṇḍadhāna, was interested, and being satisfied by personal investigation that the Elder was blameless, provided him with all necessaries, so that he need no longer go round for alms. This enabled him to concentrate his mind, and he became an arahant. Thereupon the figure of the woman disappeared.

Kuṇḍadhāna's claim to be the first among receivers of *salāka* was due

[1] A. i. 24.

to the fact that he it was who received the first food-ticket when the Buddha visited **Mahā-Subhaddā** at **Ugganagara, Culla-Subhaddā** at **Sāketa,** and also the **Sunāparanta-janapada.**[2] Only khīṇāsavas were allowed to accompany the Buddha on these visits.

Kuṇḍadhāna's determination to attain this special eminence was formed in the time of **Padumuttara** Buddha. Once he gave Padumuttara a well-ripened "comb" of bananas when the Buddha arose from a long trance. As a result he became king of the devas eleven times and king of men twenty-four times.

He was an earthbound sprite in the time of **Kassapa** Buddha. Seeing two monks, firm friends, on their way to the uposatha held by the Buddha, he had a mischievous desire to test their friendship, and when one of the monks retired into the forest leaving the other on the road, he followed the former, unseen by him, assuming the form of a woman arranging her hair, adjusting her garments, and so on. The second monk, seeing his friend return and shocked by his apparent misdemeanour, left him in disgust, refusing to perform the uposatha with him. Realising the effect of his practical joke, the sprite did all he could to make amends, but the friendship of the two monks was for ever spoilt. The sprite suffered the fears of hell for a whole Buddha-era, and even in his last birth as Kuṇḍadhāna his evil kamma pursued him, as seen above.[3]

Kuṇḍadhāna was among those to whom the Buddha preached the **Naḷakapāna Sutta,** and was therefore probably a friend of **Anuruddha** and the other Sākyan nobles present on that occasion.[4] *v.l.* **Koṇḍadhāna, Koṇṭhadhāna, Kuḍḍadhāna.**

[2] For details of these visits see *s.v.*

[3] AA. i. 146 ff.; Thag. A. i. 62 ff.; also Ap. i. 81 f.; Thag. 15. The version given in DhA. iii. 52 f. differs very slightly in certain details.

[4] M. i. 462.

Kuṇḍadhānavana.—A forest near the Koliyan village of **Kuṇḍiya.**[1] It was once the residence of the yakkha **Kuṇḍa,** who favoured offerings made to him with *kuṇḍa-dhāna* (vessels containing rice-powder ?). A woman, who was the head of a village (*gāmapatikā*), formed a settlement on a spot indicated by the yakkha and was guarded by him. She thus came to be known as **Kuṇḍiyā,** and when, later, the Koliyan nobles built a city on the same spot, the city was known as Kuṇḍiya. In the forest tract the Koliyan nobles built a monastery for the Buddha and his monks. It was while the Buddha was dwelling in this monastery that **Suppavāsā** gave birth to **Sīvalī,** after prolonged labour pains, which

[1] DhA. (iv. 192) calls it **Kuṇḍikoliya** (*v.l.* **Kuṇḍikeliya**).

only ceased after she received the Buddha's blessing.[2] *v.l.* **Kuṇḍiṭṭhāna, Kuṇḍikāna, Kuṇhāna.**

[2] Ud. ii. 8; UdA. 122; DhA. iv. 192 f.; J. i. 407.

Kuṇḍayaṅkoṭṭa(?). A locality in South India, where **Laṅkāpura** once pitched his camp.[1]

[1] Cv. lxxvi. 176.

Kuṇḍayamutta.—A Damiḷa chief, ally of **Kulasekhara.** He was defeated in battle by **Laṅkāpura.**[1]

[1] Cv. lxxvi. 94, 177.

Kuṇḍarāyana.—See **Kaṇḍarāyana.**

Kuṇḍala (*v.l.* **Kuḷakuṇḍala**) **Thera.**—An arahant. He came of a brahmin family of **Sāvatthi** and entered the Order, but from want of mental balance he could not concentrate his thoughts. Then, one day, while begging for alms, he saw how men conducted water whither they wished by digging channels, how the fletcher fixed the arrow shaft in his lathe surveying it from the corner of his eye, how the chariot-makers planed axle and tire and hub. Dwelling on these things, he soon attained arahantship.

In the past he was a park-keeper, and gave a coconut to the Buddha **Vipassī,** which the Buddha accepted while travelling through the air.[1] Perhaps he is to be identified with **Nāḷikeradāyaka** Thera of the *Apadāna.*[2] The same *Apadāna*-verses, however, are also ascribed to **Khitaka** Thera.[3] The verse attributed to Kuṇḍala in the *Theragāthā*[4] occurs twice in the *Dhammapada,* and is in the *Dhammapada Commentary* mentioned as having been preached once in reference to **Paṇḍita-Sāmaṇera,**[5] and once in reference to **Sukha-Sāmaṇera.**[6]

[1] ThagA. i. 71 f.
[2] ii. 447 f.
[3] ThagA. i. 315 f.
[4] Thag. 19.
[5] DhA. ii. 147.
[6] *Ibid.*, iii. 99.

Kuṇḍalakesā, Kuṇḍalakesī.—See **Bhaddā Kuṇḍalakesī.**

Kuṇḍalakesittheri Vatthu.—The story of **Bhaddā Kuṇḍalakesī**[1] (*q.v.*).

[1] DhA. ii. 217 ff.

Kuṇḍalinī.—The name given to the offspring of the *sārikā*(myna)-bird in the **Tesakuṇa Jātaka** (*q.v.*). She is identified with **Uppalavaṇṇā.**[1]

[1] J. v. 125.

Kuṇḍalinī-pañha.—The questions asked by the king and the answers given by **Kuṇḍalinī,** as stated in the **Tesakuna Jātaka.**[1]

[1] J. v. 120.

Kuṇḍaliya.—A Paribbājaka who visits the Buddha at the **Añjanavana** in **Sāketa.** He asks the Buddha what profit comes from the Buddha's way of living. The conversation leads to a discussion of the *bojjhaṅgas*, the *satipaṭṭhānas* and virtuous ways of behaviour. At the end of the diccussion Kuṇḍaliya becomes the Buddha's follower.[1]

[1] S. v. 73 ff.

1. **Kuṇḍalī.**—The *sārikā*-bird of the **Mahāummagga Jātaka** is identified with **Kuṇḍalī.**[1] The reference is probably to **Bhaddā Kuṇḍalakesī.**

[1] J. vi. 478.

2. **Kuṇḍalī.**—The name of the she-ass in the **Vātaggasindhava Jātaka**[1] (*q.v.*).

[1] J. ii. 338 f.

3. **Kuṇḍalī.**—The name of a *vimāna* in **Tāvatiṃsa.** In this *vimāna* was born a man who once tended **Sāriputta** and **Moggallāna** and looked after them when they stayed in a vihāra in **Kāsi.**[1]

[1] Vv. vi. 8; VvA. 295 f.

4. **Kuṇḍalī.**— A brahmin, importer of foreign goods. He was a friend of **Dīghābhaya** and lived in **Dvāramaṇḍala.**[1]

[1] Mhv. xxiii. 24.

Kuṇḍalī Sutta.—Records the visit of **Kuṇḍaliya** to the Buddha.[1]

[1] S. v. 73 ff.

Kuṇḍavana.—See **Gundāvana.**

Kuṇḍasālā.—A suburb of **Sirivaḍḍhanapura** (Kandy), on the banks of the **Mahāvāluka-gaṅgā.** It was laid out by King **Narindasīha,** who made it his favourite residence.[1] **Kittisirirājasīha** planned its garden and erected a vihāra.[2]

[1] Cv. xcvii. 34. [2] *Ibid.*, c. 216 f.

1. **Kuṇḍi, Kuṇḍiya.**—A village of the **Kurus.** Near the village was a forest where lived **Aṅganika-Bhāradvāja.** Close by was the **Uggārāma.**[1] *v.l.* **Kuṇḍikola.**

[1] ThagA. i. 339.

2. **Kuṇḍi.**—A village of the **Koliyans,** near which was the **Kuṇḍadhānavana** (*q.v.*). It was the birthplace of **Kuṇḍanagariya (Poṭṭhapāda)** Thera. Near it was the **Sānavāsīpabbata** where once **Ānanda** stayed.[1]

[1] PvA. 178.

Kuṇḍitthāna.—See **Kuṇḍadhāna.**

Kundinagariya Thera.—The name given to **Poṭṭhapāda** because he was born and brought up in **Kuṇḍi.** He lived in the **Sānavāsīpabbata** near by.[1]

[1] Pv. iii. 2; PvA. 177 ff.

Kuṇḍiyā.—See **Kuṇḍadhānavana.**

Kutūhalasālā Sutta.—**Vacchagotta** asks the Buddha how his teaching on the subject of rebirth differs from that of other teachers; for example, of **Pūraṇa Kassapa.** The Buddha explains that, according to his own teaching, rebirth comes only to a being who has fuel, the fuel being craving.[1]

The discussion arises out of a conversation which, according to Vacchagotta, took place among paribbājakas in the **Kutūhalasālā.**[2]

[1] S. iv. 398 f.

[2] Buddhaghosa says (DA. ii. 369; MA. ii. 694) that there was no special place of that name; any place where discussions were held could be so called. See also D. i. 179.

Kuttāṇḍāra.—A Damiḷa chieftain, ally of **Kulasekhara,** defeated by **Laṅkāpura.**[1]

[1] Cv. lxxvi. 182, 190.

Kuddāla Jātaka (No. 70).—The Bodhisatta was once a gardener in Benares, and because his only possession was a spade (*kuddāla*) he was known as **Kuddāla Paṇḍita.** Later he became a recluse, but six times thoughts of his spade drew him back to the world. The seventh time he threw the spade into the river and shouted for joy, winning insight. The king of Benares heard his shouts, and on knowing the reason for them, resolved to join Kuddāla as an anchorite. When the news spread, the people from twelve leagues round accompanied them, and **Sakka** sent **Vissakamma** to erect monasteries for them in the Himālaya.

The story was told in reference to **Citta-Hatthisāriputta** (*q.v.*).[1] The names of some of those who accompanied Kuddāla in his renunciation are mentioned at the end of the **Hatthipāla**[2] and the **Mūgapakkha**[3] Jātakas.

[1] J. i. 311 ff.

[2] J. iv. 490.

[3] J. vi. 30.

The same story is given in different words in the *Dammapada Commentary*.[4]

[4] DhA. i. 311 f.

Kuddāla (Kuddālaka)-paṇḍita.—See **Kuddāla Jātaka.**

He is mentioned in a list of six famous teachers of the past, who were well known for their pious and holy lives. They had numerous followers and, after death, were born in the Brahma-world.[1]

The Kuddāla-birth was one in which the perfection of *paññā* was developed.[2]

[1] A. iii. 371, 373; iv. 135.

[2] J. i. 46.

Kuddālamaṇḍala.—A village in **Rohaṇa.** Here a battle took place between the forces of **Parakkamabāhu I.** and his enemies.[1]

[1] Cv. lxxv. 16.

Kunta.—A throne (for an image) which was originally in the **Pācina-vihāra** of the **Theravādins,** and was later set up beside the Bodhi-tree of the **Abhayagiri-vihāra** by **Silākāla.**[1]

[1] Cv. xli. 31.

Kuntani Jātaka (No. 343).—In the court of the king of Benares was a heron who carried messages. Once, when she was away, the boys of the palace killed her two young ones. In revenge she persuaded a tiger to eat the boys, and told the king what she had done. She then flew away to the Himālaya because, she said, there could be no friendship between the wrong-doer and the wronged one.

The story was told in reference to a heron of the Kosala king, who acted in a similar way.[1]

[1] J. iii. 311 f.

Kuntamālaka.—A locality near **Anurādhapura** through which passed the boundary of the **Mahāvihāra.** It was the point from which the king started to mark the *sīmā*.[1] *v.l.* **Koṭṭhamālaka.**

[1] Mhv., p. 331; Mbv. 134; Dpv. xiv. 28, 33.

Kuntavarā.—The soldiers of a district in South India who fought against the Sinhalese force that invaded their territory.[1] They were subdued by the **Kesadhātu Kitti.**[2]

[1] Cv. lxxvi. 246.

[2] *Ibid.*, 259.

Kuntī.—A kinnarī, mother of the theras **Tissa** and **Sumitta.** Their father was a former inhabitant of **Pāṭaliputta.**[1]

[1] Mhv. v. 212.

Kundukāla.—A locality in South India on the tongue of land which juts out from the continent to the island of **Rāmissara.** Kundukāla is about eight miles from Rāmissāra.[1] **Laṅkāpura** built there a strong camp called **Parakkamapura,** where he had his headquarters.[2]

[1] Cv. lxxvi. 101. [2] *Ibid.*, 121.

Kupikkala.—The birthplace of the Elder **Mahā-Tissa.**[1] *v.l.* **Kuvikkala, Kubbikāla, Kuṭṭhikula.**

[1] Mhv. xxxiii. 49.

Kupuveṇa.—A village and a monastery. The story of a sāmaṇera of the monastery, as given in the *Majjhima Commentary,*[1] is similar, except in regard to the names, to the story given under **Kabupelanda** (*q.v.*).

[1] MA. ii. 700.

Kuppa Sutta.—The monk who has the four *paṭisambhidā* and has an emancipated mind realises that which is unshakable (*akuppa*).[1]

[1] A. iii. 119 f.

Kubukandanadī.—A river in Ceylon. On its banks was the **Samudda-vihāra.**[1]

[1] Mhv. xxxiv. 90.

Kubūlagalla.—A locality in **Rohaṇa.** It was one of the strongholds captured by **Vijayabāhu I.**[1]

[1] Cv. lviii. 36.

Kubera.—See **Kuvera.**

Kubbikāla.—See **Kupikala.**

Kubbugāma.—See **Kumbugāma.**

Kumā.—Wife of a householder in **Veḷukaṇḍa** in the **Avanti** country. She was the mother of **Nanda Thera,** also called **Kumāputta.**[1]

[1] ThagA. i. 100.

Kumāputta.—See **Nanda Kumāputta.**

1. **Kumāra.**—Father of **Bharaṇa.** He lived in **Kappakandara.**[1]

[1] Mhv. xxiii. 64.

2. **Kumāra.**—Name of the god Skanda. He rode on a peacock. It is said that Kumāra gave a boon to **Mānavamma.**[1]

[1] Cv. lvii. 7, 10; see also Hopkins: *Epic Mythology*, p. 227.

Kumāra Sutta. The Licchavi **Mahānāma** sees a number of **Licchavi** youths sitting by the Buddha, at the foot of a tree in the **Mahāvana** at **Vesāli**; he expresses his joy at the sight for, he says, the Licchavis are usually so mischievous. The Buddha thereupon tells Mahānāma of five things the practice of which will tend to progress: the tending of father and mother, the support of wife and children with well-gotten wealth, devotion to one's own business, honouring one's own ancestral gods, showing respect to good and holy men.[1]

[1] A. iii. 75 ff.

1. **Kumāra-Kassapa Thera.**—He was foremost among those who had the gift of varied and versatile discourse (*cittakathikānaṃ*).[1] His mother was the daughter of a banker of **Rājagaha,** and she, having failed to obtain her parent's consent to become a nun, married and, with her husband's consent, joined the Order, not knowing that she was with child. When her condition was discovered her colleagues consulted **Devadatta,** who declared that she was no true nun. The Buddha, on being consulted, entrusted the matter to **Upāli,** who had it fully investigated by **Visākhā** and other residents of **Sāvatthi,** and he gave his finding in the assembly, in the presence of the king, that the nun was innocent.[2] When the boy was born the king reared him, and the boy was ordained at the age of seven. The boy came to be called Kumāra, because he joined the Order so young and was of royal upbringing, and also because the Buddha, when sending him little delicacies such as fruit, referred to him as Kumāra Kassapa. Once when Kumāra Kassapa was meditating in **Andhavana,** an *anāgāmī* Brahmā, who had been his companion in the time of **Kassapa** Buddha, appeared before him, and asked him fifteen questions which only the Buddha could answer. This led to the preaching of the **Vammika Sutta,**[3] and after dwelling on its teachings Kassapa became an arahant.[4] His mother, too, developed insight and attained to arahantship. It is said that she wept for twelve years because she

[1] A. i. 24.

[2] For details see J. i. 148; Upāli's handling of the case won the Buddha's special commendation (see, *e.g.*, AA. i. 172).

[3] M. i. 143 ff.

[4] For Kumāja-Kassapa's story see J. i. 147 ff.; AA. i. 158 f.; ThagA. i. 322 f.; MA. i. 335 f.

could not be with Kassapa, and one day, seeing him in the street, as she ran towards him and fell, milk flowed from her breasts and wet her robe. Kassapa, realising that her great love was standing in the way of her attainments, spoke harshly to her that she might love him the less. The ruse succeeded and she became an arahant that very day.[5]

In the time of **Padumuttara** Buddha Kassapa was a learned brahmin, and having heard a monk ranked foremost in eloquence, he wished for a similar distinction and did many acts of piety towards that end. When the teachings of Kassapa Buddha were being forgotten, he, together with six others, entered the Order and lived a life of rigorous asceticism on the summit of a mountain.[6]

Two verses of deep significance ascribed to Kumāra-Kassapa are found in the *Theragāthā.*[7] Although it is said that he was a very eloquent speaker, the examples given of his preaching are extremely scanty. The *Aṅguttara Commentary*[8] states that the Buddha gave him his title from the skilful way in which he argued with **Pāyāsi,** as related in the **Pāyāsi Sutta** (*q.v.*); but this cannot be correct for, according to **Dhammapāla,**[9] the events of the Pāyāsi Sutta took place after the Buddha's death. The Sutta, however, does justify Kassapa's reputation.[10]

Kassapa's *upasampadā* took place in his twentieth year. A doubt arose as to whether this was valid because, according to the rule, twenty years must be completed for upasampadā. The Buddha held that in reckoning the age the time spent in the mother's womb could also be included.[11]

[5] DhA. iii. 147.

[6] Ap. ii. 473 f.; the details of this story are given in DhA. ii. 210-12; among Kassapa's companions were also **Pukkusāti, Dārucīriya, Dabba Mallaputta** and **Sabhiya**; see also UdA. 80 f.

[7] vv. 201. 202.

[8] i. 159.

[9] VvA. 297.

[10] For his praises see also MA. i. 500 f.

[11] Vin. i. 93; Sp. iv. 867.

2. **Kumāra-Kassapa.**—A thera in Ceylon, at whose request was written the **Dhammapadaṭṭhakathā.**[1]

[1] DhA. i. 1; Gv. 68.

Kumāra-Kassapa-thera Vatthu.—The story of **Kumāra-Kassapa** (*q.v.*) and his mother.[1]

[1] DhA. iii. 144 ff.

Kumāradhātusena (Kumāradāsa).—Son of **Moggallāna I.** and king of Ceylon (513-522 A.C.). His son was **Kittisena.**[1] Tradition tells of his

[1] Cv. xli. 1 f.

friendship with a poet **Kālidāsa.** The authorship of the Jānakīharaṇa is generally ascribed to him.[2]

[2] Cv. *Trs.* i. 51, n. 1.

Kumārapañha.—The fourth chapter of the **Khuddakapāṭha.**[1] It consists of ten questions which, according to the Commentaries,[2] the Buddha asked the young **Sopāka,** then an arahant though only seven years old, with the idea of giving him the *upasampadā*-ordination. The boy-arahant answered the questions and this conversation formed his ordination.[3] These questions were elaborated by the nun of **Kajaṅgalā**[4] (*q.v.*). The *Majjhima Commentary*[5] on the **Ambalaṭṭhika-Rāhulovāda Sutta** seems to indicate a set of questions called Kumārapañha in connection with **Rāhula** when he was seven years old.

[1] Khp. 2.
[2] KhpA. 76; ThagA. i. 479.
[3] See also Thag, v. 485; Ap. i. 64 f.
[4] See A. v. 54 ff.
[5] MA. ii. 636.

Kumārapabba.—The section of the **Vessantara Jātaka** which deals with the giving away of **Vessantara's** children to **Jūjaka.**[1]

[1] J. vi. 555.

1. **Kumārapeta Vatthu.**—A man of **Sāvatthi** abused those who gave alms to the Buddha and his monks, but his mother made him retract his words and give alms for seven days. He was born later as the son of a courtesan who left him in a graveyard. The Buddha went there and proclaimed that the boy had a great future before him. The boy was adopted by a rich man and spent his wealth in deeds of piety. After death he was born as **Sakka's** son.[1]

[1] Pv. iii. 5; PvA. 194 ff.

2. **Kumārapeta Vatthu.**—Two sons of the Kosala king committed adultery and were born as *petas.* One night they uttered loud lamentations and the inhabitants of **Sāvatthi** sought the Buddha's protection. The Buddha explained things to them, and the people gave alms and made over their merit so gained to the *petas.*[1]

[1] Pv. iv. 6; PvA. 261 f.

Kumārasīha.—Son of **Vimaladhammasūriya ;** he was adopted by King **Senāratana** and given the province of Uva. He died young.[1]

[1] Cv. xcv. 22; also Cv. *Trs.* ii. 233, n. 3.

Kumārasena.—Brother of **Dhātusena.** He helped Dhātusena to crush the Damiḷas, and was amply rewarded for his services.[1]

[1] Cv. xxxviii. 35, 53.

Kumārīpañhā.—Evidently the name given to the questions asked of the Buddha by Māra's daughters, **Taṇhā, Arati** and **Ragā**—when they visited him in order to tempt him—and the Buddha's answers. These questions and answers form the **Dhītaro Sutta** of the *Saṃyutta Nikāya*,[1] but a quotation from them given in the *Aṅguttara*[2] is mentioned as having been taken from the *Kumārīpañhā*. The Commentary[3] mentions them as being the questions of Māra's daughters (*kumārīnaṃ Māradhītānaṃ pucchā*).

[1] S. i. 124 f. [2] A. v. 46 f. [3] AA. ii. 828.

Kumārībhūta Vagga.—The eighth section of the *Bhikkhunī Pācittiya*.[1]

[1] Vin. iv. 327-37.

Kumāriya Sutta.—Few abstain from accepting women or girls, many do not.[1]

[1] S. v. 471.

1. **Kumuda.**—A niraya—strictly speaking, a period of suffering. It is equal to twelve **Padumas.**

The **Kokālika** monk was born in Kumuda-niraya.[1]

[1] S. i. 152 f.; see also SN., p. 126; SNA. ii. 476.

2. **Kumuda.**—One of the three palaces of **Sobhita** Buddha in his last lay life.[1]

[1] Bu. vii. 17.

3. **Kumuda.**—A city. There an enemy of **Piyadassī** Buddha, **Soṇa** by name, made an unsuccessful attempt to kill him by means of the elephant **Doṇamukha.**[1]

[1] Bu. xiv. 6; BuA. 174.

Kumudadāyaka Thera.—An arahant. In **Padumuttara's** time he was a bird named **Kakudha** in a lake in Himavā and offered the Buddha a lotus-flower. Sixteen hundred kappas ago he became king eight times under the name of **Varuṇa.**[1] He is probably identical with **Malitavambha.**[2]

[1] Ap. i. 180. [2] ThagA. i. 211 f.

1. **Kumudamāliya Thera.**—An arahant. In the time of **Atthadassī** he was a rakkhasa in a lake near Himavā and gave the Buddha a garland of flowers. Fifteen kappas ago he was king seven times under the name of **Sahassaratha.**[1]

[1] Ap. i. 186 f.

2. **Kumudamāliya Thera.**—An arahant. In the past he saw **Vipassī** Buddha walking in the street and gave him a garland of *kumuda*-flowers.[1]

[1] Ap. i. 257 f.

Kumba.—See **Kumbagāma.**

Kumbagāma.—A Damila stronghold near **Anurādhapura,** which was captured by **Duṭṭhagāmaṇi.** It was commanded by **Kumba.**[1]

[1] Mhv. xxv. 14.

Kumbalavāta.—A locality near **Anurādhapura;** through it passed the boundary of the **Mahāvihāra.**[1]

[1] Mhv. p. 332; Mbv. 134; Dpv. xiv. 38.

Kumbālaka.—One of the tanks built by **Mahāsena.**[1]

[1] Mhv. xxxvii. 48.

Kumbiyaṅgana.—See **Kuṭumbiyaṅgana.**

Kumbugāma (*v.l.* **Kubbugāma**).—A village in **Rohaṇa.** It is mentioned in the campaigns of **Damiḷādhakārī Rakkha.**[1]

[1] Cv. lxxv. 149, 167, 172.

Kumbha Jātaka (No. 512).—The story of how a forester, **Sura,** accidently discovered strong drink, and how, with the help of his accomplice, the ascetic **Varuṇa,** he spread abroad the discovery, thus leading to the destruction of all **Jambudīpa,** had Sakka not appeared on earth and by his exposition of the evils of drink induced **Sabbamitta,** king of **Sāvatthi,** to abstain from its use.

The story was told in answer to a question by **Visākhā** as to the origin of drink. Once during a drinking festival at **Sāvatthi** five hundred women, friends of Visākhā, visited **Jetavana** in her company. On the way they became drunk, which led to their behaving improperly in the monastery. The Buddha frightened them by his *iddhi*-power and restored them to their senses.[1]

The story of the past is also given in the *Jātakamālā* (No. 17).

[1] J. v. 11 ff.; the DhA. (iii. 100 ff.) gives a slightly different version of the doings of Visākhā's friends.

Kumbha Vagga.—The fifth chapter of the *Tikā Nipāta* of the *Jātaka Commentary*.[1]

[1] J. ii. 431-51.

1. **Kumbha Sutta.**—A pot without support is easily upset, so is it with the mind. Support for the mind is the Noble Eightfold Path.[1]

[1] S. v. 20 f.

2. **Kumbha Sutta.**—A pot, if overset, empties out its water and cannot take it in again. A monk, cultivating the Eightfold Path, empties out Ill and cannot take it in again.[1]

[1] S. v. 48.

Kumbhakaṇṇa.—A powerful Yakkha whom **Sumedha** Buddha brought under his power. His story is similar to that of **Āḷavaka.** The people brought the Yakkha a prince as sacrifice, and the Yakkha handed him over to the Buddha. Ninety crores of people realised the Truth on the occasion.[1]

[1] Bu. xii. 5; BuA. 164 f.

Kumbhakāra Jātaka (No. 408).—The Bodhisatta was a potter in Benares, and to his house came four Pacceka Buddhas—**Karaṇḍu, Naggaji, Nimi** and **Dummukha**—from **Nandamūla-pabbhāra.** He welcomed them and asked them the stories of their renunciation. Having heard them, both he and his wife wished to leave the world, but his wife, deceiving him, went before him, leaving him to look after their son and daughter. When the children were old enough he, too, became an ascetic, and though he met his wife later he refused to have anything to do with her.

The son was **Rāhula** and the daughter **Uppalavaṇṇā,** the wife being **Rāhulamātā.**

The story was related to five hundred monks who had lustful thoughts at midnight. The Buddha read their thoughts and visited them with **Ānanda.**[1] See also the **Pānīya Jātaka.**

[1] J. iii. 375 ff.

Kumbhaghosaka.—Son of the chief treasurer of **Rājagaha.** Plague breaks out in the city and attacks the chief treasurer and his wife. When about to die they bid farewell to Kumbhaghosaka, directing him to flee for his life and return later to dig up their treasure. He spends twelve years in a jungle and returns to find the treasure undisturbed; but reflecting that since he is unknown in the city he may be subjected to annoyance if he is seen digging up the treasure and spending it, he decides to earn his own living and obtains a position as foreman. One day the king, hearing his voice, exclaims: "That is the voice of some rich man." Several times this happens, and then a female servant, overhearing the king's words, offers for a consideration to make him master of the man's wealth. She obtains lodgings for herself and her daughter in Kumbhaghosaka's house and contrives to make him seduce her daughter. A marriage is arranged, and Kumbhaghosaka is obliged to dig up some of the wealth in order to defray the various expenses proclaimed by the king's orders. When the plot is complete, Kumbhaghosaka is summoned before the king, who, having heard his story, confirms him in his inheritance and gives him his own daughter as wife.

The king tells the story to the Buddha, who praises Kumbhaghosaka.[1]

[1] DhA. i. 321 ff.

1. **Kumbhaṇḍa.**—A Nigaṇṭha for whom **Paṇḍukābhaya** built a hermitage, named after him, near the **Gāmaṇi** Tank.[1]

[1] Mhv. x. 99.

2. **Kumbhaṇḍa.**—A class of spirits mentioned with Yakkhas, Asuras and Nāgas. They live in the South and **Virūḷha** is their king.[1] In the **Vidhurapaṇḍita Jātaka,**[2] **Kumbhīra** (*q.v.*) is mentioned as one of their chiefs. They had huge stomachs, and their genital organs were as big as pots, hence their name.[3]

[1] D. ii. 257; D. iii. 198. [2] J. vi. 272. [3] DA. iii. 964.

Kumbhapura.—The residence of **Kisavaccha**[1]; it is evidently another name for **Kumbhavatī** (*q.v.*).

[1] MA. ii. 599.

Kumbhavatī.—A city in the kingdom of King **Daṇḍaki. Kisavaccha** lived in the park near there.[1]

[1] J. iii. 463; v. 29, 134.

Kumbhigallaka.—A monastery in Ceylon. **Vasabha** built an uposatha-house there.[1]

[1] Mhv. xxxv. 86.

Kumbhīra.—A Yakkha who lived in the **Vepulla** mountain outside **Rājagaha.** He was present at the preaching of the **Mahāsamaya Sutta** with a train of over one hundred thousand.[1] He is called **Rājagahika** because he was born in **Rājagaha.**[2] Sometimes[3] he is spoken of as chief of the **Kumbhaṇḍas.** When **Bimbisāra** wished to visit the courtesan **Padumavatī** at **Ujjenī,** the chaplain enlisted Kumbhīra's assistance in transporting the king thither.[4]

[1] D. ii. 257.
[2] DA. ii. 686.
[3] *E.g.*, J. vi. 272.
[4] ThigA. 39.

Kumbhīla Jātaka (No. 206).—Evidently another version of the **Vānarinda Jātaka,** though the scholiast refers to another **Kumbhīla** (thus in all MSS.) **Jātaka** for particulars.[1]

[1] J. ii. 206.

Kumbhīlavānaka.—A river in Ceylon which joins the **Saṅkhavaḍḍhamānaka.**[1]

[1] Cv. lxviii. 32; see also Cv. *Trs.* i. 279, n. 4.

Kumbhīlasobbha.—A tank restored by **Vijayabāhu I.,**[1] and later by **Parakkamabāhu I.**[2]

[1] Cv. lx. 50.
[2] *Ibid.*, lxxix. 33.

1. **Kumma Sutta.**—A monk should be like the tortoise, inwardly withdrawing.[1] *v.l.* **Dukkara Sutta.**

[1] S. i. 7.

2. **Kumma Sutta.**—Gains, favours and flattery—these are the snares of **Māra,** resembling the corded harpoon with which a tortoise all unwittingly was caught of old.[1]

[1] S. ii. 226.

3. **Kumma Sutta.**—Like the tortoise who withdrew all his limbs into his shell lest the jackal should catch him, so let the monk ceaselessly guard all his senses from **Māra.**[1]

[1] S. iv. 177.

Kummāsadāyaka Thera.—An arahant. Ninety-one kappas ago, having nothing else to give, he put sour gruel into the bowl of **Vipassī** Buddha.[1] He is evidently identical with **Sīvaka Thera.**[2]

[1] Ap. ii. 415.
[2] ThagA. i. 307.

Kummāsapiṇḍa Jātaka (No. 415).—Once the Bodhisatta was servant to a rich man in Benares, and having received four portions of sour gruel for wages, gave them to four Pacceka Buddhas. After death he was born as heir to the king of Benares, and made the daughter of the Kosala king his chief queen. Remembering his previous life, he composed a song about it; the song became very popular, though no one understood its import. The queen, having been promised a boon, chose to know the meaning of the song, and the king, having summoned the people from twelve leagues round, explained the allusions. The queen, too, revealed how she had once been a slave in the court of **Ambaṭṭha** and had given alms to a holy monk. She is identified with **Rāhulamātā.**

The story was told in reference to Queen **Mallikā ;** she was a garland-maker's daughter, and one day gave three portions of sour gruel to the Buddha. That same day she became the chief queen of **Pasenadi.**[1]

[1] J. iii. 405 ff. *Cp.* the third story of the *Jātakamālā*, also *Divyāvadāna*, p. 88, and *Kathāsaritsāgara* xxvii. 79 ff.

Kuraṅgavī.—Daughter of the king of Benares. She fell in love with **Eḷakamāra** (*q.v.*) and was ultimately married to him. She misconducted herself with **Chalaṅgakumāra** and his attendant **Dhanantevāsī.**[1]

The story of Kuraṅgavī forms one of the tales related by **Kuṇāla.**

[1] J. v. 429 f.

Kuraṇḍaka.—A cave, probably in Ceylon. It contained beautiful paintings of the renunciation of seven Buddhas, but the Elder **Cittagutta** (*q.v.*), who lived in the cave for a long time, never saw them because he had never lifted his eyes. There was a great ironwood (*nāga*) tree at the entrance to the cave. The Elder, at the request of the king, once went to visit him, but after seven days, not being happy in the palace, he returned to Kuraṇḍaka.[1]

[1] Vsm. i. 38 f.

Kuraya.—See **Kuruya.**

Kuraraghara.—A town in **Avanti.** It was the residence of **Kātiyānī, Kāḷī, Soṇa Kuṭikaṇṇa,** among others. Near it was the **Papāta-pabbata.**[1] **Mahā Kaccāna** also lived there. *v.l.* **Kulaghara.**

[1] SA. ii. 188; UdA. 307; DhA. iv. 101; AA. i. 246, etc.

Kuraraghara-Papāta-pabbata.—See **Papāta-pabbata.**

Kuraragharikā.—See **Kāḷī** (2).

Kuraraghariya-Soṇa.—The name by which **Soṇa Kuṭikaṇṇa** is sometimes referred to.[1]

[1] *E.g.*, J. vi. 15.

Kuravakagalla.—A place in **Rohaṇa** where **Damiḷādhikārī Rakkha** defeated his enemies.[1]

[1] Cv. lxxv. 137.

Kuru.—A country, one of the sixteen **Mahājanapadas.**[1] Frequent references to it are found in the Pāli Canon. It is said that Kuru was originally the name of the chieftains (*rājakumārā*) of the country and that their territory was later named after them. Buddhaghosa[2] records a tradition which states that, when **Mandhātā** returned to **Jambudīpa** from his sojourn in the four Mahādīpas and in the devalokas, there were in his retinue a large number of the people of **Uttarakuru.** They settled down in Jambudīpa, and their settlement was known as **Kururaṭṭha.** It had many towns and villages.

The country seems to have had very little political influence in the Buddha's time, though, in the past, **Pañcāla, Kuru** and **Kekaka** were evidently three of the most powerful kingdoms.[3] According to the *Jātakas*,[4] the kingdom of Kuru was three hundred leagues in extent and its capital, **Indapatta,** seven leagues in circumference. The ruling dynasty at Indapatta belonged to the **Yudhiṭṭhila-gotta.**[5] Among the kings of the past, **Dhanañjaya Koravya** is mentioned several times[6] and reference is also made to a king called **Koravya**[7] whose son was the Bodhisatta **Sutasoma.** During the Buddha's time, also, the chieftain of Kuru was called Koravya, and his discussion with the Elder **Raṭṭhapāla,** who was himself the scion of a noble family of the Kurus, is recounted in the **Raṭṭhapāla Sutta.**[8] Perhaps at one time the Kuru kingdom extended as far as **Uttarapañcāla,** for in the **Somanassa Jātaka,**[9] Uttarapañcāla is mentioned as a town in the Kururaṭṭha, with **Reṇu** as its king.

Koravya had a park called **Migācīra** where Raṭṭhapāla took up his residence when he visited his parents.[10] The people of Kuru had a reputation for deep wisdom and good health, and this reputation is mentioned[11] as the reason for the Buddha having delivered some of his most profound discourses to the Kurus, for example, the **Mahānidāna,** and

[1] D. ii. 200; A. i. 213 etc.
[2] DA. ii. 481 f.; MA. i. 184 etc.
[3] See, *e.g.*, J. ii. 214.
[4] *E.g.*, J. v. 57, 484; vi. 255. Also Mtu. i. 34; ii. 419.
[5] J. iii. 400; iv. 361.
[6] J. ii. 366; iii. 400; iv. 450; vi. 260 etc.
[7] J. iv. 361; v. 457.
[8] M. ii. 65 ff.
[9] J. iv. 444.
[10] MA. ii. 725.
[11] *Ibid.*, i. 184 f.; AA. ii. 820; they were also probably reputed to be virtuous; see the **Kurudhamma Jātaka.**

the **Mahāsatipaṭṭhāna Suttas.** Among other discourses delivered in the Kuru country are the **Māgandiya Sutta,** the **Āneñjasappāya Sutta,** the **Sammosa Sutta** and the **Ariyavasā Sutta.** All these were preached at **Kammāssadhamma,** which is described as a *nigama* of the Kurūs, where the Buddha resided from time to time. Another town of the Kurūs, which we find mentioned, is **Thullakoṭṭhika,** the birthplace of Raṭṭhapāla, and here the Buddha stayed during a tour.[12] **Udena's** queen, **Māgandiyā,** came from Kuru,[13] and **Aggidatta,** chaplain to the Kosala king, lived on the boundary between Kuru and **Aṅga** and **Magadha,** honoured by the inhabitants of all three kingdoms.[14]

The Kuru country is generally identified as the district around Thānesar, with its capital Indapatta, near the modern Delhi.[15] See also **Uttarakuru.**

[12] M. ii. 54; ThagA. ii. 30.
[13] DhA. i. 199.
[14] *Ibid.*, iii. 242.
[15] CAGI. 379 f.

Kurukaccha.—Probably a wrong reading for **Bhārukaccha** (*q.v.*).

Kurukhetta.—Another name for the country of the **Kurūs.**[1]

[1] J. vi. 291.

1. **Kuruṅgamiga Jātaka** (No. 21).—Once the Bodhisatta was an antelope who used to eat the fruit of a *sepaṇṇi*-tree. One day a huntsman discovered him and lay in wait to kill him, but the Bodhisatta suspected his presence and so escaped death.

The story was told in reference to **Devadatta's** plots to kill the Buddha, the huntsman being identified with Devadatta.[1]

[1] J. i. 173 f.

2. **Kuruṅgamiga Jātaka** (No. 206).—In a forest lived three friends: an antelope, a woodpecker and a tortoise. One night the antelope was caught in a huntsman's noose, and the tortoise set about biting through the thongs of the noose while the woodpecker, uttering cries of ill-omen, kept the huntsman in his hut. The antelope escaped, but the tortoise, exhausted by his labours, was caught by the huntsman. The antelope thereupon enticed the hunter into the forest and, eluding him, released the tortoise. The antelope was the Bodhisatta, **Sāriputta** the woodpecker, **Moggallāna** the tortoise and **Devadatta** the hunter.

The story was told in reference to Devadatta's wickedness.[1]

This *Jātaka* is figured on the Bharhut Stupa.[2]

[1] J. ii. 152 ff.; DhA. iii. 152 f.
[2] Cunningham: p. 67 and Pl. xxvii. 9.

Kuruṅgamiga Vagga.—The third section of the *Eka Nipāta* of the *Jātaka Commentary.*[1]

[1] J. i. 173-98.

Kurudhamma Jātaka (No. 276).—The Bodhisatta was once born as the son of **Dhanañjaya,** king of the **Kurūs,** and, after his father's death, reigned in **Indapatta**. He observed the *Kurudhamma*—that is to say, the *pañcasīla*—as did the queen-mother, his queen-consort, the viceroy, the chaplain, the king's driver, his charioteer, the treasurer, the keeper of the royal granaries, the palace porter and the courtesan of the city. The country thus became very prosperous and its people happy. In the kingdom of **Kaliṅga** there was a drought and consequent scarcity of food. The king, acting on the advice of his ministers, sent brahmins to beg from the Bodhisatta the loan of his state elephant, **Añjanavasabha,** who was reported to bring rain. The elephant was lent willingly but no rain fell. It was thereupon decided that the prosperity of the Kurus was due to the Kurudhamma observed by the king and the others, and messengers were despatched to find out which these Kurudhammas were. From the king down to the courtesan, all had rigorously kept them, but each had unwittingly done something which he or she considered a violation of tne dhamma. The messengers, therefore, had to visit each one and take down a list of the dhamma. The incidents related by each to the messengers, explaining wherein they had transgressed the dhammas, only served to emphasise how scrupulously they had conducted themselves.

The Kaliṅga king practised the Kurudhamma and rain fell in his country.

The story was told in reference to a monk who had killed a wild goose. Two monks bathed in **Aciravatī,** and while standing on the bank, drying, they saw two geese appear. The monks took a bet as to which should hit the goose in the eye, and one of them threw a stone which pierced one eye and came out of the other. The monk was reported to the Buddha.[1]

[1] J. ii. 365 ff; DhA. iv. 86 ff; cp. Cariyāpiṭaka i. 3. With the introductory story compare that of the **Sālittaka Jātaka** (J. i. 418).

Kurundaṅkuṇḍiya.—A locality in South India.[1]

[1] Cv. lxxvi. 236, 266.

Kurundacullaka.—A pariveṇa in the **Jetavana-vihāra** in Ceylon, the residence of **Dāṭhāvedhaka.**[1]

[1] MṬ. 176.

Kurundapillaka.—A monastery in Ceylon. **Poṭṭhakuṭṭha** erected a *pāsāda* there.[1]

[1] Cv. xlvi. 21.

Kurundavāpi.—A tank built by **Aggabodhi I.**[1]

[1] Cv. xlii. 15; Cv. *Trs.* i. 66, n. 6.

Kurundavāsoka-Vihāra.—A monastery built by **Khallāṭanāga.**[1]

[1] Mhv. xxxiii. 32.

Kurunda-Vihāra.—A monastery built by **Aggabodhi I.** and dedicated to all three fraternities.[1]

[1] Cv. xlii. 15.

Kurundavelu.—A vihāra in Ceylon, where was compiled the **Kurundī-aṭṭhakathā** (*q.v.*).

Kurundiya-Vihāra.—A monastery repaired by **Vijayabāhu I.**[1]; probably identical with **Kurunda-Vihāra.**

[1] Cv. lx. 60.

Kurundī.—A village in Ceylon.[1]

[1] Cv. lxxxiii. 16; lxxxviii. 64; Cv. *Trs.* ii. 149, n. 9.

Kurundī-Aṭṭhakathā.—One of the great collections of commentaries on the Tipiṭaka used by Buddhaghosa in the compilation of his works. Tradition says[1] that it was written in Sinhalese, and was so called because it was compiled in the **Kurundavelu-Vihāra** in Ceylon. It seems to have been chiefly concerned with Vinaya rules, for we find frequent references to it, particularly in the *Samantapāsādikā*.[2] It is also called **Kurundī-gandha.**[3] In many cases its explanations appear to have been different from those of other commentaries.

[1] See, *e.g.*, Saddhamma-Saṅgaha, p. 55.
[2] *E.g.*, Sp. i. 281; ii. 319; iii. 537, 544, 545, 570, 573, 583, 597, 616, 620, 626, 627, 660, 664, 668, 688, 722, 726; iv. 745, 758, 778, 783, 789, 813, 818, 861, 920, etc.
[3] Gv. 59.

Kurundīraṭṭha.—See **Kurundī.**

Kurumba.—A Damiḷa chief, subdued by **Laṅkāpura.**[1]

[1] Cv. lxxvii. 14 f.

Kurumbāṇḍanakali.—A locality in South India, where a great battle was fought between **Laṅkāpura** and **Kulasekhara.**[1]

[1] Cv. lxxvi. 157.

Kuruvaka-tittha.—A secluded bathing-place in a large pond near the **Cittalapabbata-vihāra.**[1]

[1] MA. ii. 1025.

Kureñjiyaphaladāyaka (Kuruñjiya°) Thera.—An arahant. Thirty-one kappas ago he was a hunter, and having seen the Buddha **Sikhī** in the forest, he gave him a *kureñjiya*-fruit.[1]

He is evidently identical with **Soṇa-Seṭṭhiputta Thera.**[2]

[1] Ap. ii. 448 f. [2] ThagA. i. 316 f.

1. **Kula Sutta.**—Families consisting of many women and few men are molested by robbers; likewise a monk who has not developed emancipation of mind through love is easily molested by non-humans.[1]

[1] S. ii. 263.

2. **Kula Sutta.**—**Asibandhakaputta** visits the Buddha at the **Pāvārika-ambavana** in **Nālandā** at **Nigaṇṭha Nātaputta's** request, and tells the Buddha that he does wrong in obtaining alms from famine-stricken Nālandā. The Buddha replies that his begging does not come within the eight causes of injury to families: viz., the actions of kings and robbers, fire, water, loss of savings, slothfulness, wastrels and impermanence.

Asibandhakaputta becomes the Buddha's follower.[1]

[1] S. iv. 322 f.

3. **Kula Sutta.**—The five advantages which accrue to families visited by holy men: they cleanse their hearts and attain to heaven; they greet the monks respectfully and are born noble; they conquer greed and gain power; give alms and obtain wealth; ask questions and become wise.[1]

[1] A. iii. 244 f.

4. **Kula Sutta.**—Seven reasons for which a family is not worth visiting: they neither greet one nor show courtesy; provide no seats; hide what they have; having much, give little; what they do give they give carelessly and half-heartedly.[1]

[1] A. iv. 10.

5. **Kula Sutta.**—Similar to 4. Nine reasons are given, the additional ones being: they show no desire to hear the doctrine and take no interest when it is preached to them.[1]

[1] A. iv. 387.

Kulaghara.—See **Kuraraghara.**

Kulagharaṇī Sutta.—See **Ogāḷha Sutta.**

Kulanta-vāpi (Kulattha-vāpi).—A tank to the south of **Anurādhapura.** In the battle between the forces of **Duṭṭhagāmaṇi** and **Eḷāra** the water in the tank was dyed red with blood of the slain, hence the name.[1]

[1] Mhv. xxv. 66.

Kulaputta Sutta.—Clansmen who go forth into homelessness do so in order to gain full comprehension of the Four Noble Truths. This is true for all time.[1]

[1] S. v. 415.

" Kulaputtena-dukkhā " Suttā.—Three suttas. A clansman who goes forth should live (1) in aversion from body etc., or (2) seeing impermanence in them, or (3) seeing no soul in them.[1]

[1] S. iii. 179.

Kulavaḍḍhaka.—Given as a name used ironically to insult another.[1]

[1] Vin. iv. 8.

Kulavaddhana.—A rich merchant of **Sudassana** (Benares) who tried to stop his king, **Sutasoma,** from renouncing the world by offering him all his wealth. He is identified with **(Mahā ?) Kassapa.**[1]

[1] J. v. 185, 192.

1. **Kulasekhara.**—A Cholian king of South India. He besieged the Paṇḍyan king, **Parakkama** of **Madhurā,** and the latter sent for help to **Parakkamabāhu I.** of Ceylon. Parakkamabāhu sent an expeditionary force to South India under **Laṅkāpura,** but in the meantime the Paṇḍyan king had been slain and his capital taken. The Sinhalese force, however, landed and carried on a prolonged campaign against Kulasekhara and his allies, who seem to have been numerous and powerful. Kulasekhara was defeated, and the Paṇḍyan king's son, **Vīra Paṇḍu,** was installed in Madhurā. The Chola prisoners taken in

the war were brought to Ceylon and employed in the reconstruction of the **Mahā Thūpa** in **Anurādhapura.**[1]

[1] For details of this war see Cv. lxxvi, and lxxvii. For Kulasekhara's later history see Cv. *Trs.* ii. 100, n. 1.

2. **Kulasekhara.**—A Paṇḍu king. His general **Āriyacakkavatti** invaded Ceylon in the reign of **Bhuvanekabāhu I.** and carried off the Tooth Relic and other treasures. Later **Parakkamabāhu III.** visited Kulasekhara and retrieved the Tooth Relic.[1]

[1] Cv. xc. 47; 53 f.

Kulāvaka Jātaka (No. 31).—The Bodhisatta was born in **Macala** under the name of **Magha.** He spent his time with the heads of the other twenty-nine families in the village, engaged in various forms of social service. The headman, finding his gains diminish, made a false report to the king, who ordered Magha and his friends to be trampled by elephants; but by virtue of their *mettā* they could not be killed, and thereupon the king showed them great favour. After death they were all born in **Tāvatiṃsa,** with Magha as **Sakka.** Three of Magha's wives—**Sudhammā, Cittā** and **Nandā**—who had persuaded him to let them share in his good work, were born as Sakka's handmaidens. But **Sujātā,** who had taken no part in their activities, received no such honour.[1] At that time the **Asuras** shared Tāvatiṃsa with the **Devas,** but one day they got drunk and were hurled down to the foot of **Sineru.** They therefore declared war on the Devas, and during one of their fierce battles Sakka was defeated and fled over the sea in his chariot **Vejayanta.** When he came to **Simbalivana,** the chariot felled down the trees there, and the young **Garuḷas** were hurled into the sea. Hearing their cries of agony, Sakka made his driver, **Mātali,** turn the chariot and go back. The Asuras, seeing him return, thought it was another Sakka coming with reinforcements, and fled in terror. The **Vejayanta-pāsāda** rose from the earth, and Sakka lived in it, having fortified his city with a fivefold guard.

The story was told in reference to a monk who had drunk water without first straining it, because his friend, with whom he was travelling and with whom he had fallen out, had the only strainer available. Mātali is identified with **Ānanda.**[2]

In the version given in the *Dhammapada Commentary,*[3] the story of

[1] For the story of these women see under their names.

[2] J. i. 198 ff.; with the introductory story cp. Vin. ii. 118.

[3] i. 263 ff.; see also SA. i. 260 f.; DA. iii. 710 ff.; and SNA. ii. 484 f. According to these accounts Sakka was helped by not 29 but 33 others.

Magha is related in response to a question asked of the Buddha by the **Licchavi Mahāli.** The reason given for Sakka's flight in the Vejayanta-ratha also differs. According to this account, when Sujātā (*q.v.*) was reborn as the daughter of **Vepacitti** and the time came for her to choose a husband, Sakka went to the assembly in the guise of an aged Asura and was chosen by Sujātā. Sakka thereupon revealed himself and fled with his bride in the chariot, the Asuras in full chase.

See also **Kulāvaka Sutta.**

Kulāvaka Vagga.—The fourth chapter of the *Eka Nipāta* of the *Jātaka Commentary.*[1]

[1] J. i. 198-234.

Kulāvaka Sutta.—The story of **Sakka's** flight from the **Asuras.** When he saw the **Garuḷas** crushed under his chariot wheels, he asked his driver, **Mātali,** to turn back and risk death at the hands of the Asuras. But the Asuras fled.[1] *cp.* **Kulāvaka Jātaka.**

[1] S. i. 224.

Kulālitissa.—A monastery in Ceylon. Over the *thūpa* in the monastery King **Vohārika-Tissa** erected a parasol.[1]

[1] Mhv. xxxvi. 33.

Kuliṅga.—The name of a clan, probably Sinhalese. **Mahinda VI.** belonged to this clan.[1] The Kuliṅgas were among the tribes sent to Ceylon by **Asoka** with the Bodhi-tree.[2]

[1] Cv. lxxx. 15.
[2] Mhv. xix. 2; see also Mhv. *Trs.* 128, n. 2, and Cv. *Trs.* i. 29, n. 2, and ii. 126, n. 5.

1. **Kulupaka Sutta.**—Five qualities which make a monk disagreeable to the families he visits: he is intimate on slight acquaintance (*asanthava-vissāsī*); takes privileges without justification (*anissaravikappī*); tries to bring together estranged families (*viyatthūpasevī*); is a gossip (*upakaṇ-ṇakajappī*); and is importunate (*atiyācanako*).[1]

[1] A. iii. 136 f.

2. **Kulupaka Sutta.**—The five evil results of visiting families: sitting together in secret, and in concealed places, tendency to go uninvited, talking about women, and being filled with lustful thoughts.[1]

[1] A. iii. 258 f.

3. **Kulupaka Sutta.**—Five evil results of visiting families too often—frequent sight of women and consequent danger to celibacy in varying degrees.[1]

[1] A. iii. 259.

4. **Kulupaka Sutta.**—The Buddha says that **Mahā Kassapa** has the qualities requisite to becoming a monk worthy of visiting families. He is not vexed even if they give scantily, tardily or disrespectfully.[1]

[1] S. ii. 200.

Kulumba Sutta.—A discourse, evidently well known, but not included in the Three Rescensions (*tisso saṅgīti*).[1] The *Atthasālinī*[2] gives an extract from it and refers " to an infanticide of Kulumba." The quotation is to show that a bodily action may arise also in the mind-door.

[1] Sp. iv. 742, 743. [2] DhSA. 91.

Kulla Thera.—An arahant. He was a landowner in **Sāvatthi** and joined the Order after hearing the Buddha preach. But he was often seized by fits of lustful passion, and even when, following the Buddha's instructions, he meditated in the charnel field, he could not control the tendency. The Buddha himself went with him and bade him mark the putrefaction and dissolution of dead bodies around him. He attained first *jhāna,* developing which he won arahantship.[1] The *Theragāthā* verses[2] ascribed to him are a record of this experience.

[1] ThagA. i. 444 f. [2] 393-8.

Kuḷa Thera.—See **Kuṇḍala.**

Kuḷumbari-kaṇṇikā.—A district in Ceylon; the birthplace of **Mahā-Soṇa.**[1] According to the *Mahavaṃsa Commentary* it was in **Rohaṇa.**[2]

[1] Mhv. xxiii. 45. [2] MṬ. 45.

Kuvaṇṇā.—A Yakkha maiden, whom **Vijaya** married on his arrival in Ceylon. With her assistance he killed the Yakkhas at their feast in **Sirīsivatthu.** Later Vijaya discarded her in favour of a royal maiden from **Madhurā,** and she left, with her two children **Jīvahattha** and **Dipellā,** for **Laṅkāpura,** where she was slain as a spy. Her children fled to **Malaya** and their descendants became the **Pulindas.**[1]

Kuvaṇṇā had as companion a slave called **Sīsapātī (Sīsapātikā).**[2] *v.l.* **Kuveṇī.**

[1] Mhv. vii. 9-68. [2] MṬ. 255.

Kuvera (Kubera).—King of **Uttarakuru.** His royal residence is **Āḷakamandā** and his citadel **Visāṇa.** His messengers are **Tatolā, Tattolā, Tatotalā, Ojasi, Tejasi, Tatojasi, Sūra, Rāja, Ariṭṭha** and **Nemi.** His lotus-lake is called **Dharaṇī.** His sons are all called **Inda.**[1] He rules over the northern clime and is lord of the **Yakkhas,** with a splendid retinue.[2] He is a follower of the Buddha.[3] See **Vessavaṇa.**

He was once a brahmin called Kuvera and owned a sugar-cane farm, where he worked seven mills. The produce of one mill he gave in charity, and when his profits increased he gave alms for twenty thousand years. After death he was born as one of the **Cātummakārājika-devas.**[4]

In literature the name Kuvera signifies the god of wealth, and his city, Āḷakamandā, is said to embody all prosperity.[5] He had nine treasures.[6] The Yakkha **Puṇṇaka** calls himself the minister of Kuvera.[7] Kuvera is mentioned in a list of those who reached heaven through generosity.[8]

1 D. iii. 201 f.
2 D. ii. 257.
3 SN. v. 379.
4 DA. iii. 966; SNA. i. 369 f.
5 *E.g.*, Cv. xxxvii. 106; xxxix. 5; lxxx. 5.
6 *Ibid.*, lxxxvii. 31; see Hopkins' Epic Mythology, 142 f.
7 J. vi. 307, 325.
8 *Ibid.*, 201.

Kuveradvāra.—One of the fourteen gates of **Pulatthipura,** erected by **Parakkamabāhu I.**[1]

1 Cv. lxxiii. 161.

Kuvera-nāliṇī.—A name given to **Dharaṇī**[1] (*q.v.*).

1 D. iii. 202; DA. iii. 968.

Kusa.—The Bodhisatta, son of **Okkāka,** king of **Kusāvatī** and of his queen **Sīlavatī.** Okkāka has no heir, in spite of performing various rites. But at length, by the favour of **Sakka,** Sīlavatī miraculously gives birth to two sons. The elder, though ill-favoured, is supernaturally wise and is called Kusa. The younger, very handsome, is called **Jayampati.** Kusa consents to marry only on condition that a princess can be obtained exactly like an image which he himself has fashioned. **Pabhāvatī,** daughter of King **Madda** of **Sāgala,** is found to fulfil this condition, and is married to Kusa. The bride is not to look upon her husband's face until she has conceived, but Kusa plays various pranks upon her and she accidently discovers how ugly he is. She leaves him immediately and returns to her father's court. Thither Kusa follows her, and under a variety of menial disguises, including that of a cook, tries, but in vain, to win her affection. At length Sakka intervenes. He sends letters, purporting to come from King Madda, to seven kings, offering Pabhāvatī to each of them. They arrive in Sāgala simultaneously and threaten to destroy the city. Madda decides to cut Pabhāvatī into seven pieces, and she is only saved from immediate death by the despised husband. At his appearance the kings flee, for wherever he looks the earth trembles. Kusa returns with his wife to Kusāvatī and they live there happily.

Pleased at Kusa's victory, Sakka gives him a jewel called the **Verocaṇa-maṇi.** It was octagonal, and was evidently handed down in the succession of kings, for we are told that one of the tests, set by **Videha,** king of **Mithilā,** to discover the proficiency of **Mahosadha,** was for him to break the old thread in this gem, remove it, and insert a new one.[1] Reference is made elsewhere[2] to a *tālavaṇṭa* (fan ?) possessed by Kusa, in which could be seen the forms of all things in the world. He also possessed the **Kokanadavīṇā** (*q.v.*) given by Sakka to Sīlavatī. Kusa is called **Sīhassara,** and his shout, when he appeared before the seven kings, announcing his name, was one of the four shouts heard throughout Jambudīpa.[3] The *Dīpavaṃsa*[4] speaks of Kusa and **Mahākusa,** both descended from **Mahāsammata.**

[1] J. vi. 340; according to SA. i. 115 and DA. iii. 266, the jewel was also in the possession of **Pasenadi**; but see the **Mahāsāra Jātaka,** where no mention is made of Kusa.

[2] *E.g.*, MṬ. 552.

[3] SNA. i. 223; SA. i. 248.

[4] iii. 40.

Kusa Jātaka (No. 531).—The story of Kusa (*q.v.*). It was told in reference to a backsliding monk who fell in love with a woman in **Sāvatthi,** neglected all his duties and refused food. He was taken to the Buddha, who related this story to show how even mighty men may lose their power and come to misery through love of a woman.[1]

The story bears much resemblance to that of **Anitthigandha** (*q.v.*). See also *s.v.* **Sammillabhāsinī.**

[1] J. v. 278 ff.; the story is also given in Mtu. iii. 1 ff.; ii. 441 f.; the details differ, as do some of the names, from the Pāli version.

Kusaghara.—A city (?). The Buddha's lower robe (*nivāsana*) was deposited there after his death.[1]

[1] Bu. xxviii. 8.

Kusaṭṭhakadāyaka Thera.—An arahant. In the time of **Kassapa** Buddha he was a brahmin and gave the Buddha *kusaṭṭhaka* (eight handfuls of *kusa*-grass ?).[1] He is evidently to be identified with **Migasira Thera.**[2]

[1] Ap. ii. 416.

[2] ThagA. i. 306.

Kusanāḷi Jātaka (No. 121).—The Bodhisatta was born as a sprite, in a clump of *kusa*-grass. Hard by was a *mukkhaka*-tree in which lived a Tree-sprite. One day the king's carpenter, looking for a suitable pillar for the king's one-pillared palace, reluctantly decided to fell the *mukkhaka*. Learning of the Tree-sprite's imminent danger, the Bodhisatta assumed the shape of a chameleon and deceived the carpenter in such a way that he saw the *mukkhaka* as all rotten and of no use for his purpose.

The story was told in reference to one of **Anāthapiṇḍika's** friends. He was of low rank and poor, and Anāthapiṇḍika's other friends protested against such intimacy. But one day the poor friend saved Anāthapiṇḍika's house from being burgled. The Buddha related the story to show how each, according to his strength, could help a friend in need.[1]

Ānanda was the Tree-sprite. The story is often quoted[2] to show the value of a good friend.

[1] J. i. 441 ff. [2] *E.g.*, J. iv. 77.

Kusanāḷi Vagga.—The thirteenth chapter of the *Eka Nipāta* of the *Jātaka Commentary*.[1]

[1] J. i. 441-65.

Kusamālī.—One of the seas through which the mariner **Suppāraka** (*q.v.*) piloted his ship. It was full of emeralds and looked like an expanse of dark *kusa*-grass. Its full name was **Nīlavaṇṇa Kusamāla.**[1]

[1] J. iv. 140.

Kusamba (Kusumba).—A sage (*isi*), on the site of whose hermitage was built the city which came, for that reason, to be called **Kosambī.**[1]

[1] SNA. i. 300; MA. ii. 539; UdA. 248; PsA. 413; see also Rāmāyana i. 34.

1. **Kusalarāsi Sutta.**—The five hindrances (*nīvaraṇa*) could rightly be called a heap of demerit and the five *satipaṭṭhānas* a heap of merit.[1]

[1] S. v. 145.

2. **Kusalarāsi Sutta.**—The four *satipaṭṭhānas* could rightly be called a heap of merit.[1]

[1] S. v. 186.

1. **Kusalā Sutta.**—Conditions which are on the side of goodness have their root in earnestness (*appamāda*); the earnest monk cultivates the seven *bojjhaṅgas*.[1]

[1] S. v. 91.

2. **Kusalā Sutta.** Similar to No. 1. The conditions have their root in *yonisomanasikāra*.[1]

[1] S. v. 92.

Kusāvatī.—A city in the kingdom of the **Mallas.** In the present age it was called **Kusinārā.** Once it was the royal city of **Mahā-Sudassana** and was twelve leagues in length and twelve in breadth, prosperous and full of people, like **Āḷakamandā.**[1] It was then at the head of eighty-four towns.[2] The **Mahā-Sudassana Sutta**[3] contains a long description of the city. It was the capital of several kings of the **Mahāsammata** dynasty,[4] including **Okkāka,** father of **Kusa.**[5]

In the time of the Buddha **Metteya,** Kusāvatī will be known as **Ketumatī.**[6]

[1] D. ii. 146 f.; J. i. 392; Cyp. i. 4; Dvy. 227.
[2] S. iii. 144.
[3] D. ii. 170 f.
[4] Mhv. ii. 7; Dpv. iii. 9.
[5] J. v. 278 ff.
[6] Anāgat. v. 18.

Kusināṭā.—One of the cities of **Uttarakuru.**[1]

[1] D. iii. 200.

Kusinārā.—The capital of the **Mallas** and the scene of the Buddha's death. At that time it was a small city, " a branch-township with wattle-and-daub houses in the midst of the jungle," and **Ānanda** was, at first, disappointed that the Buddha should have chosen it for his *Parinibbāna.* But the Buddha, by preaching the **Mahā-Sudassana Sutta**, pointed out to him that in ancient times it had been **Kusāvatī,** the royal city of **Mahā-Sudassana.**[1] Between Kusinārā and **Pāvā,** three *gāvutas* away[2]—from where the Buddha came to Kusinārā on his last journey from **Rājāgaha,** stopping at various places—lay the stream of **Kakuṭṭha** on the banks of which was the **Ambavana ;** beyond that was the **Hiraññavatī** river, and near the city, in a south-westerly direction, lay the **Upavattana,** the Sāla-grove of the Mallas, which the Buddha made his last resting-place.[3]

After the Buddha's death his body was carried into the city by the northern gate and out of the city by the eastern gate; to the east of the city was **Makuṭabandhana,** the shrine of the Mallas, and there the body was cremated. For seven days those assembled at the ceremony held a festival in honour of the relics.[4]

It is said that the Buddha had three reasons for coming to Kusinārā to die: (1) Because it was the proper venue for the preaching of the Mahā-Sudassana Sutta; (2) because **Subhadda** would visit him there and, after listening to his sermon, would develop meditation and become an arahant while the Buddha was still alive; and (3) because the brahman

[1] D. ii. 146.
[2] DA. ii. 573.
[3] UdA. 238; DA. ii. 572 f.
[4] D. ii. 160 f.

Doṇa would be there, after the Buddha's death, to solve the problem of the distribution of his relics.[5] As the scene of his death, Kusinārā became one of the four holy places declared by the Buddha to be fit places of pilgrimage for the pious, the other three being **Kapilavatthu, Buddhagayā** and **Isipatana.**[6] Mention is made of other visits paid to Kusinārā by the Buddha, prior to that when his death took place. Thus, once he went there from **Āpaṇa** and having spent some time at Kusinārā, proceeded to **Ātumā.** The Mallas of Kusinārā were always great admirers of the Buddha, even though not all of them were his followers, and on the occasion of this visit they decided that any inhabitant of Kusinārā who failed to go and meet the Buddha and escort him to the city, would be fined five hundred. It was on this occasion that **Roja** the Mallan was converted and gave to the Buddha and the monks a supply of green vegetables and pastries.[7] During some of these visits the Buddha stayed in a wood called **Baliharaṇa,** and there he preached two of the **Kusinārā Suttas**[8] and the "**Kinti**" **Sutta.**[9] A third **Kusinārā Sutta** he preached while staying at Upavattana.[10]

Kusinārā was the birthplace of **Bandhula** and his wife **Mallikā.**[11] It was twenty-five yojanas from Rājagaha[12] and lay on the high road from **Aḷaka** to Rājagaha, the road taken by **Bāvarī's** disciples.[13]

This was evidently the road taken also by Maha **Kassapa** from Pāvā, when he came to pay his last respects to the Buddha.[14]

According to a late tradition, one-eighth of the Buddha's relics were deposited in a cairn in Kusinārā and honoured by the Mallas.[15]

In ancient times Kusinārā was the capital of King **Tālissara** and twelve of his descendants.[16] It was also the scene of the death of **Phussa** Buddha at the **Setārāma** (*v.l.* **Soṇārāma**).[17]

In Hiouen Thsang's day there still existed towers and Saṅghārāmas erected to mark the spots connected with the Buddha's last days and obsequies at Kusinārā. According to his account[18] Kusinārā was nineteen yojanas from **Vesāli.**

To the northern Buddhists the place was also known as Kuśigrāma (Kuśigrāmaka) and Kuśinagarī.[19]

Kusinārā is identified with the village of Kasia at the junction of the

[5] UdA. 402 f.; DA. ii. 573 f.

[6] D. ii. 140.

[7] Vin. i. 247 f.

[8] A. i. 274 f.; v. 79 f.

[9] M. ii. 238 f.

[10] A. ii. 79; for another discourse to some noisy monks at Upavattana, see Ud. iv. 2.

[11] DhA. i. 338, 349.

[12] DA. ii. 609; acc. to Fa Hsien (p. 40) it was twenty-four yojanas from Kapilavatthu.

[13] SN. v. 1012.

[14] Vin. ii. 284.

[15] D. ii. 167; Bu. xxviii. 3.

[16] Dpv. iii. 32.

[17] BuA. 195; Bu. xix. 25.

[18] Beal: *op. cit.* ii. lii. n.

[19] *E.g.*, Dvy. 152 f., 208.

river Rapti and the smaller Gondak and in the east of the Gorakhpur district.[20] A copper plate belonging to the thūpa erected at the site of the Buddha's death has recently been discovered.[21]

The people of Kusinārā are called Kosinārakā.[22]

[20] CAGI. i. 493. [21] *Ibid.*, 714. [22] *E.g.*, D. ii. 167.

Kusinārā Vagga.—The thirteenth chapter of the *Ṭikā Nipāta* of the *Aṅguttara Nikāya.*[1]

[1] A. i. 274-84; for a summary of its contents see A. v. 381.

1. **Kusinārā Sutta.**—Preached at **Baliharaṇa** in **Kusinārā.** Offerings, made to a monk by the pious, bring him no real advantage if he is slothful; he should be strenuous and vigilant.[1]

[1] A. i. 274 f.

2. **Kusinārā Sutta.**—Also preached at **Baliharaṇa.** A monk wishing to rebuke another monk, should consider five things with regard to himself—whether he is of blameless conduct in body and speech; whether he really wishes well for his colleague and is not influenced by envy; whether he is learned in the doctrine; whether his *pāṭimokkhas* are perfect. He should also consider whether his rebuke is seasonable, justified by facts, administered gently, for the other's benefit and out of compassion for him.[1]

[1] A. v. 79 f.

3. **Kusinārā Sutta.**—Preached at **Upavattana** in **Kusinārā,** in the *Sāla*-grove of the **Mallas.** The Buddha, just before his death, invites the monks to question him with regard to any doubts or misgivings they may have. They remain silent.[1] The sutta occurs also as part of the **Mahāparinibbāna Sutta.**[2]

[1] A. ii. 79 f. [2] D. ii. 137, 154.

Kusinārā Vihāra.—A monastery built by **Parakkamabāhu I.** in a suburb of **Pulatthipura,** called **Sīhapura.** It consisted of three image houses, each containing three storeys, six pāsādas, etc.[1]

[1] Cv. lxxiii. 152; lxxviii. 84; also Cv. *Trs.* ii. 18, n. 3.

1. **Kusīta Sutta.**—A woman who is faithless, shameless, unscrupulous, indolent and of weak wisdom is reborn in purgatory.[1]

[1] S. iv. 242.

2. **Kusīta Sutta.**—Eight occasions on which a monk is apt to become indolent.[1]

[1] A. iv. 332 f.

Kusima.—See **Kusumī.**

Kusumanagara.—The Pāli name for the city now known as Bassein, in Burma.[1]

Near the city was the birthplace of **Chapaṭa.**[2]

[1] Bode, *op. cit.*, 24.
[2] Sās. 74; see also pp. 41, 43, 147; Ind. Ant. 1893, xxi. 17.

Kusumapura.—See **Pāṭaliputta.**

Kusumamūlagāma.—A village near **Padumanagara,** residence of the Thera **Dhammadhara.**[1]

[1] Sās. 163.

Kusumārāma.—Another name for **Pupphārāma.**[1]

[1] Cv. ci. 7.

Kusumāsaniya Thera.—An arahant. Ninety-one kappas ago he was a learned brahman in the time of **Vipassī** Buddha, and while he was making preparations for a sacrifice, the Buddha passed his way. He spread for the Buddha a seat of flowers and offered him food. One kappa ago he was a king named **Varadassana.**[1] He is evidently identical with **Suyāma Thera.**[2]

[1] Ap. i. 160.
[2] ThagA. i. 165.

Kusumī.—A seaport in **Rāmañña** where a part of the Sinhalese expeditionary force sent by Pasakkamabāhu I. landed in five ships.[1] It is probably the same as **Kusumatittha** mentioned in the *Sāsanavaṃsa* as a seaport.[2] *v.l.* **Kusima.**

[1] Cv. lxxvi. 59.
[2] *E.g.*, pp. 66, 90.

Kuha Sutta.—Monks who are cheats, stubborn and uncontrolled, are no followers of the Buddha.[1]

[1] A. ii. 26; found also in It. 113, *cf.* Thag. 959.

Kuhaka Jātaka (No. 89).—Once a country squire, having great faith in the holiness of a matted-haired ascetic, buried some of his wealth in the hermitage he himself had provided for the ascetic. The latter, coveting the gold, hid it elsewhere, and took leave of the squire as though he were going to some other part of the country. The squire, after pressing him in vain to stay, accompanied him part of the way. Suddenly the ascetic stopped and said he had found a straw from the roof of the hermitage sticking to his hair and wished to restore it as it did not belong to him. The squire was greatly impressed by this show of non-covetousness, but another ascetic, who was the Bodhisatta, observing what happened and guessing the reason, communicated his suspicions to the squire. When they searched for the gold it could not be found, but the ascetic confessed his guilt after a sound thrashing.[1]

The occasion for the telling of the story is given in the **Uddāla Jātaka.**

[1] J. i. 375 ff.

Kuhaka Sutta.—Five qualities, such as deceitfulness, which make a monk disagreeable to his fellow monks.[1]

[1] A. iii. 111 f.

Kuhakābrāhmaṇa Vatthu.—A certain brahmin would climb a tree, grasp a branch with his feet and, swinging head downwards like a bat, demand pennies, etc., from passers by, threatening to kill himself and destroy the city if his request were refused. The Buddha hearing of this related a Jātaka story in which a false ascetic, having received some lizard meat, liked it and wished for more. He lay in wait for the king of the lizards when the latter came to pay his respects to him in order to kill him, but the lizard-king, suspecting him, escaped, reproaching him for his hypocrisy.[1]

[1] DhA. iv. 153 ff.; cp. the **Godha Jātaka;** also J. i. 480 f. and ii. 382 f.

1. **Kūṭa Sutta.**—In a peaked house (*kūṭāgāra*) all the rafters converge towards the peak; so are all wrong states fixed together in ignorance.[1]

[1] S. ii. 262.

2. **Kūṭa Sutta.**—Similar to the above; all profitable conditions have earnestness as their peak.[1]

[1] S. v. 43.

3. **Kūṭa Sutta.**—Just as all the rafters slope to the peak, so do the seven *bojjhaṅgas* tend towards *nibbāna*.[1]

[1] S. v. 75.

4. **Kūṭa Sutta.**—Two discourses of similar import, preached to **Anāthapiṇḍika.** When a peaked house is unthatched, the peak, the roof-beams

and the walls are all unprotected. When thought is unguarded all actions also are unguarded.[1]

[1] A. i. 261 f.

6. **Kūṭa Sutta.**—Of the five powers (*saddhā, hiri, ottappa, viriya, paññā*) the last is the peak.[1]

[1] A. iii. 10.

6. **Kūṭa Sutta.**—Of the five powers, (*saddhā, viriya, sati, samādhi, paññā*) the last is the peak.[1]

[1] A. iii. 12.

Kūṭatissa Vihāra.—A monastery in Ceylon. **Sena II.** gave to it a maintenance village.[1]

[1] Cv. li. 74. In the pillar inscription of Mahinda IV. in Polonnaruva it is mentioned as the *Kuṭutisa-rad-maha-veher* (Ep. Zey. ii. 50).

Kūṭadanta.—A very learned brahmin of **Khānumata,** which village had been given to him by King **Bimbisāra** as a *brahmadeyya*. The Buddha arrived at **Khānumata** when Kūṭadanta was making preparations for a great sacrifice and, wishing this sacrifice to be successful, he consulted the Buddha on the holding of sacrifices. The Buddha preached to him the **Kūṭadanta Sutta.** At the end of the discourse he became a *sotāpanna*.[1] The conversion of Kūṭadanta is considered one of the great spiritual victories won by the Buddha.[2] As a disputant, Kūṭadanta is classed with **Ambaṭṭhaka, Soṇadaṇḍa** and **Saccaka.**[3]

[1] D. i. 127 ff. [2] *E.g.*, J. vi. 329. [3] *E.g.*, MA. ii. 697.

Kūṭadanta Sutta.—Preached at **Khānumata. Kūṭadanta** consults the Buddha on the best way of making a sacrifice efficacious, and the Buddha tells him of a sacrifice held in days of yore by King **Mahā Vijitāvī,** under the guidance of his enlightened purohita. The sacrifice is undertaken with the co-operation of the four divisions of the king's subjects. The king has eight personal qualifications, as has his chaplain. No living thing is injured; all the labour is voluntary and the sacrifice is offered, not only on behalf of the king, but of all the good. No regrets are felt at any stage of the sacrifice.

The Buddha then proceeds to tell Kūṭadanta of other forms of "sacrifice" more potent than the gift of material things, and ends the sutta with a description of arahantship.

At the conclusion of the discourse Kūṭadanta declares himself to be a follower of the Buddha.[1]

[1] D. i. 127 ff.

1. **Kūṭavāṇija Jātaka** (No. 98).—The Bodhisatta was once a merchant named **Paṇḍita** and entered into partnership with a dishonest man, **Atipaṇḍita.** When the time came for dividing the profits the latter claimed a larger share, for he, as his name showed, was the "brains" of the business. To settle the dispute he hid his father in a hollow tree, and feigning to consult a Tree-sprite, referred the matter to the Tree. Paṇḍita suspecting the ruse, lighted a fire at the foot of the tree and thus exposed the cheat.

The story was related in reference to a cheating merchant of **Sāvatthi,** who is identified with Atipaṇḍita. He tried to rob his honest partner, always putting off his claims, in the hope that he would die from the hardships suffered in a long journey they had undertaken for trade.[1]

[1] J. i. 404 f.

2. **Kūṭavāṇija Jātaka** (No. 218).—A villager once deposited five hundred ploughshares with a friend in the town, but when he came to claim them, he was told that they had been eaten by mice, and was shown the dung the mice had left behind. Some time later the villager took his friend's son to bathe, hid him in a house, and reported to the townsman that the boy had been carried off by a hawk. When he was taken before the judge, who was the Bodhisatta, he protested that in a place where mice ate ploughshares a hawk could easily carry off a boy. The Bodhisatta settled their dispute.[1]

The introductory story is similar to that of No. 1 above.

[1] J. ii. 181 ff.

Kūṭavinicchayaka-peta.—One of **Bimbisāra's** judges, who was a cheat, a slanderer, and a taker of bribes, once observed the fast for half a day through a friend's persuasion. He died that night and was born as a *Vemānika-peta.* He enjoyed divine pleasures, but was condemned to eat the flesh off his own back in expiation of his evil deeds.

Nārada saw this peta and reported his story to the Buddha.[1]

[1] Pv. iii. 9; PvA. 209 f.

Kūṭāgārasālā.—A hall in the **Mahāvana** near **Vesāli.** The Buddha stayed there on several occasions, and in the books are found records of various eminent persons who visited him there and of his conversations with them. Among such visitors are mentioned several Licchavi chiefs, **Mahāli Oṭṭhatthaddha,**[1] **Nandaka,**[2] **Sunakkhatta,**[3] **Bhaddiya,**[4] **Sāḷha** and

[1] D. i. 150 ff.; S. i. 230 f.; iii. 68 f.; A. v. 86 f.; several visits of Mahāli are mentioned; for details see *s.v.* **Mahāli.** BuA. (p. 3) mentions that the Buddha spent his sixth rainy season in the Kūṭāgārasālā.

[2] S. v. 389.

[3] M. ii. 252.

[4] A. ii. 190 f.

Abhaya,[5] all attended by numerous retinues; their senāpati, **Sīha,** who went with five hundred chariots, having only decided after much hesitation to see the Buddha[6]; the Jaina **Saccaka,** whom the Buddha won only after much argumentation, as described in the **Cūḷa-** and the **Mahā-Saccaka** Suttas[7]; the householder **Ugga** of Vesāli, acclaimed by the Buddha for the possession of eight eminent qualities[8]; the upāsaka **Vāseṭṭha,**[9] the two goddesses, daughters of **Pajjunna,** both known as **Kokanadā**[10]; and the brahmin **Piṅgiyānī.**[11]

The Licchavis waited on the Buddha and ministered to him during his stay in the Kūṭāgārasālā, and it is said that they were of various hues: some blue, others yellow, etc. And Piṅgiyānī, seeing the Buddha shining in their midst, surpassing them all, once uttered the Buddha's praises in verse, winning, as reward from the Licchavis, five hundred upper garments, all of which, he, in turn, presented to the Buddha.[12] On one occasion, when the Buddha was preaching to the monks regarding the six spheres of sense contact, **Māra** arranged an earthquake to break the monks' concentration, but failed to achieve his object.[13] Several Jātakas were related by the Buddha in the Kūṭāgārasālā: the **Sigāla,**[14] the **Telovāda,**[15] the **Bāhiya,**[16] and the **Ekapanna.**[17] It was here that the Buddha finally agreed to grant the request of the five hundred Sākyan women, led by **Pajāpatī Gotamī,** that they might be ordained as nuns. They had followed the Buddha hither from **Kapilavatthu.**[18] The Buddha gave Pajāpati Gotamī, at her special request, a summary of his doctrine.[19] It was also at the Kūṭāgārasālā that the Buddha uttered his prophecy as to the ultimate downfall of the Licchavis.[20]

It was customary for the Buddha, when staying at the Kūṭāgārasālā, to spend the noonday siesta in the woods outside the **Mahāvana,** at the foot of a tree; visitors coming at that time would, if their desire to see him was insistent,[21] seek him there or be conducted to him. Sometimes he would express his desire to see no one during such a retreat, except the monk who brought him his food.

On one occasion the retreat lasted a fortnight, and on his return he found that a large number of monks had committed suicide as a result

[5] *Ibid.*, 200.

[6] A iii. 38 f.; iv. 79, 179 ff.

[7] M. i. 227 ff.; 237 ff.; the Licchavi **Dummukha** is also mentioned (M. i. 234) as having been present when Saccaka argued with the Buddha.

[8] A. iii. 49; iv. 208 f.; S. iv. 109.

[9] A. iv. 258 f.

[10] S. i. 29 f.

[11] A. iii. 237 f.

[12] A. iii. 239 f.

[13] S. i. 112.

[14] J. ii. 5.

[15] *Ibid.*, 262.

[16] J. i. 420.

[17] *Ibid.*, 504.

[18] A. iv. 274 f.; Vin. ii. 253 f.; J. ii. 392.

[19] A. iv. 280.

[20] S. ii. 267 f.

[21] See, *e.g.*, D. i. 151; A. iii. 75.

of a sermon he had preached to them before his retreat on the unloveliness of the body. He then caused the monks to be assembled, and asked them to concentrate on breathing.[22] Sometimes the Buddha would walk from the Kūṭāgārasālā to places of interest in the neighbourhood —*e.g.*, the **Sārandada-cetiya**[23] and the **Cāpāla-cetiya.**[24] It was from the Cāpāla-cetiya, during one of these walks, that he gazed for the last time on Vesāli. He then returned to the Kūṭāgārasālā, where he announced that his death would take place within three months.[25]

According to Buddhaghosa,[26] there was a monastery (*saṅghārāma*) built for the monks in the Mahāvana. Part of it consisted of a storeyed house, with a hall below surrounded only by pillars. These pillars held the gabled room which formed the main part of the Buddha's Gandhakuṭi there. The hall lay from north to south and faced east,[27] and from this hall the whole monastery came to be known as the Kūṭāgārasālā. There was a sick ward attached to the monastery, where the Buddha would often visit the patients and talk with them.[28]

The books also contain the names of others who stayed at the Kūṭāgārasālā when the Buddha was in residence—*e.g.*, **Ānanda,** who was visited there by the Licchavis **Abhaya** and **Paṇḍitakumāra**[29]; **Anuruddha,** who lived there in a forest hut[30]; **Nāgita,** the Buddha's former attendant, and Nāgita's nephew the novice **Sīha**[31]; also **Cāla, Upacāla, Kakkaṭa, Kalimbha, Nikaṭa,** and **Kaṭissaha,** all of whom left the Kūṭāgārasālā and retired to the **Gosiṅgasālavana,** when the visits of the Licchavis to the Buddha became disturbing to their solitude.[32]

In later times **Yasa Kākaṇḍakaputta** is mentioned as having stayed there.[33]

Eighteen thousand monks under **Mahā-Buddharakkhita** went from the monastery in Mahāvana in Vesāli to the foundation ceremony of the Mahā Thupa.[34]

According to the Northern books,[35] the Kūṭāgārasālā was on the banks of the lake Markaṭā (Markaṭahradatīre).

[22] S. v. 320 f.
[23] A. iii. 167.
[24] S. v. 258; A. iv. 308 f.
[25] D. ii. 119 f.; S. v. 258 ff.
[26] DA. i. 310; MA. i. 450.
[27] DA. i. 311.
[28] *E.g.*, S. iv. 210 f.; A. iii. 142.
[29] A. i. 220.
[30] S. iii. 116; iv. 380.
[31] D. i. 151.
[32] A. v. 133 f.
[33] Sp. i. 34; Mhv. iv. 12; Dpv. v. 29.
[34] Mhv. xxix. 33.
[35] Dvy. 136, 200; AvŚ. 8; Mtu. i. 300.

Kūṭāli Vihāra.—A monastery in **Rohaṇa,** founded by **Kākavaṇṇatissa.**[1] There **Malaya-Deva Thera** once preached the **Cha-Cakka Sutta,** and sixty

[1] Mhv. xxii. 23.

monks who listened to him became arahants.[2] This may be identical with the **Kuṭelitissa Vihāra** (*q.v.*).

[2] MA. ii. 1024.

Keka.—A kingdom in **Mahiṃsakaraṭṭha. Ajjuna Sahassabāhu** once ruled there. *v.l.* **Kekaya.**[1]

[1] J. v. 145.

Kekaka.—A city, regarded in ancient times as one of the three chief cities of Jambudīpa, the others being **Uttarapañcāla** and **Indapatta.** *v.l.* **Kekaya.**[1]

[1] J. ii. 213.

Kekakā.—The people of **Kekaka.**[1]

[1] J. ii. 214; v. 267, 273; vi. 280, 281.

Kekaya.—Another name for **Keka** and **Kekaka.**[1]

[1] J. ii. 214.

Kekarājā.—The king of **Kekaka.**[1]

[1] J. vi. 280, 281.

Kekkhārupupphiya.—See **Kakkāru.**

Keṇiya.—See **Keniya.**

Ketakapupphiya Thera.—An arahant. Ninety-one kappas ago he saw the Buddha **Vipassī** (?) on the banks of the **Vinatā** and gave him a *ketaka*-flower.[1] His stanzas are given in the *Theragāthā Commentary* under two names: **Abhaya** and **Kappaṭakura.**

[1] Ap. ii. 449 f.

Ketakavana.—A forest near **Naḷakapāna** in **Kosala.** There the Buddha preached the **Naḷapāna Jātaka.**[1]

[1] J. i. 170.

1. **Ketumatī.**—The future name of **Bārāṇasī.** It will be at the head of eighty-four thousand towns, the capital of the Cakkavatti **Saṅkha** and the birthplace of the Buddha **Metteyya.**[1]

[1] D. iii. 75 f.; J. vi. 594; Anāgat., vv. 8, 30; according to v. 8 it is the same as Kusāvatī.

2. **Ketumatī.**—A river in the Himālaya region. **Vessantara,** with his wife and children, had a meal on its banks, bathed and drank in the river, and from there went to **Nālika.**[1]

[1] J. vi. 518 f.

3. **Ketumatī.**—The palace of the deva **Mahāsena** (a previous birth of **Nāgasena**).[1]

[1] Mil., p. 6.

4. **Ketumatī.**—The Pāli name for the Burmese city of Taungu.[1]

Ketumatī is in **Jeyyavaḍḍhanaraṭṭha.** It was once the capital of King Mahāsirijeyyasūra who possessed a famous elephant, called Devanāga. Buddhism was established in Ketumatī by a monk from Ceylon who was named Mahāparakkama. It later became the residence of famous monks.[2]

[1] Bode: *op. cit.*, 45. [2] Sās., pp. 80, 81; see also 101, 118, 162.

Ketumā.—A Pacceka Buddha, mentioned in a list of their names.[1]

[1] M. iii. 70; ApA. i. 107.

Ketumbarāga.—The name of a Pacceka Buddha.[1]

[1] M. iii. 70; Ap. i. 107.

1. **Keniya** (*v.l.* **Keṇiya**).—A Jaṭila. He lived in **Āpaṇa,** and when the Buddha once stayed there with one thousand three hundred and fifty monks, Keniya visited the Buddha, bringing various kinds of drinks, which he gave to him and to the monks. The following day he invited the whole company to a meal and showed great hospitality. It was as a result of the drinks offered by Keniya that the Buddha laid down a rule as to which drinks were permissible for monks and which were not.[1]

According to the *Sutta Nipāta*,[2] it was owing to the elaborate preparations made by Keniya for the meal to the Buddha and the Saṅgha that the brahmin **Sela,** friend and counsellor of Keniya, came to discover the Buddha's presence in Āpaṇa. The result was the conversion and ordination of Sela and his three hundred pupils.

Buddhaghosa says[3] that Keniya was a *mahāsāla*-brahmin, and that he became a Jaṭila with the object of protecting his wealth. He bought some land from the king and built his hermitage there, and became the protector (*nissaya*) of one thousand families. In his hermitage was a

[1] Vin. i. 245 f. [2] p. 104; M. ii. 146 f.; see also ThagA. ii. 47.
[3] SNA. ii. 440; MA. ii. 779; Ap. i. 318.

palm tree which yielded a golden nut each day. Keniya was a yellow-robed ascetic by day; by night he enjoyed the pleasures of the senses. On his first visit to the Buddha he took five hundred pingo-loads of *badarapāna*[4] (? grape juice).

Keniya is mentioned[5] as an example of one of the eight classes of ascetics—those who maintain wife and children (*sa-puttabhariya*).

[4] SNA. ii. 446. [5] *E.g.*, DA. i. 270; see also DhA. i. 323; UdA. 241.

2. **Keniya.**—In the *Apadāna*[1] **Mahā Kappina** is mentioned as having belonged to the **Keniya-jāti.** Perhaps this is a wrong reading; the corresponding verse in *ThagA.* (i. 510) gives **Koliya.**

[1] ii. 469, v. 16.

Kebukā.—A river. It had to be crossed in order to reach the territory of the **Garuḍa** king who carried away the queen **Kākāti.**[1]

The scholiast says it was beyond the **Jambudīpasamudda.** Elsewhere, in the *Jātaka Commentary*,[2] *Kekuba* is a name for water.

[1] J. iii. 91, 92. [2] J. vi. 42.

Keraḷa.—A country in South India, along the Malabar coast. See **Keraḷā.**

Keraḷasīhamuttara.—A Damiḷa chief, an ally of **Kulasekhara.**[1] He later formed a friendship with **Laṅkāpura.**[2]

[1] Cv. lxxvi. 141. [2] *Ibid.*, lxxvii. 7.

Keraḷā.—The people of **Keraḷa.** The Keraḷas served as mercenary soldiers to the kings of Ceylon. They rebelled against **Mahinda V.** and governed certain parts of the country.[1] They fought in the army of **Parakkamabāhu I.** against **Gajabāhu.**[2] Later, when Parakkamabāhu's forces were employed in **Rohaṇa,** the Keraḷa mercenaries in **Koṭṭhasāra** conspired with others to capture **Rājaraṭṭha,** but their attempt was foiled.[3] The Keraḷas formed the largest part of **Māgha's** army which devastated Ceylon, and Māgha gave over to them, for their use, whatever they coveted in the conquered territory. They overran the country, carrying destruction wherever they went.[4] Later, however, they suffered severe defeat at the hands of **Parakkamabāhu II.**[5] Once a **Paṇḍu** king fled from the **Coḷa** king and took refuge among the Keraḷas.[6]

[1] Cv. lv. 5, 12.
[2] Cv. lxix. 18; lxx. 230.
[3] Cv. lxxiv. 44 f.
[4] Cv. lxxx. 61, 76; lxxi. 4.
[5] Cv. lxxxiii. 20.
[6] Cv. liii. 9; Cv. *Trs.* i. 172, n. 3.

Kelavāhā.—See **Telavāhā.**

1. **Kelāsa.**—A mountain range in **Himavā.** It is one of the five ranges which stand round **Anotatta** and is of silver colour, two hundred leagues high, bent inwards "like a crow's beak."[1] It is sixty leagues in breadth, and **Āḷavaka,** on his way to his house, having heard to his great anger that the Buddha was there, placed his left foot on **Manosilātala** and his right on **Kelāsakūṭa.** The touch of his foot sent pieces of the rock flying, and his shout "I am Āḷavaka" was heard throughout Jambudīpa.[2]

Kelāsa is often used in similes to describe an object that is perfectly white,[3] very stately,[4] or difficult to destroy.[5]

In the Mahāvastu,[6] Kailāśa is mentioned as the abode of the Kinnaras.

In Sanskrit mythology, Kailāśa is given as the abode of the gods, chiefly Śiva and Kubera.[7]

[1] SNA. ii. 437 f.; MA. ii. 585: UdA. 300; AA. ii. 759.

[2] SNA. i. 223; SA. i. 248.

[3] *E.g.*, J. iv. 232; vi. 490, 515; the horse Kanthaka (Mbv. 26); DhA. i. 192; Cv. lxxiii. 114.

[4] *E.g.*, an elephant's head or a big building (J. i. 321; v. 52, 53); Cv. lxxviii. 77.

[5] *E.g.*, J. v. 39.

[6] ii. 97, 109; see also iii. 309, 438.

[7] See, *e.g.*, Epic Mythology *passim* and Ved. Ind. *s.v.* The mountain range has been identified as belonging to the trans-Himālayan system and consisting of a group of mountains over twenty thousand feet in height (see Cv. *Trs.* i. 280, n. 4).

2. **Kelāsa.**—A vihāra in Ceylon, probably in the district of **Maṅgana.** At one time sixty thousand monks dwelt there with **Khuddatissa** at their head.[1] This is probably not the Kelāsa vihāra (in Jambudīpa ?) whence, we are told, **Suriyagotta** came with ninety thousand monks to the foundation of the **Mahā Thūpa.**[2]

[1] M. xxxii. 53.

[2] *Ibid.*, xxix. 43.

Keḷivāta.—A district or village in Ceylon. **Aggabodhi I.** built there the **Sumanapabbata-vihāra.**[1]

[1] Cv. xlii. 19.

Keḷisīla Jātaka (No. 202).—**Brahmadatta,** king of Benares, could not look upon anyone old or decrepit without playing jokes on them. He made old men roll about on the ground and played practical jokes on old women. His friends behaved likewise. All old people left his country; no parents or aged persons remained to be tended by the young, and newcomers among the gods were few in number. **Sakka** (the Bodhisatta), wishing to teach the king a lesson, once appeared before him in the guise of an old man, with two jars of butter milk in a crazy old cart, having willed that only the king should be able to see him. The king was riding his state elephant, and when he asked the old carter to move the latter dashed the two jars on the king's head and the onlookers laughed to see the milk dripping down his face. Resuming Sakka's form, the Bodhisatta admonished the king.

The story was related to account for **Lakuṇṭaka Bhaddiya's** deformity.[1]

[1] J. ii. 142-4.

1. **Kevaṭṭa** (*v.l.* **Kevaddha**).—A householder of **Nālandā.** Once when the Buddha was staying in the **Pāvārika-ambavana** at Nālandā, Kevaṭṭa visited him. The interview is recorded in the **Kevaṭṭa Sutta.**[1]

Buddhaghosa[2] speaks of him as a young householder, distinguished and wealthy, belonging to the *gahapati-mahā-sāla-kula,* with forty crores of wealth. He was possessed of very great piety, and it was his extreme devotion to the Buddha which led him to make the request contained in the Kevaṭṭa Sutta.

[1] D. i. 211 ff.

[2] DA. i. 388.

2. **Kevaṭṭa.**—Chaplain of **Cūḷani-Brahmadatta,** king of **Uttarapañcāla.** He was wise and learned and clever in device; the king followed his counsel and conquered all the territories of India except that of King **Videha** in **Mithilā.**[1] When at last Brahmadatta laid siege to Mithilā, Kevaṭṭa was responsible for the details of the siege, but his plans were upset by **Mahosadha,** who, though his junior in age, was far wiser. At one stage of the struggle Kevaṭṭa suggested that a trial of intellect be arranged between him and Mahosadha, the result of the conquest to decide the victory of Brahmadatta or Videha. The challenge was accepted, but Mahosadha, by a ruse, made Kevaṭṭa appear as though paying obeisance to him and rubbed Kevaṭṭa's head in the dust, bruising it. After the return, in disgrace, of Brahmadatta to Uttarapañcāla, Kevaṭṭa meditated revenge through the instrumentality of **Pañcāla-caṇḍī.** Kevaṭṭa visited Mithilā with a proposal that Videha should go to Uttarapañcāla and marry Pañcālacaṇḍī. During this visit, Kevaṭṭa went to visit Mahosadha, but the latter, guessing that the whole thing was a plot to kill Videha, refused to see Kevaṭṭa and caused him to be ill-treated.[2] Kevaṭṭa was everywhere defeated in his schemes by Mahosadha.[3]

[1] J. vi. 391-5.

[2] *Ibid.,* 400-19.

[3] *Ibid.,* 424, 438, 461; for details see the **Mahā Umagga Jātaka.**

Kevaṭṭa is identified with **Devadatta.**[4] He is mentioned as having belonged to the **Kosiyagotta** and is addressed as **Kosiya.**[5]

[4] J. vi. 478. [5] *Ibid.*, 418, 419.

Kevaṭṭa (*v.l.* **Kevaḍḍha**) **Sutta.**—Preached in the **Pārāvārika-ambavana** in **Nālandā. Kevaṭṭa** (1) visits the Buddha and asks him to order a monk to perform some mystic wonder in order to increase the faith of the Buddha's followers. The Buddha expresses his hatred of miracles and tells Kevaṭṭa that a greater and better wonder than any or all of them is education in the system of self-training which culminates in Arahantship. In illustration of this, he relates a legend: A monk, seeking the answer to the question "Where do the elements pass away?" goes up and up, by the power of his *iddhi*, from world to world, asking the gods for an answer. In each heaven he is referred to those who are higher up, until he comes at last to the Great **Brahmā** himself, who takes him aside and tells him that he does not know the answer. The monk seeks the Buddha, who explains to him that the question is wrongly put; it should be, "Where do the elements find no foothold; where do *nāma* and *rūpa* pass away?" And the answer is, "In the mind of the arahant, when intellect (*viññāṇa*) ceases, then *nāma* and *rūpa* cease."[1]

[1] D. i. 211 ff.; *cp.* Ud. i. 10.

Kevaṭṭagambhīra.—A village in **Rohaṇa,** given by **Dappula** to the **Nāga-vihara.**[1]

[1] Cv. xlv. 58.

Kevaṭṭadvāra.—One of the gates of Benares. The village near it bore the same name and was the residence of **Lakhumā.**[1]

[1] VvA. 97 f.

Kesa.—See **Kesi.**

Kesakambala.—See **Ajita Kesakambala.**

Kesakambala Sutta.—Just as the hair blanket is reckoned the meanest and lowest of all woven garments, even so, of all theories advanced by recluses, that of **Makkhali** is the meanest. Makkhali proclaims that there is no doing of a deed, there is nothing done and no energy to do.[1]

[1] A. i. 286 f.

Kesakārī.—A brahmin maiden of **Bārāṇasī.** Having seen a young monk begging alms, she asked her mother why men in the prime of life should renounce the world. Her mother told her of the appearance of the Buddha in the world. An upāsaka who heard the conversation told her more of the Buddha and taught her the *saraṇas* and the *sīlas*. Later he told her of the nature of the body, and she, reflecting thereon, became a *sotāpanna*. After death she became one of **Sakka's** women-attendants, and her story was related to **Moggallāna** by Sakka.[1]

[1] Vv. i. 17; VvA. 86 f.

Kesadhātu.—A very high rank bestowed by the Sinhalese kings. It appears to have corresponded to the modern Orders. It may have originated in the members of the Order being entrusted with the care of the Hair Relic (*Kesadhātu*), which was brought to Ceylon in the reign of **Moggallāna I.**[1] This duty afterwards evidently became a mere formality. The word Kesadhātu may be an abbreviation of the fuller Kesadhātunāyaka.

We first come across the term in the time of **Vijayabāhu I.**, when a Kesadhātu, **Kassapa** by name, became governor of **Rohaṇa.**[2] **Parakkamabāhu I.** conferred the title on his general, the **Daṇḍādhināyaka Rakkha.**[3]

[1] Cv. xxxix. 49. [2] *Ibid.*, lvii. 65 f. [3] *Ibid.*, lxx. 19.

Kesadhātuvaṃsa.—A book containing the history of the Buddha's Hair Relic. The Relic was brought to Ceylon from India by **Silākāla** in the reign of **Moggallāna I.** The king placed it in a crystal casket in a beautiful building with a picture of **Dīpaṅkara's** city (?) and established a festival in its honour. Silākāla was appointed custodian of the Relic.[1]

The Kesadhātuvaṃsa is not now available. It was evidently easily obtainable at the time of the writing of the first part of the *Cūlavaṃsa.*[2] It seems to have been quite distinct from the **Chakesadhātuvaṃsa** (*q.v.*).

[1] Cv. xxxix. 49 ff. [2] See, *e.g.*, Cv. xxxix. 56.

Kesaputta.—A township of the **Kosalans** and the residence of the **Kālāmas.** The Buddha once stayed there, on which occasion he preached the **Kesaputtiya Suttas.**[1]

[1] A. i. 188.

Kesaputtiya Suttā.—A group of suttas preached to the **Kālāmas** of **Kesaputta.** There need be no official tradition, no authority, no subtle reasoning or the like, in order to ascertain the true doctrine and distinguish it from the false. The noble disciple whose mind is pure has four consolations. He knows that whether there be a next world or not his happiness is secure.[1]

[1] A. i. 188 f.

Kesaputtiyā.—The people of **Kesaputta**—the **Kālāmas.**[1] It is suggested that they may be identical with the Kesins of the *Śatapatha Brāhmaṇa.*[2]

[1] A. i. 188. [2] Law: *Geog.* p. 30 n.; PHAI. 118.

Kesarapupphiya Thera.—An arahant. Ninety-one kappas ago he was a *vijjādhara* in Himavā, and having seen the Buddha **Vessabhū,** gave him three *kesara*-flowers.[1]

[1] Ap. i. 187.

1. **Kesava.**—An ascetic in Himavā. His story is given in the **Kesava Jātaka.** He is identified with **Baka Brahmā.**[1] He is sometimes addressed as **Kesi.**[2]

[1] J. iii. 145; S. i. 144; SA. i. 165; MA. i. 555. [2] *E.g.*, J. iii. 144, 362.

2. **Kesava.**—An Ascetic, also called **Nārada.** He saw the Buddha **Atthadassī** and paid him homage. He was a previous birth of **Pavittha Thera,** who is evidently identical with **Ekadaṃsaniya.**[1]

[1] Ap. i. 168; ThagA. i. 185.

3. **Kesava.**—Another name for **Vāsudeva** (*q.v.*). It is said that he was so called on account of his beautiful hair (*kesasobhanatāya*).[1]

[1] J. iv. 84; PvA. 94.

Kesava Jātaka (No. 346).—The ascetic **Kesava** lived in Himavā with five hundred pupils. The Bodhisatta, having been born as **Kappa,** a brahmin of **Kāsī,** joined him and became his senior pupil. When the ascetics went to Benares for salt and vinegar, the king lodged them in his park and fed them, and when they returned to Himavā, persuaded Kesava to stay behind. Kesava fell ill of loneliness, and the five physicians of the king could not cure him. At his own request he was taken to the Himālaya by the king's minister, **Nārada,** and there, on seeing again his familiar haunts and his pupil Kappa, he immediately recovered, though his medicine was but the broth of wild rice.

The king of the Jātaka is **Ānanda,** Nārada is **Sāriputta,** and Kesava, **Baka Brahmā.**

The story was related to **Pasenadi.** Having discovered that **Anāthapiṇḍika** daily fed five hundred monks in his house, the king gave orders that the same should be done in his palace. One day he discovered that the monks would take the food from the palace, but would eat that which was given to them elsewhere by those who served them because they loved them. When the king reported this to the Buddha, the Buddha pointed out to him that the best food was that which was given in love; love was the best flavouring for food.[1]

According to the *Dhammapada Commentary*,[2] the king personally looked after the monks for seven days, after which he forgot about them and they were uncared for. Thereupon they omitted to go to the palace.

The story of the past as given in this Commentary differs considerably from the *Jātaka*-version. Here Kesava is described as a king who had left the world and become an ascetic. The ascetics left the royal park, disliking the noise there, but they left Kappa with Kesava. Soon after, Kappa went away, and it was then that Kesava fell ill.

Kesava is identified with the Bodhisatta, Kappa with Ānanda, the king of Benares with Moggallāna, and Nārada with Sāriputta.

It was this reluctance of the Sākyan monks to accept Pasenadi's hospitality which led him to seek marriage with a Sākyan maiden; but the Sākyans gave him **Vāsabhakhattiyā** (*q.v.*).

[1] J. iii. 142-5; iii. 362; S. i. 144; SA. i. 165. [2] DhA. i. 342 ff.

Kesārāma.—A park in the city of **Sīlavatī**. The Buddha **Dhammadassī** died there.[1]

[1] Bu. xvi. 25; BuA. 185.

1. **Kesi.**—A horse-trainer. He came to see the Buddha and became his follower as a result of the interview.[1] For details see **Kesi Sutta.**

[1] A. ii. 112 f.

2. **Kesi.**—**Buddhaghosa's** father. He lived in **Ghosagāma.**[1] *v.l.* **Kesa.**

[1] Gv. 66; *Buddhaghosuppatti*, p. 38; Sās. 29.

3. **Kesi.**—A noble steed belonging to **Ekarāja.**[1]

[1] J. vi. 135.

4. **Kesi.**—See **Kesava.**

Kesi Vagga.—The twelfth chapter of the *Catukka Nipāta* of the *Aṅguttara Nikāya*.[1] The first sutta is that of **Kesi,** the horse-trainer, and most of the suttas deal with the idea of "training." The Commentary calls it **Kosiya Vagga.**

[1] A. ii. 112-21.

Kesi Sutta.—The horse-trainer **Kesi** visits the Buddha, and in answer to a question says that he trains some horses by mildness, some by harshness, and others by both; those which do not submit to his training he destroys. The Buddha says that just so does he deal with men. Some he tames by mildness—telling them what is good and showing them the way to heaven; others by harshness—condemning the evils in them; yet others by both. Those who do not submit to this discipline he destroys, by refusing to admonish them.[1]

Buddhaghosa says[2] that the Kesi Sutta should be one of those used to explain the term *purisadamma-sārathī* in reference to the Buddha.

[1] A. ii. 112 f. [2] Sp. i. 120.

1. **Kesinī.**—One of the wives of **Ekarāja.**[1]

[1] J. vi. 134.

2. **Kesinī.**—Mother of **Buddhaghosa.**[1] The *Sāsanavaṃsa*[2] calls her **Kesī.**

[1] *Buddhaghosuppatti*, p. 38. [2] p. 29.

Kesī.—See **Kesinī.**

Kehāla.—See **Kohāla.**

Keheta.—A village in Ceylon, given by **Jeṭṭhatissa III.** for the maintenance of the **Gaṅgāmāti-vihāra.**[1]

[1] Cv. xliv. 99.

Kehella.—A village in Ceylon, the revenue from which **Aggabodhi III.** gave to the *padhānaghara* called **Mahallarāja.**[1]

[1] Cv. xliv. 120.

Koka.—A hunter. While on his way to the forest with his dogs he meets a monk. He bags no game that day and blames the monk, whom he again meets on his way home. Koka sets his dogs on the monk, and when the latter climbs a tree, pierces the soles of his feet with arrows. The monk's cloak falls upon the hunter, completely covering him. The dogs, thinking that the monk has fallen from the tree, devour their own master. The monk, fearing that he is to blame, seeks the Buddha, who reassures him and relates the story of a wicked physician who cajoled a boy into catching a snake, pretending that it was a bird. When the boy discovered that it was a snake, he threw it on the physician's head, who died from its bite.

The physician is identified with Koka.[1]

[1] DhA. iii. 31 f. The story of the past is evidently derived from the **Sāliya Jātaka**, which, however, according to the *Jātaka Commentary*, was related in reference, not to Koka, but to **Devadatta** (J. iii. 202 f.).

1. **Kokanada.**—The palace of **Bodhirājakumāra** (*q.v.*), to which he invited the Buddha and the monks to a meal when the Buddha was staying at **Bhesakalāvana**; the palace was just completed.[1] The artisan who built it was blinded, in case he should build another like it.[2] According to Buddhaghosa,[3] the palace was called Kokanada (lotus), because it was built in the form of a hanging lotus.

[1] Vin. ii. 127; iii. 199; M. ii. 91.
[2] J. iii. 157; but see DhA. iii. 134 f., where it is said that, warned by Bodhi's friend, **Sanjikāputta**, the builder escaped on a magic bird.
[3] MA. ii. 739.

2. **Kokanada.**—A lute (*vinā*) given by **Sakka** to **Sīlavatī, Kusa's** mother, and afterwards used by Kusa to win back **Pabhāvatī.**[1] It was so called either from the country of its origin or from its colour.[2]

[1] J. v. 281, 290.
[2] See Jāt. *Trs.* v. 143 n.

3. **Kokanada.**—See **Kokanuda.**

1. **Kokanadā.**—Two daughters of **Pajjunna,** both called **Kokanadā,** though the younger was sometimes called **Cūḷa-Kokanadā.** They visited the Buddha at the **Kūṭāgārasālā** and spoke verses in praise of the Buddha, the Dhamma and the Saṅgha.[1]

[1] S. i. 29 f.

2. **Kokanadā.**—One of the palaces of **Siddhattha Buddha** in his last lay life.[1]

[1] Bu. xvii. 14; BuA. (185) calls it **Padumā.**

Kokanuda (Kokanada).—A Paribbājaka. He meets **Ānanda** on the banks of the **Tapodā,** where they are both bathing, and enters into conversation with him. Kokanuda asks Ānanda a series of questions, such as whether the world is eternal, whether the Tathāgata lives after death, etc., all of which, Ānanda says, are impossible to answer, not because he himself does not know these things, but because he does know them. Finally, Kokanuda asks Ānanda who he is, and, on learning his identity, asks his pardon for his questions which he had asked in all ignorance.[1]

[1] A. v. 196 f.

Kokanuda Sutta.—The conversation between **Ānanda** and **Kokanuda** (*q.v.*).

Kokavāta.—A district in Ceylon. **Mahāsena** built there a great vihāra and constructed a tank.[1]

[1] Mhv. xxxvii. 42, 47.

Kokā.—A palace occupied by **Siddattha** Buddha in his last lay-life.[1]

[1] Bu. xvii. 14.

Kokāli.—The name of a country, a town and a seṭṭhi, all connected with **Kokālika.**[1] See **Kokālika** 2.

[1] SNA. 473; J. iv. 242.

1. **Kokālika (Kokāliya).**—A monk, one of the chief partisans of **Devadatta.** Knowing the Buddha's might, he was, at first, reluctant to join in Devadatta's plot against him, but later allowed himself to be persuaded on hearing the scheme explained.[1] When the monks blamed Devadatta for his misdeeds, Kokālika was always ready to defend him.[2] When Devadatta's gains diminished, Kokālika went about praising him, his birth, accomplishments and holiness, and many believed him.[3] He was a great friend of **Thullanandā.**[4] We are told that once he expressed resentment because he had never been asked to recite the texts; so one day the monks gave him his chance. He ate his favourite soup, and at sundown, wearing a blue lower robe and an outer robe of white and carrying an elegantly carved fan, he appeared in the assembly. But when he tried to recite sweat poured from his body and he was utterly confused. Henceforth the monks knew that his claim to learning was but pretence.[5] Several Jātakas are related showing how, in previous births also, Kokālika had come to grief because of his fondness for talk and how he had been the accomplice of Devadatta. He is identified with the jackal in the **Daddara Jātaka** (ii. 65 ff.) and the **Sīhakotthuka Jātaka** (ii. 108); the ass in the lion's skin in the **Sīhacamma** (ii. 110); the talkative tortoise in the **Kacchapa** (ii. 175); the crow who praised the jackal (Devadatta) in the **Jambukhādaka** (ii. 438); the young cuckoo who lost his life because he sang, in the **Kokālika** (iii. 102); the tawny-brown brahmin in the **Takkāriya** (iv. 242; but see **Kokālika** 2); and the wicked deity in the **Samuddavāṇija** (iv. 166).

Buddhaghosa[6] says that this Kokālika was a brahmin and a pupil of Devadatta, and that he was called Mahā Kokālika to distinguish him

[1] Vin. ii. 196; iii. 171.
[2] Vin. iii. 174.
[3] J. ii. 438 f.
[4] Vin. iv. 335.
[5] J. ii. 65 f.
[6] SNA. ii. 473; AA. ii. 850; SA. i. 167.

from another Kokālika who was similarly called **Cūḷa Kokālika** (see **Kokālika** 2). There seems to be great confusions in the stories of these two men—if they were really two. In the *Jātaka Commentary*, for instance, the introductory stories of several of the Jātakas[7] refer to the Takkāriya Jātaka for details of Kokālika, obviously having in mind Devadatta's partisan; but the introductory story of the Takkāriya Jātaka is identical with that related elsewhere of Cūḷa Kokālika.

In the **Vyaggha Jātaka**[8] Kokālika is mentioned as having tried to persuade **Sāriputta** and **Moggallāna** to go with him to his own country and as having been very angry when they refused. Possibly this story also refers to Cūḷa Kokālika. See also *s.v.* **Devadatta.**

[7] See also DhA. iv. 91 f., where the story of the talkative tortoise is related to Kokālika of the Kokālika Sutta (*q.v.*) which, according to Buddhaghosa (SNA. ii. 473) refers to Cūḷa Kokālika.

[8] J. ii. 356.

2. **Kokālika (Kokāliya).**—A monk, also called **Cūḷa Kokālika** to distinguish him from **Kokālika** (1). He was the son of **Kokāli-seṭṭhi** of **Kokāli** and lived in the monastery erected by his father in Kokāli. Once the two Chief Disciples, desiring quiet, spent the rainy season with him, he promising to tell nobody of their presence. After the rains, as the Elders were about to return, Kokālika informed the inhabitants of their stay and blamed them for not showing them hospitality. The townspeople hurried to the Elders with various offerings; these were, however, refused, and Kokālika, who had expected that the gifts would be given to him, was disappointed. The Elders promised the townsmen to visit them again, and on their return were accompanied by a large following of monks to whom the townsmen showed all honour. The gifts were divided among the monks, Kokālika not receiving a share. He thereupon became abusive, and the Chief Disciples left the place. The people were annoyed, and insisted that Kokālika should either bring them back or depart himself. The Elders refused to return, and Kokālika, in great anger, sought the Buddha at **Sāvatthi,** and in spite of his injunctions spoke ill of the Chief Disciples. Having three times accused the Elders of sinful desires, he left Jetavana, but boils immediately came out on his body, swelling and bursting. Groaning with pain, he fell down at the gate of **Jetavana.** His spiritual teacher, the *anāgāmi* Brahmā, **Tudu,** hearing his cries, came to him and begged him to seek forgiveness from the Elders. But he cursed the Brahmā and refused to listen to him. Kokālika died and was born in **Paduma-niraya.**[1]

[1] S. i. 149 ff.; A. v. 171 f.; SN. 123 f.; SNA. ii. 473 f.; J. iv. 242 f.; AA. ii. 850; SA. i. 167 f.; DhA. iv. 91 f. The different sources vary in a few minor details; the Jātaka version is the fullest.

It was in reference to this incident that the **Takkāriya Jātaka** was preached.

The Brahmā **Sahampati** informed the Buddha of Kokālika's birth in the Paduma-niraya.[2]

The Kokālika Sutta was preached in reference to this Kokālika. See also Kokālika (1).

Kokālika is mentioned as an example of a person guilty of misdemeanour regarding the Buddha's disciples (*Tathāgatasāvake micchāpaṭipanno*).[3]

[2] S. i. 151; SN. p. 125.

[3] AA. i. 335, 466.

Kokālika Jātaka (No. 331).—King **Brahmadatta** was very talkative, and his minister, the Bodhisatta, sought an opportunity of admonishing him. This opportunity occurred while they were watching a crow's nest in which a cuckoo had laid an egg. The crow watched over it and fed the young cuckoo after its birth. One day the cuckoo cried before it was grown up, and the crow killed it and threw it away. The king inquired of the Bodhisatta the reason for this, and he explained that the garrulous who talk in and out of season meet with a similar fate. The king was cured of his evil habit.

The story was told in reference to **Kokālika,** who is identified with the young cuckoo.[1]

[1] J. iii. 102 f.

1. **Kokālika (Kokāliya)**[1] **Sutta.**—The story of Kokālika—according to Buddhaghosa (SnA. ii. 473), to be distinguished as **Cūḷa Kokālika.** It contains the verses preached by the Buddha to Kokālika. The verses describe the evil of back-biting and the terrors that await the back-biter after death. The *Sutta Nipāta* contains twenty-two verses (657-78). The *Sutta Nipāta Commentary* says[2] that the last two stanzas are not explained in the *Mahā Aṭṭhakathā*, and that therefore they did not belong to the original sutta. Of the remaining twenty the last fourteen (663-76) are called by Buddhaghosa the **Turitavatthugāthā,** and he says that they were uttered by **Moggallāna** as Kokālika lay dying, by way of admonition, and that, according to others, **Mahā Brahma** was the speaker. The first three stanzas (658-60) are, in the *Saṃyutta Nikāya*,[3] attributed to **Tudu.** In the *Aṅguttara Nikāya*,[4] also, Tudu speaks them; but according to this version the Buddha repeats them.

[1] See **Kokālika** (2).

[2] p. 477 f.

[3] i. 149.

[4] v. 171-4; the verses are also found in A. ii. 3 and in S. i. 149 ff.; Netti. 132.

2. **Kokālika Sutta.**—Gives the story of **Kokālika** (2) speaking ill of **Sāriputta** and **Moggallāna** before the Buddha, of Kokālika's illness and death, of his admonition by **Tudu,** and of the announcement of his death and subsequent birth in the Padumaniraya by **Sahampatī** to the Buddha. A monk questions the Buddha on the duration of suffering in the Padumaniraya, and the Buddha proceeds to instruct him by means of various illustrations. The sutta ends with the repetition by the Buddha of Tudu's verses.[1]

[1] A. v. 171-4; also S. i. 149 ff.

3. **Kokālika Sutta.**—**Subrahmā** visits the Buddha at **Sāvatthī** and utters verses in reference to **Kokālika.** The man who tries to limit the illimitable becomes confused.[1]

[1] S. i. 148.

Kokila Vagga.—The fourth section of the *Catukka Nipāta* of the *Jātaka Commentary.*[1]

[1] J. iii. 102-32.

Kokilā.—Daughter of **Ekarāja** and sister of **Candakumāra.**[1]

[1] J. vi. 134.

Koṅgamaṅgala.—A Damiḷa chief, ally of **Kulasekhara.**[1]

[1] Cv. lxxvii. 80.

Koṅgu.—The name of two districts in South India.[1] Elsewhere[2] they are spoken of as **Teṅkoṅgu** and **Vaḍakoṅgu.**

[1] Cv. lxxvi. 173. [2] *Ibid.*, 288.

Koccha.—See **Piṅgalakoccha.**

Kocchagalla.—A Sāmaṇera who went from Ceylon to **Amarapura** in 1662 of the Kaliyuga era.[1]

[1] Sās. 135.

1. **Koñca.**—See **Kañcana** (1).

2. **Koñca.**—One of the three palaces of **Vidhura-paṇḍita.**[1]

[1] J. vi. 289.

3. **Koñca.**—King of **Mantāvatī,** and father of **Sumedhā.**[1]

[1] Thig. 448; ThigA. 272 f., 281.

Koñcā.—One of the palaces occupied by **Dīpaṅkara** Buddha in his last lay life.[1]

[1] Bu. ii. 208.

Koṭa.—A Tamil general in charge of the fortification at **Koṭanagara**, which was captured by **Duṭṭhagāmaṇī** in his campaign against the Tamils.[1]

[1] Mhv. xxv. 13.

Koṭagerukapāsāda.—A building attached to the **Cittalapabbata-vihāra**. **Bhāgiṇeyya-Saṅgharakkhita** once lived there, and, during his illness, eight thousand arahants and **Sakka**, with the devas of the two deva-worlds, waited on him.[1]

[1] MṬ. 552.

Koṭapabbata (Koṭipabbata).—A mountain in **Rohaṇa**; near it was the village of **Kitti.**[1] There was a monastery on Koṭapabbatta called the **Koṭapabbata-vihāra.** This was the residence of the Sāmaṇera who was afterwards born as **Duṭṭhagāmaṇī**[2]; also of **Mahā-Summa** Thera,[3] of **Asubhakammika-Tissa** and of his teacher **Mahā-Tissa.**[4] The Vihāra was near **Mahāgāma.**[5]

The *Visuddhimagga*[6] mentions an Elder, **Tissa,** of Koṭa (Koṭi) pabbata, who, having attained arahantship through meditation on breathing, was able to limit the term of his life. According to the *Dhammapada Commentary,*[7] an Elder named **Anula** lived in the monastery during the time of Duṭṭhagāmaṇī, and the village **Bhokkanta,** residence of **Sumanā,** wife of **Lakuṇṭaka Atimbara,** was in its vicinity. It was probably the same as **Goṭapabbata**[8] (*q.v.*). The **Nāgaleṇa** was in the Koṭapabbata-vihāra.[9]

[1] Mhv. xxiii. 55.
[2] *Ibid.*, xxii. 25.
[3] *Ibid.*, xxiii. 61.
[4] MṬ. 553.
[5] *Ibid.*
[6] p. 292.
[7] iv. 50.
[8] See Mhv. xxxv. 124; MṬ. 657.
[9] DA. ii. 695.

Koṭamalaya (? more probably **Koṭṭhamalaya**).—A mountainous region in South Ceylon, whither **Duṭṭhagāmaṇī** fled from his father's wrath, and where he lived while making preparations for his campaign.[1] *v.l.* **Koṭṭamalaya, Koṭṭhamalaya, Koḷambamalaya.**

[1] Mhv. xxiv. 7; xxxii. 29; MṬ. 332, 430.

Koṭalla.—Evidently the Pāli equivalent of **Kauṭilya.** He is mentioned in the Cūḷavaṃsa as the author of a work on politics[1] and also of a work on methods of warfare.[2]

[1] Cv. lxiv. 3.
[2] *Ibid.*, lxx. 56; see also Cv. *Trs.* i. 243 n. 1 and 291, n. 3.

Koṭigāma.—A village in the vicinity of **Bhaddiyanagara.** The village was one *gāvuta* distant from the Ganges.[1] The Buddha went there from Bhaddiyanagara. **Bhaddaji** preceded the Buddha to Koṭigāma and awaited his arrival there. The people, led by **Nanduttara,** made ready a meal and provided boats in which the Buddha and the monks might cross the river. In the middle of the river, submerged in the water, stood the palace once occupied by **Mahāpanāda.**[2] During his last tour the Buddha crossed the river at **Pāṭaligāma,** went on to Koṭigāma, and remained in that village preaching to the monks. Hearing that the Buddha was there, **Ambapāli** and hosts of **Licchavis** came from **Vesāli** to visit him, and Ambapāli gave him a meal. From Koṭigāma the Buddha went to **Nādikā.**[3]

Buddhaghosa says[4] that the village was so called because it was built near the dome (*koṭi* or *thūpikā*) of Mahāpanāda's palace.

According to the *Saṃyutta Nikāya*,[5] Koṭigāma was a village of the **Vajjians.**

1 MT. 560.
2 J. ii. 332 f.; ThagA. i. 287 f.; Mhv. xxxi. 5 f.
3 Vin. i. 230 f.; D. ii. 90 f.
4 DA. ii. 542; iii. 856.
5 v. 431.

Koṭigāma Vagga.—The third chapter of the *Sacca Saṃyutta* of the *Saṃyutta Nikāya*.[1] The first sutta was preached at **Koṭigāma.**

1 S. v. 431-7.

Koṭipabbata.—See **Koṭapabbata.**

Koṭipassāva.—A monastery built by **Dhātusena.**[1] If it be identical with **Koṭipassāvana** (*q.v.*), it was merely restored by Dhātusena.

1 Cv. xxxviii. 46.

Koṭipassāvana.—A monastery erected by **Mahānāma.**[1] It is probably the same as **Koṭipassāva.**

1 Cv. xxxvii. 212.

Koṭisanthāra.—In the *Jātakas* mention is made[1] of the Buddha when he wished to address the monks of Jetavana, asking **Ānanda** to summon them to the Koṭisanthāra and ordering that a seat be prepared for him at the entrance to the **Gandhakuṭi.** Koṭisanthāra was probably the name given to that part of the Jetavana grounds just outside the Buddha's own apartments. It may have been so called in reference to the fact that **Anāthapiṇḍika** bought the land by spreading on it a crore of *kahā-*

1 *E.g.*, J. iii. 18; 375, 397; J. iv. 113.

paṇas (*kahāpaṇa-koṭi-santhārena*[2]). Or the name may have been restricted to the part actually covered by the pieces of money, for we are told[3] that the money was not sufficient to cover the whole of the ground. There were buildings in the Koṭisanthāra, the monks living in these buildings being referred to as "*Antokoṭisanthāre vasantā.*"[4] Koṭisanthāra is generally translated as The Golden Pavement,[5] which seems to be a wrong rendering.

[2] J. i. 94.
[3] Vin. ii. 159.
[4] *E.g.*, J. iv. 113.
[5] *E.g.*, Jāt. *Trs.* iii. 12; iv. 71.

Koṭisimbali Jātaka (No. 412).—A Garuḍa-king seized a Nāga-king, and when the Nāga coiled himself round a banyan-tree the Garuḍa uprooted the banyan and took it with him. He ate the Nāga's fat seated on a *koṭisimbali*-tree, and threw away the banyan and the Nāga's carcase. A bird who was in the banyan-tree left it and took up his abode in the *simbali*. The Bodhisatta, who was a tree-sprite in the simbali, trembled at the sight of the tiny bird, because the sprite knew that from the bird's droppings huge trees would spring up and kill the simbali. The Garuḍa, seeing the sprite trembling, asked the reason, and on learning it frightened the bird away. It is right to distrust where distrust is proper.

The story was related to five hundred monks who were in danger of being overcome by sinful desires.[1] *Cf.* the **Pālasa Jātaka.**

[1] J. iii. 397 ff.

Koṭisimbali-Niraya.—A Niraya where those guilty of misdemeanours, such as adultery, are born.[1]

[1] J. v. 275.

Koṭumbara.—A country celebrated for the excellence of its cloth.[1] *v.l.* **Kodumbara.**

[1] J. vi. 51 (also 47), 500, 501; Mil. 2, 331.

Koṭumbariya Thera.—An arahant. Thirty-one kappas ago he gave to **Sikkhī** Buddha seven flowers wrapped in *koṭumbara*-cloth. Twenty kappas ago he was a king named **Mahānela.**[1] *v.l.* **Koṭumbariya.**

[1] Ap. i. 192.

Koṭṭanāga-pabbata (*v.l.* for **Tobbalanāga-pabbata**[1]).

[1] MṬ. 657.

Koṭṭamālaka.—See **Kuntamālaka.**

Koṭṭha.—The drum of **Narasīha** (*q.v.*), which he gave to **Mānavamma** in order that the latter might induce the people to accompany him in the ships. When they heard the drum they thought it was beaten by Narasīha and forthwith went on board.[1]

[1] Cv. xlvii. 51.

Koṭṭhabhadda.—A great causeway on the river **Jaggarā.** It was restored by **Parakkamabāhu I.**[1] It was so called because the land on either side of it became, as a result of its construction, studded with granaries full of untrussed rice (*abaddhavīhi*).[2]

[1] Cv. lxviii. 16. [2] *Ibid.*, 31.

Koṭṭhamalaya.—See **Koṭamalaya.**

Koṭṭha(Koṭṭhi)-vāta.—A district in Ceylon in which were the villages of **Piyaṅgalla**[1] and **Devatissa.**[2]

[1] Mhv. xxx. 29. [2] Cv. xlviii. 2.

Koṭṭhasāra.—A village to the east of **Pulatthipura.** It was once the refuge of **Vikkamabāhu II.**[1] and, again, of **Gajabāhu.**[2] After Gajabāhu's death his ministers took his body to Koṭṭhasāra, and the village became the headquarters of **Mānābharaṇa.**[3] There was in the village a garrison for mercenary soldiers, specially occupied by the **Keraḷas,** and this garrison once revolted against **Parakkamabāhu I.**[4]

Later, the Damiḷas, **Māgha** and **Jayabāhu,** set up a fortification there.[5] It was evidently a point of strategic importance.

[1] Cv. lxi. 43.
[2] *Ibid.*, lxx. 355.
[3] *Ibid.*, lxxi. 6, 11.
[4] *Ibid.*, lxxiv. 44.
[5] *Ibid.*, lxxxiii. 15; see also Cv. *Trs.* i. 229, n. 1.

Koṭṭhāgāma.—A wealthy village given by **Udaya I.** (?) to the temple of the **Vaḍḍhamāna Bodhi**-tree.[1]

[1] Cv. xlix. 16.

Koṭṭhita (Koṭṭhika).—See **Mahā Koṭṭhita.**

1. **Koṭṭhita Sutta.**—A conversation between **Mahā Koṭṭhita** and **Sāriputta** as to whether or not anything exists. after the passionless ending, without remainder, of the six spheres of contact (*phassāyatanānaṃ asesavirāganirodhā*). The conversation is repeated between Mahā Koṭṭhita and **Ānanda.**[1]

[1] A. ii. 161 f.

2. **Koṭṭhita Sutta.**—**Mahā Koṭṭhita** asks **Sāriputta** a series of questions as to why the holy life (*brahmacariyā*) is lived by the Blessed One, to all of which Sāriputta answers "No." He then goes on to explain that the purpose of the holy life is the realisation of the four Ariyan truths.[1]

[1] A. iv. 382 f.

3. **Koṭṭhita Sutta.**—Three suttas. **Mahā Koṭṭhita** visits the Buddha and asks for a brief statement of the Dhamma. The Buddha answers that desire should be put away for that which is (1) impermanent, (2) Ill, (3) without a self.[1]

[1] S. iv. 145 f.

4. **Koṭṭhita Sutta.**—**Koṭṭhita** visits **Sāriputta** at **Isipatana** and asks him which is true: to say that the eye is the bond of objects or that objects are the bond of the eye? Sāriputta replies that neither is true: the bond consists in the desire and lust arising from their contact. If two men be yoked one to the other, the bond consists not in either of the men but in the yoke-tie which binds them. If this were not so, the religious life would be purposeless.[1]

[1] S. iv. 162 f.

5. **Koṭṭhita Sutta.**—A group of three suttas containing conversations between **Mahā Koṭṭhita** and **Sāriputta** on what constitutes ignorance.[1]

[1] S. iii. 175.

Koṇāgamana (Konāgamana).—The twenty-third in the list of the twenty-four Buddhas and the second Buddha to be born in the **Bhadda-kappa.** He was born in the **Subhagavatī** Park in **Sobhavatī,** the capital of King **Sobha,** his father being the brahmin **Yaññadatta** and his mother **Uttarā.** He lived in the household for three thousand years, in three palaces, **Tusita, Santusita** and **Santuṭṭha**; his chief wife was **Rucigattā** and their son was **Satthavāha.** Koṇāgamana left the world on an elephant and practised austerities only for six months, at the end of which time he was given milk-rice by the daughter of the brahmin **Aggisoma** and grass for his seat by the yavapālaka **Tinduka.** His bodhi was an *Udumbara* tree. His first sermon was preached in the Migadāya near **Sudassana-nagara,** at the foot of a *Mahā-sāla* tree. He held only one assembly of his disciples, who numbered thirty thousand. His body was thirty cubits in height. He died in the **Pabbatārāma** at the age of thirty thousand. His relics were scattered. His chief disciples were

Bhīyya and **Uttara** among monks, and **Samuddā** and **Uttarā** among nuns, his constant attendant being **Sotthiya.** His chief patrons were **Ugga** and **Somadeva** among laymen, and **Sīvalā** and **Sāmā** among laywomen. The Bodhisatta was a khattiya named **Pabbata** of **Mithilā.** He held an almsgiving, heard the Buddha preach and joined the Order.[1] The banker **Ugga** built for the Buddha a Saṅghārāma half a league in extent.[2]

On the day of the Buddha's birth a shower of gold fell all over Jambudīpa, hence he was called **Kaṇakāgamana,** Koṇāgamana being a corrupt form of that word.[3]

According to the Ceylon Chronicles,[4] Koṇāgamana visited their Island (then known as **Varadīpa**), with thirty thousand disciples, accepted the **Mahānoma** garden at **Vaḍḍhamāna,** given by King **Samiddha,** and preached the doctrine. At the conclusion of his sermon, thirty thousand people realised the Truth. At the Buddha's wish, the nun **Kantakānandā** (*v.l.* **Kanakadattā**) brought to Ceylon a branch of the Bodhi-tree. The Buddha also preached at the **Ratanamāla,** the **Sudassanamāla** and the **Nāgamālaka** and gave his girdle for the people's worship. He left **Mahāsumba** and Kantakānandā to look after the new converts.

In Koṇāgamana's time Mount **Vepulla** was known as **Vaṅkaka,** and the people living on the mountain were called **Rohitassā,** their term of life being thirty thousand years.[5] Koṇāgamana held the *uposatha* once a year.[6]

In the Northern books[7] Koṇāgamana is called Kaṇakamuni, Koṇākamuni, and Kaṇakaparvata. A Thūpa, erected on the spot where Koṇāgamana was born, is thought to have existed down to the time of **Asoka,** who rebuilt it to double its original size and worshipped it in his twentieth year.[8] Hiouen Thsang[9] says he saw thūpas at Koṇāgamana's birthplace and also at the spot where he met his father after the Enlightenment. Fa Hien[10] saw thūpas at the latter place and also at the place of the Buddha's death.

[1] D. i. 7; Bu. xxiv; BuA. 213 ff.; J. i. 42 f. (according to the Jātaka his body was twenty cubits high); Sp. i. 190.

[2] J. i. 94.

[3] BuA. 213-14.

[4] Dpv. ii. 67; xv. 25, 44, 48; xvii. 9, 17, 73: Mhv. xv. 91-124.

[5] S. ii. 191.

[6] DhA. ii. 236.

[7] *E.g.*, Dvy. 333; Mtu. i. 114; ii. 265 f., 300, 302, 304, 430; iii. 240-7, 330.

[8] Hultszch: *Inscrip. of Asoka*, p. 165.

[9] Beal, *op. cit.*, ii. 19.

[10] *Travels*, p. 36.

Koṇāgamana Sutta.—The thoughts that came to **Koṇāgamana** before his Enlightenment, regarding birth, decay and death.[1]

[1] S. ii. 9.

1. **Koṇḍañña.**—The second of the twenty-four Buddhas. After sixteen *asaṅkheyya* and one hundred thousand kappas of *pāramī*, he was born in **Rammavatī,** his father being King **Sunanda** and his mother **Sujātā.** He belonged to the **Koṇḍaññagotta** and his body was twenty-eight cubits in height. For ten thousand years he lived as a layman in three palaces—**Ruci, Suruci** and **Subha**[1]; his chief wife was **Rucidevī** and his son **Vijitasena.** He left home in a chariot, practised austerities for ten months and was given a meal of milk-rice by **Yasodharā,** daughter of a merchant in **Sunanda,** and grass for his seat by the Ājīvaka **Sunanda.** His bodhi was a *Sālakalyāṇi* tree, and his first sermon was preached to ten crores of monks in the **Devavana** near **Amaravatī.** He held three assemblies of his disciples, the first led by **Subhadda,** the second by **Vijitasena** and the third by **Udena,** all of whom had become arahants. He died at the age of one hundred thousand at **Candārāmā,** and the thūpa erected over his relics was seven leagues in height. His chief disciples were **Bhadda** and **Subhadda** among monks, and **Tissā** and **Upatissā** among nuns, his constant attendant being **Anuruddha.** His chief patrons were **Soṇa** and **Upasoṇa** among laymen and **Nandā** and **Sirimā** among laywomen.

The Bodhisatta was a king, **Vijitāvī** of **Candavatī.** He left his kingdom, joined the Order and was later reborn in the Brahma-world.[2]

[1] **Rāma, Surāmā** and **Subha,** according to BuA.

[2] Bu. iii.; BuA. 107 ff.; J. i. 30.

2. **Koṇḍañña.**—The name of a *gotta.* It was evidently common to both brahmans and khattiyas, for we find the brahman **Aññāta-Koṇḍañña** (*q.v.*) belonging to it, and elsewhere[1] it is mentioned as a *khattiya-gotta.* Among those mentioned as belonging to the Koṇḍañña-gotta are the Buddha **Koṇḍañña** (*q.v.*) (brahmin), **Candakumāra**[2] (khattiya), **Sarabhaṅga**[3] (brahmin), and the three Buddhas **Vipassī, Sikhī** and **Vessabhū,** all khattiyas.[4] In the **Kacchapa Jātaka**[5] it is said that tortoises are of the **Kassapa-gotta** and monkeys of the Koṇḍañña-gotta, and that between these two classes there is intermarriage.

[1] *E.g.*, VibhA. 464.

[2] J. vi. 137, 138.

[3] J. v. 140, 141, 142.

[4] D. ii. 3 ff. (see table in Dial. ii. 6),

[5] J. ii. 360 f.

3. **Koṇḍañña.**—The name of the apprentice in the **Vāruṇī Jātaka** (*q.v.*).

4. **Koṇḍañña.**—See also **Aññāta-Koṇḍañña, Vimala-Koṇḍañña** and **Khānu-Koṇḍañña.**

Koṇḍañña Sutta.—**Aññāta-Koṇḍañña** visits the Buddha at **Veḷuvana** after a very long interval (twelve years, says the Commentary),[1] and falling down on the ground kisses the Buddha's feet, uttering his own name, "I am Koṇḍañña, O Blessed One." **Vaṅgīsa,** who is present, having obtained the Buddha's permission, utters verses in praise of Koṇḍañña.[2]

[1] SA. i. 216. [2] S. i. 193.

Koṇdadhāna.—See **Kuṇḍadhāna.**

Koṇḍā.—See **Goṇḍā.**

Koṇḍivāsa.—A district in Ceylon.[1]

[1] Cv. l. 30.

Kotalavāpigāma.—A village in Ceylon. A story is told of how the wife of the chief householder in the village was put in bonds by the king's tax-gatherers, under the impression that she was a serving-woman.[1] *v.l.* **Kālavāpigāma.**

[1] VibhA. 441.

Kotumbariya.—See **Koṭumbariya.**

Kotūhalaka.—A poor man of **Addilaraṭṭha,** a previous birth of **Ghosakaseṭṭhi** (*q.v.*). His wife was **Kālī** and his son **Kāpi.**[1]

[1] DA. i. 317; MA. ii. 539; DhA. i. 169; the DhA. says he was of **Ajitaraṭṭha.**

Kotthumala.—A hill in the **Māyāraṭṭha** in Ceylon. The Almsbowl and the Tooth Relic of the Buddha were once buried there by **Vācissara** as a protection from enemies. Later, **Vijayabāhu III.** had them removed to **Jambuddoṇi.**[1]

[1] Cv. lxxxi. 18 ff.; see also Cv. *Trs.* ii. 137, n. 1.

Koddhaṅgulikedāra.—A place near **Nālanda** in Ceylon, mentioned in the account of **Parakkamabāhu I's** campaigns against **Gajabāhu.**[1]

[1] Cv. lxx. 221.

1. **Kodha Vagga.**—The sixteenth section of the *Duka Nipāta* of the *Aṅguttara Nikāya.*[1]

[1] A. i. 95-8.

2. **Kodha Vagga.**—The seventeenth section of the Dhammapada.

1. **Kodha Suttā.**—Two suttas on four persons showing regard to wrath, hypocrisy, gain and honour, and on the effect of these four qualities.[1]

[1] A. ii. 46.

2. **Kodha Sutta.**—A man who is given to wrath, hypocrisy, gain, and regard for honours, goes to purgatory.[1]

[1] A. ii. 84.

1. **Kodhana Sutta.**—A woman who is wrathful is reborn in purgatory.[1]

[1] S. iv. 240.

2. **Kodhana Sutta.**—Seven evil things which rivals wish for each other: ugliness, discomfort, failure in enterprises, poverty, disrepute, loss of friends, and inauspicious rebirth.[1]

[1] A. iv. 94 f.

Kontadisāvijaya.—A general of **Manābharaṇa**[1] (*q.v.* 2).

[1] Cv. lxx. 293; see Cv. *Trs.* i. 311, n. 1.

Kontiputta.—See **Tissa-kontiputta.**

Kontimārā.—A river which flowed from the hill **Ārañjara.** Alongside this river ran the road taken by men who were banished by the people of **Sibi**; the road was also taken by **Vessantara** on his way to exile.[1] The river is five leagues from **Suvaṇṇagiritāla** and five from Ārañjara.[2]

[1] J. vi. 493. [2] *Ibid.*, 514.

Konduruva.—A locality in Ceylon, where **Mānābharaṇa** (2) once took refuge.[1]

[1] Cv. lxxii. 231; see Cv. *Trs.* i. 340, n. 5.

Komāyaputta.—A brahmin; see **Komāyaputta Jātaka.**

Komāyaputta Jātaka (No. 299).—Some ascetics in Himavā failed to take their duties seriously and spent their time in eating and making merry. They had a monkey who provided them with amusement. One day when the ascetics went to the plains for salt and condiments, the Bodhisatta, who had been born as a brahmin ascetic named **Komāyaputta,** occupied their lodging; when the monkey started to play his pranks for him, the Bodhisatta snapped his fingers at him and told him to behave properly, because he lived with ascetics. The monkey thereupon became virtuous and refused to return to his evil ways, even after the arrival of his former friends.

The story was told at the **Pubbārāma,** in reference to some monks who lived there in the apartments below those of the Buddha, and who were quarrelsome and abusive. At the Buddha's request, **Moggallāna** made their house shake in order to frighten them.[1]

[1] J. ii. 447 f.

Komārabhacca (Komārabhaṇḍa).—See **Jīvaka.**

Komudī.—The full-moon day of the fourth month, **Kattika,** usually found in the phrase *Komudī Catumāsinī.*[1] The *Commentary*[2] says it was so called because then the white water-lily flowered luxuriantly (*kumudāni supupphitāni honti*).

[1] Vin. i. 155, 176 f.; D. i. 47; M. iii. 79, 80; DhA. iii. 461; J. v. 262, etc.
[2] DA. i. 139.

Komba.—Chief of the umbrella-bearers of **Gajabāhu.** He had a fortress in **Mallavāḷāna** from which he was dislodged by the Malayarāyara of **Vālikākhetta.** Later he fought a naval battle in **Muttākara.**[1]

[1] Cv. lxx. 60 f.

Korakalamba (Korakalambaka).—Younger brother of **Kapila,** the chaplain of **Apacara.**[1] See **Kapila** (3).

[1] J. iii. 454 f.

Korakkhatta (Korakkhattiya).—A naked ascetic in **Uttarakā.** He bellowed like a dog, walked on all fours, and licked up food with his mouth only. **Sunakkhatta** saw him and greatly admired him, but the Buddha prophesied that Korakkhatta would, in seven days, die of epilepsy and be born among the **Kālakañjakas.** The prophecy proved true, and Sunakkhatta learnt the truth from Korakkhatta's corpse.[1]

Buddhaghosa says[2] that Korakkhattiya was so called because his feet turned inwards (*anto vaṅkapādo*).

[1] D. iii. 6 ff.; J; i. 389 f.
[2] DA. iii. 819.

Koraṇḍaka Vihāra.—A monastery in Ceylon. The *Visuddhimagga*[1] contains the story of a young monk, nephew of the Elder of the Vihāra, who went to **Rohaṇa** for study; he later returned to the Vihāra, and for

[1] p. 91.

three months was waited on by his parents, but he did not reveal his identity, fearing that his parents would prove an impediment to him.

This monastery was once the residence of an Elder named **Mahā Saṅgharakkhita.**[2] *v.l.* **Corakaṇḍaka.**

[2] MṬ. 606.

1. **Koraṇḍapupphiya Thera.**—An arahant. Ninety-one kappas ago he saw the footprint of the Buddha **Vipassī** and offered to it a *koraṇḍa*-plant in bloom. Fifty-seven kappas ago he was a king named **Vītamala.**[1] He is probably to be identified with **Ramaṇīyavihārī.**[2]

[1] Ap. i. 206.

[2] ThagA. i. 116.

2. **Koraṇḍapupphiya Thera.**—An arahant. He was a woodsman in the time of **Tissa** Buddha, and having seen three footprints of the Buddha, he offered to him a flowering *koraṇḍa*-plant. In all subsequent births his skin was the colour of the *koraṇḍa*-flower. The same verses appear in two places in the *Apadāna* with very slight variations.[1] Perhaps these are two distinct persons, because in the *Theragātha Commentary* the verses appear twice—once under the name of **Sugandha**[2] and once under that of **Sabbamitta.**[3]

[1] Ap. ii. 383, 434.

[2] ThagA. i. 81.

[3] *Ibid.*, 270.

Koratiya.—One of the greater Yakkhas who should be invoked by a follower of the Buddha when assailed by evil spirits.[1]

[1] D. iii. 204.

Korabya, Koravya, Korabba.—Perhaps the generic name given to the king of the **Kurūs** (*cf.* **Brahmadatta**). Once in the Jātakas Koravya is given as the name of the king of **Indapatta** in the Kuru country, this king being the father of **Sutasoma.**[1] Elsewhere[2] Koravya appears as a title of **Dhanañjaya,** king of the Kurūs. Koravya may also have been used as an adjective, for we find it explained as *Kururaṭṭhavāsika.*[3] The Koravya king probably belonged to the **Yudhiṭṭhilagotta.**[4] The *Aṅguttara Nikāya*[5] mentions a king Koravya who owned a large banyan tree named **Suppatiṭṭha.** According to the **Raṭṭhapāla Sutta,**[6] in the Buddha's day, too, the ruler of Kuru was called **Koravyarājā,** and he owned a park which seems to have been called **Migācira** (*q.v.*). This king was evidently

[1] J. v. 457.

[2] J. ii. 368; iii. 400, 402; v. 59, 61, 65; vi. 256, 268, 273.

[3] *E.g.*, J. vi. 273.

[4] See J. iv. 361.

[5] iii. 369 f.

[6] M. ii. 65; see also Thag. 776. ff.; ThagA. ii. 34; for details see **Raṭṭhapāla.**

interested in religious discussion. **Thullakoṭṭhika** was his capital. The *Avadānaśataka*[7] speaks of a Kauravya of Thullakoṭṭhika.

[7] i. 67; ii. 118; see also *Camb. Hist. of India*, i. 121, which refers to a half-mythical Pañcāla king, Kraivya.

Koravyaseṭṭha.—A title used for **Sutasoma**[1] (*q.v.*).

[1] J. v. 479.

Kola.—See **Koliya.**

Kolakā.—Mentioned in a list of tribes.[1]

[1] Ap. ii. 359.

Kolañña, also called **Samaṇa-Kolañña.**—A cakkavatti, king of **Kāliṅga.** He travelled through the air, mounted on his state elephant, but he could not pass over the Bodhi-tree.[1]

[1] Mil. 256; *cp.* J. iv. 232, which evidently refers to him, though the name is not given.

Koladāyaka Thera.—An arahant. He was a hermit in the time of **Sikhī** Buddha, and, seeing the Buddha alone, gave him a *kola* (jujube)-fruit.[1] He is probably identical with **Gayā Kassapa.**[2]

[1] Ap. ii. 397. [2] ThagA. i. 417.

Koladdhajana.—An ancient work, a Commentary (probably in Sanskrit ?); it was written by a certain minister at the request of the Elder **Pāsādika.**[1]

[1] Gv., p. 63, 73.

Kolapaṭṭana.—A harbour mentioned in the *Milindapañha*[1]; it was perhaps on the Koromandel coast.[2]

[1] p. 359. [2] Questions of King Milinda, xliv.

Kolambagāmaka.—A tank built by King **Vasabha.**[1]

[1] Mhv. xxxv. 94.

Kolambatittha.—The Pāli equivalent for the modern city of Colombo.[1]

[1] Cv. xciv. 1; xcv. 4, 15.

Kolambapura.—The same as **Kolambatittha.**[1]

[1] Cv. ci. 27.

Kolambahālaka.—A village in Ceylon, where **Bhalluka** pitched his camp.[1] It is probably identical with **Kolambālaka,**[2] in which case it was near the **Titthārāma,** in the neighbourhood of the northern gate of **Anurādhapura.** There was also a monastery called **Kolambahalāka** founded by **Sūratissa,** and said to have been near **Raheraka.**[3] The **Kolambahālaka-pariveṇa** was the residence of the monk **Dāṭhāvedhaka.**[4]

[1] Mhv. xxv. 80; see also Mhv. *Trs.* 176, n. 2.
[2] Mhv. xxxiii. 42.
[3] *Ibid.*, xxi. 5.
[4] MṬ. 176.

Kolavāpi.—A tank dedicated by **Silāmeghavaṇṇa** to the stone image in the **Abhayagiri Vihāra.**[1]

[1] Cv. xliv. 69.

Kolika, Kolita.—See **Mahāmoggallāna.**

Kolita Vihāra.—A monastery, probably in Ceylon; the residence of **Catunikāyika Thera.**[1]

[1] AA. i. 343.

Kolita Sutta.—**Mahāmoggallāna** tells the monks at **Jetavana** how, when he had entered the Second Jhāna, in his effort to attain to the "Ariyan Silence," the Buddha appeared to him and exhorted him to persist in it.[1]

[1] S. ii. 273.

Kolitagāma.—The village in which **Mahāmoggallāna** (*q.v.*) was born. It was near **Upatissagāma** and not far from **Rājagaha.**[1]

[1] See, *e.g.*, SNA. i. 326; DhA. i. 73; Mtu. iii. 56.

Koliyadhītā, Koliyarājadhitā.—See **Suppavāsā.**

Koliyaputta.—An epithet of **Kakudha** (*q.v.*), **Moggallāna's** attendant.[1]

[1] Vin ii. 185; UdA. ii. 8.

Koliyā, Koḷiyā.—One of the republican clans in the time of the Buddha. The Koliyā owned two chief settlements—one at **Rāmagāma** and the other at **Devadaha.** The Commentaries[1] contain accounts of the origin of the Koliyas. We are told that a king of Benares, named **Rāma,**[2] suffered from leprosy, and being detested by the women of the court, he left the kingdom to his eldest son and retired into the forest. There, living on woodland leaves and fruits, he soon recovered, and, while

[1] DA. i. 260 f.; SNA. i. 356 f.; A. ii. 558; ThagA. i. 546; also Ap. i. 94.
[2] The Mtu (i. 353) calls him Kola and explains from this the name of the Koliyas.

wandering about, came across **Piyā,** the eldest of the five daughters of **Okkāka,** she herself being afflicted with leprosy. Rāma, having cured her, married her, and they begot thirty-two sons. With the help of the king of Benares, they built a town in the forest, removing a big *kola*-tree in doing so. The city thereupon came to be called **Kolanagara,** and because the site was discovered on a tiger-track (*vyagghapatha*) it was also called **Vyagghapajjā.** The descendants of the king were known as **Koliyā.** According to the **Kuṇālā Jātaka,**[3] when the **Sākyans** wished to abuse the Koliyans, they said that the Koliyans had once "lived like animals in a Kola-tree," as their name signified. The territories of the Sākyans and the Koliyans were adjacent, separated by the river **Rohiṇī.** The khattiyas of both tribes intermarried,[4] and both claimed relationship with the Buddha. A quarrel once arose between the two tribes regarding the right to the waters of the Rohiṇī, which irrigated the land on both sides, and a bloody feud was averted only by the intervention of the Buddha. In gratitude, each tribe dedicated some of its young men to the membership of the Order, and during the Buddha's stay in the neighbourhood, he lived alternately in **Kapilavatthu** and in **Koliyanagara.**[5]

Attached probably to the Koliyan central authorities, was a special body of officials, presumably police, who wore a distinguishing head-dress with a drooping crest (*Lambacūḷakābhaṭā*). They bore a bad reputation for extortion and violence.[6]

Besides the places already mentioned, several other townships of the Koliyans, visited by the Buddha or by his disciples, are mentioned in literature—*e.g.*, **Uttara,** the residence of the headman **Pāṭaliya**[7]; **Sajjanela,** residence of **Suppavāsā**[8]; **Sāpūga,** where **Ānanda** once stayed[9]; **Kakkarapatta,** where lived **Dīghajānu**[10]; and **Haliddavasana,** residence of the ascetics Puṇṇa **Koliyaputta** and **Seniya.**[11] **Nisabha,**[12] **Kakudha**[13] (attendant of Moggallāna), and **Kaṅkhā-Revata**[14] (and perhaps **Soṇa Koḷivisa,** *q.v.*), were also Koliyans.

After the Buddha's death the Koliyans of **Rāmagāma** claimed and obtained one-eighth of the Buddha's relics, over which they erected a thūpa.[15] See also *s.v.* **Suppavāsā.**

[3] J. v. 413.

[4] It is said that once the Koliyan youths carried away many Sākyan maidens while they were bathing, but the Sākyans, regarding the Koliyans as relatives, took no action. (DA. i. 262.)

[5] For details of this quarrel and its consequences see J. v. 412 ff.; DA. ii. 672 ff.; DhA. iii. 254 ff.

[6] S. iv. 341.

[7] *Ibid.*, 340.

[8] A. ii. 62.

[9] *Ibid.*, 194.

[10] A. iv. 281.

[11] M. i. 387; see also S. v. 115.

[12] ThagA. i. 318.

[13] SA. i. 89.

[14] Ap. ii. 491.

[15] D. ii. 167; Mhv. xxi. 18, 22 ff.

Koḷa, Koḷanagara.—See **Koḷiya.**

Koḷabhinna.—A river in Ceylon, near **Subhagiri**[1] (Yāpahu).

[1] Cv. xc. 11.

Koḷiyavessa.—See **Soṇa Koḷivisa.**

Koḷuvukkoṭṭa.—A stronghold in South India, once occupied by **Paṇḍiyāṇḍāra.**[1]

[1] Cv. lxxvi. 170, 172.

Koḷuvura.—A village in South India.[1]

[1] Cv. lxxvi. 129.

Koḷūru.—A district in South India.[1]

[1] Cv. lxxvi. 130.

Koviḷāragāma.—A village in Ceylon where a battle took place between **Mahinda II.** and the three Ādipādas who had risen against him. Mahinda was victorious.[1]

[1] Cv. xlvi. 121.

1. **Kosambaka.**—Name of a king of **Kosambī.**[1] See also **Kosambika.**

[1] See the **Kaṇhadīpāyana** Jātaka (J. iv. 28 f.).

2. **Kosambaka.**—See **Kosambiya.**

Kosambaka Vatthu.—The story of the quarrelsome monks of **Kosambī** (*q.v.*).[1]

[1] DhA. i. 44 ff.

Kosambaka Sutta.—See **Kosambiya Sutta.**

Kosambakā.—The monks of **Kosambī** (*q.v.*), who brought about schism in the Order.

Kosambakuṭi.—One of the residences at Jetavana occupied by the Buddha.[1]

[1] SNA. ii. 403.

Kosambakkhandha.—The tenth section of the *Mahāvagga* of the *Vinaya Piṭaka.*[1]

[1] Vin. i. 334-59.

Kosambika.—Name of a king of **Kosambī.**[1] See also **Kosambaka.**

[1] J. iv. 56.

Kosambika-seṭṭhi.—The banker of **Kosambī.** He adopted **Ghosaka** (*q.v.*), but later, when he had a son of his own, he tried in various ways to kill Ghosaka. All his plans failed, and he developed diarrhœa and died, even his plans of disinheriting Ghosaka having been frustrated by Ghosaka's wife. Kosambika-seṭṭhi's slave-woman, who helped in all his nefarious schemes, was called **Kāḷī.**[1]

[1] DhA. i. 174-85.

Kosambiya (Kosambaka) Sutta.—Preached at the **Ghositārāma** in **Kosambī** to the quarrelsome monks of that place. The sutta deals with amity and the six means of promoting it—acts, words and thoughts of goodwill, sharing all things with one's fellow celibates, living the higher life in its entirety, following the doctrine that leads to the destruction of Ill, and introspection, which leads to the realisation of truth.[1] The Kosambaka Sutta is given[2] as an example of a discourse originating from a quarrel.

[1] M. i. 320 ff.; cp. **Upakkilesa Sutta** (M. ii. 152 ff.).

[2] *E.g.*, in DA. i. 123.

Kosambī.—The capital of the **Vatsas** or **Vaṃsas.**[1] In the time of the Buddha its king was **Parantapa,** and after him reigned his son **Udena** (*q.v.*).[2] Kosambī was evidently a city of great importance at the time of the Buddha for we find **Ānanda** mentioning it as one of the places suitable for the Buddha's *Parinibbāna.*[3] It was also the most important halt for traffic coming to **Kosala** and **Magadha** from the south and the west.[4] The city was thirty leagues by river from Benares,[5] and the usual route from **Rājagaha** to Kosambī was up the river,[6] though there seems to have been a land route passing through **Anupiya** and Kosambī to Rājagaha.[7] In the *Sutta Nipāta*[8] the whole route is given from **Mahissati** to Rājagaha, passing through Kosambī, the halting-places mentioned being **Ujjeni, Gonaddha, Vedisa, Vanasavhya, Kosambī, Sāketa, Sāvatthi, Setavyā, Kapilavatthu, Kusinārā, Pāvā, Bhoganagara** and **Vesāli.**

[1] J. iv. 28; vi. 236.

[2] MA. ii. 740 f.; DhA. i. 164 f.

[3] D. ii. 146, 169.

[4] See, *e.g.*, Vin. i. 277.

[5] Thus we are told that the fish which swallowed **Bakkula** travelled thirty leagues through the **Yamunā,** from Kosambī to Benares (AA. i. 170; PsA. 491).

[6] This was the route taken by Ānanda when he went with five hundred others to inflict the higher punishment on **Channa** (Vin. ii. 290).

[7] See Vin. ii. 184 f.

[8] vv. 1010-13.

Near Kosambī, by the river, was Udena's park, the **Udakavana,** where Ānanda and **Piṇḍola-Bhāradvāja** preached to the women of Udena's palace on two different occasions.[9] The Buddha is mentioned as having once stayed in the **Siṃsapāvana** in Kosambī.[10] **Mahā Kaccāna** lived in a woodland near Kosambī after the holding of the First Council.[11]

Already in the Buddha's time there were four establishments of the Order in Kosambī—the **Kukkuṭārāma,** the **Ghositārāma,** the **Pāvārika-ambavana** (these being given by three of the most eminent citizens of Kosambī, named respectively, **Kukkuṭa, Ghosita** and **Pāvārika**), and the **Badarikārāma.** The Buddha visited Kosambī on several occasions, stopping at one or other of these residences, and several discourses delivered during these visits are recorded in the books.[12]

The Buddha spent his ninth rainy season at Kosambī, and it was on his way there on this occasion that he made a détour to **Kammāssa-damma** and was offered in marriage **Māgandiyā,** daughter of the brahmin **Māgandiya.** The circumstances are narrated in connection with the **Māgandiya Sutta.** Māgandiyā took the Buddha's refusal as an insult to herself, and, after her marriage to King Udena, tried in various ways to take revenge on the Buddha, and also on Udena's wife **Sāmavatī,** who had been the Buddha's follower.[13]

A great schism once arose among the monks in Kosambī. Some monks charged one of their colleagues with having committed an offence, but he refused to acknowledge the charge and, being himself learned in the Vinaya, argued his case and pleaded that the charge be dismissed. The rules were complicated; on the one hand, the monk had broken a rule and was treated as an offender, but on the other, he should not have been so treated if he could not see that he had done wrong. The monk was eventually excommunicated, and this brought about a great dissension. When the matter was reported to the Buddha, he admonished the partisans of both sides and urged them to give up their differences, but they paid no heed, and even blows were exchanged. The people of Kosambī, becoming angry at the monks' behaviour, the quarrel grew apace. The Buddha once more counselled concord, relating to the monks the story of King **Dīghīti** of **Kosala,** but his efforts at reconciliation were of no avail, one of the monks actually asking him to leave them to settle their differences without his interference. In disgust the Buddha left Kosambī and, journeying through **Bālakaloṇakāragāma** and the

[9] Vin. ii. 290 f.; SNA. ii. 514; J. iv. 375.

[10] S. v. 437.

[11] PvA. 141.

[12] For details see under these names. Thomas (*op. cit.*, 115, n. 2) doubts the authenticity of the stories connected with the Buddha's visits to Kosambī, holding that these stories are of later invention.

[13] DhA. i. 199 ff.; iii. 193 ff.; iv. 1 ff.; Ud. vii. 10.

Pācīnavaṃsadaya, retired alone to keep retreat in the **Pārileyyaka** forest. In the meantime the monks of both parties repented, partly owing to the pressure exerted by their lay followers in Kosambī, and, coming to the Buddha at Sāvatthi, they asked his pardon and settled their dispute.[14]

The Commentaries give two reasons for the name Kosambī. The more favoured[15] is that the city was so called because it was founded in or near the site of the hermitage once occupied by the sage **Kusumba** (*v.l.* **Kusumbha**). Another explanation is[16] that large and stately margossa-trees (*Kosambarukkhā*) grew in great numbers in and around the city.

Bakkula was the son of a banker in Kosambī.[17] In the Buddha's time there lived near the ferry at Kosambī a powerful Nāga-king, the reincarnation of a former ship's captain. The Nāga was converted by **Sāgata,** who thereby won great fame.[18] **Rujā** was born in a banker's family in Kosambī.[19] **Citta-paṇḍita** was also born there.[20] A king, by name **Kosambaka** (*q.v.*), once ruled there.

During the time of the **Vajjian** heresy, when the Vajjian monks of **Vesālī** wished to excommunicate **Yasa Kākaṇḍakaputta,** he went by air to Kosambī, and from there sent messengers to the orthodox monks in the different centres.[21]

It was at Kosambī that the Buddha promulgated a rule forbidding the use of intoxicants by monks.[22]

Kosambī is mentioned in the *Saṃyutta Nikāya*[23] as being "Gaṅgāya nadiyā tīre." This is either an error, or here the name Gaṅgā refers not to the Ganges but to the **Yamunā.** Kosambī is identified with the two villages of Kosam on the Jumna, about ninety miles west of Allahabad.[24]

[14] Vin. i. 337-57; J. iii. 486 ff. (cp. iii. 211 ff.); DhA. i. 44 ff.; SA. ii. 222 f.; the story of the Buddha going into the forest is given in Ud. iv. 5. and in S. iii. 94, but the reason given in these texts is that he found Kosambī uncomfortable owing to the vast number of monks, lay people and heretics. (But see UdA. 248 f., and SA. ii. 222 f.)

[15] *E.g.*, UdA. 248; SNA. 300; MA. i. 535. Epic tradition ascribes the foundation of Kosambī to a Ceḍi prince, while the origin of the Vatsa people is traced to a king of Kāśī (see PHAI. 83, 84).

[16] *E.g.*, MA i. 539; PsA. 413.

[17] MA. ii. 929; AA. i. 170.

[18] *Ibid.*, 179; but see J. i. 360, where the incident is given as happening at **Bhaddavatikā.**

[19] J. vi. 237 f.

[20] J. iv. 392.

[21] Vin. ii. 298; Mhv. iv. 17.

[22] Vin. ii. 307.

[23] S. iv. 179; but see AA. i. 170; MA. ii. 929; PsA. 491, all of which indicate that the city was on the Yamunā.

[24] CAGI. 448 f.; Vincent Smith places it further south (*J.R.A.S.* 1898, 503 ff.).

Kosambī Jātaka (No. 428).—The introductory story relates how the monks of Kosambī quarrelled and brought about great dissension among themselves because one of their number had left in a vessel the surplus water for rinsing the mouth. When the Buddha found that he could not induce the monks to live in harmony, he related to them the story of **Dīghīti,** king of **Kosala,** and when even that failed to produce the desired effect he uttered ten stanzas, standing poised in mid-air, and went away from Kosambī, leaving the monks to their fate.[1]

The Kosambī Jātaka contains only a small portion of the story of Dīghīti, scarcely more than an allusion to it. The **Dīghīti Kosala Jātaka** (*q.v.*) contains further details, but even when taken together, these two do not make the story complete. The full story is related in the *Vinaya Piṭaka.*[2]

[1] For details of the quarrel see Kosambī. [2] Vin. i. 342 ff.

Kosambī Sutta.—**Saviṭṭha,** staying in the **Ghositārāma** at **Kosambī,** asks **Musīla** about the *Paṭicca-Samuppāda*, and discovers from the answers given that Musīla is an arahant. Saviṭṭha asks **Nārada** the same questions at the latter's own request and receives the same answers; but Nārada declares that he is not an arahant. **Ānanda** is also present and joins in the discussion.[1]

[1] S. ii. 115 f.

Kosambivāsī-Tissa.—See **Tissa.**

1. **Kosala.**—A Pacceka Buddha, mentioned in a list of names.[1]

[1] M. iii. 70; ApA. i. 107.

2. **Kosala.**—A country inhabited by the **Kosalā,** to the north-west of **Magadha** and next to **Kāsī.** It is mentioned second in the list of sixteen **Mahājanapadas.**[1] In the Buddha's time it was a powerful kingdom ruled over by **Pasenadi,** who was succeeded by his son **Viḍūḍabha.** By this time Kāsī was under the subjection of Kosala, for we find that when **Bimbisāra,** king of **Magadha,** married **Kosaladevī,** daughter of **Mahākosala** and sister of Pasenadi, a village in Kāsi was given as part of the dowry.[2] Various Jātakas indicate that the struggle between Kāsi and Kosala had been very prolonged.[3] Sometimes the Kāsi king would attack Kosala, capture the king and rule over the country. At others the Kosala king would invade Kāsi and annex it to his own territory. Several Kosala kings who succeeded in doing this, are mentioned by name

[1] *E.g.*, A. i. 213; iv. 252, etc.
[2] J. ii. 237; iv. 342 f.
[3] See, *e.g.*, J. ii. 21 f.; iii. 115 f.; 211 f.; v. 316, 425.

—*e.g.*, **Dabbasena,**[4] **Dīghāvu,**[5] **Vaṅka**[6] and **Kaṃsa**; the last being given the special title of "*Bāraṇāsiggāha*,"[7] probably in recognition of the fact that he completed the conquest of Kāsi. Other kings of Kosala who came in conflict with Benares in one way or another are mentioned—*e.g.*, **Dīghiti,**[8] **Mallika,**[9] and **Chatta.**[10] Sometimes the kings of the two countries entered into matrimonial alliances.[11] With the capture of Kāsi the power of Kosala increased rapidly, until a struggle between this country and Magadha became inevitable. Bimbisāra's marriage was probably a political alliance, but it only served to postpone the evil day. Quite soon after his death there were many fierce fights between **Ajātasattu,** his successor, and Pasenadi, these fights bringing varying fortunes to the combatants. Once Ajātasattu was captured alive, but Pasenadi spared his life and gave him his daughter, **Vajirā,** in marriage and for a time all went well.[12] Later, however, after his conquest of the **Licchavis,** Ajātasattu seems to have succeeded in establishing his sway in Kosala.[13] In the sixth century B.C. the Sākyan territory of **Kapilavatthu** was subject to Kosala.[14]

At the time of the Buddha **Sāvatthi** was the capital of Kosala. Next in importance was **Saketa,** which, in ancient days, had sometimes been the capital.[15] There was also **Ayojjhā,** on the banks of the **Sarayu,** which, judging from the *Rāmāyaṇa*, must once have been the chief city; but in the sixth century B.C. it was quite unimportant. The river Sarayu divided Kosala into two parts, **Uttara Kosala** and **Dakkhiṇa Kosala.**[16] Other Kosala rivers mentioned in the books are the **Aciravatī**[17] and the **Sundarikā,**[18] while among localities spoken of as being in Kosala are **Icchānaṅgala** (A. iii. 30, 341; iv. 340, etc.), **Ukkaṭṭhā** (D. i. 87), **Ekasālā** (S. i. 111), **Opasāda** (M. ii. 164), **Kesaputta** of the **Kālāmas** (A. i. 188), **Caṇḍalakappa** (M. ii. 209), **Toraṇavatthu** (S. iv. 374), **Daṇḍakappa** (A. iii. 402), **Nagaravinda** (M. iii. 290), **Naḷakapāna** (A. v. 122; M. i. 462), **Nālandā** (S. iv. 322), **Paṅkadhā** (A. i. 236), **Venāgapura** (A. i. 180), **Veḷudvāra** (S. v. 352), **Sālā** (M. i. 285, 400; S. v. 227), **Sālāvatika** (D. i. 244), and **Setavya** (D. ii. 316).[19]

4 J. iii. 13.

5 *Ibid.*, 211 f.

6 *Ibid.*, 168.

7 J. ii. 403; v. 112.

8 J. iii. 211 f.; Vin. i. 342 f.

9 J. ii. 3.

10 J. iii. 116.

11 *E.g.*, *ibid.*, 407.

12 For details see Ajātasattu.

13 See Vincent Smith, *op. cit.*, 32 f.

14 The *Sutta Nipāta* (vs. 405) speaks of the Buddha's birthplace as belonging to the Kosalans; see also A. i. 276, where Kapilavatthu is mentioned as being in Kosala. Elsewhere (M. ii. 124) Pasenadi is reported as saying, "*Bhagavā pi Kosalako, aham pi Kosalako.*"

15 J. iii. 270; Mtu. i. 348.

16 Law: *Geog.*, p. 6.

17 D. i. 235.

18 S. i. 167; SN. p. 97; but see M. i. 39, where the river is called **Bāhukā**.

19 The Mtu. adds Droṇavastuka (iii. 377) and Mārakaraṇḍa (i. 317).

The Commentaries[20] give a curious explanation of the name Kosalā. It is said that when nothing could make **Mahāpanāda** smile, his father offered a big reward for anyone who could succeed in doing this. People, accordingly, left their work and flocked to the court, but it was not until **Sakka** sent down a celestial actor that Mahāpanāda showed any signs of being amused. When this happened the men returned to their various duties, and on their way home, when meeting their friends, they asked of each other, "*Kacci bho kusalaṃ, kacci bho kusalaṃ.*" The district where this occurred came to be called Kosalā on account of the repetition of the word *kusala*.

The Buddha spent the greater part of his time in Kosala, either in Sāvatthi or in touring in the various parts of the country, and many of the Vinaya rules were formulated in Kosala.[21] It is said[22] that alms were plentiful in Kosala, though, evidently,[23] famines, due to drought, were not unknown. Yet, though woodland tracts were numerous[24] where monks could meditate in solitude, the number of monks actually found in Kosala was not large.[25] **Bāvarī** himself was a native of Kosala,[26] yet he preferred to have his hermitage in **Dakkhiṇāpatha.**

After the Buddha's death, his *uṇṇaloma* was deposited in a thūpa in Kosala.[27] It is said that the measures used in Kosala were larger than those of Magadha—thus one Kosala *pattha* was equal to four Magadha *patthas.*[28]

Kosala is often mentioned in combination with Kāsi in the compound **Kāsi-Kosala ;** Pasenadi was king of Kāsi-Kosala[29] (*cf.* **Aṅga-Magadha**). See also *s.v.* **Pasenadi.**

20 *E.g.*, SNA. ii. 400 f.; DA. i. 239 f.
21 See Vinaya Index, *s.v.* Kosala.
22 SA. i. 221.
23 See J. i. 329.
24 See, *e.g.*, SA. i. 225.
25 VT. i. 226.
26 SN. v. 976.
27 Bu. xxviii. 9.
28 SNA. ii. 476.
29 *E.g.*, A. v. 59.

Kosala Saṃyutta.—The third section of the *Saṃyutta Nikāya.*[1] It contains discourses connected with **Pasenadi Kosala.**

1 S. i. 68-102.

1. **Kosala Sutta.**—While **Pasenadi** is visiting the Buddha, a messenger arrives and announces the death of **Mallikā.** The king is greatly grieved, but the Buddha consoles him by pointing out how it is impossible to escape old age, decay, disease, destruction.[1]

1 A. iii. 57.

2. **Kosala Sutta.**—Everything changes, even **Pasenadi,** king of **Kāsi-Kosala,** the whole universe, even **Mahā Brahmā** and the devas of the **Ābhassara** world. Instability and change are everywhere; therefore the wise loathe all, having a mind only to attain in this life the *anupādāparinibbāna.*[1]

[1] A. v. 59 ff.

3. **Kossala Sutta.**—**Pasenadi** visits the Buddha at **Jetavana** after having won a battle, and, falling at the Buddha's feet, shows great humility and does obeisance. When the Buddha asks the reason for such profound homage, the king gives various reasons for his honouring of the Buddha.[1]

[1] A. v. 65 ff.

Kosalakā.—The inhabitants of **Kosala.**[1]

[1] D. i. 150.

Kosala-devī.—Daughter of **Mahā Kosala** and sister of **Pasenadi.** She was married to **Bimbisāra,** and a village in **Kāsi** was given to her for bath-money as part of her dowry. She was the mother of **Ajātasattu.**[1] When pregnant with him, she was filled with a desire to drink blood from the right knee of her husband, and on learning from the astrologers that this presaged the birth of a patricide, she went to the park—called, on that account, **Maddakucchi** (*q.v.*)—and tried to bring about an abortion, but failed. Bimbisāra satisfied her longing. When Bimbisāra was imprisoned by Ajātasattu she waited upon him, taking him food till she was absolutely prevented from doing so. After his death she died of grief, and Pasenadi made war on Ajātasattu to avenge her death.[2]

[1] Ajātasattu is called **Videhiputta.** On this see *s.v.* Ajātasattu.
[2] J. ii. 237; 403; iii. 121 f.

Kosalanagara.—See **Sāvatthi.**

Kosalabimbavaṇṇanā.—A book containing an account of an image built by **Pasenadi,** king of Kosala, and of the merit of building images. The work was probably written about the thirteenth or fourteenth century. Quotations from it are given in the **Saddhammasaṅgaha** (*q.v.*).

Kosalarañño-parājaya Vatthu.—The story of **Pasenadi** and of his great discomfiture and disgust on being defeated three times by **Ajātasattu.**[1]

[1] DhA. iii. 259 f.

Kosalarājā.—See **Pasenadi.**

Kosalavihārī Thera.—An arahant. He was born in **Vesāli,** and was one of those who heard the Buddha preach when he came to quieten the panic which arose there, as recorded in the **Ratana Sutta** (*q.v.*). After the sermon Kosalavihārī left the world. At the conclusion of his novitiate he dwelt in a forest near a village in **Kosala.** A lay adherent seeing him camping under a tree built for him a small hut, and there the thera attained arahantship. He acquired his name from having dwelt long in Kosala.[1]

In the time of **Padumuttara** Buddha he was an ascetic in Himavā and gave the Buddha some tuberous roots. Fifty-four kappas ago he was a king named **Sumekhalisama.** He is evidently to be identified with **Bilālidāyaka** of the *Apadāna.*[2]

[1] Thag. 59; ThagA. i. 134 f. [2] Ap. i. 145.

Kosalā.—See **Kosala.**

1. **Kosika, Kosiya.**—A rock near Himavā where **Nārada Kassapa** had a hermitage.[1]

[1] Ap. ii. 381.

2. **Kosika.**—A Pacceka Buddha. He once lived in **Cittakūṭa,** and **Ukkāsatika,** in a previous birth, seeing him wandering about Himavā, lit round him at night one hundred torches and gave him alms.[1]

[1] Ap. ii. 414.

3. **Kosika.**—A king who was destroyed with his subjects for having insulted a sage.[1]

[1] ThagA. i. 368.

Kosikī.—A river, probably a branch of the Ganges. It flowed from Himavā, and on its bank was a mango-grove three leagues in extent.[1]

[1] J. v. 2, 5, 6.

Kosinārakā.—Inhabitants of **Kusinārā.**[1]

[1] *E.g.*, Vin. i. 247; AA. ii. 637.

1. **Kosiya, Kosiyagotta.**—The name of a brahmin clan. In the *Pācittiya*[1] it is given as one of the lower *gottas.* Among those mentioned as belonging to this gotta are the brahmin **Kevaṭṭa,**[2] the brahmin who

[1] Vin. iv. 8; but it is also Sakka's gotta, and is therefore generally regarded as a high one (see, *e.g.*, Thag. 415; ThagA. i. 452). [2] J. vi. 418 f.

was the father of **Soṇa Kumāra** (the Bodhisatta[3]), **Bhaddākāpilānī,** born in **Sāgala,**[4] and the banker who came to be known as **Macchariya-Kosiya** (*q.v.*). **Kātiyāna's** father was a Kosiyan, but he married a woman of the **Kātiyāna** family.[5] The **Bhūridatta Jātaka**[6] mentions a sage **Kosiya,** who taught **Ālambāyana** the Nāga-spell. The scholiast says he belonged to the Kosiyagotta. The **Sālikedāra Jātaka**[7] mentions a brahmin of **Sālindiya,** called Kosiyagotta, probably for the same reason. The **Kosiya Jātaka**[8] speaks of a **Kosiyabrāhmaṇī.** All these are either addressed or spoken of as Kosiya in their different contexts. The name Kosiya is also used twice in speaking of **Sakka**—once by the Buddha,[9] once by **Mahā Moggallāna**[10]—and again by **Guttila**[11] and by **Mahā Kassapa.**[12] The name means "belonging to the Kuśika family." It is once used of Indra in the Ṛg Veda, in what exact sense is not known. Rhys Davids[13] suggests that perhaps we have here a survival from the time when Indra was only the god of a Kuśika clan.

The word Kosiya[14] means "Owl," and is probably one of the several clan names which are also names of animals (*cf.* **Vaccha**).

[3] J. v. 319 ff.
[4] AA. i. 99; ThigA. 68; SA ii. 144.
[5] ThagA. i. 452.
[6] J. vi. 181; Mtu. ii. 49.
[7] J. iv. 278 f.
[8] J. i. 465 f.
[9] D. ii. 270.
[10] M. i. 252.
[11] J. ii. 252.
[12] Ud. iii. 7; UdA. 200; DhA. i. 429.
[13] Dial. ii. 296 f.; see also Dvy. 632; Mtu. iii. 200, 202, 315, 403.
[14] See, *e.g.*, J. ii. 208.

2. **Kosiya.**—See **Macchari-Kosiya.**

3. **Kosiya Thera.**—An arahant. He belonged to a brahmin family in **Magadha** and was called by his gotta-name. He often listened to the preaching of **Sāriputta** and, joining the Order, in due course won arahantship. He was a gate-keeper of **Bandhumatī** and in the time of **Vipassī** Buddha gave to the Buddha a piece of sugar-cane.[1] He is probably identical with **Ucchukaṇḍika** of the *Apadāna.*[2]

[1] Thag. 370-4; ThagA. i. 431 f.
[2] Ap. ii. 393.

4. **Kosiya.**—See **Kosika** (1).

5. **Kosiya.**—See **Nanda Māṇava.**

1. **Kosiya Jātaka** (No. 130).—A brahmin of Benares had a bad wife who lay in bed by day feigning sickness and spent her nights in enjoyment. The husband worked hard to supply her with dainties, and, in consequence, could not visit his teacher who was the Bodhisatta. When

the latter discovered the truth, he advised the brahmin to prepare a mess of cow-dung and other things and to insist that his wife should either swallow this medicine or get up and work. She then knew that her shamming was discovered and abandoned her evil ways.

The story was told to a brahmin of **Sāvatthi,** a pious follower of the Buddha, whose wife behaved in a similar way. The Buddha told him this story of the past and asked him to try the same remedy, for, he said, the brahmin and his wife were identical with the couple of the story.[1]

In the *atītavatthu* the woman is addressed as "Kosiyā." The scholiast[2] adds that she belonged to the **Kosiyagotta.**

[1] J. i. 463 f. [2] *Ibid.*, 465.

2. **Kosiya Jātaka** (No. 226).—The king of Benares, making war at an unseasonable time while camping in the park, saw an owl (*kosiya*) being attacked by crows. The king asked his minister the reason for this; the minister, being the Bodhisatta, said the owl had left his hiding-place too early—that is, before sunset.

The story was told to **Pasenadi,** who visited **Jetavana** on his way to quell a border rising; the time was unsuitable for such an enterprise.[1]

[1] J. ii. 208 f.

3. **Kosiya Jātaka** (No. 470).—Given under the **Sudhābhojana Jātaka** (*q.v.*).

1. **Kosiya Vagga.**—The second chapter of the *Tika Nipāta* of the *Jātaka Commentary.*[1]

[1] J. ii. 321-54.

2. **Kosiya Vagga.**—The second section of the *Nissaggiya* of the *Vinaya Piṭaka.*[1]

[1] Vin. iii. 224-42; *ibid.*, v. 10 f.

Kosiyaputta.—An arahant. He is mentioned in a list of theras who handed down the *Abhidhamma* up to the Third Council.[1]

[1] DhsA., p. 32.

Kosiyā.—The wicked wife of the **Kosiya Jātaka** 1 (*q.v.*).

Kosiyāyana.—A brahmin of **Kāsi,** his wife being called **Kosiyāyanī.** Their story is given in the **Rādha Jātaka.**[1]

[1] J. i. 495 f.

Kosumbaphaliya Thera.—An arahant. Thirty-one kappas ago he saw the Buddha **Sikhī** and gave him a *kosumba*-fruit.[1]

He is evidently identical with **Usabha Thera.**[2]

[1] Ap. ii. 449. [2] ThagA. i. 320.

Kohāla.—A tank in Ceylon, built by **Vasabha.**[1] It was near **Mahātitthapaṭṭana.**[2]

[1] Mhv. xxxv. 95. [2] MṬ. 653.

Kohombagāma.—A village near **Pulatthipura,** where a battle took place between the forces of **Gajabāhu** and those of **Parakkamabāhu I.**[1]

[1] Cv. lxx. 320.

Kyānagāma.—A village in the Malaya country, not far from **Pulatthipura. Laṅkādhikāri Kitti** once encamped there,[1] and **Parakkamabāhu I.** went there disguised as a musician.[2]

[1] Cv. lxx. 283, 300; lxxii. 207. [2] *Ibid.*, 264.

Kh

Khaggavisāna Sutta.—The third sutta of the *Uraga Vagga* of the *Sutta Nipāta,*[1] consisting of forty-one stanzas, each of which ends with the refrain: "*eko care khaggavisānakappo.*" The *Commentary*[2] divides the sutta into four vaggas and gives each a separate name (except the first), the name being generally derived from the first word of the stanza. It is said that the Buddha preached the Khaggavisāna Sutta in response to a question asked of him by **Ānanda** regarding the attainment of Enlightenment by Pacceka Buddhas; the Buddha gave details of their *abhinīhara* and *patthanā*, and illustrated them by reciting to Ānanda stanzas which had been uttered by Pacceka Buddhas of old on various occasions and at different periods as their pæans of joy (*udāna*).

Buddhaghosa[3] gives the life-story of each of the Pacceka Buddhas whose stanzas are included in this sutta. It is, however, only in the case of a few Pacceka Buddhas that the actual names are given—*e.g.*, **Brahmadatta** (v. 33), **Anitthigandha** (36), **Mahāpaduma** (39), **Ekavajjika-Brahmadatta** (40), **Ekaputtika-Brahmadatta** (41), **Cātumāsika-Brahmadatta** (44, 64), **Sītāluka-Brahmadatta** (52), **Suta-Brahmadatta** (58), **Vibhūsaka-Brahmadatta** (59), **Pādalola-Brahmadatta** (61), **Anivatta-Brahmadatta** (62), **Cakkhulola-Brahmadatta** (63), and **Mātaṅga** (74).

[1] SN. vv. 35-75. [2] SNA. i. 46 ff. [3] *Ibid.*

The rest are described as "the king of Benares," or "the son of the king," etc.

The sutta is commented on in the *Culla-Niddesa*,[4] in addition to those of the *Parāyanavagga*, an evidence of the fact that, when the *Culla-Niddesa* was composed, this was probably regarded as an independent sutta, not belonging to any particular group such as the Uragavagga, and that the comments on it were written at a time prior to the composition of the *Sutta Nipāta* as an anthology in its present form. This view is further strengthened by the fact that its mixed Sanskrit version in the *Mahāvastu*[5] is not placed in any definite group. According to the *Mahāvastu*, the Pratyeka Buddhas, five hundred in number, were living in Ṛṣipatana near Benares, and when they heard from the **Suddhāvāsa** devas of the approach of the Buddha in twelve years, they disappeared from Ṛṣipatana, each repeating one of the verses of the sutta.

The *Apadāna*[6] includes the stanzas of the Khaggavisāna Sutta in its chapter called the *Paccekabuddhāpadāna* and prefaces them with several introductory stanzas. A few stanzas are also added at the end by way of conclusion. In its exegesis the *Apadāna Commentary*[7] gives the names of several Pacceka Buddhas. They are, however, different from those given by Buddhaghosa, and correspond more nearly to those mentioned in the **Isigili Sutta.**

[4] pp. 56 ff.
[5] i. 357 f.
[6] i. 7 ff.
[7] ApA. i. 106 f.

Khajjakadāyaka Thera.—An arahant. Ninety-two kappas ago he gave a ripe *panasa*-fruit, with a coconut, to the Buddha **Tissa**; and thirteen kappas ago he was a king named **Indasoma.**[1] He is probably identical with **Setuccha Thera.**[2]

[1] Ap. i. 182.
[2] ThagA. i. 206 f.

Khajjanīya Vagga.—The eighth chapter of the *Khandha Saṃyutta* of the *Saṃyutta Nikāya.*[1]

[1] S. iii. 81-105.

Khajjanīya Sutta.—The well-taught Ariyan disciple, remembering his past lives, realises how, in the past, he has been a prey to the body, feelings, perception, activities and consciousness; how he is still their prey, and will be so in the future, too, if he be enamoured of them. Thus realising, he conceives disgust for the body, etc., is repelled by them, and obtains release from them. He thereby attains freedom and becomes aware that he is free.[1]

[1] S. iii. 86-91; this sutta is wrongly titled Sīha. in the *Samyutta text*; see KS. iii. 72, n. 3.

The sutta was also preached by **Mahinda** in the **Nandana** grove on the fifth day of his visit to Ceylon.[2]

In the *Vibhaṅga Commentary*[3] the sutta is referred to as the **Khajjanīyapariyāya.**

[2] Mhv. xv. 195. [3] VibhA. 32.

Khajjanīya-pariyāya.—See **Khajjanīya Sutta.**

Khajjūrakavaḍḍhamāna.—A tank in Ceylon.[1]

[1] Cv. lxvii. 39.

Khajjotanadī.—A river in Ceylon, tributary of the **Mahāvāḷuka-nadī.** Over it **Devappatirāja** built a bridge of thirty cubits.[1]

[1] Cv. lxxxvi. 22; see also Cv. *Trs.* ii. 173, n. 3.

Khajjopanaka Jātaka (No. 364).—See **Khajjopanaka-Pañha.**

Khajjopanaka-Pañha.—When, as a result of the conspiracy of **Senaka** and the other ministers of **Vedeha, Mahosadha** was compelled to flee from the Court and live as a potter outside the city gates, the devatā of the king's parasol, wishing to see him reinstated, appeared to the king and put to him several questions. The king consulted Senaka and his colleagues, but they could find no solution. The deity appeared again to him and said he was like a man who, wanting a fire, blows a firefly, crumbling over it cow-dung and grass, or, wanting milk, milks the cow's horn. She then threatened the king with death if her questions were not answered. In despair, the king sent for Mahosadha.[1]

It is evidently this story which is mentioned elsewhere[2] as a separate Jātaka, but no details are given, and the reader is referred to the Khajjopanaka-Pañha.

[1] J. vi. 371 f. [2] J. iii. 197.

Khañjadeva.—One of the ten chief warriors of **Duṭṭhagāmaṇī.** He was the youngest son of **Abhaya,** a householder of **Mahisadoṇika** in the **Nakulanaga** district. His name was **Deva,** but because of a slight limp he came to be known as Khañjadeva. When out hunting with the villagers, he would chase and catch buffaloes, grasp their leg with his hand, whirl them round his head and dash them on the ground, breaking their bones. **Kākavaṇṇatissa,** hearing of this, caused him to be brought to the court. Later, Khañjadeva took part in Duṭṭhagāmaṇī's campaigns.[1]

[1] Mhv. xxiii. 3, 78 ff.

Khantikakhipa.—See **Nāgita** (2).

Khaṇḍa.—The chief disciple of **Vipassī** Buddha,[1] whose step-brother he was. The Buddha preached his first sermon to Khaṇḍa and his friend **Tissa,** the chaplain's son, in the Deer Park at **Khema.** Later, Khaṇḍa became the Buddha's chief disciple[2] **Ekasaññaka,** in a previous birth, once gave alms to Khaṇḍa.[3]

1 D. ii. 11, 40; Bu. xx. 28; J. i. 41. 2 BuA. 196; AA. i. 80; DA. ii. 416; see also 457. 3 Ap. i. 121.

Khaṇḍakaviṭṭhika.—A village in Ceylon. The birthplace of **Sūranimila.**[1]

1 Mhv. xxiii. 19.

Khaṇḍacela.—A monastery (probably in Ceylon), the residence of **Padhāniya Thera.** While the Elder was once listening to the **Ariyavaṃsa** in the **Kaṇikārapadhānaghara** in the monastery, he was bitten by a snake, but bearing the pain in silence, concentrated his mind on the sermon. The poison sank to earth and he became an arahant.[1]

1 MA. i. 65.

Khaṇḍadeva.—A monk. He had been a disciple of the Buddha and was born in the **Aviha** Brahma-world, where he attained to arahantship at the moment of his birth. He is mentioned with six others, all in like circumstances, by **Ghaṭīkāra,** on the occasion of a visit he paid to the Buddha.[1]

1 S. i. 35, 60; ThigA. 222.

Khaṇḍadeviyāputta.—A monk, one of the associates of **Devadatta,** mentioned with **Kokālika, Kaṭamoraka Tissa** and **Samuddadatta.** They helped Devadatta in his attempt to cause a rift in the Saṅgha.[1] Khaṇḍadeviyāputta defended Devadatta when others blamed him[2] and was held in great esteem by **Thullanandā.**[3] The *Khuddakapāṭha Commentary*[4] mentions him in a list of wicked persons, together with those mentioned above, **Ciñcamāṇavikā,** and the brother of **Dīghavidassa.**

1 Vin. ii. 196; iii. 171.
2 *Ibid.*, iii. 174.
3 *Ibid.*, iii. 66; iv. 335.
4 KhpA. 126.

Khaṇḍaphulliya Thera.—An arahant. Ninety-two kappas ago he saw the thūpa of **Phussa** Buddha destroyed by elephants and overgrown with trees. He cleared it and restored it. Seventy-seven kappas ago he became king sixteen times under the name of **Jitasena.**[1]

1 Ap. i. 198.

Khaṇḍarāja.—A monastery in Ceylon, built by **Upatissa II.**[1]

[1] Cv. xxxvii. 186.

Khaṇḍavagga.—A district in **Rohaṇa.** The forces of the enemies of **Parakkamabāhu I.** once encamped there.[1]

[1] Cv. lxxv. 119-23.

Khaṇḍasīmā.—A sacred space in **Pulatthipura** included in the *sīmā* marked out for the Saṅgha by **Parakkamabāhu I.**[1]

[1] Cv. lxxviii. 68; see also Cv. *Trs.* ii. 110, n. 5.

Khaṇḍasumana Thera.—An arahant. He was born in **Pāvā** in the family of a **Malla** chieftain, and was called Khaṇḍasumana because, on his birthday, molasses and jasmine appeared in his house. Having heard the Buddha preach in **Cunda's** mango-grove at Pāvā, he entered the Order and became an arahant.

In the past he had built a railing of sandalwood round the thūpa of **Padumuttara** Buddha. In the time of **Kassapa** Buddha he was unable to get any flowers, the king having bought them all for his offerings; he therefore bought a *khaṇḍasumana*-flower at a great price and offered it at the thūpa of the Buddha.[1]

He is probably identical with **Saparivāriya Thera** of the *Apadāna.*[2] His *Apadāna*-verses are almost the same as those attributed to **Nandiya Thera.**[3]

[1] Thag. 96; ThagA. i. 198. [2] Ap. i. 172. [3] See ThagA. i. 82.

Khaṇḍahāla.—A brahmin; a former birth of **Devadatta.**
See the **Khaṇḍahāla Jātaka.**

Khaṇḍahāla Jātaka (No. 542).—**Khaṇḍahāla** was the chaplain of King **Ekarājā** of **Pupphavatī.** The chaplain took bribes, and the king's son, **Candakumāra,** having been told of this, once righted a wrong decision, thereby winning the applause of the people. The king appointed him judge, and Khaṇḍahāla vowed vengeance. Later the king, having dreamed of heaven, asked Khaṇḍahāla the way thither; the chaplain replied that the way lay through a sacrifice in which all the king's sons, his queens, his merchant princes, and his most treasured possessions should be offered. Khaṇḍahāla hoped thereby to bring about the death of Candakumāra. Ekarājā accepted the suggestion and made all preparations for the sacrifice. Several times the king wavered in his resolve, being interceded with by his parents, Canda and his wives, and the people. Khaṇḍahāla goaded him on, but at the moment when the sword was about to descend on the neck of Candakumāra, the latter's wife, **Candā,** daughter of the Pañcāla king, made an "act of truth," and **Sakka** appeared, brandishing a thunderbolt. Canda was saved, the crowd killed Khaṇḍahāla, and would have killed the king too but for the intervention of Sakka. The king was made an outcast and banished from the city, and Candakumāra, now the crowned king, supplied all his wants.[1]

Khaṇḍahāla is identified with **Devadatta,** Candā with **Rāhulamātā,** and Candakumāra with the Bodhisatta.

The story was told in reference to Devadatta's attempts to kill the Buddha by engaging the services of archers to shoot him.

The story is referred to as an example of a husband being saved by the virtue of his wife,[2] and also of one instance of Devadatta having greater power than the Bodhisatta.[3]

The Jātaka is sometimes called the **Candakumāra Jātaka.**

[1] J. vi. 129-57; the story is also found in the *Cariyāpiṭaka* as the **Candakumāra-cariyā.**

[2] J. iv. 47.

[3] Mil. 203.

Khaṇḍigāma.—A village in Ceylon. It contained a narrow pass where a battle took place between **Gajabāhu** and **Laṅkāpura,** in which the former was defeated. Later, the Adhikārin **Nātha** suffered defeat in the same place.[1]

[1] Cv. lxx. 216-81, 298; see also Cv. *Trs.* i. 305, n. 6.

1. **Khata Sutta.**—A man who praises and blames without scrutiny, who shows appreciation or displeasure without testing the object thereof—such a one carries with him an uprooted, lifeless self. Not so the man who has the opposite qualities.[1]

[1] A. ii 2 f.

2. **Khata Sutta.**—A man guilty of wrong conduct towards mother, father, the Tathāgata or a Tathāgata's followers is possessed of an uprooted, lifeless self.[1]

[1] A. ii. 4 f.

1. **Khattiya Sutta.**—A conversation between a *devatā* and the Buddha regarding the four best things of the world—best of bipeds, quadrupeds, of wives, and of sons.[1]

[1] S. i. 6.

2. **Khattiya Sutta.**—A conversation between **Jāṇussoṇī** and the Buddha on the ends of their efforts as envisaged by khattiyas, brahmaṇas, householders, women, thieves and recluses.[1]

[1] A. iii. 362 f.

Khattiyānī or Velāmikā.—Chief of the eighty-four thousand women who waited on the Bodhisatta when he was once a mighty king of **Kusāvatī**[1] (named **Mahāsudassana**).

[1] S. iii. 146; but see D. ii. 188.

Khadira Sutta.—It is just as impossible to destroy *dukkha* without realising the Four Noble Truths as it is to make a leaf-basket of acacia leaves, etc., or to fetch water in such a basket, or to use the leaves for a fan.[1]

[1] S. v. 438.

Khadiranganī.—A village in Ceylon. **Kitti** (afterwards **Vijayabāhu I.**) once occupied a stronghold in the village and fought a successful battle near by.[1]

[1] Cv. lvii. 72; lviii. 36.

Khadiraṅgāra Jātaka (No. 40).—Once the Bodhisatta was Treasurer of Benares, and a Pacceka Buddha, rising from a seven days' *samāpatti*, came to him at meal time. The Bodhisatta sent him some food, but **Māra** created a pit of glowing *khadira*-embers between the Pacceka Buddha and the Treasurer's house. When the Treasurer heard of this, he took the bowl of food himself and stepped into the pit, ready to die rather than to have his alms-giving thwarted. A lotus sprang up to receive his foot, the pit vanished, and Māra, discomfited, vanished

The story was related to **Anāthapiṇḍika.**

A *devatā*, who lived in the upper storey of his palace, had to come with her children down to the ground floor whenever the Buddha visited Anāthapiṇḍika. She tried to check the merchant's munificence by talking to his manager and his eldest son, but all in vain. At last, when as a result of his extreme piety Anāthapiṇḍika's wealth was exhausted, the *devatā* ventured to approach him and warn him of his impending ruin if he did not take heed. He ordered her out of the house, and she had, perforce, to obey. In despair she sought the aid of **Sakka,** who suggested that she should recover for the merchant all his debts, and reveal to him his hidden treasure which had been lost sight of. She did so, but Anāthapiṇḍika, before consenting to pardon her, took her to the Buddha, who then related this Jātaka. The **Velāmaka Sutta** was also preached on this occasion.[1] For a continuation of the story see the **Siri Jātaka.**

According to the *Dhammapada Commentary*[2] the Khadiraṅgāra Jākata was preached in reference to the two friends **Sirigutta** and **Gharadinna.** It is said[3] that at the preaching of the Jātaka eighty-four thousand beings realised the Truth.

[1] J. i. 226-34; see also the Visayha Jātaka.

[2] DhA. i. 447.

[3] AA. i. 57.

Khadiravaniya.—The name of the Bodhisatta when he was once born as a bird in a *khadira-wood.* See the **Kandagalaka Jātaka.**[1]

[1] J. ii. 162 f.

Khadiravaniya-Revata.—See **Revata.**

Khadirāvaḷi Vihāra.—A monastery in **Rohaṇa. Dappula I.** built it and offered it to the presiding deity of the place (probably **Skanda**).[1]

[1] Cv. xlv. 55; see also Cv. *Trs.* i. 94, n. 3.

Khantivaṇṇa Jātaka (No. 225)—A courtier of Brahmadatta, king of Benares, started an intrigue in the king's harem, and a servant of the courtier did likewise in his master's house. When the courtier brought the servant to the king, the king advised the master to be patient, as good servants were rare, and, said the king, he knew of a courtier who had acted in the same way, but his king did not wish to lose him.

The story was related to the king of Kosala, who had been made a cuckold by one of his young and zealous courtiers.[1]

[1] J. ii. 206 f.

Khanti Sutta.—See **Vepacitti Sutta.**

Khantivādī.—The title of the ascetic of the **Khantivādī Jātaka** (*q.v.*).

Khantivādī Jātaka (No. 313).—The Bodhisatta, under the name of **Kuṇḍaka,** was once born in a very rich family of **Kāsī.** After the death of his parents he gave away his immense wealth in charity and became an ascetic in the Himālaya. Returning later to Kāsī, he dwelt in the royal park, being tended by the commander-in-chief. One day **Kalābu,** king of Benares, visited the park with his harem and, falling into a drunken sleep, left the women to their own devices; they, wandering about and meeting the ascetic, asked him to preach to them. When the king woke he sought his women, and seeing the ascetic and being told that he had been preaching on patience (*khanti*), he gave orders that the ascetic's own patience be tested. The ascetic was subjected to various forms of ill-treatment until, becoming more and more angry at his composure, the king gave orders for him to be tortured by the cutting off of his limbs. As the king left the park the earth opened and he was swallowed in **Avīci.** The commander-in-chief, hearing what had happened, hurried off to the ascetic to ask forgiveness. The ascetic declared that he bore no malice, and died of his injuries with a blessing to the king on his lips. It is told by some that he went back to the Himālaya.

The story was related at **Jetavana** in reference to a wrathful monk.[1] Kalābu was **Devadatta** and the commander-in-chief, **Sāriputta.**

The Jātaka is frequently mentioned as an example of supreme forgiveness, the ascetic being referred to as Khantivādī.[2] The Jātaka further illustrates how a man's anger can grow towards an unoffending victim,[3] and how an angry man loses all his prosperity.[4]

[1] J. iii. 39-43.
[2] *E.g.*, DhA. i. 126; KhpA. 149; J. i. 46; iii. 178; vi. 257; BuA. 51.
[3] J. iv. 11.
[4] J. v. 113, 119.

Khanda.—Name of a god, the Pāli equivalent of the Sanskrit Skanda, mentioned with Siva in the *Udāna Commentary.*[1]

[1] UdA. 351.

1. **Khandha Sutta.**—The four *satipaṭṭhānas* must be developed in order to destroy the five *upādānakkhandas.*[1]

[1] A. iv. 458 f.

2. **Khandha Sutta.**—The four kinds of recluses—*Samaṇa-m-acala, Samaṇapuṇḍārika, Samaṇapaduma,* and *Samaṇasukhumāla*—in reference to the contemplation of the five *upādānakkhandhas.*[1]

[1] A. ii. 90 f.

3. **Khandha Sutta.**—Preached to **Rāhula.** The *khandhas* are fleeting, unhappy, and have, therefore, no *attā.*[1]

[1] S. ii. 249, 252.

4. **Khandha Sutta.**—The Four Noble Truths in respect to the five *upādānakkhandhas.*[1]

[1] S. v. 425.

Khandhakā.—The name given to a portion of the *Vinaya Piṭaka*. This is generally further divided into two parts, the **Mahāvagga** and the **Cullavagga.** It contains an attempt to give a coherent picture of the whole legal life of the Saṅgha, with detailed and connected accounts of the admission thereto, the ceremony of the uposatha, the annually recurring observances connected with the rainy season, etc. An account is given, in the case of each regulation, of the occasion on which it was formulated by the Buddha. The separate chapters are arranged in chronological order, and are intended to present a connected account of ecclesiastical history from the time of the Enlightenment of the Buddha down to that of the Second Council, convened one hundred years after the death of the Buddha.[1] In many ways the Khandhakā resemble the *Sutta Vibhaṅga* of the Vinaya, but while in the case of the Vibhaṅga the stories were added later to an original basis of regulations, the *Pātimokkha*, in that of the Khandhakā the regulations and the stories were contemporary.

The Khandhakas consist of eighty *bhāṇavāras*,[2] and are divided into twenty-two chapters, ten in the Mahāvagga and twelve in the Cullavagga. Each chapter is called a *khandhaka*. Thus, the first chapter is the Mahākhandaka; the second, the Uposathakhandhaka, and so on.

[1] See Oldenberg, *Vinaya Piṭaka* I., Introd., xxii. f.; Law, *Pāli Lit.*, i. 14 f.
[2] DA. i. 13.

Khandha Paritta.—One of the Parittas included in the collection of Parittas.[1] The text of this Paritta is given in the Aṅguttara Nikāya[2] as **Ahinda Sutta.**

[1] Mil. 150.
[2] ii. 72 f.; it is also found at Vin. ii. 109 f.; see also Khandhavatta Jātaka.

Khandha Vagga.—The third book of the *Saṃyutta Nikāya*. It consists of thirteen chapters (*Saṃyuttas*). In Burma a special *ṭīkā* was written on this section.[1]

[1] Bode, *op. cit.*, 103.

Khandha Saṃyutta.—The twenty-second chapter of the *Saṃyutta Nikāya* and the first chapter of the *Khandha Vagga*. It consists of one hundred and fifty suttas, divided into three sections. The chapter deals mainly with the five *khandhas* or constituent elements.[1]

[1] S. iii. 1-188.

Khandhaka Thūpa.—A cetiya (probably in the **Cetiyapabbata**). King **Lañjaka Tissa** caused a mantling of stone to be made for it.[1]

[1] Mhv. xxxiii. 25.

v.l. **Kaṭṭhaka, Katthaka, Kanthaka Thūpa, Kaṇṭaka Thūpa.** See also **Katthaka.**

Khandhapura.—The Pāli name for Myein Zaing in Burma.[1]

[1] Bode, *op. cit.*, 40.

Khandhavatta Jātaka (No. 203).—The Bodhisatta was once born in Kāsi, and later became an ascetic. On it being reported to him that many ascetics died of snake-bite, he gathered them together and taught them how, by cultivating love for the four royal races of snakes—the **Virūpakkhas,** the **Erāpattas,** the **Chabbyāputtas,** and the **Kaṇhagotamas**—they could prevent themselves from ever being bitten by any creature.

The story was told in reference to a monk who died of snake-bite.[1]

[1] J. ii. 144 ff.; *cf.* Vin. ii. 109 f. The story is evidently an expansion of the Khanda Paritta.

1. **Khandhā Sutta.**—The five khandhas and the five *upādānakkhandhas.*[1]

[1] S. iii. 47.

2. **Khandhā Sutta.**—It is for the full comprehension of the five *upādānakkhandhas* that the Noble Eightfold Path should be followed.[1]

[1] S. v. 60.

Khandhāvara.—The family name of **Āyasmanta.**[1] They were worshippers of the god Skanda, and were an offshoot of the **Moriyavaṃsa.**[2]

[1] Cv. lxxx. 37.

[2] According to the colophon of the Sinhalese poem, *Sälalihiṇisandesa.*

1. "**Khandhena**" **Sutta.**—All the *khandhas* are impermanent. He who has faith in the doctrine is a *saddhānusāri*; he who has understood it moderately is a *dhammānusāri*; he who knows and sees the doctrine is a *sotāpanna.*[1]

[1] S. iii. 227 f.

2. "**Khandhena**" **Sutta.**—The arising of suffering is due to the arising of the body, etc.; its cessation is brought about by their cessation.[1]

[1] S. iii. 231.

3. "**Khandhena**" **Sutta.**—Desire and lust (*chandarāga*) for body, etc., brings about corruption of the mind.[1]

[1] S. iii. 234.

1. **Khamā Sutta.**—The four modes of progress (*paṭipadā*); that which is impatient, that which is patient, that which tames, and that which calms.[1]

[1] A. ii. 152 f.

2. **Khamā Sutta.**—Similar to the above, but the practice of the *paṭipadā* is differently illustrated.[1]

[1] A. ii. 153 f.

Khambhakata Vagga.—The Third Section of the *Sekhiyā* of the *Vinaya Piṭaka.*[1]

[1] Vin. iv. 188-91.

1. **Khaya Sutta.**—Preached to **Rādha.** The body, etc., are liable to destruction. That which, by nature, is transient and perishing must be put away.[1]

[1] S. iii. 197, 199, 201.

2. **Khaya Sutta.**—All things are liable to destruction.[1]

[1] S. iv. 28.

3. **Khaya Sutta.**—The Buddha exhorts the monks to cultivate the seven *bojjhaṅgas*, which lead to the destruction of craving. In answer to a question of **Udāyī** he goes on to explain how the cultivation is pursued.[1]

[1] S. v. 86 f.

Khara.—A yakkha, friend of **Suciloma.** He was passing through **Gayā** with Suciloma when the latter questioned the Buddha on his doctrine, as recorded in the **Suciloma Sutta.**[1] Khara had been a monk in a previous birth, and had once rubbed on his body oil belonging to the Saṅgha without asking the permission of the monks. As a result his body was ugly, and his skin coarse and rough and like a " tiled roof." Whenever he wished to frighten anybody his skin would stand up like tiles on a roof. At the end of the recitation of the Suciloma Sutta, Khara became a sotāpanna, and his skin became beautiful and golden-hued.[2]

[1] S. i. 207 f.; SN., p. 47 f.; SNA. i. 302. [2] *Ibid.*, 305.

Kharadāṭhika.—A yakkha. The Bodhisatta, who became **Maṅgala Buddha** in one of his later births, left his kingdom and lived as a recluse in the forest with his wife and children. The yakkha, having heard of the Bodhisatta's generosity, came to him, begged for his two children, and on being given them ate them in the sight of their father. Even when the blood flowed from the yakkha's mouth the Bodhisatta remained unmoved, and wished that in the future there should issue from his own body rays of light, in colour like to streams of blood. As a result of this wish Maṅgala's aura always spread throughout the ten thousand world systems, while that of other Buddhas spread as a rule only one fathom from their body.[1]

[1] J. i. 31; BuA. 116 f.

Kharaputta Jātaka (No. 386).—Once **Senaka,** king of Benares, saved a Nāga-king from being beaten to death by village lads, and the Nāga in gratitude gave the king many gifts, including a Nāga maiden to minister to him, and a charm by which he might trace her if ever she went out of his sight. One day the king went with her to the park, and there Senaka found her making love to a water-snake and struck her with a bamboo. She went to the Nāga-world and complained that she had been ill-treated. The Nāga-king sent four attendants to kill Senaka, but they, overhearing the king relating the story to his queen, reported the matter to the Nāga-king. The latter confessed his error to Senaka, and in order to make amends taught him a charm which gave him the knowledge of all sounds. Senaka was told that if he taught anyone else the charm he would perish in flames. Senaka's queen discovered his possession of the charm, and did not cease to beg him to teach it to her, even though she knew that by so doing he would incur death. Unable to resist her, Senaka went with his queen to the park to teach her the charm and enter the flames. **Sakka's** throne was heated, and transforming himself and his wife into goats they waited for the king, and on the approach of his chariot began to make love. The steeds in the chariot were shocked and upbraided the goats for their stupidity, but the goats replied that the steeds were stupid to let themselves be fastened to a chariot which carried so stupid a king as Senaka. The king, hearing their conversation, alighted from the chariot and, sending the queen on, asked of Sakka how he could evade his promise. Sakka suggested that the queen be told that she would receive one hundred lashes as part of her initiation. The queen agreed to this, but, when the flogging started, wished to change her mind, but the king, remembering her selfishness, caused the flogging to be carried out.

The story was related concerning a monk who was tempted by his former wife. Senaka was identified with the monk; **Sāriputta** was the chief steed and Sakka the Bodhisatta.[1]

One of the verses in the Jātaka occurs also in the **Mahāsutasoma Jātaka.**[2]

[1] J. iii. 275 ff.

[2] J. v. 498.

Kharassara Jātaka (No. 79).—A minister of the king of Benares arranged in secret with a band of robbers that when he had collected the revenue of a border village he would march his men off to the jungle, leaving the robbers free to secure the booty. The plan was carried out, and half the booty was made over to him; but his treachery became known and he was disgraced.

The story was related in reference to a minister of the Kosala king, who was guilty of similar treachery.[1]

[1] J. i. 354 f.

Kharādiyā.—See the **Kharādiya Jātaka.**

Kharādiya Jātaka (No. 15).—The Bodhisatta was once born as a leader of deer. His sister **Kharādiyā** brought him her son that he might teach him the widsom of the deer, but the young deer was disobedient and did not attend his lessons. As a result, he was caught in a gin and killed by huntsmen.

The story was told in reference to an unruly monk. Kharādiyā is identified with **Uppalavaṇṇā.**[1]

[1] J. i. 159 f.

Khalātiya Petavatthu.—The story of a courtesan. She had beautiful hair which, however, she lost, owing to the machinations of a rival. She once stole clothes from some men who lay asleep, and on another occasion gave alms to a monk. She was later born in an ocean *vimāna* as a naked peta with lovely hair; some merchants, while going to **Suvaṇṇabhūmi,** saw her, and on learning her story gave clothes on her behalf to a pious man in their company, and as a result clothes immediately appeared on her. Later the merchants gave alms to the Buddha in her name, and she was born in **Tāvatiṃsa.**[1]

[1] Pv. i. 10; PvA. 46 ff.

1. **Khaluṅka Sutta.**—The eight defects of a horse and the corresponding eight defects of a man.[1]

[1] A. iv. 190 f.

2. **Khaluṅka Sutta.**—Three groups of three classes of horses and the corresponding three classes of men.[1]

[1] A. iv. 397 f.

Khaluggata.—See **Baluggata.**

Khalupacchā Sutta.—On the five kinds of monks found among those who refuse food offered them after the normal time ("*Khalupacchābhattikā*").[1]

[1] A. iii. 220.

Khallāṭanāga.—Son of **Saddhā-Tissa** and younger brother of **Lañjaka-Tissa.** He was king of Ceylon (50-43 B.C.). Among his religious works was the construction of the **Kurundavāsoka Vihāra.** He was killed by the general **Mahārattaka.** Khallāṭanāga's wife was **Anulā,** and his son was **Mahācūḷika.**[1]

[1] Mhv. xxxiii. 29 ff.; Dpv. xx. 12 f.

1. **Khānu.**—A Tamil general whom **Duṭṭhagāmaṇi** conquered in his campaign. His stronghold was at **Khānugāma.**[1]

[1] Mhv. xxv. 14.

2. **Khānu.**—A tank, probably at **Khānugāma,** built by **Mahāsena.**[1]

[1] Mhv. xxxvii. 47.

Khānu Koṇḍañña.—A thera. He became an arahant while living in the forest. One day, while sitting on a flat stone, he entered into a trance. A pack of thieves, mistaking him for the trunk of a tree, piled their sacks on to his head and body and slept around him. In the morning, discovering their mistake, they begged forgiveness and, having listened to his preaching, became monks. It was this incident which gained for him the name of Khānu ("stump"). The Buddha praised him on account of his achievement.[1]

Khānu Koṇḍañña's *samādhi* is classified under *vipphārā iddhi*, inasmuch as even the uproar, caused by the thieves in piling up their sacks, did not disturb it.[2]

[1] DhA. ii. 254 f.   [2] *E.g.*, BuA. 24; PsA. 497.

Khānumata.—A brahmin village of **Magadha,** presented to **Kūṭadanta** by **Bimbisāra.** The Buddha once stayed there at the **Ambalaṭṭhika** pleasance, and there he preached the **Kūṭadanta Sutta.**[1]

[1] D. i. 127.

Khārodakā.—A river in **Avīci,** flowing alongside the **Asipattavana.**[1]

[1] M. iii. 185; SNA. ii. 479.

Khiḍḍāpadosikā.—A class of devas who live in the **Cātummahārājika**-world. For ages they spend their time in laughter and in sport of sensual lusts. In consequence their self-possession is corrupted and they fall from their state.[1] They are so called because they are corrupted and are destroyed by sport (*khiḍḍāya padussanti, vinassanti*).[2] It is said that while playing about in such pleasances as **Nandanavana, Cittalatāvana** and **Phārusakavana,** they forget to eat and drink and fade away like flowers. Their death is due to self-consciousness (*attasañcetanā*).[3] They are, as it were, burnt up by their infatuation (*mohassa anudahanatāya—mohanavasena hi tesaṃ satisammoso*).[4] They were present at the preaching of the **Mahāsamaya Sutta.**[5]

v.l. **Khiḍḍāpadūsikā.**

[1] D. i. 19; PsA. 441; NidA. i. 108.
[2] DA. i. 113.
[3] AA. ii. 544
[4] VibhA. 498.
[5] D. ii. 260.

1. **Khitaka Thera.**—An arahant. He was born in a brahmin family in **Sāvatthi,** and having heard of the supernormal powers of **Mahā Moggallāna** entered the Order, wishing to attain to a like proficiency. He developed sixfold *abhiññā* and great supernormal powers.

In the time of **Padumuttara** Buddha he was a yakkha chief, and when he saw the Buddha and greeted him, the Buddha, to his great joy, preached to him. Eighty kappas ago he became king under the name of **Sumaṅgala.**[1] He is probably identical with **Supāricariya** of the *Apadāna*.[2]

[1] Thag. v. 104; ThagA. i. 209 f.
[2] Ap. i. 181.

2. **Khitaka Thera.**—An arahant. He was born in a brahmin family of **Kosala** and, having heard the Buddha preach, entered the Order, in due course winning arahantship. Later he dwelt in the forest, stirring enthusiasm in the forest-dwelling monks.

In the time of **Vipassī** Buddha he was a park-keeper, and having seen the Buddha going through the air offered him a coconut fruit, which the Buddha stopped to accept.[1]

He is probably identical with **Nāḷikeradāyaka Thera** of the *Apadāna*.[2] His *Apadāna* verses are also found under the name of **Kuṇḍala Thera.**[3]

[1] Thag. vv. 191-2; ThagA. 315 f.
[2] Ap. ii. 447 f.
[3] ThagA. i. 72.

1. **Khila Sutta.**—Fallowness of heart arises from doubt in the Buddha, the Dhamma, the Saṅgha, and the way of training (*sikkhā*), and from anger against one's fellow-celibates.[1]

[1] A. iii. 248; iv. 460; D. iii. 237; M. i. 101; Vibh. 377, etc.

2. **Khila Sutta.**—Same as the above, but here the five *vinibandhā*, which are elsewhere given as a separate section (see the **Vinibandha Sutta**), are added at the end of the *khilā*.[1]

[1] A. v. 17 ff.

Khīra Sutta.—Preached at **Sāvatthi.** Incalculable is the beginning of *saṃsāra*. The milk drunk by a being during his wanderings in *saṃsāra* is more in quantity than the water of the four seas.[1]

[1] S. ii. 180.

1. **Khīragāma.**—A village in **Rohaṇa,** where the forces of **Parakkamabāhu I.** fought a battle against the rebels.[1] In Khīragāma Queen **Ratnāvalī** was cremated, and on the spot a cetiya was erected.[2]

[1] Cv. lxxiv. 162 f. [2] *Ibid.*, lxxix. 71; see also Cv. *Trs.* ii. 36, n. 2.

2. **Khīragāma.**—See **Mahākhīragāma.**

Khīrarukkha Sutta.—Where lust, malice, and infatuation exist in a man, even trifling objects, cognisable by the senses, find their way into the mind, just as, in a sap-tree, sap flows out wherever man cuts it with an axe.[1]

[1] S. iv. 159 f.

Khīravāpikagāma.—A village in Ceylon, near the district of **Ambavana.**[1]

[1] Cv. lxvi. 85.

Khilā Sutta.—The three mental obstructions—lust, hatred, and illusion—to the comprehension of the Noble Eightfold Path.[1]

[1] S. v. 57.

Khujjanāga.—Son of **Kaniṭṭha-Tissa.** He was king of Ceylon (246-248 A.C.). He was slain by his brother **Kuñcanāga.**[1]

[1] Mhv. xxxvi. 18 f.

1. **Khujjasobhita Thera.**—An arahant. He was a brahmin of **Pāṭaliputta.** He entered the Order under **Ānanda,** after the Buddha's death, and in due course won arahantship. At the First Council held in the **Sattapaṇṇi** Cave, he was sent to bring Ānanda to the Assembly. He travelled through the earth, gave the message to Ānanda, and returning through the air announced his arrival to the Saṅgha, through the mediumship of a devatā who had been placed at the door of the cave to ward off

Māra and his followers. Sobhita was called "Khujja" because he was slightly hunchbacked.

In the time of **Padumuttara** he saw the Buddha passing with a large assembly of monks and praised him in ten stanzas.[1]

He is probably identical with **Sayampaṭibhāniya** of the *Apadāna*.[2]

[1] Thag. 234-6; ThagA. i. 350 f.

[2] Ap. ii. 410 f.

2. **Khujjasobhita Thera.**—One of the Pācīnaka ("Eastern") monks who proclaimed the ten indulgences at **Vesāli.** He was one of their representatives on the Committee of the Saṅgha appointed to settle the dispute between the monks of Vesāli and the orthodox monks.[1] According to the *Mahavaṃsa*[2] this Khujjasobhita was a disciple of Ānanda and, therefore, to be identified with Khujjasobhita (1). The latter was, however, an arahant, and therefore not likely to side with the Vesāli heretics. The identification is evidently incorrect also on other grounds, among them that of age.

[1] Vin. ii. 305; Dpv. iv. 44; v. 25, 80.

[2] iv. 57; this passage is also found in the *Samantapāsādikā* (i. 34).

Khujjuttarā.—She was born of a nurse in the house of the banker **Ghosita,**[1] and later became a slave of Queen **Sāmāvatī.** The queen gave her daily the eight pieces of money allowed to her by the king for the purchase of flowers. Khujjuttarā bought flowers with four pieces from the gardener **Sumana,** the remaining four pieces she kept. One day the Buddha visited Sumana, and Khujjuttarā, having heard the Buddha preach to him, became a *sotāpanna*. That day she spent the whole amount on flowers. The queen asked her how she had obtained so many, and she told her the whole story. From that time Sāmāvatī showed Khujjuttarā all honour, bathed her in perfumed water, and heard the Dhamma from her. Khujjuttarā became, as it were, a mother to Sāmāvatī, and going regularly to hear the Dhamma, would return and preach it to her and her five hundred attendant women. Under the instruction of Khujjuttarā they all became *sotāpannas*. When Sāmāvatī expressed a desire to see the Buddha, Khujjuttarā suggested that she should pierce holes in the walls of the palace and gaze on the Buddha as he passed along the street. After the death of Sāmāvatī, Khujjuttarā seems to have spent all her time in religious works, listening to the preaching of the Dhamma. The Buddha declared her foremost among lay women by reason of her extensive knowledge (*bahussutānaṃ*).[2]

[1] AA. i. 232.

[2] A. i. 26; DhA. i. 208 ff.; AA. i. 226, 237 f.; ItvA. 23 f.; PsA. 498 f.

Once, in the past, she was a serving-woman of the king of Benares, and one day, having seen a Pacceka Buddha who was slightly hunchbacked, she threw a blanket over her shoulder, and bending down to look like a hunchback, she imitated the Buddha's manner of walking. Therefore, in this present birth she herself was hunchbacked. On another occasion eight Pacceka Buddhas, receiving their bowls filled with rice-porridge from the palace, found the bowls so hot that they were obliged to move them from one hand to the other. Seeing this, Khujjuttarā gave them eight ivory bracelets as stands for their bowls. It is said that these bracelets are still preserved in the **Nandamūlapabbhāra.** Because of this act Khujjuttarā obtained profound wisdom in this birth, and was able to learn the Tipiṭaka by heart. In the time of **Kassapa** Buddha she was the daughter of a treasurer, and had a friend who was a nun; one day when she was adorning herself at eventide the nun visited her, and as there was no servant-girl at the time Khujjuttarā asked the nun to do various things for her. As a result she was born as a slave. Her desire to become chief among learned lay-women was formed in the time of **Padumuttara** Buddha, on her seeing a similar rank bestowed on a lay-woman.[3]

It is said that the discourses in the *Itivuttaka* are those which Khujjuttarā learned from the Buddha and later repeated to Sāmāvatī and her attendant women. Because these discourses were all preached at **Kosambī** and repeated there by her, there was no need to specify the place of their preaching; hence the formula "*Ekaṃ samayaṃ Bhagavā Kosambiyaṃ viharati*" is omitted, and instead is found "*vuttaṃ h'etaṃ Bhagavatā arahatā.*"[4]

Khujjuttarā is several times mentioned as the paragon among laywomen disciples,[5] and in the Commentaries[6] she is given as an example of *kāmabhoginiyo* (women who enjoyed the pleasures of the senses). She possessed the *paṭisambhidā* while yet a householder, but it was the *paṭisambhidā* of the probationer (*sekha*).[7]

Khujjuttarā is identified with the slave-girl in the **Uraga Jātaka**[8] and in the **Bhisa Jātaka,**[9] the nurse in the **Culla-Sutasoma Jātaka**[10] and the hunchback in the **Kusa Jātaka.**[11] Owing to her personal experience (*abhijānato*) she had the power of recalling her past births.[12]

It is said[13] that when Sāmāvatī and her companions were burnt to death, Khujjuttarā escaped because she had not participated in their

[3] DhA. i. 226 f., etc.; Dvy. 339-41.

[4] ItvA. 25.

[5] *E.g.*, A. i. 88; ii. 164; iv. 368; S. ii. 236.

[6] *E.g.*, DA. iii. 910.

[7] Vsm. 442; VibhA. 388.

[8] J. iii. 168.

[9] J. iv. 314.

[10] J. v. 192.

[11] *Ibid.*, 312.

[12] Mil. 78.

[13] UdA. 384.

previous misdeeds. At the time of the fire she was absent from the palace, some say ten leagues away.

Khudda-Aggabodhi.—The name given to Aggabodhi II.[1] He was also called Khuddarājā.[2] See **Aggabodhi** (3).

[1] Cv. xlii. 40; xliv. 2. [2] *Ibid.*, 138.

Khuddaka.—The name given to the section on *Pācittiya* which occurs in the *Sutta Vibhaṅga* of the *Vinaya Piṭaka.*[1]

[1] Vin. iv. 174, 345.

Khuddaka Nikāya.—Sometimes called **Khuddaka Gantha.** The fifth and last division of the *Sutta Piṭaka.* It consists of fifteen independent treatises, some belonging to the earlier period, while others may be ascribed to the later stratum of the Pāli Canon.[1] This Nikāya is composed for the most part in verse, and contains all the most important collections of Pāli poetry. The fifteen books are: Khuddakapāṭha, Dhammapada, Udāna, Itivuttaka, Sutta Nipāta, Vimāna-vatthu, Peta-vatthu, Theragāthā, Therīgathā, Jātaka, the Niddesas (Mahā- and Culla-), Paṭisambhidāmagga, Apadāna, Buddhavaṃsa, and Cariyāpiṭaka.[2] According to another classification the whole of the Vinaya Piṭaka and the Abhidhamma Piṭaka and all the teachings of the Buddha, not included in the remaining four Nikāyas, are regarded as forming the Khuddaka Nikāya.[3] The **Dīghabhāṇakas** refused to accept the authenticity of the Khuddakapāṭha, Cariyāpiṭaka, and the Apadāna, and included the other books as part of the Abhidhamma Piṭaka. The **Majjhimabhāṇakas** did not accept the Khuddakapāṭha but acknowledged the rest, and included them in the Sutta Piṭaka.[4] According to Burmese tradition four other later books are added to this list: Milindapañha, Suttasaṅgaha, Peṭakopadesa, and Nettippakaraṇa.[5]

[1] For details see under the different books.
[2] Sp. i. 18; DA. i. 17.
[3] *Ibid.*, 23; Sp. i. 27.
[4] DA. i. 15.
[5] Bode, *op. cit.*, 4.

Khuddaka Tissa (Khudda Tissa).—A thera credited with great *iddhi*-power. He lived in **Maṅgana,** and was one of those who shared the sour millet-gruel given by **Duṭṭhagāmaṇī** in his flight from battle. Khuddaka Tissa divided it among sixty thousand monks in the **Kelāsa Vihāra.**[1] He was one of the *pacchāgatakā* (late comers ?) to the Assemblies of **Kuddālaka, Mūgapakkha, Ayoghara,** and **Hatthipāla.**[2] He is probably identical with **Kujja Tissa** (*q.v.*).

[1] Mhv. xxxii. 53 f. [2] J. vi. 30.

Khuddakañcakuṇḍa.—A Damiḷa chief,[1] generally referred to as **Cullakañcakuṇḍa** (*q.v.*).

[1] Cv. lxxvi. 170.

Khuddakapāṭha.—One of the fifteen books of the **Khuddaka Nikāya,** generally mentioned first in this list.[1] Its rightful claim to be included as part of the Tipiṭaka was disputed both by the **Dīghabhāṇakas** and the **Majjhimabhāṇakas.**[2] It is generally acknowledged[3] that the work is of later composition and that it contains extracts from earlier works. It may have been composed in Ceylon, and it is significant that its first mention as a canonical book should occur only in the commentaries. It is not mentioned even in the *Milindapañha.*

The book consists of nine sections on texts: *Saraṇattaya, Dasasikkhāpada, Dvattiṃsākāra, Kumārapañha,* and five suttas—*Maṅgala, Ratana, Tirokuḍḍa, Nidhikaṇḍa,* and *Metta*—all found elsewhere in the canon.

According to the Commentary[4] the book derives its name from the first four texts, which are shorter than the remaining five.

[1] *E.g.,* DA. i. 17.
[2] DA. i. 15.
[3] For a discussion see Law, *Pāli Lit.,* i. 7 f.; 34 f.
[4] KhpA. 13. The Commentary was written by Buddhaghosa. See also Gv. 59, 68.

Khuddakavatthu-Khandhaka.—The fifth chapter of the *Culla Vagga* of the *Vinaya Piṭaka.*[1]

[1] Vin. ii. 105-43.

Khuddakā.—Name of a tribe.[1]

[1] Ap. ii. 359.

Khuddapārinda.—A Tamil usurper. He was the brother of **Parinda** who had usurped **Dhātusena's** throne. He reigned for sixteen years[1] (between 430 and 460 A.C.).

[1] Cv. xxxviii. 30 f.

Khuddarājā.—See **Khudda-Aggabodhi.**

Khuddarūpī.—See **Maddarūpī.**

Khuddavalikagāma.—A harbour in North Ceylon.[1]

[1] Cv. lxxxviii. 23.

Khuddasikkhā.—A Compendium of the *Vinaya,* composed by **Dhammasiri** and ascribed to a period before Buddhaghosa.[1] To this Com-

[1] *J.P.T.S.,* 1883, pp. 86 f.

pendium there exists a Sinhalese paraphrase of the eleventh century, and based on the Compendium is one *Porāṇa-ṭīkā* by **Revata** and another by **Saṅgharakkhita.**[2]

[2] For details see P.L.C., 77; Bode, *op. cit.*, 24; see also Sās. 69; Svd. 1208 f.; Gv. 62, 70; SadS. 64.

Khuradhāra.—A Niraya. Those guilty of abortion are born there.[1]

[1] J. v. 269, 274 f.

Khurappa Jātaka (No. 265).—Once the Bodhisatta was a forester, head of five hundred others. They hired themselves out to guide men through the forest. One day, while conducting a caravan, robbers fell on them and all but the Bodhisatta fled; he remained and drove the robbers off. When asked how he could do this, he replied that he who would do heroic deeds must contemn life.

The story was related in reference to a monk who had lost energy in his duties.[1]

[1] J. ii. 335 f.

Khuramāla, Khuramālī.—A sea. Once, merchants travelling from **Bhārukaccha** lost their way in it and were rescued by **Suppāraka.** In the sea were fishes with bodies like men and sharp razor-like snouts.[1]

[1] J. iv. 139.

Khulū.—Probably a wrong reading[1] for **Bhumū** (*q.v.*).

[1] D. iii. 6.

1. **Khetta Sutta.**—The eight qualities of a bad field in which to sow grain and the corresponding qualities of a good field. Similarly with the recipients of gifts.[1]

[1] A. iv. 237 f.

2. **Khetta Sutta.**—Few abstain from accepting fields; many do not.[1]

[1] S. v. 473.

Khettūpama-peta Vatthu.—The first story of the *Peta Vatthu.*[1]

[1] Pv. i. 1.

1. **Khema.**—The city in which **Sumana** Buddha was born.[1]

[1] J. i. 34; but in Bu. (v. 21) it is called **Mekhala.**

2. **Khema.**—The city in which **Tissa** Buddha was born.[1]

[1] J. i. 40. In Bu. (xviii. 16) it is called **Khemaka.**

3. **Khema.**—The city in which **Kakusandha** Buddha was born.[1] It was the capital of King **Khemaṅkara.**[2] See also No. 6 below.

[1] J. i. 42; Bu. (xxiii. 13) calls it **Khemavatī.** [2] See also Dvy. 242.

4. **Khema.**—A Khattiya, the Bodhisatta in the time of **Kakusandha** Buddha. He gave alms to the Buddha and the monks and entertained the Order.[1] He helped **Rūpanandā** to bring a branch of Kakusandha's bodhi-tree to Ceylon.[2] See also **Khemaṅkara.**

[1] D. ii. 7; J. i. 42; Bu. xxiii. 13; BuA. 211. [2] Mhv. xv. 79; MṬ. 351.

5. **Khema.**—The deer-park near **Bandhumatī.**[1] There the Buddha **Vipassī** was born, and there he preached his first sermon to his chief disciples, and later another sermon to their eighty-four thousand followers.[2]

This Khema is identical with the present **Isipatana.**[3]

[1] J. vi. 480; Bu. xx. 4; AA. i. 80, 169. [2] BuA. 196 f. [3] DA. ii. 471.

6. **Khema.**—The pleasaunce in which **Kakusandha** Buddha died.[1] It was near **Khemavatī** and was the birthplace of Kakusandha.[2]

[1] Bu. xxiii. 27. [2] BuA. 209.

7. **Khema.**—A pleasaunce near **Usabhavatī**; there the Buddha **Vessabhū** died.[1]

[1] Bu. xxii. 30; BuA. 209.

8. **Khema.**—A lake, three *gāvutas* in extent, to the north of Benares. It was constructed by King **Seyya** (*v.l.* **Saṃyama**). For details see the **Mahāhaṃsa Jātaka.**[1]

[1] J. v. 356; J. iv. 424.

9. **Khema.**—A seṭṭhiputta, nephew of **Anāthapiṇḍika.** He was very handsome and beloved of all women. Several times he was brought before the king on charges of adultery, but the king pardoned him out of regard for Anāthapiṇḍika. At the latter's request, the Buddha preached to Khema and showed him the error of his ways.

In the time of **Kassapa** Buddha he was a champion wrestler, and planted two coloured banners on the golden shrine of the Buddha and made a wish that all women, except his own kinswomen, should fall in love with him at sight.[1]

[1] DhA. iii. 481 f.

10. **Khema.**—A devaputta who visited the Buddha at **Jetavana** and spoke several verses on the desirability of leading the good life.[1]

[1] S. i. 57.

11. **Khema Thera.**—An arahant.[1] See **Khema Sutta** (2).

[1] A. iii. 358.

12. **Khema.**—A monk of Ceylon, pupil of **Dhammapālita** of **Rohaṇa.** He was well versed in the Tipiṭakā (" *tipeṭakī* "), and is mentioned among those who handed down the teaching of the Buddha in Ceylon in pupillary succession.[1]

[1] Vin. v. 3; Smp. i. 63.

13. **Khema.**—A teacher, probably of Ceylon, author of the **Khemappa-karaṇa.**[1]

[1] Gv. 61, 71; Svd. 1222; SadS. 65; Sās. 69.

14. **Khema.**—See **Khemaka** (3).

Khema Vagga.—The sixth chapter of the *Navaka Nipāta* of the *Aṅguttara Nikāya.*[1]

[1] A. iv. 455 f.

1. **Khema Sutta.**—An account of the visit paid to the Buddha at **Jetavana** by the devaputta **Khema** and the verses uttered by Khema on that occasion.[1]

[1] S. i. 57.

2. **Khema Sutta.**—Two monks, **Khema** and **Sumana,** living at **Andha-vana** near Sāvatthi, visited the Buddha. Khema stated before the Buddha that, when a monk has attained arahantship, the thought does not arise in him that he is inferior to anyone or that he has his equal. Having spoken thus, Khema took leave of the Buddha and departed; Sumana did likewise. When they were gone the Buddha declared to the monks that, by their statement, Khema and Sumana had manifested their arahantship.[1]

[1] A. iii. 358 f.

3. **Khema Sutta.**—On what is meant by having attained peace (*khema*).[1]

[1] A. iv. 455.

4. **Khema Sutta.**—The Buddha preaches peace and the path thereto.[1]

[1] S. iv. 371.

1. **Khemaka.**—A Sākyan of **Kapilavatthu,** father of **Abhirūpa-Nandā.**[1] See also **Kāḷa-Khemaka.**

[1] ThigA. 25; Ap. ii. 608.

2. **Khemaka Thera.**—An arahant. Once, when he lay very ill at the **Badarikārāmā,** near **Kosambī,** some monks, staying at the **Ghositārāma,** sent one of their number, **Dāsaka,** with a message to Khemaka, inquiring whether he managed to bear his pains. Dāsaka returned with the reply that he did not; he was sent again to ask if Khemaka had seen the self in the five *khandhas*; when Dāsaka returned with the answer that he had not, he was sent a third time to ask whether Khemaka was an arahant. "No," came the answer, and Dāsaka had to visit him a fourth time with the inquiry, What did Khemaka mean by self? In exasperation Khemaka came himself to Ghositārāma and explained how, even when the Noble Disciple has put away the five lower fetters, there still clings to him a subtle remnant of the "I" conceit. It is said that as a result of the sermon Khemaka himself and sixty others became arahants.[1]

The Commentary[2] explains that the monks wished to hear Khemaka because they knew his ability, and they also knew that if they showed keenness to learn he would come to them. They did not go to him because his hut was small, and they did not actually ask him to come to them because he was ill.

[1] S. iii. 126 ff. [2] SA. ii. 230 f.

3. **Khemaka, Khema, Khemanesāda.**—The name given to the fowler who caught the golden swan from **Cittakūṭa,** at the request of King **Seyya** (*v.l.* **Saṃyama**), as narrated in the **Mahāhaṃsa Jātaka** (*q.v.*). Khemaka received his name from the lake Khema, of which he was in charge. He is identified with **Channa.**[1]

[1] J. v. 356 ff.

4. **Khemaka.**—See **Khemavatī.**

1. **Khemaṅkara Thera.**—The constant attendant of **Sikhī Buddha.**[1] *v.l.* **Khemaṅkura.**

[1] D. ii. 6; Bu. xxi. 20; J. i. 41.

2. **Khemaṅkara.**—The king of **Khema** or **Khemavatī,** where the Buddha **Kakusandha** was born. *v.l.* **Khemākara.** His purohita was **Aggidatta,** Kakusandha's father.[1] He is sometimes also called **Khema.**[2]

[1] Bu. xxii. 13; BuA. 209; Dvy. 242. [2] MṬ. 351; D. ii. 7.

Khemappakaraṇa.—A work written by **Khema,** a thera, probably of Ceylon. The work is on the Abhidhamma and forms one of the Let-than (" Little-finger " manuals) studied in Burma. It is also known as the **Nāmarūpasamāsa.** A Commentary on it was written by **Vācissara.**[1]

[1] Gv. 61, 71; SadS. 63; for details see P.L.C. 156.

1. **Khemavatī.**—The capital of King **Khemaṅkara** and the birthplace of **Kakusandha.**[1] It is sometimes called **Khema.**[2]

[1] D. ii. 7; Bu. xxii. 13; BuA. 209; Dvy. 242.

[2] *E.g.,* J. i. 42.

2. **Khemavatī.**—The city of birth of **Tissa** Buddha.[1] There he preached the *Buddhavaṃsa* to his relatives.[2] It is sometimes also called **Khema** and **Khemaka.**

[1] Bu. xviii. 16.

[2] BuA. 190.

1. **Khemā Therī.**—An arahant, chief of the Buddha's women disciples. She was born in a ruling family at **Sāgala** in the **Madda** country, and her skin was of the colour of gold. She became the chief consort of King **Bimbisāra.** She would not visit the Buddha who was at **Veḷuvana,** lest he should speak disparagingly of her beauty with which she was infatuated. The king bade poets sing the glories of Veḷuvana and persuaded Khemā to go there. She was then brought face to face with the Buddha, and he conjured up, for her to see, a woman like a celestial nymph who stood facing him. Even as Khemā gazed on the nymph, whose extraordinary beauty far excelled her own, she saw her pass gradually from youth to extreme old age, and so fall down in the swoon of death. Seeing that Khemā was filled with dismay at the sight, the Buddha preached to her on the vanity of lust, and we are told that at that moment she attained arahantship. With the consent of Bimbisāra she entered the Order, and was ranked by the Buddha foremost among his women disciples for her great insight (*mahāpaññānaṃ aggā*).[1]

In the time of Padumuttara she was a slave, and having seen the Buddha's chief disciple, **Sujāta,** gave him three cakes, and that same day she sold her hair and gave him alms.

In **Kassapa** Buddha's time she became the eldest daughter of **Kikī,** king of Benares, and was named **Samaṇī.** With her sisters she observed celibacy for twenty thousand years and built a monastery for the Buddha. She learnt the **Mahānidāna Sutta,** having heard the Buddha preach it. In the time of **Vipassī** she became a renowned preacher of the Dhamma,

[1] A. i. 25; Dpv. xviii. 9; see also DhA. iv. 168 f.; Bu. xxvi. 19; J. i. 15, 16.

and during the time of both **Kakusandha** and **Koṇāgamana** she had great monasteries built for the Buddha and his monks.[2]

Once when Khemā was at **Toraṇavatthu,** between Sāvatthī and Sāketa, **Pasenadi,** who happened to spend one night there, heard of her presence and went to see her. He questioned her as to whether or not the Buddha existed after death. She explained the matter to him in various ways, and Pasenadi, delighted with her exposition, related it to the Buddha.[3] She is mentioned in several places[4] as the highest ideal of womanhood worthy of imitation, and is described as the nun *par excellence.*

Khemā is identified with the mother in the **Uraga Jātaka,**[5] the queen in the **Rohantamiga**[6] and in the **Haṃsa,**[7] the queen, **Khemā,** in the **Mahāhaṃsa,**[8] and the princess in the **Mahājanaka.**[9]

[2] AA. i. 187 f.; Thig. 139-44; ThigA. 126 ff.; Ap. ii. 543 ff.; DhA. iv. 57 ff.; *cf.* the story of Rūpa Nandā (DhA. iii. 113-9).

[3] S. iv. 374 ff.

[4] *E.g.*, A. i. 88; ii. 164; iv. 347; S. ii. 236.

[5] J. iii. 168.

[6] J. iv. 423.

[7] *Ibid.*, 430.

[8] J. v. 382.

[9] J. vi. 68.

2. **Khemā Therī.**—One of the two chief women disciples of **Dhammadassī** Buddha.[1]

[1] Bu. xvi. 19; J. i. 39.

3. **Khemā.**—The *Aṅguttara Commentary*[1] (on A. iv. 347) speaks of a Khemā Upāsikā in a list of lay-women. This Khemā is most probably identical with Khemā (1).

[1] AA. ii. 791.

4. **Khemā.**—Queen of **Brahmadatta,** king of Benares. She dreamed of a golden peacock preaching, and wished that her dream might come true. Though the king tried every means in his power, the wish could not be fulfilled and the queen died.[1] See the **Mora Jātaka.**

[1] J. ii. 36.

5. **Khemā.**—Chief queen of **Brahmadatta,** king of Benares. She dreamed of a golden deer preaching the Dhamma, and her wish to see her dream come true was fulfilled.[1] For details see the **Ruru Jātaka.**

[1] J. iv. 256.

6. **Khemā.**—Chief queen of **Brahmadatta,** king of Benares.[1] Her story is similar to that of **Khemā** (4). For details see the **Mahā-Mora Jātaka.**

[1] J. iv. 334.

7. **Khemā.**—Queen Consort of **Brahmadatta,** king of Benares.[1] Her story is similar to that of **Khemā** (5). She is identical with **Khemā Therī.**[2] See the **Rohantamiga Jātaka.**

[1] J. iv. 413. [2] *Ibid.*, 423.

8. **Khemā.**—Queen Consort of King **Seyya (Saṃyama)** of Benares. She saw a golden swan in a dream, and wished to see one in real life.[1] She is identified with **Khemā Therī.**[2] For details see the **Mahāhaṃsa Jātaka.**

[1] J. v. 354. [2] *Ibid.*, 382.

9. **Khemā.**—A river flowing from **Himavā.**[1]

[1] J. v. 199 f.

Khemātherī Sutta.—Records the story of the visit of **Pasenadi** to **Khemā.**[1] See **Khemā** (1).

[1] S. iv. 374 ff.

Khemābhirata.—A Pacceka Buddha mentioned in a nominal list.[1]

[1] M. iii. 70.

Khemārāma.—A locality in Ceylon. Here **Duṭṭhagāmaṇi,** having vanquished eleven Damiḷa chiefs, distributed among his troops the booty rescued from them—hence the name.[1]

[1] Mhv. xxv. 10; MṬ. 474.

Khemiyambavana.—A mango grove near Benares. **Udena** once stayed there and preached the **Ghoṭamukha Sutta.**[1]

[1] M. ii. 157.

Khemiyā.—A class of gods, present at the preaching of the **Mahā Samaya Sutta.**[1]

[1] D. ii. 261.

Khemī.—A pond,[1] probably identical with **Khema** (8).

[1] J. v. 374.

Khomadāyaka Thera.—An arahant. Ninety-one kappas ago he was a merchant in **Bandhumatī** and, having seen Vipassī Buddha in the street, gave him a linen cloth (*khoma*). Twenty-seven kappas ago he was a king named **Sindhavasandana.**[1]

[1] Ap. i. 80 f.

Khomadussa.—A (brahmin ?) township in the Sākyan country. The Buddha once stayed there and preached to an assembly of brahmin householders. It is said that the brahmins were at first hostile to the Buddha, but that he won them over.[1]

The village was so called because of the preponderance (*ussannatā*) of *khomadussā* (linen cloth).[2]

[1] S. i. 184. [2] SA. i. 207.

Khomadussa Sutta.—Records the visit of the Buddha to **Khomadussa.** The brahmins were gathered on some business, and the Buddha walked into their meeting, thus angering them. It is said that he caused a shower of rain to fall (perhaps to give him an excuse for taking shelter). When the brahmins protested against his intrusion, the Buddha told them that it was no "council" where good men were not, and where the rules of debate were not observed; this sermon pleased them.[1]

[1] S. i. 184; SA. i. 207.

Khomadussaka.—An inhabitant of **Khomadussa.**[1]

[1] S. i. 184.

Kholakkhiya.—An image of the Buddha in Ceylon. King **Udaya I.** gave for its maintenance the village of **Mahāmaga.**[1]

[1] Cv. xlix. 14.

G.

1. **Gagga.**—A monk. He became insane, and in this condition did many things unworthy of a monk. When his colleagues blamed him, the Buddha interceded on his behalf and suggested that he be given absolution for his offences, in view of his insanity. The monks acted according to the Buddha's advice.[1]

[1] Vin. i. 123; ii. 80 f.

2. **Gagga.**—A brahmin, father of **Aṅgulimāla.**[1] Gagga, whose wife was **Mantāṇī**, was chaplain to the king of **Kosala.**[2] Gagga may have been a *gotta*-name. Thus when, after his ordination, Aṅgulimāla is introduced to **Pasenadi,** the latter addresses him as **Gagga Mantāṇīputta.**[3]

[1] M. ii. 102. [2] MA. ii. 743. [3] M. ii. 102.

3. **Gagga.**—A brahmin, father of the Bodhisatta in the **Gagga Jātaka** (*q.v.*).

Gagga Jātaka (No. 155).—The Bodhisatta was once a trader's son in Kāsi. One day during their travels father and son were obliged to take lodging in a hall haunted by a yakkha. In the case of persons occupying this hall, if one of them should happen to sneeze and the other failed, thereupon, to wish him long life, the yakkha was allowed to eat them. This boon had been granted him in return for twelve years' services to **Vessavaṇa.** The two travellers from **Kāsi** took up their abode in the hall for one night, during which the father sneezed. The son, knowing nothing of his danger, said nothing, but on seeing the yakkha preparing to eat him, he guessed the reason and hastened to wish his father long life. The father acted likewise, and the yakkha was foiled in his attempt on their lives. The Bodhisatta, having heard the yakkha's story, established him in the five precepts. The story became known, and the Bodhisatta was given the post of general, while the yakkha was made tax-gatherer. In the story the Bodhisatta addresses his father as **Gagga.**

Once, when the Buddha was preaching, he sneezed, and all around him shouted " Long Life," thus interrupting his sermon. The Buddha told them that the custom was superstitious, and forbade them to follow it. On their obeying him, the common people blamed them for their lack of good manners. The Buddha, thereupon, withdrew the injunction and related this story to account for the origin of the custom.[1]

Gagga is identified with **Mahā Kassapa.**[2]

[1] J. ii. 15 f.; the introductory story is found in Vin. ii. 140.

[2] J. ii. 17.

Gaggaravāliya-aṅgana.—A locality in Ceylon. The Elder **Pītamalla** (*q.v.*) resided there with thirty other monks.[1]

[1] DA. iii. 749; the reading in the P.T.S. edition (gāravakaraṇāya) is wrong.

1. **Gaggarā.**—A lotus-pond at **Campā.** The Buddha is several times mentioned as staying on the banks of the pond. On one such occasion **Pessa** and **Kandaraka** visited him, and he preached to them the **Kandaraka Sutta.**[1] Among others who visited him there are mentioned **Bāhuna,**[2] **Vajjiyamāhita,**[3] and **Kassapagotta.**[4] On one occasion, when the Buddha was staying there, **Sāriputta** approached him with a large number of the inhabitants of Campā and asked him questions concerning the efficacy of giving alms.[5]

On another such occasion Sāriputta assembled the monks and preached to them the **Dasuttara Sutta.**[6] It was on the banks of the Gaggarā that

[1] M. i. 339.

[2] A. v. 151.

[3] *Ibid.*, 189.

[4] Vin. i. 312.

[5] A. iv. 59 ff.

[6] D. iii. 272 ff.

the Buddha preached the **Karaṇḍava Sutta** (*q.v.*) on the necessity of getting rid of evil-minded members of the Saṅgha lest they should corrupt the whole Order,[7] and the pond-bank was also the scene of the preaching of the well-known **Soṇadaṇḍa Sutta.**[8] Once, when the Buddha was at this spot with a large number of monks and lay-followers, **Vaṅgīsa** came up to him and praised him in a song, pointing out how the Buddha outshone them all.[9]

The pond was called Gaggarā because it owed its origin to a queen of that name. On its bank was a Campaka-grove where the Buddha stayed during his visits.[10] Near by was a monastery of *titthiyas.*[11] The pond, together with that at Jetavana, is given as an example of a very beautiful lotus pond.[12] Monks found it a convenient spot for meditation.[13]

[7] A. iv. 168 f.
[8] D. i. 111 f.
[9] S. i. 195; Thag. v. 1252; ThagA. ii. 210.
[10] MA. ii. 565; DA. i. 279 f.
[11] See A. v. 189.
[12] *E.g.*, AA. i. 264.
[13] SNA. i. 17.

2. **Gaggarā.**—The queen for whom the lotus pond **Gaggarā** (*q.v.*) was made.

Gaggarā Sutta.—Records the incident of **Vaṅgīsa** singing the praises of the Buddha on the banks of the **Gaggarā** pond.[1]

[1] S. i. 195; *cf.* Thag. v. 1252.

Gaggaligāma.—A village built by **Mahosadha** on the further side of the Ganges; there he stationed his elephants, horses, cattle, etc., while he had the great tunnel constructed.[1]

[1] J. vi. 431.

Gaṅgamāla.—A barber who later became a Pacceka Buddha. See **Gaṅgamāla Jātaka.**

Gaṅgamāla Jātaka (No. 421).—The Bodhisatta once took service under **Suciparivāra** of Benares, in whose household everyone kept the fast on *uposatha*-days. The Bodhisatta, not knowing this, went to work as usual on the fast day, but, on discovering that no one else was working and the reason for their abstention, he refused to take any food, and as a result of his fasting died in the night. He was reborn as son of the king of Benares, and later became king under the name of **Udaya.** On meeting **Aḍḍhamāsaka** (*q.v.*), Udaya shared the kingdom with him, but one day Aḍḍhamāsaka, discovering that he harboured a desire to kill Udaya, renounced his kingdom and became an ascetic. When

Udaya heard of this he uttered a stanza, referring to his own past life, but no one could understand the meaning of it. The queen, anxious to learn the meaning, told the king's barber **Gaṅgamāla** how he might win the king's favour, and when the king offered him a boon, Gaṅgamāla chose to have the stanza explained to him. When he learnt how Udaya had won a kingdom as a result of having kept the fast for half a day, Gaṅgamāla renounced the world and, developing asceticism, became a Pacceka Buddha. Later he visited King Udaya and preached to him and his retinue, addressing the king by name. The queen-mother took offence at this and abused Gaṅgamāla, but the king begged him to forgive her. Gaṅgamāla returned to **Gandhamādana,** though urged by Udaya to stay in the royal park.

Ānanda was Aḍḍhamāsaka, and **Rāhulamātā** was the queen.

The story was related by the Buddha to some lay-followers to encourage them in their observance of the *uposatha.*[1] Gaṅgamāla is mentioned as an example of a man who realised the evils of taṇhā and renounced desire.[2]

[1] J. iii. 444 ff.

[2] *E.g.*, J. iv. 174.

Gaṅgarājī.—A district to the east of **Anurādhapura,** where **Kaṇiṭṭhatissa** built the **Anulatissapabbata Vihāra.**[1]

[1] Mhv. xxxvi. 15.

Gaṅgalatittha.—A ford on the **Kadamba-nadī** near **Anurādhapura.** It was the starting-point of the boundary line which **Devānampiyatissa** laid down for the **Mahā Vihāra.**[1]

[1] MṬ. 361; *cf.* Mbv. 136.

1. **Gaṅgā** (Modern Ganges).—One of the five great rivers (*Mahānadī*) that water **Jambudīpa,** the others being **Yamunā, Aciravatī, Sarabhū,** and **Mahī.**[1] The Commentaries[2] give a long description of their origin. From the **Anotatta** lake flow four rivers: that from the south circles the lake three times under the name of **Āvaṭṭagaṅgā,** then as **Kaṇhagaṅgā** flows straight for sixty leagues along the surface of a rock, comes into violent contact with a vertical rock, and is thrown upwards as a column of water three *gāvutas* in circumference; this column, known as **Ākāsagaṅgā,** flows through the air for sixty leagues, falls on to the rock **Tiyaggala,** excavating it to a depth of fifty leagues, thus forming a lake which is called **Tiyaggalapokkharaṇī**; then the river, under the name of **Bahalagaṅgā,** flows through a chasm in the rock for sixty leagues, then,

[1] *E.g.*, Vin. ii. 237; S. ii. 135; v. 401; A. iv. 101; v. 22; Mil. (114) mentions ten.

[2] *E.g.*, SNA. ii. 438 f.; AA. ii. 761 ff.; MA. ii. 586; UdA. 301.

under the name of **Ummaggagaṅgā,** through a tunnel for a further sixty leagues, and finally coming upon the oblique rock **Vijjha,** divides into five streams, forming the five rivers above mentioned. Among places mentioned as being on the banks of the Gaṅgā are **Benāres, Campā, Ayojjha, Kimbhilā, Ukkāvelā, Payāga, Pāṭaliputta,** and **Saṅkassa.**[3] The Gaṅgā formed one of the most important means of communication and trade for the districts through which it flowed—*e.g.*, from **Rājagaha** to **Vesāli.** The district to the north of the river and bordering on the kingdom of **Aṅga** was called **Aṅguttarāpa.**[4] The river was five hundred leagues in length.[5]

The name of the Gaṅgā appears again and again in similes and metaphors in the Pāli books: its sands are immeasurable (S. iv. 376); its waters cannot be made bracken by adding to them a grain of salt (A. i. 250); it is full of foam, and yet its foam is empty (S. iii. 140); it were folly to wish to hold up the course of its waters with one's fist (S. iv. 298); as the river finds repose only in the ocean, so do the followers of the Buddha find repose only in nibbāna (M. i. 493); some things are as inevitable as that the Gaṅgā should flow into the sea (S. iv. 179); there is no such thing as the Gaṅgā apart from its sand, its water, and its banks; to be cast on the other side of the Gaṅgā (pāragaṅgāya) is great misfortune (see, *e.g.*, S. i. 207, SnA. i. 228). The Gaṅgā flows from west to east (*pācīnaninnā,* S. iv. 191); during the rains it is so full of water that even a crow could drink water from its bank (Vin. i. 230); sometimes the banks would be flooded and the buildings on them destroyed (SA. i. 164), and people would find difficulty in crossing; at others it was shallow and could be crossed by means of a reed bridge (SnA. i. 18); cattle could easily be driven from one bank to another (M. i. 225). At various spots were ferries where boatmen plied for hire (*e.g.*, J. iii. 230). On its banks, on the higher reaches, were numerous snakes and parrots (J. ii. 145, iii. 491), and all along the banks were hermitages (*e.g.*, J. iii. 476, v. 191, etc.). Men always bathed in the river, and on festival days even women of very good family came for water-sports, sometimes spending the whole day in the river; kings also came with their retinues (*e.g.*, J. i. 295; MA. ii. 604; DhA. iii. 199).[6] The junction of the Gaṅgā and the Yamunā is frequently referred to, and is used as a simile for perfect union (*e.g.*, J. vi. 412, 415). A tributary of the Gaṅgā is mentioned which flows from Himavā, its name being **Migasammatā** (J. vi. 72). The ford at Pāṭaliputta, where the Buddha crossed on his way from

[3] For references see *s.v.*

[4] SNA. ii. 439. [5] SA. ii. 119.

[6] Reference is also made to a Gangā-mahīkīḷā (Smp. on Vin. i. 191, and again, ii. 276). Buddhaghosa says that Mahī here refers to the earth, but Rhys Davids (VT. ii. 25, n. 3) thinks it refers to the river of that name.

Rājagaha to Vesāli, was called **Gotamatittha** (Vin. i. 230); its distance from Rājagaha was five leagues, and from Vesāli three (KhpA. 162-3). When the Buddha, after curing the plague at Vesāli, returned to Rājagaha, great festivities marked the event, and the celebration was known as the **Gaṅgārohaṇa.** The devas and the nāgas vied with each other to do honour to the Teacher, and there was a great assembly of all classes of beings, comparable to those on the occasions of the Twin Miracle and the Descent from Tusita (DhA. iii. 444). Among the nāgas who dwelt in the Gaṅgā is mentioned **Eraka** (DhA. iii. 231).

The water of the Gaṅgā was considered holy and was used for the consecration of kings, not only of India but also of Ceylon.[7]

The people on the northern bank were rough and coarse, while those on the south were pious and generous, believers in the Buddha.[8]

The upper reaches of the river were called **Uddhagaṅgā** (J. ii. 283, vi. 427) or **Uparigaṅgā** (J. iv. 230), and the lower reaches **Adhogaṅgā** (J. ii. 283, 329, v. 3).

See also **Kosikī, Bhagīrathī, Mahāgaṅgā,** and **Pāragaṅgā.**

[7] Mhv. xi. 30; MṬ. 305.

[8] DA. i. 160.

2. **Gaṅgā.**—See **Mahāvāḷukagaṅgā.**

3. **Gaṅgā.**—A lake, the residence of the Nāga king **Doṇa.**[1]

[1] BuA. 153.

Gaṅgā Sutta.—Preached to a brahmin at **Veḷuvana.** Incalculable is the beginning of *Saṃsāra*, incalculable the æons that have passed by, like the sands of the **Gaṅgā.**[1]

[1] S. ii. 183.

Gaṅgā Vīci.—One of the four kinds of waves that rise in the sea. Each wave of this class rises to a height of fifty leagues.[1]

[1] VibhA. 502.

Gaṅgātaṭa, Gaṅgātaṭaka, Gaṅgātaḷāka.—A tank in Ceylon, built by **Aggabodhi II.**[1] The country around the tank was used as a base in **Parakkamabāhu's** war against **Gajabāhu.**[2] Gajabahū lived there in comparative peace during his last days, and he also died there.[3] Later, **Māgha** and **Jayabāhu** erected fortifications in Gaṅgātaṭa.[4]

It is identified with the modern Kantalai.[5]

[1] Cv. xlii. 67.

[2] *Ibid.*, lxx. 286, 300.

[3] *Ibid.*, lxxi. 1, 5.

[4] *Ibid.*, lxxxiii. 15.

[5] See Cv. *Trs.* i. 310, n. 3.

Gaṅgātīriya Thera.—An arahant. He was a householder named **Datta** of **Sāvatthi.** On discovering that he had, though unwittingly, committed incest with both his mother and sister, he was overcome with anguish and left the world. He adopted a course of austerity, dwelling in a hut of palm leaves on the bank of the Ganges, hence his name. For a whole year he kept silence; in the second year he spoke but once to a woman who, in filling his bowl, spilt the milk, wishing to discover if he were dumb. In the third year he became an arahant.

In the time of **Padumuttara** Buddha he was a householder, and supplied drinks to monks.[1]

It is said[2] that after Gaṅgātiriya's conception his mother was driven out of her house in the absence of her husband, her mother-in-law suspecting her of infidelity. The child was born in a travellers' rest-house in **Rājagaha,** whither she had gone in search of her husband, and was taken away by a caravan leader who happened to see it when its mother was away bathing. Later the woman was carried away by a robber chief, by whom she had a daughter. One day, in a quarrel with her husband, she threw her daughter on the bed, wounding her on the head, and fearing her husband's wrath she fled to Rājagaha,where she became a courtesan and later mistress of Gaṅgātiriya, who was unaware of his relationship to her. Some time afterwards he took to wife the robber's daughter as well. One day, while looking at the young wife's head, the older one saw the wound, and as a result of her questions learnt the truth. Filled with dismay, both mother and daughter became nuns, and Gaṅgātiriya left the world as mentioned above.

Gaṅgātiriya is perhaps to be identified with **Udakadāyaka** of the *Apadāna.*[3]

[1] Thag. v. 127-8; ThagA. i. 248 f.
[2] ThigA. 195 f.; Thig. 224 f.
[3] Ap. ii. 437; but the verses are also ascribed to Mahāgavaccha (ThagA. i. 57).

Gaṅgādoṇi.—A hill in the **Maṇimekhala** district in Ceylon. The general **Saṅkha** founded a city there during **Māgha's** invasion. The hill was only two yojanas away from Māgha's capital, but provided quite a safe retreat.[1]

[1] Cv. lxxxi. 7 f.

Gaṅgāpeyyāla.—In the fifth book of the *Saṃyutta Nikāya* a repetition under the name of Gaṅgāpeyyāla occurs several times. " Just as the Gaṅgā flows to the east, slides to the east, and tends to the east, even so, a monk who cultivates the *bojjhaṅgas* (S. v. 135, 137), the *satipaṭṭhānas* (196), the *indriyas* (239, 241), the *padhānas* (244), the *balas* 249, 251), the *iddhipādas* (290), and the *jhānas* (307), slides and tends towards *nibbāna*."

Gaṅgāmāti Vihāra.—A monastery in Ceylon, to which **Jeṭṭhatissa III.** gave **Keheta** as its maintenance village.[1]

[1] Cv. xliv. 99.

Gaṅgārāma.—Also called **Rājamahā Vihāra,** a monastery founded by **Kittisirirājasīha** on the bank of the **Mahāvāḷuka-gaṅgā** near Kandy.[1] There **Rājādhirājasīha** erected a cetiya.[2]

[1] Cv. c. 202. [2] *Ibid.*, ci. 17.

Gaṅgārohaṇa Vatthu.—The account of the Buddha's visit to **Vesāli** which he paid in order to preach the **Ratana Sutta** (*q.v.*).[1]

[1] DhA. iii. 436 ff.

Gaṅgārohaṇa Sutta.—The *Culavaṃsa*[1] mentions a sutta by this name. The Commentaries on the *Dhammapada*[2] and the *Khuddakapāṭha*[3] contain accounts of the visit paid by the Buddha to Vesāli in order to drive out from there the fears of famine and pestilence, and they describe in great detail the celebrations which took place as the Buddha returned to Rājagaha along the Gaṅges. This journey is called **Gaṅgārohaṇa.** The Sutta mentioned is probably, therefore, the **Ratana Sutta** (*q.v.*) which the Buddha preached at Vesāli.

[1] Cv. xxxvii. 191. [2] DhA. iii. 436 ff. [3] KhpA. 162 ff.

Gaṅgāsiripura.—The Pāli name for the town of Gampola in Ceylon.[1] In it was an ancient vihāra, the **Nigamaggāmapāsāda.**[2] **Bhuvanekabāhu IV.** made it his capital.[3]

[1] Cv. lxxxvi. 18. [2] *Ibid.*, lxxxviii. 48. [3] *Ibid.*, xc. 107.

Gaṅgāsenakapabbata Vihāra.—A monastery in Ceylon built by **Mahāsena.**[1]

[1] Mhv. xxxvii. 41.

1. **Gaṅgeyya.**—Adjective formed from **Gaṅga.**[1] The description "Gaṅgeyya nāgarājā" in J. iii. 362 probably means a nāga king "dwelling in Gaṅga" and not "named Gaṅgeyya."

[1] J. ii. 151.

2. **Gaṅgeyya.**—One of the ten families of elephants. Each elephant had the strength of one hundred men.[1]

[1] MA. i. 262; AA. ii. 822; BuA. 37.

Gaṅgeyya Jātaka (No. 205).—Two fish, one from **Gaṅgā,** the other from **Yamunā,** once met at the confluence of the rivers and disputed as to their relative beauty. They appealed to a tortoise who was there for a decision; he said they were both beautiful, but he himself was more beautiful than either.

The story was told in reference to two monks who bragged of their good looks and quarrelled about them. They appealed to an older monk, who gave the same answer as the tortoise of the story.[1]

[1] J. ii. 151 f.

Gajakumbha Jātaka (No. 345).—The Bodhisatta was once a minister of the king of Benares. Noticing that the king was slothful, the Bodhisatta took a tortoise as an object lesson, showing him how the indolent came to misery.

The story was related in reference to a monk who was slothful regarding his duties.[1]

[1] J. iii. 139 f.

Gajakumbhakapāsāṇa.—A locality in Ceylon, through which passed the Sīmā marked out by **Devānampiyatissa** for the **Mahā Vihāra.**[1]

[1] Mhv., p. 332, v. 12; Dpv. xiv. 35; Mbv. 135.

Gajabāhu, Gajabhuja.—King of Ceylon (1137-1153). He was the son of **Vikkamabāhu II.** and succeeded his father to the throne.[1] Thus he was the grandson of **Vijayabāhu I.** and of **Tilokasundarī,** and came, therefore, of Kāliṅga stock. When he saw the increasing power of the Prince **Parakkamabāhu** (afterwards Parakkamabāhu I.), Gajabāhu sent for him with many marks of favour and welcomed him at his court. In order to win the king's confidence Parakkama gave his sister **Bhaddavatī** to be his queen, but when he saw that Gajabāhu was becoming suspicious of his power he left **Pulatthipura** and made preparations to wage war against him. In the campaign that followed, Gajabāhu suffered many reverses and, in the end, fell into the hands of Parakkama's forces. With great difficulty Parakkama saved him from death, but in the meantime **Mānābharaṇa** managed to get Gajabāhu into his power and cast him into a dungeon. From there he was rescued by Parakkamabāhu and fled to **Koṭṭhasāra.** Meanwhile, Parakkamabāhu had consolidated his power, and his officers captured Pulatthipura. Gajabāhu, being able to see no other help, implored the monks of Pulatthipura to intercede on his behalf, and, at their request, Parakkamabāhu left to Gaja-

[1] Cv. lx. 88. According to the Dimbulāgala Inscription, his mother was Sundarī.

bāhu the enjoyment of his possessions.[2] Gajabāhu took up his abode at **Gaṅgātaḷāka** and spent his last days there in comparative peace. As he had no heir and no brothers, he bequeathed his kingdom to Parakkamabāhu, and engraved his will on a stone tablet at **Maṇḍalagiri Vihāra.** He was cremated at **Koṭṭhasāra.**[3] See also *s.v.* **Gajabāhukagāmaṇi.**

[2] This is rather odd, especially in view of the fact that he invited heretical nobles to come to Ceylon (Cv. lxx. 53).

[3] Details of Gajabāhu's reign and his fights with Parakkamabāhu are contained in the *Cūḷavamsa*, particularly in chapters 63, 66, 67, 70, 71.

Gajjabāhukagāmaṇi.—Also called **Gajabāhu;** king of Ceylon (174-96 A.C.); son of **Vaṅkanāsika-Tissa.** He founded the **Mātu Vihāra** in honour of his mother, made additions to the **Abhayagiri Cetiya,** constructed the **Gamaṇitissa** tank, and built the **Rāmuka Vihāra** and the **Mahejāsanasālā.**[1]

In later chronicles he is credited with having invaded the Coḷa kingdom to avenge a raid made on Ceylon and with having introduced the cult of the goddess Pattini into Ceylon.[2]

[1] Mhv. xxxv. 115 ff.; Dpv. xxii. 13, 28, 29.

[2] See Codrington, *Short History of Ceylon*, pp. 23 f.

1. **Gajabhuja.**—An officer of **Māṇābharaṇa** (2). He was defeated by **Māyāgeha** at **Samīrakkha.**[1]

[1] Cv. lxxii. 10.

2. **Gajabhuja.**—A chieftain of Gova. He was slain by Konappu, afterwards **Vimaladhammasūriya.**[1]

[1] Cv. xciv. 2.

3. **Gajabhuja.**—See **Gajabāhu.**

Gajjagiri.—A mountain in **Aparantaka.**[1]

[1] Sās. 35.

Gaṇaka-Moggallāna.—A brahmin teacher of **Sāvatthi.** He visited the Buddha at the **Pubbārāma,** and the Buddha preached to him the **Gaṇaka-Moggallāna Sutta,** after which, it is said, he became the Buddha's follower.[1] His name and his teaching seem to indicate that he was a mathematician.

[1] M. iii. 1 ff.

Gaṇaka-Moggallāna Sutta.—The one hundred and seventh sutta of the *Majjhima Nikāya*; preached to **Gaṇaka-Moggallāna.** Moggallāna says that the brahmanical training is a thoroughly graduated system (*anupubbasikkhā anupubbakiriyā*). Can the Buddha say the same of his teaching? The Buddha says he can and proceeds to explain. It is true that not all the Buddha's disciples attain to the goal, but the fault is theirs; the Buddha accepts no responsibility, he only indicates the way.[1]

[1] M. iii. 1 ff.

Gaṇakaputta-Tissa Thera.—Probably a Commentator. **Buddhaghosa** quotes him in the *Aṅguttara Commentary*[1] as explaining the term *tisahassīmahāsahassī* differently from the commonly accepted interpretation.

[1] AA. i. 439.

Gaṇapeta Vatthu.—The story of a large number of people of **Sāvatthi** who, because of their misdeeds, had been born as petas.[1]

[1] Pv. iv. 10; PvA. 269 f.

Gaṇadevaputtā.—**Buddhaghosa** mentions[1] the palaces of the Gaṇadevaputtas (*Gaṇadevaputtānañ ca vimānāni*) among those seen by King **Nemi** as he was being conducted by **Mātali** through the deva-worlds. I cannot trace the name in the **Nimi Jātaka.** The word may be used as a collective noun.

[1] MA. ii. 737.

Gaṇānanda Pariveṇa.—A monastery at **Rājagāma** in Ceylon, the residence of the Elder Maittreya Mahā Thera.[1]

[1] P.L.C. 248.

Gaṇṭhambatittha.—A ford in the **Mahāvāḷukagaṅgā.** There an *udakakkhepasīmā* was erected by **Vimaladhammasūriya I.**[1] The name is the Pāli equivalent for the Sinhalese Gäṭambé.

[1] Cv. xciv. 17.

Gaṇṭhipupphiya Thera.—An arahant. Ninety-one kappas ago he gave a *gaṇṭhi*-flower to the Buddha **Vipassī.** Forty-one kappas ago he was a king named **Varaṇa.**[1] He is probably identical with **Hatthārohaputta.**[2]

[1] Ap. i. 162. [2] ThagA. i. 170.

Gaṇṭhimāna.—A village in Ceylon, given by **Parakkamabāhu IV.** for the maintenance of the temple at **Devapura (Devanagara).**[1]

[1] Cv. xc. 95.

Gaṇḍa.—Gardener of **Pasenadi,** king of **Kusala.** It was he who offered to the Buddha the mango, the seed of which produced the **Gaṇḍamba.**[1]

The *Apadāna Commentary*[2] calls the gardener **Gaṇḍabba,** and the *Divyāvadana*[3] calls him Gaṇḍaka.

[1] J. iv. 264. [2] i. 97. [3] p. 157.

Gaṇḍa Sutta.—The body is like a festering sore (*gaṇḍa*), full of pus, with nine openings, constantly exuding matter.[1]

[1] A. iv. 386 f.

Gaṇḍatindu Jātaka (No. 520).—**Pañcāla,** king of **Kampilla,** is a wicked monarch, and his subjects, harassed by his officers, suffer great oppression. The Bodhisatta, born as the divinity of a *gaṇḍatindu*-tree, becoming aware of this, appears in the king's bedchamber and urges him to give up his evil ways and find out for himself the condition of his subjects. The king, taking this advice, travels about in disguise with his chaplain. Everywhere he finds men, women and even the beasts cursing his very name. He returns to the capital and devotes himself to good works.[1]

The introductory story is given in the **Rājovāda Jātaka** (*q.v.*).

[1] J. v. 98 ff.

Gaṇḍamba.—The mango-tree, at the gate of **Sāvatthi,** under which the Buddha performed the **Yamaka-pāṭihāriya** (*q.v.*). The king's gardener, **Gaṇḍa,** while on his way to the palace to give the king a ripe mango-fruit from the palace gardens, saw the Buddha going on his alms-rounds and offered him the mango. The Buddha ate it immediately, and gave the seed to **Ānanda** to be planted by the gardener at the city-gate. A tree of one hundred cubits sprouted forth at once, covered with fruit and flowers. At the foot of this tree **Vissakamma,** by the order of **Sakka,** built a pavilion of the seven kinds of precious things.[1]

[1] J. iv. 264 f.; J. i. 88; DhA. iii. 206 ff.; Mil. 349.

Gaṇḍābharaṇa.—A book composed by **Ariyavaṃsa.**[1] *v.l.* **Gandhābharaṇa.**

[1] Gv. 65, 75; Sās., p. 98.

Gaṇḍāladoṇi.—A monastery in Ceylon, near the modern Kandy. The stucco work of the vihāra was carried out by **Parakkamabāhu VI.**[1]

[1] Cv. xci. 30.

Gaṇḍimitta.—See **Kaṇhamitta.**

1. **Gatasaññaka Thera.**—An arahant. In the time of **Tissa** Buddha he joined the Order at the age of seven, and threw up into the air seven *naṅgaliki*-flowers as offering to the Buddha. Eight kappas ago he became king, three times, under the name of **Aggisikha.**[1]

[1] Ap. i. 127.

2. **Gatasaññaka Thera.**—An arahant. He saw the Buddha **Siddhattha** going through the air, though only his robe was visible to him. The sight filled him with joy and he concentrated his mind thereon.[1]

[1] Ap. i. 253 f.

Gatārāpariveṇa.—A monastery in Ceylon, the residence of **Upatapassī,** author of the **Vuttamālā.**[1]

[1] PLC. 253.

Gati Sutta.—The five conditions of birth—in purgatory, among lower animals, petas, men or devas.[1]

[1] A. iv. 459.

Gatikathā.—The sixth section of the *Mahāvagga* of the *Patisambhidāmagga.*[1]

[1] Ps. ii. 73-8.

Gatipakaraṇa.—A book composed by a thera of **Pakudhanagara.**[1]

[1] Gv. 65; but see p. 75, where the author is said to belong to Ceylon.

Gatipacchedana.—A king of eighty-four kappas ago; a previous birth of **Sammukhāthavika**[1] (or **Māṇava**).[2]

[1] Ap. i. 159. [2] ThagA. i. 163.

Gatimba.—See **Mahāgatimba.**

Gatiyopañcaka Vagga.—The eleventh chapter of the *Sacca Saṃyutta* and the last chapter of the *Saṃyutta Nikāya.*[1]

[1] S. v. 474 f.

Gadāvudha.—The club wielded by **Vessavaṇa** when he was yet a *puthujjana*. It would fall on the head of many thousands of yakkhas and return to Vessavaṇa's hand.[1]

[1] SNA. i. 225.

Gadrabha.—Doorkeeper of **Āḷavaka,** the yakkha. He warned the Buddha of the yakkha's evil nature and requested him to go away, but, on finding the Buddha determined to stay, he informed the yakkha of the Buddha's arrival.[1]

[1] SNA. i. 220; AA i. 211.

Gadrabhakula.—Mentioned as one of the families in which horses are born. **Valāhaka** horses are not born in this family.[1]

[1] MA. i. 248.

Gadrabhapañha.—One of the problems set by King **Vedeha** to **Mahosadha,** in order to test him, at the instigation of the king's ministers. The king sent word to Mahosadha that while he was on his way to see him his horse had broken its leg; would Mahosadha, therefore, send him a more excellent horse ? Mahosadha, understanding the significance of the message, went to the palace, sending his father on before him. When Mahosadha entered he found his father seated, but, as had been prearranged, he obliged his father to get up and offer him his seat. On this there was a great uproar, all saying that he had slighted his father. But Mahosadha convinced the king that he was a more excellent man than his father, giving proof of this by producing before the king an ass which he had brought with him, and making the king acknowledge that a colt born of the ass through a Sindh mare would be far more valuable than the colt's sire.[1]

The story is also given as a separate Jātaka (No. 111).[2]

[1] J. vi. 342 f. [2] J. i. 424.

1. **Gaddula Sutta** (*v.l.* **Baddula**).—Incalculable is the beginning of *saṃsāra* and the untaught *puthujjana*, having wrong notions of self, revolve from birth to birth, like a dog tied by a leash to a pillar or stake round which it unceasingly chases.[1]

[1] S. iii. 149.

2. **Gaddula Sutta.**—Just as a dog tied by a leash to a strong pillar cannot escape, so the untaught *puthujjanas* cannot escape from the five *khandhas*. Mind is even more diverse than a show piece (*caraṇacitta*).

As a painter fashions all kinds of likenesses, so the *puthujjana* creates and recreates the five *khandas.*[1]

[1] S. iii. 151 f.

Ganthākara-pariveṇa.—A dwelling attached to the **Mahāvihāra** at **Anurādhapura,** where **Buddhaghosa** stayed during his sojourn in Ceylon and where he wrote his Commentaries.[1] The pariveṇa was restored by **Kassapa V.**[2]

[1] Cv. xxxvii. 243. [2] *Ibid.,* lii. 57.

Ganthisāra.—A book composed by **Saddhammajotipāla ;** it is evidently an anthology or manual composed from important texts.[1]

[1] Bode, *op. cit.,* p. 18; Gv. (p. 64) calls it Gandhasāra.

1. **Gandha.**—The name of a family of elephants; each elephant has the strength of one million men.[1]

[1] VibhA. 397; AA. ii. 822; UdA. 403, etc.

2. **Gandha.**—A seṭṭhi of Benares. On realising that his ancestors had died leaving immense wealth, which they had failed to enjoy, he started to spend large sums of money on luxuries, and one full-moon day he decorated the city and invited the people to watch him taking a meal. Among the assembled multitude was a villager, who felt that he would die unless he could obtain a morsel of Gandha's rice. When this was told to Gandha he suggested that the man should work for him for three years, taking in payment a bowl of his rice. The villager agreed and henceforth became known as **Bhattabhatika.** At the end of the three years Gandha kept his promise and gave orders that Bhattabhatika should enjoy all his master's own splendours for one day, and asked all the members of his household, except his wife **Cintāmaṇī,** to wait on him. When Bhattabhatika sat down to eat, a Pacceka Buddha appeared before him; Bhattabhatika gave his food to the Pacceka Buddha who, in sight of all those that had gathered to watch Bhattabhatika's splendour, went through the air to **Gandhamādana.** When Gandha heard of what had happened, he gave one-half of all his possessions to Bhattabhatika in return for a share of the merit he had gained.[1]

[1] DhA. iii. 87 ff.

1. **Gandha Sutta.**—See **Isayo Sutta.**

2. **Gandha Sutta.**—The scents of the world spread only along with the wind and not against it; the fragrance of a good man's virtue travels everywhere.[1]

[1] A. i. 225; *cp.* J. iii. 291; Mil. 333.

Gandhakuṭi.—The name given to the special apartment occupied by the Buddha at the **Jetavana** monastery.[1] The building, of which the Gandhakuṭi formed a part, was evidently called the **Gandhakuṭi-pariveṇa,** and there the Buddha would assemble the monks and address them.[2] The site, on which stands the bed of the Buddha in the Gandhakuṭi, is the same for every Buddha, and is one of the unalterable sites —*avijahitaṭṭhānāni.*[3]

The name Gandhakuṭi seems to have been used later in reference also to other residences of the Buddha. Thus, we are told[4] that **Visākhā** built a Gandhakuṭi for the Buddha in the **Pubbārāma** with the money she obtained by the sale of her **Mahālatāpasādhana.**

[1] J. i. 92.
[2] *E.g.,* J. i. 501; iii. 67.
[3] BuA. 247.
[4] AA. i. 226; see C.S.B., Pl. 5B. For further details see *s.v.* **Buddha.**

Gandhagata.—See **Bhadragaka.**

Gandhathūpiya Thera.—An arahant,[1] probably identical with **Gandhamāliya** (*q.v.*). The same verses are attributed to both.

[1] Ap. i. 267.

Gandhapūjaka Thera.—An arahant. In the past he put a handful of perfume on the funeral pyre of the Buddha (**Padumuttara**).[1] He is probably identical with **Hārita.**[2]

[1] Ap. ii. 406.
[2] ThagA. i. 376.

Gandhabba.—An attendant of King **Eleyya** and a follower of **Uddaka Rāmaputta.**[1]

[1] A. ii. 180.

Gandhabbakāya Saṃyutta.—The thirty-first chapter of the *Saṃyutta Nikāya.*[1]

[1] S. iii. 249-53.

Gandhabbakāyikā.—See **Gandhabbā.**

Gandhabbadvāra.—One of the gates of **Pulatthipura.**[1]

[1] Cv. lxxiii. 163.

Gandhabbarājā.—The name given to **Sakka** in the **Vidhurapaṇḍita Jātaka.**[1]

[1] J. vi. 260.

Gandhabbā.—A class of semi-divine beings who inhabit the **Cātummahārājika**-realm and are the lowest among the devas.[1] They are generally classed together with the **Asuras** and the **Nāgas.**[2] Beings are born among them as a result of having practised the lowest form of *sīla.*[3] It is a disgrace for a monk to be born in the Gandhabba-world.[4] The Gandhabbas are regarded as the heavenly musicians, and **Pañcasikha, Suriyavaccasā** and her father **Timbarū** are among their number.[5] They wait on such devas as **Sakka,** and the males among them form the masculine counterpart of the *accharā,* the nymphs. Their king is **Dhataraṭṭha,** ruler of the eastern quarter.[6] Other chieftains are also mentioned:[7] **Panāda, Opamañña,** Sakka's charioteer **Mātali, Cittasena, Nala** and **Janesabha.** The Gandhabbas are sometimes described as *vihaṅgamā* (going through the air).[8] In the **Āṭānāṭiya Sutta**[9] the Gandhabbas are mentioned among those likely to trouble monks and nuns in their meditations in solitude. The Buddha says that beings are born among the Gandhabakāyikā devā because they wish to be so; they are described as dwelling in the fragrance of root-wood, of bark and sap, and in that of flowers and scents.[10]

It is often stated that the Gandhabbas preside over conception; this is due to an erroneous translation of the word *gandhabba* in passages[11] dealing with the circumstances necessary for conception (*mātāpitaro ca sannipatitā honti, mātā ca utunī hoti, gandhabbo ca paccupaṭṭhito hoti*). The Commentaries[12] explain that here gandhabba means *tatrūpakasatta—tasmiṃ okāse nibbattanako satto*—meaning a being fit and ready to be born to the parents concerned. The *Ṭīkā* says that the word stands for *gantabba.* See also **Gandhabbarājā.**

[1] D. ii. 212.
[2] *E.g.,* A. iv. 200, 204, 207.
[3] D. ii. 212, 271.
[4] *Ibid.,* 221, 251, 273 f.
[5] *Ibid.,* 264.
[6] *Ibid.,* 257.
[7] *Ibid.,* 258.
[8] A. ii. 39; AA. ii. 506.
[9] D. iii. 203, 204.
[10] S. iii. 250 f.
[11] *E.g.,* M. i. 157, 265 f.
[12] *E.g.,* MA. i. 481 f.

Gandhabhava.—See **Bhadragaka.**

Gandhamādana.—A mountain range beyond the seven ranges of **Cullakāḷa, Mahākāḷa, Nāgapaliveṭhana, Candagabbha, Suriyagabbha, Suvaṇṇapassa** and **Himavā.** It is one of the five mountain ranges that encircle **Anotatta.** It is crowned with a tableland, is green in colour (*muggavaṇṇa*), and covered with various medicinal plants. It shines from afar " like a glowing fire on a new-moon night." In the range is an inclined slope (*pabbhāra*) named **Nandamūlaka** containing three caves, **Suvaṇṇa-, Maṇi-** and **Rajata-guhā,** which are the abodes of Pacceka Buddhas. At the entrance to Maṇiguhā is a tree named **Mañjūsaka,** one league in height and in girth; on this tree bloom all the flowers that grow both on land and in water, and especially do they bloom on the occasions of the Pacceka Buddhas' visits; round the tree is the **Sabbaratanamāla.** There the **Sammajjanakavāta** sweeps the ground, the **Samakaraṇavāta** levels the sand, and the **Siñcanakavāta** sprinkles water from Anotatta. The **Sugandhakaraṇavāta** brings all the perfumes of Himavā, the **Ocinakavāta** plucks flowers, and the **Santharaṇakavāta** spreads them. In the māla seats are always ready for the Pacceka Buddhas, who on fast days and on their own birthdays assemble there. When a new Pacceka Buddha arises in the world, he goes first to Gandhamādana and other Pacceka Buddhas, who may be in the world, assemble there to greet him, and they all sit rapt in samādhi. Then the senior among them asks the new-comer to describe how he came to be a Pacceka Buddha.[1] The Pacceka Buddhas who live on Gandhamādana will often enter into samādhi for seven days, and at the end of that period seek alms from someone on whom they wish to bestow a special favour, that he may thereby obtain merit.[2] These Buddhas will sometimes leave the mountain, and, having admonished those whom they wish to help, return again.[3] Besides Pacceka Buddhas, others are also mentioned as having resided in Gandhamādana—*e.g.*, **Nārada** (J. iv. 393), **Nalinikā** (J. v. 186), **Bahusodarī** (J. vi. 83); also the deva king **Nāgadatta** (ThagA. i. 138), and **Vessantara,** with his family, after he renounced his kingdom (J. vi. 528 f.). It is also said that **Kinnaras**[4] and **Nāgas**[5] lived on the slopes of Gandhamādana. It was among the places visited by **Khadiravaniya Revata** (AA. i. 139).

It is not explicitly mentioned that all Pacceka Buddhas die in Gandhamādana, but the inference seems to be such. Thus, once, five hundred Pacceka Buddhas led by **Mahāpaduma** died there, and their bodies were cremated.[6]

The *Jātaka Commentary*[7] explains Gandhamādana as *gandhena madakaro pabbato.*

1 SNA. i. 52, 66 f.; ii. 437; AA. ii. 759; UdA. 300, etc.; MA. ii. 585.

2 *E.g.*, DhA. iii. 368 f.; iv. 121, 199 f.; J. iv. 16.

3 *E.g.*, J. iii. 453.

4 J. iv. 438.

5 Rockhill, 169.

6 ThagA. ii. 141.

7 vi. 79.

The fragrant tree **Bhujaka** grows only in heaven and in Gandhamādana.[8]

It is said that the Buddha Metteyya will retire for a while to Gandhamādana, after spending his first rainy season.[9]

[8] VvA. 162. [9] *Anāgatavaṃsa* v. 81.

Gandhamāliya Thera.—An arahant. Ninety-four kappas ago he offered to the Buddha **Siddhattha** a *gandhathūpa* covered with *sumana*-flowers. Forty kappas ago he became king, sixteen times, under the name of **Devagandha.**[1]

[1] Ap. i. 135.

Gandhamuṭṭhiya Thera.—An arahant. One hundred thousand kappas ago he gave a handful of perfume for the construction of a (Buddha's) funeral pyre.[1]

[1] Ap. i. 292; *cp.* **Gandhapūjaka.**

Gandhara.—A mountain in **Himavā.**[1]

[1] J. vi. 579.

Gandhavaṃsa.—A late Pāli work written in Burma. It relates, in brief, the history of the Pāli Canon and gives accounts of post-canonical Pāli books written in Burma and Ceylon. The colophon states that the work was composed by a forest-dwelling Elder named **Nandapañña.** At the end of each chapter the work is referred to as **Cullagandhavaṃsa**; perhaps what we have now is an abridged edition of a larger work.[1]

[1] The work is published in *J.P.T.S.*, 1886, pp. 55-80.

Gandhavilepana Sutta.—Few are those who abstain from flowers, scents, etc.; many are those who do not.[1]

[1] S. v. 471.

Gandhābharaṇa.—See **Gaṇḍābharaṇa.**

1. **Gandhāra.**—A Pacceka Buddha mentioned in a nominal list.[1]

[1] M. iii. 69; ApA. i. 106.

2. **Gandhāra.**—One of the sixteen **Mahājanapadas.**[1] Its capital was **Takkasilā,** famous for its university; its king in the time of the Buddha was **Pukkusāti.** There was friendly intercourse between him and **Bimbisāra** of Magadha. Merchants and visitors from one country to

[1] A. i. 213; iv. 252, etc.; in the *Niddesa* and *Mahāvastu* lists Gandhāra is omitted and others substituted.

another were lodged and fed at the expense of the country's king, and no tariffs were levied on their merchandise. There was constant exchange of goods and valuables, and on one occasion Bimbisāra, wishing to send his friend a gift of particular value, despatched to him a letter containing news of the appearance in the world of the Buddha, the Dhamma and the Saṅgha. When Pukkusāti read the letter he decided to become a follower of the Buddha, and ordained himself as a monk; then, leaving his kingdom, he travelled all the way to Sāvatthi to see the Buddha.[2] This conversion of Gandhāra's king, however, does not seem to have had the effect of converting the rest of its people to the Buddha's faith. The memory of Pukkusāti was evidently soon forgotten, for we find **Moggaliputta Tissa,** at the conclusion of the Third Council, sending the thera **Majjhantika** to convert Gandhāra.[3]

According to Buddhaghosa's account, Pukkusāti's kingdom was over one hundred leagues in extent,[4] and the distance from Takkasilā to Sāvatthi was one hundred and ninety-two leagues.[5] There was evidently a well-known caravan route linking the two countries, although Gandhāra was regarded as a *paccantima-janapada.*[6]

At the time of Majjhantika's visit, the people of Gandhāra were being harassed by the Nāga-king **Aravāḷa,** and the chronicles contain details of his conversion by the monk. The Nāga-king, together with his retinue, the yakkha **Paṇḍaka** and his wife **Hāritā,** became devout followers of the Buddha. Majjhantika preached the **Āsīvisūpama Sutta,** and many thousands joined the Order.[7]

Gandhāra appears to have included **Kasmīra,** the two countries being always mentioned together as **Kasmīra-Gandhāra.** They occupied the sites of the modern districts of Peshawar and Rawalpindi in the northern Punjab.[8] In the time of Asoka the country formed part of his empire, and is mentioned as such in Rock Edict V. Before that it was subject to the Achæmenid kings. Gandhāra was always famous for its red woollen shawls (*kambala*).[9]

Another king of Takkasilā besides Pukkusāti is mentioned—namely, **Naggaji,** who was a contemporary of **Nimi,** king of Videha.[10]

One of the eye teeth of the Buddha was deposited in Gandhāra.[11]

[2] MA. ii. 979 ff.

[3] Mhv. xii. 3 ff.

[4] MA. ii. 988.

[5] *Ibid.*, 987; from Benares it was one hundred and twenty leagues (*vīsaṃyojanasata*) (J. i. 395; ii. 47).

[6] MA. ii. 982; there was also constant trade between Gandhāra and Videha (J. iii. 365 ff.). It would appear from the *Mahā Niddesa* (i. 154) that Takkasilā was a regular centre of trade.

[7] Mhv. xii. 9 ff.; Smp. i. 64 f.; Dpv. viii. 4.

[8] PHAI. p. 93.

[9] SNA. ii. 487; J. vi. 501.

[10] J. iii. 377; *cf. Ait. Brāhmaṇa* vii. 34; *Śat. Brāhmaṇa* viii. 1, 4, 10; see also **Gandhārarājā.**

[11] Bu. xxviii. 6; D. ii. 167.

Gandhāra Jātaka (No. 406).—The Bodhisatta was once king of **Gandhāra,** and he and the king of **Videha** became friends, though they never saw each other. One day the Gandhāra king saw an eclipse of the moon and, being stirred in his mind, left his kingdom and became an ascetic in Himavā.

The Videha king, hearing of this, did likewise. They met in Himavā, but failed to recognise each other until, seeing another eclipse of the moon, they exchanged reminiscences. They went out begging together, and the Videha ascetic, having once been given a large quantity of salt, stored up some of it for a saltless day. The Gandhāra ascetic, finding this out, blamed his friend for his greediness, and the latter begged his forgiveness.

The Videha ascetic is identified with **Ānanda.** The story was told in reference to the occasion of the passing of the rule forbidding monks to store medicine for more than seven days.[1]

[1] J. iii. 363 ff.; the introductory story is given in Vin. i. 206 ff.; see also *s.v.* **Pilindavaccha**; the Jātaka story is given in MA. i. 534 f.

Gandhārarājā.—The king of Gandhāra is several times[1] mentioned by this name; it is evidently a title and not a proper name.

[1] *E.g.*, J. i. 191; ii. 219 f.; iii. 364 ff.; iv. 98.

Gandhāravagga.—The second chapter of the *Satta Nipāta* of the *Jātaka Commentary.*[1]

[1] J. iii. 363-421.

Gandhāra- or **Gandhārī-vijjā.**—A charm whereby one could become invisible and multiform, pass through all obstacles, through earth and water, and touch the sun and moon.[1] Elsewhere[2] the charm is mentioned as being only useful for the purpose of making oneself invisible. The *Theragāthā Commentary*[3] distinguishes a Lesser and a Greater. **Pilindavaccha** knew the former and thought that the Buddha would teach him the other. The charm enabled him to travel through the air and read the thoughts of others.

Buddhaghosa[4] explains that the charm was so called, either because it was invented by a sage named Gandhāra, or because it originated in Gandhāra.

[1] D. i. 213.
[2] J iv. 498.
[3] I. 51 f.
[4] DA ii. 389.

Gandhodaka (-kadāyaka) Thera.—An arahant. Once, when celebrations were being held in honour of the Bodhi-tree of **Padumuttara** Buddha, he poured fragrant water from a painted pot on to the tree. There was a thunderstorm and he was killed on the spot by lightning. Being born in heaven, he uttered stanzas in praise of the Buddha and his teaching. One hundred and twenty-eight kappas ago he became a king, named **Saṃvasita.**[1]

[1] Ap. i. 105 f.

Gandhodakiya Thera.—An arahant. Ninety-one kappas ago he saw the Buddha **Vipassī** and sprinkled perfumed water on him. Thirty-one kappas ago he became king, under the name of **Sugandha.**[1] He is probably identical with **Ātuma Thera.**[2]

[1] Ap. i. 157 f. [2] ThagA. i. 160 f.

Gamika.—Father of the nun **Mahātissā.**[1]

[1] Dpv. xviii. 39.

Gamiṭṭhavāli Vihāra.—A monastery in Rohaṇa, founded by **Kākavaṇṇa-Tissa.**[1]

[1] Mhv. xxii. 23.

1. **Gambhīra.**—A seaport village, visited by **Mittavindaka** in the course of his flight from Benares.[1]

[1] J. i. 239.

2. **Gambhīra.**—A channel branching off from the **Parakkama Samudda.** It started at the point of the flood-escape known as **Makara.**[1]

[1] Cv. lxxix. 40.

Gambhīra Sutta.—Four conditions—following after the good, hearing the Dhamma, paying systematic attention thereto, and living in accordance with its precepts—which, if cultivated, lead to profound insight.[1]

[1] S. v. 412.

Gambhīracārī.—The name of one of the two otters in the **Dabbhapuppha Jātaka**[1] (*q.v.*).

[1] J. iii. 333.

Gambhīranadī.—A river, one yojana north of **Anurādhapura ;** the bricks for the **Mahā Thūpa** and for the Thupas of the three former Buddhas were prepared on its banks.[1] On its bank was **Upatissagāma.**[2]

[1] Mhv. xxviii. 7; MṬ. 508. [2] Mhv. vii. 44.

1. **Gayā.**—A pond in which people bathed, that their sins might be washed away.[1] Buddhaghosa says[2] it was a circular pond in which was a bathing ghat (*maṇḍavāpisaṇṭhānaṃ titthaṃ*). But see below, **Gayā** (2).

[1] J. v. 388 f. [2] MA. i. 145.

2. **Gayā.**—A town in India. It lay on the road between the Bodhi-tree and Benares, and was three *gāvutas* from the Bodhi-tree and fifteen yojanas from Benares.[1] It was between the Bodhimaṇḍa and Gayā that the Buddha, on his way to **Isipatana,** met **Upaka.**[2] The Buddha stayed at Gayā on several occasions: once at **Gayāsīsa,**[3] and also near the **Taṅkitamañca,**[4] the residence of **Suciloma.**

Buddhaghosa says that Gayā was the name given both to the village and a bathing ghat near to it (also called **Gayāpokkharaṇī**). Dhammapāla,[5] on the other hand, speaks of a **Gayānadī** and a **Gayāpokkharaṇī** as being two distinct bathing ghats, both commonly called **Gayātittha,** and both considered to possess the power of washing away sins. People went there, offered sacrifices to the gods, recited the Vedas, and immersed themselves in the water.

Elsewhere[6] it is stated that every year, in the earlier half of the month of Phagguna (March), people held a bathing festival at the bathing ghat at Gayā, the festival being called **Gayāphaggunī.** It was at one of these festivals that **Senaka Thera** was converted by the Buddha. This explanation of Gayāphaggu is, perhaps, not quite correct, for, according to some,[7] the river (**Nerañjarā**) which ran by Gayā was itself called Phaggu (Skt. Phalgu).

The town of Gayā is often called Brahmagayā to distinguish it from **Buddhagayā** (*q.v.*).

[1] MA. i. 387 f.; Fa Hien says the distance from the Bodhi-tree to Gayā was twenty li, or about 3½ miles.
[2] Vin. i. 8.
[3] *Ibid.*, 34; S. iv. 19; A. iv. 302.
[4] Sn. p. 47; S. i. 207, etc.
[5] UdA. 74, 75; *cp.* SNA. i. 301.
[6] ThagA. i. 388 f., 418; Thag. v. 287.
[7] *E.g.*, Cunningham: AGI. 524; Böthlinck and Roth's Dict. *s.v. Phalgu*; Neumann (Majh. N. Trans. i. 271) says that the village of Gayā itself was called Phaggu.

Gayā Sutta.—Preached at **Gayāsīsa.** The Buddha describes to the monks some of the stages through which he passed before reaching Enlightenment. At first he could only see the light from the bodies of the devas; later, through conscious striving, he could distinguish their forms, talk with them, discover how they came to be born in their different spheres; then he was able to read their past births, and at last he attained to supreme knowledge.[1]

[1] A. iv. 302 ff.

Gayā-Kassapa.—One of the three Kassapa brothers, the **Tebhātika-Jaṭilā** (*q.v.*). On leaving the world with his brothers and becoming an ascetic, he gathered round him a company of two hundred other ascetics. They all lived at **Gayāsīsa,** hence his name (*Gayāsīse pabbajito ti Gayā Kassapo nāma jāto*). When Uruvela-Kassapa was converted, Gayā-Kassapa, with his followers, joined the Order, and at the conclusion of the **Ādittapariyāya Sutta** they all became arahants.[1] Gayā-Kassapa is reported[2] to have said that he used to bathe three times a day at **Gayā-tittha,** in order to wash away his sins during the festival of **Gayāphaggu.**

In the time of **Sikhī** Buddha he was a householder, and later became a forest-dwelling hermit. One day he saw the Buddha walking alone in the forest and offered him a *kola*-fruit.[3]

He is evidently identical with **Koladāyaka** of the *Apadāna*.[4]

[1] Vin. i. 33 f.; AA. i. 165.
[2] Thag. v. 345 f.
[3] ThagA. i. 417 f.
[4] Ap. ii. 379; see also ii. 483.

Gayātittha, Gayā-phaggu, -phaggunī, Gayā-phaggunītittha.—See **Gayā** (2).

Gayāsīsa.—A hill near **Gayā.** Here the Buddha came from **Uruvelā** after converting the **Tebhātika-Jaṭilā,** and here he lived with one thousand monks. On this occasion of his coming he preached the **Ādittapariyāya Sutta.**[1] When **Devadatta** managed to win over five hundred of the monks to his side, it was to Gayāsīsa that he retired with them, and there it was that the Buddha's Chief Disciples had to go to reclaim them.[2] It is said[3] that **Ajātasattu** built a special monastery for Devadatta at Gayāsīsa.

The Commentaries[4] say that the hill was so called because it was composed of a flat stone and was shaped like an elephant's head (*gaja-sīsa-sadisa-piṭṭhipāsāno*). There was room on the rock for one thousand monks. The hill stands about one mile to the south-west of Gayā and is now called Brahmayoni. To the south-east of the hill Hiouen Thsang saw the three thūpas of the Tebhātika Jaṭilā.[5] See also **Gayā Sutta.**

[1] Vin. i. 34 f.; S. iv. 19 f.; J. i. 82; AA. i. 57, etc.; PvA. 21; Ud. i. 9; DhA. i. 72.
[2] Vin. ii. 199; DhA. i. 121; J. i. 142, 425, 490 f.; iv. 180.
[3] J. i. 185, 508; ii. 38 f.
[4] SA. iii. 4; UdA. 74.
[5] CAGI. 524 f.

Garahadinna.—A resident of **Sāvatthi** and friend of **Sirigutta.** The latter was a follower of the Buddha, and the former of the Nigaṇṭhas. Instigated by the Nigaṇṭhas, Garahadinna constantly blamed his friend for his allegiance to the Buddha, until one day, in exasperation, Sirigutta invited the Nigaṇṭhas to his house in order to prove that their claim to omniscience was false. To this end he had a ditch dug and filled with filth, ropes stretched longitudinally over the ditch, and the seats so arranged that the moment the Nigaṇṭhas sat down they would be tipped over and flung into the ditch. The Nigaṇṭhas arrived, and everything happened as Sirigutta had arranged. Garahadinna, filled with desire for revenge, hid his resentment and invited the Buddha and his disciples with the intention of humiliating them. He employed the same stratagem as his friend, except that the ditch was filled with glowing coals instead of with filth. The Buddha came, knowing all that had happened, and by an exercise of iddhi-power caused large lotus flowers to spring up from the bed of coals. Sitting thereon, he created an abundant supply of food and preached the Dhamma. Garahadinna, Sirigutta, and many others became *sotāpannas*.[1]

On this occasion was also preached the **Khadiraṅgāra Jātaka.**[2]

It is said[3] that when the Buddha preached at Garahadinna's house, eighty-four thousand beings realised the Truth.

[1] DhA. i. 434 f. [2] But see the Introductory Story of the Jātaka.
[3] Mil. 350.

Garahita Jātaka (No. 219).—Once the Bodhisatta was a monkey in the Himālayas and, having been captured by a forester, was given to the king. The king grew fond of him, and the monkey learnt the ways of men. The king set him free, and when his fellows saw him they insisted on hearing from him how men lived. He told them of men's greed for possessions, and how in each house there were two masters, one of them beardless, with long breasts and plaited hair. The monkeys, hearing of this folly, stopped their ears and went elsewhere, saying they could not bear to live in a place where they had heard such unseemly things! That place came thereafter to be called the **Garahitapiṭṭhipāsāṇa.**

The story was told in reference to a discontented monk.[1]

[1] J. ii. 184.

Garahitapiṭṭhipāsāṇa.—See **Garahita Jātaka.**

Garītara.—A tank in Ceylon constructed by **Moggallāna II.** by damming the **Kadambanadī.**[1]

[1] Cv. xli. 61.

1. **Garuḷa.**—One of the palaces occupied by **Phussa** Buddha in his last lay-life.[1] The Commentary[2] calls it **Garuḷapakkha.**

[1] Bu. xix. 15. [2] BuA. 192.

2. **Garuḍā, Garuḷā.**—A class of mythical birds generally mentioned in company with Nāgas.[1] They live in Simbali-groves[2] and are usually huge in size, sometimes one hundred and fifty leagues from wing to wing.[3] The flapping of their wings can raise a storm, known as the Garuḍa-wind.[4] This wind can plunge a whole city in darkness and cause houses to fall through its violence.[5] A Garuḷa has strength great enough to carry off a whole banyan tree, tearing it up from its roots.[6] The Garuḷas are the eternal enemies of the Nāgas[7] and live in places, such as the **Seruma** Island,[8] where Nāgas are to be found. The greatest happiness of the Nāgas is to be free from the attacks of the Garuḷas.[9] A Garuḷa's plumage is so thick that a man—*e.g.*, **Naṭakuvera**[10]—could hide in it, unnoticed by the bird. Sometimes Garuḷas assume human form; two Garuḷa kings are said to have played dice with kings of Benares and to have fallen in love with their queens, whom they took to the Garuḷa city —one of the queens being **Sussoṇḍī**[11] and the other **Kākātī.**[12] In each case the queen, being found unfaithful to her Garuḷa lover, was returned to her husband. The Garuḷas know the **Ālambāyana** spell, which no Nāga can resist.[13] It is said that in olden days the Garuḷas did not know how to seize Nāgas effectively; they caught them by the head, and the Nāgas who had swallowed big stones were too heavy to be lifted from the ground; consequently the Garuḷas died of exhaustion in trying to carry them. Later the Garuḷas learnt this secret through the treachery of the ascetic **Karambiya,** as related in the **Paṇḍara Jātaka.**[14] Garuḷas are mentioned as sometimes leading virtuous lives, keeping the fast and observing the precepts. One such was the Garuḷa king mentioned in the Paṇḍara Jātaka, and another, the son of **Vināta,** who visited the park of **Dhanañjaya Koravya** and gave a golden garland as present after hearing **Vidhurapaṇḍita** preach.[15] The Garuḷa's body was evidently considered to be specially formed for quick flight, for the ancient prototype of the aeroplane was based on the Garuḷa.[16] One of the five guards appointed by **Sakka** to protect **Tāvatiṃsa** from the Asuras was formed of Garuḷas.[17] The Bodhisatta[18] and Sāriputta[19] were both, on different occasions, born as Garuḷa kings. The Simbalī is the special tree of the Garuḷa-world.[20] The Garuḷa is often represented in art as a winged Man.[21] The Garuḷas are sometimes called **Supaṇṇas (Suvaṇṇas).**[22]

1 *E.g.*, J. iv. 181, 202.
2 *E.g.*, J. i. 202.
3 J. iii. 397.
4 J. v. 77.
5 J. iii. 188.
6 J. vi. 177.
7 J. ii. 13; iii. 103.
8 J. iii. 187.
9 J. iv. 463.
10 J. iii. 91.
11 *Ibid.*, 187.
12 *Ibid.*, 91.
13 J. vi. 178, 184.
14 *Ibid.*, 175 f.
15 *Ibid.*, 261 f.
16 DhA. iii. 135.
17 J. i. 204.
18 J. iii. 187.
19 *Ibid.*, 400.
20 Vsm. i. 206.
21 See Fergusson: Tree and Serpent Worship, pl. xxvi. 1; xxviii. 1. etc; also Gründwedel: Buddhistische Kunst, pp. 47-50.
22 VvA. 9.

Galambatittha.—A village in Ceylon, which contained a vihāra and a thūpa. King **Vasabha** repaired the thūpa, built an uposatha-house, and endowed land for the maintenance of lamps in the house.[1] The village is probably identical with that mentioned elsewhere as **Galambatitthagāma.**[2] In that case, it was in Rohaṇa and was the scene of a battle in the campaign of **Parakkamabāhu I.**

The Commentaries[3] contain references to a group of fifty monks dwelling in **Galambatittha Vihāra,** who took a vow never to address each other until they attained arahantship.

See *s.v.* **Kalambatittha.**

[1] Mhv. xxxv. 85. [2] Cv. lxxv. 7. [3] *E.g.*, SNA. i. 57; VibhA. 353.

Gallakapīṭha.—A village in Ceylon. Five hundred youths from the village were ordained by **Mahinda,** soon after his arrival in Ceylon.[1]

[1] Mhv. xvii. 59.

Gavaghātaka Sutta.—**Moggallāna** reports to the Buddha that, while descending **Gijjhakūṭa,** he saw a vast lump of flesh flying through the air. The Buddha says it was a cattle butcher of **Rājagaha,** born as a *peta.*[1]

[1] S. ii. 256.

Gavaccha.—See **Cūḷa-Gavaccha** and **Mahā-Gavaccha.**

Gavapāna.—The name of a special almsgiving held in honour of **Maṅgala** Buddha by the Bodhisatta, when he was born as the brahmin **Suruci.** The chief item of food was a kind of pudding made of milk, rice and honey.[1]

[1] Bu. iv. 11; BuA. 122.

1. **Gavampati Thera.**—An arahant. He was a son of a seṭṭhi in Benares, and one of the four lay companions of the thera **Yasa,** who, when they heard of Vasa's renunciation, imitated him and won arahantship. Later, Gavampati lived in the **Añjanavana** at **Sāketa.** One day, when the Buddha visited the Añjanavana, some of the monks accompanying him slept on the sandbanks of the **Sarabhū.** The river rose in the night and there was great dismay. The Buddha sent Gavampati to stem the flood, which he did by his *iddhi*-power. The water stopped afar off, looking like a mountain peak.

In the time of **Sikhī** Buddha he was a huntsman, and seeing the Buddha offered him flowers. Later he built a parasol and a railing for the thūpa of **Koṇāgamana.** In the time of **Kassapa** Buddha he was a rich householder possessed of many cattle. One day he saw an arahant eating his meal in the sun for lack of shade, and built for him a shelter and planted in front of it a *sirīsa*-tree. As a result he was born in the **Cātummahārājika** world, and his palace was known as **Serissaka.**[1]

Gavampati was the teacher of **Mahānāga,** son of **Madhu-Vāseṭṭha.**[2] It is said[3] that the Serissaka-vimāna, occupied by Gavampati, remained in the Cātummahārājika world even after he had left it. There Gavampati often spent his siesta and held conversations with **Pāyāsi,** who sent through him a message to the inhabitants of the earth, that they should profit by the example of him (Pāyāsi) and discriminate in the bestowal of their gifts.

The Dulvā mentions[4] that after the Buddha's death, when **Mahā Kassapa** wished to hold a Convocation of the chief monks, **Puṇṇa** was sent as a special messenger to summon Gavampati, who was then in the Serissaka-vimāna. But Gavampati did not attend, his death being imminent. Instead he sent his bowl and three robes as a gift to the Saṅgha.

Immediately afterwards he died, and Puṇṇa carried out his funeral rites.

Gavampati is evidently identical with **Girinelapūjaka** of the *Apadāna.*[5] See also **Gavampati Sutta.**

[1] Vin. i. 18 f.; Thag. v. 38; ThagA. i. 103 f.; VvA. 331 f.; DA. (iii. 814) gives a slightly different version of the origin of the Serissaka-vimāna.

[2] ThagA. i. 443.

[3] D. ii. 356 f.; DA. (iii. 814) says he went there because he found the "climate" (*utu*) more agreeable. SNA. (i. 347) says it was because he (like Piṇḍolabhāradvāja) loved his old haunts.

[4] Rockhill, p. 149 f.

[5] ii. 457.

2. **Gavampati.**—The *Sāsanavaṃsa*[1] speaks of a thera by this name, at whose request the Buddha went to **Sudhammapura** in the **Rāmañña** country to establish his religion. In a previous life Gavampati was born of an egg laid by a Nāga maiden who had relations with a *vijjādhara.* The egg was hatched and a child was born, but it died at the age of ten and was reborn at **Mithilā** as Gavampati. He joined the Order at the age of seven and became an arahant. Later he visited Sudhammapura to preach to his mother, and there King **Sīha** asked him to invite the Buddha to his country.

[1] p. 36 f.

Gavampati Sutta.—Preached by **Gavampati** at **Sahajāti** in the **Ceti** country. A number of the senior monks were talking of *dukkha,* and

Gavampati tells them that he knows from the Buddha's own self that whosoever understands *dukkha* knows all its aspects—its nature, its arising, its cessation and the path thereto.[1]

[1] S. v. 436.

Gavara.—A Tamil general of **Doṇa,** subdued by **Duṭṭhagāmaṇī.**[1]

[1] Mhv. xxv. 11.

Gavaratissa Vihāra.—A monastery in Ceylon, built by King **Bhātika-Tissa,** who also constructed for its maintenance the **Mahāmaṇi** tank.[1]

[1] Mhv. xxxvi. 3.

Gavaravāliya-aṅgaṇa.—A monastic establishment in Ceylon, the residence of **Pītamalla Thera** and thirty others.[1]

[1] MA. i. 190.

Gavesī.—A follower of **Kassapa** Buddha. Five hundred others were associated with him, and at first their spiritual life was poor. Gavesī, realising this, put forth effort and, step by step, attained greater proficiency until, at last, he became an arahant. His followers imitated him in every step of his spiritual advancement, and they, too, became arahants.

The Buddha related this story to **Ānanda** during a tour in **Kosala.** They came to a *sāla*-grove and there the Buddha smiled; when asked the reason for his smile, he replied that the grove was the scene of Gavesī's practice of the religious life.[1]

[1] A. iii. 214 ff.

Gavesī Sutta.—The story of **Gavesī** (*q.v.*).

Gavha.—See **Gahva.**

Gahapati Jātaka (No. 199).—Once, in Kāsi, the Bodhisatta's wife carried on an intrigue with the village headman. The husband, determined to catch them, pretended to leave the village, but returned as soon as the headman entered the house. The wife, seeing her husband, climbed into the granary, and professed that the headman was there to demand the price of meat which he had supplied to them during a famine, and that as there was no money he insisted on being given the value in grain, which, she said, she was determined to refuse to do. But the Bodhisatta saw through the ruse, thrashed the headman and then his wife.

The Buddha related the story to a backsliding monk to demonstrate to him how women were always sinful.[1]

[1] J. ii. 134 f.

1. **Gahapati Vagga.**—The sixth section of the *Majjhima Nikāya.*[1]

[1] M. i. 339-413.

2. **Gahapati Vagga.**—The third section of the *Aṭṭhaka Nipāta* of the *Aṅguttara Nikāya.* It contains ten suttas, including the Buddha's praises of **Ugga** of Vesāli, **Ugga** of Hatthigāma, and **Hatthaka** Āḷavaka.[1]

[1] A. iv. 208-35.

3. **Gahapati Vagga.**—The fifth chapter of the *Nidāna Saṃyutta.*[1]

[1] S. ii. 68-80.

4. **Gahapati Vagga.**—The thirteenth chapter of the *Saḷāyatana Saṃyutta.* It contains conversations between various eminent householders on the one side, and the Buddha and the monks on the other.[1]

[1] S. iv. 109-24.

Gahvaratīra.—The name of the place where the Thera **Gahvaratīriya** lived.[1]

[1] ThagA. i. 91.

Gahvaratīriya (Gavharatīriya) Thera.—He was a brahmin of **Sāvatthi,** named **Aggidatta.** Having seen **Yamakapāṭihāriya,** he entered the Order and lived in a spot called **Gahvaratīra**—hence his name—and there in due course became an arahant. On his return to Sāvatthi, his relations held a great almsgiving in his honour and requested him to live near them. But be refused this request and returned to the forest.

He was a hunter in the time of **Sikhī** Buddha, and was delighted by the sound of the Buddha's voice as he preached.[1]

He is probably identical with **Ghosasaññaka** of the *Apadāna,*[2] but the same verses are also attributed to **Dhammika.**[3]

[1] Thag. v. 31; ThagA. i. 91 f. [2] Ap. ii. 451. [3] ThagA. i. 398.

Gāthā.—A portion of the *Tipiṭaka* classified according to the matter (*aṅga*) of each one. It includes the *Dhammapada*, the *Theragāthā* and *Therīgāthā*, and those suttas, composed of stanzas only, found in the *Sutta Nipāta* and not included under the term Sutta.[1]

[1] DA. i. 23 f.; Vin. iii. 8.

Gāmakaseṭṭhi.—The name of the treasurer whose daughter was married by **Ghosakaseṭṭhi**[1] (*q.v.*).

[1] AA. i. 230; the DhA. account does not mention the man's name.

Gāmaṇi Jātaka (No. 8).—The story of Prince **Gāmaṇi.**[1] For details see the **Saṃvara Jātaka.**

[1] J. i. 136 f.

Gāmaṇi Saṃyutta.—The fifty-second *Saṃyutta* of the *Saṃyutta Nikāya.* It contains accounts of sermons preached by the Buddha to various headmen (*gāmaṇī*).[1]

[1] S. iv. 305-59.

Gāmaṇi-Caṇḍa.—A servant of **Janasandha,** king of Benares. For his story see the Gāmaṇi-Caṇḍa Jātaka.

Gāmaṇi-Caṇḍa Jātaka (No. 257).—The Bodhisatta was once born as **Ādāsamukha,** son of **Janasandha,** king of Benares. Ādāsamukha became king at the age of seven, having successfully solved the problems set him by his courtiers. Janasandha had a servant named **Gāmaṇi-Caṇḍa** who, being old, retired when Ādāsamukha came to the throne. But various mishaps befell Gāmaṇi-Caṇḍa, and he was charged on various counts by different people. As he was being brought to the king to receive punishment, he was asked by several persons to convey messages to the king, and to find out from him solutions for their troubles. The king listened to the charges brought against Gāmaṇi and to his explanation of them. Convinced of Gāmaṇi's innocence, he passed sentences which ultimately brought gain to Gāmaṇi. The king then proceeded to solve the problems contained in the messages brought by Gāmaṇi. He gave to Gāmaṇi the village in which he lived, free from all taxes, and there Gāmaṇi lived happily to the end of his days.

The story was told by the Buddha to certain monks who had been discussing his wisdom.

Gāmaṇi-Caṇḍa is identified with **Ānanda.** In the story he is referred to also as **Gāmaṇi, Caṇḍa-Gāmaṇi** and **Caṇḍa.**[1]

[1] J. ii. 297-310.

Gamaṇitissa.—A tank made by King **Gajabāhu** and given for the maintenance of the **Abhayagiri-vihāra.**[1]

[1] Mhv. xxxv. 120.

1. **Gāmaṇi.**—A Tamil general and his stronghold, subdued by **Duṭṭhagāmaṇi.**[1]

[1] Mhv. xxv. 13.

2. **Gāmaṇī.**—A prince, youngest of one hundred brothers. His story is given in the **Saṃvara Jātaka.**[1]

[1] J. iv. 130 ff.; see also J. i. 136 f.

3. **Gāmaṇī.**—One of the six brothers of **Bhaddakaccānā**; he remained behind when the others left for Ceylon.[1]

[1] MṬ. 275.

4. **Gāmaṇī.**—See also **Dīghagāmaṇī, Duṭṭhagāmaṇī** and **Āmaṇḍagāmaṇī.**

Gāmaṇīvāpi.—A tank near **Anurādhapura.** Near it was a hermitage built by **Paṇḍukābhaya.**[1]

[1] Mhv. x. 96; see Mhv. *Trs.*, p. 75, n. 1.

Gāmantapabbhāravāsī Mahā Sīva.—See **Mahā Sīva.**

Gāmeṇḍavālamahāvihāra.—A monastery in **Rohaṇa.** It was the residence of **Cūlapiṇḍapātikatissa** and of **Milakkhatissa.**[1] It was evidently within easy reach of **Cittalapabbata** and **Kājaragāma.**[2] Once **Maliyadeva Thera** recited the **Cha Chakka Sutta** at this vihāra, and at the end of the recital sixty monks became arahants.[3]

[1] AA. i. 21. [2] *Ibid.*, 22. [3] MA. ii. 1024.

Gāyikā.—One of the four wives of **Candakumāra.**[1]

[1] J. vi. 148.

Gārava Sutta.—As the Buddha sat under the **Ajapāla** Banyan tree, soon after the Enlightenment,[1] a thought came to him that he should have someone whom he could consider and honour as his teacher. But, seeing no one worthy of such honour and respect, he decided that the Dhamma should be his teacher. Thereupon **Sahampati** appeared before him and reminded him that in this decision he was acting as all Buddhas acted.[2]

[1] In the fifth week, says the Commentary (S.A i. 158). [2] S. i. 138 f.

Gālurajju.—A river in South Ceylon.[1]

[1] Cv. lxxv. 34; see also Cv. *Trs.* ii. 47, n. 1.

Gāḷhagaṅgā.—A river in South Ceylon which was once decreed to be the boundary of **Rohaṇa.** It is generally identified with **Mahāvāḷukagaṅgā.**[1]

[1] Cv. xlviii. 132; Cv. *Trs.* i. 122, n. 4.

1. **Gijjha Jātaka** (No. 164).—Once the Bodhisatta was born among the vultures on **Gijjhakūṭapabbata.** On one occasion there was a great storm of wind and rain, and the vultures were forced to seek shelter in a ditch outside Benares. A merchant, seeing them, provided them with a warm fire and food. When the weather cleared the vultures returned to their haunts, and decided to give the merchant whatever finery and jewellery they might find in their wanderings. These they dropped in the merchant's garden. The king, hearing of their depredations, set traps and caught a vulture, who confessed the truth, which was corroborated by the merchant. The vulture was set free and the goods were returned to their owners.

Ānanda was the king, and **Sāriputta** the merchant.

The story was told in reference to a monk who was charged with having supported his poor parents. The Buddha praised the man's action, saying that such gratitude was an excellent quality.[1]

[1] J. ii. 50 f.; see also the **Sāma Jātaka.**

2. **Gijjha Jātaka** (No. 399).—Once the Bodhisatta was a vulture, and supported his blind parents who lived in a cave. One day, being caught in a trap, he was heard by a hunter lamenting for his parents; the hunter set him free.

The story was told in reference to a monk who supported his mother. **Channa** was the hunter.[1]

[1] J. iii. 330 f.

3. **Gijjha Jātaka** (No. 427).—Once the Bodhisatta was a vulture in **Gijjhapabbata.** His son, **Supatta,** was king of the vultures; he was very strong and supported his parents. One day, against the advice of his father, he flew in the upper air and was dashed to death by the **Veramba**-wind.

The story was related in reference to a disobedient monk of good family, who objected to being instructed in his duties.[1]

The **Catudvāra Jātaka**[2] was related in reference to the same monk.

[1] J. iii. 483 f.; *cf.* the **Migalopa Jātaka**; see also the **Dubbaca** and the **Indasamānagotta Jātakas.**

[2] J. iv. 1 ff.

1. **Gijjhakūṭa.**—One of the five hills encircling **Rājagaha.** It was evidently a favourite resort of those who followed the religious life.[1] The Buddha seems to have been attracted by its solitude, and is mentioned as having visited it on several occasions, sometimes even in the

[1] It was so even in times gone by (see, *e.g.*, J. ii. 55).

dark, in drizzling rain, while **Māra** made unsuccessful attempts to frighten him.[2] It was on the slopes of Gijjhakūṭa, where the Buddha was wandering about, that **Devadatta** hurled at him a mighty stone to kill him, but only a splinter injured his foot.[3] It was there also that **Jīvaka Komārabhacca** administered a purgative to the Buddha.[4] Among those who visited the Buddha on Gijjhakūṭa are mentioned **Sahampati** (S. i. 153), the youth **Māgha** (Sn., p. 86), the yakkha **Inda** (S. i. 206), **Sakka** (S. i. 233; iv. 102),t he Paribbājaka **Sajjha** (A. iv. 371), the **Kassapagotta** monk (A. i. 237), **Pañcasikha** (S. iv. 103; D. ii. 220), **Sutavā** (A. iv. 369), the four kings of the **Cātummahārājika** world and their followers (D. iii. 195), **Abhayarājakumāra** (S. v. 126), **Upaka Maṇḍikāputta** (A. ii. 181), **Dhammika** (A. iii. 368), and **Vassakāra** (A. iv. 18; D. ii. 72). Several well-known suttas were preached on Gijjhakūṭa—*e.g.*, the **Māgha, Dhammika** and **Chaḷabhijāti** Suttas, the discourse on the seven **Aparihānīyadhammā** (A. iv. 21 f.), the **Mahāsāropama** and **Āṭānāṭiya** Suttas.[5] It is said[6] that in due course a vihāra was erected on Gijjhakūṭa for the Buddha and his monks; here cells were erected for the use of monks who came from afar, but these cells were so difficult of access that monks arriving late at Rājagaha would ask **Dabbamallaputta-Tissa** to find accommodation for them in Gijjhakūṭa, in order to test his capabilities.[7] Mention is made of several eminent monks who stayed at Gijjhakūṭa from time to time—*e.g.*, **Sāriputta** (M. iii. 263; A. iii. 300; S. ii. 155), **Ānanda** (A. iii. 383), **Mahā Kassapa, Anuruddha, Puṇṇa Mantāniputta, Upāli** and **Devadatta** (S. ii. 155), also **Cunda** and **Channa** (S. iv. 55). Channa fell ill there, and ultimately committed suicide.[8] **Moggallāna** and **Lakkhaṇa** are reported to have stayed there, and to have seen many inhabitants of Rājagaha reborn in Gijjhakūṭa as *petas*.[9] The **Mettiyabhummajakas** (Vin. iii. 167) and the **Chabbaggiyas** (*ibid.*, 82) were also in the habit of visiting the hill.

Several places are mentioned as having been visited by the Buddha during his sojourns on Gijjhakūṭa, and it may be inferred from accounts given of these visits that these places were within easy reach of the hill. Such, for example, are the **Paṭibhānakūṭa** (S. v. 448), the **Sītavana,** where the Buddha went to visit **Soṇa** (A. iii. 374), the river **Sappinī,** on the banks of which lived various paribbājakas, including **Sarabha**

[2] S. i. 109.

[3] Vin. ii. 193, etc.

[4] AA. i. 216.

[5] See also S. ii. 155, 185, 190, 241; iii. 121; A. ii. 73; iii. 21; iv. 160.

[6] AA. i. 412.

[7] Vin. ii. 76; DhA. iii. 321 f.

[8] Another monk is mentioned as having thrown himself down from Gijjhakūta because he was discontented with his life (Vin. iii. 82). According to one account (AA. i. 140 f.) Vakkali, too, committed suicide by throwing himself from Gijjhakūta; but see *s.v.* Vakkali.

[9] S. ii. 254; Vin. iii. 104; for Moggallāna see also A. iv. 75.

(A. i. 185; ii. 29, 176), the **Paribbājakārāma** of **Udumbarikā,** the residence of **Nigrodha,** near the **Moranivāpa** on the bank of the lake **Sumāgadhā** (D. iii. 39), and the park **Maddakucchi,** where the Buddha was removed after the injury to his foot (DhA. ii. 164). The **Sūkara-khatalena** was on the slope of Gijjhakūṭa, and there the Buddha was once visited by **Dīghanakha** (S. v. 233; M. i. 497). Jīvaka's mango-grove lay between Gijjhakūṭa and the walls of Rājagaha (DA. i. 150).

The Gijjhakūṭa was so called, either because its peak was like a vulture's beak, or because it was the resort of many vultures.[10]

Cunnungham,[11] on the authority of both Fa Hien and Hiouen Thsang, identifies Gijjhakūṭa with the modern Sailagiri, about two and a half miles to the north-east of the old town. It is also called Giriyek Hill. Gijjhakūṭa is sometimes referred to as **Gijjhapabbata**[12] and as **Gijjha.**[13]

[10] SNA. ii. 417; AA. i. 412; MA. i. 291, etc.
[11] CAGI. 534.
[12] J. ii. 50; iii. 255, 484.
[13] J. vi. 204, 212.

2. **Gijjhakūṭa.**—A tank in Ceylon, built by **Upatissa II.**[1]

[1] Cv. xxxvii. 185.

Gijjhakūṭa Sutta (commonly called **Abhaya Sutta**).—Contains an account of the visit paid by **Abhayarājakumāra** to the Buddha at **Gijjhakūṭa.** Abhaya questions the Buddha on the views of **Pūraṇa Kassapa.** The Buddha declares these to be wrong, and instructs Abhaya in the *nīvaraṇas* and the *bojjhaṅgas.*[1]

[1] S. v. 126 f.

Giñjakāvasatha.—A brick hall at **Nādikā (Ñātikā).** The Buddha stayed there on various occasions during his visits to Nādikā. It was during one of these visits that **Ambapālī** presented her park to the Buddha and the Order.[1] In the Giñjakāvasatha the Buddha preached the **Cūlagosiṅga Sutta,**[2] the **Janavasabha Sutta**[3] and several discourses on *maraṇasati*;[4] also the sermons to the Elder **Sandha** of the **Kaccānagotta**[5] and the Elder **Kaccāyana.**[6] Both in the Janavasabha Sutta and the **Giñjakāvasatha Sutta,**[7] which was preached at the same place, the Buddha is represented as having answered questions regarding the destiny and the rebirth of several residents of Nādikā. Does this perhaps mean that the people of Nādikā were more interested in this problem than the people of other

[1] Vin. i. 232.
[2] M. i. 205.
[3] D. ii. 200.
[4] *E.g.*, A. iii. 303 f.; 306 f.; 391 f.; iv. 320 f.
[5] A. v. 322 f.
[6] S. ii. 153 f.; see also S. ii. 74; iv. 90.
[7] S. v. 356 f.

places? It was by way of finding a permanent solution to these questions that the Buddha preached to **Ānanda** at Giñjakāvasatha the **Dhammādāsa** (Mirror of Truth) on his last visit to Nādikā, as described in the **Mahāparinibbāna Sutta.**[8]

The Commentaries[9] state that once the Buddha arrived at Nādikā while travelling in the Vajji country, and the people there built for him a residence entirely made of bricks (*giñjakā*), hence its name. Later, residences were also built for the monks, complete with all requirements. The bricks were evidently a special architectural feature, and this confirms the belief that buildings were generally of wood. The "Brick Hall" was, however, not designed for the Buddha and his monks alone, for we find mention of members of other sects staying there—*e.g.*, the Paribbājaka **Sabhiya Kaccāna.**[10] The building was probably a resting place for all travellers.

[8] D. ii. 91 ff.; see also S. v. 357. [9] *E.g.*, MA. i. 424. [10] S. iv. 401.

1. **Giñjakāvasatha Sutta.**—Preached at the **Giñjakāvasatha,** in answer to a question by **Kaccāyana** as to how various opinions, low, moderately good and excellent respectively, arise.[1]

[1] S. ii. 153.

2. **Giñjakāvasatha Sutta.**—A group of suttas preached at the **Giñjakāvasatha** in answer to **Ānanda's** questions regarding the destinies of various disciples, men and women, who had died at **Nādikā.** The first sutta of the group includes the **Dhammādāsa** (*q.v.*).[1]

[1] S. v. 356 ff.; *cf.* D. ii. 91 ff.

Gimhatittha.—A town in **Rohaṇa** where the **Kesadhātu Devarāja** won a victory.[1]

[1] Cv. lxxv. 22; also Cv. *Trs.* ii. 46, n. 2.

Giraggasamajjā.—A festival held from time to time (*kālānukālaṃ*) in **Rājagaha.**[1] It was held in the open air in the afternoon and was attended by all people of all grades of society from **Aṅga** and **Magadha.** Special seats were prepared for the more eminent of the audience, and the festivities seem to have consisted chiefly of nautch dances.[2] According to the *Vinaya* accounts[3] there were also singing and music, and the festival was attended not only by laymen, but also by members of religious orders, for otherwise it is unlikely that the **Sattarasavaggiyas**

[1] Perhaps elsewhere as well. The BuA. (p. 102) says it was an annual festival held all over Jambudīpa and was as old as Dīpaṅkara Buddha; see also J. iii. 538.

[2] SNA. i. 326.

[3] Vin. ii. 107 f., 150; iv. 85, 267.

and the **Chabbaggiyas** would have been there. Food was provided as well as amusements. Buddhaghosa[4] explains the name of the festival thus: *giraggasamajjo ti girimhi aggasamajjo girissa vā aggadese sammajo*, and tells us that it was announced for seven days before its commencement, and was held on level ground under a shadow of a hill and outside the city. Perhaps it was originally a pagan religious festival, a survival of old exogamic communistic dancing.[5]

It was at a Giraggasamajjā that **Sāriputta** and **Moggallāna** decided to eave the world.[6]

The Sanskrit equivalent is *Girivaggu-samāgama.*[7]

[4] Sp. iv. 831.
[5] See Dial. i. 7, n. 4; VT. iii. 71, n. 3.
[6] DhA. i. 73 f.; AA. i. 89, etc.
[7] AvŚ. ii. 24.

1. **Giri.**—A Nigaṇṭha who occupied the Nigaṇṭhārāma, later destroyed by **Vaṭṭagāmaṇī** to make room for the construction of **Abhayagiri Vihāra.** The Nigaṇṭha's name was included in that of the new Vihāra.[1]

[1] Mhv. xxxiii. 43 f., 83; Dpv. xix. 14.

2. **Giri.**—See **Giridīpa.**

3. **Giri.**—One of the palaces occupied by **Sikhī** Buddha in his last lay life.[1] The Commentary[2] calls it **Giriyasa.**

[1] Bu. xxi. 16.
[2] BuA., p. 201.

4. **Giri.**—A district in South Ceylon. Its capital was **Mahāgāma.** It included the villages of **Niṭṭhulaviṭṭhika,** birthplace of **Goṭhaimbara,**[1] and **Kutumbiyaṅgama,** birthplace of **Veḷusumana.**[2] The district was also evidently called **Girimaṇḍala.** The chieftain of Giri was **Giribhojaka,**[3] sometimes called **Girimaṇḍalika.**[4]

[1] Mhv. xxiii. 49.
[2] *Ibid.*, 68.
[3] *Ibid.*, 69, 70, 75; MṬ. 454.
[4] MṬ. 452.

5. **Giri.**—A Nigaṇṭha who lived at **Anurādhapura** during the time of **Paṇḍukābhaya.**[1] See also **Giri** (1).

[1] Mhv. x. 98.

Giri (or **Girimānanda**) **Sutta.**—Preached at **Jetavana. Ānanda** brings news to the Buddha that **Girimānanda** is ill; would the Buddha go and visit him ? The Buddha suggests that Ānanda should repeat to Girimānanda the ten ideas (*saññā*)—*aniccasaññā, anattasaññā, asubhasaññā, ādīnavasaññā, pahānasaññā, virāgasaññā, nirodhasaññā, sabbaloka-*

anabhiratisaññā, sabbasaṅkhāresu aniccasaññā, and *ānāpānasatisaññā*—and proceeds to expound them in detail. Ānanda does so and Girimānanda recovers.[1]

[1] A. v. 108 ff.

Girikaṇḍa.—A mountain occupied for some time by **Paṇḍukābhaya** during his campaign against his uncle. It was in the neighbourhood of this mountain that Paṇḍukābhaya met and married **Suvaṇṇapālī.**[1] The district around it was called Girikaṇḍa-desa, and this was later given by Paṇḍukābhaya to his father-in-law, **Girikaṇḍasiva.**[2]

[1] Mhv. x. 28 ff. [2] *Ibid.*, 82.

Girikaṇḍaka.—A vihāra in Ceylon restored by **Vijayabāhu I.**[1] The vihāra's *gocaragāma* was a village called **Vattakālaka** (*q.v.*), where lived a girl who, by reason of her great rapture, transplanted herself to the vihāra through the air.[2]

[1] Cv. lx. 60. [2] Vsm. 143; DhSA. 116.

Girikaṇḍasiva.—A chieftain, uncle of **Paṇḍukābhaya** and father of **Suvaṇṇapālī.** He had been appointed chieftain of the district of Girikaṇḍa by **Paṇḍuvāsudeva,** and refused to recognise Paṇḍukābhaya's claim to the throne.[1] When Suvaṇṇapāli was carried away by Paṇḍukābhaya, her father sent his five sons to rescue her, but they were all slain by **Canda,** son of **Paṇḍula.**[2] When Paṇḍukābhaya became king he restored the province of Girikaṇḍa to his uncle, putting him in charge of it.[3]

[1] Mhv. x. 29 f. [2] *Ibid.*, 41 f. [3] *Ibid.*, 82.

Girikassapa.—Eldest son of **Upatissa III.** He had sixteen brothers. When **Silākāla** rose in revolt, Kassapa defeated him in several contests, and in the end pursued him to his stronghold in the **Pācīnapabbata,** riding to the summit of the mountain on his elephant. This deed earned for him the title of Girikassapa. Later, while fleeing with his parents from Silākāla, he lost his way and was surrounded by his enemies. Finding no way of escape he cut his throat.[1]

[1] Cv. xli. 11 ff.

Girikālī (Girikārī).—Daughter of the chaplain of **Kākavaṇṇa-Tissa.** She became a nun, won arahantship, and became famous as an eminent teacher of the *Vinaya.*[1]

[1] Dpv. xviii. 20.

Girikumbhila.—A vihāra in Ceylon built by **Lañjitissa.**[1] At the ceremony of the dedication of the vihāra, Lañjitissa distributed to sixty thousand monks six garments each.[2]

[1] Mhv. xxxiii. 14. [2] *Ibid.*, 26.

Girigāma.—A village in Ceylon. A young novice named **Tissa** of **Pañcaggaḷalena,** travelling through the air, saw the daughter of the smith of Girigāma bathing in a lotus pond with five of her friends, and heard them singing aloud. He was so fascinated by her that he lost his power of flight.[1]

[1] SNA. i. 70; ApA. i. 128.

Girigāmakaṇṇa.—The residence of **Cūla Sudhamma Thera.**[1] It was probably a monastery near **Girigāma.**

[1] VibhA. 452.

Giriguhā.—One of the palaces occupied by **Piyadassī** Buddha in his last lay life.[1] The Commentary[2] calls it **Giribrahā.**

[1] Bu. xiv. 16. [2] BuA., p. 172.

Giritaṭa (Giritaṭāka).—A tank built by **Aggabodhi II.**[1] Near it was the village of the same name, where **Parakkamabāhu I.** once encamped with his army.[2] There the monks interviewed him on behalf of **Gajabāhu** and persuaded him to restore to the latter his kingdom.[3] Later, the village was occupied by **Mānābharaṇa** and his army.[4] The tank was among those repaired by Parakkamabāhu I., and from there he carried the canal **Kāverī,** thus joining Giritaṭa to the **Kaddūravaḍḍhamāna** tank.[5]

[1] Cv. xlii. 67.
[2] *Ibid.*, lxx. 312.
[3] *Ibid.*, 329 f.
[4] *Ibid.*, lxxii. 149.
[5] *Ibid.*, lxxix. 33, 55; see also Cv. *Trs.* i. 312, n. 3; 334 n. 1.

Giridatta Thera.—An arahant, teacher of **Vītāsoka** (*q.v.*). Giridatta was especially proficient in *Sutta* and *Abhidhamma.*[1]

[1] ThagA. i. 295.

Giridanta (*v.l.* **Giridatta, Giridattha**).—The trainer of the horse **Paṇḍava.** He was a previous birth of **Devadatta.** See the **Giridanta Jātaka.**

Giridanta Jātaka (No. 184).—King **Sāma** of Benares had a state horse **Paṇḍava,** whose trainer was the lame **Giridanta.** Observing that his trainer limped, the horse imitated him. When the king saw the horse limping, not being able to discover the reason, he asked his adviser, the

Bodhisatta, to investigate the matter. The Bodhisatta reported that it was the result of evil association, and had the trainer replaced by another. The trainer was **Devadatta.**[1]

For the introductory story see the **Mahilāmukha Jātaka.**

[1] J. ii. 98 f.

Giridāsa.—A poor caravan leader, the husband of **Isidāsī,** in a previous birth.[1]

[1] Thig. 445 f.; ThigA. 260, 265.

Giridipā.—An island near Ceylon. When the Buddha visited Ceylon he drew Giridipā up to Ceylon, told the yakkhas to go on to it, and then restored it to its former place.[1] Geiger[2] thinks that the reference is not to an island, but to the highlands (*giri*) in the interior of Ceylon.

[1] Mhv. i. 30; Dpv. i. 67 f. [2] Mhv. *Trs.*, p. 4, n. 4.

Giriddhī.—An eminent arahant Therī of the **Mahāvihāra** who taught the Vinaya in Ceylon.[1]

[1] Dpv. xviii. 14.

Girinagara (Girivhanagara).—A monastery in **Devapāli** built by **Aggabodhi V.**[1]

[1] Cv. xlviii. 3.

Girinelapūjaka Thera.—An arahant. Thirty-one kappas ago he was a hunter, and having seen **Sikhī** Buddha, he offered him a *nela*-flower.[1] He is evidently identical with **Gavampati.**[2]

[1] Ap. ii. 457. [2] ThagA. i. 104.

Girinelavāhanaka.—A vihāra to the north of **Kaṇḍanagara,** built by **Sūratissa.**[1]

[1] Mhv. xxi. 6.

Giripunnāgiya Thera.—An arahant. Ninety-four kappas ago he offered a *giripunnāga*-fruit to the Buddha **Sobhita,** then staying at the **Cittakūṭa.**[1] He is evidently identical with **Kaṇhadinna.**[2]

[1] Ap. ii. 416. [2] ThagA. i. 304.

Giribāraṭṭha.—A district in the **Dakkhiṇadesa** of Ceylon.[1]

[1] Cv. lxix. 8; lxx. 125.

Giribāvāpi.—A tank restored by **Parakkamabāhu I.**[1]

[1] Cv. lxviii. 44; for identification see Cv. *Trs.* i. 280, n. 5.

1. **Giribbaja.**—A name for **Rājagaha** (*q.v.*).

2. **Giribbaja.**—A name for **Vaṅkagiri.**[1]

[1] J. vi. 589

Giribrahā.—See **Giriguhā.**

Giribhaṇḍa.—A monastery in Ceylon restored by **Udaya I.**[1] See below, **Giribhaṇḍapūjā.**

[1] Cv. xlix. 29.

Giribhaṇḍa-(vāhana)-pūjā.—A great festival, instituted by King **Mahādāṭhika-Mahānāga** on the **Cetiyagiri** mountain. Carpets were laid from the **Kadambanadī** to the mountain, in order that people might approach the mountain with clean feet; the road was decorated and illuminated, shops were erected and largesse distributed. There were mimes, songs and music. Lamps were lit throughout the island and even on the sea for one *yojana* round.[1] It is said[2] that on the day of the festival **Māra,** wishing to spoil it, rained down a shower of coal, but an Elder created earth in the sky, thus preventing the coal from falling. The most costly offerings given during this feast to any monk—namely, a pair of garments—fell to the lot of a young novice, **Loṇagirivāsī Tissa,** in spite of the efforts of the king's ministers to get them into the hands of the older monks. It was because the novice had practised the *sārāṇīya-dhammā.*[3]

The festival was probably connected with the **Giribhaṇḍavihāra,** in which case that was the reason for the name.

[1] Mhv. xxxiv. 75 ff.; AA. i. 13.
[2] Vsm. 376; Vsm. *Trs.* ii. 436, n. 4.
[3] DA. ii. 535; AA. ii. 653 f.; MA. i. 545 f.

Girimaṇḍala.—A district in Ceylon.[1] See **Giri** (4).

[1] Cv. li. 111; for identification see Cv. *Trs.* i. 159, n. 1.

Girimānanda Thera.—He was the son of King **Bimbisāra's** chaplain and, having seen the might of the Buddha when the Buddha entered **Rājagaha,** joined the Order. He lived in a village studying, but one day, when he came to Rājagaha to visit the Buddha, the king asked him to remain, promising to look after him. The king, however, forgot his promise, and Girimānanda had to live in the open. The gods, fearing to wet him, stopped rain from falling. The king, observing the drought and discovering the reason for it, built him a hermitage wherein the Thera put forth effort and became an arahant.

In the time of **Sumedha** Buddha he was a householder, and when his wife and children died he fled into the forest in grief. There the Buddha consoled him, and he offered flowers to the Buddha and sang his praises.[1]

The **Giri Sutta** was preached in reference to Girimānanda, when he lay grievously ill.[2]

[1] Thag. vv. 325-9; ThagA. i. 409 ff.; Ap. i. 330 f.
[2] A. v. 108 ff.

Girimānanda Sutta.—See **Giri Sutta.**

Girimekhalā.—**Māra's** elephant. He was one hundred and fifty leagues in height. When **Māra** urged him to advance against the Buddha at the foot of the Bodhi-tree, he went forward and fell on his knees.[1]

[1] J. i. 72, 73, 74; MA. i. 384; Mbv. 31; Windisch, "Māra und Buddha," 199; BuA. 239; MṬ. 473.

1. **Giriya.**—A jackal, a previous incarnation of **Devadatta.**[1] See the **Manoja Jātaka.**

[1] J. iii. 322 f.

2. **Giriya.**—A Tamil general, commander of **Girilaka**; he was slain by **Duṭṭhagāmaṇī.**[1]

[1] Mhv. xxv. 47.

Giriyasa.—See **Giri** (3).

Giriyāvāpi.—A tank restored by **Parakkamabāhu I.**[1]

[1] Cv. lxviii. 46; see also Cv. *Trs.* i. 280, n. 5.

Girilaka.—A Tamil stronghold, near **Vijitapura,** commanded by **Giriya.** It was captured by **Duṭṭhagāmaṇī.**[1]

[1] Mhv. xxv. 47.

Girivaṃsa.—A royal family of Ceylon to which belonged the famous **Alagakkonāra**[1] and also the mother of **Parakkamabāhu VI.**[2]

[1] Cv. xci. 3.
[2] P.L.C. 247.

Girivāhana.—One of the palaces of **Atthadassī** Buddha in his last lay life.[1]

[1] Bu. xv. 15.

Girivihāra.—A vihāra in Ceylon erected by **Aggabodhi I.**; he gave one hundred fields for its support.[1] It was the residence of **Cullapiṇḍapātiya-**

[1] Cv. xlii. 12.

Tissa,[2] and also of a novice, pupil of **Tepitaka,** called **Culla-Summa Thera.**[3]

[2] AA. i. 367. [3] DA. ii. 514.

Girivhanagara.—See **Girinagara.**

Girisāra.—A king of eighty kappas ago; a previous birth of **Māṇava** (or **Sammukhāthavika**) **Thera.**[1] *v.l.* **Sirisāra, Hirisāra.**

[1] ThagA. i. 164; Ap. i. 159.

Girisigāmuka.—One of the tanks restored by **Parakkamabāhu I.**[1]

[1] Cv. lxviii. 49.

Girihālika.—A monastery built in an inland district of Ceylon by King **Mahallaka-Nāga.**[1]

[1] Mhv. xxxv. 125.

1. **Gilāna Vagga.**—The thirteenth chapter of the *Pañcaka Nipāta* of the *Aṅguttara Nikāya.*[1]

[1] A. iii. 142-7.

2. **Gilāna Vagga.**—The eighth chapter of the *Saḷāyatana Saṃyutta.*[1]

[1] S. iv. 46-53.

3. **Gilāna Vagga.**—The second chapter of the *Bojjhaṅga Saṃyutta.*[1]

[1] S. v. 78-83.

1. **Gilāna Sutta.**—There are three types of sick men—those who will not, in any case, recover; those who recover whether looked after or not; those who recover only if properly looked after. Even so, there are three kinds of men—those who will never, whether they hear the Dhamma or not, enter into an assurance of perfection, etc.[1]

[1] A. i. 120 f.

2. **Gilāna Sutta.**—The Buddha visits a sick novice of no reputation and talks to him. The novice, pondering on the Buddha's words, recovers.[1]

[1] S. iv. 46; *cf.* S. iii. 119.

3. **Gilāna Sutta.**—The same as the above, except that the topic is final emancipation without grasping (*anupādā parinibbāna*).[1]

[1] S. iv. 47.

4. **Gilanā Sutta.**—The Buddha visits **Mahā Kassapa** lying ill in the **Pippaliguhā,** and talks to him of the seven *bojjhaṅgas.* Delighted with the talk, **Kassapa** recovers.[1]

[1] S. v. 79.

5. **Gilāna Sutta.**—Describes a similar visit to **Mahā Moggallāna** at **Gijjhakūṭa.**[1]

[1] S. iv. 80.

6. **Gilāna Sutta.**—The Buddha lies ill in the **Kalandakanivāpa** in Veḷuvana; **Mahā Cunda** visits him, and they talk of the seven *bojjhaṅgas.* The Buddha immediately recovers.[1]

[1] S. v. 81.

7. **Gilāna Sutta.**—Once, shortly before his death, the Buddha spent the rainy season in **Beḷuva,** where he became seriously ill. By great effort of will he overcame the sickness. **Ānanda** expresses his admiration for the Buddha's strength of mind, but adds his conviction that the Buddha would not die without having made some pronouncement concerning the Order. Then follows the Buddha's famous injunction to his followers that they should take no other guide or refuge but the Dhamma and their own selves.[1]

[1] S. v. 152 f.; the sutta is found almost *verbatim* in D. ii. 98 f.

8. **Gilāna Sutta.**—The Buddha visits the sick ward in the **Kūṭāgārasāla** in **Vesāli** and talks to a sick monk, telling him that by practising five things during illness one can be sure of the speedy destruction of the *āsavas,* these things being *asubhānupassanā, āhārepaṭikūlasaññā, sabbaloke anabhiratasaññā, sabbasaṅkhāresu aniccānupassanā* and *maraṇasaññā.*[1]

[1] A. iii. 142; *cf.* **Giri Sutta.**

Gilānadassana Sutta.—When **Citta-gahapati** lies ill various *devas* approach him and urge him to aspire to be a world-ruler. He scorns the suggestion and, on being asked by his relations why he is talking to himself, he tells them and exhorts them to have faith in the Buddha, the Dhamma and the Saṅgha. Soon afterwards he dies.[1]

[1] S. iv. 302 f.

Gilāyana Sutta.—As he is about to leave the **Nigrodhārāma** in **Kapilavatthu** to start on a tour, the Buddha is visited by **Mahānāma,** who asks him how a sick lay-disciple should be admonished. The Buddha answers that he should be asked to take comfort in his loyalty to the Buddha, the Dhamma and the Saṅgha, and in his possession of the Ariyan virtues. He should be shown the futility of longing for parents, children and sensual pleasures, and should be persuaded, if possible, to aspire not after rebirth, but after emancipation.[1]

[1] S. v. 408 f.

Gilīmalaya.—A village given by **Vijayabāhu I.** for the maintenance of worship at **Samantakūṭa.**[1]

[1] Cv. lx. 65; also Cv. *Trs.* i. 221, n. 2.

Givulabā.—A village in Ceylon where the forces of **Parakkamabāhu I.** won a great victory.[1]

[1] Cv. lxxiv. 91.

Gihi Sutta.—On one occasion, when **Anāthapiṇḍika** comes to see the Buddha, the Buddha tells **Sāriputta** of the four kinds of clear consciousness (*ābhicetasikadhammā*) which come to the pious lay devotee who guards the five precepts—viz., unwavering faith in the Buddha, Dhamma and Saṅgha, and the possession of Ariyan virtues. To him comes also the confidence that he is free from birth in a *Niraya*, among beasts or *petas* or in unhappy states, and that he is a *sotāpanna.*[1]

[1] A. iii. 211 f.

Gihivinaya.—See the **Sigālovāda Sutta.**

Gihīnaya Sutta.—See **Bāḷhagilāyana Sutta.**

Gihisāmici Sutta.—The Buddha tells **Anāthapiṇḍika** of four things which constitute the householder's path of duty—he waits upon the Order with offers of robes, food, lodgings, requisites and medicines for use in sickness.[1]

[1] A. ii. 65.

Gīta Sutta.—The five evil results of preaching the Dhamma in a sing-song style (*gītassareṇa*).[1]

[1] A. iii. 251.

Guṇa.—An ājīvika of the **Kassapagotta,** who was consulted by **Aṅgati,** king of **Videha.** He is identified with the **Licchavi Sunakkhatta.**

For details see the **Mahā Nārada Kassapa Jātaka.**

Guṇa Jātaka (No. 157).—The Bodhisatta was once a Lion, and one day while out hunting he sank into a bog and remained there starving for seven days until rescued by a Jackal. To show his gratitude the Lion took the Jackal and his wife home with him, and the two animals and their wives lived together, the Lion and the Jackal going out together hunting. Later on, the Lioness grew jealous of the she-Jackal and tried to frighten her away in the absence of their husbands. When the Lion heard of this, he told his wife how the Jackal had befriended him in his hour of danger, and thenceforth they all lived happily together.

The Jackal is identified with **Ānanda**.

The story was told in reference to a gift made by Ānanda. Once, when he had been preaching to the women of **Pasenadi's** palace, they gave him five hundred new garments which the king had just presented to them. The king hearing of this was at first annoyed, but on questioning Ānanda he was satisfied that no gift presented to the Saṅgha could ever be wasted. Delighted with this discovery, the king himself gave five hundred robes to Ānanda, all of which Ānanda presented to a young monk who was very useful and helpful to him. The monk, in his turn, distributed them among his fellow celibates, who wondered why Ānanda should have singled out one monk as the recipient of his gifts. When the matter was related to the Buddha, he assured the monks that the gift was offered to the monk by Ānanda only in return for numerous services.[1]

The Jātaka is also called **Sīha Jātaka**, and probably also the **Sigāla Jātaka**.[2]

1 J. ii. 23 ff. 2 *E.g.*, in J. ii. 314.

Guṇagandha.—A scholarly monk of Burma.[1]

1 Sās. 111, 112.

Guṇamunində.—A Rājagura of Burma.[1]

1 Sās. 132, 143.

Guṇaratanadhara.—The name given by **Bhuvanekabāhu** to one of the monks who came from Ceylon to Burma to take back the pure religion[1] to Ceylon.

1 Sās. 45.

Guṇasāgara.—A monk of Burma, author of the **Mukhamattasāra** and its *Ṭīkā*.[1]

1 Gv., p. 63; Bode, *op. cit.*, 25.

Guṇasāra.—A pupil of **Guṇagandha.** He was an inhabitant of **Sahassorodhagāma.**[1]

[1] Sās. 112, 162, 164.

Guṇasiri.—A pupil of **Canda Thera** of Repinagāma. He was the teacher of **Ñāṇadhaja.**[1]

[1] Sās. 162, 163, 164.

Guṇābhilaṅkāra.—A thera of **Tunnagāma.** He was one of the originators of the **Ekaṃsika** controversy.[1] He was, later on, the incumbent of the **Jeyyabhūmi vihāra.**[2]

[1] Sās. 118.

[2] *Ibid.*, 132, 163.

Guṇārāma.—A thera of **Arimaddanapura.** King **Ujana** built for him the **Jetavana vihāra.**[1]

[1] Sās. 83.

Gutijjita.—A Pacceka Buddha, whose name occurs in a nominal list.[1]

[1] M. iii. 70; ApA. i. 107.

Gutta, Guttaka.—A Tamil usurper. He was a horse-dealer and came to Ceylon with another Tamil named **Sena.** They killed King **Sūratissa** and reigned at **Anurādhapura** for twenty-two years (177-155 B.C.). They were killed by **Asela.**[1]

[1] Mhv. xxi. 10 f.; Dpv. xviii. 47 f.

Guttasāla, Guttasālaka.—A village and a district in **Rohaṇa. Duṭṭhagāmaṇī** lived there before being crowned at **Mahāgāma.**[1] Guttasāla was thirty to thirty-five miles to the north of Mahāgāma, where the high road crossed the Māṇikagaṅga, and lay on the main route which spread from Mahāgāma to **Mutiyaṅgana,** and from there along the Mahāvālukagaṅgā to Pulatthipura; hence its strategic importance. It was the centre of several campaigns at different periods.[2] The *Atthasālinī*[3] records the story of a nun of Guttasāla; she was an arahant, and when the village was destroyed by bandits she left it with a young nun carrying her baggage. At the village gate of **Nakulanagara** she met **Mahānāga** of **Kālavallimaṇḍapa,** who offered her a meal in his own bowl, as she had none of her own. She ate the meal, washed the bowl and returned it, telling him that from the next day he would get alms without exertion; and so he did.

[1] Mhv. xxiv. 17.

[2] *E.g.*, of Mahinda (Cv. li. 109, 117); Vijayabāhu I. (*ibid.*, lxviii. 34); Jayabāhu I. (*ibid.*, lxi. 12); Parakkamabāhu I. (*ibid.*, lxxiv. 155 f.; lxxv. 15. See Cv. Trs. i. 158, n. 4.

[3] DhsA. 398 f.

1. **Guttā Therī.**—She belonged to a brahmin family of **Sāvatthi**; when she reached adolescence household life became repugnant to her owing to her *upanissaya*, and, with her parents' consent, she entered the Order under **Pajāpatī Gotamī.** For a long time she could not concentrate her mind, but, encouraged by the Buddha, she attained arahantship.[1]

Thig. vv. 163-8; ThigA. 157 f.

2. **Guttā.**—The third of the seven daughters of **Kiki,** king of Benares. She was a previous birth of **Paṭācārā.**[1]

[1] J. vi. 481; but see Ap. ii. 558, v. 15, where Paṭācārā is identified with Bhikkhunī.

Guttila.—The Bodhisatta born as a musician in Benares. He was unmarried and supported his blind parents. He had as pupil **Mūsila** from **Ujjeni,** and to him Guttila taught all he knew. Later, Guttila introduced Mūsila at the king's court where, as soon as he had the ear of the king, he arranged for a competition with his master, that the king might decide who should be the court musician. Guttila, fearing a contest in his old age, fled into the forest where **Sakka** appeared before him and promised to help him to victory. The contest was held, and when Guttila played according to Sakka's instructions, the sound of his music filled the city and heavenly nymphs descended to earth to dance. Mūsila was defeated and stoned to death by the enraged crowd. Later, Sakka sent **Mātali** to fetch Guttila to **Tāvatiṃsa** in his chariot, and as a return for his music Guttila was allowed to discover to what good deeds the inhabitants of Tāvatiṃsa owed their birth there. On returning to earth after seven days, he told the people what he had seen and exhorted them to do good.[1]

It is said that once Guttila sent a thousand to a woman, wishing to win her favour, but she would not grant it. He decked himself, and in the evening sang and played his lute outside her house. She was so enthralled by his music that she opened her window and, thinking it was a door, walked out and was killed by the fall.[2]

Guttila is mentioned[3] as one of the four human beings who went to Tāvatiṃsa even in their human body, the others being **Sādhīna, Nimi** and **Mandhātā.**

[1] J. ii. 248 ff.; VvA. 137 ff.

[2] AA. i. 16 f.; is this perhaps a different person?

[3] Mil. 115, 291.

Guttila Jātaka (No. 243).—The story of **Guttila** (*q.v.*) and his contest with **Mūsila.** Mūsila is identified with **Devadatta, Sakka** with **Anuruddha,** and the king with **Ānanda.**

The story was told in reference to Devadatta. The monks had tried to persuade him to acknowledge the Buddha as his teacher, because it was from him that he had learned the three Piṭakas and the four Jhānas. But Devadatta would not consent.[1]

[1] J. ii, 248 ff.

Guttilavimāna.—**Moggallāna** visits **Tāvatiṃsa** and, seeing thirty-six goddesses whose palaces were next to each other, questions them as to their acts in the past, and reports their answers to the Buddha. The Buddha replies that those same goddesses were in Tāvatiṃsa at the time of **Guttila's** visit; he then proceeds to give an account of Guttila.[1]

[1] Vv. iii. 5; VvA. 137 ff.

Gundāvana.—A forest in **Madhurā. Mahā Kaccāna** stayed there and was visited by **Avantiputta,** king of Madhurā, to whom he preached the **Madhurā Sutta,**[1] and by the brahmin **Kaṇḍarāyana.**[2] The full name of the forest seems to have been **Kaṇhagundāvana.**[3] *v.l.* **Kuṇḍavana.**

[1] M. ii. 83 f. [2] A. i. 67 f. [3] MA. ii. 738; *J.R.A.S.*, 1894, 349.

Gumbakabhūtā.—The slave woman of **Ummādacittā,** whose son was entrusted to her that she might bring him to safety.[1]

[1] MṬ. 280.

Gumbika, Gumbiya.—A yakkha; see the **Gumbiya Jātaka.**

Gumbiya Jātaka (No. 366).—Once the Bodhisatta was a merchant of Benares, and led a caravan of five hundred carts through the forest. He warned his men that they should not eat anything found in the forest without first consulting him. On the way they came across leaves strewn in the forest, covered with honeycomb. These had been placed there by a yakkha, named **Gumbiya,** who had put poison in the honey. Some of the men ate the honey, while others remembered the warning of the Bodhisatta as soon as they had tasted it. Those who ate died, the others were given emetics and recovered.

The story was related to a monk who, fascinated by a woman's charm, wished to become a layman. Sensuous pleasures are like honey sprinkled with deadly poison, said the Buddha. The monk became a *sotāpanna.*[1]

[1] J. iii. 200 f.; *cp.* Kimpakka Jātaka.

Guralaṭṭhakalañcha.—A locality in Ceylon, the centre of a fight between the forces of the **Damiḷādhikāri Rakkha** and his enemies.[1]

[1] Cv. lxxv. 77; Cv. *Trs.* i. 51, n. 3.

Gulissāni.—A monk living in the wilds, who once came on some business to see the monks at the **Kalandakanivāpa.** It was on his account that the **Gulissāni Sutta** was preached.[1]

[1] M. i. 469.

Gulissāni Sutta.—**Sāriputta** notices among the monks at Rājagaha an uncouth monk from the wilds who is named **Gulissāni.** Sāriputta proceeds to talk to the other monks of the duties of a bhikkhu who, coming from the wilds, starts to live in the confraternity; he should show respect and consideration to others, be correct in the matter of seats, observe certain rules in begging for alms, and keep watch over his faculties while studying the higher Dhamma and Vinaya. **Moggallāna** asks whether these duties are incumbent only on those monks who come from the wilds, and is told that they are still more so on monks living in villages.[1]

[1] M. i. 469 ff.

Guḷa.—A yakkha chief who should be invoked when unbelieving yakkhas molest any follower of the Buddha.[1]

[1] D. iii. 204.

Guḷavaṇṇa.—A horse belonging to King **Kuṭakaṇṇa-Tissa.** Once the king, on his way from **Anurādhapura** to **Cetiyapabbata,** came to the **Kadamba** river and found that his horse would not cross it. When the trainer was blamed, he explained that the horse did not wish to have his tail wet, in case the king's dress should be spoilt. The king held up the horse's tail, and he immediately crossed the stream.[1]

The story was told to illustrate the good qualities of a well-trained horse.

[1] MA. ii. 653 f.

Guhaṭṭhaka Sutta.—The second sutta of the **Aṭṭhakavagga** of the Sutta Nipāta; it was preached to **Piṇḍolabhāradvāja.** He once went to **Udakavana** in Kosambī, and there the women of King **Udena's** palace, who had come to the park with the king, left the king while he slept, and, finding the Elder, sat down and listened to his preaching. The king, awakening, went in search of them, and was angry when he discovered their whereabouts. He questioned Piṇḍola as to the solitude which he professed to seek in the park, but Piṇḍola refusing to answer, the king threatened to set red ants at him. Thereupon Piṇḍola went through the air to the Buddha's **Gandhakuti** and related the story. The Buddha was reclining on his bed and, in that position, preached this sutta to the Elder.

A man who clings to the body and to the pleasures of the senses, lives in constant fear. One should therefore cast off greed and cross the flood, unstained by the world.[1]

The sutta probably derives its name from the fact that, in the first verse, the body is spoken of as a *guhā*.

It is commented on in the *Mahā Niddesa*.[2]

[1] SN. vv. 772-9; SNA. ii. 514 ff. [2] pp. 23 ff.

Guhasīva.—King of **Kāliṅga.** At first he did not pay honour to the Tooth-relic of the Buddha which was in his capital, but later, having seen a miracle, he became a Buddhist and paid the relic all homage. Later, he sent the relic to Ceylon, through his daughter **Hemamālā** and her husband **Dantakumāra.** The whole story is given in the **Dāṭhāvaṃsa.**[1]

[1] chap. iv. ff.

Guhasela.—A palace occupied by Tissa Buddha before his final renunciation.[1]

[1] Bu. xviii. 17.

Guhānahānakoṭṭha. One of the eight stone bath-houses erected for the monks at **Pulatthipura** by **Parakkamabāhu I.**[1]

[1] Cv. lxxviii. 45.

Gūtha. One of the purgatories. It is next to the Mahā Niraya, and is the habitation of needle-mouthed creatures who rip away the skin, flesh, tendons, etc., of the victim and then devour his marrow.[1]

Those who insult their parents are born in this purgatory.[2]

[1] M. iii. 185; J. vi. 8; SNA. ii. 481. [2] DhA. iv. 34.

1. Gūthakhādaka. A peta. A householder, in a village near Sāvatthi, built a vihāra for a monk who visited his house. Other monks arrived, and the incumbent, envious of them, spoke ill of them to the householder who abused them all. As a result, he was born a peta in the cesspit of the same monastery and came under the notice of **Mahā Moggallāna.**[1]

[1] Pv. iv. 18; PvA. 266 f.; *cp.* ThagA. i. 386 f.

2. Gūthakhādaka. Same as the above, except that in this case the householder was a woman.[1]

[1] Pv. iv. 9; PvA. 269.

Gūthakhādiduṭṭhabrāhmaṇa Sutta.—Story of a peta, sunk in a dungpit. eating dung with both hands. In the time of **Kassapa Buddha,** he had invited the monks to a meal and set before them a vessel filled with dung.

The peta was seen near **Gijjhakūṭa** by both **Mahā Moggallāna** and **Lakkhaṇa.**[1]

[1] S. ii. 259.

Gūthapāṇa Jātaka (No. 227).—A dung-beetle drank some liquor dropped by merchants staying in a rest-house and returned to his dung-heap intoxicated. An elephant who came up smelt the dung and went away in disgust. The beetle, thinking the elephant was frightened of him, called after him and challenged him to a fight. The elephant returned, dropped some dung on him and, making water over him, killed him on the spot.

The story was told in reference to a monk who quelled the pride of a rowdy; the latter used to molest monks who went for alms to a village near **Jetavana,** asking them questions and insulting them so much that the monks were reluctant to go there. One day a monk, stronger than the rest, enticed the man out of the village, felled him with one blow, and threatened to teach him another lesson if he did not cease pestering the monks. After that the man decamped at the sight of a monk.[1]

[1] J. ii. 209 ff.

Gūḷhummagga, Gūḷhavessantara, Gūḷhavinaya.—Mentioned in the Commentaries[1] as *abuddhavacanāni*; they were probably books belonging to sects other than the orthodox Theravādins.

[1] *E.g.*, Sp. iv. 742.

Gūḷhatthaṭīkā.—A work, probably a glossary, written by a monk in Burma, author also of the **Bālappabodhana.**[1]

[1] Gv. 63, 73; see Vinayagandhi.

Gūḷhatthadīpanī.—A work by **Sāradassī,** explaining difficult passages in the seven books of the Abhidhamma.[1]

[1] Sās. p. 116; Bode, *op. cit.*, 56.

Geṭṭhumba.—A canal. The taxes paid for the use of its water for tillage were given by **Mahinda III.** for the repairs of the **Ratanapāsāda.**[1]

[1] Cv. xlix. 41.

Gedha Sutta.—See **Anussati Sutta.**

Geyya.—The second section of the Tipiṭaka arranged according to matter (*aṅgavasena*). It includes all the suttas composed in verse, especially the whole *Sagāthakavagga* of the Saṃyutta Nikāya.[1]

[1] DA. i. 23 f.

1. **Gelañña Sutta.**—The Buddha, staying at the **Kūṭāgārasālā** in Vesāli, visits the sick ward in the evening and talks to the sick monks. A monk, he tells them, should meet his end collected and composed. He should put away the dejection arising from craving. In whatever he does, he should act composedly. So composed and collected, he becomes free from bondage. When his body breaks up, he understands the matter and is prepared for it, for it is like a lamp which goes out when oil and wick are exhausted.[1]

[1] S. iv. 210 f.

2. **Gelañña Sutta.**—The topic is the same as in the above, but the wording differs.[1]

[1] S. iv. 213 f.

1. **Gokaṇṇa.**—A locality in Ceylon and a vihāra founded by **Mahāsena,** on the site of a Hindu temple.[1] According to the *Mahāvaṃsa Ṭīkā,*[2] it was on the east coast of Ceylon. Elsewhere,[3] the Ṭīkā speaks of a **Gokaṇṇatittha** in the neighbourhood of the estuary of the **Mahākandara-nadī,** and the Cūḷavaṃsa[4] mentions Gokaṇṇa as the last of a series of fords in **Rohaṇa,** important from a strategic point of view, along the **Mahā-vāḷkaugaṅgā,** from "Sarogāmatittha to Gokaṇṇa." In another passage,[5] Gokaṇṇa(ka) is spoken of as *mahaṇṇava* (the ocean). These facts support Geiger's conjecture[6] that Gokaṇṇa refers to the Trincomalee (Koddiyar) Bay at the estuary of the Mahāvāḷukagaṅgā.

Gokaṇṇa(ka) is twice described as the scene of magic rites, once in the case of **Mahānāga**[7] and again in that of **Mānavamma.**[8]

Aggabodhi V. built a *padhānaghara* for the **Gokaṇṇa-vihāra.**[9]

[1] Mhv. xxxvii. 41.
[2] p. 685.
[3] p. 269.
[4] lxxi. 18.
[5] Cv. xli. 79.
[6] Cv. *Trs.* i. 59, 4; n. 316, n. 2.
[7] Cv. xli. 79.
[8] *Ibid.*, lvii. 5.
[9] *Ibid.*, xlviii. 5.

2. **Gokaṇṇa.**—A general of **Gajabāhu** who defeated **Kittisirimegha;** he had his headquarters in **Kālavāpi,** of which place he was *Nagaragiri.* At a meeting between him and **Parakkamabāhu** at **Buddhagāma,** the latter won him over to his side. An amusing story is told of a dream he had after his promise of help to Parakkamabāhu.[1] He fled, there-

[1] Cv. lxvi. 47 ff.

fore, to Kālavāpi and, on various occasions, offered battle to the forces of Parakkamabāhu, but everywhere he was defeated, the worst reverse being at **Nīlagala** by the general **Māyāgeha.** After that he built a fortification in Kālavāpi, where he lived in comparative quiet. The last we hear of him is of his incitement of **Mānābharaṇa** to seize the throne.[2]

Geiger[3] thinks that Gokaṇṇa is probably a clan name.

[2] Cv. lxiii. 34; lxvi. 35 ff., 62; lxx. 68, 71, 83, 257. [3] Cv. *Trs* i. 255, n. 3.

3. **Gokaṇṇa.**—A general of **Parakkamabāhu I.** mentioned among leaders of the expedition which he sent to South India.[1]

[1] Cv. lxxvi. 253, 270, 324-6.

Gokaṇṇaka.—See **Gokaṇṇa** (1).

Gokaṇṇanāṇḍanāyaka.—A Damila chief at **Muṇḍannānaṃkoṭṭa.**[1]

[1] Cv. lxxvi. 212.

Gokulaṅkavihāra.—A monastery built by cowherds for **Dhaniya** and his wife after their ordination. Buddhaghosa says that it existed even in his day.[1]

[1] SNA. i. 46.

Gokuḷikā.—A secondary division of the **Vajjiputtakā,** their immediate parent-body being the **Mahāsaṅghikas.** Later, from the Gokulikas, sprang two other schools—the **Paññattivādins** and the **Bāhulikas** (or **Bahussutikas**).[1] Their most important heresy seems to have been that they considered all saṅkhāras, without qualification, no better than a heap of embers (*kukkuḷa*) whence the flames have died out as from an inferno of ashes. They based this view on the Buddha's declaration made in the **Adittapariyāya Sutta** ("All is on fire, bhikkhus").[2] This view was probably responsible for their other name of (**Kukkiḷikas** or **Kukkuṭikas**).[3] It may be that Kukkuḷika was their earlier name, of which Gokuḷikā was either a corruption or a derivation from the name of one of their teachers. But all Pāli records give only the "Gokuḷika" reading.

[1] Dpv. v. 40; Mhv. v. 4 f.; Mbv., p. 96.
[2] Kvu. ii. 7 (p. 208), and *Points of Controversy*, 127 f. [3] Rockhill, 186 ff.

Gocariya.—One of the ten families of elephants. It is said that a **Chaddanta**-elephant is born in a **Chaddantakula** and not in such a family as the Gocariya. *v.l.* **Kālāvaka.**[1]

[1] MA. i. 248.

Goṭapabbata.—A vihāra in South Ceylon built by **Mahallaka-Nāga.**[1] It may be that it is identical with **Koṭapabbatavihāra** and that Mahallaka merely restored it. *v.l.* **Koṭapabbata.**

[1] Mhv. xxxv. 124.

Goṭha.—See **Goṭhaimbara.**

Goṭhakasamudda.—The sea near Ceylon, the "shallow sea."[1]

[1] Mhv. xxii. 49, 85; DA. ii. 695.

1. **Goṭhakābhaya, Goṭhābhaya.**—A king of the **Rohaṇa** dynasty; son of **Yaṭṭhālayakatissa** and father of **Kākavaṇṇatissa.**[1] He is sometimes called Abhaya.[2]

[1] Mhv. xv. 170; xxii. 11.
[2] *E.g.*, Mhv. xxiii. 10, 56.

2. **Goṭhakābhaya.**—King of Ceylon (302-15 A.C.). He was a **Lambakaṇṇa** of **Mahiyaṅgana,** and having gone to **Anurādhapura** with **Saṅghatissa** and **Saṅghabodhi,** he, with their help, slew the reigning king, **Vijaya,** and they reigned in succession.[1] Goṭhakābhaya became Saṅghabodhi's treasurer but, seeing the king's weakness, he led a rebellion against him and captured the throne.[2] In addition to other religious works, he built the **Meghavaṇṇābhaya-Vihāra.** He banished from **Abhayagiri** sixty monks who had accepted the **Vetulla** heresy, but a Coḷa monk, **Saṅghamitta,** defeated in discussion the thera **Goṭhābhaya,** the king's uncle, and became the king's favourite, obtaining the position of tutor to the king's two sons, **Jeṭṭhatissa** and **Mahāsena.** The king was also known as **Meghavaṇṇābhaya.**[3]

[1] Mhv. xxxvi. 58.
[2] vv. 91, 98-117; for details see Saṅghabodhi.
[3] v. 98.

Goṭhaimbara.—One of **Duṭṭhagāmaṇi's** chief warriors. He was the son of **Mahānāga** of **Niṭṭhulaviṭṭhika** and owed his name to his dwarfish stature. He pulled up *imbara*-trees from a forest clearing, thus demonstrating his enormous strength. **Kākavaṇṇatissa,** hearing of this, sent for him to the court.[1] He took a prominent part in the attack on **Vijitapura,** using a coconut-palm as weapon.[2]

It is said[3] that in the time of **Kassapa** Buddha he gave daily milk rice to the monks.

[1] Mhv. xxiii. 49 ff.; the *Rasavāhini* (ii. 28) says he subdued a yakkha named **Jayasena.**
[2] Mhv. xxv. 27, 32, 44 f.
[3] MṬ. 452.

Goṭhābhaya.—A monk living in the **Saṅghapāla Pariveṇa.** He was the maternal uncle of King **Goṭhakābhaya II,** and tried, without success, to win the king over from the influence of **Saṅghamitta.**[1]

[1] Mhv. xxxvi. 115 f.

Goṇa (Goṇaka).—A river to the south of **Anurādhapura.** On its banks, King **Cūḷābhaya** built the **Cūḷagallaka-Vihāra,**[1] and **Vaṅkanāsika-Tissa,** the **Mahāmaṅgala-Vihāra.**[2] Once, when **Dhātusena** was fleeing from his enemies with a thera, his uncle, the river was found to be in flood, but a nāga king took them across.[3] Later, when building the **Kālavāpi,** Dhātusena dammed up the river.[4]

[1] Mhv. xxxv. 13.
[2] *Ibid.*, v. 113.
[3] Cv. xxxviii. 24.
[4] *Ibid.*, v. 42. It is identified with the modern Kalā-oya (Cv. *Trs.* i. 30, n. 3).

Goṇagāmaka.—A landing-place (*paṭṭana*) at the mouth of the **Mahākandara** river, where **Bhaddakaccānā** and her companions disembarked.[1]

[1] Mhv. viii. 25; *cf.* v. 12.

Goṇagāmuka.—A locality near the **Kālavāpi** where **Gokaṇṇa** was defeated by **Rakkhadīvāna.**[1]

Is this identical with **Goṇagāmaka ?**[2]

[1] Cv. lxx. 70.
[2] But see Cv. *Trs.* i. 293, n. 1.

Goṇaraviya Thera.—A monk of Ceylon, probably a colleague of **Mahāsīva.** It is said that Mahāsīva was explaining to him the **Mahā Saccaka Sutta,** and that when he came to the passage where the Buddha charges **Saccaka** with not understanding the training of the body, much less that of the mind, Goṇaraviya laid aside his fan and walked away, saying that the Buddha could not have said such a thing; but Mahāsiva persuaded him that it was so.[1] *v.l.* **Moraṇāḷa.**

[1] MA. i. 463.

Goṇḍā, Goṇḍamittā.—A yakkhinī, mother of **Pola-(Posa)-mittā.**[1]

[1] MṬ. 260.

Goṇḍigāma.—A tank constructed by **Upatissa II.**[1] The village belonging to it was given by **Jeṭṭhatissa III.** to the **Jetavana-vihāra.**[2] The tank was restored by **Aggabodhi V.**[3]

[1] Cv. xxxvii. 185.
[2] *Ibid.*, xliv. 97.
[3] *Ibid.*, xlviii. 9.

Goṇṇagirika.—A vihāra built by **Sūratissa** in the eastern quarter of **Anurādhapura.**[1]

[1] Mhv. xxi. 4.

1. **Gotama Thera.**—He belonged to a brahmin family of **Rājagaha** and was initiated at the age of seven. When he was seventeen, he fell into bad company, gave all he had to a courtesan and broke his vow of celibacy. He was then filled with remorse at the thought of what he had done, but the Buddha appeared before him and he entered the Order, becoming an arahant in the tonsure-hall.

He had been a householder in the time of **Vipassī** Buddha and had given to the Buddha an *āmoda*-fruit.[1]

He is evidently identical with **Āmodaphaliya** of the *Apadāna.*[2]

[1] Thag. 137 f.; ThagA. i. 256 f. [2] Ap. ii. 447.

2. **Gotama Thera.** He belonged to the Sākiyan clan and came to be known only by his gotta-name. He entered the Order when the Buddha visited his kinsfolk and, in due course, became an arahant. In the time of **Sikhī** Buddha he had offered eight *campaka*-flowers at the Buddha's thūpa.[1] He is evidently identical with **Citapūjaka** of the *Apadāna.*[2]

[1] Thag. 258-60; ThagA. i. 374 f. [2] Ap. ii. 407.

3. **Gotama Thera.**—Also called **Aparagotama.** He was older than the Buddha and belonged to an Udicca-brahmin family of Sāvatthi. He was learned in the Vedas and was an unrivalled orator. When the Buddha came to **Sāvatthi** for the dedication of **Jetavana,** he heard the Buddha preach and entered the Order, attaining arahantship in the tonsure-hall. When he returned to Sāvatthi, after a long residence in the Kosala country, many of his relations, eminent brahmins, came to him and counselled him as to the various gospels (*suddhivādā*) current among the people; he told them of the Buddha's teaching.[1]

[1] Thag. 587-96; ThagA. i. 529 f.

4. **Gotama Thera.**—An arahant, living in **Piyaṅgudīpa.** He was the teacher of **Duṭṭhagāmaṇī.**[1] When the latter, during his flight from his brother, wished to give alms to a monk before eating, Gotama knew his desire and sent a monk named **Tissa** to accept the alms. When the food was brought to **Piyaṅgudīpa,** Gotama offered morsels of it to five hundred monks[2] and, refilling the bowl with scraps of food, sent it back by air to the prince.[3]

[1] Mhv. xx. 69. [2] Twelve thousand, according to Mhv. xxxii. 55.
[3] Mhv. xxiv. 24, 30; MṬ. 465.

5. **Gotama.**—The name of the clan to which the Buddha and the Sākiyans belonged. The members of the clan, though khattiyas, claimed descent from a brahmin isi, **Gotama.**[1] Gotama and **Aṅgiras** are both enumerated in the *Pravara* ceremony as the ancestors of the Gotama clan.[2]

Late Buddhists appear to have forgotten the Vedic ṛṣi, for, according to an ancient legend, **Okkāka,** the immediate ancestor of the Sākiyans, was born of an egg formed of the coagulated blood and semen of an ascetic Gotama, as he lay impaled for the alleged murder of a courtesan. The egg was hatched by the sun.[3]

Gotama is the name by which the Buddha is addressed by brahmins and others who are not his followers. In one place, at least, the Buddha is represented as addressing the Sākiyans as "Gotamā."[4] The Gotamagotta is classed among the higher gottas, together with such gottas as **Moggallāna, Kaccāyana** and **Vāseṭṭha.**[5] According to the Theragāthā Commentary,[6] the Buddha's disciples (*e.g.*, in the case of **Vaṅgīsa**) were also called Gotama, even when they did not naturally belong to that clan. See also **Sakyā.**

[1] For an explanation of this see Thomas, *op. cit.*, 22 f.

[2] Āśvalāyana, *Śrauta-sūtra*, 12, 11, 1.

[3] Mtu. i. 338 ff.; Rockhill, Buddha, 9 f.

[4] S. iv. 183.

[5] Vin. iv. 6; DA. i. 246 f. (*uccākula-paridīpanaṃ*).

[6] ii. 204; also AA. i. 395 (*Gotama-buddhassa sāvako pi Gotamo*).

6. **Gotama.**—A brahmin sage, his full name being **Aṅgirasa Gotama.** See **Aṅgirasa** (7).

7. **Gotama.**—The name of the brahmin chaplain in the **Bhikkhāparampara Jātaka.** The scholiast adds that it was his gotta-name.[1]

[1] J. iv. 371, 372.

8. **Gotama.**—A mountain near **Himavā.**[1]

Ap. i. 162.

9. **Gotama.**—A thera in Ceylon who wrote a Sinhalese paraphrase to the **Sambandhacintā.** He belonged to the **Araññavāsī** sect and was a pupil of **Vanaratana Ānanda.**[1]

[1] P.L.C. 199, 220.

10. **Gotama.**—See **Āḷavi-Gotama.**

11. **Gotama.**[1]—The last of the twenty-five Buddhas.

He was a Sākiyan,[2] son of **Suddhodana,**[3] chief ruler of **Kapilavatthu,** and of **Mahā Māyā,** Suddhodana's chief consort, and he belonged to the **Gotama-gotta.** Before his conception he was in the **Tusita** heaven, waiting for the due time for his birth in his last existence. Then, having made the "five investigations" (*pañcavilokanāni*),[4] he took leave of his companions and descended to earth.[5] Many wondrous and marvellous events attended his conception and birth.[6] The conception takes place on the full-moon day of **Āsāḷha,** with the moon in **Uttarāsāḷha,** and Māyā has no relations with her husband. She has a marvellous dream in which the **Bodhisatta,** as a white elephant, enters her womb through her side. When the dream is mentioned to the brahmins, they foretell the birth of a son who will be either a universal monarch or a Buddha.

An earthquake takes place and thirty-two signs appear, presaging the birth of a great being. The first of these signs is a boundless, great light, flooding every corner of the ten thousand worlds; everyone beholds its glory, even the fires in all hells being extinguished. Ten months after the conception, in the month of **Visākha,** Māyā wishes to visit her parents in **Devadaha.** On the way thither from Kapilavatthu she passes the beautiful **Lumbinī** grove, in which she desires to wander; she goes to a great *sāla*-tree and seizes a branch in her hand; labour pains start immediately, and, when the courtiers retire, having drawn a curtain round her, even while standing, she is delivered of the child. It is the day of the full moon of Visākha; four Mahābrahmas receive

[1] No comprehensive account of Gotama Buddha is as yet possible. The details given in this article are those generally accepted by orthodox Theravādins and contained in their books, chiefly the Pāli Commentaries, more especially the Nidānakathā of the Jātaka and the Buddhavaṃsa Commentary. Biographical details are also found in the Mahā Vagga and the Culla Vagga of the Vinaya Piṭaka, the Buddhavaṃsa and in various scattered passages of the Nikāyas of the Sutta Piṭaka. References to these are given where considered useful. Controversy exists with regard to many of the matters mentioned; for discussion of the varying views regarding these, reference should be made to the works of Oldenberg, Rhys Davids (both Professor and Mrs. Rhys Davids), Kern, E. J. Thomas and other scholars. Further particulars of persons and places mentioned can be obtained by reference to the articles under the respective names.

[2] The Sākiyans were evidently subjects of the Kosala king; the Buddha calls himself a Kosalan (M. ii. 124).

[3] All Pāli Commentaries and Sanskrit works represent the Buddha as the son of a king, descendant of a long line of famous ancestors.

[4] See *s.v.* Buddha.

[5] According to the Lalitavistara he appointed the Bodhisatta Maitreya as king of Tusita in his place.

[6] Given in the Acchariyabbhutadhamma Sutta (M. iii. 118 f.); also D. ii. 12 f. A more detailed account is found in J. i. 47 ff.; both the Lal. and the Mtu. (ii. 14 ff.) differ as to the details given here of the conception and the birth.

the babe in a golden net, and streams of water descend from the sky to wash him. The boy stands on the earth, takes seven steps northwards and utters his lion-roar, "I am the chief in the world." On the same day seven other beings were born: the **Bodhi**-tree, Rāhula's mother (**Rāhulamātā**, his future wife), the four Treasure-Troves (described at DA. i. 284), his elephant, his horse Kanthaka, his charioteer **Channa**, and **Kāludāyī**. The babe is escorted back to Kapilavatthu on the day of his birth and his mother dies seven days later.

The isi **Asita** (or **Kāḷadevala**), meditating in the Himālaya, learns from the **Tāvatiṃsa** gods of the birth of the Buddha, visits **Suddhodana** the same day and sees the boy, whom they both worship. Asita weeps for sorrow that he will not live to see the boy's Buddhahood, but he instructs his nephew **Nālaka** (*v.l.* **Naradatta**) to prepare himself for that great day.[7] On the fifth day after the birth is the ceremony of name-giving. One hundred and eight brahmins are invited to the festival at the palace; eight of them—**Rāma, Dhaja, Lakkhana, Mantī, Koṇḍañña, Bhoja, Suyāma** and **Sudatta**—are interpreters of bodily marks, and all except Koṇḍañña prophesy two possibilities for the boy; but Koṇḍañña, the youngest, says, quite decisively, that he will be a Buddha. The name given to the boy at this ceremony is not actually mentioned, but from other passages it is inferred that it was **Siddhattha** (*q.v.*).

Among other incidents recounted of the Buddha's boyhood is that of his attaining the first jhāna under a jambu-tree. One day he is taken to the state ploughing of the king where Suddhodana himself, with his golden plough, ploughs with the farmers. The nurses, attracted by the festivities, leave the child under a jambu-tree. They return to find him seated, cross-legged, in a trance, the shadow of the tree remaining still, in order to protect him. The king is informed and, for the second time, does reverence to his son.[8]

The Bodhisatta is reported to have lived in the household for twenty-nine years a life of great luxury and excessive ease, surrounded by all imaginable comforts. He owns three palaces—**Ramma, Suramma** and **Subha**—for the three seasons.[9] When the Bodhisatta is sixteen years

[7] For details see *s.v.* **Asita**.

[8] J. i. 57 f.; MA. i. 466 f.; the incident is alluded to in the **Mahā Saccaka Sutta** (M. i. 246); the corresponding incident recounted in Mtu. (ii. 45 f.) takes place in a park, and the details differ completely. The Lal. has two versions, one in prose and one in verse and both resemble the Mtu.; but in these the Buddha is represented as being much older. The Divy (391) and the Tibetan versions (*e.g.*, Rockhill, p. 22) put the incident very much later in the Buddha's life. Other incidents are given in Lal. and Mtu.

[9] Mention is made of his luxurious life in A. i. 145; also in M. i. 504; further details are given in AA. i. 378 f.; J. i. 58. See also Mtu. ii. 115; *cf.* Vin. i. 15; D. ii. 21.

old, Suddhodana sends messengers to the Sākiyans asking that his son be allowed to seek a wife from among their daughters; but the Sākiyans are reluctant to send them, for, they say, though the young man is handsome, he knows no art; how, then, can he support a wife? When this is reported to the prince, he summons an assembly of the Sākiyans and performs various feats, chief of these being twelve feats with a bow which needs the strength of one thousand men.[10] The Sākiyans are so impressed that each sends him a daughter, the total number so sent being forty thousand. The Bodhisatta appoints as his chief wife the daughter of **Suppabuddha,** who, later, comes to be called Rāhulamātā.[11]

According to the generally accepted account, Gotama is twenty-nine when the incidents occur which lead to final renunciation. Following the prophecy of the eight brahmins, his father had taken every precaution that his son should see no sign of old age, sickness or death. But the gods decide that the time is come for the Enlightenment, and instil into Gotama's heart a desire to go into the park. On the way, the gods put before him a man showing signs of extreme age, and the Bodhisatta returns, filled with desire for renunciation. The king, learning this, surrounds him with even greater attractions, but on two other days[12] Gotama goes to the park and the gods put before him a sick man and a corpse. On the full-moon day of Āsāḷha, the day appointed for the Great Renunciation, Gotama sees a monk and hears from his charioteer praise of the ascetic life. Feeling very happy, he goes to the park to enjoy himself. **Sakka** sends **Vissakamma** himself to bathe and adorn him, and as Gotama returns to the city in all his majesty, he receives news of the birth of his son. Foreseeing in this news a bond, he decides to call the babe **Rāhula** (*q.v.*). **Kisā Gotamī** (*q.v.*) sees Gotama on the way to the palace and, filled with longing for him, sings to him a song containing the word *nibbuta*. The significance of the word (=extinguished, at peace) thrills him, and he sends to Kisā his priceless gold necklace which she, however, accepts as a token of love. Gotama enters the palace and sleeps. He wakes in the middle of the night[13] to find his female musicians sleeping in attitudes which fill him with disgust and with loathing for the worldly life, and he decides to leave it. He orders Channa to saddle Kanthaka, and enters his wife's room for a last look at her and their son.

[10] The feats with the bow are described in the **Sarabhaṅga Jātaka** (J. v. 129 f.).

[11] She is known under various names: **Bhaddakaccā** (or **Kaccānā**), **Yasodharā**, **Bimbā**, **Bimbasundarī** and **Gopā**. For a discussion see *s.v.* **Rāhulamātā.**

[12] According to some accounts, *e.g.* that of the Dīghabhāṇakas, the four omens were all seen on the same day (J. i. 59).

[13] In some versions the Renunciation takes place seven days after the birth of Rāhula (J. i. 62).

He leaves the city on his horse Kanthaka, with Channa clinging to its tail. The devas muffle the sound of the horse's hoofs and of his neighing and open the city gates for Gotama to pass. **Māra** appears before Gotama and seeks to stay him with a promise that he shall be universal monarch within seven days. On his offer being refused, Māra threatens to shadow him always. Outside the city, at the spot where later was erected the **Kanthakanivattana-cetiya,** Gotama turns his horse round to take a last look at Kapilavatthu. It is said that the earth actually turned, to make it easy for him to do so. Then, accompanied by the gods, he rides thirty leagues through three kingdoms—those of the Sākiyans, the Koliyans and the Mallas—and his horse crosses the river **Anomā** in one leap. On the other side, he gives all his ornaments to Channa, and with his sword cuts off hair and beard, throwing them up into the air, where Sakka takes them and enshrines them in the **Cūḷāmaṇicetiya** in Tāvatiṃsa. The Brahmā **Ghaṭikāra** offers Gotama the eight requisites of a monk, which he accepts and adopts. He then sends Channa and Kanthaka back to his father, but Kanthaka, broken-hearted, dies on the spot and is reborn as **Kanthaka-devaputta.**[14]

From Anomā the Bodhisatta goes to the mango-grove of **Anupiya,** and after spending seven days there walks to Rājagaha (a distance of thirty leagues) in one day, and there starts his alms rounds. **Bimbisāra's** men, noticing him, report the matter to the king, who sends messengers to enquire who this ascetic is. The men follow Gotama to the foot of the **Paṇḍavapabbata,** where he eats his meal, and they then go and report to the king. Bimbisāra visits Gotama, and, pleased with his bearing, offers him the sovereignty. On learning the nature of Gotama's quest, he wins from him a promise to visit Rājagaha first after the Enlightenment.[15] Journeying from Rājagaha,

[14] The account given here is taken mainly from the Nidānakathā (J. i. 59 ff.) and evidently embodies later tradition; *cp.* D. ii. 21 ff. From passages found in the Piṭakas (*e.g.*, A. i. 145; M. i. 163, 240; M. ii. 212 f.) it would appear that the events leading up to the Renunciation were not so dramatic as given here, the process being more gradual. I do not, however, agree with Thomas (*op. cit.*, 58) that, according to these accounts, the Bodhisatta left the world when "quite a boy." I think the word *dahara* is used merely to indicate "the prime of youth," and not necessarily "boyhood." The description of the Renunciation in the Lal. is very much more elaborate and adds numerous incidents, no account of which is found in the Pāli.

[15] This incident is also mentioned in the Pabbajjā Sutta (SN. vv. 405-24), but there it is the king who first sees Gotama. It is significant that, when asked his identity, Gotama does not say he is a king's son. The Pāli version of the sutta contains nothing of Gotama's promise to visit Rājagaha, but the Mtu. version (ii. 198-200), which places the visit later, has two verses, one of which contains the request and the other the acceptance; and the SNA. (ii. 385 f.), too, mentions the promise and tells that Bimbisāra

Gotama in due course becomes a disciple of **Āḷāra-Kālāma.** Having learnt and practised all that Āḷāra has to teach, he finds it unsatisfying and joins **Uddaka-Rāmaputta;** but Uddaka's doctrine leaves him still unconvinced and he abandons it. He then goes to **Senānīgāma** in **Uruvelā** and there, during six years, practises all manner of severe austerities, such as no man had previously undertaken. Once he falls fainting and a deva informs Suddhodana that Gotama is dead. But Suddhodana, relying on the prophecy of Kāḷadevala, refuses to believe the news. Gotama's mother, now born as a devaputta in Tāvatiṃsa, comes to him to encourage him. At Uruvelā, the **Pañcavaggiya** monks are his companions, but now, having realised the folly of extreme asceticism, he decides to abandon it, and starts again to take normal food; thereupon the Pañcavaggiyas, disappointed, leave him and go to **Isipatana.**[16]

Gotama's desire for normal food is satisfied by an offering brought by **Sujātā** to the **Ajapāla** banyan tree under which he is seated. She had made a vow to the tree, and her wish having been granted, she takes her slave-girl, **Puṇṇā,** and goes to the tree prepared to fulfil her promise. They take Gotama to be the Tree-god, come in person to accept her offering of milk-rice; the offering is made in a golden bowl and he takes it joyfully. Five dreams[17] he had the night before convince Gotama that he will that day become the Buddha. It is the full-moon day of Visākha; he bathes at **Suppatittha** in the **Nerañjarā,** eats the food and launches the bowl up stream, where it sinks to the abode of the Nāga king, **Kāla (Mahākāla).**

Gotama spends the rest of the day in a *sāla*-grove and, in the

was informed of the prophecy concerning Gotama. There is another version of the Mtu. (ii. 117-20) which says that Gotama went straight to Vaiśāli after leaving home, joining Āḷāra, and later visited Uddaka at Rājagaha. Here no mention is made of Bimbisāra. We are told in the Mhv. (ii. 25 ff.) that Bimbisāra and Gotama (Siddhattha) had been playmates, Bimbisāra being the younger by five years. Bimbisāra's father (Bhātī) and Suddhodana were friends.

[16] J. i. 66 f. The Therīgāthā Commentary (p. 2) mentions another teacher of Gotama, named **Bhaggava,** whom Gotama visited before Āḷāra. Lal. (330 [264]) contains a very elaborate account of Gotama's visits to teachers; he goes first to two brahmin women, Śākī and Padmā, then to Raivata and Rajaka, son of Trimaṇḍika, and finally (as far as this chapter is concerned) to Āḷāra at Vaiśāli. A poem containing an account of the meeting of Gotama with Bimbisāra is inserted into this account. The next chapter tells of Uddaka. An account of Gotama's visits to teachers and of the details of his austerities is also given in the Mahā Saccaka Sutta, already referred to (M. i. 240 ff.); the **Mahā Sīhanāda Sutta** (M. i. 77 ff.) contains a long and detailed account of his extreme asceticisms. See also M. i. 163 ff.; ii. 93 f.

[17] The dreams are recounted in A. iii. 240 and in Mtu. ii. 136 f.

evening, goes to the foot of the Bodhi-tree, accompanied by various divinities; there the grass-cutter **Sotthiya** gives him eight handfuls of grass; these, after investigation, Gotama spreads on the eastern side of the tree, where it becomes a seat fourteen hands long, on which he sits cross-legged, determined not to rise before attaining Enlightenment.[18]

Māra, lord of the world of passion, is determined to prevent this fulfilment, and attacks Gotama with all the strength at his command. His army extends twelve leagues to the front, right, and left of him, to the end of the Cakkavāḷa behind him, and nine leagues into the sky above him. Māra himself carries numerous weapons and rides the elephant **Girimekhala,** one hundred and fifty leagues in height. At the sight of him all the divinities gathered at the Bodhi-tree to do honour to Gotama—the great Brahmā, Sakka, the Nāga-king Mahākāla—disappear in a flash, and Gotama is left alone with the ten *pāramī*, long practised by him, as his sole protection. All Māra's attempts to frighten him by means of storms and terrifying apparitions fail, and, in the end, Māra hurls at him the **Cakkāvudha.** It remains as a canopy poised over Gotama. The very earth bears witness to Gotama's fitness to be the Enlightened One, and Girimekhala kneels before him. Māra is vanquished and flees headlong with his vast army. The various divinities who had fled at the approach of Māra now return to Gotama and exult in his triumph.[19]

Gotama spends that night in deep meditation. In the first watch he gains remembrance of his former existences; in the middle watch he attains the divine eye (*dibbacakkhu*); in the last watch he revolves in his mind the Chain of Causation (*paṭiccasamuppāda*). As he masters this, the earth trembles and, with the dawn, comes Enlightenment. He is now the supreme Buddha, and he breaks forth into a pæan of joy (*udāna*).[20]

[18] J. i. 69. The Piṭakas know nothing of Sujātā's offering or of Sotthiya's gift. Lal. (334-7 [267-70]) mentions ten girls in all who provide him with food during his austerities. Divy (392) mentions two, Nandā and Nandabalā.

[19] The whole story of the contest with Māra is, obviously, a mythological development. It is significant that in the Majjhima passages referred to earlier there is no mention of Māra, of a temptation, or even of a Bodhi-tree; but see D. ii. 4 and Thomas (*op. cit.*, n. 1). According to the Kāliṅgabodhi Jātaka, which, very probably, embodies an old tradition, the bodhi-tree was worshipped even in the Buddha's lifetime. The Māra legend is, however, to be found in the Canonical **Padhāna Sutta** of the Sutta Nipāta. This perhaps contains the first suggestion of the legend. For a discussion see *s.v.* Māra.

[20] There is great doubt as to which were these Udāna verses. The Nidānakathā and the Commentaries generally quote two verses (153, 154) included in the Dhammapada collection (*anekajāti saṃsāraṃ*, etc.). The Vinaya (i. 2) quotes three different verses (as does also DhsA. 17), and says that one verse

For the first week the Buddha remains under the Bodhi-tree, meditating on the Paṭiccasamuppāda; the second week he spends at the Ajapālanigrodha, where the "Huhuṅka" brahmin accosts him[21] and where Māra's daughters, **Taṇhā, Aratī** and **Rāgā,** appear before the Buddha and make a last attempt to shake his resolution;[22] the third week he spends under the hood of the nāga-king **Mucalinda**;[23] the fourth week is spent in meditation under the **Rājāyatana** tree;[24] at the end of this period takes place the conversion of **Tapussa** and **Bhallika.** They take refuge in the Buddha and the Dhamma, though the Buddha does not give them any instruction.

Doubts now assail the Buddha as to whether he shall proclaim to the world his doctrine, so recondite, so hard to understand. The Brahmā **Sahampati**[25] appears before him and assures him there are many prepared to listen to him and to profit by his teaching, and so entreats him to teach the Dhamma. The Buddha accedes to his request and, after consideration, decides to teach the Dhamma first to the Pañcavaggiyas at Isipatana. On the way to Benares he meets the Ājīvaka **Upaka** and tells him that he (the Buddha) is Jina. On his arrival at Isipatana the Pañcavaggiyas are, at first, reluctant to acknowledge his claim to be the Tathāgata, but they let themselves be won over and, on the full-moon day of Āsāḷha, the Buddha preaches to them the sermon which came to be known as the **Dhammacakkappavattana** Sutta.[26] At the end of the sermon Koṇḍañña becomes a sotāpanna and they all become monks.

This sermon is followed five days later by the **Anattalakkhaṇa** Sutta, at the conclusion of which all five become arahants. The following day the Buddha meets **Yasa,** whom he converts. Yasa's father, who comes seeking him, is the first to take the threefold formula of Refuge.

was repeated at the end of each watch, all the watches being occupied with meditation on the paṭiccasamuppāda. Mtu. (ii. 286) gives a completely different Udāna, and in another place (ii. 416) mentions a different verse as the first Udāna. The Tibetan Vinaya is, again, quite different (Rockhill, p. 33). For a discussion see Thomas, *op. cit.*, 75 ff.

[21] Māra now comes again and asks the Buddha to die at once (D. ii. 112).

[22] J. i. 78; S. i. 124; Lal. 490 (378).

[23] Vin. i. 3.

[24] This is the Vinaya account (Vin. i. 1 ff.); but the Jātaka (i. 77 ff.) extends this period to seven weeks, the additional weeks being inserted between the first and second. The Buddha spends one week each at the Animisa-cetiya, the **Ratanacaṅkama** and the **Ratanaghara,** and this last is where he thinks out the Abhidhamma Piṭaka.

[25] According to J. i. 81, with the gods of the thousand worlds, including Sakka, Suyāma, Santusita, Sunimmita, Vasavatti, etc.

[26] Vin. i. 4 ff.; M. i. 118 ff.; *cp.* D. ii. 36 ff. Regarding the claim of this sutta to be the Buddha's first sermon, see Thomas, *op. cit.*, p. 86; see also *s.v.* **Pañcavaggiyā.**

Yasa becomes an arahant and is ordained. The Buddha accepts a meal at his house, and Yasa's mother and one of his former wives are the first two lay-women to become the Buddha's disciples. Then four friends of Yasa and, afterwards, fifty more, enter the Order and become arahants. There are now sixty arahants besides the Buddha, and they are sent in different directions to preach the Dhamma. They return with many candidates for admission to the Order, and the Buddha, who up till now had ordained men with the "*ehi bhikkhu*" formula, now allows the monks themselves to perform the ceremony of ordination.[27]

After spending the rainy season at Benares,[28] the Buddha returns to Seṇānigāma in Uruvelā, on the way converting and ordaining the thirty **Bhaddavaggiyā.** At Uruvelā, after a long and protracted exercise of magical powers, consisting in all of three thousand five hundred miracles, the Buddha wins over the three Kassapa brothers, the **Tebhātika Jaṭilā,** with their thousand followers, and ordains them. They become arahants after listening to the **Ādittapariyāya** Sutta preached at **Gayāsīsa ;** with these followers he visits Rājagaha, where King Seniya Bimbisāra comes to see him at the **Laṭṭhivanuyyāna.** The following day the Buddha and the monks visit the palace, preceded by Sakka disguised as a youth and singing the praises of the Buddha. After the meal, the king gifts **Veḷuvana** to the Buddha and the Order. The Buddha stays for two months at Rājagaha,[29] and it is during this time that **Sāriputta** and **Moggāllana** join the Order, through the instrumentality of **Assaji.**[30] The number of converts now rapidly increases and the people of **Magadha,** alarmed by the prospect of childlessness, widowhood, etc., blame the Buddha and his monks. The Buddha, however, refutes their charges.[31]

[32]On the full-moon day of Phagguna (February-March) the Buddha, accompanied by twenty thousand monks, sets out for Kapilavatthu at the express request of his father, conveyed through Kāludāyī.[33] By slow stages he arrives at the city, where he stays at the **Nigrodhā-**

[27] Vin. i. 15 ff.; J. i. 81 f.

[28] About this time Māra twice tries to tempt the Buddha, once after he had sent the disciples out to preach and once after the Retreat (S. i. 105, 111; Vin. i. 21, 22).

[29] BuA. 4. It was probably during this year, at the beginning of the rainy season, that the Buddha visited Vesāli at the request of the Licchavis, conveyed through Mahāli. The city was suffering from pestilence and famine. The Buddha went, preached the **Ratana Sutta** and dispelled all dangers (DhA. iii. 436 ff.).

[30] Vin. i. 23 ff.

[31] Vin. i. 42 f.

[32] The account of the first twenty years of the Buddha's ministry is summarised from various sources, chiefly from Thomas's admirable account in his *Life and Legend of the Buddha* (pp. 97 ff.). The necessary references are to be found under the names mentioned.

[33] This visit is not mentioned in the Canon; but see Thag. 527-36; AA. i. 107, 167; J. i. 87; DhA. i. 96 f.; ThagA. i. 997 ff.

rāma, and, in order to convince his proud kinsmen of his power, performs the **Yamakapāṭihāriya** and then relates the **Vessantara Jātaka.** The next day, receiving no invitation to a meal, the Buddha begs in the streets of the city; this deeply grieves Suddhodana, but later, learning that it is the custom of all Buddhas, he becomes a sotāpanna and conducts the Buddha and his monks to meal at the palace. There all the women of the palace, excepting only Rāhulamātā, come and do reverence to the Buddha. **Mahāpajāpati** becomes a sotāpanna and Suddhodana a sakadāgāmi. The Buddha visits Rāhulamātā in her own apartments and utters her praises in the **Candakinnara Jātaka.** The following day the Buddha persuades his half-brother, **Nanda,** to come to the monastery, where he ordains him and, on the seventh day, he does the same with Rāhula. This is too great a blow for Suddhodana, and at his request the Buddha rules that no person shall be ordained without the consent of his parents. The next day the Buddha preaches to Suddhodana, who becomes an anāgamī. During the Buddha's visit to Kapilavatthu, eighty thousand Sākiyans join the Order, one from each family. With these he returns to Rājagaha, stopping on the way at Anupiya, where **Anuruddha, Bhaddiya, Ānanda, Bhagu, Kimbila** and **Devadatta,** together with their barber, **Upāli,** visit him and seek ordination.

On his return to Rājagaha[34] the Buddha resides in the **Sītavana.** There **Sudatta,** later known as **Anāthapiṇḍika,** visits him, is converted, and invites him to **Sāvatthi.** The Buddha accepts the invitation and journeys through **Vesālī** to Sāvatthi, there to pass the rainy season.[35] Anāthapiṇḍika gifts **Jetavana,** provided with every necessity, for the residence of the Buddha and his monks. Probably to this period belongs the conversion of **Migāra,** father-in-law of **Visākhā,** and the construction, by Visākhā, of the **Pubbārāma** at Sāvatthi. The vassa of the fourth year the Buddha spends at Veḷuvana, where he converts **Uggasena.**[36] In the fifth year Suddhodana dies, having realised arahantship, and the Buddha flies through the air, from the **Kūṭāgārasālā** in Vesāli where he was staying, to preach to his father on his death-bed. According to one account[37] it is at this time that the quarrel breaks out between the Sākiyans and the Koliyans regarding the irrigation of the river **Rohiṇī.** The Buddha persuades them to make peace, and takes up his abode in the Nigrodhārāma. Mahāpajāpatī Gotamī, with other Sākiyan women, visits him there and asks that women may be

[34] J. i. 92. The story is also told in the Vinaya (ii. 154), but no date is indicated.

[35] Vin. ii. 158; but see BuA. 3, where the Buddha is mentioned as having spent the vassa in Rājagaha.

[36] DhA. iv. 59 f.

[37] AA. i. 186; SNA. i. 357; ThigA. 141; details of the quarrel are given in J. v. 412 ff.

allowed to join the Order. Three times the request is made, three times refused, the Buddha then returning to Vesāli. The women cut off their hair, don yellow robes and follow him thither. Ānanda intercedes on their behalf and their request is granted.[38]

In the sixth year the Buddha again performs the Yamakapāṭihāriya, this time at the foot of the Gaṇḍamba tree in Sāvatthi. Prior to this, the Buddha had forbidden any display of magic powers, but makes an exception in his own case.[39]

He spends the vassa at **Maṅkulapabbata.** After the performance of the miracle he follows the custom of all Buddhas and ascends to Tāvatiṃsa in three strides to preach the Abhidhamma to his mother who is born there as a deva, and there he keeps the seventh vassa. The multitude, gathered at Sāvatthi at the Yamakapāṭihāriya, refuse to go away until they have seen him. For three months, therefore, Moggallāna expounds to them the Dhamma, while **Culla Anāthapiṇḍika** provides them with food. During the preaching of the Abhidhamma, Sāriputta visits the Buddha daily and learns from him all that has been recited the previous day. At the end of the vassa, the Buddha descends a jewelled staircase and comes to earth at **Saṅkassa,** thirty leagues from Sāvatthi.[40] It was about this time, when the Buddha's fame was at its height, that the notorious **Ciñcā-māṇavikā** was persuaded by members of some hostile sect to bring a vile accusation against the Buddha. A similar story, told in connection with a paribbājikā named **Sundarī,** probably refers to a later date.

The eighth year the Buddha spends in the country of the **Bhaggas** and there, while residing in **Bhesakalāvana** near **Suṃsumāragiri,** he meets **Nakulapitā** and his wife, who had been his parents in five hundred former births.[41]

In the ninth year the Buddha is at **Kosambī.** While on a visit to the Kuru country he is offered in marriage **Māgandiyā,** the beautiful daughter of the brahmin **Māgandiya.** The refusal of the offer, accompanied by insulting remarks about physical beauty, arouses the enmity of Māgandiyā who, thenceforward, cherishes hatred against the Buddha.[42]

[38] Vin. ii. 253 ff.; A. iv. 274 f.; for details see *s.v.* Mahāpajāpatī.

[39] DhA. iii. 199 f.; J. iv. 265, etc.

[40] For details see *s.v.* **Devorohaṇa.**

[41] A.A. i. 217. The same is told of another old couple in Sāketa. See the **Sāketa Jātaka.** The Buddha evidently stayed again at Suṃsumāragiri many years later. It was during his second visit that **Bodhirājakumāra** (*q.v.*) invited him to a meal at his new palace in order that the Buddha might consecrate the building by his presence.

[42] SN., pp. 163 ff.; SNA. ii. 542 ff.; DhA. i. 199 ff. Thomas (*op. cit.*, 109) assigns the Māgandiya incident to the ninth year. I am not sure if this is correct, for the Commentaries say the Buddha was then living at Sāvatthi.

In the tenth year there arises among the monks at **Kosambī** a schism which threatens the very existence of the Order. The Buddha, failing in his attempts to reconcile the disputants, retires in disgust to the **Pārileyyaka** forest, passing on his way through **Bālakaloṇakāragāma** and **Pācīnavaṃsadāya.** In the forest he is protected and waited upon by a friendly elephant who has left the herd. The Buddha spends the rainy season there and returns to Sāvatthi. By this time the Kosambī monks have recovered their senses and ask the Buddha's pardon. This is granted and the dispute settled.[43]

In the eleventh year the Buddha resides at the brahmin village of **Ekanālā** and converts **Kasi-Bhāradvāja.**[44] The twelfth year he spends at **Verañjā,** keeping the vassa there at the request of the brahmin **Verañja.** But Verañja forgets his obligations; there is a famine, and five hundred horse-merchants supply the monks with food. Moggallāna's offer to obtain food by means of magic power is discouraged.[45] The thirteenth Retreat is kept at **Cālikapabbata,** where **Meghiya** is the Buddha's personal attendant.[46] The fourteenth year is spent at Sāvatthi, and there **Rāhula** receives the upasampadā ordination.

In the fifteenth year the Buddha revisits Kapilavatthu, and there his father-in-law, Suppabuddha, in a drunken fit, refuses to let the Buddha pass through the streets. Seven days later he is swallowed up by the earth at the foot of his palace.[47]

The chief event of the sixteenth year, which the Buddha spent at **Ālavī,** is the conversion of the yakkha **Ālavaka.** In the seventeenth year the Buddha is back at Sāvatthi, but he visits Ālavī again out of compassion for a poor farmer who becomes a sotāpanna after hearing him preach.[48] He spends the rainy season at Rājagaha. In the next year he again comes to Ālavī from Jetavana for the sake of a poor weaver's daughter. She had heard him preach, three years earlier, on the desirability of meditating upon death. She alone gave heed to his admonition and, when the Buddha knows of her imminent death, he journeys thirty leagues to preach to her and establish her in the sotāpattiphala.[49]

The Retreat of this year and also that of the nineteenth are spent at **Cālikapabbata.** In the twentieth year takes place the miraculous conversion of the robber **Aṅgulimāla.** He becomes an arahant and dies shortly after. It is in the same year that Ānanda is appointed permanent attendant on the Buddha, a position which he holds to the end of

[43] Vin. i. 337 ff.; J. iii. 486 f.; DhA. i. 44 ff.; but see Ud. iv. 5; *s.v.* **Pārileyyaka.**

[44] SN., p. 12 f.; S. i. 172 f.

[45] Vin. iii. 1 ff.; J. iii. 494 f.; DhA. ii. 153.

[46] A. iv. 354; Ud. iv. 1.

[47] DhA. iii. 44.

[48] DhA. iii. 262 ff.

[49] *Ibid.*, 170 ff.

the Buddha's life, twenty-five years later.[50] The twentieth Retreat is spent at Rājagaha.

With our present knowledge it is impossible to evolve any kind of chronology for the remaining twenty-five years of the Buddha's life. The Commentaries state[51] that they were spent at Sāvatthi in the monasteries of Jetavana and Pubbārāma. This, probably, only implies that the Retreats were kept there and that they were made the head-quarters of the Buddha. From there, during the dry season, he went every year on tour in various districts. Among the places visited by him during these tours are the following:[52] Aggālavacetiya, Anotatta, Andhakavinda, Ambapālivana, Ambalaṭṭhikā, Ambasaṇḍā, Assapura, Āpaṇa, Icchānaṅgala, Ukkaṭṭhā (Subhagavana), Ukkācelā, Ugganagara, Ujuññā (Kaṇṇakatthaka deer-park), Uttara in Koliya, Uttarakā, Uttarakuru, Uruvelakappa, Ulumpa, Ekanālā, Opasāda, Kakkarapatta, Kajaṅgalā (Mukheluvana), Kammāssadhamma, Kalandakanivāpa (near Benares), Kimbilā, Kīṭāgiri, Kuṇḍadhānavana (near Kuṇḍakoli), Kesaputta, Koṭigāma, Kosambī (Ghositārāma and Badarikārāma), Khānumata, Khomadussa, Gosiṅgasālavana, Caṇḍalakappa, Campā (Gaggarā), Cātuma, Cetiyagiri in Vesāli, Jīvakambavana (in Rājagaha), Tapodārāma, Tindukkhānu (paribbājakārāma), Todeyya, Thullakoṭṭhita, Dakkhiṇāgiri, Daṇḍakappa, Devadaha, Desaka in the Sumbha country, Nagaraka, Nagaravinda, Nādikā (Giñjakāvasatha), Nālandā (Pāvārika mango-grove), Nāḷakapāna (Palāsavana), Paṅkadhā, Pañcasālā, Pāṭikārāma, Beluva, the Brahma world, Bhaddavatī, Bhaddiya (Jātiyāvana), Bhaganagara (Ānandacetiya), Maṇinālakacetiya, Manasākaṭa, Mātulā, Mithilā (Makhādeva mango-grove), Medatalumpa, Moraṇivāpa, Rammaka's hermitage, Laṭṭhivana, Videha, Vedhaññaambavana, Venāgapura, Verañjā, Veḷudvāra, Vesāli (also various shrines there, Udenacetiya, Gotamacetiya, Cāpalacetiya, Bahuputtakacetiya, Sattambacetiya, Sārandadacetiya), Sakkara, Sajjanela, Salalāgāraka in Sāvatthi, Sāketa (Añjanavana), Sāmagāma, Sālavatikā, Sālā, Siṃsapāvana, Silāvatī, Sītavana, Sūkarakhatalena, Setavyā, Hatthigāma, Halidavassana and the region of the Himālaya.

There is a more or less continuous account of the last year of the Buddha's life. This is contained in three suttas: the **Mahāparinibbāna**, the **Mahāsudassana** and the **Janavasabha**. These are not separate discourses but are intimately connected with each other. The only event prior to the incidents recounted in these suttas, which can be fixed

[50] For details see *s.v.* **Ānanda**.

[51] *E.g.*, BuA. 3; SNA. (p. 336 f.) says that when the Buddha was at Sāvatthi, he spent the day at the Migāramātupāsāda in the Pubbārāma, and the night at Jetavana or *vice versa*.

[52] For details of these visits see *s.v. passim*.

with any certainty, is the death of the Buddha's pious patron and supporter, **Bimbisāra,** which took place eight years before the Buddha's Parinibbāna.[53] It was at this time that **Devadatta** tried to obtain for himself a post of supremacy in the Order, and, failing in this effort, became the open enemy of the Buddha.[54] Enlisting the support of **Ajātasattu,** he tried in many ways to kill the Buddha. Royal archers were bribed to shoot the Buddha, but they were won over by his personality and confessed their intentions. Then Devadatta hurled a great rock down **Gijjhakūṭa** on to the Buddha as he was walking in the shade of the hill; the hurtling rock was stopped by two peaks, but splinters struck the Buddha's foot and caused blood to flow; he suffered great pain and had to be taken to the **Maddakucchi** garden, where his injuries were dressed by the physician **Jīvaka.**[55] The monks wished to provide a guard, but the Buddha reminded them that no man had the power to deprive a Tathāgata of his life.

Devadatta next bribed the royal elephant keepers to let loose a fierce elephant, **Nālāgiri,** intoxicated with toddy, on the road along which the Buddha would go, begging for alms. The Buddha was warned of this but disregarded the warning, and when the elephant appeared, Ānanda, against the strict orders of the Buddha, threw himself in its path, and only by an exercise of *iddhi*-power, including the folding up of the earth, could the Buddha come ahead of him. As the elephant approached, the Buddha addressed it, pervading it with his boundless love, until it became quite gentle.[56]

These attempts to encompass the Buddha's death having failed, Devadatta, with three others, decides to create a schism in the Order and asks the Buddha that five rules should be laid down, whereby the monks would be compelled to lead a far more austere life than hitherto. When this request is refused, Devadatta persuades five hundred recently ordained monks to leave Vesāli with him and take up their residence at Gayāsīsa, where he would set up an organisation similar to that of the Buddha. But, at the Buddha's request, Sāriputta and Moggallāna visit the renegade monks; Sāriputta preaches to them and they are persuaded to return. When Devadatta discovers this, he vomits hot blood and lies ill for nine months. When his end approaches, he wishes

[53] Mhv. ii. 32.

[54] Devadatta's desire to deprive the Buddha of the leadership of the Saṅgha seems to have been conceived by him, according to the Vinaya account (Vin. ii. 184), almost immediately after he joined the Order, and the Buddha was warned of this by the devaputta **Kakudha.** This account lends point to the statement contained especially in the Northern books, that even in their lay life Devadatta had always been Gotama's rival.

[55] S. i. 27.

[56] This incident, with great wealth of detail, is related in several places—*e.g.*, in J. v. 333 ff.

to see the Buddha, but he dies on the way to Jetavana—whither he is being conveyed in a litter—and is born in **Avīci.**[57]

From Gijjhakūṭa, near Rājagaha, the Buddha starts on his last journey. Just before his departure he is visited by **Vassākāra,** and the talk is of the Vajjians; the Buddha preaches to Vassākāra and the monks on the conditions that lead to prosperity. The Buddha proceeds with a large concourse of monks to **Ambalaṭṭhikā** and thence to **Nālandā,** where Sāriputta utters his lion-roar (*sīhanāda*) regarding his faith in the Buddha. The Buddha then goes to **Pāṭaligāma,** where he talks to the villagers on the evil consequences of immorality and the advantages of morality. He utters a prophecy regarding the future greatness of **Pāṭaliputta** and then, leaving by the **Gotamadvāra,** he crosses the river Ganges at **Gotamatittha.** He proceeds to **Koṭigāma** and thence to **Ñātika,** where he gives to Ānanda the formula of the *Dhammādāsa,* whereby the rebirth of disciples could be ascertained. From Ñātika he goes to Vesāli, staying in the park of the courtesan Ambapālī. The following day he accepts a meal from Ambapālī, refusing a similar offer from the Licchavis; Ambapālī makes a gift of her park to the Buddha and his monks. The Buddha journeys on to **Beluva,** where he spends the rainy season, his monks remaining in Vesāli. At Beluva he falls dangerously ill but, with great determination, fights against his sickness. He tells Ānanda that his mission is finished, that when he is dead the Order must maintain itself, taking the Dhamma alone as its refuge, and he concludes by propounding the four subjects of mindfulness.[58] The next day he begs in Vesāli and, with Ānanda, visits the **Cāpāla-cetiya.** There he gives to Ānanda the opportunity of asking him to live until the end of the kappa, but Ānanda fails to take the hint. Soon afterwards Māra visits the Buddha and obtains the assurance that the Buddha's nibbāna will take place in three months. There is an earthquake, and, in answer to Ānanda's questions, the Buddha explains to him the eight causes of earthquakes. This is followed by lists of the eight assemblies, the eight stages of mastery and the eight stages of release. The Buddha then repeats to Ānanda his conversation with Māra, and Ānanda now makes his request to the Buddha to prolong his life, but is told that it is now too late; several opportunities he has had, of which he has failed to avail himself. The monks are assembled in Vesāli, in the Service Hall, and the Buddha exhorts them to practise the doctrines he has taught, in order that the religious life may last long. He then announces his impending death.

The next day, returning from Vesāli, he looks round at the city for

[57] For further details and for references, see *s.v.* Devadatta.

[58] D. ii. 100.

the last time and goes on to **Bhaṇḍagāma**[59]; there he preaches on the four things the comprehension of which destroys rebirth—noble conduct, earnestness in meditation, wisdom and freedom.

He then passes through the villages of **Hatthigāma, Ambagāma** and **Jambugama,** and stays at **Bhoganagara** at the **Ānandacetiya.** There he addresses the monks on the Four Great Authorities (*Mahāpadesā*), by reference to which the true doctrine may be determined.[60] From Bhoganagara the Buddha goes to **Pāvā** and stays in the mango-grove of **Cunda,** the smith. Cunda serves him with a meal which includes *sūkaramaddava.*[61] The Buddha alone partakes of the *sūkaramaddava,* the remains being buried. This is the Buddha's last meal; sharp sickness arises in him, with flow of blood and violent, deadly pains, but the Buddha controls them and sets out for **Kusinārā.** On the way he has to sit down at the foot of a tree. Ānanda fetches him water to drink from the stream **Kakutthā,** over which five hundred carts had just passed; but, through the power of the Buddha, the water is quite clear. Here the Buddha is visited by **Pukkusa,** the Mallan, who is converted and presents the Buddha with a pair of gold-coloured robes. The Buddha puts them on and Ānanda notices the marvellous brightness and clearness of the Buddha's body. The Buddha tells him that the body of a Buddha takes on this hue on the night before his Enlightenment and on the night of his passing away, and that he will die that night at Kusinārā. He goes to the Kakutthā, bathes and drinks there and rests in a mango-grove. There he instructs Ānanda that steps must be taken to dispel any remorse that Cunda may feel regarding the meal he gave to the Buddha.

From Kakutthā the Buddha crosses the **Hiraññavatī** to the **Upavattana** sāla-grove in Kusinārā. There Ānanda prepares for him a bed with the head to the north. All the trees break forth into blossom and flowers cover the body of the Buddha. Divine mandārava-flowers and sandalwood powder fall from the sky, and divine music and singing sound through the air. But the Buddha says that the greater honour to him would be to follow his teachings.

The gods of the ten thousand world systems assemble to pay their

[59] According to the Commentaries (*e.g.*, DA. ii. 549), after the rainy season spent at Beluva, the Buddha goes back to Jetavana, where he is visited by Sāriputta, who is preparing for his own parinibbāna at Nālakagāma. From Jetavana the Buddha went to Rājagaha, where Mahāmoggallāna died. Thence he proceeded to Ukkācelā, where he spoke in praise of the two chief disciples. From Ukkācelā he proceeded to Vesāli and thence to Bhaṇḍagāma. Rāhula, too, predeceased the Buddha (DA. ii. 549).

[60] *Cf.* A. ii. 167 ff.

[61] There is much dispute concerning this word. See Thomas, *op. cit.*, 149, n. 3.

last homage to the Buddha, and **Upavāna,** who stands fanning him, is asked to move away as he obstructs their view.

Ānanda asks for instruction on several points, including how the funeral rites should be performed; he then goes out and abandons himself to a fit of weeping; the Buddha sends for him, consoles him and speaks his praises. Ānanda tries to persuade the Buddha not to die in a mud-and-wattle village, such as is Kusinārā, but the Buddha tells him how it was once the mighty **Kusāvatī,** capital of **Mahāsudassana.**

The Mallas of Kusināra are informed that the Buddha will pass away in the third watch of the night, and they come with their families to pay their respects. The ascetic **Subhadda** comes to see the Buddha and is refused admission by Ānanda, but the Buddha, overhearing, calls him in and converts him. Several minor rules of discipline are delivered, including the order for the excommunication of **Channa.** The Buddha finally asks the assembled monks to speak out any doubts they may have. All are silent and Ānanda expresses his astonishment, but the Buddha tells him it is natural that the monks should have no doubts. Then, addressing the monks for the last time, he admonishes them in these words: "Decay is inherent in all component things; work out your salvation with diligence." These were the Buddha's last words. Passing backwards and forwards through various stages of trance, he attains Parinibbāna. There is a great earthquake and terrifying thunder, and the Brahmā Sahampati, Sakka king of the gods, Anuruddha and Ānanda utter stanzas, each proclaiming the feeling uppermost in his mind. It is the full-moon day of the month of Visākha and the Buddha is in his eightieth year.

The next day Ānanda informs the Mallas of Kusināra of the Buddha's death, and for seven days they hold a great celebration. On the seventh day, following Ānanda's instructions, they prepare the body for cremation, taking it in procession by the eastern gate to the **Makuṭabandhana** shrine, thus altering their proposed route, in order to satisfy the wishes of the gods, as communicated to them by Anuruddha. The whole town is covered knee-deep with mandārava-flowers, which fall from the sky. When, however, four of the chief Mallas try to light the pyre, their attempt is unsuccessful and they must wait until **Mahā Kassapa,** coming with a company of five hundred monks, has saluted it. The Commentaries (*e.g.*, DA. ii. 603) add that Mahā Kassapa greatly desired that the Buddha's feet should rest on his head when he worshipped the pyre. The wish was granted: the feet appeared through the pyre, and when Kassapa had worshipped them, the pyre closed together. The pyre burns completely away, leaving no cinders nor soot. Streams of water fall from the sky to extinguish it and the Mallas pour on it scented water. They then place a fence of spears around it and continue their celebrations for seven days. At the end of that period there appear several claimants for the Buddha's relics: **Ajātasattu,** the **Licchavis** of Vesāli, the Sākiyans of Kapilavatthu, the **Bulis** of **Allakappa,** the Koliyas of **Rāmagāma,** a brahmin of **Veṭhadīpa** and the Mallas of Pāvā. But the Mallas of Kusinārā refusing to share the relics with the others, there is danger of war. Then the brahmin **Doṇa** counsels concord and divides the relics into eight equal parts for the eight claimants. Doṇa takes for himself the measuring vessel and the **Moriyas** of **Pipphalivana,** who arrive late, carry off the ashes. Thūpas were built over these remains and feasts held in honour of the Buddha.[62] It is said[63] that just before the Buddha's Sāsana disappears completely from the world, all the relics will gather together at the **Mahācetiya,** and travelling from there to **Nāgadīpa** and the **Ratanacetiya,** assemble at the Mahābodhi, together with the relics from other parts. There they will re-form the Buddha's golden-hued body, emitting the six-coloured aura. The body will then catch fire and completely disappear, amid the lamentations of the ten thousand world-systems.

The Ceylon Chronicles[64] record that the Buddha visited the Island on three separate occasions. The first was while he was dwelling at Uruvelā, awaiting the moment for the conversion of the Tebhātika Jaṭilas, in the ninth month after the Enlightenment, on the full-moon day of Phussa (Dec.-Jan.). He came to the **Mahānāga** garden, and stood in the air over an assembly of yakkhas then being held. He struck terror into their hearts and, at his suggestion, they left Ceylon and went in a body to **Giridīpa,** hard by. The Buddha gave a handful of his hair to the deva **Mahāsumana** of the **Sumanakūṭa** mountain, who built a thūpa which was later enlarged into the **Mahiyaṅgana** Thūpa. The Buddha again visited Ceylon in the fifth year, on the

[62] The concluding passage of the Mahāparinibbāna Sutta (D. ii. 167) states that the Buddha's relics were eight measures, seven of which were honoured in Jambudīpa and the remaining one in the Nāga realm in Rāmagāma. One tooth was in heaven, one in Gandhāra, a third in Kāliṅga (later taken to Ceylon), and a fourth in the Nāga world. Ajātasutta's share was deposited in a thūpa and forgotten. It was later discovered by **Asoka** (with the help of Sakka) and distributed among his eighty-four thousand monasteries. Asoka also recorded the finding of all the other relics except those deposited in Rāmagāma. These were later deposited in the Mahācetiya at Anurādhapura (Mhv. xxxi. 17 ff.). Other relics are also mentioned, such as the Buddha's collar-bone, his alms bowl, etc. (Mhv. xvii. 9 ff.; Mhv. i. 37, etc.).

[63] *E.g.*, DA. iii. 899.

[64] Mhv. i. 12 ff.; Dpv. i. 45 ff.; ii. 1 ff. etc. The Burmese claim that the Buddha visited their land and went to the Lohitacandana Vihāra, presented by the brothers Mahāpuṇṇa and Cūlapuṇṇa of Vānijagāma (*Ind. Antiq.* xxii., and Sās. 36 f.).

new-moon day of Citta (March-April), to check an imminent battle between two Nāga chiefs in **Nāgadīpa**; the combatants were **Mahodara** and **Cūḷodara,** uncle and nephew, and the object of the quarrel was a gem-set throne. The Buddha appeared before them, accompanied by the deva **Samiddhi-Sumana,** carrying a Rājayatana tree from Jetavana, settled their quarrel and received, as a gift, the throne, the cause of the trouble. He left behind him both the throne and the Rājayatana tree for the worship of the Nāgas and accepted an invitation from the Nāga-king, **Maṇiakkhika** of Kalyāṇi, to pay another visit to Ceylon. Three years later Maṇiakkhika repeated the invitation and the Buddha came to Kalyāṇi with five hundred monks, on the second day of Vesākha. Having preached to the Nāgas, he went to Sumanakūṭa, on the summit of which mountain he left the imprint of his foot.[65] He then stayed at **Dīghavāpī** and from there visited **Mahāmeghavana,** where he consecrated various spots by virtue of his presence, and proceeded to the site of the later **Silācetiya.** From there he returned to Jetavana.

Very little information as to the personality of the Buddha is available. We are told that he was golden-hued,[66] that his voice had the eight qualities of the Brahmassāra[67]—fluency, intelligibility, sweetness, audibility, continuity, distinctness, depth and resonance—that he had a fascinating personality—he was described by his opponents as seductive[68]—that he was handsome, perfect alike in complexion and stature and noble of presence.[69] He had a unique reputation as a teacher and trainer of the human heart. He was endowed with the thirty-two marks of the Mahāpurisa.[70] There is a legend that Mahā Kassapa, though slightly shorter, resembled the Buddha in appearance.[71]

Mention is often made of the Buddha's love of quiet and peace, and even the heretics respected his wishes in this matter, silencing their discus-

[65] Legend has it that other footprints were left by the Buddha, on the bank of the river **Nammadā,** on the **Saccabaddha** mountain and in **Yoṇakapura.**

[66] *E.g.*, Sp. iii. 689.

[67] *E.g.*, D. ii. 211; M. ii. 166 f. It is said that while an ordinary person spoke one word, Ānanda could speak eight; but the Buddha could speak sixteen to the eight of Ānanda (MA. i. 283).

[68] *E.g.*, M. i. 269, 275.

[69] *E.g.*, M. ii. 167.

[70] For details of these, see *s.v.* Buddha.

[71] Attempts made, however, to measure the Buddha always failed; two such attempts are generally mentioned—one by a brahmin of Rājagaha and the other by Rāhu, chief of the Asuras (DA. i. 284 f.). The Buddha had the physical strength of many millions of elephants (*e.g.*, VibhA. 397), but his strength quickly ebbed away after his last meal and he had to stop at twenty-five places while travelling three gāvutas from Pāvā to Kusinārā (DA. ii. 573).

sions at his approach.[72] Examples are given[73] of the Buddha refusing to allow noisy monks to live near him. He loved solitude and often spent long periods away from the haunts of men, allowing only one monk to bring him his meals.[74] According to one account,[75] it was his practice to spend part of the day in seclusion, but he was always ready to see anyone who urgently desired his spiritual counsel.[76]

In the **Mahā Govinda Sutta**[77] Sakka is represented as having uttered "eight true praises" of the Buddha. Perhaps the most predominant characteristics of the Buddha were his boundless love and his eagerness to help all who sought him. His fondness for children is seen in such stories as those of the two **Sopākas,** of **Kumāra-Kassapa,** of **Cūḷa Panthaka** and **Dabba-Mallaputta** and also of the novices **Paṇḍita** and **Sukha.** His kindness to animals appears, for instance, in the introductory story of the **Maccha Jātaka** and his interference on behalf of **Udena's** aged elephant, **Bhaddavatikā** (*q.v.*). The Buddha was extremely devoted to his disciples and encouraged them in every way in their difficult life. The Theragāthā and the Therīgāthā are full of stories indicating that he watched, with great care, the spiritual growth and development of his disciples, understood their problems and was ready with timely interference to help them to win their aims. Such incidents as those mentioned in the **Bhaddāli Sutta,**[78] the introduction to the **Tittha Jātaka** and the **Kañcakkhandha Jātaka,** seem to indicate that he took a personal and abiding interest in all who came under him. It was his unvarying custom to greet with a smile all those who visited him, inquiring after their welfare and thus putting them at their ease.[79] When anyone sought permission to question him, he made no conditions as to the topic of discussion. This is called *sabbaññupavāraṇa.*[80]

When he was staying in a monastery, he paid daily visits to the sick-

[72] *E.g.*, D. i. 178 f.; iii. 39; even his disciples had a similar reputation (*e.g.*, D. iii. 37).

[73] *E.g.*, M. i. 456; see also M. ii. 122, where a monk was jogged by his neighbour because he coughed when the Buddha was speaking.

[74] *E.g.*, S. v. 12, 320; but this very love of solitude was sometimes brought against him. By intercourse with whom does he attain to lucidity in wisdom? they asked. His insight, they said, was ruined by his habit of seclusion (D. iii. 38).

[75] A. i. 181.

[76] *E.g.*, A. iv. 438.

[77] D. ii. 222 f.

[78] M. i. 445.

[79] Vin. i. 313.

[80] *E.g.*, M. i. 230. When the Buddha himself asked a question of any of his interrogators, they could not remain silent, but were bound to answer; a yakkha called **Vajirapāṇi** was always present to frighten those who did not wish to do so (*e.g.*, M. i. 231). The Buddha was not over-anxious to get converts, and when his visitors declared themselves his followers he would urge them to take time to consider the matter —*e.g.*, in the case of **Acela Kassapa** and **Upāligahapati.**

ward to talk to the inmates and to comfort them.[81] The charming story of **Pūtigata-Tissa** shows that he sometimes attended on the sick himself, thus setting an example to his followers. In return for his devotion, his disciples adored him, but even among those who immediately surrounded him there were a few who refused to obey him implicitly —*e.g.*, **Lāludāyī,** the companions of **Assaji** and **Punabbasuka,** the **Chabbaggiyas,** the **Sattarasavaggiyas** and others, not to mention Devadatta and his associates.

The Buddha seems to have shown a special regard for Sāriputta, Ānanda and Mahā Kassapa among the monks, and for Anāthapiṇḍika, Mallikā, Visakhā, Bimbisāra and Pasenadi among the laity. He seems to have been secretly amused by the very human qualities of Pasenadi and by his failure to appreciate the real superiority of **Mallikā,** his wife.

The Buddha always declared that he was among the happy ones of this earth, that he was far happier, for instance, than Bimbisāra,[82] and he remained unmoved by opposition or abuse.[83]

The *Milindapañha*[84] mentions several illnesses of the Buddha: the injury to his foot has already been referred to; once when the humours of his body were disturbed Jīvaka administered a purge;[85] on another occasion he suffered from some stomach trouble which was cured by hot water, or, according to some, by hot gruel.[86] The Dhammapada Commentary[87] mentions another disorder of the humours cured by hot water obtained from the brahmin **Devahita,** through **Upavāna.** The Commentaries[88] mention that he suffered, in his old age, from constant backache, owing to the severe austerities practised by him during the six years preceding his Enlightenment, and the unsuitable meals taken during that period were responsible for a dyspepsia which persisted throughout the rest of his life,[89] culminating in his last serious illness of dysentery.

The Apadāna[90] contains a set of verses called **Pubbakammapiloti;** these verses mention certain acts done by the Buddha in the past, which resulted in his having to suffer in various ways in his last birth. He was once a drunkard named **Munāli** and he abused the Pacceka Buddha **Surabhi.** On another occasion he was a learned brahmin, teacher of five hundred pupils. One day, seeing the Pacceka Buddha **Isigaṇa,** he

[81] See, *e.g.*, *s.v.* **Kuṭāgārasālā.**

[82] *E.g.*, M. i. 94.

[83] *E.g.*, in the case of the organised conspiracy of Māgandiyā (DhA. iv. 1 f.).

[84] p. 134.

[85] Vin. i. 279.

[86] Vin. i. 210 f.; Thag. 185.

[87] DhA. iv. 232; ThagA. i. 311 f.

[88] MA. i. 465; DA. iii. 974; see also D. iii. 209, when he was preaching to the Mallas of Pāvā.

[89] SA. i. 200.

[90] Ap. i. 299 f.

spoke ill of him to his pupils, calling him "sensualist." The result of this act was the calumny against him by Sundarikā in this life.

In another life he reviled a disciple of a Buddha, named **Nanda**; for this he suffered in hell for twelve thousand years and, in his last life, was disgraced by Ciñcā. Once, greedy for wealth, he killed his step-brothers, hurling them down a precipice; as a result, Devadatta attempted to kill him by hurling down a rock. Once, as a boy, while playing on the highway, he saw a Pacceka Buddha and threw a stone at him, and as a result, was shot at by Devadatta's hired archers. In another life he was a mahout, and seeing a Pacceka Buddha on the road, drove his elephant against him; hence the attack by Nālāgiri. Once, as a king, he sentenced seventy persons to death, the reward for which he reaped when a splinter pierced his foot. Because once, as a fisherman's son, he took delight in watching fish being caught, he suffered from a grievous headache when **Viḍūḍabha** slaughtered the Sākiyans. In the time of **Phussa** Buddha he asked the monks to eat barley instead of rice and, as a result, had to eat barley for three months at Verañja. (According to the Dhammapada Commentary [iii. 257], the Buddha actually had to starve one day at **Pañcasālā,** because none of the inhabitants were willing to give him alms.) Because he once killed a wrestler, he suffered from cramp in the back. Once, when a physician, he caused discomfort to a merchant by purging him, hence his last illness of dysentery. As **Jotipāla,** he spoke disparagingly of the Enlightenment of Kassapa Buddha, and in consequence had to spend six years following various paths before becoming the Buddha. He was one of the most short-lived Buddhas, but because of those six years his Sāsana will last longer.[91]

The Buddha was generally addressed by his own disciples as Bhagavā. He spoke of himself as Tathāgata, while non-Buddhists referred to him as Gotama or Mahāsamaṇa. Other names used are Mahāmuni, Sākya-muni, Jina, Sakka (*e.g.*, Sn. vs. 345) and Brahma (Sn. vs. 91; SnA. ii. 418), also **Yakkha** (*q.v.*).

The Aṅguttara Nikāya[92] gives a list of the Buddha's most eminent disciples, both among members of the Order and among the laity. Each one in the list is mentioned as having possessed pre-eminence in some particular respect.

Among those who visited the Buddha for discussion or had interviews with him or received instruction and guidance direct from him, the following may be included in addition to those already mentioned:[93]

Aṅkura, Aggidatta, Acela-Kassapa, Ajātasattu, Ajita the paribbājaka,

[91] Sp. i. 190 f.

[92] A. i. 23 ff.

[93] This list does not pretend to be complete. Some of the names have already been mentioned in this monograph in various connections.

Ajita the Licchavi general, Attadattha, Anitthigandhakumāra, Anurā-dha, Anuruddha, Annabhāra, Abhaya-rājakumāra, Abhayā, Abhiñjaka, Abhibhūta, Abhirūpa-Nandā, Ambaṭṭha, the monk Ariṭṭha, Ariya the fisherman, Asama, Asibandhaputta, Assaji, Assalāyana, Ākotaka, Āmagandha, the yakkhas Ālavaka and Indaka, Ugga of Vesāli, Ugga the minister, Uggata-Sarīra, Uggaha, Ujjaya, Uṇṇābha, Uttara-devaputta, Uttara the Nāga king, Uttara, pupil of Pārāsariya, Uttiya, Udaya and Udāyi the brahmins, Uttara, pupil of Brahmāyu, Uttarā, daughter of Puṇṇa, Uttarā the aged nun, Upavāna, Upasāḷha, Upasena, Upāligahapati, Ubbirī, Eraka, Esakārī, Kakudha, Kandaraka, Kapila the fisherman, Kappa, Kappaṭakura, Kalārakkhattiya, Kassapa the deva, Kāṇa, Kāṇamātā, Kātiyāna, Kāpaṭhika, Kāmada, Kāraṇapāli, the Kālāmas, Kāligodhā, Kimbila, Kisāgotamī, Kukkuṭamitta the hunter, Kuṇḍadhāna, Kuṇḍaliya, Kulla, Kūṭadanta, Keṇiya the Jaṭila, Kevaddha, Kesi the horse trainer, Kokanadā, the two daughters of Pajjuna, Kokālika, Khadiravaniya-Revata, Khānu-Koṇḍañña, Khema the deva, Khemā, Gaṇaka-Moggallāna, Gavampati, Guttā, Gotama Thera, Caṅkī, Candana, Candābha, Candimā (Candimasa), Citta-Hatthasārīputta, Cunda, Cunda-Samaṇuddesa, Cundī, Culla-Dhanuggaha, Culla-Subhaddhā, Chattapāṇī, Janapada-Kalyānī-Nandā, Janavasabha, Jantu, Jambuka, Jambukhādaka, Jāṇussoṇi, Jāliya, Jīvaka-Komārabhacca, Jenta, Jotikagahapati, Tāyana, Tālapuṭa, Tikaṇṇa, Timbaruka, Tissa, cousin of the Buddha, Tissa, friend of Metteyya, Tissa of Roruva, Tudu-brahmā, Thulla-Tissa, Daṇḍapaṇī, Dāmalī, Dāsaka, Dīgha the deva, Dīghajānu, Dīghatapassī, Dīghanakha, Dīghalaṭṭhi, Dīghāvu, Dummukha, Doṇa, Dhammadinna, Dhammārāma, the Dhammika-upāsaka, Dhammika the brahmin, Nanda Thera, Nanda the herdsman, Nandana, Nandiya-paribbājaka, Nandiya the Sākiyan, Nandivisāla, Nāgita, Nālakatāpasa, Nālijaṅgha, Nigamavāsi-Tissa, Nigrodha, Niṅka, Nīta, Nhātakamuni, Paccanīkasāta, Pañcasikha, Pañcālacaṇḍa, Paṭācārā, Pasenadi, king of Kosala, Pahārāda the asura, Pāṭaliya, Pārāpariya, Piṅgala-Kaccha, Piṅgiyānī, Pilinda-Vaccha, Pilotika, Puṇṇa, Puṇṇa-Koliyaputta, Puṇṇa-Mantānīputta, Puṇṇā, Puṇṇiya, Pessa the elephant trainer, Pokkharasāti, Poṭṭhapāda, Poṭhila, Potaliya, Phagguna, Baka-brahmā, Bahuputtikā, Bāvarī and his sixteen disciples, Bāhiya-Dārucīriya, Bāhuna, Biḷālapādaka, Belaṭṭhakāni, Bojjhā, Brahmāyu, Bhagu, Bhaggava, Bhadda, Bhaddā-Kuṇḍakakesī, Bhaddāli, Bhaddiya the Licchavi, several Bhāradvājas (Akkosaka*, Aggika*, Asurinda*, Ahiṃsaka*, Kāsi*, Jaṭā*, Navakammika*, Bilaṅgika*, Suddhika*, Sundarika*), Bhāradvāja, husband of Dhanañjāni, Bhāradvāja, friend of Vāseṭṭha, Bhuñjatī, Bhumiya, Bhesika the barber, Macchari-Kosiya, Maṇibhadda, Maṇḍissa, Mahā-kappina, Mahā-Kassapa, Mahā-koṭṭhita, Mahā-Cunda, Mahādhana, Mahā-nāma, Mahā-Moggallāna, Mahāli (Oṭṭhaddha), the two Māgandiyas—one the brahmin and one the paribbājaka, Māgha, Māṇava-Gāmiya, Mānatthaddha, Mātuposaka, Māluṅkyaputta, Migajāla, Migasira, Meṇḍaka of Bhaddiya, Moliya-Phagguna, Moliya-Sīvaka, Yasoja, Raṭṭhapāla, Rādha, Rāhula, Rāsiya, Rūpānandā, Roja the Malla, Rohiṇī, Rohitassa, Lakuṇṭaka-Bhaddiya, the goddess Lājā, Lomasakaṅgiya, Lohicca, Vakkali, Vaṅgīsa, Vajjiyamāhita, Vaḍḍha the Licchavi, Vaḍḍhamāna, Vappa, Varadhara, Vassakāra, Vāraṇa, Vāseṭṭha-upāsaka, Vāseṭṭha, friend of Bhāradvāja, Visākha Pañcalaputta, Visākhā, Vīrā, Vekhanasa, Veṇḍu, Vatambari, Sakuludāyi, Sakka, Saṅkicca, the two Saṅgāravas, Saṅgharakkhita (Bhāgineyya°), Saccaka, Sajjha, Satullapa-devas, Sanaṅkumāra, Santati, Sandha, Sandhāna, Samiddhi, Sarabha, Sarabhaṅga, Sātāgira, Sātāli, Sāti, Sānu, Sikhā-Moggallāna, Sigāla, Sirimā, Siva, Sīvali, Sīha the general, Sukhā, Suciloma, Sujātā, daughter-in-law of Anāthapiṇḍika, Sudatta, Sunakkhatta, Sunīta, Sundara-Samudda, Sundarī-Nandā, the leper Suppabuddha, Suppavāsā, Subha Todeyyaputta, the two nuns named Subhā, Subhūti, the novice Sumana, Sumanā, sister of Pasenadi, Subrahmā, Surādha, Suriya, Susīma, Seniya, Seri, Sela, Soṇa-Kutikaṇṇa, Soṇa-Kolivisa, Soṇadaṇḍa, Soṇā, the two Sopākas, Hatthaka Ālavaka, Hatthaka-devaputta and Hemavata. See also *s.v.* **Buddha** and **Bodhisatta.**

1. **Gotamaka.**—A class of ascetics, enumerated in a list of such classes.[1] Rhys Davids thinks[2] they were almost certainly the followers of some other member of the Sākyan clan, as distinct from the Buddha, and suggests that it might have been **Devadatta** or possibly a brahmin of the **Gotamagotta.** The *Lalita-vistara,*[3] however, speaks of the Gautamas in a list of nine such sects; the Gotamakas and the Gautamas are evidently identical, as several of the other classes correspond with the Pāli. According to the *Lalita-vistara,* these sects existed even before the Buddha, for they are represented as meeting and addressing him in the sixth week after the Enlightenment, on his way to the **Ajapāla**-tree. We hear no more of them in subsequent history.

[1] A. iii. 276. Does *devadhammikā* in Ap. ii. 358 (vs. 11) qualify *Gotamā* ?
[2] Dial. i. 222; but see his article on Buddhist Law in ERE.; see also *Brethren* 265, n. 3.
[3] p. 492.

2. **Gotamaka.**—A yakkha. See **Gotamakacetiya.**

3. **Gotamaka.**—See **Kaṇha-Gotamaka.**

Gotamaka Sutta.—Preached to the monks at the **Gotamakacetiya.** The Buddha declares that his proclamation of a Dhamma is with full comprehension, with casual connection (*sanidānaṃ*), and accompanied by wonders. His instructions are with reason.[1]

It is said that at this pronouncement the thousandfold universe trembled.[2] The *Majjhima Commentary*[3] states that the Sutta was preached to the monks mentioned in the **Mūlapariyāya Sutta,** and that, at the end, they became arahants.

[1] A. i. 276 f. [2] Also DA. i. 130; J. ii. 259. [3] i. 49.

Gotamakacetiya.—A shrine near and to the south of **Vesāli.**[1] It was considered one of the beautiful spots of that town[2] and the Buddha stayed there several times, particularly during the first years of his ministry.[3] During one such stay, he laid down the rule which allowed monks the use of three robes; he himself felt cold during the night and had to wear extra clothing.[4]

The shrine was pre-Buddhistic and dedicated to a Yakkha named **Gotamaka.** A vihāra was later built on the spot for the Buddha and his monks.[5] There the **Gotamaka Sutta** was preached.[6] The *Divyāvadāna,*[7] in a list of noted places of Vesāli, speaks of a *Gautama-nyagrodha.* The reference is evidently to this cetiya. It has been suggested[8] that the ectiya may have been called after the Kāla (Kaṇha) Gotama Nāgas, but the suggestion appears far-fetched.

[1] D. iii. 9.
[2] *E.g.,* D. ii. 102, 118.
[3] Thus AA. i. 457.
[4] Vin. i. 288; iii. 195.
[5] UdA. 322; DhA. iii. 246; AA. i. 457; SNA. i. 344.
[6] And, according to some, also the **Hemavata Sutta** (SNA. i. 199).
[7] p. 201.
[8] See *J.P.T.S.* 1891, p. 67; Windisch: *Mara und Buddha,* p. 68; *cp.* J. ii. 145.

Gotamatittha.—The ford by which the Buddha crossed the Ganges, after leaving **Pāṭaligāma.**[1] See also **Gotamadvāra.**

[1] Vin. i. 230; Ud. viii. 6; UdA. 424; D. ii. 89.

Gotamadvāra.—The gate by which the Buddha left **Pāṭaligāma,** after having eaten there at the invitation of **Sunīdha** and **Vassakāra.**[1]

[1] Vin. i. 230, etc., as above.

Gotamā.—Mother of **Candakumāra** and chief queen of the king of Benares.[1] She is identified with **Mahāmāyā.**[2] She is sometimes also called **Gotamī.**[3]

[1] J. vi. 134. [2] *Ibid.,* 157. [3] *E.g., ibid.,* 148, 151.

1. **Gotamī, Gotamā.**—See **Mahā Pajāpatī Gotamī, Kisāgotamī,** etc.

2. **Gotamī.**—One of the chief women supporters of **Vessabhū** Buddha.[1] The Commentary[2] calls her **Kāḷigotamī.**

[1] Bu. xxii. 25. [2] BuA., p. 208.

1. **Gotamī Sutta.**—**Māra** sees **Kisā Gotamī** resting alone in the **Andhavana** and tries to frighten her, but he is forced to retire discomfited.[1]

[1] S. i. 129.

2. **Gotamī Sutta.**—The story of how **Pajāpatī Gotamī** (*q.v.*) and her companions obtained the Buddha's sanction to enter the Order and the conditions attaching to that sanction.[1]

[1] A. iv. 274 ff.

Gotamyā.—The name given to the followers of **Pajāpatī Gotamī.**[1]

[1] *E.g.*, DhA. iv. 149.

Gotta, Goda.—See **Godatta** (2).

1. **Godatta Thera.**—He belonged to a family of caravan-leaders and, on the death of his father, travelled about himself with five hundred carts, engaged in trade. One day, one of his oxen fell on the road, and seeing that his men could not get it up, Godatta went up and smote it. The ox, incensed by this cruelty, assumed a human voice and, chiding him for his base ingratitude, cursed him. Godatta, much moved, renounced all his property and joined the Order, in due course attaining arahantship.[1] The *Theragāthā*[2] contains several stanzas attributed to him, wherein he discoursed to " Ariyan " groups, both lay and religious, on *lokadhammā* (the nature of things ?), illustrating his meaning with a wealth of simile. He is probably the Godatta of the **Godatta Sutta.**

[1] ThagA. i. 555 f. [2] vs. 659-72.

2. **Godatta Thera.**—His full name was **Abhidhammika Godatta,** showing that he was considered expert in Abhidhamma. He was evidently a well-known Abhidhamma commentator and is quoted in the *Visuddhimagga*,[1] but it is said that his explanation was rejected in the Commentaries because it was only the Elder's personal view. The *Samantapāsādikā*,[2] however, relates a story showing that the Elder was recognised as an authority on the Vinaya. A monk of **Antarasamudda**

[1] p. 138. [2] ii. 307, also 478; iii. 588.

made a drinking bowl out of a coco-nut shell and, leaving it in the monastery, went to **Cetiyagiri.** Another monk, fancying the bowl, stole it and also went to Cetiyagiri, where he met the owner and was charged with theft. Unable to settle the dispute where they were, they went to the **Mahāvihāra.** There, by beating of drums, the monks were assembled near the **Mahācetiya,** and convicted the accused of theft, holding him guilty of a *pārājikā* offence. Godatta, being interviewed, pointed out that the value of the bowl was only a penny or two and that the Buddha had nowhere laid down that the theft of such an insignificant object could be held a pārājikā offence. His decision was greeted with applause, and when the report thereof reached the reigning king, **Bhātiya,** he decreed that, henceforth, in all their disputes, his subjects should abide by the decision of Godatta. *v.l.* **Godha, Godhaka, Goda, Gotta, Godanta.**

3. **Godatta Thera.**—An incumbent of **Kalyāṇi-mahāvihāra** in Ceylon. He would procure his food when the shadow of the sun was two inches long and eat it when it was but one inch. Even when no sun was to be seen, he knew the time exactly. The people discovered this by watching him and set their "clocks" by his movements.[1]

[1] MA. i. 100.

Godatta Sutta.—A conversation between **Godatta** and **Cittagahapati** at the **Ambāṭakavana** in **Macchikāsaṇḍa.** Godatta asks Citta about the different kinds of heart's release (*cetovimutti*)—*appamāṇācetovimutti, ākiñcaññācetovimutti, suññatocetovimutti* and *animittācetovimutti.* Citta explains them and points out how, according to one view, these states are diverse both in spirit and in letter and how, according to another, they are the same in spirit, though diverse in letter.[1]

[1] S. iv. 295 f.

Godāvarī.—See **Godhāvarī.**

1. **Godha, Godhaka.**—See **Godatta** (2).

2. **Godha Thera.**—A Sākiyan. A conversation between him and **Mahānāma** the Sākiyan is recorded in the **Godha Sutta**[1] (*q.v.*).

[1] S. v. 371.

1. **Godha Jātaka** (No. 138).—The Bodhisatta was once born as a lizard and paid homage to a good ascetic living near the ant-hill where he dwelt. The good ascetic left and was replaced by a wicked one,

to whom the Bodhisatta paid like homage. One day, the villagers brought a dish of lizard's flesh to the ascetic. Being attracted by its flavour, he planned to kill the Bodhisatta, that he might have more of the flesh. But the Bodhisatta discovered his intention just in time, and, making good his escape, denounced the hypocrite.

The story was told in reference to a wicked monk.[1]

[1] J. i. 480 f.

2. **Godha Jātaka** (No. 141).—The Bodhisatta was born once as an iguana, leader of many others. His son became intimate with a young chameleon, whom he used to clip and embrace. The Bodhisatta warned his son against this unnatural intimacy, but, finding his advice of no avail, and knowing that danger would come to them through the chameleon, he prepared a way of escape, should the need arise. The chameleon, growing tired of the friendship with the iguana, showed a trapper the home of the iguanas. The trapper made a fire round the hole and killed many of the iguanas as they tried to escape, but the Bodhisatta reached safety through the hole he had provided.

The story was told about a treacherous monk, identified with the young iguana.[1] For details see the **Mahilāmukha Jātaka.**

[1] J. i. 487 f.

3. **Godha Jātaka** (No. 325).—The story of the past is very similar to No. 1 above, except that there is only mention of one ascetic and he is a hypocrite. The young lizard threatened to expose the ascetic's hypocrisy and compelled him to leave the hermitage. The story was related in reference to a monk who was a cheat and a rogue.[1]

Cf. the **Kuhakabrāhmaṇa Vatthu** (DhA. iv. 154 f.).

[1] J. iii. 84 f.

4. **Godha Jātaka** (No. 333).—A prince and his wife, returning after a long journey, were greatly distressed by hunger, and some hunters, seeing them, gave them a roasted lizard. The wife carried it in her hand, hanging it from a creeper. Arriving at a lake, they sat down at the foot of a tree, and while his wife was away fetching water the prince ate the whole lizard. When his wife came back, he told her that the lizard had run away, leaving only the tail in his hand. Later, the prince became king, but his wife, though appointed queen consort, received no real honour. The Bodhisatta, who was the king's minister, wishing to see justice done to the queen, contrived that the king should be reminded of his ingratitude by allusion being made to the incident

of the roast lizard. The king thereupon realised his neglect of his dutiful wife, and conferred on her supreme power.

The story was told in reference to a couple who had been given a roast lizard, when returning from a journey undertaken to collect debts. The husband ate the whole lizard when his wife was away. She said nothing and drank some water to appease her hunger, but when they visited the Buddha, and he asked her if her husband were good and affectionate, she replied in the negative. The Buddha then told her the story of the past.[1]

[1] J. iii. 106 f.; *cf.* **Succaja Jātaka.**

Godha or Mahānāma Sutta.—**Mahānāma** visits **Godha** the Sākiyan at **Kapilavatthu** and asks him what qualities, possessed by a *sotāpanna,* will secure for him ultimate enlightenment. There are three, answers Godha—unwavering loyalty to the Buddha, the Dhamma and the Saṅgha. When Godha, in his turn, asks the same question of Mahānāma, the latter answers that there are four, and adds the possession of Āriyan virtues. The two seek the Buddha to ask his opinion. Mahānāma declares to the Buddha that he would accept the Buddha's decision in face of the opinion of everyone else in the universe. In answer to a question of the Buddha, Godha answers that of a person who holds such a view he has nothing but good to say, the conclusion evidently being that he accepts Mahānāma's opinion in preference to his own.[1]

[1] S. v. 371 f.

Godhagatta-Tissa Thera.—He it was who brought about a reconciliation between **Duṭṭhagāmaṇī** and his brother **Tissa.**[1] The Commentary[2] explains that he had a cutaneous complaint which made his skin scaly like that of a *godha* (iguana).

[1] Mhv. xxiv. 49-53. [2] MṬ. 469.

Godhapura.—See **Gonaddhapura.**

Godhā.—See **Kāligodhā.**

1. **Godhāvarī.** (*v.l.* **Godāvarī**).—A river in **Dakkhiṇāpatha,** of which it forms the southern boundary. During the Buddha's time, the **Aḷaka** (or **Mulaka**) king and the **Assaka** king (both **Andhakas**) had settlements on its northern bank, and **Bāvarī's** hermitage lay in the territory between their dominions.[1] The Commentary[2] says that near this

[1] SN. vs. 977. [2] SNA. ii. 581.

spot the Godhāvari divided into two branches, forming an island three leagues in extent, and the island was a dense forest, known as the **Kapiṭṭhavana.** Bāvarī's hermitage occupied a region of five leagues. In the past this region had been the abode of various sages, such as **Sarabhaṅga.**[3] According to the *Aṅguttara Commentary,*[4] Bāvarī's hermitage was on a bend of the river (*Godhāvarīvaṅke*). The Godhāvarī is one of the holiest rivers in Southern India, rising in Brahmagiri near the village of Triyaṅvaka and sanctified by its connection with Rāma and various saints.

[3] J. v. 132, 136; Mtu. i. 363.

[4] AA. i. 182.

2. **Godhāvarī.**—A canal, built by **Parakkamabāhu I.**, connecting the **Kāragaṅgā** and the **Parakkamasāgara.**[1]

[1] Cv. lxxix. 57.

Godhika Thera.—Son of a **Malla** chief in **Pāvā.** He went to **Kapilavatthu** with his friends, **Subāhu, Valliya** and **Uttiya,** and there he saw the Twin Miracle and joined the Order, later attaining arahantship. (But see below.) At **Rājagaha, Bimbisāra** built a hut for him but forgot the roof. The gods prevented rain from falling till this error was rectified.

Godhika and his friends had been companions in good deeds in the past, especially in the time of **Siddhattha Buddha** and of **Kassapa Buddha.** Eighty-seven kappas ago Godhika was seven times king, under the name of **Mahāsena.**[1]

According to the Saṃyutta[2] account, Godhika lived on the **Kāḷasilā** in **Isigilipassa.** There he made various vain attempts to win arahantship,[3] achieving only temporary emancipation of mind, from which he then fell away. Six times this happened and then he decided to commit suicide by cutting his throat. Māra saw this and reported it to the Buddha, but when the Buddha arrived it was too late and Godhika lay " supine on his couch with his shoulders twisted around." The Buddha, however, declared that Godhika had attained Nibbāna. The Commentary states that, after cutting his throat, Godhika so checked his final agony that he won arahantship.

[1] Thag. vs. 51; ThagA. i. 123 f.; Ap. i. 140.

[2] S. i. 120 f.; SA. i. 144 f.; also DhA. i. 431 f.

[3] The DhA. (i. 431 f.) adds that he suffered from a disease brought about by hard work.

Godhika Sutta.—Contains the story of **Godhika's** suicide, mentioned above.[1]

[1] S. i. 120 f.

Godhiya-Mahātissa Thera.—Teacher of **Dhammadinna,** of **Valaṅga-tissa-pabbata.**[1]

[1] MṬ. 606.

Godhī.—Probably the mother of **Devadatta** (*q.v.*), who is sometimes called **Godhiputta.**[1]

[1] Vin. ii. 189.

Gonaddha (Gonaddhapura).—One of the places passed by **Bāvarī's** disciples on their way from Bāvarī's hermitage to see the Buddha at **Rājagaha.** Between Gonaddha and their starting place lay **Patiṭṭhāna, Māhissati** and **Ujjeni,** and the next stopping place after Gonaddha was **Vedisā.**[1] The Commentary[2] says that Gonaddha was another name for **Godhapura.**

[1] Sn. vs. 1011. [2] SnA. ii. 583.

Gonaraṭṭha.—A district in North Ceylon, where **Māgha** and **Jayabāhu** set up fortifications.[1]

[1] Cv. lxxxiii. 17.

Gonisavihāra.—A vihāra in Ceylon where the young **Dhatusena** (*q.v.*) was brought up by his uncle, while he remained in disguise as a monk.[1] Geiger[2] thinks it was to the south of **Anurādhapura.**

[1] Cv. xxxviii. 21. [2] Cv. *Trs.* i. 30, n. 1.

Gonusuraṭṭha.—A district in North Ceylon, once occupied by **Māgha** and **Jayabāhu.**[1]

[1] Cv. lxxxiii. 17.

Gonnagāma.—A village in **Rohaṇa,** given by **Dappula** to the **Rāja-vihāra.**[1]

[1] Cv. xlv. 58.

Gonnaviṭṭhika.—A village in **Rohaṇa,** assigned by **Dappula** to the **Cittalapabbatavihāra.**[1]

[1] Cv. xlv. 59.

1. **Gopaka.**—A Thera. He once stayed at the **Kukkuṭārāma** in **Pāṭaliputta,** where he was given a set of robes.[1]

[1] Vin. i. 300.

2. **Gopaka.**—A king of ninety-one kappas ago; he offered *kaṇavera*-flowers to the Buddha. He was a previous birth of **Kaṇaverapupphiya.**[1]

[1] Ap. i. 182.

3. **Gopaka.**—A deva. He had been a Sākiyan maid of **Kapilavatthu** named **Gopikā (Gopī),** who led a virtuous life and, according to the Buddha's teaching, had cultivated the thoughts of a man. After death she was born as a *devaputta* in **Tāvatiṃsa.** There, when he saw monks reborn as **Gandhabbas,** he rebuked them for having neglected their opportunities. A series of verses attributed to Gopaka are given in the **Sakkapañha Sutta.**[1]

[1] D. ii. 271-5.

Gopaka Moggallāna.—A brahmin minister of **Ajātasattu,** in charge of some defence works in **Rājagaha.**[1] See **Gopaka Moggallāna Sutta.**

The *Theragāthā*[2] contains a stanza spoken by **Moggallāna Thera** in answer to a question by Gopaka Moggallāna. Gopaka asks Moggallāna how many of the Buddha's teachings he remembers. Eighty-four thousand, answers the latter and proceeds to explain.[3]

[1] M. iii. 7. [2] vs. 1024. [3] ThagA. ii. 130.

Gopaka Moggallāna Sutta.—Soon after the Buddha's death, **Ānanda,** on his way to **Rājagaha** for alms, visits the place where **Gopaka Moggallāna** was strengthening the city's defences. Moggallāna asks him if there were any monk in every way like the Buddha, and receives a negative answer. **Vassakāra** arrives and, on being told the topic of conversation, asks the same question and is told by Ānanda that the monks regard the Dhamma as their protector. It is true, however, that there are monks whom they hold in great esteem and reverence, and Ānanda enumerates the qualities which win for them such homage.[1]

[1] M. iii. 7 ff.

Gopaka Sivalī.—A resident of Ceylon. He built a cetiya in **Tālapiṭṭhikavihāra.** At the moment of his death, remembering this act, he was reborn in the deva-world.[1]

[1] VibhA. 156.

1. **Gopāla.**—King **Udena's** son. **Gopāla** was also the name of the father of Udena's queen consort, **Gopālamātādevī.**[1]

AA. i. 118.

2. **Gopāla.**—One of the yakkha chieftains, to be invoked by the Buddha's followers in time of need.[1]

[1] D. iii. 205.

3. **Gopāla.**—One of the four sons of the chaplain to King **Esukārī.** For their story see the **Hatthipāla Jātaka.** Gopāla is identified with **Moggallāna.**[1]

[1] J. iv. 491.

4. **Gopāla.**—A seṭṭhi, father of **Tapassu** and **Bhallika,** in the time of **Kassapa** Buddha.[1]

[1] ThagA. i. 48.

5. **Gopāla.**—A devaputta of **Tāvatiṃsa.** He was the teacher of **Uracchadamālā** and gave alms to the Buddha **Kassapa** and the monks; he heard the Dhamma but could get no special attainment. **Moggallāna** met him during a visit to Tāvatiṃsa and, in answer to the Elder's questions, Gopāla gave an account of himself. Moggallāna thereupon preached to him and he became a sotāpanna.[1]

[1] Vv. v. 14; VvA. 270 ff.

6. **Gopāla.**—A devaputta of **Tāvatiṃsa.** He had been a cowherd of **Rājagaha** and had once offered **Moggallāna** a meal of *kummāsa* (junket and rice). Immediately afterwards he was stung by a snake and died while watching the Elder eat the meal he had given him.[1]

[1] Vv. vii. 6; VvA. 308 f.

Gopālaka Sutta.—See **Cūla-Gopālaka** and **Mahā-Gopālaka Suttas.**

Gopālapabbata.—A hill near Pulatthipura, used as a landmark.[1]

[1] Cv. lxxviii. 65; for identification see Cv. *Trs.* i. 110, n. 1.

Gopālamātā.—Queen consort of **Udena.** She belonged to a poor merchant's family in **Telappanāḷi** and had long and beautiful hair, the envy of her friends. One day, **Mahā Kaccāna** and seven others visited the village, and she sold her hair for eight kahāpaṇas, that she might provide the visitors with a meal. It is said that she recovered her hair immediately on seeing Mahā Kaccāna. When the Elder reached **Ujjeni** that very day, by air, he related the incident to King Udena and the king, having sent messengers to fetch Gopālamātā, made her his chief consort. She gave birth to a son, whom she called **Gopāla,** after her own father, and thenceforth she herself was called Gopālamātā.[1]

[1] AA. i. 118; Mil. 291.

Gopī, Gopikā.—The Sākiyan maiden of **Kapilavatthu,** who was born later as **Gopaka-devaputta.** See **Gopaka** (3).

Gomagga.—A spot in **Siṃsapāvana** near **Āḷavī**. The Buddha once stayed there during the cold season and was visited by **Hatthaka Āḷavaka.**[1]

[1] A. i. 136.

Gomatakandarā.—A grotto some distance from **Veḷuvana** in **Rājagaha.** Monks coming to Rājagaha from afar were provided with lodging there, and **Dabba Mallaputta** was put in charge of these arrangements.[1]

[1] Vin. ii. 76; iii. 160.

Gomatī.—A channel built by **Parakkamabāhu I.,** branching eastwards from the **Mahāvālukagaṅgā.**[1]

[1] Cv. lxxix. 52.

Gomaya, or **Gomayapiṇḍī Sutta.**—Preached at **Jetavana.** A monk asks the Buddha whether there is any body or anything at all that is permanent and stable. The Buddha takes a pellet of cowdung in his hand and tells him that the personality in any one span of life (*attabhāva*) even as small as that pellet is unstable. The Buddha then tells the monk of the great luxuries he had enjoyed as king (**Mahā-Sudassana**) of **Kusāvatī,** and of how they all perished.[1]

This sutta was preached by **Mahinda** at the **Nandana** grove, on the sixth day after his arrival in Ceylon.[2]

[1] S. iii. 143 f. [2] Mhv. xv. 197.

Gomayagāma.—A village in **Rohaṇa.**[1]

[1] Cv. lxxv. 3.

Goyāniya.—A shortened form of **Aparagoyāna.**[1]

[1] J. iv. 278, 279; Ap. i. 18; ii. 348.

Goyogapilakkha.—A spot near Benares, visited by the Buddha on his begging rounds.[1] The Commentary[2] explains that it was near a fig tree (*pilakkha*) set up at the spot where cows were.

[1] A. i. 280. [2] AA. i. 460.

Gorimanda.—A rich man of **Mithilā.** He had no children and was ugly; when he spoke saliva flowed from his mouth, and two beautiful women, standing beside him, wiped his face with blue lilies and threw them away. When revellers had no money wherewith to buy flowers, they would stand outside Gorimanda's house and call out for him. When he leaned out of the window to ask what they wanted, his face had to be wiped with lilies and the lilies were then thrown away. The revellers picked them up, washed them, and wore them at their revels.[1]

[1] J. vi. 357 f.

Goḷakāḷa.—Husband of **Dīghatālā.** He obtained his wife after having worked seven years in a house. One day, when on his way with his wife to visit her parents, they came to a stream, and, while they were hesitating before crossing, a man named **Dīghapiṭṭhi** came along and offered to take them across, because, he said, he was well known to the denizens of the river. He took Dīghatālā first, with the sweetmeats intended for her relations, and persuaded her to come with him, leaving her husband. When Goḷakāḷa realised what had happened, he jumped into the stream in desperation, easily crossing it—because it was really very shallow—and claimed his wife. In the course of the quarrel between the two men they came to where **Mahosadha** held court, and he, having heard their respective stories, decided, with the approval of the assembled populace, in favour of Goḷakāḷa.

It is said Goḷakāḷa was so called because he was dwarfish, like a ball (*goḷa*), and black (*kāḷa*).[1]

[1] J. vi. 337, 338.

Goḷapānu.—A village given by King **Buddhadāsa** for the maintenance of the **Moraparivena.**[1]

[1] Cv. xxxvii. 173.

Goḷabāhatittha.—A ford over the **Mahāvālukagaṅgā.**[1]

[1] Cv. lxxii. 51.

Goḷahaḷā.—The soldiers of a district in South India.[1]

[1] Cv. lxxvi. 264, 259.

Govaḍḍhamāna.—A village in **Uttarāpatha,** in the dominion of King **Kaṃsa.** It was the residence of **Upasagara** and **Devagabbhā** and the birthplace of the **Andhakaveṇhudāsaputtā.**[1]

[1] J. iv. 80.

Govaraṭṭha.—A district in South India (the modern Goa). **Vimaladhammasūriya** once took refuge there.[1]

[1] Cv. xciv. 2.

Govinda.—The steward or treasurer of King **Disampati.** He had a son, **Jotipāla,** who succeeded him after his death and came to be known as **Mahā Govinda** (*q.v.*).[1] "Govinda" was evidently a title and not a name. See **Govindiya** below.

[1] D. ii. 230 f.; Mtu. iii. 204.

Govindamala.—A mountain in **Rohaṇa.** The Ādipāda **Bhuvanekabāhu** founded a town there and used it as a fortification for Rohaṇa when **Māgha's** forces overran the country.[1]

[1] Cv. lxxxi. 6; also Cv. *Trs.* ii. 135, n. 4.

Govindiya.—Evidently the title given to the High Treasurer. It occurs in the phrase *Govindiye abhisiñcissāmi*, when **Disampati** proposes to appoint **Jotipāla** to the rank of Treasurer.[1]

[1] D. ii. 232, *cp.* **Jāṇussoṇi.**

1. **Gosāla Thera.**—He came from a rich family of **Magadha** and made the acquaintance of **Soṇakuṭikaṇṇa.** When he heard that the latter had left the world, he too joined the Order and dwelt on the uplands near his native village. One day his mother gave him a meal of rice porridge with honey and sugar. After the meal, he made a great effort and won arahantship.

Ninety-one kappas ago he saw the rag robe of a Pacceka Buddha hanging from a tree trunk and offered flowers in homage.[1]

He is probably identical with **Paṃsukūlapūjaka** of the **Apadāna.**[2]

[1] Thag. vs. 23; ThagA. i. 79 f.

[2] Ap. ii. 434; but see also **Mahākāla.**

2. **Gosāla.**—See **Makkhali.**

Gosiṅga Sutta.—See **Cūlagosiṅga Sutta** and **Mahāgosiṅga Sutta.**

1. **Gosiṅgasālavanadāya.**—A forest tract near **Nādikā.** Once, when **Anuruddha, Nandiya** and **Kimbila** were living there, they were visited by the Buddha, who came from **Giñjakāvasatha.** The result of the visit was the preaching of the **Cūlagosiṅga Sutta** (*q.v.*).[1] On another occasion, when the Buddha was staying there with many eminent monks, among whom were **Sāriputta, Moggallāna** and others, their conversation led to the preaching of the **Mahāgosiṅga Sutta** (*q.v.*).[2]

[1] M. i. 205 f.

[2] *Ibid.*, 212 f.

2. **Gosiṅgasālavanadāya.**—A forest tract near **Vesāli.** When the Buddha was living in the **Kūṭāgārasāla,** in the **Mahavana,** he was visited

by many people and there was great disturbance. In order to find quiet and solitude, certain monks, among whom were **Cāla, Upacāla, Kakkaṭa, Kaḷimbha, Nikaṭa** and **Kaṭissaha,** retired into this forest.[1]

[1] A. v. 133.

Gosīsanikkhepa Thera.—An arahant. Ninety-four kappas ago he had spread *gosīsa* (sandalwood paste) outside a monastery. Seventy-five kappas ago he became a king, named **Suppatiṭṭhita.**[1]

[1] Ap. i. 245.

Gh.

Ghaṭa.—See **Ghata.**

Ghaṭa Sutta.—**Sāriputta** and **Moggallāna** are staying at the **Kalandakanivāpa** and, in the course of their conversation, it transpires that Moggallāna, exercising clairvoyance and clairaudience, had seen and heard the Buddha, then dwelling in **Jetavana.** The subject of his talk was consummate energy (*āraddhaviriya*). Sāriputta declares that, in comparison with Moggallāna, he himself is like a mound of gravel set up alongside the Himālaya. Moggallāna returns the compliment by saying that, beside Sāriputta, he is like a pinch of salt set up alongside a large jar of salt, and recalls the high praise bestowed on Sāriputta by the Buddha himself.[1]

[1] S. ii. 275 f.

Ghaṭāya.—A Sākiyan of **Kapilavatthu,** who built a monastery attached to the **Nigrodhārāma.** There the **Mahā Suññatā Sutta** was preached.[1]

[1] M. iii. 110; MA. ii. 907.

Ghaṭīkāra.—One of the great **Brahmā.** In the time of **Kassapa Buddha** he was a potter of **Vehaliṅga,** looking after his blind parents. He was a very pious and devoted follower of the Buddha, ministering to him better than anyone else, and the Buddha accepted his invitation in preference to that of the king of Benares. It is said that when the Buddha was in need of anything he would go to Ghaṭīkāra's house and take it, whether he were at home or not, so great was his confidence in Ghaṭīkāra's piety. Once, when Ghaṭīkāra was absent, the people, at the Buddha's suggestion, took away the thatch from his house to roof the hut of Tathāgata. For three months Ghaṭīkāra's house remained open to the sky, but no rain fell on it, so great was his faith.[1] According to the **Nalapāna Jātaka,**[2] no rain will ever fall on the site of Ghaṭīkāra's house as long as this kappa lasts.

The Bodhisatta, who at the time of Ghaṭīkāra was a young brahmin named **Jotipāla,** was the friend of Ghaṭīkāra but had no faith in the Buddha, and Ghaṭīkāra, having failed to persuade him to visit the Buddha, in the end took him by force. Jotipāla was converted and joined the Order, but Ghaṭikāra, as the only support of his parents, could not renounce the world. **Kikī,** king of Benares, having heard of his virtues from Kassapa Buddha, sent him five hundred cartloads of the choicest rice, etc., but Ghaṭīkāra returned the gifts, saying that he had plenty for himself.[3]

After death, Ghaṭīkāra was born as a Mahābrahmā in the **Avihā** Brahma-world, and an *anāgāmī.*[4] He provided the Buddha with the eight requisites of a monk when the Buddha, having left the world, decided to lead the life of a bhikkhu.[5] The begging bowl, then provided by him, vanished when the Buddha was given a bowl of milk rice by **Sujātā.**[6]

According to the *Saṃyutta Nikāya,*[7] Ghaṭīkāra visited the Buddha some time after the Enlightenment and the Buddha reminded him of their former friendship. Ghaṭīkāra, on that occasion, speaks of several others (besides Jotipāla) who had been his friends in Vehaliṅga—**Upaka, Phalagaṇḍa, Pukkusāti, Bhaddiya, Khaṇḍadeva, Bāhuraggi** and **Piṅgiya.** They had listened to the Buddha's teaching and, after death, were born in the Avihā-world, where he himself was. In this context the Buddha addresses him as **Bhaggava** (*q.v.*).

[1] Mil. 223 f. [2] J. i. 172.

[3] M. ii. 46 ff.; S. i. 35 f.; Bu. xxv. 41; SnA. i. 152.

[4] He was evidently already a *Sakadāgāmi* before his death (see DhA i. 380), but he did not wish his attainments to be known (AA. i. 44).

[5] J. i. 65; SnA. ii. 382; BuA. 236; VvA. 314.

[6] J. i. 69. [7] S. i. 35 f.; 60.

1. **Ghaṭīkāra Sutta.**—Preached during a tour in **Kosala.** The Buddha turned off the main road and, when he came to the spot which had once been **Vehaliṅga,** he smiled. Being asked by **Ānanda** the reason for his smile, the Buddha related to him and to the monks the story of **Ghaṭīkāra,** the potter of Vehaliṅga, as given above.[1] It is said[2] that the Buddha wished to make known to the monks the great piety of Ghaṭīkāra. The sutta was repeated at a shrine near **Todeyya,** which was being worshipped by the people without their knowing its significance. The Buddha related the sutta and explained that the shrine was the thūpa of **Kassapa** Buddha.[3]

[1] M. ii. 45 ff. [2] MA. ii. 717. [3] DhA. iii. 251.

2. **Ghaṭikāra Sutta.**—Relates the visit of **Ghaṭīkāra Mahā Brahmā** to the Buddha at **Jetavana** and the ensuing conversation.[1]

[1] S. i. 35 f., 60.

Ghaṭṭiyā.—One of the four wives of **Candakumāra.**[1]

[1] J. iv. 148.

1. **Ghata** (also called **Ghatakumāra**). The Bodhisatta, born as the king of Benares. One of his ministers misconducted himself in the royal harem and the king, catching him in the act, banished him. The minister took service with **Vaṅka,** king of **Sāvatthi,** and persuaded him to attack Benares. Ghata was captured and thrown into prison, where he entered into ecstatic meditation. But Vaṅka was seized by a burning sensation, and he ordered the release of Ghata and the restoration of his kingdom.[1] *v.l.* **Ghaṭa.**

[1] J. iii. 168 f.; *cf.* **Ekarāja.**

2. **Ghata** (also called **Ghatapaṇḍita**).—The Bodhisatta, born as the ninth of the ten **Andhakaveṇhudāsaputtā.** When a son of his brother, **Vāsudeva,** died, Vāsudeva lamented beyond all measure, and Ghata, wishing to cure him, feigned madness and went about **Dvāravatī** asking for the hare in the moon. When Vāsudeva heard of this from his courtier **Rohiṇeyya,** he hastened to Ghata and argued with him about the ridiculousness of his quest. The plan succeeded and Vāsudeva was cured of his grief.[1] *v.l.* **Ghaṭa.**

[1] J. iv. 81, 84 ff.; Pv. ii. 6; PvA. 93 f.

1. **Ghata Jātaka** (No. 355).—The story of **Ghatakumāra** (*q.v.*). It was related in reference to a minister of the Kosala king. He had been the king's favourite, but then, influenced by slanderers, the king cast him into prison, where he entered the First Path. When he was released he visited the Buddha, who told him the Jātaka story.

Ānanda is identified with King **Vaṅka** of the Jātaka.[1]

[1] J. iii. 168 ff.

2. **Ghata Jātaka** (No. 454).—The story of the **Andhakaveṇhudāsaputta**[1] (*q.v.*) and of the manner in which **Ghatapaṇḍita** (*q.v.*) assuaged the grief of his brother, **Vāsudeva.** The introductory story resembles that of the **Maṭṭhakuṇḍali Jātaka.**

Rohiṇeyya is identified with **Ānanda** and **Vāsudeva** with **Sāriputta.**[2]

[1] This **Jātaka** perhaps influenced the story of **Ummādacittā** found in the *Mahavamsa* (ix. 13); for its connection with the *Harivamsa* see ZDMG. 53, 25 ff.

[2] J. iv. 79 ff.

Ghatamaṇḍadāyaka Thera.—An arahant. Ninety-four kappas ago he saw the Pacceka Buddha, **Sucintita,** afflicted with a nervous disease and gave him ghee (*ghatamaṇḍa*). He became king of the gods fifty-four times and king of men fifty-one times.[1]

His verses are repeated elsewhere,[2] and are ascribed in the *Theragāthā Commentary* to **Ajina Thera.**[3]

[1] Ap. ii. 383 f. [2] *Ibid.*, 436. [3] ThagA. i. 250.

Ghatāsana.—Twenty kappas ago **Pupphathūpiya** (*q.v.*) became king thirty-eight times under this name.[1]

[1] Ap. i. 156.

Ghatāsana Jātaka (No. 133).—Once the Bodhisatta was king of the birds and lived with his subjects in a giant tree, whose branches spread over a lake. The Nāga king of the lake, **Caṇḍa,** enraged by the dropping of the birds' dung into the water, caused flames to dart up from the water to the tree, and the Bodhisatta, perceiving the danger, flew away with his flock.

The story was told to a monk whose hut was burnt by fire. The villagers undertook to build him another, but there was a delay of three months, during which the monk with no shelter could not proceed in his meditation. The Buddha chided him for not seeking another shelter.[1]

[1] J. i. 471 f.

Ghanasela.—A mountain in **Avanti** in the **Dakkhiṇāpatha,** where **Kāḷadevala** lived.[1]

[1] J. v. 133.

Ghanikā.—A class of spirits (cloud-gods ?).[1]

[1] Mil., p. 191.

Gharaṇī.—A woman, lay-disciple of the Buddha. She had attained the Third Fruit of the Path and when the Buddha was about to perform the Twin Miracle, she offered to perform a miracle herself—to transform the earth into water and dive about in it like a water-bird.[1]

[1] DhA. iii. 209. There was a Gharaṇī Stūpa near Suppāraka (Divy. 47).

Gharāvāsa-pañha.—The question asked by **Dhanañjaya** and answered by **Vidhura,** before he was taken away by **Puṇṇaka.** The question dealt with how a householder could so live as to get the best out of his life, both for this world and for the next.[1]

[1] J. iv. 286 f.

Ghoṭamukha.—A brahmin, probably of **Pāṭaliputta.** On coming to visit Benares, he saw **Udena** there in **Khemiyambavana** and had a conversation with him, recorded in the **Ghoṭamukha Sutta.** At the conclusion of the talk he declared himself converted and wished to offer to Udena the daily allowance of five hundred kahāpaṇas which he regularly received from the king of **Aṅga.** Udena suggested that the money might be utilised to build an assembly-hall for the Order at Pāṭaliputta. The suggestion was agreed to and the assembly-hall, when built, was called **Ghoṭamukhī.**[1]

The Commentary[2] adds that Ghoṭamukha held the view that one should seek self-glorification, even by the slaughter of one's parents, and that he was the only person born in heaven, in spite of having held that view. After his birth in heaven, having discovered the cause of his good fortune, he came to earth in disguise and, after revealing his identity to his only remaining sister, told her where his treasures were hidden and instructed her to spend some of the money on renovating an old refectory which the monks were trying to restore.

[1] M. ii. 157 ff. [2] MA. ii. 786 f.

Ghoṭamukha Sutta.—Records a conversation between **Udena** Thera and **Ghoṭamukha** at **Khemiyambavana,** after the Buddha's death. Ghoṭamukha maintains that there is a Recluse who might be called Righteous (*dhammiko paribbājo*). Does Udena know of him ? Udena describes to him the four types of individuals—those who torture themselves, those who torture others, those who torture both and those who torture neither, the last being those who live beyond appetites, consummate, unfevered and blissful. They want none of the things after which men hanker, but discarding them all go forth to homelessness. **Ghoṭamukha** admits that such are Righteous Recluses.[1]

[1] M. ii. 157 ff.

Ghoṭamukhī.—See **Ghoṭamukha.**

1. **Ghosa.**—The village in which **Buddhaghosa** was born.[1]

[1] Sās. 29.

2. **Ghosa, Ghosaka.**—A devaputta, **Kotūhalaka,** in a previous birth. Unable to make a living in his own country, he left it and came with his wife and child to a herdsman's house, where, having eaten too heartily after a long period of starvation, he died and was born as a dog in the same house, because he had envied a bitch which lived there. When the dog grew up, it used to accompany the herdsman on a visit to a Pacceka

Buddha, who had meals in his house. Sometimes, when the herdsman was unable to go himself, he would send the dog to summon the Pacceka Buddha. The road led through a forest and the dog would bark aloud to frighten away the wild beasts. One day, when the Pacceka Buddha went elsewhere, the dog died of a broken heart and was reborn in Tāvatiṃsa as the god Ghosa or Ghosaka. He was later reborn as **Ghosaka-seṭṭhi.**[1]

[1] DhA. i. 169 f.; AA. i. 227 f.; MA. i. 539 f.; DA. i. 317.

Ghosasaññaka Thera.—An arahant. Thirty-one kappas ago he was a hunter, and hearing the Buddha preach was delighted by the sound of his voice.[1] His verses are in the *Theragāthā Commentary* attributed to **Gahavaratīriya**[2] and to **Dhammika.**[3]

[1] Ap. ii. 451. [2] ThagA. i. 91. [3] *Ibid.*, p. 398.

Ghosaka-seṭṭhi (*v.l.* **Ghosita°**).—A seṭṭhi of **Kosambī.** Being born as the son of a courtesan, he is cast away on a refuse heap. A passer-by takes him home, but the Treasurer of Kosambī, knowing from an astrologer that the stars showed the birth of a very lucky boy, seeks him out and adopts him. A few days after, the Treasurer's wife bears him a son, and he therefore plans to kill Ghosaka with the help of a slave woman, **Kālī.** All his attempts having failed, he promises a potter one thousand pieces if he will kill the boy. Ghosita is sent to the potter with a message; on the way he meets his foster-brother, and gives him the message, promising to win for him a game of marbles. The foster-brother goes to the potter and is killed. The Treasurer then sends Ghosaka to the superintendent of his hundred villages with a letter ordering that he be killed. The letter is fastened to the boy's garment. On the way he stops for a meal at the house of a country-treasurer whose beautiful daughter falls in love with him. Discovering the letter, she substitutes another to the effect that Ghosaka should be married to her with great festivity and that a two-storeyed house should be built for them. The superintendent carries out these orders and the Treasurer falls ill on receiving the news. He is visited on his death-bed by Ghosaka and his wife, and while trying with his dying breath to say "I do not give him my wealth," by a slip of the tongue he says "I do." Ghosaka becomes a very pious man and is made the Treasurer of King **Udena.** Later he meets **Sāmavatī,** daughter of his friend **Bhaddavatiya,** adopts her as his daughter and, when the time comes, gives her in marriage to Udena.

In a past life Ghosaka had been **Kotūhalaka** of **Addilaraṭṭha,** but left there with his wife and child on account of great poverty. On the way he cast off the child on account of its being too heavy, but rescued it later in answer to his wife's importunities. It was as a result of that act that he was cast away in this birth. Later he was born as a dog and then as **Ghosakadevaputta**[1] (*q.v.*).

Ghosaka had two colleagues in Kosambī, **Kukkuṭa** and **Pavāriya.** For a number of years they entertained five hundred ascetics from Himavā, during the rainy season, until one year the ascetics, hearing from a tree-sprite, who had been one of **Anāthapiṇḍika's** labourers, of the arising of the Buddha, informed Ghosaka and his friends of their determination to see the Buddha at Sāvatthi. The ascetics went on ahead, followed by Ghosaka and the others, bearing all kinds of gifts. They all heard the Buddha preach, became sotāpannas, and invited the Buddha to Kosambī. On the invitation being accepted, they built residences for the Buddha and the monks at Kosambī, that built by Ghosaka being called **Ghositārāma.**[2]

Mitta[3] was the householder in charge of the refectory from which Ghosaka had food daily distributed to the needy, and **Sumana** was Ghosaka's gardener.[4]

Ghosaka is mentioned as an example of a man possessing *puññiddhi.* He could not have been killed even if stabbed in seven places.[5]

See also **Ghosita Sutta.**

[1] DhA. i. 169 ff.; PsA. 504 ff.
[2] DhA. i., 203 ff.; AA. i. 234 f.; MA. i. 539 f.; PsA. 414, etc.
[3] DhA. i. 189.
[4] *Ibid.*, 208.
[5] BuA. 24.

Ghosita.—See **Ghosaka** (2).

Ghosita Sutta.—**Ghosita-seṭṭhi** visits **Ānanda** at the **Ghositārāma** and questions him on the Buddha's teaching regarding diversity in elements (*dhātunānattaṃ*). Ānanda explains how the three kinds of feelings—pleasurable, painful and neutral—arise.[1]

[1] S. iv. 113 f.

Ghositārāma.—A monastery in **Kosambī,** built by **Ghosita** (**Ghosaka,** *q.v.*) for the use of the Buddha and the monks. The Buddha often stayed there during his visits to Kosambī and numerous incidents are mentioned in the books in connection with the monastery. It was because of a dispute between two monks of the Ghositārāma, one expert in the Vinaya and one in the Dhamma, that the first schism arose in the Order, driving the Buddha himself to seek quiet in the **Pārileyyaka** forest.[1] Even

[1] Vin. i. 337 f.; M. i. 320; DhA. i. 44 ff.; the Kosambī monks were evidently somewhat peculiar (see Vin. iv. 197).

at other times the Buddha seems to have sought solitude in this forest during his sojourns at the Ghositārāma.[2] It was here that the Buddha decreed the *ukkhepaniyakamma* for **Channa**, who refused to acknowledge and atone for his offences,[3] and here that he laid down the procedure in that connection to be followed. **Devadatta** was at Ghositārāma when he first conceived the idea of using **Ajātasattu** for his own ends.[4] The Buddha was there at the time and it is said that the devaputta **Kakudha** appeared before **Mahāmoggallāna** to warn him of Devadatta's schemes. The information was reported to the Buddha, who warned Moggallāna not to pass it on to others. The Buddha then proceeded to tell Moggallāna of the five kinds of teachers which appear in the world.[5] **Ānanda** is several times spoken of as staying in the Ghositārāma, sometimes with the Buddha, sometimes alone. On one such occasion he asks the Buddha why women should suffer from certain disabilities as compared with men.[6] And again,[7] what are the circumstances which conduce to ease (*phāsuvihāra*) in the case of monks ? Could it be said of a follower of the Buddha that his attainments depend on the length of time during which he has observed the Buddha's teachings ? Once Ānanda visits,[8] at her request, a nun living near by reported to be ill and enamoured of him. The mere sight of him causes her recovery, but he preaches to her on the impermanent nature of the body and makes her realise the truth.[9] Among those who visit Ānanda at the Ghositārāma and discuss various matters with him are mentioned **Ghosita** (S. iv. 113), **Uṇṇābha** (S. v. 271 f.), a householder, follower of the **Ājīvikas** (A. i. 217 f.), and **Bhaddaji** A. iii. 202). **Udāyi** twice visits him there, once to ask for a description of consciousness (S. iv. 169 f.), and again to quote a verse uttered by **Pañcālacaṇḍa** devaputta and to ask Ānanda to explain it (A. iv. 449). We find him also joining in a discussion which ensued on a sermon to the monks by Ānanda (A. iv. 426 f.). Udāyi preached to large audiences at the Ghositārāma and was evidently appreciated, for we find Ānanda reporting it to the Buddha and being told that it is no easy matter to preach to a large assembly with acceptance (A. iii, 184 f.). The **Yuganaddha Sutta** is a discourse preached by Ānanda to the monks at the Ghositārāma of his own accord (A. ii. 156 f.). Channa is several times mentioned in connection with incidents taking place at the Ghositārāma. Mention has already been made of the *ukkhepaniyakamma* declared on him. A devoted householder,[10] wishing to build

[2] See, *e.g.*, S. iii. 96 f.
[3] Vin. ii. 21 f.
[4] *Ibid.*, 184 f.
[5] A. iii. 122 f.
[6] A. ii. 82.
[7] *Ibid.*, iii. 132 f.
[8] *Ibid.*, iv. 37 f.
[9] *Ibid.*, ii. 144 f.
[10] Vin. iii. 155 f.; mention is made of other misdemeanours which he committed in order to have a fine vihāra (Vin. iv. 47).

a vihāra for him, asked him for a site. Channa started cutting down trees and other things, in order to clear the site, and this led to great uproar. On another occasion he is reported to the Buddha for refusing to listen to his colleagues and the Buddha chides him.[11] It was when Channa was at the Ghositārāma that Ānanda came, at the bidding of the monks, to inflict on him the *brahmadaṇḍa.*[12]

Among others mentioned as staying at the Ghositārāma are **Mūsila, Saviṭṭha, Nārada,** in the company of Ānanda (S. ii. 115), **Piṇḍola Bhāradvāja**—who converts Udena when the latter comes to see him (S. iv. 110 f.) and earns the Buddha's praises for his attainments (S. v. 224)—**Sāriputta** and **Upavāna** (S. v. 76), and **Bāhiya** and **Anuruddha** (A. ii. 239). Anuruddha is there at the time of the schism of the Kosambī monks but refuses to intervene. He indulges, instead, in his powers of clairvoyance and mention is made of a visit paid to him by the **Manāpakāyika-devas.** [13]

Dāsaka and a number of other monks were once staying in the Ghositārāma; on learning that **Khemaka** lies ill in the **Badarikārāma,** one *gāvuta* away, the others send Dāsaka several times to and fro to ask various questions of Khemaka. In the end, Khemaka himself comes to them to solve their difficulties.[14]

See also **Kosambiya Sutta, Jāliya Sutta, Sandaka Sutta, Upakkilesa Sutta** and **Sekha Sutta, Daḷhadhamma Jātaka, Kosambi Jātaka** and **Surāpāna Jātaka,** all preached while the Buddha was staying at the Ghositārāma.

Thirty thousand monks from the Ghositārāma, under the leadership of **Urudhammarakkhita,** were present at the foundation of the **Mahā Thūpa** at **Anurādhapura.**[15]

[11] Vin iii. 77, also iv. 35 f., 113. See also S. iii. 132 f.
[12] Vin. ii. 292.
[13] A. iv. 262 f.
[14] S. iii. 126 f.
[15] Mhv. xxix. 34.

C.

Cakka Peyyāla.—The seventh chapter of the *Sacca Saṃyutta.*[1] When the Buddha's teaching disappears, the *Saṃyutta Nikāya,* from the *Cakka Peyyāla* down to the *Oghataraṇa,* will be among the earliest portions to disappear.[2]

[1] S. v. 456-8.
[2] VibhA. 432

Cakka Vagga.—The fourth chapter of the *Catukka Nipāta* of the *Aṅguttara Nikāya.*[1]

[1] A. ii. 32-44.

Cakkadaha.—The home of the **Cakkaratana** (*q.v.*) of a **Cakkavatti.**[1]

[1] J. iv. 232.

Cakkana.—An *upāsaka* of Ceylon. While he was a boy, his mother once fell grievously ill and the doctors ordered her hare's flesh. Cakkana was sent by his brother into the field, where he caught a hare which, however, out of compassion he set free. His brother blamed him, but Cakkana cured his mother by a *saccakiriyā*, saying that, inasmuch as he had never deprived anything of life, by the power of that truth his mother should recover.[1] Cakkana's abstinence is one that was maintained "in spite of opportunity" (*sampattivirati*) and when he had not undertaken to observe any precept.[2]

[1] SA. ii. 112; the story is slightly different in MA. i. 165.
[2] DhsA., p. 103.

Cakkaratana.—One of the seven treasures of a **Cakkavatti** (*q.v.*). When a Cakkavatti is born into the world, the Cakkaratana appears before him from the **Cakkadaha,** travelling through the air.[1] The Cakkaratana is the Cakkavatti's chief symbol of office; on its appearance before him, he sprinkles it with water and asks it to travel to the various quarters of the world, winning them for him. This the Cakkaratana does, carrying with it through the air the Cakkavatti with his fourfold army. Wherever the Cakkaratana halts, all the chiefs of that quarter acclaim the Cakkavatti as their overlord and declare their allegiance to him. Having thus traversed the four quarters of the earth, it returns to the Cakkavatti's capital, and remains fixed as an ornament on the open terrace in front of his inner apartments.[2]

The Commentaries[3] contain lengthy descriptions of the Cakkaratana: it is shaped like a wheel, its nave is of sapphire, the centre of which shines like the orb of the moon, and round it is a band of silver. It has one thousand spokes, each ornamented with various decorations; its tyre is of bright coral; within every tenth spoke is a coral staff, hollow inside, which produces the sounds of the fivefold musical instruments when blown upon by the wind. On the staff is a white parasol, on either side of which are festoons of flowers. When the wheel moves, it appears like three wheels moving one within the other.

When a Cakkavatti dies or leaves the world, the Cakkaratana disappears from the sight of men for seven days; it gives warning of a Cakkavatti's impending death by slipping from its place some time before

[1] J. iv. 232, but see **Vepulla.** [2] D. ii. 173 f.; M. iii. 173 ff.
[3] *E.g.*, DA. ii. 617 ff.; MA. ii. 942 ff.

the event.[4] When his successor has lived righteously for seven days, it reappears.[5]

It is the most precious and the most honoured thing in the world.[6]

[4] D. iii. 59 f.; MA. ii. 885. [5] D. iii. 64. [6] UdA. 356.

Cakkavatti.—See article in the Appendix.

Cakkavatti Vagga.—The fifth chapter of the *Bojjhaṅga Saṃyutta.*[1]

[1] S. v. 98-102.

1. **Cakkavatti Sutta** (also called **Pacetana Sutta**). There was once a king called **Pacetana** who asked his wheelwright to make a pair of wheels for a battle which was to take place six months later. When but six days remained of this period, only one wheel had been made, but the other was finished within the stipulated time. Pacetana thought that both wheels were alike, but the wheelwright proved to him that the one he had made hurriedly was faulty in various ways, owing to the crookedness of its parts. The Buddha identified himself with the wheelwright and declared that one must be free from all crookedness in order not to fall away from the Dhamma and the Vinaya.[1]

[1] A. i. 109 f.

2. **Cakkavatti Sutta.**—With the appearance of a Cakkavatti there appear seven treasures in the world; similarly, with the appearance of a Tathāgata there appear the seven treasures of wisdom—mindfulness, searching of the Dhamma, energy, zest, tranquillity, concentration, equanimity.[1]

[1] S. v. 99.

Cakkavattisīhanāda Sutta.—Preached to the monks at **Mātulā.** It is a sermon on the necessity of living in accordance with the Dhamma, with the Dhamma as one's refuge. The Sutta contains the story of the Cakkavatti **Daḷhanemi** and his eldest son, and the manner in which a Cakkavatti administers the law, ruling by righteousness, over a people made virtuous by his instruction. But, later, there is a gradual corruption of morals, followed by the decay and destruction of human life with all its attendant comforts. This is followed by a gradual restoration of virtuousness, accompanied by the return of prosperity and longevity. The Sutta also records the prophecy of the coming of the Buddha **Metteyya.**[1] It is said[2] that at the end of this discourse twenty thousand monks became arahants and eighty-four thousand others realised the Truth.

[1] D. iii. 58 ff. [2] DA. iii. 858.

1. **Cakkavāka Jātaka** (No. 434).—A greedy crow, dissatisfied with the fish from the Ganges, flew to the Himālaya and there, seeing two golden-coloured geese (*cakkavāka*), asked what they fed on that they should be so beautiful. The geese replied that not food but character made people comely; the crow was too greedy ever to be beautiful.

The story was told in reference to a greedy monk who went from house to house in search of dainty food, frequenting the dwellings of the rich. The monk is identified with the crow.[1]

[1] J. iii. 520-4; *cf.* Kāka Jātaka.

2. **Cakkavāka Jātaka** (No. 451).—Similar to the above. The reason given for the colour of the crow was that his heart was full of fear and sin and that he had done evil in past lives. The greedy monk always went about looking for invitations.[1]

[1] J. iv. 70-2.

Cakkavāḷa.—The name given to a whole world-system, there being countless such systems. Each Cakkavāḷa is twelve hundred and three thousand, four hundred and fifty yojanas in extent and consists of the earth, two hundred and four thousand *nahutas* of yojanas in volume, surrounded by a region of water four hundred and eight thousand *nahutas* of yojanas in volume. This rests on air, the thickness of which is nine hundred and sixty thousand *nahutas* of yojanas. In the centre of the Cakkavāḷa is Mount **Sineru,** one hundred and sixty-eight yojanas in height, half of which is immersed in the ocean. Around Sineru are seven mountain ranges, **Yugandhara, Īsadhara, Karavīka, Sudassana, Nemindhara, Vinataka** and **Assakaṇṇa.** The mountains are inhabited by the Regent Gods (**Mahārājas**) and their followers, the **Yakkhas.** Within the Cakkavāḷa is the **Himavā** mountain, one hundred leagues high, with eighty-four thousand peaks. Surrounding the whole Cakkavāḷa is the **Cakkavāḷasilā.** Belonging to each Cakkavāḷa is a moon, forty-nine leagues in diameter, a sun of fifty leagues, the **Tāvatiṃsabhavana,** the **Asurabhavana,** the **Avīcimahāniraya** and the four *mahādīpas*—**Jambudīpa, Aparagoyāna, Pabbavideha** and **Uttarakuru,** each mahādīpa surrounded by five hundred minor *dīpas.* Between the Cakkavāḷas exist the **Lokantarikaniraya.**[1] In each Cakkavāḷa are four Regent Gods (**Cattāro Mahārājā**).[2] A sun can illuminate only one Cakkavāḷa; the rays of light from the Buddha's body can illuminate all the Cakkavāḷas.[3]

[1] SA. ii. 442 f.; DhsA. 297 f. [2] AA. i. 439. [3] *Ibid.*, 440.

1. **Cakkhu Sutta.**—Preached to **Rāhula** at **Jetavana.** The Buddha shows him how the eye and all the other senses are fleeting and lead to unhappiness. The well-taught disciple should, therefore, be repelled by the senses.[1]

[1] S. ii. 244, also 249.

2. **Cakkhu Sutta.**—The eye and all the other senses are impermanent. He who has faith in these doctrines, or has seen them moderately with his insight, is assured of perfection; he who has realised them is a stream-winner, bound for enlightenment.[1]

[1] S. ii. 225.

3. **Cakkhu Sutta.**—In the arising and the rebirth of the eye lies the origin of suffering, disease, decay and death; so also with the other senses. The cessation of these states is brought about by the cessation in the birth of the senses.[1]

[1] S. iii. 228.

4. **Cakkhu Sutta.**—The desire and lust arising in the eye and in the other senses mean corruption of the heart. By putting away such corruption can the truth be realised.[1]

[1] S. iii. 232.

Cakkhupāla Thera.—An arahant. He was the son of a landowner, **Mahā Suvanna** of **Sāvatthi,** and was called **Mahā-Pāla** (major Pāla), his brother being **Culla-Pāla.** The boys were called Pāla on account of being born through the favour of a tree deity. Mahā-Pāla heard the Buddha preach at **Jetavana** and entered the Order. After five years of novitiate he went with sixty others to a woodland spot to meditate. There he fell a victim to ophthalmia and was prescribed for by a doctor; but he neglected his eyes, devoting his whole time to the duties of recluseship. He became an arahant but lost the sight of his eyes, hence his name. Later, Cakkhupāla's colleagues returned to Sāvatthi and, at his own request, Cakkhupāla's brother sent his nephew **Pālita,** ordained as a monk, to fetch him. On the way through the forest, Pālita was attracted by the song of a woodcutter's wife and, bidding his uncle wait, went and sinned with her. When Cakkhupāla, by questioning the novice, learnt of this, he refused to be accompanied by him, even though he should die on the way. **Sakka's** throne was heated, and he led the Elder safely to Sāvatthi, where he was looked after by his brother to the end of his days.[1] It is said[2] that in a previous birth he had been a physician, and

[1] Thag. 95; ThagA. i. 195 f.

[2] DhA. i. 15 ff., where several details are given regarding Cakkhupāla which are not mentioned here.

because a woman, whose disease of the eye he had cured, tried to cheat him out of his promised reward, he gave her a drug which completely ruined her eyes.

Cakkhulola-Brahmadatta.—King of Benares. He was very fond of watching dancing and had three dancing halls where girls and women, of various ages, danced for his pleasure. One day he noticed a householder's wife who had come to watch the dance and longed to possess her. On realising the wickedness of his desire, he renounced the kingdom and became a Pacceka Buddha. His *Udānagāthā* is included in the **Khaggavisāṇa Sutta.**[1]

[1] SN. vs. 63; SNA. i. 115 f.; Ap. i., p. 11 (vs. 37); ApA. i. 160 f.

Caṅkama Sutta.—The five advantages of a *caṅkama* (cloister): it trains one to travel, encourages striving, it is healthy, it improves digestion and promotes concentration.[1]

[1] A. iii. 29.

Caṅkamadāyaka Thera.—An arahant. Eighteen kappas ago he made a magnificent cloistered walk for **Atthadassī** Buddha. For three kappas he was king of the gods and was three times Cakkavatti.[1]

[1] Ap. i. 99.

Caṇkī.—A *mahāsāla* brahmin, contemporary of the Buddha, reputed for his great learning and highly esteemed in brahmin gatherings—*e.g.*, at **Icchānaṅgala**[1] and at **Manasākaṭa.**[2] He is mentioned together with such eminent and wealthy brahmins as **Tārukkha, Pokkharasādi, Jāṇussoni** and **Todeyya.**[3] Caṅkī lived in the brahmin village of **Opasāda,** on a royal fief granted him by **Pasenadi.** When the Buddha came to Opasāda, Caṅki visited him, in spite of the protests of his friends and colleagues, and on this occasion was preached the **Caṅkī Sutta.**[4] We are not told that Caṅkī ever became a follower of the Buddha, though Buddhaghosa[5] says that he held the Buddha in great esteem.

[1] SN., p. 115.
[2] D. i. 235.
[3] *E.g.*, M. ii. 202.
[4] *Ibid.*, ii. 164 ff.
[5] MA. i. 394; this also appears from the introductory part of the Caṅkī Sutta.

Caṅkī Sutta.—**Caṅkī,** with a large company of brahmins, visits the Buddha at **Opasāda** and finds him conversing with some eminent and aged brahmins. A young brahmin, called **Kāpaṭhika,** frequently interrupts the conversation and is rebuked by the Buddha. Caṅkī tells the Buddha that the youth is a very clever scholar and obtains for him a chance of questioning the Buddha. The Buddha declares that the brahmin pretensions to possess the sole truth are vain, and goes on to explain how a man can come to have faith in truth, then gain enlightenment with regard to it, and finally attain the truth itself by means of practice and development. At the end of the discourse Kāpaṭhika declares himself a follower of the Buddha.[1]

[1] M. ii. 164 ff.

Caṅkolapupphiya Thera.—An arahant. In the time of **Vipassī** Buddha he was known as **Nārada-Kassapa** and offered the Buddha a *caṅkola*-flower. Seventy-four kappas ago he was a king named **Romasa.**[1]

[1] Ap. i. 215.

Caṅgoṭakiya Thera.—An arahant. Ninety-four kappas ago he lived near the sea, and seeing **Siddhattha** Buddha, gave him a bouquet of flowers.[1]

[1] Ap. i. 235.

1. **Caṇḍa.**—A headman (*gāmaṇi*) of **Sāvatthi.** He came to see the Buddha at **Jetavana** and asked him why some people earned the reputation of being wrathful and others of being kindly. The Buddha explained that the one man gives way to passion, resentment and illusion; therefore, others harass him; he shows vexation and comes to be called wrathful. The other shows opposite qualities and is called kindly (*sūrata*).[1] The Commentary says[2] that the name Caṇḍa was given to the *gāmaṇi* by the Elders who compiled the texts.

[1] S. iv. 305. [2] SA. iii. 99.

2. **Caṇḍa.**—See **Pañcālacaṇḍa.**

Caṇḍa Sutta.—Describes the visits of the gāmani **Caṇḍa** to the Buddha. See **Caṇḍa** (1).

Caṇḍakālī.—A nun, well known for her quarrelsome propensities. She was a friend of **Thullanandā,** during whose absence the other nuns once expelled Caṇḍakālī from their midst. This act was greatly resented by Thullanandā and Caṇḍakālī was readmitted.[1] She is several times mentioned as starting quarrels with other nuns, and when they disagreed with her she threatened to denounce the Buddha and the nuns and to join some other Order, declaring that there were other Orders which were, in every way, as good as the Buddha's. Once, when some of her colleagues asked her if she had seen something lost by them, she cursed

[1] Vin. iv. 230.

them roundly and started to weep and create a scene.[2] She was charged with frequenting gatherings of laymen,[3] and it is said[4] that she joined Thullanandā in various vicious practices. She once applied for permission to ordain nuns (*vuṭṭhāpanasammuti*) but was refused, and on discovering that other nuns had obtained this permission she became violently abusive.[5]

[2] Vin. iv. 276, 277.
[3] *Ibid.*, 293, 309.
[4] *Ibid.*, 333.
[5] *Ibid.*, 331.

Caṇḍagāmaṇi.—See **Gāmaṇicaṇḍa.**

Caṇḍa-ppajjota.—King of **Avanti** in the time of the Buddha. His name was **Pajjota,** the sobriquet being added on account of his violent temper. Once, when ill with jaundice, he asked **Bimbisāra** to lend him the services of **Jīvaka,** as no other doctor could cure him. The cure for the malady was ghee, for which Pajjota had a strong aversion. Jīvaka, therefore, decided to administer it disguised in an astringent decoction, and obtained the king's permission to use any of the royal animals or to leave the city at any time he wished, on the plea that he must go in search of various medicines. When all preparations were complete, Jīvaka gave the king the medicine and escaped on **Bhaddavatikā,**[1] the king's she-elephant, before the truth was discovered. The king sent **Kāka** in pursuit, but Jīvaka gave Kāka a purgative and so delayed his return until the medicine had taken effect on the king. Later, when Pajjota was cured, he sent Jīvaka many costly presents, including a garment of Siveyyaka cloth.[2]

King **Udena** was Pajjota's rival in splendour, and Pajjota decided to take him captive by taking advantage of his fondness for elephants. The plan succeeded and Udena was taken prisoner, but in the end Udena eloped with Pajjota's daughter, **Vāsuladattā,** and made her his queen consort.[3] Besides the she-elephant and the slave Kāka, already mentioned, Pajjota had three other fleet-footed conveyances: two mares, **Celakaṇṭhī** and **Muñjakesī,** both capable of travelling one hundred leagues a day, and an elephant, **Nālāgiri,** able to go one hundred and twenty leagues a day. In a past birth Pajjota had been the servitor of a certain chief. One day, when the chief was returning from the bath, he saw a Pacceka Buddha leaving the city, where he had begged for alms without receiving anything. The chief hurried home and, finding that his meal was ready, sent it to the Pacceka Buddha by the hand of his fleet-footed servant. The servant travelled with all possible haste and, having given the meal to the Pacceka Buddha, expressed certain wishes,

[1] The elephant could travel fifty yojanas in one day, and Kāka, sixty.
[2] Vin. i. 276 ff.; AA. i. 216.
[3] For details see *s.v.* **Vāsuladattā.**

as the result of which in this birth he gained possession of the five conveyances. He had authority equal to the power of the sun's rays.[4] His last wish was that he should partake of the Truth realised by the Pacceka Buddha.[5]

Mahā Kaccāna was the son of Pajjota's chaplain and later succeeded to his father's post. When the king heard of the Buddha's appearance in the world, he sent Kaccāna with seven others to the Buddha, to bring him to Ujjeni. But the Buddha sent Kaccāna and his companions, now become arahants, to preach to the king and establish the Sāsana in Avanti. The mission was successful. The *Theragāthā* contains stanzas uttered by the Thera in admonition to the king. It is said that the king had faith in the brahmins and held sacrifices involving the slaughter of animals; he was wicked in his deeds. One night he had a dream which frightened him and went to the Thera to have it explained. The Thera told him of the necessity for leading a virtuous life. We are told that from that day the king abandoned his evil ways and lived righteously.[6]

According to the Dulva,[7] Pajjota was the son of Anantanemi and was born on the same day as the Buddha. He was called Pajjota (Pradyota), because at the time of his birth the world was illumined as if by a lamp. He became king of Ujjeni at the time of the Buddha's Enlightenment.[8] He had a minister called Bharata, a clever mechanic.[9]

It would appear from the *Samantapāsādikā*[10] that Pajjota was born as the result of an ascetic, or some other holy person, having touched the navel of his mother.

Pajjota was the friend of Bimbisāra, and when the latter was put to death by **Ajātasattu,** Pajjota seems to have made preparations to wage war on Ajātasattu. The defences of **Rājagaha** were strengthened to meet the threatened attack, but nothing further happened.[11]

The **Sarabhaṅga Jātaka**[12] mentions a king Caṇḍapajjota, in whose dominion was **Lambacūlaka,** where lived the ascetic **Sālissara.** This either refers to another king of the same name or, more probably, it is an attempt to identify Lambacūlaka with some place in the country over which Pajjota ruled in the time of the Buddha.

[4] This may be another explanation of the nickname Caṇḍa.

[5] DhA. i. 196 ff.

[6] Thag. vs. 496-501; ThagA. i. 483 ff.; AA. i. 116 f.

[7] Rockhill, *op. cit.*, 17.

[8] *Ibid.*, 32, n. 1.

[9] *Ibid.*, 70, n. 1.

[10] Sp. i. 214.

[11] M. iii. 7.

[12] J. v. 133.

Caṇḍalakappa.—A locality in **Kosala;** it was the residence of **Dhānañjānī** and of **Saṅgārava.** The Buddha once paid a visit there and stayed in the **Todeyya-ambavana.** Saṅgārava went to see him, and on that occasion was preached the **Saṅgārava Sutta.**[1]

[1] M. ii. 209 f.

Caṇḍavajji.—The son of a minister of **Pāṭaliputta** and friend of **Siggava.** The friends entered the Order under **Soṇaka** and became very accomplished. Later, Caṇḍavajji taught **Moggaliputta-Tissa** the Sutta- and the Abhidhamma-Piṭakas.[1]

[1] Mhv. v. 99, 121, 129, 150; Dpv. iv. 46; v. 58, 70, 86; Sp. i. 36, 40, 235.

Caṇḍāla Sutta.—He who is without faith, without morals, is a diviner by curious ceremonies, believes in luck and not deeds, who seeks outside the Order for persons worthy of gifts—such a man is a *caṇḍāla* among laymen. The person possessing the opposite qualities is like a lotus.[1]

[1] A. iii. 206.

Caṇḍālatissa-mahābhaya.—According to the *Aṅguttara Commentary,*[1] there was once a period of great disaster in Ceylon, known as the Caṇḍāla-tissabhaya. There was no food to be had, and **Sakka** provided the monks with a raft on which to cross the sea. Sixty monks, however, remained in Ceylon, guarding the scriptures. Twelve years later, when the danger was past, the monks who had left the land returned and dwelt in the **Maṇḍalārāma** in **Kallagāma (Kālakagāma** ?). There the two parties of monks met and, on comparing their records of the scriptures, these were found not to differ by so much as a syllable or even a single letter.

Comparison of this story with the account given elsewhere[2] of the **Brāhmaṇatissacorabhaya** strongly suggests that both refer to the same account. For details see *s.v.* **Brāhmaṇatissa.**

[1] AA. i. 52. [2] *E.g.,* VibhA. 445 ff.

Caṇḍāsoka. The name given to **Asoka,** because he so cruelly killed his brothers. The name was later changed into **Dhammāsoka.**[1]

[1] Mhv. v. 189.

1. **Caṇḍī.**—One of the chief women supporters of **Nārada** Buddha.[1]

[1] Bu. x. 25.

2. **Caṇḍī.**—A name given to the goddess **Kālakaṇṇī,** daughter of **Virpakkha.** She was so called because of her temper.[1]

[1] J. iii. 259.

3. **Caṇḍī.**—See **Pañcālacaṇḍī.**

Caṇḍīdvāra.—One of the gates erected in **Pulatthipura** by **Parakkamabāhu I.** It was brightly painted.[1] Caṇḍī is one of the names of Durgā, Siva's wife.

[1] Cv. lxxiii. 161; lxxix. 45.

Caṇḍoraṇa.—A mountain in the Himālaya region. The Bodhisatta, as an elephant, once lived there looking after his mother.[1]

[1] J. iv. 90, 93.

Catassa Sutta.—There are four elements—earth, water, heat, air.[1]

[1] S. ii. 169.

Catukuṇḍika-niraya.—A description of the sufferings undergone by a child while in its mother's womb. The fœtus has to lie bent in four (*catukuṇḍena*), hence the name.[1]

[1] J. iii. 243 f.

Catucakka Sutta.—A deva asks how there can be escape from the body. By the destruction of craving, answers the Buddha.[1] The body is here spoken of as a "four-wheeled thing." The Commentary[2] explains that it refers to the four types of deportment—standing, sitting, lying, going.

[1] S. i. 16. [2] SA. i. 42.

Catudvāra Jātaka (No. 439).—Contains the story of **Mittavindaka** (*q.v.*). The Jātaka probably derives its name from the fact that the **Ussadaniraya,** where Mittavindaka was destined to suffer, looked like a city with four gates, surrounded by a wall. For the introductory story see the **Gijjha Jātaka.** The story is sometimes called the **Mahā Mittavindaka Jātaka.**[1]

[1] *E.g.*, J. i. 363; iii. 206.

Catunikāyika-Tissa.—A monk of Ceylon. He lived in the **Kolitavihāra,** while his elder brother, **Dattābhaya,** lived in the **Potaliyavihāra.** Once Tissa fell ill and, sending for his brother, asked for a brief formula for meditation. Dattābhaya recommended meditation on *kabaliṅkāhāra* and Tissa soon became an arahant.[1] His teacher was Mahātipiṭakatthera.[2]

[1] AA. i. 243. [2] Sp. iii. 695.

Catunikāyika-Bhaṇḍika Thera.—Evidently a well-known commentator. He is quoted as an authority in the *Saṃyutta Commentary.*[1]

[1] SA. i. 17.

1. **Catuparivaṭṭa.**—Another name for the **Bahudhātuka Sutta.**[1]

[1] M. iii. 67.

2. **Catuparivaṭṭa.**—One of the suttas not included in the Three Recensions.[1]

[1] Sp. iv. 742.

Catuposathika Jātaka.—This is given as the title of the four hundred and forty-first Jātaka and it is there stated that it will be described in the **Puṇṇaka Jātaka.**[1]

No such separate Jātaka exists and it is, probably, another name for the **Vidhurapaṇḍita Jātaka,** which, in its present form, seems to be a conglomeration of various legends which were once separate stories, each with its own title. The Catuposathika Jātaka was evidently one such story, which was later included in the Vidhura Jātaka, as its first section, and came to be known as the **Catuposathikakhaṇḍa** (see below) of that Jātaka. The first stanza of the Catuposathika Jātaka is quoted in the Catuposathika-khaṇḍa.[2]

[1] J. iv. 14. [2] J. vi. 257.

Catuposathika-khaṇḍa.—The first section of the **Vidhurapaṇḍita Jātaka.** It relates how **Sakka,** the **Nāga** king, the **Garuḷa** king, and **Dhanañjaya Koravya,** practised various virtues and asked **Vidhura** to judge as to their respective goodness.[1]

[1] J. vi. 262.

Catubhānavāra.—A compilation of twenty-seven extracts from the five *Nikāyas,* chiefly from the *Khuddaka Pāṭha.* It also includes several suttas and all the well-known **Parittas** (*q.v.*). The date of compilation and the author are not known. There is a commentary to the book called the **Sārattha-Samuccaya,** written by a pupil of **Ānanda Vanaratana** Thera, and a Sinhalese paraphrase of the eighteenth century, written by **Saranaṅkara Saṅgharāja.**[1]

[1] See Introd. to *Sārattha-Samuccaya* (H.B.S.); also Gv. 65, 75.

Catumaṭṭa Jātaka (No. 187).—Two geese from **Cittakūṭa** once used a certain tree as a perch, whenever they approached it, and became friendly with the spirit of the tree, who was the Bodhisatta. They talked together about religion until a jackal came and interrupted them. Then the geese flew away and did not return.

The story was told of an old monk who interrupted a conversation between **Sāriputta** and **Moggallāna.** The monk was the jackal.[1]

[1] J. ii. 106 f.

Caturakkha.—One of the dogs whom the goat **Meḷamātā** proposed to take with her on her visit to the jackal **Pūtimaṃsa.**[1] For details see the **Pūtimaṃsa Jātaka.** In the Ṛgveda, Caturakṣa is mentioned as one of Yama's dogs.[2]

[1] J. iii. 535. [2] Jātaka transl. iii. 318, n. 1.

Caturārakkhā.—The *Gandhavaṃsa*[1] mentions a commentary written on this work.

[1] pp. 65, 75.

Catusāmaṇera-vatthu.—A compilation by **Ñāṇābhivaṃsa Saṅgharāja.**[1]

[1] Bode, *op. cit.*, 78. For the story see DhA. iv. 176 f.

Catussālā.—A quadrangular hall, forming a part of the **Mahāvihāra** and serving as a refectory for the monks. It was erected on one of the spots where the earth trembled when sprinkled with flowers by **Mahinda.** Mahinda declared that in the time of the three previous Buddhas gifts, brought from all parts of the Island, were collected there and offered to the Buddhas and their followers.[1] It is not known who built the hall, but it was restored by **Vasabha.**[2] The *Mahāvaṃsa-Tikā* says[3] that earth from under the lintel of the Catussālā was used to make the vessels in which were placed the utensils employed in the coronation ceremony of the kings of Ceylon.

[1] Mhv. xv. 47 ff. [2] *Ibid.*, xxxv. 88. [3] p. 307.

Cattāro Mahārājāno.—See **Cātummahārājikā.**

1. **Canda.**—A king, one of the chief lay supporters of **Koṇḍañña** Buddha.[1]

[1] BuA. 114.

2. **Canda.**—Chief lay supporter of **Sikhī** Buddha.[1]

[1] Bu. xxi. 122; but BuA. (204) calls him **Nanda.**

3. **Canda.**—One of the palaces occupied by **Sumaṅgala** Buddha in his last lay life.[1]

[1] Bu. v. 22.

4. **Canda.**—A māṇava, son of a rich brahmin, **Sucindara.** Canda and his friend, **Subhadda,** became arahants at the first assembly of **Koṇḍañña** Buddha.[1]

[1] BuA. 110 f.

5. **Canda.**—The moon; generally spoken of as a deva. See **Candimā.**

6. **Canda.**—The Bodhisatta, born as a *kinnara.* For details see the **Canda-kinnara Jātaka.**

7. **Canda.**—A mountain in Himavā, where lived the kinnara, **Canda,** with his wife.[1] It is also called **Candaka**[2] and **Candapassa.**[3]

[1] J. iv. 283, 288. [2] J. v. 162. [3] *Ibid.*. 38.

8. **Canda.**—A brahmin, father of **Vidhurapaṇḍita.**[1]

[1] J. vi. 262.

9. **Canda.**—One of the palaces occupied by **Sumana** Buddha in his last lay life.[1]

[1] Bu. xxiv. 22.

10. **Canda.**—Younger brother of **Sāriputta** and a member of the Order.[1]

[1] DhA. ii. 188.

11. **Canda.**—Son of the brahmin **Paṇḍula.** He later became the chaplain of **Paṇḍukābhaya.**[1]

[1] Mhv. x. 25, 79.

12. **Canda.**—See **Candakumāra.**

Canda or **Candima Sutta.**—Just as the moon is brighter far than the stars, so is earnestness the best of profitable conditions.[1]

[1] S. v. 44.

1. **Candaka.**—Another name for **Canda (Candakumāra).**

2. **Candaka.**—The palace of King **Sivi.**[1]

[1] J. iv. 411.

3. **Candaka.**—The palace of **Aṅgati,** king of **Videha**[1] *v.l.* **Canda.**[2]

[1] J. vi. 229, 230, 231. [2] *Ibid.*, 242.

4. **Candaka.**—One of the palaces to be occupied by the future Buddha **Metteyya.**[1]

[1] Anāgatavaṃsa, vs. 46.

Candakinnara Jātaka (No. 485).—Once the Bodhisatta, born as a kinnara named **Canda,** lived with his mate **Candā** in the **Canda** mountain in Himavā. One day, while they were disporting themselves near a little stream, singing and dancing, the king of Benares, who had gone hunting, saw Candā and fell in love with her. So he shot Canda with an arrow, and when Candā lamented aloud at the sight of her dead husband, the king revealed himself and offered her his love and his kingdom. Candā scorned the offer and protested to the gods that they should have allowed harm to befall her husband. **Sakka's** throne was heated by her such great loyalty and, coming in the guise of a brahmin, he restored to Canda his life.

The king was **Anuruddha** and Candā was **Rāhulamātā.** The story was related by the Buddha when he visited his father's palace at **Kapilavatthu** and heard from **Suddhodana** how devotedly Rāhulamātā had continued to love the Buddha. He said it was not the first time that she had shown her undying affection.[1]

[1] J. iv. 282 ff.; DhA. i. 97.

1. **Candakumāra.**—The son and viceroy of **Ekarāja,** king of **Pupphavatī** (Benares). He was the Bodhisatta. For his story see the **Khaṇḍahāla Jātaka.**[1] It is also given in the *Cariyā Piṭaka*[2] as the **Candakumāra-cariyā.** Canda is sometimes referred to as **Candaka**[3] and sometimes as **Candiya.**[4]

[1] J. vi. 131 ff.
[2] p. 77.
[3] Cyp., p. 144.
[4] *Ibid.*, 137, 152, 154

2. **Candakumāra.**—Son of **Brahmadatta,** king of Benares, and brother of **Mahiṃsaka** and **Suriyakumāra.** He is identified with **Sāriputta.** For details see the **Devadhamma Jātaka.**[1]

[1] J. i. 127 ff.; DhA. iii. 73 ff.

Candakumara Cariyā.—See **Candakumāra** (1).

Candakumāra Jātaka.—Another name for the **Khaṇḍahāla Jātaka.**

Candagabbha.—One of the seven mountain ranges which must be crossed on the way to **Gandhamādana.**[1]

[1] SNA. i. 66.

Candagiri.—A vihāra in Ceylon built by **Vijayabāhu I.**[1] Geiger[2] identifies it with the Sandagiri Thūpa in the **Tissamahārāma.**

[1] Cv. lx. 61.
[2] Cv. *Trs.* i. 220, n. 2.

1. **Candagutta.**—King of **Jambudīpa.** He belonged to the **Moriya** dynasty and gained the throne through the scheming of **Cāṇakka,** who slew the rightful king **Dhanananda** and his heir **Pabbata.**[1] Candagutta reigned twenty-four years and was succeeded by his son **Bindusāra.** His grandson was **Asoka.**[2] Candagutta's senior contemporary in Ceylon was **Paṇḍukābhaya,** who died in the fourteenth year of Candagutta's reign.[3] The *Milinda*[4] mentions a soldier **Bhaddasāla,** in the service of the Nanda royal family, who waged war against Candagutta. In this war there were eighty " Corpse Dances " in which dead bodies danced. The *Theragāthā Commentary*[5] states that the father of the Thera **Tekicchakāri** incurred thed ispleasure of Candagutta, who, at the instigation of Cāṇakka, cast him into prison.

[1] The Mahāvamsaṭīkā gives details of how Cāṇakka contrived to make Candagutta king (pp. 181 ff.).
[2] Mhv. v. 16 ff.
[3] Dpv. vi. 15; Sp. i. 72; see also Dpv. v. 69, 73, 81; both the Dpv. and the Sp. talk of Pakuṇḍakābhaya (*sic*).
[4] p. 292; see also *Kathāsaritsāgara* i. 30.
[5] i., p. 440.

2. **Candagutta Thera.**—Saddhivihārika of **Mahā Kassapa** Thera. His colleague was **Suriyagutta.**[1]

[1] SA. iii. 125.

3. **Candagutta.**—One of the eight khattiyas sent by **Asoka** to accompany the Bodhi-tree to Ceylon. He took a prominent part in the celebrations when the Tree left **Pāṭaliputta,**[1] and later, on his arrival in Ceylon, was appointed by **Davānampiyatissa** to beat the golden drum at the Bodhi-tree ceremonies. He was given the office of **Malayarāja** and the **Vīrabāhujanapada** was bestowed on him for his maintenance.[2]

[1] Mbv. 152. [2] *Ibid.*, 165.

4. **Candagutta.**—An arahant Thera who came from **Vanavāsa** with 80,000 others for the foundation of the **Mahā Thūpa** in **Anurādhapura.**[1]

[1] Mhv. xxix. 42; Dpv. xix. 8.

Candatitta.—A king of twenty kappas ago, a previous birth of **Tamālapupphiya.**[1]

[1] Ap. i. 197.

Candadeva.—The third of the **Andhakaveṇhudāsaputtā.**[1]

[1] J. iv. 81.

Candadevī. See **Candā.**

Candadhara.—Name of the god **Siva.**[1]

[1] Cv. lxxiv. 193.

1. **Candana.**—A deva, vassal of the Four Regent Gods.[1] He is mentioned as one of the chief Yakkhas to be invoked by followers of the Buddha in case of need.[2] He once visited **Lomasakaṅgiya** at the **Nigrodhārāma,** questioned him regarding the True Saint, and recited to him stanzas learnt when the Buddha preached the **Bhaddekaratta Sutta** in **Tāvatiṃsa**[3] (but see below). The *Saṃyutta Nikāya*[4] records a conversation between Candana and the Buddha and a visit paid by Candana to **Mahā Moggallāna.**[5] Buddhaghosa[6] says he was an *upāsaka* in the time of **Kassapa** Buddha and offered the four requisites to the Buddha and the monks, as a result of which he became a deva. It is elsewhere stated[7] that in Kassapa's time Candana and Lomasakaṅgiya were friends and that both became monks. When Kassapa preached the Bhaddekaratta Sutta, Candana asked Lomasakaṅgiya to explain it; this he was unable to do, and so made a wish that he should be able to explain it in a future birth, Candana wishing that he should then ask the questions again. Both wishes were fulfilled. For details see **Lomasakaṅgiya** (2).

[1] D. ii. 258. [2] D. iii. 204.
[3] M. iii. 199 f.
[4] S. i. 53.
[5] S. iv. 280.
[6] MA. ii. 951.
[7] ThagA. i. 84 f. In this version not Candana, but Lomasakaṅgiya, expounds the Sutta; in M. iii. 199 f. it is Candana.

2. **Candana Thera.**—He belonged to a rich family in **Sāvatthi,** and having heard the Buddha preach, became a sotāpanna. When a son was born to him he joined the Order and took to meditating in the forest. Later he dwelt in a charnel-field near Sāvatthi. There he was visited by his wife and child who hoped to win him back, but, seeing them from afar, he made a special effort and became an arahant, preaching to his wife as she approached.[1]

Thirty-one kappas ago he was a tree-sprite, and having seen the Pacceka Buddha **Sudassana,** gave him a *kuṭaja*-flower. He is probably identical with **Kuṭajapupphiya Thera** of the *Apadāna.*[2]

[1] Thag. vs. 299-302; ThagA. i. 395 f.
[2] ii. 451; the same verses are also ascribed to **Hārita.**

3. **Candana.**—A monk of ninety-one kappas ago to whom **Upāhanadāyaka** made a gift of a pair of sandals.[1]

[1] Ap. i. 228.

1. **Candana Sutta.**—The devaputta **Candana** visits the Buddha at **Jetavana** and asks him how one can cross the flood (*ogha*) and not be drowned. By constant effort and destruction of craving, says the Buddha.[1]

[1] S. i. 53.

2. **Candana Sutta.**—**Candana** visits **Mahā Moggallāna** and asks him why some beings are born in heaven.[1]

[1] S. iv. 280.

Candanagāma.—A village in **Rohaṇa.** The nobles of the village took part in the festival of the arrival of the Bodhi-tree in Ceylon, and in the village one of the eight Bodhi-saplings was planted.[1]

[1] Mhv. xix. 54, 62; Sp. i. 100; Mbv. 161.

Candanaṅgalika.—A lay-disciple of the Buddha in **Sāvatthi.** He was present when five rājās, including **Pasenadi,** visited the Buddha and asked him which was the highest sensual pleasure. When the Buddha had answered their question, Candanaṅgalika obtained his permission and uttered a verse in his praise. The rājās thereupon gave Candanaṅgala five robes which he presented to the Buddha.[1]

The story is very similar to that of the brahmin **Piṅgiyāni** and the verse spoken is the same.[2]

[1] S. i. 81 f. [2] A. iii. 239.

Candanapāsāda.—A building in the **Maricavaṭṭivihāra** erected by **Mahinda IV.** It housed the Hair Relic of the Buddha in a jewelled reliquary.[1]

[1] Cv. liv. 40 f.

Candanapūjaka Thera.—An arahant. He was once a *kinnara* in **Candabhāgā** and lived on flowers. He offered a piece of sandalwood to **Atthadassī** Buddha.

Fourteen kappas ago he became king three times under the name of **Rohiṇi.**[1] He is probably identical with **Sīha Thera.**[2]

[1] Ap. i. 165. [2] ThagA. i. 179.

Candanamālā.—One of the residences occupied by the Buddha.[1] It was in **Sunāparanta** and was built of red sandalwood at the instigation of **Puṇṇa** of Sunāparanta. When the work was completed Puṇṇa sent a flower as message to the Buddha, who came with five hundred monks and performed the ceremony of dedication before dawn.[2] During the festival, the Buddha showed the **Yamakapāṭihāriya.**[3] *v.l.* **Candanasālā.**

[1] SNA. ii. 403. [2] ThagA. i. 158. [3] *Ibid.*, i. 312.

Candanamāliya Thera.—An arahant. He was a brahmin who entered the Order at the age of five, becoming an arahant in the tonsure-hall. In the time of **Sumedha** Buddha he was an ascetic who had renounced great wealth. Having met the Buddha, he offered him a seat and gave him mangoes, sandalwood and *sāla*-flowers. He was once king of the city of **Vebhāra.**[1] He is probably identical with **Valliya Thera.**[2]

[1] Ap. ii. 423 f.
[2] See ThagA. i. 293.

Candanasālā.—See **Candanamālā.**

Candapadumāsirī.—See **Candapadumā.**

1. **Candapadumā.**—The chief consort of the Seṭṭhi **Meṇḍaka** of **Bhaddiya,** and mother of **Dhanañjaya.**[1] She was, therefore, grandmother of **Visākhā.** She had been the wife of Meṇḍaka in a previous birth and, during a time of famine, had joined him in giving the only meal they had between them to a Pacceka Buddha. As a result of this act, the rice-pot in her home never became empty, however many people she might feed. In previous existences she had entertained the monks of various Buddhas, taking a rice-pot in one hand and a spoon in the other. Therefore, in her left hand was the sign of the lotus, covering the palm, and in her right the sign of the moon. Further, by reason of her having fetched and filtered water for the monks, on the sole of her left foot was marked a lotus and on the right a moon; hence her name, Candapadumā. When the Buddha visited Meṇḍaka's house and, after the meal, preached to the household, Candapadumā became a sotāpanna.[2] She was one of the five persons of great merit (**Mahāpuññā**).[3] The Visuddhimagga[4] calls her **Candapadumasirī.**

[1] DhA. i. 385.
[2] *Ibid.*, iii. 363-86.
[3] AA. i. 219; PsA. 509.
[4] ii. 383.

2. **Candapadumā.**—Wife of **Tiriṭavaccha** and mother of **Mahā Kaccāna.**[1]

[1] Ap. ii. 465.

Candapabbata.—See **Canda** (7).

1. **Candabhāgā.**—A river in India. It was the third river crossed by **Mahā Kappina** and his wife on their way from their own country, in the north-west, to **Sāvatthi.**[1] The river was one league deep and one wide[2] and eighteen leagues in length, with a rapid current.[3] On its bank was a large banyan-tree where the Buddha awaited Kappina's

[1] ThagA. i. 508.
[2] DhA. ii. 120.
[3] DA. iii. 877, 878.

arrival.[4] The Milinda[5] mentions it as one of the ten important rivers flowing from the **Himālaya.** The name is evidently old, as it occurs in several ancient legends.[6]

The Candabhāgā is generally identified with the Chenab (the Akesines of the Greeks).[7]

[4] AA. i. 177; SA. ii. 179.
[5] p. 114.
[6] *E.g.*, Ap. i. 75; ThagA. i. 390; ThigA. 9, etc.
[7] But see *Ps. of the Brethren* 255, n. 1.

2. **Candabhāgā.**—A canal constructed by **Parakkamabāhu I.,** flowing through the centre of the **Lakkhuyyāna.**[1]

[1] Cv. lxxix. 48.

Candabhānu.—A king of **Jāvā.** He invaded Ceylon in the eleventh year of the reign of **Parakkamabāhu II.** but was defeated in battle by **Vīrabāhu.**[1] In the reign of **Vijayabāhu IV.** he appeared once again with a large army and, landing at **Mahātittha,** marched against the king's fortress at **Subhagiri,** demanding the Tooth Relic, the Bowl Relic and the kingdom. But he was again defeated by the Sinhalese forces under Vijayabāhu and Vīrabāhu.[2]

[1] Cv. lxxxiii. 36 ff.
[2] *Ibid.*, lxxxviii. 69-83. For his later history see JA. xliii.

Candamittā.—One of the two chief women disciples of **Vipassī** Buddha.[1]

[1] Bu. xx. 29; J. i. 41.

Candamukha.—One of the descendants of **Okkāka.**[1]

[1] Dpv. iii. 42; Mhv. ii. 13.

Candamukha-Tissa.—The Majjhima Commentary contains a reference to a king of Ceylon bearing this name. He visited the Chief Elder of the **Mahāvihāra** when all the other monks were away, in order to test him. The Elder had very weak eyes, but when the king touched his feet as would a snake, he remained unafraid and asked who was there. The story is related to show that arahants know no fear.[1]

[1] MA. ii. 869.

Candamukha-Siva.—Son of **Iḷanāga** and king of Ceylon (103-112 A.C.) for eight years and seven months. His wife was **Damiḷādevī.** He was killed by his younger brother **Yasalālaka-Tissa.** Siva built a tank near

Maṇikāragāma which he gave to the **Issarasamaṇārāma.**[1] When Iḷanāga was taken captive by the **Lambakaṇṇas,** his queen sent the little Candamukhasiva to the state elephant to be killed by him, but the elephant picked him up and brought about Iḷanāga's release.[2]

[1] Dpv. xxi. 44; Mhv. xxxv. 46. [2] *Ibid.*, vs. 20 ff.

Candamukhī.—Wife of **Metteyya** Buddha in his last lay-life.[1]

[1] Anagatavaṃsa, p. 48.

1. **Candavatī.**—Wife of **Assalāyana** and mother of **Mahā Koṭṭhita.**[1]

[1] Ap. ii. 480.

2. **Candavatī.**—The city wherein, at the **Silārāma, Sujāta** Buddha died.[1]

[1] BuA. 171.

3. **Candavatī.**—The birthplace of **Anomadassī** Buddha.[1] There **Koṇḍañña** Buddha spent his first *vassa.*[2] It existed also in the time of **Sumedha** Buddha.[3] It was the capital of King **Vijitāvī.**[4]

[1] J. i. 36; Bu. viii. 17; DhA. i. 88; AA. i. 85; see also Ap. i. 76.
[2] BuA. 110.
[3] Ap. ii. 422.
[4] BuA. 111.

4. **Candavatī.**—Daughter of **Brahmadatta,** king of Benares. The king offered her to **Lomasa-kassapa** on condition that he should perform a sacrifice of beasts. Kassapa agreed but later withdrew his consent. See the **Lomasa-Kassapa Jātaka.**[1]

[1] J. iii. 515 ff.; Mil. 220.

Candasama.—See **Candūpama.**

Candasārattha-ṭīkā.—A Commentary on the **Sambandhacintā** written in the fourteenth century by **Saddhammañāṇa** of Pagān.[1]

[1] P.L.C. 198.

1. **Candā.**—Wife of **Sudinna** and mother of **Piyadassī** Buddha.[1] In the *Buddhavaṃsa*[2] she is called **Sucandā.**

[1] J. i. 39. [2] xiv. 15.

2. **Candā.**—One of the two chief women disciples of **Vipassī** Buddha.[1]

[1] J. i. 41; Bu. xx. 29.

3. **Candā.**—A *kinnarī*, wife of **Canda,** the Bodhisatta. See the **Candakinnara Jātaka.**[1] She is sometimes called **Candī.**[2]

[1] J. iv. 283 ff. [2] *E.g.*, J. iv. 284.

4. **Candā.**—Wife of **Mahāpatāpa,** king of Benares, and mother of **Dhammapāla.** She is identified with **Mahāpajāpatī Gotamī.** For details see the **Culla Dhammapāla Jātaka.**[1]

[1] J. iii. 178 ff.

5. **Candā.**—Daughter of the **Madda**-king and chief consort of the ruler of Benares. She was the mother of **Mūgapakkha (Temiya).** For details see the **Mūgapakkha Jātaka.**[1]

[1] J. vi. 1 ff.

6. **Candā.**—Chief consort of **Candakumāra** (*q.v.*). She was the daughter of the **Pañcāla** king and the mother of **Vāsula.** It was her *saccakiriyā* which saved her husband from death. She is identified with **Rāhulamātā.**[1]

[1] J. vi. 151 ff.

7. **Candā.**—Chief consort of **Sutasoma.** She is identified with **Rāhulamāta.**[1]

[1] J. v. 177, 182, 192.

8. **Candā Therī.**—An arahant. She belonged to a brahmin family which had fallen on evil days and she grew up in wretched poverty. Her kinsfolk having all died of plague, she eked out a living by begging from door to door. One day she came across **Paṭācāra** who had just finished eating. Paṭācāra, seeing her pitiable condition, gave her some food and, when she had eaten, discoursed to her. Delighted by Paṭācāra's sermon, Candā renounced the world and soon afterwards attained arahantship.[1]

[1] Thig. vs. 122-26; ThigA., p. 120 f.

9. **Candā.**—The *kinnārī*-maiden of whom **Brahmadatta** became enamoured, preferring her to his own wife, **Asitābhū.**[1]

[1] VibhA. 470 f.; the **Asitābhū Jātaka** (J. ii. 231 f.) does not mention her name.

1. **Candābha Thera.**—An arahant. He belonged to a wealthy brahmin family of **Rājagaha** and was called Candābha because from the circle of his navel proceeded a light resembling that of the moon's disk. When he grew up, the brahmins seated him in a carriage and took him about, proclaiming that whoever stroked his body would receive power and

glory. By this means they earned much money. One day, in **Sāvatthi**, a dispute arose between the brahmins and the Buddha's followers as to Candābha's supernatural powers, and finally they took him to the Buddha for him to settle the quarrel. As Candābha approached the Buddha, the light from his body disappeared and Candābha, thinking that this was owing to some charm, asked to be taught the same. The Buddha stipulated that he should join the Order. Having done so, Candābha was asked to meditate on the thirty-two constituent parts of the Body. Soon afterwards he became an arahant.

In a previous birth he was a forester and formed a friendship with a merchant to whom he supplied red sandalwood. One day, when he visited the merchant in the town, he was taken by him to the place where a shrine was being erected over the remains of **Kassapa** Buddha. The forester, making a moon-disk from sandalwood, placed it within the shrine. After death, for a whole Buddha-interval, he was in **Tāvatiṃsa** and was known as the deva **Candābha.**[1]

[1] DhA. iv. 187. ff.; the SNA. version (ii. 523 ff.) differs from this in several details.

2. **Candābha.**—Sixteen thousand kappas ago there were four kings of this name, all previous births of **Ekadīpiya.**[1]

[1] Ap. i. 189.

Candābha Jātaka (No. 135).—The Bodhisatta was once an ascetic and, at the moment of his death, answered his disciples' inquiries with the words "moonlight and sunlight." When his chief pupil (identified with **Sāriputta**) interpreted the words, his colleagues did not believe him until the Bodhisatta appeared in mid-air and said that whoever meditated on the sun and the moon would be born in the **Ābhassara** world.[1]

The Jātaka was preached about the interpretation of a problem by Sāriputta at the gates of **Saṅkassa.**

[1] J. i. 474.

Candārāma.—A monastery in **Candavatī**, where **Koṇḍañña** Buddha spent his first *vassa.*[1]

[1] BuA. 110.

Candikā.—Mother of **Candikāputta.** See below.

Candikāputta Thera.—A discourse on the teaching of **Devadatta,** delivered by **Candikāputta** to the monks, is recorded in the **Silāyūpa**

Sutta[1] (*q.v.*). The Commentary[2] says that his mother's name was **Candikā**, hence his own.

[1] A. iv. 402 f. [2] AA. ii. 808.

Candimasa Sutta.—Records the visit of the devaputta **Candimasa** to the Buddha and the conversation that ensued.[1]

[1] S. i. 51.

1. **Candimā, Candimasa, Canda.**—The name of the devaputta whose abode (*vimāna*) is the moon (**Canda**), sometimes also called Candima. The moon is forty-nine leagues in diameter and appears in the world at the wish of the **Ābhassara** Brahmas, who are the first inhabitants of the earth, hence its name (*amhākaṃ chandaṃ ñatvā viya uṭṭhito, tasmā cando hotū ti*).[1] Candimā is also included among the **Cātummahārājika** devas because he lives in their world.[2] There are other devas besides Canda who dwell in the moon.[3] According to the **Biḷārikosiya Jātaka,**[4] **Sāriputta,** having once given alms, was born as Canda, while in the **Sudhābhojana Jātaka**[5] it is **Moggallāna** who was so born. The moon cannot move in the sky without the permission of Candimā, and he can stop its movement at will.[6] It is said that once, when Candimā was seized by **Rāhu Asurinda,** he invoked the Buddha in a verse and the Buddha asked Rāhu to set him at liberty, which request was granted.[7] The deva Candimasa who is mentioned[8] as visiting the Buddha is probably identical with Candimā. The moon was worshipped when children were desired.[9] The **Sasa Jātaka** (No. 513) gives details of the story of how, as a result of the Bodhisatta's sacrifice when born as a hare, **Sakka** painted the figure of a hare on the moon, which sign will be seen throughout this *kappa.*[10]

[1] VibhA. 519; PsA. 253.
[2] *E.g.*, Mahāniddesa Cty. 108.
[3] D. ii. 269.
[4] J. iv. 63, 69.
[5] J. v. 382, 412.
[6] *E.g.*, DhA. ii. 143, 146; iii. 97.
[7] S. i. 50; this is evidently a myth connected with the lunar eclipse.
[8] S. i. 51.
[9] *E.g.*, J. iv. 1.
[10] J. i. 172.

2. **Candimā.**—One of the descendants of **Okkāka.**[1]

[1] Mhv. ii. 13; Dpv. iii. 42.

Candimā Sutta.—Records the incident of the Buddha's request to **Rāhu** to free **Candimā** (*q.v.*).[1]

[1] S. i. 50.

Candiya.—See **Candakumāra.**

Candūpama.—A king of twenty-three *kappas* ago, a previous birth of **Vaṇṇakāraka Thera.** *v.l.* **Candasama.**[1]

[1] Ap. i. 220.

Candūpama Sutta.—Monks who visit families must be like the moon, just as is **Mahā Kassapa.** They should be unobtrusive, retiring in demeanour. They should preserve their freedom and not be bound. Monks should teach the doctrine out of compassion for others, not in order to win their approval.[1]

[1] S. ii. 197 f.; see also MA. i. 14.

1. **Campaka.**—A city in the time of **Atthadassī** Buddha. The Bodhisatta, as **Susīma,** was born there.[1]

[1] BuA. 180.

2. **Campaka.**—A king of fifty-seven kappas ago, a previous birth of **Khadiravaniya Revata.**[1]

[1] Ap. i. 52; ThagA. i. 109.

3. **Campaka.**—See *s.v.* **Campā.**

1. **Campakapupphiya Thera.**—An arahant. Thirty-one kappas ago he offered seven flowers in a basket to **Vessabhu** Buddha. Two kappas later he became a king named **Vihatābhā.**[1] He is probably identical with **Belaṭṭhānika.**[2]

[1] Ap. i. 167.
[2] ThagA. i. 205.

2. **Campakapupphiya Thera.**—An arahant. Thirty-one kappas ago, while travelling through the air, he saw a Pacceka Buddha named **Sudassana,** and dropped seven flowers as offering to him.[1]

[1] Ap. i. 279.

Campakā.—See **Campā.**

1. **Campā.**—A city in India on the river of the same name; it was the capital of **Aṅga** and was celebrated for its beautiful lake, the **Gaggarāpokkharaṇī** (*q.v.*), which was excavated by Queen **Gaggarā.** On its banks was a grove of *campaka*-trees, well known for the fragrance of their marvellous white flowers, and there, in the Buddha's time, wandering teachers were wont to lodge. The Buddha himself stayed there on several

occasions.[1] **Sāriputta**[2] and **Vaṅgīsa**[3] are also said to have stayed there. The **Mahāparinibbāna Sutta**[4] mentions Campā as one of the six important cities of India, its foundation being ascribed to **Mahāgovinda.**[5] It lay at a distance of sixty yojanas from **Mithilā.**[6] In the Buddha's time the people of Campā owed allegiance to **Bimbisāra,** as king of Magadha, and Bimbisāra had given a royal fief in Campā to the brahmin **Soṇadaṇḍa.**[7] Campā was evidently an important centre of trade, and we are told that merchants travelled from there to **Suvaṇṇabhūmi** for purposes of trade.[8] Most probably it was the Indian colonists from Campā who named one of their most important settlements in Indo-China after this famous old town. The ancient name of Campā was probably Mālini or Mālina.[9]

The ninth chapter of the *Mahāvagga* of the *Vinaya Piṭaka*[10] contains several important regulations laid down by the Buddha at Campā regarding the validity and otherwise of formal acts of the Saṅgha.

Campā is mentioned as the birthplace of **Soṇa-Kolivisa, Jambugāmika, Nandaka** and **Bharata,** and among those who resided there were **Bāhuna, Vajjiyamāhita** and **Thullanandā** and her companions.

The **Soṇadaṇḍa,** the **Dasuttara,** the **Kandaraka** and the **Kāraṇḍava Suttas** were preached there.

According to Buddhaghosa,[11] Campā was so called because the whole place abounded in large Campaka-trees.

Campā is generally identified with a site about twenty-four miles to the east of the modern Bhagalpur, near the villages of Campānagara and Campāpura.[12] It was visited by Hiouen Thsang,[13] and Fa Hien calls it a great kingdom with many places of worship.[14]

The Buddha's bathing-robe was enshrined in Campā.[15]

See also **Kāla Campā,** probably another name for Campā.

[1] Vin. i. 312; S. i. 195; A. iv. 59, 168; v. 151, 189.
[2] A. iv. 59.
[3] S. i. 195.
[4] D. ii. 147.
[5] *Ibid.*, 235.
[6] J. iv. 32.
[7] D. i. 111.
[8] *E.g.*, J. vi. 539.
[9] *Campasya tu purī Campā, yā Mālinyabhavat purā* (Mbh. xii. 5, 6, 7; Matsyapurāṇa 48, 97, etc.; Law, A.G. I. 6, n. 2).
[10] Vin. i. 312 ff.; see also Vin. ii. 307.
[11] MA. ii. 565.
[12] C.A.G. I. 5.
[13] Beal, Records ii. 187 f.
[14] p. 65.
[15] Bu. xxviii. 9.

2. **Campā, Campakā.**—One of the two chief women disciples of **Kakusandha** Buddha.[1]

[1] Bu. xxiii. 21; J. i. 42.

3. **Campā, Campakā.**—Birthplace of **Paduma** Buddha.[1] Near by was the **Campaka-uyyāna.**

[1] Bu ix 16; J. i. 36.

4. **Campā.**—The river which flowed between **Aṅga** and **Magadha** (now called Chāndan). The Nāga **Campeyya** held sway over the river.[1]

[1] J. iv. 454 f.

5. **Campā.**—A channel branching off from the **Parakkama-samudda**, from the sluice near the **Caṇḍī** gate.[1]

[1] Cv. lxxix. 45.

Campeyya, Campeyyaka.—A Nāga-king who dwelt in the river **Campā.** See the **Campeyya Jātaka.**

Campeyya Cariyā.—See **Campeyya Jātaka.**

Campeyya Jātaka (No. 506).—Once the king of **Magadha,** at constant war with the king of **Aṅga,** obtaining the help of the Nāga-king who dwelt in the river **Campā,** defeated his rival. Thereafter he held an annual festival in honour of the Nāga-king. The Bodhisatta, a very poor man, saw Campeyya's splendour on his way to the feast and longed for a like greatness. As a result, after death, he was born in the Nāga-world where he became king under the name of **Campeyya.** Realising what had happened, he felt disgust at his position as a Nāga and made many attempts to observe religious vows, hoping, in this way, to gain release. But he was foiled in his efforts by his consort **Sumanā.** At last he came to the world of men, where he kept fast on certain days, lying on an ant-hill. There he was taken captive by a snake charmer who tortured him in various ways and took him about, exhibiting him for gain. By certain tokens of which Campeyya had earlier warned her, Sumanā knew that her husband had been taken captive and, after much searching, she discovered him just as the snake charmer was about to give a performance before **Uggasena,** king of Benares. The whole story was then revealed, and the snake charmer set Campeyya free. That Uggasena might be convinced of the truth of the story, he was invited to the Nāga-world, where he and his retinue were lavishly entertained.

The story was related in connection with the observance of *uposatha* vows. **Devadatta** was the snake charmer and **Sāriputta** was Uggasena. **Rahulamātā** was Sumanā.[1]

The **Campeyya-cariyā** is included in the *Cariyāpiṭaka*[2] in order to illustrate *sīlapāramitā.*

This Jātaka is often referred to[3] as one of the births in which the Bodhisatta practised *sīla* to perfection.

[1] J. iv. 454-68. [2] p. 85 f. [3] *E.g.*, J. i. 45; MA. ii. 617.

Campeyyakkhandhaka.—The ninth chapter of the *Mahāvagga* of the *Vinaya Piṭaka.*[1]

[1] Vin. i. 312 ff.

Cambuṭivāpi.—A tank built by **Vasabha.**[1]

[1] Mhv. xxxv. 95.

Cammakkhandhaka.—The fifth chapter of the *Mahāvagga* of the *Vinaya Piṭaka.*[1]

[1] Vin. i. 179 ff.

Cammasāṭaka Jātaka (No. 324).—Once a religious mendicant, clad in a leather garment, saw a ram falling back before him, and imagining that the animal was doing him obeisance, uttered its praises. The Bodhisatta, who was a merchant, hearing this, warned the ascetic that the ram was only preparing to attack him, and even as he was speaking the animal charged the mendicant and felled him to the ground.

The story was related in reference to a monk of **Sāvatthi,** to whom a similar thing happened while he was wearing a leather jerkin.[1]

[1] J. iii. 82 ff.

Cayantī-vāpi.—A tank in Ceylon built by **Vasabha.**[1] *v.l.* **Mayantī.**

[1] Mhv. xxxv. 94.

1. **Cara, Caraka.**—One of the successors of **Mahā Sammata** and a member of the **Sākya** tribe. He had a son named **Upacara.**[1]

[1] Mhv. ii. 2; Dpv. iii. 5; DA. i. 258; J. iii. 454; SnA. i. 352.

2. **Cara.**—A Yakkha chieftain to be invoked by followers of the Buddha in times of need.[1]

[1] D. iii. 205; the P.T.S. edition calls him Māṇicara as does the P.T.S. edition of the commentary (D. iii. 970); but the Sinhalese edition, both text and commentary, divides this name into two thus: Māṇi and Cara.

Cara Vagga.—The second chapter of the *Catukka Nipāta* of the *Aṅguttara Nikāya.*[1]

[1] A. ii. 13 ff.

Cara Sutta.—In every posture one must strive ardently and scrupulously against lustful, malevolent and injuring thoughts.[1]

[1] A. ii. 13; found also in *Itivuttaka,* 115.

1. **Carita Sutta.**—The four wrong practices: lying speech, spiteful speech, bitter speech, idle babble.[1]

[1] A. ii. 141.

2. **Carita Sutta.**—The four right practices: truthful speech, speech not spiteful, mild speech, wise speech.[1]

[1] A. ii. 141.

Cariyākathā.—The fifth chapter of the *Paññāvagga* of the *Paṭisambhidāmagga.*[1]

[1] Ps. ii. 225 f.

Cariyāpiṭaka.—One of the fifteen books of the **Khuddaka Nikāya,** generally placed last in the list. It contains tales in metrical verse of the Buddha's previous births, chiefly setting forth the ten *pāramī*, by which he attained Enlightenment. Each story is called a *Cariyā.* The stories told here in verse are parallel to the corresponding Jātaka stories in prose, and presuppose a familiar acquaintance with all the incidents of the prose tales. The first two *pāramī* are illustrated by ten stories each, while the remaining *pāramī* have only fifteen stories between them.

The **Dīghabhāṇakas** refused to include the Cariyāpiṭaka in their canonical books, but it was accepted by the **Majjhimabhāṇakas.**[1]

There exists a Commentary on the Cariyapiṭaka which is ascribed to **Dhammapāla** and which forms a part of the **Paramathadīpanī.**[2] According to the Commentary,[3] the Cariyāpiṭaka was preached by the Buddha at the **Nigrodhārāma,** after the conclusion of the **Buddhavaṃsa** and at the request of **Sāriputta.** It was preached by **Mahinda** at the **Nandanavana** in **Anurādhapura,** soon after his arrival in Ceylon.[4]

[1] DA. i. 15, 23.

[2] Published in the Hewavitarane Bequest Series, vol. xxvi. (1929).

[3] CypA. 1, 2.

[4] Dpv. xiv. 45; but see Mhv. xv. 179.

Carī.—Probably the name of a celestial musician, or, perhaps, of a musical instrument.[1]

[1] VvA. 94; but see note on p. 372, also p. 211, where Carī is omitted from the list.

Carukkaṭṭa.—A village in South India.[1]

[1] Cv. lxxvi. 127.

Cala.—A Sinhalese chieftain, who once joined the **Coḷas** against **Vijayabāhu I.,**[1] but who, later,[2] evidently returned to him and fought bravely on his side.

[1] Cv. lviii. 16.

[2] *Ibid.,* vs. 55; see Cv. *Trs.* i. 207, n. 3.

Calāka.—See **Talatā.**

Cāṇakka.—A brahmin of **Takkasilā,** who killed King **Dhanananda** and placed **Candagutta** on the throne.[1] In his youth **Cāṇakka** looked after his mother, and finding that she was worrying lest he, who was destined for kingly power, should leave her, he broke his tooth, having been told that there his luck resided. One day, on going for alms to Dhanananda's palace, he was insulted, and in order to avenge the insult he kidnapped the king's son, **Pabbatakumāra.** He then adopted **Candagutta** and, finding him better fitted for kingship than Pabbata, he contrived that the latter should be killed. When preparations had been made, he induced Candagutta to rise in revolt against Dhanananda, and, finally, to kill him and ascend the throne.[2]

The Theragāthā Commentary[3] states that **Tekicchāni's** father, **Subandhu,** roused the jealousy of Cāṇakka, who had him put in prison.

[1] Mhv. v. 16 f.; Mbv. 98. [2] See MṬ. 181 ff. for details, also **Candagutta.** [3] i. 440.

Cātigatikapaṭimāghara.—An image-house attached to the **Mahāthūpa** and built by **Mahādāṭhika-Mahānāga.**[1]

[1] MṬ. 634.

Cātuddisa Sutta.—Five qualities that make a monk a "four-regioner"—moving without let in the four quarters.[1]

[1] A. iii. 135.

Cātuma Sutta.—Preached at the **Āmalakīvana** in **Cātumā.** Some new members of the Order, dwelling near the Buddha, made so much noise that they were summoned and asked to leave at once. But the Sākyans of Cātumā and Brahmā **Sahampatī** interceded on their behalf and they were allowed to return. The Buddha then preached to them that just as four terrors await the man who enters the water—waves, crocodiles, whirlpools and sharks—so are there four terrors awaiting the monk—temper, gluttony, the pleasures of the senses and women.[1]

[1] M. i. 456 ff.; on this see Mil. 209.

Cātumā.—A Sākyan village containing a mote-hall; near it was the **Āmalakīvana** where the Buddha once stayed and preached the **Cātuma Sutta.**[1]

[1] M. i. 456 f.; MA. ii. 660.

1. **Cātumāsika-Brahmadatta.**—A king of Benares. Going to his park in the early summer, he rested under a *kovilāra*-tree which was thickly

covered with leaves. Going again in midsummer, he found it full of blossom. On his third visit, at the end of the season, the tree was bare and withered, and, lying under it, he realised that decay and death are the common lot of all. He thereupon became a Pacceka Buddha. His udāna is included in the **Khaggavisāna Sutta.**[1]

[1] SN. vs. 44; SNA. i. 90 f.; Ap. i. 9 (vs. 18); ApA. i. 141 f.

2. **Cātumāsika-Brahmadatta.**—King of Benares. Once in every four months he would visit his park. One day, on entering the park, he saw a *pāricchattaka*-tree covered with blossom, and picked one of the flowers. His retinue followed his example, and soon the tree was quite bare. On his return from the park he observed this, and also how another tree near by, devoid of flowers, had been spared the spoilation. He thereupon reflected how possessions led to trouble, and, renouncing his kingdom, he donned the robes of a monk, later becoming a Pacceka Buddha. His udāna is included in the **Khaggavisāna Sutta.**[1]

[1] SN. vs. 64; SnA. i. 116; ApA. i. 161.

Cātumāsinī.—Occurs in the phrase **Komudī Cātumāsinī,** probably referring to the Cātumāsya festival which is performed in the month of **Kattika,** Komudī being the full-moon day of Kattika.[1]

[1] Vin. i. 55; D. i. 47, etc.

Cātumeyyakā.—The inhabitants of **Cātumā.**[1]

[1] M. i. 457.

Cātummahārājikā.—The inhabitants of the lowest (**Cātummahārājika**) deva world. This world derives its name from the Four Great Kings (**Cattāro Mahārājāno**) who dwell there as guardians of the four quarters; **Dhataraṭṭha** of the East, **Virūḷhaka** of the South, **Virūpakkha** of the West, and **Vessaraṇa** of the North.[1] They keep large retinues consisting, respectively, of **Gandhabbas, Kumbhaṇḍas, Nāgas** and **Yakkhas,** all of whom dwell in the same world as their lords and accompany them on their travels. These kings are mentioned[2] as having undertaken the protection of the Buddha from the moment of his conception in his mother's womb, and in the **Āṭānāṭiya Sutta** (*q.v.*), they appear as protectors not only of the Buddha but also of his followers.[3]

The Four Kings appear to have been regarded as Recorders of the happenings in the assemblies of the devas.[4] On the eighth day of the lunar half-month, they send their councillors out into the world to dis-

[1] D. ii. 207 f.; iii. 194 f.

[2] D. ii. 257 f.

[3] See, *e.g.*, DhA. ii. 146; iii. 96.

[4] D. ii. 225.

cover if men cultivate righteousness and virtue; on the fourteenth day they send their sons, on the fifteenth day they themselves appear in the world, all these visits having the same purpose. Then, at the assembly of the devas, they submit their report to the gods of **Tāvatiṃsa,** who rejoice or lament according as to whether men prosper in righteousness or not.[5] These four Gods surpass the other inhabitants of their worlds in ten ways—beauty, length of life, etc.—because their merit is greater than that of the others.[6]

Besides these Regent Gods and their followers, other dwellers are to be found in their world—the **Khiḍḍāpadosikā,** the **Manopadosikā,** the **Sītavalāhakā,** the **Uṇhavalāhakā,** and the devaputtas **Candima** and **Suriya.**[7] Life in the Cātummahārājikā world lasts, according to human computation, ninety thousand years.[8] Beings are born there as a result of various acts of piety and faith which, however, are based on motives not very exalted.[9]

The Cātummahārājika world is situated half-way up Mount **Sineru.** Some of the devas of the world dwell in the mountain, others in the sky.[10]

[5] A. i. 142 f.; for more details see AA. i. 376 f.
[6] A. iv. 242.
[7] VibhA. 519; MNidA. 108.
[8] DA. ii. 472, 647, but see Kvu. 207.
[9] A. iv. 60.
[10] On these gods see Moulton: *Zoroastrianism* 22-7, 242.

Cāthamaṅgama.—A tank constructed by **Vasabha.**[1]

[1] Mhv. xxxv. 95.

Cānavela.—*v.l.* for **Tanaveli** (*q.v.*).

Cānura.—A wrestler employed by **Kaṃsa** to fight the **Andhakaveṇhudāsaputtā.** But **Baladeva** put a strap round him and, lifting him up, dashed his brains out on the ground.[1]

[1] J. iv. 81 f.

Cāpā Therī (*v.l.* **Chāvā**).—A trapper's daughter in **Vaṅkahāra** who became the wife of the Ājīvaka **Upaka** and bore him a son, **Subhadda.** When Upaka, unable to bear his wife's taunts, renounced the world and joined the Order, she followed him to **Sāvatthi,** and there, having become a nun, attained arahantship.[1]

[1] Thig. 291-311; ThigA. 220 ff.; SNA. i. 259 f.

Cāpāla.—A yakkha. See **Cāpāla-Cetiya.**

Cāpāla Vagga.—The first chapter of the **Iddhipāda Saṃyutta.**[1]

[1] S. v. 254-63.

Cāpāla-cetiya.—A shrine near **Vesālī.** Here the Buddha, three months before his parinibbāṇa, definitely decided to accede to the request of Māra that he should die. When he announced this decision the earth shook.[1] The Aṅguttara Commentary[2] states that during the first twenty years of the Buddha's ministry, he sometimes dwelt in Cāpāla-cetiya. It was once the residence of the yakkha **Cāpāla,** but, later, a vihāra was erected on the site for the use of the Buddha.[3] Fa Hsien found a pagoda there and relates a story in connection with it.[4]

[1] D. ii. 102 ff.; A. iv. 308 f.; S. v. 260 f.; Ud. vi. 1; Dvy. 201, 207; Mtu. i. 209 f.; iii. 306.

[2] i. 457.

[3] UdA. 322 f.

[4] p. 43.

Cāla Thera.—Son of **Cālā** and nephew of **Sāriputta.** He was ordained by **Khadiravaniya-Revata.**[1] He is mentioned as living at the **Kūṭāgārasālā,** which place he left when the **Licchavis** caused disturbance by their visits to the Buddha.[2] In this context he is spoken of as a very eminent Elder and was, therefore, evidently an arahant.

[1] Thag. vs. 42; ThagA. i. 110.

[2] A. v. 133.

1. **Cālā Therī.**—Daughter of **Surūpasārī** and, therefore, younger sister of **Sāriputta.** She had two sisters, **Upacālā** and **Sisūpacālā,** and all three left the world and joined the Order on hearing of Sāriputta's renunciation. In due course they attained arahantship.[1] It is said[2] that one day, when Cālā was taking her siesta in the **Andhavana, Māra** visited her, asking her various questions and trying to tempt her. Her son was **Cāla** (*q.v.*).

[1] ThigA. 162 ff.; DhA. ii. 188.

[2] Thig. 182-8; *cp*. S. i. 132.

2. **Cālā.**—Chief of the lay women supporters of **Sumaṅgala** Buddha.[1]

[1] Bu. v. 28.

3. **Cālā.**—One of the two chief women disciples of **Phussa** Buddha.[1]

[1] Bu. xix. 20; J. i. 41.

Cālā Sutta.—Records **Māra's** visit to **Cālā Therī** and their conversation.[1]

[1] S. i. 132.

Cālikapabbata.—A hill near **Cālikā** where the Buddha stayed during his visits to Cālikā. The hill was quite white in colour, and on dark nights, such as the night of the new moon, it gave the impression of moving hither and thither, hence its name.[1] But see **Cālikā.**

[1] AA. ii. 793; UdA. 217.

Cālikā.—A village near the **Cālikapabbata,** where the Buddha spent the vassas of the thirteenth, eighteenth and nineteenth years after the Enlightenment.[1] His attendant on one of these visits was **Meghiya.** Close to Cālikā was the village of **Jantu** where Meghiya went for alms. In the neighbourhood was the river **Kimikālā,** on whose banks was a mango grove.[2] Outside the city gate and all around the city was a bog (*calapaṅka*), owing to which the city gave the impression of moving, hence the name.[3] *v.l.* **Jālikā.**

[1] BuA. 3. [2] A. iv. 354; Ud. iv. 1; DhA. i. 287 f. [3] UdA. 217; AA. ii. 793.

Cāvala.—A mountain near **Himavā.**[1]

[1] Ap. i. 279; ii. 451.

Ciñcā-māṇavikā.—A paribbājikā of some ascetic Order. When the heretics of this Order found that their gains were grown less owing to the popularity of the Buddha, they enlisted the support of Ciñcā in their attempts to discredit him. She was very beautiful and full of cunning, and they persuaded her to pretend to pay visits to the Buddha at **Jetavana.** She let herself be seen going towards the vihāra in the evening, spent the night in the heretics' quarters near by, and in the morning men saw her returning from the direction of the vihāra. When questioned, she said that she had passed the night with the Buddha. After some months she simulated pregnancy by tying a disc of wood round her body and appearing thus before the Buddha, as he preached to a vast congregation, she charged him with irresponsibility and callousness in that he made no provision for her confinement. The Buddha remained silent, but **Sakka's** throne was heated and he caused a mouse to sever the cords of the wooden disc, which fell to the ground, cutting Ciñcā's toes. She was chased out of the vihāra by those present, and as she stepped outside the gate the fires of the lowest hell swallowed her up.[1]

In a previous birth, too, she had helped in various ways to harm the Bodhisatta. For details see the **Culla-** and **Mahā-Paduma,** the **Bandhanamokkha,** the **Vānarinda,** the **Vessantara,** the **Suṃsumāra** and the **Suvaṇṇakakkaṭa Jātakas.** It is stated[2] that the Buddha was subjected to the ignominy of being charged by Ciñcā with incontinence, because in a previous birth he had reviled a Pacceka Buddha. *v.l.* **Ciñcī** ; *cp.* **Sundarī.**

[1] DhA. iii. 178 f.; J. iv. 187 f.; ItA. 69. [2] Ap. i. 299; UdA. 263 f.

Ciṇṇamāla.—A king of fifty thousand kappas ago, a former birth of **Kassapa Thera** (or **Sereyyaka**).[1] *v.l.* **Cīnamāla.**

[1] ThagA. i. 178; Ap. i. 155.

Citakanibbāpaka Thera.—An arahant. Thirty-one kappas ago he sprinkled perfumed water on the pyre of **Vessabhū** Buddha and so extinguished it.[1] He is probably identical with **Abhibhūta Thera.**[2]

[1] Ap. ii. 408. [2] ThagA. i. 372 f.

1. **Citakapūjaka Thera.**—An arahant. Ninety-one kappas ago a Pacceka Buddha, named **Ānanda,** died in the forest and the Thera, who was then a deva, descended from the deva-world and burned the Pacceka Buddha's body on a pyre.[1]

[1] Ap. i. 227.

2. **Citakapūjaka Thera.**—An arahant. In the time of **Sikhī** Buddha he was a tree-sprite on a *rājāyatana*-tree. At the Buddha's death he made offerings of flowers and music and perfume at the Buddha's funeral pyre. Thirty-one kappas ago, he became king sixteen times, under the name of **Uggata.**[1]

[1] Ap. i. 151.

3. **Citakapūjaka Thera.**—An arahant. Ninety-four kappas ago, while wandering along the **Candabhāgā** River, he saw the Buddha's funeral pyre and made offering to it of seven *māluvā*-flowers. Seventy-seven kappas ago he became king seven times, under the name of **Paṭijagga.**[1]

[1] Ap. i. 237.

4. **Citakapūjaka Thera.**—An arahant. He offered *sāla*-flowers at the pyre of a Pacceka Buddha named **Jalajuttama,** one hundred thousand kappas ago.[1]

[1] Ap. i. 292 f.

1. **Citta** (called **Cittagahapati).**—A householder of **Macchikāsaṇḍa,** where he was Treasurer. He was later declared by the Buddha to be pre-eminent among laymen who preached the Doctrine.[1] On the day of his birth the whole city was covered knee-deep with flowers of various hues, hence his name. When **Mahānāma** visited Macchikāsaṇḍa, Citta, pleased with his demeanour, invited him to his park, the **Ambāṭakārāma,** and built for him a monastery there. And there the Elder preached to Citta the **Salāyatana-vibhatti** and Citta became an Anāgāmin. Thereafter many monks visited the Ambāṭakārāma and accepted Citta's hospitality. Among them was **Isidatta** (*q.v.*), a former acquaintance of Citta, but Isidatta left when he found that his identity had been discovered. Mahānāma and **Mahaka** did likewise, after having performed miracles at the request of Citta. The

[1] A. i. 26.

Citta Saṃyutta[2] contains a record of conversations between Citta and members of the Order, among whom, besides those already mentioned, were **Kāmabhū** and **Godatta.** Citta is also said to have had discussions with **Nigaṇṭha Nātaputta** and **Acela Kassapa** and to have refuted their views.

A thera named **Sudhamma** was a permanent resident in the Ambāṭakārāma and was looked after by Citta. Once, when the two Chief Disciples and several other eminent Elders came to the Ambāṭakārāma, Citta invited first these and then Sudhamma; the latter, feeling slighted, blamed Citta beyond measure, but the Buddha, hearing of this, sent Sudhamma to ask for Citta's pardon.[3]

Some time later, Citta visited the Buddha. He was accompanied by two thousand others and took with him five hundred cartloads of offerings to the Buddha and the Order. As he fell at the feet of the Buddha, flowers of five hues showered from the sky and the Buddha preached to him the **Saḷāyatana-vibhatti.** For a fortnight he continued distributing his gifts to the Order and the devas filled his carts with all kinds of valuables.[4]

When Citta lay ill just before his death, devas visited him and advised him to wish for kingship among them, but he refused to aspire to anything so impermanent, and instructed the devas and his kinsfolk gathered round him, telling them of the Buddha and his teachings.[5] He is regarded as the ideal layman.[6]

He owned a tributary village called **Migapattaka.**[7]

In the time of **Padumuttara** Buddha, Citta conceived his desire to be placed first among laymen in the teaching of the Dhamma. In the time of **Kassapa** Buddha he was a huntsman. One day, seeing a monk in a glen, and being pleased thereat, he hurried home, prepared a meal and brought it to the monk, together with flowers he had gathered on the way. After the offering, he made a wish that he should never lack for tribute and that showers of flowers should fall on him. In the deva-world he surpassed all others in his great beauty.[8] In the **Bhisa Jātaka,**[9] he is identified with the slave.

Though Citta was not an arahant, he possessed the *paṭisambhidā* of a probationer (*sekha*).[10]

2 S. iv. 282 ff.
3 Vin. ii. 15 ff.; DhA. ii. 74 f.; for details see *s.v.* Sudhamma.
4 AA. i. 210.
5 S. iv. 302 f.
6 *E.g.*, at A. i. 88; ii. 164; iii. 451.
7 SA. iii. 93.
8 AA. i. 209.
9 J. iii. 314.
10 Vsm. 442.

2. **Citta.**—The Bodhisatta born as a Caṇḍāla. For details see the **Citta-Sambhuta Jātaka.**

3. **Citta, Cittaka.**—A deer, brother of **Rohanta,** the Bodhisatta. He is identified with **Ānanda.** For details see the **Rohantamiga Jātaka.**

4. **Citta** called **Hatthirohaputta (Hatthisāriputta).**—A thera, son of an elephant trainer, who, having entered the Order, studied under the Buddha and gained special proficiency in distinguishing subtle differences in the meanings of words. Six times he left the Order and six times returned. His last quarrel was with **Mahā Koṭṭhita,** who objected to his constant interruptions of the Elder's discussions regarding the Abhidhamma.[1] It is said[2] that in the time of **Kassapa** Buddha, Citta and a friend entered the Order. When the friend expressed a desire to return to household life, Citta encouraged him to do so, coveting his belongings. This was the reason for Citta's inability to remain in the Order. He was a friend of **Poṭṭhapāda,** and when he had returned for the sixth time to a householder's life, Poṭṭhapāda brought him to the Buddha. Citta listened to their conversation and asked questions regarding personality. At the end of the discourse (recounted in the **Poṭṭhapāda Sutta**) Citta once more joined the Order, never again to leave it, for he soon after became an arahant.[3]

The **Kuddāla Jātaka**[4] gives the circumstances in which he first joined the Order. He was a youth of good family at **Sāvatthi.** One day, while on his way home from ploughing, he received from the bowl of a certain Elder some rich and dainty food. In order to gain similar food for himself, he became a monk, but soon after, lust overcame him and he left the homeless life. Even after he became an arahant his colleagues are said to have taunted him, asking when he would be leaving them, and it was only when the Buddha told them that such a time would never be were they satisfied.

The same story, except for certain details, is also found in the Dhammapada Commentary,[5] but there Citta is called **Cittahattha,** and a different explanation is given of his name: *esa cittavasiko hutvā vicarati ti Cittahatthan ti nāmaṃ kariṃsu.* It is further stated that on the last occasion of his leaving home he saw his pregnant wife lying asleep and was so filled with revolt that he returned to the Order. He started forth at once, a yellow robe tied round his waist, and as he walked to the vihāra, he became a sotāpanna. The monks were at first reluctant to reordain him, but his importunity was so great that they relented, and in a few days he became an arahant.

[1] This incident is recorded at A. iii. 392 ff.
[2] DA. ii. 378 f.; AA. ii. 688.
[3] D. i. 199 ff.
[4] J. i. 311 f.
[5] DhA. i. 305 ff.

5. **Citta.**—One of the chief lay supporters of **Sujāta** Buddha.[1]

[1] Bu. xiii. 30.

6. **Citta.**—A Thera of Ceylon. King **Mahādāṭhika Mahā-nāga** had a young and beautiful queen, named **Damiḷadevī.** One day, when she was worshipping at the **Ambatthala** at **Cetiyagiri,** Citta, who had joined the Order in his old age, fell in love with her and behaved as one mad, constantly repeating to himself "beautiful as Damiḷadevī." Even when told of her death, which took place soon after, he refused to believe the news and continued as before; he became, therefore, known as Ummattaka Citta.[1]

[1] AA. i. 13.

7. **Citta.**—A herdsman, servant of **Dīghagāmaṇi.** He was put to death by the brothers of **Ummāda-Cittā,** because he refused to promise to kill Ummāda-Cittā's child should it be a boy. He was reborn as a yakkha.[1] See **Cittarāja.**

[1] Mhv. ix. 22 f.; MṬ. 278.

8. **Citta.**—A minister, spoken of as **Cittamahāmatta.** He was very generous and kept in his house a gong, by sounding which monks could obtain the requisites at any time. Each day he spent sixty kahāpaṇas for the supply of medicines alone.[1]

[1] VibhA. 341.

9. **Citta.**—A city where **Maṅgala** Buddha performed his Twin Miracle.[1]

[1] BuA. 119.

Citta Vagga.—The third chapter of the Dhammapada.

Citta Saṃyutta.—The sixty-first section of the Saṃyutta Nikāya.[1] It contains records of discussions by **Cittagahapati** of **Macchikāsaṇḍa.**

[1] S. iv. 281-305.

Citta Sutta.—Preached in answer to a question by a deva. The world is led by thought (*citta*) and plagued by it.[1]

[1] S. i. 39; *cf.* A. ii. 177.

Cittaka Thera.—Son of a wealthy brahmin of **Rājagaha.** He heard the Buddha preach at **Veḷuvana** and, having entered the Order, practised meditation in a wooded spot, ultimately achieving arahantship.

In the time of **Vipassī** Buddha he offered him flowers in homage.[1]

He is probably identical with **Tiṇikiṅkinipupphiya Thera** of the Apadāna.[2]

[1] Thag. 22; ThagA. i. 77.

[2] Ap. ii. 433.

Cittakuṭa.—A mountain in **Himavā,** one of the five ranges round **Anotatta.** It is composed of all kinds of precious metals.[1] It is famed as the abode of golden swans living in a golden cave (**Kañcanaguhā**) on the top of the mountain, sometimes as many as ninety thousand in number.[2] There also the **Dhattaraṭṭha** swans lived.[3]

The name is sometimes[4] spelt Citrakūṭa. It is generally identified with Kāmptanāthgiri in Bundelkhand, an isolated hill on the Paisunī or Mandākinī River.[5]

1 SNA. ii. 437; AA. ii. 759; UdA. 300; Ap. i. 50, 414; PsA. 15; Vsm. 650.
2 *E.g.*, J. ii. 107; iii. 208, 247; iv. 424, etc.
3 J. v. 337.
4 *E.g.*, J. iv. 212 ; v. 338.
5 Law: *Geog. of Early Bsm.* 40.

Cittakūṭa-dvārakoṭṭhaka.—The entrance to **Tāvatiṃsa;** it formed a door into **Sudassanagiri** and was surrounded by images of **Indra.**[1]

1 J. vi. 125 f.

Cittakūṭalatāvana.—See **Cittalatāvana.**

1. **Cittagutta Thera.**—An arahant. He lived at the **Bodhimaṇḍavihāra,** and was present, with thirty thousand monks, at the foundation of the **Mahā-Thūpa.**[1]

1 Mhv. xxxix. 41; Dpv. xix. 6.

2. **Cittagutta.**—An Elder living in the **Kuraṇḍaka** Cave. In the cave was a beautiful painting of the Renunciation of the Seven Buddhas, but he never saw it, though he lived there for sixty years. Three times the king sent for him, but he refused to go until the king decreed that no infant in the country should suck milk until the Elder should visit the palace. He dwelt in the palace for seven days and always pronounced the same blessing, no matter who saluted him: "May the king be happy." On the Elder's return to the cave, the deity in the ironwood tree outside stood holding a torch and the Elder attained arahantship.[1] It may be the same Elder who is mentioned elsewhere[2] as having developed *tejo-kasina* on regarding the flame of a lamp on his return to the vihāra after listening to the Dhamma, and again *pīta-kasina* when he saw on **Cittalapabbata** a seat spread with *pattaṅga*-flowers.

1 Vsm. 38. 2 *Ibid.*, 171. 3 *Ibid.*, 173.

3. **Cittagutta.**—An arahant. He lived in **Ambapāsāṇa,** in the village of **Aṅganakola.** He was a fluent speaker, and while yet a *puthujjana*, preached the **Rathavinīta Sutta** at the **Lohapāsāda** to a gathering of twelve thousand

monks and nuns. In his explanation he referred to the glories of the Relic Chamber in the **Mahā-Thūpa.** Though he described them in great detail, yet the Elder **Mahā Tissa,** teacher of **Asathakammika-Tissa,** being present, told him that his description was incomplete.[1] The story is told to indicate the magnitude of the glories of the Relic Chamber.

[1] MṬ. 552 f.

Cittacūḷa.—A tortoise. For details see the **Bhūridatta Jātaka.**[1]

[1] J. vi. 162 f.

Cittadassī.—A mythical king, descendant of **Mahāsammata.**[1]

[1] Dpv. iii. 41.

Cittapatta.—A *kokila*-bird, a previous birth of **Lakuṇṭaka-Bhaddiya,** during the time of **Vipassī** Buddha. The bird, seeing the Buddha, gave him a ripe mango and sang to him, as he ate it, a song of joy. Hence the sweetness of Lakuṇṭaka's voice.[1]

[1] SA. ii. 173.

Cittapariyādāna Sutta.—The monk with a corrupt mind cannot achieve his purpose; the monk with a pure, well-directed mind, can.[1]

[1] A. i. 6 f.

Cittapassa.—A cave wherein **Paṇḍukābhaya,** in the presence of his people, presented his consort, the yakkhiṇī **Cetiyā.**[1]

[1] MṬ. 290.

Cittapāṭali.—A tree in the **Asurabhavana**[1] which lives for a whole æon. When the Asuras were pushed out of the deva-world into their present abode, it was the presence of this tree which revealed to them their whereabouts.[2] It is said[3] that whenever the Cittapāṭali blossomed, the Asuras thought of the **Pāricchattaka**-tree which they had left behind in Tāvatiṃsa and started making preparations for a war against **Sakka.**

[1] S. v. 238. [2] J. i. 202; SNA. ii. 485; MA. i. 476; DhA. i. 272. [3] DhA. i. 280.

Cittaratha.—A park in **Tāvatiṃsa.**[1]

[1] Thig. 374; ThigA. i. 247; Mtu. i. 32, 149, etc.; Divy. 194.

1. **Cittarāja.**—A Yakkha. It was the custom for ancient kings at the time of the Kattika Festival to deck themselves in great array and, standing on the bank of a lake "in the presence of Cittarāja,"[1] to shoot arrows to the four quarters.[2]

[1] Meaning, probably, in front of his statue. [2] J. ii. 372.

2. **Cittarāja.**—A Yakkha whom **Paṇḍukābhaya** honoured by giving him a settlement at the lower end of the **Abhaya** tank. On festival days the Yakkha occupied a seat beside the king. The Mahāvaṃsa[1] says that Cittarāja was an incarnation of the herdsman **Citta** (7) who saved Paṇḍukābhaya's life, but it is more likely that the Cittarāja mentioned here is identical with Cittarāja (1), and that the festival refers to the Kattika festival.

[1] xi. 4, 84, 87, 104.

Cittalatā Vagga.—The second chapter of the **Vimāna Vatthu.**

1. **Cittalatāvana.**—A pleasaunce, five hundred leagues in extent, in **Tāvatiṃsa.** It came into being through the good deeds performed by **Māgha's** wife, **Cittā.**[1] It is said[2] that the place was so called not only because of its association with Cittā, but also because there grew in it various creepers bearing many coloured flowers. In the pleasaunce is born the **Āsāvatī** creeper which blossoms only once in a thousand years.[3]

[1] DhA. i. 271-5; J. i. 202. [2] VvA. 94. [3] ThagA. i. 365; J. iii. 250.

2. **Cittalatāvana.**—A park laid out by **Parakkamabāhu I.**[1]

[1] Cv. lxxix. 7.

Cittalatāvimāna Vatthu.—The story of a poor man who looked after his parents, refusing to marry, and engaged in various acts of piety. After death he was born in a twelve-league vimāna in **Tāvatiṃsa.**[1]

[1] Vv. vii. 1; VvA. 299 f.

Cittalapabbata.—A mountain in **Rohaṇa** on which **Kākavaṇṇa-Tissa** built a vihāra[1] and **Vasabha** ten thūpas.[2] **Dāṭhopatissa** gave to the vihāra the village of **Gonnaviṭṭhi.**[3] The mountain is described as being healthy (*utusappāya*),[4] and sometimes there lived on it as many as twelve thousand monks.[5] Attached to the vihāra was the **Niṅkaponnapadhānaghara**[6] and the **Koṭagerukapāsāda**—the residence of Bhāgineyya **Saṅgharakkhita**[7]—and also, probably, a nunnery.[8] The Elders **Mahānāga** and **Cūḷanāga** lived at Cittalapabbata for three years.[9] The Commentaries[10] contain several stories connected with the mountain. Near by[11] was the village

[1] Mhv. xxii. 23.
[2] *Ibid.*, xxxv. 81.
[3] Cv. xlv. 59.
[4] MṬ. 552.
[5] VibhA. 445; Mhv. xxiv. 9.
[6] VibhA. 489.
[7] MṬ. 552
[8] See VibhA. 498.
[9] SA. ii. 125.
[10] *E.g.*, VibhA. 264, 498; DhsA. 351, 399; AA. i. 386; MA. i. 18, 66, 150, 223, 351, 399.
[11] AA. i. 386.

of **Kālumbara** and the bathing place of **Kuruvakatittha.**[12] It was evidently a very important monastic centre in Ceylon, and is mentioned on a par with **Abhayagiri** and **Cetiyapabbata.**[13] Cittalapabbata is sometimes called **Cittalakūṭa.**[14]

[12] MA. ii. 1024. [13] *E.g.*, DA. ii. 478. [14] *E.g.*, Mhv. xxxv. 81.

Cittalapabbata-Tissa.—A Thera. Seized by discontent, he asked his teacher's consent to leave the Order. The latter, seeing his *upanissaya*, asked him to build a hut for his use, not omitting his religious duties the while. Tissa consented, and, having finished the hut and spread the bed, he informed his teacher, who said, "Now that you have done this work with such great pains, why not spend one night in the hut?" Tissa did so, and during the night, while reflecting on what he had accomplished, his heart was filled with joy and he became an arahant.[1]

[1] AA. i. 26 f.

Citta-Sambhūta Jātaka (No. 498).—The Bodhisatta was once born as a Caṇḍāla in **Ujjeni** in the kingdom of **Avanti.** He was called **Citta** and his brother **Sambhūta.** One day, when they were out sweeping, two rich women on their way to the park noticed them and turned back. Their followers, disappointed at their loss of a picnic, beat the two Caṇḍālas. Then the brothers went to **Takkasilā** to study. Citta became very proficient, and was sent one day, in place of his teacher, to the house of a villager who had invited the teacher and his pupils. But while there, in a moment of forgetfulness, the brothers used the Caṇḍāla dialect, and having thus disclosed their caste, were driven out of Takkāsilā. In their next birth they became does and in a subsequent birth ospreys. They were always together and always met their death together. Later Citta was born as the son of the chaplain of **Kosambī,** and Sambhūta as son of the king of **Uttarapañcāla.** Citta, becoming an ascetic at the age of sixteen, remembered his past births. He waited till Sambhūta had reigned for fifty years, and knowing that he also had some recollection of his previous existences, taught a stanza to a lad and sent him to recite it before the king. Sambhūta heard the stanza, remembered his brother, and, after inquiry, visited Citta, who had then gone to the royal park. There Citta gave him counsel, and not long after Sambhūta renounced the world. After death they were both born in the Brahma world.

Ānanda is identified with Sambhūta. The story was told in reference to two monks, colleagues of **Maha-Kassapa,** who were greatly devoted to each other.

[1] J. iv. 390-401.

Cittasālā.—A hall in **Anurādhapura** to the east of **Thūpārāma,** within sight of the **Bodhi**-tree. The body of **Saṅghamittā,** as desired by her, was cremated near the hall and a thūpa was erected over the remains.[1]

[1] Mhv. xx. 52.

Cittasena.—A Gandhabba present at the preaching of the **Mahāsamaya Sutta.**[1] He is elsewhere[2] mentioned as a Yakkha chieftain who should be invoked by the Buddha's followers when troubled by evil spirits.

[1] D. ii. 258. [2] D. iii. 204.

Cittahatthisāriputta Sutta.—A number of Elders[1] were talking on the Abhidhamma in the Migadāya in **Isipatana,** when **Citta-Hatthisāriputta** (*q.v.*) broke into their talk. **Mahā Koṭṭhita** rebuked him, and, on being remonstrated with by Citta's friends, Mahā Koṭṭhita implied by means of various similes that Citta was not the wise man they thought him to be, and that he would, without doubt, return again to the lay life. This prediction proved true, but Citta came back once more to the Order, and shortly afterwards became an arahant.[2]

[1] The DA. (ii. 378) which refers to this incident says that the talk took place between Moggallāna and Koṭṭhita.

[2] A. iii. 392 ff.

1. **Cittā.**—One of the four wives of **Māgha.** Māgha and his companions erected a hall, and Cittā had a flower garden laid out close by wherein she grew every kind of flowering tree, shrub and creeper. As a result she was reborn in **Tāvatiṃsa** as **Sakka's** consort, and the **Cittalatāvana** came into being for her pleasure.[1]

[1] DhA. i. 269 f.; J. i. 201 f.

2. **Cittā.**—A Therī. She was the daughter of a leading citizen of **Rājagaha.** Hearing the Buddha preach, she entered the Order under **Pajāpatī Gotamī.** In her old age she went to **Gijjhakūṭa** and there, after meditation, she attained arahantship.

Ninety-four kappas ago she was a kinnarā on the bank of the **Candabhāgā** and there offered flowers to a Pacceka Buddha.[1] She is probably identical with **Nalamālikā** of the Apadāna.[2]

[1] Thig. vs. 27 f.; ThigA. 33 f. [2] ii. 528 f.

3. **Cittā.**—One of the five queens of **Okkāka.**[1]

[1] DA. i. 278; SNA. i. 352; MṬ. 131.

4. **Cittā.**—See **Ummāda-Cittā.**

5. **Cittā.**—One of the chief lay women supporters of **Sobhita** Buddha.[1]

[1] Bu. vii. 23.

6. **Cittā.**—A laywoman who was among the chief supporters of **Sikhī** Buddha.[1]

[1] Bu. xxi. 22.

7. **Cittā.**—Daughter of the **Madda** king and wife of **Sumitta,** son of **Sīhabāhu.**[1]

[1] MṬ. 269; Mhv. viii. 7.

Cittāgāra Vagga.—The fifth chapter of the **Bhikkhunī Pācittiya.**[1]

[1] Vin. iv. 298 ff.

Cittāpokkharaṇī.—A bathing pond in the **Dīpuyyāna,** erected by **Parakkamabāhu I.** It was adorned with gay pictures,[1] hence, probably, the name.

[1] Cv. lxxiii. 121.

Cittupaṭṭhānapāsāda.—A hall within the precincts of the king's palace in **Anurādhapura,** where the people waited on the monks with gifts. Here King **Bhātika** provided gifts for the monks.[1]

[1] Mhv. xxxiv. 65; MṬ. 633.

Citrā.—The name of certain **Supaṇṇas.**[1]

[1] D. ii. 259.

1. **Cintā Sutta.**—Unprofitable reasonings about the world, life, etc., should be abandoned. Thoughts about Ill, etc., should be cultivated.[1]

[1] S. v. 418.

2. **Cintā Sutta.**—Once a man, having left **Rājagaha,** came to the **Sumāgadhā** Lotus Pond and started speculating about the world. He then saw a whole army entering a lotus-stalk. Thinking himself mad, he returned to the town, where he told people what he had seen; they confirmed his belief in his madness. But, in fact, said the Buddha, what he saw was real; he saw the Asura-host running away from the Devas and escaping through a lotus stalk. It is, therefore, unprofitable to speculate about the world.[1]

[1] S. v. 446 f.

1. **Cintāmaṇī, Cintāmaṇikā.**—The name of a *Vijjā*, whereby the thoughts of others can be read by observing them.[1]

[1] DA. ii. 389; AA. i. 399.

2. **Cintāmaṇī.**—Wife of the Treasurer **Gandha.** When **Bhattabhatika** had fulfilled his contract with Gandha, the latter ordered that all the members of his household, with the exception of Cintāmaṇī, should wait on Bhattabhatika.[1]

[1] DhA. iii. 90.

Ciragumba.—The residence of **Ambakhādaka-Mahātissa;** it was probably a monastery.[1]

[1] Vsm. 43.

Cirappa.—A king of fifteen kappas ago, a previous birth of **Abbhañjana-dāyaka Thera.**[1]

[1] Ap. i. 236.

Ciravāsī.—The son of **Bhadragaka.** Bhadragaka visited the Buddha and told him that he was always anxiously waiting for news of Ciravāsi, who was away at school.[1]

[1] S. iv. 329; SA. iii. 103.

Cīna.—The Pāli name of China. It is several times mentioned in the Milindapañha,[1] once as a place where ships congregate.[2] **Nāgasena** speaks[3] of a contemporary Cīnarājā who could charm the ocean by an Act of Truth and could enter the ocean to a distance of one league in his chariot drawn by lions, the waves rolling back at his approach. The Apadāna[4] speaks of the Cīnaraṭṭha in a list of countries and tribes. The Commentaries[5] speak of the softness of Chinese silk (*Cīnapaṭa*).

[1] 121, 327.
[2] 359.
[3] *Ibid.*, 121.
[4] ii. 359.
[5] *E.g.*, VibhA. 159.

Cīnamāla.—See **Ciṇṇamāla.**

Cīramātikā.—An irrigation canal, the taxes from which King **Mahānāga** gave to the **Mahāvihāra.**[1] The canal probably led out of the **Cīravāpi.**

[1] Cv. xli. 100.

Cīravāpī.—A tank in Ceylon built by King **Mahāsena.**[1]

[1] Mhv. xxxvii. 49.

Cirā.—A seven-year-old novice, an arahant who offered to perform a miracle herself, so that the Buddha might be saved the trouble of performing the Twin Miracle. She offered to fetch **Sineru,** the **Cakkavāḷapabbata**

and **Himavā,** and to soar over their tops like a wild goose.[1] She is probably identical with the bhikkhunī mentioned in the Saṃyutta Nikāya[2] as having won the praise of a Yakkha.

[1] DhA. iii. 211. [2] i. 213.

Cīvara.—A teacher in Burma who wrote a ṭīkā to **Jaṅghadāsa** (*sic*).[1] Elsewhere[2] the same work is ascribed to **Vajira.**

[1] Gv. 64. [2] *Ibid.*, 67, 74.

Cīvara Sutta.—Once, when **Mahā Kassapa** was at **Veḷuvana** in **Rājagaha, Ānanda** returned from a tour in the **Dakkhiṇāgiri,** with thirty monks, mostly youths. They were ill-behaved, and Kassapa blamed Ānanda for going about with them, calling him "corn-tramper," "despoiler of families," and, finally, "a boy." Ānanda gently reminded him that being grey-haired he could hardly be called a boy, but Kassapa refused to listen. **Thulla-Nandā,** hearing of this, vented her displeasure on Kassapa by reminding him that he was once a heretical teacher. Kassapa thereupon remonstrated with Ānanda, pointing out that he was a very devoted follower and pupil of the Buddha and relating how, on one occasion, the Buddha accepted from him the gift of his soft robe, giving him, in return, the Buddha's rag-robe. Well might he, he said, claim to be a real son of the Buddha.[1]

[1] S. ii. 217 ff.

Cīvarakkhandha.—The eighth chapter of the Mahāvagga of the Vinaya Piṭaka.[1]

[1] Vin. i. 268 ff.

Cīvaracetiya.—A monastery in Ceylon. **Kitti,** queen of **Mahinda IV.,** built three bathing-tanks there.[1]

[1] Cv. liv. 51.

Cuṇṇasālā.—A district in **Rohaṇa.**[1]

[1] Cv. lvii. 46, 57.

1. **Cunda.**—A worker in metals (*kammāraputta*) living in **Pāvā.** When the Buddha reached Pāvā on his way to **Kusināra,** he stayed in Cunda's Mango grove. There Cunda visited him and invited him and the monks to a meal the next day. The meal consisted of sweet rice and cakes and *sūkaramaddava.* At the meal the Buddha ordered that he alone should be served with *sūkaramaddava,* and that what was left over should be buried

in a hole. This was the Buddha's last meal, as very soon after it he developed dysentery.[1] The Buddha, a little while before his death, gave special instructions to Ānanda that he should visit Cunda and reassure him by telling him that no blame at all attached to him and that he should feel no remorse, but should, on the contrary, rejoice, in that he had been able to give to the Buddha a meal which, in merit, far exceeded any other.[2]

The Suttanipāta Commentary[3] mentions that, at this meal, Cunda provided golden vessels for the monks' use; some made use of them, others did not. One monk stole a vessel and put it in his bag. Cunda noticed this but said nothing. Later, in the afternoon, he visited the Buddha and questioned him as to the different kinds of *samaṇas* there were in the world. The Buddha preached to him the **Cunda Sutta** (*q.v.*). The Commentary adds[4] that Cunda reached no attainment, but merely had his doubts dispelled. The Dīgha Commentary, however, says[5] that he became a Sotāpanna at the first sight of the Buddha and built for him a vihāra at the **Ambavana.** This latter incident, probably, took place at an earlier visit of the Buddha, for we are told[6] that while the Buddha was staying in Cunda's Mango grove, he was invited by the **Mallas** to consecrate their new Mote-hall, **Ubbhaṭaka.** He accepted the invitation, preached in the hall till late at night, and then requested Sāriputta to continue, which he did by preaching the **Saṅgīti Sutta.** This was soon after the death of **Nigaṇṭha Nātaputta.**[7] The Aṅguttara Nikāya[8] mentions another conversation between the Buddha and Cunda. Cunda tells the Buddha that he approves of the methods of purification (*soceyyāṇi*) laid down by the brahmins of the west (**Pacchābhūmakā**). The Buddha tells him of the teaching of the Āriyans regarding the threefold defilement and purification of the body, the fourfold defilement and purification of the speech, and the threefold defilement and purification of the mind. Cunda accepts the Buddha's explanations and declares himself his follower.

[1] D. ii. 126; Ud. viii. 5.
[2] D. ii. 135 f.
[3] SNA. i. 159.
[4] p. 166; also UdA. 399.
[5] DA. ii. 568.
[6] D. iii. 207.
[7] *Ibid.*, 210.
[8] v. 263 ff.

2. **Cunda.**—The books appear to refer to two theras by the name of Cunda, the better known being **Mahā-Cunda** and the other **Cūḷa-Cunda.** But the legends connected with them are so confused that it is not possible to differentiate clearly one from the other. Mention is also made of a **Cunda-Samaṇuddesa** whom, however, the Commentaries[1] identify with Mahā-Cunda. Mahā-Cunda is, for instance, described in the Theragāthā

[1] *E.g.*, DA. iii. 907

Commentary[2] as the younger brother of Sāriputta, under whom he joined the Order, winning arahantship after arduous and strenuous effort. In the time of Vipassī Buddha he had been a potter and had given to the Buddha a bowl made of clay. The Apadāna verses quoted in the Theragāthā Commentary are, in the Apadāna itself,[3] ascribed to a monk named **Ekapattadāyaka.** They make no mention whatever of his relationship to Sāriputta. On the other hand, there are to be found elsewhere in the Apadāna[4] certain verses ascribed to a Cunda Thera, which definitely state that he was the son of the brahmin **Vaṅganta,** and that his mother was **Sārī.** But in these verses he is called **Cūḷa-Cunda,** and mention is made of his previous birth in the time of **Siddhattha Buddha,** to whom he gave a bouquet of jasmine flowers. As a result he became king of the devas seventy-seven times and was once king of men, by name **Dujjaya.** It is further stated that he became arahant while yet a sāmaṇera and that he waited upon the Buddha and his own brother and other virtuous monks. This account goes on to say that after his brother's death, Cunda brought his relics in a bowl and presented them to the Buddha, who uttered praises of Sāriputta. This would identify Cūḷa-Cunda with Cunda Samaṇuddesa who, according to the Saṃyutta Nikāya,[5] attended Sāriputta in his last illness and, after his death, brought to the Buddha at **Jetavana** Sāriputta's bowl and outer robe and his relics wrapt in his water-strainer. Therefore if Buddhaghosa[6] is correct in identifying Cunda Samaṇuddesa with Mahā-Cunda, then all three are one and the same.

Cunda Samaṇuddesa was, for some time, the personal attendant of the Buddha,[7] and when the Buddha prepared to perform the Twin Miracle, offered to perform a miracle himself and so save the Buddha trouble and exertion.[8] Cunda's teacher was **Ānanda,** and it was to Ānanda that he first brought the news of Sāriputta's death.[9]

Mahā-Cunda was evidently a disciple of great eminence, and is mentioned by the Buddha[10] in company with the Two Chief Disciples, Mahā Kassapa, Mahā Koṭṭhita, Mahā Kaccāna and other very eminent Elders.

The Piṭakas contain several discourses[11] given to the monks by Mahā-Cunda while residing at **Sahajāti** among the **Cetis,** probably after the

[2] ThagA. i. 261; see also DhA. ii. 188 and AA. ii. 674.

[3] Ap. ii. 444.

[4] *Ibid.*, i. 101 f.

[5] S. v. 161 f.

[6] Buddhaghosa says that the monks called him Samaṇuddesa in his youth before his upasampadā, and he never lost the name (DA. iii. 907).

[7] ThagA. ii. 124; J. iv. 95, etc.

[8] DhA. iii. 211.

[9] SA. iii. 178; see also the Pāsādika Sutta and the Sāmagāma Sutta (where Cunda brings to Ānanda and then to the Buddha the news of Nigaṇṭha Nātaputta's death); see also the Sallekha Sutta.

[10] A. iii. 299; see also M. iii. 78; Ud. i. 5.

[11] A. iii. 355; v. 41, 157.

Buddha's death. Cunda (or **Cundaka** as he is called in this context) was with the Buddha in his last journey to **Kusinārā,** and spread a bed for him in the Mango grove by the **Kakutthā** River.[12] Cunda is mentioned[13] as having accompanied Sāriputta when he went to see **Channa** at the **Kalandakanivāpa** in Rājagaha, just before Channa's suicide. Once, when the Buddha lay ill in the Kalandakanivāpa, Cunda visited him and they talked of the *bojjhaṅgas.* There and then the Buddha's sickness vanished.[14]

[12] D. ii., 134 f.; Ud. viii. 5. [13] S. iv. 50 f.; M. iii. 263 f. [14] S. v. 81.

3. **Cunda.**—See **Cunda-Sūkarika.**

4. **Cunda.**—A rājakumāra, brother of **Cundī** and, therefore, son of **Bimbisāra.**[1]

[1] A. iii. 35.

1. **Cunda Sutta.**—**Cunda Kammāraputta** visits the Buddha in his Mango-grove in **Pāvā** and questions him as to how many classes of recluses there are in the world. Four, answers the Buddha—*maggajina, maggadesaka, maggajīvī* and *maggadūsī*—and proceeds to explain them.[1] The circumstances in which the sutta was preached are given *s.v.* **Cunda** (1).

[1] SN. vs. 83-90; SNA. i. 159 ff.

2. **Cunda Sutta** (also called **Mahā Cunda Sutta**).—Preached by **Mahā Cunda** at **Sahajātī** to the assembled monks. Some, who are zealous about the Dhamma, speak disparagingly of those who are given to jhāna and *vice versa.* Sometimes it happens that those who are engaged in the Dhamma praise their fellows, and similarly with those devoted to jhāna. None of these things are profitable. Dhamma-zealots should learn to praise those eager for jhāna and *vice versa.*[1]

[1] A. iii. 355 f.

3. **Cunda Sutta.**—**Mahā Cunda** tells the monks at **Sahajātī** how it is possible to distinguish true statements from false when made by a monk about himself and his attainments.[1]

[1] A. v. 41 ff.

4. **Cunda Sutta.**—**Cunda Samaṇuddesa** comes to **Jetavana** from **Nālagāmaka,** where he had attended **Sāriputta** during his last illness, and reports his death to **Ānanda,** producing, at the same time, Sāriputta's bowl and outer robe and the water-strainer containing his relics. Ānanda

accompanies Cunda to the Buddha, where he breaks the news. The Buddha praises Sāriputta's attainments and takes the opportunity of emphasising the impermanence of all things.[1]

[1] S. v. 161 ff.

Cundaka.—See **Cunda** (2).

Cundaṭṭhila.—A village near Benares, but on the other side of the river and between **Vasabhagāma** and Benares[1] (*v.l.* **Cundavīla**).

[1] Pv. iii. 1; PvA. 168, 170; Mtu. iii. 325, 327.

Cunda Sūkarika.—A pork butcher near **Veḷuvana.** For forty-five years he plied his trade, killing pigs in such a way as to retain the flavour of the flesh unimpaired. When death approached he saw before him the fires of **Avīci** and roared with pain. For seven days he grunted like a pig, crawling on all fours, and no one could prevent him. The monks told the Buddha of the noises they had heard when passing the butcher's house, and the Buddha explained how retribution had fallen on Cunda commensurate with his wickedness.[1]

[1] DhA. i. 105 ff.

Cundī.—A princess. She visited the Buddha at the **Kalandakanivāpa** in **Veḷuvana,** and he preached to her the **Cundī Sutta.**[1] According to the Commentary,[2] she was the daughter of **Bimbisāra.** The king gave her five hundred chariots for the use of herself and her companions. She was one of the three women who received this gift from their fathers, the others being **Visākhā** and the princess **Sumanā.** Cundī's brother was **Cunda.** Her name occurs in a list of eminent upāsikās.[3]

[1] A. iii. 35 f. [2] AA. ii. 596. [3] A. iv. 347.

Cundī Sutta.—**Cundī** visits the Buddha and tells him that, according to her brother, **Cunda,** those who take refuge in the Buddha, the Dhamma and the Order and refrain from the taking of life, from theft, carnal lusts, lying and liquor, will be born in a happy condition after death. She wishes to know more of this. The Buddha explains to her that the Tathāgata is the best of beings, the Doctrine which leads to Nibbāna is the best of teachings, the Tathāgata's Order is the best field of merit, and of virtues, those beloved by Ariyans are the best.[1]

[1] A. iii. 35 f.

Cumbaṭakalaha.—The name given to the quarrel between the **Sākiyans** and the **Koliyans** regarding the water of the **Rohiṇī**.[1]

[1] J. i. 208.

Culla°.—See also under **Cūla°**, and **Cūḷa°**.

Culla-Anāthapiṇḍika.—An eminent lay disciple of the Buddha. He was an Anāgāmī, and offered to perform a miracle himself before the Buddha showed the Twin Miracle.[1] Culla-Anāthapiṇḍika provided food for three months for the multitude, covering an area of twelve leagues, which had assembled at **Sāvatthi** to await the descent of the Buddha from **Tāvatiṃsa** after his preaching of the Abhidhamma Piṭaka.[2] Five hundred monks fed daily at Culla-Anāthapiṇḍika's house in Sāvatthi.[3] He was one of the seven lay disciples of the Buddha who had each five hundred followers.[4] Culla-Anāthapiṇḍika is generally mentioned[5] together with **Pasenadi, Visākhā,** and **Anāthapiṇḍika** as the Buddha's eminent lay-patrons. His personal name is not known. The sobriquet was probably given on account of his generosity, rivalling that of Anāthapiṇḍika.

[1] DhA. iii. 210.
[2] *Ibid.*, 218; AA. i. 71.
[3] DhA. i. 339.
[4] SA. iii. 223.
[5] *E.g.*, J. i. 148; ii. 287, iii. 520.

Culla-Kañcakuṇḍa.—A Damiḷa chief of South India who fought against the forces of **Parakkamabāhu I.** but was later subdued.[1] The name is closely connected with that of the districts of **Kañcakuḍiya** and **Kañcakuḍiyarājā.**[2]

[1] Cv. lxxvi. 185, 217, 220, 305.
[2] *Ibid.*, 124, 130.

Culla-Kammāsadamma.—A village in the **Kampilla** kingdom which arose on the settlement given by **Jayaddisa** to his brother, the man-eating ogre, after the latter became an ascetic.[1] For details see the **Jayaddisa Jātaka.**

[1] J. v. 35.

Cullakaseṭṭhi.—The Bodhisatta, born as a Treasurer in Benares. See the **Cullakaseṭṭhi Jātaka.**

Cullakaseṭṭhi Jātaka (No. 4).—Once the Bodhisatta was born as **Cullakaseṭṭhi** in Benares. One day, while on his way to the palace, he saw a dead mouse lying on the road, and, noticing the position of the stars, he said, " Any decent young fellow with his wits about him has only to pick up the mouse and he will be a made man." A young man of good family, called

Cullantevāsika, hearing this, picked up the mouse and sold it for a farthing to a tavern for their cat to eat. With the farthing he bought molasses and drinking water for flower-gatherers. Later, he gathered branches and leaves blown down by the wind in the king's garden and sold them to a potter for a large sum of money. He entered into friendship with a land-trader and a sea-trader and, by using the information he obtained from them, he was able to make two hundred thousand pieces by means of skilful and far-sighted business dealings. He then visited Cullaseṭṭhi to express to him his gratitude, and the seṭṭhi, on hearing of his skill, was so impressed that he gave him his daughter in marriage.

The young man is identified with **Cullapanthaka** (*q.v.*), in reference to whom the story was related.[1]

[1] J. i. 114-23. *Cf.* the story of Viṣākhila in Kathāsaritsāgara (i. 33).

Cullakāla.—A mountain in **Himavā** which must be crossed in order to reach **Gandhamādana**[1] and the **Chaddanta Lake.**[2]

[1] SNA. i. 66. [2] J. v. 38.

Culla-Kāliṅga.—Younger son of **Kāliṅga,** king of **Dantapura.** He became an ascetic, but later married the daughter of the **Madda** king, by whom he had a son **Kāliṅga** who became a cakkavatti.[1] For details see the **Kāliṅga-Bodhi Jātaka.**

[1] J. iv. 230 ff.

Cullakāliṅga Jātaka (No. 301).—**Kāliṅga,** king of **Dantapura,** anxious to make a fight, sent his four daughters of surpassing beauty into every kingdom, offering them to any man who would fight him for them. **Assaka,** king of **Potali,** with the advice of his minister **Nandisena,** accepted the challenge. Kāliṅga thereupon came with his mighty army, and the Bodhisatta who was an ascetic declared, after consultation with **Sakka,** that victory would be his. But Nandisena, undaunted, instructed Assaka as to how he should kill the tutelary deity of Kāliṅga when this deity, in the guise of a white bull, should appear on the battlefield. Nandisena led the attack of the soldiers, the white bull was killed and Kāliṅga defeated. He had to provide dowries for his daughters, and thenceforth the two kings lived as friends.

The story was related in reference to **Sāriputta** who is identified with Nandisena. Two Jains, a man and a woman, each versed in five hundred theses, met in **Vesāli** and the **Licchavis** arranged a marriage between them. They had one son, **Saccaka,** and four daughters, **Saccā, Lolā, Avavādakā** and **Paṭācārā.** After the death of their parents, the girls wandered from city to city for purposes of disputation. They came at last to Sāvatthi, where they set up at the city gate a jambu-tree, to be pulled up by anyone accepting their challenge to a discussion. Sāriputta, seeing the branch, had it removed, and when the girls came to him with a great crowd of people, answered all their questions and defeated them in debate. Thereupon they entered the Order under **Uppalavaṇṇā,** and the fame of Sāriputta increased.[1]

[1] J. iii. 1 ff.

Culla-Kuṇāla Jātaka (No. 464).—For this story reference is made to the **Kunāla Jātaka.** The opening words quoted occur at the end of several stories, related by **Kuṇāla** to illustrate the fickleness and wickedness of women. Culla-Kuṇāla is probably the name given to the last of these stories, which tells of **Piṅgiyānī** (*q.v.*), wife of **Brahmadatta.**[1]

[1] J. iv. 144.

Culla-Kuṇāla Vagga.—The fifth section of the Catukkanipāta of the Jātakaṭṭhakathā.[1]

[1] J. iii. 132-52.

Culla-Kokanadā.—The younger of the two daughters of **Pajunna,** both of whom were called Kokanadā. She visited the Buddha at the **Kuṭāgārasālā** in **Vesāli** and questioned him.[1]

[1] S. i. 30.

Culla-Kokālika.—See **Kokālika** (2).

Cullacārī.—See **Cullasārī.**

Cullatāpasa.—**Nārada,** the son of the Bodhisatta in the **Culla-Nāradākassapa Jātaka** (*q.v.*), is referred to by this title.[1]

[1] J. i. 416.

Culla-Tuṇḍila.—A pig, brother of the Bodhisatta. For details see the **Tuṇḍila Jātaka.**

Cullantevāsika.—A youth of good family who, as related in the **Cullakaseṭṭhi Jātaka,** earned money by his wits, after having listened to the counsel of **Cullakaseṭṭhi.** He is identified with **Cullapanthaka.**[1]

[1] J. i. 120 f.

Culladaddara.—A Nāga, brother of **Mahādaddara** (the Bodhisatta), and son of **Sūradaddara.** For details see the **Daddara Jātaka.**

1. **Culla-Dhanuggaha.** A brahmin of Benares, a very skilled archer. See the **Culla-Dhanuggaha Jātaka.**

2. **Culla-Dhanuggaha.**—An Udicca-brahmin. He was a clever archer, but being rather dwarfed in stature, he joined **Bimbisāra** as his page and took service under the **Andhra** king. For details see the **Bhīmasena Jātaka.** He is also referred to as **Culladhanupaṭṭhāka** and **Cullupaṭṭhāka.**[1]

[1] J. i. 357.

Culla-Dhanuggaha Jātaka (No. 374).—A young brahmin of Benares came to **Takkasilā** and became very proficient in archery. His teacher gave him his daughter in marriage and he became known as **Culla-Dhanuggaha.** When on his way with his wife to Benares, he killed a fierce elephant, and then meeting fifty bandits, slew all except the leader. He seized the leader and hurling him to the ground asked his wife for his sword. But his wife, conceiving a passion for the bandit, placed the sword's hilt in the bandit's hand, and he straightway slew Culla-Dhanuggaha. While walking away with the woman, the bandit, reflecting on her treacherousness, decided to leave her. When they came to a river he left her on the bank, and taking her ornaments across the river on the pretence of keeping them safe he deserted her. The Bodhisatta, born as **Sakka,** observing this and wishing to shame the woman, appeared before her as a jackal, with **Mātali** as a fish and **Pañcasikha** as a bird. The jackal had a piece of flesh in his mouth, but when the fish leapt up he abandoned it to catch the fish, only to find the bird flying away with it. The woman saw and understood.

The story was told in reference to a monk who wished to leave the Order because of his former wife. The monk is identified with Culla-Dhanuggaha and his wife with the woman of the story.[1]

According to the Dhammapada Commentary,[2] the story was told in reference to a young monk who, going to a house to fetch water, saw a young woman and fell in love with her. She encouraged his attentions, and the monk, desiring her, wished to leave the Order.

[1] J. iii. 219-24. [2] DhA. iv. 65 ff.

Culla-Dhammapāla Jātaka (No. 358).—Once the Bodhisatta was born as **Dhammapāla,** son of **Mahāpatāpa,** king of Benares and his queen, **Candā.** One day Candā was playing with her seven-months-old baby with whom she was so engrossed that, when the king entered the room, she omitted to rise.

This roused the king's jealousy, and he sent for the executioner and had the prince's hands and feet and head cut off and his body encircled with sword-cuts "as though with a garland." He paid no heed to Candā's lamentations, and she, in her great sorrow, fell down dead of a broken heart. Flames arose from Avīci, and wrapping Mahāpatāpa about, "as with a woollen garment," plunged him in the lowest hell.

The story was told in reference to **Devadatta's** attempts to kill the Buddha. Devadatta was Mahāpatāpa and **Mahāpajāpatī** was Candā.[1] The Jātaka is often cited[2] to illustrate how anger, when once arisen, is difficult to control.

[1] J. iii. 177-82. [2] *E.g.*, J. iv. 11; v. 113.

Cullanandaka Jātaka.—See **Cullanandiya.**

Cullanandika.—See **Cullanandiya.**

Cullanandikā.—**Talatādevī** is identified with **Cullanandikā**[1] in the present age, but nothing further seems to be known of the latter.

[1] J. vi. 478.

Cullanandiya.—A monkey, brother of **Nandiya,** the Bodhisatta. See the **Cullanandiya Jātaka.** He is identified with **Ānanda.** *v.l.* **Cullanandika.**

Cullanandiya Jātaka (No. 222)—*v.l.* **Cullanandaka.**—The Bodhisatta was once a monkey named **Nandiya** and, with his brother **Cullanandiya,** headed a band of eighty thousand monkeys. They had a blind mother, and finding that when they were away with the herd she never received the fruits they sent her, they decided to stay with her in a banyan-tree near a village. One day a brahmin, who had studied at **Takkasilā,** entered the forest with a bow and arrow. He had been warned by his teacher **Pārāsariya** to curb his wickedness, but he could find no way, apart from killing, of keeping his wife and child. Seeing the aged monkey, he prepared to shoot her, but her sons offered their lives in her stead. The brahmin killed first them and then the mother. On his way home he heard that lightning had hit his house and that his family was dead; he himself was thereupon swallowed up by the fires of hell.

The story was told in reference to **Devadatta's** wickedness. The hunter was Devadatta.[1]

[1] J. ii. 199-202.

Cullanāgatittha.—A ford in the **Mahāvāḷukagaṅgā.**[1]

[1] Cv. lxxii. 34.

Cullanārada Jātaka (No. 477)—*v.l.* **Cullanāradakassapa.**—The Bodhisatta was once a rich brahmin who, on the death of his wife, retired with his son to the Himālaya and became an ascetic. One day a girl, having been carried off by thieves, escaped from them and arrived at the ascetic's hut when the Bodhisatta was away. The son fell a victim to her charms and agreed to return with her to the haunts of men. She went on ahead and he was to follow, but his father, hearing of what had occurred during his absence, described to the youth the snares of household life in such a graphic way that he gave up the idea of following the girl.

The story was related in reference to a vain monk who succumbed to the wiles of a maiden of **Sāvatthi.** The girl's mother used her to entice the monk to become her son-in-law. The Buddha warned him that in the past the same girl had tried to destroy his spiritual life.[1]

In the Jātaka itself the Bodhisatta's son is called **Nārada,**[2] but elsewhere[3] he is referred to as **Cullatāpasa** (probably only a descriptive title). It was in reference to the same monk that the **Muṇika,** the **Udañcani,** the **Sālūka** and the **Arañña Jātakas** were related.

[1] J. iv. 219-24. [2] p. 222. [3] J. i. 416, 417.

Culla-Niddesa.—See *s.v.* **Niddesa.**

Cullapaduma Jātaka (No. 193).—The Bodhisatta was once born as **Paduma,** son of the chief queen of the Benares king. He had six brothers. The king, becoming suspicious of his sons, ordered them to leave the kingdom. They went away with their wives, and coming to a region where no food was to be had, they killed their wives one by one and ate their flesh. The Bodhisatta managed to save his wife by foregoing a share of the meal each day, and fled with her. During the flight the Bodhisatta gave his wife some of his blood to drink, she being so thirsty. Later they lived in a hut on the bank of the Ganges. One day the Bodhisatta rescued from the river a thief with his limbs cut off who was drifting down stream in a boat. At first the Bodhisatta's wife would not even look at the man, but soon she conceived a passion for him and threw her husband down a precipice. The Bodhisatta fell on a fig-tree, and after some time climbed down with the help of an iguana. He went to Benares and established his claim to his father's kingdom. His erstwhile wife, wandering from place to place with the cripple on her shoulders, gained great reputation as a devoted wife. One day she came to Benares. There the king recognised her and revealed her treachery.[1]

The story was told in reference to a backsliding monk. The details are given in the **Ummadantī Jātaka.**

Devadatta was the thief, **Ciñcā** the treacherous woman, and **Ānanda** the iguana.

[1] J. ii. 115-21.

Cullapantha.—A pariveṇa built, probably, by a Damiḷa chief in the reign of **Aggabodhi IV.**[1]

[1] Cv. xlvi. 24.

Cullapanthaka.—See **Cūlapanthaka.**

Cullapalobhana Jātaka (No. 263).—The Bodhisatta once left the Brahma-world and was born as the son of the Benares king, but would have nothing to do with women. When he grew up his father was filled with despair, and then a dancing-girl offered to seduce the prince. She sang outside his door till he was filled with desire. Eventually he came to know the joys of love, and filled with madness, ran amok through the streets, chasing people. The king banished both his son and his seducer, and they lived in a hut away down the Ganges. One day a hermit visited the hut and, seeing the woman, lost his power of flying through the air. When he saw the Bodhisatta he ran away and fell into the sea. The Bodhisatta, realising his plight, told him of the wiles of women and helped him to regain his lost power, while he himself sent the woman back to the haunts of men and became an ascetic.

The story was told in reference to a backsliding brother.[1]

[1] J. ii. 328 ff.

Cullapāla.—Son of **Mahāsuvaṇṇa** and brother of **Cakkhupāla Thera.**[1]

[1] DhA. i. 2.

Cullapiṇḍapātika-Tissa.—The young son of wealthy parents of **Rājagaha,** Having heard the Buddha preach at **Veḷuvana,** he wished to join the Order, but could only obtain his parents' consent by starving for seven days. He then went with the Buddha to **Jetavana.** On the festival day his parents made great lamentation and a slave girl offered to entice him back. She rode in a palanquin to **Sāvatthi** and took up residence in a street whither the Elder came for alms. She gradually made his acquaintance, and then, feigning illness, enticed him into her apartments. Then, having violated his chastity, she took him back to Rājagaha.[1] The Buddha, hearing of this, preached the **Vātamiga Jātaka,** in which story Tissa is identified with the antelope. He is also referred to as **Cullapiṇḍapātiya.**[2]

[1] J. i. 156 f. [2] *Ibid.*, 159.

Cullapiṇḍapātiya(°pātika)-Tissa.—A monk mentioned in the Commentaries[1] in explaining the term *mutta-muttaka.* A certain lay-woman waited on him for twelve years. One day a fire broke out in the village and burnt her house, together with those of others. The monks who were fed at neighbouring houses went there to enquire whether anything had been served, but Tissa did not arrive until the mealtime, and when given a meal which the woman had prepared with great difficulty, ate it and went away without a word. The woman, however, was not a whit disturbed by the taunts of her neighbours.

This may be the Elder who, in the Aṅguttara Commentary,[2] is mentioned as having resided in **Gāmeṇḍavālavihāra** in **Rohaṇa** and ordained **Milakkha-Tissa.** The same Commentary[3] mentions a **Cullapiṇḍapātiya-Tissa** of **Girivihāra** in (Ceylon). He, with his divine eye, saw a Tamil gate-keeper of **Madhuaṅganagāma** who, having been a fisherman for fifty years, lay dying. The Elder went to his house and made him repeat the Refuges and the Precepts. The man could not repeat beyond the first Precept, but he was born after death in the **Cātummahārājika-**world, and came to tell the Elder about it.

The Visuddhimagga[4] speaks of an Elder of the same name who had three pupils. They came to him and said they were prepared to do anything whatever for his sake, even to suffer torture and die. He thought them " possible fellows " and preached to them, whereupon they became arahants. The same Elder it may be who saw an elephant-corpse in **Kāladīghavāpi** Lake and developed his meditation on the " wormful abomination."[5]

[1] *E.g.*, MA. i. 355.
[2] AA. i. 21 f.
[3] i. 367.
[4] p. 116.
[5] *Ibid.*, p. 191.

Culla-Puṇṇa.—Brother of **Puṇṇa** of **Sunāparanta.** He was nearly shipwrecked, but was saved by Puṇṇa.[1]

[1] MA. i. 1016; SA. iii. 16.

Cullabodhi Jātaka (No. 443).—The Bodhisatta, under the name of **Bodhi,**[1] was once born in a very rich family of **Kāsi** and studied in **Takkasilā.** His

[1] He is also referred to as Culla-bodhi (J. vi. 257).

parents married him to a suitable wife but, because they had both come from the Brahma-world, they were free from passionate desire. After his parents' death, the two distributed their wealth and became ascetics. One day they came to the king's park, and there the king fell in love with the woman and carried her away by force to the palace. When he told the Bodhisatta of this, he showed no resentment whatever. In the palace the king found that he could not win the woman's love, and returned to the park, curious to know whether the ascetic really meant what he said. In the course of conversation the Bodhisatta told the king that he did not give way to anger because anger, once awakened, is difficult to curb.

The story was related in reference to a monk of violent temper. The king was **Ānanda** and the Bodhisatta's wife was **Rāhulamātā.**[2]

The story is also given in the Jātakamālā as the Khuḍḍa-bodhi Jātaka (No. xxi), and in the Cariyāpiṭaka.[3]

[2] J. iv. 22-27. *Cf.* the Ananusociya Jātaka. [3] Cyp., p. 86.

Culla-Rohita.—An ox belonging to a brahmin.[1]

[1] DhA. iv. 160.

Culla-Lohita.—An ox, brother of the Bodhisatta, **Mahā-Lohita.** He is identified with **Ānanda.** See the **Muṇika Jātaka.**

Cullavanavaṇṇanā.—The section of the **Vessantara Jātaka** which describes **Jūjaka's** journey through the forest to Vessantara's hermitage.[1]

[1] J. vi. 521-32.

Cullasutasoma Jātaka (No. 525).—The Bodhisatta was once born as the son of the king of **Sudassana** (Benares), under the name of **Soma.** Because he was fond of Soma juice and poured out libations of it, they called him **Sutasoma.** When he came of age his father gave up the throne to him, and he had sixteen thousand wives, of whom **Candādevī** was the chief consort. As time went on his family became very great, and he wished to become an ascetic as soon as a grey hair appeared on his head. Everyone in the palace tried to turn him from this resolve; rich merchants, like **Kulavaddhana,** offered him their immense wealth, but all in vain. Having handed over the kingdom to his brother, **Somadatta,** he donned the garb of an ascetic and left the city unknown to anyone. When his departure was discovered, all the inhabitants of the city left their belongings to follow him. **Sakka** sent **Vissakamma** to build for them a hermitage thirty leagues in extent.[1]

[1] J. v. 177-92.

Cullasubhaddā.—An elephant, one of the two chief consorts of **Chaddanta,** against whom she conceived a grudge because he preferred her rival to her. She gave gifts to a Pacceka Buddha and, as a result of her wish, she was born as **Subhaddā,** chief queen of the **Madda** king. She gave orders that Chaddanta's tusks be brought to her, but the hunter to whom the task was entrusted killed the elephant, and on hearing of his death Subhaddā died of a broken heart.[1]

For details see *s.v.* **Chaddanta** (4).

Cullasūka Jātaka (No. 430).—The story of the past is the same as that of the **Mahāsūka Jātaka** (*q.v.*). It was related in reference to the Buddha's visit to **Verañjā,** where, for the three months of the rainy season, he had to live on water and a modicum of the ground flour of roots, because of the evil influence of **Māra.**[1]

[1] J. iii. 494-6; Vibh. iii. 1 ff.

Cullahaṃsa Jātaka (No. 533).—The Bodhisatta was once born as **Dhataraṭṭha,** king of ninety thousand golden geese living in **Cittakūṭa.** One day some of his flock came upon Lake **Mānusiya,** near the haunts of men, and finding it a rich feeding-ground, persuaded him much against his will to go there with them. But immediately he alighted he was caught in a fowler's noose and found escape impossible. He waited till the flock had fed, then gave the cry of alarm at which all the geese flew away except his commander-in-chief, **Sumukha.** When the fowler came, Sumukha offered to give his life for his king, and thereby softened the fowler's heart. The latter set Dhataraṭṭha free and tended his wounds, and because of the man's great charity the king of the geese became whole again. When the fowler suggested that they should fly home, the two geese insisted that they should be taken to **Sakuḷa,** the king of the land, the **Mahiṃsaka** country, that they might obtain for the fowler a suitable reward. When the king heard the story he gave to the fowler a village yielding one hundred thousand annually, a chariot and a large store of gold. Dhataraṭṭha preached to the king the moral law and, after being paid great honour, returned to Cittakūṭa.

The story was related in reference to **Ānanda's** attempt to offer his life in order to save the Buddha from being killed by the elephant **Nāḷāgiri** (*q.v.*). **Channa** is identified with the fowler, **Sāriputta** with the king, and Ānanda with Sumukha.[1]

[1] J. v. 333-54; DhA. i. 119; *cf.* the **Mahāhaṃsa Jātaka** and the **Haṃsa Jātaka.**

Cullupaṭṭhāka.—See **Culladhanuggaha.**

Cūla-, Cūḷa-; see also **Culla-**.—There is a great difference of opinion as to the spelling of "Cūla," meaning "the Minor," equivalent of "Culla." I have adopted **Cūla** throughout, chiefly for the sake of convenience.

Cūla-Assapura Sutta.—Preached at **Assapura** to the assembled monks. It is not the robe that makes the recluse, nor living under a tree, nor intoning texts, bathing three times a day, etc. It is by putting away all the evil qualities that a man becomes a true bhikkhu.[1]

[1] M. i. 281-4.

Cūla-Ekasāṭaka.—See **Ekasāṭaka.**

Cūlaka Thera.—A brahmin of **Rājagaha** who, having seen the Buddha tame the elephant **Dhanapāla,** entered the Order and dwelt in the **Indasāla** cave. One day, as he sat looking down over the **Magadhakhetta,** a great storm arose and the rain came down in torrents. The peacocks danced and sang and the coolness helped Cūlaka to concentrate his mind and attain arahantship.

In the time of **Sikhī** Buddha he was a householder and gave to the Buddha a *chattapāṇi*-fruit.[1]

[1] Thag. 211 f.; ThagA. i. 333 f.

Cūla-kammavibhaṅga Sutta.—**Subha Todeyyaputta** visits the Buddha at **Jetavana** and asks him why, among mankind, some are high and some low, some long-lived and some short, some handsome and some plain, some rich and some poor, etc. It is the result of their heritage from the past, answers the Buddha; their deeds are their possessions, their parents, their kindred and their refuge; he then proceeds to explain in detail.[1] Subha acknowledges the Buddha as his teacher. The Commentary[2] calls this the **Subha Sutta.** For details of the circumstances in which the sutta was preached see *s.v.* **Subha Todeyyaputta.**

[1] M. iii. 202 ff. [2] MA. ii. 962.

1. **Cūla-Kāḷa.**—The youngest of three brothers, named **Kāḷa,** householders of **Setavyā.** He accompanied **Mahā-Kāḷa** to **Sāvatthi** with a caravan, and when Mahā-Kāḷa entered the Order he joined him. Later, as they were returning to **Setavyā,** this time with the Buddha and the monks, he was sent on ahead to arrange seats in his former house, whither the Buddha and the monks had been invited. His two erstwhile wives mocked at him and persuaded him to return to the lay-life.[1]

[1] DhA. i. 55 ff.

2. **Cūla-Kāḷa.**—A previous birth of **Aññā-Koṇḍañña.** He was a householder of **Haṃsavatī,** in the time of **Vipassī Buddha.** One day going to the rice-field, he hulled a kernel of rice, ate it and found it unusually sweet. He thereupon obtained his share of the field from his brother **Mahā-Kāḷa,** and gave to the Buddha and the monks the first-fruits of a single crop, nine times, at nine different stages.[1] He thus became the first to gain any attainment when Gotama Buddha preached his first sermon.[2]

[1] For details of the stages see DhA. i. 82. [2] The story is given in DhA. i. 8 ff.

3. **Cūla-Kāḷa.**—A lay disciple of the Buddha. He was once on his way back to **Sāvatthi,** having spent the night in listening to the Doctrine, when thieves, fleeing from their pursuers, threw their stolen goods in front of him and disappeared. When he was charged with theft, some women water-carriers, who had witnessed the incident on their way to the watering place, obtained his release.[1]

[1] DhA. iii. 157.

Cūlagaṇa.—One of the three chief buildings of the **Upāsikā Vihārā,** built by **Devānampiyatissa.** It came to be called the **Kūpayaṭṭhi-ṭhapita-ghara.**[1]

[1] Mhv. xix. 68 f.; MṬ. 409.

Cūla-Ganṭhipada.—A work on the Vinaya, attributed to **Moggallāna** and used by the **Ekaṃsikas** in their Pārupaṇa-controversy.[1]

[1] Bode, *op. cit.*, 76.

Cūlagandhāra-vijjā.—See **Gandhāra-vijjā.**

Cūlagallaka Vihāra.—A monastery built by **Cūlābhaya** on the bank of the **Goṇaka-nadī** to the south of **Anurādhapura.**[1] Attached to it was a *Padhānaghara,* built by **Aggabodhi II.**[2]

[1] Mhv. xxxv. 13. [2] Cv. xlii. 49.

Cūla-Gavaccha Thera.—A brahmin of **Kosambī.** Having heard the Buddha preach, he entered the Order. At that time the Kosambī monks had become contentious, but **Gavaccha** remained steadfast and attained to arahantship.

In the time of **Padumuttara Buddha** he was a labourer and, finding the monk **Sujāta** looking for pieces of stuff for a robe, gave him his garment.

As a result, he was king of the devas thirty-three times and king of men seven times.[1] He is, perhaps, identical with **Upaḍḍhadussadāyaka** of the Apadāna.[2]

[1] Thag. 11; ThagA. i. 55 f.

[2] Ap. ii. 435 f.; but the same verses are, in ThagA. (i. 266) also attributed to **Heraññakāni.**

Culaṅganiyapiṭṭhi.—A locality in **Rohaṇa.** There a battle was fought between **Duṭṭhagāmaṇi** and his brother, **Tissa,** when Gāmaṇi was defeated and forced to flee.[1]

[1] Mhv. xxxiv. 19; see also xxxii. 31 f.; and AA. i. 365.

Cūla Gopālaka Sutta.—Preached to the monks assembled at **Ukkācelā.** Those who will listen to and trust in the wrong kind of recluse and brahmin and who do not understand good and evil will come to grief, whereas those who hearken to teachers of the right kind will gain deliverance. The theme is illustrated by various similes drawn from the picture of a herdsman driving cattle across a ford.[1]

[1] M. i. 225 f.

Cūla Gosiṅga Sutta.—The Buddha, residing at the **Giñjakāvasatha** in **Nādikā,** visits the **Gosiṅga-Sālavana,**[1] where dwell **Anuruddha, Nandiya** and **Kimbila.** At first the keeper tries to stop the Buddha from approaching them, fearing lest he should disturb their meditation. The Buddha questions them as to their attainments and praises them. At the end of the sutta mention is made of a Yakkha, named **Dīgha,** visiting the Buddha and telling him how the fame of the three Elders had travelled even to the world of Brahmā.[2] The sutta illustrates the greatness of harmony (*sāmaggi*).[3]

[1] According to the Vinaya account (i. 350), this incident takes place in **Pācīnavaṃsadāya.**

[2] M. i. 205-11.

[3] MA. i. 361.

Cūla Cunda.—See **Cunda** (2).

Cula Janaka Jātaka (No. 52).[1]—The stories, both past and present, are the same as in the **Mahā Janaka Jātaka** (*q.v.*).

[1] J. i. 268.

Cūla Jāli.—A Pacceka Buddha mentioned in a list of these.[1]

[1] M. iii. 70; MA. ii. 890.

Cūla Tissa.—Probably a Commentator. He is called **Uruvelavāsi,** and is quoted in the Saṃyutta Commentary in reference to a discussion on *phassavedanā.*[1]

[1] SA. ii. 100.

Cūla Dukkhakkhandha Sutta.—**Mahānāma,** the Sākyan, visits the Buddha at **Nigrodhārāma** and asks him why it is that evil states of mind arise in one. The Buddha replies that it is because of certain undiscarded states of consciousness, which can be got rid of through renunciation. He proceeds to describe how he, too, failed to find satisfaction before his Enlightenment. He then tells of a conversation he once had on **Gijjhakūṭa** with some Nigaṇṭhas, who believed that suffering could be got rid of through austerities and how he told them of his happiness which was far greater even than that of **Bimbisāra,** king of **Magadha.**[1]

[1] M. i. 91 ff.

Cūla Dhammapāla.—Senior pupil of **Ānanda Vanaratana** and author of the **Saccasaṅkhepa**[1] and of an *anu-ṭīkā* to the **Abhidhamma-Mūla-ṭīkā.**[2]

[1] Gv. 60, 70; P.L.C. 113, 203 f. [2] *Ibid.*, 211 f.

Cūla Dhammasamādāna Sutta. Preached to the monks assembled at **Jetavana.** There are four ways of professing a Doctrine—one temporarily pleasant but ripening to pain thereafter; another temporarily unpleasant but ripening to pleasure, etc.—The sutta also describes the monks and recluses who follow these different ways.[1]

[1] M. i. 305 ff.

1. **Cūla Vagga.**—The second of the two volumes known as the two **Khandhakas** of the Vinaya Piṭaka. The book consists of twelve chapters or Khandhakas, and brings the ecclesiastical history of the Buddhist Order down to the Second Council, one hundred years after the Buddha's death. In the Cūla Vagga are found several references to the **Suttavibhaṅga,** which leads us to the hypothesis that the latter work was regarded as an authoritative text at the time the Cūla Vagga was finished.[1]

[1] For a discussion on the contexts of the Cūla Vagga and their historical value see Law, Pāli Lit., pp. 14 ff. and *passim.*

2. **Cūla Vagga.**—The fifth chapter of the Tika Nipāta of the Aṅguttara Nikāya.[1]

[1] A. i. 150 ff.

3. **Cūla Vagga.**—The seventh chapter of the Udāna.[1]

[1] Ud., pp. 74 ff.

4. **Cūla Vagga.**—The third chapter of the Petavatthu.[1]

[1] Pv., pp. 33 ff.

5. **Cūla Vagga.**—The second chapter of the Sutta Nipāta.[1]

[1] SN., pp. 29-72.

Cūlaccharāsaṅghāta Sutta.—If for just the duration of a finger-snap a monk indulges in a thought of goodwill and cultivates a thought of goodwill, he is verily to be called a monk. Earnestness, above all other things, encourages the arising of good states; indulgence, worst of all things, encourages evil states.[1]

It is said[2] that this sutta was preached at **Jetavana** to counteract the effects of the **Aggikkhandhopama Sutta,** which frightened many monks, causing them to revert to the lay life, the Order being thereby greatly impoverished in numbers. The present sutta was designed to reassure those who were in doubt.

[1] A. i. 10. [2] AA. i. 40.

Cūlataṇhāsaṅkhaya Sutta.—**Sakka** visits the Buddha at the **Migāramatupāsāda** and asks him how a monk can be delivered by the extirpation of cravings and become foremost among gods and men. The Buddha briefly explains, and Sakka leaves him after expressing his satisfaction. **Moggallāna,** desiring to know if Sakka has really understood the teaching, visits him and asks him the same question. Sakka evades this question and, accompanied by **Vessavaṇa,** conducts Moggallāna through his palace, **Vejayanta,** in order to demonstrate his power. Moggallāna causes the palace to quake and, seeing the agitation of Sakka, again asks him the same question; Sakka gives the Buddha's explanation, word for word, and Moggallāna is satisfied.[1]

[1] M. i. 251 ff.

Cūladeva.—A Thera, an eminent teacher of the Vinaya.[1]

[1] Vin. v. 3; Sp. i. 63.

Cūlanagaragāma.—A village near **Kāḷavallimaṇḍapa.** Two brahmins of **Pāṭaliputta,** having heard of the fame of **Mahānāga Thera** of Kāḷavallimaṇḍapa, set out to see him. One died on the way; the other went to **Anurādhapura** and, hearing there that the Thera resided in **Rohaṇa,** journeyed there and took up his abode in Cūlanagaragāma, near the vihāra.[1]

[1] AA. i. 384.

1. **Cūlanāga Thera.**—Generally referred to as **Tipiṭaka-Cūlanāga.** He was evidently a very famous commentator, and his opinions are quoted in the commentaries of Buddhaghosa.[1] **Cūlanāga** was the pupil of **Summa** Thera of **Dīpavihāra**[2] and a contemporary of **Tipiṭaka-Cūlabhaya** Thera, who seems to have differed from him most violently on certain points.[3] Cūlanāga lived in the reign of **Kuṭakaṇṇa-Tissa** (16-38 A.C.), and we are told[4] that the king held him in great respect. Once the Elder had a boil on his finger, and the king, visiting him, put the finger in his mouth to alleviate the pain. The boil burst and the king swallowed the pus therefrom. When the Elder lay dying the king carried on his head the pot containing his stools, lamenting, "The mainstay of the Dhamma is lost." The Saṃyutta Commentary[5] tells of an incident which occurred when Cūlanāga was preaching in the **Lohapāsāda.** A brahmin, listening to him, was so convinced by the sermon of the impermanence of all things, that he ran home and clasped his son to his heart, saying that he was undone. The Elder once received a bowl which it was not right for him to keep and he gave it to the Saṅgha.[6] Cūlanāga does not always seem to have agreed with his teacher in his interpretations of various matters.[7] Once when it was announced to Summa that Cūlanāga had explained the word *thūpīkata* in a certain way, he expressed great sorrow and resentment and declared that though he had seven times read the Vinaya with Cūlanāga, he had never taught him such an explanation; but Cūlanāga was able to uphold his contention.[8] Cūlanāga once preached the **Chachakka Sutta** in **Ambilahāla Vihāra,** and on that occasion the audience of men extended to a distance of one *gāvuta* and that of devas to a distance of a league. At the end of the discourse, one thousand monks became arahants.[9]

[1] *E.g.*, MA. i. 126; SA. iii. 206; DhsA. 229, 267, 284; Vm. 389; also PsA. 405.
[2] AA. ii. 845.
[3] See VibhA. 16; also DhsA. 230.
[4] VibhA. 452.
[5] SA. ii. 201.
[6] Sp. iii. 699.
[7] VibhA. 342.
[8] Sp. iv. 892; for another incident see *s.v.* **Cūla-Summa.**
[9] MA. ii. 1025.

2. **Cūlanāga.**—A Thera of **Vasāḷanagara.** With his brother **Mahānāga,** he entered the Order and, for thirty years, lived in **Cittalapabbata,** where he

attained arahantship. He refused to reveal his identity to his mother when visiting her because he did not wish to have any attachments.[1]

[1] SA. ii. 125.

3. **Cūlanāga.**—A Thera of Ceylon. An eminent teacher of the Vinaya.[1]

[1] Vin. v. 3; Sp. i. 62.

Cūlanāgapabbata.—A vihāra built in the **Huvācakaṇṇikā** (in **Rohaṇa**), by King **Mahādāṭhika-Mahānāga.**[1]

[1] Mhv. xxxiv. 90.

Cūlanāgalena.—A cave in Ceylon (**Tambapaṇṇi**). It was once the abode of five hundred monks, all of whom won arahantship, by meditating in that spot.[1]

[1] Vsm. 127.

Cūlanāgā.—An arahant therī, mentioned as an eminent teacher of the Vinaya in Ceylon.[1]

[1] Dpv. xviii. 38.

Cūla-Nidāna Sutta.—Probably another name for the **Nidāna Sutta** (*q.v.*) of the Saṃyutta Nikāya.[1]

[1] Referred to in MA. i. 225; VibhA. 267.

Cūlapanthaka Thera.—An eminent arahant, declared chief among monks skilled in creating forms by mind-power and in mental "evolution" (*cittavivaṭṭa*).[1] He was the younger son of the daughter of a rich merchant of **Rājagaha,** who developed intimacy with a slave and fled with him when her misconduct was discovered. She wished to return to her parents for the birth of her first child, but her husband always postponed the visit until, in the end, she started to go without his knowledge. He followed her, but the child was born by the wayside, and therefore they called him **Panthaka.** The same thing occurred at the birth of the second child, and he also received the name of Panthaka, he being **Cūlapanthaka** and his brother **Mahāpanthaka.** When the boys grew up they were taken to **Rājagaha,** where their grandparents took charge of them. Mahāpanthaka often accompanied his grandfather to hear the Buddha preach, and he yearned to become a monk. He easily obtained permission and entered the Order, in due course becoming an arahant. With the consent of his grandparents,

[1] A. i. 23.

he ordained Cūlapanthaka, but the latter proved to be a dullard, and in the course of four months was unable to learn a single stanza. It is said that in the time of **Kassapa Buddha** Cūlapanthaka was a clever monk, who once laughed to scorn a dull colleague who was trying to learn a passage by heart.

When Mahāpanthaka discovered his brother's stupidity, he asked him to leave the Order,[2] but Cūlapanthaka so loved the Buddha's teaching that he did not wish to return to the lay-life. One day **Jīvaka Komārabhacca,** wishing to give alms to the Buddha and the monks, asked Mahāpanthaka, who was acting as steward, to collect all the monks in the monastery. This he did, omitting only Cūlapanthaka who, he said, had made no progress in the Doctrine. Greatly grieved, Cūlapanthaka determined to leave the Order, but as he was going out the Buddha met him, took him into the **Gandhakuṭi** and comforted him, giving him a clean piece of cloth. "Sit with your face to the East," said the Buddha, "repeat the words '*rajoharaṇaṃ*' and wipe your face with the cloth." As Cūlapanthaka carried out these orders he noticed that the cloth became dirty, and as he concentrated his mind on the impermanence of all things, the Buddha sent a ray of light and exhorted him about the necessity of getting rid of the impurities of lust and other evils. At the end of the admonition Cūlapanthaka attained arahantship with the four *paṭisambhidā,* which included knowledge of all the Piṭakas.

Tradition has it that Cūlapanthaka was once a king and that while going in procession round his city he wiped the sweat from his brow with a spotless garment which he wore and noticed how the cloth was stained. His mind then grasped the idea of impermanence, hence the ease with which he did so in his last birth.

Meanwhile, the Buddha and the monks were seated in Jīvaka's house, but when the meal was about to be served the Buddha ordered it to be stopped, saying that there were other monks left in the monastery. A servant was sent to find them, and Cūlapanthaka, aware of this, contrived that the whole grove appeared full of monks engaged in various activities. When the messenger reported this, he was told to discover which of the monks was Cūlapanthaka and to bring him. But all the monks answered to this name, and the messenger was forced to return without him. "Take by the hand the first who says that he is Cūlapanthaka," ordered the Buddha; and when this was done the other figures vanished. At the conclusion of the meal, Cūlapanthaka was asked to return thanks, and "like a young lion roaring defiance" the Elder ranged over the whole of the Piṭakas in his sermon. Thenceforth his fame spread, and the Buddha, in order to prove how in

[2] On this see DhA. iv. 180 f.

previous births also Cūlapanthaka had profited by advice received, related to the monks the **Cullakaseṭṭhi Jātaka.**[3] The Dhammapada Commentary[4] gives another story of Cūlapanthaka's past. He went to **Takkasilā** to learn under a teacher, but though he did everything for his teacher he could learn nothing. The teacher, feeling sorry for him, taught him a charm: "*Ghaṭṭesi ghaṭṭesi, kiṃ kāraṇā ghaṭṭesi? ahaṃ pi taṃ jānāmi*" ("You try and try; what are you trying for? I know it too"). When he had returned home thieves entered his house, but he woke up from his sleep and repeated the charm, whereupon the thieves fled, leaving behind them even their clothes. The king of Benares, wandering about the city in disguise, seeing what had happened, sent for Cūlapanthaka the next day and learnt from him the charm after paying him one thousand. Soon afterwards the king's commander-in-chief bribed the court barber to cut the king's throat, but while the barber was sharpening his razor the king repeated the charm. The barber, thinking that his intended crime was discovered, confessed his guilt. The king, realising that the youth had saved his life, appointed him commander-in-chief in place of the traitor, whom he banished. The youth was Cūlapanthaka and the teacher was the Bodhisatta.

Cūlapanthaka was a householder in the time of **Padumuttara** Buddha, and having seen a monk exalted by the Buddha to the rank of chief among those skilled in creating mind-born forms, aspired to the same position. In the time of **Kassapa** Buddha he was a monk and practised *odātakasiṇa* for twenty thousand years.[5]

Cūlapanthaka was expert in *rūpajjhāna* and in *samādhi*, while his brother was skilled in *arūpajjhāna* and in *vipassanā*. When creating forms, other monks could produce only two or three, while Cūlapanthaka could bring into being as many as one thousand at the same time, no two being alike in appearance or action.[6]

According to the Apadāna,[7] Cūlapanthaka joined the Order at the age of eighteen. It is said[8] that when it was his turn to teach the nuns at **Sāvatthi** they expected no effective teaching, since he always repeated the same stanza. One day, at the end of the lesson, he overheard their remarks, and forthwith gave an exhibition of his magical powers and of his wide knowledge of the Buddha's teachings. The nuns listened with great admiration until after sunset, when they were unable to gain entrance to the city. The Buddha heard of this and warned Cūlapanthaka not to keep the nuns so late.

[3] Thag. 557-66; AA. i. 119 ff.; J. i. 114 ff.; DhA. i. 239 ff.; ThagA. i. 515 ff.; Vsm. 388 f.

[4] i. 250 ff.

[5] AA. i. 119.

[6] ThagA. i. 490; PsA. 276.

[7] i. 58 f.

[8] Vin. iv. 54 f.

The Udāna[9] contains a verse sung by the Buddha in praise of Cūlapanthaka, and the Milinda[10] quotes a stanza attributed to Cūlapanthaka which has so far not been traced elsewhere.

[9] v. 10; UdA. 319 f. [10] p. 368.

1. **Cūlapāsāda.**—See **Dīghasaṇḍana.**

2. **Cūlapāsāda.**—The original name of the **Dīghasaṇḍana-senāpatipariveṇa** (*q.v.*).

Cūlapuṇṇama Sutta.—Preached to the monks assembled on a full-moon night at the **Migārāmātupāsāda.** The sutta teaches how it is possible to tell a bad man and a good man through their conduct.[1]

[1] M. iii. 20 ff.

Cūla-Buddhaghosa.—An author of Ceylon to whom the Gandhavaṃsa[1] ascribes a work entitled **Jātattaginidāna,** probably a Jātaka Commentary, and a **Sotattaginidāna.**

[1] pp. 63, 67; see P.L.C. 126.

Cūlabyūha.—See **Cūlavyūha.**

Cūla-Māgandiya.—Brother of the brahmin **Māgandiya.** He took charge of **Māgandiyā** when her parents renounced the world and escorted her to **Kosambi,** where she was presented at the court of **Udena** and became the latter's wife.[1]

[1] DhA. i. 202 f.; AA. i. 236.

Cūla-Māluṅkya Sutta.—The Elder **Māluṅkyaputta** is dissatisfied, feeling that the Buddha has not expounded to him various speculations concerning life and death and the nature of the world. He visits the Buddha at **Jetavana** and tells him of his disappointment. The Buddha points out to him that no promise was made regarding the elucidation of such problems and tells him it were fitter if he were to speculate by striving for deliverance. Māluṅkyaputta sees the error of his ways.[1]

[1] M. i. 426 ff.

Cūla-Moggallāna.—See **Moggallāna II.**

Cūlayamaka Vagga.—The fifth chapter of the Majjhima Nikāya.[1]

[1] M. i. 285 ff.

Cūlaratha.—A devaputta in **Tāvatiṃsa** who excelled **Sakka** in glory.[1]

[1] DhA. i. 426.

Cūlarathavimānavatthu.—The story of Prince **Sujāta** (*q.v.*), son of the **Assaka** king.[1] He was born in **Tāvatiṃsa,** and **Cūlaratha** may have been his name there. See *s.v.* **Sujāta.**

[1] Vv. v. 13; VvA. 259 ff.

Cūla-Rahulovāda Sutta.—The Buddha realises that **Rāhula** is possessed of the qualities necessary to Deliverance and goes with him to **Andhavana** for the siesta. There the Buddha demonstrates, by means of question and answer, that all things are impermanent, and impresses on Rāhula the manner in which the disciples of the Ariyans should strive to be delivered from them. Rāhula takes the lesson to heart, and even as it is being delivered attains to arahantship.[1] Many thousands of devas are present at the preaching of the sermon, and this sutta is therefore given as an illustration of the Buddha's great compassion.[2] Among the suttas specially preached to Rāhula, this one emphasises *vipassanā.*[3] It may have been the incidents mentioned in this sutta that were illustrated in the relic-chamber of the **Mahā Thūpa.**[4]

[1] M. iii. 277 f.; this sutta is also found at S. iv. 105 ff., where it is called the Rāhula Sutta.

[2] *E.g.*, UdA. 324; MA. i. 320; also Mil. 20.

[3] AA. ii. 547.

[4] See Mhv. xxx. 83.

Cūlavaṃsa.—A Pāli chronicle of Ceylon. It is a continuation of the **Mahāvaṃsa,** but, unlike the latter, is not a homogeneous work in that it was written by different authors at different periods. It is generally agreed that chapters thirty-seven to seventy-nine were written by the **Thera Dhammakitti** in the thirteenth century. The second section, beginning with the reign of **Vijayabāhu II.** and ending with that of **Parakkamabāhu** of **Hatthiselapura** (Chaps. 80-90), seems to be the work of one author whose identity, however, remains unknown. That part of the chronicle which deals with the period from Parakkamabāhu to A.C. 1758, the death of **Kittisiri Rājasīha,** was compiled by **Tibbotuvāve** Sumaṅgala Thera, and the last chapter has been continued down to 1815 by Hikkaḍuve Siri Sumaṅgala.[1]

[1] For details see P.L.C. 141 ff.

Cūlavajira.—A grammarian, author of a work called **Atthabyakkhyāna.**[1]

[1] Gv. 60; but see p. 70, where it is ascribed to **Cūavimalabuddhi.**

Cūlavāpiyagāma.—A village given by **Aggabodhi VIII.** for the maintenance of **Rājasālavihāra.**[1]

[1] Cv. xlix. 47.

Cūlavimalabuddhi.—See **Cūlavajira,** also **Navavimalabuddhi.**

Cūlaviyūha Sutta.—Preached in connection with the **Mahāsamaya Sutta.**[1] It describes how philosophers of different schools proclaim different truths; such disputations only lead to strife in the world.[2]

[1] SNA. ii. 554. [2] SN., pp. 171-4.

Cūlavedalla Sutta.—**Visākha** visits **Dhammadinnā** and asks her a series of questions on personality, the Noble Eightfold Path, plastic forces (*saṅkhārā*), etc. Dhammadinnā explains these things to Visākha, who then consults the Buddha as to whether the explanations are correct. The Buddha tells him that he himself would have given the same answers and praises Dhammadinnā's erudition.[1] The sutta forms a kind of commentary on certain psychological terms, such as *sakkāya*, *saṅkhāra*, etc. See *s.v.* **Vedalla.**

[1] M. i. 299 f.

Cūla-Sakuladāyi Sutta.—The Buddha visits **Sakuladāyi** at the **Moranivāpa** near **Rājagaha** and their talk turns on perfection. The Buddha points out that Sakuladāyi's conception of perfection is vague and undefined, and proves, on examination, empty and faulty. In answer to Sakuladāyi's question as to what the Buddha would define as absolute bliss, the Buddha explains the four Jhānas and the destruction of the Āsavas. Sakuladāyi is converted.[1] The sutta also contains references to the teachings of **Nigaṇṭha Nātaputta.**

[1] M. ii. 29 ff.

Cūla-Saccaka Sutta.—**Saccaka Nigaṇṭhiputta** goes about **Vesāli** saying that he is unable to find his match in discussion. He meets **Assaji** and, after a preliminary debate with him, goes with a large company of **Licchavis** to seek the Buddha in the **Mahāvana.** He questions the Buddha on his method of training, and the Buddha explains this to him. The talk then turns on Self, and the Buddha points out the emptiness of Saccaka's contentions. Saccaka (here referred to as **Aggivessana**) refuses to acknowledge defeat until the Yakkha **Vajirapāṇi** threatens to smite him. Saccaka is driven to yield point after point till the sweat streams from his brow, and the Buddha shows the assembled multitude how his own skin remains quite dry. In the end, Saccaka invites the Buddha and his disciples to a meal on the next day.[1]

[1] M. i. 227 ff.

Cūlasamudda.—An Elder of Ceylon (**Tambapaṇṇi**). Once, in a time of famine, seven hundred monks came to him early in the day. Realising that he could not get alms anywhere in Ceylon, he took them across to **Pāṭaliputta** by the power of his *iddhi*. Before he started the monks asked him the time, and when he told them they said, " But, Sir, Pāṭaliputta is far off !" " Friends, aged elders seize the distance and make it near." " Where is the ocean, Sir ?" " Friends, that was the dark ditch you passed on the way !" " But, Sir, the ocean is large !" " Friends, aged elders make the great small."[1] The Majjhima Commentary[2] mentions a **Gavilaṅgana-vāsī Cūlasammuda** who, when asked what he wished for, answered, " *Lokuttara* things only."

[1] Vsm. 403. [2] ii. 758.

Cūlasāri Thera.—A co-resident of **Sāriputta.** He evidently understood medicine, and one day he administered medical treatment for a sick person, in return for which he received a portion of choice food. As he went out he met an Elder on the road to whom he offered it, telling him the circumstances in which it was obtained and offering to bring him in the future the food so obtained. The Elder listened, then walked away without a word. When the Buddha heard of this, he declared that a shameless man can, in a manner of speaking, live happily, like a crow.[1]

[1] DhA. iii. 351 f.

Cūlasāropama Sutta.—**Piṅgala-Koccha** visits the Buddha at **Jetavana** and questions him on famous teachers such as **Pūraṇa Kassapa, Makkhali Gosāla** and others. The Buddha tells him that the reward of the higher life is not to be found in presents, esteem, or good repute, nor in a life of virtue, rapt concentration, or mystic insight. Immortal deliverance only is the prize and the goal of the higher life. If a man needs the very best of wood, no other part of the tree will suffice.

Piṅgala-Koccha accepts the Buddha as his teacher.[1]

[1] M. i. 198 ff.

Cūla-Sīva.—An Elder of Ceylon. He once went to **Jambudīpa,** embarking at **Mahātittha** in a boat, in which he dwelt in seclusion. On the way across, while looking at the ocean, he developed *āpokasina.*[1]

Another thera of the same name is mentioned in the Commentaries and is described as a Saṃyuttabhāṇaka. It is said that because he dwelt in *mettā* poison had no effect on him.[2] He probably lived in the time of the **Brāhmaṇatissabhaya** (*q.v.*). His colleagues were **Isidatta** and **Mahāsoṇa.** During the time of the peril, he took leave of his colleagues and went to worship at the **Mahāvihāra.** He found it empty and started for the south, when the sprite of a neighbouring tree, assuming human form, looked after him and escorted him to a village near the **Jajjaranadī,** where he was supported by foresters (? *paṇṇakhādakamanussā*) till the peril was past.[3] The Dīgha Commentary[4] mentions another Cūla-Sīva and calls him **Tilokanagaravāsī** (*v.l.* **Lokuttaravāsī**). He was evidently a well-known commentator.

[1] Vsm. 170.
[2] *Ibid.*, 313; AA. i. 865.
[3] VibhA. 446 f.
[4] DA. iii. 883.

Cūla-Sīhanāda Sutta.—Followers of the Buddha excel those of other teachers in faith in their teacher, faith in his Doctrine, strict observance of the sīlas and in love towards their fellow-believers, laymen and monks. Their goal is the goal of men without cravings, without attachments, without facetiousness, without combative spirit, without obsessions. Their Doctrine is perfect, rightly revealed, rightly preached.[1]

[1] M. i. 63 ff.

Cūlasugandha Thera.—An arahant. In the time of **Kassapa** Buddha he belonged to a very rich family in Benares, and having heard the Buddha preach, covered the Buddha's **Gandhakuṭi** eight times with the four kinds of fragrant stuff (*catujātiyagandha*). In this age he was born in **Sāvatthī.** While he was yet in his mother's womb the perfume of sandalwood spread from her body and on the day of his birth it filled the whole city; so it was also on the day of his ordination and on that of his death. He entered the Order on seeing the Buddha convert **Sela** and his followers.[1] He is probably identical with **Subhūti Thera.**[2] His legend seems to have become confused with that of **Sugandha.**[3]

[1] Ap. ii. 508 ff. [2] ThagA. i. 405. [3] See Ap. ii. 459 and ThagA. i. 80 f.

Cūla-Suññatā Sutta.—Preached to **Ānanda** at the **Migāramātupāsāda.** True solitude is not to be found in forest-dwelling nor in the concentration of heart away from all ideas, but in attaining to deliverance from the *āsavas*.[1]

[1] M. iii. 104 ff.

Cūlasudhamma.—A Thera who lived in **Girigāmakaṇṇa.** King **Kuṭakaṇṇa(tissa)**, while staying in **Uppalavāpi,** once sent for him out of his great respect for him. The Thera came and resided in **Mālārāmavihāra.** Having discovered from the Elder's mother that Cūlasudhamma was fond of radishes (? *kanda*), the king prepared some and took them to the vihāra, but, while offering them to the Elder, he could not bring himself to look at his face. When leaving the vihāra, he asked his queen, "what did the Elder look like ?" But she replied that if he, who was the Elder's follower (*parisa*), could not look at him, how could she do so ? The king marvelled that the son of one of his subjects should have such power.[1]

[1] VibhA. 452.

Cūlasubhaddā.—Daughter of **Anāthapiṇḍika.** At the insistent request of his friend **Uggaseṭṭhi,** and after consultation with the Buddha, Anāthapiṇḍika agreed to give her in marriage to Ugga's son.[1] But he was an unbeliever, and when Nigaṇṭhas came to his house on invitation, Subhaddā refused to do obeisance to them. For this she was ordered out of the house by her father-in-law; but she convinced her mother-in-law that the reasons for her behaviour were sound, and at the suggestion of the latter she prepared a meal and invited to it the Buddha and the congregation of monks, by throwing into the air from the top storey of the house eight handfuls of jasmine. The Buddha divined her thoughts and arrived with five hundred arahants. After the meal the Buddha preached the Doctrine and Ugga and his family were converted. As a mark of favour towards Subhaddā the Buddha requested **Anuruddha** to stay behind at **Ugganagara.**[2] Cūlasubhaddā, while still in her father's house, had become a Sotāpanna, and with her sisters, **Mahāsubhaddā** and **Sumanā,** she had been entrusted with the distribution of food to the monks.[3]

[1] According to the Aṅguttara Commentary (ii. 482 ff.), the seṭṭhi's name was **Kālaka** and his city was not Ugga, but **Sāketa.**

[2] DhA. iii. 465 ff.; the story is also given in AA. ii. 482 ff., but with several variations in detail. There seems to be a comparison between the stories of Mahāsubhaddā and Cūlasubhaddā. (See also AA. i. 146 and Vsm. 390.)

[3] DhA. i. 128; J. i. 93; ApA. i. 81; see also Mil. 383, 387.

1. **Cūlasumana Thera.**—An Elder of Ceylon, master of the Tipiṭaka and a well-known commentator. His explanation, given at **Lohapāsāda,** of

the meaning of *ubhatobhāgavimutta* is regarded as the most authoritative interpretation.[1] The Visuddhimagga[2] also mentions a Cūlasumana, resident at **Niṅkaponnakapadhānaghara** on **Cittalapabbata.** He had discarded desire, and therefore the thought arose in him that he was a saint.

[1] DA. ii. 514. [2] p. 364; see also *s.v.* **Cūlasumma.**

2. **Cūlasumana.**—A householder of Ceylon who fell down dead when **Piturājā** (*q.v.*) looked at him and gnashed his teeth in anger.[1]

[1] Sp. ii. 440 f.

3. **Cūlasumana.**—A novice. In a past life he was the **Sumanaseṭṭhi,** under whom **Annabhārā** (*q.v.*) worked. In this age he was born at **Muṇḍa,** near the **Viñjhā** mountains, as the son of **Mahāmuṇḍa.** When **Anuruddha** became an arahant and looked back into his past lives he saw how Sumana had helped him. He therefore visited Mahāmuṇḍa and enjoyed his hospitality during one rainy season. At the end of his stay he obtained Muṇḍa's consent to ordain Cūlasumana, who became an arahant while his head was being shaved. Once, when Anuruddha suffered from indigestion, the novice Sumana, having discovered that the water from **Anotatta** would cure him, went there and brought the water, in spite of all the efforts of the Nāga-king **Paṇṇaka** (*q.v.*) to prevent him. Later, Paṇṇaka, realising the novice's power, asked his pardon and became his friend and servitor. When Anuruddha went with Sumana to **Sāvatthi** to visit the Buddha, some of the monks began to play with Sumana, patting his head and tweaking his ears. In order to show them Sumana's power, Anuruddha asked **Ānanda** to summon all the novices in the monastery and ask them to fetch water from Anotatta that he might wash his feet. Only Sumana, the youngest of them all, was able to do this, and his fame spread beyond all measure.[1]

[1] DhA. iv. 128 ff.

Cūlasumanā.—A Therī of Ceylon, an eminent teacher of the Vinaya.[1]

[1] Dpv. xviii. 39.

Cūlasumma.—An eminent Commentator of Ceylon, teacher of **Tipiṭaka-Cūlanāga.** The pupil seems to have disagreed with some of the explanations of his teacher—*e.g.*, as to the meaning of *ekāyanamagga.* Cūlanāga said it referred to *pubbabhāgasatipatthānamagga*, but Cūlasumma held that it referred to *missakamagga.* They could come to no decision; but while on his way to the bathing-place, Cūlasumma revolved the problem in his mind, and discovering that his pupil was right announced his mistake when Cūlanāga was preaching on the day of the first quarter. Cūlanāga, realising how even his teacher could go astray on this point, explained it at great length for the benefit of future generations.[1] The Aṅguttara Commentary[2] calls him **Dīpavihāravāsī,** while the Vibhaṅga Commentary[3] says that he dwelt in **Niṅkapoṇṇapadhānaghara** in **Cittalapabbata.** The Samantapāsādikā[4] says that he lived in **Rohaṇa.**

[1] DA. iii. 744 f.; MA. i. 187.
[2] AA. ii. 845.
[3] p. 489; probably Cūlasumma is here a misreading for **Cūlasumana** (*q.v.*).
[4] iv. 892.

Cūlahatthipadopama Sutta.—**Jāṇussoṇi,** travelling in a carriage, meets **Pilotika,** from whom he hears praise of the Buddha. He learns how Pilotika, having heard the Buddha's teachings to nobles, brahmins, householders and recluses, was convinced that the Buddha was all-enlightened, just as an expert elephant-tracker seeing a broad elephant-footprint would conclude that it indicated the track of a really large elephant. Jāṇussoṇi goes to visit the Buddha and reports his conversation with Pilotika. The Buddha tells him it would be a mistake to conclude at once from seeing a broad footprint that it belonged to a very large elephant; there are many other possibilities which should first be eliminated. He then proceeds to describe the life of a real recluse, the disciple of the Noble One, and the attainments he reaches; these he calls the Truth-finder's footprints. Following this, the disciple makes further discoveries, till his mind is completely free from the *āsavas*, and then he realises the Truth-finder's real quest. Jāṇussoṇi becomes a follower of the Buddha.[1]

This was the first sutta preached in Ceylon by **Mahinda** to **Devānampiyatissa.** At the end of the discourse the king accepts the Three Refuges.[2]

[1] M. i. 175 ff.
[2] Mhv. xiv. 22.

1. **Cūlābhaya.**—King of Ceylon (92-93 A.C.). He was the son of **Āmaṇḍagāmaṇi** and built the **Cūlagallakavihāra.** **Sivalī** was his younger sister.[1]

[1] Mhv. xxxv. 12-14; Dpv. xxi. 39 f.

2. **Cūlābhaya.**—A Thera who taught the Vinaya in Ceylon.[1]

[1] Vin. v. 3; Sp. i. 63.

3. **Cūlābhaya.**—A Thera of Ceylon and a well-known commentator; he was known as **Tipiṭaka-Cūlābhaya.** He is several times quoted in the Commentaries.[1] He had a prodigious memory. Once he shut three of

[1] *E.g.*, VibhA. 11, 16; Vsm. 69, 394, 397.

the gates of **Anurādhapura,** allowing only one door for the use of those leaving the city. As each person went out he asked his name, and each of these names he was able to repeat when the owner returned in the evening to the city.[2] He was a contemporary of **Cūlanāga,**[3] with whom he held discussions. His description (given at the **Lohapāsāda**)[4] of the details connected with the first words uttered by the Buddha after his birth, and the manner in which he walked, is accepted as authentic. He once went with a company of monks on a pilgrimage to **Nāgadīpa.** On the way he stayed in a monastery. One of his followers, who lacked self-control, made friends with another of like temperament in the vihāra, and Cūlābhaya, seeing them laugh aloud, pointed out how truly the Buddha had said in the Dhātusaṃyutta that like joins with like.[5]

[2] DA. ii. 530.
[3] DhsA. 230; SA. iii. 206.
[4] DA. ii. 442.
[5] VibhA. 457 f.

Cūlābhayasumana.—A Thera who lived in the **Mahāvihāra** in the time of King **Bhātiya.** He was an authority on the Vinaya, and a story is related in the Samantapāsādikā[1] of how he was consulted by a monk who having picked up in a crowd a robe that fell from the shoulders of another monk concealed it, but later wished to return it to the owner.

[1] Sp. ii. 305 f.

Cūlodara.—A Nāga king of Ceylon, nephew of **Mahodara.** His father was the king of **Kaṇṇavaḍḍhamāna** mountain. It was the quarrel between Cūlodara and Mahodara regarding a jewelled throne that was the cause of a visit of the Buddha to Ceylon.[1]

[1] Mhv. i. 45 ff.; Dpv. ii. 7, 29; Sp. i. 120.

Cūḷani-Brahmadatta.—King of **Uttarapañcāla,** in the country of **Kampilla.** His chaplain was **Kevaṭṭa.** For their story see the **Mahā Ummagga Jātaka.** Cūḷani is identified with **Sāriputta.**[1] He is also called **Cūḷanīya**[2] and **Cūḷaneyya.**[3]

The Petavatthu[4] contains a story of a queen of Cūḷani-Brahmadatta called **Ubbarī** (*q.v.*), whom he discovered while wandering about in his kingdom disguised as a tailor. Here the king is also referred to as **Cūḷaniputta,**[5] and the scholiast explains[6] that **Cūḷani** was his father's name; it is said[7] that there were innumerable kings of **Pañcāla** bearing that name.

[1] J. vi. 478.
[2] *E.g., ibid.,* 437, 477.
[3] *Ibid.,* 437.
[4] Pv. ii. 13; PvA. 160 ff.
[5] vs. 8. 9.
[6] PvA. 164.
[7] Pv. ii. 13, vs. 9, 10.

Cūḷāmaṇicetiya.—A cetiya in **Tāvatiṃsa** one league in height, raised by **Sakka** over the hair cut off by the Buddha when he donned an ascetic's robes on the banks of the **Anomā.**[1] After the Buddha's death, Sakka added to the hair the right collar bone taken by him from **Doṇa** (*q.v.*), who was trying to conceal it in his turban.[2]

[1] J. i. 65. [2] DA. ii. 609; MṬ. 376; BuA. 235; Mhv. xvii. 20.

Cecca.—A shortened form of **Cetiya** (*q.v.*).[1]

[1] J. v. 267, 273.

Ceta.—A kingdom through which **Vessantara** passed on his way from **Jetuttara.** Vessantara's uncle ruled in Ceta, and it was ten leagues from **Dunniviṭṭha.**[1] The women of Ceta are called **Cetiyā.**[2] Ceta is probably another name for **Cetiya.**

[1] J. vi. 514 ff.; Cyp. i. 9, vs. 38 f. [2] J. vi. 514.

Cetaka Thera.—He was the companion of **Ānanda** soon after the Buddha's death and accompanied him to **Subha's** house.[1] The Commentary[2] says he was so called because he came from the **Cetiya** country.

[1] D. i. 204. [2] DA. ii. 386; also DA. i. 7 and KhpA. 94.

1. **Cetanā Sutta.**—That which we will and intend to do and with which we are occupied, that becomes an object (*ārammaṇa*) for the persistence of consciousness (*viññāṇa*). The object being there, there comes to be a station of consciousness. Consciousness being stationed and growing, there is renewed existence with all its consequent ills.[1]

[1] S. ii. 65 f.

2. **Cetanā Sutta.**—Same as above, with " name-and-form " substituted for rebirth, and the other factors of the *paṭiccasamuppāda* following therefrom.[1]

[1] S. ii. 66.

3. **Cetanā Sutta.**—Same as (1), except that consciousness, being stationed and growing, there comes a bending (*nati*) followed, serially, by a " going to a coming " (*āgatigati*), decease, rebirth, etc.[1]

[1] S. ii. 66 f.

4. **Cetanā Sutta.**—Volitioned acts occasioned by form, sound, etc., are impermanent.[1]

[1] S. iii. 227.

5. **Cetanā Sutta.**—The arising of volitional acts is the appearing of decay-and-death; their cessation, its cessation.[1]

[1] S. iii. 230.

6. **Cetanā Sutta.**—The desire and lust that is in will, concerning shape, etc., is corruption of the heart.[1]

[1] S. iii. 233.

7. **Cetanā Sutta.**—Preached to **Ānanda.** Rebirth is due to intention (*cetanā*) and aspiration (*patthāna*) being established in a lower element because of ignorance.[1]

[1] A. i. 224.

8. **Cetanā Sutta.**—Where there is action of body, speech or mind, there arises pleasure or pain caused by intention (*cetanā*). This is due to ignorance; when ignorance is destroyed, there is no field or base for such action.[1]

[1] A. ii. 157 f.

9. **Cetanā Sutta.**—In a monk possessed of good conduct spiritual life proceeds spontaneously, not intentionally.[1]

[1] A. v. 2 f.

10. **Cetanā Sutta.**—The same, in substance, as (9).[1]

[1] A. v. 312 f.

Cetaputtā.—The name of a tribe given in a nominal list[1]; probably the inhabitants of **Ceta.**

[1] Ap. ii. 359.

1. **Cetā.**—Daughter-in-law of **Vidhura** and **Anujjā.**[1]

[1] J. vi. 290.

2. **Cetā.**—The people of **Cetiya.**[1]

[1] J. i. 256; vi. 516.

Cetāvigāma.—A village in Ceylon. When **Mattābhaya** was ordained under **Mahinda** he was followed by five hundred youths from this village.[1] The village was to the south of **Anurādhapura.**[2]

[1] Mhv. xvii. 59. [2] MṬ. 384.

1. **Ceti, Cetiya.**—One of the sixteen **Mahājanapadas,**[1] probably identical with Cedi of the older documents.[2] The people of Ceti seem to have had two distinct settlements: one, perhaps the older, was in the mountains, probably the present Nepal.[3] It is evidently this older settlement which is mentioned in the **Vessantara Jātaka;** it was passed by **Vessantara** on his way into exile in the Himālayas, and was thirty yojanas distant from **Jetuttara.**[4] The other, probably a later colony, lay near the **Yamunā,** to the east, in the neighbourhood of and contiguous to the settlement of the **Kurus;** for we are told[5] that the Buddha, having dwelt in the Ceti country, went to **Bhaddavatikā,** where, at the **Ambatittha, Sāgata** tamed a Nāga, and from there he went to **Kosambī.** This part of the country corresponds roughly to the modern Bundelkhand and the adjoining region.[6]

It was probably of the older Ceti that **Sotthivatī** was the capital, where once reigned **Apacara,** who uttered the first lie in the world.[7] The journey from Benares to Ceti lay through a forest which was infested by robbers.[8] The settlement of Ceti was an important centre of Buddhism, even in the time of the Buddha. The Aṅguttara Nikāya[9] mentions several discourses preached to the Cetis, while the Buddha dwelt in their town of **Sahajāti.** While dwelling in the **Pācīnavaṃsadāya** in the Ceti country, **Anuruddha** became an arahant after a visit which the Buddha paid to him.[10] The **Janavasabha Sutta**[11] leads us to infer that the Buddha visited the Ceti country several times. The Saṃyutta Nikāya[12] records a discussion on the four Ariyan Truths among a number of monks, including **Gavampati,** dwelling at Sahajāti (*v.l.* **Sahañcanika**).

It is said[13] that the country was called Ceti because it was ruled by kings bearing the name of **Ceti** or **Cetiya.**[14]

1 A. i. 213, etc.
2 *E.g.*, Ṛv. viii. 5, 37-9.
3 *Bud. India*, p. 26.
4 J. vi. 514, 518.
5 Vin. iv. 108 f.; J. i. 360 f.
6 Law: *Geog. of Early Bsm.*, p. 16.
7 J. iii. 454 ff. Sotthivati is probably identical with Śuktimati or Śukti-Sāhvaya of the Mahābhārata (iii. 20, 50; xiv. 83, 2); see also PHAI. 81.
8 J. i. 253, 256.
9 A. iii. 355 f.; v. 41 f.; 157 ff.
10 A. iv. 228; see also Vin. i. 300 f.
11 D. ii. 200 *and passim.*
12 S. v. 436 f.
13 *E.g.*, AA. ii. 765.
14 SNA. i. 135.

2. **Cetiya.**—A mythical king.[1] See **Ceti** (1). **Apacara** (*q.v.*) is also referred to as **Cetiya,**[2] shortened into **Cecca.**[3]

1 Mhv. ii. 3; Dpv. iii. 5; Mtu. i. 348. 2 J. iii. 457, 460, etc. 3 J. v. 267.

Cetiya Jātaka (No. 422).—Contains the story of **Apacara** (*q.v.*), king of **Ceti,** and the world's first liar. It was related in reference to the swallowing up of **Devadatta** by the earth.[1]

1 J. iii. 454 ff.

Cetiya Sutta.—The Buddha goes with **Ānanda** on his begging round in **Vesāli** and, after the meal, rests at the **Cāpāla Cetiya.** There the Buddha sings the praises of Vesāli and declares that, if he would, he could live for a whole kappa. Ānanda does not act on the hint. When Ānanda leaves him, **Māra** asks that the Buddha should die, as his disciples have been fully trained. The Buddha agrees, and declares that he will die in three months' time.[1]

[1] S. v. 258 ff.; the incident is also given in D. ii. 102 ff. and Ud. vi. 1.

Cetiyagiri.—See **Cetiyapabbata,** also **Vedisagiri.**

Cetiyapabbata.—Also called **Cetiyagiri.** The later name of the **Missaka** mountain given on account of its many shrines.[1] **Devānampiyatissa** built a vihāra there—the second vihāra in Ceylon—for **Mahinda** and those ordained under him.[2] The relics, obtained by **Sumanasāmaṇera** from **Asoka** and from **Sakka,** were deposited there until they were needed. According to the Mahāvaṃsa[3] this fact was the occasion for the name. One of the eight saplings of the Sacred Bodhi-tree at **Anurādhapura** was planted in the ārāma on Cetiyagiri.[4] Mahinda spent the last years of his life on Cetiyagiri and died there, and there his relics were enshrined.[5] Near the mountain was the village of **Dvāramaṇḍala.**[6] **Kutakaṇṇatissa** built an uposatha-hall on the mountain and planted a Bodhi-tree, while **Bhātikābhaya** supplied food daily to one thousand monks dwelling there,[7] and **Lañjakatissa** had the vihāra paved at a cost of one hundred thousand.[8] **Mahādāṭhikamahānāga** made four gateways and a road round the mountain, and held the **Giribhaṇḍapūjā** with great pomp and ceremony; it is said that in order that the people might approach the mountain with clean feet he spread carpets right up to it from the **Kadamba** River.[9] **Kanirajānutissa** had sixty monks of Cetiyapabbata put to death as traitors by flinging them into the cave called **Kanira.**[10] **Vasabha** provided four thousand lamps to be lighted on **Cetiyagiri,**[11] while **Jeṭṭhatissa** gave to the vihāra the income derived from the **Kālamattika** Tank.[12]

In the time of **Kakusandha,** Cetiyagiri was known as **Devakūṭa,** in that of **Konāgamana** as **Suvaṇṇakūṭa,** and in that of **Kassapa** as **Subhakūṭa.**[13] The **Dhammarucikas** once occupied the **Ambatthalavihāra** on Cetiyapab-

[1] See *s.v.* Missaka.
[2] Mhv. xvi. 12-17.
[3] *Ibid.*, xxii. 23 ff.
[4] *Ibid.*, xix. 62.
[5] *Ibid.*, xx. 32, 45.
[6] *Ibid.*, xxiii. 23.
[7] *Ibid.*, xxxiv. 30 f., 64.
[8] *Ibid.*, xxxiii. 25.
[9] *Ibid.*, xxxiv. 75 ff.
[10] *Ibid.*, xxxv. 11.
[11] *Ibid.*, 80.
[12] *Ibid.*, xxxvi. 130; see also Dpv. xv. 69; xvii. 90; xix. 13, and Sp. i. 82 ff.
[13] Sp. i. 86 f.

bata, it having been given to them by **Dhātusena.**[14] **Aggabodhi** supplied a permanent supply of water for the bathing-tank called **Nāgasoṇḍi,** on the top of Cetiyagiri,[15] while **Aggabodhi III.** gave to the vihāra the village of **Ambillapadara.**[16] **Aggabodhi V.** restored the ruined buildings of Cetiyapabbata at a cost of one hundred and twenty thousand pieces,[17] while the queen of **Udaya I.** built there the **Kanthakacetiya,** and her husband decorated the mountain with brightly coloured flags and streamers.[18] **Sena I.** gave to the monastery the income from the **Kāṇavāpi,**[19] and **Sena II.** provided a hospital for the use of the monks there.[20] **Kassapa VI.** built the **Hadayuṇha Pariveṇa** and gifted it to the Dhammarucikas.[21] **Parakkamabāhu I.** restored all the old buildings which had been destroyed and built sixty-four thūpas.[22]

The Commentaries relate several anecdotes connected with Cetiyapabbata. **Maliyadeva Thera** recited there the **Chachakka Sutta,** and sixty listening bhikkhus became arahants.[23] **Lomasanāga Thera** lived in the Padhānaghara in the **Piyaṅguguhā** there and overcame the cold he felt by meditating on the **Lokantarikaniraya.**[24] Cetiyapabbata was the residence of **Kālabuddharakkhita,** and King **Saddhātissa** spent some time there.[25] At the time that Fa Hsien came to Ceylon there were two thousand monks in Cetiyagiri, including a monk of great fame, called Dharmagupta.[26]

[14] Cv. xxxviii. 75
[15] *Ibid.*, xlii. 28; see Cv. *Trs.* i. 68, n. 8.
[16] Cv. xliv. 122.
[17] *Ibid.*, xlviii. 7.
[18] *Ibid.*, xlix. 23, 27.
[19] *Ibid.*, l. 72.
[20] li. 73.
[21] *Ibid.*, lii. 18.
[22] lxxviii. 108.
[23] MA. ii. 1064.
[24] *Ibid.*, i. 65.
[25] *Ibid.*, i. 469 f. See also Vsm. 20, 64; DhSA. 194, 200; AA. i. 44.
[26] Giles: p. 72.

Cetiyambatthala.—See **Ambatthala.**

Cetiyavaṃsaṭṭhakathā.—One of the sources mentioned in the Mahāvaṃsa-Ṭīkā.[1] It probably dealt with the building of the cetiyas in Ceylon, chiefly the **Mahā Thūpa.**

[1] p. 548.

Cetiyavāda.—A later offshoot of the **Mahāsaṅghika** school, through the **Paññatti** and **Bāhulika** sects of the **Gokulikavāda.**[1]

Bhavya, quoted by Rockhill,[2] says that the Caityas received their name from their having dwelt in the Caitya Mountain.

[1] Mhv. v. 7; Dpv. v. 42; Mbv. 96 f.
[2] *Op. cit.*, 183; for an account of the Cetiyavādins see de la Vallée Poussin's "The Five Points of Mahādeva" in *J.R.A.S.*, April, 1910, 413 ff. Mahādeva is considered as their founder; his points are purely speculative. They are all alleged to have been held also by the **Pubbaseliyas.**

Cetiyā.—A *yakkhiṇī* who lived in the **Dhūmarakkha** mountain near **Tumbariyaṅgana.** **Paṇḍukābhaya,** hearing of her, tried to capture her, but succeeded only after a very long and strenuous chase, in which she assumed the form of a mare. He rode her into battle, where she helped him in various ways.[1] The Mahāvaṃsa-Ṭīkā[2] says she was the wife of the Yakkha **Jutindhara,** who fell in the battle of **Sirisavatthu.**

[1] Mhv. x. 53 ff. [2] p. 289.

1. **Cetokhila Sutta.**—While the five fallows of his heart (*cetokhilā*) are left untilled—doubts about the Teacher, about the Dhamma, about the Order and the course of training, lack of ardour—and the five bondages are unshattered (attachment to sensual pleasures, to the body, to visible forms, over-eating, desire to be born among the gods)—no monk can possibly show growth and progress in the Dhamma and the Vinaya.[1]

[1] M. i. 101 ff.

2. **Cetokhila Sutta.**—The five fallows (*cetokhilā*) mentioned in (1). In order to destroy them the four *Satipaṭṭhānas* should be developed.[1]

[1] A. iv. 460.

Cetoparicca Sutta.—**Anuruddha,** questioned by some monks at **Jetavana,** tells them that by cultivating the four *Satipaṭṭhanas* he was able to read and know the minds of beings, of other persons.[1]

[1] S. v. 304.

1. **Cetovimuttiphala Sutta.**—When a monk perceives the foulness of the body, is conscious of the cloying of food, feels distaste for the world, perceives impermanence in all compounded things, and has the thought of death inwardly established in him, there come to him mind-emancipation and emancipation by way of insight and he becomes completely free.[1]

[1] A. iii. 84.

2. **Cetovimuttiphala Sutta.**—The thought of impermanence, of ill in impermanence, of no-self in ill, of renunciation and of dispassion—these things, when developed, have, as their fruit, mind-emancipation and emancipation by way of insight.[1]

[1] A. iii. 85.

1. **Cela Sutta.**—See **Ukkācela Sutta.**

2. **Cela Sutta.**—When one's turban or head is ablaze, one must put forth special effort to extinguish the fire; needless to say, such effort is also necessary for the comprehension of the four Noble Truths.[1]

[1] S. v. 440.

Celakaṇṭhī.—A mare belonging to **Caṇḍappajjota.** She could travel one hundred leagues in a day and was one of his five rapid conveyances.[1]

[1] DhA. i. 196.

Cellāra.—A village in South India.[1]

[1] Cv. lxxvi. 262.

Cokkha-brāhmaṇa.—A brahmin, referred to in the Commentaries[1]; no explanation is given of him in the references: *Diṭṭhivippayuttena pana ariyasāvako pariḷābhibhūto parilāhavūpasamattham mattahatthiparittāsito viya Cokkhabrāhmaṇo gūthaṃ kañci saṅkhāraṃ sukhato upagacchati.*

[1] MA. ii. 875; AA. i. 248.

Coḍa.—See **Coḷa.**

Codanā Sutta.—The five things to be observed by one who exhorts another —his speech should be timely, should treat of what has really happened, should be full of gentleness, should concern the good (*atthasaṃhitena*), and be uttered with a mind of amity.[1]

[1] A. iii. 196.

Codanāvatthu.—A valley (?) near **Rājagaha,** visited by the Buddha in the course of his wanderings. Here he laid down a rule, allowing monks to recite the *pāṭimokkha* under a learned monk if the leader of their own company should be inefficient.[1]

[1] Vin. i. 115 f.

Codanāvatthu-bhāṇavāra.—The twenty-seventh section of the third Khandaka of the Mahāvagga of the Vinaya.

1. **Cora Sutta.**—An evil monk is like a robber-chief, in that he relies on roughness of the way, the entanglements, the help of the powerful; he gives bribes and works alone.[1]

[1] A. iii. 128 f.

2. **Cora Sutta.**—There are eight things which lead to speedy disaster in the case of a robber—he strikes those who do not strike back, takes away everything completely, kills women, seduces maidens, robs recluses, despoils the king's treasury, carries out his activities too near, is unskilled in storing up his gain.[1]

[1] A. iv. 339.

Corakaṇḍaka.—See **Koraṇḍaka.**

Corakamahāvihāra.—A vihāra in Ceylon, the residence of **Mahāmitta.** In the vihāra was the **Kuraṇḍaka-cave** (*q.v.*).[1]

[1] Vsm. 38.

Coranāga.—King of Ceylon (3 B.C.–9 A.C.). He was the son of **Vaṭṭagāmaṇi** and his name was **Mahānāga.**[1] During the reign of **Mahācūḷi Mahātissa** he was a rebel and came to the throne after Mahācūḷi's death. He destroyed eighteen vihāras which had refused to shelter him as a rebel. He was poisoned by his queen **Anulā.**[2] It is said[3] that after death he was born in the **Lokantarikaniraya** with a body three gāvutas in height.

[1] Mhv. xxxiii. 45. [2] *Ibid.*, xxxiv. 11 ff. [3] MA. ii. 920; DA. ii. 433; AA. ii. 532.

Corambagāma.—A village in **Rohaṇa.**[1]

[1] Cv. lxxv. 15.

Corābhaya.—A brigand, who set up his stronghold between **Anurādhapura** and **Cetiyagiri.** He once came with his followers to plunder Cetiyagiri monastery, but **Dīghabhāṇaka-Abhaya Thera** (*q.v.*), hearing of his intentions, gave orders that the robbers should be given a meal of the monastery food. This so pleased Corābhaya that from that time he undertook to provide safe passage for all pilgrims to Cetiyagiri.[1]

Corābhaya is generally classed with Coranāga and, both are said to have been born after death in **Lokantarikaniraya** with bodies three gāvutas in height.[2]

[1] Sp. ii. 474. [2] AA. ii. 532; MA. ii. 920; DA. ii. 433.

Coriyassara.—A village in Ceylon.[1]

[1] VibhA. 447.

Coḷa.—A country whose people were called **Coḷā.** The country extended from the Coromandel coast of South India as far as the Penner River, its capital in mediæval times being Tanjore. The Ceylon Chronicles mention frequent invasions of Ceylon by the Coḷā chiefly for purposes of plunder. These invasions were a constant menace to the peace and prosperity of Ceylon, and helped largely in the destruction and disappearance of that country's literary and artistic works.[1]

[1] For details see Mhv. and Cv. *passim*.

Coḷakulantaka.—A village in South India.[1]

[1] Cv. lxxvii. 53, 60.

Coḷakonāra.—A Damiḷa chief, ally of **Kulasekhara.** He was slain by the forces of **Parakkamabāhu I.**[1] There may have been more than one of this name.[2]

[1] Cv. lxxvi. 145, 163. [2] See *ibid.*, vs. 181, 188; lxxvii, 77, 86.

1. **Coḷagaṅga.**—A Damiḷa chief of South India, subdued by **Laṅkāpura.**[1] He was then put to rule over the district of **Parittikkuṇḍi.**[2]

[1] Cv. lxxvi. 121. [2] *Ibid.*, lxxvii. 8.

2. **Coḷagaṅga.**—King of Ceylon (1196-7 A.C.). He was the son of King **Nissaṅka's** sister. He slew **Vikkamabāhu III.** and reigned for nine months. He was then deposed by the general **Kitti** and his eyes were put out.[1]

[1] Cv. lxxx. 29 ff.

Coḷagaṅgakumāra.—A son of **Gajabāhu.**[1]

[1] Cv. lxx. 238.

Coḷagaṅgādeva.—A Damiḷa chief, conquered by **Bhuvanekabāhu I.**[1]

[1] Cv. xc. 32.

Coḷatirikka.—A Damiḷa chief, ally of **Kulasekhara.**[1]

[1] Cv. lxxvii. 78.

Coḷarāja.—A minister of **Kassapa V.** He repaired a pariveṇa in the **Mahāvihāra** which had been destroyed.[1]

[1] Cv. lii. 34.

Coḷā.—The people of **Coḷa** (*q.v.*).

Coḷiya-Dīpaṅkara. See **Dīpaṅkara.**

Ch.

Chakesadhātuvaṃsa.—See Appendix.

Chakkhattiyakhaṇḍa.—A section of the **Vessantara Jātaka** dealing with the journey undertaken by **Sañjaya** and his army to bring back **Vessantara** and his queen. The six khattiyas referred to are Sañjaya and his queen, Vessantara and **Maddī** and **Jāli** and **Kaṇhā.**[1]

[1] J. vi. 582-7.

Chagāma, Chaggāma.—A stronghold on the sea-coast, probably in eastern **Rohaṇa.**[1]

[1] Cv. lviii. 45; lxxv. 3.

Cha-Chakkha Sutta.—Preached at **Jetavana.** The Buddha explains to the assembled monks the six "sixes"—*e.g.*, the six internal senses (hearing etc.), the six external sense-objects (form etc.), the six groups of perceptions (sight and forms, hearing and sounds, etc.), and the six groups of cravings.[1]

The Commentary[2] says that, apart from the sixty monks who became arahants when the Buddha first preached the sutta, on each occasion of its preaching, by the Chief Disciples and by the eighty chief disciples, a like number attained arahantship. In Ceylon, **Maliyadeva Thera** preached it at sixty different places, and each time sixty monks became arahants. Once, when **Tipiṭaka-Cūlanāga** preached it at the **Ambilahālavihāra,** one thousand monks attained to arahantship.[3]

[1] M. iii. 280 ff. [2] MA. ii. 1024 f. [3] *Ibid.*, 1025.

1. **Chatta.**—A youth, son of the brahmin of the **Nānacchanda Jātaka.** He received from the king a chariot drawn by lilywhite thoroughbreds.[1]

[1] J. ii. 428 f.

2. **Chatta.**—Son of the king of **Kosala.** His story is given in the **Brahāchatta Jātaka** (*q.v.*).

3. **Chatta.**—A brahmin youth of **Setavyā.** He studied under **Pokkharasāti** at **Ukkaṭṭhā** and, having finished his course, returned home for money wherewith to pay his teacher. On the way back to Setavyā he was met by the Buddha, who taught him three stanzas, on the virtues of the Buddha, the Dhamma and the Saṅgha, and made him take the five precepts. As he proceeded along his road, Chatta was attacked by robbers and killed. He was reborn in **Tāvatiṃsa,** and when all his relations, his

teacher and others were assembled for his funeral ceremony, he came into their midst, conveyed by his thirty-league *vimāna*, and made obeisance to the Buddha who was present, and declared to him his great indebtedness for his compassion. The Buddha preached to the assembled multitude, and Chatta and his parents became Sotāpannas.[1]

[1] Vv. v. 3; VvA. 229 ff.; the story is often quoted—*e.g.*, Sp. i. 172; MA. i. 256; and the stanzas taught by the Buddha, as mentioned above, have become famous—*e.g.*, DA. i. 230; MA. i. 107; AA. i. 303.

4. **Chatta.**—A Tamil general of **Eḷāra** in charge of the fort at **Mahiyaṅgana.** He was killed by **Duṭṭhagāmaṇi.**[1]

[1] Mhv. xxv. 7.

Chattaguhinda.—The Pāli name of **Kyansitthā,** son of **Anorata,** king of Pagan.[1]

[1] Sās. 75; Bode, *op. cit.* 15, n. 5.

Chattaggāhaka-vāpī.—A tank built by a parasol-bearer (*chattaggāhaka*), the husband of **Saṅghā.**[1]

[1] Cv. xxxviii. 3.

Chattadāyaka Thera.—An arahant. Ninety-four kappas ago he was a king and his son became a Pacceka Buddha. One day, while seeking his son, he came across his funeral pyre; he worshipped it and placed over it his parasol as a mark of respect. Twenty-five kappas ago he was king seven times under the name of **Mahāraha.**[1]

[1] Ap. i. 244 f.

1. **Chattapāṇi.**—An upāsaka of **Sāvatthi.**[1] Once, when listening to the Buddha's teaching, he failed to notice and do reverence to the king, **Pasenadi,** who arrived during the discourse. Later, when summoned to the king's palace, he went with every sign of respect and paid obeisance to the king. When asked why he had not so behaved on the previous occasion, Chattapāṇi replied that such an action would have been discourteous to the Buddha. Thereupon Pasenadi asked him to act as instructor in the Dhamma to the women of the palace, but he refused the invitation, deeming that such a course would be unseemly and unwise. The task was therefore given to **Ānanda.**[2]

[1] He was an Anāgāmi according to the Jātaka account (J. i. 381 f.) and a Sakadāgāmi according to the DhA. (i. 380 f.).

[2] DhA. i. 380 f.; cp. Vin. iv. 157. The story is also found in J. i. 381 f., with several variations in detail. There we are told that the Buddha, seeing that the king was displeased, made special mention to him of Chattapāṇi's attainments.

2. **Chattapāṇi.**—The barber of King **Yasapāṇi.** His story is related in the **Dhammaddhaja Jātaka** (*q.v.*). He had four virtues—he was free from envy, drank no intoxicants, had no strong desires and no wrath. In one of his previous lives he was a king whose queen carried on intrigues with sixty-four of the slaves. Having failed to tempt the Bodhisatta, she spoke calumny against him and had him put in prison. But he explained the matter to the king and was released. From that time the king gave up envy. In another birth he was a king of Benares, strongly addicted to drinking and meat-eating; one day the meat prepared for him was eaten by the palace dogs. It was fast-day, and as there was no meat in the town the cook sought the queen's advice. When the king sat down to eat, his small son, whom he much loved, was brought to him in the hope that he might forget to ask for meat. But the plan failed, and in his drunkenness he twisted his son's neck and had his flesh cooked for him to eat. Thenceforth he refrained from strong drink and meat-eating.

Two other births of Chattapāṇi are mentioned, once as **Kitavāsa** and once as **Araka** (*q.v.*). He is identified with **Sāriputta.**[1]

[1] J. ii. 186-96.

Chattapāsāda.—A building in **Anurādhapura,** probably attached to the king's palace. There King **Bhātika** distributed gifts to the monks.[1] **Sirināga** repaired the building.[2]

[1] Mhv. xxxiv. 65; MṬ. 663. [2] Mhv. xxxvi. 26.

Chattavaḍḍhi.—The spot in **Mahāmeghavana** where **Moggallāna I.** presented his parasol to the monks as a mark of homage. A pariveṇa called by the same name was built there.[1]

[1] Mhv. xxxix. 32.

Chattādhichattiya.—See **Adhichattiya.**

Chattunnatavāpi.—A tank in Ceylon, repaired by **Parakkamabāhu I.**[1]

[1] Cv. lxviii. 43.

1. **Chaddanta.**—A forest in **Himavā.** In the forest was the **Mandākinī** Lake, on the banks of which **Aññā-Koṇḍañña** lived in retirement for twelve years, waited upon by eight thousand elephants who had once ministered to Pacceka Buddhas.[1]

[1] SA. i. 217; ThagA. ii. 3, 7; AA. i. 84.

2. **Chaddanta.**—A lake, one of the seven great lakes of the Himālaya region.[1] It was fifty leagues long and fifty broad. In the middle of the lake, for a space of twelve leagues, the water was like a jewel and no weeds grew there. Around this space were seven girdles of lilies, each girdle of a different hue and each a league in extent. Round the lake were seven ranges of mountains—**Cullakāla, Mahākāla, Udaka, Candapassa, Suriyapassa, Maṇipassa** and **Suvaṇṇapassa,** the last range being seven leagues in height and of a golden hue on the side overlooking the lake. On the west side of the lake was the **Kañcanaguhā,** twelve leagues in extent, where the elephant-king lived.[2]

[1] A. iv. 101; AA. ii. 759.

[2] J. v. 37.

3. **Chaddanta.**—A tribe of elephants, of which tribe the Bodhisatta was once born as king (see No. 4). The Chaddantas and the **Uposathas** are the two highest classes of elephant.[1] The Chaddantakula sometimes provides the *hatthiratana* for a Cakkavatti, in which case it is the youngest of the tribe who so functions.[2] Of the ten tribes of elephants enumerated in the books[3] the Chaddanta is classed as the highest, and the Buddha possesses the strength of ten Chaddanta-elephants, each elephant having the strength of ten thousand million men.[4] These elephants have the power of travelling through the air and are white in hue.[5]

[1] DhA. iii. 248.

[2] KhpA. 172.

[3] *E.g.*, UdA. 403; VibhA. 397.

[4] BuA. 37.

[5] J. v. 37; Vsm. 650.

4. **Chaddanta.**—The Bodhisatta, born as king of the elephants of the **Chaddanta** tribe, eight thousand in number. His body was pure white, with red face and feet, and seven parts of his body touched the ground. He lived in the **Kañcanaguhā** on the banks of the **Chaddanta** Lake, his chief queens being **Cūlasubhaddā** and **Mahāsubhaddā.** Owing to the preference shown to Mahāsubhaddā by Chaddanta, Cūlasubhaddā conceived a grudge against him, and one day, when Chaddanta was entertaining five hundred Pacceka Buddhas, she offered them wild fruits and made a certain wish. As a result she was reborn in the **Madda** king's family and was named **Subhaddā.** Later she became chief consort of the king of Benares. Remembering her ancient grudge, she schemed to have Chaddanta's tusks cut off. All the hunters were summoned by the king, and **Sonuttara** was chosen for the task. It took him seven years, seven months and seven days to reach Chaddanta's dwelling-place. He dug a pit and covered it, and as the elephant passed over it shot at him a poisoned arrow. When Chaddanta realised what had happened, he charged Sonuttara, but, seeing

that he was clad in a yellow robe, he restrained himself. Having learnt Sonuttara's story, he showed him how his tusks could be cut off, but Sonuttara's strength was not sufficient to saw them through. Chaddanta thereupon took the saw with his own trunk and, wounded as he was and suffering excruciating pain from the incisions already made in his jaws, he sawed through the tusks, handed them over to the hunter and died. In seven days, through the magic power of the elephant's tusks, Sonuttara returned to Benares; but when Subhaddā heard that her conspiracy had resulted in the death of her former lover and husband, she died of a broken heart.[1]

Chaddanta is mentioned as one of the births in which the Bodhisatta practised *sīla-pāramitā*.[2] Chaddanta could find delight only in the lakes and forests of the Himālaya, not in the crowded city.[3] See also **Chaddanta Jātaka.**

[1] J. v. 36 ff. [2] J. i. 45. [3] Vsm. 650.

Chaddanta Jātaka (No. 514).—The story of the Bodhisatta, born as **Chaddanta,** king of elephants. It was related in reference to a nun of Sāvatthi who, while listening one day to a sermon by the Buddha, admired his extreme beauty of form and wondered if she had ever been his wife. Immediately the memory of her life as **Cullasubhaddā,** Chaddanta's consort, came to her mind and she laughed for joy; but on further recollecting that she had been the instrument of his death, she wept aloud. The Buddha related this story in explanation of her conduct.[1]

[1] J. v. 36; Speyer (ZDMG. lxxv. 2, 305 ff.) suggests an allegorical explanation of the Chaddanta Jātaka. Feer (JA. 1895 v.) gives a careful study of the story based on a comparison of five different versions—two Pāli, two Chinese and one Sanskrit. This Jātaka forms the theme of many illustrations—*e.g.*, in Barhut (Cunningham, pl. xxxvi. 6), also Ajanta Caves x. and xvii.

Chanda, Chandaka, Chandāgārika.—See **Chann°**.

" **Chandena** " **Sutta.**—A group of eighteen suttas on abandoning lust and desire for that which is impermanent, ill and without self.[1]

[1] S. iv. 148-51.

Chandosāratthavikāsinī (or **Vuttodayapañcikā**).—A Commentary on the **Vuttodaya,** written by **Saddhammañāṇa** in the fourteenth century.[1]

[1] Bode, *op. cit.*, 26.

1. **Channa.**—A Wanderer, classed among those who wore clothes (*paṭicchannaparibbājaka*). He is only mentioned once, in the Aṅguttara Nikāya,[1] where we are told that he visited **Ānanda** at **Sāvatthi** and asked him questions about the Buddha's teaching (see **Channa Sutta** below). Both the Sutta and the Commentary[2] add that he was pleased with Ānanda's explanation, and admitted that the Buddha's teachings were worthy of being followed, though it is not explicitly stated that he accepted them.

[1] A. iii. 215. [2] AA. i. 432.

2. **Channa.**—A Thera. No particulars of his early life are available. He once stayed at **Gijjhakūṭa,** dangerously ill and suffering much pain. He was visited by **Sāriputta** and **Mahā Cunda,** and when they discovered that he contemplated suicide, they tried to deter him, promising to provide him with all necessaries and to wait on him themselves. Finding him quite determined, Sāriputta discussed with him the Buddha's teachings and then left him. Soon afterwards Channa committed suicide by cutting his throat. When this was reported to the Buddha, he explained that no blame was attached to Channa, for he was an arahant at the moment of death.[1]

Buddhaghosa explains[2] that after cutting his throat, Channa, feeling the fear of death, suddenly realised that he was yet a puthujjana. This thought so filled him with anguish that he put forth special effort, and by developing insight became an arahant.

Channa had friends and relations in the **Vajjian** village of **Pubbavijjhana** (*v.l.* **Pubbavajira**), and came himself from there. *v.l.* **Chandaka.**

[1] M. iii. 263 ff.; S. iv. 55 ff. [2] MA. ii. 1012 f.; SA. iii. 12 f.

3. **Channa.**—Gotama's charioteer and companion, born on the same day as **Gotama.**[1] When Gotama left household life, Channa rode with him on the horse **Kanthaka** as far as the river **Anomā.** There Gotama gave him his ornaments and bade him take Kanthaka back to his father's palace.[2] When, however, Kanthaka died of a broken heart, Channa's grief was great, for he had suffered a double loss. It is said that he begged for leave to join Gotama as a recluse, but this leave was refused.[3] He therefore returned to **Kapilavatthu,** but when the Buddha visited his Sakyan kinsfolk, Channa joined the Order. Because of his great affection for the Buddha, however,

[1] J. i. 54; Mtu. ii. 156, 164, 189, 233; iii. 91, 262; BuA. 233; SA. ii. 231; DhsA. 34. ThagA. (i. 155) says he was the son of a servant woman of Suddhodana.

[2] A thūpa was later erected on the spot where Channa turned back; Dvy. 391.

[3] J. i. 64 f.

egotistical pride in "our Buddha, our Doctrine" arose in him and he could not conquer this fondness nor fulfil his duties as a bhikkhu.[4]

Once, when in the **Ghositārāma** in **Kosambī**, Channa committed a fault but was not willing to acknowledge it. When the matter was reported to the Buddha, he decreed that the *ukkhepaniya-kamma* be carried out against him, forbidding him to eat or dwell with the Saṅgha. He therefore changed his residence, but was everywhere "boycotted," and returned to Kosambī subdued and asking for reprieve, which was granted to him.[5] Later, in a dispute between the monks and the nuns, he deliberately sided with the latter; this was considered so perverse and so lacking in proper *esprit de corps*, that the Buddha decreed on him the carrying out of the *Brahmadaṇḍa* whereby all monks were forbidden to have anything whatsoever to do with him. This was the last disciplinary act of the Buddha, and the carrying out thereof was entrusted to **Ānanda.**[6] When Ānanda visited Channa at the Ghositārāma and pronounced on him the penalty, even his proud and independent spirit was tamed; he became humble, his eyes were opened, and dwelling apart, earnest and zealous, he became one of the arahants, upon which the penalty automatically lapsed.[7] In the past, Channa met **Siddhattha** Buddha going towards a tree, and being pleased with him, spread for him a soft carpet of leaves round which he spread flowers. Five kappas ago he became king seven times, under the name of **Tiṇasanthāraka.**[8]

He is probably identical with **Senāsanadāyaka** of the Apadāna.[9]

Channa is identified with the hunter in the **Suvaṇṇamiga** (III. 187), the **Gijjha** (III. 332), the **Rohantamiga** (IV. 423), the **Cūlahaṃsa** (V. 354), and the **Mahāhaṃsa** (V. 382) Jātakas, with the wrestler in the **Sālikedāra Jātaka** (IV. 282) and with Cetaputta in the **Vessantara Jātaka** (VI. 593). See also **Channa Sutta** (1) below.

[4] ThagA. i. 155; his verse (No. 69) quoted in Thag. does not, however, refer to any such remissness on his part.

[5] Vin. ii. 23 ff. His obstinacy and perverseness are again mentioned elsewhere—*e.g.*, Vin. iv. 35, 113, 141. A patron of his once erected a vihāra for him, but he so thatched and decked it that it fell down. In trying to repair it he damaged a brahmin's barley field (Vin. iii. 47). See also Vin. iii. 155 f., 177.

[6] D. ii. 154. It would, however, appear from DhA. ii. 110 that the Brahmadaṇḍa was inflicted on Channa for his having repeatedly reviled **Sāriputta** and **Moggallāna** in spite of the Buddha's warning. In this version other details also vary.

[7] Vin. ii. 292.

[8] ThagA. i. 155.

[9] i. 137.

Channa Vagga.—The Ninth chapter of the **Saḷāyatana Saṃyutta.**[1]

[1] S. iv. 53-70.

1. **Channa Sutta.**—Records the visit of **Channa** paribbājaka to **Ānanda,** at **Sāvatthi.** He asks Ānanda why the Buddha preaches the abandonment of *rāga, dosa, moha*; Ānanda explains and Channa goes away satisfied.[1]

[1] A. i. 215 f.

2. **Channa Sutta.**—**Channa Thera** goes from cell to cell in the monastery at **Isipatana,** asking the Elders to teach him the Dhamma. Finding that their teachings do not help him in getting rid of craving, he visits **Ānanda** at the **Ghositārāma.** Ānanda praises Channa for his new-found humility, and repeats to him a sermon which he (Ānanda) had heard the Buddha preach to the monk **Kacchānagotta,** dealing with the *paṭiccasamuppāda.* Channa expresses his delight with the exposition of Ānanda.[1] The Commentary[2] says that this account refers to Channa, the companion of the Buddha. After the infliction on him of the Brahmadaṇḍa, he was greatly affected, and wandered from place to place. In the course of these wanderings he came to Benares.

[1] S. iii. 132 ff. [2] SA. ii. 231 f.

3. **Channa Sutta.**—Records the incidents in connection with the suicide of **Channa Thera** (Channa 2).[1]

[1] S. iv. 55 f.; SA. iii. 12; *cf.* M. iii. 263 ff.

Channapatha-pañha.—The section of the **Mahāummagga Jātaka** which tells of **Mahosadha's** first meeting with **Amarādevī** and the riddle in which she indicated the way to her house.[1] It is sometimes called the **Amarādevī-pañha.**[2]

[1] J. vi. 363-5. [2] J. i. 424.

Channā.—A nun, mentioned as being specially proficient in the Vinaya.[1] *v.l.* **Chandā.**

[1] Dpv. xviii. 29.

Channāgarikā.—A secondary division of the **Vajjiputtakas.**[1]

[1] Mhv. v. 7; Dpv. v. 46; Mbv. 97.

Channovāda Sutta.—Records the same incidents as **Channa Sutta** (3).[1]

[1] M. iii. 263 ff.

Chapaṭa.—See **Saddhammajotipāla.**

Chapāṇa Sutta.—If a man were to catch six animals—a snake, a crocodile, a bird, a dog, a jackal and a monkey—and tether them with ropes, they would struggle to be free and to make off, each to his own range or pasture. So do a man's six senses. If the animals are strongly tethered, they will, with time, grow weary and rest. So will the six senses if one practises attention to the body.[1]

[1] S. iv. 197; *cp.* Vsm. 484.

Chappaccayadīpanī.—A work on Pāli prosody by **Suddhammañāṇa.**[1]

[1] Bode, *op. cit.*, 26.

Chaphassāyatanika Suttā.—A group of three suttas concerning the sixfold sphere of contact.[1]

[1] S. iv. 43 f.

Chabbaggiyā.—A group of monks, contemporary with the Buddha, frequently mentioned as being guilty of various Vinaya offences.[1]

Six monks—**Assaji, Punabbasu, Paṇḍuka, Lohitaka, Mettiya** and **Bhummaja**—were their leaders, hence their name.

There were also nuns in their following, who likewise violated the Vinaya rules in various ways.[2]

It is said that Assaji and Punabbasu had their headquarters at **Kīṭāgiri,** Mettiya and Bhummaja(ka) at **Rājagaha** and Paṇḍuka and Lohitaka at **Jetavana.**[3]

According to the Samantapāsādikā[4] they were all of **Sāvatthi** and all originally acquainted. Finding a living hard to obtain, they entered the Order under the two Chief Disciples. They decided among themselves that it was unwise for them all to live in the same place, and they therefore divided into three groups as mentioned above. Each group had five hundred monks attached to it. Of the three groups, the followers of Paṇḍuka and Lohitaka were the most virtuous. They remained near the Buddha, accompanying him on his tours. They did not, like the others, transgress Vinaya rules.

[1] Vin. i. 84 f., 104, 106, 111, 113, 114, 138, 160, 170, 185, 189, 192, 194, 203 f., 216, 285, 306, 316; ii. 73, 105 ff., 145 ff., 213 ff., 241, 262, etc.: J. i. 191, 217, 360; iii. 149; DhA. iii. 48 f., 330, 382.

[2] Vin. ii. 262, 266, 269, 271, 276.

[3] J. ii. 387.

[4] iii. 613 f.

Chabbisodhana Sutta.—On the sixfold scrutiny by which a monk can know whether he is justified in saying that for him rebirth is no more, that his heart has been absolutely delivered from the āsavas.[1]

[1] M. iii. 29-37.

Chabbyāputtā.—A royal clan of **Nāgas.**[1]

[1] Vin. ii. 110; J. ii. 145; A. ii. 72.

Chambhī.—A brahmin, chaplain of **Mahācūḷani.** He conspired with queen **Talatā** and, having poisoned **Mahācūḷani,** became king in his place. Later, fearing for his life, he wished to kill the king's son, **Cūḷani,** but Talatā (*q.v.*), by means of a ruse, saved the boy's life.[1]

[1] J. vi. 470 f.

Challūra.—A tank built by King **Mahāsena.**[1]

[1] Mhv. xxxvii. 47.

Chaḷaṅga.—A brahmin of **Haṃsavatī.** He had one thousand eight hundred pupils with whose assistance he built a bridge over the **Bhagīrathī** for the Buddha **Padumuttara** and his disciples. He was a previous birth of **Dhotaka Thera.**[1]

[1] Ap. ii. 344.

Chaḷaṅgakumāra.—A general sent by the king of Benares to instruct **Eḷakamāra** in the art of war; afterwards he became Eḷakamāra's commander-in-chief. Eḷakamāra's wife misconducted herself with Chaḷaṅgakumāra and also with his attendant **Dhanantevāsī. Kuṇāla** said it was he who was Chaḷaṅgakumāra and that, therefore, he was an incarnation of the Buddha.[1]

[1] J. v. 425, 430.

Chaḷabhijātiya Sutta.—On the six breeds declared by **Pūraṇa Kassapa**—black, blue, red, yellow, white and purest white—and the six corresponding breeds declared by the Buddha.[1]

[1] A. iii. 383 f.; *cp.* DA. i. 162; S. iii. 210; D. iii. 250 f.

Chaḷindriya Vagga.—The third chapter of the Indriya Saṃyutta.[1]

[1] S. v. 203 ff.

Chavaka Jātaka (No. 309).—The Bodhisatta was once born as a caṇḍāla. His wife, being with child, yearned to eat a mango, and he went by night to the king's garden to try and get one. But day broke before he could escape and he remained perched in the tree. While he was there, the king came with his chaplain and, sitting on a high seat at the foot of the tree, learnt the Law from the chaplain, who occupied a low seat. The

Bodhisatta climbed down from the tree and pointed out to them their error. The king, being very pleased, made him ruler of the city by night and placed round his neck the garland of red flowers which he himself was wearing. Hence the custom of the lords of the city to wear a wreath of red flowers.

The story was related in reference to the **Chabbaggiya** monks, who preached the Doctrine to those who sat on a higher seat than they themselves.[1]

[1] J. iii. 27 ff.

Chavālāta Sutta.—Some people are bent neither on their own profit nor on that of others, some only on another's profit, some only on their own, and yet others on the profit of both themselves and others. He who belongs to the first class is like a firebrand from a funeral pyre, blazing at both ends, smeared with dung in the middle, useless for any purpose.[1]

[1] A. ii. 95.

Chavasīsa.—A charm which gave the power of saying where a dead person was born, by tapping on his skull with one's finger-nail, even three years after death. **Vaṅgīsa** knew the charm.[1]

[1] ThagA. ii. 192; AA. i. 150, *cp.* **Migasira.**

Chavi Sutta.—Dire are gains, favours and flattery; they cut the skin, the flesh, right down to the marrow.[1]

[1] S. ii. 237.

Chātapabbata.—A mountain, slightly over two yojanas to the south-east of **Anurādhapura.** At the foot was a bamboo-grove in which grew three bamboo-stems, each being a waggon-pole in girth—known as *latāyaṭṭhi*, *kusumayaṭṭhi* and *sakuṇayaṭṭhi*—because of **Devānampiyatissa's** good fortune.[1] **Saddhātissa** afterwards built a vihāra there, called the **Chātavihāra.**[2] The Aṅguttara Commentary[3] has a reference to a novice dwelling in Chātapabbata who came to grief after hearing a woman's voice.

[1] Mhv. xi. 10; Dpv. xi. 15, 19; Sp. i. 74. For an explanation of these yaṭṭhis see IHQ. vi. 571 ff.

[2] MṬ. 300.

[3] i. 15.

Chāva.—See **Upaka Ājīvaka.**

1. **Chiggala Sutta.**—Once, at the **Kūṭagārasālā** in Vesāli, **Ānanda** saw **Licchavi** youths practising archery, shooting through even a small keyhole

(*chiggala*) without a miss. He reported this to the Buddha, who remarked that those who penetrate the meaning of *dukkha*, etc., do a far more difficult thing.[1]

[1] S. v. 453 f.

2. **Chiggala Sutta.**—It is more probable that a blind turtle, rising to the surface only once in a hundred years, should put his neck through a yoke (*chiggala*) with a single hole, floating about in the ocean, than that a fool who has gone to the Downfall should become a man again.[1]

[1] S. v. 455; *cp.* M. iii. 169; Thig. 500.

3. **Chiggala Sutta.**—Similar to 2. It is more probable that a turtle, etc. . . ., than that one should get birth in a human form, or that a Tathāgata should arise in the world, or that the Dhamma and Vinaya proclaimed by a Tathāgata should be shown in the world. See also **Tālacchiggala Sutta.**[1]

[1] S. v. 456.

Chindī Sutta.—**Devadatta** brought schism into the Order because his heart was possessed by gains, flattery, etc.[1]

[1] S. ii. 239.

Cheta Sutta.—See **Kassapagotta Sutta.**

Chetvā Vagga.—The eighth chapter of the **Devatā Saṃyutta.**[1] *v.l.* **Jhatvā.**[2]

[1] S. i. 41 ff. [2] On the title of the sutta see KS. i. 58, n. 1.

Chetvā Sutta.—One must destroy anger in order to be happy.[1] *v.l.* **Jhatvā.** The sutta is repeated under the same name in S. i. 237. It appears again under the names of **Māgha** (S. i. 46) and **Dhānañjānī** (S. i. 160).

[1] S. i. 41.

J.

Jagatikāraka Thera.—An arahant. In the past he set up an altar (? *jagatī*) at the thūpa of **Atthadassī Buddha.**[1]

[1] Ap. i. 221.

Jagatidāyaka Thera.—An arahant. In the time of **Dhammadassī** Buddha he set up a *jagati* at the Buddha's Bodhi-tree.[1]

[1] Ap. ii. 402.

Jagatipāla.—King of Ceylon (1047–51 A.C.). He came from **Ayojjha,** and claimed descent from the race of **Rāma.** Having slain **Vikkamapaṇḍu** he ruled in **Rohaṇa** till he himself was slain by the **Coḷas.**[1] He had a daughter named **Līlāvatī,** who later became the consort of **Vijayabāhu I.**[2]

[1] Cv. lvi. 13 f. [2] *Ibid.*, lix. 23 f.

Jagadvijaya.—A general of **Parakkamabāhu I.** He, with **Laṅkāpura,** took the most prominent part in the expedition against **Kulasekhara** and many victories are attributed to him.[1]

[1] Cv. lxxvi. 255, 292, 303, 313, 319, 332; lxxvii. 4, 45, 60, 64, 71, 82.

Jaṅghadāsa.—Probably an author of some Burmese work, to which **Vajira (Cīvara ?)** wrote a *ṭīkā.*[1]

[1] Gv. 64, 74.

Jaṅghābhāra.—A park laid out by **Parakkamabāhu I.**[1]

[1] Cv. lxxix. 9.

Jaccandha Vagga.—The sixth chapter of the **Udāna.**

Jajjaranadī.—A river in Ceylon, the present Deduru-Oya. On the river was the famous causeway known as **Koṭṭhabaddha,** restored by **Parakkamabāhu I.,**[1] who also built a dam across the river at **Dorādattika.**[2]

[1] Cv. lxviii. 16. [2] *Ibid.*, vs. 37; see also lxxix. 67.

Jaṭā Sutta.—A deva asks the Buddha how sentient beings can escape from their tangles. By the destruction of *rāga, dosa, moha,* answers the Buddha.[1] This sutta forms the basis of the **Visuddhimagga.**

[1] S. i. 13; repeated at i. 165.

Jaṭā-Bhāradvāja.—A brahmin of the **Bhāradvājagotta.** He goes to the Buddha and asks him the questions given in the **Jaṭā Sutta** (see above). The Buddha gives the same answer.[1] The Commentary[2] says that he was given this name by the Recensionists because he asked a question about *jaṭā* (tangle).

[1] S. i. 165. [2] SA. i. 179.

Jaṭika.—See **Jaṭila** (2).

1. **Jaṭila.**—A class of ascetics, so called on account of their matted hair (*jaṭilā ti tāpasā, te hi jaṭādhāriṭāya idha jaṭilā ti vuttā*[1]). These ascetics are sometimes classed under *isi*[2] and also under *muni.*[3]

[1] UdA. 74; see also 330. [2] Culla Nid. 149. [3] *Ibid.*, 513.

2. **Jaṭila.**—A governor of a province (*Mahāraṭṭhiya*) in the time of **Padummuttara Buddha.** He was the Bodhisatta.[1] *v.l.* **Jaṭika.**

[1] J. i. 37; Bu. xi. 11.

3. **Jaṭila** (*v.l.* **Jaṭilaka**).—A seṭṭhi of **Magadha,** one of the five seṭṭhis of **Bimbisāra.**[1] His mother was a seṭṭhi's daughter in Benares, who had illicit relations with a Vijjādhara, and when the child was born she placed it in a vessel which she handed to her slave, to be floated down the Ganges. Two women, while bathing, saw the vessel, discovered what it contained and each claimed the child. The dispute was settled by the king and the child was given to the woman who happened to be a disciple of **Mahā Kaccāna.** The child was called **Jaṭila** because the first time he was bathed after birth his hair became matted. When able to walk, he was given to Mahā Kaccāna to be ordained, but the thera took him to **Takkasilā** and handed him over to one of his supporters, a merchant, who adopted him as his son. Years passed, and one day the merchant, having to go on a journey, made a list of the goods which he had accumulated in his house during twelve years and asked Jaṭila to sell them if he could find buyers. Such was the lad's fortune that in one day they were all disposed of. The merchant, realising the young man's destiny, gave him his daughter in marriage and provided him with a house. As Jaṭila stepped into the house, the earth behind it was rent asunder and a mountain of gold, eighty cubits in height, appeared for his use. Thereupon the king made him a Treasurer. Later, wishing to retire from the world, Jaṭila sent out messengers to discover if there were others as rich as he, in case the king should raise objections to his going away. When news was brought back of **Meṇḍaka** and **Jotika,** he knew there would be no opposition and obtained the king's permission. He had three sons, but, having tested them, came to know that only the youngest had the necessary good fortune to enjoy his vast wealth. Jaṭila thereupon handed over to him his wealth and entered the Order, becoming an arahant within a few days. Some time afterwards the Buddha, with

[1] DhA. i. 385.

Jaṭila and other monks, was entertained for a fortnight by Jaṭila's sons, and in answer to the monks' questions Jaṭila declared that he felt no desire to re-enter household life. The monks found this hard to believe till assured by the Buddha that it was so.

In the time of **Kassapa** Buddha, Jaṭila was a goldsmith. One day, an arahant, seeking for gold wherewith to complete the shrine erected over the Buddha's remains, came to the goldsmith's house; the latter, having just quarrelled with his wife, was in a surly mood and said to the arahant, "Throw your teacher into the water and get away." His wife told him how wicked were his words, and he, realising his fault, asked pardon of the arahant and made valuable offerings at the Buddha's shrine, by way of amends. Of his three sons whom he asked, in turn, to help him with the preparations, only the youngest consented to go with him. Therefore it was that in seven successive states Jaṭila was thrown into the water on the day of his birth and only his youngest son could enjoy his wealth.[2]

Jaṭila's possession of a golden mountain is given as an example of *puññiddhi*, he being one of the five persons of great merit.[3]

[2] DhA. iv. 214 ff.; PsA. 502 f.

[3] Vsm. 383; BuA. 24.

Jaṭila Sutta.—Once when **Pasenadi** was talking with the Buddha in the loggia outside the **Migāramātupāsāda,** there passed close by thirty-five ascetics of various denominations—Jaṭilas, Nigaṇṭhas, etc.—and the king saluted them respectfully. Later, he asked the Buddha whether they were arahants or on the way to arahantship. The Buddha explained to him how hard it was for a layman, with all his encumbrances, to find an opportunity to learn the truth about arahants; much time and care and attention were necessary. The king agreed and mentioned how he gathered information through his spies.[1]

[1] S. i. 77 f.

Jaṭilagaha.—A city, the residence of **Jaṭilagāhī.**[1]

[1] AA. ii. 812.

Jaṭilagāhī.—The name given to a bhikkhunī, who, so **Ānanda** tells **Udāyī,** came to see him at the **Añjanavana** in **Sāketā.** The nun asked him for what purpose the Buddha requested that *samādhi* should be practised and Ānanda answered that it was for the purpose of obtaining insight.[1] The Commentary[2] says that the bhikkhunī was so called because she came from a city called **Jaṭilagaha.**

[1] A. iv. 427 f.

[2] AA. ii. 812.

Jatukaṇṇī (Jatukaṇṇika).—One of **Bāvarī's** disciples. His question and the Buddha's answer are found in the **Jatukaṇṇi Sutta.**[1]

In the time of **Padumuttara** Buddha, Jatukaṇṇī was a banker in **Haṃsavatī,** rich enough to lend money even to the king, **Arindama.** One day he saw the Buddha going along the street and, having invited him and twenty thousand monks, gave them a meal at his house.[2]

[1] SN. vv. 1007, 1096-1100; Dvy. 635. [2] Ap. ii. 357 ff.

Jatukaṇṇi Sutta.—Also called **Jatukaṇṇimāṇavapucchā.** Contains the question asked of the Buddha by **Jatukaṇṇī** and the Buddha's answer. It is the eleventh sutta of the **Parāyana Vagga.**[1]

[1] SN. vv. 1096-1100; SNA. ii. 598; CNid. 33 ff.

Jana Suttā.—Three suttas, in answer to questions by devas as to what brings about rebirth. Craving, answers the Buddha.[1]

[1] S. i. 37 f.

1. **Janaka.**—King of **Mithilā,** a previous birth of the Bodhisatta.[1] For his story, see the **Mahā Janaka Jātaka.**

[1] J. i. 268; J. vi. 59.

2. **Janaka.**—King of Benares.[1] His minister was **Senaka,** whose story is related in the **Sattubhasta Jātaka.**

[1] J. iii. 341, 348.

Janagāma.—See **Jantugāma.**

Janapada.—A district in Northern Malaya in Ceylon, near the frontier of the **Dakkhiṇadesa.**[1]

[1] Cv. xliv. 56, etc. For identification, see Cv. *Trs.* i. 79, n. 4; 262, n. 1.

Janapada Sutta.—Preached to the monks at **Desakā** in the **Sumbhā** country. Supposing the fairest maiden in all the countryside were to dance and sing in public, and a man were told that if he carried a bowl brimful of oil through the crowd he would win the maiden, but that if he spilt one single drop he would lose his head, that man would not turn his attention to anything else or grow slack in his efforts. In the same way should monks cultivate mindfulness relating to the body.[1]

This sutta seems also to have been called the **Janapadakalyāṇi Sutta.**[2]

[1] S. v. 169 f. [2] *E.g.*, J. i. 393 f.

Janapadakalyāṇī Nandā.—One of the three **Nandās** who became bhikkuṇīs—the others being **Nandā,** sister of **Nandatthera** and **Abhirūpa-Nandā.** Because of her very great beauty she earned the sobriquet of Janapadakalyāṇī.[1] Janapadakalyāṇi was engaged to be married to **Nanda,** but on the day fixed for the marriage the Buddha induced Nanda to join the Order, in spite of Nanda's wishes, and in due course he became an arahant. Later, when women were admitted to the Order, Janapadakalyāṇī, feeling she had nothing to look forward to, became a bhikkhuṇī under **Pajāpatī.** For a long time she would not visit the Buddha, having heard that he spoke disparagingly of physical beauty, but one day, inspired by curiosity, she accompanied her colleagues to hear the Buddha preach. He, being aware of her thoughts, created the form of a most beautiful maiden who stood fanning him. As Janapadakalyāṇī sat gazing at her, enraptured by her beauty, she saw her gradually reach extreme old age, passing through all the stages, until at last she saw her die, leaving her body to decompose and become a mass of filth. At the critical moment, the Buddha uttered the appropriate words and Janapadakalyāṇī became a *Sotāpanna.* The Buddha then preached the **Kāyavicchandanika Sutta** and she became an arahant.[2]

She seems to have been known also as **Rūpanandā.**[3]

In one of her previous lives, Janapadakalyāṇī was born as a she-mule; she sorely tempted Nanda, who was then a mule belonging to a merchant named **Kappaṭa.**[4]

Sundarī Nandā (*q.v.*) also seems to have been called Janapadakalyāṇī.

[1] The Udāna Commentary (170) gives details of her beauty, which justified her title; see also J. i. 394.

[2] Ud. iii. 2; J. i. 91; SNA. i. 241 f., 243 f., 254, 273; DhA. i. 97, 100.

[3] DhA. iii. 113 f.; but see *s.v.* Rūpanandā; perhaps here we have a confusion of legends. In the northern books she is called Bhadrā. (Rockhill, p. 55.)

[4] DhA. i. 105.

1. **Janapadakalyāṇī Sutta.**—See **Janapada Sutta.**

2. **Janapadakalyāṇī Sutta.**—Not even a *janapadakalyāṇī* (a city belle) can continuously possess the heart of a man whose mind is won over by gains, favours and flattery.[1]

[1] S. ii. 233.

Janavasabha.—A yakkha, a later birth of King **Bimbisāra.** He appears before the Buddha at the **Giñjakāvasatha** in **Ñātikā** and declares his identity. He is on his way as a messenger from **Vessavaṇa** to **Virūḷhaka** and reports to the Buddha an account of an assembly of the devas in **Tāvatiṃsa** which had taken place some time earlier, and which account he claims to have heard from Vessavaṇa. See **Janavasabha Sutta.** Janavasabha is a *Sotāpanna* and expresses a wish to be a *Sakadāgāmī.* He says he remembers fourteen lives in all.[1]

[1] D. ii. 205 f., 207, 214; *cp.* Janesabha.

Janavasabha Sutta.—Ānanda asks the Buddha at **Giñjakāvasatha** questions concerning followers of the Buddha in **Magadha.** The yakkha, **Janavasabha,** appears and says he was once King **Bimbisāra** and is now reborn into the communion of King **Vessavaṇa.** He then proceeds to relate a report he had just heard from Vessavaṇa of an assembly of the gods held in Tāvatiṃsa many years earlier, on the full-moon day of **Āsāḷhi. Sakka** presided and there were present also the Four Regent Gods. All the devas rejoiced that their numbers were increasing because so many on earth were following the teachings of the Buddha. Then there appeared in the assembly the Brahmā **Sanaṅkumāra** in the guise of **Pañcasikha ;** assuming thirty-three forms, he took his place by each god of Tāvatiṃsa and confirmed the glad tidings of the increasing number of devas. He then told them of the Four Ways of Iddhi and the Three Avenues of Bliss as taught by the Buddha, and of the seven *samādhi-parikkhārā.* Then they all sang the praises of the Buddha.[1]

[1] D. ii. 200 ff.

1. **Janasandha.**—King of Benares, father of **Ādāsamukha.** His servant was **Gāmaṇicaṇḍa.** For their story see the **Gamaṇicaṇḍa Jātaka**[1] ; Janasandha is also referred to as **Dasaratha.**[2] He was called Janasandha because he won the hearts of men by four ways of kindness (*catūhi saṅgahavatthūhi sandahanato*).[3]

[1] J. ii. 297 ff. [2] *E.g.*, p. 299. [3] J. ii. 299.

2. **Janasandha.**—A khattiya, father of **Tissa** Buddha.[1] He seems to have been called also **Saccasandha.**[2]

[1] J. i. 40; Bu. xviii. 16. [2] BuA. 188.

3. **Janasandha.**—A title given to **Dhanañjaya-Koravya,** king of **Kurukkhetta.**[1] The scholiast explains it thus: *mittaganthanena mittajanassa santhānakaro.*

[1] J. vi. 291.

4. **Janasandha.**—Son of **Brahmadatta** and king of Benares; an incarnation of the Bodhisatta. See **Janasandha Jātaka.**

Janasandha Jātaka (No. 468).—The Bodhisatta was once born as **Janasandha,** son of **Brahmadatta,** king of Benares. He studied at **Takkasilā.** On becoming king he built six almonries and there daily distributed six thousand pieces of money. He ruled righteously and his kingdom was free from all wickedness. On the fifteenth day of every month he assembled all his people, beginning with the women of his household, and preached to them the ways of righteousness.

The story was related to **Pasenadi** when he gave himself up to sin, became remiss in his duties and refrained from visiting even the Buddha for a long time.[1]

[1] J. iv. 176 ff.

Janesabha.—A **Gandhabba,** a vassal of the Four Regent Gods. He was present at the preaching of the **Mahā-Samaya.**[1]

In the Āṭānāṭiya Sutta[2] he is mentioned as a Yakkha chieftain to be invoked by the Buddha's followers in time of need.

He is probably identical with **Janavasabha.**

[1] D. ii. 258. [2] *Ibid.*, iii. 204.

Janasāna (Jarasāna, Jarasoṇa).—An **Ājīvaka.** He it was who predicted the glory of **Asoka** by explaining the prenatal desires of his mother. The queen promised him great honour if his predictions should prove true. Later, when Asoka became king and heard the story, he sent a golden palanquin to fetch Janasāna to the palace. On the way, Janasāna visited the **Vattaniya** hermitage where lived **Assagutta,** and having heard the latter talk of āyatana, his earlier kamma asserted itself and he became a monk, attaining arahantship.

In the time of **Kassapa** Buddha he was a python who died while listening to some monks reciting a chapter on the *āyatanas.*[1]

[1] MṬ. 190 ff.

Janābrahmamahārāja.—A Damiḷa chief, ally of **Kulasekhara.**[1]

[1] Cv. lxxvii. 78.

Januttama.—A king of fifty-one kappas ago, a previous birth of **Meṇḍasira Thera,** also called **Gaṇṭhipupphiya.**[1] *v.l.* **Jaluttama.**

[1] ThagA. i. 172; Ap. i. 162.

Janogha.—A city in **Uttarakuru, Kuvera's** kingdom.[1]

[1] D. iii. 201.

1. **Jantu.**—A devaputta. He saw a number of monks in a forest-lodge on the slopes of the Himālaya, muddled in mind, loose of speech and heedless. He appeared before them on an *uposatha* day and reminded them of their duties.[1]

[1] S. i. 61 f.

2. **Jantu.**—One of the five queens of **Okkāka,** founder of the third Okkāka dynasty.[1]

[1] DA. i. 258 f.; SNA. i. 352 f.; MṬ. 131.

3. **Jantu.**—Son of the third **Okkāka,** by a woman whom he appointed to be his chief queen when his first one, **Hatthā,** died. This woman was promised a boon and she asked that her son Jantu be appointed to succeed Okkāka, in preference to his other children. Okkāka first refused but was obliged to yield. His other sons and daughters thereupon left the kingdom and became the founders of the **Sākyan** race.[1]

The Mahāvastu[2] calls Jantu, Jentā, and his mother Jentī. He reigned in Sāketa.

[1] DA. 258 f; SNA. i. 352 f.; MṬ. 131. [2] i. 348.

Jantu Sutta.—Records the incident of the admonishment of the indolent monks by the devaputta **Jantu** (*q.v.*).[1]

[1] S. i. 61 f.

Jantugāma.—A village near **Cālikā**; close by was the river **Kimikālā** with the mango-grove on its banks. **Meghiya,** while staying with the Buddha at Cālikā, once went to Jantugāma for alms.[1] The Aṅguttara Commentary[2] says the village was in **Pācīnavaṃsamigadāya.** *v.l.* **Janagāma.**[3]

[1] A. iv. 354; Ud. iv. 1. [2] AA. i. 163. [3] UdA. 217.

Jambāli Sutta.—Some monks attain to release of mind, but when they apply themselves to the ending of *sakkāya* their minds do not settle down, do not stay fixed; they are like a man who grasps a branch with his hand smeared with resin. In the case of other monks, their minds abide in the release attained and stay fixed in the endeavour to destroy *sakkāya*—and they are like a man who grasps a branch with a clean hand. Some monks strive to destroy ignorance but are unsuccessful. Their minds are like a village pond (*jambālī*) which has stood for countless years with all its inlets blocked and outlets open and receiving no rain. There will be no breach in its dyke. There are other monks who break through ignorance by application of the mind—like a village pond with all its inlets open and outlets closed and with rain falling continuously into it.[1]

[1] A. ii. 165 f.

Jambāvatī.—A caṇḍālī, mother of King **Sivi** and wife of **Vāsudeva** of the **Kaṇhāyanagotta.** Vāsudeva saw her on his way to the park from **Dvāravatī,** and, in spite of her birth, married her and made her his chief queen.[1]

[1] J. vi. 421.

Jambu.—A village, in command of which was a Tamil general of the same name, whom **Duṭṭhagāmaṇī** slew.[1]

[1] Mhv. xxv. 15.

1. **Jambuka Thera.**—He was born in **Rājagaha** of rich parents but from infancy he would eat nothing but excrement. When he grew older he was ordained with the **Ājīvakas,** who pulled out his hair with a palmyra comb. When the Ājīvakas discovered that he ate filth, they expelled him and he lived as a naked ascetic, practising all kinds of austerities and accepting no offerings save butter and honey placed on the tip of his tongue with the point of a blade of grass. His fame spread far. When he was fifty-five years old, the Buddha visited him and spent the night in a cave near his abode. During the night, Jambuka saw mighty gods come to pay homage to the Buddha and was so impressed that the next day he sought the Buddha's counsel. The Buddha told him of his past evil deeds which had condemned him to practise austerities for so long and counselled him to give up his evil ways. In the course of the sermon, Jambuka grew ashamed of his nakedness and the Buddha gave him a bath-robe. At the end of the discourse Jambuka became an arahant, and when the inhabitants of **Aṅga** and **Magadha** came to him with their offerings, he performed a miracle before them and paid homage to the Buddha, acknowledging him as his teacher.

In the time of **Kassapa** Buddha, Jambuka was a monk and had a lay patron who looked after him. One day a pious monk came to his vihāra, and the layman, being pleased with him, showed him much attention. The resident monk, very jealous, reviled the visitor, saying, " It would be better for you to eat filth than food in this layman's house, to tear your hair with a palmyra comb than let his barber cut it for you, to go naked than wear robes given by him, to lie on the ground than on a bed provided by him." The Elder, not wishing to be the cause of his sinning, left the monastery the next day. Because of this act, the meditations practised by Jambuka for twenty thousand years were of no avail, and he was born in **Avīci,** where he suffered torments during an interval between two Buddhas. In this last life, too, he was condemned to suffer in many ways, as related above.[1]

In the time of **Tissa** Buddha he was a householder and made offerings at the Buddha's Bodhi-tree, fanning the Buddha's seat with a fan. He is probably identical with **Sīhāsanavījanīya** of the Apadāna.[2]

It is said[3] that when the Buddha preached to Jambuka, eighty-four thousand others realised the Truth.

[1] DhA. ii. 52-63; Thag. 283-6; ThagA. i. 386 f. [2] Ap. ii. 403. [3] Mil. 350; AA. i. 57.

2. **Jambuka.**—A parrot, an incarnation of the Bodhisatta, adopted as his son by **Brahmadatta,** king of Benares. He preached to the king on the fivefold power—of limbs, of wealth, of counsel, of caste and of wisdom—the last being the best. The king thereupon appointed him commander-in-chief.[1]

[1] J. v. 111, 120, 125.

3. **Jambuka.**—A dog, companion of the she-goat in the **Pūtimaṃsa Jātaka.**[1]

[1] J. iii. 535.

Jambuka Jātaka (No. 535).—A jackal, seeing a lion, expressed his wish to be his servant. The lion agreed and provided him with food. On growing strong, the jackal offered to kill an elephant and, in spite of the lion's warnings, was trampled to death. The lion was the Bodhisatta and the jackal **Devadatta.**

The story was related in reference to Devadatta's attempt to imitate the Buddha.[1]

[1] J. iii. 112 ff.

Jambukola.—A sea-port in **Nāgadīpa** in the north of Ceylon. Here **Mahāriṭṭha** and his companions embarked on their journey as envoys to **Dhammāsoka.**[1] Here also arrived the ship conveying **Saṅghamittā** and the branch of the sacred Bodhi-tree, welcomed by **Devānampiyatissa,** who awaited her arrival in the **Samuddapaṇṇasālā.**[2] A sapling from the Bodhi-tree was afterwards planted on the spot where it had stood after

[1] Mhv. xi. 23. [2] *Ibid.*, xix. 25 f.

landing[3] and Devānampiyatissa built a vihāra there called the **Jambukolavihāra.**[4] From Jambukola to **Tāmalitti** by sea was a seven days' voyage,[5] and it appears to have taken five days to get to **Anurādhapura** from Jambukola.[6] It was the seaport of Anurādhapura.[7]

Geiger thinks[8] that, besides the seaport, there was another locality in the interior of Ceylon bearing the same name, which he identifies with the modern Dambulla.

[3] *Ibid.*, vs. 59; Sp. i. 100; Mbv. 145-62 (*passim*).
[4] Mhv. xx. 25.
[5] *Ibid.*, xi. 23.
[6] *Ibid.*, vs. 38.
[7] *E.g.*, VibhA. 446.
[8] Cv. *Trs.* i. 293, n. 1; see Cv. lxx. 72; lxxii. 136.

Jambukola-lena.—See **Jambukola-vihāra** (2).

1. **Jambukola-vihāra.**—See **Jambukola.**

2. **Jambukola-vihāra.**—Another vihāra, with its celebrated rock-temple called the **Jambukolalena,** in the centre of Ceylon, twenty-six miles north of modern Matale. It was restored by **Vijayabāhu I.**[1] and rebuilt by **Kittinissañka,** who placed in it seventy-three golden statues of the Buddha.[2]

[1] Cv. lx. 60.
[2] *Ibid.*, lxxx. 23; see also Cv. *Trs.* ii. 128, n. 3.

Jambukhādaka.—A **Paribbājaka.** The Saṃyutta Nikāya records visits paid by him to **Sāriputta** at **Nālakagāma** and discussions between them on various topics, such as *nibbāna*, arahantship, the *āsavas*, *sakkāya*, ignorance, the Noble Eightfold Path, etc.[1]

The Commentary[2] says that he was a nephew of Sāriputta and a *channaparibbājaka*.

[1] S. iv. 251-60.
[2] SA. iii. 91.

Jambukhādaka Jātaka (No. 294).—The Bodhisatta was once a tree-sprite in a *jambu*-grove and saw how a crow, flattered by the words of a jackal sitting under the tree, dropped fruits for him to eat, praising his breeding. The sprite drove them both away as being liars.

The story was related in reference to a report that **Devadatta** and **Kokālika** were going about singing each other's praises.[1]

[1] J. ii. 438 f.; *cp.* **Anta Jātaka.**

Jambukhādaka Saṃyutta.—The thirty-eighth division of the Saṃyutta Nikaya. It records discussions between **Jambukhādaka** and **Sāriputta.**[1]

[1] S. iv. 250 ff.

Jambukhādaka Sutta.—See **Nibbāna Sutta.**

Jambugāma.—A village, probably a suburb of **Campā** (see below), which the Buddha visited during his last tour. It lay between **Ambagāma** and **Bhoganagara.**[1]

[1] D. ii. 194.

Jambugāmika (Jambugāmiya) Thera.—He was born at **Campā,** his father bearing the same name as himself.[1] He joined the Order and dwelt in the **Añjanavana** in **Sāketa.** One day, in order to test him, his father sent him a verse, and he, realising his imperfections, became an arahant.[2]

In the time of **Vessabhū** Buddha he threw three *kiṃsuka*-flowers into the air as offering to the Buddha.

He is probably identical with **Kiṃsukapupphiya** of the Apadāna.[3]

[1] He was probably chief of **Jambugāma.**

[2] Thag. 28; ThagA. i. 86 f.

[3] Ap. ii. 435; but see *s.v.* **Somamitta.**

Jambudīpa.—One of the four **Mahādīpas,** or great continents, which are included in the **Cakkavāḷa** and are ruled by a **Cakkavatti** (*q.v.*). They are grouped round Mount **Sineru.** In Jambudīpa is **Himavā** with its eighty-four thousand peaks, its lakes, mountain ranges, etc.[1] This continent derives its name from the *Jambu*-tree (also called Naga) which grows there, its trunk fifteen yojanas in girth, its outspreading branches fifty yojanas in length, its shade one hundred yojanas in extent and its height one hundred yojanas.[2] On account of this tree, Jambudīpa is also known as **Jambusaṇḍa.**[3] The continent is ten thousand yojanas in extent; of these ten thousand, four thousand are covered by the ocean, three thousand by the Himālaya mountains, while three thousand are inhabited by men.[4]

Sometimes in Jambudīpa there are as many as eighty-four thousand cities; this number is sometimes reduced to sixty thousand, forty thousand, or even twenty thousand, but never to less.[5] In the time of **Asoka** there were eighty-four thousand cities, in each of which he built a monastery.[6] In the Aṅguttara Nikāya[7] it is said that, in Jambudīpa, trifling in number are the parks, groves, lakes, etc., more numerous the steep, precipitous places, unfordable rivers, inaccessible mountains, etc.

At the time of **Metteyya** Buddha's appearance on earth Jambudīpa will be pervaded by mankind even as a jungle is by reeds and rushes. There

[1] For details see *s.v.* **Himavā.**

[2] Vin. i. 30; SNA. ii. 443; Vsm. i. 205 f.; Sp. i. 119, etc.

[3] SN. vs. 552; SNA. i. 121.

[4] *Ibid.*, ii. 437; UdA. 300.

[5] SNA. i. 59; J. (iv. 84) says sixty-three thousand; PvA. 111.

[6] Mhv. v. 176; Vsm. 201.

[7] i. 35.

will be eighty-four thousand cities with **Ketumātī** (Benares) at the head.[8]

The Buddha once declared that the people of Jambudīpa excel those of both **Uttarakuru** and **Tāvatiṃsa** in three respects—courage, mindfulness and religious life.[9]

Buddhas (and Cakkavattis) are born only in Jambudīpa.[10]

There were four sounds heard throughout Jambudīpa—the shout uttered by **Puṇṇaka** proclaiming his victory over **Dhanañjaya Koravya** in a game of dice; the bark of **Vissakamma** when taken about in the guise of a dog by **Sakka,** threatening to devour all wicked beings after the decay of **Kassapa's** *sāsana*; the roar of **Kusa,** challenging to battle the seven kings who sought the hand of **Pabhāvatī;** and the yell of **Āḷavaka,** proclaiming his name from the top of **Kelāsa,** on hearing that the Buddha had visited his abode.[11]

When opposed to **Sīhaladīpa** or **Tambapaṇṇidīpa,** Jambudīpa indicates the continent of India.[12]

For the purposes of *cārikā*, the monks divided their tours in Jambudīpa into three circuits or *maṇḍalas*—the Mahāmaṇḍala which extended over nine hundred leagues, the Majjhima which extended over six hundred, and the Antima over three hundred. Those who wish to tour the first, start after the *mahāpavāraṇa* and complete their journey in nine months, for the Majjhimamaṇḍala they start after the *Pavāraṇa*, on the full-moon day of **Kattika,** completing the tour in nine months, while for the Antimamaṇḍala they start on the first day of **Phussa** and return after seven months.[13]

In each Cakkavāla there is a Jambudīpa.[14] Mention is made in the **Kākāti Jātaka**[15] of a **Jambudīpa-samudda,** beyond which was the river **Kebuka.**

[8] D. iii. 75.
[9] A. iv. 396; Kvu. 99.
[10] BuA. 48; MA. ii. 917.
[11] SA. i. 248, etc.
[12] *E.g.*, Mhv. v. 13; xiv. 8; Cv. xxxvii. 216, 246.
[13] Sp. i. 197.
[14] A. i. 227.
[15] J. iii. 91.

Jambuddoṇi.—A mountain in the **Malayaraṭṭha** in Ceylon. **Vijayabahu III.** built on its summit a town which he made his capital. For a time the Tooth Relic and the Alms Bowl were there[1] but were later removed to **Billagiri.**[2] **Parakkamabāhu II.** also used Jambuddoṇi as his capital, but **Vijayabāhu IV.** moved the seat of government to **Pulatthipura.**[3] Later, we find **Bhuvanekabāhu I.** being crowned in Jambuddoṇi, though his capital was in **Subhagiri.**[4] **Vijayabāhu III.** built the **Vijayasundarārāma** (*q.v.*) on Jambuddoṇi.

[1] Cv. lxxxi. 15, 29. [2] *Ibid.*, lxxxii. 7 ff. [3] *Ibid.*, lxxxix. 13. [4] *Ibid.*, xc. 30.

Jambudhaja (*v.l.* **Jambudīpadhaja**).—A thera of Pagan, held in great honour by King **Ukkaṃsika.** He was the author of several works, including the **Rūpabhedapakāsanī.**[1]

[1] Bode: *op. cit.*, 55 f.

Jambuphaliya Thera.—An arahant. He once gave **Padumuttara** Buddha the firstfruits of a *jambu*-tree.[1] He is probably identical with **Nadī-Kassapa.**[2]

[1] Ap. ii. 395. [2] ThagA. i. 415.

Jambusaṇḍa.—See **Jambudīpa.**

Jambusamudda.—See **Jambudīpa.**

Jambelambiya.—A weavers' village in Ceylon, given by **Mahānāga** to the **Uttaravihāra.**[1]

[1] Cv. xli. 96.

Jayagaṅgā.—A canal flowing from the **Kalāvāpi** to **Anurādhapura.** It was restored by **Parakkamabāhu I.**[1]

[1] Cv. lxxix. 58.

Jayaṅkoṇḍāna.—A locality in South India.[1]

[1] Cv. lxxvi. 274.

Jayaddisa.—King of **Kampilla** and father of **Alīnasattu.** See **Jayaddisa Jātaka.**

Jayaddisa Jātaka (No. 513).—Twice the sons of **Pañcāla,** king of **Kampilla,** were devoured by an ogress who had conceived a hatred for his queen. On the third occasion the ogress was chased by the palace guard before she could eat the child, but she succeeded in snatching him away and brought him up as her own. He grew up to be a man-eating ogre and dwelt in a tree. The fourth son of Pañcāla was **Jayaddisa,** who succeeded his father. The ogress had died before his birth. He had a son **Alīnasattu.**

One day Jayaddisa ordered a hunt, but just as he was about to start out, **Nanda,** a brahmin from **Takkasilā,** brought him four verses worth one hundred each. Jayaddisa ordered a dwelling to be made for him and declared that he on whose side the deer escaped should pay for the verses. An antelope made straight for the king and escaped. The king pursued and killed it, but while on his way back with the carcase he came to the ogre's dwelling place and was promptly claimed as his prey. Remembering his promise to pay Nanda, Jayaddisa persuaded the ogre to let him go on condition that he would return when he had paid for the verses. Alīnasattu, hearing of this, offered to go in his father's place and this was allowed. He won over the ogre by his fearlessness, taught him the moral law and, suspecting that the ogre was his father's elder brother, proved the relationship with the help of an ascetic gifted with supernatural vision. Jayaddisa, informed of this, made a settlement for the ogre which came to be called **Cullakammāsadamma.**

The ogre was **Aṅgulimāla** and Alīnasattu the Bodhisatta.[1]

The story was related in reference to a monk who supported his mother; for details see the **Sāma Jātaka.** The story of Jayaddisa is included in the **Cariyāpiṭaka.**[2]

[1] J. v. 21-30. [2] ii. 9.

1. **Jayanta.**—King of Ceylon (then known as **Maṇḍadīpa**) at the time of **Kassapa** Buddha. His capital was **Visāla.** It was a devastating war between Jayanta and his younger brother which brought Kassapa to Ceylon.[1]

[1] Mhv. xv. 127 ff.; Dpv. xv. 60; xvii. 7; Sp. i. 87, etc.

2. **Jayanta.**—A Pacceka Buddha.[1]

[1] M. iii. 70.

1. **Jayabāhu.**—King of Ceylon (1114–1116 A.C.). He was a brother of **Vijayabāhu I.,** who made him *ādipāda* and gave him **Rohaṇa.**[1] He married his step-sister **Sumittā**[2] and was later made *uparāja.*[3] On the death of Vijayabāhu, Jayabāhu became king with the help of the Pāndyan faction of the royal family and appointed, " contrary to former custom," **Mānābharaṇa** as his *uparāja.* The latter, however, seems to have been the virtual king; his attempts to attack **Vikkamabāhu,** the lawful *uparāja,* ended in disaster, and Vikkamabāhu captured the capital, **Pulatthipura,** whereupon Jayabāhu retired to Rohaṇa. He lived there as nominal sovereign and died in obscurity.[4]

[1] Cv. lix. 12. [2] *Ibid.*, 43. [3] *Ibid.*, lx. 87. [4] *Ibid.*, lxi.

2. **Jayabāhu.**—A Tamil usurper who, with **Māgha,** seems to have been in possession of the north of Ceylon and the capital at **Pulatthipura** for many years, both before and during the reign of **Parakkamabāhu II.**[1]

[1] Cv. lxxxii. 87; lxxxiii. 15 ff.

3. **Jayabāhu.**—Youngest of the five sons of **Parakkamabāhu II.** He lived with his father and helped in the administration.[1]

[1] Cv. lxxxvii. 17; lxxxviii. 19.

4. **Jayabāhu.**—Grandson of **Parakkamabāhu VI.**, whom he is said to have succeeded, but nothing further is known of him except that he was murdered by **Bhuvanekabāhu** (vi.).[1]

[1] Cv. xcii. 1.

5. **Jayabāhu.**—A thera of Ceylon, better known as **Devarakkhita** or **Dhammakitti.** He was Saṅgharāja and composed the Nikāyasaṅgraha.[1]

[1] P.L.C. 242 f.

Jayamahālekhaka.—A rank conferred by **Devānampiyatissa** on **Sumitta**, who accompanied the Sacred Bodhi-tree to **Anurādhapura.**[1] The rank was evidently held by his descendants in perpetuity.[2]

[1] Mbv. 165. [2] *E.g.*, Cv. lxix. 12.

Jayampati.—Son of **Okkāka,** king of **Kusāvatī,** and of his wife **Sīlavatī.** He was the younger brother of **Kusa.** Whenever Kusa wished to see **Pabhāvatī** Jayampati would represent him.[1] He is identified with **Ānanda.** For details see **Kusa Jātaka.**

[1] J. v. 282, 286, 287. [2] J. v. 312.

Jayavaḍḍhanapura.—The Pāli name of the town usually known as Koṭṭe (the fort), built by **Bhuvanekabāhu V.**[1]

[1] Cv. xci. 7, 16; xciii. 1.

Jayavāpi.—See **Abhayavāpi.**

1. **Jayasena.**—Father of **Siddhattha** Buddha.[1] The Buddhavaṃsa[2] calls him **Udena.**

[1] J. i. 40; BuA. 187. [2] xvii. 13.

2. **Jayasena.**—Father of **Phussa** Buddha.[1] The Buddha preached to him and he became an arahant.[2] He was king of **Kāsī** and his wife was **Sirimā.**[3] See also **Tirokuḍḍapetavatthu.**

[1] Bu. xix. 14; J. i. 41. [2] BuA. 193. [3] PvA. 19.

3. **Jayasena.**—King of **Kapilavatthu.** His son was **Sīhahanu** and his daughter **Yasodharā.** His grandson was **Suddhodana.**[1]

[1] Mhv. ii. 15 ff.; Dpv. iii. 44; MṬ. 134; but see Mtu. i. 352, where he is called Hastikaśīrṣa. The Tibetan sources call him Dhanvadurga. (Rockhill, p. 13.)

4. **Jayasena.**—A prince who once visited the novice **Aciravata** at **Veḷuvana** in **Rājagaha** and asked him to teach the Doctrine. Reluctantly the novice did so, but at the end of the exposition Jayasena declared that he was unable to agree with it. When this was reported to the Buddha he said that Jayasena, being given up to luxury, could not be expected to appreciate renunciation.[1] A discussion which Jayasena had with his uncle **Bhūmiya Thera** is recorded in the **Bhūmiya Sutta.** In this case we are told that Jayasena was pleased with the discourse and entertained **Bhūmiya** to his own dish of rice.[2]

Buddhaghosa[3] says that Jayasena was **Bimbisāra's** own son (*Bimbisārassa putto orasako*).

[1] M. iii. 128. [2] M. iii. 138. [3] MA. ii. 932.

5. **Jayasena.**—A king who built for **Sobhita** Buddha at **Sudassana** a vihāra one league in extent.[1] Jayasena was one of the chief lay supporters of Sobhita.[2]

[1] Bu. vii. 6; BuA. 138. [2] *Ibid.*, 140; but see Bu. vii. 23.

6. **Jayasena.**—One of the theras present at the foundation of the **Mahā Thūpa.**[1]

[1] Dpv. xix. 8; MṬ. 527.

Jayasenapabbata.—A monastery built by the queen of **Udaya I.** It was probably given by her to the **Damiḷa** bhikkhu community in Ceylon.[1]

[1] Cv. xlix. 24; but see Cv. *Trs.* i. 129, n. 4.

Jarasāna.—See **Janasāna.**

Jarā.—A hunter who killed **Vāsudeva.**[1]

[1] J. iv. 88 f.

1. **Jarā Vagga.**—The sixth chapter of the *Devatā Saṃyutta.*[1]

[1] S. i. 36-9.

2. **Jarā Vagga.**—The fifth chapter of the *Indriya Saṃyutta.*[1]

[1] S. v. 216-27.

3. **Jarā Vagga.**—The eleventh section of the *Dhammapada.*

1. **Jarā Sutta.**—Once, when the Buddha was on a visit to **Sāketa,** a rich brahmin and his wife, seeing him, called him their son and ministered to him with great affection. It is said that for five hundred births they had been the parents of the Bodhisatta. At the conclusion of a meal the Buddha preached to them and they became Sotāpannas. After the Buddha left Sāketa they continued to lead pious lives and became arahants before death. At their funeral they were accorded all the honours due to arahants, and at the conclusion of the ceremonies the Buddha, who was present, preached this sutta to those assembled there.[1]

From selfishness come grief and avarice. The monk who lives away from the world, unsmeared by it, is independent and becomes purified.[2]

[1] SNA. ii. 531 ff.; DhA. iii. 317 ff.; *cp.* **Sāketa Jātaka.**
[2] SN. 804-813 explained at MNid. i. 117 ff.

2. **Jarā Sutta.**—Righteousness remains good even in old age; faith is a lucky stance, wisdom the jewel among men and merit the wealth none can steal.[1]

[1] S. i. 36.

3. **Jarā Sutta.**—Everything is subject to decay—the eye, objects, etc.[1]

[1] S. iv. 27.

4. **Jarā Sutta.**—The Buddha sits, one afternoon, outside the **Migāramātupāsāda,** warming his limbs in the sun, and **Ānanda,** while chafing the Buddha's limbs with his hands, tells him that his skin is no longer clear, his limbs are slack and his body bent. The Buddha explains that this is but natural, old age being inherent in youth and decay and death being inevitable.[1]

[1] S. v. 216.

Jarudapāna Jātaka (No. 256).—The Bodhisatta was once travelling with a large caravan. In a wood they came across a disused well and, needing water, dug it deeper. There they came across buried treasure, but the men, not being satisfied, dug deeper, in spite of the Bodhisatta's warning.

A Nāga-king who lived there was disturbed and slew all except the Bodhisatta.

The story was related in reference to some arahants of **Sāvatthi,** who, on their way back from there, after having entertained the Buddha, saw the same well and found treasure there. They, however, were satisfied with their find and reported it to the Buddha.[1]

[1] J. ii. 294 f.

Jalandhara.—See **Jutindhara** (3).

Jalasikha.—Seventy-four kappas ago there were eight kings of this name, all previous births of **Pupphacchattiya Thera.**[1]

[1] Ap. i. 265.

Jaluttama.—See **Januttama.**

Jallibāva.—A tank in Ceylon.[1]

[1] Cv. lxviii. 47.

Java, Javana.—A devaputta. **Rujā** said she could see Java making a garland ready for her birth in **Tāvatiṃsa.**[1]

[1] J. vi. 239 f.

Java Sutta.—The four qualities which make a king's thoroughbred worthy —straightness, speed, patience and docility—and the similar four qualities of a worthy monk.[1]

[1] A. ii. 113.

Javakaṇṇaka.—A family name, not considered of high social standing.[1]

[1] Vin. iv. 8, 13.

Javanahaṃsa Jātaka (No. 476).—The Bodhisatta was once king of ninety thousand geese in **Cittakūṭa.** The king of Benares, seeing him, took a great fancy to him and did him honour, desiring his friendship. When the king went to **Anotatta,** the Bodhisatta did him similar honour and friendship was established between them. One day, two of the young geese, in spite of the advice of the Bodhisatta, wished to try their speed against the sun. Their king, wishing to save them from death, went with them, rescuing them when tired. Then he himself raced the sun and was victorious, arriving at the king's palace. The king, hearing of this, wished to see an exhibition of the Bodhisatta's powers of speed, and his desire was granted. When asked whether anything was fleeter than himself, the king of the geese replied that the decay of the elements of life was a thousandfold speedier. He thereupon preached the moral law to the king. **Ānanda** is identified with the king and **Sāriputta** and **Moggallāna** with the two geese.[1]

[1] J. iv. 211-8.

Javamāla(ka)-tittha.—A ford in the **Kappakandara** river. Here **Duṭṭhagāmaṇi** gave his only food to the thera **Gotama.**[1]

[1] Mhv. xxiv. 22; MṬ. 465.

Javasakuṇa Jātaka (No. 308).—The Bodhisatta was once a woodpecker, and coming across a lion with a bone stuck in his throat he removed the bone, after having fixed a stick in the lion's mouth to prevent him from biting off the head of his rescuer. Later, he saw the lion eating the carcase of a buffalo and asked for a boon. The lion refused, saying it was enough for him to have escaped death after putting his head into a lion's jaws.

The lion is identified with **Devadatta,** and the story was related in reference to his ingratitude.[1]

[1] J. iii. 25-7; *cp.* Jātakamālā No. xxxiv.

Javahaṃsaka Thera.—An arahant. He was once a forester, and having seen **Siddhattha** Buddha he was so pleased that he paid homage to him.[1]

[1] Ap. i. 232 f.

Jahī.—A Pacceka Buddha, given in a nominal list.[1]

[1] ApA. i. 107.

Jāgara Jātaka (No. 414).—Once, the Bodhisatta was a brahmin who, having studied at **Takkasilā,** became an ascetic in the Himālaya region, living only in standing and walking attitudes. One day a tree-sprite appeared before him and asked him a riddle about waking and sleeping, which he solved to her satisfaction.

The story was related in reference to a certain layman who was a Sotāpanna. He was once travelling with a caravan along a forest road. When the caravan halted for the night it was attacked by robbers. But seeing the layman walking to and fro all night they stopped their attack and reported the matter to their leader. The layman was greatly honoured and, on arriving at **Sāvatthi,** told the Buddha of it.

The tree-sprite is identified with **Uppalavaṇṇā.**[1]

[1] J. iii. 403 f.

Jāgara Sutta.—A riddle set by a deva and answered by the Buddha, regarding the Five Spiritual Powers (*bala*) which respectively soil or cleanse, according to the spiritual health of the individual.[1]

[1] S. i. 3.

Jāṇussoṇi.—A mahāsāla brahmin, ranking with eminent brahmins such as **Caṅkī, Tārukkha, Pokkharasāti** and **Todeyya.**[1] He is mentioned as staying in **Icchānaṅgala,**[2] where he evidently took part in the periodical gatherings of brahmin leaders—and also at **Manasākaṭa.**[3] He was a follower of the Buddha, of whom he was a great admirer. He appears to have been in the habit of talking to well known teachers of other schools and hearing their opinion of the Buddha, either for the purpose of comparing his own faith in him or of discovering their views. Two such conversations are recorded —one with **Subha Todeyyaputta,**[4] the other with **Pilotika.**[5] His discussion with Pilotika he reported to the Buddha, who expanded it to form the **Culahatthipadopama Sutta.** The Buddha also preached to Jāṇussoṇi the **Bhayabherava Sutta.**[6] Jāṇussoṇi's permanent residence was **Sāvatthi,**[7] and he often visited the Buddha at **Jetavana,** consulting him on many topics, such as: results of actions (A. i. 56), *sandiṭṭhaka-nibbāna* (A. i. 157), *tevijja*-brahmins (A. i. 166), fearlessness of death (A. ii. 173), the ideals of various classes of persons (A. iii. 362), true celibacy (A. iv. 54), the **Paccārohaṇī** ceremony (A. v. 233 ff., 249 ff.), the efficacy of gifts (A. v. 269 ff.), and eternalism and annihilation (S. ii. 76). He had a white chariot with silver fittings and white trappings drawn by four pure white mares. He would drive about in this, wearing white garments, turban-cloths and sandals and fanned by a white fan. The reins, the goads and the canopy were also of white. His chariot was considered the finest in all Sāvatthi.[8] Buddhaghosa[9] says that Jāṇussoṇī was not his personal name but the name of the rank he held as chaplain to the **Kosala** king.

[1] SN. p. 115.
[2] M. ii. 196.
[3] D. i. 235.
[4] M. ii. 209.
[5] M. i. 175 ff.
[6] *Ibid.*, 16 ff.
[7] DA. ii. 399.
[8] S. v. 4 f.; *cp.* M. i. 175 and ii. 208.
[9] MA. i. 90; according to AA. (i. 308) it was the name of any noble family, members of which held this rank. *Cp. Govindiye abhisiñci* (at D. ii. 231).

Jāṇussoṇī Vagga.—The seventeenth chapter of the Dasaka Nipāta of the Aṅguttara Nikāya.[1]

[1] A. v. 249-73.

1. **Jāṇussoṇī Sutta.**—**Jāṇussoṇī** visits the Buddha and tells him that if anyone has gifts to distribute he should give them to the *tevijja* brahmins. At the Buddha's request, he describes these brahmins, and the Buddha, in his turn, tells him what is considered the threefold-lore (*tevijjā*) by the Ariyans.[1]

[1] A. i. 166.

2. **Jāṇussoṇī Sutta.**—**Jāṇussoṇī** visits the Buddha, who tells him that it is one extreme to say that everything exists, another to say nothing exists—and teaches him the Doctrine of the Middle Way, the *paṭiccasamuppāda.*[1]

[1] S. ii. 76.

Jātaka.—The tenth book of Khuddaka Nikāya of the Sutta Piṭaka containing tales of the former births of the Buddha. The Jātaka also forms one of the nine *aṅgas* or divisions of the Buddha's teachings, grouped according to the subject matter.[1] The canonical book of the Jātakas (so far unpublished) contains only the verses, but it is almost certain that from the first there must have been handed down an oral commentary giving the stories in prose. This commentary later developed into the **Jātakaṭṭhakathā** (*q.v.*). Some of the Jātakas have been included in a separate compilation, called the **Cariyā Piṭaka** (*q.v.*). It is not possible to say when the Jātakas in their present form came into existence nor how many of these were among the original number. In the time of the **Culla Niddesa,** there seem to have been five hundred Jātakas, because reference is made[2] to *pañcajātakasatāni.* Bas-reliefs of the third century have been found illustrating a number of Jātaka stories, and they presuppose the existence of a prose collection. Several Jātakas exist in the canonical books which are not included in the Jātaka collection.[3] The **Dīghabhāṇakas** included the Jātaka in the Abhidhamma Piṭaka.[4] The Jātaka consists of twenty-two sections or *nipātas.*

[1] DA. i. 15, 24.

[2] p. 80; five hundred was the number seen by Fa Hsien in Ceylon (p. 71).

[3] For a discussion on the Jātakas in all their aspects, see Rhys Davids *Buddhist India*, pp. 189 ff.

[4] DA. i. 15; the Samantapāsādikā (i. 251) contains a reference to a *Jātakanikāya.*

Jātakaṭṭhakathā.—A Commentary on the Jātaka. It comprises all the verses of the Jātaka and gives also, in prose, the stories connected with the verses. Each such story is given a framework of introductory episode, stating the circumstances in which the story was related, and each story has at the end an identification of the chief characters mentioned with the Buddha and his contemporaries in some previous birth. The whole collection is prefaced by a long introductory essay, the **Nidānakathā,** giving the Buddha's history before his birth as **Siddhattha,** and also during his last birth, up to the time of the Enlightenment.

The work is a translation into Pāli of the commentary in Sinhalese as handed down in Ceylon, but the verses of this commentary were already in Pāli. The authorship of the translation is traditionally attributed to **Buddhaghosa,** but there exists much difference of opinion on this point.[1]

[1] For a discussion see P.L.C. 123 ff.

Jātakabhāṇakavatthu.—The Commentaries[1] mention the story of a certain reciter of the Jātakas who once went begging to a house. The mistress of the house, not wishing to give, went in and returned saying she could not find any rice. The monk observed that there were other eatables in the house, and indicated to the woman, by means of a riddle, what he had seen.

[1] *E.g.*, VibhA. 484.

Jātakavisodhana.—A study of the **Jātaka,** written by **Ariyavaṃsa** of Ava.[1]

[1] Bode: *op. cit.*, 43; Gv. 65, 75.

Jātattaginidāna.—A work ascribed to **Culla-Buddhaghosa.**[1]

[1] Gv. 63.

Jātaveda.—The god of fire. The Jātakas[1] contain references to his worship. See **Aggi.** He is also called **Aggideva.**

[1] *E.g.*, J. i. 214, 494; iii. 17; v. 452; vi. 201, etc.

Jāti Sutta.—Everything is subject to rebirth—eye, objects, etc.[1]

[1] S. iv. 26.

Jātidhamma Vagga.—The fourth chapter of the *Saḷāyatana Saṃyutta.*[1]

[1] S. iv. 26 ff.

Jātipupphiya Thera.—An arahant. In a previous birth he placed a bouquet of flowers on the dead body of **Padumuttara** Buddha. As a result he was born among the **Nimmānaratī** gods.[1]

[1] Ap. i. 405 f.

Jātipūjaka Thera.—An arahant. On the day of **Vipassī** Buddha's birth many miracles occurred, and soothsayers predicted that he would be a Buddha. Jātipūjaka, hearing this, offered him jasmine flowers. Three kappas ago he became king thirty-four times under the name of **Supāricariya.**[1]

He is probably identical with **Samitigutta.**[2]

[1] Ap. i. 154.

[2] ThagA. i. 176.

Jātibhūmi occurs in the phrase *Jātabhūmakā bhikkhū.*[1]

[1] M. i. 145; but see MA. i. 346, where it is explained by *jātaṭṭhāna*.

Jātimanta.—A brahmin of **Vettavatī. Mātaṅga** incurred his wrath by throwing his toothpick so that it fell into the river and stuck in Jātimanta's hair. The latter therefore cursed Mātaṅga that his head should split in seven. Mātaṅga stopped the sun from rising till Jātimanta was forced to ask his pardon.[1]

[1] J. iv. 388 f.; in SA. (ii. 176 f.) the reason given for the curse was that Mātaṅga happened to tread on Jātimanta's head.

Jātimitta.—One of the chief disciples of **Metteyya** Buddha.[1]

[1] Anāgatavaṃsa, vs. 59.

Jātiyāvana.—A grove near **Bhaddiya.** The Buddha, when once staying there, laid down a rule about the use of slippers by monks.[1] There the banker **Meṇḍaka** visited him and provided meals for him and the monks.[2] Meṇḍaka's grandson, **Uggaha,** did likewise.[3]

The Buddha once stayed in Jātiyāvana for three months, waiting for the ripening of **Bhaddaji's** wisdom, ready for his conversion.[4] The Suttavibhaṅga[5] contains the story of an arahant on whom a woman committed a misdemeanour while he was sleeping in Jātiyāvana.

Buddhaghosa[6] says that the grove formed part of a forest track extending up to the Himālaya.

[1] Vin. i. 189 f.; DhA. iii. 451.

[2] *Ibid.*, 363; Vin. i. 242 f.

[3] A. iii. 36 f.

[4] J. ii. 331; ThagA. i. 286.

[5] Vin. iii. 37 f.

[6] AA. ii. 597.

Jālagāma.—See **Vālagāma.**

Jālaroruva.—A Niraya, one of the divisions of the **Roruva,** the other being **Dhūmaroruva.** It is filled with blood-red flowers, which enter the body of its inhabitants through the nine openings.[1]

[1] J. v. 271.

1. **Jāli.**—Son of **Vessantara** and **Maddī,** and brother of **Kaṇhajinā.** He and his sister were given to **Jūjaka** as slaves, but were later rescued by the intervention of **Sakka.** Jāli led the army which brought Vessantara back from his hermitage. He is identified with **Rāhula.**[1] See the **Vessantara Jātaka.**

Jāli is probably also the king of the same name given in a list of **Okkāka's** descendants, and stated to have succeeded Vessantara.[2]

The gift of **Jāli** as a slave is considered one of the greatest sacrifices made by the Bodhisatta.[3]

[1] J. vi. 487 ff.; *cp.* i. 9.
[2] *E.g.,* Mhv. ii. 13; Dpv. iii. 42.
[3] J. i. 77; AA. i. 64; DhA. i. 406; Mil. 275, 282, etc.

2. **Jāli.**—The name of two Pacceka Buddhas, occurring in a nominal list.[1]

[1] M. iii. 70; ApA. i. 107.

Jālikā.—See **Calikā.**

Jālina.—A Pacceka Buddha.[1]

[1] M. iii. 70; ApA. i. 107.

Jālinavana.—A forest in the dominion of the king of **Kosala.** It was the hiding-place of **Agulimāla.**[1]

[1] ThagA. ii. 58.

1. **Jālinī.**—One of the five queens of the third **Okkāka** king.[1]

[1] DA. i. 258; MṬ. 131; SNA. i. 352.

2. **Jālinī.**—A goddess of **Tāvatiṃsa,** a former wife of **Anuruddha.** Once seeing him old and feeble, she appeared before him in **Kosala** and bade him aspire to rebirth among the gods. Anuruddha told her there would be no rebirth for him.[1]

[1] S. i. 200; Thag. vs. 908; ThagA. ii. 73; SA. i. 226.

3. **Jālinī.**—See **Saddasāratthajālinī.**

Jāliya.—A paribbājaka who, with his friend **Maṇḍissa,** visited the Buddha at the **Ghositārāma.**[1] The Buddha preached to them the **Jāliya Sutta** (*q.v.*).

According to the **Pāṭika Sutta,** when **Jāliya** heard that **Pāṭika** could not come to hold a discussion with the Buddha at **Vesāli,** he went to the **Tindukkhāna-paribbājakārāma** and tried to get **Pāṭikaputta** to come. But the latter was unable to come, being fixed in his seat. Jāliya thereupon spoke insultingly to him, calling him boaster, etc.[2]

Jāliya is described as *dārupattakantevāsī*, because, says the Commentary,[3] his teacher used to beg for alms with a wooden bowl.

[1] D. i. 159. [2] *Ibid.*, iii. 22 ff. [3] DA. i. 319.

Jāliya Sutta.—Preached to **Jāliya** and **Maṇḍissa** at the **Ghositārāma** on the question as to whether body and soul are one and the same.[1] The Sutta is identical with the second part of the **Mahāli Sutta** and was once probably included in it.

[1] D. i. 159 f.

1. **Jiṇṇa Sutta.**—Two very old brahmins visit the Buddha and ask him for a teaching to cheer and comfort them. He tells them to practise self-restraint in all things.[1]

[1] A. i. 155.

2. **Jiṇṇa Sutta.**—Similar to the above. The Buddha tells them that the whole world is being burned by old age and death and that only what is saved will be useful. Meritorious deeds brings happiness after death.[1]

[1] A. i. 156.

3. **Jiṇṇa Sutta.**—**Mahā Kassapa** visits the Buddha at **Rājagaha.** The Buddha suggests that now that he is very old he should give up wearing cast-off rag robes and dwelling in the forest, and should enjoy the gifts given to him by householders. Kassapa refuses to give up his long-established austere habits of life. Being asked the reason for this method of life, Kassapa answers that it is for his own happiness and out of compassion for those that come after.[1] The Commentary[2] adds that the Buddha asked the question in order to give Kassapa an opportunity for his "lion's roar" (*kassapa-sīhanāda*).

[1] S. ii. 202. [2] SA. ii. 128.

Jita.—A Pacceka Buddha.[1]

[1] M. iii. 70; ApA. i. 107.

Jitañjaya.—See **Ajitañjaya.**

Jitamitta.—The chief disciple of **Nārada** Buddha.[1] See also **Vijitamitta.**

[1] J. i. 37.

Jitasena.—Seventy-seven kappas ago there were sixteen kings of this name, all previous births of **Khaṇḍaphulliya.**[1]

[1] Ap. i. 198.

Jitasenā.—Wife of **Nārada** Buddha in his last lay-life.[1]

[1] Bu. x. 20; BuA (151) calls her **Vijitasenā.**

Jitā.—One of the palaces occupied by **Nārada** Buddha before his Renunciation.[1]

[1] Bu x. 19.

Jitābhirāma.—A palace occupied by **Nārada** Buddha in his last lay-life.[1]

[1] BuA. 151; Bu. x. 19.

Jinacarita.—A Pāli poem of four hundred and seventy-two stanzas dealing with the life of the Buddha, written by **Vanaratana Medhaṅkara** of the **Vijayabāhu-pariveṇa.**[1]

[1] Gv. 72; P.L.C. 230 f.

Jinadattā.—A Therī. **Isidāsī** was ordained under her.[1] She is described as expert in the Vinaya.[2]

[1] ThigA. 261. [2] Thig. vs. 427.

Jinadattiya.—A fellow celibate of **Sudinna Kalandaputta.**[1]

[1] Sp. i. 206.

Jinabodhāvali.—A Pāli work composed by **Dhammakitti,** author of the **Bālāvatāra.**[1]

[1] P.L.C. 243.

Jinālaṅkāra.—A Pāli poem of two hundred and fifty verses, containing a history of the Buddha's life. Its authorship is uncertain; some attribute it to **Buddhadatta**, author of the **Mahuratthavilāsinī**, others to **Buddharakkhita**. There exists a *ṭīkā* on it.[1]

[1] Gv. 69, 72; see P.L.C. 110 f.

1. **Jīvaka-Komārabhacca.**—A celebrated physician. He was the son of **Sālavatī**, a courtesan of **Rājagaha**.[1] Directly after birth the child was placed in a basket and thrown on a dust-heap, from where he was rescued by **Abhayarājakumāra**. When questioned by Abhaya, people said "he was alive" (*jīvati*), and therefore the child was called **Jīvaka**; because he was brought up by the prince (*kumārena posāpito*), he was called **Komārabhacca**.[2] When grown up, he learnt of his antecedents, and going to **Takkasilā** without Abhaya's knowledge, studied medicine for seven years. His teacher then gave him a little money and sent him away as being fit to practise medicine. His first patient was the seṭṭhi's wife at **Sāketa**, and for curing her he received sixteen thousand kahāpaṇas, a man-servant, a maid-servant and a coach with horses. When he returned to Rājagaha, Abhaya established him in his own residence. There he cured **Bimbisāra** of a troublesome fistula and received as reward all the ornaments of Bimbisāra's five hundred wives. He was appointed physician to the king and the king's women and also to the fraternity of monks with the Buddha at its head. Other cures of Jīvaka's included that of the seṭṭhi of Rājagaha on whom he performed the operation of trepanning, and of the son of the seṭṭhi of Benares who had suffered from chronic intestinal trouble due to misplacement, and for this case Jīvaka received sixteen thousand kahāpaṇas.

When **Candappajjota**, king of **Ujjenī**, was ill, Bimbisāra lent Jīvaka to him. Candappajjota hated ghee, which was, however, the only remedy. Jīvaka prepared the medicine, prescribed it for the king, then rode away on the king's elephant **Bhaddavatikā** before the king discovered the nature of the medicine. Pajjota, in a rage, ordered his capture and sent his slave **Kāka** after him. Kāka discovered Jīvaka breakfasting at **Kosambī** and allowed himself to be persuaded to eat half a myrobalan, which purged him violently. Jīvaka explained to Kāka that he wished to delay his return; he told him why he had fled from the court and, having returned the elephant, proceeded to Rājagaha. Pajjota was cured and, as a token of his favour, sent Jīvaka a suit of **Sīveyyaka** cloth, which Jīvaka presented to the Buddha.[3] Jīvaka was greatly attracted by the Buddha. Once when the Buddha was ill, Jīvaka found it necessary to administer a purge, and he

[1] AA. (i. 216) says that Abhayarājakumāra was his father.

[2] It has been suggested, however, that Komārabhacca meant master of the Kaumārabhṛtya science (the treatment of infants); VT. ii. 184; in Dvy. (506-18) he is called Kumārabhūta.

[3] Vin. i. 268-81; AA. i. 216.

had fat rubbed into the Buddha's body and gave him a handful of lotuses to smell. Jīvaka was away when the purgative acted, and suddenly remembered that he had omitted to ask the Buddha to bathe in warm water to complete the cure. The Buddha read his thoughts and bathed as required.[4]

After Jīvaka became a Sotāpanna, he was anxious to visit the Buddha twice a day, and finding **Veḷuvana** too far away, he built a monastery with all its adjuncts in his own **Ambavana** in Rājagaha, which he gave to the Buddha and his monks.[5] When Bimbisāra died, Jīvaka continued to serve **Ajātasattu,** and was responsible for bringing him to the Buddha after his crime of parricide.[6]

Jīvaka's fame as a physician brought him more work than he could cope with. but he never neglected his duties to the Saṅgha. Many people, afflicted with disease and unable to pay for treatment by him, joined the Order in order that they might receive that treatment. On discovering that the Order was thus being made a convenience of, he asked the Buddha to lay down a rule that men afflicted with certain diseases should be refused entry into the Order.[7] Jīvaka was declared by the Buddha chief among his lay followers loved by the people (*aggaṃ puggalappasannānaṃ*).[8] He is included in a list of good men who have been assured of the realisation of deathlessness.[9]

At a meal once given by Jīvaka, the Buddha refused to be served until **Cūlapanthaka,** who had been left out of the invitation, had been sent for.[10]

It may have been the preaching of the **Jīvaka Sutta** (*q.v.*) which effected Jīvaka's conversion. One discussion he had with the Buddha regarding the qualities of a pious lay disciple is recorded in the Aṅguttara Nikāya.[11]

Sirimā was Jīvaka's youngest sister.[12]

At Jīvaka's request, the Buddha enjoined upon monks to take exercise; Jīvaka had gone to **Vesālī** on business and had noticed their pale, unhealthy look.[13]

[4] Vin. i. 279 f.; DhA. (ii. 164 f.), relates a like occurrence in another connection. When the Buddha's foot was injured by the splinter from the rock hurled by **Devadatta,** he had to be carried from **Maddakucchi** to Jīvaka's Ambavana. There Jīvaka applied an astringent, and having bandaged the wound, left the city expecting to return in time to remove it. But by the time he did return, the city gates were closed and he could not enter. He was greatly worried because he knew that if the bandage remained on all night the Buddha would suffer intense pain. But the Buddha read his thoughts and removed the bandage. See also J. v. 333.

[5] DA. i. 133; MA. ii. 590.

[6] For details see the **Sāmaññaphala Sutta;** also J. i. 508 f.; v. 262, etc.

[7] Vin. i. 71 ff.

[8] A. i. 26.

[9] *Ibid.*, iii. 451; DhA. i. 244, 247; J. i. 116 f.

[10] For details see *s.v.* **Cūlapanthaka.**

[11] A. iv. 222 f.

[12] SNA. i. 244; DhA. iii. 106.

[13] Vin. ii. 119.

2. **Jīvaka.**—Given as an example of a name.[1]

[1] J. i. 402.

3. **Jīvaka.**—A monk of the **Mahāvihāra,** at whose request **Buddhaghosa** wrote the **Manorathapūraṇī.**[1]

[1] AA. i. 874.

1. **Jīvaka Sutta.**—**Jīvaka** visits the Buddha who is staying in his Mango-grove, and asks if it is true that animals are slain expressly for the Buddha's use. The Buddha replies that he forbids the eating of meat only when there is evidence of one's eyes or ears as grounds for suspicion that the animal has been slain for one's express use. Anyone who slays an animal for the use of a monk and gives it to him commits a great evil. Jīvaka is pleased with the reply and declares himself a follower of the Buddha.[1]

[1] M. i. 368 f.

2. **Jīvaka Sutta.**—Questioned by **Jīvaka,** the Buddha explains that an *upāsaka* is one who has taken the Three Refuges and the Five Precepts, and that such a man, by reason of his qualities, works the welfare both of himself and others.[1]

[1] A. iv. 222 f.

3. **Jīvaka Sutta.**—To those who practise concentration and give themselves up to solitude things appear as they really are.[1]

[1] S. iv. 143 f.

Jīvakapañhavatthu.—The story of the bandage which **Jīvaka** applied to the Buddha's foot after his injury, and of the reading by the Buddha of Jīvaka's thoughts.[1] See **Jīvaka.**

[1] DhA. ii. 164 f.

Jīvakambavana.—A mango-grove in **Rājagaha,** belonging to **Jīvaka,** which he made over to the Buddha and his monks. He built a monastery in the grove, and there the Buddha stayed several times. On one such occasion **Ajātasattu** visited the Buddha and the **Sāmaññaphala Sutta** was preached.[1] The **Jīvaka Suttas,** mentioned above, were also preached there.

The mango-grove was near **Maddakucchi,** so thither they carried the Buddha when his foot was injured by a splinter from the rock hurled by

[1] D. i. 47 ff.

Devadatta.[2] It was in this grove that **Cūlapanthaka** attained arahantship, and, at that time, there were five hundred monks there.[3] Nuns, too, appear to have gone there for their siesta.[4]

[2] DhA. ii. 164, etc. [3] J. i. 114 f., etc. [4] ThigA. 245 f.

Jīvakambavanikā.—See **Subhā Jīvakambavanikā.**

Jīvahattha.—Son of **Vijaya,** king of Ceylon, and of the yakkhiṇī **Kuveṇī.**[1]

[1] MṬ. 264.

Jīvā.—Daughter of **Ubbirī** and the king of **Kosala.** When she died, it was her death which made Ubbirī attain to arahantship.[1] *v.l.* **Jīvanti.**

[1] Thig. vs. 51; ThigA. 53 f.

1. **Jīvita Sutta.**—One should train oneself not to lie, even at the cost of one's life.[1]

[1] S. ii. 234.

2. **Jīvita Sutta.**—There are three faculties—femininity, masculinity and vitality.[1]

[1] S. v. 204.

1. **Juṇha.**—An Elder of **Kosala.** For his story see the **Māluta Jātaka.**[1]

[1] J. i. 165 f.

2. **Juṇha.**—Son of **Brahmadatta,** king of Benares. He was the Bodhisatta. See the **Juṇha Jātaka.**[1]

[1] J. iv. 95 ff.

3. **Juṇha.**—A minister of **Pasenadi.** When Pasenadi held his **Asadisadāna,** Juṇha rejoiced in the king's generosity, but his friend **Kāḷa** was displeased at what he considered as waste. The king, hearing of this from the Buddha, asked Juṇha to use the royal revenue to give alms on his own account during seven days. This Juṇha did. He became a Sotāpanna after hearing the Buddha preach.[1]

[1] DhA. iii. 186 ff.

Juṇha Jātaka (No. 456).—Once the Bodhisatta was born as **Juṇha,** son of **Brahmadatta,** king of Benares. He studied in **Takkasilā** and, on one occasion, while walking in the dark, he ran up against a brahmin, knocking him down and breaking his bowl. Juṇha raised the brahmin to his feet and, on being asked for the price of a meal, told the brahmin who he was. He had no money with him, but requested the brahmin to remind him of the circumstance when he should become king. In due time Juṇha was anointed, and the brahmin stood one day by the road when the king was passing on his elephant. The brahmin stretched out his hand, crying, "Victory to the king." Juṇha took no notice, so the brahmin uttered a stanza to the effect that a king should not neglect a brahmin's request. Juṇha then turned back, and the man explained who he was, asking Juṇha for five villages, one hundred slave girls, one thousand ornaments and two wives, all of which Juṇha gave him.

The story was related in reference to the eight boons granted by the Buddha to **Ānanda** when the latter became his constant attendant. Ānanda is identified with the brahmin.[1] See also the **Nānacchanda Jātaka.**

[1] J. iv. 95-100.

Jutideva.—A king of seventeen kappas ago, a previous birth of **Sappidāyaka.**[1]

[1] Ap. i. 212.

1. **Jutindhara.**—A king of fifty-one kappas ago, a former birth of **Salaḷamāliya**[1] or **Samiddhi.**[2]

[1] Ap. i. 206. [2] ThagA. i. 117.

2. **Jutindhara.**—A king of ten kappas ago, a previous life of **Mandāravapūjaka**[1] or **Usabha.**[2]

[1] Ap. i. 178. [2] ThagA. i. 219.

3. **Jutindhara.**—A king of seventy-seven kappas ago, a former birth of **Kilañjadāyaka.**[1] *v.l.* **Jalandhara.**

[1] Ap. i. 219.

4. **Jutindhara.**—A Yakkha of **Udumbarapabbata,** husband of **Cetiyā.** He was killed in the fight in **Sirīsavatthu.**[1]

[1] MṬ. 289.

Jūjaka.—A brahmin of **Dunniviṭṭha** in **Kāliṅga.** He was given a young maiden in repayment of a debt, but because she was praised for her virtues, the other wives in the village grew jealous of her and mocked her as an old man's darling Thereafter she refused to go to the village well, and suggested that Jūjaka should obtain as slaves the children of **Vessantara,** then living as an ascetic in **Vaṅkagiri.** After many adventures Jūjaka found Vessantara, was allowed to have the two children, **Jāli** and **Kaṇhajinā,** and having tied their hands together, took them away. After he had travelled sixty leagues, the gods led him to **Jetuttara,** where the children's grandfather reigned as king. The king bought the children back from Jūjaka at a very great price and gave him choice foods to eat. Jūjaka, having over-eaten and being unable to digest the food, died on the spot.[1] He is identified with **Devadatta.**[2]

The wife of the brahmin who went for alms to **Bāvarī** was a descendant of Jūjaka. His descendants were still living in Dunniviṭṭha, even in the Buddha's day.[3]

[1] J. vi. 521-81. [2] *Ibid.*, 593. [3] AA. i. 183.

Jegucchi Sutta.—On the three kinds of persons—one is to be shunned as loathsome, the second to be regarded with indifference, and the third to be followed and honoured.[1]

[1] A. i. 126 f.

1. **Jeṭṭhatissa I.**—King of Ceylon (323–33 A.C.), elder son of **Goṭhābhaya,** the younger being **Mahāsena.** He slew all the ministers who were disloyal to his father and earned the title of "The Cruel." He rebuilt the **Lohapāsāda** to a height of seven storeys and renamed it the **Maṇipāsāda,** from the costly jewels he offered in it. He also built the **Pācīnatissapabbata-vihāra** and the **Ālambagāma** tank.[1]

[1] Mhv. xxxvi. 118 ff.; Dpv. xxii. 61, 66.

2. **Jeṭṭhatissa II.**—King of Ceylon, brother (?) and successor of **Sirimeghavaṇṇa.** He ruled for nine years and was a very skilful carver in ivory.[1]

[1] Cv. xxxvii. 100-4; Cv. *Trs.* i. 9, n. 1.

3. **Jeṭṭhatissa.**—Son of King **Saṅghatissa.** When **Moggallāna III.** usurped the throne Jeṭṭhatissa fled to the **Malaya** country. From there he helped **Asiggāhaka Silāmeghavaṇṇa** in his fight with Moggallāna, but on discovering that Silāmeghavaṇṇa wished to kill him also, he fled once more to Malaya. Later, he made his headquarters at **Ariṭṭhapabbata,** and from there led an army against **Aggabodhi III.,** who was then on the throne. Aggabodhi fled to **Jambudīpa,** and Jeṭṭhatissa became king as Jeṭṭhatissa III. He reigned for only five months, during which time he did several meritori-

ous works. Aggabodhi returned with an army, and in the battle which followed Jeṭṭhatissa slew himself at the sight of his army suffering defeat. His queen entered the Order and became proficient in the Abhidhamma.[1]

[1] Cv. xliv. 28, 55, 61, 70, 86-106.

Jeṭṭhamūla.—Name of a month (May-June). It came in the hot season.[1] On the fifth day of the waxing moon in Jeṭṭhamūla the Buddha's relics were divided.[2] On the full-moon day of Jeṭṭhamūla the **Aruṇavatī Sutta** was preached.[3]

[1] *E.g.*, J. v. 412. [2] DA. i. 6. [3] AA. i. 438.

Jeṭṭhā.—Chief queen of **Aggabodhi IV.** She built the **Jeṭṭhārāma**[1] (*q.v.*).

[1] Cv. xlvi. 27.

Jeṭṭhārāma.—Built by Queen **Jeṭṭhā** as an abode for the nuns. The villages of **Pattapāsāna** and **Buddhabhelagāma** were given for its maintenance and one hundred attendants were provided for its service.[1]

[1] Cv. xlvi. 27 f.

1. **Jeta.**—A prince. Owner of **Jetavana,** which he sold to **Anāthapiṇḍika** for eighteen crores. He then spent all that money on the erection of a gateway at the entrance, which he decorated with much grandeur.[1] Jeta is generally referred to as Jeta-Kumāra. According to the northern records he was the son of **Pasenadi** by the Kṣatriya princess Varṣikā.[2] He was killed by his half-brother **Viḍūḍabha** for refusing to help him in his slaughter of the Sākyans.[3] Several explanations[4] are given of his name: he was so-called either (1) because he conquered his enemies, or (2) because he was born at a time when the king had overcome his enemies, or (3) because such a name was considered auspicious for him (*maṅgalakāmyatāya*).

[1] See *s.v.* **Jetavana.**
[2] Rockhill: 48, n. 1,
[3] *Ibid.*, 121.
[4] MA. i. 50; UdA. 56; KhpA. 111, etc.

2. **Jeta.**—A Pacceka Buddha.[1]

[1] M. iii. 70.

Jetavana.—A park in **Sāvatthi,** in which was built the **Anāthapiṇḍikārāma.** When the Buddha accepted **Anāthapiṇḍika's** invitation to visit Sāvatthi the latter, seeking a suitable place for the Buddha's residence, discovered this park belonging to **Jetakumāra.**[1] When he asked to be allowed to buy it, Jeta's reply was: "Not even if you could cover the whole place with

[1] MA. i. 471 says it was in the south of Sāvatthi.

money." Anāthapiṇḍika said that he would buy it at that price, and when Jeta answered that he had had no intention of making a bargain, the matter was taken before the Lords of Justice, who decided that if the price mentioned were paid, Anāthapiṇḍika had the right of purchase. Anāthapiṇḍika had gold brought down in carts and covered Jetavana with pieces laid side by side.[2] The money brought in the first journey was found insufficient to cover one small spot near the gateway. So Anathapiṇḍika sent his servants back for more, but Jeta, inspired by Anāthapiṇḍika's earnestness, asked to be allowed to give this spot. Anāthapiṇḍika agreed and Jeta erected there a gateway, with a room over it. Anāthapiṇḍika built in the grounds dwelling rooms, retiring rooms, store rooms and service halls, halls with fireplaces, closets, cloisters, halls for exercise, wells, bathrooms, ponds, open and roofed sheds, etc.[3]

It is said[4] that Anāthapiṇḍika paid eighteen crores for the purchase of the site, all of which Jeta spent in the construction of the gateway gifted by him.[5]

Jeta gave, besides, many valuable trees for timber. Anāthapiṇḍika himself spent fifty-four crores in connection with the purchase of the park and the buildings erected in it.

The ceremony of dedication was one of great splendour. Not only Anāthapiṇḍika himself, but his whole family took part: his son with five hundred other youths, his wife with five hundred other noble women, and his daughters **Mahā Subhaddā** and **Cūla Subhaddā** with five hundred other maidens. Anāthapiṇḍika was attended by five hundred bankers. The festivities in connection with the dedication lasted for nine months.[6]

Some of the chief buildings attached to the Jetavana are mentioned in the books by special names, viz., **Mahāgandhakuṭi, Kaverimaṇḍalamāla, Kosambakuṭi** and **Candanamāla.**[7] All these were built by Anāthapiṇḍika; there was another large building erected by **Pasenadi** and called the **Salaḷa-ghara.**[8] Over the gateway lived a guardian deity to prevent all evildoers from entering.[9] Just outside the monastery was a *rājayatana*-tree, the residence of the god **Samiddhisumana.**[10] In the grounds there seems to

[2] This incident is illustrated in a bas-relief at the Bharhut Tope; see Cunningham—the Stūpa of Bharhut, Pl. lvii., pp. 84-6.

[3] Vin. ii. 158 f.

[4] MA. i. 50; UdA. 56 f.

[5] The gateway was evidently an imposing structure; see J. ii. 216.

[6] J. i. 92 ff.

[7] SNA. ii. 403. Other buildings are also mentioned—*e.g.*, the **Ambalakoṭṭhaka-āsanasālā** (J. ii. 246). According to Tibetan sources the vihāra was built according to a plan sent by the devas of Tusita and contained sixty large halls and sixty small. The Dulva also gives details of the decorative scheme of the vihāra (Rockhill: *op. cit.* 48 and n. 2).

[8] DA. ii. 407.

[9] SA. i. 239.

[10] Mhv. i. 52 f.; MṬ 105; but see DhA. i. 41, where the guardian of the gateway is called **Sumana.**

have been a large pond which came to be called the **Jetavanapokkharaṇī.**[11] The grounds themselves were thickly covered with trees, giving the appearance of a wooded grove (*araññа*).[12] On the outskirts of the monastery was a mango-grove.[13] In front of the gateway was the Bodhi-tree planted by Anāthapiṇḍika, which came later to be called the **Ānandabodhi** (*q.v.*).[14] Not far from the gateway was a cave which became famous as the **Kapallapūvapabbhāra** on account of an incident connected with **Macchariya-Kosiya.**[15]

Near Jetavana was evidently a monastery of the heretics where **Ciñcāmāṇavikā** spent her nights while hatching her conspiracy against the Buddha.[16] There seems to have been a playground just outside Jetavana used by the children of the neighbourhood, who, when thirsty, would go into Jetavana to drink.[17] The high road to Sāvatthi passed by the edge of Jetavana, and travellers would enter the park to rest and refresh themselves.[18] According to the Divyāvadāna,[19] the thūpas of **Sāriputta** and **Moggallāna** were in the grounds of Jetavana and existed until the time of Asoka. Both Fa Hien[20] and Houien Thsang[21] give descriptions of other incidents connected with the Buddha, which took place in the neighbourhood of Jetavana—*e.g.*, the murder of **Sundarikā,** the calumny of **Ciñcā,** Devadatta's attempt to poison the Buddha, etc.

The space covered by the four bedposts of the Buddha's **Gandhakuṭi** in Jetavana is one of the four *avijahitaṭṭhānāni*; all Buddhas possess the same, though the size of the actual vihāra differs in the case of the various Buddhas. For **Vipassī** Buddha, the seṭṭhi **Punabbasumitta** built a monastery extending for a whole league, while for **Sikhī,** the seṭṭhi **Sirivaḍḍha** made one covering three gāvutas. The Saṅghārāma built by **Sotthiya** for **Vessabhū** was half a league in extent, while that erected by **Accuta** for **Kakusandha** covered only one gāvuta. **Koṇagamana's** monastery, built by the seṭṭhi **Ugga,** extended for half a gāvuta, while **Kassapa's** built by **Sumaṅgala** covered sixteen karīsas. Anāthapiṇḍika's monastery covered a space of eighteen karīsas.[22]

The Buddha spent nineteen rainy seasons in Jetavana.[23] It is said that

11 AA. i. 264; here the Buddha often bathed (J. i. 329 ff.). Is this the **Pubbakoṭṭhaka** referred to at A. iii. 345? But see S. v. 220; it was near this pond that **Devadatta** was swallowed up in **Avīci** (J. iv. 158).

12 Sp. iii. 532.

13 J. iii. 137.

14 J. iv. 228 f.

15 J. i. 348.

16 DhA. iii. 179; behind Jetavana was a spot where the **Ājīvakas** practised their austerities (J. i. 493). Once the heretics bribed **Pasenadi** to let them make a rival settlement behind Jetavana, but the Buddha frustrated their plans (J. ii. 170).

17 DhA. iii. 492.

18 J. ii. 203, 341; see also vi. 70, where two roads are mentioned.

19 Dvy. 395 f.

20 Giles: p. 33 ff.

21 Beal: ii. 7 ff.

22 BuA. 2, 47; J. i. 94; DA. ii. 424.

23 DhA. i. 3; BuA. 3; AA. i. 314.

after the **Migāramātupāsāda** came into being, the Buddha would dwell alternately in Jetavana and Migāramātupāsāda, often spending the day in one and the night in the other.[24]

According to a description given by Fa Hien,[25] the vihāra was originally in seven sections (storeys ?) and was filled with all kinds of offerings, embroidered banners, canopies, etc., and the lamps burnt from dusk to dawn.

One day a rat, holding in its mouth a lamp wick, set fire to the banners and canopies, and all the seven sections were entirely destroyed. The vihāra was later rebuilt in two sections. There were two main entrances, one on the east, one on the west, and Fa Hsien found thūpas erected at all the places connected with the Buddha, each with its name inscribed.

The vihāra is almost always referred to as *Jetavane Anāthapiṇḍikassa Ārāma*. The Commentaries[26] say that this was deliberate,[27] in order that the names of both earlier and later owners might be recorded and that people might be reminded of two men, both very generous in the cause of the Religion, so that others might follow their example. The vihāra is sometimes referred to as **Jetārāma.**[28]

In the district of Saheṭh-Mabeṭh, with which the region of Sāvatthi is identified, Saheṭh is considered to be Jetavana.[29]

[24] SNA. i. 336. [25] Giles, pp. 31, 33.
[26] MA. ii. 50; UdA. 56 f., etc.
[27] At the Buddha's own suggestion (Beal: *op. cit.*, ii. 5 and Rockhill: p. 49).
[28] *E.g.*, Ap. i. 400.
[29] *Arch. Survey of India*, 1907-8, pp. 81-131.

2. **Jetavana.**—A monastery in **Anurādhapura,** situated in the **Jotivana** (*q.v.*) and founded by **Mahāsena** at the instigation of a monk named **Tissa** of the **Dakkhiṇārāma.** The monks of the **Mahāvihāra** protested against this and Jetavana was later given to them.[1] Attached to the vihāra is a large thūpa. The work was completed by **Sirimeghavaṇṇa.**[2] **Dāṭhāpabhuti** held in the vihāra the ceremony in honour of the **Dhammadhātu,**[3] while **Mahānāga** gave to it the village of **Vasabha** in **Uddhagāma** and three hundred fields, to ensure a permanent supply of rice gruel to the monks.[4] **Aggabodhi II.** crowned the thūpa with a lightning conductor (*cumbaṭa*),[5] **Jeṭṭhatissa I.** gave for its maintenance the village of **Goṇḍigāma,**[6] and **Aggabodhi III.** bestowed on it the **Mahāmaṇikagāma.**[7] **Potthasāta,** senāpati of **Aggabodhi IV.,** built in the vihāra the **Aggabodhi-pariveṇa,**[8] and **Aggabodhi IX.** made a golden image to be placed in the shrine-room.[9] **Sena I.**

[1] Mhv. xxxvii. 32 ff.
[2] Cv. xxxvii. 65.
[3] *Ibid.*, xli. 40; also Cv. *Trs.* i. 55, n. 2.
[4] *Ibid.*, xli. 97 f.
[5] *Ibid.*, xlii. 66.
[6] *Ibid.*, xliv. 97.
[7] *Ibid.*, 121.
[8] *Ibid.*, xlvi. 22.
[9] *Ibid.*, xlix. 77.

erected in the monastery grounds a mansion of several storeys.[10] **Kassapa V.** gave a village for the maintenance of the refectory,[11] while four officials of **Mahinda IV.** built four pariveṇas attached to the vihāra.[12]

The monks of Jetavana, though nominally forming part of the **Mahāvihāra** fraternity, held divergent views in regard to the teachings of the Buddha, and were considered as a separate sect (the **Sāgaliyas**) till **Parakkamabāhu I.** united all the fraternities.[13]

The thūpa at Jetavana was restored by Parakkamabāhu I. to a height of two hundred and ten feet.[14]

[10] Cv., l. 65. [11] *Ibid.*, lii. 59. [12] *Ibid.*, liv. 49. [13] *Ibid.*, lxxviii. 22. [14] *Ibid.*, 98.

3. **Jetavana.**—A monastery in **Pulatthipura,** built by **Parakkamabāhu I.** It included the building which housed the **Tivaṅka** image.[1] The **Nammadā** Canal flowed through the grounds of Jetavana.[2]

[1] Cv. lxxviii. 32, 47. [2] *Ibid.*, lxxix. 48. See also Cv. *Trs.* ii. 105, n. 5.

Jetārāma.—See **Jetavana.**

Jetuttara.—The capital of **Siviraṭṭha,** where reigned **Sivi** and **Sañjaya.** In the city was the **Vessa Street** where **Vessantara** was born.[1] The **Vessantara Jātaka**[2] gives the distances from Jetuttara to several places.

[1] J. vi. 480, 484, 486, etc. [2] *Ibid.*, 514.

Jetuyyāna.—Another name for **Jetavana.**[1]

[1] *E.g.*, Mhv. i. 56.

1. **Jenta.**—A village in **Magadha,** the birthplace of **Jenta Thera.**[1]

[1] ThagA. i. 219.

2. **Jenta.**—A thera. He was born in the village of **Jenta** as the son of a chieftain. He was thoughtful when young, and one day, having heard the Buddha preach, he entered the Order and soon became an arahant. He was a devaputta in the time of **Sikhī** Buddha and offered him *kiṅkirāta*-flowers. Five kappas ago he was a king named **Sattuttama.** *v.l.* **Sabbuttama.**

He is probably identical with **Kakkārapupphiya** of the Apadāna.[2]

[1] Thag. vs. 111; ThagA. i. 219 f. [2] Ap. i. 177.

3. **Jenta Purohitaputta.**—A thera. He was the son of the chaplain of the **Kosala** king.[1] He was intoxicated with pride over his own advantages, and one day, though visiting the Buddha, he decided not to speak unless the Buddha should address him first. The Buddha, reading his thoughts, preached a sermon, intended for him, on the evils of pride, and Jenta became a Sotāpanna. Later he entered the Order and became an arahant.[2]

Perhaps he is to be identified with **Manātthaddha** of the Saṃyutta Nikāya.[3]

[1] Was he **Aṅgulimāla's** brother ? See *s.v.* **Aṅgulimāla.**

[2] Thag. vs. 423-8; ThagA. i. 455 f.

[3] S. i. 177; KS. i. 224, n. 1.

Jentā, Jentī.—The daughter of a princely family of **Licchavis** in **Vesālī.** The rest of her story resembles that of **Abhirūpa-Nandā** (*q.v.*), and she attained arahantship after hearing the Buddha preach.[1]

[1] Thig. vs. 21 f.; ThigA. 27 f.

Jeyyapura.—The Pāli name for **Sagaing.**[1]

[1] Bode: *op. cit.*, 40, 71.

Jeyyavaḍḍhana.—The Pāli name for **Taungu** in Burma.[1]

[1] Bode: p. 40.

Jeyyasena.—A thera. He and two others, **Bhūmija** and **Abhirādhana,** were friends of **Sambhūta,** and they all left the world together.[1]

[1] ThagA. i. 47.

Jotanā.—A commentary by an unknown author.[1]

[1] Gv. 65, 75.

1. **Joti.**—A class of gods, present at the **Mahāsamaya.**[1] Buddhaghosa explains[2] that they were flaming deities, like beacon lights on mountain tops.

[1] D. ii. 261.

[2] DA. ii. 691.

2. **Joti.**—A Burmese monk, author of the **Vinayagaṇṭhipada.**[1]

[1] P.L.C. 190.

1. **Jotika, Jotiya.**—A treasurer of **Rājagaha** who later became an arahant. In the past he had been a householder of Benares who, with his elder brother,

owned a field of sugar-cane. One day, when returning from the field with some stalks of sugar-cane, he saw a Pacceka Buddha from **Gandhamādana** to whom he gave a bowl full of sugar-cane juice for him to drink, and when he had drunk it, gave him another bowlful which the Pacceka Buddha took to Gandhamādana to share with his colleagues. The householder, when proffering his gifts, wished for glory and for Nibbāna. His elder brother, hearing of this, was likewise filled with joy and he, too, wished for Nibbāna. In the time of **Vipassī** Buddha they were again brothers in a rich family of **Bandhumatī,** the elder being called **Sena** and the younger **Aparājita.** Sena entered the Order and became an arahant. At his suggestion, Aparājita[1] built for the Buddha a very costly **Gandhakuṭi,** with the seven kinds of precious things. His nephew, also called **Aparājita,** built an elephant stable in front of the Gandhakuṭi and was reborn in this age as **Meṇḍaka** (*q.v.*). The Gandhakuṭi and its surroundings contained all kinds of luxuries and splendours beyond description.[2] Within and without the chamber he caused jewels, pounded and otherwise, to be strewn knee-deep. Those who came to listen to the Buddha went away, their hands full of jewels. One day a brahmin tried to carry away a very costly jewel, which much annoyed Aparājita. On mentioning it to the Buddha, the Buddha taught him to make a wish that his property should not be taken away by thieves or lost by fire or water. For nine months Aparājita held the ceremony of dedication of the Gandhakuṭi.

In this age he was born as the son of a seṭṭhi in Rājagaha. On the day of his birth the whole city became one blaze of light, hence his name, Jotika. The king, **Bimbisāra,** gave one thousand a day for his milk-money. When the time came for his marriage, **Sakka** provided for him a palace, seven storeys high, made entirely of precious minerals. Four urns of treasure stood at the four corners and four stalks of sugar-cane made of solid gold, each the size of a palmyra tree with leaves of precious stones, to remind Jotika of his good deed in the past. Seven Yakkhas guarded the seven gates—**Yamakoḷī, Uppala, Vajira, Vajirabāhu, Kasakanda, Kaṭattha** and **Disāpāmukha**—each with numerous followers. Bimbisāra, hearing of his splendour, appointed Jotika to the rank of seṭṭhi.

The gods brought him a wife from **Uttarakuru** and lodged her in an apartment in Jotika's palace. Her name was **Satulakāyī.**[3] She brought with her a pint-pot of rice and three crystal fire-stones. Whenever they wished to eat, they would put rice over the boiler and set it over the crystals. The stones would immediately become alight and, when the meal was cooked, would extinguish themselves. The pot was inexhaustible. All who came

[1] According to DhA. iii. 364, both uncle and nephew were called **Avaroja.**

[2] For details see DhA. iv. 203 f.

[3] *Ibid.*, 223.

to visit Jotika were provided with food and were allowed to take anything they wished from the treasure, the treasure never growing less. So great were the crowds which flocked to Jotika's palace that for a long time Bimbisāra had no chance of seeing it. When Bimbisāra did in the end visit him with **Ajātasattu,** Jotika invited him to a meal which was the most dainty the king had ever tasted. After the meal Jotika presented his wife to Bimbisāra; so delicately was she nurtured that the perfume with which the king was scented hurt her eyes! There were no lamps in Jotika's house; only the light of jewels was made use of, and as a memento of Bimbisāra's visit Jotika gave him a huge jewel to be used as a lamp.[4]

Jotika was a very pious follower of the Buddha. Once, when he was away listening to the Buddha's preaching, Ajātasattu—who even when visiting the palace as a boy with his father had coveted Jotika's wealth—went with his soldiers to attack the palace in an attempt to take possession of it. But the Yakkha Yamakoḷī routed the army, and Ajātasattu fled for refuge to the vihāra where Jotika was listening to the Dhamma. On being charged by Ajātasattu with hypocrisy in that he was there listening to the Dhamma, after having charged his guards to set upon the king, Jotika's answer was that he had no need of guards since nobody could take anything of his without his sanction. He then challenged the king to remove the rings from his (Jotika's) fingers. Ajātasattu, trying with all his might, failed. Jotika then held out his hands and his rings all fell off.

Agitated by the king's desire to possess his wealth, Jotika asked for permission to become a monk. Ajātasattu agreed, hoping thus to get possession of his riches. Jotika entered the Order and soon became an arahant, but at the moment of his attainment of arahantship all his wealth and earthly glory vanished and his wife returned to Uttarakuru.[5]

Jotika is included[6] among the five persons who possessed great merit and had *puññiddhi*.

[4] This account is taken from DhA. iv. 199-213.

[5] *Ibid.*, 221-4.

[6] *Ibid.*, i. 385; Vsm. 383; PsA. 502. These five persons are described as *amitabhogā* (AA. i. 220).

2. **Jotika.**—A householder of **Rājagaha** and father of **Dīghāvu.** When Dīghāvu fell ill he sent Jotika to tell the Buddha.[1]

[1] S. v. 344 f.

Jotidāsa Thera.—A wealthy brahmin of **Pādiyattha (Pāniyattha).** One day, seeing **Mahā Kassapa** going for alms, he entertained the Elder and requested him to preach. On a hill near the village Jotidāsa built a vihāra for Kassapa and provided him with the requisites. Moved by the Elder's teaching, he left the world and soon after became an arahant. After ten years—during which he learnt the Three Piṭakas, being specially proficient in the Vinaya—while on his way to **Sāvatthi** to see the Buddha, he entered a Paribbājakārāma, and there had a discussion with the Paribbājakas on how to burn away evil. At the end of the discussion, they were ordained under him.

In the time of **Sikhī** Buddha he was a householder and, seeing the Buddha, offered him a *kāsumārika*-fruit.[1]

He is probably identical with **Kāsumāraphaladāyaka** of the Apadāna.[2]

[1] Thag. 143-4; ThagA. i. 264 f.

[2] ii. 445. But see *s.v.* **Sīvaka.**

1. **Jotipāla.**—The Bodhisatta born as the son of the chaplain of **Brahmadatta,** king of Benares. He was a great archer and became an ascetic. He is also referred to as **Sarabhaṅga.**[1] For his story see the **Sarabhaṅga Jātaka.** He is evidently identical with Jotipāla of the **Indriya Jātaka** (*q.v.*). He belonged to the **Koṇḍaññagotta.**[2]

[1] J. v. 127 ff.

[2] *Ibid.*, 140, 141, 142.

2. **Jotipāla.**—The Bodhisatta born as a brahmin of **Vehaliṅga** in the time of **Kassapa** Buddha. **Ghaṭīkāra** was his friend and invited Jotipala to accompany him to the Buddha, but Jotipāla refused to go, saying that a "shaveling recluse" could be of no use to him. But Ghaṭīkāra was very insistent, and one day, after they had bathed together in the river, seized Jotipāla by the hair and made a final appeal. This boldness on the part of an inferior (Ghaṭīkāra was a potter) caused Jotipāla to realise his extreme earnestness and he agreed to go. After hearing the Buddha preach, Jotipāla became a monk.[1]

This insulting remark made by Jotipāla regarding Kassapa Buddha led to Gotama, in his last life, having to practise austerities for a longer period than did the other Buddhas.[2] The memory of what he did as Jotipāla was one of the things that made the Buddha smile.[3]

[1] M. ii. 46 ff.; J. i. 43; Bu. xxv. 10; see also S. i. 34 f.; Mil. 221; Mtu. i. 319 ff.

[2] Ap. i. 301; UdA. 265; ApA. i. 95.

[3] DhsA. 294, 496.

3. **Jotipāla.**—A brahmin, son of **Govinda,** chaplain of **Disampati.** Jotipala was a friend of Disampati's son, **Reṇu,** who had six other nobles as companions. On the death of Govinda, Jotipāla became chaplain to Disampati. He inspired Reṇu's six companions to wait on Reṇu and make him promise to share the kingdom with them when he should come to the

throne. This promise Reṇu kept when he succeeded his father and appointed Jotipāla to carry out the division of the kingdom, which the latter duly did. All the kings wished Jotipāla to be their chaplain, and he instructed them in the art of government, teaching the mantras also to seven eminent brahmins and to seven hundred young graduates. Jotipāla himself came to be known as **Mahā Govinda.**

After some time, Jotipāla took leave of the seven kings, his disciples and his wives, and spent the four months of the rainy season in a retired spot outside the city, developing *jhāna* in order to see **Brahmā** face to face. At the end of the four months, **Brahmā Sanaṅkumāra** appeared before him and gave him a boon. Jotipāla asked to be taught the way to reach the Brahma-world, and, having listened to Sanaṅkumāra's exposition, decided to leave the world. The kings and all the others did their best to make him desist from this course, but finding their efforts of no avail they went with him into the homeless life, where all of them profited thereby.

Jotipāla was the Bodhisatta.[1] He is twice mentioned in the Aṅguttara Nikāya[2] in a list of ancient teachers with very large followings.

[1] D. ii. 232-51; Mtu. i. 197 ff. [2] A. iii. 372; iv. 135; AA. ii. 679.

4. **Jotipāla.**—A monk at whose request **Buddhaghosa** wrote the **Sāratthappakāsinī** and the **Manoratthapūraṇī.** He seems to have been a colleague of Buddhaghosa and lived with him in several places, including **Kañcīpura.**[1]

[1] Gv. 68; SA. iii. 235; AA. ii. 874.

5. **Jotipāla.**—A thera of Ceylon. He defeated in debate the adherents of the **Vetulla** school, and one of their angry followers, **Dāṭhāpabhuti,** raised his hand to strike the thera. An ulcer immediately appeared on Dāṭhāpabhuti's hand. **Aggabodhi I.** gave the Elder a dwelling in the vihāra (**Abhayagiri ?**)—where the discussion took place—and charged his nephew with his care. The king also built for the Elder the **Nīlagehapariccheda.** Later the **Kāliṅga** king came with his family to Ceylon and was ordained under Jotipāla. **Aggabodhi II.** repaired the **Thūpārāma** at Jotipāla's suggestion and deposited therein a relic of the Buddha from the **Lohapāsāda.**[1]

[1] Cv. xlii. 35, 45, 51, 60.

Jotipāsāna.—The name given to the crystals brought from **Uttarakuru** by **Jotika's** wife. When anything requiring cooking was placed on them they gleamed hot, and went out of themselves when the cooking was complete.[1]

[1] DhA. iv. 209; DA. iii. 965.

1. **Jotiya.**—See **Jotika.**

2. **Jotiya.**—A king of seventy-three kappas ago, a previous birth of **Mañjaripūjaka.**[1]

[1] Ap. i. 228.

3. **Jotiya.**—A Nigaṇṭha, for whom **Paṇḍukābhaya** built a house to the east of the Nīcasusāna at **Anurādhapura.**[1] The Mahāvaṃsa Ṭīkā[2] calls him a Nagaravaḍḍhakī. The **Abhayagiri-vihāra** was later erected on the spot occupied by Jotiya's residence.[3]

[1] Mhv. x. 97. [2] p. 296. [3] MṬ. 620.

Jotirasa.—An ascetic living near **Kañcanapabbata,** and a friend of **Vessavaṇa.** He lived in a hut called **Kañcanapatti,** and Vessavaṇa daily sent him four mangoes from his tree (**Abbhantaramba**), some of which he gave to a parrot, as related in the **Abbhantara Jātaka** (*q.v.*). He is identified with **Sāriputta.**[1]

[1] J. ii. 400.

Jotivana.—The name given to the **Nandanavana** in **Anurādhapura** after **Mahinda** had preached there, converting a large number of people.[1] It was situated immediately before the south gate of the city.[2] It was included in the boundaries of the **Mahāvihāra** and, later, **Mahāsena** built the **Jetavana-vihāra** in Jotivana.[3]

It is said[4] that when Mahinda preached at Jotivana there was an earthquake.

[1] Sp. i. 82: Mhv. xv. 202.
[2] *Ibid.*, 1, 7, 8.
[3] *Ibid.*, xxxvii. 33.
[4] DA. i. 131; see also Cv. xxxvii. 65; lii. 59.

Jh.

Jhatvā Sutta.—See **Chetvā Sutta.**

Jhāna Vagga.—The last and twentieth chapter of the Eka Nipāta of the Aṅguttara Nikāya.[1]

[1] A. i. 38-46.

1. **Jhāna Saṃyutta** (also called **Samādhi**).—The twenty-fourth Saṃyutta of the Saṃyutta Nikāya.[1]

[1] S. iii. 263-79.

2. **Jhāna Saṃyutta.**—The fifty-third Saṃyutta of the Saṃyutta Nikāya.[1]

[1] S. v. 307-10.

1. **Jhāna Sutta.**—**Anuruddha** tells his colleagues of the advantages of cultivating trance.[1]

[1] S. v. 305.

2. **Jhāna Sutta.**—Six things one must give up in order to develop *jhāna.*[1]

[1] A. iii. 428.

3. **Jhāna Sutta.**—Six other things which must be abandoned in order that *jhāna* may be developed.[1]

[1] A. iii. 428.

4. **Jhāna Sutta.**—The Buddha explains to the monks how the destruction of the *āsavas* is the result of every step taken in the sphere of contemplation.[1]

[1] A. iv. 422 f.

5. **Jhāna Sutta.**—The great benefit one derives from practising *jhāna*, even for the duration of a finger-snap, and the different methods of attaining to such practice.[1]

[1] A. i. 38 ff.

6. **Jhāna Sutta.**—On the advantages that result from the practice of mindfulness centred on the body.[1]

[1] A. i. 43 f.

Jhānasodhana Jātaka (No. 134).—The Bodhisatta was once an ascetic who, at the moment of his death, said " neither conscious nor unconscious." His chief disciple interpreted these words, but the others would not believe him until the Bodhisatta descended from the Brahma-world in order to uphold his explanation.

The story was related in reference to an explanation given by **Sāriputta** at **Saṅkassa.**[1]

This Jātaka is probably also called the **Anaṅgana Jātaka** (*q.v.*).

[1] J. i. 473.

Jhānābhiññā Sutta.—The Buddha tells the monks that **Mahā Kassapa** is able to do many of the things he himself can do.[1]

[1] S ii. 210 ff.

Ñ.

Ñāṇakathā.—The first chapter of the Mahāvagga of the Paṭisambhidāmagga.[1]

[1] Ps. i. 4-135.

Ñāṇagambhira.—A monk of Pagan, author of the **Tathāgatuppatti.**[1]

[1] Bode: *op. cit.*, 16.

Ñāṇathavika.—An arahant. One hundred thousand kappas ago he was a hermit, and, seeing the Buddha (**Padumuttara**), worshipped him with reverence and sang his praises.[1] He is probably identical with **Yasadatta Thera.**[2]

[1] Ap. ii. 392 f. [2] ThagA. i. 428.

Ñāṇathomana.—See **Ñānasaññaka.**

Ñāṇadhara (Ñāṇavara).—A king of sixty-one kappas ago, a previous birth of **Tiraṃsiya.**[1]

[1] Ap. i. 257.

Ñāṇapāla.—A leader of the fraternity of monks in **Anurādhapura** in the time of **Parakkamabāhu I.**[1]

[1] Cv. lxxviii. 8.

Ñāṇavara.—An author of Pagan. He wrote several works in Pāli, including the **Rājādhirājanāmattappakāsinī.** He was tutor to the king Mahārājādhipati. He translated the **Abhidhānappadipikā** into Burmese.[1]

[1] Bode: *op. cit.*, 66 f.

Ñāṇavilāsa.—A monk of Laos who wrote the **Saṅkhyāpakāsaka.**[1]

[1] Bode: *op. cit.*, 47.

1. **Ñāṇasaññaka Thera.**—An arahant. In a past life he met **Siddhattha** Buddha and paid him homage. Seventy-three kappas ago he became king sixteen times.[1] He is probably identical with **Subāhu.**[2]

[1] Ap. i. 140 f. [2] ThagA. i. 124.

2. **Ñāṇasaññaka Thera.**—An arahant. Ninety-one kappas ago he saw a coco-palm and, with his mind fixed on the Buddha, thought of the Buddha's

praises. Seventy-three kappas ago he was a king named **Puḷinapupphiya.**[1] He is probably identical with **Piyañjaha.**[2] *v.l.* **Ñāṇathomana.**

[1] Ap. i. 161 f. [2] ThagA. i. 169.

Ñānasāgara.—A monk of Pagan, author of the **Liṅgatthavivaraṇappakāsana.**[1]

[1] Gv. 63, 67; Bode: *op. cit.*, 22.

Ñāṇābhivaṃsa.—A leader of the Pārupaṇas in their controversy with the Ekaṃsikas in Burma.[1] He wrote several ṭikās and a Burmese translation of the Jātakas and the Rājādhirājavilāsinī.[2]

[1] Bode: *op. cit.*, 76. [2] *Ibid.*, 78; Svd. vs. 1215.

Ñānālaṅkāra.—A Burmese monk, author of the **Padavibhāga.**[1]

[1] Bode: *op. cit.*, 77.

Ñāṇodaya.—The first work written by **Buddhaghosa** while he was yet in India.[1] It was probably on some philosophical subject.

[1] Cv. xxxvii. 225.

Ñātaka Sutta.—If a well-known monk encourages others to act and speak contrary to the ordinances of the Dhamma and to have ideas contrary to them, he lives to the harm of a large number of people.[1]

[1] A. i. 106.

Ñātika (*v.l.* **Nādika, Nātika**).—A locality in the **Vajji** country on the highway between **Koṭigāma** and **Vesāli.** The Buddha first went there in the course of one of his tours, and the inhabitants, being greatly attracted by him, built for him a residence in brick, the **Giñjakāvasatha** (*q.v.*), which, in course of time, became a great vihāra.[1] The Buddha, subsequently, seems to have stayed several times in Ñātika. According to the **Cūlagosiṅga Sutta**[2] he stayed there soon after the schism of the **Kosambī** monks and sought the **Gosiṅgasālavana,** evidently in the neighbourhood where **Anuruddha, Nandiya** and **Kimbila** were in residence. The Buddha also visited Ñātika on his last journey, while on his way to **Kusinārā,** and was staying there on the day that he accepted **Ambapālī's** hospitality and her

[1] MA. i. 424.

[2] M. i. 205; but according to Vin. (i. 350 f.), which relates this incident, they were in **Pācīnavaṃsadāya** and the Buddha went there from **Bālakaloṇakāragāma.**

gift of the **Ambapāliambavana.**[3] It was evidently during this stay that **Ānanda** questioned the Buddha as to the lot of various pious inhabitants of Ñātika who had been zealous followers of the Buddha's teaching. Among them several are mentioned by name—the monk **Sāḷha,** the nun **Nandā, Sudatta, Kakudha, Kāliṅga, Nikaṭa, Kaṭissabha, Tuṭṭha, Santuṭṭha, Bhadda, Subhadda** and the upāsikā **Sugatā.** The Buddha tells Ānanda of their destiny, and informs him that more than ninety people of Ñātika had become Sakadāgāmins and more than five hundred Sotāpannas. He then proceeds to proclaim the discourse which has become famous as the **Dhammādāsa.**[4] The **Janavasabha Sutta,**[5] which was also preached at Ñātika, is evidently based on this incident and is probably an elaboration of the same. The Saṃyutta Nikāya and the Aṅguttara Nikāya record other suttas on different topics preached at Ñātika.[6] Mention is also made of discussions between the Buddha and **Kaccāyana**[7] and **Sandha,**[8] and also of a discussion between **Sabhiya Kaccāyana** and **Vacchagotta.**[9]

The books spells the name of the village in two ways: Ñātika and Nādika. This doubt as to the spelling seems to have existed from quite early times, as the apparent confusion of the etymology leads us to believe. In the Saṃyutta Commentary,[10] Buddhaghosa says "*Ñātiketi dvinnaṃ ñātakānaṃ gāme.*" In the Dīgha Commentary,[11] however, he says "*Nādikā ti etaṃ taḷākaṃ nissāya dvinnaṃ cullapitu-mahāpituputtānaṃ dve gāmā. Nādike ti ekasmiṃ ñātigāme.*" These explanations seem to support both spellings—Ñātika and Nādika—Ñātika because it was a "*ñātigāma*" and Nādika because it was near the pond Nādikā.[12] Rhys Davids[13] thinks that Nādikā (pl.) was a clan-name and Nādika the name of the clan's village. Woodward[14] also supports the reading Nādika, and suggests that the name is connected with *nadī,* and refers to Walters' Chwang (ii. 86), where reference is made to Nātaka on the Ganges between Vesāli and Patna.

[3] Vin. i. 232 f.

[4] D. ii. 91 ff.; S. v. 356 ff., also records what is evidently the same incident. Two additional names, **Asoka** and **Asoki,** occur in the Saṃyutta passage.

[5] D. ii. 200 f.

[6] See *s.v.* **Giñjakāvāsatha Sutta** and also **Ñātika Sutta;** also S. iv. 90; A. iii. 303 f., 306 f., A. iv. 316 f. and 320 f.

[7] S. ii. 153.

[8] A. v. 322 f.

[9] S. iv. 401 f.

[10] SA. ii. 56.

[11] DA. ii. 543.

[12] MA. ii. 424 definitely states that the name of the pond was also **Nādikā** (*Nādike viharati ti Nādiki nāma eka,* etc.).

[13] Dial. ii. 97, n. 1.

[14] GS. iii. 217, n. 4.

Ñātika Sutta.—Once the Buddha, while meditating in the **Giñjakāvasatha** at **Ñātika,** uttered a discourse regarding Ill, its arising and its cessation.

A certain monk stood listening, and the Buddha asked him to learn the Doctrine as he had heard it.[1]

[1] S. ii. 71; repeated at S. iv. 90.

Ñātikā (*v.l.* **Ñātikī**).—The name, probably of a pond (*taḷāka*) near the village of **Ñātika,** and/or of the clan who lived in the village. See **Ñātika.**

Ñeyyasandatī.—A Pāli work, probably by a Burmese author. There exists also *a ṭīkā* on the work.[1]

[1] Gv. 72.

Ṭ.

Ṭaṅkitamañca.—A place near **Gayā.** It was the residence of the Yakkha **Sucīloma** and the Buddha once stayed there.[1] The Sutta Nipāta Commentary[2] explains that Ṭaṅkitamañca was at **Gayātittha,** and that it was a stone-bed (*pāsāṇamañca*) formed by a stone set on the top of four other stones. The Saṃyutta Commentary[3] says it was either a house (*geha*) so-formed, or a long bed made with supports inserted under the legs of the bedstead and placed in the temples of the gods.

[1] SN. p. 47 f.; S. i. 206. [2] SNA. i. 301. [3] SA. i. 232 f.

Ṭh.

Ṭhakuraka.—The chief of the **Āriyakkhattayodhā**[1] (*q.v.*).

[1] Cv. xc. 16, 24, 27.

Ṭhapana Sutta.—Ten reasons for establishing the Pāṭimokkha.[1]

[1] A. v. 70 f.

1. **Ṭhana Sutta.**—The four kinds of persons in the world—those who live on the fruit of their efforts, not of their deeds; those who live on the fruit of their deeds, not of their efforts; those who do both; those who do neither.[1]

[1] A. ii. 135.

2. **Ṭhāna Sutta.**—A man's virtue is to be understood only by association, his integrity by living with him, his courage by watching him in time of distress, his wisdom by conversing with him.[1]

[1] A. ii. 187 ff.

3. **Ṭhāna Sutta.**—Five things that make parents desire a son—he will help them, he will do his duty by them, he will keep up tradition, worthily possess his heritage and give merit to them when they are dead.[1]

[1] A. iii. 43.

4. **Ṭhāna Sutta.**—The five unattainable states—ageing which brings no decay, sickening no disease, dying no death, wasting no destruction, ending no end.[1]

[1] A. iii. 54 f.

5. **Ṭhāna Sutta.**—Four occasions that exist—when action is unpleasant and unprofitable to the doer, when it is unpleasant but profitable, when it is pleasant but unprofitable, when it is both pleasant and profitable.[1]

[1] A. ii. 118 f.

6. **Ṭhāna Sutta.**—Five things which should often be contemplated by everyone—the possibility of old age, disease, death, separation from what is near and dear, and the fact that one is the result of one's own deeds—and the purposes of such contemplation.[1]

[1] A. iii. 71 ff.

7. **Ṭhāna Sutta.**—The special attainments of the inhabitants of **Uttarakuru, Jambudīpa** and **Tāvatiṃsa** respectively.[1]

[1] A. v. 396.

8. **Ṭhāna Sutta.**—Five conditions hard to be won by a woman who has won no merit—birth in a desirable family, marriage to a desirable person, having no other wife as rival, giving birth to a son and ability to retain the husband's affection.[1]

[1] S. iv. 249.

9. **Ṭhāna Sutta.**—The conditions that promote lust, malevolence, sloth, torpor, excitement and flurry, doubt and wavering, and the seven *bojjhaṅgas.*[1]

[1] S. v. 84 f.

10. **Ṭhāna Sutta.**—The Buddha knows how things are caused and occasioned, and the fruits of actions.[1]

[1] S. v. 304.

Ṭhānakoṅkana.—A garden in Ceylon, laid out by **Parakkamabāhu I.**[1]

[1] Cv. lxxix. 11.

Ṭhitañjaliya.—An arahant thera. In the time of **Tissa** Buddha he was a hunter, and, having seen the Buddha, worshipped him. The hunter was almost immediately afterwards killed by lightning, and at the moment of death clasped his hands once more in honour of the Buddha. Fifty-four kappas ago he was a king named **Migaketu.**[1]

[1] Ap. i. 123.

1. **Ṭhiti Sutta.**—The four kinds of people who practise meditation—those skilled in concentration but not in steadfastness, those in steadfastness but not in concentration, those in neither, those in both.[1]

[1] S. iii. 264.

2. **Ṭhiti Sutta.**—When the Buddha has passed away, the Doctrine will last if people cultivate the four *satipaṭṭhānas*, not if they do not.[1]

[1] S. v. 172.

3. **Ṭhiti Sutta.**—The Buddha praises not steadfastness in good actions, but growth in respect of them. In this sutta the Buddha explains by means of similes how this is done.[1]

[1] A. v. 96 f.

4. **Ṭhiti Sutta.**—The seven stations of consciousness (*viññāṇaṭṭhiti*).[1]

[1] A. iv. 39 f.

T.

Takka Jātaka (No. 63).—Once the Bodhisatta was an ascetic on the banks of the Ganges, from which he rescued **Duṭṭhakumārī,** daughter of the seṭṭhi of Benares, who had been thrown into the flood during a storm by her long-suffering servants. The ascetic succumbed to the wiles of Duṭṭhakumārī and took up his abode with her in a village, where they earned their living by selling *takka* (curds or dates). He therefore came to be called **Takkapaṇḍita.** One day the village was looted by robbers, and they carried the woman away together with their booty. Living happily with the robber chief, she feared that her former husband might come to claim her; she therefore sent for him with sweet words, planning to have him killed.

While being beaten by the robber-chief, Takkapaṇḍita kept repeating, " Ungrateful wretches," and, on being asked the reason, related the story. The robber thereupon killed the woman.

Ānanda is identified with the robber-chief.

The story was related to a passion-tossed monk.[1] The Jātaka is sometimes referred to[2] as the **Takkāriya Jātaka.**

[1] J. i. 295-99. [2] *E.g.*, J. v. 446 (16).

Takkapaṇḍita.—The name given to the Bodhisatta in the **Takka Jātaka** (*q.v.*).

Takkambila.—A *pāsāda* attached to a vihāra in **Rohaṇa.** It was repaired by **Dappula,** who also installed monks there.[1]

[1] Cv. xlv. 56.

Takkarā.—A city in the time of **Sumana** Buddha.[1]

[1] ThagA. i. 303; Ap. ii. 416.

Takkaru Jātaka.—See **Kakkaru Jātaka.**

Takkaḷa Jātaka (No. 446).—Once in a village lived a man called **Vasiṭṭhaka,** an only son, who looked after his father with great devotion, until the latter, much against the wishes of his son, found a wife for him. A son was born to the pair and, when seven years old, he overheard his mother planning to have the old man taken by a ruse to the cemetery and there killed and buried in a pit. The next morning, when his father set out in a cart for the cemetery, the child insisted on accompanying him. Having watched his father dig a pit, he asked what it was for, and was told that the useless old man was a burden to keep and that the pit was for him. The boy was silent, and when his father stopped to have a rest, he took up the spade and began to dig another hole. On being asked the reason, he said it was for his father when he should be too old to be supported. This remark opened Vasiṭṭhaka's eyes; he returned home and drove away his wife. He afterwards took her back on her promising to give up her treacherous ways.

The story was related to a man who had looked after his father; but the wife, whom he took at his father's wish, wanted to get rid of the old man, and suggested the idea to her husband. But his answer was that if she found the house inconvenient she could go elsewhere. The Buddha said that the characters of both stories were identical, and that he himself was the lad of the *atītavatthu.*[1]

[1] J. iv. 43-50.

Takkasilā.—The capital of **Gandhāra.** It is frequently mentioned as a centre of education, especially in the Jātakas. It is significant that it is never mentioned in the suttas, though, according to numerous Jātaka stories, it was a great centre of learning from pre-Buddhistic times. The Commentaries mention that in the Buddha's day, also, princes and other eminent men received their training at Takkasilā. **Pasenadi,** king of **Kosala, Mahāli,** chief of the **Licchavis,** and **Bandhula,** prince of the Mallas, were classmates in the university of Takkasilā.[1] Among others described as being students of Takkasilā are **Jīvaka, Aṅgulimāla, Dhammapāla** of **Avanti, Kaṇhadinna, Bhāradvāja** and **Yasadatta** (*q.v.*).

From Benares to Takkasilā was a distance of two thousand yojanas,[2] though we are told that sometimes the journey was accomplished in one day.[3] The road passed through thick jungle infested by robbers.[4] Takkasilā was, however, a great centre of trade; people flocked to it from various parts of the country,[5] not only from Benares, but also from **Sāvatthi,** from which city the road lay through **Soreyya.**[6] In ancient times students came to the university from **Lāḷa** (J. i. 447), from the **Kuru** country (DhA. iv. 88), from **Magadha** (J. v. 161), and from the **Sivi** country (J. v. 210).

The students in the university studied the three Vedas and the eighteen sciences (*vijjā*),[7] which evidently included the science of archery,[8] the art of swordmanship,[9] and elephant-craft (*hatthi-sutta*).[10] Mention is also made of the study of magic, such as the **Ālambanamanta,** for charming snakes,[11] and the **Nidhiuddharaṇamanta,** for recovering buried treasure.[12] The students were also taught the science of ritual (*manta*)[13]; but in this branch of learning Benares seems to have had a greater reputation, for we find students being sent there from Takkasilā in order to learn the mantas.[14]

The students generally paid a fee to the teacher on admission, the usual amount being one thousand gold pieces. They waited on the teacher by day and were taught by him at night. The paying students were entitled to various privileges, and lived with the teacher as members of his family, enjoying his constant company. The students seem mostly to have done

[1] DhA. i. 337.
[2] J. i. 395.
[3] J. ii. 47.
[4] DhA. iv. 66.
[5] MNid. i. 154.
[6] DhA. i. 326.
[7] J. i. 159.
[8] J. i. 356; DhA. iv. 66; also medicine and surgery (Vin. i. 269 f.)
[9] J. v. 128.
[10] J. ii. 47.
[11] J. iv. 457.
[12] J. iii. 116.
[13] J. ii. 200.
[14] DhA. iii. 445.

their own domestic work, leading a co-operate life, gathering their own firewood and cooking their meals, though mention is made of servants, both male and female, helping in the various tasks.[15]

Only brāhmaṇas and khattiyas appear to have been eligible for admission to Takkasilā.[16]

Discipline was evidently very rigorous, a breach of the rules being severely punished, irrespective of the status of the pupil, who was sometimes flogged on the back with a bamboo stick.[17] Often the most promising students were given the daughters of the teachers in marriage as a mark of very special favour.[18] Sometimes the teacher and his pupils were invited to a meal at the house of a chief man of the city.[19] The principal teacher was called Disāpāmokkhācariya; under him were assistants, usually chosen from among his students, who were called piṭṭhiācariyā.[20]

Takkasilā, being the capital of Gandhāra, was probably also the seat of government. **Bimbisāra's** contemporary in Gandhāra was **Pukkusāti.**[21] Mention is made in the Jātakas of a **Takkasilā-rājā.**[22] According to the **Kumbhakāra Jātaka** (*q.v.*), Takkasilā was the capital of **Naggaji.** The Dīpavaṃsa[23] records that twelve kings, descendants of **Dīpaṅkara,** ruled in succession at Takkasilā.

It is said in the Divyāvadāna[24] that **Bindusāra's** empire included Takkasilā. There was once a rebellion there and Asoka was sent to quell it. From the minor Rock Edict II. of Asoka it would appear that Takkasilā was the headquarters of a provincial government at Gandhāra, placed under a Kumāra or Viceroy. A rebellion broke out there again in the time of Asoka, who sent his son Kunāla to settle it.

Takkasilā is identified with the Greek Taxila, in Rawalpindi in the Punjab.

15 J. i. 319.
16 J. iv. 391.
17 J. ii. 277 f.
18 *E.g.*, DhA. iv. 66. Elsewhere (J. vi. 347) it is stated that the teacher's daughter was given to the eldest pupil.
19 J. iv. 391.
20 *E.g.*, J. ii. 100.
21 J. i. 399; ii. 218.
22 AA. i. 153; MA. i. 335; ii. 979, 987 f.
23 iii. 31.
24 p. 371.

Takkasilā Jātaka.—Apparently another name[1] for the **Telapatta Jātaka** (*q.v.*).

1 *See* J. i. 970; DhA. iv. 83.

Takkārika.—See **Takkāriya.**

Takkāriya.—The Bodhisatta as chaplain to the king of Benares. See **Takkāriya Jātaka.**

Takkāriya Jātaka (*v.l.* **Takkārika**) (No. 481).—Brahmadatta had, as chaplain, a tawny-brown brahmin who was toothless, and whose wife had a paramour possessed of the same attributes. Wishing for the death of the latter, the chaplain asked the king to build anew the southern gate of his city, and declared that on the day the gate was set up a tawny-brown brahmin should be killed and sacrificed to the guardian spirits. The king agreed, but the chaplain, unable to restrain his wife's conduct, told her about it. The news spread abroad, and all tawny-brown brahmins fled from the city, leaving, on the auspicious day, only the chaplain. The people demanded that he should be slain to avert ill-luck, and that his pupil, **Takkāriya** (the Bodhisatta), should be appointed in his place. The chaplain confessed his plan to Takkāriya, who thereupon related several stories showing how " silence is golden." In the end Takkāriya allowed the chaplain to flee from the city, and had the corpse of a goat buried under the city gates in the dead of night.[1]

The story was related in reference to **Kokālika,** who came to grief by abusing the Chief Disciples. See **Kokālika** (2).

The tawny-brown brahmin is identified with Kokālika.

The Jātaka seems also to have been called the **Takka Jātaka**[2] and the **Mahātakkāri Jātaka.**[3]

[1] J. iv. 242 ff. [2] *E.g.*, J. v. 446. [3] J. ii. 175.

Takkivīmaṃsī.—The name of a class of brahmins who might be described as sophists and researchers.[1]

[1] M. ii. 211.

Takkola.—A town mentioned in the Milindapañha[1] as a great centre of trade.

[1] p. 359.

Taṅkuttara.—A Damiḷa chieftain, ally of **Kulasekhara.**[1]

[1] Cv. lxxvi. 144.

Tagara.—A city in the time of **Dhammadassī** Buddha; it was the capital of King **Sañjaya.**[1]

[1] BuA. p. 183.

Tagarasikhī.—A Pacceka Buddha,[1] third among the five hundred sons of **Padumavatī,** all of whom became Pacceka Buddhas. **Suppabuddha,** a banker of **Rājagaha,** having seen the Pacceka Buddha on his way to a

[1] M. iii. 69; ApA. i. 106.

park, spoke insultingly to him, and, as a result, was born as a leper in this birth.[2]

The Saṃyutta Nikāya[3] contains the story of a man who often met Tagarasikhī begging for alms. One day, being attracted by him, he asked his wife to give him a meal and went on his way. His wife prepared excellent food and gave it to Tagarasikhī. The husband met Tagarasikhī on his way back to the town, and seeing the excellence of the food, was displeased with his wife's generosity, thinking to himself that it were better that slaves and workmen should have eaten the food. As a result, he was born as a very rich seṭṭhi in **Sāvatthi,** but was never able to enjoy his wealth, and died intestate, all his possessions passing to the royal treasury. The Dhammapada Commentary[4] calls him **Aputtaka.** It has been suggested[5] that the "Tagara" in Tagarasikhī was the name of a place, perhaps the modern Ter.

[2] Ud. v. 3; UdA. 291; DhA. (ii. 36) says Suppabuddha spat on the Pacceka Buddha.

[3] i. 92 f.; SA. i. 126 f.; also J. iii. 299 f. and MṬ. 597.

[4] iv. 77 f.

[5] Bud. India, p. 31.

Taṅguttavaṅka-pariveṇa.—A monastery, probably in Ceylon; the residence of **Raṭṭhapāla,** author of the original of the **Rasavāhinī.**[1]

[1] P.L.C. 224.

"Taṃ jīvaṃ taṃ sarīraṃ" Sutta.—One of the views which are held in the world, owing to the existence of the *khandhas* and the clinging to them.[1]

[1] S. iii. 215.

Tacasāra Jātaka (No. 368).—Once a poor village doctor saw some boys playing near a tree, in the hollow of which lived a snake. Hoping to make some money, he asked one of the boys, who was the Bodhisatta, to put his hand into the hollow of the tree, saying that a hedgehog lived there. The boy did so, but, feeling the snake, with great presence of mind, he seized it firmly by the neck and flung it away from him. The snake fell on the doctor and bit him so severely that he died. The boys were brought before the king and charged, but on hearing the Bodhisatta's explanation the king released them.

The story was related to show how the Bodhisatta practised *paññāpāramitā*. **Ānanda** is identified with the king.[1]

[1] J. iii. 204 ff.

Tacchakā.—A class of Nāgas present at the **Mahāsamaya.**[1]

[1] D. ii. 258.

Tacchasūkara Jātaka (No. 492).—Once a carpenter in a village near Benares picked up a young boar from a pit and took him home and reared him, calling him **Tacchasūkara** (Carpenter's Boar). The boar helped him in his work, fetching his tools and so on. When he grew up to be a big, burly beast, the carpenter let him go free in the forest. There he joined a herd of wild boars which was being harassed by a fierce tiger. Tacchasūkara made all the preparations for a counter-attack, digging pits and training all the members of the herd in their various duties, and their several positions at the time of attack. Under his guidance they succeeded in killing the tiger and greedily devouring the corpse. Tacchasūkara was told that there was a sham ascetic who had helped the tiger to eat the boars. The herd attacked the ascetic, who climbed up a fig-tree, but they uprooted the tree and devoured him. They consecrated Tacchasūkara as their king, making him sit on a fig-tree, and sprinkling water on him from a conch-shell, with its spirals turned right-wise, which the ascetic had used for drinking. Hence arose the custom of seating the king on a chair of fig-wood and sprinkling him with water from a conch-shell at his coronation.

The story was related in connection with the Thera **Dhanuggahatissa** (*q.v.*). Spies of **Pasenadi** had heard him discuss with the Thera **Datta** the plan of campaign which should be adopted if Pasenadi wished to defeat **Ajātasattu.** This was repeated to Pasenadi, who followed the suggestion and captured Ajātasattu. Dhanuggahatissa is identified with Tacchasūkara.[1]

[1] J. iv. 342 ff.

Taṭavāpi.—A locality near the **Kālavāpi.** There was a fortress there where **Gokaṇṇa** suffered defeat.[1]

[1] Cv. lxx. 165.

Taṇḍulanāli Jātaka (No. 5).—Once the Bodhisatta was appraiser to the king of Benares, with whom he always dealt fairly. The king was greedy, and thinking that his appraiser paid too much for things bought for the palace, he appointed in his place a rustic, whom he happened to see passing. This man fixed prices according to his own fancy. One day a dealer brought five hundred horses from **Uttarāpatha,** and the appraiser valued the whole lot at a single measure of rice. The horse-dealer sought the Bodhisatta's advice, who suggested that the appraiser should be asked to value a measure of rice. The horse-dealer went to the king, and, in the presence of the court, asked the appraiser the value of one measure of rice. The man replied that it was worth all Benares and its suburbs. The ministers laughed, thus putting the king to shame. He dismissed the fool and reinstated the Bodhisatta.

The story was told in reference to **Lāludāyi,** who had a dispute with **Dabba Mallaputta** regarding the distribution of food tickets. The monks thereupon asked Lāludāyi to undertake the task. This he did so badly that great confusion ensued, and the matter was reported to the Buddha, who related the above story to show that in the past, too, his stupidity had deprived others of their profit.

Lāludāyi is identified with the false appraiser.[1]

[1] J. i. 123-26.

Taṇḍulapatta.—A village in **Rohaṇa.**[1]

[1] Cv. lxxiv. 165.

Taṇḍulapāladvāra.—One of the gates of **Rājagaha.** Near the gate was the residence of the brahmin **Dhānañjāni.**[1]

[1] M. ii. 185; MA. ii. 795.

1. **Taṇhakkhaya Sutta.**—The Buddha teaches the destruction of craving, and the path thereto.[1]

[1] S. iv. 371.

2. **Taṇhakkhaya Sutta.**—**Anuruddha** tells the monks that the four *satipaṭṭhānas*, if cultivated, lead to the destruction of craving.[1]

[1] S. v. 300.

Taṇhaṅkara.—One of the four Buddhas born in the same *kappa* as **Dīpaṅkara.**[1]

[1] J. i. 44; Bu. xxvii. 1.

Taṇhā.—One of the three daughters of **Māra,** who tried to tempt the Buddha under the **Ajapālanigrodha,** soon after the Enlightenment.[1]

[1] SN. p. 163; S. i. 124 f.; J. i. 78, 469; DhA. i. 252; iii. 196, 199.

Taṇhā Vagga.—The twenty-fourth chapter of the **Dhammapada.**

1. **Taṇhā Sutta.**—On the one hundred and eight thoughts of craving—thirty-six each, of the past, the present, and the future—which, like a net, snares one, clings to one, etc.[1]

[1] A. ii. 211 f.

2. **Taṇhā Sutta.**—The four causes of the arising of craving in a monk—robes, food, lodging, success or failure in undertakings.[1]

[1] A. ii. 10.

3. **Taṇhā Sutta.**—The nine evil things which have their ultimate origin in *taṇhā*.[1]

[1] A. iv. 400 f.

4. **Taṇhā Sutta.**—Both craving and the emancipation therefrom, through knowledge, are nourished and fulfilled by something, and this something may finally be reduced to association with the bad and the good respectively.[1]

[1] A. v. 116 ff.

5. **Taṇhā Sutta.**—Preached in answer to a question by a deva. It is craving, above all things, which brings everything beneath its sway.[1]

[1] S. i. 39.

6. **Taṇhā Sutta.**—Preached to **Rāhula,** as question and answer. Craving for objects of sense is fleeting, and leads, therefore, to unhappiness.[1]

[1] S. ii. 248, 251.

7. **Taṇhā Sutta.**—Craving for body is impermanent; likewise craving for sounds, scents, savours, etc.[1]

[1] S. iii. 227.

8. **Taṇhā Sutta.**—The arising of craving for body and for things is the beginning of decay and death, its cessation, their cessation.[1]

[1] S. iii. 230.

9. **Taṇhā Sutta.**—Desire and lust for visible shape, etc.; these are a corruption of the heart.[1]

[1] S. iii. 234.

10. **Taṇhā Sutta.**—A discussion between **Sāriputta** and **Jambukhādaka** on the three kinds of craving—for sense-delight, for becoming, for not-becoming.[1]

[1] S. iv. 257.

11. **Taṇhā Sutta.**—The Noble Eightfold Path must be followed in order to get rid of the three kinds of craving.[1]

[1] S. v. 57 f.

Taṇhāsaṅkhaya Sutta.—See **Cūla°** and **Mahā°.**

Tatojasi.—A messenger of **Vessavaṇa.**[1]

[1] D. iii. 201.

Tatolā, Tatotalā, Tattalā.—Messengers of **Vessavaṇa.**[1]

[1] D. iii. 201.

Tatha.—A Pacceka Buddha.[1]

[1] M. iii. 69; ApA. i. 106.

1. **Tatha Sutta.**—There are four things that are true and unalterable—the facts of Dukkha, its arising, its cessation, the path thereto.[1]

[1] S. v. 430.

2. **Tatha Sutta.**—The Four Noble Truths. Same as above.[1]

[1] S. v. 435.

Tathāgata.—An epithet of the Buddha, used by the Buddha in referring to himself. The Commentaries[1] give eight (sometimes expanded to sixteen) explanations of the word, which shows that there was probably no fixed tradition on the point. The explanations indicate that the name can be used for any arahant, and not necessarily only for a Buddha. The term was evidently pre-Buddhistic, though it has not yet been found in any pre-Buddhistic work.

[1] DA. i. 59-67; AA. i. 58-63; MA. 39-43; UdA. 128 ff., etc.

Tathāgata Suttā.—A group of suttas in which the simile of the Tathāgata, being the chief of all creatures, is repeated.[1]

[1] S. v. 41 ff.; repeated at v. 135.

" Tathāgatena-vutta " Sutta.—Another record[1] of the first sermon preached by the Buddha, more commonly known as the **Dhammacakkappavattana Sutta** (*q.v.*). At the conclusion of the sutta, news of the establish-

[1] See Vin. i. 10 ff.

ment of the kingdom of the Dhamma was proclaimed throughout the Cakkavāḷa. **Koṇḍañña** alone, of the **Pañcavaggiyas,** understood the significance of the teaching, and became known as **Aññata-Koṇḍañña.**[2] This sutta is followed by a repetition of itself, but with the words "Tathāgatas" (plural) substituted for "Tathāgata."[3]

[2] S. v. 420 ff.; Vin. i. 10 ff. [3] S. v. 424 f.

Tadaṅga Sutta.—**Kāludāyi** asks **Ānanda,** at the **Ghositārāma,** what is meant by *Tadaṅganibbāna,* and Ānanda answers.[1]

[1] A. iv. 454.

Tadadhimutta.—A Pacceka Bhuddha.[1]

[1] M. iii. 70; ApA. i. 107.

Taddhigāma.—A chieftain of **Rohaṇa,** subdued by **Parakkamabāhu I.** He held the title of **Laṅkāpura.**[1]

[1] Cv. lxxv. 180.

Tanagaluka.—A village in **Rohaṇa.**[1]

[1] Cv. lxxiv. 165.

Tanaveḷi-vihāra.—A vihāra erected in **Bījagāma** by King **Mahallaka-Nāga.**[1] *v.l.* **Cānavela.**

[1] Mhv. xxxv. 125.

Tanasīva.—A landowner of **Mātuvelaṅga** and a supporter of **Kupikkala-Mahātissa Thera.** When **Vaṭṭagāmaṇī,** the king, was in hiding, the thera entrusted him to the care of Tanasīva, who, for fourteen years, looked after him, his queen, **Anulādevī,** and his two sons. Then, as the result of a dispute between Anulā and Tanasīva's wife, Vaṭṭagāmaṇī shot him dead.[1]

[1] Mhv. xxxiii. 52-65.

Tantavāyikacāṭikā.—A village assigned by **Potthakuṭṭha** to the *padhānaghara* at **Māṭambiya.**[1]

[1] Cv. xlvi. 20.

Tannarugāma.—A village near **Pulatthipura,** the scene of several conflicts between the forces of **Parakkamabāhu I.** and those of his enemies.[1]

[1] Cv. lxx. 313, 316, 319; lxxii. 175.

Tannitittha.—A village in Ceylon, near **Ambagāma** and **Antaravitthi.**[1]

[1] Cv. lxx. 322.

Tapakaṇṇika.—See **Tavakaṇṇika.**

Tapana.—A Niraya. Beings born there are pierced by heated stakes and they remain transfixed, motionless.[1]

[1] J. v. 266, 271, 275.

Tapassī.—An envoy sent by the king of **Rāmañña** to **Parakkamabāhu I.**[1]

[1] Cv. lxxvi. 23.

1. **Tapassu, Tapussa.**—A merchant of **Ukkala.** He and his friend, **Bhalluka (Bhalliya),** while on their way to **Rājagaha,** saw the Buddha at the foot of the **Rājāyatana** tree, in the eighth week after the Enlightenment. Urged by a deity, who had been their relation, they offered the Buddha rice-cakes and honey in a bowl provided by the Four Regent Gods. They became the first lay disciples of the Buddha, and their formula of Refuge contained no reference to the Saṅgha.[1]

According to the Theragāthā Commentary,[2] Tapassu and Bhalluka were brothers, sons of a caravan leader of **Pokkharavatī.** Some time later they visited the Buddha at Rājagaha, where he preached to them; Tapassu, thereupon, became a Sotāpanna, while Bhalluka entered the Order and became an arahant.

In the time of **Sikhī** Buddha they were brahmins of **Aruṇavatī.** Hearing that two caravan leaders, **Ujita** and **Ojita,** had given the first meal to the Buddha, they gave alms to the Buddha and his monks, and wished for a similar privilege for themselves under a future Buddha. In the time of **Kassapa** Buddha, they were sons of **Gopāla-**seṭṭhi, and for many years provided the monks with milk rice.

The Aṅguttara Commentary[3] says that the deity, who caused Tapassu and Bhalluka to give alms to the Buddha, was their mother in their previous birth. The Buddha gave them, for worship, eight handfuls of his hair, which he obtained by stroking his head. They took the hair with them to their city—which, according to this account, was **Asitañjana**—and there built a cetiya, from which rays of blue light issued on fast-days. Tapassu is called a *dvevācikaupāsaka,*[4] and is included in a list of eminent upāsakas.[5]

See also **Tapassu Sutta** below.

[1] Vin. i. 3 f.; A. i. 26; UdA. 54; J. i. 80.
[2] i. 48 f. [3] AA. i. 207 f.
[4] *Ibid.*, ii. 696.
[5] A. iii. 450. The Sanskrit books call him Trapuṣa (Dvy. 393; Mtu. iii. 303.)

2. **Tapassu.**—Chief of the lay disciples of **Dīpaṅkara** Buddha.[1]

[1] Bu. ii. 215.

Tapassu (Tapussa) Sutta.—The householder **Tapassu** visits **Ānanda** at **Uruvelakappa,** and expresses surprise that young men in the fulness of life can renounce the pleasures of household life and enter the Order. Ānanda takes Tapassu to the Buddha, who is having his siesta at the foot of a tree in the **Mahāvana,** and repeats Tapassu's remark. The Buddha tells Ānanda how he himself had attained to Buddhahood by passing through the nine successive stages, the *anupubbavihārā.* These nine stages consist of the four jhānas, the four *āyatanas* (*ākāsānañcāyatana*, etc.), and, as the crowning stage, the *saññāvedayitanirodha.*[1]

The Tapassu mentioned is evidently identical with the brother of Bhalluka mentioned above. The Commentary[2] on this passage makes no attempt to distinguish him from any other.

[1] A. iv. 438 ff. [2] AA. ii. 814.

Tapussa.—See **Tapassu.**

" Tapo-kammañca " Sutta.—As the Buddha sits under the **Ajapālanigrodha** tree, soon after the Enlightenment, rejoicing in freedom from toil, **Māra** approaches and tells him that his purity is but a delusion. The Buddha rebukes him and proves him to be wrong.[1]

[1] S. i. 103.

Tapodakandarā.—See **Tapodārāma.**

Tapodā.—A large lake below the **Vebhāra** mountain, outside **Rājagaha.** The lake was cool, but the stream flowing from it, also called **Tapodā,**[1] was hot. Around it was the **Tapodārāma** (*q.v.*). It is said[2] that the water of the river was hot because it flowed between two **Lohakumbhi-nirayas,** which existed under Rājagaha. The lake was the playground of the Nāgas who dwelt at the foot of the Vebhāra mountain. Monks and recluses were evidently in the habit of going to the Tapodā to bathe in the hot springs. Thus, we find **Samiddhi** being questioned by a deity as he dried himself after bathing in the Tapodā,[3] and the Aṅguttara Nikāya[4] records a discussion between **Ānanda** and the paribbājaka **Kokanuda,** on the banks of the Tapodā, where they had gone to bathe.

[1] Vin. iii. 108; iv. 116 f.; DA. i. 35; UdA. 110.

[2] SA. i. 30 f.; Sp. ii. 512.

[3] S. i. 8 ff.; M. iii. 192 ff.; J. ii. 56.

[4] v. 196 f.

Tapodārāma.—A grove near lake **Tapodā** (*q.v.*). In the grove was a monastery where the Buddha seems to have stayed on several occasions. It is said[1] that on one such occasion the Buddha gave **Ānanda** the chance of asking him to live for a whole *kappa*, but Ānanda failed to make use of it.

Near the Tapodārāma was the **Tapodakandārā.** They were both far from **Rājagaha,** and monks would come from afar late at night and, in order to test **Dabba Mallaputta's** powers, ask him to provide lodgings for them.[2]

[1] D. ii. 116. [2] Vin. ii. 76; iii. 159.

Tapodāvātthu.—The story of **Moggallāna** explaining the reason for the warmth of the water of the **Tapodā** and of the refusal of the monks to believe him.[1]

[1] Vin. iii. 108; Sp. ii. 512.

Tapovana.—A group of monasteries near **Anurādhapura** inhabited by the **Paṃsukūlikas.** They lay in the forest district to the west of the city.[1]

[1] Cv. lii. 22; liii. 14 ff.; also Cv. *Trs.* i. 163, n. 8.

Tabbāraṭṭha.—A district in the **Dakkhiṇadesa** of Ceylon.[1]

[1] Cv. lxix. 8.

Tabbāvāpi.—A tank in the **Dakkhiṇadesa** of Ceylon.[1]

[1] Cv. lxviii. 3.

Tamālapupphiya Thera.—An arahant. In a previous birth he owned a vimāna with eighty thousand golden pillars. He offered a *tamāla* flower to **Sikhī** Buddha. Twenty kappas ago he was a king called **Candatittha.**[1]

[1] Ap. i. 197.

Tamo Sutta.—The four types of people found in the world—those who, being in darkness, are bound for darkness, those who are in darkness, but are bound for light, etc.[1]

[1] A. ii. 85; *cf.* Pugg. p. 51; and S. i. 93, where the sutta is addressed to **Pasenadi.**

Tamonuda.—A king of ninety-one kappas ago, a previous birth of **Punnāgapupphiya.**[1]

[1] Ap. i. 180; ThagA. i. 213.

1. **Tamba.**—A king of Benares whose queen was **Sussondī.** For his story see the **Sussondī Jātaka.**[1] He is identified with Ānanda.

[1] J. iii. 187 ff.

2. **Tamba.**—A Tamil general and a fort of the same name. Both were captured by **Duṭṭhagāmaṇi** during his campaign against the Tamils. **Tamba** was an uncle of **Uṇṇama.**[1]

[1] Mhv. xxv. 14.

3. **Tamba.**—An officer of **Parakkamabāhu I.** He was chief of the **Kesadhātus.**[1]

[1] Cv. lxx. 66.

4. **Tamba.**—One of the ten families of elephants. Each elephant of this family has the strength of ten thousand men.[1]

[1] AA. ii. 822; MA. i. 262, etc.

Tambagāma.—A village in **Rohaṇa.**[1]

[1] Cv. lxxv. 90.

Tambadāṭhika.—A public executioner of **Rājagaha.** He had copper-coloured teeth and tawny skin, and his body was covered with scars. He wished to join a band of thieves, but, for some time, the ringleader refused to admit him on account of his inordinately cruel looks. In the end he was admitted; but when the thieves were captured and no one could be found willing to kill as many as five hundred of them, Tambadāṭhika agreed to do it for a reward, and slew all his colleagues. He was afterwards appointed public executioner and held the post for fifty-five years. When he became too old to behead a man with one blow, another was appointed in his place, and he was deprived of the four perquisites to which he had, for so many years, been entitled—old clothes, milk porridge made with fresh ghee, jasmine flowers, and perfumes. On the day on which he was deposed from office, he gave orders for milk porridge to be cooked, and having bathed and decked himself out, he was about to eat, when **Sāriputta,** out of compassion for him, appeared at his door. Tambadāṭhika invited the Elder in and entertained him hospitably. When Sāriputta began the words of thanksgiving, his host could not concentrate his thoughts, being worried by memories of his past wickedness. Sāriputta consoled him by representing to him that he had merely carried out the king's orders. At the end of the sermon, Tambadāṭhika developed the qualities necessary for becoming a Sotāpanna. When Sāriputta left, Tambadāṭhika accompanied him on his way, but on the way back he was gored to death by a cow.[1] The Buddha said he had been reborn in the **Tusita** world.[2]

[1] The cow was a Yakkhiṇī who also killed **Pukkusāti, Bāhiya Dāruciriya** and **Suppabuddha** (DhA. ii. 35; UdA. 289). [2] DhA. ii. 203 ff.

Tambapaṇṇi.—The name given to that district in Ceylon where **Vijaya** landed after leaving **Suppāraka.**[1] It is said to have been so called because when Vijaya's followers, having disembarked from the ship, sat down there, wearied, resting their hands on the ground, they found them coloured by the red dust that lay there. Later on Vijaya founded his capital in Tambapaṇṇi, and following that the whole island came to bear the same name.[2] Tambapaṇṇi was originally inhabited by Yakkhas, having their capital at **Sirīsavatthu** (*q.v.*). The **Valāhassa Jātaka**[3] speaks of a **Tambapaṇṇisara.** According to the Saṃyutta Commentary,[4] the **Tambapaṇṇidīpa** was one hundred leagues in extent.

Anurādhapura formed the **Majjhimadesa** in Tambapaṇṇidīpa, the rest being the **Paccantimadesa.**[5]

In Asoka's Rock Edicts II. and XIII. Tambapaṇṇi is mentioned as one of the Pratyanta deśas, together with Coḍa, Pāṇḍya, Satiyaputta, Keralaputta, and the realm of Antiyaka Yonarāja, as an unconquered territory with whose people Asoka was on friendly terms. Vincent Smith[6] identifies this, not with Ceylon, but with the river Tāmraparṇi in Tinnevelly.

[1] Mhv. vi. 47; Dpv. ix. 30.
[2] *Ibid.*, vii. 38-42. [3] J. ii. 129.
[4] ii. 83; but in VbhA. (p. 444) it is spoken of as tiyojana satika.
[5] AA. i. 265.
[6] Asoka (3rd edn.), p. 163; but see Ind. Antiq., 1919, p. 195 f.

Tambapaṇṇi.—An irrigation channel built by **Parakkamabāhu I.** It flowed northwards from the **Ambāla** tank.[1]

[1] Cv. lxxix. 50.

Tambapiṭṭha.—A village seven leagues to the east of **Anurādhapura,** on the banks of the **Mahāvālukanadī.** When **Duṭṭhagāmaṇi** made plans to build the **Mahā Thupā,** nuggets of gold appeared in Tambapiṭṭha.[1]

[1] Mhv. xxviii. 16.

Tambapupphiya.—A thera. Ninety-one kappas ago he had fled into the forest, having committed some crime. There he saw the Bodhi-tree of the Buddha **Piyadassī,** and having swept the ground around it, he scattered flowers. Three kappas ago he was a king named **Samphusita.**[1] He is probably identical with **Vanavaccha Thera.**[2]

[1] Ap. i. 176. [2] ThagA. i. 222 f.

Tambala.—A village, probably in **Rohaṇa,** where a battle was fought between **Dāṭhopatissa** and **Māṇa.**[1]

[1] Cv. xlv. 78.

Tambalagāma.—A village in **Rohaṇa,** once the headquarters of **Vijayabāhu I.**[1]

[1] Cv. lviii. 10, 38; see also Cv. *Trs.* i. 202, n. 5.

Tambaviṭṭhika.—A village in Ceylon, where the soldiers of **Vijayabāhu I.** killed the **Coḷa** king.[1]

[1] Cv. lviii. 21; see also Cv. *Trs.* i. 203, n. 3.

Tayodhamma Jātaka (No. 58).—Once **Devadatta** was born as king of the monkeys, and the Bodhisatta was his son. The monkey-king had the habit of gelding with his teeth all his male offspring, lest they should one day supersede him; but the Bodhisatta's mother left the herd before the child was born and brought him up elsewhere. When he grew up he came to see the monkey-king, and on the latter's trying to kill him by crushing him in a false embrace, the Bodhisatta showed greater strength than his sire. Then Devadatta asked him to fetch lotuses from a neighbouring lake, which was inhabited by an ogre, saying that he wished to crown his son as king. The Bodhisatta guessed the presence of the ogre and plucked the flowers by leaping several times from one bank to the other, grasping them on his way. The ogre seeing this expressed his admiration, saying that those who combine the three qualities of dexterity, valour, and resource can never be vanquished. When the monkey-king saw his son returning with the ogre, who was carrying the flowers, he died of a broken heart.

The story was related in reference to hunting.[1]

[1] J. i. 280-3.

Taracchavāpi.—A tank built by **Mahānāga.**[1]

[1] Mhv. xxii. 4.

Taracchā.—The name of a clan in Ceylon. The name is totemistic. This clan was among the tribes which accompanied the Bodhi-tree to Ceylon.[1] When **Aggabodhi I.** set up an image of **Mahinda** on the bank of the **Mahindataṭa,** the image was carried by the Taracchā.[2]

[1] Mhv. xix. 2. [2] Cv. xlii. 30; see Cv. *Trs.* i. 29, n. 2.

Taraṇa.—A king of fifty-eight kappas ago, a former birth of **Khadiravaniya Revata.**[1]

[1] Ap. i. 51; ThagA. i. 109.

1. **Taraṇiya Thera.**—An arahant. In a previous birth he took the Buddha and his monks across a river which was in flood. Thirteen kappas ago he became king five times under the name of **Sabhogavā.**[1] He is probably identical with **Sambhūta Thera.**[2]

[1] Ap. i. 204 f. [2] ThagA. i. 47.

2. **Taraṇiya Thera.**—An arahant. Ninety-one kappas ago he took the Buddha **Vipassī** and his monks across a river in a boat.[1]

[1] Ap. i. 234.

3. **Taraṇiya Thera.**—An arahant. Ninety-one kappas ago he built a bridge on an impassable road. Fifty-five kappas ago he was a king, **Samogadha** by name.[1]

[1] Ap. i. 238.

4. **Taraṇiya Thera.**—An arahant. In a previous birth he was a tortoise in the river **Vinatā,** and, seeing that the Buddha **Atthadassī** wished to cross the river, he took him on his back.[1]

[1] Ap. ii. 428 f.

Taruṇa Sutta.—In him who contemplates the enjoyment of what makes for enfettering, craving grows and a consequent mass of *dukkha,* like a sapling which is well tended; but in him who contemplates misery in all enslaving things, craving, etc., is destroyed.[1]

[1] S. ii. 88 f.

Talaṅga.—A locality in Ceylon, perhaps in **Piyaṅgudīpa.** It is known chiefly as having been the residence of the Elder **Dhammadinna.**[1]

[1] Mhv. xxxii. 52; VbhA. 389, 489; Vsm. 392, 634.

It may be the place mentioned in the Saddhammasaṅgaha[2] as the residence of **Mahādhammadinna,** under the name of **Talaṅgaratissapabbata** (elsewhere[3] called **Vālaṅgatissapabbata**). There was a cave in it called **Devarakkhitalena.** According to the Majjhima Commentary,[4] Talaṅgaratissapabbata was in **Rohaṇa,** and between it and **Tissamahārāma** lay the monasteries of **Haṅkana** and **Cittalapabbata.** *v.l.* **Talaṅka, Tālaṅkara, Tālaṅganagara.**

[2] p. 88. [3] MṬ. 606, n. 2. [4] i. 149 f.

Taladilla, Talaṇḍilla.—A port in the **Paṇḍu** kingdom, in South India. **Laṅkāpura** landed there and captured it.[1]

[1] Cv. lxxvi. 88, 92.

Talatādevī.—Mother of **Cūḷanī Brahmadatta,** king of **Pañcāla,** her husband being **Mahā Cūḷaṇī.** She was a very wise woman, wiser than the ten sages of the court. A story is related of how, in her wisdom, she managed to procure an adequate reward for a man who had saved another from drowning at the risk of his own life.[1] We are told that, while her son was still young, she committed adultery with the chaplain **Chambhī,** poisoned her husband, and made the chaplain king. Later, Chambhī wished to kill **Cūḷaṇī,** but Talatā saved his life by sending him to the royal cook.[2] She had a son by Chambī, called **Tikhiṇamantī.**[3] She is identified with **Cullanandikā.**[4]

[1] J. vi. 398. [2] *Ibid.*, 471 f. [3] *Ibid.*, 474. [4] *Ibid.*, 478.

Talanigāma-tittha.—A ford across the **Mahāvālukagaṅgā.**[1]

[1] Cv. lxxii. 4.

Taḷapuṭa.—See **Tāḷapuṭa.**

Taḷākatthalī, Taḷātthala.—A locality not far from **Pulatthipura.** It had a fortress which was once occupied by **Laṅkādhinātha Rakkha.**[1]

[1] Cv. lxx. 107, 112, 174.

Tavakaṇṇika, Tavaṇṇika, Tavakiṇṇoka.—A householder who realised Nibbāna from knowledge of the Tathāgata. He is mentioned in a list of such householders, but nothing further is known of him.[1] Is he connected with **Tikaṇṇa** (*q.v.*) ? The Commentary[2] says he was also called **Tapakaṇṇika.**

[1] A. iii. 451. [2] AA. ii. 696.

Tasiṇā Sutta.—On the three thirsts—for sensual delights, for becoming and for ceasing to become—and the way to get rid of them.[1]

[1] S. v. 58.

" Tassa-Sutaṃ " Sutta.—A group of suttas in which the Buddha is asked why beings are born among the different kinds of Nāgas. He replies that it was because men who had practised double dealing, having heard that birth among Nāgas was happy, wish to be born there.[1]

[1] S. iii. 243 f.

Tāṅgipperumāla.—A Damiḷa chieftain, ally of **Kulasekhara.**[1] He was later won over by **Laṅkāpura.**[2]

[1] Cv. lxxvi. 145. [2] *Ibid.*, 190.

Tāṇa Sutta.—The Buddha preaches the Refuge and the way thereto.[1]

[1] S. iv. 372.

Tāpana.—See **Tapana.**

Tāpanā.—The younger sister of **Kapila** and **Sodhana,** in the time of **Kassapa Buddha.** Her mother was **Sādhanī.** They all entered the Order, but introduced dissension there. Kapila was reborn as a fish in the **Aciravatī** and Tāpanā was born in the **Mahāniraya.**[1]

[1] SNA. i. 305 f., 309; DhA. iv. 37, 39.

Tāmalitti (Tāmalitthi).—The port from which the branch of the Bodhi-tree was sent to Ceylon by **Asoka.**[1] It is said[2] that Asoka came from **Pāṭaliputta,** crossed the Ganges by boat, traversed the **Vinijhāṭavi,** and so arrived at Tāmalitti. It is identified with modern Tamluk, formerly on the estuary of the Ganges, but now on the western bank of the Rūpnārāyana. When Fa Hsien came to Ceylon, he embarked at Tāmluk.[3]

[1] Mhv. xi. 38; Dpv. iii. 33. [2] Sp. i. 90 f. [3] Giles: *op. cit.* p. 65.

Tāmalinda.—One of the four companions of **Chapaṭa** and a founder of the **Sīhalasaṅgha** in Burma.[1] He later founded a sect of his own.[2]

[1] Sās., p. 65. [2] Bode: *op. cit.* 24.

Tāyana.—A devaputta. He visited the Buddha at **Sāvatthi** and uttered certain verses in the hearing of the monks, telling of the necessity of following the recluse's calling with energy and sincerity. After his departure the Buddha asked the monks to learn the verses for their own good.[1]

The Commentary[2] says that he was once a dissentient teacher, like **Nanda, Vaccha, Kisa, Saṅkicca,** etc., and taught some of the sixty-two views enumerated in the **Brahmajāla Sutta.** By the power of good deeds and by believing in Kamma, he was reborn in the heavens. Discerning from there that at length a really saving Dhamma and Order had been founded, he came to incite the Buddha's disciples.

[1] S. i. 49. [2] SA. i. 85.

Tāyana Sutta.—Records the visit of **Tāyana** (*q.v.*) to the Buddha.

Tārukkha.—One of the most eminent Mahāsāla brahmins, contemporary of the Buddha. He was present at the assemblies of the brahmins in **Icchānaṅgala** and in **Manasākaṭa.** He was the teacher of **Bhāradvāja,** companion of **Vāseṭṭha.**[1]

[1] SN., p. 115 f.; SNA. i. 372; ii. 462; D. i. 235; M. ii. 202.

Tālakkhettagāma.—A village in the **Malaya** district of Ceylon.[1]

[1] Cv. lxx. 10.

Tālaggallakavāpi.—A tank in Ceylon repaired by **Parakkamabāhu I.**[1]

[1] Cv. lxxix. 66.

Tālacchiggalūpama Sutta.—It is said that, after hearing this sutta, **Abhayarājakumāra** became a Sotāpanna.[1] The sutta is probably that of the turtle and the floating trap.[2]

[1] ThagA. i. 83. [2] *Cp.* M. iii. 169, and **Chiggala Sutta,** S. v. 455.

Tālapiṭṭhika-vihāra.—A monastery in Ceylon, where **Gopakasīvalī** built a cetiya.[1]

[1] VibhA. p. 156.

Tālapuṭa, Talapuṭa.—A *naṭagāmaṇi* (stage-manager) of **Rājagaha.** With a company of five hundred men, he gave dramatic performances of great splendour in towns and villages and in royal courts, and won much fame and favour. One day he visited the Buddha and asked if it was true that players who delight large audiences are reborn among the gods of laughter. Three times the Buddha refused to answer, but in the end allowed himself to be persuaded, and told Tālapuṭa that those who induce sensual states in others will be reborn in purgatory. Tālapuṭa wept to think that older actors should so have deceived him in telling him of their theories, and, having heard the Buddha preach, entered the Order and soon became an arahant.[1]

The Saṃyutta Commentary[2] says he obtained his name from his bright and cheerful colour, like that of a ripe palm-fruit.

[1] S. iv. 306 ff.; Thag. 1091-1145; ThagA. ii. 155 ff. [2] SA. iii. 100.

Tālaphaliya Thera.—An arahant. Ninety-four kappas ago he saw the Pacceka Buddha **Sataraṃsī** and gave him a palm-fruit.[1] He is probably identical with **Sambulakaccāyana.**[2]

[1] Ap. ii. 447. [2] ThagA. i. 314.

Tālavaṇṭadāyaka Thera.—An arahant. Ninety-two kappas ago he gave a fan made of palm leaf to the Buddha **Tissa.** Sixty-three kappas ago he became king several times under the name of **Mahārāma.**[1]

[1] Ap. i. 211.

Tālavatthu-vihāra.—A monastery in Ceylon. It was restored by **Aggabodhi V.,** who also gave to it the village of **Paṇṇabhatta.** He appears to have renamed the village **Mahāsena,** probably after its original founder.[1]

[1] Cv. xlviii. 8; Cv. *Trs.* i. 111, n. 1.

Tālavana.—See **Nāḷapana.**

Tāḷayūrunāḍu.—A district in South India.[1]

[1] Cv. lxxvi. 261.

Tāḷavelimagga.—A road lying between **Mahāgāma** and **Anurādhapura.** On this road lived the mother of **Tissa** the minister (see **Tissa** 2), and it is said that she threw down into the street a cloth worth one hundred, which had been used in her confinement.[1]

[1] Vsm. p. 63; *Path of Purity,* i. 70, n. 1.

Tālipabbata.—The brahmin who accompanied **Mahā Ariṭṭha** on his embassy from Ceylon to the court of **Asoka.**[1]

[1] MṬ. 302.

Tālissara.—A descendant of King **Dīpaṅkara,** who ruled in **Takkasilā.**[1]

[1] Dpv. iii. 32.

Tāvatiṃsa.—The second of the six deva-worlds, the first being the **Cātummahārājika** world. Tāvatiṃsa stands at the top of Mount **Sineru** (or **Sudassana). Sakka** is king of both worlds, but lives in Tāvatiṃsa. Originally it was the abode of the **Asuras** (*q.v.*); but when **Māgha** was born as Sakka and dwelt with his companions in Tāvatiṃsa he disliked the idea of sharing his realm with the Asuras, and, having made them intoxicated, he hurled them down to the foot of Sineru, where the **Asurabhavana** was later established. The chief difference between these two worlds seems to have been that the **Päricchattaka** tree grew in Tāvatiṃsa, and the **Cittapāṭali** tree in Asurabhavana. In order that the Asuras should not enter Tāvatiṃsa, Sakka had five walls built around it, and these were guarded by Nāgas, Supaṇṇas, Kumbhaṇḍas, Yakkhas and Cātummahārājika devas.[1] The entrance to Tāvatiṃsa was by way of the **Cittakūṭadvārakoṭṭhaka,** on either side of which statues of Indra (*Indapaṭimā*) kept guard.[2] The whole kingdom was ten thousand leagues in extent,[3] and contained more than one thousand *pāsādas*.[4] The chief features of Tāvatiṃsa were its parks—the **Phārusaka, Cittalatā, Missaka** and **Nandana**—the **Vejayantapāsāda,** the **Pāricchatta** tree, the elephant-king **Erāvaṇa** and the Assembly-hall **Sudhammā.**[5] Mention is also made of a park called **Nandā.**[6] Besides the **Pāricchataka** (or **Pārijāta**) flower, which is described as a **Kovilāra,**[7] the divine **Kakkāru** flower also grew in Tāvatiṃsa.[8] In the Cittalatāvana grows the **Āsāvatī** creeper, which blossoms once in a thousand years.[9]

It is the custom of all Buddhas to spend the *vassa* following the performance of the **Yamakapāṭihāriya,** in Tāvatiṃsa. Gotama Buddha went there to preach the Abhidhamma to his mother, born there as a devaputta. The distance of sixty-eight thousand leagues from the earth to Tāvatiṃsa he covered in three strides, placing his foot once on **Yugandhara** and again on **Sineru.**

The Buddha spent three months in Tāvatiṃsa, preaching all the time, seated on Sakka's throne, the **Paṇḍukambalasilāsana,** at the foot of the Pāricchattaka tree. Eighty crores of devas attained to a knowledge of the truth. This was in the seventh year after his Enlightenment.[10] It

[1] J. i. 201 ff.; also DhA. i. 272 f.
[2] J. vi. 97.
[3] DhA. i. 273.
[4] J. vi. 279.
[5] J. vi. 278; MA. i. 183; *cp.* Mtu. i. 32; for details of these see *s.v.*
[6] J. i. 204.
[7] A. iv. 117.
[8] J. iii. 87.
[9] J. iii. 250 f.
[10] J. iv. 265; DhA. iii. 216 f.; BuA. p. 3.

seems to have been the frequent custom of ascetics, possessed of iddhi-power, to spend the afternoon in Tāvatiṃsa.[11]

Moggallāna paid numerous visits to Tāvatiṃsa, where he learnt from those dwelling there stories of their past deeds, that he might repeat them to men on earth for their edification.[12]

The Jātaka Commentary mentions several human beings who were invited by Sakka, and who were conveyed to Tāvatiṃsa—*e.g.* **Nimi, Guttila, Mandhātā** and the queen **Sīlavatī.**[13] Mandhāta reigned as co-ruler of Tāvatiṃsa during the life period of thirty-six Sakkas, sixty thousand years.[14] The inhabitants of Tāvatiṃsa are thirty-three in number, and they regularly meet in the **Sudhammā** Hall.[15] A description of such an assembly is found in the **Janavasabha Sutta**. The Cātummahārājika Devas (*q.v.*) are present to act as guards. Inhabitants of other deva- and brahma-worlds seemed sometimes to have been present as guests—*e.g.* the Brahmā **Sanaṅkumāra**, who came in the guise of **Pañcasikha**. From the description given in the sutta, all the inhabitants of Tāvatiṃsa seem to have been followers of the Buddha, deeply devoted to his teachings.[16] Their chief place of offering was the **Cūḷāmaṇicetiya,** in which Sakka deposited the hair of Prince Siddhattha, cut off by him when he renounced the world and put on the garments of a recluse on the banks of the **Nerañjarā**.[17] Later, Sakka deposited here also the eyetooth of the Buddha, which **Doṇa** hid in his turban, hoping to keep it for himself.[18]

The gods of Tāvatiṃsa sometimes come to earth to take part in human festivities.[19] Thus Sakka, **Vissakamma** and **Mātali** are mentioned as having visited the earth on various occasions.[20] Mention is also made of goddesses from Tāvatiṃsa coming to bathe in the **Anotatta** and then spending the rest of the day on the **Manosilātala**.[21]

The capital city of **Tāvatiṃsa** was **Masakkasāra**.[22] The average age of an inhabitant of Tāvatiṃsa is thirty million years, reckoned by human computation. Each day in Tāvatiṃsa is equal in time to one hundred years on earth.[23] The gods of Tāvatiṃsa are most handsome; the **Licchavis,** among earth-dwellers, are compared to them.[24] The stature of some of the Tāvatiṃsa dwellers is three-quarters of a league; their undergarment is a robe of twelve leagues and their upper garment also a robe of twelve leagues. They live in mansions of gold, thirty leagues in extent.[25] The Commentaries[26] say that Tāvatiṃsa was named after **Magha** and his

[11] *E.g.*, **Nārada** (J. vi. 392); and **Kāḷadevala** (J. i. 54).
[12] VvA. p. 4.
[13] For details see *s.v.*
[14] J. ii. 312.
[15] See *s.v.* **Sudhammā** for details.
[16] D. ii. 207 ff.
[17] J. i. 65.
[18] DA. ii. 609; Bu. xxviii. 6, 10.
[19] J. iii. 87.
[20] See *s.v.*
[21] J. v. 392.
[22] *Ibid.*, p. 400.
[23] DhA. i. 364.
[24] *Ibid.*, iii. 280.
[25] *Ibid.*, p. 8.
[26] *E.g.*, SA. i. 23; AA. i. 377.

thirty-two companions, who were born there as a result of their good deeds in **Macalagāma.** Whether the number of the chief inhabitants of this world always remained at thirty-three, it is impossible to say, though some passages, *e.g.* in the Janavasabha Sutta, lead us to suppose so.

Sometimes, as in the case of **Nandiya,** who built the great monastery at **Isipatana,** a mansion would appear in Tāvatiṃsa, when an earth-dweller did a good deed capable of obtaining for him birth in this deva-world; but this mansion would remain unoccupied till his human life came to an end.[27] There were evidently no female devas among the Thirty-three. Both **Māyā** and **Gopikā** (*q.v.*) became devaputtas when born in Tāvatiṃsa. The women there were probably the attendants of the devas.[28]

There were many others besides the Thirty-three who had their abode in Tāvatiṃsa. Each deva had numerous retinues of attendants, and the dove-footed (*kakuṭapādiniyo*) nymphs (*accharā*) of Tāvatiṃsa are famous in literature for their delicate beauty. The sight of these made **Nanda,** when escorted by the Buddha to Tāvatiṃsa, renounce his love for **Janapada-kalyāṇī Nandā.**[29]

The people of **Jambudīpa** excelled the devas of Tāvatiṃsa in courage, mindfulness and piety.[30] Among the great achievements of **Asadisakumāra** was the shooting of an arrow as far as Tāvatiṃsa.[31]

Tāvatiṃsa was also known as **Tidasa** and **Tidiva** (*q.v.*).

[27] DhA. iii. 291.
[28] But see, *e.g.*, **Jālinī** and the various stories of VvA.
[29] J. ii. 92; Ud. iii. 2.
[30] A. iv. 396.
[31] J. ii. 89.

Timsamatta Sutta.—Thirty monks from **Pāvā** (described as **Pāveyyakā**), all forest-dwellers, visit the Buddha at **Rājagaha.** By means of various similes the Buddha tells them of the infiniteness of *saṃsāra*, and at the end of the sermon they become arahants.[1] The Dhammapada Commentary[2] evidently refers to the same monks, but there it is stated that the Buddha first preached to them in the **Kappāsikavanasaṇḍa** while they were searching for a woman. We seem here to have a confusion of legends. *cp.* the **Bhaddavaggiyas.**

[1] S. ii. 187 f.
[2] DhA. ii. 32 f.

Ti-ukkādhāriya Thera.—An arahant. Once in the past he lit three torches, which he stood holding, at the foot of the Bodhi-tree of **Padumuttara Buddha.**[1]

[1] Ap. ii. 404.

1. **Ti-uppalamāliya Thera.**—An arahant. In the time of **Vipassī** Buddha, he was a monkey on the banks of the **Candabhāgā,** and, having seen the Buddha, he offered him three lotuses. Shortly afterwards he fell from a rock, died, and was reborn in heaven.[1]

[1] Ap. i. 277.

2. **Ti-uppalamāliya Thera.**—An arahant. The same as (1), except that, in this case, the Buddha was **Phussa.**[1]

[1] Ap. i. 291.

Ti-kaṇikārapupphiya Thera.—An arahant. He was once a *vijjādhara*, and, having seen the Buddha **Sumedha** flying through the air, offered him three flowers which remained suspended above the Buddha's head. He was reborn as a deva in a palace in **Tāvatiṃsa** called **Kaṇikāra.**[1] He is probably identical with **Uttara Thera.**[2]

[1] Ap. ii. 441 ff. [2] ThagA. i. 241.

Ti-kiṅkinipupphiya Thera.—An arahant. Ninety-one kappas ago he gave three *kiṅkini*-flowers to **Vipassī** Buddha.[1] He is probably identical with **Cittaka Thera.**[2]

[1] Ap. ii. 433. [2] ThagA. i. 78.

Ti-campakapupphiya Thera.—An arahant. In a previous birth, ninety-one kappas ago, he saw a holy recluse under the mountain **Vikaṭa,** near Himavā, and offered him three *campaka*-flowers.[1]

[1] Ap. i. 227.

Ti-padumiya Thera.—An arahant. In the time of **Padumuttara** Buddha he was garland-maker to the king, and, seeing the Buddha, while on his way to the palace, he threw up into the air three lotuses, which formed a canopy over the Buddha. Ti-padumiya was reborn as a deva, and owned a palace called **Mahāvitthārika,** which was three hundred leagues high.[1]

[1] Ap. i. 124 ff.

Ti-saraṇāgamaniya Thera.—An arahant. In the time of **Vipassī** Buddha he was a householder in **Bandhumatī,** where he tended his blind parents. Being prevented by his parents' affliction from joining the Order, he repeated the Three Refuges under a monk, named **Nisabha,** and honoured them throughout his life of one hundred thousand years. He was eighty times born as king of the gods. In this last life he was born in a rich family in **Sāvatthi,** and, having heard the Buddha preach, became an arahant at the age of seventy-seven.[1]

[1] Ap. i. 74 f.

Tika Vagga.—The eleventh chapter of the *Chakka Nipāta* of the Aṅguttara Nikāya.[1]

[1] A. iii. 445-9.

Tikaṇṭaki Vagga.—The fifteenth chapter of the *Pañcaka Nipāta* of the Aṅguttara Nikāya.[1] *v.l.* **Tikaṇḍaki Vagga.**

[1] A. iii. 164-74.

Tikaṇṭaki Sutta.—Preached at **Tikaṇṭakivana,** on the five ways in which a monk gains poise and equanimity, being rid of both that is distasteful and that is not.[1]

[1] A. iii. 169 f.

Tikaṇṭakivana.—A grove in **Sāketa,** evidently identical with **Kaṇṭakivana** (*q.v.*).

Tikaṇḍakivana.—See **Tikaṇṭakivana.**

Tikaṇḍipupphiya Thera.—An arahant. In a previous birth he saw the Buddha **Sumaṅgala** in a grove and offered him a *tikaṇḍi* flower. Forty-six kappas ago he was a king named **Apilāpiya.**[1]

[1] Ap. i. 201 f.

Tikaṇṇa.—A brahmin. He once visited the Buddha and spoke in praise of *tevijja* brahmins. The Buddha explained to him that the threefold lore of the Ariyan disciple was a different and a far nobler thing. The brahmin accepted the Buddha as his teacher.[1]

[1] A. i. 164 f.; *cp.* D. i. 73 ff.

Tikaṇṇa Sutta.—Records the visit of **Tikaṇṇa** (*q.v.*) to the Buddha.

Tikaṇṇipupphiya.—An arahant thera. Ninety-one kappas ago he was born in heaven, and realising that this was due to the Buddha's teaching, he offered a flower in the name of **Vipassī** Buddha. Seventy-three kappas ago he became king four times under the name of **Naruttama.**[1]

[1] Ap. i. 195.

Tikicchaka Thera.—An arahant. In a previous birth he was a physician of **Bandhumatī,** and cured **Asoka,** the attendant of **Vipassī** Buddha. Eight kappas ago he was king under the name of **Sabbosadha.**[1] He is evidently identical with **Tekicchakāni Thera.**[2]

[1] Ap. i. 190. [2] ThagA. i. 442.

Tikicchā Sutta.—On emetics administered by physicians and the corresponding emetics in the discipline of the Ariyans.[1]

[1] A. v. 218 f.

Tikūṭa.—A river in **Himavā,** the resort of the **Kinnaras.**[1]

[1] J. iv. 438, 439.

Tikoṇamālatittha.—The Pāli name for Trincomali in Ceylon.[1]

[1] Cv. c. 76.

Tikhiṇamantī.—Brother of **Cūḷanī-Brahmadatta.** He was born while his mother, **Talatā,** was living with the brahmin **Chambhī,** after having killed **Mahācūḷanī.** On discovering his real parentage, he killed Chambī, and, having taken the throne, sent for his brother, Cūḷanī, who was then in exile, and crowned him king.[1] It is said[2] that, later, Cūḷanī was displeased because Tikhiṇamantī ceased to attend at the palace.

[1] J. vi. 469, 473. [2] *Ibid.,* 474.

Tiṇakaṭṭha Sutta.—Incalculable is the beginning of *saṃsāra*. If a man were to collect all the grasses and twigs of **Jambudīpa,** the number of his mothers would surpass them.[1]

[1] S. ii. 178.

Tiṇakuṭidāyaka Thera.—An arahant. Ninety-one kappas ago he was a servant, and, having been granted a day's leave by his master, he built for the Saṅgha a grass hut. As a result, he was born in **Tāvatiṃsa** after death.[1]

[1] Ap. i. 270 f.

Tiṇamuṭṭhidāyaka Thera.—An arahant. Ninety-four kappas ago he was a hunter., One day, seeing the Buddha **Tissa** (*v.l.* **Upatissa**) in the forest near **Lambaka,** he gave him a handful of grass for a seat. He was soon afterwards killed by a lion and was born in the deva-world.[1] The same story is given elsewhere[2] in somewhat different words.

This Elder is evidently to be identified with **Posiya Thera.**[3]

[1] A. i. 280 f. [2] *Ibid.*, ii. 454 f. [3] ThagA. i. 97.

Tiṇasanthāraka.—Five kappas ago there were seven kings of this name, all previous births of **Senāsanadāyaka** (or **Channa**) **Thera.**[1]

[1] Ap. i. 137; ThagA. i. 155.

Tiṇasanthāradāyaka Thera.—An arahant. In a previous birth he was a hermit living near a lake in **Himavā.** One day he saw the Buddha **Tissa** and offered him a seat of grass. He was later born among the **Nimmānarati** gods. Two kappas ago he was a king, named **Migasammata.**[1]

[1] Ap. i. 121 f.

Tiṇa-Sākiyā.—The name given to those **Sākiyans** who held reeds in their mouths in order to escape slaughter when **Viḍūḍabha** massacred the **Sākiyans.**[1]

[1] For details see DhA. i. 359.

Tiṇasūlaka Thera.—An arahant. Many kappas ago he was a householder, and, seeing a Pacceka Buddha on **Bhūtagaṇa** Mountain, offered him a *Tiṇasūla* flower. Eleven kappas ago he was a king named **Dharaṇīruha.**[1] He is evidently identical with **Dhammāsavapitu Thera.**[2]

[1] Ap. i. 179. [2] ThagA. i. 215 f.

Tiṇasūlakachādaniya Thera.—An arahant. Ninety-two kappas ago he was an ascetic on the banks of the Ganges, and meeting **Tissa** Buddha he offered him *nāga* and *tiṇasūla* flowers. He was king of the gods twenty-five times.[1]

[1] Ap. ii. 370 f.

Tiṇḍuka Jātaka.—See **Tinduka Jātaka.**

1. **Tittira Jātaka** (No. 37).—There were once three friends, a partridge (*tittira*), a monkey and an elephant. Discovering that the partridge was

the oldest of them, they honoured him as their teacher and he gave them counsel. Their conduct came to be called the **Tittiriya-brahmacariya.**

The Bodhisatta was the partridge, **Moggallāna** the elephant, and **Sāriputta** the monkey. The story was related in reference to the failure of the **Chabbaggiyas** to show due respect to Sāriputta. Once, when he visited them in company with the Buddha, they refused to provide him with lodging, and he had to sleep under a tree.[1]

[1] J. i. 217 ff.; *cp.* Vin. ii. 161; Avadāna Ś. ii. 17.

2. **Tittira Jātaka** (No. 117).—The Bodhisatta was once a leader of five hundred ascetics. One day, a talkative ascetic approached a jaundiced colleague who was chopping wood and worried him by giving him directions on how to do it. The ill man killed him with one blow of the axe. Soon after, a partridge, who used to sing on an anthill near by, was killed by a fowler. The Bodhisatta pointed out to his followers how the death of both was due to their talking too much.

The story was told in reference to **Kokalika,** who is identified with the chattering ascetic.[1]

[1] J. i. 431 f.

3. **Tittira Jātaka** (No. 319).—Once the Bodhisatta was a brahmin ascetic, and **Rāhula** a decoy partridge used by a village fowler. When the partridge uttered a cry, other partridges would flock to him, and they were killed by the fowler. The partridge was filled with remorse, fearing that he was doing wrong. One day he met the Bodhisatta who set his doubts at rest. The story was told in reference to Rāhula's readiness to profit by instruction.[1] It was related by **Moggaliputta-Tissa** to **Asoka,** to prove to him that an action becomes a crime only when performed with bad intention.[2]

[1] J. iii. 64 ff. [2] Mhv. v. 264.

4. **Tittira Jātaka** (No. 438).—Once in Benares was a famous teacher who retired into the forest. Men came from all parts to learn from him and brought him many presents. He had in his house a tame partridge, who, by listening to the teacher's exposition, learnt the three Vedas by heart. A tame lizard and a cow were given as presents to the teacher. When the teacher died, his students were in despair, but were reassured by the partridge who taught them what he knew. One day a wicked ascetic came to the hermitage and, in the absence of the students, killed the partridge,

the young lizard and the cow. The partridge had two friends, a lion and a tiger, who killed the murderer.

The ascetic was **Devadatta,** the lizard **Kisāgotamī,** the tiger **Moggallāna,** the lion **Sāriputta,** the teacher **Mahā Kassapa,** and the partridge the Bodhisatta. The story was related in reference to Devadatta's attempts to kill the Buddha.[1]

[1] J. iii. 536 f.

Tittiriya-paṇḍita.—The name given to the partridge of the **Tittira Jātaka**[1] (No. 11).

[1] J. iii. 537.

Tittiriya-brahmacariya.—See **Tittira Jātaka** (1). It consisted of observing the five precepts.[1]

[1] MA. i. 275.

Tittiriyābrāhmaṇā.—The Pāli equivalent of the Sanskrit Taittirīyā.[1]

[1] D. i. 237.

Tittha Jātaka (No. 25).—The Bodhisatta was once adviser to the king of Benares. One day, another horse was washed in the place reserved for the king's state charger, who, when taken there to bathe, refused to enter. The Bodhisatta, divining the reason, directed that the horse should be taken elsewhere, and not always bathed in the same spot, adding that a man will tire even of the daintiest food, if it never be changed. The Bodhisatta was amply rewarded for his skill in reading the horse's thoughts. The story was told in reference to a monk, a disciple of **Sāriputta.** He had been a goldsmith and the meditation on impurity, prescribed for him by Sāriputta, proved impossible for him. He was taken to see the Buddha, who asked him to gaze at a lotus in a pond near by. The monk saw the lotus fade and, developing insight, became an arahant. He marvelled at the Buddha's power of reading the thoughts and temperaments of others. The monk is identified with the state charger and **Ānanda** with the king.[1]

[1] J. i. 182 ff.

Tittha Sutta.—The Buddha examines the three beliefs held by those of other sects—that whatever is experienced is due to past action, or is the creation of a supreme deity, or is uncaused and unconditioned.[1]

[1] A. i. 173 ff.

Titthaka.—An **Ājīvaka** who gave *kusa* grass to **Phussa** Buddha before his Enlightenment.[1]

[1] BuA. 147.

Titthagāma.—A village, in the south-west of Ceylon,[1] where **Parakkamabāhu I.** established a coconut plantation.[2]

[1] Cv. lxxii. 42. [2] *Ibid.*, xc. 93.

Titthagāma-vihāra.—A vihāra in **Titthagāma,** the modern Toṭagamuva. It was erected by **Vijayabāhu IV.** and restored by **Parakkamabāhu IV.**[1]

[1] Cv. xc. 88; Cv. *Trs.* ii. 208, n. 2.

Titthamba.—A Damiḷa general of **Ambatitthaka,** who was conquered by **Duṭṭhagāmaṇi** after a four months' siege.[1] Duṭṭhagāmaṇi deceived Titthamba by promising to give him his mother in marriage.

[1] Mhv. xxv. 8; MṬ. 473.

Titthārāma.—A monastery built by **Paṇḍukābhaya** for the use of non-Buddhist monks. It was near the Nīcasusāna in **Anurādhapura. Vaṭṭagāmaṇi** demolished it and built on its site the **Abhayagiri-vihāra.**[1]

[1] Mhv. xxxiii. 42, 83.

Titthiyārāma.—A monastery of the heretics, near **Jetavana.**[1]

[1] J. ii. 415, 416; iv. 187, 188; ThigA. p. 68.

Tidasa.—A name given to **Tāvatiṃsa,** the inhabitants being called **Tidasā.**[1] The **Tidasa** devas are spoken of as being full of glory.[2]

[1] J. iii. 357, 413; vi. 168; v. 20, 390. [2] S. i. 234.

Tidiva.—A name given to **Tāvatiṃsa.**[1] See also **Tirīṭavaccha** (3).

[1] J. iv. 322, 450; v. 14, 15.

Tidivādhibhū.—A name given to **Sakka** (*q.v.*).

Tintasīsakola.—A region, thirty leagues in extent, near the spot where the stream from the **Anotatta** falls from a height of sixty leagues. The soil, being constantly sprinkled by the drops of water, is extremely soft and plastic and clay was obtained from there for the building of the **Mahā Thūpa.**[1]

[1] MṬ. 515.

Tintiṇika.—A village granted by **Mahānāga** to the **Mahāvihāra.**[1] It was once the headquarters of **Dāṭhāsiva.**[2] It evidently contained a tank which was restored by **Parakkamabāhu I.**[3]

[1] Cv. xli. 96. [2] *Ibid.*, xliv. 125. [3] *Ibid.*, lxviii. 47.

Tinduka.—A watcher of corn (*yavapālaka*), who gave grass for his seat to **Koṇāgamana** Buddha.[1]

[1] BuA. 214.

Tinduka Jātaka (No. 177).—The Bodhisatta was once the leader of eighty thousand monkeys. Near their dwelling place was a village where grew a *tinduka* tree, whose sweet fruits were eaten by the monkeys. But the people came and built a village near the tree and the monkeys could no longer take the fruit. One night, when the villagers were asleep, they crept up to the tree and began eating the fruit. A villager gave the alarm and the monkeys were in great danger of being slain when dawn came. But the Bodhisatta comforted them and kept them in good humour until they were rescued by his nephew, **Senaka,** who set fire to the village, distracting the attention of the people, thus allowing the monkeys to escape. The story was related in illustration of the Bodhisatta's sagacity.[1] Senaka is identified with **Mahānāma** the Sākyan. *v.l.* **Tiṇḍuka.**

[1] J. ii. 76 f.

Tindukakandarā.—A cave outside **Rājagaha** where lodgings were provided for visiting monks.[1]

[1] Vin. ii. 76; iii. 159.

Tindukadāyaka Thera.—An arahant. Ninety-four kappas ago he was a monkey who saw **Siddhattha** Buddha and gave him and his monks *tinduka* fruits to eat. Fifty-seven kappas ago he became king, under the name of **Upananda.**[1]

[1] Ap. i. 200 f.

Tindukaphaladāyaka Thera.—An arahant. Ninety-one kappas ago he saw the Buddha **Vessabhū** and gave him *tinduka* fruit to eat.[1]

[1] Ap. i. 281.

Tindukkhānu-paribbājakārāma.—A dwelling of **Paribbājakas,** near **Vesāli.** It was the residence of **Pāṭhikaputta.**[1]

[1] D. iii. 17.

Tipa.—A **Vanni** chieftain of Ceylon, subdued by **Bhuvanekabāhu I.**[1]

[1] Cv. xc. 33.

Tipallatthamiga Jātaka (No. 16).—Once the Bodhisatta was born as a stag, leader of a herd of deer. **Rāhula** was his sister's son and was entrusted to him, that he might learn the "deer's tricks." The young stag followed his instruction diligently and one day, being caught in a net, he feigned death and so made his escape.

The story was told in reference to Rāhula. Once, at the **Aggāḷavacetiya,** the Buddha, noticing that monks were in the habit of sleeping with novices in the preaching-hall after the sermon, he passed a rule making this a *pācittiya*-offence. As a result, Rāhula could find no lodging and spent the night in the Buddha's jakes, not wishing to transgress the rule. The Buddha, discovering this, assembled the monks and blamed them for their thoughtlessness, for if they thus treated his son, what might they not do to the other novices. The rule about lodgings was thereupon modified. The story was related to show Rāhula's diligence in following rules.[1]

The Jātaka seems also to have been called the **Sikkhākāma Jātaka.**[2]

[1] J. i. 160 ff.; *cp.* Vin. iv. 16.

[2] JA. 1876, p. 516.

Tipiṭakālaṅkāra.—A monk of Prome in Burma. He enjoyed the patronage of **Surakitti,** king of Burma, but for a time lived in retreat in **Tiriyapabbata.** Among his works are the **Yasavaḍḍhanavatthu** and the **Vinayālaṅkāraṭīkā.**[1]

[1] Sās., p. 106; Bode: *op. cit.* 53 f.

Tipucullasa.—See **Tīsucullasa.**

Tiputthulla-vihāra.—A monastery built by **Dāṭhopatissa II.** as an extension to the **Abhayagirivihāra.** The **Theravādins** objected to it, as the grounds lay within their boundary. The king refused to recognise their protest and the bhikkhus passed on him the *pattanikkujjana-kamma.*[1]

[1] Cv. xlv. 29 ff.

Tipupphiya Thera.—An arahant. In a previous birth he offered three flowers to the *Pāṭalī*, the Bodhi-tree or **Vipassī** Buddha. Thirty-three kappas ago he became king thirteen times under the name of **Samantapāsādika.**[1]

[1] Ap. i. 136.

Tibhuvanamalla, also called **Tilokamalla.**—Son of **Parakkamabāhu II.**[1] He was in command of the troops stationed between **Jambuddoṇi** and the Southern sea and he lived in **Mahāvatthalagāma.**[2]

[1] Cv. lxxxvii. 16. [2] *Ibid.*, lxxxviii. 20.

Timanda.—A monster fish of the deep sea, five hundred leagues in length. He eats only seaweed.[1]

[1] J. v. 462.

Timitimiṅgala.—A fish, one thousand leagues long, living in the deep ocean and feeding on seaweed.[1]

[1] J. v. 462; NidA. 211.

Timirapiṅgala.—A fish of the deep sea. He is one thousand leagues long and eats only seaweed.[1]

[1] J. v. 462.

1. **Timirapupphiya Thera.**—An arahant. He was once an ascetic and while walking one day along the banks of the river **Candabhāgā,** saw the Buddha **Siddhattha** and scattered over him *timira* flowers, paying him homage. Soon afterwards he was killed by a lion.[1]

[1] Ap. i. 126 f.

2. **Timirapupphiya Thera.**—An arahant. Ninety-one kappas ago he saw a Pacceka Buddha walking along the **Candabhāgā** and offered him a *timira* flower.[1]

[1] Ap. i. 288 f.

Timbaru.—A chieftain of the **Gandhabbas** and father of **Suriyavaccasā.**[1] He was present at the **Mahāsamaya.**[2]

[1] D. ii. 266, 268; see also MṬ. 576.
[2] D. ii. 258; see Hopkins: *Epic Mythology, s.v.* Tumburu.

Timbaruka.—A **Paribbājaka** who visited the Buddha at **Sāvatthi** and discussed with him the origin of pleasure and pain. The Buddha explained to him how ignorance was at the root of all conditioned existence. It it said that Timbaruka became a follower of the Buddha.[1]

[1] S. ii. 20 f.

Timbaruka Sutta.—Records the visit of **Timbaruka** (*q.v.*) to the Buddha.

Timbarutittha.—A pond at which sacrifices were offered.[1]

[1] J. v. 388, 389.

Tiyaggala.—A lake in **Himavā.**[1] The river flowing from the eastern side of **Anotatta,** after having travelled along a rocky bed for sixty leagues, falls through the air for a distance of sixty leagues, on to the rock Tiyaggala. The column of water is three gāvutas in width and, as a result of the impact, the rock is hollowed out into a lake, the **Tiyaggalapokkharaṇī,** fifty leagues wide.[2]

[1] J. v. 415; DA. i. 164. [2] SNA. ii. 439; AA. ii. 760; UdA. 302, etc.

Tiraṃsiya Thera.—An arahant. In a previous birth he was a hermit. He saw the Buddha **Siddhattha** and spoke verses in praise of him, extolling his lustre as surpassing that of the sun and of the moon. Sixty-one kappas ago he was a king named **Ñāṇadhara.**[1]

[1] Ap. i. 256 f.

Tiracchikā.—A Nāga maiden, sister of **Mahodara.** Her son was **Cūḷodara.**[1]

[1] MṬ. 104.

Tirikkāṇappera.—A locality in South India.[1]

[1] Cv. lxxvi. 302; lxxvii. 72, 82.

Tiriṇaveli.—A district in South India.[1]

[1] Cv. lxxvi. 143, 288; lxxvii. 42, 91.

Tirippāḷuru.—A locality in South India.[1]

[1] Cv. lxxvi. 309, 312.

Tiriputtūru.—A place in South India.[1]

[1] Cv. lxxvii. 16, 20.

Tirimalakka.—A village in South India.[1]

[1] Cv. lxxvii. 51, 52.

Tirivekambama.—A place in South India.[1]

[1] Cv. lxxvi. 238, 266, 276.

1. **Tirīṭavaccha.**—The Bodhisatta born as a brahmin in **Kāsi.** See the **Titīṭavaccha Jātaka.**

2. **Tirīṭavaccha.**—A seṭṭhi of **Ariṭṭhapura,** father of **Ummadantī.**[1] He is also called **Tirīṭi°.**[2]

[1] J. v. 210, 211. [2] *Ibid.*, 215; ThigA. i. 192.

3. **Tirīṭavaccha.**—A brahmin, purohita of **Candappajjota** and father of **Mahā Kaccāna.** His wife was **Candapadūmā.**[1] *v.l.* **Tidivavaccha.**

[1] Ap. ii. 465; ThagA. i. 485.

Tirīṭavaccha Jātaka (No. 259).—Once the Bodhisatta was a brahmin in **Kāsi** named **Tirīṭavaccha** and after the death of his parents he became an ascetic. The king of Benares, fleeing from his enemies, arrived at Tirīṭavaccha's hermitage, riding on an elephant. Looking for water but finding none, he let himself down into the hermit's well but was unable to get out again; the hermit rescued him and showed him every hospitality. Later the hermit visited the king, now restored to the throne, and was given a dwelling place in the royal park. The courtiers were inclined to be jealous of the attentions paid to the hermit, but the king told them of the incident in the forest and they acknowledged the hermit's claim to honour.

The story was told in reference to **Ānanda** having received five hundred robes from the women of **Pasenadi's** palace. *s.v.* **Ānanda.** The king is identified with Ānanda.[1]

[1] J. ii. 314 ff.

Tirīṭavacchagāma.—See **Milinda.**

Tirīṭivaccha.—See **Tirīṭavaccha** (2).

Tirokuḍḍa Sutta.—One of the five suttas included in the **Khuddakapāṭha.** Departed spirits haunt their old dwelling places and their compassionate kinsmen should bestow on them in due time, food, drink, etc. and also give gifts to the monks in their name. Thus will they be happy.[1] The Sutta was preached on the third day of the Buddha's visit to **Rājagaha.** On the previous night, **Petas** had made a great uproar in **Bimbisāra's** palace. In the time of **Phussa** Buddha, they had been workmen entrusted with the task of distributing alms to the Buddha and his monks, but they had been negligent in their duties and had appropriated some of the gifts for them-

[1] Khp., p. 6.

selves. As a result, they suffered for a long period in purgatory and became Petas in the time of **Kassapa** Buddha. Kassapa told them that in the future, **Bimbisāra,** who had once been their kinsman, would entertain the Buddha **Gotama** and make over the merit to them. They had long waited for this occasion and when Bimbisāra failed to fulfil their expectations, they made great outcry.

The Buddha explained this to Bimbisāra, who thereupon gave alms in the name of the Petas, thus making them happy. It was on this occasion that the Sutta was preached.[2]

[2] KhpA. 202 ff.; *cp.* PvA. 19 ff.

Tilagulla.—A village in the **Dakkhiṇadesa** of Ceylon. It is mentioned in the account of the campaigns of **Vijayabāhu I.**[1] Attached to it was a tank.[2]

[1] Cv. lviii. 43. [2] *Ibid.*, lxviii. 44; Cv. *Trs.* i. 206, n. 1.

Tilamuṭṭhi Jātaka (No. 252).—**Brahmadatta,** son of the king of Benares, was sent to **Takkasilā** to study. One day, when going to bathe with his teacher, he ate some white seeds which an old woman had spread in the sun to dry. He did this on three different days; on the third day the woman reported him to the teacher and he was beaten. When Brahmadatta ascended the throne, he sent for the teacher, wishing to avenge this insult by killing him. The teacher did not come until the king had grown older, but when he did arrive, the sight of him so rekindled the king's hatred, that he ordered him to be put to death. But the teacher spoke to him, telling him that if he had not been corrected in his youth, he would today be a highway robber. Convinced that the teacher's action had been due to a desire for his welfare, Brahmadatta asked his forgiveness and showed him all honour.

The story was told in reference to a monk who showed resentment when advised.[1]

[1] J. ii. 277-82.

Tilamuṭṭhidāyaka Thera.—An arahant. Ninety-one kappas ago he gave a handful of *tila* seeds to the Buddha, who, reading his thoughts, appeared before him in a mind-created body. Sixteen kappas ago he was a king named **Nandiya.**[1]

[1] Ap. i. 235.

Tilavatthu.—A canal which fed the **Maṇihīra** tank.[1]

[1] Cv. lx. 53.

Tilokanagara.—The residence of **Cūlasīva.**[1]

[1] So DA. (Hewavitarne edn.) ii. 641, but P.T.S. edn. (ii. 883) has **Lokuttara.**

Tilokanandana.—A garden laid out in **Pulatthipura** by **Parakkamabāhu I.**[1]

[1] Cv. lxxix. 8.

Tilokamalla.—See **Tibhuvanamalla.**

Tilokasundarī.—A **Kāliṅga** princess, the second queen of **Vijayabāhu I.** She later became his chief queen and had five daughters—**Subhaddā, Sumittā, Lokanāthā, Ratnāvalī** and **Rūpavatī**—and a son, **Vikkamabāhu.**[1]

[1] Cv. lix. 29.

Tivakka (Tavakka).—A village, administered by the brahmins of the same name. Here halted the procession bearing the Sacred Bodhi-tree from **Jambukola** to **Anurādhapura.** The brahmin, Tivakka, probably the head of the village, was present at the ceremony of the planting of the Bodhi-tree and later, one of the eight saplings from the tree was planted in the village.[1]

[1] Mhv. xix. 37, 54, 61; Mbv. p. 162; Sp. i. 100.

Tivaṅka.—An image, probably of the Buddha, installed in the **Tivaṅkaghara** in **Pulatthipura** by **Parakkamabāhu I.**[1] A similar image was found in the **Kalyāṇī-vihāra** which was restored by **Parakkamabāhu II.**[2]

[1] Cv. lxxviii. 39.
[2] *Ibid.*, lxxxv. 66; see Cv. *Trs.* ii. 105, n. 5.

Tivarā.—The name given to the inhabitants of Mount **Vepulla,** then known as **Pācīnavaṃsa,** near **Rājagaha,** in the time of **Kakusandha** Buddha. Their term of life was forty thousand years.[1]

[1] S. ii. 190.

Tisīhala.—See **Sīhala.**

1. **Tissa.**—The seventeenth of the twenty-four Buddhas. He was born in the **Anomā** pleasaunce in **Khemaka.** His father was **Janasandha** (*v.l.* **Saccasandha**) and his mother **Padumā.** He lived the household life for seven thousand years, in three palaces—**Guhāsala, Nārī (Nārisa)** and **Nisabha**—and left the world on a horse named **Soṇuttara.** For eight months he practised austerities and after a meal of milk rice given by the

daughter of **Virasetthi** of **Viragāma,** he sat on grass given by a *yavapālaka* named **Vijitasaṅgāma;** he attained Buddhahood under an *asana* tree. He preached his first sermon at **Yasavatī** to **Brahmadeva** and **Udaya** (**Udayana**) of **Haṃsavatī,** who later became his chief disciples. His attendant was **Samaṅga (Sambhava),** his chief patrons being **Sambala** and **Siri** among men and **Kisāgotamī** and **Upasenā** among women. His chief women disciples were **Phussā** and **Sudattā.** His body was sixty cubits high and after a life of one hundred thousand years he died at **Nandārāma (Sunandārāma)** in **Sunandavatī.** His body was cremated and a thūpa was erected three leagues in height.[1]

[1] Bu. xviii. 1 ff.; BuA. 188 ff.; J. i. 40.

2. **Tissa.**—The ninth future Buddha.[1]

[1] See Anāgasavaṃsa, p. 40.

3. **Tissa.**—One of the two chief disciples of **Vipassī** Buddha.[1] He was the son of the purohita **Bandhumatī,** and the Buddha's first sermon was preached to him and **Khaṇḍa.**[2]

[1] Bu. xx. 28; J. i. 41; D. ii. 4. [2] BuA. 196.

4. **Tissa.**—One of the two chief disciples of **Dīpaṅkara** Buddha.[1]

[1] Bu. ii. 213; J. i. 29; Mbv. 5.

5. **Tissa.**—An *aggasāvaka* of **Kassapa** Buddha. He was the Buddha's brother and, having renounced the household, became an ascetic. On hearing that Kassapa had become Buddha, he visited him but expressed great disappointment on discovering that he ate flesh food (*āmagandha*). The Buddha taught him that *āmagandha* was not really flesh but the *kilesas* which corrupt the heart, and he preached to him the **Āmagandha Sutta.** Tissa immediately entered the Order and became an *aggasāvaka.*[1] Tissa's father was born as **Subhadda** in this age.[2]

[1] Bu. xxv. 39; SNA. i. 280-2, 293; D. ii. 4. [2] Ap. i. 101.

6. **Tissa.**—A monk who was reborn as a **Brahmā** with great iddhi-powers. **Moggallāna** visited him soon after his birth in the Brahma-world and asked him questions about devas and Brahmas who were assured of salvation.[1] He was evidently the Tissa mentioned as being present at the **Mahāsamaya.**[2]

[1] A. iii. 331; iv. 75 ff. [2] D. ii. 261; DA. ii. 692.

7. **Tissa.**—A friend of **Metteyya.** They together visited the Buddha at **Jetavana** and, having listened to his teaching, entered the Order. Metteyya retired with his teacher into the forest and not long after became an arahant. Tissa lived in **Sāvatthi** and when his elder brother died, he went home and was persuaded by his relations to return to the lay life. Later, Metteyya, passing through the village with the Buddha, during a journey, visited Tissa and brought him once more to the Buddha. The Buddha preached to them the **Tissa-Metteyya Sutta,** at the end of which Tissa became a Sotāpanna, later attaining arahantship.[1]

[1] SN., p. 160 f.; SNA. ii. 535 f.; NidA. 184.

8. **Tissa.**—The personal name of **Metteyya,** friend of **Tissa** (7). **Metteyya** was his *gotta*-name by which he became known.[1] In the Sutta Nipāta[2] he is called **Tissa-Metteyya.**

[1] SNA. ii. 536; NidA. 184. [2] vs. 814.

9. **Tissa-Metteyya.**—A disciple of **Bāvarī.** He visited the Buddha with his colleagues and when the Buddha answered his questions, he, and his thousand pupils became arahants. Tissa was his personal name and Metteyya that of his clan.[1]

[1] SN., vs. 1040-2; SNA. ii. 588.

10. **Tissa.**—An Elder of **Sāvatthi.** He once received a length of coarse cloth as a gift and handed it to his sister to be made into a robe. She had the cloth pounded and spun into fine yarn and made of it a soft robe-cloth. At first Tissa would not accept it but was prevailed upon to do so and had it made into a soft robe by skilled robe-makers. He died on the night it was finished and, as a result of his fancy for it, was reborn as a louse in the robe. After his death, the monks wished to divide the robe but the louse started shouting. The Buddha, hearing this by his power of divine audience, asked the monks to lay the robe aside for seven days. At the end of that period, the louse was reborn in the **Tusita** world.[1]

[1] DhA. iii. 341 ff.

11. **Tissa.**—A monk. When the Buddha declared that in four months he would pass away, many monks were greatly excited, collecting in groups, not knowing what to do. But Tissa remained aloof, determined to win arahantship before the Buddha's death. The others, misunderstanding him, reported to the Buddha that Tissa had no love for him, but the Buddha, having questioned him, praised his earnestness.[1]

[1] DhA. iii. 267 f.

12. **Tissa Thera.**—An arahant. He belonged to a brahmin family of **Rājagaha** and, having attained great proficiency in the Vedas, became a teacher of five hundred young men. When the Buddha visited Rājagaha, Tissa was so struck by his majesty that he joined the Order, later winning arahantship. The Theragāthā contains verses uttered by him regarding certain monks who were jealous of his great renown.

In the time of **Piyadassī** Buddha, Tissa was an ascetic. Seeing the Buddha in *samādhi* in a forest-grove, he built over him an arbour of *sāla* flowers and for seven days paid him homage.[1]

He is evidently identical with **Sālamaṇḍapiya** of the Apadāna.[2]

[1] Thag. vv. 153-4; ThagA. i. 272 f. [2] ii. 431 f.

13. **Tissa.**—A rājā of **Roruva.** He was an "unseen" ally of **Bimbisāra** and, as such, sent him various gifts. The king sent him in return a painted panel on which was depicted the life of the Buddha and a gold plate specially inscribed with the *Paṭiccasamuppāda.* On seeing these, Tissa's mind was filled with agitation and, giving up his title, he came to **Rājagaha** as a monk and lived in the **Sappasoṇḍika** cave, from there visiting the Buddha, and soon afterwards becoming an arahant.

In the time of **Vipassī** Buddha he was a chariot-maker and gave the Buddha a stool made of sandalwood. Fifty-seven kappas ago he was four times king under the name of **Santa (Bhavanimmita)**.[1]. He is probably identical with **Phalakadāyaka** of the Apadāna.[2]

[1] Thag. 97; ThagA. i. 199 f. [2] i. 174.

14. **Tissa Thera.**—An arahant. Son of the Buddha's paternal aunt, **Amitā.** He entered the Order and dwelt in a woodland settlement, but he was proud of his rank and irritable and captious in his conduct. He once came to the Buddha in tears because his colleagues had teased him on account of his talkativeness.[1] On another occasion, the Buddha, with his celestial eye, saw Tissa sleeping with open mouth during the siesta and, sending a ray of glory, woke him. Tissa's heart was filled with anguish and when he confessed to his colleagues his mental laziness and distaste for religion, they brought him to the Buddha. The Buddha preached to him the **Tissa Sutta,** at the end of which he became an arahant.[2]

In the time of **Tissa** Buddha he swept the leaves from the foot of the Bodhi-tree. He is evidently identical with **Bodhisammajjaka** of the Apadāna.[3]

[1] S. ii. 282; MA. i. 289.
[2] Thag. v. 39; but see v. 1162; S. iii. 106 f.; ThagA. i. 105. [3] Ap. ii. 457 f.

The Dhammapada Commentary[4] calls him **Thullatissa.** He entered the Order when old and became fat through idleness. He spent most of his time in the Waiting-hall draped in rich robes. Monks, taking him for a *mahāthera*, begged the privilege of performing various services for him, such as massaging his feet. But when they discovered his attainments, they reviled him and he sought the Buddha. The Buddha, however, asked him to obtain their pardon for having failed to show them due honour, and when he refused, related to him the story of **Nārada** and **Devala.**

[4] i. 31 ff.

15. **Tissa.**—A novice. He was a gatekeeper's son and, coming with some carpenters to **Sāvatthi,** joined the Order. He was constantly finding fault with the food and other offerings, even those given by **Anāthapiṇḍika,** and he boasted of the riches enjoyed by his kinsfolk. His colleagues made enquiries and, discovering the truth about his antecedents, reported him to the Buddha who preached the **Kaṭāhaka Jātaka** (*q.v.*) to show his similar tendencies in the past.[1] Tissa was identified with **Kaṭāhaka** of the Jātaka.[2]

[1] DhA. iii. 367. [2] J. i. 455.

16. **Tissa.**—A monk. He was called **Kosambivāsī Tissa.** He spent the rainy season at **Kosambī** and, on his departure, his supporter gave him three robes and other offerings; he, however, refused them saying that he had no novice to look after them. The layman immediately gave his son, then seven years old, to be his novice. The boy attained arahantship in the Tonsure-hall. While on his way to **Sāvatthi** to see the Buddha, Tissa accidentally blinded the novice by hitting his eye with a fan at dawn. The Elder was filled with remorse and, falling at the boy's feet, asked his pardon. But the answer was that there was no fault to pardon, the accident was due to *saṃsāra*. When the matter was reported to the Buddha he said that such was the nature of arahants. They felt no resentment. At the end of the discourse, Tissa became an arahant.[1]

[1] DhA. ii. 182 ff.

17. **Tissa.**—A monk, called **Asubhakammika-Tissa.** He is mentioned in the Commentaries[1] as an example of a good friend, devoted to the contemplation of *asubha*, association with whom helps one to get rid of lust. His teacher was **Mahātissa** of **Koṭapabbata-vihāra.**[2]

[1] *E.g.*, VibhA. 270. [2] MṬ. 553.

18. **Tissa.**—A master of writing (*lekhācariya*). Even after his death he was known by reason of his writing.[1]

[1] Mil., p. 70; see *J.R.A.S.* xii. 159.

19. **Tissa.**—One of the chief lay patrons of **Padumuttara** Buddha.[1]

[1] Bu. xi. 26.

20. **Tissa.**—A monk known as **Āraddhavipassaka-Tissa.** While walking about he saw a lotus open at the rising of the sun. Immediately afterwards, he heard a slave-girl singing; her song told of how men are subject to death just as the lotus opens to the sun. Tissa thereupon developed insight and became an arahant.[1]

[1] SNA. ii. 397.

21. **Tissa.**—Uncle of **Paṇḍukābhaya.** He administered the kingdom when his elder brother, **Abhaya,** gave up the government. He was killed by **Paṇḍukābhaya.**[1]

[1] Mhv. x. 51, 70.

22. **Tissa.**—An Elder of **Asoka's** time, a disciple of **Mahāvaruṇa** and brother of **Sumitta.** He was the son of a *kinnarī* called **Kuntī,** and his name was **Tissa Kontiputta.** He died of a bite by a venomous insect. Asoka was grieved on learning that Tissa's death was due to his failure to obtain ghee in his illness.[1]

[1] Mhv. v. 213 ff.

23. **Tissa-kumāra.**—Brother of **Asoka** and his vice-regent. He once asked Asoka why monks were not joyful and gay and Asoka, in order to teach him the reason, gave him the throne for a week, saying that at the end of the week he would be put to death. Tissa then realised that monks, who had the constant consciousness of death, could not be merry.

He later became a monk under **Yonaka Mahādhammarakkhita** and lived in the **Asokārāma,** where he prevented the murder of the theras by the minister sent by Asoka to make the monks hold the *uposatha* together. He became an arahant and, on account of his love of solitude, came to be known as **Ekavihāriya.**[1]

[1] Thag. vv. 537-46; ThagA. i. 503 f.; Mhv. v. 33, 60, 154 ff., 241; SA. iii. 125.

24. **Tissa.**—King of **Kalyāṇī** and father of **Vihāramahādevī.**[1] His brother **Ayya-Uttika** entered into an intrigue with the queen and was banished. He sent the queen a letter through an attendant to an arahant who was in the habit of visiting the palace. This letter fell into the hands of the king who suspected the arahant himself, owing to a similarity in his writing to that of the intriguer. The king ordered the arahant to be killed and cast into the sea. The devas, being offended, caused the sea to overflow the land. The total destruction of the country was only averted by the king sending his daughter **Devī** (afterwards **Vihāramahadevī**), to sea in a golden boat.[2]

Tissa's father was **Muṭasiva** and his grandfather **Uttiya.**[3]

[1] Mhv. xxii. 13 ff.

[2] The Rasavāhinī, however, says he was thrown into a cauldron of boiling oil; see *s.v.* **Telakaṭāhagāthā.**

[3] MṬ 431.

25. **Tissa.**—A minister of **Duṭṭhagāmaṇī.** When the latter fled from **Saddhātissa,** Tissa joined him and he gave him his own food during the flight. But the food was ultimately given to a monk (see **Tissa** 26) who accepted their invitation to the meal.[1] It was probably the mother of this Tissa who, we are told,[2] used a cloth worth one hundred to wipe away the impurities of her son's birth, which cloth she afterwards threw out on to the **Tāḷaveli** road hoping that it might prove useful to a *pāṃsukūlika* monk.

[1] For details see Mhv. xxiv. 22 ff.; AA. i. 365;

[2] Vsm., p. 63.

26. **Tissa.**—A thera in **Piyaṅgudīpa.** He it was who accepted the meal given by **Duṭṭhagāmaṇī** while fleeing from his brother.[1]

[1] Mhv. xxiv. 25.

27. **Tissa.**—A brahmin youth of **Rohaṇa** who rebelled against **Vaṭṭagāmaṇī** in the fifth year of his reign. At that time Damiḷas invaded Ceylon and Vaṭṭagāmaṇi sent word to Tissa asking him to fight them, and take the throne for himself; Tissa did, but was conquered by them.[1] See also **Brāhmaṇa-Tissa.**

[1] Mhv. xxxiii. 38 ff.

28. **Tissa.**—A monk of **Kambugallaka;** he was very learned and helped to reconcile **Vaṭṭagāmaṇī** and his discontented ministers.[1] Later, the ministers built several vihāras—the **Mūlavokāsa,** the **Sāliyārāma,** the **Pabbatārāma** and the **Uttaratissārāma**—and handed them over to Tissa.[2]

[1] Mhv. xxxiii. 71, 75.

[2] *Ibid.*, 91.

29. **Tissa.**—A minister of **Vaṭṭagāmaṇi**; he built the **Uttaratissārāma.**[1]

[1] Mhv. xxxiii. 91.

30. **Tissa.**—Son of **Mahācūḷa** and king of Ceylon (9–12 A.D.). He was poisoned by his wife **Anulā.**[1]

[1] Mhv. xxxiv. 15 ff.

31. **Tissa.**—A paramour of Queen **Anulā.** He was a wood-carrier and was therefore called **Dārubhatika-Tissa.** He reigned for one year and one month and built a bathing-tank in the **Mahāmeghavana.** He was poisoned by **Anulā.**[1]

[1] Mhv. xxxiv. 22 ff.

32. **Tissa.**—A monk of the **Dakkhiṇārāma,** for whom **Mahāsena** built the **Jetavana-vihāra.**[1]

[1] Mhv. xxxvii. 32, 38.

33. **Tissa.**—Younger son of **Mahādāṭhika-Mahānāga** and brother of **Āmaṇḍagāmaṇi Abhaya.** He was known as **Kanirajānu-tissa**[1] (*q.v.*).

[1] Mhv. xxxv. 11 ff.; MṬ. 640.

34. **Tissa.**—Nephew of **Khallāṭanāga** and son of **Sumanadevī,** step-sister to the king. With his brothers, **Abhaya** and **Uttara,** he conspired to kill the king. But the conspiracy failed and they committed suicide.[1]

[1] MṬ. 612.

35. **Tissa.**—An artisan (*kammāraputta*), a previous incarnation of **Sāliya.** He lived in **Muṇḍagaṅgā** and receiving one day as wages the flesh of a boar, he had it cooked by his wife. When the meal was ready he announced alms; the theras **Dhammadinna, Godhiya-Mahātissa, Mahānāga** of **Samuddavihāra, Mahānāga** of **Kāḷavallimaṇḍapa, Mahāsaṅgharakkhita, Dhammagutta, Mahānāga** of **Bhātiyavaṅka** and **Maliyamahādeva** appeared to accept the alms.[1]

[1] MṬ. 605 f.

36. **Tissa.**—A monk resident in **Loṇagiri (Lenagiri).** He once saw fifty monks, on their way to **Nāgadīpa** on a pilgrimage, returning from their alms-rounds in **Mahākhīragāma,** with their bowls empty. Asking them to wait, he returned in a little while with his bowl of milk rice which proved

more than enough for the whole company. Seeing their astonishment, he explained that since he had begun to practise the *sārāṇīya-dhammā*, his bowl had never lacked food.

At the **Giribhaṇḍamahāpūjā** at **Cetiyapabbata,** Tissa wished to have for himself two shawls, the most precious things there. He declared his wish in the presence of others and the king, on being informed, determined that Tissa should not have them, but every time he put out his hand to take the robes, they slipped away, and others took their place. In the end the robes were given to Tissa.[1]

[1] DA. ii. 534 f.; MA. i. 545.

37. **Tissa.**—A thera of **Sāvatthi,** better known as **Kuṭumbiyaputta-Tissa.** He renounced forty crores of wealth and became a monk dwelling in the forest. His younger brother's wife sent five hundred ruffians to kill him. He begged them to spare his life for one night and broke his thigh-bone with a stone as token that he would not attempt to escape. During the night he overcame his pain and, dwelling on his virtues, became an arahant.[1]

[1] MA. i. 188 f.; DA. iii. 747; Vsm. 48.

38. **Tissa.**—A thera of **Sāketa.** He refused to answer questions, saying that he had no time. On being asked, "Can you find time to die ?" he felt ashamed, and going to the **Kaṇikāravālikasamudda-vihāra,** instructed monks of varying grades during the rainy season, rousing great enthusiasm among the populace by his preaching.[1]

[1] MA. i. 350 f.; DA. iii. 1061.

39. **Tissa.**—A monk of **Koṭapabbata** (*q.v.*).

40. **Tissa.**—A minister. The scholiast to the **Kaṇha Jātaka** mentions a story of an *amacca* called Tissa who, in a rage, killed his wife and all his retinue and, finally, himself.[1]

[1] J. iv. 11.

41. **Tissa.**—A novice of **Pañcaggalalena.** While travelling through the air he heard the daughter of the artisan of **Girigāma** singing, after having bathed with her companions in a lotus-pond. Being attracted by the sound, he lost his power of travelling through the air.[1]

[1] MA. i. 353; SNA. i. 70.

42. **Tissa.**—A novice of **Tissamahā-vihāra.** He complained to his teacher of his distaste for the Order and the latter took him to **Cittalapabbata.** There, with great effort, Tissa built for himself a cave and while lying there during the night, became an arahant, dying the next day. A thūpa called the **Tissa-thera-cetiya** was erected over his relics and this was still in existence in **Buddhaghosa's** day.[1]

[1] MA. i. 312 f.

43. **Tissa.**—An attendant of King **Saddhā-Tissa.** The king, wishing to eat pheasants, asked Tissa to procure some, having first tested him by threatening to have him executed if he refused to kill fowl for the king's table. Tissa, even when led to the executioner's block, refused to kill the birds. The king was thus satisfied that Tissa would not kill pheasants for him. The next day, Tissa, seeing a fowler hawking some dead pheasants, obtained them for the king.[1]

[1] SA. iii. 49 ff.; AA. i. 262.

44. See also **Kaṭamoraka-Tissa, Cullapiṇḍapātika-Tissa, Dārubhaṇḍaka-Tissa, Devānampiya-Tissa, Dhanuggaha-Tissa, Nigama-Tissa, Pabbhāravāsī-Tissa, Padhānakammika-Tissa, Padhānika-Tissa, Punabbasukuṭumbika-putta-Tissa, Pūtigata-Tissa, Maṇikārakulūpaga-Tissa, Mahātissa, Losaka-Tissa, Vanavāsika-Tissa, Saddhātissa,** etc.

1. **Tissa Sutta.**—Relates the story of the Buddha's nephew, **Tissa** (No. 14), who visits the Buddha and complains that the monks abuse him.[1]

[1] S. ii. 282.

2. **Tissa Sutta.**—The story of **Tissa** (No. 14) being taken to the Buddha because he complained of distaste for the monk's life. By means of an allegory the Buddha teaches him how he can attain *Nibbāna*, and promises to help him to do so.[1]

[1] S. iii. 106 f.

3. **Tissa Sutta.**—**Moggallāna,** hearing the Buddha report a conversation between two devatās at **Gijjhakūṭa,** visits the **Brahmā Tissa** in order to discover if the devas had knowledge of *saupādisesa* and *anupādisesa.* Tissa tells him what he knows and Moggallāna describes his visit to the Buddha. The Buddha tells him that Tissa had omitted to mention the *animittavihārī puggala,* which he then proceeds to explain.[1]

[1] A. iv. 77 f.; *cp.* A. iii. 332 f.

Tissaka Sutta.—**Subrahmā** approaches the Buddha and speaks of **Kaṭamoraka-Tissa**[1] (*q.v.*).

[1] S. i. 148.

Tissadatta.—A thera of Ceylon who had special charge of the Vinaya.[1] He may be identical with the **Tissadatta** mentioned[2] as being able to preach in eighteen different languages, explaining the text of the Tipiṭaka. On one occasion, wishing to salute the Bodhi-tree by means of his iddhi-power, he caused it to draw near to him.[3]

[1] Vin. v. 3. [2] VibhA. 387, 389; MA. i. 234. [3] Vsm. 403.

Tissabhūti.—A monk of **Maṇḍalārāma** in Ceylon, in the time of King **Vaṭṭagāmaṇi.**[1] He was evidently well versed in the Abhidhamma and it is said[2] that he once explained the **Padesavihāra Sutta** so as to include various teachings of the Abhidhamma.

Once, while on his alms-rounds, he saw something which provoked desire in his heart. He immediately returned to his teacher and asked his advice as to how to conquer his disease. The teacher sent him to **Mahāsaṅgharakkhita** of **Malaya,** who gave him the *asubhakammaṭṭhāna*. That same night Tissabhūti became an arahant at the foot of a *sepaṇṇi* tree.[3]

[1] VibhA. 448. [2] DhsA. 30. [3] AA. i. 23 f.

Tissamahārājā.—See **Saddhātissa.**

Tissamahā-vihāra.—A monastery in **Rohaṇa,** founded by **Kākavaṇṇa-Tissa.**[1] It was also called **Tissārāma.**[2] It was one of the chief monastic establishments in Ceylon and was a place of pilgrimage. Some of the Sinhalese chronicles mention that Kākavaṇṇa-Tissa built another vihāra of the same name on the east coast of Ceylon, at the place now known as Seruvila, where the Buddha's frontal bone is deposited. The **Mahāmeghavanārāma** is also sometimes called the **Tissamahārāma,**[3] and **Tissārāma.**[4] **Dappula** gave to the **Tissamahā-vihāra** the village of **Kattikapabbata.**[5]

[1] Mhv. xxii. 23.
[2] *Ibid.*, 28.
[3] *E.g.*, Mhv. xx. 25.
[4] *Ibid.*, xv. 174, 179, 203.
[5] Cv. xlv. 59.

Tissa Metteyya.—See **Tissa** (7).

Tissa-Metteyya Sutta.—Preached to **Tissa** (7) and his friend **Metteyya,** at the latter's request. It deals with the evils that follow in the train of sexual intercourse.[1]

[1] SN., p. 160 f.; SNA. ii. 535 f.

Tissa-Metteyya-māṇava-pucchā.—The question asked by **Tissa-Metteyya,** and the answer given by the Buddha.[1]

[1] SN., p. 199.

Tissarakkhā.—The second queen of **Asoka**; he married her four years before his death. She was very jealous of the attention paid by Asoka to the Bodhi-tree, and caused it to be killed by means of poisonous thorns.[1]

[1] Mhv. xx. 3 ff.

Tissarājamaṇḍapa.—The name given to the pavilions erected by **Vohārika-Tissa** in the **Mahāvihāra** and in **Abhayagiri.**[1]

[1] Mhv. xxxvi. 31; Mhv. *Trs.* 258, n. 3.

Tissavaḍḍhamānaka.—A locality in Ceylon, to the east of **Anurādhapura.**[1] It contained the **Mucela-vihāra** and a tank of the same name.[2]

[1] Mhv. xxxv. 84.

[2] *Ibid.*, xxxvii. 48.

Tissavasabha.—Probably the name of a Bodhi-tree in **Anurādhapura.** It was surrounded by a stone terrace and a wall, both built by **Sirimeghavaṇṇa.**[1]

[1] Cv. xxxvii. 91; Cv. *Trs.* i. 7, n. 3.

1. **Tissavāpi.**—A tank near **Anurādhapura,** probably built by **Devānampiyatissa.**[1] It seems to have been customary for the king to take a ceremonial bath in the Tissavāpi, after his coronation festival,[2] and, on this occasion, the **Lambakaṇṇas** formed the king's bodyguard.[3] The road from **Mahiyaṅgama** to **Anurādhapura** lay along the edge of the Tissavāpi.[4]

[1] Mhv. xx. 20.

[2] *E.g.*, Mhv. xxvi. 7; xxxv. 38; MṬ. 645.

[3] See, *e.g.*, Mhv. xxxv. 16, 38.

[4] *Ibid.*, xxxvi. 59.

2. **Tissavāpi.**—A tank in the neighbourhood of **Mahāgāma,** built by **Iḷanāga.**[1]

[1] Mhv. xxxv. 32.

Tissa-vihāra.—A monastery in **Nāgadīpa** round which **Vohāraka-Tissa** built a wall.[1]

[1] Mhv. xxxvi. 36.

1. **Tissā.**—One of the chief women disciples of **Koṇḍañña** Buddha.[1]

[1] J. i. 30; Bu. iii. 31.

2. **Tissā.**—An arahant Therī belonging to a **Sākyan** family of **Kapilavatthu.** She became a lady of the Bodhisatta's court, but later renounced the world with **Mahāpajāpatī Gotamī,** and practised insight. One day the Buddha appeared before her in a ray of glory and uttered a stanza, at the conclusion of which she became an arahant.[1]

[1] Thig. 4; ThigA. 11.

3. **Tissā.**—An arahant Therī, her story being similar to that of **Tissā** (2).[1]

[1] Thig. 5; ThigA. 12 f.

4. **Tissā.**—An *upāsikā* mentioned, together with her mother **Tissāyamātā,** in a list of pious women disciples.[1]

[1] A. iv. 348; AA. ii. 791.

5. **Tissā.**—A rival of **Mattā** (*q.v.*).[1]

[1] Pv. ii. 3; PvA. 82 f.

6. **Tissā.**—A nun of Ceylon, specially proficient in the Vinaya.[1]

[1] Dpv. xviii. 30.

7. **Tissā.**—Wife of **Mahinda** who was brother of **Sena II.** Tissā was a daughter of **Kittaggabodhi** and was the sister of **Saṅghā** and **Kitti.**[1] She had a daughter, also called **Saṅghā.**[2]

[1] Cv. l. 60. [2] *Ibid.*, li. 15.

8. **Tissā.**—Daughter of King **Kassapa IV.** and queen of **Udaya II.**[1]

[1] Cv. li. 94.

9. **Tissā.**—Daughter of Kassapa, who afterwards became **Kassapa V.** (?) and wife of **Kassapa IV.**[1]

[1] Cv. lii. 2.

1. **Tissārāma.**—Name given to the **Mahāmeghavanārāma** (*q.v.*),[1] and also to **Tissamahārāma** (*q.v.*).[2]

[1] Mhv. xv. 174, 179, 203. [2] *Ibid.*, xxii. 28.

2. **Tissārāma.**—A nunnery in **Anurādhapura,** built by **Kassapa IV.** The nuns of Tissārāma were entrusted with the care of the **Bodhi-tree** and of the **Maricavaṭṭi-vihāra.**[1]

[1] Cv. lii. 24.

Tiṇimakkulagāma.—A village in the Malaya country in Ceylon, not far from Pulatthipura.[1]

[1] Cv. lxx. 284, 301.

Tiritara.—A Tamil usurper who succeeded **Khuddapārinda** on the throne. Two months after his accession he was killed by **Dhātusena.**[1]

[1] Cv. xxxviii. 32.

Tisucullasa.—A village, probably in East Ceylon.[1] *v.l.* **Tipucullasa.**

[1] Cv. xlv. 78.

Tuṅgabhaddā.—A canal branching off from the Dakkhiṇā sluice in the **Parakkamasamudda.**[1]

[1] Cv. lxxix. 45.

Tuṭṭha.—A lay disciple of **Ñātika** who died and was reborn in the **Suddhāvāsa,** there to attain Nibbāna.[1]

[1] S. v. 358; D. ii. 92.

Tuṭṭhi Sutta.—In order to get rid of dissatisfaction, want of self-possession, and desire for much, one should cultivate the opposite qualities.[1]

[1] A. iii. 448.

Tuṇḍila.—Brother of the courtesan **Kālī.** He was a ne'er-do-well, and Kālī, having helped him with money which he proceeded to squander, refused to give him any more. But a patron of Kālī, seeing his condition, gave him his clothes on entering Kālī's house—it being the custom for those who patronised a courtesan, to be provided with clothes during their stay in her house—and had to walk away naked.[1]

[1] J. iv. 248 f.

Tuṇḍila Jātaka (No. 388).—The Bodhisatta was once born as a pig and had a brother. They were adopted by an old woman of a village near Benares and were called **Mahātuṇḍila** and **Cullatuṇḍila.** The woman loved them like her own children and refused to sell them, but, one day, some lewd men made her drunk and she agreed to sell Cullatuṇḍila. When Cullatuṇḍila discovered this, he ran to his brother, but the latter preached to him how it was the fate of pigs to be slaughtered for their flesh; he should, therefore, meet his death bravely. All Benares heard the Bodhisatta's preaching, and flocked to the spot. The king adopted the pigs as his sons and Mahātuṇḍila was appointed to the seat of judgment. On the king's death, he wrote a book of law for the guidance of future generations.

The story was related in reference to a monk who was in constant terror of the thought of death. The monk was identified with Cullatuṇḍila.[1]

It is said[2] that the lewd men were identical with the **Bhaddavaggiyā.** Having heard Mahātuṇḍila preach the five precepts, they observed them for sixty thousand years, hence their attainment of arahantship as in their last birth.

Mahātuṇḍila's preaching is referred to as the **Tuṇḍilovāda.**

[1] J. iii. 286 ff. [2] DhA. i. 83.

Tucchapoṭhila.—See **Poṭhila.**

Tudigāma.—The residence of **Subha Todeyyaputta.**[1]

[1] AA. ii. 554; MA. ii. 802. See **Todeyya.**

Tudu.—A thera. He was the teacher of **Culla Kokālika** and, having become an Anāgāmī, was born as a Pacceka Brahmā in the Brahma-world. When Kokālika was grievously ill, Tudu visited him and exhorted him to put his trust in **Sāriputta** and **Moggallāna.** But Kokālika refused to accept his advice and drove him away.[1]

[1] S. i. 149; A. v. 171; J. iv. 245; AA. ii. 852; SA. i. 167 f.; SNA. ii. 476.

Tumbarakandara.—A forest between **Upatissagāma** and **Dvāramaṇḍalaka.**[1]

[1] Mhv. x. 2; MṬ. 280.

Tumbarumālaka.—One of the *mālakas* of the **Cetiyapabbata.** The first *upsampadā* was held there by **Mahinda,** when **Mahāariṭṭha** and the others received the *upasampadā.*[1]

[1] Mhv. xvi. 16.

Tulākūṭa Sutta.—Few are they that abstain from cheating with scales and measures; many are they that do not.[1]

[1] S. v. 473.

Tulādhāra.—A mountain in the village of **Vihāravāpi.**[1] It was in **Rohaṇa,** and the vihāra on it was the residence of **Mahāpaduma,** the reciter of the **Jātakas,** from whom **Iḷanāga** heard the **Kapi Jātaka.**[2] There was also, probably, a village of the same name as the mountain, for it is mentioned[3] as having been given by **Aggabodhi IV.** for the maintenance of the *Padhānaghara* built by him.

[1] Mhv. xxiii. 90. [2] *Ibid.*, xxxv. 30. [3] Cv. xlvi. 12.

Tuvaṭaka Sutta.—The fourteenth sutta of the **Aṭṭhakavagga** of the Sutta Nipāta. It was one of the suttas preached at the **Mahāsamaya.** It deals with the qualities a monk should cultivate in order to attain emancipation.[1] It is explained in the Mahā Niddesa.[2] It is considered specially fitted for *saddhācaritas.*[3]

[1] SN., pp. 179 ff.; SNA. ii. 562 ff. [2] ii. 339 ff. [3] NidA. 223.

Tuvaradāyaka Thera.—An arahant. Ninety-one kappas ago he was a hunter who, having seen some monks in the forest, gave them a *tuvara* (?).[1]

[1] Ap. i. 222.

Tuvarādhipativeḷāra.—A Damiḷa chieftain, ally of **Kulasekhara.**[1]

[1] Cv. lxxvi. 138, 315; lxxvii. 67.

1. **Tusita.**—One of the palaces occupied by **Koṇāgamana** Buddha in his last lay life.[1]

[1] Bu. xxiv. 18.

2. **Tusita.**—The fourth of the six deva worlds.[1] Four hundred years of human life are equal to one day of the Tusita world and four thousand years, so reckoned, is the term of life of a deva born in Tusita.[2] Sometimes Sakadāgāmins (*e.g.*, **Purāṇa** and **Isidatta**) are born there.[3] It is the rule for all Bodhisattas to be born in Tusita in their last life but one; then, when the time comes for the appearance of a Buddha in the world, the devas of the ten thousand world systems assemble and request the Bodhisatta to

[1] A. i. 210, etc.
[2] *Ibid.*, 214; iv. 261, etc.
[3] A. iii. 348; v. 138; also DhA. i. 129; UdA. 149, 277.

be born among men. Great rejoicings attend the acceptance of this request.[4] **Gotama's** name, while in Tusita, was **Setaketu,**[5] and the Bodhisatta **Metteyya** (*q.v.*), the future Buddha, is now living in Tusita under the name of **Nathadeva.** The Tusita world is considered the most beautiful of the celestial worlds, and the pious love to be born there because of the presence of the Bodhisatta.[6] Tusita is also the abode of each Bodhisatta's parents.[7] The king of the Tusita world is **Santusita;** he excels his fellows in ten respects—beauty, span of life, etc.[8] Among those reborn in Tusita are also mentioned **Dhammika, Anāthapiṇḍika, Mallikā,** the thera **Tissa** (**Tissa** 10), **Mahādhana** and **Duṭṭhagāmaṇi.**[9] The Tusita devas are so-called because they are full of joy (*tuṭṭha-haṭṭhāti Tusitā*).[10]

The inhabitants of Tusita are called Tusitā. They were present at the Mahāsamaya.[11]

[4] A. ii. 130; iv. 312; DhA. i. 69 f.; J. i. 47 f.

[5] Sp. i. 161.

[6] Mhv. xxxii. 72 f.

[7] DhA. i. 110.

[8] A. iv. 243; but see Cv. lii. 47, where the Bodhisatta Metteyya is called the chief of **Tusita.**

[9] For particulars see *s.v.*

[10] VibhA. 519; NidA. 109.

[11] D. ii. 161.

Tusitā.—The inhabitants of the Tusita world. See **Tusita** (2).

Tekicchakārī (°**kāni**) **Thera.**—He was the son of the brahmin **Subandhu,** and was so-called because he was brought safely into the world with the aid of physicians. When Tekicchakārī was grown up his father, by his wisdom and policy, incurred the jealousy and suspicion of **Cāṇakka,** minister of **Candagutta,** who had him thrown into prison. Tekicchakārī, in his fright, fled, and, taking refuge with a forest-dwelling monk, entered the Order and dwelt in the open air, never sleeping and heedless of heat and cold. **Māra,** in the guise of a cowherd, tried to tempt him, but he developed insight and became an arahant.

In the time of **Vipassī** Buddha he was born in a physician's family and cured a monk, named **Asoka,** and many others. Eight kappas ago he was a king named **Sabbosadha.**[1] He is probably identical with **Tikicchaka** of the **Apadāna.**[2]

[1] Thag. 384-6; ThagA. i. 440 f.

[2] i. 190.

Tekula (?).—A thera who, with his brother **Yamelu,** asked from the Buddha permission to translate the Buddha's teachings into Sanskrit.[1]

[1] Vin. ii. 139.

Teṅkoṅgu.—A locality in South India.[1]

[1] Cv. lxxvi. 288; lxxvii. 67.

Tejasi.—One of the messengers employed by **Kuvera.**[1]

[1] D. iii. 201.

Tejodīpa.—A disciple of **Tilokaguru** and author of a *ṭīkā* on the **Paritta.**[1]

[1] Sās., p. 115.

Tennavallappalla.—A Damiḷa chief, ally of **Kulasekhara.**[1]

[1] Cv. lxxvi. 222, 231.

Tebhātika-Jaṭilā.—Three brothers, **Uruvela-Kassapa, Gayā-Kassapa** and **Nadī-Kassapa.** For their story see *s.v.* **Uruvela-Kassapa.**

Temiya.—The name of the Bodhisatta in the **Mūgapakkha Jātaka** (*q.v.*) He was so called because on the day of his birth there were great rains throughout the kingdom and he was born wet.[1]

[1] J. vi. 3.

Temiya Jātaka.—See **Mūgapakkha Jātaka.**

Tela.—One of the ambassadors sent by **Devānampiyatissa** to **Asoka.**[1] *v.l.* **Malla.**

[1] MṬ. 302.

Telakaṭāhagāthā.—A Pāli poem of eighty-eight stanzas supposed to have been uttered by **Kalyāṇiya Thera** on being thrown into a cauldron of boiling oil by King **Kalyāṇi-Tissa (Tissa** 24), who suspected him of having been accessory to an intrigue with his queen.[1]

[1] For details see P.L.C. 162 f.

Telakandarikā.—A pious and generous woman, who gave ghee in large quantities to monks. She is mentioned in a story illustrating how monks will sometimes boast of their patrons.[1]

[1] VbhA. 483; Vsm. 27.

Telakāni Thera.—An arahant. He was a brahmin of **Sāvatthi,** older than the Buddha. Having become a wandering recluse he went about questioning recluses and brahmins, but not finding satisfaction. One day he heard the Buddha preach, entered the Order and became an arahant.[1]

[1] Thag. 747-68; ThagA. ii. 24 ff.

Telagāma.—A canal, the revenue from which was given by **Aggabodhi IX.** to the monks for their rice gruel.[1]

[1] Cv. xlix. 89.

Telapakkanijjhara.—A weir forming part of the irrigation work scarried out by **Parakkamabāhu I.**[1]

[1] Cv. lxxix. 66.

Telapatta Jātaka (No. 96).—The Bodhisatta was once the youngest of one hundred sons of the king of Benares. He heard from the Pacceka Buddhas, who took their meals in the palace, that he would become king of **Takkasilā** if he could reach it without falling a prey to the ogresses who waylaid travellers in the forest. Thereupon, he set out with five of his brothers who wished to accompany him. On the way through the forest the five in succession succumbed to the charms of the ogresses, and were devoured. One ogress followed the Bodhisatta right up to the gates of Takkasilā, where the king took her into the palace, paying no heed to the Bodhisatta's warning. The king succumbed to her wiles, and, during the night, the king and all the inhabitants of the palace were eaten by the ogress and her companions. The people, realising the sagacity and strength of will of the Bodhisatta, made him their king.

The story was related in reference to the **Janapada-Kalyāṇi Sutta** (*q.v.*). The monks said it must be very hard not to look at a *janapada-kalyāṇi*, but the Buddha denied this and related the above story.[1]

The **Jātaka** seems also to have been called the **Takkasilā Jātaka.**[2]

[1] J. i. 393 ff. [2] *Ibid.*, 470.

Telappanāḷi.—A village near **Ujjeni.** When **Mahā Kaccāna** went there on his way to Ujjeni, a poor girl of noble family, seeing him return emptyhanded from his alms-round, invited him into her house, cut off her beautiful hair, sent a slave-girl to sell it, and with the price of it gave alms to Kaccāna, keeping herself out of sight. The Elder sent for her, and, at the sight of him, her hair grew as before. **Caṇḍappajjota,** hearing of the incident, sent for her and made her his queen. She gave birth to a son called, after his maternal grandmother, **Gopāla,** and his mother thereafter came to be called **Gopālamātā.**[1]

[1] AA. i. 117 f.

Telamakkhiya Thera.—An arahant. Ninety-four kappas ago he rubbed oil on the *vedikā* of **Siddhattha** Buddha's Bodhi-tree. Twenty-four kappas ago he was a king named **Succhavi.**[1]

[1] Ap. i. 230 f.

Telavāhā.—A river in the **Serivaraṭṭha,** and near **Andhapura.**[1]

[1] J. i. 111.

Telovāda Jātaka (No. 246).—Once the Bodhisatta was a brahmin ascetic. He came to a village for alms and was invited by a wealthy brahmin who, after having given him food with fish, tried to annoy him by saying that the fish had been killed specially for him. The Bodhisatta said that he himself was entirely free from blame.

The story was related in reference to **Nigaṇṭha Nāthaputta** who sneered because the Buddha had consented to eat at the house of the general **Sīha.** The wealthy brahmin is identified with **Nāthaputta.**[1]

[1] J. ii. 262 f.

Tevijja Sutta.—The thirteenth sutta of the Dīgha Nikāya, preached to **Vāseṭṭha** and **Bhāradvāja** who visited the Buddha at **Manasākaṭa.** The Buddha points out the futility of the belief that a mere knowledge of the Three Vedas leads to the attainment of reunion with **Brahmā.** Such union can, however, be attained only by the practice of the four Brahma-vihāras.[1]

[1] D. i. 235-53.

Tevijja-Vacchagotta Sutta.—The Buddha visits **Vacchagotta** at the **Paribbājakārāma** in **Vesāli** and tells him that he is called *Tevijja* (knower of the threefold lore) because he has knowledge of his former existences, possesses the divine eye, and has knowledge of the destruction of the *āsavas.*[1]

[1] M. i. 481 ff.

Tesakuṇa Jātaka (No. 521).—Once upon a time, the king of Benares had no heir, but finding three eggs in a nest—an owl's, amynah's, and a parrot's—he brought them, and when they were hatched out, adopted the birds as his children, giving them the names of **Vessantara, Kuṇḍalinī** and

Jambuka. When they had grown up in the houses of the courtiers who had charge of them, the king had them summoned one by one, and asked them for advice as to how a king should reign. Each admonished the king in eleven stanzas, and, at the suggestion of the admiring populace, they were given respectively the ranks of general, treasurer, and commander-in-chief. When the king died, the people wished to make Jambuka king, but, having inscribed rules of righteousness on a golden plate, he disappeared into the forest.

The story was related in reference to the admonitions delivered by the Buddha to the king of **Kosala.** The king of the past was **Ānanda,** Kuṇḍalinī was **Uppalavaṇā,** Vessantara, **Sāriputta** and Jambuka the **Bodhisatta.**[1]

The verses uttered by Jambuka are often quoted.[2]

[1] J. v. 109-25.   [2] *E.g.*, J. i. 177; vi. 94.

Toṇḍamāna.—A Damiḷa chieftain, ally of **Kulasekhara.** He had a mountain fortress where Kulasekhara once lay in hiding, and his wife had three brothers, all of whom helped him. He owned the villages of **Tirimalakka** and **Kattala.**[1]

[1] Cv. lxxvi. 137, 315; lxxvii. 1, 32, 39, 51, 74.

Toṇḍipāra.—A locality in South India.[1] Geiger[2] takes the name to be that of two villages, Toṇḍi and Pāra.

[1] Cv. lxxvi. 236; lxxvii. 81.   [2] Cv. *Trs.* ii. 84, n. 3.

Tondiriya.—A Damiḷa chieftain, ally of **Kulasekhara.** He was slain by **Laṅkāpura.**[1]

[1] Cv. lxxvi. 181 f.

1. **Todeyya.**—A Mahāsāla brahmin, mentioned in a list of eminent brahmins gathered together at **Icchanaṅkala** and **Manasākaṭa.**[1] Buddhaghosa says[2] that his permanent residence was at **Tudigāma;** hence his name. He was, very probably, the father of **Subha,** who is called **Todeyyaputta.**[3] Subha's father was, we know, chaplain to **Pasenadi** and, though exceedingly rich, was a great miser; after death he was born in his own house as a dog of whom Subha was very fond. When the Buddha visited Subha the dog barked, and the Buddha chided it, addressing it by the name of **Todeyya.**

Subha was greatly offended but the Buddha proved the identity of the dog by getting him to show Subha some of his father's buried treasure. The dog was later born in hell.[4]

[1] D. i. 235; Sn., p. 115.   [3] MA. ii. 802.
[2] DA. ii. 399; AA. ii. 554.   [4] Ibid., ii. 962 f.

There was in **Caṇḍalakappa** a Mango-grove belonging to the Todeyya-brahmins.[5] A Todeyya-brāhmaṇa was also the owner of the Mango-grove at **Kāmaṇḍā.**[6] The Aṅguttara Nikāya[7] mentions the pupils of the Todeyya-brahmin speaking ill of **Eḷeyya** because the latter followed the teachings of **Rāmaputta.**

[5] M. ii. 210. [6] S. iv. 121. [7] A. ii. 180.

2. **Todeyya.**—A disciple of **Bāvarī.**[1] He visited the Buddha, and his questions, with the answers given by the Buddha, are given in the **Todeyya-māṇava-pucchā.**[2] He became an arahant.[3]

[1] S., vv. 1006. [2] *Ibid.*, 1088-91. [3] SNA. ii. 597.

Todeyyagāma.—A village between **Sāvatthi** and Benares. It contained the shrine of **Kassapa** Buddha, which was honoured even in the present age. The Buddha once visited it in the company of **Ānanda.**[1]

[1] DhA. iii. 250 f.

Tobbalanāgapabbata.—A locality in **Rohaṇa.** There **Mahallakanāga** erected a vihāra.[1]

[1] Mhv. xxxv. 125.

Tompiya.—A Damiḷa chief, ally of **Kulasekhara.**[1]

[1] Cv. lxxvi. 144.

Toyavāpi.—A tank, one of the irrigation works of **Parakkamabāhu I.**[1]

[1] Cv. lxxix. 46.

Toraṇavatthu.—A locality in **Kosala,** between **Sāvatthi** and **Sāketa. Pasenadi** once stopped there and visited **Khemā,** who lived there.[1]

[1] S. iv. 374.

Tolaka-vihāra.—A monastery in **Rohaṇa** near which **Vihāramahādevī** landed after she was cast into the sea at **Kalyāṇi.**[1]

[1] MṬ. 431 (see n. 7).

Th.

Thapatayo Sutta.—The royal chamberlains, **Isidatta** and **Purāṇa,** staying at **Sādhuka,** hear that the Buddha is in the village and, waiting for him, follow him till he sits down under a tree. They tell him of their joy that he is staying near them. They are proud in telling him that in spite of the temptations placed in their way in the performance of their duties, they are free from thoughts of lust. The Buddha tells them they are possessed of the four qualities of Sotāpannas and should, therefore, be thankful for their good fortune.[1]

[1] S. v. 348 ff.

Thambāropaka Thera.—An arahant. In the past he set up a flagstaff over the cetiya of Dhammadasī Buddha and, climbing to the top of it, decked it with jasmine flowers. Ninety-four kappas ago he became king sixteen times, under the name of **Thūpasikha.**[1]

He is probably identical with **Paripuṇṇaka** Thera.[2]

[1] Ap. i. 171. [2] ThagA. i. 190.

Thalayūru.—See **Athalayūru.**

1. **Thullakoṭṭhita.**—A township in the **Kuru** country. It was the birthplace of **Raṭṭhapāla,** and it was there that the Buddha stayed during a tour among the Kurus.[1] It received its name from the fact of its granaries being always full (*thullakoṭṭhaṃ, paripuṇṇakoṭṭhāgāraṃ*). It had plenteous crops.[2]

[1] M. ii. 54; ThagA. ii. 30; AA. i. 144. [2] MA. ii. 722; also Avadāna Ś. ii. 118.

2. **Thullakoṭṭhita.**—A city in the time of **Nārada** Buddha, who preached there to **Bhaddasāla** and **Vijitamitta,** afterwards appointed as his chief disciples.[1]

[1] BuA. 154.

Thulla-Tissa.—See **Tissa** (14).

Thulla-Tissā.—A nun. She was present when **Mahā-Kassapa,** in the company of **Ānanda,** visited the nuns and preached to them. She expressed resentment that Kassapa should dare to preach in the presence of **Ānanda.** It was, she said, "as if the needle-pedlar should try to sell a needle to the needle-maker." Ānanda afterwards asked Kassapa to ignore Tissā's outburst, but she later left the Order.[1]

[1] S. ii. 215 ff.

Thulla-Nandā.—A nun, one of four sisters who all joined the Order, the others being **Nandā, Nandavatī** and **Sundarīnandā.** Thulla-Nandā appears to have had charge of a large company of nuns, all of whom followed her in various malpractices.[1] Thulla-Nandā was well-versed in the Doctrine and was a clever preacher. **Pasenadi,** king of Kosala, is mentioned as having come on two occasions to hear her preach, and was so pleased with her eloquence that he allowed her to persuade him to give her the costly upper garments he was wearing.[2] She was greedy for possessions, and was later accused of misappropriating gifts intended for other nuns.[3] She was fond of the company of men, and frequented streets and cross-roads unattended that she might not be hindered in her intrigues with men.[4] She seems to have regarded with sympathy women who succumbed to temptation and to have tried to shield them from discovery.[5] She bribed dancers and singers to sing her praises. She could brook no rival, and especially disliked **Bhaddā,** whom she deliberately annoyed on more than one occasion.[6] She was fractious and would wish for something, but when that was procured for her, would say it was something else she really wanted.[7] She was evidently an admirer of **Ānanda,** and was greatly offended on hearing that **Mahā Kassapa** had called Ānanda "boy," and gave vent to her displeasure at what she considered Kassapa's presumption. But we are told that soon after that she left the Order.[8] She befriended **Ariṭṭha** when he was cast out of the Order.[9] The **Suvaṇṇahaṃsa Jātaka** was related in reference to her, and she is identified with the brahmin's wife of the story.[10]

1 Vin. iv. 211, 239, 240, 280.
2 *Ibid.*, 254, 255, 256.
3 *Ibid.*, 245, 246, 258.
4 *Ibid.*, 270, 273.
5 *Ibid.*, 216, 225, 230 f.
6 *Ibid.*, 283, 285, 287, 290, 292.
7 *Ibid.*, 248, 250.
8 S. ii. 219 ff.
9 Vin. iv. 218.
10 J. i. 474 f.

Thusa Jātaka (No. 338).—Once the Bodhisatta was a teacher in **Takkasilā,** and the heir to the throne of Benares was his student. Foreseeing danger to the prince from his son, he taught the prince four stanzas to be repeated when his son should be sixteen years old, at the evening meal, at the time of the great levee, while ascending the palace roof, and in the royal chamber respectively. The prince in due course became king, and, as had been foreseen by his teacher, he was conspired against by his son, but saved his life by repeating the stanzas. The son was cast into prison, and set free only after the king's death.

The story was related in reference to **Bimbisāra's** great love for **Ajātasattu,** though soothsayers had predicted that the latter would kill his father.[1]

1 J. iii. 121 ff.

Thusavaṭṭhi.—A village in Ceylon where king **Buddhadāsa** effected a miraculous cure.[1] It was near **Anurādhapura**, and the sīmā of the **Mahā-vihāra** passed through it.[2]

[1] Cv. xxxvii. 124 f. [2] Mbv. 136.

Thusavāpi.—A tank near **Pulatthipura.**[1]

[1] Cv. l. 73.

Thūṇa.—A brahmin village on the western boundary of **Majjhimadesa.**[1] It was in the **Kosala** country and belonged to the **Mallas**, and was once visited by the Buddha. The people of Thūṇa were unbelievers and, hearing of the Buddha's contemplated visit, they removed all the boats of the river which the Buddha had to cross, closed all the wells except one and determined not to honour the Buddha in any way. The Buddha arrived with the monks through the air and a slave-woman, coming to fetch water, saw them and gave them to drink. For this, she was beaten by her husband and killed; but she was reborn in **Tāvatiṃsa.** The Buddha, by his power, caused the water in the wells to overflow and flood the village. The inhabitants begged his forgiveness and invited him and the monks to stay there.[2]

A city called Thūṇa is mentioned in the **Mahājanaka Jātaka.**[3]

[1] Vin. i. 197; AA. i. 56, 205; MA. 397, etc.; J. i. 49.

[2] Vv. i. 8; VvA. 45 ff. The Buddha's visit is described at Ud. vii. 9 (UdA. 377), but no mention is made there of the slave-woman.

[3] J. vi. 62, 65.

Thūṇeyyakā.—The people of **Thūṇa.**

Thūpavaṃsa.—A Pāli poem written by **Vācissara.** It has sixteen chapters, the last eight of which contain a description of the erection of the **Mahā Thūpa** by **Duṭṭhagāmaṇi** at **Anurādhapura.** The work probably belongs to the twelfth century.[1]

[1] P.L.C. 216 f.

Thūpaviṭṭhi-vihāra.—A monastery in Ceylon built by **Dhātusena.**[1]

[1] Cv. xxxviii. 48.

Thūpasikha (Thūpasikhara).—Ninety-four kappas ago there were sixteen kings of this name, all previous births of **Thambhāropaka (Paripuṇṇaka).**[1]

[1] Ap. i. 171; ThagA. i. 190.

Thūpāraha Sutta.—There are four persons worthy of a thūpa—a Buddha, a Pacceka Buddha, a Buddha's disciple and a Cakkavatti.[1]

[1] A. ii. 245.

1. **Thūpārāma.**—A monastery near the southern wall of **Anurādhapura,** erected by **Devānampiyatissa.** The spot was consecrated by the Buddha having sat there in meditation[1] and also by former Buddhas doing likewise.[2] The thūpa there was the first of its kind in Ceylon and enshrined the Buddha's collar-bone. Miracles, said to have been ordained by the Buddha himself, attended its enshrinement.[3] The monastery was built later than the thūpa, hence its name.[4] One of the eight saplings of the Bodhi-tree at Anurādhapura was planted in the grounds and exists to this day.[5] The **Cittasālā** was to the east of the Thūpārāma, and on that site **Saṅghamittā** was cremated.[6] It was the monks of Thūpārāma who helped **Thūlatthana** to become king.[7]

Lañjatissa levelled the ground between the Thūpārāma and the **Mahā Thūpa** (about four hundred yards away), made a stone mantling for the thūpa, and built a smaller thūpa to the east of it, near which he built the **Lañjakāsana-hall.**[8] **Āmaṇḍagāmaṇi** added an inner verandah to the *uposatha*-hall in the monastery,[9] while **Vasabha** placed lamps round the thūpa and built a new *uposatha*-house.[10] **Bhātika-Tissa** erected another assembly-hall, while **Goṭhābhaya** made certain restorations.[11] The **Saṅghapāla-pariveṇa** probably formed part of the monastery.[12]

Jeṭṭhatissa removed from the Thūpārāma the stone image placed there by **Devānampiyatissa** and set it up in **Pācīnatissapabbata.**[13]

The renegade monk **Saṅghamitta** once threatened to destroy the Thūpārāma but was killed in the attempt.[14] **Mahānāma** provided a gold casing for the finial of the thūpa[15] and **Dhātusena** restored the thūpa,[16] while **Aggabodhi II.** effected extensive repairs, almost rebuilding the whole structure.[17] **Dāṭhopatissa I.** did the monastery great damage, as did **Kassapa II.,** though he afterwards made amends.[18] **Dāṭhopatissa II.** gave the village of **Puṇṇali** to the Thūpārāma,[19] and **Mānavamma** built a *pāsāda.*[20] **Aggabodhi VII.**

[1] Mhv. i. 82.
[2] *Ibid.*, xv. 86.
[3] *Ibid.*, xvii. 30, 50.
[4] *Ibid.*, 62.
[5] *Ibid.*, xix. 61.
[6] *Ibid.*, xx. 52.
[7] *Ibid.*, xxxiii. 17.
[8] *Ibid.*, 23 ff.
[9] *Ibid.*, xxxv. 3.
[10] *Ibid.*, 80, 87, 91.
[11] *Ibid.*, xxxvi. 4, 106.
[12] *Ibid.*, 114.
[13] *Ibid.*, 128.
[14] Mhv. xxxvii. 27.
[15] Cv. xxxvii. 207.
[16] *Ibid.*, xxxviii. 70.
[17] *Ibid.*, xlii. 51 ff.
[18] *Ibid.*, xliv. 133, 138, 148.
[19] *Ibid.*, xlv. 28.
[20] *Ibid.*, xlvii. 66.

repaired the doors and transposed the pillars of the structure round the cetiya.[21] **Mahinda II.** placed a casing of gold and silver plates in the cetiya,[22] while **Dappula II.** covered the *thūpaghara* with golden bricks[23]; both plates and bricks were later plundered by the **Paṇḍu** king.[24] The golden plates were restored by **Udaya II.**,[25] and **Sena Ilaṅga** provided a building for the monks to the west of the Thūpārāma.[26] **Rakkha Ilaṅga** did likewise.[27] **Mahinda IV.** covered the cetiya with strips of gold and silver, provided a golden door for the vihāra and instituted a great festival.[28] **Vijayabāhu I., Parakkamabāhu I.,** and **Vijayabāhu IV.,** successively, restored the buildings and effected necessary repairs.[29] The road into Anurādhapura passed by the southern gate of the Thūpārāma, eastwards and then northwards.[30] From the **Kadambanadī** to the Thūpārāma the road lay through the gate of the **Rājamātuvihāra.**[31]

Behind the Thūpārāma was the **Mahejjāvatthu.** It is said[32] that, at the time of Devānampiyatissa, there was in the Thūpārāma a shrine dedicated to the three Buddhas previous to Gotama.

21 Cv. xlviii. 65.
22 *Ibid.*, 140.
23 *Ibid.*, xlix. 81.
24 *Ibid.*, l. 35.
25 *Ibid.*, li. 128.
26 *Ibid.*, lii. 16.
27 *Ibid.*, liii. 11.
28 *Ibid.*, liv. 42 f.
29 *Ibid.*, lx. 56; lxxviii. 107; lxxxviii. 80.
30 UdA. 238; VibhA. 449.
31 DA. ii. 572.
32 Sp. i. 86.

2. **Thūpārāma.**—The name of a building in **Pulatthipura.** The date of erection and name of the founder are unknown, but it probably existed before the time of **Parakkamabāhu I.**[1]

1 Cv. lx. 56; Cv. *Trs.* i. 220, n. 1; ii. 105, n. 5.

Thūlathana.—Second son of **Saddhātissa** and king of Ceylon (59 B.C.). On his father's death the ministers crowned him king, but after a reign of only one month and a few days his elder brother **Lañjatissa** overpowered him and seized the throne. **Thūlathana** built the **Kandara-vihāra**[1] and a cetiya on the **Sirīsamālaka.**[2]

1 Mhv. xxxiii. 15 ff.
2 MṬ. 355.

Thera.—Name of a monk in **Rājagaha.** He lived in solitude, the virtues of which state he extolled. Hearing this, the Buddha sent for him and taught him how the solitary life could be perfected in detail.[1]

1 S. ii. 282 f.

1. **Thera Vagga.**—The ninth chapter of the Pañcaka Nipāta of the Aṅguttara Nikāya.[1]

[1] A. iii. 110 ff.

2. **Thera Vagga.**—The ninth chapter of the Dasaka Nipāta of the Aṅguttara Nikāya.[1]

[1] A. v. 151-76.

3. **Thera Vagga.**—The ninth chapter of the Khandha Saṃyutta.[1]

[1] S. iii. 105-37.

1. **Thera Sutta.**—An Elder may be time-honoured, long gone forth, well-known, renowned, with a great following, a receiver of the requisites, learned, with a well-stored mind, but if he has wrong views and a perverted vision, he exists for the ill, the harm of devas and men.[1]

[1] A. iii. 114.

2. **Thera Sutta.**—Ten qualities, the possession of which will enable a monk to live happily and comfortably, wherever he may be.[1]

[1] A. v. 201.

Theragāthā.—The eighth book of the **Khuddaka-Nikāya,** a collection of poems, most of which are believed to have been composed by theras during the lifetime of the Buddha. Some poems contain life-histories of the theras, while others are pæans of joy, extolling their new-found freedom.[1]

Dhammapāla wrote a commentary on the Theragāthā, as part of the **Paramatthadīpanī.**

[1] The work has been published by the P.T.S. (1883) and translated by Mrs. Rhys Davids, as *Psalms of the Brethren.*

Theranāma Sutta.—Records the story of the Elder named **Thera.**[1]

[1] S. ii. 282 f.

Therapañha Sutta.—See **Sāriputta Sutta.**

Theraputtābhaya.—One of the ten chief warriors of **Duṭṭhagāmaṇī.** His personal name was **Abhaya.** His father was the headman of the village **Kitti** in **Rohaṇa,** and Theraputtābhaya, when sixteen, wielded a club thirty-eight inches round and sixteen cubits long. He was therefore sent to **Kākavaṇṇatissa's** court. Abhaya's father was a supporter of **Mahāsumma** and, having heard a discourse from him, became a Sotāpanna, entered the Order and soon afterwards became an arahant. His son, thereupon, came to be called Theraputtābhaya.[1] At the end of Duṭṭhagāmaṇi's campaigns, Abhaya took leave of the king and joined the Order, became an arahant, and lived with five hundred other arahants.[2] When Duṭṭhagāmaṇi lay on his deathbed Abhaya visited him and gladdened his heart by reminding him of the works of great merit he had done.[3]

In a previous birth he had given milk-rice to monks, hence his great strength.[4]

[1] Mhv. xxiii. 2, 63 ff. [2] *Ibid.*, xxvi. 2. [3] *Ibid.*, xxxii. 48 ff. [4] MṬ. 453.

Therambatthala.—See **Ambatthala.** Geiger thinks[1] that Therambatthala is the name given to the **Ambatthalathūpa,** built (on the **Cetiyagiri**) by **Mahādāṭhika Mahānāga** in memory of **Mahinda.** But, probably, the whole of this locality later came to be referred to by this name, for Therambatthala is mentioned[2] as the residence of monks, among them, **Buddha-Rakkhita** and **Mahā-Rohaṇagutta.**

[1] Mhv. *Trs.* 264, n. 3. [2] Vsm. 155, 375; DhSA 187.

Theravāda.—The name given to the Buddhist Canon as compiled by the Elders at the **Rājagaha** Council.[1] It was considered the most orthodox; from it seventeen other schools branched off from time to time in later ages, as a result of schisms in the Order.[2] The followers of Theravādā are called **Theravādins**[3] and their succession, **Theravaṃsa.**[4]

[1] Mhv. iii. 40.
[2] *Ibid.*, v. 1 ff.
[3] *E.g.*, Cv. xxxviii. 37.
[4] *E.g.*, *ibid.*, lii. 46; liv. 46.

Therānambandhamālaka.—A locality in **Anurādhapura** where **Uttiya** erected the funeral pyre of **Mahinda.** Later he erected a thūpa there over half the remains.[1]

[1] Mhv. xx. 42 f.

Therāpassaya-pariveṇa.—A building erected on the spot where **Mahinda** used to meditate, leaning against a support. [1]

[1] Mhv. xv. 210.

Therikā.—An arahant Therī. She was born in a family of **Vesāli** and was so called because of her sturdy build. She married and became a devoted wife, accepting the Buddha's teaching, after hearing him preach at Vesāli. Later she heard **Pajāpatī Gotamī** and wished to leave the world, but her husband refused his permission. One day, while cooking, she developed the thought of impermanence and became an Anāgāmī. When her husband realised this, he took her to Pajāpatī, who ordained her. In the past she had entertained **Koṇāgamana** Buddha and built for him an arbour with draped ceiling and sanded floor. In the time of **Kassapa** Buddha she was a nun.[1]

[1] Thig. 1; ThigA., p. 5.

Therīgāthā.—The ninth book of the **Khuddaka-Nikāya.** It corresponds to the **Theragāthā** and is a unique collection in the literature of the world.[1]

[1] Published by the P.T.S. (1883), and translated by Mrs. Rhys Davids as *Psalms of the Sisters.*

Theriya-parampāra.—The name given to the succession of **Theravāda** monks.[1]

[1] Mhv. v. 1.

Thomadāyaka Thera.—An arahant. Ninety-one kappas ago he was a deva, and having heard **Vipassī** Buddha preach, paid him homage.[1]

[1] Ap. i. 226.

D.

Dakapāsāṇa-vihāra.—A monastery in West Ceylon built by **Mahallaka-Nāga.**[1]

[1] Mhv. xxxv. 124.

Dakarakkhasa Jātaka (No. 517).—No story is related, but the reader is referred to the **Mahāummagga Jātaka** for details.[1] The reference is evidently to the **Dakarakkhasapañha** (*q.v.*).

[1] J. v. 75.

Dakarakkhasapañha.—At the suggestion of **Mahosadha** the ascetic **Bherī** asks King **Cūḷanī** what he would do if he were voyaging on the ocean with his mother, wife, brother, friend, chaplain, and Mahosadha, and a water-demon, seeking human sacrifice, were to seize the ship. The king answered that he would sacrifice all but the last, in the order given, and then himself, but that Mahosadha should not be sacrificed. Bherī persuaded the king to make this declaration in public, so that Mahosadha's glory might be spread far and wide.[1]

[1] J. vi. 469 ff., 477, 478.

Dakkhiṇagiri.—See **Dakkhiṇāgiri.**

Dakkhiṇajanapada.—See **Dakkhiṇāpatha.**

Dakkhiṇadesa.—A province of Ceylon, the territory west of the mountains and reaching up to the sea. It was so called from the relation of its position to that of **Anurādhapura.** At one time it was united with the **Malayaraṭṭha** and formed part of the territory governed by the king's second son.[1] Later,[2] it seems to have become the special province of the heir-apparent.

It is also referred to as **Dakkhiṇapassa**[3] and **Dakkhiṇabhāga.**[4]

Among the strongholds of Dakkhiṇadesa are mentioned **Muhunnaru, Badalatthala, Vāpināgara, Buddhagāma, Tilagulla, Mahāgalla** and **Maṇḍagalla,**[5] and among its villages, **Puṅkhagāma**[6] and **Bodhisenapabbata.**[7]

[1] *E.g.*, Cv. xli. 35; but see Cv. *Trs.* i. 54, n. 4.
[2] *E.g.*, Cv. xliii. 8; xliv. 84; lxv. 23; lxviii. 33; li. 12, etc.
[3] *E.g.*, *ibid.*, lviii. 41.
[4] *Ibid.*, *passim.*
[5] *Ibid.*, lviii. 42.
[6] *Ibid.*, lxi. 26.
[7] *Ibid.*, 33.

Dakkhiṇamalayajanapada.—The mountainous country in South Ceylon, difficult of access and providing only a hard living.[1]

[1] AA. i. 52.

Dakkhiṇamūla.—A monastery, perhaps identical with the **Dakkhiṇa-vihāra.** There **Vohārika-Tissa** erected a parasol over the Thūpa.[1] The Mahāvaṃsa Ṭīkā[2] calls it the **Dakkhiṇamūlavāsa.**

[1] Mhv. xxxvi. 33.
[2] p. 662.

Dakkhiṇamūlavāsa.—See **Dakkniṇamūla.**

Dakkhiṇa-vihāra.—A monastery built by **Uttiya,** a general of **Vaṭṭa-gāmaṇī-Abhaya,** to the south of **Anurādhapura.**[1] It was originally inhabited by monks from the **Abhayagiri-vihāra,** but later there was a schism by the **Dakkhiṇavihārakā,** as the monks of the Dakkhiṇa-vihāra were called.[2]

Āmaṇḍagamaṇī-Abhaya built for the monastery the **Mahāgāmeṇḍi-**tank,[3] while **Kaṇiṭṭhatissaka** added a mantling to the thūpa and built a

[1] Mhv. xxxiii. 88; Dpv. xix. 19.
[2] Mhv. xxxiii. 98.
[3] *Ibid.*, xxxv. 5.

refectory on some land on the boundary of the **Mahāmeghavana;** he also constructed a road to the vihāra, and moved on to one side the wall of the **Mahāvihāra** in order to do this.[4] **Vohāraka-Tissa** erected a wall round the monastery[5] and **Goṭhābhaya** restored the *uposatha* hall.[6] The thera **Tissa,** for whom **Mahāsena** built the **Jetavana-vihāra**, was an incumbent of Dakkhiṇa-vihāra, in this context called **Dakkhiṇārāma.**[7] **Aggabodhi I.** erected a splendid *pāsāda* in the vihāra.[8]

The vihāra is generally identified with what is now known as Eḷāra's tomb.[9]

[4] Mhv. xxxvi. 12 f.
[5] *Ibid.*, vs. 35.
[6] *Ibid.*, vs. 107.
[7] *Ibid.*, xxxvii. 32.
[8] Cv. xlii. 14.
[9] But see Cv. *Trs.* i. 66, n. 3.

Dakkhiṇā Sutta.—The four purities in gifts (*dakkhiṇā-visuddhi*), depending on whether giver and receiver are both virtuous, or whether only one of them.[1] It was probably also called the **Dakkhiṇā Visuddhi Sutta.**[2]

[1] A. ii. 80 f.; *cp.* M. iii. 256 f.
[2] KhpA. 222.

Dakkhiṇāgiri (*v.l.* **Dakkhiṇagiri**).—A *janapada* (district) in India, the capital of which was **Ujjeni,** and over which **Asoka** ruled as Viceroy. It also contained the city of **Vedisā.**[1]

Dakkhiṇāgiri lay to the south of **Rājagaha,** beyond the hills that surrounded the city—hence its name.[2] In the district was the brahmin village of **Ekanālā.**[3] The road from **Sāvatthi** to Rājagaha lay through Dakkhiṇāgiri, and the Buddha traversed it in the course of his periodical tours through Magadha, residing in the **Dakkhiṇāgiri-vihāra** in Ekanālā.[4] It was during one of these tours that he converted **Kasī-Bhāradvāja** and **Dhammasava** (*q.v.*) and his father. On another of these occasions the Buddha saw the **Magadhakhetta,** which gave him the idea of designing the robe of a monk to resemble a field.[5] **Ānanda** is also said to have travelled through Dakkhiṇāgiri, gathering a large number of young men into the Order, who, however, do not appear to have been very serious in their intentions, as their behaviour earned for Ānanda the censure of **Mahā Kassapa.**[6] Later, we find **Puṇṇa** with a large following in Dakkhiṇāgiri refusing to join in the findings of the **Rājagaha** Council, and preferring to follow the Dhamma according to his own lights.[7]

Dakkhiṇāgiri was the residence of **Nandamātā** of **Velukaṇṭaka** and she

[1] Sp. i. 70; Mhv. xiii. 5.
[2] SNA. i. 136; MA. ii. 795; SA. i. 188.
[3] SN., p. 13.
[4] S. i. 172; SA. ii. 133; Vin. i. 80.
[5] Vin. i. 287.
[6] S. ii. 217 f.
[7] Vin. ii. 289.

was visited both by Sāriputta and by Moggallāna during a tour in the district.[8] In Dakkhiṇāgiri, Sāriputta heard of the lack of zeal of **Dhānañjāni.**[9] The **Ārāmadūsa Jātaka** (*q.v.*) was preached in Dakkhiṇāgiri.

The **Dakkhiṇāgiri-vihāra** was, for a long time, a great monastic centre, and at the foundation of the **Mahā Thūpa** there were present from there forty thousand monks led by **Mahā Saṅgharakkhita.**[10]

[8] A. iv. 64.
[9] M. ii. 185; see J. i. 224 for another incident connected with Sāriputta's tour.
[10] Mhv. xxix. 35.

1. **Dakkhiṇāgiri-vihāra.**—See **Dakkhiṇāgiri.**

2. **Dakkhiṇāgiri-vihāra.**—A monastery built by **Saddhātissa** in Ceylon.[1] It was restored by **Dhātusena,**[2] and **Kassapa V.** granted a village for its maintenance.[3] It is probably identical with the **Dakkhiṇāgiridaḷha-vihāra,** in which **Aggabodhi I.** erected an assembly-hall.[4] It has sometimes been identified with the present Mulkirigala-vihāra.[5]

It was once the residence of **Appihā-Sāmaṇera**[6] and of **Kāḷa Buddharakkhita.**[7]

[1] Mhv. xxxiii. 7.
[2] Cv. xxxviii. 46.
[3] *Ibid.*, lii. 60.
[4] *Ibid.*, xlii. 27.
[5] Cv. *Trs.* i. 33, n. 3.
[6] MṬ. 552.
[7] MA. i. 469.

Dakkhiṇāpatha (Dakkhiṇapatha).—In the old Pāli literature the name **Dakkhiṇapatha** would seem to indicate only a remote settlement or colony on the banks of the upper **Godāvarī.** Thus, we are told that **Bāvarī** had his hermitage in Dakkhiṇāpatha territory, midway between the kingdoms of **Assaka** and **Aḷaka.**[1] Elsewhere[2] the name is coupled with **Avanti** as **Avantidakkhiṇāpatha** and seems to refer, but more vaguely, to the same limited district.

The Sutta Nipāta Commentary[3] seems to explain Dakkhiṇāpatha as the road leading to the **Dakkhiṇajanapada,** while the Sumaṅgala-Vilāsinī[4] takes Dakkhiṇāpatha to be synonymous with Dakkhiṇajanapada and says that it was the district (*janapada*) south of the Ganges (*Gaṅgāya dakkhiṇato pākaṭajanapadaṃ*).

It is clear that, in the earlier literature at any rate, the word did not mean the whole country comprised in the modern word Dekkhan. It is possible

[1] SN., vs. 976.
[2] Vin. i. 195, 196; ii. 298. In J. v. 133, however, **Avanti** is spoken of as a part of **Dakkhiṇāpatha** (*Dakkhiṇāpathe Avantiraṭṭha*), but see J. iii. 463, where **Avantidakkhiṇāpatha** is spoken of.
[3] ii. 580.
[4] DA. i. 265.

that Dakkhiṇāpatha was originally the name of the *road* which led southwards—the Aryan settlement at the end of the road, on the banks of the Godāvarī being also called by the same name—and that later the road lent its name to the whole region through which it passed.[5] In the Petavatthu Commentary[6] the **Damiḷa** country (*Damiḷavisaya*) is included in the Dakkhiṇāpatha. The Dakkhiṇāpatha is famous in literature as the birthplace of strong bullocks.[7] It held also a large number of ascetics,[8] and in the "southern districts" (*Dakkhiṇesu janapadesu*) people celebrated a feast called **Dharaṇa.**[9] See **Dharaṇa Sutta.**

[5] For a detailed description see Law: *Geog. of Early Buddhism*, pp. 60 ff.
[6] PvA., p. 133.
[7] DhSA. 141; NidA. 16; DhA. iii. 248, etc.
[8] DA. i. 265.
[9] A. v. 216.

Dakkhiṇārāma.—See **Dakkhiṇa-vihāra.**

Dakkhiṇāvibhaṅga Sutta.—Once, when the Buddha was staying at the **Nigrodhārāma** in **Kapilavatthu, Pajāpatī Gotamī** offered him two lengths of cloth woven by herself on her own loom. The Buddha asked her to present her gift to the Confraternity of monks rather than to him, for she would thereby gain greater merit. He then proceeded to describe the different kinds of recipients of gifts, the different kinds of givers and the degrees of purity in gifts.[1]

The sutta is found word for word in the Sūtrālaṅkāra[2] and is often quoted.[3]

[1] M. iii. 253 ff.
[2] Sylvan Levi: JA. 1908, xx. 99.
[3] *E.g.*, Mil. 258; MA. i. 152; also included in anthologies—*e.g.*, the Sutta-Saṅgaha.

Dakkhiṇāvisuddhi Sutta.—See **Dakkhiṇā Sutta.**

Daṭṭhabba Sutta.—The five powers—of faith, energy, mindfulness, concentration, and insight—and where they are to be seen.[1]

[1] A. iii. 12; S. v. 196.

"Daṭṭhabbena" Sutta.—He who regards pleasant feelings as ill, painful feelings as a barb, and neutral feelings as impermanence, such a one is called "rightly seeing."[1]

[1] S. iv. 207.

Daṇḍa Vagga.—The tenth chapter of the **Dhammapada.**

Daṇḍa Sutta.—Incalculable is the beginning of *saṃsāra*, not revealed; just as none knows how a stick thrown up into the air will fall, whether on its side, its tip, its butt-end, etc.[1]

[1] S. ii. 184.

Daṇḍaka Sutta.—A stick thrown into the air may fall in different ways; even so, beings fettered by craving pass from this world to the next and return again, because they fail to see the Four Noble Truths.[1]

[1] S. v. 469.

Daṇḍakappaka.—A township of the **Kosalans** near the **Aciravatī**; it was visited by the Buddha during a tour in Kosala. There he preached the **Udāna Sutta** in answer to a question by **Ānanda,** as to how the Buddha knew of the unregenerate wickedness of **Devadatta.**[1]

[1] A. iii. 402.

Daṇḍakahiraññapabbata.—A golden mountain in the **Himālaya.** The Bodhisatta was once born there as a golden peacock.[1] For details see the **Mora Jātaka.**

[1] J. ii. 33, 36, 38.

Daṇḍakārañña. The forest which overgrew **Kaliṅga** when it was laid waste through the wickedness of King **Daṇḍakī** (*q.v.*).[1] It was on the banks of the **Godāvarī** and, with the **Viñjhāṭavi,** separated the **Majjhimadesa** from the **Dakkhiṇāpatha.** It probably comprised all the forests from Bundelkhand to the river Krishnā.

[1] M. i. 378; Mil. 130.

Daṇḍakī.—King of **Kumbhavatī** in **Kaliṅga.**[1] **Kisavaccha** (*q.v.*), pupil of **Sarabhaṅga,** desiring solitude, lived in the royal park near the city, and was ill-treated by Daṇḍakī and his army while on their way to quell a rebellion, they being under the impression that insult inflicted on Kisavaccha would bring them luck. As a result the gods were greatly incensed and destroyed the king and his country, only three people escaping death: Kisavaccha, the commander-in-chief, who was a pious follower of Kisavaccha, and a man named **Rāma,** who had come from Benares to Kumbhavatī. The last named was saved from destruction owing to his care for his parents. The forest which grew on the desolate land came to be called **Daṇḍakārañña.**[1]

[1] M. i. 378; MA. ii. 599 ff.; J. iii. 463; v. 133 ff.; 267; Mtu. iii. 363 ff.

Daṇḍadāyaka Thera.—An arahant. Ninety-four kappas ago he presented to the Order a walking-stick (*ālambana*) made from a forest bamboo-tree.[1] He is probably identical with **Kumāputtasahāya.**[2]

[1] Ap. i. 283; repeated at ii. 456. [2] ThagA. i. 103.

Daṇḍanāyakabhātaro.—Two brothers, **Kitti** and **Saṅkhadhātu,** generals of **Parakkamabāhu I.** Kitti was made chief of the **Kesadhātus** and Saṅkhadhātu was made a **Nagaragalla.** These honours won from them their allegiance to the king. They took an active part in Parakkamabāhu's campaign against **Gajabāhu**[1] and also in his wars waged for the unification of the country.[2]

[1] Cv. lxx. 279, 284, 293, 301. [2] *Ibid.*, lxxii. 36, 162, 222, 272; lxxv. 181.

Daṇḍapāṇī.—A Sakyan of **Kapilavatthu,** son of **Añjana** and **Yasodharā.** His brother was **Suppabuddha** and his sisters **Māyā** and **Pajāpatī.** He was the Buddha's maternal uncle.[1] He was born in **Devadaha.**[2] According to northern sources[3] Prince Siddhattha's wife was Daṇḍapāṇī's daughter. It is recorded[4] that Daṇḍapāṇī once met the Buddha in **Kapilavatthu** and questioned him on his teachings. The Buddha explained them to him, but he was not satisfied, and went away " shaking his head, wagging his tongue, with his brow puckered into three wrinkles."

Buddhaghosa says[5] he received his name from the fact of his always being seen with a golden walking-stick and that he was a follower of **Devadatta.**

[1] Mhv. ii. 19. [3] *E.g.*, Rockhill: p. 20.
[2] MṬ. 137. [4] M. i. 108. [5] MA. i. 298.

Daṇḍasena.—A king of seventy-four kappas ago, a previous birth of **Asanabodhiya.**[1]

[1] Ap. i. 111.

Daṇḍissara.—A special grant given by kings to mendicant artists. It is first heard of in the time of **Kassapa IV.,**[1] and seems to have been kept up by **Sena III.**[2] and **Vijayabāhu I.**[3]

[1] Cv. lii. 3. [2] *Ibid.*, liii. 30. [3] *Ibid.*, lx. 22.

1. **Datta.**—A chieftain of **Dhanapiṭṭhi,** placed on the throne of Ceylon by **Potthakuṭṭha.** He reigned for only two years (674–76). Among his works of piety was a vihāra at **Dhanapiṭṭhi.**[1]

[1] Cv. xlvi. 41 ff.

2. **Datta.**—A gate-keeper, father of King **Subha.**[1]

[1] Mhv. xxxv. 51.

3. **Datta.**—See **Bhūridatta, Mantidatta,** and **Gaṅgātiriya.** Datta is given as an example of a very common name.[1]

[1] *E.g.*, DA. i. 289; AA. i. 410, etc.

Dattā.—A granddaughter of **Visākhā,** being her son's daughter. She died young, and her mother, full of grief, was comforted by the Buddha.[1]

[1] DhA. iii. 278.

Dattābhaya.—A monk, elder brother of the Catunikāyika Thera of **Kolita-vihāra.** Abhaya lived in **Potaliya-vihāra** and once, when ill, sent for his brother and asked for a formula of meditation easy to practise. The latter suggested meditation on food, and Dattābhaya became an arahant.[1] He is described as strong in appetites and dislikes, but intelligent and keen in understanding.[2]

[1] AA. i. 343.

[2] MA. ii. 527; DhSA. 268.

Daddabha Jātaka (No. 322).—Once a timid hare lying at the foot of a *vilva* tree heard a *vilva* fruit fall on a palm-leaf and, imagining that the world was collapsing, started to run. Other animals, alarmed by the sight, ran also until all the beasts of the forest were in headlong flight. The Bodhisatta, born as a lion, heard their story and calmed their fears.

The story was related in reference to a question asked of the Buddha by some monks, as to various austerities practised by ascetics.[1]

[1] J. iii. 74 ff. The Jātaka is quoted at MA. i. 313 f.

1. **Daddara (Daddarapabbata).**—A mountain in **Himavā**[1]; it is the same as the **Rajatapabbata** (*q.v.*), which was called **Daddara** on account of the thunder playing round it.

[1] J. ii. 8, 67; iii. 16; Ap. ii. 536.

2. **Daddara (Daddaranāgabhavana).**—An abode of the Nāgas at the foot of the **Daddara** mountain.[1]

[1] J. iii. 16.

3. **Daddara (Daddarapura).**—A city founded by the fifth son of King **Upacara** on a spot where two mountains rubbing together made the sound *daddara.*[1]

[1] J. iii. 461.

4. **Daddara.**—See **Mahādaddara.**

1. **Daddara Jātaka** (No. 172).—Once the Bodhisatta was a lion and dwelt with his retinue in **Rajataguhā,** while in a neighbouring cave lived a jackal. One day, when the lions were roaring and playing about, the jackal tried to imitate them and the lions became silent for very shame.

The story was told in reference to **Kokālika** who, trying to imitate the eloquence of the learned monks of **Manosilā,** failed miserably. The jackal is identified with Kokālika.[1]

[1] J. ii. 65 ff.

2. **Daddara Jātaka** (No. 304).—Once the Bodhisatta was born among the Nāgas in **Daddarapabbata.** He was called **Mahādaddara,** his father being **Sūradaddara** and his brother **Culladaddara.** Culladaddara was passionate and cruel and teased the Nāga maidens; the king wished to expel him, but he was saved by Mahādaddara. But at last the king was very angry and sent them both for three years to Benares. There the boys ill-treated them, but when Culladaddara tried to kill them his brother urged him to practise patience.

The story was related in reference to a choleric monk who is identified with Culladaddara.[1]

[1] J. iii. 15 ff.

Dadhimāla (Dadhimāli).—A sea, so called because it gleams like milk or curds. One of the seas mentioned in the **Suppāraka Jātaka.**[1]

[1] J. iv. 140.

Dadhimukha.—A Yakkha chieftain who should be invoked by disciples of the Buddha in times of need.[1]

[1] D. iii. 205.

Dadhivāhana.—King of Benares. See the **Dadhivāhana Jātaka.**

Dadhivāhana Jātaka (No. 186).—Once four brothers of **Kāsi** became ascetics in the Himālayas. The eldest died and was born as **Sakka;** he visited the others, and gave them, respectively, a magic razor-axe, which could be used as razor or axe; a drum, one side of which drove away elephants, while the other made friends of them; and a bowl from which a stream of curd flowed at its possessor's will. In a beautiful island far away lived a wild boar who owned a gem which enabled its possessor to travel through the air. A shipwrecked sailor from **Kāsi** stole this while the boar slept, and, with it, travelled to the Himālaya. There he saw the ascetics, and, in exchange for the gem, obtained from them their magic possessions, afterwards returning and killing them, so that he regained the gem. He then went to Benares and took possession of the throne, becoming known as King **Dadhivāhana,** because he destroyed his enemies by drowning them in a river of curds. In his garden grew a mango tree, sprung from a mango which had floated down from Lake **Kaṇṇamuṇḍa.** He sent fruits from this tree as presents to the neighbouring kings, but always pricked the mango stone with a thorn so that it should not bear fruit. Once, an offended king sent to Dadhivāhana a gardener whom he had bribed to destroy the flavour of the mangoes. The king gave him employment, but the gardener, by growing bitter creepers round the mango tree, destroyed the flavour of the fruit. The Bodhisatta, who was the king's councillor, discovered the plot and had the creepers uprooted.

The story was related to illustrate the effects of evil association.[1]

[1] J. ii. 101-6.

Danu.—Mother of the **Asuras,** who are, therefore, called **Dānavā.**[1]

[1] Abhidhānappadīpikā, p. 14.

Dantakumāra.—Son of the king of **Ujjeni.** He came to **Dantapura** to worship the Tooth Relic and, while there, married **Hemamālā, Guhasīva's** daughter. He brought the Tooth Relic to Ceylon in the reign of **Siri Meghavaṇṇa.**[1]

[1] Dāṭhāvaṃsa iv. 7 ff.

Dantageha (*v.l.* **Dantaroha**).—A nunnery founded by **Kuṭakaṇṇa-tissa** for his mother. She entered the Order, after having just cleaned her teeth—hence the name.[1]

[1] Mhv. xxxiv. 36; MṬ. 628.

Dantadhātuppakkarana.—See **Dantadhātubodhivaṃsa.**

Dantadhātubodhivaṃsa.—A work ascribed to **Buddhadatta,** author of the **Jinālaṅkāra.**[1] The Gandhavaṃsa[2] mentions a Dantadhātuppakaraṇa as the work of **Dhammakitti.** The reference is evidently to the **Dāṭhāvaṃsa** by that author.

[1] Buddhaghosuppati, pp. 49-51. [2] pp. 62, 65, 72, 75.

Dantapura.—Capital of the **Kaliṅga** country, reigned over by King **Sattabhu,** contemporary with **Reṇu.**[1] Other kings mentioned are **Nālikīra**[2] and **Karaṇḍu.**[3] The city is mentioned also in the **Kurudhamma Jātaka,**[4] the **Cullakāliṅga Jātaka,** and the **Kāliṅgabodhi Jātaka** (*q.v.*). The left eye-tooth of the Buddha was in Dantapura until taken to Ceylon by **Dantakumāra.** It had been handed over by **Khema Thera**[5] to **Brahmadatta,** king of Dantapura.

[1] D. ii. 235 f. [2] J. v. 144. [3] J. iii. 376 ff.
[4] Also DhA. iv. 89; see also Mtu. iii 361, 364.
[5] Dāṭhavaṃsa ii. 52, 57; for its identification see CAGI. 593.

Dantabhumi Sutta.—**Jayasena** visits the novice **Aciravata** at the Forest Hut in **Veḷuvana** and asks him to explain how a monk whose life is strenuous and purged of self can find peace in his heart. At the end of Aciravata's discourse, Jayasena leaves him, complaining that the matter is not at all clear to him. Aciravata mentions the matter to the Buddha, who says that Jayasena cannot understand such matters, being too fond of pleasure and undisciplined. He illustrates his meaning by various examples, one being a description of the catching and taming of a wild elephant.[1]

[1] M. iii. 128 ff.

Dantika.—A district in South India where **Laṅkāpura** burnt twenty-seven villages.[1]

[1] Cv. lxxvi. 172.

Dantikā.—An arahant Therī. She was daughter of the King of **Kosala's** chaplain and was born in **Sāvatthi.** She joined the Order under **Pajāpatī Gotamī.** One day, during her siesta on **Gijjhakūṭa,** she saw how a well-tamed elephant obeyed its master's commands, and developing insight on this theme, she became an arahant.

In the past she had been a *kinnarī* on the banks of the **Candabhāgā,** and having seen a Pacceka Buddha at the foot of a tree, she honoured him by offering flowers.[1]

[1] Thig. 48-50; ThigA. 51 f.

1. **Dappula.**—Second son of **Mahātissa** and **Saṅghasivā,** his brothers being **Aggabodhi** and **Maṇiakkhika.** Among his sons was **Mānavamma,** and it was with his help that he became King **Dappula I.** on the death of **Kassapa II.** But he reigned in **Anurādhapura** for only seven days, after which **Hatthadāṭha (Dāṭhopatissa II.)** captured the throne. Dappula

thereupon retired to **Rohaṇa** and ruled as king there for three years (650–3 A.C.). His wife was the daughter of **Silādāṭha (Silāmeghavaṇṇa)**.[1] Dappula was a very pious follower of the Buddha and erected many vihāras, repaired others, and made an image of **Metteyya,** fifteen cubits high.[2] He died from grief at the death of his son Mānavamma, who was killed by Hatthadāṭha.

[1] Cv. xlv, 16-22, 36 ff., 51 ff. [2] For details of his doings see Cv. xli. 53 ff.

2. **Dappula.**—Nephew of **Aggabodhi VI.** When **Mahinda II.** succeeded **Aggabodhi VII.** Dappula rose against him, but, in spite of several attempts, failed to overcome him. He thereupon retired to Rohaṇa where he ruled, having formed a treaty with **Mahinda.** Some time later, he made another attempt to win the throne and fough ta fierce battle at **Mahāummāra,** where he was defeated and forced to flee.[1]

[1] Cv. xlviii. 90, 98, 109, 122, 125, 131, 155 f.

3. **Dappula.**—Younger brother of **Aggabodhi VIII.,** whom he succeeded to the throne as **Dappula II.** (812 – 28 A.C.). He had a senāpati called **Vajira** and a daughter named **Devā.** His sister was married to **Mahinda,** ruler of **Rohaṇa,** and Dappula adopted Mahinda's sons when they were driven away by their father. Dappula rebuilt the **Hatthikucchi°**, **Vāhadīpa°** and **Lāvarāvapabbata-vihāras,** and enlarged the **Mahāpāli Hall,** in addition to various other acts of piety.[1]

[1] Cv. xlix. 65.

4. **Dappula.**—A nephew of King **Dappula II.** and brother of **Kittaggabodhi.**[1]

[1] Cv. xlix. 72.

5. **Dappula.**—Yuvarājā of **Kassapa V.,** and afterwards his successor as **Dappula III.** He reigned for only seven months (in 923 A.C.).[1]

[1] Cv. lii. 42; liii. 1.

6. **Dappula.**—Yuvarājā of **Dappula III.** and afterwards king, **Dappula IV.** (923-34 A.C.). During his reign the **Paṇḍu** king came to Ceylon to seek his help against the **Coḷas.** Dappula was willing to help him but was opposed by his mother. Dappula's commander was **Rakkhaka Ilaṅga,** who built a dwelling called after the king.[1]

[1] Cv. liii. 4-12.

Dappulapabbata.—A dwelling erected by **Udaya I.** (also probably called Dappula) in the **Ambuyyāna-vihāra.**[1] There is also mentioned a **Dappula-pabbata-vihāra** begun by one **Mahādeva** in the time of King **Dappula** (perhaps **Dappula II.**), and completed by **Sena I.**[2] There may have been two buildings of the same name.[3]

[1] Cv. xlix. 30. [2] *Ibid.*, l. 80. [3] See Cv. *Trs.* i. 126, n. 1.

Dabbapuppha Jātaka (No. 400).—There was once a jackal called **Māyāvī.** His wife had a longing to eat fresh fish, and while he was searching for it he saw two otters, **Anutīracārī** and **Gambhīracārī,** disputing as to the division of a rohita fish which they had caught between them. They appealed to Māyāvī to arbitrate, and he gave one the head, the other the tail, while he kept the middle portion for himself!

The story was related in reference to **Upananda,** who is identified with the jackal. Two old monks had received as a gift two coarse cloaks and one fine blanket, and they appealed to him to divide the gifts. He gave them each a cloak and kept the blanket for himself.[1]

[1] J. iii. 332 ff.; the story is quoted at DhA. iii. 139 ff.

Dabba-Mallaputta Thera.—An arahant. He was born at **Anupiya** in a family of the **Mallas.**[1] As a child of seven he saw the Buddha who was visiting in the Malla country, and he asked his grandmother (his mother having died at his birth) if he might join the Order under the Buddha. She brought him to the Buddha and the boy became an arahant in the Tonsure-hall. He returned with the Buddha to **Rājagaha** where, with the Buddha's sanction, and wishing to be of service to the Order, he took upon himself the task of appointing night's-lodgings to travelling monks and of directing them to meals. He performed his duties most diligently and with great intelligence, and his fame spread far and wide. Monks coming from afar, wishing to witness his skill, would deliberately arrive late and ask for lodgings in some place remote from Rājagaha; Dabba would " burst into flame " and walk ahead of them, with his finger burning to light them on the way. It was the sight of Dabba on one of these journeys which led to a slave-woman, **Puṇṇā,** being visited by the Buddha, resulting in her becoming a Sotāpanna.[2]

It once happened that meals were allotted by Dabba to the **Mettiya-Bhummajakā** at the house of a rich man, who, discovering their identity, gave orders that they were to be fed anyhow. The Mettiya-Bhummajakā were greatly offended, and believing that Dabba had intended to slight

[1] **Kusinārā,** says the Apadāna. [2] DhA. iii. 321 ff.

them, induced one of their partisans, **Mettiyā,** to accuse Dabba of having seduced her. The charge was investigated, Mettiyā was expelled, and Dabba's fame increased.[3] The Mettiya-Bhummajakā persuaded the Licchavi, **Vaḍḍha,** to make a similar charge against Dabba regarding his wife.[4] The **Taṇḍulanāli Jātaka**[5] mentions another dispute, where **Lāludāyi** charges Dabba with not performing his duties conscientiously. Thereupon Lāludāyi was appointed to the task, but proved a failure.

Dabba was given the rank of chief of those who appointed lodgings (*senāsanapaññāpakānaṃ*)[6] and was given the *upasampadā* ordination when only seven years old. He was called Dabba because he was said to be born of his mother while she was being burnt in the funeral pyre; when the flames were extinguished, the child was found lying on one of the posts of the pyre (*dabbatthambhe*).[7]

He was a seṭṭhiputta in **Haṃsavatī** in the time of **Padumuttara** Buddha, and it was then that he conceived the desire for the rank of chief apportioner of lodgings. One hundred and three times he became king among devas and one hundred and five times king of men. In the time of **Vipassī** Buddha he spoke calumny about an arahant Thera, hence the conspiracy against him by the Mettiya-Bhummajakā. In the time of **Kassapa** Buddha he, with six others, went to the top of a hill, determined not to return till they had accomplished their purpose, but five of them died before this came to pass. The other four were **Pukkusāti, Sabhiya, Bāhiya,** and **Kumārakassapa.**[8]

Dabba evidently died young. The Udāna[9] contains an account of his death. One day, returning from his alms rounds in Rājagaha, he saw that he had but a short while yet to live. He went, therefore, to the Buddha and, with his leave, showed various *iddhi*-powers and passed away.

[3] Thag. v. 5; Vin. ii. 74 ff.; iii. 158 f. 166 f., iv. 37 f.; Sp. iii. 598 f.
[4] Vin. ii. 124 f.
[5] J. i. 123 f.
[6] A. i. 24.
[7] ThagA. i. 41; AA. i. 152 f.
[8] DhA. ii. 212; ThagA. i. 44 ff.; Ap. ii. 471 f.; UdA. 81; Sp. ii. 578 f.
[9] Ud. viii. 9; UdA. 431 f.

Dabbasena.—King of **Kosala.** He captured **Ekarāja** (*q.v.*), king of Benares, and cast him into prison, but later, discovering his virtues, released him and restored his kingdom. Dabbasena is identified with **Ānanda.**[1]

[1] J. iii. 13 ff.; Cyp. xiv. 3.

Dabbila.—A Pacceka Buddha, mentioned in a nominal list.[1]

[1] M. iii. 70.

Damatha.—A king of one hundred and fifteen kappas ago, a former birth of **Bodhiupaṭṭhāyaka.**[1]

[1] Ap. i. 194.

Damiḷa.—The name of a people (Tamils) whose home was in South India. The Ceylon Chronicles[1] contain records of invasions of Ceylon by the Damiḷas, the most noteworthy being that which was repelled by **Duṭṭhagāmaṇi.** The Damiḷa leader on that occasion was **Eḷāra.** Other Damiḷas mentioned by name in the Mahāvaṃsa are **Sena, Gutta, Pulahattha, Vaṭuka** and **Niliya.** Large numbers of Damiḷas settled in Ceylon, chiefly in the north and east of the Island and, in due course, gained possession of that part of the country. They were employed as mercenary soldiers by some of the Sinhalese kings and many were brought as captives.[2] The **Damiḷa bhāsā** is mentioned among the eighteen non-Aryan languages.[3] In the **Akitti Jātaka**[4] the **Damiḷaraṭṭha** is spoken of as including also the region round **Kāvīrapaṭṭana,** while in the Petavatthu Commentary[5] it is spoken of as part of **Dakkhiṇapātha.**

[1] Mhv., Cv., and Dpv., *passim.*
[2] *E.g.,* Cv. lxx. 230; lxxv. 20, 69; lxxviii., 76, etc.
[3] *E.g.,* VibhA. 388; it was full of consonants (AA. i. 409)
[4] J. iv. 238.
[5] p. 133.

Damiḷathūpa.—A cetiya erected at **Pulatthipura** by **Parakkamabāhu I.** Its original name was the **Mahā Thūpa,** but it was renamed on account of its being built by the **Damiḷas** brought as captives from the Damiḷa kingdom. Its circumference of one thousand three hundred cubits was larger than that of all other thūpas and, according to the Chronicle, it was built without the aid of any miraculous power.[1]

[1] Cv. lxxviii. 76 ff.

1. **Damiḷādevī.**—Queen consort of **Candamukhasiva.** She gave her revenue from **Maṇikāragāma** to the **Issarasamaṇa-vihāra.**[1]

[1] Mhv. xxxv. 48.

2. **Damiḷādevī.**—Queen of **Mahādāṭhika-Mahānāga.** She was young and beautiful and when she visited **Ambatthala,** an old monk named **Citta** fell in love with her and refused to be consoled even though she died soon after.[1]

[1] AA. i. 13.

Daraga.—A locality near **Pulatthipura.**[1]

[1] Cv. lxx. 177.

Darīmukha.—A Pacceka Buddha. See **Darīmukha Jātaka.**

Darīmukha Jātaka (No. 378).—The Bodhisatta was once born as **Brahmadatta,** son of the king of **Magadha.** He studied at **Takkasilā** with his friend **Darīmukha,** son of the king's purohita. Once, while travelling, they came to Benares and there, while resting in the king's garden, Brahmadatta fell asleep and Darīmukha, who perceived certain omens which foretold kingship for his friend, left him, and having become a Pacceka Buddha, retired to **Nandamūlaguhā.** Brahmadatta became king of Benares and, in his glory, forgot Darīmukha for many, many years. When fifty years had passed Darīmukha visited the king and preached to him on Renunciation. Later, Brahmadatta also became an ascetic.

The story was related in reference to the Buddha's Renunciation.[1]

[1] J. iii. 238-46.

1. **Dalidda Sutta.**—Preached at the **Kalandakanivāpa** in **Rājagaha.** A poor man of Rājagaha, following the teaching of the Buddha, was reborn in **Tāvatiṃsa,** outshining the other gods in beauty and glory. This vexed them, but **Sakka** appealed to them saying that he who had learning, charity and wisdom, in accordance with the Buddha's teachings, was certain to obtain great bliss.[1]

[1] S. i. 231 f.

2. **Dalidda Sutta.**—The term "poor wretch" (*dalidda*) is rightly applicable to him who does not develop the seven *bojjhaṅgas.*[1]

[1] S. v. 100.

Dalla-Moggallāna.—See King **Moggallāna III.**

Daḷha Vagga.—The first chapter of the Duka Nipāta of the Jātakaṭṭhakathā.[1]

[1] J. ii. 1-40.

Daḷhadhamma.—King of Benares. See the **Daḷhadhamma Jātaka.** He is identified with **Ānanda.**[1]

[1] J. iii. 388.

Daḷhadhamma Jātaka (No. 409).—Once the Bodhisatta was born as minister to **Daḷhadhamma,** king of Benares. The king possessed a she-elephant who was of great service to him and whom he greatly honoured.

When she grew old, however, all her honours were withdrawn and she was given to the king's potter to drag his cow-dung cart. One day she saw the Bodhisatta and fell at his feet. He interceded with the king on her behalf and all her honours were restored.

The story was told in reference to Udāna's she-elephant **Bhaddavatikā** (*q.v.*). In her old age the king neglected her, but one day she complained to the Buddha, who admonished the king on the duty of gratitude to those who had once been of great service. The elephant was the same in both stories.[1]

[1] J. iii. 384 ff.

Daḷhadhamma Sutta.—Mentioned in the introduction to the **Javanahaṃsa Jātaka.**[1] This is evidently another name for the **Dhanuggaha Sutta.**[2]

[1] J. iv. 211. [2] S. ii. 266 f.

Daḷhanemi.—A **Cakkavatti** of long ago. When his cakka showed signs of disappearing, he handed the kingdom over to his eldest son and became a hermit. Later he taught his son how he, in turn, could become a cakkavatti.[1]

[1] D. iii. 59 f.

Daḷha-vihāra.—A vihāra on **Sīhagiri,** given by **Moggallāna I.** to the **Dhammarucikas.**[1]

[1] Cv. xxxix. 41.

Daḷhika.—A monk of **Sāgala.** A pupil of his once stole a turban from a shopkeeper and confessed his fault to **Daḷhika,** thinking that he would, on that account, become a *pārājika*. But the value of the turban was less than five *māsakas* and the pupil was saved from a *pārājika*-offence.[1]

[1] Vin. iii. 67.

Dasakamma Sutta.—Ten qualities the possessor of which is called an unworthy man, and abstention from which makes a man worthy.[1]

[1] A. ii. 219.

Dasakammapatha Sutta.—Ten kinds of people similarity in whose actions draws them together.[1]

[1] S. ii. 167.

Dasaganṭhivaṇṇanā.—A *ṭīkā* by **Vepullabuddhi** of Pagan, to the **Abhidhammatthasaṅgaha.**[1]

[1] Gv. 64, 74.

Dasaṅga Sutta.—The ten classes of people who flock together because of the qualities they possess in common.[1]

[1] S. ii. 168.

Dasaṇṇa.—A country in Central India. **Rujā** was once born as an ox there.[1] It was apparently a centre of the art of sword-making.[2] **Erakaccha,** a city in Dasaṇṇa, was the residence of the seṭṭhi **Dhanapāla.**[3] The kings of Dasaṇṇa are called **Dasaṇṇā.** Dasaṇṇa is mentioned in the Mahāvastu[4] as one of the sixteen mahājanapadas, and also in the Mahābhārata (ii. 5-10) and the Meghadūta (24-5). It is generally identified with Vidisā or the Bhilsa region in the Central Provinces.

[1] J. vi. 238. [2] J. iii. 338. [3] Pv. ii. 7. [4] i 34.

Dasaṇṇaka Jātaka (No. 401).—Once the Bodhisatta was born as **Senaka,** a brahmin, counsellor to King **Maddava** of Benares. Maddava, seeing that his chaplain's son was yearning for his chief queen, gave her to him for a week. But at the end of the week the queen ran away with the youth and the king became ill with longing for her. Senaka thereupon arranged for a festival, in the course of which the king was shown a man swallowing a sword. The king then asked his counsellors, **Āyura, Pukkusa** and **Senaka,** if anything could be harder to do than that. They, in turn, replied that to promise a gift, to make it, and having made it, not to regret it, these acts were, in increasing degrees, far harder than swallowing a sword made in Dasaṇṇa. The king, grasping the purport of their answers, regained his self-composure.

The story was told in reference to a monk who was tempted by his former wife.

The king was identified with the monk, Āyura with **Moggallāna,** and Pukkusa with **Sāriputta.**[1]

[1] J. iii. 336-41.

Dasabala Vagga.—The third chapter of the **Nidāna Saṃyutta.**[1]

[1] S ii. 27-47.

1. **Dasabala Sutta.**—The Buddha, possessor of the ten powers, the four confidences, etc., preaches the nature of the five *khandhas* and the arising and the passing away of *dukkha.*[1]

[1] S. ii. 27.

2. **Dasabala Sutta.**—The Buddha, possessor of the ten powers, etc., urges on his followers the desirability of putting forth supreme effort and earnestness in order to win salvation.[1]

[1] S. ii. 28 f.

3. **Dasabala Sutta.**—See **Buddha Sutta.**

Dasabala-Kassapa.—See **Kassapa Buddha.**

Dasabrāhmaṇa Jātaka (No. 495).—Once the Bodhisatta was born as **Vidhura,** counsellor to **Koravya** of the **Yudhiṭṭhila-gotta,** and king of **Indapatta.** The king's generosity was unparalleled, but he gained no satisfaction therefrom as all the recipients of his gifts were wicked men. He therefore consulted with **Vidhura** and, after having discussed with him the qualities of real virtue, obtained, with Vidhura's help, five hundred Pacceka Buddhas from the **Nandapabbata** in Himavā and entertained them for seven days.

The story was related in reference to the **Asadisadāna** of **Pasenadi.** Koravya is identified with **Ānanda.**[1]

[1] J. iv. 360-8.

Dasama.—A householder (*gahapati*) of **Aṭṭhakanagara.** One day, having finished some business which took him to **Pāṭaliputta,** he visited the **Kukkuṭārāma** to call upon **Ānanda.** Learning that Ānanda was at **Beluvagāma** near **Vesāli,** he visited him there and held a discussion with him, which is recorded in the **Aṭṭhakanāgara Sutta.** Later, assembling the monks from Pāṭaliputta and Vesāli, he entertained them and presented each with two lengths of cloth, while to Ānanda he gave a suit of three robes and built for him a cell costing five hundred pieces.[1]

Buddhaghosa says[2] that Dasama was so called because in the order of precedence with regard to aristocracy of birth and wealth, he occupied the tenth rank.

[1] M. i. 349 ff.; A. v. 342 ff.

[2] MA. ii. 571; AA. ii. 866.

Dasama Sutta.—Another name for the **Aṭṭhakanāgara Sutta** (*q.v.*).

Dasamagga Sutta.—On the tenfold way, which consists of the Eightfold Path with the addition of knowledge and reliance.[1]

[1] A. ii. 221.

1. **Dasaratha.**—Another name for **Janasandha,** king of Benares (see **Janasandha** 1). The scholiast[1] explains that he was so called because he did with his one chariot what others did with ten chariots (*dasahi rathehi kattabbaṃ attano eken'eva rathena karaṇato Dasaratho ti*).

[1] J. ii. 299.

2. **Dasaratha.**—King of Benares, identified with **Suddhodana.** See the **Dasaratha Jātaka.**

Dasaratha Jātaka (No. 461).—**Dasaratha,** king of Benares, had three children, **Rāmapaṇḍita, Lakkhaṇa** and **Sītā.** On the death of his queen he took another queen and had by her a son, **Bharata.** When Bharata was seven years old his mother claimed the kingdom for him in accordance with a boon granted her by the king. The king was horrified and fearing that she would harm his elder children, sent them into the forest for twelve years, asking them to return after his death. In the forest Rāma lived the ascetic life while Lakkhaṇa and Sītā provided him with food. Dasaratha died after nine years, and when the ministers refused to recognise Bharata as king, he went into the forest in search of Rāma. Rāma, however, refused to return until three more years had elapsed, and on Bharata refusing to occupy the throne, Rāma gave him his straw slippers to be placed on the throne in his absence. When cases were heard, if the decision given was wrong, the slippers would beat upon each other, but, if right, they would lie quiet. After three years Rāma returned and reigned from his palace of **Sucandaka** for sixteen thousand years, with Sītā as queen consort.

Dasaratha was **Suddhodana,** Bharata **Ānanda,** Lakkhaṇa **Sāriputta,** Sītā **Rāhulamātā** and Rāma the **Bodhisatta.**

The story was related to a man of Sāvatthi who greatly grieved at his father's death and neglected all his duties.[1]

[1] J. iv. 123-30.

Dasaratha-rājaputta.—A name given to **Rāma.**[1]

[1] J vi. 558.

Dasavatthu.—A Pāli treatise.[1]

[1] Gv 65, 75.

Dasavaragāthā.—The section of the **Vessantara Jātaka** containing the account of the ten boons granted by **Sakka** to **Phusatī** just before she left Sakka's world to be born as **Madda's** daughter. These ten boons were: to be chief queen of the **Sivi** kingdom, to have dark eyes and dark eyebrows, to be named Phusatī, to have a son, to keep a slim figure, to have firm breasts, not to become grey-haired, and to save the condemned.[1]

[1] J. vi. 482-4.

Dasārahā.—A group of Khattiyas, owners of the **Ānaka-drum** (*q.v.*).[1] Buddhaghosa says[2] they were so called because they took one tenth of the corn (*sassato dasabhāgaṃ gaṇhiṃsu, tasmā Dasārahā ti paññāyiṃsu*). In the **Kakkaṭa Jātaka**[3] they are referred to as the "*dasabhātikarājāno.*"

[1] S. ii. 266 f. [2] SA. ii. 167. [3] J. ii. 344.

Dasuttara Sutta.—The last (thirty-fourth) Sutta of the Dīgha Nikāya, preached by **Sāriputta** at the **Gaggarāpokkharaṇī** in **Campā**, in the presence of the Buddha. It consists of groups of doctrines—ten single doctrines, ten twofold doctrines, and so on up to ten tenfold.[1] It is said[2] that at the end of the discourse five hundred monks became arahants. The sutta is mentioned[3] as describing the *pārisuddhipadhāniyaṅga.*

[1] D. iii. 272 ff. [2] DA. iii. 1064. [3] MA. i. 330.

Dahara Sutta.—Preached at **Jetavana** to **Pasenadi.** Pasenadi hints that the Buddha is young and, as compared with other teachers, not fully enlightened. The Buddha explains to him that there are four things in the world which must not be lightly regarded on account of their youth—a noble prince, a snake, a fire, and a holy man (*bhikkhu*). It was this sutta which effected the conversion of Pasenadi.[1]

[1] S. i. 68 f. The Northern books call it the Kumāradṛṣṭānta Sūtra (Rockhill: p. 49).

Dahegallaka.—See **Rahegallaka.**

Dāṭṭha.—A thera, at whose request, according to the Gandhavaṃsa,[1] Buddhaghosa composed the **Sumaṅgalavilāsinī,** and **Dhammapāla** wrote the *ṭīkā* to the **Viduddhimagga.**

[1] Gv. 68, 69; but see *s.v.* **Dāṭhānāgā.**

1. **Dāṭhaggabodhi.**—The name of a building erected in the **Abhayuttara-vihāra** by **Aggabodhi II.** He named it after himself and his queen **Dāṭhā.**[1]

[1] Cv. xlii. 64.

2. **Dāṭhaggabodhi.**—A pariveṇa in **Mahāgāma,** built by **Aggabodhi,** son of **Mahātissa** and **Saṅghasivā.**[1]

[1] Cv. xlv. 42.

Dāṭhā.—Daughter of **Aggabodhi I.** She was given to the **Malayarājā,** the sister's son of **Aggabodhi I.,**[1] who afterwards became **Aggabodhi II.**[2] She seems to have been also called **Saṅghabhaddā.**[3]

[1] Cv. xlii. 6, 10. [2] *Ibid.*, 64. [3] *Ibid.*, 41.

Dāṭhākoṇḍañña.—A monastery in **Sīhagiri,** given by King **Moggallāna** to the **Sāgalikas.**[1]

[1] Cv. xxxix. 41.

Dāṭhādhātughara.—A building in **Anurādhapura,** in which was deposited the Tooth Relic after its arrival in Ceylon, in the reign of **Sirimeghavaṇṇa.** The building was evidently attached to the palace "in royal territory," and was originally erected by **Devānampiyatissa,** its name then being **Dhammacakka.**[1] **Dhātusena** restored it,[2] while **Aggabodhi I.** beautified it with various decorations.[3] It was burnt by the **Coḷas,** but was rebuilt by **Mahinda IV.** We are told[4] that it was situated *nagaramajjhaṃhi, i.e.*, in the heart of the royal quarters.

[1] Cv. xxxvii. 95 f.
[2] *Ibid.*, xxxviii. 70.
[3] *Ibid.*, xlii. 33.
[4] *Ibid.*, xliv. 134; liv. 45

Dāṭhādhātuvaṃsa.—A Pāli Chronicle containing the history of the Tooth Relic. It appears to have differed from the **Dāṭhāvaṃsa** and was evidently an earlier work.[1]

[1] Cv. xxxvii. 93; P.L.C. 66, 209.

1. **Dāṭhānāga Thera.**—Resident of the **Sumaṅgalapariveṇa** of the **Māhāvihāra.** At his request **Buddhaghosa** wrote the **Sumaṅgalavilāsinī.**[1]

[1] DA. ii. 780 (Hewavitame Bequest Series).

2. **Dāṭhānāga Thera.**—A forest-dwelling monk in the time of **Mahinda IV.** The king made use of his services in recitals of the Abhidhamma.[1]

[1] Cv. liv. 36.

3. **Dāṭhānāga Thera.**—A monk of Ceylon, author of the **Niruttisāramañjūsā.**[1]

[1] Svd. 1241; but see Bode: p. 29.

Dāṭhānāma.—A householder of **Ambilayāgu** and son of **Dhātusena** of **Nandivāpigāma.** Dāṭhanāma had two sons, **Dhātusena** (afterwards king) and **Silātissabodhi.**[1]

[1] Cv. xxxviii. 14.

Dāṭhāpāsāda.—A building erected by **Aggabodhi I.** at the **Hatthakucchi-vihāra.**[1]

[1] Cv. xlii. 21.

1. **Dāthāppabhuti.**—Father of King **Silākāla.** He was a **Lambakaṇṇa** and served under **Kassapa I.** Later he quarrelled with the king and retired to the **Mereliya** district.[1]

[1] Cv. xxxix. 44.

2. **Dāṭhappabhuti.**—Second son of King **Silākāla.** He was given the post of **Malayarājā** with the province of **Dakkhiṇadesa** and the care of the sea coast. On the death of Silākāla he murdered his younger brother, **Upatissa,** and became king, but his elder brother, **Moggallāna,** marched against him and challenged him to single combat. Dāṭhāppabhuti was vanquished in this conquest and committed suicide. He ruled for six months and six days[1] (in 537 A.C.).

[1] Cv. xli. 33-53.

3. **Dāṭhāppabhuti.**—An *ādipāda* (royal prince), contemporary of **Aggabodhi I.** When **Jotipāla** defeated the **Vetullavādins,** Dāṭhāppabhuti was so incensed that he raised his arm to strike the thera, but an ulcer immediately appeared on it. Dāṭhāppabhuti refused to ask Jotipāla's forgiveness and died soon after.[1]

[1] Cv. xlii. 36 f.

Dāṭhābhāra.—A general of **Gajabāhu.**[1]

[1] Cv. lxx. 104.

Dāṭhāvaṃsa.—A Pāli poem, composed in the reign of **Līlāvatī** by **Dhammakitti,** at the request of the minister **Parakkama.** It is based on an older Sinhalese Chronicle, the *Daḷadāvaṃsa,* and is an elaborate work dealing with the history of the Tooth Relic up to the time of its arrival in Ceylon.[1]

[1] Ed. by the P.T.S. (1884); for details see P.L.C. 207 f.

Dāṭhāvaḍḍhana.—A village in **Rohaṇa,** mentioned in the campaigns of **Parakkamabāhu I.**[1]

[1] Cv. lxxiv. 77.

Dāṭhāvedhaka.—The Mahāvaṃsa Ṭīkā mentions[1] two theras of this name, one a resident of the **Kurundacullaka-pariveṇa,** and the other of the **Kolambahālaka-pariveṇa.** They lived in the time of **Bhāgineyya Dāṭhopatissa,** and about fifty years after the secession of the **Sāgalikā** from the **Dhammaruci-nikāya** they set up a school of their own, in which they borrowed the Ubhato-vihaṅga from the **Dhammarucikas** and the Khandaka and Parivāra from the **Sāgalikas.**

[1] MṬ. 176.

1. **Dāṭhāsiva.**—A thera held in high esteem by **Aggabodhi I.**[1] Geiger[2] thinks he probably held some sort of position in the king's court, corresponding to that of a *purohita.*

[1] Cv. xlii. 22. [2] Cv. *Trs.* i. 67, n. 8.

2. **Dāṭhāsiva.**—Minister of **Jeṭṭhatissa III.** He was captured by the forces of **Aggabodhi III.** at **Māyetti,** but later regained his freedom and was sent by Jeṭṭhatissa to India to cut off Aggabodhi's rearward communications. When Jeṭṭhatissa committed suicide and Aggabodhi was once more king, Dāṭhāsiva returned to Ceylon, defeated Aggabodhi and became king as **Dāṭhopatissa.** But his reign was insecure and he was constantly having to flee. He was very rapacious and plundered the temples. Later, to make amends, he built the **Sākavatthu-vihāra** and restored the **Thūpārāma.** In the end he fled to India from **Kassapa II.,** but returned later and fought a battle in which he was killed.[1] He had a nephew, **Hatthadāṭha,**[2] who became known as **Bhāgineyya-Dāṭhopatissa.** The prince **Bodhi** and the princess **Lokitā** were descendants of Dāṭhopatissa.[3]

[1] Cv. xliv. 128 ff. [2] *Ibid.,* 155. [3] *Ibid.,* lvii. 40.

3. **Dāṭhāsiva.**—A thera, resident of **Nāgasālā ;** he was very learned and held in great esteem by **Aggabodhi IV.**[1]

[1] Cv. xlvi. 6.

4. **Dāṭhāsiva.**—*Uparājā* of **Aggabodhi IV.** He was captured and imprisoned by **Potthakuṭṭha.**[1]

[1] Cv. xlvi. 40.

5. **Dāṭhāsiva.**—An *ādipāda*, ruler of **Rohaṇa.** His son was **Mahinda,** who quarrelled with him and, with the king's help, drove him to India and took possession of Rohaṇa.[1]

[1] Cv. xlix. 10.

Dāṭhika.—A Damiḷa usurper. He slew **Piḷayamāra** and reigned at **Anurādhapura** for two years, till he was slain by **Vaṭṭagāmaṇi-Abhaya.**[1]

[1] Mhv. xxxiii. 59, 60, 78; Dpv. xix. 15, 16; xx. 17, 18.

Dāṭhiya.—A Damiḷa usurper who reigned at **Anurādhapura** for three years. He was then slain by **Dhātusena.**[1]

[1] Cv. xxxviii. 33.

1. **Dāṭhopatissa.**—See **Dāṭhāsiva** (2).

2. **Dāṭhopatissa.** — Also called **Bhāgineyya-Dāṭhopatissa.** See *s.v.* **Hatthadāṭha.**

Dātā Suttā.—A group of *suttas* about those who give various kinds of gifts in order to obtain corresponding kinds of happiness after death.[1]

[1] S. iii. 250 f.

1. **Dāna Vagga.**—The thirteenth chapter of the Duka Nipāta of the Aṅguttara Nikāya.[1]

[1] A. i. 91 f.

2. **Dāna Vagga.**—The fourth chapter of the Aṭṭhaka Nipāta of the Aṅguttara Nikāya.[1]

[1] A. iv. 236-48.

1. **Dāna Sutta.**—Preached at **Jetavana,** regarding an offering founded by **Velukaṇṭakī-Nandamātā** to monks, with **Sāriputta** and **Moggallāna** at their head. Her offering, says the Buddha, is complete in six ways—three on the part of the giver and three on that of the recipients. The giver is glad at heart before making the gift, is satisfied while giving, and rejoices after the gift. The recipients are either free from lust, hatred and delusion, or are on the way to such freedom. The merit obtained from such a gift is infinite.[1]

[1] A. iii. 336 f.

2. **Dāna Sutta.**—**Sāriputta,** with the lay disciples of **Campā,** visits the Buddha at the **Gaggarāpokkharaṇi** and asks him why the same offerings have, in one case, no reward, in another, great reward. The Buddha explains in detail.[1]

[1] A. iv. 59 ff.

3. **Dāna Sutta.**—On the eight kinds of alms.[1]

[1] A. iv. 236.

Dānakkhanda.—A section of the **Vessantara Jātaka** dealing with the gifts made by **Vessantara** on his way to **Vaṅkagiri,** including the chariot in which he rode.[1]

[1] J. vi. 513.

Dānavā.—Name given to the **Asuras**[1] because they were descendants of **Danu.**

[1] *E.g.*, Mil. 153.

Dānavatthu Sutta.—On eight motives from which alms are given.[1]

[1] A. iv. 236 f.

Dānaveghasā.—A class of **Asuras,** present at the **Mahāsamaya.**[1] The Commentary[2] describes them as archers (*dhanuggahaasurā*).

[1] D. ii. 259. [2] DA. ii. 689.

Dānānisaṃsa Sutta.—The five advantages of making gifts—popularity, affection, good reputation, steadfastness in the householder's duty, and happy rebirth.[1]

[1] A. iii. 41.

Dānūpapatti Sutta.—On the eight modes of rebirth of an almsgiver, according to his wish.[1]

A. iv. 239 ff.

Dāmali.—A devaputta who visits the Buddha at **Jetavana** and tells him that an arahant has to work hard for nothing. The Buddha points out to him that there is nothing left for an arahant to do.[1]

[1] S. i. 47.

Dāmali Sutta.—Records the visit of **Dāmali** (*q.v.*) to the Buddha.

Dāma-vihāra.—A pariveṇa founded by **Mahinda II.**[1]

[1] Cv. xlviii. 133.

Dāmahālaka (Dāmagallaka).—A monastery in Ceylon, the residence of the Thera **Mahādeva.**[1]

[1] Mhv. xxxvi. 68.

Dāmā.—An *aggasāvikā* of **Vessabhū** Buddha.[1]

[1] Bu. xxii. 24; J. i. 42.

Dāyagāma-vihāra.—A monastery in **Rohaṇa,** built by **Dhātusena.**[1]

[1] Cv. xxxviii. 49.

Dāyapassa.—A park near Benares. **Saṅkicca** once stayed there with his followers.[1]

[1] J. v. 264, 265.

Dārukammika Sutta.—A wood-seller visits the Buddha at **Ñātika** and tells him that, in his family, alms are given to various kinds of monks—forest-dwellers, rag-wearers, arahants, etc. The Buddha points out to him that though it is difficult to distinguish the good and bad qualities of monks, yet he should continue to give alms to the Order.[1]

[1] A. iii. 391 f.

Dārukassapa.—A minister of **Dappula II.** He started to build the **Kassaparājaka-vihāra,** but was unable to finish it.[1] He was probably a younger brother of the *ādipāda* **Kassapa,** slain by the **Paṇḍu** king.[2]

[1] Cv. l. 81. [2] Cv. *Trs.* i. 145, n. 5.

1. **Dārukkhandha Sutta.**—**Sāriputta,** coming down **Gijjhakuṭa,** sees a log of wood, and tells the monks that a wise person could see all the elements in that log.[1]

[1] A. iii. 340.

2. **Dārukkhandha Sutta.**—The Buddha, while staying at **Kosambi,** sees a great log of wood floating down the river, and tells the monks that just as the log, if it does not ground on a bank, or sink in midstream, or stick on a

shoal, or fall into human or non-human hands, or get caught in a whirlpool, or rot inwardly, will, without doubt, float down to the ocean; so will a monk, without doubt, float down to Nibbāna if he escapes the dangers on the way. The monks ask what the dangers are, and the Buddha explains them, on the analogy of the dangers besetting the log. At the end of the discourse, the cowherd **Nanda,** who had been listening, joined the Order.[1]

[1] S. iv. 179 f.

3. **Dārukkhandha Sutta.**—The same as the above, except that the place mentioned is **Kimbilā,** and the explanations are given to **Kimbila.**[1]

[1] S. iv. 181.

Dārucīriya.—See **Bāhiya-Darūcīriya.**

Dāruṇa Sutta.—Dire are gains, favours, flattery, etc., and we should train ourselves to lay them aside.[1]

[1] S. ii. 225.

Dārupattaka.—A *religieux*, teacher of **Jāliya.**[1] He was so called because he carried a wooden bowl with him.[2]

[1] D. i. 157. [2] DA. i. 319.

Dārubhaṇḍaka-Mahātissa.—A poor man of **Valliya** Street in **Mahāgāma,** so called because he earned his living by selling wood. He was very poor, and once, after consulting with his wife, offered a part of their meal to a young monk. He accepted it, but, on seeing how poor it was, threw it away. They were greatly grieved, and having obtained twelve kahapaṇas by placing their daughter in service, bought a cow and gave milk twice daily to the monks. Then, wishing to reclaim his daughter, the man worked for six months in a sugar mill, and, having obtained the necessary money, was on his way home, when he met **Piṇḍapātiyatissa** Thera of **Ambariya-vihāra.** As it was meal-time, the man looked for food, but could obtain it only by giving away all his money. The food so obtained he offered to the thera, who, on learning the man's story, was so greatly moved that he went to **Tissamahārāma,** put forth great exertion and became an arahant. Soon afterwards he died, but before his death he told his colleagues the story of his benefactor. King **Kākavaṇṇatissa** made arrangements for the thera's funeral, but it was found that the litter containing the body could not be moved until the king sent for the poor man, who lifted it. The body, thereupon, travelled through the air on to the funeral pyre, and **Dārubhaṇḍaka-Mahātissa** received great honour at the king's hands.[1]

[1] AA. i. 277 ff.

Dārubhatika-Tissa.—See **Tissa** (31).

Dārusākaṭikaputta-Vatthu.—The story of the son of a carter. His father was a heretic, but he, while playing with a Buddhist lad, had learnt to say "Praise be to the Buddha." One day he went with his father on a journey, and as his father got locked into the city at sunset, he had to spend the night all alone under the cart outside the walls of **Rājagaha.** During the night, two Yakkhas tried to eat him, but in his dream he whispered "Praise be to the Buddha" and was saved. The king, hearing the story, repeated it to the Buddha.[1]

[1] DhA. iii. 455 ff.

Dārurugāma.—A village near **Kalyāṇī** in Ceylon. Near it was **Jayavaḍḍhanakoṭṭa.**[1] The name may have been Dārugāma, the *uru* being a descriptive adjective meaning *mahā.*[2]

[1] Cv. xci. 6. [2] Cv. *Trs.* ii. 213, n. 2.

1. **Dāsaka Thera.**—He was born in **Sāvatthi** and was appointed by **Anāthapiṇḍika** to look after the vihāra. There, being impressed by what he saw and heard, he entered the Order. Some say that he was the son of a slave-woman of Anāthapiṇḍika. The seṭṭhi was pleased with him and freed him that he might become a monk. It is said that in a previous birth he had ordered an arahant to do some work for him, hence his birth as a slave.

From the time he was ordained he became slothful and fond of sleep. The Buddha admonished him, and, much agitated, he put forth effort and realised arahantship.

Ninety-one kappas ago he met the Pacceka Buddha **Ajita** and gave him some beautiful mangoes to eat. Later, in the time of **Kassapa** Buddha, he was a monk.[1]

Perhaps it is this same Dāsaka who is mentioned in the Saṃyutta Nikāya[2] as having been sent by the monks of **Kosambī** to **Khemaka,** carrying messages to and fro till he had walked up and down over two yojanas.

[1] Thag 17: ThagA. i. 68 ff [2] S. iii. 127 ff.; SA. ii. 230.

2. **Dāsaka Thera.**—Friend of **Soṇaka** and pupil of **Upāli.** He was a learned brahmin of **Vesāli,** and, meeting Upāli at the **Vālikārāma,** had a discussion with him, at the end of which he entered the Order for the purpose of studying the Doctrine. He learnt the whole of the Tipiṭaka and became an arahant. Later he ordained Soṇaka, son of the caravan-guide, and teacher of **Siggava** and **Caṇḍavajji.** After Upāli's death, Dāsaka became chief of the teachers of the Vinaya.[1]

[1] Mhv. v. 104 ff.; Dpv. iv. 28 ff.; v. 77 ff.; Vin. v. 2; Sp. i. 32, 235; but see Dvy. 3 ff.

1. **Dāsiyā.**—A nun who came from India to Ceylon; she was eminent in the knowledge of the Vinaya. She lived in **Anurādhapura.**[1]

[1] Dpv. xviii. 14.

2. **Dāsiyā.**—A nun of **Anurādhapura;** she was teacher of the **Vinaya.**[1]

[1] Dpv. xviii. 28.

Dāsī Sutta.—Few are those who abstain from accepting male and female slaves; many those who do not.[1]

[1] S. v. 472.

Dāsīvimāna.—The story of a slave-woman of **Sāvatthi.** Her master heard the Buddha preach, and gave alms every day to four monks. She was entrusted with this duty, which she discharged conscientiously. For sixteen years she observed the *sīlas*, and one day, after listening to the Dhamma, she became a Sotāpanna. After death, she was born as one of **Sakka's** companions and met **Moggallāna,** to whom she related her story.[1]

[1] vv. ii. 1; VvA. 91 ff.

Diṭṭha Sutta.—See **Diddha Sutta.**[1]

[1] See KS. ii. 156, n. 2.

Diṭṭhadhammika Sutta.—**Kāḷudāyi** asks **Ānanda,** who explains, what is meant by *diṭṭhadhammika-nibbāna.*[1]

[1] A. iv. 454.

Diṭṭhamaṅgalikā.—Daughter of a seṭṭhi in Benares and wife of **Mātaṅga.** For her story see the **Mātaṅga Jātaka.**

1. **Diṭṭhi Sutta.**—Bad conduct in deed, word and thought, and wrong views lead to purgatory; their opposites to heaven.[1]

[1] A. ii. 226.

2. **Diṭṭhi Sutta.**—The same qualities, as in the above, make one's life barren, and earn for one the censure of the wise; their opposites have the opposite effect.[1]

[1] A. ii. 228.

3. **Diṭṭhi Sutta.**—A nun who is wrong in her views and her purpose and rejects the faith goes to purgatory.[1]

[1] A. iii. 140.

4. **Diṭṭhi Sutta.**—A monk who possesses dispassionate, benevolent and harmless thinking and right views is assured of salvation.[1]

[1] A. ii. 76.

5. **Diṭṭhi Sutta.**—**Anāthapiṇḍika** visits a gathering of confessors of other tenets and confutes them by propounding to them the tenets of the Buddha, so far as they are opposed to their own.[1]

[1] A. v. 185 ff.

Diṭṭhikathā.—Second chapter of the Mahāvagga of the **Paṭisambhidāmagga.**[1]

[1] Ps. i. 135-62.

"Diṭṭhena" Sutta.—The Buddha mentions certain heresies existing in the world and explains their origin.[1]

[1] S. iii. 211.

Diddha Sutta (*v.l.* **Diṭṭha Sutta**).—Gains, favours and flatteries are like a poisoned dart to one whose mind has not attained to knowledge.[1]

[1] S. ii. 229.

Dinna.—Probably an attendant of King **Milinda.**[1]

[1] Mil., p. 56.

Dinnā.—Consort of King **Uggasena.** The lives of one hundred kings and queens who were about to be sacrificed by a king of Benares, labouring under a mistaken idea, were saved by her wisdom. In a previous birth she had killed an ewe and suffered in hell. In this age she was **Mallikā**, queen of **Pasenadi**.[1]

[1] DhA. ii. 15 ff.

Dīpadādhipati.—There were once four kings of this name, all previous births of **Sūcidāyaka** Thera.[1]

[1] Ap. i. 122.

Dīpellā.—Daughter of **Vijaya** and **Kuveṇi**.[1]

[1] MṬ. 264.

Dibbacakkhu.—A false ascetic, a previous birth of **Devadatta.** For his story see the **Somanassa Jātaka.**

Dibba-vihāra.—See **Dīpa-vihāra.**

Diyavāsa.—A brahmin. The boundary of the **Mahāvihāra** passed by his house.[1]

[1] Mbv. 135; Mhv., p. 332, vs. 14.

Divācandantabāṭava.—A forest in **Rohaṇa.**[1]

[1] Cv. lxxiv. 61.

Disampati.—A king of long ago. His son was **Reṇu** and his chief stewards were firstly **Govinda** and later **Jotipāla.**[1] His name is mentioned in the **Dīpavaṃsa.**[2] According to the Mahāvaṃsa Ṭīkā,[3] his father was **Samatha** and he reigned in Benares.

[1] D. ii. 230 f.; Mtu. i. 197 ff. [2] iii. 40. [3] p. 130.

Disā.—A slave-woman of **Okkāka.** She was the mother of **Kaṇha,** ancestor of the **Kaṇhāyana-gotta.**[1]

[1] D. i. 93.

Disāpāmukha.—A Yakkha who kept guard, with seven thousand other Yakkhas, at the seventh gate of **Jotika's** palace.[1]

[1] DhA. iv. 209.

Disāpāmokkha.—A monk of Burma. He joined the Order in his old age and studied hard, till he astonished the chief theras by his learning; and was appointed by King **Narapati** as his teacher.[1]

[1] Sās., p. 77.

1. **Dīgha.**—A Yakkha chieftain whose help should be sought by followers of the Buddha, when in distress.[1] The Buddha says[2] that Dīgha once visited him and spoke to him of the wonderful attainments of **Anuruddha, Nandiya** and **Kimbila,** and remarked how fortunate were the **Vajjians** that these three were dwelling in the **Vajji** country. Buddhaghosa[3] describes Dīgha as a *devarājā* and says that his other name was **Parajana.** His visit to the Buddha was at **Gosiṅgasālavana,** just before the Buddha left to see Anuruddha and the others.

[1] D. iii. 205. [2] M. i. 201 f. [3] MA. i. 431.

2. **Dīgha.**—A thera of Ceylon, and an expert in the Vinaya.[1]

[1] Vin. v. 3.

3. **Dīgha.**—A brahmin. He found he could not satisfy other brahmins, even though he gave five bowls of food to each. One day he went to the vihāra, and, in order to test the monks, served them with only one vessel of rice. Thirty monks partook of it and Dīgha was pleased with their great moderation.[1]

[1] AA. i. 262 f.

1. **Dīgha-Kārāyaṇa.**—Nephew of **Bandhula,** commander-in-chief of **Pasenadi.** After Bandhula's death, Dīgha was appointed in his place and accompanied the king. Once, during their travels, they came to **Naṅgaraka**[1] and, hearing that the Buddha was at **Medatalumpa,** went to see him, but Dīgha stayed outside while the Buddha talked to Pasenadi.[2] The Dhamma pada Commentary[3] adds that Dīgha went about reviling the king for the murder of his uncle, and that when Pasenadi went in to the Buddha, leaving the royal insignia in Dīgha's charge, the latter saw his chance of revenge. He left Pasenadi, hastened to **Viḍūḍabha** and crowned him king. He then returned to **Sāvatthi,** leaving for Pasenadi only a single horse and one female servant. It was this treachery which led to Pasenadi's untimely death.

[1] **Uḷumpa** says DhA. iii. 356. [2] M. ii. 118 f.; MA. ii. 753 f.; J. iv. 151. [3] i. 355 ff.

2. **Dīgha-Kārāyaṇa.**—A minister of **Bhātiya** (**Bhātikābhaya** ?). He was a very learned brahmin and was appointed by the king to settle a dispute between the residents of the **Mahāvihāra** and the **Abhayagiri,** regarding the charge brought against **Dabba-Mallaputta** by the nun **Mettiyā.** He decided in favour of the **Mahāvihāra** residents.[1]

[1] Sp. iii. 583.

Dīghagāmaṇī.—A Sākyan prince, son of **Dīghāyu** and, therefore, cousin of **Ummāda-Cittā.** Having heard of Cittā, he went to **Upatissagāma** and took service at the court of **Paṇḍuvāsudeva.** There Cittā saw him and fell in love with him and he visited her by night. When a child was conceived Cittā was given to him in marriage. This child was **Paṇḍukābhaya.** **Citta** and **Kāḷavela** were servants of Dīghagāmaṇī.[1]

[1] Mhv. ix. 13 ff.; Dpv. x. 8 f.

Dīghacaṅkamana.—A pariveṇa in **Anurādhapura,** built on the spot where **Mahinda** used to walk up and down in meditation.[1]

[1] Mhv. xv. 208.

Dīghacārika Vagga.—The twenty-third chapter of the Pañcaka Nipāta of the **Aṅguttara Nikāya.**[1]

[1] A. iii. 257-61.

Dīghacārika Suttā.—Two suttas on the five results arising from roving about.[1]

[1] A. iii. 257.

Dīghajānu.—A **Koḷiyan,** inhabitant of **Kakkarapatta.** There he visited the Buddha and asked for a teaching which would bring happiness both in this world and the next. The Buddha explained to him the four conditions of temporal welfare—*uṭṭhāna-sampadā, ārakkha-sampadā, kalyāṇamittatā* and *samajīvitā.* He then explained the four conditions of spiritual welfare —*saddhā-sampadā, sīla-sampadā, cāga-sampadā* and *pañña-sampadā.* In this discourse the Buddha addresses him as **Byagghapajja.**[1] The Commentary[2] says this was a *paveṇi-nāma,* common to all Koḷiyans.

[1] A. iv. 281 ff. [2] AA. ii. 778.

Dīghajānu Sutta.—Records the visit of **Dīghajānu** (*q.v.*) to the Buddha.

Dīghajantu (**Dīghajantuka**) *v.l.* **Dīghajayanta.**—Chief of **Eḷāra's** generals. He was slain by **Sūranimila.**[1] **Bhalluka** was his nephew.[2] He offered a red cloth (*rattapaṭa*) at the **Ākasacetiya** on **Sumanagiri.** He was born in hell, but the sight of the fires there recalled to him his offering and he was immediately born in heaven.[3]

[1] Mhv. xxv. 54, 62 f. [2] *Ibid.*, 76. [3] MA. ii. 955; AA. i. 375.

Dīghatapassī.—A Nigaṇṭha, follower of **Nātaputta.** He once visited the Buddha at **Nālandā,** and there followed a discussion on actions and their efficiency. Dīghatapassī reported this discussion to Nātaputta and **Upāli,** who was listening, went, against the advice of Dīghatapassī, to the Buddha and challenged him to a discussion, at the end of which Upāli was converted.[1] The Commentary[2] says that Dīghatapassī was long-limbed, hence his name.

[1] M. i. 371 ff. [2] MA. ii. 594.

Dīghataphala.—A yakkha resident in a palm tree outside **Rājagaha. Kālavilaṅgika's** wife, disguised as a man, taking food from the palace to an impaled man, passed under his tree and was seized as his prey. But on learning that she was the king's messenger, the yakkha released her and asked her to convey the news that Dīghataphala's wife **Kāḷī,** daughter of the god **Sumana,** had given birth to a son. In return for this service, Dīghataphala gave the messenger the treasure buried under the tree. She went about shouting the news, and Sumana, hearing it, gave her more treasure.[1]

[1] MA. ii. 818.

Dīghatālā.—Wife of **Goḷakāḷa** (*q.v.*). She ran away with **Dīghapiṭṭhi,** but **Mahosadha** restored her to her husband.[1]

[1] J. vi. 337 f.

Dīghati.—See **Dīghiti.**

Dīghathūṇikā.—The mare on which **Duṭṭhagāmaṇī** fled from **Cūlaṅgani-yapiṭṭhi.** When the king and his minister **Tissa** offered their food to the Thera **Gotāma,** the mare also gave him her share.[1]

[1] Mhv. xxiv. 20, 27.

Dīghanakha.—A paribbājaka, nephew (sister's son) of **Sāriputta.** He visited the Buddha at **Sūkarakhatalena** and the Buddha preached to him the **Dīghanakha Sutta,** at the end of which he became a sotāpanna. In the sutta he is addressed as **Aggivessana.**[1]

He was originally an Annihilationist.[2] Perhaps he is the heretic brahmin, nephew of Sāriputta, who was admonished by **Moggallāna** because he expressed great repugnance at the sight of **Kassapa.**[3]

[1] M. i. 497 f.; ThagA. ii. 95; DhA. i. 79. [2] MA. ii. 477.
[3] Thag. 1108 ff.; ThagA. ii. 180.

Dīghanakha Sutta.—Preached at **Sūkarakhatalena** to **Dīghanakha,** who tells the Buddha that no view can satisfy him. The Buddha points out to him the need for consistency in outlook and expounds to him his own doctrine. **Sāriputta** is present, fanning the Buddha. At the end of the discourse, Sāriputta becomes an arahant and Dīghanakha a sotāpanna.[1]

Elsewhere[2] the sutta is called **Vedanāpariggaha.**

[1] M. i. 497 ff.
[2] DhA. i. 79; ThagA. ii. 95; MA. ii. 862; AA. i. 92, 321; DA. iii. 882.

Dīghanikāya.—Also called **Dīghāgama** or **Dīghasaṅgaha.** It forms the first book of the Sutta Piṭaka and consists of thirty-four long suttas, divided into three vaggas—the **Sīlakkhandha,** the **Mahāvagga** and the **Pātheya** or **Pāṭikavagga.** Buddhaghosa wrote a commentary on the work called the **Sumaṅgalavilāsinī.**

Dīghapāsāṇaka.—A locality in **Anurādhapura,** through which the *sīmā* of the **Mahāvihāra** passed.[1]

[1] Mhv. Appendix, p. 332, vv. 13; Mbv. 136.

Dīghapiṭṭhi.—The man who ran away with **Dīghatālā,** wife of **Golakāla**[1] (*q.v.*).

[1] J. vi. 337 f.

Dīghapiṭṭhikā.—A class of petas whose bodies are sixty leagues in height.[1]

[1] AA. ii. 712; PsA. 79.

Dīghabāhugallaka.—A vihāra built by **Mahācūḷi-Mahātissa.**[1]

[1] Mhv. xxxiv. 9.

Dīghabhāṇakā.—Reciters of the **Dīghanikāya.** They separated the **Cariyāpiṭaka, Apadāna** and **Buddhavaṃsa** from the **Khuddakanikāya** and ascribed the remaining twelve divisions of that Nikāya to the Abhidhammapiṭaka.[1] They also held that the four omens which the Bodhisatta saw,

[1] DA. i 15.

prior to his Renunciation, were seen on one and the same day.[2] It is said that once, when the Dīghabhāṇakas recited the **Brahmajāla Sutta** at the **Ambalaṭṭhikā,** to the east of the **Lohapāsāda,** the earth shook.[3]

[2] J. i. 59.
[3] DA. i. 131; for views expressed by them see Sp. ii. 413; DhSA. 159, etc.

Dīghabhāṇaka-Mahā-Abhaya.—See **Mahā-Abhaya.**

Dīghabhāṇaka-Mahā-Siva.—See **Mahā-Siva.**

Dīghalaṭṭhi.—A devaputta who once visited the Buddha at the **Kalandakanivāpa** in **Veḷuvana** and spoke a verse.[1] The Commentary[2] says that Dīghalaṭṭhi (long-stick) was his nickname, referring to his great height while on earth.

[1] S. i. 52. [2] SA. i. 87.

Dīgharājī.—A village in **Magadha,** the residence of many **Saṃsāramocaka** heretics.[1]

[1] PvA. 67.

Dīghalaṭṭhi Sutta.—Records the visit of **Dīghalaṭṭhi** (*q.v.*) to the Buddha.

Dīghalambika.—A village, the birthplace of **Dīghāyu.** The Buddha lived there in the **Araññakuṭikā.**[1]

[1] DhA. ii. 235.

Dīghaloma Sutta.—One who yearns for gains, favours and flattery, is like a long-fleeced she-goat in a thicket of briars.[1]

[1] S. ii. 228.

Dīghavatthu.—A tank, repaired by **Vijayabāhu I.**[1]

[1] Cv. lx. 49.

Dīghavāpi.—A tank and a district in Ceylon. When the Buddha went to Ceylon he visited the village, and on the spot where he sat in meditation a cetiya was later erected.[1] It seems to have been the central post in the country lying between the Tamil kingdom and the province of **Rohaṇa.** Thus we find **Duṭṭhagāmaṇi's** brother, **Tissa,** occupying it by the order of his father. Later, on the death of his father, he retired to Dīghavāpi with his mother and the elephant **Kaṇḍula.**[2] When he made peace with his brother, he was again sent there to look after the district.

[1] Mhv. i. 78; Dpv. ii. 60; Sp. i. 89. [2] Mhv. xxiv. 2, 14 f., 48.

After the conquest of the Tamils, Tissa was again in charge of Dīghavāpi, for we find him being sent for from there at the time of Duṭṭhagāmaṇi's death.[3] Tissa (afterwards called **Saddhātissa**) founded the **Dīghavāpi-vihāra,** in connection with which he built a cetiya, to which he made valuable offerings.[4] We hear of Dīghavāpi in connection with the campaigns of **Parakkamabāhu I.**[5] Many years later **Rājasīha II.** gave the district round Dīghavāpi to the settlers who came from Holland.[6] The village of **Mahāmuni,** residence of **Sumanā,** wife of **Lakuṇṭaka Atimbara,** was in Dīghavāpi.[7] Dīghavāpi was nine leagues from **Tissamahārāma.**[8]

[3] Mhv. xxxii. 2.
[4] *Ibid.* xxxiii. 9, 14.
[5] Cv. lxxiv. 89; 98, 110, 180; lxxv. 1, 10.
[6] *Ibid.*, xcvi. 25, 28; for its identification see Cv. *Trs.* ii. 30, n. 1.
[7] DhA. iv. 50.
[8] AA. i. 386.

Dīghavidassabhātā.—The Khuddakapāṭha Commentary[1] contains a reference to a " Dīghavidassabhātā " to the effect that, for the space of four Buddha-intervals, he burnt in hell, going up and down, his body sixty leagues in height, and five hundred families who accepted his views suffered with him.

[1] KhA. 126 f.

Dīghasandana (Dīghasandanaka).—A Commander-in-chief of **Devānampiyatissa.** He built a little pāsāda " on eight pillars " for **Mahinda,** which became known as **Dīghasandasenāpati-pariveṇa,**[1] and is famous as the residence of **Mahānāma,** author of the **Mahāvaṃsa.**[2] According to the Mahāvamsa Ṭīkā,[3] Dīghasandaka was so called because he wore a long robe (*dīghasāṭakaṃ nivāsesīti Dīghasandako*), and the original name of the pariveṇa built by him was **Cūḷapāsāda.**

[1] Mhv. xv. 212 f.; also Cv. xxxviii. 16. [2] MṬ. 502. [3] p. 289.

Dīghasandasenāpati-pariveṇa.—See **Dīghasandana.**

Dīghasumana.—A thera of Ceylon, expert in the Vinaya.[1]

[1] Vin. v. 8; Sp. i. 104.

Dīghasumma.—A thera of **Kalyāṇī.** A fisherman, living at the mouth of the Kalyāṇī River, gave him alms on several occasions and remembered him at the moment of his death.[1]

[1] MA. ii. 1008; AA. ii. 522.

Dīghāgama.—See **Dīghanikāya.**

1. **Dīghābhaya.**—A son of **Kākavaṇṇatissa** by a wife other than **Vihāramahādevī.** He was in charge of the fortress at **Kacchakatittha.**[1]

[1] Mhv. xxiii. 17.

2. **Dīghābhaya.**—A Damiḷa general, in command of **Dīghābhayagallaka,** and conquered by **Duṭṭhagāmaṇī.**[1]

[1] Mhv. xxv. 12.

Dīghābhayagallaka.—A Tamil stronghold in charge of **Dīghābhaya** and captured by **Duṭṭhagāmaṇī.**[1]

[1] Mhv. xxv. 12.

1. **Dīghāyu (Dīghāvu).**—Son of **Dīghiti,** king of Kosala. After his parents had been cruelly murdered by **Brahmadatta,** king of **Kāsi,** he became the attendant of this king in order to avenge their death, but when the occasion arose he made peace with Brahmadatta. His father's kingdom was restored to him, and he married Brahmadatta's daughter.[1] He was the Bodhisatta.[2]

[1] Vin. i. 343 ff.; DhA. i. 46 f.; J. iii. 211 f., 487. [2] J. iii. 490.

2. **Dīghāyu.**—See **Āyuvaḍḍhana.**

3. **Dīghāyu.**—A Sākyan prince, grandson of **Amitodana** and brother of **Bhaddakaccānā.** He went to Ceylon and there founded a settlement which he named after himself. His son was **Dīghagāmaṇī.**[1]

[1] Mhv. ix. 10 f.; 18; Dpv. x. 6, 8.

Dīghāli.—A locality in **Rohaṇa.**[1]

[1] Cv. lxxv. 60; lxxii. 63; see Cv. *Trs.* i. 325, n. 2 and ii. 49, n. 3.

1. **Dīghāvu.**—Eldest son of King **Arindama** 1. He is identified with **Rāhula.**[1]

[1] J. v. 490.

2. **Dīghāvu.**—A householder of **Rājagaha** and son of **Jotika-gahapati.** He was a sotāpanna and, when he lay ill, he sent his father to the Buddha requesting the Buddha to visit him. The Buddha accepted the request, preached to him and consoled him. Soon afterwards Dīghāvu died and was born as an anāgāmin.[1]

[1] S. v. 344 f.

3. **Dīghāvu.**—Son of King **Mahājanaka** (*q.v.*) and his queen **Sīvalī.** He became king when Mahājanaka left the world. He is identified with **Rāhula.**[1]

[1] J. vi. 44, 61, 62, 68.

4. **Dīghāvu.**—See **Dīghāyu.**

Dīghāvu Sutta.—Records the visit of the Buddha to **Dīghāvu** (see **Dīghāvu** 2). The Buddha exhorts him to practise the six conditions which are constituent parts of knowledge (*cha vijjābhāgiyadhamme*). These are: contemplation of impermanence in the saṅkhāras, consciousness of dukkha in impermanence, of there being no self in what is dukkha, consciousness of abandoning, of dispersion, and of cessation.[1]

[1] S. v. 344 f.

Dīghāvu-bhaṇavāra.—Second chapter of the tenth Khandaka of the Mahāvagga of the Vinaya-piṭaka.[1]

[1] Vin. i. 343 ff.

Dīghāsana.—A monastery in Ceylon, in which lived **Mahānāma Thera.**[1] Geiger thinks[2] that Dīghāsana is very probably a wrong reading for **Dīghasanda.**

[1] Cv. xxxix. 42. [2] Cv. *Trs.* i. 48, n. 1.

Dīghīti, Dīghati.—A king of Kosala. His kingdom was captured by **Brahmadatta,** king of Kāsi, and he and his wife fled to Benares, where they lived in disguise in the house of a potter. His wife bore a son named **Dīghāyu** (*v.l.* **Dīghāvu**). Before his birth, his mother had a craving to see the army drawn up in battle array, its swords tempered. Dīghīti appeased her craving with the help of his friend, the chaplain of Brahmadatta. Dīghāyu was sent away from the city lest harm should befall him. Later, Dīghīti's place of refuge was discovered and he and his wife were being led to the place of execution when Dīghāyu, who was on a visit to the city, saw them. Dīghīti, recognising his son, called to him his dying advice "*mā dīghaṃ passa mā rassaṃ*" (look not too far nor too near). Dīghāyu heard and understood; he entered the service of Brahmadatta, first as an elephant-trainer, then as a musician, and finally as his personal servant. He wished to avenge the death of his parents, but when the occasion arose, he remembered his father's instructions and desisted.[1]

[1] Vin. i. 342 ff.

Dīghīti Kosala Jātaka (No. 371).—Contains the latter part of the story of **Dīghāyu**, son of **Dīghīti**, who, remembering the advice of his father, forebore from killing Brahmadatta when the occasion arose, and later benefited by this action of his.[1] It is stated in the Jātaka that the full story is given in the **Saṅghabhedaka Jātaka.** No such story is, however, to be found, unless this is another name for the **Kosambī Jātaka.** The story of Dīghīti was related in reference to the quarrelsome monks of Kosambī. Some of the stanzas found in the Jātaka story are repeated in the **Upakkilesa Sutta.**[2]

[1] J. iii. 211 f.; *cp.* Vin. i. 342 ff.; J. iii. 487. [2] M. ii. 154.

Dīpa.—A monk, probably of Ceylon, author of the **Parivārapāṭha.**[1]

[1] Vin. v. 226.

Dīpa Sutta.—A monk should cultivate in-breathing and out-breathing in order to achieve all his desires in the spiritual life. He will then understand things as they really are and, when his bodily endurance has reached its limit, he will know that it is so, like a lamp which will go out when oil and wick are used up.[1]

[1] S. v. 316 ff.

1. **Dīpaṅkara.**—The first of the twenty-four Buddhas. He was born in **Rammavatī**, his father being King **Sudeva** (*v.l.* **Sumedha**) and his mother **Sumedhā.** For ten thousand years he lived in the household, in three palaces, **Haṃsā, Koñcā** and **Mayūrā.** His wife was **Padumā** and his son **Usabhakkhandha (Samavatakkhandha).** He left home on an elephant and practised austerities for ten months. His Bodhi-tree was the Pipphalī and grass for his seat was given by an Ājīvaka named **Sunanda.** His first sermon was preached at **Nandārāma (Sunandārāma**) at **Sirighara,** where he converted the heretics. He had three great gatherings of his followers. He was always attended by eighty-four thousand arahants, and his body was eighty cubits in height. He died at Nandārāma at the age of one hundred thousand years and his thūpa was thirty-six yojanas high. **Sumaṅgala** and **Tissa** were his chief monks, **Nandā** and **Sunandā** his chief nuns, while **Sāgata** (*v.l.* **Nanda**) was his constant attendant. **Tapassu** and **Bhallika** were his chief lay patrons among men and **Sirimā** and **Soṇā** among women.

It was during the time of Dīpaṅkara Buddha that the ascetic **Sumedha** (*q.v.*), who later became **Gotama** Buddha, first declared his intention of becoming an aspirant for Enlightenment (a Bodhisatta).

After Dīpaṅkara's death, his doctrine lasted for one hundred thousand years.[1]

[1] Bu. ii. 207 ff.; BuA. 104 f.; J. i. 29; Mhv. i. 5; Dpv. iii. 31; DhA. i. 69; but see Mtu. i. 193 ff., where the details differ from those given here.

2. **Dīpaṅkara.**—See **Buddhappiya.**

Dīpaṅkara-nagara.—Probably another name for **Rammavatī.**[1]

[1] Cv. xxxix. 51.

Dīpanayā.—An eminent therī of Ceylon, resident in **Rohaṇa.** She was expert in the Dhamma and the Vinaya.[1]

[1] Dpv. xviii. 40.

Dīpanī.—Wife of **Mahinda VI.** She was a cowherd's daughter.[1]

[1] Cv. lxxx. 15.

Dīparājā.—A king of **Nāgadīpa,** son of a king of Ceylon by a younger queen. The king granted the queen a boon and she claimed the kingdom for her son. But the prince was blinded in one eye while watching a cock fight and the king refused to grant the request. So he made him king of Nāgadīpa, whence he came to be known as Dīparājā.[1]

[1] VibhA. 443 f.

Dīpavaṃsa.—The oldest extant Pāli Chronicle of Ceylon. Like the **Mahāvaṃsa,** it was based on the Aṭṭhakathā handed down in the **Mahāvihāra** of Ceylon. It gives the impression not of an evenly worked out whole, but rather of a stringing together of fragments, a composition of whole lines, sometimes whole stanzas, borrowed from the Aṭṭhakathā. It is generally agreed that the Dīpavaṃsa assumed its present form about the fourth century A.C.[1] It is stated[2] that **Dhātusena** made endowments for the regular recital of the Dīpavaṃsa.

[1] The work was edited and published by Oldenberg in 1879. For details see Geiger: *Dīpavaṃsa and Mahāvaṃsa.*
[2] Cv. xxxviii. 59.

Dīpa-vihāra.—A monastery in Ceylon, residence of **Summa Thera** (*q.v.*).[1] *v.l.* **Devī-vihāra, Dibba-vihāra.**

[1] MA. i. 126; AA. i. 319; ii. 845, etc.

Dīpāyana.—See **Kaṇhadīpāyana.**

Dīpālatittha.—A ford in the **Mahāvāluka-gaṅgā.**[1]

[1] Cv. lxxii. 54.

Dīpi Jātaka (No. 426).—Goatherds once occupied an ascetic's hut, and, on their departure, left behind a she-goat who had strayed away. As she ran to join the others, she saw a panther in the way; she showed great daring and tried to pacify him with soft words, but all in vain, for he devoured her.

The story was related in reference to a she-goat whom **Moggallāna** once saw near his mountain hut. When she, however, saw a panther, she, with great daring, jumped over his body and escaped.[1]

[1] J. iii. 479 f.

Dīpika.—See **Pañcadīpika.**

Dīpuyyāna.—A park in **Pulatthipura** laid out by **Parakkamabāhu I.** It was so called because it formed a peninsula.[1]

[1] Cv. lxxiii. 113; lxxix. 6; Cv. *Trs.* ii. 14, n. 2.

Dukūla (Dukūlaka).—A hunter's son, father of **Suvaṇṇasāma.** He is identified with **Mahā Kassapa.** For his story see the **Sāma Jātaka.**[1]

[1] See also Mil. 123; Sp. i. 214.

Dukkathā Sutta.—To five persons certain talk is ill-talk—talk on faith to the faithless, on virtue to the virtueless, on learning to one of little learning, on generosity to the mean, on insight to the foolish.[1]

[1] A. iii. 181.

1. **Dukkara** (or **Kumma**) **Sutta.**—A wise monk should withdraw within himself, like the tortoise withdrawing his limbs.[1]

[1] S. i. 7.

2. **Dukkara Sutta.**—Things difficult to do in the religious life, in varying degree.[1]

[1] S. iv. 260, 262.

1. **Dukkha Sutta.**—Dukkha arises from the contact of the senses and the objects proper to the senses, resulting in feeling, which, in turn, produces craving. By destroying this process dukkha is destroyed.[1]

[1] S. ii. 71; *cf.* S. iv. 86.

2. **Dukkha Sutta.**—All the khandhas are ill; he who realizes this destroys rebirth.[1]

[1] S. iii. 21; *ibid.*, 196.

3. **Dukkha Sutta.**—All the khandhas lead to suffering.[1]

[1] S. iii. 77.

4. **Dukkha Sutta.**—The Buddha teaches suffering, the arising thereof, the cessation, and the way to such cessation.[1]

[1] S. iii. 158.

5. **Dukkha Sutta.**—That which is suffering and of the nature of suffering must be put away.[1]

[1] S. iv. 199.

6. **Dukkha Sutta.**—**Sāriputta** tells **Jambukhādaka** of the three kinds of suffering, caused by pain, by the activities and by the changeable nature of things.[1]

[1] S. iv. 259.

7. **Dukkha Sutta.**—A monk without faith is unconscientious, has no fear of blame, is indolent and lacking in insight, lives ill at ease in this world and will suffer in the next.[1]

[1] A. iii. 3.

8. **Dukkha Sutta.**—If a monk has brooding on sense-desires, ill-will, cruelty and conjures up thoughts of these things, he will live ill at ease now and also after death.[1]

[1] A. iii. 429.

9. **Dukkha Sutta.**—It is impossible that a monk who sees happiness in any phenomenon shall live in harmony and peace.[1]

[1] A. iii. 442.

Dukkhakhandha Sutta.—See **Cūḷadukkhakhandha Sutta** and **Mahādukkhakhandha Sutta.**

Dukkhatātissa Sutta.—On the three forms of suffering, caused by pain, by the activities and by the changeable nature of things.[1]

[1] S. v. 56; *cp.* **Dukkha Sutta 6 above.**

Dukkhadhamma Sutta.—When a monk knows the arising and the destruction of all states of ill, he realizes the nature of sensual pleasures and has no longing for them. This is explained by various similes.[1]

[1] S. iv. 188 ff.

"Dukkham-ajjhatta" Sutta.—The eye is Ill, so are the other senses, and therefore void of self.[1]

[1] S. iv. 2.

"Dukkham-bāhira" Sutta.—Forms seen by the eye are Ill, so are the things perceived by other senses. They are void of self.[1]

[1] S. iv. 4.

Dukkhamūla.—A Pacceka Buddha, mentioned in a nominal list.[1]

[1] ApA. i. 107; M. iii. 70.

Dukkhalakkhaṇa Vatthu.—The story of five hundred monks who, in the time of **Kassapa** Buddha, had practised meditation on the characteristics of suffering. In the present age they became arahants immediately on hearing a stanza on suffering.[1]

[1] DhA. iii. 406.

"Dukkhāni" Sutta.—The five ills of a recluse: he is not content with any of the four requisites and finds no delight in the holy life.[1]

[1] A. iii. 146

"Dukkhena" Sutta.—Desire should be put away for that which has suffering inherent in it.[1]

[1] S. iii. 178.

Duggata Sutta.—Whenever one sees a hardship or a hard lot one should remember that one, too, has suffered likewise in some life or other. Incalculable is the course of saṃsāra.[1]

[1] S. ii. 186.

Duggati Sutta.—The Ariyan who has unwavering faith in the Buddha, the Dhamma and the Saṅgha and is possessed of virtue, is free from an unhappy condition of existence.[1]

[1] S. v. 364.

Duccarita Vagga.—The twenty-fifth chapter of the Pañcaka Nipāta of the Aṅguttara Nikāya.[1]

[1] A. iii. 267-70.

1. **Duccarita Sutta.**—The four bad habits of speech—falsehood, slander, bitter speech, idle babble ; and the four good habits—truthful speaking, speaking well of others, soft speech and wise speech.[1]

[1] A. ii. 228.

2. **Duccarita Sutta.**—Five disadvantages of evil conduct—self-upbraiding, dispraise by the wise, evil reputation, death as a lunatic, unhappy rebirth.[1]

[1] A. iii. 267.

3. **Duccarita Sutta.**—A monk once came to the Buddha and asked for a brief teaching. The Buddha asked him to abandon wrong conduct with regard to body, feelings, mind and mind-states, and to cultivate the four satipaṭṭhānas.[1]

[1] S. v. 188.

4. **Duccarita Sutta.**—Three conditions—wicked conduct in deed, word and thought—and their opposites.[1]

[1] A. iii. 446.

Dujīpa.—A king who lived to the age of one thousand. He reigned for five hundred years and, at the end of that period, gave alms to the brahmins, renounced his kingdom and became an ascetic.[1]

He is probably identical with **Dudīpa,** king of Benares, who is mentioned[2] as having given away great wealth, and as a result reached heaven. *v.l.* **Dudīpa.**

[1] J. vi. 203. [2] J. vi. 99.

Dujjaya.—A king of a past age, a previous birth of **Cūla-Cunda Thera.**[1]

[1] Ap. i. 102.

1. **Duṭṭha,** called **Duṭṭhakumāra,** king of Benares.—A former birth of **Devadatta.**[1] His story is given in the **Saccaṅkira Jātaka** (*q.v.*).

[1] J. i. 327.

2. **Duṭṭha.**—Also called **Duṭṭhakumāra,** the son of **Kitavāsa.** At his birth soothsayers foretold his death from thirst, and Kitavāsa had lakes and ponds dug in various parts of the capital and waterpots placed everywhere. One day Duṭṭha saw a Pacceka Buddha begging for alms and dashed his bowl to the ground. He was seized with thirst, and all the water in the city was dried up. He died, and was reborn in **Avīci.**[1]

[1] J. ii. 194 f.

3. **Duṭṭha.**—Son of the king of Benares; a previous birth of the cruel **Licchavi** prince on whose account the **Ekapaṇṇa Jātaka** (*q.v.*) was preached.[1]

[1] J. i. 506.

Duṭṭhakumārī.—Daughter of a banker of Benares. For her story see the **Takka Jātaka.**

Duṭṭhagāmaṇī-Abhaya.—King of Ceylon (101-77 B.C.) He was the son of **Kākavaṇṇatissa** (ruler of **Mahāgāma**) and of **Vihāradevī,** and was called **Gāmaṇi-Abhaya.** The antenatal cravings of his mother showed that he would be a great warrior, and his father gathered at his court the most famous warriors of the land skilled in various ways. Chief among them were **Nandhimitta, Sūranimila, Mahāsoṇa, Goṭhaimbara, Theraputtābhaya, Bharaṇa, Veḷusumana, Khañjadeva, Phussadeva** and **Labhiyavasabha.** Abhaya early showed signs of an adventurous disposition, and resented the confined limits of his father's kingdom, bounded on the north by the **Mahāvāḷuka-nadī,** on the further bank of which lay the Sinhalese country ruled by the Damiḷas. Abhaya was constantly refused permission by his father to fight the Damiḷas and fled in anger to the hills, whence he sent his royal father a woman's garment, to indicate that he was no man. This earned for him the nickname of Duṭṭha, which always stuck to him. At his father's death he had to fight with his brother **Tissa** (afterwards **Saddhā-Tissa**) for the possession of the throne. He was first defeated at **Cūḷaṅganiyapiṭṭhi,** but later he was victorious, and the Saṅgha brought about a reconciliation between the brothers. When fully prepared, Duṭṭhagāmaṇī marched against the Damiḷa king, **Eḷāra.** He rode his state elephant, **Kaṇḍula,** born on the same day as himself. He commenced operations at **Mahiyaṅgana,** capturing fort after fort, manned by Eḷāra's followers, and fought his way down to Mahāvāluka-nadī, where he pitched his camp at **Kandhāvārapiṭṭhi,** near **Vijitapura,** where were concentrated the Damiḷas. After a siege of four months Vijitapura fell, and Duṭṭhagāmaṇī advanced through **Girilaka** and **Mahelanagara** to **Kāsapabbata** near **Anurādhapura,** the capital.[1] There he waited for the onset of Eḷāra and, in the battle that ensued, Eḷāra was defeated and fled towards the capital, but he was pursued by Duṭṭhagāmaṇī and slain by him in single combat close to the southern gate of the city. Eḷāra's body was burnt with royal honours, and Duṭṭhagāmaṇī built a tomb over the ashes and decreed that no music should be played by people passing it, a decree that was for long honoured. This act of chivalry, so much in contrast

[1] Mhv. xxv. 75. It is said that in the course of his journey from Mahāgāma to Anurādhapura he captured thirty-two fortresses manned by the Damiḷas.

with the usual conduct of victors, earned for Duṭṭhagāmaṇī great honour. Later, he defeated reinforcements from India under **Bhalluka,** nephew of Eḷāra, and thus became sole monarch of Laṅkā.

On the seventh day after his final victory, he celebrated a water festival at the **Tissavāpi** and, at its conclusion, built the **Maricavaṭṭhi-thūpa** (*q.v.*) on the spot where his spear, containing the relic of the Buddha, given by the monks at **Tissamahārāma,** remained firmly embedded, no one being able to remove it. From now onwards, consoled by the arahants of **Piyaṅgudīpa,** who absolved him from blame for the slaughter of his enemies, he began his great works of piety, after having distributed largesse to his generals and soldiers. He first built the **Lohapāsāda** (*q.v.*) of nine stories, resembling the palace of **Bīraṇī,** the plan of which was brought to him from **Tusita** by arahants. He then began his greatest achievement, the **Mahā Thūpa,** erected on a site visited by the Buddha during his third visit to Ceylon. The devas, led by **Sakka,** provided the necessary materials, discovered in various parts of the island, and he began work immediately, on the full-moon day of **Vesākha.** Great celebrations marked the inauguration of the mighty task, plans of various builders were inspected before the final choice and no free work was allowed to be done. After the relics, obtained by the arahant **Soṇuttara** from the Nāga-world, had been enshrined in unparalleled splendour and with great feasting, but before the *chatta* of the cetiya and the plaster work could be finished, Duṭṭhagāmaṇī fell ill. Saddhā-Tissa was summoned from **Dīghavāpi,** and he covered the cetiya with white cloth and crowned it with a spire of bamboo, that the king, before his death, might visualize his great work in its complete form. **Theraputtābhaya,** a former general, now become an arahant, and living in the **Pañjalipabbata,** was at the king's side at the time of his death and consoled him with reminders of the great merit he had accumulated during his life. A record of the king's good deeds was read by his secretary, from which it would appear that the king had erected ninety-nine other vihāras, besides the buildings already mentioned. He had once tried to preach in the Lohapāsāda, but was so overcome by nervousness that, realizing how difficult was the task of the preacher, he ordered special benefactions for those who preached the Doctrine. Two gifts made by him are recorded as of very special merit—one was the sale of his special earrings to procure food for five theras during the **Akkhakkhāyika** famine, the other was his gift of food during his flight from Cūḷaṅganiya-piṭṭhi.[2] He was starving, and his minister Tissa procured a meal for him, but as he never ate without offering some of the food to the monks, he wished for a monk to appear before him. When a thera did so appear, he gave him all he had. He was told later, on his death bed, by Thera-

[2] For details see Mhv. xxxii. 49 ff.; also AA. i. 365 f.

puttābhaya, that this food was divided among many thousands of arahants so that the merits of the donor might increase manifold.

It is said that after death Duṭṭhagāmaṇi was born in the Tusita-world, there to await the appearance of **Metteyya Buddha.** He will then become the chief disciple of that Buddha, and his parents will be the parents of Metteyya. Before his birth, as the son of Kākavaṇṇatissa, he was a sāmaṇera of **Koṭapabbata-vihāra.** He fell ill through his hard work on behalf of the Saṅgha at the **Ākāsa-cetiya** near **Cittalapabbata**, and as he lay dying in the **Silāpassaya-pariveṇa, Vihāradevī** visited him at the suggestion of an arahant thera, and after much difficulty persuaded him to be reborn in this world as her son.[3]

Duṭṭhagāmaṇī is regarded as the hero of the **Mahāvaṃsa** epic. His son was **Sāliya,** who, however, did not succeed him, preferring to marry a caṇḍāla maiden, **Asokamālā.** Duṭṭhagāmaṇī's successor, therefore, was Saddhātissa.

The Dhammapada Commentary[4] mentions a minister of Duṭṭhagāmaṇī called **Lakuṇṭaka-atimbara,** whose wife was **Sumanā.**

Duṭṭhagāmaṇī lived to the age of sixty-eight.[5]

Once, after his conquest of the Damiḷas, he was unable to sleep for a whole month, then, at the suggestion of the monks, he took the fast of the eight vows and eight monks chanted to him the **Cittayamaka.** He fell asleep during the chanting.[6]

[3] These particulars relating to Duṭṭhagāmaṇī are summarised from Mhv. chaps. xxii.-xxxii.; Dpv. xviii. 53; xix. 1 ff.; Sp. i. 102.

[4] DhA. iv. 50.

[5] Mhv. xxiv. 47.

[6] DA. ii. 640.

Duṭṭhaṭṭhaka.—The third Sutta of the **Aṭṭhakavagga** of the Sutta Nipāta.[1] The sutta was preached in reference to the calumny raised against the Buddha by the heretics who used the female ascetic **Sundarī** to further their ends.[2] Commentarial explanation of this is included in the Mahāniddesa.[3] The burden of the sutta is that he who praises his own virtue and is dependent upon varying dogmas of philosophy is constantly censured. The *muni* is one who has shaken off all systems of philosophy.

[1] SN. vs. 780-87. [2] SNA. ii. 518 f. [3] i. 62 ff.

1. **Dutiya Sutta.**—On the four modes of progress: painful with sluggish intuition and with swift intuition, and pleasant, with the same two varieties of intuition.[1]

[1] A. ii. 154.

2. **Dutiya Sutta.**—Questions asked by a deva and the Buddha's reply thereto. "What has a good man as his companion?" is one question, and the reply thereto is "faith."[1]

[1] S. i. 38.

Dutiyapalāyi Jātaka (No. 230).—The Bodhisatta was once king of Benares, and the **Gandhāra** king of **Takkasilā** besieged his capital. The Bodhisatta appeared before him and threatened to crush his forces, and the Gandhāra king fled.

The story was told in reference to an ascetic who visited **Jetavana** in order to argue with the Buddha; but on seeing the Buddha seated in the hall expounding the Doctrine, his courage forsook him and he ran away with a crowd at his heels. He is identified with the Gandhāra king.[1]

[1] J. ii. 219-21.

Dutiyamakkaṭa Jātaka.—See **Dūbhiyamakkaṭa.**

Dutiyasela-vihāra.—A monastery in Ceylon (Sinhalese, *Devanagala*). **Kittisirirājasīha** gave to the vihāra the village of **Ratanadoṇi.**[1]

[1] Cv. c. 232.

Dudīpa.—See **Dujīpa.**

Duddada Jātaka (No. 180).—*v.l.* **Dudda, Dudada.** Once the Bodhisatta was a brahmin of Kāsi and, after being educated in **Takkasilā,** became an ascetic in the Himālaya. When he and his fellow ascetics visited Benares for salt and seasoning, the people gathered together and gave them food.

The story was told in reference to two young men who made a collection in **Sāvatthi** to feed the Buddha and his monks.[1]

[1] J. ii 85 f.

Dundubhissara Thera.—An arahant. After the Third Council he accompanied the Thera **Majjhima** to the region at the foot of the **Himālaya.**[1] In the Dīpavaṃsa[2] he is called **Durabhisāra.**

[1] Sp. i. 68; MṬ. 317; Mbv. 115. [2] viii. 10.

Dunniviṭṭha.—A brahmin village in the **Kāliṅga** country. It lay on the road (along which **Vessantara** journeyed to **Vaṅkagiri**) from **Jetuttara** to the **Ceti** kingdom, five leagues from **Arañjaragiri** and ten from the Ceti country. It was the residence of **Jūjaka** and **Amittatāpanā.**[1]

[1] J. vi. 521, 541.

1. **Duppañña Sutta.**—One who is an unbeliever, immoral, indolent and of weak wisdom, is born in purgatory.[1]

[1] A. ii. 227.

2. **Duppañña Sutta.**—One who has the above qualities is censured by the wise and gathers much demerit.[1]

[1] A. ii. 227.

3. **Duppañña Sutta.**—A monk asks the Buddha as to who can be called a witless imbecile, and the answer is, he who fails to practise the seven bojjhaṅgas.[1]

[1] S. v. 99.

Duppasaha.—A king of long ago, descendant of **Mahāsammata.** He was the last of fifty kings who ruled in **Ayujjha.** Sixty of his descendants reigned in Benares.[1]

[1] Dpv. iii. 16; MṬ. 127.

Dubbaca Jātaka (No. 116).—The Bodhisatta was once a very skilled acrobat and travelled about with his teacher who knew the dance of the four javelins. One day the teacher, in a drunken fit of boasting, announced that he would do the dance of the *five* javelins—which he did not know—and insisted on doing it against the advice of the Bodhisatta. The result was that the boaster was impaled on the fifth javelin.[1] For the introductory story see the **Gijjha Jātaka** (No. 42).

[1] J. i. 430 f.

Dubbaṇṇiya Sutta.—Once an ill-favoured yakkha came to be seated on **Sakka's** throne. The gods of **Tāvatiṃsa** were greatly vexed on seeing him, but the greater their annoyance, the handsomer grew the yakkha. Then Sakka came up and showed great humility before the yakkha, and the greater his humility the uglier did the yakkha become, until he disappeared.[1]

[1] S. i. 237.

Dubbalakaṭṭha Jātaka (No. 105).—Once an elephant, caught in the Himālaya, while being trained by the king's trainers, broke away from his chains and escaped to the mountains. There he lived in a constant state of terror until the Bodhisatta, who was a tree-sprite, dispelled his fears.

The story was told in reference to a monk who was always in fear of death. He is identified with the elephant.[1]

[1] J. i. 414-6.

Dubbalavāpitissaka-vihāra.—A monastery in Ceylon, founded by **Saddhātissa.**[1] **Kaṇiṭṭhatissa** built for it an uposatha-hall.[2]

[1] Mhv. xxxiii. 8. [2] *Ibid.*, xxxvi. 17.

Dubbinoda Sutta.—Five things are hard to push against: ill-will, infatuation, ostentation and vagrant thoughts.[1]

[1] A. iii. 184.

Dumasāra.—A cakkavatti of four kappas ago, a former birth of **Saññaka Thera.**[1]

[1] Ap. i. 120.

Dumbara.—A district in the **Malaya** country of Ceylon.[1]

[1] Cv. lxx. 5, 8.

1. **Dummukha.**—A Licchavi chieftain. He was present at the discussion of the Nigaṇṭha **Saccaka** with the Buddha, and seeing Saccaka discomfited in the debate, Dummukha compared him to a crab pulled out of a pond and ill-treated by village boys.[1]

The Commentary says[2] that Dummukha just happened to be his name. He was in reality quite handsome.

[1] M. i. 234. [2] MA. i. 459.

2. **Dummukha.**—King of **Kampilla** in **Uttarapañcāla.** One day, while looking from his window down on to the palace yard, he saw several bulls setting upon a cow in lust, and one bull, stronger than the rest, killed another with his horns. The king, realizing the evil nature of lust, entered into a trance and became a Pacceka Buddha.[1]

[1] J. iii. 379, 381.

1. **Dummedha Jātaka** (No. 50).—The Bodhisatta was once born as **Brahmadatta,** king of Benares. Seeing that his subjects were much given to offering sacrifices to the gods in course of which animals were killed and other sins committed, he made proclamation, soon after becoming king, that he had made a vow to offer in sacrifice all those of his subjects who were addicted to the Five Sins and walked upon the ten paths of unrighteousness. His ministers were sent to look for such people, and the proclamation had the desired effect.[1]

For the introductory story see the **Mahākaṇha Jātaka.**

[1] J. i. 259 f.

2. **Dummedha Jātaka** (No. 122).—The Bodhisatta was once the state elephant of the **Magadha** king of **Rājagaha.** When the king rode in procession, the people had eyes only for the elephant, and the king, in envy, schemed to have the elephant thrown down a precipice. The mahout discovering this, flew on the elephant's back to Benares. The king of Benares welcomed them and, with their help, obtained the sovereignty of all India.

The story was told in reference to **Devadatta's** envy of people's praise of the Buddha. Devadatta is identified with the Magadha king, **Sāriputta** with the king of Benares and **Ānanda** with the mahout.[1]

[1] J. i. 444 f.

1. **Duyyodhana.**—The Bodhisatta, born as king of **Magadha.** He was later born as king of the Nāgas, under the name of **Saṅkhapāla.** For his story see the **Saṅkhapāla Jātaka.**[1]

[1] S. v. 162 ff.

2. **Duyyodhana.**—The Pāli form of the Sanskrit Duryodhana.[1]

[1] *E.g.*, Cv. lxiv. 43.

Durājāna Jātaka (No. 64).—A young brahmin student of **Takkasilā** fell in love with a woman and married her. She was very capricious and her husband neglected his duties. The teacher instructed his student to take no notice of his wife's moods.

The story was related to a devout layman of **Sāvatthi** who had as wife a capricious woman. She worried him so much that he neglected his visits to the Buddha. The couple were identical in both stories.[1]

[1] J. i. 299-301.

Dullabha Sutta.—Three persons are hard to find in the world: a Tathāgata, one who can expound the Dhamma and Vinaya of a Tathāgata, and a grateful person.[1]

[1] A. i. 266.

Duḷudesa.—A country, probably in South India.[1]

[1] Cv. lvi. 11.

Duvera or **Anāthapiṇḍika Sutta.**—**Anāthapiṇḍika** visits the Buddha, who tells him of the five guilty fears—that begotten by killing, by stealing, by wrong indulgence of sensual lust, by evil speaking, and by the drinking of intoxicants—freedom from which, together with possession of the Noble Insight, enables a man to say that he is destined for Enlightenment.[1]

[1] S. v. 387 f.

Dussa-thūpa.—A thūpa built in the Brahma-world by **Ghaṭīkāra,** enshrining the garments worn by the Buddha at the time of his Renunciation. It was built of gems and was twelve yojanas high.[1] Among the wonders performed by **Bhaddaji** one was to carry it on his outstretched palm and show it to the multitude.[2]

[1] Dāthāvaṃsa, vs. 35. [2] Mhv. xxxi. 11; MṬ. 562.

Dussadāyaka Thera.—An arahant. Ninety-four kappas ago he was a khattiya, and having received some garments as a tribute, gave them to the Buddha **Siddhattha.** Sixty-seven kappas ago he was a king named **Parisuddha.**[1]

[1] Ap. i. 185.

Dussanta.—The Pāli form of the Sanskrit Duṣyanta.[1]

[1] *E.g.*, Cv. lxiv. 44.

Dussapāvārika.—A seṭṭhi of **Nālandā** who owned a mango-grove near the city. Having heard the Buddha preach, he became his follower and built for him and his Order a monastery in his mango-grove, which came to be called **Pāvārikambavana.**[1]

[1] DA. iii. 873; MA. ii. 594; SA. iii. 169.

Dussalakkhaṇa.—A brahmin of **Rājagaha** who claimed to be able to prognosticate by looking at pieces of cloth. For his story see the **Maṅgala Jātaka.**[1]

[1] J. i. 373.

Dussārāma.—A monastery in **Sīlavatī** where the Buddha **Sikhī** died.[1] The Commentary[2] calls it **Assārāma.**

[1] Bu. xxi. 28. [2] BuA. 204.

Dussāvudha.—One of the four most effective weapons found in the world. It belonged to **Āḷavaka.** If he threw it up into the sky, no rain would fall for twelve years; if he let it fall on the earth, all plants and trees would die and nothing would grow for twelve years; if he threw it into the sea, the sea would completely dry up; it could make **Sineru** crumble into pieces. Āḷavaka hurled it at the Buddha, but it fell at the Buddha's feet and remained there as a rug. It is also called **Vatthāvudha,** and was evidently made of cloth.[1]

[1] SNA. i. 225 f.

1. **Dussīla Sutta.**—For the wicked who lack virtue, right concentration is perforce destroyed, and this ultimately leads to the destruction of emanci-

pated knowledge and insight, just as a tree devoid of branches and leaves is ultimately destroyed.[1]

[1] A. iii. 19.

2. **Dussīla Sutta.**—A woman who is faithless, shameless, unscrupulous, immoral and of weak wisdom, is born in purgatory.[1]

[1] S. iv. 242.

1. **Dussīlya** or **Anāthapiṇḍika Sutta.**—**Anāthapiṇḍika,** grievously ill, sends for **Sāriputta,** who visits him with **Ānanda.** Sāriputta reminds Anāthapiṇḍika of his virtuous qualities, such as his loyalty to the Buddha, the Dhamma and the Saṅgha, his freedom from immorality and the like, from wrong views, aims, etc. Immediately Anāthapiṇḍika's pains vanish, he serves the two monks from his own cooking-pot, and they take their leave. Ānanda reports the incident to the Buddha, who praises Sāriputta's wisdom.[1]

[1] S. v. 380 ff.

2. **Dussīlya** or **Anāthapiṇḍika Sutta.**—The same as the first, but here it is **Ānanda** who admonishes and reminds Anāthapiṇḍika that he possesses all the qualities of a sotāpanna.[1]

[1] S. v. 385 f.

1. **Dūta Jātaka** (No. 260).—Once the Bodhisatta was king of Benares. He was very dainty as to food, and spent so much on it that he came to be known as **Bhojanasuddhika** (Dainty-food). He always ate in a decorated pavilion in full view of his people. One day, a greedy man seeing him eat and wishing to taste the food, rushed up to him with clasped hands, saying that he was a messenger (*dūta*), messengers having free access to the king. Approaching the table, he snatched some food and thrust it into his mouth. The king's attendants wished to behead him, but the king invited him to share his meal, and, at the conclusion, enquired as to his message. He said he was the messenger of Lust and of the Belly, and told the king how great was the power of these two. The king was pleased with him and gave him one thousand cows.

The story was told in reference to a greedy monk.[1]

[1] J. ii. 318-21.

2. **Dūta Jātaka** (No. 478).—The Bodhisatta was once a brahmin of **Kāsi.** He studied at **Takkasilā,** and wandered about begging for gold to pay his teacher. He collected a few ounces, but on his way back he was forced to cross the Ganges, and the gold fell into the river. He then thought

out a plan and sat fasting on the bank of the river, refusing to speak to anybody until the king of Benares himself came. To him he told his story, pointing out that it would have been useless to tell the others, they being unable to help him. The king gave him twice the original quantity of gold.

The story was related in reference to a discussion by the monks as to the Buddha's great resourcefulness.[1]

[1] J. iv. 224-8.

1. **Dūteyya Sutta.**—Eight qualities which make a monk a suitable messenger. **Sāriputta** possesses these eight qualities.[1]

[1] A. iv. 196.

2. **Dūteyya Sutta.**—Few are those who abstain from sending messengers, or from serving as such; many those who do not.[1]

[1] S. v. 473.

Dūratissaka-vāpi.—A tank in **Rohaṇa,** near **Mahāgāma. Meghavaṇṇābhaya,** minister of **Mahāsena,** leading a revolt against the king, once encamped on its bank.[1] **Saddhātissa** built a vihāra near by.[2] **Mahānāga** gave to the ascetics one thousand fields watered by the tank,[3] and **Parakkamabāhu I.** repaired the tank.[4] Geiger thinks[5] that Dūratissa-vāpi is probably identical with **Dūravāpi.**

[1] Mhv. xxxvii. 18.
[2] *Ibid.*, xxxiii. 9.
[3] Cv. xli. 99; see Cv. *Trs.* i. 62, n. 1.
[4] *Ibid.*, lxxix. 32.
[5] Mhv. *Trs.* 248, n. 5.

Dūravāpi.—A tank built by **Iḷanāga,**[1] probably identical with **Dūratissavāpi** (*q.v.*).

[1] Mhv. xxxv. 32.

Dūrenidāna.—The story of the Bodhisatta from the time of the announcement made by **Dīpaṅkara** regarding his Enlightenment to his birth in the **Tusita** world. This forms part of the Nidānakathā of the Jātaka Commentary.[1]

[1] J. i. 2-47.

Dūsī.—Name of **Māra** in the time of **Kakusandha** Buddha. He was, in that birth, son of **Kāḷī,** sister of **Moggallāna.** He first incited the brahmin householders to revile Kakusandha's monks, chief of whom were **Vidhura** and **Sañjīva;** when that effort failed owing to the thoughts of goodwill, pity, sympathy and equanimity, developed by the monks, he next incited the brahmins to show great honour to the monks, hoping, in that way, to tempt them. But, owing to the intervention of Kakusandha, Dūsī's attempts failed and he was born in the Mahā Niraya. The story is given in the **Māratajjaniya Sutta.**[1] Dūsī is mentioned[2] as having died early because his life was cut off by kamma.

[1] M. i. 333 ff.; also Thag. 1187-91; ThagA. ii. 183. [2] Vsm. 229.

Demaṭavala.—A locality of **Rohaṇa.**[1]

[1] Cv. lxxiv. 139.

Demaṭṭhapādatthāli.—A village in the **Malaya** district of Ceylon.[1]

[1] Cv. lxx. 11.

Demaliyagāma.—A locality in Ceylon, mentioned in the campaigns of **Gajabāhu.**[1]

[1] Cv. lxvii. 45.

1. **Deva.**—Aggasāvaka of **Sujāta** Buddha. He was a chaplain's son, and the Buddha's first sermon was addressed to him and his friend **Sudassana.**[1] He is also called **Sudeva.**[2]

[1] J. i. 38; BuA. 168, 170. [2] Bu. xiii. 25.

2. **Deva.**—A devaputta, son of **Virūpakkha** and brother of **Kālakaṇṇi.**[1]

[1] J. iii. 261.

3. **Deva.**—A monk, resident in **Kappukagāma** (*v.l.* **Kambugāma**). **Vohārikatissa** heard him preach and restored for him five buildings.[1]

This may be the thera whom **Saṅghatissa** heard preaching the **Andhakavinda Sutta.** The king, being very pleased with him, set up an offering of gruel to the monks of the **Mahāvihāra.**[2]

[1] Mhv. xxxvi. 29; Dpv. xxii. 41. [2] Dpv. xxii. 50.

4. **Deva.**—A thera of Ceylon at whose request **Upasena** wrote the Mahā Niddesa Commentary.[1]

[1] MNidA. i. 1.

5. **Deva.**—See also **Maliya(Malaya-)-deva** and **Mahādeva.**

6. **Deva.**—A thera of Ceylon, who, according to the Gandhavaṃsa,[1] wrote the **Sumanakūṭavaṇṇanā.** This work is, however, generally ascribed to **Vedeha.**[2]

[1] Gv. p. 63. [2] P.L.C. 223 f.; Svd. 1263.

7. **Deva.**—Senāpati of **Kittisirimegha.** He was stationed at **Badalatthalī,** and accompanied **Ratnāvalī** when he took the young **Parakkamabāhu** to Kittisirimegha.[1]

[1] Cv. lxvii. 82.

8. **Deva.**—**Laṅkādhināyaka.** A general of **Gajabāhu II.**[1]

[1] Cv. lxx. 104, 324.

9. **Deva.**—A general of **Parakkamabāhu I.** He took part in the campaigns against **Gajabāhu,** and later was sent to his rescue in **Pulatthipura.** Deva was imprisoned there, and Parakkamabāhu sent housebreakers to release him, after which he was despatched with an army to **Gaṅgātaṭāka,** where he defeated **Mānābharaṇa.** At **Hedillakhaṇḍagāma** he defeated **Mahinda.** The last we hear of him is that he fell into his enemy's power at a village called **Surulla.** Parakkamabāhu went to rescue him, but had to abandon the effort. It is possible that he was ransomed and became **Laṅkāpura.**[1] (See below.)

[1] Cv. lxx. 123, 153-7, 245, 285, 300, 316; lxxii. 45, 75, 82, 122, 137 f.

10. **Deva.**—A general of **Parakkamabāhu I.,** called **Laṅkāpura,** probably identical with 9. He fought against **Sūkarabhātu,** and later took part in the Sinhalese expedition to South India and fought in fierce battles at Tirippāḷuru and Rājinā, capturing the latter place.[1]

[1] Cv. lxxv. 130; lxxvi. 250, 310, 324, 326.

11. **Deva.**—A minister of **Āyasmanta.** He was sent to erect a vihāra at **Valligāma.**[1]

[1] Cv. lxxx. 38.

12. **Deva.**—A seṭṭhi of **Vedisagiri.** His daughter **Devī** was married to **Asoka,** who met her while staying at her father's house on his way to **Ujjeni.**[1]

[1] MṬ. 324; Sp. i. 70.

Deva Sutta.—The struggle of the devas and the asuras is typical of that of the monks with **Māra**; victory is sometimes on one side, sometimes on the other, until the enemy is completely crushed and rendered ineffective.[1]

[1] A. iv. 432 f.

Devakaṭasobbha.—A pool near **Kosambī.** Close by was the **Pilakkhaguhā** and the Paribbājakārāma, where **Ānanda** once visited **Sandaka** and held a discussion with him.[1]

[1] M. i. 513; MA. ii. 687.

1. **Devakūṭa.**—The name of the **Cetiyapabbata** in the time of the Buddha **Kakusandha.** The Buddha visited it, and all the people of **Ojadīpa** (as Ceylon was then called) paid him homage.[1]

[1] Mhv. xv. 63; Sp. i. 86; Dpv. xv. 38; xvii. 14, 32.

2. **Devakūṭa.**—A hill in India where **Sumedha** Buddha preached to a very large concourse.[1]

[1] Bu. xii. 9.

Devagajjita.—A king of thirty-six kappas ago; a previous birth of **Aṅkolaka Thera.**[1]

[1] Ap. i. 199.

Devagandha.—Fourteen kappas ago there were sixteen kings of this name, all previous births of **Gandhamāliya Thera.**[1]

[1] Ap. i. 135.

Devagabbha.—A yakkha. When **Candagutta** died, the yakkha entered into his dead body and pretended that the king was yet alive. **Bindusāra** thereupon cut off his head.[1]

[1] MṬ. 188 f.; *cp.* J. vi. 474.

Devagabbhā.—Daughter of **Mahākaṃsa,** king of **Asitañjana.** It was predicted that her son would destroy the lineage of Kaṃsa; she was therefore imprisoned in a room built on a single pillar. With the help of her serving woman, **Nandagopā,** she entered into an intrigue with **Upasāgara,** whom she afterwards married. They had ten sons—the notorious **Andhakaveṇhudāsaputtā** (*q.v.*)—and one daughter, **Añjanā.**[1]

[1] J. iv. 79 ff.; PvA. 99 ff.

Devacārika Suttā.—A group of three suttas describing how **Moggallāna** visits the deva-worlds and learns from the devas how they attained happiness through following the Buddha's teaching.[1]

[1] S. v. 366 f.

1. **Devatā Vagga.**—The fourth chapter of the Chakka Nipāta of the Aṅguttara Nikāya.[1]

[1] A. iii. 329-44.

2. **Devatā Vagga.**—The seventh chapter of the same.[1]

[1] A. iii. 421-9.

3. **Devatā Vagga.**—The fourth chapter of the Sattaka Nipāta of the Aṅguttara Nikāya.[1]

[1] A. iv. 27-39.

Devatā Saṃyutta.—First division of the Saṃyutta Nikāya. It contains records of visits paid to the Buddha by various deities and the conversations which ensued.[1]

[1] S. i. 1-45.

1. **Devatā Sutta.**—A devatā visits the Buddha at **Jetavana** and tells him of six things necessary for a monk's spiritual development: reverence for the Buddha, the Dhamma and the Saṅgha, reverence for the discipline, grace in speech and good friendship. The Buddha reports this visit to the monks, and **Sāriputta** explains why these particular qualities were mentioned by the devatā.[1]

[1] A. iii. 423.

2. **Devatā Sutta.**—The Buddha tells the monks how, on various occasions, devas had visited him and told him that they had felt remorse after their death because they had not honoured recluses during their life as human beings. Others who had honoured recluses had obtained happiness.[1]

[1] A. iv. 390 f.

Devatāpañha, Devatāpañha Jātaka.—Jātaka No. 350 is called Devatāpañha Jātaka,[1] and the Commentary states that the story will be explained in the **Ummagga Jātaka.** The Ummagga Jātaka contains a series of questions asked of King **Vedeha** by the goddess who lived in his parasol, because she wished to restore **Mahosadha** to the king's favour. Vedeha inquired of all his wise men, but they could find no answers, and, in the end, he was compelled to send for Mahosadha. The questions, in the nature of riddles, were put to him and he solved them all.[2]

[1] J. iii. 152. [2] vi. 370 f.; the riddles with answers are found in pp. 376 f.

Devatissa.—A village in **Koṭṭhavāta,** given to the **Dhammarucikas** by **Aggabodhi V.**[1]

[1] Cv. xlviii. 2.

Devadatta.—Son of the Sākyan **Suppabuddha** (maternal uncle of the Buddha) and his wife **Amitā.** He had a sister **Bhaddakaccānā,** who married

Prince **Siddhattha.**[1] When the Buddha visited **Kapilavatthu** after the Enlightenment and preached to the Sākyans, Devadatta was converted together with his friends **Ānanda, Bhagu, Kimbila, Bhaddiya, Anuruddha,** and their barber, **Upāli,** and he sought the Buddha at Anupiyā and entered the Order.[2] During the rainy season that followed, Devadatta acquired the power of *iddhi* possible to those who are yet of the world (*puthujjanika-iddhi*).[3] For some time he seems to have enjoyed great honour in the Order, and in one passage[4] he is mentioned in a list of eleven of the chief Elders of all of whom the Buddha speaks in praise. Devadatta was later suspected of evil wishes.[5] About eight years before the Buddha's death,[6] Devadatta, eager for gain and favour and jealous of the Buddha's fame, attempted to win over **Ajātasattu.** He assumed the form of a child having a girdle of snakes, and suddenly appeared on Ajātasattu's lap, frightening him. He then resumed his own form, and Ajāsattu, much impressed, paid him great honour and, it is said, visited him morning and evening with five hundred chariots and sent him daily five hundred dishes of food.[7] This encouraged Devadatta in his schemes, and he conceived the idea of taking he Buddha's place as leader of the Saṅgha. As soon as this thought ccurred to him, his *iddhi*-power disappeared.

The Koliyan **Kakudha,** follower of **Moggallāna,** reborn as a *manomaya-kāyikadeva*, divined Devadatta's plan and informed Moggallāna. The latter repeated the matter to the Buddha, but the Buddha said it was unnecessary to discuss it as Devadatta would ultimately betray himself.

[1] Mhv. ii. 22; MṬ. 136; DhA. iii. 44. The Dulva (Rockhill, p. 13) calls him the son of Amitodana and brother of Ānanda. This is supported by Mtu. (ii. 69), which says that after the Buddha's renunciation, Devadatta tried to tempt Bhaddakaccānā. In one passage in the Vinaya (ii. 189), Devadatta is spoken of as Godhiputta. Does this mean that his mother's name was Godhī? The Sanskrit books (*e.g.*, Mtu) give several stories of his youth which show his malice. When Siddhattha was about to show his skill in the arts, a white elephant was being brought for him, and Devadatta, out of envy, killed it. The carcase blocked the city gates till Siddhattha threw it outside. The Pāli Commentaries (*e.g.*, SA. i. 62) say that Devadatta had the strength of five elephants. On another occasion he quarrelled with Siddhattha, who protested against his shooting a goose.

[2] Vin. ii. 182.

[3] *Ibid.*, 183; for particulars see Rockhill, p. 85.

[4] Ud. i. 5. Again in Vin. (ii. 189) Sāriputta is mentioned as having gone about Rājagaha singing Devadatta's praises; see also DhA. i. 64 f.

[5] *E.g.*, S. ii. 156.

[6] The following account is summarised from various passages in the books, chiefly Vin. ii. 184 ff.; iii. 171 f.; 174 f.; iv. 71; DhA. i. 112 ff.; iii. 154; A. iii. 123, 402; ii. 73; iv. 160; J. i. 113, 142, 185, 490; iv. 37, 158; v. 333 ff.; vi. 129 f., etc.

[7] According to J. i. 186, 508, Ajāsattu built for him a monastery at Gayāsīsa and sent him, daily, five hundred pots of three-year-flavoured rice and the choicest dishes. These meals were so tempting that some of the Buddha's followers would go there to eat them and return stealthily.

Sometime later, Devadatta went to the Buddha and suggested that the leadership of the Order should be handed over to him in view of the Buddha's approaching old age. The Buddha scorned the suggestion, saying, "Not even to Sāriputta or Moggallāna would I hand over the Order, and would I then to thee, vile one, to be vomited like spittle ?"[8] Devadatta showed great resentment and vowed vengeance. Thereupon, at the Buddha's suggestion, a proclamation was issued to the Saṅgha that in anything done by Devadatta in the name of the Buddha, the Dhamma and the Saṅgha, none but Devadatta was to be recognised.

It was at this time that Devadatta incited Ajātasattu to kill his father, **Bimbisāra,** while he himself prepared to kill the Buddha.[9]

Ajātasattu agreed, and provided Devadatta with royal archers to shoot the Buddha. These were placed on different paths, one on one path, two on another, and so on up to sixteen, and the plan was so laid that not one of them would survive to tell the tale. But when the Buddha approached the first man, he was terrified by the Buddha's majesty, and his body became stiff. The Buddha spoke kindly to him, and the man, throwing away his weapons, confessed his intended crime. The Buddha thereupon preached to him and, having converted him, sent him back by a different path. The other groups of archers, tired of waiting, gave up the vigil and went away one after the other. The different groups were led to the Buddha by his *iddhi*-power, and he preached to them and converted them. The first man returned to Devadatta saying that he was unable to kill the Buddha because of his great *iddhi*-power.

Devadatta then decided to kill the Buddha himself. One day, when the Buddha was walking on the slopes of **Gijjhakūṭa,** he hurled down on him a great rock. Two peaks sprang up from the ground, thereby arresting its rushing advance, but a splinter struck the Buddha's foot, causing the blood to flow. Being in great pain, he was carried to **Maddakucchi,** and from there to Jīvaka's Ambavana, where **Jīvaka** attended him. After this event, the monks wished the Buddha to have a guard, but this he refused, saying that it was impossible for anyone to deprive a Tathāgata of his life.

Devadatta's next attempt on the Buddha's life was to persuade elephant-keepers to let loose a fierce elephant, **Nalāgiri** (or **Dhanapāla**), drunk with toddy, on to the road by which the Buddha would pass. The news spread rapidly, and the Buddha was warned, but refused to turn

[8] Vin. ii. 188. This incident is referred to in the Abhayarājakumāra Sutta (M. i. 393).

[9] The Ap. (ii. 300 f.) explains that all these plans of Devadatta to harm the Buddha were the result of the Buddha's previous evil deeds.

back. As the elephant advanced he pervaded it with love, and thus completely subdued it.

This outrage made Devadatta very unpopular, and even Ajātasattu was compelled by the force of public opinion to withdraw his patronage from Devadatta,[10] whose gain and honour decreased. Thereupon he decided, with the help of several others, **Kokālika, Kaṭamoraka-tissa, Khaṇḍadeviyāputta** and **Samuddadatta,** to bring about a schism in the Order. These five went accordingly to the Buddha and asked for the imposition of five rules on all members of the Saṅgha: (1) that monks should dwell all their lives in the forest, (2) that they should accept no invitations to meals, but live entirely on alms obtained by begging, (3) that they should wear only robes made of discarded rags and accept no robes from the laity, (4) that they should dwell at the foot of a tree and not under a roof, (5) that they should abstain completely from fish and flesh. The Buddha's reply was that those who felt so inclined could follow these rules—except that of sleeping under a tree during the rainy season—but he refused to make the rules obligatory. This refusal delighted Devadatta, who went about with his party, declaring that the Buddha was prone to luxury and abundance. He was believed by the foolish, and in spite of the Buddha's warning against the dire sin of causing schism in the Order, Devadatta informed Ānanda of his intention of holding an uposatha meeting without the Buddha, and, having persuaded five hundred newly ordained monks from Vesāli to join him, he went out to **Gayāsīsa.**[11] Among the followers of Devadatta were also some nuns, chief of whom was **Thullanandā,** who never tired of singing his praises.[12] The mother of **Kumārakassapa** (*q.v.*), also, first entered the Order under Devadatta, but when he denounced her, following the discovery of her pregnancy, she sought refuge with the Buddha. Some of the Sākyans, too, seem to have preferred Devadatta to the Buddha—*e.g.*, **Daṇḍapāṇi.**[13] The Buddha sent Sāriputta and Moggallāna to Gayāsīsa to bring back the deluded ones. Devadatta, believing that they had come to join him, rejoiced, and, in spite of Kokālika's warning, welcomed them. That night he preached very late to the monks, and, wishing for rest, asked Sāriputta to address the assembly. Sāriputta and Moggallāna preached to such effect that they persuaded the five hundred monks to return with them. Kokālika kicked Devadatta on the chest to awaken him and tell him the news. When Devadatta discovered what had happened, hot blood came from his mouth, and

[10] Sp. iv. 811. At this time, Kokālika was very useful to Devadatta (J. ii. 438).

[11] On this occasion he tried to imitate the Buddha, keeping two chief disciples beside him (DhA. i. 122). Three suttas, the two Devadatta, and the Mahāsāropama, were preached after this event.

[12] Vin. iv. 66, 335.

[13] MA. i. 298.

for nine months he lay grievously ill.[14] As his end drew near, he wished to see the Buddha, though the latter had declared that it would not be possible in this life. Devadatta, however, started the journey on a litter, but on reaching Jetavana, he stopped the litter on the banks of the pond and stepped out to wash. The earth opened and he was swallowed up in **Avīci,** where, after suffering for one hundred thousand kappas, he would be reborn as a Pacceka Buddha called **Aṭṭhissara.**[15] It is said[16] that at the moment of being swallowed by the earth, Devadatta uttered a stanza in which he declared that he had no refuge other than the Buddha. It is this last act of Devadatta's which the Buddha had in view when he agreed to ordain Devadatta. The Dhammapada Commentary[17] contains a graphic account of the tortures of Devadatta in Avīci. In previous births, also, he had been swallowed by the earth, as King **Kalābu** and as **Mahāpatāpa.**

When the people heard of Devadatta's death, they held a great festival, as they had done of yore at the death of **Piṅgala,** who was an incarnation of Devadatta.[18]

The Jātaka Commentary contains numerous stories showing that Devadatta's enmity towards the Buddha was not confined to this life. It had existed during many kappas, and though sometimes he was foiled in his attempts to harm the Bodhisatta, in many cases he succeeded in working his will.[19] The beginning of this enmity, which increased with time, is described in the **Serivāṇija Jātaka.**

Devadatta's wickedness and his hatred of the Bodhisatta are illustrated in various Jātakas besides those already mentioned—*e.g.*, the **Kakkara,** the **Kapi,** the **Kukkura,** the **Kuruṅga,** the **Kuruṅga-miga,** the **Khaṇḍahāla,** the **Godha,** the **Campeyya,** the **Cūla-Nandiya,** the **Chaddanta,** the **Taccha-sūkara,** the **Tayodhamma,** the **Tittira,** the **Dummedha,** the **Dhammaddhaja,** the **Dhonasākha,** the **Paṇḍara,** the **Bhūridatta,** the **Maṇicora,** the **Mahā-ummagga,** the **Mahākapi,** the **Mahā-Nāradakassapa,** the **Mahāpaduma,** the **Mahāsīlava,** the **Romaka,** the **Laṭukika,** the **Vānara,** the **Vānarinda,** the **Vessantara,** the **Saccaṅkira,** the **Sattigumba,** the **Sāliya,** the **Suṃsu-māra,** and the **Suvaṇṇakakkaṭa.** In the **Dhamma Jātaka,** Devadatta

[14] The Vinaya account omits the kicking, but it is mentioned in DhA. i. 121 and in J. i. 491.

[15] The Saddharmapuṇḍarika (chap. xi.) says he will be a Buddha named Devarāja.

[16] DhA. i. 125; see also Mil. 108. He was one of five people who were swallowed by the earth in the Buddha's time. Mil. 101.

[17] DhA. i. 125; also PSA. 79. His body in hell is one hundred leagues long.

[18] DhA. i. 126 f.

[19] One of the Milinda dilemmas (200 ff.) is as follows: "Why should Devadatta, who was so wicked, have been, time after time, superior in power to the Bodhisatta ?" A list of such instances is given. Nāgasena's reply is that Devadatta did several good deeds, such as protecting the poor, building bridges, etc.

is spoken of as having been the very incarnation of unrighteousness, **Adhamma.** In several stories his craftiness is emphasised—*e.g.*, as the jackal in the **Sigālā Jātaka,** as the drunken sot in the **Sigāla** (No. 2) and also in the **Manoja.** In the **Kālabāhu Jātaka** he is represented as very envious, and his falsehood and duplicity are emphasised in the **Cetiya,** the **Kakkāra** and the **Somanassa Jātakas.** His ingratitude is illustrated in such stories as those of the **Anta,** the **Amba,** the **Asampadāna,** the **Upāhana,** the **Guttila,** the **Javasakuṇa,** the **Dūbhiya-makkaṭa,** the **Nigrodha,** the **Mahākapi,** the **Ruru** and the **Sīlavanāga Jātakas,** while others, such as the **Apannaka,** the **Ubhatobhaṭṭha,** the **Kandagalaka,** the **Kāsāva,** the **Giridanta,** the **Jambuka,** the **Jambukhādaka,** the **Parantapa,** the **Lakkhaṇa,** the **Vinīlaka,** the **Virocana,** the **Vīraka,** the **Sabbadāṭha,** the **Sammuddavānija,** the **Sammodamāna Jātakas,** speak of his folly and inefficiency.

It is stated[20] that in spite of the great hatred shown by Devadatta towards him, the Buddha did not harbour, on his part, one single feeling of ill-will.

Only once is mention made[21] of the text of a sermon by Devadatta. **Candikāputta** reports this to Sāriputta, who makes it an occasion for a talk to the monks.

[20] *Eg.*, Mil. 410. [21] A. iv. 402 f.

1. **Devadatta Sutta.**—Preached to the monks at **Gijjhakūṭa** soon after **Devadatta** left the Order. Love of gain, favours and flattery came upon Devadatta for his undoing, like fruit to a plaintain or a bamboo tree, etc.[1]

[1] A. ii. 73; see No. 3 below; *cp.* Vin. ii. 187 f. and S. ii. 242.

2. **Devadatta Sutta.**—Preached in the same circumstances as the above. It gives eight reasons for Devadatta's downfall, and urges upon the monks the necessity for reflection on the good and bad fortune which overtake oneself and others from time to time.[1]

[1] A. iv. 160 f.; *cp.* Vin. ii. 202.

3. **Devadatta Sutta.**—Brahmā **Sahampati** visits the Buddha at **Gijjhakūṭa** soon after Devadatta had left the Order, and utters the stanza contained in No. 1 above.[1]

[1] S. i. 153.

1. **Devadaha.**—A township (*nigama*) of the Sākyans. The Buddha stayed there during his tours and preached to the monks on various topics.[1] According to the Commentaries[2] it was the city of the birth of the Buddha's

[1] S. iii. 5 f.; iv. 124 f.; M. ii. 214.
[2] J. i. 52; BuA. 226; MA. ii. 924, 1021, etc.; ThigA. 182.

mother and of **Pajāpatigotamī** and of their companions, who married the Sākyans of **Kapilavatthu.** The **Lumbinīvana,** where the Buddha was born, was near Devadaha. The name was originally that of a lake, so called either because kings held their sports in it (*devā vuccanti rājāno tesaṃ maṅgaladaho*), or because it came into existence without human intervention, hence divine (*sayañjāto vā so daho, tasmā pi Devadaho*). The name was later transferred to the village near by.[3] Devadaha was the residence of **Devadaha Sakka**[4] and of **Pakkha Thera.**[5]

[3] SA. ii. 186; also MA. ii. 810. Acc. to the Dulva (Rockhill, p. 12), the city was founded by Sākyans from Kapilavatthu, when they grew very numerous. The spot was pointed out by a deva, hence its name. **Suppabuddha** of Devadaha was a contemporary of Suddhodana (p. 14).

[4] Mhv. ii. 17; MṬ. 87.

[5] ThagA. i. 114.

2. **Devadaha.**—A Sākyan chief called **Devadaha-Sakka.** His children were **Añjana** and **Kaccānā.** **Māyā** and **Pajāpatī,** respectively mother and step-mother of the Buddha, were daughters of **Añjana.**[1]

[1] Mhv. ii. 17; MṬ. 87.

1. **Devadaha Vagga.**—The eleventh section of the Majjhima Nikāya (suttas 101-10), the **Devadaha Sutta** being its first sutta.[1]

[1] M. ii. 214 ff.

2. **Devadaha Vagga.**—The fourteenth chapter of the Saḷāyatana Saṃyutta.[1]

[1] S. iv. 124 ff.

1. **Devadaha Sutta.**—Preached to the monks at **Lumbinīvana,**[1] in **Devadaha.** It deals with the teaching of the **Nigaṇṭhas,** that whatsoever the individual experience, it comes from former actions. The sutta also gives ten beliefs of the Nigaṇṭhas, which, the Buddha says, are to be condemned. In contrast to these, ten statements are made respecting the Tathāgata, which are intrinsically true.[2]

[1] MA. ii. 810. [2] M. ii. 214 ff.

2. **Devadaha Sutta.**—Preached to the monks at **Devadaha.** Some monks, going to reside in the western districts, come to the Buddha to take leave of him. He advises them, before starting, to visit **Sāriputta,** whom he extols. This they do, and Sāriputta explains to them the fundamental teachings of the Buddha, in order that they may be ready to answer any questions which may be put to them.[1]

[1] S. iii. 6 ff.

Devadahakkhaṇa Sutta.—Arahants need not strive earnestly in respect of the sixfold sphere of sense, but those who are yet students (*sekhā*) must do so. The reasons for this are given.[1]

[1] S. iv. 124.

Devadūta Vagga.—The fourth chapter of the Tika Nipāta of the Aṅguttara Nikāya.[1]

[1] A. i. 132-50.

Devadūta Sutta.—Deals with the three warning messengers of death—the sight of old age, the sight of illness and the sight of death. The man who fails to pay heed to these messengers and is guilty of unrighteousness is condemned by **Yama** to the tortures of the **Mahānirayas,** which are described in detail.[1]

The same sutta, with several variations, is given at greater length in the Majjhima Nikāya,[2] where five messengers are spoken of, the first and fourth being the sight of a new-born babe and the sight of a guilty robber being punished for his offences respectively. The sutta is referred to for a description of **Avīci.**[3] It was preached by **Mahādeva** to the people of **Mahisamaṇḍala,**[4] and by **Mahinda** at **Anurādhapura,** on the first day of the latter's arrival there, when one thousand people became sotāpannas.[5]

The Majjhima version of the sutta is given[6] as an example of a discourse where the Buddha starts the sermon with a simile and then preaches the Doctrine.

[1] A. i. 138 f.; *cp. Makhādeva Jātaka.*
[2] M. iii. 178 ff.
[3] DhA. i. 107; also AA. i. 21.
[4] Mhv. xii. 29; Mbv. 114.
[5] Mhv. xiv. 63.
[6] *E.g.,* MA. i. 135.

Devadhamma Jātaka (No. 6).—Once the Bodhisatta was born as **Mahiṃsāsa,** son of the king of Benares. His brother was **Canda** and his step-brother **Suriya.** Suriya's mother, having been granted a boon, claimed for him the kingdom. Mahiṃsāsa and Canda thereupon went into exile, but they were accompanied by Suriya. Arrived in Himavā, Mahiṃsāsa sent his two brothers to fetch water from a pool. There, first Suriya and then Canda, were seized by a demon who had been allowed by **Vessavaṇa** to eat anyone entering the pond, provided he did not know the Devadhamma. Mahiṃsāsa then went himself to the pond, and on being questioned by the demon, preached to him the Devadhamma—which is to shrink from sin. The demon was pleased, and offered to release one of his victims. Mahiṃsāsa chose Suriya, and gave as his reason that he was afraid of being blamed by others. Thereupon the demon gave up both his brothers and showed the Bodhisatta great honour. The Bodhisatta converted him and he gave up his evil ways.

The story was related in reference to a rich man of **Sāvatthi** who joined the Order after his wife's death. But he continued to enjoy all kinds of luxuries until, arraigned before the Buddha, he pulled off his robes and stood only in his waist-cloth. The Buddha told him it was not the first time he had had to show him the error of his ways. He is identified with the water demon, **Ānanda** with Suriya, and **Sāriputta** with Canda.[1]

The **Nacca Jātaka** was preached in reference to the same monk.

[1] J. i. 126 ff.; DhA. iii. 74-6.

Devadhammika.—A class of ascetics (?) mentioned in a nominal list. They are doomed to purgatory.[1]

[1] A. iii. 277; see also Dial. i. 222.

Devanagara.—Also called **Devapura.** A town at the southern point of Ceylon, the modern Dondra. An old vihāra, repaired by **Vijayabāhu I.,** existed there.[1] Devanagara is mentioned in the campaigns of **Parakkamabāhu I.** as a scene of conflict.[2] There was a temple at Devanagara built[3] in honour of the god **Uppalavaṇṇa.** Here **Vīrabāhu** celebrated a sacrifice after his victory over the Jāvakas.[4] **Parakkamabāhu II.** found the shrine in great decay and rebuilt it with great splendour, and inaugurated a festival which is celebrated every year, even up to the present day, in the month of Āsāḷha.[5] **Parakkamabāhu IV.** built a long-shaped temple of two storeys for the recumbent image of the Buddha, which is found in the vihāra.[6]

[1] Cv. lx. 59.
[2] *Ibid.*, lxxv. 47.
[3] By Dappulasena acc. to the Sinhalese poem Pärākumbā-Sirita.
[4] Cv. lxxxiii. 49.
[5] *Ibid.*, lxxxv. 85.
[6] *Ibid.*, xc. 94.

Devapa.—A king of twenty-five kappas ago; a previous birth of **Aḍḍhacandiya.**[1]

[1] Ap. i. 231.

Devapada Sutta.—The four paths that lead to the devas: unwavering loyalty to the Buddha, to the Dhamma, to the Saṅgha, and the cultivation of virtues dear to the Ariyans.[1]

[1] S. v. 392.

Devapāli.—A village in Ceylon in which **Aggabodhi V.** built the **Giriṇagara-vihāra.**[1]

[1] Cv. xlviii. 3.

Devaputta Saṃyutta.—The second section of the Saṃyutta Nikāya. It contains accounts of visits paid by various devas to the Buddha.[1]

[1] S. i. 46 ff.

Devaputta-māra.—See **Māra.**

Devaputtaraṭṭha.—A district, evidently in Ceylon, the residence of an Elder named **Piṇḍapātika-Tissa.**[1]

[1] Vsm. 292.

Devapura.—See **Devanagara.**

Devappatirāja.—A minister of **Parakkamabāhu II.** To him were entrusted, by the king, various acts of piety, such as building the road to the shrine at **Sumanakūṭa.** In making this road the minister constructed several bridges, and, at the top of the peak, he placed an image of the god **Sumana.** He also built a three-storeyed pāsāda at **Hatthavanagalla-vihāra.** The village of **Mahālābugaccha** was given to his family in perpetuity, and he was entrusted with the special care of the Tooth Relic.[1] He was evidently a great patron of learning.[2]

[1] For a detailed account of his doings, see Cv. lxxxvi. 4 ff. [2] P.L.C. 214, 219.

Devabhūti.—Thirty kappas ago there were five kings of this name, all previous births of **Pupphacaṅgotiya.**[1]

[1] Ap. i. 118.

Devamantiya.—One of the nobles of King **Milinda.** He it was who took the king to **Nāgasena** and who was asked to invite Nāgasena to the palace.[1] The name is considered[2] to be a corruption of the Greek **Demetrius.**

[1] Mil. 22 f. 29. [2] Mil. *Trans.* vol. i. p. xix, etc.

Devamalla.—Son of **Kitti** of **Makkhakudrūsa.** He came to **Kitti** (afterwards **Vijayabāhu I.**) with a large following from **Rohaṇa** and offered his services, asking to be made ādipāda. Later, he retired to **Hiraññamalaya** and built a stronghold in **Remuṇa.**[1]

[1] Cv. lvii. 59.

1. **Devarāja.**—A general of **Parakkamabāhu I.** He held the office of **Kesadhātu** and lived in **Pañcayojana.** He won a great victory at **Gimhatittha.**[1]

[1] Cv. lxxv. 21.

2. **Devarāja.**—A vihāra in **Rohaṇa,** the residence of **Piyadassī,** author of the **Padasādhana.** Devarāja formed part of the Rambhā-vihāra.[1]

[1] P.L.C. 205.

1. **Devala.**—An ascetic who once came from the region of **Himavā** in search of vinegar and honey and took refuge for the night in a potter's house. Another ascetic, **Nārada** (the Bodhisatta), arrived later at the hut and, with the permission of Devala, stayed there. During the night, Nārada, going out of the hut, trod on the locks of Devala who lay right across the doorway. He asked for pardon, and returning, passed by what he took to be Devala's feet, but Devala had turned round and Nārada again trod on his hair. Devala thereupon cursed him, saying that, at sunrise, his head would split in seven pieces; but Nārada stopped the sun from rising. The king enquired as to what had happened, and, on learning the story, forced Devala to ask Nārada's pardon. As he did not do this of his own free will, he was taken, at Nārada's suggestion, to a pond and made to stand up to his neck in water with a lump of clay on his head. As soon as the sun rose the lump of clay split in seven pieces and Devala swam away. Devala is identified with **Thulla-Tissa.**[1]

[1] DhA. i. 32 ff.

2. **Devala.**—See **Kāḷadevala.**

3. **Devala.**—Cousin of **Padumuttara** Buddha and later his aggasāvaka. Padumuttara's first sermon was addressed to him and his brother **Sujāta.**[1]

[1] Bu. xi. 24; BuA. 159; Ap. i. 106.

4. **Devala.**—An ascetic in **Himavā.** He lived before the time of **Padumuttara** Buddha, who was yet in **Tusita,** but realizing in his mind the qualities of previous Buddhas, Devala built a cetiya on the bank of a river and made offerings to it in the name of the Buddha. Later, he was born in the Brahma-world. He was a previous birth of **Sirimatthera** (**Puḷinuppādaka**).[1]

[1] ThagA. i. 280; Ap. ii. 426.

5. **Devala.**—A Pacceka Buddha. When **Upāli** was once born as **Sunanda,** the king's son, one day, when riding on an elephant, he saw Devala and insulted him. It was for this reason that he was born in a low caste in his last life.[1]

[1] ThagA. i. 368.

Devalā.—A Sinhalese princess, sister of **Lokitā.**[1]

[1] Cv. lvii. 27.

Devarakkhita.—Another name for **Dhammakitti,** author of the Nikāya Saṅgraha.[1]

[1] P.L.C. 243.

Devarakkhitalena.—The residence of **Talaṅgara-tissa-pabbata-vāsī Mahādhamma Thera.**[1]

[1] Sad., p. 88.

Deva-vihāra.—A vihāra in **Antarasobbha,** built by **Aggabodhi V.**[1]

[1] Cv. xlviii. 4.

1. **Devasabha Thera.**—An arahant. He was the son of the ruler of a province and succeeded to the title when quite young. He visited the Buddha, and after hearing him preach, entered the Order, attaining arahantship shortly afterwards.

In the time of **Sikhī** Buddha he was a dove, and, having seen the Buddha, offered him a *piyāla*-fruit. He was three times king under the name of **Piyālī.**[1] He is probably identical with **Piyālaphaladāyaka** of the Apadāna.[2]

[1] Thag. v. 100; ThagA. i. 187 f. [2] Ap. i. 169 f.

2. **Devasabha Thera.**—An arahant. He was a Sākyan of **Kapilavatthu.** He witnessed the Buddha settle the quarrel between the Sākyans and the Koliyans and was established in the Refuges. Later he visited the Buddha at the **Nigrodhārāma** and entered the Order, afterwards attaining arahantship.

In the time of **Sikhī** Buddha he was a householder and offered the Buddha *bandhujīvaka*-flowers. Seven kappas ago he was a king named **Samantacakkhu.**[1]

He is probably identical with **Bandhujīvaka** of the Apadāna.[2]

[1] Thag. v. 100; ThagA. i. 203 f. [2] Ap. i. 175 f.

Devaseṭṭhi.—See **Deva** 12.

Devasūta.—One of the yakkha chiefs mentioned in the **Āṭānāṭiya Sutta.**[1]

[1] D. iii. 204.

Devahita.—A brahmin of **Sāvatthi.** Once when the Buddha was ill with cramp and desired hot water Upavāna obtained from Devahita hot water and molasses, which he sent on a pingo by a serving man. Hot fomentations and the administering of molasses cured the Buddha's complaint. Devahita came later to the Buddha, and after some conversation he was converted.[1] Devahita was said to be a friend of **Upavāna.**[2]

The Saṃyutta Commentary[3] adds that Devahita earned his living from the provision of water heated on his row of ovens and of cosmetics for those who came to bathe. On hearing of the Buddha's illness, he gave to Upavāna a kind of treacle to be administered in water.

[1] S. i, 174 f.; DhA. iv. 232. [2] ThagA. i. 311 f. [3] SA. i. 201.

Devahita Sutta.—Records the incident related above about **Devahita.**[1]

[1] S. i. 174 f.

1. **Devā.**—A class of beings. As a title the word *Deva* is attributed to any being regarded, in certain respects, as being above the human level. Thus it is used for a king. In a late classification[1] there are three kinds of Devā: *sammutidevā* (conventional gods—*e.g.*, kings and princes); *visuddhidevā* (beings who are divine by the purity of their great religious merit—arahants and Buddhas); and *uppattidevā* (beings who are born divine). Under the third category various groups are enumerated, the commonest number being seven: **Cātummahārājikā, Tāvatiṃsā, Yāmā, Tusitā, Nimmānaratī, Paranimmitavasavattī** and **Brahmakāyikā.**[2] The longest list is that of the Majjhima Nikāya,[3] which contains the names of twenty-five groups. The popular etymology of the word connects it with the root *div* in the sense of playing, sporting, or amusing oneself, sometimes also of shining: *dibbantī ti devā, pañcahi kāmaguṇehi kīḷanti, attano vā siriyā jotantī ti attho.*[4] The word implies possession of splendour and power of moving at will, beauty, goodness and effulgence of body, and, as such, is opposed to the dark powers of mischief and destruction—such as the Asuras, Petas and Nerayikas. The Devas are generally regarded as sharing kinship and continuity of life with humans; all Devas have been men and may again be born among men. They take interest in the doings of men, especially the Cātummahārājikā and the gods of Tāvatiṃsa. They come to earth to worship the Buddha and to show reverence to good men. **Sakka** (*q.v.*) is usually spoken of as chief of the gods—*devānam indo*. All Devas are themselves in *saṃsāra*, needing salvation. They are subject to death, their life-spans varying according to the merit of each individual deva. They are born in the full flower of youth and are free from illness till the moment of their death. Devas die from one of the following

[1] CNid. 307; KhA. 123, etc.

[2] *E.g.*, D. i. 216; A. i. 210, etc.

[3] i. 289; iii. 100. The Divyāvadāna (p. 266) contains a list of twenty-two.

[4] KhA. 123.

causes: exhaustion of life, merit or food; failing, through forgetfulness, to eat; and jealousy at the glory of another, which leads to anger.[5] When a deva is about to die five signs appear on him: his clothes get soiled, flowers worn by him fade, sweat exudes from his armpits, his body loses its colour and he becomes restless on his seat.[6]

[5] DhA. 1. 173. For other particulars regarding devas see the article in the NPD.

[6] DA. ii. 427 f.; DhSA, 33, etc.

2. **Devā.**—Daughter of **Udaya I.** and wife of **Mahinda,** son of the **Ādipāda Dāṭhāsiva.**[1]

[1] Cv. xlix. 12.

3. **Devā.**—Daughter of **Dappula II.** and wife of **Kittaggabodhi.**[1]

[1] Cv. xlix. 71.

4. **Devā.**—Wife of **Kassapa V.** and mother of **Sakkasenāpati.** She built, for the monks living in the wilderness, a vihāra called after herself, and adorned the Buddha-image at **Maricavaṭṭi.**[1]

[1] Cv. lii. 52, 61, 64 ff.

1. **Devā** or **Vatapada Sutta.**—The seven rules of conduct observed by **Sakka,** whereby he obtained celestial sovereignty.[1]

[1] S. i. 227.

2. **Devā Sutta.**—Explains the various names of **Sakka**-Magha, Purindada, Vāsava, Sahassakkha, Sujampati and Devānam-inda.[1]

[1] S. i. 228.

3. **Devā Sutta.**—**Mahāli** visits the Buddha at the **Kūṭāgārasālā** and asks if he has seen **Sakka.** The Buddha answers that he has and that he knows many things about Sakka. He then repeats what is given in Nos. 1 and 2 above.[1]

[1] S. i. 229.

Devātideva.—The seventh of the future Buddhas.[1]

[1] Anāgat., p. 40.

Devānampiyatissa.—King of Ceylon (247-207 B.C.). He was the second son of **Muṭasiva.** It is said that on the day of his coronation many wonderful treasures miraculously appeared, some of which he resolved to send as tokens of esteem to his contemporary **Dhammāsoka** of India, with whom he had long been on terms of friendship. An embassy, led by his nephew **Mahāriṭṭha,** was despatched to **Pāṭaliputta,** and the emperor showed the ambassadors every mark of honour. He sent back with them all the requisites for a coronation, with instructions to celebrate the inauguration of the Sinhalese king, whom he invited to embrace Buddhism. On the return of the embassy, the king was solemnly crowned a second time.[1]

The chief event in the reign of Devānampiyatissa was the arrival of **Mahinda** in Ceylon. He arrived at the head of a mission in the year of the king's second coronation. Mahinda met the king hunting on the full-moon day of Jeṭṭha. The king welcomed him with great honour and speedily embraced the new religion, to which Asoka had already drawn his attention. His conversion was the direct result of Mahinda's preaching of the **Cūlahatthipadopama Sutta.** His earlier religion is not known, it may have been Jainism. His example was followed by a large number of his subjects, many of whom entered the Order. Devānampiyatissa dedicated to their use the **Nandana** park and the **Mahāmeghavana,** which he himself had laid out a little earlier. In the Mahāmeghavana he built the famous **Mahā-Vihāra** which, for many centuries, remained the centre of the orthodox religion in Ceylon. The dedication of the Mahā-Vihāra took place in the two hundred and thirty-sixth year after the death of the Buddha. The king's next pious work was the erection of the **Cetiyapabbata-vihāra** and he, later, built the **Thūpārāma,** containing the Buddha's right collar-bone.

When the women of the palace, led by **Anulā,** wife of the sub-king, **Mahānāga,** expressed a desire to become nuns, Devānampiyatissa sent another embassy to Asoka asking him to send **Saṅghamittā,** together with the right branch of the sacred Bodhi-tree. This branch miraculously severed itself from the parent tree and, together with Saṅghamittā, was conveyed down the Ganges and arrived in **Jambukola,** where it was received with all honour by Devānampiyatissa. From Jambukola it was taken in procession to **Anurādhapura,** where it was planted in the Mahāmeghavana, the king instituting in its honour a festival, which was observed for many centuries. For the use of Saṅghamittā and the nuns the king erected various buildings, the chief of which was the **Hatthāḷhaka-vihāra** and the **Upāsikā-vihāra** with its twelve mansions.[2] Among other works of Devānampiyatissa we are told of the building of the **Issarasamaṇa-** and the **Vessagiri-vihāras,** the refectory called **Mahāpāli,** the **Jambukola-vihāra**

[1] This confirmation of Devānampiyatissa's sovereignty under the ægis of Asoka may have been due either to the commanding position of Asoka or for the strengthening of family connections. Asoka was a Moriyan (a branch of the Sākyans) and Devānampiyatissa had Sākyan blood.

[2] This account is summarised from the Mahāvaṃsa (chaps. xi., xiii.-xx.); also Dpv. xi. 14 ff.; xii. 7; xvii. 92.

in **Nāgadīpa,** the **Tissamahā-vihāra,** the **Pācīnārāma** and the **Paṭhamathūpa.** He also built the **Tissavāpi** at Anurādhapura.[3]

Mahinda survived him by eight years. Devānampiyatissa seems to have died without issue, for he was succeeded by four of his brothers.

[3] The Cv. (xxxvii. 94) mentions also the **Dhammacakka** as having been built by Devānampiyatissa. It later became the Temple of the Tooth at Anurādhapura.

Deviyāpaṭṭana.—A village in South India, captured by **Laṅkāpura.**[1]

[1] Cv. lxxvi. 169.

Devila.—A **Kesadhātu,** an officer of **Parakkamabāhu I.** He was in charge of the district of **Mahāniyyāma.**[1]

[1] Cv. lxxii. 57.

Devinda.—A minister of King **Vedeha.** His story is given in the **Mahāummagga Jātaka.** He is identified with **Pilotika.**[1]

[1] J. vi. 478.

Devi-vihāra.—See **Dīpa-vihāra.**

Devī.—Mother of **Mahinda** and **Saṅghamittā** and wife of **Asoka.** She was the daughter of **Deva** of **Vedisagiri.** Asoka met and married her while on his way to **Ujjeni,** there to become Viceroy. When he became king, Devī continued to live at Vedisagiri.[1] She is sometimes called **Vedisa-devī.**[2]

[1] Mhv. xiii. 6 ff.; Dpv. vi. 16; Sp. i. 70.

[2] MṬ. 324.

Devuttara.—Thirty-six kappas ago there were sixteen kings of this name all previous births of **Muṭṭhipupphiya (Añjavaniya).**[1]

[1] Ap. i. 142; ThagA. i. 128.

Desaka.—A township in **Sumbharaṭṭha,** where the Buddha preached the **Telapatta Jātaka**[1] and the **Udaya Sutta.**[2] *v.l.* **Sedaka.**

[1] J. i. 393.

[2] S. v. 89.

Desakittiya Thera.—An arahant. Ninety-two kappas ago he was a brahmin named **Upasālaka** who, seeing the Buddha in the forest, worshipped him.[1]

[1] Ap. i. 246.

Desanā or **Bhāvanā Sutta.**—On the psychic power, its basis, and the practice which leads to its cultivation.[1] The sutta corresponds, word for word, with a passage in Aśvaghoṣa's Sūtrālaṅkāra.

[1] S. v. 276.

Desapūjaka Thera.—An arahant. He once saw **Atthadassī** Buddha passing through the air and, much pleased, offered homage in his direction. In another birth he was a king named **Gosujāta.**[1]

[1] Ap. i. 183.

1. **Doṇa.**—A brahmin. He was at **Kusinārā** at the time of the Buddha's death, and it was his intervention which prevented a quarrel among the kings who assembled there to claim the Buddha's relics. He pointed out to them the impropriety of a quarrel over anything connected with the Buddha, the teacher of Peace. The claimants thereupon asked Doṇa to undertake the distribution of the relics. He divided them into eight parts, one of which he gave to each king. He himself kept the vessel used for collecting and dividing the relics, and over it he built a thūpa, celebrating a feast in its honour.[1]

Doṇa first met the Buddha on the road between **Ukkaṭṭhā** and **Setavyā.** He saw the Buddha's footprints and, following them, he came upon the Buddha seated at the foot of a tree. Doṇa asked him various questions as to his identity and the Buddha explained to him his Buddhahood.[2] The Commentary[3] states that Doṇa was a teacher with a large following, and that the Buddha's journey to Setavyā was undertaken for the purpose of meeting him. At the end of the Buddha's discourse, Doṇa became an anāgāmī and composed a poem of twelve thousand words in praise of the Buddha. This poem became known as the **Doṇagajjita.** Doṇa was held in very high esteem as a teacher, and it is said[4] that at some time or other practically all the chiefs of Jambudīpa had sat at his feet. Therefore he was able to dissuade them from quarrelling over the Buddha's relics. On that occasion he stood on a hill and recited the Doṇagajjita. At first his voice could not be heard through the uproar, but, by degrees, they recognised his voice and listened with wrapt attention.

At the distribution of the relics, Doṇa, watching his opportunity, hid, in his turban, the right eye-tooth of the Buddha, but **Sakka** saw this, and thinking that Doṇa was incapable of rendering suitable honour to this relic, removed it and placed it in the **Cūḷāmaṇi-cetiya.**[5]

[1] D. ii. 166 f.; Bu. xxviii. 4; UdA. 402.
[2] A. ii. 37 f.
[3] AA. ii. 505 f.
[4] DA. ii. 607 f.
[5] *Ibid.*, 609.

2. **Doṇa.**—A Nāga king. See **Mahādoṇa.**

3. **Doṇa.**—A bathing place in **Jambudīpa,** where sacrifice was offered to the gods.[1]

[1] J. v. 388 f.

4. **Doṇa.**—A Tamil stronghold captured by **Duṭṭhagāmaṇī.** It was commanded by **Gavara.**[1]

[1] Mhv. xxv. 11.

Doṇa Sutta.—A brahmin, **Doṇa** (probably identical with **Doṇa** 1 above), visits the Buddha and asks if it be true that the Buddha does not honour brahmins. The Buddha tells him that there are five kinds of brahmins—the Brahma-like, the deva-like, the bound, the breaker of bonds, and the brahmin-outcast—and, at Doṇa's request, describes these in detail.[1] The classification of brahmins given in this sutta is often referred to.[2]

[1] A. iii. 223 ff.

[2] *E.g.*, SNA. i. 318, 325, etc.

Doṇa-gajjita.—A poem composed by the brahmin **Doṇa** (*q.v.*), in honour of the Buddha.

Doṇapāka Sutta.—Once **Pasenadi,** uncomfortable and short of breath after a heavy meal, visited the Buddha. The Buddha admonished him on the evils of gluttony and taught the young **Sudassana,** who came with Pasenadi, a verse to be repeated whenever food was placed before the king. The king paid the young man one hundred kahāpaṇas daily for this service. Pasenadi profited by the lesson and became healthy.[1]

[1] S. i. 81; DhA. iii. 264 f. gives a fuller version of this story. There Sudassana is described as the king's nephew. This is also probably the incident mentioned at DhA. iv. 15 f.; but the youth there is called **Uttara.**

Doṇamukha.—The elephant sent by Prince **Mahāpāduma** of **Kumuda-nagara,** at **Soṇa's** request, to kill **Piyadassī** Buddha. The Buddha spoke to the elephant and so won him over.[1] *Cf.* **Nālāgiri.**

[1] Bu. xiv. 6; BuA. 174 f.

Doṇavatthu.—A brahmin village near **Kapilavatthu,** the residence of **Puṇṇā-Mantānīputta** and of **Aññākoṇḍañña.**[2]

[1] ThagA. i. 37.

[2] *Ibid.*, ii. 1; AA. i. 81, 84, 114.

Doṇivagga.—A village mentioned in the campaigns of **Parakkamabāhu I.**[1] It stood in a depression twelve miles from the modern Ratnapura, and the name is preserved in a stream flowing through it, the Denavaka.[2]

[1] Cv. lxxv. 69, 72.

[2] Cv. *Trs.* ii. 50, n. 3.

Dorādattika.—A locality on the **Jajjarā-nadī.** At this spot **Parakkamabāhu I.** built a dam across the river and constructed a canal from there to **Sūkaranijjhara.**[1]

[1] Cv. lxviii. 37.

Dolāmaṇḍapa.—A building erected by **Parakkamabāhu I.** in the **Dīpuyyāna.** It was so called because it contained a swing hung with minute golden bells.[1]

[1] Cv. lxxiii. 116.

Doḷapabbata.—Also called **Doḷaṅgapabbata.** A mountain in Ceylon, to the south of the **Mahāvāḷukanadī,** where **Paṇḍukābhaya** had his stronghold for four years.[1]

[1] Mhv. xi. 44; MṬ. 287.

Dovaca Sutta.—To get rid of unruliness, evil friendship and being tossed about in mind, one should cultivate the opposite qualities.[1]

[1] A. iii. 448.

Dovārikamaṇḍala.—See **Dvāramaṇḍala.**

Dohaḷakhaṇḍa.—A section of the **Vidhurapaṇḍita Jātaka.** It deals with **Vimalā's** plan for seeing **Vidhura.**[1]

[1] J. vi. 262-74.

Dohaḷapabbata.—A mountain in Ceylon, probably in the district of **Janapada. Silāmeghavaṇṇa** once occupied it.[1] Near to it was an image house of the Buddha, called **Sūkara.**[2]

[1] Cv. xliv. 56; Cv. *Trs.* i. 79, n. 4. [2] Cv. c. 294.

Dvattiṃsākāra.—The third section of the **Khuddakapāṭhaka**—on the thirty-two component parts of the body.[1]

[1] Khp. p. 2; KhpA. 37 ff.

1. **Dvaya Sutta.**—The various "duals" which exist—eye and object, ear and sound, etc.[1]

[1] S. iv. 67.

2. **Dvaya Sutta.**—Owing to the "duals," mentioned above, arise the different kinds of consciousness, etc.—*e.g.*, owing to the eye and objects arise eye-consciousness, etc.[1]

[1] S. v. 167 f.

Dvayakārī Sutta.—Double dealers are born, after death, among the egg-born harpies.[1]

[1] S. iii. 247.

Dvayatānupassanā Sutta.—A dissertation delivered by the Buddha, outside the **Migārāmātupāsāda,** on a full-moon day. He tells of the two-fold insight—the insight of dukkha and its cause, nirodha and the way thereto. He then proceeds to explain the origin of dukkha, from *upadhi*, *avijjā*, etc.[1]

[1] SN. p. 139 ff.

Dvādasasahassaka.—A district in **Rohaṇa,** the modern Giruvā-pattu. The meaning of the name is the province of the twelve thousand villages.[1]

[1] Cv. lxi. 22; lxxv. 160, 166; Cv. *Trs.* i. 227, n. 2.

Dvāraka.—See **Dvāravatī.**

Dvārakathā.—The name of a book.[1]

[1] Gv. 65, 75.

Dvāranāyaka.—A village in Ceylon, given by **Aggabodhi IV.** for the maintenance of the *padhānaghara* built by him for **Dāṭhāsiva.**[1]

[1] Cv. xlvi. 13.

Dvārapālaka Vimāna.—The story of a man who was engaged by a pious man of **Rājagaha** to guard his gate. The gate had to be kept shut for fear of thieves and, as a result, monks had often to go away without receiving any alms. A man was therefore engaged to see that the monks' needs were satisfied. The gate-keeper was born after death in **Tāvatiṃsa.**[1]

[1] Vv. v. 5; VvA. 246 f.

Dvāramaṇḍala.—A village in Ceylon. When **Paṇḍukābhaya** was young, he lay there in concealment and escaped various attempts on his life.[1] It was near the **Cetiyapabbata,** and **Kuṇḍalī,** friend of **Dīghābhaya,** lived there.[2] Five hundred young men from this village were ordained by **Mahinda.**[3]

[1] Mhv. x. 1; Dpv. x. 9. [2] Mhv. xxiii. 23. [3] *Ibid.*, xvii. 59.

1. **Dvāravatī (Dvāraka).**—A city in India. It had the sea on one side and a mountain on the other. The **Andhakaveṇhudāsaputtā** tried to take it but in vain, because when the goblin, guarding the city, gave the alarm, the city would rise up in the air and settle on the sea till the enemy dis-

appeared. They then sought **Kaṇhadīpāyana's** advice and fixed the city down with chains. This enabled the Andhākaveṇhudāsaputtā to capture it and make it their capital.[1] It was also the capital of King **Sivi.**[2] The Petavatthu and its Commentary[3] speak of Dvāravati as a city of **Kamboja.** It may be Kaṃsabhoja which is meant, the country of the Andhakaveṇhudāsaputtā.

[1] J. iv. 82 ff. [2] J. vi. 421. [3] Pv. ii. 9; PvA. 113.

2. **Dvāravatī.**—A city in the time of **Siddhattha** Buddha.[1]

[1] Ap. i. 200.

Dvedhāvitakka Sutta.—Preached at **Jetavana.** The Buddha tells the monks how, before the Enlightenment, he divided his thoughts into two groups—the first being of pleasures of sense, of harm and of hurt, and the other thoughts of renunciation. He then proceeds to explain how this ultimately led to Enlightenment.[1]

[1] M. i. 114 ff.

Dvebhāra.—A king of twenty-five centuries ago, a previous birth of **Sukatāveḷiya.**[1] *v.l.* **Vebhāra.**

[1] Ap. i. 217.

Dvemātikā.—A late compilation, made in Burma, from the Pāli texts. It contains the Bhikkhu- and Bhikkhunī-pātimokkha, and extracts from the Parivāra and other Vinaya texts.[1]

[1] Bode, *op. cit.*, 6, n. 2.

Dveratanīya Thera.—An arahant. In the time of **Vipassī** Buddha he was a hunter, and, seeing the Buddha in a forest, gave him a piece of flesh. Four kappas ago he was a king named **Mahārohita.**[1]

[1] Ap. i. 214.

Dh.

Dhaja.—One of the eight brahmins who recognised the signs at the Buddha's birth.[1] The Milindapañha[2] speaks of him as one of the Buddha's first teachers.

[1] J. i. 56. [2] p. 236.

Dhajagga Sutta.—Relates the story of how, when **Sakka** led his forces into battle, he told them that should any panic arise in their heart, they should look at the crest of his banner and their fears would immediately vanish. Or they should look at the banners of **Pajāpati** or **Varuṇa** or **Isāna.** Similarly should any fear arise in the mind of a monk he should recall to mind the excellences of the Buddha, or the Dhamma, or the Saṅgha, and peace would come to him.[1]

This sutta is also included among the Parittas and is called the **Dhajagga Paritta.**[2]

[1] S. i. 218 f.

[2] *E.g.*, Mil. 150.

1. **Dhajadāyaka Thera.**—An arahant. He set up a standard at the foot of **Padumuttara's** Bodhi-tree and swept the ground around it. He was once a king named **Uggata,** and again a king named **Megha.**[1]

[1] Ap. i. 108 f.

2 **Dhajadāyaka Thera.**—An arahant. Ninety-two kappas ago he saw **Tissa** Buddha and set up a flag in his honour.[1]

[1] Ap. i. 277 f.

Dhajaviheṭha Jātaka (No. 391).—A wizard was wont to come at midnight in order to corrupt the queen of Benares. She complained to the king and, at his request, she set the mark on her hand with vermillion on his back. By day the man was an ascetic, and when he found that he was discovered he fled through the air. The king thereupon suspected all ascetics and ordered them all to leave the kingdom. The king became a heretic. The Bodhisatta who was born as Sakka, seeing all this, came to Benares with an old Pacceka Buddha and stood close to the palace, showing him great reverence. When the king came out Sakka revealed his identity, telling him that even the ruler of the gods honoured pious men. The king saw his error and mended his ways.

The origin of the story is given in the **Mahākaṇha Jātaka.** The king is identified with **Ānanda.**[1]

[1] J. iii. 303-7. More or less the same story is given at greater length and with several variations in detail in both the **Cullahamsa** and the **Mahāhamsa Jātakas.**

Dhañña Sutta.—Few are they who refrain from accepting uncooked grain, many those who do not.[1]

[1] S. v. 471.

1. **Dhaññavatī.**—The city of birth of **Nārada** Buddha.[1]

[1] Bu. x. 20.

2. **Dhaññavatī.**—A city in the time of **Paduma** Buddha. It was the residence of **Sudhaññaseṭṭhi,** whose daughter, also called **Dhaññavatī,** offered a meal of milk rice to Paduma, just before his Enlightenment.[1]

[1] BuA. 147.

3. **Dhaññavatī.**—A city in the time of **Vipassī** Buddha.[1]

[1] Ap. i. 160; ThagA. i. 164.

1. **Dhataraṭṭha.**—One of the **Cātummahārājikā,** the ruler of the Eastern Quarter. His followers are the **Gandhabbas.** He has numerous sons called **Indra.**[1] He was present at the preaching of the **Mahāsamaya Sutta** and the **Āṭānāṭiya Sutta.** The name of his daughter is **Sirī.**[2]

[1] D. ii. 207, 220, 257 f.; iii. 197.

[2] J. iii. 257.

2. **Dhataraṭṭha.**—A mythical king, mentioned in a list of kings—with **Vessāmitta, Aṭṭhaka, Yāmataggi, Usinnara** and **Sivi**—as having entered **Sakka's** heaven by virtue of his righteousness and his waiting on pious men.[1]

[1] J. vi. 251.

3. **Dhataraṭṭha.**—There were two kings of this name, contemporaries and vassals of **Reṇu.** One of these two was king of **Aṅgā** with his capital in **Campā,** and the other of the **Kāsis** with his capital in Benares.[1]

[1] D. ii. 235 f.

4. **Dhataraṭṭha.**—A Nāga king. Thanks to the scheming of the tortoise **Cittacūla,** he married **Samuddajā,** daughter of the king of Benares. They had four sons: **Sudassana, Bhūridatta, Subhaga** and **Kāṇāriṭṭha.** His kingdom was beneath the **Yamunā.** Dhataraṭṭha is identified with **Suddhodana.**[1]

[1] J. vi. 162 ff., 171. 186, 200, 219. For details see the **Bhūridatta Jātaka.**

5. **Dhataraṭṭha.**—The Bodhisatta born as king of the haṃsas. He lived in **Cittakūṭa,** at the head of ninety thousand haṃsas. One day he was caught in a snare on the lake **Khemā,** set by the orders of King **Bahuputtaka.** Dhataraṭṭha's friend, **Sumukha,** refused to leave him while he was caught. The two friends melted the heart of the hunter when he came to take Dhataraṭṭha, and later they were brought before the king. Dhataraṭṭha preached the Doctrine to the king and to his queen, **Khemā,** who longed to hear a haṃsa preach.[1] Dhataraṭṭha is often referred to[2] as a king surrounded by a splendid following.

[1] J. iv. 425 ff.; for details see the **Haṃsa Jātaka.**

[2] *E.g.,* DA. i. 40; MA. ii. 576; UdA. 57, 412; PvA. 171.

6. **Dhataraṭṭha.**—The family of haṃsas to which belonged **Dhataraṭṭha,** king of the haṃsas. The members of this family are called **Dhataraṭṭhā.** They were golden-coloured and lived in **Cittakūṭa.** The **Mahā-Sutasoma Jātaka**[1] contains a story of the complete destruction of these haṃsas. They lived in **Kañcanaguhā,** and during the four months of the rainy season would not leave their cave, in case their wings should be drenched with water and they fell into the sea. A spider, as big as a cartwheel, used to weave a thick web at the entrance to the cave, but the Dhataraṭṭha geese sent one of their young ones, who had received two portions of food, to cut through the web. One season, however, the rains lasted for four months, and the haṃsas became cannibals and thus lost their strength. When, at the end of the rains, they tried to break through the web, they failed, and the spider cut off their heads one by one and drank their blood. This was the end of the Dhataraṭṭha haṃsas.

[1] J. v. 345, 355, 357. [2] *Ibid.*, 469 f.

7. **Dhataraṭṭha.**—A class of Nāgas, descendants of the Nāga king **Dhataraṭṭha** and of **Samuddajā,**[2] and possessed great power. They dwell in the **Sattasīdantara-samuda.**[3]

[1] D. ii. 259. [2] J. vi. 219. [3] SA. ii. 254.

1. **Dhana.**—A banker of **Rājagaha,** grandfather of **Mahā-** and **Cūla-panthaka.**[1]

[1] ThagA. i. 491, 515.

2. **Dhana.**—A banker of Benares, a previous birth of **Anuruddha.** His original name was **Annabhāra,** but one day he entertained the Pacceka Buddha, **Upariṭṭha,** and, as a result, won the favour of the king, who conferred on him the rank of seṭṭhi.[1]

[1] ThagA. ii. 66.

3. **Dhana.**—See **Mahādhana.**

Dhana Vagga.—The first chapter of the Sattaka Nipāta of the Aṅguttara Nikāya.[1]

[1] A. iv. 1 ff.

1. **Dhana Sutta.**—On the five treasures—faith, virtue, learning, charity, and insight.[1]

[1] A. iii. 53.

2. **Dhana Sutta.**—On the seven treasures—the five given above, and fear and shame.[1]

[1] A. iv. 4 f.

3. **Dhana Sutta.**—The same as No. 2, but the "treasures" are explained in detail.[1]

[1] A. iv. 5 f.

1. **Dhanañjaya.**—King of Benares. For his story see the **Kālabāhu Jātaka.**[1]

[1] J. iii. 97 f.

2. **Dhanañjaya.**—King of **Indapatta** in the **Kuru** country.[1] He was the father of **Dhanañjaya** 3.

[1] J. ii. 366.

3. **Dhanañjaya Koravya.**—King of the **Kurus.** He was the Bodhisatta and preached the five Kurudhammā. For his story see the **Kurudhamma Jātaka.**[1] His state elephant was **Añjanavasabha.** Dhanañjaya was one of the births in which the Bodhisatta practised *dānapāramitā.*[2]

[1] J. ii. 368 ff. [2] J. i. 45.

4. **Dhanañjaya.**—King of the **Kurus,** called **Koravya-rājā.** He reigned in **Indapatta** and belonged to the **Yudhiṭṭhila-gotta.** For his story see the **Sambhava Jātaka.**[1] He is identified with **Ānanda.**

[1] J. v. 57 ff.

5. **Dhanañjaya.**—Also called **Koravya,** king of the **Kurus,** with his capital at **Indapatta.** His minister was **Vidhurapaṇḍita.** He was fond of games of dice and was defeated by **Puṇṇaka.** For his story see the **Vidhurapaṇḍita Jātaka.**[1] He is identified with **Ānanda.** He is probably also the king mentioned in the **Dhūmakāri Jātaka** (*q.v.*).[2]

[1] J. vi. 255 ff.; SNA. i. 223. [2] J. iii. 400 ff.

6. **Dhanañjaya.**—A seṭṭhi of **Bhaddiyanagara;** he was the son of **Meṇḍaka** and **Candapadumasirī.** His wife was **Sumanadevī,** and their children were **Visākhā** and **Sujātā.** He was lent by **Bimbisāra** to **Pasenadi,** for the latter's kingdom held no person of great merit. Dhanañjaya and his family built the city called **Sāketa,** seven leagues from **Sāvatthi,** and settled down there. Dhanañjaya is included among the five persons of great merit (**Mahāpuññā**), contemporary with the Buddha, and he was a sotāpanna.[1]

[1] DhA. i. 384 ff.; iii. 363; J. ii. 347; Vsm. 383, etc.

7. **Dhanañjaya.**—One of the chief lay supporters of **Phussa** Buddha.[1]

[1] Bu. xix. 21.

8. **Dhanañjaya.**—A pleasaunce near **Dhaññavatī** where **Paduma** Buddha first preached.[1] **Nārada** Buddha was born there.[2]

[1] Bu. ix. 20; BuA. 147. [2] *Ibid.*, 151.

9. **Dhanañjaya.**—A city in the time of **Sikhī** Buddha. There the Buddha converted the householder **Dhanapālaka.**[1]

[1] BuA. 202.

Dhanañjaya Jātaka (No. 413).—**Dhanañjaya,** king of **Indapattana,** was wont to neglect his old warriors and to show favour only to newcomers. The result was that he once suffered defeat in a rebellion. On his return from the battle he consulted his chaplain **Vidhurapaṇḍita** (the Bodhisatta), who told him of a goatherd of yore, called **Dhūmakāri.** Once, when Dhumakāri was tending his goats, a herd of golden deer came from the Himālaya, and he looked after them and neglected his own goats. In the autumn the deer went back to the mountains and he found that his goats had died of starvation.

The story was told to **Pasenadi** who, like Dhanañjaya, suffered a defeat, and for the same reasons. Pasenadi sought the consolation of the Buddha, who told him this ancient tale. See Appendix.

Dhanañjaya is identified with **Ānanda** and Dhumakāri with Pasenadi.[1]

[1] J. iii. 400 ff.

Dhanañjānī.—See **Dhānañjānī.**

Dhanada.—See **Kuvera.**

Dhanananda.—The youngest of the nine **Nandas,** sons of **Kālāsoka.** He was killed by **Cāṇakka,** who raised **Candagutta** to the throne.[1] He incurred Cāṇakka's wrath by insulting him in the alms-hall. Cāṇakka stole his son **Pabbata,** put him to death, adopted Candagutta as his protégé, and stole Dhanananda's treasures which he had discovered. With the money thus obtained he raised an army for Candagutta and defeated Dhanananda.[2]

[1] Mhv. v. 17. [2] MṬ. 181 ff.

Dhanantevāsī.—An attendant of **Chaḷaṅgakumāra** (*q.v.*). **Kuruṅgavī** misconducted herself with **Dhanantevāsī.**[1]

[1] J. v. 225, 231.

1. **Dhanapāla (Dhanapālaka).**—Another name for **Nālāgiri**[1] (*q.v.*).

[1] J. i. 66; iii. 293, etc.

2. **Dhanapāla.**—A seṭṭhi of **Erakaccha** in **Dasaṇṇa.** He was a miser and, after death, was born as a peta. Some merchants, travelling to **Uttarāpatha,** saw his sufferings and, at his request, gave alms to the Buddha on his behalf.[1]

[1] Pv. ii. 7; PvA. 99 ff.

Dhanapālaka.—A householder of **Dhanañjaya,** who was converted by **Sikhī** Buddha.[1]

[1] BuA. 202.

Dhanapāla-Gajjita.—Mentioned[1] in reference to the subjugation of the elephant **Dhanapāla** by the Buddha. Gajjita is probably the name given to the stanzas spoken by the Buddha to the elephant on that occasion (*Mā kuñjara, nāgam āsado,* etc.).[2]

[1] *E.g.,* J. iii. 293.

[2] See J. v. 336.

Dhanapālī.—A slave-girl who, in spite of her name, was ill-treated by her master and mistress. The incident is mentioned as illustrating the small importance of a name.[1]

[1] J. i. 402.

Dhanapiṭṭhi.—A locality in Ceylon. In the time of **Aggabodhi IV.** its chief was **Datta.** He erected there a vihāra called by his name.[1]

[1] Cv. xlvi. 41, 43.

Dhanavatī.—A brahmin lady, mother of **Kassapa** Buddha. Her husband was **Brahmadatta.**[1]

[1] D. ii. 7; J. i. 43; Bu. xxv. 34; SNA. i. 280.

Dhanavāpī.—One of the three tanks constructed by **Moggallāna II.** through damming up the **Kadambanadī.**[1]

[1] Cv. xli. 62.

Dhanika.—See **Dhaniya.**

Dhaniṭṭha.—A king of thirteen kappas ago, a previous birth of **Saṇṭhita.**[1]

[1] Ap. i. 210.

Dhaniṭṭhaka.—An example of a low family name.[1]

[1] Vin. iv. 6, 13.

1. **Dhaniya.**—**Dhanika.** A herdsman living on the bank of the river **Mahī.** He was a seṭṭhiputta of **Dhammakoṇḍa** in **Pabbataraṭṭha,** which belonged to the kingdom of **Videha.** He had thirty thousand oxen and twenty thousand cows. He had seven sons and seven daughters and numerous retainers. In the dry season he lived on an island formed by the two forks of the river Mahī, and in the rainy season in a house on the upland. One day, while he was in this house, having finished his preparations for the approach of the rains, he sat meditating on his comfortable circumstances and broke forth into song in token of his happiness. The Buddha heard the song at **Sāvatthi,** seven hundred leagues away, and having travelled through the air, stood over Dhaniya's dwelling. As Dhaniya proceeded with his song, the Buddha added a verse to each one of Dhaniya's. At the end of this song Dhaniya, his wife, and two of his daughters, became sotāpannas. The Buddha then revealed himself and Dhaniya and his wife entered the Order. Later they became arahants and the cowherds erected for their use a monastery, which came to be called the **Gokulaṅka-vihāra.**[1]

[1] SN. vv. 18 ff.; SNA. i. 26 ff.

2. **Dhaniya.**—A potter of **Rājagaha.** In his house the Buddha taught **Pukkusāti** the **Cha-dhātu-vibhaṅga Sutta.** Dhaniya, hearing that Pukkasāti had died an arahant the same night, was so impressed by the power of the Dhamma, that he entered the Order.[1] He once made a grass hut on the slopes of **Isigili** and lived there with several others during the rains. He continued to live there after the others had left. While he was away begging for alms, his hut was pulled down by women searching for straw and firewood, but he rebuilt it. Three times this happened, until, in exasperation, Dhaniya very skilfully made bricks and tiles and built a hut both strong and splendid, with tiles of shining crimson which gave out a bell-like sound when tapped. The Buddha, seeing this, chided Dhaniya and ordered the hut to be pulled down. Dhaniya then built a hut of wood which he obtained from a guild of timber merchants, suppliers of wood to the king, giving them to understand that he had the king's permission. **Vassakāra,** hearing of this, reported the matter to **Bimbisāra,** who sent for Dhaniya. Dhaniya maintained that the king, by royal proclamation, had permitted the monks to use the royal supplies of wood and other materials. Bimbisāra admitted the proclamation, but said it referred only to supplies straight from the forest, and he sent Dhaniya away with a warning. The matter created a great uproar and the Buddha blamed Dhaniya.[2]

[1] Thag. v. 228-30; ThagA. i. 347 f.

[2] Vin. iii. 41-5; Sp. ii. 286.

Dhaniya later changed his ways and became an arahant. In the time of **Sikhī** Buddha he was a householder and gave the Buddha a reed-chain (? *naḷamālā*). He is probably identical with **Naḷamāliya** of the Apadāna.[3]

[3] Ap. ii. 412.

Dhaniya (Dhaniyagopāla) Sutta.—Records the conversation between the herdsman Dhaniya (*q.v.*) and the Buddha.[1]

[1] SN. vv. 18 ff.

Dhanuggaha.—See **Culla-Dhanuggaha.**

Dhanuggaha Sutta.—A man, who can simultaneously sieze the arrows shot by four expert bowmen from the four quarters, is possessed of great speed. Far speedier than he are the sun and the moon, but the change taking place in all things surpasses all these in speed.[1]

This seems also to have been called the **Daḷhadhamma Sutta.**[2]

[1] S. i. 265. [2] *E.g.*, at J. iv. 211.

Dhanuggaha-Tissa.—An Elder. One night, while staying with his friend **Utta (Datta** ?) in a monastery in **Kosala,** he awoke and, lighting a fire, started talking to him. Their conversation turned on the war which **Pasenadi** was waging against **Ajātasattu.** Tissa, maintaining that Pasenadi was ignorant of the arts of war, proceeded to describe in detail what Pasenadi should do if he wished for victory. Some courtiers, overhearing the conversation, reported it to Pasenadi, who, profiting by it, re-entered the battle and captured Ajātasattu alive. When the matter was reported to the Buddha, he related the **Vaḍḍhaki-sūkara Jātaka** (*q.v.*) to show that in the past, too, Tissa had been skilled in the art of warfare.[1] The **Taccha-sūkara Jātaka**[2] was also related in this connection.

[1] J. ii. 403 f. [2] J. iv. 343, 354.

Dhanumaṇḍala.—A locality in the hill-district of Ceylon. In the time of **Gajabāhu** its chief was **Otturāmallaka.**[1] It was subdued for **Parakkamabāhu I.** by the Adhikārin **Mañju.**[2]

[1] Cv. lxx. 17. [2] *Ibid.*, lxxiv. 166.

Dhanuvillaka.—A locality in the **Malaya** district of Ceylon.[1]

[1] Cv. lxx. 15.

Dhanusekha (Dhanusekhavā).—Son of the cook of Queen **Talatā.** He was born on the same day as **Cūḷani** (*q.v.*), who was sent to the cook's house as a refuge from **Chambhī.** The two boys became playmates. When

Cūḷani became king, Dhanusekhavā remained his constant companion, even visiting him unbidden, thus becoming a nuisance, as Cūḷani confessed to **Bherī.**[1]

[1] J. v. 469, 471, 475.

1. **Dhamma.**—The Bodhisatta, born as a devaputta in the Kāmāvacara-world. See the **Dhamma Jātaka.** In the Milandapañha[1] he is called a yakkha.

[1] p. 212.

2. **Dhamma.**—The palace built by **Vissakamma** for **Mahāsudassana,** by order of **Sakka.**[1]

[1] D. ii. 180 ff.

3. **Dhamma.**—The lake in front of the palace mentioned above.[1]

[1] D. ii. 184.

Dhamma Jātaka (No. 457).—The Bodhisatta once became a Kāmāvacara-god, named **Dhamma,** and **Devadatta** became **Adhamma.** On uposatha-days Dhamma would appear among men and urge them to lead virtuous lives, while Adhamma encouraged them in wickedness. One day, their two chariots meeting in mid-air, they each claimed the right of way. But at the end of the argument Adhamma's chariot fell headlong to earth, where he was swallowed up into hell. The story was related in reference to Devadatta's being swallowed up in Avīci.[1]

[1] J. iv. 100-4.

Dhamma Vagga.—The ninth chapter of the Duka Nipāta of the Aṅguttara Nikāya.[1]

A. i. 83 f.

1. **Dhamma Sutta.**—On the four kinds of preachers : those who speak little and cannot persuade the audience and those who can; those who speak much and cannot persuade the audience and those who can.[1]

[1] A. ii. 138.

2. **Dhamma Sutta.**—On ten matters to be continually considered by an ascetic.[1]

[1] A. v. 87 f.

3. **Dhamma Sutta.**—**Devadatta** brought schism into the Order because, in him, the conditions of good karma came to be extirpated.[1]

[1] S. ii. 240.

4. **Dhamma Sutta** (or **Sajjhāya Sutta**).—Once a certain monk retired to a forest track in **Kosala.** His life had been one of great diligence, but later he lived at ease, resigned and given to silence. A deva asked him the reason for this change, and he replied that he had realised the Pure and the Holy.[1]

[1] S. i. 202.

5. **Dhamma Sutta.**—See **Nāvā Sutta.**

1. **Dhammaka.**—A king, one of the chief supporters of **Anomadassī** Buddha.[1]

[1] BuA. 145.

2. **Dhammaka.**—A mountain in the neighbourhood of **Himavā,** where **Sumedha** had his hermitage.[1]

[1] J. i. 6; Bu. ii. 29.

Dhammakathika Vagga.—The twelfth chapter of the Khandha Saṃyutta.[1]

[1] S. iii. 162-70.

Dhammakathika Sutta.—A monk questions the Buddha as to who is a real teacher of the Dhamma and the Buddha replies.[1]

[1] S. ii. 18.

Dhammakathī.—See **Mahādhammakathī.**

1. **Dhammakitti.**—One of the Sinhalese envoys of **Parakkamabāhu I.** to the king of **Rāmañña.** The king insulted him and sent him, together with **Vāgissara,** back to Ceylon in a leaky ship.[1]

[1] Cv. lxxvi. 32 ff.

2. **Dhammakitti.**—A monk of **Tambaraṭṭha. Parakkamabāhu II.,** hearing of his great virtues and holiness, sent him offerings of piety, inviting him to Ceylon. The Elder came and was much honoured by the king.[1] It is commonly believed[2] that this was the monk who wrote the continuation of the Mahāvaṃsa (the Cūlavaṃsa) dealing with the period from the reign of Mahāsena to that of **Parakkamabāhu II.**

[1] Cv. lxxxiv. 11. [2] *E.g., J.R.A.S.*, 1896, pp. 202 ff.

3. **Dhammakitti.**—A thera in the time of **Vīravikkama** (*circa* 1542). The king appointed him head of the Order and held the ceremony of ordination under him.[1]

[1] Cv. xcii. 21.

4. **Dhammakitti.**—Author of the **Dāṭhāvaṃsa.** He wrote this book in the reign of **Līlāvatī,** at the request of her minister **Parakkama,** who was his patron. Dhammakitti speaks of himself as a pupil of **Sāriputta** (of **Pulatthipura**).[1] He is perhaps, identical with Dhammakitti 1.[2]

[1] P.L.C. 207 f.; Gv. 62, 67. [2] P.L.C. 215.

5. **Dhammakitti.**—A thera of Ceylon, author of the Sinhalese prose work, the Saddharmālaṅkāra, in the fourteenth century, which is an enlarged translation of the **Rasavāhinī.** He was Saṅgharāja in the time of **Bhuvanekabāhu V.** His teacher was also called Dhammakitti and was a member of the **Puṭabhattasela** fraternity. This teacher was probably the author of the Pāli poem the **Pāramīmahāsataka.** In addition to the Saddharmālaṅkāra, his pupil wrote several other works, the **Saṅkhepa,** the **Jinabodhāvalī** and the **Bālāvatāra**; also the Sinhalese chronicle, the Nikāyasaṅgraha.[1]

[1] P.L.C. 226, 240, 243.

6. **Dhammakitti.**—Called **Dhammakitti Mahāsāmi,** author of the **Saddhamasaṅgaha.** His teacher was also called Dhammakitti, well-known in Ceylon. Dhammakitti Mahāsāmi came to Ceylon from **Yodhapura** (Ayojjha ?) and, having acquired much merit, returned there, where he lived in the **Laṅkārāma,** built by Paramarāja.[1]

[1] *J.P.T.S.*, 1890, p. 90.

Dhammakoṇḍa.—A city in **Pabbataraṭṭha** in **Videha.** There the herdsman Dhaniya was born as a seṭṭhiputta.[1]

[1] SNA. i. 26.

Dhammagaṇārāma.—A monastery built by King **Uggata** in **Mekhalā** for the use of **Sobhita** Buddha.[1]

[1] BuA. 139.

Dhammagutta Thera.—An arahant. He lived in the **Kalyāṇika-vihara** and was known as the "earth-shaker" (*paṭhavicālaka*). He was among those who received a share of the meal given by **Duṭṭhagāmaṇī** when the latter fled from **Cūlaṅganiyapiṭṭhi.** He shared his portion with five hundred others.[1] According to the Jātaka Commentary,[2] he was among those who joined in the assemblies (*samāgama*) known as Kuddalasamāgama, Mūgapakkhasamāgama, Ayogharasamāgama and Hatthipalasamāgama. The Mahāvaṃsa Ṭīkā[3] mentions him as being one of those

[1] Mhv. xxxii. 50; xxiv. 24 ff. [2] J. iv. 490. [3] p. 606.

who accepted the meal of pork given by **Sāliya** and his wife, when they were blacksmiths, in their birth immediately preceding the last.

1. **Dhammaguttā, Dhammaguttikā.**—A secondary division of the **Mahiṃsāsakas,**[1] probably an offshoot of the **Sabbatthivādins.** They had a special Vinaya of their own. According to Tibetan sources,[2] they were called after their leader, Dharmagupta. Their fundamental doctrines were these: that the Buddha is not comprised in the Saṅgha; that while there is great reward for offerings made to the Buddha, there is none for offerings to the Saṅgha; that a life of brahmacariya exists also among the devas; and that there are worldly laws as opposed to spiritual.

[1] Dpv. v. 47; Mhv. v. 8; Mbv., p. 96. [2] Rockhill, pp. 185, 192.

2. **Dhammaguttā.**—A Vemanika-peta, mentioned as having the power of travelling through the air.[1]

[1] Vsm. 382.

Dhammacakka-kathā.—The seventh chapter of the Yuganaddhavagga of the Paṭisambhidāmagga.[1]

[1] Ps. ii. 159-66.

Dhammacakka-geha.—A building in **Anurādhapura,** erected by **Devānampiyatissa.**—It was attached to the royal palace, and when the Tooth Relic was brought to Ceylon it was deposited in this building.[1]

[1] Cv. xxxvii. 95.

Dhammacakkappavattana Vagga.—Second chapter of the Sacca Saṃyutta.[1] The first sutta is known as the Dhammacakkappavattana, *q.v.*

[1] S. v. 420-31.

Dhammacakkappavattana Sutta.—Name of the first sermon, preached by the Buddha, to the **Pañcavaggiyas** at the **Migadāya** in **Isipatana,** on the full-moon day of Āsāḷha. The sutta contains the fundamental principles of the Buddha's teaching—the avoidance of the two extremes of asceticism and luxury and the four Ariyan truths including the Ariyan Eightfold Way.

There was great rejoicing throughout the Cakkavāḷa at the preaching of the sermon, and at its conclusion **Kondañña** attained to realisation of the Truth—hence his name, **Aññā-Kondañña.**[1]

[1] Vin. i. 10 f.; the sutta is also given in S. v. 420 ff.; in neither context is the name of the sutta given as such; the name occurs only in the Commentaries—*e.g.*, J. i. 82; DA. i. 2; AA. i. 69, etc.; the Sanskrit version is found in Lal. 540 (416) f., and in Mtu. iii. 330 f.

The sermon was later preached by the thera **Majjhima** in the Himālaya country, when eighty thousand crores of beings understood the Doctrine.[2] It was also preached by **Mahinda** in Ceylon in the **Nandanavana,** when one thousand persons were converted.[3]

[2] Mhv. xii. 41; Dpv. viii. 11. [3] Mhv. xv. 200; Dpv. xiv. 46, etc.

Dhammacakkika (*v.l.* **Dhammacakkadāyaka**) **Thera.**—An arahant. Ninety-four kappas ago he placed a Dhammacakka in front of the seat of **Siddhattha** Buddha. Eleven kappas ago he became king eight times under the name of **Sahassarāja.**[1]

[1] Ap. i. 90.

Dhammacariya Sutta.—See **Kapila Sutta.**

Dhammacāri.—A Burmese monk of the twelfth century; he was a pupil of **Chapaṭa,** who wrote the **Suttaniddesa** at his request.[1]

[1] Gv. 74; Bode: *op. cit.*, 18.

Dhammaceti.—King of Pegu (A.C. 1460-91); a very enlightened monarch. He was first a monk; he then gave up his robes and became first the minister and later the son-in-law and successor of Queen Shin-san-bu. He sent a mission to Ceylon, where a body of **Rāmañña** monks were ordained at the **Kalyāṇi-sīmā.** These returned to Rāmañña and were known as the **Sīhalasaṅgha.**[1]

[1] For details see Bode: *op. cit.*, 38 f.

Dhammacetiya Sutta.—**Pasenadi** and **Dīgha-Kārāyaṇa** were staying once at **Naṅgaraka** and, hearing that the Buddha was residing at **Medataḷumpa,** three leagues away, the king went to visit him. He was deeply impressed by the silence surrounding the Buddha and, falling at his feet, he kissed them and showed great reverence. On being asked by the Buddha why he did so, the king replied that he perceived the marvellous effects of the Buddha's teaching on his disciples. They were well controlled, yet joyful, buoyant, with hearts as free as those of wild creatures; and he added that he knew of no such discipline outside the Buddha's teaching. He then proceeded to tell the Buddha of his own servants, **Isidatta** and **Purāṇa,** and of their great devotion to the Buddha, reminding the Buddha that they were both Kosalan nobles of about the same age. On the king's departure, the Buddha commended the king's words to the monks, asking them to remember them, for they formed a monument (*cetiya*) to the results of the Dhamma.[1]

[1] M. ii. 118-25.

According to the Commentary[2] this was the last occasion on which Pasenadi saw the Buddha, for during his absence Dīgha-Kārāyaṇa set up **Viḍūdabha** on the throne.

Pasenadi went to Rājagaha to seek **Ajātasattu's** aid, but died in a hut by the wayside.

[2] MA. ii. 753 ff.; J. iv. 151 ff.

Dhammajoti.—A Sinhalese monk of the eighteenth century who wrote a Sinhalese paraphrase (*sanne*) to the **Bālavatāra,** called the Okandapoḷa-sanne, because it was written in Okandapola-vihāra.[1]

[1] P.L.C. 244, 284.

Dhammaññu Sutta.—On seven qualities—such as knowing the Dhamma, moderation, etc.—which make a monk worthy of homage and of gifts.[1]

[1] A. iv. 113 ff.

Dhammaṭṭha Vagga.—The nineteenth chapter of the Dhammapada.

Dhammatāpasā.—An eminent therī of **Anurādhapura,** expert in the Vinaya.[1]

[1] Dpv. xviii. 15.

1. **Dhammadassī.**—The fifteenth of the twenty-four Buddhas. He was born in the **Saraṇa** pleasaunce in the city of **Saraṇa,** his father being a khattiya named **Saraṇa,** and his mother **Sunandā.** It is said that on the day of his birth all unjust laws disappeared from the law-books, hence his name. For eight thousand years he lived in the household, in three palaces—**Araja, Viraja** and **Sudassana.** His chief wife was **Vicitolī** and his son **Puññavaḍḍhana.** He left the world travelling in his palace, accompanied by all his retinue. For seven days he practised austerities; his wife gave him a meal of milk-rice, and a yavapālaka, named **Sirivaḍḍha,** gave grass for his seat; his bodhi-tree was a *bimbijāla*-tree. His first sermon was preached at **Isipatana.** Later he preached to King **Sañjaya** of **Tagara,** and to **Sakka,** who was the Bodhisatta. The Buddha's half-brothers, **Paduma** and **Phussadeva,** became his chief disciples, and **Hārita** was chief of those who practised the *dhutaṅgas.* The Buddha's personal attendant was **Sunetta,** his chief women disciples being **Khemā** and **Sabba-(Sacca)-dinnā. Subhadda** and **Kaṭisaha** were the chief among men of his lay patrons, and **Sāliyā** and **Vaḷiyā** among women. The Buddha's body was eighty cubits high and he lived to be one hundred thousand years old, dying at the **Kesārāma** in **Sālavati.**[1]

[1] Bu. xvi. 1 ff.; BuA. 182 ff.; J. i. 38, 39, 40, 44.

2. **Dhammadassī.**—A monk of Pagan, author of the Pāli grammar, **Vaccavācaka.**[1]

[1] Bode: *op. cit.*, p. 22.

Dhammadāyāda Sutta.—The Buddha exhorts the monks at **Jetavana** to strive earnestly to be heirs, not of the world's goods, but of the Doctrine. On the Buddha's departure the monks gather round **Sāriputta** and ask him how the Buddha expects them to cultivate the inner life with the same aloofness as does the Buddha himself, and Sāriputta delivers a discourse.[1] This sutta is often referred to[2] as teaching the virtues of contentment.

[1] M. i. 12 ff.

[2] *E.g.*, Mil. 242; Sp. iii. 694.

1. **Dhammadinna Thera.**—Also called **Mahādhammadinna.** An arahant. He resided at **Talaṅga-(Talaṅgatissa-pabbata)** (*q.v.*). He was one of the monks who partook of the meal of sour gruel given by **Duṭṭhagāmaṇī** when in dire distress for want of food. Dhammadinna distributed his share among ten thousand monks in **Piyaṅgudīpa.**[1] He is also mentioned[2] as having accepted a meal given by **Sāliya** and his wife when they were blacksmiths in a previous birth. Dhammadinna had a nephew who became an arahant in the tonsure-hall. Dhammadinna read to him the three Piṭakas, and he learnt them all on that occasion.[3] Dhammadinna's teacher was **Mahānāga** of **Uccatalaṅka** (*v.l.* **Uccavālika**). Dhammadinna visited him in his old age, knowing that, though he himself thought he had attained arahantship, this was not the case. By a display of *iddhi*-power, Dhammadinna convinced Mahānāga of his error and gave him a subject of meditation. Almost immediately after, the Elder became an arahant.[4] Once, while preaching the **Apaṇṇaka Sutta,** at **Tissamahārāma,** Dhammadinna pointed his fan downwards, whereupon the earth opened to the depth of **Avīci,** revealing all that was there. Similarly, he showed all things to the height of the **Brahma-**world. During his sermon he frightened the audience with the fear of hell and lured them with the bliss of heaven.[5]

The Majjhima Commentary[6] records that soon after the ordination of Dhammadinna many monks, on his advice, became arahants. Hearing of this, the monks of Tissamahārāma sent a number of their colleagues to fetch him. He preached to them, and they attained arahantship and remained with him. Three times this happened. On the fourth occasion an aged monk was sent. He gave the message of the monks and Dhammadinna started at once to go to them. On the way, at **Haṅkana** (*v.l.* **Taṅ-**

[1] Mhv. xxxii. 52.

[2] MṬ. 606.

[3] VibhA. 389.

[4] *Ibid.*, 489; Vsm. 634 f.

[5] *Ibid.*, 392.

[6] MA. i. 149 ff. A variation of what is evidently the same story is found in AA. i. 25.

gana) and at **Cittalapabbata,** he persuaded two monks, who thought they were arahants, to display their *iddhi*-power, and, thereby convinced them of their error; thereupon he gave them topics of meditation. On his arrival at Tissamahārāma, the monks failed to pay him their respects. He thereupon made the earth tremble and returned to his own vihāra. The Saddhammasaṅgaha[7] relates the story of a blind rat-snake who heard Dhammadinna recite the satipaṭṭhānas and was later born as **Tissāmacca,** minister of Duṭṭhagāmaṇī.

[7] p. 88 f.

2. **Dhammadinna.**—An eminent lay-follower of the Buddha. He once came with five hundred upāsakas to the Buddha at **Isipatana** and asked him to give them a lesson which might profit them, for, said he, it is difficult for a householder encumbered with a family and the luxuries of household life to comprehend the Buddha's teachings in their fulness. The Buddha answers that they should practise the four limbs of sotāpatti: loyalty to the Buddha, the Dhamma and the Saṅgha, and the cultivation of Ariyan virtues. Dhammadinna answers that they already possess these limbs. The Buddha then expresses his great satisfaction.[1]

The Commentary[2] says that Dhammadinna was one of seven laymen with followings of five hundred—the others being **Visākha, Ugga, Citta, Hatthaka Āḷavaka** and **Cūḷa-** and **Mahā-Anāthapiṇḍika.**

[1] S. v. 406 ff. [2] SA. iii. 223.

Dhammadinna Sutta.—Records the visit of the householder **Dhammadinna** (*q.v.*) to the Buddha at **Isipatana.**[1]

[1] S. v. 406 ff.

1. **Dhammadinnā.**—One of the two chief women disciples of **Piyadassī** Buddha.[1]

[1] Bu. xiv. 21; J. i. 39.

2. **Dhammadinnā.**—One of the chief supporters, among lay women, of **Piyadassī** Buddha.[1]

[1] Bu. xiv. 22.

3. **Dhammadinnā.**—An eminent Therī, ranked foremost among nuns who possessed the gift of preaching.[1] She was the wife of **Visākha** of **Rājagaha,** and when he, having heard the Buddha preach, became an anāgāmin, she left the world with the consent of her husband who sent her to the nunnery in a golden palanquin.[2] Dwelling in solitude, she soon attained arahant-

[1] A. i. 25. [2] MA. (i. 515) says this was provided by **Bimbisāra.**

ship with the four paṭisambhidā.[3] She later returned to Rājagaha to worship the Buddha, and there Visākha asked her questions on the Dhamma, which she answered "as easily as one might cut a lotus-stalk with a knife." The questions and answers are given in the **Cūla Vedalla Sutta.**[4] Visākha reported this interview to the Buddha, who praised her great wisdom and commended her eloquence.

In the time of **Padumuttara** Buddha she was a servant, and one day saw the Buddha's disciple, **Sujāta,** begging alms and gave him a curry.[5] Her master, seeing this, made her his daughter-in-law. Later, while on a visit to the vihāra, she saw a nun declared to be chief of preachers and wished for similar eminence.

In the time of **Phussa** Buddha she obtained merit by giving to the Buddha's half-brother double the gift prescribed by her husband.[6]

In the time of **Kassapa** Buddha she was born as **Sudhammā,** the sixth of the seven daughters of **Kiki,** king of Benares; for twenty thousand years she lived in celibacy.[7]

Dhammadinnā was the teacher of **Sukhā.**[8]

[3] See Thig. (v. 12) for a stanza uttered by her.

[4] M. i. 299 ff.

[5] The ThigA. (p. 15) says Sujāta had just risen from samādhi.

[6] Details of this are given in PvA., p. 21.

[7] Her story is given in ThigA. 15 ff.; Ap. ii. 567 f.; AA. i. 196 f.; MA. i. 515 ff.; DhA. iv. 229 ff.

[8] ThigA. 58.

Dhammaddhaja.—The Bodhisatta born as the chaplain of **Yasapāṇi,** king of Benares. For his story see the **Dhammaddhaja Jātaka.**

1. **Dhammaddhaja Jātaka** (No. 220).—The Bodhisatta was once born as **Dhammaddhaja,** chaplain to **Yasapāṇi,** king of Benares. One day the king's captain, **Kāḷaka,** who was wont to take bribes, gave a wrong decision in a case, and the Bodhisatta, being appealed to, reheard the case and decided in the plaintiff's favour. The people applauded greatly and the king made him judge. But Kāḷaka, wishing for an excuse to put Dhammaddhaja to death, persuaded the king that he was getting too popular, and the king gave him various impossible tasks. Dhammaddhaja, with the help of **Sakka,** performed them all. One day the king ordered him to find a park-keeper with four virtues, and once again, with the aid of Sakka, the Bodhisatta discovered **Chattapāṇi,** the king's barber. On being questioned, Chattapāṇi told the king that he was free from envy, drank no wine, had no strong desires, never gave way to anger; he then related stories of his past lives,[1] the experiences of which had made him renounce these evils. The king, at length, discovered Kāḷaka's perfidy and had him put to death.

[1] For details see *s.v.* **Chattapāṇi** (2).

The Jātaka was related in reference to **Devadatta's** attempts to kill the Buddha. Devadatta is identified with Kāḷaka and **Sāriputta** with Chattapāṇi.[2]

[2] J. ii. 186-96.

2. **Dhammaddhaja Jātaka** (No. 384).—The Bodhisatta was once born as leader of a flock of birds on an island. Certain merchants of Benares started on a voyage taking with them, to aid them on the way, a much travelled crow. The ship was wrecked and the crow flew to the island. There he pretended to the other birds that he was a holy person, practising austerities and living on air. The birds, being deceived by him, left him in charge of their eggs and young ones, which he proceeded to eat each day. One day the Bodhisatta kept watch and thus discovered his villainy. The birds collected round the crow and pecked him to death.

The story was related in reference to a deceitful monk, who is identified with the crow.[1]

[1] J. iii. 267-70.

Dhammantarī.—A celebrated physician (the Sanskrit Dhanvantarī), mentioned together with **Vetaraṇī** and **Bhoja,** in the *Jātaka Commentary*[1] and with **Nārada, Aṅgirasa, Kapila, Kaṇḍaraggisāma, Atula** and **Pubba Kaccāyana,** in the *Milindapañha.*[2]

[1] J. iv. 496, 498. [2] Mil. 272.

Dhammapada.—The second book of the Khuddaka Nikāya of the Sutta Piṭaka. It is probably a later anthology than the Thera-Therī-Gāthā, and its earliest mention by name is in the Milinda-pañha.[1] It includes gāthas collected together from various books in the Canon, but contains hardly any from the Jātaka collection, or directly derived from the Sutta Nipāta. The present text of the Dhammapada contains four hundred and twenty-three verses divided into twenty-six vaggas. So far, five recensions of the Dhammapada have been discovered.[2] A commentary on it exists called the **Dhammapadaṭṭhakathā.**

[1] p. 408. [2] For details see Law: *Pāli Lit.*, pp. 215 f.

Dhammapada Sutta.—On four righteous things which are always held in esteem—freedom from covetousness, from envy, right mindfulness and right concentration of mind.[1]

[1] A. ii. 29.

Dhammapadaṭṭhakathā.—The Commentary on the **Dhammapada,** containing stories similar to those of the Jātakas and explaining the occasions on which the **Dhammapada**-stanzas were uttered. A considerable number of these stories are found in the Four Nikāyas and the Vinaya, and more than fifty are either directly derived from the Jātaka Commentary or are closely parallel to them. The work is usually ascribed to **Buddhaghosa,** and in the prelude to the book it is stated that he translated the work from Sinhalese at the request of a monk named **Kumārakassapa.**[1]

[1] For a discussion see P.L.C., pp. 95 ff.; and Law: *Pāli Lit.*, pp. 449 ff.

1. **Dhammapāla Thera.**—An arahant. He was a brahmin of **Avanti** and studied in **Takkasilā.** While returning from there after completing his studies, he saw a monk dwelling apart and, having heard the Dhamma from him, entered the Order and became an arahant. We are told that one day, while meditating, he saw two novices climbing a tree in the vihāra to pick flowers. The bough broke and they fell, but he, with his *iddhi*-power, caught them and put them down unhurt.

In the time of **Atthadassī** Buddha he gave to the Buddha a *pilakkha*-fruit.[1] He is probably identical with **Pilakkhaphaladāyaka** of the *Apadāna.*[2]

[1] Thag. vs. 203 f.; ThagA. i. 326 f. [2] Ap. i. 298.

2. **Dhammapāla.**—A brahmin, son of the Bodhisatta. See **Mahā-Dhammapāla.**

3. **Dhammapāla.**—The Bodhisatta born as the son of **Mahā-Dhammapāla.** For his story see the **Mahā-Dhammapāla Jātaka.**

4. **Dhammapāla.**—The Bodhisatta born as the son of King **Mahāpatāpa.** For his story see the **Culla-Dhammapāla Jātaka.**

5. **Dhammapāla.**—A name given to **Vidhurapaṇḍita.**[1]

[1] J. vi. 289, 291.

6. **Dhammapāla Kumāra.**—The son of **Vidhurapaṇḍita** (*q.v.*).[1] He is identified with **Rāhula.**[2]

[1] J. vi. 290, 300. [2] *Ibid.*, 329.

7. **Dhammapāla.**—The name of the family (*kula*) of **Dhammapāla,** and the village in **Kāsi** where he lived.[1] See the **Mahā-Dhammapāla Jātaka.**

[1] J. iv. 50; PvA. 61.

8. **Dhammapāla.**—A celebrated author, generally referred to as Ācariya. Various works are attributed to him, but as there seem to have been

several authors of the same name,[1] it is difficult to assign their works separately. The best known, distinguished by the name of Ācariya, is said[2] to have written fourteen books. The Sāsanavaṃsa[3] records that he lived at **Badaratittha** in South India. His works show that he was a native of **Kāñcipura.** His period is uncertain, though it is generally agreed that he is posterior to **Buddhaghosa.** He seems to have studied in the **Mahāvihāra,** because he mentions this fact in the introduction to his books (*e.g.*, the Petavatthu Commentary). It is quite likely that he studied the Tamil Commentaries as well and that he wrote at Badaratittha.[4] The **Khuddaka Nikāya** was his chief study, and seven of his works are commentaries on the books of poetry preserved in the Canon—the Thera- and Therī-Gāthā, Udāna, Vimāna- and Peta-vatthu, Itivuttaka and Cariyāpiṭaka. His other works are a commentary on the Netti, and on the Visuddhimagga (called the **Paramatthamañjūsā**), ṭīkās (called **Līnatthavaṇṇanā**) on Buddhaghosa's Commentaries to the Four Nikāyas and another on the Jātakaṭṭhakathā. He is also credited with having written a ṭīkā on the Buddhavaṃsa Commentary and on the Abhidhammatthakathā.

[1] Gv. (p. 66 f.) mentions four.
[2] Gv. p. 69.
[3] p. 33.
[4] Hiouen Thsang- (Beal. ii. 229) says that Dhammapāla was a clever youth of Kāñcipura and that the king gave him his daughter. But Dhammapāla, not wishing to marry, prayed before an image of the Buddha. The gods took him to a place far away where he was ordained by the monks.

9. **Dhammapāla.**—A thera of Ceylon, generally called **Culla-Dhammapāla.** He was the senior pupil of **Vanaratana Ānanda** and wrote the **Saccasaṅkhepa.** He is also credited with ṭīkās on several works, including a Līnathavaṇṇanā on Ānanda's Mūlaṭīkā.[1]

[1] Gv. 60, 70; also P.L.C., 203 f., 211.

10. **Dhammapāla.**—A Burmese scholar of **Arimaddana.**[1]

[1] Gv. 67.

Dhammapāla Jātaka.—See **Culladhammapāla** and **Mahādhammapāla Jātakas.**

Dhammapālā, Dhammapālī, Therī.—An arahant. She was the preceptor (*upajjhāya*) of **Saṅghamittā.**[1]

[1] Mhv. v. 208; Sp. i. 51.

Dhammapālita.—A thera in **Rohaṇa,** expert in the Vinaya. His pupil was **Khema.**[1]

[1] Vin. v. 3.

Dhammapāsāda.—The palace built by **Vissakamma** at **Sakka's** request for **Mahā-Sudassana.**[1]

[1] For details of its construction see D. ii. 181 f.

Dhammabhaṇḍāgārika.—A name given to **Ānanda** (*q.v.*).

Dhammamitta.—A monk of the **Sitthagāma-pariveṇa.** He wrote a Commentary on the Abhidhamma at the request of **Mahinda IV.**[1]

[1] Cv. liv. 35.

1. **Dhammarakkhita.**—A Yona Thera sent by the Third Council to **Aparantaka.** There he preached the **Aggikkhandhopama Sutta** and converted thirty-seven thousand persons.[1]

[1] Mhv. xii. 4, 34 f.

2. **Dhammarakkhita.**—See **Mahā-Dhammarakkhita** and **Yonaka-Mahā-Dhammarakkhita.**

3. **Dhammarakkhita.**—A thera in Ceylon in the time of **Kittisirirājasīha.**[1]

[1] Cv. c. 299.

4. **Dhammarakkhita.**—A Thera at whose request **Ācariya Dhammapāla** wrote the Commentary on the Netti.[1]

[1] Gv. 69.

5. **Dhammarakkhita.**—Mentioned as a high-class name.[1]

[1] *E.g.*, Vin. iv. 8; Sp. ii. 448, 480.

6. **Dhammarakkhita.**—A monk of **Asokārāma** in **Pāṭaliputta,** under whom **Nāgasena** studied the Tipiṭaka.[1]

[1] Mil. 16, 18.

Dhammaramma.—A tank in Ceylon built by **Mahāsena.**[1]

[1] Mhv. xxxvii. 47.

1. **Dhammaruci.**—One of the heterodox sects of Ceylon which branched off from the **Theravāda.**[1] According to the *Nikāya Saṅgraha*[2] this secession

[1] Mhv. v. 13. [2] p. 11.

took place four hundred and fifty-four years after the death of the Buddha, and in the fifteenth year of the reign of **Vaṭṭagāmaṇi Abhaya.** The *Nikāya Saṅgraha* gives an account of the origin of this sect. A monk called **Mahā-Tissa,** incumbent of **Abhayagiri,** was convicted of living in domestic intercourse and expelled by the **Mahāvihāra** fraternity. He thereupon left with his followers and lived apart at Abhayagiri. They were strengthened by the arrival of some monks from **Pallarārāma** in South India, descendants of the **Vajjiputtakas.** Their teacher was **Dhammaruci,** and when they joined the Abhayagiri monks, Mahā-Tissa himself took the name of Dhammaruci and his followers became known as Dhammarucikas. The Mahāvaṃsa Ṭīkā[3] says that Dhammarucika was the name given to the monks of Abhayagiri when they seceded from the Mahāvihāra, and gives elsewhere[4] the points on which they differed from the Theravādins. These points concerned minor teachings of the Vinaya. The Dhammarucikas became active in the time of **Meghavaṇṇābhaya,** and the king, after an enquiry into the matter, sent sixty of them into exile. They again became powerful in the time of **Mahāsena,** through the influence of **Saṅghamitta,** and almost succeeded in destroying the Mahāvihāra. But this disaster was averted by the intervention of the king's friend and counsellor, **Meghavaṇṇābhaya,** and Saṅghamitta was killed by one of the queens.[5]

In spite of Saṅghamitta's untimely end, the Dhammarucikas seem to have enjoyed favour in Ceylon during a long period. **Dhātusena** gave over to them the **Ambatthala-vihāra,** which he built on **Cetiyapabbata,**[6] and **Kassapa I.** bestowed on them the vihāra he built in the **Niyyanti** garden, and made all provisions for their comfort.[7] **Moggallāna I.** gave over to them the **Daḷha-vihāra**[8] and **Aggabodhi V.** the **Rājinādīpika-vihāra.**[9] **Sena Ilaṅga,** general of **Kassapa IV.,** built for them the **Dhammārāma** and the **Hadayuṇha-pariveṇa.**[10]

The **Sāgaliyas** were an offshoot of the Dhammarucikas.

[3] p. 176.
[4] p. 676 f.
[5] Mhv. xxxvii. 17 ff.
[6] Cv. xxxviii. 75.
[7] *Ibid.*, xxxix. 17.
[8] *Ibid.*, 41.
[9] *Ibid.*, xlviii. 1.
[10] *Ibid.*, lii. 17, 18.

2. **Dhammaruci Thera.**—An arahant. In the time of **Dīpaṅkara** Buddha he was a young man named **Megha,** and on hearing the Buddha's declaration regarding **Sumedha,** he entered the Order under the latter. But, owing to wrong association, he left the Order and murdered his mother. For this he suffered in **Avīci** and was later born as a fish. One day he heard some shipwrecked sailors calling on the name of **Gotama** Buddha for protection, and, remembering Dīpaṅkara's prophecy, the fish died. He

was then born in **Sāvatthi,** and hearing the Buddha preach at **Jetavana,** he entered the Order and became an arahant.[1]

[1] Ap. ii. 429 f.

3. **Dhammaruci.**—A Nāga king who gave grass to **Atthadassī** Buddha for his seat.[1]

[1] BuA. 178.

Dhammavādi.—A monk who lived in the time of **Kassapa** Buddha. After the Buddha's death, another monk, **Adhammavādi,** was charged with having violated the rules of the Vinaya, and Dhammavādi decided against him. But Adhammavādi succeeded in getting two others to give a verdict in his favour. These two monks were later born as **Hemavata** and **Sātāgira.**[1]

[1] SNA. i. 195 f.

Dhammavādi Sutta.—**Sāriputta** says, in answer to a question by **Jambukhādaka,** that those who preach the doctrine of abandoning lust and hatred and illusion are real preachers. To be able to do this, they must practise the doctrine which they preach, and the method of such practice is the Ariyan Eightfold Path.[1]

[1] S. iv. 252; *cp.* 261 f.

Dhammavilāsa.—See **Sāriputta** 3.

Dhammavihārī Suttā.—Two suttas on the same theme. The monk worthy to be called a *dhammavihārī* is not one who has mastered the Dhamma nor one who teaches it to others, neither is he one who repeats it by heart nor who reflects on it, but he is one who, having learnt the Dhamma, dwells apart and devotes himself to attaining calmness of self.[1]

[1] A. iii. 86.

Dhammasaṅgaṇi.—The first book, in the accepted order of precedence, of the Abhidhamma Piṭaka. It deals with more or less the same topics as the Nikāyas, differing only in methods of treatment; the chief subject is that of ethics, the enquiry thereinto being conducted from a psychological standpoint. The book enumerates and defines a number of categories of terms occurring in the Nikāyas. There is in existence a commentary on the book, written by **Buddhaghosa** and called the **Atthasālinī.** King **Vijayabāhu I.** of Ceylon translated the Dhammasaṅgaṇi into Sinhalese,[1] but this translation is now lost. The work has been translated into English.[2]

The Dhammasaṅgaṇi appears to have been also called **Dhammasaṅgaha.**[3]

[1] Cv. lx. 17.

[2] The text is published by the P.T.S. (1885), and the translation (by Mrs. Rhys Davids) is published by the R.A.S., under the title of *A Buddhist Manual of Psychological Ethics.*

[3] DA. i. 17.

Dhammasaṅgaṇi-geha.—A building in the centre of the citadel of **Anurādhapura.** It was evidently built by **Kassapa V.,** who placed therein a copy of the **Dhammasaṅgaṇi** adorned with manifold jewels, and caused a festal procession to be held in its honour.[1] **Mahinda IV.** restored the building.[2]

[1] Cv. lii. 50 f.

[2] *Ibid.*, liv. 45.

Dhammasaṅgaha.—Evidently another and earlier name for the **Dhammasaṅgaṇi.** The name occurs in the Sumaṅgalavilāsini[1] in the classification of the Abhidhamma books. Its Commentary is also referred to[2] as the **Dhammasaṅgahaṭṭhakathā.**

[1] DA. i. 17.

[2] *E.g.*, VibhA. 39 f., 43, 105, 518; PSA. 405.

Dhammasaṅgāhaka Therā.—The name given to the Elders who took part in the Three Councils. These Elders sometimes inserted in the Canon additional information by way of explanation or of summarising what has gone before.[1]

[1] *E.g.*, D. ii. 128, 134, 135, 167; as explained by DA. ii. 568, etc.

Dhammasaññaka Thera.—An arahant. Once, during a festival in honour of **Vipassī** Buddha's bodhi-tree, he heard the Buddha preach and paid him homage. Thirty-three kappas ago he was a cakkavatti named **Sutavā.**[1]

[1] Ap. i. 249.

Dhammasattha.—Name given to the codes of law drawn up from time to time in Burma, with the assistance of the monks. **Dhammavilāsa** (or **Sāriputta**) was the author of the oldest of these known by name.[1]

[1] Bode: *op. cit.*, p. 33.

Dhammasamādāna Sutta.—See **Culla- and Mahā-Dhammasamādāna Sutta.**

Dhammasava Thera.—An arahant. He was a brahmin of **Magadha** who, having heard the Buddha preach at **Dakkhiṇāgiri,** entered the Order.

In the time of **Padumuttara** Buddha he was a brahmin ascetic named **Suvaccha**, versed in the three Vedas. The Buddha appeared before him, and he paid him homage by scattering *nāga*-flowers in his path. Thirty-one kappas ago he was a king named **Mahāratha.**[1] He is probably identical with **Nāgapupphiya** of the Apadāna.[2]

[1] Thag. 107; ThagA. i. 214 f. [2] Ap. i. 179.

Dhammasavaṇiya.—A thera who attained arahantship at the age of seven, having heard the Buddha preach the stanza beginning with "*anicca vata saṅkhārā.*" In the time of **Padumuttara** Buddha he was a Jaṭila who, while flying through the air, was forced to descend where the Buddha sat preaching, it being impossible to fly over him. He was afterwards born in **Tāvatiṃsa.**[1]

[1] Ap. i. 273 f.

Dhammasavana Sutta.—The five advantages of hearing the Dhamma: hearing things not heard, purging things heard, dispelling doubt, straightening one's views, calmness of heart.[1]

[1] A. iii. 248.

Dhammasava-pitā.—Father of **Dhammasava.** He was one hundred and twenty years old when his son joined the Order and, being impressed by his son's renunciation while yet young, he followed his example and soon after became an arahant. Once, in the past, he saw a Pacceka Buddha on the **Bhūtagaṇa** mountain, and honoured him with *tiṇasūla*-flowers. Eleven kappas ago he was a king called **Dharaṇipati (Dharaṇiruha).**[1] He is probably identical with **Tiṇasūlaka** of the Apadāna.[2]

[1] Thag. 108; ThagA. i. 215 f. [2] Ap. i. 179.

Dhammasāmi.—The fourth future Buddha.[1]

[1] Anāgat., p. 40.

Dhammasāla-vihāra.—A vihāra in **Rohaṇa** where **Aggabodhi,** son of **Mahātissa,** erected some buildings.[1]

[1] Cv. xlv. 46.

Dhammasiri.—A monk of **Anurādhapura,** author of the **Khuddasikkhā.** He probably lived about the fourth century A.C.[1]

[1] Gv. 61, 70; Svd. 1206; P.L.C. 77.

1. **Dhammasena.**—Son of the chaplain of **Kaṇṇakujja.** He later became the chief disciple of **Phussa** Buddha.[1]

[1] Bu. xix. 19; BuA. 193; J. i. 41.

2. **Dhammasena.**—The chief disciple of **Maṅgala** Buddha. He was a resident of **Mekhala.**[1]

[1] Bu. xxii. 23; BuA. 120; J. i. 41; Mtu. (i. 248) calls him Dharmadeva.

3. **Dhammasena Thera.**—An arahant of **Isipatana.** He was present, with twelve thousand others, at **Anurādhapura,** at the foundation of the **Mahā-Thūpa.**[1]

[1] Mhv. xxix. 31; Dpv. xxix. 5.

4. **Dhammasena.**—A monk of Ceylon of the thirteenth century. He translated a large part of the **Dhammapada** Commentary into Sinhalese, which work he called the Saddharmaratnāvalī.[1]

[1] P.L.C. 97.

1. **Dhammasenāpati.**—A title given to **Sāriputta** (*q.v.*).

2. **Dhammasenāpati.**—A monk of the **Ānanda-vihāra** in Pagan. He probably started as a nobleman and later joined the Order. He wrote a Pāli grammatical work called **Kārikā.**[1]

[1] Bode: *op. cit.*, 15 f.; Gv. 63, 73.

Dhammahadayavibhaṅga Sutta.—In the **Sutta-Saṅgaha,** a portion of the Dhammahadayavibhaṅga of the Vibhaṅgappakaraṇa[1]—dealing with birth in the Kāmāvacara worlds, the good deeds that lead to birth therein, and the span of life in each world—has been taken as a separate sutta (No. 14) and called by this name.

[1] Vibh. 422 f.

1. **Dhammā Therī.**—She belonged to a respectable family in **Sāvatthi** and was given in marriage to a suitable husband. Having heard the Doctrine, she wished to join the Order, but her husband refused his permission. After his death she became a nun, and one day, while returning from her alms round, she slipped and fell. Meditating on this, she became an arahant.[1]

[1] Thig. vs. 17; ThigA. 23 f.

2. **Dhammā.**—The chief woman disciple of **Atthadassī** Buddha.[1]

[1] Bu. xv. 20; J. i. 39.

3. **Dhammā.**—The fifth of the seven daughters of **Kikī,** king of Benares. For twenty thousand years she lived the life of celibacy. She is identified with **Kisāgotamī.**[1]

[1] J. vi. 431; Ap. ii. 565.

4. **Dhammā.**—Wife of **Bindusāra** and mother of **Asoka.** She had two sons, Asoka and **Tissa.**[1]

[1] MṬ. 189, 193; the "*Kambodian*" *Mahāvaṃsa* (vs. 1129) calls her Siridhammā.

5. **Dhammā.**—An eminent Therī of **Anurādhapura,** an expert teacher of the Vinaya.[1]

[1] Dpv. xviii. 14.

1. **Dhammādāsa-pariyāya.**—One of the titles given to the **Bahudhātuka Sutta.**[1]

[1] M. iii. 67.

2. **Dhammādāsa-pariyāya.**—The name given to a sermon preached by the Buddha at **Ñātikā,** showing how the rebirth of a disciple can be predicted.[1]

[1] D. ii. 93 f.; S. v. 357.

Dhammānanda.—A monk who wrote several Pāli grammatical works. The Gandhavaṃsa[1] assigns to him the **Kaccāyanasāra** together with its ṭīkā, and also the **Kaccāyanabheda.**

[1] p. 74 (also Svd. 1250); but see under these names.

Dhammānusāraṇī.—A Pāli commentarial work.[1]

[1] Gv. 68, 72.

Dhammābhinandī.—An author mentioned in a list of names.[1]

[1] Gv. 67.

1. **Dhammārāma.**—A monastery where lived **Anomadassī** Buddha.[1]

[1] Bu. viii. 29; BuA. 145.

2. **Dhammārāma.**—A monastery in which **Paduma** Buddha died.[1]

[1] Bu. ix. 29.

3. **Dhammārāma Thera.**—We are told that when the Buddha announced that he would die in four months, a large number of monks wandered about distracted, in small groups, not knowing where to turn. But Dhammārāma dwelt apart, meditating. This was reported to the Buddha and, on being questioned, Dhammārāma confessed that he wished to become an arahant while yet the Buddha was alive. The Buddha praised him and asked the other monks to follow his example.[1]

[1] DhA. iv. 93 ff.

4. **Dhammārāma.**—A monastery in Ceylon, founded for the **Dhammarucikas** by **Sena Ilaṅga,** general of Kassapa IV.[1]

[1] Cv. lii. 17.

1. **Dhammāsoka.**—See **Asoka.**

2. **Dhammāsoka.**—A king of Ceylon (1208-9 A.C.). He was of royal blood, and was three months old on his accession. He was killed by the **Mahādīpāda Anīkaṅga.**[1]

[1] Cv. lxxx. 42, 44; also Cv. *Trs.* ii. 131, n. 1.

1. **Dhammika Thera.**—A brahmin of **Kosala** who was converted at the presentation of **Jetavana** and entered a village vihāra. As he became irritated when monks visited the vihāra they desisted, and he became sole master of the vihāra. When this was reported to the Buddha by a layman, the Buddha sent for him and preached to him the **Rukkhadhamma Jātaka,** showing that in the past, too, he had been guilty of similar conduct. Dhammika concentrated on the verses of the Jātaka and, developing insight, became an arahant. In the time of **Sikhī** Buddha he had been a hunter and had listened to the Buddha preaching to an assembly of the gods in a forest.[1]

He may be identical with **Ghosasaññaka** of the Apadāna.[2]

[1] Thag. 303-6; ThagA. i. 396 ff. According to A. iii. 366 ff. Dhammika had to leave seven lodgings, one after the other, because the lay supporters of the lodgings could not tolerate his insulting ways. He therefore sought the Buddha and complained to him. The Rukkhadhamma Jātaka mentioned here is evidently not the story of the same name mentioned in the Jātaka Commentary (i. 327 ff.). The story is given in full in the Aṅguttara Nikāya (*loc. cit.*). There the Buddha is said to have related to him stories of several past teachers, showing the evil effects of reviling others.

[2] Ap. ii. 451.

2. **Dhammika.**—A householder of **Sāvatthi** who led a very holy life. One day he felt the wish to become a monk and spoke of it to his wife, but she begged him to wait until after the birth of their child. He waited till the child was able to walk and then spoke again to her, but she then wished him to wait until the child should be of age. To this he would not agree, but joined the Order and soon after became an arahant. Later, he visited his family and preached to his son, who became a monk and attained arahantship. His mother, left alone, joined the nuns, becoming an arahant herself.[1]

[1] DhA. ii. 157-9.

3. **Dhammika.**—An eminent lay disciple of **Sāvatthi,** a very learned man and an anāgāmin. He had five hundred followers, all anāgāmins, who, like himself, could travel through the air.[1] He was one of those who possessed *sekhapaṭisambhidā.*[2] See also **Dhammika Sutta** 2.

[1] SNA. i. 367. [2] Vsm. 442; VibhA. 388.

4. **Dhammika.**—One of the chief lay supporters of **Piyadassī** Buddha.[1]

[1] Bu. xiv. 22.

5. **Dhammika.**—King of Siam, contemporary of **Kittisirirājasīha** of Ceylon. He welcomed the delegation sent from Ceylon to Siam to bring back some monks, and gave it every help. On two occasions he sent groups of monks to Ceylon to re-establish ordination in that country, and the king of Ceylon, to show his gratitude, sent him a replica of the Tooth Relic and various other gifts.[1]

[1] Cv. c. 66, 136, 151, 157.

6. **Dhammika.**—See DhA. i. 129 ff. The "*dhammika upāsaka*" mentioned there is probably merely "a righteous lay disciple" and not an upāsaka "named Dhammika."

7. **Dhammika.**—Name of a jackal in the **Biḷāra Jātaka** (*q.v.*).

Dhammika Vagga.—The fifth chapter of the Chakka Nipāta of the Aṅguttara Nikāya.[1]

[1] A. iii. 344 ff.

1. **Dhammika Sutta.**—**Dhammika Thera** is driven out by the lay disciples of seven settlements in succession, because he insulted and reviled visiting monks. He, thereupon, seeks the Buddha at **Gijjhakūṭa** and reports the matter to him. The Buddha relates to him a story of the past connected with the observance of Rukkha-dhamma, and exhorts him to observe the dhamma of a recluse. He also tells Dhammika of various teachers of the past whose disciples, by accepting their teaching, were born in happy states.[1]

[1] A. iii. 366 ff.; the teachers are **Sunetta, Mūgapakkha, Araṇemi, Kuddālaka** and **Jotipāla.** These names occur in the Jātakas; see *s.v.* for details. Perhaps the stories were pre-Buddhistic. Compare the list with that at A. iv. 135, where the name of **Araka** is added.

2. **Dhammika Sutta.**—**Dhammika Upāsaka,** with five hundred others, visits the Buddha at **Jetavana,** singing his praises and asking what should be the life of a monk and what that of a householder. The Buddha pro-

ceeds to lay down the course of conduct to be followed by a monk and the virtues to be cultivated by a layman.[1]

The Commentary adds[2] that these upāsakas were all anāgāmins who, on the day in question, had taken the uposatha vows. During the middle watch the question of the difference between the life of a monk and that of a layman occurred to them and they sought the Buddha.

[1] SN. vv. 376-404. [2] SNA. i. 367 f.

Dhammika-Tissa.—See **Saddhā-Tissa.**

Dhammikasilāmegha.—A title of King **Mahinda III.**[1]

[1] Cv. xlix. 39.

Dhammuttarā, Dhammuttarikā, Dhammuttariyā.—A secondary division of the **Vajjiputtakas.**[1] It is said[2] that they are so called after their teacher, **Dhammuttara.** Their fundamental doctrine[3] is: in birth is ignorance, in the arresting of birth is the arresting of ignorance.

[1] Mhv. v. 7; Dpv. v. 46; Mbv. 97. [2] Rockhill: *op cit.*, 184. [3] *Ibid.*, 194.

Dharaṇa.—See **Varaṇa.**

Dharaṇī.—A lake in **Kuvera's** city.[1]

[1] D. iii. 201.

Dharaṇīpati.—*v.l.* for **Dharaṇīruha** (*q.v.*).

Dharaṇīruha.—A king of eleven kappas ago, a former birth of **Tiṇasūlaka.**[1]

[1] Ap. i. 179.

Dhavajālikā.—A vihāra on **Saṅkheyyaka-pabbata** in **Mahisavatthu.** A monk, named **Uttara,** once lived there and was visited by **Sakka.**[1] The vihāra was so named because it was surrounded by a *dhava*-forest.[2]

[1] A. iv. 162 ff. [2] AA. ii. 739.

Dhavalaviṭṭhika.—A village in Ceylon in which was a tank, repaired by **Parakkamabāhu I.**[1]

[1] Cv. lxviii. 47.

Dhavalā.—A channel flowing eastward from the **Aciravatī,** a canal of the **Mahāvālukanadī.**[1]

[1] Cv. lxxix. 53.

Dhātaraṭṭhā.—A tribe of Nāgas, followers of **Dhataraṭṭha** (*q.v.*).[1]

[1] J. vi. 219.

Dhātā.—A deva who was born in the deva-world because of his gifts to brahmins.[1]

[1] J. vi. 201 f.

Dhātusaṃyutta.—The fourteenth division of the Saṃyutta Nikāya.[1]

[1] S. ii. 140-68.

1. **Dhātu Sutta.**—On the diversity in *dhātu*—*e.g.*, the *dhātu* of eye, of visible-object, of eye-consciousness, the ear, etc.[1]

[1] S. ii. 140.

2. **Dhātu Sutta.**—On the diversity in *dhātu*—*e.g.*, object-*dhātu*, sound *dhātu*, odour-*dhātu*, etc.[1]

[1] S. ii. 143.

3. **Dhātu Sutta.**—Taught to **Rāhula.** All *dhātus* are fleeting.[1]

[1] S. ii. 248.

4. **Dhātu Sutta.**—Preached at **Sāvatthi.**[1] Same as No. 3.

[1] S. iii. 227.

5. **Dhātu Sutta.**—The appearing of the *dhātus* is the appearing of decay and death. Their cessation is also simultaneous.[1]

[1] S. iii. 231.

6. **Dhātu Sutta.**—Desire and lust after the *dhātus* is a corruption of the heart.[1]

[1] S. iii. 234.

7. **Dhātu Sutta.**—The three principles (*dhātu*) of *kāma*, *vyāpāda* and *vihiṃsā*, and how to get rid of them.[1]

[1] A. iii. 447.

Dhātukathā.—One of the seven books of the Abhidhamma Piṭaka. It seems to have been designed as a supplement to the **Dhammasaṅgaṇi,** and discusses, chiefly, the mental characteristics found in converted and earnest persons. It is divided into fourteen sections and possesses a Commentary by **Buddhaghosa.**[1]

[1] Published by the P.T.S.

The Sarvāstvādins call the Dhātukathā the Dhātukāyapada. There seems to have existed in Ceylon another work called the Mahādhātukathā, claimed by the Vitaṇḍavādins as an Abhidhamma-work, but rejected by the orthodox as uncanonical.[2]

[2] DhSA. 4.

Dhātukathāyojanā.—A Pāli work by **Sāradassī** of Pagan.[1]

[1] Bode: *op. cit.*, 67.

1. **Dhātupūjaka.**—An arahant thera. In the past he obtained a relic of **Siddhattha** Buddha, which he honoured for five years.[1]

[1] Ap. i. 224.

2. **Dhātupūjaka Thera.**—An arahant. When **Siddhattha** Buddha died he summoned his relations and paid obeisance to the Buddha's relics.[1]

He is probably identical with **Uttara Thera.**[2]

[1] Ap. ii. 425.

[2] ThagA. i. 284.

Dhātubhājanīyakathā.—The last chapter of the **Buddhavaṃsa.** It contains details of the distribution of the relics of **Gotama** Buddha.[1] The Commentary makes no comments on this.

[1] Bu. xxviii.

Dhātumañjūsā.—See **Kaccāyanadhātumañjūsa.**

Dhātuvaṃsa.—See **Lalāṭadhātuvaṃsa.**

Dhātuvibhaṅga Sutta.—Preached to **Pukkusāti,** whom the Buddha met at the house of **Bhaggava** the potter. It deals with the six elements of earth, water, fire, air, space and consciousness.

Pukkusāti recognised the Buddha by his preaching and, at the end of the sermon, wished to be ordained. The Buddha asked him to fetch a bowl and robe. On his way to fetch these, Pukkusāti was killed by a mad cow.[1]

This sutta forms the suttanta counterpart of the Vibhaṅga.

[1] M. iii. 248 ff.

1. **Dhātusena.**—A householder of **Nandivāpigāma,** father of **Dāṭhānāma.**[1]

[1] Cv. xxxviii. 14.

2. **Dhātusena.**—King of Ceylon (460-78 A.C.). He was the son of **Dāṭhānāma** and brother of **Silātissabodhi.** He seems to have had another

brother, **Kumārasena** (*q.v.*). Dhātusena belonged to the **Moriyavaṃsa.** He became a monk under his uncle, the incumbent of **Dīghasaṇḍasenāpati-pariveṇa,** and remained with him till preparations for his campaign were made. Then he returned to the lay life, killed the Pāndyan, **Tiritara,** then reigning at **Anurādhapura,** and became king. His chief work was the construction of the **Kālavāpi,** which he carried out by damming the **Goṇa-nadī.** He built eighteen vihāras and eighteen tanks. He showed great favour to the monks and did many works of piety. The **Ambatthala-vihāra** he gave to the **Dhammarucikas.**

He had two sons—**Moggallāna** and **Kassapa.** Kassapa rebelled against his father at the instigation of his brother-in-law—who had been punished for ill-treating the king's daughter—and seized Dhātusena in the hope of securing his treasure. The king asked to be taken to Kālavāpi, saw the Thera who had been his teacher, and announced that his whole treasure was the Kālavāpi. Kassapa then had him buried alive.

Among Dhātusena's gifts is mentioned that of one thousand gold pieces spent by him for an interpretation (?) of the **Dīpavaṃsa** (*dīpetuṃ Dīpavaṃsaṃ*).[1]

[1] Cv. xxxviii. 14 f., 30 ff.

3. **Dhātusena.**—A vihāra. See **Uttaradhātusena.**

Dhātusenapabbata.—A vihāra built by **Mahāsena** and restored by **Dhātusena,** in the west of Ceylon.[1]

[1] Mhv. xxxvii. 42; Cv. xxxviii. 47.

1. **Dhānañjāni** (*v.l.* **Dhanañjāni**).—A brahmin of **Taṇḍulapāladvāra** in **Rājāgaha.** He was a minister of the king and oppressed the people in order to get rich. **Sāriputta,** hearing of his fall from the ways of earnestness—after the death of his first pious wife and his marriage to another—visited Dhānañjāni and pointed out to him that if he departed from equity and righteousness he could not hope to be excused on the plea that his fall was due to force of circumstances. Dhānañjāni profited by the discourse, and later, when he was ill, he sent word to Sāriputta, told him of his dire illness, and expressed his wish to be born in one of the Brahma-worlds. Sāriputta taught how union with Brahmā could be attained. Soon after, Dhānañjāni died, and the Buddha said that he was born in one of the lower Brahma-worlds.[1]

[1] M. ii. 184 ff.

2. **Dhānañjāni.**—A brahminee, probably of **Rājagaha.** She was married to a brahmin of the **Bhāradvāja-gotta.** One day, while serving her husband's dinner, she sang the praises of the Buddha, the Dhamma and the Order. The brahmin, very annoyed, threatens to go to the Buddha and abuse him. His wife encourages him to go. He goes, has a discussion with the Buddha, and is converted. Later, he joins the Order and, in due course, becomes an arahant.[1]

Buddhaghosa[2] says the brahminee was a sotāpanna and that she would constantly sing the praises of the Buddha while engaged in her duties and that the brahmin closed his ears to it. One day he invited a large number of his friends to a banquet, and, on the eve of the great day, asked her to promise not to offend his brahmin friends by her *udāna.* She refused to give any such promise, even when he threatened to cut her with a dagger. She declared herself ready to suffer, and sang five hundred verses on her theme. The brahmin surrendered. While waiting on the guests, her impulse became too great for her, and, laying down bowl and spoon, she started repeating her song of praise. The scandalised guests hurried away, spitting out the food, defiled by the presence of a heretic, and her husband scolded her for the spoiled feast. She may be the woman who was responsible for the visit of **Saṅgārava** (*q.v.*) to the Buddha. The latter is, however, stated to have lived in **Caṇḍalakappa.**[3]

[1] S. i. 159 f. [2] SA. i. 175 ff. [3] M. ii. 209.

3. **Dhānañjāni.**—Buddhaghosa[1] says that this was the name of a brahmin clan of great pride of birth, claiming descent from the head of **Brahmā,** whereas the other brahmins were born from his mouth.

[1] SA. i. 175.

1. **Dānañjāni Sutta.**—Records the story of **Dhānañjāni** of **Taṇḍulapāladvāra**[1] (*q.v.*).

[1] S. ii. 184 ff.

2. **Dhānañjāni Sutta.**—Records the story of how **Bhāradvāja,** husband of the brahminee **Dhānañjāni** (*q.v.*), became an arahant.[1]

[1] S. i. 159 ff.

Dhāraṇighara.—A building in **Pulatthipura** erected by **Parakkamabāhu I.** for the recital of incantations by brahmins.[1]

[1] Cv. lxxiii. 71.

Dhītaro Sutta.—When **Māra** retires discomfited in his struggle with the Buddha, his daughters, **Taṇhā, Aratī** and **Ragā,** undertake to seduce the

Buddha. They appear before him in various forms and guises, but all their attempts are in vain, and they report their failure to Māra.[1] See also **Palobhana Sutta.**

[1] S. i. 124 f. The sutta is referred to as **Kumāripañha** at A. v. 46; *cp.* DhA. i. 202.

1. **Dhītā Sutta.**—**Pasenadi** visits the Buddha and grumbles because **Mallikā** has given birth to a daughter. The Buddha points out to him that a woman may prove a better offspring than a male.[1]

[1] S. i. 86.

2. **Dhītā Sutta.**—Incalculable is *saṃsāra,* and it is impossible to find one who, in his wanderings, has not lost a daughter.[1]

[1] S. ii. 190.

Dhīrā.—Two Therīs of this name are mentioned, both belonging to the Sākyans of **Kapilavatthu.** They were members of the Bodhisatta's court, at the time when he became the Buddha. They left home with **Pajāpatī Gotamī,** entered the Order and became arahants.[1]

[1] Thig. 6, 7; ThigA. 12.

Dhuva Sutta.—The Buddha teaches stability and the path leading thereto.[1]

[1] S. iv. 370.

Dhūpadāyaka Thera.—An arahant. Ninety-four kappas ago he burnt incense in the cell of **Siddhattha** Buddha.[1]

[1] Ap. i. 78.

Dhūmakāri.—A brahmin goatherd. For his story see the **Dhūmakāri Jātaka.** He is identified with **Pasenadi,** king of Kosala.[1] *Cp.* **Vāseṭṭha.**

[1] J. iii. 402.

Dhūmakāri Jātaka.—See **Dhanañjaya Jātaka.**

Dhūmaketu.—Thirteen kappas ago there were eight kings of this name, all previous births of **Tivaṇṭipupphiya.**[1]

[1] Ap. i. 196.

Dhūmarakkha.—A mountain in Ceylon, not far from **Kacchakatittha,** no the right bank of the **Mahāvālukanadī.** There **Paṇḍukābhaya** defeated his uncles and occupied their fortified camp for two years. The mountain was the abode of yakkhas, and it was here that Paṇḍukābhaya captured the yakkhinī **Cetiyā,** near the pond **Tumbariyaṅgana** in the vicinity of the mountain.[1] King **Mahānāma** built a vihāra there.[2]

According to the Mahāvaṃsa Ṭīkā,[3] the mountain was also called **Udumabarapabbata** (or **-giri**). There seems[4] to have lived at Udumbaragiri a fraternity of forest-dwelling monks who produced from among their number several scholars of great repute and monks of great piety—*e.g.*, **Kassapa** and **Medhaṅkara.**

The mountain is identified[5] with the present " Gunners' Quoin " on the right bank of the Mahāvaligaṅgā.

1 Mhv. x. 46, 53, 58 ff.
2 Cv. xxxvii. 213.
3 p. 289.
4 See P.L.C., *s.v.* Udumbaragiri.
5 Ep. Zey. ii. 194 ff.

Dhūmaroruva.—A Niraya. The eyes of beings born there are put out with fierce smoke.[1]

1 SNA. ii. 480; J. v. 271.

Dhūmasikha.—Mentioned wuth **Apalāla, Cūlodara, Mahodara, Aggisikha** and **Dhanapāla,** as a beast tamed by the Buddha and converted to the faith.[1]

1 Sp. i. 120.

Dhotaka.—One of **Bāvarī's** disciples; he was among those who visited the Buddha at Bāvarī's request.[1] The questions he asked of the Buddha on this occasion, and the answers given, are found in the **Dhotakamāṇavapucchā.**[2]

He became an arahant.

In the time of **Padumuttara** Buddha he was a brahmin teacher named **Chalaṅga,** with a large following, and he built a bridge over the **Bhagīrathī** for the Buddha and his monks to cross in comfort.[3]

1 SN. p. 194.
2 *Ibid.*, p. 204 f.; explained at SNA (ii. 592 f.) and also CNid. (19 ff.).
3 Ap. ii. 343 ff.

Dhotodana.—Son of **Sīhahanu** and brother of **Suddhodana.**[1] In the Tibetan books[2] he is called Dhonodana, and is said to have been the father of **Mahānāma** and **Anuruddha.**

1 Mhv. ii. 20; SNA. ii. 357.
2 Rockhill: p. 13.

Dhonasākha Jātaka (No. 353).—Once a prince of Benares, named **Brahmadatta,** learned the arts from the Bodhisatta, then a teacher at **Takkasilā.** The teacher (**Pārāsariya),** having observed his character, warned him against harshness and counselled him to be gentle. In due course, Brahmadatta became king, and on the advice of his chaplain, **Piṅgiya,** went out at the head of a large army and captured alive one thousand kings. He could not, however, take Takkasilā, and Piṅgiya suggested that a sacrifice be offered, to take the form of blinding the captive kings and letting their blood flow round the rampart. This was done; but when Brahmadatta went to bathe, a yakkha tore out his right eye, and, as he lay down, a sharp-pointed bone, dropped by a vulture, blinded his left eye. He died in agony and was born in hell.

The story was related in reference to **Bodhirājakumāra** (*q.v.*) who blinded **Kokanada,** the architect of his palace, lest he should build another as grand.

Bodhi is identified with Brahmadatta and **Devadatta** with Piṅgiya.[1]

[1] J. iii. 157, 161.

Dhovana Sutta.—On the difference between the purification (*dhovana*) practised by people of the southern countries and that practised by the Āriyans.[1]

The Commentary[2] explains that in the south people do not burn their dead, but bury them. When the corpse has decayed, they remove the bones, wash them, arrange them in due order, and, on feast days, offer to them flowers and incense and lamentations.

[1] A. v. 216 f.

[2] AA. ii. 858.

End of Volume I.

DICTIONARY
OF
PALI PROPER NAMES

DICTIONARY OF PALI PROPER NAMES

G. P. MALALASEKERA

IN TWO VOLUMES
VOLUME TWO
N - H

ISBN : 978-93-5324-398-2 (Set)

ISBN : 978-93-5324-400-2 Vol. 2 (PB)

First Published, London, 1937-38

Published, 2020

Published by

Facsimile Publisher
12 Pragati Market
Ashok Vihar, Ph-2
Delhi-110052
E-mail: books@facsimilepublisher.com

Printed at: G. Print Process, Delhi.

Dictionary of Pali Proper Names

Author: G. P. Malalasekera

INDIAN TEXTS SERIES

DICTIONARY
OF
PALI PROPER NAMES

BY

G. P. MALALASEKERA, M.A., PH.D.(LOND.)

HEAD OF THE DEPARTMENT OF INDO-ARYAN STUDIES AT
THE CEYLON UNIVERSITY COLLEGE

VOL. II.

N — H

LONDON

JOHN MURRAY, ALBEMARLE STREET, W. 1

PUBLISHED FOR THE GOVERNMENT OF INDIA

1938

TO

MY TEACHER AND FAR MORE THAN TEACHER

CAROLINE A. F. RHYS DAVIDS

IN REVERENT AFFECTION AND INTENSE GRATITUDE

"Paṭipādesi me maggaṃ tava ñāṇena, cakkhumā."

GENERAL NOTE

One of my abiding memories of the days in the Nineties, when work under and with Rhys Davids became an essential part of my married life, was the foreground-presence of three interleaved volumes. These were Robert H. Childers's Pali Dictionary (a copy bequeathed by him to my husband) and the Pali Text Society's *Journal* for 1888, almost monopolized by an Index of Pali Names by the Swiss scholar Edward Müller-Hess. Daily those interleaved pages were becoming ever more filled, to say nothing of marginal additions, so keenly did Rhys Davids record as soon as it appeared the New—or shall I say, the Newly-risen from the Once-had-been.

Even then the question of loyal collaborators in the new Dictionary and that of raising funds to print it were exercising energy and patience. The Names Dictionary, as less yet otherwise important, he consigned to a list of desirable publications worthy to be included in the programme of the Indian Texts Series, a subvention which he had persuaded Lord Curzon, at a Calcutta interview, to make. In that list, to give prior place to the works of other men, he gave it a place so low down that its publication could not come within his lifetime. Others would garner and arrange what he had reaped.

I did not find the assigning of this an easy task. For a scholar in the best sense the work was not creative enough. For the analytical scholar its range was too scattered in space and time. And the scholar is a hopeful animal who will accept work he has neither time nor serious intention to take up without delay. Meanwhile I had to nurse impatience and wait.

Then a keen and gifted student, once my pupil, consented to fill the breach. With Dr. Malalasekera, to undertake is to will to begin work there and then. And now, working as men-of-will work, in the leisure intervals of an educational appointment, with yet another large task on his shoulders—the *Mahāvaṃsa-Ṭīkā*, published in 1935—unbaffled by a temporary breakdown through over-work, he has come as editor of the Names Dictionary to see land ahead.

He has naturally not rested content with the materials collected by Rhys Davids. That collecting came to an end with the end of an earth-life in 1922. Since that date the Pali Text Society has published 28 volumes of first editions of texts, and some 14 annotated translations. And this is to say nothing of other contributions made elsewise, referring to names associated with Buddhist history. Nor is there yet an end to all that. For yet a few years the collecting of addenda will be necessary. None the less the hour for the book's appearance is come, and I am happy to have been yet here to say so.

C. A. F. RHYS DAVIDS.

LIST OF ABBREVIATIONS

P.T.S. means published by the Pāli Text Society.
SHB. means published in the Simon Hewavitarne Bequest Series (Colombo).
A=Aṅguttara Nikāya, 5 vols. (P.T.S.).
AA.=Manorathapūraṇī, Aṅguttara Commentary, 2 vols. (S.H.B.).
AbhS.=Abhidhammatthasaṅgaha (P.T.S. *Journal*, 1884).
Anāgat.=Anāgatavaṃsa (P.T.S. *Journal*, 1886).
Ap.=Apadāna, 2 vols. (P.T.S.).
ApA.=Apadāna Commentary (S.H.B.).
AvŚ.=Avadāna Śataka, ed. Speyer (Bibl. Buddhica).
Barua: History of Pre-Buddhist Indian Philosophy (Calcutta).
Beal: Romantic Legend of the Buddha (Kegan Paul).
Beal: Buddhist Records of the Western World (Kegan Paul).
Bode: The Pāli Literature of Burma (R.A.S.).
Brethren=Psalms of the Brethren, by Mrs. Rhys Davids (P.T.S.).
Bu.=Buddhavaṃsa (P.T.S.).
BuA.=Buddhavaṃsa Commentary (S.H.B.).
CAGI.=Cunningham's Anct. Geography of India, ed. Majumdar (Calcutta).
CNid.=Culla-Niddesa (P.T.S.).
Codrington: Short History of Ceylon.
Compendium=Compendium of Philosophy (P.T.S.).
Cv.=Cūlavaṃsa, ed. Geiger, 2 vols. (P.T.S.).
Cv. *Trs.*=Cūlavaṃsa, translated by Geiger, 2 vols. (P.T.S.).
Cyp.=Cariyāpiṭaka (P.T.S.).
CypA.=Cariyāpiṭaka Commentary (S.H.B.).
D.=Dīgha Nikāya, 3 vols. (P.T.S.).
DA.=Sumaṅgala Vilāsinī, 3 vols. (P.T.S.).
Dāṭh=Dāṭhāvaṃsa (P.T.S. *Journal*, 1884).
DhA.=Dhammapadaṭṭhakathā, 5 vols. (P.T.S.).
DhS.=Dhammasaṅgani (P.T.S.).
DhSA.=Atthasālinī (P.T.S.).
Dial.=Dialogues of the Buddha, 3 vols. (Oxford).
Dpv.=Dīpavaṃsa, ed. Oldenberg (Williams and Norgate).
Dvy.=Divyāvadāna, ed. Cowell and Neill (Cambridge).
Ep. Zey.=Epigraphia Zeylanica (Oxford).
ERE.=Encyclopædia of Religion and Ethics.

Giles: Travels of Fa Hsien (Cambridge).
GS.=Gradual Sayings, 5 vols. (P.T.S.).
Gv.=Gandhavaṃsa (P.T.S. *Journal*, 1886).
I.H.Q.=Indian Historical Quarterly (Calcutta).
Ind. Ant.=Indian Antiquary.
Itv.=Itivuttaka (P.T.S.).
ItvA.=Itivuttaka Commentary (P.T.S.).
J.=Jātaka, ed. Fausböll, 5 vols.
JA.=Journal Asiatique.
J.P.T.S.=Journal of the Pāli Text Society.
J.R.A.S.=Journal of the Royal Asiatic Society.
KhpA.=Khuddakapāṭha Commentary (P.T.S.).
KS.=Kindred Sayings, 5 vols. (P.T.S.).
Knv.=Kaṅkhāvitaraṇī (S.H.B.).
Kvu.=Kathāvatthu (P.T.S.).
Lal.=Lalita Vistara, ed. S. Lefmann.
Law: Kṣatriya Clans in Buddhist India.
Law: Geography of Early Buddhism.
M.=Majjhima Nikāya, 3 vols. (P.T.S.).
MA.=Papañca Sūdanī, Majjhima Commentary, 2 vols. (Aluvihāra Series, Colombo).
Mbv.=Mahābodhivaṃsa (P.T.S.).
Mhv.=Mahāvaṃsa, ed. Geiger (P.T.S.).
Mhv. *Trs.*=Mahāvaṃsa Translation, by Geiger (P.T.S.).
Mil.=Milindapañha, ed. Treckner (Williams and Norgate).
MNid.=Mahā Niddesa, 2 vols. (P.T.S.).
MNidA.=Mahā Niddesa Commentary (S.H.B.).
MṬ.=Mahāvaṃsa Ṭīkā (P.T.S.).
Mtu.=Mahāvastu, ed. Senart, 3 vols.
Netti.=Nettippakaraṇa (P.T.S.).
NidA. See MNidA.
NPD.=P.T.S. Pali-English Dictionary.
PHAI.=Political History of Anct. India, by Chavdhuri, 2nd ed. (Calcutta).
P.L.C.=The Pali Literature of Ceylon, by Malalasekera (R.A.S.).
PS.=Paṭisambhidāmagga, 2 vols. (P.T.S.).
PSA.=Paṭisambhidāmagga Commentary (S.H.B.).
Pug.=Puggalapaññatti (P.T.S.).
Pv.=Petavatthu (P.T.S.).
PvA.=Petavatthu Commentary (P.T.S.).
Ras.=Rasavāhinī, 2 vols. (Colombo).
Rockhill: Life of the Buddha (Kegan Paul).
S.=Saṃyutta Nikāya, 5 vols. (P.T.S.).

SA.=Sāratthappakāsinī, Saṃyutta Commentary.
SadS.=Saddhammasaṅgha (P.T.S. *Journal*, 1890).
Sās.=Sāsanavaṃsa (P.T.S.).
Sisters=Psalms of the Sisters, by Mrs. Rhys Davids (P.T.S.).
Sp.=Samantapāsādikā, 4 vols. (P.T.S.).
SN.=Sutta Nipāta (P.T.S.).
SNA.=Sutta Nipāta Commentary, 2 vols. (P.T.S.)
Svd.=Sāsanavaṃsadīpa, by Vimalasāra Thera (Colombo, 1929).
Thag.=Theragāthā (P.T.S.).
ThagA.=Theragāthā Commentary, 2 vols. (S.H.B.).
Thig.=Therīgāthā (P.T.S.).
ThigA.=Therīgāthā Commentary (P.T.S.).
Thomas: The Life of Buddha (Kegan Paul).
Ud.=Udāna (P.T.S.).
UdA.=Udāna Commentary (P.T.S.).
VibhA.=Sammoha-Vinodanī, Vibhaṅga Commentary (P.T.S.).
Vin.=Vinaya Piṭaka, 5 vols, ed. Oldenberg (Williams and Norgate).
Vsm.=Visuddhimagga, 2 vols. (P.T.S.).
VT.=Vinaya Texts, trs. by Rhys Davids and Oldenberg, 3 vols. (Sacred Books of the East).
Vv.=Vimānavatthu (P.T.S.).
VvA.=Vimānavatthu Commentary (P.T.S.).
ZDMG.=Zeitschrift der Deutschen Morgenländischen Gesellschaft.

NOTE ON THE USE OF THE DICTIONARY

An effort has been made to avoid repetition as far as possible. Generally speaking, the information appearing under any particular word should not, therefore, be regarded as complete until reference has also been made to the words given in that article in **Clarendon type.** Reference should likewise be made to the Appendix given at the end of this Volume.

The arrangement of words is purely alphabetical—*i.e.*, according to the Pāli alphabet. Cerebral ḷ follows dental l. There is great discrepancy in the texts regarding the use of cerebrals, especially ḷ and ṇ. Thus, a word not appearing in its place under the cerebral letter may be found under the corresponding dental and *vice versa*.

There has been a certain amount of unavoidable confusion in the arrangement of words beginning with the Pāli equivalent for the prefix meaning "junior," as opposed to **Mahā.** Reference should be made under all three heads, **Cūla, Cūḷa** and **Culla,** before the search for a word is abandoned.

There is also lack of uniformity in the texts regarding the use of the prefix **Mahā.** Sometimes it is an integral part of the word, sometimes merely an honorific. It is necessary, therefore, to look—*e.g.*, under both **Saṅgharakkhita** and **Mahā**°—before the list of possible Saṅgharakkhita's is exhausted.

Potential trouble also lurks with regard to the hyphen. Generally speaking, the names of Jātakas and Suttas are given without a hyphen—*e.g.*, **Kapi Jātaka, Kavi Sutta**—and these words follow the usual order. Thus **Kapi Sutta** is given before **Kapiṭṭha** and **Kavi Sutta** before **Kaviṭṭha-vana.** When a word is hyphened, either because it is a true compound or merely for convenience, it is regarded as a single word. The presence or absence of a hyphen affects the order, and a certain amount of circumspection is, therefore, requested in looking for compound names, or those that appear to be so.

The regnal years given for the rulers of Ceylon are taken from the chronological table in Geiger's Translation of the *Cūlavaṃsa*, Vol. II., pp. ix-xv, and should be regarded as only provisional. A.C.=After Christ.

DICTIONARY OF PĀLI PROPER NAMES

" Na jīrati " Sutta.—A series of questions asked by a deva and the Buddha's answers. The first question is, " What doth decay and what doth not ?" The answer is that material shapes of mortals decay, but not their name.[1]

[1] S. i. 43.

" Na tumhā " Sutta.—The body is not yours nor is it any other's. It is brought about by actions in the past, etc. Thus does the Ariyan disciple comprehend the causal law.[1] This sutta influenced **Pītamalla Thera** to join the Order.[2]

[1] S. ii. 64. [2] MA. i. 190.

" Na tumhāka " Vagga.—The fourth chapter of the **Khandha Saṃyutta.**[1]

[1] S. iii. 33-42.

1. **" Na tumhākaṃ " Sutta.**—" None of the *khandhas* belong to you, therefore they should be put away. The putting of them away will be for your profit and welfare."[1]

[1] S. iii. 33-4.

2. **" Na tumhākaṃ " Sutta.**—" The eye is not yours, nor objects, nor eye-consciousness—even so with the other senses. They should therefore be put away. Such putting away is for your profit and welfare."[1]

[1] S. iv. 81-2.

" Na dubbhiya " Sutta.—**Sakka** once made up his mind not to betray even his enemy. Soon after, **Vepacitti,** discerning his thoughts, approached him. Sakka wished to take him prisoner, but Vepacitti undertook to show him no treachery.[1]

[1] S. i. 225.

" Na santi " Sutta.—A set of verses spoken before the Buddha by a number of **Satullapa** devas on how to escape sense-desires. **Mogha-**

rāja was present, and, by asking a question of the Buddha, he helped to clear away a possible misunderstanding.[1]

[1] S. i. 22 f.; SA. i. 50.

"Na hoti Tathāgata" Sutta.—One of the many views existing in the world due to want of enlightenment.[1]

[1] S. iii. 215.

Nakānibiḷu.—A Damiḷa chief, ally of **Kulasekhara.**[1]

[1] Cv. lxxvii. 75.

1. **Nakula.**—Second of the five sons of King **Paṇḍu,** the others being **Ajjuna, Bhīmasena, Yudhiṭṭhila** and **Sahadeva.** All of them became husbands of **Kaṇhā** (*q.v.*).[1]

[1] J. v. 424, 426.

2. **Nakula.**—A Damiḷa chief, ally of **Kulasekhara.**[1]

[1] Cv. lxxvi. 139.

3. **Nakula.**—One of the chief lay supporters of **Atthadassī Buddha.**[1]

[1] Bu. xv. 21.

4. **Nakula.**—Son of **Nakulapitā** and **Nakulamātā.** There is nothing further recorded of him.[1]

[1] SA. ii. 181.

Nakula Jātaka (No. 165).—The Bodhisatta was once an ascetic in the Himālayas. Near his walk lived a mongoose and a snake who were always quarrelling. He preached to them the virtues of amity and dispelled their suspicions of each other.

The story was related to two of **Pasenadi's** officers, who were always quarrelling. For details see the **Uraga Jātaka** (No. 154). The two noblemen are identified with the two animals.[1]

[1] J. ii. 52 ff.

1. **Nakula Sutta.**—Records the incident of the grievous illness of **Nakulapitā,** when his wife admonished him to be calm and collected, saying there was no reason to be fretful.[1]

[1] A. iii. 295.

2. **Nakula Sutta.**—**Nakulamātā** visits the Buddha at **Bhesakaḷāvana.** The Buddha tells her of eight qualities which will secure for a woman birth among the **Manāpakāyika**-devas.[1]

[1] A. iv. 268 f.; *cp. ibid.*, 265 f.

Nakulanagara.—A village in Ceylon, near **Guttasāla.** When Guttasāla was destroyed by bandits, an arahant therī, with a young nun, came to this village, and there she was seen by Thera **Mahānāga** of **Kāḷavallimaṇḍapa,** sitting at the foot of a tree. The thera offered her food, but she had no bowl, and the thera lent her his. We are told that, as a result, he never had trouble in obtaining alms.[1]

[1] DhSA. 298 f.

Nakulanigama.—The village in which lived **Nakulā** (3).[1]

[1] BuA. 163.

Nakulapitā and **Nakulamātā.**—A man and his wife, householders of **Suṃsumāragiri** in the **Bhagga**-country. When the Buddha visited the village and stayed at **Bhesakaḷāvana,** they went to see him. They immediately fell at his feet, calling him " son " and asking why he had been so long away. It is said that they had been the Bodhisatta's parents for five hundred births and his near relations for many more. The Buddha preached to them and they became sotāpannas. The Buddha visited their village once more when they were old. They entertained him, telling of their devotion to each other in this life and asking for a teaching which should keep them likewise together in after-life. The Buddha referred to this in the assembly of the Saṅgha, declaring them to be the most intimate companions (*vissāsikā*) among his disciples.[1]

Once, when Nakulapitā lay grievously ill, his wife noticed that he was fretful with anxiety. She assured him there was no need for anxiety on his part, either on behalf of her or his children. She spoke with such conviction that Nakulapitā regained his composure of mind and grew well. Later he visited the Buddha and told him of this, and was congratulated by the Buddha on having such an excellent wife.[2]

The Saṃyutta Nikāya[3] contains records of conversations between Nakulapitā and the Buddha. Both husband and wife are mentioned in lists of eminent disciples.[4]

[1] A. i. 26; ii. 61 f.; AA. i. 216 f., 246; ii. 514; SA. ii. 182.

[2] A. iii. 295 ff.

[3] S. iii. 1 ff.; iv. 116; A. iv. 268 contains a sermon preached to Nakulamātā. (See **Nakula Sutta 2.**)

[4] *E.g.*, A. iii. 465; iv. 348.

It is said that[5] Nakulapitā's desire for eminence was first conceived in the time of **Padamuttara** Buddha. He was then a householder of **Haṃsavatī,** and was present at an assembly where the Buddha declared someone to be chief of the *vissāsikas.*

[5] *E.g.*, A. i. 216.

Nakulapitā Vagga.—The first chapter of the **Khandha Saṃyutta.**[1]

[1] S. iii. 1-21.

1. **Nakulapitā Sutta.**—**Nakulapitā** visits the Buddha at **Bhesakaḷāvana** and asks for a teaching to comfort him since he is now old and always ailing. The Buddha advises him to train his mind. Nakulapitā then visits **Sāriputta** and asks him to explain the Buddha's teaching on this point. Sāriputta explains in detail that training of the mind implies the getting rid of thoughts of self with regard to the *khandhas.*[1]

[1] S. iii. 1 ff.

2. **Nakulapitā Sutta.**—**Nakulapitā** visits the Buddha at **Bhesakaḷāvana** and asks him why some beings are wholly set free in this very life, while others are not. This has to do with grasping, says the Buddha, and then proceeds to explain it.[1]

[1] S. iv. 107, 116.

1. **Nakulā.**—The chief woman disciple of **Sobhita** Buddha.[1]

[1] Bu. vii. 22; J. i. 35.

2. **Nakulā.**—Chief of the lay women who supported **Sobhita** Buddha.[1]

[1] Bu. vii. 23.

3. **Nakulā.**—Daughter of the seṭṭhi of **Nakulanigama.** She gave a meal of milk-rice to **Sumedha** Buddha just before his Enlightenment.[1]

[1] BuA. 163.

Nakkhatta Jātaka (No. 49).—Two parties, having arranged a marriage, fix a day for it to take place. The bridegroom's party consult their family ascetic who, piqued at not having been asked before, declare that the chosen day is unlucky. The bride's family, after waiting a while, give their daughter to another. When the first bridegroom comes later to claim her, he is charged with lack of common courtesy and a wrangle ensues, which is settled by a wise man who points out that all the trouble is due to the foolish habit of consulting stars.

The story is related in reference to two parties of **Sāvatthi** whose plans are similarly thwarted by a naked ascetic. The characters in both stories are the same, says the Buddha.[1]

[1] J. i. 257 ff.

1. **Nakhasikhā Sutta.**—Preached at **Jetavana.** Even as the mighty earth is many times greater than the pinch of dust taken on the tip of one's finger-nail, so also is the Ill, destroyed by the Ariyan disciple of vision and understanding, greater than the Ill which remains undestroyed.[1]

[1] S. ii. 133.

2. **Nakhasikhā Sutta.**—Simile the same as the above. Even so are the beings born elsewhere and not among humans greater by far than those born among humans.[1]

[1] S. ii. 263.

3. **Nakhasikhā Sutta.**—No material form, even as much as can be taken up on the tip of the finger-nail, is impermanent. It is the same with the other *khandhas*. Therefore is the holy life set forth for the utter destruction of suffering.[1]

[1] S. iii. 147.

4. **Nakhasikhā Sutta.** Same as No. 1.[1]

[1] S. v. 459.

Nakhā-cetiya.—A holy shrine in Ceylon (at **Anurādhapura** ?). It is mentioned among places at which festivals were held by **Kittisirirājasīha.**[1]

[1] Cv. xcix. 38.

Nagara.—The name of King **Madda's** capital (?).[1]

[1] J. v. 310.

Nagara Sutta.—The Buddha tells the monks how, before his Enlightenment, he was worried by the existence of birth, old age, decay and death in the world, and how, gradually, he discovered the conditions that caused their coming-to-be and their cessation. Thereupon knowledge arose in him and insight. Just as, when a man, faring through a forest, comes upon an ancient city and announces his discovery to the king, who has the city restored, so did the Buddha see the ancient path traversed by the Enlightened Ones of the past and declare it to many, to devas and to men.[1]

[1] S. ii. 104 ff.

Nagaraka (*v.l.* **Naṅgaraka**).—A Sākyan township near **Medataḷumpa.** From there **Pasenadi,** accompanied by **Dīgha-Kārāyaṇa,** paid his last visit to the Buddha, as recorded in the **Dhammacetiya Sutta.**[1]

The Buddha evidently once stayed in Nagaraka, for in the **Cūḷa-Suññatā Sutta,**[2] **Ānanda** is reported as reminding the Buddha that once, while staying at Nagaraka, the Buddha had remarked that he lived "with the Void a great deal."

[1] M. ii. 118. [2] *Ibid.*, iii. 104.

Nagarakhaṇḍa.—A section of the **Bhūridatta Jātaka,** dealing with the marriage of **Samuddajā** to **Dhataraṭṭha.**[1]

[1] J. vi. 167.

Nagaragalla.—A village in Ceylon gifted by **Mahinda I.** for the maintenance of a nunnery built by him.[1]

[1] Cv. xlviii. 36.

Nagarapavesana-khaṇḍa.—A section of the **Bhūridatta Jātaka,** which deals with the capture of the Bodhisatta by **Ālambāyana** and his ultimate release by **Sudassana** and **Accimukhī.**[1]

[1] J. vi. 197.

Nagaravinda.—A brahmin village in **Kosala** where the Buddha once stayed during a tour and where he preached the **Nagaravindeyya Sutta.**[1]

[1] M. iii. 290.

Nagaravindeyya Sutta.—Preached to the brahmins of **Nagaravinda.** One should honour and reverence only such Wanderers as have shed lust and hate and folly, have a tranquil heart, and walk in the paths of righteousness. Such Wanderers dwell in remote solitudes where there exists nothing which might excite their senses.[1]

[1] M. iii. 290 ff.

Nagarūpama Sutta.—The seven defences and the four kinds of supplies which make a king's frontier fortress unassailable by enemies and the corresponding qualities in a noble disciple which render him unassailable by **Māra.**[1]

[1] A. iv. 106 ff.

Nagga Vagga.—The third section of the Pācittiya in the **Bhikkhunī Vibhaṅga.**[1]

[1] Vin. iv. 278-88.

Naggaji.—A king of **Kasmīra-Gandhāra,** his capital being **Takkasilā.** One day, while sitting on the terrace of his palace, he saw a woman grinding perfume, wearing a jewelled bracelet on each hand. After a while, she put both bracelets on one hand and they started jingling. This set the king thinking on the virtues of solitude, and he became a Pacceka Buddha. He joined **Karaṇḍu, Dummukha** and **Nimi,** who also became Pacceka Buddhas.[1]

[1] J. iii. 377, 381.

Naggadīpa.—An island where the children of Vijaya and of his companions landed on being expelled from **Lāḷa.**[1]

[1] Mhv. vi. 45; Dpv. ix. 13.

Naṅgaraka.—See **Nagaraka.**

Naṅgalakula Thera.—An arahant. He was originally a very poor man. A monk of Jetavana, seeing him clad in a loin-cloth, carrying a plough on his shoulder, suggested to him that he should become a monk. He was ordained, and, at his teacher's suggestion, hung his loin-cloth and plough on a tree near the monastery. He was called Naṅgalakula (ploughman) on account of his former calling. Whenever he felt discontented with monastic life, he would go to the tree and blame himself for his shamelessness in harbouring thoughts of returning to his former life. On being asked where he went, he would say "to my teacher." One day he became an arahant, and when asked why he no longer went to his teacher, he answered that the need was no more. This was reported to the Buddha, who praised the monk for his self-admonition.[1]

[1] DhA. iv. 115-17.

Naṅgalīsa Jātaka (No. 123).—Once the Bodhisatta was a brahmin teacher, and among his five hundred pupils was a very foolish but devoted youth, who had a knack of saying the wrong thing. Hoping to cure him, the Bodhisatta asked him to report anything which he saw.

One day the youth saw a snake, and on being asked by the Bodhisatta how it looked, he answered, "like the shaft of a plough" (*naṅgalīsa*). The Bodhisatta thought the simile good, but when it was used again about an elephant, a sugar-cane, molasses and even curds and milk, he realized that the boy was hopeless. The story was told in reference to **Lāḷudāyī,** who never made an appropriate remark. Lāḷudāyī is identified with the youth.[1]

[1] J. i. 446 ff.

Naṅguṭṭha Jātaka (No. 144).—Once the Bodhisatta was born in a brahmin family in the North Country, and on the day of his birth his parents lit for him a sacrificial fire. When he grew up, family life having no attractions for him, he took the fire to a hermitage in the forest and there tended it. One day he was given a cow in lieu of fee, and, wishing to sacrifice it to the Lord of Fire, he left it by the fire and went to the village in search of salt. When he returned he found that thieves had eaten the cow, leaving only the hide and the tail. Disgusted that the Lord of Fire could not even guard his own possessions, he put out the fire and became a recluse.

The story was related in reference to a question as to whether the Ājīvikas—some of whom lived behind **Jetavana**—obtained any merit through the practice of their difficult penances.[1]

[1] J. i. 493 ff.

Nacca Jātaka (No. 32).—When the world was yet young, a golden swan, who had been elected king of the birds, had a lovely daughter, and to her he promised the boon of being allowed to choose her own husband. When all the birds were assembled, she gazed on them, and, by reason of his beautiful colouring, chose the peacock. Overjoyed by his good fortune, the peacock spread his feathers and began to dance, thus exposing himself, and feeling no shame. The swan-king was so shocked by this lack of modesty that he gave his daughter to a young swan.

The story was related in reference to a monk who was charged before the Buddha with possessing too many clothes. On being questioned by the Buddha, he removed all his clothes and stood naked in the assembly. The people expressed disgust at his behaviour, and he became a layman. He is identified with the peacock of the story.[1]

[1] J. i. 206 ff. The story is sculptured in Bharhut; see Stūpa of Bharhut. Pl. xxvii. (11).

Nacca Sutta.—Few are they who abstain from witnessing exhibitions of dancing and singing, more numerous they who do not.[1]

[1] S. v. 470.

Najjūpama.—Ninety-four kappas ago there was five hundred kings of this name, all previous births of **Uppalahatthiya (Valliya)** Thera.[1] *v.l.* **Sabbūpasama.**

[1] Ap i. 141; ThagA. i. 125.

Naṭakuvera.—A musician of the king of Benares, whose queen was **Kākātī.** For details see the **Kākātī Jātaka.**[1]

Naṭakuvera is identified with the discontented monk with reference to whom the Jātaka was preached.

[1] J. iii. 91 ff.; v. 424.

Naṭapubbaka.—The name given to two monks who were once mimes. Later, they joined the Order and became arahants.[1]

[1] DhA. iv. 224, 225.

Nataṃdaḷha Vagga.—The sixth chapter of the Duka Nipāta of the Jātaka Commentary.[1]

[1] J. ii. 139-64.

" Natthi " Sutta.—A discussion on the annihilation views—elsewhere ascribed to **Ajita Kesakambala** (*q.v.*)—that there is no value in doing good, there are no holy men, etc. The Buddha explains that such views disappear when the Ariyan disciple gets rid of his doubts and becomes a sotāpanna.[1]

[1] S. iii. 206 f.

" Natthi-putta-sama " Sutta.—Records a conversation between a deva and the Buddha. The deva mentions certain things considered as unique and the Buddha gives a different list.[1]

[1] S. i. 6.

1. **Nadī Sutta.**—Just as a man who, when carried away by a mountain torrent, clings to grasses and reeds growing on the bank, which, however, break and he is destroyed, so does the man, who clings to various wrong beliefs—such as that the body is self—come by his undoing.[1]

[1] S. iii. 137.

2. **Nadī Sutta.**—It is as impossible to persuade a monk, devoted to detachment, to return to the lower life, as it would be to make the eastward-flowing Ganges to flow westward.[1]

[1] S. v. 53; *cp.* iv. 191; v. 136, 300.

Nadī-Kassapa.—Brother of **Uruvela-Kassapa** and one of the **Tebhātika-Jaṭilā.** He received his name from living on the bank of the **Nerañjarā** at the head of three hundred ascetics.[1] For his story see *s.v.* **Uruvela-Kassapa.**

[1] Thag. 340-44; ThagA. i. 434, etc.

Nadībhaṇḍagāma.—A village in **Rohaṇa,** mentioned in the campaigns of **Parakkamabāhu I.**[1]

[1] Cv. lxxv. 104; see also Cv. *Trs.* ii. 55, n. 1.

1. **Nanda Thera.**—Son of **Suddhodana** and **Mahāpajāpatī,** and therefore half-brother of the Buddha.[1] On the third day of the Buddha's visit to **Kapilavatthu,** after the Enlightenment, the Buddha went to Nanda's house, where festivities were in progress in honour of Nanda's coronation and marriage to **Janapadakalyāṇī Nandā.** The Buddha wished Nanda good fortune and handed him his bowl to be taken to the vihāra. Nanda, thereupon, accompanied the Buddha out of the palace. Janapadakalyāṇī, seeing him go, asked him to return quickly. Once inside the vihāra, however, the Buddha asked Nanda to become a monk, and he, unable to refuse the request, agreed with reluctance. But as the days passed he was tormented with thoughts of his beloved, and became very downcast and despondent, and his health suffered. The Buddha suggested that they should visit the Himālaya. On the way there, he showed Nanda the charred remains of a female monkey and asked him whether Janapadakalyāṇī were more beautiful than that. The answer was in the affirmative. The Buddha then took him to **Tāvatiṃsa** where **Sakka,** with his most beautiful nymphs, waited on them. In answer to a question by the Buddha, Nanda admitted that these nymphs were far more attractive than Janapadakalyāṇī, and the Buddha promised him one as wife if he would live the monastic life. Nanda was all eagerness and readily agreed. On their return to **Jetavana** the Buddha related this story to the eighty chief disciples, and when they questioned Nanda, he felt greatly ashamed of his lust-

[1] He was only a few days younger than the Buddha, and when the Buddha's mother died, Pajāpatī gave her own child to nurses and suckled the Buddha herself (AA. i. 186).

fulness. Summoning all his courage, he strove hard and, in no long time, attained arahantship. He thereupon came to the Buddha and absolved him from his promise.[2] When the Buddha was told of Nanda's arahantship by a devatā, he related the **Saṅgāmāvacara Jātaka** (*q.v.*) to show how, in the past, too, Nanda had been quick to follow advice. He also related the story of **Kappaṭa** (*q.v.*) and his donkey to show that it was not the first time that Nanda had been won to obedience by the lure of the female sex. The male donkey in the story was Nanda and the female donkey Janapadakalyāṇī.[3] Nanda is identified with the sub-king (*uparājā*) in the **Kurudhamma Jātaka** (*q.v.*).

Later, on seeing how eminently Nanda was trained in self-control, the Buddha declared him chief among his disciples in that respect (*indriyesu guttadvārāṇaṃ*). Nanda had aspired to this eminence in the time of **Padumuttara** Buddha. In the time of **Atthadassī** Buddha he was a tortoise in the river **Vinatā,** and, seeing the Buddha on the bank waiting to cross, he took him over to the other side on his back.[4] He is said to have been called Nanda because his birth brought joy to his kinsmen. The Apadāna[5] says he was of golden hue, as reward for a gift of a costly robe given by him to Padumuttara. One hundred thousand kappas ago he became king four times under the name of **Cela.** Sixty thousand kappas ago he was again king in four births, under the name of **Upacela.** Later, five thousand kappas ago, he was four times cakkavatti, and his name then, too, was **Cela.**

Nanda was very beautiful, and was only four inches shorter than the Buddha. He once wore a robe made according to the dimensions of the Buddha's robe. Discovering this, the Buddha chided him for his presumption.[6] The Aṅguttara Nikāya[7] contains a discourse in which the Buddha discusses Nanda's claim to have achieved self-control in all things.

He is probably to be identified with **Taraṇiya** Thera of the Apadāna.[8]

[2] Thag. 157 f.; J. i. 91; ii. 92 ff.; Ud. iii. 2; DhA. i. 96-105; UdA. 168 ff.; SNA. 273 f.

[3] DhA. i. 103 f.

[4] A. i. 25; AA. i. 174 f.; ThagA. i. 276 ff.

[5] i. 57.

[6] Vin. iv. 173; perhaps this is another version of the story found at S. ii. 281. There, Nanda is said to have donned a robe which was pressed on both sides, painted his face, and gone to see the Buddha, carrying a bright bowl. The Buddha chided him, and Nanda thereupon became a forest-dweller and a rag-robeman. Buddhaghosa (SA. ii. 174) says that Nanda dressed himself up in order to evoke some comment from the Buddha—either approval, so that he might dress thus for the remainder of his life, or censure, in which case he would put on rag robes and dwell in the forest.

[7] A. iv. 166 f.

[8] ii. 428; *cp.* ThagA. i. 277.

2. **Nanda.**—Called **Nanda-māṇava.** One of the chief disciples of Bāvarī; he visited the Buddha. His conversation with the Buddha is recorded in the **Nanda-māṇavapucchā** (*q.v.*). Later, he became an arahant.[1]

[1] SN. vs. 1007, 1124.

3. **Nanda.**—Called **Nanda-Gopālaka.** He was a cowherd of **Kosambī.** One day he heard the Buddha preach to the monks, using as simile a log of wood—how, in certain circumstances, it finds its way direct to the sea—and how, similarly, a monk may reach nibbāna. Nanda asked permission to join the Order. But the Buddha insisted that he should first return the cattle, for which he was responsible, to their owners. Nanda did so, and was then ordained, becoming an arahant soon after.[1]

[1] S. iv. 181.

4. **Nanda Thera.**—An arahant. In the past he was once a hunter, and, while wandering in the forest, he saw a Pacceka Buddha named **Anuruddha.** He built for the Buddha a hut thatched with lotus-flowers, and, having listened to the Buddha's preaching, became a monk. Soon after he fell ill, died, and was born in **Tusita.** He possessed the power of travelling through the air and of walking over the sea. In this birth he visited the Buddha and questioned him regarding the "further shore." At the end of the conversation he became an arahant.[1]

He is probably identical with No. 3 above.[2]

[1] Ap. ii. 350 f.

[2] See DA. i. 122, where Nanda-Gopālaka's questions are given; these seem to correspond with Nanda Thera's questions about the "further shore."

5. **Nanda.**—A herdsman of **Anāthapiṇḍika,** living in **Sāvatthi.** He was rich and tended the king's cattle as well. He often went to Anāthapiṇḍika's house with gifts, and there he saw and heard the Buddha. He invited the Buddha to his house, but his invitation was not accepted for some time, until his wisdom should be ripe. But at last the Buddha paid him a visit, lasting seven days, and Nanda entertained him and his monks with the choicest foods. On the seventh day the Buddha preached to him and he became a sotāpanna. He accompanied the Buddha part of the way back to the vihāra, but, on his return journey, was killed by a hunter's arrow.[1]

[1] DhA. i. 322 f.

6. **Nanda-māṇava.**—A former incarnation of **Subhūti Thera** (*q.v.*) in the time of **Padumuttara** Buddha. He was a *mahāsāla*-brahmin of **Haṃsavatī,** and later became an ascetic at the head of forty-four thousand Jaṭilas. After thirty thousand years, Padumuttara visited him in the forest, and, later, ten thousand of his followers joined the Buddha. Nanda provided them all with seats made of heavenly flowers, the Buddha's being one league in height. Nanda stood by the Buddha for seven days, holding an umbrella made of flowers. Nanda and the rest of his disciples joined the Order, and all except Nanda became arahants, he being born in the Brahma-world after death. Later, for five hundred births he was a forest-dweller living alone on Mount **Nisabha** in Himavā. He was king of the devas for eighty births.[1] He evidently belonged to the **Kosiya-gotta.**[2]

[1] Ap. i. 67; ThagA. i. 17 f.; AA. i. 124 f. [2] Ap. i. 67.

7. **Nanda.**—A disciple of a Pacceka Buddha named **Sabbābhibhū.** The Bodhisatta was then a drunkard, named **Munāli,** and abused Nanda. It was a result of this that **Ciñcā** slandered the Buddha (**Gotama**).[1]

[1] Ap. i. 299; UdA. 264.

8. **Nanda.**—A devaputta who visited the Buddha and had a conversation with him.[1]

[1] S. i. 62.

9. **Nanda.**—One of the three palaces occupied by **Vipassī** Buddha in his last lay-life.[1]

[1] Bu. xx. 24.

10. **Nanda.**—One of the chief lay supporters of **Sikhī** Buddha.[1] *v.l.* **Canda.**

[1] BuA. 204.

11. **Nanda.**—King of Benares, a former birth of **Mahā Kassapa.** He belonged to a poor family, but, owing to his merit in having covered **Kassapa** Buddha's cetiya with a golden coverlet, he came to be crowned king of Benares. He had a *kapparukkha*, which provided him and his subjects with divine robes. With the help of his queen—who became **Bhaddakapilā** in this life—he held a great almsgiving to five hundred Pacceka Buddhas, led by **Mahāpaduma,** and entertained them up to the time of their death. Nanda was away, quelling a frontier rebellion, at the time of their death. On his return, he gave over his kingdom

to his eldest son and became an ascetic.[1] Nanda's wealth was proverbial.[2]

[1] Ap. ii. 582; ThagA. ii. 139 ff.; SA. ii. 140 f.; the story is also found at PvA. 73 ff.; there it is said that Nanda was granted divine clothes because he had once given his shawl to a Pacceka Buddha for a robe; see also ThigA. 72.

[2] *E.g.*, Pv. ii. 1 (vs. 16), iii. 2 (vs. 16).

12. **Nanda.**—One of the chief lay supporters of **Maṅgala** Buddha.[1]

[1] Bu. xxii. 25.

13. **Nanda.**—Generally known as **Nanda Vaccha.** Mentioned in a list of well-known leaders of the **Ājīvakas.** They were declared by **Pūraṇa Kassapa,** in his classification of the *chaḷabhijātas,* to be *parama-sukkābhijātas.*[1] There seems to be some uncertainty as to Nanda's name. The list in which the name occurs runs as follows: Nanda Vaccho, Kiso Saṅkicco, Makkhali Gosālo. The Sutta Nipāta Commentary[2] seems to treat Nanda and Vaccha as two distinct persons. The Majjhima Commentary,[3] however, says that Nanda was his personal name and Vaccha that of his gotta.

The austerities practised by Nanda Vaccha are detailed in the **Mahā Saccaka Sutta.**[4] Elsewhere[5] the Buddha is reported as saying that though the Ājīvakas had existed for a long time, they had only produced three distinguished leaders: Nanda Vaccha, Kisa Saṅkicca and Makkhali Gosāla.

[1] A. iii. 384; DA. i. 162; SNA. i. 372, etc.; but see MA. ii. 632, where they rank lower than the Ājīvakas, who are there considered as the *parama-sukkābhijātas.*

[2] SNA. i. 372.

[3] MA. i. 463; see also M. i. 524.

[4] M. i. 238.

[5] *Ibid.,* 524.

14. **Nanda.**—A slave, born in this life as the co-resident of **Sāriputta.** For his story see the **Nanda Jātaka.**

15. **Nanda.**—A brahmin of **Takkasilā,** learned in the Vedas, who supported his parents. He related four verses to **Jayaddisa,** seated on a throne, and earned four thousand pieces of money. For details see the **Jayaddisa Jātaka.**[1]

This is evidently the same story as that related in the **Mahā Sutasoma Jātaka.**[2] There Nanda is said to have learnt the stanzas from **Kassapa** Buddha, and to have come expressly to **Indapatta** in order to teach them to **Sutasoma.** Nanda is identified with **Ānanda.**[3]

[1] J. v. 23 ff.

[2] J. v. 476 f., 483.

[3] *Ibid.,* 511. For details see Mahā Sutasoma Jātaka.

16. **Nanda.**—Called **Nandakumāra.** A brahmin ascetic, brother of the Bodhisatta in his birth as **Sona.** Nanda is identified with **Ānanda.** For details see **Sona-Nanda Jātaka.**[1]

[1] J. v. 312 ff.

17. **Nanda.**—A brahmin, mentioned in the *Milindapañha*[1] as having been swallowed up by the earth for having insulted the Buddha and his disciples.

[1] p. 101. This probably refers to the brahmin **Ānanda** (*q.v.*) who raped **Uppalavaṇṇā** (DhA. ii. 49); this is confirmed by MA. ii. 814, where Uppalavaṇṇā's seducer is called **Nanda-māṇavaka.**

18. **Nanda.**—See **Nandopananda.**

19. **Nanda Kumāputta Thera.**—He was born in **Veḷukaṇḍa** in **Avanti** and his mother was **Kumā.** Having heard **Sāriputta** preach, he entered the Order, visiting the Buddha later. From the Buddha he obtained a formula of meditation and became an arahant.[1] He had a friend named **Sudanta** (also called **Vāsula**) who, too, became an arahant.[2] In the time of **Vipassī** Buddha, Nanda was an ascetic, and, having seen the Buddha in the royal park at **Bandhumatī,** gave him oil to massage his feet. He is probably to be identified with **Abbhañjanadāyaka** of the Apadāna.[3]

[1] Thag. vs. 36; ThagA. i. 100. [2] *Ibid.*, 101. [3] Ap. ii. 456.

20. **Nanda.**—Nine kings, called the **Nava-Nandā,** reigned in India after the dynasty of **Kālāsoka** and his sons.[1] The first of the Nava-Nandā was a bandit who captured the throne. Their names are given in the *Mahābodhivaṃsa*[2] as follows: Uggasena-Nanda, Panduka-Nanda, Paṇḍugati-Nanda, Bhūtapāla-Nanda, Raṭṭhapāla-Nanda, Govisāṇaka-Nanda, Dasasiddhaka-Nanda, Kevaṭṭa-Nanda and Dhana-Nanda. The last was killed by **Candagutta** with the help of **Cāṇakka,** and his throne was seized. The nine Nandas together reigned for twenty-two years.

[1] Mhv. v. 15. [2] p. 98; for details see MṬ. 177-9.

21. **Nanda.**—There were once two butchers named **Nanda.** One day they killed a cow, and the younger asked that he might take the head and the tail as he had many children. The elder refused and was killed by the other. But the murderer had no peace of mind thereafter, and, on his death, was born in hell.[1]

[1] ItvA. 82; also AA. i. 295; but here the names are not mentioned.

22. **Nanda.**—A distinguished monk in the time of **Parakkamabāhu I.** He lived in the **Selantara** monastery, and was appointed Head of the three fraternities in **Rohaṇa.**[1]

[1] Cv. lxxviii. 10.

23. **Nanda.**—A butcher who killed cattle for fifty years. One day, having no meat, he cut off the tongue of a living ox, fried it and started eating it. His own tongue fell on to his plate. He died in great agony and was born in hell.[1]

[1] MA. ii. 814.

24. **Nanda.**—The **Isigili Sutta** mentions four Pacceka Buddhas of this name.[1]

[1] M. iii. 70.

25. **Nanda.**—See *s.v.* **Nandaka.**

Nanda Jātaka (No. 39).—The Bodhisatta was once born as a squire, and he had as friend another squire who was old and whose young wife bore him a son. In order that the son might not be deprived of his wealth, the old squire took his slave **Nanda** into his confidence and buried the money, charging Nanda to deliver it to his son after his death. The old man died and, at his mother's suggestion, the son asked Nanda to show him where the wealth was buried. Nanda took him to the place in the forest, but as soon as he started digging, the thought of being able to get the money for himself so elated him that he started abusing his master. The young man pretended not to hear, and said they would go some other time. Several times the same thing happened, and at last the son decided to consult his father's friend, the Bodhisatta. The latter told him to note where Nanda started digging, and then to dig there himself and so get the treasure. This he did and found the money, which he made Nanda carry home.

The story was related in reference to a co-resident of **Sāriputta.** He was by nature very modest, but when he went on tour the attentions he received made him proud and insolent. He is identified with Nanda of the Jātaka.[1]

[1] J. i. 224 ff.

Nanda Vagga.—The third chapter of the Udāna.[1]

[1] Ud. 21-33.

1. **Nanda Sutta.**—**Nanda-devaputta** visits the Buddha and recites a stanza to the effect that men should acquire merit in order to obtain bliss. The Buddha tells him that men should rather aspire to final peace.[1]

[1] S. i. 62; *cp.* S. i. 2, where the same verses are given.

2. **Nanda Sutta.**—Records the incident of the chiding of **Nanda Thera** (see **Nanda** 1) by the Buddha for wearing attractive robes and painting his eyes.[1]

[1] S. ii. 281.

3. **Nanda Sutta.**—The Buddha relates how **Nanda Thera** is eminent in his restraint of the senses, his moderation in food, his wakefulness and his mindfulness.[1]

[1] A. iv. 166 ff.

1. **Nandaka** (*v.l.* **Nanda**) **Thera.**—A householder of **Sāvatthi.**[1] Having entered the Order after hearing a sermon of the Buddha, he developed insight and soon attained arahantship. Once, at the Buddha's request, he preached a sermon to the nuns; on the first day they became sotāpannas, and, on the second, five hundred of them attained arahantship. From that time the Buddha declared him foremost among exhorters of the nuns.[2] The *Theragāthā*[3] contains several verses uttered by him to a woman to whom he was once married. She met him begging alms in Savatthi and smiled to him with sinful heart.

His aspiration after eminence was formed in the time of **Padumuttara** Buddha, when he heard a disciple of that Buddha declared foremost among exhorters of nuns. He offered the Buddha a very costly robe and illuminated his bodhi-tree. In the time of **Kakusandha** Buddha he was a *karavīka*-bird and delighted the Buddha with his song. Later, he was a peacock, and sang three times daily at the door of a Pacceka Buddha's cell.[4]

[1] The Apadāna (ii. 499) says he belonged to a rich clan of merchants and that he entered the Order at the ceremony of dedication of Jetavana.

[2] A. i. 25. The sermon he preached is known as the **Nandakovāda Sutta** (*q.v.*). The Aṅguttara Commentary (i. 173) says that the nuns were Sākyan maidens who had entered the Order with Pajāpatī. At first Nandaka was reluctant to preach to them, they having been his wives in a previous birth when he was king, and he feared the calumny of his colleagues who might suggest that he wished to see his former companions. He, therefore, sent another monk in his place; but the Buddha, knowing that only Nanda's preaching would effect the nuns' release, insisted on his going.

[3] vs. 279-82.

[4] ThagA. i. 384 f. The Apadāna verses given in this context differ from those given in the Apadāna itself (ii 499 f.).

The Aṅguttara Nikāya attributes two discourses to Nandaka. The first[5] was preached at the **Migāramātupasāda** and takes the form of a discussion with **Sāḷha,** Migāra's grandson, and **Rohaṇa, Pekkhuṇiya's** grandson—on greed, covetousness, malice and delusion, and the benefits following their destruction. The second discourse is a sermon addressed to the monks at the waiting-hall at Jetavana. It is said that the Buddha was attracted to the spot by the sound of Nandaka's preaching, and, finding the door locked, stood for a long time outside, listening.[6] When his back began to ache he knocked at the door, and, having entered, told Nandaka that he had been waiting until the end of his discourse to speak to him. Nandaka expressed his regret that he should have kept the Buddha waiting and pleaded ignorance of his presence. The Buddha, conscious of Nandaka's remorse, went on to praise his sermon, and said that the preaching of such sermons was the duty of all pious monks. When the Buddha left, Nandaka resumed his sermon, and told his audience of the five results of listening to the Dhamma in due season.

The Majjhima Commentary[7] states that Nandaka was once the leader of a guild of five hundred slaves of Benares and that **Pajāpatī Gotamī** was his wife. One day, while fetching water, his wife noticed five hundred Pacceka Buddhas enter the city, and, on her return, she witnessed their departure. On enquiry, she learnt that they had applied to a merchant for lodgings for the rainy season, but that he had been unable to help. She undertook the care of them and, having enlisted the support of all her companions and their husbands, she and her husband ministered to the Pacceka Buddhas. As a result, they were born together as man and wife for many births, as were their helpers. In one birth Nandaka was king, and all the women became his wives. In this birth, the women were born as Pajāpatī's companions, and they left the world in her company. To them was the **Nandakovāda Sutta** preached.

[5] A. i. 193 f. See *s.v.*, **Sāḷha.**

[6] A. iv. 358 ff.; throughout the three watches of the night says the Commentary (AA. ii. 794; also MA. i. 348).

[7] ii. 1019.

2. **Nandaka Thera.**—A householder of **Campā** and younger brother of **Bharata Thera.** When these two heard that **Soṇa Koḷivisa** had left the world—and he so delicate—they too renounced household life. Bharata soon acquired sixfold *abhiññā*, and, wishing to help Nandaka, came to him and discoursed on insight. A caravan passed by, and an ox, unable to pull his cart through a boggy place, fell down. The caravan leader had him released and fed with grass

and water. He was then able to pull the cart out. Bharata drew Nandaka's attention to the incident, and the latter, making that his subject of meditation, soon attained arahantship.[1]

In the time of **Sikhī** Buddha, Nandaka was a woodsman, and one day, while wandering about, he saw the Buddha's cloistered walk. Pleased with its appearance, he scattered sand over it.[2]

[1] Thag. 173 f.; ThagA. i. 299 f.

[2] Ap. ii. 418.

3. **Nandaka.**—A yakkha. One day, while travelling through the air with his friend, he saw **Sāriputta** sitting in samādhi, his head newly shaved. Ignoring his friend's warning, Nandaka knocked Sāriputta on the head; the former immediately fell down, his body aflame, and was swallowed up in hell.[1]

[1] MA. ii. 814; Mil. 100; the incident is related at Ud. iv. 4 (UdA. 244 ff.) and referred to in ThagA. ii. 116, but the yakkha's name is not given. The blow was hard enough to kill an elephant seven or eight cubits high or shatter a rock. Sāriputta was outside **Kapota-Kandarā, Moggallāna** being near by.

4. **Nandaka.**—A minister of the **Licchavis.** See **Nandaka Sutta** (2).

5. **Nandaka.**—General of **Piṅgala,** king of **Suraṭṭha,** who reigned some two hundred years after the Buddha's death. Nandaka was a Nihilist, and, after death, was born as a *vemānikapeta* in the **Vindhyā** forest. His daughter, **Uttarā,** was a pious woman, and gave alms in his name to an arahant monk. Thereupon Nandaka attained celestial happiness. Wishing to liberate Piṅgala from his Nihilist views, Nandaka waited for him on his return from a conference with **Dhammāsoka,** and, having led the king to his abode, ministered to him. Then, revealing his identity, Nandaka advised the king to follow the Buddha's teaching.[1]

[1] Pv. iv. 3; PvA. 244 ff.

1. **Nandaka Sutta.**—Records the incident of the Buddha listening to the preaching of **Nandaka** and the continuation of Nandaka's sermon.[1] See **Nandaka** (1).

[1] A. iv. 358 ff.

2. **Nandaka** (or **Licchavi**) **Sutta.**—**Nandaka,** minister of the **Licchavis,** visits the Buddha at the **Kūṭāgārasālā** in **Vesāli.** The Buddha tells him that the Ariyan disciple, possessed of unwavering loyalty to the Buddha, the Dhamma and the Saṅgha, and having Ariyan virtues, is assured of enlightenment and happiness. During the conversation, a man comes to tell Nandaka that his bath is ready. Nandaka sends

him away, saying that the inner washing—loyalty to the Buddha—is far more important.[1]

[1] S. v. 389.

Nandakovāda Sutta.—Preached at the **Rājakārāma,** at the Buddha's special request, by **Nandaka** (*q.v.*), to five hundred nuns led by **Pajāpatī.** The first part of the sermon is a catechism, the second is more explanatory, and contains various similes illustrating the impermanence of the senses and of sense-objects. The sermon ends with the seven *bojjhaṅgas.* After the sermon the nuns visit the Buddha who, seeing that their minds are not quite ripe, asks Nandaka to repeat the sermon to them the next day. Nandaka does so, and their enlightenment is assured.[1]

[1] M. iii. 270 ff.; *cf.* J. ii. 392, where it says the nuns became arahants at the conclusion of the sermon.

Nandagopā.—A serving-woman of **Devagabbhā.** Her husband was **Andhakaveṇhu.** She bore ten daughters, their births coinciding with those of ten sons to Devagabbhā, and exchanged her daughters for the latter's sons. These, because they were adopted by her husband, came to be known as **Andhaveṇhudāsaputtā.**[1]

[1] J. iv. 79 ff.

"Nandati" Sutta.—A deva visits the Buddha and tells him of various sources of gladness—children, cattle and sense-pleasures. The Buddha replies that these are really all sources of sorrow.[1]

[1] S. i. 6; *cp. ibid.,* 107.

Nandatissārāma.—A monastery in Ceylon built by **Kaṇiṭṭhatissa.**[1]

[1] Mhv. xxxvi. 14.

Nandana.—A devaputta who visited the Buddha at **Sāvatthi** and asked him questions regarding virtue, wisdom, etc. The Buddha answered them, and he went away satisfied.[1]

[1] S. i. 52.

Nandana Vagga.—The second chapter of the **Devatā Saṃyutta.**[1]

[1] S. i. 5-13.

1. **Nandana Sutta.**—The Buddha tells the monks at **Jetavana** how once a deva, surrounded by celestial sensuous enjoyments in **Nandanavana,** declared that no one, who had not seen the Nandana-grove,

understood real bliss. But another deva, standing by, reminded him that all saints had declared such enjoyments to be vain and impermanent.[1]

[1] S. i. 5.

2. **Nandana Sutta.**—Records the conversation between the devaputta **Nandana** and the Buddha.[1]

[1] S. i. 52.

3. **Nandana Sutta.**—Same as "**Nandati**" **Sutta** (*q.v.*), except that here it is **Māra** who utters the first verse.[1]

[1] S. i. 107.

Nandana-pariveṇa.—A monastery built in **Devanagara** by **Vīrabāhu,** nephew of **Parakkamabāhu II.**[1]

[1] Cv. lxxxiii. 50.

Nandana-pokkharaṇī.—A lake of great splendour in **Nandanavana,** having one hundred bathing-places and one thousand inlets, and covered with the five kinds of lotus.[1]

[1] J. ii. 189; *cp.* **Nandā-pokkharaṇī.** Elsewhere (*e.g.*, J. vi. 333) it is called **Nandanavana-pokkharaṇī.**

1. **Nandanavana.**—The chief of the parks in **Tāvatiṃsa,** where the inhabitants of Tāvatiṃsa, headed by **Indra,** go for their amusement.[1] Cakkavatti-kings are born in Tāvatiṃsa after death and spend their time in Nandanavana.[2] It is said[3] that there is a Nandanavana in each deva-world. The devas go there just before their death and disappear in the midst of their revels. Thus, the Bodhisatta went to Nandanavana in the **Tusita**-world before his "descent" into **Mahāmāyā's** womb.[4] In Nandanavana is a lake called **Nandana** (*q.v.*),[5] and evidently also a palace called **Ekapuṇḍarīkavimāna.**[6] Nandanavana was so called because it awoke delight in the hearts of all who visited it.[7] Sometimes ascetics, like **Nārada,**[8] possessed of great *iddhi*-power, would spend their siesta in the shadow of the grove.

[1] *E.g.*, DhA. ii. 266; A. iii. 40; J. vi. 240; VvA. 7, 34, 61, etc.; PvA. 173, 176, 177, etc.; Mtu. i. 32, etc.

[2] S. v. 342.

[3] *E.g.*, J. i. 49.

[4] J. i. 50; see also J. vi. 144.

[5] J. ii. 189.

[6] MṬ. 568.

[7] J. v. 158.

[8] *Ibid.*, 392.

2. **Nandanavana.**—A park in **Anurādhapura** between the **Mahāmeghavana** and the southern wall of the city. **Mahinda** preached there,

to the assembled populace, the **Bālapaṇḍita Sutta,** the day after his arrival in Anurādhapura. Later, on successive days, he preached the **Āsīvisūpama,** the **Anamatagga,** the **Khajjanīya,** the **Gomayapiṇḍī** and the **Dhammacakkappavattana Suttas.** On the occasions of the preaching of these various suttas, thousands of people attained to various fruits of the Path, and, because the park was the first centre from which Mahinda radiated a knowledge of the Buddha's teaching, it came to be called the **Jotivana,** by which name it was known later.[1]

[1] Mhv. xv. 1, 4, 176, 178, 186, 195, 197, 199, 202; Dpv. xiii. 11, 12, 14, 15; xiv. 12, 17, 44, 46; Sp. i. 80-82.

3. **Nandanavana.**—A private park in **Pulatthipura,** laid out by **Parakkamabāhu I.**[1]

[1] Cv. lxxiii. 97; lxxix. 2.

Nandanavimāna Vatthu.—A story of a man who looked after his parents and continued to do so after his marriage. He was later born in **Tāvatiṃsa,** where he was visited by **Moggallāna.**[1]

[1] Vv. vii. 2; VvA. 300 f.

Nandamāṇava-pucchā.—The questions asked of the Buddha by **Nandamāṇava,** pupil of **Bāvarī,** and the Buddha's replies thereto. It forms the seventh sutta of the **Parāyaṇa Vagga**[1] and is commented upon in the **Cullaniddesa.**[2]

[1] SN. vs. 1077-83.

[2] CNid. 26 ff.

Nandamātā.—See **Uttarā Nandamātā** and **Velukaṇṭakī Nandamātā.**

Nandamātā Sutta.—Gives the story of the encounter between **Velukaṇṭakī Nandamātā** (*q.v.*) and **Vessavaṇa.**[1]

[1] A. iv. 63 ff.

Nandamāla.—An eminent Buddhist monk of Burma in the latter half of the eighteenth century. He took a prominent part in the Pārupaṇa-Ekaṃsika controversy and was appointed by the king Mahādhammarājādhirāja as Head of the Buddhist Saṅgha. He wrote the **Sāsanasuddhidīpikā.**[1]

[1] Bode: *op. cit.*, 73.

Nandamūlapabbhāra.—A mountain cave in **Gandhamādana.** It is the residence of Pacceka Buddhas and has three caves: **Suvaṇṇaguhā,**

Maṇiguhā and **Rajataguhā.** In front of the Maṇiguhā stands the **Mañjūsaka**-tree.[1] The mountain is in the northern Himālayas.[2]

[1] SNA. i. 66; DhA. i. 226; J. ii. 195; etc. [2] J. iv. 367.

Nandarājā and **Nandarājadevī.**—See **Nanda** (11).

Nandarāmā.—One of the chief women supporters of **Paduma Buddha.**[1]

[1] Bu. ix. 23.

Nandavaccha.—See **Nanda** (13).

Nandavatī.—A nun, sister of **Thullanandā.** Her other two sisters were **Nandā** and **Sundarīnandā.** They were all married to the same brahmin and all left the world after his death.[1]

[1] Vin. iv. 211, 259.

Nandasārathī.—Chief warrior of **Eḷāra.** He was killed by **Veḷusumana.**[1]

[1] MṬ. 315.

Nandasena.—An Upāsaka of a village near **Sāvatthi.** His wife, **Nandā,** was a wicked woman and, after death, became a peta. When she revealed herself to him Nandasena gave alms in her name, and she gained happiness.[1]

[1] Pv. ii. 4; PvA. 89 ff.

1. **Nandā.**—Chief woman disciple of **Dīpaṅkara** Buddha.[1]

[1] Bu. ii. 214; J. i. 29.

2. **Nandā.**—One of the four wives of **Magha.** When Magha and his friends built their hall, **Nandā** had a pond built in the grounds. As a result, she was reborn as the mate of **Sakka,** and the **Nandāpokkharaṇī** came into existence on account of her merit.[1]

[1] J. i. 201 ff.; DhA. i. 269 f.

3. **Nandā.**—Three daughters of the Bodhisatta in one of his births. For details see the **Suvaṇṇahaṃsa Jātaka.**

4. **Nandā.**—Daughter of **Candakumāra.**[1]

[1] J. vi. 134.

5. **Nandā.**—A nun, sister of **Thullanandā** (*q.v.*). Her other two sisters were **Nandavatī** and **Sundarīnandā.**[1]

[1] Vin. iv. 211, 259.

6. **Nandā Therī.**—Declared by the Buddha[1] to be foremost among nuns in meditative power (*jhāyīnaṃ*). She was the daughter of **Suddhodana** and **Pajāpatī** and was therefore sister of **Nanda Thera.**

She is evidently to be identified with **Sundarīnandā** (*q.v.*).

There were three therīs[2] of the name of Nandā who were ordained with Pajāpatī: Nandā, sister of Nanda Thera (also evidently called **Sundarīnandā** and sometimes **Rūpanandā** and even **Janapadakalyāṇīnandā**),[3] **Abhirūpānandā** (daughter of **Khema** the Sākyan)[4] and **Janapadakalyāṇīnandā** (evidently sometimes also called Rūpānandā).[5] The legends about them seem to have been confused from very early times.

[1] A. i. 25.
[2] SNA. i. 241.
[3] *E.g.*, AA. i. 198; and ThigA. 80.
[4] See *s.v.*
[5] *E.g.*, DhA. iii. 113 f.

7. **Nandā.**—A nun (evidently distinct from No. 6) mentioned as having died at **Ñātika** and having been reborn spontaneously in the **Suddhāvāsā,** there to pass away, never to return.[1]

[1] D. ii. 91; S. v. 356 f.

8. **Nandā.**—One of the chief women supporters of **Kakusandha Buddha.**[1]

[1] Bu. xxiii. 22.

9. **Nandā.**—Daughter of King **Ānanda** of **Haṃsavatī** and half-sister of **Padumuttara** Buddha. She was a previous birth of **Sakulā (Pakulā) Therī** (*q.v.*).[1]

[1] ThigA. 91, 92.

10. **Nandā Therī.**—An arahant. Sister of King **Kālāsoka.** She was instrumental in winning the king's support for the orthodox monks, when he was inclined to favour the heretics.[1]

[1] Mhv. iv. 38 ff.; probably the same as Dpv. xviii. 10.

11. **Nandā.**—Wife of **Nandasena** (*q.v.*).

12. **Nandā.**—One of the palaces occupied by **Paduma** Buddha in his last lay life.[1]

[1] Bu. ix. 17.

13. **Nandā.**—A palace occupied by **Sujāta** Buddha in his last lay life.[1]

[1] Bu. xiii. 21.

14. **Nandā.**—Probably the name of a celestial female musician, attendant of **Indra.**[1]

[1] Vv. ii. 10; iv. 25; but see PvA. (372), note on p. 93 (l. 23).

15. **Nandā.**—The collective name of the nine **Nandas** (see **Nanda** 20) who ruled after the ten sons of **Kālāsoka.**[1]

[1] Mhv. v. 15.

Nandādevī.—Chief queen of **Cūḷani-Brahmadatta,** king of **Pañcāla.** She is identified with **Yasassikā.**[1]

[1] J. vi. 434 ff., 478; for details see **Mahāummagga Jātaka.**

Nandāpokkharaṇī.—A lake, five hundred leagues in extent, in the **Nandanavana** in **Tāvatiṃsa,** which arose there as the result of the merit of **Nandā,** wife of **Magha.**[1] *v.l.* **Nandanapokkharaṇī** (*q.v.*).

[1] J. i. 204, 205; vi. 132, 232, 531; DhA. i. 275.

Nandāmūlakagāma.—A village in Ceylon near **Āḷisāra,** mentioned in the campaigns of **Parakkamabāhu I.** There was a castle there captured by **Māyāgeha.**[1]

[1] Cv. lxx. 164.

1. **Nandārāma.**—The pleasaunce in which **Dīpaṅkara** Buddha preached his first sermon. It was also the scene of his death.[1] *v.l.* **Sunandārāma.**

[1] Bu. ii. 212, 220.

2. **Nandārāma.**—The place where **Padumuttara** Buddha died.[1]

[1] Bu. xi. 31.

3. **Nandārāma.**—A pleasaunce in **Sunandavatī** where **Tissa** Buddha died.[1] *v.l.* **Sunandārāma.**

[1] Bu. xviii. 28; BuA. 192.

Nandika.—A Damiḷa chieftain of **Nandigāma.**[1]

[1] Mhv. xxv. 14.

Nandikkhaya Vagga.—The sixteenth chapter of the **Saḷāyatana Saṃyutta.**[1]

[1] S. iv. 142-8.

1. **Nandikkhaya Suttā.**—Two discourses on the destruction of the lure of lust, through realizing the impermanence of the khandhas.[1]

[1] S. iii. 51.

2. **Nandikkhaya Suttā.**—Four discourses on the destruction of the lure of lust, through realizing the impermanence of sense-organs and the objects of sense.[1]

[1] S. iv. 142.

Nandigāma.—A village, evidently near **Kacchakatittha,** on the **Mahāvālukanadī.**[1] There was once a **Damiḷa** stronghold there, guarded by **Nandika.** **Duṭṭhagāmaṇī** killed Nandika and captured the fort.[2] Later, **Subha** erected a vihāra there.[3] The stronghold is also mentioned in the account of the campaigns of **Parakkamabāhu I.**[4]

[1] MṬ. 472.
[2] Mhv. xxv. 14.
[3] *Ibid.*, xxxv. 58.
[4] Cv. lxxii. 44.

Nandicakka.—An Elder who came to Ceylon at the head of a chapter of monks from **Rakkhaṅga,** at the request of King **Vimaladhammasūriya,** in order to confer the *upasampadā* ordination on the monks of Ceylon.[1]

[1] Cv. xciv. 15.

Nandipadmara.—A Damiḷa chief, ally of **Kulasekhara;** he was captured by the Sinhalese forces.[1]

[1] Cv. lxxvii. 86.

Nandimitta.—See **Nandhimitta.**

1. **Nandiya Thera.**—He belonged to a Sākyan family of **Kapilavatthu,** and was called Nandiya because his birth brought bliss. He left the world at the same time as **Anuruddha, Kimbila** and the others, and he soon attained arahantship. Thereafter he dwelt with his companions in the **Pācīnavaṃsamigadāya.**[1] It is said that **Māra** appeared before him in a terrible form, but Nandiya drove him away.

In the time of **Padumuttara** Buddha, Nandiya built an altar of sandalwood at the Buddha's *cetiya* and held great celebrations. Fifteen kappas ago Nandiya was eight times born as king under the name of **Samatta (Samagga).**[2] He is probably identical with **Saparivāriya** (*q.v.*) of the *Apadāna.*[3]

According to the *Mahāvastu*[4] Nandiya (Nandika) was the son of Śukrodana.

He was a special friend of **Kimbila.**[5]

[1] Vin. i. 350 f. It was to them that the Upakkilesa Sutta was preached (M. iii. 155). Later, they seem to have lived in the Gosiṅgasālavana (M. i. 205).
[2] Thag. 25; ThagA. 82 f.
[3] i. 172.
[4] iii. 177.
[5] ThagA. i. 275.

2. **Nandiya.**—A Sākyan layman, evidently to be distinguished from the above. He visited the Buddha at the **Nigrodhārāma** in **Kapilavatthu** and had a discussion with him on the different kinds of Ariyan disciple, the one who dwells in remissness and the one who is earnest.[1] Later, when the Buddha returned to **Sāvatthi** for the rainy season, Nandiya also went there, finding some business to do, and from time to time he visited the Buddha. At the end of the rains, when the Buddha and the monks were about to start on tour, Nandiya went to the Buddha and was taught the eleven conditions which lead to the destruction of evil.[2]

[1] S. v. 397 ff.; see also p. 403. [2] A. v. 334 ff.

3. **Nandiya.**—A householder of Benares. He was very pious and looked after his parents. When they wished him to marry **Revatī,** he refused because she belonged to a family of unbelievers. But when Revatī offered to help Nandiya in all his work, he agreed and they were married. When Nandiya's parents died, leaving him very rich, he used the money to feed the poor and needy. Later he built a quadruple hall in the great monastery at **Isipatana** and furnished it with great splendour. On the day of its dedication to the Buddha and the monks, as the water of donation fell on the Buddha's hand, there arose in **Tāvatiṃsa** a celestial mansion, measuring twelve leagues in each direction, for Nandiya's use. During one of **Moggallāna's** visits to Tāvatiṃsa he saw this mansion, and was told by many nymphs that they were awaiting Nandiya's arrival.[1] The Vimānavatthu Commentary[2] goes on to say that after a life devoted to good deeds Nandiya died, and was born in his celestial mansion, and that Revatī, on the death of her husband, stopped the gifts of alms, abused the monks, and was cast alive into the **Ussada-niraya** by the orders of **Vessavaṇa.**

[1] DhA. iii. 290 ff. [2] VvA. 222 f.

4. **Nandiya.**—A Paribbājaka who visits the Buddha at Jetavana and asks him the conditions for the attainment of nibbāna. The Buddha teaches him the Noble Eightfold Path.[1]

[1] S. v. 11.

5. **Nandiya.**—The Bodhisatta born as a monkey. For his story see the **Cūla-Nandiya Jātaka.**[1] He is also called **Mahā-Nandiya** to distinguish him from his brother.

[1] J. ii. 199 ff.

6. **Nandiya.**—The Bodhisatta born as a deer. See the **Nandiyamiga Jātaka.**[1]

[1] J. iii. 270 ff.

7. **Nandiya.**—A king of sixteen kappas ago; a former birth of **Tilamuṭṭhidāyaka.**[1]

[1] Ap. i. 235.

1. **Nandiya Sutta.**—The Paribbājaka **Nandiya** (see **Nandiya** 4) visits the Buddha and is instructed in the Noble Eightfold Path.[1]

[1] S. v. 11.

2. **Nandiya Sutta.**—The Sākyan **Nandiya** (**Nandiya** 2) visits the Buddha and learns the difference between the Ariyan disciple who is remiss and the one who is earnest.[1]

[1] S. v. 397 ff.

3. **Nandiya Sutta.**—**Nandiya,** the Sākyan, is taught by the Buddha hat the Ariyan disciple who is possessed of unwavering loyalty to the Buddha, the Dhamma and the Saṅgha, and who has the Ariyan qualities, is bound for enlightenment.[1]

[1] S. v. 403.

4. **Nandiya Sutta.**—Relates the visit of **Nandiya,** the Sākyan (**Nandiya** 2) to **Sāvatthi,** to be near the Buddha, and the instruction he receives from the Buddha at the end of the rainy season.[1]

[1] A. v. 334 ff.

Nandiyamiga Jātaka (No. 385).—The Bodhisatta was once born as a deer named **Nandiya** and looked after his parents. The king of **Kosala** was very fond of hunting, and his subjects, that they might be left in peace, planned to drive deer from the forest into a closed park where the king might hunt. Nandiya, seeing the men come, left his parents in the thicket and joined the deer who were being driven into the park so that his parents might not be seen. The deer agreed each to take his turn in being killed by the king. The Bodhisatta stayed on—even in spite of a message brought by a brahmin from his parents—though he could have escaped. But he wished to show his gratitude to the king who had supplied the deer with food and drink. When his turn came to be killed, he appeared fearlessly before the king, and by the power of his virtue the king's bow refused to shoot. The king thereupon realized Nandiya's goodness and granted him a boon. Nandiya asked for security for all living beings, and established the king in the path of virtue.

The story was related in reference to a monk who was blamed for looking after his parents. But the Buddha praised him.

The king of the story was **Ānanda,** and the brahmin who brought the message was **Sāriputta.**[1]

[1] J. iii. 270 ff.

Nandiyāvaṭṭa.—The name of a huge fish dwelling in the ocean.[1]

[1] AA. i. 265.

Nandivaḍḍha.—One of the chief lay supporters of **Anomadassī** Buddha.[1]

[1] Bu. viii. 24.

Nandivāpigāma.—A village in Ceylon, residence of **Dhātusena,** father of **Dāṭhānāma.**[1] **Gokaṇṇa,** officer of **Gajabāhu,** was once defeated there.[2] The village is perhaps identical with **Nandigāma.**

[1] Cv. xxxviii. 14. [2] *Ibid.*, lxx. 72.

1. **Nandivisāla.**—The Bodhisatta born as a bull. See the **Nandivisāla Jātaka.**

2. **Nandivisāla.**—A deva who visits the Buddha and converses with him on the nature of the body and its riddance.[1]

[1] S. i. 63; *cp. ibid.*, 15.

Nandivisāla Jātaka (No. 28).—Once the Bodhisatta was born as a bull in **Gandhāra** and was named **Nandivisāla.** When quite young, he was given to a brahmin, who fed him on delicacies and looked after him. When Nandi grew up, in order to show his gratitude to the brahmin, he suggested that he should draw one hundred carts for a wager. The brahmin boasted to his friends and had a wager with them. On the appointed day he loaded one hundred carts, lashed them together, and having tied Nandivisāla to the first, took his seat on the pole and, flourishing his goad, shouted, "Now, you rascal, pull." The bull, very offended, would not stir, and the brahmin lost his money. As he lay groaning in bed, Nandivisāla went to him and said that he should not have abused him. He then asked him to wager two thousand, and said that this time he would win. This the brahmin did, and the next day, having tied one hundred carts together, he yoked Nandivisāla to the first and stroked his back saying, "Now then, my fine fellow, pull." With one heave, Nandivisāla pulled the carts, and the last stood where the first had been. Nandivisāla's master received many presents in addition to the wager.

The story was related in reference to the taunts uttered by the **Chabbaggiyas** against the virtuous monks.

Ānanda was the brahmin of the story.[1] It was also related in connection with the **Yamakapāṭihāriya.**[2]

[1] J. i. 191 ff.; the story is also given at Vin. iv. 5. [2] DhA. iii. 213.

Nandivisāla Sutta.—Records the visit of the deva **Nandivisāla** (2) to the Buddha.[1]

[1] S. i. 63.

1. **Nandisena.**—Minister of **Assaka,** king of **Potali.** Nandisena is identified with **Sāriputta.** For details see the **Culla-Kāliṅga Jātaka.**[1]

[1] J. iii. 1 ff.

2. **Nandisena.**—Father of **Suppatiṭṭhitabrahmā,** and minister of **Duṭṭhagamaṇī.** His wife was **Sumanā.**[1]

[1] Dpv. xix. 9; MṬ. 528.

1. **Nanduttara.**—A brahmin, a former incarnation of **Soṇuttara** (*q.v.*). He lived in **Koṭigāma,** a league from **Payāga,** and offered hospitality to the Buddha and his monks. He saw the miracle performed by **Bhaddaji** in raising up the sunken palace of **Mahāpanāda** and showing the **Dussa-Thūpa,** and expressed the wish to possess similar power to procure relics held by others.[1]

[1] Mhv. xxxi. 5 ff.; *cf.* MṬ. 560.

2. **Nanduttara.**—Son of **Nārada** Buddha in his last lay-life. When the Buddha preached to him, eighty crores of people realized the Truth.[1]

[1] Bu. x. 9, 20.

Nanduttarā Therī.—She belonged to a brahmin family of **Kammāssadamma** and entered the Order of the **Nigaṇṭhas.** She was a renowned speaker and travelled about India, challenging others to discussion. In the course of her wanderings she met **Moggallāna,** and was defeated in discussion by him. Acting on his advice, she became a bhikkhuṇī, and, soon after, an arahant.[1]

[1] Thig. vs. 87-91; ThigA. 87.

1. **Nandopananda.**—A Nāga-king, tamed by **Moggallāna.** The Buddha and five hundred monks, on their way to **Tāvatiṃsa** one morning, travelled over the Nāga-king's abode as he was having a meal. In anger, the Nāga coiled round **Sineru** and covered the road to Tāvatiṃsa.

Thereupon several members of the Buddha's retinue, including **Raṭṭhapāla, Bhaddiya** and **Rāhula,** offered to quell the Nāga's power, but the Buddha would not agree until Moggallāna sought permission to do so. It is said that no other monk had the power to face *all* the dangers created by the Nāga and remain unscathed. Moggallāna and Nandopananda vied with one another in the exhibition of their *iddhi*-power, and, in the end, Nandopananda had to acknowledge defeat. He was thereupon conducted to the Buddha, whose follower he became. When **Anāthapiṇḍika** heard of Moggallāna's victory, he celebrated it by holding a great alms festival, lasting for seven days, for the Buddha and his monks.[1]

In the Divyāvadāna[2] Nanda and Upananda are spoken of as two Nāga-kings.

[1] ThagA. ii. 188 f.; J. v. 126. [2] p. 395.

2. **Nandopananda.**—One of the **Lohakumbhi-Nirayas.**[1]

[1] SA. i. 111.

Nandhimitta (Nandimitta).—One of the chief warriors of **Duṭṭhagāmaṇī.** He was the nephew of **Mitta,** one of **Eḷāra's** generals. His genitals were hidden in his body, and he had the strength of ten elephants. When he was a baby, he was wont to wander about, and so was tied to a mill-stone by a strap (*nandhi*), but he dragged the stone after him. In **Anurādhapura** he slew the Damiḷas who desecrated the temples, but later he joined the Sinhalese soldiers in **Rohaṇa** and fought in Duṭṭhagāmaṇī's campaigns.[1]

[1] Mhv. xxiii. 2 ff.; xxv. 21 ff.; MA. ii. 688; DA. i. 90.

Namuci.—A name for **Māra** (*q.v.*), given because he does not allow either gods or men to escape from his clutches, but works them harm.[1]

[1] SNA. ii. 386.

1. **Nammadā.**—A river in India,[1] the modern Nerbudda. It was regarded as the boundary between **Uttarāpatha** and **Dakkhiṇāpatha.** There the Buddha left his footprint to be worshipped by the Nāgas. This footprint is covered by high tide but visible at low tide.[2]

[1] J. ii. 344; iv. 392, 397. [2] MA. ii. 1018; for details see *s.v.* **Puṇṇa.**

2. **Nammadā.**—A Nāga-king who dwelt in the river **Nammadā.** When the Buddha returned after his visit to **Puṇṇa** (*q.v.*) and reached the Nammadā river, the Nāga-king invited the Buddha to his abode and

there showed the Buddha and his monks great honour. At the Nāga's request, the Buddha left his footprint on the bank of the river for the Nāgas to worship.[1]

[1] MA. ii. 1018; SA. iii. 18.

3. **Nammadā.**—A canal flowing from the **Puṇṇavaddhana** tank through the **Jetavana-vihāra** in **Pulatthipura.**[1]

[1] Cv. lxxix. 48.

Nayanāyudha.—One of the four most powerful weapons in the world. It belongs to **Yama,** and seems to be comparable to Siva's third eye. At a glance from this "weapon" many thousands of *kumbhaṇḍas* are shattered to bits.[1]

[1] SNA. i. 225.

Nayanussava.—A garden in **Pulatthipura,** laid out by **Parakkamabāhu I.**[1]

[1] Cv. lxxix. 8.

Naratuṅgabrahmā.—A Damiḷa chieftain of South India, defeated by the forces of **Parakkamabāhu I.,** near **Rāmissara.**[1]

[1] Cv. lxxvi. 98.

1. **Naradeva.**—A yakkha who, once a fortnight, took possession of **Kāvinda** and made him bark like a dog. When this happened Kāvinda's son shut him up indoors.[1]

[1] J. vi. 383, 387.

2. **Naradeva.**—A man-eating yakkha who lived in a lake near **Khemavatī.** The Buddha **Kakusandha** visited him and converted him.[1]

[1] Bu. xxiii. 5 ff.; BuA. 210 f.

3. **Naradeva.**—A yakkha, who went about from city to city, killing the kings and taking possession of their harems. When his identity was discovered by the women, he would eat them and go elsewhere. When he came to the city of **Sunanda,** the Buddha **Kassapa** preached to him and converted him.[1]

[1] Bu. xxv. 7 ff.; BuA. 219.

4. **Naradeva.**—The last of the descendants of **Bhaddadeva** who reigned in **Kaṇṇagoccha.** Seven of his descendants reigned in **Rojanagara.**[1]

[1] Dpv. iii. 27.

Naradevagāthā.—A set of verses in praise of the Buddha, compiled by a Sinhalese monk.[1]

[1] Gv. p. 65.

Narapati-Sithu.—King of Pagan (1167-1202 A.C.). He was a very enlightened monarch and a great patron of learning. His tutor was **Aggavaṃsa.**[1]

[1] For details see Bode: *op. cit.*, 16, 20, 21, 23, 31.

Naramittā.—An eminent Therī of **Anurādhapura.**[1]

[1] Dpv. xviii. 15.

Naravāhana.—One of the palaces occupied by **Padumuttara** Buddha in his last lay life.[1]

[1] Bu. xi. 20.

1. **Narasīha.**—King of India, ruler of **Kaṇḍuveṭhi,** and friend of **Mānavamma.** The latter helped him to defeat the **Vallabha king,** and was rewarded by Narasīha's help in acquiring the throne of Ceylon.[1]

[1] Cv. xlvii. 4-49.

2. **Narasīha.**—The eighth future Buddha.[1]

[1] Anāgat. p. 40.

Narasīhagāthā.—Ten verses praising the Buddha's beauty, said to have been uttered by **Rāhulamātā** when Suddhodana announced to her that the Buddha was begging alms in his own city of **Kapilavatthu.** Each verse ends with the word "narasīha."[1]

[1] ApA. i. 79; J. i. says there were only 8 verses.

Narasīhadeva.—An officer of **Kulasekhara.**[1]

[1] Cv. lxxvi. 95, 174.

Narasīhapadmara.—An ally of **Kulasekhara.** He was captured by **Laṅkāpura.**[1]

[1] Cv. lxxvii. 76, 86.

Narinda.—A Nāga-king, who gave grass for his seat to **Vessabhū** Buddha.[1]

[1] BuA. 205.

Naruttama.—Seventy-three kappas ago there were four kings of this name, all previous births of **Tikaṇṇapupphiya.**[1]

[1] Ap. i. 195.

Naḷa.—A Gandhabba chieftain[1] to be invoked by followers of the Buddha in time of need.[2]

[1] D. ii. 258. [2] *Ibid.*, iii. 204.

Naḷa Vagga.—The first chapter of the **Saṃyutta Nikāya.**[1]

[1] S. i. 1-5.

Naḷaka.—The personal name of **Mahā Kaccāna** (*q.v.*), **Kaccāna** being his gotta-name.

Naḷakapāna.—A village in **Kosala,** where the Buddha once stayed and preached the **Naḷakapāna Sutta.**[1] The village received its name from the **Naḷakapāna-pokkharaṇī.**[2] The reason for the name of this pond, which was in the village, is given in the **Naḷapāna Jātaka** (*q.v.*). There were two groves near the village, the **Ketakavana** and the **Palāsavana;** in the latter, **Sāriputta** preached two sermons at the request of the Buddha.[3]

[1] M. i. 462. [2] MA. ii. 664 f.; AA. ii. 843. [3] A. v. 122 f., 125 f.

1. **Naḷakapāna Sutta.**—Preached at the **Palāsavana** in **Naḷakapāna.** The Buddha asks the assembled monks—among whom are many distinguished members, such as **Anuruddha, Kimbila, Nandiya** and others—if they feel they have realized the aim for which they have given up household life ? On their assenting, he proceeds to tell them that when he claims that he has destroyed the āsavas and that his disciples have gained various attainments through his teaching, he does so, not in order to cajole or to delude others, nor to gain fame and profit for himself, but to hearten and fill with enthusiasm believing young men, that they may concentrate with their whole hearts and follow the example of his disciples.[1]

[1] M. i. 462 ff.

2. **Naḷakapāna Sutta.**—The Buddha, having preached to the monks in **Palāsavana** in **Naḷakapāna** till late at night, asks **Sāriputta** to continue, as he has pain in his back and wishes to rest. **Sāriputta** thereupon takes up the sermon and tells the monks of the necessity for *saddhā, hiri, ottappa, viriya* and *paññā*, for the performance of good works. The Buddha returns and praises Sāriputta.[1]

[1] A. v. 122 ff.

3. **Naḷakapāna Sutta.**—The circumstances are the same as in (2), but the qualities mentioned by **Sāriputta** differ—*saddhā, hiri, ottappa, viriya,*

sotāvadhāna, *dhammadhāraṇā*, *atthupaparikkhā*, *dhammānudhammapaṭipatti*, and *appamāda*.[1]

[1] A. v. 125 ff.

Naḷakalāpiya Sutta.—A discussion between **Sāriputta** and **Mahā Koṭṭhita** at the Migadāya in **Isipatana.** Sāriputta says that each link in the chain of causation depends upon the one next to it. It is as if two sheaves of reeds stand, leaning one against the other; if one is pushed, the other must fall.[1]

[1] S. ii. 112 f.

Naḷakāra.—The Bodhisatta, born as a deva in **Tāvatiṃsa.** In his previous life he had been a farmer in Benares. One day, while going to his fields, he saw a Pacceka Buddha. Thereupon he turned back, took the Pacceka Buddha home, fed him, and, with his son, built for him a hut with reed walls, on the banks of the Ganges, looked after him in the rains and gave him robes to wear. When **Sumedhā,** queen of **Suruci,** yearned for a son, Naḷakāra agreed to be born as her son, at Sakka's request; he then came to be called **Mahāpanāda**[1] (*q.v.*). Regarding his son, see *s.v.* **Saṅkha.**[2]

[1] J. iv. 318-23.
[2] DA. iii. 806 f.

Naḷakāragāma.—A village mentioned in the **Subha Sutta**[1] as being not far from **Sāvatthi.**

[1] M. ii. 206.

Naḷakuṭidāyaka Thera.—An arahant. Thirty-one kappas ago he built a house of reeds near **Bhārika (Hārita)** in **Himavā,** for the Pacceka Buddha **Nārada,** thatched it with reeds and made a covered walk near by. When he was born in **Tāvatiṃsa** he had a palace sixty leagues in extent.[1] He is probably identical with **Valliya Thera.**[2] The same verses are attributed to **Naḷagārika** (see below).

[1] Ap. ii. 440.
[2] ThagA. i. 247.

Naḷannaru.—A tank in Ceylon, repaired by **Parakkamabāhu I.**[1]

[1] Cv. lxviii. 47.

Naḷapāna Jātaka (No. 20).—The Bodhisatta is born as leader of a herd of monkeys. He has given strict injunctions that none of his followers should eat or drink in a strange place without his consent. One day the monkeys are very thirsty and arrive at a lake in the forest, but will not drink until their leader arrives. He examines the lake and discovers that it is haunted by an ogre. He then provides all his followers with long reeds which, by the power of his virtue, immediately become hollow throughout. Thenceforth all the reeds round that lake are hollow, and the lake itself comes to be known as **Naḷakapānapokkharaṇī.** This is one of the four miracles which will endure throughout the kappa. The story was related by the Buddha in the village of Naḷakapāna to explain the hollowness of the canes which grew round the lake. The ogre in the story is identified with **Devadatta.**[1]

[1] J. i. 170 ff.

Naḷamāla, Naḷamālī.—An ocean passed by **Suppāraka** and his crew on their way from **Bharukaccha.** It looked like an expanse of reeds or a grove of bamboos. The scholiast explains that the sea was red like "scorpion-reeds" or "crab-weeds," which are red in colour. The sea contained coral (*veḷu*) in its bed, and some of this Suppāraka hauled into his ship.[1]

[1] J. iv. 140, 141.

Naḷamālikā Therī.—An arahant. Ninety-four kappas ago she was a *kinnarā* on the banks of the **Candabhāgā** and, having seen the Buddha, offered him a garland of flowers. She was queen of the devas thirty-six times and queen among men in ten lives.[1] She is probably identical with **Cittā Therī.**[2]

[1] Ap. ii. 528 f. [2] ThigA. 33 f.

1. **Naḷamāliya Thera.**—An arahant. Once he gave a fan, made of reeds, to **Padumuttara** Buddha, who praised his gift. He became king many times under the name of **Subbata** and eight times under that of **Māluta**[1] He is probably identical with **Kuṭivihāriya Thera.**[2]

[1] Ap. i. 143 f. [2] ThagA. i. 131.

2. **Naḷamāliya Thera.**—An arahant. Thirty-one kappas ago he saw **Sikhī** Buddha and gave him a garland of reed-flowers.[1] He is probably identical with **Dhaniya Thera.**[2]

[1] Ap. ii. 412. [2] ThagA. i. 347.

Naḷasākiyā.—A branch of the **Sākiyas.** When **Viḍūḍabha** waged war on the Sākiyas, he gave orders that all those calling themselves by the name of Sākiya should be slain. His men went about asking for those who were called Sākiyas. Some of these therefore took blades of grass in their teeth and others reeds. When asked if they were Sākiyas, the former said "not *sāka*" (potherb) but "grass," (*tiṇa*), and the latter "not *sāka*" (potherb) but "reed" (*naḷa*). Owing to this play on their name they escaped death. Thenceforth they were known respectively as **Tiṇasākiyā** and **Naḷasākiyā.**[1]

[1] DhA. i. 358 f.

Naḷāgārika Thera.—An arahant. In the time of **Nārada** Buddha, he built for the Buddha a hut of reeds near the **Hārita** mountain and thatched it with grass. Seventy-four times he became king of the devas and seventy-seven times king of men.[1] He is probably identical with **Valliya Thera.**[2]

[1] Ap. i. 178 f.

[2] ThagA. i. 247.

Naḷāṭa.—See **Laḷāṭa.**

Naḷinakesariya Thera.—An arahant. Ninety-two kappas ago he was a water-fowl, who, having seen the Buddha **Tissa** travelling through the air, took a lotus-flower in his beak and offered it to him. Seventy-three kappas ago he was a king named **Satapatta.**[1]

[1] Ap. i. 223.

Naḷiṇi Jātaka.—See **Naḷinikā Jātaka.**

Naḷinikā.—Daughter of the king of **Kāsi.** She seduced **Isisiṅga.** For her story see **Naḷinikā Jātaka.**

Naḷinikā Jātaka (No. 526).—The Bodhisatta was once an ascetic in Himavā. A doe drank water in which his semen had fallen and conceived a son, whom he adopted and named **Isisiṅga.** Isisiṅga was a sage of such austerity that **Sakka** trembled at his power. In order to destroy his virtue, Sakka caused a drought in **Kāsi,** lasting three years. When the inhabitants complained to the king, Sakka appeared before him and suggested that if the king's daughter, **Naḷinikā,** would seduce Isisiṅga and destroy his virtue, rain would fall. Naḷinikā was, accordingly, sent to the Himālaya and arrived in Isisiṅga's hut dressed in the ascetic's garb, when the Bodhisatta was absent. Pretending to have been wounded by a bear, she played on the simplicity of the guileless young man (much as Venus did on that of Adonis). Through her seductions his virtue was overcome and his mystic meditation broken off. Delighted with the outcome of his plot, Sakka caused rain to fall on Kāsi, and Naḷinikā left the hermitage. When the Bodhisatta returned and heard of the visit of the youthful ascetic and of all that followed, he admonished Isisiṅga and warned him for the future. The story was told in reference to a monk who was seduced by the wife of his worldly days. Isisiṅga is identified with the monk and Naḷinikā with his wife.[1] *v.l.* **Naḷinī Jātaka**.

[1] J. v. 193-209. It is probably a variation of the same story which is found in Mtu. iii. 143 ff.

Naḷinī.—The kingdom of **Vessavaṇa.**[1]

[1] J. vi. 313; but VvA. (339, 340) explains Nalinī as a *kīḷanaṭṭhāna*. This agrees with D. iii. 202, where mention is made of a **Kuvera-naḷinī** as one of the beauties of Vessavaṇa's kingdom.

Naḷira. One of the palaces occupied by **Sobhita** Buddha in his last lay life.[1]

[1] Bu. vii. 17.

Naḷerupucimanda.—A grove near **Verañjā** where the Buddha spent part of his time on his visit to **Nerañjā.**[1] Buddhaghosa explains[2] that the chief tree to be found there was a *pucimanda* or *nimba*-tree at the foot of which was a shrine dedicated to a yakkha named **Naḷeru.** The tree was shady and beautiful to look upon. The road northwards (to **Uttarakuru** ?) went past this tree.[3]

[1] Vin. iii. 1; A. iv. 172, 197. [2] Sp. i. 108 f. [3] *Ibid.*, 184.

Nava Sutta.—Once a novice, returning from his alms round, entered his cell and sat down in silence and at ease, not helping the monks with the robe-making. This was reported to the Buddha, who sent for the monk. The Buddha discovered his abilities, and told the monks to leave him alone as he was one who could win, without toil, the four *jhānas.*[1]

[1] S. ii. 277 f.

Navakammika-Bhāradvāja.—One of the **Bhāradvājas** (*q.v.*). Once, when the Buddha was staying in a forest in **Kosala,** Navakammika, who was there seeing about some timber-work, saw the Buddha at the foot of a tree and asked him what pleasure he found in his contemplations. When the Buddha explained to him how he had found liberty, the brahmin was pleased and accepted the Buddha as his teacher.[1]

The Commentary[2] explains that this brahmin had forest trees cut, and out of the timber had the framework for gables, roof-terraces, etc., fitted, and these were then carried to the town and sold.

[1] S. i. 179. [2] SA. i. 205.

Navakammika Sutta.—Records the conversation between the Buddha and **Navakammika Bhāradvāja** (*q.v.*).[1]

[1] S. i. 179.

Navagāmapura.—A locality in Ceylon mentioned in an account of the campaigns of **Parakkamabāhu I.**[1]

[1] Cv. lxxii. 137.

Navanavatiya.—A city in **Uttarakuru.**[1]

[1] D. iii. 201.

Navapūraṇa Vagga.—The fifteenth chapter of the **Saḷāyatana Saṃyutta.**[1]

[1] S. iv. 132-42.

Navayojanaraṭṭha.—A district in **Rohaṇa.**[1]

[1] Cv. lxxii. 60, 61, 72; see also Cv. *Trs.* i. 324, n. 7.

Navaratha.—One of the descendants of King **Mahāsammata.**[1]

[1] Dpv. iii. 40.

Navavimalabuddhi.—See **Vimalabuddhi.**

1. **Nāga.**—An eminent thera of Ceylon, a teacher of the Vinaya.[1]

[1] Vin. v. 3.

2. **Nāga.**—Third of the ten sons of **Muṭasīva,** and therefore a brother of **Devānampiyatissa.**[1]

[1] Dpv. xi. 6; xvii. 75.

3. **Nāga.**—A thera of Ceylon during the pillage by **Brahmaṇa-Tissa.** His sister was an arahant therī named **Nāgā** (*q.v.*).[1]

[1] For their story see MA. i. 546 f.; AA. ii. 654 f.

4. **Nāga.**—An Elder of **Kāraḷiyagiri** in Ceylon. For eighteen years he gave up teaching the Dhamma, but later he taught the *Dhātukathā,* and his memory of the contents was perfect.[1]

[1] Vsm. 96.

5. **Nāga.**—See **Coranāga, Mahānāga,** etc.

Nāga Vagga.—The twenty-third chapter of the **Dhammapada.**

Nāga Saṃyutta.—The nineteenth section of the **Saṃyutta Nikāya.**[1]

[1] S. iii. 240-6.

1. **Nāga Sutta.**—Once, when the Buddha was seated under the **Ajapāla** Banyan-tree, soon after his Enlightenment, **Māra** assumed the form of a fearsome elephant and tried to frighten him. But the Buddha recognised Māra and sent him away discomfited.[1]

[1] S. i. 103 f.

2. **Nāga Sutta.**—A certain novice was in the habit of spending too much time in clansmen's houses. When warned against this, he answered that he could not understand how he was to blame when he saw many senior monks acting in the same way. He was reported to the Buddha, who related the story of an elephant who dwelt by a great lake. He plunged into the lake, pulled up lotus-stalks, cleaned them and then, by eating them, gained strength and beauty. But when the baby elephants tried to follow his example, they could not clean the stalks, and eating them with mud and dirt, they grew sick, some of them even dying.[1]

[1] S. ii. 268 f.

3. **Nāga Sutta.**—Snakes which dwell in the Himālaya, when grown and strong, find their way into the sea, where they grow even greater. Even so do monks, who develop the Noble Eightfold Path.[1]

[1] S. v. 47.

4. **Nāga Sutta.**—An elephant, to be fit for the royal stalls, should have four qualities: he should be a good listener (*sotā*), a good slayer (*hantā*), full of patience (*khantā*), and a good goer (*gantā*). A monk should have the corresponding qualities in order to be fit for the respect and gifts of the world.[1]

[1] A. ii. 116 f.

5. **Nāga Sutta.**—The Buddha goes to the bathing-place near the **Migāramātupāsāda** with **Ānanda,** bathes there, and, while drying his limbs, sees **Pasenadi's** elephant, **Seta,** coming out of the bathing-place, attended by great ceremony. People, seeing him, express their wonder and admiration of the noble animal. **Udāyi,**[1] who is near by, asks the Buddha if it is only the elephant whom people praise for his bulk or do they praise other bulky things as well ? They do, says the Buddha, praise all huge things—horses, bulls, snakes, trees, and big men, calling them Nāgas,

[1] **Kāludāyi,** says the Commentary (AA. ii. 669).

but really, the best Nāga is he who commits no enormity in word or thought (*āguṇ na karoti, taṃnāgo*). Thereupon Udāyī breaks forth into song, praising the Buddha's teaching, comparing the Buddha to an elephant, each limb representing a different virtue.[2]

This sutta is also called **Nāgopama Sutta.**[3]

[2] A. iii. 345 ff. [3] ThagA. ii. 7.

6. **Nāga Sutta.**—Sometimes it happens that a forest-dwelling elephant gets bored with the company of his fellows, his women-folk and the young elephants who get in his way and interfere with his freedom. Thereupon he breaks away from them and retires into solitude. So should the monk, wearied of the haunts of men, resort to loneliness and there rid himself of the *āsavas*.[1]

[1] A. iv. 435 ff.

Nāgakesariya Thera.—An arahant. In the past he was a hunter, and, while wandering in the forest, he saw a full-blown *nāga*-flower and offered it with both hands to **Tissa** Buddha. Seventy-seven kappas ago he was a king named **Pamokkharaṇa.**[1]

[1] Ap. i. 222.

Nāgacatukka.—A locality near **Ambatthala.** While seated here, **Devānampiyatissa** heard the novice **Sumana** announce the time for the preaching of the Dhamma, to be heard all over Ceylon.[1] Geiger[2] identifies it with the modern Nāgapokuṇa (but see **Nāgasoṇḍi**). According to the Dīpavaṃsa[3] (which has a *v.l.* **Nagaracatukka**) it was a pond at the foot of the **Missakapabbata** and was made out of rock.

[1] Mhv. xiv. 36. [2] Mhv. *Trs.* 94, n. 1. [3] Dpv. xiv. 58; also Mhv. xvi. 6.

1. **Nāgadatta Thera.**—He once lived in a forest tract in **Kosala** and was inclined to be indolent. A deva, noticing this, admonished him, and it is said that Nāgadatta paid heed to the warning.[1]

[1] S. i. 200.

2. **Nāgadatta.**—A deva, living, according to one account,[1] in **Kelāsapabbata;** according to another,[2] in **Gandhamādana. Anuruddha,** when residing in the **Chaddantavana,** used to pass by his dwelling, and the deva gave him milk-rice with lotus-honey. When **Sīvalī** visited Gandhamādana with five hundred monks, the deva gave them milk-rice one day and clarified butter the next. When the monks inquired how

[1] SA. i. 217. [2] ThagA. i. 138; AA. i. 139.

he could get milk and ghee, he told them that this was the result of a gift of milk-rice given by him in the time of **Kassapa** Buddha.

Nāgadatta Sutta.—Records the admonition given by a deva to **Nāgadatta Thera**[1] (*q.v.*).

[1] S. i. 200.

Nāgadāsaka.—King of **Magadha** and son of **Muṇḍa.** He slew his father and ruled for twenty-four years. The people deposed him and made **Susunāga** king in his place.[1]

[1] Mhv. xvi. 4 ff.; Sp. i. 73; Dpv. iv. 41; v. 78; xi. 10, where he is called **Dāsaka.** But see DA. i. 153, where his father is called **Anuruddha.**

Nāgadīpa.—A province of Ceylon, identified with the modern Jaffna peninsula and the north-west of Ceylon. The Buddha's second visit to Ceylon was to Nāgadīpa, to settle a dispute between two Nāgas, **Mahodara** and **Cūḷodara.**[1] **Jambukola** (*q.v.*) was a harbour in Nāgadīpa, and there a vihāra was built by **Devānampiyatissa**[2] and later restored by **Kaniṭṭhatissa.**[3] This vihāra was probably called **Tissa-vihāra.**[4] Another vihāra, called **Sālipabbata,** was built by **Mahallaka-Nāga.**[5] The **Uṇṇalomaghara,** the **Rājāyatana-dhātucetiya** and the **Āmalacetiya** were probably all places of worship in Nāgadīpa.[6] The **Valāhassa Jātaka**[7] says that the coast of Ceylon, from the river **Kalyāṇī** to Nāgadīpa, was once infested by yakkhiṇīs. Once[8] Nāgadīpa was known as **Serumadīpa,** and near by was **Karadīpa,** earlier known as **Ahidīpa.**[9] An old story, given in the Commentaries,[10] speaks of a king called **Dīparāgā,** who reigned over Nāgadīpa in great splendour. Nāgadīpa was once an important centre of Buddhism in Ceylon[11] and contained many places of pilgrimage. There is a legend[12] which relates that, when the Buddha's *sāsana* comes to an end, all the Buddha's relics in Ceylon will gather together at the **Mahācetiya** and travel to the Rājāyatanacetiya in Nāgadīpa, and then from there to the Mahābodhi tree at **Gayā.**

[1] Mhv. i. 47. [2] *Ibid.*, xx. 25.
[3] *Ibid.*, xxxvi. 9.
[4] See *ibid.*, 36.
[5] *Ibid.*, xxxv. 124.
[6] Cv. xlii. 62.
[7] J. ii. 128.
[8] J. iii. 187.
[9] J. iv. 238.
[10] *E.g.*, VibhA. 444.
[11] *E.g.*, *ibid.*, 446, 457; AA. i. 422. MA. i. 545; see also *J.R.A.S.*, vol. xxvi.
[12] DA. iii. 899; VibhA. 433.

Nāgadeva.—One of the descendants of **Mahāsammata.** He reigned in **Campā,** and twenty-five of his descendants reigned in **Mithilā.**[1]

[1] Dpv. iii. 29.

Nāgapaṭṭana.—The port from which **Buddhaghosa** sailed for Ceylon.[1]

[1] SadS. 53.

Nāgapabbatagāma.—A village in the province of **Malaya** in Ceylon.[1]

[1] Cv. lxx. 10.

Nāgapaliveṭhana.—One of the seven mountain ranges which must be crossed in order to reach **Gandhamādana.**[1]

[1] SNA. i. 66.

1. **Nāgapupphiya Thera.**—An arahant. In the time of **Padumuttara** Buddha he was a brahmin teacher, named **Suvaccha.** One day he saw the Buddha travelling through the air and, marvelling at the miracle, sprinkled *nāga*-flowers along his route. Thirty-one kappas ago he was a king named **Mahāratha.**[1] He is probably identical with **Dhammasava Thera.**[2]

[1] Ap. i. 179. [2] ThagA. i. 214.

2. **Nāgapupphiya Thera.**—An arahant. Probably identical with **Lomasakaṅgiya.**[1] Ninety-one kappas ago he saw the Buddha (**Vipassi** ?) walking along the street and offered him *nāga*-flowers.[2]

[1] ThagA. i. 84. [2] Ap. ii. 450.

Nāgapeta-vatthu.—In a brahmin family of Benares, the two sons and the daughter heard the Doctrine from **Saṅkicca Thera** and became believers. The parents were anxious to give their daughter to their nephew, but he had joined the Order. Later, however, wishing to marry his cousin, he asked his teacher's permission to become a layman. The latter withheld his consent for some time, and, while he hesitated, the house in which the family lived fell down and they were all killed. The two sons and the daughter were born among the *bhumma*-devas and the parents became *petas*. The young monk's teacher showed them to him one day as he passed behind the monastery at **Isipatana,** and having heard their story from their own lips, the monk caused alms to be given in the name of the *petas*, and they were freed from their sufferings.[1]

[1] Pv. i. 11; PvA. 53 ff.

Nāgamaṇḍala-paritta (or **Nāgamaṇḍalamanta**). Mentioned as a charm possessing the power of bringing blessings on others.[1]

[1] VibhA. 410, 411.

Nāgamahāvihāra.—A monastery in **Rohaṇa,** built by **Mahānāga,** ruler of **Mahāgāma** and brother of **Devānampiyatissa.**[1] **Iḷanāga** restored it and bestowed land for its maintenance.[2] A story is related of a monk of this vihāra who cut down a *nāga*-tree near the monastery. The devatā living in the tree was annoyed, and announced to the thera that the king who looked after him would die in seven days. The thera mentioned this in the palace; seven days passed and, as nothing happened, the king had the thera's hands and feet cut off.[3] Near the monastery was a village named **Kelakacchagāma** (*v.l.* **Kāḷagacchagāma**).[4] **Dappula** gave the village of **Kevaṭṭagambhīra** to the vihāra.[5]

[1] Mhv. xxii. 9.
[2] *Ibid.*, xxxv. 31; MṬ. 469.
[3] VibhA. 407.
[4] MA. ii. 1025.
[5] Cv. xlv. 58.

Nāgamālaka.—A locality in **Anurādhapura** to the north of **Sirīsamāla. Koṇāgamana** Buddha preached the Dhamma there and twenty thousand people realized the truth. To the north was the **Asokamālaka.**[1] In Nāgamālaka was the **Silāsobbhakaṇḍaka-cetiya,** and, near it, **Thūlatthana** built another *cetiya.*[2]

[1] Mhv. xv. 118, 153.
[2] MṬ. 355.

Nāgamittā.—An eminent therī of **Anurādhapura,** a teacher of the Vinaya.[1]

[1] Dpv. xviii. 34.

Nāgamuṇḍā.—A female slave, mistress of **Mahānāma** the Sākyan. She was the mother of **Vāsabhakhattiyā.**[1]

[1] J. i. 133; iv. 145.

Nāgalena.—A cave in **Koṭipabbata-vihāra.** A novice once recited there the **Mahāsamaya Sutta,** and a goddess, in the *nāga*-tree outside, applauded him. She had been present when the Buddha preached the sutta when, she said, the concourse of devas was so great that she could get a foothold only in the sea near **Mahāgāma** in Ceylon; yet she could see and hear the Buddha distinctly.[1]

[1] DA. ii. 695.

Nāgavaḍḍhana.—A monastery in Ceylon, on which **Udaya I.** bestowed many maintenance villages.[1]

[1] Cv. xlix. 21.

Nāgavana.—A pleasaunce near **Hatthigāma,** belonging to **Uggagahapati.** It was there that he first met the Buddha and was converted.[1]

[1] A. iv. 213; AA. ii. 762.

1. **Nāgavimāna-Vatthu.**—The story of **Yasuttarā**[1] (*q.v.*).

[1] Vv. iv. 3; VvA. 181 ff.

2. **Nāgavimāna-Vatthu.**—The story of a man who, having offered eight flowers at the thūpa of **Kassapa** Buddha, was born in **Tāvatiṃsa,** where he rode a white elephant. He had procured the flowers with great difficulty. **Moggallāna** saw him on one of his journeys and heard from him his story.[1]

[1] Vv. v. 10; VvA. 252 ff.

Nāga-vihāra.—See **Nāgamahā-vihāra.**

1. **Nāgasamāla Thera.**—He was a Sākyan and entered the Order when the Buddha visited his kinsmen at **Kapilavatthu.** For some time he was the Buddha's personal attendant—*e.g.*, when the Buddha preached the **Mahāsīhanāda Sutta** (or the **Lomahaṃsapariyāya**).[1] One day, when entering the city for alms, he saw a nautch-girl gaily dressed, dancing to the accompaniment of music and contemplated her as the snare of **Māra.** Making this his topic of thought, he developed insight into the perishableness of life and became an arahant.[2] Another day (evidently earlier than the previous incident), while walking with the Buddha, they came to a cleft in the road, and the Buddha wished to go along one way, while Nāgasamāla wished to go along another, in spite of the Buddha's warning that it was dangerous. In the end, he put the Buddha's begging-bowl and robe on the ground and left him. Brigands waylaid him and ill-treated him, breaking his bowl and threatening to kill him. Thereupon he turned back to the Buddha and asked his forgiveness.[3]

Nāgasamāla was a householder in the time of **Padumuttara** Buddha, and, seeing the Buddha walking in the sun, he gave him an umbrella. After that, wherever he went a white parasol appeared over his head. For thirty kappas he was king of the gods. He is probably to be identified with **Ekachattiya** of the Apadāna.[4]

[1] M. i. 83; MA. i. 283; AA. i. 163; UdA. 217; J. iv. 95.
[2] Thag. vs. 267-70; ThagA. i. 378.
[3] Ud. viii. 7; UdA. 425 f.
[4] Ap. ii. 405.

2. **Nāgasamāla Thera.**—An arahant. The Apadāna[1] distinguishes him from the above, whom it calls Ekachattiya. Thirty-one kappas ago he placed a *pāṭali*-flower on the thūpa of **Sikhī** Buddha. Fifteen kappas ago he was a king named **Bhūmiya.**

[1] Ap. i. 119.

The Apadāna Commentary says, however, that this thera was the *pacchāsamaṇa* (personal attendant) of the Buddha for some time and that he was called Nāgasamāla because his body was tender as *nāga*-buds.

Nāgasamālā.—One of the two chief women disciples of **Sujāta** Buddha.[1]

[1] Bu. xiii. 26; J. i. 38.

Nāgasālā.—A monastic building, once the residence of a monk named **Mahādhammakathī. Kassapa II.** found the buildings dilapidated, and, during their restoration, he persuaded the Elder to live in a large pāsāda attached to the **Maricavaṭṭi-vihāra.** The Elder was proficient in the Abhidhamma, and the king caused the Abhidhamma and the Commentaries to be recited by him. The village of **Mahāniṭṭhula** was given to him for his maintenance.[1] Nāgasālā was also the residence of **Dāṭhāsiva.**[2] A pariveṇa, called the **Nāgasāla-parivena,** was built by **Aggabodhi,** ruler of Malaya and minister to the king, in the reign of **Sena III.,** who gave a village for its maintenance.[3]

[1] Cv. xliv. 149 ff.; xlv. 2. [2] *Ibid.*, xlvi. 6. [3] *Ibid.*, liii. 36.

1. **Nāgasena Thera.**—An arahant, celebrated for his discussions with King **Milinda.** He was the son of the brahmin **Soṇuttara,** in the village of **Kajaṅgala** in the Himālaya. He was well versed in the Vedas, and entered the Order under **Rohaṇa** to learn the Buddha's teaching. Later he went to **Assagutta** of the **Vattaniya-senāsana** and studied under him. There, one day, at the conclusion of a meal, while giving thanks to a lay woman who had looked after Assagutta for more than thirty years, Nāgasena became a Sotāpanna. Then he was sent to **Pāṭaliputta,** where he studied under **Dhammarakkhita,** and there he attained arahantship. Subsequently he went to the **Saṅkheyya-pariveṇa** in **Sāgala,** where he met Milinda. It is said that in his previous birth he was a deva, named **Mahāsena,** living in **Tāvatiṃsa,** in a palace called **Ketumatī,** and that he consented to be born among men at the insistent request of **Sakka** and the arahants led by Assagutta. In an earlier life he had made an aspiration to be able to defeat Milinda in discussion.[1]

[1] For further details see Milindapañha, 6 ff.

2. **Nāgasena.**—A king of **Jambudīpa,** descendant of **Mahāsammata.**[1]

[1] Dpv. iii. 40.

Nāgasoṇḍi.—A bathing tank in **Cetiyapabbata,** restored by **Aggabodhi I.**[1] It is probably the modern Nāgapokuṇa where, hewn in the face of the rock, the heads of a cobra (*nāga*) seem to rise out of the water.[2]

[1] Cv. xlii. 28. [2] Cv. *Trs.* i. 68, n. 8.

1. **Nāgā.**—Chief woman disciple of **Sujāta** Buddha.[1]

[1] J. i. 38; Bu. xiii. 26.

2. **Nāgā.**—One of the chief women supporters of **Phussa** Buddha.[1]

[1] Bu. xix. 21.

3. **Nāgā.**—A former birth of **Asokamālā,** when she was the wife of **Tissa** (later **Sāliya**), an artisan of **Muṇḍagaṅgā.**[1]

[1] MṬ. 605.

4. **Nāgā Therī.**—An arahant of **Bhātaragāma.** During the pillage of **Brāhmaṇa-Tissa,** when all the villagers had fled, she went with her colleagues to a banyan tree, the presiding deity of which provided them with food. She had a brother, **Nāga;** when he visited her she gave him part of her food, but he refused to accept food from a bhikkhuṇī.[1]

[1] MA. i. 546; AA. ii. 654.

5. **Nāgā.**—A class of beings. See Appendix.

6. **Nāgā.**—An eminent therī of Ceylon.[1]

[1] Dpv. xviii. 35.

1. **Nāgita Thera.**—An arahant. He belonged to a Sākyan family in **Kapilavatthu** and entered the Order after hearing the preaching of the **Madhupiṇḍika Sutta.**

In the time of **Padumuttara** Buddha he was a brahmin, named **Nārada,** and uttered three stanzas in praise of the Buddha. He was once a king named **Sumitta.**[1] He is probably identical with **Atthasandassaka** of the Apadāna.[2]

[1] Thag. vs. 86; ThagA. i. 183 f. [2] Ap. i. 168.

2. **Nāgita Thera.**—For some time the personal attendant of the Buddha.[1] He was the maternal uncle of the novice **Sīha,** who is said to have addressed him by the name of **Kassapa,** his gotta-name. He was fat and, therefore, lazy; he got most of his work done by Sīha.

[1] D. i. 151; DA. i. 310; A. iii. 31, 341; iv. 341; J. iv. 95, etc.

3. **Nāgita Thera.**—A thera of Ceylon, author of the **Saddasāratthajālinī.**[1]

[1] Gv. p. 74; Svd. vs. 1249.

1. **Nāgita Sutta.**—Once, when the Buddha went to **Icchānaṅgala,** the brahmin householders there came, in large numbers, to pay him their respects and made great uproar outside. When **Nāgita,** the Buddha's personal attendant at the time, told him the cause of the clamour, the Buddha replied that he had nothing to do with homage; his concern was with renunciation. He went on to state five inevitable things: whosoever eats and drinks must answer the calls of nature; whosoever loves is destined to sorrow and despair; whosoever dwells on the *asubha* must feel disgust for the *subha*; whosoever sees impermanence in the six spheres of contact feels disgust for contact; whosoever sees the rise and fall in the five kinds of attachment, must feel disgust for attachment.[1]

[1] A. iii. 31 ff.

2. **Nāgita Sutta.**—The circumstances are the same as those of No. 1. The Buddha tells **Nāgita** that he is pleased with monks who do not live in the village, but who seek the forest and stave off gains and flattery, but to him the best is to walk on the highway unattached.[1]

[1] A. iii. 341 ff.; *cp. ibid.*, iv. 341 ff.

Nāgindapalliya.—An eminent thera of Ceylon in the time of **Parakkamabāhu I.;** he was the leader of the monks in **Dakkhiṇadesa.**[1]

[1] Cv. lxxviii. 9.

Nāgopama Sutta.—See **Nāga Sutta** (5).

Nāṭapuriya.—A city in **Uttarakuru.**[1]

[1] D. iii. 200.

Nātaputta, Nāthaputta.—See **Nigaṇṭha Nātaputta.**

1. **Nātha.** Called **Adhikārī,** a general of King **Māṇābharaṇa.**[1]

[1] Cv. lxx. 298; lxxii. 123, 126.

2. **Nātha.**—Called **Nātha Laṅkāgiri.** A general of King **Māṇābharaṇa,** killed in battle.[1]

[1] Cv. lxxii. 124 f.

3. **Nātha Nagaragiri.**—General of **Parakkamabāhu I.** He held the title of **Saṅkhanāyaka.**[1]

[1] Cv. lxx. 318; lxxii. 31, 107; lxxv. 75.

Nātha Vagga.—The second chapter of the Dasaka Nipāta of the Aṅguttara Nikāya.[1]

[1] A. v. 15-32.

Nātha Suttā.—Two suttas on the qualities which give protection to a monk: virtue, learning, good friends, affability, skill in performance of duties, fondness for truth, energy, contentment, mindfulness, wisdom.[1]

[1] A. v. 23 f., 25 f.

Nāthadeva.—A name given to Viṣṇu as the protector (*nātha*) of Ceylon.[1]

[1] Cv. c. 248; Cv. *Trs.* ii. 243, n. 6.

Nāthaputtiyā.—The followers of **Nigaṇṭha Nāthaputta.**[1]

[1] D. iii. 117.

Nādikā.—See **Ñātikā.**

Nānacchanda Jātaka (No. 289).—Once the Bodhisatta was king of Benares, and while walking about the city in disguise, he fell one night into the hands of drunken thieves. He pleaded poverty, gave them his robe and escaped. In the city lived his father's former chaplain who had been dismissed. He told his wife how, as he watched the stars that night, he had seen the king fall into hostile hands and then escape. The king heard all this in the course of his wanderings and the following morning sent for his astrologers. They had not observed any such thing in the stars. He dismissed them therefore, appointed the other in their place, and gave him a boon. When the chaplain went home to consult his family as to what boon he should beg, his wife, his son **Chatta,** and his slave **Puṇṇā,** each wanted something different. He reported this to the king, who gave to each what he had desired.

The circumstances leading to the story are given in the **Juṇha Jātaka** (*q.v.*). The brahmin is identified with **Ānanda.**[1]

[1] J. ii. 426 ff.

Nānatta Vagga.—The first chapter of the **Dhātu Saṃyutta.**[1]

[1] S. ii. 140-9.

Nānātitthiya Vagga.—The third chapter of the **Devaputta Saṃyutta.**[1]

[1] S. i. 56-68.

Nānātitthiya Sutta.—Various devaputtas—followers of different teachers—come to the Buddha and sing the praises of their respective teachers—**Asama** the praises of **Pūraṇa-Kassapa, Sahali** of **Makkhali-Gosāla, Niṅka** of **Nigaṇṭha Nātaputta** and **Ākoṭaka** of all three. **Veṭambarī** makes rejoinder to Ākoṭaka and **Māra** agrees with him, while **Māṇava-Gāmiya** sings the Buddha's praises.[1]

[1] S. i. 65 ff.

Nānādhimuttiya Sutta.—**Anuruddha** tells his colleagues that by cultivating the four *satipaṭṭhānas* he has come to know the divers characters of beings.[1]

[1] S. v. 305.

Nābhasa.—A lake, the residence of Nāgas called **Nābhasā.**[1]

[1] DA. ii. 688.

Nābhasā.—A class of **Nāgas** living in the lake **Nābhasa**[1]; they were present at the **Mahāsamaya.**[2]

[1] DA. ii. 688. [2] D. ii. 258.

Nāma Sutta.—Preached in answer to a deva's question—*nāma*, more than anything else, brings everything beneath its sway.[1]

[1] S. i. 39.

Nāmarūpa Sutta.—In him who contemplates the enjoyment of all that makes for fettering there comes descent of name-and-shape. The remaining links in the chain of causation follow on this.[1]

[1] S. ii. 90.

Nāmarūpaparicccheda.—An Abhidhamma-treatise in verse, in thirteen chapters, by **Anuruddha** of **Kāñcipura.** There are two ṭīkās on it, one by **Vācissara** and the other by **Sumaṅgala.**[1]

[1] Gv. 61, 71; Sās. 69; P.L.C. 173 f.

Nāmarūpasamāsa.—Also called the **Khemppakaraṇa.** An Abhidhamma treatise by **Khema Thera.** A ṭīkā on it was written by **Vācissāra.**[1]

[1] Gv. 61, 71; P.L.C. 155 f.; published in *J.P.T.S.* 1915.

Nāmasiddhi Jātaka (No. 97).—Once the Bodhisatta was a famous teacher of **Takkasilā,** and among his pupils was one named **Pāpaka.** He, wishing for a less ill-omened name, consulted his teacher. The Bodhisatta suggested that Pāpaka should travel and find a suitable name. He came back a wiser man, for he discovered that "Jīvakas" died and that "Dhanapālīs" grovelled in poverty—the name signified nothing.

The story was related in reference to a monk called Pāpaka who wished to change his name. The two are identical.[1]

[1] J. i. 401 ff.

Nāmācāradīpanī.—An Abhidhamma-treatise, probably composed by **Chapaṭa.**[1]

[1] Bode: *op. cit.*, 18.

1. **Nārada.**—The ninth of the twenty-four Buddhas; he was born in the **Dhanañjaya** park at **Dhaññavatī,** his father being king **Sudeva** and his mother **Anomā.** For nine thousand years he lived as a layman in three palaces: **Jitā, Vijitā** and **Abhirāmā.**[1] His wife was **Jitasenā** (*v.l.* **Vijitasenā**), and his son **Nanduttara.** He made his Renunciation on foot accompanied by his retinue. He practised austerities for only seven days, then, having accepted a meal of milk-rice from his wife, he sat at the foot of a *mahāsoṇa*-tree, on grass given by the park-keeper **Sudassana.** His first sermon was preached in the **Dhanañjaya** Park. His body was eighty-eight cubits high, and his aura always spread round him to a distance of one league. He died at the age of ninety thousand years in **Sudassana,** and his thūpa was four leagues high. **Bhaddasāla** and **Jitamitta** were his chief monks and **Uttarā** and **Phaggunā** his chief nuns. **Vāseṭṭha** was his personal attendant, and chief among his patrons were **Uggarinda** and **Vasabha,** and **Indavarī** and **Caṇḍī.** Among his converts were the Nāga-kings **Mahādona** and **Verocana.** The Bodhisatta was a Jaṭila in Himavā, and the Buddha, with his followers, visited his hermitage, where they were fed for seven days and received gifts of red sandalwood.[2]

[1] BuA. calls them **Vijita, Vijitāvī** and **Jitābhirāma.**

[2] Bu. x. 1 ff.; BuA. 151 ff.; J. i. 35 f.

2. **Nārada.**—The personal attendant of **Sujāta** Buddha.[1]

[1] Bu. xiii. 25.

3. **Nārada.**—A brahmin in the time of **Padumuttara** Buddha, who praised the Buddha in three stanzas. He was a former birth of **Nāgita** (or **Atthasandassaka) Thera.**[1]

[1] ThagA. i. 185; Ap. i. 168.

4. **Nārada.**—A brahmin in the time of **Atthadassī** Buddha, a former birth of **Paviṭṭha** (or **Ekadaṃsanīya**) **Thera.** He was also called **Kesava.**[1]

[1] ThagA. i. 185; Ap. i. 168 f.

5. **Nārada.**—Minister of **Brahmadatta,** king of Benares. He was entrusted with escorting the ascetic **Kesava,** when he fell ill, to **Kappa's** hermitage in Himavā. Nārada is identified with **Sāriputta.** For details see the **Kesava Jātaka.**[1]

[1] J. iii. 143 ff., 362; DhA. i. 344.

6. **Nārada.**—A sage, younger brother of **Kāḷadevala** and pupil of **Jotipāla (Sarabhaṅga).** He lived in the **Majjhimapadesa** in **Arañjaragiri.** He became enamoured of a courtesan, and was saved only through the intervention of Sarabhaṅga. For details see the **Indriya Jātaka.**[1]

[1] J. iii. 463 ff.; v. 133 f.

7. **Nārada.**—An ascetic, son of the ascetic **Kassapa.** He was tempted by a maiden fleeing from brigands, but his father came to his rescue. For details see the **Culla-Nārada Jātaka.**[1]

[1] J. iv. 220 ff.

8. **Nārada.**—King of **Mithilā,** seventh in direct descent from **Sādhīna.** He is identified with **Ānanda.** For details see the **Sādhīna Jātaka.**[1]

[1] J. iv. 355 ff.

9. **Nārada.**—A brahmin sage, called a *devabrāhmaṇa*, and **Nāradadeva.** One day, having wandered about in **Tāvatiṃsa,** he was returning to his dwelling in **Kañcanaguhā** holding a **Pāricchattaka-**flower over his head, when the four daughters of **Sakka—Āsā, Saddhā, Sirī** and **Hirī**—asked him to give it to them. He agreed to give it to that one among them whom they should choose as their queen. They sought the advice of their father, who directed them to **Macchariya-Kosiya.** Kosiya decided in favour of Hirī. Nārada is identified with **Sāriputta.** For details see the **Sudhābhojana Jātaka.**[1] It is probably this same Nārada who is mentioned as being present when **Kuṇāla** (*q.v.*) delivered his famous diatribe against women. He is described as possessing the *pañcābhiññā* and as being attended by ten thousand ascetics. When Kuṇāla had finished his discourse, Nārada supplemented it with all he knew of the vices of women.[2] He is also mentioned as having admonished **Mahā-**

[1] J. v. 392 ff. [2] *Ibid.*, 424, 450 ff., 456.

Janaka when the latter renounced the world. In that context, Nārada is described as belonging to the **Kassapa-gotta.**[3]

[3] J. vi. 56, 58, 68. In SNA. ii. 359 he is called **Narāda-Devala.** This may be a wrong reading for **Nāradadeva.**

10. **Nārada.**—The Bodhisatta born as a Mahā Brahmā. He helped **Rujā** to convince her father, **Aṅgati,** of the truth as declared by her. He came down to earth and frightened Aṅgati by revealing to him the horrors of hell. In this context he is described as belonging to the **Kassapa-gotta.** For details see the **Mahānāradakassapa Jātaka.**[1]

[1] J. vi. 220, 242 ff.; Ap. ii. 483.

11. **Nārada.**—A celebrated physician,[1] probably identical with the famous sage, No. 9, above.

[1] Mil. 272.

12. **Nārada.**—The fifth future Buddha.[1]

[1] Anāgat. p. 40.

13. **Nārada.**—A Thera, mentioned once as staying at the **Ghositārāma** in **Kosambī,** with **Mūsila, Saviṭṭha,** and **Ānanda.** In the course of discussion he declares that, though aware of the nature of nibbāna, he is not an arahant.[1] Elsewhere[2] he is mentioned as staying in the **Kukkuṭārāma** in **Pāṭaliputta.** At that time King **Muṇḍa** was grieving over the death of his wife, **Bhaddā,** to the neglect of everything else, and his treasurer, **Piyaka,** suggested that he should visit Nārada. The king agreed, and Nārada preached to him on the inevitableness of old age, disease, death, etc. Muṇḍa was consoled, and buried the body of his wife which he had till then preserved.

He may be identical with the Thera mentioned in the Petavatthu Commentary[3] as finding out from various petas the stories of their deeds, and in the Vimānavatthu Commentary[4] as visiting various vimānas in the course of his wanderings among the deva-worlds (*devacārikā*). He is stated as having repeated the stories he learnt to the *dhammasaṅgāhakas* to be embodied in their rescensions.

[1] S. ii. 115 f.
[2] A. iii. 57 f.
[3] PvA. 2, 10, 11, 14, 204, 208, 210, 211.
[4] VvA. 165, 169, 203.

14. **Nārada.**—The Bodhisatta born as an ascetic. For his story see *s.v.* **Devala.**

15. **Nārada.**—A Yakkha who presided over **Nāradakūṭa.** Offerings, which included a man from each village, were brought to him once a year. **Dīpaṅkara** Buddha visited him and, after performing many miracles, converted him. He, with ten thousand other Yakkhas, became a sotāpanna.[1]

[1] Bu. ii. 199; BuA. 101 f.

16. **Nārada.**—A class of devas mentioned, with the **Pabbatas,** as being wise.[1]

[1] SN. vs. 543; SNA. ii. 435; see also J. vi. 568, 571; Mtu. iii. 401.

17. **Nārada.**—An ascetic, also called **Kassapa.** A former birth of **Caṅkolapupphiya**[1] (*q.v.*).

[1] Ap. i. 215.

18. **Nārada.**—An ascetie, also called **Kassapa,** a former birth of **Ekāsanadāyaka**[1] (*q.v.*).

[1] Ap. ii. 381.

Nāradakūṭa.—A mountain, the dwelling-place of the Yakkha **Nārada** 15 (*q.v.*).[1]

[1] Bu. ii. 199.

1. **Nārāyana.**—The name of a god (Viṣṇu).[1]

[1] *E.g.*, Cv. xlvii. 25.

2. **Nārāyana.**—A general of **Parakkamabāhu I.,** in charge of **Anurādhapura.** He rose in rebellion against the king and was slain in battle.[1]

[1] Cv. lxxii. 65.

3. **Nārāyana.**—A Damiḷa chief, one of the three Vīrapparāyaras. He was an ally of **Laṅkāpura,** general of **Parakkamabāhu I.**[1]

[1] Cv. lxxvii. 6.

Nārāyana-saṅghāṭa-bala.—The name given to a certain measure of physical strength. It was the equivalent of the strength of ten **Chaddanta** elephants and was the strength of the Buddha.[1]

[1] VibhA. 397; SNA. ii. 401.

Nārivaḍḍhana.—One of the palaces occupied by **Sumaṅgala** Buddha in his last lay life.[1]

[1] BuA. 125; but see Bu. v. 22, where other names are given.

Nārivana.—A grove in **Himavā** where grew flowers shaped like the bodies of women.[1]

[1] J. v. 152.

Nārivasabha.—One of the palaces occupied by **Sikhī** Buddha in his last lay life.[1]

[1] BuA. 201; but Bu (xxi. 16) gives other names.

1. **Nārivāhana.**—Son of **Sujāta.** He lived in **Nārivāhananagara,** and when the Buddha **Tissa** came there, he entertained him and the monks for seven days, and at the end of that time handed the kingdom over to his son and joined the Order.[1]

[1] BuA. 190.

2. **Nārivāhana.**—A city, capital of King **Nārivāhana,** in the time of **Tissa** Buddha (see above) and of **Upasanta,** in the time of **Vessabhū** Buddha.[1]

[1] BuA. 206.

Nārisa.—See **Nārī.**

Nārī.—One of the palaces occupied by **Tissa** Buddha in his last lay life.[1]

[1] Bu. xviii. 17; BuA (188) calls it **Nārisa.**

Nāla, Nālaka, Nālika (also **Nāḷa,** etc.).—A brahmin village **in Magadha,** not far from **Rājagaha.** It was the township of the **Upatissas** (hence also called **Upatissagāma**), and it was there that **Sāriputta** and other members of his family were born.[1] It was also the birthplace of **Mahā-Gavaccha.**[2] **Sāriputta** seems to have continued to reside there from time to time, even after he joined the Order,[3] and when his death drew near, he went back to Nālakagāma and, having made his mother a sotāpanna, died in the room where he was born.[4]

[1] SA. ii. 172; ThagA. i. 108; ii. 93; ThigA. 162; VvA. 149, 156, 158, 164; Mtu (iii. 56) calls it Nālanda.

[2] ThagA. i. 57.

[3] See his discussions with **Jambukhādaka** (S. iv. 251) and with **Sāmaṇḍakāni** (A. v. 120, 121); DhA. iv. 164 f.

[4] S. v. 161; J. i. 391; v. 125; UdA. 322, etc.

Nālaka.—Nephew of **Asita (Kāḷadevala).** When Asita realized that he would not live to see the Buddha, he sought out Nālaka and asked him to leave the world at once and become an ascetic and hold himself in readiness to profit by the Buddha's Enlightenment. This Nālaka did, though possessing eighty thousand crores of wealth, and he spent his time in Himavā. When the time came, he visited the Buddha seven days after the Buddha's first sermon and questioned him on the **Moneyya-paṭipadā** (also called the **Nālakapaṭipadā,** because it is included in the **Nālaka Sutta**). Nālaka retired once more into Himavā and there attained arahantship. There he spent seven months leaning against a golden rock, practising *paṭipadā* in its highest form. After his death the Buddha, with his monks, visited the scene of his death, cremated his remains, and had a cetiya built over them.

It is said that Nālaka's aspiration to learn and practise the Moneyya-paṭipadā was made in the time of **Padumuttara** Buddha.[1]

[1] J. i. 55; SNA. ii. 483 ff., 501. The story as drawn from Thibetan sources differs greatly from this story. (See, *e.g.*, Rockhill: *op. cit.*, p. 18, 45 f.). In the Mahāvastu (iii. 380, 387) he is called Kātyāyana.

Nālaka Sutta.—Preached, seven days after the first sermon, to **Nālaka** (*q.v.*), nephew of **Asita.** The sutta itself is a discourse on the state of a recluse (*Moneyyapaṭipadā*), but there are twenty introductory verses (called *Vatthugāthā*) giving the story of Asita and Nālaka.[1]

The sutta is also called **Nālaka-paṭipadā.**[2]

[1] SN. vs. 679-723; SNA. ii. 501.

[2] J. i. 55.

Nālagāma.—A village in the **Malaya** district in Ceylon.[1]

[1] Cv. lxx. 296.

1. **Nālandā.**—A town near **Rājagaha,** (according to Buddhaghosa[1]) one league away. The Buddha is mentioned as having several times stayed there during his residence in **Pāvārika's** mango-grove, and while there he had discussions with **Upāli-gahapati** and **Dīghatapassī,**[2] with **Kevaṭṭa,**[3] and also several conversations with **Asibandhakaputta.**[4] The Buddha visited Nālandā during his last tour through Magadha, and it was there that **Sāriputta** uttered his "lion's roar," affirming his faith in the Buddha, shortly before his death.[5] The road from Rājagaha to Nālandā passed through **Ambalaṭṭhikā,**[6] and from Nālandā it went on to **Pāṭaligāma.**[7] Between Rājagaha and Nālandā was situated the **Bahuputta-cetiya.**[8] According to the **Kevaṭṭa Sutta,**[9] in the Buddha's time Nālandā was already an influential and prosperous town, thickly populated, though it was not till later that it became the centre of learning

[1] DA. i. 35.

[2] S. ii. 110; M. i. 376 ff.

[3] D. i. 211 ff.

[4] S. ii. 311-23.

[5] D. ii. 81 f.; iii. 99 ff.; S. v. 159 ff.

[6] D. ii. 81; Vin. ii. 287.

[7] D. ii. 84.

[8] S. ii. 220.

[9] D. i. 211.

for which it afterwards became famous. There is a record in the Saṃyutta Nikāya,[10] of the town having been the victim of a severe famine during the Buddha's time.

Nālandā was the residence of **Soṇṇadinnā.**[11] **Nigaṇṭha Nātaputta** (*q.v.*) is several times mentioned as staying at Nālandā, which was evidently a centre of activity of the **Nigaṇṭhas** (*q.v.*).

Hsouien Thsang[12] gives several explanations of the name Nālandā. One is that it was named after the Nāga who lived in a tank in the middle of the mango-grove. Another—and accepted by him—is that the Bodhisatta once had his capital here and gave "alms without intermission," hence the name.

Nālanda is, in the northern books, given as the name of Sāriputta's birthplace (see Nālaka). Nālanda is identified with the modern Baragaon.[13]

[10] S. iv. 322.
[11] VvA. 144.
[12] Beal: *op. cit.*, ii. 167 f.
[13] CAGI. 537.

2. **Nālandā.**—A village in the central province of Ceylon. Once **Parakkamabāhu I.** occupied a camp there, and it is several times mentioned in the accounts of his campaigns.[1]

[1] Cv. lxx. 167, 207; lxxii. 169.

1. **Nālandā Sutta.**—A conversation between the Buddha and **Upāligahapati** in **Pāvārika's** mango-grove, as to why some beings attain full freedom in this world while others do not.[1]

[1] S. iv. 110.

2. **Nālandā Sutta.**—**Sāriputta's** affirmation of faith in the Buddha—there never was, nor is, nor shall be, anyone possessing higher wisdom than the Buddha.[1]

[1] S. v. 159 f.; *cp.* D. ii. 81 and D. iii. 99 ff.

1. **Nālā.**—A village in **Magadha,** near the Bodhi-tree at **Gayā.** It was the birthplace of **Upaka.**[1] The Buddhavaṃsa Commentary[2] speaks of a brahmin village Nālā where the Buddha spent his eleventh rainy season.

[1] Thig. 294; ThigA. 225.
[2] p. 3.

2. **Nālā.**—Wife of the **Ādipāda Udaya.** She was the daughter of his maternal uncle and was under the protection of King **Sena I.,** but Udaya married her during an absence of the king and took her to **Pulatthinagara.** The king, however, forgave him.[1]

[1] Cv. l. 9; see also Cv. *Trs.* i. 138, n. 3.

Nālāgiri.—An elephant of the royal stalls at **Rājagaha.** **Devadatta,** after several vain attempts to kill the Buddha, obtained **Ajātasattu's** consent to use Nālagiri as a means of encompassing the Buddha's death. The elephant, he said, knows nothing of the Buddha's virtues and will have no hesitation in destroying him. Nālagiri was a fierce animal, and in order to increase his fierceness, Devadatta instructed his keeper to give him twice his usual amount of toddy. Proclamation was made, by the beating of drums, that the streets of the city should be cleared as Nālāgiri would be let loose upon them. When the Buddha was informed of this and warned against going into the city for alms, he ignored the warning, and went into Rājagaha with the monks of the eighteen monasteries of the city. At the sight of Nālāgiri all the people fled in terror. **Ānanda,** seeing the elephant advancing towards the Buddha, went, in spite of the Buddha's orders to the contrary, and stood in front of the Buddha, who had to make use of his supernatural power to remove him from his place. Just then, a woman, carrying a child, saw the elephant coming and fled, in her terror dropping the child at the Buddha's feet. As the elephant was about to attack the child, the Buddha spoke to him, suffusing him with all the love at his command, and, stretching out his right hand, he stroked the animal's forehead. Thrilling with joy at the touch, Nālāgiri sank on his knees before the Buddha, and the Buddha taught him the Dhamma. It is said that had the elephant not been a wild beast he would have become a sotāpanna. Marvelling at the sight, the assembled populace threw all their ornaments on the elephant's body, covering it entirely, and henceforth the elephant was known as **Dhanapāla (Dhanapālaka).** The Buddha returned to **Veḷuvana,** and that day, at eventide, preached the **Cullahaṃsa Jātaka** in praise of Ānanda's loyalty to himself.[1] It is said[2] that nine hundred million living beings, who saw the miracle, realized the Truth.

The Bodhisatta, in a past life, was once riding an elephant when he saw a Pacceka Buddha. Intoxicated by his own glory, he made the elephant charge the Pacceka Buddha. It was as a result of this action that the Buddha, in this birth, was charged by Nālāgiri.[3] *cp.* **Doṇamukha.**

[1] Vin. ii. 194 f.: J. v. 333 ff.; Avadānaś i. 177.

[2] Mil. 349.

[3] UdA. 265; Ap. i. 300.

Nālika.—A mountain in Himavā, on the way to the **Mucalinda Lake.** **Vessantara** passed it on his way to **Vaṅkagiri.**[1]

[1] J. vi. 518, 519.

Nālikera.—An island, with many attendant islands. When the country of King **Bharu** (*q.v.*) was destroyed because he took bribes, those who had blamed him for his unrighteousness were saved and found shelter in the islands round Nālikera.[1]

[1] J. ii. 173.

Nālikeradāyaka Thera.—An arahant. Ninety-one kappas ago he was a park-keeper in **Bandhumatī** and gave to the Buddha a *nālikera*-fruit.[1] He is probably identical with **Kuṇḍala Thera**[2] or with **Khitaka Thera.**[3]

[1] Ap. ii. 447 f. [2] ThagA. i. 72 [3] *Ibid.*, 315.

Nālikeramahāthambha.—A tank in Ceylon, restored by **Parakkamabāhu I.**[1]

[1] Cv. lxxix. 33.

Nālikeravatthutittha.—A ford in the **Mahāvāḷukagaṅgā.**[1]

[1] Cv. lxxii. 14.

Nāḷaka Thera.—Given as an example of an *ugghaṭitaññūpuggala*. After hearing, only once, the teaching of Pacceka Buddhas, he became himself a Pacceka Buddha.[1]

[1] AA. i. 354.

Nāḷika.—A Damiḷa general, in charge of **Nāḷisobbha.** He was defeated by **Duṭṭhagāmaṇi.**[1]

[1] Mhv. xxv. 11.

Nāḷikīra (Nāḷikera).—King of **Dantapura** in **Kāliṅga.** Once, a holy ascetic came with five hundred others and took up his abode in the royal park. Nāḷikīra visited the ascetic and was displeased with the questions he was asked as to whether he ruled his people righteously. He therefore invited the ascetics to his palace, filled their bowls with filth, and had them beaten and attacked by dogs. The earth opened and swallowed the king. He was born in the **Sunakha-niraya,** where he had to undergo various kinds of tortures. His kingdom was destroyed and became a waste.[1] The story was evidently widely current in India.

[1] J. v. 119, 143, 144 f.; MA. ii. 602 ff.; Mtu. iii. 361, 368, 369.

Nāḷijaṅgha.—A brahmin, whom **Mallikā** sent to the Buddha to find out if it were true that the Buddha had said that loved ones brought sorrow and tribulation.[1]

[1] M. ii. 108.

Nāḷisobbha.—A Damiḷa stronghold in charge of **Nāḷika,** and captured by **Duṭṭhagāmaṇi.**[1]

[1] Mhv. xxv. 11.

1. **Nāvā Sutta,** also called **Dhamma Sutta.**—It was preached in reference to **Sāriputta's** habit when he was on tour of worshipping the direction in which his teacher, **Assaji,** lived. Others noticed this and said it was a relic of his old brahmanic habit of worshipping the different quarters. But the Buddha said there was no need of Sāriputta to do that, for even the devas themselves worshipped him. In the sutta the wise man is compared to a ship (*nāvā*) which takes many others across.[1]

[1] SN. vs. 316-23; SNA. i. 325 ff.

2. **Nāvā Sutta.**—See **Vāsijaṭa Sutta.**

3. **Nāvā Sutta.** If a sea-going vessel is left stranded on the bank, it is dried up by the wind and sun in the dry season and rotted by water in the rains—so are the fetters in the case of a monk who cultivates the Ariyan Eightfold Path.[1]

[1] S. v. 51.

Nāvāgirisa.—A village in Ceylon, where **Parakkamabāhu I.** spent some time before coming to the throne.[1]

[1] Cv. lxvi. 92.

Nāvindakī.—One of King **Eḷeyya's** guards. He was a follower of **Rāmaputta.**[1]

[1] A. ii. 180.

Nāsinnagāma.—A village in the **Āḷisāra** district of Ceylon.[1]

[1] Cv. lxx. 172.

"**Nāsenti**" **Sutta.**—The five powers of woman—beauty, wealth, kindred, sons and virtue. But if she has no virtue, the possession of other qualities will not prevent her from being cast out.[1]

[1] S. iv. 247.

1. **Nikaṭa.**—An upāsaka of **Ñātikā.** After death he was born in the **Suddhāvāsā,** there to pass away.[1]

[1] S. v. 358 f.; D. ii. 91 f.

2. **Nikaṭa.**—One of several eminent theras mentioned as staying in the **Kūṭāgārasāla** in **Vesāli.** When the Buddha came there, **Licchavis** crowded out the place with all their retinues, and Nikaṭa and his colleagues, desiring solitude, retired to the **Gosiṅgasālavana.**[1]

[1] A. v. 133 f.

Nikaṭṭha Sutta.—Four kinds of people in the world: those with debased bodies and noble minds, with noble bodies and debased minds, with both mind and body noble, with both debased.[1]

[1] A. ii. 137 f.

Nikapennaka-padhānaghara.—A building on the **Cittalapabbata,** the residence of **Cūḷasumana.**[1]

[1] Vsm. ii. 634; see also **Niṅkapoṇṇa,** below.

Nikumba.—The name of a country.[1]

[1] Mil. 327.

Nikkhanta Sutta.—Once **Vaṅgīsa,** soon after his ordination, was staying at the **Aggālava-cetiya** with his tutor, **Nigrodha-Kappa.** During his tutor's absence, a number of gaily-dressed women came to the vihāra, and Vaṅgīsa was greatly perturbed in mind. But he put forth great effort, and thinking of the loyalty he owed to the Buddha, conquered his disaffection.[1]

[1] S. i. 185 f.; the verses are also found in Thag. (1209-13).

Nigaṇṭha-Nāta(Nātha-)-putta.—One of six eminent teachers, contemporary with the Buddha; he is described as a heretic (*aññatitthiya*[1]). He was leader of a sect known as the **Nigaṇṭhā,** and a summary of his teachings is found in the **Sāmaññaphala Sutta.**[2] "A Nigaṇṭha is restrained with a fourfold restraint (*cātuyāma-saṃvara*)—he is restrained as regards all water, restrained as regards all evil, all evil has he washed away, and he lives suffused with the sense of evil held at bay. And, because of this fourfold restraint, he is called a *Nigaṇṭha* (free from bonds), *gatatta* (one whose heart has been in the attainment of his aim), *yattata* (one whose heart is under command) and *ṭhitatta* (one whose heart is fixed)."[3]

[1] *E.g.*, S. i. 66.

[2] D. i. 57; DA. i. 166.

[3] The meaning of this fourfold restraint is not clear; for a discussion of this *cātuyāma-saṃvara,* see Barua: *Pre-Bhuddhistic Indian Philosophy,* pp. 378 f. The first is evidently the well-known rule of the Jains against drinking cold water, as it contains "souls" (*cp.* Mil. 259 ff.). The Buddha taught a corresponding fourfold restraint, which consisted of observing the four precepts against injury, stealing, unchastity and lying (D. iii. 48 f.).

Nātaputta is also stated[4] to have claimed omniscience—to be all-knowing, all-seeing, to have all-comprising (*aparisesa*) knowledge and vision. "Whether I walk or stand or sleep or wake," he is mentioned as saying, "my knowledge and vision are always, and without a break, present before me." He taught that past deeds should be extirpated by severe austerities, fresh deeds should be avoided by inaction. By expelling through penance all past misdeeds and by not committing fresh misdeeds, the future became cleared. From the destruction of deeds results the destruction of *dukkha*; this leads to the destruction of **vedanā**. Thus all *dukkha* is exhausted and one passes beyond (the round of existence). It is said[5] that Nātaputta did not employ the term **kamma** in his teaching; he used, instead, the word *daṇḍa*; and that, according to him, the *daṇḍa* of deed was far more criminal than the *daṇḍas* of word and mind. He is said to have shown no hesitation in declaring the destinies of his disciples after death[6]; but **Sakuludāyi** says[7] that when asked a question as to the past, he skipped from one matter to another and dismissed the question, evincing irritation, bad temper and resentment.

Only one discussion is recorded between Nātaputta and a follower of the Buddha, and that was with **Citta-gahapati** at **Macchikā-Saṇḍa.**[8] He praises Citta at the outset of the discussion, holding him up as an example to his own flock, and agreeing with Citta that knowledge is more excellent than faith. But later, when Citta claims knowledge of the four *jhānas*, Nātaputta is represented as condemning him for a deceitful man. Citta, thereupon, asks him ten questions[9] and, getting no answer, leaves him.

The **Devadaha Sutta**[10] contains a detailed analysis and criticism, attributed to the Buddha, of the beliefs and teachings of the Nigaṇṭhas. He there selects for his condemnation ten of their operative utterances, major and minor, and proves that the efforts and strivings of the Nigaṇṭhas are fruitless.

[4] *E.g.*, M. ii. 31; A. i. 220; M. i. 92 f.; also M. ii. 214 ff. It is curious, in view of this statement of Nātaputta's doctrine of inaction, that the main ground on which he is stated to have objected to **Sīha's** visit to the Buddha, was that the Buddha was an *akiriyavādī* (A. iv. 180).

[5] M. i. 371. *Daṇḍa* probably means sins or hurtful acts. Buddhaghosa says (MA. ii. 595 ff.) that the Jain idea was that *citta* (the *manodaṇḍa*) did not come into bodily acts or into words—which were irresponsible and mechanical, like the stirring and sighing of boughs in the wind.

[6] S. iv. 398.

[7] M. ii. 31; also *ibid.*, i. 93; and ii. 214 f.; the Nigaṇṭhas admit they did not know of the past.

[8] S. iv. 298 ff.

[9] The Commentary (SA. iii. 99) explains that the questions Citta asked were the same as the **Kumārapañhā** (*q.v.*).

[10] M. ii. 214; *cp.* **Cūla-Dukkhakkhandha Sutta** (M. i. 91 ff.; also A. v. 150; D. iii. 119).

Nātaputta is said[11] to have claimed miraculous powers, but he did not, in fact, possess them. When, for instance, the **Rājagaha-seṭṭhi** offered his bowl of red sandal-wood to anybody who could remove it from its perch, Nātaputta tried to obtain it by a ruse, but was unable to deceive the seṭṭhi.

The books contain the names of several disciples of Nātaputta, among them a deva called **Niṅka.**[12] Nātaputta is so convinced of the truth and the irrefutableness of his own doctrines, that he actually encourages his disciples to hold discussions with the Buddha. Some, like **Dīgha Tapassī,** come away unscathed, without having carried the discussion to any conclusion; others are mentioned as being convinced by the Buddha in the end and as becoming his disciples. Such, for instance, are **Asibandhakaputta**[13] and **Abhayarājakumāra.**[14] Nātaputta tries, without success, to dissuade **Sīha,** general of the Licchavis, from visiting the Buddha.[15] Sīha goes and is converted. The next day he holds an almsgiving, on a grand scale, to the Buddha and his monks, at which flesh is served. It is said that Nātaputta went about **Vesāli,** sneering at the Buddha for encouraging slaughter. The Buddha, hearing of this, relates the **Telovāda Jātaka** (*q.v.*),[16] to show that in the past, too, Nātaputta had sneered at him for a similar reason. Nātaputta is identified with the rich man of the Jātaka. In the **Bāveru Jātaka**[17] he is identified with the crow who lost all his honour and glory when approached by the peacock, who was the Bodhisatta.

But the greatest blow to Nātaputta was when **Upāli-gahapati**[18] joined the Buddha. Nātaputta had allowed Upāli to visit him in spite of the warning of Dīgha-Tapassī as to the Buddha's arresting personality. But Nātaputta thought Upāli would be proof against it, and, on hearing that he had renounced his allegiance to the Nigaṇṭhas, refused to believe it until he could verify the information himself. The discovery of the apostasy of Upāli prostrated him with grief; he vomited hot blood and had to be carried away on a litter from **Bālaka,** where he was then living, to **Pāvā.** There, soon after, he died, and immediately great dissensions arose among his followers. When the Buddha heard of the quarrels, he remarked that it was only to be expected.[19]

Nigaṇṭha-Nātaputta is the name by which the Jaina teacher, Mahāvīra, was known to his contemporaries. He was also called

11 DhA. iii. 201.

12 S. i. 66; the Buddha's own paternal uncle, **Vappa** (*q.v.*), was a follower of the Nigaṇṭhas.

13 S. iv. 317 ff.

14 M. i. 392 ff.

15 A. iv. 180 ff.

16 J. ii. 262 f.; Vin. i. 233 ff.

17 J. iii. 126 f.

18 M. i. 373 ff.

19 *Ibid.*, ii. 243 f.; D. iii. 117, 210; it is stated that the quarrel was deliberately fostered by Nātaputta before his death. See *s.v.* **Nigaṇṭhā.**

Vardhamāna. Nāta (or Nāya) was the name of his clan,[20] which belonged to Vesāli. According to Jaina tradition, his father's personal name was Siddhatha, and he was a Kṣatriya, his mother being Triśālā.[21]

[20] SNA. (ii. 423) says Nāta was the name of his father.

[21] For an account of Mahāvīra's life and philosophy, see Barua: *op. cit.*, pp. 372 ff.

Nigaṇṭhā.—The name given to the Jains, the followers of **Nigaṇṭha Nātaputta.** Unlike the **Acelakas,** they wore one garment, a covering in front. But when praised for their modesty, they answered that their reason for wearing a garment was to prevent dust and dirt from falling into their alms-dishes. For even dust and dirt are actual individuals and endowed with the principle of life.[1] The chief precepts of the Nigaṇṭhā are included in the *cātuyāmasaṃvara*—the fourfold restraint.[2] The chief centres of the Nigaṇṭhas, in the time of the Buddha, seem to have been **Vesāli**[3] and **Nālandā,**[4] though they had settlements in other important towns, such as **Rājagaha.**[5] The books contain several names besides that of Nātaputta of distinguished members of the Nigaṇṭha Order—*e.g.*, **Dīgha-Tapassī,** and **Saccaka** (*q.v.*), and also of several women, **Saccā, Lolā, Avavādakā** and **Paṭācārā.**[6] The lay followers of the Nigaṇṭhas wore white garments.[7]

In the Chaḷabhijāti-classification of **Pūraṇa Kassapa,** the Ekasāṭaka-Nigaṇṭhas occupied the third rank, the red.[8] The Buddha condemned the Nigaṇṭhas as unworthy in ten respects: they were without faith, unrighteous, without fear and shame, they chose wicked men as friends, extolled themselves and disparaged others, were greedy of present gain, obstinate, untrustworthy, sinful in their thoughts, and held wrong views.[9] Their fast resembled a herdsman looking after the kine by day, which were restored to their owners at eventide.[10] The Nigaṇṭhas were so called because they claimed to be free from all bonds (*aṃhākaṃ ganthanakileso palibujjhanakileso natthi, kilesagaṇṭhirahitā mayan ti evam vāditāya laddhanāmavasena Nigaṇṭho*).[11]

The Buddhist books record[12] that there was great dissension among the Nigaṇṭhas after the death of Nātaputta at **Pāvā.** The Commentaries

[1] DhA. iii. 489.

[2] For their beliefs and practices see *s.v.* **Nigaṇṭha Nātaputta.**

[3] *E.g.*, J. iii. 1; M. i. 228.

[4] M. i. 371. The chief patrons of the Buddha's time were Sīhasenāpati in Vesāli, Upaligahapati in Nālandā and Vappa the Sakyan in Kapilavatthu (AA. ii. 751).

[5] *E.g.*, at **Kālasilā,** on the slopes of **Isigili** (M. i. 92).

[6] J. iii. 1.

[7] M. ii. 244.

[8] A. iii. 384.

[9] A. v. 150.

[10] *Ibid.*, i. 205 f.

[11] *E.g.*, MA. i. 423.

[12] M. ii. 243 f.; D. iii. 117, 210.

state[13] that Nātaputta, realizing on his death-bed the folly and futility of his teaching, wished his followers to accept the Buddha's teaching. In order to bring this about, he taught his doctrine in two different ways to two different pupils, just before his death. To the one he said that his teaching was Nihilism (*uccheda*), and to the other that it was Eternalism (*sassata*). As a result, they quarrelled violently among themselves, and the Order broke up.[14]

There is evidence in the Jātakas to show that the Nigaṇṭha Order was in existence prior to the life of the Buddha. **Saccatapāvī,** mentioned in the **Kuṇāla Jātaka,**[15] is described as a *setasamaṇī*, and may well have belonged to the Order of the Śvetambaras, while in the **Mahābodhi Jātaka**[16] mention is made of a teacher who is identified with Nigaṇṭha Nātaputta himself.

There seems to have been a settlement of Nigaṇṭhas in Ceylon from very early times. When **Paṇḍukābhaya** laid out the city of **Anurādhapura,** he built also hermitages for several Nigaṇṭhas—**Jotiya, Giri** and **Kumbhaṇḍa.**[17] These continued to be inhabited even after the establishment of Buddhism in the Island, for we hear of them in the reign of **Vaṭṭagāmaṇī** (*circa* 44 A.C.). When Vaṭṭagāmaṇī pulled down the residence of the Nigaṇṭha Giri, because of his disloyalty to the king, he built on its site the **Abhayagiri-vihāra.**[18]

[13] DA. iii. 906; MA. ii. 831.

[14] That the Nigaṇṭhas lasted till, at least, the time of **Nāgasena,** is admitted (Mil. p. 4) by the fact that Milinda was asked to consult a teacher called Nigaṇṭha Nātaputta, who, if at all historical, was probably the direct successor to the teacher of the same name, contemporary with the Buddha.

[15] J. v. 427.

[16] J. v. 246.

[17] Mhv. x. 97 f.

[18] *Ibid.*, xxxiii. 42 f.

Nigamaggāmappāsāda.—A monastery in **Gaṅgāsiripura,** restored by **Vijayabāhu IV.**[1]

[1] Cv. lxxxviii. 49.

Nigamavāsī-Tissa.—A thera of a market-town (*nigama*) near **Sāvatthi.** He had the reputation of being contented, purged and pure; he went for his alms only in the village of his kinsmen. When it was reported to the Buddha that Tissa lived in intimate association with his relations, the Buddha questioned him and accepted his explanation, praising him, and remarking that Tissa's good qualities were the result of association with himself; he then related the **Mahāsuka Jātaka.**[1]

[1] DhA. i. 283-6. The introductory story of the Jātaka (*q.v.*), however, gives a different reason for its recital (J. ii. 490 f.).

Nigaya.—A Damiḷa chief, ally of **Kulasekhara,** subdued by **Laṅkāpura.**[1]

[1] Cv. lxxvi. 316; lxxvii. 69.

Nigaḷadha.—A Damiḷa chief, ruler of **Velaṅkuṇḍi** and ally of **Kulasekhara.** He was won over by **Laṅkāpura.**[1]

[1] Cv. lxxvi. 138; lxxvii. 10 f.; 89 ff.

Niguṇḍivālukā-tittha.—A ford in the **Mahāvālukanadī.**[1]

[1] Cv. lxxii. 37.

1. **Nigguṇḍipupphiya Thera.**—An arahant. Ninety-one kappas ago he was the monastery attendant (*ārāmika*) of **Vipassī** Buddha, and once gave a *nigguṇḍi* flower to the Buddha. Thirty-five kappas ago he was king, under the name of **Mahāpatāpa.**[1] He is probably identical with **Vīra Thera.**[2]

[1] Ap. i. 205.

[2] ThagA. i. 50 f.

2. **Nigguṇḍipupphiya Thera.**—An arahant. In the past he had been an inhabitant of the deva-world and listened to the preaching of a disciple of **Padumuttara** Buddha, called **Sumana.** He then offered a *nigguṇḍi* flower on the seat of the Buddha. In this life he entered the Order at the age of seven, and after listening to a sermon by **Ānanda** became an arahant. He was sixteen times king, under the names of **Abbuda** and **Nirabudda.**[1]

[1] Ap. i. 262 f.

1. **Nigrodha.**—A Paribbājaka. Once, when he was staying with a large number of colleagues at the **Udumbarikārāma** near **Rājagaha, Sandhāna,** on his way to see the Buddha, stopped him and entered into conversation. The Buddha, by his divine ear, hearing their talk, approached them and continued the discussion with Nigrodha; this discussion is recorded in the **Udumbarika Sīhanāda Sutta** (*q.v.*).[1]

[1] D. iii. 36 ff.; this discussion is also referred to in the **Kassapa-Sīhanāda** Sutta (D. i. 175 f.). There Nigrodha is said to have felt great joy, but this is not mentioned in the Udumbarika-Sīhanāda (see D. iii. 57).

2. **Nigrodha.**—The Bodhisatta born as the son of a Banker in **Rājagaha,** later becoming king of Benares. For details see the **Nigrodha Jātaka.**

3. **Nigrodha Thera.**—He belonged to an eminent brahmin family of **Sāvatthī.** On the day of the dedication of **Jetavana,** he saw the majesty of the Buddha and entered the Order, becoming an arahant soon after. Eighteen kappas ago, in the time of **Piyadassī** Buddha, he left great riches and became an ascetic, dwelling in a *sāla* grove. Once, seeing

the Buddha wrapped in *samādhi*, he built a bower over him, and stood there with clasped hands until the Buddha awoke from his *samādhi*. Then, at the Buddha's wish, the Saṅgha too came to the *sāla* grove, and in their presence the Buddha predicted the ascetic's future.[1]

Nigrodha is probably identical with **Sālamaṇḍapiya** of the Apadāna.[2]

[1] ThagA. i. 74 f.; Thag. 21.

[2] Ap. ii. 431 f.; but the same Apadāna verses are also given under **Tissa Thera** (ThagA. i. 273).

4. **Nigrodha.**—See **Nigrodhamiga** and **Vattabbaka-Nigrodha.**

5. **Nigrodha.**—A **Sākyan**, owner of the **Nigrodhārāma** (*q.v.*).[1]

[1] J. i. 88.

6. **Nigrodha.**—Commonly known as **Nigrodha-sāmaṇera.** He was the son of **Sumana,** the eldest of **Bimbisāra's** children, and his mother was **Sumanā.** When **Asoka** slew Sumana, his wife, who was with child, fled to a caṇḍāla village, where the guardian deity of a nigrodha tree built her a hut. Here she gave birth to her son, whom she named after her benefactor. The chief caṇḍāla looked after them. When Nigrodha was seven years old, the Thera **Mahāvaruṇa** ordained him, and he became an arahant in the tonsure hall. One day, while walking near the palace, Asoka saw him and, because of their connection in a past life, was attracted by him. Nigrodha had been one of the three brothers who gave honey to a Pacceka Buddha in a past life.[1] Nigrodha had called the Pacceka Buddha a caṇḍāla, hence he was born in a caṇḍāla village. Asoka invited Nigrodha to the palace and entertained him, and Nigrodha preached to him the **Appamāda Vagga.** The king was greatly pleased, and offered to give food daily at the palace to thirty-two monks in Nigrodha's name. It was this visit of Nigrodha to Asoka which ulti mately resulted in the conversion of the latter to the faith of the Buddha.[2] It is said[3] that Asoka paid great honour to Nigrodha throughout his life. Three times a day he sent to Nigrodha gifts of robes carried on the backs of elephants, with five hundred measures of perfume and five hundred caskets of garlands. All these Nigrodha would distribute among his colleagues, and most of the monks of Jambudīpa at that time wore robes which were the gift of Nigrodha.

[1] For the story see *s.v.* **Asoka** and Mhv. v. 49 ff.

[2] For details see *ibid.*, 37-72; Dpv. vi. 34 ff.; vii. 12, 31; Sp. i. 45 ff.

[3] MA. ii. 931.

7. **Nigrodha.**—Called **Māragiri.** A general of **Parakkamabāhu I.** He was stationed at **Uddhavāpi.**[1]

[1] Cv. lxxii. 164, 174.

Nigrodha Jātaka (No. 445).—A king, named **Magadha,** once reigned in **Rājagaha.** His son married a rich merchant's daughter, but she, because she was barren, lost favour. Thereupon she pretended to be with child, and when her time drew near, she journeyed to her home with an old nurse who was in the secret. On the way she found a child deserted by its mother, and, greatly rejoicing, she claimed it as her own. The child was the Bodhisatta and was called **Nigrodha.** His father found for him two companions: **Sakhā,** son of a merchant, and **Pottika,** son of a tailor. These three grew up together and were educated in **Takkasilā.** In the course of their travels, while his companions lay sleeping, Pottika heard a cock say that whoever ate its fat would become king, the flesh of its body commander-in-chief, and the flesh near its bones treasurer. Pottika killed the cock, gave to **Nigrodha** the fat, to Sākha the flesh of the body, while he himself ate the flesh near the bones. Immediately after, men, in search of a successor to the throne of Benares, chose Nigrodha, while the others accompanied him as commander-in-chief and treasurer. One day Nigrodha, wishing to have his parents near him, sent Pottika to fetch them from Rājagaha. On the way back he called at Sākha's house, but Sākha, who had a grievance against him for having given the cock's fat to Nigrodha, insulted him. When Pottika reported this to Nigrodha, he wished to have Sākha killed, but Pottika intervened on his behalf.

The story was related in reference to **Devadatta's** ingratitude. Sākha is identified with Devadatta and Pottika with **Ānanda.**[1]

[1] J. iv. 37 ff.

Nigrodha-aṅgana.—A locality in **Anurādhapura,** through which the *sīmā* of the **Mahāvihāra** passed.[1]

[1] Dpv. xiv. 34; Mbv. 136; Mhv. p. 332. vs. 14.

Nigrodha-Kappa Thera.—He was the preceptor (*upajjhāya*) of **Vaṅgīsa,** and together they lived in **Aggālava-cetiya,**[1] where Kappa died. When Vaṅgīsa questioned the Buddha as to the destiny of Kappa, the Buddha's answer was that he had completely passed away.[2] It is said[3] that Vaṅgīsa was away when Kappa died, and had also seen him sleeping with his hands curled up. This was unlike a *khīṇāsava,* but, in Kappa's case, it was due to long-continued habit. Vaṅgīsa, not knowing this, was assailed with doubts as to his teacher's attainments. Kappa was a *vihāragaruka*—that is, he attached importance to keeping to his cell. When he came back from his alms rounds, he would enter his cell and not

[1] S. i. 185.
[2] Thag. vs. 1263 ff.; SN. vs. 343 ff.
[3] ThagA. ii. 211; SNA. i. 346.

leave it again until evening or the next day. This caused disaffection in Vaṅgīsa's heart, which the latter quelled by force of reasoning.[4]

In Nigrodhakappa, Kappa was the thera's personal name, but the prefix Nigrodha was given because he attained arahantship at the foot of a *nigrodha* (banyan) tree.[5]

[4] S. i. 186; SA. i. 208.

[5] SNA. i. 346; because he dwelt under a banyan, says SA. i. 207.

Nigrodhapiṭṭhi.—A vihāra in Ceylon, the residence of **Mahāsīva Thera.**[1]

[1] MṬ. 555.

Nigrodhamāragallaka.—A place in **Rohaṇa,** mentioned in the campaigns of **Parakkamabāhu I.**[1]

[1] Cv. lxxv. 182.

Nigrodhamiga Jātaka (No. 12).—(Also called **Nigrodha Jātaka.**) Once the Bodhisatta was born as king of the deer and was called **Nigrodha.** With him was the leader of another herd, and he was called **Sākha.** There was an agreement between these two leaders that, on alternate days, a deer from their herd should offer itself to be killed by the king of Benares. One day the turn fell on a pregnant doe of Sākha's herd, and when she asked to be allowed to wait until she had brought forth her young she was refused by Sākha. She then appealed to Nigrodha, who took her turn on himself. Immunity had been granted to Nigrodha, and when his act was reported to the king, he came in person to enquire into the matter. On hearing the story, he was greatly moved, and promised immunity both to Nigrodha and the doe. But Nigrodha was not satisfied till the king promised immunity to all living beings. Later, on discovering that the deer, taking advantage of this, were destroying men's crops, Nigrodha gave orders to his herd to refrain from doing so.

The story was related in reference to the mother of **Kumāra Kassapa** (*q.v.*). She had joined the Order under **Devadatta,** not knowing that she was pregnant. On discovering her condition, Devadatta expelled her from the Order. She appealed to the Buddha, who caused an enquiry to be held, and, having been assured of her innocence, he restored her to all honour. When Kumāra Kassapa was born he, too, was admitted to the Order.

Devadatta is identified with Sākha, Kumāra Kassapa with the doe's young one, his mother with the doe, and the king with **Ānanda.**[1]

[1] J. i. 145 ff.; DhA. iii. 148 f. The story is figured in the Bharhut Stūpa (Cunningham: pl. xxv. (1) and xliii. (2). It is given in Mtu. (i. 359 ff.) with several variations in detail.

Nigrodhasāla.—A mound in **Rohaṇa,** near which **Veḷusumana** killed **Eḷāra's** giant **Nandasārathi.**[1]

[1] MṬ. 441.

1. **Nigrodhārāma.**—A grove near **Kapilavatthu,** where a residence was provided for the Buddha when he visited the city in the first year after his Enlightenment.[1] It belonged to a Sākyan named **Nigrodha,** who gave it to the Order. In order to convince his proud kinsmen of his attainments, the Buddha performed there the **Yamakapāṭihāriya,** and when, at the conclusion of the miracle, a shower of rain fell, wetting only those who wished to be wetted, he related to them the **Vessantara Jātaka.**[2] It was during this visit that **Mahāpajāpatī Gotamī** first asked permission for women to enter the Order. This was refused, and from there the Buddha went on to **Vesāli.**[3] The Buddha stayed at the Nigrodhārāma on several other occasions, and several Vinaya rules are mentioned as being first promulgated there.[4] Various Sākyans[5] came to see the Buddha at the Nigrodhārāma, among them, **Mahānāma, Godha, Sarakāni, Nandiya** and **Vappa.** The Buddha himself visited **Kāḷigodhā** during his residence there. It was during a discussion with Mahānāma that the **Cula-Dukkhakkhandha Sutta** (*q.v.*) was preached. During one of the Buddha's residences in Nigrodhārāma, the Sākyans invited him to consecrate their new Mote Hall, which he did by preaching there far into the night and then asking **Moggallāna** to continue his discourse.[6] On another occasion the Buddha is mentioned as having spent a period of convalescence at Nigrodhārāma[7]; he was there also when the quarrel broke out between the Sākyans and the Koliyans regarding the water of the **Rohiṇī.**[8] It seems to have been the Buddha's custom, when staying at Nigrodhārāma, sometimes to spend the noonday siesta in the **Mahāvana** near by.[9]

Among others mentioned as having stayed at Nigrodhārāma are **Anuruddha**[10] and **Lomasakaṅgiya.**[11]

Near Nigrodhārāma was once the site of the dwelling of a hermit

[1] MA. i. 289.

[2] Vin. i. 82; J. i. 88 f.; vi. 479; BuA. 22; DhA. iii. 163; also Mtu. iii. 101, 107, 114, 138, 141, 179.

[3] Vin. ii. 253; A. iv. 274.

[4] *E.g.*, Vin. iii. 235, 244; iv. 55, 101, 167, 181, 262, 314.

[5] S. v. 369-78; 395-7, 403-4, 408; A. ii. 196; iii. 284; iv. 220; v. 83, 328, 332, 334.

[6] S. iv. 182 ff.; also M. i. 353 (Sekha Sutta).

[7] A. i. 219 f.

[8] SNA. i. 357; but see J. v. 413, where he is said to have been in Sāvatthi.

[9] *E.g.*, S. iii. 91 f.

[10] DhA. iii. 295.

[11] M. iii. 200; a deva called **Candana** there taught him the **Bhaddekaratta Sutta.** Is this Lomasakaṅgiya the same as **Lomavaṅgisa,** who is also mentioned (S. v. 327) as having lived in Nigrodhārāma ?

(*isi*) called **Kaṇha.** The Buddha, remembering this, once smiled, and, when asked the reason for his smile, related the **Kaṇha Jātaka.**[12]

There is a tradition[13] that the Cariyā Piṭaka and the Buddhavaṃsa were preached by the Buddha to **Sāriputta** during his first stay in Nigrodhārāma. It was probably there that Anuruddha's sister built, at his request, an assembly hall of two storeys for the Saṅgha.[14] Buddhaghosa says[15] that **Kāḷa-Khemaka,** the Sākyan, built a special vihāra near Nigrodhārāma, on one side of the grounds.

[12] J. iv. 6.
[13] CypA. 1, 7; BuA. 3.
[14] DhA. iii. 295 f.
[15] MA. ii. 906; M. iii. 109 f.

2. **Nigrodhārāma.**—A grove in **Rājagaha.** The Buddha says that there he once gave **Ānanda** the chance of asking him to live for a whole æon, but Ānanda missed his opportunity.[1]

[1] D. ii. 116.

Nighaṇḍu.—A yakkha chieftain, to be invoked by followers of the Buddha when in distress.[1] He was present at the **Mahāsamaya.**[2]

[1] D. iii. 204.
[2] *Ibid.*, ii. 258.

Nighā Sutta.—The three pains—of lust, hatred and illusion. For their full comprehension the Noble Eightfold Path must be cultivated.[1]

[1] S. v. 57.

Niṅka (Nika).—A deva who visits the Buddha in the company of several other devas and utters a verse in praise of **Nigaṇṭha Nātaputta.**[1]

[1] S. i. 65 f.

Niṅkapaṇṇa-padhānaghara.—A building on **Cittalapabbata,** the residence of **Cūḷasumma.**[1] It is probably identical with **Nikapennaka** (*q.v.*).

[1] VibhA. 489.

Niceluvana.—A grove of mucalinda trees in **Kimbilā.**[1]

[1] A. iii. 247. (The P.T.S. Ed. reads Veḷuvana.) AA. ii. 642.

Niccavinodavāṇava.—A Damiḷa chief, ally of **Kulasekhara.**[1]

[1] Cv. lxxvi. 144; lxxvii. 76.

"Nicchavitthiaticāriṇī" Sutta.—**Mahāmoggallāna** reports to the Buddha that while descending **Gijjhakūṭa** he saw a flayed woman going through the air. The Buddha replies that the woman was an adulteress of **Rājagaha.**[1]

[1] S. ii. 259.

Nicchavorabhi Sutta.—Similar to the above; a flayed man, a sheep butcher of **Rājagaha.**[1]

[1] S. ii. 256.

Nijjarā Sutta.—Ten things which are brought to nought by the cultivation of their opposites.[1]

[1] A. v. 215 f.

Niṭṭhā Sutta.—Five conditions which are consummated in this life and five in the next.[1]

[1] A. v. 119 f.

Niṭṭhulaviṭṭhika.—A village in the district of **Giri** in Ceylon, the birthplace of **Goṭhaimbara.**[1] It is probably identical with the village (**Niṭṭhulaveṭṭhi**) given by **Pottakuṭṭha** for the **Māṭambiya-padhānaghara.**[2]

[1] Mhv. xxiii. 49. [2] Cv. xlvi. 20.

Nidāna Vagga.—The second division of the **Saṃyutta Nikāya.**[1]

[1] Vol. II. of the P.T.S. Edition.

Nidāna Saṃyutta.—The twelfth section of the Saṃyutta Nikāya.[1]

[1] S. ii. 1-133.

1. **Nidāna Sutta.**—The three means by which deeds are heaped up: greed, hatred and delusion.[1]

[1] A. iii. 338.

2. **Nidāna Sutta.**—Preached at **Kammāsadamma. Ānanda** tells the Buddha that though the Paṭiccasamuppāda is so deep, yet, to him, it is so plain. The Buddha warns him against such an idea, because all *saṃsāra* is due to lack of understanding of the Causal law.[1] This sutta was probably called the **Cūḷanidāna Sutta**[2] as opposed to the **Mahānidāna Sutta.**

[1] S. ii. 92. [2] *E.g.*, MA. i. 225; VibhA. 267.

1. **Nidāna Suttā.**—Two suttas on the three originating causes of action: lust, malice and delusion.[1]

[1] A. i. 134 f.

2. **Nidāna Suttā.**—The three causes of action: lust, malice and delusion.[1]

[1] A. i. 263.

3. **Nidāna Suttā.**—Absence of lust, malice and delusion prevents the arising of actions.[1]

[1] A. i. 264.

4. **Nidāna Suttā.**—Actions are originated by desire for things which, in the past, were based on desire, for the like things in the future and at the present time.[1]

[1] A. i. 265.

5. **Nidāna Suttā.**—The opposite of No. 4.[1]

[1] A. i. 266.

Nidānakathā.—The introductory chapter of the Jātaka Commentary. It gives the story of the Buddha in three sections: the Dūrenidāna from the time of his birth, as **Sumedha,** up to his birth in the **Tusita** world; the Avidūrenidāna from his death in Tusita and his birth as **Siddhattha,** son of **Suddhodana,** up to his Enlightenment; and the Santikenidāna, which contains his story up to the dedication of Jetavana by **Anāthapiṇḍika.**[1]

[1] J. i. 1-94.

Nidānuddesa.—One of the five divisions of the **Pāṭimokkha.**

1. **Niddasavatthu Sutta.**—The seven constituent qualities of a *niddasa* (*khīṇāsava*).[1]

[1] A. iv. 15.

2. **Niddasavatthu Sutta.**—The same, preached in answer to a question by **Sāriputta** as to whether it is right to say that one who has observed celibacy for twelve years could be called a *niddasa.*[1]

[1] A. iv. 34 ff.

3. **Niddasavatthu Sutta.**—Similar to No. 2, but the questioner is **Ānanda** and the qualities are differently stated.[1]

[1] A. iv. 37 f.

Niddā.—An *upāsikā* who was born as a *vemānika* peta.[1]

[1] Vv. ii. 8; VvA. 117.

Niddātandi Sutta.—Preached in answer to the question of a deva: sloth, drowsiness and surfeit of food prevent understanding of the Noble Eightfold Path.[1]

[1] S. i. 7.

Niddesa.—A commentarial work included in the Canon as part of the **Khuddaka Nikāya.** It is generally divided into two books: the **Culla-Niddesa** and the **Mahā-Niddesa.** The Culla Niddesa contains comments on the **Khaggavisāna Sutta** and the sixteen suttas of the **Parāyaṇa Vagga** of the **Sutta Nipāta,** while the Mahā-Niddesa deals with the sixteen suttas of the **Aṭṭhaka Vagga.** It is significant that the Culla-Niddesa contains no comments on the fifty-six (*Vatthugāthā*) introductory stanzas which preface the Parāyaṇa Vagga as at present found in the Sutta Nipāta. This lends support to the suggestion that at the time the Culla-Niddesa was written the Parāyaṇa Vagga was a separate anthology, and that the Khaggavisāna Sutta did not belong to any particular group. Similarly with the Mahā-Niddesa and the Aṭṭhaka Vagga. The comments in the Niddesa seem to have been modelled on exegetical explanations such as are attributed here and there in the Piṭakas to **Mahā Kaccāna**[1] and to **Sāriputta.**[2]

There is a tradition[3] which ascribes the authorship of the Niddesa to Sāriputta. There exists a Commentary on it, called the **Saddhamma-pajjotikā,** by **Upasena.** It was written in Ceylon at the request of a monk called **Deva Thera.**

[1] *E.g.,* **Madhupiṇḍika Sutta** (M. i. 110 f.); also S. iii. 9.

[2] *E.g.,* **Saṅgīti Sutta** (D. iii. 207 f.).

[3] NidA. p. 1.

Niddhamana Sutta.—Ten things which are burnt out by the possession of their opposites.[1]

[1] A. v. 220 f.

Nidhikaṇḍa Sutta.—One of the suttas of the **Khuddakapāṭha.**[1] A man buries treasure that he may use it later, but very often he loses it; not so is the treasure laid up by the doing of good deeds.

[1] Khp. p. 7.

Nipaññañjalika.—See **Paññañjalika.**

Nipannapaṭimāguhā.—A cave forming part of the **Uttarārāma** (*q.v.*) built in **Pulatthipura** by **Parakkamabāhu I.**[1]

[1] Cv. lxxviii. 75.

Nipura.—See **Sinipura.**

1. **Nibbāna Sutta.**—The Buddha explains to **Jāṇussoṇi** the meaning of "seeing" nibbāna in this life.[1]

[1] A. i. 158.

2. **Nibbāna Sutta.**—**Sāriputta** explains to **Ānanda** why some beings do not attain nibbāna in this very life.[1]

[1] A. ii. 167.

3. **Nibbāna Sutta.**—It is impossible that one who sees sorrow in nibbāna shall live in harmony and patience.[1]

[1] A. iii. 442.

4. **Nibbāna Sutta.**—**Sāriputta** explains to **Udāyi** (**Lāludāyi,** according to the Commentary)[1] how nibbāna is happiness, though in it there is no "experiencing" (*vedayitaṃ*).[2]

[1] AA. ii. 810. [2] A. iv. 414 f.

5. **Nibbāna Sutta.**—Preached at **Nālaka. Sāriputta** explains to **Jambukhādaka** the meaning of nibbāna and the way thereto.[1]

[1] S. iv. 251.

6. **Nibbāna Sutta.**—Preached at **Ukkācelā. Sāriputta** explains to **Sāmaṇḍaka** the meaning of nibbāna and the way thereto.[1]

[1] S. iv. 261 f.

1. **Nibbidā Sutta.**—The seven *bojjhaṅgas*, if cultivated, lead to revulsion, calm and nibbāna.[1]

[1] S. v. 82.

2. **Nibbidā Sutta.**—The same as above but with the four *iddhipādas.*[1]

[1] S. v. 255.

3. **Nibbidā Sutta.**—Five things, the perception of which leads to revulsion: foulness of the body, cloying of food, distaste of the world, impermanence in all things and the thought of death.[1]

[1] A. iii. 83.

4. **Nibbidā Sutta.**—Calling to mind the Buddha, the Dhamma, and the Saṅgha, etc., conduces to revulsion and to nibbāna.

[1] A. i. 30.

Nibbindā.—A channel, branching eastwards from the **Aciravatī** canal of the **Mahāvālukagaṅgā.**[1]

[1] Cv. lxxix. 53.

Nibbedha Sutta.—The Buddha tells **Udāyi** that a monk who cultivates the seven *bojjhaṅgas* will penetrate and break through lust, hatred and illusion.[1]

[1] S. v. 87 f.

Nibbedhika Sutta.—Four things that lead to penetration: association with the good, listening to the doctrine, reflection, observance of the Dhamma.[1]

[1] S. v. 419.

Nibbedhikapariyāya.—A comprehensive discourse addressed to the monks on sense-desires, their source, their variety, their fruit, and the steps leading thereto.[1]

[1] A. iii. 410 f.; it is often quoted, *e.g.*, UdA. 176; DhSA. 369.

1. **Nimi.**—The Bodhisatta born as king of **Mithilā.** See **Nimi Jātaka.**

2. **Nimi.**—A Pacceka Buddha. He was king of **Mithilā.** One day he saw a hawk, which was flying with some meat, attacked by vultures. The hawk dropped the meat, which was then taken up by another bird and he, in his turn, was attacked. This process continuing for some time, the king realized that possessions bring sorrow and suffering. He thereupon renounced his sixteen thousand women, and reflecting on his renunciation, became a Pacceka Buddha, and joined three others, who had also become Pacceka Buddhas: **Karaṇḍu, Naggaji** and **Dummukha.**[1]

[1] J. iii. 378 f.

Nimi Jataka (No. 541).—Once the Bodhisatta was born as the son of the king of **Mithilā**, in the **Videha** country. He was a rebirth of **Makhādeva,** who came down among men from the **Brahma-**world in order to bring the number of his family, who renounced the world, up to eighty-four thousand. And because the boy was born to round off the family, like the hoop of a chariot, he was called **Nemi** (" hoop "). On his father's renunciation, he came to the throne and engaged himself and all his subjects in righteousness and generosity. Once, when doubt arose in his mind as to which was more fruitful—holy life or giving alms—**Sakka** himself appeared before him to answer and encourage him. His fame spread to **Tāvatiṃsa,** and when the gods desired to see him, **Sakka** sent his chariot, with **Mātali,** to fetch him. On the way to Tāvatiṃsa, Mātali showed the king various hells and heavens and the palaces of various gods and goddesses. Arriving at the **Sudhammā** Hall, Nimi discoursed to the assembled gods. After staying in Tāvatiṃsa for seven days, he returned to Mithilā to tell his subjects what he had seen. When, later, his barber told him of the appearance of the first white hair on his head, he, like all his predecessors, handed over the throne to his son and became an ascetic. His son, **Kaḷārajanaka,** was the last of the eighty-four thousand kings of Makhādeva's dynasty.

The story was told by the Buddha when he visited Mithilā. He smiled when he came to the site of Makhādeva's palace, and when asked why he smiled he related the Jātaka.

Anuruddha is identified with Sakka and **Ānanda** with Mātali.[1]

This story forms the basis of the Makhādeva Sutta[2] and is included in the Cariyapiṭaka.[3]

[1] J. vi. 95-129.
[2] M. ii. 74 ff.; in Dpv. (iii. 35) the king is called **Nemiya.**
[3] Cyp. i. 6; CypA. 42 ff.

Nimitta Vagga.—The eighth chapter of the Duka Nipāta of the Aṅguttara Nikāya.[1]

[1] A. i. 82 f.

Nimittavyākaraṇīya Thera.—An arahant. Ninety-two kappas ago he was an ascetic in **Himavā,** at the head of fifty-four thousand pupils. Having seen the miracles preceding the birth of a Buddha (**Tissa** ?), he was glad at heart and told of it to others.[1] He is probably identical with **Vāraṇa Thera.**[2]

[1] Ap. ii. 411 f. [2] ThagA. i. 353 f.

Nimittasaññaka Thera.—An arahant. Ninety-four kappas ago he was a hermit on the banks of the **Candabhāgā,** and, seeing a golden deer wandering in the forest, his mind turned to thoughts of the Buddhas. Twenty-seven kappas ago he was a king named **Araññasatta.**[1]

[1] Ap. i. 261.

Nimokkha Sutta.—A deva questions the Buddha on deliverance and detachment and the Buddha answers him.[1]

[1] S. i. 2.

Nimmala.—An officer in the service of **Parakkamabāhu I.**[1]

[1] Cv. lxvi. 124.

Nimmānarati.—A class of devas, inhabiting the fifth of the six deva-worlds.[1] They are so called because they delight in their own creations. They can create any form in any colour.[2]

[1] D. i. 218; M. i. 289, etc.; S. i. 133, etc.; A. i. 210, etc. For their life-span see *Compendium* 140 f.
[2] NidA. 109; ItA. 234; VibhA. 519.

Nimmita.—Nineteen kappas ago there were sixteen kings of this name, all previous births of **Vaṭaṃsakiya (Abhaya) Thera.**[1]

[1] Ap. i. 174; ThagA. i. 201.

Nimmitapura.—A park in **Pulatthipura** laid out by **Parakkamabāhu I.**[1]

[1] Cv. lxxix. 9.

Niyama.—A district in South India.[1]

[1] Cv. lxxvii. 15, 101.

Niyarāya.—A Damiḷa chief, ally of **Kulasekhara.**[1]

[1] Cv. lxxvii. 79.

Niyasa.—See **Yasa.**

Niyelatissārāma.—A vihāra in Ceylon, built by king **Kaniṭṭhatissa.**[1]

[1] Mhv. xxxvi. 15.

Niyyanti-uyyāna.—A park, probably near **Sīhagiri,** where **Kassapa I.** built a vihāra for the **Dhammarucikas.**[1]

[1] Cv. xxxix. 14.

Niraggala.—A sacrifice in which alms are given with wide-open, boltless doors.[1]

[1] ItvA. 75.

1. **Nirabbuda.**—A **Niraya** ; really a period of suffering equal to twenty **Abbudas** (*i.e.*, twenty thousand Ninnahutas).[1]

[1] SN. p. 126; S. i. 149; SNA. 477; AA. ii. 853.

2. **Nirabbuda.**—Twenty-five thousand kappas ago there were eight kings of this name, all previous births of **Niggaṇḍipupphiya.**[1]

[1] Ap. i. 263.

Niraya.—Various lists of Nirayas are found in the books. In the Jātaka Commentary[1] occurs the following: **Sañjīva, Kālasutta, Saṅghāta, Jālaroruva, Dhūmaroruva, Mahāvīci, Tapana, Patāpana.** The Saṃyutta and Aṅguttara Nikāyas and the Sutta Nipāta contain a different list: **Abbuda, Nirabbuda, Ababa, Aṭaṭa, Ahaha, Kumuda, Sogandhika, Uppala, Puṇḍarīka, Paduma.**[2] The Commentaries explain[3] that these are not separate Nirayas but specified periods of suffering in Avīci. The **Devadūta Sutta**[4] of the Majjhima Nikāya contains yet another list: **Gūtha, Kukkuḷa, Simbalivana, Asipattavana** and **Khārodakanadī.** Other names, also, occur sporadically—*e.g.*, **Khuradhāra** (J. v. 269), **Kākola** (J. vi. 247), **Sataporisa** (J. v. 269) and **Sattisūla** (J. v. 143). The most fearful of the Nirayas is, however, the Avīcimahāniraya (see *s.v.* **Avīci**).

[1] J. v. 266, 271; the same list is found in Dvy. (67), except that Raurava is substituted for Jalaroruva and Mahāraurava for Dhūmaroruva.

[2] S. i. 149; A. v. 173; SN. p. 126; see also Dvy. 67.

[3] *E.g.*, AA. ii. 853.

[4] M. iii. 185.

Niraya Vagga.—The twenty-second chapter of the Dhammapada.

1. **Niraya Sutta.**—Five things that lead to hell: destruction of life, theft, lust, falsehood, liquor.[1]

[1] A. iii. 170; also 204.

2. **Niraya Sutta.**—Six things that lead to hell: taking life, theft, living carnally, falsehood, evil desires and wrong views.[1]

[1] A. iii. 432.

Nirayarūpa Sutta.—Four kinds of persons which exist in the world.[1]

[1] A. ii. 71.

Nirāmisa Sutta.—See **Suddhika Sutta.**

Nirāsa Sutta.—Three kinds of persons existing in the world: he who longs not, he who longs, and he who has done with longing.[1]

[1] A. i. 107 f.

Nirutti.—A work on exegesis, ascribed to **Mahā Kaccayāna** and divided into two parts: **Cūlanirutti** and **Mahānirutti.**[1] Aṭīkā on it exists, the **Niruttisāramañjūsā,** written by **Saddhammaguru.**[2]

[1] Gv. 59, 65; Svd. 1233 f.

[2] Bode, p. 29; Gv. 60.

Niruttipatha Sutta.—On three modes of reckoning: matter that has ceased is reckoned as "has been," not as "is" or "will be"; the same with the other *khandhas*.[1]

[1] S. iii. 71 f.

Niruttisāramañjūsā.—A ṭīkā on the **Nirutti**; also a ṭīkā on the **Nyāsa** by **Dāṭhānāga.**[1]

[1] Bode, *op cit.*, p. 55; Svd. 1241.

Nirodha Vagga.—The eighth chapter of the **Bojjhaṅga Saṃyutta.**[1]

[1] S. v. 132 ff.

1. **Nirodha Sutta.**—**Sariputta** tells **Ānanda** that he has attained to a state of cessation of perception and feeling.[1]

[1] S. iii. 238.

2. **Nirodha Sutta.**—**Sāriputta** tells the monks that one, who has achieved virtue, concentration and insight, may both enter the cessation of perception and feeling and also emerge therefrom. **Udāyin (Lāludāyī),** who is present, contradicts this three times, but none upbraids him. Sāriputta's words are repeated before the Buddha, and Udāyin acts similarly. The Buddha rebukes Ānanda for not admonishing Udāyin. Later, the Buddha talks of the matter to **Upavāna** and tells him of five qualities which a monk should possess.[1]

[1] A. iii. 192 ff.

Nilavāsī.—A Thera mentioned as staying at the **Kukkuṭārāma** in **Pāṭaliputta.**[1]

[1] Vin. i. 300.

Niliya.—A Damiḷa brahmin, purohita in the palace. He became the paramour of **Anulā** and occupied the throne for six months, until she poisoned him.[1]

[1] Mhv. xxxiv. 24 ff.; Dpv. xx. 29.

Nilīya.—A hunter.[1]

[1] J. iii. 330.

Nivattagiri.—The name of the city built on the spot where **Kaṇḍula,** the elephant, turned back in order to capture **Mahelanagara.**[1]

[1] MṬ. 480.

Nivattacetiya.—A cetiya near the **Kadamba-nadī,** built on the spot where **Mahinda,** at **Devānampiyatissa's** invitation, turned back on the way to **Missakapabbata.**[1]

[1] Mhv. xv. 10.

Nivāpa Sutta.—Preached at **Jetavana**; a parable of **Māra** as trapper. He sets up various gins and snares to trap the unwary, and many are caught in them. It is, however, possible to find a retreat, where Māra and his train cannot penetrate; and the Buddha proceeds to explain how this may be found.[1]

[1] M. i. 150 ff.

Nisanti Sutta.—**Ānanda** tells **Sāriputta** how a monk who is apt at *attha, dhamma, vyañjana, nirutti* and *pubbāparānusandhi*, comes speedily to grasp things and does not forget about that which he has grasped.[1]

[1] A. iii. 201.

1. **Nisabha.**—One of the two chief disciples of **Anomadassī** Buddha.[1] **Pañcasīlasamādāniya Thera** took the precepts from him in the time of Anomadassī Buddha.[2]

[1] Bu. viii. 22; J. i. 36; DhA. i. 88. [2] Ap. i. 76; also 74 (?).

2. **Nisabha.**—One of the chief lay supporters of **Atthadassī Buddha.**[1]

[1] Bu. xv. 21.

3. **Nisabha.**—Also called **Mahānisabha,** chief among the *dhutaṅgadharas* in the time of **Padumuttara** Buddha. It was his example that prompted **Mahā Kassapa** to strive for a similar honour.[1]

[1] ThagA. ii. 134 f.; SA. ii. 135 f.; AA. i. 85 f.

4. **Nisabha Thera.**—He was born in a Koliyan family, and, having seen the Buddha's wisdom and power in the fight between the Sākyans and the Koliyans, he entered the Order and became an arahant. Two verses uttered by him in admonition of a fellow-worker are found in the Therāgathā.[1] In time of **Vipassī** Buddha he was a householder, and gave to the Buddha a *kapiṭṭha*-fruit.[2] He is probably identical with **Kapiṭṭhaphaladāyaka** of the Apadāna.[3]

[1] vs. 195 f. [2] Thag. i. 318. [3] Ap. ii. 449; but see also ThagA. i. 73.

5. **Nisabha.**—A mountain in **Himavā.**[1]

[1] J. vi. 204, 212; Ap. i. 67.

Nisabhā.—One of the palaces occupied by **Tissa** Buddha is his last lay life.[1]

[1] Bu. xviii. 17.

Nisinnapaṭimālena.—A cave in **Pulatthipura,** forming part of the **Uttarārāma** built by **Parakkamabāhu I.**[1]

[1] Cv. lxxviii. 75.

Nissaggiya.—The fourth division of the Pārājikā of the Sutta Vibhaṅga.

Nissaṅka.—See **Kittinissaṅka.**

Nissaya Vagga.—The first chapter of the Ekādasaka Nipāta of the Aṅguttara Nikāya.[1]

[1] A. v. 311-28.

1. **Nissaya Sutta.**—The Buddha explains to a monk how one can be called *nissayasampanna.*[1]

[1] A. iv. 353 f.

2. **Nissaya Sutta.**—The Buddha explains to **Upāli** what qualities a monk needs to give *nissaya.*[1]

[1] A. v. 73.

Nissayaṭṭhakathā.—A Commentary on the **Saccasaṅkhepa** by **Mahābodhi Thera.**[1]

[1] P.L.C. 205.

Nissaraṇiya Sutta.—A monk, who is not obsessed by thoughts of lust, ill-will, hurt, form and his own body (*sakkāya*), possesses the five elements of escape.[1]

[1] A. iii. 245 f.

Nisseṇikkhetta.—A district in the **Malaya** province of Ceylon.[1]

[1] Cv. lxx. 18.

Nisseṇidāyaka Thera.—An arahant. In the time of **Kondañña** Buddha he built a stairway for the Buddha by which he might ascend to his cell. Thirty-one kappas ago he was king three times, under the name of **Pahasambahula.**[1]

[1] Ap. i. 187.

Nīta Thera.—He was a brahmin of **Sāvatthi** and joined the Order, believing that there he would find pleasure and comfort. He was lazy and indolent, but the Buddha, discerning his antecedents, admonished him, and Nīta, developing insight, became an arahant.

In the time of **Padumuttara** Buddha he was a brahmin teacher named **Sunanda.** One day, as he prepared a Vājapeyya sacrifice, the Buddha visited him and walked through the air above him. Sunanda threw flowers in the sky, and they formed a canopy over the whole town. He became king thirty-five times under the name of **Abbhasa** (*v.l.* **Ambaraṃsa**).[1]

He is probably identical with **Puppachadaniya** of the Apadāna.[2]

[1] Thag. vs. 84; ThagA. i. 180 f. [2] Ap. i. 166.

Nītha.—A Pacceka Buddha, mentioned in a nominal list.[1]

[1] M. iii. 69; ApA. 106.

1. **Nīla.**—A friend of **Mahinda I.** He died early, and Mahinda refused the kingship out of sorrow for his friend.[1]

[1] Cv. xlviii. 27 ff.

2. **Nīla Thera.**—He belonged to a family of flower-sweepers. He joined the Order and became an arahant in the tonsure-hall. When he came to **Sāvatthi** in search of a rag-robe a Mahābrahmā saw him and stood worshipping him. Other brahmas heard of this, and all worshipped him.[1]

[1] SA. ii. 217.

1. **Nīlagalla.**—A monastery in Ceylon, built by **Udaya I.**[1]

[1] Cv. xlix. 31.

2. **Nīlagalla** or **Nīlagiri.**—A locality in the **Malaya** district of Ceylon, mentioned in the account of the campaigns of **Parakkamabāhu I.**[1]

[1] Cv. lxx. 14, 16, 20, 83; lxxii. 12.

Nīlagallaka.—An officer of **Parakkamabāhu I.**[1]

[1] Cv. lxx. 67.

Nīlagiri.—See **Nīlagalla** (2), also **Rāmanīlagiri.**

Nīlageha.—A building (*pariccheda* : cell ?) erected by **Aggabodhi II.** for the Thera **Jotipāla.**[1]

[1] Cv. xlii. 39.

Nīlapokkharaṇī.—A pond, probably in **Anurādhapura.** It was one of the places from which clay was taken for the vessels which held the paraphernalia used in royal coronations.[1]

[1] MṬ. 307.

Nīlavālatittha.—A locality in **Rohaṇa,** identified with the modern Mātara.[1]

[1] Cv. lxxv. 48; Cv. *Trs.* ii. 48, n. 2.

Nīlavāhanā.—One of the three rivers crossed by **Mahā Kappina** on his way from **Kukkuṭavatī** to see the Buddha.[1]

[1] DhA. ii. 120.

Nīlavāhinī.—A channel branching off from the **Mālatīpuppha** sluice in the **Parakkamasamudda.**[1]

[1] Cv. lxxix. 42.

Nīlārāma.—A monastery in Ceylon to which **Udaya I.** gave the village of **Kāḷussa.**[1]

[1] Cv. xlix. 16.

1. **Nīvaraṇa Vagga.**—The sixth chapter of the Pañcaka Nipāta of the Aṅguttara Nikāya.[1]

[1] A. iii. 63-79.

2. **Nīvaraṇa Vagga.**—The fourth chapter of the **Bojjhaṅga Saṃyutta.**[1]

[1] S. v. 91-8.

1. **Nīvaraṇa Sutta.**—The five *nivaraṇas* make one blind, the seven *bojjhaṅgas* give one light and wisdom.[1]

[1] S. v. 97 f.

2. **Nīvaraṇa Sutta.**—The four *satipaṭṭhānas* are to be practised in order to get rid of the five *nīvaraṇas.*[1]

[1] A. iv. 457 f.

Nīvaraṇapahāna Vagga.—The second chapter of the Eka Nipāta of the Aṅguttara Nikāya.[1]

[1] A. i. 3 ff.

Nīvaraṇāni Sutta.—The five *nīvaraṇas*: sensual desire, malevolence, sloth and torpor, excitement and flurry, and doubt and wavering.[1]

[1] S. v. 60.

Neṭṭāru.—A locality in South India.[1]

[1] Cv. lxxvi. 189.

Nettippakaraṇa.—Also called **Nettigantha.** An exegetical work on the Piṭakas, traditionally ascribed to **Mahā Kaccāna.** There exists a Commentary on it by **Dhammapāla.**[1] **Ñaṇābhivaṃsa** wrote a ṭīkā on it.[2]

[1] Gv. 59, 60; SadS. 65.

[2] Svd. 1215.

Netti.—A yakkha chieftain.[1]

[1] D. iii. 204.

1. **Nemi.**—See **Nimi.**

2. **Nemi.**—A servitor of **Kuvera.**[1]

[1] D. iii. 201.

3. **Nemi.**—A Pacceka Buddha,[1] perhaps the same as **Nimi** (*q.v.*).

[1] M. iii. 70.

4. **Nemi.**—Forty-three kappas ago there were sixteen kings of this name, all previous births of **Vimala-Koṇḍañña.**[1]

[1] ThagA. i. 146; Ap. i. 150.

Nemindhara (*v.l.* **Nimindhara**).—One of the seven mountain ranges round **Sineru.**[1]

[1] J. vi. 125; Sp. i. 119; SNA. ii. 443; Dvy. 217; Mtu. ii. 300.

1. **Nerañjarā.**—A river. After the Enlightenment, the Buddha lived under the **Ajapāla-Nigrodha** (*q.v.*) at **Uruvelā,** on the banks of this river. There **Māra** tempted him, and, later, **Brahmā** persuaded him to preach the Dhamma.[1]

The Commentaries say[2] that when the Buddha, having realized the futility of austerities, left the **Pañcavaggiyas,** he retired to Uruvelā, on the banks of the Nerañjarā, and there, just before the Enlightenment, **Sujātā** gave him a meal of milk-rice, taking him to be a god. Before eating the food, he bathed in the ford called **Suppatiṭṭha.** Under the bed of the river lay the abode of the Nāga-king, **Kāla.** There was a *sāla* grove on the banks, where the Buddha spent the afternoon previous to the night of the Enlightenment.

[1] Vin. i. 1 ff.; SN. vs. 425 ff.; *cp.* Mtu. ii. 238; Lal. 327 (261); S. i. 103 f.; 122, 136 ff.; v. 167, 185, 232; Ud. i. 1-4; ii. 1; iii. 10; A. ii. 20. f.; D. ii. 267.

[2] *E.g.*, J. i. 68 ff.; DhA. i. 71; BuA. 238.

Three explanations are given of the name: (1) Its waters are pleasant (*nelaṃ jalaṃ assā ti = nelañjalā*, the *r* being substituted for the *l*); (2) it has blue water (*nīla-jalāyā ti vattabbe Nerañjarāyā ti vuttaṃ*); (3) it is just simply the name of the river.[3]

Nadī-Kassapa's hermitage was on the bank of the Nerañjarā.[4]

Nerañjarā is identified with the modern Nīlājanā with its source in Hazaribagh, which, together with the Mohanā, unites to form the river Phalgu.[5]

[3] UdA. 26 f. [4] ThagA. i. 45. [5] CAGI. 524.

2. **Nerañjarā.**—A channel that branched northwards from the **Puṇṇavaḍḍhana** tank.[1]

[1] Cv. lxxix. 49.

1. **Neru.**—The name of a king of India, descendant of **Mahāsammata.** He was the son of **Mahāsudassana** and father of **Mahā-Neru.**[1]

[1] Mhv. ii. 5; Dpv. iii. 8.

2. **Neru.**—A mountain in **Himavā.** All birds settling there become golden.[1]

[1] J. iii. 247; *cp.* **Kākaneru, Mahāneru, Sineru, Meru.**

Neru Jātaka (No. 379).—Once, the Bodhisatta was a golden swan living on **Cittakūṭa** with his brother. One day, while flying homewards, they saw Mount **Neru** and settled down there. All the birds there looked golden by virtue of the lustre of the mountain, and no one paid honour to the Bodhisatta and his brother; so they flew away.

The story was related in reference to a monk of a frontier village. At first he was honoured by the people who, however, later, transferred their favours elsewhere. But the monk, though very unhappy, contrived to stay on. When the Buddha heard of this, he rebuked the monk for remaining where he was not appreciated.[1]

[1] J. iii. 246 ff.

Nesāda.—A brahmin, a previous birth of **Sattapaduminiya.**[1]

[1] Ap. i. 254.

Nesādaka.—A hill where the thera **Mahānāma** practised meditation.[1]

[1] ThagA. i. 227.

Nehātakamuni Thera.—He was a brahmin of **Rājagaha,** who had become proficient in Vedic lore. Having become an ascetic, he dwelt in a forest glade, three leagues from Rājagaha, living on wild rice and worshipping fire. There the Buddha visited him and was entertained for three days. The Buddha taught him the Doctrine, and the ascetic became a sotāpanna and, later, an arahant. He continued to live in the jungle, and the Buddha visited him again when he fell ill of cramp.[1]

[1] Thag. vs. 435-40; ThagA. i. 459 f.

Nyāsa. A grammatical treatise by **Vimalabuddhi.** It is also called **Mukhamattadīpanī.** Vimalabuddhi Thera also wrote a glossary on it.[1]

[1] Gv. 72; Bode, *op. cit.*, 21; see also Svd. 1240.

P

Paṃsu Sutta.—The five classes of *paṃsukūlikas*, corresponding to the five kinds of *āraññakas*.[1] (See **Arañña Sutta.**)

[1] A. iii. 219.

Paṃsukūladhovana Jātaka.—The **Sumaṅgala-Vilāsinī**[1] mentions a Jātaka by this name, together with the **Vessantara Jātaka,** and says that the earth trembled at the preaching of these Jātakas. Faüsboll's edition contains no Jātaka of this name, nor have I been able to trace it elsewhere. It may have some connection with the *Paṃsukūladhovana pāṭihāriya*, which formed one of the fifteen hundred miracles that assisted the conversion of **Uruvela-Kassapa.**[2]

[1] DA. i. 130. [2] See Vin. i. 29.

Paṃsukūlapūjaka Thera.—An arahant. Ninety-one kappas ago he saw a *paṃsukūla* robe hanging over the mountain **Udaka (Uraga),** and being pleased with the sight, he offered before it three *kiṇkhaṇi* flowers.[1] His Apadāna verses are mentioned in the Theragātha Commentary in connection both with **Gosāla Thera**[2] and with **Mahākāla Thera.**[3]

[1] Ap. ii. 434. [2] ThagA. i. 79. [3] *Ibid.*, 272.

Paṃsukūlasaññika Thera.—An arahant. He was a hunter in the time of **Tissa** Buddha, and, one day, seeing in the forest a *paṃsukūla* robe of the Buddha, he worshipped it.[1] He is probably identical with **Puṇṇamāsa Thera.**[2]

[1] Ap. ii. 418 f. [2] ThagA. i. 297 ff.

Paṃsukūlī, Paṃsukūlino, Paṃsukūlikā.—A sect of ascetics in Ceylon, whose particular observance was probably the use of rag robes (*paṃsukūla*). Their early origin is not known. **Mānavamma** is said to have built for them a *pāsāda* in the **Thūpārāma.**[1] They also occupied the **Rājamātika-vihāra** and enjoyed the special favour of both **Aggabodhi V.** and of **Aggabodhi VII.**[2] **Vajira,** senāpati of **Aggabodhi IX.,** built for them the **Kacchavāla-vihāra.**[3] **Sena I.** established for them headquarters on the **Ariṭṭha-pabbata** and also made special provision for them at **Pulatthipura.**[4] They seem to have originally belonged to the congregation of the **Abhayagiri-vihāra,** and continued to do so up to the reign of **Sena II.,** when they separated off and formed special groups.[5] Later, **Sena Ilaṅga,** general of **Kassapa IV.,** built the **Samuddagiri-pariveṇa,** in the **Mahā-vihāra** for their use, and it is said that he dispensed rice and clothing to the mothers of the Paṃsukulikas.[6] In the time of **Udaya III.** various officials of the court fled to the *tapovana* occupied by the Paṃsukulikas, but were pursued thither by the king and his viceroy and beheaded. Incensed by this act, the Paṃsukulikas left the *tapovana,* which stood on land granted by the king, and went to **Rohaṇa.** The people rose in rebellion, and those who had perpetrated the crime in the *tapovana* visited the Paṃsukulikas in Rohaṇa, asked their forgiveness, and persuaded them to return.[7] **Mahinda IV.** also showed them great honour.[8] We hear of them last in the reign of **Vikkamabāhu II.,** when that king deprived them of their lands, and they, in anger, retired again to Rohaṇa.[9] Thenceforth we hear no more of the sect, and it probably ceased to exist.

It is mentioned in the Aṅguttara Commentary[10] that, after the depredations of **Caṇḍāla-Tissa,** when the religion was at a very low ebb, a discussion arose between the Paṃsukulikas and the **Dhammakathikas** as to which was the more important branch of the *sāsana—pariyatti* or *paṭipatti.* The Paṃsukulikas voted for *paṭipatti,* but were defeated by the others.

1 Cv. xlvii. 66.
2 *Ibid.*, xlviii. 4, 16, 73.
3 *Ibid.*, xlix. 80.
4 *Ibid.*, l. 63, 76.
5 *Ibid.*, li. 52.
6 *Ibid.*, lii. 21.
7 *Ibid.*, liii. 14 ff., 21 ff.
8 *Ibid.*, liv. 18, 24 f.
9 *Ibid.*, lxi. 59 f.
10 AA. i. 52 f.

Paṃsudhovaka Sutta.—The process of getting rid of the impurities found in gold ore is a very gradual one, involving many stages; so is the progress in ecstatic meditation, the first step in which is the removal of the gross sins.[1]

1 A. i. 253.

Paṃsupabbata-vihāra.—A monastery in Ceylon, mentioned as the residence of **Bhuvenakabāhu Thera.**[1]

[1] P.L.C. 247.

Paṃsupisācakā.—A class of *pisācas*, born in filth.[1] The word is used as a term of contempt.[2]

[1] MA. ii. 713, 921; UdA. 247.

[2] *E.g.*, AA. i. 438; MA. ii. 610, 611.

Pakudha-Kaccāyana (Pakudha-Kātiyāna, Kakudha-Kaccāyana, Kakuda-Kātiyāna).—Head of one of the six heretical sects of the Buddha's time. In the **Sāmaññaphala Sutta,**[1] **Ajātasattu** is said to have visited him and obtained from him an exposition of his teaching, which was to the effect that the four elements—earth, fire, air, water; pleasure, pain, and the soul—these seven things were eternally existent and unchangeable in their very nature; that there is no volitional activity of consciousness in them. His doctrine is, therefore, one of non-action (*akiriya-vāda*). When one, with a sharp sword, cleaves a head in twain, no one is thereby deprived of life, a sword has merely penetrated into the interval between seven elementary substances.[2] In other words, there is no such act as killing, or hearing, or knowing, etc.; no conceptions of, or distinction between, good and bad, knowledge and ignorance, etc.[3]

Buddhaghosa adds[4] that Pakudha avoided the use of cold water, using always hot; when this was not available, he did not wash. If he crossed a stream he would consider this as a sin, and would make expiation by constructing a mound of earth. This is evidence of the ascetic tendency in his teaching on matters of external conduct. His teaching is, however, described as *nissirikaladdhi*.

We are told[5] that Pakudha's followers did not hold him in high esteem, in contrast to the devotion felt for the Buddha by his followers. Pakudha did not welcome questions, and displayed annoyance and resentment when cross-examined. Elsewhere,[6] however, he is spoken of as having been highly honoured by the people, a teacher of large and well-reputed schools, with numerous followers. But he did not lay claim to perfect enlightenment.[7]

Pakudha-Kaccāyana's name is spelt in several ways. Some texts

[1] D. i. 56.

[2] *Cf.* the doctrine of the Cartesians, that there is no sin in taking the life of lower animals because they have no soul.

[3] Pakudha's teachings are also referred to in the **Sandaka Sutta** (M. i. 517), and there described at even greater length, but here his name is not mentioned.

[4] DA. i. 144.

[5] M. i. 250; ii. 4.

[6] *E.g.*, M. i. 198; S. i. 66; SN. p. 91.

[7] S. i. 68.

give his personal name as Kakudha, or Kakuda. In the Praśnopaniṣad,[8] mention is made of a Kakuda Kātyāna, a younger contemporary of Pippalāda. There he is called Kabandhiṇ, which name, like Kakuda, means that he had a hump on his neck or shoulder. Buddhaghosa says[9] that Pakudha was his personal name and Kaccāyana that of his gotta. The Kaccāyana (or Kātiyāna, as it is sometimes called) was a brahmin gotta.

Pakudha is mentioned as having been, in a past life, one of the five *diṭṭhigatikas* mentioned in the **Mahābodhi Jātaka.**[10] He is also mentioned in the Milindapañha[11] as one of the teachers visited by **Milinda.** The whole account is either a plagiarism of the Sāmaññaphala Sutta or else the teachers referred to only belonged to the same respective schools of thought.

[8] Barua: *Prebuddhistic Indian Philosophy,* 281; see also Dvy. 143; Mtu. i. 253, 256, 259; iii. 383.

[9] DA. i. 144; SA. i. 102.

[10] J. v. 246.

[11] p. 8.

Pakudhanagara.—A city, evidently in Burma, once the centre of great literary activity.[1]

[1] See Gv. 65; but elsewhere (Gv. 67) the works attributed to the residents of Pakudhanagara are stated to have been written in **Kāñcipura.** See also Gv. 75, where reference is made to a Makuranagara, *v.l.* Pakuta. Perhaps this is the same as Pakudha.

Pakiṇṇaka Nipāta.—The fourteenth section of the Jātakaṭṭhakathā.[1]

[1] J. iv. 276, 374.

Pakiṇṇaka Vagga.—The twenty-first chapter of the Dhammapada.

Pakulā.—See **Sakulā.**

Pakkanta Sutta.—The Buddha addresses the monks at **Gijjhakūṭa,** soon after **Devadatta** had seceded from the order, and tells them that Devadatta's gain was his ruin, in the same way as the flowering of the plaintain, the bamboo and the rush.[1]

[1] S. ii. 241.

Pakkha Thera.—An arahant. He was a **Sākyan** of **Devadaha** and was called **Sammoda,** but in his boyhood he suffered from rheumatism (*vātaroga*) and was crippled for some time; hence he came to be called Pakkha (cripple) even after his recovery. When the Buddha visited his kinsfolk he entered the Order and lived in the forest. One day he saw a kite flying up into the sky with some flesh, from which first one kite and then another grabbed a piece. Reflecting that worldly desires were like the flesh taken by the kite, he developed insight and attained arahantship.

In the time of **Vipassī** Buddha he had been a yakkha-senāpati with a retinue of eighty-four thousand and had given the Buddha a divine robe.

Fifteen kappas ago he was sixteen times cakkavatti under the name of **Suvāhana (Vāhana).**[1]

He is evidently identical with **Mahāparivāra** of the Apadāna.[2]

[1] Thag. vs. 63; ThagA. i. 144 f. [2] Ap. i. 146 f.

Paṅkadhā.—A township in **Kosala,** the residence of a monk named **Kassapa** of the **Kassapagotta.** The Buddha is mentioned as having once stayed there during his tours in Kosala.[1]

[1] A. i. 236; AA. i. 446.

Paṅkadhā Sutta.—When the Buddha stayed at **Paṅkadhā** during one of his tours and instructed the monks there, **Kassapa** of the **Kassapagotta** disapproved of his teaching, thinking that he was too scrupulous. But later, when the Buddha returned to **Rājagaha,** Kassapa, filled with remorse, followed him thither, and confessing his transgression, begged for forgiveness. The Buddha praised him for having made confession, and said that only those monks who were zealous in the practice of religion deserved praise, but others did not.[1]

[1] A. i. 236 f.

Paṅkavela.—A village in Ceylon where **Vikkamabāhu II.** defeated **Jayabāhu I.** and his brothers.[1]

[1] Cv. lxi. 16; see also Cv. *Trs.* i. 226, n. 2.

Paṅga.—The name of a Pacceka Buddha, found in a nominal list.[1]

[1] M. iii. 70; ApA. i. 107.

Paṅgura-vihāra.—A monastery in **Hatthibhogajanapada** in the south of Ceylon. In front of its refectory stood a *paṅgura* tree. One day the devatā of the tree heard a novice recite the **Mahādhammasamādāna Sutta** and applauded the recital. On being questioned by the novice, he told him that he had heard the Buddha preach the sutta but had been unable to see him, there being so many deities present more important than himself. It is said that the devatā became a sotāpanna on the very day of this conversation.[1]

[1] MA. i. 530 f.

Pagata Sutta.—A conversation between **Sāriputta** and **Mahā Koṭṭhita** as to whether or not the Tathāgata exists after death.[1]

[1] S. iv. 384 f.

Pacalā Sutta.—Once, when the Buddha was at **Suṃsumāragiri,** he saw with his divine eye that **Moggallāna** was at **Kallavāḷamuttagāma,** and that he was nodding (*pacalāyamāno*) very sleepily. He thereupon visited him and instructed him in the various ways of overcoming somnolence. Some other miscellaneous subjects are also dealt with in this sutta, such as the proper way of entering a house, the benefits of dwelling in solitude, the advantages of practising *mettā.*[1]

[1] A. iv. 85 ff.

Pacāyika Sutta.—Few are they that pay respect to the elders of the clan; more numerous those that do not.[1]

Both the text and the *uddāna* call this sutta Pacāyika, but the correct name is **Apacāyika,** and it should be altered to this.

[1] S. v. 468.

Pacuruyyāna.—A park in Ceylon, laid out by **Parakkamabāhu I.**[1]

[1] Cv. lxxix. 12.

Pacetana.—A king of old, whose wheelwright was the Bodhisatta.[1] See **Cakkavatti Sutta.**

[1] A. i. 110.

Pacetana Sutta.—See **Cakkavatti Sutta.**

Paceli-vihāra.—A monastery in **Soṇṇagiripāda,** residence of **Soṇaka Thera,** son of the hunter.[1]

[1] MA. ii. 887.

Paccaṇīka Sutta.—Once the brahmin **Paccanīkasāta** of **Sāvatthi** visited the Buddha and asked him to recite a doctrine. But the Buddha refused, saying that there was no use in trying to teach one whose heart was corrupt and full of animosity. This refusal seems to have pleased the brahmin.[1]

[1] S. i. 179.

Paccaṇīkasāta.—A brahmin of **Sāvatthi,** to whom the Buddha refused to preach (see **Paccanīka Sutta**). Buddhaghosa says[1] that the brahmin

[1] SA. i. 205.

was so called (" Gainsayer ") because he took delight in opposing everything that anyone else said.

Paccanta Sutta.—Few are those born in the **Majjhimadesa;** more numerous those born in the **Paccanta-janapada,** among unreasoning barbarians.[1]

[1] S. v. 466.

Paccantajanapada.—In the texts contrast is often drawn between the Paccantajanapada and the **Majjhimadesa.** In the latter the fortunate ones are born, and it is a great disadvantage to be born outside it; for, then, the possibilities of hearing of the Buddha and his teaching become remote.[1] The boundaries of the Majjhimadesa are given in several places, and the Paccantajanapada lies beyond these boundaries. They are: in the east, **Kajaṅgala** and **Mahāsālā**; in the south-east, the river **Salalavatī**; in the south, **Setakaṇṇikā**; in the west, **Thūna**; and in the north, **Usīraddhaja (pabbata).**[2] The Vinaya rules were relaxed in the case of those who lived in the Paccantajanapada, where it is said that the Buddha never spent a night.[3]

[1] *E.g.*, DhA. iii. 248, 489; KhA. 133. [2] Vin. i. 197; J. i. 49; *cp.* Dvy. 21 f. [3] MA. ii. 982.

1. **Paccaya Thera.**—An arahant. He belonged to a noble family of **Rohī** (**Rohiṇī**) and succeeded to his father's estate. Once, when he was holding a ceremonial oblation, a great number of people assembled, and the Buddha, arriving among them, preached from the sky, seated in a jewelled pavilion made for him by **Vessavaṇa.** Paccaya heard the preaching and renounced the world, attaining arahantship in a few days, and not leaving his cell till he had developed insight.

It is said that in the time of **Kassapa** Buddha, Paccaya was a monk who refused to leave the vihāra till he gained insight, but he died before his purpose was fulfilled. Earlier, ninety-one kappas ago, he had come across the Buddha **Vipassī,** on the banks of the **Vinatā,** and had offered him a fig (*udumbara*).[1] He is probably identical with **Udumbaraphaladāyaka** of the Apadāna.[2]

[1] Thag. vss. 222-4; ThagA. i. 341 f. [2] Ap. i. 295.

2. **Paccaya.**—The state elephant of **Vessantara,** brought to the stall by a female flying elephant, on the day of his birth, and deposited there. He was white in colour, and was called Paccaya because he supplied a need of Vessantara.[1]

[1] J. vi. 485.

Paccaya Sutta.—An explanation of the teaching regarding *Paṭicca-samuppāda.*[1]

S. ii. 25 f.

Paccayasaṅgaha.—A compilation by **Vācissāra.**[1]

[1] Gv. 71.

Paccarī.—See **Mahāpaccarī.**

Paccāgamanīya Thera.—An arahant. In the time of **Vipassī** Buddha he was a *cakkavāka* dwelling on the banks of the river **Sindhu.** One day, seeing the Buddha travelling through the air, the bird offered him a *sāla* flower in its beak. Seventeen kappas ago he was king eighteen times under the name of **Sucārudassana.**[1] He is probably identical with **Puṇṇamāsa Thera.**[2]

[1] Ap. i. 113. [2] ThagA. i. 53 f.

Paccuggamanīya Thera.—An arahant. Ninety-four kappas ago he saw **Siddhattha** Buddha and followed him with rapt gaze. Twenty-seven kappas ago he was a king called **Saparivāra.**[1]

[1] Ap. i. 240.

Paccupaṭṭhānasaññaka Thera.—An arahant. In the time of **Atthadassī** Buddha he was a yakkha, and, learning that the Buddha had died before he could pay him homage, he was filled with grief. The Buddha's disciple, **Sāgara,** advised him to honour the Buddha's *thūpa,* and this he did for five years. Seven kappas ago he became king four times under the name of **Bhūripañña.**[1] He is probably identical with **Ekūdānīya Thera.**[2]

[1] Ap. i. 153. [2] ThagA. i. 153 f.

Pacceka Buddha.—The name given to one who is enlightened by and for himself—*i.e.*, one who has attained to supreme and perfect insight, but who dies without proclaiming the truth to the world—hence the equivalent " Silent Buddha " sometimes found in translations. Pacceka Buddhas practise their *pāramī* for at least two thousand *asaṅkheyya* kappas. They are born in any of the three kulas: *brāhmaṇa, khattiya,* or *gahapati* only in a *vivattamāna kappa,* during which Buddhas are also born, but they never meet a Buddha face to face. They cannot instruct others; their realization of the Dhamma is " like a dream seen by a deaf mute." They attain to all the *iddhi, samāpatti* and *paṭisanbhidā* of the Buddhas, but are second to the Buddhas in their spiritual development. They do ordain others; their admonition is only in reference to good and proper conduct' (*abhisamācārikasikkhā*). Sometimes (*e.g.*, at J. iv. 341) it is stated that a Pacceka Buddha's knowledge and comprehension of ways and means is less than that of a Bodhisatta. They hold their uposatha in the **Ratanamālaka,** at the foot of the **Mañjūsarukkha** in **Gandhamādana.** It is possible to become a Pacceka Buddha while yet a layman, but, in this case, the marks of a layman immediately disappear. Three caves in the **Nandamūlakapabbhāra**—**Suvaṇṇaguhā, Maṇiguhā** and **Rajataguhā**—are the dwelling-places of Pacceka Buddhas. Round the Ratanamālaka, *q.v.* (or Sabbaratanamālaka), seats are always ready to receive the Pacceka Buddhas. When a Pacceka Buddha appears in the world, he immediately seeks the Ratanamālaka, and there takes his appointed seat. Then all the other Pacceka Buddhas in the world assemble there to meet him, and, in reply to a question by the chief of them, he relates the circumstances which led to his enlightenment. Similarly, all the Pacceka Buddhas assemble at the same spot when one of them is about to die. The dying one takes leave of the others, and, after his death, they cremate his body and his relics disappear.[1] But, according to another account, they die on the mountain called **Mahāpapāta** (*q.v.*). There does not seem to be any limit to the number of Pacceka Buddhas who could appear simultaneously. In one instance, five hundred are mentioned as so doing, all sons of **Padumavatī** (*q.v.*), at the head of whom was **Mahāpaduma.** In the **Isigili Sutta**[2] appears a long list of Pacceka Buddhas who dwelt on the **Isigili** Mountain (*q.v.*), and after whom the mountain was named. According to Buddhaghosa,[3] the names in this list belonged to the five hundred sons of Padumavatī, but the number of the names is far less than five hundred. This discrepancy is explained by saying that as many as twelve bore the same name. Other names are found scattered over different texts, such as the Jātakaṭṭhakathā.[4] The name occurring most frequently in the texts is that of **Tagarasikhī** (*q.v.*). Mention is also made of the Pacceka Buddhas going among men for alms and spending the rainy season in dwellings provided by men.[5]

Among the teachings preserved of the Pacceka Buddhas, the mos important is the **Khaggavisāṇa Sutta** (*q.v.*). For the definition of a Pacceka Buddha see **Puggalapaññatti** (p. 14; *cf.* p. 70). There he is

[1] These details are given in SNA. i. 47, 51, 58, 63; KhA. 178, 199; ApA. i. 125; see also *s.v.* **Gandhamādana.**

[2] M. iii. 68 ff.

[3] MA. ii. 889 ff.

[4] *E.g.*, **Darimukha** (J. iii. 240), **Sonaka** (v. 249); see also DhA. iv. 120, etc.

[5] *E.g.*, DhA. ii. 112 f.; iii. 91, 368; iv. 200. Their *patthanā* (SNA. 51). Their wisdom less than that of a Bodhisatta (J. iv. 341).

described as one who understands the Truth by his own efforts, but does not obtain omniscience nor mastery over the Fruits (*phalesu vasībhāvaṃ*).

Pacceka Brahmā.—Mention is made in one or two places in the books of Brahmas who are described as Pacceka Brahmā—*e.g.*, **Subrahmā, Suddhāvāsa** and **Tudu.**[1] I have not come across any explanation of this term. It may designate a Brahmā who does not live in any recognized Brahmā-world, but in a world of his own.

[1] See *s.v.*

Paccorohaṇī Vagga.—The twelfth section of the Dassaka Nipāta of the Aṅguttara Nikāya.[1] One of the suttas deals with the " spiritual coming down again " (*paccorohaṇi*); hence, probably, the name of the Vagga.

[1] A. v. 222-37.

Paccorohaṇī Sutta.—**Jānussoṇī** tells the Buddha how, on certain fast days, the brahmins perform a ceremony called *paccorohaṇī*, when they bathe and purify themselves and worship the fire three times during the night. He then asks the Buddha whether the Ariyans have a corresponding observance, and the Buddha answers him.[1]

[1] A. v. 233 ff.

Pacchābhumma (Pacchābhūma).—The name given to the district to the west (of the Majjhimadesa).[1] Mention is also made of the **Pacchābhūmaka** brahmins, who are carriers of water-pots, fire-worshippers, and who claim to be able to send a man heavenward after death.[2]

[1] S. iii. 5, 6; SA. ii. 186. [2] *E.g.*, A. v. 263; see also S. iv. 311.

Pacchābhū Thera.—The teacher of **Malitavambha**[1]; the word perhaps means " born in the west "; see below.

[1] Thag. vs. 105; ThagA. i. 211.

Pacchābhūmaka Sutta(=Mataka Sutta).—Once, when the Buddha was at the **Pāvārika-ambavana, Asibandhakaputta** visits him and asks if he claims to be able to send men heavenwards as do the **Pacchābhūmaka** brahmins. The Buddha explains to him that a man's destiny depends on the life he leads; no one else can send him to heaven or to a place of suffering.[1]

[1] S. iv. 311 f.

Pacchāsamaṇa Sutta.—The five qualities which should be lacking in a monk who is taken as an attendant (*pacchāsamaṇa*).[1]

[1] A. iii. 137.

Pacchidāyaka Thera.—See **Sajjhadāyaka.**

Pacchimadesa, Pacchimadisā, Pacchimapassa.—A province in Ceylon, probably in the west.[1] In the province was the **Vallipāsāṇa-vihāra,** residence of **Mahā-Nāgasena.**[2]

[1] Cv. xliv. 88 f.; but see Cv. *Trs.* i. 82, n. 4.

[2] MṬ. 552.

Pacchimārāma.—A monastery, probably to the west of **Pulatthipura.** It was founded by **Parakkamabāhu I.** and contained twenty-two pariveṇas and numerous other buildings.[1]

[1] Cv. lxxviii. 70 ff.

Pajāka.—A king. **Lambacūḷaka** was in his kingdom and **Meṇḍissara** (*q.v.*) lived there with his followers.[1] But, elsewhere,[2] we are told that Lambacūḷaka was in the kingdom of **Caṇḍappajota.** Does this mean that the kingdom of Caṇḍapajjota was identical with that of Pajāka ?

[1] J. iii. 463.

[2] J. v. 133.

1. **Pajāna Sutta.**—It is impossible to destroy Ill without understanding the eye, the nose, etc.[1]

[1] S. iv. 89.

2. **Pajāna Sutta.**—Ill cannot be destroyed without understanding of objects, sounds, savours, etc.[1]

[1] S. iv. 90.

1. **Pajāpati.**—A name given to **Māra,** because he uses his power over all creatures.[1]

[1] M. i. 2; MA. i. 28.

2. **Pajāpati.**—One of the kings of the devas, mentioned with **Sakka, Varuṇa, Isāna,** etc.[1] Buddhaghosa says[2] that he, among the gods, was like Sakka in looks and that he lived to the same age, but in the assembly he occupied the second seat. He is sometimes mentioned with **Brahmā,** as distinct from him.[3] In the **Āṭānāṭiya Sutta**[4] he is mentioned among the Mahāyakkhas, to be invoked by followers of the Buddha in times of danger.

[1] S. i. 219; D. i. 244; in J. v. 28 he is mentioned with Varuṇa and Soma; see also D. ii. 274; DA iii. 709.

[2] SA. i. 262.

[3] J. vi. 568, 571; M. i. 140, 327, 329.

[4] D. iii. 204.

3. **Pajāpati.**—See **Mahā-Pajāpatī Gotamī.**

Pajjamadhu.—A Pāli poem of one hundred and four stanzas, by **Coḷiya Dīpaṅkara** or **Buddhapiya,** on the beauty of the Buddha's person, of his teaching and of the Saṅgha.[1]

[1] P.L.C. 222; Svd. 1260.

Pajjaraka.—The name of a disease which afflicted **Abhayapura** (capital of Ceylon) in the time of **Kakusandha** Buddha. It was due to the influence of the yakkha **Puṇṇakāla.** Kakusandha visited the Island to dispel the disease. It is defined as an *uṇhasīsābādha.*[1]

[1] Mhv. xv. 63; MṬ. 349.

Pajjuna.—The eighth of the ten **Andhakaveṇhudāsaputtā,** sons of **Devagabbhā.**[1]

[1] J. iv. 81; PvA. 93, 111.

Pajjunna.—A devarāja, the god of rain. He was subject to the will of **Sakka,** and the books contain instances of his causing rain to fall at the command of Sakka.[1] He was also influenced by the exercise of *saccakiriyā* (protestation of truth).[2] Buddhaghosa[3] describes him as **Vassavalāhaka,** and says that he was an inhabitant of the **Cātummahārājika** world. **Kokanadā** and **Culla Kokanadā** were his daughters.[4] Pajjunna is mentioned among the Mahāyakkhas to be invoked in time of need,[5] and he was present at the preaching of the **Mahāsamaya Sutta.**[6]

[1] J. i. 330; Mhv. xxi. 31; J. iv. 253;

[2] *E.g.,* J. i. 331 f.

[3] SA. i. 64.

[4] S. i. 29 f.

[5] D. iii. 205.

[6] *Ibid.,* ii. 260.

1. **Pajjunnadhītā Sutta.**—**Kokanadā,** daughter of **Pajjunna,** visits the Buddha at the **Mahāvana** in **Vesāli** and praises him and his teaching.[1]

[1] S. i. 29.

2. **Pajjunnadhītā Sutta.**—**Culla-Kokanadā,** daughter of **Pajjunna,** visits the Buddha at the **Mahāvana** in **Vesāli** and, after paying homage to him and his teaching, utters a summary of the Dhamma.[1]

[1] S. i. 30.

1. **Pajjota.**—See **Caṇḍappajjota.**

2. **Pajjota.**—A tank near **Kāsapabbata,** built by **Duṭṭhagāmaṇī.** Near it was the city of **Pajjotanagara.**[1]

[1] Mhv. xxv. 51; M. i. 346.

1. **Pajjota Sutta.**—The four splendours: of the moon, the sun, fire, and wisdom.[1]

[1] A. ii. 140.

2. **Pajjota Sutta.**—The four things that give light: the sun, the moon, fire, and the Buddha, the Buddha being the best.[1]

[1] S. i. 15.

3. **Pajjota Sutta.**—A series of questions asked by a deva, and the Buddha's answers; the first being on radiance—wisdom gives radiance to all the world.[1]

[1] S. i. 44.

Pañca Sutta.—See **Anattalakkhaṇa Sutta.**[1]

[1] S. iii. 66.

Pañcaka.—See **Paṇḍaka** and **Pañcikā.**

Pañcakaṅga.—The Thapati of **Pasenadi,** king of Kosala. He was a devoted follower of the Buddha and loved discussion. The **Bahuvedaniya Sutta**[1] is based on a discussion between him and **Mahā-Udāyi,** which discussion **Ānanda** overheard and repeated to the Buddha. On another occasion, Pañcakaṅga related to the Buddha the conversation he had had with the Paribbājaka **Uggāhamāna Samaṇamaṇḍikāputta,** and the Buddha preached to him the **Samanamaṇḍikā Sutta.**[2] The **Anuruddha Sutta**[3] contains a discussion between **Anuruddha** and **Abhiya Kaccāna,** which took place at Pañcakaṅga's house, whither he had invited them. The discussion was started by a question asked by Pañcakaṅga. Buddhaghosa says[4] that Pañcakaṅga was the Thapati's personal name, and that he was so called ("Five-tools") because he carried the five tools of a carpenter: *vāsīpharasu* (adze), *nikhādana* (chisel), *daṇḍa* (measuring stick), *muggara* (gavel), and *kāḷasutta* (blackened thread). He explains Thapati by *vaḍḍhakī-jeṭṭha.*

[1] M. i. 396 ff.; see also S. iv. 223 f.
[2] M. ii. 23 ff.
[3] M. iii. 144 ff.
[4] MA. ii. 629; SA. iii. 86.

Pañcakaṅga Sutta.—See **Bahuvedanīya Sutta.**

Pañcagati Suttā.—A series of suttas in which the Buddha declares that, through not understanding the four Ariyan truths, beings continue to be born in one or other of the five conditions: as humans, animals, petas, devas, or in the nirayas.[1]

[1] S. v. 474 ff.

Pañcagativaṇṇanā.—The name of a Commentary.[1]

[1] Gv. 65, 75.

Pañcagaru Jātaka (No. 132)=**Bhīruka Jātaka.**—The Bodhisatta was once the youngest of the hundred sons of Brahmadatta, king of Benares. He had, as far as could be seen, no chance of being king, but, on seeking the counsel of a Pacceka Buddha and following his advice, he became king on his father's death. For details reference is invited to the "Takkasilā Jātaka," this evidently being another name for the **Telapatta Jātaka** (*q.v.*).

This Jātaka was related in reference to the attempts made by **Māra's** daughters to tempt the Buddha as he sat under the **Ajapāla-nigrodha.**[1]

[1] J. i. 469 ff.

Pañcaggadāyaka.—A brahmin, so called because he gave the first-fruits of his harvest in five stages: when it was ripe, when it was being threshed, when it was put into tubs, when it was put in the boiler, and when it was heaped on the dish. One day, the Buddha went to his house and stood at the door, while the brahmin was having his meal, his wife serving him. The wife, seeing the Buddha, and fearing that her husband would give away his food, made a sign to the Buddha to go. But the Buddha made a gesture of refusal and sent a radiance in the direction of the brahmin. The wife laughed at the Buddha's obstinacy, and, at that moment, the brahmin saw the Buddha and brought to him the remnant of his meal, which the Buddha accepted. He then preached to the brahmin and his wife, both of whom became anāgāmins.[1]

[1] DhA. iv. 98 ff.; the story is also found at SNA. i. 270, but there the brahmin and his wife only become sotāpannas.

Pañcaggaḷalenavāsī-Tissa.—A young novice who could travel through the air. One day, while so journeying, he heard the daughter of the chief artisan of **Girgāma** singing in a lotus pond while bathing with five hundred friends. He was attracted by her voice and lost his concentration of mind.[1]

[1] SNA. i. 70.

Pañcaṅgika Vagga.—The third section of the Pañcaka Nipāta of the Aṅguttara Nikāya.[1]

[1] A. iii. 14-32.

Pañcaṅguliya Thera.—An arahant. Ninety-two kappas ago he approached **Tissa** Buddha, who was entering the Gandhakuṭi, and offered him a handful of perfume. Seventy-two kappas ago he was a king called **Sayampabhā.**[1]

[1] Ap. i. 186.

Pañcacūḷaka.—The name of **Sanankumāra** when he was born as a human in a former birth. He practised the jhānas, and having died in that state, was born in the brahma-world.[1] More probably, Pañcacūḷaka here is not a name but a description meaning " while he was yet a lad with his hair tied in five knots."

[1] MA. ii. 584.

Pañcacūḷakagāmadāraka.—The disguise assumed by **Vissakamma** when, acting on **Sakka's** orders, he went with **Asoka** to fetch the relics for his cetiyas. These relics lay buried, and no one had been able to find them.[1]

[1] DA. ii. 614; see **Pañcacūḷaka** above for more probable explanation.

Pañcacchiddageha.—A brahmin and his wife wished to give alms to four brahmins; the brahmin went to the monastery to fetch them. With him returned four arahant-sāmaṇeras: **Saṅkicca, Paṇḍita, Sopāka** and **Revata.** The wife was angry at the sight of them and sent the man back. He brought, in turn, **Sāriputta** and **Moggallāna,** both of whom turned back on seeing the novices. **Sakka's** throne was heated, as the novices sat hungry, and he came in the guise of a brahmin, entered the house, and sat down after worshipping the novices. The brahmin and his wife tried to turn him out; but failing in this, they fed all their five guests. Each of them made an opening in some part of the house, through which he departed. Henceforth the house was known as the **Pañcacchiddageha.**[1]

[1] DhA. iv. 176 ff.

Pañcattaya Sutta.—Preached at **Jetavana.** It deals with various schools of thought and their doctrines regarding the future. Some say the self is conscious, others deny this; some teach annihilation, others deny that. The Buddha does not support any of these speculations.[1]

[1] M. ii. 228 ff.

Pañcadīpadāyikā Therī.—An arahant. One hundred thousand kappas ago she was a recluse wandering from one monastery to another. One dark night she sat at the foot of the bodhi-tree and wished that the tree should shine in radiance. Her wish was granted, and for seven days she sat there, and on the ninth day she lit five lamps under the tree. After death she was born in **Tāvatiṃsa,** and her palace was known as **Pañcadīpī.**

She had the power of seeing in all directions without turning her head. She was eighty times queen of the king of the devas. In her last life she attained arahantship at the age of seven.[1]

The same story is told in identical words under the name of another therī, called **Pañcadīpikā.**[2] The verses are also attributed in the Therīgāthā Commentary to the Therī **Selā.**[3]

[1] Ap. ii. 527 f. [2] *Ibid.*, ii. 519 f. [3] ThigA. 62 f.

Pañcadīpika Thera.—An arahant. He was once a follower of **Padumuttara** Buddha and lit a lamp under his bodhi-tree. Thereby he obtained the power of being able to see through all obstacles. Thirty-four kappas ago he was king, under the name of **Satacakkhu.**[1]

[1] Ap. i. 108.

Pañcadīpikā.—See **Pañcadīpadāyikā.**

Pañcadīpī.—See **Pañcadīpadāyikā.**

Pañcanadī, Pañcamahānadī.—In several places in the texts five rivers are mentioned as the five great rivers of India, and they are used in various similes and metaphors. These rivers are: **Gaṅgā, Yamunā, Aciravatī, Sarabhū** and **Mahī.**[1]

[1] *E.g.*, Vin. ii. 239; A. iv. 101; S. ii. 135; Ud. v. 4; also Mil. 380.

Pañcanikāyamaṇḍala.—An assembly hall in the **Lohapāsāda,** where the monks living to the north of the **Mahāvālukanadī** used regularly to assemble at the end of the rainy season.[1]

[1] DA. ii. 581.

Pañcanīvaraṇa Sutta.—On the five *nīvaraṇas*, their evil results and the means of getting rid of them.[1]

[1] A. i. 3 ff.

Pañcapaṇḍita Jātaka (No. 508).—Also called **Pañcapaṇḍitapañha** and **Paṇḍitapañha.** The name given to a section of the **Mahā-Ummagga Jātaka,** which deals with the plot of **Senaka, Pukkusa, Kāvinda** and **Devinda,** to have **Mahosadha** killed by informing the king that Mahosadha has a guilty secret which he did not desire anyone to know of. But Mahosadha learnt their secrets and defeated their intentions.[1]

[1] J. iv. 473; v. 81; vi. 379, 389.

Pañcapariveṇamūla.—A monastery in Ceylon. At one time **Abhaya** was head of the monks there and interceded with the chief of the **Kuṭhārasabhā** in settling the differences between **Kittisirimegha** and the prince (who afterwards became **Parakkamabāhu I.**).[1] A **Pañcapariveṇādhipati** was author of the Pāli medical work, the **Bhesajjamañjūsā,** in the reign of **Parakkamabāhu IV.** of **Jambuddoṇi.**[2]

[1] Cv. lxvii. 61. [2] P.L.C. 244.

Pañcapāpā.—Daughter of a poor man of Benares. Her hands, feet, mouth, eyes and nose were hideous, hence her name ("the Five Defects"); but her touch was ecstatic. The reason of all this was that in a previous birth she had given clay to a Pacceka Buddha with which to tidy his dwelling, but, on first sight, she had looked angrily at him. One day she happened to touch **Baka,** king of Benares, and he became infatuated with her. He visited her home in disguise and married her. Later, wishing to make her his chief consort, but fearing the mockery of others because of her ugliness, he devised a plan by which the citizens should become aware of her divine touch. Afterwards, owing to the jealousy of the other queens, she was cast adrift in a vessel and claimed by King **Pāvāriya.** Baka, hearing of this, wished to fight Pāvāriya, but they agreed to compromise, and from that time Pañcapāpā lived for a week at a time in the house of each king. The story forms one of the tales related by **Kuṇāla,** who is identified with Baka.[1]

[1] J. v. 440 ff.

Pañcappakaraṇa.—Name given to the collection of the books of the Abhidhammapiṭaka, with the exception of the **Dhammasaṅgaṇi** and the **Vibhaṅga.** There is a Commentary on these by **Buddhaghosa** and **Ānanda Vanaratana.**[1]

[1] P.L.C. 210; Gv. 64. 75.

Pañcambaṅgana.—A place in **Mahāmeghavana** in **Anurādhapura.** Here **Dārubhatika-Tissa** had a pond made, which was later filled up by **Dhātusena,** who had a series of cells built there.[1]

It is probably identical with **Pañhambamālaka** (*q.v.*).

[1] Mhv. xxxiv. 23; MṬ. 626.

Pañcayojanaraṭṭha.—A district in the **Dakkhiṇadesa** of Ceylon, the modern Pasyodunkorala. It is mentioned in various campaigns, and was irrigated and made fertile by **Parakkamabāhu I.** In it was the **Bhīmatittha-vihāra,** once the repository of the Tooth Relic.[1]

[1] Cv. lvii. 71; lxi. 35; lxviii. 51; lxxii. 57; lxxv. 21; lxxxv. 81.

"Pañcarājāno" Sutta.—Once five rājās, with **Pasenadi** as their chief, were indulging in various forms of amusement and they fell to discussing among themselves as to which of the sense-pleasures was the highest. Unable to come to any decision, they sought the Buddha, who explained that the highest pleasure, in the case of any of the senses, was the limit-point in anyone's enjoyment. A lay disciple, **Candanaṅgalika,** who was present, thereupon rose from his seat and uttered a stanza in praise of the Buddha. The five rājās wrapped their robes around the disciple, and he, in turn, presented these to the Buddha.[1]

[1] S. i. 79 ff.

Pañcala-vihāra.—A monastery in **Soṇṇagiripāda** (in Ceylon); the residence of the monk **Soṇa,** the son of a hunter.[1]

[1] AA. i. 255.

Pañcavaggiyā.—The name given to the five monks—**Koṇḍañña, Aññā-Koṇḍañña), Bhaddiya, Vappa, Mahānāma** and **Assaji**—to whom the Buddha preached his first sermon at **Isipatana.** Of these, Koṇḍañña was the youngest of the eight brahmins who read the signs on Gotama's body on the day of the name-giving festival. The four others were children of four of the other brahmins. They had been advised by their fathers to watch Gotama's career and to join him should he renounce the world. This they did, and all five joined in the austerities of Gotama at **Uruvelā.** When he abandoned his austerities and started to follow the Middle Way, they left him in disappointment. But after the Enlightenment, the Buddha visited them and preached to them. At first they refused to pay heed to him, but gradually his powers of persuasion won their hearts and they became his first disciples.[1] It is noteworthy that, although warned by their fathers of the great destiny awaiting Gotama, they were yet reluctant to accept the Buddha's claim to Enlightenment.

[1] J. i. 57, 67, 81, 82; DhA. i. 87, etc. For details of the members of the group, see under their several names; see also article by Mrs. Rhys Davids in *J.R.A.S.* for 1927 on them as the "Unknown co-founders of Buddhism," where she suggests that the members of this group were responsible for certain tendencies in the Buddha's teaching.

Pañcavihāra.—A place near **Pulatthinagara** to which **Parakkamabāhu I.** and his followers retreated while awaiting a favourable opportunity to advance against **Mānābharaṇa.**[1]

[1] Cv. lxxii. 116 f.

Pañcaverabhaya Sutta.—Preached at **Jetavana** to **Anāthapiṇḍika.** The Ariyan disciple is free from the fivefold guilty dread: he knows that he is not guilty of taking life, of theft, of wrong indulgence of the senses, of falsehood, of the use of intoxicants, and he is free from dread of the guilt attaching to these. He is also possessed of unwavering faith in the Buddha, the Dhamma and the Saṅgha, and sees the Ariyan truth of the Causal Law. He thus begets confidence regarding his ultimate destiny.[1]

[1] S. ii. 68 ff.

Pañcasataraṭṭha.—A district in Ceylon (the modern Pansiyapattu to the North-east of Kandy) where King **Senāratna** once deposited the Tooth Relic to guard it from his enemies.[1]

[1] Cv. xcv. 9.

Pañcasatikakhandhaka.—The eleventh section of the Cullavagga of the Vinaya Piṭaka.

Pañcasatikā.—The name given to the First Council, which was held under the presidency of **Mahā Kassapa.** Five hundred monks took part in it, hence its name.[1]

[1] MṬ. 151.

Pañcasattatimandira.—A building erected in **Pulatthipura** by **Parakkamabāhu I.** for " the reception of the magic water and the magic thread given him by the yellow-robed ascetics."[1] Geiger suggests[2] that the building was used for *paritta*-ceremonies.

[1] Cv. lxxiii. 73. [2] Cv. *Trs.* ii. 9, n. 2.

Pañcasālā.—A brahmin village of **Magadha.**[1] For an episode connected with it see **Piṇḍa Sutta.**

[1] S. i. 113; DhA. iii. 257; Mil. 154.

Pañcasikha.—A **Gandhabba.** His favourite instrument was the **Beḷuvapaṇḍuvīṇā** (*q.v.*). He was considered a favourite of the Buddha,[1] and when **Sakka** visited the Buddha at the **Indasālaguhā** in order to ask him certain questions, he sent Pañcasikha in advance, that he might obtain permission for the interview.[2] Pañcasikha approached the Buddha and, playing on his *vīṇā*, sang of the beauties of the Buddha, the Doctrine, Arahants and Love. The verses really formed a love-poem addressed

[1] DA. iii. 699.
[2] The episode is given in full in the **Sakkapañha Sutta** (D. ii. 263 ff.).

to his beloved, **Bhaddā Suriyavaccasā,** daughter of the Gandhabba **Timbarū.** The Buddha praised his music and song and questioned him about the poem. He confessed that when the Buddha was staying under the **Ajapāla-nigrodha,** before the Enlightenment, he (Pañcasikha) had met Suriyavaccasā going with her father to dance before Sakka. Pañcasikha thereupon fell in love with her; but she favoured the suit of **Sikhaṇḍi,** son of **Mātali.** Pañcasikha thereupon composed a song, which he sang to her. She was greatly pleased with the references in the song to the Sākyan sage of whom she had heard when she went to the **Sudhammāsabhā,**[3] and she consented to marry **Pañcasikha.** It is said that Sakka blessed the marriage in return for Pañcasikha's intercession with the Buddha on his behalf.

In the **Janavasabha Sutta**[4] it is stated that when Brahmā **Sanaṅkumāra** appeared before the assembly of the gods of **Tāvatiṃsa** and materialized himself he assumed the form of Pañcasikha. Buddhaghosa says,[5] by way of explanation, that all the devas loved Pañcasikha and wished to resemble him. In the **Mahāgovinda Sutta**[6] Pañcasikha is represented as conveying to the Buddha a full report of the happenings in the assembly of the devas, when Sakka spoke the Buddha's praises.

No really satisfactory explanation is found in the Commentaries of Pañcasikha's name. Buddhaghosa says[7] *Pañcasikho ti pañcacūḷo, pañcakuṇḍaliko,* and goes on to say that Pañcasikha was born once as a human being, and, while yet a boy wearing his hair in five knots[8] (*pañcacūḷakadāraka-kāle*), he became chief of those who tended the calves. Together with other lads he engaged in works of public utility, such as repairing roads, digging wells, building rest-houses, etc., and he died while young. He was reborn in the **Cātummahārājika** world, destined to live for ninety thousand years, his body three gāvutas in height. He wore on his person one hundred cartloads of ornaments and rubbed nine pots of perfume on his body. He wore red robes, and on his head a chaplet of red gold, round which his hair was arranged in five locks

[3] On this occasion Sakka pronounced his 8-fold eulogy of the Buddha (contained in the **Mahāgovinda Sutta**), says Buddhaghosa (DA. ii. 704).

[4] D. ii. 211; also in the Mahāgovinda Sutta (D. ii. 230).

[5] DA. ii. 640.

[6] D. ii. 220; *cp.* Mtu. iii. 197 ff.

[7] DA. ii. 647.

[8] This is done even now in Ceylon, where young boys' hair is tied round their heads in several knots. But in one place (DA. i. 296) Buddhaghosa says that one way of insulting a man was to shave his head, leaving him five locks of hair (*garahāyā ti pañcasikhā muṇḍakaraṇaṃ*). And, again (SA. i. 171), he mentions that Sanaṅkumāra retained his eternal youth because in a previous life he had developed *jhāna* while yet a lad (*pañcasikhakumārakāle*). See also J. vi. 496, where a traitor had his hair tied in five knots as a sign of disgrace.

(*kuntalikehi*), which fell back as in the case of a young boy (*pañcacūḷikadārakaparihāreṇ' eva*).

It was Pañcasikha who first received from the king of the Cātummahārājika worlds and their ministers reports of good-deeds done by human beings. These he would pass on to **Mātali**, who, in his turn, presented them to Sakka.[9] On the day of the **Devorohaṇa**, when the Buddha descended from Tāvatiṃsa, Pañcasikha was present to render honour to the Teacher in song and music.[10] According to the legends[11] he was present with the Buddha on other occasions as well.

Pañcasikha was evidently not only the name of a person, but also of an office (like Sakka), for in the **Biḷārakosiya Jātaka** (*q.v.*) **Ānanda** is said to have been born as Pañcasikha and to have helped Sakka and others to make of Biḷārakosiya a generous man.[12] Similarly, in the **Sudhābhojana Jātaka** (*q.v.*), **Anuruddha** is identified with Pañcasikha.[13]

[9] DA ii. 650.
[10] DhA. iii. 225; AA. i. 72; Vsm. i. 392.
[11] *E.g.*, Mhv. xxx. 75; xxxi. 82.
[12] J. iv. 69.
[13] J. v. 412.

Pañcasikha Sutta.—**Pañcasikha** visits the Buddha at **Gijjhakūṭa** and asks how it is that some beings are wholly set free in this very life, while others are not. The Buddha enlightens him.[1]

[1] S. iv. 103 f.

Pañcasikkhāpada Sutta.—On account of a common element those who commit the five evils—take life, steal, etc.—consort with those who do likewise.[1]

[1] S. ii. 167.

Pañcasīla Sutta.—The five things, being possessed of which makes women to be born in purgatory—the taking of life, theft, wrong sensuous indulgence, falsehood, the use of intoxicants. These are to be guarded against.[1]

[1] S. iv. 245.

Pañcasīlasamādāniya Thera.—An arahant. He belonged to a family of Māhāsāla brahmins in **Vesāli** and became an arahant at the age of five. It is said that he heard his parents take the five precepts, and remembered his own actions of a past life when, in the time of **Anomadassī** Buddha, he was a ferryman on the **Candavatī** and took the five precepts from the Buddha's disciple **Nisabha,** keeping them for one hundred thousand years. Thirty times he was king of the devas and five hundred times king of men.[1]

[1] Ap. i. 76 f.

1. **Pañcahatthiya Thera.**—An arahant. He once saw the Buddha **Sumedha,** to whom he offered five handfuls of lilies, which formed a canopy over the Buddha's head. Later, he was king five times under the name of **Hatthiya.**[1]

[1] Ap. i. 97 f.

2. **Pañcahatthiya Thera.**—An arahant. Ninety-two kappas ago he saw **Tissa** Buddha passing along the street with his followers and scattered five handfuls of lilies on his path. Thirteen kappas ago he was king five times under the name of **Sabhāsammata.**[1]

[1] Ap. i. 193.

1. **Pañcāla, Pañcālajanapada, Pañcālaraṭṭha, Pañcālā.**—One of the sixteen **Mahājanapadas.**[1] It consisted of two divisions: **Uttara-Pañcāla** and **Dakkhiṇa-Pañcāla.** The river **Bhagīrathī** (*q.v.*) formed the boundary between the divisions. According to the **Kumbhakāra Jātaka,**[2] the capital of Uttara-Pañcāla was **Kampillanagara,** where a king named **Dummukha** once reigned. Pañcāla was to the east of the **Kuru** country, and, in ancient times, there seems to have been a constant struggle between the Kurus and the Pañcālas for the possession of Uttara-Pañcāla. Thus, sometimes, Uttara-Pañcāla was included in the Kuru kingdom,[3] but at other times it formed a part of **Kampillaraṭṭha,**[4] Kampilla probably being the capital of Dakkhiṇa-Pañcāla. So it happened that sometimes the kings of Kampillaraṭṭha had their capital in Uttara-Pañcāla-nagara, while at others the kings of Uttara-Pañcāla-nagara had their capital in Kampilla-nagara. **Cūlaṇī-Brahmadatta** (*q.v.*) is described in the **Mahā-Ummagga Jātaka**[5] as king of Pañcāla, with his capital in Kampilla. There seems to have been a chieftain (*rājā*) of Pañcāla even in the Buddha's day, for we are told[6] that **Visākha Pañcāliputta** (*q.v.*) was the son of the daughter of the "Pañcāla-rājā." Pañcāla is generally identified[7] with the country to the north and west of Delhi, from the foot of the Himālaya to the river Chambal.

[1] A. i. 213; iv. 252, etc.

[2] J. iii. 379; also Mtu. iii. 26; but the Dvy. (435) calls the capital Hastināpura. According to the Mahābhārata (i. 138, 73-4), the capital was Ahicchatra or Chatravatī, while the capital of Dakṣiṇa-Pañcāla was Kāmpilya.

[3] *E.g.*, J. v. 444; also Mahābhārata i. 138.

[4] *E.g.*, J. iii. 79; v. 21, 289.

[5] J. vi. 329, 396, etc.; also PvA. 161; see also Uttarādhiyayana Sūtra (SBE. xlv. 57-61) and the Rāmāyaṇa (i. 32). Similarly Sambhūta was king of Uttara-Pañcāla (J. iv. 392 ff.). Sometimes the king of Pañcāla is merely spoken of as Pañcāla—*e.g.*, J. iv. 430, v. 98. See also **Jayaddisa.**

[6] ThagA. i. 331.

[7] Law: *Geog. of Early Buddhism*, p. 19.

Pañcāla Vagga.—The fifth section of the Navaka Nipāta of the Aṅguttara Nikāya.[1]

[1] A. iv. 449-54.

Pañcāla Sutta.—A discussion between **Ānanda** and **Udāyi** (**Kāḷudāyi**) regarding a verse uttered by the devaputta **Pañcālacaṇḍa**[1] as to what constitutes obstacles (*sambādha*) in the world and what release therefrom (*okāsādhigama*). Udāyi says that the five sensuous pleasures are the *sambādha*, and that *okāsadhigama* consists in the attainment of the *jhānas*.[2]

[1] See S. i. 48. [2] A. iv. 449 f.; AA. ii. 815.

1. **Pañcālacaṇḍa.**—A devaputta who visited the Buddha at **Jetavana** and uttered a verse to the effect that the man who understands *jhāna* finds room even among crowding obstacles. The Buddha corrects him, saying that those who are mindful and self-possessed know the way to Nibbāna.[1] This discussion forms the basis for the **Pañcāla Sutta** (above.) It is probably this same deva who is mentioned as a Mahāyakkha in the **Āṭānāṭiya Sutta**[2] who is to be invoked by the Buddha's followers in time of need.

[1] S. i. 48. [2] D. iii. 205.

2. **Pañcālacaṇḍa.**—A handsome brahmin youth with whom the queen of a Kosala king misconducted herself on various occasions. She first saw and fell in love with him when on the way to visit her son; thereafter she found various excuses for coming to the city where he lived. This is one of the stories related by **Kuṇāla.**[1]

[1] J. v. 425, 430 f.

3. **Pañcālacaṇḍa.**—A former birth of **Kuṇāla.** He was the chaplain of **Kaṇḍari,** king of Benares, and helped the king in discovering the love intrigues of his queen, **Kinnarā,** with a misshapen cripple. When Kaṇḍari wished to have the queen beheaded, Pañcālacaṇḍa interceded on her behalf and convinced the king, by recalling to his mind several experiences they had lived through together, that the queen's sin was due to her nature as woman.[1]

[1] J. v. 437 ff.

4. **Pañcālacaṇḍa.**—Son of **Cūḷanī Brahmadatta.** He was sent by **Mahosadha** to be kept as hostage to King **Videha,** when Cūḷanī threatened to harm the latter; but Videha treated him like a younger brother. **Pañcālacaṇḍī** was sister to Pañcālacaṇḍa.[1]

[1] J. vi. 434, 435, 454, 462, 466.

Pañcālacaṇḍa Sutta.—Recounts the discussion between the Buddha and the devaputta **Pañcālacaṇḍa** (1).[1]

[1] S. i. 48.

Pañcālacaṇḍī.—Daughter of **Cūḷanī Brahmadatta.** Her marriage with King **Videha,** which was accomplished by the wisdom and diplomacy of **Mahosadha,** forms the main theme of the **Mahā Ummagga Jātaka.** She bore a son to Videha, who succeeded him ten years after the marriage. Pañcālacaṇḍī is identified with **Sundarī-(Nandā).**[1]

[1] J. vi. 409, 410, 426, 427, 434, 438, 445, 453, 454, 466, 478.

Pañcālī.—Wife of **Esukārī,** king of Benares. When Esukārī longed for wealth, she showed him the folly of covetousness and persuaded him to become an ascetic, later entering to ascetic life herself. The story is related in the **Hatthipāla Jātaka** (*q.v.*). Pañcālī is identified with **Mahāmāyā.**[1] The scholiast says[2] that she was called Pañcālī because she was the daughter of the Pañcāla king.

[1] J. iv. 491. [2] *Ibid.*, 486.

Pañcāliputta.—See **Visākha Pañcāliputta.** According to Buddhaghosa,[1] Visākha's mother was a brahmin called **Pañcālī;** but the Theragāthā Commentary says[2] that Visākha's mother was the daughter of the rājā of Pañcāla.

[1] AA. ii. 511. [2] ThigA. i. 331 f.

Pañcavudha Jātaka (No. 55).—The story of **Pañcāvudha-kumāra,** given below. The ogre is identified with **Aṅgulimāla.** The story was related in reference to a monk who had renounced all effort.[1]

[1] J. i. 272 ff.

Pañcāvudha-kumāra.—The Bodhisatta born as king of Benares. He was the son of Brahmadatta, and was so named because eight hundred brahmins prophesied that he would win glory through prowess in arms. He studied in **Takkasilā,** and, at the end of his course, his teacher gave him a set of five weapons. On the way home he had a conflict with an ogre named **Silesaloma,** against whom his weapons were of no avail, as they could not penetrate the ogre's hair. But he fought on, and the ogre, marvelling at his courage and his fearlessness, set him free. He thereupon preached to the ogre and converted him. Pañcāvudha later became king of Benares.[1]

[1] J. i. 272 ff.

Pañcikā.—See **Moggallāna-Pañcikā.**

Pañcuddharaṭṭha.—The name of the districts lying round the modern city of Kandy.[1]

[1] Cv. xciv. 4; xcv. 23, 24; xcvi. 17; see Geiger, Cv. *Trs.* ii. 233, n. 2.

Pañcuposatha Jātaka (No. 490).—Once four animals—a wood pigeon, a snake, a jackal, and a bear—lived on friendly terms with the Bodhisatta, who was an ascetic, add, with him as their teacher, they all kept the *uposatha* to rid themselves of their sins and desires. The pigeon had yearned too much after his mate, who was killed by a hawk; the snake had killed a bull, which trod on it; the jackal had lost his hair by clinging too long to an elephant's corpse; the bear had received many blows when he visited a village for food; while the ascetic himself had been proud until visited by a Pacceka Buddha, who pointed out to him the folly of pride.

Anuruddha was the pigeon, **Kassapa** the bear, **Moggallāna** the jackal, and **Sāriputta** the snake.

The Jātaka was related to five hundred *upāsakas* to encourage them to keep the fast days.[1]

[1] J. iv. 325 ff.

Pañjalipabbata.—A mountain in South Ceylon, at the source of the **Karindanadī.** Here **Theraputtābhaya** lived after he renounced the world and became an arahant.[1] *v.l.* **Pañcalipabbata, Pajjalitapabbata.**

[1] Mhv. xxxii. 14; Thūpavaṃsa 77.

Pañña Jātaka.—See **Pāniya Jātaka.**

Pañña Vagga.—The third section of the **Paṭisambhidāmagga.**

1. **Paññā Sutta.**—On the four powers: wisdom, energy, innocence (*anavajja*) and collectedness or kindness (*saṅgāha*).[1]

[1] A. ii. 142.

2. **Paññā Sutta.**—On eight reasons and causes which strengthen elementary wisdom (*ādibrahmacariyikā paññā*).[1]

[1] A. iv. 151 ff.

Paññatti Sutta.—On four types of beings and their chiefs: of those who have bodies, **Rāhu** is chief; of those who enjoy pleasures of sense,

Mandhātā is chief; of those who have lordship, **Māra** is chief; but the Tathāgata is chief of the whole world of devas, Māras, etc.[1]

[1] A. ii. 17.

Paññattivādā (*v.l.* **Pannatti°**).—A secondary division of the **Gokulikas.**[1] Their main doctrine was that suffering is no *skandha*, that there are no perfect *āyatanas*, that the *saṃskāras* are all bound together, that suffering is absolute, that what proceeds from the mind is not the way, that there is no untimely death, that there is no human agency, and that all suffering comes from *karma.*[2]

[1] Dpv. v. 41; Mhv. v. 4; Mbv. p. 96. [2] Rockhill: *op. cit.*, 189.

Paññavā Sutta.—A monk who cultivates the seven factors of wisdom can be called intelligent.[1]

[1] S. v. 467.

Paññā Sutta.—Few are they blessed with insight; more numerous they that are not.[1]

[1] S. v. 467.

Paññāvuddhi Sutta.—The four states which conduce to growth in wisdom: association with the good, hearing the Doctrine, right reflection, and right behaviour in accordance with the Dhamma.[1]

[1] A. ii. 245.

Paññhamaṇḍapaṭṭhāna.—A place near the **Abhayavāpi** in **Anurādhapura.**[1]

[1] SA. iii. 151.

Paññhambamālaka.—A place in **Anurādhapura,** where **Devānampiyatissa** offered **Mahinda** a mango, which he ate on the spot, and caused the seed to be planted. Immediately there sprouted from it a tall tree, bearing mangoes. This place later became the centre of distribution of various gifts to the monks.[1] After Mahinda's death, the bier containing his body was placed here for a week, and many honours were shown to it prior to its cremation.[2] This is probably the same as **Pañcambamālaka** (*q.v.*).

[1] Mhv. xv. 38. [2] *Ibid.*, xx. 39.

1. **Paṭācārā Therī.**—An arahant. She was the daughter of a banker of **Sāvatthi,** and, when grown up, formed an intimacy with a servant. When her parents wished to marry her to a youth of her own rank, she ran away with her lover and lived in a hamlet. As the time for her confinement drew near, she wished to return to her parents, but the husband, on

various pretexts, put off the visit. One day when he was out she left a message with the neighbours and started for Sāvatthi. Her husband followed her, but on the way she gave birth to a son, and they returned home. The same happened when her second child was born, but soon after its birth a great storm broke, and her husband went to cut some sticks and grass in the jungle with which to make a shelter. He was bitten by a snake and died. The wife spent the night in misery, lying on the ground hugging her children. In the morning she discovered her husband's body, and started off to go to her parents. On the way she had to cross a river, and, because it was in flood, she could not carry both her children across at the same time. She therefore left the younger on some leaves on the bank and started wading across with the other. In midstream she looked back and saw a hawk swoop down and carry away the babe. In her excitement she dropped the child she was carrying and it was swept away by the flood. Distracted, she went on towards Sāvatthi, but on the way she learnt that the house in which her parents and brother lived had fallen on them in the night and that they had been burnt on one pyre. Mad with grief, she wandered about in circles, and because, as she circled round, her skirt-cloth fell from her, she was called **Paṭācārā** ("cloak-walker"). People drove her from their doors, till one day she arrived in **Jetavana,** where the Buddha was preaching. The people round him tried to stop her from approaching, but the Buddha called her to him and talked to her. By the potency of his gentleness, she regained presence of mind and crouched on the earth. A man threw her his outer robe, and she, wearing it, drew close to the Buddha, and worshipping at his feet, told him her story and begged for his help. The Buddha spoke to her words of consolation, making her realize the inevitableness of death; he then taught her the Truth. When he finished speaking, she became a *sotāpanna* and asked for ordination. Her request was granted, and one day, while washing her feet, she noticed how the water trickled, sometimes only to a short distance, sometimes further, and she pondered "even so do mortals die, either in childhood, in middle age, or in old age." The Buddha sent her a ray of glory and appeared before her, speaking and confirming her thoughts. When he had finished speaking, Paṭācārā won arahantship. She later became a great teacher, and many women, stricken with grief, sought her guidance and her consolation.[1] She was declared by the Buddha to be the best among therī's who knew the Vinaya.[2]

In the time of **Padumuttara** Buddha, she was born in a clansman's family, and having heard the Buddha speak of a nun as first among those who knew the rules of the Order, she aspired to a similar rank for herself.

[1] See, *e.g.*, ThigA. 47, 117, 122. [2] A. i. 25.

In the time of **Kassapa** Buddha, she became a bhikkuṇī, and was third of the seven daughters of **Kikī,** king of Benares. She built a cell for the Order and lived a celibate life for twenty thousand years.[3]

Paṭācārā is given as an example of one whose grief was assuaged by listening to the Dhamma.[4]

[3] Thig. 112-16; ThigA. 108 ff.; Ap. ii. 557 f.; AA. ii. 194 ff.; DhA. ii. 260 ff.; iii. 434 f.; J. vi. 481.

[4] DA. iii. 746; MA. i. 188; UdA. 127.

2. **Paṭācārā.**—One of the five children of two Jain disputants, a man and a woman, of **Vesāli;** they married at the suggestion of the **Licchavis** in order that their children might inherit the skill of both. Paṭācārā and her three sisters and one brother were later converted by **Sāriputta** and became arahants. Paṭācārā is identified with one of the daughters of the Kaliṅga king in the **Cullakāliṅga Jātaka.**[1] Her brother was the Nigaṇṭha **Saccaka.**[2]

[1] J. iii. 1 ff.

[2] MA. i. 450.

Paṭikkūla Sutta.—The idea of the repulsiveness of food, if cultivated and encouraged, conduces to great profit.[1]

[1] S. v. 132.

Paṭicchanna Sutta.—Three things which are practised in secret: the ways of women, the chants of brahmins, the views of perverse men; and three others which are there for all to see: the sun, the moon, and the *dhammavinaya* of a Tathāgata.[1]

[1] A. i. 282.

Paṭijagga.—Sixty-seven kappas ago there were seven kings of this name, all previous incarnations of **Citakapūjaka Thera.**[1]

[1] Ap. i. 237.

Paṭidesanīya Vagga.—One of the sub-divisions of the Pācittiya.[1]

[1] Vin. iii. 175 ff.

Paṭipatti Vagga.—The fourth chapter of the **Magga Saṃyutta.**[1]

[1] S. v. 23 ff.

Paṭipatti Sutta.—Preached at **Sāvatthi,** on wrong conduct and right conduct.[1]

[1] S. v. 23.

1. **Paṭipadā Sutta.**—The Buddha teaches of both the wrong way and the right way.[1]

[1] S. ii. 4.

2. **Paṭipadā Sutta.**—The Buddha teaches both the way that leads to the arising of the condition of the body and also the way leading to the cessation of such a condition.[1]

[1] S. iii. 43.

3. **Paṭipadā Sutta.**—The Buddha teaches both wrong practice and right practice.[1]

[1] S. v. 18.

4. **Paṭipadā Sutta.**—The Buddha does not praise wrong practice, but he praises right practice.[1]

[1] S. v. 18 f.

1. **Paṭipanna Sutta.**—The Buddha teaches about those that are wrongly conducted and those that are rightly conducted.[1]

[1] S. v. 23.

2. **Paṭipanna Sutta.**—By the completion and the fulfilment of the five indriyas one becomes an arahant; their cultivation in a less degree brings lower attainments.[1]

[1] S. v. 202.

Paṭiyārāma.—The name of the **Thūpārāma** in the time of **Kakusandha** Buddha.[1]

[1] Sp. i. 86; Dpv. xvii. 11.

Paṭiyāloka.—A place near **Rājagaha.**[1]

[1] Vin. iv., 79, 131.

Paṭibhāna Sutta.—The four kinds of people in the world: he who replies to the point, not diffusely; he who replies diffusely; etc.[1]

[1] A. ii. 135.

Paṭimā-vihāra.—A monastery probably in **Kāṇagāma,** where **Agga-bodhi,** ruler of **Rohaṇa,** set up a large stone image of the Buddha.[1]

[1] Cv. xlv. 43.

Paṭirūpa Sutta.—The Buddha was once staying in **Ekasālā** in **Kosala,** and there preached to a large congregation. **Māra** warned the Buddha not to teach, lest he should suffer both from the zeal of his supporters and the anger of his opponents. The Tathāgatha is unmindful of both, answered the Buddha.[1]

[1] S. i. 111.

Paṭilābha Sutta.—A description of the five indriyas.[1]

[1] S. v. 199 f.

Paṭisaṅkhāra.—Thirty kappas ago there were thirteen kings of this name, all previous births of **Sudhāpiṇḍiya Thera.**[1]

[1] Ap. i. 133.

1. **Paṭisambhidā Sutta.**—Five qualities which make a monk become that which he should: the four paṭisambhidā and knowledge of all things, great and small, which must be done for his fellow-celibates.[1]

[1] A. iii. 113.

2. **Paṭisambhidā Sutta.**—Seven qualities which enable a monk to realize, unaided, the four *paṭisambhidā.*[1]

[1] A. iv. 32 f.

Paṭisambhidākathā.—The sixth section of the Yuganaddhavagga of the **Paṭisambhidāmagga.**[1]

[1] Ps. ii. 147-158.

Paṭisambhidāmagga.—The twelfth " book " of the **Khuddaka Nikāya.** It really belongs to the literature of the Abhidhamma type, and describes how analytical knowledge can be acquired by an arahant. It presents a systematic exposition of certain important topics of Buddhism. It is possible that, before the development of the extant Abhidhammapiṭaka, it passed as one of the Abhidhamma treatises. The book consists of three vaggas—Mahāvagga, Yuganaddhavagga and Paññāvagga—and each vagga contains ten topics (*kathā*). The treatment of the various topics is essentially scholastic in character, and whole passages are taken *verbatim* from the Vinaya and from various collections of the Sutta Piṭaka, while a general acquaintance with the early Buddhist legends is assumed.[1]

A commentary exists, written by **Mahānāma,** a thera of Ceylon, and called **Saddhammappakāsinī.**

[1] **Published by the P.T.S. There is an index in *J.R.A.S.*, 1908.**

Paṭisallāna Sutta.—The Buddha exhorts the monks to apply themselves to solitude, because the solitary man knows things as they really are.[1]

[1] S. iii. 15; iv. 80; v. 414.

Paṭisāraṇīya Sutta.—Eight kinds of disqualifications in a monk, which entitle the Order to censure him.[1]

[1] A. iv. 346 f.

Paṭṭi.—A Damiḷa chieftain, ally of **Kulasekhara.**[1]

[1] Cv. lxxvi. 144.

Paṭṭhānagaṇānaya.—An Abhidhamma treatise ascribed to **Saddhammajotipāla.**[1]

[1] Gv. 64, 74.

Paṭṭhānappakaraṇa.—The last "book" of the Abhidhammapiṭaka. It might be described as the book of "causes," and deals with the twenty-four *paccayas* or modes of relations between things, mental and material.[1] Its Commentary was written by **Buddhaghosa** at the request of a monk called **Culla Buddhaghosa.**

[1] Published by the P.T.S.

Paṭṭhānasāradīpanī.—A work by a monk named **Saddhammālaṅkāra.**[1]

[1] Sās. 48; Bode, *op. cit.*, 47.

Paṭhama-Cetiya.—A cetiya built by **Devānampiyatissa,** on the spot where **Mahinda** alighted on his first visit to **Anurādhapura** and the king's palace.[1] One of the eight Bodhi saplings was planted there.[2]

[1] Mhv. xiv. 45; xx. 20; Sp. i. 79. [2] Mhv. xix. 61.

Paṭhamasambodhi.—The name of a book.[1]

[1] Gv. 65, 75.

Paṭhavicālaka-Dhammagutta.—See **Dhammagutta.**

Paṭhavidundubhi.—A king of ninety-one kappas ago, a previous birth of **Māṇava (Sammukhāthavika).**[1]

[1] ThagA. i. 163; Ap. i. 159.

1. **Paṭhavindhara.**—A Nāga-king, a previous birth of **Rāhula.**[1]

[1] AA. i. 142, etc.; but see *s.v.* **Rāhula.**

2. **Paṭhavindhara.**—Son of **Kiki,** king of Benares. He built one of the gateways of the Dhātughara of **Kassapa** Buddha.[1]

[1] SNA. i. 194.

Paṭhamasuddhiya Sutta.—The four jhānas, which, when cultivated, flow to Nibbāna, just as the Ganges flows to the east.[1]

[1] S. v. 307.

Paḍāvī.—A locality in Ceylon where **Udaya I.** built a large hall for the sick.[1]

[1] Cv. xlix. 19.

Paṇanagara.—A village in Ceylon which was one of the centres of the campaigns of **Paṇḍukābhaya.**[1]

[1] Mhv. x. 27.

Paṇiva.—A locality in South India.[1]

[1] Cv. lxxvi. 184, 186.

Paṇihita-acchanna Vagga.—The fifth section of the Eka Nipāta of the Aṅguttara Nikāya.[1]

[1] A. i. 8-10.

Paṇītatara Sutta.—The four kinds of birth among the Nāgas and the pre-eminent among them.[1]

[1] S. iii. 240.

1. **Paṇḍaka.**—A monk, friend of **Kapila,** who lived in a village near Kosambī. He was found guilty of having taken what did not belong to him and also of unchastity.[1]

[1] Vin. iii. 67.

2. **Paṇḍaka.**—A yakkha of the **Himālaya** region. He, his wife **Hāritā,** and his five hundred sons, became sotāpannas when **Majjhantika** preached to **Aravāḷa.**[1]

[1] Mhv. xii. 21.

1. **Paṇḍara, Paṇḍaraka.**—A Nāga-king. See **Paṇḍara Jātaka.**

2. **Paṇḍara.**—The name of the horse ridden by **Maṅgala** Buddha when he left household life.[1]

[1] BuA. 116.

3. **Paṇḍara.**—A clan of elephants, each having the strength of one thousand men.[1]

[1] UdA. 403; VibhA. 397; AA. ii. 822.

5. **Paṇḍara.**—The name of a *gotta*. An ascetic of this clan, hearing **Phussa Thera** preach, asked him a question which led to a long explanation by Phussa.[1] It is said that the *gotta* had, as ancestor, a sage named **Paṇḍara.** *v.l.* **Paṇḍarasa.**

[1] Thag. vs. 949; ThagA. ii. 82 ff.

Paṇḍara Jātaka (No. 518).—A ship was once wrecked in mid-ocean and only a man called **Karambiya** survived. He was cast upon an island, where he wandered about naked and destitute. The people thought he was an ascetic and built him a hermitage. Among his followers were a Garuḍa-king, and also a Nāga-king named **Paṇḍara** (or **Paṇḍaraka**). One day, at the instigation of the Garuḍa, the ascetic wheedled out of Paṇḍara the secret of how the Nāgas prevented themselves from being carried off by the Garuḍas. They swallowed large stones, thus making themselves very heavy. If the Garuḍas seized them by their tails, they would have to disgorge the stones and could easily be carried off. Karambiya betrayed this secret to the Garuḍa-king who, thereupon, seized Paṇḍara in the right way and carried him away. Paṇḍara begged for mercy, and the Garuḍa set him free, warning him never again to tell his secret. Thereafter the Garuḍa and Paṇḍara lived as friends. Paṇḍara cursed Karambiya and his head split in seven pieces.

The story was related in reference to the wickedness of **Devadatta,** who is identified with Karambiya. Paṇḍara was **Sāriputta** and the Garuḍa the Bodhisatta.[1]

[1] J. v. 75 ff.; vi. 177.

Paṇḍaraṅga.—A sect of brahmin ascetics; they are mentioned in the time of the Buddha[1] and also in that of **Asoka.**[2] Perhaps they covered their bodies with ashes.

[1] *E.g.*, DhA. iv. 8. [2] *E.g.*, Dpv. viii. 35; Sp. i. 44.

Paṇḍarakā.—The name of a river which is mentioned with **Mallaṅgiri** and **Tikūṭa** as a haunt of **Kinnarī's.**[1]

[1] J. iv. 438, 439.

Paṇḍarasa.—See **Paṇḍara** (5).

1. **Paṇḍava.**—The horse of **Sāma,** king of Benares; his trainer was **Giridanta.**[1] See **Giridanta Jātaka.**

[1] J. ii. 98.

2. **Paṇḍava.**—A hill near **Rājagaha,** under the shadow of which the Buddha ate his meal when he begged alms in Rājagaha, soon after leaving home.[1] It is said[2] that ascetics lived on its eastern slope. It seems formerly to have borne another name.[3] Paṇḍava was one of the halting-places of **Sīvalī Thera** when on his way to the **Himālaya.**[4]

[1] J. i. 66; SN. vs. 414; DhA. i. 70; Thag. vs. 41, 1167; Mtu. ii. 198, etc.
[2] SNA. ii. 383 f.
[3] See M. iii. 68.
[4] AA. i. 139.

3. **Paṇḍava.**—Adjective from **Paṇḍu.**[1]

[1] *E.g.*, Cv. lxxxvii. 29.

Paṇḍavavāpī.—A tank and a monastery in Ceylon, restored by **Vijayabāhu I.**[1] The tank was later enlarged by **Parakkamabāhu I.** and converted into the **Parakkamasamudda.**[2]

[1] Cv. lx. 48, 58.
[2] *Ibid.*, lxviii. 39; for its identification see Cv. *Trs.* i. 219, n. 1.

Paṇḍavāvana.—A park laid out by **Parakkamabāhu I.**[1]

[1] Cv. lxxix. 12.

1. **Paṇḍita.**—The Bodhisatta born as a merchant. See the **Kūṭavāṇija Jātaka.**

2. **Paṇḍita.**—One of the four novices invited by the brahmin whose house came later to be known as the **Pañcachiddageha** (*q.v.*).[1] In the time of **Kassapa** Buddha he was known as **Mahāduggata** (*q.v.*). In his last birth his mother was the daughter of a rich merchant of **Sāvatthi.** During her pregnancy, she had a longing to give to five hundred monks, headed by **Sāriputta,** the choicest portions of red fish, to don yellow robes, to sit in the outer circle of the monks' seats, and to partake of the food left over by the monks. This longing was satisfied, and seven times she held similar festivities. When the child was born he was called Paṇḍita because, from the day of his conception, various people of the household who had been stupid or deaf or dumb recovered their faculties. When seven years old, he was filled with the desire to become a monk, and was ordained by Sāriputta, a constant visitor to the house. For seven days his parents held a festival in honour of his ordination. On the eighth day he went, with Sāriputta, into the village for alms; on the way, certain things which he saw—a ditch, arrow-makers, carpenters—made him wish to strive for arahantship. Thereupon, with the leave of Sāriputta, he returned to the monastery requesting the Elder to

[1] DhA. iv. 176 ff.

bring him some red fish on his return from the alms-round. In the monastery, **Sakka** stilled all noises and held back the sun and the moon, lest Paṇḍita should be disturbed. The Buddha, seeing this, detained Sāriputta back on his way to the monsatery, and engaged him in conversation until Paṇḍita should have succeeded in his effort. After a while, Paṇḍita became an arahant and the whole world rejoiced.[2]

[2] *Ibid.*, ii. 139 ff.

3. **Paṇḍita.**—A Pacceka Buddha, mentioned in a nominal list.[1]

[1] M. iii. 70; ApA. i. 107.

Paṇḍita Vagga.—The sixth chapter of the Dhammapada.

Paṇḍita Sutta.—On three things enjoined by the wise and the good: charity, going into homelessness, and support of parents.[1]

[1] A. i. 151.

Paṇḍitakumāraka.—A **Licchavi** who, with **Abhaya,** visited **Ānanda** at the **Mahāvana** in **Vesāli** and held a discussion regarding ascetic practices.[1]

[1] A. i. 220 f.

Paṇḍitapañha.—See **Pañcapaṇḍitapañha.**

Paṇḍimaṇḍalanāḍālvara.—A Damiḷa chief.[1]

[1] Cv. lxxvi. 179.

Paṇḍiyarāyara.—A Damiḷa chief.[1]

[1] Cv. lxxvi. 174, 178.

1. **Paṇḍu.**—Ancestor of the **Pāṇḍavas.**[1] The name is also for those who claimed to belong to that dynasty—*e.g.*, in the case of the kings of **Madhurā.**[2] See also **Paṇḍurājā.**

[1] Cv. lxiv. 43.

[2] *E.g.*, Mhv. vii. 50. See also **Paṇḍū.**

2. **Paṇḍu.**—A Sākyan, son of **Amitodana;** he was the father of **Bhaddakaccānā** and her six brothers. On learning from soothsayers of the impending destruction of the Sāykans by **Viḍūḍabha,** Paṇḍu left the Sākyan country and settled beyond the Ganges.[1] His wife was **Susīmā.**[2]

[1] Mhv. viii. 18 f.; Dpv. x. i.

[2] MṬ. 275.

3. **Paṇḍu.**—See **Paṇḍuputta.**

1. **Paṇḍuka.**—One of the **Chabbaggiyā.** He and **Lohitaka** were leaders af a special group called the **Paṇḍukalohitakā,** who are mentioned as having been guilty of various offences against Vinaya rules.[1] Paṇḍuka and Lohitaka lived at **Jetavana** and encouraged heretics by upholding their views. The **Satapatta Jātaka** was preached in reference to these two.[2] They were the least evil of the Chabbaggiyī.[3]

[1] Vin. ii. 1, 5, 6. [2] MA. ii. 668; J. ii. 387. [3] Sp. iii. 614.

2. **Paṇḍuka.**—A Damiḷa usurper. He killed **Mittasena** and reigned for five years over Ceylon (433-8 A.C.), during which time he was unsuccessful in his attempts to kill **Dhātusena,** the rightful heir. Paṇḍuka's son was **Pariṇḍa.**[1]

[1] Cv. xxxviii. 11, 21, 29.

Paṇḍukaṇṇa.—A juggler (*nāṭaka*) who was among those who tried, but without success, to make **Mahā-Panāda** laugh. He entered with his troupe into a blazing fire and there remained until it burnt out. The people sprinkled the ashes with water, and Paṇḍukaṇṇa and his troupe rose up, wearing flowers and dancing.[1]

[1] J. iv. 324.

Paṇḍukambalasilāsana.—The throne of **Sakka,** which stands under the **Pāricchattaka-Kovilāra** tree and is sixty leagues long, fifty broad and fifteen deep. Sakka, sitting on it, sinks as far as the middle of his body. It is the colour of the *jayasumana* flower.[1] The Buddha occupied the seat when he visited Tāvatiṃsa to preach to his mother. It is said that Sakka feared the seat might prove too high for the Buddha, but the Buddha, perceiving his thoughts, sat on it, covering the whole with a fold of his robe.[2] Mention is also made[3] of the Buddha occupying the seat on a subsequent visit to Tāvatiṃsa. Distinguished guests of Sakka, such as **Sādhīna,**[4] were allowed to sit on the throne by Sakka's side. When Sakka's span of life draws near its end, or his merit is exhausted, or a righteous being is in danger and needs his help, the Paṇḍukambalasilāsana becomes heated, thus attracting his attention.[5] It is so called because it resembled a red blanket (*rattakambala*).[6]

[1] DA. ii. 482.
[2] DhA. iii. 217; iv. 80.
[3] J. ii. 93. [4] J. iv. 357.
[5] *E.g.*, J. iv. 8 f., 238, 323; iii. 53; v. 92, etc.
[6] MNidA. 313.

Paṇḍukābhaya.—King of Ceylon (377-307 B.C.). He was the son of **Dīghagāmaṇī** and **Ummāda-Cittā** and was protected from death in infancy by **Citta** and **Kāḷavela,** who afterwards became yakkhas. He was brought up by a man in **Dvāramaṇḍalaka,** but several times his uncles, discovering his whereabouts, tried to kill him, for it had been foretold that he would slay his uncles in order to obtain possession of the kingdom. At the age of sixteen he was apprenticed to the brahmin **Paṇḍula,** who taught him various arts and provided him later with the necessary money for an army. Paṇḍula's son, **Canda,** was given as friend and counsellor to Paṇḍukābhaya. Paṇḍukābhaya married, by force, a maiden named **Suvaṇṇapālī,** and declared war upon his uncles, all of whom, except the eldest, **Abhaya,** had determined to slay him. With the help of the yakkhiṇī **Cetiyā,** who dwelt in **Dhūmarakkhapabbata,** Paṇḍukābhaya made all preparations for a final campaign against his uncles. For four years he lived in Dhūmarakkha, and then for seven in **Ariṭṭhapabbata.** Following the counsel of Cetiyā, he enticed his uncles into a trap, and slew them and their followers at **Lābugāmaka.** He then proceeded to **Anurādhagāma,** where he set up his capital, which, thenceforward, came to be called **Anurādhapura.** His uncle, Abhaya, was made Nagaraguttika, and to him was given over the government of the city by night.

After establishing peace in the land, Paṇḍukābhaya proceeded to lay out his capital as a city, and among the buildings which he erected were hermitages for the Nigaṇṭhas **Jotiya, Giri** and **Kumbhaṇḍa,** and dwellings for the **Ājīvakas,** the brahmins, etc. He also marked out the boundaries of the villages throughout the island. He ruled for seventy years, and died at the age of 107. He was succeeded by his son **Muṭasīva.**[1]

[1] Mhv. ix. 28; x. 1 ff.; xi. 1; Dpv. v. 69, 81; x. 9; xi. 1-12.

Paṇḍunādukoṭṭāna.—A locality in South India.[1]

[1] Cv. lxxvii. 105.

Paṇḍuputta.—An **Ājīvaka.** He came of a wagon-building stock of bygone days. In the **Anaṅgana Sutta,**[1] **Moggallāna** tells **Sāriputta** that, one day, when begging alms in **Rājagaha,** he came to the house of **Samīti,** the wagon builder who was shaping a felloe. Standing by was Paṇḍuputta, watching him and wishing that he should shape it without blemish. When Samīti did so, Paṇḍuputta expressed his joy, saying that Samīti had read his thoughts.

Buddhaghosa says[2] that Paṇḍuputta was so called because he was the son of **Paṇḍu.**

[1] M. i. 31 f.

[2] MA. i. 124.

Paṇḍupura.—A village near **Sāvatthi.**[1]

[1] DhA. iii. 449.

1. **Paṇḍurājā.**—The ancestor of the **Paṇḍavas. Ajjuna, Nakula, Bhīmasena, Yudhiṭṭhila** and **Sahadeva** are called the sons of Paṇḍurājā and are said to belong to the Paṇḍurājāgotta.[1]

[1] J. v. 426.

2. **Paṇḍurājā.**—A king of **Madhurā.**[1] This is probably a descriptive name and means that he belonged to the Pāṇḍyan dynasty.

[1] Mhv. vii. 50, 69, 72.

3. **Paṇḍurājā.**—A Damiḷa chief, ally of **Kulasekhara.**[1]

[1] Cv. lxxvi. 126.

Paṇḍula.—A brahmin of **Paṇḍulagāma,** rich and learned in the Vedas. He taught **Paṇḍukābhaya,** advised him in the choice of a wife, gave him one hundred thousand with which to raise an army, and allowed his son **Canda** to accompany him as his friend and counsellor.[1]

[1] Mhv. x. 20 ff.

Paṇḍulagāma.—The residence of **Paṇḍula** (*q.v.*); it was to the south of **Anurādhapura.**[1]

[1] Mhv. x. 20.

Paṇḍuvāsudeva.—King of Ceylon (444-414 B.C.). He was the youngest son of **Sumitta,** brother of **Vijaya.** He came to Ceylon at Vijaya's request, and having succeeded him to the throne, reigned in **Upatissagāma.** He married **Bhaddakaccānā,** who bore him ten sons and one daughter. He reigned for thirty years.[1]

[1] Mhv. viii. 10 ff.; ix. 1 ff., 28; x. 29; Dpv. iv. 41; x. 2, 7, 8; xi. 8 ff.

Paṇḍuvijaya.—A village founded by **Parakkamabāhu I.** in memory of his conquest of the **Paṇḍu** country.[1]

[1] Cv. lxxvii. 105.

Paṇḍū.—A nation in South India, the Pāṇḍiyas. Their country comprised the greater part of the Madura and Tinnevelly, with its capital first at Kolkai and later at Madhurā.[1] Ceylon was in constant communication with this country, both peaceful and otherwise. Marauding bands of Paṇḍūs often came to Ceylon and, having deposed the rightful sovereign, ruled over the country. Chief among these invasions were the following: (*a*) for fourteen years, when **Vaṭṭagāmaṇī** lay in hiding; (*b*) for twenty-seven years, after the death of **Mahānāma** and until **Dhātusena** established his authority; (*c*) in the time of **Sena I.**; (*d*) after the death of

Mahinda V. They also came with **Māgha** and **Candabhānu,** and, later, with **Āryacakkavattin,** who succeeded in carrying the Tooth Relic away to the Pāṇḍyan court; this was later rescued by **Parakkamabāhu III.** Sometimes the Sinhalese kings would make reprisals by invading the Pāṇḍyan territory—*e.g.*, in the reign of **Sena II.,** and, perhaps also, under **Nissaṅka Malla. Parakkamabāhu I.** sent an army under his general **Laṅkāpura** to help the Pāṇḍyan king **Parākrama Pāṇḍya** against the Coḷa king, **Kulasekhara.** This, according to the Mahāvaṃsa account, brought great joy to the Sinhalese.

Mention is made in the chronicles of several marriages between members of the Pāṇḍyan and the Sinhalese royal families. **Vijaya** himself took his consort from the Pāṇḍyan king at **Madhurā,** and later, **Mittā,** sister of **Vijayabāhu I.,** married a Pāṇḍyan prince who became the grandfather of Parakkamabāhu I. This led to the establishment of a " Pāṇḍyan party " in Ceylon which was not always loyal to the reigning monarch —*e.g.*, in the case of **Vikkamabāhu III. Parakkama Paṇḍu,** who deposed **Līlāvatī,** evidently belonged to this party and probably also **Vijaya III.** The Pāṇḍyaṇ kings claimed descent from the Lunar race.[1]

[1] Codrington, *op. cit.*, 15. For other references, see under the names mentioned. Reference should also be made to the Index at the end of the Cūḷavaṃsa, *s.v.* Paṇḍū.

Paṇṇaka.—A Nāga king living in **Anotatta** lake. When **Cūla-Sumana** (*q.v.*) went to the lake to fetch water for his teacher, Paṇṇaka refused to let him take it. There ensued a great struggle of iddhi-power between them, in view of the many hosts of deities invoked by Sumana. In the end, Sumana trod with his heel on the head of the Nāga, water squirted forth from the folds of the Nāga's hood and he was overcome. Ashamed of his defeat, Paṇṇaka complained to Sumana's teacher that the novice had stolen the water. But, on the teacher's advice, Paṇṇaka begged forgiveness of Sumana and promised to fetch water from Anotatta whenever he should need it. Sumana visited him again at the Buddha's instigation, in order that his power might be manifest to others.[1]

[1] DhA. iv. 129 ff.

Paṇṇakata.—A city in **Esikāraṭṭha.**[1]

[1] Pv. iv. 7; PvA. 195 ff.

Paṇṇattivāda.—See **Paññattivāda.**

1. **Paṇṇadāyaka Thera.**—An arahant. In the time of **Siddhattha** Buddha he was an ascetic wearing bark robes and eating raw leaves.

One day the Buddha came to him as he ate and he gave the Buddha a handful of leaves. Twenty-seven kappas ago he was a king named **Yadatthiya.**[1]

[1] Ap. i. 228 f.

2. **Paṇṇadāyaka Thera.**—An arahant. Ninety-four kappas ago he gave a handful of the leaves he was eating to **Siddhattha** Buddha and spread for him a seat of leaves.[1]

[1] Ap. i. 239.

Paṇṇabhatta.—A village given by **Aggabodhi V.** for the maintenance of the **Tālavatthu** (or **Mahāsena)-vihāra.**[1]

[1] Cv. xlviii. 8.

Paṇṇavallakabhūta.—A monastery in Ceylon, built by **Dhātusena.**[1]

[1] Cv. xxxviii. 47.

Paṇṇasālaka.—A village in Ceylon. **Kalyāṇavatī,** the first queen consort of **Kitti-Nissaṅka,** was fond of this village and built a vihāra there, endowing it with all manner of possessions.[1]

[1] Cv. lxxx. 35.

Paṇṇika Jātaka (No. 102).—A greengrocer of Benares had a pretty daughter who was always laughing. Before agreeing to give her in marriage, her father wished to test her virtue, lest she should bring disgrace on his name. He took her into the forest and whispered to her words of love. When she expressed her horror, he was convinced of her innocence and agreed to the marriage. The Bodhisatta was a Tree-sprite and witnessed the incident. The story was related to a greengrocer in **Sāvatthi** who treated his daughter in a similar way. He later visited the Buddha and told him the story. The characters were identical in both cases.[1]

[1] J. i. 411 f.

Patāpa.—A mythical king, descendant of **Mahāsammata.** His father was **Mahāruci** (or **Suruci**) and his son was **Mahāpatāpa.**[1]

[1] Dpv. iii. 7; Mhv. ii. 44.

Patāpana.—A Niraya,[1] so called because its heat was excessive (*ativiya tāpetī ti Patāpano*).[2]

[1] J. v. 266, 453. [2] J. v. 271.

Patikolamba.—A cook. He refused to listen to **Sattigumba** who suggested killing the **Pañcāla** king.[1] See the **Sattigumba Jātaka.**

[1] J. iv. 431 f.

Patiṭṭhāna.—The capital of **Aḷaka,** the first place to be passed by **Bāvarī's** disciples on their way to **Sāvatthi.**[1] It is identified with the Baithana or Paitana of Ptolemy.

[1] SN. vs. 1011.

Patiṭṭhāraṭṭha.—Another name for **Rājaraṭṭha** (*q.v.*), a division of Ceylon.

Patiṭṭhita Sutta.—On how a monk may establish earnestness in the five *indriyas.*[1]

[1] S. v. 232.

Patipūjikā.—A woman of **Sāvatthi,** who once had belonged to the retinue of the god **Mālābhārī,** and passed out of her deva-existence while sitting on the branch of a tree picking flowers for him. She remembered her former existence, and yearned to rejoin Mālābhārī even after she was married, hence her name. With this object in view she did many good deeds, and is said to have developed simultaneously the fifty-six qualities of goodness. She gave birth to four sons, and dying one day of a sudden illness, was reborn into the retinue of Mālābhārī. He was greatly agitated on hearing her story and realizing how short is the span of human life.[1]

[1] DhA. i. 363 ff.

Patilīna Sutta.—A monk, who has shaken off various speculations, has given up searching for sense pleasures and going on other quests and has obtained calm by abandoning pleasure and pain, such a one is called *patilīna* (withdrawn).[1]

[1] A. ii. 41 f.

Patoda Sutta.—Four kinds of thoroughbred steeds in the world and the corresponding four kinds of thoroughbred men. The first kind of thoroughbred steed is stirred at the very sight of the shadow of the goad-stick, similarly thoroughbred men are agitated at the news of another's affliction.[1]

[1] A. ii. 114 f.

1. **Patta Vagga.**—The third chapter of the Nissaggiya of the Vinaya Piṭaka.

2. **Patta Vagga.**—The third section of the Parivāra of the Vinaya Piṭaka.

1. **Patta Sutta.**—Eight reasons for which the Order is entitled to turn their begging bowls upside down (as a mark of censure), or to hold them up (showing their good will) on entering a layman's house.[1]

[1] A. iv. 344 f.

2. **Patta Sutta.**—The Buddha was once preaching a sermon to the monks on the five *upādānakkhandhā*, and **Māra,** wishing to disturb their thoughts, appeared in the shape of a bullock and wandered about among the bowls which had been placed to dry. But he was recognized and had to retire discomfited.[1]

[1] S. i. 112 f.

Pattakamma Vagga.—The seventh chapter of the Catukka Nipāta of the Aṅguttara Nikāya.[1]

[1] A. ii. 65-76.

Pattakamma Sutta.—Preached to **Anāthapiṇḍika.** Four things are difficult to acquire in the world: wealth lawfully obtained, good report, long life, happy rebirth. Four things conduce to their attainment: perfection of faith, of virtue, of generosity and of wisdom.[1]

[1] A. ii. 65 ff.

Pattadāyaka Thera.—An arahant. Ninety-four kappas ago he gave a bowl to **Siddhattha** Buddha.[1]

[1] Ap. i. 224.

Pattapāsāṇa.—A district of Ceylon, given for the maintenance of the **Jeṭṭhārāma,** by **Jeṭṭhā,** chief queen of **Aggabodhi IV.**[1]

[1] Cv. xlvi. 28.

Pattapāsāṇavāpi.—A tank in Ceylon, formed by **Moggallāna II.** by the damming up of the **Kadambanadī.**[1] It was restored by **Vijyabāhu I.**[2] and again by **Parakkamabāhu I.**[3]

[1] Cv. xli. 61. [2] *Ibid.*, lx. 50. [3] *Ibid.*, lxxix. 34.

Pattipupphiya Thera.—An arahant. He offered a *patti* flower to the body of **Padumuttara** Buddha as it was being taken in the procession for cremation.[1]

[1] Ap. i. 291.

Patthodanadāyaka Thera.—An arahant. Ninety-four kappas ago he was a forester, and one day, when wandering in the forest with his basket of rice, he saw the Buddha (Siddhattha ?) and offered him the food.[1]

[1] Ap. ii. 376 f.

1. **Pathavī Sutta.**—Seven small balls of clay, as big as jujube kernels, are infinitely smaller than the earth. So with the Ariyan disciple—when he has won understanding, the *dukkha* that remains is infinitely smaller than that which he has destroyed.[1]

[1] S. ii. 135 f.; repeated at S. v. 462 f.

2. **Pathavī Sutta.**—The same as the above.[1]

[1] S. ii. 136.

3. **Pathavī Sutta.**—Incalculable is *saṃsāra*. The number of parents a man has had would be greater than the number of balls, each the size of a *kola* (jujube) kernel, that could be made of the clay of the earth.[1]

[1] S. ii. 179.

1. **Pada Sutta.**—Just as all the foot-characteristics of roaming creatures are united in the foot of the elephant, and included in it, so, of all profitable conditions which are rooted in earnestness, earnestness is reckoned the chief.[1]

[1] S. v. 43.

2. **Pada Sutta.**—The simile is the same as the above; but it illustrates the fact that of all the elements which conduce to wisdom, the controlling faculty of insight is reckoned the chief.[1]

[1] S. v. 231.

Padakusalamāṇava Jātaka (No. 432).—Once the queen of a Benares king, having sworn a false oath, became a horse-faced yakkha. She served **Vessavaṇa** for three years and was given leave to eat people within a certain range. One day she caught a rich and handsome brahmin, and, falling in love with him, made him her husband. When she went out she shut him up, lest he should escape. The Bodhisatta was born as their son, and, on learning his father's story, discovered from the yakkha how far her power extended, and then escaped with his father. The yakkha followed, but they were outside her territory and would not be persuaded to return. She gave her son a charm enabling him to trace the footsteps of any person, even after the lapse of twelve years. On the strength of his charm, the lad entered the service of the king of

Benares. One day, the king and his chaplain, wishing to test him, stole some treasure, took it away by devious paths, and hid it in a tank. The youth recovered it quite easily, tracing their footsteps even in the air. The king wished the names of the thieves to be divulged, but this the boy would not do. But he related to the king various stories, showing that he knew the real culprits. The king, however, insisted on the thieves being denounced, and when the boy revealed their names, the assembled populace murdered the king and his chaplain and crowned the Bodhisatta as king.

The story was related in reference to a seven-year-old boy of **Sāvatthi** who could recognize footsteps. His father put him through a severe test, and then went to the Buddha, where the boy found him. When the Buddha heard the story he revealed that of the past. The father of the story of the past is identified with **Mahā Kassapa.**[1]

[1] J. iii. 501-14.

Padakkamana.—See **Padavikkamana.**

Padapūjaka.—See **Pādapūjaka.**

Padaratittha-vihāra.—A monastery in the Damiḷa country in South India. It was the residence of **Ācariya Dhammapāla.**[1] *v.l.* **Badaratittha.**

[1] Sās. 33; Svd. 1194.

Padarūpavibhāvana.—A commentary on **Nāmarūpapariccheda.**[1]

[1] Gv. 71.

Padarūpasiddhi.—See **Rūpasiddhi.**

Padalañchana.—A village in Ceylon where **Vajirā,** queen of **Kassapa V.,** built a monastery for the **Theravādins.**[1] Mention is made[2] of a temple of four cetiyas in Padalañchana, which was burnt down by the **Coḷas** and restored by **Mahinda IV.**

[1] Cv. lii. 63. [2] *Ibid.*, liv. 44.

Padavāraṣuññakaṇḍa.—A district in the **Dakkhiṇadesa** of Ceylon.[1]

[1] Cv. lxvi. 10.

Padavikkamana.—A king of eighty-two kappas ago, a previous birth of **Māṇava (Sammukhāthavika) Thera.**[1] *v.l.* **Padakkamana.**

[1] ThagA. i. 164; Ap. i. 159.

Padavibhāga.—A grammatical work by a monk named **Ñāṇa.**[1]

[1] Bode, *op. cit.*, 71.

Padasaññaka Thera.—An arahant. Ninety-two kappas ago he happened upon the footprint of **Tissa** Buddha and was overjoyed at the sight. Seven kappas ago he was a king named **Sumedha.**[1]

[1] Ap. i. 119.

Padasādhana.—A Pāli grammar belonging to the **Moggallāna** school, by **Piyadassī. Vanaratana Ānanda** wrote a Sinhalese paraphrase on it, and there also exists a Ṭīkā on it called the **Buddhippasādanī.** The book is also called **Moggallānasaddattharatnakāra.**[1]

[1] P.L.C. 201, 205.

Padīraṭṭha.—A district in Ceylon, where **Māgha** and **Jayabāhu** set up fortifications.[1]

[1] Cv. lxxxiii. 16; see also lxxxviii. 64; and Cv. *Trs.* ii. 149, n. 9.

Padīvāpī.—A tank restored by **Parakkamabāhu II.**[1]

[1] Cv. lxxix. 34. See also Cv. *Trs.* ii. 119, n. 2.

1. **Paduma.**—The eighth of the twenty-four Buddhas. He was born in **Campaka.** His father was the Khattiya **Asama**[1] and his mother **Asamā.** For ten thousand years he lived as a householder in three palaces: **Nandā, Suyasā** and **Uttarā.**[2] His wife was **Uttarā** and his son **Ramma.** He left home in a chariot and practised austerities for eight months. **Dhaññavatī** gave him milk-rice, and an Ajīvaka, named **Titthaka,** spread grass for his seat under his bodhi-tree, which was a *Mahāsona.* He preached his first sermon in **Dhanañjuyyāna.** His chief disciples were his younger brothers **Sāla** and **Upasāla** and his attendant was **Varuṇa. Rādhā** and **Surādhā** were his chief women disciples, and his chief patrons were **Bhiyya** and **Asama** among men and **Rucī** and **Nandarāmā** among women. His body was fifty-eight cubits high, and he lived for one hundred thousand years. He died in **Dhammārāma** and his relics were scattered. The Buddhavaṃsa Commentary states that his full name was **Mahāpaduma,** that he was so called because on the day of his birth a shower of lotuses fell over **Jambudīpa,** and that, at that time, the Bodhisatta was a lion.[3]

[1] But see J. i. 36, where he is called **Paduma.**

[2] BuA. calls them **Uttarā, Vasuttarā** and **Yasuttarā.**

[3] Bu. ix.; BuA. 146 ff.; J. i. 36; Mhv. i. 7; DhA. i. 84.

2. **Paduma.**—One of the chief lay disciples of **Revata** Buddha.[1]

[1] Bu. vi. 23.

3. **Paduma.**—One of the three palaces occupied by **Sobhita** Buddha in his last lay life.[1]

[1] Bu. vii. 17.

4. **Paduma.**—Step-brother of **Dhammadassī** Buddha. The Buddha preached to him at **Saraṇa**, and he later became the Buddha's chief disciple.[1]

[1] Bu. xvi. 18; BuA. 183; J. i. 39.

5. **Paduma.**—A palace occupied by **Siddhattha** Buddha.[1]

[1] BuA. 185; but see Bu. xvii. 14.

6. **Paduma.**—A Pacceka Buddha to whom **Anūpama** (or **Aṅkolapupphiya**) **Thera** offered some *ākulī* flowers.[1]

[1] ThagA. i. 335; Ap. i. 287; see also M. iii. 70 and PvA. 75.

7. **Paduma.**—A cakkavatti of eight kappas ago; a previous birth of **Piṇḍola-Bhāradvāja.**[1]

[1] Ap. i. 50.

8. **Paduma.**—A cetiya built by **Mahā Kaccāna,** in a previous birth, for **Padumuttara** Buddha.[1] The Apadāna Commentary explains that the building was, in fact, a gandhakuṭi, which was called a cetiya as a mark of respect (*pūjanīyabhāvena*), and that it was called Paduma because it was shaped like a lotus and was covered with lotuses.

[1] Ap. i. 84.

9. **Paduma Thera.**—An arahant. He once threw a lotus to **Padumuttara** Buddha as he was travelling through the air, and the Buddha accepted it. For thirty kappas Paduma was king of the devas, and for seven hundred king of men.[1]

[1] Ap. i. 109 f.

10. **Paduma.**—A Niraya. The Sutta Nipāta explains that it was not a separate Niraya but only a period of suffering. The monk **Kokālika** was born there.[1]

[1] SN. p. 126; J. iv. 245; AA. ii. 853; DhA. iv. 91.

11. **Paduma.**—A rock near **Himavā.**[1]

[1] Ap. ii. 362.

12. **Paduma.**—One of the Theras who assisted at the foundation-laying ceremony of the **Mahā Thūpa.**[1]

[1] Dpv. xix. 8; MṬ. (524) calls him **Mahāpaduma.**

13. **Paduma.**—The Bodhisatta born as king of Benares. See the **Culla Paduma Jātaka.**

14. **Paduma.**—The Bodhisatta born as son of the king of Benares. See the **Mahā-Paduma Jātaka.**

15. **Paduma.**—See **Mahāpaduma.**

Paduma Jātaka (No. 261).—The Bodhisatta was once the son of a rich merchant in Benares. In the town was a tank tended by a leper who had lost his nose. One feast-day the Bodhisatta with his two brothers went to the tank to fetch some lotuses. The brothers tried to flatter the leper, thereby making him angry, but the Bodhisatta, being honest, was given a whole bunch of lotuses.

The story was related in reference to **Ānanda.** Some monks once wandered all over the Lotus-street to find some lotuses to offer at the **Ānanda-bodhi** (*q.v.*). But they found none, and Ānanda, hearing of it, went himself to the Lotus-street and returned with many handfuls of blue lotus. The incident was reported to the Buddha who related the story of the Jātaka.[1]

[1] J. ii. 321 ff.

Padumakūṭāgāriya Thera.—An Arahant. In the time of **Piyadassī** Buddha he was a hunter and, having seen the Buddha, built for him a gabled hut covered with lotuses, which the Buddha occupied for seven days. Then, at the Buddha's wish, his attendant monk **Sudassana** came with thousands of monks, and the Buddha declared the future in store for the hunter.[1]

[1] Ap. i. 326 f.

Padumakesariya Thera.—An arahant. Ninety-one kappas ago he was an elephant and, seeing the Buddha **Vipassī,** scattered lotus-pollen over him.[1]

[1] Ap. i. 248.

Padumaghara.—A building in **Anurādhapura,** where gifts were presented to the monks.[1] It was in the palace grounds and was near the **Padumapokkharaṇī.**[2]

[1] Mhv. xxxiv. 65. [2] MṬ. 633.

Padumacchadaniya Thera. An arahant. He offered a lotus at the pyre of **Vipassī** Buddha. Forty-seven kappas ago he was a king named **Padumissara.** Wherever he went a canopy of lotuses spread itself over him.[1]

[1] Ap. i. 98.

Padumaccharā.—A name given to the nymphs who danced in the lotus blossoms which grew in the ponds between the tusks of **Erāvaṇa.**[1]

[1] SNA. i. 369.

Padumadhāriya Thera.—An arahant. Thirty-one kappas ago he offered a lotus to a Pacceka Buddha named **Sambhava.**[1]

[1] Ap. ii. 453 f.; in Ap. i. 279 the same verses are attributed to **Padumapūjaka**; see also ThagA. i. 399.

Padumanahānakoṭṭha.—A bathing-pool in the form of a lotus, built in Pulatthipura by **Parakkamabāhu I.**[1]

[1] Cv. lxxviii. 45.

Padumapuppha (or **Puṇḍarīka**) **Sutta.**—Once a monk, living in a forest tract in **Kosala,** returned from his alms-round and, plunging into a lotus pool, deeply inhaled the perfume of the lotus. A deva of the forest, wishing to agitate him, called him a thief, and engaged him in conversation.[1]

[1] S. i. 204 f.

Padumapupphiya Thera.—An arahant. Ninety-two kappas ago, while picking lotuses, he saw **Phussa** Buddha and offered him a flower. He later joined the Order. Forty-eight kappas ago he was king eighteen times under the name of **Padumabhāsa.**[1]

[1] Ap. i. 132.

1. **Padumapūjaka Thera.**—An arahant. Ninety-one kappas ago he lived in **Romasa,** near **Himavā,** and offered a lotus to the Pacceka Buddha **Sambhava.**[1] In the Theragāthā Commentary[2] his verses are attributed to **Sappaka Thera,** and it is said there that in the time of Sambhava he was a Nāga-king.

[1] Ap. i. 279 f.; see also **Padumadhāriya.** [2] i. 399.

2. **Padumapūjaka Thera.**—An arahant. Ninety-one kappas ago he was an ascetic in **Gotama,** near **Himavā,** and, together with his pupils,

he called to mind the Buddha's virtues and offered lotuses in his name. Fifty-one kappas ago he was a king named **Jaluttama.**[1] He is probably identical with **Meṇḍasira.**[2]

[1] Ap. i. 162 f. [2] ThagA. i. 172.

Padumapokkharaṇī.—A pond in **Anurādhapura** in the palace grounds. Near by was the **Padumaghara.**[1]

[1] MṬ. 633.

1. **Padumavatī.**—Mother of five hundred Pacceka Buddhas. She was once a householder's daughter in a village near Benares; one day, while guarding her father's field, she saw a Pacceka Buddha, and gave him a lotus with five hundred grains of fried rice (*lājā*), making a wish to have five hundred sons. At that moment, five hundred hunters who stood by gave honey and flesh to the Pacceka Buddha and expressed their wish to be her sons. Later, she was born in a lotus-pond, within a lotus. An ascetic, seeing her, brought her up. Wherever she went, lotuses sprang up at her every footstep. The King of Benares, hearing of her. made her his chief consort. She gave birth to five hundred sons, the eldest being **Mahāpaduma.** All of them became Pacceka Buddhas.[1]

The Aṅguttara Nikāya Commentary[2] mentions that Padumavatī was a previous birth of the therī **Uppalavaṇṇā,** and gives her story with much greater detail.

[1] MA. ii. 889. [2] i. 188 ff.; see *s.v.* **Uppalavaṇṇā,** also Thig A. 185 ff.

2. **Padumavatī.**—A courtesan of **Ujjenī,** who later became the therī **Abhayamātā** (*q.v.*).

Padumassara.—A park in Anurādhapura laid out by King **Kuṭakaṇṇa-Tissa.**[1]

[1] Mhv. xxxiv. 35.

Padumissara.—A king of forty-seven kappas ago; a former birth of **Padumacchadaniya Thera.**[1]

[1] Ap. i. 98.

1. **Padumā.**—Chief of the women patrons of **Anomadassī** Buddha.[1]

[1] Bu. viii. 24.

2. **Padumā.**—Chief of the lay women supporters of **Sujāta** Buddha.[1]

[1] Bu. xiii. 30.

3. **Padumā.**—Mother of **Tissa** Buddha.[1]

[1] Bu. xviii. 16.

4. **Padumā.**—Chief of women patrons of **Phussa** Buddha.[1]

[1] Bu. xix. 21; J. i. 40.

5. **Padumā.**—One of the chief women disciples of **Sikhī** Buddha.[1]

[1] Bu. xxi. 21; J. i. 41.

6. **Padumā.**—Wife of **Dīpaṅkara** Buddha, in his last lay life.[1]

[1] Bu. ii. 209; Mbv. p. 4.

7. **Padumā.**—One of the most distinguished lay-women, followers of the Buddha.[1] She was the wife of **Meṇḍaka** and her full name was **Candapadumā** (*q.v.*).

[1] A. iv. 347.

8. **Padumā.**—A distinguished therī of Ceylon.[1]

[1] Dpv. xviii. 24.

9. **Padumā.**—One of the chief women disciples of **Metteyya** Buddha.[1]

[1] Anāgat., vs. 98.

1. **Padumuttara.**—The tenth of the twenty-four Buddhas. He was born in **Haṃsavatī,** of the khattiya **Ānanda** and his wife **Sujātā.** At the moments of his birth and his Enlightenment, a shower of lotuses fell in the ten thousand worlds, hence his name. He lived as a householder for ten thousand years in three palaces: **Naravāhana, Yasa** (or **Yasavatī**) and **Vasavatti.** His wife was **Vasudattā,** by whom he had a son, **Uttara.**[1] He left home in his palace (Vasavatti), and practised austerities only for seven days. A maiden of **Ujjeni,** called **Rucinandā,** gave him milk-rice, and the Ājīvaka **Sumitta** gave him grass for his seat. His bodhi-tree was a *salala,* under which he spent a week, and when he touched the ground with his foot, huge lotus flowers sprang out of the earth, covering his body completely with their pollen. (The Saṃyuttabhāṇakas give this as the reason for his name.) His first sermon was preached to his cousins **Devala** and **Sujāta,** who later became his chief disciples. The spot where the sermon was preached was **Mithiluyyāna.** Sumana was Padumuttara's personal attendant, **Amitā** and **Asamā** his chief women disciples, **Vitiṇṇa** and **Tissa** his chief patrons among men, and **Hatthā** and **Vicittā** among women. His body was fifty-eight cubits high, and his

[1] According to SNA. i. 341, his son was **Uparevata.**

aura spread for twelve yojanas. He died in **Nandārāma** at the age of one hundred thousand, and a thūpa twelve leagues in height was erected over his relics. In his time, the Bodhisatta was governor of a province (*raṭṭhika*) called **Jaṭika (Jaṭila)**.[2] It is said[3] that in the time of Padumuttara there did not exist a single heretic.

Many of the eminent disciples of **Gotama** Buddha are said to have first conceived their desire for their respective positions in the time of Padumuttara Buddha, after seeing similar rank conferred on Padumuttara's various disciples in acknowledgment of their special attainments—*e.g.*, **Aññākoṇḍañña, Mahā Kassapa, Anuruddha, Bhaddiya, Piṇḍola-Bhāradvāja, Puṇṇa Mantāniputta, Mahā Kaccāna, Culla Panthaka, Subhūti, Khadiravaniya-Revata, Kaṅkhā-Revata, Soṇa-Koḷivisa, Soṇa-Kuṭikaṇṇa, Sīvalī, Vakkali, Rāhula, Raṭṭhapāla, Kuṇḍadhāna, Vaṅgīsa, Upasena Vaṅgantaputta, Dabba Mallaputta, Pilinda Vaccha, Bāhiya Dārucīriya, Kumāra-Kassapa, Mahā Koṭṭhita, Ānanda, Uruvela-Kassapa, Kāḷudāyī, Sobhita, Upāli, Nanda, Mahā Kappina, Sāgata, Rādha, Mogharājā, Vappa, Upavāna, Mahāpajāpatī Gotamī, Khemā, Uppalavaṇṇā, Paṭācārā, Dhammadinnā, Sundarī-Nandā, Soṇā, Sakulā, Bhaddā Kuṇḍalakesā, Bhaddā-Kapilānī, Bhaddā-Kaccānā, Kisāgotamī** and **Sigālakamātā**.[4]

[2] Bu. xi. 1 ff.; BuA. 157 ff.; J. i. 37, 44; DhA. i. 99, 417; iii. 146, etc.; also Ap. i. 57, 63, 101, 107; Mtu. ii. 58.

[3] *E.g.*, MṬ. 59.

[4] For details see *s.v.*

2. **Padumuttara.**—A Pacceka Buddha.[1]

[1] M. iii. 70.

1. **Padesa Sutta.**—A conversation between **Sāriputta, Anuruddha** and **Moggallāna** in the **Ketakivana** in **Sāketa**, regarding the meaning of the word "*sekha.*" A *sekha* is one who has only partially cultivated the four *satipaṭṭhānas*.[1]

[1] S. v. 174 f.

2. **Padesa Sutta.**—Whoever cultivates psychic power, partially, can only do so by cultivating and developing the four bases of psychic power (*iddhipādā*).[1]

[1] S. v. 255.

Padesavihāra Sutta.—The Atthasālinī[1] refers to a sutta of this name and quotes from it. The reference is, evidently, to the **Vihārā Sutta** (1) of the Saṃyutta.[2]

[1] p. 30.

[2] S. v. 12.

Padyapadoruvaṃsa.—The name given to the **Mahāvaṃsa** by the author of the **Mahāvaṃsa-Ṭīkā** (*q.v.*). *v.l.* **Padyapadānuvaṃsa.**

1. **Padhāna Sutta.**—The four kinds of effort: to restrain, to abandon, to develop, and to preserve.[1]

[1] A. ii. 74.

2. **Padhāna Sutta.**—Four qualities which show that their possessor has entered on the path to surety, and that he is definitely bent on the destruction of the āsavas: virtue, learning, ardent energy, wisdom.[1]

[1] A. ii. 76.

3. **Padhāna Sutta.**—The Buddha describes how, when he gave himself up to meditation in order to win Enlightenment, **Māra (Namuci)** came to tempt him with his eightfold army of lust, discontent, hunger and thirst, craving, cowardice, doubt, hypocrisy and stupour. But the Buddha was firm, and Māra retired discomfited.[1]

[1] SN. vs. 425-49.

4. **Padhāna Sutta.**—The four right efforts: for the non-arising of evil, for the abandoning of evil, for the arising of profitable states, and for the increase and fulfilment of such states.[1]

[1] A. ii. 15; cp. D. ii. 120; M. ii. 11, etc.

Padhānakammika-Tissa Thera.—Five hundred monks of **Sāvatthi** retire into the forest to meditate; one (**Tissa**) falls away, the rest attain arahantship. They return to the Buddha, who has a word of praise for all but Tissa. The latter renews his determination to become an arahant and walks up and down the cloister all night long, thereby earning his nickname. Becoming drowsy, he stumbles over a stone and breaks his thigh. As his colleagues are on the way to receive their alms at the house of a certain layman they hear his groans, and stopping to minister to him, are prevented from receiving their gifts. The Buddha tells them that this is not the first time that Tissa has so stood in their way and relates the **Varaṇa Jātaka** (*q.v.*), a discourse on the evils of procrastination.[1]

[1] DhA. iii. 407 ff.; in the Varaṇa Jātaka, however, the name of the monk is given as **Kuṭumbiya-Tissa** (*q.v.*); perhaps the two are identical.

Padhānaghara.—See **Mahāpadhānaghara.**

Padhānarakkha.—A monastery in Ceylon where **Mānavamma** erected the **Sepaṇṇipāsāda.**[1]

[1] Cv. xlvii. 64.

Padhānika-Tissa Thera.—He went with five hundred others to meditate in the forest, and, having instructed his fellows to apply themselves diligently to meditation, he himself spent the night in sleep. When the others discovered his deceit, they complained to the teacher, who related the **Akālarāvi-Kukkuṭa Jātaka** (*q.v.*), identifying Tissa with the cock of that story.[1]

[1] DhA. iii. 142 ff.

Panayamāra or **Panayamāraka.**—A Damiḷa ursurper who slew **Bāhiya,** another ursurper, and reigned in **Anurādhapura** for seven years (between 439 and 454) till he, in turn, was slain by his commander-in-chief **Piḷayamāra.**[1]

[1] Mhv. xxxiii. 57 ff.; Dpv. xix. 15; xx. 16.

Panasaphaladāyaka Thera.—An arahant. Ninety-one kappas ago he saw the Pacceka Buddha **Ajjuna** in **Himavā** and offered him a ripe jak-fruit as large as a pot on a platter of leaves.[1]

[1] Ap. i. 297; *cf. ibid.*, ii. 446.

Panasabukka.—A village in the **Guttahāla** district of Ceylon.[1]

[1] Cv. lxi. 12.

Panasiyarāja.—A Damiḷa chief, ally of **Kulasekhara.**[1]

[1] Cv. lxxvi. 99.

1. **Panāda.**—A mythical king, who succeeded **Mahāpatāpa** and was himself succeeded by **Mahāpanāda.**[1]

[1] Mhv. ii. 4; Dpv. iii. 7.

2. **Panāda.**—One of the chief Yakkhas to be invoked by the Buddha's followers in time of need.[1] He is also mentioned in the **Mahāsamaya Sutta.**[2] Buddhaghosa says[3] that Panāda was a **Gandhabba.**

[1] D. iii. 204. [2] *Ibid.*, ii. 258. [3] DA. ii. 688.

3. **Panāda.**—See **Mahāpanāda.**

1. **Panthaka.**—See **Cūla-Panthaka** and **Mahā-Panthaka.**

2. **Panthaka.**—Mentioned as the name of a man.[1]

[1] J. i. 403.

Pandriya.—A Damiḷa chief, ally of **Kulasekhara.**[1]

[1] Cv. lxxvi. 184.

Pannañjalika Thera.—An arahant. Ninety-two kappas ago he lay grievously ill at the foot of a tree in the forest. The Buddha **Tissa,** in his compassion, came to him, and **Pannañjalika,** unable to rise, clasped his hands above his head and worshipped the Buddha. Five kappas ago he was king five times, under the name of **Mahāsikha.**[1]

[1] Ap. i. 128.

Pannaṭṭaṅkoṭṭa.—A locality in South India, mentioned in the account of **Laṅkāpura's** campaigns.[1]

[1] Cv. lxxvi. 313.

Papañcasūdanī.—**Buddhaghosa's** Commentary on the Majjhima Nikāya. The colophon states that it was written at the request of the monk **Buddhamitta** of **Mayūrapaṭṭana.** The work is quoted in the **Samanta-pāsādikā.**[1]

[1] Sp. iv. 870.

Papatita Sutta.—He who does not possess the virtue, the concentration, the wisdom and the release of the Ariyans, is said to have fallen away from the *Dhamma-vinaya.*[1]

[1] A. ii. 2.

Papāta Vagga.—The fifth chapter of the Sacca Saṃyutta.[1]

[1] S. v. 446 ff.

Papāta Sutta.—The Buddha once went with some monks to **Paṭibhānakūṭa** for the siesta, and a certain monk, seeing the precipice below them, asked if any precipice were deeper than that. Yes, answered the Buddha, the precipice of ignorance of the nature of *dukkha.*[1]

[1] S. v. 448 f.

Papātapabbata.—A mountain in **Avantī,** near **Kuraraghara.** It was a favourite spot of **Mahā Kaccāna,** and we are told of several discussions having taken place there.[1] Mahā Kaccāna's attendant was, at that time, **Soṇa Kuṭikaṇṇa** (*q.v.*), yet a layman. He later became a monk, and the ten monks necessary for his ordination were found with great difficulty.[2]

[1] *E.g.*, S. iii. 9 ff.; iv. 115 f.; A. v. 46 f. [2] Vin. i. 194 f.; Ud. v. 6; DhA. iv. 101 f.

Pappaṭa.—A grove near the modern Colombo. **Parakkamabāhu VI.** erected there the **Sunetta-pariveṇa** in memory of his mother.[1]

[1] Cv. xci. 24; see also Cv. *Trs.* ii. 216, n. 3 and 4.

Papphālama.—A landing place in **Rāmañña** where the forces of **Damiḷādhikarin** landed.[1]

[1] Cv. lxxvi. 63.

Pabbajjā Sutta.—When **Gotama,** after leaving home, entered **Giribbaja** (**Rājagaha**) for alms, **Bimbisāra** saw him go and sent messengers to discover his whereabouts. They reported that Gotama was taking his meal under the shadow of the **Paṇḍavapabbata.** There Bimbisāra visited him and requested him to share his kingdom. Gotama told Bimbisāra of his antecedents, that he was a Sākyan of Kosala and had renounced all pleasures, seeing ill in them.[1]

Buddhaghosa explains[2] that the Sutta was preached by **Ānanda** at Jetavana, because he desired to give an account of the renunciation of the Buddha, similar to that of **Sāriputta** and others. The Commentary adds[3] that at the end of the talk with the Buddha, Bimbisāra asked him to visit Rājagaha as soon as he had attained Enlightenment.

[1] SN. vs. 405-24. [2] SNA. ii. 381. [3] p. 386.

Pabbajita Sutta.—On how a monk should develop and cultivate his mind, filling it with thoughts of how to get rid of evil, of thoughts of transiency, selflessness, etc.[1]

[1] A. v. 107 f.

1. **Pabbata.**—A Pacceka Buddha, mentioned in a nominal list.[1]

[1] M. iii. 70.

2. **Pabbata.**—The name of the Bodhisatta in the time of **Koṇāgamana** Buddha. He was king of **Mithilā** and entertained the Buddha and his monks.[1]

[1] J. i. 43; BuA. 9; Bu. xxiv. 215.

3. **Pabbata.**—A sage, the chief disciple of **Sarabhaṅga.** For details see the **Indriya Jātaka.**[1] Pabbata is identified with **Anuruddha.**

[1] J. iii. 463 ff.; see also J. v. 133, 151.

4. **Pabbata.**—A minister of **Vaṭṭagāmaṇi,** who built a monastery called **Pabbatārāma,** which he presented to **Kupikkala Mahā Tissa.**[1]

[1] Mhv. xxxiii. 91.

5. **Pabbata.**—A **Laṅkāpura** who fought against **Parakkamabāhu I.** and was captured alive.[1]

[1] Cv. lxxv. 180, 184.

6. **Pabbata.**—A class of gods (**Pabbatā**) mentioned with the Nāradas.[1] The Commentary says[2] that they were wise (*paññavanto*).

[1] SN. vs. 543. [2] SNA. ii. 435.

Pabbata Vagga.—The first chapter of the Bojjhaṅga Saṃyutta.[1]

[1] S. v. 63 ff.

1. **Pabbata Sutta.**—The sāla trees on the Himālaya grow in branch, leaf and flower, in bark and shoots, in softwood and pith; similarly the folk in a devout man's house grow in faith, virtue and wisdom.[1]

[1] A. i. 152.

2. **Pabbata Sutta.**—An æon is longer than the time taken by a man to waste away a mountain one league high, one long, and one wide, by stroking it once in every hundred years with a Kāsī-cloth.[1]

[1] S. ii. 181.

Pabbatakumāra.—The son of **Dhananda.** He was kidnapped by **Cāṇakka,** who brought him up with his protégé, **Candagutta.** On discovering that Pabbata was the weaker, he contrived to have him murdered as he slept.[1]

[1] For details see MṬ. 183 ff.

Pabbatachinnā.—An eminent nun of Ceylon.[1]

[1] Dpv. xv. 78; in xviii. she is called Pabbatā.

Pabbatanta.—A canal built by **Mahāsena** from the **Mahāvālukagaṅgā.**[1]

[1] Mhv. xxxvii. 50.

Pabbatabbhantara.—The Pāli name for the Burmese Taung-dwin-gyī.[1]

[1] Bode, *op. cit.*, 43.

Pabbataraṭṭha.—A district in the centre of **Videharaṭṭha.** In it was the city of **Dhammakoṇḍa,** the residence of **Dhaniya.**[1]

[1] SNA. i. 26.

Pabbata-vihāra.—A monastery built by **Moggallāna I.** and given over to the Thera **Mahānāma** of the **Dīghāsana** (? **Dīghasaṇḍa**)-**vihāra.**[1]

[1] Cv. xxxix. 42.

Pabbatārāma.—A monastery built by **Pabbata,** minister of **Vaṭṭagāmaṇī.** It is probably the same that is mentioned in the Mahāvaṃsa Ṭīkā[2] as lying to the south of **Vessagiri-vihāra** and near the village of **Silāsobbhakaṇḍaka.**

Mhv. xxxiii. 90. [2] p. 616.

Pabbatūpatthara Jātaka (No. 195).—Once, Brahmadatta, king of Benares, discovered one of his courtiers intriguing in his harem. But being fond both of the man and the woman concerned, he asked advice of his counsellor, the Bodhisatta, in a riddle—that a pretty lake at the foot of a hill was being used by a jackal, while the lion lay quiet through it all. The counsellor's answer was that all creatures drink at will of a mighty river, yet the river is a river for all that. The king understood the answer and advised both those concerned.

The story was related to the king of **Kosala** who had detected a similar happening in his court.[1]

[1] J. ii. 125 ff.

1. **Pabbatūpama Sutta.**—**Pasenadi** comes to the Buddha and tells him that he has been much occupied with kingly matters. The Buddha reminds him by means of a parable that old age and death are ceaselessly rolling on upon him, like mighty mountains crushing everything in their way. Against such an advance his counsellors and his armies would be useless, and the king admits that leading the righteous life is the only way.[1]

The Commentary adds[2] that on the occasion of this visit the king had been attacked by bandits lying in wait for him in the **Andhavana.** He had, however, been warned, and, having surrounded the wood, destroyed the bandits.

[1] S. i. 100 f. [2] SA. i. 131 f.

2. **Pabbatūpama Sutta.**—The *dukkha* which one Ariyan disciple who has won understanding has destroyed, placed beside the *dukkha* which remains to be destroyed, would be like the whole **Himālaya** beside seven grains of gravel the size of mustard seeds.[1]

[1] S. v. 464.

3. **Pabbatūpama Sutta.**—Same as (2) above, except that the simile used is that of the **Himālaya** as it is, compared with what it would be if it

were wasted away to the size of seven grains of gravel the size of mustard seeds.[1]

[1] S. v. 465.

Pabbhāradāyaka Thera.—An arahant. He once cleaned the shed (*pabbhāra*) in which **Piyadassī** Buddha kept his drinking water and provided him with a pot. Twenty-two kappas ago he was a king named **Susuddha.**[1]

[1] Ap. i. 252.

Pabbhāravāsi-Tissa Thera.—Having received a topic of meditation from the Buddha, he went into the forest. Seeing a cave, he dwelt there, a woman from the neighbouring village supplying him with food. The deity in the cave found the Elder's presence inconvenient, but could think of no excuse for asking him to go away, his life having been spotless. But after much thinking, she hit upon a plan; she took possession of the body of the youngest son of the woman who supplied the Elder, and wrung his neck, telling the mother that he would be cured if she could get certain things from the Elder as medicine. This the woman refused to do, but, in the end, she consented to throw on the head of her son, with the Elder's permission, the water used for washing the latter's feet. When the Elder returned to his cave the deity addressed him as "physician." He could not understand this until she had told him the story. Then realizing how blameless his life had been, he was filled with joy and attained arahantship. But because the deity had tried to bring calumny on him, he asked her to leave the forest.[1]

[1] DhA. iii. 169 ff.

Pabhaṅkara Thera.—An arahant. He once saw the cetiya of **Padumuttara** Buddha covered with trees and creepers and quite inaccessible. He cleared it and made it ready for worship.[1]

[1] Ap. i. 269-70.

Pabhaṅgu Sutta.—The Buddha teaches that which has the nature of crumbling away and that which has not. Body crumbles, but the sinking of the body to rest does not.[1]

[1] S. iii. 32.

Pabhassara.—A king of long ago, a previous birth of **Mahā Kaccāna.**[1]

[1] Ap. i. 84.

Pabhassara Sutta.—The mind is luminous, but is defiled by taints from without. It can, however, be cleansed of these taints.[1]

[1] A. i. 10.

1. **Pabhāvatī.**—Mother of **Sujāta** Buddha.[1]

[1] Bu. xiii. 20; J. i. 38.

2. **Pabhāvatī.**—Mother of **Sikhī** Buddha.[1]

[1] Bu. xxi. 15; J. i. 41; D. ii. 6; AA. i. 436.

3. **Pabhāvatī.**—Daughter of King **Madda** of **Sāgala** and wife of **Kusa.** For her story see the **Kusa Jātaka.**[1]

[1] J. v. 283 ff.; Mtu. ii. 441 f. calls her Sudarśanā and her father Mahendraka.

4. **Pabhāvatī.**—Daughter of **Māṇābharaṇa** (1) and sister of **Parakkamabāhu I.**[1] She married **Mānābharaṇa** (2), son of **Sirivallabha.**[2]

[1] Cv. lxii. 3. [2] *Ibid.*, lxiv. 24.

Pabhedavatthu, Pabhejavatthu.—See **Mahejjāvatthu.**

Pamatta.—Fifteen kappas ago there were eight kings of this name all previous births of **Saparivāriya Thera.**[1] *v.l.* **Samatta, Somagga.**

[1] Ap. i. 172.

Pamāda Vagga.—The ninth chapter of the Eka Nipāta of the Aṅguttara Nikāya.[1]

[1] A. i. 15 f.

Pamāda Sutta.—Two Pacceka Brahmās, **Subrahmā** and **Suddhāvāsa,** came to see the Buddha, but finding him engaged in meditation, decided to visit a certain infatuated (*pamatta*) Brahmā in a certain Brahma-world. On their suggesting to him that he should visit the Buddha, he reproduced himself one thousand times and said he had greater iddhi-power than the Buddha. But Subrahmā reproduced himself two thousand times, and pointed out that the Buddha's iddhi-power exceeded theirs. It is said that the infatuated Brahmā visited the Buddha later.[1]

[1] S. i. 146 f.

Pamādavihārī Sutta.—The difference between him who dwells in heedlessness and him who dwells in earnest.[1]

[1] S. iv. 78.

Pamitā.—One of the seven children of the Sākyan **Sīhahanu,** and therefore a sister of Suddhodana.[1] *v.l.* **Pālitā.**

[1] Mhv. ii. 20; MṬ. 135; she is not mentioned in Dpv. (see iii. 46).

Pamokkharaṇa.—A king of seventy-seven kappas ago, a previous birth of **Nāgakesariya Thera.**[1]

[1] Ap. i. 222.

Payāga, Payāgatittha, Payāgapatiṭṭhāna.—A ford on the Ganges, on the direct route from **Verañjā** to **Benares,** the road passing through **Soreyya, Saṅkassa** and **Kaṇṇakujja,** and crossing the Ganges at **Payāga.**[1] It was one of the river-ghats where people did ceremonial bathing to wash away their sins.[2] It was here that the palace occupied by **Mahāpanāda** (*q.v.*) was submerged. The Buddha passed it when visiting the brahmin **Nanduttara,** and **Bhaddaji,** who was with him, raised the palace once more above the water. Bhaddaji had once been Mahāpanāda.[3] Buddhaghosa says[4] the bathing-place was on the spot where the palace stairs had stood. Reference is made to Payāga even in the time of **Padumuttara** Buddha.[5] It is identified with the modern Allahabad, at the confluence of the Gaṅgā and the Yamunā.

[1] Vin. iii. 11.
[2] M. i. 39; J. vi. 198.
[3] Mhv. xxxi. 6 ff.
[4] MA. i. 145; DA. iii. 856.
[5] AA. i. 126.

Payogasiddhi.—A Pāli grammatical work, belonging to the **Moggallāna** school, by **Vanaratana Medhaṅkara.**[1]

[1] P.L.C. 230 f.

Parakusināṭā.—One of the cities of **Uttarakuru,** described as having been built on an airy base.[1]

[1] D. iii. 200.

Parakkantabāhu, Parakkantabhuja.—See **Parakkamabāhu.**

1. **Parakkama (Parakkanta).**—A Paṇḍyan king, probably the son of **Vikkamapaṇḍu,** who ruled over Ceylon for two years (1051-52). He was slain by the **Coḷas.**[1]

[1] Cv. lvi. 16.

2. **Parakkama.**—A Paṇḍu king of **Madhurā.** When attacked by **Kulasekhara,** he appealed for assistance to **Parakkmabāhu I.** of Ceylon. Parakkamabāhu sent an army under **Laṅkāpura** to help him, but by the time the Sinhalese forces arrived, Kulasekhara had slain the king and his family and seized Madhurā. Parakkama's youngest son, who escaped death, was **Vīrapaṇḍu.**[1] Parakkama was killed in the village of **Tirimalakka.**[2]

[1] Cv. lxxvi. 76 ff., 142, 193, 200.
[2] *Ibid.*, lxxvii. 52.

3. **Parakkama.**—The general and minister of Queen **Līlāvatī.** He belonged to the family of the **Kālanāgaras** and was responsible for the queen's accession. He seems to have been slain by the Paṇḍu king **Parakkama**[1] (4)—see below. This Parakkama was a patron of learning, and the **Dāṭhāvaṃsa** (*q.v.*) was written at his request.

[1] Cv. lxxx. 49, 52.

4. **Parakkama.**—A Paṇḍu king who deposed Queen **Līlāvatī** and captured the throne of Ceylon. He ruled in **Pulatthinagara,** but was captured by **Māgha** and tortured to death.[1]

[1] Cv. lxxx. 52 ff., 71.

Parakkamataḷāka.—A tank built by **Parakkamabāhu I.**[1] See **Parakkamabāhu.**

[1] Cv. lxxix. 27.

Parakkamapaṇḍu.—One of the three **Vīrapperayaras** whom **Laṅkāpura** won over with gifts to alliance with **Vīrapaṇḍu.**[1]

[1] Cv. lxxvii. 6.

1. **Parakkamapura.**—A town built by **Parakkamabāhu I.** It was evidently another name for **Pulatthinagara,** which Parakkambāhu laid out and embellished in various ways.[1]

[1] Cv. lxxiv. 15; see also lxxii. 151; for the identification see Cv. *Trs.* ii. 22, n. 1.

2. **Parakkamapura.**—A stronghold in South India, built at **Kundukāla** by the general **Laṅkāpura.** The Chronicle contains a vivid account of a battle which took place just outside the gates of the stronghold between the forces of **Laṅkāpura** and of **Kulasekhara.** But no more is heard of the stronghold; it may have been abandoned in favour of another.[1]

[1] Cv. lxxvi. 121, 133, 147, 150.

1. **Parakkamabāhu I.**—King of Ceylon (1153-86). He was the son of the eldest of the three brothers, **Mānābharaṇa, Kittisirimegha** and **Sirivallabha,** who ruled over **Dakkhiṇadesa** and **Rohaṇa.** He was born at **Puṅkhagāma** in the **Dakkhiṇadesa,** where **Mānābharaṇa** was ruler. His birth was accompanied by various miracles. **Vikkamabāhu II.,** the then reigning king at **Pulatthipura,** hearing of this, wished to bring the boy up at his own court and make him his heir in place of his own son. But Mānābharaṇa refused to consent to this, and soon after died. Thereupon his brother Kittisirimegha took over Dakkhiṇadesa and left

Rohaṇa to Sirivallabha, who brought Mānābharaṇa's widow **Ratnāvalī** with her two daughters **Mittā** and **Pabhāvatī** and her son **Parakkama,** to his capital of **Mahānāgakula.** Meanwhile Vikkamabāhu dies and is succeeded by his son **Gajabāhu,** who maintains his position in spite of the attacks of Kittisirimegha and Sirivallabha. Parakkama, finding no scope for his talents in Rohaṇa, seeks his uncle Kittisirimegha, who receives him joyfully and takes him to live in his capital at **Saṅkhatthalī.** There Parakkama finishes his education, and his coming of age is celebrated under the direction of the Senāpati **Saṅkha** of **Badalatthalī.** Sirivallabha dies in Rohaṇa and is succeeded by his son, the younger Mānābharaṇa. Parakkama's ambitious spirit makes him restless, and he is discontented at the prospect of serving a petty principality. He wishes to seek royal dignity in **Rājaraṭṭha,** and refuses to listen to his uncle's dissuasion, who assures him that he is only influenced by his love for him and fears for his safety. But Parakkama leaves Saṅkhatthalī secretly and goes to Badalatthalī, where the general Saṅkha is slain because he informed the king of Parakkama's flight. Parakkama then goes to **Buddhagāma** near the frontiers of the Rājaraṭṭha. The inhabitants make repeated attempts to check his advance, but he repels these by his valour.

Meanwhile Kittisirimegha, after consultation with his ministers, sends a stronger force to try and overcome him, but the force is ambushed by the prince and completely routed after a night assault in **Khīravāpī.** Parakkama then goes to **Rājaraṭṭha,** where messengers with gifts from Gajabāhu meet him, the latter following to greet him in person and bring him to the capital. Parakkama lives at the court in Pulatthipura, but spends his time in spying out the country and intriguing with his host's subjects. In order to lull the suspicions of Gajabāhu, he gives him his sister **Bhaddavatī** in marriage, keeping her dowry in his own hands. Later, feeling his position insecure, he returns to Dakkhiṇadesa, meeting on the way with all kinds of adventures which put his courage to the test. Kittisirimegha, delighted to hear of his return, sends messengers to **Saraggāma** to meet him. But Parakkama hesitates to enter the capital until persuaded by his mother to do so. Shortly after, Kittisiremegha dies and Parakkama succeeds to the throne. He consolidates his position by various captures, including that of Gajabāhu, which follows on the storming of Pulatthipura. But Mānābharaṇa comes to the rescue, defeats Parakkama's army, and sets Gajabāhu free; but the latter, finding him unbearable, appeals to Parakkama for help. War ensues, and Gajabāhu, again at liberty, flees, while his officers fight with Parakkama. Ultimately he abdicates in favour of the latter, and dies at **Gaṅgātaṭa.** His ministers, however, send for Mānābharaṇa, while

Parakkama hastens to Pulatthipura, where he is crowned. A campaign of varying fortunes ensues ending in the defeat of Mānābharaṇa, who flees to his own country, where he dies. Parakkama is then crowned a second time. Parakkama is now sole monarch, but his rule is not universally acceptable. In the fourth year of his reign, **Sugalā,** mother of Mānābharaṇa, raises the standard of revolt in Rohaṇa. The campaign against her is a protracted one and is conducted by the general **Rakkha.** In the early part of the campaign the Tooth and Bowl Relics are recovered and brought with great ceremony to Pulatthipura. The rebels are gradually cornered and defeated. Sugalā is captured, and the revolt collapses. Rohaṇa is quiet for a time, but rises again after some years.

In the twelfth year of his reign, Parakkama goes to war with the king of **Rāmañña,** disputes having arisen about the elephant trade and the treatment of the Sinhalese ambassadors, the crowning offence being the seizing of a princess who was being sent from Ceylon to **Kamboja.** A fleet is collected at **Pallavavaṅka,** and the soldiers are landed at the port of **Kusumī,** with the **Nagaragiri Kitti** at their head, a further attack being made by the **Damiḷādhikarin Ādicca** at **Papphālama.** After five months the Rāmañña king is slain and peace again restored.

Soon after, the Paṇḍu king Parakkama being besieged by the Coḷa king **Kulasekhara,** appeals for help from Ceylon. Parakkamabāhu sends an army under his general **Laṅkāpura,** but, in the meantime, the Paṇḍu king has been slain and his capital **Madhurā** taken. The Sinhalese army, however, landed on the opposite coast and carried on a war against the Coḷas, and built a fortress called **Parakkamapura.** As a result of this campaign, Kulasekhara was defeated and the Paṇḍu king's son, **Vīrapaṇḍu,** was crowned in the ancient capital. The Coḷa prisoners were sent to Ceylon and employed in repairing the **Ratanavāluka-cetiya.** The village of **Paṇḍuvijaya** was founded by Parakkama to commemmorate the victory. The ultimate outcome of this expedition is not certain. The Coḷa records claim that Laṅkāpura was defeated, and that his head was nailed to the gates of Madhurā together with those of his generals. The war of the Paṇḍyan succession did not end there.

Parakkamabāhu now engaged in more peaceful pursuits and, after some trouble, he succeeded in reconciling the three sects of monks—the **Mahāvihāra,** the **Abhayagiri** and the **Jetavana**—and held a convocation under a thera called **Mahā Kassapa.** The **Vaitulya** heresy now finally disappeared from Ceylon. The king built for the use of the monks the **Jetavanārāma,** including a round Temple of the Tooth, in the vicinity of the royal palace, and, further to the north, he constructed the **Āḷāhana-Pariveṇa,** the **Laṅkātilaka-vihāra** and the **Baddhasīmāpāsāda.** He also built the **Pacchimārāma,** the **Uttarārāma** and the **Mahā Thūpa** (or **Damila Thūpa**).

In the three suburbs he built the **Isipatana,** the **Kusinārārāma** and the **Veḷuvana-vihāras,** and, in addition, the **Kapila-vihāra,** while he restored the shrines at **Anurādhapura.**

Parakkamabāhu also enlarged and fortified Pulatthipura and adorned the city with numerous palaces and pleasure-gardens. He paid great attention to irrigation, opening the **Ākāsagaṅgā** and forming or improving a system of irrigation, its centre being in the **Parakkama-samudda,** and building numerous tanks throughout the country.

The internal peace of the latter half of his reign was disturbed only by a rebellion near **Mahātittha,** this being easily quelled.

Parakkamabāhu I. was succeeded by his sister's son, **Vijayabahu II.** According to the Nikāyasaṅgraha, Parakkama was born after death as the god Naradeva in the Himālaya.[1]

[1] Chaps. 62-79 of the Cv. are devoted to a description of Parakkamabāhu and his reign. The above is a very concise account of the contents of these chapters.

2. **Parakkamabāhu.**—Son of **Vijayabāhu III.** and brother of **Bhuvanekabāhu.** He was born at **Sirivaḍḍhana,** and, in his youth, was entrusted to the care of the monks under **Saṅgharakkhita.** On the death of his father he ascended the throne, and reigned for thirty-three years (1236-68), at **Jambuddoṇi,** as **Parakkamabāhu II.** On account of his profound erudition, he received the sobriquet of *Kalikāla-Sāhicca-sabbaññupaṇḍita* (" the scholar entirely familiar with literature in the Dark Age "). The first act of his reign was the bringing of the Tooth Relic from the **Billa** mountain to the capital, amidst the exhibition of various miracles. He then set about regaining Pulatthipura from the Tamils, with **Māghinda** and **Jayabāhu** at their head, and this was accomplished by 1244. In the eleventh year of his reign Ceylon was invaded by a Jāvaka (Javanese) named **Candabhānu,** probably a sea-robber with a large force. The attack was repulsed by **Vīrabāhu,** the king's nephew, but Candabhānu appeared again later. The rest of Parakkama's life was devoted to pious works. He invited Coḷa monks over to Ceylon and held a convocation, with the object of reforming the priesthood, and showed special honour to **Dhammakitti,** a monk of **Tambaraṭṭha.** Among buildings erected by him were the **Bhuvenakabāhu-pariveṇa** at **Billasela** and the **Mahāmahindabāhu-pariveṇa** at **Hatthiselapura.** He also restored the vihāras at **Kalyāṇi** and at **Hatthavaṅgalla.** He added to the **Sirivijayasundara-vihāra** built by his father and inaugurated a yearly festival in **Devanagara.** He made a pilgrimage to **Samantakūṭa** and erected a bridge, so that pilgrims might reach it more easily. In all these works he was assisted by his minister **Devappatirāja.** Parakkama had five sons: **Vijayabāhu, Bhuvanekabāhu, Tibhuvanamalla, Parakkamabāhu** and **Jaya-**

bāhu. In his old age he abdicated in favour of his son Vijayabāhu, who, because of his piety, was called Bodhisatta.[1]

[1] Cv., chaps. 81-9.

3. **Parakkamabāhu.**—One of the five sons of **Parakkamabāhu II.** Nothing further is known of him.[1]

[1] Cv. lxxxvii. 16.

4. **Parakkamabāhu.**—Son of **Vijayabāhu IV.** and grandson of **Parakkamabāhu II.** He became king about 1302 A.C., but the length of his reign is not known. He paid a visit to the Pāṇḍyan king and recovered the Tooth and Bowl Relics which had been carried away by **Ariyacakkavatti.** They were restored to **Pulatthipura.**[1] It may be conjectured that Parakkama secured the Relics at the price of vassalage to the Pāṇḍyan court.

[1] Cv. xc. 48 ff.

5. **Parakkamabāhu.**—Son of **Bhuvanekabāhu II.** He became king in **Hatthiselapura** as Parakkamabāhu IV. in about 1325 A.C. The length of his reign is unknown. He paid great honour to the Tooth Relic and is said to have written, in Sinhalese, a work called the Ceremonial of the Tooth Relic (*Dāṭhādhātucāritta*).[1]

[1] Cv. xc. 64 ff.

6. **Parakkamabāhu V.**—King of Ceylon.[1] He was, perhaps, the brother of **Bhuvanekabāhu IV.,** and, probably, had his capital at **Gaṅgāsiripura.** The period of his reign is not definitely known, but it was somewhere between 1348 and 1360 A.C.

[1] Cv. xc. 1; see Codrington, *op. cit.*, 83, 89, and Cv. *Trs.* ii. 212, n. 1.

7. **Parakkamabāhu VI.**—King of Ceylon.[1] He ruled at **Jayavaḍḍhaṇapura.** The Cūḷavaṃsa tells us nothing of importance except that his mother was **Sunettā.** We gather from other sources that his father was **Vijayabāhu,** but the authenticity of this information is doubtful. The date of his accession is also uncertain. Some place it at 1412 A.C., others at 1415 A.C. At the beginning of his reign he lived for three years at **Rājagāma,** moving later to Jayavaḍḍhaṇapura. Among his religious works were the restoration of the monasteries at **Gaṇḍāladoṇi** and **Laṅkātilaka,** and the building of a temple of the Tooth in his capital, also the founding of the **Sunettā-pariveṇa** in honour of his mother. He

[1] Cv. xci. 16 ff.; see also Cv. *Trs.*, ii. 215, n. 1; and Codrington, *op. cit.*, 90 f.

abdicated in favour of his sister's son, **Vīra Parakkamabāhu,** and died after a reign of fifty-five years. His reign is noted for a great output of Sinhalese literature, particularly of poetry.

8. **Parakkamabāhu VII.**—Also called **Paṇḍita Parakkamabāhu,** son of **Bhuvanekabāhu VI.**[1] He reigned for four years (*circa* 1480-84 A.C.), and was slain by his uncle who became king as **Vīra-Parakkamabāhu.**[2]

[1] Cv. xcii. 3. [2] Codrington, *op. cit.*, 94.

9. **Parakkamabāhu VIII.**—Also called **Vīra-Parakkamabāhu,** uncle of **Parakkamabāhu VII.**[1] He seems to have ruled from about 1484-1509 A.C. He had constant trouble with his relations. His successor's name is uncertain.[2]

[1] Cv. xcii. 3. [2] Codrington, *op. cit.*, 94 f.

10. **Parakkamabāhu IX.**—Also called **Dhamma-Parakkamabāhu.** He is not mentioned in the Cūḷavaṃsa, but probably ruled somewhere about 1509-28 A.C.[1]

[1] Codrington, *op. cit.*, 95 f.

Parakkamabāhupāsāda.—A monastic building attached to the **Valligāma-vihāra** and erected by **Parakkamabāhu IV.**[1]

[1] Cv. xc. 96.

1. **Parakkasamudda.**—A tank built by **Parakkamabāhu I.,** by the enlargement of the **Paṇḍavāpī.**[1]

[1] Cv. lxviii. 40.

2. **Parakkamasamudda.**—A tank built by **Parakkamabāhu I.** and attached to the river system of the **Kāragaṅgā.** It was, probably, in the neighbourhood of **Pulatthipura** and had many canals branching off: the **Gambhīra, Hemavatī, Nīlavāhinī, Salaḷavatī, Vettavatī, Maṅgalagaṅgā** and **Campā**; and contained many sluices: **Makara, Mālatīpuppha, Vettavatī, Dakkhiṇā, Maṅgala** and **Caṇḍī.** The canal connecting it with the Kāragaṅgā was called the **Ākāsagaṅgā.**[1]

[1] Cv. lxxix. 26 f., 40 ff.; see also Cv. *Trs.* ii. 117, n. 5.

Parakkamasāgara.—A tank built by **Parakkamabāhu I.** It was connected with the **Kāragaṅgā** by the **Godāvarī** Canal.[1]

[1] Cv. lxxix. 28, 57.

Paraṅgī.—The Pāli name for the Portuguese, who invaded Ceylon.[1]

[1] *E.g.*, Cv. xcv. 5, 96; xcviii. 80.

Paragāma-vihāra.—A monastery in Ceylon, restored by **Vijayabāhu I.**[1]

[1] Cv. lx. 61.

Paradārika Sutta.—About a man of **Rājagaha,** an adulterer, born as a peta in a dung-pit and seen by **Mahā Moggallāna.**[1]

[1] S. ii. 258.

Paranimmita-Vasavattī.—A class of devas, inhabitants of the highest stage of the sensuous universe (*kāmaloka*). They are described[1] as "beings who desire the creation of others, in order to get them into their power." The Commentary[2] explains that the objects of their desires are created by other devas who know their weakness, just as a cook, knowing the king's favourite dishes, will prepare them for him. It adds that, according to some authorities, their desires are fulfilled by a mere look, a smile, an embrace, but this statement is rejected by the ancient Commentary.

[1] *E.g.*, A. i. 210, etc.; S. v. 410, 423; D. ii. 91; iii. 218.

[2] DA. iii. 1001; ItvA. 243 f.; see also MNidA. 109; PSA. 441; VibhA. 519.

1. **Parantapa.**—King of **Kosambī** and father of **Udena.**[1]

[1] DhA. i. 164.

2. **Parantapa.**—An attendant of the king of Benares. For his story see the **Parantapa Jātaka.**

Parantapa Jātaka (No. 416).—The Bodhisatta was once born as the son of the king of Benares. He came to understand the speech of animals, and thus learned from a she-jackal whom he had offended that a hostile king with whom he would have to fight would march on to the city. His father bore him no love, and sent him to fight this king when he arrived. But all the citizens followed the prince, and his father, very alarmed, retired into the forest with his queen, his chaplain, and a servant, named **Parantapa,** and lived in a hut. When the king and the chaplain went for fruit, the queen, though with child by the king, sinned with Parantapa and instigated him to kill the king while on his way to bathe in the river. The chaplain watched this deed but said nothing, and on his return feigned to have been suddenly blinded by a snake's breath. The queen bore a son, and when he was sixteen, the chaplain told him of what had happened and taught him the use of a sword. Soon after, the boy killed

Parantapa and returned with his mother and the chaplain to Benares, where the Bodhisatta made him his viceroy.

The story was told in reference to **Devadatta's** attempts to kill the Buddha. Devadatta is identified with the old king.[1]

[1] J. iii. 415-21.

Parantapabbata.—One of the ambassadors sent by **Devānampiyatissa** to **Asoka.**[1]

[1] Dpv. xi. 29, 31.

Parappasādaka Thera.—An arahant. Ninety-four kappas ago he was a brahmin named Sena, who, seeing Siddhattha Buddha, praised him in four stanzas. Fourteen kappas ago he was king four times under the name of Uggata.[1] He is probably identical with Bhūta Thera.[2]

[1] Ap. i. 113 f. [2] ThagA. i. 494.

Paramatta.—A Brahmā who was present at the **Mahāsamaya.**[1]

[1] D. ii. 260.

Paramaṭṭhaka Sutta.—The fifth sutta of the Aṭṭhaka Vagga of the Sutta Nipāta. It was preached in reference to the divergence of views held by various teachers in **Sāvatthi.** The king, on hearing of their constant disputes, gave orders that a company of blind men be collected and an elephant placed before them. They were then asked to touch the elephant. and each one described what it appeared like to him. Each described that part which he had touched. The king told the heretics that their divergent views were as unreliable as the blind men's descriptions of the elephant. The Buddha, hearing of this, preached the sutta in order to confirm the king's judgment.

One should not give oneself up to philosophical speculations which lead nowhere and promote wrangles.[1] The sutta is commented upon in the Mahā Niddesa.[2]

[1] SN. vs. 796-803; SNA. ii. 529 ff. [2] MNid. 102 ff.

Paramatthajotikā.—**Buddhaghosa's** Commentary on the **Khuddakapāṭha, Dhammapada, Sutta Nipāta** and **Jātaka.**

Paramatthadīpa.—Another name for the **Khemappakaraṇa** (*q.v.*).

Paramatthadīpanī.—**Dhammapāla's** Commentary on the **Udānā, Itivuttaka, Vimānavatthu, Petavatthu, Theragāthā** and **Therīgāthā.**[1] It seems also to have been called **Vimalavilāsinī.**[2]

[1] Gv. 60. [2] P.L.C. 114, n. 4.

Paramatthabindu.—A grammatical work on Pāli, by King Kyocvā of Pagan. There is a Ṭīkā on it by **Mahā Kassapa.**[1]

[1] Bode, *op. cit.*, 25.

1. **Paramatthamañjūsā.**—**Dhammapāla's** Commentary (Ṭīkā) on the **Visuddhimagga.**[1]

[1] P.L.C. 113.

2. **Paramatthamañjūsā.**—An Abhidhamma treatise by **Vepullabuddhi.**[1]

[1] Bode, *op. cit.*, 28.

Paramatthavinicchaya.—A treatise on the Abhidhamma written by **Anuruddha** of **Kāñcipura.** There exists a Ṭīkā on it by **Māhābodhi Thera.**[1]

[1] P.L.C. 173 f.; Gv. 61, 71; Svd. 1226, 1230; Sās. 69.

Paramannadāyaka Thera.—An arahant. Ninety-one kappas ago he invited **Vipassī** Buddha to his house, where he served him with excellent food.[1]

[1] Ap. i. 249.

Paramarāja.—A king of **Ayodhya** (in India ?) who built a monastery, called the **Laṅkārāma,** for the Elder **Dhammakitti.**[1]

[1] P.L.C. 245.

Paramassāsa Sutta.—A conversation between **Sāriputta** and **Jambukhādaka** on what constitutes supreme comfort.[1]

[1] S. ii. 254; *cp.* iv. 261.

Parammaraṇa Sutta.—**Mahā Kassapa** explains to **Sāriputta** that the Buddha has omitted to say anything of his existence or otherwise after death, because such a discussion would be fruitless; but he has taught of *dukkha* and its cessation, because that is fruitful.[1]

[1] S. ii. 222 f.

1. **Parābhava Sutta.**—The sixth sutta of the **Sutta Nipāta,** preached on the day after that of the preaching of the **Maṅgala Sutta.** In the latter the Buddha had spoken of the ways of progress; the devas then wished to hear how beings deteriorated, and, at their request, **Sakka** sent a deva to ask the Buddha who, thereupon, preached this discourse. It is said that at the conclusion of the sutta countless beings realized the Truth.[1]

[1] SNA. i. 169-74.

The sutta deals with various causes which lead to the decay and corruption of beings. Having well considered all the various ways of destruction, the wise man avoids them and, being endowed with insight, attains to happiness.[2]

[2] SN. vs. 91-115.

2. **Parābhava Sutta.**—Seven conditions that bring about loss.[1]

[1] A. iv. 26 f.

Parikuppa Sutta.—Five kinds of persons who lie festering (*parikuppa*) in hell: those who kill mother, father, or arahant, maliciously draw blood from the Buddha, or create dissension in the Order.[1]

[1] A. iii. 146.

Parikkhāra Sutta.—The seven requisites for the attainment of *samādhi*—the first seven stages of the Noble Eightfold Path.[1]

[1] A. iv. 40.

Parijāna (or **Abhijāna**) **Sutta.**—By not thoroughly knowing or understanding the five *khandhas* one is unfit for the destruction of suffering.[1]

[1] S. iii. 26 f.

Parijānana Sutta.—Without comprehending and detaching himself from the all—eye, nose, etc.—a man is incapable of extinguishing suffering.[1]

[1] S. iv. 17.

1. **Pariññā Sutta.**—The five *khandhas* are things to be understood (*pariññeyyā dhammā*).[1]

[1] S. iii. 26.

2. **Pariññā Sutta.**—The teaching for the comprehension of all attachment: from eye and object arises eye-consciousness, the union of these is contact; from contact comes feeling; similarly with regard to the other senses.[1]

[1] S. iv. 32 f.

3. **Pariññā** (or **Addhāna**) **Sutta.**—The five *indriyas*, if developed, conduce to comprehension of the way out.[1]

[1] S. v. 236.

Pariññāya Sutta.—By fully understanding body, feeling, etc., deathlessness is realized.[1]

[1] S. v. 182.

Pariññeyya Sutta.—The All should be fully known.[1]

[1] S. iv. 29.

1. **Pariññeyyā Sutta.**—The five *khandhas* should be understood, and their understanding consists in the destruction of lust, hatred and illusion.[1]

[1] S. iii. 159.

2. **Pariññeyyā Sutta.**—Preached to **Rādha**; the same as the above, with the addition that the person who has so understood should be called "*arahā.*"[1]

[1] S. iii. 191.

Paritta, Parittā.—A collection of texts taken from the Khuddakapāṭha, the Aṅguttara Nikāya, the Majjhima Nikāya and the Sutta Nipāta, and recited on special occasions to ward off illness and danger. The word "*paritta*" means protection. The Milindapañha[1] gives a list of the chief Parittas: **Ratana Sutta, Khandha-paritta, Mora-paritta, Dhajagga-paritta, Āṭānāṭiya-paritta** and **Aṅgulimāla.**[2] To these are generally added, in the extant collection of Parittas, the **Maṅgala Sutta** and the **Metta Sutta.** The word *paritta* first occurs in the Culla Vagga[3] in connection with the Khandha-paritta, which was allowed by the Buddha as a watch, a guard, a protection for oneself, for the use of the Order. The occasion of the delivery of this general injunction was the death of a monk from snake-bite. The Milindapañha states (see above) that the recital of the Paritta had the Buddha's express sanction.

The collection of Parittas is, to this day, more widely known by the laity of Burma and Ceylon than any other Pāli book, and is generally used in times of danger or of sickness, both individual and national. Thus, **Sena II.,** king of Ceylon, made the community of monks recite the Paritta, and by sprinkling the water charmed with Paritta he made the people free from illness, and so removed the danger of plague from the country. He also decreed that this practice should continue every year.[4] **Kassapa V.** is said to have had a Paritta-ceremony performed by the three fraternities of monks to protect his people from danger and plague and bad harvest.[5] Bode says[6] that in the days of King **Anorata** of Burma

[1] 150 f.

[2] For particulars of these see *s.v.*; also Dial. iii. 185.

[3] Vin. ii. 110.

[4] Cv li. 80.

[5] *Ibid.*, lii. 80; in the recent (1935) epidemic of malaria in Ceylon, monks were taken in carts through the badly affected areas reciting the Paritta and sprinkling water. The ceremony is held on most diverse occasions such as the inauguration of a new house, the starting of a journey, of a new business, etc. For a discussion on the Paritta see Dial. iii. 180 ff.; also P.L.C. 75 f.

[6] *Op. cit.*, 4.

corrupt and cynical monks used the recital of the Paritta as an easy means of clearing man's guilty conscience from all wrong-doing, even from matricide.

Buddhaghosa is mentioned[7] as having once attempted to compile a **Parittaṭṭhakathā.** Geiger[8] calls this a commentary on the Paritta, but it is more probable that paritta is here used as an adjective, meaning short, concise, and that what is meant is a short or concise commentary on the Piṭakas.

[7] Cv. xxxvii. 226. [8] Cv. *Trs.* i. 24, 3.

Parittasubhā.—A class of devas belonging to the **Subhas.**[1] Beings are born among them after attaining the third *jhāna.*[2] Their life-span is sixteen kappas.[3]

[1] M. iii. 102. [2] VibhA. 507. [3] AbhS. 23.

Parittābhā.—A class of devas included among the **Ābhā** gods.[1] They belong to the plane of the second *jhāna.*[2] Beings are born there by virtue of absorbing the idea of lesser brilliancy.[3] Their life-span is two kappas.[4]

[1] M. iii. 102.
[2] VibhA. 520.
[3] M. iii. 147.
[4] AbhS. 22.

Parittikuṇḍiyāra.—A Damiḷa chief, ally of **Kulasekhara.**[1]

[1] Cv. lxxvi. 137, 221.

Parittikkuṇḍiraṭṭha.—A district in South India. It was given over to **Coḷagaṅgara** in return for his allegiance to **Parakkamabāhu I.**[1]

[1] Cv. lxxvii. 9.

1. **Parinibbāna Sutta.**—An account of the death of the Buddha at **Kusinārā.** It contains the last words of the Buddha and stanzas of **Sahampati, Sakka** and **Anuruddha,** uttered immediately after his death.[1]

[1] S. i. 157; *cp.* D. ii. 156 f.; on their difference, see KS. i. 196, n. 1.

2. **Parinibbāna Sutta.**—On the complete passing away.[1]

[1] A. iv. 254.

Parinda.—A Damiḷa usurper, son of King **Paṇḍu.** He ruled in **Anurādhapura** for three years between 433 and 460, and was succeeded by his youngest brother, **Khudda-Parinda.**[1]

[1] Cv. xxxviii. 29.

Paripuṇṇaka Thera.—He belonged to a **Sākyan** family of **Kapilavatthu**, and was so called because of the completeness of his gifts and fortune. His means allowed him to enjoy, at all times, food of one hundred essences. On hearing that the Buddha lived on very simple diet, he renounced the world, and, entering the Order, became an arahant.

He had been a householder in the time of **Dhammadassī** Buddha and had offered various gifts at his shrine. Ninety-four kappas ago he was king sixteen times under the name of **Thūpasikhara.**[1] He is probably identical with **Ṭhambhāropaka** of the Apadāna.[2]

[1] Thag. vs. 91; ThagA. i. 190 f. [2] Ap. i. 171.

Paribbājaka Vagga.—The eighth chapter of the Majjhima Nikāya, containing suttas 71-80.[1]

[1] M. i. 481 ff.

1. **Paribbājaka Sutta.**—A brahmin paribbājaka asks the Buddha how far the Dhamma is *sandiṭṭhiko, akāliko, ehipassiko, opanayiko,* and *paccattaṃ veditabbo viññūhi.* The Buddha explains.[1]

[1] A. i. 157 f.

2. **Paribbājaka Sutta.**—The Buddha visits the Paribbājakārāma on the banks of the **Sappinikā** and converses with a number of distinguished Paribbājakas—**Annabhāra, Varadhara, Sakuludāyī** and others. The Buddha tells them that there are four factors of Dhamma which no discerning recluse or brahmin can despise—not-coveting, not-malice, right mindfulness, and right concentration.[1]

[1] A. ii. 31 f.

Paribbājakā.—The name given to the ascetics and recluses (not otherwise classified) of the Buddha's time. They were not exclusively brahmin. Their presence seems to have been recognized and respected from earlier times. Generally speaking, their creed is formulated as a belief in perfect bliss after death for the self purged from evil, and as a conviction that this bliss can be won by *brahmacariyā*, by freedom from all evil in acts, words, aims, and mode of livelihood.[1] All these four standards of conduct were bodily incorporated in the Buddha's Noble Eightfold Path, and the last of the four gave to the **Ājīvakas** (*q.v.*) their specific name as a separate sect. The Paribbājakas claimed to be identical with the followers of the Buddha in their tenets and teaching,[2] but the Buddha maintained that the two teachings were quite distinct. This is clearly indicated[3] in connection with the conversion of **Sāriputta**

[1] See, *e.g.*, M. ii. 24. [2] *E.g.*, M. i. 64 f., 84 f. [3] *E.g.*, Vin. i. 39.

and **Moggallāna,** who were Paribbājakas under **Sañjaya.** The goal of the Paribbājakas was deathlessness (*amata*) which, to them, probably meant birth in the world of Brahmā. Their conversion to the Buddha's Doctrine followed the recognition that Gotama dealt, not with effects but with causes, and that he went to the root of the matter by teaching how casual states of consciousness arose and how they could be banished for ever.[4]

The Paribbājakas were not ascetics except in so far as they were celibates; some of them were women. They were teachers or sophists who spent eight or nine months of every year wandering from place to place for the purpose of engaging in friendly, conversational discussions on matters of ethics and philosophy, nature-lore and mysticism. They differed very much in intelligence, earnestness, and even in honesty. Some of the views discussed in the **Brahmajāla Sutta,** for instance, and described as those of "Eel-wrigglers" and "Hair-splitters," were undoubtedly truly thus described. The books mention halls erected for the accommodation of the Paribbājakas, such as those in **Mallikā's** park at Sāvatthi,[5] and the **Kūtāgārasālā** (*q.v.*) at **Vesāli.** Sometimes special places were set apart for them in the groves near the settlements, as at **Campā** on the bank of the **Gaggarā** lake,[6] at the **Moranivāpa** in **Rājagaha,**[7] and on the banks of the **Sappinikā.**[8] It was in such places that the Paribbājakas met each other, and in the course of their journeys they would visit each other in order to exchange greetings of courtesy and to engage in profitable discussion. The utmost cordiality seems to have prevailed on these occasions, intercourse and discussions were free, there were no restrictions of creed, caste or pride. Thus **Dīghanakha** calls on the Buddha,[9] the Buddha on **Sakuladāyī**[10] and **Sarabha.**[11] **Vekhanassa** calls on the Buddha,[12] as do **Timbaruka,**[13] **Vacchagotta,**[14] and **Sivaka Moḷiya.**[15] **Poṭaliputta** calls on **Samiddhi,**[16] **Susīma** on **Ānanda,**[17] and **Jambukhādaka** on **Sāriputta.**[18] The inhabitants of the towns and villages, near which the Paribbājakas stopped, visited them, both to show their respect and to benefit by their teachings. The names of a considerable number of Paribbājakas, besides those already mentioned, who were well known in the time of the Buddha, are given in the texts

[4] Chalmers: Further Dialogues i. Introd. xxi. For discussions on the views of the Paribbājakas as compared with those of the Buddha, see also A. iv. 35 ff., 378; i. 215.

[5] D. i. 178.

[6] *Ibid.*, 111.

[7] A. v. 326.

[8] *Ibid.*, i. 185; ii. 176.

[9] M. i. 497.

[10] *Ibid.*, ii. 29; also A. ii. 175 ff.

[11] *Ibid.*, i. 185.

[12] M. ii. 40.

[13] S. ii. 22.

[14] *Ibid.*, iii. 257.

[15] *Ibid.*, iv. 230.

[16] M. iii. 207.

[17] S. ii. 119.

[18] *Ibid.*, iv. 251.

(*e.g.*, **Annabhāra, Varadhara,** etc.),[19] also **Sāmaṇḍaka**[20] and the Paribbājikā **Sucimukhī.**[21] In most cases they are represented as having large followings, so that they were evidently regarded as distinguished teachers.

[19] A. ii. 175. [20] S. iv. 26. [21] S. iii. 238 f.

Paribhutta.—A city in the time of **Sikhī** Buddha, where the Bodhisatta was born as King **Arindama.**[1]

[1] BuA. 203.

Parimaṇḍala Vagga.—The first section of the Sekhiyā.[1]

[1] Vin. iv. 185-7.

Parimucchita Sutta.—One who does not regard the body, etc., as "I" and "mine" and as "self" will not have a hereafter.[1]

[1] S. iii. 165.

Pariyādinna Suttā.—Two suttas on how attachments arise and on how they can be completely exhausted.[1]

[1] S. iv. 33 f.

Pariyāya Sutta.—Followers of other teachers might say that their teaching was the same as that of the Buddha regarding the five hindrances and the seven limbs of wisdom. But there is a method in the teaching of the Buddha whereby five become ten and seven fourteen. Other teachers cannot satisfactorily explain this method.[1]

[1] S. v. 108 f.

Pariyesanā Sutta.—On four quests that are un-Ariyan and four that are Ariyan.[1]

[1] A. ii. 247.

Pariḷāha.—A niraya where all objects of the senses, even when really attractive, appear quite repulsive to those experiencing them.[1]

[1] S. v. 450.

Pariḷāha Sutta.—Not to understand *dukkha* and its cessation is far more fearsome than to be born in the **Pariḷāha-niraya.**[1]

[1] S. v. 450.

Parivārapāṭha (or **Parivāra**).—The concluding part of the Vinaya Piṭaka. It is a digest of the other parts of the Vinaya and consists of nineteen chapters. The colophon states that the book was the work of a monk named **Dīpa,** probably of Ceylon. The Commentaries,[1] however, speak of the Soḷasa-Parivāra as having formed part of the Vinaya when it was rehearsed at the First Council. Perhaps the Parivāras correspond to the *mātikā* of the Abhidhamma and were enlarged later on.

[1] *E.g.*, DA. i. 17; Sp. i. 18.

Parivīmaṃsana Sutta.—A monk, when pondering on *dukkha*, realizes that it is the result of birth, and he practises according to the Dhamma to bring about its cessation. He ponders further and gets at the root cause of all things; he then realizes a state free from birth, decay, old age and death, and he becomes aware of its realization.[1]

[1] S. ii. 80 ff.

Pariveṇa-vihāra.—A vihāra in **Rohaṇa,** built by **Aggabodhi,** ruler of **Rohaṇa** (Aggabodhi 6).[1]

[1] Cv. xlv. 45.

Parisā Vagga.—The fifth chapter of the Duka Nipāta of the Aṅguttara Nikāya.[1]

[1] A. i. 70.

1. **Parisā Sutta.**—The four corrupters of a company: a monk, a nun, a male disciple and a female disciple, if they are immoral.[1]

[1] A. ii. 225.

2. **Parisā Sutta.**—On the three companies: the company trained in bombast, the company trained in enquiry, and the company trained according to its bent.[1]

[1] A. i. 285.

3. **Parisā Sutta.**—On the eight assemblies: khattiya, brāhmaṇa, householder, samaṇa, Cātummahārājika, Tāvatiṃsa, Māra and Brahma. The Buddha visits them all and preaches to them.[1]

[1] A. iv. 307 f.

Parisuddha.—A king of sixty-seven kappas ago, a previous birth of **Dussadāyaka Thera.**[1]

[1] Ap. i. 185.

Parisuddha Vagga.—The thirteenth chapter of the Dasaka Nipāta of the Aṅguttara Nikāya.[1]

[1] A. v. 237-40.

Parisuddha Sutta.—Eight conditions—the factors of the Noble Eightfold Path—which are absolutely pure and which come into being only on the appearance of a Tathāgata.[1]

[1] S. v. 15.

Parisuddhābhā.—A class of devas included among the **Ābhā** gods. Beings are born among them as a result of absorbing the idea of untarnished brilliancy.[1] They belong to the plane of the third *jhāna*,[2] and their life-span is sixteen kappas.[3]

[1] M. iii. 102, 147. [2] VbhA. 520. [3] AbhS. 23.

1. **Parihāna Sutta.**—**Sāriputta** tells the monks of the qualities which lead to their deterioration—not listening to the Dhamma, not having clear ideas about it, not practising it, and not obtaining fresh knowledge thereof. He who wishes to progress should train himself to know both his own mind and the minds of others; he should practise introspection.[1]

[1] A. v. 102 ff.

2. **Parihāna Sutta.**—On eight conditions which lead to the degeneration of a learner, and their opposites.[1]

[1] A. iv. 331 f.

3. **Parihāna Sutta.**—On the six stations of mastery (*cha abhibhāyatanāni*) which prevent a monk from falling away. Seeing an object with the eye, he does not allow evil and unprofitable states to arise in his mind, memories and hopes akin to fetters that bind. Likewise with the other senses.[1]

[1] S. iv. 76 f.

4. **Parihāna Sutta.**—A conversation between **Ānanda** and **Bhadda** at the **Kukkuṭārāma** in **Pāṭaliputta,** regarding decay and non-decay.[1]

[1] S. v. 173.

Parihāni Sutta.—**Sāriputta** tells the monks of four qualities that bring about "falling off": abundance of lust, hatred, and delusion, and want of wisdom in profound matters.[1]

[1] A. ii. 143 f.

Parosata Jātaka (No. 101).—This story is analogous in all respects to the **Parosahassa Jātaka** (*q.v.*).

Parosata Vagga.—The eleventh chapter of the Eka Nipāta of the Jātakaṭṭhakathā.[1]

[1] J. i. 410-24.

Paresa Sutta.—On three qualities essential for one who teaches others the Dhamma.[1]

[1] A. i. 151.

Parosahassa Jātaka (No. 99).—Once the Bodhisatta was an ascetic in the **Himālaya,** leader of five hundred ascetics. His chief disciple was away at the time of his (the Bodhisatta's) death, and when his other disciples asked him, just before his death, what excellence he had won, he answered "Nothing," meaning, "insight into the nothingness of things." But they did not understand, and therefore neglected to pay him the customary honours at his cremation. When the chief disciple returned and heard of this, he tried to explain matters to them, but they would not hearken until the Bodhisatta himself appeared from the Brahma-world and convinced them of their folly. "Far better than a thousand fools," he said, "is one who, hearing, understands." The story was told in reference to **Sāriputta's** great wisdom. He is identified with the chief disciple.[1] See also **Sarabhaṅga Jātaka.**

[1] J. i. 406 ff.

Parosahassa Sutta.—Relates how once, when the Buddha was at **Jetavana** with twelve hundred and fifty monks, instructing them and inciting them by means of a sermon on Nibbāna, **Vaṅgīsa,** who was in the assembly, after obtaining the Buddha's permission, extolled him in a number of verses.[1]

[1] S. i. 192.

Palaṅkoṭṭa.—A locality in South India, mentioned in the account of **Laṅkāpura's** campaign against **Kulasekhara.**[1]

[1] Cv. lxxvii. 58, 64, 66.

Palandīpa.—A country in South India. **Vīradeva** was once its king.[1]

[1] Cv. lxi. 36.

Palannagara.—A village and a monastery in Ceylon. **Aggabodhi II.** built a *padhānaghara* attached to the monastery in honour of the Thera **Jotipāla.**[1]

[1] Cv. xlii. 50.

Palāyi Jātaka (No. 229).—Once the Bodhisatta was king of **Takkasilā.** Brahmadatta, king of Benares, marched on his city with a large army, hoping to capture it; but on seeing the towers on the city gates, he took fright and fled.

The story was told in reference to a mendicant who loved arguing.

He could find no one to contradict him until he came to **Sāvatthi,** where was the Buddha. Forthwith he set off for Jetavana; but on seeing the gate-towers, he fled.[1] See also **Dutiya-Palāyi Jātaka.**

[1] J. ii. 216 ff.

1. **Palāsa Jātaka** (No. 307).—Once a poor brahmin paid great honour to a judas tree (*palāsa*), hoping thereby to get some benefit. One day, the tree sprite appeared before him in disguise and asked why he honoured the tree. Pleased with his answer, the sprite revealed his identity and helped the brahmin to obtain the treasure which lay buried beneath the tree. The story was related to **Ānanda** as he stood weeping, leaning against the lintel, when the Buddha lay dying. The Buddha sent for him and told him not to grieve as his services to the Buddha would not be fruitless. Ānanda is identified with the poor brahmin.[1]

[1] J. iii. 23 ff.

2. **Palāsa Jātaka** (No. 370).—Once the Bodhisatta was a golden goose living in **Cittakūṭa.** On his way to and fro from the **Himālaya,** he rested on a *palāsa*-tree and a friendship sprang up between him and the tree-sprite. One day a bird dropped a banyan-seed in the fork of the *palāsa*-tree from which a sapling sprang. The goose advised the sprite to destroy it, but he paid no heed, and by and by the banyan grew up and destroyed the *palāsa*.

The story was related by the Buddha to the monks in order to illustrate that sins should be uprooted however small they may be.[1]

[1] J. iii. 208 ff.

Palāsavana.—A wood near **Naḷakapāna** in **Kosala.** The Buddha stayed there,[1] and it was there that the **Naḷakapāna Sutta** was preached.[2]

[1] A. v. 122. [2] M. i. 462.

Palāsinā Sutta.—One should put away what is not his—eye, ear, etc.[1]

[1] S. iv. 128 f.

Paluṭṭhagiri.—A locality in **Rohaṇa,** the scene of two fierce battles against the **Coḷas,** in both of which they were defeated, once in the reign of **Mahinda V.,**[1] and again in the twelfth year of the reign of **Vijayabāhu I.**[2]

[1] Cv. lv. 28. [2] *Ibid.*, lviii. 18.

Paloka Sutta.—The Buddha tells **Ānanda** that the world (*loka*) is so called from its transitory nature (*palokadhamma*). In the teachings of the Ariyans the world consists of eye, objects, etc.[1]

[1] S. iv. 53.

Palobhana Sutta.—Mention is made of a sutta of this name in the **Pañcagaruka Jātaka,**[1] but no sutta has been traced by that name. The reference is probably to the **Dhītaro Sutta** (*q.v.*).

[1] J. i. 469.

Pallaṅkadāyaka Thera.—An arahant. He once gave a couch (*pallaṅka*), with cushions, etc., to the Buddha **Sumedha.** Twenty thousand kappas ago he was king three times under the name of **Suvaṇṇābha.**[1] He is probably identical with **Uttiya Thera.**[2]

[1] Ap. i. 175. [2] ThagA. i. 202 f.

Pallaṅka-vimāna-vatthu.—The story of a woman of **Sāvatthi** who was married to a youth of equal rank, with whom she lived a virtuous life. After death she was born in **Tāvatiṃsa,** where **Moggallāna** met her and learned her story.[1]

[1] Vv. iii. 3; VvA. 128 ff.

Pallava.—A Damiḷa chief, ally of **Kulasekhara.**[1]

[1] Cv. lxxvii. 55, 73.

Pallavakā.—The name of a tribe, occurring in a nominal list.[1]

[1] Ap. ii. 359.

Pallavabhogga.—A country from which came **Mahādeva,** together with four hundred and sixty thousand monks, for the foundation ceremony of the **Mahā Thūpa.**[1] Geiger thinks the reference is to Persia.[2]

[1] Mhv. xxix. 38. [2] Mhv. *Trs.* 194, n. 2.

Pallavavaṅka.—A harbour in Ceylon, the starting-place of the expeditionary force sent by **Parakkamabāhu I.** against the king of **Kamboja.**[1]

[1] Cv. lxxvi. 46.

Pallavavāla.—A locality in Ceylon occupied by **Mānābharaṇa** in his campaign against **Parakkamabāhu I.**[1]

[1] Cv. lxxii. 178, 220.

Pallikavāpi.—A locality where **Gokaṇṇa,** general of **Gajabāhu,** was once defeated.[1]

[1] Cv. lxx. 73.

Pavattanī Sutta.—Religious talk is profitable when they who teach the Dhamma are separately and together able to penetrate the spirit and the letter of the Dhamma.[1]

[1] A. i. 151.

Pavattā.—A Pacceka Buddha.[1]

[1] M. iii. 70; MA. ii. 890.

Pavarā.—One of the five daughters of **Vessavaṇa,** appointed, with her sisters, to dance before **Sakka.**[1]

[1] Vv. iii. 4; VvA. 131.

Pavāraṇa Sutta.—The Buddha was once staying at the **Migāramātupāsāda,** and on the day of the *pavāraṇa* he summoned the five hundred arahants who were with him and asked if they had any fault to find with him. **Sāriputta,** speaking for them, uttered the Buddha's praises, and the Buddha, in his turn, spoke of Sāriputta's greatness and of the blamelessness of the arahants. Thereupon **Vaṅgīsa,** also present, extolled the Buddha in verse.[1]

[1] S. i. 190 f.; also Thag. vs. 1234 ff.

Pavāraṇakkhandha.—The fourth section of the Mahāvagga of the Vinaya Piṭaka.

Paviṭṭha Thera.—A brahmin of **Magadha** who, following his own inclination, became a **Paribbājaka.** His training ended, he wandered forth and heard of **Upatissa** and **Kolita** joining the Buddha's Order. Impressed by their example, he became a monk and, soon after, an arahant. In the time of **Atthadassī** Buddha, he was an ascetic named **Narādakesava** and paid homage to the Buddha. Seventeen kappas ago he was a king named **Amittatāpana.**[1] He is evidently identical with **Ekadaṃsaniya** of the Apadāna.[2]

[1] Thag. vs. 87; ThagA. i. 185 f.

[2] Ap. i. 168 f.

Paviveka Sutta.—Teachers of other schools teach three forms of aloofness: from robes, from food, from lodging. The Buddha's teachings give three other forms of aloofness: from immorality, from wrong views, from the *āsavas.*[1]

[1] A. i. 240 f.

Pavesana Sutta.—Ten evil results of a monk visiting the king's harem.[1]

[1] A. v. 81 ff.; *cp.* Vin. iv. 159.

Pasayha Sutta.—Five powers—beauty, wealth, kin, sons, virtue—the possession of which enables a woman to live at home, overpowering (*pasayha*) her husband.[1]

[1] S. iv. 246.

1. **Pasāda Sutta.**—Eight qualities of a monk which promote devotion towards him in the minds of his lay disciples.[1]

[1] A. iv. 345 f.

2. **Pasāda Sutta.**—The four best faiths: in the Buddha, the Noble Eightfold Path, the Dhamma, which is passionless, and the Order of monks.[1]

[1] A. ii. 34 f.; *cf. ibid.*, iii. 36 f.; quoted in Vsm. i. 293; it is found in Itv. 87.

Pasādapāsāda.—A monastic building erected in the **Selantarasamūha-vihāra** by **Yasodharā,** daughter of **Vijayabāhu I.**[1]

[1] Cv. lx. 84.

Pasūra.—A **Paribbājaka.** He was a great debater who wandered from place to place, carrying a *jambu*-branch, which he set up where he stopped, challenging anyone, who wished to engage him in disputation, to dislodge it. When he came to **Sāvatthi, Sāriputta,** seeing the branch, ordered its removal. Pasūra, followed by a large crowd, went to Sāriputta's lodgings and had a discussion with him, in which he suffered defeat.[1] Later, he joined the Order under **Lāludāyī,** whom he defeated in discussion, and having returned in his monk's robes to the dwelling of the heretics, he started off in these same robes to visit the Buddha and hold a discussion with him. But as he entered **Jetavana,** the deity presiding over the gate made him dumb, and he had to sit before the Buddha, unable to utter a single word in answer to his questions. The Buddha thereupon preached the **Pasūra Sutta** before the assembled people.[2]

[1] *Cf.* **Paṭācārā.**

[2] SNA. ii. 538 ff.

Pasūra Sutta.—The eighth sutta of the Aṭṭhaka Vagga of the Sutta Nipāta. Preached to **Pasūra** at **Jetavana.** Disputants quarrel with each other and call each other fools; they wish for praise and, failing to get it, become discontented. No one is purified by dispute.[1] This sutta is commented on in the Mahā Niddesa.[2]

[1] SN. vs. 824, 834.

[2] pp. 161 ff.

Pasenadi.—King of **Kosala** and contemporary of the Buddha. He was the son of **Mahā Kosala,** and was educated at **Takkasilā** where, among his companions, were the **Licchavi Mahāli** and the **Malla** prince **Bandhula.** On his return home his father was so pleased with his proficiency in the various arts that he forthwith made him king.[1] As ruler, Pasenadi

[1] DhA. i. 338; for his genealogy see Beal: Records ii. 2, n. 3.

gave himself wholeheartedly to his administrative duties[2] and valued the companionship of wise and good men.[3] Quite early in the Buddha's ministry,[4] Pasenadi became his follower and close friend, and his devotion to the Buddha lasted till his death.

But Pasenadi's conversion did not prevent him from extending his favour, with true Indian toleration, to the members of other religious orders. Mention is even made of a great animal sacrifice which he once prepared, but which he abandoned on the advice of the Buddha, whom he sought at **Mallika's** suggestion.[5] He frequently visited the Buddha and discussed various matters with him.[6] The whole of the Third Saṃyutta (**Kosala Saṃyutta**), consisting of twenty-five anecdotes, each with a moral bias, is devoted to him. The topics discussed are many and varied. The Buddha and Pasenadi were equals in age, and their talks were, therefore, intimate and frank.[7] On one occasion we find the Buddha telling him to eat less and teaching his nephew

[2] *E.g.*, S. i. 74, 100; the Commentary (SA i. 109 f.) adds that the king tried to put down bribery and corruption in his court, but his attempt does not appear to have been very successful.

[3] Thus he showed his favour to **Pokkharasâdi** and **Caṅkī**, by giving them, respectively, the villages of **Ukkaṭṭhā** and **Opasāda** free of all taxes. It is said that his alms-halls were always open to everyone desiring food or drink (Ud. ii. 6). Even after becoming the Buddha's follower, he did not omit to salute holy men of other persuasions (Ud. vi. 2).

[4] According to Tibetan sources, Pasenadi's conversion was in the second year of the Buddha's ministry (Rockhill, p. 49). We find the king referring to the Buddha, at their first meeting, as being young in years (S. i. 69). Their first meeting and conversation, which ended in Pasenadi's declaring himself an adherent of the Buddha, are recorded in the **Dahara Sutta** (*q.v.*).

[5] S. i. 75; for details see the **Mahāsupina** and **Lohakumbhī Jātakas.** It is said (SA. i. 111) that the king fell in love with a woman while riding round the city; on discovering that she was married, he ordered her husband to go, before sunset, and fetch clay and lilies from a pond one hundred leagues away. When the man had gone, the king ordered the gate-keepers to shut the gates early and not on any account to open them. The husband returned in the evening, and finding the gates shut, went to Jetavana, to seek protection from the king's wrath. The king spent a sleepless night owing to his passion and had bad dreams. When the brahmins were consulted they advised a great animal sacrifice. The story is also found at DhA. ii. 1 ff., with several variations in detail.

[6] It is said that he went three times a day to wait on the Buddha, sometimes with only a small bodyguard. Some robbers, knowing this, arranged an ambush in the **Andhavana.** But the king discovered the plot, of which he made short work.

[7] Pasenadi was extremely attached to the Buddha, and the books describe how, when he saw the Buddha, he bowed his head at the Buddha's feet, covering them with kisses and stroking them (M. ii. 120). The Chinese records say (Beal, xliv.) that when the Buddha went to Tāvatiṃsa, Pasenadi made an image of the Buddha in sandalwood, to which he paid honour. He was very jealous of the Buddha's reputation, and put down with a firm hand any attempt on the part of heretics to bring discredit on him—*e.g.*, in the case of **Sundarī-Nandā** (*q.v.*). In the **Aggañña Sutta** (D. iii. 83 f.),

Sudassana (or **Uttara**) a verse on the advantages of moderation, to be repeated to the king whenever he sat down to a meal. This advice was followed and the king became slim.[8] Pasenadi's chief consort was **Mallikā,** daughter of a garland-maker.[9] He loved her dearly and trusted her judgment in all things. When in difficulty he consulted her, realizing that her wisdom was greater than his own.[10] There is an account given[11] of Pasenadi seeking a confession from her that she loved him more than her own soul (*attā*) as a confirmation of their mutual trust. But the queen was pious and saw into the reality of things, and declared that nothing was dearer to her than her own soul. Piqued by this answer, Pasenadi sought the Buddha, who comforted him by explaining the true import of Mallikā's words. On another occasion, Pasenadi expressed to the Buddha his disappointment that Mallikā should have borne him a daughter instead of a son; but the Buddha pointed out to him that there was much, after all, to be said for daughters.[12]

Mallikā predeceased Pasenadi[13]; he had also other wives, one of them being the sister of **Bimbisāra,**[14] and another **Ubbirī** (*q.v.*). The Kaṇṇakatthala Sutta[15] mentions two others who were sisters: **Somā** and **Sakulā.**[16]

---

the Buddha explains why Pasenadi honours him. For Pasenadi's own explanation as to why people honoured the Buddha even more than the king, see M. ii. 123; see also A. v. 65 ff. Pasenadi was also jealous of the reputation of the Order, and if anything arose which seemed likely to bring discredit on it, he took prompt steps to have the matter remedied —*e.g.*, in the case of **Kuṇḍadhāna** (*q.v.*) and **Kumāra Kassapa's** mother (*q.v.*). Pasenadi's palace overlooked the **Aciravatī,** and when he once saw some monks sporting in the river in an unseemingly way, he made sure that the Buddha knew of it (Vin. iv. 112). The story of the blind man and the elephant shows that he was anxious to justify the Buddha's teaching as against that of other sects (SNA. ii. 529).

8 S. i. 81; DhA. iii. 264 f.; iv. 6 f.; the Saṃyutta Commentary (SA. i. 136) states that the bowl out of which he ate (**paribhogapāti**) was the size of a cartwheel. Pasenadi was always conscious of his own dignity—*e.g.*, the incident with Chattapāṇi (*q.v.*); but see Vin. iv. 157 f., which probably refers to the same story.

9 See *s.v.* **Mallikā** for details of her marriage with the king.

10 *E.g.*, in the Asadisadāna.

11 S. i. 74.

12 S. i. 83.

13 A. iii. 57.

14 DhA. i. 385; Pasenadi's relations with Bimbisāra were very cordial. Bimbisāra had five millionaires in his kingdom—**Jotiya, Jaṭila, Meṇḍaka, Puṇṇaka** and **Kākavaliya**—while Pasenadi had none. Pasenadi therefore visited Bimbisāra and asked for one to be transferred to him. Bimbisāra gave him **Dhanañjaya,** Meṇḍaka's son, and Pasenadi settled him in **Sāketa** (DhA. i. 385 ff.).

15 M. ii. 125.

16 In the Saṃyutta Nikāya (v. 351), the king's chamberlains, **Isidatta** and **Purāṇa,** speak of his harem. When he went riding in the park he took with him his favourite and lovely wives on elephants, one before and one behind. They were sweetly scented—"like caskets of scent"—and their hands were soft to the touch.

It is stated that Pasenadi wished to associate himself with the Buddha's family so that their relationship might be even closer. For seven days he had given alms to the Buddha and one thousand monks, and on the seventh day he asked the Buddha to take his meals regularly at the palace with five hundred monks; but the Buddha refused the request and appointed **Ānanda** to take his place. Ānanda came daily with five hundred others, but the king was too busy to look after them, and the monks, feeling neglected, failed to come any more, only Ānanda keeping to his undertaking. When the king became aware of this he was greatly upset, and determined to win the confidence of the monks by marrying a kinswoman of the Buddha. He therefore sent messages to the Sākyan chiefs, who were his vassals, asking for the hand of one of their daughters. The Sākyans discussed the proposition in their Mote-Hall, and held it beneath the dignity of their clan to accede to it. But, unwilling to incur the wrath of their overlord, they sent him **Vāsabha-khattiyā,** daughter of **Mahānāma** and of a slave-woman, **Nāgamuṇḍā.** By her, Pasenadi had a son **Viḍūḍabha.** When the latter visited **Kapilavatthu,** he heard by chance of the fraud that had been practised on his father and vowed vengeance. When he came to the throne, he invaded the Sākyan territory and killed a large number of the clan without distinction of age or sex.[17] It is said that when Pasenadi heard of the antecedents of Vāsabhakhattiyā, he withdrew the royal honours which had been bestowed on her and her son and reduced them to the condition of slaves. But the Buddha, hearing of this, related to Pasenadi the **Kaṭṭhahārika Jātaka,** and made him restore the royal honours to the mother and her son. Mention is made of another son of Pasenadi, named **Brahmadatta,** who entered the Order and became an arahant.[18]

Pasenadi's sister, **Kosaladevī,** was married to Bimbisāra. **Mahākosala** gave her a village in Kāsi as part of her dowry, for her bath-money. When **Ajātasattu** killed Bimbisāra, Kosaladevī died of grief, and Pasenadi confiscated the Kāsi village, saying that no patricide should own a village which was his by right of inheritance. Angered at this, Ajātasattu declared war upon his aged uncle. At first, victory lay with Ajātasattu, but Pasenadi had spies who reported to him a plan of attack suggested by the Thera **Dhanuggaha-Tissa,** in the course of a conversation with his colleague **Mantidatta,** and in the fourth campaign Pasenadi took Ajātasattu prisoner, and refused to release him until he renounced his claim to the throne. Upon his renunciation, Pasenadi

[17] DhA. i. 339 ff.; J. i. 133 f.; iv. 144 ff.

[18] ThagA. i. 460; the Dulva says that Jeta, owner of Jetavana, was also Pasenadi's son (Rockhill, p. 48).

not only gave him his daughter **Vajirā** in marriage, but conferred on her, as a wedding gift, the very village in dispute.[19]

Three years later, Viḍūḍabha revolted against his father. In this he was helped by the commander-in-chief, **Dīghakārāyaṇa,** nephew of **Bandhula** (*q.v.*). Bandhula, chief of the Mallas, disgusted with the treachery of his own people, had sought refuge with his former class-mate, Pasenadi, in Sāvatthi. Bandhula's wife, **Mallikā,** bore him thirty-two sons, brave and learned. Pasenadi, having listened to the tales of his corrupt ministers, contrived to have Bandhula and all his sons killed while they were away quelling a frontier rebellion. Bandhula's wife was a devout follower of the Buddha's faith, and showed no resentment against the king for this act of treachery. This moved the king's heart, and he made all possible amends. But Dīghkārāyaṇa never forgave him, and once when Pasenadi was on a visit to the Buddha at **Medatalumpa (Uḷumpa),** leaving the royal insignia with his commander-in-chief, Dīghakārāyaṇa took advantage of this opportunity, withdrew the king's bodyguard, leaving behind only one single horse and one woman-servant, hurried back to the capital and crowned Viḍūḍabha king. When Pasenadi heard of this, he hurried on to Rājagaha to enlist Ajātasattu's support; but as it was late, the city gates were closed. Exhausted by his journey, he lay down in a hall outside the city, where he died during the night.

When Ajātasattu heard the news, he performed the funeral rites over the king's body with great pomp. He wished to march at once against Viḍūḍabha, but desisted on the advice of his ministers.[20]

Pasenadi had a sister, **Sumanā,** who was present at his first interview with the Buddha and decided to enter the Order, but she delayed doing so as she then had to nurse their aged grandmother. Pasenadi was very fond of his grandmother, and was filled with grief when she died in her one hundred and twentieth year. After her death, Sumanā became a nun and attained arahantship.[21] The old lady's possessions were given over to the monks, the Buddha giving special permission for them to be accepted.[22]

Among the king's most valued possessions was the elephant **Seta**[23]; he had two other elephants, **Bhadderaka** (or **Pāveyyaka**)[24] and **Puṇḍarīka.**[25] Mention is also made[26] of a pet heron which lived in the palace and conveyed messages. Tradition says[27] that Pasenadi had in his possession

[19] J. ii. 237, 403; iv. 342 f.

[20] M. ii. 118; MA. ii. 753 ff.; DhA. i. 353 ff.; J. iv. 150 ff.

[21] ThigA. 22; S. i. 97; A. iii. 32.

[22] Vin. ii. 169.

[23] A. iii. 345.

[24] DhA. iv. 25.

[25] *Ibid.*, ii. 1.

[26] J. iii. 134 f.

[27] SA. i. 115; J. i. 382 ff.

the octagonal gem which **Sakka** had given to **Kusa.** He valued it greatly, using it as his turban jewel, and was greatly upset when it was reported lost; it was, however, recovered with the help and advice of Ānanda. The Jātaka Commentary[28] records that Pasenadi built a monastery in front of Jetavana. It was called the **Rājakārāma,** and the Buddha sometimes stayed there. Pasenadi's chaplain, **Aggidatta** (*q.v.*) had originally been Mahākosala's chaplain. Pasenadi therefore paid him great respect. This inconvenienced Aggidatta, and he gave his wealth to the poor and renounced the world.[29] Pasenadi's minister, **Santati** (*q.v.*), who was once allowed to reign for a week in the king's place as reward for having quelled a frontier dispute, did likewise.[30] The king was always ready to pay honour to those who had won the praise of the Buddha, as in the case of **Kāṇā,**[31] **Culla-Eka-Sāṭaka,**[32] or **Aṅgulimālā**[33]; on the other hand, he did not hesitate to show his disapproval of those who disregarded the Buddha's teaching—*e.g.*, **Upananda.**[34]

Pasenadi liked to be the foremost in gifts to the Buddha and his Order. This was why he held the **Asadisadāna** (*q.v.*) under the guidance and inspiration of Mallikā; but he was hurt when the Buddha's sermon of thanksgiving did not seem to him commensurate with the vast amount (fourteen crores) which he had spent. The Buddha then explained to him that this lack of enthusiasm was out of consideration for the king's minister **Kāḷa.** When the king learned that Kāḷa disapproved of the lavish way in which money had been spent at the almsgiving, he banished him from the court, while he allowed the minister **Juṇha,** who had furthered the almsgiving, to rule over the kingdom for seven days.[35]

Pasenadi seems to have enjoyed discussions on topics connected with the Dhamma. Reference has already been made to the Kosala Saṃyutta, which records several conversations which he held with the Buddha when visiting him in Sāvatthi; even when Pasenadi was engaged in affairs of state in other parts of the kingdom, he would visit the Buddha and engage him in conversation if he was anywhere in the neighbourhood. Two such conversations are recorded in the **Dhammacetiya Sutta** (*q.v.*) and the **Kaṇṇakatthala Sutta** (*q.v.*). If the Buddha was not

[28] J. ii. 15. According to Hiouen Thsang, Pasenadi also built a monastery for **Pajāpatī Gotamī** (Beal, Records ii. 2).

[29] DhA. iii. 241 ff.; SNA. (580) says that **Bāvarī** was Mahākosala's chaplain and Pasenadi studied under him. When Pasenadi came to the throne, Bāvarī declared his wish to leave the world. The king tried to prevent him but failed; he did, however, persuade Bāvarī to live in the royal park. Bāvarī, after staying there for some time, found life in a city uncongenial. The king thereupon detailed two of his ministers to establish a suitable hermitage for Bāvarī.

[30] DhA. iii. 28 ff.

[31] *Ibid.*, ii. 150 ff.

[32] *Ibid.*, iii. 2 ff.

[33] M. ii. 100.

[34] S. i. 153 f.

[35] DhA. iii. 188 ff.

available, he would seek a disciple. Thus the **Bāhitika Sutta** (*q.v.*) records a discussion between Pasenadi and Ānanda on the banks of the **Aciravatī.** Once when Pasenadi was in **Toraṇavatthu,** midway between **Sāketa** and **Sāvatthi,** he heard that **Khemā Therī** was there, and went at once to visit and talk to her.[36] Rhys Davids thinks[37] that Pasenadi was evidently an official title[38] and that the king's personal name was Agnidatta. He bases this surmise on the fact that in the Divyāvadāna (p. 620) the king who gave **Ukkaṭṭhā** to **Pokkarasādi** is called Agnidatta, while in the Dīgha Nikāya (i. 87) he is called Pasenadi, and that Pasenadi is used as a designation for several kings.[39] The evidence is, however, insufficient for any definite conclusion to be drawn.

According to the Anāgatavaṃsa,[40] Pasenadi is a Bodhisatta. He will be the fourth future Buddha.

[36] S. iv. 374 ff.

[37] *Buddhist India*, p. 10.

[38] The UdA. (104) explains Pasenadi as "*paccantaṃ parasenaṃ jināti ti = Pasenadi.*" According to Tibetan sources he was so called because the whole country was illuminated at the time of his birth (Rockhill, p. 16).

[39] *E.g.*, in Dvy. 369, for a king of Magadha and again in the *Kathāsaritsāgara* i. 268, 298.

[40] *J.P.T.S.* 1886, p. 37.

Passaddhi Sutta.—On tranquillity—a conversation between **Ānanda** and **Udāyī.**[1]

[1] A. iv. 455.

Passika Thera.—A brahmin of **Kosala** who, after seeing the Twin Miracle, entered the Order. He fell ill, but was attended and cured by his own people. Putting forth great energy, he became an arahant, and, travelling through the air to his kinsmen, he converted them.

In the time of **Atthadassī** Buddha he was a householder and gave the Buddha some *pilakkha*-fruits.[1] He is probably identical with **Pilakkhaphaladāyaka Thera** of the Apadāna.[2]

[1] Thag. vs. 240-42; ThagA. i. 355.

[2] Ap. i. 296; *cp.* ii. 410.

Passī.—A Pacceka Buddha mentioned in a nominal list.[1]

[1] M. iii. 70; ApA. i. 107; MA. ii. 890.

Pahasambahula.—Thirty-one kappas ago there were three kings of this name, all previous births of **Nisseṇidāyaka Thera.**[1] *v.l.* **Sambahula.**

[1] Ap. i. 187.

1. **Pahātabba Sutta.**—Everything must be cast away.[1]

[1] S. iv. 29.

2. **Pahātabba Sutta.**—The six *nivāraṇas* must be given up by those who wish to achieve right views.[1]

[1] A. iii. 438.

Pahāna Sutta.—The higher life (*brahmacariyā*) is for the purpose of getting rid of the seven fetters (*sanyojanāni*).[1]

[1] A. iv. 7.

Pahārāda.—An **Asura** chief.[1] Buddhaghosa says[2] he was one of the three leaders of the Asuras, the others being **Vepacitti** and **Rāhu.** He first conceived a wish to see the Buddha on the day of the Enlightenment; but this wish was not fulfilled until eleven years later, when he visited the Buddha at Verañjā. The conversation which then took place is recorded in the **Pahārāda Sutta** (*q.v.*).

[1] D. ii. 259. [2] AA. ii. 758.

Pahārāda Sutta.—Preached at the **Naḷerupucimandamūla** in **Verañjā** where **Pahārāda** (*q.v.*) visited the Buddha. In answer to a question, Pahārāda tells the Buddha that there are eight wonderful characteristics of the ocean, on account of which Asuras delight in it. The Buddha tells him of eight similar qualities in his own teaching and discipline, wherefore monks find joy in them.[1]

[1] A. iv. 197 ff.

Pahāsa.—A niraya in which stage-players are born after death. **Tālapuṭa** maintained that after death they were born among the **Pahāsadevā.** The Buddha contradicts this and says that their rebirth is in a Niraya and not in any deva-world.[1] Buddhaghosa explains[2] that Pahāsa is not a special Niraya but rather a section of **Avīci,** where beings suffer while wearing the form of singers or dancers.

[1] S. iv. 305 f.; ThagA. ii. 156. [2] SA. iii. 100.

Pahīna Sutta.—The six *nivāraṇas* are given up by those who have achieved right views.[1]

[1] A. iii. 438.

Pahecivatthu.—See **Mahejjāvatthu.**

Pākatindriya (or **Sambahulā Sutta**).—Once, a company of monks, staying in a forest-track in **Kosala,** were muddled in mind, noisy and uncontrolled in their senses. The deva, who haunted the forest, admonished them, which agitated them.[1]

[1] S. i. 203 f.

Pākasāsana.—A name for **Indra.**[1]

[1] Cv. lxxii. 186; Abhidhānappadīpikā 20.

Pācittiya.—One of the two main divisions of the Sutta Vibhaṅga of the Vinaya Piṭaka. It contains Vinaya rules connected with the Pāṭimokkha, the violation of which can be expiated in some way.

Pācīna Suttā.—A group of three suttas, in all of which it is stated that just as certain rivers (*e.g.* **Gaṅgā, Yamunā, Aciravatī,** etc.) tend to flow eastward, so the monk who cultivates the Noble Eightfold Path tends to Nibbāna.[1]

[1] S. v. 38 f.

Pācīnakambaviṭṭhi.—A monastery in Ceylon, built by **Dhātusena.**[1]

[1] Cv. xxxviii. 48.

Pācīnakā.—By this name are described the **Vajjiputtaka** monks who raised the Ten Points which occasioned the Second Council.[1] They were so called because they belonged to the East.[2]

[1] Mhv. iv. 47, 48.

[2] MṬ. 165, 166.

Pācīnakhaṇḍarājī.—A district in Ceylon near **Cittapabbata**[1] in which was the **Vettavāsa-vihāra,** given by **Aggabodhi II.** to the **Kaliṅga** minister who was ordained by **Jotipāla Thera.**[2] The road to the district lay to the south of **Anurādhapura,** past the Potters' Village. The Visuddhimagga[3] speaks of it as a prosperous place. The Aṅguttara Commentary[4] has a story of a monk of the vihāra who was a paṃsukulika and became an arahant.

[1] Mhv. xxiii. 4; see Mhv. *Trs.* 155, n. 3 and Cv. *Trs.* i. 71, n. 2.

[2] Cv. xlii. 48.

[3] p. 90 f.

[4] AA. ii. 489; also DA. iii. 1010.

Pācīnatissapabbata-vihāra.—A monastery in Ceylon, built by **Jeṭṭhatissa** and given to the monks of the "five settlements." The stone image set up by **Devānampiyatissa** in the **Thūpārāma** was transferred to this vihāra by Jeṭṭhatissa.[1] **Mahāsena** had it brought from there to the **Abhayagiri-vihāra.**[2] Near the monastery was the mountain, **Pācīnatissapabbata,** where an engagement took place between **Kassapa,** son of **Upatissa III.,** and **Silākāla.**[3] Later, at the same spot, took place the decisive battle between **Saṅghatissa** and **Moggallāna III.**[4]

[1] Mhv. xxxvi. 127, 129.

[2] *Ibid.,* xxxvii. 14.

[3] Cv. xli. 14.

[4] *Ibid.,* xliv. 14 ff.

Pācīnadīpa.—An island off the coast of Ceylon. While on a journey there in order to eat *jambu*-fruit, **Saṅghatissa** was killed by the enraged islanders.[1] The Mahāvaṃsa Ṭīkā explains[2] that it was situated in the sea off **Mahātittha,** in which case it is one of the islands between the north point of Ceylon and the Indian continent.[3]

[1] Mhv. xxxvi. 70 f. [2] p. 666. [3] Mhv. *Trs.* 261, n. 4.

Pācīnadesa.—The Eastern Province of Ceylon. It was less important than the **Dakkhiṇadesa.**[1] It is also called the **Pubbadesa**[2] and the **Puratthimadesa.**[3]

[1] See, *e.g.*, Cv. xlviii. 33, 41. [2] *E.g.*, *ibid.*, xlv. 21. [3] *Ibid.*, xli. 33.

Pācīnapabbata.—A monastery in Ceylon, on the **Vaṅguttarapabbata,** and built by **Sūratissa.**[1]

[1] Mhv. xxi. 5.

Pācīnavaṃsa.—The name of Mount **Vepulla** in the time of **Kakusandha** Buddha. The inhabitants were called **Tivarā,** and it took them four days to climb the mountain and four days to descend.[1]

[1] S. ii. 190.

Pācīnavaṃsa(miga)dāya.—A park in the **Cetiya**-kingdom.[1] The Buddha visited it during his tours, and once, while staying there with **Meghiya,** the latter stopped in a mango-grove in the village of **Jantugāma,** refusing to go any farther.[2] The park lay between **Bālakaloṇakāragāma** and the **Pārileyyakavana.**[3] **Anuruddha, Nandiya** and **Kimbila** were living there during the time of the quarrel of the monks at **Kosambī,** and the Buddha visited them on his way to Pārileyyaka.[4] It was there that Anuruddha became an arahant.[5] Buddhaghosa explains[6] that the park was so called because it was to the east of where the Buddha lived (?) and it was covered with green bamboos.

[1] A. iv. 228 f.
[2] *Ibid.*, 163.
[3] DhA. i. 47.
[4] Vin. i. 350 f.; *cp.* M. i. 205 ff.
[5] A. iv. 228 f.; AA. i. 108.
[6] *Ibid.*, ii. 765.

Pācīnārāma.—A monastery to the east of **Anurādhapura,** built by **Devānampiyatissa** in the first year of his reign.[1] Its site was one of the resting-places of the Bodhi-tree on the way from **Jambukola** to **Anurādhapura.** There **Mahinda** and the monks were given a morning meal, and Mahinda preached on the subduing of the Nāgas by the Buddha.[2]

[1] Mhv. xx. 25. [2] *Ibid.*, xix. 34 f.

1. **Pāṭala.**—A dancer. He lived in a village near Benares. One day, having earned some money in a fête in the city, he sat down on the bank of the river, eating and drinking with his wife. He became drunk, and fastening his lute round his neck, he went with his wife down to the river. The water filled his lute and he began to sink. His wife thereupon let go of his hand and came out of the river. Seeing him about to drown, the wife begged of him one song wherewith to earn her living. He sang her a stanza to the effect that the water of the Ganges, which was the salvation of many, proved to be his bane.

This story was among those related by the Bodhisatta in the **Padakusalamāṇava Jātaka.**[1]

[1] J. iii. 507 f. The Pārupaṇas made use of this story in poking fun at the Ekaṃsikas, because the texts chosen by the Ekaṃsikas to prove their case proved just the contrary (see Bode, *op cit.*, 76, n. 3.).

2. **Pāṭala.**—A tank restored by **Parakkamabāhu I.**[1]

[1] Cv. lxviii. 44.

Pāṭali.—A headsman of **Uttara** who visited the Buddha and questioned him regarding his power of magic. Several conversations he had with the Buddha, on various topics, are given in the Saṃyutta Nikāya.[1]

[1] S. iv. 340 ff.

Pāṭali or **Mānapa Sutta.**—A series of discussions between **Pāṭali** and the Buddha, on various topics.[1]

[1] S. iv. 340 ff.

Pāṭaligāma, Pāṭaliputta.—The capital of **Magadha** and situated near the modern Patna. The Buddha visited it shortly before his death. It was then a mere village and was known as Pāṭaligāma. At that time **Ajātasattu's** ministers, **Sunīdha** and **Vassakāra,** were engaged in building fortifications there in order to repel the **Vajjīs.** The Buddha prophesied the future greatness of Pāṭaligāma, and also mentioned the danger of its destruction by fire, water, or internal discord. The gate by which the Buddha left the town was called **Gotamadvāra,** and the ferry at which he crossed the river, **Gotamatittha.**[1]

The date at which Pāṭaliputta became the capital is uncertain. Hiouen Thsang seems to record[2] that it was **Kālāsoka** who moved the seat of government there. The Jains maintain that it was **Udāyi,** son of Ajātasattu.[3] The latter tradition is probably correct as, according to the Aṅguttara Nikāya,[4] even **Muṇḍa** is mentioned as residing at Pāṭa-

[1] Vin. i. 226-30; D. ii. 86 ff.
[2] Beal: Records ii. 85, n. 11.
[3] Vin. Texts ii. 102, n. 1.
[4] iii. 57.

liputta. It was, however, in the time of **Asoka** that the city enjoyed its greatest glory. In the ninth year of his reign Asoka's income from the four gates of the city is said to have been four hundred thousand kahāpanas daily, with another one hundred thousand for his sabhā or Council.[5]

The city was known to the Greeks as Pālibothra, and Megasthenes, who spent some time there, has left a vivid description of it.[6] It continued to be the capital during the greater part of the Gupta dynasty, from the fourth to the sixth century A.C. Near Pāṭaliputta was the Kukkuṭārāma, where monks (*e.g.* **Ānanda, Bhadda** and **Nārada**) stayed when they came to Pāṭaliputta.[7] At the suggestion of **Udena Thera,** the brahmin **Ghoṭamukha** built an assembly-hall for the monks in the city.[8]

Pāṭaligāma was so called because on the day of its foundation several *pāṭali*-shoots sprouted forth from the ground. The officers of Ajātasattu and of the **Licchavi** princes would come from time to time to Pāṭaligāma, drive the people from their houses, and occupy them themselves. A large hall was therefore built in the middle of the village, divided into various apartments for the housing of the officers and their retainers when necessary. The Buddha arrived in the village on the day of the completion of the building, and the villagers invited him to occupy it for a night, that it might be blessed by his presence. On the next day they entertained the Buddha and his monks to a meal.[9]

Pāṭaliputta was also called Pupphapura[10] and Kusamapura.[11] The journey from **Jambukola,** in Ceylon, to Pāṭaliputta took fourteen days, seven of which were spent on the sea voyage to **Tāmalitti.**[12] The **Asokārāma** built by Asoka was near Pāṭaliputta.[13] The Buddha's water-pot and belt were deposited in Pāṭaliputta after his death.[14] The Petavatthu Commentary[15] mentions that trade was carried on between Pāṭaliputta and **Suvaṇṇabhūmi.**

[5] Sp. i. 52.
[6] Buddhist India 262 f.
[7] M. i. 349; A. v. 341; A. iii. 57; S. v. 15 f., 171 f.
[8] M. ii. 163.
[9] Ud. viii. 6; UdA. 407 ff.
[10] Mhv. iv. 31, etc.; Dpv. xi. 28.
[11] Mbv. p. 153.
[12] *E.g.*, Mhv. xi. 24.
[13] *Ibid.*, xxix. 36.
[14] Bu. xxviii. 9.
[15] p. 271.

Pāṭaliputta.—A paribbājaka; see **Potaliputta,** for which it is a wrong reading.

Pāṭaliputtaka-brahmin.—A brahmin of **Pāṭaliputta.** He and a friend, both of that city, having heard of the virtues of **Mahānāga Thera** of **Kāḷavallimaṇḍapa** in Ceylon, came by ship to **Mahātittha.** One died on the way, the other went to **Anurādhapura,** and from there to **Rohaṇa,** where he took up his abode in **Cullanagaragāma** and visited the Elder in his monastery. Under him he entered the Order and became an arahant.[1]

[1] AA. i. 384.

Pāṭaliputta-peta.—A man of **Pāṭaliputta,** having gone to **Suvaṇṇabhūmi** for trade, fell in love with a woman there, and was born after death as a vimāna-peta on an island. After some time, the woman passed the island in a ship, and he managed to stop the vessel and to get her marooned. He lived with her for a year, and then, at her request, took her back to Pāṭaliputta.[1]

[1] Pv. iv. 11; PvA. 271 f.

Pāṭalipupphiya Thera.—An arahant. Ninety-two kappas ago he was a seṭṭhi-putta who, seeing Tissa Buddha, offered him a lapful of *pāṭali*-flowers. Sixty-three kappas ago he was a king named **Abhisammata.**[1]

[1] Ap. i. 122 f.

1. **Pāṭalipūjaka Thera.**—An arahant. Thirty-one kappas ago he carried some *pāṭali*-flowers on his head and offered them to **Vessabhū** Buddha.[1]

[1] Ap. i. 224 f.

2. **Pāṭalipūjaka Thera.**—An arahant. In the past, while going from **Bandhumatī** to bathe in the river, with three *pāṭali*-flowers in his waist, he saw **Vipassī** Buddha entering the city and offered him the flowers.[1]

[1] Ap. i. 290.

Pāṭaligāmiya Vagga.—The eighth section of the Udāna.[1]

[1] Ud., pp. 80 ff.

1. **Pāṭika.**—Father of **Pāṭikaputta** (*q.v.*).

2. **Pāṭika.**—Chief of the Vinayadharas in the time of **Padumuttara** Buddha.[1]

[1] Thag. i. 362, 365; but see Ap. i. 38.

Pāṭika Vagga (or **Pāṭiya Vagga).**—The third and last section of the Dīgha Nikāya, the first sutta of the section being the **Pāṭika Sutta.**

Pāṭika Sutta.—The twenty-fourth sutta of the Dīgha Nikāya. The Buddha visits the hermitage of the paribbājaka **Bhaggava** at **Anupiya** and the conversation turns on the **Licchavi Sunakkhatta's** reason for leaving the Order. Sunakkhatta was dissatisfied because the Buddha would not work mystic wonders for him nor reveal to him the beginnings of things. Mention is also made of **Korakkhattiya, Kandaramasuka** and **Pāṭikaputta,** whom Sunakkhatta held in great esteem for their austerities, but whose spiritual development was insignificant. The Buddha is shown as holding the practice of miracles not entirely worthy.

The second part of the sutta, which is a kind of appendix, deals with the beginnings of things.[1]

[1] D. iii. 1 ff.; for a discussion on the sutta, see Dial. iii. 1 ff.

Pāṭikaputta.—A naked ascetic of **Vesāli** who went about claiming to have greater mystic powers than the Buddha, and thereby much impressed **Sunakkhatta.** Pāṭikaputta had prophesied that, after death, the Licchavi general **Ajita** would be born in **Mahā Niraya,** but Ajita was born in **Tāvatiṃsa** and accused Pāṭikaputta of being a liar. Later, the Buddha visited the hermitage of Pāṭikaputta, with a large following, in order to refute his claims, but Pāṭikaputta avoided him and went to the **Tindukhānuparibbājakārāma.** A message was sent to him asking him to come as the Buddha was at his hermitage, but Pāṭikaputta was unable to arise from his seat. Thereupon, a Licchavi minister, and, after him, **Jāliya Dārupattikantevāsi,** went to fetch him, but on discovering that he could not rise, they reviled him for his boastfulness.[1]

[1] D. iii. 13 ff.

Pāṭikārāma.—A park near **Vesāli,** where the Buddha was staying, when **Sunakkhatta,** having failed to impress him as to the greatness of **Korakkhattiya,** left the Order and went about abusing the Buddha.[1]

[1] J. i. 389; *cp. ibid.*, 77.

Pāṭibhoga Sutta.—Four things against which there can be no surety: decay, disease, death and rebirth.[1]

[1] A. ii. 172; *cp.* iii. 54; Kvu. 457.

Pāṭimokkha, Pātimokkha.—The name given to a set of two hundred and twenty-seven rules to be observed by members of the Buddhist Order. The rules are not ethical but mainly economic, regulating the behaviour of the members of the Order towards one another in respect of clothes, dwellings, furniture, etc., held in common. In four cases out of the two hundred and twenty-seven the punishment for infringement of a rule is exclusion from the Order; in all the remaining cases, it is merely suspension for a time.

The rules are arranged in seven sections,[1] corresponding very roughly to the degree of weight attached to their observance. The Pāṭimokkha is not included in the extant Buddhist Canon. The rules are included, in the Sutta Vibhaṅga (" sutta " here meaning " rule "), which contains besides the rules themselves, an old Commentary explaining them and a new Commentary containing further supplementary information concerning them. The rules are divided into two parts: one for the monks (Bhikkhu-pāṭimokkha) and the other for the nuns (Bhikkhuṇī-pāṭimokkha). It is a moot point whether the rules originally appeared with the explanatory notes (as in the Vibhaṅga), the Pāṭimokkha being subsequently extracted, or whether the Pāṭimokkha alone was the older portion, the additional matter of the Vibhaṅga being the work of a subsequent revision.[2] It is sometimes suggested[3] that the original number of Pāṭimokkha rules numbered only about one hundred and fifty. A passage in the Aṅguttara Nikāya[4] is quoted in support of this suggestion (sādhikaṃ *diyaḍḍhasikkhāpadasataṃ*). According to this theory the seventy-five Sekhiyā rules were added later.[5] The rules were recited at the gatherings of members of the Order[6] in their respective districts on *uposatha*-days (the fourteenth and fifteenth days of the month). Each section of the rules is recited and, at the end of such recital, the reciter asks the members of the Order who are present if any one of them has infringed any of the rules. Silence implies absence of guilt.[7]

The word pāṭimokkha is variously explained, the oldest explanation being that the observance of the rules is the face (*mukhaṃ*), the chief (*pamukhaṃ*) of good qualities. The Sanskritised form of the word being *prātimokṣa*, this led to a change in its significance, the completion of the recital being evidence that all those who have taken part are pure in respect of the specified offences—*pātimokkha* thus meaning acquittal, deliverance or discharge. But in most contexts the word simply means code—*i.e.*, code of verses for the members of the Order.[8]

[1] *Pārājikā° Dhammā - pāṭimokkha, Saṅghādisesā-pāṭimokkha, Aniyatā-pātimokkha, Nissaggiyāpācittiyā-pātimokkha, Pācittiyā-pāṭimokkha, Paṭidesanīyā-pāṭimokkha*, and *Sekhiyā-pāṭimokkha.*

[2] For a discussion of this, see Vin. i. Introd. xvi; Law: Pāli. Lit. 2 ff.; Hastings: Encyclopædia under Pātimokkha.

[3] Law: *op. cit.*, p. 2.

[4] i. 231, 232.

[5] See Law: *op. cit.*, 19 f.; Law's argument, however, that the Pāṭimokkha rules were among the texts *not* recited at the First Council, is due to a wrong understanding of the Sumaṇgala Vilāsinī passage (i. 17).

[6] The **Uposatha-khandha** of the Mahāvagga (Vin. i. 101-36) gives details of the procedure at these gatherings.

[7] This practice of interrupting the recital seems to have been changed later (see Vin. ii. 240 ff.) even though the old formula, asking the members to speak, continued as a part of the recital.

[8] For a detailed account of the Pāṭimokkha rules see Law: Pāli Literature, 49 ff.

Pāṭimokkha Sutta.—A monk asks the Buddha for a brief teaching. The Buddha tells him that he should dwell in the self-control of the **Pāṭimokkha,** well equipped in his range of practice (*ācāragocarasampanno*), seeing danger in the minutest faults and undertaking the precepts. Thus will he be able to develop the four *satipaṭṭhānas.*[1]

[1] S. v. 187.

Pāṭimokkhaṭhapana-Khandaka.—The ninth chapter of the Culla Vagga of the Vinaya Piṭaka.

Pāṭimokkhalekhana.—A book for Vinaya students, by **Ñāṇavara.**[1]

[1] Bode, *op cit.*, 67.

Pāṭimokkhavisodhanī.—A commentary by **Saddhammajotipāla.**[1]

[1] Gv. p. 64.

Pāṭihāriyakathā.—The sixth chapter of the Paññāvagga of the Paṭisambhidāmagga.

Pāṭihīrasaññaka Thera.—An arahant. In the past he had seen the miracles attending the entry of **Padumuttara** Buddha into his city and marvelled thereat.[1]

[1] Ap. ii. 392.

Pāṭhika (Pāṭhiya).—An **Ājīvaka** of **Sāvatthi.** He was looked after by a woman of Sāvatthi who, hearing one day her neighbours praise the Buddha, wished to invite him to her home. Pāṭhika dissuaded her from so doing; but one day, unbeknown to him, she sent her son to invite the Buddha. The boy called at Pāṭhika's hermitage on the way, and the ascetic tried to dissuade him from going. Failing to do so, he told him not to tell the Buddha where to find the house, hoping that thus they would be able to eat themselves all the food prepared for the Buddha. The boy did as he was told, and the next day he and Pāṭhika hid in a room at the back of the house. The Buddha came, and, after the meal, thanked the woman. But when Pāṭhika heard her applaud the Buddha's sermon, he could no longer forbear and rushed forth to abuse her.[1]

[1] DhA. i. 376 ff.

Pāṭhīna.—A monastery in Ceylon, restored by **Vijayabāhu I.**[1]

[1] Cv. lx. 58.

Pāṭheyyakā.—See **Pāveyyakā.**

Pāṇa Sutta.—Few are they who abstain from taking life, more numerous they who do not.[1]

[1] S. v. 468.

1. **Pāṇā Sutta.**—Just as whatsoever creatures adopt the four postures do so in dependence on the earth, so does a monk develop the seven bojjhaṅgas, dependent on virtue.[1]

[1] S. v. 78.

2. **Pāṇā Sutta.**—Supposing a man were to collect all the grass, sticks, etc., in **Jambudīpa,** and after making sticks of various sizes were to impale on them all the creatures of the ocean, creatures of all sizes, even so a majority of the minute animals would remain free, being too small to be impaled. Even thus widespread is the ruin of things, yet from such widespread ruin will be saved those who have the gift of realizing the Four Noble Truths.[1]

[1] S. v. 441.

Pātapata.—A locality in South India, mentioned in the account of the campaigns of **Laṅkāpura.**[1]

[1] Cv. lxxvi. 224, 234.

Pātāla Sutta.—The worldlings speak of a bottomless pit (*pātāla*) in the mighty ocean. But the real *pātāla* is painful bodily feeling, which brings about weeping and wailing and lamentation.[1]

[1] S. iv. 206 f.

Pāti Sutta.—Dire are gains, favours and flattery. They tempt even a man, otherwise incorruptible, to lie for the sake of a silver bowl filled with gold dust, or a golden bowl filled with silver dust.[1]

[1] S. ii. 233.

Pātimokkha.—See **Pāṭimokkha.**

Pātubhava Sutta.—Six things, the manifestation of which in this world is rare.[1]

[1] A. iii. 441.

Pāttanallūra.—A fortress in South India, once occupied by **Jagadvijaya.**[1]

[1] Cv. lxxvi. 304, 306; lxxvii. 71.

Pādañjali Jātaka (No. 247).—Brahmadatta, king of Benares, had a son **Pādañjali,** who was an idle loafer. When the king died, the courtiers, headed by the Bodhisatta who was the chaplain, went to test him. At everything the boy sneered with a superior air, whether it were right or wrong; and the Bodhisatta was made king in his stead.

The story was related in reference to **Lāḷudāyī,** who once curled his lip in scorn when the two chief disciples were praised. Lāḷudāyī is identified with Pādañjali.[1]

[1] J. ii. 263 f.

Pādapāvara.—Seven kappas ago there were four kings of this name, previous births of **Sattapaduminiya Thera.**[1]

[1] Ap. i. 254.

Pādapīṭhiya Thera.—An arahant. In the past he made a footstool for the seat of **Sumedha** Buddha.[1]

[1] Ap. ii. 400.

1. **Pādapūjaka Thera.**—An arahant. In the past he scattered seven jasmine-flowers on the feet of **Siddhattha** Buddha. Five kappas ago he was king thirteen times under the name of **Samantagandha (Samantabhadda).**[1] He is probably identical with **Uttiya Thera.**[2]

[1] Ap. i. 141 f. [2] ThagA. i. 125.

2. **Pādapūjaka Thera.**—An arahant. Ninety-one kappas ago he was a kinnara who, seeing **Vipassī** Buddha, gave him sandalwood, *tagara* and other perfumes.[1]

[1] Ap. i. 246.

Pādalola-Brahmadatta.—King of Benares. He loved dancing, and had three houses in which young, middle-aged, and old women danced respectively. One day he passed from one house to the other, and though the dancers put forth all their skill, the king failed to find satisfaction. Realizing that this discontent was the result of his craving, he left the world, developed insight, and became a Pacceka Buddha. His verse is included in the **Khaggavisāna Sutta.**[1]

[1] SN. vs. 61; SNA. i. 113 f.; ApA. i. 158.

Pādiyattha.—A district, the birthplace of **Jotidāsa Thera.**[1] *v.l.* **Pāniyattha.**

[1] ThagA. i. 264.

Pādulaka.—A tank built by **Dhātusena.**[1]

[1] Cv. xxxviii. 50.

Pānadhidāyaka Thera.—An arahant. Ninety-one kappas ago he gave a couch (*pānadhi* ?) to a forest-dwelling sage. Seventy-seven kappas ago he was eight times king under the name of **Suyāna.**[1]

[1] Ap. i. 208 f.

Pānīya Jātaka (No. 459).—The story of how six persons became Pacceka Buddhas by feeling remorse for sins committed and by developing supernatural insight. The Jātaka derives its name from the first of these, who was a villager of Kāsi. He went with his friend into the fields, each carrying a flask of water. From time to time they drank, but the first drank out of the other's flask, wishing to save the water in his own. In the evening remorse seized him, and as he stood reflecting on his wickedness he became a Pacceka Buddha.

The Pacceka Buddhas met at **Nandamūlapabbhāra** and together visited the king of Benares who was the Bodhisatta. On hearing their stories he renounced the world, and, in spite of the efforts of his consort to stop him, became an ascetic.

The story was related in reference to five hundred householders of **Sāvatthi** who became monks. They lived in the monastery but indulged in thoughts of sin. The Buddha sent **Ānanda** to summon them, and admonished them saying that no matter how small a sin it was, it must be checked.[1] The queen consort of the story was **Rāhulamātā.**

[1] J. iv. 113 ff.

Pānīyadvāra.—One of the gates of **Pulatthipura** erected by **Parakkamabāhu I.**[1]

[1] Cv. lxxiii. 162.

Pāpa Vagga.—The ninth section of the Dhammapada.

Pāpa Sutta.—The wicked man is he who takes life, steals, etc., and is of malicious heart; more than wicked is he who encourages others in these things. Just so with the good and the more than good.[1]

[1] A. ii. 222 f.

Pāpaka.—A monk who, believing that his name was of ill omen, wished to change it. The Buddha preached to him the **Nāmasiddhi Jātaka** (*q.v.*) to show that a name has no importance.[1]

[1] J. i. 401 f.

1. **Pāpaṇika Sutta.**—The shopkeeper who neglects his duties at early dawn, at midday, and at eventide, does not prosper; nor does the monk who similarly neglects his duties.[1]

[1] A. i. 115.

2. **Pāpaṇika Sutta.**—The shopkeeper who is shrewd, supremely capable, and who inspires confidence, soon attains to greatness and increase of wealth; a monk will in like manner attain to spiritual development.[1]

[1] A. i. 115 f.

Pāpadhamma Sutta.—On the man who is wicked by nature and the one who is more than wicked; also on him who is of goodly nature and the one who is more than goodly.[1]

[1] A. ii. 223.

Pāpanivāriya Thera.—An arahant. In the time of **Piyadassī** Buddha he had cleaned the cloistered walk of the Buddha and shown great exertion in the fulfilment of religious practices. Eleven kappas ago he was a king, named **Aggideva.**[1]

[1] Ap. i. 212 f.

Pāyāgā.—A class of Nāgas.[1] The Commentary explains[2] that they lived in **Pāyāgapatiṭṭhāna.**

[1] D. ii. 258. [2] DA. ii. 688.

Pāyāsadāyaka Thera.—An arahant. Ninety-one kappas ago he offered a bronze bowl filled with milk-rice to **Vipassī** Buddha. Forty-one kappas ago he was a king named **Buddha.**[1] He is probably identical with **Vacchapāla Thera.**[2]

[1] Ap. i. 157. [2] ThagA. i. 159 f.

Pāyāsi.—A chieftain (*rājañña*) of **Setavyā,** who lived on a royal domain gifted by **Pasenadi.** He held the view that there was no world other than this, no fruit of actions and no rebirth. But after a discussion with **Kūmara-Kassapa,** who was staying in the **Siṃsapāvana** near by, he was convinced of the error of his views. Thereupon he instituted an almsgiving to all who sought his generosity. The gifts were, however, coarse and unpalatable. A young brahmin named **Uttara,** who came to the almsgiving and was passed over, spoke scornfully of the gifts. Hearing of this, Pāyāsi appointed him to supervise the distribution. After death, Pāyāsi was born among the **Cātummahārājika** gods while Uttara was born in **Tāvatiṃsa.** **Gavampati** met Pāyāsi in the deva-world, and Pāyāsi instructed him to teach men to give their gifts with thoroughness and with their own hands.[1] Pāyāsi-devaputta was also known as **Serīsaka-devaputta** because he lived in the **Serīsaka-vimāna.** For details see **Serīsaka-devaputta.**

[1] D. ii. 316 ff.; VvA. 297 f., 331 f.

Pāyāsi Vagga.—The sixth chapter of the Vimānavatthu.

Pāyāsi Sutta.—The twenty-third sutta of the Dīgha Nikāya. It contains a discussion on rebirth and karma between **Pāyāsi** and **Kumāra-Kassapa** in the **Siṃsapāvana** at **Setavyā.**[1] The incidents mentioned in the sutta took place, according to Dhammapāla,[2] after the Buddha's death and the erection of thūpas over his relics.

[1] D. ii. 316 ff.

[2] VvA. p. 297.

Pāra Sutta.—The Buddha teaches of the further shore (beyond *saṃsāra*) and the path leading thereto.[1]

[1] S. iv. 369.

Pāragaṅgā.—The region beyond the Ganges,[1] to be exiled into which was a great punishment.[2]

[1] *E.g.*, J. ii. 333; vi. 427.

[2] *E.g.*, SN. pp. 32, 47.

Pāragā.—A class of devas.[1]

[1] D. ii. 260.

Pāramīmahāsataka.—A Pāli poem of one hundred verses, in twelve sections, dealing with the ten *pāramitā*, written by **Dhammakitti Saṅgharāja.** The poem is based on the Jātaka and the Cariyā Piṭaka.[1]

[1] P.L.C. 242.

Pārājikā.—The first of the two divisions of the Sutta Vibhaṅga of the Vinaya Piṭaka.

Pārājikākaṇḍa.—The first chapter of the Pārājikā.

Pārājikuddesa.—The third of the five divisions of the Pāṭimokkha.

Pārāpata Jātaka.—See **Romaka Jātaka.**

Pārāyana Vagga.—The fifth and last division of the Sutta Nipāta.[1] It consists of sixteen suttas preceded by an introduction of fifty-six *Vatthugāthā*. The Vatthugāthā describe how **Bāvarī** (*q.v.*) first heard of the coming of the Buddha from a devotee and sent sixteen of his pupils to visit the Buddha and find out if his claims to Enlightenment were true. A description of the route taken by them is also given. The sixteen suttas give the questions asked by Bāvarī's disciples and the answers given by the Buddha. The Culla Niddesa comments on the sixteen suttas, but makes no mention of the Vatthugāthā. Perhaps, at one time, the **Khaggavisāna Sutta** (*q.v.*) was attached to the Pārāyana Vagga. The Pārāyana Vagga is mentioned in the Aṅguttara Nikāya[2] and in the Saṃyutta Nikāya,[3] which is evidence of its having been one of the oldest collections. The Pārāyanaka-Samiti is among the incidents represented in the **Mahā Thūpa.**[4] It is said[5] that at the end of the discourses contained in the Pārāyaṇa Vagga, fourteen crores of beings realized nibbāna.

Buddhaghosa says[6] that the Pārāyana was so called because it leads to nibbāna (*nibbānasaṅkhātaṃ pāraṃ ayanato Pārāyanā ti laddhavohāraṃ dhammaṃ*).

1 SN. vs. 976 ff.
2 A. i. 133, 134; ii. 45; iv. 63.
3 S. ii. 49.
4 Mhv. xxx. 84.
5 *E.g.*, AA. i. 57.
6 AA. ii. 717.

Pārāyana Sutta.—The Buddha teaches the goal (*pārāyana*) and the path leading thereto.[1]

1 S. iv. 373.

Pārāyanikabrāhmaṇā.—The name given to the sixteen disciples of **Bāvarī** (*q.v.*). Each of them had one thousand followers. At the end of the suttas contained in the **Pārāyana Vagga,** they all expressed their desire to join the Order, and the Buddha ordained them by the "*ehi-bhikkhu-pabbajjā.*"[1]

1 Sp. i. 241.

Pārāpara.—The name of a family. See **Pārāpariya.**

Pārāpariya Thera.—An arahant. He was the son of a very eminent brahmin of **Sāvatthi,** and was so called because the name of his family was **Pārāpara.** One day he went to **Jetavana** to hear the Buddha preach, and the Buddha, seeing him, preached the **Indriyabhāvanā Sutta.**[1] After

1 This probably refers to M. iii. 298 ff., which deals with the views of the brahmin teacher **Pārāsariya,** and then gives the method of developing the indriyas as taught in the Ariyan Vinaya. The sutta, however, was preached at **Kajaṅgalā** and *not* at Sāvatthi, the questioners being **Uttara,** a pupil of Pārāsariya, and **Ānanda.** See *Brethren* 295, n. 1.

learning the sutta, Pārāpariya pondered on its meaning and won arahantship.[2] The Theragāthā[3] contains a number of verses spoken by Pārāpariya after the Buddha's parinibbāna and immediately before his own death.

[2] Thag. vs. 726 ff.; ThagA. ii. 17 f. [3] vs. 920-48; ThagA. ii. 74 ff.

Pārāsara.—The name of a family. See **Pārāsariya.**

1. **Pārāsariya Thera.**—A brahmin of **Rājagaha,** expert in the three Vedas. He belonged to the family of **Pārāsara,** hence his name. He was a teacher of many brahmins up to the time of his witnessing the miracles attending the Buddha's visit to Rājagaha. Thereupon he joined the Order and shortly after became an arahant.

In the time of **Piyadassī** Buddha he was a hunter, and while hunting in the forest, he saw the Buddha in meditation, and erected a hut over him, covering it with lilies. For seven days he renewed the supply of flowers. On the seventh day a large concourse of humans and devas assembled to hear the Buddha preach. The hunter listened to the sermon, and was born after death in the deva-world.[1] He is probably identical with **Padumakūṭāgāriya** of the Apadāna.[2] *v.l.* **Pārāpariya.**

[1] Thag. vs. 116; ThagA. i. 229 ff. [2] Ap. i. 326 ff.

2. **Pārāsariya.**—A brahmin teacher mentioned in the **Indriyabhāvanā Sutta.** He is said, by his pupil **Uttara,** to have taught that those who have developed their *indriyas* could neither see forms with their eyes nor hear sounds with their ears.[1] He is perhaps identical with **Pārāpariya Thera.**

[1] M. iii. 298.

3. **Pārāsariya.**—A brahmin teacher of **Takkasilā,** mentioned in the **Cūlānandiya Jātaka.**[1]

[1] J. ii. 202.

4. **Pārāsariya.**—The Bodhisatta born as a teacher of **Takkasilā.**[1] His family name was Pārāsariya.[2] For details see the **Dhonasākha Jātaka.**

[1] J. iii. 160. [2] *Ibid.*, 161.

Pārikā, Pārī.—A hunter's daughter, wife of **Dukūlaka** and mother of **Suvaṇṇasāma** (the Bodhisatta).

For details see the **Sāma Jātaka.** Pārikā was a former birth of **Bhaddā Kāpilānī.**[1]

[1] J. vi. 95; Mil. 123.

Pāricchattaka.—A tree in **Tāvatiṃsa,** which grew in the **Nandanavana** as the result of the *Koviḷāra*-tree planted by **Magha** outside the **Sudhammāsālā.** It is one hundred leagues in circumference and at its foot is the **Paṇḍukambalasilāsana.**[1] The **Cittapāṭali** in the **Asura** world corresponds to the Pāricchattaka in Tāvatiṃsa, but the flowers are different.[2] The colour of the flowers is visible fifty leagues away, while their perfume travels one hundred leagues. The devas eagerly watch each stage of development of leaf and flower, and each stage is marked by great rejoicings.[3] When the flowers are fully open they shine like the morning sun. They are never plucked; a wind arises and sweeps away the faded flowers and scatters fresh ones on the seats of **Sakka** and the other gods of Tāvatiṃsa. The bodies of the devas are completely covered with the sweetly scented pollen, making them resemble golden caskets. The ceremony of playing with the flowers lasts four months.[4] The Pāricchattaka is one of the seven trees which last throughout the kappa.[5]

The Pāricchattaka is generally described as a Kovilāra.[6] It is also called the Pārijāta, the Sanskrit name being Pāriyātra.[7]

[1] DhA. i. 273.
[2] *Ibid.*, 280; SNA. 485.
[3] A. iv. 117 f.
[4] AA. ii. 730 f.
[5] AA. i. 264.
[6] *E.g.*, VvA. 174.
[7] *E.g.*, Dvy. 184, 195, 219.

Pāricchattaka Vagga.—The third chapter of the Vimāna Vatthu.

Pāricchattaka-Vimāna Vatthu.—Once a pious follower of the Buddha, living at **Sāvatthi,** invited the Buddha to a meal and showed him great honour. A woman who had gone to **Andhavana** to gather firewood picked some asoka-flowers on the way, and, passing the Buddha, gave them to him and worshipped him. She was born after death in **Tāvatiṃsa** and questioned by **Moggallāna.**[1]

[1] Vv. iii. 10; VvA. 172 ff.

Pāricchattaka Sutta.—Just as the devas in **Tāvatiṃsa** rejoice on seeing the **Pāricchattaka** tree gradually growing and putting forth flowers, and hold celebrations at each stage, so do they rejoice when the householder leaves the world and joins the Order, finally attaining to nibbāna. His fame spreads from world to world, even up to the Brahma-world.[1]

The sutta was evidently also known as the **Pāricchattakopama.**[2]

[1] A. iv. 117 ff.
[2] *E.g.*, AA. i. 32; MA. i. 14.

Pārileyya, Pārileyyaka.—A town (*nagara*) near **Kosambī.** When the Buddha found that he could not persuade the **Kosambī** monks to refrain from quarrelling, he left Kosambī alone and unattended, and passing through **Bālakloṇakāragāma** and **Pācīnavaṃsadāya,** went to Pārileyyaka, where he stayed at the foot of **Bhaddasāla** in the **Rakkhitavanasaṇḍa.** There a certain elephant who, finding communal life distasteful, had left his herd, waited on the Buddha, ministering to all his needs. From Pārileyyaka the Buddha went on to **Sāvatthi.**[1] This was in the tenth year after the Enlightenment.[2] The Commentaries[3] say that the elephant's name was Pārileyya, and describe in vivid detail the perfect manner in which he looked after the Buddha, omitting nothing, even to the extent of finding hot water for his bath. There was also there a monkey who offered the Buddha a honeycomb. Soon after, the monkey fell on a tree-stump and died and was born in **Tāvatiṃsa.** Later, when **Ānanda** came with five hundred others to invite the Buddha to return to Sāvatthi, Pārileyyaka provided them all with food. He died of a broken heart when the Buddha left the forest, and was born in Tāvatiṃsa in a golden palace, thirty leagues high, where he came to be known as **Pārileyyaka-devaputta.**

This elephant is identified with the elephant of the **Bhisa Jātaka.**[4]

[1] Vin. i. 352 f.; S. iii. 95; Ud. iv. 5; J. iii. 489; M. i. 320.

[2] BuA., p. 3.

[3] *E.g.*, DhA. i. 48 ff.; iv. 26 ff. UdA. 250 f.; see Thomas, *op. cit.*, 117 n.

[4] J. iv. 314.

Pārileyyaka Sutta.—When the Buddha was staying in a forest near **Pārileyya,** some monks asked **Ānanda** to take them to him. This he did, and the Buddha, reading the thoughts of certain monks, preached a sermon on the destruction of the *āsavas* by the full realization of impermanence and the absence of any self.[1]

[1] S. iii. 95 ff.

Pārivāsika Khandha.—The second section of the Culla Vagga of the Vinaya Piṭaka.

Pārupaṇā.—The name given to one of the two parties of disputants in a controversy which arose in Burma in the eighteenth century, regarding the manner in which the robe should be draped by Buddhist monks. The Pārupaṇas held that both shoulders should be covered, while their opponents, the **Ekaṃsikas,** maintained that it was sufficient to drape one shoulder.[1]

[1] For a fairly full account of the controversy, see Sās. pp. 117 ff.

Pāla.—See **Cullapāla, Mahāpāla,** and **Cakkhupāla.**

Pālikapāsāda.—A building erected by **Kassapa V.**[1]

[1] Cv. lii. 66; see also Cv. *Trs.* i. 168, n. 8.

1. **Pālita (Pālika).**—Nephew of **Cakkhupāla.** When **Cullapāla,** brother of Cakkhupāla, heard of the latter's blindness, he sent Pālita to fetch him, and, in order to protect him from danger on the way, had him ordained before he set forth. While returning with Cakkhupāla, Pālita heard the song of a woman collecting firewood, and, making some excuse, left Cakkhupāla and had intimacy with her. When Cakkhupāla heard what had happened, he refused to go any further with him.[1]

[1] ThagA. i. 197 f.

2. **Pālita.**—A rājakumāra of **Sumaṅgala** city. He and his friend, **Sabbadassī,** son of the chaplain, visited the Buddha **Piyadassī** and entertained him for seven days, after which they entered the Order, becoming arahants in due time. Later, they became the chief disciples of Piyadassī Buddha.[1]

[1] Bu. xiv. 20; BuA. 176; J. i. 39.

3. **Pālita.**—The constant attendant of **Maṅgala** Buddha.[1]

[1] Bu. vi. 23; J. i. 34.

4. **Pālita.**—A Nāga-king in the time of **Padumuttara Buddha,** a previous birth of **Rāhula** (*q.v.*).[1]

[1] SA. iii. 26; MA. ii. 722, 1023; but see SNA. i. 341, where he is called **Saṅkha.** At AA. i. 143 his name is given as **Paṭhavindhara.**

Pālimuttaka-Vinayavinicchaya.—See **Vinayavinicchaya.**

Pālī.—See **Mahapālī** and **Suvaṇṇapālī.**

Pāvā.—A city of the **Mallas** which the Buddha visited during his last journey, going there from **Bhogagāma** and stopping at Cunda's mango-grove.

Cunda lived in Pāvā and invited the Buddha to a meal, which proved to be his last.[1] From Pāvā the Buddha journeyed on to **Kusinārā,** crossing the **Kakkuṭṭhā** on the way.[2] According to the **Saṅgīti Sutta,**[3] at the time the Buddha was staying at Pāvā, the Mallas had just com-

[1] It was on this occasion that the **Cunda Sutta** (1) was preached (SNA. i. 159).

[2] D. ii. 126 ff.; Ud. viii. 5; the road from Pāvā to Kusināra is mentioned several times in the books—*e.g.*, Vin. ii. 284; D. ii. 162.

[3] *q.v.*

pleted their new Mote-hall, **Ubbhaṭaka,** and, at their invitation, the Buddha consecrated it by first occupying it and then preaching in it. After the Buddha had finished speaking, **Sāriputta** recited the Saṅgīti Sutta to the assembled monks.

Pāvā was also a centre of the **Nigaṇṭhas** and, at the time mentioned above, **Nigaṇṭha Nāthaputta** had just died at Pāvā and his followers were divided by bitter wrangles.[4] **Cunda Samaṇuddesa** was spending his rainy season at Pāvā, and he reported to the Buddha, who was at **Sāmagāma,** news of the Nigaṇṭhas' quarrels.[5]

The distance from Pāvā to Kusinārā was three gāvutas. It is said[6] that on the way between these two places, the Buddha had to stop at twenty-five resting-places, so faint and weary was he.

Mention is made in the Udāna[7] of the Buddha having stayed at the **Ajakapālaka-cetiya** (*q.v.*) in Pāvā. This may have been during a previous visit.

After the Buddha's death, the Mallas of Pāvā claimed a share in his relics. **Doṇa** satisfied their claim, and a thūpa was erected in Pāvā over their share of the relics.[8]

The inhabitants of Pāvā are called **Pāveyyakā** (*q.v.*). Pāvā was the birthplace of **Khaṇḍasumana** (*q.v.*).

[4] D. iii. 210.
[5] *Ibid.*, 117 f.; M. ii. 243 f.
[6] UdA. 403.
[7] i. 7.
[8] D. ii. 167; Bu. xxviii. 3.

1. **Pāvārika, Pāvāriya.**—A king. When **Pañcapāpā** (*q.v.*) was sent down the river by her husband **Baka,** Pāvāriya rescued her and took her as his wife. Baka, hearing of this, threatened war, and it was arranged by the ministers of the two kings that Pañcapāpā should live as the wife of them both, spending one week in the house of each.[1]

[1] J. v. 443 f.

2. **Pāvārika.**—A seṭṭhi of **Kosambī,** friend of **Ghosita** and **Kukkuṭa.** When these three went to Sāvatthi to invite the Buddha to Kosambī, they erected three monasteries to accommodate the Buddha and his monks. The one built by Pāvārika was in his Mango-grove (*ambavana*) and is referred to as **Pāvārikārāma** and **Pāvārikambavana.**[1]

[1] DA i. 319; AA. i. 234 f.; MA. i. 541; DhA. i. 203 ff.

3. **Pāvārika.**—See **Dussapāvārika.**

1. **Pāvārikambavana.**—The Mango-grove of **Pāvārika** (*q.v.*) of **Kosambī.**

2. **Pāvārikambavana.**—A Mango-grove at **Nālandā** where the Buddha stayed when on a visit there.[1] It was there that he preached the **Kevaṭṭa Sutta**, the **Sampasādanīya Sutta** and the **Upāli Sutta**. Among those who visited the Buddha there are mentioned **Kevaḍḍha, Upāligahapati** and **Asibandhakaputta.**[2]

The grove belonged to a seṭṭhi named **Pāvārika,** who is distinguished from the seṭṭhi of the same name at Kosambī by being described as **Dussapāvārika.**[3] (? **Pāvārika** the milliner, *q.v.*).

[1] *E.g.*, D. ii. 81.
[2] For details see *s.v.*
[3] *E.g.*, DA. ii. 873; MA. i. 540; SA. iii. 169.

Pāvārikārāma.—See **Pāvārika** (2).

Pāveyyaka.—An elephant. See **Baddheraka.**

Pāveyyaka Sutta.—See **Tiṃsamatta Sutta.**

Pāveyyakā.—The name given to the inhabitants of Pāvā—*e.g.*, Pāveyyakā Mallā.[1] Pāvā was evidently a centre of Buddhist activity even during the lifetime of the Buddha, and mention is made of Pāveyyaka monks in the Vinaya.[2] During the time of the **Vajjiputta** heresy, it was the Pāveyyakā who upheld the true doctrine, their leaders being **Revata, Sambhūta-Sāṇavāsī, Yasa Kākaṇḍakaputta** and **Sumana.**[3] In this connection the Pāveyyakā are also described as "**Pacchimikā**" in opposition to the Vajjiputtakas who are called "**Pācīnakā.**" It is explained[4] that the Pāveyyakā were called "Pacchimikā" because they lived to the west.[5]

The Burmese MSS. seem to spell Pāveyyakā as Pāṭheyyakā.

[1] *E.g.*, D. ii. 165.
[2] *E.g.*, Vin. i. 253.
[3] *Ibid.*, ii. 301 ff.; Mhv. iv. 17 ff.
[4] *E.g.*, MṬ. 166.
[5] West of Kosala, according to Buddhaghosa, on Mahāvagga (vii. 1.).

Pāsa.—A locality in South India, captured by **Laṅkāpura.**[1]

[1] Cv. lxxvi. 236.

1. **Pāsa Sutta.**—Preached at the Migadāya in **Isipatana.** The Buddha tells the monks that he realized supreme emancipation by means of *yonisomanasikāra*, and asserts that he is free from Māra's snares.[1]

[1] S. i. 105.

2. **Pāsa Sutta.**—Preached at **Isipatana.** The Buddha declares that he is free from all snares, both celestial and human, and admonishes the

monks to wander about for the good of the many. He himself was going to **Senānigama** in **Uruvelā** to preach.[1]

[1] S. i. 106.

Pāsarāsi Sutta.—Another name for the **Ariyapariyesanā Sutta** (*q.v.*).[1]

[1] See also MA. ii. 740.

Pāsāṇa Sutta.—Once when the Buddha was in **Gijjhakūṭa** on a dark and rainy night, **Māra** sent many rocks crashing down in order to frighten him, but the Buddha was quite calm.[1]

[1] S. i. 109.

Pāsāṇaka-cetiya.—A shrine near **Rājagaha,** where the disciples of **Bāvarī** met and questioned the Buddha.[1] The Buddha went there from **Sāvatthi,** knowing it to be the best place in which to meet them. Bāvarī's disciples followed him thither. The cetiya was originally a shrine dedicated to some divinity (*devaṭṭhāna*) and built on a great rock, hence its name. Later, it was converted into a vihāra for the Buddha, being within easy reach of the town. **Sakka** built there a great hall (*maṇḍapa*) for the Buddha.[2] This hall was evidently behind the cetiya (*piṭṭhi-pāsāṇe*).[3]

[1] SN. vs. 1013. [2] SNA. 583, 584. [3] AA. i. 184.

Pāsāṇachātaka.—See **Akkhakkhāyika.**

Pāsāṇagāmavāpī.—A tank restored by **Parakkamabāhu I.**[1]

[1] Cv. lxxix. 36.

Pāsāṇatittha.—A ford across the **Kadambanadī.** From this ford the sīmā of the Mahāvihāra started, returning to the same spot. In Pāsāṇatittha was the **Kuḍḍavāṭakapāsāṇa.**[1]

[1] Mbv. 134, 135.

Pāsāṇadīpa.—A vihāra in **Rohaṇa,** built by **Mahādāṭhika-Mahānāga,** who gave to it a tract of land spreading for half a league round in honour of a sāmaṇera who lived there and had given the king a draught of water.[1] **Silādāṭha** heard the Elder of this vihāra preach the sacred texts, and, very pleased with him, built for him the **Rohaṇa-vihāra.**[2]

[1] Mhv. xxxiv. 91. [2] Cv. xlv. 53.

Pāsāṇapabbata.—A hill near **Anurādhapura,** to the north of the Nīcasusāna, laid out by **Paṇḍukābhaya.**[1]

[1] Mhv. x. 35.

Pāsāṇalekha Sutta.—Three kinds of persons: like carvings on rock, on the ground and on water. The first is easily angered and his anger lasts long; that of the second does not last long; the third is easily reconciled.[1]

[1] A. i. 283.

Pāsāṇasinna.—A locality in Ceylon where **Dhātusena** built the **Dhātusenapabbata-vihāra.**[1]

[1] Cv. xxxviii. 47.

Pāsādakampana Vagga.—The second chapter of the Iddhipāda Saṃyutta.[1] It derives its name from the **Pāsādakampana** (or **Moggallāna**) **Sutta** (*q.v.*).

[1] S. v. 263 ff.

Pāsādakampana Sutta.—The Theragāthā Commentary[1] says that the incident of **Moggallāna** rocking the **Migāramātupāsāda** with his thumb, at the command of the Buddha, in order to frighten some novices who indulged in worldly talk—is recounted in the **Pāsādākampana Sutta.** This incident is recounted in the **Moggallāna Sutta** of the Saṃyutta Nikāya.[2] It is also related in the Sutta Nipāta Commentary,[3] as an introduction to the **Uṭṭhāna Sutta.**

[1] ThagA. ii. 184. [2] S. v. 269 f. [3] SNA. i. 336 f.

Pāsādabahula.—A brahmin of **Sāvatthi** who was so delighted with the preaching of the Buddha that he gave meals regularly at his house to sixteen monks, always addressing them as "Arahant." This displeased both the Arahants and the non-Arahants, and they ceased going there. When the Buddha heard of it, he admonished the monks.[1]

[1] DhA. iv. 138 f.

Pāsādika Sutta.—The twenty-ninth sutta of the Dīgha Nikāya. **Cunda Samaṇuddesa,** who had been spending the rainy season at **Pāvā,** returns and reports to **Ānanda** the death of **Nigaṇṭha Nātaputta** and the consequent wrangling which had broken out among the **Nigaṇṭhas.** Together they visit the Buddha at **Sāmagāma** and tell him of it. He replies that this is to be expected from the character of Nātaputta and from the doctrine which he taught. The Buddha then proceeds to give in detail the qualities of the perfect teacher and the perfect teaching. The Tathāgata is such a teacher and the Dhamma such a teaching.[1]

In the Pāsādika Sutta the threefold training is called *brahmacariyā.*[2]

[1] D. iii. 117-41. [2] DA. i. 179; MA. i. 275.

1. **Piṅgala.**—See **Mahā-Piṅgala.**

2. **Piṅgala.**—A cow-killing huntsman, a former birth of **Alāta.**[1]

[1] J. vi. 227.

3. **Piṅgala.**—King of **Suraṭṭha,** contemporary of **Dhammāsoka,** whose adviser he was. One day, as Piṅgala was returning from Dhammāsoka's court, the peta **Nandaka,** father of **Uttarā,** revealed himself and instructed him to follow the Buddha's teaching.[1]

[1] Pv. iv. 3; PvA. 244 ff.

4. **Piṅgala.**—A race of elephants,[1] each having the strength of one hundred thousand men.[2]

[1] MA. i. 262; VibhA. 397; UdA. 403; AA. ii. 822. [2] BuA. 37.

Piṅgalakoccha.—A brahmin of **Sāvatthi.** He visited the Buddha at **Jetavana** and the Buddha preached to him the **Cūla-Sāropama Sutta,** at the end of which he declared himself the Buddha's follower.[1] Buddhaghosa says[2] that the man's name was **Koccha,** and that he was called Piṅgala because he was tawny (*piṅgaladhātuko*).

[1] M. i. 198 ff. [2] MA. i. 422.

Piṅgala-Buddharakkhita.—A monk of Ceylon, incumbent of the **Ambariya-vihāra.** The upāsaka of **Uttara-**(or **Antara-**)**vaḍḍhamānaka** took the precepts from him and was soon after seized by a snake. The upāsaka made up his mind not to break the precepts, and the snake set him free.[1] Piṅgala-Buddharakkhita's monastery was near **Uttaragāma (Uttaravaḍḍhamāna** ?) and there were one hundred houses in the village, all of which he visited, and there was not one single house at the door of which he had not developed *samāpatti.*[2]

[1] MA. i. 165; SA. ii. 113; DhSA. 103, etc. [2] MA. ii. 978.

Piṅgalā.—A slave who, having made an assignation with her lover, as soon as her work was finished, waited outside her master's house, expecting his arrival. At the end of the middle watch, she gave up waiting and slept peacefully. This is one of the incidents mentioned in the **Sīlavīmaṃsa Jātaka.**[1]

[1] J. iii. 101.

1. **Piṅgiya.**—Chaplain to Brahmadatta, king of Benares. He was a former birth of **Devadatta.**[1] His story is given in the **Dhonasākha Jātaka** (*q.v.*).

[1] J. iii. 161.

2. **Piṅgiya.**—Called **Piṅgiya-māṇava,** nephew and pupil of **Bāvarī.** At the time that he visited the Buddha with the other disciples he was 120 years old and very feeble. At the end of his discussion with the Buddha, as recorded in the **Piṅgiya Sutta,**[1] because of his feebleness, he failed to reach any attainment. Thereupon he praised the Buddha and begged of him to go on. The Buddha preached to him further, and he became an anāgamī, failing, however, to attain arahantship because his mind wandered to his maternal uncle, Bāvarī. His one thousand pupils, however, became arahants. Later, with the Buddha's leave, he visited Bāvarī and told him the glad tidings, describing the Buddha's glory.[2] At the end of his statement, the Buddha, seeing that the minds of both of them were mature, sent forth a ray of light from Sāvatthi and, appearing before them, preached to them. Thereupon Bāvarī became an anāgamī and Piṅgiya an arahant.[3]

Piṅgiya was called **māṇava,** even at the age of 120.[4]

[1] SN. vs. 1120-23.
[2] *Ibid.*, 1131-45.
[3] SNA. ii. 603 ff.
[4] *Ibid.*, 413.

3. **Piṅgiya.**—One of the seven anāgamins born in the **Avihā**-world, in the company of **Ghaṭīkārā.**[1] He is described as a *bhikkhū*, and is therefore probably identical with **Piṅgiya** (2). The story of the latter having attained arahantship must, in that case, have been a later legend. It is also possible that Piṅgiya is a variant reading for **Piṅgiyānī** (*q.v.*).

[1] S. i. 35, 60.

4. **Piṅgiya.**—A dog, mentioned in the **Pūtimaṃsa Jātaka.**[1]

[1] J. iii. 535.

1. **Piṅgiyānī.**—A brahmin of **Vesālī.** The Aṅguttara Nikāya records a conversation between him and **Kāraṇapālī.** The latter meets Piṅgiyānī and, on learning that he was returning from a visit to the Buddha, asks him about the Buddha's wisdom. Piṅgiyānī utters the Buddha's praises with a wealth of simile and metaphor. Kāraṇapāli is impressed, and declares himself the Buddha's follower.[1] On another occasion, Piṅgiyānī is present when five hundred **Licchavis** come to pay honour to the Buddha at the **Kūṭāgārasālā.** The sight of the Buddha, sitting in their midst, outshining them all, inspires Piṅgiyānī and he bursts into song. The Licchavis give him five hundred upper garments, all of which he presents to the Buddha.[2]

[1] A. iii. 236 ff.
[2] *Ibid.*, 239 f.

Buddhaghosa says[3] that Piṅgiyānī was an anāgāmī. He went daily to the Buddha, with flowers and perfumes. See also **Piṅgiya** (3).

[3] AA. ii. 636.

2. **Piṅgiyānī.**—Wife of **Brahmadatta.** One day when opening her window she saw a royal groom, with whom she fell in love, and when the king fell asleep, she climbed down through the window, lay with the groom, and climbed back again, after which she perfumed herself and lay down beside the king. The king eventually discovered her misdemeanour and proclaimed it to his ministers, depriving her of her royal rank.

The story is one of those related by **Kuṇāla,** who is identified with Brahmadatta.[1] It is perhaps this story which is referred to as the **Culla-Kuṇāla Jātaka** (*q.v.*).

[1] J. v. 444.

Piṅgiyānī Sutta.—The story of the brahmin **Piṅgiyānī** (*q.v.*) uttering the Buddha's praises before the **Licchavīs.** When Piṅgiyānī ended his song of praise, the Buddha told the Licchavīs of the five kinds of rare treasures: the Tathāgata, one who can teach the Dhammavinaya, one who recognises the Dhamma, one who follows the Dhamma, and one who is grateful.[1]

[1] A. iii. 239 ff.

Piṅguttara.—A lad of **Mithilā** who studied in **Takkasilā** and was given in marriage his teacher's beautiful daughter. But he was unlucky and intensely disliked his wife, avoiding her whenever possible. On the way to Mithilā, when his wife climbed up a fig-tree in order to assuage her hunger, he put thorns round the tree and left her there. King **Videha** of Mithilā rescued her and married her, naming her **Udumbarā.** Some time later she saw Piṅguttara mending the road, and smiled at her own good fortune. The king was ready to kill her out of jealousy, but **Mahosadha** saved her life.[1]

[1] J. vi. 347 f.

Piṭakattayalakkhaṇa.—A treatise ascribed by the **Pārupaṇas** to **Buddhaghosa.**[1]

[1] P.L.C. 189; Bode, *op. cit.*, 75.

Piṭṭhigāma.—A monastery built in **Kārapiṭṭhi** by **Moggallāna III.**[1]

[1] Cv. xliv. 50.

Piṇḍa Sutta.—Once the Buddha was at **Pañcasālā** when the day came for all young people to send gifts to each other. The Buddha went to the village for alms, but the villagers, influenced by **Māra,** gave him nothing, and he returned with his empty bowl. Māra tried to influence the Buddha to go a second time, but this he refused to do.[1] The Commentary says[2] that Māra did not want the Buddha to accept the gifts of the maidens and to preach to them, because then they would pass beyond his evil influence.

[1] S. i. 113; the incident is also found at DhA. iii., p. 257 f. [2] SA. i. 141.

Piṇḍapātadāyaka-Tissa.—One of the four names given to **Vanavāsi-Tissa** (that being the last), because, when he came to **Sāvatthi,** the citizens vied with one another to do him honour, and in two days he was given one thousand bowls of alms and one thousand garments, all of which he gave to the Order. This was due to his having given in a previous birth a piece of cloth to an Elder.[1]

[1] DhA. ii. 88.

Piṇḍapātapārisuddha Sutta.—Preached at **Veḷuvana** in **Rājagaha. Sāriputta** visits the Buddha and tells him that most of his time is spent aloof. The Buddha praises him and says that all monks should practise constant review and self-questioning when they go begging for alms, and should rid themselves of the evils they have and develop those virtues they already possess.[1]

[1] M. iii. 293 ff.

Piṇḍapātika Thera.—An arahant. Ninety-two kappas ago he was in the **Tusita**-world in the time of **Tissa** Buddha and, leaving there, he gave alms to the Buddha.[1]

[1] Ap. i. 285.

Piṇḍapātika-Tissa.—An Elder of the kingdom of **Devaputta.** He is mentioned in a list of arahants, who, having become arahants by the development of *ānāpāṇasati*, could limit the term of their lives.[1]

[1] Vsm. 292.

Piṇḍapātiya-Tissa.—A monk resident in **Ambariya-vihāra.**[1] For his story see **Dārubhaṇḍaka-Mahātissa.**

[1] AA. i. 276 f.

Piṇḍasakuṇiya Sutta.—The story of a fowler of **Rājagaha,** born as a peta.[1]

[1] S. ii. 256.

Piṇḍika Sutta.—The five kinds of persons who eat only out of one bowl.[1]

A. iii. 220.

Piṇḍola.—A Pacceka Buddha, given in a nominal list.[1]

[1] M. iii. 69; ApA. i. 106.

Piṇḍola Sutta.—The Buddha explains to some monks at the **Ghositārāma** that **Piṇḍola-Bhāradvāja** had realized truth through having cultivated three controlling faculties: mindfulness, concentration, and insight. These accomplish the destruction of birth, old age, and death.[1]

[1] S. v. 224 f.

Piṇḍola-Bhāradvāja.—The son of the chaplain of King **Udena** of **Kosambī.** He belonged to the **Bhāradvāja-gotta.** He learnt the Vedas and became a successful teacher, but, finding his work distasteful, he went to **Rājagaha.** There he saw the gifts and favours bestowed on the Buddha's disciples and joined the Order. He was very greedy, and went about with a large bowl made of dried gourd, which he kept under his bed at night and which made a scraping sound when touched; but the Buddha refused to allow him a bag for it until it should be worn down by constant contact. Later he followed the Buddha's advice, conquered his intemperance in diet, and became an arahant. He then announced before the Buddha his readiness to answer the questions of any doubting monks, thus uttering his "lion's roar." The Buddha declared him chief of the "ḷion-roarers."[1] The Udāna[2] contains the praise uttered by him of the Buddha, because of his perfected self-mastery.

Piṇḍola was in the habit of taking his siesta in Udena's park at Kosambī. (He had been king in a former birth and had spent many days in that park.) One day Udena's women, who had come to the park with him, left him asleep and crowded round Piṇḍola to hear him preach. Udena, noticing their absence, went in search of them, and, in his anger, ordered a nest of red ants to be put on Piṇḍola's body. But Piṇḍola vanished and returned to Sāvatthi, where the Buddha related the **Mahānāga Jātaka**[3] and also the **Guhaṭṭhaka Sutta.**[4] Later,[5] we find Udena consulting him at the same spot and following his advice regarding

[1] A. i. 23; AA. i. 112 f.; ThagA. i. 245 f.; UdA. 252; SA. iii. 26.

[2] iv. 6.

[3] J. iv. 375 ff.; SA. iii. 26 says that when the king went to fetch the red ants from an asoka-tree, the ants fell on him and started to sting him. The women, under pretence of helping him, picked up the ants that fell from him and replaced them on his body, because they were angry at his rudeness to Piṇḍola.

[4] SNA. ii. 514 f.

[5] S. iv. 110 f.; SA. iii. 26.

the control of the senses. In the Vinaya[6] we find the Buddha rebuking Piṇḍola for performing a cheap miracle. The seṭṭhi of Rājagaha had placed a sandal-wood bowl on a high pole and challenged any holy person to bring it down. Piṇḍola heard of this and, at **Moggallāna's** suggestion, rose in the air by magic power and brought it down. The Buddha blamed him for using his great gifts for an unworthy end. The bowl was given to the monks to be ground into sandal-paste.

In the time of **Padumuttara** Buddha, Piṇḍola had been a lion in **Himavā**. The Buddha visited the lion in his cave, who waited on him for seven days, paying him great honour. Later, the lion died and was reborn in **Haṃsavatī**, where he heard the Buddha preach and declare one of his disciples chief of the "lion-roarers." Eight kappas ago he was a king named **Paduma.**[7]

The Theragāthā contains two verses[8] of Piṇḍola, uttered by him to a former friend, to convince him that he was no longer greedy and self-seeking. The Milindapañha[9] contains two other verses not traced elsewhere.

Dhammapāla says[10] that Piṇḍola was so called because he entered the Order from love of food (*piṇḍaṃ ulamāno pariyesamāno pabbajito ti, Piṇḍolo.*)

[6] Vin. ii. 110 f.; the story is given in greater detail at DhA. iii. 201 ff.; see also J. iv. 263.

[7] AA. i. 111 f.; Ap. i. 50 f.; ThagA. i. 244 f.; the last seems to identify him with Piyālaphaladāyaka of the Apadāna (ii. 444).

[8] vs. 123-4.

[9] pp. 398, 404.

[10] UdA. 252; see also SA. iii. 26.

Piṇḍolya Sutta.—The Buddha retires for his siesta to the **Mahāvana,** near **Kapilavatthu,** and the thought occurs to him that he should admonish the monks and look after them tenderly as some of them had only lately joined the Order. **Sahampatī** appears before him and confirms his intention. The Buddha thereupon goes to the **Nigrodhārāma,** makes the monks come to him in ones and twos, and talks to them. The life of a recluse is the meanest of callings—to be called a "scrap-gatherer." It is entered on by householders solely as a means of escaping from woe. The man who leaves the world and who yet does not fulfil the life of a recluse, is like a faggot from a funeral pyre, burnt at both ends and smeared with filth. Therefore should the monks shun thoughts of lust, ill-will and hurt, and practise the four *satipaṭṭhānas*. Thus will they obtain release.[1]

[1] S. iii. 91 ff.

Pitirājā.—See **Vaṭṭagāmaṇī.**

Pippali-māṇava.—See **Pipphali-māṇava.**

Pipphaligūhā.—A cave near **Rājagaha,** evidently a favourite haunt of **Mahā Kassapa.** Once when he lay there grievously ill, the Buddha visited him and cheered him by talking to him of the seven *bojjhaṅgas.*[1] On another occasion, Mahā Kassapa spent several days there in a trance, and when, at the end of that period, he entered Rājagaha for alms, **Sakka,** with **Sujātā,** waited for him in the guise of a weaver, and his wife gave him a meal. When Kassapa discovered this, he asked Sakka not to do such a thing again; but the Buddha heard Sakka's song of triumph when his meal was accepted and praised him for his gift.[2] On another occasion, when Kassapa was in the Pipphaliguhā, he had two novices waiting on him. One was lazy and a liar and took the credit for the work, all of which was done by the other. Kassapa admonished him, and he then set fire to the Elder's hut and ran away.[3] One day, as Kassapa sat in the Pipphaliguhā, he tried to contemplate the rising and falling of living beings, but the Buddha discouraged him, saying that such a task was beyond his abilities.[4] The goddess **Lājā** (*q.v.*), who had been born in **Tāvatiṃsa** as a reward for a meal which she once gave to Kassapa, attempted to sweep his cell in the Pipphaliguhā and to look after it, but Kassapa rejected her services.[5]

[1] S. v. 79.
[2] Ud. iii. 7; UdA. 195 f.; DhA. i. 427 f.; see also Ud. i. 6.
[3] DhA. ii. 19 f.
[4] *Ibid.*, i. 258 f.
[5] *Ibid.*, iii. 6 ff.

Pipphali-māṇava, Pipphalī-kumāra, Pipphalī-brāhmaṇa.—The name of **Mahā Kassapa** in a previous birth. The correct form is probably **Pippali-māṇava.**

Pipphali-vihāra.—A monastery in **Soṇagiripāda** in Ceylon. It was the residence of a monk named **Soṇa**[1] (*q.v.*). *v.l.* **Sabbagiri-vihāra.**

[1] VibhA. 439.

Piya Vagga.—The sixteenth chapter of the Dhammapada.

1. **Piya Sutta.**—A monk who is virtuous, learned, lovely in speech, who cultivates the four jhānas and possesses emancipation in mind and through insight—such a monk is pious and pleasing in *brahmacariyā.*[1]

[1] A. iii. 262.

2. **Piya Sutta.**—**Pasenadi** visits the Buddha and tells him of certain thoughts which had arisen in his mind regarding self. Those whose

conduct in deed, word, and thought is evil, for them the self is a hateful enemy, because that which one enemy would do to another, that they do to the self. For those whose conduct is virtuous, the self is a dear friend. The Buddha approves of the king's exposition.[1]

[1] S. i. 71 f.

3. **Piya Sutta.**—On seven qualities which make a monk beloved of his fellows.[1]

[1] A. iv. 1 f.

4. **Piya Sutta.**—Seven other similar qualities.[1]

[1] A. iv. 2.

5, 6. **Piya Sutta.**—Eight similar qualities.[1]

[1] A. iv. 155 f., 156.

Piyaka.—The treasurer (*Kosārakkha*) of King **Muṇḍa.** When Muṇḍa abandoned himself to grief at the death of his wife **Bhaddā,** Piyaka arranged for him to visit **Nārada** at the **Kukkuṭārāma.** After the visit, Muṇḍa was consoled and ordered Piyaka to build a thūpa for Bhaddā's remains.[1]

[1] A. iii. 57 ff.

Piyaketa.—One of the three palaces of **Vidhurapaṇḍita.**[1]

[1] J. vi. 289.

Piyaṅkara.—A little boy-yakkha. While his mother, with him on her hip, was seeking for food at night, she came unexpectedly to **Jetavana** where **Anuruddha** was reciting some verses. The sound pleased her and she stood " smitten to the marrow, like a post," hushing to sleep her child who was whimpering for food.[1]

[1] S. 209; also Vsm. 382; DA. ii. 509; and PSA. 79, where she is called a vimāna-peta.

Piyaṅkara Sutta.—Records the incident, above related, of **Piyaṅkara's** mother.

Piyaṅga-pariveṇa.—A building attached to the **Mahāvihāra.**[1] *v.l.* **Ciṅgara-pariveṇa.**

[1] VibhA. 292.

Piyaṅgalla.—A village of Ceylon, in the **Koṭṭhivāta** district. The Mahāvaṃsa relates an incident of a monk of this village who wished to have a share in the building of the **Mahā Thūpa,** in spite of the orders of **Duṭṭhagāmaṇī.**[1]

[1] Mhv. xxx. 29 ff.

Piyaṅgudīpa.—An island, probably near Ceylon, the monks of which enjoyed a reputation for extreme holiness. When **Duṭṭhagāmaṇī,** fleeing from **Cūlaṅganiyapiṭṭhi,** wished to give alms though having so little food, an arahant Thera came from Piyaṅgudīpa to accept it as soon as the time of the almsgiving was announced by the minister **Tissa.**[1] Again, when **Duṭṭhagāmaṇī,** after his conquest of the **Damiḷas,** was filled with remorse for his slaughter of men, arahants of Piyaṅgudīpa read his thoughts and came to console him.[2] Mention is made of as many as twelve thousand monks living on Piyaṅgudīpa.[3]

[1] Mhv. xxiv. 24 ff. [2] *Ibid.*, xxv. 104 ff. [3] *Ibid.*, xxxii. 55.

Piyajātika Sutta.—The Buddha tells a householder, who is mourning for his son, that dear ones always bring sorrow and tribulation. The man, however, disagreed with this view and did not scruple to say so wherever he went. **Pasenadi** taunted **Mallikā** with this, and she sent **Nālijaṅgha** to the Buddha to ask if these were his words. The Buddha convinced him by means of various examples that the statement was true, and when this was reported to Mallikā, she was able to prove to Pasenadi that the Buddha's teaching was in accordance with facts.[1]

[1] M. ii. 106 ff.

Piyajālī.—A teacher of the Abhidhamma who handed it down in pupillary succession.[1]

[1] DhSA., p. 32.

Piyañjaha Thera.—He belonged to the family of a **Licchavi** nobleman of **Vesālī** and, when he grew up, his chief interest was war, hence his name ("ever destroying what is dear to his enemies"). When the Buddha visited Vesāli, Piyañjaha found faith in him, joined the Order and became an arahant, dwelling in the forest.

In the time of **Vipassī** Buddha he had been a tree-sprite, and, standing on the edge of a concourse of devas because his influence was small, he had heard the Buddha preach. One day seeing a bank of pure sand by a beautiful river, he reflected that the Buddha's virtues were more numerous than even the grains of sand. Seventy-three kappas ago he was a king named **Pulinapupphiya.**[1] He is probably identical with **Ñāṇasaññaka** of the Apadāna.[2]

[1] Thag. vs. 76; ThagA. i. 168 f. [2] Ap. i. 161.

1. **Piyadassī.**—The thirteenth of the twenty-four Buddhas. He was born in **Sudhañña (Sudassana)** and his mother was **Sucandā (Candā).** He was called Piyadassī because he showed many pleasing miracles. For nine thousand years he lived as a layman in three palaces: **Sunimala, Vimala** and **Giriguhā (Giribrahā).** His wife was **Vimalā** and his son **Kañcanavela (Kañcana).** He left home in a chariot and practised austerities for six months. He was given milk-rice by **Vasabha's** daughter and grass for his seat by the **Ājīvaka Sujāta.** His bodhi was a *Kakudha* tree. Among his converts were the deva-king **Sudassana** and the elephant **Doṇamukha.** A monk named **Soṇa** conspired with Prince **Mahāpaduma** to kill the Buddha, Doṇamukha being the elephant they used in their unsuccessful plot. *cp.* **Nālāgiri.**

Piyadassi's chief disciples were **Pālita** and **Sabbadassī** among monks and **Sujātā** and **Dhammadinnā** among nuns, his constant attendant being **Sobhita. Sannaka** and **Dhammika** were his chief lay patrons among men, and **Visākhā** and **Dhammadinnā** among women. He lived for ninety thousand years and died at **Assatthārāma,** his thūpa being three leagues in height. The Bodhisatta of that time was a brahmin named **Kassapa,** and he built a monastery for the Buddha at a cost of one hundred thousand crores.[1]

[1] Bu. xiv. 1 ff.; BuA. 172 ff.; J. i. 38 f., etc.

2. **Piyadassī.**—A Pacceka Buddha.[1]

[1] M. iii. 69; Ap. i. 106.

3. **Piyadassī Thera.**—An arahant. He was present with sixty thousand others, from **Jetārāma,** at the foundation ceremony of the **Mahā Thūpa.**[1] He stood on the north-east side at the ceremony, and at the close of it he preached to **Duṭṭhagāmaṇī.**[2]

[1] Dpv. xix. 15; Mhv. xxix. 32. [2] *Ibid.*, 65; MṬ. 531.

4. **Piyadassī.**—A seṭṭhi of **Sudassananigama,** whose daughter gave milk-rice to **Sikhī** Buddha.[1]

[1] BuA. 201.

5. **Piyadassī.**—A Thera of Ceylon, incumbent of the **Devarāja-vihāra.** He was a pupil of the grammarian **Moggallāna** and wrote the Pāli grammar, **Padasādhana.**[1]

[1] P.L.C. 205.

6. **Piyadassī.**—A name for **Dhammāsoka** (*q.v.*)

Piyapāla.—A teacher of the Abhidhamma.[1]

[1] DhSA., p. 32.

Piyā.—The eldest of the five daughters of the third **Okkāka,** her mother being **Hatthā.** She developed a skin disease, and her brothers, not wishing to be near her, took her into the forest and left her near a pond. There she met **Rāma,** king of Benares, who, afflicted with a similar disease, was living in exile in the forest. After hearing Piyā's story, he married her, and they had thirty-two children, who became the ancestors of the **Koliyans.**[1]

[1] SNA. i. 352 f., 355 f.; DA. i. 258; MṬ. 131.

Piyālapupphiya Thera.—An arahant. Ninety-one kappas ago he was a hunter who, seeing the Buddha **Vipassī,** threw a *piyāla*-flower on the path whereon he had trodden.[1]

[1] Ap. i. 220.

Piyālaphaladāyaka Thera.—An arahant. Thirty-one kappas ago he was a hunter, and seeing the Buddha **Nārada,** he offered him a *piyāla*-fruit.[1] He is probably identical with **Piṇḍola-Bhāradvāja.**[2] See also **Phaladāyaka.**

[1] Ap. i. 440 f. [2] ThagA. i. 245.

Piyālī.—Fifteen kappas ago there were three kings of this name, previous births of **Devasabha Thera.**[1]

[1] ThagA. i. 188; but see Ap. i. 170, where they are called **Mālabhī.**

Pilakkhaguhā.—A cave near **Kosambī.** The **Paribbājaka Sandaka** is said to have stayed there. Near by was the **Devakaṭasobbha.**[1] The cave was so called because a *pilakkha*-tree grew in front of it.[2]

[1] M. i. 513. [2] MA. ii. 687.

Pilakkhaphaladāyaka Thera.—An arahant. Eighteen kappas ago he met the Buddha **Atthadassī** and gave him a *pilakkha*-fruit.[1] His Apadāna verses are, in the Theragāthā Commentary, attributed both to **Dhammapāla**[2] and to **Passika.**[3] There may have been two of the same name.

[1] Ap. i. 296, repeated at Ap. ii. 410. [2] ThagA. i. 326. [3] *Ibid.*, 355.

Pilavasu.—A fortress erected by **Parakkamabāhu I.**[1]

[1] Cv. lxx. 93, 97.

Pilaviṭṭhi.—A locality in the **Dakkhiṇadesa** of Ceylon, where there was a fortress.[1] It is perhaps identical with **Pillaviṭṭhi.**

[1] Cv. lxix. 8; lxx. 71.

Piliṃvatthu.—A village near **Badalatthalagāma.**[1]

[1] Cv. lxv. 5.

Pilicchakoḷi.—A locality in Ceylon.[1]

[1] SA. ii. 169.

Pilinda, Pilindī.—The personal name of **Pilinda-Vaccha** (*q.v.*).

Pilindagāma.—Another name for **Ārāmikagāma** (*q.v.*).

Pilinda-Vaccha, Pilindi-Vaccha, Pilindiya-Vaccha.—He was a brahmin of **Sāvatthi,** born before the Buddha's Enlightenment. Pilinda was his personal name, Vaccha being that of his family. He became a recluse and learnt the **Cūla-Gandhāra-vijjā,** but, when the Buddha appeared, the charm refused to work. Having heard that the **Mahā-Gandhāra** prevented the working of the **Cūla-Gandhāra** and having concluded that the Buddha knew the former, he entered the Order at the Buddha's suggestion, in order to acquire it. The Buddha gave him exercises in meditation, and he became an arahant.

Certain devas who had been born in the deva-world as a result of Pilinda's guidance in a former birth, out of gratitude, waited on him morning and evening. He thus became famous as being dear to the devas, and was declared by the Buddha to be chief among such monks.[1]

In the time of **Padumuttara** Buddha, he was a rich householder of **Haṃsavatī** and wished to become a monk beloved of the devas. In the time of **Sumedha Buddha** he was born in the world of men and paid great honour to the Buddha's thūpa. In a later existence he was a cakkavattī, named **Varuṇa,** and established his subjects in righteousness, so that after death they were born in heaven.[2]

Pilinda had a habit of addressing everyone as *Vasala* (outcaste). When this was reported to the Buddha he explained that this was because Pilinda had, for one hundred lives, been born among Vasalavādī brahmins.[3] One day, on entering **Rājagaha,** Pilinda met a man carrying a bowl of *pipphalī* (long pepper). "What's in thy bowl, Vasala?" he asked, and the man, in anger, said, "The dung of mice." "So be it,"

[1] A. i. 24. [2] ThagA. i. 51 f. [3] Ud. iii. 6; DhA. iv. 181 f.

said Pilinda, and the pepper turned into dung. The man was horrified, and, seeking Pilinda, persuaded him to right the matter.[4]

The Vinaya Piṭaka[5] mentions that on several different occasions Pilinda suffered from various ailments and the Buddha had to give permission for the provision of suitable remedies. Once **Bimbisāra** found Pilinda clearing a cave in order to provide a cell for himself. The king promised to build a monastery for him if he could obtain the Buddha's sanction. The permission was obtained and was reported to the king, but he forgot the matter until one hundred days later. On remembering, he made ample amends, gave Pilinda five hundred attendants to look after the monastery, and granted for their maintenance a village, which came to be called **Ārāmikagāma** or **Pilindagāma.** One day, while in the village for alms, Pilinda went into a house where a girl was weeping because the day was a feast-day and she had no ornament to wear, her parents being too poor to afford any. Pilinda gave her a roll of grass to put round her head and it turned instantly into solid gold. The king's officers, hearing of this wreath, suspected the family of theft and cast them into prison. The next day Pilinda, discovering what had happened, visited the king and convinced him of his *iddhi*-powers by turning the whole palace into gold. The family was released, and the king and his courtiers gave to Pilinda large quantities of the five medicaments, all of which Pilinda distributed among those who wished for them.[6]

Another story is related[7] of Pilinda's *iddhi*-powers. Once a family of Benares, which was wont to minister to Pilinda, was attacked by robbers and two girls were kidnapped. Pilinda, by his *iddhi*-power caused them to be brought back, and the monks complained of this to the Buddha, but the Buddha held that no wrong had been done. The Apadāna[8] has two sets of verses ascribed to Pilinda, the second very much longer than the first, thus supporting the view mentioned earlier (see *note* [5]), that there were two Theras named Pilindavaccha. In any event, there has evidently been a confusion of legends, and it is no longer possible to separate them. It is the first set of Apadāna verses which is quoted in the Theragāthā Commentary.[9] In the second set we are told that in

[4] AA. i. 154 f.

[5] Vin. i. 204 f.; some hold (*e.g., Brethren* 14, n. 4) that the Thera of Rājagaha, mentioned in the following stories, was distinct from the Thera of Sāvatthi. See below.

[6] Vin. i. 206 ff.; iii. 248 ff. This was the occasion for the forming of the rule that all medicaments required by a monk should be used within seven days. It was in reference to this that the **Gandhāra Jātaka** (J. iii. 363 ff.) was preached. The incident of the palace being turned into gold is referred to at Kvu. 608.

[7] Vin. iii. 67.

[8] i. 59 f.; 302-16.

[9] *Loc. cit.*

the time of **Padumuttara** Buddha, Pilinda was a very wealthy *dovārika.* He took many precious gifts to **Ānanda,** Padumuttara's father, and won from him a boon. He asked, as his boon, that he should be allowed to entertain the Buddha. The king refused to grant this, but the *dovārika* appealed to the judges and they gave the verdict in his favour. Thereupon he held a great almsgiving of unparalleled splendour for seven days and gave away all manner of gifts. As a result he was born one thousand times as king of the devas and one thousand times also as king of men. In his last birth he suffered from neither heat nor cold, dust did not adhere to his body, and the rain did not wet him.

Piliya.—A seṭṭhi of Benares, a previous birth of **Devadatta.** For his story see **Asampadāna Jātaka.**[1]

[1] J. i. 466 ff.

Piliyakkha.—A king of Benares, a former birth of **Ānanda.** For his story see the **Sāma Jātaka.**[1]

[1] J. vi. 71 ff.; also Mil. 198; Mtu. ii. 212, 216, 226.

1. **Pilotika.**—A **Paribbājaka. Jānussoṇi** once met him returning from **Jetavana,** where he had gone early to wait on the Buddha. Pilotika, on being questioned, spoke very highly of the Buddha. It is this conversatiou which, on its being repeated by Jānussoṇi to the Buddha, led to the preaching of the **Cullahatthipadopama Sutta.**[1] Jānussoṇi addresses Pilotika as **Vacchāyana,** which, according to the Commentary,[2] was the name of his clan. From the same source we gather that the Paribbājaka's own name was **Pilotikā;** he was young, of a golden colour, and loved ministering to the Buddha and the Buddha's eminent disciples. He is spoken of, together with **Sabhiya,**[3] as a wise Paribbājaka. Pilotika is identified with **Devinda** of the **Mahā-Ummagga Jātaka.**[4]

[1] M. i. 175 ff.
[2] MA. i. 393.
[3] SA. ii. 188.
[4] J. vi. 478.

2. **Pilotika Thera.**—**Ānanda** once saw a poor youth going along in a ragged garment, a potsherd in his hand. Ānanda took him to the monastery and ordained him. The youth hung his garment and the potsherd on the branch of a tree and practised meditation. After a time he became fat and discontented and wished to return to the lay life. But on noticing his rag and his potsherd, he realized his folly and, admonishing himself, returned to his meditation. Three times the same thing happened, but in the end he became an arahant. He used to speak of the rag as his "teacher."[1]

[1] DhA. iii. 84 f.

Pilotikakamma.—A chapter in the Apadāna[1] which mentions various incidents in the lives of the Bodhisatta, as a result of which the Buddha, in his last life, had to suffer physical ailments and calumny. See **Pubba-kammapiloti.**

[1] Ap. i. 299 f.; repeated in UdA. 263 f.

Pillaviṭṭhi.—A village near the **Kālavāpi,** mentioned in the account of the campaigns of **Parakkamabāhu I.**[1] It is very probably identical with **Pilaviṭṭhi.**[2]

[1] Cv. lxxii. 163, 170. [2] Cv. *Trs.* i. 335, n. 4.

Piḷayamāra.—A Damiḷa usurper, the senāpati of **Panayamāra,** whom he slew. He, in his turn, was slain by his own senapāti **Dāṭhika.** Piḷa-yamāra reigned for seven years (between 44-29 B.C.).[1]

[1] Mhv. xxxiii. 58; Dpv. xix. 15; xx. 16.

Pihita Sutta.—The world is shut in by death.[1]

[1] S. i. 40.

Piṭha Jātaka (No. 337).—The Bodhisatta was once an ascetic in the Himālaya. One day, having gone to Benares for salt and vinegar, he entered the city for alms and went to the house of a merchant with a reputation for piety. But the merchant was away at the court, and as the ascetic saw no one in the house, he turned and went away. On the way he was met by the merchant, who apologised for his absence and invited him to return to his house.

The story was told to a monk, who, on joining the Order, inquired who looked after the monks. On being told that **Anāthapiṇḍika** and **Visakhā** did so, he went to their houses very early the next day. It was so early that no one attended to him. When he returned later it was too late and the food had all gone. Thereupon he started abusing the two families.[1]

[1] J. iii. 118 ff.

Pīṭha Vagga.—The first chapter of the Vimānavatthu.

Piṭhiya.—A Damiḷa usurper who ruled at **Anurādhapura** for seven months, in the time of **Dhātusena.**[1]

[1] Cv. xxxviii. 34.

Pītavimānavatthu.—The story of a woman of **Rājagaha.** When **Ajātasattu** erected a thūpa over the Buddha's relics at Rājagaha, she started early one morning with four *kosātakī*-flowers to offer at the thūpa. On the way there she was gored to death by a cow, and was reborn in **Tāvatiṃsa,** wearing yellow garments. There **Moggallāna** met her and learned her story.[1]

[1] Vv. iv. 9; VvA. 200 f.

Pīti Sutta.—**Sāriputta** tells **Ānanda** how, by the fading away of zest (*pīti*), he had dwelt in the third *jhāna*.[1]

[1] S. iii. 236.

Pītimalla, Pītimallaka, Pītamallaka.—A thera. Having won the flags of three countries, he went on a visit to Ceylon and was honoured by the king. While passing the door of the **Kiñjakāsanasālā,** he heard a monk reciting the "**Na-tumhāka**" **Vagga,** and, touched thereby, he went to the Mahāvihāra and joined the Order. Having learnt the two Mātikā, he went with thirty others to **Gavaravāliya-aṅgana,** and there practised meditation while walking up and down. When his legs ached he walked about on his knees. One day a hunter, mistaking him for an animal, shot at him. The dart pierced him, but he filled the wound with herbs, lay down on a slab of rock, developed insight and attained arahantship. To the monks who gathered round him he expressed his great joy at having succeeded in his quest, and they said that had the Buddha been alive he would have stroked his head.[1] His story is given[2] as an example of a monk striving amid great discomfort.

[1] MA. i. 190.

[2] *E.g.*, AA. i. 29; SA. ii. 216.

Pīlapiṭṭhi.—A monastery in Ceylon, built by king **Kaniṭṭhatissa.**[1]

[1] Mhv. xxxvi. 15.

Pukkāma.—A city in Burma (**Arimaddana**).[1]

[1] Cv. lxvii. 74.

1. **Pukkusa.**—A counsellor of **Maddava,** king of Benares. For details see the **Dasaṇṇaka Jātaka.** Pukkusa is identified with **Sāriputta.**[1]

[1] J. iii. 341.

2. **Pukkusa.**—One of the four ministers of **Vedeha,** king of **Mithilā.** He joined with his three companions in a conspiracy against **Mahosadha,** stealing a golden necklace from the king's palace in order to try and implicate Mahosadha. The details are given in the **Mahāummagga**

Jātaka.[1] On Pukkusa's thigh was a leprous spot, which he hid from the king because the king loved to lay his head on Pukkusa's lap. Only his younger brother knew of this secret; but it was discovered later by Mahosadha, and Pukkusa was sent to prison. Pukkusa is identified with **Poṭṭhapāda.**[2]

[1] J. vi. 330 ff. [2] *Ibid.*, 478.

3. **Pukkusa.**—A **Mallarājaputta.** He was a disciple of **Āḷāra Kālama,** and one day, while on his way from **Kusinārā** to **Pāvā,** he saw the Buddha seated under a tree by the roadside and stayed to talk to him. He mentioned that once five hundred carts had passed by where Āḷāra sat, and yet so deep was he in meditation that he had failed to notice them. The Buddha told him how, when he himself was in **Ātumā** in the **Bhusāgāra,** there was a great thunderstorm which killed two peasants and four oxen, but that he had heard and seen nothing, so deep was his concentration. Pukkusa was greatly impressed by this statement, and, having declared himself a follower of the Buddha, he gave to the Buddha two robes of cloth of gold, one of which, at the Buddha's suggestion, he handed to **Ānanda.** When Pukkusa had left, Ānanda draped one robe over the Buddha, and was greatly astonished at its pale appearance in comparison with the deep gold of the Buddha's body.[1]

Buddhaghosa says[2] that Pukkusa was a merchant, and was the owner of the five hundred carts which had crossed the **Kakkuṭṭhā** (*q.v.*) shortly before the incident above mentioned.

[1] D. ii. 130 ff. [2] DA. ii. 569.

4. **Pukkusa.**—The name of a caste, classified among the despised castes.[1] The Commentary explains[2] them as "those who sweep up flowers which are offered at shrines and are not removed by the devotees who have given them." The word Pukkusa was evidently not despised as a personal name because, in the case of **Pukkusa** (3), for instance, the person bearing the name was a khattiya.

[1] *E.g.*, A. ii. 85; M. ii. 152. [2] *E.g.*, AA. ii. 523.

Pukkusāti.—A young monk whom the Buddha met at the house of **Bhaggava,** the potter, in **Rājagaha.** Pukkusāti was already occupying the guest-room of the house, and the Buddha asked to be allowed to share it, to which Pukkusāti readily agreed. They sat together for some time in silence, and then the Buddha preached the **Dhātuvibhaṅga Sutta.** Pukkusāti recognised the Buddha at the end of the sermon and begged his forgiveness for not having paid him due honour; he then begged to have the *upasampadā* conferred on him. The Buddha consented and sent him to procure a begging bowl and a robe. On the way Pukkusāti was gored to death by a mad cow. When this was reported to the Buddha, he said that Pukkusāti was an Anāgāmin and had been born in the realms above, never more to return.[1]

In his comments on the Dhātuvibhaṅga Sutta, Buddhaghosa[2] gives a long account of Pukkusāti. He had been the king of **Takkasilā,** contemporary of **Bimbisāra** and of about the same age. A friendly alliance was established between the two kings through the medium of merchants who travelled between the two countries for purposes of trade. In the course of time, although the two kings had never seen each other, there grew up between them a deep bond of affection. Pukkusāti once sent to Bimbisāra, as a gift, eight priceless garments in lacquered caskets. This gift was accepted at a special meeting of the whole court, and Bimbisāra having nothing of a material nature which he considered precious enough to send to Pukkusāti, conceived the idea of acquainting Pukkusāti with the appearance in the world of the Three Jewels (*ratanāni*)—the Buddha, the Dhamma, and the Saṅgha. He had inscribed on a golden plate, four cubits long and a span in breadth, descriptions of these Three Jewels and of various tenets of the Buddha's teachings, such as the *satipaṭṭhānā*, the Noble Eightfold Path, and the Thirty-seven factors of Enlightenment. This plate was placed in the innermost of several caskets of various precious substances, and was taken in procession on the back of the state elephant up to the frontier of Bimbisāra's kingdom. Similar honours were paid to it by the chiefs of other territories, through which lay the route to Takkasilā. When Pukkusāti, in the solitude of his chamber, read the inscription on the plate, he was filled with boundless joy and decided to renounce the world. He cut off his hair, donned the yellow robes of a monk, and left the palace alone amid the lamentations of his subjects. He travelled the one hundred and ninety-two leagues to **Sāvatthi,** passing the gates of **Jetavana ;** but having understood from Bimbisāra's letter that the Buddha was at Rājagaha, he omitted to enquire for him at Jetavana, and travelled on forty-five leagues more to Rājagaha, only to find that the Buddha was all the time in Sāvatthi. As it was then evening, he took lodging in Bhaggava's house. The Buddha, with his divine eye, saw what was in store for Pukkusāti, and travelling *on foot* from Sāvatthi, reached Bhaggava's house at sundown, and, waiting his opportunity, engaged Pukkusāti in talk and preached to him the Dhātuvibhaṅga Sutta, as related above. After his untimely

[1] M. iii. 237-47. In this context Pukkusāti is spoken of as a *kulaputta* (iii. 238); see also J. iv. 180 and DhA. ii. 35.

[2] MA. ii. 979 ff. *Cp.* the story of **Tissa,** king of **Roruva** (ThagA. i. 199 f.).

death,[3] Pukkusāti was born in the **Avihā** world, where, together with six others, he became an arahant at the moment of his birth.[4]

Pukkhusāti was one of seven monks who, in the time of **Kassapa** Buddha, decided to abstain from eating until they should attain arahantship. They lived on the top of a mountain. The senior monk attained arahantship, the second became an anāgāmin, but the remaining five died of starvation and were reborn in **Tusita.** In this age they became, respectively, **Pukkusāti, Kumāra-Kassapa, Dāruciriya, Dabba-Mallaputta** and **Sabhiya.**[5]

[3] The cow that killed Pukkusāti is said to have been a yakkhiṇī who was a cow in one hundred births. In her last birth as a cow, she killed, in addition to Pukkusāti, **Bāhiya Dāruciriya, Tambadāṭhika,** and **Suppabuddha** the leper (DhA. ii. 35).

[4] See S. i. 35, 60, for the names of the others.

[5] Ap. ii. 473; DhA. ii. 212; UdA. 81; but see MA. i. 335, where only three are mentioned (Pukkusāti, Dāruciriya, and Kassapa).

Puggala Vagga.—Several sections of the Aṅguttara Nikāya are called by this name: the sixth of the Duka Nipāta (A. i. 76-80), the third of the Tika (A. i. 118-31), the fourteenth of the Catukka (ii. 133-39), the sixteenth of the Dasaka (v. 247-49), and the twentieth of the Dasaka (v. 281-2).

1. **Puggala Sutta.**—Seven kinds of persons who are worthy of gifts and homage.[1]

[1] A. iv. 10 f.

2. **Puggala Sutta.**—Nine kinds of persons who exist in the world: those who have attained the Four Fruits of the Path, those who are on the way thereto, and putthijjanas.[1]

[1] A. iv. 372.

3. **Puggala Sutta.**—Preached at **Sāvatthi,** to **Pasenadi,** on the four kinds of persons: those that are joined to darkness and fare to light, those that are joined to darkness and fare to darkness, those that are joined to light and fare to darkness, those that are joined to light and fare to light.[1]

[1] S. i. 93 ff.; cp. D. iii. 233; A. ii. 85; Pugg. iv. 19.

4. **Puggala Sutta.**—Incalculable is the beginning of *saṃsāra.* The bones of a single person faring on for an æon, if collected, would be a pile as great as **Vepulla.**[1]

[1] S. ii. 185.

Puggalapaññatti.—The fourth (in the present order) of the seven books of the Abhidhamma Piṭaka. It is, however, generally considered to be the earliest of the Abhidhamma books. Its subject matter is the *puggala* (person). The author first gives a table of contents of the whole work, and then follows the method of the Aṅguttara Nikāya, grouping human types first under one term, then under two, and so on up to ten. Several of the sections are found, almost complete, in the corresponding sections of the Aṅguttara. Others are found in the **Saṅgīti Sutta.**[1]

[1] For details see Morris' edition in the P.T.S. series (Introd. x-xi).

Puggalappasāda Sutta.—On the five disadvantages of devotion to a person.[1]

[1] A. iii. 270.

Puṅkoṇḍa.—A Damiḷa chief, ally of **Kulasekhara;** he fought against **Mālavacakkavatti** and captured **Semponmāri.** Later, he surrendered to **Laṅkāpura** and received much honour; but he then deserted Laṅkāpura, who had his palace burnt down. The last we hear of him is of his alliance with **Nigaḷadha.**[1]

[1] Cv. lxxvi. 139, 240, 273, 277, 278, 280, 299, 301; lxxvii. 57, 92.

Puṅkhagāma.—A village in the **Dakkhiṇadesa** of Ceylon, where **Mānābharaṇa** lived under the name of **Vīrabāhu**[1] and where **Parakkamabāhu I.** was born.[2] Parakkamabāhu subsequently erected there the **Sūtigharacetiya,** one hundred and eighty feet high, on the site of the house in which he was born.[3]

[1] Cv. lxi. 26. [2] *Ibid.*, lxxii. 18. [3] *Ibid.*, lxxix. 61.

Pucimanda Jātaka (No. 311).—Once the Bodhisatta was the sprite of a *nimba* tree in a cemetery, and one day, when a robber with stolen goods came in front of the tree, he drove him off, lest he should be discovered and impaled on a stake from the tree. When the king's officials came to find the robber, he had disappeared, and they went away. Nearby was a bodhi-tree whose sprite was **Sāriputta.**

The story was related to **Moggallāna,** who saw a man lurking near his cell, and, feeling suspicious, drove him away. Later, his suspicions were confirmed by the arrival of the king's men.[1]

[1] J. iii. 33 ff.

Pucimanda Vagga.—The second section of the Cātukka Nipāta of the Jātakaṭṭhakathā.

Pucchārāma.—A monastery, rebuilt by **Udaya I.**[1]

[1] Cv. xlix. 28. It is probably identical with the **Pubbārāma** (*q.v.*); Cv. *Trs.* i. 130 n. 2, and 144, n. 4.

Puñña-cetiya.—A cetiya attached to the monastery where **Ariyavaṃsa** wrote the **Maṇisāramañjūsā.**[1]

[1] Bode, *op. cit.*, 42.

Puññalakkhaṇā.—Wife of **Anāthapiṇḍika.**[1] *v.l.* **Puṇṇalakkhaṇā.**

[1] J. ii. 410, 415; iii. 435.

Puññavaḍḍhana.—Son of **Dhammadassī** Buddha.[1] See also **Puṇṇavaḍḍhana.**

[1] Bu. xvi. 14.

1. **Puññābhisanda Vagga.**—The sixth chapter of the Cātukka Nipāta of the Aṅguttara Nikāya.[1]

[1] A. ii. 54-65.

2. **Puññābhisanda Vagga.**—The fourth chapter of the Sotāpatti Saṃyutta.[1]

[1] S. v. 391 f.

Puṭa Sutta.—**Tālapuṭa** visits the Buddha and asks him if there be any truth in the tradition that stage-actors are born, after death, among the **Pahāsadevā.** The Buddha refuses at first to answer the question, but, on being pressed, he says that the truth is that actors are born in the **Pahāsa-niraya.** Tālapuṭa thereupon starts to weep to think that he should have been so long deceived. He enters the Order and, in due course, becomes an arahant.[1]

[1] S. iv. 306 f.

Puṭadūsaka Jātaka (No. 280).—The Bodhisatta was once a householder, and one day, on going to the park, he saw the gardener picking large leaves and throwing them on the ground for pottles, and the chief monkey who lived in the park destroying them as they fell. The monkey, on being questioned, said it was his nature to destroy these things; thereupon the Bodhisatta drove him away.

The story was related in reference to the young son of a gardener of **Sāvatthi.** The owner of the garden invited the monks to his park, and there they saw the gardener picking leaves for pottles and his son tearing them up. The monkey is identified with the boy.[1]

[1] J. ii. 390 ff.

Puṭabhatta Jātaka (No. 223).—**Brahmadatta,** king of Benares, had a son whom he feared, so he sent the son away with his wife, and these two lived in a village in **Kāsi.** When the king died they returned to Benares, and on the way someone gave the prince a bowl of food asking him to share it with his wife; but he ate it all, and even when he became king and she his queen, he showed her very little honour. The Bodhisatta, who was the king's counsellor, perceiving this, asked the queen to speak to the king about his neglect of her. The king confessed his fault, and thereafter showed the queen great honour.

The story was related to a landowner of Sāvatthi who once went with his wife into the country to collect a debt. On the way back, when they were famishing, someone gave a meal to be shared by them. But the man, deceiving his wife, sent her on ahead and ate the food himself. The wife, on visiting the Buddha, spoke to him of this. The two couples were identical.[1]

[1] J. ii. 202 ff. *Cp.* **Godha Jātaka.**

Puṭabhattasilā, Puṭabhattasela.—A mountain in Ceylon where **Parakkamabāhu I.** built a monastery for the **Araññavāsī** fraternity.[1] This was the residence of several well-known scholars, such as **Dhammakitti.**[2]

[1] Cv. lxxxiv. 24. [2] P.L.C. *s.v.*

1. **Puṇḍarīka.**—One of the state elephants of **Pasenadi.**[1]

[1] DhA. ii. 1.

2. **Puṇḍarika.**—A Niraya; it is a period of suffering in **Avīci,** equal to twenty **Uppalakā.**[1]

[1] S. i. 152; SN., p. 126; SNA. ii. 476.

3. **Puṇḍarīka.**—One of the four treasure-troves left behind by the Buddha when he renounced the world.[1]

[1] DA. i. 284.

Puṇḍarīka Sutta.—A monk, staying in a forest tract in **Kosala,** once entered a lotus-pool and inhaled the scent of a lotus. The deva of the forest, desirous of his welfare, called him "scent-thief" and engaged him in conversation, whereby he was greatly agitated.[1]

[1] S. i. 204 f.

Puṇḍarīkā.—A class of nymphs who provided music for **Sakka,** or, perhaps, the name of some musical instruments.[1]

[1] See VvA. 93, 96, 211; and 372 f.

1. **Puṇṇa, Puṇṇaka Thera.**—He was born in the family of a householder of **Suppāraka** in the **Sunāparanta** country. When he was grown up, he went with a great caravan of merchandise to **Sāvatthi** where, having heard the Buddha preach, he left the world and joined the Order. He won favour by attention to his duties. One day he asked the Buddha for a short lesson so that, having learnt it, he might go back to dwell in Sunāparanta. The Buddha preached to him the **Puṇṇovāda Sutta** (*q.v.*). So Puṇṇa departed, and, in Sunāparanta, he became an arahant. There he won over many disciples, both male and female, and having built for the Buddha a cell out of red sandalwood (**Candanāsālā**), he sent him a flower by way of invitation. The Buddha came with five hundred arahants, spent a night in the cell, and went away before dawn.

Ninety-one kappas ago, when there was no Buddha alive, Puṇṇa was a learned brahmin, and later became a hermit in **Himavā.** Near his abode a Pacceka Buddha died, and at the moment of his death there appeared a great radiance. The ascetic cremated the body and sprinkled scented water on the pyre to extinguish the flames. A deva, witnessing the event, prophesied his future greatness. His name throughout his many lives was Puṇṇa or Puṇṇaka.[1]

In Sunāparanta he first lived at **Ambahatthapabbata,** but, on being recognised by his brother, he went to **Samuddagiri-vihāra,** where was a magnetised walk which none could use. The waves of the sea breaking made great noise, and, in order to help him to concentration, Puṇṇa caused the sea to be quiet. From there he went to **Mātulagiri,** where the incessant cries of birds disturbed him; he finally went to **Makulakagāma.** While he was there, his brother **Cūla-Puṇṇa,** with five hundred others, sailed in a trading ship, and, before embarking, he visited Puṇṇa, took the precepts from him, and asked for his protection during the voyage. The ship reached an island where red sandalwood grew; with this the merchants filled the ship, and the spirits of the island, angered by this, raised a great storm and appeared before the sailors in fearful forms. Each merchant thought of his guardian deity and Cūla-Puṇṇa of his brother. Puṇṇa, sensing his brother's need, travelled through the air to the ship, and, at sight of him, the spirits disappeared. In gratitude for their deliverance, the merchants gave to the Elder a share of their sandalwood. It was with this material that the **Candanasālā,** above referred to, was built.

Kuṇḍadhāna was the first among the arahants to be chosen to accompany the Buddha to Sunāparanta. **Sakka** provided five hundred palanquins for the journey, one of which was empty. This was subsequently taken by the ascetic **Saccabandha,** whom the Buddha converted

[1] Thag. vs. 70; ThagA. i. 156 ff.; Ap. ii. 341.

and ordained on the way. On his return journey, the Buddha stopped at the river **Nammadā,** and was entertained there by the Nāga-king.[2]

[2] MA ii. 1014 ff.; SA. iii. 14 ff.; KhA. 149.

2. **Puṇṇa, Puṇṇaka.**—A seṭṭhi of **Rājagaha,**[1] father of **Uttarā-Nandamātā.** He had been a poor man and had worked for the seṭṭhi **Sumana.** One feast day, though his master offered him a holiday, he went to work in the field, because he was too poor to be able to enjoy himself. While he was in the field **Sāriputta** came to him, and Puṇṇa gave him a toothstick and water. Puṇṇa's wife, coming with her husband's food, met Sāriputta as he was coming away, and offered him the food she carried. She cooked fresh rice and took it to her husband, who was overjoyed to hear of her gift to Sāriputta. After the meal, he rested his head for a while on his wife's lap, and, on awaking, he found that the field he had ploughed had turned into gold. He reported the matter to the king, who sent carts to fetch the gold; but as soon as his men touched it, saying that it was for the king, it turned again into earth. The gold was, therefore, gathered in Puṇṇa's name, and the king conferred on him the rank of **Bahudhana-seṭṭhi.** He built a new house, and, at the feast of inauguration, held a great almsgiving to the Buddha and the monks. When the Buddha thanked him, he and his wife and his daughter **Uttarā** (*q.v.*) became sotāpannas.[2]

It is this Puṇṇa, described as *bhataka*, that is mentioned in the Milindapañha[3] among the seven people whose acts of devotion brought reward in this very life.

[1] DhA. i. 385; iii. 104.

[2] MA. ii. 812; DhA. iii. 302 ff.; also VvA. 62 ff., where Puṇṇaka's wife is called Uttarā. In the Aṅguttara Commentary (i. 240 ff.) the man's name is given as Puṇṇasīha, of which Puṇṇa is the shortened form.

[3] pp. 115, 291; see also MA. ii. 812.

3. **Puṇṇa.**—Slave of **Meṇḍaka** (*q.v.*). He was one of the five persons of Great Merit (**Pañca-Mahāpuññā**).[1] When he ploughed the field with a single plough he made fourteen furrows, seven on each side.[2]

[1] AA. i. 219; DhA. i. 385. [2] Vsm. 383.

4. **Puṇṇa.**—A servitor (*dabbigāhaka*) who held the oblation-ladles for the seven sages, mentioned in the **Assalāyana Sutta**[1]; they were rebuked by **Asita Devala** for their pretensions regarding the superiority of brahmins.

[1] M. ii. 157; MA. ii. 785.

5. **Puṇṇa-Koliyaputta.**—A naked ascetic (*Acela*) who visited the Buddha at **Haliddavasana,** together with **Seniya Kukkuravatika.** Puṇṇa

questioned the Buddha regarding the practices of Seniya, while Seniya did likewise regarding those of Puṇṇa. The discussion is recorded in the **Kukkuravatika Sutta** (*q.v.*). At the end of the discussion, Puṇṇa declared himself a follower of the Buddha. He is called **Govatika** (one who behaved like a cow).[1] Buddhaghosa says[2] that, in order to support his bovine character, he wore horns and a tail and browsed on the grass in the company of cattle.

[1] M. i. 387 ff. [2] MA. ii. 624.

6. **Puṇṇa-Mantāniputta Thera.**—He belonged to a brahmin family of **Donavatthu** near **Kapilavatthu.** His mother was **Mantānī,** sister of **Aññākondañña.** While the Buddha was at **Rājagaha,** whither he had gone after preaching the **Dhammacakkappavattana Sutta,** Aññākoṇḍañña went to Kapilavatthu and ordained Puṇṇa. Koṇḍañña then returned to Rajagaha, whence, having taken leave of the Buddha, he retired to live on the banks of the **Chaddantadaha.** But Puṇṇa remained in Kapilavatthu, intent on his practices, and soon after became an arahant. He gathered round him five hundred clansmen who all became monks, and he taught them the ten bases of discourse (*dasa kathāvatthūni*), which he himself had learnt, and they became arahants. When they wished to visit the Buddha, Puṇṇa sent them on in advance to Rājagaha, asking them to pay homage to the Buddha in his name. Later, when the Buddha came from Rājagaha to Sāvatthi, Puṇṇa visited him and was taught the Dhamma in the Buddha's own **Gandhakuṭi. Sāriputta,** hearing of the fame of Puṇṇa, wished to meet him, and went to **Andhavana,** where Puṇṇa was spending his siesta. Sāriputta questioned him on the seven acts of purity, and Puṇṇa answered him. The two monks found great joy in each other's words.[1] Later, the Buddha declared Puṇṇa to be pre-eminent among those who preached the Dhamma.[2]

In the time of **Padumuttara** Buddha, Puṇṇa was born in a rich brahmin family of **Haṃsavatī,** before the birth of the Buddha. When grown up, he one day visited the Buddha, and as he sat on the edge of a large crowd, hearing him preach, the Buddha declared one of his monks pre-eminent among preachers, and Puṇṇa, wishing for a like honour under a future Buddha, paid great homage to Padumuttara.[3]

In the Aṅguttara Commentary,[4] however, we are told that in the time of Padumuttara Buddha, Puṇṇa was named **Gotama** and was expert in the Vedas. But he found no solace in the teaching of the Vedas and

[1] The interview with Sāriputta is given in the **Rathavinīta Sutta** (M. i. 146 ff.). Buddhaghosa says (MA. i. 362) that the two Elders had many things in common.

[2] A. i. 23; S. ii. 156.

[3] ThagA. i. 37 ff.

[4] AA. i. 113 ff.

became an ascetic with a following of eighteen thousand Jaṭilas, all of whom, under his guidance, developed great *iddhi*-powers. Puṇṇa was already old when Padumuttara attained Enlightenment. One day the Buddha visited Gotama's hermitage, and Gotama and his disciples entertained him to a meal. Afterwards the Buddha wished his chief disciple **Mahādeva** to come to the hermitage with one hundred thousand monks; this he did, and the ascetics provided flowers for their seats. For seven days the Buddha and his monks remained in trance on their seats, at the end of which period the Buddha asked the most pre-eminent preacher to render thanks. At the conclusion of the sermon, all except Gotama became arahants. Gotama wished to gain pre-eminence in preaching under a future Buddha, and Padumuttara proclaimed that his wish would find fulfilment. The Apadāna[5] contains yet another version, according to which Puṇṇa's name in the time of Padumuttara was **Sunanda.**

Besides the **Rathavinīta Sutta** mentioned above (n. 1), which bears testimony to Puṇṇa's skill as a preacher, another Sutta, of the Saṃyutta Nikāya,[6] represents **Ānanda** as saying to the assembled monks that Puṇṇa was of great help to himself and others when they were yet novices; Puṇṇa had preached to them on causation, and they were able to understand the Doctrine because of his skilful exposition.

It is, perhaps, this Puṇṇa who is identified with the gate-keeper (*dovārika*) of the **Kurudhamma Jātaka**[7] and with one of the seven brothers of the **Bhisa Jātaka.**[8] The Mahāvastu[9] contains twenty verses attributed to Pūrṇa Maitrayānīputra.

[5] Ap. i. 38, quoted at ThagA. i. 362.
[6] S. iii. 105 f.; according to ThagA. ii. 124, Ānanda became a sotāpanna after hearing a sermon by Puṇṇa.
[7] J. ii. 381.
[8] J. iv. 314.
[9] iii. 382.

7. **Puṇṇa.**—See also *s.v.* **Puṇṇaka.**

Puṇṇa Sutta.—Another name for the **Puṇṇovāda Sutta** (*q.v.*).

1. **Puṇṇaka.**—One of the stallions of Ekarāja.[1]

[1] J. vi. 135.

2. **Puṇṇaka.**—One of the sixteen disciples of **Bāvarī,** who visited the Buddha.[1] His conversation with the Buddha is given in the **Puṇṇakamāṇavapucchā.**[2] At the end of the interview Puṇṇaka and his one thousand followers became arahants.[3]

[1] SN. vs. 1006.
[2] *Ibid.*, 1043-48.
[3] SNA. ii. 590.

3. **Puṇṇaka.**—A yakkha chief, nephew of **Vessavaṇa.**[1] The story of how he won the Nāga maiden **Irandatī** is related in the **Vidhurapaṇḍita Jātaka** (*q.v.*). In his previous birth he had been a young man named **Kaccāyana** in the **Aṅga** country.[2] He is also referred to as **Puṇṇaka-rājā.**[3] He is evidently identical with the yakkha-chieftain mentioned in the **Āṭānāṭiya Sutta**[4] among those to be invoked by followers of the Buddha in times of tribulation. The gem used by Puṇṇaka as a stake in his gambling with **Koravya** was such that all things in the world could be seen in it.[5] The shout of victory uttered by Puṇṇaka when he defeated Koravya was one of the four shouts heard throughout **Jambudīpa.**[6]

[1] J. vi. 255.
[2] *Ibid.*, 273 f.; he is also called **Kātiyāna** (**Kaccāna**).
[3] J. iv. 182.
[4] D. iii. 204.
[5] MṬ. 552.
[6] SNA. i. 223.

4. **Puṇṇaka.**—A king of twenty-five kappas ago, a former birth of **Asanabodhiya Thera.**[1]

[1] Ap. i. 111.

5. **Puṇṇaka.**—Puṇṇaka was evidently not a name of high station.[1]

[1] *E.g.*, J. vi. 273.

6. **Puṇṇaka.**—See also *s.v.* **Puṇṇa.**

Puṇṇaka Jātaka.—Another name for the **Vidhurapaṇḍita Jātaka.**

Puṇṇaka(māṇava)-pucchā (or **-pañha**). — The questions asked by **Puṇṇaka,** pupil of **Bāvarī** (*q.v.*), and the Buddha's answers thereto. Those who make sacrifices and exert themselves for gain of pleasure and praise do not succeed in escaping birth and decay. Only the calm and the free can so escape.[1]

[1] SN. vs. 1043-48. They are explained in CNid. 11 ff. The questions are referred to at A. i. 133.

Puṇṇakāla.—A yakkha who, in the time of **Kakusandha** Buddha, spread in Ceylon a pestilence called **Pajjaraka.**[1]

[1] MṬ. 349.

Puṇṇaji.—One of the four friends of **Yasa** who, on hearing of his ordination by the Buddha, visited him and were taken to the Buddha. The Buddha talked to them and they became arahants. They were among the first eleven arahants, and were ordained by the "*ehi bhikkhu pabbajjā.*"[1]

[1] Vin. i. 18 f.

Puṇṇanadī Jātaka (No. 214).—The Bodhisatta was once chaplain at the court of **Brahmadatta,** king of Benares. But the king, listening to his enemies, sent the Bodhisatta away from the court, and he dwelt in a village of **Kāsi.** Later, the king, remembering his chaplain's goodness, composed a verse, wrote it on a leaf, and sent it to him, together with cooked crow's flesh. The Bodhisatta understood the message and returned to the court.

The story was related in reference to the great wisdom of the Buddha. **Ānanda** is identified with the king.[1] The Jātaka derives its name from the first two words of the verse composed by the king.

[1] J. ii. 173-5.

Puṇṇa-pariveṇa.—See **Pūjā-pariveṇa.**

Puṇṇapāti Jātaka (No. 53).—The Bodhisatta was once Treasurer of Benares, and some rogues, wishing to rob him of his money, conspired together and drugged some liquor, which they offered him as he was on his way to the palace. The Treasurer suspected them, and promised to join them on his way back from the palace. But on his return the vessels which contained the liquor were still quite full; he therefore charged the men with the intent to poison him, or they would have drunk some of the liquor during his absence. They then ran away.

The story was told to **Anāthapiṇḍika,** who had a similar experience. But in this case he was returning from the palace, and challenged the rogues to taste their own liquor first.[1]

[1] J. i. 268 ff.

Puṇṇabhadda.—The Mahā Niddesa,[1] in its explanation of *vattasuddhikā*, mentions, among others, **Puṇṇabhaddavattika, Vāsudevavattika, Baladevavattika** and **Maṇibhaddavattika.** Puṇṇabhadda is, therefore, probably the name of a yakkha like **Vāsudeva** and **Baladeva.**[2]

[1] pp. 89, 92.

[2] The N.P.D., *s.v.* Puṇṇa, suggests Puṇṇabhadda was the father of the yakkha **Harikesa.** The Mahābhārata (i. 35, 1557) gives Pūrṇabhadra as the name of a serpent.

Puṇṇamā Sutta.—Once, when the Buddha was staying in the **Migārāmātupāsāda,** a certain monk asked him a series of questions regarding the five *upādānakkhandhā*—their origin and nature, their definitions, the cause of their arising, etc. The Buddha answered his questions. At the end of the sutta is an explanation of *attā*.[1]

[1] S. iii. 100 ff.

1. **Puṇṇamāsa Thera.**—He was born in **Sāvatthi** as the son of a brahmin, named **Samiddhi;** he was called Puṇṇamāsa because, on the day of his birth, all the empty vessels in the house were filled with golden pennies. He left the world after a son had been born to him, and, having entered the Order under the Buddha, took the formula of the five impurities (*tacapañcaka*) as topic of meditation and became an arahant. His former wife adorned herself and came with her child, seeking to seduce him, but without success.

In the time of **Vipassī** Buddha he was a partridge (*cakkavāka*), and, pleased with the appearance of the Buddha, offered him a *sāla*-flower, holding it in his beak. Seventeen kappas ago he became king eight times under the name of **Sucārudassana.**[1]

He is evidently identical with **Paccāgamaniya** of the Apadāna.[2]

[1] Thag. vs. 10; ThagA. i. 53 f. [2] Ap. i. 113.

2. **Puṇṇamāsa Thera.**—He was born at **Sāvatthi** in a landowner's family. He was named Puṇṇamāsa because, on the day of his birth, all the empty vessels in the house became filled with gold and silver coins. He left the world after the birth of a son, and, dwelling near the village, put forth effort, till he became an arahant. Then going to Sāvatthi, he paid homage to the Buddha and dwelt in a charnel-field. Meanwhile his son died, and his wife, wishing to prevent the king from taking the property which was now left without an heir, went, with a large company, to her husband in order to persuade him to return to the lay-life.

In the time of **Tissa** Buddha he was wandering about the forest, bow in hand, when he saw the Buddha's robe hanging on a branch outside his cell. He immediately threw away his bow and, recalling the Buddha's virtues, paid homage to the robe.[1] He is probably identical with **Paṃsukūlasaññika** of the Apadāna.[2]

[1] Thag. vs. 171, 172; ThagA. i. 297 f. [2] Ap. ii. 418 f.

1. **Puṇṇamukha.**—One of the merchants (*seṭṭhi*) of King **Ekarāja,** whom he proposed, at the suggestion of **Khaṇḍahāla,** to sacrifice for his own welfare.[1]

[1] J. vi. 135.

2. **Puṇṇamukha.**—A royal cuckoo (*phussakokila*). For his story see the **Kuṇāla Jātaka.** He is identified with **Udāyī Thera.**[1]

[1] J. v. 456.

Puṇṇalakkhaṇadevī.—See **Puññalakkhaṇadevī.**

1. **Puṇṇavaḍḍhana.**—Son of **Migāra** and husband of **Visākhā**[1] (*q.v.*).

[1] AA. i. 220; DhA. i. 387; UdA. 158, etc.

2. **Puṇṇavaḍḍhana.**—One of the gardens laid out by **Parakkamabāhu I.** in **Pulatthipura.**[1] In it was a tank which was connected with the **Toyavāpī** by the **Sarassatī** Canal. From this branched off, to the west, the **Yamunā** Canal.[2]

[1] Cv. lxxix. 9. [2] *Ibid.*, 46, 47.

3. **Puṇṇavaḍḍhana.**—The name given to a kind of precious garment. **Kuṇḍalī** of **Dvāramaṇḍala** sent several of these garments to **Dīghābhaya** through **Sūranimila,** and Dīghābhaya gave a pair himself to Sūranimila.[1] Puṇṇa was probably another variation of the name.[2]

[1] Mhv. xxiii. 33, 37; MṬ. 450. [2] *E.g.*, *ibid.*, 538.

Puṇṇavallika.—A locality in Ceylon, the residence of **Mahātissa.**[1]

[1] Vsm. 143; DhSA. 116.

Puṇṇasīha.—Father of **Uttarā Nandamātā.**[1] See **Puṇṇa** (1).

[1] AA. i. 240.

1. **Puṇṇā.**—Slave-girl of **Sujātā**[1] (*q.v.*).

[1] J. i. 69; AA. i. 218.

2. **Puṇṇā Therī.**—An arahant. She was born in a householder's family of **Sāvatthi,** and, at the age of twenty, having heard **Pajāpatī Gotamī** preach, she left the world. One day, while meditating, the Buddha appeared before her in a ray of glory and she became an arahant.

In the past she was a kinnarī on the banks of the **Candabhāgā,** and, having seen a Pacceka Buddha, worshipped him with a wreath of reeds.[1]

She is perhaps identical with **Tiṇinalamālikā** of the Apadāna.[2]

[1] Thig. vs. 3; ThigA. 9 f. [2] Ap. ii. 515.

3. **Puṇṇā Therī** (*v.l.* **Puṇṇikā**).—An arahant. She was born in **Anāthapiṇḍika's** household, as the daughter of a domestic slave. She was called **Puṇṇā** because, with her birth, the number of children in the household reached one hundred.

On the day on which she heard the **Sīhanāda Sutta** she became a sotāpanna. She converted the brahmin **Sotthiya,** who believed in purification through water,[1] and thereby won the esteem of Anāthapiṇḍika,

[1] The conversation is recorded in Thig. vs. 236-51.

so that he freed her. Thereupon she entered the Order and in due course became an arahant.

In the time of **Vipassī** Buddha she was born in a clansman's family and entered the Order. She learned the three Piṭakas and became a distinguished preacher. She did the same under five other Buddhas—**Sikhī, Vessabhū, Kakusandha, Koṇāgamana** and **Kassapa**—but, owing to her tendency to pride, she was unable to root out the defilements.[2]

Buddhaghosa, however, says of this Therī[3] that she was a slave-girl of **Anāthapiṇḍika.** On one occasion, when the Buddha was about to set out on a tour, Anāthapiṇḍika and the other chief patrons of the Buddha, loth to lose him for several months, begged him to remain with them. But the Buddha declined this request, and Puṇṇā, seeing Anāthapiṇḍika very dejected and learning the reason, offered to persuade the Buddha to stay. So she approached him and said that she would take the Three Refuges with the Five Precepts if he would postpone his tour. The Buddha at once agreed, and Puṇṇā was freed and adopted as Anāthapiṇḍika's daughter. She later joined the Order, and became an arahant after listening to an admonition[4] of the Buddha, who appeared before her in a ray of glory. Here we undoubtedly have a confusion of legends. See **Puṇṇā** (2).

It may be this same Puṇṇā who is mentioned in the Milindapañha[5] as one of the seven people whose acts of devotion brought them recompense in this very life.

[2] ThigA. 199 ff.; Ap. ii. 611.

[3] MA. i. 347 f.; the story, with very different details, is given in AA. ii. 716 f.

[4] The stanza being that which is mentioned in the Therīgāthā (vs. 3) about **Puṇṇā** (2).

[5] p. 115.

4. **Puṇṇā.**—The slave-girl of the brahmin soothsayer of the **Nānacchanda Jātaka** (*q.v.*). When asked what boon she desired, she answered, "A pestle and mortar and a winnowing basket."[1]

[1] J. ii. 428, 429.

5. **Puṇṇā.**—A slave-woman of **Rājagaha.** Late one night, when standing outside the house, cooling herself after having pounded a large quantity of rice, she saw **Dabba Mallaputta** taking some monks to their lodgings. She thought to herself that she had to work and therefore could not sleep early, but why should monks, who are free from care, be sleepless? She concluded that one of them was sick or had been bitten by a snake. At dawn the next day she went down to the bathing-ghat, taking a cake made of rice-dust and baked over charcoal, meaning to eat it after the bath. On the way she met the Buddha and offered

him the cake, though she did not expect he would eat it. But the Buddha, who was with **Ānanda,** accepted the gift and sat down to eat it, while **Puṇṇā** stood watching. When the meal was over, the Buddha asked her what she had thought of the monks, and she told him. The Buddha pointed out to her that monks could not sleep till late for they had to be watchful and assiduous. At the end of the discourse Puṇṇā became a sotāpanna. It was in reference to this Puṇṇā that the **Kuṇḍakasindhavapotaka Jātaka** was preached.[1] (But see *s.v.*)

[1] DhA. iii. 321 ff.

6. **Puṇṇā.**—A slave-woman. The Commentaries mention[1] that the Buddha once made a rag-robe (*paṃsukūla*) out of a garment cast off by her in a cemetery overgrown with weeds (*atimuttakasusāna*). When the Buddha donned the robe the earth trembled in wonder. It was this robe that the Buddha exchanged with **Mahā Kassapa;** when the Buddha picked it up from the cemetery where Puṇṇā had cast it off it was covered with insects.[2]

[1] *E.g.*, MA. ii. 696. [2] SA. ii. 149.

1. **Puṇṇikā.**—A slave-girl of **Pokkharasāti.**[1]

[1] M. ii. 201.

2. **Puṇṇikā.**—See *s.v.* **Puṇṇā** (3).

Puṇṇiya.—A monk. He is mentioned as visiting the Buddha and asking him under what conditions a sermon presents itself to the mind of a Tathāgata.[1]

[1] A. iv. 337 f.; v. 154 f.

1. **Puṇṇiya Sutta.**—The Buddha tells **Puṇṇiya** of eight conditions under which a sermon presents itself to the mind of a Tathāgata.[1]

[1] A. iv. 337 f.

2. **Puṇṇiya Sutta.**—Same as above (1), but two conditions are added.[1]

[1] A. v. 154 f.

Puṇṇeli.—A village granted by **Dāṭhopatissa II.** to the **Thūpārāma.**[1]

[1] Cv. xlv. 28.

Puṇṇovāda Sutta.—**Puṇṇa** (of **Sunāparanta**) visits the Buddha and asks him for a teaching that he may follow it and be purged of self. The Buddha tells him to avoid finding delight in the pleasures of the senses.

On learning that Puṇṇa proposes to live in Sunāparanta, the Buddha warns him that the people of that part are fierce and violent. Puṇṇa declares that even should they kill him, he would not bear them ill-will, but would rejoice to be of use to them. He leaves for Sunāparanta, with the Buddha's approval, and there gather around him five hundred disciples of either sex who have won arahantship. After Puṇṇa's death, the monks question the Buddha about him, and the Buddha tells them that he had realised nibbāna.[1]

[1] M. iii. 267 ff.; S. iv. 60 ff.

1. **Putta Sutta.**—An *upāsikā* should teach her only son to be like **Cittagahapati, Hatthaka-Āḷavaka,** or **Sāriputta** and **Moggallāna.**[1]

[1] S. ii. 235.

2. **Putta Sutta.**—Five things that make parents desire a son.[1]

[1] A. iii. 44.

Puttatissa.—An astrologer (*gaṇaka*), one of the four envoys sent by **Devānampiyatissa** to the court of **Asoka.**[1]

[1] Dpv. xi. 29, 31; *cp.* MṬ. 302, where he is called Tissa.

Puttabhāga-vihāra.—A vihāra in Ceylon, restored by **Vohāratissa.**[1]

[1] Mhv. xxxvi. 36.

Puttamaṃsa Sutta.—The four kinds of food—material food, contact, will, and consciousness—and how they should be regarded. Material food should be eaten only to maintain existence, as parents might eat the flesh of their own son in the desert. Contact should be regarded as a cow with a sore hide—exposed always to creatures and insects who devour her. Will should be regarded as a pit of glowing coal; and consciousness as a robber, brought before the king and smitten with darts at morning, noon, and evening.[1]

[1] S. ii. 97 ff.

Puthu Sutta.—Following after the good, hearing the Dhamma, systematic attention thereto, and living according to its precepts—these four conduce to increase of insight.[1]

[1] S. v. 412.

Puthujjana.—A king of old, who, though he gave great gifts, could not attain to beyond the realms of sense.[1]

[1] J. vi. 99.

Puthuvindhara.—King of Benares and son of **Kiki.** His son was Suyāma.[1]

[1] ThagA. i. 151.

1. **Punabbasu.**—A young yakkha.[1] He became a sotāpanna.[2] See **Punabbasumātā.**

[1] S. i. 210. [2] SA. i. 239.

2. **Punabbasu.**—One of the **Chabbaggiyā.** His followers were called **Punabbasukā,** and, together with the followers of **Assaji,** they were called **Assaji-Punabbasukā** (*q.v.*).

Punabbasu Sutta.—Records an incident relating to Punabbasumātā[1] (*q.v.*).

[1] S. i. 210.

Punabbasukuṭumbikaputta-Tissa Thera.—He was of Ceylon, and crossed over to India, where he studied under **Yonaka Dhammarakkhita.** On his way home by sea he felt doubtful of one word, and returned all the way, one hundred leagues, to consult his teacher. On the way from the port he mentioned the word to a householder, who was so pleased with him that he gave him a blanket and one hundred thousand. This blanket Tissa gave to his teacher, but the latter cut it up and used it as a spread, as an example to others (not to desire luxuries). Tissa had his doubts set at rest and returned to **Jambukola.** There, at the **Vālikārāma,** as he was sweeping the courtyard of the cetiya, other monks asked him questions in order to vex him. But he was able to answer all these, having attained the *paṭisambhidā.*[1]

[1] VibhA. 389.

Punabbasumātā.—A yakkhiṇī, mother of **Punabbasu.** One evening towards sunset, when the Buddha was at **Jetavana,** she, with her daughter **Uttarā** on her hip and the boy's hand in hers, came to the grove in search of food. She saw the silent monks seated round the Buddha while he preached, and having hushed her babe to silence she and Punabbasu listened to the Buddha. At the end of the sermon, both mother and son became sotāpannas, Uttarā being too young to understand.[1]

Punabbasumātā is quoted as an example of a yakkhiṇī who could travel through the air.[2] She was a vemānikapeta.[3]

[1] S. i. 210 f.; SA. i. 239 f. [2] PSA. 79. [3] DA. ii. 509.

1. **Punabbasumitta.**—A rich merchant in the time of **Vipassī** Buddha. He built a monastery, one yojana in extent, on the site of **Jetavana,** the ground of which he bought by covering the whole with golden bricks.[1]

[1] J. i. 94; Bu. xx. 30; DA. ii. 424.

2. **Punabbasumitta.**—Son of **Sumedha** Buddha.[1]

[1] BuA. 163; the Bu. (xii. 20) calls him **Sumitta.**

Punnāgapupphiya Thera.—An arahant. Ninety-two kappas ago he was a hunter who, while wandering in the forest, saw a flower, which he offered on a heap of sand in the name of the Buddha **Tissa.** Ninety-one kappas ago he was a king named **Tamonuda.**[1] He is probably identical with **Suhemanta Thera.**[2]

[1] Ap. i. 180. [2] ThagA. i. 212.

1. **Puppha Thera.**—An eminent teacher of the **Vinaya.**[1]

[1] Vin. v. 3.

2. **Puppha.**—One of the five horses of King **Kappina,** used by him in sending messages.[1]

[1] DhA. ii. 117.

1. **Puppha Vagga.**—The fourth section of the Dhammapada.

2. **Puppha Vagga.**—The tenth chapter of the Khandha Saṃyutta.[1]

[1] S. iii. 137-57.

Puppha (or **Vaḍḍha**) **Sutta.**—The Buddha declares that he upholds only that which is upheld in the world of sages (*paṇḍitānaṃ*)—viz., that the *khandhas* are impermanent, subject to woe and decay. The Buddha has thoroughly penetrated the world-condition (*lokadhamma*) of the world of *saṅkhāras.* He is like a lotus, sprung from the water and come to full growth therein, yet unspotted by it.[1]

[1] S. iii. 138 f.

1. **Pupphaka.**—The palace of **Sutasoma.**[1]

[1] J. v. 187.

2. **Pupphaka.**—A parrot, discovered in a bed of flowers, hence his name. He was the Bodhisatta. For his story see **Sattigumba Jātaka.**[1]

[1] J. iv. 431 ff.

Pupphacaṅgotiya Thera.—An arahant. Thirty-one kappas ago he took a casket of flowers which he sprinkled over **Sikhī** Buddha. He was five times king, under the name of **Devabhūti.**[1]

[1] Ap. i. 118.

Pupphachattiya Thera.—An arahant. Ninety-four kappas ago he made a parasol of lotus-flowers, which he held over **Siddhattha** Buddha. Seventy-four kappas ago he was king nine times, under the name of **Jalasikha.**[1]

[1] Ap. i. 264 f.

Pupphachadaniya.—In the very distant past there were five kings of this name, all previous births of **Maggadattika Thera.**[1]

[1] Ap. i. 189.

Pupphathūpiya Thera.—An arahant. In the time of **Vipassī** Buddha he was a brahmin ascetic on **Kukkurapabbata** with a large number of disciples. Hearing of the Buddha's appearance in the world, he wished to visit him, but fell ill on the way. He thereupon erected a thūpa of flowers in the Buddha's name and died soon after. Forty-four kappas ago he was king sixteen times under the name of **Aggisama,** and thirty-eight times under that of **Ghatāsana.**[1]

[1] Ap. i. 155 f.

Pupphadhāraka.—Ninety-one kappas ago he was an ascetic wearing bark and antelope-skin. Seeing **Vipassī** Buddha, he held over him a canopy of *pāricchattaka*-flowers. Eighty-seven kappas ago he was a king, named **Samantadharaṇa.**[1]

[1] Ap. i. 244.

Pupphapura.—Another name for **Pāṭaliputta**[1] (*q.v.*).

[1] *E.g.*, Dpv. xi. 28; Mhv. xxix. 36.

Pupphabhāṇī Sutta.—The three kinds of people in the world: the tricky-tongued (*gūthabhāṇī*), the fair-spoken (*pupphabhāṇī*), and the honey-tongued (*madhubhāṇī*).[1]

[1] A. i. 127.

Puppharatta Jātaka (No. 147).—Once, during the Kattika Festival in Benares, the wife of a poor man insisted on having a pair of garments dyed with safflower to wear at the festival. Urged by her desire, the husband stole at night into the king's conservatories to get the safflowers.

He was caught by the guard and impaled alive. He died lamenting the non-fulfilment of his wife's desire and was born in hell. The Bodhisatta was, at that time, a Spirit of the Air.

The story was told to a passion-tossed monk who longed for the wife of his lay life. The couple are identified with that of the story.[1]

[1] J. i. 149 f.

Pupphavati.—An old name for Benares, when **Ekarāja,** father of **Candakumāra,** was its king.[1]

[1] J. iv. 131; iv. 119; Cyp. i. 7.

Pupphārāma.—A central monastic establishment in **Sirivaḍḍhanapura** (modern Kandy) in Ceylon. It formed the headquarters of the Siamese monks under **Upāli,** who came to Ceylon at the invitation of the king **Kittisirirājasīha.**[1]

[1] Cv. c. 86, 141.

Pupphāsaniya Thera.—An arahant. Ninety-four kappas ago he saw **Siddhattha** Buddha, and, following him to his hermitage, made for him a seat of flowers.[1]

[1] Ap. i. 254 f.

Pupphita.—Seventeen kappas ago there were three kings of this name, all previous births of **Kuṭajapupphiya Thera.**[1]

[1] Ap. i. 191.

1. **Pubba** (or **Hetu**) **Sutta.**—The Buddha tells the monks of how, even before the Enlightenment, he cultivated the four *iddhipādas*, and of how their development brought various attainments, such as clairvoyance, etc.[1]

[1] S. v. 263 ff.

2. **Pubba** (or **Pariyesanā**) **Sutta.**—The Buddha tells the monks how, before his Enlightenment, he wondered as to what was the satisfaction in the world, what its misery and what the escape therefrom, and how, in the end, he thoroughly comprehended all these.[1]

[1] A. i. 258 f.

Pubba-Kaccāyana.—See **Kaccāyana.**

Pubbakammapiloti.—A chapter in the Apadāna[1] which gives incidents from several lives of the Bodhisatta in explanation of the reason for which

[1] Ap. i. 299 ff.

the Buddha suffered in various ways during his last life—*e.g.*, from persecutions at the hands of his enemies and from various bodily ills. Most of the incidents mentioned are not to be found in the Jātakas. This chapter is described as a Buddhāpadāna,[2] but there is no reference either to it or to the incidents recounted in the chapter entitled Buddhāpadāna which is found at the beginning of the Apadāna. See also **Pilotikamma.**

[2] *Ibid.*, 301.

Pubbakoṭṭhaka.—See below **Pubbakoṭṭhakā.**

Pubbakoṭṭhaka Sutta.—The Buddha, while staying at **Pubbakoṭṭhaka** in **Sāvatthi,** asks **Sāriputta** if he believes that the five *indriyas* (of *saddhā*, etc.) if cultivated, lead to Deathlessness. Sāriputta answers that he not only believes it, but has actually realized and understood it by insight.[1]

[1] S. v. 220 f.

Pubbakoṭṭhakā.—A bathing-place in **Sāvatthi,** near the **Migāramātupāsāda,** and therefore to the east of the city. Mention is made[1] of the Buddha having bathed there. It was evidently extensive, for Pasenadi's state elephant **Seta** also bathed there to the accompaniment of music. The Commentary calls it[2] a nadī. The bathing-place was probably near the **Pubbakoṭṭhaka** (? Eastern Gatehouse) of Sāvatthi, where the Buddha is said to have stayed.[3] Public bathing-places were generally near the city gates.

[1] A. iii. 345.
[2] AA. ii. 668.
[3] S. v. 220; the bathing-place seems also to have been called **Pubbakoṭṭhaka.** Near by was the hermitage of the brahmin **Rammaka** (M. i. 161).

Pubbaṅgama Sutta.—Just as the dawn precedes sunrise, so do right views (*samādiṭṭhi*) precede good actions.[1]

[1] A. v. 236 f.

Pubbaṅgamaniya Thera.—An arahant. Ninety-four kappas ago he was a leader of eighty-four thousand religieux and waited upon holy ones.[1]

[1] Ap. i. 243.

Pubbajira (*v.l.* **Pubbavicira**).—A village of the **Vajjians** which was the constant dwelling-place of **Channa.** The people there were blamed for his suicide.[1] The village seems to have been also called **Pubbavijjhana.**[2]

[1] M. iii. 266. [2] S. iv. 59.

Pubbaṇha Sutta.—Those that practise righteousness at morn, at noon, and at eve, are always happy.[1]

[1] A. i. 294.

Pubbadesa.—See **Pācīnadesa.**

Pubbayogāvacara Sutta.—One of the suttas preached to **Ānanda** as introduction to the **Khaggavisāna Sutta.** It dealt with the five advantages of *pubbayogāvacara*.[1]

[1] SNA. i. 47.

Pubbavicira, Pubbavijjhana.—See **Pubbajira.**

Pubbavideha.—The eastern of the four continents (*mahādīpā*) which compose a Cakkavāḷa.[1] It is seven thousand leagues in extent[2] and its chief tree is the Acacia (*Sirīsa*).[3] It is the first mahādīpa visited by a **Cakkavatti** when on tour.[4] See also *s.v.* **Videha.**

[1] A. i. 227; v. 59.
[2] SNA. 443; 8,000 says BuA. 112.
[3] AA. i. 264; MA. ii. 947; Vsm. i. 206, etc.
[4] BuA. 131.

Pubbaseliyā.—One of the seventeen heterodox sects which arose in **Jambudīpa** in the second century after the Buddha's death.[1] According to the Kathāvatthu Commentary[2] they belonged to the **Andhaka** school. Their views seem to have been similar to those of the **Cetiyavādins.**[3] According to Tibetan sources[4] they were so called because they lived on the Pūrva Mountain.

[1] Mhv. v. 12; Dpv. v. 55.
[2] See Points of Controversy xli. 104, 108, 115.
[3] *J.R.A.S.* 1910, p. 413 ff.
[4] Rockhill: *op. cit.*, 184.

1. **Pubbārāma.**—A park outside the eastern gate of **Sāvatthi.** It was the custom of the Buddha to spend his siesta there after eating at the house of **Anāthapiṇḍika.**[1] In the Pubbārāma, **Visākhā** erected the **Migāramātupāsāda** (*q.v.*), the site costing her nine crores and the building another nine.[2] The Pubbārāma in Sāvatthi corresponded to the **Uttamadevī-vihāra** in **Anurādhapura.**[3] It was while staying at the Pubbārāma that the Buddha sent the novice **Sumana** to fetch water from **Anotatta.**[4] The **Vighāsa Jātaka**[5] was also preached there.

[1] DhA. i. 413; see also MA. i. 369.
[2] DhA. i. 413.
[3] UdA. 158; MA. i. 471.
[4] DhA. iv. 120.
[5] J. iii. 310.

2. **Pubbārāma.**—A monastery in Ceylon, built by **Sena I.** and his consort **Saṅghā.**[1] **Parakkamaābhu I.** is said to have restored it.[2]

[1] Cv. l. 69; see also Cv. *Trs.* i. 144, n. 4. [2] SadS. 58.

1. **Pubbārāma Sutta.**—Preached at the **Pubbārāma.** The winning of insight means the destruction of the *āsavas.*[1]

[1] S. v. 222.

2. **Pubbārāma Sutta.**—The cultivation of Ariyan insight (*paññā*) and Ariyan release (*vimutti*) leads to the destruction of the *āsavas.*[1]

[1] S. v. 223.

3. **Pubbārāma Sutta.**—The cultivation of the four indriyas (*viriya, sati, samādhi* and *paññā*) leads to the destruction of the *āsavas.*[1]

[1] S. v. 224.

4. **Pubbārāma Sutta.**—The same as 4 with *saddhā* added to the indriyas.[1]

[1] S. v. 224.

Puratthimadesa.—See **Pācīnadesa.**

Puradeva.—A god, evidently the tutelary deity of **Anurādhapura.** There was a shrine erected to him within the precincts of the **Mahāvihāra.** Near this shrine a battle took place between **Duṭṭhagāmaṇī** and **Bhalluka. Kaṇḍula** considered it a lucky spot and led Duṭṭhagāmaṇī's forces up to it.[1] The shrine was to the north of the Mahāsusāna.[2]

[1] Mhv. xxv. 87. [2] MṬ. 486.

1. **Purāṇa.**—A monk who lived in **Dakkhiṇāgiri.** It is said that when he visited Rājagaha after the holding of the First Council, he was asked to give his approval to the " findings " of the same. His answer was that he preferred to remember what he himself had heard and learnt from the Buddha.[1]

[1] Vin. ii. 189 f.

2. **Purāṇa.**—A chamberlain (*thapati* ? equerry) of **Pasenadi.** He was the brother of **Isidatta** and the father of **Migasālā.** In his later years he lived the life of a celibate and was reborn in **Tusita** as a sakadāgāmī.[1] A conversation he had with the Buddha, in the company of Isidatta, at **Sādhuka** (*q.v.*), is recorded in the Saṃyutta Nikāya.[2] In the **Dhammacetiya Sutta**[3] Pasenadi speaks of the great loyalty of these two men

[1] A. iii. 348 ff.; v. 138 ff. The SA. (iii. 215), however, says that Purāṇa was a sotāpanna.

[2] S. v. 349 ff.

[3] M. ii. 123.

towards the Buddha. After discussing the Doctrine till late at night, they would sleep with their heads towards the spot where the Buddha was staying and their feet towards the king. Purāṇa is mentioned[4] as an ideal layman.

[4] *E.g.*, at A. iii. 451.

Purāṇagāma.—One of the four villages granted by **Parakkamabāhu IV.** for the maintenance of the special pariveṇa built for **Medhaṅkara.**[1]

[1] Cv. xc. 87.

Purābheda Sutta.—The tenth sutta of the Aṭṭhaka Vagga of the Sutta Nipāta. It was among the suttas preached at the **Mahāsamaya** in answer to the questions asked of the Buddha by the created-Buddha.[1] It is a long disquisition on the characteristics of a calm sage (*upasanta*). He is free from craving, anger, etc., is equable and thoughtful, possessed of calm, and walks in the path of righteous men.[2] The sutta was preached for the benefit of the *buddhi-caritā.*[3]

[1] SNA. ii. 548. [2] SN. vs. 848-61. [3] SNA. i. 361; MNid. 223.

Purindada.—A name for **Sakka,** because, as a human being, he bestowed gifts from town to town (*pure pure dānaṃ adāsi*).[1]

[1] S. i. 229; DhA. i. 264; *cp.* Sanskrit *purandara* (destroyer of cities).

Purisa Sutta.—The Buddha, in answer to a question of **Pasenadi,** tells him that three kinds of inward experience arise in a man for his bane—greed, hate, and dullness.[1]

[1] S. i. 70.

Purisagati Sutta.—On the seven conditions of a person (*purisagatiyo*), and an explanation of *anūpādā parinibbāna.*[1]

[1] A. iv. 70 ff.

Purisarūpa Sutta.—Nothing so enslaves a woman as the form, etc., of a man.[1]

[1] A. i. 2.

1. **Pulacceri.**—A park laid out by **Parakkamabāhu I.**[1]

[1] Cv. lxxix. 11.

2. **Pulacceri.**—A landing-place in Ceylon where **Māgha** and **Jayabāhu** set up fortifications.[1]

[1] Cv. lxxxiii. 17.

Pulatthi-nagara(-pura).—A capital of the Sinhalese kings. It is first heard of in the reign of **Aggabodhi III.,** who built in the town the **Mahāpānadīpa-vihāra.**[1] But it was probably an important centre even earlier, and **Vijitapura,** wrested from the Tamils by **Duṭṭhagāmaṇī,** was probably near by.[2] **Sena I.** first made Pulatthipura the capital,[3] though even before his time it seems to have been used as a royal residence—*e.g.*, by **Aggabodhi IV.,**[4] **Aggabodhi VII.,**[5] and **Udaya I.,**[6] who built a hospital there.[7] **Mahinda II.** built in the city the **Dāmavihāra-pariveṇa** and the **Sannīratittha-vihāra.**[8] **Sena I.** reigned in Pulatthipura for twenty years and erected there several buildings, including the **Senaggabodhi-shrine** near the **Thusavāpi.**[9] The successors of Sena I. found in Pulatthipura a certain amount of protection from the inroads of the **Coḷas** and the **Pāṇḍiyans;** but in the time of **Sena V.** the town fell into the hands of the **Damiḷas**, through the treachery of Sena's mother and his commander-in-chief, Sena. But Sena V. recovered the city by making a treaty with his commander-in-chief.[10] About 1017 A.C. the Coḷas overran the country, captured Pulatthipura, and made the reigning king, **Mahinda V.,** their prisoner. He died, after twelve years, as a prisoner in India.[11] During this period many of the Hindu shrines in the city were erected.

For many years the Coḷas held the sovereignty of the city, though the Sinhalese made several vain attempts to drive them out. The Coḷas named the city **Jananāthapura** and put down all rebellion with a strong hand. Finally, a young prince named **Kitti,** born about 1039 A.C., assumed the title of **Vijayabāhu** and determined to rescue Pulatthipura. His first attempts failed, partly owing to rebellion among his own people; but finally, civil war broke out in the Coḷa country itself, and thus, about 1070, he captured Pulatthipura after a great deal of fierce fighting both on sea and land. But, owing to dissensions among his subjects, it was only several years later that he was able to hold his coronation.[12] He renamed the city **Vijayarājapura,** and erected there many religious buildings, chief among which was the Temple of the Tooth Relic.[13] It was not, however, till the time of **Parakkamabāhu I.** that Pulatthipura reached the pinnacle of its greatness. He enlarged it to the size of four gāvutas in length and seven in width and called it **Parakkamapura.** The city had three suburbs—**Rāvjavesībhujaṅga, Rājakulantaka** and **Vijita**—

[1] Cv. xliv. 122.
[2] See Codrington, *op. cit.*, 20.
[3] Cv. l. 9, 46, 85.
[4] Cv. xlvi. 34.
[5] *Ibid.*, xlviii. 74.
[6] *Ibid.*, xlix. 9, 18.
[7] Kassapa iv. is also mentioned as building a hospital against an epidemic (Cv. lii. 25).
[8] Cv. xlviii. 134.
[9] *Ibid.*, l. 73.
[10] *Ibid.*, liv. 64, 68.
[11] *Ibid.*, lv. 22 ff.
[12] Cv. lvii. 66; lviii. 22 ff.; lix. 6 ff.
[13] *Ibid.*, lx. 2 ff.

and fourteen gates. Parakkama adorned it with various parks, chief of which were the **Nandanavana** and the **Dīpuyyāna,** and with ponds and numerous buildings, both secular and religious.[14] **Kittinissaṅka** added a stone temple for the Tooth Relic.[15] In the reign of **Līlavatī, Lokissara** captured the city and ruled there for nine months. He was ousted by the general **Parakkama,** and later **Parakkamapaṇḍu** ruled as king, till he was deposed about 1215 A.C. by **Māgha** of the Kaliṅga race, who, coming with a large host of Keralas and Malabars, captured the city and mercilessly plundered its possessions.[16] From this spoliation the city never completely recovered, and it gradually lost its importance, though **Parakkamabāhu II., Vijayabāhu IV.** and **Parakkamabāhu III.** made attempts to restore it to its original splendour.[17]

14 For details see chiefly Cv. lxxiii. 1 ff.; lxxviii. 44 ff.

15 *Ibid.*, lxxx. 19.

16 *Ibid.*, lxxxiii. 15 ff.

17 *Ibid.*, lxxxvii. 67; lxxxviii. 28, 35, 89, 92, 120 f.; lxxxix. 1.

Pulavaka Sutta.—The idea of a worm-eaten corpse, if cultivated, leads to great profit.[1]

1 S. v. 131.

Pulinacaṅkamiya Thera.—An arahant. Thirty-one kappas ago he was a hunter who, seeing the covered walk (*caṅkama*) of **Sikhī** Buddha, scattered sand over it.[1] He is probably identical with **Nandaka Thera.**[2]

1 Ap. ii. 418.

2 ThagA. i. 299.

Pulinathūpiya Thera.—An arahant. Once, in the past, he was a Jaṭila named **Nārada,** with fourteen thousand followers, living near the rock called **Samaṅga.** He erected, on the bank of the **Amarikā,** a thūpa of sand as an object of worship for himself. In his last birth he was of parents who were devout followers of the Buddha and worshipped at a shrine erected in the Buddha's name. When the boy was seven years old he saw the shrine and, recalling his past, became an arahant.[1] He is perhaps to be identified with **Vasabha Thera** (*q.v.*).[2]

1 Ap. ii. 437 ff.

2 ThagA. i. 258 f.

Pulinapupphiya.—A Cakkavatti of ninety-one kappas ago, a former birth of **Ñāṇasaññaka** (or **Piyañjaha**) **Thera.**[1]

1 Ap. i. 161 f.; ThagA. i. 169.

1. **Pulinapūjaka Thera.**—An arahant. Ninety-one kappas ago he cleared the foot of **Vipassī** Buddha's bodhi-tree and scattered fresh sand around it. Fifty-three kappas ago he was a king named **Mahāpulina.**[1]

1 Ap. i. 79.

2. **Pulinapūjaka Thera.**—An arahant. Ninety-one kappas ago he saw **Vipassī** Buddha and, gladdened by the sight, worshipped him and strewed sand on his path.[1]

[1] Ap. i. 259.

Pulinuppādaka Thera.—An arahant. One hundred thousand kappas ago he was an ascetic named **Devala** with eighty thousand followers. He erected a thūpa of sand and honoured it in the name of the Buddha.[1] He is probably identical with **Sirima Thera.**[2]

[1] Ap. ii. 426 ff.

[2] ThagA. i. 280 f.

Pulindā.—The name given to the wild tribes of Ceylon, evidently to be identified with the present Veddas. Their ancestry is traced to **Jīvahattha** and **Dīpellā,** the son and daughter of **Vijaya** by **Kuveṇī.**[1]

[1] Mhv. vii. 58; MṬ. 264, 266.

Puḷahattha.—A Damiḷa usurper who reigned for three years at **Anurādhapura** in the time of **Vaṭṭagāmaṇī.** He was slain by his general **Bāhiya.**[1]

[1] Mhv. xxxiii. 56 f.; Dpv. xix. 15; xx. 15.

Pūgadaṇḍakāvāṭa.—A stronghold in **Rohaṇa,** mentioned in the account of the campaigns of **Parakkamabāhu I.**[1]

[1] Cv. lxxv. 86, 95, 143.

Pūjā-pariveṇa.—A monastery in **Anurādhapura** to which the Nāgas followed **Sonuttara** when he brought the relics from the Nāga-world in order to deposit them in the **Mahā Thūpa.** From Pūjā-pariveṇa the Nāgas were induced to return by being given a few of the relics.[1] *v.l.* **Puṇṇa-pariveṇa.**

[1] Mhv. xxxi. 4; MṬ. 575.

Pūtigatta-Tissa.—A young man of **Sāvatthi,** of good family. After he joined the Order an eruption broke out on him which covered his whole body with sores. His fellow-monks, unable to look after him, abandoned him. When the Buddha discovered this, he boiled some water and washed Tissa with his own hands and cleaned and dried his garments. When Tissa felt comforted the Buddha preached to him, and Tissa became an arahant. In a past birth he had been a fowler and had killed many birds, of which he sometimes first broke the bones to prevent them from flying away. One day he had given alms to an arahant.[1]

[1] DhA. i. 319 ff.

Pūtimaṃsa.—A jackal, the mate of **Veṇī.** For their story see **Pūtimaṃsa Jātaka.**

Pūtimaṃsa Jātaka (No. 437).—Once, on the slopes of the Himālaya, lived a jackal called **Pūtimaṃsa,** with his mate **Veṇī.** Near by dwelt a flock of wild goats. Pūtimaṃsa formed a device for killing the goats one by one and eating their flesh, till only a she-goat, called **Meḷamātā,** was left. Wishing to devour her as well, Pūtimaṃsa suggested to Veṇī that he should pretend to be dead and that Veṇī should then entice Meḷamātā into the cave by asking her to assist in the funeral rites. But the goat was wise and observant and discovered the ruse. Veṇī went to her later and saying that Pūtimaṃsa had recovered consciousness at the very sight of her, invited her to join them in a feast to celebrate his recovery. Meḷamātā agreed, saying that she would bring with her a large escort of her friends, fierce dogs, including **Maliya, Piṅgiya, Caturakkha** and **Jambuka,** in order that the celebration might be a great one. At this suggestion Pūtimaṃsa and Veṇī fled from their cave, taking rescue elsewhere.

The story was told to the monks in order to impress on them the necessity for keeping guard over their senses.[1]

[1] J. iii. 532 ff.

Pūtimukha.—A peta who had been a monk in the time of **Kassapa** Buddha and who had brought a dissension between two holy monks by carrying tales from one to the other.[1]

[1] Pv. i. 3; PvA. 12 ff.

Pūṇagāma.—A ford on the **Mahāvālukagaṅgā.**[1]

[1] Cv. lxxii. 6.

Pūraṇa-Kassapa.—One of the six well-known teachers, contemporaneous with the Buddha. He is said to have taught the doctrine of non-action (*akiriya*), denying the result of good or bad actions.[1] Elsewhere,[2] however, he is mentioned as an *ahetuvādin*, denying *hetupaccaya* (condition and cause—*i.e.*, the efficacy of kamma), which teaching, in the **Sāmaññaphala Sutta,**[3] is attributed to **Makkhali-Gosāla.** Buddhaghosa says[4]

[1] D. i. 52 f.; probably the more correct description of Kassapa's teaching would be *niṣkriyavāda*—*i.e.*, an affirmation that the soul is passive, unaffected by the good or the bad done by us, the ultimate reality lying beyond good or evil.

[2] S. iii. 69; v. 126.

[3] D. i. 53; see also A. iii. 383, where the teaching of *Chalabhijātiyo* is also attributed to Pūraṇa.

[4] DA. i. 142; he could not have been a slave. Kassapa is a brahmin-gotta. The SNA (372) calls him an *ājīvaka*.

that Pūraṇa-Kassapa came by his name from the fact that as a result of his birth the number of slaves in a certain household reached one hundred. Owing to this fact he was never found fault with, even when he failed to do his work satisfactorily. But, in spite of this, he was dissatisfied and fled from his masters. He then had his clothes stolen by thieves and went about naked. His gotta name was **Kassapa.** He had a following of five hundred, among whom was the deva-putta **Asama.**[5] (See also **Ajātasattu**). He was consulted by the **Licchavis Abhaya**[6] and **Mahāli**[7] and by the wanderer **Vacchagotta.**[8] He claimed to be omniscient.[9] A story in the Dhammapada Commentary[10] states that when the heretics were unable to prevent the Buddha from performing the Twin Miracle under the **Gaṇḍamba,** they fled discomfited. Pūraṇa-Kassapa was among them, and in the course of his flight, he came across one of his followers, a farmer, who was on his way to see him, carrying a vessel of broth and a rope. Pūraṇa took the vessel and the rope, and going to the banks of the river near Sāvatthi, tied the vessel round his neck and threw himself into the stream. There was a circle of bubbles on the water and Pūraṇa was reborn in **Avīci.** The Milindapañha[11] also mentions a Pūraṇa Kassapa, contemporary with **Milinda.** This perhaps refers to a teacher descended from the same school who is credited with the view that the earth rules or sustains the world. *v.l.* **Purāṇa.**

[5] S. i. 65.
[6] *Ibid.*, v. 126.
[7] *Ibid.*, iii. 68.
[8] *Ibid.*, iv. 398.
[9] A. iv. 428; here we probably have a more correct explanation of his name, Pūraṇa—*i.e.*, in his claim to have attained perfect wisdom (*pūraṇañāṇa*).
[10] DhA. iii. 208; for a different version see Rockhill: *op. cit.*, 80. According to this legend, Kassapa must have died in the sixteenth year of the Buddha's ministry. This is hardly reconcilable with the statement that Ajātasattu consulted him.
[11] p. 4 f.

Pūraḷāsa Sutta.—Another name[1] for **Sundarikabhāradvāja Sutta** (*q.v.*).

[1] SNA. ii. 400.

Pekhuṇiya.—Grandson of **Rohaṇa** (*q.v.*), who is, therefore, called **Pekhuṇiyanattā.**[1] The Commentary[2] calls Pekhuṇiya a *seṭṭhi.*

[1] A. i. 193.
[2] AA. i. 419.

Pecchadāyaka.—See **Mañcadāyaka.**

Pejalaka.—See **Sejalaka.**

Peṭakopadesa.—A treatise on textual and exegetical methodology, generally ascribed to **Mahā Kaccāyana**[1] and included (by the Burmese)

[1] Gv. 59.

in the Khuddaka Nikāya.[2] A ṭīkā on this work is ascribed to a teacher named **Udumbara** (?).[3]

[2] Bode, *op. cit.*, 5. [3] Gv. 65.

Peṭakālaṅkara.—A ṭīkā by **Ñāṇābhivaṃsa** on the **Nettippakaraṇa.**[1]

[1] Sās. 134.

Peṇṇākaṭa.—See **Bheṇṇākaṭa.**

Petavatthu.—The seventh book of the Khuddaka Nikāya. It consists of stories of persons born in the *peta*-world owing to various midseeds.[1] **Dhammapāla** wrote on it a Commentary, called the Petavatthuvaṇṇanā or Petavatthu-Aṭṭhakathā, and forming a part of the **Vimalavilāsinī.**[2] **Mahinda** preached the Petavatthu to **Anulā** and her companions on the day of his entry into **Anurādhapura.**[3]

[1] Published by the P.T.S. 1889. [2] Gv. 60. [3] Mhv. xiv. 58.

Pettaṅgavāḷika.—A monastery built by **Saddhā-Tissa.**[1]

[1] Mhv. xxxiii. 8.

Petteyya Sutta.—Few are they who show reverence to their fathers.[1]

[1] S. v. 467.

Penambaṅgana.—See **Setambaṅgana.**

1. **Pema Sutta.**—Of affection can be born both affection and ill-will; likewise of ill-will. Freedom from these states is acquired by the development of the jhānas.[1]

[1] A. ii. 213 ff.

2. **Pema** (or **Sāriputta-Koṭṭhita**) **Sutta.**—A conversation between **Sāriputta** and **Koṭṭhita** as to why the Buddha has said nothing regarding the existence or otherwise of a Tathāgata after death.[1]

[1] S. iv. 387.

Peraddoṇī.—A town in Ceylon, the modern Peradeṇiya.[1]

[1] Cv. xci. 2.

Perumpalaya.—A village in South India.[1]

[1] Cv. lxxvi. 287.

Peḷagāma-vihāra.—A monastery in Ceylon, built by **Kuṭakaṇṇa-Tissa.**[1]

[1] Mhv. xxxiv. 32; see also Mhv. *Trs.* 240, n. 1.

Peḷahāla.—A village in Ceylon, granted by **Aggabodhi IV.** for the maintenance of the Padhānaghara built by him for **Dāṭhāsiva.**[1]

[1] Cv. xlvi. 13.

Peḷivāpikagāma.—A village seven leagues to the north of **Anurādhapura.** When **Duṭṭhagāmaṇī** was looking for material for the building of the **Mahā Thūpa,** four gems were discovered by a hunter near the tank of this village.[1]

[1] Mhv. xxviii. 39; Mhv. *Trs.* 190, n. 1.

Pesakāradhītuvatthu.—The story of a weaver's daughter of **Āḷavi.** She heard the Buddha preach at the **Aggāḷava-cetiya** on the necessity of meditating constantly on the inevitableness of death and, though she was only sixteen, she was the only one to profit by the sermon. Three years later the Buddha again visited Āḷavi. The citizens entertained him, but the Buddha would not preach his thanksgiving sermon till the weaver's daughter, having finished the tasks required of her by her father, was able to be present. On her arrival the Buddha asked her questions so that her wisdom might be known to the assembled populace, and, at the conclusion of the Buddha's discourse, she became a sotāpanna. That same day she was killed by an accident to her loom, and her father joined the Order, attaining arahantship in due course.[1]

[1] DhA. iii. 170-6.

Pesalā-atimaññanā Sutta.—Once when **Vaṅgīsa** was at **Aggāḷava-cetiya** with his tutor, **Nigrodhakappa,** he found himself despising his friendly colleagues, proud of his own skill of improvisation. This discovery made him repent of his conceit and admonish himself.[1]

[1] S. i. 187 f.

Pesuna Sutta.—Few are they who abstain from slander.[1]

[1] S. v. 469.

Pessa.—An elephant trainer of **Campā.** He visited the Buddha at **Gaggarāpokkharaṇī** where **Kandaraka** was also present, and his conversation on that occasion is recorded in the **Kandaraka Sutta.** When Pessa had left, the Buddha is reported to have said that he was a man of great understanding, and that had he stayed longer he could have taken away with him something which would have proved precious to him.[1]

[1] M. i. 339-42.

Pokkhara.—A musical instrument, or, perhaps, a divine musician.[1]

[1] VvA. 93; see also note on p. 372.

Pokkharakkhī.—One of the wives of **Candakumāra** (the Bodhisatta).[1]

[1] J. vi. 148.

Pokkharaṇiyā.—A vihāra in **Sāmagāma** where the Buddha is said once to have stayed.[1]

[1] A. iii. 309; AA. ii. 660. The translator (G.S. iii. 220) calls it a lotus pond; the Commentary definitely calls it a Vihāra.

Pokkharaṇī Sutta.—The ill which remains to an Ariyan disciple who has won insight compared to the ill which he has destroyed, is as the water taken up by the tip of a blade of grass compared to the water left behind in a tank fifty yojanas in length, breadth and depth.[1]

[1] S. ii. 134; *ibid.*, v. 460.

Pokkharapāsaya.—A tank in Ceylon, built by **Upatissa II.**[1]

[1] Cv. xxxvii. 185.

Pokkharavatī.—A city, the birthplace of **Tapussa** and **Bhalliya.**[1]

[1] ThagA. i. 48.

Pokkharasāti, Pokkharasādi.—A **Mahāsāla** brahmin of great wealth and learning who lived in **Ukkaṭṭhā,** on a royal demesne given by **Pasenadi. Ambaṭṭha** was the pupil of Pokkharasāti, who sent him to the Buddha at **Icchānaṅgala** to discover if the report of the Buddha's greatness were true. When Pokkharasāti heard later that Ambaṭṭha had been rude to the Buddha, he sought the Buddha by night and begged for his forgiveness. The next day he invited the Buddha to a meal, and having listened to his teaching, declared himself his follower and became a sotāpanna.[1] Owing to his eminence, he was present at the meetings of the brahmins held in **Manasākaṭa**[2] and Icchānaṅgala.[3] **Vaseṭṭha,** of the **Vāseṭṭha Sutta,** was also his pupil.[4] In the **Subha Sutta,**[5] **Subha-Todeyyaputta,** another disciple, is reported to have said that Pokkharasāti—here described as **Opamañña** (of the **Upamañña** clan) and lord of **Subhagavana (Subhagavanika)**—treated as empty boasts the claims of brahmins and recluses to transcend ordinary human bonds and rise to the height

[1] D. i. 87 f., 106 ff.
[2] *Ibid.*, 235.
[3] SN. p. 115.
[4] *Ibid.*, vs. 594.
[5] M. ii. 200 ff.; the Vimānavatthu gives the name of another of his disciples, **Chattamāṇava** (*q.v.*), who was killed while bringing presents to his teacher. (Vv. v. 3; VvA. 229 ff.)

of Ariyan knowledge. This evidently refers to a time prior to his conversion. The same Sutta mentions a slave-girl of Pokkharasāti, **Puṇṇikā** by name.

The Commentaries[6] dwell at length on Pokkharasāti's attractive personality. His body was of the colour of the white lotus, like a silver pandal in heaven, his hair the colour of sapphire, his eyes like blue lotus, etc. He evidently was of true regal appearance.

In the time of **Kassapa** Buddha he was a brahmin versed in the three Vedas who, having heard the doctrine and given alms, was reborn in the deva-world. Thereafter, scorning birth in the womb of a woman, he sprang to life in a lotus which grew in a pond in **Himavā.** An ascetic saw the lotus, adopted the boy, and taught him the Vedas. The king was pleased with his great learning, and gave him Ukkaṭṭhā as a mark of great favour. The name of Pokkharasāti was given to him owing to his birth in a lotus.

The Divyāvadāna[7] calls him Puṣkarasārī, and tells a story of his daughter Prakṛti.

[6] DA. i. 244 f.; MA. ii. 804; SNA. 462.

[7] p. 616 ff., 620.

Poṭiriya.—See **Selissariya.**

1. **Poṭṭhapāda.**—A **Paribbājaka.** A discussion between him and the Buddha on trance and on the soul, which took place in **Mallikārāma** in **Sāvatthi,** is reported in the **Poṭṭhapāda Sutta.** Poṭṭhapāda, accepting the Buddha's views, was jeered at by his companions for doing so. Two or three days later he again visited the Buddha with **Citta Hatthisāriputta** (*q.v.*), when the Buddha continued the earlier discussion on personality and the soul. At the end of the discourse Poṭṭhapāda became the Buddha's follower.[1] Poṭṭhapāda is identified with **Pukkusa** of the **Mahā Ummagga Jātaka.**[2]

[1] D. i. 178 ff.

[2] J. vi. 478.

2. **Poṭṭhapāda.**—The Bodhisatta born as a parrot. For his story see the **Rādha Jātaka** (1).[1]

[1] J. i. 495 f.

3. **Poṭṭhapāda.**—A parrot, younger brother of **Rādha,** the Bodhisatta. Poṭṭhapāda is identified with **Ānanda.** For his story see the **Rādha Jātaka** (2).[1]

[1] J. ii. 132 ff.

4. **Poṭṭhapāda.**—A parrot born as the younger brother of the Bodhisatta and identified with **Ānanda.** For their story see **Kālabāhu Jātaka.**[1]

[1] J. iii. 97 ff.; see also J. iv. 129.

5. **Poṭṭhapāda Thera.**—In the past he was born as **Sunetta,** son of King **Kitava,** and because he insulted a Pacceka Buddha he was reborn in **Avīci.** Later he was born in a family of fishermen near **Kuṇḍinagara,** but, remembering his past lives, he refused to take part in any fishing. His parents therefore cast him out, but **Ānanda,** finding him starving, gave him food, and, at the Buddha's suggestion, ordained him. He soon became an arahant and dwelt with twelve others in **Sānavāsipabbata.** Poṭṭhapāda's kinsmen became petas, and his parents sent to him a brother, of whom Poṭṭhapāda was specially fond, to plead for his intervention. He therefore begged alms, and offered them to his colleagues in the name of his kinsmen, who thus regained happiness.[1]

[1] Pv. iii. 2; PvA. 177 ff.

Poṭṭhapāda Sutta.—A discussion between the Buddha and the Paribbājaka **Poṭṭhapāda,** held at the **Mallikārāma.**[1] It deals with the question of trances and of the soul, and also with the infinity and eternalism of the world. This sutta is significant as containing a list of the topics which **Paribbājakas** appear to have discussed at their meetings.

[1] D. i. 178-203.

Poṭhila, Poṭṭhila Thera.—During the dispensation of seven Buddhas, he was learned in the Tipiṭaka and preached to large numbers of monks, but he failed to win any attainment for himself. Wishing to rouse him to exert himself, the Buddha constantly referred to him as "Tuccha-Poṭhila." Poṭhila took the hint, and, travelling one hundred and twenty leagues, arrived at a forest hermitage where lived thirty monks. He asked their leader to help him, but he referred him to a junior monk, who, in his turn, referred him on, and so on, until at last he was forced to apply to the seven-year old novice who sat doing needlework. With his pride humbled, Poṭhila asked him for advice. In order to test him, the novice asked him to jump into a pool with his robes on. This Poṭhila did, and the novice, satisfied as to his earnestness, taught him how, in the case of an anthill with six holes into which a lizard entered, anyone, wishing to capture the lizard, would close up five of the holes. So with the six doors of the senses; close five doors, and concentrate on the door of the mind. At the end of the discourse, the Buddha appeared before

Poṭhila in a ray of light and Poṭhila became an arahant.[1] Two verses, addressed to him by **Moggallāna,** are given in the Theragāthā.[2]

[1] DhA. iii. 417-21. [2] vs. 1174-5.

Pota, Potana, Potala, Potali.—A city in **Kāsiraṭṭha,** the capital of the **Assaka** king.[1]

[1] J. ii. 155 f.; J. iii. 3; see also VvA. 259. It was probably near the residence of **Bāvarī** (see SNA. ii. 581).

Potaliputta.—A **Paribbājaka** who visited **Samiddhi** at the **Veḷuvana** in **Rājagaha** and said that he had heard the Buddha declare that all action and speech were vain, and that what passed in the mind was the only thing of importance. A stage could be reached in which there was no feeling whatever. Samiddhi protested that Potaliputta misinterpreted the Buddha's teaching, and Potaliputta then asked him questions regarding experience, which Samiddhi answered. Potaliputta, showing neither approval nor disapproval, walked away. When the Buddha heard from **Ānanda** of Potaliputta's questions and Samiddhi's answers he blamed Samiddhi for his hasty reply.[1]

[1] For details see **Mahākammavibhanga Sutta.** (M. iii. 207 ff.)

1. **Potaliya.**—A householder of **Āpaṇa.** Meeting the Buddha in a wood outside the town, he greeted him, and was addressed by the Buddha as "householder," at which he was very angry, for he had, so he said, handed over his wealth to his sons, and possessed only his food and clothing. But the Buddha told him that true retirement from the household meant far more than that, and, at the request of Potaliya, he proceeded to explain his words. At the end of the discourse Potaliya declared himself the Buddha's follower.[1]

[1] M. i. 359 ff.

2. **Potaliya.—**A wanderer (**Paribbājāka**) probably identical with the above (1). A conversation he had with the Buddha is recorded in the Aṅguttara Nikāya. At the end of the discussion he declares himself the Buddha's follower.[1]

[1] A. ii. 100 f.

1. **Potaliya Sutta.**—A discussion between the householder **Potaliya** and the Buddha as to what constitutes true retirement from household life. The Buddha shows, by means of various similes, that the pleasures of the senses are unsatisfying and dangerous, and should be avoided. Such renunciation brings higher knowledge.[1]

[1] M. i. 359 ff.

2. **Potaliya Sutta.**—The Buddha tells the **Paribbājaka Potaliya,** who visits him, of four kinds of persons found in the world: those who praise and dispraise rightly and seasonably, and those who praise and dispraise wrongly and unseasonably.[1]

[1] A. ii. 100 ff.

Pottika, Pottiya.—The son of a tailor and the friend of **Nigrodha-kumāra** and **Sākha-kumāra.** When Nigrodha became king, Pottika was appointed Treasurer. For their story see the **Nigrodha Jātaka** (No. 445). Pottika is identified with **Ānanda.**[1]

[1] J. iv. 37 ff.

Potthaka Sutta.—Quite new fibre-cloth is of an ill colour, painful to handle and of little worth; so is one of middling wear and one worn out. Men use worn-out fibre-cloth for wiping cooking pots or they throw it away. So are a novice, a monk of middle standing, or a senior monk, any of whom is immoral, of "ill colour." Their followers suffer because of them; hence they are painful to handle, and because gifts to them produce no good they are of little worth.[1]

[1] A. i. 246 f.

Potthakuṭṭha.—A Damiḷa in the service of **Aggobodhi IV.** He erected and endowed the **Māṭambiyapadhānaghara,** and built houses in the **Kuppurā-pariveṇa,** the **Kurundapillaka-vihāra** and the **Mahārājaghara.** When the king died, he administered the kingdom, threw the sub-king **Dāṭhāsiva** into prison and set **Datta of Dhanapiṭṭhi** on the throne. When Datta died, Potthakuṭṭha had **Hatthadāṭha** crowned king. Later, when **Mānavamma** rebelled against him, he ate poisoned food, provided by his friend, the chief of **Merukandara,** and died.[1]

[1] Cv. xlvi. 19, 39, 44; xlvii. 55, 61.

Potthadāyaka Thera.—An arahant. Ninety-one kappas ago he gave a gift of bark (? *pottha*) in the name of the Buddha, the Dhamma and the Saṅgha.[1]

[1] Ap. i. 237.

Potthasāta.—The senāpati of **Aggobodhi IV.** He built the **Aggabodhi-pariveṇa** in the **Jetavanārāmā** at **Anurādhapura.**[1]

[1] Cv. xlvi. 22.

Potthā.—Wife of **Vasabha's** uncle, the senāpati **Subha.** She saved the life of **Vasabha** and, later, when he became king, he made her his queen.[1] She built a thūpa and a temple attached to the **Catussāla** in the **Mahāvihāra.**[2]

[1] Mhv. xxxv. 70. [2] *Ibid.*, vs. 90.

Ponamaravatī.—A locality in South India, mentioned in the account of the campaigns of **Laṅkāpura.**[1]

[1] Cv. lxxvii. 20, 22, 92.

Porāṇavaṃsa.—A chronicle, probably of Ceylon, mentioned in the Gandhavaṃsa.[1]

[1] p. 70.

Porogāhali.—A district in the **Dakkhiṇadesa** of Ceylon.[1]

[1] Cv. lxvi. 108.

Polajanaka.—The younger son of **Mahājanaka.** For his story see the **Mahājanaka Jātaka.**[1]

[1] J. vi. 30 ff.

Polonnarutala.—A tank in Ceylon, restored by **Parakkamabāhu I.**[1]

[1] Cv. lxviii. 49.

Polamittā (*v.l.* **Posamittā**).—A yakkhiṇī, wife of **Mahākālasena.** She was from **Laṅkapura** and her mother was **Goṇḍā.**[1]

[1] MṬ. 259 f.

Posāla.—One of **Bāvari's** pupils. His question to the Buddha and the answer thereto are given in the **Posālamāṇava-pucchā** (or **Posāla Sutta**) of the **Parayana Vagga.**[1]

[1] SN. vs. 1006, 1112-5.

Posāla Sutta, or **Posālamāṇava-puccha.**—See **Posāla.**

Posiya Thera.—The son of a very rich banker in **Sāvatthi** and the younger brother of **Saṅgāmajita.** When grown up, he married and had a son. Soon after, he left the world to join the Order and, dwelling alone in the forest, became an arahant. Once, when he went to **Sāvatthi** to worship the Buddha, he visited his home. His former wife entertained him, but when he saw that she was trying to tempt him, he hurried away.

In the time of **Tissa** Buddha he was a hunter. The Buddha, out of compassion for him, went to the forest and stood near him. He provided the Buddha with a seat of grass and paid him homage. Soon after, he was killed by a lion.[1] He is probably identical with **Tiṇamuṭṭhidāyaka** of the Apadāna.[2]

[1] Thag. vs. 34; ThagA. i. 96 ff. [2] Ap. i. 280; see also ii. p. 455.

Ph.

1. **Phagguna.**—A monk. In the Saṃyutta Nikāya[1] he is represented as asking the Buddha if it were possible, by means of any of the senses, to recognize and proclaim the past Buddhas. The Buddha replies in the negative. It is probably the same monk who is mentioned in the Aṅguttara Nikāya[2] as having been visited during his illness by the Buddha on the suggestion of **Ānanda.** The Buddha found Phagguna in bed and grievously ill, and he talked to him and comforted him. Phagguna died soon after, having attained arahantship.

[1] S. iv. 52. [2] A. iii. 379 ff.

2. **Phagguna.**—See **Moḷiya-Phagguna.**

1. **Phagguna Sutta.** — A conversation between the Buddha and **Phagguna** (1) on the possibility of recognizing, by means of the senses, the Buddhas of the past.[1]

[1] S. iv. 52.

2. **Phagguna Sutta.**—Contains an account of the Buddha's visit to **Phagguna** (1) when the latter lay ill. At the end of the sutta is a list of six advantages of hearing the Dhamma and of testing its goodness in time.[1]

[1] A. iii. 379 ff.

3. **Phagguna Sutta.**—A discussion between the Buddha and **Moḷiya-Phagguna** as to whether anyone feeds on consciousness, exercises contact, feels, has craving, etc. The Buddha says that the question is badly formed; all these activities are conditioned by other activities, and so on.[1]

[1] S. ii. 12 ff.

Phaggunī.—One of the two Aggasāvikā of **Nārada** Buddha.[1]

[1] Bu. x. 24; J. i. 37.

Phandana Jātaka (No. 475).—A lion acquired the habit of going to lie under a *phandana*-tree, but one day a branch fell on his shoulder and hurt him. The lion thereupon conceived an enmity against the tree, and when a carpenter came in search of wood for a cartwheel, suggested to him that he should cut down that very tree as the wood would be excellent for his purpose. The deity of the tree, discovering this, appeared before the carpenter and told him that if he placed four inches of the hide of a lion on the rim of his wheel its value would be greatly enhanced. The carpenter, adopting both suggestions, killed the lion and cut down the tree.[1] This was one of the stories related by the Buddha in the course of the quarrel between the **Sākyans** and the **Koliyans.**[2]

[1] J. iv. 207 ff. [2] SNA. i. 358.

Phala Jātaka (No. 54).—The Bodhisatta was once a caravan leader, and, while travelling along a road which led through a forest, advised his followers to eat neither fruit, flower nor leaf, without first obtaining his leave. Near a village, on the outskirts of the forest, grew a *kimpakka*-tree which, in every respect, resembled a mango-tree. Some of the men ate of it, and their leader, when he knew this, gave them medicine which cured them. The next day the villagers rushed up to the tree hoping to find all the members of the caravan dead, like those of former caravans, leaving the villagers to rob their goods. They were amazed on finding these men alive.

The story was told in reference to a gardener employed by a squire in **Sāvatthi.** He took some monks round the garden and was amazed to find that they could tell the condition of a mango by looking at the tree.[1]

[1] J. i. 270 ff.

1. **Phala Sutta.**—The cultivation of the five indriyas leads to one of two results: either realization in this life, or the state of anāgāmī.[1]

[1] S. v. 236.

2. **Phala Sutta.**—Same as (1), only substituting the four *iddhipādas* for the five *indriyas.*[1]

[1] S. v. 285 f.

3. **Phala Sutta.**—On seven fruits to be obtained from the cultivation of the four *iddhipādas.*[1]

[1] S. v. 285.

4. **Phala Sutta.**—Four conditions which, if cultivated, lead to the Four Fruits of the Path.[1]

[1] S. v. 410 f.

Phalakadāyaka Thera.—An arahant. Ninety-one kappas ago he was a waggon-builder (*yānakāra*), and gave a plank of sandal-wood to the Buddha **Vipassī.** Fifty-seven kappas ago he was king four times under the name of **Bhavanimmita** (*v.l.* **Santa**).[1] He is probably identical with **Tissa Thera** (No. 13).[2]

[1] Ap. i. 174. [2] ThagA. i. 199 f.

Phalagaṇḍa.—One of the seven human beings born in the **Avihā**-world, where they will pass completely away.[1]

[1] S. i. 35, 60, etc.

Phalagga-pariveṇa.—A building in **Anurādhapura,** erected by **Devānampiyatissa** on the spot where **Mahinda** sat wrapt in meditation.[1]

[1] Mhv. xv. 209.

1. **Phaladāyaka Thera.** — An arahant. Ninety-two kappas ago he was an ascetic in **Himavā,** and gave a handful of fruit to **Phussa** Buddha.[1]

[1] Ap. i. 130.

2. **Phaladāyaka Thera.**—An arahant. In the time of **Padumuttara** Buddha he was an ascetic well versed in the Vedas who, seeing the Buddha, gave him a *puṇḍarīka*-fruit. One hundred and seven kappas ago he was a king named **Sumaṅgala.**[1] He is probably identical with **Susārada Thera.**[2]

[1] Ap. i. 160 f. [2] ThagA. i. 167.

3. **Phaladāyaka Thera.**—An arahant. Also called **Piyālaphaladāyaka.** In the time of **Sikhī** Buddha he was a pigeon who gave to the Buddha a *piyāla*-fruit. Fifteen kappas ago he was a king called **Mālabhi.**[1] He is probably identical with **Devasabha.**[2]

[1] Ap. i. 169 f. [2] ThagA. i. 187 f.

4. **Phaladāyaka Thera.**—An arahant. Ninety-four kappas ago **Siddhattha** Buddha came to him for alms after having arisen from *samādhi*, and he gave the Buddha various fruits. Fifty-seven kappas ago he was a king named **Ekajjha.**[1]

[1] Ap. i. 239.

5. **Phaladāyaka Thera.**—An arahant. In the time of **Vipassī** Buddha he was an ascetic living on the banks of the **Bhāgīrathī** and gave to the Buddha all the fruits he had gathered for his own meal.[1]

[1] Ap. i. 250.

Phaladāyaka-vimāna Vatthu.—The story of a gardener of **Bimbisāra.** The king expressed a desire to eat mangoes out of season, and the gardener, having promised to satisfy this desire, worked very hard and succeeded in making one of the trees bear four fruits. While on his way to the palace with these fruits, he saw **Moggallāna** and gave them to him, prepared to bear the king's wrath. Moggallāna gave the fruits to the Buddha, who gave one each to **Sāriputta, Mahā Kassapa** and **Moggallāna.** When Bimbisāra heard of what his gardener had done he was greatly pleased, and granted him a village and made him other presents. After death the gardener was born in **Tāvatiṃsa,** where he met Moggallāna.[1]

[1] Vv. vi. 3; VvA. 288 ff.

Pharusa Sutta.—Few are those who abstain from harsh speech.[1]

[1] S. v. 469.

Phalika.—One of the peaks of the **Himālaya.**[1] **Phalikaguhā** was evidently in this peak.[2]

[1] J. v. 415.

[2] J. ii. 6, 7, 8.

Phalikasandāna.—One of the Theras dwelling in the **Kukkuṭārāma** in **Pāṭaliputta** in the time of the Buddha.[1]

[1] Vin. i. 300.

Phaḷudhiya.—A Damiḷa chief, ally of **Kulasekhara.**[1]

[1] Cv. lxxvi. 99.

1. **Phassa Sutta.**—Because of diversity in elements arises diversity of perceptions, etc.[1]

[1] S. ii. 146.

2. **Phassa Sutta.**—Eye-contact is impermanent, changeable; so is it with the others.[1]

[1] S. iii. 226.

3. **Phassa Sutta.**—The arising of contact by the six senses is the arising of decay and death; and, similarly, its cessation.[1]

[1] S. iii. 230.

4. **Phassa Sutta.**—The desire and lust which is in the contact of the six senses is a corruption of the heart.[1]

[1] S. iii. 233.

Phassamūlaka Sutta.—Three things are rooted in, and conditioned by, contact: feeling pleasant, painful and neutral.[1]

[1] S. iv. 215.

Phassāyatanika Sutta.—The Buddha explains how necessary is the right understanding of the arising and destruction, the satisfaction and misery, and the escape from the sixfold sphere of contact.[1]

[1] S. iv. 43 f.

Phārusa, Phārusaka.—One of the parks of **Tāvatiṃsa.**[1]

[1] J. vi. 278; VibhA. 439; PSA. 259, etc.

Phārusaka.—A garden in Ceylon, laid out by **Parakkamabāhu I.**[1]

[1] Cv. lxxix. 10.

Phārusaphaladāyaka Thera.—An arahant. Ninety-one kappas ago he saw **Vipassī** Buddha and offered him a *phārusa*-fruit.[1]

[1] Ap. i. 296.

Phālakāla.—The name of three generals of **Rohaṇa** who were subdued by the forces of **Parakkamabāhu I.**[1]

[1] Cv. lxxv. 180, 183.

1. **Phāsu Sutta.**—The five abodes of comfort: the four *jhānas* and final emancipation of mind through insight.[1]

[1] A. iii. 119.

2. **Phāsu Sutta.**—The five comfortable abodes: living in amity with one's fellows in act of deed, in act of word, in act of mind, maintaining whole and unbroken the virtues, praised by the wise and living in accordance with the Ariyan view.[1]

[1] A. iii. 132; *cf.* D. ii. 88.

Phāsuvihāra Vagga.—The eleventh section of the Pañcaka Nipāta of the Aṅguttara Nikāya.[1]

[1] A. iii. 127 ff.

Phudhamanakamanta.—Mentioned among the *dhammika-vijjā.*[1]

[1] VibhA. 410.

Phulla.—Ninety-two kappas ago there were seven kings of this name, all previous births of **Saṅgharakkhita (Kadambapupphiya) Thera.**[1] *v.l.* **Puppha.**

[1] ThagA. i. 217; Ap. i. 217.

Phusatī.—Daughter of the **Madda** king and chief queen of the **Sivi** king **Sañjaya** and mother of **Vessantara.** She had been **Sudhammā,** daughter of **Kikī,** and was born in **Tāvatiṃsa** because of an offering of sandal-wood made by her to **Vipassī** Buddha. When she left Tāvatiṃsa, Sakka gave her ten boons: to be chief queen, to have dark eyes, dark eyebrows, to be named Phusatī, to have a son, to keep a slim figure, to have firm breasts, hair always dark, to have soft skin, and to save the condemned. She was called Phusatī because on the day of her birth her body smelt of sandal-wood. She was a previous birth of **Mahāmāyā.**[1]

[1] J. iv. 480 ff., 593; Cyp. i. 9.

"Phusatī" Sutta.—To him who toucheth not comes no touch. A wicked man's actions recoil upon him.[1]

[1] S. i. 13.

1. **Phussa.**—The eighteenth of the twenty-four Buddhas. He was born in the **Sirimāuyyāna** in **Kāsī,** his father being the khattiya **Jayasena**[1] and his mother **Sirimā.** He lived for six thousand years in three palaces: **Garuḷa, Haṃsa** and **Suvaṇṇabhara.** His wife was **Kisāgotamī** and his son **Ānanda** (or **Anūpama**). His body was fifty-eight cubits high. He left the world riding an elephant, and practised austerities for six months. A seṭṭhi's daughter, **Sirivaḍḍhā,** gave him milk-rice, while an ascetic, named **Sirivaḍḍha,** gave him grass for his seat, under an *āmaṇḍa*-(or *āmalaka*-)tree. His chief disciples were **Sukhita** (or **Surakkhita**) and **Dhammasena** among men and **Cālā** (or **Sālā**) and **Upacālā (Upasālā)** among women. His personal attendant was **Sambhiya. Dhanañjaya** and **Visākha** among men, and **Padumā** and **Nāgā** among women, were his chief lay patrons. The Bodhisatta was a khattiya named **Vijitāvī** of **Arimanda.** The Buddha lived for ninety thousand years and died at the **Sonārāma (Setārāma)** in **Kusinārā.** His relics were scattered.[2] **Ambapālī** was his sister.[3]

[1] AA. (i. 144) says that his father was **Mahinda** and that he had three step-brothers. One of them was **Uruvela Kassapa** (i. 165) in this birth.

[2] Bu. xix. 1 ff.; BuA. 192 f.; PvA. 19 f.

[3] Ap. ii. 613.

2. **Phussa Thera.**—He was the son of a ruler of a province and was trained in all accomplishments. Having heard a great Thera preach,

he left the world and joined the Order. He practised *jhāna* and became an arahant. One day an ascetic named **Paṇḍarassagotta** heard him preach and questioned him on the future progress of *bhikkhus*. Phussa's reply is contained in the Theragāthā.[1]

[1] vs. 949-80; ThagA. ii. 82 f.

1. **Phussadeva.**—One of the two chief disciples of **Dhammadassī** Buddha.[1]

[1] J. i. 39; Bu. xvi. 18.

2. **Phussadeva Thera.**—An eminent teacher of the Vinaya[1] in Ceylon. He was a contemporary of **Upatissa,** from whose views his own often differed.[2]

[1] Vin. v. 3. [2] See Sp. i. 263; ii. 456, 495; iii. 651, 653; iv. 890.

3. **Phussadeva Thera.**—An incumbent of **Kaṭakandhakāra** in Ceylon. He was among those taking part in the assemblies mentioned in **Kuddālaka, Mūgapakkha, Ayoghara** and **Hatthipāla Jātakas.**[1] Once **Māra,** assuming the form of the Buddha, tried to tempt him, but the Elder, seeing this form and deriving joy from its contemplation, became an arahant.[2]

[1] J. iv. 490; vi. 30. [2] Vsm. 263.

4. **Phussadeva.**—One of the chief warriors of **Duṭṭhagāmaṇī.** He was born in the village of **Gaviṭa** and his father was **Uppala.** Once, having gone to the vihāra with other boys, he saw a conch-shell offered at the bodhi-tree and blew on it. All those who heard him stood as if stunned, and he came to be called **Ummāda-Phussadeva.** His father was an archer, and he himself became very skilled in this art,[1] the best archer in the island.[2] In Duṭṭhagāmaṇī's fight with **Bhalluka,** Phussadeva sat behind the king on the elephant and shot Bhalluka. His arrow grazed the king's ear, causing the blood to flow. In expiation, Phussadeva cut off the lobe of his own ear and showed it to the king. Later the king planted Phussadeva's arrow on the floor, and covering it to its full height with *kahāpaṇas,* gave the money to Phussadeva.[3]

[1] Mhv. xxiii. 82 f. [2] *Ibid.*, xxv. 82. [3] *Ibid.*, 91 ff.

Phussamitta.—A monk of the **Kurundaka-vihāra** in Ceylon; he was evidently a commentator.[1]

[1] AA. i. 31.

Phussamittā.—A denizen of purgatory (*vinipātikā*) who had the power of travelling through the air.[1]

[1] Vsm. 382; PSA. 79.

Phussā.—One of the two chief women disciples of **Tissa** Buddha.[1]

[1] J. i. 40; Bu. xviii. 22.

Pheggū.—A Therī of **Jambudīpa** who came to Ceylon, where she taught the Vinaya.[1]

[1] Dpv. xviii. 12.

Phena Sutta.—Like a lump of foam, a water-bubble or a mirage, the trunk of a plantain tree, and the vision conjured up by a magician are, respectively, the body, feelings, perception, activities and consciousness, unreal, having no excuse. The sutta was preached at **Ayojjhā,** on the bank of the Ganges.[1]

[1] S. iii. 140 f.

B.

1. **Baka.**—A **Brahmā.** When the Buddha was once staying at **Ukkaṭṭhā** in the **Subhagavana,** he read the thoughts of Baka, who had conceived the idea that this world was permanent and free from decay and death; and the Buddha visited him in order to point out his error. Baka welcomed the Buddha but, owing to the influence of **Māra,** refused to acknowledge his error, until the Buddha, by the exercise of his magical power, prevented Baka from disappearing from sight, while he himself dissolved into complete darkness. The Buddha then proceeded to tell him of four incidents connected with his previous birth as **Kesava.**[1] Baka was once born in a noble family, but he renounced the world and became an ascetic named Kesava. One day, seeing a caravan in distress in the desert, by his supernatural power he turned a river into the desert, thereby rescuing the members of the caravan. On another occasion, while staying on the banks of the river **Eṇī,** near a frontier village, he found the village being attacked by dacoits, whom he drove away by causing them to see a vision of the royal police approaching, with himself at their head. On another day he saw people floating down the river in boats, making merry, singing and drinking. The Nagā of the river, incensed at their behaviour, appeared before them, threatening destruction. Kesava, assuming the form of a Garuḍa, frightened the

[1] M. i. 326 ff.; S. i. 142 ff.

Nāga away. The fourth incident is related in the **Kesava Jātaka** (*q.v.*). The Bodhisatta, known as **Kappa,** was the pupil of Kesava. Kesava, practising meditation, developed the fourth *jhāna* and was born in the **Vehapphala**-world. While there he developed the third *jhāna* and was born in the **Subhakiṇha** world. Thence he descended to the **Ābhassara** world, and, later, by practising the first *jhāna*, he was reborn in the same world, but with a span of life of only a single kappa.[2] See also **Baka-brahma Sutta.**

[2] J. iii. 358 ff.; SA. i. 164 f.; MA. i. 553 ff.

2. **Baka.**—The Bodhisatta, born as the king of Benares. For his story see *s.v.* **Pañcapāpā.**[1]

[1] J. v. 440 ff.

1. **Baka Jātaka** (No. 38).—A crane, living near a pond, where the water dried up in summer, offered to carry the fish to a distant pond where water was plentiful. The fish, very suspicious, sent one of their number with the crane to verify his words, and when he returned with a favourable report, they accepted the crane's offer. One by one the fish were carried off and eaten by the crane, till only a crab was left. The wily crab agreed to go too, but he clung round the crane's neck while being carried along and cut off his head with his pincers when he discovered the crane's intentions.

The story was told in reference to a monk of Jetavana who was a clever robe-maker. He could make robes of rags, which he dyed so skilfully that they looked new and costly. Visiting monks, on seeing them, would exchange their new robes for his old ones and not discover their folly till later. A similar robe-maker lived in a hamlet at some distance from Jetavana, who, hearing of the Jetavana monk, succeeded in cheating him. The monk was the crane and the hamlet-dweller the crab of the story.[1]

[1] J. i. 220 ff.

2. **Baka Jātaka** (No. 236).—The Bodhisatta was once the leader of a large shoal of fish. A crane, who wished to eat them, stood on the bank of the pond with outstretched wings, gazing vacantly into space. The fish were impressed by his pious demeanour, but were warned against him by the Bodhisatta.

The story was told in reference to a hypocrite who is identified with the crane.[1]

[1] J. ii. 233 f.

Bakagalluddhavāpī.—A locality in **Rohaṇa,** mentioned in the account of the campaigns of **Parakkamabāhu I.**[1]

[1] Cv. lxxv. 124.

Bakabrahma Jātaka (No. 405).—Relates the story of the Buddha's visit to **Baka Brahma** (*q.v.*) and the incidents mentioned regarding Baka's previous birth as **Kesava.**[1]

[1] J. iii. 358 ff.

Bakabrahma Sutta.—Relates the story of the Buddha's visit to **Baka** and the conversation between Baka and the Buddha on that occasion. The incidents of Baka's previous life are referred to but without detail.[1] *Cp.* **Brahmanimantika Sutta.**

This sutta cannot be identical with the **Bakabrahma Sutta** mentioned in Theragāthā Commentary and quoted there in full.[2] It is stated there that once when the Buddha was at **Jetavana** a certain Brahmā conceived the view that no monk or recluse could come to his world. The Buddha, aware of this, went to the Brahma world and stood in the air enveloped in flame. He was followed by **Moggallāna, Kassapa, Kappina** and **Anuruddha.** Moggallāna asked the Brahmā if he still held the same view, to which he replied that he no longer thought that he was eternal. (This shows that the Brahmā of the story was most probably Baka.) When the Buddha and his followers had departed, the Brahmā sent one of his retinue to Moggallāna to find out if there were other disciples of the Buddha as mighty as he. Moggallāna's answer was that there were many such.[3]

[1] S. i. 142 f.

[2] ii. 185 f.

[3] The sutta is given at S. i. 144 ff., but there the name given is "**Aparādiṭṭhi**" **Sutta.**

Bakkula, Bākula, Vakkula Thera.—He was born in the family of a councillor of **Kosambī,** and, while being bathed by his nurse in the waters of the Yamunā, he slipped into the river and was swallowed by a fish. The fish was caught by an angler and sold to the wife of a Benares councillor.[1] When the fish was split open the child was discovered unhurt, and cherished by the councillor's wife as her own son. On discovering his story, she asked permission of his parents to keep him. The king decided that the two families should have him in common, hence his name Bākula ("two-families, bi-kin").[2] After a prosperous

[1] This preservation of Bakkula was due to the power of the sanctity of his last life; it was a case of psychic power diffused by knowledge (*ñāṇavipphārā iddhi*), PS. ii. 211; Vsm. 379.

[2] *Cp.* the explanation of *bakkula* in *J.P.T.S.* 1886, pp. 95 ff.

life, at the age of eighty, Bakkula heard the Buddha preach and left the world. For seven days he remained unenlightened, but on the dawn of the eighth day he became an arahant. Later, the Buddha declared him to be foremost in good health.[3]

In the time of **Anomadassī** Buddha, he was a learned brahmin who became a holy hermit. He heard the Buddha preach and became his follower, and when the Buddha suffered from stomach trouble, he cured him and was reborn later in the Brahma world. In the time of **Padumuttara** Buddha, he was a householder of **Haṃsavatī,** and, hearing a monk acclaimed as most healthy, he wished for a similar honour in a future life. Before the appearance of **Vipassī** Buddha, he was born in **Bandhumatī,** where he became a hermit. Later, he saw the Buddha, acknowledged him as teacher, and cured a monk of *tiṇapupphakaroga* (? hay fever). In the time of **Kassapa Buddha,** he renovated an old vihāra and provided the monks with medicaments.[4] Bakkula lived to a very old age,[5] and shortly before his death ordained **Acela Kassapa,** who had been his friend in his lay days.[6] Bakkula was one of the four who had great *abhiññā* (*mahābhiññappattā*) in the time of **Gotama Buddha,** the others being the two chief disciples and **Bhaddā Kaccānā.**[7] He is often mentioned[8] as an example of a monk who practised asceticism without preaching it to others. Fifty-five kappas ago he was a king named **Anoma** (*v.l.* **Araṇemī**).[9]

[3] A. i. 25; for a problem connected with this, see Mil. 215 ff.

[4] AA. i. 168 ff.; MA. ii. 928 ff.; ThagA. i. 434 ff.; Ap. i. 328 ff.; PSA. 491.

[5] AA. ii. 596; according to the **Bakkula Sutta** (M. iii. 125), he was eighty years a monk. This is confirmed by DA. ii. 413, where his age is given as 160.

[6] See **Bakkula Sutta** below. The Thag. contains three verses (225-7) which he spoke when about to pass away.

[7] AA. i. 204.

[8] *E.g.*, MA. i. 348.

[9] Ap. i. 329.

Bakkula Sutta.—Bakkula's friend, **Acela Kassapa,** visits him at **Veḷuvana** in **Rājagaha.** Bakkula tells him of his life during the eighty years of monkhood, and Kassapa wishes to be ordained under him. Soon after, Kassapa becomes an arahant, and Bakkula passes away as he sat on his pyre.[1]

[1] M. iii. 124 ff.

Badaguṇa.—A locality in **Rohaṇa,** mentioned in the account of the campaigns of **Parakkamabāhu I.**[1]

[1] Cv. lxxiv. 124.

Badaratittha.—See **Padaratittha.**

Badaravallī.—The scene of a battle between the forces of **Mānābharaṇa** and those of **Parakkamabāhu I.**[1]

[1] Cv. lxxii. 96.

Badarikārāma.—A park about three miles from **Kosambī**[1] where **Khemaka** stayed during his illness. He was visited by monks from the **Ghositārāma.**[2] The Buddha is said to have stayed there and to have preached the **Tipallatthamiga Jātaka**[3] and the **Tittira Jātaka**[4] regarding **Rāhula** (*q.v.*), who spent a whole night in the Buddha's jakes at the Badarikārāma because he was unwilling to violate the rule laid down by the Buddha that no novice should share the room of an ordained monk.[5]

[1] S. iii. 126. [2] SA. ii. 230. [3] J. i. 160. [4] J. iii. 64. [5] See also Vin. iv. 16.

Badarībhātikamāna.—A locality in Ceylon, mentioned in the account of the campaigns of **Parakkamabāhu I.**[1]

[1] Cv. lxx. 148.

Badalatthala, Badalatthalī.—A locality in the **Dakkhiṇadesa** of Ceylon.[1] It was the abode of the senāpati **Saṅkha,** who was killed there.[2] Nearby was **Pilimvatthu**[3]; it was to Badalatthala that the young **Parakkamabāhu** first came when he escaped from his custodians. From there he went to **Buddhagāma,**[4] and later returned to Baddalatthala in order to meet his mother, **Ratanāvalī,** and the senāpati **Deva,** that he might visit his father with them.[5]

[1] Cv. lviii. 42; lxv. 26. [2] *Ibid.*, lxiv. 9. [3] *Ibid.*, lxv. 4. [4] *Ibid.*, lxvi. 19. [5] lxvii. 81.

Baddula Sutta.—See **Gaddula Sutta.**

Baddhaguṇa-vihāra.—A monastery in Ceylon. The cetiya there, destroyed by the **Coḷas,** was restored by **Vīrabāhu,** viceroy of **Vijayabāhu I.**[1]

[1] Cv. lx. 80.

Baddheraka.—An elephant of the king of **Kosala.** He was once very strong, but as he grew old he became weak and, one day, stuck fast in the mire. The elephant-trainer, by the king's orders, went to the elephant arrayed as for battle and caused the battle-drum to be beaten. The elephant's pride was roused and he rose from the mire.[1] *v.l.* **Pāveyyaka.**

[1] DhA. iv. 25 f.

Baddhasīmāpāsāda.—A twelve-storied uposatha-house built in **Pulatthipura** by **Parakkamabāhu I.**[1]

[1] Cv. lxxviii. 56, 67.

Bandha Sutta.—See **Vaccha Sutta.**

1. " **Bandhati** " **Sutta.**—Eight ways in which a woman attracts a man.[1]

[1] A. iv. 196 f.

2. " **Bandhati** " **Sutta.**—Eight ways in which a man attracts a woman.[1]

[1] A. iv. 197.

1. **Bandhana Sutta.**—The world is bound by pleasure; by abandoning craving, the world will become free.[1]

[1] S. i. 39.

2. **Bandhana Sutta.**—The Buddha once heard that **Pasenadi** had taken men prisoners and had bound them in chains. He thereupon declared that the bonds of passion were stronger than any chains.[1] The Commentary says[2] that the incident was connected with the loss of the king's turban diadem.

[1] S. i. 76. [2] SA. i. 115; *cp.* **Bandhanāgāra Jātaka.**

Bandhanamokkha Jātaka (No. 120).—The Bodhisatta was once chaplain to King **Brahmadatta.** While the king was absent, quelling a frontier rebellion, his queen sinned with all the messengers sent by the king to inquire after her welfare. On the day of the king's return, the chaplain, while decorating the palace, entered the queen's apartments, and she asked him to satisfy her lust. When he refused the queen (feigning illness) charged him with having ill-treated her. Thereupon the king ordered that the chaplain be beheaded, but the latter begged to be brought before the king, where he protested his innocence and proved, by the testimony of the king's messengers, the queen's wickedness. The king wished to put to death the queen and all the messengers, but the chaplain interceded on their behalf and they were pardoned. He himself retired to the Himālaya, where he became an ascetic.

The story was told in reference to the attempt of **Ciñcā** to bring calumny upon the Buddha. The queen is identified with Ciñcā and the king with **Ānanda.**[1]

[1] J. i. 437 ff.

Bandhanā Sutta.—Those who regard the body, feelings, perceptions, etc., as self, are fettered by bonds; those who do not are free.[1]

[1] S. iii. 164.

Bandhanāgāra Jātaka (No. 201).—The Bodhisatta was once born in a poor family and supported his mother. Having provided him with a wife, much against his will, she died soon after. When his wife was with child, he wished to go away and became an ascetic, but his wife persuaded him to stay. On her second conception he ran away and, becoming an ascetic, rejoiced in his freedom from the bonds of wife and family.

The story was related when some monks reported to the Buddha that a gang of thieves had been taken captive by **Pasenadi** and put in chains. No chains were stronger than those of passion, said the Buddha.[1]

[1] J. i. 139 ff.; *cp.* **Bandhana Sutta** (2); the verses given in the Jātaka are also found there.

1. **Bandhujīvaka Thera.**—An arahant. Thirty-one kappas ago he strung *bandhujīvaka* flowers together and offered them to **Sikhī Buddha.** Seven kappas ago he was a king named **Samantacakkhu.**[1] He is probably identical with **Devasabha.**[2]

[1] Ap. i. 175 f. [2] ThagA. i. 203 f.

2. **Bandhujīvaka Thera.**—An arahant. He met **Siddhattha Buddha** in the forest ninety-four kappas ago and offered him lotuses and *bandhujīvaka* flowers. Fourteen kappas ago he was a king named **Samuddakappa.**[1]

[1] Ap. i. 192.

1. **Bandhumatī.**—The city of birth of **Vipassī Buddha.**[1]

[1] J. i. 41; Bu. xx. 23; D. i. 7, etc.

2. **Bandhumatī.**—Wife of King **Bandhumā** and mother of **Vipassī Buddha.**[1]

[1] J. i. 41; Bu. xx. 23; D. i. 7, etc.

3. **Bandhumatī.**—A river near **Bandhumatī.**[1]

[1] SNA. i. 190.

1. **Bandhumā.**—King of **Bandhumatī** and father of **Vipassī Buddha.** His wife was **Bandhumatī.**[1] He had two daughters who, in their later lives, were **Mahāmāyā** and **Uracchadā.**[2] See also **Ekasāṭaka** and **Mettā Therī.**

[1] J. i. 41, etc. [2] J. vi. 480 f.

2. **Bandhumā.**—A Pacceka Buddha.[1]

[1] M. iii. 70; ApA. i. 107.

1. **Bandhura Thera.**—Son of the seṭṭhi of **Sīlavatī.** Having gone to **Sāvatthi** on business and heard the Buddha preach, he entered the Order, winning arahantship in due course. He later returned to Silāvatī and preached to the king, who became a convert, and built for him a vihāra called **Sudassana** and paid him great honour. Bandhura gave the vihāra to the monks and returned to Sāvatthi, saying that he had no need of possessions.

In the time of **Siddhattha Buddha** he was a watchman in the king's palace and offered *kaṇavera* flowers to the Buddha and his monks.[1]

He is probably identical with **Kaṇaverapupphiya** of the Apadāna.[2] *v.l.* **Sandhaya, Sandhava.**

[1] Thag. vs. 103; ThagA. 207 f.

[2] Ap. i. 182.

2. **Bandhura.**—The chief groom of the elephant house of the king of Benares. Bandhura had only one eye. A crow built her nest over the doorway of the elephant house, laid there her eggs and hatched out her young. But every time Bandhura entered or left the stable on the back of the elephant, he struck the crow's nest with his hook, thus destroying it. The crow, in despair, made complaint, and her cry was one of the sounds mentioned in the **Aṭṭhasadda Jātaka** (*q.v.*). When the king discovered how Bandhura was acting, he rebuked him and dismissed him from his service.[1]

[1] J. iii. 430 f.

Bandhula.—Son of a chieftain of the **Mallas** in **Kusinārā.** He studied at **Takkasilā** with **Mahāli** and **Pasenadi.** On his return home, he wished to give an exhibition of his skill, and the princely families of the Mallas bound sticks of bamboo in bundles of sixty, inserting a strip of iron in each bundle; they then suspended the bundles in the air and challenged Bandhula to cut them down. He leapt up in the air and smote them with his sword, but on discovering the treachery of his kinsmen, he threatened to kill them all; his parents, however, dissuaded him, and he went to live in Sāvatthi, where Pasenadi appointed him Senāpati. Bandhula's wife was **Mallikā** (known as **Bandhula-Mallikā** in order to distinguish her from the wife of Pasenadi). As she bore no children, Bandhula wished to send her back to her people; but when she went to bid farewell to the Buddha before her departure, he asked her to return to her husband. He accepted her, thereby showing his faith in the Buddha. Soon after she conceived a child, and her pregnancy-longing was to enter the lotus tank used by the princes of **Vesāli** on their coronation and to drink its water. Bandhula took her to Vesāli, drove away the strong guards who were posted at the lotus tank, and let Mallikā enjoy it to her heart's content. When the **Licchavi** princes heard of this, they were greatly enraged and pursued Bandhula's chariot, in spite of the warning of Mahāli. When the chariots of the Licchavis came into line, Bandhula, in order to frighten them, twanged his bow; but as they still pursued him, he shot a single arrow, which pierced each of the five hundred Licchavis through his girdle without their being aware of the wound. Bandhula told them of their plight; but they refused to believe him until they loosed the girdle of the foremost and he fell down dead. Thereupon they returned to their homes, bade farewell to their families, and fell dead on the moment of loosening their armour.

Mallikā bore twin sons sixteen times; each of them became perfect in the various arts, and each had a retinue of one thousand men. One day, Bandhula retried a case which had been unjustly decided by the judge and his decision was greatly applauded. The king, hearing the applause and learning the reason, appointed him judge.[1] But the former judges poisoned the king's mind against Bandhula, and the king, listening to them, sent Bandhula and his sons to quell a frontier rebellion, giving orders that they should all be murdered on the way home. This was done, and the news of the massacre was brought to Mallikā while she was entertaining five hundred monks led by the two Chief Disciples.[2] Mallikā read the message, and placing it in a fold of her dress, went on with her duties. **Sāriputta** discovered her fortitude at the end of the meal and greatly praised her. Mallikā, sending for her daughters-in-law, broke the news to them, urging them to harbour no resentment against the king. The king's spies, discovering this, brought the news to Pasenadi. The king was greatly moved, and having sent for Mallikā, begged her forgiveness and granted her a boon. She chose as her boon that she and her thirty-two daughters-in-law should be allowed to return home to **Kusinārā.** Bandhula's nephew, **Dīghakārāyāṇa,** was appointed commander-in-chief, but he never forgave the injury to Bandhula, and, in the end, brought about Pasenadi's deposition and consequent death.[3]

Bandhula is sometimes referred to as **Bandhulamalla.**[4]

Bandhula's wife, Mallikā, was one of the three persons possessing the **Mahālatāpasādhana,** the others being **Visākhā** and **Devadāniyacora.**[5]

1 It is probably this incident which is referred to at S. i. 74 (**Aṭṭhakaraṇa Sutta**); see also KS. i. 101, n. 3.

2 According to MA. (ii. 753) the Buddha was also present.

3 DhA. i. 228 f., 349-56; J. iv. 148 ff.; MA. ii. 753 f.

4 *E.g.*, J. iv. 148.

5 But see DhA. i. 412, where the daughter of Bārāṇasīseṭṭhi is substituted for Devadāniya.

From the time of her husband's death Mallikā laid aside the pasādhana, but, on the day on which the Buddha's body was being removed for cremation, she washed the pasādhana in perfumed water and placed it on the body, which it completely covered. She expressed the wish that, as long as she remained in *saṃsāra*, her body should need no ornament.[6]

[6] DA. ii. 597.

Babbarā.—Name of a tribe.[1]

[1] Ap. ii. 359.

Babbu Jātaka (No. 137).—There was once a rich merchant of **Kāsi** who amassed forty crores of gold. His wife died and, because of her love of money, was reborn as a mouse dwelling over the family treasure. In due course the rest of the family died and the village was deserted. The Bodhisatta was a stone-cutter, working a quarry near the mouse's residence. She, liking him, brought him one day a coin, suggesting that, with a part of it, he should buy her some meat. The Bodhisatta agreed, and this continued for some time. One day the mouse was caught by a cat, but she obtained her release by promising him some of her food. She was later caught by three other cats, but was let free on the same terms. The mouse thus had only one fifth of her food and grew very thin. The Bodhisatta noticed this, and when she told him the reason, he put her inside a crystal box and suggested that when the cats came she should refuse to have anything to do with them. The first cat arrived and, on being reviled by the mouse, jumped on the crystal box and was crushed to death. The same fate overtook the other cats. The mouse thus became free, and in gratitude to the Bodhisatta, showed him all the treasure.

The story was told in reference to **Kāṇā** (*q.v.*), who lost her husband owing to four monks. The monks were the cats and Kāṇā the mouse.[1]

[1] J. i. 477-80.

Barabbala.—A locality in Ceylon, mentioned in the account of the campaigns of **Parakkamabāhu I.**[1]

[1] Cv. lxxiv. 51.

1. **Bala Vagga.**—The second chapter of the Pañcaka Nipāta of the Aṅguttara Nikāya.[1]

[1] A. iii. 9-14.

2. **Bala Vagga.**—The third and eighth chapters of the **Bala Saṃyutta.**[1]

[1] S. v. 250, 252.

Bala Saṃyutta.—The sixth section of the Mahā Vagga of the Saṃyutta Nikāya.[1]

[1] S. v. 249-53.

1. **Bala Sutta.**—The four powers: energy, mindfulness, concentration and wisdom.[1]

[1] A. ii. 252.

2. **Bala Sutta.**—On the five powers: faith, self-respect (*hiri*), fear of blame, energy and wisdom.[1]

[1] A. iii. 248.

3. **Bala Sutta.**—On the six powers: faith, energy, mindfulness, concentration, insight, destruction of the āsavas.[1]

[1] A. iii. 280.

4. **Bala Sutta.**—On the seven powers: the five in Sutta 2 (above) to which are added mindfulness and concentration.[1]

[1] A. iv. 3.

5. **Bala Sutta.**—On the ten powers of an arahant, whereby he knows that his *āsavas* have come to an end.[1]

[1] A. v. 174 f.

6. **Bala Sutta.**—The five powers (*saddhā, viriya, sati, samādhi, paññā*) constitute the path which leads to the Uncompounded.[1]

[1] S. iv. 361.

7. **Bala Sutta.**—The practice of these five powers (see 6) is the path to the Uncompounded.[1]

[1] S. iv. 366.

8. **Bala Sutta.**—The eight powers of eight beings: weeping in children, anger in women, weapons with thieves, power in kings, discontent with fools, understanding with the wise, consideration with the learned, forgiveness with ascetics and recluses.[1]

[1] A. iv. 223.

9. **Bala Sutta.**—Just as all deeds requiring strength are done with the earth as their support, even so a monk, supported by virtue, cultivates the Noble Eightfold Path.[1]

[1] S. v. 45=S. v. 135.

Balakathā.—The ninth chapter of the Yuganandha Vagga of the Paṭisambhidāmagga.

Balakaraṇīya Vagga.—Several sections of the Mahā Vagga of the Saṃyutta Nikāya bear this name—*i.e.*, S. v. 45, 135, 138, 191, 240, 242, 246, 291, 308.

Balakkāra.—A **Kāliṅga** prince, kinsman of **Tiloka-Sundarī.** He came to Ceylon and was given honour and gifts by **Vijayabāhu I.**[1]

[1] Cv. lix. 46.

"**Balataṃ**" **Sutta.**—Six qualities, the possession of which destroys strength in concentration.[1]

[1] A. iii. 427.

Baladatta.—A king, last of the dynasty of **Brahmadeva,** who reigned in **Ekacakkhu.**[1]

[1] Dpv. iii. 25; MṬ. 128.

Baladeva.—The second of the sons of **Devagabbhā,** the brothers known as the **Andhakaveṇhuputtā.** Baladeva killed **Cānura** and **Muṭṭhika.** The latter, when dying, vowed vengeance and, having been born as a goblin in the **Kāḷamattikā** forest, assumed the form of a wrestler when Baladeva passed that way and killed and ate him.[1]

[1] J. iv. 81, 82, 88; PvA. 11, 93.

Baladevavattikā.—Followers of a certain cult who hoped for purification by their practices.[1]

[1] MNid. 89.

Balapāsāna.—A locality in **Rohaṇa,** mentioned in the account of the campaigns of **Parakkamabāhu I.**[1]

[1] Cv. lxxiv. 178; lxxv. 3, 5.

Balasena.—A king of fifty-seven kappas ago; a previous birth of **Upaṭṭhāyaka Thera.**[1]

[1] Ap. i. 241.

"**Balāni**" **Sutta.**—The four powers of faith, energy, mindfulness, concentration.[1]

[1] A. ii. 141 f.

Balibhojakā.—Probably the totemistic name of a Sinhalese clan; they are mentioned in connection with the celebrations in honour of the Tooth Relic in the reign of **Parakkamabāhu II.**[1]

[1] Cv. lxxxv. 51; see also Cv. *Trs.* i. 29, n. 2.

Balivadda Sutta.—On four kinds of oxen: those that are fierce to the cows of their own herd, to cows of other herds, those that are fierce to neither their own nor others; and the four corresponding kinds of men.[1]

[1] A. ii. 108.

Balisa Sutta.—Dire are gains, favours and flattery, like to a flesh-baited hook, **Māra** being the fisherman.[1]

[1] S. ii. 226.

Baliharaṇa.—A forest-tract (*vanasaṇḍa*) near **Kusinārā** where the Buddha is said to have stayed.[1] It was so called because the people there made offerings to various spirits.[2] The **Kinti Sutta** was preached there.[3]

[1] A. i. 274; v. 79. [2] AA. i. 457; MA. ii. 826. [3] M. ii. 238.

Baluggata.—Fifteen kappas ago there were twelve kings of this name, previous births of **Ugga Thera.**[1] *v.l.* **Khaluggata.**

[1] ThagA. i. 175; Ap. i. 165.

Bahalagaṅgā.—The name given to a portion of the river flowing from the south of **Himavā.** The section is that which flows between the **Tiyaggalapokkharaṇī** and the **Ummaggagaṅgā.** It flows through a rock for a distance of sixty leagues.[1]

[1] SNA. ii. 439; AA. ii. 760; UdA. 302; MA. i. 586.

Bahalamassu-Tissa Thera.—He was a pupil of **Mahātissa,** and when the latter was expelled by the **Mahāvihāra** monks for misdemeanour, Bahalamassu-Tissa left the Mahāvihāra in anger and, dwelling in **Abhayagiri,** formed there a separate faction.[1]

[1] Mhv. xxxiii. 96.

Bahukā.—A river to which sacrifices were offered.[1] *v.l.* **Bāhukā.**

[1] M. i. 39; J. v. 388 f.

Bahukāra Sutta.—Three persons who are very helpful to one another he who leads to the Three Refuges, he through whom one understands Ill, etc., and he who leads one to the destruction of the *āsavas.*[1]

[1] A. i. 123.

Bahucintī.—A fish. See the **Mitacintī Jātaka.**[1]

[1] J. i. 427 f.

"**Bahutarā-Sattā**" **Vagga.**—The tenth chapter of the Sacca Saṃyutta.[1]

[1] S. v. 473.

Bahudhanaseṭṭhi.—The name conferred by the king of **Rājagaha** on **Puṇṇa,** when the latter was raised to the rank of seṭṭhi.[1] See **Puṇṇa** (No. 2).

[1] DhA. iii. 307.

Bahudhātuka Sutta.—Preached at **Jetavana.** It contains a series of questions asked by **Ānanda** and the Buddha's answers. The Buddha describes various ways in which the monk can achieve mastery of the elements (*dhātu*), the senses, the chain of causation, the rationally possible and the rationally impossible. Other names for the sutta are **Catuparivaṭṭa, Dhammādāsa, Amatadundubhi** and **Anuttara-Saṅgāmavijaya.**[1]

[1] M. iii. 61 ff.

Bhudhīti.—A brahmin of the **Bhāradvājagotta** who had seven widowed daughters and was much in debt. One day he lost fourteen oxen, and, after searching for them for six days, he came across the Buddha in a forest-tract. He spoke the praises of the Buddha's freedom, unperturbed by the anxieties to which he himself was a prey—for the Buddha had no nagging wife, no creditors, no vermin disturbing his sleep. The Buddha agreed with him, and he was so pleased with the Buddha's words that he asked to be ordained. The Buddha ordained him[1]; the Commentary adds[2] that he took the newly ordained to **Pasenadi** to whom he related what had happened. The king summoned the man's creditors and paid them off, and having sent for his wife and daughters he took them under his protection. The man soon after became an arahant.

[1] S. i. 170 f. [2] SA. i. 187 ff.

Bahudhīti Sutta.—Relates the story of **Bahudhīti Bhāradvāja.**[1]

[1] S. i. 170 f.

Bahunandi.—See **Bāhuraggi.**

Bahuputta, Bahuputtaka.—King of Benares and husband of **Khemā.** He is identified with **Sāriputta.** For details see the **Haṃsa Jātaka.**[1]

[1] J. iv. 423 ff.; *cp.* **Seyya.**

Bahuputta-, Bahuputtaka-cetiya.—A shrine in the neighbourhood of **Vesāli,** to the north of that city.[1] The Buddha is said to have stayed there.[2] It was a pre-Buddhistic shrine and, according to the Commentaries,[3] was a many-branched *nigrodha* tree where persons prayed for sons to the deva of the tree. Hence its name.

Mahā Kassapa says that while yet a "learner" he paid homage to the Buddha at a **Bahuputtaka-nigrodha** where the Buddha had gone to meet him. The Buddha taught him of the training to be followed and, profiting by the lesson, eight days later Mahā Kassapa became an arahant. This nigrodha, however, was on the road from **Rājagaha** to **Nālandā** and was three leagues from **Rājagaha.**[4] It cannot, therefore, have been identical with the tree which gave its name to the Bahuputta-cetiya.

1 D. iii. 9.
2 *Ibid.*, ii. 118; Ud. vi. 1; S. v. 259.
3 *E.g.*, UdA. 323; SA. ii. 128, etc.
4 S. ii. 220; see *s.v.* **Mahā Kassapa.** It was here that the Buddha exchanged his robe for that of Kassapa, SA. ii. 128; ThagA. ii. 145; AA. i. 102; Mtu. iii. 50.

Bahuputtaka-nigrodha.—See **Bahuputtaka-cetiya.**

Bahuputtikā.—See **Soṇā Therī.**

Bahumaṅgala-cetiya.—A shrine in **Anurādhapura** in the image-house of which **Dhātusena** erected Bodhisatta figures. He also provided a diadem of rays for the Buddha images in the cetiya. These images were known as **Kālaselasatthā** and **Upasumbha.**[1] The cetiya is probably identical with the **Maṅgala-cetiya** (*q.v.*).

1 Cv. xxxviii. 65.

Bahubhāṇi Jātaka.—Evidently another name[1] for the **Kacchapa Jātaka** (No. 215) (*q.v.*).

1 Given in DhA. iv. 92.

Bahubhāṇī Sutta.—The five disadvantages of excessive talking: liability to falsehood, malice, harshness, babbling and suffering after death.[1]

1 A. iii. 254.

Bahula Sutta.—Four conditions which conduce to the growth of insight.[1]

1 S. v. 412.

Bahulikā, Bāhulikā.—A heretical sect among the Buddhists, an offshoot of **Gokulikā.**[1] The Dīpavaṃsa[2] calls the adherents of this sect **Bahu-**

1 Mhv. v. 5; Mbv. p. 97.
2 Dpv. v. 41.

suttakā. According to Tibetan sources[3] they derived their name from their teacher, Bahuśrutiya. In addition to the five propositions held by the **Mahāsaṅghikas,** they considered it as a fundamental doctrine that there is no mode of life leading to real salvation, that the truth of suffering is the Noble Truth, that to perceive the suffering of the *saṃskāras* is to enter perfect purity, that there is no way of seeing the misery of suffering and the misery of change; the Saṅgha is but subject to worldly laws and conditions, arahants acquire the doctrine of others, there is a rightly preached way and a right entry into *samāpatti.*[4]

[3] Rockhill, p. 183.
[4] *Ibid.*, 189.

Bahuvedanīya Sutta.—**Pañcakaṅga** asks **Udāyi**[1] how many kinds of feelings the Buddha mentions. Udāyi answers that there are three: pleasant, unpleasant and indifferent. Pañcakaṅga, however, insists that there are but two: pleasant and unpleasant. **Ānanda,** overhearing the conversation, reports it to the Buddha, who says that both Pañcakaṅga and Udāyi are correct because he himself classified feelings in various ways; sensual pleasures might be pleasant, but are not the highest pleasures; far better and more excellent are the pleasures enjoyed by a monk who develops the four *jhānas*, the plane of infinity of consciousness and the plane of nought.[2]

[1] **Paṇḍita-Udāyi,** says MA. ii. 629.
[2] M. i. 396 ff.; the sutta is repeated at S. iv. 223 ff., under the name of **Pañcakaṅga Sutta.**

Bahusodarī.—A goddess (*devadhītā*) living in **Gandhamādana.**[1] See the **Sāma Jātaka.**

[1] J. vi. 83.

Bahussuta Sutta.—Five qualities which make a man learned and wise.[1]

[1] S. iv. 244.

Bahussutakā.—Another name[1] for **Bāhulikā** (*q.v.*).

[1] Dpv. v. 41.

Bahūpakāra Sutta.—Five things which make a monk of great service to his residence.[1]

[1] A. iii. 263.

Bākula.—See **Bakkula.**

Bārāṇasī.—The capital of **Kāsi-janapada.** It was one of the four places of pilgrimage for the Buddhists—the others being **Kapilavatthu, Buddha-**

gayā and **Kusinārā**—because it was at the Migadāya in **Isipatana** near Bārāṇasī that the Buddha preached his first sermon to the **Pañcavaggiyā.**[1] This was the spot at which all Buddhas set in motion the Wheel of the Law (**Dhammacakka**). It is the custom of Buddhas to travel by air from the Bodhi-tree to the scene of their first sermon, a distance of eighteen leagues,[2] but the present Buddha did all the journey on foot in order to be able to meet on the way the **Ājīvaka Upaka** (*q.v.*).

Benares was an important centre of trade and industry. There was direct trade between there and **Sāvatthi,**[3] (the road passing through **Bhaddiya,**[4]) and between there and **Takkasilā.**[5] It was the custom for enthusiastic young men of Benares to go to the university at Takkasilā,[6] but there seem to have been educational institutions at Benares also, some of which were older than even those of Takkasilā.[7] From **Verañjā** to Benares there seem to have been two routes: one rather circuitous, passing through **Soreyya,** and the other direct, crossing the Ganges at **Payāgatittha.** From Benares the road continued to Vesāli.[8] On the road from Benares to Rājagaha was **Andhakavinda.**[9] There seems to have been friendly intercourse between the chieftains of Benares and the kings of **Magadha,** as shown by the fact that **Bimbisāra** sent his own physician, **Jīvaka,** to attend to the son of the Treasurer of Benares.[10] The distance from **Kosambī** to Benares was thirty leagues by river.[11]

The extent of the city of Benares, including its suburbs, at the time when it was the capital of an independent kingdom, is often stated[12] to have been twelve leagues. The names of several kings are mentioned in the Jātakas, among them being those of **Aṅga, Uggasena, Udaya, Kikī, Dhanañjaya, Mahāsīlava, Vissasena,** and **Saṃyama.**[13] The name which occurs most frequently, however, is that of **Brahmadatta,** which seems to have been the dynastic name of the Benares kings. In the **Mahāgovinda Sutta,** the foundation of Bārāṇasī is attributed to **Mahāgovinda,** its first king being **Dhataraṭṭha,** contemporary of **Reṇu.**[14] The Ceylon Chronicles[15] mention the names of others who reigned in Benares —*e.g.*, **Duppasaha** and sixty of his descendants; **Asoka,** son of **Samaṅkara,**

[1] D. ii. 141.
[2] MA. i. 388; BuA. 242, etc.
[3] DhA. iii. 429.
[4] Vin. i. 189.
[5] DhA. i. 123.
[6] See, *e.g.*, J. ii. 4; DhA. i. 250.
[7] KhA. 198; see also DhA. iii. 445, where **Susīma, Saṅkha's** son, goes from Takkasilā to Benares for purposes of study.
[8] Sp. i. 201.
[9] Vin. i. 220.
[10] *Ibid.*, 275 f.
[11] MA. ii. 929.
[12] *E.g.*, J. iv. 377; vi. 160; MA. ii. 608.
[13] For details see *s.v.* The SNA. on the **Khaggavisāṇa Sutta** contains the names of several kings of Benares who renounced the world and became Pacceka Buddhas.
[14] D. ii. 235 f.
[15] MṬ. 127, 129, 130.

and eighty-four thousand of his descendants; also sixteen kings, ancestors of **Okkāka.** The city itself had been known by different names at different periods; thus, in the time of the **Udaya Jātaka** it was called **Surundhana**; in that of the **Sutasoma, Sudassana**; in that of the **Soṇanaṇḍa,** Brahmavaddhana; in that of the **Khaṇḍahāla, Pupphavatī**; in that of the **Yuvañjaya, Rammanagara**[16]; and in that of the **Saṅkha, Molinī.**[17] It was also called **Kāsinagara** and **Kāsipura,**[18] being the capital of Kāsi. The **Bhojājānīya Jātaka**[19] says that "all the kings around coveted the kingdom of Benares." In the **Brahāchatta Jātaka,**[20] the king of Benares is mentioned as having captured the whole of **Kosala.** At the time of the Buddha, however, Benares had lost its great political importance. Kosala was already the paramount power in India, and several successful invasions of Kāsi by the Kosalans under their kings **Vaṅka, Dabbasena** and **Kaṃsa,** are referred to. The final conquest would seem to be ascribed to Kaṃsa because the epithet **Bārāṇasiggaha** (conqueror of Benares) is an established addition to his name.[21]

Later, when **Ajātasattu** succeeded in establishing his sway over Kosala, with the help of the **Licchavis,** Kāsī, too, was included in his kingdom. Even in the Buddha's time the city of Benares was wealthy and prosperous and was included in the list of great cities suggested by **Ānanda** as suitable places for the Parinibbāna of the Buddha.[22]

Mention is also made of a **Bānārasīseṭṭhi**[23] and a **Santhāgārasālā** (Mote Hall), which was then, however, no longer being used so much for the transaction of public business as for public discussions on religious and philosophical questions.[24] Near Benares was a grove of seven *sirīsaka*-trees where the Buddha preached to the Nāga-king **Erakapatta,**[25] and also the **Khemiyambavana** where **Udena** met **Ghoṭamukha**[26]; on the other side of the river was **Vāsabhagāma,** and beyond that another village called **Cundaṭṭhila.**[27]

The Buddha is several times spoken of as staying in Benares, where he preached several sermons[28] and converted many people including **Yasa,** whose home was in Benares,[29] and his friends **Vimala, Subāhu, Puṇṇaji** and **Gavampati,** all members of eminent families.[30] Isipatana (*q.v.*) became a monastic centre in the Buddha's time and continued so

16 J. iv. 119 f.

17 J. iv. 15.

18 *E.g.*, J. v. 54; vi. 165; DhA. i. 87.

19 J. i. 178.

20 J. iii. 116.

21 J. ii. 403.

22 D. ii. 146.

23 *E.g.*, DhA. i. 412; iii. 87, 365.

24 *E.g.*, J. iv. 74; ascetics who came to the city found lodging for the night in the Potters' Hall (*e.g.*, DhA. i. 39).

25 DhA. iii. 230.

26 M. ii. 158.

27 PvA. 168.

28 *E.g.*, A. i. 110 f., 279 f.; iii. 392 ff., 399 ff.; S. i. 105; v. 406; Vin. i. 189, 216 f., 289.

29 Vin. i. 15.

30 *Ibid.*, 19.

for long after. From there came twelve thousand monks under the leadership of **Dhammasena** to be present at the ceremony of the foundation of the **Mahā Thūpa.**[31]

In the past, Bārāṇasī was the birthplace of **Kassapa Buddha.**[32] In the time of **Metteyya Buddha,** Bārāṇasī will be known as **Ketumatī,** at the head of eighty-four thousand towns. Saṅkha will be Cakkavatti there, but he will renounce the world and will become an arahant under Metteyya.[33] Bārāṇasī evidently derives its name from the fact that it lies between the two rivers Barṇā and Asi.[34]

[31] Mhv. xxix. 31.
[32] Bu. xxv. 33.
[33] D. iii. 75 f.
[34] CAGI. 499 f.

Bārāṇasīseṭṭhi.—See **Mahādhana.**

1. **Bāla Vagga.**—The fifth section of the Dhammapada.

2. **Bāla Vagga.**—The third chapter of the Duka Nipāta of the Aṅguttara Nikāya.[1]

[1] A. i. 59-61.

3. **Bāla Vagga.**—The tenth chapter of the Duka Nipāta of the Aṅguttara Nikāya.[1]

[1] A. i. 84-6.

4. **Bāla Vagga.**—The first chapter of the Tika Nipāta of the Aṅguttara Nikāya.[1]

[1] A. iii. 101-5.

Bālaka.—See below, **Bālakaloṇakāragāma.**

Bālakaloṇakārāma, Bālakaloṇakārāgama.—A locality near **Kosambī.** When the monks of Kosambī started quarrelling, the Buddha left them and went to Bālakaloṇakārāma, where he visited **Bhagu** and preached to him on the virtues of solitude. From there the Buddha proceeded to **Pācīnavaṃsadāya.**[1] The readings of the texts are uncertain, and it is impossible to say whether a village (*gāma*) is meant or only a grove (*ārāma*). The reading Bālakaloṇakāragāma occurs in the Majjhima Commentary[2]; but even here two explanations are given: one to the effect that **Bālaka** was the name of a village of salt-makers (? *loṇakāragāma*) belonging to **Upāli-gahapati.** When the inhabitants of the village came to Upāli with their taxes, he went with them (*bālakagāmavāsiniyā*

[1] Vin. i. 350; M. iii. 154; DhA. i. 47; J. iii. 489.
[2] MA. ii. 596.

. . . *parisāya*) to see **Nigaṇṭha Nātaputta.** The other explanation is that the word *bālakiniyā* in the text is an adjective meaning "composed of fools" (*bālavatiyā bālussannāya*).[3] The confusion seems, therefore, to have arisen very early. Upāli's village (of Bālaka), if such a place existed, was probably near **Nālandā.**

[3] *Cp.*, J. i. 246, where mention is made of *bālagāmikamanussā* who were obviously fools.

Bālacittapabodhanī.—The name of a *Ṭīkā.*[1]

[1] Gv. 65, 67.

Bālanakkhatta.—A festival lasting for seven days, during which people smeared their bodies with ashes and cow-dung and went about talking coarsely. They respected no one, and when they visited at a house where their conversation was not appreciated, they received one penny to go away. Once when the festival was being held in **Sāvatthi,** the Buddha's followers requested him not to leave the monastery, and provided him and the monks with all requisites so that they did not have to go out.[1]

[1] DhA. i. 256 f.

Bālapaṇḍita Sutta.—The 129th sutta of the Majjhima Nikāya, preached at **Jetavana.** It deals with the disabilities of folly and the pain and anguish resulting therefrom, also with the advantages of wisdom and the bliss to which it leads. It contains, besides, descriptions of the horrors of the hells, expressed by means of various similes.[1] The sutta forms a kind of prose background to the **Bāla Vagga** and the **Paṇḍita Vagga** of the Dhammapada. **Mahinda** preached this sutta at the **Nandanavana** in **Anurādhapura,** and one thousand women, who listened to him, became sotāpannas.[2]

[1] M. iii. 163 ff.; *cp.* S. ii. 23 f.

[2] Mhv. xv. 4.

Bālava.—A maintenance village, given by **Aggabodhi V.** to the padhānaghara of Dāṭhāsiva.[1]

[1] Cv. xlvi. 13.

Bālādicca.—A monastery in South India, the residence of **Coḷiya Dīpaṅkara (Buddhappiya),** author of the **Rūpasiddhi.**[1]

[1] P.L.C. 220.

Bālappabodhana.—A Pāli work, probably a Commentary.[1] There exists a Ṭīkā on it.[2]

[1] Gv. 63, 73.

[2] *Ibid.*, 65, 75.

Bālāvatāra.—A Pāli grammar in seven chapters, by **Dhammakitti** (or **Vācissara**), written in the fourteenth century. It is based on the **Kaccāyana** and forms an extremely good summary of Pāli grammar. There are to be found several Sinhalese paraphrases of the work and two ṭīkās in Pāli.[1]

[1] For details see P.L.C. 243 ff.

Bālisika Sutta.—Like baited hooks cast by a fisherman are the "objects" cognisable by the external sense-spheres. He who avoids them has escaped from the clutches of **Māra.**[1]

[1] S. iv. 158.

Bāḷhagilāyana (or **Gihīnaya**)[1] **Sutta.**—A number of monks visit **Anuruddha,** who lies grievously ill in the **Andhakavana,** and ask him how it is that painful feelings make no impression on his mind. He answers that it is because he is well grounded in the four *satipaṭṭhānā.*[2]

[1] But see KS. v. 268, n. 2. [2] S. v. 302.

Bāvarī.—A brahmin ascetic who went from **Sāvatthi** to **Dakkhiṇāpatha** and lived on the banks of the **Godhāvarī** in a hermitage which lay half in the territory of **Assaka** and half in that of **Aḷaka.** He received the revenue of a village near by and held a great sacrifice, spending all he possessed. Then to him came a brahmin of terrible mien, demanding five hundred pieces.[1] When Bāvarī told him of his poverty, the brahmin cursed him saying that his head would split in seven pieces. Bāvarī was greatly distressed, but a devatā,[2] seeing his trouble, reassured him by saying that the brahmin knew neither the meaning of "head" nor of "the splitting of it." "Who then knows it?" asked Bāvarī, and the devatā told him of the appearance in the world of the Buddha. Forthwith he sent his sixteen pupils—**Ajita, Tissametteyya, Puṇṇaka, Mettagū, Dhotaka, Upasīva, Nanda, Hemaka, Todeyya, Kappa, Jatukaṇṇī, Bhadrāvudha, Udaya, Posāla, Mogharāja** and **Piṅgiya**—to Sāvatthi to see the Buddha and to find out if his claims to Buddhahood were justified. The pupils went northward, through **Aḷaka, Patiṭṭhāna, Māhissati, Ujjeni, Gonaddha, Vedisā, Vanasavhya** (or **Tumbava,** *v.l.* **Vanasāvatthi**), **Kosambī, Sāketa** and **Sāvatthi;** then, finding that the Buddha had gone to **Rājagaha,** they followed him there to the **Pāsāṇaka-cetiya,** passing through **Setavyā, Kapilavatthu, Kusinārā, Pāvā, Bhoganagara** and **Vesāli.** When

[1] He was a brahmin of Dunniviṭṭha. His wife was a descendant of the family of Jūjaka and was constantly nagging at him. It was she who sent him to Bāvarī (AA. i. 183).

[2] His mother in a previous birth (AA. i. 183).

they arrived before the Buddha, they greeted him in the name of Bāvarī, and being satisfied that he bore the characteristic signs of a Great Being,[3] Ajita asked Bāvarī's question of the Buddha, and when that had been answered, each of the pupils asked him a question in turn, to which the Buddha replied.[4]

According to the Commentary,[5] all Bāvarī's disciples and their sixteen thousand followers whom they had gathered on their way, became arahants at the conclusion of the Buddha's sermon, save only Piṅgiya, Bāvarī's nephew, who became an anāgāmī, because he had been thinking of Bāvarī when the Buddha preached. Piṅgiya took leave of the Buddha and returned to Bāvarī, to whom he recounted all these events. At the end of his recital, the Buddha appeared before them in a ray of glory and preached to them. Piṅgiya thereupon became an arahant and Bāvarī an anāgāmī.

In the time of **Kassapa Buddha** Bāvarī was King **Kaṭṭhavāhana** (*q.v.*). Hearing of the Buddha from his friend, the king of Benares, he sent messengers, including his nephew, to find out about the Buddha and to report to him. But the nephew returned with the news of the Buddha's death which had taken place before their arrival at Benares. Thereupon, Kaṭṭhavāhana, having accepted the Buddha's teaching, engaged in various good deeds and was reborn after death in the *Kāmāvacara*-deva-world. From there he was born in the family of **Pasenadi's** chaplain and was the teacher of Pasenadi's boyhood. Unwilling to remain longer in the court, he took leave of the king and lived in the royal park as an ascetic. Then, wishing for greater peace, he retired to an island (*antara-dīpa*) in the Godhāvarī where the two kings Assaka and Aḷaka gave him a tract of land, five leagues in extent, the residence of the sages of old. It was from there that he sent his disciples to the Buddha.[6] At that time he was one hundred and twenty years old. Bāvarī was the name of his gotta. He bore on his body three of the marks of a Great Being.[7]

[3] For a problem arising out of the manner in which some of the marks were seen, see Mil. 168 f.; DA. i. 275 f.

[4] This account is given in SN. vs. 976-1148.

[5] SNA. 603 f.

[6] SNA. 575 ff.; AA. i. 182 ff.

[7] SN. vs. 1019.

Bāveru.—A kingdom outside India, beyond the sea. Trade was carried on between Bāveru and India. See the **Bāveru Jātaka.** Bāveru is identified with Babylon.[1]

[1] *E.g.*, Buddhist India, p. 104.

Bāveru Jātaka (No. 339).—Once some merchants sailed from **Bārāṇasī** to **Bāveru** with a crow on board to help them in finding land. There were then no birds in Bāveru, and the people, marvelling at the sight, bought the bird, after much bargaining, for one hundred pieces and paid it great honour. On another voyage, the same merchants brought with them a peacock (the Bodhisatta), and this bird, after much show of reluctance on the part of the merchants, was sold to the people of Bāveru for one thousand pieces. From the time of the arrival of the more beautiful peacock, the crow was entirely neglected and flew away on to a refuse heap.

The story was told in reference to the fact that from the time the Buddha appeared in the world, the heretics lost all their glory.[1]

[1] J. iii. 126 ff.; *cp.* Ud. vi. 10.

Bāhika.—See **Bāhiya.**

1. **Bāhiya Dārucīriya.**—An arahant. He was born in the family of a householder of **Bāhiya**[1]—hence his name—and engaged himself in trade, voyaging in a ship. Seven times he sailed down the Indus and across the sea and returned safely home. On the eighth occasion, while on his way to **Suvaṇṇabhūmi,** his ship was wrecked, and he floated ashore on a plank, reaching land near **Suppāraka.** Having lost all his clothes, he made himself a bark-garment, and went about, bowl in hand, for alms in Suppāraka. Men, seeing his garment and struck with his demeanour, paid him great honour. Though they offered him costly robes and many other luxuries, he refused them all and his fame increased. Because of his bark-garment he was known as **Dārucīriya.** In due course he came himself to believe that he had attained arahantship, but a devatā,[2] reading his thoughts and wishing him well, pointed out to him his error and advised him to seek the Buddha at **Sāvatthi.** By the power of the devatā, Bāhiya reached Sāvatthi in one night, a distance of one hundred and twenty leagues, and was told that the Buddha was in the city begging alms. Bāhiya followed him thither and begged to be taught something for his salvation. Twice he asked and twice the Buddha refused, saying that it was not the hour for teaching.[3] But Bāhiya insisted, saying that life was uncertain and that the Buddha or he might die. The

[1] Ap. ii. 476 says he was born in **Bhārukaccha.**

[2] A Suddhāvāsa-brahmā, who had been his fellow-celibate in the time of Kassapa Buddha, says the Commentary. See below and also MA. i. 340.

[3] The Commentaries say that Bāhiya was excited by his meeting with the Buddha and that the Buddha wished to give him time to regain his calm, hence his refusal. The Buddha knew of his impending death and of his *upanissaya* for arahantship. He was a *pacchimabhavika.*

Buddha then taught him the proper method of regarding all sense-experiences—namely, as experiences and no more. Even as he listened, Bāhiya became an arahant and the Buddha left him. Shortly after, Bāhiya was gored to death by a cow with calf.[4] The Buddha, seeing his body lying on the dung heap, asked the monks to remove it and to have it burnt, erecting a thūpa over the remains. In the assembly he declared Bāhiya to be foremost among those who instantly comprehended the Truth (*khippābhiññāṇaṃ*).[5]

Bāhiya's resolve to attain to this eminence was made in the time of **Padumuttara Buddha** when he heard the Buddha declare a monk foremost in instantaneous comprehension. In the time of **Kassapa Buddha,** when the Buddha's teachings were fading from the minds of men, Bāhiya was one of seven monks who climbed a rock, determined not to leave it until they had attained their goal. Their leader became an arahant and the second an anāgāmī—passing into the Suddhāvāsa-world; the rest were reborn in this age as **Pukkusāti, Kumāra-Kassapa, Dabba-Mallaputta, Sabhiya** and **Bāhiya.** Although Bāhiya had kept the precepts in previous births, he had never given a bowl or a robe to a monk. For this reason the Buddha did not, at the end of his sermon, ordain him by the "*ehi bhikkhu-pabbajā.*" The Buddha knew that Bāhiya had not sufficient merit to obtain divine robes. Some say that he was once a brigand and had shot a Pacceka Buddha with an arrow and had taken possession of the Pacceka Buddha's begging-bowl and robe. Bāhiya met his death while searching for a robe in which to be ordained.[6] The cow which killed Bāhiya was identical with the one which killed Pukkusāti, **Tambadāṭhika** and **Suppabuddha.**[7]

[4] *Cp.* the story of **Pukkusāti.**
[5] A. i. 24; Ud. i. 10.
[6] UdA. 77 ff.; AA. i. 156 ff.; DhA. ii. 209 ff.; Ap. ii. 475 ff.
[7] For her story see DhA. ii. 35 f.

2. **Bāhiya.**—A Damiḷa usurper who reigned in **Anurādhapura** for two years (between 43 and 29 B.C.). He was commander-in-chief of **Puḷahattha** whom he slew, being himself, in turn, slain by his own commander-in-chief, **Panayamāra.**[1]

[1] Mhv. xxxiii. 56 ff.; Dpv. xx. 15.

3. **Bāhiya.**—A monk. He is said to have come to the Buddha asking for a teaching in brief and the Buddha told him to dwell on the impermanence of the senses and of sense-objects. Profiting by the lesson, Bāhiya dwelt apart and, putting forth effort, soon became an arahant.[1] It is perhaps the same monk—called **Bāhiya** or **Bāhika**—who is mentioned

[1] S. iv. 63 f.

elsewhere[2] as asking for the Buddha for a lesson and being told to meditate on the four *satipaṭṭhānas*. This contemplation led to arahantship.

[2] S. v. 165 f.

4. **Bāhiya.**—A monk, fellow-dweller of **Anuruddha** at the **Ghositārāma.** He seems to have taken a prominent part in the disputes of the **Kosambī** monks, helping them, but Anuruddha let him take his own way, not protesting at all.[1]

[1] A. ii. 239; *cf.* KhA. 115.

5. **Bāhiya, Bāhika.**—The name of a country, residence of **Bharata,** the hunter mentioned in the **Aṭṭhasadda Jātaka.**[1] See also **Bāhiya Jātaka.**

[1] J. iii. 432.

Bāhiya Jātaka (No. 108).—Once **Brahmadatta,** king of Benares, saw from his window a fat and badly dressed woman relieving nature modestly and decently as she passed the courtyard of the palace when pressing need came upon her. The king was pleased with her quickness and decency, and having sent for her made her his chief queen. Their son became a Cakkavatti.

The story was told in reference to the fat wife of a **Licchavi** prince. The monks expressed surprise that he should love her, but the Buddha pointed out that she was healthy and cleanly in her house.[1]

In the course of the Jātaka, the woman is referred to as a *bāhiyā*, which the scholiast explains by *bahijanapadavāsī*. Bāhiya here, therefore, probably means "rustic."

[1] J. i. 420 ff.

1. **Bāhiya Sutta.**—Relates the incident of **Bāhiya** (3) asking the Buddha for a lesson.[1]

[1] S. iv. 63.

2. **Bāhiya Sutta.**—The same as the above, but the lesson given is on the *satipaṭṭhānas*.[1]

[1] S. v. 165.

Bāhukā.—See **Bahukā.**

Bāhuna.—A monk who is said to have asked the Buddha, while on the banks of the **Gaggarā** Lake in **Campā,** about the conditions from which the Tathāgata is released and emancipated. The Buddha enumerated ten such.[1]

[1] A. v. 151 f.

Bāhuna Sutta.—The questions asked by **Bāhuna** (*q.v.*) and the Buddha's answers thereto.[1]

[1] A. v. 151 f.

Bāhumatī.—A holy river where men bathe in order to expiate their sins.[1]

[1] M. i. 39; MA. i. 145.

Bāhuraggi.—One of seven beings born in the **Avihā**-world, there to pass away entirely. *v.l.* **Bahunandi.**[1]

[1] S. i. 35, 60; ThigA. 222.

Bindumatī.—A courtezan of **Pāṭaliputta.** She was present when **Asoka,** sailing up the Ganges, asked his ministers and the people if there were any person who could make the river flow backwards. Bindumatī performed an act of Truth (*saccakiriyā*) and the river rolled back.[1]

[1] Mil. 121 f.

Bindusāra.—King of **Magadha** and father of **Asoka.** He was the son of **Candagutta** and reigned for twenty-eight years. He had one hundred sons—the eldest being **Sumana**—ninety-nine of whom were killed by Asoka.[1] Bindusāra patronised the brahmins and provided constant meals for sixty thousand brahmins of various sects.[2] His mother was Candagutta's maternal cousin and chief queen. One day, while Bindusāra was yet unborn, she was eating with Candagutta and he fed her with some food prepared for himself. The food contained poison, placed there by the orders of Candagutta's minister, **Cāṇakka,** that the king might gradually be made immune from poison. Cāṇakka entered as she was about to swallow the food, and, anxious to save the unborn child, he cut off the queen's head with a sword before the food could travel down into her stomach, opened her womb, removed the child, and placed it in the womb of a freshly slaughtered goat. For seven days the child lay in the womb of a goat, each day a fresh one, until, at the end of these seven days, the child was ready for birth. Because of this, Bimbisāra's body was spotted in various places from the blood of the goats, and from this he obtained his name.[3] Bindusāra's chief queen was **Dhammā** (*q.v.*) of the **Moriya** clan. She bore two sons, Asoka and **Tissa.**[4] Bindusāra had to kill the yakkha **Devagabbha** (*q.v.*) before he could ascend the throne.[5]

[1] Mhv. v. 18 f., 38 f.; Dpv. v. 101; vi. 15; some accounts (*e.g.*, MṬ. 324) say he had one hundred and one sons.

[2] Sp. i. 44.

[3] MṬ. 187 f.

[4] *Ibid.*, 189, 324.

[5] *Ibid.*, 188.

Bimbasundarī.—Probably another name for **Bimbādevī** (*q.v.*). She is identified with **Amarādevī** of the **Mahā Ummagga Jātaka.**[1]

[1] J. vi. 478.

Bimbādevī.—See *s.v.* **Rāhulamātā.**

Bimbijāliya Thera.—An arahant. In the past he gave a *bimbijālika* flower to **Padumuttara Buddha.** Sixty-eight kappas ago he was king four times under the name of **Kiñjakesara.**[1]

[1] Ap. i. 225.

Bimbisāra.—King of **Magadha** and patron of the Buddha. He ascended the throne at the age of fifteen and reigned in **Rājagaha** for fifty-two years. The Buddha was five years older than Bimbisāra, and it was not until fifteen years after his accession that Bimbisāra heard the Buddha preach and was converted by him. It is said[1] that the two were friends in their youth owing to the friendship which existed between their fathers.[2] But according to the **Pabbajā Sutta**[3] the first meeting between the Buddha and Bimbisāra took place in Rājagaha under the **Paṇḍavapabbata,** only after the Buddha's Renunciation. The king, seeing the young ascetic pass below the palace windows, sent messengers after him. On learning that he was resting after his meal, Bimbisāra followed him and offered him a place in his court. This the Buddha refused, revealing his identity. The Commentary adds[4] that Bimbisāra wished him success in his quest and asked him to visit first Rājagaha as soon as he had attained Enlightenment. It was in fulfilment of this promise that the Buddha visited Rājagaha immediately after his conversion of the **Tebhātika Jaṭilā.** He stayed at the **Supatiṭṭha-cetiya** in **Laṭṭhivanuyyāna,** whither Bimbisāra, accompanied by twelve *nahutas* of householders, went to pay to him his respects. The Buddha preached to them, and eleven *nahutas*, with Bimbisāra at their head, became sotāpannas. On the following day the Buddha and his large retinue of monks accepted the hospitality of Bimbisāra. **Sakka,** in the guise of a young man, preceded them to the palace, singing songs of glory of the Buddha. At the conclusion of the meal, Bimbisāra poured water from a golden jar on the Buddha's hand and dedicated **Veḷuvana**

[1] Mhv. ii. 25 ff.; Dpv. iii. 50 ff.

[2] Bimbisāra's father was called **Bhāti** (MṬ. 137; Dpv. iii. 52); according to Thibetan sources (Rockhill, *op. cit.*, 16) he was called Mahāpaduma and his mother Bimbī.

[3] SN. vs. 405 ff.; also J. i. 66 and DhA. i. 85; also Rockhill, p. 27.

[4] SNA. ii. 386.

for the use of him and of his monks.[5] From this moment up till the time of his death, a period of thirty-seven years, Bimbisāra did all in his power to help on the new religion and to further its growth. He set an example to his subjects in the practice of the precepts by taking the uposatha vows on six days of each month.[6]

Bimbisāra's chief queen was **Kosaladevī** (*q.v.*), daughter of **Mahākosala** and sister of **Pasenadi.** On the day of her marriage she received, as part of her dowry, a village in **Kāsi,** for her bath-money. Her son was **Ajātasattu**[7] (*q.v.*). Bimbisāra had other wives as well; **Khemā,** who, at first, would not even visit the Buddha till enticed by Bimbisāra's descriptions of the beauties of Veḷuvana; and the courtezan **Padumavatī,** who was brought from **Ujjenī,** with the help of a yakkha, so that Rājagaha might not lack a *Nagarasobhinī.* Both these later became nuns. Padumavatī's son was **Abhaya.** Bimbisāra had another son by **Ambapālī,** known as **Vimala Koṇḍañña,** and two others, by different wives, known as **Sīlava** and **Jayasena.** A daughter, **Cundī,** is also mentioned.[8]

Bimbisāra's death, according to the Commentaries,[9] was a sad one. Soothsayers had predicted, before the birth of Ajātasattu, that he would bring about the death of his father, for which reason his mother had wished to bring about an abortion. But Bimbisāra would not hear of this, and when the boy was born, treated him with the greatest affection.[10] When the prince came of age, **Devadatta,** by an exhibition of his iddhi-power, won him over to his side and persuaded him to encompass the death of his father, Bimbisāra's patronage of the Buddha being the greatest obstacle in the path of Devadatta. The plot was discovered, and Bimbisāra's ministers advised him to kill Ajātasattu, Devadatta and their associates. But Bimbisāra sent for Ajātasattu and, on hearing that he desired power, abdicated in his favour. Devadatta chided Ajātasattu for a fool. " You are like a man who puts a skin over a drum in which is a

[5] Vin. i. 35 ff. It was this gift of Veḷuvana which formed the model for **Devānampiyatissa's** gift of the **Mahāmeghavana** to Mahinda (Mhv. xv. 17). The gift of Veḷuvana was one of the incidents sculptured in the Relic chamber of the Mahā Thūpa (Mhv. xxx. 80). It may have been in Veḷuvana that the king built for the monks a storeyed house, fully plastered (Vin. ii. 154). With the attainment of sopātatti, the king declared that all the five ambitions of his life had been fulfilled: that he might become king, that the Buddha might visit his realm, that he might wait on the Buddha, that the Buddha might teach him the doctrine, that he might understand it (Vin. i. 36). According to BuA. (p. 18 f.) the king became a sotāpanna after listening to the **Mahā Nārada Jātaka.**

[6] PvA. 209.

[7] Also J. iii. 121.

[8] For details of the names in this paragraph see *s.v.*

[9] *E.g.*, DA. i. 135 ff.; see also Vin. ii. 190 f.

[10] For details see *s.v.* **Ajātasattu.**

rat," and he urged on Ajātasattu the need for the destruction of Bimbisāra.

But no weapon could injure Bimbisāra[11]; it was therefore decided that he should be starved to death, and with this end in view he was imprisoned in a hot-house (*tāpanageha*) with orders that none but the mother of Ajātasattu should visit him. On her visits she took with her a golden vessel filled with food which she concealed in her clothes. When this was discovered she took food in her head-dress (*molī*), and, later, she was obliged to take what food she could conceal in her footgear. But all these ways were discovered, and then the queen visited Bimbisāra after having bathed in scented water and smeared her person with *catumadhura* (the four kinds of sweets). The king licked her person and that was his only sustenance. In the end the visits of the queen were forbidden; but the king continued to live by walking about his cell meditating. Ajātasattu, hearing of this, sent barbers to cut open his feet, fill the wounds with salt and vinegar, and burn them with coals. It is said that when the barbers appeared Bimbisāra thought his son had relented and had sent them to shave him and cut his hair. But on learning their real purpose, he showed not the least resentment and let them do their work, much against their will. (In a previous birth he had walked about in the courtyard of a cetiya with shoes on, hence this punishment !) Soon after, Bimbisāra died, and was reborn in the **Cātummahārājika**-world as a yakkha named **Janavasabbha,** in the retinue of **Vessavaṇa.** The **Janavasabha Sutta** records an account of a visit paid by Janavasabha to the Buddha some time after.

A son was born to Ajātasattu on the day of Bimbisāra's death. The joy he experienced at the birth of his son made him realize something of the affection his own father must have felt for him, and he questioned his mother. She told him stories of his childhood, and he repented, rather belatedly, of his folly and cruelty. Soon after, his mother died of grief, and her death gave rise to the protracted war between Ajātasattu and Pasenadi, as mentioned elsewhere.[12]

The books contain no mention of any special sermons preached by the Buddha to Bimbisāra nor of any questions asked by him of the Buddha.[13] Perhaps, like **Anāthapiṇḍika,** his equal in devotion to the

[11] Probably because he was a sotāpanna. He also had the power of judging the status of anyone by his voice—*e.g.*, in the case of **Kumbhaghosa** (DhA. i. 233).

[12] See *s.v.* also J. ii. 237, 403.

[13] When he heard that the Buddha intended to perform a miracle, although he had ordered his disciples to refrain from doing so, Bimbisāra had doubts about the propriety of this and questioned the Buddha who set his doubts at rest (DhA. iii. 204; J. iii. 263 f.). It was also at the request of Bimbisāra that the Buddha established the custom of the monks assembling on the first, eighth, fourteenth and fifteenth days of each month (Vin. i. 101 f.).

Buddha, he refrained from giving the Buddha extra trouble, or perhaps the affairs of his kingdom, which was three hundred leagues in extent,[14] did not permit him enough leisure for frequent visits to the Buddha. It is said that he once visited four monks—**Godhika, Subāhu, Valliya** and **Uttiya**—and invited them to spend the rainy season at Rājagaha. He built for them four huts, but forgot to have them roofed, with the result that the gods withheld the rains until the king remembered the omission.[15]

Bimbisāra's affection for the Buddha was unbounded. When the **Licchavis** sent **Mahāli,** who was a member of Bimbisāra's retinue, to beg the Buddha to visit **Vesāli,** Bimbisāra did not himself try to persuade the Buddha to do so, but when the Buddha agreed to go he repaired the whole road from Rājagaha to the Ganges—a distance of five leagues—for the Buddha to walk upon; he erected a rest-house at the end of each league, and spread flowers of five different colours knee-deep along the whole way. Two parasols were provided for the Buddha and one for each monk. The king himself accompanied the Buddha in order to look after him, offering him flowers and perfume and all requisites throughout the journey, which lasted five days. Arrived at the river, he fastened two boats together decked with flowers and jewels and followed the Buddha's boat into the water up to his neck. When the Buddha had gone, the king set up an encampment on the river bank, awaiting his return; he then escorted him back to Rājagaha with similar pomp and ceremony.[16]

Great cordiality existed between Bimbisāra and Pasenadi. They were connected by marriage, each having married a sister of the other. Pasenadi once visited Bimbisāra in order to obtain from him a person of unbounded wealth (*amitabhoga*) for his kingdom. Bimbisāra had five such—**Jotiya, Jaṭila, Meṇḍaka, Puṇṇaka** and **Kākavaliya ;** but Pasenadi had none. The request was granted, and Meṇḍaka's son, **Dhanañjaya,** was sent back to Kosala with Pasenadi.[17]

Bimbisāra also maintained friendly relations with other kings, such as **Pukkasāti**, king of **Takkasilā, Caṇḍappajjota,** king of **Ujjenī,** to whom

[14] DhA. iii. 205; the kingdom included eighty thousand villages (*gāma*) (Vin. i. 179).

[15] ThagA. i. 125. He similarly forgot his promise to give **Pilindavaccha** a park-keeper, if the Buddha would sanction such a gift. Five hundred days later he remembered his promise, and, to make amends, gave five hundred park-keepers with a special village for their residence, called **Ārāmikagāma** or **Pilindagāma** (Vin. i. 207 f.).

[16] DhA. iii. 438 ff.

[17] DhA. i. 385 f.; AA. i. 220. Some of these were richer than Bimbisāra—*e.g.*, **Jotiya** (*q.v.*), whose house was built entirely of jewels while the king's palace was of wood; but the king showed no jealousy (DhA. iv. 211).

he sent his own physician **Jīvaka** to tend in his illness—and Rudrāyaṇa of Roruka.[18]

Among the ministers and personal retinue of Bimbisāra are mentioned **Soṇa-Koḷvisa,** the flower-gatherer **Sumana** who supplied the king with eight measures of jasmine-flowers, the minister **Koliya,** the treasurer **Kumbhaghosaka** and his physician **Jīvaka.** The last named was discovered for him by the prince Abhaya when he was suffering from a fistula. The king's garments were stained with blood and his queens mocked him. Jīvaka cured the king with one single anointing; the king offered him the ornaments of the five hundred women of the palace, and when he refused to take these, he was appointed physician to the king, the women of the seraglio and the fraternity of monks under the Buddha.[19]

When **Dhammadinnā** wished to leave the world, Bimbisāra gave her, at her husband's request, a golden palanquin and allowed her to go round the city in procession.[20]

Bimbisāra is generally referred to as **Seniya Bimbisāra.** The Commentaries[21] explain Seniya as meaning " possessed of a large following " or as " belonging to the Seniyagotta," and Bimbisāra as meaning " of a golden colour," *bimbī* meaning gold.

In the time of **Phussa Buddha,** when the Buddha's three step-brothers, sons of **King Jayasena,** obtained their father's leave to entertain the Buddha for three months, Bimbisāra, then head of a certain district, looked after all the arrangements. His associates in this task were born as petas, and he gave alms to the Buddha in their name in order to relieve their sufferings.[22]

During his lifetime, Bimbisāra was considered the happiest of men, but the Buddha declared[23] that he himself was far happier than the king.

The kahāpana in use in Rājagaha during Bimbisāra's time was the standard of money adopted by the Buddha in the formation of those rules into which the matter of money entered.[24]

Bimbisāra had a white banner and one of his epithets was **Paṇḍaraketu.**[25] Nothing is said about his future destiny, but he is represented in the **Janavasabha Sutta**[26] as expressing the wish to become a Sakadāgāmī, and this wish may have been fulfilled.

[18] Dvy. 545.

[19] Vin. i. 272 f.

[20] MA. i. 516.

[21] *E.g.*, UdA. 104. According to Thibetan sources, Bimbī was the name of his mother, and from this his own name was derived; but another reason was that he was radiant like the morning sun (Rockhill 16).

[22] See **Tirokudda Sutta,** also PvA. 21 ff.; for his intercession on behalf of another peta see PvA. 89.

[23] *E.g.*, M. i. 95.

[24] Sp. ii. 297.

[25] Thag. vs. 64; ThagA. i. 147.

[26] D. ii. 206.

Bimbi.—An eminent laywoman, follower of the Buddha.[1]

[1] A. iv. 347; AA. ii. 791.

Bilaṅgika-Bhāradvāja.—One of the **Bhāradvāja** brothers. On hearing that the eldest of the clan had entered the Order, he went to the Buddha, and, unable to speak for rage, sat on one side, sulking. The Buddha preached to him, and he was pleased and entered the Order, becoming an arahant in due course.[1]

The Commentary expains[2] that he had earned large profits by running a shop for different kinds of excellently prepared "congey" (*kañjikā*). The name Bilaṅgika (*bilaṅga* being another name for such preparations) was given him by the Recensionists at the Third Council.

[1] S. i. 164; DhA. iv. 163. [2] SA. i. 178 f.

Bilaṅgika-Bhāradvāja Sutta.—Relates the story of the conversion of **Bilaṅgika-Bhāradvāja.**[1]

[1] S. i. 164.

Billagāmatittha.—A ford in the **Mahāvālukagaṅgā,** mentioned in the account of the campaigns of **Parakkamabāhu I.**[1]

[1] Cv. lxxii. 48, 122.

Billaphaliya Thera.—An arahant. He was an ascetic living on the banks of the **Candabhāgā** in the time of **Kakusandha Buddha.** One day he gave the Buddha a *billa*-fruit (wood-apple) from the tree which grew in his grove.[1]

[1] Ap. ii. 397.

Billasela.—A mountain in Ceylon. **Vijayabāhu III.** built, on its summit, a temple for the Tooth Relic.[1] From there the Relic was removed by **Parakkamabāhu II.** to **Jambuddoṇi.**[2]

[1] Cv. lxxxi. 33; see also Cv. *Trs.* ii. 138, n. 4. [2] Cv. lxxxii. 7.

Billasela-vihāra.—A monastery on **Billasela,** where **Bhuvanekabāhu,** brother of **Parakkamabāhu II.,** erected, under the king's orders, a pariveṇa called the **Bhuvanekabāhu-pariveṇa.**[1]

[1] Cv. lxxxv. 59.

1. **Biḷāra Jātaka** (No. 128).—The Bodhisatta was once born as a big rat, leader of a troop of rats. A roving jackal, wishing to eat them, took up his stand near their home, poised on one leg, feigning great holiness. Impressed by his austerities, the Bodhisatta and his troop worshipped

him, and each day the jackal ate the rat which was hindmost when they turned to leave him. Seeing their number diminish, the Bodhisatta suspected the reason, and one day he himself came last, behind the others. When the jackal pounced on him, he sprang at his throat and killed him, the other rats eating the body.

The story was told in reference to a monk who was a hypocrite.[1]

[1] J. i. 460 f.

Biḷāra Sutta.—A cat once stood on the refuse heap of a house-drain, and when the mouse who lived there came out, pounced on her and ate her. But the mouse gnawed the guts of the cat so that she died. Such will be the fate of monks who go among the dwellings of householders with unrestrained senses. The sutta was preached to a recalcitrant monk.[1]

[1] S. ii. 270.

Biḷārikosiya.—A rich miser whom **Sakka** converted into a generous donor. See the **Biḷārikosiya Jātaka.**

Biḷārikosiya Jātaka (No. 450).—The Bodhisatta was once a rich merchant of Benares who built an almonry and distributed much alms On his deathbed, he asked his son to continue with the alms, and, after death, he was reborn as **Sakka.** His son followed him and became the the god **Canda.** His son **Suriya,** Suriya's son **Mātalī,** and **Mātalī's** son **Pañcasikha,** all followed in the same path. But the sixth of the line, **Biḷārikosiya,** became a miser and burnt the almonry. Sakka and the others then came separately, in the guise of brahmins, to visit him and to ask for alms. Kosiya refused their request until each one uttered a little verse, when he was asked to enter and receive a small gift. Kosiya asked the servant to give each a little unhusked rice. This was refused, and in the end he was obliged to give the brahmins cooked rice, meant for cows. Each swallowed a mouthful, but then let it stick in his throat and lay down as if dead. Kosiya, very frightened, had a meal prepared, which he put into their bowls, and then, calling in the passers-by, asked them to note how the brahmins, in their greed, had eaten too much and died. But the brahmins arose, spat out the rice, and publicly shamed Kosiya by showing up his miserliness and the manner in which he had disgraced his ancestors. Then each revealed his identity and departed. Biḷārikosiya mended his ways and became most generous.

The story was related to a monk reputed for his great generosity; he would not even drink a cup of water without sharing it. The monk is identified with Biḷārikosiya, and the Buddha related the story in order to show how he had changed his ways. **Sāriputta** was Canda, **Moggallāna** Suriya, **Kassapa** Mātalī and **Ānanda** Pañcasikha.[1]

[1] J. iv. 62-9.

Biḷālapādaka.—A rich man of **Sāvatthi.** Once a resident of Sāvatthi invited the Buddha and all his monks to a meal and went from house to house asking the householders to share in the almsgiving. Biḷālapādaka, annoyed at the request, gave only as much as could be grasped by three fingers—hence his name—(" catfoot "). The man took the gifts and added them to the others, but Biḷālapādaka, suspecting that he might be disgraced in public, went to the almsgiving with a knife concealed on his person, ready to kill the man if he should mention his gift in ridicule. But he heard the man offer the alms to the Buddha, expressing the wish that all who had joined in the almsgiving should receive a rich reward. Moved by the man's largeness of heart, Biḷālapāda fell at his feet, confessing his guilty intentions and begging for pardon. The Buddha thereupon preached to Biḷālapāda, who, at the conclusion of the sermon, became a sotāpanna.[1]

[1] DhA. iii. 17 ff.

1. **Biḷālidāyaka Thera.**—An arahant. In the time of **Padumuttara Buddha** he was an ascetic in the **Himālaya** and offered the Buddha some biḷāli-tubers. Fifty-four kappas ago he was a king called **Sumekhali**[1] (*v.l.* **Sumelaya**). He is probably identical with **Kosalavihārī Thera.**[2]

[1] Ap. i. 145. [2] ThagA. i. 134 f.

2. **Biḷālidāyaka Thera.**—An arahant. Fifty-four kappas ago he gave some biḷāli-tubers to a recluse at the foot of the mountain **Romasa.**[1]

[1] Ap. i. 232.

1. **Bīja Sutta.**—The five sorts of seed, if unspoilt and planted in good soil, and nourished by wind and water, will sprout and grow. Like to the five kinds of seed are the five kinds of consciousness; like to the earth the four *satipaṭṭhānas*, like to water the lure of lust.[1]

[1] S. iii. 54 f.

2. **Bīja Sutta.**—Just as earth is essential to all seed and vegetation, so is virtue essential to the practice of the Noble Eightfold Path.[1]

[1] S. v. 54 f.

3. **Bīja Sutta.**—Perverted view is the most fertile soil for the development of evil states.[1]

[1] A. i. 30.

4. **Bīja Sutta.**—Just as bitter seed produces bitter fruit, so do false views produce evil and suffering. It is the opposite with sweet seeds and right views.[1]

[1] S. v. 212 ff.

Bījaka.—The son of **Sudinna Kalandakaputta** by the wife of his lay days. He was conceived after Sudinna had already been ordained. His wife came to him during her period and begged him to give her an offspring (*bījaka*). As the rule against unchastity had not then been promulgated, Sudinna yielded to her importunities, thus becoming guilty of the first *pārājikā*. The son was called Bījaka, and so Sudinna came to be called **Bījakapitā** and the mother **Bījakamātā.** Both Bījaka and his mother later left the world and became arahants.[1]

[1] Vin. iii. 17-19; Sp. i. 215 f.

2. **Bījaka.**—A slave of **Videha,** present when the ascetic **Guṇa** expounded his doctrine to King **Aṅgati,** and it was approved by **Alāta.** Bījaka also agreed that Guṇa's teaching accorded with his own experience. He remembered his previous life, when he had been born as **Bhāvaseṭṭhi** of **Sāketa** and had done many acts of virtue and piety. But at present he was the son of a poor prostitute leading a wretched life. Even so, he always gave half his food to any who might desire it, kept the fast, and led, in every way, a virtuous life. But virtue, he said, was useless; it bore no fruit. So saying, he wept. When **Rujā** (*q.v.*) heard this, she said that Bījaka's sufferings were due to evil actions done in the past in earlier lives.[1] The scholiast explains[2] that in the time of **Kassapa Buddha,** while Bījaka was seeking a lost ox, a monk enquired of him the way which he had lost. Bījaka was angry and abused the monk, calling him a slave. His birth as Bhāvaseṭṭhi was due to some earlier good done by him, but in this birth he became a slave. Bījaka is identified with **Moggallāna.**[3]

[1] J. vi. 227, 228, 229, 233, 235. [2] *Ibid.*, 228. [3] *Ibid.*, 255.

Bījagāma.—A village in Ceylon where **Mahallaka-Nāga** built the **Tānaveli-**(or **Canavela-**)**vihāra.**[1]

[1] Mhv. xxxv. 125.

Bīraṇatthambhaka Vagga.—The seventh chapter of the Duka Nipāta of the Jātakaṭṭhakathā.[1]

[1] J. ii. 164 ff.

Bīrāṇī.—A goddess (*devadhītā*). She had a palace in the **Cātummahārājika**-world which **Nimi** saw on his visit to heaven when he learnt her story from **Mātali.** In the time of **Kassapa** Buddha she had been a slave in a brahmin's house. The brahmin, whose name was **Asoka,** invited eight monks to feed daily at his house and asked his wife to arrange to feed them at a cost of one *kahāpaṇa* each. This she refused to do as did also his daughters; but their slave agreed to carry out this work, and she did it most conscientiously and with great devotion. As a result she was reborn in heaven.[1] Her palace was twelve leagues in height and one in extent; it possessed nine storeys and one thousand rooms. When **Duṭṭhagāmaṇī** wished to erect the **Lohapāsāda,** he asked the monks for a plan, and eight arahants went to the deva-world and returned with a plan of Bīraṇī's palace.[2]

[1] J. vi. 117 f.

[2] Mhv. xxvii. 9 ff.

Budalaviṭṭhi.—A village in Ceylon where **Vijayabāhu I.** erected five dwelling-places for the monks on the spot where his parents had been cremated.[1]

[1] Cv. lx. 57.

1. **Buddha.**—A generic name, an appellative—but not a proper name—given to one who has attained Enlightenment[1]; a man superior to all other beings, human and divine, by his knowledge of the Truth (*Dhamma*). The texts mention two kinds of Buddha: viz., **Pacceka Buddhas** (*q.v.*)—*i.e.*, Buddhas who also attain to complete Enlightenment but do not preach the way of deliverance to the world; and Sammāsambuddhas, who are omniscient and are teachers of Nibbāna (*Satthāro*). The Commentaries, however,[2] make mention of four classes of Buddha: *Sabaññu-Buddhā*, *Pacceka-Buddhā*, *Catusacca-Buddhā* and *Suta-Buddhā*. All arahants (*khīṇāsavā*) are called *Catusacca-Buddhā* and all learned men *Bahussuta-Buddhā*. A Pacceka-Buddha practises the ten perfections (*pāramitā*) for two asaṅkheyyas and one hundred thousand kappas, a Sabbaññu Buddha practises it for one hundred thousand kappas and four or eight or sixteen asaṅkheyyas, as the case may be (see below).

[1] *Na mātarā kataṃ, na pitarā kataṃ—vimokkhantikaṃ etaṃ buddhānaṃ bhagavantānaṃ bodhiyā mūle . . . paññatti* (MNid. 458; Ps. i. 174.)

[2] *E.g.*, SA. i. 20; AA. i. 65.

Seven Sabbaññu-Buddhas are mentioned in the earlier books[3]; these are **Vipassī, Sikhī, Vessabhū, Kakusandha, Koṇāgamana, Kassapa** and **Gotama.** This number is increased in the later books. The *Buddhavaṃsa* contains detailed particulars of twenty-five Buddhas, including the last, Gotama, the first twenty-four being those who prophesied Gotama's appearance in the world. They are the predecessors of Vipassī, etc., and are the following[4]: **Dīpaṅkara, Koṇḍañña, Maṅgala, Sumana, Revata, Sobhita, Anomadassī, Paduma, Nārada, Padumuttara, Sumedha, Sujāta, Piyadassī, Atthadassī, Dhammadassī, Siddhattha, Tissa** and **Phussa.** The same poem, in its twenty-seventh chapter, mentions three other Buddhas—**Taṇhaṅkara, Medhaṅkara** and **Saranaṅkara**—who appeared in the world before Dīpaṅkara. The *Lalitavistara* has a list of fifty-four Buddhas and the *Mahāvastu* of more than a hundred. The **Cakkavatti Sīhanāda Sutta**[5] gives particulars of **Metteyya Buddha** who will be born in the world during the present kappa. The *Anāgatavaṃsa* gives a detailed account of him. Some MSS. of that poem[6] mention the names of ten future Buddhas, all of whom met Gotama who prophesied about them. These are **Metteyya, Uttama, Rāma, Pasenadi Kosala, Abhibhū, Dīghasoṇī, Saṅkacca, Subha, Todeyya, Nāḷāgiripalaleyya** (*sic*).

The **Mahāpadāna Sutta**[7] which mentions the seven Buddhas gives pariculars of each under eleven heads (*paricchedā*)—the kappa in which he is born, his social rank (*jāti*), his family (*gotta*), length of life at that epoch (*āyu*), the tree under which he attains Enlightenment (*bodhi*), the names of his two chief disciples (*sāvakayuga*), the numbers present at the assemblies of arahants held by him (*sāvakasannipāta*), the name of his presonal attendant (*upaṭṭhākabhikkhu*), the names of his father and mother and of his birthplace. The Commentary[8] adds to these other particulars—the names of his son and his wife before his Renunciation, the conveyance (*yāna*) in which he leaves the world, the monastery is which his **Gandhakuṭi** was placed, the amount of money paid for its purchase, the site of the monastery, and the name of his chief lay patron. In the case of Gotama, the further fact is stated that on the day of his birth there appeared also in the world **Rāhulamātā, Ānanda, Kanthaka, Nidhikumbhi** (Treasure Trove), the **Mahābodhi** and **Kāludāyī.** Gotama was conceived under the asterism (*nakkhatta*) of **Uttarāsāḷha,** under which asterism he also made his Renunciation,[9]

[3] *E.g.*, D. ii. 5 f.; S. ii. 5 f.; *cp*. Thag. 491; J. ii. 147; they are also mentioned at Vin. ii. 110, in an old formula against snake-bites. Beal (*Catena*, p. 159) says these are given in the Chinese Pāṭimokkha. They are also found in the Sayambhū Purāṇa (Mitra, Skt. Buddhist Lit. of Nepal, p. 249).

[4] See *s.v.*

[5] D. iii. 75 ff.

[6] *J.P.T.S.* 1886, p. 37.

[7] D. ii. 5 f.

[8] DA. ii. 422 ff.

[9] *Ibid.*, 425.

preached his first sermon and performed the Twin Miracle. Under the asterism of **Visākha** he was born, attained Enlightenment and died; under that of **Māgha** he held his first assembly of arahants and decided to die; under **Assayuja** he descended from **Tāvatiṃsa.**

The *Buddhavaṃsa Commentary* says[10] that in the Buddhavaṃsa particulars of each Buddha are given under twenty-two heads, the additional heads being the details of the first sermon, the numbers of those attaining realization of truth (*abhisamaya*) at each assembly, the names of the two chief women disciples, the aura of the Buddha's body (*raṃsi*), the height of his body, the name of the Bodhisatta (who was to become Gotama Buddha), the prophecy concerning him, his exertions (*padhāna*) and the details of each Buddha's death. The Commentary also says that mention must be made of the time each Buddha lived as a householder, the names of the palaces he occupied, the number of his dancing women, the names of his chief wife, and his son, his conveyance, his renunciation, his practice of austerities, his patrons and his monastery.

There are eight particulars in which the Buddhas differ from each other (*aṭṭhavemattāni*). These are length of life in the epoch in which each is born, the height of his body, his social rank (some are born as khattiyas, others as brahmins), the length of his austerities, the aura of his body (thus, in the case of Maṅgala, his aura spread throughout the ten thousand world systems, while that of Gotama extended only one fathom[11]); the conveyance in which he makes his renunciation, the tree under which he attains Enlightenment, and the size of the seat (*pallaṅka*) under the Bodhi tree.[12]

In the case of all Buddhas, there are four fixed spots (*avijahitaṭṭhānāni*). These are: the site of the seat under the Bodhi-tree (*bodhipallaṅka*), the Deer Park at Isipatana where the first sermon is preached, the spot where the Buddha first steps on the ground at **Saṅkassa** on his descent from **Tusita** (**Tāvatiṃsa** ?), and the spots marked by the four posts of the bed in the Buddha's Gandhakuṭi in **Jetavana.** The monastery may vary in size; the site of the city in which it stands may also vary, but not the site of the bed. Sometimes it is to the east of the vihāra, sometimes to the north.[13]

Thirty facts are mentioned as being true of all Buddhas (*samatiṃsavidhā dhammatā*). In his last life every Bodhisatta is conscious at the moment of his conception; in his mother's womb he remains cross-legged

[10] BuA. 2 f.

[11] But when he wishes, a Buddha can spread his aura at will (BuA. 106).

[12] Only the first five are mentioned in DA. ii. 424; also at BuA. 105; all eight are given at BuA. 246 f., which also gives details under each of the eight heads, regarding all the twenty-five Buddhas.

[13] DA. ii. 424; BuA. 247.

with his face turned outwards; his mother gives birth to him in a standing posture; the birth takes place in a forest grove (*araññe*); immediately after birth he takes seven steps to the north and roars the "lion's roar"; he makes his renunciation after seeing the four omens and after a son is born to him; he has to practise austerities for at least seven days after donning the yellow robe; he has a meal of milk-rice on the day of his Enlightenment; he attains to omniscience seated on a carpet of grass; he practises concentration in breathing; he defeats Māra's forces; he attains to supreme perfection in all knowledge and virtue at the foot of the Bodhi-tree; **Mahā Brahmā** requests him to preach the Dhamma; he preaches his first sermon in the Deer Park at Isipatana; he recites the **Pāṭimokkha** to the fourfold assembly on the full-moon day of **Māgha ;** he resides chiefly in **Jetavana,** he performs the Twin Miracle in **Sāvatthi ;** he preaches the Abhidhamma in **Tāvatiṃsa ;** he descends from there at the gate of **Saṅkassa ;** he constantly lives in the bliss of *phalasamāpatti*; he investigates the possibility of converting others during two *jhānas*; he lays down the precepts only when occasion arises for them; he relates Jātakas when suitable occasions occur; he recites the Buddhavaṃsa in the assembly of his kinsmen; he always greets courteously monks who visit him; he never leaves the place where he has spent the rainy season without bidding farewell to his hosts; each day he has prescribed duties before and after his meal and during the three watches of the night; he eats a meal containing flesh (*maṃsarajabhojana*) immediately before his death; and just before his death he enters into the twenty-four crores and one hundred thousand *samāpattī*. There are also mentioned four dangers from which all Buddhas are immune: no misfortune can befall the four requisites intended for a Buddha; no one can encompass his death; no injury can befall any of his thirty-two **Mahāpurisalakkhaṇā** or eighty *anubyañjanā*; nothing can obstruct his aura.[14]

A Buddha is born only in this **Cakkavāḷa** out of the ten thousand Cakkavāḷas which constitute the jātikkhetta.[15] There can appear only one Buddha in the world at a time.[16] No Buddha can arise until the *sāsana* of the previous Buddha has completely disappeared from the world. This happens only with the *dhātuparinibbāna* (see below). When a Bodhisatta takes conception in his mother's womb in his last life, after leaving Tusita, there is manifested throughout the world a wonderful radiance, and the ten thousand world systems tremble.[17]

[14] BuA. 248.

[15] AA. i. 251; DA. iii. 897.

[16] D. ii. 225; iii. 114; the reasons for this are given in detail in Mil. 236, and quoted in DA. iii. 900 f.

[17] Similar earthquakes appear when he is born, when he attains Enlightenment, when he preaches the first sermon, when he decides to die, when he finally does so (D. ii. 108 f.; *cp.* DA. iii. 897).

The **Mahāpadāna Sutta**[18] and the **Acchariyabbhutadhamma Sutta**[19] contain accounts of other miracles which attend the conception and birth of a Buddha. Later books[20] have greatly enlarged these accounts. They describe how the Bodhisatta, having practised the thirty *pāramī*, and made the five great gifts (*pañcamahāpariccāgā*), and thus reached the pinnacle of the threefold cariyā—*ñātatthacariyā*, *lokatthacariyā* and *buddhicariyā*—gives the seven *mahādānā*, as in the case of **Vessantara,** making the earth tremble seven times, and is born after death in Tusita. The Bodhisatta, who later became Vipassī Buddha, remained in Tusita during the whole permissible period—fifty-seven crores and sixty-seven thousand years. But most Bodhisattas leave Tusita before completing the full span of life there. Five signs appear to warn the *devaputta* that his end is near[21]; the gods of the ten thousand worlds gather round him, beseeching him to be born on earth that he may become the Buddha. The Bodhisatta thereupon makes the five investigations (*pañcamahā-vilokanāni*).

Sometimes only one Buddha is born in a kappa, such a kappa being called **Sārakappa ;** sometimes two, **Maṇḍakappa ;** sometimes three, **Varakappa ;** sometimes four, **Sāramaṇḍakappa ;** rarely five, **Bhadda-kappa.**[22] No Buddha is born in the early period of a kappa, when men live longer than one hundred thousand years and are thus not able to recognize the nature of old age and death, and therefore not able to benefit by his preaching. When the life of man is too short, there is no time for exhortation and men are full of *kilesa*. The suitable age for a Buddha is, therefore, when men live not less than one hundred years and not more than ten thousand. The Bodhisatta must first consider the continent and the country of birth. Buddhas are born only in **Jambudīpa,** and there, too, only in the **Majjhimadesa** (*q.v.*). He must then consider the family; Buddhas are born only in brahmin or khattiya families, whichever is more esteemed during that particular age. Then he must think of the mother: she must be wise and virtuous and her life must be destined to end seven days after the Buddha's birth.

Having made these decisions, the Bodhisatta goes to **Nandanavana** in Tusita, and while wandering about there " falls away " from Tusita and takes conception. He is aware of his death but unaware of his *cuticitta* or dying thought. The Commentators seem to have differed as to whether there is awareness of conception. When the Bodhisatta is conceived, his mother has no further wish for indulgence in sexual pleasure. For seven days previously she observes the *uposatha* vows,

[18] D. ii. 12-15.
[19] M. iii. 119-124.
[20] *E.g.*, J. i.
[22] BuA. 158 f.
[21] See *s.v.* Deva.

but there is no mention of a virgin birth; the birth might be called parthenogenetic.[23]

On the day of the actual conception, the mother, having bathed in scented water after the celebration of the **Asāḷha**-festival, and having eaten choice food, takes upon herself the uposatha vows and retires to the adorned state-bedchamber. As she sleeps, she dreams that the Four Regent Gods raise her with her bed, and, having taken her to the Himālaya, bathe her in Lake **Anotatta,** robe her in divine clothes, anoint her with perfumes and deck her with heavenly flowers.[24] Not far away is a silver mountain and on it a golden mansion. There they lay her with her head to the east. The Bodhisatta, assuming the form of a white elephant, enters her room, and after circling rightwise three times round her bed, smites her right side with his trunk and enters her womb. She awakes and tells her husband of her dream. Soothsayers are consulted, and they prophesy the birth of a Cakkavatti or of a Buddha.

The two suttas mentioned above speak of the circumstances obtaining during the time spent by the child in his mother's womb. It is said[25] that the Bodhisatta is born when his mother is in the last third of her middle age. This is in order that the birth may be easy for both mother and child. Various miracles attend the birth of the Bodhisatta. The Commentaries expound, at great length, the accounts of these miracles given in the suttas. Immediately after birth the Bodhisatta stands firmly on his feet, and having taken seven strides to the north, while a white canopy is held over his head, looks round and utters in fearless voice the lion's roar: "*Aggo 'ham asmi lokassa, jeṭṭho 'ham asmi lokassa, seṭṭho 'ham asmi lokassa, ayam antimā jāti, natthi dāni punabbhavo.*"[26] To the later Buddists,[27] not only these acts of the Bodhisatta, but every item of the miracles accompanying his birth, have their symbolical meaning. There seems to have been a difference of opinion among the Elders of the Saṅgha as to what happened when the Bodhisatta took his seven strides northwards. Did he walk on the earth or travel through the air ? Did people see him go ? Was he clothed ? Did he look an infant or an adult ? **Tipiṭaka Cuḷābhaya,** preaching on the first floor of the **Lohapāsāda,** settled the question by suggesting a

[23] See Mil. 123.

[24] According to the Nidānakathā (J. i. 50.), it is their queens who do these things. *Re* the Bodhisatta assuming the form of an elephant, see Dial. ii. 116 n.

[25] DA. ii. 437.

[26] D. ii. 15.

[27] See, *e.g.*, DA. ii. 439; thus, standing on the earth means the attaining of the four *iddhipādas;* facing north implies the spiritual conquest of multitudes; the seven strides are the seven bojjhaṅgas; the canopy is the umbrella of emancipation; looking round means unveiled knowledge; fearlessness denotes the irrevocable turning of the Wheel of the Law; the mention of the last birth, the arahantship he will attain in this life, etc.

compromise: the Bodhisatta walked on earth, but the onlookers felt he was travelling through the air; he was naked, but the onlookers felt he was gaily adorned; he was an infant, but looked sixteen years old; and after his roar he reverted to infancy ![28]

After birth, the Bodhisatta is presented to the soothsayers for their prognostications and they reassert that two courses alone are open to him—either to be a Cakkavatti or a Buddha. They also discover on his body the thirty-two marks of the Great Man (**Mahāpurisa,** *q.v.*).[29] The Bodhisatta has also the eighty secondary signs (*asīti anubyañjana*) such as copper-coloured nails glossy and prominent, sinews which are hidden and without knots, etc.[30] The **Brahmāyu Sutta**[31] gives other particulars about Gotama, which are evidently characteristic of all Buddhas. Thus, in walking he always starts with the right foot, his steps are neither too long nor too short, only his lower limbs move; when he gazes on anything, he turns right round to do so (*nāgavilokana*). When entering a house he never bends his body[32]; when sitting down, accepting water to wash his bowl, eating, washing his hands after eating, or returning thanks, he sits with the greatest propriety, dignity and thoroughness. When preaching, he neither flatters nor denounces his hearers but merely instructs them, rousing, enlightening and heartening them.[33] His voice possesses eight qualities: it is frank, clear, melodious, pleasant, full, carrying, deep and resonant; it does not travel beyond his audience.[34] A passage in the Aṅguttara[35] says that a Buddha preaches in the eight assemblies—of nobles, brahmins, householders, recluses, devas of the Cātummahārājika-world, and of Tāvatiṃsa, of Māras and of Brahmās. In these assemblies he becomes one of them and their language becomes his.

The typical career of a Buddha is illustrated in the life of Gotama (*q.v.*). He renounces the world only after the birth of a son. This, the Commentary explains,[36] is to prevent him from being taken for other than a human being. He sees the four omens before his Renunciation: an old man, a sick man, a dead man, and a recluse. Some Buddhas see all four on the same day, others, like Vipassī, at long intervals.[37] On the night before the Enlightenment, the Bodhisatta dreams five dreams.[38] After the Enlightenment the Buddha does not preach till asked to do so by Mahā Brahmā. This is on order that the world may pay greater

[28] DA. ii. 442.

[29] These are given at D. ii. 17-19; also M. ii. 136 f.

[30] The list is found in Lal. 121 (106).

[31] For details see M. ii. 137 f.

[32] *Cp.* DhA. ii. 136.

[33] M. ii. 139.

[34] For details concerning his voice see DA. ii. 452 f.; and MA. ii. 771 f.

[35] A. iv. 308.

[36] DA. ii. 422.

[37] *Ibid.*, 457.

[38] These are given at A. iii. 240.

attention to the Buddha and his teaching.[39] A Buddha generally travels from the Bodhi-tree to Isipatana for his first sermon, through the air, but Gotama went on foot because he wished to meet Upaka on the way.[40]

The Buddha's day is divided into periods, each of which has its distinct duties.[41] He rises early, and having attended to his bodily functions, sits in solitude till the time arrives for the alms round. He then puts on his outer robe and goes for alms, sometimes alone, sometimes with a large following of monks. When he wishes to go alone he keeps the door of his cell shut, which sign is understood by the monks.[42] Occasionally he goes long distances for alms, travelling through the air, and then only *khīṇāsavā* are allowed to accompany him.[43] Sometimes he goes in the ordinary way (*pakatiyā*), sometimes accompanied by many miracles. After the meal he returns to his cell; this is the *pure-bhattakicca.*

Having washed his feet, he would emerge from his cell, talk to the monks and admonish them. To those who ask for subjects of meditation, he would give them according to their temperament. He would then retire to his cell and, if he so desire, sleep for a while. After that, he looks around the world with his divine eye, seeking whom he may serve, and would then preach to those who come to him for instruction. In the evening he would bathe, and then, during the first watch, attend to monks seeking his advice. The middle watch is spent with devas and others who visit him to question him. The last watch is divided into three parts: the first part is spent in walking about for exercise and meditation; the second is devoted to sleep; and the third to contemplation, during which those who are capable of benefiting by the Buddha's teaching, through good deeds done by them in the past, come into his vision. Only beings that are *veneyyā* (capable of benefiting by instruction) and who possess *upanissaya,* appear before the Buddha's divine eye.[44] The Buddha gives his visitors permission to ask what they will. This is called *Sabbaññupavāraṇa,* and only a Buddha is capable of holding to this promise to answer any question.[45] Except during the rains, the Buddha spends his time in wandering from place to place, gladdening men and inciting them to lead the good life. This wandering is called *cārikā* and is of two kinds—*turita* and *aturita.* The first is used for a long journey accomplished by him in a very short time, for the benefit of some particular person. Thus Gotama travelled three gāvutas to meet **Mahā Kassapa,** thirty yojanas to see **Āḷavaka** and **Aṅgulimāla,**

[39] DA. ii. 467.
[40] *Ibid.,* 471.
[41] These are detailed at DA. i. 45 f.; SNA. i. 131 f., etc.
[42] *Ibid.,* 271.
[43] ThagA. i. 65.
[44] DA. ii. 470.
[45] SNA. i. 229.

forty-five yojanas to see **Pukkusāti,** etc. In the case of *aturita-cārikā* progress is slow. The range of a Buddha's cārikā varies from year to year. Sometimes he would tour the *Mahāmaṇḍala* of nine hundred yojanas, sometimes the *Majjhimamaṇḍala* of nine hundred yojanas, sometimes only the *Antomaṇḍala* of six hundred yojanas. A tour of the Mahāmaṇḍala occupies nine months, that of the Majjhimamaṇḍala eight, and that of the Antomaṇḍala from one to four months.[46]

The Buddha is omniscient, not in the sense that he *knows* everything, but that he *could* know anything should he so desire.[47] His *ñāña* is one of the four illimitables.[48] He converts people in one of three ways: by exhibition of miraculous powers (*iddhipāṭihāriya*), by reading their thoughts (*ādesanāpāṭihāriya*), or teaching them what is beneficial to them according to their character and temperament (*anusāsanīpāṭihāriya*). It is the last method which the Buddha most often uses.[49] Though the Buddha's teaching is never really lost on the listener, he sometimes preaches knowing that it will be of no immediate benefit.[50] It is said that wherever a monk dwells during the Buddha's time, in the vicinity of the Buddha, he would always have ready a special seat for the Buddha because it is possible that the Buddha would pay him a special visit.[51] Sometimes the Buddha will send a ray of light from his **Gandhakuṭi** to encourage a monk engaged in meditation and, appearing before him in this ray of light, preach to him. Stanzas so preached are called *obhāsa-gāthā*.[52]

Every Buddha founds an Order; the first *pāṭimokkhuddesagāthā* of every Buddha is the same.[53] The attainment of arahantship is always the aim of the Buddha's instruction.[54] Beings can obtain the four *abhiññā* only during the lifetime of a Buddha.[55] A Buddha has ten powers

[46] Details of the *cārikā* and the reasons for them, are given at length in DA. i. 240-3. When the Buddha cannot go on a journey himself, he sends his chief disciples (SNA. ii. 474). The Buddha announces his intention of undertaking a journey two weeks before he starts, so that the monks may get ready (DhA. ii. 167).

[47] See MNid. 178, 179; see also MNidA. 223; SNA. i. 18.

[48] Neither can the Buddha's body be measured for purposes of comparison with other bodies (MA. ii. 790).

[49] BuA. 81; the Buddha's rivals say that he possesses the power of fascination (*āvattanīmāyā*); but this is untrue, as sometimes (*e.g.*, in the case of the **Kosambi** monks) he cannot make even his own disciples obey him. Some beings, however, can be converted only by a Buddha. They are called *buddha-veneyyā* (SNA. i. 331). Some are pleased by the Buddha's looks, others by his voice and words, yet others by his austerities, such as the wearing of simple robes, etc.; and finally, those whose standard of judgment is goodness, reflect that he is without a peer (DhA. iii. 113 f.).

[50] See, *e.g.*, **Udumbarikasīhanāda Sutta** (D. iii. 57).

[51] DA. i. 48.

[52] SNA. i. 16, 265.

[53] DA. ii. 479.

[54] *Ibid.*, iii. 732.

[55] AA. i. 204.

(*balāni*) which consist of his perfect comprehension in ten fields of knowledge,[56] and physical strength equal to that of one hundred thousand crores of elephants.[57] He alone can digest the food of the devas or food which contains the *ojā* put into it by the devas. No one else can eat with impunity the food which has been set apart for the Buddha.[58] Besides these excellences, a Buddha possesses the four assurances (*vesārajjāni*),[59] the eighteen *āveṇikadhammā*,[60] and the sixteen *anuttariyas*.[61] The remembrance of former births a Buddha shares with six classes of purified beings, only in a higher degree. This faculty is possessed in ascending scale by *titthiyā, pakatisāvakā, mahāsāvakā, aggasāvakā, pacceka-buddhā* and *buddhā*.[62]

Every Buddha holds a **Mahāsamaya** (*q.v.*), and only a Buddha is capable of preaching a series of suttas to suit the different temperaments of the mighty assembly gathered there.[63]

A Buddha is not completely immune from disease (*e.g.*, **Gotama**). Every Buddha has the power of living for one whole *kappa*,[64] but no Buddha does so, his term of life being shortened by reason of climate and the food he takes.[65] No Buddha, however, dies till the sāsana is firmly established.[66] There are three *parinibbānā* in the case of a Buddha: *kilesa-parinibbāna, khandha-parinibbāna* and *dhātu-parinibbāna*. The first takes place under the Bodhi-tree, the second at the moment of the Buddha's death, the third long after.[67] Some Buddhas live longer than others; those that are *dīghāyuka* have only *sammukhasāvakā* (disciples who hear the Doctrine from the Buddha himself), and at their death their relics are not scattered, only a single thūpa being erected over them.[68] Short-lived Buddhas hold the uposatha once a fortnight; others (*e.g.* Kassapa Buddha) may have it once in six months; yet others (*e.g.*

[56] A. v. 32 f.; M. i. 69, etc. At S. ii. 27 f., ten similar powers are given as consisting of his knowledge of the *Paṭiccasamuppāda*. The powers of a disciple are distinct from those of a Buddha (Kvu. 228); they are seven (see, *e.g.*, D. iii. 283).

[57] BuA. 37.

[58] SNA. i. 154.

[59] Given at M. i. 71 f.

[60] Described at Lal. 183, 343, Buddhaghosa also gives (at DA. iii. 994) a list of eighteen *buddhadhammā*, but they are all concerned with the absence of *duccarita* in the case of the Buddha.

[61] Given by Sāriputta in the **Sampasādaniya Sutta** (D. iii. 102 ff.).

[62] *E.g.*, Vsm. 411.

[63] D. ii. 255; DA. ii. 682 f.

[64] The Commentary explains (DA. ii. 554 f.) that *kappa* here means *āyukappa*, the full span of a man's life during that particular age. Some, like **Mahāsīva Thera,** maintained that if the Buddha could live for ten months, overcoming the pains of death, he could as well continue to live to the end of this **Bhaddakappa.** But a Buddha does not do so because he wishes to die before his body is overcome by the infirmities of old age.

[65] DA. ii. 413.

[66] D. iii. 122.

[67] DA. iii. 899 f.; for the history of Gotama's relics see *s.v.* Gotama.

[68] SNA. 194, 195.

Vipassī) only once in six years.[69] After the Buddha's death, his Doctrine is gradually forgotten. The first Piṭaka to be lost is the **Abhidhamma,** beginning with the **Paṭṭhāna** and ending with the **Dhammasaṅgaṇi.** Then, the **Aṅguttara Nikāya** of the Sutta Piṭaka, from the eleventh to the first Nipāta; next the **Saṃyutta Nikāya** from the **Cakkapeyyāla** to the **Oghataraṇa**; then the **Majjhima,** from the **Indriyabhāvanā Sutta** to the **Mūlapariyāya Sutta,** and then the **Dīgha,** from the **Dasuttara** to the **Brahmajāla.** Scattered *gāthā* like the **Sabhiyapucchā,** and the **Āḷavakapucchā,** last much longer, but they cannot maintain the *sāsana.* The last Piṭaka to disappear is the **Vinaya,** the last portion being the *mātikā* of the **Ubhatovibhaṅga.**[70]

When a Buddha dies, his body receives the honours due to a monarch.[71] It is said[72] that on the night on which a Buddha attains Enlightenment, and on the night during which he dies, the colour of his skin becomes exceedingly bright. At all times, where a Buddha is present, no other light can shine.[73]

No Buddha is born during the *saṃvaṭṭamānakappa,* but only during the *vivaṭṭamānakappa.*[74] A Bodhisatta who excels in *paññā* can attain Buddhahood in four asaṅkheyyas; one who excels in *saddhā,* in eight, and one whose *viriya* is the chief factor, in sixteen.[75] When once a being has become a Bodhisatta there are eighteen conditions from which he is immune.[76] The Buddha is referred to under various epithets. The Aṅguttara Nikāya[77] gives one such list. There he is called *Samaṇa, Brāhmaṇa, Vedagū, Bhisaka, Nimmala, Vimala, Ñāṇī* and *Vimutta.* The Buddha generally speaks of himself as *Tathāgata.*[78] His followers usually address him as *Bhagavā,* while others call him by his name (Gotama). In the case of Gotama Buddha, we find him also addressed as *Sakka,*[79] *Brahma,*[80] *Mahāmuni*[81] and *Yakkha.*[82] Countless other epithets occur in the books, especially in the later ones. One very famous formula, used by Buddhists in their ritual, contains nine epithets, the formula being: *Bhagavā arahaṃ sammāsambuddho, vijjācaraṇasampanno, sugato, lokavidū, anuttaro, purisadammasārathi, satthā devamanussānaṃ, Buddho*

69 ThagA. i. 62.

70 VibhA. 432.

71 These are detailed at D. ii. 141 f.

72 *Ibid.,* 134. Here we have the beginning of a legend which later grew into an account of an actual "transfiguration" of the Buddha.

73 SNA. ii. 525.

74 *Ibid.,* i. 51.

75 *Ibid.,* 47 f.

76 For details see SNA. i. 50.

77 C. iv. 340; Buddhaghosa gives seven others: *Cakkhumā, Sabbabhūtānukampī, Vihātaka, Mārasenappamaddī, Vusitavā, Vimutto* and *Aṅgirasa* (DA. iii. 962 f.).

78 This term is explained at great length in the Commentaries — *e.g.,* DA. i. 59 f.

79 SN. vs. 345; perhaps the equivalent of Sākya.

80 SN. p. 91; SNA. ii. 418.

81 BuA. 38.

82 M. i. 386; see also KS. i. 262.

Bhagavā.[83] It is maintained[84] that the Buddha's praises are limitless (*aparimāṇa*). One of his most striking characteristics, mentioned over and over again, is his love of quiet.[85] In this his disciples followed his example.[86] The dwelling-place of a Buddha is called **Gandhakuṭi** (*q.v.*). His footprint is called *Padacetiya*, and this can be seen only when he so desires it. When once he wishes it to be visible, no one can erase it. He can also so will that only one particular person shall see it.[87] It is also said[88] that his power of love is so great that no evil action can show its results in his presence. A Buddha never asks for praise, but if his praises are uttered in his presence he takes no offence.[89] When the Buddha is seated in some spot, none has the power of going through the air above him.[90] He prefers to accept the invitations of poor men to a meal.[91]

See also *s.v.* **Gotama** and **Bodhisatta.** Also the article on Buddha in the N.P.D.

83 These words are analysed and discussed in Vsm. 198 ff.

84 *E.g.*, DA. i. 288.

85 *E.g.*, D. i. 178 f.; he is also fond of solitude (*paṭisallāna*), (D. ii. 70; A. iv. 438 f.; S. v. 320 f., etc.). When he is in retirement it is usually *akāla* for visiting him (D. ii. 270). There are also certain accusations which are brought against a Buddha by his rivals, for this very love of solitude. "It is said that his insight is ruined by this habit of seclusion. By intercourse with whom does he attain lucidity in wisdom? He is not at his ease in conducting an assembly, not ready in conversation, he is occupied only with the fringe of things. He is like a one-eyed cow, walking in a circle" (D. iii. 38).

86 D. iii. 37.

87 DhA. iii. 194.

88 SNA. ii. 475.

89 ThagA. ii. 42.

90 SNA. i. 222.

91 DhA. ii. 135.

2. **Buddha.**—A king of forty-one kappas ago, a previous birth of **Vacchapāla (Pāyāsadāyaka) Thera.**[1]

1 ThagA. i. 160; Ap. i. 157.

3. **Buddha.**—A minister of **Mahinda V.** He was a native of **Māragallaka** and, in association with **Kitti,** another minister, vanquished the **Coḷa** army at **Paluṭṭhagiri.** He received as reward his native village.[1]

1 Cv. lv. 26-31.

4. **Buddha.**—A Kesadhātu, general of **Parakkamabāhu I.** He inflicted a severe defeat on **Mānābharaṇa** at **Pūnagāmatittha.**[1]

1 Cv. lxxii. 7.

5. **Buddha.**—See **Buddhanāyaka.**

1. **Buddha Vagga.**—The fourteenth chapter of the Dhammapada.

2. **Buddha Vagga.**—The first chapter of the Nidāna Saṃyutta.[1]

[1] S. ii. 1-11.

Buddha Sutta.—See **Arahaṃ Sutta** (5).

Buddhakula.—The family of the brahmin of **Sāketa** mentioned in the Commentary to the **Jarā Sutta.** He and his wife had been the parents of the Buddha in five hundred births, and when they saw him at Sāketa they greeted him like a long-lost son. Thenceforth they were known as **Buddhapitā** and **Buddhamātā** and their family as **Buddhakula.**[1]

[1] SNA. ii. 531 ff.; see also the **Sāketa Jātaka** and *Avadāna Śataka* ii. 41.

Buddhagāma.—A village and district in the **Dakkhiṇadesa** of Ceylon. It is mentioned in the account of the campaigns of **Parakkamabāhu I.**[1]

[1] Cv. lviii. 43; lxvi. 19, 25, 39, 62; lxix. 9; lxx. 311; lxxii. 178; for its identification see Cv. *Trs.* i. 206, n. 1.

Buddhagāmakanijjhara.—A tank restored by **Parakkamabāhu I.**[1]

[1] Cv. lxviii. 45.

Buddhagāma-vihāra.—A monastery in Ceylon for the maintenance of which **Sena II.** gifted a village.[1]

[1] Cv. li. 74.

1. **Buddhaghosa Thera.**—The greatest of Commentators on the Tipiṭaka. He was a brahmin[1] born in a village near **Buddhagayā** and became proficient in the Vedas and allied branches of knowledge. One day he met a monk, named **Revata,** and on being defeated by him in controversy, entered the Order to learn the Buddha's teachings. Because his speech was profound, like that of the Buddha, and because his words spread throughout the world (like those of the Buddha), he came to be called Buddhaghosa. While dwelling with Revata, he wrote the **Ñāṇodaya** and the **Atthasālinī,** and also began to write a **Parittaṭṭhakathā** (a concise commentary) on the Tipiṭakas. In order to complete his task, he came over to Ceylon at the suggestion of Revata[2] and studied the Sinhalese

[1] The Sās. (p. 29) says his father was a purohita named **Kesa,** his mother being **Kesī.** Gv. (66) says his father was the purohita of King **Saṅgāma.**

[2] Sās. (p. 29) says he was sent to Ceylon as punishment for thinking himself wiser than his teachers.

Commentaries at the **Mahāvihāra,** under **Saṅghapāla.** When his studies were ended he wrote the **Visuddhimagga,** and having thereby won the approval of the Elders of the Mahāvihāra, he rendered the Sinhalese Commentaries into Pāli. During this peroid he lived in the **Ganthākara-vihāra,**[3] and on the accomplishment of his task he returned to **Jambudīpa.**[4]

Besides the above-mentioned works of Buddhaghosa, we have also the **Samantapāsādikā** and the **Kaṅkhāvitaraṇī** on the Vinaya Piṭaka; the **Sumaṅgalavilāsinī,** the **Papañcasūdanī,** the **Sāratthappakāsinī** and the **Manorathapūranī** on the Sutta Piṭaka. He is also said to have compiled Commentaries on the **Khuddakapāṭha** and the **Sutta Nipāta** (called the **Paramatthajotikā**) and on the Dhammapada. He also wrote a series of Commentaries on the Abhidhamma Piṭaka (the **Atthasālinī,** the **Sammohavinodanī** and the **Pañcappakaraṇaṭṭhakathā**). Some ascribe to him the **Jātakaṭṭhakathā.**[5]

[3] Burmese tradition says he obtained his copy of the Tipiṭaka and the Commentaries from the **Āloka-Vihāra.**

[4] But see P.L.C. 83, n. 1.

[5] For details of these works see *s.v.* For further particulars relating to Buddhaghosa, see Law's "Life and work of Buddhaghosa" and P.L.C. 79 ff. The account of his life given here is taken from Cv. xxxvii. 215 ff. For a list of works ascribed to Buddhaghosa see Gv., pp. 59 and 68.

2. **Buddhaghosa.**—Called **Culla-Buddhaghosa** to distinguish him from the greater. He was a native of Ceylon,[1] and two works are ascribed to him[2]—the Jātattagīnidāna and the Sotattagīnidāna. The former probably refers to the Jātakaṭṭhakathā.[3] It was at his request that **Buddhaghosa** (1) wrote his Commentaries to the Abhidhamma.[4]

[1] Gv. 67. [2] *Ibid.*, 63. [3] P.L.C. 126. [4] Gv. 68.

Buddhaghosuppatti.—A very late account of the life of Buddhaghosa; it is more a romance than a historical chronicle.[1]

[1] For an account of this see Law, Pāli Lit. 558 f. The work has been translated and edited by Gray (London).

1. **Buddhadatta Thera.**—He lived in **Uragapura** in South India and wrote his works in the monastery of **Bhūtamaṅgalagāma** in the **Coḷa** country, his patron being **Accutavikkama.** He studied, however, at the **Mahāvihāra** in **Anurādhapura.** Tradition says[1] that he met **Buddhaghosa.** Buddhadatta's works include the **Vinaya-Vinicchaya,** the **Uttaravinicchaya,** the **Abhidhammāvatāra** and the **Rūpārūpavibhāga.** The **Madhuratthavilāsinī** and the **Jinālaṅkāra** are also sometimes ascribed to him.[2]

[1] *E.g.*, SadS., p. 55.

[2] Svd. 1195, 1199; Gv. 59, 66, 69. Fo details see P.L.C. 105 ff. and also *s.v.* for the books mentioned.

2. **Buddhadatta.**—Head of a dynasty of twenty-five kings who reigned in **Rājagaha.** His ancestors reigned in **Mithilā.**[1]

[1] Dpv. iii. 30; the MṬ. (p. 129) calls him **Samuddadatta.**

Buddhadāsa.—King of Ceylon for twenty-nine years (between 362 and 409 A.C.) He was the son of **Jeṭṭhatissa** and led a very pious life. He was renowned as a great physician, and various miraculous cures are attributed to him, even snakes seeking his assistance. A jewel which he received from a snake in gratitude for a cure, he placed in the stone image in the **Abhayagiri-vihāra.** A medical work, the **Sāratthasaṅgaha,** in Sanskrit, is ascribed to him.[1] It is said that he appointed a royal physician for every ten villages, and established hospitals for the crippled and for the dumb and also for animals. He appointed preachers to look after the people's spiritual welfare. Among religious buildings erected by him was the **Moraparivepa.** He extended his patronage to a holy monk, named **Mahādhammakathī,** who translated the suttas into Sinhalese. Buddhadāsa had eighty sons, named after the Buddha's eminent disciples, the eldest being **Upatissa II.,** who succeeded him.[2]

[1] But see Cv. *Trs.* 13, n. 7.

[2] Cv. xxxvii. 105 ff.

Buddhadeva Thera.—A member of the **Mahiṃsāsaka** sect. He was one of the three monks—the others being **Atthadassī** and **Buddhamitta**—at whose suggestion the **Jātakaṭṭhakathā** was written.[1]

[1] J. i. 1.

Buddhanāga Thera.—A disciple of **Sāriputta** of Ceylon. He wrote the **Vinayatthamañjūsā** on the **Kankhāvitaranī** at the request of a monk named **Sumedha.**[1]

[1] Gv. 61 f., 71; SadS. 65; Svd. 1212; P.L.C. 201.

Buddhanāyaka, Buddhanātha.—A general of **Mānābharaṇa** (2). He was defeated at **Nāla** by the **Kesadhātu Rakkha.** Later, during eight days, he fought at **Pillaviṭṭhi** a battle against the forces of **Parakkamabāhu I.** and again against the **Adhikārin Rakkha.** He was killed in the last-named conflict. [1]

[1] Cv. lxx. 296; lxxii. 171, 266, 270. See Cv. *Trs.* i. 311, n. 2.

Buddhapakiṇṇakhandha.—The twelfth chapter of the Buddhavaṃsa.

Buddhapitā.—See **Buddhakula.**

1. **Buddhappiya Thera.**—He was a native of **Coḷa,** but studied in Ceylon under **Ānanda Vanaratana.** He was the head of **Bālādicca-vihāra** and wrote two books, the **Rūpasiddhi** and the **Pajjamadhu.** He is also known as **Coḷiya Dīpaṅkara.**[1]

[1] P.L.C. 220 f.; Svd. 1239, 1260; SadS. 65.

2. **Buddhappiya.**—A monk, one of those who requested **Buddhaghosa** to write the **Jātakaṭṭhakathā.**[1]

[1] Gv. 68; but see J. i. 1, where his name does not occur.

Buddhabhelagāma.—A village in Ceylon given by **Jeṭṭhā,** wife of **Aggabodhi IV.,** for the maintenance of the **Jeṭṭhārāma.**[1]

[1] Cv. xvli. 28.

Buddhamātā.—See **Buddhakula.**

1. **Buddhamitta Thera.**—A colleague of **Buddhaghosa** and one of those at whose request he wrote the **Jātakaṭṭhakathā.**[1] He is also mentioned as having requested Buddhaghosa to write the Majjhima Commentary. It is said that he lived with Buddhaghosa at the **Mayūrarūpapaṭṭana.**[2]

[1] J. i. 1; Gv. 68.

[2] MA. ii. 1029.

2. **Buddhamitta.**—A monk. It was at his request that **Ānanda** wrote the **Mūlaṭīkā** on the **Abhidhammaṭṭhakathā.**[1]

[1] Gv. 69.

1. **Buddharakkhita Thera.**—A monk of Ceylon, an eminent teacher of the Vinaya.[1]

[1] Vin. v. 3; Sp. i. 62.

2. **Buddharakkhita.**—A monk of Ceylon. He was once, with thirty thousand others, ministering to the Elder **Mahārohaṇagutta** of **Therambatthala,** when he saw the king of the Supaṇṇas dashing across the sky to seize the Nāga-king who was offering rice-gruel to the Elder. Buddharakkhita immediately created a mountain into which he made the Elder enter, thus saving the Nāga-king.[1]

[1] Vsm. 154 f., 376.

3. **Buddharakkhita.**—A monk of Ceylon to whom is sometimes ascribed the **Jinālaṅkāra.** He is supposed to have lived about 426 B.C. on the west coast of Ceylon, at the head of a congregation of monks.[1] According to others,[2] he is said to have written both the Jinalaṅkāra and its Ṭīkā.

[1] P.L.C. 18.

[2] *E.g.,* Gv. 72.

4. **Buddharakkhita.**—See **Mahā Buddharakkhita.**

Buddharāja.—A powerful man of **Rohaṇa** who is said to have quarrelled with **Loka,** ruler of **Kājaragāma.**[1]

[1] Cv. lvii. 45.

Buddhavaṃsa.—The fourteenth book of the **Khuddaka Nikāya.**[1] The **Dīghabhāṇakas** excluded it from the canon, but it was accepted by the **Majjhimabhāṇakas.**[2] It contains, in verse, the lives of the twenty-five Buddhas, of whom **Gotama** was the last. The name of the Bodhisatta under each Buddha is also given. The last chapter deals with the distribution of Gotama's relics. It is said[3] that the Buddhavaṃsa was preached, at **Sāriputta's** request, at the **Nigrodhārāma** in **Kapilavatthu,** after the Buddha had performed the miracle of the **Ratanacaṅkama.** The Commentary on the Buddhavaṃsa is known as the **Madhurattha-vilāsinī** (*q.v.*).

The Gandhavaṃsa[4] speaks of a Buddhavaṃsa written by an author named **Kassapa.** This is probably not the same work. Mention is also made[5] of a Ṭīkā to the Buddhavaṃsa, Paramatthadīpāni by name.

[1] DA. i. 17.
[2] *Ibid.*
[3] Bu. i. 74. The Bu. has been published by the P.T.S. (1882).
[4] p. 61.
[5] Gv. 60.

Buddhavīmaṃsaka-māṇava.—See **Uttara** (9).

1. **Buddhasaññaka Thera.**—An arahant. In the time of **Vipassī Buddha** he was an earth-bound deva, and when, at the death of the Buddha, the earth trembled, he realized the Buddha's might and honoured him in his heart. Fourteen kappas ago he was a king named **Samita.**[1] He is probably identical with **Meghiya Thera.**[2]

[1] Ap. i. 151 f.
[2] ThagA. i. 149 f.

2. **Buddhasaññaka Thera.**—Ninety-four kappas ago he saw **Siddhattha Buddha** and his heart was gladdened.[1]

[1] Ap. i. 252.

3. **Buddhasaññaka.**—A hermit in the time of **Siddhattha Buddha.** Having heard from his pupils of the birth of the Buddha, he set forth from his hermitage to visit him. But he fell ill while yet one hundred and fifty leagues away, and he died full of faith in the Buddha.[1] He is probably identical with **Vītasoka Thera.**[2]

[1] Ap. ii. 420.
[2] ThagA. i. 295 f.

Buddhasiri. A monk of the **Mahāvihāra,** at whose request **Buddhaghosa** wrote the **Samantapāsādikā.**[1]

[1] Sp. i. 2.

Buddhasīha.—A monk of Ceylon, pupil of **Buddhadatta.** It was at his request that **Buddhadatta** (1) wrote the **Rūpārūpavibhāga.**[1] According to one tradition[2] Buddhasīha himself was the author of the work, but the colophon to the book states otherwise.

[1] P.L.C. 108. [2] SadS. 30.

Buddhasoma.—A monk of Ceylon, friend of **Ānanda,** the author of the **Saddhammopāyana.** The work was composed by **Ānanda** to be sent as a religious gift to Buddhasoma.[1]

[1] P.L.C. 212.

Buddhā.—Wife of Prince **Bodhi** and, later, of **Moggallāna.** By Bodhi she had a daughter **Lokitā** and by Moggallāna four children: **Kitti** (afterwards **Vijayabāhu I.**), **Mittā, Mahinda** and **Rakkhita.**[1]

[1] Cv. lvii. 40.

Buddhālaṅkāra.—A Pāli poem based on the **Sumedhakathā** by **Sīlavaṃsa.**[1]

[1] Bode, p. 43.

Buddhija, Buddhiya.—Personal attendant of **Kakusandha Buddha.**[1]

[1] Bu. xxiii. 20; J. i. 42; D. ii. 6.

Buddhippasādinī.—A Ṭīkā on the **Padasādhana** by Śrī Rāhula of the fifteenth century.[1]

[1] P.L.C. 205.

Buddhupaṭṭhāka Thera. — An arahant. Ninety-one kappas ago he blew a conch-shell in honour of **Vipassī Buddha.** Twenty-four kappas ago he became king sixteen times under the name of **Mahānigghosa.**[1] He is probably identical with **Vimala Thera.**[2]

[1] Ap. i. 138 f. [2] ThagA. i. 122 f.

Buddhūpaṭṭhāyaka Thera.—An arahant. Thirty-one kappas ago he was named **Veṭambarī** and his father dedicated him to the service of the Buddha (? **Sikhī**). Twenty-three kappas ago he became king four times under the name of **Samaṇūpaṭṭhaka.**[1]

[1] Ap. i. 242.

Bubbula.—A village in Ceylon, mentioned in the account of the campaigns of **Parakkamabāhu I.**[1]

[1] Cv. lxx. 99; see Cv. *Trs.* i. 295, n. 4.

Bumū.—The name of a gotta. The village of **Uttarakā** belonged to them, and when the Buddha was staying there with **Sunakkhatta,** the latter was greatly taken up with the practices of **Korakkhattiya.**[1] *v.l.* **Thulū** and **Khulū.** The editors of the Sumaṅgala Vilāsinī[2] have adopted the reading Khulū.

[1] D. ii. 6. [2] DA. iii. 819.

Burudatthalī.—A ford across the **Mahāvālukagaṅgā.**[1]

[1] Cv. lxxii. 36.

Bulī.—The name of a gotta. They claimed one-eighth share of the Buddha's relics and raised a thūpa over them in their city of **Allakappa.**[1] Their territory was probably near **Veṭhadīpa,** because the king of Allakappa is mentioned[2] as being in intimate relationship with the king of Veṭhadīpa.

[1] D. ii. 167. [2] DhA. i. 161.

Būkakalla.—A village in Ceylon near which was the **Ambavāpī** given by **Potthakuṭṭha** to the **Māṭambiya-padhānaghara.**[1]

[1] Cv. xlvi. 20.

Belaṭṭha.—Father of **Sañjaya**[1] (*q.v.*).

[1] SNA. ii. 423.

Belaṭṭha-Kaccāna.—A sugar-dealer. On his way from **Andhakavinda** to **Rājagaha** he met the Buddha seated at the foot of a tree, and, with his permission, presented a pot of sugar (*guḷakumbha*) to the monks. When the monks had shared as much of the sugar as they wished, much was left over, and the Buddha asked Kaccāna to throw it into the water. This he did, and the water crackled. The Buddha preached to Kaccāna who accepted his teaching.[1]

[1] Vin. i. 224 ff.

Belaṭṭhaputta.—See **Sañjaya Belaṭṭhaputta.**

Belaṭṭhasīsa Thera.—An arahant, preceptor of **Ānanda.** He was once afflicted with scurvy and his robes clung to him. The monks thereupon applied water to the robes, but when the Buddha heard of it he made a rule allowing necessary therapeutic measures.[1] At one time this Thera would lie in the forest where he kept a store of dried boiled rice. When he needed food, after samāpatti he would sprinkle water on the rice and eat it instead of going for alms. When this was reported to the Buddha, he blamed Belaṭṭhasīsa for storing up food and promulgated a rule forbidding this.[2] The Dhammapada Commentary,[3] however, states that the offence was committed after the rule was laid down, and, because the food was stored, not because of greed but through lack of covetousness, the Buddha declared Balaṭṭhasīsa free from guilt.

Belaṭṭhasīsa was a brahmin of **Sāvatthi** who had left the world under **Uruvela-Kassapa** before the Buddha's Enlightenment and was converted when Uruvela-Kassapa became a follower of the Buddha. He had been a monk in the time of **Padumuttara Buddha,** but could achieve no attainment. He once gave a *mātuluṅga*-fruit to **Vessabhū** Buddha.[4] He is probably identical with **Mātuluṅgaphaladāyaka** (*q.v.*) of the Apadāna.[5]

1 Vin. i. 202, 295 f.
2 *Ibid.*, iv. 86.
3 DhA. ii. 171.
4 ThagA. i. 67 ff.; Thag. vs. 16.
5 Ap. ii. 446.

Belaṭṭhānika (Belaṭṭhakāni) Thera.—He belonged to a brahmin family of **Sāvatthi,** and, after hearing the Buddha preach, he entered the Order. While meditating in a forest tract in **Kosala,** he grew slothful and rough in speech. One day the Buddha, seeing his maturing insight, appeared before him in a ray of glory and admonished him with a verse. Belaṭṭhānika was filled with agitation and soon after became an arahant.

In the time of **Vipassī Buddha** he was a brahmin teacher, and, while wandering about with his pupils, he saw the Buddha and offered him seven flowers. Twenty-nine kappas ago he became king under the name of **Vipulābhāsa.**[1] He is probably identical with **Campakapupphiya** of the Apadāna.[2]

1 Thag. vs. 101; ThagA. i. 205 f.
2 Ap. i. 167.

Beluva.—A village near **Vesāli,** where the Buddha spent his last *vassa*.[1] He fell grievously ill during this period, but, by a great effort of will, overcame his sickness.[2] It was at this time that the Buddha, in answer to a question by **Ānanda,** said that he had kept nothing back from his disciples and had no special instructions for the Order to follow after his death. Each disciple must work out his own salvation.[3]

1 This was ten months before his death (SA. iii. 198). According to the Commentaries (*e.g.*, UdA. 322; SA. iii. 172) the Buddha did not go straight from Beluva to Vesāli, but turned back to Sāvatthi.

2 During this sickness **Sakka** ministered to the Buddha, waiting on him and carrying on his head the Buddha's stools when he suffered from acute dysentery (DhA. iii. 269 f.).

3 D. ii. 98 ff.; S. v. 151 ff.

Ānanda is also mentioned as having stayed at Beluva after the Buddha's death. The householder **Dasama** of **Aṭṭhakanagara** sought him there, and their conversation is recorded in the **Aṭṭhakanagara Sutta.**[4] Beluva was a small village, and when the Buddha was there the monks stayed in **Vesāli.** Beluva was just outside the gates of Vesāli[5] and was to the south of this city.[6]

The Theragāthā[7] states that **Anuruddha** died at **Veluvagāma** in the **Vajjī** country. This probably refers to Beluvagāma, in which case Veluva is a *varia lectio.*

[4] M. i. 349 ff.; A. v. 342 ff.
[5] SA. iii. 165.
[6] MA. ii. 571.
[7] vs. 919.

Beluvapaṇḍuvīṇā.—The lute carried by **Pañcasikha** (*q.v.*); it belonged originally to **Māra.** When **Māra,** after wasting seven years trying in vain to discover some shortcoming in the Buddha—six years before the Enlightenment and one year after it—left the Buddha in disgust and weariness, the lute which he carried slung on his shoulder slipped and fell. **Sakka** picked it up and gave it to Pañcasikha. It was so powerful that when plucked with the fingers the lovely music produced echoed on for four months.[1] The *vīṇā* was three gāvutas in length[2] and had fifty trestles.[3] The **Sumaṅgala Vilāsinī**[4] describes it at length. It was pale yellow, like a ripe *beluva*-fruit. Its base (*pokkhara*) was of gold, its stem of sapphire its strings of silver, and its knots (*veṭhikā*) of coral. The vīṇā was probably so called partly because its base was made of a *bilva*-fruit, instead of the usual gourd, and partly because of its colour.

[1] SNA. ii. 393 f.
[2] BuA. 239.
[3] AA. i. 72.
[4] DA. iii. 699.

Bokusala.—A village in **Rohaṇa,** mentioned in the account of the campaigns of **Parakkamabāhu I.**[1]

[1] Cv. lxxiv. 169.

Bojjhaṅga Saṃyutta. — The second section (forty-sixth Saṃyutta) of the Mahāvagga of the Saṃyutta Nikāya.[1]

[1] S. v. 61 ff.

1. **Bojjhaṅga Sutta.**—Among the four kinds of deeds—dark with a dark result, dark with a bright result, bright with a bright result and bright with a dark result—the seven kinds of wisdom (*bojjhaṅga*) are neither dark nor bright, and conduce to the waning of deeds.[1]

[1] A. ii. 236 f.

2. **Bojjhaṅga Sutta.**—The seven bojjhaṅgas lead to the Uncompounded (*Asaṅkhata*).[1]

[1] S. iv. 361.

3. **Bojjhaṅga Sutta.**—Describes how concentration on breathing leads to the cultivation of the seven *bojjhaṅgas*.[1]

[1] S. v. 312.

Bojjhaṅgakathā.—The third chapter of the Yuganaddha Vagga of the Paṭisambhidāmagga.

Bojjhaṅgakosalla Sutta. — One of the sections of the Bojjhaṅga Saṃyutta.[1]

[1] VibhA. 229, 231; the reference is to S. v. 112 f.

Bojjhaṅga-Sākacca Vagga. — The sixth chapter of the **Bojjhaṅga Saṃyutta.**[1]

[1] S. v. 102 ff.

Bojjhā, Bocchā.—An eminent *upāsikā.* The Aṅguttara Nikāya[1] records a visit paid by her to the Buddha at **Jetavana.** The Buddha then preached to her on the *uposatha* and the advantages of keeping the fast.

[1] A. iv. 259, also 347.

Bojjhā Sutta.—Records the visit of **Bojjhā** (*q.v.*) to the Buddha and the sermon preached to her on the *uposatha*.[1]

[1] A. iv. 259 ff.

Bodhanā Sutta.—The Buddha explains to a monk, in answer to his question, that the *bojjhaṅgas* are so called because they conduce to wisdom.[1]

[1] S. v. 83.

Bodhāhārakula, Bodhidhārakula.—That name given to the descendants of the eight families who brought the branch of the Bodhi-tree from **Pāṭaliputta** to Ceylon.[1] The heads of the families were brothers of **Vedisadevī,** wife of **Asoka,** and they were led by **Sumitta** and **Bodhigutta.**[2] The others[3] were **Candagutta, Devagutta, Dhammagutta, Suriyagutta, Gotama** and **Jutindhara.** They were entrusted with the ceremonies in connection with the Bodhi-tree at **Anurādhapura** and each was given a special office.

[1] Mhv. xix. 67. [2] Mbv. p. 154. [3] *Ibid.*, p. 165 f.

1. **Bodhi,** called **Bodhirājakumāra.**—He lived at **Suṃsumāragiri** in the **Bhagga** country and built a palace called **Kokanada** (*q.v.*). When the palace was completed, the Buddha was staying at **Bhesakalāvana** near by, and Bodhi sent a message by **Sañjikāputta,** inviting the Buddha to the palace, that he might bless it by being its first occupant. The Buddha agreed to come and, the next day, arrived with the monks for a meal. Bodhi came, with his retinue, to meet them at the foot of the steps and asked the Buddha to step on to the carpeting which was spread there. Three times the request was made, three times the Buddha kept silence. Thereupon **Ānanda** asked for the carpeting to be removed, saying that the Buddha's refusal to step thereon was as an example to future generations. After the meal, Bodhi had a discussion with the Buddha,[1] recorded in the **Bodhirājakumāra Sutta** (*q.v.*).

The Commentary adds[2] that one of the reasons for the Buddha's refusal to step on the carpet was that he knew the thoughts of Bodhi. Bodhi was saying to himself: "If I am to have a son, the Buddha will step on this carpet, if not, he will not." The Buddha knew also that Bodhi was not destined to have a son because in a previous life he and his wife had lived on an island and eaten young birds.

Bodhi was the son of **Udena,** king of **Kosambī,** and his mother was the daughter of **Caṇḍappajjota** (*q.v.*). Bodhi was skilled in the art of managing elephants,[3] which art he learned from his father, a master in this direction. It is said[4] that, while Bodhi was yet in his mother's womb, she visited the Buddha at the **Ghositārāma** in Kosambī and declared that whatever child was born to her it would accept the Buddha, his teaching and the Order, as its abiding refuge. Later, after Bodhi's birth, his nurse took him to the Buddha at Bhesakalāvana and made a similar declaration. When, therefore, Bodhi acknowledged the Buddha as his teacher, at the conclusion of the Bodhirājakumāra Sutta, he was seeking the Buddha's refuge for the third time.

Some accounts[5] of the building of Bodhi's palace add that, as it was being completed, Bodhi conceived the idea of killing the architect or of blinding him so that he could never design a similar house for anyone else. He confided this idea to Sanjikāputta, who warned the architect. The latter, therefore, obtained special timber from Bodhi, saying it was

[1] Vin. ii. 127 f.; M. ii. 91 ff.

[2] MA. ii. 739 ff.; DhA. (iii. 137 ff.) adds that the Buddha actually told Bodhi of the non-fulfilment of his wish for a son, and related to him the story of his past life in which he and his wife ate birds' eggs.

[3] See also M. ii. 94.

[4] *Ibid.*, 97.

[5] *E.g.*, DhA. iii. 134 ff.; in J. iii. 157 it is stated briefly that Bodhi did actually blind the architect. In a previous birth he put out the eyes of one thousand warriors. See the **Dhonasākha Jātaka.**

for the palace, and made out of it a wooden bird large enough to hold himself and his family. When it was ready, he made it fly out of the window, and he and his family escaped to the Himālaya country, where he founded a kingdom and came to be known as King **Kaṭṭhavāhana.**

2. **Bodhi.**—One of the eight brahmins who recognised the signs at the birth of the Buddha.[1]

[1] J. i. 56; in the Milinda (236) he is called **Subodhi.**

3. **Bodhi.**—Called **Bodhikumāra.** The Bodhisatta born as an ascetic. For his story see the **Cullabodhi Jātaka.**[1]

[1] J. iv. 22 ff.

4. **Bodhi.**—Also called **Mahābodhi**; the Bodhisatta born as an ascetic. See the **Mahābodhi Jātaka.**[1]

[1] J. v. 227 ff.

5. **Bodhi.**—A monk of Ceylon. At his request **Silāmeghavaṇṇa** proclaimed a regulative act against the undisciplined monks of **Abhayagiri-vihāra.** The monks, expelled under the act, conspired together and killed Bodhi. But the king renewed his exertions and, in memory of Bodhi, succeeded in purifying the Order.[1]

[1] Cv. xliv. 75.

6. **Bodhi.**—A descendant of **Dāṭhopatissa.** He married **Buddhā** (*q.v.*), and had by her a daughter named **Lokitā.**[1]

[1] Cv. lvii. 40.

7. **Bodhi.**—**Laṅkādhinātha Bodhi.** General of **Mānābharaṇa** (2). He was slain in battle.[1]

[1] Cv. lxx. 294, 309.

Bodhi Vagga.—The first chapter of the Udāna.

Bodhi Sutta.—On the seven *bojjhaṅgas* as the seven things that cause not decline (*aparihāniyā dhammā*).[1]

[1] A. iv. 23.

Bodhiāvāṭa.—A village in **Rohaṇa** mentioned in the accounts of the campaigns of **Parakkamabāhu I.**[1]

[1] Cv. lxxv. 97, 146.

Bodhiupaṭṭhāyaka Thera.—An Arahant. Eighteen kappas ago he was born in **Rammavatī** under the name of **Muraja** and paid great homage to the Bodhi-tree. Fifteen kappas ago he was a king named **Damatha.**[1]

[1] Ap. i. 174.

Bodhigāmavara.—A village and district in the **Dakkhiṇadesa** of Ceylon, mentioned in the account of the campaigns of **Parakkamabāhu I.**[1]

[1] Cv. lxvi. 78; lxix. 9; lxx. 88; for its identification see Cv. *Trs.* i. 259, n. 1.

Bodhigutta.—Brother of **Vedisadevī.** He belonged to the Sākyan clan, and with **Sumitta** was leader of the retinue sent by **Asoka** to escort the branch of the Bodhi-tree to **Anurādhapura.** At the conclusion of the planting of the tree, Bodhigutta was taken by the king to **Morapāsāda** and there invested with the rank of **Laṅkājayamahālekhaka** (*q.v.*) amid great pomp and ceremony. He was given a house near the Bodhi-tree. Later he married **Sunandā,** sister of **Bodhiguttā,** and had two children—**Mahinda** and **Vidhurinda.**[1]

[1] Mbv. 154 f., 163 f., 169.

Bodhiguttā.—A nun of the **Hatthāḷhakārāma** in **Anurādhapura,** colleague of **Saṅghamittā.** She belonged to the **Moriya** clan and was the elder sister of **Sunandā,** wife of **Bodhigutta.**[1]

[1] Mbv. 169.

Bodhighariya Thera.—An Arahant. Ninety-four kappas ago he built a pavilion by the Bodhi-tree of **Siddhattha Buddha.** Sixty-five kappas ago he became king in **Kāsika,** which city was built for him by **Vissakamma,** ten leagues long and eight broad. His palace was called **Maṅgala.**[1]

[1] Ap. ii. 401.

Bodhitalagāma.—A village on the road from **Gaṅgāsiripura** to **Samantakūṭa** where **Devappatirāja** built a bridge.[1]

[1] Cv. lxxxvi. 21.

Bodhitissa.—A chieftain, probably of **Malaya.** He built the **Bodhitissavihāra.**[1]

[1] Cv. xlvi. 30.

Bodhitissa-vihāra.—See **Bodhitissa.**

Bodhimaṇḍa.—The name given to the spot under the Bodhi-tree where the Buddha attained Enlightenment and where he sat for one week after the Enlightenment.[1] A monastery was later erected there called the **Bodhimaṇḍa-vihāra.** Thirty thousand monks, under **Cittagutta,** came from there to the foundation ceremony of the **Mahā Thūpa.**[2] It was near here that **Buddhaghosa** was born,[3] and here **Silākāla** entered the Order.[4] See also *s.v.* **Bodhirukkha.**

[1] Vin. i. 1; but according to DhA. i. 71 he spent seven weeks there.
[2] Mhv. xxix. 41.
[3] Cv. xxxvii. 215.
[4] *Ibid.*, xxxix. 47.

Bodhimaṇḍa-vihāra.—See **Bodhimaṇḍa.**

Bodhimātu-Mahātissa Thera.—He came through the air to receive from **Duṭṭhagāmaṇī** (*q.v.*) a share of the food which the latter had obtained while fleeing from **Cuḷaṅganiyapiṭṭhi.**[1] Accodring to other accounts the Thera's name was **Kuṭumbiyaputta-Tissa** (*q.v.*).

[1] AA. i. 366.

Bodhirājakumāra Sutta.—Records the visits of the Buddha to Prince **Bodhi** (1) and the discussion which ensued. The Buddha refutes **Bodhi's** view that true welfare comes only through unpleasant things, and declares that if a monk has confidence in the Buddha and also the necessary qualities of head and heart, he can master the Dhamma without delay.[1]

[1] M. ii. 91 ff.

Bodhirukka.—The generic name given to the tree under which a Buddha attains Enlightenment.[1] The tree is different in the case of each Buddha. Thus, for **Gotama** and also for **Koṇḍañña** it was an *assattha*; for **Dīpaṅkara** a *sirīsa*; for **Maṅgala, Sumana, Revata** and **Sobhita** a *nāga*; for **Anomadassī** an *ajjuna*; for **Paduma** and **Nārada** a *mahāsoṇa*; for **Padumuttara** a *salala*; for **Sumedha** a *nimba*; for **Sujāta** a bamboo; for **Piyadassī** a *kakudha*; for **Atthadassī** a *campaka*; for **Dhammadassī** a *bimbajāla*; for **Siddhattha** a *kaṇikāra*; for **Tissa** an *asana*; for **Phussa** an *āmaṇḍa*; for **Vipassī** a *pāṭalī*; for **Sikhī** a *puṇḍarīka*; for **Vessabhū** a *sāla*; for **Kakusandha** a *sirīsa*; for **Koṇāgamma** an *udumbara*; for **Kassapa** a banyan.[2] The site of the Bodhi-tree is the same for all Buddhas,[3] and it forms the navel of the earth[4] (*puthuvinābhi*). No other place can support the weight of the Buddha's attainment.[5]

[1] DA. ii. 416.
[2] See *passim*; the details differ somewhat at BuA. 247.
[3] BuA. 247.
[4] J. iv. 233.
[5] *Ibid.*, 229.

When no Bodhi-tree grows, the **Bodhimaṇḍa** (ground round the Bodhi-tree), for a distance of one royal *karīsa*, is devoid of all plants, even of any blade of grass, and is quite smooth, spread with sand like a silver plate, while all around it are grass, creepers and trees. None can travel in the air immediately above it, not even **Sakka.**[6]

When the world is destroyed at the end of a kappa, the Bodhimaṇḍa is the last spot to disappear; when the world emerges into existence again, it is the first to appear. A lotus springs there bringing it into view and if during the kappa thus begun a Buddha will be born, the lotus puts forth flowers, according to the number of Buddhas (DA. ii. 412).

In the case of Gotama Buddha, his Bodhi-tree sprang up on the day he was born.[7] After his Enlightenment, he spent a whole week in front of it, standing with unblinking eyes, gazing at it with gratitude. A shrine was later erected on the spot where he so stood, and was called the **Animisalocana-cetiya** (*q.v.*). The spot was used as a shrine even in the lifetime of the Buddha, the only shrine that could be so used. While the Buddha was yet alive, in order that people might make their offerings in the name of the Buddha when he was away on pilgrimage, he sanctioned the planting of a seed from the Bodhi-tree in **Gayā** in front of the gateway of Jetavana. For this purpose **Moggallāna** took a fruit from a tree at **Gayā** as it dropped from its stalk, before it reached the ground. It was planted in a golden jar by **Anāthapiṇḍika** with great pomp and ceremony. A sapling immediately sprouted forth, fifty cubits high, and in order to consecrate it the Buddha spent one night under it, wrapt in meditation. This tree, because it was planted under the direction of **Ānanda,** came to be known as the **Ānanda-Bodhi.**[8]

According to the Ceylon Chronicles,[9] branches from the Bodhi-trees of all the Buddhas born during this kappa were planted in Ceylon on the spot where the sacred Bodhi-tree stands today in **Anurādhapura.** The branch of Kakusandha's tree was brought by a nun called **Rucānandā, Koṇagamana's** by **Kantakānandā** (or **Kanakadattā**), and **Kassapa's** by **Sudhammā. Asoka** was most diligent in paying homage to the Bodhi-tree, and held a festival every year in its honour in the month of **Kattika.**[10] His queen, **Tissarakkhā,** was jealous of the Tree, and three years after she became queen (*i.e.*, in the nineteenth year of Asoka's reign), she caused the tree to be killed by means of *maṇḍu*-thorns.[11] The tree, however, grew again, and a great monastery was attached to the Bodhimaṇḍa. Among those present at the foundation of the

[6] J. iv., 232 f.
[7] DA. ii. 425; BuA. 248.
[8] J. iv. 228 ff.
[9] *E.g.*, Mhv. xv.
[10] *Ibid.*, xvii. 17.
[11] *Ibid.*, xx. 4 f.

Mahā Thūpa are mentioned thirty thousand monks, from this Vihāra, led by **Cittagutta.**[12]

Kittisirimegha of Ceylon, contemporary of Samudragupta, erected with the permission of Samudragupta, a Saṅghārāma near the **Mahābodhi-vihāra**, chiefly for the use of the Sinhalese monks who went to worship the Bodhi-tree. The circumstances in connection with the Saṅghārāma are given by Hiouen Thsang[13] who gives a description of it as seen by himself. It was probably here that **Buddhaghosa** met the Elder **Revata** who persuaded him to come to Ceylon.

In the twelfth year of Asoka's reign the right branch of the Bodhi-tree was brought by **Saṅghamittā** to **Anurādhapura** and placed by **Devānampiyatissa** in the **Mahāmeghavana.** The Buddha, on his death-bed, had resolved five things, one being that the branch which should be taken to Ceylon should detach itself.[14] From **Gayā,** the branch was taken to **Pāṭaliputta,** thence to **Tāmalittī,** where it was placed in a ship and taken to **Jambukola,** across the sea; finally it arrived at Anurādhapura, staying on the way at **Tivakka.** Those who assisted the king at the ceremony of the planting of the Tree were the nobles of **Kājaragāma** and of **Candanagāma** and of **Tivakka.** From the seeds of a fruit which grew on the tree sprang eight saplings, which were planted respectively at **Jambukola,** in the village of **Tivakka,** at **Thūpārāmā,** at **Issarasamaṇārāma,** in the court of the **Paṭhamacetiya,** in **Cetiyagiri,** in **Kājaragāma** and in **Candanagāma.**[15] Thirty-two other saplings, from four other fruits, were planted here and there at a distance of one yojana. Ceremonies were instituted in honour of the Tree, the supervision of which was given over to **Bodhāhārakula,** at the head of which were the eight ministers of Asoka who, led by **Bodhigutta** and **Sumitta,**[16] were sent as escorts of the Tree. Revenues were provided for these celebrations.

Later, King **Dhātusena** built a Bodhighara or roof over the Tree[17] while **Silākāla** made daily offerings at the shrine,[18] and **Kittisirimegha** had the Bodhighara covered with tin plates.[19] **Mahānāga** had the roof of the Bodhighara gilded, built a trench round the courtyard and set up Buddha images in the image-house.[20] **Aggabodhi I.** erected a stone terrace round the Tree and placed, at the bottom of it, an oil-pit to receive the oil for illuminations on festival days.[21] **Aggabodhi II.** had a well dug for the use of pilgrims,[22] and **Moggallāna III.** held a great celebration in the Tree's

[12] Mhv. xxix. 41.

[13] Beal, *op. cit.*, 133 ff.

[14] Mhv. xvii. 46 f.

[15] *Ibid.*, xix. 60 ff.; for details in connection with the bringing of the Bodhi-tree, see Mbv. 144 ff.

[16] See *ibid.*, 165 f., for the names of the others.

[17] Cv. xxxviii. 431.

[18] See Cv. *Trs.* i. 32, n. 6; Cv. xli. 29.

[19] *Ibid.*, 65

[20] *Ibid.*, 94.

[21] *Ibid.*, xlii. 19.

[22] *Ibid.*, 66.

honour.[23] **Aggabodhi VII.** found the Bodhighara in ruins and had it rebuilt[24]; **Mahinda II.** instituted a regular offering in its honour,[25] and **Udaya III.** gave a village near Anurādhapura to the service of the Bodhi-tree.[26]

[23] Cv. xliv. 45.
[24] *Ibid.*, xlviii. 70.
[25] *Ibid.*, 124.
[26] *Ibid.* liii. 10.

Bodhivandaka Thera.—An arahant. Ninety-one kappas ago he saw the *pāṭali*-bodhi of **Vipassī Buddha** and worshipped it.[1]

[1] Ap. i. 290.

Bodhivaṃsa.—See **Mahābodhivaṃsa.**

Bodhivāla.—A village in **Rohaṇa,** mentioned in the account of the campaigns of **Kitti (Vijayabāhu I.)**.[1]

[1] Cv. lvii. 54.

Bodhisatta.—The name given to a being who aspires to *Bodhi* or Enlightenment.[1] The word can therefore be used in reference to all those who seek Nibbāna, including Buddhas, Pacceka-Buddhas, and the disciples of Buddhas (*Buddhapaccekabuddhabuddhasāvakā*), but is commonly used only of those beings who seek to become Buddhas. The word may have been used originally only in connection with the last life of a Buddha, in such contexts as " in the days before my Enlightenment, when as yet I was only a Bodhisatta."[2] But already in the Kathāvatthu[3] the previous lives of Gotama Buddha and other saints had begun to excite interest and speculation.

In the developed form of the ideas regarding Bodhisattas, a Bodhisatta's career started with his making a resolution before a Buddha (*abhinīhārakaraṇa* or *mūlapanidhāna*) to become a Buddha for the welfare and liberation of all creatures. In later literature, the *abhinīhāra* is preceded by a period during which the Bodhisatta practises *manopanidhi,* when he resolves in his mind to desire to become a Buddha without declaring this intention to others.

For the *abhinīhāra* to be effective, eight conditions should be fulfilled[4]: the aspirant should be (1) a human being, (2) a male, (3) sufficiently de-

[1] The Commentaries (*e.g.*, DA. ii. 427) define the word thus: *Bodhisatto ti paṇḍitasatto bujjhanakasatto; bodhisaṅkhātesu vā catusu maggesu āsatto laggamānaso ti Bodhisatto.* See also AA. i. 453. For a discussion of the meaning of the word see Har Dayal: *The Bodhisattva Doctrine*, pp. 4 ff.

[2] *E.g.*, M. i. 17, 114, 163; so also in the **Mahāpadāna Sutta** (D. ii. 13) and the **Acchariyaabbhutadhamma Sutta** (M. iii. 119).

[3] *E.g.*, 283-90, 623.

[4] Bu. ii. 59; explained at BuA. 75 f. and SNA. i. 48 f.

veloped to become an arahant in that very birth, (4) a recluse at the time of the declaration, (5) he should declare his resolve before a Buddha, (6) should be possessed of attainments such as the *jhānas*, (7) be prepared to sacrifice all, even life, and (8) his resolution should be absolutely firm and unwavering. In the case of Gotama Buddha, his *abhinīhāra* was made at **Amaravātī** in the presence of **Dīpaṅkara Buddha.** His name at that time was **Sumedha** (*q.v.*). The Buddha, before whom the *abhinīhāra* is made, looks into the future and, if satisfied, declares the fulfilment of the resolve, mentioning the particulars of such fulfilment. This declaration is called *vyākaraṇa*, and is made also by all subsequent Buddhas whom the Bodhisatta may meet during his career. Having received his first *vyākaraṇa*, the Bodhisatta proceeds to investigate the qualities which should be acquired by him for the purposes of Buddhahood (*buddhakārakadhammā*), in accordance with the custom of previous Bodhisattas. These he discovers to be ten in number, the Ten Perfections (*dasapāramī*): *dāna, sīla, nekkhamma, paññā, viriya, khanti, sacca, adiṭṭhāna, mettā* and *upekhā.*[5] He also develops the four Buddhabhūmi (*catasso buddhabhūmiyo*)—*ussāha, ummagga, avatthāna* and *hitacariyā*—explained respectively as zealousness (*viriya*), wisdom (*paññā*), resolution (*adhiṭṭhāna*) and compassion (*mettā-bhāvanā*). He cultivates the six *ajjhāsayas* which conduce to the maturing of Enlightenment (*bodhiparipākiyā saṃvattanti*), these six being: *nekkhammajjhāsaya, pavivekajjhāsaya, alobhajjhāsaya, adosajjhāsaya, amohajjhāsaya* and *nissaraṇajjhāsaya.*[6]

A Bodhisatta, during his career, escapes from being born in eighteen inauspicious states (*aṭṭhārasa abhabbaṭṭhānāni*). He is never born blind, deaf, insane, slobbery (*eḷamūga*) or crippled, or among savages (*milakkhesu*), in the womb of a slave, or as a heretic. He never changes his sex, is never guilty of any of the five *ānantarikakammas*, and never becomes a leper. If born as an animal, he never becomes less than a quail or more than an elephant. He is never born either among various classes of petas nor among the **Kālakañjakas,** neither in **Avīci** nor in the *lokantaraka-nirayas*, neither as **Māra,** nor in worlds where there is no perception (*asaññībhava*), nor in the **Suddhāvāsas,** nor in the **Arūpa-**worlds, nor ever in another **Cakkavāḷa.**[7]

[5] Bu. ii. 116 ff. Sometimes thirty *pāramī* are spoken of, each of the ten being divided into three, varying in kind and degree. Thus, in the case of *dāna*, the *dānapāramī* consists in giving one's limbs, *dāna-upapāramī* in giving away one's external possessions and *dāna-paramatthapāramī* in giving one's life, this last being the most excellent. In the case of Gotama Buddha, examples of births in which the ten *pāramī* were practised to the highest degree are as follows: the **Ekarāja, Khantivādī, Cūla-Saṅkhapāla, Mahājanaka, Mahāsutasoma, Mūgapakkha, Lomahaṃsa, Sattubhattaka, Sasa,** and **Sutasoma Jātakas** (BuA. 50; J. i. 44 f.).

[6] SNA. i. 50.

[7] SNA. i. 50 f.

Besides practising the (thirty) *pāramī*, all Bodhisattas must make the five great sacrifices (*mahāpariccāgā*)—giving up wife, children, kingdom, life and limb[8]—and must fulfil the three kinds of conduct (*cariyā*) *ñātatthacariyā*, *lokatthacariyā* and *buddhiatthacariyā*—and the seven *mahādānas* as practised by **Vessantara,** which caused the earth to quake seven times.[9]

The length of a Bodhisatta's career varies; some practice the *pāramī* for at least four asaṅkheyyas and one hundred thousand kappas, others for at least eight asaṅkheyyas and one hundred thousand kappas, and yet others for sixteen asaṅkheyyas and one hundred thousand kappas. The first of these periods is the very least that is required and is intended for those who excel in wisdom (*paññā*). The middle is for those who excel in faith (*saddhā*); and the last and highest for those whose chief feature is perseverance (*viriya*).[10]

In their penultimate life all Bodhisattas are born in Tusita,[11] where life lastsf or fifty-seven crores and six million years, but most Bodhisattas leave Tusita before completing their life-span.[12]

As the time for the announcement of their last birth approaches, all is excitement because of various signs appearing in the ten thousand world systems. The devas of all the worlds assemble in Tusita and request the Bodhisatta to seek birth as a human being, that he may become the Buddha. The Bodhisatta withholds his reply until he has made the Five Great Investigations (*pañcamahāvilokanā*) regarding time, continent, place of birth, his mother and the life-span left to her. Buddhas do not appear in the world when men live to more than one hundred thousand years or to less than one hundred. They are born only in **Jambudīpa** and in the **Majjhimadesa,** and only of a khattiya or brahmin clan. The Bodhisatta's mother in his last birth must not be passionate or given to drink; she should have practised the *pāramī* for one hundred thousand kappas, have kept the precepts inviolate from birth, and should not be destined to live more than ten months and seven days after the conception of the Bodhisatta.

Having satisfied himself as to these particulars, the Bodhisatta goes with the other devas to **Nandanavana** in Tusita, where he announces his departure from their midst and disappears from among them while playing. On the day of his conception, the Bodhisatta's mother takes the vows of fasting and celibacy at the conclusion of a great festival,

[8] J. vi. 552.

[9] DA. ii. 427; DhA. iii. 441; the BuA. (116 f.) gives a story about **Maṅgala Buddha** which corresponds to that of **Vessantara** in regard to Gotama Buddha. See *s.v.* **Kharadāṭhika.**

[10] SNA. i. 47 f.

[11] See *s.v.* **Buddha.**

[12] **Vipassī,** *e.g.*, was among the exceptions (DA. ii. 427).

and when she has retired to rest, she dreams that the Four Regent Gods take her with her bed, bathe her in the Anotatta Lake, clad her in divine garments, and place her in a golden palace surrounded by all kinds of luxury. As she lies there the Bodhisatta in the form of a white elephant enters her womb through her right side. The earth trembles and all the ten thousand world systems are filled with radiance. Immediately the Four Regent Gods assume guard over mother and child. Throughout the period of pregnancy, which lasts for ten months exactly, the mother remains free from ailment and sees the child in her womb sitting crossed-legged.[13] At the end of the ten months she gives birth to the child, standing in a grove, never indoors. Suddhāvāsa brahmins, free from all passion, first receive the child in a golden net, and from them the Four Regent Gods take him on an antelope-skin and present him to his mother. Though the Bodhisatta is born free of the mucous otherwise present at birth, two showers of water—one hot, the other cold—fall from the sky and bathe mother and child. The child then takes seven strides to the north, standing firmly on his feet, looks on all sides, and seeing no one anywhere to equal him, announces his supremacy over the whole world and the fact that this is his last birth.[14] Seven days after birth his mother dies. She dies because she must bear no other being. The Bodhisatta's time of conception is so calculated that the mother's destined life-span completes itself seven days after his birth. From the Commentary[15] account it would appear that the age of the Bodhisatta's mother at the time of his birth is between fifty and sixty (*majjhimavayassa pana dve koṭṭhāsā atikkamma tatiye-koṭṭhāse*).

The Bodhisatta's last birth is attended by various miracles.[16] Soothsayers, being summoned, see on the child's body the thirty-two marks of a Great Man (*mahāpurisa*),[17] and declare that the child will become either a **Cakkavatti** or a **Buddha.** His father, desiring that his child shall be a Cakkavatti rather than a Buddha, brings him up in great luxury, hiding from him all the sin and ugliness of the world. But the destiny of a Bodhisatta asserts itself, and he becomes aware of the presence in the world of old age, disease, death and the freedom of mind

[13] Like a preacher on a dais, says the Commentary (DA. ii. 436).

[14] Gotama Buddha as the Bodhisatta, spoke, in three different births, as soon as born—as **Mahosadha,** as **Vessantara,** and in his last birth (J. i. 53).

[15] DA. ii. 437; UdA. 278.

[16] The Commentaries see, in the various incidents connected with the Bodhisatta's last birth, signs of various features which came, later, to be associated with the Buddha and his doctrine; for details see DA. ii. 439 ff.

[17] For details of these see D. ii. 17 ff.; M. ii. 136 f. The reasons for these marks are given at D. iii. 145 ff.

to be found in the life of a Recluse.[18] Urged by the desire to discover the cause of suffering in the world and the way out of it, the Bodhisatta leaves the world on the day of his son's birth. Some Bodhisattas leave the world riding on an elephant (*e.g.*, Dīpaṅkara, Sumana, Sumedha, Phussa, Sikhī and Koṇāgamana), some on a chariot (*e.g.*, Koṇḍañña, Revata, Paduma, Piyadassī, and Kakusandha), some on a horse (*e.g.*, Maṅgala, Sujāta, Atthadassī, Tissa, Gotama), and some in a palanquin (*e.g.*, Anomadassī, Siddhattha and Vessabhū). Some, like Nārada, go on foot, while Sobhita, Dhammadassī and Kassapa travelled in the palaces of their lay-life.

Having left the world, the Bodhisatta practises the austerities, the period of such practices varying. In the case of Dīpaṅkara, Koṇḍañña, Sumana, Anomadassī, Sujāta, Siddhattha and Kakusandha it was ten months; for Maṅgala, Sumedha, Tissa and Sikhī it was eight; for Revata seven; for Piyadassī, Phussa, Vessabhū and Koṇāgamana six; for Sobhita four; for Paduma, Atthadassī and Vipassī two weeks; for Nārada, Padumuttara, Dhammadassī and Kassapa one week; and for Gotama six years.[19] On the day the Bodhisatta attains to Buddhahood, he receives a meal of milk-rice (*pāyāsa*) from a woman and a gift of kusa-grass, generally from an **Ājīvika,** which he spreads under the Bodhi-tree[20] for his seat. The size of this seat varies; the seats of Dīpaṅkara, Revata, Piyadassī, Atthadassī, Dhammadassī and Vipassī were fifty-three hands in length; those of Koṇḍañña, Maṅgala, Nārada and Sumedha fifty-seven hands; that of Sumaṇa sixty hands; those of Sobhita, Anomadassī, Paduma, Padumuttara and Phussa thirty-eight; of Sujāta thirty-two; of Kakusandha twenty-six; of Koṇāgamana twenty; of Kassapa fifteen; of Gotama fourteen.[21] Before the Enlightenment the Bodhisatta has five great dreams: (1) that the world is his couch with the Himālaya as his pillow, his left hand resting on the eastern sea, his right on the western, and his feet on the southern; (2) that a blade of *tiriyā*(*kusa*)-grass growing from his navel touches the clouds; (3) that white worms with black heads creep up from his feet, covering his knees; (4) that four birds of varied hues from the four quarters of the world fall at his feet and become white; (5) that he walks to and fro on a heap of dung, by which he remains unsoiled.[22]

The next day the Bodhisatta sits cross-legged on his seat facing the

[18] In the case of some Bodhisattas (*e.g.*, **Vipassī**) these four signs (*nimittāni* as they are called) are seen by them at different times, but in the case of others on one and the same day (DA. ii. 457).

[19] For the reason for this great length in the last case, see *s.v.* Gotama.

[20] The Bodhi-tree (*q.v.*) is different for each Bodhisatta.

[21] BuA. 247.

[22] For the explanations of these dreams see A. iii. 240 f.; these dreams are referred to at J. i. 69.

east, determined not to rise till he has attained his goal. The gods of all the worlds assemble to do him honour, but **Māra** (*q.v.*) comes with his mighty hosts and the gods flee. All day, the fight continues between Māra and the Bodhisatta; the *pāramī* alone are present to lend their aid to the Bodhisatta, and when the moment comes, the Goddess of the Earth bears witness to his great sacrifices, while Māra and his armies retire discomfited at the hour of sunset, the gods then returning and singing a pæan of victory. Meanwhile the Bodhisatta spends the night in deep concentration; during the first watch he requires knowledge of past lives, during the second watch he develops the divine eye, while during the last watch he ponders over and comprehends the Paṭicca-samuppāda doctrine. Backwards and forwards his mind travels over the chain of causation and twelve times the earth trembles. With sunrise, omniscience dawns on him, and he becomes the Supremely Awakened Buddha, uttering his udānā of victory, while the whole world rejoices with him.[23]

The above is a brief account, as given in the books, of certain features common to all Bodhisattas. In addition to these, particulars of the personal career of the Bodhisatta who became Gotama, are found, chiefly in the Buddhavaṃsa and the Jātakaṭṭhakathā. It has already been stated that each Bodhisatta receives the *vyākaraṇa* from every Buddha whom he meets, and Gotama was no exception. He received his first *vyākaraṇa* as the ascetic Sumedha, from Dīpaṅkara; and then, as a cakkavatti, from Koṇḍañña; as the brahmin **Suruci**, from Maṅgala; as the Nāga-king **Atula,** from Sumana; as the brahmin **Atideva,** from Revata; as the brahmin **Ajita,** from Sobhita; as a yakkha chief, from Anomadassī; as a lion, from Paduma; as an ascetic (*isi*) from Nārada; as a governor (*Mahāraṭṭhiya*) Jaṭila, from Padumuttara; as the youth **Uttara,** from Sumedha; as a Cakkavatti, from Sujāta; as the youth **Kassapa,** from Piyadassī; as the ascetic **Susīma,** from Atthadassī; as **Sakka,** from Dhammadassī; as the ascetic **Maṅgala,** from Siddhattha; as **Sujāta,** from Tissa; as King **Vijitāvī,** from Phussa; as the Nāga-king **Atula,** from Vipassī; as King **Arindama,** from Sikhī; as King **Sudassana,** from Vessabhū; as King **Khema,** from Kakusandha; as King **Pabbata,** from Koṇāgamana; and as the youth **Jotipāla,** from Kassapa.

The Jātakaṭṭhakathā gives particulars of other births of the Bodhisatta[24]—*e.g.*, as Akitti, Ajjuna, Aṭṭhisena, Anitthigandha, Ayoghara,

[23] For the Paṭicca-Samuppada see D. ii. 31 ff.; for the other details see J. i. 56 ff., where the story of Gotama is given. DA. ii. 462 ff. gives similar details regarding Vipassī; BuA. 248 says it is the same for all Bodhisattas.

[24] To the births given below and taken from the Jātakaṭṭhakathā should be added those given in the Pubbapilotikhaṇḍa of the Apadāna (i. 299 ff.; also UdA.) and given *s.v.* Gotama.

Araka, Arindama, Alīnacitta, Alīnasattu, Asadisa, Ādāsamukha, Udaya, Udayabhadda, Kaṭṭhavāhana, Kaṇhadīpāyana, Kaṇhapaṇḍita, Kapila, Kappa, Kassapa, Kāraṇḍiya, Kāliṅgabhāradvāja, Kuṇāla, Kuṇḍakumāra, Kuddālaka, Kusa, Komāyaputta, Khadiravaniya, Guttila, Ghata, Canda, Candakumāra, Campeyya, Cittapaṇḍita, Cullaka-seṭṭhi, Culladhanuggaha, Chaddanta, Chaḷaṅgakumāra, Janasandha. Juṇha, Jotipāla (= Sarabhaṅga), Takkapaṇḍita, Takkāriya, Tirīṭavaccha, Temiya (= Mūgapakkha), Dīghāvu, Duyyodhana, Dhanañjaya, Dhamma, Dhammaddhaja, Dhammapāla (prince and brahmin), Nārada, Nigrodha, Nimi, Pañcālacaṇḍa, Pañcāvudha, Paṇḍita, Padumakumāra, Baka, Bodhikumāra, Brahmadatta (in several births), Bhaddasāla, Bharata, Bhallāṭiya, Bhūridatta, Bhojanasuddhika, Makhādeva, Magha, Mandhātā, Mahākañcana, Mahājanaka, Mahādhana, Mahābodhi (= Bodhi), Mahāsīlava, Mahāsudassana, Mahiṃsāsa, Mahosadha, Mātaṅga, Mūgapakkha (= Temiya,) Yuvañjaya, Rakkhita, Rāma, Lomasakassapa, Vacchanakha, Vidhura, Visayha, Vessantara, Saṅkicca, Saṅkha, Santusita, Sambhava, Sarabhaṅga, Sādhīna, Siri, Suciparivāra, Sujāta, Sutana, Sutasoma, Suppāraka, Suvaṇṇasāma, Susīma, Senaka, Seruva, Sona, Soma, Somadatta, Somanassa, Hatthipāla and Hārita.

In these and other births the Bodhisatta occupied various stations in life, such as that of an acrobat (Dubbaca Jātaka); ājīvaka (Lomahaṃsa Jātaka); ascetic (numerous births); barber (Illīsa Jātaka); caravan leader (Kimpakka and Mahāvāṇija Jātakas); carpenter (Samuddavāṇija Jātaka); chaplain (various births); conch-blower (Saṅkhadhamana Jātaka); councillor (Kacchapa, Kalāyamuṭṭhi, Kukku, Giridanta, Dhūmakāri, Pabbatūpatthara, Pādañjali, Puṭabhatta, Vālodaka Jātakas); courtier (Bāhayi, Sālittaka, etc., Jātakas); dice-player (Litta Jātaka); drummer (Bherivāda Jātaka); elephant-trainer (Saṅgāmāvacara Jātaka); farmer (Kañcanakkhandha, Kummāsapiṇḍa, Sīhacamma, Suvaṇṇakakkaṭa Jātakas); forester (Khurappa Jātaka); gardener (Kuddālaka Jātaka); goldsmith (Kuṇāla Jātaka); hawker (Seriva Jātaka); horse-dealer (Kuṇḍakakucchisindhava Jātaka); householder (Gahapati and Jāgara Jātaka, also as Kuṇḍaka, Sutana and Hārita); judge (Kūṭavāṇija, Rathalatthi Jātakas); king (numerous births, *e.g.* Arindama, Ādasamukha, etc.); mariner (Suppāraka Jātaka); merchant (several births, *e.g.* as Paṇḍita, etc.); minister (numerous births, *e.g.* as Senaka, Vidhura); musician (Guttila); physician (Kāma, and Visavanta Jātakas); potter, (Kacchapa, Kumbhakāra Jātakas); robber[25] (Kaṇavera, Sata-

[25] The scholiast (J. ii. 389) explains that when a Bodhisatta is born as a wicked man it is due to a fault in his horoscope!

patta Jātakas); smith (Sūci Jātaka); squire (*e.g.*, Nanda Jātaka); stone-cutter (Babbu Jātaka); teacher (numerous births, *e.g.* Anabhirati, Durājāna, Losaka Jātakas); treasurer (*e.g.* as Cullaka, Visayha, Saṅkha and Suciparivāra); tumbler (Ucchiṭṭhabhatta Jātaka); and valuer (Taṇḍulanāli Jātaka). The Bodhisatta was born as a caṇḍāla in several births (*e.g.*, as Citta and Mātaṅga); in several instances as Sakka, (*e.g.* in the Kāmanīta, Kelisīla, Mahāpanāda and Vaka Jātakas). He was born several times in the deva-world (*e.g.* as Dhamma and Bhaddasāla, also in the Kakkāru, Kāmavilāpa and Mittavinda Jātakas.) He was a Brahmā of the Ābhassara-world (Candābha and Janasodhana Jātakas); and a Mahābrahmā (Parosahassa and Mahānārada-Kassapa), in the latter his name was Nārada. He was an air-sprite (Puppharatta Jātaka) and a mountain-sprite (*e.g.* Kāka and Samudda Jātakas); a tree-sprite in numerous births (*e.g.* Āyācitabhatta, Baka, Matakabhatta, Rukkhadhamma Jātakas); and a forest-sprite (Kaṇḍina and Gūthapāṇa Jātakas). Many Jātakas mention the birth of the Bodhisatta among animals—*e.g.*, as buffalo (Mahisa Jātaka); bull (as Ayyakāḷaka, Nandivisāla, Mahālohita, Sārambha); cock (in the two Kukkuṭa Jātakas, Nos. 383, 448); crow (as Vīraka and Supatta and in Kāka Jātaka); dog (Kukkura Jātaka); elephant (*e.g.*, Chaddanta and Sīlava Jātakas); fish (Mitacintī); frog (Haritamāta Jātaka); garuḍa (*e.g.*, Sussoṇḍi Jātaka); goose (*e.g.* Ulūka, Cakkavāka, Neru, Palāsa Jātakas); hare (Sasa Jātaka); horse (Ājañña, Bhogājānīya Jātakas and as Vātaggasindhava); iguana (Godha Jātaka); jackal (Sigāla Jātakas); kinnara (as Canda); lion (*e.g.*, Guṇa, Sigāla Jātaka (No. 152), Sūkara Jātakas); mallard (Nacca Jātaka); monkey (Kapi, Nalapāna, Mahākapi, Suṃsumāra Jātakas and as Nandyia); parrot (*e.g.* as Jambuka, Pupphaka, Poṭṭhapāda, and Rādha); peacock (Nos. 42, 375, Mora, Bāveru, and Mahāmora Jātakas); pig (Mahātuṇḍila Jātakas); pigeon (Kapota, Kāka No. 395, Romaka, Lola Jātakas); quail (the three Vaṭṭaka and Sammodamāna Jātakas); rat (Aggika and Biḷāra Jātakas); snake—*nāga*—(as Cāmpeyya, Bhuridatta, Mahādaddara, Saṅkhapāla); vulture (as Aparaṇṇa and in the three Gijjha Jātakas, Nos. 164, 399, 427), and woodpecker (as Khadiravaniya and in Javasakuna Jātaka).

The Bodhisatta was born several times in the purgatories.[26] The wishes of Bodhisattas are generally fulfilled,[27] chiefly because of their great wisdom[28] and zeal.[29] The wisdom of a Bodhisatta is greater than that of a Pacceka Buddha[30]. See also *s.v.* **Buddha.**

26 Ap. i. 299 ff.

27 J. iii. 283; v. 282, 291; vi. 401, 405, etc.

28 J. iii. 282.

29 *Ibid.*, 425.

30 J. iv. 341.

Bodhisammajjaka Thera.—An arahant. In the past he picked up leaves from the courtyard of a Bodhi-tree and cleaned it.[1] He is probably identical with **Tissa Thera.**[2]

[1] Ap. ii. 457. [2] ThagA. i. 105 f.

Bodhisiñcaka Thera.—An arahant. Ninety-one kappas ago, when a great festival was being held in honour of the Bodhi-tree of **Vipassī** Buddha, he sprinkled perfumed water on the tree. Thirty-three kappas ago he became king eight times under the name of **Udakāsecana.**[1] *v.l.* **Bodhisaññaka.**

[1] Ap. i. 131.

Bodhisenapabbatagāma.—A village in the **Dakkhiṇadesa** of Ceylon where **Vikkamabāhu II.** defeated **Mānābharaṇa** and his two brothers.[1]

[1] Cv. lxi. 33.

1. **Bodhī.**—Daughter of **Kassapa I.**[1]

[1] Cv. xxxix. 11.

2. **Bodhī Therī.**—A friend of **Isidāsī,** who related the story of her own past lives at the request of **Bodhī.**[1]

[1] ThigA. p. 261.

Bodhī-Uppalavaṇṇā-Kassapagiri.—The name given to the enlarged monastery at **Issarasamaṇārāma** built by **Kassapa I.**[1]

[1] Cv. xxxix. 11; see also Cv. *Trs.* i. 43, n. 7.

Bolagāma.—A village mentioned in the account of the campaigns of **Parakkamabāhu I.**[1]

[1] Cv. lxxv. 6.

Brahāchatta Jātaka (No. 336).—Once Brahmadatta, king of Benares, captured Kosala with its king, and brought all its treasures to Benares, where he buried them in iron pots in the royal park. **Chatta,** the Kosala king's son, escaped, and became an ascetic near **Takkasilā** with a following of five hundred. Later he came with his followers to Benares, won the heart of the king by his demeanour, and lived in the royal park. There, by means of a spell, he discovered the buried treasure, and taking his followers into his confidence, took the treasure to **Sāvatthi** and made the city impregnable. When Brahmadatta discovered his loss and its results, he was disconsolate, but was comforted by his minister, who was the Bodhisatta, and who pointed out to him that Chatta had but taken what belonged to him.

The story was told in reference to a knavish monk, identified with **Chatta.**[1]

[1] J. iii. 115 ff.

Brahmakāyikā-devā.—See **Brahmaloka.**

1. **Brahmacariya Sutta.**—*Brahmacariyā* is practised for nought else but self-restraint and cessation of Ill.[1]

[1] A. ii. 26.

2. **Brahmacariya Sutta.**—The best practice is the Noble Eightfold Path. Its fruits are sotāpatti, etc.[1]

[1] S. v. 26.

3. **Brahmacariya Sutta.**—The best practice is the Noble Eightfold Path Its aim is the destruction of lust, hatred, and illusion.[1]

[1] S. v. 26 f.

Brahmajāla Sutta.—The first sutta of the **Dīgha Nikāya.** It was preached to the paribbājaka **Suppiya** and his disciple **Brahmadatta.** It first explains the *sīlā*, or moral precepts, in three successive sections—*cūla* (concise), *majjhima* (medium), and *mahā* (elaborate)—and then proceeds to set out in sixty-two divisions various speculations and theories regarding the " soul."[1] Other names for it are **Atthajāla, Dhammajāla, Diṭṭhijāla,** and **Saṅgāmavijaya.** At the end of the discourse the ten world-systems trembled.[2] It is said that once when **Piṇḍapātiya Thera** recited this sutta at the **Kalyāṇiya-vihāra,** his mind concentrated on the Buddha, the earth trembled; the same phenomenon occurred when the **Dīghabhāṇaka Theras** recited it at the **Ambalaṭṭhikā,** to the east of the **Lohapāsāda.**[3]

The Brahmajāla was the first sutta preached in **Suvaṇṇabhūmi,** when **Soṇa** and **Uttara** visited it as missionaries.[4]

The sutta is often quoted, sometimes even in the Canon.[5]

[1] D. i. 46.
[2] *Ibid.*
[3] DA. i. 131.
[4] Mhv. xii. 51.
[5] *E.g.*, S. iv. 286, 287.

1. **Brahmañña Sutta.**—The highest life is the Noble Eightfold Path, and the fruits thereof are sotāpatti, etc.[1]

[1] S. v. 26

2. **Brahmañña Sutta.**—The highest life is the Noble Eightfold Path, and its aim is the destruction of lust, hatred, and illusion.[1]

[1] S. v. 26; *cf.* **Brahmacariya Sutta** (3).

3. **Brahmañña Sutta.**—Few are they who reverence brahmins, many they who do not.[1]

[1] S. v. 468.

1. **Brahmadatta.**—King of **Kāsi.** He captured **Kosala** and murdered its king **Dīghiti** and Dīghiti's wife, but made peace later with Dīghiti's son, **Dīghāvu,** restored to him his father's kingdom, and gave him his own daughter in marriage.[1]

[1] Vin. i. 342 ff.; DhA. i. 56 f.

2. **Brahmadatta.**—King of the **Assakas** and friend of **Reṇu.** When **Mahāgovinda** divided Jambudīpa into seven equal portions for Reṇu and his six friends, Brahmadatta was given the kingdom, of the Assakas, with **Potana** as his capital.[1]

[1] D. ii. 235 f.

3. **Brahmadatta.**—In the Jātaka Commentary this is given as the name of numerous kings of Benares. In most cases we are told nothing further of them than that they reigned at Benares at the time of the incidents related in the story. Brahmadatta was probably the dynastic name of the kings of Benares. Thus, for instance, in the **Gaṅgamāla Jātaka**[1] **Udaya,** king of Benares, is addressed as Brahmadatta. In the **Gaṇḍatindu Jātaka,**[2] however, **Pañcāla,** king of **Uttarapañcāla,** is also called Brahmadatta; in this case it was evidently his personal name. It was also the name of the husband of **Piṅgiyānī** (*q.v.*). He was a king, but we are not told of what country. He is identified[3] with **Kuṇāla.**

[1] J. iii. 452. [2] J. v. 102, 103, 104, 105, 106. [3] *Ibid.*, 444.

4. **Brahmadatta Thera.**—He was the son of the king of **Kosala,** and, having witnessed the Buddha's majesty at the consecration of Jetavana, he entered the Order and in due course became an arahant. One day, while going for alms, he was abused by a brahmin, but kept silence. Again and again the brahmin abused him, and the people marvelled at the patience of Brahmadatta, who then preached to them on the wisdom of not returning abuse for abuse. The brahmin was much moved and entered the Order under Brahmadatta.[1]

[1] Thag. vs. 441-6; ThagA. i. 460 ff.

5. **Brahmadatta.**—Head of a dynasty of thirty-six kings, all of whom ruled at **Hatthipura.** His ancestors ruled at **Kapilanagara.**[1]

[1] MṬ. 127; Dpv. iii. 18.

6. **Brahmadatta.**—A Pacceka Buddha. In the time of **Kassapa Buddha** he had been a monk and had lived in the forest for twenty thousand years. He was then born as the son of the king of Benares. When his father died he became king, ruling over twenty thousand cities with Benares as the capital, but, wishing for quiet, he retired into solitude in the palace. His wife tired of him and committed adultery with a minister who was banished on the discovery of his offence. He then took service under another king and persuaded him to attack Brahmadatta. Brahmadatta's minister, much against his will, and having promised not to take life, made a sudden attack on the enemy and drove them away. Brahmadatta, seated on the field of battle, developed thoughts of *mettā* and became a Pacceka Buddha.[1]

[1] SNA. i. 58 ff.

7. **Brahmadatta.**—A brahmin, father of **Kassapa Buddha.**[1]

[1] J. i. 43; Bu. xxv. 34.

8. **Brahmadatta.**—Pupil of the Paribbājaka **Suppiya.** A conversation between these two led to the preaching of the **Brahmajāla Sutta.**[1]

[1] D. i. 1.

9. **Brahmadatta.**—A monk, sometimes credited with having supplied the illustrations to the aphorisms in **Kaccāyana's** grammar.[1]

[1] P.L.C. 180.

10. **Brahmadatta.**—See also **Ekaputtika°**, **Catumāsika°**, **Cūḷani°**, and **Sāgara°**; and below, *s.v.* **Brahmadatta-kumāra.**

Brahmadatta Jātaka (No. 323).—Once, the Bodhisatta, after studying at **Takkasilā,** became an ascetic in the **Himālaya,** visited **Uttarapañcāla,** and resided in the garden of the **Pañcāla** king. The king saw him begging for alms, invited him into the palace and, having shown him great honour, asked him to stay in the park. When the time came for the Bodhisatta to return to the Himālaya, he wished for a pair of single-soled shoes and a leaf parasol. But for twelve years he could not summon up enough courage to ask the king for these things! He could only get as far as telling the king he had a favour to ask, and then his heart failed him, for, he said to himself, it made a man weep to have to ask and it made a man weep to have to refuse. In the end the king noticed his discomfiture and offered him all his possessions; but the ascetic would take only the shoes and the parasol, and, with these, he left for the Himālaya. The king is identified with **Ānanda.**[1]

[1] J. iii. 78 ff.

1. **Brahmadatta-kumāra.**—Son of **Brahmadatta,** king of Benares. He was the Bodhisatta. For his story see **Dummedha Jātaka.**[1]

[1] J. i. 259 ff.

2. **Brahmadatta-kumāra.**—See **Rājovāda Jātaka.**[1]

[1] J. ii. 2 ff.

3. **Brahmadatta-kumāra.**—Brother of **Asadisa;** see the **Asadisa Jātaka.**[1]

[1] J. ii. 87 ff.

4. **Brahmadatta-kumāra.**—See the **Asitābhū Jātaka.**[1]

[1] J. ii. 229 ff.

5. **Brahmadatta-kumāra.**—See the **Tilamuṭṭhi Jātaka.**[1]

[1] J. ii. 277 ff.

6. **Brahmadatta-kumāra.**—See the **Dhonasākha Jātaka.**[1]

[1] J. iii. 158 ff.

7. **Brahmadatta-kumāra.**—See the **Susīma Jātaka.**[1]

[1] J. iii. 391 ff.

8. **Brahmadatta-kumāra.**—See the **Kummāsapiṇḍa Jātaka.**[1]

[1] J. iii. 407 ff.

9. **Brahmadatta-kumāra.**—See the **Aṭṭhāna Jātaka.**[1]

[1] J. iii. 475 ff.

10. **Brahmadatta-kumāra.**—See the **Lomasakassapa Jātaka.**[1]

[1] J. iii. 514 ff.

11. **Brahmadatta-kumāra.**—See the **Suruci Jātaka.**[1]

[1] J. iv. 315 ff.

12. **Brahmadatta-kumāra.**—See the **Saṅkicca Jātaka.**[1]

[1] J. v. 263 ff.

13. **Brahmadatta-kumāra.**—See the **Mahāsutasoma Jātaka.**[1]

[1] J. v. 457 ff.

14. **Brahmadatta-kumāra.**—See the **Bhūridatta Jātaka.**[1]

[1] J. vi. 159 ff.

1. **Brahmadeva.**—One of the two chief disciples of **Revata Buddha.**[1]

[1] Bu. vi. 21; J. i. 35.

2. **Brahmadeva.**—A khattiya of **Haṃsavatī** to whom **Tissa** Buddha preached his first sermon.[1] He later became the Buddha's chief disciple.[2]

[1] BuA. 189. [2] Bu. xviii. 21.

3. **Brahmadeva Thera.**—The son of a brahmin woman. Having joined the Order, he dwelt in solitude and became an arahant. One day he went to **Sāvatthi** for alms, and, in due course, arrived at his mother's house. She was in the habit of making an oblation to **Brahmā,** but, on that day, **Sahampatī** appeared before her and told her to bestow her gifts on her son.[1]

[1] S. i. 140 f.

4. **Brahmadeva.**—Aggasāvaka of **Metteyya Buddha.**[1]

[1] Anāgatavaṃsa, vs. 97.

Brahmadeva Sutta.—Records the story of **Brahmadeva Thera** (*q.v.* 3) and his mother.[1]

[1] S. i. 140 ff.

Brahmanimantanika Sutta.—Preached at **Jetavana.** The Buddha tells the monks of his visit to **Baka Brahmā,** who holds the view that this world is eternal. The Buddha tells Baka that his view is false, whereupon **Māra,** having taken possession of one of the Brahmās, protests and urges the Buddha not to be recalcitrant. Baka himself agrees with the Buddha, who tells him of planes of existence of which Baka knows nothing. Baka then says that he will vanish from the Buddha's presence, but finds himself unable to do so. The Buddha then vanishes and repeats a stanza for the Brahmās to hear. Baka admits defeat, but Māra again enters into a Brahmā and asks the Buddha not to communicate his doctrine to others. The Buddha refuses to agree to this. The sutta is so called because it was preached on account of Baka Brahmā's challenge.[1] *Cp.* **Bakabrahma Sutta.**

[1] M. i. 326 ff.

Brahmapārisajja, Brahmapurohita.—See **Brahmaloka.**

Brahmaloka.—The highest of the celestial worlds, the abode of the Brahmas. It consists of twenty heavens: the nine ordinary Brahma-worlds, the five **Suddhāvāsā,** the four Arūpa-worlds, the **Asaññasatta** and the **Vehapphala.**[1] All except the four Arūpa-worlds are classed among the Rūpa-worlds (the inhabitants of which are corporeal). The inhabitants of the Brahma-worlds are free from sensual desires.[2] The Brahma-world is the only world devoid of women[3]; women who develop the jhānas in this world can be born among the **Brahmapārisajjā** (see below), but not among the Mahābrahmas.[4] Rebirth in the Brahma-world is the result of great virtue accompanied by meditation.[5] The Brahmas, like the other celestials, are not necessarily sotāpannā or on the way to complete knowledge (*sambodhiparāyaṇā*); their attainments depend on the degree of their faith in the Buddha, the Dhamma and the Saṅgha.[6] The Jātakas contain numerous accounts of ascetics who practised meditation, being born after death in the Brahma-world.[7] Some of the Brahmas —*e.g.*, **Baka** (*q.v.*)—held false views regarding their world, which, like all other worlds, is subject to change and destruction.[8] When the rest of the world is destroyed at the end of a kappa, the Brahma-world is saved,[9] and the first beings to be born on earth come from the **Ābhassara Brahma-**world.[10] Buddhas and their more eminent disciples often visit the Brahma-worlds and preach to the inhabitants.[11] If a rock as big as the gable of a house were to be dropped from the lowest Brahma-world it would take four months to reach the earth travelling one hundred thousand leagues a day. Brahmas subsist on trance, abounding in joy (*sappītikajjhāna*), this being their sole food.[12] Anāgāmins, who die before attaining arahantship, are reborn in the **Suddhāvāsā** Brahma-worlds and there pass away entirely.[13] The beings born in the lowest Brahma-world are called **Brahmapārisajjā;** their life-term is one-third

[1] *E.g.*, VibhA. 521; for details see *s.v.*

[2] But see the **Mātaṅga Jātaka** (J. iv. 378), where **Diṭṭhamaṅgalikā** is spoken of as **Mahābrahmabhariyā,** showing that some, at least, considered that Mahābrahmas had wives.

[3] DhA. i. 270.

[4] VibhA. 437 f.

[5] Vsm. 415.

[6] See, *e.g.*, A. iv. 76 f.; it is not necessary to be a follower of the Buddha for one to be born in the Brahma-world; the names of six teachers are given whose followers were born in that world as a result of listening to their teaching (A. iii. 371 ff.; iv. 135 ff.).

[7] *E.g.*, J. ii. 43, 69, 90; v. 98, etc.

[8] M. i. 327.

[9] Vsm. 415; KhpA. 121.

[10] Vsm. 417.

[11] *E.g.*, M. i. 326 f.; ThagA. ii. 184 ff.; **Sikhī Buddha** and **Abhibhū** are also said to have visited the Brahma-world (A. i. 227 f.). The Buddha could visit it both in his mind-made body and his physical body (S. v. 282 f.).

[12] SA. i. 161; food and drinks are offered to Mahābrahmā, and he is invited to partake of these, but not of sacrifices (SA. i. 158 f.).

[13] See, *e.g.*, S. i. 35, 60, and Compendium v. 10.

of an asaṅkheyya-kappa; next to them come the **Brahma-purohitā,** who live for half an asaṅkheyya-kappa; and beyond these are the Mahā Brahmas who live for a whole asaṅkheyya-kappa.[14]

The term **Brahmakāyikā-devā** seems to be used as a class-name for all the inhabitants of the Brahma-worlds.[15] The Mahā-Niddesa Commentary[16] says that the word includes all the five (?) kinds of Brahmā (*sabbe pi pañca vokāraBrahmāno gahitā*). The BuA.[17] thus defines the word Brahmā: *brūhito tehi tehi guṇavisesahī ti=Brahmā. Ayaṃ pana Brahmasaddo Mahā - Brahma - brāhmaṇa-Thathāgata-mātāpitu-seṭṭhādisu dissati.* The Samantapāsādikā[18] speaks of a Mahā Brahmā who was a *khiṇāsava,* living for sixteen thousand kappas. When the Buddha, immediately after his birth, looked around and took his steps northward, it was this Brahmā who seized the babe by his finger and assured him that none was greater than he.

The names of several Brahmās occur in the books—*e.g.,* **Tudu, Nārada, Ghaṭikāra, Baka, Sanaṅkumāra** and **Sahampatī.**[19] These are described as Mahā Brahmās. Mention is also made of Pacceka Brahmās—*e.g.,* **Subrahmā** and **Suddhavāsa.**[20] Tudu is also sometimes described as a Pacceka Brahmā.[21] Of the Pacceka Brahmās, Subrahmā and Suddhavāsa are represented as visiting another Brahmā, who was infatuated with his own power and glory, and as challenging him to the performance of miracles, excelling him therein and converting him to the faith of the Buddha.[22] Tudu is spoken of as exhorting **Kokālika** to put his trust in **Sāriputta** and **Moggallāna.**[23]

No explanation is given of the term Pacceka-Brahmā. Does it mean Brahmās who dwelt apart, by themselves ? *Cp.* **Pacceka-Buddha.**

The Brahmās are represented as visiting the earth and taking an interest in the affairs of men. Thus, Nārada descends from the Brahma-world to dispel the heresies of King Aṅgati.[24] When the Buddha hesitates to preach his doctrine, because of its profoundity, it is **Sahampatī** (*q.v.*) who visits him and begs him to preach it for the welfare of the

[14] Compendium, v. 6; but see VibhA. 519 f., where Mahā-Brahmās are defined.

[15] A. i. 210; v. 76 f.

[16] p. 109.

[17] BuA., p. 10.

[18] i. 131.

[19] For details, see *s.v.*; to these should be added the names of seven Anāgāmīs resident in **Avihā** and other Brahma-worlds —**Upaka, Phalagaṇḍu, Pukkusāti, Bhaddiya, Khaṇḍadeva, Bāhuraggi** and **Piṅgiya** (S. i. 35, 60; SA. i. 72 etc.). **Baka** speaks of seventy-two Brahmās, living, apparently, in his world, as his companions (S. i. 142). See also **Tissa Brahmā.**

[20] S. i. 146 f.

[21] *E.g., ibid.,* 149.

[22] See *s.v.*

[23] *Loc. cit.*

[24] J. vi. 242 f.

world.[25] Sahampatī is mentioned as visiting the Buddha several times subsequently, illuminating Jetavana with the effulgence of his body. It is said that with a single finger he could illuminate a whole **Cakkavāḷa.**[26] **Sanaṅkumāra** (*q.v.*) was also a follower of the Buddha. The Brahmās appear to have been in the habit of visiting the deva-worlds too, for Sanaṅkumāra is reported as being present at an assembly of the **Tāvatiṃsa** gods and as speaking there the Buddha's praises and giving an exposition of his teaching. But, in order to do this, he assumed the form of **Pañcasikha.**[27]

The books refer[28] to the view held, at the Buddha's time, of Brahmā as the creator of the universe and of union with Brahmā as the highest good, only to be attained by prayers and sacrifices. But the Buddha himself did not hold this view and does not speak of any single Brahmā as the highest being in all creation.[29] There are Mahā Brahmās, mighty and powerful (*abhibhū anabhibhūto aññadatthudaso vasavattī*), but they too, all of them, and their world are subject to the laws of *Kamma.*[30] To the Buddha, union with Brahmā seems to have meant being associated with him in his world, and this can only be attained by cultivation of those qualities possessed by the Brahmā. But the highest good lay beyond, in the attainment of Nibbāna.[31]

The word Brahma is often used in compounds meaning highest and best —*e.g.*, Brahmacariyā, Brahmassara; for details see *s.v.* Brahma in the New Pāli Dictionary.

[25] The explanation given (*e.g.*, at SA. i. 155) is that the Buddha waited for the invitation of Sahampati that it might lend weight to his teaching. The people were followers of Brahmā, and Sahampati's acceptance of the Buddha's leadership would impress them deeply.

[26] SA. i. 158.

[27] D. ii. 211 ff.

[28] *E.g.*, at D. i. 18, where Brahmā is described as *vasavattī issaro kattā nimmātā*, etc.

[29] See, however, A. v. 59 f., where Mahā Brahmā is spoken of as the highest denizen of the Sahassalokadhātu (*yāvatā sahassalokadhātu, MahāBrahmā tattha aggaṃ akkhāyati*); but he, too, is impermanent (*MahāBrahmuno pi . . . atthi eva aññathattaṃ, atthi viparināmo*).

[30] *E.g.*, at S. v. 410 (*Brahmaloko pi āvuso anicco adhuvo sakkāyapariyāpanno sādhāyasmā Brahmalokā cittaṃ vuṭṭhāpetvā sakkāyanirodhacittaṃ upasaṃharāhi*). See also A. iv. 76 f., 104 f., where **Sunetta,** in spite of all his great powers as Mahā Brahmā, etc., had to confess himself still subject to suffering.

[31] Thus in the **Tevijjā Sutta**; see also M. ii. 194 f.

Brahmavatī.—A brahminee, the mother of **Metteyya Buddha.**[1]

[1] Vsm. 434; DhSA. 415; Dvy. 60; Anāgatavaṃsa, vs. 96.

1. **Brahmavaddhana.**—An old name for **Bārāṇasī.**[1] A king named **Manoja** reigned there. For details see the **Sona-Nanda Jātaka.**[2]

[1] J. iv. 119.

[2] J. v. 312 ff.

2. **Brahmavaddhana.**—Son of **Metteyya Buddha** before his Renunciation.[1]

[1] Anāgatavaṃsa, vs. 48.

Brahmā.—See **Brahmaloka.**

Brahmā Saṃyutta.—The sixth section of the Saṃyutta Nikāya.[1]

[1] S. i. 136-59.

1. **Brahmā Sutta.**—The Buddha is under the **Ajapālanigrodha,** soon after the Enlightenment, pondering on the four *satipaṭṭhānas* as the only way to Nibbanā. **Sahampati** visits him and agrees with his sentiments.[1]

[1] S. v. 167.

2. **Brahmā Sutta.**—The scene is the same as in the above. The Buddha is reflecting on the five *indriyas* (*saddhā*, *sati*, etc.), as the way to Nibbāna, and **Sahampati** visits him and agrees with him, relating how, when he was a monk named **Sahaka,** in the time of **Kassapa Buddha,** he developed the five *indriyas* and was born in the Brahma-world.[1]

[1] S. v. 232 f.

Brahmāyu.—A brahmin, foremost in **Mithilā** in his knowledge of the Vedas. On hearing of the Buddha at the age of one hundred and twenty, he sent his pupil **Uttara** to discover if the Buddha had on his body the marks of a **Mahāpurisa.** Uttara therefore visited the Buddha and, having seen the thirty-two marks, resolved to observe the Buddha in his every posture and, to this end, followed him about for seven months. He then returned to Brahmāyu and told him of the result of his investigations. Brahmāyu folded his palms reverently and uttered the praises of the Buddha. Soon after, the Buddha came to Mithilā and took up his residence in the **Makhādeva-ambavana.** Brahmāyu, having sent a messenger to announce his arrival, visited the Buddha. It is said that all those present rose to greet him, but Brahmāyu signed to them to be seated. He satisfied any remaining doubts he had as to the marks on the Buddha's body and then proceeded to ask him questions on various topics. At the end of the discussion he fell at the Buddha's feet, stroking them and proclaiming his name. The Buddha asked him to compose himself, and preached to him on "progressive" discourse. Brahmāyu invited the Buddha and his monks to his house, where he entertained them for a week. His death occurred not long after, and the

Buddha, when told of it, said that Brahmāyu had become an Anāgāmī.[1] Brahmāyu's salutation of the Buddha is described as *paṇipāta*.[2]

[1] M. ii. 133 ff. [2] ItvA. 177.

Brahmāyu Sutta.—Records the story of the conversion of **Brahmāyu** (*q.v.*). The Sutta contains a description of the thirty-two marks of the Mahāpurisa[1] and also particulars of the Buddha's conduct in various circumstances—such as walking, eating, meditating, preaching, etc. That is an example of a sutta in which the word "*dhammacakkhu*" means the three Paths leading to *anāgāmiphala*.[2]

[1] *Cp.* Lakkhaṇa Sutta. [2] MA. ii. 617.

Brahmāli Thera.—He belonged to a brahmin family of **Kosala,** and, through association with spiritually-minded friends and his own realization of the ills of *saṃsāra,* he entered the Order. Dwelling in the forest he soon developed insight and acquired arahantship. In the time of **Vipassī Buddha** he was a householder, and, seeing the Buddha going on his alms-rounds, he gave him a *vāra*-fruit.[1]

[1] Thag. vs. 205-6; ThagA. i. 327 f.

1. **Brāhmaṇa Vagga.**—The tenth section of the Majjhima Nikāya, suttas 91-100.

2. **Brāhmaṇa Vagga.**—The sixth chapter of the Tika Nipāta of the Aṅguttara Nikāya.[1]

[1] A. i. 155-73.

3. **Brāhmaṇa Vagga.**—The twentieth chapter of the Pañcaka Nipāta of the Aṅguttara Nikāya.[1]

[1] A. iii. 221-46.

4. **Brāhmaṇa Vagga.**—See also **Yodhājīva Vagga** (2).

5. **Brāhmaṇa Vagga.**—The twenty-sixth section of the Dhammapada.

Brāhmaṇa Samyutta.—The seventh section of the Saṃyutta Nikāya.[1]

[1] S. i. 160-84.

1. **Brāhmaṇa Sutta.**—**Ānanda** sees, on his begging round, **Jānussoni's** white chariot, drawn by four white mares, the people crowding round it and declaring it the best and most beautiful of chariots. He goes to

the Buddha and asks him if such a description could be used of the Buddha. The Buddha says that the Noble Eightfold Way can be so described.[1]

[1] S. v. 4 f.

2. **Brāhmaṇa Sutta.**—A brahmin visits the Buddha at **Jetavana** and asks why it is that the Buddha's Doctrine will disappear soon after his death. The Buddha says it is because of the failure of men to realize the four *satipaṭṭhānas.*[1]

[1] S. v. 174.

3. **Brāhmaṇa Sutta.**—The brahmin **Uṇṇābha** visits **Ānanda** at the **Ghositārāma** and questions him. Ānanda tells him that the life of a recluse has for its object the abandonment of desire and that this is brought about by the cultivation of the four *iddhipādas.* That would be a task without end, says Uṇṇābha; but Ānanda proves to him that once the purpose is accomplished, there remains nothing more to do. Uṇṇābha accepts Ānanda as his teacher.[1]

[1] S. v. 271 f.

4. **Brāhmaṇa Sutta.**—The Buddha explains to the monks how the teachings of the brahmins differ from his on the practice leading to prosperity.[1]

[1] S. v. 361.

5. **Brāhmaṇa Sutta.**—The Buddha explains, in answer to the question of a brahmin, how the Dhamma can be described as *sandiṭṭhika.*[1]

[1] A. i. 156.

6. **Brāhmaṇa Sutta.**—Two brahmins, skilled in *lokāyata,* visit the Buddha and say that, according to **Pūraṇa Kassapa,** the world is finite, while, according to **Nigaṇṭha Nātaputta,** it is infinite, and that both teachers claim omniscience. How can one know which teaching is true ? The Buddha dismisses their question and teaches them that it is not by trying to walk to the end of the world that the end of the world can be reached, but by understanding the five strands of sense-desire (*kāmaguṇa*). This can be accomplished by the cultivation of the *jhānas.*[1]

[1] A. iv. 428 f.

Brāhmaṇagāma.—A village in Ceylon, near which **Mahāsena** built the **Kalandavihāra.**[1]

[1] MṬ. 685.

Brāhmaṇagāmavāpi.—A tank in Ceylon, restored by **Parakkamabāhu I.**[1]

[1] Cv. lxxix. 32.

Brāhmaṇatissa-cora, Brāhmaṇatissabhaya.—Reference is made in the Ceylon Chronicles and in some of the Commentaries to a period of great distress in Ceylon, owing to the activities of a *cora* (? brigand) called **Brāhmaṇatissa** in the time of **Vaṭṭagāmaṇī-Abhaya (Pitirājā).** According to the Mahāvaṃsa and the Mahāvaṃsa Ṭīkā,[1] Tissa was a brahmin youth of **Rohaṇa.** One day he heard a brahmin-soothsayer announce that if a brigand were to commence his activities under a certain combination of planets, he would conquer the whole of Ceylon. Tissa, acting on this idea, turned robber and sent word to the king that he should hand over his throne to him. At the same time seven **Damiḷas,** with their followers, arrived in **Mahātittha** with the same demand. The king thereupon sent word to Tissa that the kingdom would be his if he could defeat the Damiḷas. Tissa agreed to this and marched against them, but was taken captive in a battle near **Saṅketahāla.** The Pāli Commentaries give further details. Tissa plundered the land for twelve long years; food became so scarce that, owing to starvation, people lost even their sexual desires, and the birth of a child was such a rare occurrence that all the land rejoiced over such a birth.[2] Tissa's activities were at their height when **Vaṭṭagāmaṇī** was in hiding. The stores of food in **Cittalapabbata-vihāra** and in **Tissamahārāma** were laid waste by enormous rats and the monks could obtain no food, Tissa having ravished the land. They therefore sent eight Theras to **Sakka,** begging him to rid the country of Tissa; but Sakka sent reply that he was powerless, and suggested that the monks should go over the seas. Some took his advice and sailed from **Jambukola,** but the leaders of the community—**Saṃyuttabhāṇaka-Cūlasīva, Isidatta** and **Mahāsoṇa**—remained behind awaiting better times.[3] The **Mahāvihāra** at **Anurādhapura** was deserted; the **Mahā Thūpa** was overgrown with trees. The monks had to live on lotus-stalks and fruit-rinds thrown away by the people. When Brāhmaṇatissa died, Vaṭṭagāmaṇī once more came to the throne.[4] *v.l.* **Brāhmaṇatiya-cora** (from which the Ceylon Chronicles derive the form Bäminitiyā.[5]) See also **Caṇḍāla-Tissa (Caṇḍāla-Tiya)** which evidently refers to this same "*bhaya.*"

[1] Mhv. xxxiii. 37 ff.; MṬ. 613.

[2] SA. ii. 83.

[3] See also *s.v.* **Nāgā Therī,** whose story given in AA. ii. 654 f.; also MA. i. 546.

[4] VibhA. 445-51.

[5] About the date of the *Bäminisāya* (the brahmin famine as it was called in Sinhalese), see Cv. *Trs.* Introd. xvii., section 4.

Brāhmaṇadhammika Sutta.—Several old and decrepit but wealthy (*Mahāsāḷa*) brahmins of **Kosala,** visit the Buddha at **Jetavana** and ask him if the practices of the brahmins of their own day are in conformity with those of old. The Buddha answers in the negative and describes in detail the high moral standard of the lives of ancient brahmins. In course of time, however, the brahmins were disturbed by the sight of the king's wealth and adorned and bejewelled women, and became covetous of these. They thereupon induced the king to make offerings and hold sacrifices of animals that these might be for their own gain. Thus righteousness decayed and disease became prevalent among men.

The brahmins, pleased with the Buddha's sermon, declared themselves his followers.[1]

[1] SN. pp. 50-55.

Bh.

Bhagandha-Hatthaka Sutta.—See **Bhadragandha-Hatthaka Sutta.**

Bhagalavatī.—A place in **Uttarakuru** where the **Yakkhas** assemble. The Dīgha Nikāya[1] speaks of it as a hall (*sabhā*), while the Sutta Nipāta Commentary[2] says it is a mountain in **Himavā** where the devas assemble every month for eight days in order to settle disputes. The Yakkha leaders also attend these assemblies. The Sumaṅgalavilāsinī,[3] however, says that it is a jewelled pavilion (*ratanamaṇḍapa*) twelve leagues in extent, on the banks of the **Dharaṇī** Lake. It is surrounded by a creeper named Bhagalavatī, hence, probably, its name.

[1] D. iii. 201. [2] SNA. i. 197. [3] DA. iii. 967.

1. **Bhaginī Sutta.**—It would not be easy to find a person who has not been one's sister during *saṃsāra.*[1]

[1] S. ii. 189.

2. **Bhaginī Sutta.**—There are men who would not lie, even for a sister's sake.[1]

[1] S. ii. 243.

Bhagīrathī, Bhagīrasī.—See **Bhāgīrathī.**

Bhagīrasa.—A king of old, mentioned as having held great sacrifices; he could not, however, advance beyond the *peta*-world.[1]

[1] J. vi. 99.

1. **Bhagu.**—A famous sage (*isi*) of old.[1] He was one of the teachers who composed runes combined with the teachings of **Kassapa Buddha.**[2]

[1] Vin. i. 245; D. i. 104, 238, 243; M. ii. 169, 200; A. iii. 224; iv. 61.
[2] DA. i. 273, etc.

2. **Bhagu Thera.**—He was born in a Sākyan family, and having left the world with his clansmen **Anuruddha** and **Kimbila,** he dwelt in the village of **Bālakaloṇa.** One day, having left his cell in order to drive away his drowsiness, he fell as he was stepping on to the terrace, and, urged thereby to further effort, he accomplished self-mastery and won arahantship. Later, when he was living in the bliss of fruition, the Buddha came to congratulate him on his solitude.[1] It is said[2] that, on this occasion, the Buddha, after his meal, preached to Bhagu for a whole day and a whole night. The next day Bhagu accompanied the Buddha on his alms-round, and turned back when the Buddha proceeded to **Pācīnavaṃsa-migadāya** to see Anuruddha and the others.

In the time of **Padumuttara Buddha,** Bhagu was a householder, and, after the Buddha's death, offered flowers to his relics. As a result he was born among the **Nimmānaratī** gods.[3]

He is probably identical with **Jātipupphiya** of the Apadāna.[4]

A monk named Bhagu is mentioned[5] as staying with **Jātipupphiya** at the **Kukkuṭārāma** in **Pāṭaliputta,** but he is probably a different person.

[1] Thag., vss. 271-4; ThagA. i. 380 f.; *cf.* M. iii. 155; Vin. i. 350, ii. 182; DhA. i. 56, 133; J. i. 140, iii. 489; Mil. 107.
[2] SA. ii. 222; this sermon is referred to as the **Kilesiya Sutta** (*q.v.*).
[3] ThagA. i. 380.
[4] Ap. ii. 405 f.
[5] Vin. i. 300.

1. **Bhaggava.**—A teacher to whom the Buddha went after leaving **Rājagaha,** and before seeking **Āḷāra** and **Uddaka.**[1]

[1] ThigA., p. 2.

2. **Bhaggava.**—Father of **Aṅgulimāla** and chaplain of the king of **Kosala.** Bhaggava was a brahmin.[1]

[1] ThagA. ii. 57.

3. **Bhaggava.**—A potter in **Rājagaha** in whose dwelling the Buddha met and conversed with **Pukkusāti.**[1] Bhaggava seems to have been a generic name for all potters, perhaps a special form of address used towards members of the *kumbhakāra* "caste." Thus we find in the books several instances of potters being addressed as "Bhaggava."[2] In the Saṃyutta

[1] M. iii. 237.
[2] *E.g.*, DhA. i. 33; J. ii. 80, iii. 382. At J. iii. 382 the potter's wife is addressed as "**Bhaggavī.**"

Nikāya[3] the Buddha addresses **Ghaṭīkāra Brahmā** as "Bhaggava"; he had been a potter of **Vehaliṅga** in his previous birth and the name "Ghaṭīkāra" itself means "jar-maker." The Commentaries give no explanation of the word; perhaps the potters claimed their descent from Bhṛgu. Bhaggava is sometimes given as an example of a *gotta*.[4] See also **Bhaggavagotta.**

[3] S. i. 36, 60. [4] *E.g.*, Sp. i. 160 (with **Gotama**).

Bhaggavagotta.—A clothed Wanderer (*channaparibbājaka*),[1] who lived in a pleasaunce near **Anupiyā.** He was a friend of **Sunakkhatta** (*q.v.*). The Buddha once visited him, and their conversation is recorded in the **Pāṭika Sutta** (*q.v.*).[2] He was evidently so called because he belonged to the gotta named Bhaggava (? potters).

[1] DA. iii. 816. [2] D. iii. 1 ff.

Bhaggavī.—See **Bhaggava** (3).

Bhaggā.—The name of a tribe and a country, the capital of which was **Suṃsumāragiri** (*q.v.*). The Buddha went there several times in the course of his wanderings[1] and three rules for the monks were laid down there.[2] **Bodhirājakumāra** (*q.v.* 1), son of **Udena** of **Kosambi,** lived there, apparently as his father's viceroy, in which case the Bhaggā were subject to Kosambī.[3] The Bhagga country lay between **Vesāli** and **Sāvatthi.**

It was while sojourning in the Bhagga-country that **Moggallāna** was attacked by **Māra** entering into his stomach,[4] and it was there that he preached the **Anumāna Sutta.**[5] **Sirimaṇḍa** and the parents of **Nakula** were inhabitants of the Bhagga-country, and **Sigālapitā**[6] went there in order to meditate; there he became an arahant.

In the Apadāna[7] the Bhaggā are mentioned with the Kārusā.

[1] *E.g.*, A. ii. 61, iv. 85, etc.; Vin. ii. 127; iv. 115, 198. [2] Vin. v. 145. [3] The C.H.I. (i. 175) says that the Bhaggā were members of the Vajjian confederacy. [4] M. i. 332. [5] *Ibid.*, 95. [6] ThagA. i. 70. [7] Ap. ii. 359.

Bhañña.—The word occurs in the compound **Ukkalā(Okkalā)-Vassa-Bhaññā,**[1] a group described as *ahetuvādā, akiriyavādā, natthikavādā,* but who, nevertheless, agreed that the *khandhas* might be divided into past, present and future and who accepted the teaching of the Great Forty (see **Mahācattārīsaka Sutta**). They also accepted non-covetousness, non-malice, right mindfulness and right concentration as worthy. The Commentaries[2] explain that Vassa and Bhañña were two people (*dve janā*) (? tribes).

[1] S. iii. 73; M. iii. 78; A. ii. 31.
[2] AA. ii. 497; MA. ii. 894; SA. (ii. 204) says, *dve pi te mūladiṭṭhigatikā.*

Bhaṇḍa, Bhaṇḍu Thera.—A colleague of **Ānanda** whom **Kassapa** reported to the Buddha at **Veḷuvana** for disputing with **Abhiññjaka,** colleague of **Anuruddha.** The Buddha sent for the disputants and rebuked them for their contentiousness. They confessed their fault and were pardoned.[1]

[1] S. ii. 204 f.

Bhaṇḍakucchi.—One of the gate-keepers (*dovārikā*) of **Maṇḍavya,** who were ordered to cast **Mātaṅga** out.[1]

[1] J. iv. 382.

Bhaṇḍagāma.—A **Vajjian** village between **Vesāli** and **Hatthigāma** and near the former. The Buddha visited it during his last tour, and while there he talked to the monks on four conditions which lead to Nibbāna: righteousness, earnest thought, wisdom, and freedom.[1]

[1] D. ii. 123; A. ii. 1 ff.

Bhaṇḍagāma Vagga.—The first chapter of the Catukka Nipāta of the Aṅguttara Nikāya.[1]

[1] A. ii. 1-12.

1. **Bhaṇḍana Sutta.**—The Buddha says it is unpleasant for him even to think of a place where monks are given to dispute, but far worse to go to it. Strife is due to the abandonment of dispassionate, benevolent and harmless thinking. Monks who dwell in harmony cultivate these things.[1]

[1] A. i. 275 f.

2. **Bhaṇḍana Sutta.**—Five disadvantages which come to those who encourage strife and disputes.[1]

[1] A. iii. 252.

3. **Bhaṇḍana Sutta.**—The Buddha rebukes some monks at **Jetavana** who were engaged in disputation and tells them to reflect on ten things which conduce to kindness, peace and concord.[1]

[1] A. v. 88 ff.

? **Bhaṇḍāgāra-amacca.**—Given as an example of a handsome person.[1]

[1] AA. ii. 596.

Bhaṇḍika.—An eminent Thera, well-versed in the four Nikāyas (*catunikāyika*). He was evidently an esteemed Commentator.[1]

[1] See, *e.g.*, SA. i. 17.

Bhaṇḍikā-pariveṇa.—A building attached to the **Abhayagiri-vihāra** and built by **Kassapa V.**[1] It evidently received its name in honour of the king's mother.[2]

[1] Cv. lii. 58. [2] Cv. *Trs.* i. 167, n. 6.

1. **Bhaṇḍu, Bhaṇḍuka.**—An Anāgāmi upāsaka, son of a sister of **Devī**, and therefore cousin of **Mahinda** and **Saṅghamittā**. He accompanied Mahinda to Ceylon, and was ordained, on the day of their arrival, at **Ambatthala.** He attained arahantship immediately after.[1]

[1] Mhv. xiii. 16, 18; xiv. 29, 31 f.; Dpv. xii. 26, 39, 62, 63.

2. **Bhaṇḍu.**—See **Bhaṇḍa.**

Bhaṇḍukaṇṇa.—A juggler, who tried to make **Mahāpanāda** laugh. He made a mango-tree, the **Atulamba,** grow before the palace door and climbed it with the help of a string. **Vessavaṇa's** slaves chopped him up and threw the pieces down, and the other jugglers joined the pieces together and poured water over them. Bhaṇḍukaṇṇa then donned upper and under garments of flowers and started dancing again. But he could not make Mahāpanāda laugh.[1]

[1] J. iv. 324.

Bhatta Sutta.—The five disadvantages which come to a family who wait to eat till the sun has fully risen.[1]

[1] A. iii. 260.

Bhattabhatika.—A labourer who, in return for three years' work, obtained the privilege of enjoying the luxuries of the Treasurer **Gandha** (*q.v.*). When he was ready to eat, however, a Pacceka Buddha appeared and Bhattabhatika gave him all his food. When Gandha discovered this, he made over to Bhattabhatika one-half of all his possessions, and they became firm friends. The king made Bhattabhatika a Treasurer. After death he was born in the deva-worlds, whence he was reborn in **Sāvatthi** as **Sukhakumāra.**[1]

[1] DhA. iii. 87 ff.; for the rest of the story see *s.v.* **Sukha.**

Bhattabhuttavaḷāhaka.—The name given to the spot where **Duṭṭhagāmaṇi** took his meal after crossing the **Mahāvālukagaṅgā,** in his advance against the **Damiḷas.**[1]

[1] MṬ. 476.

Bhattasūpagāma.—A village in **Rohaṇa,** where a great battle was fought between the forces of **Parakkamabāhu I.** and the rebels who wished to take possession of the Buddha's Tooth Relic and Alms Bowl. Parakkama's forces were victorious.[1]

[1] Cv. lxxiv. 135.

Bhattā.—See **Hatthā.**

1. **Bhadda.**—A lay disciple of **Nādikā** who, the Buddha declared, had destroyed the five *orambhāgiyasaṃyojanā* and had been born in the highest deva-worlds, thence to pass away entirely.[1]

[1] D. ii. 92.

2. **Bhadda Thera.**—He was born in the family of a seṭṭhi of **Sāvatthi.** His parents had gone to the Buddha before his conception, and had told him that if they had a child they would give him to the Buddha as his servant. When he was seven years old, they took him, arrayed in his best, to the Buddha, in fulfilment of their promise. The Buddha asked **Ānanda** to ordain him. This he did and instructed him, and the same night Bhadda became an arahant. The Buddha called to him saying, "Come, Bhadda," and that was his *upasampadā*.

In the time of **Padumuttara Buddha** he had offered hundreds of thousands of robes, etc., to the Buddha and his monks.[1]

[1] Thag. vss. 473-9; ThagA. i. 474 f.

3. **Bhadda Thera.**—Perhaps to be identified with **Bhadda** (2). He is mentioned as staying at the **Kukkuṭārāma** in **Pāṭaliputta** in the company of **Ānanda,** with whom he discussed the righteous and the unrighteous life[1] and the cultivation of the *satipaṭṭhānas.*[2]

[1] S. v. 15 f. [2] *Ibid.*, 171 f.

4. **Bhadda.**—One of the two chief disciples of **Koṇḍañña Buddha.**[1]

[1] J. i. 30; Bu. iii. 304.

5. **Bhadda.**—Commander-in-chief of **Sena I.** He built the **Bhaddasenāpatipariveṇa** and endowed it with servants and revenues.[1]

[1] Cv. l. 82.

Bhaddaka Sutta.—**Sāriputta** tells the monks that he who delights and engages himself in worldly activities meets with a luckless fate, while he who renounces such meets with a lucky fate.[1]

[1] A. iii. 293.

Bhaddakaccā, Bhaddākaccā, Bhaddakaccānā, also **Subhaddakaccānā.** See **Rāhulamātā.**

Bhaddakaccānā.—The youngest of the children of **Paṇḍu,** the Sākyan. She was so beautiful that seven kings begged to be allowed to marry her. Her father, unable to decide between her suitors, put her in a boat with thirty-two companions and launched the boat upon the Ganges. The boat arrived in the course of the following day at **Goṇagāmaka** in Ceylon, where the women landed, dressed as nuns. In due course they came to **Upatissagāma,** where the king, **Paṇḍuvāsudeva,** warned by soothsayers, awaited their arrival and married Bhaddakaccānā. Later, six of her brothers came to Ceylon and settled in different parts; the brothers were **Rāma, Uruvela, Anurādha, Vijita, Dīghāyu** and **Rohaṇa.** The seventh brother, **Gāmaṇī,** stayed at home.

Bhaddakaccānā had ten children, the eldest being **Abhaya** and the youngest **Ummādacittā.**[1]

[1] Mhv. viii. 18 ff.; ix. 1, 9 f.; Dpv. x. 1 ff.

Bhaddakappa.—A *kappa* such as the present in which five Buddhas are born.[1]

[1] BuA. 159.

Bhaddaji Thera.—The son of a seṭṭhi in **Bhaddiya.** He was worth eighty crores, and was brought up in luxury like that of the Bodhisatta in his last birth. When Bhaddaji was grown up, the Buddha came to Bhaddiya to seek him out, and stayed at the **Jātiyāvana** with a large number of monks. Thither Bhaddaji went to hear him preach. He became an arahant, and, with his father's consent, was ordained by the Buddha. Seven weeks later he accompanied the Buddha to **Koṭigāma,** and, while the Buddha was returning thanks to a pious donor on the way, Bhaddaji retired to the bank of the Ganges outside the village, where he stood wrapt in *jhāna,* emerging only when the Buddha came by, not having heeded the preceding chief theras. He was blamed for this; but, in order to demonstrate the attainments of Bhaddaji, the Buddha invited him to his own ferry-boat and bade him work a wonder. Bhaddaji thereupon raised from the river bed, fifteen leagues into the air, a golden palace twenty leagues high, in which he had lived as **Mahāpanāda** (*q.v.*). On this occasion the **Mahāpanāda** or **Suruci Jātaka** was preached. The Mahāvaṃsa account[1] says that, before raising Mahāpanāda's palace, Bhaddaji rose into the air to the height of seven palmyra-trees, holding the **Dussa Thūpa** from the Brahma-world in his hand. He then dived into the Ganges and returned with the palace. The brahmin **Nanduttara,** whose hospitality the Buddha and his monks had accepted, saw this miracle of Bhaddaji, and himself wished for similar power by which he

[1] xxxi. 37 ff.

might procure relics in the possession of others. He was reborn as the novice **Soṇuttara** (*q.v.*), who obtained the relics for the thūpas of Ceylon.

In the time of **Padumuttara** Buddha, Bhaddaji was a brahmin ascetic who, seeing the Buddha travelling through the air, offered him honey, lotus-stalks, etc. Soon after he was struck by lightning and reborn in **Tusita.** In the time of **Vipassī Buddha** he was a very rich seṭṭhi and fed sixty-eight thousand monks, to each of whom he gave three robes. Later, he ministered to five hundred Pacceka Buddhas. In a subsequent birth his son was a Pacceka Buddha, and he looked after him and built a cetiya over his remains after his death.[2]

Bhaddaji is identified with **Sumana** (*q.v.*) of the **Mahānārada-Kassapa Jātaka.**[3]

He is probably identical with **Bhisadāyaka** of the Apadāna.[4] Bhaddaji is mentioned among those who handed down the Abhidhamma to the Third Council.[5] See also **Bhaddaji Sutta.**

[2] Thag. vs. 163 f.; ThagA. i. 285 ff.; also J. ii. 331 ff., where the details vary slightly; J. iv. 325; also MṬ. 560 f.

[3] J. vi. 255.

[4] Ap. ii. 420 f.

[5] DhSA. 32.

Bhaddaji Sutta.—A discussion between **Bhaddaji** and **Ānanda** at the **Ghositārāma.** In answer to Ānanda's questions, Bhaddaji says that **Brahmā** is the best of sights; the best of sounds is that of Radiant Devas shouting "Joy, joy," etc. Ānanda says that such is the talk of *puthujjanas.* The best sight, in his view, is that of the destruction of the *āsavas*; the best sound that of their destruction, etc.[1]

[1] A. iii. 202 f.

Bhaddanahānakoṭṭha.—A bathing-place in **Pulatthipura,** built by **Parakkamabāhu I.**[1]

[1] Cv. lxxviii. 45.

Bhaddayānikā.—An offshoot of the **Vajjiputtaka** heretics.[1] Their doctrines resembled those of the **Dhammuttariyas ;** In birth is ignorance and in the arresting of birth is the arresting of ignorance.[2] They also held the view that the corruptions were put away by slices.[3]

[1] Mhv. v. 7; Dpv. v. 46.

[2] Rockhill, *op. cit.*, 194.

[3] Mrs. Rhys Davids, *Points of Controversy*, p. 130.

Bhaddavaggiyā.—A group of thirty young men, converted by the Buddha. They had gone picnicing with their wives in a forest-glade between **Bārāṇasī** and **Uruvelā.** One of them had no wife, and for him they found a courtezan; but she awaited the opportunity and ran away with their goods. While seeking for her, they saw the Buddha and enquired if he had seen a woman. But he answered, should they not rather seek the " self " than a woman. They all agreed thereto, and he preached to them. At the end of the sermon they realized the Truth and were ordained.[1] Their conversion was one of the subjects sculptured in the Relic Chamber of the **Mahā Thūpa.**[2]

[1] Vin. i. 23 f.; DhA. ii. 33 f. [2] Mhv. xxx. 79.

Bhaddavatikā.—A market-town near **Kosambī.** The Buddha went there and was warned by cowherds and others not to approach **Ambatittha** as a fierce Nāga dwelt there. **Sāgata Thera,** hearing this, went to Ambatittha and subdued the Nāga, afterwards rejoining the Buddha at Bhaddavatikā.[1] The town is probably identical with **Bhaddavatī** (*q.v.*), and was in the **Cetiya** Country.[2]

[1] Vin. iv. 108 f.; J. i. 360 f. [2] Vin. iv. 108.

Bhaddavatiya.—Father of **Sāmāvatī** ; he was a seṭṭhi of **Bhaddavatī.** He formed a close friendship with **Ghositaseṭṭhi** of **Kosambī,** through the medium of traders and, when Bhaddavatī was attacked by plague, he left with his wife and daughter to visit Ghositaseṭṭhi. But he died of starvation outside the city before he could reach him.[1]

[1] DhA. i. 187 f.

1. **Bhaddavatī.**—A city, the residence of **Bhaddavatiyaseṭṭhi,** father of **Sāmāvatī.** Trade was carried on between **Kosambī** and Bhaddavatī.[1] See also **Bhaddavatikā.**

[1] DhA. i. 187.

2. **Bhaddavatī, Bhaddavatikā.**—A female elephant belonging to King **Udena.** She had belonged originally to **Caṇḍappajjota.** She could travel fifteen leagues in a day.[1] Udena made use of her in his elopement with **Vāsuladattā.**[2] At first the king paid her great honour, declaring that his life, queen and kingdom were all due to her; her stall was smeared with perfumed earth and hung with coloured hangings, a lamp burned perfumed oil and a dish of incense was set on one side. She stood on a coloured carpet and ate royal food of many flavours. But when she grew old she was neglected and became destitute. One day she saw the Buddha entering the city for alms, fell at his feet, and complained of the king's neglect. The Buddha reported the matter to the notice of Udena, and all former honours were restored to Bhaddavatī. This incident led to the preaching of the **Daḷhadhamma Jātaka.**[3]

[1] DhA. i. 196. [2] *Ibid.*, 198. [3] J. iii. 384 f.

3. **Bhaddavatī.**—A princess, sister of **Parakkamabāhu I.**[1]

[1] Cv. lxvi. 147.

1. **Bhaddasāla.**—One of the chief disciples of **Nārada Buddha.**[1] He was a brahmin of **Thullakoṭṭhita** and, together with his friend **Vijitamitta,** he went in search of the Lake of Immortality (*Amatarahada*). During their travels they met Nārada Buddha and entered the Order under him, later becoming arahants.[2]

[1] J. i. 37; Bu. x. 23. [2] BuA. 154.

2. **Bhaddasāla.**—A dryad; see the **Bhaddasāla Jātaka.**

3. **Bhaddasāla Thera.** — An arahant. He accompanied **Mahinda** to Ceylon.[1] **Sirimeghavaṇṇa** made an image of him and placed it in a shrine near his palace.[2] *v.l.* **Bhaddanāma.**

[1] Mhv. xii. 7; Dpv. xii. 12, 38; Sp. i. 62, 70. [2] Cv. xxxvii. 87.

4. **Bhaddasāla.**—A tree in the **Rakkhitavanasaṇḍa** in the Pārileyyaka forest where the Buddha stayed during his retirement.[1]

[1] Ud. iv. 5; Vin. i. 352.

5. **Bhaddasāla.**—A general of King **Nanda**; he waged war against **Candagutta.** In that war took place eighty Corpse Dances, where headless corpses arose and danced in frenzy over the battle-field.[1]

[1] Mil. 292.

6. **Bhaddasāla Thera.**—A monk of Ceylon. **Mahāsiva** was greatly devoted to him, and built for him the **Nagaraṅgana-vihāra** to the east of **Anurādhapura.**[1]

[1] Mhv. xxi. 2.

Bhaddasāla Jātaka (No. 465).—**Brahmadatta,** king of Benares, wishing to have a palace built on one column, sent his carpenters to find a suitable tree. They found many such in the forest, but no road by which to transport them. At last they discovered a lordly *sāla*-tree in the king's park and made preparations to cut it down. The deity of the tree (**Bhaddasāla** 2), who was the Bodhisatta, was greatly distressed at the prospect of the destruction of his children. He, therefore, visited the king by night and begged him not to have the tree cut down. When the king refused this request, Bhaddasāla asked that the tree should be cut down in pieces, so that in its fall it might not damage its kindred round about. This feeling of Bhaddasāla for his kinsmen touched the king, and he desisted from his purpose of destroying the tree.

The story was related in reference to the Buddha's interference with **Viḍūḍabha** (*q.v.*) when he wished to destroy the **Sākyans.**

Ānanda is identified with the king.[1] On this occasion was preached also the **Kukkura Jātaka** (No. 22), the **Kāka Jātaka** (No. 140), and the **Mahākapi Jātaka** (No. 407).

[1] J. iv. 153-7.

Bhaddasena.—Son of **Ekarāja** and brother of **Candakumāra.**[1] He is identified with **Moggallāna.**[2]

[1] J. vi. 134. [2] *Ibid.*, 157.

Bhaddasenāpati-pariveṇa.—A monastic building erected and endowed by **Bhadda,** general of **Sena I.**[1]

[1] Cv. l. 82.

1. **Bhaddā.**—One of the two chief women disciples of **Revata Buddha.**[1]

[1] J. i. 35; Bu. vi. 22.

2. **Bhaddā.**—One of the chief women patrons of **Kassapa Buddha.**[1]

[1] Bu. xxv. 41.

3. **Bhaddā.**—Wife of King **Muṇḍa.** At her death the king placed her body in a vessel of oil and mourned for her until his friend **Piyaka** took him to **Nārada Thera** at the **Kukkuṭārāma,** and there made him realize the folly of mourning.[1]

[1] A. iii. 57 ff.

4. **Bhaddā.**—A woman of **Kimbila;** she was the wife of **Rohaka.** She became famous in the city as a virtuous woman (*bhadditthī*) on account of her goodness and was admired even by the gods. One festival day, while her husband was away in **Takkasilā** on business, she greatly longed to be with him. The spirit of the house conveyed her thither, and from their union a child was born. Her virtue was doubted by her relations, but she convinced them by arresting a flood with an "Act of Truth." Her husband was also suspicious, but she convinced him by producing a signet ring which he had given her in Takkasilā. Thus she became famous through her virtue. After death she was born in **Tāvatiṃsa,** where she met the Buddha on his visit there, and at his request related to him her story.[1]

[1] Vv. ii. 5; VvA. 109 ff.

Bhaddā-Kaccāna.—See **Bhadda-Kaccāna.**

Bhaddā Kapilānī Therī.—The daughter of a **Kosiyagotta** brahmin[1] of **Sāgala,** in the **Madda** country. When the messengers sent by the parents of **Pipphali-māṇava** (Mahā Kassapa, *q.v.*) were wandering about seeking for a wife for him to resemble the image they carried with them, they discovered Bhaddā and informed Pipphali's parents. The parents arranged the marriage without the knowledge of the young people and Bhaddā went to Pipphali's house. There they lived together, but, by mutual consent, the marriage was never consummated. It was said that she brought with her, on the day of her marriage, fifty thousand cartloads of wealth. When Pipphali desired to leave the world, making over to her his wealth, she wished to renounce it likewise, and together they left the house in the guise of recluses, their hair shorn, unobserved by any. In the village, however, they were recognized by their gait, and the people fell down at their feet. They granted freedom to all their slaves, and set forth, Pipphali leading and Bhaddā following close behind. On coming to a fork in the road, they agreed that he should take the right and she the left. In due course she came to the Titthiyārāma (near **Jetavana**), where she dwelt for five years, women not having yet been admitted to the Buddha's Order. Later, when **Pajāpatī Gotamī** had obtained the necessary leave, Bhaddā joined her and received ordination, attaining arahantship not long after. Later, in the assembly, the Buddha declared her foremost of nuns who could recall former lives.

In the time of **Padumuttara Buddha** she was the wife of **Videha,** a seṭṭhi of **Haṃsavatī,** and having heard a nun proclaimed in the first rank of those who could recall former lives, she resolved to acquire a similar rank, while her husband (Mahā Kassapa in this life) resolved to be chief among those who practise austere vows (*dhutavādīnaṃ*). Together they did many good deeds and were reborn in heaven. In the time of **Vipassī Buddha,** the husband was the brahmin **Ekasāṭaka** and she was his wife. In his next birth he was king of Benares and she his chief queen. Together they entertained eight Pacceka Buddhas on a very lavish scale. In the interval between the appearance in the world of **Koṇāgamana** and **Kassapa Buddha,** the husband was a clansman and she his wife. One day a quarrel arose between her and her sister-in-law. The latter gave alms to a Pacceka Buddha and Bhaddā, thinking "She will win glory for this," took the bowl from her hand and filled it with mud. But later she was filled with remorse, took back the

[1] Ap. ii. 583 (vs. 57) says that her mother was **Sucīmatī** and her father **Kapila,** whence, probably, her title of Kāpilānī.

bowl, emptied it, scrubbed it with scented powder and, having filled it with the four sweet foods, sprinkled over the top ghee of the colour of a lotus-calyx. Handing it back to the Pacceka Buddha, she prayed to herself " May I have a shining body like this offering."

In a later birth, Bhaddā was born as the daughter of a wealthy treasurer of Benares; she was given in marriage, but her body was of such evil odour that she was repulsive to all and was abandoned by several husbands. Much troubled, she had her ornaments made into an ingot of gold and placed it on the shrine of Kassapa Buddha, which was in process of being built, and did reverence to it with her hands full of lotuses.[1] Her body immediately became fragrant and sweet, and she was married again to her first husband.[2] Later, she was the queen of **Nanda,** king of Benares,[3] with whom she ministered to five hundred Pacceka Buddhas, sons of **Padumavatī.** When they passed away she was greatly troubled and left the world to give herself up to ascetic practices. She dwelt in a grove, developed *jhāna,* and was reborn in the Brahma-world.[4]

Bhaddā-Kāpilānī's name is mentioned several times[5] in the Vinaya rules in connection with her pupils who were found guilty of transgressing them. She and **Thullanandā** were both famous as preachers, and the latter, being jealous of Bhaddā, went out of her way to insult her.[6] Once Bhaddā sent word to **Sāketa** asking Thullanandā if she could find her a lodging in **Sāvatthi.** Nandā agreed to do this, but made things very unpleasant for Bhaddā when she arrived.[7]

Bhaddā Kāpilānī is identified with the brahmin woman in the **Hatthipāla Jātaka**[8] and with **Sāma's** mother in the **Sāma Jātaka.**[9]

[2] The Apadāna account mentions two other lives: one when she was the wife of **Sumitta** and gave a blanket to a Pacceka Buddha,' and again when she was born among the Koliyans and attended on one hundred Pacceka Buddhas of **Koliya.**

[3] **Brahmadatta,** according to the Apadāna, which gives King Nanda as the name of her husband in another life.

[4] ThigA. 67 ff.; Ap. ii. 578 ff.; AA. ii. 93 ff., 203 f.; A. i. 25; Thig. vs. 63-6.

[5] *E.g.,* Vin. iv. 227, 268, 269, etc.

[6] Vin. iv. 290.

[7] *Ibid.,* 292.

[8] J. iv. 491.

[9] J. vi. 95.

Bhaddā-Kuṇḍalakesā.—A Therī. She was foremost among nuns, of swift intuition, and was born in the family of a treasurer of **Rājagaha.** On the same day, a son was born to the king's chaplain under a constellation favourable to highwaymen, and was therefore called **Sattuka** (*q.v.*). One day, through her lattice, Bhaddā saw Sattuka being led by the city-guard to execution on a charge of robbery. She fell at once in love with him and refused to live without him. Her father, out of his love for her, bribed the guard to release Sattuka, let him be bathed in perfumed water, and brought him home, where Bhaddā, decked in jewels, waited upon him. Very soon, Sattuka began to covet her jewels and told her that he had made a vow to the deity of the Robbers' Cliff that, should he escape, he would bring him an offering. She trusted him and, making ready an offering, went with him arrayed in all her ornaments. On arriving at the top of the cliff, he told her of his purpose, and she, all undaunted, begged of him to let her embrace him on all sides. He agreed to this, and then, making as if to embrace him from the back, she pushed him over the cliff. The deity of the mountain praised her presence of mind saying that men were not in all cases wiser than women.

Unwilling to return home after what had happened, she joined the Order of the white-robed **Nigaṇṭhas.** As she wished to practise extreme austerities, they dragged out her hair with a palmyra comb. Her hair grew again in close curls, and so they called her **Kuṇḍalakesā** ("Curly-hair"). Dissatisfied with the teaching of the Nigaṇṭhas, she left them, and going to various teachers, became very proficient in discussion and eager for debate. She would enter a village and, making a heap of sand at the gate, set up the branch of a rose-apple saying, "Whoever wishes to enter into discussion with me, let him trample on this bough." One day, **Sāriputta,** seeing the bough outside **Sāvatthi,** ordered some children to trample on it. Bhaddā then went to **Jetavana** accompanied by a large crowd whom she had invited to be present at the discussion. Sāriputta suggested that Bhaddā should first ask him questions; to all of these he replied until she fell silent. It was then his turn, and he asked "One—what is that ?"[1] She, unable to answer, asked him to be her teacher. But Sāriputta sent her to the Buddha, who preached to her that it were better to know one single stanza bringing calm and peace than one thousand verses bringing no profit. At the end of this sermon, Bhaddā attained arahantship, and the Buddha himself ordained her.

In the time of **Padumuttara Buddha,** she had heard him preach and place as foremost among nuns one whose intuition was swift (*khippā-bhiññā*). She vowed that this rank should one day be hers. Later, when **Kassapa** was Buddha, she was one of the seven daughters of **Kikī,** king of Benares, and was named **Bhikkhadāyikā** (*v.l.* **Bhikkhu-dāsikā**). For twenty thousand years she remained celibate and built a dwelling for the Order.[2]

1 Probably meaning "state any *one* fact true for everyone."

2 A. i. 25; AA. i. 200 ff.; ThigA. 99 ff.; Ap. ii. 560 ff. The DhA. account (ii. 217 ff.) differs in various details. There Bhaddā is shut up by her parents at the top of a seven-storeyed building with only a single woman to wait on her, for "girls when young, burn for men !" It was thus that she saw the robber.

In the Therīgāthā[3] are included several verses spoken by her when she had been a nun for fifty years, wandering about in **Aṅga, Magadha, Kāsi** and **Kosala,** living on the people's alms.

[3] Thig. vss. 107-11.

Bhaddāli Thera.—When the Buddha, at **Jetavana,** laid down the rule that monks should eat one meal a day and that in the morning, Bhaddāli protested and refused to keep this rule because he said that, in so eating, he would be a prey to scruples and misgivings. For three months he avoided the Buddha, until, just before the Buddha was starting on a journey, Bhaddāli, acting on the advice of his fellow-monks, confessed his fault to the Buddha and begged for forgiveness.[1] The Buddha praised this action and preached to him the **Bhaddāli Sutta** (*q.v.*).

It is said[2] that, in a previous birth, Bhaddāli had been a crow, therefore in this life he was always hungry and was known among his fellows as the Great Eater (**Mahāchātaka**).

Thirty kappas ago he met **Sumedha Buddha** in the forest, wrapt in meditation, and, having tidied the place where the Buddha was sitting, he erected over him a pavilion.[3]

[1] M. i. 437 ff. [2] MA. ii. 648. [3] Ap. ii. 365 f.

Bhaddāli Sutta.—Preached to **Bhaddāli** (*q.v.*) when he confessed his fault. The monk, who believes in the Buddha and obeys his instructions, will ultimately understand *dukkha* and will bring it to an end. The sutta also contains the parable of the *Ajāniya*-horse. A horse, schooled by an expert trainer and put through the various stages of training, becomes endowed with ten qualities, and is fit to be regarded as a treasure by a king. Similarly, a man who has developed the Noble Eightfold Path and obtained right knowledge and right deliverance, becomes the richest field in which the seed of merit may be sown.[1]

[1] M. i. 437 ff.

Bhaddā-Suriyavaccasā.—Daughter of the Gandhabba **Timbarū** and beloved of **Pañcasikha** (*q.v.*).

Bhaddika.—See **Bhaddiya** (3).

Bhadditthivimāna-vatthu.—The story of **Bhaddā,** wife of **Rohaka.** See **Bhaddā (4).**

1. **Bhaddiya Thera.**—An *anāgāmī*, one of seven persons who became arahants as soon as they were born in **Avihā.**[1]

[1] S. i. 35, 60; ThigA. 222, etc.

2. **Bhaddiya Thera.**—Called **Kāḷigodhāputta,** chief among monks of aristocratic birth (*uccakulikānaṃ*).[1] He belonged to a family of the Sākyan rājas of **Kapilavatthu** and entered the Order in the **Anupiya** Mango-grove with **Anurudha** and the others, soon afterwards attaining to arahantship. Dwelling in the bliss of Nibbāna, under a tree in a lonely spot, Bhaddiya used to exclaim "*Aho sukhaṃ, aho sukhaṃ.*" When this was reported to the Buddha, he questioned Bhaddiya, who answered that when he was ruling his principality he was well protected, yet was ever fearful and nervous, whereas now, having remounced all, he was free from all fear.[2] This incident was the occasion for the preaching of the **Sukhavihārī Jātaka** (*q.v.*).

Bhaddiya was the son of **Kāḷigodhā,** the senior Sākyan lady of her time. For five hundred births Bhaddiya had been king, hence his eminence in this life, though there were others more aristocratic.[3] His resolve to gain this distinction was formed in the time of **Padumuttara Buddha,** when he was born in a very rich family and did various good deeds towards that end. In the interval between **Kassapa Buddha** and **Gotama Buddha,** he was a householder of Benares and, discovering that **Pacceka** Buddhas took their meals on the banks of the Ganges, placed seven stone planks for them to sit on.[4] When Bhaddiya was ruling his Sākyan principality he had as general **Soṇa-Poṭiriyaputta,** who later joined the Order.[5] Anuruddha was Bhaddiya's great friend, and when Anuruddha wished to renounce the world, his mother agreed only on condition that Bhaddiya should accompany him, hoping, in this way, to hold him back. But Anuruddha overcame all Bhaddiya's objections and persuaded him to renounce the household life within a week. It is said[6] that Bhaddiya attained arahantship in the first rainy season after his ordination.

[1] A. i. 23.
[2] Thag. vss. 842-65; UdA. ii. 10; Vin. i. 183 f.; J. i. 140.
[3] AA. i. 109.
[4] ThagA. ii. 55 f.; Ap. i. 95 f.
[5] ThagA. i. 316.
[6] Vin. ii. 182 f.

3. **Bhaddiya.**—A city in the **Aṅga** kingdom.[1] The Buddha visited there several times and stayed sometimes at the **Jātiyāvana** where **Meṇḍaka** (*q.v.*), who lived there, came to see him.[2] It was there that the precept was laid down forbidding monks to wear sandals.[3] Bhaddiya

[1] DhA. i. 384; also iii. 363.
[2] Vin. ii. 242; DhA. iii. 363; also A. iii. 36.
[3] Vin. i. 190; DhA. iii. 451 f.; also another ruling *re* the *Pārājikā* (Vin. iii. 37 f.).

was also the residence of **Bhaddaji Thera**[4] and **Visākhā** (*q.v.*). *v.l.* **Bhaddika.**

[4] J. ii. 331, etc.; Dvy. (123 ff.) calls it Bhadraṅkara.

4. **Bhaddiya.**—A seṭṭhi, father of **Bhaddaji Thera** (*q.v.*).

5. **Bhaddiya.**—See **Lakuṇṭaka Bhaddiya.**

6. **Bhaddiya.**—One of the four chief merchants of **Ekarāja,** king of **Pupphavatī** (Benares).[1]

[1] J. vi. 135.

7. **Bhaddiya.**—A **Licchavī** who visited the Buddha at the **Kūṭāgārasālā** and asked if it were true that the Buddha was a magician who, by a glamorous trick, enticed away the followers of others. The Buddha advised Bhaddiya not to be led away by hearsay but to judge for himself; and he then proceeded, by means of question and answer, to convince Bhaddiya that his teachings were truly founded on fact and, if accepted and practised, would benefit not only human beings but the very trees of the forest.[1]

The Commentary adds[2] that, at the conclusion of the discourse, Bhaddiya became a sotāpanna.

[1] A. ii. 190 ff.

[2] AA. ii. 558.

1. **Bhaddiya Sutta.**—Records the visit of the Licchavi **Bhaddiya** to the Buddha and also their conversation.[1]

[1] A. ii. 190 ff.

2. **Bhaddiya Sutta.**—Preached in reference to **Lakuṇṭaka Bhaddiya** (*q.v.*). Though hunchbacked and unsightly, yet, says the Buddha, he was highly gifted, of a lofty nature, having achieved his goal. Even a puny boy, if wise, is truly great, feared by men as the lion is by animals.[1]

[1] S. ii. 279.

3. **Bhaddiya Sutta.**—The Buddha tella **Bhaddiya Thera** (2) that the Noble disciple who is a sotāpanna is pleased with four things: unwavering loyalty to the Buddha, to the Dhamma, to the Saṅgha, and virtues that are dear to the Noble Ones.[1]

[1] S. v. 403.

Bhaddekaratta Sutta.—Preached at **Jetavana.** The true saint is he who does not hanker after the past and does not long for the future. He is not swept away by present states of consciousness, but, scanning his heart with insight, he struggles unceasingly to win eternal Changelessness.[1] This sutta was learned by **Ānanda** and used by him in an exposition to his colleagues. This exposition was approved by the Buddha and came to be called the **Ānanda-Bhaddekaratta Sutta.**[2] One day, as **Samiddhi** was drying himself after bathing at **Tapodā** in **Rājagaha,** a deity questioned him on this sutta, and he had to confess his ignorance. Samiddhi then went to the Buddha and asked him about the sutta, and the Buddha preached to him only the verses, with no explanation. The monks, who were present, thereupon asked **Mahā Kaccāna** for a detailed exposition. He gave it, and the monks referred it to the Buddha who advised them to remember it. This exposition came to be called the **Mahā Kaccāna-Bhaddekaratta Sutta.**[3] Similarly, **Lomasakaṅgiya** was asked about the sutta by the god **Candana** when he was staying in the **Nigrodhārāma** at **Kapilavatthu.** He, in his turn, had to confess his ignorance, and Candana taught him the verses, which, he said, were uttered by the Buddha during his visit to **Tāvatiṃsa.**[4] Lomasakaṅgiya learnt the verses, and, going to the Buddha, questioned him concerning them. The Buddha made them clear to him. This account is called the **Lomasakaṅgiya-Bhaddekaratta Sutta.**[5] Extracts from the Bhaddekaratta Sutta are uttered by speakers in the **Hatthipāla Jātaka**[6] and the **Mahākapi Jātaka.**[7]

[1] M. iii. 187 ff.
[2] *Ibid.*, 189.
[3] *Ibid.*, 192 ff.
[4] When he went to preach the Abhidhamma. The Commentary (MA. ii. 962) explains that the Buddha preached this sutta for the benefit of devas who could not understand the Abhidhamma.
[5] M. iii. 199 ff.
[6] J. iv. 481.
[7] J. v. 66.

Bhadra, or ? **Bhagandha-Haṭṭhaka Sutta.**—The headman **Bhadragaka** visits the Buddha at **Uruvelakappa** and asks for a teaching about *dukkha.* The Buddha says he will talk neither of the future nor of the past, but only of the present. By means of questioning Bhadragaka, the Buddha makes him realize that sorrow and suffering come only through desire. For example, he would grieve if anything happened to his friends in Uruvelakappa, or to his son **Ciravāsi,** or to his wife; but he would not worry about those who were unknown to him and therefore unloved by him.[1]

The Commentary says[2] that in this sutta *vaṭṭadukkha* (? the sorrow of transmigration) is described.

[1] S. iv. 327 f.
[2] SA. iii. 103.

Bhadrakāra.—Son of **Vidhura** and eldest brother of **Sambhava** (the Bodhisatta). For details see the **Sambhava Jātaka.** Bhadrakāra is identified with **Moggallāna.**[1]

[1] J. v. 67.

Bhadragaka.—A headman of **Uruvelakappa** and father of **Ciravāsī.**[1] See **Bhadra Sutta.**

[1] S. iv. 327.

Bhadraghaṭa Jātaka (No. 291).—Once the Bodhisatta was a rich merchant with an only son. He did great good and was born as **Sakka.** The son squandered all his wealth in drinking and amusements and fell into poverty. Sakka took pity on him and gave him the **Bhadraghaṭa** (Wishing Cup), asking him to take care of it. But one day, when the son was drunk, he threw the cup into the air and smashed it, thus reducing himself once again to misery.

The story was told in reference to a ne'er-do-well nephew of **Anāthapiṇḍika.** His uncle helped him again and again, but he squandered everything, and one day Anāthapiṇḍika had him turned out of his house. The two squanderers were the same.[1]

[1] J. ii. 431 f.

Bhadravanasaṇḍa.—The name given to the grove near the **Bodhi**-tree where the Buddha took his noonday rest after the meal of milk-rice provided by **Sujātā.**[1]

[1] SNA. ii. 391.

Bhadrā Therī.—She belonged to a clan of the Sākyans, and left the world with **Pajāpatī Gotamī.** While she was meditating, the Buddha sent her a ray of glory and she attained arahantship.[1]

[1] Thig. vs. 9; ThigA. 13.

Bhadrāvudha.—One of the sixteen disciples of **Bāvarī,** who, at his request, visited the Buddha.[1] He questioned the Buddha as to how a man could get over attachment and cross the flood. By grasping after nothing in the world, answered the Buddha, for **Māra** follows the man who clings to things. This question and answer are contained in the **Bhadrāvudhamāṇava-puccha,**[2] which is explained in the Culla Niddesa.[3] At the end of the discourse, Bhadrāvudha and his pupils became arahants and joined the Order.[4]

[1] SN. vs. 1008.
[2] *Ibid.*, 1101-4.
[3] CNid. 36 f.
[4] SNA. ii. 599.

Bhaya Vagga.—The thirteenth chapter of the Catukka Nipāta of the Aṅguttara Nikāya.[1]

[1] A. ii. 121-33.

1. **Bhaya Sutta.**—There are three terrors that part mother and son: a great fire, a great flood, and a raid by robbers. They are also parted by old age, disease, and death. The practice of the Noble Eightfold Path will avoid these terrors.[1]

[1] A. i. 178 f.

2. **Bhaya Sutta.**—" Fear " is a name for sense-desires; likewise " pain," " disease," " blain," " bondage " and " bog." Impassioned by the senses and bound by them, both in this world and in the next, men are subject to fear, etc.[1]

[1] A. iii. 310 f.

3. **Bhaya Sutta.**—The same as No. 2, with the addition of " womb " to the list.[1]

[1] A. iii. 311.

4. **Bhaya Sutta.**—There are four fears: birth, old age, disease, and death.[1]

[1] A. ii. 121.

5. **Bhaya Sutta.**—Four other fears : fire, water, kings, bandits.[1]

[1] A. ii. 121.

6. **Bhaya** or **Bhikkhu Sutta.**—In the Ariyan disciple the five kinds of guilty dread are allayed; he is possessed by the four limbs of sotāpanna, and the Ariyan method is, by him, well seen and penetrated by insight.

[1] S. v. 389.

Bhayabherava Sutta.—**Jāṇussoṇi** visits the Buddha at **Jetavana** and asks him how it is that young men who have left the world under him should be able to live in solitude, in the depths of the forest, a joyless life. The Buddha answers that while yet a Bodhisatta he was assailed by the same doubts. Fear comes only to him whose heart is filled with desire and longing, and who is restless, witless, and drivelling. But the man who is pure, resolute, and free from corruptions of the heart, lives in confidence in the forest and develops the *jhānas*. The Buddha then describes how he passed through these stages of development before becoming the Enlightened One.[1] This sutta contains an account of the " threefold lore " (*tisso vijjā*) of the Buddha[2] and praises of the *Saraṇā*[3] (Refuges).

[1] M. i. 16 ff. [2] See Sp. i. 116. [3] *Ibid.*, 172.

1. **Bhayasīva.**—A member of the **Moriya**-clan in Ceylon, contemporary of **Silākāla.** His son was **Aggabodhi** and his nephew King **Mahānāga.**[1]

[1] Cv. xli. 69 f.

2. **Bhayasīva.**—A Pacceka Buddha.[1]

[1] M. iii. 69; ApA. i. 106.

Bhayoluppala.—A tank in Ceylon, made by **Kuṭakaṇṇatissa.**[1] The name was later corrupted into **Bahuppala.**[2]

[1] Mhv. xxxiv. 33. [2] MṬ. 628.

Bharaṇa.—One of the chief warriors of **Duṭṭhagāmaṇi.** He was the son of **Kumāra** of **Kappalakandara** and was very fleet of foot. At the age of ten or twelve he could chase hare and elk, seize them and dash them on the ground.[1]

[1] Mhv. xxiii. 64 ff.

Bharaṇḍu Sutta.—Records the visit of the Buddha to the hermitage of Bharaṇḍukālāma (*q.v.*).[1]

[1] A. i. 276 ff.

Bharaṇḍukālāma.—A recluse, once a co-disciple of the Buddha in the holy life. Once, when the Buddha visited **Kapilavatthu** and wanted lodging for the night, **Mahānāma** suggested that he should go to the hermitage of **Bharaṇḍu.** The Buddha acted on this suggestion and spent the night there. When Mahānāma arrived the next morning, the Buddha talked to him about the three kinds of teachers: those who have full comprehension of sense-desires only but not of objects of sense or of feelings; those who have full comprehension of sense desires and of objects of sense; and those who have comprehension of all three. Would their conclusions coincide, or would they differ ? Here Bharaṇḍu chimed in and asked Mahānāma to say they would be the same. But the Buddha contradicted him, whereupon Bharaṇḍu said they would be different; but the Buddha again contradicted him, and even, also, a third time. Grieved at being slighted by the Buddha in the presence of Mahānāma, an important Sākyan, Bharaṇḍu left Kapilavatthu, never to return.[1]

The Commentary explains[2] that he had lived in the same hermitage as the Buddha, when they were both pupils of **Āḷārakālama.**

Bharaṇḍu had the reputation of being able to secure the best and choicest alms in the city.

[1] A. i. 276 f. [2] AA. i. 458.

1. **Bharata.**—A sage of old who, as a result of living the holy life, was born in the Brahma-world.[1]

[1] J. vi. 99.

2. **Bharata.**—The Bodhisatta born as the king of **Roruva** and husband of **Samuddavijayā**. For his story see the **Āditta Jātaka.**[1]

[1] J. iii. 470 ff.

3. **Bharata.**—A hunter who brought from the **Himālaya** the chief of a herd of monkeys whose cry was one of the noises mentioned in the **Aṭṭhasadda Jātaka** (*q.v.*).[1]

[1] J. iii. 432.

4. **Bharata Thera.**—He was a householder of **Campā,** and, having heard that **Soṇa Kolivisa** had left the world, he, too, with his brother, **Nandaka,** entered the Order, soon afterwards becoming an arahant. Later, he helped his more slow-witted brother to obtain insight.

In the past Bharata gave to **Anomadassi Buddha** a pair of comfortable and very beautiful sandals.[1]

[1] Thag. vss. 175, 176; ThagA. i. 300 f.

5. **Bharata.**—King of the **Sovīras** in the time of **Reṇu.** His capital was in **Roruva.**[1]

[1] D. ii. 235 f.

6. **Bharata.**—A king of Benares, belonging to the dynasty of **Okkāka.** He was the father of **Dasaratha** (*q.v.*).[1]

[1] MṬ. 130.

7. **Bharata.**—A scion of the **Mahāsammata**-race and son of **Sāgaradeva.** He was the father of **Aṅgīrasa.**[1]

[1] Mhv. ii. 4; Dpv. iii. 6.

Bharatakumāra.—Son of the second queen of **Dasaratha** and step-brother of **Rāma** and **Lakkhaṇa.** For his story see the **Dasaratha Jātaka.** He is identified with **Ānanda.**[1]

[1] J. iv. 124 ff.

Bharattāla.—A village in Ceylon, given by **Aggabodhi IV.** for his maintenance of the **Dāṭhāsiva-padhānaghara.**[1]

[1] Cv. xlvi. 12.

Bharu.—The name of a king, a country, and its capital. See the **Bharu Jātaka** and **Bharukaccha.** The name of the king and the country in the **Suppāraka Jātaka** (*q.v.*) are also identical.

Bharu Jātaka (No. 213).—Once the Bodhisatta was leader of a band of five hundred ascetics in **Himavā.** One day they came to the city of **Bharu** for salt and vinegar, and took up their residence under a banyan-tree to the north of the city. A similar group remained under a tree to the south. Next year, the tree to the south of the city was found to have withered away, and the group who had lived there, having arrived first, took possession of the other tree, to the north. This led to a dispute between the two groups, and they sought the intervention of **Bharu,** king of the Bharu country. He decided in favour of one group, but being bribed by the other, he changed his mind. Later, the ascetics repented of their greed and hastened back to Himavā. The gods, angry with the king, submerged the whole of Bharu, three hundred leagues in extent, under the sea.

The story was told to **Pasenadi,** king of **Kosala,** who took bribes from some heretics and gave permission for them to build a centre near **Jetavana.** When the Buddha heard of it, he sent monks to interview the king, but the latter refused to receive even the Chief Disciples. The Buddha then went himself and dissuaded the king from giving permission for an act which would lead to endless dissensions.[1]

[1] J. ii. 169 ff.; the story is also given at SA. iii. 218 f., which says further that Pasenadi built the **Rājakārāma** to make amends for his fault.

1. **Bharukaccha.**—A seaport in the country of **Bharu.**[1] Mention is made of merchants going by sea from there to **Suvaṇṇabhūmi.**[2] Bharukaccha was the residence of **Vaḍḍhamātā Therī**[3] and **Malitavambha Thera.**[4] In the Mahāniddesa,[5] Bharukaccha is mentioned in a list of places to which men went for trade. **Vijaya** lived there for three months before sailing for Ceylon.[6] Bharukaccha is the modern Broach in Kathiawar. The people of Bharukaccha are called **Bharukacchakā.**[7]

[1] J. iv. 137.

[2] *E.g.*, J. iii. 188.

[3] ThigA. 171.

[4] ThagA. i. 211.

[5] MNid. i. 155; see also Mil. 331.

[6] Dpv. ix. 26; the Dvy. (586) says the city was founded by Bhiru, one of the three people who escaped from the kingdom of Sikhaṇḍi, the parricide ruler of Sauvīra, when this was destroyed by a heavy fall of sand, following on the murder of Rudrāyana, king of Roruka. Bharukaccha is, according to this account, a corruption of Bhīrukaccha (Marsh of Bhiru). But Brahmanized tradition ascribes its foundation to the sage Bhṛgu. It is identical with Barygaza of Ptolemy and the Periplus of the Erythrean Sea.

[7] *E.g.*, DhSA. 305.

2. **Bharukaccha.**—A park in Ceylon laid out by **Parakkamabāhu I.**[1]

[1] Cv. lxxix. 11.

Bharukacchaka Vatthu.—The story of a monk of **Bharukaccha** who having (in his dream) lain with a woman, thought he was guilty of a *pārājikā* offence. But **Upāli** ruled that he was blameless.[1]

[1] Vin. iii. 39; Sp. i. 283.

Bhallatittha.—A landing-place in Ceylon where **Abhayanāga** once lived.[1]

[1] Mhv. xxxvi. 43.

Bhallāṭiya.—King of Benares. See the **Bhallāṭiya Jātaka.**

Bhallāṭiya Jātaka (No. 504).—The Bodhisatta was once born as **Bhallāṭiya,** king of Benares. Desirous of eating venison cooked on charcoal, he gave the kingdom in charge of his courtiers and went to the **Himālaya** on a hunting expedition. While wandering about near **Gandhamādana,** among pleasant streams and groves, he came across two kinnaras fondly embracing each other and then weeping and wailing most pitifully. The king quieted his hounds, laid down his weapons, and approached the kinnaras. In answer to his questions, the female told him that one day, while she was picking flowers on the opposite bank for a garland for her lover, it grew late and a storm arose. The stream which separated the two lovers swelled in flood and they had to spend the night apart from each other. The memory of one night, thus passed in separation, had filled them with sorrow for six hundred and ninety-seven years, and they still wept whenever they thought of it.

The story was told in reference to a quarrel between **Pasenadi** and **Mallikā** about conjugal rights. They were sulky and refused to look at each other. The Buddha visited the palace and reconciled them. The two kinnaras were identified with the king and the queen.[1]

[1] J. iv. 437 ff.

Bhallātakadāyaka Thera.—An arahant. Eighteen kappas ago he was an ascetic and, seeing the **Buddha Atthadassī** going through the air, invited him to his hermitage. There he gave the Buddha a *bhallātaka*-fruit.[1]

He is probably identical with **Vijitasena.**[2]

[1] Ap. ii. 398.

[2] ThagA. i. 426.

Bhallātaka-vihāra. A monastery in Ceylon, built by **Dhātusena**[1] and restored by **Vijayabāhu I.**[2]

[1] Cv. xxxviii. 47. [2] *Ibid.*, lx. 61.

1. **Bhallika, Bhalliya, Bhalluka Thera.**—The younger brother of **Tapassu,** their father being a caravan leader of **Pokkharavatī** in **Ukkalā.**[1] While they were going along with five hundred trading carts, these stopped near the **Rājāyatana**-tree where the Buddha was sitting, eight weeks after his Enlightenment. When they investigated the cause for their carts thus stopping, a deity, their kinsman in a former life (their mother according to one account),[2] pointed out to them the Buddha and asked them to give him a meal as he had eaten nothing for seven weeks. Not waiting to cook, the merchants gave the Buddha some butter and honey in a bowl provided by the Four Regent Gods. At the end of the meal the Buddha talked to them. They accepted the Buddha and the Dhamma as their Refuge,[3] and obtained from the Buddha a few hairs as an object of worship. Later, when the Buddha was in **Rājagaha** after the preaching of his First Sermon, the merchants visited him and listened to his preaching. Tapassu became a sotāpanna, and Bhallika entered the Order and became an arahant.

In the past, Bhallika had given fruit to a Pacceka Buddha, named **Sumana.** During this life of **Sikhī Buddha,** he was a brahmin of **Aruṇavatī,** and hearing that **Ujita** and **Ojita** had given the Buddha his first meal, he and his friend invited the Buddha to eat at their house, and resolved to win a similar distinction for themselves in the future. They were herdsmen in the life of **Kassapa Buddha,** and for many years supplied milk-rice to the Buddha and the monks.[4]

The Theragāthā[5] contains a verse spoken by Bhallika when **Māra** tried to frighten him by assuming a hideous form.

It is said[6] that the hair (eight handfuls) given by the Buddha was deposited in a cetiya in **Asitañjana** and that on fast days blue rays shone from the cetiya.

[1] AA. i. 207 calls their birthplace **Asitañjana.**

[2] AA. i. 207.

[3] The *Dvevācikasaraṇa.* They thus became the Buddha's first lay disciples; A. i. 26.

[4] ThagA. i. 48 f.; AA. i. 207 f.; Vin. i. 3 f.; J. i. 80. Mhv. iii. 303 f.

[5] vs. 7.

[6] AA. i. 208. There is a tradition in Ceylon (recorded in the *Pūjāvaliya*) that Tapassu and Bhalluka visited the east coast of Ceylon and built a cetiya there. An inscription makes a similar record.

2. **Bhallika, Bhalluka.**—One of the chief lay patrons of **Dīpaṅkara Buddha.**[1]

[1] Bu. ii. 215.

Bhalluka.—Nephew of **Dīghajantu.**—He received a message from **Eḷāra,** in consequence of which he landed at **Mahātittha** in Ceylon with sixty thousand men, only to find that Eḷāra was dead and had been cremated seven days earlier. Bhalluka thereupon marched on **Anurādhapura** and pitched his camp at **Kolambahālaka. Duṭṭhagāmaṇī** marched against him, and a battle took place in the precincts of the **Mahāvihāra.** Bhalluka shot an arrow at the king, and, believing that it had pierced his mouth, set up a great shout, but **Phussadeva,** who was seated on **Kaṇḍula** immediately behind the king, shot at Bhalluka, who thereupon fell dead prostrate at the feet of the king.[1]

[1] Mhv. xxv. 77 ff.

1. **Bhava Sutta.**—A discussion between **Sāriputta** and **Jambukhādaka** on " becoming."[1]

[1] S. iv. 258.

2. **Bhava Sutta.**—On the three kinds of *bhava*—in the *kāma*-world, the *rūpa*-world, and the *arūpa*-world.[1]

[1] S. v. 56.

3. **Bhava Sutta.**—There are three kinds of *bhava: kāma, rūpa,* and *arūpa*; these can be given up by training in further virtue, further thought, and further insight.[1]

[1] A. iii. 444.

4. **Bhava Sutta.**—**Ānanda** asks the Buddha to what extent there is " becoming." There will be " becoming " as long as there are worlds of sense, of form, and of formlessness; action is the field, consciousness the seed, and craving the moisture which bring about rebirth in these worlds.[1]

[1] A. i. 223 f.

Bhavagga.—The name given to the highest point of existence (among the gods),[1] but, more often, to the highest point in the universe as opposed to **Avīci,** the lowest.[2]

[1] *E.g.*, Vibh. 426; Mil. 132. [2] *E.g.*, J. iv. 182; J. vi. 354; Mil. 336.

Bhavanimmita.—Fifty-seven kappas ago there were four kings of this name, previous births of **Phalakadāyaka Thera.**[1] *v.l.* **Santanāmika.**

[1] Ap. i. 174.

Bhavanetti Sutta.—The Buddha tells **Rādha** that that which leads to rebirth is lust for the body, for feelings, etc.[1]

[1] S. iii. 190.

1. **Bhāgineyya Saṅgharakkhita Thera.**—He was the nephew of the Elder **Saṅgharakkhita,** hence his name. Once, at a certain monastery he was given two sets of robes, and immediately put away the better set to be given as a present to his uncle and teacher. At the end of the rains, he went to the monastery of his uncle, and, having waited upon him, offered his gift. But his uncle refused it in spite of the youth's repeated request. Thereupon the nephew became sulky, and while fanning the Elder, started to think what he could do if he became a layman. He would sell his robe, buy a she-goat, get rich thereby, marry, and have a son. While taking the child out for a walk, he would ask to be allowed to carry him, his wife would refuse and carry him herself. Then she would drop the child and her husband would hit her. So thinking, in his absent-mindedness, the youth hit the Elder with the fan. The Elder read his thoughts and rebuked him. The youth then started to run away, but the monks caught him and brought him before the Buddha. The Buddha preached to him on the difficulty of keeping the mind in check. At the end of the sermon the youth became a sotāpanna.[1]

[1] DhA. i. 300 ff.

2. **Bhāgineyya Saṅgharakkhita.**—A novice who ate hot food and burnt his tongue. His teacher warned him against such lack of restraint, and the novice, developing insight on that topic, became an arahant.[1]

[1] Vsm., p. 45.

3. **Bhāgineyya Saṅgharakkhita.**—A monk who lived in the **Koṭageru-kapāsāda** during his illness. His cell could accommodate just one bed, yet the devas of two deva-worlds, led by **Sakka,** were present there to wait upon him.[1]

[1] MṬ. 552.

4. **Bhāgineyya-Upali.**—See **Upāli** (2).

1. **Bhāgīrathī.**—A name for the Ganges.[1] The river was so called because the sage **Bhagīratha** filled up the ocean with the Ganges whom he made his daughter.[2] It may also be the name of a separate river flowing from the **Himālaya** and forming one of the chief sources of the Ganges. The river flowed past **Haṃsavatī.**[3] *v.l.* **Bhagīrasī, Bhagīrathī.**

[1] *E.g.*, J. v. 93, 255; Ap. ii. 436.
[2] *Mahābhārata*, iii. 107, 9961; v. 178, 7096.
[3] *E.g.*, Ap. i. 51; ii. 343.

2. **Bhāgīrathī.**—A channel, branching off from the **Anotatta-vāpī** in Ceylon, and forming part of the irrigation scheme of **Parakkamabāhu I.**[1]

[1] Cv. lxxix. 49.

Bhājanadāyaka Thera.—An arahant. Ninety-one kappas ago he was a potter of **Bandhumatī** and supplied pots to the monks. Fifty-three kappas ago he was a king named **Anantajāli.**[1]

[1] Ap. i. 218.

Bhātaragāma.—A village in Ceylon, residence of **Nāgā Therī.**[1]

[1] AA. ii. 654; MA. i. 546.

Bhātā Sutta.—It is not easy to find one who has not been a brother in the long faring of *saṃsāra.*[1]

[1] S. ii. 189.

Bhāti, Bhātiya.—King of **Magadha,** father of **Bimbisāra.**[1]

[1] Dpv. iii. 52 f.; MṬ. 137.

Bhātikatissa.—Son of **Mahallanāga** and king of Ceylon for twenty-four years (203-227 A.C.). He built a wall round the **Mahāvihāra.** He erected the **Gavaratissa** and **Bhātikatissa-vihāras** and built the **Mahāmaṇi** tank, and also built an *uposatha*-hall in the **Thūpārāma.** He was succeeded by his younger brother, **Kaṇiṭṭhakatissa.**[1]

[1] Mhv. xxxvi. 1 ff.; Dpv. xxii. 18, 20, 30, 31.

Bhātikatissa-vihāra.—A vihāra built by **Bhātikatissa** (*q.v.*).

Bhātikābhaya.—Also called **Bhātika** or **Bhātiya.** Son of **Kuṭakaṇṇatissa** and king of Ceylon for twenty-eight years (38-66 A.C.). He was called Bhātika or Bhātiya because he was the elder brother of **Mahādāṭhika Mahānāga.** He was very pious, and once had the whole of the **Mahā-Thūpa** covered with sandalwood paste in which were embedded sweet-smelling flowers. On another occasion he covered the whole thūpa with flowers and sprinkled them with water drawn by machines from the **Abhaya-vāpi.** He made a plaster covering for the **Mahā-Thūpa** into which were mixed many cartloads of pearls. A net of coral was made and thrown over the cetiya, and in its meshes were fastened lotus-flowers of gold, as large as waggon-wheels. One day the king heard the sound of the chanting of arahants in the relic-chamber of the Mahā-Thūpa, and he lay down resolving not to rise until he had seen them. The theras made a door by which he could enter, and, having seen the glories of the chamber, he described them for the benefit of the people, making figures in illustration of his descriptions. Bhātikābhaya did many other works of merit, held **Vesākha**-festivals, organized offerings for the **Bodhi**-tree, and showed great hospitality to the monks at various places. He was succeeded by his brother **Mahādāṭhika-Mahānāga.**[1]

Bhātikābhaya once heard of a skilful judgment being given by **Ābhidhammika-Godha Thera** and laid down a rule that all disputes should be taken to the Elder for settlement.[2] On another occasion he appointed a brahmin minister, named **Dīghakārāyaṇa,** to settle a controversy between the monks of **Abhayagiri** and those of the **Mahāvihāra.**[3] He had a queen called **Sāmadevī** who was the daughter of a cattle-butcher. A large number of cattle-butchers were once brought before the king, but as they were unable to pay the fine demanded, he appointed them as scavengers in the palace. One of them had a beautiful daughter, and the king fell in love with her and married her. Owing to her, her kinsmen, too, lived in happiness.[4]

Bhātikābhaya once heard a Sutta[5] in which the Buddha had declared that, of all perfumes, that of jasmine was the strongest. In order to test this the king filled a room with the four kinds of perfume and then placed in it handfuls of various flowers, including jasmine. He then left the room and shut the door. After a while he entered again, and the first scent which greated him was that of jasmine. Convinced of the truth of the Buddha's statement, he fell prostrate and worshipped him.[6] It is said[7] that the king once asked a reciter to tell him of an auspicious stanza (*jayamaṅgala*) connected with all the Three Jewels. After thinking for a while, he recited the stanza beginning *divā tapati ādicco, ratti ābhāti candimā.*[8] At the end of the first *pāda*, the reciter saluted the setting sun, at the end of the second the rising moon, at the end of the third the Saṅgha, and at the end of the stanza he stretched his hands upwards in salutation of the **Mahā Thūpa.** The king asked him to hold his hands there and placed in them one thousand pieces.

1 For details see Mhv. xxxiv. 38 ff.; MṬ. 553 f.
2 Sp. ii. 307.
3 *Ibid.*, iii. 583.
4 VibhA. 440.
5 See A. v. 21 f.
6 AA. ii. 819.
7 SA. ii. 180.
8 S. ii. 284.

Bhātiyavaṅka-vihāra.—A monastery in Ceylon. A monk of the monastery, who once went to worship at the **Mahā Thūpa,** saw there some devatās also worshipping; they had been born in heaven as a result of having participated in the building of the thūpa.[1] In the time of **Duṭṭhagāmaṇi,** the chief incumbent of the vihāra was **Mahānāga.**[2]

1 Mhv. xxx. 46 f.
2 MṬ. 606.

Bhāra Vagga.—The third chapter of the **Khandha Saṃyutta.**[1]

1 S. iii. 25-33.

Bhāra Sutta.—The burden is the five *upādānakkhandhas*, the burden-bearer is the person (*puggala*), the taking up of the burden is the lust that leads to rebirth, the laying down of the burden is passionless ceasing of craving.[1]

[1] S. iii. 25 f.

Bhārata.—A title by which **Pañcāla,** king of **Uttarapañcāla,** is addressed in the **Sattigumba Jātaka**[1]; also the king of Benares, in the **Saṅkhapāla Jātaka,**[2] and **Manoja,** king of Benares, in the **Sona-Nanda Jātaka.**[3] The scholiast explains[4] the word by "*raṭṭhabhāradhāritāya.*"

[1] J. iv. 435.
[2] J. v. 170.
[3] *Ibid.*, 317, 326.
[4] *Ibid.*, 317.

Bhāratayuddha.—Evidently refers to the story of the Mahābhārata. It is reckoned among the sinful topics of conversation.[1]

[1] *E.g.*, VibhA. 490.

1. **Bhāradvāja.**—One of the two chief disciples of **Kassapa Buddha.**[1]

[1] J. i. 43; Bu. xxv. 39; SNA. i. 293.

2. **Bhāradvāja Thera.**—He belonged to the **Bhāradvājagotta** and was a brahmin of **Rājagaha.** He sent his son **Kaṇhadinna** to **Takkasilā,** to study under a certain teacher, but, on the way there, the boy met a Thera, entered the Order, and became an arahant. Bhāradvāja, too, heard the Buddha preach at **Veḷuvana,** became a monk, and attained arahantship. Later, when Kaṇhadinna visited the Buddha at Rājagaha, he met his father and learnt from him of his attainments.

Thirty-one kappas ago, Bhāradvāja met the Pacceka Buddha **Sumana** and gave him a *vallīkāra*-fruit.[1] He is, perhaps, identical with **Vallīkāraphaladāyaka** of the Apadāna.[2]

[1] Thag. vss. 177-8; ThagA. i. 302 f.
[2] Ap. ii. 416; but the same Apadāna verses are given under **Bhalliya** (ThagA. i. 49).

3. **Bhāradvāja Thera.**—He was the eldest of a clan of **Bhāradvājas** living in **Rājagaha** and his wife was a **Dhanañjāni** brahminee. The wife was a devout follower of the Buddha, and constantly sang the praises of the Buddha, of his teachings, and of the Order. Annoyed at this, Bhāradvāja went to the Buddha and asked a question. He was so pleased with the answer that he joined the Order and not long after became an arahant,[1] several of his brothers following his example. (See No. 5, below.)

[1] S. i. 160 f.

4. **Bhāradvāja.**—A young brahmin, pupil of **Tārukkha.** A discussion between him and **Vāseṭṭha** led to the preaching of the **Tevijja Sutta** (*q.v.*),[1] and also the **Vāseṭṭha Sutta** (*q.v.*).[2] Bhāradvāja later became the Buddha's follower.[3] The **Aggañña Sutta** was preached to him and to Vāseṭṭha when they were undergoing the probationary period prior to their becoming fully ordained monks.[4] Buddhaghosa says[5] that they accepted the Buddha as their teacher at the conclusion of the Vāseṭṭha Sutta and entered the Order at the end of the Tevijja Sutta. Later, while meditating on the teachings of the Aggañña Sutta, they became arahants.[6] According to Buddhaghosa,[7] Bhāradvāja belonged to a noble family worth forty-five crores.

[1] D. i. 235.
[2] SN., p. 115 ff.; M. ii. 197 f.
[3] D. i. 252; SN., p. 123.
[4] D. iii. 80.
[5] DA. iii. 860.
[6] *Ibid.*, 872.
[7] *Ibid.*, 860.

5. **Bhāradvāja.**—The name of a brahmin clan; about twenty individuals belonging to this clan are mentioned in the Piṭakas. In one family, living at **Rājagaha,** the eldest was married to a **Dhanañjāni** brahminee and later became an arahant. (See above, No. 3.) His brothers, **Akkosaka-Bhāradvāja, Asurindaka-Bhāradvāja, Bilaṅgika-Bhāradvāja** and **Saṅgārava-Bhāradvāja,** followed him.[1] Several other Bhāradvājas living in **Sāvatthi** visited the Buddha there, and joined the Order and became arahants; viz., **Ahiṃsaka-Bhāradvāja, Jaṭā-°** and **Suddhika-; Aggika-°** joined the Order at **Veḷuvana, Sundarika-°** on the banks of the **Sundarikā,** and **Bahudhītika-°** in a forest tract in **Kosala. Kasī-Bhāradvāja, Kaṭṭhahāra-°** and **Navakammaki-°** became lay disciples.[2] The Elder **Piṇḍola** (*q.v.*) also belonged to the Bhāradvājagotta; so did **Kāpaṭhika.**[3] The gotta was evidently considered to be very ancient. Mention is made in the books of a **Bhāradvāja-isi** among the authors of the runes of the brāhmaṇas.[4] The **Kāliṅgabodhi Jātaka** (*q.v.*) speaks of a **Kāliṅgabhāradvāja** brahmin, while the brahmin carpenter in the **Phandana Jātaka** (*q.v.*) belongs to the same clan. The purohita **Sucīrata,** of **Dhanañjaya Koravya** (in the **Sambhava Jataka,** *q.v.*), is a Bhāradvāja, as is also **Jūjaka** of the **Vessantara Jātaka** (*q.v.*). In a Vinaya passage[5] the Bhāradvājagotta is mentioned together with the **Kosiya** as a low clan (*hīnagotta*).

[1] S. i. 160 ff.; SA. i. 175 ff.; MA. ii. 808.
[2] For particulars of the names mentioned here, see *s.v.*
[3] M. ii. 169 f.
[4] *E.g.*, D. i. 242; M. ii. 169, 200; A. iii. 224; iv. 61, etc.
[5] Vin. iv. 6; but see DA. iii. 860.

6. **Bhāradvāja.**—A brahmin of the **Bhāradvāja-gotta** living at **Kammāssadhamma.** The Buddha once stayed there and slept on a mat in his fire-hut, and there he met the **Paribbājaka Māgandiya.**[1]

[1] M. i. 501 ff.

7. **Bhāradvāja.**—A yakkha chief to whom disciples of the Buddha should make appeal in time of need.[1]

[1] D. iii. 204.

8. **Bhāradvāja.**—A Pacceka Buddha.[1]

[1] M. iii. 70.

Bhāradvāja Sutta.—**Udena** visits **Piṇḍola-Bhāradvāja** at the **Ghositārāma** and asks how it is that young men in their prime should leave the world and yet live to the full the righteous life. Piṇḍola answers that these young men regard all women as mothers, sisters, or daughters. They regard the body as full of manifold impurities, and abide watchful over the doors of the senses. Udena is pleased with the explanation and accepts the Buddha's teaching.[1]

[1] S. iv. 110 f.

Bhāvaseṭṭhi.—A previous birth of **Bijaka** (2).[1]

[1] J. vi. 228.

1. **Bhāvāna Sutta.**—A monk may wish to be free from the *āsavas* and from attachment, but his wish will be fruitless unless he develops the four *satipaṭṭhānas*, the four *sammappadhānas*, the four *iddhipādas*, the five *indriyas*, the five powers, the seven *bojjhaṅgas*, and the Eightfold Noble Path. Without these he resembles one who waits for eggs to hatch out when there is no hen. But if the monk develops these qualities he will wear away the *āsavas*, etc., and be aware that they are worn away, like a carpenter who knows when the handle of his adze is worn away; all these things will weaken and rot away like a ship out of the water all the winter, exposed to wind and rain.[1]

[1] A. iv. 125 f.

2. **Bhāvanā Sutta.**—The four *satipaṭṭhānas*, if cultivated, conduce to the state in which no further and no hither shore exist.[1]

[1] S. v. 180.

3. **Bhāvanā Sutta.**—The cultivation of the four *satipaṭṭhānas* consists in contemplation of body, feelings, mind, and mind states.[1]

[1] S. v. 182.

4. **Bhāvanā Sutta.**—On psychic (*iddhi-*) power, its basis, its cultivation, and the practice which leads to its cultivation.[1]

[1] S. v. 276.

1. **Bhāvitatta.**—One of the two chief disciples of **Sumana Buddha.**[1] He was the purohita in Sumana's city of birth, and was one of those to whom Sumana preached his first sermon.[1]

[1] J. i. 34; Bu. v. 26. [2] BuA. 126.

2. **Bhāvitatta.**—A king who heard **Paduma Buddha** preach, and became a monk with a retinue of one hundred thousand crores.[1]

[1] BuA. 148.

3. **Bhāvitatta.**—The name of two Pacceka Buddhas.[1]

[1] M. iii. 69.

Bhikkhaka Sutta.—A mendicant brahmin of **Sāvatthi** asks the Buddha if there be any difference between the Buddha and himself, they both being mendicants. Mere mendicancy does not make a "*bhikkhu,*" answers the Buddha; the true *bhikkhu* is he who has cast out all wickedness.[1]

[1] S. i. 182.

Bhikkhadāyaka Thera.—An arahant. Ninety-four kappas ago he gave a spoonful of food to **Siddhattha Buddha.** Eighty-seven kappas ago he was king seven times under the name of **Mahāreṇu.**[1] He is probably identical with **Godhika Thera.**[2]

[1] Ap. i. 140. [2] ThagA. i. 124.

Bhikkhadāyī.—See **Bhikkhudāsī.**

Bhikkhādāyaka.—Once a man of **Rājagaha** had just sat down to eat when he saw a monk, who had travelled far, standing outside his house. He emptied his food into the monk's bowl. When he died he was reborn in **Tāvatiṃsa** in a golden palace twelve yojanas in height.[1]

[1] Vv. vi. 6; VvA. 292 f.

1. **Bhikkhādāyikā.**—A woman of **Uttaramadhurā.** The Buddha visited that city for her special benefit. Seeing him as she was returning from her bath, she invited him to her house and gave him a meal. She died soon after and was reborn in **Tāvātiṃsa,** where **Moggallāna** saw her and learnt her story.[1]

[1] Vv. ii. 10; VvA. 118 f.

2. **Bhikkhādāyikā.**—A similar story of a woman of **Rājagaha** who gave alms to an arahant monk and was reborn in **Tāvatiṃsa.**[1]

[1] Vv. ii. 11; VvA. 119 f.

Bhikkhāparampara Jātaka (No. 496).—Once **Brahmadatta,** king of Benares, travelled about his kingdom in disguise seeking for some one who would tell him of a fault possessed by him. One day, in a frontier village, a very rich landowner saw him, and, pleased with his appearance, brought him a very luxurious meal. The king took the food and passed it to his chaplain; the latter gave it to an ascetic who happened to be by. The ascetic placed it in the bowl of a Pacceka Buddha sitting near them. The Pacceka Buddha proceeded, without a word, to eat the meal. The landowner was astonished and asked them the reason for their action, and, on learning that each one was progressively greater in virtue than the king, he rejoiced greatly.

The story was told in reference to a landowner of **Sāvatthi,** a devout follower of the Buddha. Being anxious to honour the Dhamma also, he consulted the Buddha, and, acting on his advice, invited **Ānanda** to his house and gave him choice food and three costly robes. Ānanda took them and offered them to **Sāriputta,** who, in his turn, made a gift of them to the Buddha.

Ānanda was the king of the story, Sāriputta the chaplain, while the ascetic was the Bodhisatta.[1]

[1] J. iv. 369 ff.

1. **Bhikkhu Vagga.**—The seventh section of the **Majjhima Nikāya,** containing suttas 61-70.

2. **Bhikkhu Vagga.**—The twenty-fifth section of the **Dhammapada.**

Bhikkhu Vibhaṅga.—The first division of the Sutta Vibhaṅga of the Vinaya Piṭaka. It is also called the **Mahā Vibhaṅga.**

Bhikkhu Saṃyutta.—The twenty-first section of the Saṃyutta Nikāya.[1]

[1] S. ii. 273-86.

1. **Bhikkhu Sutta.**—Gains, favours and flattery are a danger even to an arahant unless the freedom of his will is unshakable.[1]

[1] S. ii. 238.

2. **Bhikkhu Sutta.**—Once **Moggallāna** and **Lakkhaṇa** saw a bhikkhu, born as a peta, going through the air, his body, robes, etc., on fire. He had been a sinful monk in the time of **Kassapa Buddha.**[1]

[1] S. ii. 260.

3. **Bhikkhu Sutta.**—A monk asks for a teaching in brief and the Buddha tells him that that for which a monk has bias, by that is he reckoned (*i.e.*, he has to give up all bias). The monk dwells in solitude, reflecting on this, and becomes an arahant.[1]

[1] S. iii. 34 f.

4. **Bhikkhu Sutta.**—Ignorance consists in ignorance of the nature of the body, its arising, its cessation and the way thereto; wisdom is wisdom with regard to these things. The same with the other khandhas.[1]

[1] S. iii. 162 f.

5. **Bhikkhu Sutta.**—The Buddha agrees with a group of monks that if when questioned by other sectarians as to the object of their holiness, they answer that it is the full knowledge of *dukkha*, their answer is right; he proceeds to tell them what should be their answer if questioned as to what is *dukkha*.[1]

[1] S. iv. 50 f.

6. **Bhikkhu Sutta.**—The Buddha tells a monk about feelings, their arising and cause, their cessation and the way thereto, etc.[1]

[1] S. iv. 232.

7. **Bhikkhu Sutta.**—A monk asks for a teaching in brief, and the Buddha tells him that he must have truly pure virtue and straight view. Standing on sure virtue, he should cultivate the four *satipaṭṭhānas*; thus will he reach his goal. The monk follows this teaching and becomes an arahant.[1]

[1] S. v. 142 f.

8. **Bhikku Sutta.**—It is by cultivating the four *iddhipādas* that a monk destroys the *āsavas*.[1]

S. v. 284.

9. **Bhikkhu Sutta.**—See **Bhaya Sutta** (6).

10. **Bhikkhu Sutta.**—The Buddha tells the monks at **Gijjhakūṭa** of seven things, the maintenance of which among the monks will conduce to their progress and save them from desire.[1]

[1] A. iv. 216.

11. **Bhikkhu Sutta.**—See also **Bhikkhū Sutta.**

Bhikkhudāsikā, Bhikkhadāyikā.—The fourth of the seven daughters of **Kikī,** king of Benares, in the time of **Kassapa Buddha.** She lived in celibacy for twenty thousand years and erected a building for the use of the monks. She was a previous birth of **Bhaddā Kuṇḍalakesā.**[1]

[1] Ap. ii. 561; ThigA. 104; J. vi. 481, however, says she was **Gotamā** (**Pajāpatī Gotamī**).

1. **" Bhikkhunā " Sutta.**—In the Buddha's method of explaining Dhamma, there feelings are divided into various categories of 2, 3, 5, 6, 18, 30, 108, etc.[1]

[1] S. iv. 228.

2. **" Bhikkhunā " Sutta.**—Same as **Bhikkhu Sutta** (6).

Bhikkhuṇī.—The third of the seven daughters of **Kikī** (*q.v.*), king of Benares. She was a previous birth of **Paṭācārā.**[1]

[1] *E.g.*, Ap. ii. 546, 561; ThigA. 114; but see J. vi. 481, where bhikkhuṇī is given as a common noun. I am inclined to think that this latter reading is wrong.

Bhikkhuṇī Vibhaṅga.—The second section of the **Sutta Vibhaṅga** of the Vinaya Piṭaka, also called **Cūla-Vibhaṅga.**

Bhikkhuṇī Saṃyutta.—The fifth section of the **Saṃyutta Nikāya.**[1]

[1] S. i. 128-35.

1. **Bhikkhuṇī Sutta.**—The same as **Bhikkhu Sutta** (2), substituting " nun" for " monk."[1]

[1] S. ii. 261.

2. **Bhikkuṇī Sutta.**—Once a nun, being enamoured of **Ānanda,** sent a message asking him to visit her, saying that she was ill. Ānanda came and preached to her on the body, how food should be taken only to sustain it, how craving for food should be abandoned together with pride and desire for sexual relations. The nun was overcome with shame at her intended deception and, falling at Ānanda's feet, begged his forgiveness.[1]

[1] A. ii. 144 f.

Bhikkhuṇī-khandhaka.—The tenth section of the **Culla Vagga** of the Vinaya Piṭaka.

Bhikkhuṇīvāsaka Sutta.—**Ānanda** visits a settlement of nuns at **Sāvatthi** and is told that the nuns who have cultivated the four *satipaṭṭhānas* have attained to greater excellence of comprehension than before. Ānanda says that is how it should be. Later, he visits the Buddha and reports to him the incident. The Buddha tells him how to develop the *satipaṭṭhānas* and of the advantages resulting therefrom. The sutta ends with an exhortation to earnestness and diligence. There are plenty of places suitable for meditation, one should not therefore be remiss with regard to this.[1]

[1] S. v. 154 f.

Bhikkhupāṭimokkha.—See **Anumāna Sutta.**

1. **Bhikkhū Sutta.**—A monk who knows decay and death, birth, becoming, grasping, craving, etc., their arising, their cessation and the way thereto—such a monk stands knocking at the door of Deathlessness.[1]

[1] S. ii. 43.

2. **Bhukkhū Sutta.**—Whatever monks have destroyed the *āsavas* by personal knowledge and insight, have done so by cultivating and developing the four *iddhipādas.* It is the same for the past, present and future.[1]

[1] S. v. 257.

3. **Bhikkhū Sutta.**—The Buddha explains to a group of monks psychic power and its cultivation.[1]

[1] S. v. 287.

4. **Bhukkhū Sutta.**—The Buddha tells a group of monks about the seven *bojjhaṅgas* and their cultivation.[1]

[1] S. v. 334 f.

5. **Bhikkhū or Suddhika Sutta.**—Four conditions, the possession of which makes of a disciple a *sotāpanna.*[1]

[1] S. v. 403.

Bhinnālavanagāma.—A village in **Rohaṇa,** mentioned in the account of the campaigns of **Parakkamabāhu I.**[1]

[1] Cv. lxxv. 97.

Bhinnorudīpa.—A monastery in Ceylon built by **Aggabodhi I.** for the Elder (probably **Dāṭhāsiva**) who was living in the **Mahāpariveṇa.** The revenue from **Vaṭṭākārapiṭṭhi** was given for its maintenance.[1]

[1] Cv. xlii. 26.

Bhiyya.—One of the chief lay patrons of **Paduma Buddha.**[1]

[1] Bu. ix. 23.

Bhiyyasa (Bhīya).—One of the two chief disciples of **Koṇāgamana Buddha.**[1] He was a royal prince, and the Buddha preached to him and to his companion, **Uttara,** together with their thirty thousand followers, at **Sundaravatī.**[2]

[1] J. i. 43; Bu. xxiv. 22; D. ii. 5, etc. [2] BuA. 215.

Bhīma.—The name of a celestial musician or a musical instrument.[1]

[1] VvA. 93, 96, 211, 372.

Bhīruka Jātaka.—See **Pañcagaru Jātaka.**

Bhillivāna-vihāra.—A monastery in Ceylon built by **Dhātusena.**[1]

[1] Cv. xxxviii. 50.

Bhisa.—A king of three kappas ago, a previous birth of **Bhisāluvadāyaka.**[1]

[1] Ap. i. 120.

Bhisa Jātaka (No. 488).—Once the Bodhisatta was born into a family which had eighty crores. He was called **Mahā Kañcana** and had six younger brothers (the eldest of them being **Upakañcana**) and a sister, **Kañcanadevī**. None of them would marry, and, on the death of their parents, they distributed their wealth, and, together with a servant man and maid, they went into the **Himālaya** and became ascetics, gathering wild fruits for food. Later, they agreed that Mahā Kañcana, Kañcanadevī and the maid should be spared the task of collecting fruit and that the others should do this in turn. Each day the fruits collected were divided into lots and the gong was sounded. The ascetics would then come one by one and take each his or her share. By the glory of their virtues, **Sakka's** throne trembled. In order to test them, for three days in succession he caused Mahā Kañcana's share to disappear. On the third day, Mahā Kañcana summoned the others and asked the reason for this. Each protested his innocence and swore an oath that heavy curses should attend them if any were guilty of stealing so much as a lotus-stalk (*bhisa*). In each case punishment was to be that in their next birth they should have lands, possessions and other encumbrances—which, from an ascetic's point of view, would be a grievous thing. At this gathering were also present the chief deity of the forest, an elephant escaped from a stake, a monkey who had once belonged to a snake-charmer, and Sakka, who remained invisible. At the end of their protestations of innocence, Sakka inquired of Mahā Kañcana why they all so dreaded possessions; on hearing the explanation, he was greatly moved and asked pardon of the ascetics for his trick.

The story was related in the same circumstances as the **Kusa Jātaka** (*q.v.*).

Sāriputta, Moggallāna, Puṇṇa, Kassapa, Anuruddha and **Ānanda** were the Bodhisatta's brothers, **Uppalavaṇṇā** the sister, **Khujjuttarā** the maid, **Citta-gahapati** the servant, **Sātāgiri** the forest deity, **Pārileyya** the elephant, **Madhuvāseṭṭha** the monkey and **Kāludāyi**, Sakka.[1]

The **Bhisacariyā** is included in the **Cariyā-Piṭaka**,[2] and the story is also found in the Jātakamālā.[3]

[1] J. iv. 304-14. [2] iii. 4. [3] No. 19.

1. **Bhisadāyaka Thera.**—An arahant. In the past, while gathering lotus-stalks for food, he saw **Padumuttara Buddha** travelling through the air and asked him to accept some stalks. The Buddha did so. Soon after, the man was struck by lightning and reborn in **Tusita.**[1]

He is probably identical with **Bhaddaji Thera.**[2]

[1] Ap. ii. 420 f. [2] ThagA. i. 286.

2. **Bhisadāyaka Thera.**—An arahant. Thirty-one kappas ago he was an elephant, and seeing **Vessabhū Buddha** in the forest, he gave him lotus-stalks to eat. Thirteen kappas ago he was born sixteen times as king under the name of **Samodhāna.**[1]

[1] Ap. i. 114.

Bhisapuppha Jātaka (No. 392).—The Bodhisatta was born once as an ascetic, and one day a goddess, having seen him smell a lotus in bloom, upbraided him, telling him he was a thief to smell a lotus which did not belong to him. Near by was a man digging up lotus plants for their fibres, but to him the goddess said nothing. When questioned, her answer was that in a man like the Bodhisatta, seeking for purity, a sin even as large as a hair-tip showed like a dark cloud in the sky. The Bodhisatta, greatly impressed, thanked her.

The goddess is identified with **Uppalavaṇṇā.**

The story was told in reference to a monk who was upbraided by a deity in a forest tract in **Kosala** for smelling a lotus. In great agitation, he went and consulted the Buddha, who told him the above story.[1]

[1] J. iv. 307 ff.

Bhisamuḷāladāyaka Thera.—An arahant. Ninety-two kappas ago he met **Phussa Buddha** alone in the forest and gave him lotus-stalks and petals.[1]

[1] Ap. i. 286 f.

Bhisāluvadāyaka Thera.—An arahant. Ninety-one kappas ago he gave some lotus-stalks and water to **Vipassī Buddha.** Three kappas ago he was a king named **Bhisa.**[1]

[1] Ap. i. 120.

Bhīta Sutta.—The Buddha, in answer to a deva's question, says that if a man be pure in word, deed and thought, has faith, and is generous, he need not fear life in another world.[1]

[1] S. i. 42.

Bhīma.—A sage of old who possessed the five *abhiññā* and great *iddhi*-powers. The Bodhisatta, at that time, was a learned brahmin, and, having met Bhīma, said that he was a sensualist (*kāmabhogī*), and his disciples agreed with him. It was for this reason the Buddha and five hundred monks suffered calumny at the hands of **Sundarikā.**[1]

[1] Ap. i. 299; UdA. 264.

Bhīmatittha-vihāra.—A monastery in the **Pañcayojana** district of Ceylon (the modern Bentoṭa). In the time of **Parakkamabāhu II.** a tooth of **Mahā Kassapa** was enshrined in the vihāra, and the king visited the vihāra and held a three days' festival in honour of the relic.[1]

Kittinissaṅka laid out a garden of fruit trees in the vihāra-precincts, and later **Devappatirāja,** minister of Parakkamabāhu II., laid out, on the king's orders, a great grove of cocopalm, a *yojana* broad, from the vihāra up to **Kālanadītittha.**[2]

[1] Cv. lxxxv. 81. [2] *Ibid.*, lxxxvi. 16, 40, 44.

1. **Bhīmaratha.**—One of the vassal kings of **Daṇḍakī** who sinned against **Kisavaccha.** When Daṇḍakī and his kingdom were destroyed, **Kāliṅga, Aṭṭhaka** and **Bhīmaratha,** in the company of **Sakka,** sought **Sarabhaṅga.** Sarabhaṅga preached to them and they became free from sensuality.[1]

[1] J. v. 135, 137, 149.

2. **Bhīmaratha.**—A king and a city of the same name. **Siddhattha Buddha** preached to the king, and ninety crores of beings understood the Truth.[1]

[1] Bu. xvii. 4; BuA. 186.

3. **Bhīmaratha.**—A king of seventy-seven kappas ago, a previous birth of **Sirivaḍḍha (Kiṅkiṇipupphiya) Thera.**[1]

[1] Ap. i. 204; ThagA. i. 107.

Bhīmarāja.—A **Kāliṅga** prince of **Sīhapura,** brother of **Tilokasundarī.** He came to Ceylon and **Vijayabāhu I.** gave him suitable maintenance.[1]

[1] Cv. lix. 46.

1. **Bhīmasena.**—A weaver; see the **Bhīmasena Jātaka.**

2. **Bhīmasena.**—One of the five **Pāṇḍavas,** sons of King Paṇḍu; he was the husband of **Kaṇhā** (*q.v.*).[1]

[1] J. v. 424, 426.

Bhīmasena Jātaka (No. 80).—The Bodhisatta was once a very skilful archer, educated at **Takkasilā** and famed as **Culla-Dhanuggaha.** He was a crooked little dwarf and, lest he should be refused employment on account of his size, he persuaded a tall, well-built weaver, called **Bhīmasena,** to be his stalking-horse. Bhīmasena went with him to the king of Benares and obtained the post of royal archer. Onee, the kingdom was attacked by a tiger and Bhīmasena was sent to kill it. Following the advice of the Bodhisatta, he went with a large band of country men, and when the tiger was sighted he waited in a thicket and lay flat on his face. When he knew that the tiger had been killed, he came out of the thicket trailing a creeper in his hand and blamed the people, saying that he had meant to lead the tiger like an ox to the king and had gone into the wood to find a creeper for that purpose. "Who has killed the tiger and spoilt all my plans ?" he asked. "I will report all of you to the king." The terrified people bribed him heavily and said no word as to who had killed the tiger. The king, believing that Bhīmasena himself had killed it, rewarded him handsomely. The same thing happened with a buffalo. Bhīmasena grew rich and began to neglect the Bodhisatta. Soon after, a hostile king marched on Benares. Bhīmasena went with a large army riding on an elephant, the Bodhisatta behind him, but at the sight of the battlefield Bhīmasena was so terrified that he fouled the elephant's back. The Bodhisatta taunted him and sent him home, while he himself captured the enemy king and brought him to the king of Benares, who showed him all honour.

The story was related in reference to a monk who, although of low family, used to boast of that family's greatness. The truth was discovered and his pretensions exposed. He is identified with Bhīmasena.[1]

[1] J. i. 355-9.

Bhujaka.—A tree with fragrant wood, found only in **Gandhamādana.**[1]

[1] VvA. 162.

Bhujaṅgadvāra.—One of the gates of **Pulatthipura.**[1]

[1] Cv. lxxiii. 162.

Bhuñjati.—Wife of **Vessavaṇa** and a devout follower of the Buddha. Once, when **Sakka** went to see the Buddha at the **Salalāgāra,** he found the Buddha engaged in meditation, Bhuñjatī waiting on him and worshipping him with clasped hands. Sakka asked her to salute the Buddha in his name when he should awake from his meditation.[1] Buddhaghosa adds[2] that Bhuñjatī had reached the second Fruit of the Path and found no pleasure in the luxuries of heaven.

[1] D. ii. 270 f. [2] DA. iii. 705.

Bhummaja.—One of the **Chabbaggiyā** (*q.v.*). His followers were called **Bhummajakā.**

Bhummā.—A class of devas, earth-bound deities. They belong to the lowest category of devas.[1]

[1] *E.g.*, A. iv. 119.

1. **Bhuvanekabāhu.**—A Sinhalese ruler (*Ādipāda*) who founded a town at **Govindamala** in **Rohaṇa** and dwelt there after **Māgha's** forces had devastated Ceylon.[1]

[1] Cv. lxxxi. 6.

2. **Bhuvanekabāhu.**—The younger son of **Vijayabāhu III.** When **Parakkamabāhu II.** came to the throne, Bhuvanekabāhu was made Yuvarāja. By the king's orders he learnt the Tipiṭaka, in which he became well versed, and later instructed the Theras therein.[1] See also **Bhuvanekabāhu-pariveṇa.**

[1] Cv. lxxxi. 68; lxxxii. 4; lxxxiv. 29.

3. **Bhuvanekabāhu.**—The second of the five sons of **Parakkamabāhu II.** He was entrusted (by Vijayabāhu IV.) with the defence of the north of Ceylon with his headquarters at **Sundarapabbata.** He later built a town there where he settled. When Vijayabāhu died and **Mitta** usurped the throne, Bhuvanekabāhu fled from the capital (**Jambuddoṇi**) and narrowly escaped death on the way. But soon after, the Āriya-soldiers revolted against Mitta and restored Bhuvanekabāhu to the throne, where he ruled for eleven years (1237-84 A.C.) as Bhuvanekabāhu I. Among other acts of piety, he appointed scribes to copy the whole of the Tipiṭaka, and gave copies to the chief vihāras of Ceylon.[1]

[1] Cv. lxxxvii. 16; lxxxviii. 24, 79; xc. 4, 28 ff.

4. **Bhuvanekabāhu.**—Son of **Bhuvanekabāhu I.** He succeeded **Parakkamabāhu III.** and had his capital at **Hatthiselapura.** Every year, in the month of Jeṭṭhamūla, he held a great festival to celebrate his coronation and to admit new members into the Order. He ruled for eleven years (1291-1302 A.C.). [1]

[1] Cv. xc. 59 ff.

5. **Bhuvanekabāhu III.**—Also called **Vanni-Bhuvanekabāhu.** He succeeded **Parakkamabāhu IV.**[1]

[1] Cv. xc. 105.

6. **Bhuvanekabāhu IV.**—He succeeded **Vijayabāhu V.** and ruled at **Gaṅgāsiripura** (*c.* 1346-53 A.C.).[1]

[1] Cv. xc. 107 ff.

7. **Bhuvanekabāhu V.** (1360-91 A.C.).—He reigned at **Jayavaḍḍhanakoṭṭa.** Among other pious acts, he made a very costly casket for the Tooth Relic.[1]

[1] Cv. xci. 9 ff.

8. **Bhuvanekabāhu VI.**—He came to the throne by murdering **Jayabāhu II.** and ruled for seven years (1473-80 A.C.).[1]

[1] Cv. xcii. 1 f.

9. **Bhuvanekabāhu VII.** (1521-50 A.C.).—He succeeded **Vijayabāhu VI.**[1]

[1] Cv. xcii. 4 f.

10. **Bhuvanekabāhu Thera.**—An eminent monk of Ceylon in the fifteenth century. He was the teacher of the author of the **Anāpattidīpanī.**[1]

[1] P.L.C. 247, 254.

Bhuvanekabāhu-pariveṇa.—A monastic building in the **Billaselavihāra** in **Hatthiselapura,** erected by **Bhuvanekabāhu,** younger brother of **Parakkamabāhu II.**[1] Bhuvanekabāhu was cremated there, and **Vijayabāhu IV.** erected a three-storeyed building on the spot, with a Buddha-image. He also set up a statue of Bhuvanekabāhu with all ornaments and gave a maintenance village for the vihāra.[2]

[1] Cv. lxxxv. 59. [2] *Ibid.*, lxxxviii. 54 ff.

Bhusāgāra.—The threshing floor in **Ātumā** where the Buddha stayed on his visit there.[1] Once while he was meditating there, a thunderstorm

[1] Vin. i. 249.

broke out and two peasants and four oxen were killed near him, but so wrapt in thought was he that he knew nothing of it.[2]

[2] D. ii. 131 f.

1. **Bhūta Thera.**— The son of a very wealthy councillor of **Sāketa,** his last and only child, the others having been devoured by a Yakkha. The child was, therefore, well guarded at his birth, but the Yakkha had meanwhile gone to wait on **Vessavaṇa** and had not returned. The boy was called Bhūta so that non-humans might protect him. He grew up in great luxury, but, like **Yasa,** having heard the Buddha preach at **Sāketa,** he entered the Order and dwelt on the banks of the **Ajakaraṇī,** where he attained arahantship. Later, when visiting his relations, he stayed in the **Añjanavana.** They besought him to remain there, but this he refused to do.

In the time of **Siddhattha Buddha** he was a brahmin and, seeing the Buddha, he sang his praises in four verses. Fourteen kappas ago he became king four times under the name of **Uggata.**[1]

He is probably identical with **Parappasādaka Thera** of the Apadāna.[2]

[1] Thag. vs. 518-26; ThagA. i. 493 ff. [2] Ap. i. 113 f.

2. **Bhūta.**—An officer of **Parakkamabāhu I.** He bore the title **Bhaṇḍārapotthakī,** and later came to be called **Adhikārī.**[1]

[1] Cv. lxxii. 196; lxxiv. 72, 119, 136; lxxv. 196.

3. **Bhūta.**—The son of a householder of **Sāvatthi,** his mother being **Tissā** and his step-mother **Mattā** (*q.v.*).[1]

[1] PvA. 82.

Bhūtagana.—A mountain near **Himavā.**[1]

[1] Ap. i. 179; ThagA. i. 215.

Bhūta-pariveṇa.—A monastic building erected by **Aggabodhi VIII.**[1] It was probably attached to the **Bhūtārāma** (*q.v.*).

[1] Cv. xlix. 46.

1. **Bhūtapāla.**—An example of one who possessed *ñāṇavipphāra-iddhi.*[1] He was the child of a poor man of **Rājagaha,** and went one day with his father in a cart to the forest to collect firewood. By the time they returned to the town-gate, evening had fallen. The cart was halted awhile, and the oxen, having got free from the yoke, entered the town. Telling the child to sit near the cart, the father set off after the oxen. Before he could return, the gate was shut, and the child owed his escape during the night from wild beasts and demons to his *ñāṇavipphāra-iddhi.*[1]

[1] PS. ii. 211.

Although the place where he slept was near to a cemetery, no evil spirit could harm the boy as that birth was destined to be his last. He later joined the Order and became an arahant, being famed as Bhūtapāla Thera.[2]

[2] PSA. 493 f.; Vsm. 379 f.

2. **Bhūtapāla.**—The Vibhaṅga Commentary[1] in explaining the term *kāsāvapajjota* says that it means "resplendent with the colour of orange, completely (*ekobhāsinī*) like the family of Bhūtapālaseṭṭhi" (*Bhūtapālaseṭṭhikulasadisānī*).[1]

[1] VibhA. 342; see also **Bhūtavālika.**

Bhūtamaṅgalagāma.—A village in the **Coḷa** country in South India. **Buddhadatta** lived there in a monastery built by **Veṇhudāsa.**[1]

[1] P.L.C. 107.

Bhūtavālika.—A seṭṭhiputta, held up as an example of a devout follower of the Buddha.[1] He is probably identical with **Bhūtapālaseṭṭhi.**

[1] AA. i. 335.

Bhūmicāla Vagga.—The seventh chapter of the Aṭṭhaka Nipāta of the Aṅguttara Nikāya.[1]

[1] A. iv. 293-313.

Bhūmicāla Sutta.—It records the incident, at the **Cāpāla-cetiya** in **Vesāli,** of the Buddha giving **Ānanda** a last chance of asking him to prolong his life. When Ānanda fails to take advantage of this opportunity, the Buddha announces to **Māra,** who asks him to finish his life, that he will die at the end of three months. At this announcement there was a great earthquake, the reason for which Ānanda enquires of the Buddha, who enlightens him.[1]

[1] A. iv. 308 ff.; D. ii. 102 f.; S. v. 259; Ud. vi. 1.

Bhūmija Thera.—Uncle of Prince **Jayasena.** He was a friend of **Sambhuta** (*q.v.*), and, when the latter left the household, he was accompanied by his friends **Bhūmija, Jeyyasena** and **Abhirādhana,** all of whom joined the Order.[1] See **Bhūmija Sutta.**

[1] M. iii. 138 ff.

Bhūmija Sutta.—**Bhūmija** once went to the house of his nephew **Jayasena** in **Rājagaha.** Jayasena questioned him about the Buddha's teaching, and, pleased with what he heard, entertained Bhūmija to a meal. Bhūmija reported this to the Buddha, who approved of what he had said to Jayasena and further developed the theme. Right outlook is absolutely essential to the winning of the fruits of the higher life; it is just as impossible to get oil out of sand or milk from a cow's horn as it is to obtain the fruits of higher life with a wrong outlook.[1]

[1] M. iii. 138 ff.

Bhūmiya. A king of fifteen kappas ago; a previous birth of Nāgasamāla.[1]

[1] Ap. i. 119.

Bhūri Sutta. Four conditions which, if developed, lead to extensive insight.[1]

[1] S. v. 412.

Bhūridatta.—The Bodhisatta born as the son of the Nāga king, **Dhataraṭṭha.** See the **Bhūridatta Jātaka.**

Bhūridatta Jātaka (No. 543).—Prince **Brahmadatta,** son of the king of Benares, lived on the banks of the **Yamunā,** exiled from his father's kingdom. He wore the garb of an ascetic, but his heart was not in the ascetic life, and, when a Nāga-maiden tried to seduce him, he easily succumbed. Their children were **Sāgara-Brahmadatta** and **Samuddajā.** When the king of Benares died, Brahmadatta returned with his children to the kingdom and his Nāga wife returned to the Nāga-world. While playing about in a lake specially prepared for them, the children of Brahmadatta discovered a tortoise, **Cittacūla,** and were much frightened. Cittacūla was brought before the king and was ordered to be cast into the Yamunā, that being the direst penalty the king could envisage. Caught in a whirlpool, Cittacūla was carried to the realm of the Nāga-king **Dhataraṭṭha,** and, when questioned, had the presence of mind to say that he had been sent from Benares to propose a marriage between Dhataraṭṭha and Samuddajā. Nāga messengers were sent to the Benares court to make arrangements, and they laid their proposal before the king. Cittacūla had meanwhile spirited himself away. Brahmadatta was horrified at the proposals of the messengers, and did not fail to say so, whereupon Dhataraṭṭha was so incensed at the insult offered to him that he laid siege to Benares with his Nāga hosts. To avert the total destruction of the city, Samuddajā was given to Dhataraṭṭha, with whom she dwelt for a long time without discovering that she was in the Nāga-world, everyone, at the king's orders, having assumed human form. Samuddajā had four children—**Sudassana, Datta, Subhaga** and **Ariṭṭha (Kāṇāriṭṭha)**—and one step-daughter, **Accimukhī.** Datta, who was the Bodhisatta, used to visit **Virūpakkha,** the ruler of the Nāga hosts, and one day went with him to pay homage to **Sakka.** In the assembly a question arose which only Datta could answer, and Sakka was so pleased with him that he gave him the name of **Bhūridatta** (wise Datta). Anxious to be born in Sakka's company, Bhūridatta took the vows and observed the fast, lying on the top of an ant-hill. At the end of the fast, Nāga maidens would come and take him back.

One day a brahmin villager and his son, **Somadatta,** went hunting in the forest and spent the night on a banyan tree near where Bhūridatta lay. At dawn, these two saw the Nāga maidens come for Bhūridatta and witnessed their song and dance, which Bhūridatta, having laid aside his snake-form, much enjoyed. Discovering the presence of the villagers, Bhūridatta entered into conversation with them, and invited them to the Nāga-world, where they passed a whole year, enjoying great luxury. Owing to lack of merit, the villagers grew discontented and wished to return to the world of men on the pretext that they wished to become ascetics. Bhūridatta offered them a wish-conferring jewel, but this they refused, saying that they had no use for it. Once in the world of men, Somadatta and his father took off their ornaments to bathe, but these divine ornaments disappeared to the Nāga-world.

Some time later, while father and son were wandering about in the forest, having returned from stalking deer, they met a brahmin called **Ālambāyana,** who possessed a Nāga jewel. He was a poor man of Benares who had fled into the forest to escape his creditors. There he had met an ascetic, **Kosiya,** to whom a Garuḍa king had taught the Ālambāyana spell which was potent to tame Nāgas. The Garuḍa had torn up a banyan-tree which shaded the ascetic's walk. A Nāga, which the Garuḍa had seized, coiled itself round the tree, but the Garuḍa carried the tree with the Nāga on it. When he discovered that he had done the ascetic an injury in pulling up the tree, he felt repentant and taught the ascetic the Ālambāyana spell by way of atonement. The ascetic, in turn, taught it to the poor brahmin, hoping it would help him. The brahmin, now called Ālambāyana, left the ascetic and, while wandering about, came across some Nāgas, carrying Bhūridatta's jewel. They heard him recite the spell and fled in terror, leaving behind them the jewel, which he picked up.

When Somadatta and his father met the brahmin, they saw the jewel, and the father schemed to steal it. He told Ālambāyana of the difficulties connected with guarding the jewel and of how dangerous it might prove, if not duly honoured. If Ālambāyana would give him the jewel, he would show him the abode of Bhūridatta, whom the brahmin might then capture, making money with his help. When Somadatta realised his father's treachery, he rebuked him and fled from him. Ālambāyana went with the villager and captured Bhūridatta and crushed his bones. Having thus rendered the Nāga helpless. Ālambāyana put him in a basket and travelled about making him dance before large audiences. The jewel, which Ālambāyana gave to the treacherous villager, slipped from the latter's hand and returned to the Nāga-world.

On the day of the capture of Bhūridatta, his mother had a terrifying dream, and later, when Bhūridatta had been absent for a month, she grew very anxious and lamented piteously. A search was instituted—Kāṇāriṭṭha was sent to the deva-world, Subhaga to Himavā, Sudassana and Accimukhī to the world of men. Sudassana went disguised as an ascetic, and Accimukhī, assuming the form of a frog, hid in his matted hair. They found Ālambāyana making ready to give an exhibition of Bhūridatta's dancing before the king of Benares. Sudassana took up his stand at the edge of the crowd, and Bhūridatta, seeing him, went up to him. The crowd retreated in fear. When Bhūridatta was back in his basket, Sudassana challenged Ālambāyana to prove that his magic powers were greater than those of Sudassana. This challenge was accepted, and Sudassana called out to Accimukhī who, uttering the frog's cry, stood on his shoulder, and having spat drops of poison on to his palm, went back into his hair. Saying that the country would be destroyed if the poison fell on the earth, Sudassana had three holes dug, and filled the first with drugs, the second with cowdung, and the third with heavenly medicines. He poured the poison into the first hole; a flame instantly burst out, spread to the second, and, having travelled on to the third, consumed all the medicines and was extinguished. Ālambāyana was standing near the last hole: the heat of the poison smote him, the colour of his skin changed, and he became a leper. Filled with terror, he set the Nāga free. Bhūridatta assumed a radiant form, decked with all ornaments; so did Sudassana and Accimukhī. The king, on discovering that they were the children of Samuddajā, rejoiced greatly and entertained them. Bhūridatta returned to the Nāga-world, the king accompanying him. The king stayed there for some days and then returned to his kingdom.

Subhaga, in the course of his wanderings, came across Somadatta's father, and, on discovering that it was he who had betrayed Bhūridatta, snatched him away into the Nāga-world, after first nearly drowning him in the whirlpools of the Yamunā. Kāṇāriṭṭha, who was guarding the entrance to the room where Bhūridatta lay ill and tired after his experiences, protested against Subhaga's ill-treatment of a brahmin, and described the greatness of the brahmins and the importance of holding sacrifices and of learning the Vedas. The Nāgas, who were listening, were greatly impressed, and Bhūridatta, seeing them in danger of accepting false doctrine, sent for Kāṇāriṭṭha, confuted his arguments, and converted the Nāgas to the right view. Some time after, Bhūridatta, with his retinue, and followed by Dhataraṭṭha, Samuddajā, and their other children, visited his grandfather Brahmadatta, who had become an ascetic. There they met Sāgara-Brahmadatta, now king of Benares, and great was the rejoicing over their reunion. Samuddajā then returned with her family to the Nāga-world, where they lived happily to the end of their days.

The story was related in reference to some laymen of Sāvatthi who kept the fast diligently.

Devadatta is identified with Ālambāyana, **Ānanda** with Somadatta, **Uppalavaṇṇā** with Accimukhī, **Sāriputta** with Sudassana, **Moggallāna** with Subhaga, and **Sunakkhatta** with Kāṇāriṭṭha.[1]

The story of Bhūridatta is found also in the Cariyāpiṭaka[2] as the **Bhūridatta-cariyā,** to illustrate *Sīlapāramitā*. In the fifteenth century **Raṭṭhasāra,** a monk of Ava, wrote a metrical version of the Bhūridatta Jātaka.[3]

[1] J. vi. 157-219. [2] Cyp. ii. 2. [3] Sās. 99.

Bhūripañña.—One hundred and seven kappas ago there were four kings of this name, previous births of **Paccupaṭṭhānasaññaka (Ekūdāniya).**[1]

[1] Ap. i. 153; ThagA. i. 153.

Bhūripañha Jātaka (No. 452).—The name given to a section of the **Mahā Ummagga Jātaka,** which describes how **Mahosadha,** having lost the king's favour, lived with a potter. The deity of the king's parasol put several questions to the king, but his wise men (**Senaka** and others) were unable to answer them. The king then sent messengers with gifts to look for Mahosadha; they found him in the potter's hut and brought him back. The king expressed surprise that Mahosadha should have borne him no resentment. Mahosadha pointed out to him that wise men were incapable of ingratitude or meanness.[1]

[1] J. vi. 372-6.

Bheṇṇākaṭa.—A locality where **Rujā** lived as a castrated goat.[1]

[1] J. vi. 237.

Bherapāsāṇa-vihāra.—A monastery in **Rohaṇa.** A story is told of a man who lived there, named **Uttara.** He once went with some young novices into the forest to fetch grass for the fireplace; he had agreed to carry a certain load and they cheated him into taking a larger one.[1]

[1] AA. i. 442 f.

Bheravāya.—A rock-cave, near **Himavā,** where **Sambula-kaccāna** dwelt in meditation.[1]

[1] ThagA. i. 314.

Bherivāda Jātaka (No. 59).—The Bodhisatta was once a drummer, and having gone one day, with his son, to a great festival where he had earned much money, was returning through a forest infested by robbers. The boy kept on beating the drum, though his father tried to stop him, saying, " Beat it only now and again, as if some great lord were passing by." At first the robbers were scared away, but they soon discovered that the two were alone and robbed them of their money.

The story was told to a self-willed monk who is identified with the youth of the story.[1]

[1] J. i. 283-4.

Bherī.—A female ascetic who was often invited to the palace of King **Videha,** where she heard of the wisdom of **Mahosadha** and wished to meet him. One day she met him on her way to the palace and questioned him by means of dumb signs, to which Mahosadha replied in the same way. Queen **Nandā's** confidantes saw this, and reported to the king that Mahosadha and Bherī were conspiring to kill him. But the king questioned each of the two separately, and, satisfied with their innocence, appointed Mahosadha commander-in-chief.[1] Bherī is identified with **Uppalavaṇṇā.**[2]

[1] J. vi. 467 f. [2] *Ibid.*, 478.

Bheruva.—A city, the residence of **Asayhaseṭṭhi.**[1]

[1] PvA. 112, 118, 119.

Bhesakalā.—A yakkhiṇī. See **Bhesakalāvana.**

Bhesakalāvana.—A grove in the **Bhagga** country. It contained a Deer Park wherein the Buddha stayed, on **Suṃsumāragiri.** Near by was the house in which lived **Nakulapitā** and **Nakhulamātā.**[1] Once, when the Buddha was at Bhesakalāvana, he saw, with his divine eye, **Anuruddha** dwelling in the **Pācīnavaṃsadāya** in the **Ceti** country, and appeared

[1] A. ii. 61; iii. 295; S. iii. 1; iv. 116.

before him to encourage him in his meditations.[2] The palace **Kokanada,** built for Prince **Bodhi,** was in the neighbourhood of the grove.[3]

It was while staying in this grove that **Mahā Moggallāna** was molested by **Māra,** and he preached the **Māratajjanīya Sutta.**[4] **Siṅgālapitā** is said to have retired to Bhesakalāvana for his meditations.[5]

The grove received its name from the fact that its presiding spirit was a yakkhiṇī called **Bhesakalā.**[6]

According to the Buddhavaṃsa Commentary,[7] the Buddha spent the eight *vassa* at Bhesakalāvana. The Divyāvadāna calls it Bhīsanikāvana.[8]

[2] A. iv. 228 ff.; J. iii. 157.
[3] Vin. ii. 127; DhA. iii. 134, etc.
[4] M. i. 332.
[5] ThagA. i. 70.
[6] SA. ii. 181.
[7] BuA. 3.
[8] Dvy. 182.

Bhesajja-anuññāta-bhāṇavāra.—The thirteenth chapter of the sixth Khandaka of the Mahāvagga of the Vinaya Piṭaka.

Bhesajjamañjūsā.—A Pāli medical work written in the time of **Parakkamabāhu II.** by a monk of Ceylon. The author is referred to as **Pañcapariveṇādhipati. Saranaṅkara** wrote a Sinhalese Commentary on it.[1]

[1] Cv. xcvii. 59; Svd. 1265.

Bhesikā.—The barber of **Lohicca** (*q.v.*).[1]

[1] D. i. 224.

Bhokkanta.—A village in the **Dakkhiṇadesa** of Ceylon. Till deserted by its inhabitants,[1] it was the residence of **Sumanā,** wife of **Lakuṇṭaka Atimbara.**[2]

[1] Probably through fear of the Damiḷas.
[2] DhA. iv. 50.

Bhoga Sutta.—The five disadvantages of riches and also the five advantages of the same.[1]

[1] A. iii. 259.

Bhogagāmanagara.—A village in the **Vajji** country, where the Buddha stayed on his last journey, in the **Ānanda-cetiya,** and where he preached a sermon on the four **Mahāpadesā** (the "Great Authorities").[1] From Bhoga he went on to **Pāvā.**[2] Bhoga was one of the places passed by **Bāvarī's** pupils on their way to **Rājagaha.** It lay between Pāvā and **Vesāli.**[3]

[1] D. ii. 124 f.; A. ii. 167 ff.
[2] D. ii. 126.
[3] SN. vs. 1013.

Bhogavatī.—A palace in the Nāga-world, the residence of the Nāga king **Varuṇa,** father of **Irandatī.**[1]

[1] J. vi. 269, 270.

Bhogasaṃhara-petavatthu.—The story of a woman of **Rājagaha** who, having earned money by selling things with false measures, was born in the peta-world.[1]

[1] Pv. iv. 14; PvA. 278 f.

1. **Bhoja.**—A brahmin, one of the eight who read the auspicious marks on the Buddha's body on the fifth day after his birth.[1]

[1] J. i. 56; in the Milinda (p. 236) he is called **Subhoja.**

2. **Bhoja.**—A physician of old.[1]

[1] J. iv. 496, 498.

3. **Bhoja.**—A country. See **Bhojaputta.**

Bhojakagiri.—A vihāra in **Kāliṅga,** built by **Asoka,** at the cost of one crore, for his brother **Tissa (Ekavihārika).**[1]

[1] ThagA. i. 506, 507.

Bhojana Vagga.—The fourth section of the Pācittiya of the Vinaya Piṭaka.[1]

[1] Vin. iv. 69-90.

1. **Bhojana Sutta.**—He who gives food gives four things to the receiver thereof: life, beauty, comfort, and strength.[1]

[1] A. ii. 64.

2. **Bhojana Sutta.**—In giving a meal, the giver gives five things: life, beauty, comfort, strength, and ready understanding (*paṭibhāṇa*), and he himself also becomes a partaker of these things.[1]

[1] A. iii. 42.

Bhojanadāyaka Thera.—An arahant. Thirty-one kappas ago he gave a meal to **Vessabhū Buddha.** Twenty-five kappas ago he was a king named **Amitābha.**[1]

[1] Ap. i. 253.

Bhojanasuddhika.—The Bodhisatta born as the king of Benares. See the **Dūta Jātaka.**[1]

[1] J. ii. 319, 321.

Bhojaputta.—Evidently the name for a resident of the **Bhoja** country. In the Saṃyutta Nikāya[1] the devaputta **Rohitassa** says that he was a Bhojaputta in his previous birth. The Jātakas[2] mention sixteen Bhojaputtā. Bhoja is modern Berar.[3]

[1] S. i. 6 f. [2] J. i. 45; v. 163. [3] Law: Geog. 62.

Bhojājānīya Jātaka (No. 23).—The Bodhisatta was once born as a thoroughbred horse and was made the destrier of the king of Benares. He was given every kind of luxury and was shown all honour. All the king's around coveted the kingdom of Benares, and seven kings encompassed the city. At the suggestion of his ministers, the king sent out a knight on the royal destrier. Mounted on the noble steed, the knight destroyed six camps, when his horse was wounded. He thereupon took it to the gate, loosened its armour, and prepared to arm another horse. But the animal, knowing that no other horse could accomplish what awaited him, insisted on attacking the seventh camp. Then when they brought him back to the king's gate, the king came out to look upon him, and the horse died with a counsel for mercy towards the captive kings.

The story was told in reference to a monk who had given up persevering. **Ānanda** is identified with the king.[1] *Cp.* the **Ājañña Jātaka.**

[1] J. i. 178-81.

M.

Maṃsa Jātaka (No. 315).—The four sons of four rich merchants of Benares were once sitting at the cross-roads, and, seeing a deer-stalker hawking venison in a cart, one of them proposed to get some flesh from him. So he went up to the man and said, "Hi! my man! give me some meat," and the hunter gave him some skin and bone; the second, going up to him addressed him as "Elder Brother" and was given a joint; but the third cajoled him, calling him "Father," and received a savoury piece of meat; while the fourth (the Bodhisatta) addressed him as "Friend," and was given the whole of the rest of the deer, and the meat was conveyed to his house in the man's cart.

The story was related in reference to **Sariputta.** Some monks of **Jetavana,** having taken oil as a purgative, wished for some dainty food. They sent their attendants to beg in the cooks' quarters, but these had to come back empty-handed. Sāriputta met them, and, having heard their story, returned with them to the same street; the people gave him a full measure of dainty fare, which was distributed among the sick monks. Sāriputta is identified with the hunter of the story.[1]

[1] J. iii. 48-51.

Maṃsa Sutta.—Few are those who abstain from accepting gifts of uncooked flesh, many who do not.[1]

[1] S. v. 471.

Makara.—A floodgate in the **Parakkamasāmudda** from which ran the **Gambhīra** Canal.[1]

[1] Cv. lxxix. 40.

Makaraddhaja.—A name for the god Kāma.[1]

[1] Cv. lii. 68.

Makasa Jātaka (No. 44).—Once, in a border village in **Kāsi,** there lived a number of carpenters. One day, one of them, a bald, grey-haired man, was planing some wood when a mosquito settled on his head and stung him. He asked his son who was sitting by to drive it away. The boy raised an axe, and meaning to drive away the mosquito, cleft his father's head in two, killing him. The Bodhisatta, a trader, saw this incident. " Better an enemy with sense than such a friend," said he.

The story was related in reference to some inhabitants of a hamlet in **Magadha** who were worried by mosquitoes when working in the jungle. One day they armed themselves with arrows, and while trying to shoot the mosquitoes, shot each other. The Buddha saw them outside the village greatly disabled because of their folly.[1]

[1] J. i. 246-48.

Makākarañjiya.—A monastery, the residence of the Elder **Mahātissa.**[1]

[1] Vsm. 292.

Makuṭa-cetiya.—A monument erected by **Sakka** on the summit of **Sineru,** enshrining a lock of hair cut off by **Dīpaṅkara** Buddha, when he renounced the world and became a monk.[1]

[1] BuA. 68.

Makuṭabandhana.—A " shrine " of the **Mallas** to the east of **Kusinārā,** where the Buddha's body was cremated.[1] Buddhaghosa explains that the Makuṭabandhana was a Hall in which the Malla-chiefs put on their

[1] D. ii. 160-1.

ornaments on festival days. It was called a *cetiya* because it was decorated (*cittakatatthena pan'esa cetiyaṃ*).[2]

[2] DA. ii. 596; see also Dvy. 201. Hiouen Thsang's description (Beal, *op. cit.*, ii. 37) of the stūpa erected at what is evidently Makuṭabandhana suggests a different explanation. It was there that the Mallas laid aside their diamond maces (? *makuṭa*) and fell prostrate on the ground with grief at the Buddha's death.

Makuṭamutta-sālā.—A hall built in Anurādhapura on the spot where the dancing maidens laid aside their ornaments immediately after the death of **Duṭṭhagāmaṇī.**[1]

[1] Mhv. xxxii. 78; MṬ. 601.

Makulaka.—A vihāra in Ceylon, to the east of **Ariṭṭhapabbata,** built by **Sūratissa.**[1]

[1] Mhv. xxi. 6.

Makkaṭa Jātaka (No. 173).—Once the Bodhisatta was a learned brahmin of **Kāsi,** and, when his wife died, he retired with his son to the **Himālaya,** where they lived the ascetic life. One day during a heavy shower of rain, a monkey, wishing to gain admission to the ascetics' hut, put on the bark dress of a dead ascetic and stood outside the door. The son wished to admit him, but the Bodhisatta recognised the monkey and drove him away. The boy is identified with **Rāhula.**[1]

The circumstances in which the story was related are given in the **Uddāla Jātaka** (*q.v.*).

[1] J. ii. 68 f.

Makkaṭa Sutta.—In certain tracts of the **Himālaya** where monkeys resort, hunters set up traps of pitch to catch the monkeys. Wise monkeys avoid the traps, but the foolish ones handle the pitch and their paws stick in it, one after another, and finally their muzzles, in their struggles to escape. So it is with foolish men who allow their senses to roam in wrong pastures—the objects of the senses.[1]

[1] S. v. 148.

Makkarakaṭa.—A locality in **Avanti. Mahā Kaccāna** once stayed there in a forest hut and was visited by **Lohicca** and his pupils.[1] The Commentary[2] calls Makkarakaṭa a town (*nagara*).

[1] S. iv. 116 f.

[2] SA. iii. 29.

Makkhakudrūsa.—A village in **Rohaṇa,** the residence of **Kitti** and **Loka.**[1]

[1] Cv. lv. 26; lvii. 1, 59.

Makkhali Vagga.—The ninth chapter of the Eka Nipāta of the Aṅguttara Nikāya.[1]

[1] A. i. 33-5.

Makkhali (or Micchādiṭṭhika) Sutta.—A man with perverted view leads many people away from righteousness and plants them in unrighteousness.

There is no other thing so greatly to be blamed as wrong view. Like a fish-trap set at a river mouth is **Makkhali**, existing for the distress and destruction of many beings. He who urges adherence to a doctrine and discipline rightly expounded, he whom he thus urges, and he who, thus urged, walks therein accordingly, all alike beget much merit.[1]

[1] A. i. 33 f.

Makkhali-Gosāla.—One of the six heretical teachers contemporaneous with the Buddha. He held[1] that there is no cause, either ultimate or remote, for the depravity of beings or for their rectitude. The attainment of any given condition or character does not depend either on one's own acts, nor on the acts of another, nor on human effort. There is no such thing as power or energy or human strength or human vigour. All beings (*sattā*), all lives (*pāṇā*), all existent things (*bhūtā*), all living substances (*jīvā*),[2] are bent this way and that by their fate, by the necessary conditions of the class to which they belong, by their individual nature; it is according to their position in one or other of the six classes (*abhijāti*) that they experience ease or pain. There are fourteen hundred thousands of principle genera or species (*pamukhayoniyo*), again six thousand others and again six hundred. There are five hundred kinds of *kamma*—there are sixty-two paths (or modes of conduct), sixty-two periods, six classes among men, eight stages of a prophet's existence (*aṭṭhapurisabhūmi*),[3] forty-nine hundred kinds of occupation, forty-nine hundred Ājīvakas, forty-nine hundred Wanderers (Paribbājakā), forty-nine

[1] D. i. 53 f. **Makkhali, his views and his followers are also referred to at M. i. 231, 238, 483, 516 f.; S. i. 66, 68; iii. 211; iv. 398; A. i. 33 f., 286; iii. 276, 384; also J. i. 493, 509; S. iii. 69 ascribes the first portion of the account of Makkhali's views (as given in D. i. 53)—that there is no cause, no reason for depravity or purity—to Pūraṇa Kassapa. A. i. 286 apparently confounds Makkhali with Ajita Kesakambala, and A. iii. 383 f. represents Pūraṇa Kassapa as though he were a disciple of Makkhali.**

[2] Buddhaghosa (DA. i. 160 ff.) gives details of these four classes showing how they are meant to include all that has life on this earth, from men down to plants. But the explanation is very confused and makes the terms by no means mutually exclusive.

[3] Buddhaghosa gives them as babyhood, playtime, trial time, erect time, learning time, ascetic time, prophet time, and prostrate time, with (very necessary) comments on each.

hundred Nāga abodes (or species), two thousand sentient existences (*vīse indriyasate*), three thousand infernal states, thirty-six celestial, mundane or passionate grades (*rajodhātuyo*), seven classes of animate beings (*saññigabbhā*), or beings with the capacity of generating by means of separate sexes, seven of inanimate production (*asaññigabbhā*), seven of production by grafting (*niganṭhagabbhā*), seven grades of gods, men, devils, great lakes, precipices, dreams. There are eighty-four thousand periods during which both fools and wise alike, wandering in transmigration, shall at last make an end of pain. This cannot be done by virtue, or penance, or righteousness. Ease and pain, measured out as it were with a measure, cannot be altered in the course of transmigration (*saṃsāra*); there can be neither increase nor decrease thereof—both fools and wise alike, wandering in transmigration, exactly for the allotted term, shall then, and then only, make an end of pain.

Makkhali's views as given in the Buddhist books are difficult to understand, the Commentators themselves finding it a hopeless task. He seems to have believed in infinite gradations of existence; in his view, each individual thing has eternal existence, if not individually, at least in type. He evidently had definite conceptions of numerous grades of beings, celestial, infernal and mundane, as also of the infinity of time and the recurrent cycles of existence. He seems to have conceived the world as a system in which everything has a place and a function assigned to it, a system in which chance has no place and which admits of no other cause whatever, of the depravity or purity of beings, but that which is implied in the word Fate or Destiny (*niyati*). All types of things and all species of beings, however, are individually capable of transformation, that is of elevation or degradation in type. His theory of purification through transmigration (*saṃsārasuddhi*) probably meant perfection through transformation (*pariṇatā*)—transformation which implies not only the process of constant change, but also a fixed orderly mode of progression and retrogression. All things must, in course of time, attain perfection.[4] Makkhali's followers are known as the **Ājīvakas** (*q.v.*).

According to the books, the Buddha considered Makkhali as the most dangerous of the heretical teachers: "I know not of any other single person fraught with such loss to many folk, such discomfort, such sorrow to devas and men, as Makkhali, the infatuate."[5] The Buddha also considered his view the meanest—"just as the hair blanket is reckoned the meanest of all woven garments, even so, of all

[4] For a discussion on Makkhali and his doctrines see Barua: *Pre-buddhistic Indian Philosophy*, 297 ff.

[5] A. i. 33.

the teachings of recluses, that of Makkhali is the meanest."[6] Buddhaghosa[7] draws particular distinction between the moral effect of Makkhali's doctrine on the one hand and that of the doctrines of **Pūraṇa Kassapa** and **Ajita** on the other. **Pūraṇa,** by his theory of the passivity of the soul, denied action; Ajita, by his annihilationistic theory denied retribution; whereas Makkhali, by his doctrine of fate or non-causation, denied both action and its result.

Very little is known of the name and the life of Makkhali. The Buddhist records call him Makkhali-Gosāla. Buddhaghosa explains[8] that he was once employed as a servant; one day, while carrying an oil-pot along a muddy road, he slipped and fell through carelessness, although warned thus by his master: "Mā khali," (stumble not)—hence his name. When he found that the oil-pot was broken, he fled; his master chased him and caught him by his garment, but he left it and ran along naked. He was called Gosāla, because he was born in a cow-shed. According to Jaina records,[9] he is called Gosāla Maṅkhaliputta; he was born at Saravana near Sāvatthi, his father's name being Maṅkhali and his mother's Bhaddā. His father was a Maṅkha—*i.e.*, a dealer in pictures—and Gosāla followed this profession until he became a monk.

The philosopher's true name[10] seems to have been Maskarin, the Jaina-Prakrit form of which is Maṅkhali and the Pāli form Makkhali. "Maskarin" is explained by Pāṇini[11] as "one who carries a bamboo staff" (*maskara*). A Maskarin is also known as Ekadaṇḍin. According to Patañjali,[12] the name indicates a School of Wanderers who were called Maskarins, not so much because they carried a bamboo staff as because they denied the freedom of the will. The Maskarins were thus fatalists or determinists.

[6] A. i. 286.
[7] DA. i. 166 f.
[8] *Ibid.*, 143 f.; MA. i. 422.
[9] See, *e.g.*, Uvāsaga-dasāo, p. 1.
[10] Barua, *op. cit.*, 298.
[11] VI. i. 154.
[12] Mahābhāṣya iii. 96.

1. **Makhādeva.**—King, son of **Sāgaradeva,** in the direct line from **Mahāsammata.** He was a great and liberal ruler, and his sons and grandsons, eighty-four thousand in number, reigned in **Mithilā,** the last of them being **Nemiya,** son of **Kalārajanaka.**[1] His dynasty was followed by that of **Okkāka,** so that he is one of the ancestors of the **Sākyans.**[2] See also **Makhādeva Jātaka** and **Makhādeva Sutta.** Makhādeva is identified with the Bodhisatta. In a later birth he became **Nimi** (*q.v.*). *v.l.* **Maghādeva.**

[1] Dpv. iii. 34 f.; Mhv. ii. 10; MṬ. 129; DA. i. 258 calls him the son of **Upacara**; also SNA. i. 352.
[2] DA. i. 258; SNA. i. 352.

2. **Makhādeva.**—A yakkha, identified with **Aṅgulimāla.** For his story see **Sutana Jātaka.**[1]

[1] J. iii. 325 ff.

Makhādeva Jātaka (No. 9).—The Bodhisatta was once born as **Makhādeva,** king of **Mithilā** in **Videha.** For successive periods of eighty-four thousand years each he had respectively amused himself as prince, ruled as viceroy, and reigned as king. He one day asked his barber to tell him as soon as he had any gray hairs. When, many years later, the barber found a gray hair, he pulled it out and laid it on the king's palm as he had been requested. The king had eighty-four thousand years yet to live, but he granted the barber a village yielding one hundred thousand, and, on that very day, gave over the kingdom to his son and renounced the world as though he had seen the King of Death. For eighty-four thousand years he lived as a recluse in the **Makhādeva-ambavana** and was reborn in the Brahma-world. Later, he became once more king of Mithilā under the name of **Nimi,** and in that life, too, he became a recluse.

The barber is identified with **Ānanda** and the son with **Rāhula.** The story was related to some monks who were talking one day about the Buddha's Renunciation.[1]

[1] J. i. 137 ff.; *cp.* M. ii. 74 ff., and J. vi. 95. See Thomas: *op. cit.*, 127.

Makhādeva Sutta.—The Buddha visits the **Makhādeva-ambavana,** and, at a certain spot, smiles. In reply to **Ānanda's** question, he tells him the story of **Makhādeva,** of how he renounced the world when gray hairs appeared on his head and became a recluse, enjoining on his eldest son to do likewise when the time came. Makhādeva developed the four Brahmavihārā and was reborn in the Brahma-world. Eighty-four thousand of his descendants, in unbroken succession, followed the tradition set by him; the last of the kings to do this was **Nimi,** and his virtue having been remarked by the gods of **Tāvatiṃsa, Sakka** invited him there. Nimi accepted the invitation, but later returned to earth to rule righteously and to observe the four fast days in each month. Nimi's son was **Kalārajanaka,** who broke the high tradition and proved the last of the line.

Makhādeva's tradition led only to the Brahma-world, but the teachings of the Buddha lead to Enlightenment and Nibbāna.

Makhādeva is identified with the Buddha.[1]

[1] M. ii. 74 ff.; *cp.* **Makhādeva Jātaka** and **Nimi Jātaka.**

Makhādeva-ambavana.—A mango-grove in **Mithilā** where **Makhādeva** lived in meditation after retiring from household life.[1] This grove existed even in the time of the Buddha, and during his stay there with **Ānanda** he preached the **Makhādeva Sutta.**[2] Buddhaghosa explains[3] that the garden was originally planned by Makhādeva, and that other kings, from time to time, replaced trees which had died.

[1] J. i. 138 f.; vi. 95. [2] M. ii. 74. [3] MA. ii. 732; see also Mtu. iii. 450.

1. **Makhilā.**—A city near the Deer Park at **Isipatana** close to where **Kakusandha Buddha** preached his first sermon.[1]

[1] BuA. 210.

2. **Makhilā.**—One of the two chief women disciples of **Sikhī Buddha.**[1]

[1] J. i. 41; BuA. 204; see also **Akhilā.**

3. **Makhilā.**—One of the chief female lay patrons of **Atthadassī Buddha.**[1]

[1] Bu. xv. 21.

4. **Makhilā.**—Wife of **Sobhita Buddha** in his last lay life; she gave him a meal of milk-rice just before his Enlightenment.[1]

[1] BuA. 137; but Bu (vii. 18) calls her **Samaṅgī.**

Magadha.—One of the four chief kingdoms of India at the time of the Buddha, the others being **Kosala,** the kingdom of the **Vaṃsas** and **Avanti.** Magadha formed one of the sixteen **Mahājanapadas**[1] and had its capital at **Rājagaha** or **Giribbaja** where **Bimbisāra,** and after him **Ajātasattu,** reigned. Later, **Pāṭaliputta** became the capital. By the time of **Bimbisāra, Aṅga,** too, formed a part of Magadha, and he was known as king of Aṅga-Magadha.[2] But prior to that, these were two separate kingdoms, often at war with each other.[3] Several kings of Magadha are mentioned by name in the Jātakas—*e.g.*, **Arindama** and **Duyyodhana.** In one story[4] the Magadha kingdom is said to have been under the suzerainty of Aṅga. In the Buddha's day, Magadha (inclusive of Aṅga) consisted of eighty thousand villages[5] and had a circumference of some three hundred leagues.[6]

Ajātasattu succeeded in annexing Kosala with the help of the **Licchavis,** and he succeeded also in bringing the confederation of the latter under his sway; preliminaries to this struggle are mentioned in the books.[7]

[1] *q.v.*

[2] See, *e.g.*, Vin. i. 27 and ThagA. i. 544, where Bimbisāra sends for **Soṇa Koḷivisa,** a prominent citizen of **Campā,** capital of Aṅga.

[3] *E.g.*, J. iv. 454 f.

[4] J. vi. 272.

[5] Vin. i. 179.

[6] DA. i. 148.

[7] *E.g.*, D. ii. 73 f., 86.

Under Bimbisāra and Ajātasattu, Magadha rose to such political eminence that for several centuries, right down to the time of **Asoka,** the history of Northern India was practically the history of Magadha.[8]

At the time of the Buddha, the kingdom of Magadha was bounded on the east by the river **Campā,**[9] on the south by the Vindhyā Mountains, on the west by the river **Soṇa,** and on the north by the Ganges. The latter river formed the boundary between Magadha and the republican country of the Licchavis, and both the Māgadhas and the Licchavis evidently had equal rights over the river. When the Buddha visited **Vesāli,** Bimbisāra made a road five leagues long, from Rājagaha to the river, and decorated it, and the Licchavis did the same on the other side.[10]

During the early Buddhist period Magadha was an important political and commercial centre, and was visited by people from all parts of Northern India in search of commerce and of learning. The kings of Magadha maintained friendly relations with their neighbours, Bimbisāra and **Pasenadi** marrying each other's sisters. Mention is made of an alliance between **Pukkusāti,**[11] king of **Gandhāra** and Bimbisāra. When **Caṇḍappajjota** of **Ujjeni** was suffering from jaundice, Bimbisāra sent him his own personal physician, **Jīvaka.**[12]

In Magadha was the real birth of Buddhism,[13] and it was from Magadha that it spread after the Third Council. The Buddha's chief disciples, **Sāriputta** and **Moggallāna**, came from Magadha.[14] In Asoka's time the income from the four gates of his capital of Pāṭaliputta was four hundred thousand kahāpaṇas daily, and in the Sabhā, or Council, he would daily receive another hundred thousand kahāpaṇas.[15] The cornfields of Magadha were rich and fertile,[16] and each Magadha field was about one gāvuta in extent.[17]

The names of several places in Magadha occur in the books—*e.g.*, **Ekanālā, Nālakagāma, Senāṇigāma, Khānumata, Andhakavindha, Macala, Mātulā, Ambalaṭṭhikā, Pāṭaligāma, Nālandā** and **Sālindiya.**[18]

Buddhaghosa says[19] that there are many fanciful explanations (*bahudhā*

[8] A list of the kings from Bimbisāra to Asoka is found in Dvy. 369; cp. DA. i. 153; Mbv. 96, 98.

[9] Campā flowed between Aṅga and Magadha; J. iv. 454.

[10] DhA. iii. 439 f.; the Dvy. (p. 55) says that monks going from Sāvatthi to Rājagaha could cross the Ganges in boats kept either by Ajātasattu or by the Licchavis of Vesāli.

[11] See *s.v.*

[12] For details see *s.v.*

[13] See, *e.g.*, the words put in the mouth of **Sahampati** in Vin. i. 5 (*pātur ahosi Magadhesu pubbe dhammo*, etc.).

[14] See *s.v.*

[15] Sp. i. 52.

[16] Thag. vs. 208.

[17] Thus AA. ii. 616 explains the extent of **Kakudha's** body which filled two or three Māgadha village-fields (A. iii. 122).

[18] See *s.v.*

[19] SNA. i. 135 f.

papañcanti) of the word Magadha. One such is that king **Cetiya,** when about to be swallowed up by the earth for having introduced lying into the world, was thus admonished by those standing round—" *Mā gadhaṃ pavisa* ;" another that those who were digging in the earth saw the king, and that he said to them: " *Mā gadhaṃ karotha.*" The real explanation, accepted by Buddhaghosa himself, seems to have been that the country was the residence of a tribe of khattiyas called Magadhā.

The Magadhabhāsā is regarded as the speech of the Āriyans.[20] If children grow up without being taught any language, they will spontaneously use the Magadha language; it is spread all over Niraya, among lower animals, petas, humans and devas.[21]

The people of Aṅga and Magadha were in the habit of holding a great annual sacrifice to Māha Brahmā in which a fire was kindled with sixty cartloads of firewood. They held the view that anything cast into the sacrificial fire would bring a thousandfold reward.[22] Magadha was famous for a special kind of garlic[23] and the Magadha *nāḷa* was a standard of measure.[24]

Magadha is identified with the modern South Behar. See also **Magadhakhetta.**

[20] *E.g.*, Sp. i. 255.
[21] VibhA. 387 f.
[22] SA. i. 269; but it is curious that in Vedic, Brāhmaṇa and Sūtra periods, Magadha was considered as outside the pale of Ariyan and Brahmanical culture, and was therefore looked down upon by Brahmanical writers. But it was the holy land of the Buddhists. See VT. ii. 207; Thomas: *op. cit.*, 13, 96.
[23] Sp. iv. 920.
[24] *E.g.*, AA. i. 101.

Magadhakhetta.—Mention is made in the books of the Magadhakhetta, probably an extensive rice-field which at once caught the eye on account of its terraces. It could be seen from the **Indasāla-guhā.**[1] The contour of the field struck the Buddha's imagination and he asked **Ānanda** to design a robe of the same pattern. Ānanda did this very successfully, and this pattern has been adopted for the robes of members of the Order ever since.[2]

The **Suvaṇṇakakkaṭa Jātaka**[3] mentions a field of one thousand *karīsas* (about eight thousand acres) in a brahmin village called **Sālindiya** to the east of **Rājagaha.** Magadhakhetta may sometimes have been used as another name for **Magadha.**[4]

[1] ThagA. i. 333.
[2] Vin. i. 287.
[3] J. iii. 293; also iv. 277.
[4] See, *e.g.*, AA. i. 126, where **Nālakagāma** is mentioned as having been in Magadhakhetta.

Magga Vagga.—The twentieth section of the **Dhammapada.**

Magga Saṃyutta.—The forty-fifth section of the Saṃyutta Nikāya.[1]

[1] S. v. 1-62.

1. **Magga Sutta.**—The Buddha tells the monks how, as he meditated under the **Ajapāla-nigrodha,** the conviction came to him that the only way to Nibbāna was the cultivation of the four *satipaṭṭhānas.* The Brahmā **Sahampatī** read his thoughts, and, appearing before him, confirmed this view.[1]

[1] S. v. 167 f.; 185 f.

2. **Magga Sutta.**—The Buddha tells the monks how, while yet a Bodhisatta, he discovered the method of cultivation of the *iddhipādas.*[1]

[1] S. v. 281.

3. **Magga Sutta.**—Wrong view, wrong aim, wrong speech and wrong action lead one to purgatory, their opposites to heaven. Likewise with livelihood, effort, mindfulness and concentration.[1]

[1] A. ii. 227.

4. **Magga Sutta.**—The man who has wrong view, aim, speech and action, is censured by the wise.[1]

[1] A. ii. 229.

Maggakathā.—The ninth division of the Mahāvagga of the Patīsambhidāmagga.

Maggasira.—The name of a month.[1]

[1] DA. i. 241.

Maggadattika Thera.—An arahant. He once saw **Atthadassī Buddha** wandering about and scattered flowers in his path. Twenty thousand kappas ago he was king five times under the name of **Pupphachadaniya.**[1]

[1] Ap. i. 189.

Maggadāyaka Thera.—An arahant. Ninety-four kappas ago he saw **Siddhattha Buddha** walking in the forest, and, with basket and hoe, made a path for him. Fifty-seven kappas ago he was a king named **Suppabuddha.**[1] He is probably identical with **Eraka Thera.**[2]

[1] Ap. i. 173. [2] ThagA. i. 193 f.

Maggasaññaka Thera.—An arahant. In the time of **Padumuttara Buddha** he was a devaputta in **Himavā,** and, coming across some monks who had lost their way in the forest, he entertained them and set them on the right road. One hundred and five kappas ago he was king twelve times under the name of Sacakkhu.[1] He is probably identical with **Ekadhammasavaṇiya.**[2]

[1] Ap. i. 152 f.

[2] ThagA. i. 151 f.

"Maggena" Sutta.—The Noble Eightfold Path goes to the Uncompounded (*asaṅkhata*). The Buddha has shown it to his disciples for their welfare.[1]

[1] S. iv. 361.

Magha.—The name **Sakka** bore in a previous birth[1] when he was born as a man in **Macalagāma** in **Magadha.** His story is given in the **Kulāvaka Jātaka** (*q.v.*).[2] Because of his birth as Magha, Sakka came to be known as **Maghavā.** Maghavā was, perhaps, not the personal name of any particular Sakka, but a title of all Sakkas, because the Sakka who was the real Magha is identified with the Bodhisatta,[3] while the Buddha says[4] that the Sakka, who visited him, and whose conversation is recorded in the **Sakkapañha Sutta,** was also known as Maghavā. The title probably originated from the time when Magha became Sakka.

The Saṃyutta Commentary,[5] however, says that Magha was not the Bodhisatta, but that his life was like that of a Bodhisatta (*Bodhisatta-cariyā viyassa cariyā ahosi*); in which case the name Maghavā belongs only to the present Sakka. Magha took upon himself seven vows (*vatapadāni*), which brought him birth as Sakka: to maintain his parents, to revere his elders, to use gentle language, to utter no slander, to be free from avarice, to practise generosity and open-handed liberality and kindness, to speak the truth, to be free from anger.[6]

For this and other titles of Sakka, see *s.v.* **Sakka.**

[1] The usual form of the name is a derivative—*e.g.*, J. vi. 212; he is often called **Maghavā Sujampati**—*e.g.*, J. iii. 146; iv. 403; v. 137, 139; vi. 102, 481, 573; or **Maghavā Sakko**—*e.g.*, J. v. 141; see also Mtu. i. 165, 167 (*sahaśranetro Maghavān va śobhase*) and Mtu. iii. 366 (*Śakro āha : Maghavān ti me āhu manuśyaloke*).

[2] For a slightly different version see DhA. i. 264 ff.

[3] J. i. 207.

[4] S. i. 231; DhA. i. 264; see also n. 1 above.

[5] SA. i. 267; this is supported by the story as given in DA. iii. 710 ff. and DhA. i. 264 ff., where no mention is made of the Bodhisatta.

[6] S. i. 227 f.; SA. i. 267.

Maghavapupphiya Thera.—An arahant. Ninety-one kappas ago he saw the Buddha (? Vipassī) seated in meditation on the banks of the Nammudā, and honoured him by placing a maghava-flower near him.[1]

[1] Ap. i. 240 f.

Maghavā.—See **Magha.**

Maghādeva.—See **Makhādeva.**

Maṅkura.—One of the four ministers of **Milinda** who were sent to fetch **Nāgasena** to the palace.[1]

[1] Mil., p. 29 f.

Maṅkulakārāma.—A monastery in **Sunāparanta** where **Puṇṇa Thera** lived (*q.v.*) and where the Buddha visited him. Near by was a village of merchants where Puṇṇa went for his alms and where lived his brother **Culla-Puṇṇa.** After the merchants had been saved from death by the intervention of Puṇṇa, they gave him a share of the red sandalwood they had obtained in the course of their travels, and with this they built a *maṇḍalamāla* in the vihāra and dedicated it to the Buddha. The Buddha lived there for seven days.[1]

[1] SA. iii. 15 ff.

Maṅkulapabbata.—A locality where the Buddha spent his sixth *vassa.*[1] The reference is perhaps to the **Maṅkulakārāma** (*q.v.*), but there the Buddha is said to have stayed only seven days of the rainy season.

[1] BuA. 3.

Maṅgana.—A locality, probably a monastery in Ceylon, the residence of an arahant, **Khuddaka-Tissa (Kujjaka-Tissa).**[1] The place was five leagues from **Anurādhapura** and was visited by **Saddhātissa.**[2] A **Maṅgana-vihāra** is mentioned among the religious buildings erected by **Dhātusena.**[3] This was probably a restoration of the original.

[1] Mhv. xxxii. 53; J. vi. 30. [2] AA. i. 384. [3] Cv. xxxviii. 48.

1. **Maṅgala.** The third of the twenty-four Buddhas. He was born sixteen asaṅkheyyas and one hundred thousand kappas ago in the Uttaramadhura Park, in the city of **Uttara,** his father being a khattiya named **Uttara** and his mother **Uttarā.** It is said that from the day of her conception, an aura shed its rays night and day from her body, to a distance of eighty hands—hence his name. He surpassed other Buddhas in glory of body. In his last birth as a human being (corresponding to that of **Vessantara** in the case of **Gotama**) he lived with his family as an ascetic. A man-eating yakkha, named **Kharadāṭhika,** took from him his two children and ate them in his presence, " crunching them as though they

were yams," while the blood dripped from his mouth.[1] The Bodhisatta stood firm in his resolve and repented not of his gift to the yakkha, but registered a desire that in future births his body should emit light as bright as the blood which flowed down the yakkha's face. In a previous birth, Maṅgala paid honour to the cetiya of a Buddha by wrapping his body in cloth drenched with oil, setting fire to it and walking round the cetiya throughout the night, carrying on his head a golden bowl filled with scented oil and lighted with one thousand wicks. Not a hair on his body suffered damage.

For nine thousand years Maṅgala lived in the household in three palaces, **Yasavā, Sucimā** and **Sirimā,** with his wife **Yasavatī,** by whom he had one son, **Sīvala.** He left the world on a horse and practised austerities for eight months. Just before his Enlightenment he ate a meal of milk-rice given by a maiden, **Uttarā,** daughter of **Uttarasetṭhi** in **Uttaragāma ;** an Ājīvaka, named **Uttara,** gave him grass for his seat. His Bodhi was a Nāga-tree. After his Enlightenment he lived for ninety thousand years, and for all that time the aura from his body spread throughout the ten thousand world systems, shutting out sun, moon and stars. People knew the times and the seasons by the cries of the birds and the blooming of the flowers.

Maṅgala's first sermon was preached in the **Sirivaruttama** Grove, near **Sirivaḍḍha.** His chief disciples among men were **Sudeva** and **Dhammasena,** and his chief nuns **Sīvalā** and **Asokā. Pālita** was his constant attendant.[2] **Nanda** and **Visākha** were his chief patrons among lay men and **Anulā** and **Sutanā** among lay women. In Maṅgala's time the Bodhisatta was the brahmin **Suruci** (*q.v.*). Maṅgala's body was eighty cubits high; he held three assemblies: the first at the preaching of the Dhammacakka, the second at **Cittanagara,** when he preached to **Sunanda,** king of **Surabhinagara,** and his son **Anurāja,** and the third at **Mekhala** to Sudeva and Dhammasena who later became his chief disciples.

He died in the park of **Vessara,** and a cetiya, thirty leagues high, was erected over his ashes.[3] It is said[4] that all Maṅgala Buddha's personal disciples attained arahantship before their death.

[1] It is probably this incident which is referred to at J. iv. 13.

[2] BuA. (124) calls him Uttara.

[3] Bu. iv. 1 ff.; BuA. 115 ff.; J. i. 30 ff.; the particulars found in Mtu. (i. 248-50) are slightly different.

[4] Bu. iv. 29.

2. **Maṅgala.**—The Bodhisatta born as an ascetic in the time of **Dhammadassī Buddha.**[1]

[1] J. i. 40; but Bu. xvi. 9 says he was then born as Sakka.

3. **Maṅgala.**—The Bodhisatta born as an ascetic in the time of **Siddhattha Buddha.**[1] He was a very rich brahmin of **Surasena,** and later gave away all his wealth and became an ascetic. On one occasion, by his *iddhi*-power, he obtained fruit which grew on the jambu-tree (which gave its name to Jambudīpa) and offered it at the **Surasena-vihāra** to Siddhattha Buddha and ninety crores of monks.[2]

[1] Bu. xvii. 8; M.Ṭ. 62. [2] BuA. 187.

4. **Maṅgala Thera.**—An arahant. He was present at the Foundation-ceremony of the **Mahā Thūpa.**[1] See **Mahāmaṅgala.**

[1] Dpv. xix. 8.

5. **Maṅgala.**—A flood-gate in the **Parakkamasamudda** from which branched off the **Maṅgala-Gaṅgā.**[1]

[1] Cv. lxxix. 45.

6. **Maṅgala.**—A locality in South India mentioned in the account of the campaigns of **Parakkamabāhu.**[1]

[1] Cv. lxxvi. 297.

7. **Maṅgala.**—A tribe of elephants, each of which had the strength of ten million men.[1]

[1] MA. i. 262; AA. ii. 822; BuA. 37, etc.

8. **Maṅgala.**—A monk of Pagan, probably of the fourteenth century, author of a grammatical work called the **Gandhatthi.**[1]

[1] Bode, *op. cit.*, 26.

9. **Maṅgala.**—A Thera of Ceylon, preceptor of **Vedeha.**[1]

[1] P.L.C. 223.

10. **Maṅgala.**—A young man in the time of **Vipassī Buddha,** who came from **Tāvatiṃsa** and held a *mandārava*-flower over the Buddha as he sat meditating. Maṅgala was a previous birth of **Ekamandāriya Thera.**[1]

[1] Ap. i. 286.

11. **Maṅgala.**—A Pacceka Buddha.[1]

[1] M. iii. 70.

Maṅgala Jātaka (No. 87).—The Bodhisatta was once an Udicca-brahmin who, having entered the ascetic life, lived in **Himavā.** He one day visited **Rājagaha,** and the king invited him to stay in the Royal Park. While he was there, a brahmin who believed in omens as shown by clothes (*Dussalakkhaṇa-brāhmaṇa*) found a garment in his chest which had been gnawed by mice, and, fearing disaster, wished to have it thrown out into the charnel-ground. Unwilling to entrust the job to anyone else, he gave the clothes to his son to throw away. The Bodhisatta saw the garment and picked it up in spite of the grave warnings of the old brahmin, saying that no wise man should believe in omens.

The story was told in reference to a superstitious brahmin of Rājagaha who had his clothes thrown away in the manner related above. The Buddha was waiting in the charnel-field and picked up the garments. When the brahmin protested, he related to him the story and preached to him on the folly of paying heed to superstitions. At the end of the sermon, father and son became sotāpannas. The characters in both stories are the same.[1]

[1] J. i. 371 ff.

Maṅgala Vagga.—The fifteenth chapter of the Tika Nipāta of the Aṅguttara Nikāya.[1]

[1] A. i. 292-4.

Maṅgala Sutta.—Preached at **Jetavana** in answer to a question asked by a deva as to which are the auspicious things (*maṅgalāni*) in the world. The sutta describes thirty-seven *maṅgalāni*, including such things as the avoidance of fools, association with the wise, honouring those worthy of honour, etc.[1] The Commentary[2] explains that at the time the sutta was preached there was great discussion over the whole of **Jambudīpa** regarding the constitution of *maṅgala*. The devas heard the discussion and argued among themselves till the matter spread to the highest Brahma-world. Then it was that **Sakka** suggested that a devaputta should visit the Buddha and ask him about it.

In the Sutta Nipāta[3] the sutta is called **Mahāmaṅgala.** It is one of the suttas at the preaching of which countless devas were present and countless beings realized the Truth.[4]

The sutta is often recited, and forms one of the commonest of the **Parittas.** To have it written down in a book is considered an act of great merit.[5] It is said[6] that once **Duṭṭhagāmaṇi** attempted to preach the Maṅgala Sutta at the **Lohapāsāda,** but he was too nervous to proceed. The preaching of the Maṅgala Sutta was one of the incidents of the

[1] Khp. pp. 2 ff.
[2] KhpA. vii.; SNA. i. 300.
[3] SN., pp. 46 f.
[4] SNA. i. 174; BuA. 243; AA. i. 57, 320.
[5] MA. ii. 806.
[6] Mhv. xxxii. 43.

Buddha's life represented in the Relic Chamber of the **Mahā Thūpa.**[7] See also **Mahāmaṅgala Jātaka.**

[7] Mhv. xxx. 83.

Maṅgala-gaṅgā.—A channel branching off from the sluice called Maṅgala in the **Parakkama Samudda.** See **Maṅgala** (5).[1]

[1] Cv. lxxix. 45.

Maṅgalaṅkoṭṭa.—A locality in South India, mentioned in the account of the campaigns of **Parakkamabāhu I.**[1] It is probably identical with **Maṅgala** (6).

[1] Cv. lxxvii. 38.

Maṅgalagiri.—A spot where the Buddha was staying when **Kāḷudāyi** visited him at **Suddhodana's** request.[1]

[1] Ap. ii. 501.

Maṅgalacetiya.—A religious building, probably in **Anurādhapura. Upatissa II.** erected a thūpa to the north of it and also an image house containing an image.[1] It is probably identical with **Bahumaṅgala-cetiya** (*q.v.*).[2]

[1] Cv. xxxvii. 183.   [2] Cv. *Trs.* i. 36; n. 1.

Maṅgaladīpanī.—A commentary on the **Maṅgala Sutta,** written by **Sirimaṅgala** of Laos.[1]

[1] Bode, *op. cit.*, 47.

Maṅgalapabbata.—See **Maṅgalappadesa.**

Maṅgalapāsāda.—A palace in **Kāsika,** erected by **Vissakamma** and inhabited by **Bodhighariya** in a previous birth sixty-five kappas ago.[1]

[1] Ap. ii. 401.

Maṅgalapokkharaṇī.—A bathing-place in the garden of **Parakkama-bāhu I.**[1]

[1] Cv. lxxiii. 110.

Maṅgalappadesa (Maṅgalapabbata).—A place in the south of Ceylon which formed the limit of the estate given to **Sāliya** by **Duṭṭhagāmaṇī.**[1]

[1] MṬ. 607.

Maṅgalabegāma.—A place near **Pulatthipura,** mentioned in the account of the campaigns of **Parakkamabāhu I.**[1]

[1] Cv. lxvii. 52; lxx. 178, 283, 297; lxxii. 160, 207.

Maṅgalavitāna.—A place in the west of Ceylon, near **Vallipāsāna-vihāra.**[1]

[1] MṬ. 552.

Maṅgalāna.—A minister of **Kittisirimegha** (2).[1]

[1] Cv. lxvi. 66; see Cv. *Trs.* i. 258, n. 2.

Macala.—A village in **Magadha,** residence of **Magha**[1] (*q.v.*).

[1] J. i. 199; SA. i. 267; DhA. i. 265; SNA. ii. 484.

Macala Vagga.—The ninth chapter of the Catukka Nipāta of the Aṅguttara Nikāya.[1]

[1] A. ii. 83-91.

1. **Maccha Jātaka** (No. 34).—Some fishermen once cast their net into a river, and a great fish, swimming along, toying amorously with his wife, was caught in the net, while his wife escaped. The fishermen hauled him up and left him on the sand while they proceeded to light a fire and whittle a spit whereon to roast him. The fish lamented, saying how unhappy his wife would be, thinking he had gone off with another. The Bodhisatta, who was the king's priest, coming along to the river to bathe, heard the lament of the fish and obtained his freedom from the fishermen.

The story was related to a passion-tossed monk who longed for the wife of his lay days. The two fish were the monk and his seducer.[1]

[1] J. i. 210-12.

2. **Maccha Jātaka** (No. 75).—Once the Bodhisatta was born as a fish in a pond; there was a great drought, the crops withered, and water gave out in tanks and ponds and there was great distress. Seeing this, the Bodhisatta approached **Pajjuna,** god of rain, and made an Act of Truth, begging for rain. The request succeeded, and heavy rain fell.

The story was told in reference to a great drought in **Kosala.** Even the pond by the gate of **Jetavana** was dry, and the Buddha, touched by the universal suffering, resolved to obtain rain. On his way back from the alms-round, he sent **Ānanda** to fetch the robe in which he bathed. As he was putting this on, **Sakka's** throne was heated, and he ordered Pajjuna to send rain. The god filled himself with clouds, and then bending his face and mouth, deluged all Kosala with torrents of rain. The Pajjuna of the earlier story is identified with **Ānanda.**[1]

[1] J. i. 329-32; *cp.* Cyp. iii. 10.

3. **Maccha Jātaka** (No. 216).—The story very much resembles **Maccha Jātaka** (1).[1]

[1] J. ii. 178 f.

Maccha Sutta.—Once, during a tour in **Kosala** with a large number of monks, the Buddha saw a fisherman selling fish. Sitting down at the foot of a tree by the wayside, the Buddha pointed out to the monks how no fisherman enjoyed a happy life because his mind was for ever engaged in slaughter. It was the same, he said, with those who killed other creatures; those guilty of killing would suffer greatly after death.[1]

[1] A. iii. 301 f.

Macchatittha.—The name of two villages and two monasteries of Ceylon.[1]

[1] Cv. xlviii. 24; Ep. Zey. i. 216, 221, 227.

Macchadāyaka Thera.—An arahant. Ninety-four kappas ago he was a hawk on the banks of the **Candabhāgā** and once gave a large fish to **Siddhattha Buddha.**[1]

[1] Ap. i. 232.

Maccharaṭṭha.—See **Macchā.**

1. **Maccharikosiya.**—A *seṭṭhi*, worth eighty crores, of **Sakkhara** near **Rājagaha.** His real name was **Kosiya,** but as he was too miserly to give away even a drop of oil, he came to be called Maccharikosiya. One day, when returning from the palace, he saw a half-starved yokel eating a round cake filled with sour gruel. The sight made him hungry, but fearing to spend his money, he told no one, but lay on his bed in great distress, till his wife found him. Having discovered the reason for his misery, she said she would bake cakes sufficient for everyone in Sakkhara. "But that would be such extravagance," said Kosiya, and persuaded his wife to bake just one cake, using only broken grains of rice. Fearful lest someone should ask for a piece of his cake, he retired with her to the seventh storey of his house and there made her start the cooking after bolting all the doors.

The Buddha saw him with his divine eye and sent **Moggallāna** to him; Moggallāna stood poised in mid-air just outside Kosiya's window and indicated his wish to have something to eat, but Kosiya blustered and threatened, and, after refusing to give him anything, bade his wife cook another little cake for him. But each cake she baked grew bigger than the previous one, and when she tried to take a single cake from the basket, they all stuck together. In despair, Kosiya presented cakes and basket to the Elder. Moggallāna then preached on the importance of generosity, and transported Kosiya, his wife and the cakes to Jetavana. There the cakes were offered to the Buddha and five hundred monks, and even after they had all eaten, there was no end to the cakes. The spot where the remaining ones were thrown away at the gates of Jetavana was known as **Kapallapūvapabbhāra.** The Buddha preached to Kosiya and his wife and they became sotāpannas. Kosiya then spent all his wealth in the service of the Buddha and his religion. It was in reference to him that the **Illīsa Jātaka** was preached, **Illīsa** being identified with Maccharikosiya.[1]

[1] DhA. i. 367 ff.; J. i. 345 ff.

2. **Maccharikosiya.**—See the **Sudhābodhana Jātaka.**

1. **Maccharī Sutta.**—On the five disadvantages of staying too long in one place—one grudges sharing one's lodging, the families who provide alms, one's provisions, one's fame, or the Dhamma.[1]

[1] A. iii. 258.

2. **Maccharī Sutta.**—A monk who grudges sharing his lodging, the families who provide him with food, the gifts he receives, his fame, and who frustrates gifts offered in faith—such a monk is destined to hell.[1]

[1] A. iii. 266.

3. **Maccharī Sutta.**—The same as the above except that the fifth quality is given as stinginess with regard to Dhamma.[1]

[1] A. iii. 266 f.

4. **Maccharī Sutta.**—The same as (3) except that " nun " is substituted for " monk."[1]

[1] A. iii. 139.

5. **Maccharī Sutta.**—A group of **Satullapa**-devas visit the Buddha at **Jetavana** and four of them speak, each one verse, before him on the evils of avarice and the blessings of generosity. The Buddha utters a verse to the effect that gifts given should be well gotten.[1]

[1] S. i. 18 f.

6. **Maccharī Sutta.**—A deva visits the Buddha and asks him questions as to what kind of person is a miser and what awaits the generous man. The Buddha replies.[1]

[1] S. i. 34.

7. **Maccharī Sutta.**—Seven fetters must be destroyed in order that the good life may be led: complying, resisting, wrong views, uncertainty, conceit, envy, meanness.[1]

[1] A. iv. 8.

8. **Maccharī Sutta.**—The five forms of meanness: in sharing lodgings, the services of a family, gains, fame and Dhamma.[1]

[1] A. iv. 459.

" Maccharena " Sutta.—A woman who is faithless, shameless, stingy, and of weak wisdom, is destined to suffering.[1]

[1] S. iv. 24.

Macchā.—A country, with its people, included in the traditional list of the sixteen **Mahājanapadas.**[1] The Macchā are generally mentioned with the **Sūrasenā.**[2] In the **Vidhura Paṇḍita Jātaka**[3] the Macchā are mentioned among those who witnessed the game of dice between the king of the Kurus and Puṇṇaka.

The Macchā country lay to the south or south-west of Indraprastha and to the south of Sūrasena. Its capital was Virāṭanagara or Vairāṭ, so called because it was the city of King Virāṭa.[4]

[1] A. i. 213; iv. 252, 256, 260.
[2] *E.g.*, D. ii. 200; *cp.* **Kāsikosalā, Vajjimallā.**
[3] J. vi. 280.
[4] Rv. vii. 6, 18; Law: Anct. Geog. of India, p. 19.

Macchikāsaṇḍa.—A township in **Kāsī,** the residence, among others, of **Cittagahapati.**[1] It contained the **Ambāṭakavana,** which Citta presented as a monastery for the monks, at the head of whom was **Mahānāma.**

Sudhamma Thera also lived there, and the place was visited by **Sāriputta** and **Moggallāna**[2] and also by **Acela Kassapa.**[3] The books contain, besides these, the names of several monks who lived at **Macchikāsaṇḍa**—*e.g.*, **Isidatta, Mahaka, Kāmabhū** and **Godatta.**[4] The place

[1] S. iv. 281.
[2] For details see DhA. ii. 74 f.; according to Vin. ii. 15 f., they were accompanied by **Mahākaccāna, Mahākoṭṭhita, Mahākappina, Mahācunda, Anuruddha, Revata, Upāli, Ananda** and **Rāhula**; these all went there while travelling in the Kāsi kingdom.
[3] S. iv. 300.
[4] See *s.v.* for details.

may also have been a centre of the Nigaṇṭhas, for **Nigaṇṭha Nātāputta** is mentioned as having gone there with a large following.[5] It was thirty leagues from **Sāvatthi**,[6] and near by was the village of **Migapathaka** (*q.v.*).

[5] S. iv. 298. [6] DhA. ii. 79.

Macchikāsaṇḍika.—An epithet of **Cittagahapati**, because he lived in **Macchikāsaṇḍa.**[1]

[1] A. i. 26; AA. i. 209; ThagA. i. 238.

Maccutthala.—A locality in **Rohaṇa**, where **Vijayabāhu I.** once set up a camp.[1]

[1] Cv. lviii. 35.

Macchuddāna Jātaka (No. 288).—The Bodhisatta was once the son of a landed proprietor, and, after his father's death, he and his younger brother went to a village to settle some business. On their way back, they had a meal out of a leaf-pottle, and, when they had finished, the Bodhisatta threw the remains into the river for the fish, giving the merit to the river-spirit. The power of the river-spirit increased and she discovered the cause. The younger brother was of a dishonest disposition, and when the elder was asleep, he packed a parcel of gravel to resemble the money they were carrying and put them both away. While they were in mid-river he stumbled against the side of the boat and dropped overboard what he thought to be the parcel of gravel, but what was really the money. He told the Bodhisatta about it who said, "Never mind, what's gone has gone." But the river-spirit out of gratitude to the Bodhisatta made a fish swallow the parcel. The fish was later caught and hawked about, and, owing again to the influence of the spirit, the fisherman asked one thousand pieces and seven annas for it, and the people laughed at what they thought was a joke. But when they came to the Bodhisatta's house, they offered him the fish for seven annas. The fish was bought and cut open by his wife, and the money was given to him. At that instant the river-spirit informed him of what she had done and asked him to have no consideration for his brother, who was a thief and was greatly disappointed at the failure of his trick. But the Bodhisatta sent him five hundred pieces.

The story was told in reference to a dishonest merchant who is identified with the cheat.[1]

[1] J. ii. 423-6.

Majjha.—See **Megha.**

Majjhantika Thera.—An arahant. He recited the *kammavācā* (or ecclesiastical act) at the ordination of **Mahinda,** on whom he later conferred the *upasampadā* ordination.[1] Later, at the conclusion of the Third Council, Majjhantika went as preacher to **Kasmīra-Gandhāra.** There, by his great *iddhi*-powers, he overcame the Nāga-king **Aravāḷa** and converted him to the Faith, while **Paṇḍaka** and his wife **Hāritā** and their five hundred sons became sotāpannas. Majjhantika preached the **Āsīvisopama Sutta** to the assembled concourse and later ordained one hundred thousand persons.[2] The sermon preached by Majjhantika is referred to in the Scholiast to the **Sarabhaṅga Jātaka.**[3]

This same Elder is referred to elsewhere[4] as an example of one who practised *pariyatti-appicchatā.* He was the leader of the assembly of monks (*saṅghathera*). On the day of the dedication of **Asoka's** vihāra, the Thera was a *khīṇāsava* and was present, but his begging bowl and robe were hardly worth a farthing. People, seeing him there, asked him to make way; but he sank into the earth, rising to receive the alms given to the leader of the monks, knowing that he alone was fit to accept it.[5]

1 Mhv. v. 207; Sp. i. 51; Dpv. vii. 24.

2 Mhv. xii. 3, 9 ff.; Sp. i. 64 ff.; Dpv. viii. 4; Mbv. 113; for the Tibetan version see Rockhill, *op. cit.*, 167 ff.

3 J. v. 142.

4 SNA. ii. 494; DA. iii. 1061, but at AA. i. 263 he is called **Majjhantika-Tissa.**

5 The story is given at AA. i. 43; MA. i. 350.

Majjhantika or **Saṇika Sutta.**—Once a monk dwelt in a forest-tract in **Kosala** and was told by a deva of the forest how the noonday silence frightened him. But the monk replied that to him it was enchanting.[1]

1 S. i. 203.

Majjhantika-Tissa.—See **Majjhantika.**

Majjhapalli-vihāra.—A vihāra in Ceylon restored by the monk **Saṅgharakkhita** in the reign of **Kittisirirājasīha.** The king showed the monk great honour and gave the village of **Mālāgāma** for the maintenance of the vihāra.[1]

1 Cv. c. 234. (Sinhalese *Medapola.*)

Majjhavela-vihāra.—A monastery in Ceylon built by **Vaṭṭagāmaṇī** and restored by **Kittisirirājasīha,** who gave for its maintenance the village of **Siṅgatthala.**[1]

1 Cv. c. 230. (Sinhalese *Medavala.*)

Majjhima.—An Arahant. He went, after the Third Council, as preacher to the Himālaya country,[1] accompanied by four others: **Kassapagotta, Durabhissara, Sahadeva,** and **Mūlakadeva.**[2] Majjhima preached the Dhammacakkappavattana Sutta and eighty crores of persons became sotāpannas. The five Elders, separately, converted five kingdoms, and each of them ordained one hundred thousand persons.[3]

[1] Mhv. xii. 6.

[2] Dpv. viii. 10; MṬ. (317) has **Dundubhissara** for **Durabhissara**; Mbv. (115) agrees with MṬ., but has **Sahassadeva**; Sp. (i. 68) gives their names as **Kassapagotta, Ālokadeva, Dundubhissara,** and **Sahadeva.**

[3] Mhv. xii. 41 ff.

Majjhima Nikāya.—The second "book," or collection, of the Sutta Piṭaka, containing discourses of medium length. It consists of eighty *bhāṇavāras* and is divided into three sections of fifty suttas each (*paṇṇāsa*), the last *paṇṇāsa* containing fifty-two suttas. At the First Council the duty of learning the Majjhima Nikāya and of handing it down intact was entrusted to the "school" of **Sāriputta.**[1] **Buddhaghosa** wrote a commentary to the Majjhima Nikāya, which is called the **Papañca-Sūdanī,** and Sāriputta of Ceylon wrote its *ṭīkā.* The Majjhima Nikāya was also called the **Majjhima Saṅgīti.**[2] When the Sāsana disappears, the Majjhima predeceases the Dīgha Nikāya.[3]

[1] DA. i. 15. [2] *E.g.*, MA. i. 2; MṬ. 193, 305. [3] MA. ii. 881.

Majjhima-Kāḷa.—The second of three brothers, all named **Kāḷa,** of Setavyā. **Culla-Kāḷa** and **Mahā-Kāḷa,** the youngest and the oldest, used to travel about with caravans and procure goods which were sold for them by **Majjhima-Kāḷa.**[1] He had four crores.[2]

[1] DhA. i. 66. [2] *Ibid.*, 73.

Majjhimagāma.—A village in **Rohaṇa,** mentioned in the account of the campaigns of **Parakkamabāhu I.**[1]

[1] Cv. lxxiv. 83.

Majjhima-janapada.—See **Majjhimadesa.**

Majjhimaṭīkā.—The second of three Commentaries on the **Saddatthabhedacintā.**[1]

[1] Gv. 63, 73.

Majjhimadesa.—The country of Central India which was the birthplace of Buddhism and the region of its early activities. It extended in the east to the town of **Kajaṅgala,** beyond which was **Mahāsāla;** on the south-east to the river **Salalavatī**; on the south-west to the town of **Satakaṇṇika**; on the west to the brahmin village of **Thūna**; on the north to the **Usīraddhaja** Mountain.[1] The Majjhimadesa was three hundred yojanas in length, two hundred and fifty in breadth, and nine hundred in circumference.[2] It contained fourteen of the sixteen **Mahājanapadas** (*q.v.*), that is to say all but **Gandhāra** and **Kamboja**, which belonged to the **Uttarāpatha**. The people of Majjhimadesa were regarded as wise and virtuous.[3] It was the birthplace of noble men (*purisājanīyā*) including the Buddhas,[4] and all kinds of marvellous things happened there.[5] The people of Majjhimadesa considered peacocks' flesh a luxury.[6]

[1] Vin. i. 197; J. i. 49, 80; Mbv. 12; Dvy. (21 f.) extends the eastern boundary to include Puṇḍavardhana, roughly identical with North Bengal. It is interesting to note that in early Brahminical literature (*e.g.* the Dharmaśūtra of Baudhāyana), Āryāvarta, which is practically identical with what came to be called Madhyadeśa, is described as lying to the east of the region where the Sarasvatī disappears, to the west of the Kāḷakavana, to the north of Pāripātra, and to the south of the Himālaya. This excludes the whole of **Magadha** (*Baudhāyana* i. 1, 2, 9, etc.). It is also noteworthy that in the Commentaries the Majjhimadesa is extended to include the whole of **Jambudīpa**, the other continents being **Paccantima-janapadā**. The term came also to be used in a generic sense. Thus, in Ceylon (**Tambapaṇṇidīpa**) **Anurādhapura** came to be called the Majjhimadesa (AA. i. 165).

[2] DA. i. 173.

[3] J. iii. 115, 116.

[4] DhA. iii. 248; AA. i. 265.

[5] SNA. i. 197.

[6] VibhA. 10.

Majjhimabhāṇakā.—The "reciters" of the **Majjhima Nikāya** (*q.v.*), those who learned it and handed it down, probably the "school" of **Sāriputta.** This "school" included the Cariyāpiṭaka, Apadāna and Buddhavaṃsa in the Khuddaka Nikāya, and ascribed the whole Nikāya to the Sutta Piṭaka.[1]

[1] DA. i. 15; Mil. 341.

Majjhimavagga.—A district in the Malaya country of Ceylon, mentioned in the account of the campaigns of **Parakkamabāhu I.**[1]

[1] Cv. lxx. 20, 21, 23; see Cv. *Trs.* i. 289, n. 1.

Mañcakkuṇḍi.—A locality in South India mentioned in the account of the campaigns of **Parakkamabāhu I.**[1]

[1] Cv. lxxvii. 87.

1. **Mañcadāyaka Thera.**—An arahant. In the time of **Siddhattha Buddha** he was a Caṇḍāla, and made a lintel which he offered to the

Order. He was fifty times king of the gods and eighty times king of men.[1]

[1] Ap. ii. 377 f.

2. **Mañcadāyaka.**—An arahant thera. Ninety-one kappas ago he gave a bed to **Vipassī Buddha.**[1] He is probably identical with **Sāmaññakāni Thera.**[2] *v.l.* **Pecchadāyaka.**

[1] Ap. ii. 455.
[2] ThagA. i. 99.

Mañjarīpūjaka Thera.—An arahant. Ninety-two kappas ago, while walking in the street with a spray of flowers in his hand, he saw the Buddha (? **Tissa**) and offered him the flowers. Seventy-three kappas ago he was a king, named **Jotiya.**[1]

[1] Ap. i. 228.

Mañju.—An officer of **Parakkamabāhu I.** He was sent to fight against **Sūkarabhātu,** and defeated him at **Sāpatagamu.** He was put in charge of the campaign in **Rohaṇa,** his colleagues being **Kitti** and **Bhūta.** Mañju practised great cruelty in order to instil terror into the hearts of the people. He seems to have been replaced by Bhūta.[1]

[1] Cv. lxxiv. 129, 144; lxxv. 150, 152, 185, 196.

Mañjūsaka.—A tree in **Gandhamādana** in front of the **Maṇiguhā.** It is one yojana in height and one in girth, and bears all the flowers which bloom both on land and in water, on earth and in heaven. Around the tree is the **Sabbaratanamāla,** where the **Pacceka Buddhas** hold their assembly. The place of meeting seems also to have been called the **Mañjūsakamāla.**[1]

[1] SNA. i. 66, 67; VvA. 175.

1. **Mañjeṭṭhaka Vagga.**—The fourth section of the **Vimāna Vatthu.**

2. **Mañjeṭṭhaka-vimāna.**—The abode in **Tāvatiṃsa** of a woman who once spread over the Buddha's seat a bouquet of flowers which she had gathered in **Andhavana.**[1]

[1] Vv. iv. 1; VvA. 176 f.

Mañjerika.—The name of the Nāga kingdom (Nāgabhavana). It is five hundred leagues in extent and is the residence of **Mahākāḷa,** the Nāga king.[1] When the urn containing the Buddha's relics, deposited

[1] J. i. 72; J. vi. 264; BuA. 239.

in **Rāmagāma,** was washed away, it was taken to the Mañjerika Nāgabhavana, and remained there till taken by **Soṇuttara** to be enshrined in the **Mahā Thūpa.**[2]

[2] Mhv. xxxi. 27; see also *J.R.A.S.* 1885, p. 220.

Maññamāna Sutta.—One who lets his imagination play on the body, feeling, etc., becomes **Māra's** bondsman.[1]

[1] S. iii. 74.

Maṭṭakuṇḍali, Maṭṭhakuṇḍali.—The only son of the brahmin **Adinnapubbaka.** His father loved him dearly, but was a great miser, and made for him, with his own hands, a pair of burnished ear-rings in order to save the goldsmith's fee; the boy thus came to be called Maṭṭakuṇḍali (burnished ear-rings). When he was sixteen he had an attack of jaundice. His father refused to call in a physician, and prescribed for him himself till the boy was beyond all cure. Then he carried him out and laid him on the terrace, lest those who came to prepare for the funeral should see his wealth.

The Buddha saw Maṭṭakuṇḍali as he lay dying, and, out of compassion, came to the door of his father's house. Too weak to do anything else, the boy conjured up devout faith in the Buddha; he died soon after, and was born among the gods in a golden mansion thirty leagues in extent. When he surveyed his past birth, he saw his father in the charnel-ground, weeping and lamenting and preparing to cremate his body. Assuming the form of Maṭṭakuṇḍali, he went himself to the charnel-ground and, standing near, started to weep. When questioned by Adinnapubbaka, he said he wanted the moon, and in the course of conversation he revealed his identity and censured his father. Adinnapubbaka invited the Buddha to a meal the next day, and, when it was over, asked if it were possible to attain to heaven by a mere act of faith. In order to convince him, the Buddha made Maṭṭakuṇḍali appear before him and confirm his statement that this was so. At the conclusion of the Buddha's sermon, both Adinnapubbaka and Maṭṭakuṇḍali became sotāpannas,[1] and eighty thousand persons realized the Truth.[2]

[1] DhA. i. 20 ff.; Vv. vii. 9; VvA. 322 ff.; Pv. ii. 5; PvA. 92; the stanzas found in Maṭṭakuṇḍali's story occur also in the Maṭṭakuṇḍali Jātaka (*q.v.*), but the introductory story is quite different.

[2] Mil. 350.

Maṭṭakuṇḍali Jātaka (No. 449).—The son of a wealthy brahmin died at the age of sixteen and was reborn among the devas. From the time of his son's death, the brahmin would go to the cemetery and walk round the heap of ashes, moaning piteously. The deva visited him and admonished him, as in the story of Maṭṭakuṇḍali. The brahmin followed his advice and gave up his grief.

The story was told in reference to a rich landowner of **Sāvatthi,** a devout follower of the Buddha, who lost his son. The Buddha, knowing of his great grief, visited him in the company of **Ānanda** and preached to him. At the conclusion of the sermon, the landowner became a sotāpanna.[1]

[1] J. iv. 59 ff.

Maṭṭhara.—See **Māṭhara.**

Maṇamekkuṇḍi.—A locality of South India pillaged by **Laṅkāpura.**[1]

[1] Cv. lxxvii. 87.

Maṇi.—A yakkha chief, to be invoked by Buddhists in time of need.[1]

[1] D. iii. 205.

2. **Maṇiakkhi, Maṇiakkhika.**—A Nāga king of **Kalyāṇi,** maternal uncle of **Mahodara.** He came to take part in the battle between Mahodara and **Cūḷodara,** and having heard the Buddha preach on that occasion, begged him to visit his kingdom. The Buddha agreed, and, three years later, went to Kalyāṇi in the eighth year after the Enlightenment on the full-moon day of **Vesākha.** The Nāga entertained him and his five hundred monks on the spot where, later, the **Kalyāṇi-cetiya** was built.[1]

[1] Mhv. i. 63 ff.; xv. 162; Dpv. ii. 42, 52; it is said that Maṇikkhika went to **Jambudīpa** to bring the Buddha to Ceylon (MṬ. 111).

2. **Maṇiakkhika.**—The youngest of the three sons of **Mahātissa** and **Saṅghasivā.**[1]

[1] Cv. xlv. 40.

Maṇiupaṭṭhāna.—One of the places appointed by King **Bhātika** for the dispensing of hospitality to the monks of Ceylon.[1]

[1] Mhv. xxxiv. 65; the MṬ. (633) calls it **Maṇiupaṭṭhāna-pāsāda.**

Maṇikaṇṭha.—A Nāga king. See **Maṇikaṇṭha Jātaka.** The king was so called because he wore round his neck a wish-conferring gem.[1]

[1] Sp. iii. 565.

Maṇikaṇṭha Jātaka (No. 253).—The Bodhisatta and his younger brother, after the death of their parents, lived as ascetics in leaf-huts on the Ganges, the elder being higher up the stream than the younger. One day, the Nāga king **Maṇikantha,** while walking along the river in the guise of a man, came to the hut of the younger ascetic and became his friend. Thereafter he called daily and their friendship grew apace. Maṇikaṇṭha finally became so fond of the ascetic that he put off his disguise, and encircling the other in his folds, lay thus for a short while each day, until his affection was satisfied. But the ascetic was afraid of his Nāga shape and grew thin and pale.

The Bodhisatta noticing this, suggested that the next time Maṇikaṇṭha came, his brother should ask for the jewel which he wore round his throat. On the morrow, when the ascetic made this request, Maṇikaṇṭha hurried away. Several times this happened, and then he came no more. The ascetic was much grieved by his absence, but was comforted by the Bodhisatta.

The Buddha related this story at the **Aggāḷava-cetiya** near **Āḷavī.** The monks of Āḷavi became so importunate with their requests for building materials from the householders that at the mere sight of a monk the householders would hurry indoors. **Mahā Kassapa** discovered this and reported it to the Buddha, who admonished the monks against begging for things from other people.[1]

On the same occasion were preached the **Brahmadatta Jātaka** and the **Aṭṭhisena Jātaka** (*q.v.*).

[1] J. ii. 282-6; also Vin. iii. 146 f., where the details of the story of the past are slightly different.

Maṇikā.—The name of a *vijjā*, whereby thoughts can be read.[1]

[1] DA. ii. 389.

Maṇikārakulūpaga-Tissa.—An Elder who ate for twelve years at the house of a jeweller of **Sāvatthi.** One day when the jeweller was chopping some meat, **Pasenadi** sent him a certain precious stone to be cleaned and threaded. The jeweller took the stone without wiping his hands and put it in a box. While he went to wash his hands, his pet heron, thinking it was a piece of meat, swallowed it. Tissa was present and saw this happen. The jeweller, finding his jewel had disappeared, suspected Tissa and questioned him. The Elder denied having taken the stone, but said nothing about the heron in case it should be killed. The jeweller became very angry, and, convinced that Tissa was the thief, proceeded to torture him, in spite of the protests of his wife. As the blood flowed from the Elder's body, the heron came to drink it, but the jeweller kicked him and he fell down dead. Then Tissa told the jeweller what had happened. The heron's crop was cut open and the jewel recovered. The jeweller was full of remorse and begged Tissa's pardon, which was readily granted, but, soon after, Tissa passed away into Nibbāna. The heron was reborn in the womb of the jeweller's wife. She became a deva after death, but the jeweller was reborn in hell.[1]

[1] DhA. iii. 34 ff.

Maṇikāragāma.—A village in Ceylon near which **Candamukhasiva** constructed a tank, the revenues from which he gave to the **Issarasamaṇa-vihāra.**[1]

[1] Mhv. xxxv. 47.

Maṇikuṇḍala Jātaka (No. 351).—The Bodhisatta, born as king of Benares, discovering that one of his ministers had intrigued in his harem, expelled him from the kindgom. The minister took up service under the king of **Kosala,** and, as a result of his conspiracy, the Bodhisatta was taken captive and cast into prison.[1] For the rest of the story see **Ekarāja Jātaka.**

The story was related in reference to a councillor of **Pasenadi** who was guilty of misconduct in the harem.

[1] J. iii. 153 ff.

Maṇikuṇḍala Vagga.—The thirty-sixth chapter of the Jātakaṭṭhakathā. It forms the first chapter of the Pañca Nipāta.[1]

[1] J. iii. 153 ff.

Maṇikhaṇḍa.—A section of the **Vidhurapaṇḍita Jātaka** which contains a description of the marvellous jewel offered by **Puṇṇaka** as a stake in the dice-play with **Koravya.**[1]

[1] J. vi. 275-9.

Maṇiguhā.—One of the three caves in the **Nandamūlakapabbhāra.** In front of the cave was the **Mañjūsaka** tree (*q.v.*).[1]

[1] SNA. i. 66.

Maṇicūḷa Sutta.—In the royal palace at **Rājagaha,** the report once arose among the retinue that Sākyan recluses were allowed to take gold and silver. The headman **Maṇicūḷaka,** who was present, denied this, but, being unable to convince his audience, he sought the Buddha, who assured him that these monks were allowed neither to seek nor to accept gold and silver.[1]

[1] S. iv. 325 f.; *cp.* Vin. ii. 296 f.

Maṇicūḷaka.—A headman of **Rājagaha.** See **Maṇicūḷa Sutta.**

Maṇicora Jātaka (No. 194).—The Bodhisatta was once a householder in a village near Benares and he had a most beautiful wife, named **Sujātā.** One day, at her request, they prepared some sweetmeats, and, placing them in a cart, started for Benares to see her parents. On the way Sujātā was seen by the king of Benares, and, wishing to possess her, he ordered the jewel of his diadem to be introduced into the Bodhisatta's cart. The cry of "thief" was then set up, and the Bodhisatta arrested and taken off to be executed. But **Sakka's** throne was heated by Sujātā's lamentations, and, descending to earth, Sakka made the king and the Bodhisatta change places. The king was beheaded, and Sakka, revealing himself, set the Bodhisatta on the throne.

The story was related in reference to **Devadatta's** attempts to kill the Buddha. The king is identified with Devadatta, Sakka with **Anuruddha,** and **Rāhulamātā** with Sujātā.[1] The story gives the case of a man getting happiness through a virtuous woman.[2]

[1] J. ii. 121-5. [2] J. iv. 77.

Maṇithūnavimāna.—A palace in **Tāvatiṃsa,** the abode of a deva who had been a resident of **Sāvatthi** and cleared a path leading from the forest to Sāvatthi, in order to make it easy for the many monks who went to and fro.[1]

[1] Vv. vii. 3; VvA. 301 f.

Maṇidīpa.—A sub-commentary (*anuṭīkā*) to the **Atthasālinī,** by **Ariyavaṃsa.**[1]

[1] Gv. 65, 75; Bode, *op. cit.*, 42.

Maṇināgapabbata.—A vihāra in the **Kālāyana-Kaṇṇikā** in **Rohaṇa,** built by **Mahādāṭhika-Mahānāga.**[1]

[1] Mhv. xxxiv. 89; MṬ. 637.

Maṇipabbata, Maṇipassapabbata.—A mountain range of the **Himālaya.**[1]

[1] J. ii. 92; v. 38, 415; SNA. i. 358.

Maṇipāsāda.—The name given to the **Lohapāsāda,** after it had been rebuilt in seven storeys by **Jeṭṭhatissa.** He offered to the building a jewel worth sixty thousand, hence its name. The building was worth one crore.[1] The **Coḷas** burnt it down, and **Udaya IV.** tried to rebuild

[1] Mhv. xxxvi. 125.

it, but died before the work was completed.[2] This was done by **Mahinda IV.**[3]

[2] Cv. liii. 51. [3] *Ibid.*, liv. 48.

1. **Maṇipūjaka Thera.**—An arahant. Ninety-four kappas ago he was an ascetic, and, having seen the Buddha (? **Padumuttara**), gave him a jewelled seat. Twelve kappas ago he was king eight times under the name of **Sataraṃsī.**[1]

[1] Ap. i. 190.

2. **Maṇipūjaka Thera.**—An arahant. He was once a Nāga king in a lake in **Himavā,** and, having seen **Padumuttara** Buddha travelling through the air, he offered him the jewel which he wore round his throat, that being the only thing he had.[1] He is probably identical with **Mātaṅgaputta Thera.**[2]

[1] Ap. ii. 413 f. [2] ThagA. i. 349.

Maṇippabhāsa.—One hundred and sixteen kappas ago there were thirty-two kings of this name, all previous births of **Vedikāraka (Vijaya) Thera.**[1]

[1] Ap. i. 171; ThagA. i. 192.

Maṇibhadda.—A yakkha who visited the Buddha at the **Maṇimālaka-cetiya** and held a conversation with him regarding hate and the release therefrom.[1]

[1] S. i. 208; *cf.* Avadānaś. ii. 179.

Maṇibhadda Sutta.—Records the conversation between the Buddha and **Maṇibhadda** (*q.v.*).

Maṇibhaddavattikā.—A class of ascetics and recluses who, perhaps, worshipped **Maṇibhadda**[1] (*q.v.*). The Maṇibhaddā are mentioned in the Milindapañha,[2] together with tumblers, jugglers, actors, etc.

[1] MNid. 89. In the Mahābhārata, Maṇibhadda is mentioned among the yakśas in Kuvera's palace (ii. 10, 397). He is the tutelary deity of travellers and caravans (iii. 65, 2553).

[2] p. 191.

Maṇimālaka.—A Cetiya where the Buddha stayed and where he was visited by the yakkha **Maṇibhadda.**[1]

[1] S. i. 208.

Maṇimekhala-pāsāda.—A monastic building in Ceylon, probably belonging to the Mahāyānists. It held statues of the Bodhisattas which were restored by **Sena II.**[1]

[1] Cv. li. 77.

1. **Maṇimekhalā.**—A goddess who presided over the ocean where she was placed by the **Cātummahārājikā** to protect virtuous people who might suffer shipwreck.[1]

[1] J. iv. 17; vi. 35.

2. **Maṇimekhalā.**—A dam erected by **Aggabodhi I.** across the **Mahāvālukagaṅgā.**[1] It was restored by **Sena II.**[2]

[1] Cv. xlii. 34. [2] *Ibid.*, li. 72.

3. **Maṇimekhalā.**—A district in Ceylon, founded by the general **Saṅkha** during the time that the usurper **Māgha** ruled at **Pulatthipura.**[1]

[1] Cv. lxxxi. 7.

Maṇisāramañjūsā.—A Commentary on the **Abhidhammatthavibhāvanī,** by **Ariyavaṃsa.**[1]

[1] Gv. 65, 75; Bode, *op. cit.*, 42.

Maṇisūkara Jātaka (No. 285).—The Bodhisatta lived in the Himālaya as an ascetic, and near his hut was a crystal cave in which lived thirty boars. A lion used to range near the cave in which his shadow was reflected. This so terrified the boars that one day they fetched mud from a neighbouring pool with which they rubbed the crystal; but because of the boars' bristles, the more they rubbed, the brighter grew the crystal. In despair they consulted the Bodhisatta, who told them that a crystal could not be sullied.

The story was told in reference to an unsuccessful attempt by the heretics to accuse the Buddha of having seduced **Sundarī** (*q.v.*) and then brought about her death.[1]

[1] J. ii. 415-8.

Maṇisomārāma.—Probably another name for the **Somārāma** (*q.v.*). **Kaṇiṭṭha-Tissa** built a *pariveṇa* there.[1] **Goṭhābhaya** restored the vihāra and built there an **uposatha** house.[2]

[1] Mhv. xxxvi. 8. [2] *Ibid.*, 106 f.

1. **Maṇihīra.**—A vihāra built by **Mahāsena.**[1]

[1] Mhv. xxxvii. 40.

2. **Maṇihīra.**—A tank built by **Mahāsena.**[1] **Aggabodhi** built a canal leading out of it[2]; so did **Sena II.**[3] Among the canals flowing into the tank was the **Tilavatthuka,** restored by **Vijayabāhu I.**[4] **Parakkamabāhu I.** rebuilt the tank,[5] and constructed the **Kālindī** Canal to carry away the overflow from the south side.[6] It was near this tank that **Saṅghatissa** was taken prisoner by the followers of **Moggallāna III.**[7]

[1] Mhv. xxxvii. 47.
[2] Cv. xlii. 34.
[3] *Ibid.*, li. 72.
[4] *Ibid.*, lx. 53.
[5] *Ibid.*, lxxix. 31.
[6] *Ibid.*, 54.
[7] *Ibid.*, xliv. 30.

Maṇḍakappa.—A kappa in which two Buddhas are born.[1]

[1] BuA. 158; J. i. 38, 39, 41, 42.

Maṇḍagalla.—A village near **Anurādhapura,** mentioned in the account of the campaigns of **Parakkamabāhu I.**[1]

[1] Cv. lviii. 43; Cv. *Trs.* i. 206, n. 5.

Maṇḍagāma.—A village in **Rohaṇa,** given by **Aggabodhi,** son of **Mahātissa,** to the monks, in gratitude for a meal which they had given him.[1]

[1] Cv. xlv. 47; Cv. *Trs.* i. 93, n. 5.

Maṇḍadīpa.—The name of Ceylon in the time of **Kassapa Buddha;** its capital was **Visāla** and its king **Jayanta.** The **Mahāmeghavana** was called **Mahāsāgara.**[1]

[1] Mhv. xv. 127; Dpv. i. 73; ix. 20; xv. 57, etc.

Maṇḍapadāyikā Therī.—An arahant. She built a pavilion for **Koṇāgamana Buddha.**[1]

[1] Ap. ii. 514; ThigA. 6.

Maṇḍapeyyakathā.—The tenth chapter of the Mahāvagga of the Paṭisambhidāmagga.

Maṇḍalagiri-vihāra.—A monastery in Ceylon, built by **Kaṇiṭṭhatissa.**[1] The ruler of the province of Malaya in the time of **Aggabodhi IV.** built a relic-house for the cetiya there,[2] while **Sena II.** gave to it several maintenance villages[3] and **Vijayabāhu I.** restored it.[4] It was while living there that **Gajabāhu** made his peace with **Parakkamabāhu I.** and

[1] Mhv. xxxvi. 17.
[2] Cv. xlvi. 29.
[3] *Ibid.*, li. 75.
[4] *Ibid.*, lx. 58.

set up an inscription to that effect in the vihāra.[5] *v.l.* **Maṇḍalagirika, Maṇḍaligiri.**

[5] Cv. lxxi. 3; for its identification see Cv. *Trs.* i. 100, n. 3.

Maṇḍalamandira.—A building erected by **Parakkamabāhu I.** at **Pulatthipura.** It was used by the teacher specially appointed by him to recite Jātaka stories.[1]

[1] Cv. lxxiii. 72; see Cv. *Trs.* ii. 9, n. 1.

Maṇḍalārāma.—A monastery in Ceylon, probably near the village of **Bhokkanta.** It was the residence of the Elder **Mahā Tissa,** reciter of the **Dhammapada. Sumanā,** wife of **Lakuṇṭaka Atimbara,** recited there, in the assembly of the monks, the story of her past lives.[1] According to the Vibhaṅga Commentary[2] the monastery was in the village of **Kālakagāma,** and, in the time of **Vaṭṭagāmaṇī,** it was the residence of many monks, at the head of whom was **Tissabhūta.** It was also the residence of **Maliyadeva Thera.**[3]

[1] DhA. iv. 51. [2] VibhA. 448; also DhSA. 30; AA. i. 52. [3] AA. i. 22.

Maṇḍavāṭaka.—A tank in Ceylon, restored by **Vijayabāhu I.**[1]

[1] Cv. lx. 49.

Maṇḍavāpi-vihāra.—A monastery built by **Mahā-Cūḷi-Tissa.**[1] **Mahādāṭhika-Mahānāga** gave land for the monks of this vihāra out of gratitude to a *sāmaṇera* who lived there.[2]

[1] Mhv. xxxiv. 8. [2] *Ibid.*, 93.

1. **Maṇḍavya.**—An ascetic. For his story see the **Kaṇhadīpāyana Jātaka.**

2. **Maṇḍavya.**—Son of **Mātaṅga** and **Diṭṭhamangalikā.** For his story see the **Mātaṅga Jātaka.** Maṇḍavya is given as an example of conception by umbilical attrition.[1]

[1] Mil. 123 f.; Sp. i. 214.

Maṇḍika.—A tank in Ceylon restored by **Parakkamabāhu I.**[1]

[1] Cv. lxviii. 44; see Cv. *Trs.* i. 280, n. 5.

Maṇḍikā.—Mother of **Maṇḍikāputta** (*q.v.*).

Maṇḍikāputta.—See **Upaka Maṇḍikāputta.** He was so called because he was the son of **Maṇḍikā.**[1] See also **Samaṇa Maṇḍikāputta.**

[1] AA. ii. 554; KhpA. 105.

Maṇḍissa.—A Paribbājaka of **Kosambi,** friend of **Jāliya.** It was to them that the **Jāliya Sutta** (*q.v.*) was preached. *v.l.* **Muṇḍiya.**

Maṇḍūka.—A deva. In his previous birth he was a frog on the banks of the **Gaggarā,** and, hearing the Buddha preach, was attracted by his voice. A cowherd, who stood leaning on a stick, drove it unwittingly into the frog's head and it died immediately, to be reborn in **Tāvatiṃsa** in a palace twelve yojanas in extent. Having discovered his previous birth, he appeared before the Buddha, revealed his identity and worshipped him. The Buddha preached to him, and the deva became a *sotāpanna*. Eighty-four thousand others realized the Truth.[1]

[1] Vv. v. 1; VvA. 216 ff.; Vsm. 208 f.; Sp. i. 121; Mil. 350.

Maṇṇaya.—A Damiḷa chief, ally of **Kulasekhara.**[1] He later joined **Laṅkāpura.**[2]

[1] Cv. lxxvi. 141.

[2] *Ibid.*, lxxvii. 7, 35.

Mataka Sutta.—See **Pacchābhūmika Sutta.**

Matakabhatta Jātaka (No. 18).—Once a brahmin, well versed in the Vedas, wished to slay a goat at the Feast of the Dead (*Matakabhatta*), and sent his pupils to bathe the goat in the river. After the bath, the goat remembered its past lives and knew that after its death that day it would be free from misery. So it laughed for joy. But it saw also that the brahmin, through slaying it, would suffer great misery, and this thought made it weep. On being questioned as to the reason for its laughing and its weeping, it said the answer would be given before the brahmin. When the brahmin heard the goat's story, he resolved not to kill him; but that same day, while the goat was browsing near a rock, the rock was struck by lightning and a large splinter cut off the goat's head. The Bodhisatta, who was a tree-sprite, saw all this and preached the Law to the assembled multitude.

The story was told in reference to a question by the monks as to whether there was any good at all in offering sacrifices as Feasts for the Dead, which the people of **Sāvatthi** were in the habit of doing.[1]

[1] J. i. 166 ff.

Matarodana Jātaka (No. 317).—The Bodhisatta was once born in a family worth eighty crores. When his parents died, his brother managed the estate. Some time later the brother also died, but the Bodhisatta shed no tear. His relations and friends called him heartless, but he convinced them that he did not weep because he knew that all things are transient.

The story was related to a landowner of **Sāvatthi** who gave himself up to despair on the death of his brother. The Buddha visited him and preached to him, and the man became a *sotāpanna*.[1]

[1] J. iii. 56-8.

1. **Matta.**—One of the seven children of **Paṇḍuvāsudeva** and **Bhaddakaccānā.**[1]

[1] Dpv. x. 3.

2. **Matta.**—A householder in the **Vihāravāpi** village near the **Tulādhāra** Mountain; he was the father of **Labhiya-Vasabha.**[1]

[1] Mhv. xxiii. 90.

3. **Matta.**—A hunter who discovered four marvellous gems near **Peḷavāpikagāma,** seven leagues to the north of **Anurādhapura.** He reported his discovery to **Duṭṭhagāmaṇī,** and the gems were used for the **Maha Thūpa.**[1]

[1] Mhv. xxviii. 39; MṬ. 512.

Mattakela.—One of the eleven children of **Paṇḍavāsudeva** and **Bhaddakaccānā.**[1]

[1] Dpv. x. 3.

Mattapabbata.—A monastery in Ceylon where **Aggabodhi II.** built a *padhānaghara* for **Jotipāla Thera.**[1]

[1] Cv. xlii. 46.

1. **Mattā.**—A Therī who came to Ceylon from **Jambudīpa** and taught the Vinaya at **Anurādhapura.**[1]

[1] Dpv. xviii. 12.

2. **Mattā.**—A *petī.* In her previous life she was married to a householder of **Sāvatthi,** but, because she was barren, her husband married another woman, named **Tissā,** by whom he had a child called **Bhūta.** One day, when Tissā and her husband were talking together, **Mattā** was

seized with jealousy and threw a heap of dirt on Tissā's head. After death, Mattā was born as a petī and suffered grievously. She appeared before Tissā, and, at her request, Tissā gave alms to eight monks, giving the merit to Mattā. Mattā immediately won heavenly bliss.[1]

[1] Pv. ii. 3; PvA. 82 ff.

Mattābhaya.—Younger brother of **Devānampiyatissa.** He witnessed the miracles which attended the arrival of the Buddha's Relics in Ceylon, and, with one thousand others, entered the Order.[1] When **Mahā-Ariṭṭha** recited the Vinaya at the **Thupārāma** and held the Saṅgīti at the suggestion of **Mahinda,** Mattābhaya, with five hundred others, was charged with the duty of learning the Vinaya from him.[2]

[1] Mhv. xvii. 57 f. [2] Sp. i. 103.

Mattikāvāṭatittha.—A landing-place in Ceylon, the scene of the embarkment of part of the army sent by **Vijayabāhu** to the **Coḷa** kingdom.[1]

[1] Cv. lx. 34.

Mattikāvāpi.—A village in the **Āḷisāra** district of Ceylon, where **Māyāgeha** captured an entrenchment.[1]

[1] Cv. lxx. 172.

Matteyyā Sutta.—Few are they who abstain from intoxicating liquor; many they that do not.[1]

[1] S. v. 467.

Matthalā.—The name of a tribe mentioned in a nominal list.[1]

[1] Ap. ii. 359.

Mathurā.—See **Madhurā.**

Madagu.—A tank in Ceylon, restored by **Parakkamabāhu I.**[1]

[1] Cv. lxxix. 37.

Madda.—The name of a country and its people **(Maddā).** In the **Kusa Jātaka** (*q.v.*), **Kusa,** son of **Okkāka,** king of **Kusāvatī** in the **Malla** country, is mentioned as having married **Pabhāvatī,** daughter of the king of Madda, and the capital of the Madda king was **Sāgala.**[1] In the similar story of **Anitthigandha,** a prince of Benares contracts a marriage with a daughter of the king of **Sāgala**—his name being **Maddava ;** but

[1] J. v. 283 ff.; Kusāvatī was one hundred leagues from Sāgala (J. v. 290), *cp.* Mtu. ii. 441 f.

the girl dies on the way to her husband.[2] The **Chaddanta Jātaka**[3] also mentions a matrimonial alliance between the royal houses of Benares and Sāgala, while in the **Kālingabodhi Jātaka**[4] the Madda king's daughter marries a prince of **Kāliṅga** while both are in exile. **Cūḷani,** son of **Talatā,** also married a princess of Madda.[5] According to the Mahāvaṃsa,[6] **Sumitta,** son of **Sīhabāhu** and king of **Sīhapura,** married the daughter of the Madda king and had three sons by him, the youngest of whom, **Paṇḍuvāsudeva,** became king of Ceylon.

Bhaddā-Kāpilānī, wife of **Pippalimāṇava (Mahā Kassapa),** was the daughter of a **Kosiyagotta** brahmin of **Sāgala** in the Madda country. Men went there in search of a wife for him because it was famed for the beauty of its women (*Maddaraṭṭhaṃ nāma itthāgāro*).[7] **Anojā,** wife of **Mahā Kappina** of **Kukkuṭavatī,** also came from the royal household of Madda,[8] as did **Khemā,** wife of **Bimbisāra.**[9] The wife of a Cakkavattī comes either from Uttarakuru or from the royal family of Madda.[10]

For the identification of Madda see *s.v.* **Sāgala.**

2 SNA. i. 68 f.; *cp.* DhA. iii. 281, about the other **Anitthigandha** of **Sāvatthi** of the Buddha's days, who also married a Madda princess.

3 J. v. 39 f.; so also in the **Mūgapakkha Jātaka** (J. vi. 1), the wife of the Kāsi king was the daughter of the king of Madda, **Candadevī** by name; while **Phusatī,** wife of **Sañjaya** of **Jetuttara** in the **Sivi** kingdom and mother of **Vessantara,** was also a Madda princess (J. vi. 480); likewise **Maddī,** wife of Vessantara.

4 J. iv. 230 f.

5 J. vi. 471.

6 Mhv. viii. 7; this probably refers to Madras and not to the Madda country, whose capital was Sāgala.

7 ThagA. ii. 142; ThigA. 68.

8 DhA. ii. 116.

9 ThigA. 127.

10 MA. ii. 950; DA. ii. 626; KhA. 173.

Maddakucchi.—A park near **Rājagaha,** at the foot of **Gijjhakūṭa.** It was a preserve (*migadāya*) where deer and game could dwell in safety. When **Devadatta,** wishing to kill the Buddha, hurled a rock down **Gijjhakūṭa,** it was stopped midway by another rock, but a splinter from it fell on the Buddha's foot, wounding it severely. As the Buddha suffered much from loss of blood, the monks took him on a litter to Maddakucchi, and from there to the **Jīvaka-ambavana,** where he was treated by **Jīvaka.**[1] It is said[2] that seven hundred devas of the **Satullapa** group visited the Buddha there and told him of their great admiration for his qualities. **Māra** tried to stir up discontent in the Buddha, but had to retire discomfited.[3]

According to the Commentaries,[4] Maddakucchi was so called because it was there that **Bimbisāra's** queen, mother of **Ajātasattu,** tried to bring about an abortion when she was told by soothsayers that the child in

1 Vin. ii. 193 f.; DhA. ii. 164 ff.; J. iv. 430; Mil. 179.

2 S. i. 27 f.

3 *Ibid.*, 110; this visit of Māra is referred to at D. ii. 116.

4 *E.g.*, S.A. i. 61; *cp.* J. iii. 121 f.

her womb was destined to bring about Bimbisāra's death. She went into the park unknown to the king and violently massaged her womb, but without success. The king heard of this and forbade her to visit the park.

Once when **Mahā Kappina** was at Maddakucchi, doubts arose in his mind as to the necessity of joining the assembly of monks for the holding of *uposatha*, he himself being pure. The Buddha read his thoughts, appeared before him, and urged upon him the necessity of so doing.[5]

Maddakucchi was difficult of access; monks who came from afar late at night, wishing to put **Dabba Mallaputta's** powers to the test, would often ask him to provide lodging there for them.[6]

[5] Vin. i. 105. [6] *Ibid.*, ii. 76; iii. 159.

Maddarūpī.—Daughter of **Okkāka** and wife of **Kaṇha,** ancestor of **Ambaṭṭha.**[1] *v.l.* **Khuddarūpī.**

[1] D. i. 96 f.

1. **Maddava.**—King of Benares. The Bodhisatta was his councillor **Senaka.** See the **Dasaṇṇaka Jātaka.**[1]

[1] J. iii. 337.

2. **Maddava.**—King of **Sāgala** in the **Madda** country. His daughter was given in marriage to **Anitthigandha** of Benares, but she died on the way to her husband's house.[1]

[1] SNA. i. 69.

Maddā.—The people of **Madda** (*q.v.*).

Maddīpabba.—The section of the **Vessantara Jātaka** which deals with the search of **Maddī** for her children, and finally with her joy on learning the purpose of **Vessantara's** gift.[1]

[1] J. vi. 568.

Maddī.—Wife of **Vessantara** whose first cousin she was, being the daughter of the Madda king. When Vessantara went into exile, she, with her two children, **Jāli** and **Kaṇhājinā,** accompanied him. At **Vaṅkagiri** she and the children occupied one of the hermitages provided for them by **Vissakamma,** at **Sakka's** orders. While she was getting fruit and leaves, **Jūjaka** obtained from Vessantara the two children as slaves. Maddī the previous night had had a dream warning her of this, but Vessantara had consoled her. When she came back from her quest for food later than usual, the gods having contrived to detain her, she found the children missing, and searched for them throughout the night. It was at dawn the next day, on her recovery from a deathlike swoon, that Vessantara told her of the gift of the children, describing the miracles which had attended the gift and showing how they presaged that he would reach Enlightenment. Maddī, understanding, rejoiced herself in the gift.

The next day Sakka appeared in the guise of a brahmin and asked Vessantara to give him Maddī as his slave. Seeing him hesitate, Maddī urged him to let her go, saying that she belonged to him to do as he would with her. The gift was made and accepted by Sakka. He then, however, gave her back, with praises of Vessantara and Maddī.[1]

Maddī is identified with **Rāhulamātā.**

[1] For these details see the Vessantara Jātaka; see also Cyp. i. 9; Mil. 117, 281 f.; J. i. 77; DhA. i. 406.

Maddha.—A locality in Ceylon, probably a vihāra, residence of **Mahānāga Thera.**[1]

[1] J. vi. 30.

Madhukaṇṇava.—A **Kāliṅga** prince, brother of **Tilokasundarī,** queen of **Vijayabāhu I.** He came to Ceylon, and the king paid him great honour.[1]

[1] Cv. lix. 46.

Madhukavanagaṇṭhi.—A locality in Ceylon.[1]

[1] Cv. lxx. 325.

Madhitthala.—A fortress in **Rohaṇa** where **Damiḷādhikārin** defeated the rebels.[1]

[1] Cv. lxxv. 147.

Madhutthala-vihāra.—A vihāra restored by **Vijayabahu I.**[1]

[1] Cv. lx. 58; also Cv. *Trs.* i. 220, n. 2.

Madhudāyaka Thera.—An arahant. Once in the past he was a hermit living on the banks of the **Sindhu,** and, having seen **Sumedha Buddha,** he gave him some honey. It is said that on the day of his birth there was a shower of honey.[1] He is probably identical with **Mahānāma Thera.**[2]

[1] Ap. i. 325.

[2] ThagA. i. 228.

Madhudīpanī.—A *ṭīkā* on the **Visuddhimagga.**[1]

[1] Sās. 33.

Madhupādapatittha.—A landing place, probably in the north of Ceylon. It was used as a stronghold by **Māgha** and **Jayabāhu.**[1]

[1] Cv. lxxxiii. 18.

Madhupiṇḍika Sutta.—**Daṇḍapāṇi** meets the Buddha at the **Mahāvana** near **Kapilavatthu** and questions him as to his tenets. The Buddha explains that his tenets are such that they avoid all strife and make a man dwell above all pleasures of sense, etc. Daṇḍapāṇi shakes his head and walks on, without comment.

Later in the evening the Buddha visits the **Nigrodhārāma** and tells the monks there briefly how to get rid of all obsessions, so that all evil and wrong states of mind are quelled and pass away entirely. After the Buddha's departure the monks seek **Mahā Kaccāna** and ask him to expound in detail what the Buddha has told them in brief. Kaccāna explains that where there is eye and visible form, visual consciousness arises, this begets contact, contact conditions feeling, what a man feels he perceives, what he perceives he reasons about, and this leads to obsession. It is the same with the other senses. The monks report this explanation to the Buddha, who approves of it and praises Kaccāna's earning and insight. **Ānanda** praises the discourse, comparing it to a honeyed pill of delicious savour, and the Buddha suggests that the sutta should be remembered by that name (*Madhupiṇḍika*).[1]

Nāgita was among those present when the sutta was preached. He was thereby persuaded to enter the Order, and soon after became an arahant.[2]

[1] M. i. 108-14. [2] ThagA. i. 183.

Madhupiṇḍika Thera.—An arahant. In the time of **Siddhattha Buddha** he was a hunter, and, meeting the Buddha in the forest, he offered him a honey cake, when he rose from *samādhi*. Thirty-four kappas ago he was king four times under the name of **Sudassana,** and at his birth showers of honey fell.[1]

[1] Ap. i. 136 f.

Madhubhaṇḍapūjā.—A ceremony held by **Bhātikābhaya** in honour of the **Mahā Thūpa.** It consisted of offerings of vessels filled with honey, and of lotus-flowers strewn ankle-deep in the courtyard, of lighted lamps filled with fragrant oil, etc.[1]

[1] Mhv. xxxiv. 52 ff.; MṬ. 631.

Madhumaṃsadāyaka Thera.—An arahant. Ninety-one kappas ago, in the time of **Vipassī Buddha**, he was a pig-sticker of **Bandhumatī**, and one day gave as alms to an Elder a bowl of tender flesh. He was reborn after death in **Tāvatiṃsa.**[1]

[1] Ap. ii. 372.

1. **Madhura Sutta.**—**Avantiputta,** king of **Madhurā,** visits **Mahā Kaccāna,** who is staying at the **Gundāvana** in **Madhurā,** some time after the Buddha's death, and questions him regarding the brahmin claims to superiority over other castes. Kaccāna points out that wealth confers power on all, not only on brahmins. A brahmin experiences the result of his actions both good and bad, in this world and in the next, just as do members of other castes. A brahmin ascetic receives no more homage than an ascetic of other castes. Avantiputta accepts the Buddha's Faith.[1]

[1] M. ii. 83-90; *cp.* **Ambaṭṭha Sutta**; for a discussion see Dial. i. 105.

2. **Madhura Sutta.**—On the five disadvantages of **Madhurā**: the ground is uneven, there is much dust, there are fierce dogs and bestial yakkhas, and alms are obtained with difficulty.[1] The Commentary explains[2] that the Buddha, during a tour, once entered **Madhurā,** and was on his way to the inner city. But a certain heretic yakkhiṇī stood before him naked, stretching out her arms, her tongue out. The Buddha thereupon turned back and went to the vihāra, where the people entertained him and the monks.

[1] A. iii. 256. [2] AA. ii. 646.

Madhurakā.—The people of **Madhurā,** mentioned in a list of tribes.[1]

[1] Ap. i. 359; also Mil. 331.

Madhuratthavilāsinī.—A Commentary on the **Buddhavaṃsa** written by **Buddhadatta Thera** of **Kāvīrapaṭṭana** at the request of **Buddhasīha.**[1]

[1] Gv. 60; BuA. 249; Svd. 1195.

Madhuraddhamakkāra.—A district in South India, the forces of which were among the allies of **Kulasekhara.**[1]

[1] Cv. lxxvii. 2.

Madhurapācikā.—A woman of **Sāvatthi,** wife of a man who joined the Order in his old age with his friends. All these friends used to eat at his house, where they were well looked after. But the wife died, and they all lamented greatly. The Buddha heard of this, and sent for them and recited to them the **Kāka Jātaka** (*q.v.*).[1] At the end of the discourse the aged monks all became *sotāpannas*.[2]

[1] J. i. 497 ff. [2] DhA. iii. 422 ff.

Madhurammāṇavīra.—A fortress in South India subdued by **Jagadvijaya.**[1]

[1] Cv. lxxvi. 304.

Madhurasasavāhinī.—See **Rasavāhinī.**

1. **Madhurā.**—The capital of **Surasena,** situated on the **Yamunā.** Its king, soon after the death of **Bimbisāra,** was **Avantiputta,**[1] who, judging by his name, was probably related to the royal family of **Ujjeni.** Madhurā was visited by the Buddha,[2] but there is no record of his having stayed there. In fact, the **Madhura Sutta** (2) (*q.v.*) states that he viewed the city with distinct disfavour. But **Mahā Kaccāna** evidently liked it, for he stayed there in the **Gundāvana,** and was visited there by the king of the city, Avantiputta,[3] and the brahmin **Kaṇḍarāyana.**[4] One of the most important suttas on caste, the **Madhura Sutta** 1 (*q.v.*), was preached to Avantiputta by Mahā Kaccāna at Madhurā. Perhaps it was through the agency of Mahā Kaccāna that Buddhism gained ground in Madhurā. Already in the Buddha's time there were, in and around Madhurā, those who accepted his teachings, for the Aṅguttara Nikāya[5] mentions that once when he was journeying from Madhurā to **Verañjā** and stopped under a tree by the wayside, a large number of householders, both men and women, came and worshipped him. Later, about 300 B.C., Madhurā became a **Jain centre,**[6] but when Fa Hsien[7] and Hiouen Thsang[8] visited it, Buddhism was flourishing there, and there were many *saṅghārāmas* and *stūpas*. From **Saṅkassa** to Madhurā was a distance of four yojanas.[9]

Madhurā is sometimes referred to as **Uttara-Madhurā,** to distinguish it from a city of the same name in South India. Thus, in the Vimānavatthu Commentary,[10] a woman of Uttara-Madhurā is mentioned as having been born in **Tāvatiṃsa** as a result of having given alms to the Buddha.

[1] M. ii. 83.
[2] A. ii. 57; iii. 256.
[3] M. ii. 83.
[4] A. i. 67.
[5] *Ibid.*, ii. 57.
[6] CHI. i. 167.
[7] Giles, p. 20.
[8] Beal. i. 179 ff.; for a prophecy (attributed to the Buddha) regarding the future greatness of Madhurā, see Dvy. 348 ff.
[9] Thus in Kaccāyana's Grammar, iii. 1.
[10] VvA. 118 f.

The **Ghaṭa Jātaka**[11] speaks of **Mahāsāgara** as the king of Uttara-Madhurā, and relates what is evidently the story of **Kaṃsa's** attempt to tyrannize over Madhurā by overpowering the Yādavas and his consequent death at the hands of Kṛṣṇa, a story which is found both in the Epics and in the Purāṇas. This Jātaka confirms the brahmanical tradition as to the association of **Vasudeva's** family with Madhurā.[12]

There is a story[13] of a king called **Mahāsena** of **Pāṭaliputta,** who was very generous in feeding the monks, and once thought of giving alms by cultivating a piece of land himself. He, therefore, went to Uttara Madhurā in disguise, worked as a labourer, and held an almsgiving with the gains so obtained.

Madhurā is generally identified with Maholi, five miles to the south-east of the present town of Mathurā or Muttra. It is the Modura of Ptolemy and the Methoras of Pliny.[14]

The Milindapañha[15] refers to Madhurā as one of the chief cities of India. In the past, **Sādhina** and twenty-two of his descendants, the last of whom was **Dhammagutta,** reigned in Madhurā.[16]

[11] J. iv. 79 ff.
[12] PHAI., p. 89.
[13] Cv. xcii. 23 ff.
[14] CAGI. 427 f.
[15] p. 331.
[16] Dpv. iii. 21.

2. **Madhurā.**—A city in South India, in the Madras Presidency, and now known as Madura. It is generally referred to as Dakkhiṇa-Madhurā, to distinguish it from **(Uttara-)Madhura** on the **Yamunā.** Dakkhiṇa-Madhurā was the second capital of the Paṇḍyan kingdom,[1] and there was constant intercourse between this city and Ceylon. From Madhurā came the consort of **Vijaya,** first king of Ceylon, and she was accompanied by many maidens of various families who settled in Ceylon.[2] **Sena II.** sent an army to pillage Madhurā, and set upon the throne a Paṇḍu prince who had begged for his support.[3] Later, Madhurā was attacked by **Kulasekhara,** and its king, **Parakkama,** sought the assistance of **Parakkamabāhu I.** of Ceylon. The latter sent an army under his general **Laṅkāpura,** but in the meantime the **Pāṇḍyan** king had been slain and his capital taken. The Sinhalese army, however, landed on the opposite coast and carried on a war against the **Coḷas,** and built a fortress near **Rāmnād,** which they called **Parakkamapura.** They managed to defeat Kulasekhara and restore the crown of Madhurā to the Pāṇḍyan king's son, **Vīra-Paṇḍu.** The captives taken by the army were sent to Ceylon.[4]

[1] Their first being Korkai (Vincent Smith, EHI. 335 ff.).
[2] Mhv. vii. 49 ff.
[3] Cv. li. 27 ff.
[4] For details see Cv. lxxvi. 76 ff.; lxxvii. 1 ff.; see also Cv. *Trs.* ii. 100, n. 1.

Rājasīha II. is said to have obtained wives from Madhurā,[5] as did his successors **Vimaladhammasūriya II.**, **Narindasīha** and **Vijayarājasīha.**[6]

[5] Cv. xcvi. 40. [6] *Ibid.*, xcvii. 2, 24; xcviii. 4.

Madhurindhara.—King of **Rādhavatī. Anomadassī Buddha** preached to him, and he and seven thousand of his followers became arahants.[1]

[1] BuA. 144.

Madhuvāseṭṭha.—A brahmin of **Sāketa,** father of **Mahānāga Thera.**[1] It is probably he who is identified with the ape in the **Bhisa Jātaka.**[2]

[1] ThagA. i. 442. [2] J. iv. 314.

Madhusāratthadīpanī.—A Commentary on the Abhidhammaṭīkā compiled by **Ānanda** of **Haṃsavatī.**[1]

[1] Sās. 48.

Manasākaṭa.—A brahmin village in **Kosala** on the banks of the **Aciravatī.** It was in a beautiful spot, and eminent brahmins would collect there from time to time in order to find rest and quiet and recite their mantras.[1] The Buddha stayed in the Mango-grove to the north of the village, and, during one such stay, preached the **Tevijja Sutta.**[2]

[1] DA. ii. 399. [2] D. i. 235.

"**Manasi**" **Sutta.**—If, for just the space of a finger-snap, a monk indulges a thought of goodwill, such a one is to be called a monk.[1]

[1] A. i. 11.

Manasikāra Sutta.—**Ānanda** asks the Buddha, and the Buddha explains how far it is possible to be without any distinct perception and apperception and yet possess perception and apperception.[1]

[1] A. v. 321 f.

Manāpakāyikā.—A class of devas possessing lovely forms. Once a large number of them visited **Anuruddha** at the **Ghositārāma** and announced to him that in a trice they could assume any colour they desired, produce any sound, and obtain any happiness. Anuruddha tested their claims and found them to be true. Some of them sang, some danced, some clapped, some played on various musical instruments, but, finding that their entertainment was lost on Anuruddha, they left him. Anuruddha told the Buddha of their visit, and the Buddha explained to him the eight qualities, the possession of which enabled women to be born among the Manāpakāyikā.[1]

[1] A. iv. 265 ff., also *ibid.*, 268, where the Buddha speaks of them to **Visākhā**; *cf.* AA. ii. 773.

Manāpadāyī Sutta.—**Ugga,** a householder of **Vesāli,** having heard from the Buddha that the giver of good things (*manāpadāyī*) gains the good, invites the Buddha to his house and gives him various things which he himself is very fond of—gruel from sal-flowers, flesh of pigs with jujube-fruit, oily tube-like vegetables, rice with curries and condiments, muslin from Benares and a sandalwood plank (in place of a luxurious couch, which, Ugga knew, the Buddha could not accept). Out of compassion for Ugga, the Buddha accepted these gifts and blessed him. Later, Ugga died and was reborn in a mind-born world (*manomayakāya*). He visited the Buddha at **Jetavana** and told him that his hopes had been realized.[1]

[1] A. iii. 49 f.

"**Manāpāmanāpā**" **Sutta.**—Five qualities that make a woman attractive to a man: she is beauteous in form, possessed of wealth, moral, vigorous, and has offspring. Absence of these qualities robs her of this claim. Likewise for a man.[1]

[1] S. iv. 238 f.

Manu.—An Indian sage of old who wrote a work for the guidance of kings in good government.[1]

[1] *E.g.*, Cv. lxxx. 9, 55; lxxxiii. 6; lxxxiv. 2; xcvi. 26.

Manujā.—An eminent *upāsikā* mentioned in a list.[1]

[1] A. iv. 347; AA. ii. 791.

1. **Manoja.**—King of **Brahmavaddhana** (Benares). He is identified with **Sāriputta.**[1] For his story see the **Sona-Nanda Jātaka.**

[1] J. v. 332.

2. **Manoja.**—A lion. See the **Manoja Jātaka.**

Manoja Jātaka (No. 397).—The Bodhisatta was once a lion and had a son called **Manoja.** One day Manoja, in spite of his father's warnings, made friends with a jackal called **Giriya.** Acting on **Giriya's** suggestion, Manoja went in search of horse-flesh and attacked the king's horses. The king engaged the services of an archer, who shot Manoja as he was making off with a horse. Manoja managed to reach his den, but there he fell down dead.[1]

The circumstances in which the story was related are similar to those of the **Mahilāmukha Jātaka** (*q.v.*).

[1] J. iii. 321 ff.

Manojava.—A sage of old mentioned in a nominal list.[1]

[1] J. vi. 99.

Manonivāraṇa Sutta.—Preached in answer to the question of a deva as to where the mind should be checked and where developed.[1]

[1] S. i. 14.

Manopadosikā (Manopadūsikā).—A class of devas living in the **Cātummahārājika-world.**[1] They burn continually with envy one against another,[2] and their hearts become ill-disposed and debauched. Their bodies thus become feeble and their minds imbecile, and, as a consequence, they fall from their state.[3]

The Manopadosikā were among those present at the preaching of the **Mahāsamaya Sutta.**[4] They are so called because their minds are debauched by envy (*dosassa anudahanatāya*).[5]

[1] DA. i. 114; AA. ii. 544; MNid. 108.
[2] Buddhaghosa relates a story illustrating this (DA. i. 114).
[3] D. i. 20; iii. 32.
[4] *Ibid.*, ii. 260.
[5] VibhA. 498.

Manomaya.—A Pacceka Buddha.[1]

[1] M. iii. 70; ApA. i. 107.

Manorathapūraṇī.—**Buddhaghosa's** Commentary on the Aṅguttara Nikāya, written at the request of **Jotipāla** and **Jīvaka.**[1]

[1] AA. ii. 874; Gv. 59, etc.

Manosattā.—A class of devas. Beings who die devoted to some idea are born in their world—*e.g.*, a **Nigaṇṭha** who will take only warm water and would rather die than take it cold.[1]

[1] M. i. 376; MA. ii. 597.

Manosilātala.—A locality in **Himavā.** When **Āḷavaka** threatened the Buddha he stood with his left foot on Manosilātala and his right on **Kelāsa.**[1] Manosilātala was near **Anotatta,** and those who bathed in the lake dried and robed themselves there.[2] It was also a resort of lions[3] and was sixty leagues in extent.[4] Above it was the **Kañcanaguhā**[5] and below it the **Kālapabbata.**[6]

[1] SNA. i. 223.
[2] *E.g.*, J. i. 232; iii. 379.
[3] J. ii. 65.
[4] *Ibid.*, 92, 219.
[5] J. v. 392.
[6] J. vi. 265.

Manohara.—A park laid out by **Parakkamabāhu I.**[1]

[1] Cv. lxxix. 9.

Manoharī.—A king of Thaton who later became a vassal of **Anorata** of Burma. It is said that flames issued from his mouth when he spoke, till Anorata made him eat food taken from a holy shrine. Manoharī, confounded by the loss of his power, sold a gem and erected two great images of the Buddha.[1]

[1] Sās. 64; Bode, *op. cit.*, 13, 14, 15.

Manohāra.—A ṭīkā written by **Dhammasenāpati Thera.**[1]

[1] Gv. 63, 73.

1. **Mantānī.**—Sister of **Aññākoṇḍañña** and mother of **Puṇṇa Mantāniputta** (*q.v.*). She lived in **Rājagaha.**

2. **Mantānī.**—A brahminee, mother of **Aṅgulimāla;** her husband was **Gagga.**[1]

[1] M. ii. 102; ThagA. ii. 58.

Mantāvatī.—A city, the birthplace of **Sumedhā Therī,** its chieftain being **Koñca.**[1]

[1] Thig. vs. 448; ThigA. 272.

Mantidatta Thera.—He was once an officer of **Pasenadi,** but later left the world. A conversation between him and **Dhanuggahatissa** it was which, overheard by Pasenadi's spies, led to Pasenadi changing his tactics and defeating **Ajātasattu.**[1] In the conversation Mantidatta is addressed as Datta, which was evidently his personal name, the prefix Manti being given him as the king's minister and to distinguish him from other Dattas.

[1] J. iv. 343; but see J. ii. 403, where Dhanuggatissa's companion is called **Utta,** which is probably a wrong reading of Datta.

Manti.—A brahmin well versed in reading auspicious signs. He was one of the brahmins consulted by **Suddhodana** when **Gotama Buddha** was born.[1]

[1] J. i. 56; Mil. 236.

Mandākinī.—One of the seven great lakes of the **Himālaya.**[1] It is in the **Chaddantavana** and is fifty leagues in extent, of which twenty-

[1] Their names are given at J. v. 415; A. iv. 101; SNA. ii. 407; DA. i. 164; UdA. 300; AA. ii. 759. At Vsm. 416, the name **Tiyaggalā** is substituted for Mandākinī.

five leagues is of crystal water, free from moss or weeds. For the next twenty-five leagues, the water is but waist-deep and is covered with white lotus, spreading for half a league around the lake; beyond that are red lotus, red lilies, etc., rice-fields, fruit-trees, a grove of sugar-cane—each cane being as big as a palm tree—banana, jak, mango, rose-apple, etc. On the bank of the lake is a spot where **Pacceka Buddha's** generally live; but **Aññā-Koṇḍañña** lived there for twelve years attended by **Chaddanta,** the elephant and **Nāgadatta,** a devaputta. They ministered to all his needs, and he only left there to take leave of the Buddha before his death. He then returned to Mandākinī, where he died and was cremated, his relics being later deposited at the gateway of **Veḷuvana,** where a cetiya was erected over them.[2] The Mandākinī-lake never grows hot and dries up only at the end of the *kappa.*[3]

[2] SA. i. 217 ff.; but see ThagA. ii. 3, where he is said to have lived on the bank of the **Chaddantadaha;** Mandākinī may have been another name for the same lake.

[3] SNA. ii. 407.

Mandāra.—A mountain in **Himavā,** mentioned together with **Meru** and **Daddara.**[1]

[1] Ap. ii. 536, 86; according to the *Abhidhānappadīpikā* (606), it is the western mountain, behind which the sun sets.

Mandāravapūjaka Thera.—An arahant. In the time of **Sikhī Buddha** he was a devaputta, and offered the Buddha some *mandārava*-flowers, which remained like a canopy over the Buddha's head for seven days. Ten kappas ago he was a king named **Jutindhara.**[1] He is probably identical with **Usabha Thera.**[2]

[1] Ap. i. 178.

[2] ThagA. i. 219.

Mandiyaputta.[1]—See **Meṇḍiya,** for which it is a wrong reading.

[1] DA. i. 181.

Mandī.—A general of **Parakkamabāhu I.,** mentioned among those who led his campaigns.[1] He is titled "**Jīvitapotthakī.**"[2]

[1] Cv. lxx. 318; lxxii. 161.

[2] See Cv. *Trs.* i. Introd. xxix. for an explanation of the title.

Mandhātā.—A primeval king, descended from **Mahāsammata, Roja, Vararoja, Kalyāṇa, Varakalyāṇa** and **Uposatha,** the last named being his father. He was thus an ancestor of the **Sākyans.**[1] He had the

[1] J. ii. 311; iii. 454; Mtu. ii. 2; Dpv. iii. 5; but see SNA. i. 352, where the genealogy is slightly different.

seven Jewels of a **Cakkavatti** and his four Supernatural Powers. When he clenched his left hand and touched it with his right, a shower of the seven kinds of jewels fell knee-deep from the sky. For eighty-four thousand years he was a prince, for eighty-four thousand a viceroy, and for eighty-four thousand more a king. His life-span was an asaṅkheyya. But he grew discontented, and, at the suggestion of his ministers, visited the deva-world. First he went to the **Cātummahārājika**-world, where he ruled; but still unsatisfied, he went to **Tāvatiṃsa.** There **Sakka** welcomed him and gave him half his kingdom. Mandhātā ruled there during the lifetime of thirty-six Sakkas, each Sakka's life lasting for thirty-six million years and sixty times one hundred thousand. As time went on, Mandhātā's craving increased; he wished to kill Sakka and gain the whole kingdom. Because of his greed his power waned, and he fell from heaven into his park. The gardener announced his arrival to the royal family, and they provided a resting-place for him and there he lay dying. When asked for a message for his people, he wished them to know how even he, in spite of his great pomp and power, had to die.[2]

Mandhātā is identified with the Bodhisatta.[3] His son was **Varamandhātā,** whose son was **Cara** and grandson **Upacara** (or **Apacara**).[4] Mandhātā ruled at **Rajagaha,**[5] and is named[6] as one of the four persons who attained, while yet in their earthly bodies, to the glory of the gods. He is considered as chief of those given up to the pleasures of the senses[7] and as an example of one whose desires could never be satisfied.[8]

When Mandhātā went to the deva-world he was accompanied by inhabitants of all the four continents. After his return to earth, however, the Cakkaratana stuck fast in the ground, and the others could not return to their homes. They thereupon begged for the intervention of the minister (*Parināyaka*), who was carrying on the government with Mandhātā's shoes on the throne. He gave them lands in **Jambudīpa.** There those who came from **Pubba-Videha** called their land **Videharaṭṭha ;** those from **Apara-goyāna** called it **Aparantajanapada,** and those from **Uttarakuru** dwelt in what afterwards came to be known as **Kururaṭṭha.**[9]

[2] J. ii. 311 ff.; DA. ii. 481 f.; MA. i. 182 f.; *cp.* Dvy. 210 ff.

[3] J. ii. 314.

[4] J. iii. 454; Dpv. iii. 6.

[5] SNA. ii. 413; DA. i. 132.

[6] Mil. 115, 291; MA. ii. 737 f. ; the others being **Guttila, Sādhina** and **Nimi.**

[7] A. ii. 17; AA. ii. 474; *e.g.*, VibhA. 506.

[8] Thig. 486.

[9] DA. ii. 482; MA. i. 183 f.

Mandhātu Jātaka (No. 258).—The story of King **Mandhātā.** It was told to a backsliding monk who, while travelling in **Sāvatthi** for alms, saw an attractively-dressed woman and fell in love with her. This was reported to the Buddha, who told him this story to show that lust could never be satisfied.[1] At the end of the discourse the monk, with many others, became a *sotāpanna*.[2]

[1] DhA. iii. 240 gives a different occasion for the story; but that, too, refers to a discontented monk.

[2] J. ii. 310 ff.

Mannāya.—A Damiḷa chief, among the immediate retinue of **Kulasekhara.**[1]

[1] Cv. lxxvi. 220.

Mannāra.—A village in Ceylon (the modern Mannar) near **Mahātittha.** There **Vīradeva** defeated **Vikkamabāhu.**[1] The village possessed a harbour, where **Māgha** and **Jayabāhu** set up fortifications.[2]

[1] Cv. xli. 39 ff.

[2] *Ibid.*, lxxxiii. 16.

Manyāgāma.—A village in the **Dakkhiṇadesa** of Ceylon, mentioned in the account of the campaigns of **Parakkamabāhu I.**[1]

[1] Cv. lxx. 133, 134.

Mayanti.—A tank built by King **Subha.**[1] *v.l.* **Cayanti.**

[1] Mhv. xxxv. 94.

Mayūra.—One of the three palaces of **Vidhurapaṇḍita.**[1]

[1] J. vi. 289.

Mayūra-pariveṇa.—A building attached to the **Mahāvihāra** and built by King **Buddhadāsa.** Two villages, **Samaṇa** and **Goḷapānu,** were given for its maintenance.[1] The building was twenty-five cubits high; **Dhātusena** removed it and replaced it by a building twenty-one cubits high.[2] It was restored by **Mahānāga,**[3] while **Dāṭhopatissa II.** gave to it the village of **Kesagāma.**[4] *v.l.* **Morapariveṇa.**

[1] Cv. xxxvii. 172; also Cv. *Trs.* i. 16, n. 2.

[2] Cv. xxxviii. 52.

[3] *Ibid.*, xli. 100.

[4] *Ibid.*, xlv. 28.

Mayūrapāsāna.—A locality in Ceylon, mentioned in the account of the campaigns of **Parakkamabāhu I.**[1]

[1] Cv. lxxii. 73.

Mayūrarūpaṭṭana.—A place where **Buddhaghosa** once stayed with his colleague **Buddhamitta.**[1]

[1] MA. ii. 1029.

Mayettikassapāvāsa.—A monastic building in Ceylon. **Jeṭṭhatissa** gave to it the village of **Sahannanagara,**[1] and **Aggabodhi III.** that of **Sālaggāma.**[2]

[1] Cv. lxiv. 100. [2] *Ibid.*, 121.

Mayettivāpi.—A tank, enlarged by **Udaya II.**[1]

[1] Cv. li. 130.

Mayhaka.—A bird, see the **Mayhaka Jātaka.**

Mayhaka Jātaka (No. 390).—The Bodhisatta was once born in a very wealthy family, and he built an alms-hall and gave away generously. He married, and, on the birth of a son, he entrusted wife and child to his younger brother and became an ascetic. When the boy began to grow up, the brother drowned him in the river lest he should claim half the estate. The Bodhisatta saw this with his divine eye and called on his brother, to whom he pointed out the folly of covetousness—" You are like the bird, Mayhaka, who sits on the pipal-tree and keeps on crying ' Mine, mine,' while the other birds eat the fruit."

The story was told in reference to a wealthy man of **Sāvatthi,** a stranger who settled down there. He neither enjoyed his wealth nor gave it to others, living in poverty, eating rice-dust and sour gruel, and travelling in a broken-down chariot with a parasol of leaves. He died without issue and his money passed to the king. When the king told the Buddha of this, the Buddha explained to him that the miser had, in a previous birth, met the Pacceka Buddha **Tagarasikhī** begging for alms and had sent word to his wife to give the food prepared for himself. This the wife gladly did. But the man saw Tagarasikhī with his bowl full of sweet foods and repented of his generosity. Therefore, in this birth, though possessing much wealth, he never enjoyed it. He was childless because he was the very man who had drowned the Bodhisatta's son.[1]

[1] J. iii. 299-303.

1. **Maraṇasati Sutta.**—The Buddha tells the monks at **Nādika** that mindfulness of death, if properly cultivated, leads to great advantages. Various monks thereupon claim that they practise such mindfulness, but the Buddha tells them their practice is not sufficiently diligent and instructs them how to improve it.[1]

[1] A. iv. 317 f.

2. **Maraṇasati Sutta.**—Preached at **Nādika.** A monk must ever remember that death may overtake him at any instant. He must, therefore, examine himself day and night and put away any evil states that may remain in him.[1]

[1] A. iv. 320 f.

Maravarā.—The soldiers of a certain district in India. They were employed by **Kulasekhara** against **Laṅkapura.**[1]

[1] Cv. lxxvi. 130, 246.

Maricavaṭṭi.—A cetiya in **Anurādhapura** and a monastic building attached to it. The cetiya was built by **Duṭṭhagāmaṇī** on the spot where the king's spear, containing the Buddha's relic given to him by the monks,[1] was planted, when Duṭṭhagāmaṇī went to the **Tissavāpi** for his ceremonial bathing after his consecration. When the king's men attempted to remove the spear they found it impossible, and the king, after consultation with the monks, decided to build a cetiya enclosing the spot with a vihāra attached. The work was completed in three years and a great ceremony of dedication was held, the building and the ceremony costing nineteen crores. The vihāra was called Maricavaṭṭi because it was intended by the king as an expiation for having once eaten a pepper-pod (*maricavaṭṭi*) without sharing it with the monks, thus violating the vow of his childhood.[2]

Vohārika-Tissa renovated the vihāra,[3] while **Goṭhābhaya** built an *uposatha*-hall[4] and **Vasabha** provided a mantling for the thūpa.[5]

Kassapa II. built a pāsāda in the vihāra and gave it to the Thera who, at one time, lived in **Nāgasālā.**[6] **Kassapa IV.** entrusted the care of the Bodhi-tree at Maricavaṭṭi to the bhikkhunīs at the **Tissārāma,** which he built for them,[7] while **Kassapa V.** restored the whole vihāra, gave it to the **Theravādins** and granted five hundred maintenance villages.[8] **Devā,** mother of **Sakkasenāpati,** provided a diadem-jewel for the Buddha-image in the vihāra, also a halo, an umbrella and a garment.[9] **Dappula III.** gave a maintenance village to the vihāra,[10] while **Mahinda IV.** started to build in it a pāsāda called **Candana,** which does not seem to have been completed.[11] **Parakkamabāhu I.** found the thūpa destroyed by the Damiḷas and rebuilt it to the height of eighty cubits.[12]

[1] See Mhv. xxv. 1.

[2] For the building of the vihāra, see Mhv. xxvi. 1 ff.; the vow is mentioned at Mhv. xxii. 80; the Dpv. makes no mention of Maricavaṭṭi.

[3] Mhv. xxxvi. 33, 36.

[4] *Ibid.*, 107.

[5] *Ibid.*, xxxv. 121.

[6] Cv. xliv. 149.

[7] *Ibid.*, lii. 24.

[8] *Ibid.*, 45.

[9] *Ibid.*, 65.

[10] *Ibid.*, liii. 2.

[11] *Ibid.*, liv. 40.

[12] *Ibid.*, lxxviii. 99.

Marugaṇa-pariveṇa.—A building in **Anurādhapura,** erected on the spot where hosts of gods visited **Mahinda** to pay obeisance to him.[1]

[1] Mhv. xv. 211.

Marutta-pokkharaṇī.—A tank in **Anurādhapura,** north of the royal palace, in the time of **Devānampiyatissa.** When **Mahinda** scattered flowers on it the earth trembled, and Mahinda prophesied that it would become the **Jantāghara-pokkhoraṇī,** situated to the east of the gateway of the **Kālapāsāna-pariveṇa.** It had disappeared by the time the Mahāvaṃsa Ṭīkā was written.[1] The *sīmā* of the **Mahāvihāra** passed through the tank.[2]

[1] MṬ. 344 f. [2] Mbv. 135, 136.

Maruthukoṭṭa.—A locality in South India.[1]

[1] Cv. lxxvi. 180.

Maruthūpa.—A village in South India mentioned in the account of the campaigns of **Parakkamabāhu I.**[1]

[1] Cv. lxxvi. 129.

Maruppiya.—See **Devānampiyatissa.**

Marumabatittha.—A locality in **Anurādhapura,** through which passed the *sīmā* of the **Mahāvihāra.**[1]

[1] Mbv. 135, 136.

Mala Vagga.—The twenty-first chapter of the **Dhammapada.**

Mala Sutta.—On the three stains: lust, hatred, and illusion. They are comprehended by the Noble Eightfold Path.[1]

[1] S. v. 57.

Malatā.—See **Mallā.**

1. **Malaya.**—A mountainous district in South India.[1]

[1] *E.g.*, J. iv. 327; Cv. lxxvi. 195.

2. **Malaya.**—The mountainous country of Ceylon, originally the home of the **Pulindā.**[1] When **Duṭṭhagāmaṇī** fled from his father's wrath, it was in Malaya that he hid.[2] In Malaya was the **Ambaṭṭhakolalena,** from

[1] Mhv. vii. 68; see Mhv. *Trs.* 60, n. 5. [2] Mhv. xxiv. 7.

which **Duṭṭhagāmaṇī** obtained silver for the **Mahā Thūpa.**[3] The hill-country provided protection from marauders who invaded Ceylon,[4] and also from those causing danger to the rightful ruler.[5] When Buddhism was threatened by the activities of unbelievers who had obtained possession of **Anurādhapura,** it was to Malaya and to **Rohaṇa** that the monks fled in order to save themselves and their teaching.[6] Malaya also afforded shelter to rebels against the government both during preparations for attack and, if necessary, during their flight.[7]

In later times Malaya was treated as a special province, and was in charge of an official called **Malayarāja,** who was generally the king's younger son, the elder being viceroy in charge of the Eastern Province (**Pācīnadesa**). The district of **Dakkhiṇadesa** was included in Malaya,[8] but it was later separated.[9] The Yuvarāja himself was sometimes Malayarājā, particularly when the other provinces were in the hands of enemies.[10] Mention is also made[11] of a Malayarājā who was in charge of a Damiḷa army (probably of mercenaries). In times of war the people of Malaya usually gave a great deal of trouble as the country was difficult of access.[12] Some of the villages in Malaya were composed of only one house.[13]

[3] Mhv. xxviii. 20.
[4] *E.g.,* in the case of Vaṭṭagāmaṇī; Mhv. xxxiii. 62; also xxxv. 26.
[5] *E.g., ibid.,* xxxvi. 50; Cv. xli. 20; l. 20.
[6] *E.g.,* Mhv. xxxvii. 6.
[7] *E.g.,* Cv. xli. 10; xliv. 62; xlviii. 98; li. 112 f.; lvii. 47, 57.
[8] See Cv. xli. 33 ff.; lii. 68; Cv. *Trs.* i. 54, n. 4; but see Cv. xlii. 6, 10; xliv. 43; li. 13; liii. 36.
[9] Cv. li. 8.
[10] *E.g., ibid.,* lviii. 7.
[11] *Ibid.,* lxix. 6.
[12] *E.g., ibid.,* lxx. 30.
[13] Sp. ii. 298.

3. **Malaya.**—The mountainous district of **Rāmañña.**[1]

[1] Cv. lxxvi. 22.

Malayappa.—A Damiḷa chief, ally of **Kulasekhara.**[1]

[1] Cv. lxxvii. 18, 55, 91; MṬ. 593.

Malaya-Mahādeva (*v.l.* **Maliya-Mahādeva, Maliyadeva**) **Thera.**—An arahant. During the **Akkhakkhāyika** famine, **Duṭṭhagāmaṇī** provided him and four others with a dish of sour millet-gruel, which was purchased with the proceeds of the sale of the king's earrings.[1] Mahādeva took his portion to **Sumanakūṭa** and shared it with nine hundred others.[2] He was also among the eight arahants who accepted a meal of pork from **Sāliya** in his previous birth as a blacksmith.[3] He was probably so called because he lived at **Koṭapabbata** in the **Malaya** country.[4]

[1] Mhv. xxxii. 30.
[2] *Ibid.,* xxxii. 49.
[3] MṬ. 606.
[4] At MṬ. 606 he is called **Koṭapabbatavāsika.**

It is said that for three years after his ordination Mahādeva[5] lived in the **Maṇḍalārāmaka-vihāra.** One day, while going for alms in **Kallagāma,** near by, he was invited by an *upāsikā* to her dwelling, where she gave him a meal, and, regarding him as a son, invited him to take all his meals at her home. The invitation was accepted, and each day, after the meal, he would return thanks with the words "May you be happy and free from sorrow" (*sukhaṃ hotu, dukkhā mucca*). At the end of the rainy season he became an arahant, and the chief incumbent of the Vihāra entrusted him with the task of preaching to the assembled people on the Pavāraṇa-Day. The young novices informed the upāsikā that her "son" would preach that day, but she, thinking they were making fun of her, said that not everyone could preach. But they persuaded her to go to the vihāra, and, when the turn of Maliyadeva came, he preached all through the night. At dawn he stopped, and the upāsikā became a sotāpanna.

Maliyadeva once preached the **Cha Chakka Sutta** in the **Lohāpāsāda,** and sixty monks, who listened to him, became arahants. He also preached the same sutta in the **Mahāmaṇḍapa,** in the **Mahāvihāra,** at **Cetiyapabbata,** at **Sākiyavaṃsa-vihāra,** at **Kuṭāli-vihāra,** at **Antarasobbha, Mutiṅgana, Vātakapabbata, Pācīnagharaka, Dīghavāpī, Lokaṇḍara,** and **Gameṇḍavāḷa,** and, at each place, sixty monks attained arahantship. At Cittalapabbata he saw a monk of over sixty preparing to bathe at **Kuruvakatittha,** and asked permission to bathe him. The Elder, discovering from his conversation that he was Maliyadeva, agreed to let him do so, though, he said, no one had ever touched his body during sixty years. Later in the day, the Elder begged Maliyadeva to preach to him, and this he did. Sixty monks, all over sixty, were among the audience, and at the conclusion of the Cha Chakka Sutta they all became arahants. The same thing happened at **Tissamahāvihāra, Kalyāṇi-vihāra, Nāgamahāvihara, Kalacchagāma,** and at other places, sixty in all.[6]

Malaya-Mahādeva was among those various large groups who renounced the world in the company of the Bodhisatta: the **Kuddāla-samāgama, Mūgapakkha-samāgama, Cūḷasutasoma-samāgama, Ayogharapaṇḍita-samāgama** and **Hatthipāla-samāgama.**[7]

It is said[8] that two monks once asked Malaya-Mahādeva for a subject of meditation, and that he gave them the formula of the thirty-two parts of the body. Though versed in the three Nikāyas, the monks

[5] Called **Maliyadeva** in the context (AA. i. 22), but further on in the same passage (p. 23) he is addressed as **Mahādeva.**

[6] MA. ii. 1024 f.

[7] J. iv. 490; also vi. 30, where **Mahāmaliyadeva** is called **Kāḷavelavāsī.**

[8] Vsm. 241.

could not become sotāpannas until they had recited the formula for a period of four months.

Malayavāsī Mahāsaṅgharakkhita.—See **Mahāsaṅgharakkhita.**

"Malāni" Sutta.—On eight stains—non-repetition in the case of a mantra, late rising, sluggishness in beauty, carelessness in a guard, misconduct in a woman, etc., and ignorance, which is the greatest sta in.[1]

[1] A. iv. 195; *cp.* Dhp. vs. 241 f.; see also **Mala Sutta.**

Malitavambha Thera.—He was the son of a brahmin of **Bhārukaccha** and entered the Order under **Pacchābhū Thera.** It is said that he preferred to live where no conveniences, except food, were available, and before long he became an arahant.

In the time of **Padumuttara Buddha** he was a bird named **Kakudha** living on a lake, and, seeing the Buddha walking along the edge of the lake, he offered him *kumudu*-flowers. One hundred and sixteen kappas ago he was king eight times under the name of **Varuṇa.**[1] He is probably identical with **Kumudadāyaka** of the Apadāna.[2]

[1] Thag. vs. 105; ThagA. i. 210 f.

[2] Ap. i. 180.

Maliya.—Perhaps the name of a dog, or it may be an adjective describing its colour.[1]

[1] See J. iii. 535.

Maliyadeva.—See **Malaya-Mahādeva.**

Malla.—See **Tela.**

Mallaka.—An Elder. As he stood one day looking at a ploughed field a sign arose in him of the size of the field. He enlarged it, induced the five *jhānas*, and, developing insight, became an arahant.[1] He is mentioned as consulting **Dīghabhāṇaka Abhaya** on some problem connected with *jhāna.*[2]

[1] Vsm. 123.

[2] *Ibid.*, 265 f.

Mallagiri, Mallāgiri, Mallaṅgiri.—A mountain in the **Himālaya,** the abode of Kinnaras.[1]

[1] J. iv. 438, 439.

Mallaputta.—See **Dabba.**

Mallavāta.—A monastery in Ceylon, built by **Aggabodhi VII.**[1] **Aggabodhi VIII.** gave to it a maintenance village.[2]

[1] Cv. xlviii. 70. [2] *Ibid.*, xlix. 47.

Malavāḷāna.—A district of Ceylon, mentioned in the account of the campaigns of **Gajabāhu. Komba** built a fortress there which was captured by the **Malayarāja,** and later by the **Nagaragiri Mahinda.**[1]

[1] Cv. lxx. 60 ff., 89.

Mallā.—The name of a people and their country. The country is included in the sixteen **Mahājanapadas** (*q.v.*) of the Buddha's time. The kingdom, at that time, was divided into two parts, having their respective capitals in **Pāvā** and **Kusinārā.** The Mallas of Pāvā were called **Pāveyyaka-Mallā,** those of Kusināra, **Kosinārakā.** That these were separate kingdoms is shown by the fact that after the Buddha's death at Kusināra, the Mallas of Pāvā sent messengers to claim their share of the Buddha's relics.[1] Each had their Mote Hall. In the **Saṅgīti Sutta** we are told that the Buddha, in the course of one of his journeys, came with five hundred followers to Pāvā and stayed in the Ambavana of **Cunda** the smith. A new Mote Hall, called **Ubbhaṭaka,** had just been completed for the Mallas of Pāvā, and the Buddha was invited to be the first to occupy it that it might be consecrated thereby. The Buddha accepted the invitation, and preached in the Hall far into the night. It was also at Pāvā that the Buddha took his last meal, of *Sūkaramaddava,* at the house of Cunda.[2] From there he went to Kusinārā, and there, as he lay dying, he sent **Ānanda** to the Mallas of Kusināra, who were assembled in their Mote Hall to announce his approaching death. The Mallas thereupon came to the **Upavattana** Sāla-grove where the Buddha was, in order to pay him their last respects. Ānanda made them stand in groups according to family, and then presented them to the Buddha, announcing the name of each family. After the Buddha's death, they met together once more in the Mote Hall, and made arrangements to pay him all the honour due to a **Cakkavatti.** They cremated the Buddha's body at the **Makuṭa-bandhana-cetiya,** and then collected the relics, which they deposited in their Mote Hall, surrounding them with a lattice-work of spears and a rampart of bows till they were distributed among the various claimants by **Doṇa.**[3] The Mallas, both of Pāvā and Kusināra, erected thūpas over their respective shares of the relics and held feasts in their honour.[4]

[1] D. ii. 165.
[2] *Ibid.*, 126 f.
[3] *Ibid.*, 166.
[4] *Ibid.*, 167.

The Malla capital of Kusinārā was, in the Buddha's day, a place of small importance. Ānanda contemptuously refers to it as a "little wattle-and-daub town in the midst of a jungle, a branch township," quite unworthy of being the scene of the Buddha's Parinibbāna. But the Buddha informs Ānanda that it was once **Kusāvatī** (*q.v.*), the mighty capital of **Kusa** and **Mahāsudassana.** This shows that the Mallas had, at first, a monarchical constitution, but in the sixth century B.C. they were regarded, together with the **Vajjis,** as a typical example of a republic (*saṅgha, gaṇa*).[5] The chief Mallas administered the state in turn. Those who were free from such duties engaged in trade, sometimes undertaking long caravan journeys.[6]

Both the Buddha and **Nigaṇṭha Nātaputta** appear to have had followers among the Mallas. Pāvā was the scene of Nātaputta's death, just as Kusinārā was of the Buddha's.[7] Several followers of the Buddha among the Mallas are mentioned by name—*e.g.*, **Dabba, Pukkusa, Khaṇḍasumana, Bhadragaka, Rāsiya, Roja** and **Sīha** (*q.v.*). The Mallas seem to have lived at peace with their neighbours, though there was apparently some trouble between them and the **Licchavis,** as shown by the story of **Bandhula Malla** (*q.v.*). Both the Mallas and the Licchavis were khattiyas, belonging to the **Vasiṭṭha-gotta,** because in the books both tribes are repeatedly referred to as **Vāseṭṭhā** (*q.v.*).[8] There is reason to believe that the Malla republic fell into the hands of **Ajātasattu,** as did that of the Licchavis.[9]

The Mallas are generally identified with the Malloi mentioned in the Greek accounts of Alexander's invasion of India. The Malloi were a warlike tribe who, for some time, successfully resisted Alexander's attack. Their territory must have been situated in or near the Panjab.

Other places in the Malla country, besides Pāvā and Kusinārā, are mentioned where the Buddha stayed—*e.g.*, **Bhoganagara, Anupiyā** and **Uruvelakappa,**[10] near which was the **Mahāvana,** a wide tract of forest.

Bandhula went from Kusināra to **Takkasilā** for purposes of study. *v.l.* **Mālā**[11] and **Malatā,**[12] evidently both wrong readings.

[5] M. i. 231.

[6] DA. ii. 569.

[7] See *s.v.* Pāvā.

[8] Manu says that both Licchavis and Mallas had kṣatriya parents, but their fathers were Vrātyas—*i.e.*, had not gone through the ceremony of Vedic initiation at the proper time.

[9] Bhandarkar, *Carmichael Lectures*, 1918, p. 79.

[10] See *s.v.*

[11] *E.g.*, UdA. 377.

[12] *E.g.*, AA. ii. 814.

2. **Mallā.**—A bhikkhunī who came to Ceylon from **Jambudīpa;** she was an eminent teacher of the Vinaya at **Anurādhapura.**[1]

[1] Dpv. xviii. 12.

Mallika.—A king of **Kosala,** identified with **Ānanda.** See the **Rājovāda Jātaka.**[1]

[1] J. ii. 2 ff.

1. **Mallikā.**—Chief queen of **Pasenadi,** king of **Kosala.** She was the daughter of the chief garland-maker of Kosala, and was very good and beautiful. When she was sixteen she was, one day, on her way to the garden with some companions, carrying with her three portions of sour gruel in a basket. Meeting the Buddha, she offered them to him and worshipped him. The Buddha, seeing her wrapt in joy, smiled, and, in answer to **Ānanda's** question, said she would be chief queen of Kosala that very day.[1]

It happened that Pasenadi, having suffered defeat at the hands of **Ajātasattu** that very day, was passing by and entered the flower garden, attracted by Mallikā's voice. Mallikā, seeing him coming, and noting his weariness, seized his horse's bridle. The king, discovering that she was unmarried, dismounted, and, having rested awhile, his head on her lap, entered the town with her and took her to her own house. In the evening he sent a chariot for her, and with great honour and pomp brought her from her own home, set her on a heap of jewels and anointed her chief queen. From that day onward she was the beloved and devoted wife of the king and an undeviating follower of the Buddha.[2] The king found her sagacious and practical-minded and consulted her and accepted her advice when in difficulty—*e.g.*, in the **Asisadisa-dāna** (*q.v.*), wherein he wished to excel his subjects, and again when he was troubled by evil dreams as narrated in the **Mahāsupina Jātaka** (*q.v.*).[3] The Jātaka states how Mallikā saved many innocent lives from being sacrificed, and the Buddha declared that in a past life too, as **Dinnā** (*q.v.*), she had saved the lives of a large number of people by her wisdom.[4]

Both Mallikā and Pasenadi's other queen, **Vāsabhakhattiyā,** desired to learn the Dhamma, and, at their request conveyed through Pasenadi, the Buddha asked Ānanda to visit the palace regularly and teach them the Doctrine. Ānanda found in Mallikā an apt and ready pupil, conscientious in her work; Vāsabhakhattiyā was not so devoted to her duties.[5] Mallika's knowledge of the Dhamma made her wiser than Pasenadi

[1] J. iii. 405; SA. i. 110 ff. It was to explain Mallikā's good fortune that the **Kummāsapiṇḍa Jātaka** (*q.v.*) was preached.

[2] DhA. iii. 121 f.

[3] DhA. ii. 8 ff. says that Mallikā called the king a simpleton for putting his faith in brahmins and took him to the Buddha, and while the king sat trembling, asked the questions for him and had them explained.

[4] DhA. ii. 15 f.

[5] *Ibid.*, iii. 382 f. For an incident connected with Ānanda's visit to the palace, see Vin. iv. 158 f.

would have desired, and he once, in a moment of great affection, asked if *anyone* were dearer to her than her own "self." "No, Sire," was the answer; the king was evidently greatly disappointed, for he sought the Buddha, who explained to him that Mallikā, in making that answer, had uttered a great truth.[6] Mallikā, though an exemplary wife, was not without lapses. Reference is made to the quarrels she had with her husband, once, at least, on the question of conjugal rights,[7] as a result of which they both sulked and had to be reconciled by the Buddha. The Dhammapada Commentary[8] relates a ridiculous story about her misbehaviour with a dog in the bath-house. Pasenadi was a witness of this scene, but she was able to convince him that it was the fault of the lighting of the bath-house. Nevertheless, it is said that at the moment of her death she recollected this misdeed, and, as a result, was reborn in **Avīci.** The king was overcome by grief at Mallika's death, and, after the funeral rites, went to the Buddha to ask where she had been reborn. The Buddha, not wishing him to know, caused the king to forget the question, every time he came to the vihāra, for a whole week, till Mallikā's suffering in Avīci was over; then he allowed the question to be asked, and he was able to assure Pasenadi that she had been reborn in **Tusita** and to console him in his grief. It is said[9] that Pasenadi was on a visit to the Buddha when a man came with the whispered message that the queen was dead. It was a terrible shock, "his shoulders drooped, his mouth fell, and he sat brooding, unable to speak."

Mallikā had a daughter by Pasenadi[10]; no mention is made of a son. He is said to have been disappointed on hearing that the child was a girl; but the Buddha assured him that women were sometimes wiser than men.[11]

Mallikā is mentioned[12] as one of seven persons whose acts of devotion bore fruit in this life and whose fame reached even to the gods. Only one instance is on record of Mallikā asking a question of the Buddha. She wished to know why some women are plain, others beautiful, some rich, others poor. And the Buddha explained to her the reasons for these discrepancies.[13]

In the **Piyajātika Sutta**[14] Pasenadi is said to have taunted her because

[6] S. i. 75; Ud. v. 1.

[7] J. iv. 437; also J. iii. 20; in these quarrels the king was probably more to blame than Mallikā; it is said that until reconciled by the Buddha he ignored her very existence, saying that prosperity had turned her head.

[8] DhA. iii. 119 ff.

[9] A. iii. 57.

[10] Probably **Vajirī** (*q.v.*), who is spoken of as the king's *only* daughter (M. ii. 110).

[11] S. i. 86 f.

[12] Mil. 115, 291.

[13] See **Mallikā Sutta** 1.

[14] M. ii. 106 ff.

"her recluse Gotama" had said that dear ones bring sorrow and tribulation. "If the Lord says so, it must be so," she replies; but secretly sends **Nāḷijaṅgha** to find out from the Buddha himself if he had said so and why. Having learnt the facts, she faces Pasenadi again, and convinces him too that the Buddha is right.

Mallikā had a garden, called the **Mallikārāma,** in which was a Hall among the Deispyros-trees (*tindukācīra*) set apart for religious discussions between members of various sects (*samayappavādaka*).[15]

Mallikā is identified with **Sujātā** of the **Sujāta Jātaka,**[16] the Kinnarī in the **Bhallāṭiya Jātaka**[17] and **Sambulā** in the **Sambula Jātaka.**[18] In all three births Pasenadi was her husband.

Mallikā is included in a list of eminent upāsikās.[19]

15 M. ii. 22; MA. 710; D. i. 178; see *s.v.* **Ekasālā.**
16 J. iii. 22.
17 J. iv. 444.
18 J. v. 98.
19 A. iv. 348.

2. **Mallikā.**—Wife of **Bandhula** (*q.v.*). She is called **Mallarājaputtā,**[1] and belonged, evidently, to a **Malla** clan.

1 VvA. 165.

1. **Mallikā Sutta.**—**Mallikā** visits the Buddha and asks him why some women are beautiful, others plain, some rich, others poor. The Buddha explains that if a woman be ill-tempered and irritable, jealous and slow to give alms, such a one becomes poor and of ill favour, wherever she may happen to be born. A woman, however, who never becomes angry or agitated even under great provocation, and is generous, such a one becomes beautiful and rich.

Mallikā declares her determination for the future, to be gentle in temper, never revengeful or harbouring a grudge, but always amiable and generous.[1]

1 A. ii. 202 ff.

2. **Mallikā Sutta.**—Pasenadi asks **Mallikā,** as they sit on the upper terrace of the palace, if anyone is dearer to her than her own "self"; she says "No one." He says that the same is true of him, but is evidently piqued, for he seeks the Buddha; the Buddha tells him that Mallikā has spoken truly and well.[1]

1 S. i. 75.

Mallikārāma.—A pleasaunce in **Sāvatthi** belonging to Queen **Mallikā.** It is described as "*Samayappavādakatindukācīra*-(*v.l. tindukākhīra*)-*ekasalaka*."[1] The Commentary[2] says it was called *Samayappavādaka*

1 D. i. 178; M. ii. 22, etc.; Sp. i. 107, etc.
2 MA. ii. 710; *cf.* DA. ii. 365.

because teachers holding various views used to gather there and discourse on their doctrines. It was surrounded by *tindukakhīra* (*timbaru*) trees, hence *tindukācīra* (*sic*); at first it possessed only one hall, but later many were erected through the good fortune of **Poṭṭhapāda**—hence its epithet *Ekasālāka*.

Mallikāvimāna-vatthu.—The story of **Mallikā,** wife of **Bandhula,** who, after death, was born in a wonderful palace in **Tāvatiṃsā,** surrounded by all manner of luxuries. This was chiefly as a result of her having offered her **Mahālatāpasādhana** in honour of the Buddha, after his death. **Moggallāna** met her in Tāvatiṃsa and heard her story.[1]

[1] Vv. iii. 8; VvA. 165 ff.

Mallī.—A **Malla** woman.[1]

[1] Vin. ii. 268.

Masakkasāra.—A name given to **Tāvatiṃsa,** the abode of **Vāsava** (**Sakka**).[1] The scholiast explains[2] that Masakkasāra is really the name of Mount **Sineru,** so called because it is immoveable (*Masakkasāro vuccati osakkana-parisakkanābhāvena-ghanasāratāya ca Sinerupabbarājā*), and Tāvatiṃsa came to be known as Masakkasāra because it was built on Sineru.

[1] J. v. 167; vi. 272, 289, 400; VvA. 350. [2] J. v. 168; vi. 272.

Masāra.—A hill from which the *masāragalla* stones are obtained.[1]

[1] See Rhys Davids, Milinda *Trs.* i. 117, n. 6.

1. **Mahaka.**—A novice, pupil of **Upananda,** who is mentioned as having been guilty of an unnatural offence with **Kaṇḍaka,** another novice.[1]

[1] Vin. i. 70.

2. **Mahaka Thera.**—An arahant. See **Mahaka Sutta.**

Mahaka Sutta.—Once a number of monks staying in the **Ambāṭaka-grove** in **Macchikāsaṇḍa** were entertained by **Citta-gahapati** to a sumptuous meal. At the end of the meal, Citta escorted them back to the monastery. On the way the monks were overcome by the heat, and **Mahaka,** the junior monk, with the permission of his senior, made by his magic power a cool wind to blow and wrought a thunderstorm accompanied by gentle rain. Citta was greatly impressed, and, seeking Mahaka in his cell, asked him to perform some miracle. Mahaka told him to put his cloak on the verandah and to scatter a bundle of grass on it. Then he retired to his cell, locked the door, and caused a flame to dart through the keyhole and burn the grass without damaging the cloak. Citta was overcome with surprise, and promised to supply Mahaka with all requisites. Mahaka thanked him, but soon after left Macchikāsaṇḍa never to return.[1]

[1] Because he did not wish to enjoy gains won by a display of *iddhi*-power; S. iv. 288 ff.; the story is also referred to at Vsm. 393.

Mahaṇṇavāpi.—A tank restored by **Parakkamabāhu I.**[1]

[1] Cv. lxxix. 34.

Mahanta.—A stone image of the Buddha set up in the **Paṭimā-vihāra** in **Kāṇagāma** by **Aggabodhi,** son of **Mahātissa** and ruler of **Rohaṇa.**[1]

[1] Cv. xlv. 44.

Mahanta-pariveṇa.—A monastic building erected by a corporation (*pūga*) in **Bandhumatī** in the time of **Vipassī Buddha.**[1]

[1] Ap. ii. 493 (vs. 19).

Mahapphala Sutta.—The four *iddhipādas,* if developed, bear great fruit.[1]

[1] S. v. 267.

Mahārivara.—A stronghold in **Rohaṇa,** mentioned in the account of the campaigns of **Parakkamabāhu I.**[1]

[1] Cv. lxxiv. 121.

Mahallaka-Nāga, Mahalla-Nāga.—Father-in-law and commander-in-chief of **Gajabāhuka-Gāmaṇi.** After Gajabāhu's death he became king of Ceylon and reigned for six years (196-202 A.C.). He built seven vihāras: **Sejalaka, Goṭapabbata, Dakapāsāṇa, Sālipabbata, Tanaveli, Tobbalanāgāpabbata** and **Girihālika.** He was succeeded by his son **Bhātika-Tissa.**[1]

[1] Mhv. xxxv. 123 ff.; xxxvi. 1; MṬ. 657; Dpv. xxii. 15 ff., 29.

Mahallarāja.—A padhānaghara erected by **Aggabodhi III.** and his viceroy **Māna.** The villages of **Hankāra** and **Sāmugāma** were given for its maintenance.[1]

[1] Cv. xliv. 119.

Mahā-aṅgaṇa.—A locality in **Anurādhapura** through which the *sīmā* of the **Mahāvihāra** passed; it was so called because of a large *aṅgaṇa*-tree which stood there.[1]

[1] Mbv. 135, 136.

Mahāaṭṭhakathā.—The oldest and most important of the Commentaries on the Tipiṭaka, brought, according to tradition, to Ceylon by **Mahinda,** who translated it into Sinhalese.[1] It thus came to be called the *Sīhalaṭṭhakathā*. Besides exegetical material on the Pāli Canon, it contained also historical materials on which were later based the Pāli Chronicles, the **Mahāvaṃsa** and the **Dīpavaṃsa.**[2] The Mahāaṭṭhakathā was the chief source from which **Buddhaghosa** drew his materials for his Commentaries and is often referred to in his works, particularly in the **Samantapāsādikā.**[3] The Mahāaṭṭhakathā was in charge of the monks of the **Mahāvihāra** at **Anurādhapura.** It was superseded by the Commentaries of Buddhaghosa, **Dhammapāla** and others, and is not now extant. It is often referred to merely as *Aṭṭhakathā.*[4]

[1] Cv. xxxvii. 228 f.

[2] For a description see Geiger's Dīpavaṃsa and Mahavaṃsa, pp. 44, 63, etc.

[3] *E.g.*, Sp. i. 2; ii. 494; 265; iii. 537, 616, 617, 627, 701, 716, 718, 726; iv. 744, 776, 783, 817, 863, 914, 923; DhSA. 157; DA. i. 180, etc.

[4] *E.g.*, VibhA. 56, 155, 200, etc.

Mahā-Anāthapiṇḍika.—See **Anāthapiṇḍika.** He was evidently so called in some contexts to distinguish him from **Culla-Anāthapiṇḍika.**[1]

[1] *E.g.*, DhA. iii. 145; J. i. 148.

Mahā-Anula Thera.—He once saw a number of monks, who had obtained only dry food, eating it on the banks of a river. Anula resolved that the river water should turn into butter-cream and made a sign to the novices, who then took the cream in cups and gave it to the monks.[1]

[1] Vsm. 404.

1. **Mahā-Abhaya.**—See **Abhaya-giri.**

2. **Mahā-Abhaya Thera.**—Usually called **Dīghabhāṇaka-Abhaya.** He was evidently an eminent Thera. It is said[1] that when news arrived that the brigand **Abhaya** was coming to **Cetiyagiri** to pillage it, the patrons of the vihāra informed Abhaya Thera of this. He asked them to collect various kinds of food and drink wherewith to entertain the brigand. The latter was greatly pleased, and, on learning that this hospitality

[1] Sp. ii. 474 f.; referred to at DhSA. 399.

was shown him at the instigation of Abhaya Thera, he visited the Elder and took upon himself the protection of the vihāra from all danger. Later the monks questioned the right of the Elder to entertain a robber with what belonged to the vihāra, but he convened an assembly of the monks and convinced them that he was guiltless, as his act had been solely for the protection of the belongings of the Saṅgha. This story shows that the Elder lived at Cetiyagiri.

On another occasion[2] Abhaya Thera preached the **Mahā-ariyavaṃsa paṭipadā,** and the whole village (? **Mahāgāma**) came to hear him. After the sermon he received great honour. An elderly monk was full of envy and abused him, saying that under guise of preaching he had filled the night with noise. The two monks had to travel along the same road for the distance of a gāvuta, and all the way the old monk abused Abhaya. When their roads separated, Abhaya worshipped the monk and took leave of him and said, when asked later, that he had heard none of the abuse because he had been all the time engaged in meditation. One day, a certain woman who had come all the way from **Ullabha-kolakaṇṇikā,** a distance of five leagues, to hear Abhaya preach the **Ariyavaṃsa,** found that he was about to arise without finishing the sermon, and reminded him that he was omitting the most important part. The monk praised her and continued to preach till dawn, when the woman became a sotāpanna.[3] It is said that once Abhaya wanted to know if a certain *piṇḍapātika* monk were a *putthujjana* or not. While this monk was bathing at the mouth of the **Kalyāṇī** River, Abhaya told a novice to dive into the water and catch hold of his foot. The monk, thinking it was a crocodile, screamed with fear, and Abhaya knew that he was a *puthujjana.*[4] Thieves once bound an Elder with creepers and made him lie down. A jungle fire spread to him, but before the creepers could be cut, he established insight and died an arahant. Abhaya, coming along with five hundred others, saw the body, cremated it, and had a shrine built over the remains.[5]

Abhaya's opinion was evidently greatly respected, and he is mentioned as having been consulted by **Maha-Dhammarakhita**[6] and **Mallaka**[7] on problems connected with the Abhidhamma.

Abhaya is mentioned among those who could remember very early incidents in their lives. When he was only nine days old, his mother bent down to embrace him, but her hair became loose and the *sumana-*flowers she wore on her head fell on him, hurting him. In later life he could remember this incident.[8]

[2] MA. i. 65 f.
[3] AA. i. 386.
[4] MA. ii. 869.
[5] Vsm. 36.
[6] VibhA. 81.
[7] Vsm. 266.
[8] DA. ii. 530; MNidA. 234.

Mahā-Ariṭṭha.—Nephew of **Devānampiyatissa.** He was the king's chief minister, and led the embassy which was sent to **Asoka** soon after Devānampiyatissa ascended the throne.[1] Asoka conferred on him the title of Senāpati.[2] It is said that he had fifty-five elder and younger brothers who all joined the Order at **Cetiyagiri** at the end of a sermon by **Mahinda** on the **Vassūpanāyikakhandha.**[3] This was before the commencement of the rainy season, but elsewhere[4] it is said that Ariṭṭha was sent in the month of Assayuja—*after* the *pavāraṇa*, when the rains were over—to **Pāṭaliputta** to fetch **Saṅghamittā** and the Bodhi-tree from the court of Asoka, and that he agreed to go only on condition that he should join the Order on his return. The king consented, and, his mission successfully concluded, he entered the Order with five hundred others and attained arahantship.[5] He died in the reign of **Uttiya.**[6] The Samantapāsādikā[7] gives an account of a recital (*saṅgīti*) held in Ceylon by Mahā-Ariṭṭha. The scene was the pariveṇa of the minister **Meghavaṇṇābhaya** in the **Thūpārāma,** where sixty-eight thousand monks were assembled. A seat, facing south, was provided for Mahinda, Ariṭṭha's seat, the *dhammāsana*, facing north. Ariṭṭha occupied this seat at Mahinda's request, and sixty-eight Mahātheras, led by Mahinda, sat around him. Devānampiyatissa's younger brother, **Mattābhaya Thera,** with five hundred others, were present in order to learn the Vinaya, the king also being present. When Ariṭṭha began his recital of the Vinaya, many miracles occurred. This was on the first day of the *pavāraṇa*-ceremony in the month of Kattika.

Mahā-Ariṭṭha's chief disciples were **Tissadatta, Kālasumana** and **Dīghasumana** (*q.v.*).

1 Mhv. xi. 20.
2 *Ibid.*, 25.
3 *Ibid.*, xvi. 10.
4 *Ibid.*, xviii. 3; perhaps here we have to deal with two different traditions.
5 Mhv. xix. 5, 12, 66.
6 *Ibid.*, xx. 54.
7 Sp. i. 102 ff.

Mahāariyavaṃsa Sutta.—On the four Ariyan lineages, reckoned as ancient and pure, and held in esteem by discerning recluses and brahmins of all times. A monk is content with any kind of robe; he does not, for the sake of robes, resort to unseemly conduct; he is free from either selfishness or greed with regard to robes; neither does he exalt himself because of his contentment. So it is with other requisites. He also delights in abandoning and in *bhāvanā*. A monk possessed of these four *Ariyavaṃsā* verily becomes a sage, praised by Brahmā himself.[1]

This sutta was evidently a favourite topic for a sermon.[2] The Commentary explains[3] how, for instance, anyone who preaches on the first

1 A. ii. 27 ff.
2 AA. i. 385, 386.
3 *Ibid.*, ii. 494.

three *Ariyavaṃsā* (*catupaccayasantosa*) could bring the whole Vinaya Piṭaka to bear on the discussion, while a discussion on the *bhāvanārāma-ariyavaṃsa* could include the two other Piṭakas, chiefly the *nekkhamma-pāli* of the Paṭisambhidāmagga, the **Dasuttara Sutta** of the Dīgha Nikāya, the **Satipaṭṭhāna Sutta** of the Majjhima Nikāya, and the Niddesapariyāya of the Abhidhamma.

The full name of the sutta seems to have been *Catupaccayasantosa-bhāvanārāma-Mahāariyavaṃsa Sutta.*[4] It was also probably called **Vaṃsa Sutta** for short.

It is probably this Mahāariyavaṃsa Sutta which was held in such high esteem by **Vohāraka Tissa,** that he ordered almsgiving throughout Ceylon whenever the " Ariyavaṃsa " was read.[5] It is said that people would journey five yojanas to hear a monk preach the Ariyavaṃsa,[6] and mention is made of **Mahāariyavaṃsabhāṇakā,** who, judging from the stories of them,[7] were extremely able and eloquent preachers.

[4] *E.g.*, *ibid.*, i. 385.
[5] Mhv. xxxvi. 38; but see Mhv. *Trs.* 258, n. 6.
[6] *E.g.*, AA. i. 386.
[7] *E.g.*, SA. iii. 151.

Mahā-Avīci.—See **Avīci.**

Mahā-Assapura Sutta.—Preached at **Assapura** in the **Aṅga** country. Since monks are called recluses (*samaṇā*) they must train themselves to be true *samaṇas* and *brāhmaṇas*; they should be conscientious and scrupulous, pure in deed, word and thought, guarding the portals of the senses, moderate in eating, ever vigilant, mindful and self-possessed, striving to put off the five *nivaraṇā* and cultivating the *jhānā*. Such an almsman can truly be called a samaṇa, a brahmin, a *nahātaka, vedagū, sotthiya, ariya,* and arahant. He is an ideal recluse.[1]

[1] M. i. 271-80.

Mahā-Assāroha Jātaka (No. 302).—The Bodhisatta was once king of Benares, and having been defeated in some frontier disturbance, he fled on his horse till he reached a certain village. At sight of him all the people disappeared except one man, who made enquiries, and, on finding that he was no rebel, took him home and entertained him with great honour, looking well after his horse. When the king left, he told the man that his name was **Mahā-Assāroha,** and asked him to visit his home if ever he should be in the city. On reaching the city himself, he gave orders to the gate-keepers that if anyone should come enquiring for Mahā-Assāroha, he should be brought at once to the palace. Time passed and the man failed to appear. The king, therefore, constantly increased the taxes of the village, until the villagers asked their neighbour to visit his friend Mahā-Assāroha and try to obtain some relief. So he prepared presents for Mahā-Assāroha and his wife, and taking a cake baked in his own house he set forth. Arrived at the city gates, he was conducted by the gate-keeper to the palace. There the king accepted his presents, showed him all the honours due to a king, and, in the end, gave him half of his kingdom. When the ministers complained, through the medium of the king's son, that a mere villager had been exalted to the rank of king, the Bodhisatta explained that real friends who help one in time of adversity should be paid every honour.

The story was related in reference to the good offices of **Ānanda,** who is identified with the villager.[1]

[1] J. iii. 8-13.

Mahā-āsana.—A spot in **Anurādhapura** where the fruit from the Bodhi-branch, brought by **Saṅghamittā,** was planted in a golden vase by **Devānampiyatissa.** Immediately eight saplings sprang from the fruit.[1]

[1] Mhv. xix. 57; Mbv. 162.

Mahā-Ukkusa Jātaka (No. 486).—Not far from a certain village settlement a hawk lived on the south shore of a lake. He courted a female hawk on the western shore, and, at her suggestion, made friends with an osprey on the west side, a lion on the north and a tortoise on an island in the lake. Later, the hawks had two sons, who lived on the island. One day, some men, wandering about in search of food, lay down under the tree where the hawks lived and kindled a fire to keep away the insects. The smoke disturbed the young ones and they set up a cry. The men, hearing this, wished to get the birds for their food. But the she-hawk, perceiving the danger, sent her husband to summon their friends. First came the osprey who brought water in his wings and quenched the fire every time it was lighted; when he was tired, the tortoise sent his son with mud from the lake, which he put on the fire. The men caught the tortoise and tied it with creepers, but he plunged into the water, dragging the men with him. Then the lion appeared, and at his first roar the men fled, and the friends rejoiced over the firmness of their friendship.

The story was told in reference to **Mittagandhaka** (*q.v.*) and his wife. They were the hawks of the story. **Rāhula** was the young tortoise and **Moggallāna** the father tortoise. **Sāriputta** was the osprey and the Bodhisatta the lion.[1]

[1] J. iv. 288-97.

Mahā-Udāyī.—See **Udāyī.**

Mahā-Ummagga Jātaka (No. 546).—The Bodhisatta was once born in **Mithilā** as the son of **Sirivaḍḍhaka** and **Sumanādevī.** The child was born with a medicinal plant in his hand, and was therefore called **Mahosadha.** He talked immediately after birth, and it is said that, on the day of his conception, **Videha,** king of Mithilā, dreamed a dream which presaged the birth of a sage. From early childhood Mahosadha gave evidence of unusual ability, and one of his first acts was to build a large hall and lay out a garden with the help of his companions. The king wished to have him in the court though he was only seven years old, but was dissuaded by his wise men. But he sent a councillor to watch the boy and report of his doings from time to time. When the king was fully convinced[1] that Mahosadha was undoubtedly endowed with unusual wisdom, he sent for him in spite of the counsel of his ministers—**Senaka, Pukkusa, Kāvinda** and **Devinda**—and appointed him as his fifth councillor. One day, Mahosadha saved the queen **Udumbarā** (*q.v.*) from the unjust wrath of the king, and ever after she was his firm and loyal friend. After his entry into the court, Mahosadha was on many occasions called upon to match his wit against that of the senior councillors, and on each occasion he emerged triumphant.[2] When aged sixteen he married **Amarādevī.** She was a wise woman, and frustrated many attempts of Mahosadha's enemies to embroil him with the king. Once they stole various things from the palace and sent them to her. She accepted them, and made assignations with each of the donors. When they arrived she had them seized, their heads shaved, and themselves thrown into the jakes, where she tormented them, and then arraigned them before the king with the stolen goods. Mahosadha, aware of the plots against him, lay in hiding, and the deity of the king's parasol put several questions to the king, knowing that none but Mahosadha could answer them. The king sent men to seek him, and he was discovered working for a potter. The king showed him all honour, and obtained from him the answers to the deity's questions.

But his enemies continued to plot against him, until orders were given by the king that he should be killed the next day. Udumbarā discovered this and warned him. But in the meantime he had discovered the guilty secrets of his enemies: Senaka had killed a courtesan, Pukkusa had a leprous spot on his thigh, Kāvinda was possessed by a yakkha named **Naradeva,** and Devinda had stolen the king's most precious gem. Mahosadha posted these facts everywhere in the city, and the next day

[1] The Jātaka gives an account of nineteen problems solved by Mahosadha.

[2] *E.g.*, in the **Meṇḍakapañha** (*q.v.* and the **Sirimandapañha** (*q.v.*).

went boldly into the palace. The king professed innocence of any evil intentions against him; but Mahosadha exposed the schemes of them all, and Senaka and the others were only saved from severe punishment by the intervention of Mahosadha himself. Thenceforward Mahosadha was Videha's trusted councillor, and took various measures to increase his royal master's power and glory. Spies were sent to every court, whence they brought home reports. Mahosadha also had a parrot whom he employed to ferret out the most baffling secrets. While returning from a visit to **Saṅkhapala,** king of **Ekabala,** the parrot passed through **Uttarapañcāla** and there overheard a conversation between **Cūḷani-Brahmadatta,** king of **Kampilla,** and his purohita **Kevaṭṭa,** wherein the latter unfolded a scheme for capturing the whole of **Jambudipa.** Kevaṭṭa was too wise to allow Brahmadatta to attack Mithilā, knowing of Mahosadha's power, but Mahosadha deliberately provoked Brahmadatta by sending his men to upset a feast he had prepared, during which he had planned to poison the hundred princes whom he had brought under subjection. Brahmadatta then set out to attack Mithilā. He laid siege to the city, and adopted various ways of compelling the citizens to surrender. But Mahosadha was more than a match for him, and found means of defeating all his plans. In the end Mahosadha engaged the services of **Anukevaṭṭa,** who, pretending to be a traitor to Mithilā, went over to the army of Brahmadatta and, gaining the king's confidence, informed him that Kevaṭṭa and all the other counsellors of Brahmadatta had accepted bribes from Mahosadha. The king listened to him, and on his advice raised the siege and fled to his own city.

But Kevaṭṭa planned revenge, and, a year later, he persuaded Brahmadatta to send poets to Videha's city, singing songs of the peerless beauty of the daughter of Brahmadatta, **Pañcālacaṇḍī.** Videha heard the songs and sent a proposal of marriage, and Kevaṭṭa came to Mithilā to arrange the day. Videha suggested that Kevaṭṭa should meet Mahosadha to discuss the plans, but Mahosadha feigned illness, and when Kevaṭṭa arrived at his house, he was grossly insulted by Mahosadha's men. When Kevaṭṭa had left, Videha consulted Mahosadha, but would not be dissuaded from his plan to marry Pañcālacaṇḍī. Finding that he could do nothing with the king, Mahosadha sent his parrot **Maṭṭhara** to find out what he could from the maynah bird which lived in Brahmadatta's bedchamber. Maṭṭhara used all his wits and won the favour of the maynah and learnt from her of Kevaṭṭa's plan, which he repeated to Mahosadha.

With Videha's leave, Mahosadha went on Uttarapañcāla to, as he said, make preparations for the wedding. But he gave orders for a village to be built on every league of ground along the road, and gave instructions to the shipwright, **Ānandakumāra,** to build and hold ready three hundred ships. At Uttarapañcāla he was received with great honour, and obtained the king's permission to build in the city a palace for Videha. The king gave him a free hand, and he immediately started to threaten to pull down houses belonging to various people, from the queen-mother downwards, and obtained money from them as bribes to spare their houses. Having reported to the king that no suitable spot was available within the city, he obtained his consent to erect a palace outside the city, between that and the Ganges. All access was forbidden to the site on penalty of a large sum, and having first erected a village called **Gaggali** for his workmen, elephants, etc., Mahosadha started to dig a tunnel, the mouth of which was in the Ganges. The tunnel, a marvellous place, was duly constructed, fitted with all manner of machinery, and beautifully decorated. A smaller tunnel was dug, leading into the larger, one opening, which was, however, concealed, giving access to the king's palace. The task occupied four months, and when all preparations were complete, Mahosadha sent word to Videha.

Videha arrived at Brahmadatta's court, and a great feast was held in his honour at **Upakārī,** the palace which had been prepared for his residence. While the feast was in progress, Mahosadha sent men by the smaller tunnel to the palace and bade them fetch **Talatā** (the queen-mother), the queen **Nandā,** and Pañcālacaṇḍī, on the pretext that they had been sent for by Brahmadatta to take part in the festivities as Videha and Mahosadha had both been killed, according to plan. Meanwhile Brahmadatta had given orders that the whole city should be surrounded. Videha was overcome with fright on discovering what was happening, but he put himself into Mahosadha's hands. The latter led him into the large tunnel, and there he was brought face to face with the members of Brahmadatta's family, who had already been conducted thither. Pañcālacaṇḍī was placed upon a heap of treasure and married to Videha. On emerging from the tunnel, they were placed on board a waiting ship, with Tālatā and Nandā, and sent away into safety, escorted by the other ships, Mahosadha himself remaining behind in Uttarapañcāla.

The next day, Brahmadatta came with his army to Upakāri, hoping to capture Videha. There Mahosadha revealed to him what had happened, and, in due course, persuaded him to forget his wrath and inspect the tunnel. While in the tunnel Brahmadatta expressed his remorse for having listened to the evil advice of Brahmadatta, and he and Mahosadha swore eternal friendship. Mahosadha returned to Mithilā, taking with him Brahmadatta's dowry for his daughter; the members of Brahmadatta's family returned to Uttarapañcāla, and the two kings lived in great amity.

Videha died ten years later, and in fulfilment of a promise made to Brahmadatta, Mahosadha went to Uttarapañcāla. There Nandā, who had never forgiven him, tried to poison the king's mind against him; but this plot was frustrated by a religious woman, **Bherī** (*q.v.*), and Brahmadatta remained his firm friend, loving him, as he confessed to Bherī, more than any of his own family.

The Jātaka was related to illustrate the Buddha's great wisdom. **Uppalavaṇṇā** is identified with Bherī, **Suddhodana** with **Sirivaḍḍhaka, Mahamāyā** withh **Sumanādevī, Bimbādevī** with Amarā, **Ānanda** with Maṭṭhara, **Sāriputta** with Cūḷaṇi-Brahmadatta, **Devadatta** with Kevaṭṭa, **Culla-Nandikā** with Talatā, **Sundarī** with Pañcālacaṇḍī, **Yasassikā** with Nandī, **Ambaṭṭha** with Kāvinda, **Poṭṭhapāda** with Pukkusa, **Pilotika** with Devinda, **Saccaka** with Senaka, **Diṭṭhamaṅgalikā** with Udumbarā, **Kuṇḍalī** with the maynah bird, and **Lāḷūdāyī** with King Videha.[3]

[3] The story occupies J. iv., pp. 329-478, in Fausböll's edition; what is given here is merely an extremely short summary; *cp.* Mtu. ii. 83-9.

Mahā-Kaṃsa.—King of **Asitañjana** in **Kaṃsabhoga** in **Uttarāpatha.** His children were **Kaṃsa, Upakaṃsa** and **Devagabbhā.**[1]

[1] J. iv. 79; PvA. 111.

Mahā-Kaccāna, Kaccāyana.—One of the most eminent disciples of the Buddha, considered chief among expounders in full of the brief saying of the Buddha (*saṅkhittena bhāsitassa vitthāreṇa atthaṃ vibhajantānaṃ*).[1] He was born at **Ujjenī** in the family of the chaplain of King **Caṇḍappajjota,** and was called Kaccāna both because of his golden colour and because Kaccāna was the name of his gotta. He studied the Vedas, and, on the death of his father, succeeded him as chaplain. With seven others he visited the Buddha, at the request of Caṇḍappajjota, to invite him to come to Ujjenī. Kaccāna and his friends listened to the Buddha's sermon, and having attained arahantship, joined the order. He then conveyed the king's invitation to the Buddha, who pointed out that it would now suffice if Kaccāna himself returned to Ujjenī.

Kaccāna accordingly set out for Ujjenī with his seven companions, accepting alms on the way at the house of a very poor girl of **Telappanāḷi,** who later became Caṇḍappajjota's queen.[2]

Arrived in Ujjenī, Kaccāna lived in the royal park, where the king showed him all honour. He preached constantly to the people, and, attracted by his discourses, numerous persons joined the Order, so that the whole city was one blaze of orange robes. It is said that after having

[1] A. i. 24.

[2] For details see *s.v.* **Telappanāḷi.**

duly established the sāsana in **Avantī**, Kaccāna returned once more to the Buddha.[3] Caṇḍappajjota consulted him on various occasions, and among the verses attributed to him in the Theragāthā,[4] are several addressed to the king himself.

It was in the time of **Padumuttara Buddha** that Kaccāna had made his resolve to win the eminence he did, after listening to Padumuttara's praise of a monk, also named Kaccāna, for similiar proficiency. Kaccāna was then a *vijjādhara*,[5] and offered the Buddha three *kaṇikāra*-flowers. In the time of **Kassapa Buddha** he was a householder of Benares, and offered a golden brick, worth one hundred thousand, to the cetiya which was being built over the Buddha's remains, and then made a vow that in future births his body should be golden.[6]

According to the Apadāna,[7] Kaccāna's father was called **Tirīṭivaccha** (or **Tidivavaccha**), and his mother **Candapadumā**. There is another account of Mahā-Kaccāna in the Apadāna,[8] in which it is said that in the time of Padumuttara Buddha he built a *gandhakuti* named **Paduma** in the shape of a lotus and covered with lotus-flowers, and that thirty kappas later he became king under the name of **Pabhassara.**

Three suttas are mentioned[9] as having obtained for Kaccāna his title of eminence—the **Madhupiṇḍika**, the **Kaccāyana** and the **Parāyaṇa;** several instances are given of people seeking Mahā-Kaccāna's assistance, for a detailed explanation of something said in brief by the Buddha—*e.g.*, **Hāliddikāni, Kāḷī, Samiddhi, Uttara** and **Valliya.**[10] Among Kaccāna's pupils and followers and those who consulted him were **Sonakuṭikaṇṇa, Isidatta, Avantiputta, Lohicca, Ārāmadaṇḍa,** and **Kaṇḍarāyaṇa.**[11]

In Avanti, Kaccāna is said to have stayed, not in the king's park, where he lived soon after his return from the Buddha, but chiefly in the **Kuraraghara-papātā**[12] and in a hut in **Makkarakaṭa**-forest.[13] Mention is also made of his staying at **Varaṇā** on the bank of **Kaddamadaha**[14]; at the **Gundāvana** in **Madhurā**[15]; at **Tapodā** in **Rājagaha,**[16] in **Soreyya,**[17] and in **Kosambī.**[18] It is said[19] that even when Kaccāna was living at Avanti,

[3] Thus, the explanation of the Madhupiṇḍika Sutta was given at **Kapilavatthu.**

[4] Thag. vss. 494-501.

[5] So says the Apadāna ii. 463, but ThagA. says he was a *vijjādhara* in the time of **Sumedha Buddha.**

[6] ThagA. i. 483 f.; AA. i. 117 f.

[7] Ap. ii. 465.

[8] i. 84 f.

[9] AA. i. 118.

[10] For details see *s.v.*; see also A. iii. 314, 321; v. 225; M. iii. 223.

[11] See *s.v.*

[12] *E.g.*, S. iii. 9; A. v. 46; Ud. v. 6; Vin. i. 194; DhA. iv. 101.

[13] S. iv. 116; see also VvA. 259, according to which he stayed near **Potali.**

[14] A. i. 65. [15] *Ibid.*, 67; M. ii. 83.

[16] *Ibid.*, iii. 192.

[17] DhA. i. 325; for a curious incident connected with Kaccāna's visit to Soreyya, see *s.v.* **Soreyya.**

[18] PvA. 140; according to Dvy. (551, 585, 586) he also stayed in Roruka.

[19] DhA. ii. 176.

a long distance away, he went regularly to hear the Buddha preach, and when the chief theras took their places in the assembly, they always left room for him. On one such occasion **Sakka** showed him great honour, falling at his feet, and the Buddha explained that this was because Mahā-Kaccāna kept his senses well guarded.

The Majjhima Commentary[20] records a curious story in reference to Kaccāna. **Vassakāra,** minister of **Ajātasattu,** saw Kaccāna descending **Gijjhakūṭa** and said he looked like a monkey. The Buddha read Vassakāra's thoughts, and warned him that after death he would be born as a monkey in **Veḷuvana.** He believed the Buddha, and made provision in Veḷuvana for his future comfort as monkey. And this he did indeed become, living in Veḷuvana and answering to the name of Vassakāra!

Kaccāna is identified with the charioteer in the **Kurudhamma Jātaka,**[21] and with **Devala** in the **Sarabhaṅga Jātaka.**[22]

According to tradition, Kaccāna was the author of the **Nettippakaraṇa,** the Pāli grammar bearing his name, and of the **Peṭakopadesa.** It is probable that these works were the compilations of a school which traced its descent to Mahā-Kaccāna.

See also **Madhura Sutta.**

[20] MA. ii. 854. [21] J. ii. 381. [22] J. v. 151.

Mahā-Kaccāna Vatthu.—The story of **Sakka's** honouring of **Mahā-Kaccāna** (*q.v.*).[1]

[1] DhA. ii. 176 f.

Mahā-Kaccāna-Bhaddekaratta Sutta.—**Samiddhi** was once drying himself after bathing at **Tapodā** in **Rājagaha,** when a deity appeared before him and asked if he knew the **Bhaddekaratta Sutta.** On his replying in the negative, the deity asked him to learn it, and the next day Samiddhi sought the Buddha and learnt the verses of the sutta. Samiddhi and his colleagues then went to **Mahā-Kaccāna** and urged him to explain the sutta in detail. This he did, for which they were very grateful. They repeated Kaccāna's exposition to the Buddha, who greatly approved of it.[1]

[1] M. iii. 192 ff.

Mahā-Kāñcana.—The Bodhisatta born as the son in a rich brahmin family, and later becoming an ascetic. See the **Bhisa Jātaka.**[1]

[1] J. iv. 305 ff.

Mahākaṇha.—The name assumed by **Mātali** when he became a dog. See the **Mahākaṇha Jātaka.**

Mahākaṇha Jātaka (No. 469).—In the past, when the teachings of **Kassapa Buddha** were already forgotten, there ruled a king named **Usīnara.** Monks and nuns lived in wickedness, and men followed evil paths, being born, after death, in the **Niraya. Sakka,** finding no one entering the deva-worlds from among men, decided to scare the men into virtue. Assuming the guise of a forester and leading **Mātali** disguised as a black fierce-looking dog called **Mahākaṇha,** Sakka came to the city gates and cried aloud that the world was doomed to destruction. The people fled in terror into the city and the gates were shut. But the forester leapt over the city wall with his dog, the latter scaring everyone he saw. The king shut himself up in his palace, but the dog put his forefeet on the palace window and set up a roar which was heard from the hells to the highest heavens. The forester said the dog was hungry, and the king ordered food to be given him. But he ate it all in one mouthful and roared for more. Usīnara then asked the forester what kind of dog it was, and was told that the animal ate up all those who walked in unrighteousness, and described who the unrighteous were. Then having terrified everyone, Sakka revealed himself and returned to his heaven. The king and his people became virtuous, and Kassapa's religion lasted for one thousand years more.

The story was told in reference to a conversation among the monks to the effect that the Buddha was always working for the good of others, never resting, never tiring, his compassion extended towards all beings. Mātali is identified with **Ānanda.**[1]

The barking of Mahākaṇha was among the four sounds heard throughout **Jambudīpa.**[2]

[1] J. iv. 180-6. [2] SNA. i. 223; see J. iv. 182, where only three are mentioned.

Mahākanda.—The name of a Damiḷa and of a pariveṇa built by him in the reign of **Aggabodhi IV.**[1]

[1] Cv. xlvi. 23.

Mahākandara.—A river in Ceylon, at the mouth of which **Paṇḍuvāsudeva** and his retinue landed from India.[1]

[1] Mhv. viii. 12.

1. **Mahākapi Jātaka** (No. 407).—The Bodhisatta was once a monkey, leader of eighty thousand. In the grove where they lived was a mango-tree (some say a banyan) growing on a river bank bearing fruit of divine flavour, and the monkeys were always careful to let no fruit drop into the river. But one day a fruit, which had been hidden by an ants' nest,

fell into the water, and was picked up at Benares, where the king was bathing. The king tasted it, and being seized with a desire to eat more, had many rafts made, and ascended the river with a company of foresters. They found the tree, and the king, having eaten his fill, lay down at the foot. At midnight the Bodhisatta came with his retinue and started eating the mangoes. The king was disturbed, and gave orders to his archers that the wood should be surrounded and all the monkeys shot at daybreak. But the Bodhisatta was a real leader; he ascended a straight-growing branch and, with one leap, reached the river-bank. He then marked the distance, and having cut off a bamboo shoot of the required length, fastened one end to a tree on the bank and the other end round his waist. On leaping back, he found he had not allowed for the length which went round his waist, but grasping a branch firmly with both hands, he signalled to his followers to cross the bridge so formed. The eighty thousand monkeys thus escaped; but the monkey who was **Devaddatta,** coming last, saw a chance of injuring the Bodhisatta, and taking a spring into the air, fell on the Bodhisatta's back, breaking it. There the Bodhisatta hung in agony, and the king who had seen all this caused him to be brought down and covered with a yellow robe and ministered to. But nothing could be done, and the Bodhisatta died after having admonished the king. A funeral pyre was made with one hundred wagon-loads of timber, and the dead monkey was paid all the honours due to a king. A shrine was built on the spot where the cremation took place, while the skull was inlaid with gold and taken to Benares, where a great feast was held in its honour for seven days. Afterwards it was enshrined and offerings were made to it.

The story was told concerning good works towards one's relations, as narrated in the introduction to the **Bhaddasāla Jātaka. Ānanda** is identified with the king.[1]

The Jatāka is also called the **Rājovāda Jātaka.** It is probably this story which is said to have greatly impressed **Iḷanāga** when he heard it from the Thera **Mahāpaduma,** who lived in **Tulādhāra.**[2]

[1] J. iii. 369-75; *cf.* **Jātakamālā,** No. 27; the story is sculptured in the stūpa of Bharhut, Cunningham, pl. xxxiii. 4.

[2] Mhv. xxxv. 30.

2. **Mahākapi Jātaka** (No. 516).—The Bodhisatta was once a monkey, and one day, in the forest, he came across a man who had fallen into a pit while looking for his oxen and had lain there starving for ten days. The Bodhisatta pulled him out and then lay down to sleep. But the man, very hungry, and wishing to eat him, struck his head with a stone, grievously wounding him. The monkey at once climbed a tree in order to escape, but realising that the man would be unable to find his way out

of the forest, he jumped from tree to tree (in spite of his intense pain) and showed him the way out. The man became a leper, and wandered about for seven years till he came to the **Migācira Park** in Benares and told his story to the king. At the end of his recital the earth opened and he was swallowed up in **Avīci.**

The story was related in reference to **Devadatta's** attempt to kill the Buddha by hurling a stone upon him. The leper was Devadatta.[1]

The story is also called the **Vevaṭiyakapi Jātaka.**

[1] J. v. 67-74; *cf.* **Jātakamāla,** No. 24.

Mahā-Kappina Thera.—One of the most eminent disciples of the Buddha, considered foremost among those who taught the monks (*bhikkuovādakānaṃ*).[1] He was older than the Buddha, and was born in a frontier kingdom three hundred yojanas in extent, in the city of **Kukkuṭavatī.** On the death of his father he became rājā under the name of **Mahā-Kappina.** His chief wife was **Anojā** (*q.v.*), from **Sāgala** in the **Madda** kingdom. She had been his companion in good works in past births. Every morning Mahā-Kappina would send men out of the four gates of the city to stop any scholarly or learned men who might happen to pass along the road, and then to return and tell him of them. He owned five horses: **Vāla, Puppha, Vālavāhana, Pupphavāhana** and **Supatta.** Supatta he alone rode, the others were used by his messengers. One day, after the Buddha's appearance in the world, traders came from **Sāvatthi** to Kukkuṭavatī and, after disposing of their goods, went to see Mahā-Kappina. He received them and asked them about their country and the teaching (*sāsana*) which they followed. "Sire," they replied, "we cannot tell you with unwashed mouths." A golden jug of water was brought, and with cleansed mouths and clasped hands they told the king of the appearance of the Buddha. At the word "Buddha" Kappina's body was suffused with rapture. He made them utter the word three times, giving them one hundred thousand pieces. The men told him also of the Dhamma and the Saṅgha, and he trebled his gifts and forthwith renounced the world, followed by his ministers. They set forth to find the Buddha, and reached the bank of a river which they crossed by an "Act of Truth," saying, "If this teacher be a *Sammāsambuddha,* let not even a hoof of these horses be wetted." In this manner they crossed three rivers: the **Aravacchā,** the **Nīlavāhana** (*q.v.*), and the **Candabhāgā.** The Buddha perceived them with his divine eye, and after he had eaten at Sāvatthi, went through the air to the banks of the Candabhāgā[2] and sat down under the great banyan-tree facing the

[1] A. i. 25.

[2] One hundred and twenty yojanas, says J. iv. 180; see also SNA. ii. 440.

landing stage of the river, sending forth Buddha-rays. Kappina and his men saw him and prostrated themselves. The Buddha taught them the Doctrine, and they became arahants and joined the Order,[3] the formula " *Ehi bhikkhu* " being their sanction and their ordination.

Anojā and the wives of Kappina's ministers hearing that their husbands had renounced the world and gone to see the Buddha, determined to do likewise. They crossed the river in the same way as Kappina and his retinue, and approached the Buddha as he sat under the banyan-tree on the banks of the Candabhāgā. The Buddha made the husbands and wives invisible to each other and preached to the latter. They became sotāpannas and were ordained by **Uppalavaṇṇā,** the Buddha taking the monks to **Jetavana.** Mahā-Kappina spent his days in the ecstasy of *jhāna*, and so full of happiness was he that he constantly repeated " *aho sukhaṃ, aho sukhaṃ,*" which made the monks suspect that he was longing for the pleasures of kingship which he had left behind, until the Buddha dispelled their doubts.

One day the Buddha discovered that Kappina lived inactively,[4] enjoying his happiness, and that he never taught anybody. He sent for him and asked him to teach the Doctrine to his associates. This Kappina did, and at the end of a single sermon one thousand listening recluses became arahants, hence the title conferred on him.

In the time of **Padumuttara Buddha,** Kappina had registered a vow to become chief among admonishers of monks, having seen a similar honour conferred on a disciple of the Buddha. He was at that time an assessor (*akkhadassa*) of **Haṃsavatī,** and having invited the Buddha and his monks entertained them with great honour. In another birth he was a **Koliyan,** and waited upon five hundred Pacceka Buddhas and gave them robes.[5] In the time of **Kassapa Buddha,** he was the leader of a guild of

[3] But see Vsm. 393, where it says that at the end of the sermon Kappina became only an anāgāmin and his followers sotāpannas.

[4] Vin. i. 105 records that when Kappina was in the Deer Park at **Maddakucchi** he wondered whether he need attend the *uposatha*-ceremonies, since he himself was pure. The Buddha appeared before him, telling him to go.

[5] The story of the entertainment of the Pacceka Buddhas is given at length in DhA. ii. 112 ff., and the number given there is one thousand. They came to Benares, but the king, occupied with the ploughing festival, asked them to return on the third day. The wife of the senior weaver of a village near by heard this and invited the Pacceka Buddhas to her village, where there were one thousand artisans. On the invitation being accepted, she returned quickly to the village, told the people of what she had done, and they all made the necessary preparations, each family looking after one Pacceka Buddha. The Pacceka Buddhas, by their own wish, stayed on for three months, the same woman seeing to all their comforts. At the end of their visit, she persuaded each family to give a set of robes to its own Pacceka Buddha. The senior weaver was Kappina and his wife Anojā.

one thousand men and built a great *pariveṇa* containing one thousand rooms.[6]

It is said[7] that once Kassapa Buddha was preaching and that all the householders of Benares, with their families, went to hear him. Scarcely had they entered the monastery when there was a heavy downpour of rain. Those who had friends among the novices and monks found shelter in their cells, the others were unprotected. The senior householder then suggested that they should build a great monastery so that all might be sheltered in future; the others agreeing, he himself gave one thousand, each of the other men five hundred, and each woman two hundred and fifty. The monastery had one thousand pinnacles, and when money ran short, each gave half as much again. At the dedication ceremony the festival lasted for seven days. The senior householder's wife, Anojā, offered the Buddha a casket of *anoja*-flowers and placed at his feet a garment of the colour of the flowers worth one thousand, and made a wish that in future births her body should be of the colour of the *anoja*-flower.

Although Kappina was famed as a teacher of monks, the Theragāthā, curiously enough, contains verses in which he admonishes the nuns (*bhikkhuṇiyo*).[8]

Kappina is described by the Buddha as pale (? *odāta*), thin, and having a prominent nose (*tanukaṃ tuṅganāsikaṃ*). He possessed great *iddhi*-powers[9] and had attained every *samāpatti* which could be attained.[10] It has been remarked[11] that the verses attributed to him are, for the most part, more gnomic sayings of popular philosophy than genuine Dhamma, and that they would have befitted an early Greek Pagan. Mrs. Rhys Davids[12] has an interesting theory that Kappina was **Assaji's** teacher.

Mahā-Kappina was quite often in the company of **Sāriputta,** and it is said[13] that once, seeing the profound homage the gods payed to his colleague, he smiled by way of congratulation.

See also **Kappina Sutta.**

[6] AA. i. 175 ff.; ThagA. i. 507 ff.; SA. ii. 172 ff.; DhA. ii. 117 ff. gives a more detailed and slightly different version; *cp.* Avadānaś. ii. 102 f.

[7] DhA. ii. 115 f.

[8] Thag. vss. 547-556; ThagA. i. 511.

[9] It was owing to his *iddhi*-powers that he was able to follow the Buddha to the Brahma-world (S. i. 145); see also S. v. 315, where he is described as *samādhibhāvanīya*.

[10] J. ii. 284.

[11] Brethren, p. 257 n. 2.

[12] *J.R.A.S.* 1927, ii. p. 206 f.; also *Sākya*, p. 140.

[13] Thag. vs. 1086.

Mahā-Kappina Thera Vatthu.—Describes the good deeds done by Kappina and Anoja in the time of **Kassapa Buddha.** See **Maha-Kappina.**[1]

[1] DhA ii. 112-27.

Mahā-Kammavibhaṅga Sutta.—**Potaliputta** comes to **Samiddhi** in his forest hut, near **Veḷuvana** in **Rājagaha,** and tells him that the Buddha has declared that all one says or does is vain; the only thing of importance is that which passes in one's mind. Samiddhi protests against this, and when Potaliputta says, "Tell me, what does a man experience who acts of set purpose?" gives his own explanation. Potaliputta then goes away without further talk and seeks **Ānanda,** to whom he reports the incident. Ānanda takes him to the Buddha, remarking that Samiddhi should not have given a single direct reply to a question which required careful qualifications in the answer. **Lāḷudāyi** interrupts and is rebuked by the Buddha, who explains that the question was essentially a triple one and should have been so answered. If a man's purposeful act is calculated to produce a pleasant feeling, his experience is pleasant; if an unpleasant feeling, unpleasant; if neither pleasant nor unpleasant, it is neither. Ānanda asks him to explain further, and this he does. A man may be wicked in this world and yet, at death, pass either into heaven or into hell, he may be good yet go into hell or into heaven. But one should not rush to conclusions from this truth, because the consequence of man's action, good or bad, may be felt either here and now, in the next birth, or at some other time. Kamma can be divided into four classes: (1) not only in operation, but also having the appearance of being so; (2) in operation, though not appearing so; (3) in operation, and appearing so; (4) not in operation, and not appearing so.[1]

[1] M. iii. 207-15.

Mahā-Kammāsadamma.—See **Kammāsadamma.**

Mahākalyāṇa.—Another name for **Varakalyaṇa** (*q.v.*).

1. **Mahā-Kassapa Thera.**—One of the Buddha's most eminent disciples, chief among those who upheld minute observances of form (*dhutavādānaṃ*).[1] He was born in the brahmin village of **Mahātittha** in **Magadha,** and was the son of the brahmin **Kapila,** his mother being **Sumanādevī**[2]; he himself was called **Pippali.** When he grew up he refused to marry in spite of the wishes of his parents; but in the end, to escape from their importunities, he agreed to marry if a wife could be found resembling a statue which he had made. **Bhaddā Kāpilānī** (*q.v.*) was found at **Sāgala** to fulfil these conditions, and though the young people wrote to each other suggesting that somebody else should be found as a match for each, their letters were intercepted and they were married. By mutual consent, however, the marriage was not consummated, the two spending the night separated by a chain of flowers. Pippali had

[1] A. i. 23. [2] At Ap. ii. 583, vs. 56; but there his father is called Kosiyagotta.

immense wealth; he used twelve measures of perfumed powder daily, each measure a *Magadhanāli*, for his person alone. He had sixty lakes with water-works attached, and his workmen occupied fourteen villages, each as large as **Anurādhapura.** One day he went to a field which was being ploughed and saw the birds eating the worms turned up by the plough. On being told that the sin therein was his, he decided to renounce all his possessions. At the same time, Bhaddā had been watching the crows eating the little insects which ran about among the seamsum seeds that had been put out to dry, and when her attendant women told her that hers would be the sin for their loss of life, she also determined to renounce the world.

The husband and wife, finding that they were of one accord, took yellow raiments from their wardrobe, cut off each other's hair, took bowls in their hands, and passed out through their weeping servants, to all of whom they granted their freedom, and departed together, Pippali walking in front. But soon they agreed that it was not seemly they should walk thus together, as each must prove a hindrance to the other. And so, at the cross roads, he took the right and she the left and the earth trembled to see such virtue.

The Buddha, sitting in the **Gandhakuṭi** in **Veḷuvana,** knew what the earthquake signified, and having walked three *gāvutas*,[3] sat down at the foot of the **Bahuputtaka Nigrodha,** between **Rājagaha** and **Nālandā,** resplendent in all the glory of a Buddha. Pippali (henceforth called **Mahā Kassapa**)[4] saw the Buddha, and recognising him at once as his teacher, prostrated himself before him. The Buddha told him to be seated, and, in three homilies,[5] gave him his ordination. Together they returned to Rājagaha, Kassapa, who bore on his body seven of the thirty-two marks of a Great Being, following the Buddha. On the way, the Buddha desired to sit at the foot of a tree by the roadside, and Kassapa folded for him his outer robe (*pilotikasaṅghāṭi*) as a seat. The Buddha sat on it and, feeling it with his hand, praised its softness. Kassapa asked him to accept it. " And what would you wear ?" inquired the Buddha. Kassapa then begged that he might be given the rag-robe worn by the Buddha. " It is faded with use," said the Buddha,

[3] This journey of the Buddha is often referrred to—*e.g.*, MA. i. 347, 357.

[4] No explanation is to be found anywhere as to why he is called Kassapa; it was probably his gotta-name, but see n. 2 above.

[5] The three homilies are given at S. ii. 220, " Thus Kassapa must thou train thyself: (1) 'There shall be a lively sense of fear and regard (*hirotappa*) towards all monks, seniors, novices, and those of middle status.' (2) 'Whatever doctrine I shall hear bearing upon what is good, to all that I will hearken with attentive ear, digesting it, pondering it, gathering it all up with my will.' (3) 'Happy mindfulness with respect to the body shall not be neglected by me.' "

but Kassapa said he would prize it above the whole world and the robes were exchanged.[6] The earth quaked again in recognition of Kassapa's virtues, for no ordinary being would have been fit to wear the Buddha's cast-off robe. Kassapa, conscious of the great honour, took upon himself the thirteen austere vows (*dhutaguṇā*) and, after eight days, became an arahant.

In the past Kassapa and Bhaddā had been husband and wife and companions in good works in many births. In the time of **Padumuttara Buddha,** Kassapa was a very rich householder named **Veheda** and married to Bhaddā, and very devoted to the Buddha. One day he heard the Buddha's third disciple in rank (**Nisabha**) being awarded the place of pre-eminence among those who observed austere practices, and registered a wish for a similiar honour for himself in the future. He learnt from the Buddha of the qualities in which Nisabha excelled the Buddha himself, and determined to obtain them. With this end in view, during birth after birth, he expended all his energies in goods deeds. Ninety-one kappas ago, in the time of **Vipassī Buddha,** he was the brahmin **Ekasāṭaka** (*q.v.*) and Bhaddā was his wife. In the interval between **Koṇāgamana** and **Kassapa Buddhas** he was a *setthiputta.* He married Bhaddā, but because of an evil deed she had done in the past,[7] she became unattractive to him and he left her, taking her as wife again when she became attractive. Having seen from what had happened to his wife how great was the power of the Buddhas, the *seṭṭhiputta* wrapped Kassapa Buddha's goldern cetiya with costly robes and decked it with golden lotuses, each the size of a cartwheel.[8] In the next birth he was **Nanda** (*q.v.*), king of Benares, and, because he had given robes in past lives, he had thirty-two *kapparukkhas,* which provided him and all the people of his kingdom with garments. At the suggestion of his queen, he made preparations to feed holy men, and five hundred Pacceka Buddhas, sons of **Padumā,** came to accept his gift. In that life, too, Nanda and his queen renounced the world and became ascetics, and having developed the *jhānas,* were reborn in the Brahma-world.[9]

[6] This incident Kassapa always recalled with pride, *e.g.*—S. ii. 221. It is said that the Buddha paid him this great honour because he knew that Kassapa would hold a recital after his death, and thus help in the perpetuation of his religion, SA. ii. 130.

[7] For details see *s.v.* **Bhaddā Kāpilānī.**

[8] The Therī Apadāna (Ap. ii. 582. vs. 47-51) gives an account of two more of his lives, one as **Sumitta** and the other as **Koliyaputta,** in both of which he and his wife ministered to Pacceka Buddhas.

[9] This account of Kassapa's last life and his previous life is compiled from AA. i. 92 ff.; SA. ii. 135 ff.; ThagA. ii. 134 ff.; Ap. ii. 578 ff. Ap. i. 33 ff. gives other particulars—that he made offerings at Padumuttara's funeral pyre and that he was once a king named **Ubbiddha** in the city of **Rammaka;** see *s.v.*, also ApA. i. 209 f.

Kassapa was not present at the death of the Buddha; as he was journeying from **Pāvā** to **Kusinārā** he met an **Ājīvaka** carrying in his hand a *mandārava*-flower picked up by him from among those which had rained from heaven in honour of the Buddha, and it was he who told Kassapa the news. It was then the seventh day after the Buddha's death, and the **Mallas** had been trying in vain to set fire to his pyre. The arahant theras, who were present, declared that it could not be kindled until Mahā Kassapa and his five hundred companions had saluted the Buddha's feet. Mahā Kassapa then arrived and walked three times round the pyre with bared shoulder, and it is said the Buddha's feet became visible from out of the pyre in order that he might worship them. He was followed by his five hundred colleagues, and when they had all worshipped the feet disappeared and the pyre kindled of itself.[10] It is said[11] that the relics of the Buddha which fell to **Ajātasattu's** share were taken to Rājagaha by Kassapa, in view of that which would happen in the future. At Pāvā (on the announcement of the Buddha's death), Kassapa had heard the words of **Subhadda,** who, in his old age, had joined the Order, that they were " well rid of the great *samaṇa* and could now do as they liked." This remark it was which had suggested to Kassapa's mind the desirability of holding a Recital of the Buddha's teachings. He announced his intention to the assembled monks, and, as the senior among them and as having been considered by the Buddha himself to be fit for such a task, he was asked to make all necessary arrangements.[12] In accordance with his wishes, all the monks, other than the arahants chosen for the Recital, left Rājagaha during the rainy season. The five hundred who were selected met in Council under the presidency of Kassapa and recited the Dhamma and the Vinaya.[13] This recital is called the **Therasaṅgīti** or **Theravāda** (*q.v.*).

The books contain numerous references to Mahā Kassapa—he is classed with **Moggallāna, Kappina** and **Anuruddha** for his great *iddhi*-powers.[14] The Buddha regarded him as equal to himself in exhorting the monks to lead the active and zealous lives,[15] and constantly held him up as an example to others in his great contentment[16] and his ability to win over families by his preaching.[17] The Buddha also thought him

[10] D. ii. 163 f.

[11] Mhv. xxxi. 20 f.; see also Vsm. 430.

[12] See, *e.g.*, DA. i. 3.

[13] *Ibid.*, 3 f.; 5 ff.; Sp. i. 4 ff.; Mhv. iii. 3 ff.

[14] *E.g.*, S. i. 114; but his range of knowledge was limited; there were certain things which even Kassapa did not know (DhA. i. 258).

[15] S. ii. 205.

[16] *Ibid.*, 194 f.

[17] The Buddha compares him to the moon (*candopama*), unobtrusive; his heart was free from bondage, and he always taught others out of a feeling of compassion. S. ii. 197 ff. Kassapa's freedom from any kind of attachment was, as the Buddha pointed out to the

equal to himself in his power of attaining the jhānas and abiding therein.[18]

Kassapa was willing to help monks along their way, and several instances are given of his exhortations to them[19]; but he was evidently sensitive to criticism, and would not address them unless he felt them to be tractable and deferential to instruction.[20] He was very reluctant to preach to the nuns, but on one occasion he allowed himself to be persuaded by **Ānanda,** and accompanied by him he visited the nunnery and preached to the nuns. He was probably not popular among them, for, at the end of his discourse, **Thullatissā** openly reviled him for what she called his impertinence in having dared to preach in the presence of Ānanda, "as if the needle-pedlar were to sell a needle to the needle-maker."[21] Kassapa loved Ānanda dearly, and was delighted when Ānanda attained arahantship in time to attend the First Recital, and when Ānanda appeared before the arahants, it was Kassapa who led the applause.[22] But Kassapa was very jealous of the good name of the Order, and we find him[23] blaming Ānanda for admitting into the Order new members incapable of observing its discipline and of going about with them in large numbers, exposing the Order to the criticism of the public. "A corn-trampler art thou, Ānanda," he says, "a despoiler of families, thy following is breaking up, thy youngsters are melting away," and ends up with "The boy, methinks, does not know his own measure." Ānanda, annoyed at being called "boy," protests—"Surely my head is growing grey hairs, your reverence." This incident, says the Commentary[24] took place after the Buddha's death, when Ānanda, as a new arahant and with all the honour of his intimacy with the Buddha, whose bowl and robe he now possessed, had become a notable personage. **Thullanandā** heard Kassapa censuring Ānanda and raised her voice in protest, "What now? Does Kassapa, once a heretic, deem that he can chide the learned sage Ānanda?" Kassapa was hurt by her words, and complained to Ānanda that such

---

monks, due to the earnest wish he had made for that attainment in the past. "He has no attachment to requisites or households or monasteries or cells; but is like a royal swan which goes down into a lake and swims there, while the water does not adhere to his body" (DhA. ii. 169 f.).

18 S. ii. 210 ff.

19 *E.g.*, Thag. vss. 1051-57, 1072-81, and his long sermon at A. v. 161 ff.

20 *E.g.*, S. ii. 203 ff.; and at 219, when Thullanandā finds fault with him for blaming Ānanda. See below. Kassapa had good reason for not wishing to address recalcitrant monks. The **Kuṭidūsaka Jātaka** relates how one of his disciples, **Uluṅka-Saddaka,** angered by some admonition from Kassapa, burnt the latter's grass hut while he was away on his alms round (J. iii. 71 f.).

21 S. ii. 215 f.

22 DA. i. 10 f.

23 S. ii. 218 f.

24 SA. ii. 133; Ānanda regarded Kassapa in some sort of way as a teacher, and held him in great respect, not daring to mention even his name, lest it should imply disrespect (see Vin. i. 92 f.).

things should be said of him who had been singled out by the Buddha for special honour.

Kassapa viewed with concern the growing laxity among members of the Order with regard to the observance of rules, even in the very lifetime of the Buddha, and the falling off in the number of those attaining arahantship, and we find him consulting the Buddha as to what should be done.[25] Kassapa himself did his utmost to lead an exemplary life, dwelling in the forest, subsisting solely on alms, wearing rag-robes, always content with little, holding himself aloof from society, ever strenuous and energetic.[26] When asked why he led such a life, he replied that it was not only for his own happiness but also out of compassion for those who came after him, that they might attain to the same end. Even when he was old and the Buddha himself had asked him to give up his coarse rag-robe and to dwell near him, he begged to be excused.[27] Once, when Kassapa lay grievously ill at **Pipphaliguhā,** the Buddha visited him and reminded him of the seven *bojjhaṅgas* which he had practised.[28] The knowledge that he had profited by the Master's teaching, we are told,[29] calmed his blood and purified his system, and the sickness fell away from him "like a drop of water from a lotus leaf." He disdained being waited upon by anybody, even by a goddess such as **Lājā** (*q.v.*), lest he should set a bad example.[30]

Owing to his great saintliness, even the gods vied with each other to give alms to Kassapa. Once when he had risen from a trance lasting seven days, five hundred nymphs, wives of **Sakka,** appeared before him; but, snapping his fingers, he asked them to depart, saying that he bestowed his favours only on the poor.[31] When Sakka heard of

[25] S. ii. 224 f. At the First Council, when Ānanda stated that the Buddha had given leave for the monks to do away with the minor rules of the Order, Kassapa was opposed to any such step, lest it should lead to slackness among the monks and contempt from the laity (Vin. ii. 287 f.).

[26] See also the **Mahāgosinga Sutta** (M. i. 214), where Kassapa declares his belief in the need for these observances; that his example was profitable to others is proved by the case of **Somamitta** (*q.v.*) who, finding his own teacher **Vimala** given up to laziness, sought Kassapa and attained arahantship under his guidance.

[27] S. ii. 202 f.; but see *s.v.* **Jotidāsa,** who is said to have built a vihāra for Kassapa, and entertained him.

[28] S. v. 78.

[29] SA. iii. 128.

[30] DhA. iii. 6 ff.

[31] The story of **Kāḷavilaṅgika** is an example of Kassapa's compassion for the poor. Once, after a seven days' trance, he went to the house of Kāḷavilaṅga and received alms from his wife, which he gave to the Buddha for their greater benefit. The Buddha took a portion of this and gave the rest to five hundred monks. **Kāḷavilaṅgika** received only a mouthful of the food left. The Buddha said that as a result he would be a seṭṭhi within seven days. Kāḷavilaṅgika told this to his wife. It happened that a few days later the king saw a man impaled alive in the place of execution; the man begged him for some food, which he agreed to

this, he disguised himself as a weaver worn with age, and accompanied by **Sujātā,** transformed into an old woman, appeared in a weaver's hut along the lane where Kassapa was begging. The ruse succeeded and Kassapa accepted their alms; but, later, he discovered the truth and chided Sakka. Sakka begged forgiveness, and, on being assured that in spite of his deception the almsgiving would bring him merit, he flew into the air shouting, "*Aho dānaṃ, mahā danaṃ, Kassapassa patiṭṭhitaṃ.*" The Buddha heard this and sympathised with Sakka in his great joy.[32] But on one occasion so great was the importunity with which the monks of **Ālavi** had wearied the people, that even Mahā Kassapa failed to get alms from them.[33] The Visuddhimagga[34] relates a story of how once, when Kassapa was begging for alms in Rājagaha. in the company of the Buddha, on a festival day, five hundred maidens were going to the festival carrying cakes, "round like the moon." They saw the Buddha but passed him by, and gave their cakes to Kassapa. The Elder made all the cakes fill just his single bowl and offered it to the Buddha.[35]

Sāriputta seems to have held Kassapa in great esteem, and the **Kassapa Saṃyutta** contains two discussions between them: one on the necessity for zeal and ardour in the attainment of Nibbāna,[36] and the other on the existence of a Tathāgata after death.[37] This regard was mutual, for when Kassapa saw the great honour paid to Sāriputta by the devas he rejoiced greatly and broke forth into song.[38]

Kassapa lived to be very old, and, when he died, had not lain on a bed for one hundred and twenty years.[39] He is several times referred to in the Jātakas. Thus, he was the father in the **Gagga Jātaka** (ii. 17), the brahmin in the **Kurudhamma** (ii. 381), one of the devaputtas in the

send. At night, when eating, the king remembered his promise, but could find no one bold enough to go to the cemetery. On the offer of one thousand pieces, Kāḷavilaṅgika's wife agreed to go in the guise of a man. On the way she was stopped by the yakkha **Dīghataphala** (*q.v.*), who, however, later released her and gave her treasure, as did also the yakkha's father-in-law, the deva **Sumana.** The man ate the food and, when wiping his mouth, recognised her as a woman and caught hold of her hair. But she cut off her hair, and proved to the satisfaction of the king that her mission had been accomplished. She then recovered the treasure given her by the yakkha and Sumana; when the king discovered her wealth, she and her husband were raised to the rank of seṭṭhi (MA. ii. 812 ff.).

32 DhA. i. 423 ff.; *cp*. Ud. iii. 7.

33 J. ii. 282.

34 403.

35 This is probably the incident referred to at Vsm. 68.

36 S. ii. 195 f.

37 *Ibid.*, 222 f.

38 Thag. vs. 1082-5.

39 DA. ii. 413; AA. ii. 596; he was one hundred and twenty at the time of the First Recital (SA. ii. 130). According to northern sources, Kassapa did not die; he dwells in the Kukkuṭagiri Mountains, wrapt in *samādhi*, awaiting the arrival of Metteyya Buddha (Beal, *op. cit.*, ii. 142 f.). A tooth of Mahā Kassapa was enshrined in the **Bhīmatittha-vihāra** in Ceylon (Cv. lxxxv. 81).

Kakkāru (iii. 90), **Meṇḍissara** in the **Indriya** (iii. 469), and in the **Sarabhaṅga** (v. 151), the father in the **Padakusalamāṇava** (iii. 514), the teacher in the **Tittira** (iii. 545), **Mātali** in the **Biḷārakosiya** (iv. 69), one of the seven brothers in the **Bhissa** (iv. 314), the bear in the **Pañcuposatha** (iv. 332), the chaplain in the **Hatthipāla** (iv. 491), **Vidhura** in the **Sambhava** (v. 67), the senior ascetic in the **Saṅkhapāla** (v. 177), **Kulavaddhana-seṭṭhi** in the **Cullasutasoma** (v. 192), **Suriya** in the **Sudhābhojana** (v. 412), the tree-sprite in the **Mahāsutasoma** (v. 511), the father in the **Sāma** (vi. 95), and **Sūra Vāmagotta** in the **Khaṇḍahāla** (vi. 157).

Mahā Kassapa was so called to distinguish him from other Kassapas,[40] and also because he was possessed of great virtues (*mahanti hi sīlakkhanda hi Samannāgatattā*).

[40] BuA. 42; chiefly Kumāra-Kassapa (VibhA. 60).

2. **Mahā Kassapa.**—An eminent thera of Ceylon, incumbent of **Udumbaragirivihāra,** who, as the most senior monk, was in charge of the reform of the Saṅgha carried out by **Parakkamabāhu I.**[1]

[1] Cv. lxxviii. 6, 16, 57; Cv. *Trs.* ii. 102, n. 2.

Mahā Kassapa Thera-piṇḍapāta Vatthu.—The story of **Sakka** giving alms to **Mahā Kassapa** (*q.v.*) in the disguise of a weaver.[1]

[1] DhA. i. 423 ff.

Mahā-Kassapa-saddhi-vihārika Vatthu.—The story of the pupil of Mahā Kassapa (*q.v.*) who set fire to his hut.[1]

[1] DhA. ii. 19 ff.; see also the **Kuṭidūsaka Jātaka.**

Mahākālasena.—The chief yakkha of **Sirīsavatthu** who married **Polamittā** of **Laṅkāpura.**[1] *v.l.* **-kāḷa-.** See **Kāḷasena** (2).

[1] MṬ. 259 f.

1. **Mahākāḷa Thera.**—He belonged to a merchant family of **Setavyā,** and, while on a journey to **Sāvatthi** with five hundred carts, he heard the Buddha preach at **Jetavana** and entered the Order. He lived in the charnel field meditating, and, one day, the crematrix **Kāḷā,** noticing him, arranged the limbs of a recently cremated body near the Thera that he might gaze at them. With these as a topic of meditation, he soon became an arahant.[1]

[1] Thag. vss. 151 f.; his story is given in much greater detail at DhA. i. 66 ff.; there he is said to have been the eldest of three brothers, of whom the others were **Majjhimakāḷa** and **Cūlakāḷa.** He went with the latter to **Sāvatthi,** where both of them joined the Order. After becoming an arahant, Mahākāḷa went

Ninety-one kappas ago, while wandering near the mountain **Urugaṇa**, he saw the rag-robe of an ascetic and offered three *kiṅkiṇika*-flowers in its honour.[2] He is probably identical with **Paṃsukūlapūjaka Thera** of the Apadāna.[3]

with the Buddha to Setavyā and dwelt in the **Siṃsapā-grove**, Cūlakāḷa accompanying him. Cūlakāḷa's wives invited the Buddha and the other monks to a meal, and he himself went on earlier to make arrangements. His wives disrobed him. At the end of the meal, Mahākāḷa was left behind by the Buddha to make the thanksgiving. His eight wives surrounded him and stripped him of his robes, but, knowing their intention, he disappeared through the air.

[2] ThagA. i. 271 f.

[3] Ap. ii. 434; but see ThagA. i. 79, where the same Apadāna verses are quoted.

2. **Mahākāḷa.**—An upāsaka of **Savatthi** who was a *sotāpanna.* One day he took the *uposatha*-vows and, having listened throughout the night to the preaching, was washing his face in the pool near **Jetavana** early the next morning, when thieves who had broken into a house and were being pursued put their stolen goods near him and ran away. He, being taken for a thief, was beaten to death. When this was reported to the Buddha, he related a story of the past in which Mahākāḷa had been a forest-guard of the king of Benares. One day he saw a man entering the forest road with his beautiful wife and, falling in love with the wife, invited them to his house. He then had a gem placed in the man's cart, and the latter was beaten to death as a thief.[1]

[1] DhA. iii. 149 ff.

3. **Mahākāḷa.**—A Naga-king who dwelt in the **Mañjerika Nāgabhavana.** When the Buddha, after eating the meal given by **Sujātā,** launched the bowl up-stream, it travelled a short way and then stopped, having reached the Nāga's abode under the **Nerañjarā,** and then came into contact with the bowls similarly launched by the three previous Buddhas of this kappa. To the Nāga because of his long life it seemed that the previous Buddha had died only the preceding day, and he rejoiced to think that another had been born. He went therefore to the scene of the Buddha's Enlightenment with his Nāga maidens and they sang the Buddha's praises.[1] Kāḷa's life-span was one *kappa*; therefore he saw all the four Buddhas of this kappa, and when **Asoka** wished to see the form of the Buddha, he sent for Mahākāḷa, who created for him a beautiful figure of the Buddha, complete in every detail.[2]

When the Buddha's relics, deposited at **Rāmagāma,** were washed

[1] J. i. 70, 72; this incident is among those sculpturally represented in the Relic Chamber of the **Mahā Thūpa** (Mhv. xxxi. 83); see also Dvy., 392; Mtu. ii. 265, 302, 304.

[2] Mhv. v. 87 f.; Sp. i. 43, etc.

away, Mahākāḷa took the basket containing them into his abode and there did them honour till they were removed, against his will, by **Soṇuttara.**[3]

[3] Mhv. xxxi. 25 ff.

4. **Mahākāḷa.**—A householder of **Bandhumatī** in the time of **Vipassī Buddha.** He was a previous birth of **Aññā-Koṇḍañña.** He and his brother **Cūlakāḷa** gave the firstfruits of their harvest, in nine stages of its growth, to the Buddha.[1]

[1] AA. i. 79 ff.; ThagA. ii. 1 f.

5. **Mahākāḷa.**—One of the seven mountains surrounding **Gandhamādana.**[1]

[1] SNA. i. 66; J. v. 38.

Mahākāḷasena.—See **Kāḷasena** (2).

Mahākāliṅga.—King of **Dantapura** and brother of **Cullakāliṅga.** For their story see the **Kāliṅgabodhi Jātaka.**[1]

[1] J. iv. 230 ff.

Mahākālī.—An eminent Therī of Ceylon.[1]

[1] Dpv. xviii. 39.

Mahākirāḷavāpi.—A tank restored by **Parakkamabāhu I.**[1]

[1] Cv. lxviii. 46.

Mahākusa.—A king of **Jambudīpa,** descendant of **Mahāsammata.** His father was **Kusa** and his son **Navaratha (Bharata).** They reigned in **Kapilavatthu.**[1]

[1] Dpv. iii. 40; MṬ. 130.

Mahākokālika.—See **Kokālika** (1).

Mahākoṭṭha.—A Damiḷa chief of **Antarāsobbha,** whom **Duṭṭhagāmaṇī** subdued in the course of his campaigns.[1]

[1] Mhv. xxv. 11.

Mahā-Koṭṭhita (Mahā-Koṭṭhika) Thera.—One of the foremost disciples of the Buddha, ranked foremost among masters of logical analysis (*paṭisambhidappattānaṃ*).[1] He was born into a very wealthy brahmin family of **Sāvatthi,** his father being **Assalāyana** and his mother **Candavatī.**

[1] A. i. 24; Dpv. iv. 5; v. 9.

He gained great proficiency in the Vedas and, after hearing the Buddha preach,[2] entered the Order and, engaging in meditation, soon became an arahant.

He was extremely skilled in knowledge of the Paṭisambhidā, on which were based all his questions to the Buddha and his own colleagues.

In the time of **Padumuttara Buddha** he was a rich householder, and, hearing the Buddha praise a monk as foremost among those skilled in the Paṭisambhidā, he wished for similar eminence for himself in the future. To this end he visited the Buddha and his monks and entertained them for seven days, giving them three robes each at the conclusion of his almsgiving. Owing to the skill showed by him in the **Mahā Veddha Sutta** (*q.v.*), the Buddha declared him foremost among those skilled in the Paṭisambhidā.[3]

Several instances are given of discussions between Koṭṭhita and other eminent theras—*e.g.*, the **Naḷakalāpiya Sutta** on kamma,[4] the **Sīla Sutta** on religious discipline,[5] three suttas on *samudayadhamma* (the nature of arising), two on *assāda* (satisfaction),[6] two on *samudaya* (arising)[7] and three on *avijjā* and *vijjā*.[8] Another similar sutta is on sense and sense objects,[9] and there is a series of suttas on matters not revealed by the Buddha (*avyākatāni*).[10] All these suttas took the form of discussions with **Sāriputta,** in which Mahā-Koṭṭhita is the questioner and Sāriputta the instructor.

One sutta[11] records a "lesson" given by the Buddha to Koṭṭhita on conceptions of *anicca, dukkha* and *anattā*. The Aṅguttara Nikāya[12] records a discussion at Jetavana between **Saviṭṭha,** Koṭṭhita and Sāriputta, as to who is best: one who has testified to the truth with body, one who has won view, or one released by faith. Another discussion[13] takes place between Sāriputta and Koṭṭhita as to whether anything continues to exist after the ending of the six spheres of contact (Nibbāna). Once there was a dispute between Koṭṭhita and **Citta-Hatthisāriputta;** Citta was constantly interrupting the elder monks who were gathered at **Isipatana** for the discussion of the Abhidhamma, and was asked by

[2] To his father, says the Apadāna account.

[3] Thag. vs. 2; ThagA. i. 29 ff.; AA. i. 159; Ap. ii. 479; also Avadānaś ii. 195.

[4] S. ii. 112 f.

[5] *Ibid.*, iii. 165 ff.

[6] *Ibid.*, 172-7.

[7] S. iii. 173.

[8] S. iii. 17.

[9] *Ibid.*, iv. 162-5.

[10] *Ibid.*, 384-91; Mrs. Rhys Davids suggests (KS. i. 79, n. 1) that all these suttas were compiled rather as "lessons" to be learnt than as genuine inquiries by Koṭṭhita. The pre-eminent monks were "playing" at teacher and pupil in order to aid Koṭṭhita to win proficiency as a teacher. Another such "lesson" is given at A. iv. 382 ff., as to the motives guiding those who live the *bahmacariya*-life.

[11] S. iv. 145-7.

[12] See the **Kāyasakkhi Sutta** (A. i. 118 f.).

[13] A. ii. 161 f.

Koṭṭhita to abide his time and not interrupt. Citta's friends protested that Citta was well qualified to take part in the discussion; but Koṭṭhita declared that, far from being wise enough, Citta would, not long after, renounce the Order. And so it happened.[14]

Sāriputta evidently had a great regard for Koṭṭhita; the Theragāthā[15] contains three stanzas in which Sāriputta proclaims his excellence.

[14] A. iii. 392 ff. [15] Thag. vss. 1006-8; ThagA. ii. 117.

Mahākosala.—King of **Kosala.** He was the father of **Pasenadi,** and his daughter, **Kosaladevī,** was given in marriage to **Bimbisāra,** who re-received a village in **Kāsi** for her bath-money.[1] **Aggidatta** was the purohita of Mahākosala.[2]

[1] J. ii. 237, 403; iv. 342; SA. i. 120, etc. [2] DhA. iii. 241.

Mahākhandaka.—The first chapter of the Mahāvagga of the Vinaya Piṭaka.

Mahākhīragāma.—A village near **Nāgadīpa** in Ceylon; it was the residence of **Loṇagirivāsī-Tissa.**[1]

[1] AA. ii. 653; MA. i. 545.

Mahākhetta.—A locality in **Rohaṇa,** mentioned in the account of the campaigns of **Parakkamabāhu I.**[1]

[1] Cv. lxxv. 50; Cv. *Trs.* ii. 49, n. 3.

Mahāgaṅgā.—See **Gaṅgā** and **Mahāvālukagaṅgā.**

Mahāgaṇa.—One of the three chief buildings of the **Upāsikā-vihāra** (*q.v.*). It was later called **Piyaṭhapitaghara.**[1]

[1] MṬ. 408, 409.

Mahāgatimba-Abhaya Thera.—Mentioned among those who could remember early incidents in their lives. When he was five days old he saw a crow pecking at some milk-rice prepared for a ceremony and made a sound to drive it away. This was the earliest recollection of the Thera.[1] He had a beautiful complexion.[2]

[1] DA. ii. 530; MNidA. 234. [2] AA. ii. 596.

Mahāgatimbiya-Tissadatta (*v.l.* **Mahāgatigamiya-Tissadatta**).—A Thera. He once went over from Ceylon to India to worship the Bodhi-tree. While crossing, seeing only the waters round him, he fell to wondering which was the more extraordinary, the sound of the ocean waves or the method of the twenty-four divisions of the Paṭṭhāna. The limits of the great ocean then became apparent to him.[1]

[1] DhSA., p. 11.

1. **Mahāgallaka.**—A village in **Dakkhiṇadesa** of Ceylon where **Saṅghatissa** once camped.[1] **Dāṭhopatissa II.** gave the village to the *Padhānaghara* in the **Kassapa-vihāra.**[2] The village is mentioned in the account of the campaigns of **Parakkamabāhu I.**[3]

[1] Cv. xliv. 3.
[2] *Ibid.*, lxv. 27.
[3] *Ibid.*, lviii. 43; see also Cv. *Trs.* i. 74, n. 2; 206, n. 1.

2. **Mahāgallaka.**—A tank built by **Mahāsena.**[1] **Parakkamabāhu I.** repaired it and constructed a canal from the tank to **Sūkaranijjhara.**[2]

[1] Mhv. xxxvii. 49.
[2] Cv. lxviii. 34, 43; lxxix. 66; see also Cv. *Trs.* i. 279, n. 5.

Mahāgavaccha Thera.—He was the son of **Samiddhi,** a brahmin of **Nāḷaka** in **Magadha.** Mahāgavaccha admired **Sāriputta** greatly, and on learning that he had joined the Order, he followed Sāriputta's example, becoming an arahant in due course.

In the past he gave a drink of water to **Padumuttara Buddha** and was a devout follower of **Sikhī Buddha.**[1] He is probably identical with **Udakadāyaka** of the Apadāna.[2]

[1] Thag. vs. 12; ThagA. i. 57.
[2] Ap. ii. 437; but the same verses are attributed to **Gaṅgātiriya** (ThagA. i. 249).

1. **Mahāgāma.**—The capital of **Rohaṇa. Duṭṭhagāmaṇī** was born there, and ruled there till he started on his campaign against the **Damiḷas.**[1] Throughout history Mahāgāma remained the most important place in Rohaṇa. Near by were the **Tissamahārāma** and the **Anurārāma** built by **Subha.** It is first mentioned[2] as the residence of **Devānampiyatissa's** younger brother, **Mahānāga,** who founded the Rohaṇa dynasty, but, as a settlement, it probably dates back to the most ancient times. **Mahānāga** built in it the **Nāgamahā-vihāra. Mahātissa** built the **Mahāpāli Hall** in Mahāgāma and attached to it the **Dāṭhaggabodhi-pariveṇa.**[3] The Damiḷas (probably in the time of **Mahinda IV.**) destroyed Mahāgāma, but the buildings were restored by **Vijayabāhu I.**[4]

[1] Mhv. xxviii. 8, 59, etc.; Cv. xlv. 42, etc.; see also Mhv. *Trs.* 146, n. 5.
[2] Mhv. xxii. 8.
[3] Cv. xlv. 42.
[4] *Ibid.*, lx. 56.

2. **Mahāgāma.**—A tank built by **Mahāsena.**[1]

[1] Mhv. xxxvii. 47.

Mahāgāmanāga-Vihāra.—A monastery in **Rohaṇa** where **Vohārika-Tissa** crowned the thūpa with a parasol.[1] The vihāra is probably identical with the **Nāgamahā Vihāra,** built by **Mahānāga** (*q.v.*).

[1] Mhv. xxxvi. 34; MṬ. 662.

Mahāgāmeṇḍivāpi.—A tank built by **Āmaṇḍagāmaṇi-Abhaya** to the south of **Anurādhapura** and gifted to the **Dakkhiṇa-Vihāra.**[1]

[1] Mhv. xxxv. 5; Mhv. *Trs.* 246, n. 4.

Mahāgirigāma.—A village on the road to **Nāgadīpa,** near the residence of **Loṇagirivāsi-Tissa.**[1]

[1] DA. ii. 534.

Mahāgopālaka Sutta.—Preached to the monks at **Jetavana.** A herdsman who is ignorant of form, has no eye for marks, does not get out ticks, does not dress sores, does not smoke out lairs, knows nothing either of fords or watering-places, roads or pastures, milks the cows dry, and fails to pay special attention to the leaders of the herd—such a herdsman cannot look after his herd nor promote its increase. A monk who has the corresponding eleven bad qualities is not capable of showing growth and progress in the Dhamma and the Vinaya.[1]

[1] M. i. 220 ff.; A. v. 347 ff.

1. **Mahāgovinda.**—A primæval king, mentioned with **Mandhātā** as reigning in **Rājagaha.**[1]

[1] SNA. ii. 413; DA. i. 132, etc.; VvA. (p. 82) speaks of a **Mahāgovindapaṇḍita** by whom **Rājagaha** was planned and built; see **Jotipāla.**

2. **Mahāgovinda.**—See **Jotipāla.**

Mahāgovinda Sutta.—**Pañcasikha** visits the Buddha at **Gijjhakūṭa** and tells him of a meeting once held in **Tāvatiṃsa.** At this meeting **Sakka** rejoices with the devas of Tāvatiṃsa over the increase in their numbers, owing to the appearance in their midst of new devas produced by the good kamma of the followers of the new view of life put forward by the Buddha. Sakka expresses his joy in a song and then utters an eulogy on the eight qualities of the Buddha. Brahmā **Sanaṅkumāra** appears and desires to hear the eulogy, which is, accordingly, repeated for his benefit. Sanaṅkumāra says that the Buddha has ever been thus wise, and tells the story of **Disampati** and his son **Reṇu.** Disampati has a *purohita* called **Govinda,** and when he dies Disampati is distressed, but, at the suggestion of Reṇu, appoints Govinda's son **Jotipāla** in his place.

On the death of Disampati Reṇu becomes king, and, with Jotipāla's help, divides his kingdom into seven to be shared by himself and six of his friends, the divisions of the kingdom being **Dantapura, Potana, Māhissati, Roruka, Mithilā, Campā** and **Bārāṇasi ;** and the kings, respectively, are: **Sattabhū, Brahmadatta, Vessabhū, Bharata, Reṇu,** and two **Dhataraṭṭhas.** Jotipāla, now called **Mahāgovinda** by virtue of his post, trains seven others to fill the posts of stewards to the seven kings. Mahāgovinda acquires the reputation of having seen Brahmā face to face, and, in order to justify this reputation, he takes leave of Reṇu and practises meditation for four months. During his meditation, Sanaṅkumāra appears before him and tells him that he may see Brahmā face to face and attain communion with him. Here we have the teaching regarding the ideal brahmin. Mahāgovinda decides to leave the world and carry out the teachings of Sanaṅkumāra. Having obtained the leave of his master, he enters the homeless life, where he practises the four ecstasies of love, pity, sympathy in joy and equanimity. He teaches these to his disciples, and, after death, they are all born into the Brahma-world.

At the end of Pañcasikha's recital, the Buddha tells him that he himself was Mahāgovinda and therefore remembers all that life.[1]

In the Mahāgovinda Sutta, *brahmacariyā* is explained as the four infinities (*appamaññā*), infinite love, etc.[2]

[1] D. ii. 220-51; *cp.* **Janavasabha Sutta,** also Mtu. iii. 197 ff.

[2] DA. i. 178; MA. i. 275.

Mahāgosiṅga Sutta.—A discussion in **Gosiṅgasālavana,** between **Sāriputta, Mahā Moggāllāna, Mahā-Kassapa, Anuruddha, Revata** and **Ānanda.** Sāriputta is visited by the others in the evening, and asks them what type of monk would illumine the Gosiṅga-wood. Ānanda speaks of one who treasures what he has been taught and learns by heart the doctrines which declare the higher life in all its perfection and purity; Revata of one who delights in meditation and lives in solitude; Anuruddha of one who possesses the celestial eye; Mahā-Kassapa of one living in the forest a strenuous life, recommends that life; Moggallāna of one who holds discussions with another on the Abhidhamma; Sāriputta of a monk who is master of his heart and is not under its mastery. They all seek the Buddha and ask for his opinion. He praises the opinion of each of the Elders, but he himself would choose a monk who is delivered from the *āsavas.*[1]

[1] M. i. 212-19.

Mahācattārīsaka Sutta.—Preached at **Jetavana.** The Buddha explains to the monks the meaning of Right Concentration—the focussing of the heart with the sevenfold equipment of Right Views, Right Thoughts—Right Mindfulness. In all things, Right Views come first.[1]

[1] M. iii. 71-8.

Mahācanda.—A river. See *s.v.* **Candabhāgā.**

Mahā-Cunda.—See **Cunda.**

Mahā-Cunda Sutta.—See **Cunda Sutta.**

Mahācūḷa-(Cūḷika-)Mahātissa.—Son of **Khallāṭanāga** and **Anulādevī. Vattagāmaṇi** adopted him (thereby earning the title of **Pitirājā**) and took him with him when forced to flee from the **Damiḷas.**[1] Mahācūḷa succeeded Vaṭṭagāmaṇi as king of Ceylon and ruled for fourteen years (17-3 B.C.). He worked in a rice-field, disguised as a labourer, and with the wages so earned gave alms to **Mahāsumma.** For three years he laboured in a sugar-mill near **Soṇṇagiri** and built the vihāras known as **Maṇḍavāpi, Abhayagallaka, Vaṅkāvaṭṭakagalla, Dīghabāhugallaka,** and **Jālagāma.** He was succeeded by **Coranāga.**[2] Mahācūḷa had two sons, **Tissa** (poisoned by the notorious **Anulā**) and **Kuṭakaṇṇatissa.**[3]

[1] Mhv. xxxiii. 35, 45; Dpv. xx. 22 f., 31.
[2] Mhv. xxxiv. 1 ff.
[3] *Ibid.*, 15, 28.

Mahā-Cūlani.—King, father of **Cūlani-Brahmadatta.** His wife was **Talatā,** who intrigued with his purohita **Chambhī** and poisoned her husband.[1]

[1] J. vi. 470.

Mahācetiya.—See **Mahā Thūpa.**

Mahācora Sutta.—A robber chief carries on his activities through relying on the inaccessible, the impenetrable and the powerful. Inaccessible are mountains, etc.; impenetrable are jungles, etc.; powerful are chieftains and their ministers, ready to speak in his defence. Similarly, a depraved monk depends on crooked actions, wrong views and influential friends.[1]

[1] A. i. 153.

Mahāchātaka.—A nickname given to **Bhaddāli** (*q.v.*), because he was always eating.[1]

[1] MA. ii. 648.

1. **Mahājanaka.**—King of **Mithilā** in **Videha.** He had two sons, **Ariṭṭhajanaka** and **Polajanaka.**[1]

[1] J. vi. 30.

2. **Mahājanaka.**—Son of **Ariṭṭhajanaka.** See the **Mahājanaka Jātaka.**

Mahājanaka Jātaka (No. 539).—**Mahājanaka,** king of **Mithilā** in **Videha,** had two sons, **Ariṭṭhajanaka** and **Polajanaka.** On his death, the elder came to the throne and made his brother viceroy, but, later, suspecting him of treachery, had him put in chains. Polajanaka escaped, and, when he had completed his preparations, laid siege to the city, killed Ariṭṭhajanaka, and seized the throne. Ariṭṭhajanaka's wife escaped in disguise, taking with her a lot of treasures. She was pregnant, and as her child was the Bodhisatta, **Sakka's** throne was heated, and he appeared before her as a charioteer and took her to **Kālacampā.** There she was adopted by an Udicca brahmin as his sister and the child was born. When he played with other boys they mocked at him, calling him the widow's son. He asked his mother what this meant, but she put him off with evasive answers until one day he bit her on the breast and insisted on being told the truth. When he was sixteen, she gave him half the treasures, and he embarked on a ship going to **Suvaṇṇabhūmi** for trade. The ship was wrecked in mid-ocean, but nothing daunted, Mahājanaka (as the boy was called) swam valiantly for seven days, till **Maṇimekkhalā,** goddess of the sea, admiring his courage, rescued him and placed him in the mango-grove in Mithilā.

Meanwhile Polajanaka had died and left orders that the throne should go to one who could find favour in the eyes of his daughter, should know which is the head of a square bed, could string the bow that required the strength of one thousand men, and could draw out the sixteen great treasures. No one seemed forthcoming who was able to fulfil these conditions; the ministers thereupon decked the state chariot with the five insignia of royalty and sent it out, accompanied by music. The car left the city gates, and the horses went to the mango-grove and stopped at the spot where Mahājanaka lay asleep. The chaplain, seeing the auspicious marks on his feet, awoke him, and explaining to him his mission, crowned him king. When he entered the palace, **Sīvalī** (the late king's daughter) was immediately won over by his appearance, and willingly agreed to be his queen. He was told of the other conditions mentioned by the dead king; he solved the riddles contained in some and fulfilled them all.

In time Sīvalī bore him a son, **Dīghāvukumāra,** whom, in due course,

Mahājanaka made viceroy. One day Mahājanaka went into his park, and noticing how a mango-tree which bore fruit had been plundered by his courtiers while another which was barren was left in peace, he realised that possessions meant sorrow, and retiring into a room, lived the ascetic life. His life-span was ten thousand years, of which three thousand still remained to him. After living for four months in the palace, he resolved to renounce the world, and having made his preparations, secretly left the palace. The queen met him on the stairs, but did not recognise him in his ascetic garb. On discovering his absence, she ran after him and tried by many devices to persuade him to return, but in vain. She then urged his people to follow him, but he turned them back. She, however, would not obey him, and for sixty leagues she and the people followed Mahājanaka.

The sage **Nārada,** dwelling in **Himavā,** saw Mahājanaka with his divine eye and encouraged him in his resolve, as did another ascetic, **Migājina,** who had just risen from a trance. Thus they journeyed on till they reached the village of **Thūṇā.** There the king saw a dog running away with a morsel of roasted flesh, which it dropped in its flight. The king picked it up, cleaned it, and ate it. The queen, very disgusted, felt that he was not worthy to be a king. Further on they saw a girl shaking sand in a winnowing basket; on one arm she wore a single bracelet, on the other arm, two. The two bracelets jingled, while the single one was noiseless. Mahājanaka pointed out the moral of this to Sīvalī, and she agreed to go a different way, but soon came running back to him and followed him till they came across a fletcher, straightening an arrow, looking at it with one eye only. On being questioned by the king, he answered that the wide horizon of two eyes served but to distract the view. But Sīvalī still refused to leave him till, on the edge of a forest, he told her there could be no more intercourse between them, and she fell senseless. The king rushed into the forest, while the ministers revived the queen. When she recovered the king was no more to be seen, and she returned to the city. Thūpas were erected on various spots connected with the king's renunciation, and the queen lived as an ascetic in the royal garden of Mithilā.

The story was told in reference to the Buddha's Renunciation. Maṇimekhālā is identified with **Uppalavaṇṇā,** Nārada with **Sāriputta,** Migājina with **Moggallāna,** the girl with **Khemā,** the fletcher with **Ānanda,** Sīvalī with **Rahulamātā,** Dīghāvu with **Rāhula,** while Mahājanaka was the Bodhisatta.[1] The Jātaka exemplifies *viriya-pāramitā.*[2]

[1] J. iii. 30-68. [2] BuA. 51.

Mahājanapadā.—The books frequently mention[1] the sixteen Mahājanapadas or countries, which existed in the time of the Buddha. They are **Kāsī, Kosala, Aṅga, Magadha, Vajji, Malla, Cetiya, Vaṃsa, Kuru, Pañcāla, Maccha, Sūrasena, Assaka, Avanti, Gandhāra** and **Kamboja.** The first fourteen are included in the **Majjhimadesa,** the two last being in **Uttarāpatha.**

[1] *E.g.*, A. i. 213; iv. 252, 256, 260; a list of twelve is found at D. ii. 200, in which the last four are omitted. The Niddesa adds the **Kaliṅgas** to the sixteen and substitutes Yona for the Gandhāra (CNid., p. 37). For details of the countries mentioned see *s.v.* The Jaina *Bhagavatī sutra* gives a slightly different list: Aṅga, Baṅga, Magadha, Malaya, Mālava, Accha, Vaccha, Kocchaka, Pāḍha, Lāḍha, Bajji, Moli, Kāsi, Kosala, Avaha and Sambhuttara (PHAI., p. 60).

Mahājāli.—A Pacceka Buddha mentioned in a list of names.[1]

[1] M. iii. 70.

Mahātakkāri Jātaka.—See **Takkāriya Jātaka.**

Mahātaṇhāsankhaya Sutta.—**Sāti Thera,** a fisherman's son, went about saying that, according to the Buddha's doctrine, one's consciousness runs on and continues without break of identity. Hearing this, several monks protested, but failed to convince him of his error. Sāti was therefore brought before the Buddha and acknowledged that he had spread such a view. The Buddha explains that he had always taught that consciousness arises only by causation and that, without assignable condition, consciousness does not come about. There are four substances (*āhārā*) which either maintain existing organisms or help those yet to be: material substance, contact, cogitation, and perception. The derivation and birth of all four substances is craving—craving arises from feeling and so on. Three things must combine for a conception to take place: the coitus of the parents, the menstruation, at the time, of the mother, and the presence of a being awaiting rebirth (*gandhabba*).[1]

[1] M. i. 256-71.

Mahātālitagāma.—A village in **Uttaradesa,** in Ceylon, where the **Paṇḍu** king who invaded Ceylon in the reign of **Sena I.** occupied an armed camp.[1]

[1] Cv. l. 14.

1. **Mahātittha.**—A brahmin village in **Magadha,** the birthplace of **Mahā-Kassapa.**[1]

[1] ThagA. ii. 141; AA. i. 99; SA. ii. 143.

2. **Mahātittha.**—The name of **Mahāmeghavana** in the time of **Kakusandha Buddha.** It was presented to the Buddha by king **Abhaya,** who planted in it a branch of the Bodhi-tree brought by **Rucānandā.**[1]

[1] Mhv. xv. 58, 73 f., 83.

3. **Mahātittha.**—A landing-place on the west coast of Ceylon. The wives brought from **Madhurā** for **Vijaya** and his companions landed there, hence the name.[1] There landed also in later times **Bhalluka,** from South India,[2] the **Damiḷas** and others who invaded Ceylon.[3] It was probably the chief port for vessels plying between South India and Ceylon.[4] It was a convenient place for preparations to be made before advancing on the capital, or merely journeying thither.[5] It was a place of strategic importance, and when **Māgha** and **Jayabāhu** invaded Ceylon, they set up fortifications there.[6]

[1] Mhv. vii. 58; see Mhv. *Trs.* 60, n. 1.

[2] Mhv. xxv. 79.

[3] *E.g., ibid.,* xxxiii. 39; Cv. lviii. 14; xi. 37; lxxxviii. 63.

[4] Thus, it was from there that **Sakkasenāpati** embarked for the **Paṇḍu** country (Cv. lii. 73), and there that the Paṇḍu king landed from **Coḷa** (liii. 5). The expeditionary force of **Vijayabāhu I.** embarked there for Coḷa (lx. 34), as did the forces of **Parakkamabāhu I.,** under **Laṅkāpura** (lxxvi. 85).

[5] Thus Cv. lxviii. 81; li. 28.

[6] *Ibid.,* lxxxiii. 16.

Mahātitthadvāra.—One of the gates of **Pulatthipura,** erected by **Parakkamabāhu I.**[1]

[1] Cv. lxxiii. 163.

1. **Mahātissa.**—A thera who lived in **Bhaggari** in Ceylon. He was an arahant, and is mentioned as being among the last of those who took part in various assemblies that followed the departure of the Bodhisatta during different births, such as the **Kuddālaka-Samāgama, Mūgapakkha,** etc.[1]

[1] J. vi. 30.

2. **Mahātissa.**—Called **Vanavāsī-Mahātissa.** He was a colleague of **Ālindakavāsī-Mahāphussadeva** of Ceylon, and witnessed **Sakka** and other deities waiting on the latter in recognition of his holiness. Mahātissa perceived only the radiance of the devas and questioned Phussadeva, who did not, however, give a direct answer.[1]

[1] SNA. i. 55 f.; VibhA. 352.

3. **Mahātissa Thera.**—Called **Ambakhādaka-Mahātissa.** He lived at **Ciragumba,** and is mentioned as an example of a monk who refused to

eat food which came to him as a result of signifying in words that he desired it.[1]

[1] Vsm. 43.

4. **Mahātissa Thera.**—He lived in **Cetiyagiri,** and one day, while on his way to **Anurādhapura,** saw a woman who was leaving her husband, having quarrelled with him. She was beautifully dressed, and seeing the Elder, smiled at him, in order to show her perfect teeth. The Elder looked at her, and acquiring the perception of "the foul" through thinking of the bones of her teeth, became an arahant. The husband followed his wife and asked the Elder if he had seen her. The Elder replied, "I know not if it was man or woman, but I saw a lump of bones."[1]

[1] Vsm. 20 f., 194.

5. **Mahātissa Thera.**—Of **Puṇṇavallika.** One full-moon day, at evening, he went to the courtyard of the **Mahā Thūpa,** saw the moonlight, and turning towards the shrine, entered into rapture, the Buddha being his object of thought. He habitually recalled this experience thenceforth until, one day, he was able to travel through the air to the Mahā Thūpa.[1]

[1] Vsm. 143; DhSA. 116.

6. **Mahātissa.**—An Elder of the **Mahākarañjiya-Vihāra.**—He became an arahant by developing *ānāpāṇasati,* and was thus able to limit his life-term.[1]

[1] Vsm. 292.

7. **Mahātissa Thera.**—While begging for alms in **Kalyāṇigāma** his mind was defiled by the sight of an "uncommon" form (*visabhāgarūpa,* ? naked woman).[1]

[1] SNA. i. 6 f.

8. **Mahātissa Thera.**—An incumbent of the **Maṇḍalārāma** near **Bhokkantagāma.** He was a reciter of the **Dhammapada. Sumanā,** wife of **Lakuṇṭaka Atimbara,** related the story of her past in the assembly of monks in association with this thera.[1]

[1] DhA. iv. 51.

9. **Mahātissa.**—A man of the **Okkāka** race, father of **Dappula I.** His wife was **Saṅghasivā,** and they had two other sons, **Aggabodhi** and **Maṇiakkhika,** and one daughter.[1]

[1] Cv. xlv. 38.

10. **Mahātissa Thera.**—Incumbent of **Koṭapabbata Vihāra** and teacher of **Asubhakammika Tissa.**—He was an arahant, and heard, with his divine ear, the description given in the **Lohapāsāda** by **Cittagutta Thera** of the marvels of the **Mahā Thūpa.** Mahātissa told Cittagutta that the description was not full enough.[1]

[1] MṬ. 552 f.

11. **Mahātissa Thera.**—Incumbent of **Kambugallaka Vihāra.** He was a colleague of **Kupikkala-Mahātissa,** and interceded on behalf of **Vaṭṭagāmaṇī** when that king's ministers wished to leave him. Later, the ministers appointed him to look after all the monasteries built by them.[1]

[1] Mhv. xxxiii. 76, 89 ff.; MṬ. 619, 622.

12. **Mahātissa Thera.**—Incumbent of **Kupikkala Vihāra.** When **Vaṭṭagāmaṇī** was in hiding in the forest of **Vessagiri,** the Elder once provided him with a meal, and the king, out of gratitude, made him a grant of land.[1] Later, the ministers wanted to revolt against the king on account of his cruelty to **Tanasīva,** but the Elder and his colleague Mahātissa from **Kambugallaka,** prevented them from doing so.[2] When Vaṭṭagāmaṇī built the **Abhayagiri Vihāra,** he gave it into the charge of Mahātissa.[3]

[1] Mhv. xxxiii. 49. [2] *Ibid.*, 76. [3] *Ibid.*, 83.

13. **Mahātissa Thera.**—An incumbent of the **Mahāvihāra.** He was expelled by reason of his association with families. His pupil **Bahalamassutissa** thereupon seceded from the Mahāvihāra and established a new sect in **Abhayagiri.**[1]

[1] Mhv. xxxiii. 95 ff.

14. **Mahātissa Thera.**—Incumbent of **Anurārāma. Vohārika-Tissa** was so pleased with him that he ordered alms to be regularly given to him in the **Mucelapaṭṭana.**[1]

[1] Mhv. xxxvi. 30.

15. **Mahātissa Thera.**—Even when sixty years old he did not realise that he was a puthujjana. Then, one day, his pupil **Dhammadinna** of **Talaṅgara** came to him, asking for his company in a journey to **Tissamahāvihāra,** where he had been asked to preach. Mahātissa greeted him, and in the course of conversation, Dhammadinna discovered that his teacher was under the false impression that he was an arahant. Wishing to show him his error, he persuaded Mahātissa, by his *iddhi*-power, to

create a pond, and in the pond a lotus, which a young girl was picking. At the sight of the girl, Mahātissa was possessed by lust, and realized that he was no arahant. Dhammadinna withdrew, and that same day Mahātissa put forth effort and attained arahantship.[1]

[1] AA. i. 25.

16. **Mahātissa.**—An incumbent of **Cittalapabbata.** He was troubled by lustful thoughts and consulted his teacher. The thera asked him to prepare a cell for him, which he did with great care. The thera then asked him to occupy it for one night, since he had taken so much trouble over it. That night Mahātissa put forth effort and became an arahant.[1]

[1] AA. i. 26.

Mahātissabhūti Thera.—An incumbent of the **Maṇḍalārāma.** While begging for alms in the village, his mind was defiled by an unusual sight. He therefore returned to the vihāra, but, even in his sleep, he was haunted by what he had seen, and, greatly agitated, he went to **Mahāsangharakkhita** and obtained from him a formula of meditation with which to counteract the lustful feelings. With this formula he went into a thicket and lay on his *paṃsukūla* robe and became an *anāgāmin.*[1]

[1] MA. i. 55.

Mahātissā.—An eminent Therī of Ceylon.[1]

[1] Dpv. xviii. 38.

Mahātuṇḍila.—The Bodhisatta born as a pig. See the **Tuṇḍila Jātaka.**

Mahāthala.—A village in which **Aggabodhi V.** built the **Kadambagona-vihāra.**[1]

[1] Cv. xlviii. 3.

Mahā-Thupa.—The great Thūpa in **Anurādhapura,** built by **Duṭṭhagāmaṇi.** The site on which it was erected was consecrated by the visit of all the four Buddhas of this kappa and was at the upper end of the **Kakudhavāpi.** It was one of the spots at which **Mahinda** scattered *campaka*-flowers by way of homage, and the earth trembled. When Mahinda informed **Devānampiyatissa** of the great sanctity of the spot and of its suitability for a Thūpa, Tissa immediately wished to build the Thūpa himself, but Mahinda bade him desist, telling him that the work would be carried out in the future by Duṭṭhagāmaṇi. Tissa recorded this prophecy on a pillar of stone.[1] When Duṭṭhagāmaṇi had won his victory over the Damiḷas and had brought peace to the country, he saw the prophecy inscribed on the stone pillar, but was unwilling to start the work as the people were too crippled with regard to money to be able to support such an immense undertaking. But the devas read his thoughts and provided him with all the necessaries for the building of the Thūpa. Prepared bricks were found on the banks of the **Gambhīranadī,** copper near **Tambapiṭṭha,** silver in the **Ambaṭṭhakolaleṇa,** pearls at **Uruvelā,** and gems in a cave near **Peḷivāpigāma.** The building was started on the full-moon day of **Visākha.** The foundation stone was laid on the fourteenth day of the bright half of the month of **Āsāḷha.** Great celebrations marked the event, arrangements for which were in the hands of the ministers **Visākha** and **Sirideva.** Monks were present not only from all over Ceylon but from many other places: eighty thousand under **Indagutta** from **Rājagaha,** twelve thousand under **Dhammasena** from **Isipatana,** sixty thousand under **Piyadassī** from **Jetavanārāma,** eighteen thousand under **Mahā-Buddharakkhita** from **Mahāvana** in **Vesāli,** thirty thousand under **Mahā-Dhammarakkhita** from **Ghositārāma** in **Kosambī,** forty thousand under **Mahā-Saṅgharakkhita** from **Dakkhiṇāgiri** in **Ujjeni,** one hundred and sixty thousand under **Mittinna** from **Asokārāma** in **Pāṭaliputta,** two hundred and eighty thousand under **Uttinna** from **Kasmīra,** four hundred and sixty thousand under **Mahādeva** from **Pallabhogga,** thirty thousand under **Yonamahā-Dhammarakkhita** from **Alasandā,** sixty thousand under **Uttara** from **Viñjhāṭavī,** thirty thousand under **Cittagutta** from **Bodhimaṇḍa-vihāra,** eighty thousand under **Candagutta** from **Vanavāsa,** and ninety-six thousand under **Suriyagutta** from **Kelāsa-vihāra.** Of arahants alone ninety-six crores were present.

As the king stepped into the space left open for him, he expressed the desire that, if his worship were to have a happy result, theras bearing the names of the Buddha, his Dhamma and his Saṅgha, should take their places on the east, south, and west sides respectively, and a thera bearing the name of **Ānanda** on the north side, each thera to be surrounded by a group bearing the same name. The king's wish was fulfilled; the theras in question and their companions were called **Mahā-Buddharakkhita, Mahā-Dhammarakkhita, Mahā-Saṅgharakkhita** and **Mahānanda.** As the king was about to mark the space to be covered by the cetiya, the Thera **Siddhattha,** looking into the future, told him to define only a moderate space for the Thūpa. This the king did; then, looking at the theras immediately around him, he inquired their names and rejoiced to find them so auspicious, they being **Siddhattha, Maṅgala, Sumana, Paduma,**

[1] Mhv. xv. 51 ff., 167 ff.

Sīvalī, Candagutta, Suriyagutta, Indagutta, Sāgara, Mittasena, Jayasena, and **Acala.** He then laid the first foundation stone on the east side on sweet-smelling clay prepared by **Mittasena** and sprinkled with water by **Jayasena; Mahāsumana** placed jasmine flowers on the stone. Immediately the earth trembled in wonder. The minister who helped the king to mark out the area of the cetiya was **Suppatiṭṭhitabrahmā,** son of **Nandisena** and **Sumanadevī.** At the end of the ceremony, **Piyadassī** preached to the assembled populace, and many attained to various fruits of the Path.

The Thūpa was like a water-bubble in shape; its architect was **Sirivaḍḍha** and his assistant **Acala.** Orders were given that no unpaid work should be done in the construction of the cetiya. Arahants caused the three terraces of flower-offerings to the Thūpa (*pupphādhānā*) to sink nine times into the earth, in order, as they explained, to strengthen the foundations. The cetiya was one hundred and twenty cubits high, and for the ten flower terraces alone ten crores of bricks were used.

The Relic Chamber was of unparalleled magnificence, and consisted of four *medavaṇṇapāsāṇā*, each eighty cubits in length and in breadth and eight inches thick. These were brought from **Uttarakura** by two sāmaṇeras, **Uttara** and **Sumana.** In the Chamber were placed sculptural representations of the chief events connected with the Buddha's life[2] as well as pictures of several Jātakas, including the **Vessantara.** The work of the Relic Chamber was under the personal supervision of **Indagutta Thera,** of great *iddhi*-power. When the Chamber was ready for the enshrining of the Relics, **Soṇuttara** of **Pūjā-pariveṇa** was entrusted with the task of obtaining them. In a previous birth, as **Nanduttara,** he had vowed to have the power of doing this, and now was his opportunity. He went to **Mañjerika Nāga-bhavana,** where the Relics, washed away from the Thūpa at **Rāmagāma,** were in the custody of the **Nāga Mahākāla,** and by a display of *iddhi*-power obtained them from the Nāga against his desire. They represented one *doṇa* of the Buddha's Relics, and the Buddha had predicted that they would ultimately be placed in the Mahā Thūpa. These Relics were enshrined on the fifteenth *uposatha*-day in the light half of the month of Āsāḷha, under the constellation of **Uttarāsāḷha.** Many devas and brahmas and nāgas were present as on the day of the Buddha's Enlightenment, and ninety-six crores of arahants attended the ceremony. As the king, after passing three times round the cetiya, ascended it on the east side, and was about

[2] For list see Mhv. xxx. 71 ff.; the MṬ (549 ff.) contains a long disquisition to prove that there is no reason to doubt the account given of the contents of the Relic Chamber, for in its construction the power (*iddhi*) of the king, of devas, and of arahants came into play.

to descend into the Relic Chamber, bearing on his head the Casket of Relics, the casket opened and the Relics rose out of it, and taking on the form of the Buddha, performed the Twin Miracle, as at the foot of the **Gaṇḍamba.** When the Relics were placed on the couch prepared for them they assumed, as the king had desired, the form of the Buddha as he lay on his death-bed. For a whole week the celebrations lasted, and during this period the king offered to the Relics the dominion of Ceylon, and Indagutta decreed that the people of Ceylon, wherever they might be, should be able immediately to visit the Thūpa should they desire to do so. At the end of the seven days, the two sāmaṇeras, Uttara and Sumana, closed the Chamber with the *medavaṇṇapāsānā* set apart for the purpose, while arahants pronounced that flowers offered in the Relic Chamber should not wither, nor scents dry up; the lamps should not be extinguished nor anything whatever perish.[3] The treasures enshrined in the Mahā Thūpa were worth twenty crores, the rest cost one thousand crores.[4]

Before the parasol of the Mahā Thūpa and the plaster work could be completed, Duṭṭhagāmaṇi fell ill, and his brother, **Saddhātissa,** summoned from **Dīghavāpi,** contrived with great skill to make the Thūpa look complete, that the king might see it before he died. After the king's obsequies had been performed, in a place within sight of the Mahā Thūpa,[5] Saddhātissa finished the work yet remaining and established celebrations to be performed three times daily at the Mahā Thūpa.[6] **Lañjatissa** levelled the ground between the Mahā Thūpa and the **Thūpārāma** and built three stone terraces at the cost of three hundred thousand.[7] **Khallāṭanāga** made the courtyard of sand, surrounded by a wall.[8] **Bhātika** constructed two *vedikā* round the courtyard.[9] It is said[10] that Bhātika was taken by the arahants into the Relic Chamber, and he held great celebrations in its honour.[11] **Mahādāṭhika-Mahānāga** converted the sand courtyard into a wide court laid out with *kiñcakkha*-stones on plaster,[12] while **Āmaṇḍagāmaṇi** erected a parasol over the cetiya[13] and **Iḷanāga** made the **Lambakaṇṇas** construct a roadway leading up to the Mahā Thūpa.[14] **Sirināga** had the whole Thūpa gilded and crowned with a new parasol,[15] this work being undertaken again later by **Saṅghatissa,**[16] while **Saṅghabodhi** made rain to pour down by means of prostrating

[3] The building of the Māha Thūpa is described in Mhv. chaps xxviii.-xxx.; MṬ. 514-83; Dpv. xix. 1 ff.; also Thūpavaṃsa (pp. 66 ff.).
[4] Mhv. xxxii. 18.
[5] *Ibid.*, 58.
[6] *Ibid.*, xxxii. 60; xxxiii. 5.
[7] *Ibid.*, 22 f.
[8] *Ibid.*, 31.
[9] *Ibid.*, xxxiv. 39.
[10] See MṬ. 553 f.
[11] See *s.v.*, Bhātikābhaya.
[12] Mhv. xxxiv. 69.
[13] *Ibid.*, xxxv. 2.
[14] *Ibid.*, 17.
[15] *Ibid.*, xxxvi. 24.
[16] *Ibid.*, 65.

himself in the courtyard.[17] **Jeṭṭhatissa** offered two precious gems to the Thūpa,[18] while **Aggabodhi I.** placed on the Thūpa a golden umbrella.[19] From this time onward the country passed through very troublous times and the Mahā Thūpa was neglected. But it was restored by **Parakkamabāhu I.**[20] and again by **Kittinissaṅka**[21]; it was later pillaged by **Māgha,**[22] and remained neglected till the time of **Parakkamabāhu II.,** who started the work of reconstruction,[23] which was completed by his son **Vijayabāhu IV.**[24]

The Mahā Thūpa has been a place of pilgrimage for Buddhists from the time of its building down to the present day, even when the place was deserted and its courtyards overgrown with creepers.[25] There seems to have been a hall for pilgrims to the west of the cetiya.[26] When the Buddha's *sāsana* disappears, all the Relics of the Buddha deposited in various cetiyas all over Ceylon will gather together at the Mahācetiya, and from there will go to the **Rajāyatana-cetiya** in **Nāgadīpa,** thence to the **Mahābodhipallaṅka,** where all the Relics, assembled from everywhere, will take the form of the Buddha seated at the foot of the Bodhi-tree. Then they will be consumed by self-generated flames.[27]

The Mahā Thūpa is known by other names: **Mahācetiya, Ratanavāluka,**[28] **Ratanavāli,**[29] **Soṇṇamāli**[30] **(Hemamāli),** and **Hemavāluka.**[31]

17 *Ibid.*, 75.
18 *Ibid.*, 126.
19 Cv. xlii. 32.
20 *Ibid.*, lxxiv. 10; lxxvi. 106 f.; lxxviii. 97.
21 *Ibid.*, lxxx. 20.
22 *Ibid.*, 68.
23 *Ibid.*, lxxxvii. 66.
24 *Ibid.*, lxxxviii. 83; after this, the cetiya once more fell into disrepair and has so continued till recently, when an attempt is being made to rebuild it.
25 See, *e.g.*, VibhA. 446.
26 *Ibid.*, 446.
27 *Ibid.*, 433.
28 Cv. lxxvi. 106.
29 *Ibid.*, lxxx. 68.
30 Mhv. xxvii. 3.
31 Cv. li. 82.

1. **Mahādatta.**—A thera of **Ariyakoṭiya.** He was once sitting at the foot of a tree to meditate, but because of the great power of his virtue, the children of the tree-deity grew restless, and the deity tried to frighten him away but failed. She then appeared before the thera in disguise and told him of her trouble. He asked her to take her family somewhere else for that day only as he did not wish it to be thought that she had scared him away.[1]

1 MA. i. 131.

2. **Mahādatta Thera.**—An incumbent of **Haṅkanaka** who wrongly believed that he was an arahant because of the inoperation of the corruptions.[1]

1 Vsm. 634; VibhA. 489.

3. **Mahādatta.**—An Elder of **Moravāpi,** an eminent commentator whose opinions are quoted in the Commentaries.[1]

[1] *E.g.*, DhSA. 230, 267, 284, 286; PSA. 405.

4. **Mahādatta.**—A *senāpati.* He was a follower of the brāhmaṇas, and at the moment of his death he saw before him a picture of hell. The brahmins who were round him asked him what he saw, and he said that he saw a house blood-red in colour. They assured him that that was the Brahma-world, but after death he was born in hell.[1]

[1] MA. ii. 803.

Mahādaddara.—The Bodhisatta born as a Nagā-king, son of **Sūradaddara.**[1] See the **Daddara Jataka.**

[1] J. iii. 16 ff.

Mahādāṭhika-Mahānāga.—Younger brother of **Bhātikābhaya** and king of Ceylon for twelve years (67-79 A.C.). He made a courtyard of *kiṅcikkha*-stones on plaster round the **Mahā Thūpa,** and built the **Ambatthala-thūpa,** making it firm at the risk of his own life. He placed chairs for the preachers in all the vihāras of Ceylon, and laid out the grounds round **Cetiyagiri,** holding a great celebration called the **Giribhaṇḍapūjā** (*q.v.*). From the **Kadambanadī** to Cetiyagiri he laid carpets for the comfort of pilgrims. He built the **Maṇināgapabbata,** the **Kalanda,** the **Samudda,** and the **Cūḷānāgapabbata-Vihāras,** and gave land for the use of monks in **Pāsāṇadīpaka** and **Maṇḍavāpi Vihāras** in gratitude for favours shown him by novices of these monasteries. He had two sons, **Āmaṇḍagāmaṇi Abhaya** and **Kaṇirajānutissa,** both of whom succeeded to the throne.[1] He had a queen called **Damiḷadevī** (apparently a Tamil lady) who died young.[2]

[1] Mhv. xxxiv. 68 ff.; xxxv. 1, 9; Dpv. xxi. 34. [2] AA. i. 13.

Mahādāragalla.—A tank built by **Mahāsena.**[1] It was repaired by **Vijayabāhu I.** and later by **Parakkamabāhu I.**[2]

[1] Mhv. xxxvii. 49. [2] Cv. lx. 50; lxxix. 31.

Mahādāragiri.—A village (probably near **Mahādāragallaka**) given by **Jeṭṭhatissa II.** to the **Abhayagiri-vihāra.**[1]

[1] Cv. xliv. 96.

" **Mahādiṭṭhena** " **Sutta.**—The great heresy: that the four elements and weal and woe are stable and permanent, that weal and woe are allotted to each person and do not wax and wane.[1] Some of these views are elsewhere attributed to **Pakudha Kaccāyana** and others to **Makkhali Gosāla.**

[1] S. iii. 211 f.

Mahādīpanī.—A Commentary.[1]

[1] Gv. 65, 75.

Mahādukkhakkhandha Sutta.—Some monks once visited a Paribbājakārāma near **Sāvatthi** and were told by the Paribbājakas that they, as well as the Buddha, understood how to transcend pleasures of sense, visible forms and feelings; what then was the difference between themselves and the Buddha? The monks repeated this to the Buddha, who said that none save himself knew the satisfaction, the perils, and the deliverance which attend pleasures of sense, etc.; he then proceeded to explain the pleasures of the senses, the perils that attend them, and the deliverance therefrom, which is to shed all desire and appetite therefor. It is the same with feelings.[1]

[1] M. i. 83 ff.

Mahāduggata.—A very poor man of Benares in the time of **Kassapa Buddha.** The citizens of Benares once invited the Buddha and his monks and went about asking people to help in their entertainment. In spite of their extreme poverty, Mahāduggata and his wife undertook to look after one monk; they both worked hard to earn the necessary money and then prepared a simple meal. **Sakka,** knowing what was to come, came in the guise of a labourer to help them. When the time came for the meal it was found that in allotting the monks to their several hosts, Mahāduggata's house had been overlooked. Mahāduggata wrung his hands and burst into tears, but somebody pointed out to him that nobody was yet entertaining the Buddha. He, therefore, went to the vihāra and invited the Buddha, who accepted the invitation, while princes and nobles waited outside wishing to conduct him to their own palaces. The Buddha ate the food prepared by Mahāduggata and Sakka and returned thanks. That same day, by the power of Sakka, the seven kinds of jewels fell from the sky and filled Mahāduggata's house, and when it was reported to the king that he was the wealthiest man in the city, he was appointed Treasurer. Mahāduggata built a new house and discovered many hidden treasures while digging the foundations. With the money from these he entertained the Buddha and his monks for seven days, and, after death, was reborn in heaven. He is identified with **Paṇḍitasāmaṇera.**[1]

[1] DhA. ii. 127-38.

Mahāduggala.—A monastery and cetiya built by **Kākavaṇṇatissa.** At its inauguration twelve thousand monks from **Cittalapabbata** were present.[1] *v.l.* **Mahānuggala.**

[1] Mhv. xxiv. 8 ff.

Mahādundubhi.—Thirty thousand kappas ago there were sixteen kings of this name, previous births of **Vappa** (or **Saraṇāgamaniya**) **Thera.**[1]

[1] Thag. i. 141; Ap. i. 149.

1. **Mahādeva Thera.**—The Chief Disciple of **Padumuttara Buddha.**[1]

[1] AA. i. 114; but Bu. xi. 24 calls him **Devala.**

2. **Mahādeva Thera.**—A disciple of **Kakusandha Buddha,** whom he accompanied to Ceylon, and who was left behind by the Buddha to look after the converts.[1]

[1] Mhv. xv. 89; Dpv. xv. 38, 43; xvii. 25; Sp. i. 86.

3. **Mahādeva Thera.**—He conferred the *pabbajā*-ordination on **Mahinda.**[1] After the Third Council he went as apostle to **Mahisamaṇḍala,** where he preached the **Devadūta Sutta,** converting forty thousand people and conferring ordination on forty thousand more.[2]

[1] Mhv. v. 206; Dpv. vii. 25.

[2] Mhv. xii. 3, 29; Dpv. viii. 5; Sp. i. 66.

4. **Mahādeva.**—A minister of **Asoka,** whose counsel was followed by Asoka in the arrangements for the despatch of a branch of the Bodhi-tree to Ceylon.[1]

[1] Mhv. xviii. 20.

5. **Mahādeva Thera.**—He was from **Pallavabhogga,** and was present with four hundred and sixty thousand monks at the Foundation Ceremony of the **Mahā Thūpa.**[1]

[1] Mhv. xxix. 38.

6. **Mahādeva Thera.**—He was an incumbent of **Bhaggari,** and was among those who were the last to become arahants after renouncing the world with the Bodhisatta in previous births.[1]

[1] J. iv. 490.

7. **Mahādeva Thera.**—From **Dāmahālaka.** King **Saṅghatissa** heard him one day preach the merits of giving rice-gruel, and thereupon instituted an abundant gift of rice-gruel to the monks at the gates of **Anurādhapura.**[1]

[1] Mhv. xxxvi. 68.

8. **Mahādeva.**—A minister of **Dappula II.** He built the **Dappulapabbata-vihāra.**[1]

[1] Cv. l. 80.

9. **Mahādeva.**—See **Maliya Mahādeva.**

Mahādevarattakurava.—A vihāra in the district of **Kāsikhaṇḍa** in Ceylon; the **Anurārāma** was a building attached to it.[1]

[1] Cv. xli. 101.

Mahādevī.—An eminent Therī of Ceylon.[1]

[1] Dpv. xviii. 24.

Mahādoṇa.—A Nāga king of the city of **Mahādoṇa** on the bank of the **Gaṅgārahada.** He used to destroy the districts of those who did not pay him tribute. **Nārada Buddha** preached to him and vanquished him.[1]

[1] Bu. x. 7; BuA. 153.

1. **Mahādhana.**—The son of the Treasurer of Benares. His parents possessed eighty crores, and, for all education, he learnt music and singing. He married the daughter of an equally rich family and of similar education. After the death of their parents, they were very rich. One night, as the husband was on his way from the palace, some knaves tempted him to drink. He soon fell a victim to the habit and all his wealth was squandered. Then he spent his wife's money, and finally sold all his belongings, and used to go about begging, a potsherd in his hand. One day the Buddha, seeing him waiting outside the refectory for leavings of food, smiled. In answer to **Ānanda,** who asked him the reason for his smile, the Buddha said that there was a man who had had the power of becoming chief Treasurer or attaining arahantship, if he did but use his opportunities, but he was now reduced to beggary, like a heron in a dried-up pond.[1]

[1] DhA. iii. 129 ff.

2. **Mahādhana.**—A merchant of **Sāvatthi.** Five hundred thieves once attempted unsuccessfully to enter his house, but hearing that he was about to travel through a forest with five hundred carts laden with goods, they lay in wait for him. The merchant took with him five hundred monks and entertained them in a village at the entrance to the forest. As he tarried there several days, the thieves sent a man to find out when he might be setting out, which he learnt would be soon. The villagers

warned the merchant of the thieves' intention, and he gave up the idea of the journey and decided to return home. But on hearing that the thieves were lying in ambush on the homeward road, he stayed in the village. The monks returned to **Jetavana** and told the Buddha, who taught them that men should avoid evil even as Mahādhana avoided thieves.[1]

[1] DhA. iii. 21 f.

3. **Mahādhana.**—A merchant of Benares. On his way to **Sāvatthi** with five hundred carts filled with cloth of the colour of safflower, he came to the river and unyoked his oxen, thinking to cross on the morrow. In the night it rained and there was a flood. For seven days the rain continued, and Mahādhana decided to stay until his wares were sold and then return home. The Buddha, on his begging rounds, saw him and smiled. When asked the reason by **Ānanda,** he said that the man, in spite of all his plans, had only seven days to live. With the Buddha's permission, Ānanda warned Mahādhana, who thereupon invited the Buddha and his monks and entertained them. At the end of the meal the Buddha preached to him and he became a sotāpanna. Shortly after he was seized with pain in the head and died immediately, to be re-born in **Tusita.**[1]

[1] DhA. iii. 429 f.

4. **Mahādhana.**—A very rich man of **Rājagaha.** He had only one son, to whom he taught nothing, in case he should weary of learning. The boy, when grown up, married a woman likewise of no education. After the death of his father, he squandered all his wealth and sought refuge in a destitute's home (*anāthasālā*). Thieves saw him there, and as he was young and strong enlisted his services. One night the thieves broke into a house, but the owner awoke and pursued them, catching Mahādha's son, who was brought before the king. The king ordered him to be beheaded. The courtesan of the city, **Sulasā,** saw him being led to execution, and remembering their past friendship, gave him sweetmeats and drink, bribing the guard to let him have them. At that moment **Moggallāna,** seeing the youth's fate with his divine eye, appeared before him and was given some sweetmeats. After execution, the man was born as a tree-sprite, and one day carried Sulasā off as she was walking in the park and kept her for a week. Sulasā's mother consulted Moggallāna on her disappearance, and was told she would return to **Veḷuvana** at the end of a week. When the time came, the sprite brought Sulasā back and left her on the edge of the crowd which was listening to the Buddha's preaching at Veḷuvana. Sulasā was recognised, and recounted

what had happened. The Buddha made this a topic for a sermon, which benefited many beings.[1]

[1] Pv. i. 1; PvA. 3 ff.

5. **Mahādhana.**—Sixty-five kappas ago there were four kings of this name, all previous births of **Tiṇasanthāradāyaka Thera.**[1]

[1] Ap. i. 198.

Mahādhanaka.—A seṭṭhi of Benares identified with **Devadatta.** For his story see the **Ruru Jātaka.**[1]

[1] J. iv. 255 ff.

Mahādhana-kumāra.—The Bodhisatta born as the son of the Treasurer of Benares.[1] For his story see the **Aṭṭhāna Jātaka.**

[1] J. iii. 475 ff.

1. **Mahādhammakathī Thera.**—In the time of king **Buddhadāsa** he translated the Pāli Suttas into Sinhalese.[1]

[1] Cv. xxxvii. 175; he is evidently referred to by Fa Hsien (Giles, p. 72).

Mahādhammakathī Thera.—An incumbent of **Nāgasāla-vihāra. Kassapa II.** showed him great honour and induced him to preach the Dhamma.[1]

[1] Cv. xlv. 2.

Mahādhammapāla Jātaka (No. 447).—In **Dhammapāla,** a village of **Kāsi,** there lived a family whose head was **Mahādhammapāla.** The Bodhisatta was his son, and was called **Dhammapala-kumāra.** He went to study at **Takkasilā.** There the teacher's eldest son died, but among all the lamentations it was noticed that Dhammapāla did not weep. When questioned by his fellows as to how he could refrain, he answered that as it was impossible for anybody young to die, he did not believe his friend was dead. The teacher asked him about this, and found that in Dhammapāla's family no one died young. Wishing to know if this were true, he left Takkasilā and went to the home of Dhammapāla, carrying with him the bones of a goat. After his welcome had subsided, he announced to Dhammapāla that his son was dead, and begged him not to grieve. But Dhammapāla clapped his hands and laughed, saying that such a thing could never be as no member of their family ever died young. He then told the brahmin, in answer to his query, that they owed their longevity to the fact that they lived good lives.

The story was related to **Suddhodana,** who told the Buddha how, when the Buddha was practising severe penances, some gods came to him (Suddhodana) and said that he was dead. But he refused to believe them. Suddhodana was Mahādhammapāla and the teacher **Sāriputta.**[1] At the conclusion of the Jātaka Suddhodana became an *anāgāmi* and **Mahāpajāpatī Gotamī** a *sotāpanna.*[2]

[1] J. iv. 50-55. [2] DhA. i. 99; J. i. 92.

1. **Mahādhammarakkhita Thera.**—An arahant. He lived at **Asokārāma.** Once, **Tissa,** brother of **Asoka,** saw him seated at the foot of a tree meditating, fanned by a Nāga with a *sāla*-branch. Tissa was later ordained by him.[1] After the Third Council he was sent as messenger of Buddhism to **Mahāraṭṭha.** There he preached the **Mahānārada-Kassapa Jātaka,** and eighty-four thousand people were converted, thirteen thousand joining the Order.[2]

[1] Mhv. v. 161, 167; ThagA. i. 505; but see Sp. i. 561, according to which it was **Yonaka Mahādhammarakhita** who ordained Tissa; also SA. iii. 125.

[2] Mhv. xii. 5, 37; Dpv. viii. 8; Sp. i. 67.

2. **Mahādhammarakkhita.**—An ancient Commentator, generally called **Tipiṭaka-Mahādhammarakkhita,** who is quoted several times in the Commentaries. He was a contemporary of **Dīghabhāṇaka-Abhaya.**[1]

[1] *E.g.*, DhSA. 267, 278, 286 f.; VibhA. 81; PSA. 405.

3. **Mahādhammarakkhita.**—An Elder of **Tulādhāra-vihāra** in **Rohaṇa. Tipiṭaka-Cūḷābhaya** went to him from the **Mahāvihāra** in order to learn from him the Doctrine. At the end of the teaching, Dhammarakkhita asked Abhaya to give him a subject for meditation, for, he said, Abhaya had a greater knowledge than he of that matter. The subject was given, and soon after Dhammarakkhita attained Nibbāna, and died while preaching at the **Lohapāsāda.**[1]

[1] Vsm. 96 f.

4. **Mahādhammarakkhita.**—See **Yonaka-Mahādhammarakkhita.**

Mahādhammasamādāna Sutta.—On professions and living up to them. There are four ways of professing a Doctrine: the first is unpleasant at the time and ripens to pain thereafter, the second is pleasant at the time but also ripens to pain, the third is unpleasant at the time but ripens to pleasure, while the fourth is pleasant both at the time and thereafter. The Buddha then explains in detail these four classes of profession.[1]

[1] M. i. 309-17.

Mahādhātukathā.—See **Dhātukathā.**

Mahānadī.—A river, dammed up by **Udaya II.**[1]

[1] Cv. li. 127; Cv. *Trs.* i. 159, n. 3.

Mahānanda.—An author of **Haṃsavatī,** to whom some authorities ascribe the authorship of the **Madhusāratthadīpanī** in the Abhidhamma.[1]

[1] Bode, *op. cit.*, 47, n. 6.

Mahānandana.—See **Nandana.**

1. **Mahānāga Thera.**—The son of **Madhuvāseṭṭha** of **Sāketa.** While the Buddha was at **Añjanavana,** Mahānāga saw the wonder wrought by **Gavampati** and entered the Order under him, attaining to arahantship in due course. In the past he had given a *dāḍima*(pomegranate)-fruit to **Kakusandha Buddha.**[1] Several verses uttered by him in admonition of the **Chabbaggiyā,** because of their failure to show regard for their co-religionists, are found in the Theragāthā.[2]

[1] ThagA. i. 442 f. [2] Thag. vss. 387-92.

2. **Mahānāga.**—Son of **Muṭasīva** and viceroy of **Devānampiyatissa.** His wife was **Anulā,** for whose ordination **Saṅghamittā** came over from **Jambudīpa.**[1] His second wife was a foolish woman who tried to poison him in order to get the throne for her son. While he was building the **Taraccha-tank,** she sent him some mangoes, the top one of which, intended for him, was poisoned. But it was her son who ate the mango and died. Mahānāga thereupon went to **Rohaṇa,** where he founded the dynasty of that name at **Mahāgāma.** His son was **Yaṭṭhālayaka-Tissa.** Mahānāga built the **Nāgamahā-vihāra** and the **Uddhakandara-vihāra.**[2]

[1] Mhv. xiv. 56; Dpv. xi. 6; xvii. 75. [2] Mhv. xxii. 2 ff.

3. **Mahānāga.**—A resident of **Niṭṭhulaviṭṭhika** in **Girijanapada.** He was the father of **Goṭhaimbara.**[1]

[1] Mhv. xxiii. 49.

4. **Mahānāga.**—Son of **Vaṭṭagāmaṇī.**[1] He later came to be known as **Coranāga** (*q.v.*).

[1] Mhv. xxxiii. 45.

5. **Mahānāga.**—See **Māhādāṭhika-Mahānaga.**

6. **Mahānāga Thera.** Incumbent of **Bhūtārāma.** As a mark of favour, **Kaṇiṭṭhatissa** built for him the **Ratanapāsāda** at **Abhayagiri-vihāra.**[1]

[1] Mhv. xxxvi. 7.

7. **Mahānāga Thera.**—Incumbent of **Samudda-vihāra.** He was among those who accepted the gift of a meal by Prince **Sāliya,** in his birth as a blacksmith.[1]

[1] MṬ. 606.

8. **Mahānāga Thera.**—Incumbent of **Kālavallimaṇḍapa.** He was among those who accepted the meal given by **Sāliya** in his previous birth.[1] He was one of the last to attain arahantship among those who left the world with the Bodhisatta in various births.[2] He did not sleep for seven years, after which he practised continual meditation for sixteen years, becoming an arahant at the end of that time.[3]

His fame was great, and there is a story of a brahmin who came all the way from **Pāṭaliputta** to Kālavallimaṇḍapa in Rohaṇa to visit him. The brahmin entered the Order under him and became an arahant.[4] Once, while Mahānāga was begging alms at **Nakulanagara,** he saw a nun and offered her a meal. As she had no bowl, he gave her his, with the food ready in it. After she had eaten and washed the bowl, she gave it back to him saying, "Henceforth there will be no fatigue for you when begging for alms." Thereafter the Elder was never given alms worth less than a *kahāpaṇa*. The nun was an arahant.[5]

[1] MṬ. 606.
[2] J. iv. 490.
[3] SNA. i. 56; MA. i. 209; SA. iii. 155.
[4] AA. i. 384.
[5] DhSA. 399.

9. **Mahānāga Thera.**—Incumbent of **Bhātiyavaṅka-vihāra.** He received alms from **Sāliya** in his previous birth.[1]

[1] MṬ. 606.

10. **Mahānāga Thera.**—Incumbent of **Maddha(?)-vihara.** He was one of the last to become arahant among those who left the world with the Bodhisatta in various births.[1]

[1] J. vi. 30.

11. **Mahānāga Thera.**—He and his brother, **Cūḷanāga,** householders of **Vasāḷanagara,** renounced the world and became arahants. One day, while visiting their own village, they went to their mother's house for alms. The mother, not quite sure who they were, asked if they were her sons. But they, not wishing for any bonds of affection, gave an evasive reply.[1]

[1] SA. ii. 125.

12. **Mahānāga Thera.**—He lived in **Uccatalaṅka (Uccavālika). Talaṅkavāsi-Dhammadinna** (*q.v.*) was his pupil and became an arahant through his intervention.[1]

[1] VibhA. 489; Vsm. 634.

13. **Mahānāga Thera.**—He once went to his mother's house for alms and while sitting there entered into trance. The house caught fire and all the others fled. When the fire was put out the thera was discovered unhurt, and the villagers did him great honour. Finding his attainments discovered, he rose into the air and went to **Piyaṅgudīpa.**[1]

[1] Vsm. 706.

14. **Mahānāga.**—A king of Ceylon, mentioned in the **Dhammasaṅgaṇi** Commentary.[1] While travelling to India from Ceylon he won the favour of an Elder, and on his return became king. Out of gratitude he established gifts of medicine in **Setambaṅgana** for as long as he lived.[1]

[1] DhSA. 399.

15. **Mahānāga.**—Teacher of **Saṅgharakkhitasāmaṇera** (*q.v.*). He was called **Sāmuddika-Mahānāga.**[1]

[1] DA. ii. 558.

16. **Mahānāga.**—Nephew of **Bhayasiva.** During a time of famine he sold his upper garment and obtained food for a man learned in magic spells. The latter, in gratitude, took him to the **Gokaṇṇasamudda,** and there, having conjured up a Nāga, prophesied Mahānāga's future. Mahānāga entered **Silākāla's** service, and was sent by him to collect revenue in **Rohaṇa.** Later he was made *Andhasenāpati*, and he established himself master of Rohaṇa. He once attempted to fight against **Dāṭhāpabhuti,** but soon gave up the attempt. Taking advantage of the confusion in **Kittisirimegha's** dominions, Mahānāga advanced against him, killed him, and seized the throne. Among his benefactions was the grant of the village of **Jambalambaya** to **Uttara-vihāra, Tintinika** to **Mahāvihāra,** and **Vasabha** in **Uddhagāma** to **Jetavana-vihāra,** together with three hundred fields for the supply of rice-soup. He also gave **Cīramātikavāra** to **Mahāvihāra** and instituted a gift of rice-soup. He renovated the **Mayūrapariveṇa** and **Anurārāma** in the **Mahādevarattakuruva-vihāra** in **Kāsikhaṇḍa.** He reigned for only three years (556-9 A.C.), and was succeeded by his nephew, **Aggabodhi I.,**[1] who built a vihāra in his memory and assigned it to an Elder versed in the Tipiṭaka.[2]

[1] Cv. xli. 69 ff.

[2] *Ibid.*, xlii. 24; Cv. *Trs.* i. 68, n. 2.

Mahānāgakula.—See **Mahānāgahula.**

Mahānāgatissa-vihāra.—A monastery in Ceylon where **Vohārika-Tissa** erected a parasol over the thūpa.[1]

[1] Mhv. xxxvi. 34.

Mahānāgapabbata.—A vihāra in Ceylon where **Aggabodhi I.** built an *uposatha*-hall.[1]

[1] Cv. xlii. 27.

1. **Mahānāgavana.**—An open space in Ceylon, on the banks of the **Mahāvālukagaṅgā.** It was three yojanas long and one wide and was the meeting-place of the Yakkhas. The Buddha went there on his first visit to Ceylon, and in it was later built the **Mahiyaṅgana Thūpa.**[1]

[1] Mhv. i. 22 f.

2. **Mahānāgavana.**—A park near **Anurādhapura.** It was there that the relics brought by **Sumana** for the **Thūpārāma** were first received by **Devānampiyatissa.**[1]

[1] Mhv. xvii. 7, 22 f.

1. **Mahānāga-vihāra.**—See **Nāgamahā-vihāra.**

2. **Mahānāga-viharā.**—A monastery built by **Aggabodhi I.** in memory of King **Mahānāga**[1] (see **Mahānāga** 16). **Jeṭṭhatissa III.** assigned the villages of **Mātulaṅgana** and **Odumbaraṅgana** to the *padhānaghara* there.[2]

[1] Cv. xlii. 24.
[2] *Ibid.*, xliv. 98.

Mahānāgasena.—An Elder who lived in **Indasālakalena** in **Vallipāsāṇa-vihāra.** When he lay ill, eight thousand arahants and the devas of the two deva-worlds, led by **Sakka,** came to wait upon him.[1]

[1] MṬ. 552.

Mahānāgahula, Mahānāgasula, Mahānāgakula.—A town in **Rohaṇa** in **Dvādasasahassakaraṭṭha.** It is first mentioned in the account of the campaigns of **Vijayabāhu I.**[1] His ādipāda, **Vikkamabāhu,** made it his capital and lived there,[2] as did **Kittisirimegha,** brother of **Mānābharaṇa.**[3] Later, **Sirivallabha** lived there with his queen **Ratnāvalī,** her two daughters and the young **Parakkamabāhu.**[4] When **Parakkamabāhu** became king as Parakkamabāhu I., he wished to bring the city under his power, and

[1] Cv. lviii. 39.
[2] *Ibid.*, lx. 90.
[3] *Ibid.*, lxi. 23.
[4] *Ibid.*, lxiii. 4.

sent **Damiḷādhikari-Rakkha** and **Rakkha-Kañcukināyaka** to subdue it. This they did only after much difficulty, owing to the severe resistance of the rebels of Rohaṇa. After its capture, Damiḷādhikāri-Rakkha held a great festival in celebration of his victory, and the place was made the headquarters of Parakkamabāhu's forces in Rohaṇa.[5]

[5] Cv. lxxv. 19, 70, 115 ff.; 162 f. For its identification see Cv. *Trs.* i. 205, n. 3.

1. **Mahānāma Thera.**—He was born in a brahmin family of **Sāvatthi,** and, after hearing the Buddha preach, entered the Order. Taking a formula of meditation, he dwelt on the hill called **Nesādaka.** Unable to prevent the rising of evil thoughts, he was disgusted with himself, and climbing a steep crag, made as if to throw himself down, and evoking insight became an arahant.

In the time of **Sumedha Buddha** he was a brahmin teacher skilled in the Vedas, and the Buddha visited him in his hermitage on the banks of the **Sindhū** and was given honey by him.[1] Mahānāma is probably identical with **Madhudāyaka Thera** of the Apadāna.[2]

[1] ThagA. vs. 115; ThagA. i. 227 ff.

[2] Ap. ii. 325 f.

2. **Mahānāma Thera.**—One of the **Pañcavaggiyā.**[1] He became a *sotāpanna* on the third day after the preaching of the **Dhammacakkappavattana Sutta.** He became an arahant on the day of the preaching of the **Anattalakkhaṇa Sutta,** together with the other Pañcavaggiyā.[2] Mahānāma once visited **Macchikāsaṇḍa,** and there **Cittagahapati,** seeing him beg for alms and pleased with his bearing, invited him to his house, gave him a meal, and listened to a sermon by him. Citta was greatly pleased, and offered his pleasure garden of **Ambāṭakavana** to Mahānāma as a gift to the Order and built there a great monastery.[3]

[1] J. i. 82.

[2] AA. i. 84; MA. i. 390.

[3] DhA. ii. 74.

3. **Mahānāma.**—A Sākyan rājā, son of **Amitodana;** he was elder brother of **Anuruddha** and cousin of the Buddha. When the Sākyan families of **Kapilavatthu** sent their representatives to join the Order of their distinguished kinsman, Mahānāma allowed Anuruddha to leave the household, he knowing nothing of household affairs.[1] Mahānāma showed great generosity to the Saṅgha, and was proclaimed best of those who gave choice alms to the monks.[2] Once, with the Buddha's permission, he

[1] Vin. ii. 180 f.; DhA. i. 133; iv. 124, etc.; but according to Northern sources (Rockhill, p. 13) he was son of Dronodana; according to ThagA. (ii. 123) Ānanda was a brother (or, at least, a step-brother) of Mahānāma, for there Ānanda's father is given as Amitodana. But see MA. i. 289, where Mahānāma's father is called **Sukkodana** and Ānanda's Amitodana.

[2] A. i. 26.

supplied the Order with medicaments for three periods of four months each. The **Chabbaggiyā,** always intent on mischief, tried in vain to discourage him.[3] Mahānāma was a devoted follower of the Buddha and wished to understand the Doctrine. The books record several conversations between him and the Buddha, and **Ānanda, Godha,** and **Lomasavaṅgīsa.**[4] Once when the Buddha arrived at Kapilavatthu he asked Mahānāma to find him lodging for the night. Mahānāma tried everywhere without success, and finally suggested that the Buddha should spend the night in the hermitage of **Bharaṇḍu Kālāma.**[5] This he did, and was joined there the next morning by Mahānāma; as a result of the discussion between the Buddha, Mahānāma and Bharaṇḍu, the last-named left Kapilavatthu never to return.[6] On another occasion, Mahānāma visited the Buddha at **Nigrodhārāma** where the Buddha was convalescing after a severe illness, and at once Mahānāma asked a question as to whether concentration followed or preceded knowledge. **Ānanda,** who was present, not wishing the Buddha to be troubled, took Mahānāma aside and explained to him the Buddha's teachings on the subject.[7]

Mahānāma had a daughter **Vāsābhakhattiyā,** born to him by a slave-girl named **Nāgamuṇḍā,** and when **Pasenadi** asked the Sākyans to give him in marriage a Sākyan maiden they met in the Mote Hall, and, following the advice of Mahānāma, sent Vāsabhakhattiyā to him. In order to allay any suspicions, Mahānāma sat down to a meal with her, taking one mouthful from the same dish; but before he could swallow it a messenger arrived, as secretly arranged, and summoned him away. He left, asking Vāsabhakhattiyā to continue her meal.[8]

See also the **Cūla-Dukkhakkhandha Sutta** and **Sekha Sutta,** both preached to Mahānāma.

His resolve to attain to eminence as the best distributor of pleasant food to the monks was made in the time of **Padumuttara Buddha.** He was then a householder of **Haṃsavatī** and heard the Buddha confer a similar rank on a monk.[9]

Mahānāma is included in a list of exemplary lay-devotees.[10] The Samantapāsādikā[11] adds that Mahānāma was one month older than the Buddha and that he was a *sakadāgāmī.*

[3] Vin. iv. 101; AA. (i. 213) adds that this was during the period of want experienced by the Buddha and his monks at **Verañjā.** At the end of the year, Mahānāma wished to continue the supply of good food to the Buddha and his monks, but the Buddha refused his permission.

[4] See *s.v.* **Mahānāma Sutta** below. See also *s.v.* **Lomasavaṅgīsa.**

[5] S. v. 327 f.

[6] For details see *s.v.* **Bharaṇḍu.**

[7] See **Sakka Sutta** (S. i. 219 f.).

[8] DhA. i. 345 f.; J. i. 133; iv. 145 f.

[9] AA. i. 213.

[10] A. iii. 451.

[11] Sp. iv. 857.

4. **Mahānāma.**—A **Licchavi.** One day while walking about in the **Mahāvana** in **Vesāli** he saw some young Licchavis paying homage to the Buddha and accused them of inconsistency.[1]

[1] For deatils see the **Kumāra Sutta** (A. iii. 75 ff.).

5. **Mahānāma.**—King of Ceylon. He was the younger brother of **Upatissa II.** and was for some time a monk, but he carried on an intrigue with Upatissa's wife, and she killed her husband. Then Mahānāma became a layman, assumed the sovereignty, and married Upatissa's queen. He built refuges for the sick, enlarged the **Mahāpāli Hall,** and erected the **Lohadvāra-, Ralaggāma-,** and **Koṭipassāvana-vihāras,** which he gave to the monks of **Abhayagiri.** A vihāra which he built on the **Dhūmarakkha** mountain, he gave, at the instigation of his queen, to the monks of **Mahāvihāra.** He ruled for twenty-two years (409-31 A.C.). It was during his reign that **Buddhaghosa** arrived in Ceylon and wrote his Commentaries, dwelling in a vihāra given by the king.[1]

[1] Cv. xxxvii. 209 ff.; see also P.L.C. 96. The king seems to have also been called Sirinivāsa and Sirikuḍḍa.

6. **Mahānāma Thera.**—Incumbent of **Dīghasaṇḍa** (or **Dīghāsana**) **Vihāra.**[1] He is generally identified with the uncle of **Dhātusena** mentioned elsewhere.[2] **Moggallāna I.** built for him the **Pabbata-vihāra.**[3] Mahānāma is generally regarded as the author of the older part of the **Mahāvaṃsa.**[4]

[1] Cv. xxxix. 42.
[2] *Ibid.*, xxxviii. 16.
[3] *Ibid.*, xxxix. 42.
[4] MṬ. 687; *e.g.*, in Gv. 61, 66; Svd. 1266; for a discussion on this see P.L.C. 139 ff.

7. **Mahānāma Thera.**—Author of the **Saddhammappakāsanī** Commentary on the **Paṭisambhidāmagga.**[1] The colophon to the book[2] states that he lived in the **Uttaramanti-pariveṇa** in the **Mahāvihāra** and finished his work in the third year after the death of **Moggallāna** (probably **Moggallāna I.**). The Gandhavaṃsa[3] says that the work was written at the request of an *upāsaka,* also named Mahānāma.

[1] Gv. 61; Svd. 1196.
[2] PSA. 526.
[3] Gv. 70.

8. **Mahānāma.**—See **Mahānanda.**

1. **Mahānāma Sutta.**—**Mahānāma** the Sākyan visits the Buddha at **Nigrodhārāma** and confesses his worry as to where he would be reborn if he were to meet with an accident while passing through the crowded streets of **Kapilavatthu!** The Buddha assures him that he need not

distress himself as he has for long practised faith and virtue, learning, renunciation and insight. His mind will soar aloft like a jar of butter or of oil, broken in a deep pool of water, where the fragments of the jar will sink but the butter and the oil float.[1]

[1] S. v. 370.

2. **Mahānāma Sutta.**—The circumstances are similar to those of the above sutta. The noble disciple, possessed of unwavering loyalty to the Buddha, the Dhamma and the Saṅgha, and who cultivates virtues dear to the Ariyans, such a one is destined to Nibbāna. Mahānāma is such a one.[1]

[1] S. v. 371; 404.

3. **Mahānāma Sutta.** See **Godha Sutta.**

4. **Mahānāma Sutta.**—**Mahānāma** asks the Buddha, at **Nigrodhārāma,** as to how a man becomes a disciple, how virtuous and a believer, how far is he given to generosity and blessed with insight? The Buddha answers his questions.[1]

[1] S. v. 395 f.

5. **Mahānāma Sutta.**—The Buddha tells **Mahānāma,** in answer to his question, that the noble disciple who has won the fruit (*āgataphala*) and grasped the teaching (*viññātasāsana*), lives a life of abundance, his mind occupied with thoughts of the Buddha, the Dhamma and the Saṅgha, the virtues he practises, his liberality and the devas. Thus among uneven folk he lives evenly and untroubled.[1]

[1] A. iii. 284 ff.

6. **Mahānāma Sutta.**—On six qualities which are developed in a monk who is faithful, energetic, mindful, concentrated and wise. His thoughts dwell on the Tathāgata, the Dhamma and the Saṅgha, on his own generosity and on the devas. Thus his mind is free from thoughts of ill-will, lust, folly; it is direct, and he realises the *attha* and *dhamma* and the joy associated with *dhamma*; his body is serene and his mind filled with joy.[1]

[1] A. v. 328 ff.; cp. No. 5 above.

7. **Mahānāma Sutta.**—Very similar to sutta No. 6.[1]

[1] A. v. 332 ff.

Mahānāmamatthaka.—A tank restored by **Parakkamabāhu I.**[1]

[1] Cv. lxxix. 35.

Mahānāmasikkhāpada.—A rule formulated by the Buddha regarding the advisability of those not actually ill receiving medicaments.[1]

[1] Sp. iv. 842; see Vin. iv. 102.

Mahānāradakassapa Jātaka (No. 544).—**Aṅgati,** king of **Mithilā** in **Videha,** is a good ruler. One full-moon night he consults his ministers as to how they shall amuse themselves. **Alāta** suggests new conquests; **Sunāma** suggests that they shall seek pleasure in dance, song and music; but **Vijaya** recommends that they shall visit some samaṇa or brahmin. Aṅgati falls in with the views of Vijaya, and in great state goes to **Guṇa** of the **Kassapa-gotta,** an ascetic who lives in the park near the city. Guṇa preaches to him that there is no fruit, good or evil, in the moral life; there is no other world than this, no strength, no courage; all beings are predestined and follow their course like the ship her stern. Alāta approves of the views of Guṇa; he remembers how, in his past life, he was a wicked councillor called **Piṅgala ;** from there he was born in the family of a general, and now he is a minister. A slave, **Bījaka,** who is present, can remember his past life and says he was once **Bhavaseṭṭhi** in **Sāketa,** virtuous and generous, but he is now the son of a prostitute. Even now he gives away half his food to any in need, but see how destitute he is !

Aṅgati is convinced that Guṇa's doctrine is correct, and resolves to find delight only in pleasure. He gives orders that he shall not be disturbed in his palace; **Candaka,** his minister, is deputed to look after the kingdom. Fourteen days pass in this manner. Then the king's only child, his beloved daughter **Rujā,** comes to him arrayed in splendour, attended by her maidens, and asks for one thousand to be given the next day to mendicants. Aṅgati protests; he will deny his daughter no pleasure or luxury, but has learnt too much to approve of her squandering money on charity or wasting her energy in keeping the fasts.

Rujā is at first amazed, then tells her father that his councillors are fools, they have not taken reckoning of the whole of their past, but remember only one birth or two; they cannot therefore judge. She herself remembers several births; in one she was a smith in Rājagaha and committed adultery, but that sin remained hidden, like fire covered with ashes, and she was born as a rich merchant's only son in **Kosambī.** There she engaged in good works, but, because of previous deeds, she was born after death in the **Roruva-niraya** and then as a castrated goat in **Bheṇṇākaṭa.** In her next birth she was a monkey, and then an ox among the **Dasaṇṇas;** then a hermaphrodite among the **Vajjians,** and later a nymph in **Tāvatiṃsa.** Once more her good deeds have come round, and hereafter she will be born only among gods and men. Seven births hence she will be a male god in Tāvatiṃsa, and even now the god **Java** is gathering a garland for her.

All night she preaches in this way to her father, but he remains unconvinced. The Bodhisatta is a Brahmā, named **Nārada Kassapa,** and, surveying the world, sees Rujā and Aṅgati engaged in conversation. He therefore appears in the guise of an ascetic, and Aṅgati goes out to greet and consult him. The ascetic praises goodness, charity, and generosity, and speaks of other worlds. Aṅgati laughs, and asks for a loan which, he says, he will repay twice over in the next world, as the ascetic seems so convinced that there is one. Nārada tells him of the horrors of the hell in which Aṅgati will be reborn unless he mends his ways, and mentions to him the names of former kings who attained to happiness through good lives. The king at last sees his error and determines to choose new friends. Nārada Kassapa reveals his identity and leaves in all majesty.

The story was related in reference to the conversion of **Uruvela Kassapa.** He came, after his conversion, with the Buddha to **Laṭṭhivana,** and the people wondered if he had really become a follower of the Buddha. He dispelled their doubts by describing the folly of the sacrifices which he had earlier practised, and, laying his head on the Buddha's feet, did obeisance. Then he rose seven times into the air, and, after having worshipped the Buddha, sat on one side. The people marvelled at the Buddha's powers of conversion, which, the Buddha said, were not surprising since he possessed them already as a Bodhisatta.

Aṅgati is identified with Uruvela Kassapa, Alāta with **Devadatta,** Sunāma with **Bhaddiya,** Vijaya with **Sāriputta,** Bījaka with **Moggallāna,** Guṇa with the **Licchavi Sunakkhatta,** and Rujā with **Ānanda.**[1]

[1] J. vi. 219-55; see also J. i. 83.

Mahānikkaḍḍhika.—One of the villages given by **Aggabodhi IV.** for the maintenance of the *Padhānaghara*, which he built for **Dāṭhasiva.**[1]

[1] Cv. xlvi. 13.

Mahānikkhavaṭṭivāpi.—A tank built by King **Vasabha.**[1]

[1] Mhv. xxxv. 94.

Mahānigaṇṭha.—See **Nigaṇṭha Nātaputta.**

Mahānigama.—A minister of **Mahānāma** ; he built the **Ganthakāra-pariveṇa.**[1]

[1] P.L.C. 96.

Mahānigghosa.—Twenty-four kappas ago there were sixteen kings of this name, previous births of **Vimala** (or **Buddhupaṭṭhāka**) **Thera.**[1]

[1] ThagA. i. 122; Ap. i. 139.

Mahāniṭṭhilagāma.—A village given by **Kassapa II.** for the incumbent of the **Nāgasāla-vihāra.**[1]

[1] Cv. xliv. 151.

Mahānidāna.—Seventy-two kappas ago there were eight kings of this name, previous births of **Vātātapanivāriya Thera.**[1]

[1] Ap. i. 207.

Mahānidāna Sutta.—The fifteenth sutta of the **Dīgha Nikāya,** preached to **Ānanda** at **Kammāssadamma** in the **Kuru** country. Ānanda says that the doctrine of events as arising from causes is quite clear to him; that it only *appears* deep. "Say not so," warns the Buddha, and proceeds to give a detailed exposition of the *Paṭiccasamuppāda*, or Chain of Causation, as it comes later to be called, explaining how each link in the chain of *saṃsāra* is both the effect of one factor and the cause of another. The sutta also discusses the idea of "soul," the seven resting-places of cognition (*viññāṇaṭṭhiti*), the two spheres (*āyatana*), and the eight kinds of deliverance (*vimokkha*).[1]

Khemā had heard the Mahānidāna Sutta in the time of **Kassapa Buddha.**[2] On hearing it again, preached by **Gotama,** she revived her memory and became an arahant.[3]

[1] D. ii. 55-71; Thomas : *op. cit.*, 197. [2] Ap. ii. 546 (vs. 34). [3] Ap ii. 549 (vs. 72).

Mahāniddesa.—See *s.v.* **Niddesa.** One of the books of the **Khuddaka Nikāya.**

Mahāniyyāmaraṭṭha.—A district in Ceylon, mentioned in the account of the campaigns of **Parakkamabāhu I.**[1]

[1] Cv. lxxii. 57; Cv. *Trs.* i. 324, n. 2.

1. **Mahānipāta.**—The twenty-second section of the Jātakaṭṭhakathā.[1]

[1] J. vi. 1-593.

2. **Mahānipāta.**—The last section of the **Theragāthā** and the **Therīgāthā.** The former contains the verses attributed to **Vaṅgīsa** and the latter those attributed to **Sumedhā.**[1]

[1] See *s.v.*

Mahāniraya.—See **Avīci.**

Mahānirutti.—One of the books attributed to **Mahā Kaccāna.**[1] This probably refers to the tradition which ascribes the Kaccāyana Grammar to Mahā Kaccāna (*q.v.*).

[1] Gv. 59.

Mahānisabha.—See **Nisabha.**

Mahānissara.—A work ascribed to **Ariyavaṃsa** of Ava.[1] The correct reading is probably **Mahānissaya,** and refers to the *atthayojanā* written by him on the Abhidhamma.

[1] Gv. 65.

Mahānīpa.—A place in **Anurādhapura** through which the *sīmā* of the **Mahāvihāra** passed.[1] It probably received its name from a *nīpa*-tree growing there.

[1] Mbv. 134, 135.

Mahānuggala.—See **Mahāduggala.**

Mahānettapabbata.—A monastery in Ceylon where **Sena I.** built a refectory (*mahāpāli*).[1]

[1] Cv. l. 74.

Mahānettappāsāda.—A monastery in Ceylon, for the incumbent of which **Vijayabāhu I.** built a vihāra in **Vātagiri.**[1] Among the incumbents of Mahānettappāsāda was an Elder known as **Vīdāgama Thera,** author of several Sinhalese works.[2]

[1] Cv. lxxxviii. 46. [2] P.L.C. 253.

Mahānettādipādika.—A series of cells built for the **Dhammaruci** monks by **Aggabodhi IV.**[1]

[1] Cv. xlviii. 2.

1. **Mahāneru.**—A mountain.[1] Another name for **Meru (Sumeru)** *q.v.*

[1] M. i. 338; D. iii. 199; J. iii. 210.

2. **Mahāneru.**—A primæval king, descendant of **Mahāsammata**; he lived for the space of one *asaṅkheyya.*[1]

[1] Dpv. iii. 8; Mhv. ii. 5; MṬ. 124.

Mahānela.—A king of twenty kappas ago, a previous birth of **Koṭumbarīya Thera.**[1]

[1] Ap. i. 192.

Mahānoma.—The name of the **Mahāmeghavana** in the time of **Koṇagamana Buddha.** The capital, **Vaḍḍhamāna,** lay to the south of it, and the park was given by King **Samiddha** to the Buddha.[1]

[1] Mhv. xv. 92, 107 ff.

Mahāpakaraṇa.—Another name for the **Paṭṭhānappakaraṇa** (*q.v.*) of the Abhidhamma.

Mahāpaccarī.—An old Commentary on the Tipiṭaka, used by **Buddhaghosa** in the compilation of his works. It is often referred to in the **Samantapāsādika** and its comments quoted.[1] Tradition has it that it was so called because it was compiled on a raft.

[1] *E.g.*, Sp. i. 283; iii. 527, 536, 553, 615; iv. 763, 770, 776, 778, 782, 803, 806, 807, 813, 861, 914, 923, etc.

Mahāpajāpatī Gotamī.—An eminent Therī. She was born at **Devadaha** in the family of **Suppabuddha**[1] as the younger sister of **Mahāmāyā.** At the birth of each sister, interpreters of bodily marks prophesied that their children would be *cakkavattins.* King **Suddhodana** married both the sisters, and when Mahāmāyā died, seven days after the birth of the Buddha, Pajāpatī looked after the Buddha and nursed him. She was the mother of **Nanda,** but it is said that she gave her own son to nurses and herself nursed the Buddha. The Buddha was at **Vesāli** when Suddhodana died, and Pajāpatī decided to renounce the world, and waited for an opportunity to ask the permission of the Buddha.[2] Her opportunity came when the Buddha visited **Kapilavatthu** to settle the dispute between the Sākyans and the Koliyans as to the right to take water from the river **Rohiṇī.** When the dispute had been settled, the Buddha preached the **Kalahavivāda Sutta,** and five hundred young Sākyan men joined the Order. Their wives, led by Pajāpatī, went to the Buddha and asked leave to be ordained as nuns. This leave the Buddha refused, and he went on to **Vesāli.** But Pajāpatī and her companions, nothing daunted, had barbers to cut off their hair, and

[1] Ap. (ii. 538) says her father was **Añjana-Sakka** and her mother **Sulakkhaṇā.** Mhv. (ii. 18) says her father was Añjana and her mother **Yasodharā. Daṇḍapāṇi** and **Suppabuddha** were her brothers; *cp.* Dpv. xviii. 7 f.

[2] Pajāpatī was already a *sotāpanna.* She attained this eminence when the Buddha first visited his father's palace and preached the **Mahādhammapāla Jātaka** (DhA. i. 97).

donning yellow robes, followed the Buddha to Vesāli on foot. They arrived with wounded feet at the Buddha's monastery and repeated their request. The Buddha again refused, but **Ānanda** interceded on their behalf and their request was granted, subject to eight strict conditions.[3]

After her ordination, Pajāpatī came to the Buddha and worshipped him. The Buddha preached to her and gave her a subject for meditation. With this topic she developed insight and soon after won arahantship, while her five hundred companions attained to the same after listening to the **Nandakovāda Sutta.** Later, at an assembly of monks and nuns in **Jetavana,** the Buddha declared Pajāpatī chief of those who had experience (*rattaññūnaṃ*).[4] Not long after, while at Vesāli, she realized that her life had come to an end. She was one hundred and twenty years old; she took leave of the Buddha, performed various miracles, and then died, her five hundred companions dying with her. It is said that the marvels which attended her cremation rites were second only to those of the Buddha.

It was in the time of **Padumuttara Buddha** that Pajāpatī made her resolve to gain eminence. She then belonged to a clansman's family in **Haṃsavatī,** and, hearing the Buddha assign the foremost place in experience to a certain nun, wished for similar recognition herself, doing many good deeds to that end. After many births she was born once more at Benares, forewoman among five hundred slave-girls. When the rains drew near, five Pacceka Buddhas came from **Nandamūlaka** to **Isipatana** seeking lodgings. Pajāpatī saw them after the Treasurer had refused them any assistance, and, after consultation with her fellow-slaves, they persuaded their several husbands to erect five huts for the Pacceka Buddhas during the rainy season and they provided them with all requisites. At the end of the rains they gave three robes to each Pacceka Buddha. After that she was born in a weaver's village near Benares, and again ministered, this time to five hundred Pacceka Buddhas, sons of **Padumavatī.**[5]

It is said that once Pajāpatī made a robe for the Buddha of wonderful material and marvellously elaborate. But when it came to be offered to the Buddha he refused it, and suggested it should be given to the Order as a whole. Pajāpatī was greatly disappointed, and Ānanda

[3] For details see Vin. ii. 253 ff.; also A. iv. 274 ff. There was some question which arose later as to the procedure of Pajāpatī's ordination, which was not formal. When the nuns discovered this some of them refused to hold the *uposatha* with her. But the Buddha declared that he himself had ordained her and that all was in order (DhA. iv. 149). Her *upasampadā* consisted in acquiescing in the eight conditions laid down for nuns (Sp. i. 242).

[4] A. i. 25.

[5] ThigA. 140 ff.; AA. i. 185 f.; Ap. ii. 529-43.

intervened. But the Buddha explained that his suggestion was for the greater good of Pajāpatī, and also as an example to those who might wish to make similar gifts in the future. This was the occasion for the preaching of the **Dakkhiṇāvibhaṅga Sutta.**[6] The Buddha had a great love for Pajāpatī, and when she lay ill, as there were no monks to visit her and preach to her—that being against the rule—the Buddha amended the rule and went himself to preach to her.[7]

Pajāpatī's name appears several times in the Jātakas. She was the mother monkey in the **Cūḷa-Nandiya Jātaka,**[8] **Candā** in the **Culla-Dhammapāla,**[9] and **Bhikkhudāyikā** (or **Bhikkhudāsikā**) daughter of **Kiki,** king of Benares.[10]

Mahāpajāpatī was so called because, at her birth, augerers prophesied that she would have a large following; Gotamī was her *gotta*-name.[11]

There is a story related of a nurse employed by Pajāpatī and born in Devadaha. She renounced the world with Pajāpatī, but for twenty-five years was harassed by thoughts of lust till, at last, she heard **Dhammadinnā** preach. She then practised meditation and became an arahant.[12]

[6] M. iii. 253 ff.; MA. ii. 1001 ff.; this incident is referred to in the Milinda (p. 240 f.).
[7] Vin. iv. 56.
[8] J. ii. 202.
[9] J. iii. 182.
[10] J. vi. 481.
[11] MA. i. 1001; *cp.* AA. ii. 774.
[12] ThigA. 75 f.

Mahāpajāpatī Sutta.—Contains details of the events which led to the admission of women into the Order.[1]

[1] A. iv. 274 ff.; *cp.* Vin. ii. 253 ff.

Mahāpaññākathā.—The first chapter of the Paññāvagga of the **Paṭisambhidāmagga.**

1. **Mahāpañha Sutta.**—A series of questions and answers forming an epitome of the Buddha's teachings; each question contains one statement (*uddesa*) and one exposition (*veyyākaraṇa*), and so on, up to ten, which consists of ten subjects (*dasa akusalakammapathā*) put in one group.[1] It is probably this sutta which is referred to as the Mahāpañhā in the Aṅguttara Nikāya.[2]

[1] A. v. 48 ff.
[2] A. v. 54.

2. **Mahāpañha Sutta.**—A number of lay devotees of **Kajaṅgalā** visit the **Kajaṅgalā-bhikkhunī** (*q.v.*) and ask her to explain in detail the *Mahāpañhā* as stated by the Buddha. She answers that she has heard neither the explanation of the Buddha nor that of the arahants, but she

will explain them according to her own lights, and proceeds to do so. The devotees report her explanation to the Buddha, who praises her wisdom and declares that his own explanation would have been identical.[1]

[1] A. v. 54 ff.

Mahāpañhā.—A series of questions referred to in the Aṅguttara Nikāya.[1] See **Mahāpañha Sutta** 1.

[1] A. v. 54.

Mahāpaṭhavī.—The name of the Bodhisatta once born as a monkey. In that birth **Devadatta** was a man who earned his living by winnowing grain; he was therefore superior to the Bodhisatta.[1]

[1] Mil. 201.

1. **Mahāpatāpa, Mahāpatāpana.**—King of Benares, father of the Bodhisatta in the **Culla Dhammapāla Jātaka** (*q.v.*). He is identified with **Devadatta.**[1] He was swallowed up by the earth.[2]

[1] J. iii. 182. [2] DhA. i. 129.

2. **Mahāpatāpa.**—A king of thirty-five kappas ago, a former birth of **Vīra** (or **Nigguṇḍipupphiya**) **Thera.**[1]

[1] ThagA. i. 50; Ap. i. 205.

3. **Mahāpatāpa.**—A king of twenty-seven kappas ago; a former birth of **Vaṭamsakiya Thera.**[1]

[1] Ap. i. 216.

4. **Mahāpatāpa.**—A primæval king, descendant of **Mahāsammata.**[1]

[1] Dpv. iii. 7; Mhv. ii. 5; *cp.* Mtu. i. 348.

Mahāpadāna Sutta.—The fourteenth sutta of the **Dīgha Nikāya.** It gives an account of the general events attendant on the advent of a Buddha, and gives various facts connected with the Buddhas, with details of seven Buddhas by way of illustration. But it is only the life of **Vipassī,** the first of the seven Buddhas preceding **Gotama,** which is at all elaborately treated. The sutta was preached at the **Karerimaṇḍapa** in **Jetavana,** and was the result of a conversation among the monks, in which they expressed the desire to know something of the births of previous Buddhas.[1] It is noteworthy that the **Cullaniddesa**[2] cites the sutta as a typical example of the earlier Jātakas. Some regard it as

[1] D. ii. 6-54. [2] p. 80.

the basis of the Mahāvastu. The sutta is held in great esteem and is called in the Commentaries[3] the "King of Suttas" (*Suttantarājā*), because no other sutta contains so many *bhāṇvāras* (one hundred and twenty-six).

[3] *E.g.*, DA. ii. 480.

1. **Mahāpaduma.**—A **Pacceka Buddha,** chief of five hundred Pacceka Buddhas, all sons of **Padumavatī.** He alone was born of his mother's womb, the others being *saṃsedajā*. After Padumavatī's rivals[1] had placed the children in caskets which they launched down-stream, they announced to the king that Padumavatī was a non-human and had given birth to a log of wood. He expelled her from the palace, and as she wandered about in the streets, deprived of all her glory, an old woman had pity on her, took her home, and looked after her. The king was bathing in the river when the caskets containing the children got entangled in his nets, and, having taken them out and unlocked them, he found the babes inside, together with a letter from **Sakka** saying that they were the children of Padumavatī. The king hastened back to his palace and issued a proclamation that anyone finding Padumavatī would receive one thousand as reward. On Padumavatī's suggestion, the old woman, her protector, offered to find her, and Padumavatī then revealed herself. She was conducted back to the palace in all glory, and her five hundred rivals were given to her as slaves. She had them freed, and appointed them as nurses to look after her children, except Paduma (called Mahāpaduma), whom she nursed herself. When Mahāpaduma and his brothers reached the age of sixteen, they went one day to the park, where they were impressed by the appearance of old and faded lotus among the fresh ones growing in the pond, and developing this topic of thought, they became Pacceka Buddhas and went to **Nandamūla**-cave. Padumavatī died of grief at the loss of all her sons and was reborn in a labourer's family. She married, and, one day, while taking gruel to her husband, she saw eight Pacceka Buddhas (her sons in a previous birth) travelling through the air and descending near to where she stood. She gave them the food intended for her husband and invited them for the next day. The next day all the five hundred came to do honour to their mother and to accept her entertainment. She fed them all and offered flowers to them.[2] Afterwards Mahāpaduma and his brothers were entertained by **Nanda,** king of Benares, and his queen (who in their last birth were **Mahā Kassapa** and **Bhaddā Kāpilānī**).

[1] For the earlier part of their story see *s.v.* **Uppalavaṇṇā.**

[2] ThigA. 185 ff.

They stayed in the royal park during the rains, and, one day, when the king was away, the queen visited them and found them dead.[3]

[3] ThagA. ii. 140 f.; SA. ii. 142; AA. i. 98, 190 ff.; MA. ii. 889.

2. **Mahāpaduma.**—A prince of **Kumudanagara. Soṇa Thera**—who harboured enmity against **Piyadassī Buddha,** just as **Devadatta** did against **Gotama**—persuaded Paduma to kill his father, and devised various schemes for killing the Buddha, all of which failed. In the end he sent his elephant **Doṇamukha,** drunk with toddy, to attack the Buddha, who, however, subdued the animal.[1]

[1] BuA. 174; *cp.* **Ajātasattu.**

3. **Mahāpaduma.**—A **Pacceka Buddha.** In the time of **Kassapa Buddha** he was a monk, but was later reborn as a Treasurer of Benares, in which life he committed adultery and was reborn in hell. Later, he became the daughter of a treasurer and was given in marriage. But, owing to her former misdeeds, her husband did not care for her and went with another woman to the fair. One day, however, she begged her husband to take her, and he told her to make preparations. This she did, and on the day of the feast, hearing that her husband had already gone to the park, she followed him with her servants, taking the food and drink she had prepared. On the way she met a Pacceka Buddha, descended from her carriage, filled his bowl with food, placing a lotus on the top, and then offered him a handful of lotus. When her gift was accepted, she made a vow that she should be born in a lotus and be of a lotus colour, should become a man and attain the deliverance of Nibbāna. Her body instantly became beautiful, and her husband, who suddenly remembered her, sent for her, and from then on loved her exceedingly. After death she was born in a lotus in the deva-world and was called **Mahāpaduma.** In his next birth, at the suggestion of **Sakka,** he was born in a lotus in the park of the king of Benares, whose queen was childless. She saw the lotus in the pond, and conceiving a great affection for it, picked it and found the child within as if in a casket. She adopted the child and brought him up in great luxury. One day, while playing outside the palace gates, he saw a Pacceka Buddha and warned him not to enter the palace as they pressed all who entered to eat and drink. The Pacceka Buddha turned away, and the boy was filled with remorse at the idea that the Pacceka Buddha should be offended, and went to his lodging, riding on an elephant, to ask his forgiveness. On the way he descended from the elephant and went on foot. Arrived near the dwelling of the Pacceka Buddha, he dismissed his attendants and went

on alone. He found the Pacceka Buddha's cell empty, and, sitting down, developed insight and became a Pacceka Buddha. When his attendants came for him, he declared his attainment. His verse is included in the **Khaggavisāna Sutta.**[1]

[1] SN. vs. 39; SNA. i. 76 ff.

4. **Mahāpaduma.**—An elephant, belonging to **Devānampiyatissa,** which, with **Kuñjara,** drew the plough that marked the boundaries of the **Mahāvihāra.**[1]

[1] Mbv. 134.

5. **Mahāpaduma Thera.**—Preacher of **Jātakas** (*Jātakabhāṇaka*). When **Iḷanāga** was in **Rohaṇa,** after fleeing from the capital, he heard the **Kapi Jātaka** from Mahāpaduma, who lived in **Tulādhāra-vihāra,** and was greatly pleased.[1]

[1] Mhv. xxxv. 30.

6. **Mahāpaduma.**—One of the chief Theras present at the Foundation Ceremony of the **Mahā Thūpa.**[1] See also **Paduma.**

[1] MṬ. 524.

7. **Mahāpaduma Thera.**—Of Ceylon. Famous for his knowledge of the Vinaya. He was a pupil of **Upatissa** and colleague of **Mahāsumma.**[1] Mahāpaduma's opinions are often quoted in the **Samantapāsādikā.**[2]

Once, when **Vasabha's** queen was ill, a woman of the court was sent to Mahāpaduma for a remedy, he being evidently skilled in medicine. The Thera would not prescribe, but explained to his fellow-monks what should be done in the case of such an illness. The remedy was applied in the case of the queen and she recovered. Later, she visited the Thera, and offered him three robes and a medicine chest containing three hundred *kahāpaṇas*; this she placed at his feet, requesting that he should offer flowers in her name. The Elder accepted the gift and spent the money on offerings of flowers.[3]

[1] Sp. i. 263.

[2] i. 184, 283; ii. 368, 471; iii. 536, 538, 588, 596, 609, 644, 651, 683, 715; iv. 819, 827, etc.

[3] Sp. ii. 471.

8. **Mahāpaduma.**—The Bodhisatta. See the **Mahāpaduma Jātaka.**

Mahāpaduma Jātaka (No. 472).—The Bodhisatta was once born as **Mahāpaduma,** son of **Brahmadatta,** king of Benares. When Paduma's mother died, his father took another wife. On one occasion the king had to leave the city to quell a border rising, and, thinking the dangers too great to take his queen with him, he entrusted her to the care of Paduma. The campaign was victorious. In the course of making arrangements for the celebration of his father's return, Paduma entered the queen's apartments. She was struck by his amazing beauty, and fell in love with him, inviting him to lie with her. On his indignant refusal, she feigned illness, and, on the return of the king, falsely accused him of having ill-treated her. The king gave orders, in spite of the protestations of the people, that Paduma should be thrown from the "Robbers' Cliff." The deity of the mountain saved his life and entrusted him to the care of the Nāga-king, who took him to his abode, where he stayed for one year. Paduma then went to the **Himālaya** and became an ascetic. The king heard of this and went to offer him the kingdom, but it was refused by Paduma. The king, convinced of the falsity of the charge brought against Paduma, caused the queen to be flung from the Robbers' Cliff.

The story was related in reference to **Ciñcamāṇavikā's** false accusations against the Buddha. Ciñcā was the wicked queen, **Devadatta** the king, **Sāriputta** the deity, and **Ānanda** the Nāga.[1]

[1] J. iv. 187-96; DhA. iii. 181 ff.

Mahāpadesa Sutta.—Preached at the **Ānanda-cetiya** in **Bhoganagara.** The Buddha tells the monks of the four *mahāpadesā* to be respected by them. If a monks says he has a certain teaching direct from the Buddha himself, his statement should be compared with the rest of the Vinaya and Dhamma; if these do not agree, it should be rejected; if they do, accepted. The same applies to that which is said to have been learnt from a group of monks led by a Thera from a body of senior monks residing in a certain place, or from a single senior monk, proficient in the Dhamma, the Vinaya, and the *Mātikā.*[1]

[1] A. ii. 167 ff.; the sutta is incorporated in the **Mahāparinibbāna Sutta** (D. ii. 123 ff.).

Mahāpadhānaghara.—A monastic building in **Anurādhapura,** where **Buddhaghosa** went to learn the Sinhalese Commentaries under **Saṅghapāla.**[1] **Dāṭhopatissa II.** gave the village of **Mahāgalla** for its maintenance.[2]

[1] Cv. xxxvii. 232. [2] *Ibid.*, xlv. 27.

1. **Mahāpanāda.**—Son of **Suruci** and king of **Mithilā.** He owned a palace one hundred storeys high, all of emerald; it was one thousand bowshots (twenty-five leagues) high and sixteen broad and held six thousand musicians. Mahāpanāda was a previous birth of **Bhaddaji.** See the **Mahāpanāda Jātaka** and also *s.v.* **Kosalā.**

2. **Mahāpanāda.**—A primæval king, descendant of **Mahāsammata.**[1]

[1] Mhv. ii. 4; Dpv. iii. 7.

Mahāpanāda Jātaka (No. 264).—The story of **Mahāpanāda,** given in the **Suruci Jātaka** (*q.v.*).[1]

[1] *Cp.* Dvy. 56 ff.

Mahāpanālagāma.—A village of **Rohaṇa** in Ceylon, mentioned in the account of the campaigns of **Parakkamabāhu I.**[1]

[1] Cv. lxxv. 47.

Mahāpanthaka Thera.—The elder brother of **Cūḷapanthaka** (*q.v.*) and grandson of **Dhanaseṭṭhi** of **Rājagaha.** He went with his grandfather to hear the Buddha preach, won faith, and entered the Order. He became skilled in the Doctrine, and, in due course, received higher ordination and became an arahant, with special proficiency in the four *arūpajhānas.* Later, he was declared pre-eminent among those skilled in the evolution of consciousness (*saññāvivaṭṭakusalānaṃ*).[1]

His resolve to win such eminence was made in the time of **Padumuttara Buddha** when he heard a monk similarly honoured by the Buddha.[2]

A set of verses uttered by him in the joy of attainment is included in the Theragāthā.[3]

[1] A. i. 24.
[2] ThagA. i. 490 f.; AA. i. 118 f.; details about Mahāpanthaka are given *s.v.* **Cūḷapanthaka.** They are to be found in J. i. 114 ff.; DhA. i. 241 ff.
[3] Thag. vss. 510-17.

Mahāpapāta.—A mountain in the **Himālaya** where all **Pacceka Buddhas** die. When the time comes for a Pacceka Buddha to die, he goes there, throws into the precipice below the bones of the Pacceka Buddha who died last, and then sits down on the special seat to die himself.[1]

[1] SNA. i. 129.

1. **Mahāpabbata.**—The state elephant of **Eḷāra.**[1]

[1] Mhv. xxv. 57.

2. **Mahāpabbata.**—A mountain in **Rohaṇa** in Ceylon, mentioned in the account of the campaigns of **Parakkamabāhu I.**[1]

[1] Cv. lxxv. 158.

Mahāparakkama Thera.—He belonged to Taungu in Burma, and settled the dispute regarding the monks being allowed to drink the fermented juices of the coconut palm. He wrote the **Surāviniechaya,** a book dealing with this subject.[1]

[1] Sās., p. 81.

Mahāparinibbāna Sutta.—The sixteenth sutta of the **Dīgha Nikāya.** It contains a more or less detailed account of the last year of the Buddha's life. It also contains, besides other matter, a prophecy of the greatness of **Pāṭaliputta** and the contemplated attack on the **Vajjians** by **Ajātasattu,** details of the seven conditions of welfare of the Order, the lineage of faith (*ariyavaṃsa*), eight causes of earthquake, the last meal of the Buddha, the four places of pilgrimage, the four great authorities (*mahāpadesa*), the obsequies of a king, the erection of cetiyas, the previous history of **Kusinārā,** the Buddha's death and cremation, the distribution of the Relics by **Doṇa,** and the erection of the Thūpas over the Relics.[1]

[1] D. ii. 72 ff.

Mahāparivāra Thera.—An arahant. In the time of **Vipassī Buddha** he was a Yakkha chief and, seeing the Buddha enter Bandhumatī with a large following of monks, offered his upper garment and worshipped him. The earth trembled with the force of his wish. Fifteen kappas ago he was king sixteen times under the name of **Vāhana.**[1] He is probably identical with **Pakkha Thera.**[2]

[1] Ap. i. 146 f. [2] ThagA. i. 144 f.

Mahāpariveṇa.—A building attached to the **Jetavana-vihāra** at **Anurādhapura.**[1] **Aggabodhi I.** built the **Bhinnorudīpa-vihāra** and gave it, with endowments, to an incumbent of the Mahāpariveṇa[2] while **Aggabodhi VII.** enlarged the pariveṇa by the addition of a *pāsāda.*[3] This was later destroyed by fire and rebuilt by **Sena I.**[4]

[1] Cv. l. 67. [2] *Ibid.*, xlii. 26. [3] *Ibid.*, xlviii. 65. [4] *Ibid.*, l. 67.

Mahāpalobhana Jātaka (No. 507).—The story is the same in all details as that of the **Cullapalobhana Jātaka** (*q.v.*). The name of the Bodhisatta is **Anitthigandha.**[1]

[1] J. iv. 468-73.

Mahāpaharaṇī.—A channel branching off from the **Mahāvālukagaṅgā** and constructed by **Parakkamabāhu I.**[1]

[1] Cv. lxxix. 52.

Mahāpānadīpa.—A monastery in **Pulatthipura** built by **Aggabodhi III.**[1]

[1] Cv. xliv. 122.

Mahāpāragā.—A class of devas present at the preaching of the **Mahāsamaya Sutta.**[1]

[1] D. ii. 26.

Mahāpāla.—The original name of **Cakkhupāla**[1] (*q.v.*).

[1] DhA. i. 4.

1. **Mahāpāli.**—A refectory built by **Devānampiyatissa** at **Anurādhapura,** for the use of the monks.[1] Various kings provided special food to be distributed there—*e.g.*, **Upatissa II.,** who sent food prepared for him in the palace,[2] and himself ate of the food left over after the distribution.[3] **Mahānāma** enlarged the building,[4] as did **Silāmeghavana**[5] and **Udaya II.**[6] **Dhātusena** instituted distribution of rice,[7] while **Aggabodhi II.** added to the hall and set up a stone-canoe (*bhattanāvaṃ*) for the distribution of rice.[8] After his victory, **Kassapa II.,** by way of celebration, held a special almsgiving at the Mahāpāli.[9] **Dāṭhopatissa II.** distributed there clothing, rice, sour milk, milk and milk-rice on *uposatha* days.[10] **Mahinda I.** gave ten cartloads of food,[11] and **Aggabodhi IX.** distributed daily an amount of rice equal in weight to his own body.[12] The **Coḷiyans** burnt down the building, and the last we hear of it is its restoration by **Mahinda IV.**[13]

[1] Mhv. xx. 23.
[2] Cv. xxxvii. 181; so did King **Silākāla** (Cv. xli. 28).
[3] *Ibid.*, xxxvii. 203.
[4] *Ibid.*, 211.
[5] *Ibid.*, xliv. 65.
[6] *Ibid.*, li. 132.
[7] *Ibid.*, xxxviii. 41.
[8] *Ibid.*, xlii. 67; **Aggabodhi I.** had already given a canoe of bronze (Cv. xlii. 33).
[9] *Ibid.*, xlv. 1.
[10] *Ibid.*, 25.
[11] *Ibid.*, xlviii. 34.
[12] *Ibid.*, lxix. 78.
[13] *Ibid.*, liv. 45.

2. **Mahāpāli.**—A monastic building, probably a refectory, built by **Aggabodhi,** son of **Mahātissa,** at **Mahāgāma.**[1]

[1] Cv. xlv. 42.

Mahāpiṅgala.—King of Benares, father of the Bodhisatta. He is identified with **Devadatta.** See the **Mahāpiṅgala Jātaka.**

Mahāpiṅgala Jātaka (No. 240).—**Mahāpiṅgala** was once king of Benares; he was extremely wicked and quite pitiless. When he died the people were delighted, and burnt his body with one thousand cartloads of wood amidst great festivity. They then elected his son, the Bodhisatta, as king. He noticed that while all others rejoiced, the palace doorkeeper wept, and inquired the reason. The man replied that Mahāpiṅgala would strike him on the head in passing eight times a day. He was sure, he would treat **Yama** in like fashion, and would be banished from hell and return to his palace where he would again start to assault him. The Bodhisatta told the man it would be quite impossible for Mahāpiṅgala to rise from hell.

The story was told in reference to the great joy shown by multitudes of people at the death of **Devadatta.** Devadatta is identified with Mahāpiṅgala.[1]

[1] J. ii. 239 ff.; DhA. i. 126 f.

Mahāpiṭaka Thera.—Of Ceylon. He was an eminent Thera and was teacher of **Catunikāyika-Tissa Thera.** At the time of the great disturbance in the country (*mahābhaya*, probably the **Brāhmaṇatissamahābhaya**) there was only one monk who knew the **Mahāniddesa,** and Mahāpiṭaka asked his colleague, **Mahārakkhita,** to learn it from him. But the latter refused on the plea of the wickedness of the monk possessing this knowledge; but in the end he acquiesced, on condition that Mahāpiṭaka himself would be present at the lessons. On the day of the last lesson he discovered a woman hidden under the teacher's bed.[1]

[1] Sp. iii. 695.

Mahāpuññā.—Five persons of the Buddha's day considered the most lucky: the seṭṭhi **Meṇḍaka,** his chief wife **Candapadumā,** his son **Dhanañjaya,** his daughter-in-law **Sumanādevī,** and his servant **Puṇṇa.**[1]

[1] *E.g.*, AA. i. 219.

Mahāpuṇṇa.—A village in Ceylon where **Lakuṇṭaka Atimbara** lived with his wife **Sumanā.** It was near **Koṭapabbata-vihāra.**[1]

[1] DhA. i. 117.

Mahāpuṇṇama Sutta.—Preached at the **Migāramātupāsāda** on a full-moon night. A monk asks the Buddha a series of questions regarding the five *upādānakkhandhā*, their origin, their definition, and also as to how notions of self come about (*sakkāyadiṭṭhi*). The Buddha answers him, and shows how deliverance can be attained by realization that there is no self in any khandhas. It is said that sixty monks, who heard the sutta, became arahants.[1]

[1] M. iii. 15-20.

Mahāpurisa.—The name given to a Great Being, destined to become either a Cakkavatti or a Buddha. He carries on his person the following thirty-two marks (*Mahāpurisalakkhaṇāni*)[1]: he has feet of level tread;

[1] These are given at D. ii. 17 f.; iii. 142 ff.; M. ii. 136 f.

on his soles are marks of wheels with spokes, felloes and hubs; his heels project; his digits are long; his hands and feet are soft; his fingers and toes straight; his ankles like rounded shells; his legs like an antelope's; standing, he can touch his knees without bending; his privities are within a sheath; he is of golden hue; his skin so smooth that no dust clings to it; the down on his body forms single hairs; each hair is straight, blue-black and at the top curls to the right; his frame is straight; his body has seven convex surfaces; his chest is like a lion's; his back flat between the shoulders; his sheath is the same as his height; his bust is equally rounded; his taste is consummate; he has a lion's jaws; has forty teeth; they are regular, and continuous; lustrous; his tongue is long; his voice like that of a karavīka bird; his eyes intensely black; his eyelashes like a cows; between his eyelashes are soft, white hairs like cotton-down; his head is like a turban.

The theory of Mahāpurisa is pre-Buddhistic. Several passages in the Piṭakas[2] mention brahmins as claiming that this theory of the Mahāpurisa and his natal marks belonged to their stock of hereditary knowledge. The Buddhists, evidently, merely adopted the brahmin tradition in this matter as in so many others. But they went further. In the **Lakkhaṇa Sutta**[3] they sought to explain how these marks arose, and maintained that they were due entirely to good deeds done in a former birth and could only be continued in the present life by means of goodness. Thus the marks are merely incidental; most of them are so absurd, considered as the marks of a human being, that they are probably mythological in origin, and a few of them seem to belong to solar myths, being adaptations to a man, of poetical epithets applied to the sun or even to the personification of human sacrifice. Some are characteristic of human beauty, and one or two may possibly be reminiscences of personal bodily peculiarities possessed by some great man, such as **Gotama** himself.

Apart from these legendary beliefs, the Buddha had his own theory of the attributes of a Mahāpurisa as explained in the **Mahāpurisa Sutta**[4] and the **Vassakāra Sutta.**[5]

Buddhaghosa says[6] that when the time comes for the birth of a Buddha, the **Suddhāvāsa Brahmās** visit the earth in the guise of brahmins and teach men about these bodily signs as forming part of the Vedic teaching so that thereby auspicious men may recognize the Buddha. On his death this knowledge generally vanishes. He defines a Mahāpurisa as one who is great owing to his *paṇidhi*, *samādāna*, *ñāna* and *karuṇā*. A Mahāpurisa can be happy in all conditions of climate.[7]

2 *E.g.*, D. i. 89, 114, 120; A. i. 163; M. ii. 136; SN. vs. 600, 1,000, etc.

3 D. iii. 142 ff.

4 S. v. 158.

5 A. ii. 35 f.

6 MA. ii. 761.

7 DA. ii. 794.

Bāvarī had three Mahāpurisalakkhaṇā; he could touch his forehead with his tongue, he had a mole between his eyebrows (*uṇṇā*), and his privities were contained within a sheath.[8]

[8] SN. vs. 1022.

Mahāpurisa Sutta.—**Sāriputta** asks the Buddha who is a "*mahāpurisa.*" The Buddha answers that it is one who has won emancipation of mind, which can be attained by practising the four *satipaṭṭhānas.*[1]

[1] S. v. 158.

Mahāpurisavitakka Sutta.—The books say[1] that **Anuruddha** became an arahant after listening to this sutta. There is no sutta of this name, but the reference is evidently to the **Anuruddha Sutta** (*q.v.*),[2] which the Buddha preached to Anuruddha who was then dwelling among the **Cetis** in **Pācīnavaṃsamigadāya.** Anuruddha was meditating on the seven *purisavitakkā*, and the Buddha appeared before him and taught him the eighth—that the Dhamma is for the precise and for one who delights in exactness, not for the diffuse or for him who delights in diffuseness. The Buddha later addresses the monks of **Suṃsumāragiri** and tells them of the eight *mahāpurisavitakkā.*

[1] *E.g.*, DhA. i. 117.

[2] A. iv. 227 ff.

Mahāpuḷina.—A king of fifty-three kappas ago, a previous birth of **Puḷinapūjaka Thera.**[1]

[1] Ap. i. 79.

Mahāppamāda Sutta.—One of the **Appamāda Suttas** (*q.v.*). It was preached by **Mahinda** in the **Mahāmeghavana,** on the thirteenth day of the bright half of **Āsāḷha.**[1]

[1] Mhv. xvi. 3.

Mahāphussadeva Thera.—Generally called **Ālindakavāsī-Mahāphussadeva.** For twenty-one years he practised meditation on his way up and down to the village for alms (*gatapaccāgatikavatta*). People working in the fields, seeing him constantly stop and walk back again, would wonder why he did so. But he did not heed their curiosity, and after twenty years he became an arahant. That night the deity at the end of his walk illuminated it with the radiance of her fingers, and **Sakka, Brahmā,** and other gods came to do him honour. His colleague, **Vanavāsī-Mahātissa,** asked him the next day the reason for all the light, but he evaded the question.[1] It is said[2] that during the period of his

[1] SA. iii. 154 f.; VibhA. 352; MA. i. 208 f.; SNA. i. 55 f.

[2] MA. i. 524.

meditations, he wept every *pavāraṇa*-day to see that he was yet a "learner."

1. **Mahābodhi.**—See **Bodhirukkha.**

2. **Mahābodhi.**—See **Bodhirājakumāra.**

3. **Mahābodhi Thera.**—He belonged to the **Mahāvihāra,** and wrote the Commentaries on the **Paramatthavinicchaya** and the **Saccasaṅkhepa.**[1]

[1] P.L.C. 174.

Mahābodhi Jātaka (No. 528).—The Bodhisatta was born in an Udicca-brahmin family, and, on growing up, renounced the world. His name was **Bodhi.** Once, during the rains, he came to Benares, and, at the invitation of the king, stayed in the royal park. The king had five councillors, unjust men, who sat in the judgment-hall giving unjust judgments. One day a man, who had been very badly treated by them, asked Bodhi to intervene. Bodhi reheard the case and decided in his favour. The people applauded, and the king begged Bodhi to dispense justice in his court. Bodhi reluctantly agreed and twelve years passed. The former councillors, deprived of their gains, plotted against Bodhi and constantly poisoned the king's mind against him; they first decreased all the honours paid to Bodhi, and when this failed to drive him away, obtained the king's permission to kill him. A tawny dog, to whom Bodhi used to give food from his bowl, overheard the plot, and, when Bodhi approached the palace the next day, bared his teeth and barked as a warning of the conspiracy. Bodhi understood, returned to his hut, and, in spite of the king's expression of remorse, left the city, promising to return later, and dwelt in a frontier village. The councillors, nervous lest Bodhi should return, informed the king that Bodhi and the queen were conspiring to slay him. Believing their words, he had the queen put to death. The queen's four sons thereupon rose in revolt, and the king was in great danger and fear. When Bodhi heard of this, he took a dried monkey-skin, went to Benares, and stayed again in the royal park. The king came to do him honour, but Bodhi sat silent, stroking the monkey-skin. The king asked him why he did so. He answered, "This monkey was of the greatest service to me; I travelled about on its back, it carried my water-pot, swept out my dwelling, and performed various other duties for me; in the end, through its simplicity, I ate its flesh and now I sit and lie on its skin." (He had used the skin for his garment, hence "I sat on the monkey's back"; he had the skin on his shoulder, whence his water-pot was suspended, hence "it carried the water-pot"; he had swept the cell with the skin, hence "swept my dwelling-place"; he had eaten the flesh of the monkey, hence "I ate its flesh"). The councillors who were present made great uproar, calling him a murderer and a traitor. But Bodhi knew that of these councillors, one denied the effect of all kamma, one attributed everything to a Supreme Being, one believed that everything was a result of past actions, one believed in annihilation, and one held the *khattiya* doctrine that one should secure one's interests, even to the extent of killing one's parents. He, therefore, argued with one after another, and proved that in accordance with their doctrines no blame whatever attached to him for having killed the monkey. Having thus completed their discomfiture, he exhorted the king not to trust in slanderers, and asked the king's sons to obtain their father's pardon. The king wished the councillors to be killed, but Bodhi intervened, and they were disgraced and exiled from the kingdom, their hair fastened in five locks.

The story was related in the same circumstances as the **Mahāummagga Jātaka** (*q.v.*). The five ministers are identified with **Pūraṇa Kassapa, Makkhali Gosāla, Pakudha Kaccāna, Ajita Kesakambala** and **Nigaṇṭha Nātaputta**; the dog was **Ānanda.**[1]

[1] J. v. 227-46; *cp.* Jātakamālā xxiii.

Mahābodhivaṃsa.—A Pāli translation of a Sinhalese original, giving the history of the arrival of the Bodhi-tree in Ceylon. It was written about the tenth century and is ascribed to **Upatissa,**[1] who wrote it at the request of **Dāṭhānāga. Saranaṅkara Saṅgharāja** wrote a paraphase on it, the *Madhurārthaprakāśinī.*[2]

[1] Svd. vs. 1262. [2] For details see P.L.C. 156 ff.

Mahābyūha Sutta.—Philosophers praise only themselves and their views, and disparage others. Their disputations cannot lead to purity. The true brahmin is he who has overcome all disputes and is confident in his knowledge. He is indifferent to learning, for he is calm and peaceful.[1]

The sutta was one of those preached on the occasion of the **Mahāsamaya,**[2] and is specially recommended for those inclined to confusion of mind (*mohacaritānaṃ*).[3]

[1] SN. vss. 895-914. [2] SNA. ii. 557. [3] MNidA. 222.

Mahābrahmā.—See **Brahmaloka.**

Mahāmagagāma.—A village given by **Udaya I.** for the celebrations in honour of the **Kholakkhiya**-image of the Buddha.[1]

[1] Cv. xlix. 15.

Mahāmaṅgala Thera.—A monk present at the foundation ceremony of the **Mahā-Thūpa.**[1]

[1] MṬ. 524.

Mahāmaṅgala Jātaka (No. 453).—The Bodhisatta, called **Rakkhita,** was born in a wealthy brahmin family. He married, and then, having distributed all his wealth, became an ascetic with five hundred followers. During the rains, his disciples went to Benares and dwelt in the king's park, while Rakkhita stayed in the hermitage. At that time there was a great discussion going on among men as to what constituted auspiciousness, and Rakkhita's disciples, on being consulted, said that Rakkhita would solve the problem. They, therefore, went to Rakkhita's hermitage and asked him the question, which he answered in a series of eight verses.[1] The disciples, having learnt the verses, returned to Benares, where they expounded them, thus setting all doubts at rest.

The story was related in reference to the preaching of the **Mahāmaṅgala Sutta.** It happened that in **Rājagaha** there was a large assembly at the *Santhāgāra*, and a man rose and went out, saying, "This is a day of good omen." Some one, hearing this, inquired the meaning of "good omen." One said, "The sight of a lucky thing is a good omen." But this was denied, and then began the discussion on omens, which, in the end, was carried to **Sakka,** and referred by him to the Buddha.[2]

The senior disciple of Rakkhita is identified with **Sāriputta.**[3]

[1] The *maṅgalas* enumerated in these verses differ from those given in the **Maṅgala Sutta.**

[2] *cp.* **Maṅgala Sutta.**

[3] J. iv. 72-9.

Mahāmaṅgala Sutta.—See **Maṅgala Sutta.**

Mahāmaṅgala-vihāra.—A monastery built by **Vaṅkanāsikatissa** on the banks of the **Goṇanadī.**[1]

[1] Mhv. xxxv. 113.

Mahāmaṇi.—A tank constructed by **Bhātikatissa,** and given by him to the **Gavaratissa-vihāra.**[1] It was restored by **Mahāsena.**[2]

[1] Mhv. xxxvi. 3.

[2] *Ibid.,* xxxvii. 47.

Mahāmaṇikagāma.—A village granted by **Aggabodhi III.** to the **Jetavana-vihāra.**[1]

[1] Cv. xliv. 121.

Mahāmaṇḍapa.—A palace in **Anurādhapura,** probably in the **Mahāvihāra,** used by preachers. **Maliyadeva Thera** preached there the *Cha Chakka Sutta,* when sixty monks became arahants.[1]

[1] MA. ii. 1024.

Mahāmattā.—Wife of King **Vaṅkanāsikatissa.** She was the daughter of King **Subha,** and was given to a friend of his, a brickworker, who adopted her as his daughter. She used to bring him food at midday. One day, seeing an ascetic in a *kadamba*-thicket, she gave him the food. The brick-worker was glad, and asked her to give food regularly to the monk, who prophesied that she would be the queen, and asked her not to forget the *kadamba*-thicket. She had auspicious signs on her body, on account of which she was chosen to be the wife of Vaṅkanāsika. She later remembered the thera's words and built a vihāra on the site of the *kadamba*-thicket.[1]

[1] Mhv. xxxv. 101 ff.

Mahāmaliyadeva.—See **Malayamahādeva.**

Mahāmalla.—Younger brother of **Sena,** general of **Sena V.** He committed an offence with his mother and the king had him killed.[1]

[1] Cv. liv. 60.

Mahāmallaka.—A nunnery built by **Mahinda IV.** for the **Theravāda**-nuns.[1]

[1] Cv. liv. 47.

Mahāmahinda.—See **Mahinda.**

Mahāmahindabāhu-pariveṇa.—A monastic building, probably in **Hatthiselapura,** erected by **Bhuvanekabāhu,** at the request of his brother, **Parakkamabāhu II.**[1]

[1] lxxxv. 63.

Mahāmāyā.—See **Māyā.**

Mahāmāladeva.—A general of **Manābharaṇa** (2) stationed at **Kālavāpi.**[1]

[1] Cv. lxxii. 171.

Mahāmāluṅkyā Sutta.—On the five bonds that chain uninstructed men to the lower life: delusion as to personality, doubt, attachment to rites, lusts of the flesh, and malevolence. The path to the destruction of these bonds is the cultivation of the *jhānas*.[1]

The Sutta is so called because it was preached in contradiction of a wrong answer given by **Māluṅkyāputta** to a question of the Buddha. The Buddha pointed out his error, and **Ānanda** requested the Buddha to give the correct answer.

This is one of the suttas which teach *samathavipassānā*.[2]

[1] M. i. 432-7. [2] MA. ii. 572.

Mahāmittavindaka.—See the **Catudvāra Jātaka.**

Mahāmucala.—A primæval king, descendant of **Mahāsammata.**[1]

[1] Dpv. iii. 6; Mhv. ii. 3; Mtu. i. 348.

Mahāmucalamālaka.—A locality in **Mahāmeghavana,** where stood the *uposatha*-hall for monks.[1] It was outside the enclosure of the Bodhi-tree.[2]

[1] Mhv. xv. 36. [2] MṬ. 346.

1. **Mahāmuṇḍa.**—See **Muṇḍa.**

2. **Mahāmuṇḍa.**—A lay disciple of **Muṇḍa,** in Viñjhaṭavi. He was the friend and patron of **Anuruddha** and had two children, **Mahāsumana** and **Cullasumana.** Anuruddha visited him because he wished to ordain **Cullasumana** (*q.v.*).[1]

[1] DhA. iv. 128.

Mahāmuni.—A village in Ceylon, in the **Dīghavāpi** district. **Sumana,** father of **Sumanā,** who was the wife of **Lakuṇṭaka Atimbara,** lived there.[1]

[1] DhA. iv. 50.

1. **Mahāmeghavana.**—A park to the south of **Anurādhapura.** Between the park and the city lay **Nandana** or **Jotīvana.** The park was laid out by **Muṭasīva,** and was so called because at the time the spot was chosen for a garden, a great cloud, gathering at an unusual time, poured forth rain.[1] **Devānampiyatissa** gave the park to **Mahinda** for the use of the Order,[2] and within its boundaries there came into being later the **Mahāvihara** and its surrounding buildings. The fifteenth chapter of the

[1] Mhv. xi. 2 f. [2] *Ibid.*, xv. 8, 24; Dpv. xviii. 18; Sp. i. 81.

Mahāvaṃsa[3] gives a list of the chief spots associated with the religion, which came into existence there. Chief among these are the sites of the **Bodhi**-tree, the thirty-two *mālakas*, the **Catussālā**, the **Mahā Thūpa**, the **Thūpārāma**, the **Lohapāsāda**, and various *pariveṇas* connected with **Mahinda**: **Suṇhāta**, **Dīghacaṅkamana**, **Phalagga**, **Therāpassaya**, **Marugana** and **Dīghasandasenāpati**. Later, the **Abhayagiri-vihāra** and the **Jetavanārāma** were also erected there. The Mahāmeghavana was visited by **Gotama Buddha**,[4] and also by the three Buddhas previous to him. In the time of **Kakusandha** it was known as **Mahātittha**, in that of **Koṇagamana** as **Mahānoma**, and in that of **Kassapa** as **Mahāsāgara**.[5] The Mahāmeghavana was also called the **Tissārāma**, and on the day it was gifted to the Saṅgha, Mahinda scattered flowers on eight spots contained in it, destined for future buildings, and the earth quaked eight times.[6] This was on the day of Mahinda's arrival in Anurādhapura. The first building to be erected in the Mahāmeghavana was the **Kālapāsāda-pariveṇa** (*q.v.*) for the use of Mahinda. In order to hurry on the work, bricks used in the building were dried with torches.[7] The boundary of the Mahāmeghavana probably coincided with the *sīmā* of the Mahāvihāra, but it was later altered by **Kaniṭṭhatissa**, when he built the **Dakkhiṇa-vihāra**.[8]

[3] Mhv. xv. 27 ff.
[4] *Ibid.*, i. 80; Dpv. ii. 61, 64.
[5] Mhv. xv. 58, 92, 126.
[6] *Ibid.*, 174.
[7] *Ibid.*, 203.
[8] *Ibid.*, xxxvi. 12.

2. **Mahāmeghavana**.—A park laid out by **Parakammabāhu I**.[1]

[1] Cv. lxxix. 7, 41.

Mahāmetta.—A Bodhi-tree, planted in the **Mahāvihāra** by **Jeṭṭhatissa III**.[1]

[1] Cv. xliv. 96.

Mahā Moggallāna Thera.—The second of the Chief Disciples of the Buddha. He was born in **Kolitagāma** near **Rājagaha**, on the same day as **Sāriputta** (they were both older than the Buddha), and was called **Kolita** after his village. His mother was a brahminee called **Moggalī** (**Moggallānī**), and his father was the chief householder of the village. Moggallāna's and Sāriputta's families had maintained an unbroken friendship for seven generations, and so the children were friends from their childhood. Sāriputta had five hundred golden palanquins and Moggallāna five hundred carriages drawn by thoroughbreds. One day the two friends went together to see a mime play (*giraggasamajjā*), and there, realizing the impermanence of things, decided to renounce the world. They first lived as disciples of **Sañjaya** (*q.v.*), and then wandered all over **Jambudīpa,** discussing with all learned men, but finding no satisfaction. Then they separated, after agreeing that whoever first succeeded in finding what they sought should inform the other.

After some time, Sāriputta, wandering about in Rājagaha, met **Assaji,** was converted by him to the faith of the Buddha, and became a *sotāpanna.* He found Moggallāna and repeated the stanza he had heard from Assaji (*ye dhammā hetuppabhavā, etc.*), and Moggallāna also became a sotāpanna. The two then resolved to visit the Buddha at **Veḷuvana,** after an unsuccessful attempt to persuade Sañjaya to accompany them. Sañjaya's disciples, however, five hundred in number, agreed to go, and they all arrived at Veḷuvana. The Buddha preached to them, and ordained them by the "*ehi-bhikkhu-pabbajjā.*" All became arahants except Sāriputta and Moggallāna. Moggallāna went to the hamlet of **Kallavāla**[1] in Magadha, and there, on the seventh day after his ordination, drowsiness overcame him as he sat meditating. The Buddha knew this, and appearing before him, exhorted him to be zealous. That very day he attained arahantship.

On the day that Sāriputta and Moggāllana were ordained, the Buddha announced in the assembly of monks that he had assigned to them the place of Chief Disciples and then recited the **Pāṭimokkha.** The monks were offended that newcomers should be shown such great honour. But the Buddha told them how these two had for a whole *asaṅkheyya* and one hundred thousand years strenuously exerted themselves to win this great eminence under him. They had made the first resolve in the time of **Anomadassī Buddha.** Moggallāna had been a householder, named **Sirivaḍḍha,** and Sāriputta a householder, called **Sarada.** Sarada gave away his immense wealth and became an ascetic. The Buddha visited him in his hermitage, where Sarada and his seventy-four thousand pupils showed him great honour. Anomadassī's chief disciple, **Nisabha,** gave thanks, and Sarada made a vow that he would become the chief disciple of some future Buddha. Anomadassī saw that his wish would be fulfilled and told him so.

After the Buddha's departure, Sarada went to Sirivaḍḍha, and, announcing the Buddha's prophecy, advised Sirivaḍḍha to wish for the place of second disciple. Acting on this advice, Sirivaḍḍha made elaborate preparations and entertained the Buddha and his monks for seven days. At the end of that time, he announced his wish to the Buddha, who declared that it would be fulfilled. From that time, the two friends, in that and subsequent births, engaged in good deeds.[2]

[1] For details see **Pacala Sutta** (A. iv. 85 f.) where the village is called **Kallavāḷamutta.**

[2] AA. i. 84 ff.; Ap. ii. 31 ff.; DhA. i. 73 f.; SNA. i. 326 ff.; the story of the present is given in brief at Vin. i. 39 ff.

Sāriputta and Moggallāna are declared to be the ideal disciples, whose example others should try to follow.[3] In the **Saccavibhaṅga Sutta**[4] the Buddha thus distinguishes these "twin brethren" from the others: "Sāriputta is as she who brings forth and Moggallāna is as the nurse of what is brought forth; Sāriputta trains in the fruits of conversion, Moggallāna trains in the highest good. Sāriputta is able to teach and make plain the four Noble Truths; Moggallāna, on the other hand, teaches by his *iddhipātihāriya*."[5] Moggallāna's pre-eminence lay in his possession of *iddhi*-power.[6] He could create a living shape innumerable times and could transfer himself into any shape at will.[7] Several instances are given of this special display of *iddhi*. Once, at the Buddha's request, with his great toe he shook the **Migāramātupāsāda,** and made it rattle in order to terrify some monks who sat in the ground floor of the building, talking loosely and frivolously, regardless even of the fact that the Buddha was in the upper storey.[8]

On another occasion, when Moggallāna visited **Sakka** to find out if he had profited by the Buddha's teaching, he found him far too proud and obsessed by the thought of his own splendour. He thereupon shook Sakka's palace, **Vejayanta,** till Sakka's hair stood on end with fright and his pride was humbled.[9] Again, Moggallāna is mentioned as visiting the Brahma-world in order to help the Buddha in quelling the arrogance of **Baka-Brahmā.** He himself questioned Baka in solemn conclave in the **Sudhammā**-Hall in the Brahma-world and made him confess his conviction that his earlier views were erroneous.[10] In the **Māratajjaniya Sutta**[11] we are told how **Māra** worried Moggallāna by entering into his belly, but Moggallāna ordered him out and told him how he himself had once been a Māra named **Dūsī** whose sister **Kālī** was the mother of the present Māra. Dūsī incited the householders against **Kakusandha Buddha** and was, as a result, born in purgatory.

[3] *E.g.*, S. ii. 235; A. i. 88. [4] M. iii. 248.

[5] BuA. 31. [6] A. i. 23.

[7] Thag. vs. 1183; he is recorded as saying that he could crush **Sineru** like a kidney bean (DhA. iii. 212), and, rolling the earth like a mat between his fingers, could make it rotate like a potter's wheel, or could place the earth on Sineru like an umbrella on its stand. When the Buddha and his monks failed to get alms in **Verañjā,** Moggallāna offered to turn the earth upside down, so that the essence of the earth, which lay on the under surface, might serve as food. He also offered to open a way from **Nalerupucimanda** to **Uttarakuru,** that the monks might easily go there for alms; but this offer was refused by the Buddha (Vin. iii. 7; Sp. i. 182 f.; DhA. ii. 153).

[8] See **Pasādakampana Sutta** (S. v. 269 ff.; also the **Uṭṭhāma Sutta,** SNA. i. 336 f.).

[9] See **Cūlataṇhāsaṅkhaya Sutta** (M. i. 251 ff.).

[10] Thag. vs. 1198; ThagA. ii. 185; S. i. 144 f.; other visits of his to the Brahma-world are also recorded when he held converse with **Tissa Brahmā** (A. iii. 331 ff.; iv. 75 ff.; *cp.* Mtu. i. 54 ff.)

[11] M. i. 332 ff.

But, according to the Commentaries,[12] Moggallāna's greatest exhibition of *iddhi*-power was the subjugation of the Nāga **Nandopananda.** No other monk could have survived the ordeal because no other was able to enter so rapidly into the fourth *jhāna*; which was the reason why the Buddha would give permission to no other monk but Moggallāna to quell the Nāga's pride. Similar, in many ways, was his subjection of the Nāga who lived near the hermitage of **Aggidatta**[13] (*q.v.*). Moggallāna could see, without entering into any special state of mind, petas and other spirits invisible to the ordinary mortal eye.[14] He would visit various worlds and bring back to the Buddha reports of their inhabitants,[15] which the Buddha used in illustration of his sermons. The **Vimānavatthu**[16] contains a collection of stories of such visits, and we are told[17] that Moggallāna's visits to the deva-worlds—*e.g.*, that to **Tāvatiṃsa**—were very welcome to the devas.

Though Moggallāna's pre-eminence was in *iddhi*-power, yet in wisdom, too, he was second only to Sāriputta. These two could answer questions within the range of no other disciple of the Buddha.[18] The Buddha paid a compliment to Moggallāna's powers of preaching, when, having preached himself to the **Sākyans** in their new Mote Hall at **Kapilavatthu,** he asked Moggallāna, after their departure, to talk to the monks, as he himself was weary. And Moggallāna spoke to them of lusts and of the means of getting rid of them. At the end of the sermon the Buddha praised him warmly.[19] Mention is made elsewhere[20] of eloquent sermons preached by him on the *jhānas*, on qualities which lead to true emancipation,[21] and of visits paid to him by Sakka in company with numerous other gods in order to hear him preach. Other devas also went to hear him—*e.g.*, **Candana, Suyāma, Santusita, Sunimitta** and **Vasavatti.**[22] He was also consulted by those, such as **Vacchagotta,**[23] and **Vappa,**[24] eager to learn from him the teachings of the Buddha. When the Buddha went to preach the Abhidhamma in Tāvatiṃsa, it was to Moggallāna that he entrusted the task of preaching to the people who were waiting for his return. Moggallāna, therefore, provided for these people spiritually, while **Anāthapiṇḍika** looked after their bodily needs.[25] When the time drew near for the Buddha's return, Moggallāna, at the request of the people, went to Tāvatiṃsa, diving into the earth and climbing

[12] *E.g.*, ThagA. ii. 188 ff.

[13] DhA. iii. 242.

[14] See, *e.g.*, DhA. ii. 64; iii. 60, 410 f., 479; S. ii. 254 ff.; where he saw petas while in the company of **Lakkhaṇa**; *cp.* Avadānaś i. 246 ff.

[15] See also Mtu. i. 4 ff. regarding his visit to the Nirayas.

[16] See also DhA. iii. 291 (*re* **Nandiya**) and iii. 314.

[17] S. v. 366 f.

[18] DhA. iii. 227.

[19] S. iv. 183 ff.

[20] *Ibid.*, 262-9.

[21] A. v. 155 ff.

[22] S. iv. 269-80.

[23] *E.g.*, S. iv. 391 ff.

[24] A. ii. 196 ff.

[25] DhA. iii. 219.

Sineru, in full view of them all, in order to find out what the Buddha intended doing, so that the people might be kept informed.[26] No task, which he might be told by the Buddha to perform, seemed to Moggallāna too insignificant. Thus we find him employed by the Buddha as messenger to the arahant **Uggasena,** telling him that the Buddha wished to see him.[27] He was also sent to **Sakkhara,** to **Macchariya-Kosiya,** to check his miserliness and bring him to **Jetavana**[28]; and to **Sīlavā,** whom **Ajātasattu** was plotting to kill.[29] When **Visakhā** was building the Migāramātupāsāda and the Buddha was away on one of his journeys, Moggallāna, because of his *iddhi*-power, and five hundred monks were left to supervise the work, which was carried through without difficulty.[30]

The Buddha placed great faith in his two chief disciples and looked to them to keep the Order pure.[31] Their fame had reached even to the Brahma-world, for we find **Tudu-Brahmā** singing their praises, much to the annoyance of the **Kokālika** monk.[32] When **Devadatta** created a schism among the monks and took five hundred of them to **Gayāsīsa,** the Buddha sent Sāriputta and Moggallāna to bring them back. They were successful in this mission.[33] **Kakudha Koliyaputta,** once servant of Moggallāna and later born in a huge *manomayakāya*, had warned Moggallāna of Devadatta's intrigues against the Buddha, but the Buddha ignored this information carried to him by Moggallāna.[34] When **Rāhula,** the Buddha's son, was ordained, Sāriputta was his preceptor and Moggallāna his teacher.[35] Moggallāna seems to have carried out diligently the charge laid on him by the Buddha of looking after the monks' welfare. Among the verses, attributed to him in the Theragāthā, are several containing exhortations to his colleagues[36]; some of the colleagues are mentioned by name—*e.g.*, **Tissa, Vaḍḍhamāna** and **Poṭṭhila.**[37] Elsewhere[38] mention is made of his living at **Kāḷasilā,** with a company of five hundred monks, watching over them and discovering

26 *Ibid.*, 224; J. iv. 265; *cp.* Dvy. 375.

27 *Ibid.*, iv. 62.

28 *Ibid.*, i. 369 f.; J. i. 347.

29 ThagA. i. 536.

30 DhA. i. 414 f.

31 There is one instance recorded of Moggallāna seizing a wicked monk, thrusting outside and bolting the door (A. iv. 204 ff.). Once, when a monk charged Sāriputta with having offended him as he was about to start on a journey, Moggallāna and Ānanda went from lodging to lodging to summon the monks that they might hear Sāriputta vindicate himself (Vin. ii. 236; A. iv. 374).

32 Kokālika had a great hatred of them —*e.g.*, A. v. 170 ff.; SN., p. 231 ff.; SNA. ii. 473 ff.

33 DhA. i. 143 ff.; see also DhA. ii. 109 f., where they were sent to admonish the Assajipunabbasukā.

34 Vin. ii. 185; A. iii. 122 ff.

35 J. i. 161; see SNA. i. 304 f., where the account is slightly different. There Moggallāna is spoken of as Rāhula's kammavācācariya.

36 Thag. vss. 1146-9, 1165 f.

37 *Ibid.*, 1162, 1163, 1174 f.

38 S. i. 194 f.

that all were arahants. **Vaṅgīsa** witnessed this and praised Moggallāna in verse before the Buddha.

The love existing between Moggallāna and Sāriputta was mutual, as was the admiration. Sāriputta's verses in praise of Moggallāna[39] are even more eloquent than those of Moggallāna in praise of Sāriputta.[40] Their strongest bond was the love of each for the Buddha; when away from him, they would relate to each other how they had been conversing with him by means of the divine ear and the divine eye.[41] In the **Mahāgosiṅga Sutta**[42] we find them staying in the **Gosiṅgasālavana** in the company of **Mahā Kassapa, Ānanda, Revata** and **Anuruddha,** engaged in friendly discussion, referring their conclusions to the Buddha for his opinion. Sariputta, Moggallāna, and Anuruddha are again mentioned[43] as staying in the **Ketakīvana** in **Sāketa.** Among discussions between Anuruddha and Moggallāna is recorded one in which Anuruddha speaks of the value of cultivating the four *satipaṭṭhānas.*[44] It seems to have been usual for Sāriputta and Moggallāna, in their journeys, to travel together at the head of the monks, and lay disciples, who gave alms to the monks, were anxious to include them in their invitations.[45]

Moggallāna died before the Buddha, Sāriputta dying before either. The Theragāthā contains several verses attributed to Moggallāna regarding Sāriputta's death.[46] Sāriputta died on the full-moon day of Kattika and Moggallāna two weeks later, on the new-moon day.[47] According to the Commentaries[48] his death resulted from a plot of the **Nigaṇṭhas.** Moggallāna used to visit various worlds and return with his report that he had discovered that those who followed the Buddha's teaching reached happy worlds, while the followers of the heretics were reborn in woeful conditions. These statements diminished the number of the heretics and they bribed brigands to kill Moggallāna.

[39] Thag. vss. 1178-81.

[40] *Ibid.*, 1176 f.

[41] *E.g.*, S. ii. 275 ff.; Moggallāna elsewhere also (S. ii. 273 f.) tells the monks of a conversation he held with the Buddha by means of these divine powers. For another discussion between Sāriputta and Moggallāna, see A. ii. 154 f.

[42] M. i. 212.

[43] S. v. 174 f., 299.

[44] *Ibid.*, 294 ff.

[45] **Veḷukaṇḍakī** in **Dakkhiṇagiri** (A. iii. 336; iv. 63); and **Cittagahapati** in **Macchikāsaṇḍa** (DhA. ii. 74 f.).

[46] vs. 1158-61.

[47] SA. iii. 181.

[48] J. v. 125 ff.; the account in DhA. iii. 65 ff. differs in several details. The thieves tried for two months before succeeding in their plot and, in the story of the past, when the blind parents were being beaten, they cried out to the supposed thieves to spare their son. Moggallāna, very touched by this, did not kill them. Before passing into Nibbāna, he preached to the Buddha, at his request, and performed many miracles, returning to Kāḷasilā to die. According to the Jātaka account his cremation was performed with much honour, and the Buddha had the relics collected and a thūpa erected in **Veḷuvana.**

They surrounded the Elder's cell in **Kāḷasilā**, but he, aware of their intentions, escaped through the keyhole. On six successive days this happened; on the seventh, they caught him and beat him, crushing his bones and leaving him for dead. Having recovered consciousness, with a great effort of will, he dragged himself to the Buddha in order to take his leave, and there he died, to the sorrow of the deva-worlds. This sad death is said to have been the result of a sin committed by him in a previous birth. Acting on the instigation of his wife, he had taken his blind parents into a forest, where, pretending that they were attacked by thieves, he had beaten them to death. For this deed he suffered in hell for innumerable years, and in his last birth lost his life by violence.

Moggallāna's body was of the colour of the blue lotus or the rain cloud.[49] There exists in Ceylon an oral tradition that this colour is due to his having suffered in hell in the recent past!

Moggallāna is connected with characters in several Jātakas: thus, he was **Kisavaccha** in the **Indriya Jātaka** (J. iii. 469), **Sakka** in the **Illisa** (i. 354), one of the devas in the **Kakkāru** (iii. 90), the tortoise in the **Kuruṅgamiga** (ii. 155), **Candasena** in the **Khaṇḍahāla** (vi. 157), the senāpati in the **Cullasutasoma** (v. 192), the youngest bird in the **Javanahaṃsa** (iv. 218), the elephant in the **Tittira** (i. 220), the tiger in the **Tittira** (iii. 543), **Āyura** in the **Dasaṇṇaka** (iii. 341), the jackal in the **Pañcūposatha** (iv. 332), **Suriya** in the **Biḷārikosiya** (iv. 69), one of the brothers in the **Bhisa** (iv. 314), **Subhaga** in the **Bhūridatta** (vi. 219), the old tortoise in the **Mahāukkusa** (iv. 297), **Migājina** in the **Mahājanaka** (vi. 68), **Bījaka** in the **Mahānāradakassapa** (vi. 255), the king's charioteer in the **Rājovāda** (ii. 5), the tiger in the **Vaṇṇāroha** (iii. 193), the Garuḷa-king in the **Vidhurapaṇḍita** (vi. 329), the tiger in the **Vyaggha** (ii. 358), the rat in the **Saccaṅkara** (i. 32), **Bhadrakāra** in the **Sambhava** (v. 67), **Kisavaccha** in the **Sarabhaṅga** (v. 151), the jackal in the **Sasa** (iii. 56), **Canda** in the **Sudhābhojana** (v. 412), and **Gopāla** in the **Hatthipāla** (iv. 491).

[49] Bn. i. 58.

Mahāyañña Vagga.—The fifth section of the Sattaka Nipāta of the **Aṅguttara Nikāya.**[1]

[1] A. iv. 39-67.

Mahāyamaka Vagga.—The fourth section of the **Majjhima Nikayā,** containing suttas 21-30.

Mahāyasa Thera.—Of Thāton, author of the **Kaccāyanabheda** and the **Kaccāyanasāra.** He probably belonged to the fourteenth century.[1]

[1] Bode, *op. cit.*, 36 f.; Svd. 1250.

1. **Mahārakkhita Thera.**—He went after the Third Council to the **Yona** country, and there preached the **Kālakārama Sutta.** One hundred and seventy thousand people adopted the Buddha's faith and ten thousand entered the Order.[1]

[1] Mhv. xii. 5, 39; Dpv. viii. 9; Sp. i. 64, 67.

2. **Mahārakkhita.**—An ascetic in **Himavā.** See the **Somanassa Jātaka.** He is identified with **Sāriputta.**[1]

[1] J. iv. 454.

3. **Mahārakkhita Thera.**—Incumbent of **Uparimaṇḍalaka.**[1] See **Mahā-Saṅgharakkhita** (3).

[1] J. vi. 30.

4. **Mahārakkhita Thera.**—When told by his patron that the latter had given a robe to a certain monk, he praised him; when the man offered to give him one, he praised that likewise.[1]

[1] MA. ii. 666.

1. **Mahāraṭṭha.**—A country where **Mahādhammarakkhita** went after the Third Council.[1] It is generally identified with the country of the Marāṭhī at the source of the Godāvarī.

[1] Mhv. xii. 5, 37; Dpv. viii. 8; Sp. i. 64, 67.

2. **Mahāraṭṭha.**—A district in Ceylon, near **Kālavāpi,** to the east. It held the village of **Pillavaṭṭhi.**[1]

[1] Cv. lxxii. 141, 163, 190, 199; also Cv. *Trs.* i. 333, n. 3.

1. **Mahāratha.**—A king of thirty-one kappas ago; a former birth of **Dhammasava (Nāgapupphiya) Thera.**[1]

[1] ThagA. i. 215; Ap. i. 179.

2. **Mahāratha.**—A devaputta in **Tāvatiṃsa.** As a result of his good deeds, he excelled in majesty **Sakka** himself.[1]

[1] DhA. i. 426; UdA. i. 199.

Mahāratha Vagga.—The fifth section of the **Vimānavatthu.**

Mahāratha-vimānavatthu.—The story of the devaputta **Gopāla.**[1]

[1] Vv. v. 14; VvA. 270 ff.

Mahārājaghara.—A monastery enlarged by **Potthakuṭṭha.**[1]

[1] Cv. xlvi. 21.

Mahārājapabba.—A section of the **Vessantara Jātaka.**[1]

[1] J. vi. 582.

Mahārājāno.—See **Cattāro Mahārājāno.**

Mahārāma.—A king of sixty-three kappas ago, a previous birth of **Tālavaṇṭadāyaka Thera.**[1]

[1] Ap. i. 211.

Mahārāmetti.—A tank constructed by **Vasabha.**[1]

[1] Mhv. xxxv. 94.

Mahārāhulovāda Sutta.—The Buddha and **Rāhula** are on their way to the village for alms, and the Buddha tells Rāhula that all *rūpa* should be regarded as *anattā*, and not only *rūpa*, but also the other *khandhas.* Rāhula stops and sits under a tree meditating. **Sāriputta** approaches and suggests that he should develop *ānāpānasati.* Later in the evening Rāhula asks the Buddha how he can do this. The Buddha describes how it is done by regarding all the elements—earth, water, fire, air and space, both personal and external—with disgust and loathing of heart. One should not allow sensory impressions to lay hold of one's heart, just as the earth remains impassive whatever may be thrown upon it. It is so with the other elements. One should grow in lovingkindness, compassion, in gladness over the welfare of others, in equanimity, contemplation of the body's corruption, perception of the fleeting nature of things, and in the mindfulness which comes from ordered breathing.[1]

[1] M. i. 420-6; it is perhaps a part of this sutta which is quoted at Mil. 385, 388; see Mil. *Trs.* ii. 312, n. 1.

1. **Mahāruci.**—A primæval king, descendant of **Mahāsammata.**[1]

[1] Dpv. iii. 7.

2. **Mahāruci.**—A king of thirty-eight kappas ago, a previous birth of **Sucintita Thera.**[1]

[1] Ap. i. 133.

Mahārukkha Sutta.—In him who contemplates enjoyment in things which make for grasping (*upādāna*), craving grows with its consequent round of suffering, like juice which travels upwards from the roots of a tree. If he contemplates the misery of such things, craving ceases, like the growth of a tree which is cut in pieces and burnt to ashes.[1]

[1] S. ii. 87 f.

Mahārukkhatittha.—A ford in the **Mahāvālukagaṅgā.**[1]

[1] Cv. lxxii. 11; Cv. *Trs.* i. 320, n. 1.

Mahāruhā.—A nun, skilled in the *Saddhammavaṃsa*; she came from India to Ceylon.[1]

[1] Dpv. xviii. 31.

Mahāreṇu.—Eighty-seven kappas ago there were seven kings of this name, previous births of **Godhika (Bhikkhadāyaka) Thera.**[1]

[1] ThagA. i. 124; Ap. i. 140.

Mahāroruva.—One of the **Nirayas.**[1]

[1] S. i. 92; DhA. iv. 79.

Mahārohaṇagutta Thera.—Of **Therambatthala.** When he was ill, thirty thousand monks of great power came to minister to him. The king of the Nāgas was also present, and as he offered rice-gruel to the Elder, the king of the **Supaṇṇas** dashed across the sky to seize him. But **Buddharakkhita** created a mountain, into which he made the Elder and the Nāga enter.[1]

[1] Vsm. 155, 375; DhSA. 187.

Mahārohita.—A king of four kappas ago; a previous birth of **Dverataniya Thera.**[1]

[1] Ap. i. 214.

Mahālatā-pasādhana (°pilandhana).—A very costly ornament of gold. In the time of the Buddha it was possessed only by three persons: **Bandhula's** wife, **Mallikā, Visākhā** and **Devadāniyacora.**[1] Visākhā once left it behind in the monastery, where she had gone to hear the Buddha preach, and when she sent her slave-girl for it **Ānanda** had already put it away. She, thereupon, refused to take it back and had it sold. It was worth nine crores, the workmanship being worth one hundred thousand. No one was found able to buy it, so Visākhā herself paid the price for it, and, with the proceeds, erected the **Migāramātupāsāda.**[2] **Mallikā,** after the death of her husband, refused to wear her jewels, and,

[1] DA. ii. 599; at DhA. i. 412 the daughter of the treasurer of Benares is substituted for Devadāniya.

[2] DhA. i. 411 ff.

when the Buddha's body was being taken for cremation, she washed her ornament in scented water and placed it on the Buddha's bier with the following resolve: "May I, in future births, have a body that shall need no ornaments, but which shall appear as though it always bore them."[3]

The making of Visākhā's ornament took four months, with five hundred goldsmiths working day and night. In its construction were used four pint-pots (*nāli*) of diamonds, eleven of pearls, twenty-two of coral, thirty-three of rubies, one thousand *nikkhas* of ruddy gold, and sufficient silver. The threadwork was entirely of silver, the parure was fastened to the head and extended to the feet. In various places, seals of gold and dies of silver were attached to hold it in position. In the fabric itself was a peacock with five hundred feathers of gold in either wing, a coral beak, jewels for the eyes, the neck-feathers and the tail. As the wearer walked the feathers moved, producing the sound of music.[4] Only a woman possessed of the strength of five elephants could wear it.[5]

[3] DA. ii. 597. [4] DhA. i. 393 ff. [5] MA. i. 471.

Mahālabujagaccha.—A forest cleared by **Devappatirāja.** He built a village there, and planted a large grove of jak-trees near by.[1] This village was among those given to Devappatirāja by **Parakkamabāhu II.**, to be held in perpetuity.[2]

[1] Cv. lxxxvi. 49. [2] *Ibid.*, 53.

Mahālānakitti.—A usurper (1041-44 A.C.). He murdered **Kitti,** the successor of **Vikkamabāhu I.,** and ruled in **Rohaṇa,** but was defeated in the third year of his reign by the **Coḷas,** and, with his own hand, cut his throat.[1]

[1] Cv. lvi. 7.

1. **Mahāli.**—A **Licchavi** chief, mentioned as having visited the Buddha at the **Kūṭāgārasālā** to ask if he had seen **Sakka**[1] and also to beg information as to the teachings of **Pūraṇa Kassapa.**[2] (See **Mahāli Sutta.**) Mahāli was educated at **Takkasilā.** After his return to **Vesāli,** he devoted himself to the education of the young Licchavi men, but, through overexertion, lost his sight. He continued to instruct them, however, and was given a house by the gate which led from **Sāvatthi** into Vesāli. The revenue from this gate, worth one hundred thousand, was given to him.[3] When **Bandhula** came to Vesāli, to satisfy the pregnancy-longings of

[1] S. i. 230; DhA. (i. 263 ff.) adds that the Buddha here related to him the story of Magha. This conversation resulted from Mahāli having heard the Sakkapañha Sutta.

[2] S. iii. 68.

[3] DhA. i. 338.

his wife **Mallikā,** Mahāli, hearing the rumble of his chariot, instantly recognised it. He warned the Licchavis not to interfere with Bandhula, and, finding that they insisted on pursuing him, urged them to turn back when they saw Bandhula's chariot sink up to the nave, or at least when they heard a sound like the crash of a thunderbolt, or when they saw a hole in the yokes of the chariot. But they paid no heed to his warnings and were killed.[4]

When the Licchavis decided to invite the Buddha to Vesāli, to rid the city of its plagues, Mahāli it was who went with the son of the purohita to **Veḷuvana** to intercede with **Bimbisāra,** that he might persuade the Buddha to come. Mahāli was a favourite of Bimbisāra and a member of his retinue. He had attained *sotāpatti* at the same time as the king.[5]

This Mahāli is perhaps identical with the Mahāli mentioned in the Apadāna[6] as the father of **Sīvalī.** His wife was **Suppavāsā.**

[4] DhA. i. 350 f.; J. iv. 148 f. [5] DhA. iii. 438. [6] Ap. ii. 494 (vs. 28).

2. **Mahāli.**—See **Oṭṭhaddha.**

3. **Mahāli.**—A **Sākyan** prince, one of seven grandsons of **Amitodana.** They were brothers of **Bhaddakaccānā,** wife of **Paṇḍuvāsadeva,** and came to Ceylon, where they settled.[1]

[1] Dpv. x. 6. See Mhv. ix. 6, 9.

1. **Mahāli Sutta.**—The Licchavi **Oṭṭhaddha (Mahāli)** visits the Buddha at the **Kuṭāgārasālā** and reports to him a conversation he had had with **Sunakkhatta,** who claimed to be able to see heavenly forms but not to hear heavenly sounds. Mahāli inquires how such a faculty can be acquired, and the Buddha tells him, but explains that it is not for the sake of acquiring these powers that people join the Order. Asking what then is their object, he gradually leads the conversation on to the question of arahantship, along the Eightfold Path. The Buddha then raises a quite different question, as to whether the soul and the body are identical. The discourse on this again leads to the question of arahantship (*cp.* **Jāliya Sutta**), but it is significant that the Buddha leaves this last question unanswered.[1]

Buddhaghosa explains[2] that the Buddha raised the point of body and soul, because he knew that Mahāli harboured the heretical belief that a soul exists and that it has form.

[1] D. i. 150-8. [2] DA. i. 316.

2. **Mahāli Sutta.**—The Licchavi **Mahāli** visits the Buddha at the **Kūṭāgārasālā** and questions him regarding the doctrine of **Pūraṇa**

Kassapa that there is no cause or condition for the impurity of beings. The Buddha contradicts this view, and explains that it is because beings take delight in the body, etc., that they become impure. When they feel revulsion towards the body, etc., they become pure.[1]

[1] S. iii. 68 f.

3. **Mahāli Sutta.**—The Buddha, in answer to a question of **Mahāli,** says that greed, ill-will, dulness cause the continuance of evil action, and right reflection and a well-poised mind cause the continuance of good. The existence of these two different sets of qualities cause the good and evil in the world.[1]

[1] A. v. 86 f.

Mahālekha.—A *pariveṇa* in the **Abhayagiri-vihāra ;** it was built by **Mahinda II.**[1]

[1] Cv. xlviii. 135.

Mahālekhapabbata.—A *pariveṇa* in the **Mahāvihāra ;** it was founded by the **Mahālekha Sena,** in the time of **Kassapa IV.**[1]

[1] Cv. lii. 33.

Mahālohita.—The Bodhisatta born as a bull; see the **Muṇika** and **Sālūka Jātakas.**

Mahāvaṃsa.—The great Chronicle of Ceylon. The first part of the work—*i.e.*, to the time of King **Mahāsena**—is attributed to **Mahānāma Thera.**[1] The continuation of the Chronicle is called the **Cūlavaṃsa.** The first portion of the Cūlavaṃsa—*i.e.*, from Mahāsena to the reign of **Parakkamabāhu II.**—is traditionally ascribed to a thera named **Dhammarakkhita.**[2] The next section—*i.e.*, to the time of **Kittisiri-Rājasīha**—was written by Tibbaṭuvāve Thera, Mahānāyaka of **Pupphārāma,** at the invitation of the king, who obtained for him copies of the Chronicle from Siam.[3] From there it was continued till the time of the British occupation (1815 A.C.) by Hikkaḍuve Sumaṅgala Thera.[4]

There is a Commentary on the Mahāvaṃsa called the **Vaṃsatthappakāsinī** (*q.v.*).

[1] MṬ. 687.
[2] Cv. *Trs.* ii. 155, n. 3.
[3] Cv. xcix. 78 f.; Cv. *Trs.* ii. 263, n. 1.
[4] P.L.C. 310.

Mahāvaṃsaka-Tissa Thera.—Of Ceylon. Mentioned among the last of the arahants. He was among those who took part in various "assemblies"—the **Kuddālaka, Mūgapakkha, Ayoghara** and **Hatthipāla.**[1]

[1] J. vi. 30.

1. **Mahāvagga.**—A section of the Vinaya Piṭaka, divided into chapters called *Khandhakas.* The introductory chapters give an account of the incidents immediately following the Buddha's Enlightenment, leading up to the foundation of the Order of the Saṅgha. It then gives various rules for members of the Saṅgha, together with the circumstances which led to the formulation of each rule.

2. **Mahāvagga.**—The second section of the **Dīgha Nikāya,** containing suttas XIV.-XXIII.

3. **Mahāvagga.**—The third section of the **Sutta Nipāta,** containing twelve suttas.

4. **Mahāvagga.**—The first section of the **Paṭisambhidāmagga.**

5. **Mahāvagga.**—The fifth section of the **Saṃyutta Nikāya.**

6. **Mahāvagga.**—The seventh section of the Tika Nipāta, the twentieth of the Catukka, the sixth of the Chakka, the seventh of the Sattaka, the second of the Aṭṭhaka, and the third of the Dasaka Nipāta of the **Aṅguttara Nikāya.**

Mahāvacchagotta Sutta.—The Paribbājaka **Vacchagotta** visits the Buddha at **Veḷuvana** and asks him to expound right and wrong. The Buddha does so, and adds that those who follow his teaching are sure of deliverance and of birth in happy worlds and are destined for Nibbāna. Vacchagotta is very pleased and seeks admission to the Order, but the Buddha says that he must first pass four months as a probationer. At the end of that time he enters the Order, and the Buddha further expounds the Doctrine to him. Shortly after he becomes an arahant.[1]

[1] M. i. 489-97.

Mahāvajirabuddhi.—A monk of Ceylon, author of **Vinayagaṇṭhi (Vinayagandhi)** or **Vajirabuddhiṭīkā** on the Vinaya Commentaries.[1] He was a contemporary of King **Dhammaceti** of Burma, and presented him with a copy of his work.[2]

[1] Gv. 60, 66. [2] Bode, *op. cit.*, 39 f.

Mahāvatthalagāma.—A village on the southern sea coast of Ceylon, where **Tilokamalla** lived.[1]

[1] Cv. lxxxviii. 22; Cv. *Trs.* ii. 184, n. 2.

1. **Mahāvana.**—A wood near **Vesāli.** It was partly natural, partly man-made, and extended up to the **Himālaya.**[1] See *s.v.* **Kūṭāgārasālā.**

[1] MA. i. 298; DA. i. 309.

2. **Mahāvana.**—The wood near **Kapilavatthu.** It was virgin forest, and reached from the edge of Kapilavatthu to the **Himālaya** on one side and to the sea on the other.[1] In this wood was preached the **Mahāsamaya Sutta** (for etails see *s.v.* **Mahāsamaya**) and also the **Madhupiṇḍika Sutta** (*q.v.*).

[1] MA. i. 298, 449.

3. **Mahāvana.**—A forest on the outskirts of **Uruvelakappa,** where the Buddha retired for his noonday rest after his meal at **Uruvelakappa.** It was in that grove that **Ānanda** took **Tapussa** to see him.[1]

[1] A. iv. 437 f.

4. **Mahāvana.**—A forest on the banks of the **Nerañjarā.**[1]

[1] DhA. i. 86; DhSA. 34, etc.; J. i. 77.

Mahāvaruṇa Thera.—He ordained **Nigrodha-Sāmaṇera**[1] and also **Tissa** and **Sumitta,** the two sons of the kinnarī **Kuntī.**[2]

[1] Sp. i. 46; Mhv. v. 45. [2] *Ibid.*, 214.

Mahāvalligotta-vihāra.—A monastery built by **Vasabha** and given to the incumbent of the **Valliyera-vihāra.**[1]

[1] Mhv. xxxv. 82.

Mahāvācakāla.—A man who lived on the banks of the **Mahāvālukagaṅgā.** For thirty years he meditated on the thirty-two impurities of the body in the hope of becoming a *sotāpanna.* But at the end of that period he gave up his meditations, renouncing the Buddha's Doctrine as futile. After death he was born as a crocodile in the river, and one day sixty carts laden with stone pillars started crossing the river at **Kacchakatittha.** The crocodile ate bulls, carts, and pillars.[1]

[1] AA. i. 367.

Mahāvāṇija Jātaka (No. 493).—A company of merchants once went astray in the forest without food or water, and, seeing a huge banyan-tree with moist branches, they cut off a branch and water poured out, from another branch came food, from another a company of girls, and from the fourth various precious things. Overcome by greed, they wished to cut the tree from its roots in order to get more. Their leader, the Bodhisatta, tried to prevent this, but they refused to listen. Then the Nāga-king, who lived in the tree, ordered his followers to slay all the merchants except the leader. Him the Nāgas escorted to his home with all the treasures.

The story was told in reference to a company of merchants from **Sāvatthi,** followers of the Buddha, who had a similar experience. But having moderate desires, they made no attempt to cut down the tree. Then they returned to Sāvatthi, and, offering some of the precious things to the Buddha, made over the merit thereof to the deity of the tree. The Buddha praised them for their moderation. **Sāriputta** is identified with the Nāga-king.[1]

[1] J. iv. 350 ff.

Mahāvālukagaṅgā, Mahāgaṅgā, Mahāvālukanadī.—The chief river of Ceylon, the modern *Mähāveligaṅga.* Viewed from the city of **Anurādhapura,** the right bank was called *pāragaṅgā* and the left *oragaṅgā.* The river was of great strategic importance, and is mentioned in various accounts of campaigns between opposing armies. It was always regarded as the boundary between North Ceylon, with **Anurādhapura** (and later, Pulatthipura) as the centre, and the South-east province of **Rohaṇa.** Various fords on this river are mentioned in the books, the chief among these being **Kacchakatittha, Gaṇṭhambatittha, Mahārukkhatittha, Mālāgāmatittha, Yakkhasūkaratittha, Sarogāmatittha, Sahassatittha** and **Suvaṇṇatthambhatittha.** There were evidently other fords at the bends of the river with no particular names.[1] The kings of Ceylon constructed various canals branching off from the river to help in their irrigation schemes. One such was the **Pabbatanta Canal,** built by **Mahāsena**[2]; while the **Aciravatī,** the **Gomatī,** and the **Malāpaharaṇī** were constructed by **Parakkamabāhu I.**[3] **Dhātusena** irrigated the surrounding fields by means of damming up the river,[4] as did **Sena II.** by the construction of the **Maṇimekhala** dam.[5] In the time of **Parakkamabāhu II.,** and, later, of **Vijayabāhu IV.,** great ordination ceremonies were held on the river at Sahassatittha,[6] and again at Gaṇṭhambatittha in the time of **Vimaladhammasūriya I.**[7] The river rises in **Samantakūṭa.**[8] The **Mahānāgavana** of the Yakkhas, where, later, was erected the **Mahiyaṅgathūpa,** was on the right bank of the river.[9]

[1] See, *e.g.*, Cv. lxxii. 285.
[2] Mhv. xxxvii. 50.
[3] Cv. lxxix. 51 f.
[4] *Ibid.*, xxxviii. 12.
[5] *Ibid.*, li. 72.
[6] *Ibid.*, lxxxvii. 72; lxxxix. 70 f.
[7] *Ibid.*, xciv. 17; also **Vimaladhammasūriya II.** (Cv. xcvii. 12).
[8] *Ibid.*, c. 82.
[9] *Ibid.*, lxxxix. 70; Mhv. *Trs.*, p. 3, n. 9.

Mahāvālukagāma.—A village on the south coast of Ceylon. It is mentioned in the account of the campaigns of **Parakkamabāhu I.**[1] *c.p.* **Vālukagāma.**

[1] Cv. lxxv. 36 f., 40, 45.

Mahāvijita.—A king of long ago, whose exemplary sacrifice, held under the direction of his chaplain, is narrated in the **Kūṭadanta Sutta** (*q.v.*).

Mahāvitthārika.—A palace in heaven, occupied by **Tiṇipadumiya Thera** in a previous birth.[1]

[1] Ap. i. 124.

Mahāvinayasaṅgahapakaraṇa.—Another name for the **Vinayavinicchaya** (*q.v.*).

Mahāvibhaṅga.—The first part of the **Sutta Vibhaṅga** of the Vinaya Piṭaka, also called the **Bhikkhu-vibhaṅga.**

Mahāvimalabuddhi.—See **Vimalabuddhi.**

Mahāvisuddhācariya.—See **Visuddhācariya.**

Mahāvihāra.—The great monastery at **Anurādhapura,** for many centuries the chief seat of Buddhism in Ceylon. It was founded by **Devānampiyatissa,** on the counsel of **Mahinda,** and included the **Mahāmeghavana.** The Mahāmeghavanārāma henceforth came to be included in the Mahāvihāra. The boundary of the vihāra was marked out by the king ploughing a circular furrow starting from near the **Gaṅgalatittha** on the **Kadambanadī** and ending again at the river.[1] A list is given in the Mahābodhivaṃsa[2] of the places through which the *simā* (boundary) of the Mahāvihāra passed—Pāsāṇatittha, Kuddavāṭakapāsāṇa, **Kumbhakāraāvāṭa,** the Mahānīpa-tree, Kakudhapāli, Mahāaṅgana-tree, Khujjamātula-tree, **Marutta-pokkharaṇī,** the northern gate of the Vijayārāma park, Gajakumbhakapāsāṇa, then passing Avaṭṭimajjha, Bālakapāsāṇa on the Abhayavāpi, Mahāsusāna, Dīghapāsāṇa, the left side of Caṇḍalagāma, the Nīcasusāna to the left of Kammāradeva, Sīmānigrodha, Veḷuvaṅgana, round the hermitages of the Nigaṇṭhas Jotiya Giri and Kumbhaṇḍa, to the right of the various hermitages of the Paribbājakas, by Hiyagalla, along the shrine of the brahmin Dīyavāsa,

[1] Mhv. xv. 188 ff.; MṬ. 361; Mbv. 135, 136 says that the ford on the Kadambanadī was Pāsāṇatittha.

[2] pp. 135 f.

through Telumapāli, Tālacatukka, to the right of the stables (*assa-maṇḍala*), on to Sasakapāsāṇa and Marumbatittha. It then proceeded up the river to Sīhasinānatittha, on to Pāsāṇatittha, ending at Kuddavāṭakapāsāṇa.

The Mahāvihāra contained thirty-two *Mālakas*[3] and had numerous buildings attached to it, apart from sacred shrines, such as the Mahābodhi-tree, **Thūpārāma, Mahā Thūpa,** etc. In its early period, the precincts of the Mahāvihāra contained other buildings besides those dedicated to the service of Buddhism—*e.g.*, the hermitages of the Nigaṇṭhas and the Paribbājakas (as mentioned above) and the shrine of the guardian deity of Anurādhapura.[4]

In the time of **Vaṭṭagāmaṇī,** the Mahāvihāra monks divided into two factions, and one party occupied **Abhayagiri,** built by the king.[5] At first the differences between these two factions were trivial, but, as time went on, Abhayagiri grew in power and riches and proved a formidable rival to the older monastery.

From time to time various kings and nobles made additions and restorations to the Mahāvihāra. Thus **Vasabha**[6] built a row of cells, and **Bhātikatissa** erected a boundary wall,[7] while **Kaṇiṭṭhatissa** removed the boundary wall and constructed the **Kukkuṭagiri-pariveṇa,** twelve large pāsādas, a refectory, and a road leading from Mahāvihāra to **Dakkhiṇa-vihāra.**[8] **Vohārikatissa** appointed a monthly gift of a thousand to the monks of Mahāvihāra,[9] while **Sirisaṅghabodhi** built a *salāka*-house.[10] **Goṭhābhaya** erected a stone pavilion and made a *padhānabhūmi* to the west of the vihāra.[11]

Towards the latter part of Goṭhābhaya's reign, a dispute arose between the Mahāvihāra and Abhayagiri on matters of doctrine, and sixty monks of Abhayagiri, who had adopted the **Vetulyavāda,** were banished. They obtained the assistance of a **Coḷa** monk, named **Saṅghatissa,** and at a solemn assembly of the monks concerned, at Thūpārāma, Saṅghamitta expounded his heretical doctrine, refuting the opposition of the Mahāvihāra monks, and succeeded in winning over the king, who was present, in spite of the efforts of his uncle, Goṭhābhaya Thera, to bring him round to the orthodox party. Saṅghamitta became tutor to the king's sons, and when one of these, **Mahāsena,** became king, he prompted him to destroy the Mahāvihāra. A royal decree was issued forbidding the giving of alms to the Mahāvihāra. The monks thereupon left the monastery, and for nine years it remained deserted. Many of the build-

[3] Mhv. xv. 214.
[4] *Ibid.*, xxv. 87.
[5] *Ibid.*, xxxiii. 97 f.
[6] *Ibid.*, xxxv. 88.
[7] *Ibid.*, xxxvi. 2.
[8] *Ibid.*, 10 ff.
[9] *Ibid.*, 32.
[10] *Ibid.*, 74.
[11] *Ibid.*, 102, 105.

ings were destroyed, and various possessions belonging to the Mahāvihāra were removed to Abhayagiri; but the people, led by the king's minister and friend, **Meghavaṇṇābhaya,** revolted against the impious deeds of Mahāsena and his admirers, Saṅghamitta and **Soṇa,** and the king was forced to yield. Saṅghamitta and Soṇa were slain by one of the queens, and the king, with the help of Meghavaṇṇābhaya, rebuilt several *pariveṇas* and restored some of the possessions which had been removed. But Mahāsena's allegiance to the Mahāvihāra teaching was not lasting; acting on the advice of a monk named **Tissa,** he built the **Jetavana-vihāra** in the grounds of the Mahāvihāra, against the wish of the monks there; the latter left again for nine months as a sign of protest against the king's attempts to remove the boundary of the vihāra. This attempt, however, he was forced to abandon.[12]

Mahāsena's son, **Sirimeghavaṇṇa,** on coming to the throne, exerted himself to undo the damage which had been wrought by his father. He rebuilt the **Lohapāsāda** and restored all the demolished *pariveṇas,* together with their endowments.[13] Mahāvihāra had, by now, become famous as a seat of learning; it was the centre of **Theravāda** Buddhism, and was the repository of various Commentataries, of which the chief were the **Sīhalaṭṭhakathā** on the Pāli Canon. Thither, therefore, came scholars from various countries, among them **Buddhaghosa** (*q.v.*), who resided in the **Ganthākara-pariveṇa** and compiled his Pāli Commentaries.[14]

When Dhātusena became king he had the walls of the Mahāvihāra painted with various ornamental designs.[15] The **Dhammaruccikas** seem to have been favourites of this king and to have occupied the Mahāvihāra, later moving to **Ambatthala-vihāra.**[16] **Mahānāga** instituted a permanent distribution of soup to the inhabitants of the Mahāvihāra,[17] and **Jeṭṭhatissa III.** planted another Bodhi-tree there, called the **Mahāmetta.**[18] **Udaya I.** built a new *salāka*-hall.[19] **Aggabodhi IX.** discontinued the habit of the monks of the smaller vihāras surrounding Anurādhapura from coming to Mahāvihāra for their supply of medicines and made other arrangements for their distribution.[20] **Sena I.** and his queen **Saṅghā** erected and endowed the **Saṅghasena-pariveṇa,**[21] while **Kassapa IV.** built the **Samuddagiri-pariveṇa** and gave it for the use of the **Paṃsukūlikas,** while for the forest-dwelling monks of Mahāvihāra he built forest dwellings.[22] Kassapa's kinsman, the general **Rakkha,** built a

[12] Mhv. xxxvi. 110 f.; xxxvii. 1-37.
[13] Cv. xxxvii. 54 ff.
[14] *Ibid.*, 215 ff.
[15] *Ibid.*, xxxviii. 43.
[16] *Ibid.*, 75 f.
[17] *Ibid.*, xli. 99.
[18] *Ibid.*, xliv. 96.
[19] *Ibid.*, xlix. 14.
[20] *Ibid.*, 88.
[21] *Ibid.*, l. 70.
[22] *Ibid.*, lii. 21 f.; Cv. *Trs.* i. 163, n. 8.

vihāra in the village of **Savāraka** and gave it to the incumbents of Mahāvihāra, to be used as a *padhānaghara,* while **Mahālekhasena** built, in Mahāvihāra itself, the **Mahālekhapabbata.**[23] **Udaya IV.** gave a diadem of jewels to the Buddha-image in Mahāvihāra, while his wife **Vidurā** added to it a network of rays made of precious stones.[24]

During the invasions of the **Coḷas** and the **Paṇḍus** from South India, and owing to the consequent confusion prevailing in the country, the Mahāvihāra seems to have been neglected. Many of the buildings were destroyed and their priceless possessions plundered. Discipline among the monks became slack and there were many dissensions. Later, when **Parakkamabāhu I.** had restored peace, he wished to purify the religion, but met with great opposition, and it was only after strenuous efforts that he brought about a reconciliation between the different parties.[25] It is said[26] that the king could not find one single pure member of the Order. He, therefore, held a special ordination ceremony, admitting many monks into the Order. After the removal of the capital from Anurādhapura to **Pulatthipura,** Mahāvihāra lost its importance; the centre of activity was now at Pulatthipura, and later, at other capitals, and the Mahāvihāra fell into neglect and decay, from which it has never recovered.

[23] Cv. lii. 31 ff.
[24] *Ibid.*, liii. 49 f.
[25] Cv. lxxviii. 11 ff.
[26] *Ibid.*, 25.

Mahāvedalla Sutta.—A series of questions asked by **Mahā Koṭṭhita** on psychological topics—*e.g.*, understanding, consciousness, feeling, perception, pure mental consciousness (*manoviññāṇa*), isolated from the five faculties of bodily sense—the eye of understanding, right outlook, types of rebirth, first *jhāna,* etc.—and **Sāriputta's** answers thereto.[1] The sutta was probably originally compiled rather as a " lesson " for learners than as a genuine enquiry by Koṭṭhita. This sutta it was which obtained for Koṭṭhita the rank of pre-eminence among those possessing the *paṭisambhidā.*[2]

[1] M. i. 292-8.
[2] AA. i. 159.

Mahāvessantara Jātaka.—See **Vessantara.**

Mahāvyaggha Thera.—An arahant of **Ukkanagara-vihara.** He received a portion of sour millet-gruel given by **Duṭṭhagāmaṇi,** and distributed his share among seven hundred monks.[1]

[1] Mhv. xxxii. 54.

Mahāvyūha.—A gabled chamber erected by **Mahāsudassana** into which he could retire during the heat of the day. It was made of silver.[1]

[1] D. ii. 182; DA. ii. 632; see Dial. ii. 214, n. 1.

Mahāvyūha Sutta.—See **Mahābyūha.**

Mahāsakuludāyī Sutta.—The Buddha visits the hermitage of **Sakuludāyī** near **Rājagaha** Sakuludāyī tells him that the Buddha, unlike other religious teachers, is honoured by his disciples, and gives it as his opinion that this is because the Buddha eats sparingly, is content with any raiment, accepts any alms, is satisfied with any lodging, lives in seclusion, and counsels others to do likewise. The Buddha answers that if the esteem shown him depends on these qualities, he has numerous disciples more austere than himself with regard to these practices, and gives five other qualities which have won for him esteem: he has the higher virtues, outstandingly keen vision, super-eminent intellect, he teached his disciples the Noble Truths, and shows them the way in which to develop the four *satipaṭṭhānas.* He has taught them, besides, the *sammappadhāna*, the four *iddhipādas*, the five *indriyas*, the five *balas*, the seven *bojjhaṅgas*, the Noble Eightfold Path, the eight Deliverances, the eight spheres of mastery (*abhibhāyatanas*), the ten *kasināyatanas*, the four *jhānas*, the sixfold *abhiññā.* It is for these reasons that his disciples esteem him.[1]

[1] M. ii. 1-22.

1. **Mahā Saṅgharakkhita Thera.**—An arahant. He came, with forty thousand others, from **Dakkhiṇāgiri-vikāra** in **Ujjeni,** to the Foundation Ceremony of the **Mahā Thūpa**[1] and took up his position at the western entrance.[2]

[1] Mhv. xxix. 35. [2] MṬ. 530.

2. **Mahā Saṅgharakkhita.**—A monk of **Corakaṇḍaka-vihāra;** one of those who accepted the meal given by Prince **Sāliya** in his previous birth as a blacksmith.[1]

[1] MṬ. 606.

3. **Mahā Saṅgharakkhita.**—Called **Malayavāsi-Mahā Saṅgharakkhita** or **Uparimaṇḍalakamalayavāsī.** Tissabhūti went to him, on finding his mind corrupted by sinful thoughts, and having received from Saṅgharakkhita a topic of meditation, he attained to arahantship.[1] He was one of the last of the arahants.[2] **J. L. Makārakkhira.**

[1] AA. i. 23 f.; MA. i. 55. [2] J. iv. 490; vi. 30.

4. **Mahā Saṅgharakkhita.**—Mentioned in the Commentaries as being free from impurities.[1]

[1] *E.g.*, MA. i. 525; Vsm. 104; DhSA. 268.

5. **Mahā Saṅgharakkhita Thera.**—When over sixty years old and about to die, his companions questioned him on his transcendental attainment. "I have none," he replied. A young monk who waited on him said that people had come from twelve yojanas round in the belief that he had attained Nibbāna. He then asked that he should be raised up and left alone. As soon as the others left him, he snapped his fingers to show that he had attained arahantship. He confessed that he had never done anything without mindfulness and understanding. His nephew also attained arahantship only after fifty years of age.[1]

[1] Vsm. 47 f.

Mahāsaṅghikā, Mahāsaṅgītikā.—One of the Buddhist schools which separated out from the **Theravādins** at the Second Council. The members rejected the **Parivāra,** the six sections of the Abhidhamma, the **Paṭisambhidāmagga,** the **Niddesa** and some portions of the **Jātakas.**[1] The school was so called owing to the great number of its followers, which made a great assembly or "Mahāsaṅgītī." They were counted among the Anātmavādins, and later gave rise to the following schools: the **Mahāsaṅghika, Pubbasela, Aparasela, Rājagiriyā, Hemavatas, Cetiyavādins, Saṅkantivādins** and **Gokulikas.** Originally they had only two divisions—the **Ekabbohārikas** and **Gokulikas.**[2] Their separation from the orthodox school was brought about by the **Vajjiputta monks,** and was probably due to difference of opinion on the ten points[3] held by the Vajjiputta monks. According to Northern sources, however, the split occurred on the five points raised by Mahādeva: (1) An arahant may commit a sin under unconscious temptation; (2) one may be an arahant and unconscious of the fact; (3) an arahant may have doubts on matters of doctrine; (4) one cannot attain arahantship without the help of a teacher; (5) the "Noble Way" may begin with some such exclamation as "How sad!" uttered during meditation.[4] These articles of faith are found in the **Kathāvatthu,**[5] attributed to the Pubbaselas and the Aparaselas, opponents of the Mahāsaṅghika school. According to Hiouen Thsang,[6] the Mahāsaṅghikas divided their canon into five parts: Sūtra, Vinaya, Abhidhamma, Miscellaneous and Dhāraṇī. Fa Hsien took from Pāṭali-

[1] KvuA., p. 4; Dpv. v. 32 ff.
[2] Rockhill, *op. cit.*, 182 ff.
[3] For these see Vin. ii. 294. f.
[4] *J.R A.S.* 1910, p. 416; cf. MṬ 173.
[5] 173 ff., 187 ff., 194, 197.
[6] Beal. ii. 164.

putta to China a complete transcript of the Mahāsanghika Vinaya.[7] The best known work of the Mahāsaṅghikas is the Mahāvastu. Their headquarters in Ceylon were in **Abhayagiri-vihāra,** and **Sena I.** is said to have built the **Vīraṅkurārāma** for their use.[8]

[7] Giles, p. 64, Nañjio's Catalogue mentions a Mahāsaṅghika Vinaya and a Mahāsaṅghabhiksunī Vinaya in Chinese translations (Cols. 247, 253. Ms. No. 543).

[8] Cv. l. 68.

Mahāsaccaka Sutta.—Saccaka visits the Buddha at the **Kūṭāgārasālā** and questions him on the disciplining of the body and the mind. The Buddha describes to him the training he underwent from the time of leaving the world to that of his Enlightenment, stopping at no exertion, avoiding no austerities till, in the end, wisdom came to him, and he realized that bliss could not be experienced with an emaciated body. The **Pañcavaggiyas,** who had been with him till then, left him in disgust. But he persevered, and, in the end, destroyed the *āsavas.* Saccaka, addressed in the sutta as **Aggivessana,** expresses great admiration for the Buddha and acknowledges his superiority over other teachers.[1]

[1] M. i. 237-51; see Thomas: *op. cit.*, 58.

Mahāsaṭṭhivassa Thera.—A resident of **Katthakasālā-pariveṇa.** King **Vasabha** went to the monastery, as the monk lay dying, intending to worship him, but at the door he heard the groans of the ill man, and disgusted that, after sixty years of monastic life, he should not be able to conquer his pain, he did not enter. This was reported to the Elder, and putting forth great effort, he subdued his pain and sent word to the king to come to him. Vasabha entered, and prostrating himself before the Elder, said, " I worship you, not for your arahantship, but for the exertion you put forth while yet a *puthujjana.*"[1]

[1] DA. i. 291.

Mahāsatipaṭṭhāna Sutta.—Preached at **Kammāssadamma** in the **Kuru** country. The Buddha tells the monks that the one and only path leading to Nibbāna is that of the Four Bases of Mindfulness. These, in brief, are the four ways of directing the mind to the impurities and the impermanency of body: (1) *kāya,* physical structure and activities; (2) *vedanā,* the emotional nature, first as bare feeling, then as having ethical implications; (3) *citta,* conscious life or intelligence, considered under ethical aspects; (4) *dhamma,* considered under the five hindrances; the five groups (*khandhas*), the six spheres of sense, the seven *bojjhaṅgas,* and the four Ariyan Truths.[1]

[1] D. ii. 290-315.

The sutta is considered as one of the most important in the Buddhist Canon. It has been translated into various languages, and several commentaries on it are in existence. Its mere recital is said to ward off dangers and to bring happiness, and it is the desire of every Buddhist that he shall die with the Satipaṭṭhāna Sutta on his lips, or, at least, with the sound of it in his ears.

The materials found in the Mahāsatipaṭṭhāna Sutta are found also in the **Majjhima Nikayā,** broken up into two portions, each representing a separate discourse—the **Satipaṭṭhāna Sutta** and the **Saccavibhaṅga Sutta.**

1. **Mahāsamaya Sutta.**—Preached at **Mahāvana** in **Kapilavatthu,** where the Buddha was staying with five hundred arahants. The gods of the ten thousand world systems had come to visit the Buddha and the monks, and were joined by four gods from the **Suddhāvāsā,** who saluted the Buddha in verse. The Buddha then addressed the monks and recited this sutta.[1] It is possible to divide the discourse into three parts. The first contains a list of the devas[2] and other beings present to worship the Buddha. It is a long list of strange names given in verses, mostly doggerel. Many of the beings mentioned are to us now mere names, with no special information attached. Most of them were probably local deities, the personification of natural phenomena, guardian spirits, fairies, harpies, naiads, dryads, and many others, who are here represented as adherents of the Buddha, come to do him honour. It is noteworthy that even the most important gods—*e.g.*, **Soma, Varuṇa** and **Brahmā**—are only incidentally mentioned, added to the list, as it were, without special distinction.

The second part of the sutta is the framework of the words attributed to the Buddha, introducing the list of devas, giving the Buddha's warning to the monks to beware of **Māra** and Māra's declaration that he had no power over them as arahants are free from fear.

The third part of the sutta may be called the prologue, the verses of greeting spoken by the devas from **Suddhāvāsā.**[3]

This prologue is elsewhere preserved as a separate episode.[4]

The Commentaries give long accounts of the preaching of the Mahāsamaya.[5] The arahants mentioned are **Sākyan** and **Koliyan** youths, representatives of Sākyan and Koḷiyan families, sent to join the Order

[1] D. ii. 253-62.

[2] A similar list is found in the Mahāvastu (i. 245; iii. 68, 77); the addition of Siva to this list is significant. The list of gods given in the Mahāsamaya should be compared with that given in the **Āṭānāṭiya Sutta.**

[3] Rhys Davids, Dial. ii. 282 f.

[4] S. i. 27.

[5] *E.g.*, SNA. 357 ff.; DA. ii. 672 ff.

as a sign of gratitude to the Buddha for having averted the quarrel between the two families regarding the water of the **Rohiṇī.** On that occasion the Buddha had preached to the opposing armies the **Attadaṇḍa Sutta** and the **Phandana, Laṭukika** and **Vaṭṭaka Jātakas.**[6] He then related the story of their origin, showing that both families were descended from a common stock. When the quarrel was thus settled, two hundred and fifty young men from each family entered the Order and the Buddha dwelt with them in Mahāvana. But the wives of the men tried to entice them back; the Buddha, therefore, took them to **Himavā,** where he preached to them the **Kuṇāla Jātaka** on the banks of the **Kuṇāla** Lake. At the conclusion of the sermon they attained to various fruits of the Path, from *anāgāmiphala* to *sotāpatti.* He then returned with them to Mahāvana, where they developed insight and became arahants. They assembled to pay homage to their teacher on the evening of the full-moon day of Jeṭṭhamāsa, and to the assembly came the devas of the ten thousand world systems. The Buddha told the monks the names of the devas present (as given in the Mahāsamaya), and, surveying the assembly, saw that it consisted of two kinds of beings, one capable of benefiting by his teaching (*bhabbā*), and the other not so capable (*abhabbā*). The *bhabbā*, he saw, could be divided into six groups—the *rāgacaritā* and the *dosa-moha-vitakka-saddhā-buddhi-caritā,* according to temperament. To these, respectively, he preached six suttas, calculated to benefit each separate class, and, in order that each sutta might take the form of question and answer, he created a Buddha-form to ask questions, while he himself answered them. The six suttas, so preached, were the **Purābheda, Kalahavivāda, Cūlavyūha, Mahāvyūha, Tuvaṭaka** and **Sammāparibbājaniya.** Countless numbers of beings realized the Truth.[7]

The preaching of the Mahāsamaya Sutta was among the incidents of the Buddha's life sculptured in the Relic Chamber of the **Mahā Thūpa.**[8]

[6] *Ibid.*, 674 adds the **Paṭhaviuddriyana** and the **Rukkhadhamma Jātakas.**

[7] AA. i. 173, 320; Mil. 20, 350; SNA. i. 174.

[8] Mhv. xxx. 83.

2. **Mahāsamaya Sutta.**—See the **Sammāparibbājaniya Sutta.**

Mahāsammata.—A king who lived in the beginning of this present age. The Pāli Chronicles[1] mention him as the original ancestor of the **Sākyan** family, to which the Buddha belonged, and gives a list of the dynasties from his day to the time of the Buddha, to prove that the line was "unbroken." Mahāsammata belonged to the Solar Race and is identified with the Bodhisatta, who was born among men after sojourn

[1] Mhv. ii. 1 ff.; Dpv. iii. 1 ff.; MṬ. 122 ff.; also J. ii. 311; iii. 454, etc.

in the Brahma-worlds.[2] He was called Mahāsammata, because, on the arising of wickedness in the world, he was chosen by the people[3] to show indignation against and disapproval of those worthy of blame. In return for his services, he was given a portion of their harvest. It is said[4] that in the dynasty of Mahāsammata the idea of meting out punishments, such as torture, fining, expulsion, was unknown. These were invented later with the advance of civilisation! The **Vimānavatthu** Commentary[5] explains that Mahāsammata is the name given in the sacred books (*sāsane*) for Manu. Some, at least, of the Ceylon kings traced their descent from Mahāsammata.[6]

[2] MṬ. 121 f.
[3] "*sannipatitvā samaggajātehi mahājanehi sammannitvā kato Mahāsammato;*" MṬ. 122; *cp.* D. iii. 92 f.; Mtu. i. 248; DhSA. 390, 392.
[4] J. iv. 192.
[5] p. 19.
[6] See, *e.g.*, Cv. xlvii. 2.

Mahāsarā.—The books contain a list of seven great lakes, situated in the **Himālaya.** They form the sources of the five great rivers and dry up only when four suns appear in the world. These seven lakes are **Anotatta, Sīhapapāta, Rathakāra, Kaṇṇamuṇḍā, Kunāla, Chaddanta** and **Mandākinī.**[1] Sometimes[2] **Haṃsapātana** is given in place of **Mandākinī.**

[1] A. iv. 101; also at J. v. 415; SNA. 407; DA. i. 164; UdA. 300; AA. ii. 759.
[2] *E.g.*, Vsm. 416.

Mahāsalāyatana, Mahāsaḷāyatanika Sutta.—The Buddha instructs the monks on the necessity of acquiring the right kind of knowledge of the sense organs, their objects, their perception, their contact and the feelings arising therefrom. Such knowledge enables a monk to traverse the Noble Eightfold Path to its perfected development and to the realization of transcendant knowledge, which is understanding and deliverance.[1]

[1] M. iii. 287-90.

Mahāsākyamuni Gotama Sutta.—The Buddha describes how, before reaching Enlightenment, he traced back, step by step, the cause of Ill in the world and the Way of escape therefrom.[1]

[1] S. ii. 10 f.

1. **Mahāsāgara.**—A king of **Uttaramadhurā; Sāgara** and **Upasāgara** were his sons.[1]

[1] J. iv. 79.

2. **Mahāsāgara.**—The name of **Mahāmeghavana** (*q.v.*) in the time of **Kassapa Buddha.**[1]

[1] Mhv. xv. 126 ff.

1. **Mahāsāmi.**—A name given by his people to **Dappula,** governor of **Rohaṇa** and father of **Mānavamma.**[1]

[1] Cv. xlv. 50.

2. **Mahāsāmi.**—A title given to **Moggallāna,** ruler of **Rohaṇa,** and father of **Kitti** (afterwards **Vijayabhāhu I.**).[1]

[1] Cv. lvii. 30, 49.

3. **Mahāsāmi.**—A Thera of Ceylon, to whom tradition ascribes the authorship of the **Mūlasikkhā.**[1]

[1] P.L.C. 77.

4. **Mahāsāmi Thera.**—Author of the new *ṭikā* on the **Nāmarūpaparicchedа.**[1]

[1] Sās. 69.

Mahāsāmi Thera.—Author of a *ṭikā* on the **Subodhālaṅkāra.**[1]

[1] Gv. 62.

Mahāsāra Jātaka (No. 92).—The Bodhisatta was once minister of **Brahmadatta,** king of Benares. One day the king went with his queens to the park and the latter took off their ornaments for bathing. A female monkey, watching her opportunity, stole a pearl necklace. On the loss being discovered, the king had every person and every place searched. A rustic, seeing the commotion, took to his heels and was chased and captured by the guards. When questioned, he confessed to having stolen the necklace, thinking that the best way of saving his life, and said he had given it to the Treasurer. The Treasurer said he had given it to the chaplain, the chaplain to the chief musician, the musician to the courtesan. As it was by this time late, the matter was put off till the next day, the alleged accomplices being imprisoned. The Bodhisatta, doubting their words, obtained the king's leave to investigate the matter. He had the prisoners watched, and knew, from their reported conversations, that they were innocent. He then decided that it had been stolen by a monkey, and gave orders that a number of monkeys should be captured and turned loose again with strings of beads round their necks, wrists, and ankles. The monkey, who had stolen the necklace, on seeing the others with their beads, was filled with jealousy and produced the necklace. The guard frightened her, and so she dropped it, and the Bodhisatta was greatly praised for his wisdom.

The story was told in reference to **Ānanda. Pasenadi's** wives wished for someone to preach to them in the palace. Pasenadi went to the Buddha and from him heard the praises of **Chattapāṇī.** Later, he met him and asked him to preach in his harem. But Chattapāṇī was unwilling, saying that it was the prerogative of the monks. Thereupon the king asked the Buddha to appoint someone, and the Buddha appointed Ānanda. One day Ānanda found all the women of the palace very dejected, and learnt that the jewel of the king's turban had been lost and everyone was most distracted. Ānanda, therefore, went to the king and asked that each suspect should be given a wisp of straw on a lump of clay and asked to place it somewhere, the idea being that the thief would leave the jewel in one of these lumps. The ruse, however, did not succeed, and orders were then given that a water-pot be set in a retired corner of the courtyard behind a screen and that everyone should be asked to wash his hands. When all had washed, the pot was emptied and the jewel found inside it.

Ānanda is identified with the king of the Jātaka.[1]

[1] J. i. 381-7.

Mahāsārappakāsinī.—The name of a Commentary.[1]

[1] Gv. 75.

Mahāsāropama Sutta.—Preached at **Gijjhakūṭa,** soon after **Devadatta's** secession. Some young men leave the household, being lured by the life of a monk. As monks, they receive presents, esteem, and repute. These things so please them and satisfy their aspirations that they become conceited and disparage others. Thus they grow remiss and a prey to Ill. Their case resembles that of a man who, needing the best of timber, goes into a forest and is satisfied with cutting off the leafy foliage or the bark of the trees, knowing nothing of the grades of wood. On the other hand, the monk who is satisfied only when he reaches the end of Ill is like a man who takes only the choicest timber, passing over the other.[1]

[1] M. i. 192-7.

1. **Mahāsāla Sutta.**—A rich brahmin asks the Buddha why there is an apparent decrease of human beings. The Buddha answers that it is because the world is ablaze with unlawful lusts, wrong doctrines, and depraved longings. There is no reasonable rain, harvests are poor, and men die easily.[1]

[1] A. i. 159 f.

2. **Mahāsāla** or **Lūkhapāpuraṇa Sutta.**—A wealthy brahmin, looking worn and wearing a coarse garment, visits the Buddha at **Sāvatthi** and tells him that his four sons, aided by their wives, have shown him the door. The Buddha teaches him several verses illustrating the ingratitude of his sons to be recited in the *Santhāgārasālā*. He recited these and his sons, who are in the assembly, take him home and look after him. Later he goes to the Buddha and asks him to accept a set of garments which his sons have given him. The Buddha accepts it out of compassion.[1]

The Commentary says that the man had immense wealth in his house, some eighty crores. He found wives for his sons and divided half his wealth among them. His wife died, and his sons, fearful lest he should marry again and they should lose the rest of their patrimony, pet him and look after him, and he gives them all except his wrap. He goes to live with his eldest son, but is driven out by his daughter-in-law; the rest of the family treat him likewise. He enters the order of the **Paṇḍaraṅgas** and suffers the greatest privations, till he finally throws himself on the reputed kindness and graciousness of the Buddha. When the people discover the disloyalty of the sons they threaten to kill them, and then the sons take the old man back and nurse him. Later the mem ers of the family become *sotāpannas*.[2]

[1] S. i. 175 f. [2] SA. i. 202 ff.

Mahāsālā.—A village to the east of **Kajaṅgalā;** the eastern boundary of **Majjhimadesa** passed through it.[1]

[1] Vin. i. 197; J. i. 49, where it is called **Mahāsāla.**

Mahāsikha.—Five kappas ago there were five kings of this name, previous births of **Pannañjalika Thera.**[1]

[1] Ap. i. 128.

Mahāsineru.—See **Sineru.**

Mahāsīlava.—The Bodhisatta born as king of Benares. See the **Mahāsīlava Jātaka.**

Mahāsīlava Jātaka (No. 51).—The Bodhisatta was once king of Benares under the name of **Mahāsīlava.** He built six almonries and ruled in all goodness. One of his ministers, having intrigued with a member of his harem, was expelled and took service under the king of **Kosala.** He caused several bands of ruffians to invade the territory of Mahāsīlava at different times. When they were caught and brought before Mahāsīlava, the latter gave them money and sent them away, telling them to act differently in the future. In this way the king of Kosala was easily persuaded by his minister that Mahāsīlava's kingdom could easily be captured. He therefore set out with an army, and as the people of Mahāsīlava were allowed to offer no resistance, the king and his ministers were captured alive and buried up to their necks in the cemetery. In the night, when jackals approached to eat them, Mahāsīlava fastened his teeth in the neck of the jackal that came to him. The jackal started howling and his companions fled. In his struggles to get free, the jackal loosened the earth round Mahāsīlava, who managed to free himself and then his companions.

In the cemetery two Yakkhas were having a dispute about a dead body, and they asked Mahāsīlava to settle it. But he wished first to bathe, and they fetched him water and perfumes and food from the usurper's table in Benares and also his sword of state. With this he cut the body in half, giving half to each Yakkha, and, with their aid, he entered the usurper's room where he slept. When the latter showed signs of terror, Mahāsīlava told him of what had happened and granted him forgiveness. His kingdom was then restored, and Mahāsīlava exhorted his subjects on the virtues of perseverance.

The story was related to a backsliding monk. **Devadatta** is identified with the treacherous minister of the Jātaka.[1]

[1] J. i. 261-8.

1. **Mahāsiva.**—King of Ceylon; he was the son of **Muṭasīva** and the younger brother of **Uttiya,** whom he succeeded. He reigned for ten years (197-87 B.C.) and built the **Nagaraṅgana-vihāra** for **Bhaddasāla Thera.** He was succeeded by **Sūratissa.**[1]

[1] Mhv. xxi. 1 ff.

2. **Mahāsīva Thera.**—Resident of **Vāmantapabbhāra.** He was among the last of the arahants, and had taken part in various assemblies led by the Boddhisatta.[1] It is probably this Thera who is referred to as **Gāmantapabbhāravāsī Mahāsīva** in the Aṅguttara Commentary.[2] He lived in **Tissamahārāma** at **Mahāgāma,** and was the teacher of eighteen groups of monks. One of his pupils became an arahant, and, being aware that his teacher was yet a *puthujjana,* went to him and asked his leave to be taught a stanza. But Mahāsīva said his pupils were so numerous that he had no time to give him a stanza. The pupil waited

[1] J. iv. 490; vi. 30. [2] AA. i. 24, 29.

for a whole day and night, and then getting no chance of learning, said, "If you are so busy now how will you find time to die?" Mahāsīva heard and understood, and exerted himself strenuously for thirty long years, at the end of which time he became an arahant.

3. **Mahāsīva.**—A famous Commentator, sometimes called **Dīghabhāṇaka-Mahāsīva.** His interpretations are quoted, with respect, in the Commentaries.[1]

[1] *E.g.*, DA. ii. 430, 511, 543, 554, 805, 881, 883; SA. iii. 171, 198; Sp. iii. 711; DhSA. 405; PSA. 80; AA. ii. 490.

4. **Mahāsīva Thera.**—An incumbent of **Bhātivaṅka,** during the reign of **Duṭṭhagāmaṇī.** One day he went to worship at the **Mahā Thūpa,** and there he saw two devatās offering flowers. In their previous lives they were two women who had worked for hire on the Mahā Thūpa.[1]

[1] Mhv. xxx. 46 ff.

5. **Mahāsīva Thera.**—Incumbent of **Nigrodhapiṭṭhi** and expert in the Tipiṭaka. Once, while preaching the **Sīhanāda Sutta** in King **Vasabha's** palace, he described the splendours of the Relic Chamber in the **Mahā Thūpa** and the king expressed some difficulty in believing the report, but the Elder was able to convince the king that nothing was impossible where there was a combination of *rājiddhi*, *deviddhi* and *ariyiddhi*. The king was pleased, conveyed the Elder under the white umbrella to the **Mahā Vihāra** and made great offerings, lasting for seven days, to the Mahā Thūpa.[1]

[1] MṬ. 555.

6. **Mahāsīva Thera.**—Mentioned as an eminent teacher of the Vinaya.[1] He is probably identical with one of the foregoing.

[1] Vin. v. 3; Sp. i. 63.

7. **Mahāsīva Thera.**—It was for him that **Aggabodhi I.** built a *pariveṇa* and also the **Kurunda-vihāra** with a tank and a grove of cocopalms.[1]

[1] Cv. xlii. 11, 16.

Mahāsīvalī Thera.—A commentator, evidently of Ceylon, referred to by **Buddhaghosa.**[1]

[1] *E.g.*, MA. ii. 797.

Mahāsīhanāda Sutta.—Preached at the **Mahāvana** in **Vesālī. Sāriputta** tells the Buddha that **Sunakkhatta,** who had recently left the Order, went about saying that there was nothing marvellous about the Buddha's knowledge and insight and that his teachings did not lead to the end of Ill. The Buddha says that Sunakkhatta is a man of wrath and folly and incapable of appreciating the good either of the Tathāgata or of his teachings. He then issues his challenge to the effect that no one can deny to the Tathāgata the possession of ten powers, (*balā*)—which are enumerated—and the four confidences (*vesārajjā*). The Tathāgata can attend any of the eight assemblies without fear; he knows the various classifications of beings, the birth of beings, the way to Nibbāna; he can read the minds of men and the five destinies which await different beings. He has lived the fourfold higher life—being foremost in his practice of asceticism, in loathliness, in scrupulosity, in solitude. No one has surpassed him in the practice of these things. He has discovered, by experimentation, the futility of the claims of those who maintain that purity comes by way of food, or offering, or ritual. Though eighty years old and his body broken down, yet his powers of mind are at their prime; even if he must be carried on a litter, yet will his mind retain its powers.[1]

Nāgasamāla, who is by, asks the Buddha for a title for the discourse, and the Buddha gives it the name of **Lomahaṃsapariyāya.** *cp.* **Lomahaṃsa Jātaka.**

[1] M. i. 68-83.

Mahāsuka Jātaka (No. 429).—The Bodhisatta was once king of the parrots and lived in a fig-tree grove in the **Himālaya.** After some time the fruits of the trees on which he lived came to an end, but he still lived on there, eating bark or shoots or whatever else he could find. **Sakka's** throne was heated, and Sakka, assuming the form of a goose and accompanied by **Sujā,** visited the parrot and asked why he did not go elsewhere. The parrot answered that he did not wish to forsake old friends, and Sakka, pleased with this answer, promised him a boon. The parrot asked that the fig-tree be made fruitful again, and this Sakka did.

The story was told in reference to a monk who had a pleasant dwelling-place near a village, but who found alms difficult to get, the villagers becoming very poor. He became very discontented, but the Buddha asked him not to forsake his dwelling.

The Sakka of the story is identified with **Anuruddha.**[1] According to the Dhammapada Commentary,[2] the story was related to **Nigamavāsī Tissa** (*q.v.*) and Sakka is identified with **Ānanda.**

[1] J. iii. 490-4. [2] DhA. i. 283 ff.

Mahāsuññatā Sutta.—Preached at **Nigrodhārāma** in **Kapilavatthu.** The Buddha was staying in the cell erected by **Kāḷakhemaka,** and near by, in the cell erected by **Ghaṭāya, Ānanda,** with many monks, was making robes. The Buddha knew from the number of pallets outside the cells of Kāḷakhemaka that many monks were in residence there. He therefore addressed Ānanda, telling him of the joys of tranquillity and solitude. A monk should dwell apart and concentrate his heart internally and thus develop the four *jhānas*. He then knows that, whatever his posture, he will be free from evil dispositions, his speech will be free from faults, his thoughts pure. A monk should always search his heart to discover if he has any traffic with pleasures of sense. A disciple should follow his master's footsteps, not in order to obtain interpretations of canonical law, but solely to hear words which conduce to passionlessness, illumination, Nibbāna.[1]

The sutta is also called **Gaṇabheda,** because it tends to break up crowds. Once, in the **Vālikapiṭṭhi-vihāra, Ābhidhammika-Abhaya** recited this sutta with several others, and, understanding its import, dwelt apart and attained arahantship during the rains.[2]

[1] M. iii. 109-18.   [2] MA. ii. 907.

Mahāsutasoma Jātaka (No. 537).—**Brahmadatta,** king of Benares, was much addicted to meat. One *uposatha*-day the meat which had been prepared for him was eaten by dogs, and the cook, unable to buy any more, cut a piece from a human body recently dead and cooked it. Brahmadatta had been a Yakkha in a former birth and therefore enjoyed the dish. Having discovered what the meat was, he developed a taste for human flesh, and, in due course, came to having his subjects murdered in order to supply him with food. His crime was discovered and his guilt brought home by his commander-in-chief, **Kāḷahatthi,**[1] but the king refused to give up his cannibalism and was driven out of the kingdom. He dwelt in the forests with his cooks, eating all the travellers they were able to seize. The day arrived when he killed the cook himself and ate his flesh. Some time after he fell upon a brahmin travelling through the forest with a large retinue, and they gave chase to the king. As he ran an acacia splinter pierced his foot, causing him great pain. Seeing a banyan tree, he made a vow to bathe its trunk with the blood of one hundred and one princes if his foot were healed in seven days. The foot did heal within that time, and with the assistance of a Yakkha, who had been his friend in a previous birth, he managed to capture one

[1] Kāḷahatthi relates various stories to the king, showing the folly of his behaviour—*e.g.*, the story of the fish **Ānanda,** of **Sujāta**'s son, of the geese who lived in **Cittakūṭa** and of the **Uṇṇābhi** spider. For details see *s.v.*

hundred kings whom he hung on the tree by means of cords passed through their hands.

The deity of the tree was alarmed and, on the advice of **Sakka,** appeared before the man-eater (who is called in the context *porisāda*) and demanded that he should bring **Sutasoma,** Prince of **Kuru,** to complete the number of his victims. Sutasoma had been the man-eater's friend and private tutor (*piṭṭhācariya*) at **Takkasilā.** Anxious to appease the deity, the man-eater went to Sutasoma's park and there waited for him hidden in the pond, when Sutasoma came to take his ceremonial bath on the festival-day of Phussa. On the way to the park, Sutasoma met a brahmin, **Nanda,** who offered, for four thousand pieces, to teach him four verses learnt from **Kassapa Buddha.** Sutasoma promised to learn them on his return from the park, but there he was caught by the *porisāda*. Promising to return to the *porisāda*, Sutasoma obtained leave to keep his appointment with Nanda. This promise fulfilled, Sutasoma returned to the *porisāda* and went with him to the banyan-tree. There he told the *porisāda* of the verses he had learnt from Nanda, reciting them to him, and discoursing on the virtues of Truth. The *porisāda* was greatly pleased and offered Sutasoma four boons. Sutasoma chose as his first boon that the *porisāda* should live for one hundred years; as his second, that the captive kings should be released; as his third, that their kingdoms should be restored; and as his fourth, that the *porisāda* should give up his cannibalism. Only very reluctantly did the *porisāda* agree to the fourth. Sutasoma then took him back to Benares, where he restored to him his kingdom, having first assured the people that the king would never return to his former vicious habits. Sutasoma then returned to **Indapatta.** In gratitude for the tree-sprite's intervention, a lake was dug near the banyan-tree and a village founded near by, whose inhabitants were required to make offerings to the tree. This village, built on the spot where the *porisāda* was converted, came to be called **Kammāsadamma.**

The story was related in reference to the Buddha's conversion of **Aṅgulimāla,** with whom the man-eater is identified. Kāḷahatthi was **Sāriputta,** Nanda was **Ānanda,** the tree-sprite was **Kassapa,** Sakka was **Anuruddha,** and Sutasoma the **Bodhisatta.**[2]

[2] J. v. 456-511; *cp.* Jātakamāla xxxi. The *Sutasomacariyā* is given in the Cariyāpiṭaka iii. 12.

Mahāsudassana.—The Bodhisatta born as king of **Kusāvatī.**[1] See the **Mahāsudassana Sutta.**

[1] J. i. 45; Dpv. iii. 8; Mhv. ii. 5; Mtu. i. 348.

Mahāsudassana Jātaka (No. 95).—Relates the story of the death of **Mahāsudassana.** For the rest of the king's story, reference is suggested to the **Mahāsudassana Sutta.** Mahāsudassana's queen is called **Subhaddā** and is identified with **Rāhulamātā.**[1]

[1] J. i. 391-3.

Mahāsudassana Sutta.—Preached between the twin Sāla-trees in **Upavattana,** the grove of the **Mallas. Ānanda** asks the Buddha not to die in the "little wattle-and-daub" town of **Kusinārā,** but in some important city, such as **Campā, Rājagaha** or **Sāvatthi.** The Buddha tells him that Kusinārā was once **Kusāvatī,** the royal city of King **Mahāsudassana,** and was surrounded by seven ramparts, a city containing all the characteristics of a great capital.

Mahāsudassana possessed the seven treasures of a **Cakkavatti** (*q.v.*): the *cakka-ratana*, the *hatthi-ratana* (named **Uposatha),** the *assa-ratana* (named **Valāhaka),** the *maṇi-ratana*, the *itthi-ratana* (pearl among women), the *gahapati-ratana*, and the *parināyaka-ratana*. He also possessed four *iddhi*-powers: he was handsome, long-lived, free from disease, and beloved by all classes of people. He had lotus ponds made all over his kingdom, food and clothing being placed on their banks for any who might require them. With the money brought to the king by the people, **Vissakamma,** under **Sakka's** orders, built the **Dhammapāsāda** Palace, filled with all splendour and luxury. The king possessed a gabled hall called **Mahāvyūha,** where he spent the hot part of the day. In front of the Dhammapāsāda was the **Dhammapokkharaṇī.**

Having realized that his power and glory were the result of past good deeds, Mahāsudassana practised generosity, self-conquest and self-control, and developed the four *jhānas*, suffusing all quarters with thoughts of love and pity and sympathy and equanimity.

Mahāsudassana had eighty-four thousand cities, the chief of which was Kusāvatī; eighty-four thousand palaces, the chief being Dhammapāsāda; eighty-four thousand gabled houses, the chief being Mahāvyūha; eighty-four thousand state elephants, led by Uposatha; and eighty-four thousand horses, led by Valāhaka. He had eighty-four thousand chariots led by **Vejayanta,** and eighty-four thousand wives, of whom Subhaddā was the chief. One day, the king realized that his death was approaching, and, when Subhaddā visited him to try and induce him to enjoy his pleasures, he stopped her, telling her to speak to him of the impermanence of things and the need for giving up all desire. While she talked to him of these things, he died and was reborn in the **Brahma**-world. For eighty-four thousand years he had been a prince, a viceroy and a king respectively, and later, for forty-eight thousand years, a devout layman in the Dhammapāsāda. Mahāsudassana is identified with the Buddha.[1]

In the time of **Kassapa Buddha,** Sudassana had been a forester. He met a monk in the forest and built a hut for him. He also requested the monk to receive alms every day at his house or, at least, to eat there. The monk agreed, and Sudassana made his hut comfortable in every way, constructing walks, bathing-places, gardens, etc., outside. He also gave him innumerable gifts, of various kinds and descriptions.[2]

[1] D. ii. 169-99; the story is also referred to at S. iii. 144. [2] DA. ii. 631 f.

Mahāsupina Jātaka (No. 77).—**Pasenadi,** king of **Kosala,** had, one night, sixteen bad dreams, and his brahmins, on being consulted, said that they presaged harm either to his kingdom, his life, or his wealth, and prescribed all manner of sacrifices in order to avert the danger.[1] **Mallikā,** the king's wife, heard of this and suggested that the Buddha should be consulted. The king followed her advice, and the Buddha explained the dreams. The first dream was of wild bulls entering the royal courtyard to fight but retiring after roaring and bellowing. This, said the Buddha, meant that, in future, when wicked kings rule, rain-clouds will gather, but there will be no rain. The second dream was of trees and shrubs sprouting from the earth which flowered and bore fruit when only about one span high. This foretold a time when men would be short-lived owing to their lusts. In the third dream cows sucked calves which were hardly a day old. This showed that, in the future, the young would refuse respect to the old. The fourth dream was of sturdy draught oxen standing by, while young steers tried to draw loads. This signified a time when the administration of affairs will be entrusted to the young and inexperienced, while the wise and old stand by. The fifth dream was of a horse which ate from two mouths, one on either side of its body, which foretold a time when the king's justices will take bribes from contending parties and give themselves to corruption. The sixth dream was of people holding a very valuable golden bowl and asking a jackal to stale therein. This shows that, in the future, kings will exalt the low-born and noble maidens will be mated with upstarts. The seventh dream was of a man holding a rope which he trailed at his feet, while a she-jackal kept on eating it. This foretold a time when women will lose their sense of modesty and behave badly. In the eighth dream was a big pitcher at the palace gates filled with water and surrounded by empty ones. This foretold a time when kings will be poor and set the whole country working for them, the people being left in extreme poverty. The ninth dream

[1] It is perhaps this sacrifice which is referred to at S. i. 75.

was of a deep pool with sloping banks overgrown with lotus. Men and beasts entered the pond; the middle was muddy, but at the edges was crystal water. This meant that in the future there would be unrighteous kings oppressing the people, who would leave the capital and take refuge in the frontier districts. The tenth dream was of rice cooking in a pot, which rice, instead of cooking evenly, remained in three parts: some sodden, some raw, some well cooked; this showed that in the future men of all classes, even brahmins and sages, will be wicked, the very forces of nature will be against them, and their harvest will be spoiled. The eleventh dream was of men bartering butter-milk for precious sandal-wood, and presaged a time when the Dhamma would decay and its votaries clamour for money and gifts. The twelfth dream was of empty pumpkins sinking in the water; the world will be reversed: the low-born will become great lords and the noble sink into poverty. In the thirteenth dream solid blocks of rock floated in the water; nobles and wise men will be scorned while upstarts shall have their own way. In the fourteenth dream tiny frogs chewed huge snakes and ate them; a time will come when men, because of their lusts, will become the slaves of their wives and be ruled by them. The fifteenth dream was of a wicked village crow attended by mallards; kings will arise, ignorant and cowardly, who will raise to power, not their peers, but their footmen, barbers, and the like; nobles will be reduced to waiting on these upstarts. In the sixteenth dream goats chased panthers, devouring them; the lowborn will be raised to lordship and nobles will sink into obscurity and distress; when the latter plead for their rights, the king's minions will have them cudgelled and bastinadoed.

Having thus explained the dreams, the Buddha told Pasenadi a story of the past. A king of Benares, named Brahmadatta, had dreams similar to those of Pasenadi. When he consulted the brahmins, they began to prepare sacrifices. A young brahmin protested, saying that animal sacrifice was against the teaching of the Vedas, but they would not listen. The Bodhisatta, who was a hermit in the **Himālaya,** possessed of insight, became aware of what was happening, travelled through the air and took his seat in the park. There he was seen by a young brahmin, who brought the king to the park. The Bodhisatta heard the king's dreams and explained them to his satisfaction.

Ānanda was the king and **Sāriputta** the young brahmin.[2]

[2] J. i. 334-45.

1. **Mahāsubhaddā.**—Chief wife of the Bodhisatta when he was the elephant king **Chaddanta.**[1]

[1] J. v. 37, 39.

2. **Mahāsubhaddā.**—Eldest daughter of **Anāthapiṇḍika.** Before her marriage she waited on the monks who came to her father's house and became a *sotāpanna.*[1] According to the Aṅguttara Commentary[2] she married an unbeliever, a householder of **Ugganagara,** and the Buddha, at her request, went to her house with five hundred monks (chief among whom was **Kuṇḍadhāna**) to receive alms. But see *s.v.* **Cūla-Subhaddā.**

[1] DhA. i. 128; J. i. 93. [2] AA. i. 146, 148 f.

3. **Mahāsubhaddā.**—Chief queen of **Mahāsudassana** (*q.v.*).[1]

[1] D. ii. 189; S. iii. 145; J. i. 392, calls her **Subhaddā.**

1. **Mahāsumana.**—The presiding deity of **Sumanakūṭa.** He was a *sotāpanna,* and on the Buddha's first visit to Ceylon obtained from him a handful of hair, which he placed in a sapphire shrine. This shrine was later known as **Mahiyaṅgana Thūpa.**[1]

[1] Mhv. i. 33 ff.

2. **Mahāsumana.**—Elder son of **Mahāmuṇḍa.** He waited upon **Anuruddha** at his father's house and his father offered to have him ordained. But Anuruddha preferred his brother **Cullasumana.**[1]

[1] DhA. iv. 128 f.

3. **Mahāsumana.**—A Thera, present at the Foundation Ceremony of the **Mahā Thūpa;** when the foundation was laid, he offered *jātisumana* flowers.[1]

[1] MṬ. 524, 527, 528.

Mahāsumanā.—One of the pre-eminent nuns of Ceylon.[1]

[1] Dpv. xviii. 39.

Mahāsumba Thera.—A disciple of **Koṇāgamana Buddha;** he came to Ceylon at the Buddha's request. He, with one thousand others, was left behind to look after the new converts.[1]

[1] Mhv. xv. 123.

1. **Mahāsumma Thera.**—An incumbent of **Koṭapabbata-vihāra.** The father of **Theraputtābhaya** was his supporter and was ordained by him.[1]

[1] Mhv. xxiii. 60 f.

2. **Mahāsumma Thera.**—A monk of Ceylon. King **Mahācūli-Mahātissa** laboured in a rice harvest, and, with the wages thus received, gave him alms.[1]

[1] Mhv. xxxiv. 3.

3. **Mahāsumma Thera.**—Pupil of **Upatissa.** After reading the Vinaya Piṭaka nine times, he went to live beyond the river (**Mahāvālukagaṅgā**).[1] His views are quoted in the **Samantapāsādikā.**[2]

[1] Sp. i. 263 f.
[2] *E.g.*, ii. 368; iii. 535, 538, 556, 588, 596, 609, 644, 646, 647, 651, 683, 698, 715, 719, etc.

Mahāsuvaṇṇa.—Father of **Cakkhupāla.**[1]

[1] ThagA. i. 195; DhA. i. 2.

Mahāsuvaṇṇadīpa.—Son of **Parakkamabahalarājā** and ācariya of Queen **Sīvalī** of **Haṃsavatī,** in Pegu. He was author of the **Apheggusāradīpanī.**[1]

[1] Bode, *op. cit.*, 36, n. 2.

1. **Mahāsena.**—A *deva* living in **Ketumatī** Palace to the east of **Vejayanta.** At the request of **Sakka** and of members of the Order, led by Assagutta, he was born in the world of men as **Nāgasena.**[1]

[1] Mil. 6 f.

2. **Mahāsena.**—A brahmin, friend of **Vaṅganta,** father of **Sāriputta.** He was poor, and, out of compassion for him, Sāriputta came to his house for alms. Twice Mahāsena hid himself, having nothing to give, but, one day, receiving a bowl of rice porridge and a small piece of cloth, he thought of Sāriputta. The Elder had just risen from a trance, and, becoming aware of Mahāsena's desire, he visited him, and was given the porridge and the piece of cloth with a prayer from Mahāsena, " May I realize the Truth you have seen." After death, Mahāsena was born as the novice and was called **Vanavāsī Tissa.**[1]

[1] DhA. ii. 84.

3. **Mahāsena.**—Younger son of King **Goṭhābhaya.** He became king of Ceylon (334-361 A.C.), and under the advice of his teacher **Saṅghamitta** and his minister **Soṇa,** he despoiled **Mahāvihāra** and enriched **Abhayagiri.** He issued a decree that no one should give alms to the monks of Mahāvihāra. But, later, his friend and minister, **Meghavaṇṇābhaya,** convinced him of his error, and he became a supporter of Mahāvihāra. Soon after, however, he fell under the influence of a monk, named **Tissa,**

and built **Jetavanavihārā** in the precincts of Mahāvihāra, despite the protests of the monks. Tissa was later expelled from the Order. The king built the **Maṇihīra, Gokaṇṇa, Erakāvilla, Kalandagāma, Migagāma, Gaṅgāsenakapabbata, Dhātusenapabbata, Kokavāta, Rūpārāma,** and **Hulapiṭṭhi-vihāras** and two nunneries—**Uttara** and **Abhaya.** He also built sixteen tanks and a great canal called **Pabbatanta.**[1]

Sirimeghavaṇṇa was the son of Mahāsena.[2]

[1] Dpv. xxii. 66-76; Mhv. xxxvii. 1 ff. [2] Cv. xxxvii. 53.

4. **Mahāsena.**—A king of India who ruled in **Pāṭaliputta.** He fed one thousand monks daily; but, not satisfied with that, he went to **Uttaramadhurā,** where he laboured in disguise, giving alms with the wages so earned.[1]

[1] Cv. xcii. 23 ff.

Mahāsenagāma.—A village in **Rohaṇa,** whose vihāra was restored by **Vijayabāhu I.**[1] The village is mentioned in the account of the campaigns of **Parakkamabāhu I.**[2]

[1] Cv. lx. 62. [2] *Ibid.*, lxxv. 109; Cv. *Trs.* ii. 55, n. 2.

Mahāsena-vihāra.—A vihāra called after King **Mahāsena,** to which **Aggabodhi V.** gave the village of **Paṇṇabhatta.**[1] In the vihāra was a Buddha-image, and **Sena II.** granted it a village and appointed watchmen to look after it.[2]

[1] Cv. xlviii. 8; Cv. *Trs.* i. 111, n. 1. [2] Cv. li. 76.

Mahāsela.—See **Sela.**

1. **Mahāsoṇa.**—An evil-natured horse of **Brahmadatta,** king of Benares. ee the **Suhanu Jātaka.**

2. **Mahāsoṇa.**—One of the ten chief warriors of **Duṭṭhagāmaṇī.** He was born in **Hunadarīvāpī** in the **Kuḷumbarī** district as the eighth son of a man named Tissa. He was as strong as ten elephants, and took a prominent part in the attack on **Vijitapura.**[1]

[1] Mhv. xxiii. 2, 46 ff.; xxv. 27 f.; 44 f.

3. **Mahāsoṇa.**—A monk in the time of **Vaṭṭagāmaṇi-Abhaya.** During the troubles caused by the brigand **Brāhmaṇatissa,** he travelled about in the company of **Isidatta Thera,** maintaining themselves on whatever they could find. One day a maiden made three balls of food, gave one

to Isidatta, the second to Mahāsoṇa, and wished to give the third to Isidatta; but her hand turned, and the food fell into Mahāsoṇa's bowl. Later, he lived with five hundred others in **Maṇḍalārāma-vihāra.** One day, while in **Kālakagāma** for alms, they were entertained by a pious devotee. The latter asked for Mahāsoṇa and showed him special honour, though Mahāsoṇa was only a junior monk. Some time after, Mahāsoṇa returned to the **Mahāvihāra** in **Anurādhapura** and received many gifts, which he distributed among the Saṅgha.[1]

[1] VibhA. 446 ff.

Mahāsoṇā Therī.—A teacher of the Vinaya in Ceylon.[1]

[1] Dpv. xviii. 27.

Mahāhaṃsa Jātaka (No. 534).—**Khemā,** wife of **Saṃyama,** king of Benares, had a dream, after which she longed to see a golden haṁsa preach the law from the royal throne. When the king came to know this, he consulted various people, and, acting on their advice, had a pond dug to the north of the city in the hope of enticing a golden haṃsa there, and appointed a fowler, who came to be called **Khemaka,** to look after the pond.

The plan succeeded. Five different kinds of geese came: the grass geese, the yellow geese, the scarlet geese, the white geese, and the *pāka* geese.

Dhataraṭṭha, king of the golden geese, who lived in **Cittakūṭa,** had taken as wife a *pakā* goose, and at the repeated suggestion of his minister, **Sumukha,** arrived with his flock of ninety thousand, to see the wonderful pond at Benares. Khemaka saw them and waited his opportunity. On the seventh day he found it, and set a snare in which Dhataraṭṭha was caught. At his cry of alarm the flock fled, with the exception of Sumukha, who stayed and asked Khemaka for permission to take Dhataraṭṭha's place. When Sumukha heard why they had been caught, he asked that both he and Dhataraṭṭha should be taken before Saṃyama. When Saṃyama heard of Sumukha's devotion he was greatly touched, and showed the haṃsas every possible honour, after asking their forgiveness for the way they had been treated. Dhataraṭṭha preached to the queen and the royal household, and, having exhorted the king to rule righteously, returned to Cittakūṭa.

The story was told in reference to **Ānanda's** attempt to sacrifice his own life for that of the Budda, when **Nālāgiri** (*q.v.*) was sent to kill him.

Khemaka was **Channa,** Khemā the Therī **Khemā,** the king **Sāriputta,** Sumukha **Ānanda,** and Dhataraṭṭha the Bodhisatta.[1]

[1] J. v. 354-82; *cp.* Cullahaṃsa Jātaka.

Mahāhatthipadopama Sutta.—**Sāriputta** addresses the monks at **Jetavana** and tells them that, just as the foot of every creature will fit in the elephant's footprint, even so are all right states of mind comprised within the Four Noble Truths. He then goes on to explain that *dukkha* consists of the five *upādānakkhandhas*—visible shapes, feelings, perception, saṅkhāras and consciousness. The constituents of these attachments are the four principle elements: earth, water, fire, and air. Each element is of two kinds—personal (*ajjhatta*) and external (*bahiddhā*)—and each is transient and subject to decay. The chain of causation entails all that makes up the five attachments. Where there is eye intact, on which external shapes come to focus, and where there is developed pertinent material to sustain it, there is developed a manifestation of the pertinent section of consciousness. Thus arises the *upādānakkhandha* of form; similarly with the others.[1]

[1] M. i. 184-91.

Mahiṃsaka.—A kingdom mentioned in the **Saṅkhapāla Jātaka** as being near Mount **Candaka.** There lived the Bodhisatta, in a hermitage on the bend of the river **Kaṇṇapaṇṇā,** where it left Lake **Saṅkhapāla.**[1] **Keka** is mentioned as the capital of Mahiṃsaka, where a king named **Ajjuna** once ruled[2]; also a city, called **Sakuḷa,** capital of King Sakuḷa. Near Sakuḷa was a lake, called **Mānusiya.**[3] In the **Bhīmasena Jātaka**[4] the Bodhisatta is mentioned as living for some time in Mahiṃsaka in his birth as **Cūḷadhanuggaha-paṇḍita.** Mahiṃsaka is mentioned[5] as an example of a country where cold weather frequently occurs.

The country is generally identified with Malayagiri, the Malabar Ghats. See also **Mahisamaṇḍala.**

[1] J. v. 162. [2] *Ibid.*, 145. [3] *Ibid.*, 337. [4] J. i. 356. [5] *E.g.*, VibhA. 4.

Mahiṃsāsa.—The Bodhisatta, born as the son of the king of Benares. For details see the **Devadhamma Jātaka.**[1]

[1] J. i. 127 ff.; DhA. iii. 73.

Mahiṃsāsaka.—An heretical sect, which broke off from the **Theravādins** at the same time as the **Vajjiputtakas.** The sect was later divided into the **Sabbatthivādins** and the **Dhammaguttikas.**[1] They held that the truth of *nirodha* had two aspects.[2] **Buddhadeva Thera,** at whose request the **Jātakaṭṭhakathā** was written, belonged to the **Mahiṃsāsaka-vaṃsa.**[3] Fa Hsien found a group of monks belonging to this sect in Ceylon.[4]

[1] Mhv. v. 6, 8; Dpv. v. 45, 47; MṬ. 174 f.; Mhv. 96.

[2] Kvu. ii. 11; see also viii. 9; xviii. 6; xix. 8; xx. 5; and Rockhill, *op. cit.*, 182, 183, 184, 185, 186, 191, 192.

[3] J. i. 1. [4] Giles, *op. cit.*, p. 76.

Mahiddhi, or **Samaṇabrāhmaṇa Sutta.**—All recluses or brahmins possessed of *iddhi* power, whether of the past, present or future, must obtain it through the development of the four *satipaṭṭhānas*.[1]

[1] S. v. 273 f.

1. **Mahinda Thera.**—Son of **Asoka** and brother of **Saṅghamittā.** He was fourteen at the time of the coronation of his father and was ordained at the age of twenty, his perceptor being **Moggaliputtatissa.** The ordination was performed by **Mahādeva,** while **Majjhantika** recited the *kammavācā*. Mahinda became an arahant on the day of his ordination.[1] He spent three years in study of the Doctrine under his preceptor, and, later, when the latter retired to **Ahogaṅgā,** he left his one thousand disciples for seven years under the care of Mahinda.[2] When the Third Council was held, Mahinda had been for twelve years a monk and was charged with the mission of converting Ceylon. But he delayed for six months, until **Devānampiyatissa** became king. He then went to **Dakkhiṇāgiri** and from there to his birthplace, **Vedisagiri,** staying in **Vedisagiri-vihāra** and visiting his mother, the queen **Devī.** Still one more month he tarried, teaching the Doctrine to **Bhaṇḍuka,** and then, on the full-moon day of Jeṭṭha, at the request of **Sakka,** he went, in company with **Iṭṭhiya, Uttiya, Sambala, Bhaddasāla, Sumanasāmaṇera** and **Bhaṇḍuka,** to Ceylon, where he converted Devānampiyatissa by preaching to him the **Cūlahatthipadopama Sutta.** Later, on the same day, he preached the **Samacitta Sutta.** The next day, at the request of the king, he visited **Anurādhapura,** travelling through the air and alighting on the site of the (later) **Paṭhamacetiya.** After a meal at the palace he preached the **Petavatthu,** the **Vimānavatthu** and the **Sacca Saṃyutta,** and **Anulā** and her five hundred companions became *sotāpannas*. Later, in the elephant-stables, he preached the **Devadūta Sutta** to the assembled people, and, in the evening, the **Bālapaṇḍita Sutta,** in **Nandanavana.** The night he spent in **Mahāmeghavana,** and on the next day the king gave the park to Mahinda, on behalf of the Order.

Mahinda pointed out to the king various spots destined to be connected with the growth of the *sāsana* in Ceylon, offering flowers at the same, and at the site of the (later) **Mahā Thūpa,** he described the visits of the Four Buddhas of this *kappa* to Ceylon. On the fourth day he preached the **Anamatagga Sutta** in Nandanavana and helped the king in defining the boundaries of what later became the **Mahāvihāra.** On the fifth day he preached the **Khajjanīya Sutta,** on the sixth the **Gomayapiṇḍī Sutta,** and on the seventh the **Dhammacakkappavattana Sutta.**

[1] Mhv. v. 204 ff.; Dpv. v. 24 f.; Sp. i. 51. [2] Mhv. v. 233; Sp. i. 52.

The *pāsāda* first built for the residence of Mahinda was called **Kāḷapāsāda-pariveṇa.** Other buildings associated with him were the **Suṇhāta-pariveṇa,** the **Dīghacaṅka-pariveṇa,** the **Phalagga-pariveṇa,** the **Therāpassaya-pariveṇa,** the **Marugaṇa-pariveṇa,** and the **Dīghasandasenāpati-pariveṇa.**[3]

Twenty-six days Mahinda stayed in Mahāmeghavana, and on the thirteenth day of the bright half of Āsāḷha, after having preached the **Mahāppamāda Sutta,** he went to **Missakapabbata,** to spend the *vassa.* The king had sixty-eight rock-cells built in the mountain and gave them to the theras on the full-moon day. On the same day Mahinda ordained sixty-two monks, who attained arahantship, at **Tumbarumālaka.** After the full-moon day of Kattika, at the conclusion of the *pavāraṇa* ceremony, Mahinda held a consultation with Devānampiyatissa and sent Sumanasāmaṇera to **Pāṭaliputta** to bring the relics of the Buddha from Dhammāsoka and other relics from Sakka. These relics were brought and placed on the Missakapabbata, which from then onwards was called **Cetiyagiri.** The collar-bone from among the relics was deposited in the **Thūpārāma** (*q.v.*), which was built for the purpose. It was at Mahinda's suggestion that Devānampiyatissa sent an embassy headed by **Mahāarittha** to Asoka, with a request that **Saṅghamittā** should come to Ceylon with a branch of the Bodhi-tree. The request was granted, and Saṅghamittā arrived in Ceylon with the branch. Devānampiyatissa, during the later part of his reign, acting on the advice of Mahinda, built numerous vihāras, each one yojana from the other; among them were **Issarasamaṇaka** and **Vessagiri.**

Mahinda is said to have taught the Commentaries to the Tipiṭaka in the Sinhalese language, after translating them from the Pāli.[4]

The **Samantapāsādikā**[5] mentions a recital held by Mahinda under the presidency of Mahāariṭṭha.

Mahinda continued to live for the first eight years of the reign of **Uttiya,** who succeeded Devānampiyatissa. Then, at the age of sixty, he died on the eighth day of the bright half of Assayuja, in Cetiyagiri, where he was spending the rainy season. His body was brought in procession, with every splendour and honour, to the Mahāvihāra and placed in the **Pañhambamālaka,** where homage was paid to it for a whole week. It was then burnt on a pyre of fragrant wood on the east of the **Therānambandhamālaka,** to the left of the site of the Mahā Thūpa. A cetiya was erected on that spot over half the remains, the other half being distributed in thūpas built on Cetiyagiri and elsewhere. The place of cremation was called *Isibhūmaṅgana,* and there for many centuries were cremated

[1] See *s.v.* for details. [4] Cv. xxxvii. 228 ff. [5] pp. 102 ff.

the remains of holy men who lived within a distance of three yojanas.[6]

Later, King **Sirimeghavaṇṇa** had a life-size image of Mahinda made of gold; this he took to the **Ambatthalacetiya.** For eight days a festival was held in its honour; on the ninth day the image was taken from Ambatthala, carried by the king himself at the head of a large and splendid procession, and placed for three days in **Sotthiyākara-vihāra.** On the twelfth day it was taken with all splendour to Anurādhapura, to the Mahāvihāra, where it was left for three months in the courtyard of the Bodhi-tree. From there it was removed to the inner city and deposited in a magnificent image-house to the south-east of the palace. An endowment was set up for the annual performance of ceremonies in honour of the image, and this custom was continued for many centuries. The image was brought from the inner town to the (Mahā)vihāra on the *pavāraṇa*-day, and every year an offering was made on the thirteenth day.[7]

Dhātusena had the image brought to the place where Mahinda's body was cremated and there held a great festival,[8] while **Aggabodhi I.** set up the image on the banks of the tank called **Mahindataṭa,** and ensured that the special task of carrying the image to the dyke of the tank was the task of the **Taracchas.**[9]

[6] For details of Mahinda see Mhv. xiii.-xx.; Dpv. vii. 57 f., xii., xiii., xiv., xv.; Sp. i. 61, 69 ff., 79 ff., 83 ff., 90 ff., 103, etc.

[7] Cv. xxxvii. 66 ff.

[8] *Ibid.*, xxxviii. 58.

[9] *Ibid.*, xlii. 30.

2. **Mahinda.**—See **Indra** (= **Sakka**).

3. **Mahinda.**—King, father of **Phussa Buddha.**[1] Elsewhere he is called **Jayasena.** See *s.v.* **Phussa.**

[1] AA. i. 165; SA. iii. 4; DhA. i. 84.

4. **Mahinda.**—A king of old, descendant of **Mahāsammata,** and last of a dynasty which ruled at **Rojanagara.** Twelve of his sons and grandsons ruled in **Campā.**[1]

[1] Dpv. iii. 28.

5. **Mahinda I.**—Brother of **Kassapa III.** and king of Ceylon (724-27 A.C.). He refused to be crowned, out of sorrow for the death of his friend **Nīla,** and administered the government as *ādipāda*. He thus came to be known as **Ādipāda Mahinda.** His brother's son, **Aggabodhi,** was his viceroy, while his own son was made ruler of **Dakkhiṇadesa.**

He gave ten cartloads of food to the **Mahāpāli** and would eat nothing without first giving of it to beggars. He built a nunnery for the bhikkhuṇīs (called **Mahindaupassaya**) and gave to it the village of **Nagaragalla.** He also built the **Mahindataṭa-vihāra.**[1]

[1] Cv. xlviii. 26 ff.

6. **Mahinda.**—Son of **Aggabodhi VII.** He was made viceroy, but died young.[1]

[1] Cv. xlviii. 69, 75.

7. **Mahinda.**—Son of **Silāmegha (Aggabodhi VI.)**.[1] Aggabodhi made him senāpati and gave over the government to him. But when Aggabodhi VI. died and **Aggabodhi VII.** came to the throne, Mahinda went to **Mahātittha.** Later, on the death of Aggabodhi VII., Mahinda quelled all disturbances and put the queen in chains because she conspired to kill him. His cousin **Dappula** rose against him, but was defeated after much fighting. Mahinda then married the queen of Aggabodhi VI. and became king as **Mahinda II.,** when a son was born to him. Dappula again rose in revolt, but Mahinda made a treaty with him and gave him part of **Rohaṇa** with the **Gāḷhagangā** as boundary.

Among Mahinda's benefactions was the erection of the **Dāmavihāra-pariveṇa** and the **Sannīratittha-vihāra** in **Pulatthipura,** also the costly **Ratanapāsāda,** containing a golden image of the Buddha. To the **Silāmegha** nunnery Mahinda gave a silver Bodhisatta statue. He had the Abhidhamma recited by the monks of **Hemasāli-vihāra,** and built many shrines and helped those who were poor or in trouble. To the lame he gave bulls and to the Damiḷas horses. He strengthened the weir of the **Kālavāpi.** He reigned for twenty years (772-92 A.C.) and was succeeded by his son **Udaya I.**[2]

[1] Cv. xlviii. 42, 76. [2] *Ibid.*, 83 ff.

8. **Mahinda.**—Son of the **Ādipāda Dāṭhāsīva** of **Rohaṇa.** He quarrelled with his father, took service under **Udaya I.** and married his daughter **Devā.** He was later sent to Rohaṇa, where he drove out his father. His two sons revolted against him, and, with Udaya's help, led an army against him. Mahinda defeated them, but was killed in a fight with another kinsman.[1]

[1] Cv. xlix. 10 ff.; 66 ff.

9. **Mahinda.**—Son of **Udaya I.;** he was, however, known by the name of **Dhammikasilāmegha** and was a very pious man. He gave the income

from the **Geṭṭhumba** Canal to be used in repairs of the **Ratanapāsāda.** He became king as **Mahinda III.** and reigned for four years (797-801 A.C.).[1]

[1] Cv. xlix. 38 ff.

10. **Mahinda.**—Son of **Mahinda III.** When **Aggabodhi IX.** came to the throne, contrary to the laws of succession, Mahinda fled to India.[1] He was afterwards slain by **Sena I.**[2]

[1] Cv. xlix. 84 f. [2] *Ibid.*, l. 4.

11. **Mahinda.**—Younger brother of **Sena I.** and his viceroy. He quelled the rising of **Udaya** against the king, his brother. When the **Paṇḍu** king invaded Ceylon, Mahinda led an army against him, and, on the defeat of his forces, he cut his own throat.[1]

[1] Cv. l. 6, 10, 21 ff.

12. **Mahinda.**—Eldest son of **Kittaggabodhi,** ruler of **Rohaṇa.** He was killed by Kittaggabodhi's sister.[1]

[1] Cv. l. 51.

13. **Mahinda.**—Son of the **Ādipāda Kassapa** and brother of **Sena II.** He married **Tissā** and **Kittī.** He became viceroy under **Sena II.** and ruled in **Dakkhiṇadesa.** Later he was discovered guilty of an intrigue in the king's harem, and fled, unrecognised, with his family, to **Malaya.** Afterwards, however, he regained his honours and continued as viceroy, his daughter **Saṅghā** being married to **Kassapa,** son of Sena II. Mahinda built a temple under the Bodhi-tree, and, in the course of its construction, a workman discovered that one of the beams would harm a branch of the tree. Mahinda, on being informed of this, came and made a *sacca-kiriyā*, as a result of which the branch of the tree straightened itself during the night, leaving the building free. Mahinda also built the **Mahindasena-pariveṇa,** and died in the twenty-third year of Sena's reign.[1] **Ādipāda Kittaggabodhi** was his son.[2]

[1] Cv. l. 59; li. 7, 13, 15 ff., 53 ff. [2] *Ibid.*, 94.

14. **Mahinda.**—Son of **Kassapa V.**, and brother of **Sena II.** and **Saṅghā.** When the **Ādipāda Kittaggabodhi** raised a rebellion in **Rohaṇa** against **Udaya II.**, the latter sent Mahinda to quell it with the help of the general **Vajiragga.** The expedition was completely successful and Kittaggabodhi taken prisoner. Mahinda stayed in **Mahāgāma** and ruḷed over Rohaṇa justly and well. Among his works was the construction of a dam across

the **Mahānadī.**[1] When **Kassapa IV.** became king, Mahinda revolted against him, but the king, through the influence of Mahinda's father, persuaded him to desist. Later, Mahinda returned to **Anurādhapura** at the request of the monks, and, after having married the king's daughter, went back to Rohaṇa, where, evidently, he died.[2]

[1] Cv. li. 99 ff. [2] *Ibid.*, lii. 4 ff.

15. **Mahinda.**—Viceroy of **Sena IV.** and probably his brother. He afterwards became king as **Mahinda IV.** (956-72 A.C.). He married a **Kāliṅga** princess. During his reign, the **Vallabha** king invaded Ceylon, but was defeated by the general **Sena** and entered into a treaty with Mahinda. Mahinda showed great favour to the **Paṃsukulikas** and the **Lābhavāsins** and decreed that the incomes derived from vihāras should not be taxed. His good acts were many. He had a Commentary to the Abhidhamma written by the Thera **Dhammamitta** in the **Sitthagāma-pariveṇa** and the Abhidhamma recited by the Thera **Dāṭhānāga.**

He made great offerings at the **Mahā Thūpa** and started to build the **Candanapāsāda,** where he had preserved the Hair Relic of the Buddha. He restored the temple of the four cetiyas in **Padalañchana** as well as the Temple of the Tooth, the **Dhammasaṅganigeha** and the **Mahāpāli.** He built the **Mahāmallaka** for the **Theravāda** nuns and completed the **Maṇipāsāda.** Mahinda's wife was **Kittī** (*q.v.*), who, herself, engaged in various works. Their son was **Sena (Sena V.)**.[1]

[1] Cv. liv. 1 ff.; Cv. *Trs.* i. 178, n. 2; 179, n. 2; 183, n. 2.

16. **Mahinda.**—Younger brother of **Sena V.** He succeeded Sena as **Mahinda V.** and ruled for ten years at **Anurādhapura** under great difficulties. He was weak and powerless, and the **Kerala** soldiers in his employ mutinied for better salaries. Mahinda escaped to **Rohaṇa** by means of an underground passage, and lived at **Sīdupabbatagāma** with his brother's wife as queen, later marrying his brother's daughter. Their son was **Kassapa,** and afterwards they lived in **Kappagallaka.** In the thirty-sixth year of Mahinda's reign, the **Coḷas,** taking advantage of the discontent in Ceylon, invaded the country, capturing the king, the queen, and all the royal regalia. They ruled for many years with **Pulatthinagara** as base, and Mahinda died in Coḷa after a captivity lasting for twelve years.[1] **Lokitā** and **Devalā** were his maternal cousins.[2]

[1] Cv. lv. 1 ff. [2] *Ibid.*, lvii. 27.

17. **Mahinda.**—Son of **Moggallāna** and **Lokitā** and brother of **Kitti** (afterwards **Vijayabāhu I.**).[1]

[1] Cv. lvii. 42.

18. **Mahinda.**—Son of **Vikkamabāhu II.** and brother of **Gajabāhu.** He fought against **Deva,** general of **Parakkamabāhu I.**, at **Hedillakhaṇḍagāma,** but was defeated, and fled to **Billagāma.** From there he went to **Vallitittha,** and was again defeated. Later he joined **Māṇābharaṇa,** and was sent by him to **Moravāpi,** thence to **Anurādhapura,** where he defeated **Mahālekha-Rakkha** and **Bhaṇḍārapotthakī,** who marched against him. From Anurādhapura, Mahinda proceeded to **Kālavāpi** where, for three months, he fought against **Bhaṇḍārapotthakī Bhūta,** and was finally defeated by him. This is the last we hear of him.[1]

[1] Cv. lxii. 59; lxxii. 46, 82, 123 ff., 176 ff., 191 f., 198 ff.

19. **Mahinda.**—An officer of **Kittisirimegha,** sent by him to fetch the young **Parakkamabāhu.**[1]

[1] Cv. lxvi. 66.

20. **Mahinda.**—A **Lambakaṇṇa** in the **Moriya** district, an officer of **Parakkamabāhu I.** He was a **Nagaragiri,** and was sent by Parakkamabāhu to **Mallavāḷāna,** where he conducted a victorious campaign against Uttararaṭṭha. Later he took **Anurādhapura,** and was one of those responsible for the capture of Gajabāhu at Pulatthipura.[1]

[1] Cv. lxix. 13; lxx. 89, 146 ff.; 158, 199 ff.

21. **Mahinda Mahālekha.**—An officer of **Māṇābharaṇa.** He was defeated by the **Kesadhātu Rakkha** at **Sarogāmatittha** and again by the troops of **Parakkamabāhu I.** at **Janapada.**[1]

[1] Cv. lxxii. 1 ff., 166.

22. **Mahinda.**—A minister and kinsman of **Parakkamabāhu I.** He lived in the palace and erected at **Pulatthipura** a *pāsāda* for the Tooth Relic.[1]

[1] Cv. lxxiii. 124 ff.

23. **Mahinda.**—A man of the **Kuliṅga** clan, whose wife was a cowherd's daughter called **Dīpanī.** He killed **Vijayabāhu II.** and reigned for five days, but was slain by **Kittinissaṅka.**[1]

[1] Cv. lxxx. 15 ff.

24. **Mahinda.**—Son of **Sumanadevī** and **Bodhigutta.** He came among the escort of the Bodhi-tree. **Devānampiyatissa** conferred on him the rank of **Cullajayamahālekhaka.**[1]

[1] Mbv. 169.

Mahindaupassaya.—A nunnery built by **Mahinda I.** The village of **Nagaragalla** was just outside its boundary, and this he gave for its maintenance.[1]

[1] Cv. xlviii. 36.

Mahindaguhā.—The cave occupied by **Mahinda** in the **Cetiyagiri-vihāra.**[1] It was on the **Hatthikucchipabbhāra,** covered by forest, at the entrance to a deep valley.[2]

[1] Mhv. xx. 16; MṬ. 416. [2] Vsm., p. 110.

Mahindataṭa.—A monastery built by **Mahinda I.**[1]

[1] Cv. xlviii. 37.

Mahindataṭavāpi.—A tank built by **Aggabodhi I.** The image of **Mahinda Thera** (*q.v.*) was taken there by the **Taracchas** and set up on its dyke at the time of the Mahinda festival.[1]

[1] Cv. xlii. 29.

Mahindataḷāka.—A tank built by **Parakkamabāhu I.**[1] It is perhaps identical with **Mahindataṭa** (above), in which case the king merely restored it.

Cv. lxxix. 28.

Mahindasena.—A *pariveṇa* built and endowed by **Mahinda,** viceroy of **Sena II.**[1]

[1] Cv. li. 60.

Mahindasenavāsa.—A building erected in the **Uttara-vihāra (Abhayagiri)** by **Saṅghā,** wife of **Sena I.**[1] It was later destroyed, and afterwards restored by **Parakkamabāhu I.**[2]

[1] Cv. l. 79. [2] *Ibid.*, lxxviii. 105.

Mahiyaṅgana.—A locality in the old **Mahānāga** garden, on the banks of the **Mahāvālukagaṅgā.** It was there that the Buddha hovered in the air on his first visit to Ceylon, in order to frighten the **Yakkhas.** Later, **Mahāsumana** built there a shrine seven cubits in diameter, all of sapphire, and containing the hair given to him by the Buddha. After the Buddha's death, **Sarabhū,** a disciple of **Sāriputta,** brought there the collar-bone of the Buddha, which he deposited in the thūpa, increasing the height of the thūpa to twelve cubits. **Uddhacūḷābhaya** raised it to thirty cubits, while **Duṭṭhagāmaṇī,** dwelling there during his campaign against the **Damiḷa Chatta,** increased it to eighty cubits.[1] **Vohārika Tissa** erected a parasol over the thūpa.[2] Attached to the thūpa was a vihāra, near which lived the three **Lambakaṇṇas, Saṅghatissa, Saṅghabodhi** and **Goṭhābhaya.**[3]

In later times, **Sena II.** gave maintenance villages to the vihāra,[4] as did also **Kasssapa IV.**[5] **Vijayabāhu I.** found the vihāra in a bad state of decay and had it restored,[6] while **Parakkamabāhu VI.** carried out repairs to the thūpa.[7] King **Vīravikamma** went from his capital to Mahiyaṅgana, a distance of seven gāvutas on foot, and held a great festival in honour of the thūpa.[8] King **Narindasīha** is mentioned as having visited Mahiyaṅgana three times—once alone and twice with his army—and as having held magnificent festivals in its honour.[9] **Vijayarājasīha** held a festival there,[10] as did **Kittisirirājasīha,** who made a pilgrimage to the spot[11]; he also made arrangements for travellers from Siam to Ceylon to visit the spot and hold celebrations there.[12] **Rājasīha II.** was born in Mahiyaṅgana, while his parents were staying there for protection from their enemies.[13]

1 Mhv. i. 24, 33 ff.; xxv. 7; Cv. *Trs.* i. 154, n. 3.
2 Mhv. xxxvi. 34.
3 *Ibid.*, 58.
4 Cv. li. 74.
5 *Ibid.*, lii. 14.
6 *Ibid.*, lx. 59.
7 *Ibid.*, xci. 29.
8 *Ibid.*, xcii. 17.
9 *Ibid.*, xcvii. 27 ff.
10 *Ibid.*, xcviii. 85.
11 *Ibid.*, xcix. 38.
12 *Ibid.*, c. 125 ff.
13 *Ibid.*, xcv. 12.

Mahilā.—An eminent therī of Ceylon who kept the *dhutaṅgas.*[1]

1 Dpv. xviii. 15.

Mahilādīpa.—An island off the coast of India where the women, who were exiled with **Vijaya,** landed.[1]

1 Mhv. vi. 45.

Mahilāmukha.—The state elephant of **Brahmadatta,** king of Benares. See the **Mahilāmukha Jātaka.**

Mahilāmukha Jātaka (No. 26).—**Brahmadatta,** king of Benares, owned a state elephant, called **Mahilāmukha,** who was gentle and good. One day thieves sat down outside his stable and started talking of their plans for robbery, and murder. Several days in succession this happened, until at last, by dint of listening to them, Mahilāmukha became cruel and began to kill his keepers. The king sent his minister, the Bodhisatta, to investigate the matter. He discovered what had happened, and made good men sit outside the stables who talked of various virtues. The elephant regained his former goodness and gentleness.

The story was related in reference to a monk who was persuaded by a friend to eat at the monastery of **Gayāsīsa,** built for **Devadatta** by **Ajātasattu.** The monk would steal off there at the hour of the meal and then return to **Veḷuvana.** After some time his guilty secret was discovered, and he was admonished by the Buddha. He is identified with Mahilāmukha and the king with **Ānanda.**[1]

[1] J. i. 185-8; see also Giridanta and Manoja Jātakas.

Mahisa Jātaka (No. 278).—The Bodhisatta was born once as a buffalo in **Himavā**. One day, as he stood under a tree, a monkey fouled him, and taking hold of his horn pulled him about. But the buffalo showed no resentment. This happened several times, and on being asked by the spirit of the tree why he endured it, the buffalo answered that it was by virtue of his goodness. Later the monkey tried his games on another buffalo, who killed him.

The story was told in reference to a monkey who, in the same way, fouled an elephant of **Sāvatthi** and escaped unhurt owing to the patience of the elephant. On another day a fierce elephant came from the stables and the monkey was trampled to death.[1]

[1] J. i. 385-7.

Mahisadoṇika.—A village in the **Nakulanagara** district; the birthplace of **Khañjadeva.**[1]

[1] Mhv. xxiii. 77.

Mahisamaṇḍala.—A country, converted by the **Thera Mahādeva,** who preached there the **Devadūta Sutta.**[1]

The country is generally regarded as the modern Mysore. *v.l.* **Mahiṃsamaṇḍala.**[2]

[1] Mhv. xii. 4, 29; Dpv. viii. 5; Sp. i. 63.

[2] But see *J.R.A.S.* 1910, 429 ff., where the author says that **Māhissati** was its capital and that it was an island in the Narbadā River; see also Mhv. *Trs.* 84, n. 5.

Mahisamanta.—Long ago there were thirty-eight kings of this name, previous births of **Isimuggadāyaka Thera.**[1]

[1] Ap. i. 194.

Mahisavatthu.—A place on the **Saṅkheyya** Mountain where **Uttara** is said to have stayed, in **Dhavajālika** (vihāra).[1]

[1] A. iv. 162; AA. ii. 739.

1. **Mahī.**—One of the five great rivers of India, all of which have a common origin.[1] **Aṅguttarāpa** was to the north of the **Mahī.**[2] It is also called **Mahāmahī.**

[1] Vin. ii. 237; A. iv. 101; v. 22; S. ii. 135; v. 38; Mil. 20, 104; Vsm. 10, etc.
[2] SNA. ii. 437 ff.

2. **Mahī.**—A **Laṅkāgiri,** an officer of **Parakkamabāhu I.,** stationed at **Assamaṇḍala-tittha.**[1]

[1] Cv. lxxii. 27.

Mahīpālaraṭṭha.—A district in the **Dakkhiṇadesa** of Ceylon.[1]

[1] Cv. lxix. 8.

Mahummāra, Mahāummāra.—A village in which **Mahinda II.** once occupied an armed camp.[1] Later his son had a hand-to-hand fight there with **Dappula,** defeating him.[2] The queen of **Udaya I.** gave the village for the maintenance of **Jayasenapabbata-vihāra.**[3]

[1] Cv. xlviii. 120. [2] *Ibid.*, 156 [3] *Ibid.*, xlix. 24.

Maheja.—See **Mahejjāghara.**

Mahejjāghara, Mahejjāgharavatthu, Mahejjāgharāsanasālā. A building in **Anurādhapura,** near the west gate. The grounds of the building were laid out by **Paṇḍukābhaya.**[1] **Gajabāhu I.** first erected the **Mahejjāsanasālā.**[2] The Mahāvaṃsa Ṭīkā[3] explains that Mahejavatthu is a shrine (*devaṭṭhāna*) dedicated to the Yakkha **Maheja.**

Mhv. x. 90; xvii. 30. [2] *Ibid.*, xxxv. 122. [3] p. 378.

Mahelanagara.—A Damiḷa stronghold, subdued by **Duṭṭhagāmaṇi** after a four months' siege. Its commander was called **Mahela.**[1] The Mahāvaṃsa Ṭīkā[2] explains that the city lay off the road leading from **Vijitapura** to **Anurādhapura.** It was the king's elephant, **Kaṇḍula,** who led the way thither.

The city erected on the spot where the elephant turned off the main road was called **Nivattagirinagara.**

[1] Mhv. xxv. 48 f. [2] 479 f.

Mahodara.—A Nāga-king who reigned over a kingdom by the sea in Ceylon. His younger sister was married to the Nāga on **Vaḍḍhamānapabbata** and her son was **Cūlodara.** There was a war between uncle and nephew regarding a gem-set throne, and it was to settle this dispute that the Buddha paid his second visit to Ceylon.[1]

[1] Mhv. i. 45 ff.

Mahosadha.—The Bodhisatta born as minister to King **Videha.** For details see the **Mahāummagga Jātaka.**

Māgadha.—The name of a gotta.[1]

[1] J. iii. 339.

Māgadhā.—The people of **Magadha** (*q.v.*).

1. **Māgandiya.**—A brahmin of the **Kuru** country. He had a very beautiful daughter, called **Māgandiyā.** Many men of high station sought her hand, but the brahmin did not consider them worthy. The Buddha, one day, became aware that both Māgandiya and his wife were ready for conversion, so he visited their village. Māgandiya saw him, and, noting the auspicious marks on his body, told him of his daughter and begged him to wait till she could be brought. The Buddha said nothing, and Māgandiya went home and returned with his wife and daughter arrayed in all splendour. On arriving, they found the Buddha had gone, but his footprint was visible, and Māgandiya's wife, skilled in such matters, said that the owner of such a footprint was free from all passion. But Māgandiya paid no attention, and, going a little way, saw the Buddha and offered him his daughter. The Buddha thereupon told them of his past life, his renunciation of the world, his conquest of **Māra,** and the unsuccessful attempts of Māra's very beautiful daughters to tempt him. Compared with them, Māgandiyā was, he said, a corpse, filled with thirty-two impurities, an impure vessel painted without; he would not touch her with his foot. At the end of the discourse, Māgandiya and his wife became *anāgāmins.*[1] It is said that they gave their daughter into the charge of her uncle, **Culla-Māgandiya,** retired from the world, and became arahants.[2]

According to the Aṅguttara Commentary,[3] Māgandiya's village was **Kammāsadamma,** and the Buddha went there on his journey to **Kosambī** at the invitation of **Ghosita, Kukkuṭa** and **Pāvārika.** He turned off the main road to visit Māgandiya. See also **Māgandiya** (2), **Māgandiya Sutta,** and **Māgandiyapañha.**

[1] DhA. iii. 193 ff.; SNA. ii. 542 f.; *cp.* Dvy. 515 ff., where the name is given as Mākandika and he is called a *parivrājaka.* The daughter's name is given as Anūpamā and the wife's Sākalī.

[2] DhA. i. 202.

[3] AA. i. 235. f.

2. **Māgandiya.**—A **Paribbājaka.** The Buddha was once staying in the fire-hut of the brahmin **Bhāradvājaggotta** at **Kammāsadamma** and **Māgandiya** came to the hut. Seeing the grass mat on which the Buddha slept at night, he inquired whose it was, and, on being told, he was very annoyed, calling the Buddha a rigid repressionist (*bhunahu*). Bhāradvāja protested, whereupon Māgandiya offered to repeat his charge to the Buddha's face. The Buddha, aware of this conversation, entered the hut in the evening and had a discussion with Māgandiya, who ended by joining the Order, later becoming an arahant.[1]

Buddhaghosa explains[2] that this Māgandiya was the nephew of **Māgandiya** (1).

[1] M. i. 502 ff.; Mil. 313. [2] MA. ii. 681.

1. **Māgandiya Sutta.**—The conversation between **Māgandiya** and the Buddha after the former had offered the Buddha his daughter in marriage. Māgandiya expresses the view that purity comes from philosophy, from disputations and discussions, learning and austerities. The Buddha denies this, and says that purity comes from inward peace. The sage (*muni*) is a confessor of peace and does not indulge in disputes.[1]

[1] SN. vs. 835-47.

2. **Māgandiya Sutta.**—Records the conversation between the Buddha and the paribbājaka **Māgandiya.** Māgandiya says the Buddha is a repressionist (*bhunahu*) and this the Buddha denies, saying that he teaches only the subjugation of the senses, knowing their origin and their cessation; he has discarded all craving after them and dwells with his heart at peace. He then relates how, in his youth, he had enjoyed the greatest and most luxurious kinds of sensuous pleasures and had renounced them. He could no more crave for them than a leper, cured of his disease, craves for his old sores. Both the Buddha and teachers of other persuasions are convinced that health is the greatest boon and Nibbāna the highest bliss. But the Buddha's conception of health and Nibbāna differs from that of other teachers. Their knowledge is as that of a blind man, taken on trust. Māgandiya listens and is convinced. He enters the Order and becomes an arahant.[1]

[1] M. i. 501-13; Thomas: *op. cit.*, 115.

Māgandiyapañhā.—The name given to the questions asked of the Buddha by the brahmin **Māgandiya.**[1] See **Māgandiya Sutta** (1).

[1] S. iii. 12.

Māgandiyā.—Daughter of the brahmin **Māgandiya** (*q.v.*). When the Buddha rejected her father's offer of marriage with her, her parents joined the Order, giving her in charge of her uncle, **Culla-Māgandiya.** The latter took her to **Udena,** king of **Kosambī,** who made her his chief consort, giving her five hundred ladies-in-waiting. Māgandiyā was incensed against the Buddha for having called her a "vessel of fiḷth," and, when he came to Kosambī, she planned her revenge. Having discovered that Udena's other queen, **Sāmāvatī,** and her companions were in the habit of watching for the Buddha through windows in the walls of their rooms, she told the king that Sāmāvatī and her friends were conspiring to kill him. For some time the king refused to believe this, but when the holes were shown to him, he had them closed up and the windows built higher.

This plan having failed, Māgandiyā hired a slave to revile and abuse the Buddha in the streets. **Ānanda** suggested to the Buddha that they should go elsewhere. The Buddha answered, "I am like the elephant who has entered the fray, I must endure the darts that come upon me." After seven days the abuse ceased. Māgandiyā then persuaded her uncle to send eight live cocks to the palace and sent a page with them to the king's drinking-place. When the king asked what should be done with them, she suggested that Sāmāvatī and her friends should be asked to cook them for him. This the king agreed to do, but the women refused to deprive an animal of its life. Māgandiyā said they should be tested, and sent word by the page that the cocks were to be cooked for the Buddha. The page was bribed to change the live cocks for dead ones on the way, and Sāmāvatī and her companions then cooked them and sent them to the Buddha. But even then the king, though not knowing of the exchange, would not be convinced of Sāmāvatī's disloyalty.

Māgandiyā then obtained a snake from her uncle with its fangs removed. This she inserted in the shell of the flute which Udena carried about, closing the hole with a bunch of flowers. Udena was in the habit of spending a week in turn with each of his three consorts. When he announced his intention of going to Sāmāvatī, Māgandiyā begged of him not to go, saying she had had a dream and feared for his safety. But the king went and Māgandiyā went with him. As he lay asleep with the lute under his pillow she pulled out the bunch of flowers, and the snake lay coiled on his pillow. Māgandiyā screamed and accused Sāmāvatī of designs on the king's life. This time Udena believed her, and placing Sāmāvatī and her friends in a line one behind the other, he sent for his bow, which could only be strung by one thousand men, and shot an arrow at Sāmāvatī's breast. But by the power of her goodness the arrow failed to pierce her. Convinced of her innocence, the king pleaded for her forgiveness and gave her a boon. She chose that the Buddha should be invited to come to the palace every day, but the Buddha would not accept the invitation and sent **Ānanda** in his place.

Once more Māgandiyā conspired with her uncle against Sāmāvatī. They had all the pillars of Sāmāvatī's house wrapt in cloth, soaked in oil, and, when she and her women were inside, the house was set fire to. Sāmāvatī saw the flames spreading and exhorted her women to be self-possessed, and they attained to various fruits of the Path. Udena questioned Māgandiyā very carefully, and became convinced of her share and that of her uncle in the crime. He then sent for all Māgandiya's relations saying that he wished to reward them. He buried them waist-deep in the palace grounds and covered them with straw; the straw was then set fire to, and when it was burnt he had their bodies ploughed with an iron plough. Pieces of flesh were ripped from Māgandiyā's body, fried like cakes in oil, and Māgandiyā was then forced to eat them.[1]

[1] DhA. i. 201 f., 210 ff.; UdA, 383 f.; *cf.* Dvy., 515 ff., where Māgandiyā is called Anūpamā.

1. **Māgha.**—A sage of old.[1]

[1] J. vi. 99.

2. **Māgha.**—A youth of **Rājagaha.** He visited the Buddha at **Gijjhakūṭa** and asked if he would gain greatly by the gifts he made to various people, gifts which were rightly obtained. The Buddha answered that his gifts would bear great fruit. At the end of the Buddha's discourse, Māgha became his follower.[1]

[1] SN. pp. 86 ff.; SNA. ii. 413 ff.

3. **Māgha.**—See **Sakka** and **Magha.**

4. **Māgha.**—A usurper from **Kāliṅga** who came to Ceylon with a band of **Keraḷa** warriors in about 1215 A.C., deposed the reigning king, **Parakkamapaṇḍu II.,** blinded him, and occupied the throne at **Pulatthipura.** Being a bigoted Hindu, he destroyed the Buddhist religious buildings and burnt their books. He persecuted the people in various ways and distributed their land among his warriors. He ruled for twenty-one years, and seems to have been succeeded at Pulatthipura by **Jayabāhu** (*q.v.*).[1] During part of his reign, **Vijayabāhu III.** (*q.v.*) ruled over a portion of Ceylon.[2]

[1] Cv. lxxx. 58 ff.

[2] *Ibid.*, lxxxi. 10 ff.

Māgha Sutta.—Records the conversation between **Māgha** (1) and the **Buddha.**

Māṭambiya.—A *Padhānaghara* built by the Damiḷa **Potthakuṭṭha.** He gave for its maintenance the **Ambavāpi** at **Būkakalla** and the villages of **Tantavāyikacāṭikā** and **Niṭṭhilaveṭṭhi,** together with slaves.[1]

[1] Cv. xlvi. 19 f.; Cv. *Trs.* i. 100, n. 1.

Māṭhara (*v.l.* **Maṭṭhara**).—A parrot belonging to **Mahosadha.** When Mahosadha wished to find out the plans of **Cūḷaṇī Brahmadatta,** he sent Māṭhara to the mynah that lived in Cūḷaṇī's bedchamber. Māṭhara made love to her, pretending that he had come from **Ariṭṭhapura** to ask her to marry him, because his first wife (also a mynah) had been killed by a hawk. He related the stories of **Vāsudeva** and **Jambāvatī** and of **Vaccha** and **Rattavatī,** to prove that husband and wife need not be equal in birth. Having won her heart and discovered Cūḷaṇī's secrets, Māṭhara flew back to Mahosadha.[1] He is identified with **Ānanda.**[2]

[1] J. vi. 418 ff. [2] *Ibid.*, 478.

Māṇava Thera.—He belonged to a rich brahmin family of **Sāvatthi.** When on his way to the park one day, at the age of seven, he saw, for the first time, persons afflicted with old age, disease, and death. These filled him with horror, and he went to the monastery, heard the Buddha preach, and, with his parents' consent, entered the Order. He was called " Māṇava " because he left the world so young.

In the time of **Vipassī Buddha** he was a physiognomist, and, having seen the child, declared that he would certainly become a Buddha, and worshipped him. In subsequent lives he became king many times under the names of **Sammukhāthavika, Paṭhavīdundubhi, Obhāsa, Sadinacchedana, Agginibbāpaka, Vātasama, Gatipacchedana, Ratanapajjala, Padakkamana, Vilokana** and **Girisāra.**[1]

He is evidently identical with **Sammukhāthavika Thera** of the Apadāna.[2]

[1] ThagA. vs. 73; ThagA. i. 162 ff. [2] Ap. i. 158 f.

Māṇavagāmiya, Māṇavagāmika.—A devaputta. He visited the Buddha in the company of **Asama, Sahali, Ninka, Ākoṭaka** and **Veṭambarī,** and while these all spoke in praise of their own teachers, Māṇavagāmiya sang the glories of the Buddha.[1] It is said[2] that in his previous birth he was a body-servant of the Buddha.

[1] S. i. 65, 67; Mil. 242. [2] SA. i. 101.

Māṇicara.—A yakkha chief to be invoked by followers of the Buddha in time of need.[1]

[1] See DA. iii. 970; D. iii. 205; but see **Cara** (2).

1. **Mātaṅga.**—The Bodhisatta born as a caṇḍāla. See the **Mātaṅga Jātaka.**

2. **Mātaṅga.**—A Pacceka Buddha.[1] He was the last of the Pacceka Buddhas and lived near **Rājagaha.** At the last birth of the Bodhisatta the devas, on their way to do him honour, saw Mātaṅga and told him, "Sir, the Buddha has appeared in the world." Mātaṅga heard this as he was issuing from a trance, and, going to Mount **Mahāpapāta** where Pacceka Buddhas die, he passed away.[2]

[1] M. iii. 70; ApA. i. 107. [2] *Ibid.*, 170; SNA. i. 128 f.; Mtu. i. 357.

3. **Mātaṅga.**—A hermit. One day he arrived in Benares and went to a potter's hall for the night. He found the place already occupied by another hermit named **Jātimā,** and was told by the potter that he could only stay there with Jātimā's permission. Jātimā agreed to his staying, but, on finding that Mātaṅga was a caṇḍāla, he wished him to occupy a place apart. During the night Mātaṅga wished to go out, and, not knowing where Jātimā was lying, trod on his chest. When Mātaṅga returned he took the other way with the idea of passing near Jātimā's feet, but meanwhile Jātimā had changed his position, and Mātaṅga again trod on his chest. Jātimā thereupon cursed him, saying that his head would split in seven pieces at sunrise. Mātaṅga thereupon stopped the sun from rising.[1]

The rest of the story is as in the **Mātaṅga Jātaka.** It may be a variety of the same legend. *cp.* also **Nārada** and **Devala.**

[1] SA. ii. 176 f.

4. **Mātaṅga.**—Father of **Mātaṅgaputta** (*q.v.*).

Mātaṅga Jātaka (No. 497).—The Bodhisatta was once born in a Caṇḍāla village outside Benares and was named **Mātaṅga.** One day, when **Diṭṭhamaṅgalikā,** the daughter of a rich merchant, was on her way to the park with a group of friends, she saw Mātaṅga coming towards the city, and thinking the sight inauspicious, washed her eyes with perfumed water and turned back home. Her companions, annoyed at being deprived of their fun, beat Mātaṅga and left him senseless. On recovering consciousness, he determined to get Diṭṭhamaṅgalikā as wife and lay down outside her father's house refusing to move. Seven days he lay thus until her relations, fearing the ignominy of having a caṇḍāla die at their door, gave Diṭṭhamaṅgalikā to him as wife.

Knowing her pride to be quelled by this act, Mātaṅga decided to bring her great honour. He, therefore, retired into the forest and, in seven days, won supernatural power. On his return he told her to proclaim abroad that her husband was not a caṇḍāla but Mahābrahmā, and that seven days later, on the night of the full-moon, he would come to her, breaking through the moon's disk. She did as he said and so it happened. The people thenceforth honoured her as a goddess; the water in which she washed her feet was used for the coronation of kings, and in one single day she received eighteen crores from those who were allowed the privilege of saluting her. Mātaṅga touched her navel with his thumb, and, knowing that she had conceived a son, admonished her to be vigilant and returned to the moon.

The son was born in the pavilion, which the people had constructed for the use of Diṭṭhamaṅgalikā, and was therefore called Maṇḍavya. At the age of sixteen he knew all the Vedas and fed sixteen thousand brahmins daily. On a feast day Mātaṅga came to him, thinking to turn him from his wrong doctrines, but Maṇḍavya failed to recognize him, and had him cast out by his servants, **Bhaṇḍakucchi, Upajjhāya,** and **Upajotiya.** The gods of the city thereupon grew angry and twisted the necks of Maṇḍavya and all the brahmins so that their eyes looked over their shoulders. When Diṭṭhamaṅgalikā heard of this she sought Mātaṅga, who had left his footsteps so that she might know where he was. He asked her to sprinkle on the brahmins water in which were dissolved the leavings of his food; to Maṇḍavya himself was given some of the food. On recovering and seeing the plight of the brahmins, he realized his error. The brahmins recovered, but were shunned by their colleagues; they left the country and went to live in the kingdom of **Mejjha.**

On the bank of the **Vettavatī** lived a brahmin called **Jātimanta,** very proud of his birth. Mātaṅga went thither to humble the pride of Jātimanta and lived higher up-stream. One day he nibbled a tooth-stick and threw it into the river, where, lower down, it got entangled in Jātimanta's hair. He was greatly annoyed and went up-stream, where he found Mātaṅga and told him that, if he stayed there any longer, at the end of seven days his head would split into seven pieces. On the seventh day Mātaṅga stopped the sun from rising. On discovering the cause, the people dragged Jātimanta to Mātaṅga and made him ask forgiveness, falling at Mātaṅga's feet. Jātimanta's head was covered with a lump of clay, which was immersed in the water as the sun rose.

Mātaṅga then went to the kingdom of Mejjha, where the exiled brahmins reported against him to the king, saying that he was a juggler and a mountebank. The king's messengers surprised Mātaṅga as he was eating his food beside a well, and cut off his head. He was born in the Brahma-world. The gods were angry and wiped out the whole kingdom of Mejjha by pouring on it torrents of hot ashes. Before his meeting with Diṭṭhamaṅgalikā the Bodhisatta was a mongoose-tamer (*koṇḍadamaka*).[1]

The story was told in reference to the attempt of King **Udena** (*q.v.*) to torture **Piṇḍolabhāradvāja.** Udena is identified with Maṇḍavya.[2]

[1] But in SNA. i. 186, he is called a *sopākajīvika*.

[2] J. iv. 375-90; the story is found also at SNA. i. 184-93, with alterations in certain details—*e.g.*, for Vettavatī we have Bandhumatī; see also Mil. 123 ff.

Mātaṅgaputta Thera.—The son of **Mātaṅga,** a landowner of **Kosala.** He was idle, and, when rebuked, joined the monks, hoping thus to have an easy life. But one day he heard the Buddha preach, entered the Order, and not long after became an arahant.

In the time of **Padumuttara Buddha** he was a mighty Nāga king, and, seeing the Buddha travelling through the air, he honoured him by giving him his throat-jewel.[1] He is probably identical with **Maṇipūjaka Thera** of the Apadāna.[2]

[1] Thag. vss. 231-3; ThagA. i. 348 ff.

[2] Ap. ii. 413 f.

Mātaṅgārañña.—Another name for **Mejjhārañña** (*q.v.*).[1]

[1] See Mil. 130; MA. ii. 615.

1. "**Mātari**" **Sutta.**—Sometimes a man who would not lie, even for his mother's sake, has been won over by flattery and bribes.[1]

[1] S. ii. 241.

2. "**Mātari**" **Sutta.**—Six things—such as killing his mother, father, etc.—which a man who possesses right view will never do.[1]

[1] A. iii. 439.

Mātali.—The name given to the chariot-driver (*saṅgāhaka*) of **Sakka.** The Mātali of the present age had a son, **Sikhaṇḍhi,** with whom **Bhaddā Suriyavaccasā,** daughter of **Timbarū,** was in love; but later she transferred her affections to **Pañcasikha.**[1] Mātali is Sakka's constant companion and accompanies him everywhere, more as a confidant than as a servant.[2] Thus, he was by Sakka's side in the war against the **Asuras**

[1] D. ii. 268.

[2] See, *e.g.*, the conversation reported at S. i. 221, 224, 234 ff.; and Vv. iv. 9.

and drove his chariot when he fled with his bride **Sujātā.** The chariot is called **Vejayanta-ratha** and is drawn by one thousand Sindh horses.[3] Mātali often accompanied Sakka on his journeys to the world of men, changing his form—*e.g.*, to that of a fish in the **Culladhanuggaha Jātaka,** a brahmin in the **Bilārakosiya Jātaka** and in the **Suddhābhojana Jātaka,** and a big black dog in the **Mahākaṇha Jātaka.** On several occasions he was sent by Sakka to fetch human beings to **Tāvatiṃsa**—*e.g.*, **Guttila, Nimi, Makhādeva** and **Sādhīna**—and he proved an excellent guide, pointing out to the visitors the places of interest passed on the way.[4]

When the Buddha descended from Tāvatiṃsa, after preaching there the Abhidhamma, he was accompanied, on the left, by Mātali, offering celestial scents, garlands and flowers.[5] Both in the Bilārakosiya and the Sudhābhojana Jātakas (*q.v.*) Mātali is spoken of as the son of **Suriya. Ānanda** is said to have been Mātali during several lives[6]; so also **Mahā Kassapa.**[7] In the **Mahāsamaya Sutta,**[8] Mātali is described as a **Gandhabba** chief, while in the **Āṭānāṭiya Sutta**[9] he is mentioned among the chief Yakkhas to be invoked by followers of the Buddha in time of need.

[3] DhA. i. 279 f.; J. i. 202 f.
[4] For details of the incidents mentioned in this paragraph, see *s.v.*
[5] DhA. iii. 226.
[6] See J. i. 206; iv. 180; v. 412; vi. 129.
[7] J. iv. 69.
[8] D. ii. 258.
[9] *Ibid.*, iii. 204.

Mātikaṭṭhakathā.—Another name for the **Kaṅkhāvitaraṇī** (*q.v.*).

Mātikatthadīpanī.—A work on the Abhidhamma, ascribed to **Chapaṭa.**[1]

[1] Gv. 64; Bode, *op. cit.*, 19.

Mātikapiṭṭhaka.—A vihāra in Ceylon, built by the sword-bearer of **Aggabodhi II.**[1]

[1] Cv. xlii. 43.

Mātikā.—A portion of the Vinaya Piṭaka in its arrangement according to *Dhammakkhandhas.*[1]

[1] DA. i. 24.

Mātugāma Saṃyutta.—The thirty-seventh section of the **Saṃyutta Nikāya.**[1]

[1] S. iv. 238-60.

Mātugāma Sutta.—No woman can persistently possess the heart of a man who is influenced by gains and flattery.[1]

[1] S. ii. 234.

Mātuputtika Sutta.—Once a mother and her son—a monk and a nun—spent the rainy season at **Sāvatthi.** They saw much of each other and, in course of time, became guilty of incest. When this was reported to the Buddha, he declared that nothing ensnares the heart of a man as does a woman; she is indeed a noose of **Māra.**[1]

[1] A. iii. 67 f.

Mātuposaka Jātaka (No. 455).—The Bodhisatta was once born as an elephant in the **Himālaya** and looked after his blind mother, who lived near Mount **Caṇḍoraṇa.** One day he met a forester who had lost his way, and, feeling sorry for him, the elephant set him on the right path, carrying him on his back. But the forester was wicked, and, on his return to Benares, told the king about the elephant. The king asked him to fetch the elephant, who, seeing the forester approaching, meekly followed him lest his virtue be impaired. The elephant was received in the city with great pomp and placed in the royal stables as the state elephant, but he would touch no morsel of food. The king enquired into this and learnt of the elephant's blind mother. Thereupon the elephant was set free, and returned to the Himālaya amid the applause of the people. The king built a town near the elephant's dwelling, where he showed him great honour, and later, when, at his mother's death, the elephant went away to the **Karaṇḍaka** monastery to wait on the ascetics there, the king did the same for them.

The story was related in reference to a monk who tended his mother. For details see the **Sāma Jātaka.** **Ānanda** is identified with the king, whose name is given as **Vedeha,** and **Mahāmāyā** with the mother-elephant.[1]

The Dhammapada Commentary[2] calls this the **Mātuposaka-Nāgarāja Jātaka** and gives the name of the elephant as **Dhanapāla.** It was related to the four sons of a brahmin who waited on their aged father. The audience shed floods of tears, so greatly were they moved, and the brahmin and his sons became sotāpannas.

[1] J. iv. 90-5. [2] DhA. iv. 13.

Mātuposaka Sutta.—A brahmin of **Sāvatthi** visits the Buddha and, having told him that he supports his mother with food obtained from begging, asks if his action is worthy. The Buddha declares his action to be very good and one which will bring him birth in heaven.[1] See also the **Sāma Jātaka.**

[1] S. i. 181.

Mātuposaka-Rāma.—See **Rāma.**

Mātulagiri.—A place in **Sunāparanta** where **Puṇṇa Thera** lived for some time.[1]

[1] MA. ii. 1015; SA. iii. 15.

Mātulaṅgaṇa.—A village assigned by **Jeṭṭhatissa III.** to **Mahānāga-vihāra.**[1]

[1] Cv. xliv. 97.

Mātularaṭṭha, Mātulajanapada.—One of the provinces of Ceylon,[1] the modern Mātale. The name is found only in the latest part of the **Cūḷavaṃsa.** In the earlier parts it is called **Mahātila.**[2] Near by is **Āloka-vihāra.**

[1] Cv. xcv. 22; xcvi. 4; xcviii. 65. [2] *E.g.*, *ibid.*, lxvi. 71.

Mātulā.—A village in **Magadha,** where the Buddha stayed and where he preached the **Cakkavattisīhanāda Sutta.**[1]

[1] D. iii. 58.

Mātuluṅgaphaladāyaka Thera.[1]—Evidently identical with **Belaṭṭha-sīsa**[2] or **Surādha**[3] (*q.v.*).

[1] Ap. ii. 446. [2] ThagA. i. 67. [3] *Ibid.*, 255.

1. **Mātuvihāra.**—A vihāra built by King **Saddhātissa.**[1]

[1] Mhv. xxxiii. 9.

2. **Mātuvihāra.**—A vihāra built by the mother of **Gajabāhukagāmaṇī,** on the spot where, in a thicket of flowering *kadambas,* she had met an ascetic rising from a trance of seven days and had given him food which she was taking to her father the brick-worker. As a result of this gift she became the queen of **Vaṅkanāsikatissa.** Later she bought the piece of land for one thousand and built there the vihāra. Gajabāhukagāmaṇī built a stone thūpa connected with it and gave lands to the monks of the vihāra.[1] The full name of this vihāra seems to have been **Rājamātu-vihāra** (*q.v.*).[2]

[1] Mhv. xxxiii. 104 ff., 115 ff. [2] MṬ. 656.

Mātuvelaṅga.—A locality near **Sāmagalla,** where lived **Kupikkalama-hātissa Thera.**[1]

[1] Mhv. xxxiii. 51.

Mādhava.—A Damiḷa chief, ally of **Kulasekhara.**[1]

[1] Cv. lxxvii. 77, 79.

Mādhuraka.—The classifying name for an inhabitant of Madhurā.[1]

[1] *E.g.*, Mil. 331.

1. **Māna.**—Youngest brother and viceroy of **Aggabodhi III. (Sirisaṅghabodhi).** He was governor of **Dakkhiṇadesa.** He was later found guilty of an offence in the women's apartments of the palace and was treacherously killed by the court officers.[1]

[1] Cv. xliv. 84, 123 f.

2. ***Māna.**—Eldest son of **Kassapa II.**[1] His full name was **Mānavamma.** He was very young when his father died, and, when the government fell into the hands of **Dappula I.** and later of **Dāṭhopatissa II.,** he left **Uttaradesa,** where he was living in retirement with his wife **Saṅghā,** and went to **Jambudīpa,** there to take service under the **Pallava** king, **Narasīha.**[2] He won the king's favour and very loyally helped him to defeat the **Vallabha** king. He then raised an army with the help of **Narasīha,** landed in Ceylon, and recovered the kingdom from **Dāṭhopatissa.** But later his army deserted him on hearing tidings of Narasīha's illness and Māna returned once more to Jambudīpa. Some time after he came again to Ceylon with a large army and defeated **Hatthadāṭha,** the reigning king, and his general **Potthakuṭṭha.** In the confusion which followed, Hatthadāṭha was killed and Potthakuṭṭha was poisoned at **Merukandara.** Māna thereupon became king and did many acts of merit, including the erection of the **Padhānarakkha-** and the **Sirisaṅghabodhi-vihāras,** also the **Sepaṇṇi-** and **Sirī-pāsādas.** Māna was a supporter of the **Paṃsukūlins.**[3]

[1] Cv. xlv. 6.
[2] For details see Cv. xlvii. 9 ff., 15 ff.
[3] *Ibid.*, xlvii. 1 ff. Mānavamma reigned *circa* 676-711 A.C.

3. ***Māna** (also called **Mānavamma).**—He was the nephew of **Kassapa II.** and the son of **Dappula I.** Kassapa handed over the kingdom to him at the time of his death, his own children being very young. When Kassapa died, the **Damiḷas** attacked Ceylon, but Māna, with his father's help, repulsed them and crowned his father king. When **Hatthadāṭha** heard of this, he came with a large force and seized the throne under the name of **Dāṭhopatissa II.** Māna went to the Eastern Province, while Dappula returned to **Rohaṇa.** Later, Māna led a rebellion against Dāṭhopatissa and was killed in battle.[1] His mother was the sister of Kassapa II. and the daughter of King **Silāmeghavaṇṇa.**[2]

[1] Cv. xlv. 11 ff.; 52, 77 ff.
[2] Cv. *Trs.* i. 94, n. 1.

4. **Māna.**—Called **Mūlapotthakī.** He was an officer of **Parakkamabāhu I.** and, in one campaign, defeated **Lokagalla Vikkama** at **Mahāgāma.**[1]

[1] Cv. lxxv. 139 f.

---

* Regarding these names, **Māna** and **Mānavamma,** see Cv. *Trs.* i. 192, n. 3.

Mānakapiṭṭhi.—A village in **Rohaṇa,** mentioned in the account of the campaigns of **Parakkamabāhu I.**[1]

[1] Cv. lxxv. 47.

"Mānakāma" Sutta.—The praises spoken of the Buddha by a deva at **Jetavana** regarding his freedom from all vain conceits.[1]

[1] S. i. 4.

Mānaggabodhi.—A monastery built by **Aggabodhi VII.**[1]

[1] Cv. xlviii. 64.

Mānacchidda.—A **Pacceka Buddha.**[1]

[1] M. i. 70; ApA. i. 107.

1. **Mānatthaddha.**—A brahmin of **Sāvatthi** who, because of his great pride respected no one. One day he came upon the Buddha preaching to a large crowd of people and stood near, on one side. The Buddha, seeing him, preached on the vanity of pride; Mānatthaddha understood, and, falling at the Buddha's feet, worshipped him. And then, in answer to his question, the Buddha told him of those to whom respect should be shown, among whom the arahants are perfect. Mānatthaddha became the Buddha's follower.[1]

[1] S. i. 177 f.; *cp.* **Jenta.**

2. **Mānatthaddha.**—A **Pacceka Buddha** mentioned in a nominal list.[1]

[1] M. iii. 71; ApA. i. 107.

Mānatthaddha Sutta.—Records the visit of the brahmin **Mānatthaddha** (*q.v.*) to the Buddha.[1]

[1] S. i. 177 f.

Mānadiṇṇa.—A householder of **Rājagaha.** When he lay ill he was visited by **Ānanda,** to whom he confessed that even in his illness he practised the four *satipaṭṭhānas.* He was quite free from the five *orambhāgiyasaṃyojanā.*[1]

[1] S. v. 178.

Mānadiṇṇa Sutta.—Records the visit of **Ānanda** to **Mānadiṇṇa** (*q.v.*).[1]

[1] S. v. 178.

Mānabhūsaṇa.—See **Mānābharaṇa.**

Mānamatta.—A village, probably in North Ceylon; one of the spots where the **Damiḷas,** under **Māgha** and **Jayabāhu,** set up fortifications.[1]

[1] Cv. lxxxiii. 16.

1. **Mānavamma.**—See **Māna,** Nos. 2 and 3.

2. **Mānavamma.**—Elder brother of **Māna** (**Māna** 2) and son of **Kassapa II.** Once, as he made an incantation, the god **Kumāra** appeared before him, riding his peacock; the bird, finding nothing to drink, flew at Mānavamma's face. He, thereupon, offered the peacock his eye, of which the bird drank. Kumāra promised him the fulfilment of his wish, but he did not aspire to royal power, and retired in favour of his younger brother Māna.[1]

[1] Cv. lvii. 5 ff.

Mānavīramadhurā.—A place in South India mentioned in the account of the campaigns of **Laṅkāpura.**[1]

[1] Cv. lxxvi. 213.

1. **Mānābharaṇa, Mānabhūsaṇa.**—Nephew of **Vijayabāhu I.** His father was king of **Paṇḍu** and his mother, **Mittā,** was Vijayabāhu's sister. He had two brothers, **Kittisirimegha** and **Sirivallabha.** He married **Ratanāvalī,** daughter of Vijayabāhu.[1] When Vijayabāhu died, **Jayabāhu I.** became king and Mānābharaṇa was made viceroy. When the rightful heir, **Vikkamabāhu,** rose in revolt, Mānābharaṇa seized from him **Rohaṇa** and **Dakkhiṇadesa** and lived in **Puṅkhagāma,** under the name of **Vīrabāhu.**[2] He seems to have lived in constant conflict with Vikkamabāhu. Later, when he had already two daughters, **Mittā and Pabhāvatī,** he gave over the government to his ministers and retired from the world. But seven or eight months later he had a dream in the temple of Indra and hurried back to Puṅkhagāma because the dream presaged the birth of a mighty son. This son was **Parakkamabāhu I.**[3]

[1] Cv. lix. 42 ff. [2] *Ibid.*, lxi. 21 ff. [3] *Ibid.*, lxii. 3 ff.

2. **Mānābharaṇa.**—Son of **Sirivallabha** and **Sugalā. Līlāvatī** was his sister.[1] He married **Mittā,** daughter of Mānābharaṇa I., and also her sister, **Pabhāvatī,** and by the latter he had a son, **Kittisirimegha.**[2] Mānābharaṇa reigned in **Rohaṇa** as an independent king.[3] When the throne was captured by **Gajabāhu,** Mānābharaṇa tried several times to wrest it from him, but, failing in these attempts, made an alliance with Gajabāhu through the intervention of the monks; later, however, finding

[1] Cv. lxii. 2. [2] *Ibid.*, lxiv. 19, 23, 24. [3] See *ibid.*, lxvii. 95.

Parakkamabāhu growing in power, he went over to him.[4] When Gajabāhu was captured and detained at **Pulatthinagara,** the soldiers started to pillage the city, despite the orders of Parakkamabāhu. The people were enraged and invited Mānābharaṇa to come. On his arrival at Pulatthipura, he captured Gajabāhu and threw him into a dungeon, seized all the treasures, including the Tooth Relic and Alms-bowl, and took counsel with his mother to kill Gajabāhu. On hearing of this, Parakkamabāhu sent his forces against Mānābharaṇa and defeated the latter's followers at various places. Mānābharaṇa then fled to Rohaṇa, taking with him some of the treasures.[5] From there he again tried to ally himself with Gajabāhu; but the latter did not so desire, though his ministers were in favour of it. Relying on their support, Mānābharaṇa advanced from Rohaṇa. He was, however, severely defeated at **Pūnagāma** and other places and Parakkamabāhu's forces assailed him from all sides. The campaign brought varying success to the opposing armies, and Mānābharaṇa proved a skilful warrior. He was helped by various chieftains and fought bitterly and valiantly to the end,[6] but, as he lay dying, he summoned his children and ministers and counselled them to join Parakkamabāhu. Even after his death his queen **Sugalā** encouraged intrigues against Parakkamabāhu.[7]

[4] Cv. lxx. 179 ff.
[5] *Ibid.*, 255 ff.
[6] For details see *ibid.*, lxxii. 148-309.
[7] *Ibid.*, lxxiv. 29 ff.

3. **Mānābharaṇa.**—A general of **Māgha,** for whose coronation he was responsible.[1]

[1] Cv. lxxx. 73.

4. **Mānābharaṇa.**—A **Damiḷa** chief, ally of **Kulasekhara.**[1]

[1] Cv. lxxvi. 146.

Māpamādakandarā.—A cave, probably not very far from **Rājagaha.** When the Buddha went on tour with the monks, some of the latter accompanied him as far as this cave and then turned back. To such monks the Buddha would say, "*Mā pamajjittha*" (Be not heedless). From this fact the cave took its name.[1]

[1] DhA. ii. 167.

Māyā, Mahāmāyā.—The mother of the **Buddha.**[1] Her father was the Sākyan **Añjana** of **Devadaha,** son of **Devadahasakka,** and her mother **Yasodharā,** daughter of **Jayasena.**[2] **Daṇḍapāṇi** and **Suppabuddha** were

[1] D. ii. 52; see Thomas: *op. cit.*, 25.
[2] Mhv. ii. 17 ff.; elsewhere her father is called **Mahā-Suppabuddha** (ThigA. 141), while the Apadāna (ii. 538) gives the name of her mother as **Sulakkhaṇā.**

her brothers, and **Mahā Pajāpatī** her sister. Both the sisters were married to **Suddhodana** in their youth, but it was not till Māyā was between forty and fifty that the Buddha was born.[3] She had all the qualities necessary for one who was to bear the exalted rank of being the mother of the Buddha: she was not too passionate, she did not take intoxicants, she had practised the *pāramī* for one hundred thousand kappas, and had not, since her birth, violated the five *sīlā*. On the day of her conception she kept her fast, and in her sleep that night she had the following dream: the four **Mahārāja**-gods took her in her bed to **Himavā** and placed her under a *sāla*-tree on *Manosilātala*. Then their wives came and bathed her in the **Anotatta** Lake and clad her in divine robes. They then led her into a golden palace and laid her on a divine couch; there the Bodhisatta, in the form of a white elephant, holding a white lotus in his gleaming trunk, entered into her right side. This was on the day of the Uttarāsāḷhanakkhatta, after a festival lasting seven days, in which she had already taken part.

From the day of her conception she was guarded by the Four Regent Gods; she felt no desire for men, and the child in her womb could be seen from outside. At the end of the tenth month she wished to return to her people in Devadaha, but, on her way thither, she stopped at the *sāla*-grove in **Lumbinī** and there her child was born as she stood holding on to the branch of a *sāla*-tree.[4] Seven days later Māyā died and was reborn as a male in the Tusita-world, under the name of **Māyādevaputta.**[5] The Buddha visited **Tāvatiṃsa** immediately after the performance of the Twin-Miracle at the foot of the **Gaṇḍamba**-tree, on the full-moon day of Āsāḷha, and there, during the three months of the rainy season, the Buddha stayed, preaching the Abhidhamma Piṭaka to his mother (who came there to listen to him), seated on **Sakka's Paṇḍukambala-silāsana,** at the foot of the **Pāricchattaka**-tree. (It is said that, during this time, at certain intervals, the Buddha would return to earth, leaving a seated image of himself in Tāvatiṃsa to continue the preaching while he attended to his bodily needs, begging alms in **Uttarakuru** and eating his food on the banks of **Anotatta,** where **Sāriputta** waited on him and learnt of what he had been preaching to the devas.[6])

The Commentaries[7] state the view, held by some, that had Māyā been alive the Buddha would not have shown such reluctance to bestow ordination on women. This view, says Dhammapāla,[8] is erroneous. It would have made no difference, for it is the *dhammatā* of all Buddhas that women shall be ordained, but subject to certain important re-

[3] VibhA. 278.
[4] J. i. 49 ff.
[5] Thag. vss. 533 f.; ThagA. i. 502.
[6] DhSA. i. 15; DhA. iii. 216 f.
[7] UdA. 276 f.
[8] *Ibid.*

strictions. The mothers of all Buddhas die very soon after the birth of their son, because no other child is fit to be conceived in the same womb as a Buddha.

Māyā is mentioned in several Jātakas as the mother of the Bodhisatta —*e.g.*, in the **Alīnacitta,** the **Kaṭṭhahāri,** the **Kurudhamma,** the **Kosambī,** the **Khaṇḍahāla,** the **Dasaratha,** the **Bandhanāgāra,** the **Mahāummagga,** the **Mātuposaka,** the **Vessantara,** the **Susīma,** the **Somanassa** and the **Hatthipāla.** According to some contexts, after her birth as **Phusatī** in the Vessantara Jātaka, Māyā became one of the daughters of King **Kikī** (*q.v.*).

Māyā's resolve to be the mother of a Buddha was formed ninety-one kappas ago in the time of **Vipassī Buddha.**[9] She was then the elder daughter of King **Bandhumā.** One of the king's vassals sent him a piece of priceless sandalwood and a golden wreath, worth one hundred thousand. The sandalwood the king gave to his elder daughter and the wreath to the younger. The elder powdered the sandalwood and took it in a golden casket to the Buddha. Some of the powder she offered to the Buddha to be rubbed on his body, and the rest she scattered in his cell. It was the sight of the Buddha's golden body that inspired her with the desire to be the mother of such a being. Her sister later became **Uracchadā** (*q.v.*).

[9] J. vi. 480 f.

Māyā Sutta.—Once, **Vepacitti,** ruler of the **Asuras,** was ill. He was visited by **Sakka,** who was requested by the Asuras to heal him. Sakka agreed to do this if Vepacitti would teach him the **Sambaramāyā.** But Vepacitti wished to consult the Asuras on this matter and was advised against it.[1]

[1] S. i. 238.

Māyāgeha.—An officer of **Parakkamabāhu I.,** mentioned in the account of his campaigns. He fought against **Gokaṇṇa** at **Nilagala.** Later, he was in charge of the successful campaign in **Āḷisāra,** and then was stationed in **Ambavana,** where the king confided to him his plan to attack **Pulatthinagara.** In recognition of his services, Parakkamabāhu conferred on him the rank of **Adhikārī.**[1] The last mention made of him[2] is of his being appointed to guard the ford at **Samīrukkha** and crushing there the army of **Gajabāhu.**

[1] Cv. lxx. 83, 162, 170, 191, 278. [2] *Ibid.*, lxxii. 10.

Māyādvāra.—One of the gates of **Pulatthipura.**[1]

[1] Cv. lxxiii. 162.

1. **Māyādhanu.**—The youngest brother of **Bhuvanekabāhu VII.** and father of **Rājasīha I.** He reigned over a part of Ceylon with his capital at **Sītāvaka** (1521-81 A.C.). His reign was marked by a series of severe and fluctuating struggles against his brother and against the Portuguese then in Colombo. He is said to have been succeeded by his son, Rājasīha.[1]

[1] Cv. xciii. 3 ff.; Cv. *Trs.* ii. 224, n. 1; 225, n. 3.

2. **Māyādhanu.**—The name of a district in Ceylon, between the coast and the mountains. Its capital was **Sītāvaka,** founded by **Parakkamabāhu IV.** There was in it a village called **Udakagāma.**[1]

[1] Cv. xc. 100; c. 213; Cv. *Trs.* ii. 209, n. 8.

Māyāvī.—A jackal, for whose story see the **Dabbapuppha Jātaka.** He is identified with **Upananda.**[1]

[1] J. iii. 336.

Māyetti.—A village in Ceylon in the time of **Jeṭṭhatissa III.**[1]

[1] Cv. xliv. 90.

Māyettikassapāvāsa.—A vihāra in Ceylon, to which **Jeṭṭhatissa III.** gifted the village of **Sahannanagara.**[1]

[1] Cv. xliv. 100.

Māra.—Generally regarded as the personification of Death, the Evil One, the Tempter (the Buddhist counterpart of the Devil or Principle of Destruction). The legends concerning Māra are, in the books, very involved and defy any attempts at unravelling them. In the latest accounts, mention is made of five Māras—Khandha-Māra, Kilesa-Māra, Abhisaṅkhāra-Māra, Maccu-Māra and Devaputta-Māra—as shown in the following quotations: *pañcannam pi Māranaṃ vijayato jino* (ThagA. ii. 16); *sabbāmitteh khandhakilesābhisaṅkhāramaccudevaputtasaṅkhāte sabbapaccatthike* (ThagA. ii. 46); *saṅkhepato vā pañcakilesakhandhābhisaṅkhāradevaputtamaccumāre abhañji, tasmā . . . bhagavā ti vuccati* (Vsm. 211). Elsewhere, however, Māra is spoken of as one, three, or four. Where Māra is one, the reference is generally either to the *kilesas* or to Death. Thus: *Mārenāti kilesamārena* (ItvA. 197); *Mārassa visaye ti kilesamārassa visaye* (ThagA. ii. 70); *jetvāna maccuno senaṃ vimokkhena anāvaran ti lokattayābhibyāpanato diyaḍḍhasahassādi-vibhāgato ca vipulattā aññehi avārituṃ paṭisedhetuṃ asakkuṇeyyattā ca maccuno, Mārassa, senaṃ vimokkhena ariyamaggena jetvā* (ItvA. 198); *Mārāsenā ti ettha satte anatthe niyojento māretīti Māro* (UdA. 325); *nihato Māro bodhimūle ti* *vihato samucchinno kilesamāro bodhirukkhamūle* (Netti Cty. 235); *vasaṃ Mārassa gacchatīti kilesamārassa ca sattamārassa* (?) *ca vasaṃ gacchi* (Netti, p. 86); *tato sukhumataram Mārabandhanan ti kilesabandhanaṃ pan' etaṃ tato sukhumataraṃ* (SA. iii. 82); *Māro māro ti maraṇaṃ pucchati, māradhammo ti maraṇadhammo* (SA. ii. 246).

It is evidently with this same significance that the term Māra, in the older books, is applied to the whole of the worldly existence, the five *khandhas*, or the realm of rebirth, as opposed to Nibbāna. Thus Māra is defined at CNid. (No. 506) as *kammābhisaṅkhāravasena paṭisandhiko kandhamāro dhātumāro, āyatanamāro.* And again: *Māro Māro ti bhante vuccati katamo nu kho bhante Māro ti? Rūpaṃ kho, Rādha, Māro, vedanāmāro, saññāmāro, saṅkhāramāro viññāṇam Māro* (S. iii. 195); *yo kho Rādha Māro tatra chando pahātabbo. Ko ca Rādha Māro? Rūpaṃ kho Rādha Māro . . . pe . . . vedanāmāro. Tatra kho Rādha chando pahātabbo* (S. iii. 198); *sa upādiyamāno kho bhikku baddho Mārassa, anupadiyamāno mutto pāpimato* (S. iii. 74); *evaṃ sukhumaṃ kho bhikkhave, Vepacittibandhanaṃ; tato sukhumataraṃ mārabandhanaṃ; maññamāno kho bhikkhave baddho Mārassa, amaññamāno mutto pāpimato* (S. iv. 202); *labhati Māro otāraṃ, labhati Māro ārammaṇaṃ* (S. iv. 85); *santi bhikkhave cakkhuviññeyyarūpā . . . pe . . . tañ ce bhikkhu abhinandati . . . pe . . . ayaṃ vuccati bhikkhave bhikkhu āvāsagato Mārassa, Mārassa vasaṃ gato* (S. iv. 91); *dhunātha maccuno senaṃ naḷāgāraṃ va kuñjaro ti paññindriyassa padaṭṭhānaṃ* (Netti, p. 40); *rūpe kho Rādha sati Māro vā assa māretā vā yo vā pana mīyati. Tasmā he tvaṃ Rādha rūpaṃ māro ti passa māretā ti passa mīyatīti passa . . . ye naṃ evaṃ passanti te sammā passanti* (S. iii. 189); *Mārasaṃyogan ti tebhūmakavaṭṭaṃ* (SNA. ii. 506).

The Commentaries also speak of three Māras: *bodhipallaṅke tiṇṇaṃ Mārāṇaṃ matthakaṃ bhinditvā* (DA. ii. 659); *aparājitasaṅghan ti ajj' eva tayo Māre madditvā vijitasaṅgāṇaṃ matthakaṃ madditvā anuttaraṃ sammāsambodhiṃ abhisambuddho* (CNidA. p. 47). In some cases the three Māras are specified: *yathayidaṃ bhikkhave mārabalan ti yathā idaṃ devaputtamāra-maccumāra-kilesamārāṇaṃ balaṃ appasahaṃ durabhisambhavaṃ* (DA. iii. 858); *maccuhāyino ti maraṇamaccu-kilesamaccu-devaputtamaccu hāyino, tividham pi taṃ maccuṃ hitvā gāmino ti vuttaṃ hoti* (SNA. ii. 508; *cp.* MA. ii. 619); *na lacchati Māro otāraṃ; Māro ti devaputtmāro pi maccumāro pi kilesamāro pi* (DA. iii. 846); but elsewhere five are mentioned—*e.g.*, *ariyamaggakkhaṇe kilesamāro abhisaṅkhāramāro, devaputtamāro ca carimaka-cittakkhaṇe khandhamāro maccumāro ti pañcavidhamāro abhibhūto parājito* (UdA. 216). Very occasionally four Māras are mentioned: *catunnaṃ Mārāṇaṃ matthakaṃ madditvā anuttaraṃ sammāsambodhiṃ abhisambuddho* (MNid. 129); *indakhīlopamo catubbidhamāraparavādigaṇehi akampiyaṭṭhena* (SNA. i. 201); *Mārasenaṃ sasenaṃ abhibhuyyāti kilesasenāya anantasenāya ca sasenaṃ anavasiṭṭhaṃ catubbidhaṃ pi māraṃ abhibhavitvā devaputtamārassā pi hi guṇamāraṇe sahāyabhāvūpagamanato kilesā senā ti vuccanti* (ItvA. 136). The last quotation seems to indicate that the four Māras are the five Māras less Devaputta-Māra.

A few particulars are available about Devaputta-Māra: *Māro ti Vasavattibhūmiyaṃ aññataro dāmarikadevaputto. So hi taṃ ṭhānaṃ atikkamitukāmaṃ janaṃ yaṃ sakkoti taṃ māreti, yaṃ na sakkoti tassa pi maraṇaṃ icchati, tenā Māro ti vuccati* (SNA. i. 44); *Māro yeva pana sattasaṅkhātāya pajāya adhipatibhāvena idha Pajāpatīti adhippeto. So hi kuhiṃ vasatīti? Paranimmittavasavattidevaloke. Tatra hi Vasavattirājā rajjaṃ kāreti. Māro ekasmiṃ padese attano parisāya issariyaṃ pavattento rajjapaccante dāmarikarājaputto viya vasatī ti vadanti* (MA. i. 28); *so hi Māro opapātiko kāmāvacarissaro, kadāci brahmapārisajjānampi kāye adhimuccituṃ samattho* (Jinālaṅkāra Ṭīkā, p. 217).

In view of the many studies of Māra by various scholars, already existing, it might be worth while here, too, to attempt a theory of Māra in Buddhism, based chiefly on the above data. The commonest use of the word was evidently in the sense of Death. From this it was extended to mean "the world under the sway of death" (also called *Māradheyya—e.g.*, A. iv. 228) and the beings therein. Thence, the *kilesas* also came to be called Māra in that they were instruments of Death, the causes enabling Death to hold sway over the world. All Temptations brought about by the *kilesas* were likewise regarded as the work of Death. There was also evidently a legend of a *devaputta* of the **Vasavatti** world, called Māra, who considered himself the head of the *Kāmāvacara*-world and who recognized any attempt to curb the enjoyment of sensual pleasures, as a direct challenge to himself and to his authority. As time went on these different conceptions of the word became confused one with the other, but this confusion is not always difficult to unravel.

Various statements are found in the Piṭakas connected with Māra, which have, obviously, reference to Death, the *kilesas*, and the world over which Death and the *kilesas* hold sway. Thus: Those who can restrain the mind and check its propensities, can escape the snares of Māra (Dhp. Yamaka, vs. 7). He who delights in objects cognisant to the eye, etc., has gone under Māra's sway (S. iv. 91). He who has attachment is entangled by Māra (S. iii. 73). Māra will overthrow him who is unrestrained in his senses, immoderate in his food, idle and weak (Dhp. Yamaka, vs. 8). By attaining the Noble Eightfold Path one can be free from Māra (Dhp. vs. 40). The Saṃyutta (i. 135) records a conversation between Māra and **Vajirā**. She has attained arahantship and tells Māra: "There is no *satta* here who can come under your control; there is no being but a mere heap of saṅkhāras (*suddhasaṅkhārarapuñja*).

The later books, especially the Nidānakathā of the Jātaka Commentary[1] and the Buddhavaṃsa Commentary,[2] contain a very lively and detailed description of the temptation of the Buddha by Māra, as the Buddha sat under the Bodhi-tree immediately before his Enlightenment. These accounts describe how Māra, the devaputta, seeing the Bodhisatta seated, with the firm resolve of becoming a Buddha, summoned all his forces and advanced against him. These forces extended to a distance of twelve yojanas to the front of the Bodhisatta, twelve to the back, and nine each to the right and to the left. Māra himself, thousand-armed, rode on his elephant, **Girimekhala,** one hundred and fifty leagues in height. His followers assumed various fearsome shapes and were armed with dreadful weapons. At Māra's approach, all the various Devas, Nāgas and others, who were gathered round the Bodhisatta singing his praises and paying him homage, disappeared in headlong flight. The Bodhisatta was left alone, and he called to his assistance the ten *pāramī* which he had practised to perfection.

Māra's army is described as being tenfold, and each division of the army is described, in very late accounts,[3] with great wealth of detail. Each division was faced by the Buddha with one *pāramī* and was put to flight. Māra's last weapon was the *Cakkāvudha* (*q.v.*). But when he hurled it at the Buddha it stood over him like a canopy of flowers. Still undaunted, Māra challenged the Buddha to show that the seat on which he sat was his by right. Māra's followers all shouted their evidence that the seat was Māra's. The Buddha, having no other witness, asked the Earth to bear testimony on his behalf, and the Earth roared in response. Māra and his followers fled in utter rout, and the Devas and others gathered round the Buddha to celebrate his victory. The sun set on the defeat of Māra. This, in brief, is the account of the Buddha's conquest of Māra, greatly elaborated in later chronicles and illustrated in countless Buddhist shrines and temples with all the wealth of riotous colour and fanciful imagery that gifted artists could command.

That this account of the Buddha's struggle with Māra is literally true, none but the most ignorant of the Buddhists believe, even at the present day. The Buddhist point of view has been well expressed by Rhys Davids.[4] We are to understand by the attack of Māra's forces, that all the Buddha's "old temptations came back upon him with renewed force. For years he had looked at all earthly good through the medium

[1] J. i. 71 ff.; *cp.* MA. i. 384.

[2] p. 239 f.

[3] Especially in Sinhalese books.

[4] Article on Buddha in the Ency. Brit.

of a philosophy which had taught him that it, without exception, carried within itself the seeds of bitterness and was altogether worthless and impermanent; but now, to his wavering faith, the sweet delights of home and love, the charms of wealth and power, began to show themselves in a different light and glow again with attractive colours. He doubted and agonized in his doubt, but as the sun set, the religious side of his nature had won the victory and seems to have come out even purified from the struggle." There is no need to ask, as does Thomas, with apparently great suspicion,[5] whether we can assume that the elaborators of the Māra story were recording "a subjective experience under the form of an objective reality," and did they know or think that this was the real psychological experience which the Buddha went through? The living traditions of the Buddhist countries supply the adequate answer, without the aid of the rationalists. The epic nature of the subject gave ample scope for the elaboration so dear to the hearts of the Pāli rhapsodists.

The similar story among Jains, as recorded in their commentarial works—*e.g.*, in the *Uttarādhyayana Sūtra*[6]—bears no close parallelism to the Buddhist account, but only a faint resemblance.

There is no doubt that the Māra legend had its origin in the **Padhāna Sutta** (*q.v.*). There Māra is represented as visiting **Gotama** on the banks of the **Nerañjarā**, where he is practising austerities and tempting him to abandon his striving and devote himself to good works. Gotama refers to Māra's army as being tenfold. The divisions are as follows: the first consists of the Lusts; the second is Aversion; the third Hunger and Thirst; the fourth Craving; the fifth Sloth and Indolence; the sixth Cowardice; the seventh Doubt; the eighth Hypocrisy and Stupidity; Gains, Fame, Honour and Glory falsely obtained form the ninth; and the tenth is the Lauding of oneself and the Contemning of others. "Seeing this army on all sides," says the Buddha, "I go forth to meet Māra with his equipage (*savāhanaṃ*). He shall not make me yield ground. That army of thine, which the world of devas and men conquers not, even that, with my wisdom, will I smite, as an unbaked earthen bowl with a stone." Here we have practically all the elements found in the later elaborated versions.

The second part of the Padhāna Sutta[7] is obviously concerned with later events in the life of Gotama, and this the Commentary[8] definitely tells us. After Māra had retired discomfited, he followed the Buddha for seven years, watching for any transgression on his part. But the quest was in vain, and, "like a crow attacking a rock," he left Gotama

[5] Thomas, *op. cit.*, 230.
[6] ZDMG. vol. 49 (1915), 321 ff.
[7] SN. vs. 446 f.; *cf.* S. i. 122.
[8] SNA. ii. 391.

in disgust. "The lute of Māra, who was so overcome with grief, slipped from his arm. Then, in dejection, the yakkha disappeared thence." This lute, according to the Commentary,[9] was picked up by **Sakka** and given to **Pañcasikha.** Of this part of the sutta, more anon.

The Saṃyutta Nikāya[10] also contains a sutta (**"Dhītaro" Sutta**) in which three daughters of Māra are represented as tempting the Buddha after his Enlightenment. Their names are **Taṇhā, Arati** and **Ragā,** and they are evidently personifications of three of the ten forces in Māra's army, as given in the Padhāna Sutta. They assume numerous forms of varying age and charm, full of blandishment, but their attempt is vain, and they are obliged to admit defeat.

Once Māra came to be regarded as the Spirit of Evil all temptations of lust, fear, greed, etc., were regarded as his activities, and Māra was represented as assuming various disguises in order to carry out his nefarious plans. Thus the books mention various occasions on which Māra appeared before the Buddha himself and his disciples, men and women, to lure them away from their chosen path.

Soon after the Buddha's first *vassa*, Māra approached him and asked him not to teach the monks regarding the highest emancipation, he himself being yet bound by Māra's fetters. But the Buddha replied that he was free of all fetters, human and divine.[11] On another occasion Māra entered into the body of **Vetambarī** and made him utter heretical doctrines.[12] The **Māra Saṃyutta**[13] contains several instances of Māra's temptations of the Buddha by assailing him with doubts as to his emancipation, feelings of fear and dread, appearing before him in the shape of an elephant, a cobra, in various guises beautiful and ugly, making the rocks of Gijjhakūṭa fall with a crash; by making him wonder whether he should ever sleep; by suggesting that, as human life was long, there was no need for haste in living the good life; by dulling the intelligence of his hearers.[14] Once, when the Buddha was preaching to the monks, Māra came in the guise of a bullock and broke their bowls, which were standing in the air to dry; on another occasion he made a great din so that the minds of the listening monks were distracted. Again, when the Buddha went for alms to **Pañcasālā,** he entered into the brahmin householders and the Buddha had to return with empty bowl. Māra approached the Buddha on his return and tried to persuade him to try

[9] SNA. ii. 394.

[10] S. i. 124 f.; given also at Lal. 490 (378); *cp.* A. v. 46; see also DhA. iii. 195 f.

[11] Vin. i. 22.

[12] S. i. 67; *cp.* DhA. iv. 141, where Māra asks the Buddha about the further shore. In the **Brahmanimantanika Sutta** (M. i. 326) Māra is spoken of as entering the hearts even of the inhabitants of the Brahma-world.

[13] S. i. 103 ff.

[14] *E.g.*, at **Ekasālā**; *cf.* **Nigrodha** and his fellow Paribbājakas (D. iii. 58).

once more; this was, says the Commentary, a ruse, that he might inspire insult and injury in addition to neglect. But the Buddha refused, saying that he would live that day on *pīti*, like the **Ābhassara** gods.[15] Again, as the Buddha was preaching to the monks on Nibbāna, Māra came in the form of a peasant and interrupted the sermon to ask if anyone had seen his oxen. His desire was to make the cares of the present life break in on the calm and supramundane atmosphere of the discourse on Nibbāna. On another occasion he tempted the Buddha with the fascination of exercising power that he might rescue those suffering from the cruelty of rulers. Once, at the Sākyan village of **Silāvatī,** he approached the monks who were bent on study, in the shape of a very old and holy brahmin, and asked them not to abandon the things of this life, in order to run after matters involving time. In the same village, he tried to frighten **Samiddhi** away from his meditations. Samiddhi sought the Buddha's help and went back and won arahantship.[16] Māra influenced **Godhika** to commit suicide and tried to frighten **Rāhula** in the guise of a huge elephant.[17] In the account of Godhika's suicide,[18] there is a curious statement that, after Godhika died, Māra went about looking for his (Godhika's) consciousness (*paṭisandhicitta*), and the Buddha pointed him out to the monks, " going about like a cloud of smoke." Later, Māra came to the Buddha, like a little child (*khuddadārakavaṇṇī*),[19] holding a *vilva*-lyre of golden colour, and he questioned the Buddha about Godhika. (This probably refers to some dispute which arose among the monks regarding Godhika's destiny.)

The books mention many occasions on which Māra assumed various forms under which to tempt bhikkhunīs, often in lonely spots—*e.g.*, **Āḷavikā, Kisāgotamī, Somā, Vijayā, Uppalavaṇṇā, Cālā, Upacālā, Sisūpacālā, Selā, Vajirā** and **Khemā.**[20] To the same category of temptations belongs a story found in late commentaries[21]: when Gotama was leaving his palace on his journey of Renunciation, Māra, here called **Vasavattī,** appeared before him and promised him the kingdom and the whole world within seven days if he would but turn back. Māra's

[15] The incident is related at length in SA. i. 140 f. and DhA. iii. 257 f.; the Commentaries (*e.g.*, Sp. i. 178 f.) state that the difficulty experienced by the Buddha and his monks in obtaining food at **Verañja** (*q.v.*) was also due to the machinations of Māra.

[16] *Cp.* the story of **Nandiya Thera.** Buddhaghosa says (DA. iii. 864) that when **Sūrambaṭṭha,** after listening to a sermon of the Buddha, had returned home, Māra visited him there in the guise of the Buddha and told him that what he (the Buddha) had preached to him earlier was false. Sūrambaṭṭha, though surprised, could not be shaken in his faith, being a *sotāpanna*.

[17] DhA. iv. 69 f.

[18] S. i. 122.

[19] SA. i. 145.

[20] See *s.v.* for details.

[21] *E.g.*, J. i. 63.

temptations were not confined to monks and nuns; he tempted also lay men and women and tried to lure them from the path of goodness—*e.g.*, in the story of **Dhaniya** and his wife.[22]

Mention is made, especially in the **Mahāparinibbāna Sutta,** of several occasions on which Māra approached the Buddha, requesting him to die; the first of these occasions was under the **Ajapala** Banyan-tree at **Uruvelā,** soon after the Enlightenment, but the Buddha refused to die until the *sāsana* was firmly established. Can it be that here we have the word Māra used in the sense of physical death (*Maccumāra*), and that the occasions referred to were those on which the Buddha felt the desire to die, to pass away utterly, to "lay down the burden"? Perhaps they were moments of physical fatigue, when he lay at death's door, for we know[23] that the six years he spent in austerities made inroads on his health and that he suffered constantly from muscular cramp, digestive disorders and headache. At **Beluvagāma,** shortly before he finally decided to die, we are told[24] that "there fell upon him a dire sickness, and sharp pains came upon him even unto death." But the Buddha conquered the disease by a strong effort of his will because he felt it would not be right for him to die without addressing his followers and taking leave of the Order. Compare with this Māra's temptation of the Buddha at **Maddakucchi** (*q.v.*), when he lay suffering from severe pain after the wounding of his foot by a splinter. It may have been the physical weariness, above referred to, which at first made the Buddha reluctant to take upon himself the great exertions which the propagation of his Dhamma would involve.[25] We know of other arahants who actually committed suicide in order to escape being worried by physical ills—*e.g.*, **Godhika, Vakkali, Channa.** When their suicide was reported to the Buddha, he declared them free from all blame.

Can it be, further, that with the accounts of Māra, as the personification of Evil, came to be mixed legends of an *actual* devaputta, named Māra, also called **Vasavatti,** because he was an inhabitant of the **Paranimmita-vasavatti deva** world? Already in the Aṅguttara Nikāya,[26] Māra is

[22] SNA. i. 44; see also J. i. 231 f.

[23] See *s.v.* **Gotama.** It is true that in the **Mahāsaccaka Sutta** (M. i. 240 ff.), which contains an account of the events leading up to the Enlightenment, there is no mention whatsoever of any temptation by Māra, nor is there any mention of the Bodhi-tree. But to argue from this, that such events did not form part of the original story, might be to draw unwarranted inferences from an *argumentum e silentio.*

[24] D. ii. 99; *cp.* Dvy. 203.

[25] See, *e.g.*, Vin. i. 4 f.

[26] A. ii. 17. Even after the Buddha's death Māra was regarded as wishing to obstruct good works. Thus, at the enshrinement of the Buddha's relics in the **Mahā Thūpa, Indagutta Thera** (by supernatural power) made a parasol of copper to cover the universe, in order that it might ward off the attentions of Māra (Mhv. xxxi. 85).

described (*aggo ādhipateyyānaṃ iddhiyā yasasā jalaṃ*) as the head of those enjoying bliss in the *Kāmāvacara*-worlds and as a *dāmarika devaputta* (as mentioned earlier). Can it be that ancient legends represented him as looking on with disfavour at the activities of the Buddha ? Buddhaghosa says[27] that Māradevaputta, having dogged the Buddha's footsteps for seven years, and having found no fault in him, came to him and worshipped him. Is it, then, possible that some of the conversations which the Buddha is reported to have had with Māra—*e.g.*, in the second part of the **Padhāna Sutta** (see above)—were originally ascribed to a real personage, designated as Māradevaputta, and later confused with the allegorical Māra ? This suggestion gains strength from a remark found in the **Māratajjaniya Sutta,**[28] uttered by **Moggallāna,** that he too had once been a Māra, **Dūsī** by name; **Kāḷā** was his sister's name, and the Māra of the present age was his nephew. In the sutta, Dūsī is spoken of as having been responsible for many acts of mischief, similar to those ascribed to the Māra of Gotama's day. According to the sutta, Māradevaputta was evidently regarded as a being of great power, with a strong bent for mischief, especially directed against holy men. This suggestion is, at all events, worthy of further investigation.[29]

Māra bears many names in Pāli Literature, chief of them being **Kaṇha, Adhipati, Antaka, Namuci** and **Pamattabandhu.**[30] His usual standing epithet is *pāpimā*, but other words are also used, such as *anattha-kāma, ahitakāma*, and *ayogakkhemakāma.*[31]

Māra is called Namuci because none can escape him—*Namucī ti Māro ; so hi attano visayā nikkhamitukāme devamanusse na muñcati antarāyaṃ tesaṃ karoti tasmā Namucī ti vuccati.*[32] In the **Mahāsamaya Sutta,** Namuci is mentioned[33] among the Asuras as being present in the assembly. The Commentary explains[34] that Namuci refers to Māradevaputta and accounts for his presence among the Asuras by the fact that he was temperamentally their companion (*te pi acchandikā abhabbā, ayaṃ pi tādiso yeva, tasmā dhātuso saṃsandamāno āgato*). Buddhaghosa says[35] that Māra is so called because he destroys all those who seek to evade him—

[27] MA. i. 533.

[28] M. i. 333; *cp.* D. iii. 79.

[29] See also **Mārakāyikā-deva.**

[30] MNid. ii. 489; for their explanation see MNidA. 328; another name of Māra was **Pajāpati** (MA. i. 28).

[31] *E.g.*, M. i. 118.

[32] SNA. ii. 386.

[33] D. ii. 259; elsewhere in the same sutta (p. 261 f.) it is said that when all the devas and others had assembled to hear the Buddha preach, Māra came with his "swarthy host" and attempted to blind the assembly with thoughts of lust, etc. But the Buddha, seeing him, warned his followers against him and Māra had to depart unsuccessful. At the end of the sutta, four lines are traditionally ascribed to Māra. They express admiration of the Buddha and his followers. In this sutta Māra is described as *mahāsena* (having a large army).

[34] DA. ii. 689.

[35] SA. i. 133; *cp.* MNidA. 328.

attano visayaṃ atikkamituṃ paṭipanne satte māretī ti Māro; he is called **Vasavatti**[36] because he rules all—*Māro nāma vasavattī sabesaṃ upari vasaṃ vattati.*

[36] SA. i. 158.

Māra Saṃyutta.—The fourth section of the **Saṃyutta Nikāya.**[1]

[1] S. i. 103-27.

Māra Sutta.—**Rādha** asks the Buddha as to what is meant by "*Māra.*" Anything that perishes, says the Buddha, such as body, feeling, perceptions, etc.[1]

[1] S. iii. 188.

Mārakāyika-devā.—A group of devas, evidently followers of **Māra,** who were credited by the **Pubbaseliyas** and **Aparaseliyas** with making arahants discharge seminal fluid, though neither the arahants nor the devas themselves were guilty of physical impurity.[1] One of these devas once entered the bodies of five hundred women, friends of **Visākhā,** made them drunk, and caused them to commit gross improprieties in the presence of the Buddha.[2]

[1] Kvu. 164 f. [2] DhA. iii. 102.

Māragalla.—A village in **Rohaṇa,** the birthplace of the minister **Buddha.**[1] It is probably identical with **Mārapabbata** mentioned in the account of the campaigns of **Mahinda II.**[2]

[1] Cv. lv. 26. [2] *Ibid.*, xlviii. 129.

Māratajjaniya Sutta.—The fiftieth sutta of the **Majjhima Nikāya.** While **Moggallāna** is living at **Bhesakalāvana, Māra** enters his belly and worries him. When Māra realizes that Moggallāna has discovered him and can read his thoughts, he leaves his body and perches on the door bar of his cell. Moggallāna then addresses him and tells him how, once, he himself was a Māra named **Dūsī,** and roused the brahmin householders against **Kakusandha Buddha** and his disciples. As a result of this, Dūsī was born in **Mahāniraya** and suffered great torments. Moggallāna warns Māra against assailing holy men lest he suffer a similar fate. Māra retires discomfited.[1]

[1] M. i. 332-8.

Māradhamma Sutta.—The Buddha admonishes **Rādha** and says that desire for whatever is perishable, such as the body, etc., must be put away.[1]

[1] S. iii. 195, 198, 200.

Mārapāsa Sutta.—Māra's noose encircles him who finds delight in objects, sounds, etc.[1]

[1] S. iv. 91, 92.

Mārapabbata.—See **Māragalla.**

Mālatīpuppha.—A sluice-gate of the **Parakkamasamudda,** from which flowed the **Nīlavāhinī** Canal.[1]

[1] Cv. lxxix. 42.

Mālabhāri, Mālābhāri.—A devaputta, husband of **Patipūjakā** (*q.v.*).

Mālabhī.—See **Piyālī.**

Mālavatthu.—A village in **Rohaṇa,** given by **Dappula** to the **Ariyākari-vihāra.**[1] It is mentioned[2] in the account of the campaigns of **Parakkamabāhu I.**

[1] Cv. xlv. 60. [2] *Ibid.,* lxx. 66.

Mālavallī.—A tank in **Dakkhiṇadesa** repaired by **Parakkamabāhu I.**[1] It was the scene of a battle between the forces of **Gajabāhu** and those of Parakkamabāhu I.[2]

[1] Cv. lxviii. 45. [2] *Ibid.,* lxx. 66.

Mālā.—An eminent Therī of Ceylon.[1]

[1] Dpv. xviii. 30

Mālāgāma.—A village in Ceylon, given by **Kittisirirājasīha** to **Majjhapallivihāra.**[1]

[1] Cv. c. 236; Cv. *Trs.* ii. 293, n. 5.

Mālāgāmatittha.—A ford in the **Mahāvālukagaṅgā,** mentioned in the account of the campaigns of **Parakkamabāhu I.**[1]

[1] Cv. lxii. 50; Cv. *Trs.* i. 323, n. 2.

Mālāgiri.—A mountain in the **Himālaya.** This and other mountains were formed out of the brick collected by the king of Benares as mentioned by **Kāṇāriṭṭha** in the **Bhūridatta Jātaka.**[1]

[1] J. vi. 204, 212.

Mālārāma.—A vihāra in Ceylon, near **Uppalavāpi,** in the time of King **Kuṭakaṇṇa (tissa).** The **Thera Cūlasudhamma** lived there.[1]

[1] VibhA. 452.

Mālāvaratthalī.—A place in **Rohaṇa,** the scene of a campaign of **Parakkamabāhu I.**[1]

[1] Cv. lxxv. 66 ff.

Māliya.—One of the dogs mentioned in the **Pūtimaṃsa Jātaka** (*q.v.*).

Māliyaunna.—A vihāra in Ceylon. **Muṇḍagaṅgā** was a village in its neighbourhood.[1]

[1] MṬ. 605.

Mālunkyā.—See **Māluṅkyāputta.**

Mālunkyāputta Thera (*v.l.* **Māluṅkyaputta, Mālukyaputta).**—Son of the assessor (*agghāpanika*) of the king of **Kosala,** his mother being **Māluṅkyā.** He was religious by nature, and, when he came of age, became a **Paribbājaka.** Later, he heard the Buddha preach and joined the Order, becoming an arahant.[1] The Theragāthā contains two sets of verses attributed to him : one[2] spoken on his visit to his home after attaining arahantship when his people tried to lure him back by a great display of hospitality; the other[3] in connection with a brief sermon preached to him by the Buddha before he became an arahant. The Thera asked the Buddha for a doctrine in brief and the Buddha gave him one. The verses contain a detailed account of the stanzas which were only outlined to him by the Buddha.

In the **Majjhima Nikayā** are two suttas—the **Cūla-Māluṅkyā**[4] and the **Mahā-Māluṅkyā**—both evidently preached before Māluṅkyāputta's attainment of arahantship, because in both the Buddha speaks disparagingly of him.

[1] ThagA. i. 446 f. [2] vv. 399-404.
[3] vv. 794-817; the reference is probably to the **Māluṅkyāputta Sutta** of A. ii. 248; see also S. iv. 72, where the verses are quoted in full. There the monk is described as a broken-down old man, far on in years. The Commentators (AA. ii. 582 and SA. iii. 20) add that he had, in his youth, neglected the detailed teaching and fallen back, through love of possessions.
[4] This is referred to at Mil. 144.

Māluṅkyāputta Sutta.—**Māluṅkyāputta** comes to the Buddha in his old age and asks for a teaching in brief. The Buddha first chides him for having wasted his opportunities, but then tells him of the four ways in which craving arises and the advantages of destroying it.

Mālunkyāputta retires into the forest and shortly after becomes an arahant.[1]

[1] A. ii. 248 f.; AA. ii. 582 f.; *cp.* S. iv. 72 f. and SA. iii. 20 f.

Māluta.—Twenty-nine thousand kappas ago there were eight kings of this name, previous births of **Nalamāliya (Kuṭivihāriya) Thera.**[1]

[1] Ap. i. 144; ThagA. i. 132.

Māluta Jātaka (No. 17).—Once, two friends, a lion and a tiger, lived in a cave. They had a dispute as to which was the cold part of the month, the dark half or the light, and they referred the matter to a hermit (the Bodhisatta), who said that the cold was caused by wind and not by light or darkness.

The story was told to two forest-dwelling monks of **Kosala, Kāḷa** and **Juṇha,** who consulted the Buddha in a similar dispute. The lion and the tiger are identified with the monks.[1]

[1] J. i. 164 ff.

Māḷava.—The name of various Damiḷa chiefs, allies of **Kulasekhara.**[1] Two of them were called **Lambakaṇṇas.**[2]

[1] Cv. lxxvi. 132, 137, 210, 235, 265 ff., 284.

[2] *Ibid.*, lxxvii. 27.

Māhissati.—A city in the Buddha's day, mentioned as lying on the route from **Bāvari's** hermitage to **Sāvatthi.**[1] According to the **Mahāgovinda Sutta**[2] it was the capital of **Avanti** and was founded at the same time as **Campā.** It was probably the capital of Southern Avanti, **Avanti Dakkhiṇāpatha,** the capital of Northern Avanti being **Ujjenī.**[3]

[1] SN. vs. 1011.

[2] D. ii.

[3] In the Māhābhārata (ii. 31, 10) Avanti and Māhiśmati are spoken of as two different countries.

Miga.—A king of the two kappas ago, a previous birth of **Tiṇasanthāradāyaka.**[1]

[1] Ap. i. 122; the name is probably **Migasammata.**

Migaketu.—A king of fifty-four kappas ago, a former birth of **Ṭhitañjaliya Thera.**[1]

[1] Ap. i. 123.

Migagāma-vihāra.—A monastery in Ceylon, founded by **Mahāsena.**[1]

[1] Mhv. xxxvii. 41.

Migajāla Thera.—Son of **Visākhā.** Having heard the Dhamma during his frequent visits to the vihāra, he entered the Order and in due time became an arahant.[1]

The **Saṃyutta Nikāya**[2] contains two discussions which he had with the Buddha; the second was a teaching in brief which he learned before going to the forest to live in solitude prior to his attainment of arahantship.

[1] Thag. 417-22; ThagA. i. 452 f. [2] S. iv. 35 f.

Migajāla Vagga.—The second chapter of the **Saḷāyatana Saṃyutta.**[1]

[1] S. iv. 35-83.

Migajāla Sutta.—**Migajāla** visits the Buddha and asks for a brief teaching before going to live in the forest. The Buddha tells him how lure arises from various objects of the senses and how the destruction of this lure means the destruction of *dukkha.* Migajāla profits by the lesson and, contemplating it, becomes an arahant.[1]

[1] S. iv. 37 f.

"**Migajālena**" **Sutta.**—**Migajāla** visits the Buddha and asks what is meant by an *ekavihārī* (lone-dweller) and what by a *sadutiyavihārī* (living with a mate). The Buddha answers that he who is enamoured of objects of sense is a *sadutiyavihārī,* while the lone-dweller is he who has cast off craving.[1]

[1] S. iv. 35 f.

Migapathaka.—A village near **Macchikāsaṇḍa,** behind **Ambātakavana.** It was a tributary village of **Cittagahapati.**[1]

[1] S. iv. 281; SA. iii. 93

Migapotaka Jātaka (No. 372).—Once a certain ascetic in **Himavā** adopted a young deer which had lost its dam. The deer grew up most comely but died from over-eating. The ascetic lamented greatly till **Sakka** (the Bodhisatta) appeared before him and pointed out the folly of his sorrow.

The story was told in reference to an old man of **Sāvatthi** who looked after a novice very devotedly. The novice died and the old man abandoned himself to grief. The characters in both stories were identical[1]

[1] J. iii. 213-15.

Migalaṇḍika.—An undesirable monk (*samaṇakuttaka*). When the Buddha had once been preaching to the monks in **Mahāvana** in **Vesāli** regarding the defilement and filth of the body, and had retired into solitude, many of the monks, in disgust with their bodies, put an end to their lives. Some of them sought out Migalaṇḍika and asked him to cut off their heads. This he did with a sword, but on his way to the River **Vaggamudā**, to wash his sword, he was seized with remorse. A **Mārakāyika-devatā**, however, appeared before him in the river and assured him he was doing a service to the monks by helping them to commit suicide. This encouraged him, and he put to death many more monks, until the Buddha, discovering the facts, intervened.[1] *v.l.* **Migaladdhika.**

[1] Vin. iii. 68 ff.; Sp. ii. 399 ff.

Migaludda-petavatthu.—The story of a hunter of **Rājagaha** who, acting on the advice of a holy friend, refrained from hunting at night. He was reborn as a *vemānika-peta*. **Nārada** came across him in the course of his wanderings and learnt his story.[1]

[1] Pv. iii. 7; PvA. 204 ff.

Migasammata.—See **Miga.**

Migasammatā.—A river which rose in **Himavā** and flowed into the Ganges. On its bank was the hermitage of **Sāma.**[1]

[1] J. vi. 72, etc.

Migasiṅga.—See **Isisiṅga.**

1. **Migasira Thera.**—He belonged to a brahmin family of **Kosala,** and was so called because he was born under the constellation of Migasira. He acquired brahmin-culture and practised the skull-spell (*chavasīsamanta*), by which he could tap with his nail on the skull and declare the destiny of the dead person. Later, he became a **Paribbājaka** and visited the Buddha at **Sāvatthi.** The Buddha, having been told of his claims to knowledge, gave to him the skull of an arahant. Migasira tried his art, but had to confess himself beaten. The Buddha thereupon offered to teach him if he would join the Order. Migasira agreed and soon became an arahant.

In the time of **Kassapa Buddha** he was a brahmin, and, seeing the Buddha, offered him eight handfuls of *kusa*-grass (? *kusaṭṭha*).[1]

He is evidently identical with **Kusaṭṭhakadāyaka Thera** of the Apadāna.[2] *v.l.* **Migasīsa.**

[1] Thag. vss. 181 f.; ThagA. i. 305 ff.

[2] Ap. ii. 416.

2. **Migasira.**—The name of a constellation and the month named after it.[1]

[1] *E.g.*, DA. i. 241.

Migasālā.—A woman, follower of the Buddha. She was the daughter of **Pūraṇa,** chamberlain of **Pasenadi,** and neice of **Isidatta.**[1] See below.

[1] A. iii. 347; v. 137.

Migasālā Sutta.—**Ānanda** visits **Migasālā** in her home and is questioned as to why both **Pūraṇa** and **Isidatta,** the former of whom was a *brahmacārī* and the latter not, should both have been born in Tusita as sakadāgāmins. Ānanda offers no explanation, but consults the Buddha, who declares that Migasālā is but a foolish, frail, motherly body with none but mother-wit; how, then, could she understand the diversity in the person of man? (*purisapuggalaparopariyañāṇa*). The Buddha then goes on to divide men into six classes according to their capabilities and attainments. It is not possible for anyone, save a Tathāgata, to measure persons.[1]

[1] A. iii. 347 ff.; v. 137 ff.

Migasīsa.—See **Migasira.**

1. **Migācira.**—A park in Benares.[1] This seems to have been an old name for **Isipatana,** for it was the scene of **Sikhī Buddha's** first sermon,[2] and all Buddhas preach their first sermon in the same place.[3]

[1] J. v. 68, 476, 506. [2] BuA. 205. [3] See *s.v.* **Buddha.**

2. **Migācira.**—A park near **Indapatta,** which once belonged to **Dhanañjaya Korabba.**[1] It existed even in the time of the Buddha, for **Raṭṭhapāla Thera** is mentioned as having stayed there.[2]

[1] J. vi. 256. [2] M. ii. 65; MA. ii. 725, 730; but ThagA. ii. 34 calls it **Migājina.**

Migājina.—An ascetic in **Himavā.** When **Mahājanaka** renounced the world he was followed by a great crowd, and there was danger that he might be turned from his noble purpose. **Migājina,** who had just risen from an ecstatic trance, saw this and, appearing before him, exhorted him to be earnest and determined.[1] Migājina is identified with **Moggallāna.**[2]

[1] J. vi. 58 ff. [2] *Ibid.*, 68.

1. **Migāra.**—A seṭṭhi of **Sāvatthi.** His son, **Puṇṇavaddhana,** married **Visākhā.** He was evidently not as rich as Visākhā's father, **Dhanañjaya,**

for he drove back, on the plea that he could not afford to feed them, the large retinue who wished to follow Visākhā to her new home. Migāra was a follower of the **Nigaṇṭhas,** and was angry when Visākhā refused to wait on them and pay homage to them when they visited his house. One day, while Migāra was eating and Visākhā was standing by his side fanning him, a monk stopped at their door, and Visākhā stepped aside that Migāra might see him. But Migāra refused to notice the monk, whom, therefore, Visākhā asked to go away, saying that Migāra ate "stale food" (*purāṇaṃ*). This greatly annoyed Migāra, and he ordered her to be cast out of the house. But the servants refused to carry out his orders, and he was obliged to agree to Visākhā's suggestion that the matter should be submitted for arbitration to the eight householders who had accompanied her to enquire into disputes of such a nature. To them, therefore, Migāra recited a list of all his grievances against Visākhā, but she was adjudged quite innocent and threatened to return at once to her father. Migāra begged her to stay, and she agreed on condition that he invited the Buddha and his monks for a meal. He did so, but the Nigaṇṭhas would not allow him to wait upon the Buddha. At the conclusion of the meal, however, out of politeness, he insisted on listening to the Buddha's sermon, if only from behind a screen. At the conclusion of the sermon Migāra became a *sotāpanna,* and, realizing the error of his ways, adopted Visākhā as his mother by sucking her breast. Henceforth Visākhā was called **Migāramātā.** The next day, again, the Buddha was invited, and Migāra's wife became a *sotāpanna.* From that day onwards they kept open house for the Buddha and his monks. As a token of his gratitude, Migāra held a great festival in honour of Visākhā, to which the Buddha and his monks were invited. She was bathed in sixteen pots of perfumed water and presented with a jewelled ornament called **Ghanamaṭṭhakapasādhana.**[1] It is probably this same Migāra whose grandson was called **Sāḷha** (*q.v.*) **Migāranattā**; but see **Migāra** (2).

[1] DhA. i. 387 ff.; AA. i. 220; MA. i. 471 f.

2. **Migāra.**—Son of **Visākhā** and **Puṇṇavaddhana.**[1]

[1] DhA. i. 407; AA. i. 313 says he was their eldest son.

3. **Migāra Rohaṇeyya.**—A very rich seṭṭhi of **Sāvatthi. Ugga, Pasenadi's** minister, mentions him during a visit to the Buddha and remarks on his immense wealth. But the Buddha reminds him that Migāra's treasure is not real treasure in that it is subject to various dangers—fire, water, kings, robbers, enemies and heirs.[1]

[1] A. iv. 7.

The Commentary says[2] that Migāra was called **Rohaṇeyya** because he was the grandson of **Rohaṇaseṭṭhi.** He is probably to be distinguished from **Visākhā's** son.

[2] AA. ii. 697.

4. **Migāra.**—A general of **Kassapa I.** He built a *pariveṇa* called after himself and a house for an image of **Abhiseka** Buddha, for which he also instituted a festival.[1]

[1] Cv. xxxix. 6, 40.

Migāranattā.—See **Sāḷha.**

Migārapariveṇa.—See **Migāra** (4).

Migāramātā.—A name of **Visākhā.** See **Migāra** (1).

Migāramātupāsāda.—The name given to the monastery erected by **Visākhā Migāramātā** in the **Pubbārāma,** to the east of **Sāvatthi.** It is said[1] that, one day, when Visākhā had gone to the monastery to hear the Dhamma and afterwards attend on the sick monks and novices, she left in the preaching hall her **Mahālatāpasādhana,** and her servant-girl forgot to remove it.[2] Later, on going to fetch it, she found that **Ānanda** had put it away, and Visākhā, being told of this, decided not to wear it again. She had it valued by goldsmiths, who declared that it was worth nine crores and one hundred thousand. She had the ornament put in a cart and sent round for sale. But there was none in Sāvatthi rich enough to buy it, and Visākhā herself bought it back. With the money thus obtained she built the Migāramātupāsāda at the Budha's suggestion. The site for the pāsāda on the Pubbārāma cost nine crores, the buildings costing another nine. While the building was being erected, the Buddha went on one of his journeys and, at Visākhā's request, **Moggallāna** was left to supervise the work with five hundred other monks. Moggallāna made use of his *iddhi*-powers in order to expedite and facilitate the work. The building had two floors with five hundred rooms in each, the whole structure being surmounted by a pinnacle of solid gold, capable of holding sixty water-pots. The work was completed in nine months, and the celebration of its dedication was held on the Buddha's return. These celebrations lasted for four months and cost a further nine crores. On the last day, Visākhā gave gifts of

[1] DhA. i. 410 ff.; SNA. ii. 502; UdA. 158; DA. iii. 860; SA. i. 116, etc.

[2] This incident is referred to at Vin. iv. 161 f., as the cause of the institution of a Vinaya rule.

cloth to the monks, each novice receiving robes worth one thousand. The building was so richly equipped that one of Visākhā's friends, wishing to spread a small carpet, worth one hundred thousand, wandered all over the building, but could find no place of which it was worthy. Ānanda found her weeping in disappointment, and suggested that it should be spread between the foot of the stairs and the spot where the monks washed their feet.

During the last twenty years of his life, when the Buddha was living at Sāvatthi, he divided his time between the **Anāthapiṇḍikārāma** at **Jetavana** and the **Migāramātupāsāda,** spending the day in one place and the night in the other and *vice versâ*.[3]

It is, therefore, to be expected that numerous suttas were preached there; chief among these were the **Aggañña,** the **Uṭṭhāna,** the **Ariyapariyesana,** and the **Pāsādakampana.**[4] It was at Migāramātupāsāda that the **Vighāsa Jātaka** (*q.v.*) was preached, and the Buddha gave permission for the Pāṭimokkha to be recited in his absence.[5]

[3] SNA. i. 336.
[4] See also S. i. 77, 190 (=Ud. vi. 2); iii. 100; v. 216, 222 f.; A. i. 193 f.; ii. 183 f.; iii. 344 f.; (*cp* Thag. vss. 689-704); iv. 204 f., 255, 265, 269; Ud. ii. 9; DhA. iv. 142 f.; iv. 176.
[5] Sp. i. 187.

Migālopa.—See the **Migālopa Jātaka.**

Migālopa Jātaka (No. 381).—The Bodhisatta was once born as a vulture, **Aparaṇṇagijjha,** and lived with his son, **Migālopa,** in **Gijjhapabbata.** Migālopa used to fly much higher than the others in spite of his father's warning, and he was, one day, dashed to pieces by the **Verambha** winds.

The story was told in reference to an unruly monk who is identified with Migālopa.[1]

[1] J. iii. 255 f.; *cp.* **Gijjha Jātaka** (No. 427).

Micchatta Vagga.—The third chapter of the **Magga Saṃyutta.**[1]

[1] S. v. 17-23.

1. **Micchatta Sutta.**—Wrong views, etc., are perversion (*micchatta*) and their opposites perfection (*sammatta*).[1]

[1] S. v. 17.

2. **Micchatta Sutta.**—Perversion leads to failure (*virādhanā*) and not to success (*ārādhanā*) because it encourages evil states.[1]

[1] A. v. 211 f.

Micchā Sutta.—Wrong views arise because of clinging to body, feelings, etc., because they are impermanent.[1]

[1] S. iii. 184.

1. **Micchādiṭṭhi Sutta.**—Wrong view is abandoned by realizing that eye, objects, seeing, etc., are all impermanent.[1]

[1] S. iv. 147.

2. **Micchādiṭṭhi Sutta.**—See **Makkhali Sutta.**

Miṅgala.—One of the great fishes that live in the deep ocean.[1]

[1] J. v. 462.

Miñjavaṭaṃsakiya Thera.—An arahant.—Thirty-one kappas ago he made offerings at the Bodhi-tree of **Sikhī Buddha.** Twenty-six kappas ago he was a king named **Meghabbha.**[1]

[1] Ap. i. 216 f.

Mita.—A stronghold in Ceylon, mentioned in the account of the campaigns of **Parakkamabāhu I.**[1]

[1] Cv. lxx. 134.

Mitacintī.—A fish, see the **Mitacintī Jātaka.**

Mitacintī Jātaka (No. 114).—There were once three fishes—**Bahucintī, Appacintī** and **Mitacintī**—who, one day, left their haunts and came to where men dwelt. Mitacintī (the Bodhisatta) saw the danger and warned the others, but they would not listen and were caught in a net. Then Mitacintī splashed about and deceived the fishermen into thinking that the other two had escaped. They thereupon raised the net by one single corner and the other two escaped.

The story was told in reference to two aged monks who spent the rainy season in the forest, wishing to go to the Buddha. But they constantly postponed their visit, and it was not till three months after the end of the rains that they finally arrived at **Jetavana.** The two monks are identified with the thoughtless fish.[1]

[1] J. i. 426-8.

1. **Mitta.**—A general of King **Eḷāra.** He was governor of a village (**Khaṇḍarājī**) in East Ceylon. **Nandimitta** was his nephew.[1]

[1] Mhv. xxxiii. 4 ff.

2. **Mitta.**—One of the ten sons of **Muṭasīva.**[1]

[1] Dpv. xi. 7.

3. **Mitta.**—A general of **Vijayabāhu IV.** He slew **Vijayabāhu** and occupied the throne for a few days at **Jambuddoṇi,** but the Āriyan mercenaries refused him their allegiance, and their leader, **Ṭhakuraka,** cut off his head as he sat on the throne.[1]

[1] Cv. xc. 2 ff.

4. **Mitta.**—A householder of **Kosambī** who later adopted **Sāmāvatī** (*q.v.*).[1]

DhA. i. 189.

5. **Mitta.**—A common name.[1]

[1] *E.g.*, J. iv. 478; VibhA. 138; MA. i. 454, etc.

1. **Mitta Sutta.**—On what constitutes a good friend in various circumstances.[1]

[1] S. i. 37.

2. **Mitta Sutta.**—A real friend is he who gives what is hard to give, does what is hard to do, and bears what is hard to bear.[1]

[1] A. i. 286.

3. **Mitta Sutta.**—Five qualities which make a man a bad friend.[1]

[1] A. iii. 171.

4. **Mitta Sutta.**—A monk who is a bad friend will never follow the course of training which leads to all destruction of lust and passion.[1]

[1] A. iii. 422.

Mittaka.—See **Mittavindaka.**

Mittakālī, Mittakālikā Therī.—She came of a brahmin family of **Kammāsadamma** and entered the Order after hearing the Buddha preach the **Mahā Satipaṭṭhāna Sutta.** For seven years she showed a craving for gifts and honours and was quarrelsome. But later she put forth effort and became an arahant.[1] Some verses ascribed to her are found in the Therīgāthā.[2]

[1] ThigA. i. 89. [2] vs. 92-6.

Mittagandhaka.—The child of a decayed family of **Sāvatthi.** He sent a companion to offer marriage to a young girl of good family and the question was asked whether he had any friends. The answer being in the negative, he was asked to make some. This advice was taken, and he struck up a friendship with the four gate-keepers and, through them, with the town-warders, astrologers, nobles, commander-in-chief, viceroy, king, various monks and, finally, the Buddha himself. He therefore came to be known as Mittagandhaka (" man of many friends "). The king showed him great favour and arranged for the celebration of his marriage. He received numerous presents from people in the highest circles, and on the seventh day the young married pair invited the Buddha and five hundred monks to a meal at their house. At the end of the meal the Buddha preached to them and they became *sotāpannas*.[1]

The **Mahā Ukkusa Jātaka** was preached in reference to them.

[1] J. iv. 288 f.

1. **Mittavinda Jātaka** (No. 82).[1]—This is evidently a fragmentary continuation of the story of **Mittavinda,** as given in the **Catudvāra Jātaka** (*q.v.*).

[1] J. i. 363.

2. **Mittavinda Jātaka** (No. 104).[1]—An additional fragment of the **Catudvāra Jātaka.**

[1] J. i. 413 f.

3. **Mittavinda Jātaka** (No. 369).[1]—Evidently another fragmentary version of the **Catudvāra Jātaka.**

[1] J. iii. 206 ff.

1. **Mittavindaka.**—A previous birth of **Losaka Tissa.** For his story see the **Losaka Jātaka.**

2. **Mittavindaka.**—The son of a very rich merchant of Benares in the days of **Kassapa Buddha.** His parents were *sotāpannas,* but he himself was an unbeliever. When his father died, Mittavindaka stopped all alms. His mother bribed him one full-moon day to keep the fast by promising him one thousand. He agreed to do this, and went to the monastery where he slept all night, and then, on his return to the house, refused to eat until he was given the money. Later, he wished to go on a trading voyage, and, when his mother tried to restrain him, he knocked her down. In mid-ocean the ship refused to move, and when lots were cast, the lot fell three times on Mittavindaka. He was,

therefore, fastened to a raft and cast adrift. The raft was cast up on an island where lived four female spirits of the dead. They passed seven days in bliss and then seven in woe. He lived with them for the seven days of bliss, and when they departed to do their penance, he left them and came to several islands, one after the other, each one greater than the last in prosperity and in its number of women. He then went on the **Ussada-niraya,** which appeared to him as a most beautiful city. There he saw a man supporting on his head a wheel as sharp as a razor, but to Mittavindaka it appeared as a lotus bloom. He asked the man for it, and insisted on getting it in spite of the man's warning. No sooner had he taken the wheel on his head than he started suffering the torments of hell. At that time the Bodhisatta, born as a deva, was going round Ussada with his retinue. He saw Mittavindaka, who asked him the reason for his torture, and the Bodhisatta told him that it was the result of his greed and his wickedness to his mother. There would be no salvation for him till his sins were expiated.[1]

The story is given in the **Catudvāra Jātaka** (*q.v.*).

Mittavindaka is an example of a person who behaved wrongly towards his mother.[2]

[1] J. iv. 1 ff.; see also **Losaka** and the three **Mittavinda Jātakas** (Nos. 82, 104, 369); *cp.* VibhA. 471; Avadānaś iii. 6 (36) and Dvy. 603 f. [2] AA. ii. 466.

1. **Mittasena Thera.**—One of the eminent monks who took a leading part in the Foundation Ceremony of the **Mahā Thūpa.**[1]

[1] Dpv. xix. 8; MṬ. 525, 527.

2. **Mittasena.**—A thief (? *vīhicora*) who succeeded **Sotthisena** and ruled for one year (432-33 A.C.) at **Anurādhapura,** after the murder of Sotthisena by **Saṅghā.** He restored some of the cetiyas and was slain by the **Damiḷa Paṇḍu.**[1]

[1] Cv. xxxviii. 5 ff.

1. **Mittā** (*v.l.* **Mettā**) **Therī.**—Ninety-one kappas ago, in the time of **Vipassī Buddha,** she was one of the consorts of King **Bandhumā** and won meritorious *kamma* by bestowing food and costly raiment on an arahant Therī. After death she was born in **Tāvatiṃsa** and was wife of the king of the gods thirty times, and then chief queen of twenty kings of men. In this age she belonged to a Sākyan family of **Kapilavatthu** and left the world with **Pajāpatī Gotamī,** winning arahantship soon after.[1]

She is evidently identical with **Ekapiṇḍadāyikā** of the Apadāna.[2]

[1] Thig. vs. 31 f. [2] ThigA. 36 f.; Ap. ii. 515 f.

2. **Mittā.**—Younger sister of **Vijayabāhu I.** She married the **Paṇḍu** king and had three sons, **Mānābharaṇa, Kittisirimegha** and **Sirivallabha.**[1]

[1] Cv. lix. 41; lxi. 1; lxii. 1.

3. **Mittā.**—Daughter of **Mānābharaṇa** (1), her sister being **Pabhāvatī.** She married **Mānābharaṇa,** son of **Sirivallabha.**[1]

[1] Cv. lxii. 3; lxiii. 6; lxiv. 19.

1. **Mittā Sutta.**—Those whom one holds in affection one should admonish and establish in the *satipaṭṭhānas.*[1]

[1] S. v. 189.

2. **Mittā Sutta.**—The same as 1, with the four Ayrian Truths.[1]

[1] S. v. 434.

1. **Mittāmitta Jātaka** (No. 197).—The Bodhisatta was once the leader of a band of ascetics, and one of these, disregarding the advice of the Bodhisatta, adopted a young elephant whose dam was dead. The elephant grew up and slew its master.

The story was told in reference to a monk who took a piece of cloth belonging to his teacher and made with it a shoe-bag, feeling sure that his teacher would not mind. The latter, however, flew into a rage and struck him.[1]

[1] J. ii. 130 ff.

2. **Mittāmitta Jātaka** (No. 473).—The Bodhisatta was once the minister of **Brahmadatta,** king of Benares. At that time the other ministers were slandering a certain courtier who was upright. The king consulted the Bodhisatta, who pointed out to him the marks of a friend as opposed to those of a foe.

The story was told to the king of **Kosala,** who consulted the Buddha on a similar matter.[1]

[1] J. iv. 496 ff.

Mittiṇṇa.—The chief of the monks at **Asokārāma** in **Pāṭaliputta.** He came with one hundred and sixty thousand monks to the Foundation Ceremony of the **Mahā Thūpa.**[1]

[1] Mhv. xxix. 36; Dpv. xix. 5.

1. **"Mittenamaccā" Sutta.**—All intimate friends should be advised on and established in the four limbs of *sotāpatti.*[1]

[1] S. v. 364.

2. "**Mittenamaccā**" **Sutta.**—It is impossible that a *sotāpanna* should be born in hell, or as an animal or a *peta*. Therefore, all those dear to one should be advised on and established in the four limbs of *sotāpatti*.[1]

[1] S. v. 365.

Mithilā.—The capital of the **Videha** country. The city was very ancient, and, according to the **Mahāgovinda Sutta,**[1] was founded by **Mahāgovinda,** steward of King **Reṇu.** It was also the capital of **Makhādeva**[2] and eighty-four thousand of his descendants, and of various other kings mentioned in the Jātakas—*e.g.*, **Aṅgati** (vi. 220), **Ariṭṭhajanaka** (vi. 30), **Nimi** (iii. 378), **Videha** (ii. 39), **Vedeha** (vi. 330), **Mahājanaka** (vi. 30 f.), **Sādhīna** (iv. 355), and **Suruci** (ii. 333). The size of the city is frequently given[3] as seven leagues in circumference, and the **Mahājanaka Jātaka**[4] contains a description of it. There was a road leading from **Campā** to Mithilā, a distance of sixty leagues.[5]

According to the **Mahāummagga Jātaka**[6] there were four market towns at the four gates of Mithilā, each being known by the name of **Yavamajjhaka.** The Buddha is mentioned as having stayed in Mithilā and having preached there the **Makhādeva Sutta**[7] and the **Brahmāyu Sutta.**[8] It was also in Mithilā that the **Therī Vāseṭṭhī**[9] first met the Buddha and entered the Order, after having heard him preach. After the Buddha's death, the **Videhas** of Mithilā claimed a part of his relics and obtained them.[10] In the time of **Koṇāgamana Buddha** Mithilā was the capital of King **Pabbata,** and the Buddha preached there on his visit to the city.[11] **Padumuttara Buddha** preached his first sermon to his cousins, **Devala** and **Sujāta,** in the park of Mithilā,[12] and later to King **Ānanda** and his retinue in the same spot.[13]

Mithilā is generally identified with Janakapura, a small town within the Nepal border, north of which the Mazaffarpur and Darbhaṅga districts meet.[14]

In the Indian Epics[15] Mithilā is chiefly famous as the residence of King Janaka.

[1] D. ii. 235.
[2] M. ii. 72 f.; MṬ. 129; see also Dpv. iii. 9, 29, 35.
[3] *E.g.*, J. iii. 365.
[4] J. vi. 46 f.
[5] *Ibid.*, 32.
[6] *Ibid.*, 330 f.
[7] M. ii. 74.
[8] *Ibid.*, 133.
[9] Thig. vs. 135; see also Dvy., p. 60.
[10] Bu. xxviii. 11.
[11] BuA. 215.
[12] Bu. xi. 23; BuA. 159.
[13] *Ibid.*, 160.
[14] CAGI., p. 718.
[15] *E.g.*, Rāmāyana i. 48.

Mithiluyyāna.—A park in **Mithilā** where **Padumuttara Buddha** preached his first sermon.[1]

[1] Bu. xi. 23; BuA. 159.

Minelapupphiya.—See **Vinelapupphiya.**

Milakkha-Tissa Thera.—He was a hunter who lived near **Gāmeṇḍavāla-vihāra** in **Rohaṇa.** One day he caught an animal, which he killed and cooked, and then was filled with a great thirst. Looking for water, he came to the vihārā. There he drank ten pots of water, but his thirst was still unquenched, and while he complained bitterly about the absence of water, **Cūlapiṇḍapātika-Tissa Thera** heard him and, looking about, saw plenty of water. He then knew that the man's evil kamma was asserting itself. The Elder poured water on to the man's hands, but it all dried up. The man, realizing his wickedness, was greatly alarmed, and went and set all the captive animals free and destroyed his traps. He then returned to the monastery and asked to be ordained. His request was granted, and the Elder gave him a formula for meditation. One day, while learning the **Devadūta Sutta,** Tissa wished to know how fierce were the fires of hell, and his teacher showed him how one spark of the fire could reduce to ashes a whole heap of wood. This induced Tissa to put forth even greater effort, and he spent all his time in meditation living sometimes in **Cittalapabbata-vihāra** and sometimes in **Gāmeṇḍavāla-vihāra** with a wet blanket round his head and his feet in water. Then, one day, he heard a novice recite the **Aruṇavatī Sutta,** and he became an *anāgāmin,* attaining arahantship in due course.[1]

He is quoted as an example of one who strove hard to rid himself of sloth and torpor.[2]

[1] AA. i. 21 f.; SA. ii. 199 f.

[2] *E.g.,* AA. i. 29; SNA. i. 236.

Milakkhā or **Milakkhukā.**—The name given to the people of non-Ariyan origin, the Mlecchas.[1] Their language is called **Milakkhabhāsā.**

[1] *E.g.,* D. iii. 264; A. i. 35, etc.

Milānakkhetta.—A locality near **Pulatthipura,** mentioned in the campaigns of **Parakkamabāhu I.**[1]

[1] Cv. lxx. 176.

Milinda.—King of **Sāgala.** He was born in **Kalasi** in **Alasandā.** His discussions with the Buddhist Elder **Nāgasena** are recorded in the **Milindapañha.** It is said there that the king embraced Buddhism.[1]

[1] For a discussion on the facts connected with Milinda, and his identification with the Baktrian king Menander, see *Questions of King Milinda,* vol. i., introd. xviii ff.

Milindapañha.—Records the conversation between **Milinda** and **Nāgasena.** It is believed[1] that the book was compiled later than the time of the conversation and that many of the recorded conversations are spurious. There is a Sinhalese translation to it, which is called the *Saddharmādāsaya*, written in the eighteenth century by a monk[2] named **Sumaṅgala.**

[1] For a discussion see *Questions of King Milinda*, vol. i. xxv f. [2] P.L.C. 274.

Missakauyyāna.—A park in Ceylon, laid out by **Parakkamabāhu I.**[1]

[1] Cv. lxxix. 7.

Missakapabbata.—A mountain near **Anurādhapura,** the present Mihintale. It was while hunting the elk on this mountain that **Devānampiyatissa** met **Mahinda** who had come with his companions to convert the Island to Buddhism. It was on **Silākūṭa,** the northern peak of the mountain, that Mahinda alighted after his journey through the air from India, while the conversation between him and the king took place in **Ambatthala,** the small tableland below the peak.[1] The mountain later came to be called **Cetiyagiri** (*q.v.*).[2]

[1] Mhv. xiii. 14, 20; xiv. 2; Dpv. xii. 28, 37 ff. [2] Mhv. xvii. 23; Dpv. xiv. 56.

Missakavana.—A park in **Tāvatiṃsa.**[1] It is generally mentioned together with **Nandana, Phārusaka** and **Cittalatāvana.**[2]

[1] J. vi. 278; Dvy. 194, 195; Mtu. ii. 451. [2] *E.g.*, Sp. i. 164; VibhA. 439; Vsm. 425.

Missakā.—A class of devas present at the preaching of the **Mahāsamaya Sutta.**[1]

[1] D. ii. 260.

Missakesī.—A nymph (*accharā*), a heavenly musician of **Sakka.**[1]

[1] Vv. ii. 1; iv. 12; VvA. 93, 96, 211; see also p. 372 f.

Missā.—A name for **Alambūsā** (*q.v.*). The scholast explains[1] that it is a generic name for women—"*purise kilesamissanena missanato.*"

[1] J. v. 153.

Mihiraṇabibbila.—A village in Ceylon, mentioned in the account of the campaigns of **Parakkamabāhu I.**[1]

[1] Cv. lxxii. 232, 271.

Mīḷhaka Sutta.—A monk who prides himself on the fact that he gets great gains is like a dung-beetle who boasts that he is stuffed with dung.[1] *v.l.* **Piḷhaka.**

[1] S. ii. 228.

Mīḷhābhaya Thera.—An Elder who never lay down on a bed to sleep. The people, seeing this, made for him a seat with a back support and a hand support on either side.[1]

[1] Vsm. 79.

Mukkhamattadīpanī, also called **Nyāsa.** A commentary on the **Kaccāyanayoga** by **Vimalabuddhi,** a monk of Ceylon according to some, of Pagan according to others. There is a *ṭīkā* on the work, also ascribed to a **Vimalabuddhi Thera.**[1]

[1] Gv. 60, 70; Bode, *op. cit.*, 21.

Mukhamattasāra.—A Pāli grammatical work by **Sāgara** or **Guṇasāgara** of Pagan, written at the request of King Kyocvā's preceptor. There is a *ṭīkā* on it ascribed to **Sāgara.**[1]

[1] Sās. 76; Gv. 63, 67, 73; Bode, *op. cit.*, 25.

Mukheluvana.—A grove in **Kajaṅgalā.** It was there that the Buddha preached the **Indriyabhāvanā Sutta.**[1] The Commentary explains[2] that the grove consisted of *mukhelu*-trees.

[1] M. iii. 298.   [2] MA. ii. 1028.

Mucala.—A legendary king, descendant of **Mahāsammata.**[1] He was son of **Upacaraka.**[2]

[1] Mhv. ii. 3; Dpv. iii. 6.   [2] MṬ. 125; Mtu. i. 348.

1. **Mucalinda.**—A legendary king, descended from **Mahāsammata.**[1]

[1] Mhv. ii. 3; Dpv. iii. 6; Mtu. i. 348.

2. **Mucalinda.**—A tree near the **Ajapālanigrodha** in **Uruvelā.** The Buddha spent there the third week after the Enlightenment. There was a great shower of rain, and the Nāga-king, **Mucalinda,** of the tree, sheltered the Buddha by winding his coils seven times round the Buddha's body and holding his hood over the Buddha's head.[1] The Udāna Commentary[2] adds that the space provided by the Nāga's coils was

[1] Vin. i. 3; J. i. 80; BuA. 8, 241; Ud. ii. 1; Mtu. iii. 300, 302; DhSA. 35.
[2] 100 f.; see also MA. i. 385.

as large as the floor-space of the **Lohapāsāda** and that the Nāga king lived in a pond near the tree.

3. **Mucalinda.**—A king of long ago. He is mentioned[1] in a list of those who, in spite of having given great gifts, could not penetrate beyond the realms of sense. He is, perhaps, identical with **Mucalinda** (1), and probably also with **Mujalinda** (*q.v.*).

[1] J. vi. 99.

4. **Mucalinda.**—A lake in **Himavā,** north of **Nāḷicapabbata. Vessantara** and his family passed it on their way to **Vaṅkagiri,** which was near by.[1] It seems also to have been called **Sumucalinda.**[2] Mucalinda is one of the great lakes of Himavā.[3]

[1] J. vi. 518, 519, there is a description of it at J. vi. 534 and again at 539.

[2] *E.g.*, J. vi. 582.

[3] D. i. 164.

5. **Mucalinda.**—One of the chief Yakkhas to be invoked by the Buddha's followers in time of need.[1]

[1] D. iii. 205.

6. **Mucalinda.**—A mountain.[1]

[1] Ap. ii. 536 (verse 86).

Mucalinda Vagga.—The second chapter of the Udāna.

Mucelapaṭṭana.—Perhaps a place in Ceylon, where **Vohārika-Tissa** instituted alms.[1] The MṬ.,[2] however, says that Mucelapaṭṭana was a metal boat in which various gifts were kept for distribution among the monks.

[1] Mhv. xxxvi. 30.

[2] p. 661 f.

Mucela-vihāra.—A monastery in **Tissavaḍḍhamānaka,** in the eastern province of Ceylon. It was built by King **Vasabha.**[1]

[1] Mhv. xxxv. 84; MṬ. 652.

Mucelupaṭṭhāna.—A building in **Anurādhapura,** where gifts were regularly distributed to the monks.[1]

[1] Mhv. xxxiv. 65; MṬ. 633.

Mujalinda.—A king of Benares, who went to heaven as a reward for his great sacrifices.[1]

[1] J. vi. 202; *cp.* **Mucalinda** (3).

Muñjakesi.—One of the two horses of King **Udena**; it was capable of travelling one hundred leagues a day.[1]

[1] DhA. i. 196.

Muṭasīva.—King of Ceylon, senior contemporary of **Asoka.** He was the son of **Paṇḍukābhaya** and **Suvaṇṇapālī**, and reigned for sixty years (307-247 B.C.). Among his works was the laying out of the **Mahāmeghavana.** He had ten sons and two daughters,[1] and was succeeded by his second son, **Devānampiyatissa.**[2] The Dīpavaṃsa[3] says that the sixth year of Asoka's reign corresponded with the forty-eighth of Muṭasīva's. Muṭasīva was crowned in the fourteenth year of **Candagutta's** reign and was still alive when the Third Council was held, when **Mahinda** was entrusted with the conversion of Ceylon; but Mahinda waited for the death of Muṭasīva before carrying out his mission.[4]

[1] For their names see Dpv. xi. 5 and xvii. 25 f., also MṬ. 425: **Abhaya, Tissa** (Devānampiyatissa), **Nāga (Mahānāga), Uttiya, Mattābhayā, Mitta, Sīva (Mahāsīva), Asela, Tissa, (Sūratissa), Kira, Anulā** and **Sīvalī.**

[2] Mhv. xi. 1 ff.; xiii. 2.

[3] v. 82; but see xi. 13.

[4] Mhv. xi. 12.

1. **Muṭṭhasati Sutta.**—A woman who is muddle-headed is born in purgatory.[1]

[1] S. iv. 242.

2. **Muṭṭhasati Sutta.**—Five disadvantages to one who falls asleep forgetfully, without self-possession.[1]

[1] A. iii. 251.

Muṭṭhika.—A wrestler employed by **Kaṃsa** to destroy the **Andhakavenhudāsaputtā.** He was, however, killed by **Baladeva** and reborn as a Yakkha in **Kāḷamattiya** Forest. There, later, he ate up Baladeva "like a radish-bulb."[1]

[1] J. iv. 81 f., 88.

Muṭṭhipupphiya Thera.—An arahant. In the time of **Padumuttara Buddha** he was a garland-maker, named **Sudassana,** and offered the Buddha a handful of jasmine-flowers. Thirty-six kappas ago he became king sixteen times under the name of **Devuttara.**[1] He is evidently identical with **Añjanavanīya.**[2]

[1] Ap. i. 142.

[2] ThagA. i. 128.

Muṭṭhipūjaka Thera.—An arahant. In the time of **Sumedha Buddha,** while the Buddha was practising austerities, he gave him a handful of *girinela*-flowers. Twenty-three kappas ago he was a king named **Sunela.**[1]

[1] Ap. i. 201.

Muṇayadha.—A Damiḷa chief, ally of **Kulasekhara.**[1]

[1] Cv. lxxvi. 146; lxxvii. 40.

Muṇika.—A pig; see the **Muṇika Jātaka.**

Muṇika Jātaka (No. 30).—The Bodhisatta was once an ox, called **Mahālohita,** in a householder's family, where his brother **Cullalohita** and he did all the work. When their master's daughter was about to be married, a pig, named **Muṇika,** was brought and fattened on all kinds of luxuries. Cullalohita protested to his brother, but the latter warned him of Muṇika's fate. And soon after Muṇika was killed and eaten.

The origin of the story is the same as that of the **Culla-Nāradakassapa Jātaka.** The passion-tost monk was **Muṇika,** and **Ānanda** the younger ox.[1]

[1] J. i. 196 ff.

Muṇḍa.—A king of **Magadha,** great-grandson of **Ajātasattu** and son of **Anuruddha.** He slew his father and came to the throne, but, in turn, he was slain by his son **Nāgadāsaka.**[1]

It is probably this same king who is referred to in the **Aṅguttara Nikāya.**[2] His wife **Bhaddā** died, and Muṇḍa gave himself up to complete despair and mummified the queen's body. The king's Treasurer, **Piyaka,** consulted the Elder **Nārada** who lived at **Kukkuṭārāma** in **Pāṭaliputta** and persuaded him to visit the king. Nārada preached to him, and his sorrow vanished.

[1] Mhv. iv. 2 ff.; DA. i. 153; Dvy. 369. [2] iii. 57 ff.

Muṇḍakā.—Name of a tribe, mentioned in a nominal list.[1]

[1] Ap. ii. 359.

Muṇḍagaṅgā.—A village in Ceylon, near **Māliyaunna-vihāra.** It was the residence of **Sāliya,** in his previous birth as artisan.[1]

[1] MṬ. 605.

Muṇḍanigama.—A village on the slopes of the Vindhyā Mountains. It was the residence of a lay devotee named **Mahāmuṇḍa.**[1]

[1] DhA. iv. 128.

Muṇḍannānaṅkoṇḍa.—A place in South India, mentioned in the account of the campaigns of **Laṅkāpura.**[1]

[1] Cv. lxxvi. 212.

Muṇḍarāja Vagga.—The fifth chapter of the Pañcaka Nipāta of the **Aṅguttara Nikāya.**[1]

[1] A. iii. 45-62.

Muṇḍikāputta.—See **Maṇḍikāputta.**

Muṇḍikkāra.—A place in South India, mentioned in the account of the campaigns of **Laṅkāpura.**[1]

[1] Cv. lxxvi. 208, 211, 267, 270.

Muṇḍiya.—See **Maṇḍissa.**

Mutiyaṅgana.—A cetiya in Ceylon, erected, according to tradition, by **Devānampiyatissa,**[1] on a spot consecrated by the Buddha on his third visit to Ceylon.[2] It was restored by **Jeṭṭhatissa.** It is, perhaps, the monastery attached to this cetiya that is mentioned in the **Majjhima Commentary**[3] as **Mutiṅgana. Maliyadeva Thera** preached there the **Cha-Cakka Sutta** and sixty monks became arahants.

[1] Codrington, *op. cit.*, 28. [2] Sp. i. 89. [3] MA. ii. 1024.

1. **Muttā.**—A Therī. She belonged to an eminent brahmin family of **Sāvatthi** and, in her twentieth year, renounced the world under **Pajāpatī Gotamī.** One day, as she meditated after her return from the alms round, the Buddha appeared before her in a ray of glory and exhorted her in a verse. Not long after she became an arahant. In the past, she had seen **Vipassī Buddha** walking along the street and, gladdened by the sight, had rushed out and thrown herself at his feet.[1] She is evidently identical with **Saṅkamanattā** of the Apadāna.[2]

[1] Thig. vs. 2; ThigA. 8 f. [2] Ap. ii. 514.

2. **Muttā Therī.**—She was the daughter of **Oghātaka,** a poor brahmin of **Kosala,** and was given in marriage to a hunch-backed brahmin. Unwilling to live with him, she persuaded him to allow her to join the Order, where she soon became an arahant.

In the time of **Padumuttara Buddha,** she showed the Buddha great honour when he visited her city.[1]

[1] Thig. vs. 11; ThigA. 14 f.

3. **Muttā.**—An eminent *upāsikā*, mentioned in a list of such.[1]

[1] A. iv. 347; AA. ii. 791.

Muttākara.—A locality on the sea coast of Ceylon.[1]

[1] Cv. lxx. 63; see. Cv. *Trs.* i. 292, n. 3.

Muttāpabbata.—A village in Ceylon, given by **Kittisirirājasīha** for the maintenance of festivals.[1]

[1] Cv. c. 43.

Mutti Sutta.—The Buddha teaches release and the path thereto.[1]

[1] S. iv. 372.

Muttima.—The Pali name for Martaban in Burma.[1]

[1] Bode, *op. cit.*, 33.

Muttolamba.—Probably the name of a pāsāda repaired by **Dappula.**[1]

[1] Cv. xlv. 56; see Cv. *Trs.* i. 94, n. 4.

Mudita Thera.—He belonged to a commoner's family in **Kosala,** and when, for some reason, his clan fell into disfavour with the king, Mudita ran away into the forest and came across the dwelling of an arahant. The latter, noting Mudita's terror, comforted and ordained him at his request. Mudita practised insight, and refused to leave his cell till he had attained arahantship.

In the time of **Vipassī Buddha** he was a householder and gave the Buddha a bed.[1] He is identified with **Mañcadāyaka** (wrongly called **Sajjhadāyaka**) of the Apadāna.[2]

[1] Thag. vs. 311-14; ThagA. i. 401 f.

[2] Ap. i. 284 f.

Muditā.—Daughter of **Cadakumāra,** son of **Vasavattī.**[1]

[1] J. vi. 134.

Muditā Sutta.—The idea of joy, if cultivated, leads to great bliss.[1]

[1] S. v. 131.

Mudukā.—A celebrated musician or, perhaps, a divine musical instrument.[1]

Vv. ii. 1; VvA. 94, 211; see also p. 372.

Mudupāṇi Jātaka (No. 262).—The Bodhisatta was once king of Benares and had a daughter whom he was anxious to marry to his nephew; later, however, he changed his mind. But the young people loved each other, and the prince bribed the princess's nurse to help her to escape. The nurse, while combing the girl's hair, indicated, by scratching her head with the comb, that the prince was in love with her. The princess then taught her a stanza to be repeated to the prince: "A soft hand, a well-trained elephant and a black rain-cloud will give you what you want." The prince understood, and, one night in the dark fortnight, when his preparations were complete, a heavy shower of rain fell as he waited outside the princess's window, accompanied by a page boy seated on the king's elephant. The princess slept in the same room as the king, and realizing that the prince was there, she told the king that she wished to bathe in the rain. The king led her to the window and bade her step outside on to the balcony while he held her hand. As she bathed she held out the other hand to the prince, who removed the bangles from it and placed them on the page's arm. Then, lifting the boy, he placed him beside her. The princess took his hand and placed it in her father's, who thereupon let go of her other arm. This process was repeated, and, in the darkness, the king took the page inside thinking it was his daughter and put him to sleep while the lovers escaped. When the king discovered the plot, he was convinced of the futility of trying to guard women and forgave the lovers.

The story was related to a monk who became a backslider owing to a woman's wiles. The monk became a *sotāpanna*.[1]

[1] J. ii. 323-7.

Mudulakkhaṇa Jātaka (No. 66).—The Bodhisatta was once an ascetic, named **Mudulakkhaṇa,** of great spiritual attainments, living in the **Himālaya.** On one occasion he came to Benares where the king, pleased with his demeanour, invited him to the palace and persuaded him to live in the royal park. Sixteen years passed, and the king, leaving the city to quell a border rising, left his wife in the care of the ascetic. The next day the ascetic visited the palace, and having seen the queen, fell instantly in love with her, losing all his *iddhi*-powers. When the king returned he found the ascetic disconsolate, and, on learning the reason, agreed to give him the queen. But he secretly asked the queen, whose name was **Mudulakkhaṇā,** to think of some device by which she might save the ascetic's holiness. Together the ascetic and the queen left the palace and went to a house which the king had given them and which was generally used as a jakes. The queen made the ascetic clean the house and fetch water and do one hundred other things. The ascetic then realized his folly and hastened back to the king, surrendering the queen.

The story was related to a young man of rich family belonging to **Sāvatthi,** who became a monk and practised meditation. One day, while going for alms, he saw a beautiful woman and was seized with desire. He thereupon gave up his practices, and was brought before the Buddha, who told him this story, at the conclusion of which he became an arahant. **Ānanda** was the king and **Uppalavaṇṇā** the queen.[1]

[1] J. i. 302-6.

Mudulakkhaṇā.—Queen of **Brahmadata.** See the **Mudulakkhaṇa Jātaka,** above.

Mudusītala.—Thirty-seven kappas ago there were seven kings of this name, previous births of **Ārāmadāyaka Thera.**[1]

[1] Ap. i. 251.

Muddhaphālanapañha.—The name given to the questions formulated by **Bāvarī** (*q.v.*) and given to his disciples to be put to the Buddha. The questions were so named evidently because they were suggested by the curse uttered upon Bāvarī by the brahmin, whose request for money he had to refuse.[1]

[1] AA. i. 183.

Munaru.—A tank restored by **Parakkamabāhu I.**[1]

[1] Cv. lxviii. 48.

Munāli.—The Bodhisatta born as a gamester (*dhutta*). He abused a Pacceka Buddha, named **Surabhi,** and this was why when he became Buddha he was insulted by **Sundarikā.**[1]

[1] Ap. i. 299; UdA. 264.

Muni Sutta.—The twelfth sutta of the **Sutta Nipāta.**[1] It defines the *muni* as one who lives the homeless life, free of encumbrances, devoid of strife and covetousness, firm, self-restrained, thoughtful, and delighting in meditation. He has overcome all obstacles and knows all things. He is as different from a householder as a peacock from a fast-flying swan. According to the Commentary[2] the sutta is a composite one made up of stanzas preached on various occasions; thus, the first four

[1] SN., pp. 35-8. [2] SNA. i. 254 f.

verses had reference to a mother and a son who joined the Order, met frequently, and, owing to their affection for each other, fell into sin.[3] The fifth was in reference to **Upaka's** attainment of *anāgāmiphala*; the sixth to **Khadiravaniya Revata**; the seventh was preached to **Suddhodana** to explain why the Buddha had renounced his luxuries. The ninth was in reference to **Ciñcā's** attempt to malign the Buddha; the tenth was preached to the daughter of a **Sāvatthi** *seṭṭhi*. Seeing a weaver's spindle and reflecting on it, she realized the crookedness of beings and was disgusted with the worldly life. The Buddha, reading her thoughts, appeared before her in a ray of light and preached to her. The eleventh was preached to the seven-year-old daughter of a weaver of **Āḷavi,** who became a *sotāpanna* and died soon after.[4] The twelfth was preached to the brahmin **Pañcaggadāyaka**; and the thirteenth was in reference to a treasurer of Sāvatthi who joined the Order and left it three times; on the fourth time of joining he became an arahant. The fourteenth was in reference to the Buddha's cousin **Nanda,** who was being teased by the monks even after he had attained arahantship. The last was in defence of a monk for whom a hunter conceived a friendship, providing him with alms; the monk was a forest-dweller, and men blamed him saying that he told the hunter of the animals' haunts.

[3] *Cp.* Mātuputtika Sutta.

[4] See DhA. iii. 170 ff.

Mundrannaddhāna.—A place in South India mentioned in the account of the campaigns of **Laṅkāpura.**[1]

[1] Cv. lxxvi. 296.

Muraja.—An inhabitant of **Rammavatī.** He was a previous birth of **Bodhi-upaṭṭhāyaka Thera.**[1]

[1] Ap. i. 194.

Muluttagāma.—A village in **Rohaṇa,** mentioned in the account of the campaigns of **Parakkamabāhu I.**[1]

[1] Cv. lxxv. 6.

Muvarāyara.—A Damiḷa chief, ally of **Kulasekhara.**[1]

[1] Cv. lxxvi. 140, 216.

Musā Vagga.—The first section of the Pācittiya of the Vinaya Piṭaka.

Musā Sutta.—A man guilty of lying is born in purgatory.[1]

[1] A. ii. 83.

Musāvāda Sutta.—Few are they that abstain from lying, many they that do not.[1]

[1] S. v. 469.

Musīla.—See **Mūsila.**

Muhunnaruggāma.—A village which formed a stronghold of the **Coḷas** in the time of **Vijayabāhu I.**[1]

[1] Cv. lviii. 42.

Mūgapakkha.—Another name for **Temiyakumāra,** son of the king of **Kāsi.** See the **Mūgapakkha Jātaka.**

Mūgapakkha Jātaka (No. 538).—Also called **Temiya Jātaka. Candādevī,** wife of the king of **Kāsi,** had, to her great grief, no son. **Sakka's** throne was heated by her piety, and he persuaded the Bodhisatta, then in **Tāvatiṃsa,** to be born as her son. The Bodhisatta reluctantly agreed. Great were the rejoicings over his birth. He was called **Temiya** because on the day of his birth there was a great shower throughout the kingdom and he was born wet. When he was one month old, he was brought to the king, and, as he lay in his lap, he heard grievous sentences passed on some robbers brought before the king. Later, as he lay in bed, Temiya recollected his past births and remembered how he had once reigned for twenty years as king of Benares, and, as a result, had suffered in **Ussada-niraya** for twenty thousand years. Anguish seized him at the thought of having to be king once more, but the goddess of his parasol, who had once been his mother, consoled him by advising him to pretend to be dumb and incapable of any action. He took this advice, and for sixteen years the king and queen, in consultation with the ministers and others, tried every conceivable means of breaking his resolve, knowing him to be normal in body. But all their attempts failed, and at last he was put in a chariot and sent with the royal charioteer, **Sunanda,** to the charnel-ground, where he was to be clubbed to death and buried. At the queen's urgent request, however, Temiya was appointed to rule over Kāsi for one week before being put to death, but the enjoyment of royal power did not weaken his resolve. The charioteer, under the influence of Sakka, took Temiya to what he considered to be the charnel-ground and there, while Sunanda was digging the grave, Temiya stole up behind him and confided to him his purpose and his resolve to lead the ascetic life. Sunanda was so impressed by Temiya's words that he immediately wished to become an ascetic himself, but Temiya desired him to inform his parents of what had happened. When the king and queen heard Sunanda's news, they went with all their retinue to Temiya's hermitage and there, after hearing Temiya preach, they all became ascetics. The inhabitants of the three kingdoms adjacent to Benares followed their example, and great was the number of ascetics. Sakka and **Vissakamma** provided shelter for them. The crowds who thus flocked together were called the **Mūgapakkha-samāgama.** With the death of **Malayamahādeva Thera** (*q.v.*) came the end of those who participated in this great collection of ascetics.

Temiya's parents are identified with the parents of the Buddha, Sunanda with **Sāriputta,** and the goddess of the parasol with **Uppalavaṇṇā.** The story was told in reference to the Buddha's Renunciation.[1] It is often referred to[2] as giving an example of the Bodhisatta's great determination. The **Dhammika Sutta** (*q.v.*) mentions **Mūgapakkha** in a list of teachers of old.

[1] J. vi. 1-30; the story of Temiya is also given in **Temiyacariyā** in Cyp. iii. 6.
[2] *E.g.*, BuA. 51.

Mūgasenāpati-vihāra.—A monastery in Ceylon built by **Aggabodhi I.** who gave for its maintenance the village of **Lajjaka.**[1]

[1] Cv. xlii. 22.

Mūla.—A minister of King **Vaṭṭagāmaṇi.** He built the **Mūlavokāsa-vihāra.**[1]

[1] Mhv. xxxix. 89; Dpv. xix. 18, 19.

1. **Mūla Sutta.**—When a man is overcome by gains and flattery, the root of good kamma is extirpated in him.[1]

[1] S. ii. 240.

2. **Mūla Sutta.**—See **Mūlaka Sutta.**

Mūlaka Sutta.—The Buddha tells the monks that, should they be questioned by followers of other religions, they should answer that all things have desire (*chanda*) as their root. They originate in attention, they are caused by contact, their confluence is feeling, concentration is their chief state—of all things, emancipation is the most precious.[1]

[1] A. v. 106 f.= A. iv. 338, where it is called Mūla Sutta.

Mūlakadeva.—See **Alakadeva.**

Mūlaṭikā.—A sub-Commentary on the Abhidhamma Piṭaka written by **Ānanda Thera** of Ceylon.[1] It was so called because it was the first of the ṭīkās.[2] The *anuṭīkā* on this is called the **Līnatthavaṇṇanā.**[3]

[1] Gv. 60, 69; Svd. 1217. [2] Sās. 33. [3] Gv. 60.

Mūladeva.—A robber, mentioned as having great power.[1]

[1] MA. ii. 688; DA. i. 89.

Mūlanāgasenāpati-vihāra.—A monastery in Ceylon round which **Vohārakatissa** built a wall.[1]

[1] Mhv. xxxvi. 35.

Mūlapariyāya Jātaka (No. 245).—The Bodhisatta was once a brahmin teacher of great fame. Among his pupils were five hundred brahmins, versed in the three Vedas, who thought they knew as much as their teacher. The Bodhisatta, aware of this, gave them a riddle to solve: " Time consumes all, even itself, but who can consume the all-consumer ?" For a whole week they tried to find a solution and then owned defeat. The Bodhisatta rebuked them, saying that they had holes in their ears but no wisdom. Their pride was quelled, and from that time they honoured their teacher.

The story was told in reference to some monks to whom the **Mūlapariyāya Sutta** was preached. The disciples are the same in both cases.[1]

[1] J. ii. 259-262.

Mūlapariyāya Sutta.—The first sutta of the **Majjhima Nikāya.** It was preached in the **Subhagavana** in **Ukkaṭṭhā,** and is claimed as striking the keynote of the entire doctrine of the Buddha (*sabbadhammamūlapariyāya*). In the sutta the Buddha explains various contemporary systems of philosophy and points out the differences between these and his own system. It also deals with the theory of the soul and of Nibbāna.[1]

The Commentary states[2] that the five hundred monks to whom the sutta was addressed found no pleasure in listening to it. The Buddha, realizing this, preached to them the **Mūlapariyāya Jātaka** (*q.v.*).[3] Their pride was thereby vanquished, and they begged the Buddha for a subject of meditation. Later, when the Buddha was away journeying, staying at the **Gotamaka-cetiya** in **Vesāli,** he preached to them the **Gotamaka Sutta** and they became arahants.

[1] M. i. 1-6.

[2] MA. ii. 46 ff.; see also AA. i. 457 and J. ii. 259, where it is stated that at the end of the **Gotamaka Sutta** the earth trembled.

[3] But in the introduction to the Jātaka itself, it is stated that the Jātaka was related, not *to* them, but *in reference* to them, after they had become arahants.

Mūlavārikavāpi.—A tank in Ceylon, repaired by **Parakkamabāhu I.**[1]

[1] Cv. lxviii. 49.

Mūlavokāsa-vihāra.—A monastery in Ceylon, built by the minister **Mūla.**[1]

[1] Mhv. xxxiii. 89.

Mūlasālā.—A village in **Rohaṇa,** where **Kitti** (afterwards **Vijayabāhu I.**), lived in his youth.[1]

[1] Cv. lvii. 44.

Mūlasikkhā.—A compendium of Vinaya rules, chiefly in verse. According to tradition, it was compiled about two hundred years after the Buddha's death,[1] but the language shows it to be much later. The work is generally ascribed to a monk named **Mahāsāmi.**[2] There exists a *ṭīkā* on it.

[1] *J.P.T.S.* 1882, p. 87. [2] See P.L.C. 76.

Mūlasoma-vihāra.—A monastery in which **Anuruddha,** author of the **Abhidhammattha-saṅgaha,** was an incumbent.[1]

[1] P.L.C. 168.

Mūlānagāma.—A village in **Rohaṇa,** mentioned in the account of the campaigns of **Parakkamabāhu I.**[1]

[1] Cv. lxxv. 16.

Mūluppalavāpi.—A village in Ceylon. A story is told of a monk[1] who lived in the vihāra near by.[2] He was an arahant, and was one day invited to a meal at the house of one of the king's ministers. At the end of the meal the minister's daughter sat near him talking to him. Another monk, seeing them, thought they were on the same seat, and when the Elder returned to the vihāra, the monk showed his displeasure in various ways. Realizing the reason of the monk's strange behaviour, the Elder convinced him that, as an arahant, he was incapable of such conduct as was attributed to him.[2]

[1] According to some MSS., his name was Revata. [2] MA. i. 536.

Mūsika Jātaka (No. 373).—The Bodhisatta was once a world-famed teacher. Among his pupils was **Yava,** son of the king of Benares. He was a good student, and when he was about to leave, the Bodhisatta, foreseeing danger for him, taught him three verses.[1] The first two were

[1] The verses are in the nature of conundrums, with double meaning.

based on incidents seen by the Bodhisatta—a horse killing the mouse that worried the sore place in his foot and throwing him into the well; and the same horse, later, trying to eat barley by putting its head through the fence; the third was made of his own accord. Later, Yava became king, and his son, when sixteen years old, made three attempts on his life. But they all failed because Yava repeated the stanzas taught him by the Bodhisatta. On each occasion the uttering of the stanzas made the boy feel that he was discovered, and he confessed his guilt, whereupon he was cast into chains.

The story was related in reference to **Ajātasattu.**[2] For details see the **Thusa Jātaka.**

[2] J. iii. 215-9.

Mūsikā.—A slave-woman of King **Yava** (see the **Mūsika Jātaka**). One day, on going to prepare the king's bath, she saw his son, sword in hand, waiting to kill him. When the prince found he was discovered, he cut Mūsikā in two and threw her into the lake.[1]

[1] J. iii. 217.

1. **Mūsila** (*v.l.* **Musila, Musila**).—**Devadatta** born as the chief musician of **Ujjeni.** For his story see the **Guttila Jātaka.**

2. **Mūsila Thera.**—A monk. A conversation is recorded in the **Saṃyutta Nikayā**[1] between him and **Saviṭṭha,** which is said to have taken place in **Ghositārāma** in **Kosambī,** regarding the *paṭiccasamuppāda.*

[1] S. ii. 115 f.

Mekalā.—Name of a tribe, occurring in a nominal list.[1]

[1] Ap. ii. 359; the reading is, however, very uncertain.

Mekhala.—The city of birth of **Sumana Buddha** and the scene of his first sermon to **Saraṇa** and **Bhāvitatta.**[1] It was there that **Maṅgala Buddha** converted his chief disciples, **Sudeva** and **Dhammasena.**[2] **Revata Buddha** once preached there to an assembly of one thousand crores of people,[3] while later, King **Uggata** built, for **Sobhita Buddha,** the **Dhammaganārāma** in the same city.[4]

[1] Bu. v. 21; BuA. 125 f. [2] *Ibid.*, 120. [3] *Ibid.*, 134. [4] *Ibid.*, 139.

Mekhaladāyikā.—An arahant Therī. Ninety-four kappas ago she offered her *mekhalā* for the restoration of the *thūpa* of **Siddhattha Buddha.**[1] She is probably identical with **Mettikā Therī.**[2]

[1] Ap. ii. 513 f. [2] ThigA. 35.

1. **Megha.**—A youth in the time of **Dīpaṅkara Buddha.** Hearing the Buddha prophesy the future of **Sumedha,** Megha entered the Order with him. He was a former birth of **Dhammaruci Thera.**[1]

[1] Ap. ii. 430.

2. **Megha** (*v.l.* **Majjha).**—He was treasurer of **Sāketa** and father of **Anopamā Therī.**[1]

[1] ThigA. 138.

3. **Megha.**—A king of long ago; a previous birth of **Dhajadāyaka Thera.**[1]

[1] Ap. i. 109.

1. **Megha Sutta.**—Just as a raincloud makes all the dust in the air vanish, so does the practice of the Noble Eightfold Path destroy evil states.[1]

[1] S. v. 50.

2. **Megha Sutta.**—Just as a strong wind disperses rainclouds, so does the Noble Eightfold Path disperse all Ill.[1]

[1] S. v. 50.

Meghabba (*v.l.* **Meghava).**—A king of twenty-six kappas ago, a previous birth of **Miñjavaṭaṃsakiya Thera.**[1]

[1] Ap. i. 216.

Meghamāla.—A robber of great fame.[1]

[1] DA. i. 89; MA. ii. 688.

1. **Meghavaṇṇābhaya.**—Another name for King **Goṭhakābhaya** (*q.v.*).

2. **Meghavaṇṇābhaya.**—A minister of King **Mahāsena.** He was an intimate friend of the king, but when the latter attempted to destroy the **Mahāvihāra,** he showed his displeasure by raising a revolt in **Malaya.** The king went out to fight him and pitched his camp near **Dūratissavāpi.** During the night, Meghavaṇṇābhaya visited the king alone, taking some delicacies which he had obtained, wishing to share them with him. At their meeting they begged each other's forgiveness, and, with the king's help, Meghavaṇṇābhaya restored the **Mahāvihāra.**[1] According to the **Samantapāsādikā,**[2] one of the pariveṇas built by Meghavaṇṇābhaya seems to have borne his name. It was built on the site where, in the time

[1] Mhv. xxxvii. 17 ff.

[2] Sp. i. 102; also SadS. 43.

of **Devānampiyatissa,** a recital of the Dhamma was held under the presidency of the **Thera Mahā-Ariṭṭha.**

Meghavaṇṇābhaya-vihāra.—A monastery founded by King **Goṭhābhaya (Meghavaṇṇābhaya).** At the festival of its consecration the king distributed six garments each to thirty thousand monks.[1]

[1] Mhv. xxxvi. 108.

Meghavana.—See **Mahāmeghavana.**

Meghalatā.—Among the decorations of the Relic Chamber of the **Mahā Thūpa** are mentioned " *Meghalatā vijjukumāri,*" which is explained in the Mahāvaṃsa Ṭīkā[1] as " *Meghalatānāma vijjukumāriyo.*"

[1] p. 549.

Meghiya Thera.—He belonged to a **Sākyan** family of **Kapilavatthu,** and having joined the Order, was for some time the personal attendant of the Buddha. Once, when the Buddha was staying with him at **Cālikā,**[1] Meghiya went to **Jantugāma** for alms, and, on his return, was much attracted by a mango-grove on the banks of the river **Kimikālā.** He asked the Buddha's permission to dwell there in meditation. Twice the Buddha refused, but, on his third request, let him go. There, however, Meghiya was consumed by evil thoughts and returned to the Buddha. The Buddha preached to him on the five things which make the heart ripe for emancipation—good friends, virtuous life, profitable talk, zealous exertion, insight—and admonished him. Meghiya thereupon attained arahantship.[2]

Ninety-one kappas ago, on the death of **Vipassī Buddha,** there was a great earthquake. The people were very frightened, but **Vessavaṇa** explained to them the reason for it and dispelled their fears. Meghiya was then a householder, and having thus heard of the Buddha's qualities, was filled with joy. Fourteen kappas ago he was a king named **Samita.**[3] He is evidently to be identified with **Buddhasaññaka** of the Apadāna.[4]

[1] This was in the thirteenth year after the Enlightenment (BuA. 3).

[2] A. iv. 354 ff.; Ud. iv. 1; Thag. vs. 66; AA. ii. 794; DhA. i. 289 says, however, that at the end of the Buddha's sermon Meghiya became a *sotāpanna.*

[3] UdA. 217 ff.; ThagA. i. 149 f.

[4] Ap. i. 151 f.

Meghiya Vagga.—The fourth section of the **Udāna.**

Meghiya Sutta.—Preached to **Meghiya** (*q.v.*) on the five factors which make the heart ripe for emancipation.[1]

[1] A. iv. 354 ff.

Meghiya-Thera Vatthu.—The story of **Meghiya Thera** (*q.v.*).[1]

[1] DhA. i. 287 ff.

Mejjha.—A king and his country. The sixteen thousand brahmins who had enjoyed the patronage of **Maṇḍavya** (*q.v.*), after they had lost caste through having eaten the leavings of **Mātaṅga,** went to live in Meghiyaraṭṭha, and Mātaṅga himself proceeded thither that he might humble their pride. The brahmins saw him and reported to the king that Mātaṅga was a juggler and a mountebank. The king, therefore, sent messengers to seize him. They found him sitting on a bench eating, and, approaching him from behind, struck him dead with their swords. The gods were enraged, and pouring down hot ashes on the kingdom utterly destroyed it.[1] The country became a wilderness known as **Mejjhārañña.**[2]

The scene of the **Vighāsa Jātaka** is said to have been in Mejjhārañña.[3] The wilderness was also known as **Mātaṅgārañña,** being connected with Mātaṅga.[4]

[1] J. iv. 388 f.; MA. ii. 613 ff.

[2] *E.g.*, M. i. 378; J. v. 114, 267; Mil. 130.

[3] J. iii. 310.

[4] MA. ii. 615.

Mejjhārañña.—See **Mejjha.**

Meṇḍaka.—A very rich householder of **Bhaddiyanagara** in **Aṅga.** He was the father of **Dhanañjaya** and, therefore, the grandfather of **Visākhā.** He was one of the five Treasurers of **Bimbisāra.** When the Buddha visited Bhaddiya, Meṇḍaka, with the help of Visākhā, entertained him and the monks, and, after listening to the Buddha, he became a *sotāpanna.*[1] It is said[2] that when he went to his granaries after his ceremonial bath, as he stood at the door, showers of grain would fall from heaven and fill the stores. His wife, **Candapadumā,** would cook one measure of rice and one curry and serve the food, ladle in hand. As long as there were people coming to receive the food, so long would the food cooked be unexhausted. Meṇḍaka's son, Dhanañjaya, would put one thousand pieces into a purse and give money from this purse to all who needed it, and at the end of the day the purse would remain full. His daughter-in-law, **Sumanadevī,** would sit by a basket containing four *doṇas* of seed paddy and distribute from this supply

[1] DhA. i. 384 ff.; he had been earlier a follower of the heretics. The heretics tried in vain to stop him from visiting the Buddha; AA. i. 219 f.

[2] Vin. i. 240 f.; also PSA. 509; DhA. iii. 372 f.; Vsm. 383; the accounts differ slightly.

among the servants, enough to last for six months, but the supply of paddy would remain unexhausted. Meṇḍaka's slave, **Puṇṇaka,** ploughed his fields with a golden plough. With every furrow so ploughed, six other furrows would appear, three on either side, each one *ammaṇa* wide. These five people came to be known as the five very lucky ones (*Pañcamahāpuññā*). When Bimbisāra heard of this, he sent his minister to **Bhaddiya** with a fourfold army and discovered that it was true.

When the Buddha left Bhaddiya for **Anguttarāpa,** Meṇḍaka gave orders to his servants and followed the Buddha with abundant provisions of all sorts, entertaining the Buddha and his monks with luxurious food and fresh milk. At the end of the meal, Meṇḍaka provided the monks with ghee and butter for their journey. At first the monks were unwilling to accept the gifts, but the Buddha, at Meṇḍaka's request, allowed them to do so.[3]

Meṇḍaka was so called ("Ram") because, behind his house, in a yard eight *karīsas* in extent, some golden rams pranced up and down, as big as elephants, horses or bulls, hoofing the earth, smiting each other back to back. Whenever Meṇḍaka needed food or garments or money, he would place balls of coloured thread in the mouths of the rams, and when he pulled these out, there would follow them all that he needed.[4]

All this was because of good deeds done in the past by Meṇḍaka. In the time of **Vipassī Buddha,** he was a householder named **Avaroja.** He had an uncle of the same name, and when the latter proposed building a **Gandhakuṭi** for the Buddha, his nephew wished to help with it. But the uncle refused his help. He therefore built an Elephant Hall (*kuñjarasālā*) opposite the Gandhakuṭi. In the middle of the hall was a jewelled pavilion with a seat for preaching, which contained a foot-rest, all this supported by golden rams. At the festival of dedication, he gave alms for four months to sixty-eight hundred thousand monks and presented them with sets of three robes each, the robes given to the novices being worth one hundred thousand. After many births, he was born in this age as seṭṭhi of Benares.

One day, when on his way to the palace, he met the purohita, who told him that there would be a famine in three months. Profiting by this warning, the Treasurer exerted himself to collect all possible grain and store it in every available place. The famine came, and for many months the Treasurer and his retinue lived on the stored grain, but, in the end, the supplies were exhausted, and most of them, acting on his advice, went to the mountains in search of food. He, his wife, his son and daughter-in-law and a slave remained behind. One day, his wife cooked a *nāḷi* of rice which she had hidden away and divided it into

[3] Vin. i. 243 ff.

[4] PSA. 504; BuA. 24.

five portions. As the family were about to eat, a Pacceka Buddha came to the door for alms; they all gave him their portions of food and made various wishes. As a result of these earnest wishes, Meṇḍaka and the members of his family and his slave possessed the supernatural powers above mentioned. During the afternoon, after the Pacceka Buddha had had the food, the Treasurer felt very hungry and asked his wife if there were any lumps of rice sticking to the bottom of the pot. She went into the kitchen to the pot and found it full of fragrant food. From that time their supply of food never failed.[5] Mendaka's grandson was **Uggaha** (*q.v.*).

[5] DhA. iii. 363 ff.; but according to DhA. iv. 203, Meṇḍaka's name in the time of Vipassī Buddha was **Aparājita.** He was a nephew of that Aparājita who, in this life, became **Jotiya-seṭṭhi.** (See also Divyāvadāna, pp. 123 ff., 131 ff.)

Meṇḍaka Jātaka.—Another name for **Meṇḍakapañha** (*q.v.*).

Meṇḍakapañha.—One of the questions set by King **Videha** to his five ministers, after having noticed a strange friendship between a ram and a dog. The ram was beaten by the elephant-keepers because he took the grass from the stalls, while the dog had suffered at the hands of the cook for stealing meat from the kitchen. They met and agreed that the dog should go to the stalls and the ram to the kitchen, in order to avoid suspicion. The king saw this and set the question to his ministers. Only **Mahosadha** knew the solution and he told it to the others. The king was pleased and gave to each a chariot, a she-mule and various other gifts.[1]

[1] J. vi. 349 ff.

Meṇḍasira (*v.l.* **Meṇḍasīsa**).—An arahant Thera. He was born in the family of a burgher of **Sāketa** and was so called because his head resembled that of a ram. When the Buddha was staying in **Añjanavana** in **Sāketa,** Meṇḍasira heard him preach and entered the Order, attaining arahantship in due course.

In the time of **Vipassī Buddha,** he lived near Mount **Gotama** in **Himavā** with a large following of ascetics. There they met the Buddha and offered him lotus-flowers. Fifty-one kappas ago he was a king named **Januttama (Jaluttama).**[1] He is evidently to be identified with **Padumapūjaka** of the Apadāna.[2]

[1] Thag. vs. 78; ThagA. i. 171 f.

[2] Ap. i. 162 f.

Meṇḍissara.—One of the chief disciples of **Jotipāla (Sarabhaṅga).** He lived with many ascetics, in the country of King **Pajaka,** near the town of **Lambacūḷaka.** He helped Sarabhaṅga to convince **Nārada** of the error of his ways.[1] Meṇḍissara is identified with **Mahā Kassapa.**[2]

[1] See the **Indriya Jātaka** (J. iii. 463 ff.). In the Sarabhaṅga Jātaka (v. 133), however, Meṇḍissara is stated as living on the banks of the **Sātodikā.** But see *s.v.* **Sālissara.**

[2] J. v. 151; iii. 469.

1. **Metta Sutta.**—One should be diligent and upright, gentle and not vain-glorious, free from deceit. Let none, out of anger, or through resentment, wish misery to another. A person should cherish boundless goodwill towards all beings, like a mother fostering her only son.[1]

This sutta was preached by the Buddha to five hundred monks who had obtained from him a formula for meditation and dwelt in a region in the **Himālaya.** The gods there were alarmed by the goodness of the monks and tried to frighten them away. The monks, constantly harassed, sought the Buddha at **Sāvatthi.** He preached this sutta to them and admonished them on the practice of goodwill. They followed his advice, and the gods, understanding, left them in peace.[2] The sutta is included in the **Parittas.**

[1] SN. vss. 143-52; also Khp. p. 8 f.; where it is called **Karaṇīyametta Sutta,** by which name it is more popularly known.

[2] KhpA. 232 ff.; *cp.* DhA. i. 313 ff.

2. **Metta Sutta.**—Once when the Buddha was at **Haliddavasana,** a discussion arose between some monks and some **Paribbājakas** as to whether there was any difference between their respective doctrines since they both inculcated the practice of goodwill, compassion, sympathy, and equanimity. The monks consulted the Buddha, who told them that the **Paribbājakas** were ignorant of how to cultivate these qualities, of what was their goal and their excellence, their fruit and their ending.

He then proceeded to explain to them that these are cultivated through the seven *bojjhaṅgas*; goodwill has the " beautiful " for its excellence, compassion the infinity of space, sympathy the infinity of consciousness, and equanimity the sphere where nought exists.[1]

[1] S. v. 115 f.

Mettagū Thera.—One of the sixteen disciples of **Bāvari** who visited the Buddha. His question (*pucchā*) to the Buddha was as to how various ills originated in the world, and the Buddha's answer that it was through *upadhi*. At the end of the sermon Mettagū and his thousand followers attained arahantship.[1] According to the Apadāna,[2] he gave away alms worth sixty crores of gold before joining Bāvarī.

In the time of **Sumedha Buddha** he was an ascetic living near Mount

[1] SN. vss. 1006, 1049-60; SNA. ii. 592.

[2] ii. 342 f.

Asoka in **Himavā,** in a hermitage built for him by **Vissakamma.** There the Buddha visited him, and the ascetic gave him a bowl filled with ghee and oil. As a result, he was eighteen times king of the gods and fifty-one times king of men.

Mettagū-pucchā and Sutta.—See **Mettagū.**

Mettaji Thera.—He belonged to a brahmin family of **Magadha,** and, when he grew up, became a forest-dwelling monk. Hearing of the Buddha's advent, Mettaji visited him, and questioned him concerning progress and regress (*pavattiyo*), and, believing, he entered the Order and attained arahantship.

In the time of **Anomadassī Buddha** he was a householder and built a wall round the Bodhi-tree. One hundred kappas ago he was a king named **Sabbagghana (Sabbosana).**[1] He is evidently identical with **Anulomadāyaka Thera** of the Apadāna.[2]

[1] Thag. vs. 94; ThagA. i. 194 f. [2] Ap. i. 173.

Mettā Therī.—She belonged to a **Sākyan** family of **Kapilavatthu** and renounced the world with **Pajāpatī Gotamī,** gaining arahantship in due course.

Ninety-one kappas ago, in the time of **Vipassī Buddha,** she was one of the wives of **Bandhumā,** king of **Bandhumatī,** and, pleased with a certain nun, entertained her to a meal and gave her a pair of very costly robes.[1] She is probably identical with **Ekapiṇḍadāyikā** of the Apadāna.[2]

[1] Thig. vs. 31 f.; ThigA. 36 f. [2] Ap. ii. 515 f.

Mettā Vagga.—The first chapter of the Aṭṭha Nipāta of the **Aṅguttara Nikāya.**[1]

[1] A. iv. 150-72.

1. **Mettā Sutta.**—On four kinds of persons to be found in the world —those who irradiate all quarters with goodwill, compassion, sympathy and equanimity. These are born after death in various Brahma-worlds; if they happen to be disciples of the Buddha, they will no more return to the world of men.[1]

[1] A. ii. 128.

2. **Mettā Sutta.**—Very similar to the above. Such persons are born, after death, in the **Suddhāvāsā.**[1]

A. ii. 129.

3. **Mettā Sutta.**—When a man has developed emancipation of the mind through goodwill, compassion, sympathy and equanimity, by the signless (*animitta*) and getting rid of the thought "I am," it cannot be said of him that he has failed to find escape from the opposite qualities.[1]

[1] A. iii. 290 f.

4. **Mettā Sutta.**—Nine qualifications which, if they accompany the observance of the fast-days, make such observance fruitful—the eight precepts (abstention from killing, etc.), and irradiating the world with thoughts of goodwill.[1]

[1] A. iv. 388 f.

5. **Mettā Sutta.**—Eleven advantages which come from the development of goodwill towards all beings.[1]

[1] A. v. 342.

6. **Mettā Sutta.**—The idea of goodwill, if cultivated, leads to much profit.[1]

[1] S. v. 131.

Mettākathā.—The fourth chapter of the **Yuganandha Vagga** of the **Paṭisambhidāmagga.**

Mettākāyikā.—A class of devas present at the preaching of the **Mahāsamaya Sutta.**[1]

[1] D. ii. 259.

Mettikā Therī.—She was born in a rich brahmin family of **Rājagaha** and joined the Order under **Pajāpatī Gotamī.** One day, in her old age, while meditating on the top of a peak, her insight expanded and she became an arahant.

In the time of **Siddhattha Buddha,** she belonged to a burgher's family and offered her *mekhalā* at the Buddha's cetiya.[1] She is evidently identical with **Mekhaladāyikā** of the Apadāna.[2]

[1] Thig. vss. 29, 30; ThigA. 35 f. [2] Ap. ii. 513.

Mettiya Thera.—One of the six leaders of the **Chabbaggiyā** (*q.v.*).

Mettiyabhummajakā.—A group of monks, followers of **Mettiya** and **Bhummajaka,** forming part of the **Chabbaggiyā** (*q.v.*). They lived near **Rājagaha.**[1] Twice they brought an unfounded charge of breach of

[1] Sp. iii. 614; J. ii. 387; Sp. iii. 579 says they were the chief leaders of the Chabbaggiyā.

morality against **Dabba Mallaputta,** who seems to have earned their special dislike. Dabba was in charge of the distribution of alms at the *ārāma* where they stayed, and one day it was their turn to receive alms from a certain householder who had a reputation for providing good food. When, however, the man heard from Dabba that it was the turn of the Mettiyabhummajakā to receive his hospitality, he was much displeased, and ordered his female slave to look after them. The monks were greatly annoyed, and accused Dabba of having slandered them to the householder. They, therefore, persuaded a nun named **Mettiyā** to go to the Buddha and accuse Dabba of having violated her chastity. The charge was investigated and proved false and the nun expelled from the Order.[2]

On another occasion, these monks persuaded a **Licchavi,** named **Vaḍḍha,** who was their patron and friend, to go to the Buddha and charge Dabba with having had relations with his wife. This, too, was proved false, and other monks refused to accept alms from Vaḍḍha until he had confessed his guilt.[3] One day, while descending from **Gijjhakūṭa,** the Mettiyabhummajakā monks saw a heifer with a she-goat and the idea occurred to them of calling the heifer Dabba and the she-goat Mettiyā and then of spreading the story that they had seen Dabba mating with Mettiyā[4] !

[2] Vin. ii. 76 ff.; iii. 160 ff.

[3] *Ibid.*, ii. 124 ff.

[4] *Ibid.*, iii. 166 ff.; see also iv. 37 f., Dhammapāla mentions a tradition, but contradicts it, that the persecution of Dabba by the Mettiyabhummakajakā was so persistent that in the end he committed suicide to escape from it (UdA. 431). In any case, they managed to bring him into disfavour with the laity, and the Buddha had to take special steps to reinstate him in their esteem (UdA. 434). The incident regarding the charge brought by Mettiyā seems to have given much trouble to later commentators. Sp. iii. 582 says that there was a great dispute about this between the monks of the **Mahāvihāra** and those of **Abhayagiri.** In the end, King **Bhātikatissa** intervened and had the matter settled by **Dīghakārāyaṇa.**

Mettiyā.—A nun who, at the instigation of the **Mettiyabhummajakā** (*q.v.*), charged **Dabba Mallaputta** with having violated her chastity. She was expelled from the Order for this offence.

1. **Metteyya.**—The future Buddha, the fifth of this kappa.[1] According to the **Cakkavatti-Sīhanāda Sutta,** he will be born, when human beings will live to an age of eighty thousand years, in the city of **Ketumatī** (present Benares), whose king will be the **Cakkavattī Saṅkha.** Saṅkha will live in the fairy palace where once dwelt King **Mahāpanadā,** but

[1] Bu. xxvii. 21.

later he will give the palace away and will himself become a follower of Metteyya Buddha.[2]

The **Anāgatavaṃsa**[3] gives further particulars. Metteyya will be born in a very eminent brahmin family and his personal name will be **Ajita.** Metteyya is evidently the name of his gotta. For eight thousand years he will live the household life in four palaces—**Sirivaḍḍha, Vaḍḍhamāna, Siddhattha** and **Candaka**—his chief wife being **Candamukhī** and his son **Brahmavaddhana.** Having seen the four signs while on his way to the park, he will be dissatisfied with household life and will spend one week in practising austerities. Then he will leave home, travelling in his palace and accompanied by a fourfold army, at the head of which will be eighty-four thousand brahmins and eighty-four thousand Khattiya maidens. Among his followers will be **Isidatta** and **Pūraṇa,** two brothers, **Jātimitta, Vijaya, Suddhika** and **Suddhanā, Saṅgha** and **Saṅghā, Saddhara, Sudatta, Yasavatī** and **Visākhā,** each with eigty-four thousand companions. Together they will leave the household and arrive on the same day at the Bodhi-tree. After the Enlightenment the Buddha will preach in **Nāgavana** and King Saṅkha will, later, ordain himself under him. Metteyya's father will be **Subrahmā,** chaplain to King Saṅkha, and his mother **Brahmavatī.** His chief disciples will be **Asoka** and **Brahmadeva** among monks, and **Padumā** and **Sumanā** among nuns. **Sīha** will be his personal attendant and his chief patrons **Sumana, Saṅgha, Yasavatī** and **Saṅghā.** His Bodhi will be the *Nāga*-tree. After the Buddha's death, his teachings will continue for one hundred and eighty thousand years. According to the **Mahāvaṃsa,**[4] **Kākavaṇṇatissa** and **Vihāramahādevī,** father and mother of **Duṭṭhagāmaṇi,** will be Metteyya's parents, **Duṭṭhagāmaṇi** himself will be his chief disciple and **Saddhātissa** his second disciple, while Prince **Sāli** will be his son.

At the present time the future Buddha is living in the **Tusita** deva-world.[5] There is a tradition that **Nātha** is the name of the future Buddha in the deva-world.

The worship of the Bodhisatta Metteyya seems to have been popular in ancient Ceylon, and **Dhātusena** adorned an image of him with all the equipment of a king and ordained a guard for it within the radius of seven yojanas.[6]

Dappula I. made a statue in honour of the future Buddha fifteen cubits high.[7] It is believed that Metteyya spends his time in the deva-world, preaching the Dhamma to the assembled gods, and, in emulation of his example, King **Kassapa V.** used to recite the Abhidhamma in the

[2] D. iii. 75 ff.

[3] *J.P.T.S.* 1886, pp. 42, 46 ff., 52; DhSA. 415 gives the names of his parents.

[4] Mhv. xxxii. 81 f.; see Mil. 159.

[5] Mhv. xxxii. 73.

[6] Cv. xxxviii. 68.

[7] *Ibid.*, xlv. 62.

assemblies of the monks.[8] **Parakkamabāhu I.** had three statues built in honour of Metteyya,[9] while **Kittisirirājasīha** erected one in the **Rajatavihāra** and another in the cave above it[10] It is the wish of all Buddhists that they meet Metteyya Buddha, listen to his preaching and attain to Nibbāna under him.[11]

[8] Cv. lii. 47. [9] *Ibid.*, lxxix. 75. [10] *Ibid.*, c. 248, 259. [11] See, *e.g.*, J. vi. 594; MṬ. 687; DhSA. 430.

2. **Metteyya Thera.**—An arahant, friend of **Tissa,** of the **Tissa-Metteyya Sutta.**[1] His personal name, too, was Tissa, but he was better known by his gotta-name of Metteyya.[2] In a verse in the **Suttanipāta**[3] he is referred to as **Tissa Metteyya.**

[1] See. *s.v.* **Tissa** (7). [2] SNA. ii. 536. [3] SN. vs. 814.

Metteyyapañha.[1]—Evidently another name for **Tissametteyya-pucchā** (*q.v.*).

[1] A. iii. 399.

Methuna Sutta.—Preached to **Jāṇussoṇi** in answer to a question as to what constitutes *brahmacariyā* (chastity). There are seven "sex-bonds" mentioned, subjection to any of which is violation of *brahmacariyā*. The Buddha claims that he has destroyed them all.[1]

[1] A. iv. 54 f.

Methula.—A **Pacceka Buddha,** whose name appears in a nominal list.[1]

[1] M. iii. 70; ApA. i. 106.

Medakathalikā.—The pupil of a "bamboo-acrobat" (*caṇḍālavaṃsika*)[1] of long ago. His master called to him one day and asked him to climb the bamboo and to stand on his shoulder. Then the master suggested that they should watch and look after each other during their performances. But Medakathalikā said that each should look after himself,[2] which would be the better way. The Buddha related this story at **Desakā,** in the **Sumbha** country, to the monks, and said that, in the same way, each monk should look after himself; by guarding oneself, one guards another; this is done by the cultivation of the four *satipaṭṭhānas*.[3]

The name Medakathalikā, though feminine in inflection, is used for a male.[4]

[1] See KS. v. 148, n. 3

[2] The Commentary (SA. iii. 182) adds that, in this performance, the end of the pole rests on the forehead or throat. The man who thus holds it must watch the balance closely and not attend to the man at the end of the pole.

[3] S. v. 168 f. [4] SA. iii. 181.

Medataḷumpa.—A **Sākyan** village three leagues from **Naṅgaraka.**[1] **Pasenadi** when staying there with **Dīgha Kārāyaṇa,** heard that the Buddha was there and visited him. On this occasion was preached the **Dhammacetiya Sutta** (*q.v.*). This was the last time that Pasenadi saw the Buddha.

The Dhammapada Commentary, however, in its record[2] of the king's visit, calls the place **Uḷumpa.** On the other hand, the Majjhima Commentary[3] confirms the reading Medataḷumpa, and says that it was so called because *medavaṇṇa* stones were visible there on the surface of the earth (*medavaṇṇā pāsāṇā kir'ettha ussannā ahesuṃ, tasmā Medataḷumpan ti saṅkhaṃ gataṃ*).

[1] M. ii. 119. [2] DhA. i. 356. [3] MA. ii. 753.

1. **Medhaṅkara.**—A Buddha of very long ago, belonging to the same *kappa* as **Dīpaṅkara.**[1]

[1] Bu. xxvii. 1.; J. i. 44.

2. **Medhaṅkara Thera.**—He lived in Ceylon, and was the author of a Sinhalese work called *Vinayārthasamuccaya.*[1]

[1] P.L.C. 202.

3. **Medhaṅkara Thera.**—Called **Araññaka Medhaṅkara.** He presided over the Council held by **Parakkamabāhu III.**[1]

[1] P.L.C. 213.

4. **Medhaṅkara Thera.**—He was entrusted by **Parakkamabāhu IV.** with the translation of the **Jātakas** into Sinhalese. The king built for him a *pariveṇa* called the **Parakkamabāhu-pariveṇa,** and gave for its maintenance the villages of **Purāṇagāma, Sannīrasela, Labujamaṇḍaka** and **Moravaṅka.**[1]

[1] Cv. xc. 86.

5. **Medhaṅkara Thera** (called **Vanaratana Medhaṅkara**).—He wrote the **Jinacarita** and the **Payogasiddhi** and lived in the time of **Bhuvanakabāhu I.** He was an incumbent of the **Vijayabāhu-pariveṇa,** built by **Vijayabāhu II.**[1]

[1] Gv. 62, 72; P.L.C. 230 f.

6. **Medhaṅkara.**—A Burmese author of the fourteenth century. He was the royal preceptor of Queen **Bhaddā,** mother of **Setibhinda,** king of **Muttimanagara.** He studied for a time in Ceylon and afterwards wrote the **Lokadīpasāra.**[1]

[1] Sās. p. 42; Bode, *op. cit.*, 35 f.

Medhārāma.—The park wherein **Sumedha Buddha** died.[1]

[1] Bu. xii. 31.

Meru.—See **Sineru.**

Merukandara.—A district in **Malaya** (in Ceylon) often sought as a place of refuge—*e.g.*, by **Kassapa,** son of **Upatissa III.**[1]; **Jeṭṭhatissa,** son of **Asiggāhaka Saṅghatissa**[2] and **Potthakuṭṭha.**[3] **Vijayabāhu I.** gave Merukandara as dowry to his daughter, **Yasodharā,** who married **Vīravanna.**[4] The village of **Vacāvāṭaka** was in Merukandara.[5]

[1] Cv. xli. 19. [2] *Ibid.*, xliv. 28. [3] *Ibid.*, xlvii. 58. [4] *Ibid.*, lix. 27. [5] *Ibid.*, lxx. 282.

Merumajjara.—A forest in Ceylon, where King **Asiggāhaka Saṅghatissa** fled with his son and minister after his defeat by **Moggallāna III.**[1]

[1] Cv. xliv. 21.

Mereliya.—A district in Ceylon, where **Dāṭhāpabhuti,** father of **Silākāla,** lived for some time.[1]

[1] Cv. xxxix. 45.

Melamaṅgala.—A district in South India, mentioned in the account of the campaigns of **Laṅkāpura.**[1]

[1] Cv. lxxvi. 209 (211).

Meḷajina Thera.—He belonged to a nobleman's family of Benares, and, becoming distinguished in various branches of knowledge, visited the Buddha at **Isipatana.** There, gaining faith, he entered the Order, becoming an arahant in due course.

Ninety-four kappas ago, in the time of **Sumedha Buddha,** he was a householder, and, seeing the Buddha begging for alms, gave him an *āmoda*-fruit.[1]

[1] Thag. vs. 131 f.; ThagA. i. 252 f.

Meḷamātā.—A she-goat. See the **Pūtimaṃsa Jātaka.**

Moggali.—A brahmin of **Pāṭaliputta,** father of **Moggaliputta-Tissa.** He was converted by **Siggava.**[1]

[1] Mhv. v. 102, 133.

Moggaliputta-Tissa Thera.—President of the Third Council. In his penultimate birth he was a **Brahmā,** called **Tissa,** and consented to be born in the world of men at the urgent request of the arahants who held the Second Council, in order to prevent the downfall of the Buddha's religion. He was born in the home of the brahmin **Moggali** of **Pāṭaliputta. Siggava** and **Caṇḍavajji** had been entrusted with the task of converting him. From the time of Tissa's birth, therefore, for seven years, Siggava went daily to the house of Moggali, but not even one word of welcome did he receive. In the eighth year someone said to him, "Go further on." As he went out he met Moggali, and, on being asked whether he had received anything at his house, he said he had. Moggali inquired at home and the next day charged Siggava with lying. But hearing Siggava's explanation, he was greatly pleased and thereafter constantly offered Siggava hospitality at his house. One day, young Tissa, who was thoroughly proficient in the Vedas, was much annoyed at finding Siggava occupying his seat and spoke to him harshly. But Siggava started to talk to him and asked him a question from the **Cittayamaka.** Tissa could not answer it, and, in order to learn the Buddha's teachings, he entered the Order under Siggava, becoming a *sotāpanna* soon after. Siggava instructed him in the Vinaya and Caṇḍavajji in the Sutta and Abhidhamma Piṭakas. In due course he attained arahantship and became the acknowledged leader of the monks at Pāṭaliputta.[1]

At the festival of dedication of the **Asokārāma** and the other vihāras built by Asoka, Moggaliputta-Tissa informed Asoka, in answer to a question, that one becomes a kinsman of the Buddha's religion only by letting one's son or daughter enter the Order. Acting on this suggestion, Asoka had both his children ordained. Moggaliputta acted as Mahinda's *upajjhāya.*[2] Later, because of the great gains which accrued to the monks through Asoka's patronage of the Buddha's religion, the Order became corrupt, and Moggaliputta committed the monks to the charge of Mahinda, and, for seven years, lived in solitary retreat on the **Ahogaṅgā-pabbata.** From there Asoka sent for him to solve his doubts as to what measure of sin belonged to him owing to the murder of the monks by his minister. But Moggaliputta would not come until persuaded that his services were needed to befriend the religion. He travelled by boat to Pāṭaliputta, and was met at the landing-place by the king who helped him out by supporting him on his arm.[3] The

[1] Mhv. v. 95 ff., 131 ff.; Dpv. v. 55 ff.; Sp. i. 35-41.

[2] Mhv. v. 191 ff.; Sp. i. 50 f.

[3] According to Sp. i. 58, the king had a dream on the preceding night which the soothsayers interpreted to mean that a great ascetic (*samaṇanāga*) would touch his right hand. As the Thera touched the king's hand the attendants were about to kill him, for to do this was a crime punishable by death. The king, however, restrained them. The Thera took the king's hand as a sign that he accepted him as pupil.

king, having led him to **Rativaḍḍhana** Park, begged him to perform a miracle. This the Thera consented to do and made the earth quake in a single region. To convince the king that the murder of the monks involved no guilt for himself, the Thera preached to him the **Tittira Jātaka.** Within a week, with the aid of two yakkhas, the king had all the monks gathered together and held an assembly at the Asokārāma. In the presence of Moggaliputta, Asoka questioned the monks on their various doctrines, and all those holding heretical views were expelled from the Order, Moggaliputta decreeing that the **Vibhajjavāda** alone contained the teaching of the Buddha. Later, in association with one thousand arahants, Moggaliputta held the Third Council at Asokārāma, with himself as President, and compiled the **Kathāvatthuppakaraṇa,** in refutation of false views. This was in the seventeenth year of Asoka's reign and Moggaliputta was seventy-two years old.[4] At the conclusion of the Council in nine months, Moggaliputta made arrangements, in the month of Kattika, for monks to go to the countries adjacent to India for the propagation of the religion.[5] Later, when the request came from Ceylon for a branch of the Bodhi-tree, Asoka consulted the Elder as to how this could be carried out, and Moggaliputta told him of the five resolves made by the Buddha on his death-bed.[6]

The **Dīpavaṃsa** says[7] that Moggaliputta-Tissa's ordination was in the second year of **Candagutta's** reign, when Siggava was sixty-four years old. Candagutta reigned for twenty-four years, and was followed by **Bindusāra,** who reigned for thirty-seven years, and he was succeeded by Asoka. In the sixth year of Asoka's reign, Moggaliputta was sixty-six years old, and it was then that he ordained Mahinda. He was eighty years old at the time of his death and had been leader of the Order for sixty-eight years. He died in the twenty-sixth year of Asoka's reign.

[4] Mhv. v. 231-81; Dpv. vii. 16 ff., 39 ff.; Sp. i. 57 ff.

[5] For a list of these, see Mhv. xii. 1 ff.; Dpv. viii. 1 ff.; Sp. i. 63 ff.

[6] Mhv. xviii. 21 ff.

[7] Dpv. v. 68 ff., 82, 94, 96, 100 f. 107 f.; also vii. 23 ff.

Moggalī.—The name of **Mahāmoggallāna's** mother.[1]

[1] ThagA. ii. 93; AA. i. 88; DhA. i. 73; but SNA. i. 326 calls her **Moggallānī**

Moggalla.—A man in the retinue of King **Eḷeyya.** He was a follower of **Uddaka Rāmaputta.**[1]

[1] A. ii. 187; AA. ii. 554.

1. **Moggallāna.**—See **Mahāmoggallāna.**

2. **Moggallāna.**—A celebrated Pāli grammarian of the twelfth century.[1]

[1] P.L.C. 179 f.

3. **Moggallāna.**—Thera of Ceylon, author of the Abhidhānappadīpikā.[1]

[1] P.L.C. 187 ff.

4. **Moggallāna.**—Younger son of **Dhātusena.** When his brother, **Kassapa,** took **Dhātusena** captive, Moggallāna fled to **Jambudīpa.** He collected troops, and, in the eighteenth year of Kassapa's reign, landed in Ceylon with twelve friends, counting on the support of the **Nigaṇṭhas.** He lived for a time at **Kuṭhāri-vihāra** in **Ambaṭṭhakola,** making preparations. Kassapa came out of **Sīhagiri** to meet him, and, being defeated in battle, committed suicide. Moggallāna thereupon became king as **Moggallāna I.,** making **Anurādhapura** once more the capital. At first he showed great cruelty to his father's enemies, earning the title of "*Rakkhasa,*" but later he became gentle and engaged himself in good works. He patronized the **Dhammaruci** and **Sāgalika** schools and gave them the **Daḷha-** and **Dāṭhakoṇḍañña-vihāras** at **Sīhagiri.** To **Mahānāma,** incumbent of **Dīghāsana-(? Dīghāsaṇḍa)-vihāra,** he gave the **Pabbata-vihāra,** and the **Rājinī** nunnery to the Sāgalika nuns. In Moggallāna's reign, **Silākāla (Amba-Sāmaṇera)** brought the Buddha's Hair-relic to Ceylon. Moggallāna instituted celebrations in its honour and gave them into the charge of Silākāla, who left the Order and became his sword-bearer (*asiggāhaka*). **Migāra** and **Uttara** were two of his generals. He reigned for eighteen years[1] (496-513 A.C.). Moggallāna's sister married **Upatissa III.**[2]

[1] Cv. xxxviii. 80, 86 ff., 96, 108; xxxix. 20 ff. [2] *Ibid.*, xli. 6.

5. **Moggallāna.**—Eldest son of **Ambasāmaṇera-Silākāla.** He was made *Ādipāda* and put in charge of the Eastern Province. He had two brothers, **Dāṭhāpabhuti** and **Upatissa.** On the death of Silākāla the former seized the throne and murdered Upatissa. **Moggallāna** marched against him with an army and challenged him to single combat. The challenge was accepted, and the brothers fought, each on an elephant. Dāṭāpabhuti was defeated and killed himself, and Moggallāna became king as **Moggallāna II.,** also known as **Culla-Moggallāna.** He was a great poet and a very good man. He held recitals of the Piṭakas and the Commentaries in various parts of the Island and encouraged the study of the Dhamma. He once composed a poem in praise of the Dhamma and recited it while seated on the back of his elephant.

By means of damming up the **Kadamba** River, he constructed three tanks—**Pattapāsāṇa, Dhanavāpi** and **Garītara.** He ruled for twenty years (537-56), and was succeeded by his son **Kittisirimegha.**[1]

[1] Cv. xli. 33 f., 43-63.

6. **Moggallāna.**—A general of **Aggabodhi II.** He revolted against **Saṅghatissa,** and, after some reverses, defeated him, with the help of the treacherous senāpati, at **Pācīnatissapabbata.** He then became king as **Moggallāna III.** and was known as **Dabba-Moggallāna.**[1] He did many good deeds, among them being the construction ot the **Moggallāna-, Piṭṭhigāma-** and **Vaṭagāma-vihāras.** He made Saṅghatissa's senāpati ruler of **Malaya,** but later quarrelled with him and had his hands and feet cut off. The senāpati's son rose in revolt and killed the king near **Sīhagiri.** Moggallāna ruled for six years (511-17 A.C.).[2]

[1] Cv. xliv. 63. [2] *Ibid.*, xliv. 3-62.

7. **Moggallāna.**—Son of **Lokitā** and **Kassapa. Loka** was his brother. Moggallāna was known by the title of *Mahāsāmi*[1] and lived in **Rohaṇa.** He married **Lokitā,** daughter of **Buddhā,** and had four sons: **Kitti** (afterwards **Vijayabāhu I.**), **Mitta, Mahinda** and **Rakkhita.**[2]

[1] On this see Cv. *Trs.* i. 195, n. 5. [2] Cv. lvii. 29 f., 41 f.

8. **Moggallāna.**—An eminent Thera who was associated with **Mahā Kassapa** in the Council held at **Pulatthipura** under the patronage of **Parakkamabāhu I.** for the purification of the Order.[1]

[1] Cv. lxxviii. 9.

9. **Moggallāna.**—See **Sikha-Moggallāna.** Also **Gaṇaka Moggallāna** and **Gopaka Moggallāna.**

Moggallāna Saṃyutta.—The fortieth chapter of the **Saṃyutta Nikāya.**[1]

[1] S. iv. 262-81.

1. **Moggallāna Sutta.**—**Vaṅgīsa** sings the praises of **Mahā Moggallāna** before the Buddha and a company of five hundred arahants.[1]

[1] S. i. 194 f.; cf. Thag. vs, 1249-51.

2. **Moggallāna Sutta.**—Another name for the **Pāsādakampana Sutta** (*q.v.*).

3. **Moggallāna Sutta.**—The Buddha holds up **Mahā Moggallāna** as an example of a monk who, by cultivating the four *iddhipādas*, obtained magic power and majesty.[1]

[1] S. v. 288.

4. **Moggallāna** or **Āyatana Sutta.**—**Vacchagotta** asks **Mahā Moggallāna** a series of questions as to whether the world is eternal or finite, and Moggallāna replies that these matters have not been revealed by the Buddha because the Buddha's point of view is different from that of other teachers. Vacchagotta seeks the Buddha, asks the same questions, and receives the same answers and the same explanation.[1]

[1] S. iv. 291.

5. **Moggallāna Sutta.**—**Mahā Moggallāna** wonders how many devas have become *sotāpannas* and are assured of Nibbāna. In order to discover this, he visits **Tissa Brahmā,** who had once been a monk. Tissa welcomes him and tells him that only those devas who have faith in the Buddha, the Dhamma, and the Saṅgha have such assurance.[1]

[1] A. iii. 331 f.

Moggallāna-vihāra.—A monastery built by **Moggallāna III.** in **Kārapiṭṭhi.**[1]

[1] Cv. xliv. 50.

Moggallānī.—See **Moggalī.**

Mogharāja Thera.—He belonged to a brahmin family and studied under **Bāvarī** as an ascetic. He was one of the sixteen pupils sent by Bāvarī to the Buddha. When Mogharāja had asked his question of the Buddha and had received the answer, he attained arahantship. He then attained distinction by wearing rough cloth which had been thrown away by caravaners, tailors, and dyers, and the Buddha declared him foremost among wearers of rough clothing.[1] Later, through want of care and former *kamma*, pimples and the like broke out over his body. Judging that his lodging was infected, he spread a couch of straw in the **Magadha** field and lived there even during the winter. When the Buddha asked him how he fared in the cold, he replied that he was extremely happy.[2]

In the time of **Padumuttara Buddha,** Mogharāja first resolved to win the eminence which was his. In the time of **Atthadassī Buddha** he was a brahmin teacher, and one day, while teaching his students, he saw the Buddha, and having worshipped him with great solemnity, he uttered six verses in his praise and offered him a gift of honey. Later, after sojourn in the *deva*-worlds, he became a minister of King **Kaṭṭhavāhana,** and was sent by him, with one thousand others, to visit **Kassapa Buddha.** He heard the Buddha preach, entered the order, and lived the life of a monk

[1] See also A. i. 25. [2] Thag. vs. 207 f.

for twenty thousand years.[3] The **Saṃyutta Nikāya**[4] contains a stanza spoken by Mogharāja and the Buddha's answer thereto.

Buddhaghosa explains[5] that Mogharāja was present during the discussion of **Pasuraparibbājaka** (*q.v.*) with **Sāriputta.** At the end of Sāriputta's explanation, Mogharāja wished to settle the matter and uttered this stanza.

Mogharāja is given as an example of one who attained arahantship by the development of investigation (*vimāṃsaṃ dhuraṃ katvā*).[6]

The Apadāna contains two sets of verses in reference to Mogharāja. They seem to be parts of the same Apadāna which have become separated. The first set[7] gives an account of the meeting of Mogharāja with **Atthadassī Buddha** (see above) and includes the verses uttered by Mogharāja in praise of the Buddha. The second set[8] contains an account of his meeting with **Padumuttara Buddha** and the resolves he made before him. It further mentions that, for one thousand years, in a later birth, Mogharāja suffered in hell, and that for five hundred births he suffered from skin diseases. This was because he had lighted a fire in the Buddha's cloister and had made the floor black. In his last birth, too, he suffered from a *kuṭṭharoga* and could not sleep at night, hence his name (*mogharajjasukhaṃ yasmā Mogharājā tato ahaṃ*). These verses also include the **Mogharājamāṇava-pucchā.**

In the Milindapañha[9] appears a stanza attributed to Mogharāja, but not found in the stanzas mentioned in connection with him either in the Sutta Nipāta or in the Theragāthā. See also **Mogharājamāṇava-pucchā.**

[3] ThagA. i. 181 ff.; SN. vs. 1006.
[4] S. i. 23. [5] SA. i. 49 f.
[6] SA. iii. 201.
[7] Ap. i. 87 f.
[8] *Ibid.*, ii. 486 f.
[9] p. 412.

Mogharāja-māṇava-pucchā.—**Mogharāja** asks the Buddha how he should regard the world in order to escape death. The Buddha replies that the world should be regarded as empty (*suññato*) and one must get rid of the thought of self (*attānudiṭṭhi*).[1] It is said[2] that Mogharāja tried twice before to ask the question, once at the conclusion of the preaching of the **Ajita Sutta** and again at the end of the recitation of the **Tissa-metteyya Sutta**; but the Buddha, knowing that he was not yet ready for conversion, did not give him an opportunity.

[1] SN. vss. 1116-19; the Buddha's answer is quoted at Kvu. p. 64.
[2] SN. vs. 1116; SNA. ii. 601 f.

Monasīhakā.—A totemistic clan of the Sinhalese. They were employed by **Mitta** against **Bhuvanekabāhu I.**[1]

[1] Cv. xc. 7; see. Cv. *Trs.* i. 29, n. 2.

Moneyya Sutta.—On the three perfections of a saint (*moneyyāni*), perfection of body, speech and mind.[1]

[1] A. i. 273.

Mora Jātaka (No. 159).—The Bodhisatta was once born as a golden peacock and lived on a golden hill in **Daṇḍaka.** He used to recite one spell in honour of the sun and another in praise of the Buddhas, and thus he was protected from all harm. **Khemā,** queen of Benares, saw in a dream a golden peacock preaching. She longed for the dream to come true and told it to the king. He made enquiries, and sent hunters to catch the golden peacock, but they failed. Khemā died of grief, and the king, in his anger, inscribed on a golden plate that anyone eating the flesh of the golden peacock would be immortal. His successors, seeing the inscription, sent out hunters, but they, too, failed to catch the Bodhisatta. Six kings in succession failed in this quest. The seventh engaged a hunter who, having watched the Bodhisatta, trained a peahen to cry at the snap of his finger. The hunter laid his snare, went with the peahen and made her cry. Instantly, the golden peacock forgot his spell and was caught in the snare. When he was led before the king and told the reason for his capture, he agreed with the king that his golden colour was owing to good deeds done in the past as king of that very city, and that he was a peacock owing to some sin he had committed. The eating of his flesh could not make anyone young or immortal, seeing that he himself was not immortal. Being asked to prove his words, he had the lake near the city dredged, when the golden chariot in which he used to ride was discovered. The king thereupon paid him great honour and led him back to Daṇḍaka.

The story was told to a backsliding monk who was upset by the sight of a woman magnificently attired.

Ānanda is identified with the king of Benares.[1] See also **Moraparitta.**

[1] J. ii. 33-8; the story is alluded to at J. iv. 414.

Morakavāpi.—See **Moravāpi.**

Moragalla.—The later name of **Sāmagalla.**[1]

[1] MṬ. 616.

Moraṇāla.—See **Goṇaravīya.**

Moranivāpa.—A grove in **Veḷuvana** at **Rājagaha.** It contained a **Paribbājakārāma,** the resort of recluses of various denominations. The

Udumbarikā Sīhanāda, the **Mahā Sakuladāyi** and the **Culla Sakūladāyi** Suttas were preached there.[1]

The place was so called because peacocks were protected there and food was provided for them.[2]

The Moranivāpa was on the bank of the **Sumāgadhā** and the Buddha is mentioned[3] as walking there. Not far away was the park of the Queen **Udumbarikā.**[4] See also **Moranivāpa Sutta,** 1 and 2.

[1] D. iii. 36 ff.; M. ii. 1, 29.
[2] DA. iii. 835; MA. ii. 694.
[3] D. iii. 39.
[4] *Ibid.*, 36.

1. **Moranivāpa Sutta.**—Preached at **Moranivāpa** on the qualities which make a monk fully proficient in the holy life—the aggregate of the virtues, concentration and insight, belonging to the adept.[1]

[1] A. i. 291.

2. **Moranivāpa Sutta.**—Preached at the **Paribbājakārāma** in **Moranivāpa.** It enumerates several groups of qualities the possession of which make a monk fully proficient in the higher life. Three of the groups are triads and the fourth a dyad. A stanza, attributed to **Sanaṅkumāra,** is also quoted.[1]

[1] A. v. 326 ff.

Moraparitta.—One of the **Parittas** (*q.v.*). The name is given to the spells found in the **Mora Jātaka.**[1]

[1] J. ii. 33 f.

Morapariveṇa.—See **Mayūra-pariveṇa.**

Moramaṇḍapa.—A pavilion erected by **Parakkamabāhu I.** in his **Dīpuyyāna.**[1]

[1] Cv. lxxiii. 118.

Moravaṅka.—One of the four villages given by **Parakkamabāhu I.** for the maintenance of the *pariveṇa* which he built for **Medhaṅkara.**[1]

[1] Cv. xc. 87.

Moravāpi.—A tank in Ceylon, built by **Mahāsena** and repaired by **Parakkamabāhu I.**[1] The district round it was called by the same name.[2] In Parakkamabāhu's campaign against **Gajabāhu,** the officers in charge of the district were **Nīlagallaka**[3] and, later, the **Nagaragiri Mahinda.**[4]

[1] Mhv. xxxvii. 47. MṬ. 680; Cv. lxviii. 44.
[2] *Ibid.*, lxix. 8.
[3] *Ibid.*, lxx. 67.
[4] *Ibid.*, 200.

The place seems to have had some strategic importance[5] and to have been situated to the south of **Anurādhapura** and the west of **Kālavāpi.**[6]

Moravāpi was the residence of the Elder **Mahādatta,** who was called **Moravāpivāsī.**[7]

[5] See *e.g.*, *ibid.*, lxii. 177, 201.

[6] Cv. *Trs.* i. 336, n. 4.

[7] *E.g.*, DhSA. 267, 284, 286.

Morahatthiya Thera.—An arahant. Another name for **Senaka Thera** (*q.v.*).[1]

[1] Ap. ii. 403.

Moriyaraṭṭha.—A district in the **Dakkhiṇadesa** of Ceylon. It was once the residence of several families of **Lambakaṇṇas.**[1]

[1] Cv. lxix. 13.

Moriyā.—A *khattiya* clan of India. Among those claiming a share of the Buddha's relics were the Moriyas of **Pipphalivana.** They came rather late and had to be satisfied with a share of the ashes.[1] **Candagutta,** grandfather of **Asoka,** was also a Moriyan.[2]

The Mahāvaṃsa Ṭīkā[3] contains an account of the origin of the name. According to one theory they were so called because they rejoiced in the prosperity of their city (*attānaṃ nagarasiriyā modāpīti, ettha sañjātā ti, dakārassa rakāraṃ katvā Moriyā ti laddhavohārā*). They lived in a delightful land. Another theory connects the name with *mora* (peacock). The city which they founded had buildings of blue stone, like the neck of the peacock, and the place always resounded with the cries of peacocks. It is said that the Moriyans were originally **Sākyan** princes of **Kapilavatthu,** who escaped to the **Himālaya** regions to save themselves from the attacks of **Viḍūḍabha,** and established a city there. Thus Asoka was a kinsman of the Buddha, for Candagutta was the son of the chief queen of the Moriyan king. The king was killed by a neighbouring ruler and the city pillaged.[4] Asoka's mother, **Dhammā,** was also a Moriyan princess.[5]

Mention is also made of the Moriyans as a Sinhalese clan.[6] Whether these had any connection with the Moriyans of India is not known.

[1] D. ii. 166; Bu. xxviii. 4.

[2] Mhv. v. 16; Dpv. vi. 19.

[3] MṬ. 180.

[4] *Ibid.*, 183; but according to the Mudrārākṣasa (Act iii.) Candragupta was a Vṛṣala, a person of low birth, an illegitimate son of the last Nanda king by a Śūdra woman, Murā.

[5] MṬ. 189.

[6] Cv. xxxviii. 13; xli. 69; see also Cv. *Trs.* i. 29, n. 2.

Molinī.—An old name for Benares. See the **Saṅkha Jātaka.**

Moliyagāma —A village. The story is told of a monk who went there for alms.[1]

[1] AA. i. 398.

Moliya-Phagguna Thera.—He was always friendly with the nuns and stood up for them in discussions with the monks. This was reported to the Buddha, who sent for him and preached the **Kakacūpama Sutta.**[1] In the **Saṃyutta Nikāya**[2] is recorded a discussion between Moliya-Phagguna and the Buddha, regarding the consciousness-sustenance (*viññāṇāhāra*). Moliya asks a question as to who feeds on consciousness. The Buddha rejects the question as being wrongly put and similar questions follow, which the Buddha puts in a different form and to which he provides the answers. In another context,[3] in the same collection, **Kalārakhattiya** is reported as saying to **Sāriputta** that Moliya-Phagguna had reverted to the lay life. Buddhaghosa[4] explains that the man's name was Phagguna and that he was given the title of *Moli* because he wore a large knot of hair on the top of his head while he was a layman, and that the name persisted after he joined the Order. See also **Phagguna.**

[1] M. i. 122 ff.
[2] S. ii. 12 f.
[3] S. ii. 50.
[4] SA. ii. 22; MA. i. 315.

Moliyasivaka.—A **Paribbājaka.** He once visited the Buddha at **Veḷuvana** and questioned him regarding predestination. The Buddha explains to him that suffering arises from various causes—bile, phlegm, wind, bodily humour, change of season, stress of untoward happenings, sudden attacks from without and also from one's *kamma*—and to say that these are all predestined is to go too far. Sīvaka expresses his approval and declares himself the Buddha's follower.[1] Another conversation he had with the Buddha is recorded in the **Aṅguttara Nikāya.**[2] There he asks the Buddha if the claims made with regard to the Dhamma are justified. The Buddha proves to him, by illustration, that they are.

Buddhaghosa explains[3] that the Paribbājaka's name was **Sīvaka,** his sobriquet being due to his having worn his hair in a topknot.

[1] S. iv. 230 f.; this sutta is quoted at Mil. 137.
[2] A. iii. 356.
[3] SA. iii. 87.

Mohavicchedanī.—An Abhidhamma treatise by Kassapa Thera[1].

[1] Gv. 60, 70; Svd. 1221; Sās. 69; P.L.C. 160, 179.

Y.

Yakkha.—A class of non-human beings generally described as *amanussā.* They are mentioned with *Devas, Rakkhasas, Dānavas, Gandhabbas, Kinnaras,* and *Mahoragas* (? *Nāgas*).[1] In other lists[2] they range immediately above the *Petas*; in fact, some of the happier Petas are called Yakkhas. Elsewhere[3] they rank, in progressive order, between *manussā* and *gandhabbā.* They are of many different kinds: spirits, ogres, dryads, ghosts, spooks. In the early records, yakkha, like nāgā, as an appelative, was anything but depreciative. Thus not only is **Sakka,** king of the gods, so referred to,[4] but even the Buddha is spoken of as a yakkha in poetic diction.[5] Many gods, such as Kakudha, are so addressed.[6] According to a passage in the Vimānavatthu Commentary,[7] which gives illustrations, the term is used for Sakka, the Four Regent Gods (**Mahārājāno**), the followers of **Vessavaṇa,** and also for *puriso* (individual soul ?). In the scholiast to the **Jayadissa Jātaka,**[8] the figure of the hare in the moon is also called yakkha. Of these above named, the followers of Vessavaṇa appear to be the Yakkhas proper. The term yakkha as applied to *purisa* is evidently used in an exceptionally philosophical sense as meaning " soul " in such passages as *ettāvatā yakkhassa suddhi,*[9] or *ettāvat' aggaṃ no vadanti h' ekā, yakkhassa suddhiṃ idha pāṇḍitāse.*[10] In the Niddesa,[11] *yakkha* is explained by *satta, nara, māṇava, posa, puggala, jīva, jagu, jantu, indagu, manuja.* The last term is significant as showing that yakkha also means " man."

The cult of yakkhas seems to have arisen primarily from the woods and secondarily from the legends of sea-faring merchants. To the latter origin belong the stories connected with *vimānas* found in or near the sea or in lakes. The worship of trees and the spirits inhabitating them is one of the most primitive forms of religion. Some, at least, of the yakkhas are called *rukkha-devatā*[12] (spirits of trees), and others *bhummadevatā,*[13] (spirits of the earth), who, too, seem to have resided in trees. Generally speaking, the Yakkhas were decadent divinities, beings half-deified, having a deva's supernormal powers, particularly as regards influencing people, partly helpful, partly harmful. They are sometimes called *devatā,*[14] or *devaputtā.*[15] Some of these, like **Indakūṭa** and **Suciloma,**

1 *E.g.*, J. v. 420.
2 *E.g.*, PvA. 45, 55.
3 *E.g.*, A. ii. 38.
4 M. i. 252; J. iv. 4; DA. i. 264.
5 M. i. 386.
6 S. i. 54.
7 VvA. 333.
8 J. v. 33.
9 SN. vs. 478.
10 *Ibid.*, 875.
11 MNid. 282.
12 *E.g.*, J. iii. 309, 345; Pv. i. 9; PvA. 5.
13 *Ibid.*, 45, 55.
14 *E.g.*, S. i. 205.
15 *E.g.*, PvA. 113, 139.

are capable of intelligent questioning on metaphysics and ethics. All of them possess supernatural powers; they can transfer themselves at will, to any place, with their abodes, and work miracles, such as assuming any shape at will. An epithet frequently applied is *mahiddhika*.[16] Their appearance is striking as a result of former good *kamma*.[17] They are also called *kāmakāmī*, enjoying all kinds of luxuries,[18] but, because of former bad *kamma*, they are possessed of odd qualities, thus they are shy, they fear palmyra leaf and iron. Their eyes are red and they neither wink nor cast a shadow.[19] Their abode is their self-created palace, which is anywhere, in the air, in trees, etc. These are mostly *ākasaṭṭha* (suspended in the air), but some of them, like the abode of **Āḷavaka**, are *bhumaṭṭha* (on the ground) and are described as being fortified.[20] Sometimes whole cities—*e.g.*, **Āḷakamandā**—stand under the protection of, or are inhabited by, Yakkhas.

In many respects they resemble the Vedic Piśācas, though they are of different origin. They are evidently remnants of an ancient demonology and have had incorporated in them old animistic beliefs as representing creatures of the wilds and the forests, some of them based on ethnological features.[21]

In later literature the Yakkhas have been degraded to the state of red-eyed cannibal ogres. The female Yakkhas (*yakkhiṇī*) are, in these cases, more fearful and evil-minded than the male. They eat flesh and blood (J. iv. 549; v. 34); and devour even men (D. ii. 346; J. ii. 15 ff.) and corpses (J. i. 265). They eat babies (J. v. 21; vi. 336) and are full of spite and vengeance (DhA. i. 47; ii. 35 f.). The story of **Bhūta Thera** is interesting because his elder brothers and sisters were devoured by a hostile Yakkha, so the last child is called Bhūta to propitiate the Yakkha by making him the child's sponsor !

Ordinarily the attitude of the Yakkhas towards man is one of benevolence. They are interested in the spiritual welfare of the human beings with whom they come in contact and somewhat resemble tutelary genii. In the **Āṭānāṭiya Sutta,**[22] however, the Yakkha-king, **Vessavaṇa,** is represented as telling the Buddha that, for the most part, the Yakkhas believe neither in the Buddha nor in his teachings, which enjoin upon his followers abstention from various evils and are therefore distasteful

16 *E.g.*, Pv. ii. 9; J. vi. 118.

17 Pv. i. 2, 9; ii. 11; iv. 3, etc.

18 *Ibid.*, i. 3.

19 J. iv. 492; v. 34; vi. 336, 337; these various characteristics are, obviously, not found in all Yakkhas. The Yakkhas are evidently of different grades—as is the case with all classes of beings—the highest among them approximate very nearly to the devas and have deva-powers, the lowest resemble petas. The Yakkhas are specially mentioned as being afraid of palm-leaves (J. iv. 492).

20 SNA. i. 222.

21 See Stede: Gespenstergeschichten des Petavatthu v. 39 ff.

22 D. iii. 194 f.

to some of the Yakkhas. Such Yakkhas are disposed to molest the followers of the Buddha in their woodland haunts.[23] But the Mahā Yakkhas,[24] the generals and commanders among Yakkhas, are always willing to help holy men and to prevent wicked Yakkhas from hurting them. Among Yakkhas are some beings who are *sotāpannas*—*e.g.*, **Janavasabha, Sucîloma** and **Khara** (*s.v.*). Some Yakkhas even act as messengers from another world, and will save prospective sinners from committing evil.[25] The case of the Yakkha **Vajirapāṇi** is of special interest.[26] He is represented as a kind of mentor, hovering in the air, threatening to kill **Ambaṭṭha,** if he does not answer the Buddha's question the third time he is asked. In many cases the Yakkhas are "fallen angels" and come eagerly to listen to the word of the Buddha in order to be able to rise to a higher sphere of existence—*e.g.*, **Piyaṅkaramātā** and **Punabbasumātā,** and even **Vessavaṇa,** listening to **Veḷukandakī Nandamātā** reciting the **Parāyaṇa Vagga.**[27] At the preaching of the **Mahāsamaya Sutta** (*q.v.*) many hundreds of thousands of Yakkhas were present among the audience.[28]

It has been pointed out[29] that the names of the Yakkhas often give us a clue to their origin and function. These are taken from (*a*) their bodily appearance—*e.g.*, **Kuvaṇṇā, Khara, Kharaloma, Kharadāṭhika, Citta, Cittarāja, Silesaloma, Sūciloma** and **Hāritā;** (*b*) their place of residence, attributes of their realms, animals, plants, etc.—*e.g.*, **Ajakalāpaka, Āḷavaka** (forest-dweller), **Uppala, Kakudha** (name of plant), **Kumbhīra, Gumbiya, Disāmukha, Yamamoli, Vajira, Vajirapāṇi** or **Vajirabāhu, Sātāgira, Serīsaka;** (*c*) qualities of character, etc.—*e.g.*, **Adhamma, Kaṭattha, Dhamma, Puṇṇaka, Māra, Sakaṭa;** (*d*) embodiments of former persons—*e.g.*, **Janavasabha** (lord of men = **Bimbisāra**), **Dīgha, Naradeva, Paṇḍaka, Sīvaka, Serī.**

Vessavaṇa (*q.v.*) is often mentioned as king of the Yakkhas. He is one of the four Regent Gods, and the Āṭānāṭiya Sutta[30] contains a vivid description of the Yakkha-kingdom of **Uttarakuru,** with its numerous cities, crowds of inhabitants, parks, lakes and assembly-halls. Vessavaṇa is also called **Kuvera,** and the Yakkhas are his servants and messengers. They wait upon him in turn. The Yakkhiṇīs draw water for him, and often are so hardworked that many die in his service.[31] No one, ap-

[23] *Cp.* the story of the Yakkha who wished to kill **Sāriputta** (Ud. iv. 4).

[24] The Sutta contains a list of such Mahāyakkhas (D. iii. 204 f.).

[25] *E.g.*, Pv. iv. 1.

[26] D. i. 95. The Commentary (DA. i. 264) says he is not an ordinary Yakkha, but Sakka himself.

[27] A. iv. 63.

[28] *s.v.*

[29] Stede, *op. cit.*

[30] D. iii. 199 ff.

[31] *E.g.*, J. iv. 492. Mention is also made (*e.g.*, DA. ii. 370) of Yakkhadāsīs who have to dance and sing to the devas during the night. Early in the morning they drink a cup of toddy (*surā*) and go off into a deep sleep, from which they rise betimes in the evening ready for their duties.

parently, is free from this necessity of waiting upon the king—even **Janavasabha** has to run errands for Vessavaṇa.[32] Among the duties of Vessavaṇa is the settling of disputes between the devas, and this keeps him much occupied.[33] In this work he is helped by the Yakkhasenāpati, whose business it is to preside over the courts during eight days of each month.[34] The Yakkhas hold regular assemblies on **Manosilātala** on the **Bhagalavatīpabbata.**[35] As followers of Kuvera, lord of riches, the Yakkhas are the guardians and the liberal spenders of underground riches, hidden treasures, etc., with which they delight men.[36]

It is difficult to decide whether the Yakkhas, who are the aborigines of Ceylon **(Laṅkā)**, were considered human or non-human. **Kuveṇī,** one of their princesses, and her maid, can both assume different forms, but **Vijaya** marries Kuveṇi and has two children by her.[37] The Yakkhas are invisible, and **Vijaya** is able to kill them only with the help of Kuveṇi[38]; but their clothes are found fit for Vijaya and his followers to wear.[39] Again, **Cetiyā** (*q.v.*) could make herself invisible and assume the form of a mare, but **Paṇḍukābhaya** lived with her for four years and she gave him counsel in battle. Later, when he held festivities, he had the Yakkha **Cittarāja** on the throne beside him.[40] In all probability these Yakkhas were originally considered as humans, but later came to be confused with non-humans. Their chief cities were **Laṅkāpura** and **Sirīsavatthu**.

The commonly accepted etymology of Yakkha is from the root √*yaj*, meaning to sacrifice. Thus: *yajanti tattha baliṃ upaharantī ti yakkha* (VvA. 224), or *pūjanīyabhāvato yakkho, ti uccati* (VvA. 333).

[32] D. ii. 207. [33] J. vi. 270.
[34] SNA. i. 197.
[35] *Ibid.*, 187; *cp.* D. iii. 201 and DA. iii. 967.
[36] *E.g.*, Pv. ii. 11; PvA. 145; Pv. iv. 12; PvA. 274. These were seven yakkhas who guarded the wealth of **Jotiyaseṭṭhi** (DhA. iv. 208 f.).
[37] *Cp.* Vin. iii. 37; iv. 20; where sexual intercourse with a Yakkha is forbidden.
[38] Mhv. vii. 36 [39] *Ibid.*, 38.
[40] Mhv. x. 87.

Yakkha Saṃyutta.—The tenth chapter of the **Saṃyutta Nikāya.**[1]

[1] S. i. 206 ff.

Yakkhasūkaratittha.—A ford on the *Mahāvāluka-gaṅgā.*[1]

[1] Cv. lxxii. 21; Cv. *Trs.* i. 321, n. 1.

Yagālla.—A place in Ceylon, mentioned in the account of the campaigns of **Parakkamabāhu I.**[1]

[1] Cv. lxx. 105.

Yajamāna Sutta.—**Sakka** asks the Buddha how best to offer gifts, so as to gain great reward. The Buddha replies that the gifts should be offered to the Order of monks.[1]

[1] S. i. 233.

Yañña.—See **Aññata-Koṇḍañña.**[1]

[1] Mil. 236.

Yañña Sutta.—Preached in reference to an animal sacrifice which **Pasenadi** proposed to hold on the advice of the brahmins in order to avert the effects of his evil dreams. The Buddha, hearing of it, declares that such sacrifices never produce good results. There are other "sacrifices" which harm no one and by which the celebrants are blessed and the gods pleased.[1]

[1] S. i. 75.

1. **Yaññadatta.**—A brahmin, father of **Koṇāgamana Buddha.**[1]

[1] D. ii. 7; J. i. 43; Bu. xxiv. 17.

2. **Yaññadatta.**—Son of **Āṇi-Maṇḍavya.** While he was playing, his ball rolled into an anthill, and, all unsuspecting, he put his hand in and was bitten by a snake. He was cured by "Acts of Truth" performed by his parents and by **Kaṇha Dīpāyana.**[1] See the **Kaṇhadīpāyana Jātaka.** He is identified with **Rāhula.**[2]

[1] J. iv. 30 f. [2] *Ibid.*, 37.

Yaññabhedavāda.—A poem of twenty-one stanzas in which **Bhūridatta** describes to his brother **Ariṭṭha** the various kinds of sacrifices and their futility.[1]

[1] J. vi. 205 ff.

Yaṭṭhālatissa, Yaṭṭhālayakatissa.—Son of **Mahānāga,** who was a brother of **Devānampiyatissa.** His son was **Goṭhabhaya** and his grandson **Kākavaṇṇatissa,** father of **Duṭṭhagāmaṇī.**[1] He was born in the **Yaṭṭhālavihāra**[2] and ruled in **Rohaṇa.** Among his works was the construction of the five-storeyed *pāsāda* at **Kalyāṇī.**[3]

[1] Mhv. xv. 170. [2] *Ibid.*, xxii. 10. [3] Cv. lxxxv. 64.

Yaṭṭhālaya-vihāra.—A vihāra in **Rohaṇa,** where **Yaṭṭhālayatissa** was born.[1]

[1] Mhv. xxii. 10.

Yaṭṭhikaṇḍa.—A district in **Malaya** in Ceylon, mentioned in the account of the wars between **Gajabāhu** and **Parakkamabāhu I.**[1]

[1] Cv. lxx. 7, 9

1. " **Yathābhata** " **Sutta.**—Five qualities which lead a monk to hell: he is faithless, unconscientious, reckless of blame, indolent and without insight.[1]

[1] A. iii. 3.

2. " **Yathābhata** " **Sutta.**—Similar groups of five qualities. See (1).[1]

[1] A. iii. 264.

Yadatthīya.—A king of twenty-seven kappas ago, a former birth of **Paṇṇadāyaka.**[1]

[1] Ap. i. 229.

1. " **Yad-anicca** " **Sutta.**—The *khandhas* are impermanent, what is impermanent is suffering, and what is suffering is void of self. Thus does the Noble Disciple comprehend things.[1]

[1] S. iii. 22.

2. " **Yad-anicca** " **Sutta.**—The eye is impermanent, it is *dukkha* and without the self, whether of the past, present, or future, so also are objects of sight. It is the same with all other senses.[1]

[1] S. iv. 152 ff.

Yama.—The god of death.[1] When beings die they are led before him to be judged according to their deeds. Birth, old age, illness, punishment for crime and death, are regarded as his messengers, sent among men as a warning to abstain from ill and do good. Yama questions beings brought before him as to whether they have seen these messengers and profited by them. If the answer is in the negative, the *nirayapālas* take them away to the different hells.[2] In the **Mahāsamaya Sutta**[3] mention is made of two Yamas (*duve Yamā*), which the Commentary explains[4] by " *dve Yamakadevatā* " (the twins, whom Rhys Davids[5] calls the Castor and Pollux of Indian Mythology). Elsewhere[6] Buddhaghosa speaks of four Yamas (*na c' esa eko va hoti, catusu pana dvāresu cattāro janā honti*) at the four gates (of the Nirayas ?). He says that Yama is a *Vemānikapetarājā*, who sometimes enjoys all the pleasures of heaven, in a celestial mansion, surrounded by *kapparukkhas*, and at other times experiences the fruits of his *kamma*. He is a good king.

[1] See, *e.g.*, DhA. iii. 337; *Yamassa santikaṃ* = *Maraṇasantikaṃ*.
[2] M. iii. 179 ff.
[3] D. ii. 259.
[4] DA. ii. 690.
[5] Dial. ii. 290, n. 1.
[6] AA. i. 374; MA. ii. 953.

In the Jātakas[7] the Nirayas are particularly mentioned as Yama's abode (*Yamakkhaya, Yamanivesana, Yamasādana,* etc.); but, more generally, all *Saṃsāra* is considered as subject to Yama's rule, and escape from *saṃsāra* means escape from Yama's influence, Yama being the god of Death. It is evidently in this sense that Yama is called **Vesāyī** (*q.v.*).[8] Yama is sometimes mentioned[9] with **Indra, Varuṇa, Soma, Pajāpati,** etc., as a god to whom sacrifices are offered. There is a tradition[10] that once Yama longed to be born as a human being and to sit at the feet of a Tathāgatha.

Yama's **Nayanāyudha** is mentioned[11] among the most destructive of weapons.

[7] *E.g.*, J. ii. 318; iv. 273; v. 268, 274, 304. The **Vetaraṇī** is mentioned as forming the boundary of Yama's kingdom (i. 21; J. ii. 317; iii. 472; but see ii. 318). At J. iv. 405, Yama's abode is called **Ussadaniraya.** DhA. i. 334 explains *Yamaloka* by *Catubbidhaṃ apāyalokaṃ*. *Cp.* PvA. 33 (*Yamaloko ti petaloko*); *ibid.*, 107 (*Yamavisayaṃ = Petalokaṃ*).

[8] J. ii. 317, 318.

[9] *E.g.*, J. vi. 201; D. i. 244; at Mil. 37 the list includes **Kuvera, Suyāma** and **Santusita**; *cp.* Mtu i. 265; iii. 68, 77; 77, 307.

[10] A. i. 142.

[11] SNA. i. 225.

1. **Yamaka.**—The sixth book of the Abhidhammapiṭaka. It is divided into ten chapters (called **Yamaka**)—**Mūla, Khandha, Āyatana, Dhātu, Sacca, Saṅkhārā, Anusaya, Citta, Dhamma** and **Indriya.** The method of treatment of each of the ten divisions tends to be threefold. Firstly, a *Paññattivāra or* section deliminating the term-and-concept, divided into an *Uddesavāra*, stating the inquiries only, and a *Niddesavāra*, wherein the inquiries are repeated with their several answers. Secondly, and mainly, there is the *Pavattivāra*, referring not to procedure generally, but to living processes, and, lastly, the *Pariññāvāra*, dealing with the extent to which a given individual (*i.e.*, a class of beings) understands the category under consideration.[1] There is a Commentary to the Yamaka by **Buddhaghosa,** which is included in the **Pañcappakaraṇaṭṭhakathā.**

[1] See P.T.S. edn., i. xix ff.; the Yamaka has been published by the P.T.S. 1911, 1913.

2. **Yamaka.**—A Thera holding heretical views, refuted by **Sāriputta.** See **Yamaka Sutta.**

3. **Yamaka.**—A man belonging to the retinue of King **Eḷeyya.** He was a follower of **Uddaka Rāmaputta.**[1]

[1] A. ii. 180; AA. ii. 554.

1. **Yamaka Vagga.**—The first section of the **Dhammapada.**

2. **Yamaka Vagga.**—The eight chapter of the Aṭṭhaka Nikāya of the **Aṅguttara Nikāya.**[1]

[1] A. iv. 314-35.

3. **Yamaka Vagga.**—The seventh chapter of the Dasaka Nipāta of the **Aṅguttara Nikāya.**[1]

[1] A. v. 113-31.

4. **Yamaka Vagga.**—The second chapter of the **Saḷāyatana Saṃyutta.**[1]

[1] S. iv. 6-15.

Yamaka Sutta.—The Thera **Yamaka** held the view that, in so far as a monk has destroyed the *āsavas*, he is broken up and perishes at the break-up of the body and becomes not after death. Yamaka's colleagues tried to correct this erroneous view[1] but failed, and so reported him to **Sāriputta.** Sāriputta visited Yamaka and argued with him that if it were false to say of anybody that he existed in truth, in reality, even in this very life, how much more so to speak of *someone* existing or not existing after death. Yamaka thereupon confessed his error. Sāriputta further elucidated the matter by using the simile of a man who enters the service of a rich householder with the intent to murder him. Such a man would always be a murderer, even though his master knew him not to be so. Even so, the disciple who regards body, etc., as permanent and so on, harbours a murderous view, even though he knows it not as such.[2] The sutta is often referred to.[3] It is sometimes[4] called the **Yamakovāda Sutta.**

[1] The heresy lies in the implication that "a being is broken up and perishes"; SA. ii. 226.

[2] S. iii. 109 ff.

[3] *E.g.*, VibhA. 32; Vsm. 479; *cp. ibid.*, 626 (*Yamakato sammasana*). Does Yamakato here mean "according to the Yamaka Sutta"?

[4] *E.g.*, Netti, p. 30.

Yamaka-pāṭihāriya.—The miracle of the "double appearances." When the Buddha laid down a rule forbidding the exercise of supernatural powers by monks—following on the miracle performed by **Piṇḍola-Bhāradvāja** (*q.v.*)—the heretics went about saying that henceforth they would perform no miracles except with the Buddha. **Bimbisāra** reported this to the Buddha, who at once accepted the challenge, explaining that the rule was for his disciples and did not apply to himself. He, therefore, went to **Sāvatthi**, the place where all Buddhas perform the Miracle. In reply to **Pasenadi,** the Buddha said he would perform the miracle at the foot of the **Gaṇḍamba-**tree on the full-moon day of

Asāḷha.[1] The heretics therefore uprooted all mango-trees for one league around, but, on the promised day, the Buddha went to the king's garden, accepted the mango offered by **Gaṇḍa,** and caused a marvellous tree to sprout from its seed. The people, discovering what the heretics had done, attacked them, and they had to flee helter-skelter.[2] The multitude, assembled to witness the miracle, extended to a distance of thirty-six leagues. The Buddha created a jewelled walk in the air by the side of the Gaṇḍamba. When the Buddha's disciples knew what was in his mind, several of them offered to perform miracles and so refute the insinuations of the heretics. Among such disciples were **Gharaṇī, Culla Anāthapiṇḍika, Cirā, Cunda, Uppalavaṇṇā** and **Moggallāna.** The Buddha refused their offers and related the **Kaṇhausabha** and **Nandivisāla Jātakas.** Then, standing on the jewelled walk, he proceeded to perform the **Yamakapāṭihāriya** (Twin Miracle), so called because it consisted in the appearance of phenomena of opposite character in pairs—*e.g.*, producing flames from the upper part of the body and a stream of water from the lower, and then alternatively. Flames of fire and streams of water also proceeded alternatively from the right side of his body and from the left.[3] From every pore of his body rays of six colours darted forth, upwards to the realm of **Brahmā** and downwards to the edge of the **Cakkavāḷa.** The Miracle lasted for a long while, and as the Buddha walked up and down the jewelled terrace he preached to the multitude from time to time. It is said that he performed miracles and preached sermons during sixteen days, according to the various dispositions of those present in the assembly. At the conclusion of the Miracle, the Buddha, following the example of his predecessors, made his way, in three strides, to **Tāvatiṃsa,** there to preach the Abhidhamma Piṭaka to his mother, now born as a devaputta.[4]

It is said[5] that two hundred millions of beings penetrated to an understanding of the Dhamma at the conclusion of the Miracle.

The Twin Miracle can only be performed by the Buddha.[6]

[1] This was in the seventh year after the Enlightenment (DA. i. 57).

[2] It was during this flight that **Pūraṇa Kassapa** (*q.v.*) committed suicide.

[3] DA. i. 57; DhA. iii. 214 f. explains how this was done.

[4] The Twin Miracle is described at DA. i. 57, and in very great detail at DhA. iii. 204; see also J. iv. 263 ff. The DhA. version appears to be entirely different from the Jātaka version; the latter is very brief and lacks many details, especially regarding Piṇḍola's miracle and the preaching of the Abhidhamma in Tāvatiṃsa. The account given in Dvy. (143-66) is again different; the Miracle was evidently repeatedly performed by the Buddha (see, *e.g.*, *s.v.* **Candanamālā**), and it is often referred to—*e.g.*, J. i. 77, 88, 193; Ps. i. 125; SNA. i. 36; AA. i. 71; MA. ii. 962; Mil. 349; Vsm. 390; PvA. 137; Dāthāvaṃsa i. 50. The miracle was also performed by the Buddha's relics; see, *e.g.*, Mhv. xvii. 52 f.; Sp. i. 88, 92.

[5] Mil. 349.

[6] *Ibid.*, 106.

Yamakapāṭihāriya Vatthu.—The story of the **Yamakapāṭihāriya.**[1]

[1] DhA. iii. 199-230.

Yamakoḷi.—A Yakkha who, with one thousand others, stood guard over the first gate of **Jotika's** palace.[1] When **Ajātasattu** attempted to take the palace the Yakkha drove him away.[2]

[1] DhA. iv. 208.

[2] *Ibid.*, 222.

Yamataggi.—A sage of old who led a good life and persuaded his followers to do likewise. He was among the originators of the Vedic hymns.[1]

[1] Vin. i. 245; D. i. 238, 239; M. ii. 169, 200; A. iii. 224, 229; iv. 61; also J. vi. 251, where he is called **Yāmataggi** and is described as a king of old. *Cp. Vedic Index, s.v.* Jamadagni.

1. **Yamunā.**—The second of the five great rivers of **Jambudīpa,**[1] which are often used in similes. On its banks were **Kosambī** and **Madhurā** (*q.v.*). For its origin see *s.v.* **Gaṅgā.** It is stated in the story of **Bakkula**[2] that newly-born children were bathed in the waters of the Yamunā for their health. The river was evidently the special resort of the **Nāgas.**[3] It is said[4] that the fish of the Yamunā considered themselves more beautiful than those of the Gaṅgā. The waters of the Gaṅgā mix very easily with those of the Yamunā.[5]

[1] Vin. ii. 237; A. iv. 101, 198, 202; v. 22; S. ii. 135; v. 401, etc.; Ud. v. 5; Mil. 114 (where ten rivers are mentioned); Mtu. iii. 203, 363.

[2] ThagA. i. 344.

[3] See, *e.g.*, D. ii. 259; J. vi. 158, 161 ff., 164, 197.

[4] J. ii. 151 ff. (under the river was the realm of the Nāga king, **Dhataraṭṭha** (J. vi. 200).

[5] J. v. 496; vi. 412, 415.

2. **Yamunā.**—A channel branching off westward from the **Puṇṇavaddhana Tank.**[1]

[1] Cv. lxxix. 47.

Yava.—Son of **Brahmadatta** and afterwards king of Benares. For his story see the **Mūsika Jātaka.**

Yavakalāpiya Thera.—An arahant. He was a barley-reaper (? *yavasika*) in the time of **Sikhī Buddha,** and one day, seeing the Buddha on the road, he spread a sheaf of barley for his seat.[1]

[1] Ap. i. 282.

Yavakalāpiya Sutta.—If six men, armed with flails, were to beat out a sheaf of corn, it would be thoroughly threshed. Thus are *putthujjanas* threshed by objects, etc.; thoughts of a future birth thresh them even more thoroughly.

Once **Vepacitti** and the **Asuras** were defeated by **Sakka** and the **Devas** and Vepacitti was bound hand and foot. But when Vepacitti thought that the Devas were righteous, his bonds slackened. Subtle were the bonds of Vepacitti, but more subtle are those of **Māra.** He who possesses conceits of *taṇhā-diṭṭhi-māṇa* is Māra's bondsman.[1]

[1] S. iv. 201 ff.

Yavapālakavimāna Vatthu.—The story of a *yavapālaka* of **Rājagaha** who gave a meal of sour gruel (*kummāsa*) to an arahant, and, as a result, was born in **Tāvatiṃsa** where **Moggallāna** met him and learnt his story.[1]

[1] Vv. iv. 7; VvA. 294.

Yavamajjhaka.—A village near **Mithilā,** the residence of **Amarādevī,** wife of **Mahosadha.**[1]

[1] J. vi. 365, 366; *ibid.*, 330 says there were villages of this name on the four sides of Mithilā.

Yameḷutekulā.—Two brahmins, probably named **Yameḷu** and **Tekuḷa,** who proposed to the Buddha that the Dhamma should be put into Sanskrit (*chandasi*). The Buddha refused their request.[1]

[1] Vin. ii. 139.

1. **Yasa Thera.**—He was the son of a very wealthy treasurer of Benares, and was brought up in great luxury, living in three mansions, according to the seasons and surrounded with all kinds of pleasures. Impelled by antecedent conditions, he saw one night the indecorum of his sleeping attendants, and, greatly distressed, put on his gold slippers and left the house and the town, non-humans opening the gates for him. He took the direction of **Isipatana,** exclaiming: "Alas! what distress! Alas! what danger!" The Buddha saw him in the distance and called to him, "Come Yasa, here is neither distress nor danger." Filled with joy, Yasa took off his slippers and sat beside the Buddha. The Buddha preached to him a graduated discourse, and when he had finished teaching the Truths, Yasa attained realization of the Dhamma. To Yasa's father, too, who had come in search of his son, the Buddha preached the Doctrine, having first made Yasa invisible to him.[1] At the end of the sermon he acknowledged himself the Buddha's follower,[2] and Yasa, who

[1] This is given as an example of the Buddha's *iddhi*-power, Vsm. 393.

[2] He thus became the first *tevācika upāsaka*.

had been listening, became an arahant. When, therefore, Yasa's presence became known to his father, who asked him to return to his grieving mother, the Buddha declared that household life had no attractions for Yasa and granted his request to be admitted to the Order. The next day, at the invitation of Yasa's father, he went, accompanied by Yasa, to his house, and there, at the conclusion of the meal, he preached to Yasa's mother and other members of the household, who all became his followers, thus becoming the first *tevācikā upāsikā*. When Yasa's intimate friends, **Vimala, Subāhu, Puṇṇaji** and **Gavampati,** heard of Yasa's ordination they followed his example and joined the Order, attaining arahantship in due course, as did fifty others of Yasa's former friends and acquaintances.[3]

In the time of **Sumedha Buddha,** Yasa was a king of the **Nāgas** and invited the Buddha and his monks to his abode, where he showed them great honour and hospitality. He then gave costly robes to the Buddha, and to each monk a pair of valuable robes. In the time of **Siddhattha Buddha** he was a Treasurer, and offered the seven kinds of jewels at the Bodhi-tree. In the time of **Kassapa Buddha** he was a monk. For eighteen thousand kappas he was a deva-king and one thousand times he was king of men. Wherever he went he had a gold canopy, and in his last life over his funeral pyre was a gold canopy.[4] He is evidently identical with **Sabbadāyaka** of the Apadāna.[5] A verse attributed to him is found in the **Theragāthā.**[6]

Yasa is often quoted as one who enjoyed great luxury in his lay life.[7]

The Dhammapada Commentary[8] states that, in a past life, Yasa and his four companions wandered about engaged in various acts of social service. One day they came across the dead body of a pregnant woman, which they took to the cemetery to be cremated. There the others went away, leaving Yasa to finish the work. While burning the corpse his mind was filled with thoughts of the foulness of the human body; he drew the attention of his friends to this idea, and, later, of his parents and wives, all of whom approved of what he said. For this reason Yasa felt revulsion against the household life, and his friends and members of his family were able to realize the Dhamma early in the Buddha's career.

The ordination of Yasa was one of the scenes of the Buddha's life to be sculptured in the Relic Chamber of the **Mahā Thūpa.**[9]

According to the Aṅguttara Commentary,[10] **Sujātā Senānidhitā** (who gave the Buddha a meal of milk-rice just before his Enlightenment) was

[3] Vin. i. 15-20; DhA. i. 72.
[4] ThagA. i. 232 f.
[5] Ap. i. 333 f.
[6] vs. 117.
[7] AA. ii. 596.
[8] DhA. i. 82 f.
[9] Mhv. xxx. 79.
[10] AA. i. 218 f.

Yasa's mother. She became a *sotāpanna* after listening to the Buddha's sermon.

2. **Yasa.**—Called **Kākaṇḍakaputta.** He was the son of the brahmin **Kākaṇḍaka** and was a pupil of **Ānanda.** It is said he was fortunate enough to see the Buddha alive.[1] When he arrived at the **Kūṭāgārasālā** in the **Mahāvana,** he discovered that the **Vajjian** monks had raised the "Ten Points" (*dasavatthu*) contrary to the Buddha's teachings, and that they were publicly asking for money from their lay disciples. Yasa thereupon protested against such misdemeanours, and the Vajjian monks, hoping to win him over, offered him a share of the money they had collected. This offer he rejected with scorn, and the monks passed on him the *Paṭisāraṇiyakamma* (craving of pardon from lay folk). This necessitated that Yasa should be sent among the laymen, accompanied by a messenger, presumably to ask their pardon for having misinformed them. But instead of this, Yasa told the lay people that the behaviour of the Vajjian monks was completely at variance with the rules laid down by the Buddha, and quoted the Buddha's discourses to prove his charge. When the Vajjian monks heard of this, they pronounced on him the *Ukkhepaniya-Kamma* (Act of Suspension), but when they assembled to carry it out, Yasa disappeared through the air to **Kosambī,** from where he sent messengers to the monks of **Avanti,** of the west (**Pātheyyakā** or **Pāveyyakā**) and of the south (**Dakkhiṇāpatha**), asking for their assistance in checking the corruption of the religion. With them he visited **Sambhūta Sāṇavāsī** at **Ahogaṅgapabbata,** and there they decided to consult **Revata** who lived in **Soreyya.** Yasa, therefore, went to Revata, following him through **Saṅkassa, Kaṇṇakujja, Udumbara, Aggalapura** and **Sahajāti.** Having found Revata, he questioned him regarding the ten points, and obtained from him promise of assistance. Together they returned to **Vesāli,** where lived **Sabbakāmī,** the oldest Thera of the day. After obtaining his opinion on the matter, an assembly of the monks was held and a committee was appointed (to settle the matter by an *Ubbāhikā*) of four from the East: **Sabbakāmī, Sāḷha, Khujjasobhita,** and **Vāsabhagāmika** ; and four from the West: **Revata, Sambhūta-Sāṇavāsī, Yasa** and **Sumana.** They debated the question at the **Vālikārāma,** Revata acting as questioner and Sabbakāmī answering his questions. At the end of the enquiry the decision was given against the ten points of the Vajjian monks, and this decision was conveyed to the assembly. Then the recital of the Vinaya was held in which seven hundred monks participated; this recital was called the **Sattasatī.**[2] The

[1] Mhv. iv. 57 f.

[2] Vin. ii. 294 ff.; Mhv. iv. 9 ff.; Dpv. iv. 45 ff.; v. 23. The Mhv. says that at first the king (**Kālāsoka**) was inclined to support the Vajjians, but his sister, **Nandā Therī,** warned him against this (iv. 37 ff.).

monks who refused to accept the findings of the committee held another convocation, which was called the **Mahāsaṅgīti.**[3] The Sattasatī Recital (also called The Second Recital) was also named[4] **Yasathera-saṅgīti,** evidently because of the prominent part played by Yasa.

Yasa is ranked[5] among the great benefactors of the religion.

[3] Dpv. v. 30 ff. [4] *E.g.*, AA. i. 251; MA. ii. 880. [5] See, *e.g.*, DA. ii. 525.

3. **Yasa.**—A deva, present at the preaching of the **Mahā Samaya Sutta.**[1]

[1] D. ii. 259; perhaps the name is **Yasasa** (DA. ii. 690).

4. **Yasa.**—A monk, author of the *Porāṇaṭīkā* on the **Khuddasikkhā.**[1] See also **Mahāyasa.**

[1] Svd. 1208.

5. **Yasa.**—A king of twenty-nine kappas ago; a previous birth of **Rāmaṇeyya Thera.**[1]

[1] ThagA. i. 121.

6. **Yasa.**—A palace occupied by **Padumuttara Buddha** in his last lay-life.[1]

[1] Bu. xi. 10; BuA. (158) calls it **Yasavatī.**

7. **Yasa.**—A palace occupied by **Kassapa Buddha.**[1]

[1] Bu. xxv. 35; BuA. (217) calls it **Yasavā.**

Yasa Sutta.—Once when the Buddha is staying at **Icchānaṅgala,** with **Nāgita** as his attendant, the brahmins of Icchānaṅgala come to pay him homage with various kinds of offerings and make a great noise and uproar as they wait outside the gate. The Buddha is disturbed by their noise and expresses his disapproval, whereupon, Nāgita begs of him to accept their homage and their gifts. The Buddha answers that he has no need for them; he has attained the happiness of renunciation, of insight, of awakening, of calm; happiness proceeding from gains and flattery is dung-like. He knows of monks who joke and make merry, who eat their bellies full and give themselves up to languor and torpor, or live on the outskirts of some village. They do not please him, but a forest-dwelling monk pleases him because he knows that, some day, that monk will find emancipation.[1]

[1] A. iv. 340 ff.

Yasadatta Thera.—He belonged to a family of **Malla** chieftains and was educated at **Takkasilā,** where he attained great proficiency. Later, while journeying in the company of **Sabhiya,** he came to **Sāvatthi,** where he was present at the discussion between Sabhiya and the Buddha. It was his purpose to try and discover flaws in the Buddha's argument. The Buddha knew what was in his mind, and at the end of the **Sabhiya Sutta** admonished him in five verses.[1] Yasadatta was greatly moved and entered the Order, winning arahantship in due course.

In the time of **Padumuttara Buddha,** he had been a very learned brahmin, living as an ascetic in the forest. One day he saw the Buddha, and, with clasped hands, praised his virtues.[2] He is evidently identical with **Ñāṇathavika** of the Apadāna.[3]

[1] The verses occur in the Thag. 360-4. [2] ThagA. i. 427 f. [3] Ap. ii. 392 f.

Yasapāṇi.—King of Benares. See the **Dhammaddhaja Jātaka.**

Yasava.—One of the chief lay supporters of **Sumedha Buddha.**[1]

[1] Bu. xii. 25.

Yasalālaka-Tissa.—Younger brother of **Candamukha-Siva.** He killed Siva at the festival sports at **Tissavāpi** and ruled as king for seven years and eight months (112-20 A.C.). His gate-watchman, **Subha,** bore a strong resemblance to him, and Tissa would sometimes deck Subha in all his royal ornaments and place him on the throne, where all the nobles of the court paid him homage, thinking him to be the king, Tissa, meanwhile, enjoying the fun, as watchman. One day, as Tissa stood at the door, laughing to himself, Subha charged him with impertinence and ordered the guard to slay him.[1]

[1] Mhv. xxxv. 49 ff.; Dpv. xxi. 46.

Yasavaḍḍhanavatthu.—A book by **Tipiṭakālaṅkāra Thera,** written at the request of Nyaung Ram Min.[1]

[1] Bode, *op. cit.*, 53.

1. **Yasavatī.**—Wife of **Supatita (Suppatīta),** and mother of **Vessabhū Buddha.**[1]

[1] Bu. xxii. 18; J. i. 42; D. ii. 7.

2. **Yasavatī.**—Wife of **Maṅgala Buddha** in his last lay life.[1]

[1] Bu. iv. 20.

3. **Yasavatī.**—Chief of the women patrons of **Revata Buddha.**[1]

[1] Bu. vi. 23.

4. **Yasavatī.**—Sister of **Akitti** (*q.v.*).[1]

[1] J. iv. 237.

5. **Yasavatī.**—One of the chief women supporters of **Metteyya Buddha.** She will be one of the leaders of the women who will accompany Metteyya on his Renunciation.[1]

[1] Anāgat. vs. 63, 99.

6. **Yasavatī.**—The city in whose park **Tissa Buddha** preached his first sermon. It was the capital of **King Sujāta.**[1]

[1] BuA. 189, 190.

7. **Yasavatī.**—See *s.v.* **Yasa** (6).

8. **Yasavatī.**—A Therī. The Apadāna contains a set of verses attributed to a group of nuns, at the head of whom was **Yasavatī.**[1]

[1] Ap. ii. 597.

9. **Yasavatī.**—Wife of **Okkāmukha** and mother of **Devadahasakka.**[1]

[1] MṬ. 135.

Yasavanta.—See **Yasavā** (1).

1. **Yasavā.**—A khattiya of **Candavatī,** father of **Anomadassī Buddha.**[1]

[1] Bu. viii. 17; J. i. 36; DhA. i. 105 calls him **Yasavanta.**

2. **Yasavā.**—One of the palaces occupied by **Maṅgala Buddha.**[1]

[1] BuA. 116.

Yasasa.—See **Yasa** (3).

Yassasī.—The name of a **Pacceka Buddha.**[1]

[1] M. iii. 69; ApA. i. 106; MA. ii. 890.

1. **Yasuttarā.**—One of the palaces occupied by **Paduma Buddha** in his last lay life.[1]

[1] BuA. 146; but see *s.v.* **Paduma.**

2. **Yasuttarā.**—A devatā of **Tāvatiṃsa.** She had been a resident of **Bārāṇasī.** She once spun two robes, and, having washed them, she offered them to the Buddha. The Buddha accepted the gift and preached

to her and she became a *sotāpanna*. After death she was born in Tāvatiṃsa as Yasuttarā and was much loved by **Sakka.** When she realized that her good fortune was due to her faith in the Buddha, she visited him at **Jetavana** and told him her story. It is said that, owing to the power of her merit, she owned a most marvellous elephant.[1]

[1] Vv. iv. 3; VvA. 181 ff.

Yasoja (*v.l.* **Yasojoti**) **Thera.**—He was born outside the gates of **Sāvatthi** in a fishing village, where his father was the headman of five hundred families. When he came of age, he was fishing one day in the **Aciravatī,** and, casting his net, caught a large golden-coloured fish. Yasoja and his companions took the fish to **Pasenadi** who sent them to the Buddha. The Buddha told them that the fish had been a wicked monk in the time of **Kassapa Buddha,** and had since suffered in purgatory, where his mother and sisters still were. He then preached to them the **Kapila Sutta,** and Yasoja and his companions, greatly moved, renounced the world.[1]

The Udāna mentions[2] how, later, Yasoja and five hundred of his companions went to see the Buddha at **Jetavana.** There they stood talking to the monks who lived there and made a great uproar. The Buddha, sending **Ānanda** to fetch them, asked them to remove themselves from his presence, as they were behaving like fishermen. Taking his admonition to heart, they returned to the banks of the **Vaggumudā** in the **Vajji**-country, and there they determined to lead such lives as would commend them to the Buddha. During the rainy season, they all put forth effort and attained arahantship. Some time after, the Buddha visited **Vesāli** during a journey and asked Ānanda to send for Yasoja and his friends as he desired to see them. Ānanda sent a message. When the monks arrived, they found the Buddha lost in meditation, and they, too, seated themselves and entered into *samādhi*, remaining thus throughout the night. Ānanda could not understand why the Buddha, having sent for Yasoja and his companions, should have sunk into *samādhi* without greeting them,[3] and three times during the night he tried to remind the Buddha of their arrival; but the Buddha ignored his warnings and in the morning explained to him that it was more joy for them all to live in the bliss of *samādhi* than to indulge in mere conversation. It is said[4] that when Yasoja and the others visited the Buddha at Vesāli, they were very thin and had grown uncomely through their austerities. The Buddha commended their self-denial in a verse, and

[1] ThagA. i. 356 f.

[2] Ud. iii. 3.

[3] It is said (UdA. 185) that the Buddha spent the night in *samādhi* in order to show Yasoja and his companions that he regarded them as equals.

[4] ThagA. i. 357.

Yasoja, appreciating the Buddha's praise, uttered two other verses, exalting the love of solitude.[5]

In the time of **Vipassī Buddha** Yasoja belonged to a family of park-keepers (*ārāmagopakā*), and one day seeing the Buddha travel through the air, he gave him a *labuja*-fruit.[6] In the time of **Kassapa Buddha,** Yasoja was the leader of a band of five hundred robbers. They were pursued by the villagers and fled into the forest for safety. There they saw a monk sitting on a stone and asked him for protection. He advised them to take the five precepts, and when they had done so, he exhorted them never to violate these precepts even if keeping them meant the loss of their lives. Soon after, they were captured and killed. But remembering the monk's admonition at the moment of death, they harboured no hatred against anyone, and after death were reborn in the deva-world.[7]

The Vinaya relates[8] how once, when Yasoja was ill, drugs were brought for his use, but as the Buddha had forbidden the use of a special place for storing such things (*kappiyabhūmi*) they were left out of doors and were partly eaten by vermin, the remainder being carried away by robbers. When the matter was reported to the Buddha, he allowed the use of a duly-chosen *kappiyabhūmi.* The Apadāna verses ascribed to Yasoja in the Theragāthā are, in the Apadāna itself, found in two places: one under **Labujadāyaka**[9] and the other, with slight variations, under **Labujaphaladāyaka.**[10]

[5] These verses are given in Thag. vss. 243-5.

[6] ThagA. i. 356.

[7] UdA. 179 f.

[8] Vin. i. 239.

[9] Ap. ii. 409.

[10] *Ibid.*, i. 295.

Yasoja Sutta.—The story of **Yasoja** (*q.v.*) as given in the Udāna.[1]

[1] SNA. i. 312.

1. **Yasodhara.**—A king of fifty-five kappas ago; a previous birth of **Ukkhepakaṭavaccha (Ekatthambhika) Thera.**[1]

[1] ThagA. i. 148; Ap. i. 56.

2. **Yasodhara.**—There were once seventy-seven kings of this name, all previous births of **Soṇa Koḷivisa.**[1]

[1] ThagA. i. 546; Ap. i. 94.

3. **Yasodhara.**—A brahmin, father of **Subhadda,** who became one of the chief disciples of **Koṇḍañña Buddha.**[1]

[1] BuA. 110.

4. **Yasodhara.**—A preacher in the time of **Kassapa Buddha.**[1] See *s.v.* **Andhavana.**

[1] SA. i. 148.

1. **Yasodharā.**—See **Rāhulamātā.**

2. **Yasodharā.**—The daughter of the Treasurer of **Sunandagāma**; she offered a meal of milk-rice to **Koṇḍañña Buddha.**[1]

[1] BuA. 108.

3. **Yasodharā.**—Wife of the *khattiya* **Yasavā** and mother of **Anomadassī Buddha.**[1]

[1] J. i. 36; DhA. i. 105; Bu. viii. 17; AA. i. 85.

4. **Yasodharā.**—Daughter of King **Jayasena.** She married **Añjana** the Sākyan, and their children were **Māyā** and **Pajāpatī,** and **Daṇḍapāṇī** and **Suppabuddha.**[1] Yasodharā was the sister of **Sīhahanu.**[2]

[1] Mhv. ii. 16 ff. [2] MṬ. 135; see also Mtu. i. 355.

5. **Yasodharā.**—Daughter of **Vijayabāhu I.** and **Līlāvatī.** She married **Vīravamma** and had two daughters, **Līlāvatī** and **Sugalā.**[1] She was later raised to the rank of *rājinī* (? queen) by Vijayabāhu, and erected a massive building, called **Pāsādapāda,** in the **Kappūramūlāyatana.**[2]

[1] Cv. lix. 26. [2] *Ibid.*, lx. 83.

6. **Yasodharā.**—One of the chief women supporters of **Sumedha Buddha.**[1]

[1] Bu. xii. 25.

" Yassam-disaṃ " Sutta.—Five qualities, the possession of which makes a king honoured wherever he rules—pure descent, great wealth, strong armies, a wise minister and great glory; and five similar qualities—virtue, learning, active energy, insight and emancipation—which enable a monk to live free in heart wherever he resides.[1]

[1] A. iii. 151 ff.

Yāgu Sutta.—The five advantages of gruel: it satisfies hunger, keeps off thirst, regulates wind, cleanses the bladder, and digests raw remnants of food.[1]

[1] A. iii. 250.

Yāgudāyaka Thera.—An arahant. Thirty thousand kappas ago, while on his way home laden with gifts, he found the river impassable and took his evening meal at a monastery. There he was pleased with the demeanour of the monks and gave them a meal of gruel with five savouries (? *pañcanna-yāgu*). After death, he was born in **Tāvatiṃsa**, and was king of gods thirty-three times and king of men thirty times.[1]

[1] Ap. ii. 375 f.

Yācitagāma.—A ford in the **Mahāvāluka-gaṅgā.**[1]

[1] Cv. lxxii. 39.

Yādhava.—A Damiḷa chief, ally of **Kulasekhara.**[1]

[1] Cv. lxxvi. 163, 173, 177.

Yābālagāma.—One of the villages given by **Aggabodhi IX.** for the supply of medicinal gruel to the smaller monasteries of **Anurādhapura.**[1]

[1] Cv. xlix. 89.

Yāmataggi.—See **Yamadaggi.**

Yāmuna, Yāmuneyya.—Derivatives of **Yamunā** (*q.v.*).

Yāmahanu.—One of the seven sages who lived the holy life and were reborn in the Brahma-world.[1]

[1] J. vi. 99.

1. **Yāmā.**—A class of Devas, mentioned in lists of *devas* between those of **Tāvatiṃsa** and those of **Tusita.**[1] Two hundred years of human life are but one day to the Yāma-devā, and two thousand years, composed of such days, form their life-period.[2] **Sirimā,** sister of **Jīvaka,** was born after death in the Yāma-world and became the wife of **Suyāma,** king of **Yāmabhavana.** From there she visited the Buddha with five hundred others.[3]

The meaning of Yāmā is explained in the Commentaries[4] as "those that have attained divine bliss" (*dibbaṃ sukhaṃ yātā payātā sampattā ti Yāmā*). Other explanations are "misery-freed" or "governing gods."[5]

[1] *E.g.*, Vin. i. 12; A. i. 228; iii. 287; M. ii. 194; iii. 100, etc.

[2] A. i. 213; iv. 253.

[3] SNA. i. 244 f.; see also VvA. 246 for an *upāsaka* born in the Yāma-world. In the **Hatthipāla Jātaka** (J. iv. 475) mention is made of four Yāma-devas who were reborn as men.

[4] *E.g.*, VibhA. 519; PSA. 441.

[5] *Compendium*, p. 138, n. 2.

2. **Yāmā.**—In some contexts, Yāmā seems to have been derived from **Yama,** king of the underworld—*e.g.*, in such expressions as "*Yāmato yāva Akaniṭṭhaṃ*" (From the underworld to the highest heaven).[1]

[1] KhA. 166.

Yuganaddha (or **Yuganandha**) **Sutta.**—**Ānanda** tells the monks at **Ghositārāma,** in **Kosambī,** that those who have attained arahantship have done so in one of four ways: by developing insight preceded by calm, or calm preceded by insight, or calm and insight together, or by having a mind utterly devoid of perplexities about the Dhamma.[1]

[1] A. ii. 157.

Yuganandha-kathā.—The first chapter of the second section of the **Paṭisambhidāmagga.**[1]

[1] Ps. ii. 98 ff.

Yuganandha Vagga.—The second section of the **Paṭisambhidāmagga.**[1]

[1] Ps. ii. 98 ff.

1. **Yugandhara.**—One of the mountains of the **Himālaya.**[1] It forms the first of the seven ranges round **Sineru.**[2]

A **Yugandharasāgara**[3] is also sometimes mentioned, and was probably a sea between Yugandhara and the next mountain range. When the Buddha reached **Tāvatiṃsa** in three strides, his first stride was from the earth to Yugandhara.[4] It was on the summit of Yugandhara that **Assagutta** convened an assembly of the monks in order to discuss their plan of campaign against **Milinda.**[5] The sun is mentioned as first rising over Yugandhara,[6] hence the expression "Like the morning sun over Yugandhara."[7]

[1] J. i. 119, 232; iv. 213; vi. 125; DhA. i. 249; Vsm. 206.

[2] SNA. ii. 443; but according to J. vi. 125 it is the fourth range.

[3] *E.g.*, J. i. 64; vi. 43.

[4] DhA. iii. 216.

[5] Mil. p. 6.

[6] *E.g.*, SA. ii. 165.

[7] *E.g.*, PvA. 137.

2. **Yugandhara.**—One of the chief **Yakkhas** to be invoked by the Buddha's followers in time of need.[1]

[1] D. iii. 205.

Yudhañjaya.—See **Yuvañjaya.**

Yudhañjaya Vagga.—The third section of the **Cariyāpiṭaka.**

1. **Yudhiṭṭhila.**—Son of the **Paṇḍu** king and one of the five husbands of **Kaṇhā.**[1]

[1] J. v. 424, 426.

2. **Yudhiṭṭhila.**—Son of **Sabbadatta,** king of **Ramma,** and younger brother of the Bodhisatta, born as **Yuvañjaya.** He is identified with **Ānanda.** See the **Yuvañjaya Jātaka.**

3. **Yudhiṭṭhila.**—The name of a gotta to which **Dhanañjaya,** king of the **Kurus,** belonged.[1] Mention is made also of a **Koravyarājā** of the **Yudhiṭṭhilagotta.**[2] Probably the kings of the Kurus (*q.v.*) belonged mostly to a dynasty that claimed its descent from Yudhiṭṭhila (Yudhiṣṭhira ?).

[1] J. iii. 400; v. 59, etc.

[2] J. iv. 361.

Yuvañjaya.—The Bodhisatta born as the son of King **Sabbadatta.** See the **Yuvañjaya Jātaka.** *v.l.* **Yudhañjaya.**

Yuvañjaya Jātaka (No. 460).—The Bodhisatta was once born as **Yuvañjaya,** son of **Sabbadatta,** king of **Ramma** (Benares). He was the eldest of one thousand sons, and **Yudiṭṭhila** was his younger brother. After he came of age he was on his way early one morning to the park, and saw all around him dew. In the evening, as he returned home, the dewdrops were no more to be seen. His charioteer explained that the sun had dried them up. Reflecting on this, the prince realized the impermanence of life and asked his father's leave to renounce the world. Both his parents tried to dissuade him but they failed, and he and **Yudhiṭṭhila** built a hermitage in the **Himālaya,** where they became ascetics.

Yudhiṭṭhila is identified with **Ānanda.** This story was told in reference to the Buddha's Renunciation, to some monks who marvelled at the Buddha's great sacrifice.[1]

[1] J. iv. 119 ff.; the story of Yuvañjaya (Yudhañjaya) is also given in the Cariyāpiṭaka iii. 1; CypA. 143 ff.

1. **Yūthikapupphiya Thera.**—An arahant. Ninety-four kappas ago he saw the Buddha (? **Siddhattha**) on the banks of the **Candabhāgā,** and offered him a *yūthika* (jasmine)-flower. Sixty-seven kappas ago he was a king named **Samuddhara.**[1]

[1] Ap. i. 184.

2. **Yūthikapupphiya.**—An arahant Thera. In a previous birth he saw **Padumuttara Buddha** and offered him a *yūthika* (jasmine)-flower. Fifteen kappas ago he was a king name **Samitanandana.**[1]

[1] Ap. i. 202.

1. **Yoga Sutta.**—The four bonds—sensual desire, becoming, wrong view, ignorance—for the comprehension of which the Noble Eightfold Path must be followed.[1]

[1] S. v. 59.

2. **Yoga Sutta.**—On details regarding the four kinds of bonds: of passion, of becoming, of (wrong) views, of ignorance.[1]

[1] A. ii. 10 f.

Yogakkhema Vagga.—The eleventh chapter of the **Saḷāyatana Saṃyutta.**[1]

[1] S. iv. 85 ff.

Yogakkhema Sutta.—The Tathāgata has won security from bondage, because he has abandoned desire for objects, etc.[1]

[1] S. iv. 85.

Yogavinicchaya.—A Commentary by **Vācissara.**[1]

[1] Gv. 68; P.L.C. 202.

1. **Yodha Sutta.**—Three qualities which make a soldier serviceable to a king: he must be a long-distance shot, a rapid (like lightning) shot, and a piercer of huge objects; and three similar qualities (details of which are given) which make a monk worthy of homage and gifts.[1]

[1] A. i. 284 f.

2. **Yodha Sutta.**—Similar to (1), but four qualities are given, the fourth being that the soldier must be skilled in the knowledge of points of vantage.[1]

[1] A. ii. 170 f.

Yodhājīva.—A headman (*gāmaṇī*) who visited the Buddha and asked if it was true that men who fall fighting in battle are reborn among the **Sārañjita** devas. At first the Buddha refused to answer the question, but finding that Yodhājīva insisted, explained to him that fighting men were reborn after death either in the **Sārājita-niraya** or among animals. The headman became the Buddha's follower.[1]

[1] S. iv. 308.

1. **Yodhājīva Vagga.**—The fourteenth chapter of the Ṭikā Nipāta of the **Aṅguttara Nikāya.**[1]

[1] A. i. 284-92.

2. **Yodhajīvā Vagga.**—The nineteenth chapter of the Catukka Nipāta of the **Aṅguttara Nikāya.**[1] The Commentary calls it **Brāhmaṇa Vagga.**[2]

[1] A. ii. 170-84. [2] AA. 552 f.

3. **Yodhājīva Vagga.**—The eight chapter of the Pañcaka Nipāta of the **Aṅguttara Nikāya.**[1]

[1] A. iii. 84-110.

1. **Yodhājīva Sutta.**—On five kinds of warriors: those who are frightened by a cloud of dust, by the sight of a flag, by tumult, by conflict, and those who fight victoriously; and on five similar kinds of monks.[1]

[1] A. iii. 87 f.

2. **Yodhājīva Sutta.**—On five kinds of warriors: those who go down into the thick of the fight where thay are overpowered, those who are wounded and die on the way to their home, those who survive for some time but die of their wounds, those who are cured of their wounds, those that are victorious in battle and continue to fight. There are five corresponding kinds of monks.[1]

[1] A. iii. 94 ff.

3. **Yodhājīva Sutta.**—Records the visit of the headman **Yodhājīva** to the Buddha.[1]

[1] S. iv. 308.

1. **Yonaka-Dhammarakkhita Thera.**—He was sent to **Aparantaka** at the conclusion of **Moggaliputtapissa's** Council.[1] There he preached the **Aggikkhandhopama Sutta** and converted thirty-seven thousand beings.[2]

[1] Mhv. xii. 4. [2] *Ibid.*, 34 f.; Dpv. viii. 7; Sp. i. 67.

2. **Yonaka-Dhammarakkhita.**—Teacher of **Punabbasukuṭumbika-putta-Tissa** (*q.v.*).

Yona-Mahādhammarakkhita Thera.—With thirty thousand others, he came from **Alasandā** to the Foundation Ceremony of the **Mahā Thūpa.**[1]

[1] Mhv. xxix. 39.

Yonā, Yavanā, Yonakā.—A country and its people. The name is probably the Pāli equivalent for Ionians, the Baktrian Greeks.[1] The country was converted by the Thera **Mahārakkhita,** who was sent there after the Third Council.[2] In the time of **Milinda** the capital of the Yona country was **Sāgala.**[3] It is said[4] that at the Foundation Ceremony of the **Mahā Thūpa,** thirty thousand monks, under **Yona-Mahādhamma-rakkhita,** came from **Alasandā** in the Yona country. Alasandā was evidently the headquarters of the Buddhist monks at that time. Alasandā is generally identified[5] with the Alexandria founded by the Macedonian king (Alexander) in the country of the Paropanisadae near Kābul.

In the **Assalāyana Sutta,**[6] Yona and **Kamboja** are mentioned as places in which there were only two classes of people, masters and slaves, and the master could become a slave or *vice versa*. The Commentary[7] explains this by saying that supposing a brahmin goes there and dies, his children might consort with slaves, in which case their children would be slaves. In later times, the name Yavanā or Yonā seems to have included all westerners living in India and especially those of Arabian origin.[8] Yonaka statues, holding lamps, were among the decorations used by the Sākyans of **Kapilavatthu.**[9] The language of the Yavanas is classed with the **Milakkhabhāsā.**[10] The Aṅguttara Commentary[11] records that from the time of **Kassapa Buddha** the Yonakas went about clad in white robes, because of the memory of the religion which was once prevalent there.

[1] The Yonas are mentioned with the Kambojas in Rock Edicts v. and xii. of Asoka, as a subject people, forming a frontier district of his empire.
[2] Mhv. xii. 5; Dpv. viii. 9; Sp. i. 67.
[3] Mil. 1.
[4] Mhv. xxix. 39.
[5] See, *e.g.*, Geiger, Mhv. *Trs.* 194, n. 3.
[6] M. ii. 149.
[7] MA. ii. 784.
[8] Cv. *Trs.* ii. 87, n. 1.
[9] MA. ii. 575.
[10] *E.g.*, DA. i. 276; VibhA. 388.
[11] AA. i. 51.

1. "**Yoniso**" **Sutta.**—Just as the dawn is harbinger of the sun, so is *yonisomanasikāra* the harbinger of the Noble Eightfold Path.[1]

[1] S. v. 31 f.

2. "**Yoniso**" **Sutta.**—Mindfulness comes by *yonisomanasikāra* and goes through it to fulfilment.[1]

[1] S. v. 93 f.

"**Yo no cedam**" **Sutta.**—If there were no satisfaction from the earth-element, beings would not lust after it; if there were no misery in it, they would not be repelled by it; if there were no escape from it, beings would not so escape; when all these things are fully known, beings will live aloof from the world.[1]

[1] S. ii. 172.

R.

Raṃsimuni.—The sixth future Buddha.[1]

[1] Anāgat, p. 40.

1. **Raṃsisaññaka Thera.**—An arahant. He was an ascetic in **Himavā,** and seeing Vipassī Buddha radiating light, he paid him homage.[1]

[1] Ap. i. 129.

2. **Raṃsisaññaka.**—An arahant Thera. Ninety-two kappas ago he was an ascetic, and seeing **Phussa Buddha** in trance, was overjoyed at the sight.[1]

[1] Ap. i. 130.

3. **Raṃsisaññaka.**—An arahant Thera. Thirty thousand kappas ago he saw a Buddha seated on a rock suffusing all the place with his aura, and was gladdened by the sight. Fifty-seven kappas ago he was a king named **Sujāta.**[1]

[1] Ap. i. 210.

1. **Rakkha.**—A general of **Parakkamabāhu I.** He was originally the **Daṇḍādhināyaka** (? general) of **Gajabāhu,** but Parakkamabāhu won him over and put him in charge of the conquest of the **Malaya** country. He accomplished this with the help of his younger brother, after fighting many battles and subduing the chiefs of the various districts.[1] The king thereupon conferred on him the rank of **Kesadhātu.** Later, he subdued the district of **Merukandara** and was sent against the **Mahālekha Mahinda,** whom he defeated at **Sarogāmatittha.** He was associated with **Nagaragiri Nātha** in the fight against **Mānābharaṇa** near **Badaravallī.** After this he is referred to as **Adhikārī Rakkha,** and the war against Mānābharaṇa seems to have been chiefly in his charge. He was in command of the army at **Maṅgalabegāma** and **Mihiraṇabibbila,** and decisively defeated Mānābharaṇa's general, **Buddhanāyaka** at **Rajatakedāra.** Later, when Queen **Sugalā** raised a revolt in **Rohaṇa,** it was Rakkha who was sent to crush it. He was by now commander-in-chief, and was helped in the

[1] For details see Cv. lxx. 5 ff.

subjugation of Rohaṇa by the general **Bhūta.** They fought a battle at **Lokagalla** and advanced to **Majjhimagāma** and occupied **Uddhanadvāra,** where Rakkha was helped by the two **Kittis,** the **Adhikāri** and the **Jīvapotthakī.** From there they marched to **Mahārīvara,** and at **Badaguṇa** crushed Sugalā's forces, thus gaining possession of the Sacred Bowl and the Sacred Tooth which these forces were carrying. In a last onslaught at **Demaṭavala,** Rakkha put the enemy to flight and marched on to **Sappanārukokilla,** where he died of an attack of dysentery.[2]

[2] Cv. lxx. 5, 15, 19, 282, 295; lxxii. 2 ff., 107, 160, 207, 232, 265 ff.; lxxiv. 41 ff. 55, 72 ff., 111 ff., 136 ff.

2. **Rakkha,** called **Laṅkādhinātha.**—A general of **Parakkamabāhu I.** He helped **Lokajitvāna** to defeat **Hukitti,** and was later sent to **Janapada** to fight against **Gajabāhu's** forces. He was successful, and occupied **Yagālla** and **Taḷātthala.** Gajabāhu tried to win him over with bribes, but Rakkha mutilated the envoys and sent the presents to Parakkamabāhu. He fought at **Āḷigāma** against Gajabāhu's general, **Sīka,** and, proving victorious, held a great celebration. Later he was in charge of the successful attack on **Pulatthipura,** when the city was captured and Gajabāhu taken prisoner. He was then sent to **Maṅgalabegāma** against **Mānābharaṇa,** and fought so fiercely that the latter was forced to flee to **Rohaṇa.** Rakkha was placed in charge of the ford at **Niguṇḍivālukā.** He was, however, greatly offended by the favour shown by **Parakkamabāhu** to his rival, the Senāpati **Deva,** and no longer showed himself zealous in war. An officer of Gajabāhu who was with Rakkha, noticing this, sent word to Mānābharaṇa to come at once and take advantage of Rakkha's lethargy. Mānābharaṇa followed this advice and advanced against Rakkha, whom he killed in the course of a fierce battle.[1]

[1] Cv. lxx. 24, 98 ff., 115 ff., 174, 232, 283, 297, 306; lxxii. 37, 75 ff.

3. **Rakkha,** called **Mahālekha.**—He was an officer of **Parakkamabāhu I.** and took part in the campaigns against **Mānābharaṇa,** being stationed at **Maṅgalabegāma,** at **Pillaviṭṭhi.** At this place he fought a battle, which lasted for eight days, against **Buddhanāyaka** and **Mahāmāladeva,** and brought the district of **Kālavāpi** under his power.[1]

[1] Cv. lxxii. 161, 170 ff., 182, 206.

4. **Rakkha,** called **Damiḷādhikāri.**—He was an officer of **Parakkamabāhu I.,** and was one of those chiefly responsible for the subjugation of **Rohaṇa.** He fought battles at **Doṇivagga, Guralaṭṭhakalañcha, Pūgadaṇḍakāvāṭa, Bodhiāvāṭa, Bhinnālavanāgāma** and several other places, and inflicted severe defeats on the rebel forces, dealing them a

severe blow at **Mahāsenagāma,** where **Laṅkāpura Rakkha** was killed. This enabled him to take possession of **Mahānāgahula.** In order to bring the province completely under his control he had to fight further at **Bakagalla-Uddhavāpi, Saṅghabhedakagāma, Kuravakagalla** and **Mahāpabbata,** and he thus won full possession of **Dvādasasahassaka,** where he seems to have spent the rest of his days.[1]

[1] Cv. lxxv. 20, 69 ff., 74 ff., 87-159.

5. **Rakkha Kañcukīnāyaka.**—An officer of **Parakkamabāhu I.**, associated with **Damiḷādhikārī Rakkha.** He fought victorious battles at **Mahāvālukagāma, Devanagara, Kammāragāma, Mahāpanālagāma, Mānakapiṭṭhi, Nīlavalā Ford** and **Kadalīpatta,** and marching then through **Mārāvaratthali,** he assisted Damiḷādhikārī Rakkha in the capture of **Mahānāgahula.**[1]

[1] Cv. lxxv. 20 ff., 35 ff., 52 ff., 116.

6. **Rakkha Laṅkāpura.**—One of the leaders of the rebels in **Rohaṇa** in the time of **Parakkamabāhu I.** He was later made their commander-in-chief. He advanced with his forces to **Nadībhaṇḍagāma,** and was killed in the battle at **Mahāsenagāma,** fighting against **Damiḷādhikārī Rakkha.** His place in the army was taken by his elder brother.[1]

[1] Cv. lxxv. 70, 103, 112, 134.

1. **Rakkhaka.**—A general of **Vikkamabāhu II.,** he was captured by **Vīradeva.**[1]

[1] Cv. lxi. 42.

2. **Rakkhaka Ilaṅga.**—A general of **Dappula IV.** He built a dwelling-house near the **Thūpārāma,** which was named after the king.[1]

[1] Cv. liii. 11.

3. **Rakkhaka Saṅkhanāyaka.**—An officer of **Parakkamabāhu I.,** who stationed him at **Hillapattakakhaṇḍa.**[1]

[1] Cv. lxxii. 41.

Rakkhaṅga.—A country (modern Arakan) from which **Vimaladhammasūriya I.** obtained a number of monks, headed by **Nandicakka,** in order to re-establish the *upasampadā* in Ceylon.[1] **Vimaladhammasūriya II.** did likewise[2]; so did **Vijayarājasīha.**[3] The last two were helped in their enterprise by the Dutch. **Kittisirirājasīha**[4] is mentioned as having paid special honour to the monks from Rakkhaṅga.

[1] Cv. xciv. 15.

[2] *Ibid.*, xcvii. 10; see also Cv. *Trs.* ii. 239, n. 1.

[3] Cv. xcviii. 89; see also Cv. *Trs.* ii. 253, n. 2.

[4] Cv. xcix. 25.

Rakkhacetiyapabbata.—A vihāra in Ceylon, restored by **Vijayabāhu I.**[1] It is probably identical with **Rakkha-vihāra** (*q.v.*).

[1] Cv. lx. 58.

Rakkhadīvāna.—A general of **Parakkamabāhu I.** who defeated **Nagaragiri Gokaṇṇa** at **Goṇagāmuka.**[1]

[1] Cv. lxx. 70.

Rakkhapāsāṇakaṇṭha.—A place in **Rājaraṭṭha.** It was the limit of the **Coḷa** territory in Ceylon in the time of **Mahinda V.**[1] It was evidently a frontier post.[2]

[1] Cv. lv. 22. [2] *Ibid.*, lvii. 67.

Rakkhamāna.—A tank, repaired by **Parakkamabāhu I.**[1]

[1] Cv. lxviii. 46.

Rakkha-vihāra.—A monastery in Ceylon in which **Moggallāna III.** built a cetiya.[1] It was probably identical with **Rakkhacetiyapabbata.**

[1] Cv. xliv. 51.

Rakkhasa.—A minister of **Sena I.** He built a dwelling-house, called after him, in the **Abhayuttara-vihāra.**[1]

[1] Cv. l. 84.

Rakkhasadvāra.—One of the gates of **Pulatthipura.**[1]

[1] Cv. lxxiii. 161.

Rakkhasā.—A class of demons, chiefly nocturnal and harmful. They usually have their haunt in the water and devour men when bathing there. Some of them live in the sea.[1]

[1] *E.g.*, Thag. v. 931; SN. vs. 310; J. i. 127; vi. 469; DhA. i. 367; iii. 74; Mhv. xii. 45, etc.

1. **Rakkhita Thera.**—He was born in a noble **Sākyan** family of **Vedeha-nigama** (? **Devadaha**) and was one of the five hundred youths given by the Sākyan and **Koliyan** chiefs to provide an escort to the Buddha, as an acknowledgement of his having prevented war between them. When the Buddha preached the **Kuṇāla Jātaka,** Rakkhita, realising the dangers of sensuality, developed insight, and later became an arahant.

In the time of **Padumuttara Buddha** he heard the Buddha preach and praised his erudition.[1] He is evidently identical with **Sobhita Thera** of the Apadāna.[2]

[1] Thag. vs. 79; ThagA. i. 173. [2] Ap. i. 163 f.

2. **Rakkhita Thera.**—He was sent to the **Vanavāsa** country to convert it at the end of the Third Council. Floating in the air amid the people, he preached the **Anamatagga Saṃyutta.** Sixty thousand people embraced the new religion and thirty-seven thousand joined the Order, five hundred vihāras being founded.[1]

[1] Mhv. xii. 4, 31 ff.; Dpv. viii. 7; Sp. i. 63, 66.

3. **Rakkhita.**—See **Mahārakkhita** in the **Somanassa Jātaka.**

4. **Rakkhita.**—The Bodhisatta born as an ascetic. See **Mahāmaṅgala Jātaka.**

5. **Rakkhita.**—Son of **Lokitā** and **Moggallāna** and brother of **Kitti** (afterwards **Vijayabāhu I.**).[1]

[1] Cv. lvii. 42.

6. **Rakkhita Thera.**—See **Buddharakkhita.**

Rakkhitatala.—A locality in the **Himālaya.** It was there that the arahants met and discussed as to what they should do to solve the questions put by **Milinda.**[1]

[1] Mil. p. 6.

Rakkhita-vanasaṇḍa.—A forest tract near the village of **Pārileyya.** There the Buddha retired and lived at the foot of the **Bhaddasāla,** when unable to settle the dispute among the **Kosambī** monks. The elephant Pārileyya lived there and waited upon the Buddha.[1] It is said[2] that the place derived its name from the fact that Pārileyya looked after the Buddha, guarding him throughout the night, wandering about the forest till dawn, a stick in his trunk, in order to ward off danger.

[1] Vin. i. 352 f.; Ud. iv. 5; DhA. i. 47; iv. 26; UdA. 250. [2] DhA. i. 49.

Ragā.—One of **Māra's** three daughters, who sought to tempt the **Buddha.**[1]

[1] SN. vs. 835; S. i. 124 ff.; J. i. 78; DhA. i. 201; iii. 196, 199, etc.

Rajakatthala.—A village dedicated by **Kittisirirājasīha** to celebrations in honour of the Tooth Relic.[1]

[1] Cv. c. 43.

Rajakamatasambādha.—A place near **Pulatthipura** where **Laṅkādhinātha Rakkha** and **Jīvitapotthakī Sukha** fought a battle against the forces of **Gajabāhu.**[1]

[1] Cv. lxx. 175.

Rajata Sutta.—Few are they who abstain from taking silver, many they who do not.[1]

[1] S. v. 471.

Rajatakedāra.—A locality in Ceylon, mentioned in the account of the battle between the forces of **Parakkamabāhu I.** and those of **Mānābharaṇa.**[1]

[1] Cv. lxxii. 257, 269.

Rajataguhā.—A cave in the **Himālaya.**[1]

[1] J. ii. 67.

Rajatapabbata.—A mountain range in the **Himālaya.**[1]

[1] J. i. 50; ii. 6, 7, 92.

Rajatamayalena.—A cave in **Ambilajanapada** in which lived five hundred arahants. One day one of these was suffering from stomach trouble and ten thousand of his colleagues came by air to minister to him. They all found room in the cave because of their *iddhi*-power.[1]

[1] MṬ. 552.

Rajata-Rajatalena-(Rajatamaya)-vihāra.—A monastery in Ceylon, built by **Āmaṇḍagāmaṇī Abhaya.**[1] It was in **Ambaṭṭhakolalena,** where silver was discovered for use in the construction of the **Mahā Thūpa.**[2] **Kittisirirājasīha**[3] visited the vihāra and paid it great honour and gave it to a *sāmaṇera* called **Siddhattha.**[4] The vihāra is now called *Ridī-vihāra* and is near the modern Kurunegala.

[1] Mhv. xxxv. 4; but see Cv. c. 238, where **Duṭṭhagāmaṇī** is stated to have built it.

[2] Mhv. *Trs.* 188, n. 1.

[3] Cv. xcix. 41.

[4] *Ibid.*, c. 238.

Rajanīya Sutta.—A monk who is enticed by the enticing, corrupted by the corrupting, infatuated by the infatuating, angered by the angry and maddened by the maddening—such a one is not respected by his fellows.[1]

[1] A. iii. 110.

Rajanīyasaṇṭhita Sutta.—The *khandhas* have lust inherent in them. Desire for them must be put away.[1]

[1] S. iii. 79.

Rajja Sutta.—Once the Buddha was thinking compassionately of those suffering from the cruelty of rulers and wondering if it were possible to rule without causing suffering. **Māra** approaches and tries to make him absorbed in the fascination of exercising power, suggesting that if the Buddha wished he could change even the **Himālaya** into a mass of gold. But, says the Buddha, he has seen suffering and its source and will not, therefore, incline to sense-desires.[1]

[1] S. i. 116.

Rajju Sutta.—Gains, favours and flattery are like a cord cutting through a man's skin right to his marrow.[1]

[1] S. ii. 238.

Rajjumālā.—A slave in the village of **Gayā.** Her mistress disliked her and ill-treated her in every way. One day, in order to escape being pulled by her hair, she had her head shaved; but her mistress then had a rope tied round her head, with which she pulled her about; hence her name. Unable to bear her life any longer, the slave went into the village near by, intending to commit suicide, but there she found the Buddha waiting for her, and he preached to her. Rajjumālā became a *sotāpanna,* and then returned to her mistress, who, having heard her story, visited the Buddha and became his follower. The Buddha explained that the two women had had their positions reversed in a previous birth, and that the then slave, who was the mistress in the present birth, had vowed vengeance for the cruelty inflicted upon her. Rajjumālā was freed and was born after death in **Tāvatiṃsa.**[1]

[1] Vv. iv. 12; VvA. 206 ff.

1. **Raṭṭhapāla Thera.**—Chief of those who had left the world through faith (*saddhāpabbajitānaṃ*).[1] He was born at **Thullakoṭṭhita** in the **Kuru** country as the son of a very wealthy councillor and was called by his family name of Raṭṭhapāla.[2] He lived in great luxury, and, in due course, married a suitable wife. When the Buddha visited Thullakoṭṭhita, Raṭṭhapāla went to hear him preach and decided to leave the world. His parents would not, however, give their consent till he threatened to

[1] A. i. 24.

[2] Given to the family because it retrieved the fortunes of a disrupted kingdom, says the Commentary.

starve himself to death. Realizing then that he was in earnest, they agreed to let him go on condition that he would visit them after his ordination. Raṭṭhapāla accompanied the Buddha to **Sāvatthi,** and there, dwelling alone, he attained arahantship within a short time.[3] Then, with the Buddha's permission, he returned to Thullakoṭṭhita and dwelt in the deer-park of the Kuru king. The day after his arrival, while begging for alms, he came to his father's house. His father was in the entrance hall having his hair combed, but, failing to recognize his son, he started to abuse him, taking him for an ordinary monk, one of those who had robbed him of his son. Just at that moment the slave-girl of the house was about to throw away some stale rice, which Raṭṭhapāla begged of her. The girl recognized his voice, gave him the rice and told his parents who he was. When his father came to look for his son, he found him eating stale rice as though it were ambrosia.[4] Having already finished eating, when invited to enter the house, he would not do so, but on the next day he went again, and his father tried to tempt him by making a display of the immense wealth which would be his should he return to the lay life, while his former wives, beautifully clothed, asked him about the nymphs, for whose sake he led the homeless life. "For the sake of no nymphs, Sisters," he said, and they fell fainting under the shock of being addressed as "Sisters." Growing impatient at the conduct of his family, he asked for his meal, ate it, preached to them[5] on the impermanence of all things, the futility of wealth, the snare of beauty, etc., and returned to **Migācira.**[6] There the Kuru king, who was feasting there, and had often heard of Raṭṭhapāla's fame, visited him. Their conversation is recorded in the **Raṭṭhapāla Sutta.** Raṭṭhapāla then returned to the Buddha.[7]

In a previous birth, before the appearance of **Padumuttara Buddha,** Raṭṭhapāla was one of two rich householders of **Haṃsavatī,** both of whom spent their wealth in good deeds. They once waited on two companies of ascetics from **Himavā;** the ascetics left, but their leaders remained, and the two householders looked after them till they died. After death, one of them (Raṭṭhapāla) was reborn as **Sakka,** while the other was born

[3] But MA. (ii. 725) says he took twelve years, during which time he never slept on a bed (DA. iii. 236).

[4] This eating of stale rice made of him an *uggaariyavaṃsika* (Sp. i. 208; MA. ii. 726).

[5] Buddhaghosa says that according to the Commentators of India (*parasamuddavāsītherānaṃ*) he preached standing. The stanzas so preached are given in M. i. 64 f. and again in Thag. (769-75).

[6] Through the air, says the Commentary (ThagA. ii. 34; MA. ii. 730), because his father put bolts on the house and tried to keep him there. He also sent men to remove his yellow robes and clothe him in white.

[7] Raṭṭhapāla's story is given in M. ii. 54 ff.; MA. ii. 722; ThagA. ii. 30 ff.; AA. i. 144 ff.; *cp.* Avadaś. ii. 118 ff.; Mtu. iii. 41, n. 1.

as the Nāga-king **Pālita** (*v.l.* **Paṭhavindhara**), who, in this Buddha-age, became **Rāhula.** At Sakka's request, Pālita gave alms to Padumuttara and wished to be like the Buddha's son, **Uparevata.** Sakka himself entertained the Buddha and his monks for seven days and wished to resemble the monk Raṭṭhapāla, whom Padumuttara Buddha had declared to be foremost among those who had joined the Order through faith. Padumuttara declared that the wish of both would be fulfilled in the time of **Gotama Buddha.**[8]

Raṭṭhapāla is mentioned[9] with **Soṇa-seṭṭhiputta** as one who enjoyed great luxury as a householder. He is an example[10] of one who attained to the higher knowledge through resolution (*chandaṃ dhuraṃ katvā*). The Vinayapiṭaka[11] contains a stanza quoted by the Buddha, in which Raṭṭhapāla's father enquires of his son why the latter never asked him for anything. "Because begging is a degrading thing," says Raṭṭhapāla.

[8] MA. ii. 722; ThagA. (ii. 30) differs in many details; it makes no mention of Pālita, and says that in Padumuttara's time, too, the householder's name was Raṭṭhapāla. The name of the monk, disciple of Padumuttara, whose example incited the householder to wish for similar honour, is not given. This account adds (see also AA. i. 143 f.) that in the time of **Phussa Buddha** (*q.v.*) he was one of those in charge of the almsgiving held in the Buddha's honour by his three step-brothers. **Bimbisāra** and **Visākha** were his colleagues (AA. i. 165). The Ap. (i. 63 f.) is again different. It says that in Padumuttara's time the householder gave the Buddha an elephant with all its trappings, and then, buying it back, built with the money a *saṅghārāma* containing fifty-four thousand rooms. As a result he was king of the gods fifty times and **Cakkavatti** fifty-eight times. AA. i. 141 gives the story at greater length, some of the minor details varying.

[9] *E.g.*, SNA. i. 232; at AA. ii. 596 Yasa's name is added.

[10] DA. ii. 642; SA. iii. 201; VibhA. 306; DhA. iv 195.

[11] Vin iii. 148; Raṭṭhapāla is here called a *kulaputta*. The incident probably refers to his lay-life.

2. **Raṭṭhapāla.**—A monk in the time of **Padumuttara Buddha.** He was declared foremost among those who left the world through faith.[1]

[1] But see **Raṭṭhapāla** (1), n. 8.

3. **Raṭṭhapāla.**—The name of the family into which **Raṭṭhapāla** (1) was born.[1]

[1] See Raṭṭhapāla (1), n. 2.

4. **Raṭṭhapāla Thera.**—A monk of Ceylon, author of the **Madhura-Rasavāhinī** (*q.v.*).

Raṭṭhapāla Sutta.—The eighty-second sutta of the **Majjhima Nikāya.** It contains an account of **Raṭṭhapāla's** admission into the Order, his visits to his parents after attaining arahantship, and his conversation with the **Kuru** king in the latter's Deer Park. This last conversation forms the chief theme. The king asks Raṭṭhapāla why he has left his home when he suffers neither from old age, failing health, poverty, nor death of kinsfolk. Raṭṭhapāla answers that his reason for leaving it was his conviction of the truth of the four propositions enunciated by the Buddha—that the world (1) is in a state of continual flux and change; (2) there is no protector or preserver; (3) in it, we own nothing, but must leave all behind us; (4) it lacks and hankers, being enslaved by craving.[1] He explains the meaning of these statements to the satisfaction of the king and summarizes his statements in a series of stanzas.[2]

The Raṭṭhapāla Sutta[3] is mentioned as an example of a discourse in which the *rūpakammaṭṭhāna* is given first, leading on through *vedanā* to the *arūpakammaṭṭhāna*.

[1] These four propositions are referred to as *Cattāro dhammuddesā* (MA. i. 361).

[2] M. ii. 54-74. The stanzas included in the sutta are found in Thag. vss. 769-75 (those preached to Raṭṭhapāla's father), and 776-93.

[3] VibhA. 267; MA. i. 225; what this means is not quite clear; this sutta makes no mention of *kammaṭṭhāna*; another sutta of the same name is probably meant.

Raṭṭhapāla-gajjita.—An unorthodox Buddhist work, whose views were rejected by the **Theravādins** as beings contrary to the teachings of the Buddha (*abuddhavacana*).[1]

[1] *E.g.*, Sp. iv. 742; SA. ii. 150.

Raṭṭhasāra.—A monk of **Ava.** He wrote metrical versions of various Jātakas and recited them, for which reason he was censured by his colleagues.[1]

[1] Sās, p. 99; Bode, *op. cit.*, 44.

Ratana Paritta.—See **Ratana Sutta** (1).

Ratana Vagga.—The ninth section of the **Pācittiya** of the Vinaya Piṭaka.

1. **Ratana Sutta.**—One of the suttas of the **Khuddakapāṭha.**[1] It was preached at **Vesāli,** on the occasion of the Buddha's visit there at the invitation of the **Licchavis,** who begged him to rid the city of the various dangers which had fallen upon it. According to the Commentaries,[2] the Buddha first taught the sutta to **Ānanda** and asked him to go round the city, accompanied by the Licchavi princes, reciting the sutta and sprinkling water from the Buddha's bowl. Immediately all the evil

[1] It is also included in the Sutta Nipāta (vss. 222-38); see also Gaṅgārohaṇa Sutta.

[2] SNA. i. 278 ff.; DhA. iii. 436 ff.; KhpA. 164 f.

spirits fled from the city and the people recovered from their diseases. They then gathered at the Mote-hall with various offerings and thither they conducted the Buddha. In the assembly were present not only all the inhabitants of Vesāli, but also the devas of two deva-worlds, with **Sakka** at their head. The Buddha preached the Ratana Sutta to this great crowd. Another account, quoted by Buddhaghosa,[3] says that in the assembly the Buddha preached only the first five stanzas, the rest having been earlier recited by Ānanda. Because this sutta was first preached to ward off the evil from Vesāli, it became the most famous of Buddhist Ward-runes (**Parittā**) *q.v.*

The sutta consists of seventeen verses: the first two contain a request to the devas to receive the homage and offerings of men and protect them in their danger; then follow twelve verses, descriptive of the virtues of the Buddha, the Dhamma and the Saṅgha. It ends with three verses purporting[4] to have been spoken by Sakka on behalf of all the devas, expressing their adoration of the Buddha, his Dhamma and his Saṅgha. It is also said[5] that during this visit the Buddha stayed at Vesāli for two weeks, preaching the sutta on seven consecutive days; on each day eighty-four thousand beings realized the Truth. The Sutta seems also to have been known as the **Gaṅgārohaṇa Sutta.**[6] When Ceylon was troubled by famine and plague in the reign of **Upatissa II.**, the king had the sutta preached by monks while walking in the streets of the city. All troubles vanished, and he decreed that his successors should do likewise in times of need.[7] **Sena II.** had the whole sutta inscribed on a golden plate and held a great festival in its honour.[8]

The sutta is given in the Mahāvastu,[9] where it is described as Svastyanagāthā.

[3] DhA. iii. 165. [4] *Ibid.*, 195. [5] *Ibid.*, 196. [6] Cv. xxxvii. 191. [7] *Ibid.*, 195 ff. [8] *Ibid.*, li. 79. [9] i. 290 ff.

2. **Ratana Sutta.**—The Dīgha Commentary[1] refers the reader to a Ratana Sutta of the **Bojjhaṅga Saṃyutta** for details of the seven gems of a Cakkavatti. The reference is evidently to the **Cakkavatti Sutta** (*q.v.*).[2]

[1] DA. i. 250. [2] S. v. 98.

Ratanagāma.—A village in Ceylon given by **Aggabodhi I.** as a maintenance village to the **Unnavalli-vihāra.**[1]

[1] Cv. xlii. 18; it is probably identical with the modern Ratnapura; see Cv. *Trs.* i. 67, n. 4.

Ratanagghi.—One of the three palaces occupied by **Revata Buddha** in his last lay life.[1]

[1] Bu. vi. 17.

Ratanaghara-cetiya.—A shrine erected on the site of the Jewelled Hall (**Ratanaghara**), which was created by the gods to the north-west of the **Bodhi**-tree. There the Buddha sat during the fourth week after the Enlightenment, revolving in his mind the Abhidhamma Piṭaka.[1]

[1] J. i. 78; BuA. 8, 241.

Ratanacaṅkama-cetiya or **Ratna-cetiya.**—A shrine erected near the **Animisa-cetiya** close to the **Bodhi**-tree, to mark the spot on which the Buddha spent the third week after the Enlightenment, walking to and fro in the Jewelled Walk (*Ratanacaṅkama*).[1]

[1] J. i. 78; BuA. 8, 241.

Ratanacaṅkamana-khaṇḍa.—The Introductory Chapter of the **Buddha Vaṃsa.**

Ratanadoṇi.—A village in Ceylon, given by **Kittisirirājasīha** for the maintenance of the **Dutiyasela-vihāra.** The village had originally belonged to the vihāra but had been taken away.[1]

[1] Cv. c. 232.

Ratanapajjala (Ratanapattala).—A Cakkavatti of eighty kappas ago, a former birth of **Sammukhāthavika** (or **Māṇava**) **Thera.**[1]

[1] Ap. i. 159; ThagA. i. 164.

Ratanapāsāda.—A building in the **Abhayagiri-vihāra,** erected by King **Kaniṭṭhatissa** for **Mahānāga Thera.**[1] **Mahinda II.** evidently rebuilt it at a cost of three hundred thousand kahāpaṇas, and installed in it a Buddha-image worth sixty thousand. At the dedication festival, the king offered his whole kingdom to the image.[2] **Mahinda III.** gave the revenue from the **Geṭṭhumba** Canal for the repairs of the *pāsāda.*[3] In the reign of **Sena I.** the **Pāṇḍiyas,** who invaded Ceylon, plundered the *pāsāda* and removed the jewels from the eyes of the image.[4] **Sena II.** found the image itself removed from its pedestal and taken to **Madhurā,** and, after his victory over the Pāṇḍiyas, he had it restored.[5] When the people rose in rebellion against **Udaya III.,** he took refuge in the Ratana-paāsād with his colleagues, but the people surrounded the building and they were forced to flee.[6]

[1] Mhv. xxxvi. 8; for its identification see Cv. *Trs.* i. 123, n. 2.
[2] Cv. xlviii. 135 f.
[3] *Ibid.*, xlix. 41.
[4] *Ibid.*, l. 34.
[5] *Ibid.*, li. 22, 49.
[6] *Ibid.* liii. 17.

Ratanapura.—The Pāli name for Ava.[1]

[1] Bode, *op. cit.*, 29.

Ratanamālaka.—A platform in **Gandhamādana,** at the foot of the **Mañjūsa**-tree, where **Pacceka Buddhas** assemble on special occasions such as the *uposatha.*[1] It seems also to have been called **Sabbaratnamāla.**[2]

[1] SNA. i. 52. [2] *E.g., ibid.*, 66.

Ratanavāluka.—Another name for the **Mahā Thūpa.** *Cp.* **Ratanāvalicetiya.**

Ratana-vihāra.—A nunnery in Ceylon, built by the queen of **Aggabodhi II.** for the use of the **Kāliṅga** queen, who came to Ceylon with her husband and renounced the world under **Jotipāla Thera.**[1]

[1] Cv. xlii. 47.

Ratanasiriñāṇa Thera.—Author of the **Saddatthacintā** (*q.v.*).[1]

[1] Svd. 1246.

Ratanākara.—A district in the **Dakkhiṇadesa** of Ceylon.[1]

[1] Cv. lxix. 31; for its identification see Cv. *Trs.* i. 286, n. 3.

Ratanadāṭha.—Nephew (sister's son) of **Dāṭhopatissa II.** He was the king's *Mahādipāda.*[1]

[1] Cv. xliv. 136.

1. **Ratanāvali-cetiya.**—Another name for the **Mahā Thūpa** (*q.v.*).

2. **Ratanāvali-cetiya.**—A thūpa in **Pulatthipura.** It was probably built by **Parakkamabāhu I.** and restored and crowned with a golden finial by **Kittinissaṅka.**[1]

[1] Cv. lxxx. 20; also Cv. *Trs.* ii. 128, n. 1; 107, n. 3.

3. **Ratanāvali-cetiya.**—A thūpa erected in **Khīragāma** by **Parakkamabāhu I.** on the site of his mother's pyre.[1]

[1] Cv. lxxix. 71; Cv. *Trs.* ii. 122, n. 7.

Ratanāvalī.—One of the five daughters of **Vijayabāhu I.** and **Tilokasundarī.**[1] Soothsayers predicted that she alone, of these daughters, would bear a son and would thus become the king's favourite child. Later she married **Mānābharaṇa,** by whom she had two daughters—

[1] Cv. lix. 31.

Mittā and **Pabhāvatī**—and a son who later became famous as **Parakkamabāhu I.**[2] After her husband's death, she lived with her children in **Mahānāgahula,** protected by her husband's brother, **Sirivallabha.**[3] Later, she went and lived at the court of his elder brother, **Kittisirimegha.**[4] She died at **Khīragāma** and was cremated there. Parakkamabāhu erected the **Ratanāvali-cetiya** in her memory.[5]

[2] Cv. lix. 34 ff., 44; lxii. 3, 12 ff.
[3] *Ibid.*, lxiii. 4.
[4] *Ibid.*, lxvii. 75 ff.
[5] *Ibid.*, lxxix. 71.

1. **Rativaḍḍhana.**—One of the three palaces of **Vessabhū Buddha** in his last lay life.[1]

[1] BuA. 205; the Bu. (xxii. 19) calls it **Vaḍḍhana.**

2. **Rativaḍḍhana.**—A palace of **Kakusandha Buddha** in his last lay life.[1]

[1] BuA. 209; but BuA. (xxiii. 16) calls it **Vaḍḍhana.**

3. **Rativaḍḍhana.**—A palace of King **Sabbadatta** in the city of **Ramma** (Benares).[1]

[1] J. iv. 122.

4. **Rativaḍḍhana.**—A palace in **Mithilā.** It was the special residence provided for **Rujā** by her father **Aṅgati.**[1]

[1] J. iv. 231, 232.

5. **Rativaḍḍhana.**—A pleasure-park of **Asoka.** The king led **Moggaliputtatissa** there on his arrival from **Ahogaṅgapabbata,** and, at the king's request, the Elder caused a partial earthquake.[1]

[1] Mhv. v. 257 ff.

Ratī.—One of the daughters of **Māra** (*q.v.*).

"**Rato**" **Sutta.**—A monk who keeps guard over the door of his faculties, is moderate in eating and given to watchfulness, dwells in happiness in this life and has strong help in the destruction of the *āsavas.* The sutta gives details of these faculties.[1]

[1] S. iv. 175 ff.

Rattakara.—A district in the **Dakkhiṇadesa** of Ceylon.[1]

[1] Cv. lxviii. 23; lxix. 6.

Rattakkhi.—A **Yakkha** who worried Ceylon in the time of **Sirisaṅghabodhi.** All those who saw him or heard of him developed a fever (*jararoga*) accompanied by redness of the eyes and died of the disease, the Yakkha devouring their bodies. The king heard of this, and, by the power of his goodness, compelled the Yakkha to come to him, and persuaded him to abandon his evil influence. In return, the king promised to have offerings (*bali*) placed for the Yakkha at the entrance to every village.[1]

[1] Mhv. xxxvi. 82 ff.; Attanagaluvaṃsa, p. 16.

Rattapāṇi.—The name of a dyer; perhaps a class name.[1]

[1] M. i. 385.

Rattabeduma.—A place in the **Malaya** country of Ceylon, mentioned in the account of the campaigns of **Parakkamabāhu I.**[1]

[1] Cv. lxx. 15.

Rattamāla-kaṇḍaka.—A tank in Ceylon, built by King **Mahāsena.**[1]

[1] Mhv. xxxvii. 48; Mhv. *Trs.* 271, n. 7.

Rattamālagiri.—A mountain in Ceylon. **Sena Iḷaṅga,** general of **Kassapa IV.,** built there a monastery for ascetics.[1]

[1] Cv. lii. 20.

Rattipupphiya Thera.—An arahant. In the time of **Vipassī Buddha** he was a hunter, and, seeing the Buddha in the forest, he offered him some flowers which bloom by night (*rattikaṃ pupphaṃ*). Eight kappas ago he was a king named **Suppasanna.**[1]

[1] Ap. i. 188.

Rattiya Sutta.—A monk who desires much, is fretful and discontented with his requisites, has no faith or virtue, is indolent, forgetful, and lacking in insight—such a one falls away in goodness " come day, come night."[1]

[1] A. iii. 434.

Rattivihāra.—A locality in Ceylon; it was once the encampment of King **Saṅghatissa.**[1]

[1] Cv. xliv. 5.

Rathakāra, Rathakārī.—One of the seven great lakes (**Mahāsarā,** *q.v.*) in the **Himālaya.**

Rathakāra Vagga.—The second chapter of the Tika Nipāta of the **Aṅguttara Nikāya.**[1]

[1] A. i. 106-118.

Rathalaṭṭhi Jātaka (No. 332).—The chaplain of the king of Benares, while on his way to his village estate, came upon a caravan in a narrow road, and, becoming impatient, threw his goad at the driver of the first cart. The goad, however, struck the yoke of his own chariot, and, rebounding, hit him on the forehead, where a lump appeared. He turned back in a rage and complained to the king, who, without any enquiry, confiscated the property of the caravan-owner. But the Bodhisatta, who was the king's chief judge, had the order reversed.

The story was told in reference to the chaplain of the king of **Kosala,** who was guilty of a similar offence, but, in this case, the king had the case examined by his judges and the chaplain was proclaimed guilty.[1] The stanzas of the Jātaka are quoted elsewhere.[2]

[1] J. iii. 104 ff.

[2] *E.g.*, at J. iv. 30, 451; vi. 375.

Rathavaṅka.—See **Ravivaṭṭa.**

Rathavatī.—A *kinnarī*, the handmaiden of the hermit **Vaccha** (*q.v.*).

Rathavinīta Sutta.—The twenty-fourth sutta of the **Majjhima Nikāya. Sāriputta** visits **Puṇṇa Mantāṇiputta** in **Andhavana** and asks him why he lives the higher life. To attain absolute Nibbāna, answers Puṇṇa, and, on being questioned further as to the nature of Nibbāna, he explains that Nibbāna is the goal and can only be attained by passing through various successive stages—purity of life, purity of heart, purity of view, purity through dispelling doubts, purity through full insight into paths, right and wrong, into the path to be followed, and the purity which arises from insight. It may be compared to a journey of **Pasenadi** from **Sāvatthi** to **Sāketa,** by means of relays of seven carriages.

It is said in the introduction to the sutta that Sāriputta had been awaiting the opportunity of a discussion with Puṇṇa ever since he heard the monks at **Veḷuvana** in Rājagaha speak of him to the Buddha in terms of the highest praise. But this opportunity did not arise until later, when Puṇṇa visited Sāvatthi. Puṇṇa was unaware of the identity of Sāriputta until the end of his discourse.[1]

The **Mahāvaṃsa Ṭīkā** mentions[2] that once **Ambapāsāṇavāsī Cittagutta** preached this sutta to a very large assembly of monks and nuns at the **Lohapāsāda** in **Anurādhapura,** and in his exposition of the sutta included a short account of the relics enshrined in the **Mahā Thūpa.**

It has been suggested by Dr. Neumann that the *upatisapasina* mentioned in Asoka's Bhabru Edict, refers to this sutta.[3]

[1] M. i. 145-51.

[2] MṬ. 552 f.

[3] But see Rhys Davids, *J.R.A.S.* 1893, and Mukherji, *Asoka*, 118 f., n. 8.

Randhakaṇḍaka.—A tank in Ceylon, built by **Bhātikatissa.**[1]

[1] Mhv. xxxvi. 4.

Ramaṇā.—The Pāli name for the inhabitants of **Rāmañña.**[1]

[1] Cv. lxxvi. 66.

Ramaṇīyakuṭika Thera.—An arahant. He was a nobleman of **Vesālī** and left the world after hearing the Buddha preach the **Ratana Sutta.** After ordination, he dwelt in a pleasant hut in a beautiful forest, where he won arahantship. One day some women tried to tempt him, but in vain.[1]

His first desire to attain liberation was made in the time of **Padumuttara Buddha.** Later he gave a beautiful seat to **Atthadassī Buddha** and offered him flowers in homage. One hundred and seventy kappas ago he was a king named **Sandimā (Sannibbāpaka).** He is probably identical with **Āsanūpaṭṭhāyaka** of the Apadāna.[2]

[1] Thag vs. 58; ThagA. i. 122 f. [2] Ap. i. 144.

Ramaṇīya-vihāra.—A monastery in **Amarapura** in Burma.[1]

[1] Sās. 132, 143.

Ramaṇīyavihārī Thera.—An arahant. He was the son of a banker of **Rājagaha** and lived a dissolute life, till one day, on witnessing the arrest of an adulterer, he was very agitated and joined the Order. As a monk, too, he lived in luxury, in a well-furnished room—hence his name. Later, seized with remorse, he wandered out of his cell. On the way he saw a carter refresh a weary bull and then reyoke him. Determined to take up his duties as a monk, he sought **Upāli,** and, with his help, attained arahantship. In the past he had offered *koraṇḍa*-flowers to **Vipassī Buddha.**[1]

He is probably identical with **Koraṇḍapupphiya Thera** of the Apadāna. Fifty-seven kappas ago he was a king named **Vitamala.**[2]

[1] Thag. vs. 45; ThagA. i. 115 f. [2] Ap. i. 206.

1. **Ramma.**—One of the chief lay patrons of **Sobhita Buddha.**[1]

[1] Bu. vii. 23; but see *s.v.* **Sobhita.**

2. **Ramma.**—Son of **Paduma Buddha** in his last lay life. He joined the Order and later became an arahant. Eighty crores of beings realized the Truth when the Buddha preached to him.[1]

[1] Bu. ix. 5, 18; BuA. 147.

3. **Ramma.**—One of the chief lay patrons of **Vessabhū Buddha.**[1]

[1] Bu. xxii. 25.

4. **Ramma, Rammaka.**—The name of Benares at the time recorded in the **Yuvañjaya Jātaka.**[1]

[1] J. iv. 119 ff.

5. **Ramma, Rammavatī.**—The city of birth of **Dīpaṅkara Buddha.** It was while Dīpaṅkara was on a visit to this city that **Sumedha** met him and was declared by him to be a **Bodhisatta.** At that time the Buddha was living in a monastery called **Sudassana-mahāvihāra.**[1]

[1] J. i. 11, 13, 29; iv. 119; DhA. i. 69; Bu. ii. 207; BuA. 65 calls it **Rammavatī.**

6. **Ramma.**—A nine-storeyed palace occupied by **Gotama Buddha** in his last lay life.[1]

[1] BuA. 230; Bu. (xxvi. 14) calls it Rāma.

1. **Rammaka.**—A brahmin whose hermitage was in **Sāvatthi,** near the **Pubbakoṭṭhaka.** It was a great resort of the monks, and there the Buddha preached the **Ariyapariyesana Sutta.**[1]

[1] M. i. 160.

2. **Rammaka.**—A city where, sixty thousand kappas ago, **Mahā Kassapa** reigned as King **Ubbiddha.**[1]

[1] Ap. i. 34.

3. **Rammaka.**—See *s.v.* **Ramma** (4).

1. **Rammavatī.**—The birthplace of **Koṇḍañña Buddha.**[1] There **Bodhiupaṭṭhāyaka Thera** was born as **Muraja.**[2]

[1] J. i. 30; Bu. iii. 25.

[2] Ap. i. 194.

2. **Rammavatī.**—A city in the time of **Revata Buddha,** where lived **Atideva** (*q.v.*).[1]

[1] BuA. 134.

3. **Rammavatī.**—See also **Ramma** (5).

Rammā.—One of the chief lay women supporters of **Siddhattha Buddha.**[1]

[1] Bu. xvii. 20.

Ralaggāma.—A monastery in Ceylon, built by King **Mahānāma.**[1]

[1] Cv. xxxvii. 212.

Ravavaṭṭisālā.—A hall in **Anurādhapura,** built on the spot where the people started wailing when the body of **Duṭṭhagāmaṇī** was laid on the funeral pyre.[1] *v.l.* **Rathavaṅka.**

[1] Mhv. xxxii. 79; MṬ. 601.

Ravideva.—A Sinhalese chief. He fought with the **Coḷas** against **Vijayabāhu I.,** but, later, appears to have joined Vijayabāhu.[1]

[1] Cv. lviii. 16, 65; Cv. *Trs.* i. 203, n. 3.

Rasavāhinī.—A collection of stories in Pāli, by **Vedeha,** a monk of the **Vanavāsī** fraternity in Ceylon. The work probably belongs to the early part of the fourteenth century, and seems to be a revision of an old Pāli translation made from an original Sinhalese compilation by **Raṭṭhapāla Thera** of the **Mahāvihāra.** The present text consists of one hundred and three stories, forty relating to incidents occurring in **Jambudīpa** and the rest to Ceylon. There exists a glossary on the work called the *Rasavāhinīgaṇṭhi.*[1] *v.l.* **Madhurarasavāhinī.**

[1] P.L.C. 210; Svd. 1264.

Rahada Sutta.—The mind is like a pool of water; no understanding is possible unless the mind is clear.[1]

[1] A. i. 9.

Rahera, Raheraka.—The name is frequently mentioned in the Pāli Chronicles, sometimes as a locality, sometimes as a mountain,[1] apparently situated[2] to the north of, and not far from, **Anurādhapura.** It is also given as the name of a tank, repaired by **Parakkamabāhu I.,**[3] and also as that of an irrigation canal (*dakavāra*), given by **Silākāla** to the monks of **Abhayagiri.**[4] Near Raheraka was the **Kolambahālaka-vihāra** (*q.v.*).

[1] *E.g.*, Mhv. xxi. 5; Cv. xli. 44; xliv. 7.
[2] Mhv. *Trs.* 176, n. 2.
[3] Cv. lxxix. 33.
[4] *Ibid.*, xli. 31.

1. **Rahogata Vagga.**—The second chapter of the **Vedanā Saṃyutta.**[1]

[1] S. iv. 216-30.

2. **Rahogata Vagga.**—The first chapter of the **Anuruddha Saṃyutta.**[1]

[1] S. v. 294 ff.

1. **Rahogata Sutta.**—While in solitude a monk thinks of the three kinds of feelings, and, visiting the Buddha, questions him. The Buddha tells him that the statement " Whatsoever is experienced is joined with *dukkha* " is made concerning the impermanence of compounded things. The ceasing of activities is gradual, so is their mastery.[1]

[1] S. iv. 216 f.

2. **Rahogata Suttā.**—Two Suttas. **Moggallāna** visits **Anuruddha,** as the latter is meditating in solitude in **Jetavana,** and asks for details as to how a monk should practise the four *satipaṭṭhānas.* Anuruddha explains.[1]

[1] S. v. 294 ff.

Rāga Sutta.—In order to get rid of passion, cultivate the idea of foulness; to get rid of hatred, cultivate amity; to get rid of delusion, insight.[1]

[1] A. iii. 445.

1. **Rāja Vagga.**—The ninth section of the **Majjhima Nikāya** (Suttas 81-90).[1]

[1] M. ii. 44 ff.

2. **Rāja Vagga.**—The fourteenth chapter of the Pañcaka Nipāta of the **Aṅguttara Nikāya.**[1]

[1] A. iii. 147-64.

1. **Rāja Sutta.**—Five good qualities in a king—pure descent, great wealth, strong army, wise minister, glory—which make him secure in his conquest; five similar qualities in a monk—virtuous conduct, wide and deep learning, active energy, insight, release—which bring him emancipation.[1]

[1] A. iii. 149 ff.

2. **Rāja Sutta.**—On the eighth day of the lunar fortnight, the ministers of the **Cātummahārājāno** visit the earth, on the fourteenth day their sons, on the fifteenth day the kings themselves. They report what they find at the assembly of the gods in **Sudhammā**-hall and rejoice if men have done good, sorrowing if they have done evil.[1]

[1] A. i. 142 f.

3. **Rāja Sutta.**—Men should keep their fast, not in order to be **Sakka,** who is not rid of passion, malice or delusion, but to be arahants.[1]

[1] A. i. 143 f.

4. **Rāja Sutta.**—**Pasenadi** asks the Buddha if there is any born thing which is free from decay and death. No, answers the Buddha, not even the arahants.[1]

[1] S. i. 71.

5. **Rāja Sutta.**—Just as all petty princes follow in the train of a universal monarch, so do all profitable states follow earnestness.[1]

[1] S. v. 44.

Rājakārāma.—A monastery in **Sāvatthi,** near **Jetavana,** built by **Pasenadi.**[1] It was to the south-east of the city, corresponding to **Thūpārāma** in **Anurādhapura.**[2] It was there that the **Nandakovāda Sutta** was preached.[3] This was probably the monastery built for nuns by Pasenadi, at the Buddha's suggestion, after the assault on **Uppalavaṇṇā** in **Andhavana,** referred to in the Dhammapada Commentary.[4] The **Saṃyutta Commentary,**[5] however, gives a different account. It states that the heretics, jealous of the Buddha and his popularity, desired to build a monastery for themselves in close proximity to **Jetavana,** and, in order that he might raise no objections, they presented Pasenadi with one hundred thousand. When the Buddha discovered their intentions, owing to the great uproar they made while preparing the preliminaries of the building, he sent **Ānanda** to the king, asking to have it stopped. But Pasenadi refused to see him or **Sāriputta** or **Moggallāna.** (It was as a punishment for this discourtesy that he lost the throne before his death.) Thereupon the Buddha went himself. Pasenadi received him and entertained him to a meal, at the end of which the Buddha preached to him the **Bharu Jātaka** (*q.v.*) on the evils of bribery and of creating an opportunity for virtuous people to quarrel among themselves. Pasenadi was filled with remorse; he had the heretics expelled, and, realizing that he had never built a monastery, proceeded to construct the **Rājakārāma.**

The Saṃyutta Nikāya[6] contains several sermons preached by the Buddha at the Rājakārāma.

[1] J. ii. 15.
[2] MA. ii. 1021.
[3] M. iii. 271.
[4] DhA. ii. 52.
[5] SA. iii. 218 f.; the introductory story of the Bharu Jātaka (J. ii. 170) gives the same account but omits the statement that the king built a vihāra.
[6] S. v. 360 ff.

Rājakārāma Vagga.—Also called **Sahassaka.** The second chapter of the **Sotāpatti Saṃyutta.**[1]

[1] S. v. 360-69.

Rājakulantaka.—The name given to one of the suburbs (*sākhānagarā*) of **Pulatthipura.**[1] Geiger[2] thinks that this is identical with **Sīhapura,** mentioned elsewhere[3] as a suburb of Pulatthipura.

[1] Cv. lxxiii. 153. [2] Cv. *Trs.* ii. 18, n. 3. [3] Cv. lxxviii. 79 ff.

Rājakulavaḍḍhana.—See **Sarāja°.**

Rājagaha.—A city, the capital of **Magadha.** There seem to have been two distinct towns; the older one, a hill fortress, more properly called **Giribbaja,** was very ancient and is said[1] to have been laid out by **Mahāgovinda,** a skilled architect. The later town, at the foot of the hills, was evidently built by **Bimbisāra.**[2] But both names were used indiscriminately,[3] though Giribbaja seems, as a name, to have been restricted to verse passages. The place was called Giribbaja (mountain stronghold) because it was surrounded by five hills—**Paṇḍava, Gijjhakūṭa, Vebhāra, Isigili** and **Vepulla**[4]—and **Rājagaha,** because it was the seat of many kings, such as **Mandhātā** and **Mahāgovinda.**[5] It would appear, from the names given of the kings, that the city was a very ancient royal capital.[6] The Commentaries[7] explain that the city was inhabited only in the time of Buddhas and Cakkavatti kings; at other times it was the abode of Yakkhas who used it as a pleasure resort in spring. The country to the north of the hills was known as **Dakkhiṇāgiri.**[8]

Rājagaha was closely associated with the Buddha's work. He visited it soon after the Renunciation, journeying there on foot from the River

[1] VvA. p. 82; but *cp.* D. ii. 235, where seven cities are attributed to his foundation.

[2] Hiouen Thsang says (Beal, ii. 145) that the old capital occupied by Bimbisāra was called Kuśāgra. It was afflicted by frequent fires, and Bimbisāra, on the advice of his ministers, abandoned it and built the new city on the site of the old cemetery. The building of this city was hastened on by a threatened invasion by the king of Vesāli. The city was called Rājagṛha because Bimbisāra was the first person to occupy it. Both Hiouen Thsang and Fa Hsien (Giles: 49) record another tradition which ascribed the foundation of the new city to Ajātasattu.

Pargiter (*Ancient Ind. Historical Tradition,* p. 149) suggests that the old city was called Kuśāgrapura, after Kuśāgra, an early king of Magadha. In the Rāmāyaṇa (i. 7, 32) the city is called Vasumatī. The Mahābhārata gives other names—Bārhadrathapura (ii. 24, 44), Varāha, Vṛsabha, Ṛṣigiri, Caityaka (see PHAI., p. 70). It was also called Bimbisārapurī and Magadhapura (SNA. ii. 584).

[3] *E.g.,* S.N. vs. 405.

[4] SNA. ii. 382; it is said (M. iii. 68) that these hills, with the exception of Isigili, were once known by other names—*e.g.,* **Vaṅkaka** for Vepulla (S. ii. 191). The Saṃyutta (i. 206) mentions another peak near Rājagaha—**Indakūṭa.** See also **Kāḷasilā.**

[5] SNA. ii. 413.

[6] In the **Vidhurapaṇḍita Jātaka** (J. vi. 271), Rājagaha is called the capital of **Aṅga.** This evidently refers to a time when Aṅga had subjugated Magadha.

[7] *E.g.,* SNA. *loc. cit.*

[8] SA. i. 188.

Anomā, a distance of thirty leagues.[9] Bimbisāra saw him begging in the street, and, having discovered his identity and the purpose of his quest, obtained from him a promise of a visit to Rājagaha as soon as his aim should be achieved.[10] During the first year after the Enlightenment, therefore, the Buddha went to Rājagaha from **Gayā,** after the conversion of the **Tebhātika Jaṭilas.** Bimbisāra and his subjects gave the Buddha a great welcome, and the king entertained him and a large following of monks in the palace. It is said that on the day of the Buddha's entry into the royal quarters, **Sakka** led the procession, in the guise of a young man, singing songs of praise of the Buddha. It was during this visit that Bimbisāra gifted **Veḷuvana** to the Order and that the Buddha received Sāriputta and Moggallāna as his disciples.[11] Large numbers of householders joined the Order, and people blamed the Buddha for breaking up their families. But their censure lasted for only seven days. Among those ordained were the **Sattarasavaggiyā** with **Upāli** at their head. The Buddha spent his first *vassa* in Rājagaha and remained there during the winter and the following summer. The people grew tired of seeing the monks everywhere, and, on coming to know of their displeasure, the Buddha went first to **Dakkhiṇāgiri** and then to **Kapilavatthu.**[12] According to the Buddhavaṃsa Commentary,[13] the Buddha spent also in **Rājagaha** the third, fourth, seventeenth and twentieth *vassa*. After the twentieth year of his teaching, he made **Sāvatthi** his headquarters, though he seems frequently to have visited and stayed at Rājagaha. It thus became the scene of several important suttas—*e.g.*, the **Āṭānāṭiya, Udumbarika** and **Kassapasīhanāda, Jīvaka, Mahāsakuladāyī,** and **Sakkapañha** (*q.v.*).[14] Many of the Vinaya rules were enacted at Rājagaha. Just before his death, the Buddha paid a last visit there. At that time, **Ajātasattu** was contemplating an attack on the **Vajjians,** and sent his minister, **Vassakāra,** to the Buddha at Gijjhakūṭa, to find out what his chances of success were.[15]

After the Buddha's death, Rājagaha was chosen by the monks, with **Mahā Kassapa** at their head, as the meeting-place of the First Convocation. This took place at the **Sattapaṇṇiguhā** (*q.v.*), and Ajātasattu extended to the undertaking his whole-hearted patronage.[16] The king also erected at Rājagaha a cairn over the relics of the Buddha, which he had obtained as his share.[17] According to the **Mahāvaṃsa,**[18] some time later, acting

[9] J. i. 66.

[10] See the **Pabbajjā Sutta** and its Commentary.

[11] Details of this visit are given in Vin. i. 35 ff.

[12] *Ibid.*, 77 ff.

[13] p. 3.

[14] For other incidents in the Buddha's life connected with Rājagaha, see *s.v.* **Gotama.** The most notable of these was the taming of **Nālāgiri** (*q.v.*).

[15] D. ii. 72.

[16] Vin. ii. 285; Sp. i. 7 f.; DA. i. 8 f., etc.

[17] D. ii. 166.

[18] Mhv. xxxi. 21; MṬ. 564.

on the suggestion of Mahā Kassapa, the king gathered at Rājagaha seven *doṇas* of the Buddha's relics which had been deposited in various places—excepting those deposited at **Rāmagāma**—and built over them a large *thūpa*. It was from there that **Asoka** obtained relics for his vihāras.

Rājagaha was one of the six chief cities of the Buddha's time,[19] and as such, various important trade routes passed through it. The road from **Takkasilā** to Rājagaha was one hundred and ninety-two leagues long and passed through Sāvatthi, which was forty-five leagues from Rājagaha. This road passed by the gates of **Jetavana.**[20] The **Parāyaṇa Vagga**[21] mentions a long and circuitous route, taken by **Bāvarī's** disciples in going from **Patiṭṭhāna** to Rājagaha, passing through **Māhissati, Ujjeni, Gonaddha, Vedisā, Vanasavhaya, Kosambī, Sāketa, Sāvatthi, Setavyā, Kapilavatthu, Kusinārā,** on to Rājagaha, by way of the usual places (see below). From Kapilavatthu to Rājagaha was sixty leagues.[22] From Rājagaha to **Kusinārā** was a distance of twenty-five leagues,[23] and the **Mahāparinibbāna Sutta**[24] gives a list of the places at which the Buddha stopped during his last journey along that road—**Ambalaṭṭhikā, Nālandā, Pāṭaligāma** (where he crossed the Ganges), **Koṭigāma, Nādikā, Vesāli, Bhaṇḍagāma, Hatthigāma, Ambagāma, Jambugāma, Bhoganagara, Pāvā,** and the **Kakuttha** River, beyond which lay the Mango grove and the **Sāla** grove of the **Mallas.** From Rājagaha to the Ganges was a distance of five leagues, and when the Buddha visited Vesāli at the invitation of the **Licchavis,** the kings on either side of the river vied with each other to show him honour.[25] The distance between Rājagaha and Nālandā is given as one league, and the Buddha often walked between the two.[26]

The books mention various places besides Veḷuvana, with its **Kalandaka-nivāpa-vihāra** in and around Rājagaha—*e.g.*, **Sītavana, Jīvaka's Amba-vana, Pipphaliguhā, Udumbarikārāma, Moranivāpa** with its **Paribbāja-kārāma, Tapodārāma, Indasālaguhā** in **Vediyagiri, Sattapaṇṇiguhā, Laṭṭhivana, Maddakucchi, Supatiṭṭhacetiya, Pāsāṇakacetiya, Sappasoṇḍi-kapabbhāra** and the pond **Sumāgadhā.**

At the time of the Buddha's death, there were eighteen large monasteries in **Rājagaha.**[27] Close to the city flowed the rivers **Tapodā** and **Sappinī.**[28] In the city was a Potter's Hall where travellers from far distances spent the night.[29] The city gates were closed every evening,

[19] The others were **Campā, Sāvatthi, Sāketa, Kosambī** and Benares (D. ii. 147).

[20] MA. ii. 987; SA. i. 243.

[21] SN. vss. 1011-3.

[22] AA. i. 115; MA. i. 360.

[23] DA. ii. 609.

[24] D. ii. 72 ff.

[25] DhA. iii. 439 f.; also Mtu. i. 253 ff.; according to Dvy. (p. 55) the Ganges had to be crossed between Rājagaha and Sāvatthi, as well, by boat, some of the boats belonging to the king of Magadha and others to the Licchavis of Vesāli.

[26] DA. i. 35.

[27] Sp. i. 9.

[28] For details of these see *s.v.*

[29] *E.g.*, **Pukkusāti** (MA. ii. 987); it had also a Town Hall (J. iv. 72).

and after that it was impossible to enter the city.[30] In the Buddha's time there was constant fear of invasion by the Licchavis, and Vassakāra (*q.v.*) is mentioned as having strengthened its fortifications. To the north-east of the city were the brahmin villages of **Ambasaṇḍā**[31] and **Sālindiya**[32]; other villages are mentioned in the neighbourhood, such as **Kiṭāgiri, Upatissagāma, Kolitagāma, Andhakavinda, Sakkhara** and **Codanāvatthu** (*q.v.*). In the Buddha's time, Rājagaha had a population of eighteen crores, nine in the city and nine outside, and the sanitary conditions were not of the best.[33] The Treasurer of Rājagaha and **Anāthapiṇḍika** had married each other's sisters, and it was while Anāthapiṇḍika (*q.v.*) was on a visit to Rājagaha that he first met the Buddha.

The people of Rājagaha, like those of most ancient cities, held regular festivals; one of the best known of these was the Giraggasamajjā (*q.v.*). Mention is also made of troupes of players visiting the city and giving their entertainments for a week on end.[34]

Soon after the death of the Buddha, Rājagaha declined both in importance and prosperity. **Sisunāga** transferred the capital to Vesāli, and **Kālāsoka** removed it again to **Pāṭaliputta,** which, even in the Buddha's time, was regarded as a place of strategical importance. When Hiouen Thsang visited Rājagaha, he found it occupied by brahmins and in a very dilapidated condition.[35] For a long time, however, it seems to have continued as a centre of Buddhist activity, and among those mentioned as having been present at the foundation of the **Mahā Thūpa** were eighty thousand monks led by **Indagutta.**[36]

[30] Vin. iv. 116 f.; the city had thirty-two main gates and sixty-four smaller entrances (DA. i. 150; MA. ii. 795). One of the gates of Rājagaha was called **Taṇḍulapāla** (M. ii. 185). Round Rājagaha was a great *peta*-world (MA. ii. 960; SA. i. 31).

[31] D. ii. 263.

[32] J. iii. 293.

[33] SA. i. 241; DhA. ii. 43; it was because of the city's prosperity that the **Mettiya-Bhummajakas** made it their headquarters (Sp. iii. 614). The city was not free from plague (DhA. i. 232).

[34] See, *e.g.*, the story of **Uggasena.**

[35] Beal, *op. cit.*, ii. 167.

[36] Mhv. xxix. 30.

Rājagahaseṭṭhi.—Evidently not a proper name, but the title of the Treasurer of **Rājagaha.**[1] In the time of the Buddha, the seṭṭhi was the brother-in-law of **Anāthapiṇḍika** and was a devout follower of the Buddha; he was responsible for the meeting between the Buddha and Anāthapiṇḍika.[2] He had a slave-girl named **Puṇṇā**[3] and a slave **Puṇṇa,** who later became a seṭṭhi, and whose daughter, **Uttarā,** was given in marriage to the son of the Rājagahaseṭṭhi. This latter was an unbeliever, but was later converted and became a *sotāpanna.*[4]

[1] See, *e.g.*, DhA. i. 232.

[2] For details see *s.v.* **Anāthapiṇḍika.**

[3] DhA. iii. 321 ff.

[4] See VvA. 63 ff. for details.

Rājagāma.—A town in Ceylon in the time of **Parakkamabāhu IV.** In it was the **Sirighanānanda-pariveṇa.**[1]

[1] Cv. xc. 93.

Rājagiri.—One of the elephants of **Candakumāra** (*q.v.*).[1]

[1] J. vi. 135.

Rājagiriyā.—One of the heterodox Buddhist sects which branched off in the second century after the death of the Buddha.[1] They formed a part of the **Andhaka** sect.[2]

[1] Dpv. v. 54; Mhv. v. 12. [2] Points of Controversy, p. 104.

Rājadatta Thera.—An arahant. He belonged to a caravan-leader's family of **Sāvatthi,** and was so called because he was born through the favour of **Vessavaṇa.** When he came of age he took a caravan of five hundred carts to **Rājagaha.** Then, having squandered all his money, he went to **Veḷuvana,** and, after hearing the Buddha preach, entered the Order and lived in a charnel-field. While wandering about, he saw the mangled body of a murdered courtesan, and only with a great effort saved himself from distraction of mind. Later, he induced *jhāna* and won arahantship.

Fourteen kappas ago he had seen a **Pacceka Buddha** at the foot of a tree and had given him an *ambāṭaka*-(mango ?) fruit.[1]

He is probably identical with **Ambāṭaka Thera.**[2]

[1] Thag. vss. 315-19; ThagA. i. 402 f. [2] Ap. i. 394.

Rājadvāra.—One of the gates of **Pulatthipura.**[1] It was probably to the south of the city.[2]

[1] Cv. lxxiii. 160. [2] Cv. *Trs.* ii. 39, n. 4.

Rājanārāyaṇa.—A park in Ceylon, laid out by **Parakkamabāhu I.**[1]

[1] Cv. lxxix. 7.

Rājamaṇicūḷa-cetiya.—A cetiya in Sagaing.[1]

[1] Bode, *op. cit.*, 55.

Rājamahāvihāra.—A monastery in Ceylon, built by **Kaniṭṭhatissa.**[1]

[1] Mhv. xxxvi. 16.

Rājamātikā.—A monastery in Ceylon, dedicated by **Aggabodhi V.** to the **Paṃsukūlins.**[1]

[1] Cv. xlviii. 4.

Rājamātu-vihāra.—A monastery in **Anurādhapura,** probably identical with **Mātuvihāra** (2). It was on the road from the **Kadambanadī** to the **Thūpārāma.**[1]

[1] DA. ii. 572; SA. i. 173.

Rājamālaka.—A courtyard outside the precincts of the monastery where the body of **Duṭṭhagāmaṇī** was burnt.[1]

[1] Mhv. xxxii. 80.

Rājamittaka.—A village in Ceylon where **Silāmeghavaṇṇa** defeated **Sirināga.**[1]

[1] Cv. xliv. 72.

Rājaraṭṭha.—The name given to the northern part of Ceylon, with **Pulatthipura** as centre, as opposed to **Rohaṇa**[1] and **Dakkhiṇadesa.**[2] Later, the name was changed to **Patiṭṭhāraṭṭha.**[3] Rājaraṭṭha was the scene of many conflicts between the Sinhalese and the invaders who came from time to time from South India, till, in the end, it was abandoned, and the Sinhalese capital moved southwards. Rājaraṭṭha was also called **Rājinoraṭṭha.**[4]

[1] *E.g.*, Cv. lxx. 184 f.
[2] *Ibid.*, lxxii. 176-9.
[3] *E.g.*, *ibid.*, lxxxii. 26.
[4] *E.g.*, *ibid.*, lii. 4.

Rājarājakalappa.—A Damiḷa chief, ally of **Kulasekhara.**[1]

[1] Cv. lxxvii. 74.

Rājavaṃsasaṅkhepa.—A historical work by **Aggadhammālaṅkāra.**[1]

[1] Bode, *op. cit.*, 57.

Rājavasatikhaṇḍa.—One of the sections of the **Vidhurapaṇḍita Jātaka.**[1]

[1] J. vi. 298.

Rājavihāra.—A monastery in **Rohaṇa** to which **Silādāṭha** assigned the village of **Gonnagāma.**[1]

[1] Cv. xlv. 58.

Rājavesibhujaṅga.—A building attached to the palace of **Parakkamabāhu I.,** at **Pulatthipura.** It was painted and consisted of three storeys.[1] The name was also given to one of the suburbs (*sākhānagara*) of Pulatthipura,[2] in which the king built the **Isipatana-vihāra.**[3]

[1] Cv. lxxiii. 87 f.
[2] *Ibid.*, 153.
[3] *Ibid.*, lxxviii. 79; but see Cv. *Trs.* ii. 112, n. 3.

Rājavesibhujaṅga-Silāmegha.—A title conferred by **Laṅkāpura** on **Ilaṅkiya.**[1]

[1] Cv. lxxvi. 192.

Rājasālā.—A monastery in Ceylon, to which **Aggabodhi VIII.** gave the village of **Cūlavāpiyagāma.**[1]

[1] Cv. xlix. 47.

1. **Rājasīha I.**—King of Ceylon (1581-93 A.C.). He was the son of **Māyādhanu.** It is said that at the age of eleven he was distinguished for his bravery. He gained the throne by defeating the Portuguese. His capital was at **Sītāvaka.** Later, he slew his father, and, when the monks declared that it was impossible to atone for such a heinous crime, he turned against them, gave the revenues from **Sumanakūṭa** to the Saivite priests, slew the monks, and burned their sacred books.[1]

[1] Cv. xciii. 3 ff.; he was held in great fear and is now worshipped as a god; Cv. *Trs.* ii. 226, n. 1.

2. **Rājasīha II.**—Youngest son of King **Senāratana.** He dispossessed his brother and became king; many stories of his prowess are related.[1] He reigned for fifty-two years (1635-87 A.C.), and his capital was at **Sirivaḍḍhanapura.** He obtained wives from the royal family at **Madhurā.** In his time, the Dutch came to Ceylon and exacted tribute. His son was **Vimaladhammasūriya.**[2]

[1] *E.g.*, Cv. xcvi. 7 ff. [2] *Ibid.*, xcv. 23; xcvi. 3 ff.; xcix. 109.

Rājasīhamahāḷa.—A village in South India.[1]

[1] Cv. lxxvi. 286.

Rājā.—A **Yakkha,** one of the messengers of **Kuvera.**[1]

[1] D. iii. 201; DA. iii. 967.

Rājādhirājasīha.—Brother of **Kittisirirājasīha** and king of Ceylon (1780-98 A.C.). He was a man of piety and learning, and was author of a Sinhalese poem, the *Asadisajātaka.*[1]

[1] Cv. ci. 1 ff.

" Rājāno " Sutta.—Kings do not punish beings who practise goodness; they punish only criminals.[1]

[1] A. iii. 208 f.

Rājāyatana.—The name of a tree, at the foot of which the Buddha received a gift of wheat and honey from the merchants **Tapassu** and **Bhallika** in the eighth week after the Enlightenment.[1] A *thūpa* was later erected on the site of the tree.[2]

[1] Vin. i. 3 f.; J. i. 80; BuA., p. 9. [2] Beal, *op. cit.*, 129.

Rājāyatanadhātu.—Probably identical with **Rājāyatana-cetiya** in **Nāgadīpa. Aggabodhi II.** built for it the **Uṇṇalomaghara-vihārā.**[1] The cetiya was perhaps erected in honour of the Rājāyatana-tree, which was brought by **Samiddhisumana** from **Jetavana** when he came with the Buddha to Ceylon.[2] It is said[3] that when the Buddha's religion disappears, all the relics of the Buddha in Ceylon will gather together at the **Mahācetiya,** proceed from there to the Rājāyatana-cetiya in Nāgadīpa, and from there, finally, to the Bodhi-tree.

[1] C. xlii. 62. [2] See Mhv. i. 52, 57 f. [3] DA. iii. 899.

Rājāyatana-cetiya.—See **Rājāyatanadhātu.**

Rājinā.—A town in South India, captured from **Kulasekhara** by **Laṅkāpura** and **Jagadvijaya.**[1]

[1] Cv. lxxvi. 317 ff.

1. **Rājinī.**—Queen of **Kassapa V.** She once had the whole of the **Hemamālikacetiya** covered with cloth. She had a son named **Siddhattha.**[1]

[1] Cv. lii. 67.

2. **Rājinī.**—A nunnery in Ceylon, built by **Moggallāna I.** for the **Sāgalika** nuns.[1]

[1] Cv. xxxix. 43.

Rājinīdīpika.—A monastery in Ceylon, presented by **Aggabodhi V.** to the **Dhammaruci** monks.[1]

[1] Cv. xlviii. 1.

Rājininijjhara.—A weir in a river in **Dakkhiṇadesa,** restored by **Parakkamabāhu I.**[1]

[1] Cv. lxxix. 66.

Rājindabrahma.—A Damiḷa chief, ally of **Kulasekhara,** captured by **Laṅkāpura.**[1]

[1] Cv. lxxvii. 77, 86.

Rājindarājābhidheyyadīpanī.—A treatise (on the naming of kings) by **Ratnākara** Thera of Burma eulogizing various kings.[1]

[1] Sās, p. 102; Bode, *op. cit.*, 52.

Rājuppala.—A tank in Ceylon, built by **Vasabha**[1] and repaired by **Upatissa II.**[2]

[1] Mhv. xxxv. 94. [2] Cv. xxxvii. 185.

1. **Rājovāda Jātaka** (No. 151).—Two kings, **Brahmadatta** of Benares (the Bodhisatta) and **Mallika** of Kosala, while journeying in disguise, in order to discover if anyone in their respective kingdoms could tell them of any faults which they (the kings) possessed, meet in a narrow path, and a dispute arises among the charioteers as to who should give place. It is discovered that both are of the same age and power. Each driver sings the praises of his own master, but then they discover that Mallika is good to the good and bad to the bad, while Brahmadatta is good to both the good and the bad. Mallika's charioteer acknowledges Brahmadatta as the superior and gives place.

The story is related to **Pasenadi,** who comes to the Buddha after having had to decide a difficult case involving moral turpitude. He is satisfied that he has done well, and the Buddha agrees with him that to administer justice with impartiality is the way to heaven.

Mallika is identified with **Ānanda** and his driver with **Moggallāna,** while Brahmadatta's driver is **Sāriputta.**[1]

[1] J. ii. 1 ff.

2. **Rājovāda Jātaka** (No. 334).—Once the king of Benares, wishing to discover if he ruled justly, travelled about in disguise, and, in the course of his wanderings, came to the **Himālaya,** where the Bodhisatta lived as an ascetic. The ascetic gave him ripe figs, and, when asked why they were so sweet, explained that the king of the country was evidently a just ruler. The king returned to his kingdom and ruled for a while unjustly; and returning again to the hermitage, he found that the figs had become bitter.

The story was related to **Pasenadi,** in order to show the importance of a king ruling wisely and justly. **Ānanda** is identified with the king of the story.[1]

[1] J. iii. 110-12; *cp.* Mahākapi Jātaka (No. 407).

Rājovāda Sutta.—Probably this name, mentioned in the introduction to the **Sumaṅgala Jātaka,**[1] is a descriptive title and not the name of any particular sutta preached by the Buddha to **Pasenadi.**

[1] J. iii. 439.

1. **Rādha.**—A parrot, brother of **Poṭṭhapāda,** the Bodhisatta. See the **Rādha Jātaka** (1). He is identified with **Ānanda.**[1]

[1] J. i. 496.

2. **Rādha.**—The Bodhisatta born as a parrot. See the **Rādha Jātaka** (2).

3. **Rādha.**—The Bodhisatta born as a parrot. See the **Kālabāhu Jātaka.**

4. **Rādha Thera.**—He was a brahmin of **Rājagaha** who, being neglected by his children in his old age, sought ordination. The monks refused his request on the ground of his age, so he sought the Buddha who, seeing his *upanissaya*, asked **Sāriputta** to admit him.[1] Soon after he won arahantship. He stayed near the Buddha, and, by reason of his skill, the Buddha declared him foremost among those who could inspire speech in others (? *paṭibhāṇakeyyānaṃ*).[2] He thereby earned the name of **Paṭibhāṇiya Thera.**[3] The Theragāthā[4] contains two verses spoken by him in praise of concentration of the mind. The Rādha Saṃyutta[5] contains a large number of suttas preached by the Buddha in answer to Rādha's questions on various topics. It is said that when the Buddha saw Rādha he felt the inclination to talk on matters dealing with subtle topics, illustrating them with various similes.[6]

[1] It is probably this incident which is referred to at ThagA. ii. 114, where Sāriputta is said to have ordained a poor brahmin named Rādha, but no mention is made of any order from the Buddha. If the reference is to this same thera, Rādha was, for some time, the attendant (*pacchāsamaṇa*) of Sāriputta, and there is a verse in Thag. (993) spoken to him by Sāriputta, who was pleased with Rādha's gentle manner. DhA. ii. 104 ff. gives more details of the ordination of Rādha. There we are told that he went to the monastery where he performed various duties. But the monks would not admit him into the Order, and, owing to his disappointment, he grew thin. One day the Buddha, seeing him with his divine eye, went to him, and hearing of his wish to join the Order, summoned the monks and asked if any of them remembered any favour done by Rādha. Sāriputta mentioned that he had once received a ladleful of Rādha's own food while begging in Rājagaha. The Buddha then suggested that Sāriputta should listen to Rādha's request for ordination. After ordination, Rādha grew weary of the food of the refectory, but Sāriputta constantly admonished him and found him most humble; later, he spoke highly of Rādha's obedience, and the Buddha praised him. It was on Rādha's account that the **Alīnacitta Jātaka** (*q.v.*) was preached. AA. i. 179 f. agrees, more or less, with the account given above; so does Ap. ii. 485 f.

[2] A. i. 25; ThagA. i. 253 f.

[3] SA. ii. 246.

[4] vss. 133-4.

[5] S. iii. 188-201; see also Rādha Sutta.

[6] SA. ii. 246; this was because of Rādha's wealth of views (*diṭṭhisamudācāra*) and unwavering faith (*okappaniyasaddhā*); AA. i. 179; also ThagA. i. 254.

In the time of **Padumuttara Buddha,** Rādha was a householder of **Haṃsavatī** and held a great almsgiving in honour of the Buddha, wishing to gain pre-eminence in the power of inspiring others to speak. He gave ripe mangoes to **Vipassī Buddha**[7] and, as a result, was born in heaven.

Surādha Thera (*q.v.*) was his younger brother. Rādha was, for some time, the Buddha's attendant.[8]

[7] ThagA. i. 253; AA. i. 180; Ap. ii. 484.
[8] AA. i. 163.

1. **Rādha Jātaka** (No. 145).—The Bodhisatta was once born as a parrot, named **Poṭṭhapāda,** and his brother was **Rādha.** They were brought up by a brahmin of **Kāsi.** When the brahmin was away, his wife admitted men to the house and her husband set the birds to watch. Rādha wished to admonish her, but his brother said it was useless and they must await the brahmin's return. Having told him what had happened, the two parrots flew away, saying they could not live there any longer.

Rādha is identified with **Ānanda.**[1] The introductory story is identical with that of the **Indriya Jātaka** (No. 423).

[1] J. i. 495 f.

2. **Rādha Jātaka** (No. 198).—The Bodhisatta was once born as a parrot, brother to **Poṭṭhapāda.** They were brought up by a brahmin in Benares. When the brahmin went away, he told the birds to watch his wife and report to him any misconduct. But Poṭṭhapāda, in spite of his brother's warning, admonished the woman, who, in a rage, while pretending to fondle him, wrung his neck and threw him into the fire. When the brahmin returned, Rādha said he did not wish to share his brother's fate, and flew away.

Poṭṭhapāda is identified with **Ānanda.** The story was told in reference to a monk who became a backslider owing to a woman.[1]

[1] J. ii. 132 ff.; *cf.* the **Kālabāhu Jātaka.**

Rādha Saṃyutta.—The twenty-third section of the **Saṃyutta Nikāya.** It contains various suttas preached by the Buddha in answer to **Rādha's** questions.[1]

[1] S. iii. 188-201.

1. **Rādha Sutta.**—**Rādha** asks the Buddha if ideas of " I " and " mine " are completely absent in him who knows and sees, regarding the body, consciousness and external objects. The Buddha answers in the affirmative.[1]

[1] S. iii. 79.

2. **Rādha Sutta.—Rādha,** before becoming an arahant, goes to the Buddha and asks for a teaching in brief. The Buddha tells him to abandon desire for what is impermanent—*i.e.*, the eye, objects, eye-consciousness, etc.[1]

[1] S. iv. 48 f.

Rādhatheravatthu.—Gives a detailed account of **Rādha's** admission into the Order and **Sāriputta's** praise of him.[1]

[1] DhA. ii. 104 ff.

Rādhavatī.—A city where **Anomadassī Buddha** preached to King **Madhurindhara.**[1]

[1] BuA. 144.

Rādhā.—One of the two chief women disciples of **Paduma Buddha.**[1]

[1] Bu. ix. 22.

1. **Rāma.**—A brahmin, skilled in physiogmony. He was one of the eight consulted by **Suddhodana** regarding his son, the future Buddha.[1]

[1] J. i. 56; Mil. 236.

2. **Rāma.**—King of Benares. He suffered from a virulent skin disease, and, leaving his kingdom to his eldest son, went into the forest, where he was cured by eating medicinal herbs. In the forest he met and married **Piyā,** the eldest daughter of **Okkāka.** She suffered from the same complaint, and was cured by him. They lived in the forest with their thirty-two children. A forester recognized Rāma in the forest, and, on his return to the city, told the news to the king. The king went to the forest with his retinue and begged his father to return to the kingdom. He refused to do so, and, at his own suggestion, a city was built for him in the forest which was called **Koliya** or **Vyagghapajja.** Rāma thus became the ancestor of the **Koliyans.**[1]

[1] DA. i. 260 ff.; SNA. 355 f.; *cf.* Mtu. i. 355, where he is called Kola.

3. **Rāma.**—A brahmin, father of the Buddha's teacher, **Uddaka-Rāmaputta** (*q.v.*).[1]

[1] J. i. 66; M. i. 165.

4. **Rāma.**—The Bodhisatta born as the eldest son of **Dasaratha,** king of Benares. He is also called **Rāmapaṇḍita.** He married his sister **Sītā,** and her devotion to him became proverbial.[1] For Rāma's story see

[1] *E.g.*, J. iv. 559, 560; Cv. lxxiii. 137.

the **Dasaratha Jātaka.** Certain ruling princes of Ceylon claimed descent from Rāma—*e.g.*, **Jagatīpāla** (*q.v.*). Rāma's fight with **Rāvaṇa** and the incidents recounted in the *Rāmāyaṇa* are mentioned only in the later Pāli Chronicles, such as the **Cūlavaṃsa.**[2]

[2] *Ibid.*, lxiv. 42; lxviii. 20; lxxv. 59; lxxxiii. 46, 69, 88.

5. **Rāma.**—A Sākyan prince, brother of **Bhaddakaccānā.** He came to Ceylon, where he founded the settlement of **Rāmagoṇa.**[1]

[1] Mhv. ix. 9; Dpv. x. 4 ff.

6. **Rāma.**—Called **Mātuposaka-Rāma.** He was an inhabitant of Benares and greatly loved his parents. He once went on business to **Kumbhavatī,** in the country of **Daṇḍakī,** and there, when the country was being destroyed owing to the wickedness of the king, **Rāma** thought of the goodness of his parents. The devas were moved by the power of this thought and conveyed him safely to his mother.[1] He was one of the three survivors of the disaster which overtook Daṇḍakī's kingdom.[2]

[1] J. v. 29.

[2] MA. ii. 602.

7. **Rāma.**—One of the palaces of **Koṇḍañña Buddha** in his last lay life.[1]

[1] BuA. 107; but see Bu. iii. 26.

8. **Rāma.**—One of the generals of **Gajabāhu.** Rāma was once defeated by the general **Deva,**[1] but later won a victory at the **Mahārakkha-**ford. Rāma received the title of **Nīlagiri,** which was evidently the name of his district.[2]

[1] Cv. lxx. 137, 142.

[2] *Ibid.*, lxxii. 12; Cv. *Trs.* i. 299, n. 1; 320, n. 2.

9. **Rāma.**—The second of the future Buddhas.[1]

[1] Anāgatavaṃsa, p. 40.

10. **Rāma.**—See **Ramma.**

Rāmaka, or **Rāmuka.**—A vihāra in Ceylon, built by **Gajabāhukagāmaṇi** in the last year of his reign.[1] *v.l.* Bhamuka.

[1] Mhv. xxxv. 122.

Rāmakula.—An elephant used by **Parakkamabāhu I.** in his youth.[1]

[1] Cv. lxvii. 33.

Rāmagāma.—A Koliyan village on the banks of the Ganges. Its inhabitants claimed and obtained a share of the Buddha's relics, over which they erected a *thūpa.*[1] This *thūpa* was later destroyed by floods, and the urn, with the relics, was washed into the sea. There the **Nāgas,** led by their king, **Mahākāla,** received it and took it to their abode in **Mañjerika** where a *thūpa* was built over them, with a temple attached, and great honour was paid to them. When **Duṭṭhagāmaṇi** built the **Mahā Thūpa** and asked for relics to be enshrined therein, **Mahinda** sent **Soṇuttara** to the Nāga-world to obtain these relics, the Buddha having ordained that they should ultimately be enshrined in the Mahā Thūpa. But Mahākāla was not willing to part with them, and Soṇuttara had to use his *iddhi*-power to obtain them. A few of the relics were later returned to the Nāgas for their worship.[2]

[1] D. ii. 167; Bu. xxviii. 3; Dvy. 380.

[2] For details see Mhv. xxxi. 18 ff.

Rāmagoṇa.—A settlement in Ceylon, founded by **Rāma,** brother of **Bhaddakaccānā.**[1]

[1] Mhv. ix. 9.

Rāmagoṇaka-vihāra.—A monastery in Ceylon, built by **Kaniṭṭhatissa.**[1]

[1] Mhv. xxxvi. 14.

Rāmañña.—The Pāli name for Burma, referring particularly to the maritime provinces. After the conversion of Rāmañña to Buddhism, there was a constant intercourse between that country and Ceylon.[1] **Vijayabāhu I.** sent an embassy to **Anuruddha,** king of Rāmañña, and obtained from him learned and pious monks to re-establish the Saṅgha in Ceylon.[2] The kings of Rāmañña seem to have been in the habit of giving a special maintenance to Sinhalese envoys sent to their country. The chief trade between the two countries was in elephants; the king of Rāmañña made a gift of an elephant to every vessel bringing gifts from foreign lands. In the time of **Parakkamabāhu I.,** relations were strained between the two countries as a result of insults paid by the king of Rāmañña, and Parakkamabāhu sent a punitive expedition under the **Damiḷādhikārin, Ādicca.** This expedition started from **Pallavaṅka,** and some of the forces landed at **Kusumī** in Rāmañña and the others at **Papphālama.** It is said that in a battle fought at **Ukkama,** the Sinhalese forces killed the Rāmañña king. Thereafter, through the intervention of the monks, peace was restored between the two countries, and the

[1] So says also Cv. lxxvi. 10 f.

[2] *Ibid.*, lxviii. 8; lx. 5 ff.; but see Cv. *Trs.* i. n. 4.

Ramaṇas, as the people of Rāmañña were called, sent a yearly tribute to the king of Ceylon.[3]

[3] For details of this expedition see Cv. lxxvi. 10 ff.; also Cv. *Trs.* ii. 69, n. 3.

Rāmaṇeyyaka Thera.—An arahant. He belonged to a wealthy family of **Sāvatthi,** and left the world impressed by the presentation of **Jetavana.** Dwelling in the forest, he practised meditation, and, because of his attainments and charm, he was called **Rāmaṇeyyaka.** Once **Māra** tried to frighten him, but without success. The verse he uttered on that occasion is included in the Theragāthā.[1]

In the time of **Sikhī Buddha,** he had offered him flowers. Twenty-nine kappas ago he was king under the name of **Sumedhayasa** (*v.l.* **Sumeghaghana**).[2] He is probably identical with **Minelapupphiya** of the Apadāna.[3]

[1] Thag. vs. 49. [2] ThagA. i. 120 f. [3] Ap. i. 203 f.

Rāmaṇeyyaka Sutta.—**Sakka** visits the Buddha at **Jetavana** and asks him what it is which, by situation, is enjoyable. The Buddha replies that whatever place is occupied by the arahants that is the most enjoyable.[1]

[1] S. i. 232; *cp.* DhA. ii. 195; the verse here ascribed to the Buddha is, in the Thag. (vs. 991) attributed to **Sāriputta.** Both there and in DhA. (see above) the verse is uttered in reference to Sāriputta's brother, **Revata.**

Rāmaputta.—See **Uddaka-Rāmaputta.**

1. **Rāmā.**—One of the two chief women disciples of **Paduma Buddha.**[1]

[1] J. i. 36; Bu. ix. 22, calls her **Rādhā.**

2. **Rāmā.**—One of the two chief women disciples of **Sumedha Buddha.**[1]

[1] J. i. 38; Bu. xii. 24.

Rāmāyaṇa.—Reference to this Epic Poem does not occur in the Piṭakas or in the early books. Even in the Commentaries reference thereto is rare,[1] and then it is only condemned as " purposeless talk " (*niratthakakathā*). Only in the later Chronicles, such as the **Cūḷavaṃsa,**[2] is the work actually mentioned by name. See also *s.v.* **Rāma** (5).

[1] *E.g.*, DA. i. 76; MA. i. 163, as **Sītāharaṇa.** [2] *E.g.* Cv. lxiv. 42.

Rāhu.—An **Asura** chieftain (**Asurinda**).[1] The Saṃyutta Nikāya[2] says that on one occasion when he seized **Candimā** (Moon-god), and on another **Suriya** (Sun-god), both these invoked the aid of the Buddha. The Buddha then instructed Rāhu to let them free. Rāhu immediately

[1] *Cp.* Mtu. iii. 138, 254. [2] S. i. 49 f.

let them go and ran to **Vepacitti,** "trembling and with stiffened hair." This incident evidently refers to the Indian myth of the eclipses, and the legend has been annexed by the Buddhists to illustrate the Buddha's power and pity.

Elsewhere[3] Rāhu is spoken of as the chief of those possessing personality (*attabhāva*). The Commentaries[4] explain that he is four thousand eight hundred leagues in height, and that the breadth of his chest is one thousand two hundred yojanas. His hands and feet are two hundred leagues long, each finger-joint measuring fifty leagues, the space between the eyebrows also measuring fifty leagues. His forehead is fifty leagues broad, and his head nine hundred leagues in height. His face measures one hundred leagues, his nose three hundred, and the depth of his mouth one hundred. He is jealous of the gods of the Sun and the Moon, and stands in their paths with wide-open mouth. When they fall into his mouth, the gods abandon their abodes and flee for their lives. Sometimes he caresses their abodes with his hand only, or with the lower part of his jaw, or with his tongue. Sometimes he takes them up and places them against his cheek; but he cannot stop the course of either the Sun or the Moon; if he attempts to do so, he will meet with disaster. So he journeys along with them.

The seizure of the Moon by Rāhu and the escape from him is often used as a simile.[5] Rāhu is one of the four "stains" (*upakkilesā*) of the Sun and the Moon, preventing them from shining in all their glory.[6] He is further mentioned as one of the five causes of lack of rain (*vassassa antarāya*). When he gathers water into his hands and spills it into the ocean, there is no rain.[7] The idea seems to be that he gathers up the rain-water which is in the sky in order to cool his body.

To bring Rāhu down from the sky is mentioned as one of the impossible tasks.[8]

It is said[9] that for a long time Rāhu did not visit the Buddha, he thought that being so tall he would fail to see the Buddha. One day, however, he decided to go, and the Buddha, aware of his intention, lay on a bed when he arrived, and, by his *iddhi*-power, contrived to make himself so tall that Rāhu had to crane his neck to see his face. Rāhu, thereupon, confessed his folly and accepted the Buddha as his teacher.

Rāhu is mentioned[10] as being among the Asuras who were present at the **Mahāsamaya** and as blessing that assembly. In this context he

[3] A. ii. 17.

[4] *E.g.*, AA. ii. 474; DA. ii. 487 f.; MA. ii. 790; SA. i. 86, contains more details and differs slightly.

[5] *E.g.*, SN. vs. 465; J. i. 183, 274; iii. 364, 377; iv. 330; v. 453; DhA. iv. 19, etc.

[6] A. ii. 53; Vin. ii. 295; *cp.* J. iii. 365.

[7] A. iii. 243.

[8] J. iii. 477.

[9] DA. i. 285; MA. ii. 790 f.

[10] D. ii. 259.

is called **Rāhubhadda.** When Rāhu steps into the ocean, the water of the deepest part reaches only to his knees.[11] Rāhu is also called **Veroca,** and **Bāli's** hundred sons were called after him, he being their uncle.[12] The name **Rāhumukha** is given to a form of torture,[13] in which the victim's mouth is forced open by a stake and fire or spikes are sent through the orifice of the ear into the mouth, which becomes filled with blood.[14]

11 DA. ii. 488.
12 *Ibid.*, 689.
13 *E.g.*, M. i. 87; iii. 164; Nid. 154; Mil. 197, 358.
14 AA. i. 293.

1. **Rāhula Thera.**—Only son of **Gotama Buddha.** He was born on the day on which his father left the household life.[1] When the Buddha visited **Kapilavatthu** for the first time after his Enlightenment and accepted **Suddhodana's** invitation, Rāhula's mother (**Rāhulamātā**) sent the boy to the Buddha to ask for his inheritance (*dāyajja*). The Buddha gave him no answer, and, at the conclusion of the meal, left the palace. Rāhula followed him, reiterating his request, until at last the Buddha asked **Sāriputta** to ordain him.[2] When Suddhodana heard of this he protested to the Buddha, and asked as a boon that, in future, no child should be ordained without the consent of his parents, and to this the Buddha agreed.[3]

It is said[4] that immediately after Rāhula's ordination the Buddha preached to him constantly (*abhiṇhovādavasena*) many suttas for his guidance. Rāhula himself was eager to receive instruction from the Buddha and his teachers and would rise early in the morning and take a handful of sand, saying: " May I have today as many words of counsel from my teachers as there are here grains of sand !" The monks constantly spoke of Rāhula's amenability, and one day the Buddha, aware of the subject of their talk, went amongst them and related the **Tipallatthamiga Jātaka**[5] and the **Tittira Jātaka**[6] to show them that in past births, too, Rāhula had been known for his obedience. When Rāhula was seven years old, the Buddha preached to him the **Ambalatthika-Rāhulovāda Sutta** (*q.v.*) as a warning that he should never lie, even in fun. Rāhula used to accompany the Buddha on his begging rounds,[7] and noticing that he harboured carnal thoughts fascinated by

1 J. i. 60; AA. i. 82, etc.; *cf.* J. i. 62.

2 According to SNA. (i. 340), **Moggallāna** taught him the *kammavācā*; see also J. ii. 393.

3 Vin. i. 82 f.; the story of Rāhula's conversion is also given at DhA. i. 98 f.

4 AA. i. 145.

5 J. i. 160 ff.

6 J. iii. 64 ff.

7 Sometimes he would accompany **Sāriputta** on his begging rounds. He was present when Sāriputta went to his (Sāriputta's) mother's house, where he was roundly abused by her for having left her. DhA. iv. 164 f.

his own physical beauty and that of his father, the Buddha preached to him, at the age of eighteen, the **Mahā Rāhulovāda Sutta** (*q.v.*). Two other suttas, also called **Rāhulovāda**, one included in the **Saṃyutta** and the other in the **Aṅguttara** (see below), formed the topics for Rāhula's meditation (*vipāssanā*).[8] Later, the Buddha, knowing that Rāhula's mind was ripe for final attainment, went with him alone to **Andhavana**, and preached to him the **Cūla-Rāhulovāda Sutta.** At the end of the discourse, Rāhula became an arahant, together with one hundred thousand crores of listening devas.[9] Afterwards, in the assembly of monks, the Buddha declared Rāhula foremost among those of his disciples who were anxious for training (*sikkhākāmānaṃ*).[10]

In the time of **Padumuttara Buddha,** both Rāhula and **Raṭṭhapāla** were rich householders of **Haṃsavatī,** who, realizing the vanity of riches, gave all away to the poor. One day they entertained two ascetics of great power. The ascetic to whom Rāhula ministered was in the habit of visiting the abode of the Nāga-king, **Paṭhavindhara,** and had been impressed by its magnificence. Therefore, in returning thanks to Rāhula for his hospitality, he wished that his host might resemble Paṭhavindhara. Rāhula remembered this, and after death he was born in the Nāga-world as Paṭhavindhara, his friend being born as **Sakka.** He was, however,

[8] To these Suttas Buddhaghosa (MA. i. 635) adds the **Sāmaṇera,** or **Kumārapañhā,** and proceeds to enumerate the different purposes which the Buddha had in view in preaching these suttas; see also AA. ii. 547. SNA. i. 340 says, about the **Rāhula Sutta** (*q.v.*), that the Buddha constantly preached it to Rāhula. See also the **Rāhula Saṃyutta.**

[9] SA. iii. 26 says these devas were among those who, in the time of **Padumuttara Buddha,** had heard Rāhula's wish to be born as the son of a future Buddha. They were subsequently born in various deva-worlds, but on this day they all assembled at Andhavana in order to be present at the fulfilment of Rāhula's wish. This scene was one of the incidents sculptured in the Relic Chamber of the **Mahā Thūpa,** as was also the ordination of Rāhula. Mhv. xxxi. 81, 83.

[10] A. i. 24; the Vinaya (iii. 16) gives a story illustrating Rāhula's extreme conscientiousness in the observance of rules. He arrived one evening at **Kosambī,** when the Buddha was staying there in the **Badarikārāma.** Rāhula was told there of a new rule which had been laid down to the effect that no novice should sleep under the same roof as a fully ordained monk. Unable to find any resting-place which did not violate this rule, Rāhula spent the night in the Buddha's jakes. When the Buddha discovered him there the next morning, he modified the rule. This incident and Rāhula's keenness in observing rules, are described again in greater detail at J. i. 161 f. There the Buddha is said to have found fault with Sāriputta for his neglect of Rāhula (see also Sp. iv. 744). On another occasion, finding no place in which to sleep because monks who had arrived late had taken his sleeping-place, Rāhula spent the night in the open, in front of the Buddha's cell. **Māra,** seeing him there, assumed the form of a huge elephant and trumpeted loudly, hoping to frighten him. But the plot failed. This was eight years after Rāhula had attained arahantship (DhA. iv. 69 f.).

dissatisfied with his lot, and one day when, with **Virūpakkha,** he was on a visit to Sakka, Sakka recognized him, and finding out that he was dissatisfied, suggested to him a remedy. Paṭhavindhara invited the Buddha to his abode. The Buddha, attended by **Sumana** and one hundred thousand arahants, came and was entertained by him. In the company of monks was **Uparevata,** the Buddha's son, seated next to him, and Paṭhavindhara was so fascinated by him that he could not take his eyes off him. Discovering who he was, Paṭhavindhara expressed a wish that he, too, might be born as the son of a future Buddha. Later, in the time of **Kassapa Buddha,** Rāhula was born as **Paṭhavindhara,** the eldest son of King **Kiki,** later becoming his viceroy. His seven sisters built seven residences for the Buddha, and, at their suggestion, Paṭhavindhara built five hundred residences for the monks.[11]

Four verses uttered by Rāhula are included in the **Theragāthā.**[12]

It is said that the news of Rāhula's birth was brought to the Bodhisatta when he was enjoying himself in his pleasaunce on the banks of the royal pond after being decked by **Vissakamma.** As soon as the news was announced, he made up his mind to renounce the world without delay, for he saw, in the birth of a son, a new bond attaching him to household life ("*Rāhulajāto, bandhanaṃ jātaṃ*"—the word *rāhula* meaning bond).[13]

According to the Dīgha and Saṃyutta Commentaries,[14] Rāhula predeceased the Buddha and even Sāriputta, and the place of his death is given as **Tāvatiṃsa.** For twelve years he never lay on a bed.[15]

In numerous Jātakas, Rāhula is mentioned as having been the Bodhisatta's son—*e.g.*, in the **Uraga, Kapi** (No. 250), **Kumbhakāra, Khaṇḍahāla, Culla-Sutasoma, Daddara, Bandhanāgāra, Makkaṭa, Makhadeva, Mahājanaka, Mahāsudassana, Vidhurapaṇḍita, Vessantara, Sihakoṭṭhuka** and **Sonaka.**[16] He was also **Yaññadatta,** son of **Maṇḍavya**

[11] The story of the past as given here is taken from AA. i. 141 ff.; part of it is given in MA. ii. 722 under **Raṭṭhapāla,** but the account differs in details. There the Nāga-world is called **Bhumindhara,** and the Nāga-king, **Pālita.** SNA. i. 341 differs again and calls the king **Saṅkha.** See also ThagA. ii. 30 on Raṭṭhapāla, where no mention is made of Rāhula. The Apadāna (i. 60 f.) gives a different version altogether. There Rāhula gave Padumuttara Buddha a carpet (*santhara*), as a result of which, twenty-one kappas ago, he was born as a khattiya named **Vimala,** in **Reṇuvati.** There he lived in a palace, **Sudassana,** specially built for him by **Vissakamma.**

[12] vv. 295-98; Mil. 413 contains several other stanzas attributed to Rāhula.

[13] J. i. 60; DhA. i. 70. The Ap. Commentary, however, derives Rāhula from Rāhu; just as **Rāhu** obstructs the moon, so would the child be as obstruction to the Bodhisatta's Renunciation.

[14] DA. ii. 549; SA. iii. 172.

[15] DA. iii. 736.

[16] For Rāhula's condition and name (where it is given) in these various births, see *s.v.*

(*Sāriputta*) and the young tortoise in the **Mahāukkusa.**[17] The Apadāna[18] says that in many births **Uppalavaṇṇā** and Rāhula were born of the same parents (*ekasmiṃ sambhave*) and had similar tendencies (*samānacchandamānasā*).

Rāhula was known to his friends as **Rāhulabhadda** (Rāhula, the Lucky). He himself says[19] that he deserved the title because he was twice blest in being the son of the Buddha and an arahant himself. Mention is often made in the books[20] that, though Rāhula was his own son, the Buddha showed as much love for **Devadatta, Aṅgulimāla** and **Dhanapāla** as he did for Rāhula.

Asoka built a thūpa in honour of Rāhula, to be specially worshipped by novices.[21]

17 *q.v.*
18 ii. 551.
19 Thag. vs. 295 f.
20 DhA. i. 124; MA. i. 537; Mil. 410 attributes this statement to Sāriputta; SNA. i. 202 expands it to include others.
21 Beal, Records i. 180, 181.

2. **Rāhula.**—One of the four monks who accompanied **Chapaṭa** to Ceylon. These monks later became the founders of the **Sīhalasaṅgha** in Burma. Later, at one of the festivals of King **Narapati, Rāhula** fell in love with an actress and went with her to **Malayadīpa,** where he taught the king the **Khuddasikkhā** and its Commentary. With the money given to him by the king he became a layman.[1]

1 Sās. 65; Bode, *op. cit.*, 23 f.

Rāhula Saṃyutta.—The eighteenth section of the **Saṃyutta Nikāya.** It consists of a series of lessons given by the Buddha to **Rāhula,** showing him the fleeting nature of all things.[1] Buddhaghosa says[2] that these suttas were preached on various occasions, from the time Rāhula entered the Order, to the time of his attainment of arahantship. They contain mention of qualities which mature emancipation.[3]

1 S. ii. 244-56. 2 MA. ii. 635 f. 3 *vimuttiparipācaniyadhammā* (SA. ii. 159).

1. **Rāhula Sutta.**—The Buddha tells **Rāhula** that a monk should cultivate the thought that, in the four elements, either in one's own body or in external objects, there is neither self nor what pertains to the self.[1]

Buddhaghosa says[2] that the Buddha here declares *catukoṭikasuññatā* (emptiness in the four things—*i.e.*, elements).

1 A. ii. 164; this same topic is discussed in greater detail in the **Ambalaṭṭhika-Rāhulovāda Sutta.** 2 AA. ii. 547.

2. **Rāhula Sutta.**—**Rāhula** visits the Buddha and asks him how to get rid of the insidious idea of " I " and " mine," both with regard to one's own body and with all external objects. The Buddha replies that one should see things as they really are, that in none of the five *khandhas* is there any " I " or " mine." This is right insight.[1]

[1] S. iii. 135; this sutta is given at S. ii. 252 as **Anusaya Sutta.** Buddhaghosa describes both this sutta and the next as **Rāhulovāda-vipassanā** (AA. ii. 547).

3. **Rāhula Sutta.**—Similar to No. 2. **Rāhula** asks how one's mind can be removed from such vain conceits.[1]

[1] S. iii. 136. This sutta is given at S. ii. 253 as the **Apagata Sutta.**

4. **Rāhula Sutta.**—The discourse which brings about the attainment of arahantship by **Rāhula.**[1] It is the same as the **Cūla-Rāhulovāda Sutta** (*q.v.*).

[1] S. iv. 105 f.

5. **Rāhula Sutta.**—A series of stanzas which, according to Buddhaghosa,[1] were frequently recited by the Buddha for the guidance of **Rāhula.** The Buddha reminds him that he (Rāhula) is a follower of " the torch-bearer among men." He has left the world to put an end to sorrow. He should, therefore, associate with good friends, in good surroundings. He should be free from attachment to food or clothes. He should tree his mind from all evil tendencies and fill it with thoughts of renunciation.[2]

[1] SNA. i. 340.

[2] SN. vv. 335-42. Buddhaghosa says (MA. ii. 532, 635) that the purpose of this sutta was to emphasize the value of good association (*kalyāṇamittūpanissaya*).

Rāhulabhadda.—See **Rāhula.**

Rāhulamātā.—The name, generally given in the texts, of **Rāhula's** mother[1] and **Gotama's** wife. She is also called **Bhaddakaccā,**[2] and, in later texts, **Yasodharā,**[3] **Bimbādevī**[4] and, probably, **Bimbāsundarī.**[5] The Northern texts[6] seem to favour the name of Yasodharā, but they call her the daughter of **Daṇḍapāṇī.** It is probable that the name of Gotama's wife was **Bimbā,** and that **Bhaddakaccā, Subhaddakā, Yosadhāra** and the others, were descriptive epithets applied to her, which later became

[1] *E.g.*, Vin. i. 82.

[2] *E.g.*, Bu. xxvi. 15; Mhv. ii. 24 calls her Bhaddakaccānā; but see Thomas, *op. cit.*, 49; she is also called Subhaddakā, this being probably a variant of Bhaddakaccānā.

[3] BuA., p. 245; Dvy. 253.

[4] J. ii. 392 f.; DA. ii. 422.

[5] J. vi. 478 (12).

[6] See also Rockhill, *op. cit.*, where various other names are given as well.

regarded as additional names. It is also possible that in Gotama's court there was also a Yasodharā, daughter of Daṇḍapāṇī, and that there was a later confusion of names. The Commentarial explanation,[7] that she was called **Bhaddakaccānā** because her body was the colour of burnished gold, is probably correct. To suggest[8] that the name bears any reference to the **Kaccānagotta** seems to be wrong, because the Kaccāna was a brahmin gotta and the **Sākyans** were not brahmins.

Rāhulamātā was born on the same day as the Bodhisatta.[9] She married him (Gotama) at the age of sixteen,[10] and was placed at the head of forty thousand women, given to Gotama by the Sākyans, after he had proved his manly prowess to their satisfaction. Gotama left the household life on the day of the birth of his son Rāhula.[11] It is said that just before he left home he took a last look at his wife from the door of her room, not daring to go nearer, lest he should awake her. When the Buddha paid his first visit to **Kapilavatthu** after the Enlightenment, and on the second day of that visit, he begged in the street for alms. This news spread, and Rāhulamātā looked out of her window to see if it were true. She saw the Buddha, and was so struck by the glory of his personality that she uttered eight verses in its praise. These verses have been handed down under the name of **Narasīhagāthā** (*q.v.*); on that day, after the Buddha had finished his meal in the palace, which he took at the invitation of **Suddhodana,** all the ladies of the court, with the exception of Rāhulamātā, went to pay him obeisance. She refused to go, saying that if she had any virtue in her the Buddha would come to her. The Buddha went to her with his two chief Disciples and gave orders that she should be allowed to greet him as she wished. She fell at his feet, and clasping them with her hands, put her head on them. Suddhodana related to the Buddha how, from the time he had left home, Rāhulamātā had herself abandoned all luxury and had lived in the same manner as she had heard that the Buddha lived—wearing yellow robes, eating only once a day, etc. And the Buddha then related the **Candakinnara Jātaka** (*q.v.*), to show how, in the past, too, her loyalty had been supreme.

On the seventh day of the Buddha's visit, when he left the palace at the end of his meal, Rāhulamātā sent Rāhula to him saying, "That is your father, go and ask him for your inheritance." Rāhula followed the Buddha, and, at the Buddha's request, was ordained by **Sāriputta.**[12]

[7] *E.g.*, AA. i. 204.

[8] *E.g.*, Thomas, *op. cit.*, 49.

[9] J. i. 54; BuA. 106, 228.

[10] The following account is taken chiefly from J. i. 58 ff.

[11] According to one account, referred to in the Jātaka Commentary (i. 62), Rāhula was seven days old.

[12] The account of this event is given in Vin. i. 82; this is probably the only passage in the Piṭakas where Rāhulamātā is mentioned by name.

Later, when the Buddha allowed women to join the Order, Rāhulamātā became a nun under **Mahāpajāpatī Gotamī.**[13]

Buddhaghosa identifies[14] Rāhulamātā with Bhaddakaccānā who, in the Aṅguttara Nikāya,[15] is mentioned as chief among nuns in the possession of supernormal powers (*mahābhiññappattānaṃ*). She was one of the four disciples of the Buddha who possessed such attainment, the others being **Sāriputta, Moggallāna** and **Bakkula.** She expressed her desire for this achievement in the time of **Padumuttara Buddha.**

In this account Bhaddakaccānā is mentioned as the daughter of the Sākyan Suppabuddha and his wife Amitā.[16] She joined the Order under Pajāpatī Gotamī in the company of **Janapadakalyāṇī (Nandā),** and in the Order she was known as **Bhaddakaccānā Therī.** Later, she developed insight and became an arahant. She could, with one effort, recall one *asaṅkheyya* and one hundred thousand kappas.[17]

In the Therī Apadāna[18] an account is found of a Therī, Yasodharā by name, who is evidently to be identified with Rāhulamātā, because she speaks of herself (vvs. 10, 11) as the Buddha's *pajāpatī* before he left the household (*agāra*), and says that she was the chief (*pāmokkhā sabbaissarā*) of ninety thousand women.

In the time of **Dīpaṅkara Buddha,** when the Bodhisatta was born as **Sumedha,** she was a brahmin-maiden, **Sumittā** by name, and gave eight handfuls of lotuses to Sumedha, which he, in turn, offered to the Buddha. Dīpaṅkara, in declaring that Sumedha would ultimately become the Buddha, added that Sumittā would be his companion in several lives. The Apadāna account[19] mentions how, just before her death, at the age of seventy-eight, she took leave of the Buddha and performed various miracles. It also states[20] that eighteen thousand arahants nuns, companions of Yasodharā, also died on the same day.

The **Abbhantara Jātaka**[21] mentions that Bimbādevī (who is called the chief wife of Gotama and is therefore evidently identical with Rāhulamātā) was once, after becoming a nun, ill from flatulence. When Rāhula, as was his custom, came to visit her, he was told that he could not see her, but that, when she had suffered from the same trouble at home, she had been cured by mango-juice with sugar. Rāhula reported

[13] AA. i. 198.

[14] *Ibid.*, 204 f.

[15] A. i. 25.

[16] *Cf.* Mhv. ii. 21 f. It is said (DhA. iii. 44 f.) that Suppabuddha did not forgive the Buddha for leaving his daughter; Devadatta was Bhaddakaccānā's daughter, and it has been suggested that Devadatta's enmity against the Buddha was for reasons similar to her father's.

[17] AA. i. 205.

[18] Ap. ii. 584 ff.

[19] vvs. 1 ff.

[20] Ap. ii. 592 f.

[21] J. ii. 392 f.; *cf.* the **Supatta Jātaka,** where Sāriputta, at Rāhula's request, obtained for her from Pasenadi rice with ghee, flavoured with red fish. This was for abdominal pain (J. ii. 433).

the matter to his preceptor, Sāriputta, who obtained the mango-juice from **Pasenadi.** When Pasenadi discovered why the mango-juice had been needed, he arranged that from that day it should be regularly supplied. The Jātaka relates how, in a past birth too, Sāriputta had come to Rāhulamātā's rescue.

Numerous stories are found in the Jātaka Commentary in which Rāhulamātā is identified with one or other of the characters—*e.g.*, the queen consort in the **Abbhantara, Sammillabhāsinī** in the **Ananusociya, Samuddavijayā** in the **Āditta, Udayabhaddā** in the **Udaya,** the potter's wife (? **Bhaggavī,** *q.v.*) in the **Kumbhakāra,** the queen in the **Kummāsa,** the queen consort in the **Kurudhamma, Pabhāvatī** in the **Kusa, Candā** in the **Khaṇḍahāla,** the queen in the **Gaṅgamāla,** the female in the two **Cakkavāka Jātakas, Candā** in the **Candakinnara, Sumanā** in the **Campeyya,** the woman ascetic in the **Cullabodhi, Candā** in the **Culla Sutasoma,** the queen in the **Jayaddisa, Sītā** in the **Dasaratha,** the queen in the **Pānīya,** the wife in the **Bandhanāgāra, Sujātā** in the **Maṇicora, Manoja's** mother in the **Manoja, Sīvalī** in the **Mahājanaka, Subhaddā** in the **Mahāsudassana,** the mother-deer in the **Lakkhaṇa, Visayha's** wife in the **Visayha, Maddī** in the **Vessantara, Suphassā** in the **Supatta,** the queen in the **Susīma,** and the smith's wife in the **Sūci.**

Rāhulovāda Sutta.—See **Cūla-Rahulovāda, Mahā-Rāhulovāda** and **Ambalaṭṭhika-Rāhulovāda.** The **Cūla-Rāhulovāda** is the one generally referred to as **Rāhulovāda.**

Rukkha.—An officer of **Kassapa IV.** He built a vihāra in **Savāraka** which he handed over to the **Mahāvihāra.** He also laid down rules for the guidance of the monks.[1] *v.l.* **Rakkha.**

[1] Cv. lii. 31.

Rukkha Vagga.—The sixth chapter of the **Nidāna Saṃyutta.**[1]

[1] S. ii. 80-94.

1. **Rukkha Sutta.**—Of those who sit at the foot of trees, he who does so because he desires seclusion and his needs are few, is the best.[1]

[1] A. iii. 219.

2. **Rukkha Sutta.**—On four kinds of trees and four corresponding kinds of men. Some men are evil and their company is evil, some are good and their company is evil, etc.[1]

[1] A. ii. 109.

3. **Rukkha Sutta.**—Just as a tree, which leans towards the east, falls to the east when cut down, so does a monk who cultivates the Eightfold Path incline to Nibbāna.[1]

[1] S. v. 47.

4. **Rukkha Sutta.**—Mighty trees, grown from tiny seeds, overspread other trees and kill them; so are householders destroyed by their lusts. There are five hindrances (*nīvaraṇa*) that overspread the heart; the seven *bojjhaṅgas* are not like them.[1]

[1] S. v. 96 f.

Rukkhadhamma Jātaka (No. 74).—The Bodhisatta was once a tree-sprite in a *sāla*-grove. A new king **Vessavaṇa** was appointed by **Sakka,** and the king gave orders to the tree-sprites to choose their abodes. The Bodhisatta advised his kinsmen to choose trees near his own. Some did not follow his advice and dwelt in the lonely trees. A tempest came and uprooted the lonely trees, leaving the trees in the grove unscathed.

This story was one of those related by the Buddha to the **Sākyans** and **Koliyans,** who fought for the waters of the **Rohiṇī.** He wished to show them the value of concord.[1]

For another Jātaka, not found in the Jātaka Commentary, but quoted in the Aṅguttara Nikāya and sometimes[2] referred to as the **Rukkhadhamma Jātaka,** see *s.v.* **Suppatiṭṭha.**

[1] J. i. 327 ff.

[2] *E.g.*, ThagA. i. 397.

Rukkhopama Sutta.—This sutta is included in a list of suttas[1] dealing with *arūpakammaṭṭhāna*. No such title has so far been traced. The name probably refers to one of the above **Rukkha Suttas.**

[1] *E.g.*, VibhA. 267.

Rucagatti.—Wife of **Koṇāgamana Buddha** in his last lay life.[1]

[1] DA. ii. 422; but Bu. xxiv. 19 calls her **Rucigattā.**

Rucānandā.—A nun in the time of **Kakusandha Buddha.** She came to Ceylon at the Buddha's wish with five hundred other nuns, bringing a branch of the **Bodhi**-tree.[1]

[1] Mhv. xv. 78; Dpv. xvii. 16, 51 ff.

1. **Ruci.**—A king of the **Mahāsammata** dynasty. He was the son of **Aṅgīrasa** and the father of **Suruci.**[1]

[1] Mhv. ii. 4; *cf.* Dpv. iii. 7.

2. **Rucī.**—A king of thirty-eight kappas ago; a previous birth of **Sucintita Thera.**[1]

[1] Ap. i. 134.

3. **Ruci.**—A palace occupied by **Vessabhū Buddha** when he was yet a layman.[1]

[1] Bu. xxii. 19.

4. **Ruci.**—One of the three palaces of **Kakusandha Buddha** before he left the world.[1]

[1] Bu. xxiii. 16.

5. **Ruci.**—See **Suruci.**

Rucigattā.—The wife of **Koṇāgamana Buddha.**[1] *v.l.* **Rucagattī.**

[1] Bu. xxiv. 19.

Rucidevī.—Wife of **Koṇḍañña Buddha** in his last lay life.[1]

[1] Bu. iii. 26.

Rucinandā.—A seṭṭhi's daughter of **Ujjenī,** who gave a meal of milk-rice to **Padumuttara Buddha** just before his Enlightenment.[1]

[1] BuA. 158.

Rucirā.—A class of devas present at the preaching of the **Mahāsamaya Sutta.**[1]

[1] D. ii. 260.

Rucira Jātaka (No. 275).—The story of a pigeon (the Bodhisatta) and a greedy crow. The story is identical with that of the **Lola Jātaka** (*q.v.*).

1. **Rucī.**—One of the chief lay women supporters of **Paduma Buddha.**[1]

[1] Bu. ix. 23.

2. **Rucī.**—An *upāsikā,* held up as an example to others.[1] *v.l.* **Rūpī.**

[1] A. iv. 347; AA. ii. 791.

Rujā.—The daughter of **Aṅgati,** king of **Mithilā.** Her story is given in the **Mahā-Nāradakassapa Jātaka** (*q.v.*). She is identified with **Ānanda.**[1]

[1] J. vi. 255.

Ruṇṇa Sutta.—In the discipline of the Āriyans, singing is a lamentation, dancing a madness, and immoderate laughter childishness.[1]

[1] A. i. 261.

Ruru(miga) Jātaka (No. 482).—Once, in Benares, there lived **Mahādhanaka,** son of a rich man. His parents had taught him nothing, and after their death he squandered all their wealth and fell into debt. Unable to escape his creditors, he summoned them and took them to the banks of the Ganges, promising to show them buried treasure. Arrived there, he jumped into the river. He lamented aloud as he was being carried away by the stream. The Bodhisatta was then a golden-hued deer living on the banks of the river, and, hearing the man's wailing of anguish, he swam into the stream and saved him. After having ministered to him, the deer set him on the road to Benares and asked him to tell no one of the existence of the Bodhisatta.

The day the man reached Benares, proclamation was being made that the Queen Consort, **Khemā,** having dreamed of a golden deer preaching to her, longed for the dream to come true. Mahādhanaka offered to take the king to such a deer and a hunt was organized. When the Bodhisatta saw the king with his retinue, he went up to the king and told him the story of Mahādhanaka. The king denounced the traitor and gave the Bodhisatta a boon that henceforth all creatures should be free from danger. Afterwards the Bodhisatta was taken to the city, where he saw the queen. Flocks of deer, now free from fear, devoured men's crops; but the king would not go against his promise and the Bodhisatta begged his herds to desist from doing damage.

The story was told in reference to **Devadatta's** ingratitude and wickedness. Devadatta was Mahādhanaka and **Ānanda** the king.[1]

[1] J. iv. 255-63; the story is included in the Jātakamālā (No. 26).

Rudradāmaka.—Mentioned in connection with different kinds of coins.[1]

[1] Sp. ii. 297.

Ruhaka.—Chaplain of the king of Benares. See the **Ruhaka Jātaka.**

Ruhaka Jātaka (No. 191).—**Ruhaka** was the chaplain of the Bodhisatta, born as king of Benares. The king gave him a horse with rich trappings, and, when he rode him, everybody was lost in admiration. Ruhaka's wife was a foolish old woman who, on hearing of the people's praise, declared that their excitement was due, not to the qualities of the animal, but to its trappings, and that if Ruhaka would go out wearing the horse's trappings, he would be similarly applauded. Ruhaka agreed to the suggestion and suffered great humiliation; he went home in anger, determined to punish his wife, but she had escaped and had sought the king's protection. The king persuaded Ruhaka to forgive her because "all womankind is full of faults."[1]

The occasion for the story is given in the **Indriya Jātaka** (No. 423) (*q.v.*).

[1] J. ii. 113 ff.

Ruhaka Vagga.—The fifth section of the Duka Nipāta of the Jātaka.[1]

[1] J. ii. 113-38.

Rūpa Vagga.—The first chapter of the Eka Nipāta of the Aṅguttara Nikāya.[1]

[1] A. i. 1, 2.

1. **Rūpa Suttā.**—Two of a group of suttas preached to **Rāhula,** to show him that all things are fleeting, unhappy and changeable.[1]

[1] S. ii. 245, 251.

2. **Rūpa Sutta.**—He who realizes the impermanence of the body and the other *khandhas* becomes a *sotāpanna.*[1]

[1] S. iii. 225.

3. **Rūpa Sutta.**—The cessation of suffering, disease, decay and death, is identical with the cessation of the five sense-objects—forms, sounds, etc.[1]

[1] S. iii. 229.

4. **Rūpa Sutta.**—Desire and lust, which arise from forms, sounds, etc., are corruption of the heart; the getting rid of them leads to higher knowledge.[1]

[1] S. iii. 232.

Rūpanandā.—Called **Janapadakalyāṇī Rūpanandā.**[1] She is evidently identical with **Janapadakalyāṇī Nandā**[2] (*q.v.*), and is described as a sister (? step-sister) of the Buddha. The person referred to as her husband (*bhattā*) is probably **Nanda** (*q.v.*), the Buddha's step-brother; strictly speaking, he joined the Order without having married her, though the wedding had been announced and all preparations were being made.

[1] DhA. iii. 113 ff.

[2] At AA. i. 198 she is actually identified with her. But see *s.v.* **Sundarī Nandā.**

Rūpabhedapakāsinī.—A little grammatical treatise by a Burmese monk called **Jambudhaja.**[1]

[1] Bode, *op. cit.*, 55.

Rūpamālā.—A short treatise on the declension of Pāli nouns, with numerous paradigms and examples; written by **Saraṇaṅkara** of Ceylon in order to facilitate the study of Pāli.[1]

[1] P.L.C. 281.

1. **Rūpavatī.**—Daughter of **Vijayabāhu I.** and **Tilokasundarī.** She had four sisters, and a brother called **Vikkamabāhu.**[1] She died young and unmarried.[2]

[1] Cv. lix. 31. [2] *Ibid.*, 45.

2. **Rūpavatī.**—Queen of **Parakkamabāhu I.** She was a descendant of King **Kittisirimegha.** She is mentioned as having erected a "golden" thūpa in **Pulatthipura.**[1]

[1] Cv. lxxiii. 137, 142 ff. The thūpa has been identified with the modern *Pabuḷu Vehera* (Arch. Survey of Ceylon, vi. 1014, p. 6).

Rūpavatīcetiya.—A thūpa in **Pulatthipura,** built by **Parakkamabāhu I.**[1]

[1] Cv. lxxviii. 51; see also Cv. *Trs.* ii. 107, n. 3. The thūpa is probably the modern *Kiri Vehera.*

Rūpasārī.—Mother of **Sāriputta,** who was called after her, his personal name being **Upatissa.**[1] Her husband was the brahmin **Vaṅganta,**[2] and she became the mother of seven children, all of whom became arahants—**Sāriputta, Upasena, Mahācunda, Revata-Khadiravaniya, Cālā, Upacālā** and **Sisūpacālā.**[3] Both she and her husband were unbelievers, and she was very sad when, one after another, her children, giving up wealth worth eighty crores, joined the Order. She wished to keep at least the youngest of the boys, **Revata,** for herself, and had him married at the age of seven, but her plot miscarried.[4] This embittered her against the monks, and, though she gave them alms when they came to the house, she blamed them for having enticed her children away. Once when Sāriputta visited her with five hundred monks, among whom was **Rāhula,** she invited them in and gave them food, but did not fail to abuse her son, calling him "eater of leavings" (*ucchiṭṭhakhādaka*).[5] She outlived Sāriputta, who visited her just before his death, at **Nāḷakagāma,** in the

[1] SNA. i. 326; DhA. i. 73, etc.; in Sanskrit texts (*e.g.*, Dvy. 395) Sāriputta is called Śāradvatīputra.

[2] DhA. ii. 84.

[3] *Ibid.*, 188; SA. iii. 172.

[4] See *s.v.* **Revata.**

[5] DhA. iv. 164 f.

house where he was born. There she provided lodging for him and his five hundred companions. Sāriputta fell ill of a violent attack of dysentery on the night of his arrival, and she saw various gods, including even **Mahā Brahmā,** come to wait on him. Learning their identity from Mahā Cunda, she was amazed and went to see Sāriputta to have Mahā Cunda's words confirmed. Sāriputta told her how Mahā Brahmā was a follower of the Buddha and talked to her about the marvellous virtues of his teacher. At the end of his talk, she became a *sotāpanna.* Sāriputta died the next day at dawn, and she made elaborate arrangements for his cremation.[6]

She seems to have also been called **Surūpasārī.**[7]

[6] SA. iii. 172 ff.; for details see *s.v.* **Sāriputta.** [7] *E.g.*, ThigA. 162.

Rūpasiddhi.—A Pāli grammar by **Buddhappiya** (or **Dīpaṅkara**) **Thera** (*q.v.*). It is based on **Kaccāyana's** grammar, in its general outlines, and its full name is **Pada-rūpasiddhi.** There is a *ṭīkā* on it ascribed to Buddhappiya himself.[1]

[1] P.L.C., p. 220 f.

Rūpāramma-vihāra.—A monastery in Ceylon built by **Mahāsena.**[1] *v.l.* **Thūpārāma.**

[1] Mhv. xxxvii. 43; MṬ. 684.

Rūpārūpavibhāga.—An Abhidhamma treatise by **Buddhadatta Thera.**[1]

[1] P.L.C., 108.

Rūpī.—An eminent lay woman disciple of the Buddha.[1] *v.l.* **Ruci.**

[1] A. iv. 347; *cf.* AA. ii. 791.

" Rūpī attā " Sutta, " Arūpī atta " Suttā, " Rūpī ca arūpī ca attā " Sutta.—It is owing to the presence of the five khandhas that the view arises that the self has a form, is without sickness after death, or that it is formless, or that it both has form and is formless.[1]

[1] S. iii. 218 f.

1. **Reṇu.**—Son and successor of King **Disampati.** On the death of his father Reṇu, with the advice and co-operation of his chief steward (**Mahāgovinda**) **Jotipāla,** who was also his great friend, divided his kingdom into seven parts and shared it with his friends—**Sattabhu, Brahmadatta, Vessabhu, Bharata,** and the two **Dhataraṭṭhas.** The seven divisions of the kingdom were called **Kalinga, Assaka, Avanti,**

Sovīra, Videha, Aṅga and **Kāsi;** their capitals were, respectively, **Dantapura, Potana, Māhissatī, Roruka, Mithilā, Campā** and **Bārāṇasī.** Renu himself occupied the central kingdom.[1]

[1] D. ii. 228-36; Reṇu probably reigned in Benares, though the account given in the **Mahāgovinda Sutta** does not make it clear which was his kingdom; see Dial. ii. 270 n.; also Mtu. iii. 197-209; and **Reṇu** (2).

2. **Reṇu.**—Son of **Disampati,** king of Benares.[1] He is probably identical with **Reṇu** (1).

[1] Dpv. iii. 40; MṬ. 130.

3. **Reṇu.**—King of **Uttarapañcāla,** the capital of the **Kurus.** He was the father of **Somanassa.** For details see the **Somanassa Jātaka.**[1]

[1] J. iv. 444 ff.

4. **Reṇu.**—A king of forty-five kappas ago, a previous birth of **Vajjiputta (Reṇupūjaka) Thera.**[1]

[1] ThagA. i. 143=Ap. i. 146.

Reṇupūjaka Thera.—An arahant. Ninety-one kappas ago he saw **Vipassī Buddha** and offered him the pollen (*reṇu*) of *nāga*-flowers. Forty-five kappas ago he was a king named **Reṇu.**[1] He is evidently identical with **Vajjiputta Thera.**[2]

[1] Ap. i. 146. [2] ThagA. i. 143.

Reṇuvatī.—A city, capital of the Cakkavatti **Vimala** (*q.v.*).

Remuṇasela.—A rock in the **Hiraññamalaya** in Ceylon. **Kitti** (afterwards **Vijayabāhu I.**) once occupied a stronghold there.[1]

[1] Cv. lvii. 62.

Rerupallika.—A district in the **Malayaraṭṭha** of Ceylon, mentioned in the account of the campaigns of **Gajabāhu.**[1]

[1] Cv. lxx. 25.

1. **Revata.**—The fifth of the twenty-four Buddhas. He was born in **Sudhaññaka (Sudhaññavatī),** his father being the *khattiya* **Vipula** and his mother **Vipulā.** For six thousand years he lived in the household and then renounced the world, travelling in a chariot, leaving his wife **Sudassanā** and their son **Varuṇa.** The three palaces occupied by him in his lay life were **Sudassana, Ratanagghi** and **Āvela.** He practised austerities for seven months and attained Enlightenment under a *Nāga*-tree,

having been given milk-rice by **Sādhudevī** and grass for his seat by the **Ājīvaka Varuṇindhara.** His first sermon was preached at **Varuṇārāma.** The Bodhisatta was a brahmin of **Rammavatī,** named **Atideva,** who, seeing the Buddha, spoke his praises in one thousand verses. Among the Buddha's converts was King **Arindama** of **Uttaranagara.** The Buddha's chief disciples were **Varuṇa** and **Brahmadeva** among monks and **Bhaddā** and **Subhaddā** among nuns. His constant attendant was **Sambhava.** His chief lay patrons were **Paduma** and **Kuñjara,** and **Sirimā** and **Yasavatī.** His body was eighty hands in height, and his aura spread uninterruptedly to a distance of one yojana. He died in the **Mahāsāra** pleasaunce at the age of sixty thousand, and his relics were scattered.[1]

[1] Bu. vi. 1 ff.; BuA. 131 ff.; J. i. 30, 35, 44.

2. **Revata.**—A monk, the personal attendant of **Siddhattha Buddha.**[1]

[1] Bu. xvii. 18; J. i. 40.

3. **Revata** (called **Khadiravaniya**).—An arahant Thera. An eminent disciple of the Buddha, declared by him foremost among forest-dwellers (*araññakānaṃ*).[1] He was the youngest brother of **Sāriputta,** and a marriage was arranged for him by his mother who was miserable at seeing her children desert her one after another to join the Order, and wished to keep the youngest at home. He was only seven years old, and, on the wedding day, the relations of both bride and bridegroom showered blessings on the couple and said to the bride: "May you live as long as your grandmother." Revata asked to see the grandmother, and was shown a woman of one hundred and twenty, decrepit, and showing all the signs of advanced old age. Realizing that his wife would probably share the same fate, he left the bridal procession on some pretext on the way home, and ran away to a place where lived some monks. Sāriputta, foreseeing this, had instructed the monks to ordain his brother without reference to his parents, and, when Revata revealed his identity, the monks at once admitted him into the Order.

When Sāriputta heard this, he wished to visit his brother, but was persuaded by the Buddha to wait. Revata, after waiting a long time for the visit from Sāriputta, obtained from his teachers a formula of meditation and himself set out to see the Buddha. On the way he stopped at a *khadiravana* (acacia forest) during the rainy season and there won arahantship.

At the end of the rains the Buddha, accompanied by Sāriputta and **Ānanda** with five hundred other monks, started out to visit Revata.

[1] A. i. 24.

There were two routes leading to the *khadiravana*, of which the shorter was thirty leagues long, straight, but infested with evil spirits. This the Buddha chose because **Sīvalī Thera** (*q.v.*) was in the company of monks, and the Buddha knew that the deities of the forest would provide the monks with all they needed because of Sīvali's presence. When Revata knew that the Buddha was approaching, he created, by his magic power, splendid dwellings for him and his monks. The Buddha spent two months in the forest and then returned to the **Pubbārāma** in **Sāvatthi.** There he found that **Visākhā** (*q.v.*) had heard contradictory accounts of the dwelling erected by Revata for the monks who had accompanied the Buddha. He dispelled Visākhā's doubts and spoke of Revata's powers.[2]

Some time after, Revata returned to his native village and brought away with him his three nephews, sons of his three sisters, **Cālā, Upacālā** and **Sisūpacālā. Sāriputta** heard of this and went to see Revata. Revata, knowing that he was coming, exhorted his nephews to be particularly heedful, and Sāriputta expressed his pleasure at their behaviour.[3]

The ThagA.[4] mentions another incident which took place during Revata's old age. He was in the habit of visiting the Buddha and Sāriputta from time to time after returning to his home in the *khadira vana*. Once, during a visit to Sāvatthi, he stayed in a forest near the city. The police, on the track of some thieves, came upon him, and, finding him near the booty which the thieves had dropped in their flight, arrested him and brought him before the king. When the king questioned him, the Elder spoke a series of verses,[5] demonstrating the impossibility of his committing such an act, and also by way of teaching the king the Dhamma. It is said[6] that at the conclusion of the stanzas he sat cross-legged in the sky until his body burnt itself out.

Revata loved solitude, and, on one occasion,[7] a lay disciple named **Atula,** hearing that he was in Sāvatthi, went with five hundred others

[2] DhA. ii. 188 ff.; it was on this occasion that the Buddha related the story of **Sīvali's** past; see also DhA. iv. 186 f. One of the stanzas (No. 212), of the **Muni Sutta** was also preached to the monks, according to Buddhaghosa (SNA. i. 261 f.), in connection with Revata. This was immediately after the Buddha's talk to Visākhā, mentioned above. The story of Revata's ordination is also given at AA. i. 126 ff., with some variations in detail. The account given in ThagA. i. 108 ff. is much shorter; no mention is made of the Buddha's visit to the *khadiravana*. Here it is said that, after winning arahantship, Revata went to Sāvatthi to greet the Buddha and Sāriputta.

[3] ThagA. i. 110; his admonitory verse is given at Thag. vs. 43; two verses uttered by Sāriputta in praise of Revata are given at Thag. vss. 991-2.

[4] i. 551 f.

[5] Thag. vss. 646-58; Mrs. Rhys Davids speaks of Revata as a teacher of the Jain doctrine of *ahiṃsā* (*Gotama the Man*, p. 116).

[6] ThagA. i. 555.

[7] DhA. iii. 325 f.

to hear him preach. But Revata said that he delighted in solitude and refused to address them, and Atula went away complaining.

Revata's delight in solitude was sometimes misunderstood. For instance, the Elder **Sammuñjani** went about continually sweeping, and, seeing Revata sitting cross-legged, thought him an idler. Revata read his thoughts and admonished him.[8]

In the time of **Padumuttara Buddha,** Revata was a boatman at **Payāga** on the Ganges, and once took the Buddha and his thousand followers across the river in a boat decked with canopies, flowers, etc. On that occasion he heard the Buddha declare one of the monks highest among forest-dwellers, and wished for a similar honour for himself under a future Buddha.[9] Later, he was born in deva-worlds. Fifty-eight kappas ago he was a king named **Tāraṇa,** and a kappa later another king named **Campaka.**[10]

[8] For details see *s.v.* **Sammuñjani.** [9] ThagA. i. 108; AA. i. 126. [10] Ap. i. 51 f.

4. **Revata.**—The DhpA.[1] mentions a novice **Revata,** with three others —**Saṅkicca, Paṇḍita** and **Sopāka**—all four of whom became arahants at the age of seven. The Revata referred to is, very probably, the Revata (3) above. For their story see *s.v.* **Pañcachiddageha.**

[1] iv. 176 f.

5. **Revata.**—See **Kaṅkhā-Revata.**

6. **Revata.**—Called **Soreyya-Revata.** He was one of the Elders who took a prominent part in the Second Council. He lived in **Soreyya,** and, on discovering (by means of his divine ear) that the orthodox monks, led by **Sambhūta Sāṇavāsī** and **Yasa Kākaṇḍakaputta,** were anxious to consult him, Revata left Soreyya, and, travelling through **Saṅkassa, Kaṇṇakujja, Udumbara** and **Aggalapura,** reached **Sahajāti.** There the monks met him and consulted him regarding the "Ten Points." He enquired into these, and, after condemning them as wrong, decided to end the dispute. The **Vajjiputtakas** (*q.v.*), too, had tried to win Revata over to their side, but on failing to do so, persuaded Revata's pupil, **Uttara,** to accept robes, etc., from them, and speak to his teacher on their behalf. Uttara did this, but was dismissed by Revata as an unworthy pupil.

Revata suggested that the dispute should be settled in **Vesāli,** and the monks having agreed, he visited **Sabbakāmī**—who was the oldest monk then living and a pupil of **Ānanda**[1]—during the night, and talked to him

[1] According to Mhv. iv. 57, 60, Revata himself was a pupil of Ānanda and had seen the Buddha; *cp.* Dpv. iv. 49.

on matters of doctrine. During the conversation, **Sāṇavāsī** arrived and questioned Sabbakāmī regarding the Ten Points, but the latter refused to express an opinion in private. On Revata's suggestion a jury of eight, four from either side, was appointed to go into the question. Revata himself was a member of this jury, and he it was who questioned Sabbakāmī during the meeting, held in **Vālikārāma,** regarding the Ten Points. All the Ten Points were declared to be wrong, and, at the end of the questions, seven hundred monks—chosen from one hundred and twelve thousand, at the head of whom was Revata—held a recital of the Dhamma, which recital therefore came to be called **Sattasatī** (" Seven Hundred "). This recital, according to the Mhv.,[2] lasted for eight months.

[2] Vin. ii. 299 ff. The Mhv. (iv. 1 ff.) gives an account of this Council, which account differs in numerous details. In both accounts it is Revata who takes the most prominent part in settling the dispute. The Mhv. introduces **Kālāsoka** (*q.v.*) as the patron of the Second Council; *cp.* Dpv. iv. 46 ff.; v. 15 ff.; Sp. i. 33 f.; it would appear from the Dpv. account that the heretics refused to accept the decision of Revata's Council and separated off, to the number of ten thousand, forming a new body called the **Mahāsaṅghikas.**

7. **Revata.**—An Elder of Ceylon. He was a **Majjhimabhāṇaka,** and, once, going to **Revata** (8) who lived in the **Malaya** country of Ceylon, he asked him for a subject of meditation. The latter knowing that the former was a Majjhimabāṇake spoke to him of the difficulties facing such a one in meditation. The other at once agreed not to recite the Majjhima until his meditations should prove fruitful. He was given a topic of meditation, and attained arahantship nineteen years later. But when, at the end of that time, he again started to recite the Majjhima, he was never in doubt as to a single consonant.[1]

[1] Vsm. i. 95.

8. **Revata.**—An Elder of Ceylon, living in the **Malaya** country of Ceylon. See **Revata** (7).

9. **Revata.**—Teacher of **Buddhaghosa.** He was very proficient in the Vedas, and, when Buddhaghosa visited him in his vihāra and recited the Vedas, he was able to speak with contempt of Buddhaghosa's knowledge. Buddhaghosa then became his pupil, and was later sent by him to Ceylon to translate the Sinhalese Commentaries into Pāli.[1]

[1] Cv. xxxvii. 218 ff.

10. **Revata.**—See **Mahāyasa.**[1]

[1] P.L.C. 180, 199, 221.

Revatā.—A nun of Ceylon, a well-known teacher of the Vinaya. She was a daughter of **Somanadeva.**[1]

[1] Dpv. xviii. 29.

1. **Revatī.**—Wife of **Nandiya** (*q.v.*). Her story is given in DhA. iii. 290 ff. and also at VvA. 220 ff.[1] According to the VvA. version, Nandiya was born after death in **Tāvatiṃsa,** but Revatī, on the death of her husband, stopped the gift of alms which he had instituted, abused the monks, and was cast alive into hell.

[1] The story is also referred to in PvA. 257.

2. **Revatī.**—An *upāsikā*, probably of **Nāḷaka.** She was a patron of **Sāriputta,** and, on his death, she brought three vases filled with golden flowers to be offered at the pyre. **Sakka** came, with his great retinue, to do honour to the Elder, and in the crush caused by his arrival Revatī was trampled to death. She was immediately reborn with a body three *gāvutas* in height in **Tāvatiṃsa,** and, on discovering the cause of her happiness, she appeared with her followers before the people and declared her homage to Sāriputta.[1]

[1] SA. iii. 177 f.

3. **Revatī.**—Another name, according to the Dīpavaṃsa,[1] for **Sīvalī,** daughter of King **Āmaṇḍagāmaṇi-Abhaya.** She was the sister of **Cūlābhaya** and succeeded him for a period of four months, when she was dethroned by **Iḷanāga.**[1]

[1] xxi. 40 f.; *cp.* Mhv. xxxv. 14 f.

Roga Sutta.—There are those beings in the world who can be free of bodily disease for varying periods, but only those who have destroyed the *āsavas* are free from mental disease, even for one moment.[1]

[1] A. ii. 142 f.

Roguva.—See **Roruva.**

Rocanī.—Wife of **Kakusandha Buddha** in his last lay life.[1] Elsewhere[2] she is called **Virocamānā.**

[1] BuA. 210; DA. ii. 422.

[2] Bu. xxiii. 17.

1. **Roja.**—A **Malla,** inhabitant of **Kusinārā.** When the Buddha and **Ānanda** visited Kusinārā, the Malla chieftains decreed that whoever failed to pay homage to the Buddha would be fined five hundred coins. Roja

was Ānanda's friend,[1] and Ānanda was pleased when he arrived to pay homage to the Buddha, but when Roja said that he did so only out of regard for his kinsmen's decree, Ānanda was bitterly disappointed and asked the Buddha to discover some means by which Roja could be made to become his follower. The Buddha agreed to do this, and by means of the power of his compassion, Roja was induced to visit him again. The Buddha preached to Roja, who asked, as a boon, that the monks should accept hospitality only from him. This request was refused by the Buddha, who said that Roja must take his turn with others in showing hospitality to him and his monks. Finding that he had long to wait for his turn, Roja made enquiries, and, discovering that the monks had no supply of green vegetables (*ḍāka*) or pastry (*piṭṭakhādaniya*), he consulted Ānanda, and, with the Buddha's sanction, offered these things to the Buddha and his monks.[2] It is said[3] that Roja once invited Ānanda to his house, and, after entertaining him lavishly, tried to induce him to leave the Order by offering him half his wealth. But Ānanda refused this offer, explaining to him the miseries involved in household life. Later, Ānanda repeated this conversation to the Buddha, who related the **Vacchanakha Jātaka** (*q.v.*) to show that Roja and Ānanda had been friends in a past life too.

[1] Once he forced on Ānanda a linen-cloth (*khomapilotikā*); Ānanda had need of it, and accepted it with the Buddha's permission (Vin. i. 296).

[2] *Ibid.*, 274 ff.

[3] J. ii. 231 f.

2. **Roja.**—A primeval king, son of **Mahāsammata,** and, therefore, an ancestor of the **Sākyans.** Roja's son was **Vararoja.**[1]

[1] J. ii. 311; iii. 454; SNA. i. 353; Dpv. iii. 4; Mhv. ii. 2; MṬ. 124; *cp.* Mtu. i. 384 where he is called Rava.

3. **Roja.**—A city in India, the capital of **Naradeva** and six of his descendants.[1] *v.l.* **Roma, Jāna.**

[1] MṬ. 128; Dpv. iii. 27 calls it **Rojanā.** The KMv. calls it **Thūna.**

Rojā.—A class of devas, present at the preaching of the **Mahāsamaya Sutta.**[1]

[1] D. ii. 260.

Roma.—There were four kings of this name sixty thousand kappas ago, all previous births of **Sataraṃsika Thera.**[1]

[1] Ap. i. 104.

Romaka Jātaka (No. 277)—*v.l.* **Pārāpata.**—The Bodhisatta was once born as king of a flock of pigeons. For a long time they visited regularly a good ascetic in a cave near by, until, one day, he left and his place was taken by a sham ascetic. The pigeons continued their visits, till one day the villagers served the ascetic with a dish of pigeon's flesh, and he, liking the flavour, conceived the desire to kill the pigeons. The Bodhisatta, suspecting his intentions, warned his followers and charged the ascetic with hypocrisy.[1]

[1] J. ii. 382-4; *cp.* **Godha Jātaka** (No. 325).

Romamukkharaṭṭha.—A country mentioned in the Mahāvaṃsa Commentary as a place rich in coral; it was from there that **Bhātikābhaya** (*q.v.*) obtained the coral for the net which he threw over the **Mahā Thūpa.**[1]

[1] MṬ. 630.

1. **Romasa.**—A mountain in **Himavā.**[1]

[1] Ap. i. 232, 453; ThagA. i. 399.

2. **Romasa.**—A **Pacceka Buddha** of ninety-four kappas ago.[1]

[1] Ap. i. 238, 281.

3. **Romasa.**—A *Dānava* (? **Asura**) of ninety-four kappas ago, a previous birth of **Ambapiṇḍiya Thera.**[1]

[1] Ap. i. 247.

4. **Romasa.**—A king of seventy-four kappas ago, a previous birth of **Caṅkolapupphiya Thera.**[1]

[1] Ap. i. 215.

1. **Roruka.**—A city, capital of the **Sovīras,** established by **Jotipāla,** chaplain of **Reṇu.** Its king was **Bharata.**[1] In the **Āditta Jātaka**[2] it is called **Roruva.**

[1] D. ii. 235; *cp.* Mtu. iii. 208; see also Dvy. 544 ff. [2] J. iii. 470.

2. **Roruka.**—Capital of King **Seri**[1] (*q.v.*).

[1] SA. i. 90.

1. **Roruva.**—See **Roruka** (1).

2. **Roruva.**—A Niraya. Beings were presumably born there as a result of casting aspersions on the Dhamma,[1] miserliness,[2] or adultery.[3] Some-

[1] S. i. 30. [2] See, *e.g.*, J. iii. 299. [3] J. vi. 237.

times[4] two Roruvas are mentioned which the scholiast[5] explains as being **Jālaroruva** and **Dhūmaroruva;** in the first beings have red hot flames blown into their bodies, and in the second, noxious gases (*khāradhūma*).

Buddhaghosa says[6] that Jālaroruva is another name for **Avīci,** and that the Niraya is so called because beings shout while being burnt there (*aggiṃhi jalante punappunaṃ ravanti*).

[4] J. v. 266. [5] *Ibid.*, 271. [6] SA. i. 64.

Rolika.—See **Heḷigāma.**

Rohaka.—A householder of **Kimbila;** he was the husband of **Bhaddā.**[1] See **Bhaddā** (4).

[1] VvA. 109.

1. **Rohaṇa.**—Grandfather of **Migāra Rohaṇeyya** (*q.v.*).[1]

[1] AA. ii. 697.

2. **Rohaṇa.**—A brahmin, grandson of **Pekkhuṇiya.** He was a friend of the **Licchavi Sāḷha,** and a visit paid by both of them to **Nandaka** is recorded in the Aṅguttara Nikāya.[1]

[1] A. i. 193 f.

3. **Rohaṇa.**—A **Sākyan** prince, one of the brothers of **Bhaddakaccānā.** He went over to Ceylon and there founded a settlement which was named after him.[1]

[1] Mhv. ix. 10; Dpv. x. 6.

4. **Rohaṇa.**—One of the three main provinces of early Ceylon comprising the south-eastern part of the island, the **Mahāvālukanadī** forming its northern boundary. It was probably colonized by **Rohaṇa** (3). The capital of the province was **Mahāgāma.** When the northern parts of the island were in the hands of foreigners or usurpers, the Sinhalese court, its nobles and loyalists, often sought refuge in Rohaṇa. It seems, for the most part, to have been very little controlled from the capital, and many rebellions against the ruler of the capital originated in Rohaṇa.[1] In times of persecution and scarcity the Buddhist monks found patronage and shelter among the inhabitants of Rohaṇa.[2] Even till about 600 A.C., Rohaṇa was regarded as a separate kingdom, holding, or at least claiming to hold, an independent position beside **Anurādhapura.**[3]

[1] See *s.v.* **Duṭṭhagāmaṇī** and **Vijayabāhu;** also, *e.g.*, Mhv. xxiii. 13; xxxiii. 37; xxxv. 27 f., 67, 125; Cv. xxxviii. 12, 39; xli. 89 ff.; xliv. 54; xlviii, 59, etc.

[2] *E.g.*, Mhv. xxxvii. 6.

[3] See, *e.g.*, Cv. xlv. 41.

5. **Rohaṇa.**—See **Rohanta.**

6. **Rohaṇa Thera.**—When **Assagutta** summoned the heads of the Order to a conference regarding the heresy of **Milinda,** Rohaṇa was lost in meditation, and a messenger had to be sent to fetch him. As punishment for this, he was charged with the task of persuading **Nāgasena** to join the Order. To achieve this purpose, Rohaṇa had to visit the house of Nāgasena's father, **Soṇuttara,** during seven years and ten months, without ever receiving even a kind word, till, at last, one day Soṇuttara was pleased with his kindness and courtesy and gave him food daily at the house. When Nāgasena grew up and learnt the Vedas, Rohaṇa engaged him in discussion, as a result of which Nāgasena joined the Order under Rohaṇa, who, as his first preceptor, taught him the Abhidhamma. One day, Nāgasena thought lightly of his teacher, and Rohaṇa, reading his thoughts, chided him. Nāgasena begged his forgiveness, but Rohaṇa said he would forgive him only if he succeeded in refuting Milinda's heretical views.[1]

[1] Mil. 7 ff.

7. **Rohaṇa.**—Headman of the village of **Kitti** and father of **Thera-puttābhaya.** Rohaṇa was a supporter of **Mahāsumma Thera,** and, having heard him preach at the **Koṭapabbata-vihāra,** he became a *sotāpanna* and joined the Order, later attaining arahantship.[1]

[1] Mhv. xxiii. 55 ff.

Rohaṇagutta.—See **Mahā-Rohaṇagutta.**

Rohaṇa-vihāra.—A monastery in **Rohaṇa,** built by **Silādāṭha** for the incumbent of the **Pāsāṇadīpa-vihāra.**[1]

[1] Cv. xlv. 54.

Rohaṇā.—The name of a tribe.[1]

[1] Ap. ii. 359.

1. **Rohanta.**—A lake in **Himavā.**[1]

[1] J. iv. 413.

2. **Rohanta.**—The Bodhisatta born as king of deer. See the **Rohanta-miga Jātaka.**

Rohantāmiga Jātaka (No. 501).—The Bodhisatta was once born as **Rohanta,** a golden deer, king over eighty thousand deer, near Lake

Rohanta. He had a brother, **Cittamiga,** and a sister **Sutanā.** One day **Khemā,** wife of the king of Benares, dreamed that a golden deer preached to her and begged the king to make the dream come true. The king offered great rewards, and a hunter, who was aware of Rohanta's existence, undertook to bring him to the court. He set a trap in the ford where the deer drank and Rohanta was caught in it. When Rohanta gave the alarm, all the deer fled except Cittamiga and Sutanā. They told the hunter that they would die with their brother rather than leave him, and the hunter, touched by their devotion, set Rohanta free. When Rohanta discovered why he had been caught, he offered to go to Benares, but was dissuaded by the hunter owing to the risks he would run. Rohanta then taught the Law to the hunter and sent him back with a golden hair from his body. The hunter related the story to the king and queen and preached to them the Law. Then rejecting the rewards they offered him, he became an ascetic in the **Himālaya.**

The story was related in reference to **Ānanda's** attempt to throw himself before the elephant **Dhanapāla,** who was sent to kill the Buddha. Ānanda is identified with Cittamiga, **Channa** with the hunter, **Sāriputta** with the king and **Uppalavaṇṇā** with Sutanā.[1]

[1] J. iv. 413 ff.; some of the verses of this Jātaka are found also in the **Tesakuṇa Jātaka** (J. v. 123 f.).

1. **Rohiṇī Therī.**—She was the daughter of a prosperous brahmin of **Vesālī.** When the Buddha visited Vesāli, she heard him preach and became a *sotāpanna,* taught the Doctrine to her parents, and, with their permission, entered the Order, where she became an arahant.

Ninety-one kappas ago she saw **Vipassī Buddha** begging in **Bandhumatī,** and, filling his bowl with meal cakes, paid him homage.[1]

The Therīgāthā[2] contains a set of verses spoken by her in exaltation, when, after becoming an arahant, she recalled to mind the discussion she had had with her father while she was yet a *sotāpanna.*

It is said[3] that the last stanza of the series was spoken by her father, who later himself joined the Order and became an arahant.

[1] ThagA. 214 f. [2] vss. 271-90. [3] ThigA. 219 f.

2. **Rohiṇī.**—Sister of **Anuruddha Thera.** When he visited his family at **Kapilavatthu,** she refused to see him because she was suffering from a skin eruption. But Anuruddha sent for her, and when she came, her face covered with a cloth, he advised her to erect an assembly hall for the monks. She consented to do this, sold her jewels, and erected a hall of two storeys, the building of which was supervised by **Anuruddha.** At the dedication ceremony she entertained the Buddha and the monks. At

the conclusion of the meal the Buddha sent for her. She was reluctant to go to him owing to her disease, but was persuaded, and he told her the story of her past.

Long ago she had been the chief consort of the king of Benares, and being jealous of a dancing-girl whom the king loved, she contrived to get powdered scabs on the girl's body, clothes and bed. The girl developed boils and her skin was ruined.

At the conclusion of the Buddha's sermon, Rohiṇī's disease vanished and her body took on a golden colour, while she herself was established in the First Fruit of the Path. After death, Rohiṇī was born in **Tāvatiṃsa,** at the meeting-point of the boundaries of four deities. Because of her beauty, each deity claimed her as his, and they referred their quarrel to **Sakka.** Sakka, too, became enamoured of her, and when he confessed his desire, they agreed to let him take her, and she became his special favourite.[1]

[1] DhA. iii. 295 ff.

3. **Rohiṇī.**—A small river dividing the **Sākyan** and **Koliyan** countries. A dam was constructed across the river, and the people on the two sides used the water to cultivate their fields. Once, in the month of Jeṭṭhamūla, there was a drought, and a violent quarrel arose between the two peoples for the use of the water. A battle was imminent, when the Buddha, seeing what was about to happen, appeared in the air between the opposing forces in the middle of the river and convinced them of the folly of killing each other for the sake of a little water. It is said that he preached on this occasion the **Attadanda Sutta** and the **Phandana,** the **Laṭukika** and the **Vaṭṭaka Jātakas.**

To show their gratitude to the Buddha for his timely intervention, the Sākyans and the Koliyans gave two hundred and fifty young men from each tribe to be ordained under him.[1]

The Rohiṇī is identified[2] with a small stream which joins the Rapti at Goruckpore. It is now called the Rowai or Rohwaini.

Dhammapāla says[3] that the Rohiṇī flows from north to south and that **Rājagaha** lies to the south-east of it.

[1] SNA. i. 358; *cp.* J. v. 412; DhA. iii. 254 ff. The accounts differ in details; the Jātaka account, which is the longest, mentions other Jātakas: **Daddabha** and **Rukkhadhamma.** DA. ii. 672 f. and SA. i. 53 ff. substitute **Paṭhavudriyana** for **Daddabha.** But see under these Jātakas.

[2] For details see Cunningham, Arch. Survey of India xii. 190 ff.

[3] ThagA. i. 501.

4. **Rohiṇī.**—An asterism.[1] The planting of the Bodhi-tree in Ceylon was performed under this constellation.[2]

[1] MA. ii. 783; SNA. ii. 456.

[2] Mhv. ix. 47.

5. **Rohiṇī.**—A city which was the birthplace of **Paccaya Thera.** *v.l.* **Rohī.**[1]

[1] ThagA. i. 341.

6. **Rohiṇī.**—A slave woman of **Anāthapiṇḍika.** See the **Rohiṇī Jātaka.**

7. **Rohiṇī.**—See **Rohita.**

Rohiṇī Jātaka (No. 45).—Once the Bodhisatta was the Lord High Treasurer of Benares and he had a slave-woman named **Rohiṇī.** One day, when Rohiṇī was pounding rice, her mother lay down near her and flies settled on her and stung her. When she asked her daughter to drive them away, the latter lifted her pestle and hit her with it, thinking thus to kill the flies. But instead of the flies she killed her mother.

The story was related to **Anāthapiṇḍika** in reference to a slave girl of his also named **Rohiṇī,** who killed her mother in the same way. The mother and daughter are the same in both stories.[1]

[1] J. i. 248 f.

Rohiṇīkhattiyakaññā Vatthu.—The story of **Rohiṇī,** sister of **Anuruddha.** See **Rohiṇī** (2).

1. **Rohiṇeyya.**—See **Migāra Rohiṇeyya.**

2. **Rohiṇeyya.**—Minister of King **Vāsudeva** and brother of **Ghatapaṇḍita.** It was he who brought to the king the news of Ghata's feigned insanity.[1] He is identified with **Ānanda.**[2]

[1] J. iv. 84; PvA. 94; for details see the **Ghata Jātaka.** [2] J. iv. 89.

1. **Rohita.**—Fourteen thousand kappas ago there were thirteen kings of this name, all previous births of **Sīha** (or **Candanapūjaka**) **Thera.**[1] *v.l.* **Rohiṇī.**

[1] ThagA. i. 182; Ap. i. 165.

2. **Rohita.**—See **Rohitassa** (1).

1. **Rohitassa.**—A devaputta. He once visited the Buddha at **Jetavana** and asked if one could, by travelling, reach the end of the world where there would be no birth, old age, death, etc. The Buddha said that such was not possible. The devaputta then confessed that he had, in a previous life, been a sage called **Rohitassa,** a **Bhojaputta** of great psychic

powers, able in one stride to cross from the western ocean to the eastern.[1] With such a stride, he had travelled for one hundred years, and yet failed to reach the world's end, where there was no birth, old age, death, etc. That was true, agreed the Buddha; in this fathom-long body is the world, its origin, its making and end, likewise the practice which leads to such end.[2]

[1] The Commentary (SA. i. 92) adds that he would wash in the **Anotatta Lake** and go to eat in **Uttarakuru**.

[2] S. i. 61 f.; repeated at A. ii. 47 f.

2. **Rohitassa.**—A sage, described as **Bhojaputta.** See **Rohitassa** (1).

Rohitassa Vagga.—The fifth chapter of the Catukka Nipāta of the Aṅguttara Nikāya.[1]

[1] A. ii. 44-54.

1. **Rohitassa Sutta** (also called **Rohita Sutta**).—A conversation between the **Buddha** and **Rohitassa** (1).[1]

[1] S. i. 61 f.; A. ii. 47 f.

2. **Rohitassa Sutta.**—The Buddha tells the monks of his conversation with **Rohitassa.**[1]

[1] A. ii. 49 f.

Rohitassā.—The legendary inhabitants of **Rājagaha,** in the time of **Koṇāgamana Buddha.** At that time, Mount **Vipula** was called **Vaṅkaka.** The life of a Rohitassa was thirty thousand years. The people took three days to climb Vipula and three to descend it.[1]

[1] S. ii. 191.

Rohī.—See **Rohiṇī** (5).

L.

Lakuṇṭaka-Atimbara.—One of the chief ministers of **Duṭṭhagāmaṇī.** He was the husband of **Ubbarī,** when, in her last birth, she was reborn as **Sumanā.**[1]

[1] For the story see under **Ubbarī** (1).

Lakuṇṭaka-Bhaddiya Thera.—He was born in a wealthy family of **Sāvatthī** and was given the title of **Lakuṇṭaka** (Dwarf) owing to his very small stature.[1] Having heard the Buddha preach, he entered the Order

[1] He was, nevertheless, beautiful in body, says the ApA.; but see below.

and became learned and eloquent, teaching others in a sweet voice. Once, on a festival day, a woman of the town, driving with a brahmin in a chariot, saw the Elder and laughed, showing her teeth. The Elder, taking the teeth as his object, developed *jhāna* and became an *anāgāmin.* Later, after being admonished by **Sāriputta,**[2] he developed mindfulness regarding the body and became an arahant.

In the time of **Padumuttara Buddha** he was a very rich householder of **Haṃsavatī,** and, having heard the Buddha describe one of his monks as the sweetest-voiced among them all, he wished for a similar distinction for himself under a future Buddha. In the time of **Phussa Buddha** he was a *cittapattakokila,* named **Nanda,** who, seeing the Buddha in the royal park, placed in his bowl a ripe mango.[3] In **Kassapa Buddha's** day he was the chief architect entrusted with the building of the *thūpa* over the Buddha's relics, and, when a dispute arose as to how big the *thūpa* should be, he decided in favour of a small one; hence his small stature in his last life.[4]

In the assembly of monks the Buddha ranked him as foremost among sweet-voiced monks[5] (*mañjussarānaṃ*). Several stories connected with Bhaddiya are recorded in the books. Because of his shortness and his youthful appearance he was sometimes mistaken for a novice.[6] Elsewhere[7] it is said that, because he was ugly and hunch-backed, he was despised by his companions, and the Buddha had to proclaim to them his greatness and hold him up as an example of a man who, though small, was of great power. Another account[8] relates how novices used to pull his hair and tweek his ears and nose saying, " Uncle, you tire not of religion ? You take delight in it ?" But he showed no resentment and took no offence.

It was in reference to Bhaddiya that the Buddha preached two famous riddle-stanzas in the Dhammapada,[9] where he describes the arahant as one who has killed father and mother and two kings and destroyed a kingdom, but who yet goes scatheless—the words having a metaphorical meaning.

[2] The Udāna (vii. 1, 2) makes reference to the admonitions of Sāriputta and to the Buddha's joy when these had the desired effect. The Commentary (UdA. 360 f.) gives details.

[3] The Ap. (*loc. infra*) says he was the king's general.

[4] ThagA. i. 469 ff.; Ap. ii. 489 f.; the account in AA. i. 110 f. is slightly different; the **Keḷisīla Jātaka** (*q.v.*) gives a different reason for his shortness.

[5] A. i. 25.

[6] DhA. iii. 387.

[7] S. ii. 279; *cp.* Ud. vii. 5.

[8] DhA. ii. 148; the introduction to the Keḷisīla Jātaka (J. ii. 142) speaks of thirty monks from the country who, seeing Bhaddiya at Jetavana, pulled him about until they were told by the Buddha who he was.

[9] Nos. 294, 295; for the explanation of the riddle see DhA. iii. 454.

Several stanzas uttered by Bhaddiya in the **Ambāṭakavana,** as he sat there enjoying the bliss of arahantship, are included in the Theragāthā.[10] In the *Avadānaśataka*[11] he is called Lakuñcika.

[10] Thag. vss. 466-72. [11] See Avś. ii. 152-60.

Lakkhakhaṇḍa.—The fourth section of the **Vidhura Jātaka,** which describes the play of dice between **Dhanañjaya** and **Puṇṇaka,** ending in the defeat of the former.[1]

[1] J. iv. 280-92.

1. **Lakkhaṇa.**—Son of **Dasaratha** and brother of **Rāma, Sītā** and **Bharata.** He is identified with **Sāriputta.**[1]

[1] J. iv. 130; for details see the **Dasaratha Jātaka.**

2. **Lakkhaṇa.**—One of the eight brahmins who recognized the auspicious signs at the birth of the Buddha.[1] The Milinda[2] speaks of him as one of the Buddha's first teachers.

[1] J. i. 56. [2] Mil. 236.

3. **Lakkhaṇa Thera.**—Mentioned as having stayed with **Mahā Moggallāna** on **Gijjhakūṭa.** Once, when they were going down to **Rājagaha** for alms, Lakkhaṇa noticed that at a certain spot Moggallāna smiled; on asking him why, he was told to wait till they saw the Buddha. When the question was repeated in the Buddha's presence, Moggallāna said that he had smiled on seeing various *Petas* with gruesome forms flying through the air. From the text[1] it would appear that these visions were seen again on several occasions.

The Commentary[2] explains that Lakkhaṇa was one of the thousand Jaṭilas ordained by the Buddha (when he converted the **Tebhātika Jaṭilas**). He attained arahantship at the conclusion of the preaching of the **Ādittapariyāyadesanā.** He was called Lakkhaṇa because of his marvellous personality, "like unto Brahmā's" (*brahmasamena*). It adds further that Lakkhaṇa's failure to see the *Petas* was not because he lacked the divine eye but because he was not giving attention (*anāvajjento*), as a clairvoyant must. It is said[3] that when Moggallāna related his vision, some of the monks blamed him for claiming superhuman powers (*uttarimanussadhamma*), but the Buddha declared him free from blame.

[1] S. ii. 254; Vin. iii. 104 ff.; the stories of some of the *Petas* seen and of their past lives are given in detail in DhA. ii. 68 ff.; iii. 60 ff.; 410 ff., 479.
[2] SA. ii. 159. [3] Vin. iii. 105.

4. **Lakkhaṇa.**—A deer, son of the Bodhisatta, identified with **Sāriputta.** For his story see the **Lakkhaṇa Jātaka.**

Lakkhaṇa Jātaka (No. 11).—The Bodhisatta was once a deer and had two sons, **Lakkhaṇa** and **Kāḷa.** When the time came for gathering the crops, he told his sons to seek refuge in the mountain tracts with their herds. They agreed, but Kāḷa, being ignorant, kept his deer on the tramp early and late, and men, coming upon them, destroyed most of them. Lakkhaṇa, however, moved his deer only in the dead of night and reached the forest without losing any of his herd. The same thing happened on their return four months later, and the Boddhisatta praised Lakkhaṇa's intelligence.

The story was related in reference to **Devadatta** and **Sāriputta.** Devadatta had persuaded five hundred monks to secede from the Buddha and go with him, but Sāriputta visited them and brought them all back. Devadatta is identified with Kāḷa and Sāriputta with Lakkhaṇa.[1]

[1] J. i. 142 f.; the story is referred to at DhA. i. 122.

Lakkhaṇa Saṃyutta.—The nineteenth section of the **Saṃyutta Nikāya.** It contains account of the *Petas* seen by **Moggallāna** when in the company of **Lakkhaṇa Thera.**[1]

[1] S. ii. 254-63.

Lakkhaṇa Sutta.—The thirtieth sutta of the **Dīgha Nikāya.** It gives an account of the thirty-two special marks of the superman (*mahāpurisalakkhaṇāni*) which signify that their possessor will be either a world-emperor (*Cakkavatti*) or a Buddha. The sutta definitely states that these marks are entirely due to good deeds done in former births and can only be maintained in the present life by goodness.[1]

[1] D. iii. 142-79; the sutta is quoted in Mil. p. 405.

Lakkhadhammā.—An illustrious nun of Ceylon.[1]

[1] Dpv. xviii. 40.

1. **Lakkhī.**—The Pāli equivalent of Lakṣmī, goddess of beauty and fortune. The name is found usually only in later works.[1]

[1] *E.g.*, Cv. lxxii. 101; lxxvi. 233; J. ii. 413; iii. 306 (explained as being equal to *paññā*); v. 113; the word **Lacchī,** however, probably equivalent to **Lakkhī** (1), is found in Thig. vs. 419, but the passage is obscure. See *Sisters* 159, n. 2.

2. **Lakkhī.**—Daughter of **Dhataraṭṭha.** She is generally called **Sirī.** For her story see the **Sirikālakaṇṇī Jātaka.**

Lakkhuyyāṇa.—A park in Ceylon, laid out by **Parakkamabāhu I.** for the benefit of the monks. The **Candabhāgā** Canal flowed through it.[1]

[1] Cv. lxxix. 3, 48.

Lakhumā.—A woman who lived near **Kevattadvāragāma,** near Benares. She was pious and gave alms to several holy monks, listened to their preaching, and became a *sotāpanna*. After death she was born in a *vimāna* in **Tāvatiṃsa** and there had a conversation with **Moggallāna,** at the end of which she became a *sakadāgāmī*.[1]

[1] Vv. ii. 2; VvA. 97 f.

Laṅkā, Laṅkādīpa, Laṅkātala.—Pāli names for Ceylon, found in the Chronicles—*e.g.*, Dīpavaṃsa, Mahāvaṃsa and the Commentaries. An ancient tradition recorded in the Mahāvaṃsa,[1] and in the Samantapāsādikā,[2] gives the names of the Island in the times of the three previous Buddhas, the names of the capital cities, the different names of **Mahāmeghavana,** and of the kings contemporary with these Buddhas. Thus, in the time of **Kakusandha,** the Island was called **Ojadīpa,** the king was **Abhaya,** the capital **Abhayapura** and **Mahāmeghavana, Mahātittha.** In the time of **Koṇāgamana,** the Island was **Varadīpa,** the capital **Vaḍḍhamāna,** the king **Samiddha** and the park **Mahānoma.** In the time of **Kassapa,** the Island was **Maṇḍadīpa,** the king **Jayanta,** the capital **Visālā** and the park **Mahāsāgara.** Besides Mahāmeghavana, the other physical feature of Ceylon, mentioned in these accounts, is the mountain known in the present age as **Sumanakūṭa,** whereon the Buddha Gotama placed his footprint. During the ages of the three previous Buddhas, it was known, respectively, as **Devakūṭa, Sumanakūṭaka** and **Subhakūṭa.** Gotama paid three visits to Ceylon, while the other three Buddhas came only once.[3] During their visits they consecrated various spots by spending there a short time wrapt in meditation.

Laṅkā was once inhabited by **Yakkhas.** Gotama Buddha obliged them to leave the Island and seek shelter in the neighbouring **Giridīpa.** Laṅkādīpa was later colonised by **Vijaya** and his three hundred companions. Two cities of the Yakkhas are mentioned: **Sirīsavatthu** and **Laṅkāpura.**[4]

[1] Mhv. xv. 57 ff.
[2] Sp. i. 86 ff.
[3] Details are given under each name.
[4] For details see *s.v.*

Laṅkāgiri.—A title in use at the time of **Parakkamabāhu I.** Among those mentioned as having borne it are **Mahī, Nātha** and **Sora.**[1]

[1] See. Cv. lxxii. 27, 124; lxxvi. 250.

Laṅkāgiripabbata.—A hill in the mountainous central province of Ceylon, in the district once known as **Bodhigāmavara.**

It is mentioned in the account of the campaigns of **Parakkamabahu I.**[1]

[1] Cv. lxvi. 90; lxx. 88; for identification with modern Laggala, see Cv. *Trs.* i. 259, n. 3.

Laṅkājayamahālekhaka.—A title conferred by **Devānampiyatissa** on **Bodhigutta,** leader of the embassy which brought the Bodhi-tree from India to Ceylon. The title was a higher one than that of **Jayamahālekhaka,** which was conferred on **Sumitta.**[1] It was, evidently, continued in later times, because one of the officers of **Parakkamabāhu I.** was called **Laṅkāmahālāna,**[2] which appears to be a corruption of "*Laṅkāmahālekhakanāyaka.*"

[1] See Mbv., p. 164 f., for a description of the ceremony of investiture. [2] Cv. lxix. 12.

1. **Laṅkātilaka.**—An image-house in **Pulatthipura,** built by **Parakkamabāhu I.** The standing image of the Buddha (also built by the king), which it contained, bore the name of Laṅkātilaka too.[1]

[1] Cv. lxxviii. 53 f., 63; for identification see Cv. *Trs.* ii. 108, n. 2, 4.

2. **Laṅkātilaka.**—A park in Ceylon, laid out by **Parakkamabāhu I.**[1]

[1] Cv. lxxix. 9.

3. **Laṅkātilaka.**—A monastery near the modern Kandy, restored by **Parakkamabāhu VI.**[1] It was built by **Bhuvanekabāhu IV.**[2]

[1] Cv. xci. 30. [2] Codrington: *op. cit.*, 83.

Laṅkādhikāri.—A title in use in the time of **Parakkamabāhu I.** It was higher than either **Saṅkhanāyaka** or **Laṅkādhināyaka,** and was conferred on the two officers, **Kitti**[1] and **Rakkha.**[2]

[1] Cv. lxx. 278. [2] *Ibid.*, 306.

Laṅkādhināyaka, Laṅkādhinātha, Laṅkānātha.—A title in use in the time of **Parakkamabāhu I.,** held both by **Kitti** and **Rakkha,**[1] who later became **Laṅkādhikāri.**

[1] Cv. lxx. 24, 205.

Laṅkānagara, Laṅkāpura.—One of the chief cities of the **Yakkhas** in Ceylon. **Polamittā,** wife of **Mahākālasena,** the chief Yakkha of Ceylon, was a princess of Laṅkāpura.[1] **Kuveṇī** herself was evidently from

[1] Mhv. vii. 33; MṬ. 260.

Laṅkāpura, because it was there she went when she was abandoned by **Vijaya.**[2]

[2] Mhv. vii. 62; MṬ. 265.

1. **Laṅkāpura.**—See **Laṅkānagara.**

2. **Laṅkāpura Daṇḍanātha.**—A general of **Parakkamabāhu I.** He was probably[1] the son of the **Laṅkādhinātha Kitti.** We first hear of him as having parried the attack of **Gajabāhu's** forces, at the pass of **Khaṇḍigāma.** He was later sent in command of the expedition against **Kulasekhara,** to help the **Paṇḍu** king, **Parakkama** of **Madhurā.** He landed at the Paṇḍu port of **Taladilla** and occupied **Rāmissara.** From there he advanced to **Kundukāla.** The prisoners whom he sent to Ceylon were used to help in the restoration of the **Ratanavāluka-cetiya.** At Kundukāla, Laṅkāpura built the fortress of **Parakkamapura.** He defeated Kulasekhara and his numerous allies in several battles, and won over some of his allies, such as **Iḷaṅkiyarāyara, Mālavarāyara** and **Coḷagaṅgara,** by gifts and honours, and captured, among other places, the fortress of **Semponmāri.** He was assisted by **Laṅkāpura Deva** and **Laṅkāgiri Sora,** the general **Gokaṇṇa,** the **Kesadhātus Loka** and **Kitti,** and an officer named **Jagadvijaya.** He then captured **Muṇḍikkāra** and several other fortresses and occupied **Rājinā.** He subdued the **Coḷa** and **Paṇḍu** countries, and is said to have issued coins bearing the name of Parakkamabāhu I., while he restored the Paṇḍu kingdom to **Vīrapaṇḍu.** The village of **Paṇḍu-vijaya** was founded by the king to commemorate the victory of Laṅkāpura.[2]

It is curious that no mention is made in the Ceylon Chronicles of Laṅkāpura's return to Ceylon, nor of any honours bestowed on him by the king. South Indian inscriptions relate that Laṅkāpura was defeated, and that his head, with those of his officers, was nailed to the gates of Madhurā.[3]

[1] Cv. lxx. 218; Cv. *Trs.* 305, n. 5.

[2] The account of Laṅkāpura's exploits is found in Cv. lxxvi. 76 ff.; lxxvii. 1 ff.

[3] Codrington, *op. cit.*, 62, 74; also Smith, *Early History of India*, p. 340.

3. **Laṅkāpura.**—The name seems to have been used also as a title and was conferred on **Kaḍakkuḍa,**[1] **Rakkha,**[2] and **Deva.**[3]

[1] Cv. lxxii. 39. [2] *Ibid.*, lxxv. 70. [3] *Ibid.*, 130.

Laṅkāmahālāna.—See **Laṅkājayamahālekhaka.**

Laṅkārāma.—A monastery in **Ayodhyā** where lived the author of the **Saddhammasaṅgaha** (*q.v.*).

Laṅkā-vihāra.—A monastery near **Mahāgāma;** it was near there that **Kākavaṇṇatissa** found **Vihāradevī** when she landed from the sea.[1] But this is probably a wrong reading.[2]

[1] Mhv. xxii. 22. [2] See MṬ. 432, where the place is called **Tolaka-vihāra.**

Lacchī.—See **Lakkhī.**

Lajjika.—A village in Ceylon given by **Aggabodhi I.** for the maintenance of the **Mūgasenāpati-vihāra.**[1]

[1] Cv. xlii. 23.

Lajjitissa.—See **Lañjatissa.**

Lañjakāsanasālā.—A building in Ceylon, erected by **Lañjatissa** for the use of the monks.[1]

[1] Mhv. xxxiii. 24.

Lañjatissa, Lañjakatissa, Lajjitissa.—King of Ceylon (59-50 B.C.). He was the eldest son of **Saddhātissa,** but, when his father died, the ministers and monks crowned his younger brother, **Thūlatthana,** king. Lañjatissa killed Thūlatthana after one month, and ruled for nine years and fifteen days. At first he was very indifferent towards the monks, but later made amends. He built the **Ariṭṭha** and **Kuñjarahīnaka-vihāras,** the **Lañjakāsanasālā** and a stone mantling for the **Kanthakathūpa,** in addition to other good works.[1]

[1] Mhv. xxxiii. 14 ff.

Laṭukika Jātaka (No. 357).—A quail once laid her eggs in the feeding ground of the elephants. When the young ones were hatched, the Bodhisatta, the leader of the elephants, passed along that way with the herd, and, at the request of the mother quail, carefully avoided the young ones. But a rogue elephant, who came after, though warned in the same way, trod on the nest and fouled it. The quail swore revenge, and got a crow to put out the elephant's eyes and a fly to put maggots in them, and when the elephant, in great pain, looked for water, she persuaded a frog to croak on the mountain top and thus to lead the elephant into a precipice down which he fell and was killed.

The story was told in reference to **Devadatta** who was identified with the rogue-elephant.[1]

In the accounts[2] of the quarrel between the **Sākyans** and the **Koliyans,** this Jātaka is said to have been one of those preached by the Buddha

[1] J. iii. 174-77. [2] See *s.v.* **Rohiṇī.**

on that occasion, showing that even such a weak animal as a quail could sometimes cause the death of an elephant. Perhaps the story was related on more than one occasion.[3] See also below, **Laṭukikopama Sutta.**

[3] See DhA. i. 46, where it is related to the **Kosambi** monks to show the danger of quarrelling.

Laṭukikopama Sutta.—Preached to **Udāyi**[1] in a wood near **Āpaṇa.** Udāyi recalls the rules made by the Buddha regarding the hours for meals, how such rules were added to, until, in the end, any meal out of hours was forbidden; and he mentions how, though at first these rules involved hardship, in the end they were very helpful in dispelling unhappy states of consciousness and in implanting happy ones. The Buddha agrees, but adds that many people are foolish, and consider such sacrifices insignificant, growing discontented when asked to make them. But this insignificant thing develops into a bond strong enough to hold them fast. Some people are like quails caught in traps, unable to escape from their bonds, others like mighty elephants, bursting their bonds and going where they wish. Thus there are four types of individuals, differing according as to whether they are attached to their bonds or detached from them.[2]

[1] This is **Mahā-Udāyi,** says the Commentary.

[2] M. i. 447-56; MA. ii. 656-60.

Laṭṭhivana, Laṭṭhivanuyyāna.—A grove to the south-west of **Rājagaha.** In it was the **Supatiṭṭha-cetiya,** where the Buddha stayed during his first visit to Rājagaha from **Gayāsīsa,** after the Enlightenment. There **Bimbisāra** visited him with twelve *nahutas* of followers, and **Uruvela Kassapa** dispelled their doubts by declaring his acceptance of the Buddha as his teacher. It was during this visit that Bimbisāra gifted **Veḷuvana** to the Buddha and his Order.[1] Eleven *nahutas,* with Bimbisāra at their head, became *sotāpannas* at the end of the Buddha's sermon, which included the **Mahānārada Kassapa Jātaka.** The remaining *nahuta* was established in the Refuges.[2] The grove evidently received its name from its green liquorice creepers, hence its description as *Laṭṭhimadhukavana.*[3] Hiouen Thsang[4] calls it Yaṣṭivana and describes it as a grove of bamboos, giving accounts of its origin and various stories connected with it.

[1] Vin. i. 35 ff.; DhA. i. 72; AA. i. 166; BuA. 18, etc.

[2] J. i. 84; AA. i. 57; also J. vi. 219.

[3] *E.g.,* J. i. 68.

[4] Beal, *op. cit.,* 145 f.; see VT. 136.

Latā.—A woman of **Sāvatthi.** She was good and holy, and after death was born as a daughter of **Vessavaṇa.** Her sisters were **Sajjā, Pavarā,**

Acchimatī and **Sutā**. **Sakka** married them all, and when a dispute arose as to which was the most skilled in dance and song, a contest was held on the banks of the **Anotatta**, in which Latā won. Sutā asked Latā how she acquired her great talents, and the latter gave an account of her good deeds as a human being. Later, the story was related to **Moggallāna** on one of his visits to the deva worlds, and was repeated by him to the Buddha.[1]

[1] Vv. iii. 4; VvA. 131 ff.

Ladagāma.—A village assigned by **Jeṭṭhatissa** for the maintenance of **Kālavāpi-vihāra.**[1]

[1] Cv. xliv. 101.

Labujagāma.—A village in Ceylon, in the province of **Saparagamu.** Once, for a short period, the Tooth Relic of the Buddha was placed in the monastery there, after being taken from **Jayavaddhanapura,**[1] and **Vimaladhammasūriya** removed it from there to **Sirivaḍḍhanapura.**[2]

[1] *Cp.* Cv. xci. 17 f.

[2] *Ibid.*, xciv. 11 f.

Labujadāyaka Thera.—An arahant.[1] It was evidently the same as **Yasoja** (*q.v.*).

[1] Ap. ii. 409.

Labujaphaladāyaka Thera.—An arahant.[1] The story given is identically the same as that of **Labujadāyaka** (*q.v.*).

[1] Ap. i. 295.

Labujamaṇḍaka.—One of four villages given by **Parakkamabāhu IV.** for the maintenance of the *pariveṇa* built by him for **Medhaṅkara Thera.**[1]

[1] Cv. xc. 87.

Labhiya-Vasabha.—See **Vasabha.**

Lambaka.—A rock near **Himavā.**[1]

[1] ThagA. i. 97; Ap. i. 15, 280; ii. 454.

Lambakaṇṇā.—A gotta, mentioned in the Chronicles as being among the inhabitants of Ceylon. The Lambakaṇṇas had, probably, certain duties to perform in connection with the consecration of a king,[1] for we

[1] This was perhaps the reason why **Parakkamabāhu I.** gave them a prominent place in the ceremonies held in honour of the Tooth Relic (Cv. lxxiv. 213); see also below, in the text.

find that **Iḷanāga,** when he went to take his ceremonial bath in **Tissavāpi,** was enraged on finding that the Lambakaṇṇā were not there. As a punishment, he ordered them to work at the remaking of a road along the bank of the tank, leading to the **Mahā Thūpa,** and set caṇḍalas to supervise them. Full of anger, the Lambakaṇṇas rose in revolt and seized the throne. Three years later the king returned from exile, and, having defeated the Lambakaṇṇas, made them drag his chariot in triumphal procession. When he proposed to behead them his mother intervened, and he contented himself with having their noses and toes cut off.[2]

The Lambakaṇṇas were evidently a powerful clan, and several members of the clan ruled as kings of Ceylon—*e.g.*, **Vasabha, Saṅghatissa, Saṅghabodhi** and **Goṭhābhaya,** the last three of whom came from **Mahiyaṅgana** and seized the throne from **Vijayakumāra.**[3] Between the reign of **Kittisirimegha** and the Coḷiyan conquest in 1017 A.C.—*i.e.*, between the third and the eleventh centuries—out of thirty-six kings who occupied the throne of Ceylon the majority belonged to either the **Moriyā** or the **Lambakaṇṇā.** A clan of Lambakaṇṇas lived also in South India in the twelfth century. When **Laṅkāpura,** acting under the orders of **Parakkamabāhu I.,** crowned **Vīrapaṇḍu** as king of **Paṇḍu,** three Lambakaṇṇa chiefs were asked to carry out "the duties of the Lambakaṇṇas" (*Lambakaṇṇadhuraṃ*).[4]

The name may have had a totemistic origin, but according to some Sinhalese Chronicles[5] the Lambakaṇṇas of Ceylon were a branch of the Moriyas. They claimed descent from **Sumitta**—a prince of the Moriyan clan, who formed one of the escort that brought the Bodhi-tree from India—and **Sumanā,** a princess of the same race, who was at one time a nun, ordained under **Saṅghamittā.** According to these Chronicles most of the kings of Ceylon down to the time of **Parakkamabāhu VI.** were scions of this clan.

In Ceylon, the Lambakaṇṇas had settlements in **Rohaṇa.**[6]

[2] Mhv. xxxv. 18 ff.
[3] *Ibid.*, xxxvi. 58 ff.
[4] Cv. lxxvii. 27 f.
[5] *E.g.*, the *Saddharmaratnākara* and the *Pärakumbā-Sirita*.
[6] See, *e.g.*, AA. i. 262.

Lambacūḷaka.—A town in the domain of King **Pajaka,**[1] and, therefore, in **Avanti.** Elsewhere[2] it is mentioned as having been in the domain of **Caṇḍappajjota,** probably again referring to Avanti.

[1] J. iii. 463.
[2] J. v. 133.

Lambītakā.—A class of devas present at the preaching of the **Mahāsamaya Sutta.**[1]

[1] D. ii. 261.

Laḷātadhātuvaṃsa.—A Pāli work containing the history of the frontal bone relic of the Buddha.[1]

[1] For a discussion see P.L.C. 255.

Lasuṇadāyaka Thera.—An arahant. In the time of **Vipassī Buddha** he was an ascetic living on garlic (*lasuṇa*). Pleased with the Buddha and his monks, he once gave a whole pingo-load of garlic to the monastery.[1]

[1] Ap. i. 89.

1. **Lahu Sutta.**—Four conditions, the cultivation of which leads to buoyant (*lahu*) insight.[1]

[1] S. v. 412.

2. **Lahu Sutta.**—There is no other single thing so quick to change (*lahuparivatta*) as mind.[1]

[1] A. i. 10.

Lahulla.—A village in Ceylon, near **Nālandā.**[1]

[1] Cv. lxx. 214.

Lājā.—A goddess (*devadhītā*). She was once the watcher of a field of paddy-rice in **Rājagaha,** and when **Mahā Kassapa,** out of compassion, approached her, she took some of the parched rice and, with devout heart, poured it into his bowl. Almost immediately she was bitten by a snake, and was reborn after death in **Tāvatiṃsa.** Realizing that it was to Kassapa that she owed her good fortune, she decided to wait on him, sweep his cell, etc. As soon as Kassapa discovered this, he forbade her to come near him any more. Lājā was much distressed, and the Buddha, noting her despair, sent a ray of light to console her.[1]

[1] DhA. iii. 6 ff.

Lābugāmaka.—A village in Ceylon where **Paṇḍukābhaya** vanquished his uncles. Their heads were collected and lay "like a heap of gourds," hence the name of the village.[1] Its original name was **Nagaragāma.**[2]

[1] Mhv. x. 72; see also Mhv. *Trs.* 73, n. 2. [2] MṬ. 292.

Lābhagaraha Jātaka (No. 287).—The Buddha was once a famous teacher of the Vedas with five hundred pupils. One pupil asked him how people could obtain gain in this world. His teacher answered that in a world full of fools the man who slanders, possesses the tricks of an actor and carries evil talk, gains prosperity. The pupil expressed his disappointment and continued his religious life.

The story was related in reference to a colleague who asked **Sāriputta** the same question and received the above answer.[1]

[1] J. ii. 420-3.

Lābhavāsī.—A group of ascetic monks within the Buddhist Order in Ceylon. **Mahinda IV.** showed them special favour,[1] while **Vijayabāhu I.** gave for their maintenance the villages of **Antaraviṭṭhi, Saṅghātagāma** and **Sirimaṇḍagalagāma,** and provided them with necessaries.[2]

[1] Cv. liv. 27. [2] *Ibid.*, lx. 68, 72.

Lābhasakkāra Saṃyutta.—The seventeenth section of the **Saṃyutta Nikāya.**[1]

[1] S. ii. 225-44.

Lāmaseṭṭhā.—A class of devas present at the preaching of the **Mahāsamaya Sutta.**[1]

[1] D. ii. 261; DA. ii. 691.

Lāḷa.—A country in India, the capital of which was **Sīhapura;** it was the birthplace of **Vijaya,** founder of the Sinhalese dynasty.[1] The country is now generally identified with the modern Gujerat, the Larika of Ptolemy.

[1] Dpv. ix. 5; Mhv. vi. 5, 36.

Lāḷudāyī Thera.—An Elder who possessed the knack of saying "the wrong thing." He would go to a place where people were enjoying a holiday and recite stanzas suitable to a funeral and *vice versâ.*[1] When the Buddha heard of this he related the **Somadatta Jātaka** (*q.v.*), showing that in past births, too, Lāḷudāyī had possessed the same propensity. He is identified with the foolish father **(Agnidatta)** of the story.[2] We also read of his jealousy of the praises bestowed on **Sāriputta** and **Moggallāna** for their knowledge and exposition of the Law, and he claimed that he possessed knowledge equal to theirs. But one day when asked to preach, he sat on a seat holding a painted fan, but found nothing to say. He thereupon agreed to preach in the evening; but the same thing happened, and he barely escaped with his life, so furious was his audience. The Buddha, on hearing of this, related the **Sūkara Jātaka** (*q.v.*) (in which Lāḷudāyī was the pig), showing that in the past, too, he

[1] DhA. iii. 123 ff. [2] J. ii. 167; DhA. iii. 125.

had covered himself with disgrace because of his boastfulness.[3] On another occasion, he had a dispute with **Dabba Mallaputta** regarding the allotment of the rice tickets, and the monks, in order to teach him a lesson, handed him the tickets to distribute. But he created such confusion that there was a great uproar, and **Ānanda** was sent by the Buddha to find out what was happening. When Ānanda returned with this story, the Buddha related the **Taṇḍulanāli Jātaka** (*q.v.*) to show that in the past Lāḷudāyī had been a foolish appraiser.[4] The **Naṅgalīsa Jātaka** gives another example of his folly and ineptitude[5]; so does also the **Padañjali Jātaka**,[6] where he is identified with **Padañjali**, an idle, lazy loafer. In the **Mahāummagga Jātaka**[7] he is identified with the somewhat foolish king, **Vedeha.**

Lāḷudāyī once had a discussion with **Pasūra**, who, at first, thought him to be clever and wise, and accepted him as teacher, being ordained by him. But, later, Pāsura easily defeated him in discussion.[8] Others, too, visiting **Jetavana**, and seeing him in the Preacher's seat, mistook him for an eminent Elder, but soon discovered their mistake.[9]

On one occasion[10] Lāḷudāyī even dared to contradict Sāriputta regarding birth among the *manomayadevā*. Three times Sāriputta repeated his statement and three times Lāḷudāyī contradicted him, and, there being no monk in the assembly who supported Sāriputta, he took Lāḷudāyī to the Buddha, where he three times repeated the same statement, being three times contradicted. Then the Buddha called Lāḷudāyī " a witless fool " and silenced him. Ānanda was witness to the dispute, but took no part in it, thereby winning the Buddha's censure.

Elsewhere,[11] however, we find Lāḷudāyī listening in all humility to a discourse by Sāriputta on Nibbāna, as the happiness which is not sensed (*avedayitasukha*). Though Udāyī's knowledge of the Dhamma was not profound, he did not hesitate to take part in a discussion, even with the Buddha himself, when occasion arose. We find him twice censured by the Buddha for this exhibition of his ignorance, once in the **Mahākamma-vibhaṅga Sutta**[12] and once again in a discussion on *anussati*.[13] In both instances Ānanda is present, and, in the discussion on *anussati*, he earns the Buddha's praise for his knowledge compared with Udāyī's ignorance. This annoyed Udāyī, for we find him confronting Ānanda with the fact that though he had been in the constant society of the

[3] J. ii. 344 ff.; but according to the introductory story of the Jātaka itself (in J. ii. 9 ff.), Lāḷudāyī's name is not mentioned, and the incident described differs somewhat.

[4] J. i. 123 ff.

[5] *Ibid.*, 446 ff.

[6] J. ii. 263 f.

[7] J. vi. 478.

[8] SNA. ii. 540.

[9] *E.g.*, DhA. ii. 31.

[10] A. iii. 192 f.; AA. ii. 628.

[11] A. iv. 414 f.; AA. ii. 810.

[12] M. iii. 208.

[13] A. iii. 322 f.

Buddha he had not profited by it, a remark which earned the censure of the Buddha and his assurance that Ānanda would certainly reach perfection in that very life.[14]

Buddhaghosa[15] calls Lāḷudāyī **Kovarlyaputta.** It is not clear whether this means that his father was called **Kovarlya.** The Vinaya[16] mentions a monk called Udāyī who was a colleague of **Seyyasaka.** He persuaded Seyyasaka to commit the first *Saṅghādisesa* offence, saying that he himself acted likewise. For this the *Mānatta* penalty was imposed on him. According to the Commentaries,[17] this Udāyī is to be identified with Lāḷudāyī, and if this be correct, it was perhaps the same monk who was guilty of several Vinaya offences attributed to Udāyi—see **Udāyi** (2)—though the Vinaya Commentary does not elsewhere[18] definitely so identify him, except once,[19] where he is mentioned as having made an embroidered robe for a nun, which he persuaded her to wear in the assembly of the nuns ! Was this because the Commentator regarded the two Udāyis as distinct persons ?[20]

Lāḷudāyī is given as an example of a person who did no good either to himself or to others (*neva attahitāya paṭipanno no parahitāya*). Buddhaghosa elsewhere[21] describes him as "*bhantamigasappaṭibhāgo niddārāmatādiṃ anuyuttānaṃ aññataro lolabhikkhu.*"

[14] A. i. 228; AA. i. 441.
[15] ThagA. ii. 7; some of the MSS. read *nāṭakācariyaputta*.
[16] Vin. iii. 110.
[17] Sp. iii. 517; DhA. iii. 5.
[18] *E.g.*, Sp. iii. 541, 549, 552, where he is simply called Udāyi.
[19] Sp. iv. 804.
[20] *E.g.*, MA. i. 348.
[21] Sp. iii. 517.

1. **Lāḷudāyīthera Vatthu.**—The story of **Lāḷudāyī's** past life as **Aggidatta.**[1] *Cp.* the **Somadatta Jātaka.**

[1] DhA. iii. 123 ff.

2. **Lāḷudāyīthera Vatthu.**—The story of **Lāḷudāyī's** futile attempt to excel **Sāriputta** and **Moggallāna** in the power of preaching.[1]

[1] DhA. iii. 344 ff.

Lāvarāvapabbata.—Probably a monastery in Ceylon rebuilt by **Aggabodhi IX.**[1]

[1] Cv. xlix. 76.

Liṅgatthavivaraṇa.—A Pāli grammatical work by **Subhūtacandana,** a monk of Pagan. Two Commentaries on it were written, the **Liṅgatthavivaraṇappakāsaka** by **Ñāṇasāgara** and the **Liṅgatthavivaraṇaṭīkā** by

Uttama. A work called **Liṅgatthavivaraṇavinicchaya,** by an unknown author, is also mentioned.[1]

[1] Gv. 63, 65, 67, 72, 73, 75; Bode, *op. cit.*, 22, n. 1.

Licchavi Sutta.—See the **Nandaka Sutta.**

Licchavibhāṇavāra.—The second bhāṇavāra of the sixth khandhaka of the **Mahāvagga.**[1]

[1] Vin. i. 210-33.

Licchavī.—A powerful tribe of India in the time of the Buddha. They were certainly *khattiyas,* for on that ground they claimed a share of the Buddha's relics.[1] Their capital was **Vesāli,** and they formed a part of the Vajjian confederacy, being often referred to as the **Vajjīs** (*q.v.*). Their strength lay in their great unity; if one Licchavi fell ill, all the others would visit him. The whole tribe would join in any ceremony performed in the house of Licchavi, and they would all unite in honouring any distinguished visitors to their city.[2] They were beautiful to look at and wore brilliantly coloured garments, riding in brightly painted carriages.[3] The Buddha once compared them to the gods of **Tāvatiṃsa.**[4]

Though this would seem to indicate that they were very prosperous and rich, they do not appear to have lived in luxury and idleness. They are, on the contrary, spoken of[5] as sleeping on straw couches, being strenuous and diligent and zealous in their service.[6] They also practised seven conditions of welfare (*aparihānīyadhammā*), which the Buddha claimed to have taught them at the **Sārandada cetiya:** (1) They held frequent public meetings of their tribe which they all attended; (2) they met together to make their decisions and carried out their undertakings in concord; (3) they upheld tradition and honoured their pledges; (4) they respected and supported their elders; (5) no women or girls were allowed to be taken by force or abduction; (6) they maintained and paid due respect to their places of worship; (7) they supported and fully protected the holy men (arahants) among them.[7]

The young men among the Licchavis were evidently fond of archery, for mention is made[8] of large numbers of them roving about in the **Mahāvana,** with bows and arrows, the strings set, and surrounded by hounds. They were a martial people and fond of " sport," but we find one

[1] D. ii. 165; according to the Mtu. (i. 283, etc.) they belonged to the *Vāsiṣṭha gotta*; *cp.* the **Mallas** (*q.v.*), who are called **Vāseṭṭhas.**

[2] DA. ii. 519.

[3] D. ii. 96; A. iii. 239; *cp.* Mtu. i. 259.

[4] D. ii. 96; also DhA. iii. 280.

[5] S. ii. 267 f.

[6] As skilful hardy archers, says the Commentary.

[7] D. ii. 73 f.; A. iv. 15 f.

[8] *Ibid.*, iii. 76.

of their Elders, **Mahānāma**,[9] complaining of them to the Buddha: "The Licchavi youths are quick tempered, rough and greedy fellows; such presents as are sent by the members of their tribe—sugar-cane, jujubes, sweet cakes, sweetmeats, etc.—they loot and eat; they slap the women and girls of their tribe on the back." Violation of chastity was considered a serious offence among the Licchavis, and the assembly would even give its consent to a husband's request that his unfaithful wife should be murdered.[10]

According to the Buddhist books, the Licchavis were devout followers of the Buddha and held him in the highest esteem.[11] Even careless boys, referred to above as wandering about with hounds and bows and arrows, would lay aside their arms when they saw the Buddha seated under a tree and would surround him with clasped hands, eager to hear him.[12] There were numerous shrines in Vesāli itself, several of which are mentioned by name: **Cāpāla, Sattambaka, Bahuputta, Gotama, Sārandada** and **Udena.**[13] Buddhaghosa says[14] that these shrines were originally Yakkha cetiyas, where various Yakkhas were worshipped, but that they were later converted into monasteries for the Buddha and his Order. It is, however, apparent from the Buddhist books themselves,[15] that Vesāli was also a stronghold of the Jains. The Buddha visited Vesāli at least three times,[16] and is frequently mentioned as staying in **Kūṭāgārasālā** (*q.v.*) in Mahāvana. There the Licchavis visited him in large numbers, sometimes[17] disturbing the calm of the spot and obliging resident monks to seek peace in **Gosiṅgasālāvana** near by. Once, five hundred Licchavis invited the Buddha to a discussion held by them at the Sārandada-cetiya regarding the five kinds of treasures. The Buddha went and gave his opinion.[18]

But not all the Licchavis were followers of the Buddha. When **Saccaka** the **Nigaṇṭha** visited the Buddha at Mahāvana, he was accompanied by five hundred Licchavis, who did not all salute the Buddha as their teacher, but showed him only such respect as was due to an honoured stranger.[19] Several eminent Licchavis are specially mentioned by name as having visited and consulted the Buddha; among whom are **Mahānāma,**

[9] A. iii. 76, the *Lalitavistara* is even more condemnatory.

[10] Vin. iv. 225.

[11] Five hundred Licchavis once gave a garment each to **Piṅgiyāni,** because he recited a verse in praise of the Buddha (A. iii. 239).

[12] A. iii. 76.

[13] For details see *s.v.*

[14] *E.g.*, UdA. 322 f.

[15] *E.g.*, in the story of the general **Sīha** (*q.v.*).

[16] The first visit was in order to destroy the threefold panic of drought, sickness and non-human foes. It was probably this act which earned for the Buddha the gratitude of the Licchavis.

[17] *E.g.*, A. v. 133 f.

[18] A. iii. 167 f.

[19] M. i. 229; MA. i. 454 gives their reasons.

Sīha, Bhaddiya, Sāḷha, Abhaya, Paṇḍitakumāra, Nandaka, Mahāli and **Ugga.** Several Licchavis, both men and women, joined the Order—*e.g.*, the famous courtesan **Ambapālī, Jentī, Sīhā** and **Vāsiṭṭhī,** and, among monks, **Añjanavaniya, Vajjiputta** and **Sambhūta.**[20]

The Licchavis were greatly admired for their system of government. It was a republic (*gaṇa, saṅgha*), all the leading members of which were called *rājā.*[21] They held full and frequent assemblies at which problems affecting either the whole republic or individual members were fully discussed. When the assembly drum was heard, all left other duties and assembled immediately in the *Santhāgārasālā.*[22] Sometimes, as appears from the story of the conversion of Sīha, religion was also discussed at these meetings. The rules of procedure adopted[23] evidently resembled those followed in the *upasampāda* ordination of a monk.[24] Besides the *rājās* there were also numerous *uparājās, senāpatis,* and *bhaṇḍāgārikas.*[25] There was an elaborate judicial procedure by which any person charged with an offence was handed over, in turn, to the *Vinicchayamahāmattas* (inquirers), the *Vohārikas* (experts in law), *Suttadharas* (experts in tradition), the *Aṭṭhakulakas* (probably a judicial committee), the *Senāpati,* the *Uparājā,* and finally to the *Rājā,* who would inflict the proper sentence according to the *paveṇipotthaka.*[26]

In their political relationships with their neighbours, the Licchavis seem to have been on friendly terms with **Bimbisāra** (*q.v.*), king of **Magadha,** and with **Pasenadi,** king of **Kosala.**[27] Generally speaking, they were friendly also with the **Mallas,** though the story of **Bandhula** (*q.v.*) shows that a certain amount of rivalry existed between the two tribes.

After the death of Bimbisāra, **Ajātasattu,** in his desire for the expansion of Magadha, resolved to destroy the Licchavis. He was probably partly influenced by his fear of his foster-brother **Abhayarājakumāra** (*q.v.*), who had in him Licchavi blood. Buddhaghosa[28] gives another story. There was a port on the Ganges, extending over one yojana, half of which territory belonged to Ajātasattu, and the other half to the Licchavis. Near by was a mountain, from which much fragrant material (? *gandhabhaṇḍa*) flowed into the river. While Ajātasattu was making preparations to claim his portion of this material, the Licchavis would go before him

[20] For details see *s.v.*

[21] According to Mtu. i. 271, there were 68,000 rājās in Vesāli; the Jātakas (i. 504; iii. 1) speak of 7707; see also DhA. iii. 436.

[22] DA. ii. 517 f.

[23] See D. ii. 76 f., where the Buddha enjoins on the monks the observance of the same habits as practised by the Licchavis.

[24] These are given at Vin. i. 56 (VT. i. 169 f.).

[25] J. iii. 1.

[26] DA. ii. 519.

[27] See, *e.g.*, M. ii. 101, where Pasenadi says this.

[28] DA. ii. 526 f.; AA. ii. 705; was the port Pāṭaligāma ? see UdA. 408.

and remove it all. This happened on several occasions, and Ajātasattu vowed vengeance. In order to discover what the Buddha thought of his chances of success, he sent to him his minister **Vassakāra.** The Buddha predicted[29] that as long as the Licchavis remained united they were proof against any foe. Ajātasattu then decided to bring about disunion among them. He was successful in this, with the aid of Vassakāra.[30] When Ajātasattu arrived at the gates of Vesāli, the Licchavis, owing to their disunion, were unable to put up any opposition, and Ajātasattu captured the city without further trouble.[31] The degeneration may have set in earlier among the Licchavis, for we find reference[32] to their giving up their earlier austere habits and to their fondness for soft pillows, long sleep and other luxuries. Their power and prosperity were probably also weakened by the plague and drought which had ravaged Vesāli.

The Commentaries[33] contain a mythical account of the origin of the Licchavis. The queen of Benares gave birth to a lump of flesh, and, wishing to avoid disgrace, her ladies-in-waiting put it in a sealed casket and threw it into the Ganges. A deva wrote the king's name on the casket, which was picked up by an ascetic, who tended the embryo until two children, a boy and a girl, emerged from it. The ascetic fed them with milk. Whatever entered the stomachs of the children could be seen as though the stomach were transparent, so that they appeared skinless (*nicchavi*); some said the skin was so thin (*līnachavī*) that the stomach and whatever entered it appeared as though sewn together. From this the children came to be called Licchavi, and, as they grew, were brought up by the villagers living near the hermitage. The other children disliked them, saying they were to be avoided (*vajjitabbā*) because of their quarrelsome disposition. When they were sixteen years old the villagers obtained land for them from the king, founded a town, and married them together. Their country came to be called **Vajji.** They had sixteen pairs of twins, and their city had to be greatly enlarged —hence its name, **Visālā** or **Vesāli.**

[29] D. ii. 72 ff.

[30] For details see *s.v.* Vassakāra.

[31] DA. ii. 524.

[32] S. ii. 268; see also DhA. iii. 280, where they quarrel over a woman; *cp.* Sp. i. 284.

[33] MA. i. 258; KhpA. etc.; for a very comprehensive account of the Licchavis, see Law, Kṣatriya Clans in Buddhist India, pp. 1 ff.

Litta Jātaka (No. 91).—The Bodhisatta was once a dice-player, and used to play with a sharper who, when he saw that he was losing, would put one of the dice in his mouth, pretending that it was lost. The Bodhisatta discovered this, and one day brought dice smeared with dried poison. The sharper played his usual tricks, and suffered great pain from the poison. The Bodhisatta then cured him, thus teaching him to be honest in future. The story was told in reference to certain monks who were careless in the use of various requisites given to them.[1]

[1] J. i. 379 f.

Litta Vagga.—The tenth chapter of the Eka Nipāta of the Jātaka.[1]

[1] J. i. 379-410.

Līnatthadīpanī.—A *ṭīkā* by **Vācissara** on the **Paṭisambhidāmagga.**[1]

[1] P.L.C. 217.

1. **Līnatthappakāsinī,** or **Līnatthavaṇṇanā.**—A series of *ṭīkās* on the four Nikāyas and the Jātaka. They are ascribed to **Dhammapāla.**[1]

[1] Gv. 60, 69; also P.L.C. 192.

2. **Līnatthappakāsinī.**—A *ṭīkā* on the **Kaṅkhāvitaraṇī,** by an unknown author.[1]

[1] Gv. 62, 72.

Līnatthavaṇṇanā.—See **Līnatthappakāsinī** (1).

Līnatthavisodhanī.—A Commentary on the **Saddabindu** by **Ñāṇavilāsa** of Pagan.[1]

[1] Bode, *op. cit.*, 25, n. 4.

1. **Līlāvatī.**—A **Coḷa** princess, daughter of **Jagatīpāla.** She escaped with her father to Ceylon, where she became the queen ot **Vijayabāhu I.**[1]

[1] Cv. lix. 24 f.

2. **Līlāvatī.**—Daughter of **Vīravamma** and **Yasodharā,** the latter being the daughter of **Vijayabāhu I.** and his queen **Līlāvatī.** She married **Vikkamabāhu.**[1]

[1] Cv. lix. 28, 50. See **Vikkamabāhu** (2).

3. **Līlāvatī.**—Daughter of **Sirivallabha** and **Sugalā** and sister of **Māṇābharaṇa.**[1] She was the first queen of **Parakkamabāhu I.,** and after his death, she ruled over Ceylon for three years (1197-1200 A.C.), with the help of the general **Kitti,** till she was expelled by **Sāhasamalla.** Then she reigned again for one year, this time with the help of **Vikkantacamūnakka. Lokissara** deposed her and ruled for nine months, when the

[1] Cv. lxii. 2.

general **Parakkama** once more restored Līlāvatī to the throne, which, this time, she occupied for about seven months.[2]

[2] *Ibid.*, lxxx. 31, 46, 50; also Cv. *Trs.* ii. 131, n. 5.

Lumbinī.—A park, situated between **Kapilavatthu** and **Devadaha.** It was there that the Buddha was born.[1] A pillar now marks the spot of **Asoka's** visit to Lumbinī. According to an inscription on the pillar, it was placed there by the people then in charge of the park to commemorate Asoka's visit and gifts.[2] The park is now known as Rummindei, inside the Nepal frontier and two miles north of Bhagavanpura.

In the Sutta Nipāta[3] it is stated that the Buddha was born in a village of the Sākyans, in the *Lumbineyya Janapada.* The Buddha stayed in Lumbinīvana during his visit to Devadaha and there preached the **Devadaha Sutta.**[4]

[1] J. i. 52, 54; Kvu. 97, 559; AA. i. 10; MA. ii. 924; BuA. 227; Cv. li. 10, etc.

[2] See Mukerji: Asoka, p. 27; see p. 201 f. for details.

[3] vs. 683.

[4] MA. ii. 810.

Lumbineyya.—See **Lumbinī.**

Lūkhapāpuraṇa Sutta.—A very rich brahmin once visited the Buddha clad in a coarse cloak. When asked why he was thus clothed, he said that his four sons, with their wives, had thrown him out of his house. The Buddha taught him a series of verses to be recited at the brahmin assembly, when his sons would be present. The sons realized their folly and took him home and looked after him well. The brahmin went back to thank the Buddha.[1]

[1] S. i. 175 f.

Lena-vihāra.—See **Loṇagiri.**

1. **Loka.**—A general, inhabitant of **Makkhakudrūsa.** He ruled for six years over **Rohaṇa,** his seat of government being in **Kājaragāma.** A chieftain named **Buddharāja** quarrelled with him and fled to **Cuṇṇasālā,** where he was joined by **Kitti** (afterwards **Vijayabāhu I.**). Loka marched against their combined forces, was defeated in **Remuṇa,** and died soon after.[1]

[1] Cv. lvii. 1, 45-64.

2. **Loka.**—Son of **Kassapa** (afterwards **Vikkamabāhu I.**) and **Lokitā.** His brother was **Moggallāna.**[1]

[1] Cv. lvii. 29; Cv. *Trs.* i. 195, n. 3.

3. **Loka Kesadhâtu.**—An officer of **Parakkamabāhu I.**[1] He served under the generals **Damiḷādhikāri Rakkha**[2] and **Laṅkāpura**[3] and took a prominent part in the campaign against **Kulasekhara,** particularly in the capture of **Rājinā.**[4]

[1] Cv. lxxii. 57.
[2] *Ibid.*, lxxv. 75.
[3] *Ibid.*, lxxvi. 253, 269.
[4] *Ibid.*, lxxvi. 324, 327.

Loka Vagga.—The thirteenth chapter of the **Dhammapada.**

1. **Loka Sutta.**—The origin and continuance of the world depends on the six senses.[1]

[1] S. i. 41.

2. **Loka Sutta.**—The Buddha tells **Pasenadi** that greed, hate and delusion make for trouble and suffering in the world.[1]

[1] S. i. 98.

3. **Loka Sutta.**—The origin and passing away of the world depend on the senses and their objects.[1]

[1] S. ii. 73.

4. **Loka Sutta.**—The world is so called because it crumbles away (*lujjati*).[1]

[1] S. iv. 52.

5. **Loka Sutta.**—Because of eye and object arises eye-consciousness. Thence comes contact, feeling, craving, grasping and becoming. Thus is the world originated; with their cessation the world ceases.[1]

[1] S. iv. 87.

6. **Loka Sutta.**—**Anuruddha** tells **Sāriputta** that his knowledge of the universe is due to the cultivation of the four *satipaṭṭhānas.*[1]

[1] S. v. 175.

7. **Loka Sutta.**—**Anuruddha** tells his companions that he knows the world and its divers shapes and forms through the *satipaṭṭhānas.*[1]

[1] S. v. 304.

8. **Loka Sutta.**—In this world of many kinds of beings, the Tathāgata is an Āriyan.[1]

[1] S. v. 435.

9. **Loka Sutta.**—The world and its arising are fully known by a Tathāgata and he is released from both; he also knows the ending of it and the way thereto. He speaks as he does; he is unconquered in the world.[1]

[1] A. ii. 23.

Lokakāmaguṇa Vagga.—The twelfth chapter of the **Saḷāyatana Saṃyutta.**[1]

[1] S. iv. 91-109.

Lokagalla.—An important strategic position in **Rohaṇa,** mentioned in the account of the campaigns of **Parakkamabāhu I.**[1]

[1] Cv. lxxiv. 79, 81, 83, 166.

Lokajitvāṇa.—A general of **Parakkamabāhu I.**[1]

[1] Cv. lxx. 24.

Lokadīpasāra.—A collection of chapters on different subjects—hell, animal kingdom, etc.—written by **Medhaṅkara** of **Muttimanagara.**[1]

[1] Gv. 64, 74; Bode, *op. cit.*, 35 f.

Lokanāthā.—One of the five daughters of **Vijayabāhu I.** and **Tilokasundarī.** She married **Kittisirimegha.**[1]

[1] Cv. lix. 31, 44.

Lokantaranirayā.—A series of hells, each one being bound by three *cakkavāḷas.*[1] Each hell is eight thousand leagues in extent. Beings are born there as a result of heinous crimes, "like those of **Coranāga,** or **Corābhaya,** both of **Tambapaṇṇidīpa.**" Their bodies are three gāvutas in height and with their long nails they cling to the *cakkavāḷapabbata.* Sometimes they fall into the world-bearing water (*lokasandhārakaudaka*) and are dried up because of its great salinity.[2] Elsewhere[3] they are said to suffer from extreme cold. Those holding wrong views are also born there.[4] According to the Buddhavaṃsa Commentary,[5] Lokantara is the hell of the **Asurakāyā.**

[1] *Cp.* Sp. i. 120; SNA. ii. 443.
[2] AA. ii. 532.
[3] NidA. 8; SNA. i. 59.
[4] J. vi. 247.
[5] BuA., p. 26.

Lokandara.—A monastery, evidently in Ceylon. **Maliyadeva Thera** preached the **Cha Chakka Sutta** there and sixty monks became arahants.[1]

[1] MA. ii. 1024.

Lokapaññatti.—A Pāli treatise by an unknown author.[1]

[1] Gv. 62, 72.

Lokapālā.—The name given to the kings of the **Cātummahārājikadevā** (*q.v.*).

Lokappasādaka, Lokappasādana.—See **Lokavivaraṇa.**

Lokabyūha.—A class of devas. One hundred thousand years before the end of the world-cycle (*kappuṭṭhāna*) they wander about among men with dishevelled hair, weeping, wearing red garments, ugly in form, announcing the approach of doom. This is called *kappakolāhala.*[1]

[1] BuA. 224 f.; J. i. 47 f.

1. **Lokavipatti Sutta.**—On eight worldly conditions which obsess the world and round which it revolves: gain and loss, fame and obscurity, blame and praise, contentment and pain.[1]

[1] A. iv. 156.

2. **Lokavipatti Sutta.**—Average people are obsessed by the eight worldly conditions mentioned in Sutta 1; not so the Ariyan disciple who knows their impermanence.[1]

[1] A. iv. 157.

Lokavivaraṇa.—The name of a miracle (*pāṭihāriya*). It enables all beings, from the **Akaniṭṭhā** world above to **Avīci** below, to see each other, because the whole universe is illuminated. It is also called **Lokappasādaka** or **Lokappasādana.**[1] It was performed by **Sāriputta** in honour of the Buddha, before the preaching of the **Buddhavaṃsa,**[2] and again by the arahants, led by **Indagutta,** to enable **Dhammāsoka** to see simultaneously the celebrations held at the dedication of his eighty-four thousand vihāras.[3]

[1] BuA. 40; MṬ. 226 f. confines it to this world only.

[2] Bu. i. 47.

[3] Mhv. v. 188; MṬ. 226 f.

Lokāyata.—Name of a branch of brahmin learning[1]; the name signifies that which pertains to the ordinary view (of the world)—*i.e.*, common or popular philosophy—much the same as *lokakkhāyika* (popular philosophy).[2]

[1] D. i. 11, etc.

[2] For a discussion of the word see Dial. i. 166-72.

Lokāyatika Sutta.—A brahmin, well versed in **Lokāyata** (*q.v.*), asks the Buddha a series of questions regarding the world and existence. The

Buddha ignores them and teaches him the *paticcasamuppāda*, which he accepts.[1]

[1] S. ii. 77 f.

1. **Lokitā.**—A Sinhalese princess, sister of **Devalā.** She married the son of her paternal aunt, **Kassapa** (later **Vikkamabāhu I.**), and had two sons, **Moggallāna** and **Loka.**[1]

[1] Cv. lvii. 27 f.

2. **Lokitā.**—A princess, daughter of **Bodhi** and **Buddhā.** She married **Moggallāna** and had by him four children: **Kitti** (afterwards **Vijayabāhu I.**), **Mittā, Mahinda** and **Rakkhita.**[1]

[1] Cv. lvii. 41.

Lokissara.—A Damiḷa chief who came from India with a spear wound on his shoulder. He defeated **Līlāvatī** in Ceylon and reigned there for nine months (1210-11 A.C.), till he was defeated by the general **Parakkama.**[1]

[1] Cv. lxxx. 47 f.

Lokuttarakathā.—The eight chapter of the Yuganandha Vagga of the **Paṭisambhidāmagga.**

Lokuppatti.—A Pāli work by **Aggapaṇḍita** of Pagan.[1]

[1] Gv. 64, 74; Bode, *op. cit.*, 21.

"**Loke Sutta.**"—**Doṇa** notices the footprints of the Buddha on the road between **Ukkaṭṭhā** and **Setavyā,** and, following them, comes upon the Buddha. Doṇa asks the Buddha who he is—*deva, yakkha, gandhabba,* etc. ?—and the Buddha explains to him that he is a "Buddha."[1]

[1] A. ii. 37 f.

1. **Loṇagiri.**—A vihāra on the banks of the **Ajakaraṇī,** where **Sabbaka (Sappaka)** attained arahantship.[1] *v.l.* **Lena-vihāra.**

[1] ThagA. i. 399.

2. **Loṇagiri.**—A vihāra in Ceylon, near **Mahākhīragāma** (*v.l.* **Mahāgirigāma**). In the Commentaries[1] we find two stories about a monk named **Tissa,** who lived there. Once, five hundred monks, on their way to **Nāgadīpa,** reached Khīragāma and went into the village for alms, but returned with empty bowls. When Tissa discovered this, he went into

[1] AA. ii. 653 f.; M.A. i. 545 f.; DA. ii. 534 f.

the village, whence he shortly returned with his bowl full of milk-rice, which he served to the five hundred monks, keeping some for himself. When asked whether he possessed supernormal power, Tissa replied that he practised *Sārāṇīyadhammā*, as a result of which his bowl was never empty even after he had served as many as one thousand monks from it.

The other story relates how, when Tissa was still a novice, he went to the **Giribhaṇḍa**-festival. There, having heard that the costliest offering was a pair of robes, he openly wished that he should get them. The king heard of this and tried to prevent Tissa from having the robes, but this effort was unsuccessful. The king was amazed, and, on questioning Tissa, the reply was to the same effect as that of the first story. *v.l.* **Lenagiri.**

Loṇaphala Vagga.—The tenth chapter of the Ṭīkā Nipāta of the **Aṅguttara Nikāya.**[1]

[1] A. i. 239-58.

Loṇaphala Sutta.—There are certain persons, careless in habits of body and thought, without insight—even a small offence takes such persons to hell, while others expiate a similar small offence in this very life. A grain of salt cast into a small cup of water renders it undrinkable, but such is not the case if it be cast into a river. The same idea is illustrated with other similes.[1]

[1] A. i. 248 ff.

Loṇambila Sutta.—Given as an example of a sutta in which the Buddha expands the meaning by means of similes.[1] The reference is, perhaps, to the **Loṇaphala Sutta** (*q.v.*).

[1] AA. i. 32.

Lomasakaṅgiya Thera.—An arahant. In the time of **Kassapa Buddha** he had been a monk. After Kassapa Buddha had preached the **Bhaddekaratta Sutta,** a certain monk had talked about it to Lomasakaṅgiya, who, unable to understand it, said, " May I, in the future, be able to teach thee this sutta !" And the other answered " May I ask thee !"

In the present age, Lomasakaṅgiya was born in a Sākyan family of **Kapilavatthu,** while the other monk became the deva **Candana.**

Lomasakaṅgiya (so called because he was delicate and the soles of his feet were covered with hair[1]) did not go with the Sākyan young men who joined the Order. Noticing this, Candana appeared before him and questioned him on the Bhaddekaratta Sutta. Lomasakaṅgiya did not

[1] MA. ii. 961 says he was so called because he had only a little down on his body (*kāyassa īsakalomasākāratāya*).

know it, and Candana reminded him of his past wish. Lomasakaṅgiya, therefore, went to consult the Buddha, and, later, wished to join the Order. He was sent back to obtain his parents' consent. His mother, fearing for his health, would not agree, but he uttered a verse[2] which convinced her. After his ordination, he went into a forest, and, when his companions warned him against the cold, he repeated the verse, and, being devoted to meditation, soon won arahantship.[3]

According to the **Lomasakaṅgiya-Bhaddekaratta Sutta,**[4] Candana visited Lomasakaṅgiya in the **Nigrodhārāma** in Kapilavatthu, where he lived after his ordination, and questioned him on the Bhaddekaratta Sutta. When Lomasakaṅgiya again confessed his ignorance, Candana taught him the verses, and then the former packed his bedding and went to **Sāvatthi,** where the Buddha, at his request, taught him the Sutta.

In the time of **Vipassī Buddha,** he offered *nāga*-flowers to the Buddha.[5] See also **Lomasavaṅgīsa.**

[2] This verse is included in Thag. (vs. 27).

[3] ThagA. i. 84; the story given in Ap. ii. 504 f., both of the past and the present, differs in several details.

[4] M. iii. 199 f.; *cf.* Ap. ii. 505, according to which, it was this sutta which led to his becoming an arahant.

[5] ThagA. i. 84; Ap. ii. 504; *cf.* Ap. ii. 450 (**Nāgapupphiya**); it is these latter Apadāna verses which are quoted in ThagA.

Lomasakaṅgiya-Bhaddekaratta Sutta.—The **Bhaddekaratta Sutta** (*q.v.*) as it was preached to **Lomasakaṅgiya** (*q.v.*).

Lomasakassapa.—The Bodhisatta born as an ascetic. See the **Lomasakassapa Jātaka.**

Lomasakassapa Jātaka (No. 433).—The Bodhisatta was once born as **Kassapa,** son of the chaplain to the king of Benares. He and the king's son shared a teacher and became friends. When the prince became king, Kassapa, having no desire for power, left him and became an ascetic. Because of the thick hair on his body, men called him **Lomasakassapa. Sakka** grew frightened of Kassapa's power, and, wishing to destroy it, appeared before the king at midnight and suggested to him that if he could persuade Kassapa to offer a sacrifice of slain beasts, he should be king over all India. The king, therefore, sent his minister, **Sayha,** to fetch Kassapa to him. When Kassapa heard of the proposal he refused to go, but Sakka appeared again before the king and said that if the king's daughter, **Candavatī,** were offered as reward, Kassapa would come. This proposal was agreed to, and Kassapa, tempted by the princess's beauty, agreed to come. The people gathered at the place of sacrifice and tried to dissuade Kassapa from slaying the animals, but he refused to listen. Many beasts were slain, and as he raised his sword to cut off the head of the royal elephant the latter raised a cry in which all the animals joined. Roused by this uproar, Kassapa remembered his asceticism and was filled with remorse. He admonished the king, and, sitting cross-legged in the air, developed transcendental power, which enabled him to fly through the air.

The story was related to a passion-tossed monk. Sayha is identified with **Sariputta.**[1]

[1] J. iii. 514 ff.; the story forms one of the dilemmas of the Milindapañha, p. 219. There Kassapa is stated to have performed the *Vājapeyya* sacrifice.

Lomasanāga.—A monk of Ceylon who lived in the *Padhānaghara* in the **Piyanguguhā** on **Cetiyapabbata.** He is given as an example of a monk who did not abandon his meditations in spite of extreme cold or heat.[1]

[1] MA. i. 65.

Lomasa-Vaṅgīsa.—The Saṃyutta Nikāya mentions an interview between an Elder of this name and the Sākyan **Mahānāma.** Mahānāma asks the Elder if the learner's way of life is identical with that of the Tathāgata. Vaṅgīsa answers that it is not so; learners only abandon the five hindrances; arahants have completely destroyed them from the root.

The interview took place in the **Nigrodhārāma** at **Kapilavatthu.** The name Lomasavaṅgīsa is, probably, a wrong or variant reading for **Lomasakaṅgiya** (*q.v.*).[1]

[1] S. v. 327 f.

Lomahaṃsa.—A **Pacceka Buddha,** mentioned in a nominal list.[1]

[1] M. iii. 70; ApA. i. 107.

Lomahaṃsa Jātaka (No. 94).—The Bodhisatta once became an **Ājīvaka** and practised all manner of austerities in order to test the efficiency of asceticism, enduring extremes of heat and cold. He realized his error as he lay dying, and was reborn in the deva-world.

The story was told in reference to **Sunakkhatta,** who, having left the Order and joined **Korakkhattiya,** went about **Vesāli,** vilifying the Buddha and declaring that his doctrines did not lead to the destruction of suffering. When Sāriputta reported this to the Buhda, the Buddha declared that he had tested the efficacy of asceticism ninety kappas ago and had found it wanting.[1]

[1] J. i. 389-91.

The story is also referred to in the **Cariyāpiṭaka**[2] as the **Mahālomahaṃsacariyā,** where it exemplifies the practice of *upekkhā.*[3]

[2] iii. 15. [3] J. i. 47.

Lomahaṃsapariyāya.—Another name, given by the Buddha himself to the **Mahāsīhanāda Sutta**[1] (*q.v.*).

[1] M. i. 83.

Lola Jātaka (No. 274).—The story of the Bodhisatta born as a pigeon and of his friendship with a greedy crow. The story is practically the same as that of the **Kapota Jātaka** (No. 42) (*q.v.*), and was related in reference to a greedy monk who was reported to the Buddha. The crow is identified with the monk.[1]

[1] J. ii. 361 ff.

Lolā.—A **Paribbājikā,** sister of **Saccaka** (*q.v.*).[1] See also the **Cullakāliṅga Jātaka.** After the discussion which she and her sisters had with **Sāriputta,** in which they were defeated, she joined the Order with the others and became an arahant.[2]

[1] J. iii. 1. [2] MA. i. 450 f.

Losaka Jātaka (No. 41).—In the time of **Kassapa Buddha** there lived a monk who was maintained by a rich man of the district. Into the monastery belonging to this rich man there came one day an arahant, and the former, liking his appearance, asked him to stay in the monastery, promising to look after him. The arahant agreed, but the incumbent of the monastery grew jealous and told their patron that the arahant was lazy and good for nothing. Some food sent by the patron for the arahant the incumbent threw into the embers. The arahant, reading his thoughts, left and went elsewhere. The monk was seized with remorse and was reborn in hell. In five hundred successive births he was a **Yakkha,** with never enough to eat; during a further five hundred births he was a dog. Then he was born, under the name of **Mittavindaka,** in a poor family in **Kāsi.** Because of him, dire misfortune befell the family, and he was driven out. In Benares he became a charity scholar under the Bodhisatta, who was a teacher there, but he was so quarrelsome that he was sent away. He married a poor woman and had two children. For a while he was a teacher, but the village in which he lived earned the king's displeasure seven times, their houses caught fire and the water dried up. Having discovered the cause, the villagers drove out Mittavindaka and his family. In a haunted forest the wife and children were eaten up by demons.

In his wanderings Mittavindaka came to a coastal village, **Gambhīra,** where he took service in a ship. On the seventh day of the voyage the ship suddenly stopped sailing. Lots were cast, and seven times the lot fell on Mittavindaka, so they put him on a raft and lowered him overboard. He was cast ashore on an island where lived four *vimāna*-petas in palaces of crystal, and he enjoyed happiness with them for seven days. From there he went to an island where lived eight goddesses in palaces of silver, thence to another where lived sixteen in palaces of jewels, thence to another still where lived thirty-two in palaces of gold. In each he stayed seven days. From the last he went to an island of ogres. There he seized an ogress wandering about in the shape of a goat, and, when she kicked him, he was hurled into the dry moat of Benares. There goatherds were keeping watch for thieves, and when Mittavindaka seized a goat, hoping to be kicked back to his original place, he was caught. As he was being led away, the Bodhisatta saw and recognized him and persuaded the goatherds to allow him to have him as a slave.

The story was told in reference to **Losaka-Tissa,** with whom Mittavindaka is identified.[1]

[1] J. i. 234-46.

Losaka-Tissa Thera.—He was the son of a fisherman of **Kosala.** In his village lived one thousand families, and on the day of his conception they all had to starve and various misfortunes gradually befell them. By a process of exclusion, they discovered that their misfortunes were due to Losaka's family, and therefore drove them out. As soon as Losaka could walk, his mother put a potsherd into his hand and sent him to beg. He wandered about uncared for, picking up lumps of rice like a crow. One day, when he was seven years old, **Sāriputta** saw him and, feeling pity for him, ordained him. But he was always unlucky; wherever he went, begging for alms, he received but little and never had a real meal. In due course he became an arahant, and when the time came for him to die Sāriputta determined that he should have a proper meal. He went with Losaka to **Sāvatthi,** but no one would even notice them. He then took Losaka back to the monastery and, having collected food himself, sent it to Losaka, but the messengers entrusted with it ate it all themselves. It was afternoon when Sāriputta discovered this; he therefore went to the king's palace and, having obtained a bowl filled with *catumadhura* (honey, ghee, butter and sugar), took it to Losaka and asked him to eat out of the bowl as he (Sāriputta) held it, in case the food should disappear. That night Losaka died, and a shrine was erected over his ashes.[1] When the Buddha was asked why Losaka was so unlucky, he related the **Losaka Jātaka** (*q.v.*). Losaka is identified with **Mittavindaka** of that story.

[1] J. i. 234 f.

Lohakumbha, Lohakumbhī, Lohitakumbhiya.—A **Niraya.** Beings born there suffer from excessive heat.[1] The Niraya extends under the whole of the earth and is four *nahutas* and one hundred thousand *yojanas* in depth. It is like a cauldron filled up to the brim with molten metal.[2]

It is said[3] that when **Kālāsoka** attempted to extend his patronage to the **Vajjiputtaka** monks, the devas frightened him with a dream that he had been cast into Lohakumbhī. See also the **Lohakumbhi Jātaka.**

[1] SNA. i. 59; J. iii. 22; v. 269. [2] SNA. ii. 480. [3] Mhv. iv. 38.

Lohakumbhi Jataka (No. 314).—The Bodhisatta was once an ascetic of great power. The king of Benares, having heard at night four sounds—*du, sa, na, so*—uttered by four beings who dwelt in hell, was greatly frightened. When he consulted his *purohita,* the latter ordained a fourfold sacrifice. The Bodhisatta, seeing the fate that lay in wait for numerous creatures, went to the king's park and there, with the help of the *purohita's* chief disciple—not himself in favour of the sacrifice—explained to the king the meaning of the sounds and had the sacrificial animals released. The *purohita's* disciple is identified with **Sāriputta.**

The story was told in reference to **Pasenadi,** who one night heard four syllables uttered by four inhabitants of hell. These had once been nobles of Sāvatthi, guilty of adultery. After death they were born in four iron cauldrons. After sixty thousand years they had gradually come to the top of these cauldrons and had uttered these syllables in their attempt to proclaim their misery. The king, very frightened, consulted his priests, who ordered a sacrifice. But **Mallikā** intervened and sent the king to see the Buddha, who explained the matter and allayed the king's fears.[1]

[1] J. iii. 43-8; the stories, both of the past and present, appear also at DhA. ii. 5 ff. and PvA. 279 ff. In both places the introductory story gives greater details. Pasenadi heard the sounds while lying sleepless, because he contemplated putting a helpless man to death in order to obtain his beautiful wife. There are also other differences in the two accounts. For details see Burlinghame: *Buddhist Legends* ii. 100, n. 1.

Lohadvāra.—A monastery in Ceylon, built by King **Mahānāma.**[1]

[1] Cv. xxxvii. 212.

Lohapāsāda.—A building at **Anurādhapura,** forming the *uposatha*-hall of the **Mahāvihāra.** It was originally built by **Devānampiyatissa,**[1] but it was then a small building erected only to round off the form of Mahāvihāra (*vihāraparipuṇṇamattasādhakaṃ*).[2] Later, **Duṭṭhagāmaṇi** pulled it down and erected on its site a nine-storeyed building, one hundred cubits square and high, with one hundred rooms on each storey. The building was planned according to a sketch of the **Ambalaṭṭhikapāsāda**[3] in **Biraṇī's** palace which eight arahants obtained from the deva-world. The building was roofed with copper plates, hence its name. The nine storeys were occupied by monks, according to their various attainments, the last four storeys being reserved for arahants. In the centre of the hall was a seat made in the shape of **Vessavaṇa's Nārīvāhana** chariot.[4] The building was visible out at sea to a distance of one league.[5] Once Duṭṭhagāmaṇi attempted to preach in the assembly-hall of the Lohapāsāda, but he was too nervous to proceed. Realizing then how difficult was the task of preachers, he endowed largesses for them in every vihāra.[6] Duṭṭhagāmaṇi had always a great fondness for the Lohapāsāda, and as he lay dying he managed to have a last view of it.[7] Thirty crores were spent on its construction; in **Saddhātissa's** day it caught fire from a lamp, and he rebuilt it in seven storeys at a cost of nine millions.[8]

Khallāṭanāga built thirty-two other pāsādas round the Lohapāsāda for its ornamentation,[9] while **Bhātikābhaya** carried out various repairs to the building,[10] and **Āmaṇḍagāmaṇī** added an inner courtyard and a verandah (*ājira*).[11] **Sirināga I.** rebuilt it in five storeys,[12] **Abhayanāga** built a pavilion in the courtyard and **Goṭhābhaya** had the pillars renewed.[13] He evidently started to rebuild the structure, because we are told[14] that, after his death, his son **Jeṭṭhatissa** completed up to seven storeys the Lohapāsāda which had been left unfinished (*vippakata*) by his father. The building was worth one crore, and Jeṭṭhatissa offered to it a jewel worth sixty thousand, after which he renamed it **Maṇipāsāda.** Afterwards **Soṇa,** a minister of his brother, the renegade king **Mahānāma,** acting on the advice of heretical monks led by **Saṅghamitta,** destroyed the pāsāda and carried away its wealth to enrich **Abhayagiri-vihāra.**[15]

Mahānāma's son, **Sirimeghavaṇṇa,** had the pāsāda restored to its

[1] See Mhv. xv. 205.
[2] MṬ. 364.
[3] The actual **Ambalaṭṭhikā** (*q.v.*) of the Lohapāsāda was to the east of the building (DA. ii. 635).
[4] For details see Mhv. xxvii. 1 ff.
[5] MṬ. 505.
[6] Mhv. xxxii. 42 ff.
[7] *Ibid.*, 9.
[8] *Ibid.*, xxxiii. 6.
[9] Mhv. xxxii. 30.
[10] *Ibid.*, xxxiv. 39.
[11] *Ibid.*, xxxv. 3.
[12] *Ibid.*, xxxvi. 25, 52.
[13] *Ibid.*, 102.
[14] *Ibid.*, xxxvi. 124 f.
[15] *Ibid.*, xxxvii. 10 f., 59.

original form,[16] and, later, **Dhātusena** renovated it,[17] as did **Aggabodhi I.**, who distributed the three garments to thrity-six thousand monks at the festival of dedication and assigned a village to provide for its protection.[18] His successor, **Aggabodhi II.**, deposited in the pāsāda the Buddha's right collar-bone, which relic was later transferred to the **Thūpārāma.**[19] In the reign of **Aggabodhi IV.**, the ruler of **Malaya** repaired the central pinnacle,[20] while **Mānavamma** provided a new roof.[21] **Sena II.** completely restored the pāsāda and placed in it an image of the Buddha in gold mosaic. The building was evidently not in use at the time, but he provided for its upkeep and assigned villages for its protection, and decreed that thirty-two monks should be in constant residence.[22] **Sena IV.** was in the habit of preaching in the Lohapāsāda periodical sermons to the monks[23] which were based on the suttas, but, after his death, the place again fell into disrepair and was destroyed by the **Coḷas. Parakkamabāhu I.** restored it once again,[24] but it was soon after pillaged again and fell into ruin, in which state it remains to this day. There are now sixteen hundred monolithic stone columns (the same number as in the time of Parakkamabāhu I.), which evidently formed the framework of the lowest storey.

Frequent mention is made in the books of sermons preached in the lowest storey of the Lohapāsāda, at which very large numbers were present. Once, when **Ambapāsāṇavāsī Cittagutta** preached the **Rathavinita Sutta,** there were twelve thousand monks and one thousand nuns.[25] On another occasion, **Bhātikābhaya** described the contents of the Relic-chamber of the **Mahā Thūpa** to all the monks of the Mahāvihāra assembled in the Lohapāsāda.[26]

Buddhaghosa says[27] that, up to his day, it was customary for all the monks of Ceylon, who lived to the north of the **Mahāvālukanadi,** to assemble in the Lohapāsāda twice a year, on the first and last days of the *vassa*, while those to the south of the river assembled at the **Tissamahāvihāra.** When disputes arose as to the interpretation of various rules or teachings, the decision was often announced by a teacher of repute from the lowest storey of the Lohapāsāda.[28]

The hood of the Nāga-king **Mucalinda** was of the same size as the storehouse (*bhaṇḍāgāragabbha*) of the Lohapāsāda.[29] A mass of rock, as big as the seventh storey of the Lohapāsāda, if dropped from the Brahmaworld, would take four months to reach the earth.[30]

[16] Mhv. xxxvii. 62.
[17] *Ibid.*, xxxviii. 54.
[18] *Ibid.*, xlii. 20.
[19] *Ibid.*, 53, 59.
[20] *Ibid.*, xlvi. 30.
[21] *Ibid.*, xlvii. 65.
[22] *Ibid.*, li. 69 f.
[23] *Ibid.*, liv. 4.
[24] *Ibid.*, lxxviii. 102.
[25] MṬ. 552 f.
[26] *Ibid.*, 555.
[27] DA. ii. 581.
[28] DA. ii. 442, 514.
[29] UdA. 101.
[30] DA. ii. 678.

Loharūpa.—The name given to an image of the Buddha, one of several in **Anurādhapura.**[1]

[1] Cv. xlix. 17.

1. **Lohicca.**—A brahmin of **Makkarakaṭa** in **Avanti.** Once when **Mahā Kaccāna** was living there in a forest hut, a number of **Lohicca's** pupils came there and began abusing the monks, calling them shavelings, menials, etc. Kaccāna talked to them, telling them how degenerate were the brahmins, differing from brahmins of old, the present ones being backsliders, mere reciters, doing things for trifling gains. The pupils went back to Lohicca and told him this. Lohicca visited Kaccāna and discussed with him these statements, and, at the end of the talk, declared himself Kaccāna's follower.[1]

[1] S. iv. 117 ff.

2. **Lohicca.**—A brahmin of **Sālāvatikā.** He once conceived the idea that a *samaṇa* or recluse who had reached a good state of mind should tell no one else of it, lest he should entangle himself in new bonds. When the Buddha went to Sālāvatikā Lohicca sent the barber, **Bhesikā,** to invite the Buddha and the monks in his name. The Buddha accepted the invitation, and, at the end of the meal, questioned Lohicca regarding his views. At the end of the discussion Lohicca became the Buddha's follower.[1]

[1] D. i. 224 ff.

1. **Lohicca Sutta.**—The account of the visit of **Lohicca** (1) (*q.v.*) of **Makkarakaṭa** to **Mahā Kaccāna.**[1]

[1] S. iv. 117 ff.

2. **Lohicca Sutta.**—The twelfth sutta of the **Dīgha Nikāya,** containing the discussion between the Buddha and **Lohicca** of **Sālāvatikā.** The underlying argument of the sutta is that everyone should be allowed to learn; that everyone possessing certain attainments should be allowed to teach; but that if he does teach, he should teach all and to all, keeping nothing back, shutting no one out. But no man should take upon himself to teach unless he has first taught himself, and has acquired the faculty of imparting to others the truth he has gained himself.[1]

[1] D. i. 224 ff.

Lohitaka.—One of the **Chabbaggiyā** (*q.v.*). The followers of **Lohitaka** and **Paṇḍu** were not as undesirable as the other heretics.[1] See *s.v.* **Paṇḍu-Lohitakā.**

[1] Sp. iii. 4, 6.

Lohitavāsī.—A class of devas present at the preaching of the **Mahāsamaya Sutta.**[1]

[1] D. ii. 260.

Lohitavāhakhaṇḍa.—The field of battle on which **Canda,** son of **Pandula,** slew the five brothers of **Suvaṇṇapālī.**[1]

[1] Mhv. x. 43.

V.

Vaṃsa Sutta.—See **Ariyavaṃsa Sutta.**

Vaṃatthappakāsinī.—The Commentary on the **Mahāvaṃsa,** traditionally ascribed to a Thera named **Mahānāma,** and probably written about the ninth century.[1]

[1] For details see P.T.S. edition, Introd.

Vaṃsabhūmi, Vaṃsaraṭṭha.—The country of the **Vaṃsā** (*q.v.*).

Vaṃsarājā.—See **Udena.**

Vaṃsā.—The Vaṃsas and their country. It lay to the south of **Kosala,** and its capital was **Kosambī**[1] on the **Yamunā. Udena,** son of **Parantapa,** also called **Vaṃsarājā,**[2] was its king in the time of the Buddha. **Avanti** lay to the south of the Vaṃsa country. The Vaṃsā were also called **Vatsā.**[3] The country formed one of the sixteen **Mahājanapadā** (*q.v.*). The district of **Bhagga,** in which was **Suṃsumāragiri,** seems to have been subject to the Vaṃsā in the Buddha's time, for we find Udena's son, **Bodhi,** living there.[4] In nominal lists[5] the Vaṃsā are generally mentioned with the **Ceti.**

[1] *E.g.*, J. iv. 28.
[2] *E.g.*, *ibid.*, 370, 390.
[3] Bud. India, 3, 27; Mtu. i. 34.
[4] J. iii. 157, also Mahābhārata ii. 30, 10 f.
[5] *E.g.*, D. ii. 200.

Vaka Jātaka (No. 300).—A wolf once lived on a rock near the Ganges. The winter floods came and surrounded the rock, and the wolf, unable to escape, decided to keep the holy day. The Bodhisatta, who was **Sakka,** appeared before him in the guise of a he-goat, and the wolf, forgetting his holy day, chased him round and round the rock. Finding he could not succeed in catching him, the wolf expressed his joy that his holy day had not been violated! Sakka, hovering above him, rebuked him for his weakness.

The story was related in reference to some monks, followers of **Upasena** (**Vaṅgantaputta**) (*q.v.*). Being aware of the permission granted by the Buddha to the monks who practised the thirteen *dhutaṅgas* to visit him even during his periods of solitude, these monks would practise them for a short while and then visit him. But, the visit over, they would at once throw off their rag-robes and don other garments. The Buddha discovered this and related the Jātaka.[1]

[1] J. ii. 449 ff.; *cp.* Vin. iii. 231 f., where no mention is made of the Jātaka.

1. **Vakkali Thera.**—He belonged to a brahmin family of **Sāvatthi** and became proficient in the three Vedas. After he once saw the Buddha he could never tire of looking at him, and followed him about. In order to be closer to him he became a monk, and spent all his time, apart from meals and bathing, in contemplating the Buddha's person. One day the Buddha said to him, " The sight of my foul body is useless; he who sees the Dhamma, he it is that seeth me " (*yo kho dhammaṃ passati so maṃ passati; yo maṃ passati so dhammaṃ passati*).[1] But even then Vakkali would not leave the Buddha till, on the last day of the rains, the Buddha commanded him to depart. Greatly grieved, Vakkali sought the precipices of **Gijjhakūṭa.** The Buddha, aware of this, appeared before him and uttered a stanza; then stretching out his hand, he said: " Come, monk." Filled with joy, Vakkali rose in the air pondering on the Buddha's words and realized arahantship.[2]

According to the Theragāthā Commentary,[3] when Vakkali was dismissed by the Buddha he lived on Gijjhakūṭa, practising meditation, but could not attain insight because of his emotional nature (*saddhā*). The Buddha then gave him a special exercise, but neither could he achieve this, and, from lack of food, he suffered from cramp. The Buddha visited him and uttered a verse to encourage him. Vakkali spoke four verses[4] in reply, and, conjuring up insight, won arahantship. Later, in the assembly of the monks, the Buddha declared him foremost among those of implicit faith (*saddhādhimuttānaṃ*).[5] In the **Pārāyanavagga**[6] the

[1] *Cp.* Itv. sec. 92.

[2] AA. i. 140 f.; the Apadāna account (Ap. ii. 465 f.) is similar. It says that the Buddha spoke to him from the foot of the rock. Vakkali jumped down to meet the Buddha, a depth of many cubits, but he alighted unhurt. It was on this occasion that the Buddha declared his eminence among those of implicit faith; also DhA. iv. 118 f. The DhA. reports three verses uttered by the Buddha in which he assures Vakkali that he will help him and look after him.

[3] ThagA. i. 420.

[4] These are included in Thag, vss. 350-4.

[5] *cp.* A. i. 25; also Dvy. 49 and VibhA. 276; Vsm. i. 129.

[6] SN. vs. 1146.

Buddha is represented as holding Vakkali up to **Piṅgiya** as an example of one who won emancipation through faith.

The **Saṃyutta** account[7] gives more details and differs in some respects from the above. There, Vakkali fell ill while on his way to visit the Buddha at **Rājagaha,** and was carried in a litter to a potter's shed in Rājagaha. There, at his request, the Buddha visited him and comforted him. He questioned Vakkali, who assured him that he had no cause to reprove himself with regard to morals (*sīlato*); his only worry was that he had not been able to see the Buddha earlier. The Buddha told him that seeing the Dhamma was equivalent to seeing him, and because Vakkali had realized the Dhamma, there would be no hereafter for him. After the Buddha had left, Vakkali asked his attendants to take him to **Kālasilā** on **Isigili.** The Buddha was on Gijjhakūṭa and was told by two devas that Vakkali was about to " obtain release." The Buddha sent word to him: " Fear not, Vakkali, your dying will not be evil." Vakkali rose from his bed to receive the Buddha's message, and sending word to the Buddha that he had no desire or love for the body or the other *khandhas,* he drew a knife and killed himself. The Buddha went to see his body, and declared that he had obtained Nibbāna and that **Māra's** attempt to find the consciousness of Vakkali would prove useless.

The Commentary adds that Vakkali was conceited and blind to his remaining faults. He thought he was a *khīṇāsava,* and that he might rid himself of bodily pains by death. However, the stab with the knife caused him such pain that at the moment of dying he realized his *puthujjana* state, and, putting forth great effort, attained arahantship.

His resolve to become chief among the *saddhādhimuttas* had been made in the time of **Padumuttara Buddha,** when he saw a monk also named Vakkali similarly honoured by the Buddha.[8]

[7] S. iii. 119 ff.; SA. ii. 229.

[8] Ap. ii. 465 f.; AA. i. 140.

2. **Vakkali.**—A monk in the time of **Padumuttara Buddha,** declared chief of those having implicit faith.[1]

[1] ThagA. i. 422; Ap. ii. 466.

Vakkali Sutta.—The account, given in the **Saṃyutta Nikāya,**[1] of the attainment of arahantship and death of **Vakkali** (1) (*q.v.*).

[1] S. iii. 119 ff.

Vakkula.—See **Bakkula.**

Vaggumudā.—A river in the **Vajji** country (*v.l.* **Vattamudā**). On its banks lived **Yasoja** and his five hundred companions.[1]

[1] Ud. iii. 3; ThagA. i. 357.

Vaggamudātiriyā.—Monks who lived on the banks of the **Vaggumudā**, evidently distinct from **Yasoja** (*q.v.*) and his companions. When there was scarcity of food in the **Vajji** country these monks went about praising each other's superhuman qualities so that the laymen, deceived by their pretensions, kept them in great luxury. When the Buddha discovered this, he rebuked them strongly and laid down the rules concerning the fourth **Pārājikā** offence.[1]

[1] Vin. iii. 87 ff.; Sp. ii. 481 ff.; DhA. iii. 480.

Vaṅka.—A king of **Sāvatthi.** For his story see the **Ghata Jātaka** (No. 355). He is identified with **Ānanda.**[1]

[1] J. iii. 170.

Vaṅkaka.—The name of Mount **Vepulla** in the time of **Koṇāgamana Buddha.**[1]

[1] S. ii. 191.

Vaṅkagiri, Vaṅkapabbata, Vaṅkatapabbata.—A mountain in **Himavā** to which **Vessantara** was banished with his family. It was thirty leagues from the **Ceta** country and sixty leagues from **Jetuttara,** the way passing through **Suvaṇṇagiritāla,** over the river **Kontimāra,** through **Arañjaragiri, Dunniviṭṭha,** northwards beyond **Gandhamādana,** over Mt. **Vipula,** across the **Ketumatī** River, through Mount **Nālika** and the **Mucalinda** Lake.[1] Vessantara and his family lived there in a hermitage built by **Vissakamma** at **Sakka's** suggestion.[2] **Sañjaya** later built a road, eight usabhas wide, from Jetuttara to Vaṅka.[3]

[1] Cyp. i. 9; J. vi. 514, 518, 519. [2] *Ibid.*, 520. [3] *Ibid.*, 580.

Vaṅkanāsika-Tissa.—King of Ceylon (171-4 A.C.). He was the son of **Vasabha** and his wife was the daughter of King **Subha.** He built the **Mahāmaṅgala-vihāra,** and his wife built the **Mātu-vihāra** in honour of a monk who had given her his blessing. Vaṅkanāsika's son was **Gajabāhukagāmaṇī.**[1]

[1] Mhv. xxxv. 108 ff.; Dpv. xxii. 12, 27 f.

Vaṅkahāra, Vaṅgahāra.—A district in India, the birthplace of the Therī **Cāpā.**[1] It was probably to the south of **Magadha.**[2] **Upaka** lived

[1] ThigA. 220; but see SNA. i. 259, where the *janapada* is called Vaṅga, not Vaṅkahāra. [2] *Sisters.* 132 f.

there for some time, first as an **Ājīvaka** and later as Cāpā's husband. The place is said to have been infested with fierce flies.[3]

[3] MA. i. 388.

Vaṅkāvaṭṭakagalla.—A monastery in Ceylon, built by **Mahācūli-Mahātissa.**[1]

[1] Mhv. xxxiv. 9.

Vaṅga, Vaṅgā.—The name of a people and their country, the modern Bengal. It is nowhere mentioned in the four Nikāyas, nor included among the **Mahājanapadas.** The mother of **Sīhabāhu** and **Sīhasīvalī** was a Vaṅga princess, the daughter of the Vaṅga king who had married the daughter of the king of **Kaliṅga.**[1] The Milinda[2] mentions Vaṅga as a trading-place to be reached by sea.

[1] Mhv. vi. 1 ff.; Dpv. ix. 2. [2] p. 359.

Vaṅganta.—A brahmin, father of **Sāriputta**[1] (*q.v.*) and husband of **Rūpasārī.**[2] The brahmin **Mahāsena** was his friend, and the son of another friend became Sāriputta's attendant.[3] See **Kiṃsīla Sutta.**

[1] SNA. i. 331; UdA. 266. [2] Ap. i. 102. [3] DhA. ii. 84.

Vaṅgantaputta.—The epithet applied to **Sāriputta's** brother **Upasena** (*q.v.*), to distinguish him from others of the same name.

Vaṅgīsa Thera.—He belonged to a brahmin family and was proficient in the Vedas. He gained repute by tapping on skulls with his finger-nail and telling thereby where the owners of the skull were reborn. During three years he thus gained much money. Then, in spite of the protests of his colleagues, he went to see the Buddha,[1] who gave him the skull of an arahant. Vaṅgīsa could make nothing of this and joined the Order to learn its secret. He was ordained by **Nigrodhakappa,** and, meditating on the thirty-two constituents of the body, he won arahantship. He then visited the Buddha again and praised him in various verses, full of similes and metaphors. This brought him reputation as a poet (*Kāvya-citta* or *Kāveyyamatta*). Later the Buddha declared him foremost among those pre-eminent in ready expression (*paṭibhānavantānaṃ*). His resolve to attain to this position was made in the time of **Padumuttara Buddha.**[2]

The Theragāthā[3] contains numerous verses spoken by him on various

[1] According to the Apadāna, he saw Sāriputta first and learnt from him about the Buddha.

[2] A. i. 24; Dpv. iv. 4; ThagA. ii. 192 ff.; AA. i. 149 ff.; DhA. iv. 226 f.; SNA. i. 345 f.; Ap. ii. 495 ff.

[3] Thag. vss. 1208-79; most of these are repeated at S. i. 185 ff.

occasions—some of them (1209-18) uttered about himself, his attempts to suppress desires excited by the sight of gaily dressed women[4]; others (1219-22) were self-admonitions against conceit because of his facility of speech; some were spoken in praise of sermons preached by the Buddha —*e.g.*, the **Subhāsita Sutta** (1227-30), a sutta on Nibbāna (1238-45), and a sutta preached at the *Pavāraṇa* ceremony (1234-7). Several verses were in praise of his colleagues—*e.g.* **Sāriputta** (1231-3), **Aññā-Koṇḍañña** (1246-8), and **Moggallāna** (1249-51). One of Vaṅgīsa's long poems (vvs. 1263-74) is addressed to the Buddha, questioning him as to the destiny of his (Vaṅgīsa's) teacher Nigrodhakappa. The Commentary[5] explains that when Nigrodhakappa died Vaṅgīsa was absent and wished to be assured by the Buddha that his teacher had reached Nibbāna. But the poem is more than a question. It is really a eulogy of the Buddha. Another verse (1252) describes the Buddha as he sat surrounded by his monks on the banks of the **Gaggarā** at **Campā.**

The Saṃyutta[6] devotes one whole section to Vaṅgīsa, dealing with the incidents connected with his life and giving poems made by him on these occasions. The Milinda[7] also contains a poem attributed to Vaṅgīsa in praise of the Buddha. According to the Apadāna,[8] he was called Vaṅgīsa, both because he was born in Vaṅga and also because he was master of the spoken word (*vacana*). See also **Vaṅgīsa Sutta** and **Subhāsita Sutta.**

[4] *Cf.* S. i. 185; on one such occasion, he confessed his disaffection to **Ānanda,** who admonished him.

[5] ThagA. ii. 211.

[6] S. i. 185 ff.; SA. i. 207 ff.

[7] p. 390.

[8] Ap. ii. 497 (vs. 27).

1. **Vaṅgīsa Sutta.**—Preached by the Buddha at **Aggāḷava-cetiya. Vaṅgīsa's** teacher, **Nigrodhakappa,** had just died there, and Vaṅgīsa asks the Buddha if he had attained Nibbāna. Vaṅgīsa's question is really a poem in itself, containing ten verses, in praise of the Buddha. The Buddha says that Kappa has won Nibbāna, because he had severed all the bonds of **Māra.** Vaṅgīsa then declares that Kappa attained that state because he followed the Buddha's teaching.[1]

In the Commentary[2] the sutta is called **Nigrodhakappa Sutta.**

[1] SN. pp. 59 ff.; the verses of the sutta are included in the Theragāthā (1263-79).

[2] SNA. i. 345.

2. **Vaṅgīsa Sutta.**—A set of ten verses, spoken by **Vaṅgīsa** at **Jetavana,** soon after winning arahantship, as he sat experiencing the bliss of emancipation. He congratulates himself on having become a disciple of the Buddha.[1]

[1] S. i. 196; the verses are included in Thag. 1253-62.

Vaṅgīsa-Thera Vatthu.—The story of **Vaṅgīsa's** conversion, his entry into the Order, and his attainment of arahantship.[1]

[1] DhA. iv. 226 f.

Vaṅgīsa-Thera Saṃyutta.—The eigth section of the **Saṃyutta Nikāya,**[1] dealing with incidents connected with **Vaṅgīsa Thera** (*q.v.*).

[1] S. i. 185-96.

Vaṅguttara.—A mountain in Ceylon on which was built the **Pācīna-pabbata-vihāra** by **Sūratissa.**[1] The Mahāvaṃsa Ṭīkā[2] explains that Vaṅguttara was at the foot of **Ekadvārikapabbata.**

[1] Mhv. xxi. 5. [2] p. 424.

Vacana Sutta.—See **Vanaropa Sutta.**

Vacanatthajoti, Vacanatthajotikā.—A glossary on the **Vuttodaya** by **Vepullabuddhi Thera.**[1]

[1] Sās., p. 75; Bode, *op. cit.*, 28, n. 5.

Vacāvāṭaka.—A village in the **Merukandara** district, mentioned in the account of the campaigns of **Parakkamabāhu I.**[1]

[1] Cv. lxx. 282, 295.

Vaccavācaka.—See **Vācavācaka.**

1. **Vaccha.**—A brahmin ascetic of long ago, near whose hut lived some Kinnaras. A spider used to weave his web around them, crack their heads and drink their blood. The Kinnaras sought Vaccha's assistance, but Vaccha refused to kill the spider, till tempted by the offer of a Kinnara-maiden named **Rathavatī** as his servant. Vaccha killed the spider and lived with Rathavatī as his wife.

This story was among those related by **Mahosadha's** parrot **Māṭhara** to the mynah-bird of the **Pañcāla** king's palace, to show her that in love there is no unlikeness—a man may well mate with a Kinnari, a parrot with a mynah.[1]

[1] J. vi. 422.

2. **Vaccha.**—See **Kisavaccha, Nandavaccha, Pilindavaccha, Tiriṭa-vaccha, Vacchagotta,** etc. Also **Ukkhepakatavaccha** and the two **Vanavacchas.**

Vaccha or **Bandha Sutta.**—A conversation between the Buddha and **Vacchagotta Paribbājaka.** Vacchagotta asks, and the Buddha explains, why, unlike the various Paribbājakas, the Buddha does not say whether the world is eternal or not, or make various similar statements. Vacchagotta puts the same question to **Moggallāna** and receives the same answer. Vacchagotta expresses his admiration of the fact that teacher and pupil should agree so closely.[1]

[1] S. iv. 395 f.; *cp.* S. iii. 257 f.

1. **Vacchagotta.**—A **Paribbājaka,** who later became an arahant Thera. Several conversations he had with the Buddha are mentioned in the books. For details see the **Tevijja Vacchagotta°, Aggi Vacchagotta°, Mahā Vacchagotta°, Vaccha°** and **Vacchagotta Suttas.** Some of these suttas are quoted in the **Kathāvatthu.**[1] The **Saṃyutta Nikāya**[2] contains a whole section on **Vacchagotta;** his discussions were chiefly concerned with such mythical questions as to whether the world is eternal, the nature of life, the existence or otherwise of the Tathāgata after death, etc. The three Vacchagotta Suttas of the **Majjhima Nikāya** seem to contain the story of Vacchagotta's conversion, in due order: at the conclusion of the Tevijja-Vacchagotta (No. 72) it is merely stated that "the Paribbājaka Vacchagotta rejoiced in what the Blessed One has said." At the end of the next, the Aggi-Vacchagotta, he is mentioned as having accepted the Buddha as his teacher. In the third, the Mahā-Vacchagotta, he seeks ordination from the Buddha at **Rājagaha,** and receives it after the requisite probationary period of four months. He returns to the Buddha after two weeks and tells him that he has attained all that is to be attained by a non-arahant's understanding and asks for a further exposition of the Doctrine. The Buddha tells him to proceed to the study of calm and insight, whereby sixfold *abhiññā* may be acquired. Vacchagotta profits by the lesson and soon after becomes an arahant. He thereupon sends news of his attainment to the Buddha through some monks, and the Buddha says he has already heard the news from the devas.[3]

This story definitely identifies the Paribbājaka with the Thera of the same name, whose verse of ecstasy is included in the **Theragāthā.**[4] According to the Commentary,[5] he belonged to a rich brahmin family of the **Vaccha**-clan (Vacchagotta). His personal name is not given. He

[1] *E.g.*, p. 267, 505.

[2] S. iii. 257 ff.; see also S. iv. 391 ff., for several discussions of Vacchagotta with **Moggallāna, Ānanda** and **Sabhiya Kaccāna** on similar topics.

[3] M. i. 493-97.

[4] vs. 112.

[5] ThagA. i. 221.

became an expert in brahmin learning, but failing to find therein what he sought, he became a Paribbājaka, joining the Buddha's Order later.

In the time of **Vipassī Buddha** he was a householder of **Bandhumatī,** and one day, when the Buddha and his monks were invited to the king's palace, he swept the street along which the Buddha passed and set up a flag as decoration. As a result he was born, four kappas ago, as a rājā, **Sudhaja** by name. He is probably identical with **Vīthisammajjaka** of the Apadāna.[6]

[6] Ap. i. 177.

2. **Vacchagotta.**—A **Paribbājaka.** He is mentioned in the Aṅguttara Nikāya[1] as visiting the Buddha at **Venāgapura,** where he was at the head of the brahmins. He is possibly to be identified with **Vacchagotta** (1). In this context, however, he is called **Venāgapurika.** Vacchagotta (1) (*q.v.*) was a native of **Rājagaha,** but seems to have travelled widely, for we find him visiting the Buddha at **Vesāli,**[2] at **Sāvatthi,**[3] and at **Ñātikā,**[4] in addition to his visits to Rājagaha.[5] The Commentary,[6] moreover, explains Venāgapuraka by "*Venāgapuravāsī,*" which may mean that he merely lived at Venāgapura and was not necessarily a native of that place. Vacchagotta's question was as to how the Buddha looked so shining and his colour so clear? Was it because he slept on a luxurious bed? The Buddha answered that his bed was luxurious and comfortable, but from quite a different point of view. At the end of the discourse, Vacchagotta declares himself a follower of the Buddha.

[1] A. i. 180 f.
[2] M. i. 481.
[3] *Ibid.*, 483; S. iii. 257.
[4] S. iv. 401.
[5] M. i. 489.
[6] AA. i. 410.

3. **Vacchagotta.**—A brahmin of **Kapilavatthu,** father of **Vanavaccha Thera** (*q.v.*).[1]

[1] ThagA. i. 58.

Vacchagotta Sutta.—The **Paribbājaka Vacchagotta** asks the Buddha if it be true that the Buddha discourages the giving of alms to other than his own followers. The Buddha says that, in his eyes, even pot-scourings or dregs from cups thrown into a pool or cesspool, to feed the creatures living there, would be a source of merit. But gifts made to the good are more fruitful than those made to the wicked. The good are those who have abandoned lust, malevolence, sloth-and-torpor, excitement-and-flurry and doubt-and-wavering.[1]

[1] A. i. 160 f.

Vacchanakha.—The Bodhisatta born as a **Paribbājaka.** See the **Vacchanakha Jātaka.**

Vacchanakha Jātaka (No. 235).—The Bodhisatta was once born as **Vacchanakha,** an anchorite living in the **Himālaya,** and on one occasion, having gone to Benares for salt and seasoning, he stayed in the king's garden. A rich man saw him and, pleased with his looks, attended to his wants. A friendship soon grew up between them, and the rich man invited the hermit to give up his robes and share his wealth. But this offer the hermit refused, pointing out the disadvantages of household life.

The story was told in reference to an attempt of **Roja,** the **Malla,** friend of **Ānanda,** to tempt the latter back to the worldly life by offering him half his possessions. Roja is identified with the rich man of the story.[1]

[1] J. ii. 231 ff.

Vacchapāla Thera.—An arahant. He belonged to a rich brahmin family of **Rājagaha.** He witnessed the miracles performed by **Uruvela-Kassapa** and his self-submission to the Buddha when they visited **Bimbisāra** together, and marvelling thereat, entered the Order. Within a week he developed insight and became an arahant.

In the past he had been a brahmin, expert in brahmin-lore, and one day, while seeking a suitable person to whom he might give a large vessel of milk-rice left over from the sacrifice, he saw **Vipassī Buddha** and offered it to him. Forty-one kappas ago he became a king named **Buddha.**[1] He is probably identical with **Pāyāsadāyaka** of the Apadāna.[2]

[1] Thag. vs. 71; ThagA. i. 159 f. [2] Ap. i. 157.

Vacchāyana.—See **Pilotika.** Buddhaghosa says[1] this was the name of Pilotika's *gotta.*

[1] MA. i. 393.

Vajagaragiri-vihāra.—A monastery, probably in Ceylon, the residence of **Kāḷadeva Thera** (*q.v.*).[1]

[1] MA. i. 100.

1. **Vajira.**—A *senāpati* of **Dappula II.** He built **Kacchavāla-vihāra** for the **Paṃsukūlins.**[1]

[1] Cv. xlix. 80.

2. **Vajira.**—A minister of **Sena I.** He built for the monks a dwelling-house called **Vajirasenaka.**[1]

[1] Cv. l. 84.

3. **Vajira.**—A teacher who wrote a commentary to the work of **Jaṅghadāsaka.**[1]

[1] Gv. 74.

4. **Vajira.**—One of the seven **Yakkhas,** guardians of **Jotiya's** palace. He stood at the third gate and had a retinue of three thousand.[1]

[1] DhA. iv. 209.

Vajirakumārī, Vajirā.—Daughter of **Pasenadi.** When peace was established between Pasenadi and **Ajātasattu,** Pasenadi gave Vajirā in marriage to Ajātasattu, and gave, as part of her dowry, the village in Kāsi which had been the cause of their quarrel.[1] In the **Piyajātika Sutta**[2] she is called **Vajirī.** She was Pasenadi's only daughter.[3]

[1] J. ii. 404; iv. 343; DhA. iii. 266. [2] M. ii. 110. [3] MA. ii. 751.

Vajiragga.—A general of **Udaya II.** He helped in the subjugation of **Rohaṇa** and in the capture of the **Ādipāda Kittaggabodhi,** who had rebelled against the king.[1]

[1] Cv. li. 105, 118, 126.

Vajirapāṇi.—A **Yakkha.** It is said that whoever, even up to the third time of being asked, refuses to answer a reasonable question put by a Buddha, his head will split into pieces on the spot. It was Vajirapāṇi's duty to frighten such people by appearing before them in the sky, armed with a thunderbolt, which he was ready to hurl if necessary. He was visible only to the Buddha and the person in question. Two instances of this are given in the books—once in the case of **Ambaṭṭha,**[1] and again in that of **Saccaka Nigaṇṭhaputta.**[2] Buddhaghosa says[3] that Vajirapāṇi is identical with **Sakka,** and proceeds to describe the fierce appearance assumed by him on these occasions. This arrangement was made in fulfilment of a promise made by Sakka, in the presence of **Mahā Brahmā,** when the Buddha was reluctant to preach the Dhamma,[4] that if the Buddha would establish his rule of the Dhamma (*Dhammacakka*), Sakka would afford it the necessary protection. In some places,[5] **Vajirapāṇi's** conquest of the **Asuras** is alluded to, thus establishing his identity with Indra. See also **Vajirahattha.**

[1] D. i. 95; *cf.* the story in the **Ayakūṭa Jātaka.**

[2] M. i. 231.

[3] DA. i. 264; MA. i. 457; *cp.* Dvy. 130.

[4] See Vin. i. 5 f.

[5] *E.g.*, Cv. xcvi. 37; see also *J.R.A.S.* 1916, p. 733 f.

Vajirabāhu.—A **Yakkha** who, with four thousand others, kept guard at the fourth gate of **Jotiya's** palace.[1]

[1] DhA. iv. 209.

Vajirabuddhi.—See **Culla-Vajirabuddhi** and **Mahā-Vajirabuddhi.**

Vajirabuddhiṭīkā.—Also called **Vinayagandhi** or **Vinayagaṇṭhi.** A *ṭīkā* or explanation of difficult passages in the Vinaya Commentaries by **Mahāvajirabuddhi Thera** of Ceylon.[1]

[1] Gv. 60, 66.

Vajiravāpi.—A tank in Ceylon near which was a fortress, once occupied by **Gokaṇṇa.**[1]

[1] Cv. lxx. 72.

Vajiravutti.—See **Vajirā** (3).

Vajirasama.—Ninety-one kappas ago there were seven kings of this name, all previous births of **Sucidāyaka Thera.**[1] *v.l.* **Vajirāsakha.**

[1] Ap. i. 135.

Vajirasena.—A building in the **Abhayagiri-vihāra,** erected by **Vajira,** minister of **Sena I.**[1]

[1] Cv. l. 84.

Vajirahattha.—A deva, conqueror of the **Asuras.**[1] Buddhaghosa[2] identifies him with **Indra.**

[1] D. ii. 259. [2] DA. ii. 689.

1. **Vajirā.**—See **Vajirakumārī.**

2. **Vajirā Therī.**—The **Saṃyutta Nikāya**[1] relates that one day, when she was taking her siesta in **Adhavana** at **Sāvatthi, Mārā** questioned her as to the origin of " being " (*satta*), its creator, its origin, its destiny. Vajirā answers that there is no such thing as " being," apart from certain conditioned factors, like a chariot, which exists only because of its parts. Māra retires discomfited.

Vajirā's verses are often quoted[2] both in the Canon and in later works, but they are not included in the **Therīgāthā,** nor do we know anything else about her.

[1] S. i. 134 f. [2] *E.g.*, Kvu. 240, 626; Mil. p. 28; Vsm. ii. 593.

3. **Vajirā.**—A city in which reigned twenty-six kings, descendants of **Deva.** The last of them was called **Sādhina.**[1] The Mahāvaṃsa Ṭīkā[2] calls the city **Vajiravutti.** According to the Buddhavaṃsa,[3] the Buddha's bowl and staff were deposited, after his death, in Vajirā.

[1] Dpv. iii. 20. [2] p. 128, 130. [3] Bu. xxviii. 8.

4. **Vajirā.**—Wife of **Sakkasenāpati,** the son of **Kassapa V.** She built a *pariveṇa*, which was named after her.[1]

[1] Cv. lii. 52, 62.

Vajirā Sutta.—An account of the conversation between **Vajirā Therī** (*q.v.*) and **Māra.**[1]

[1] S. i. 134 f.

Vajirāvudha.—The weapon of **Sakka.** If he were to strike with it the **Sinerupabbata,** the weapon would pierce right through the mountain, which is one hundred and sixty-eight thousand yojanas in height.[1]

[1] SNA. i. 225.

Vajirindha.—A brahmin of **Sucirindha,** whose daughter gave a meal of milk-rice to **Kakusandha Buddha** just before his Enlightenment.[1]

[1] BuA. p. 210.

Vajirī, Vājirī.—See **Vajirakumārī.**

Vajjabhūmi.—See **Vajjī.**

Vajjita Thera.—He belonged to a retainer's (*ibbha*) family in **Kosala,** and, because he had come from the Brahma-world, he wept whenever a woman took him in her arms. Since he thus avoided the touch of women, he came to be called "Vajjita." When of age, he saw the Buddha's Twin Miracle, entered the Order, and on that same day attained arahantship with sixfold *abhiññā*. Sixty-five kappas ago he was born in a remote village as a woodsman, and seeing the Pacceka Buddha, **Upasanta,** he offered him a *campaka*-flower.[1] Two verses spoken by him are included in the Theragāthā.[2]

He is evidently identical with **Ekacampakapupphiya** of the Apadāna.[3]

[1] ThagA. i. 336. [2] vss. 215-6. [3] Ap. i. 288.

1. **Vajjiputta Thera.**—He belonged to the family of a minister of **Vesāli,** and, seeing the majesty of the Buddha who visited the city, he joined the Order and lived in a wood near by. A festival took place in

Vesāli, with much singing and dancing and gaiety. This distracted Vajjiputta, and he expressed his disgust in a verse spoken in scorn of the forest-life. A woodland sprite heard him and upbraided him, saying, "Though you spurn life in the forest, the wise, desiring solitude, think much of it," and she then uttered a verse praising it.[1] Urged on by the sprite's words, Vajjiputta developed insight and became an arahant.

Ninety-one kappas ago he had been a householder and had paid homage to **Vipassī Buddha,** with pollen from *nāga*-flowers. Forty-five kappas ago he was a king, named **Reṇu.**[2]

Vajjiputta's story is also given in the Dhammapada Commentary.[3] There he is called a *rājā*, and is said to have renounced his kingdom when his turn came to rule. On the day of the festival, on the full-moon day of Kattika, he was filled with discontent. After his conversation with the woodland sprite, he sought the Buddha, who preached to him. He attained arahantship at the end of the Buddha's sermon.

He is evidently to be identified with **Reṇupūjaka** of the Apadāna.[4]

[1] This verse, which the monk afterwards repeated, is included in Thag. vs. 62.

[2] ThagA. i. 142 f. Vajjiputta's story is given very briefly in S. i. 201 f.

[3] DhA. iii. 460 f.; see also SA. i. 228, where also he is called rājā. There may be some confusion between Vajjiputta (1) and (2).

[4] Ap. i. 146.

2. **Vajjiputta Thera.**—He belonged to a **Licchavi** *rājā's* family, and while still young, and learning various arts, such as training elephants, he was filled with the desire for renunciation. One day he went to a vihāra where the Buddha was preaching, entered the Order, and not long after became an arahant.

After the Buddha's death, when the chief Elders were living in various places prior to their agreed meeting for the recital of the Dhamma, he saw **Ānanda,** still a learner (*sekha*), teaching the Doctrine to a large assembly. Wishing to urge him to higher attainment, Vajjiputta uttered a verse, and this verse was among those which led to Ānanda's attainment of arahantship.[1]

Ninety-four kappas ago, Vajjiputta had seen a Pacceka Buddha begging for alms and had given him plantain fruits.[2]

[1] The verse is found in Thag. vs. 119. In S. i. 199 the verse is attributed to a forest deva who wished to agitate Ānanda. In Rockhill (*op. cit.*, 155 f.), Vajjiputta was Ānanda's attendant at the time and preached to the people while Ānanda meditated.

[2] ThagA. i. 236 f.

Vajjiputta or **Vesāli Sutta.**—Contains the story of the discontent of **Vajjiputta** (1) (*q.v.*).[1]

[1] S. i. 201 f.

Vajjiputtaka Sutta.—A **Vajjian** monk visits the Buddha at the **Kūṭāgārasālā** in **Vesālī,** and complains that he has to recite over two hundred and fifty rules twice a month. "I cannot stand such training," he says. The Buddha then asks him if he can train himself in three particulars. The monk agrees to do this and is told to develop higher morality, the higher thought and higher insight (*adhisīla, adhicitta, adhipaññā*). The monk develops these, and, as a result, gets rid of lust, malice, and delusion.[1]

[1] A. i. 230 f.

Vajjiputtakā, Vajjiputtiyā.—The name of a large group of monks belonging to the Vajjian clan and dwelling in **Vesālī,** who, one century after the Buddha's death, brought forward Ten Points (*dasa vatthūni*) as being permissible for members of the Order. These points are as follows: (1) The storing of salt in a horn (*siṅgiloṇakappa*); (2) the eating of food when the shadow of the sun had passed two fingers' breadth beyond noon (*duvaṅgulakappa*); (3) to eat once and then go again to the village for alms (*gāmantarakappa*); (4) the holding of the *uposatha* separately by monks dwelling in the same district (*āvāsakappa*); (5) the carrying out of an official act when the assembly is incomplete (*anumatikappa*); (6) the following of a practice because it is so done by one's tutor or teacher (*āciṇṇakappa*); (7) the eating of sour milk by one who has already had his midday meal (*amathitakappa*); (8) the use of strong drink before it has fermented (*jalogikappa*); (9) the use of a rug which is not of the proper size (*nisīdanakappa*); (10) the use of gold and silver (*jātarūparajatakappa*). The orthodox monks refused to agree to these points, and one of their leaders, **Yasa Kākaṇḍakaputta,** publicly condemned the action of the Vajjiputtakas. Yasa then left **Kosambī,** and, having summoned monks from **Pāvā** in the west and **Avanti** in the south, sought **Sambhūta Sāṇavāsī** in **Ahogaṅga.** On his advice they sought **Soreyya-Revata,** and together they consulted **Sabbakāmī** at **Vālikārāma.** In the Council that followed the Ten Points were declared invalid, and this decision was conveyed to the monks. Soon after was held a recital of the Doctrine in which seven hundred monks took part under the leadership of Soreyya-Revata. The recital lasted eight months.[1]

The Vajjiputtakas refused to accept the finding of Revataïs Council

[1] The story of the Vajjiputtaka heresy is given in the twelfth chapter of the **Cullavagga** (Vin. ii. 294 ff.); the Mhv. (iv. 9 ff.) gives more details in certain respects; see also Dpv. iv. 48 ff.; v. 17 ff.; 32 ff. It is noteworthy that even during the Buddha's life five hundred monks, described as **Vajjiputtakā,** seceded from the Order and joined **Devadatta** though they were later brought back by **Sāriputta** and **Moggallāna** (Vin. ii. 199 f.). Buddhaghosa actually (Sp. i. 228) identifies the heretics as belonging to the same party. For the part played by Yasa Thera see **Yasa** (2).

and formed a separate sect, the **Mahāsaṅghikas**,[2] numbering ten thousand monks, who held a recital of their own.

[2] For details see *s.v.*

Vajjiya Sutta.—The story of the visit of **Vajjiyamāhita** (*q.v.*) to the Buddha.[1]

[1] A. v. 189 ff.

Vajjiyamāhita.—A householder of **Campā**, a devout and skilled follower of the Buddha. Once, when on his way to see the Buddha at **Gaggarā** Lake, he found he had arrived too early and went into the **Paribbājakārāma** near by. The **Paribbājakas** asked him if it was true that the Buddha ridicules all forms of asceticism and austerity. They spoke of the Buddha as a teacher of a discipline which he himself did not follow, a nihilist (*venayika*) and a visionary (? *appaññattika*).[1] Vajjiyamāhita refuted their arguments, maintaining that the Buddha declared what was good and what was bad, and that the truth of his teachings could be proved. Having thus silenced them, he sought the Buddha, to whom he repeated the conversation. The Buddha praised him, and said it was untrue that he discouraged all austerity and asceticism; such penances as led to the destruction of evil states and the promotion of good states, he welcomed and encouraged. When Vajjiyamāhita had left him, the Buddha held him up to the monks as an example of a good householder, capable of profitable discussion with followers of other persuasions.[2]

[1] For explanation of these terms, see AA. ii. 854.

[2] A. v. 189 ff., see also A. iii. 451.

Vajjirājā.—See **Vajjī.**

Vajjihārā.—The name of a tribe.[1]

[1] Ap. ii. 359 (vs. 19).

Vajjī.—The name of a country and of its people. It was one of the sixteen **Mahājanapadas** (*q.v.*). The inhabitants appear to have consisted of several confederate clans[1] of whom the **Licchavī** (*q.v.*) and the **Videhā** (*q.v.*) were the chief. As time went on the Licchavī became the most

[1] A passage in the Commentaries (*e.g.*, DA. ii. 519)—which states that among those responsible for the administration of justice in the Vajji country (see *s.v.* **Licchavī**) were the *Aṭṭhakulakā*—has given rise to the conjecture that Aṭṭhakulakā meant heads of eight clans composing the Vajjian confederacy. There is no other evidence regarding the number of the clans. The Aṭṭhakulakā were probably a judicial committee.

powerful of these clans (*Licchavī Vajjiraṭṭhavāsīhi pasatthā*),[2] and the names Vajjī and Licchavī were often synonymous.[3] **Vesāli** was the capital of the Licchavis and **Mithilā** of the Videhas. In the time of the Buddha, both Vesāli and Mithilā were republics, though Mithilā had earlier been a kingdom under **Janaka.**

In the time of the Buddha, and even up to his death, the Vajjians were a very prosperous and happy community. The Buddha attributed this to the fact that they practised the seven conditions of welfare taught to them by himself in the **Sārandada-cetiya.**[4] But soon after the Buddha's death,[5] **Ajātasattu,** with the help of his minister **Vassakāra** (*q.v.*), sowed dissension among the Vajjians and conquered their territory.

The Buddha travelled several times through the Vajjian country, the usual route being through **Kosala, Malla, Vajji, Kāsi, Magadha,** and thus back,[6] and he preached to the people, mostly in the **Kūṭāgārasālā** in Vesāli. Among other places besides Vesāli visited by the Buddha, are mentioned **Ukkācelā, Koṭigāma,**[7] **Nādikā** (in which were **Giñjakāvasatha** and **Gosingasālavana** (*q.v.*), **Beḷuvagāma** (or **Veḷuvagāma**), **Bhandagāma, Bhogagāma** and **Hatthigāma. Pubbavijjhana,** the birthplace of **Channa,** is also mentioned as a village of the Vajjians.[8] The **Vaggumudā** river flowed through Vajjian territory.[9]

In one context[10] Dhammapāla describes **Udena** as *Vajjirājā*. This is probably a mistake, for nowhere is Udena, who was king of the **Vatsas** (or **Vaṃsas**), called the king of the Vajjis. The Vajjī are mentioned in the **Mahānāradakassapa Jātaka** (*q.v.*). It is significant that the first great schism in the Buddhist Order arose in Vajji, when the **Vajjiputtakā** (*q.v.*) brought forward their Ten Points. Even during the Buddha's lifetime some monks of Vajji joined **Devadatta.**[11] According to Hiouen Thsang,[12] who visited it, the Vajji (Vriji) country was broad from east to west and narrow from north to south. The people of the neighbouring

[2] *E.g.*, MA. i. 394.

[3] See *s.v.* **Licchavi**; in the *Trikandasesa*, quoted by Cunningham (AGI. 509), Licchavi, Vaideha and Tirabhukti were synonymous. In one passage (A. iii. 76) the Licchavi, **Mahānāma,** seeing that a band of young Licchavis who had been out hunting were gathered round the Buddha, is represented as saying, "These Licchavis will yet become Vajjians" (*bhavissanti Vajjī*). This probably only means that there was great hope of these young men becoming true Vajjians, practising the seven conditions of welfare taught by the Buddha, conditions which ensured their prosperity. But see G. S. iii. 62, n. 1 and 3.

[4] The details of this teaching, and various other matters connected with the Vajji, are given under **Licchavi** (*q.v.*).

[5] Three years after the Buddha's last visit to Vesāli, according to Buddhaghosa (DA. ii. 522).

[6] See, *e.g.*, S. v. 348.

[7] See, *e.g.*, J. ii. 232, where it is called a village of the Vajjians, on the Ganges.

[8] S. iv. 59.

[9] Ud. iii. 3.

[10] UdA., p. 382.

[11] Vin. ii. 199 f.

[12] Beal: *op. cit.*, 77.

countries were called *Saṃvajji*, or United Vajjis.[13] The Commentaries contain a mythical account of the origin of the name Vajjī.[14]

[13] For details see Cunningham, AGI. 512 ff. [14] See *s.v.* **Licchavī.**

Vajjī Vagga.—The third chapter of the Sattaka Nipāta of the Aṅguttara Nikāya.[1]

[1] A. iv. 16 ff.

1. **Vajjī Sutta.**—Records the visit of **Uggagahapati** (*q.v.*) to the Buddha at **Hatthigāma.**[1]

[1] S. iv. 109.

2. **Vajjī Sutta.**—Evidently another name for the **Sārandada Sutta** (*q.v.*).[1]

[1] See. DA. ii. 524.

Vañña.—Belonging to the **Vanni** (*q.v.*).

Vaṭaṃsa.—One of the three palaces of **Sumana Buddha** in his last lay life.[1]

[1] Bu. v. 22.

Vaṭaṃsaka.—A **Pacceka Buddha** of the future. A man once offered a *vaṭaṃsaka*-flower to the Buddha as he was begging for alms in **Sāvatthi.** The Buddha accepted the gift and smiled. When **Ānanda** asked the reason for the smile, the Buddha replied that the man would enjoy bliss for eighty-four kappas and would then become a Pacceka Buddha named Vaṭaṃsaka.[1]

[1] Netti, p. 138 f.

1. **Vaṭaṃsakiya Thera.**—An arahant,[1] probably identical with **Abhaya Thera;** see **Abhaya (1).**

[1] Ap. i. 174.

2. **Vaṭaṃsakiya Thera.**—An arahant. Thirty-one kappas ago, while riding on an elephant, he saw **Sikhī Buddha** and offered him a *vaṭaṃsaka*-flower. Twenty-seven kappas ago he became king under the name of **Mahāpatāpa.**[1]

[1] Ap. i. 216.

Vaṭaṃsikā.—The wife of **Sumana Buddha** before his Renunciation. **Anupama** was their son.[1]

[1] Bu. v. 23.

Vaṭagāma.—A monastery in Ceylon, built by **Moggallāna III.** He gave for its maintenance the village of the same name, which was attached to it.[1]

[1] Cv. xliv. 50.

Vaṭarakkhatthali.—A village in Ceylon, mentioned in the account of the campaigns of **Parakkamabāhu I.**[1]

[1] Cv. lxxiv. 76.

Vaṭuka.—A **Damiḷa,** paramour of **Anulā.** He reigned for one year and two months and was then poisoned by her. He was originally a carpenter in **Anurādhapura.**[1]

[1] Mhv. xxxiv. 19 f.; Dpv. xx. 27.

1. **Vaṭṭaka Jātaka** (No. 35).—The Bodhisatta was once born as a quail, and before he was old enough to fly, fire broke out in the forest wherein was his nest. Seeing no means of escape, he made an Act of Truth (*saccakiriyā*), calling to mind the holiness of the Buddhas and their doctrines. The fire retreated to a distance of sixteen lengths and then extinguished itself. The story was related in reference to a fire which broke out in the jungle when the Buddha was travelling in **Magadha** with a large company of monks. Some of the monks were frightened and suggested various methods for putting out the fire, while others said they should seek the Buddha's protection. This they did, and the Buddha took them to a certain spot, where he halted. The flames came no nearer than sixteen lengths from where they were standing, and in approaching the spot extinguished themselves. When the monks marvelled at the great power of the Buddha, he told them the story of the past and said that, owing to his Act of Truth as a quail, that spot would never be harmed by flames during the whole of this kappa.[1]

[1] J. i. 212 ff.; *cp.* i. 172.

2. **Vaṭṭaka Jataka** (No. 118).—The Bodhisatta was once born as a quail, and was caught by a fowler who sold birds after fattening them. The Bodhisatta, knowing this, starved himself, and when the fowler took him out of the cage to examine his condition the quail flew away and rejoined his companions.

The story was told in reference to a young man of **Sāvatthi** called **Uttaraseṭṭhiputta.** He had descended from the Brahma-world and had no desire for women. Once, during the Kattika-festival, his friends sent him a gaily-decked woman to entice him, but he gave her some money and sent her away. As she came out of his house, a nobleman saw her and took her with him. When she failed to return, her mother complained to the king, and the seṭṭhiputta was told to restore her. On failing to do so, he was taken off for execution. He resolved that if by any means he could escape execution he would become a monk. The girl noticed the crowd following the young man, and on learning the reason she revealed her identity and he was set free. He, thereupon, joined the Order and soon after became an arahant.[1]

[1] J. i. 432 ff.

3. **Vaṭṭaka Jātaka** (No. 394).—The Bodhisatta was once a forest-quail living on rough grass and seeds. A greedy crow of Benares, who was in the forest, saw the quail and thought that the good condition of his body was due to rich food. The quail, seeing the crow, talked to him, and then the crow discovered that the quail had a beautiful body not because he ate rich food, but because he had contentment of mind and freedom from fear.

The story was related in reference to a greedy monk who is identified with the crow.[1]

[1] J. iii. 312 f.

4. **Vaṭṭaka Jātaka.**—See also the **Sammodamāna Jātaka,** which is evidently also referred to as the **Vaṭṭaka Jātaka.**[1]

E.g., J. v. 414; DhA. i. 46; SNA. ii. 358.

Vaṭṭakakārapiṭṭhi.—A village granted by **Aggabodhi I.** for the maintenance of the **Bhinnorudīpa-vihāra.**[1]

[1] Cv. xlii. 26.

Vaṭṭagāmaṇī Abhaya.—King of Ceylon (29-17 B.C.). He was the son of **Saddhātissa,** and came to the throne by killing the usurper **Mahārattaka** (*v.l.* **Kammahārattaka**). He married **Anulā,** wife of **Khallāṭanāga,** and adopted **Mahācūlika** as his own son; because of this Vaṭṭagāmaṇī came to be known as **Pitirājā.**[1] Vaṭṭagāmaṇī had a second wife, **Somadevī,** and also a son of his own, called **Coranāga.** In the fifth month of his reign a brahmin, named **Tissa,** rose against him, but was defeated by seven Damiḷas who landed at **Mahātittha.** After that, the Damiḷas waged war against the king and defeated him at **Kolambālaka.** It was a remark made by the **Nigaṇṭha Giri** to Vaṭṭagāmaṇī, as he fled from the battle, that led later to the establishment of **Abhayagiri** (*q.v.*). The king

[1] This name occurs several times in the Commentaries—*e.g.*, VibhA. *passim*, see *s.v.* **Pitirājā.**

hid in the forest in **Vessagiri** and was rescued by **Kupikkala Mahātissa,** who gave him over to the care of **Tanasīva.** In his flight he left Somadevī behind, and she was captured by the Damiḷas. For fourteen years Vaṭṭagāmaṇī and his queen Anulā lived under the protection of Tanasīva, and, during this time, five Damiḷas ruled in succession at **Anurādhapura;** they were **Puḷahattha, Bāhiya, Panayamāra, Piḷayamāra** and **Dāṭhika.** After a time, Anulā quarrelled with Tanasīva's wife, and the king, in his resentment, killed Tanasīva. Later, when he also killed **Kapisīsa,** his ministers left him in disgust, but were persuaded by Mahātissa to return. When his preparations were complete, the king attacked **Dāṭhika,** slew him, and took the throne. He then founded **Abhayagiri-vihāra** and recovered Somadevī. He also built the **Silāsobbhakaṇḍaka-cetiya.** He had seven ministers who themselves built several vihāras; among them **Uttiya, Mūla, Sāliya, Pabbata** and **Tissa** are mentioned by name. It was in the reign of Vaṭṭagāmaṇī that the Buddhist Canon and its Commentaries were first reduced to writing in Ceylon, according to tradition, in **Āloka-vihāra.**[2] The foundation of Abhayagiri-vihāra formed the beginning of dissensions in the ranks of the monks.[3] Vaṭṭa-gāmaṇi was, however, regarded by later generations as a great protector of the faith.[4] Various monasteries, chiefly rock-temples, are traditionally ascribed to Vaṭṭagāmaṇī, and said to have been built by him during his exile; among these is the modern *Dambulla-vihāra.* The **Cūḷavaṃsa** calls him the founder of the **Majjhavela-vihāra.**[5]

[2] For details of Vaṭṭagāmaṇī's reign see Dpv. xx. 14 ff.; Mhv. xxxiii. 34 ff.

[3] Cv. lxxiii. 18.

[4] *Ibid.*, lxxxii. 23.

[5] *Ibid.*, c. 229.

Vaṭṭanahānakoṭṭha.—One of the eight bath-houses erected in **Pulatthipura by Parakkamabāhu I.**[1]

[1] Cv. lxxviii. 45.

Vaḍakoṅgu.—A place in South India in charge of which was a maternal uncle of **Kulasekhara.** It is mentioned with **Tenkoṅgu.**[1]

[1] Cv. lxxvi. 288; lxxvii. 43.

Vaḍamaṇamekkuṇḍi.—A locality in South India burnt by **Laṅkāpura.**[1]

[1] Cv. lxxvii. 87.

Vaḍali.—A village in South India where **Laṅkāpura** killed **Āḷavanda,** and which he occupied after severe fighting.[1]

[1] Cv. lxxvi. 134, 169.

Vaḍavalathirukka.—A Damiḷa chief, ally of **Kulasekhara.**[1]

[1] Cv. lxxvi. 94.

1. **Vaḍḍha.**—A **Licchavi.** He was a friend of the **Mettiyabhummajakā** (*q.v.*), and, at their instigation, charged **Dabba Mallaputta** with having committed adultery with his wife. Dabba repudiated the charge, and the Buddha ordered the monks to proclaim the *pattanikkujjana* on Vaḍḍha. When **Ānanda** visited Vaḍḍha and told him this news he fell in a faint, and, later, visited the Buddha with his family to ask for forgiveness. He was ordered to go before the Saṅgha and confess his error, after which the sentence was revoked.[1]

He is probably identical with **Vaḍḍhamāna Thera** (*q.v.*).

[1] Vin. ii. 124 ff.

2. **Vaḍḍha Thera.**—He belonged to a householder's family of **Bhārukaccha.** His mother (**Vaḍḍhamātā**) left the household, entrusting him to her kinsfolk, joined the Order and became an arahant. Vaḍḍha became a monk under **Veludatta** and developed into an eloquent preacher. One day he visited his mother alone and without his cloak, and was rebuked by her. Agitated by this, he returned to his monastery, and, during his siesta, developed insight, attaining arahantship.[1]

[1] ThagA. i. 413 f. Six of his verses appear in Thag. (335-9); *cp.* Thig. 210-12.

Vaḍḍhakisūkara Jātaka (No. 283).—A carpenter of a village near Benares was once wandering in the forest, and having found a young boar in a pit, took him home and brought him up. The boar was well-mannered and helped the carpenter in his work, and so he came to be called **Vaḍḍhakisūkara** ("Carpenter-boar"). When he grew up, the carpenter took him back to the forest, and there he came across some boars who lived in mortal fear of a tiger. The young boar drilled his army of boars, arranged them in battle array, and awaited the tiger. When he arrived, the boars, under their leader's instructions, mimicked the tiger in all he did. The tiger, thereupon, sought the advice of a false ascetic who shared his prey, and, following his counsel, made a leap at the boar-leader and fell into a pit which had been dug for him. There the boars attacked him and ate him, and those who were unable to get any of the flesh sniffed at the others' mouths to see how "tiger" tasted. Then they set off after the false ascetic, and when he climbed a fig-tree they dug it up and it fell to the ground. The man was torn to pieces and his body licked clean. The boars then placed their leader on the tree-trunk, consecrated him king with water, which they fetched in the dead man's skull, and made a young sow his consort. (This is how kings came to be consecrated with water from shells and seated on a throne of fig-planks.) The Bodhisatta who was then a tree-sprite sang the boar's praises.

The story was told in reference to **Dhanuggahatissa** (*q.v.*), who was responsible for **Pasenadi's** victory over **Ajātasattu.**[1]

[1] J. ii. 403 ff.

Vaḍḍhagāma.—See **Veḷugāma.**

1. **Vaḍḍhana.**—A palace occupied by **Vessabhū Buddha** before his Renunciation.[1]

[1] Bu. xxii. 19; BuA. (p. 205) calls it **Rativaḍḍhana.**

2. **Vaḍḍhana.**—A palace occupied by **Kakusandha Buddha** before his Renunciation.[1]

[1] Bu. xxiii. 16.

Vaḍḍhanavāpi.—A tank repaired by **Parakkamabāhu I.**[1]

[1] Cv. lxxix. 36.

Vaḍḍhamātā Therī.—An arahant, mother of **Vaḍḍha Thera.** After the birth of Vaḍḍha (*q.v.*) she heard a monk preach, joined the Order, and became an arahant. She rebuked Vaḍḍha when he visited her alone and without his cloak, and, later, when he asked for her advice, gave it to him and encouraged him. Then Vaḍḍha developed insight and became an arahant.[1]

[1] ThigA. 171 f.; her conversation with Vaḍḍha and his declaration to her after becoming an arahant are included in the Thig. (vs. 204-12).

1. **Vaḍḍhamāna Thera.**—An arahant. He belonged to a **Licchavi** rājā's family in **Vesāli** and was a devoted follower of the Buddha, delighting in waiting upon him and in making gifts to the monks. Later, because of an offence he had committed, the Buddha passed on him the sentence of *pattanikkujjana.* He was much grieved and begged the forgiveness of the Saṅgha,[1] and, because of his agitation, he renounced the world and joined the Order. But he was given up to sloth and torpor, till the Buddha admonished him in a verse.[2] He then put forth effort and became an arahant.

[1] He is probably to be identified with **Vaḍḍha** (1), though no mention is made of Vaḍḍha having entered the Order.

[2] This verse is found in the Thag. (vs. 40); elsewhere (Thag. vs. 1162) this verse is ascribed to **Moggallāna** as having been spoken by him to a monk named Tissa and again repeated (vs. 1163) by him to Vaḍḍhamāna.

In the time of **Tissa Buddha** he had been a householder and had given the Buddha beautiful mango-fruits.[3]

[3] ThagA. i. 106.

2. **Vaḍḍhamāna.**—The capital of Ceylon (**Varadīpa**) in the time of **Koṇāgamana Buddha.** Its king was **Samiddha.**[1]

[1] Mhv. xv. 92; Dpv. xv. 48; xvii. 6; Sp. i. 86.

3. **Vaḍḍhamāna.**—A city (*nagara*) in **Mahāgāma,** over which **Gāmaṇi-Abhaya** (afterwards **Duṭṭhagāmaṇī**) was appointed chief soon after his birth.[1]

A story is related[2] of a hunter of **Vaḍḍhamāna** who, in the name of his dead kinsman, gave alms to a wicked monk. Three times he did this, till the spirit of the *peta* cried out against it. He then gave alms to a good monk. The *peta* benefited by his gift.

[1] MṬ. 443.
[2] AA. ii. 522.

4. **Vaḍḍhamāna.**—The name of a Bodhi-tree in Ceylon. Attached to it was a temple, restored by **Aggabodhi IV.**[1] and again by **Udaya I.**[2]

[1] Cv. xlviii. 5.
[2] *Ibid.*, xlix. 15.

5. **Vaḍḍhamāna.**—A palace to be occupied by the future **Buddha Meteyya.**[1]

[1] Anāgat. vs. 46.

Vaḍḍhamānaka.—See **Vaḍḍha-vihāra.**

Vaḍḍha-vihāra.—A monastery in Ceylon, built by **Dhātusena.**[1] Its name was probably **Vaḍḍhamānaka.**

[1] Cv. xxxviii. 46.

1. **Vaḍḍhī Sutta.**—An Ariyan woman disciple increases in five things: faith, virtue, learning, generosity and wisdom.[1]

[1] S. iv. 250=A. iii. 80.

2. **Vaḍḍhī Sutta.**—The same as Sutta (1), but as applied to a man.[1]

[1] A. iii. 80.

3. **Vaḍḍhī Sutta.**—The Ariyan disciple grows in ten ways: in lands and fields, wealth and possessions, wife and family, servitors and retinue, beasts of burden, faith, virtue, learning, generosity and wisdom.[1]

[1] A. v. 137.

Vaṇijjagāma-vihāra.—A monastery in Ceylon, built by **Kassapa III.**[1]

[1] Cv. xlviii. 24.

1. **Vaṇijjā Sutta.**—The Buddha explains to **Sāriputta,** in answer to his question, why it is that some people succeed in their trade and others do not, while in the case of yet others they prosper even beyond their hopes.[1]

[1] A. ii. 81 f.

2. **Vaṇijjā Sutta.**—The five trades which should not be plied by a lay-devotee: trade in weapons, human beings, flesh, spirits, poisons.[1]

[1] A. iii. 208.

Vaṇṇa Sutta.—One who praises and blames wrongly, without scrutiny, and who fails to blame or praise rightly, suffers in purgatory.[1]

[1] A. ii. 84.

Vaṇṇaka.—An irrigation channel (*mahāmātika*) constructed by **Kuṭakaṇṇatissa.**[1]

[1] Mhv. xxxiv. 32; see also Mhv. *Trs.* 240, n. 1.

Vaṇṇakāraka Thera.—An arahant. Thirty-one kappas ago he was a painter (*vaṇṇakāra*) in **Aruṇavatī** and painted the drapery of the Buddha's *cetiya*. Twenty-three kappas ago he was a king named **Candūpama.**[1]

[1] Ap. i. 220.

Vaṇṇanā Sutta.—A nun who, without test or scrutiny, praises the unworthy and blames the worthy, shows faith in things unbelievable and disbelief in things believable and rejects the gift of faith—such a one goes to purgatory.[1]

[1] A. iii. 139.

Vaṇṇanītigandha.—One of the six treatises ascribed to **Kaccāyana** (*q.v.*).[1]

[1] Gv. 59.

Vaṇṇapiṭaka.—A compilation condemned by the orthodox as *abuddha-vacana.*[1]

[1] *E.g.*, SA. ii. 150; Sp. iv. 742.

Vaṇṇabodhana.—A treatise on the Pāli language by **Ukkaṃsamāla** of **Ava.**[1]

[1] Sās, p. 120; Bode, *op. cit.*, 65.

Vaṇṇāroha Vagga.—The second chapter of the **Jātakaṭṭhakathā.**[1]

[1] J. iii. 191-210.

Vaṇṇāroha Jātaka (No. 361).—Once a lion, **Sudāṭha,** and a tiger, **Subāhu,** who lived in a forest, became friends. A jackal, who lived on their leavings, wishing to make them quarrel, told each that the other spoke evil of him. The lion and tiger discovered his plot and he had to flee.

The story was told in reference to a man who lived on the broken food of **Sāriputta** and **Moggallāna** and tried to set them at variance with each other. The attempt failed and the man was driven away. He is identified with the jackal.[1]

[1] J. iii. 191 ff.; *cp.* the **Sandhibheda Jātaka.**

Vaṇṇupatha Jātaka (No. 2).—The Bodhisatta was once the leader of a caravan of five hundred carts. One night, while crossing a desert of sixty leagues, in the last stage of a journey, the pilot fell asleep and the oxen turned round. All the wood and water was finished, but the Bodhisatta made the men dig a well. After digging sixty cubits down they came upon a rock. The men were filled with despair, but the Bodhisatta had the rock broken through by a serving-lad who still showed courage and thus obtained water.

The story was related about a young man of **Sāvatthi** who entered the Order and practised meditation, but was unable to attain insight. He was filled with despair and his companions took him to the Buddha. He is identified with the serving-lad of the story.[1]

[1] J. i. 106-110.

Vaṇṇūpama.—See **Candūpama.**

Vatapada or "**Devā**" **Sutta.**—The Buddha tells the monks of seven rules of conduct, the observance of which won for **Sakka** his celestial sovereignty. There are the maintenance of parents, reverence for the head of the family, the use of gentle language, avoidance of slander, delight in renunciation, generosity and amiability, the speaking of truth and avoidance of anger.[1]

[1] S. i. 228.

Vatta Sutta.—**Sāriputta** addresses the monks at **Sāvatthi** on the seven *bojjhaṅgas* and of his ability to abide in any of these according to his desire; just as a nobleman possessed of many robes can don whichever he desires.[1]

[1] S. v. 70 f.

Vattakālaka.—A village near **Girikaṇḍaka-vihāra.** A girl of this village soared into the sky by the power of her rapture when thinking of the Buddha. Her parents went to the monastery, leaving her at home as she was unfit to walk. From her home she saw the monastery lighted up and heard the monks chanting, and was so filled with rapture that she was transported to the vihāra.[1]

[1] Vsm. i. 143 f.; DhSA. 116.

Vattakkhandhaka.—The eighth section of the **Cullavagga.**[1]

[1] Vin. ii. 207-31.

Vattaniya.—A hermitage (*senāsana*) where lived Rohaṇa **Nāgasena's** teacher, by whom he was ordained, and **Assagutta,** with whom he spent a *vassa* in order to train himself for debate.[1] Assagutta, who ordained the **Ājīvaka Janasāna** (*q.v.*), is also said to have been " *Vattaniyasenāsane.*"[2] At the ceremony of the **Mahā Thūpa** foundation, the **Thera Uttara** came from " *Vattaniyasenāsana* " in **Viñjhāṭavī** with sixty thousand others.[3] Both the Visuddhimagga and the Atthasālinī[4] mention a Thera named **Assagutta,** evidently a visitor, who, seeing the monks at Vattaniyasenāsana eating dry food, resolved " Every day before meals may the pool of water take on the taste of milk curds." From that day the pool water tasted of curds before the meal and became natural water again after the meal.

[1] Mil. 10, 12, 14; from the context it would appear as though these two residences were not identical, but were far away from each other. Was *Vattaniyasenāsana* rather a generic than a proper name ?

[2] MṬ. 192.

[3] Mhv. xxix. 40.

[4] Vsm. 430; DhSA. 419.

Vattabbaka-Nigrodha.—A famous Elder in the time of **Pitirājā (Vaṭṭagāmaṇī).** He was a *sāmaṇera*, and, during the prevalence of the **Brahmaṇatissabhaya** (*q.v.*), looked after his teacher at the risk of his own life, once even climbing a palmyra-tree in order to get him some nuts. Later, feeling that the care of an old and feeble man was too much for him, his teacher advised him to go away alone. The teacher was later eaten by cannibals.

The *sāmaṇera* became famous as a *Tipiṭakadhara*, and when the Tissabhaya had disappeared, monks came from overseas to visit him. He thus became the leader of a large company, and once when he visited **Anurādhapura,** he received gifts of three robes in nine different places.[1]

[1] See VibhA. 449 f., where the story is given in great detail.

Vattalagāma.—A village in which **Vijayabāhu III.** built the **Vijayabāhu-vihāra.**[1]

[1] Cv. lxxxi. 58; see also Cv. *Trs.* ii. 140, n. 3.

Vattita-Sutta.—On the eight proper ways of dealing with a monk guilty of some offence, against whom proceedings have been taken.[1]

[1] A. iv. 347; *cp.* Vin. ii. 86; M. ii. 249.

Vatra.—An **Asura.**[1] See **Vatrabhū.**

[1] J. v. 153; *cp.* Sanskrit Vṛtra.

Vatrabhū.—A name for **Indra (Sakka).**[1] Buddhaghosa[2] explains it as "*sveva vattena aññe abhibhavitvā devissariyapatto ti Vatrabhū, Vatranāmakaṃ vā asuraṃ abhibhavatī ti.*"

[1] J. v. 153; S. i. 47. [2] SA. i. 83.

1. **Vattha Sutta.**—Benares cloth is of good colour, pleasant to handle and of great worth when new or of middling wear, or even when worn out. So is a good monk, whether he be a novice, of middle standing, or a senior.[1]

[1] A. i. 247; *cp.* Pugg. 34.

2. **Vattha Sutta.**—See **Vatthūpama.**

Vatthadāyaka Thera.—An arahant. In the time of **Atthadassī Buddha,** he was a *Garuḷa*, and, seeing the Buddha on his way to **Gandhamādana,** he offered him a garment. Thirty-six kappas ago he was king seven times under the name of **Aruṇaka.**[1]

[1] Ap. i. 116.

1. **Vatthu Sutta.**—The Buddha declares, in answer to a deva's question, that children are a man's support, wife his supreme comrade, and the spirits of the rain sustain all earthbound creatures.[1]

[1] S. i. 37.

2. **Vatthu Suttā.**—Two suttas, one of the ten causes of malice (*āghāta*), and the other on the ten remedies for the same.[1]

[1] A. v. 150 f.

Vatthugāthā.—The introductory stanzas (976-1031) of the **Pārāyaṇa-vagga,** which give the story of **Bāvarī,** the circumstances which led to his sending his students to the Buddha and their journey to **Rājagaha.**[1] The **Cullaniddesa,** which comments on the Parāyaṇavagga,[2] does not comment on these stanzas.

[1] SN., pp. 190-7. [2] p. 6 ff.

Vatthūpama Sutta.—The seventh sutta of the **Majjhima Nikāya.**[1] The Buddha says that, even as a dirty piece of cloth takes dyes badly, so in an impure heart bliss is not to be found. He then proceeds to enumerate the heart's impurities and to show how they can be cleansed. **Sundarika-Bhāradvāja,** who is present, asks the Buddha if he has bathed in the **Bāhukā.** The Buddha then gives a list of places whose waters are considered holy, and declares that the real cleansing is the cleansing of the heart—" to love all that lives, speak truth, slay not nor steal, no niggard be but dwell in faith." Bhāradvāja seeks ordination and becomes an arahant.

It is evidently this sutta which is referred to in the **Sumaṅgalavilāsinī**[2] as the **Vattha Sutta.**

[1] M. i. 36 ff. [2] DA. i. 50, 123.

Vatsā.—See **Vaṃsā.**

Vaddha (or **Puppha**) **Sutta.**—The Buddha states that he has no quarrel with the world; the world quarrels with him. He teaches only what is upheld by the world of sages and proceeds to describe what this teaching is. Like a lotus which, though it arises and grows in the water, is yet unspotted by it, so a Tathāgata, arisen and grown in the world, is yet unspotted by it.[1]

[1] S. iii. 138 f.

Vadha-ālopa-sāhasakāra Sutta.—Few are they who abstain from torture, highway robbery and violent deeds; it is because they do not see the Four Noble Truths.[1]

[1] S. v. 473.

Vadhagāmakapāsāṇa.—A village in **Rohaṇa,** mentioned in the account of the campaigns of **Parakkamabāhu I.**[1]

[1] Cv. lxxv. 6.

Vadhukā Sutta.—When a young wife is first led home she is full of fear and bashfulness, not only towards her relations but also towards the servants. So is a monk who has just entered homelessness full of fear and bashfulness, even before novices of the monastery. As time goes on, this feeling, in both cases, gives place to boldness. But a monk should always be like a newly-wed wife.[1]

[1] A. ii. 78 f.

Vana Saṃyutta.—The ninth section of the **Saṃyutta Nikāya.**[1]

[1] S. i. 197-205.

Vanakoraṇḍiya Thera.—An arahant. Ninety four kappas ago he gave a *vanakoraṇḍa*-flower to **Siddhattha Buddha.**[1]

[1] Ap. i. 404.

Vanagāma.—A locality in Ceylon where **Sugalā** was captured.[1]

[1] Cv. lxxv. 174.

Vanaggāmapāsāda.—A monastery built by **Vijayabāhu IV.,** to which was attached the **Abhayarāja-pariveṇa.**[1]

[1] Cv. lxxxviii. 51.

Vananadī.—A river in **Rohaṇa.**[1]

[1] Cv. lxxv. 156; identified with *Velaveyaṅga* (Cv. *Trs.* ii. 59, n. 4).

Vanapattha Sutta.—On the principles which should guide a monk's life wherever he lives—in the forest, village, town, or with another person. He should quit his dwelling-place only if he fails to develop mindfulness, stedfastness of heart, etc., and not because he finds it difficult to procure food, etc.[1]

[1] M. i. 104 ff.

1. **Vanappavesanakhaṇḍa.**—The third section of the **Bhūridatta Jātaka,** which deals with the return of **Alambāyana** and **Somadatta** from the **Nāga**-world and their entering the forest for their livelihood.[1]

[1] J. vi. 170-7.

2. **Vanappavesanakhaṇḍa.**—A section of the **Vessantara Jātaka,** dealing with the journey of **Vessantara** and his family from **Jetuttara** to **Vaṅkapabbata** and their life in the hermitage prior to the arrival of **Jūjaka.**[1]

[1] J. vi. 513-21.

Vanaratana.—See **Medhaṅkara** (5).

Vanaratana-Tissa.—See **Ānanda** (11).

Vanaropa (or **Vacana**) **Sutta.**—The Buddha says, in answer to a deva's question, that those who plant groves and fruitful trees and build causeways, dams and wells, and give shelter to the homeless, increase in merit every day.[1]

[1] S. i. 33.

1. **Vanavaccha Thera.**—He was the son of **Vacchagotta,** a brahmin of **Kapilavatthu,** and was born in the forest, his mother having longed to see it and having been taken in travail while wandering there. His name was Vaccha; but because of his love for the woods, he was called Vanavaccha. He left the world soon after the Buddha's Renunciation, and led the ascetic life till he heard of the Buddha's Enlightenment. Then he joined the Order, and it was in the forest that he strove and won arahantship. When he returned to Kapilavatthu with the Buddha, his companions asked him why he so loved the forest, and he spoke a verse in praise of forest-life.[1]

In the time of **Atthadassi Buddha,** he was a large tortoise living in the **Vinatā.** Seeing the Buddha about to cross the river, he took him on his back. Many hundreds of times afterwards he lived as an ascetic in the forest. In the time of **Kassapa Buddha** he became a dove, and his heart was gladdened by the sight of a monk practising compassion. Later he was born as a householder in Benares and renounced the world[2]

[1] This verse is included in Thag. (vs. 13).

[2] ThagA. i. 58 f.; Ap. ii. 506 f.

2. **Vanavaccha Thera.**—The son of a rich brahmin of **Rājagaha ;** he joined the Order, impressed by the majesty of the Buddha's visit to **Bimbisāra.** Soon after, he attained arahantship and, devoted to detachment, dwelt in the woods—hence his name. When he went to Rājagaha his kinsmen asked him to live near them, but he said he preferred the lonely life of the forest.[1]

In the time of **Vipassī Buddha** he was a labourer, and, having committed a crime, while fleeing from justice he saw a Bodhi-tree. Pleased with the look of the tree, he gathered masses of *asoka*-flowers and heaped them up round the tree. When his pursuers reached him, he remained as he was, looking at them, with no hatred in his heart. They hurled him into a precipice, and he died with the thought of the Bodhi-tree in his heart. Three kappas ago he was a king named **Santusita.**[2] He is perhaps identical with **Tambapupphiya** of the Apadāna.[3]

[1] This verse is included in Thag. (vs. 113).

[2] ThagA. i. 222 f.

[3] Ap. i. 176.

Vanavāsa.—A district, probably Northern Kanara, in South India. After the Third Council, **Rakkhita Thera** was sent there to convert the people, and he preached the **Anamatagga Saṃyutta** poised in mid-air. It is said that sixty thousand persons embraced the faith, thirty-seven thousand joined the Order, while fifty vihāras were established in the country.[1]

[1] Mhv. xii. 4, 30 f.; Sp. i. 63, 66; Dpv. viii. 6. The Vanavāsī are mentioned in the Mahābhārata (6. 366) and the Harivaṃsa (5232) as a people of S. India. The Sās (p. 12) also mentions a country called Vanavāsī, which, however, is the country round Prome in Lower Burma.

1. **Vanavāsī (Vanavāsika) Tissa.**—A monk. In his previous birth he was the brahmin **Mahāsena** (*q.v.*). During pregnancy his mother invited **Sāriputta,** with five hundred monks, to her house, and fed them on milk-rice. She herself put on yellow robes and ate of the rice left by the monks. On the day of his naming, he presented Sāriputta with his blanket. He was called **Tissa** after Sāriputta, whose personal name was **Upatissa.** At the age of seven Tissa joined the Order and his parents held a festival lasting for seven days, distributing porridge and honey to the monks. On the eighth day, when Tissa went for alms in **Sāvatthi,** he received one thousand bowls of alms and one thousand pieces of cloth, all of which he gave to the monks. This earned for him the name of **Piṇḍapātadāyaka.** One day, in the cold season, he saw monks warming themselves before fires and, discovering that they had no blankets, he, accompanied by one thousand monks, went into the city. Wherever he went people gave him blankets; one shopkeeper had hidden two of his very costly blankets, but on seeing Tissa he gave them willingly. Tissa thus got one thousand blankets and was thereafter called **Kambaladāyaka.**

Having discovered that, at **Jetavana,** his young relations came too often to see him, he obtained a formula of meditation and went into the forest to a distance of twenty leagues from Sāvatthi. At the request of the inhabitants of the village near by, he spent the rainy season in the forest hermitage, going into the village for alms. There, at the end of two months, he attained arahantship. Because he was so devoted to the forest, he was given the name of **Vanavāsī.** At the end of the *vassa,* all the Buddha's chief disciples, with a retinue of forty thousand monks, visited Tissa in his hermitage, arriving there in the evening. The villagers, recognizing Sāriputta, asked him to preach the Dhamma, saying that Tissa, their teacher, knew only two sentences—"May you be happy, may you obtain release from suffering!"—which sentences he repeated whenever anyone made him a gift. Thereupon Sāriputta asked him to explain the meaning of the two sentences, and the novice preached till sunrise, summarizing the whole of the Buddha's teaching "even as a thunderstorm rains incessantly upon the four great continents."

At the end of the discourse Tissa's supporters were divided into two camps, some were offended that he should not have preached to them before, while others marvelled at his saintliness and skill. The Buddha, aware of this disagreement, went himself to the village. The villagers gave alms to the Buddha and the monks, and, in returning thanks, the Buddha told them how fortunate they were that, owing to Tissa, they had been able to see himself and his chief disciples. They were then all satisfied.

On the way back to Sāvatthi, Tissa walked beside the Buddha and pointed out to him the various beautiful spots. The Buddha preached the **Upasāḷhaka Jātaka** to show that there was no spot on earth where men had not at some time died. In answer to a question of the Buddha, Tissa said that he never felt afraid of the animals in the forest, but only a greater love for the forest at the sound of their voices. He then recited fifty stanzas in praise of life in the wilds. Arrived at the outskirts of the forest, he took leave of the Buddha and Sāriputta and returned to live in his forest hermitage.[1]

[1] DhA. ii. 84-102. The visit of the Buddha is also reported at DA. i. 240 and MA. i. 357, though the details are different. There the Buddha is accompanied by Sāriputta and the chief disciples and twenty thousand arahants.

2. **Vanavāsī Thera.**—The Theragāthā Commentary[1] mentions a **Vanavāsī Thera** as the teacher of **Tekicchakāni.** This is probably not a proper name but only a descriptive epithet.

[1] i. 440

Vanavāsī Nikāya.—See **Araññavāsī.**

Vanavāsī Mahātissa.—A monk, probably distinct from **Vanavāsī-Tissa**—see **Vanavāsī** (1). On the day that **Ālindakavāsī Mahā Phussadeva Thera** attained arahantship, the devas stood by him, illuminating all the forest. **Mahātissa** saw the light, and the next day asked **Phussadeva** the reason for it, but his question was evaded.[1]

[1] SA. iii. 154 f.

Vanasa (Vanasāvhaya ?).—A city, lying between **Vedisā** and **Kosambī,** on the road taken by **Bāvarī's** disciples.[1] The Commentary states[2] that

[1] SN. vs. 1011.

[2] SNA. ii. 583.

this was another name for **Tumbavanagara** (*v.l.* **Pavana**), and that it was also called **Vanasāvatthi.**

Vanasāvatthi.—See **Vanasa.**

Vantajīvakā.—A group or sect of Buddhist ascetics. **Vijayabāhu I.** provided them with necessaries and granted maintenance villages to their relations.[1] *cp.* **Lābhavāsī.**

[1] Cv. lx. 69.

Vandanavimāna Vatthu.—The story of a woman who, seeing monks on their way to visit the Buddha at **Sāvatthi,** worshipped them with great devotion, watching them pass out of sight. She was later reborn in **Tāvatiṃsa** where **Moggallāna** saw her and heard her story.[1]

[1] Vv. iv. 11; VvA. 205 f.

1. **Vandanā Sutta.**—There are three kinds of homage: homage done with body, with speech, and with mind.[1]

[1] A. i. 294.

2. **Vandanā Sutta.**—**Sakka** and **Brahmā Sahampati** visit the Buddha and each stands leaning against a doorpost. Sakka recites a verse in worship of the Buddha, emphasizing the Buddha's emancipation. Sahampati recites another in which he begs of the Buddha to teach the Dhamma to the world.[1]

[1] S. i. 233.

Vannibhuvanekabāhu.—See **Bhuvanekabāhu III.**

Vannī.—The name of a people inhabiting the north-east of Ceylon. They are first mentioned in the Chronicles,[1] in the reign of **Vijayabāhu III.** (1232-36), who, with their help, gained the throne of Ceylon. They appear to have inhabited the frontier country between Jaffna and the Sinhalese kingdom and were either subjects of one or other of these states, or affected complete independence, according to the strength of their neighbours. **Vijayabāhu IV.** made friends with the Vanni chiefs and gave into their hands the protection of **Anurādhapura.**[2] They seem to have been a warlike people. Today they occupy a few small villages in the North Central Province of Ceylon and go in largely for hunting. Their origin is unknown, though they are called **Sīhalā.**[3] Several of

[1] Cv. lxxxi. 11. [2] *Ibid.*, lxxxviii. 87. [3] *E.g.*, *ibid.*, lxxxiii. 10.

their chieftains are mentioned by name, as having been overcome by **Bhuvanekabāhu I.**—*e.g.*, **Kadalīvāṭa, Āpāna, Tipa, Himiyānaka.**[4] The adjective from Vannī is **Vañña.**[5]

[4] *Ibid.*, xc. 33. [5] See, *e.g.*, *ibid.*, lxxxiii. 10; lxxxvii. 26.

1. **Vappa Thera.**—One of the **Pañcavaggiyā.** He was the son of **Vāseṭṭha,** a brahmin of **Kapilavatthu.** When **Asita** declared that Prince **Siddhattha** would become the Buddha, Vappa and four other brahmins, headed by **Koṇḍañña,** became recluses. Vappa was with the Buddha during the six years of his ascetic practices, but being disappointed when the Buddha began taking solid food, he left him and went to **Isipatana,** where the Buddha, after his Enlightenment, preached to him and the others the **Dhammacakkappavattana Sutta.** On the fifth day after,[1] Vappa and his companions became arahants, at the end of the **Anattalakkhaṇa Sutta.** Vappa's resolve to be among the first of the Buddha's followers was taken in the time of **Padumuttara Buddha.** In the past, he was sixteen times king, under the name of **Mahādundubhi.**[2]

[1] Vappa became a *sotāpanna* on the second day of the quarter (AA. i. 84); *pāṭipadadivase*, says ThagA. (*loc. infra*) and MA. (i. 390).

[2] ThagA. i. 140 f.; a verse attributed to him is found in Thag. (vs. 61); see also J. i. 82; Dpv. i. 32; Vin. i. 12.

2. **Vappa.**—A **Sākyan,** disciple of the **Nigaṇṭhas.**[1] He visits **Moggallāna** and they talk of the *āsavas*. The Buddha joins them and tells Vappa how the *āsavas* can be completely destroyed so that the monk who has so destroyed them will abide in the six *satata-vihāras* with equanimity, mindful and comprehending. Vappa is convinced of the superiority of the Buddha's teaching and becomes his follower.[2]

[1] AA. ii. 559 says he was the Buddha's uncle (*cūlapitā*) and a Sākyan rājā. He was a disciple of **Nigaṇṭha Nātaputta.** [2] A. ii. 196 f.

Vappa Sutta.—The conversation between **Vappa,** the Sākyan, and the **Buddha.**[1] See **Vappa** (2).

[1] A. ii. 196 f.

Vamana Sutta.—Like a physician who administers an emetic for the curing of sickness, so does the Buddha administer the Ariyan emetic to cleanse beings of birth, old age, etc. Thus, right belief cleanses them from wrong belief, etc.[1]

[1] A. v. 219 f.

Vammika Sutta.—A deity appeared before **Kumārakassapa** in **Andhavana** and propounded a riddle: " There is an anthill burning day and night. The brahmin said: 'Take your tool, Sumedha (sage), and dig.' As the brahmin dug, he came across, successively, a bar, a frog, a forked passage, a strainer, a tortoise, a cleaver, a joint of meat—all of which he was told to cast out and dig on. He then came across a cobra, which he was asked not to harm, but to worship." At the suggestion of the deity, Kassapa related the story to the Buddha, who solved the riddle. The anthill is the body, the brahmin the arahant, the tool wisdom, digging perseverance, the bar ignorance, the forked passage doubting, the strainer the five *nīvaraṇas*, the tortoise the fivefold *upādānakkhandhas*, the cleaver the fivefold pleasures of sense, the joint of meat passion's delights (*nandīrāga*), and the cobra (*nāga*) the arahant monk.[1]

According to the Commentary,[2] Kumārakassapa was not an arahant at the time of the preaching of the sutta. The deity was a deity of the **Suddhāvāsa-brahma** world. He was one of five friends who, in the time of **Kassapa Buddha,** had entered the Order and who, in order to meditate uninterruptedly, had climbed a rock by means of a ladder which they had then removed, thus cutting off their return. The eldest became an arahant in three days, the second (*anuthera*) was this deity, who had become an *anāgāmī*. The third was **Pukkusāti,** the fourth **Bāhiya Dāruciriya** and the last Kumārakassapa. This deity was responsible for the arahantship both of Bāhiya and Kassapa, for Kassapa took the Vammīka Sutta as the subject of his meditations and thus developed insight.

1 M. i. 142 ff.

2 MA. i. 340.

Vaya Sutta.—That which is transient by nature must be put away.[1]

1 S. iii. 197.

Vayiga.—A river in South India.[1]

1 Cv. lxxvi. 307.

Varakappa.—The name of a *kappa* in which three Buddhas are born in the world.[1]

1 BuA. 158 f.

Varakalyāṇa.—A primæval king, son of **Kalyāṇa.** His son was **Uposatha.**[1]

1 Dpv. iii. 4; Mhv. ii. 2; J. ii. 311; iii. 454; but, according to DA. i. 258 and SNA. i. 342, Varakalyāṇa's son was **Mandhātā.**

Varañāṇamuni.—A Thera. One of the two theras appointed to lead the delegation of monks who left **Ayyojhā** (in Siam) to go to Ceylon, for the furtherance of the Order in Ceylon, in the reign of **Kittisirirājasīha.** He was expert in the Dhamma and the Vinaya and taught them to the monks of Ceylon.[1]

[1] Cv. c. 138, 174.

Varaṇa.—A **Cakkavatti** of forty-one kappas ago, a previous birth of **Kusumāsaniya (Suyāma) Thera.**[1]

[1] Ap. i. 162; ThagA. i. 171.

Varaṇa Jātaka (No. 71).—The Bodhisatta was once a teacher of **Takkasilā,** with five hundred brahmin pupils. One day he sent the pupils into a forest to gather wood, but one of them was lazy and went to sleep, and when his companions woke him he climbed on to a tree and broke off some green branches. One of the boughs hit him in the eye and wounded him. The next day the pupils had been invited to a meal in a distant village and a servant-girl was told to make them some gruel early, before their start. She lit a fire with the green wood which lay on the top of the firewood, and the fire would not burn. The green wood had been thrown there last by the lazy pupil who had been the last to return. The pupils could not start in time and the journey had to be abandoned.

The story was told in reference to **Kuṭumbikaputta-Tissa** (*q.v.*), with whom the brahmin youth is identified.[1]

[1] J. i. 316 ff.

Varaṇa Vagga.—The eighth chapter of the Eka Nipāta of the **Jātakaṭṭhakathā.**[1]

[1] J. i. 316-59.

Varaṇā.—A city on the banks of the **Kaddamadaha,** where **Ārāmadaṇḍa** visited **Mahā Kaccāna.**[1]

[1] A. i. 65; AA. i. 322.

Varadassana.—A **Cakkavatti** of one kappa ago, a previous birth of **Kusumāsaniya (Suyāma) Thera.**[1]

[1] Ap. i. 160; ThagA. i. 166.

Varadīpa.—The name given to Ceylon in the time of **Koṇāgamana Buddha.** Its capital was **Vaḍḍhamāna** and its king **Samiddha.**[1]

[1] Sp. i. 86; Mhv. xv. 93; Dpv. i. 73; ix. 20; xv. 45, etc.

Varadhara.—A noted **Paribbājaka** in the time of the Buddha. He lived with **Annabhāra, Sakuludāyī** and others in the **Paribbājakārāma,** on the banks of the **Sappinikā,**[1] and again in the **Moranivāpa** in **Rājagaha.**[2]

[1] A. ii. 29, 176. [2] M. ii. 1.

Varamandhātā.—A primæval king, son of **Mandhātā.** His son was **Cara.**[1]

[1] J. iii. 454, but according to DA. i. 258 and SNA. i. 352, his son was **Uposatha.**

1. **Vararoja.**—A primæval king, son of **Roja;** his son was **Kalyāṇa.**[1]

[1] Dpv. iii. 4; Mhv. ii. 2; J. ii. 311, etc.

2. **Vararoja.**—Buddhaghosa says[1] that the heretics once paid **Vararoja** one thousand to speak ill of the Buddha's person. Vararoja went to see the Buddha and was struck by the perfection of every feature; he spoke the Buddha's praises in a verse of over one thousand lines.

[1] DA. ii. 656.

Varavāraṇā.—A class of long-lived deities. Hearing that the Buddha was to be born, they started to make garlands to put on him on the day of his birth, but even on the day of his death these garlands were not finished, because, according to their computation, the time had passed so quickly. When they heard that the Buddha was about to die, they brought the unfinished garlands, but could not get anywhere within the Cakkavāḷa. They therefore remained in the sky, singing the praises of the Buddha.[1]

[1] DA. ii. 576 f.

1. **Varuṇa.**—One of the chief lay disciples of **Sumana Buddha.**[1]

[1] Bu. v. 28.

2. **Varuṇa.**—Son of **Revata Buddha** and also his chief disciple. His mother was **Sudassanā.**[1] Once, when he was ill, large numbers of people came to see him, and he preached to them on the three signata, ordaining one hundred thousand persons by the "*ehi bhikkhu*" ordination.[2]

[1] Bu. vi. 18, 21; J. i. 35. [2] BuA. 134.

3. **Varuṇa.**—The personal attendant of **Anomadassī Buddha.**[1]

[1] J. i. 36; Bu. viii. 22; DhA. i. 88, etc.

4. **Varuṇa.**—The personal attendant of **Paduma Buddha.**[1]

[1] Bu. ix. 21; J. i. 36.

5. **Varuṇa.**—Sixteen kappas ago there were eight kings of this name, all previous births of **Malitavambha (Kumudadāyaka) Thera.**[1]

[1] ThagA. i. 211; Ap. i. 180.

6. **Varuṇa.**—A disciple of **Piyadassī Buddha.**[1]

[1] ThagA. i. 75, 273.

7. **Varuṇa.**—A brahmin, a former birth of **Suppiya Thera.**[1]

[1] ThagA. i. 93; Ap. ii. 452.

8. **Varuṇa.**—A king of fifty-one kappas ago, a previous birth of **Sayanadāyaka Thera.**[1]

[1] Ap. i. 99.

9. **Varuṇa.**—One hundred and sixty kappas ago there were two kings of this name, previous births of **Sucintita Thera.**[1]

[1] Ap. i. 115.

10. **Varuṇa.**—A king of forty kappas ago, a previous birth of **Ekasaññaka Thera.**[1]

[1] Ap. i. 121.

11. **Varuṇa.**—A king in the time of **Atthadassī Buddha,** a previous birth of **Sīvali (Ekāsaniya) Thera.**[1]

[1] Ap. i. 149 calls him *devarājā*; ThagA. i. 139 calls him *ekarājā.*

12. **Varuṇa.**—A *yavapāla* who gave grass to **Siddhattha Buddha** for his seat.[1]

[1] BuA. 185.

13. **Varuṇa.**—A brahmin village, residence of the brahmin **Vasabha.**[1]

[1] BuA. 172.

14. **Varuṇa.**—A king of twenty-five kappas ago, a former birth of **Pilindavaccha Thera.**[1]

[1] ThagA. i. 52; Ap. i. 59.

15. **Varuṇa.**—A Nāga-king in the time of **Anomadassī Buddha,** a previous birth of **Mahāmoggallāna.** He played music to the Buddha and entertained him in his abode.[1]

[1] Ap. i. 31.

16. **Varuṇa.**—An ascetic who, together with the hunter **Sura,** discovered intoxicating liquor. This came to be called *Vāruṇī.*[1]

[1] See **Kumbhakāra Jātaka,** J. v. 12 f.

17. **Varuṇa.**—A Nāga-king. His wife was **Vimalā** and their daughter was **Irandatī.** For details see **Vidhurapaṇḍita Jātaka.** Varuṇa is identified with **Sāriputta.**[1]

[1] J. vi. 329.

18. **Varuṇa.**—A king of the devas, mentioned as the companion of **Sakka, Pajāpati** and **Isāna.** In battle against the **Asuras,** the devas of **Tāvatiṃsa** were asked to look upon the banner of Varuṇa in order to have all their fears dispelled.[1] In the **Tevijja Sutta**[2] Varuṇa is mentioned with **Indra, Soma, Isāna, Pajāpati, Yama** and **Mahiddhi,** as the gods invoked by brahmins. In the **Āṭānāṭiya Sutta**[3] he is mentioned with **Indra** and others as a **Yakkha** chief. Buddhaghosa says[4] that Varuṇa is equal in age and glory (*vaṇṇa*) with Sakka and takes the third seat in the assembly of devas.

See also **Varuṇā** and **Vāruṇī.**

[1] S. i. 219.
[2] D. i. 244; *cf.* J. v. 28; vi. 20; also Mil. 22.
[3] D. iii. 204.
[4] SA. i. 262.

Varuṇadeva.—The sixth son of **Devagabbhā** (*q.v.*).

Varuṇā.—A class of deities present at the preaching of the **Mahāsamaya Sutta.**[1] They probably form the retinue of **Varuṇa** (18).

[1] D. ii. 259, 260.

Varuṇindhara.—An **Ājīvaka** who gave grass for his seat to **Revata Buddha.**[1]

[1] BuA., p. 132.

Valaṅgatissapabbata-vihāra.—See **Talaṅgatissapabbata-vihāra.**

Valāha Saṃyutta.—The thirty-second section of the **Saṃyutta Nikāya.**[1]

[1] S. iii. 254-57; *cf.* A. ii. 102 ff.

1. **Valāhaka.**—A family of horses from which the Assaratana of a **Cakkavatti** is supplied.[1] He is best among animals, because he takes

[1] KhpA. 172; M. iii. 174.

his rider away from all danger.[2] Noble chargers come from the **Valāhaka** stock.[3]

[2] MA. ii. 616. [3] DhA. iii. 248.

2. **Valāhaka.**—The name of the horse of **Mahāsudassana.** He is all white, with a crow-black head and a dark mane.[1]

[1] D. ii, 174; *cp.* S. iii. 145.

Valāhaka Vagga.—The eleventh chapter of the Catukka Nipāta of the **Aṅguttara Nikāya.**[1]

[1] A. ii. 102-111; *cp.* S. iii. 254 ff.

1. **Valāhaka Sutta.**—There are four kinds of rain-clouds: those which produce thunder but no rain; those which produce rain but no thunder; those which produce neither; those which produce both. There are four similar kinds of persons: those that speak but do not act; those that act but do not speak; those that do neither; and those that do both.[1]

[1] A. ii. 102.

2. **Valāhaka Sutta.**—There are four kinds of rainclouds (as above) and four kinds of people: those that know the Dhamma but do not understand it; those that do not know it but understand it; those that do neither; those that do both.[1]

[1] A. ii. 103.

Valāhakāyikādevā.—A class of deities, spirits of the skies, divided into **Uṇhavalāhakā, Sītavalāhakā, Abbhavalāhakā, Vātavalāhakā** and **Vassavalāhakā**—the cloud spirits of heat, cold, air, wind and rain. The changes of weather are due to these spirits.[1]

[1] S. iii. 254 f.

Valāhassa Jātaka (No. 196).—Once, in **Tambaṇṇidīpa,** was a **Yakkha**-city called **Sirīsavatthu,** peopled by Yakkhiṇīs. When shipwrecked sailors were cast on the shore from the River **Kalyāṇī to Nāgadīpa,** the yakkhiṇīs would assume human form and entice them and use them as their husbands. On the arrival of other castaways, they would eat their former husbands and take the new arrivals as their lovers. Once five hundred merchants were cast ashore there and became the husbands of the yakkhiṇīs. In the night the yakkhiṇīs left them and ate their former husbands. The eldest merchant discovered this and warned the others, but only half of them were willing to attempt an escape. Now it happened that the Bodhisatta was a horse of the **Valāhaka** race and was flying through the air from the **Himālaya** to **Tambapaṇṇi.** There, as he passed over the banks and fields, he asked in a human voice: " Who wants to go home ?" and the two hundred and fifty traders begged to be taken. They climbed on the horse's back and tail and he took them to their own country. The others were eaten by the yakkhiṇīs.

The story was told in reference to a monk who had become a backslider from running after a beautifully-dressed woman.[1]

[1] J. ii. 127 ff.

Valāhassavāpi.—A tank in Ceylon, built by **Upatissa II.**[1] and repaired by **Aggabodhi II.,**[2] **Vijayabāhu I.**[3] and **Parakkamabāhu I.**[4]

[1] Cv. xxxvii. 185.
[2] *Ibid.*, xlii. 67.
[3] *Ibid.*, lx. 50.
[4] *Ibid.*, lxxix. 36.

Vallakkuttāra.—A district in South India.[1]

[1] Cv. lxxvi. 247, 260.

Vallabhā.—A South Indian tribe. Their ruler is described in the Chronicles simply as the **Vallabha. Mānavamma** once joined **Narasīha** against the Vallabha king and defeated him.[1] On another occasion, the Vallabha king sent a force to subdue **Nāgadīpa** in the reign of **Mahinda IV.** The latter sent an army under the general **Sena,** defeated the Vallabhas and made a friendly treaty with them.[2]

[1] Cv. xlvii. 15 ff.
[2] *Ibid.*, liv. 12 ff.

Valliggāma.—A village in South Ceylon. In the reign of Queen **Kalyāṇavatī** (1202-8), the regent, **Āyasmanta,** sent the **Adhikārin Deva** to the village, where a vihāra was erected[1] by him. Later, **Parakkamabāhu IV.** built the **Parakkamabāhu-pāsāda** attached to the vihāra and gave for its maintenance the village of **Sāligiri.**[2]

[1] Cv. lxxx. 38.
[2] *Ibid.*, xc. 96.

Vallitittha.—A ford in the **Mahāvālukagaṅga.**[1]

[1] Cv. lxxii. 82.

Vallipāsāṇa-vihāra.—A monastery to the west of **Anurādhapura,** near **Maṅgalavitāna.** It held the **Indasālakalena,** where once lived **Mahānāgasena.**[1]

[1] MṬ. 552.

Valliphaladāyaka Thera.—An arahant,[1] evidently identical with **Visākha-Pañcāliputta** (*q.v.*).

[1] Ap. i. 296.

1. **Valliya Thera.**—He was the son of a **Malla** chieftain of **Pāvā** and joined the Order with his companions, **Godhika, Subāhu** and **Uttiya,** when they went on some embassy to Kapilavatthu and saw the **Yamakapāṭihāriya** in **Nigrodhārāma. Bimbisāra** later built huts for them, but he forgot to roof them, and so there was no rain till the roofs were added.

In the time of **Siddhattha Buddha,** Valliya offered him a handful of flowers.[1]

[1] ThagA. i. 123; his verse is included in the Thag. (vs. 53).

2. **Valliya Thera.**—He was the son of an eminent brahmin of **Sāvatthi,** and, owing to his good friends, he met the Buddha and joined the Order, soon after attaining arahantship. Thirty-one kappas ago he saw the **Pacceka Buddha Nārada** at the foot of a tree, and built for him a hut of reeds, which he thatched with grass, together with a cloistered walk strewn with sand. He was seventy-one times king of the devas and thirty-four times king of men.[1]

He is probably identical with **Naḷāgārika** of the Apadāna.[2]

[1] ThagA. i. 247; two verses in the Thag. (125-6) are attributed to him.
[2] Ap. i. 278 f.

3. **Valliya Thera.**—He belonged to a brahmin family of **Vesāli,** and was named **Gaṇḍimitta** (*v.l.* **Kaṇhamitta**). Much struck by the Buddha when he came to Vesāli, he joined the Order under **Mahā Kaccāyana.** Because he was dull of insight and depended too much on his colleagues, he was called *Valliya* (creeper), like the ivy which must lean on something in order to grow. Later, following the advice of **Venudatta Thera,** he developed insight.

In the time of **Sumedha Buddha** he was a rich brahmin, well versed in learning. Later, he renounced eighty crores of wealth, and, after becoming an ascetic, lived on a river bank. There the Buddha visited him, and, seated on an antelope skin, preached the Doctrine. The ascetic paid him great honour and gave him mangoes and perfume and flowers.

In the Apadāna verses, quoted in ThagA., it is said that Valliya was born in the city of **Vebhāra,** built by **Vissakamma,** and that he left the household at the age of five.[1]

He is probably identical with **Candanamāliya** of the Apadāna.[2]

[1] ThagA. i. 292 f.; two verses addressed by him to Venudatta are included in the Thag. (167-8).
[2] Ap. ii. 423 f.

Valliyavīthi.—A street in **Mahāgāma.**[1]

[1] AA. i. 279.

Valliyera-vihāra.—A monastery in **Rohaṇa.** For the use of an Elder who lived there, King **Vasabha** built the **Mahāvalligotta-vihāra.**[1]

[1] Mhv. xxxv. 82; MṬ. 652.

Vallī-vihāra.—A monastery near **Uruvelā,** in Ceylon, built by King **Subha.**[1]

[1] Mhv. xxxv. 58.

Vaḷabhāmukha.—A sea (*samudda*), the last of those seen by **Suppāraka** on his voyage. Here the water is sucked away and rises on every side, leaving in the centre what looks like a deep pit. **Suppāraka,** by an Act of Truth, prevented his ship from being sunk there.[1] It is also called **Vaḷabhāmukhī.**[2]

[1] For details see the **Suppāraka Jātaka.**

[2] J. iv. 142.

Vaḷiyā.—One of the chief women supporters of **Dhammadassī Buddha.**[1]

[1] Bu. xvi. 20.

Vaḷuṭṭhi.—A Damiḷa chief of South India, won over to **Laṅkāpura's** side with gifts.[1]

[1] Cv. lxxvi. 237.

Vasa Sutta.—Seven things, skill in which enables a monk to turn his mind according to his wish and not to turn himself according to his mind.[1]

[1] A. iv. 34.

Vasantaguhā.—A cave in the park of **Parakkamabāhu I.** in **Pulatthipura.**[1]

[1] Cv. lxxiii. 112.

1. **Vasabha.**—A householder of **Kuṭumbiyaṅgaṇa** and father of **Veḷusumana.**[1]

[1] Mhv. xxiii. 68.

2. **Vasabha.**—King of Ceylon (127-171 A.C.). He was a **Lambakaṇṇa** of **Uttarapassa** and served under his uncle, the general of King **Subha.** As it was declared by the soothsayers that one named Vasabha would be king, Subha ordered the slaughter of all bearing that name and Vasabha's uncle took him to the court to surrender him. But the general's wife,

Potthā, gave her husband betel without lime to take with him, and, on the way to the palace, Vasabha was sent back to fetch the lime. There Potthā told him of the plot against his life, gave him one thousand pieces and helped him to escape. When his plans were ready, he fought against Subha, killed both him and his uncle in battle and became king. Potthā was made his queen. Soothsayers told him that he would live only twelve years, and, after consultation with the monks, Vasabha did many acts of merit in order to prolong his life; he reigned for forty-four years. Among the buildings erected by him were the **Mahāvalligotta-vihāra,** the **Anurārāma-vihāra** and the **Mucela-vihāra.** He also built twelve tanks and raised the wall of **Anurādhapura.** His son and successor was **Vaṅkanāsikatissa.**[1]

It is said[2] that once Vasabha listened to **Dīghabhāṇaka** monks reciting the **Mahāsudassana Sutta** in the **Ambalaṭṭhika-pāsāda,** near **Lohapāsāda,** and applauded the Buddha's statement contained in the sutta that all things are transient. On another occasion he went to the **Katthakasāla-pariveṇa** to worship an Elder named **Mahāsaṭṭhivassa** (this may be only a descriptive title), but as he approached the door of his cell, he heard the Elder's groans of pain, and, disappointed that he had not yet developed the power of suppressing pain even after sixty years of monastic life, the king turned away. The Elder was told of this by his attendant, and, putting forth great effort, attained arahantship; he thereupon sent for the king. The king lay at full length on the ground and worshipped him, saying, "It is not your arahantship I worship, but the *sīla* you observed as a *puthujjana.*"[3]

Another story is related of Vasabha, of how once, in order to test a monk, he sat near him and began to crush a jujube fruit. The monk's mouth watered, and Vasabha knew that he was not an arahant.[4]

Once when Vasabha's queen was ill, she was cured by medicines suggested by **Mahāpaduma Thera.**[5]

[1] For details of Vasabha's reign and works, see Dpv. xxii. 1 ff. and Mhv. xxxv. 59 ff.

[2] DA. ii. 635.

[3] *Ibid.*, i. 291.

[4] MA. ii. 869.

[5] Sp. ii. 471.

3. **Vasabha.**—A brahmin of **Varuṇa**-village. His daughter gave milk-rice to **Piyadassī Buddha** before his Enlightenment.[1]

[1] BuA. 172.

4. **Vasabha.**—One of the chief lay supporters of **Nārada Buddha.**[1]

[1] Bu. x. 25; J. i. 37.

5. **Vasabha Thera.**—He belonged to a family of a **Licchavi-rājā** of **Vesāli** and joined the Order when the Buddha visited that town,[1] winning arahantship in due course. Out of compassion for his patrons, he enjoyed what he received from them; the common-minded thereupon deemed him self-indulgent. Near him lived a fraudulent monk who deceived the people by pretending to live the simple life and was greatly honoured by them. **Sakka,** discerning this, visited Vasabha and questioned him concerning the ways of an impostor. The Elder replied in two verses,[2] and Sakka then warned the impostor and departed.

In the past, when the world was without a Buddha, Vasabha was a **Jaṭila** named **Nārada** on **Samaggapabbata,** with a retinue of fourteen thousand. Seeing no one deserving of his worship, he made a cetiya of sand on the bank of the River **Apadikā,** in the name of the Buddhas, gilded it and offered it his homage. Eighty times he was king of devas and three hundred times king of men.[3] He is evidently to be identified with **Pulinathūpiya** of the Apadāna.[4]

[1] According to the Apadāna verses quoted, he was born in **Sāvatthi** and was ordained under **Sāriputta** at the age of seven.

[2] Included in Thag. (139-40).

[3] ThagA. i. 257 ff.

[4] Ap. ii. 437 f.

6. **Vasabha.**—Called **Labhiya Vasabha.** One of the famous warriors of **Duṭṭhagāmaṇi.** He was called *Labhiya* because his body was noble in form, " straight like a stick (*yaṭṭhi*)."[1] When he was twenty years old, he started to build a tank with some friends, and he threw away masses of earth which would have needed ten or twelve ordinary men to move them. **Kākavaṇṇatissa** heard of this and summoned him to the court. The village irrigated by the tank was given to him, and it came to be called **Vasabhodakavāra.**[2]

[1] MṬ. 459.

[2] Mhv. xxiii. 90 ff.

7. **Vasabha.**—A mountain near **Himavā.**[1]

[1] ThagA. i. 182; Ap. i. 166.

Vasabhagāma.—A village in **Uddhagāma,** given by **Mahānāga** to the **Jetavana-vihāra.**[1]

[1] Cv. xli. 97.

Vasabhodakavāra.—See **Vasabha** (6).

Vasala, Vassala.—A mountain near **Himavā,** where lived **Sudassana Pacceka Buddha.**[1]

[1] ThagA. i. 88, 395; Ap. ii. 451 calls it Cāvala.

Vasala Sutta.—The seventh sutta of the **Uragavagga** of the **Sutta Nipāta.** It was preached at **Sāvatthi** to the brahmin **Aggikabhāradvāja,**[1] who reviled the Buddha, calling him outcaste (*vasala*) when the Buddha went to his house for alms. The Buddha replied that the brahmin knew neither the meaning of *vasala*, nor what makes a man such. At the request of the brahmin he preached this sutta, the burden of which is that it is not by birth that one is an outcaste or a brahmaṇa, but by one's deeds.[2] The Sutta is also included in the **Parittas** (*q.v.*).

[1] It is thus also called the **Aggikabhāradvāja Sutta** (SNA. 174). [2] SN., pp. 21 f.

1. **Vasavattī.**—A name given to **Māra**[1] (*q.v.*).

[1] *E.g.*, J. i. 63, 232; iii. 309; MA. ii. 538, etc.

2. **Vasavattī.**—One of the palaces of **Padumuttara Buddha** before his Renunciation.[1]

[1] Bu. xi. 20.

3. **Vasavattī.**—A devaputta, king of the devas of the **Parinimmita-vassavatti-world.**[1] Because of his generosity and virtue practised in past births, he surpasses the devas of his world in ten things: divine life, beauty, happiness, pomp and power, divine shapes, sounds, perfumes, tastes and touch.[2] **Māra** also rules over a part of this world, but more as a recalcitrant vassal.[3]

[1] D. i. 219. [2] A. iv. 243. [3] MA. i. 28.

4. **Vasavattī.**—An epithet of **Mahā Brahmā:** "*Sabbaṃ janaṃ vase vattemī.*"[1]

[1] DA. i. 111.

5. **Vasavattī.**—King of **Pupphavatī,** father of **Candakumāra.** For his story see the **Khaṇḍahāla Jātaka.**[1]

[1] J. vi. 131 ff.

Vasavattī Sutta.—**Vasavattī** devaputta visits **Moggallāna** with five hundred other devaputtas and agrees with Moggallāna in singing the praises of the Buddha, the Dhamma and the Saṅgha.[1]

[1] S. iv. 280.

Vasāḷanagara.—A village in Ceylon, probably near **Cittalapabbata.** It was the residence of two brothers, **Cūḷanāga** and **Mahānāga,** who later became monks.[1]

[1] SA. ii. 125.

Vasiṭṭhaka.—The father of the Bodhisatta in the **Takkaḷa Jātaka** (*q.v.*).[1]

[1] J. iv. 44 ff.

Vasiṭṭhī.—See **Vāseṭṭha.**

Vasī.—An epithet of **Mahābrahmā.**[1]

[1] *E.g.*, J. vi. 201.

Vasuttara.—One of the palaces of **Paduma Buddha** before his Renunciation.[1]

[1] BuA., p. 146; but see *s.v.* **Paduma.**

Vasudattā.—Wife of **Padumuttara Buddha** in his last lay life.[1]

[1] Bu. xi. 21.

Vasū.—A class of devas of whom **Sakka** is the chief. See **Vāsava.**[1]

[1] D. ii. 260; DA. ii. 690.

Vasulokī or **Vāsula.**—See **Sudanta.**

Vassa.—Mentioned with **Bhañña** in the compound **Vassabhaññā,** as dwellers of **Ukkala** and as " denying cause, consequence and reality." There were certain aspects of the Buddha's teaching which even they would accept.[1] Buddhaghosa explains[2] Vassabhaññā as "*Vasso ca Bhañño cāti dve janā.*"

[1] *E.g.*, S. iii. 73; A. ii. 31; M. iii. 78.
[2] AA. ii. 497; MA. ii. 894.

1. **Vassa Sutta.**—A monk asks the Buddha why it sometimes rains. It rains when the **Vassavalāhaka** devas wish to revel their bodies answers the Buddha.[1]

[1] S. iii. 257.

2. **Vassa Sutta.**—Just as rain, falling on mountain tops, flows into gullies, pools, great lakes and rivers and from there into the ocean, so do the virtues of the Ariyan disciple flow onwards and lead to the destruction of the āsavas.[1]

[1] S. v. 396.

3. **Vassa Sutta.**—On five things which stop rain: the fiery element raging in the upper air, the windy element, Rāhu, the indolence of the rainclouds, the wickedness of men.[1]

[1] A. iii. 243.

Vassakāra.—A brahmin, chief minister of **Ajātasattu.** He and **Sunidha**[1] were in charge of the fortifications of **Pāṭaligāma,** built against the **Vajji.** At Ajātasattu's suggestion, Vassakāra visited the Buddha to discover, indirectly, whether, in the Buddha's view, there were any chance of Ajātasattu conquering the Vajjians in battle. The Buddha said that as long as the Vajjians practised the seven conditions of prosperity which he had taught them at **Sārandada-cetiya,** they would prosper rather than decline, and this gave Vassakāra the idea that the downfall of the Vajjians could be brought about by diplomacy (*upalāpana*) or disunion (*mithubheda*). He thereupon conspired with the king[2] and, by agreement, the latter expelled him on the charge of showing favour to the Vajjians during discussions in the assembly. Vassakāra then went to the Vajjian country, and the **Licchavis,** all unsuspecting, welcomed him and appointed him as the teacher of their children. By means of cunning and questioning the children in secret, he made them quarrel with each other, and these quarrels soon spread to the elders. In three years the Licchavis were completely disunited, and when the assembly drum was beaten, they failed to appear. Vassakāra then sent a message to Ajātasattu, who was able to capture **Vesālī** without meeting any resistance.

In the **Gopaka-Moggallāna Sutta,**[3] Vassakāra is represented as arriving in the middle of a conversation, which **Gopaka-Moggallāna** was holding with **Ānanda,** having been sent to inspect the works at **Rājagaha,** which were in charge of Moggallāna. Having asked the subject of conversation, he inquired whether the Buddha himself or the Order had chosen a leader for the Saṅgha after the Buddha's death. Ānanda explains that the Buddha did not do so, that no special leader has been appointed, but that there were monks to whom they showed honour and reverence because of their virtue and insight. Vassakāra admits this as good, as does also **Upananda,** the Senāpati, who is present. Vassakāra asks Ānanda where he lives, and is told, in **Veḷuvana.** Vassakāra thinks this a good place for the practice of *jhāna*, and tells Ānanda of a conversation he once had with the Buddha regarding *jhāna*. Ānanda remarks that all *jhānas* are not equally praiseworthy, and Vassakāra takes his leave.

Buddhaghosa says[4] that Vassakāra knew well of Ānanda's residence at Veḷuvana, but that as the place was under his special protection, he wished to hear his work praised. Then follows a curious tale. Vassakāra once saw **Mahā Kaccāna** descending **Gijjhakūṭa** and remarked that

[1] Vin. i. 228; Ud. viii. 6; the Dīgha account (D. ii. 72 ff.) omits Sunidha. The Vinaya account omits Vassakāra's questions to the Buddha; *cf.* AA. ii. 705 ff.

[2] For details see D.A. ii. 522 ff.

[3] M. iii. 8 ff.

[4] MA. ii. 854.

he was just like a monkey. The Buddha, hearing of this, said that, unless Vassakāra begged the Elder's forgiveness, he would be born as a monkey in Veḷuvana. Vassakāra, feeling sure that the Buddha's prophecy would come true, had various fruit and other trees planted in Veḷuvana, to be of use to him as a monkey. After death he was actually reborn as a monkey and answered to the name of Vassakāra.

Three conversations between the Buddha and Vassakāra are recorded in the Aṅguttara Nikāya, all three taking place at Veḷuvana.[5]

Vassakāra had a daughter whom he wished to give in marriage to **Uttara,** but the latter refused the proposal as he wished to join the Order. Vassakāra was angry, and contrived to take his revenge even after Uttara had become a monk.[6] Buddhaghosa says[7] that Vassakāra was envious by nature, and, on discovering that a certain forest official had given tribute to **Dhaniya** without the king's special leave, he reported the man to the king and had him punished.[8] In this context we find that Vassakāra was *Mahāmatta* (? prime minister) to **Bimbisāra** as well.

[5] See **Vassakāra Suttas** (1) and (2), and **Suta Sutta.** Another Sutta, also called **Vassakāra** (3), repeats the conversation recorded in the Dīgha regarding the possibility of Ajātasattu defeating the Vajjians.

[6] ThagA. i. 240; see *s.v.* **Uttara.**

[7] Sp. ii. 295.

[8] The incident is repeated at Vin. iii. 42 ff.

1. **Vassakāra Sutta.**—**Vassakāra** visits the Buddha at **Veḷuvana** and tells him that, among brahmins, a man is considered great and wise if he understands a thing as soon as uttered, has a good memory, is skilled and diligent in business, and resourceful and capable in investigation. The Buddha mentions four other qualities of greatness: to be given up to the welfare of many, to be master of the mind in the domain of thought (*cetovasippatta*), to be able to enter into the four *jhānas* at will, to have comprehended Nibbāna by the destruction of the *āsavas.* The Buddha acknowledges, in answer to Vassakāra's question, that he himself possesses these four qualities.[1]

[1] A. ii. 35 f.

2. **Vassakāra Sutta.**—**Vassakāra** visits the Buddha at **Veḷuvana** and asks him a series of questions. The Buddha, in answer, says that a bad man cannot, as a good man can, recognize either a good man or a bad man as such. Vassakāra then relates how, once, the followers of the brahmin **Todeyya** spoke ill of **Eḷeyya** and his retinue for showing homage to **Rāmaputta;** he now understands why they honour Rāmaputta; it is because he is wiser than they.[1]

[1] A. ii. 179 f.

3. **Vassakāra Sutta.**—**Vassakāra** visits the Buddha at **Gijjhakūṭa,** at the request of **Ajātasattu,** and tells him of the latter's desire to destroy the **Vajjians.** The Buddha tells him that as long as the Vajjians practise the seven conditions of welfare, taught by him at **Sārandada-cetiya,** they will not decline, but rather prosper. Ajātasattu can achieve victory, not by battle, but by causing disunity.[1]

[1] A. iv. 17 ff.; *cf.* D. ii. 72 f.

Vassavalāhakā.—One of the **Valāhaka** devas (*q.v.*). See also **Pajjuna.** One of them once visited an arahant Thera in the **Himālaya,** and, revealing his identity, said that he could cause rain at will. The Elder wished to test this claim, but even before he could enter his hut the deva sang a song, raised his hand, and rain fell to a distance of three leagues. There are causes for rain: the power of nāgas, of supaṇṇas, of devas, of an Act of Truth, of change of weather, of **Māra,** and of *iddhi*-power.[1]

[1] SA. ii. 255 f.

Vassavuṭṭha Sutta.—A monk, who had spent the *vassa* at **Sāvatthi** with the Buddha, goes to **Kapilavatthu,** where he is visited by the Sākyans who wish to learn of the welfare of the Buddha and his disciples and of the teaching of the Buddha during the *vassa.* The monk tells them of a statement made by the Buddha, to the effect that only few in the world become arahants, *anāgāmins, sakadāgāmins* or even *sotāpannas.*[1]

[1] S. v. 405.

Vassāvāsabhāṇavāra.—The first chapter of the **Vassūpanāyikakhandha** of the **Mahāvagga.**[1]

[1] Vin. i. 137-48.

Vassika Sutta.—Just as of all scented flowers the jasmine (*vassika*) is the chief, so of all profitable conditions earnestness is the chief.[1]

[1] S. v. 44.

Vassūpanāyikakhandha.—The third chapter of the **Mahāvagga** of the Vinayapiṭaka.[1] It was preached by **Mahinda** to **Devānampiyatissa** to show the necessity of a monastery in **Cetiyagiri.**[2]

[1] Vin. i. 137 ff. [2] Mhv. xvi. 9.

Vahana.—One of the three palaces of **Sikhī Buddha** before his Renunciation.[1]

[1] Bu. xxi. 16; but BuA. (p. 201) calls it **Nārivasabha.**

Vahavāpi.—A tank built by **King Vasabha.**[1]

[1] Mhv. xxxv. 94; Dpv. xxii. 7.

Vahiṭṭha.—A Damiḷa chief, conquered by **Duṭṭhagāmaṇī.** His fortress bore his name.[1]

[1] Mhv. xxv. 13.

Vāgissara.—One of the Sinhalese envoys sent by **Parakkamabāhu I.** to **Rāmañña.** His companion was **Dhammakitti.** The Rāmañña king put them into a leaky vessel and sent them home.[1]

[1] Cv. lxxvi. 32.

Vācakopadesa.—A treatise on **Kaccāyana's** grammar by **Vijitāvī,** a monk of Burma.[1] There is also a *ṭīkā* on it by another **Vijitāvī.**[2]

[1] Sās., p. 90. [2] Bode, *op. cit.*, 46, and n. 4.

Vācavācaka or **Vaccavācaka.**—A grammatical treatise by **Dhammadassī** of Pagan.[1] There are several commentaries on it, the best known being by **Saddhammanandi.** Others are called **Vaccavācakavaṇṇanā, Vacavācakaṭīkā** and **Vaccavācakadīpanī.**

[1] Sās., p. 75; Bode, *op. cit.*, 22, and n. 6.

1. **Vācā Sutta.**—A nun who is wrong in speech, wrong in action, and who rejects the gift of faith, is destined for purgatory.[1]

[1] A. iii. 141.

2. **Vācā Sutta.**—Speech is good if spoken in season, in truth, softly, about the good and in amity.[1]

[1] A. iii. 243.

1. **Vācissara.**—A Sinhalese monk who wrote Commentaries to **Buddhadatta's** works: the **Abhidhammāvatāra,** the **Vinayavinicchaya,** the **Uttaravinicchaya** and the **Khemappakaraṇa.** He probably belonged to the twelfth century, and was also the author of the **Rūpārūpavibhāga** and the **Sīmālaṅkāra** (*q.v.*).[1]

[1] P.L.C. 108 f., 156, 174, 202; also Gv. 62, 71.

2. **Vācissara.**—A monk of Ceylon, pupil of **Sāriputta.** Numerous works are assigned to him, among them commentaries on the various books of grammar: the **Sambandhacintā-ṭīkā,** the **Subodhālaṅkāra-ṭīkā** and the **Vuttodayavivaraṇa.** He also wrote the **Sumaṅgalapasādanī**

on the **Khuddasikkhā** and a commentary on the **Moggallānavyākaraṇa.**[1] He seems also to have written the Pāli **Thūpavaṃsa** and several books in Sinhalese.[2]

[1] P.L.C. 204. [2] *Ib d.*, 217; also Gv. 62, 71.

3. **Vācissara Thera.**—Probably identical with (2) above. He was at the head of the Saṅgha in the reign of **Vijayabāhu III.**, and had hidden the Alms-bowl and Tooth-relic of the Buddha in **Kotthumala,** in order to preserve them. After that, he went to South India for protection. Later, he was sent for by Vijayabāhu, whom he helped in the reformation of the Saṅgha.[1]

[1] Cv. lxxxi. 18 ff.

Vājapeyya.—A sacrificial offering; the Commentaries[1] give it two interpretations: (1) Greeting people kindly with soft and pleasant speech (*peyyavajjaṃ, piyavācatā*); (2) a sacrifice in which *Soma* (*Vāja*) is drunk. In the second seventeen animals are offered seventeen times.

[1] *E.g.*, ItvA. 75, 76.

Vājirīya.—A heretical sect of Buddhists, one of the seventeen schools which branched off one hundred years after the Buddha's death.[1]

[1] Mhv. v. 13; Mbv. p. 97; Dpv. v. 54 calls them **Apararājagirikā.**

Vājirī.—See **Vajirakumārī.**

Vāta Sutta.—It is because of clinging to body, etc., that such views arise as that winds do not blow, pregnant women do not bring forth, the sun and moon neither rise nor set; but all these things are stable as a pillar. These vanish with the Ariyan disciple's doubts regarding suffering, its cause, its cessation, and the way to such cessation.[1]

[1] S. iii. 202 f.

Vātakapabbata.—A place in Ceylon where **Maliyadeva Thera** preached the **Cha Chakka Sutta** and sixty monks became arahants.[1]

[1] MA. ii. 1024.

Vātakālaka.—An executioner of **Rājagaha** who worked for fifty years and then retired because of old age. As he had no time for luxuries during his years of work, on the day of his retirement he asked his wife to cook milk-rice and went to bathe. On his way home, clad in clean garments, his body perfumed, he met **Sāriputta,** invited him to his house, and gave him various delicacies. At the end of the meal he accompanied the Elder for some distance, and, on his return, was gored to death by a cow with calf. After death he was reborn in **Tāvatiṃsa.**[1]

[1] AA. i. 368.

Vātagiri.—A mountain in the **Dakkhiṇadesa** of Ceylon, a point of strategic importance, providing a safe place of refuge.[1]

[1] Cv. lviii. 31; lx. 39; lxxxviii. 43; see also Cv. *Trs.* i. 204, n. 2.

Vātaggasindhava.—The Bodhisatta born as the state horse of the king of **Benares.** See the **Vātaggasindhava Jātaka.**

Vātaggasindhava Jātaka (No. 266).—The Bodhisatta was once born as the state horse of the king of Benares, his name being **Vātaggasindhava.** A she-ass, **Kundalī,** fell in love with him and refused to eat. Her son discovered this, and made the horse agree to come and see her after his bathe. But when the horse came, Kundalī, not wishing to make herself cheap, kicked him on the jaw and nearly killed him. The horse was ashamed and did not repeat his visit, and Kundalī died of love.

The story was told to a landowner of **Sāvatthi,** with whom a beautiful woman fell desperately in love. Her friends, with great difficulty, persuaded him to visit her one night, but she was capricious and rejected his advances. He went away never to return, and she died of love. When he heard of her death, he sought the Buddha, who told him the story. The she-ass is identified with the woman.[1]

[1] J. ii. 337 ff.

Vātamaṅgana.—See **Cittamaṅgana.**

Vātamiga Jātaka (No. 14).—The Bodhisatta was once born as **Brahmadatta,** king of Benares. He had a gardener named **Sañjaya.** A *vātamiga* used to visit the royal park, and the king asked Sañjaya to catch it. Sañjaya put honey on the grass where the animal fed, and, in due course, the animal came to eat out of his hand. He was thus able to entice it right into the palace, where he shut the door on it. The king marvelled that a *vātamiga,* who was so shy that if it once saw a man it would not visit the same place for a week after, should allow itself to be caught by greed.

The story was related in reference to **Cullapiṇḍapātika-Tissa** (*q.v.*), who was enticed back to the lay-life by a slave girl. Sañjaya is identified with the slave and the *vātamiga* with the monk.[1]

[1] J. i. 156 ff.

According to the Dhammapada Commentary,[2] however, it was with reference to **Sundarasamudda** that the story was told.

[2] DhA. iv. 199.

Vātavalāhakā.—See **Valāhakā.**

Vātasama.—A **Cakkavatti** of long ago, a previous birth of **Māṇava (Sammukhāthavika) Thera.**[1]

[1] ThagA. i. 164; Ap. i. 159.

Vātātapanivāriya Thera.—An arahant.[1]

[1] Ap. i. 207.

Vātīyamaṇḍapa.—A village mentioned in the account of the campaigns of **Parakkamabāhu I.**[1]

[1] Cv. lxxii. 32.

" Vādino " Sutta.—No dogmatists, no matter where from, can make a monk who understands suffering, its cause, etc., quake or waver. He is like a stone column sixteen cubits long, half of its length buried under the earth. No wind can make it tremble.[1]

[1] S. v. 445.

Vādī Sutta.—There are four kinds of expounders (*vādī*): those that know the meaning of a passage but not the letter, those that know the letter but not the meaning, those that know neither, those that know both.[1]

[1] A. ii. 138.

Vānara Jātaka (No. 342).—The Bodhisatta was a young monkey living on a river bank. A female crocodile in the river longed to eat his heart, and her husband persuaded the monkey to go for a ride on his back in search of wild fruits. In midstream he began to sink and revealed his purpose, and the monkey, nothing daunted, said that monkeys did not keep their hearts in their bodies for fear of their being torn to pieces on the trees, but that they hung them on trees, and, pointing to a ripe fig-tree, showed the crocodile what he said was his heart. The crocodile took him to the tree, and the monkey jumped ashore and laughed at him.

The story was told in reference to **Devadatta's** attempt to kill the Buddha.[1]

[1] J. iii. 133 f.; *cf.* **Suṃsumāra Jātaka** (No. 208).

Vānaragāma.—A village in **Rohaṇa,** mentioned in the account of the campaigns of **Parakkamabāhu I.**[1]

[1] Cv. lxxv. 7.

Vānarākara.—A park in Ceylon, laid out by **Parakkamabāhu I.**[1]

[1] Cv. lxxix. 8.

Vānarinda Jātaka (No. 57).—The Bodhisatta was once a monkey living on a river bank. On his way from one bank to another, he used to jump off and on a rock in midstream, and a female crocodile, living in the river, longed to eat his heart and asked her husband to get it. So the crocodile lay on the rock, ready to catch the monkey as he jumped. The monkey noticing that, in spite of there being no tide, the rock was higher than usual, spoke to it and received no reply. His suspicions were then confirmed, and he said again, " O rock, why don't you talk to me today ?" The crocodile then revealed both his identity and his purpose, and the monkey resolved to outwit him. So he asked him to open his mouth, knowing that when a crocodile does this he shuts his eyes. So the crocodile did this, and the monkey jumped on to its back and from there to the other bank.

The story was related in reference to **Devadatta's** attempt to kill the Buddha.[1]

[1] J. i. 278 f.; *cp.* **Kumbhila Jātaka.**

Vāpāraṇi.—A monastery built by **Aggabodhi VI.**[1]

[1] Cv. xlviii. 64.

Vāpinagara.—A stronghold mentioned in the account of the campaigns of **Vijayabāhu I.**[1]

[1] Cv. lviii. 43.

Vāpivāṭaka.—A locality in the **Malaya** province of Ceylon, mentioned in the account of the campaigns of **Gajabāhu.**[1]

[1] Cv. lxx. 21.

Vāmaka.—One of the great sages held in esteem by the brahmins.[1]

[1] Vin. i. 245; D. i. 104, 238; M. ii. 169, 200; A. iii. 224, etc.; *cf.* Vaṃsa in Ṛgveda x. 99.

Vāmagotta.—See **Sūra Vāmagotta.**

Vāmadeva.—One of the great sages honoured by the brahmins as authors of hymns, etc.[1]

[1] Vin. i. 245; D. i. 104, etc.; see *s.v.* **Vāmaka**; *cf.* Ṛgveda iv. 26; Rāmāyana i. 7, etc.

Vāmantapabbhāra.—A glen in Ceylon, where lived **Mahāsiva Thera** (*q.v.*).[1]

[1] J. vi. 30; iv. 490.

Vāyāma Sutta.—A nun who speaks carelessly in praise of the unworthy and in blame of the praiseworthy, who is wrong in mindfulness and rejects the gifts of the faith, is destined for hell.[1]

[1] A. iii. 141.

Vāyu.—A deity, whose son was **Vijjādhara.** See the **Samugga Jātaka.**

Vāyussaputta.—See the **Samugga Jātaka.**

Vāyodevā.—A class of deities present at the preaching of the **Mahāsamaya Sutta.**[1]

[1] D. ii. 259.

Vāraṇa.—A Thera. He was born in a brahmin family of **Kosala,** and having heard a forest-dwelling monk preach, entered the Order. One day, when on his way to visit the Buddha, he saw a fight between snakes and mongooses, in which many of them perished. Distressed by the sight of their hatred for each other, he sought the help of the Buddha, who preached to him three stanzas.[1] At the end of the recitation, Vāraṇa developed insight and became an arahant. Ninety-two kappas ago he was born in the family of the brahmin **Sumedha,** and becoming expert in brahmin lore, he entered the ascetic life. As he sat teaching hymns to his pupils there was an earthquake, marking the conception of **Tissa Buddha.** People, in terror, sought the sage, who explained it to them, thereby himself experiencing great joy in contemplating the glory of the Buddha.[2] He is evidently identical with **Nimittivyākaraṇīya** of the Apadāna.[3]

[1] These are included in Thag. (vss. 237-9).

[2] ThagA. i. 353 f.

[3] Ap. ii. 411 f.

Vāraṇavatī.—The capital of **Anikaratta,** the king to whom **Sumedhā** (*q.v.*) was to be given in marriage.[1]

[1] ThigA. 272.

Vāruṇā.—A class of deities, followers of **Varuṇa,** who were present at the preaching of the **Mahāsamaya Sutta.**[1]

[1] D. ii. 259.

Vāruṇī.—The name given to slave women, attendants of **Varuṇa.** They live in dread of him.[1]

[1] J. vi. 500, 501. At J. vi. 586 Vāruṇī is explained as *yakkhāviṭṭhā ikkhaṇikā* (fortune-tellers possessed by a Yakkha, the Yakkha being perhaps Varuṇa).

Vāruṇī Jātaka (No. 47).—The Bodhisatta once had a friend who was a tavern keeper. One day the tavern keeper made ready a supply of strong spirits and went to bathe, leaving his apprentice, **Koṇḍañña,** in charge. The latter, who had seen customers send for salt and jagghery to make their drink more appetizing, pounded some salt and put it in the liquor, hoping to improve it.

The story was told in reference to a friend of **Anāthapiṇḍika** who was a tavern keeper, whose apprentice did likewise.[1]

[1] J. i. 251 ff.

Vālakkoṇḍa.—A place in South India.[1]

[1] Cv. lxxvi. 187.

Vālagāma.—See **Jālagāma.**

Vālikagāma.—A village in Ceylon, evidently a seaport, where the Damiḷas, under **Māgha** and **Jayabāhu,** once had a fort.[1]

[1] Cv. lxxxiii. 17.

Vālikapiṭṭhi-vihāra.—A monastery, probably in Ceylon, the residence of **Ābhidhammika-Abhaya Thera.** At the commencement of the *vassa* he, with a large number of his colleagues, recited the **Mahāsuññatā Sutta,** and, as a result, they lived apart from each other during the *vassa,* attaining arahantship before the end of the season.[1]

[1] MA. ii. 907.

Vālika-vihāra.—A monastery in **Jambukolapaṭṭana,** once the residence of **Punabbasu-kuṭumbikaputta-Tissa.**[1]

[1] VibhA. 389.

Vālikākhetta.—A village mentioned in the account of the campaigns of **Gajabāhu.**[1]

[1] Cv. lxx. 62; also Cv. *Trs.* i. 292, n. 2.

Vālikārāma.—A monastery in **Vesālī,** where the question of the Ten Points raised by the **Vajjiputta** monks (*q.v.*) was settled.[1] It was also the dwelling-place of **Upāli, Dāsaka's** teacher.[2] *v.l.* **Vālukārāma.**

[1] Vin. ii. 306; Mhv. iv. 50, 63; according to Dpv. v. 29 this was done in the **Kuṭāgārasālā.**

[2] Mhv. v. 107.

Vālivāsaragāma.—A village in **Rohaṇa,** mentioned in the account of the campaigns of **Parakkamabāhu I.**[1]

[1] Cv. lxxiv. 177.

Vālukagāma.—A village in **Rohaṇa,** mentioned in the account of the campaigns of **Parakkamabāhu I.**[1]

[1] Cv. lxxv. 18; *cf.* **Mahāvālukagāma.**

Vālukapatta.—A village near **Pulatthipura.**[1]

[1] Cv. lxx. 318.

Vālukārāma.—See **Vālikārāma.**

Vālodaka Jātaka (No. 183).—Once **Brahmaddata,** king of Benares, went with a large army to quell a frontier rebellion, and, on his return, ordered that his horses be given some grape juice to drink. The horses drank and stood quietly in their stalls. There was a heap of leavings empty of all goodness, and the king ordered that these be kneaded with water, strained, and given to the donkeys who carried the horses' provender. The donkeys drank it, and galloped about braying loudly. The king asked his courtier (the Bodhisatta) the reason for this, and he answered that the lowborn lack self-control.

The story was told in reference to some boys, attendants of devotees, at **Sāvatthi.** The devotees themselves were calm and collected, but the boys would eat and then scamper about the banks of the **Aciravatī,** making great uproar. They are identified with the donkeys.[1]

According to the Dhammapada Commentary[2] the story was related after the monks returned to **Sāvatthi** from **Verañjā.** Their attendants had been quiet in Verañjā, where there was little to eat, but in Sāvatthi they ate the remnants of the monks' food and made a great noise.

[1] J. ii. 95 f. [2] DhA. ii. 154 f.

Vāḷa.—A horse belonging to King **Kappina.**[1]

[1] DhA. ii. 117.

Vāḷavāhana.—A horse belonging to King **Kappina.**[1]

[1] DhA. ii. 117.

Vāḷugāma.—A village in South India which **Laṅkāpura** laid waste and rebuilt.[1]

[1] Cv. lxxvi. 286.

Vāsabhakkhattiyā.—Daughter of **Mahānāma** the **Sākyan** by a slave-woman.[1] When **Pasenadi** asked for a Sākyan girl in marriage, she was given to him. Mahānāma went through the pretence of eating with her in order to allay Pasenadi's suspicions. It is said[2] that Mahānāma sat down to eat with her, but that as he was about to take the first mouthful, a messenger arrived, as prearranged, and brought him an urgent letter. He, thereupon, left the food uneaten in order to read the letter, and asked Vāsabhakkhattiyā to finish her meal.

Viḍūḍabha was her son. It was this deceit practised on Pasenadi which made Viḍūḍabha take his revenge on the Sākyans.[3] It is said[4] that when Pasenadi discovered Vāsabhakkhattiyā's servile origin, he degraded both her and her son from their rank, and that they never went outside the palace. When the Buddha heard of this, he visited the king, preached to him the **Kaṭṭhahāri Jātaka** (*q.v.*), and had the queen restored to honour.

1 Named **Nāgamuṇḍā** (J. i. 133).
2 J. iv. 145.
3 DhA. i. 345 f.; J. iv. 145 f.
4 J. i. 133 f.; iv. 148; see also M. ii. 110, where she is called **Vāsabhā.**

Vāsabhagāma.—A village in **Kāsi.** It was once the residence of **Kassapa Thera** (*q.v.*).[1] Beyond this village was another, called **Cundaṭṭhila,** between Vāsabhagāma and Benares.[2]

1 Vin. i. 312 f.
2 Pv. iii. 1; PvA. 168, 170.

Vāsabhagāma-bhāṇavāra.—The fourth chapter of the **Campeyya-khandhaka** of the **Mahāvagga.**[1]

1 Vin. i. 312-22.

Vāsabhagāmī, Vāsabhagāmika.—A Thera, pupil of **Anuruddha Thera.** He was one of the four **Pācinaka** monks appointed to the committee (*ubbāhikā*) which considered the Ten Points raised by the **Vajjiputtakā.** His fellow-pupil was **Sumana,** and they had both seen the Buddha.[1]

1 Vin. ii. 305; Dpv. iv. 51; v. 22, 24; Sp. i. 35; Mhv. iv. 48, 58.

Vāsabhā.—See **Vāsabhakhattiyā.**

Vāsava.—A name of **Sakka.**[1] Several explanations are given of the title. In the **Saṃyutta Nikāya**[2] it is said that when he was a human being, in his previous birth, he gave dwelling-places (*āvasathaṃ adāsi*)—hence the name.

1 S. i. 221, 223, 229-30, 234-7; D. ii. 260, 274; SN. vs. 384; DhA. iii. 270; J. i. 65, etc.; Cv. xxxvii. 151, etc.
2 S. i. 229; *cp.* DhA. i. 264.

According to the Dīgha Nikāya, however,[3] he is Vāsava because he is chief of the **Vasū** (*Vasūnaṃ seṭṭho*), whom Buddhaghosa[4] calls **Vasudevatā.**

[3] D. ii. 260. [4] DA. ii. 690.

Vāsavanesī.—A class of devas, present at the preaching of the **Mahāsamaya Sutta.**[1]

[1] D. ii. 260.

Vāsijaṭa (or **Nāvā**) **Sutta.**—The *āsavas* are destroyed only by self-training, not by merely wishing for their destruction. A hen may wish for her chicks to break through their eggs with foot, or claw, or mouth, or beak, but they will not do so till they are fully warmed, fully brooded over by the hen. When they are ready to break through, they will do so, irrespective of the hen's wish. A carpenter knows that his adze handle has worn away, not by looking at the finger marks on the handle, but just by its wearing away.

A seagoing vessel, stranded without water and beaten on by wind and sun, will fall to pieces easily and without effort. So will the *āsavas* in a monk who dwells attentive to self-training.[1]

[1] S. iii. 152 f.; *cp.* A. iv. 126 f.

Vāsiṭṭhā, Vāsiṭṭhī.—See **Vāseṭṭhā, Vāseṭṭhī.**

Vāsidāyaka Thera.—An arahant. Ninety-four kappas ago he was an artisan (*kammāra*) in **Tivarā** and gave a razor to the Buddha.[1]

[1] Ap. i. 221.

Vāsudeva.—The eldest of the **Andhakaveṇhudāsaputtā** (*q.v.*). The **Ghata Jātaka** (No. 454) relates how, when Vāsudeva's son died and Vāsudeva gave himself up to despair, his brother **Ghatapaṇḍita** (*q.v.*) brought him to his senses by feigning madness. Vāsudeva's minister was **Rohiṇeyya.** Vāsudeva is addressed[1] as **Kaṇha** and again as **Kesava.** The scholiast explains[2] that he is called Kaṇha because he belonged to the **Kaṇhāyanagotta,** and Kesava because he had beautiful hair (*kesasobhanatāya*). These names, however, give support to the theory[3] that the story of Vāsudeva was associated with the legend of Kṛṣṇa. In the **Mahāummagga Jātaka**[4] it is stated that **Jambāvatī,** mother of King **Sivi,** was the consort of **Vāsudeva Kaṇha.** The scholiast identifies this

[1] J. iv. 84; he is called Kaṇha at J. vi. 421.

[2] J. iv. 84.

[3] See *s.v.* **Andhakaveṇhudāsaputtā,** No. 1.

[4] J. vi. 421.

Vāsudeva with the eldest of the Andhakaveṇhudāsaputtā, and says that Jambāvatī was a *caṇḍalī*. Vāsudeva fell in love with her because of her great beauty and married her in spite of her caste. Their son was **Sivi,** who later succeeded to his father's throne at **Dvāravatī.** Vāsudeva is identified with **Sāriputta.**[6]

[6] J. iv. 89.

Vāsudevavattikā.—Probably followers of **Vāsudeva** (? Kṛṣṇa); they are mentioned with **Baladevavattikā** and others in a list of *samaṇabrāhmaṇā-vattasuddhikā.*[1]

[1] Nid. i. 89; *cf.* *Vāsudevāyatana* at DhSA., p. 141.

Vāsula.—Son of **Candakumāra** (*q.v.*)[1]; he is identified with **Rāhula.**[2]

[1] J. vi. 143. [2] *Ibid.*, 157.

Vāsuladatta.—A Nāga of **Mañjerikabhavana.** He was the nephew of **Mahākāla,** and when **Soṇuttara** went to the Nāga-world to obtain the Buddha's relics for the **Mahā Thūpa,** Mahākāla signed to Vāsuladatta to hide them. Vāsuladatta assumed a huge Nāga-form, three hundred leagues long, with a head one league in extent, and having swallowed the casket containing the relics, lay down at the foot of **Sineru.** But Soṇuttara, by his *iddhi*-power, put his hand into the Nāga's stomach and removed the invisible relics.[1]

[1] Mhv. xxxi. 52 ff.

Vāsuladattā.—Wife of **Udena,** king of **Kosambī.** She was the daughter of **Candappajjota.** When Pajjota heard that Udena's splendour surpassed his own, he resolved to capture him. He was told that Udena could charm elephants with his magic lute, and had a wooden elephant made in which he placed sixty men. A woodsman was sent to inform Udena of the new elephant which had appeared in the forest, and he set out to capture it. The men inside the elephant caused it to run, and, in the course of the chase, Udena was separated from his retinue and taken captive. For three days Pajjota feasted in celebration of his victory, and Udena asked him either to release him or order his death. Pajjota promised release if Udena would teach him the elephant charm; but Udena would teach only to one who paid him homage as a teacher, and this Pajjota would not do. Then Pajjota contrived that Udena should teach it to Vāusladattā. A curtain was hung between them, Udena was told that his pupil was a hunch-backed woman of the court, while Udena was described to the princess as a leper who knew a priceless charm. For many days Udena tried to teach the charm, but the princess could not learn it. In impatience, Udena said: "Dunce of a hunchback, thy lips are too thick and thy cheeks too fat; I've a mind to beat thy face in." And the princess replied: "Villain of a leper, what meanest thou by calling me hunchback?" Udena lifted the fringe of the curtain and they saw each other. From that moment they planned to escape and marry. There was no more learning of charms nor giving of lessons. When their plans were complete, Vāsuladattā told her father that she needed a conveyance and the use of a gate in the city wall. To work the charm, she explained, a certain herb was necessary, which must be obtained at night, at a time indicated by the stars. Thus she secured the use of Pajjota's female elephant, **Bhaddavatī,** and permission to use a certain door at any time. And one day, when Pajjota was out on pleasure, the two filled several bags with gold and silver coins and they started off on Bhaddavatī. The harem guards gave the alarm and the king sent men in pursuit. Udena opened first a sack of gold and then one of silver, scattering the coins, which delayed his pursuers, greedy for the coins. He, meanwhile, hurried on and reached the stockade where his soldiers awaited him. They conducted him and Vāsuladattā to **Kosambī,** where she was made Udena's chief consort.[1]

[1] DhA. i. 191-6, 198 f.

1. **Vāseṭṭha.**—The constant attendant of **Nārada Buddha.**[1]

[1] J. i. 37; Bu. x. 23.

2. **Vāseṭṭha, Vāsiṭṭha.**—The name of an old *ṛṣi* held in high esteem for his knowledge. He was one of the originators of the Vedic runes.[1]

[1] Vin. i. 245; D. i. 104; M. ii. 164, 200; Mil. 162, etc.; *cf.* Vasiṣṭha in Vedic Index.

3. **Vāseṭṭha.**—Name of a *gotta*, probably tracing its descent to the sage **Vāseṭṭha** (Skt. *Vasiṣṭha*). In the **Mahāparinibbāna Sutta**[1] we find the **Mallas** of **Kusinārā** addressed as **Vāseṭṭhā,** as well as the **Mallas** of **Pāvā.**[2] It was a *gotta* held in esteem (*ukkaṭṭha*).[3]

[1] D. ii. 147, 159. [2] *Ibid.*, iii. 209. [3] *E.g.*, Vin. iv. 8.

4. **Vāseṭṭha.**—A young brahmin who, with his friend **Bhāradvāja,** visited the Buddha and held discussions with him. These discussions are recorded in the **Tevijja Sutta,** the **Vāseṭṭha Sutta,** and the **Aggañña Sutta.**[1] Buddhaghosa says[2] that Vāseṭṭha was the chief disciple of **Pokkharasāti.** According to him again,[3] Vāseṭṭha's first visit to the

[1] For details see *s.v.*

[2] DA. ii. 399; SNA. ii. 463; *cf.* SN., p. 116.

[3] DA. ii. 406; *cf.* iii. 860, 872.

Buddha was on the occasion of the preaching of the Vāseṭṭha Sutta, at the conclusion of which he accepted the Buddha as his teacher. He again did so, when, at his next visit, the Buddha preached to him the Tevijja Sutta. Soon after, he entered the Order, and, at the conclusion of the preaching of the Aggañña Sutta, he was given the higher ordination and attained arahantship. He belonged to a very rich family and renounced forty crores when he left the world. He was an expert in the three Vedas.

5. **Vāseṭṭha.**—A lay disciple, evidently distinct from **Vāseṭṭha** (3). He visited the Buddha at the **Kūṭāgārasālā** in **Vesālī** and the Buddha preached to him.[1] See **Vāseṭṭha Sutta** (2). He is mentioned among the Buddha's eminent lay disciples.[2]

[1] A. iv. 258. [2] *Ibid.*, iii. 451.

6. **Vāseṭṭha.**—A brahmin; see **Dhūmakārī.** The scholiast explains[1] that he belonged to the **Vāseṭṭhagotta.**

[1] J. iii. 402.

7. **Vāseṭṭha.**—A brahmin of **Kapilavatthu,** father of **Vappa Thera.**[1]

[1] ThagA. i. 140.

8. **Vāseṭṭha.**—A very rich brahmin, father of **Sela Thera.**[1]

[1] Ap. i. 318.

1. **Vāseṭṭha Sutta.**—The young brahmins, **Vāseṭṭha** and **Bhāradvāja,** fell to discussing one day, at **Icchānaṅkala,** as to what makes a true brahmin. Bhāradvāja maintained that it was pure descent from seven generations of ancestors, with neither break nor blemish in the lineage, whereas Vāseṭṭha contended that virtue and moral behaviour made a true brahmin. As neither could convince the other, they agreed to refer the matter to the Buddha, who said it was not birth but deeds which made the true brahmin.[1]

[1] M. ii. 196 ff. The sutta also occurs in SN., p. 115 ff.; many of the verses are included in the **Brāhmaṇa Vagga** of the Dhammapada.

2. **Vāseṭṭha Sutta.**—The lay disciple **Vāseṭṭha** visits the Buddha at the **Kūṭāgārasālā** in **Vesālī** and states that it would be a good thing for them, for many a day, if his kinsmen, brahmins, tradesfolk, labourers, etc., kept the *uposatha* with the eightfold qualifications. The Buddha

agrees, and says, further, that it would be good if not only gods and men but even the trees were to keep it.[1]

[1] A. iv. 258.

1. **Vāseṭṭhī.**—A brahminee, wife of King **Esukī's** chaplain. She was the mother of **Hatthipāla** (the Bodhisatta), and is identified with **Mahāmāyā.**[1]

[1] J. iv. 483, 491.

2. **Vāseṭṭhī Therī.**—She was born in **Vesāli,** and after being happily married bore a son. The child died very young, and his mother was mad with grief. One day she ran away from home, and, in the course of her wanderings, came to **Mithilā,** where she saw the Buddha, who calmed her grief. He taught her the Doctrine and had her ordained at her own request. She soon after became an arahant.[1] It is said[2] that the brahmin **Sujāta,** father of **Sundarī** (*q.v.*), met Vāseṭṭhī (probably in Benares), and, hearing her story, himself sought the Buddha at Mithilā, where he joined the Order, becoming an arahant at the end of three days.

[1] The story of her child's death and her subsequent history are contained in Thig. vs. 133-8; see also ThigA. 124 f.

[2] Thig. 312-24; ThigA. 228 f.; according to Thig. 312 Vāseṭṭhī would seem to have lost "seven children," but the Commentary explains this as a rhetorical phrase.

Vāha.—The name of **Eḷāra's** state-horse, stolen by **Veḷusumana** (*q.v.*).[1]

[1] MṬ. 440.

Vāhadīpa.—A monastery in Ceylon, to which **Aggabodhi VI.** added a *pāsāda,*[1] and **Udaya I.** another, called the **Senaggabodhipabbata-pāsāda,**[2] which was later repaired by **Dappula II.**[3]

[1] Cv. xlviii. 65. [2] *Ibid.*, xlix. 33. [3] *Ibid.*, 76.

Vāhanavāpi.—A tank built by King **Mahāsena.**[1]

[1] Mhv. xxxvii. 48.

Vikaṭa.—A mountain near **Himavā.**[1]

[1] Ap. i. 227.

Vikaṇṇaka Jātaka (No. 233).—The Bodhisatta was once king of Benares, and, one day, while dallying near a lake in his park, he noticed that fishes and tortoises flocked to him. He learnt, on enquiry, that these animals were attracted by his music, and ordered that they should be fed regularly. On finding that some of them failed to appear, he made arrangements for a drum to be sounded at the feeding-time. Later, finding that a crocodile came and ate some of the fish, the king ordered him to be harpooned. The crocodile escaped capture, but died soon after.

The story was related to a backsliding monk. Desire always leads to suffering, said the Buddha; it was desire that caused the death of the crocodile.[1]

[1] J. ii. 227 f.

Vikāla Sutta.—Few are they who abstain from eating at unseasonable hours, many they who do not.[1]

[1] S. v. 470.

Vikkantacāmunakka.—General of **Anīkaṅga,** whom he slew. He acted for one year (1209 A.C.) as regent for Queen **Līlāvatī.**[1]

[1] Cv. lxxx. 45.

Vikkantabāhu.—See **Vikkamabāhu.**

Vikkama.—A **Lokagalla.** He was a general of **Rohaṇa** and was defeated by the **Mūlapotthakī Māna.**[1]

[1] Cv. lxxv. 138.

Vikkamacoḷappera.—A stronghold in South India, occupied by **Paṇḍiyarāyara.** It was captured by **Laṅkāpura.**[1]

[1] Cv. lxxvi. 178.

Vikkamapaṇḍu.—Son of **Mahālānakitti.** He was staying in the **Duḷu** country when he heard of the events in Ceylon, and, going to the province of **Rohaṇa,** he carried on the government at **Kālatittha** for one year (1046 A.C.), till he was slain by **Jagatīpāla.**[1]

[1] Cv. lvi. 11 ff.

Vikkamapura.—A town in **Dakkhiṇadesa,** once used as headquarters by **Parakkamabāhu I.,** before his capture of the throne. It was near **Kyānagāma.**[1]

[1] Cv. lxxii. 147, 263. Geiger suggests (Cv. *Trs.* i. 333, n. 3) that it was the town attached to the fortress of **Sīhagiri** (*q.v.*).

1. **Vikkamabāhu, Vikkamabhuja, Vikkantabāhu.**—Surnames of King **Kassapa VI.** See **Kassapa** (21).

2. **Vikkamabāhu.** Son of **Vijayabāhu I.** and **Tilokasundarī.** He had two wives, **Sundarī** and **Līlāvatī.**[1] He was made *Ādipāda* by **Vijayabāhu I.**, and, when his son **Gajabāhu** was born, the king gave the province of **Rohaṇa** for his welfare. Vikkamabāhu lived there with **Mahānāgahula** as his capital.[2] When Vijayabāhu died, some of Vikkamabāhu's relations, **Jayabāhu** and the three sons of **Mittā** (**Māṇābharaṇa, Kittisirimegha** and **Sirivallabha**) conspired to keep him out of the succession, but he defeated them in various battles and took possession of the capital **Pulatthipura,** losing, however, **Dakkhiṇadesa** and his former province of **Rohaṇa.**[3] A year later his enemies again rose in revolt, led by **Māṇābharaṇa,** and, as Vikkamabāhu advanced to **Kalyaṇī** to fight them, **Vīradeva** of **Palandīpa** (*q.v.*) landed in **Mannāra,** and his attention was diverted. In the first engagements, Vikkamabāhu was defeated by Vīradeva and forced to flee to **Koṭṭhasāra,** but Vīradeva was later defeated and slain at **Antaraviṭṭhika.** From then onwards Vikkamabāhu and the three sons of Mittā (see above) lived each in his province, but became unpopular both with the saṅgha and the laity owing to their greed and lust. Following the death of Jayabāhu and the Queen Mittā, Vikkamabāhu appears to have been acknowledged king (Vikkamabāhu II.); and it was evidently as such that the birth of his nephew, the prince who after became **Parakkamabāhu I.,** was reported to him. Vikkamabāhu had two sons, **Mahinda** and **Gajabāhu,** but asked that his nephew should be sent to the court; this request, however, was not granted.[4] Vikkamabāhu reigned, till his death, for twenty-one years (1116-1137 A.C.), and was succeeded by his son Gajabāhu.[5]

[1] Cv. lix. 32, 49 f. [2] *Ibid.*, lx. 88 f.
[3] For details see *ibid.*, lxi. 2 ff.
[4] *Ibid.*, lxii. 58 f.
[5] *Ibid.*, lxiii. 18.

3. **Vikkamabāhu.**—Son of **Gajabāhu** and brother of **Coḷagaṅgakumāra.**[1]

[1] Cv. lxx. 238.

4. **Vikkamabāhu.**—Younger brother of King **Kittinissaṅka.** He became king on the death of **Vīrabāhu I.,** but reigned for only three months (in 1196 A.C.), after which he was slain by **Coḍagaṅga.**[1]

[1] Cv. lxxx. 28.

5. **Vikkamabāhu.**—The king who succeeded **Parakkamabāhu V.** He was himself succeeded by **Bhuvenakabāhu V.**[1]

[1] Cv. xci. 1, 3; he seems to have reigned for eighteen years (1347-75 A.C.). See Cv. *Trs.* ii. 212, n. 2.

Vikkamabhuja.—See **Vikkamabāhu.**

Vikkamarājasīha.—The last king of Ceylon. He was the son of the sister of **Rājādhirājasīha,** whom he succeeded. He ruled for eighteen years (1798-1815 A.C.), but the people rebelled against him, and he was obliged to abdicate in favour of the **Ingirisī** (English).[1]

[1] Cv. ci. 19 ff.

Vigatānanda.—A king of twenty-four kappas ago, a former birth of **Ekanandiya Thera.**[1]

[1] Ap. i. 217.

Vigatāsoka.—See **Vītāsoka.**

Viggāhita Sutta.—The Buddha exhorts the monks not to engage in wordy warfare, such talk being neither profitable nor conducive to Nibbāna. They should converse about *dukkha,* its cause, etc.[1]

[1] S. v. 419.

Vighāsa Jātaka (No. 393).—Once seven brothers of a **Kāsi** village renounced the world and lived as ascetics in **Mejjhārañña,** but they were given up to various amusements. The Bodhisatta, who was **Sakka,** saw this, and, assuming the form of a parrot, visited them and sang the praises of the ascetic life. They expressed their joy at being thus praised, but the parrot went on to make them understand that their lives were useless; they were mere refuse-eaters and not ascetics.

The story was related in reference to the monks mentioned in the **Pāsādakampana Sutta** (*q.v.*). The monks are identified with the seven ascetics.[1]

[1] J. iii. 310 f.

Vicakkhaṇā.—A class of devas, present at the preaching of the **Mahāsamaya Sutta.**[1]

[1] D. ii. 261.

Vicitoli (Vicikoli).—Wife of **Dhammadassī Buddha** in his last lay life. Their son was **Puññavaḍḍhana.**[1] Vicitoli gave milk-rice to the Buddha just before his **Enlightenment.**[2]

[1] Bu. xvi. 15. [2] BuA. 182.

Vicittā.—One of the chief lay women supporters of **Padumuttara Buddha.**[1]

[1] Bu. xi. 26.

Vicchidaka Sutta.—The idea of a fissured corpse, if cultivated, leads to great profit.[1]

[1] S. v. 131.

Vijambhavatthu.—A place of residence for monks in the **Vattaniya-senāsana**, where **Rohaṇa** took **Nāgasena** to admit him into the Order.[1]

[1] Mil. p. 12.

1. **Vijaya.**—The first Ariyan king of Ceylon. He was the eldest of the thirty-two sons of **Sīhabāhu**, king of **Lāḷa**, and of **Sīhasīvalī**. Because of his evil conduct he, with seven hundred others, was deported by the king, with their heads half shaved. Their wives and children were deported with them. The children landed at **Naggadīpa** and the women at **Mahilādīpaka.**[1] Vijaya and the other men landed at **Suppāraka**, but was obliged to leave owing to the violence of his supporters.[2] They reached Ceylon on the day of the Buddha's death, received the protection of the deva **Uppalavaṇṇa**, and thus escaped destruction by the **Yakkhas**. The yakkhiṇī, **Kuveṇī**, fell in love with Vijaya, and he, with her assistance, killed the Yakkhas of **Laṅkāpura** and **Sirīsavatthu**, and founded the city of **Tambapaṇṇi**. Vijaya's chief ministers, **Anurādha**, **Upatissa**, **Ujjena**, **Uruvela** and **Vijita**, founded separate colonies, named after themselves.

Vijaya had two children by Kuveṇī, **Jīvahattha** and **Dīpellā**; but when he wished to be consecrated king, he sent for and obtained, for his wife, a daughter of the **Paṇḍu** king of **Madhurā**. Kuveṇī, thereupon, left him and was killed by the Yakkhas. Vijaya reigned for thirty-eight years and was succeeded by **Paṇḍuvāsudeva.**[3]

Ajātasattu and **Vijaya** were contemporaries, Ajātasattu's twenty-fourth year of kingship corresponding to Vijaya's sixteenth year.[4]

[1] MṬ. 264.

[2] According to Dpv. ix. 26, Vijaya went from Suppāraka to **Bhārukaccha**, where he stayed for three months.

[3] For details of Vijaya's life, see Mhv. vi. 38 ff.; vii. 6 ff.; viii. 1-3; Dpv. ix. 6 ff.

[4] *Ibid.*, iv. 27; v. 77.

2. **Vijaya.**—See **Vijayakumāra.**

3. **Vijaya.**—Minister of **Aṅgati**, king of **Videha**. For details see the **Mahānāradakassapa Jātaka**. He is identified with **Sāriputta.**[1]

[1] J. vi. 255.

4. **Vijaya.**—A king of Benares, descended from **Mahāsammata**. His son was **Vijitasena.**[1]

[1] Dpv. iii. 39.

5. **Vijaya.**—A householder, mentioned as an exemplary layman.[1]

[1] A. iii. 451.

6. **Vijaya Thera.**—He was born in **Sāvatthi** and was versed in brahmin lore. Then he became an ascetic and lived in the forest. Having heard of the Buddha, Vijaya visited him and joined the Order, becoming an arahant in due course. In the time of **Piyadassī Buddha** he was a rich householder and built a jewelled cornice (*vedikā*) round the Buddha's *thūpa*. Sixteen kappas ago he became king thirty-six times, under the name of **Maṇippabhāsa.**[1] He is probably identical with **Vedikāraka Thera** of the **Apadāna.**[2]

[1] Thag. vs. 92; ThagA. i. 191f. [2] Ap. i. 171.

7. **Vijaya.**—Mentioned with **Jātimitta,** as a patron of **Metteyya Buddha.**[1]

[1] Anāgat. vs. 59.

Vijaya Sutta.—The eleventh sutta of the **Sutta Nipāta.** According to Bhuddhaghosa,[1] this sutta was preached on two occasions: once to **Janapadakalyāṇī-Nandā,** following her attainment of *sotāpatti*, in order to help her to higher attainment—and again when the Buddha took the monks to the funeral of **Sirimā,** sister of **Jīvaka.** The sutta is also called the **Kāyavicchandanika Sutta.**

The sutta is a discourse on the foul nature of the body, full of impurities flowing in nine streams; when dead, nobody cares for it. Only a monk, possessed of wisdom, understands it and reflects on its worthlessness.[2]

[1] SNA. i. 241 f. [2] SN. vs. 193-206; *cf.* J. i. 146.

Vijayakumāra.—Son of **Sirināga II.,** and king of Ceylon for one year (302-3 A.C.). He was killed in his palace by the three **Lambakaṇṇas: Saṅghatissa, Saṅghabodhi** and **Goṭhābhaya.**[1]

[1] Mhv. xxxvi. 57 f.; Dpv. xxii. 51.

Vijayapāla.—Son of **Vimaladhammasūriya I.** and his queen, Dona Catherina. He was governor of the province of **Mātula.**[1]

[1] Cv. xcv. 22.

Vijayapura.—The Pāli name for the city of Panyā in Burma.[1]

[1] Bode, *op. cit.*, 27, 40.

1. **Vijayabāhu.**—King of Ceylon (**Vijayabāhu I.,** 1059-1114 A.C.). His earlier name was **Kitti;** his parents were **Moggallāna** and **Lokitā,**[1] and

[1] Cv. lvii. 42 f.; but see Cv. *Trs.* i. 201, n. 1.

from his thirtieth year he lived in **Mūlasālā.** Later, without the knowledge of his parents, he left home, defeated the general **Loka,** and became *Ādipāda* of **Malaya** after bringing this province under his power. At the age of sixteen he defeated **Kassapa,** chief of the **Kesadhātus,** and became ruler of **Rohaṇa** as well, assuming the title of *Yuvarāja* and the name of Vijayabāhu. At this time the **Coḷas** were in possession of the government at **Pulatthipura,** and they made efforts to stem the advance of Vijayabāhu. They were at first successful, owing to the disunion among the Sinhalese themselves, but Vijayabāhu conquered the Coḷa armies near **Paluṭṭhapabbata** and marched to Pulatthipura. He was helped by forces sent by the king of **Rāmañña,** to whom he sent an embassy with various presents. He had, however, to bide his time, and retreated to **Vātagiri.** From there he went, in due course, to **Mahānāgahula,** his officers having, in the meantime, crushed all opposition in **Dakkhiṇadesa** and captured the province of **Anurādhapura** and the district round **Mahātittha.** When he felt the right moment had arrived, Vijayabāhu marched once more to Pulatthipura and captured it after a siege of one and a half months. From there he advanced to Anurādhapura, spent three months in the city and returned to Pulatthipura. This was fifteen years after he became Yuvarāja. In the eighteenth year he crowned himself king, under the title of **Sirisaṅghabodhi,** making his younger brother **Vīrabāhu** Yuvarāja and governor of Dakkhiṇadesa, and his other brother, **Jayabāhu,** Ādipāda and governor of Rohaṇa. The king had several queens, among whom was **Līlāvatī,** a Coḷa princess and daughter of **Jagatīpāla;** by her he had a daughter **Yasodharā.** Another of his queens was a Kāliṅga princess, **Tilokasundarī,** by whom he had five daughters—**Subhaddā, Sumittā, Lokanāthā, Ratanāvalī** and **Rūpavatī**—and a son called **Vikkamabāhu.** Vijayabāhu gave his younger sister, **Mittā,** in marriage to the king of **Paṇḍu,** refusing an offer of marriage made by the Coḷa king.

When peace had been established, Vijayabāhu sent messengers to **Anuruddha,** king of **Rāmañña,** and fetched monks from that country to help in the reformation of the Saṅgha in Ceylon. He gave over the whole district of **Āḷisāra** for the use of the monks and built many vihāras. He translated the **Dhammasaṅgaṇī** and held an annual **Daṇḍissara** offering. He also had the Tipiṭaka copied, and presented the copies to various monks. Because the Sinhalese envoys sent to **Kaṇṇāṭa** were insulted and maimed, the king prepared to send a punitive expedition to Coḷa, but the **Velakkāra** troops revolted, captured Mittā and her children, and burned the king's palace. The king was forced to retreat to **Dakkhiṇadesa,** but, with the help of **Vīrabāhu,** he defeated the rebels. In the forty-fifth year of his reign he took an army to Coḷa and stopped at a seaport in that country; but as the Coḷa king refused to accept his challenge to fight, he returned to his own country. He repaired many tanks and restored many vihāras in various parts of the country. He provided facilities for pilgrims journeying to **Samantakūṭa,** and patronized the **Lābhavāsī** and the **Vantajīvaka** monks. He ruled for fifty-five years. Vīrabāhu died before him, and he made Jayabāhu Uparāja in his place.[2]

[2] For details of Vijayabāhu's reign, see Cv. chaps. lviii-lx.

2. **Vijayabāhu.**—Sister's son of **Parakkamabāhu I.** and king of Ceylon (**Vijayabāhu II.,** 1186-87 A.C.). He succeeded his uncle. Among his acts was the grant of an amnesty to all those imprisoned by Parakkamabāhu I., and the despatch of an embassy to the king of **Arimaddana** with a letter in Pāli, composed by himself. He was a good king, but was slain at the end of one year's reign by **Mahinda** (afterwards **Mahinda VI.**). His viceroy was **Kittinissaṅka.**[1]

[1] Cv. lxxx. 1-18.

3. **Vijayabāhu.**—King of Ceylon (**Vijayabāhu III.,** 1232-36 A.C.). He claimed descent from King **Sirisaṅghabodhi I.** and was lord of the **Vannī.** He found the government of Ceylon in the hands of the **Damiḷas,** and, after defeating them, he established the seat of government in **Jambuddoṇi.** He sent for the monks, who, with **Vācissara** at their head, had left Ceylon during the preceding disturbed period and had deposited the Buddha's Alms-bowl and Tooth Relic in the rock fortress at **Billasela.** The king did much for the reform of the priesthood and built various monasteries, chief of which was the **Vijayasundarārāma** and the **Vijayabāhu-vihāra.** He had two sons, **Parakkamabāhu** and **Bhuvanekabāhu.** He appointed the Elder **Saṅgharakkhita** as head of the Order in Ceylon.[1]

[1] Cv. lxxxi. 10 ff.

4. **Vijayabāhu.**—King of Ceylon (**Vijayabāhu IV.,** 1271-72 A.C.). He was the eldest of the five sons of **Parakkamabāhu II.,** his brothers being **Bhuvanekabāhu, Tibhuvanamalla, Parakkamabāhu** and **Jayabāhu.** With the consent of the monks, Parakkamabāhu II. handed over the government, before his death, to Vijayabāhu, who was evidently very popular, and was known among his subjects as a **Bodhisatta.**[1] He restored **Pulatthipura** and built and renovated numerous monasteries, among them the vihāra at **Titthagāma.** During his reign, **Candabhānu** invaded Ceylon, but was defeated by the king with the help of his Ādipāda, **Vīrabāhu.** Vijayabāhu built a city near **Subhagiri** and made it his seat of government. He restored the **Ratnāvalī-cetiya** and gave

[1] See, *e.g.*, Cv. lxxxviii. 35.

Anurādhapura into the charge of the **Vanni** chiefs. Later, when **Vīrabāhu** had completely restored Pulatthipura, the king was consecrated there in the presence of his father, who came over from **Jambuddoṇi.** Then, at the desire of his father, he held, on the **Mahāvālukagaṅgā,** at **Sahassatittha,** a festival for admission into the Order. The celebrations lasted a fortnight, and the king conferred on the monks various ranks, such as *mahāsāmipāda, mūlatherapāda, pariveṇathera,* etc. Two years after the death of Parakkamabāhu, Vijayabāhu was slain by a treacherous general, named **Mitta.**[2] Vijayabāhu's son was **Parakkamabāhu III.**[3]

[2] For details regarding Vijayabāhu, see Cv. lxxxvii. 14-xc. 1. [3] *Ibid.,* xc. 48.

5. **Vijayabāhu.**—King of Ceylon (**Vijayabāhu V.**). He succeeded **Vannibhuvanekabāhu,** and was himself succeeded by **Bhuvanekabāhu IV.**[1]

[1] Cv. xc. 105; he was among the successors of **Parakkamabāhu IV.,** and reigned somewhere between 1302 and 1346 A.C.

6. **Vijayabāhu.**—King of Ceylon (**Vijayabāhu VI.**). He was one of the successors of **Parakkamabāhu VI.** His immediate predecessor was **Vīraparakkamabāhu.**[1]

[1] Cv. xcii. 4; his reign was somewhere between 1405 and 1411 A.C.

Vijayabāhu-pariveṇa-vihāra.—A monastery built by King **Vijayabāhu III.** in **Vattalagāma.**[1] A monk, named **Kāyasatti,** was its chief incumbent in the time of **Parakkamabāhu IV.**[2]

[1] Cv. lxxxi. 58. [2] *Ibid.,* xc. 91.

Vijayabhuja.—See **Vijayabāhu.**

Vijayasundārāma.—A monastery built by **Vijayabāhu III.**[1]

[1] Cv. lxxxi. 51; see also P.L.C. 209.

Vijayā Therī.—She belonged to a household in **Rājagaha** and was a friend of **Khemā.** When Khemā left the world, Vijayā went to her, and, having listened to her teaching, joined the Order under her, attaining arahantship soon afterwards.[1] She may be identical with the Vijayā, mentioned in the *Saṃyutta Nikāya,*[2] a bhikkhuṇī whom **Māra,** assuming the form of a young man, tried unsuccessfully to tempt.

[1] ThigA. 159 f.; her *Udāna* verses are included in Thig. 169-74. [2] S. i. 130.

Vijayā Sutta.—Contains the story of **Māra's** temptation of **Vijayā Therī.**[1]

[1] S. i. 130.

Vijayārāma.—A garden in **Anurādhapura,** through which the boundary of the **Mahāvihāra** passed.[1] A monastery was built there (probably later), which came to be called the **Vijayārāma-vihāra.** Once, an arahant monk, teaching a *kammaṭṭhāna* to two monks, spoke of *samuddha* instead of *samudda.* One of the monks pointed out his error, and was sent by the arahant to the **Mahāvihāra** with a message that he had paid more attention to letters than to their meaning. The monk went to the Mahāvihāra and later attained Nibbāna, after solving various difficult questions in the presence of the assembly.[2]

[1] Mbv. p. 136. [2] MA. ii. 827.

Vijayuttara.—**Sakka's** conch-trumpet, which he blew at the moment of the Buddha's Enlightenment. It was one hundred and twenty hands in length.[1] He also blew it on the occasion of the enshrinement of relics in the **Mahā Thūpa**[2] and on the day of the coronation of **Candakumāra.**[3]

[1] J. i. 72; BuA. 239. [2] Mhv. xxx. 74. [3] J. vi. 157.

1. **Vijita.**—A Pacceka Buddha.[1]

[1] M. iii. 70; ApA. i. 107.

2. **Vijita.**—One of the ministers of **Vijaya,** and founder of **Vijitapura.**[1]

[1] Mhv. vii. 45; Dpv. ix. 32.

3. **Vijita.**—A Sākyan prince, brother of **Bhaddakaccānā.** He went to Ceylon, where he founded **Vijitagāma.**[1]

[1] Mhv. ix. 10.

4. **Vijita.**—A suburb of **Pulatthipura,** in which was **Veḷuvana-vihāra.**[1]

[1] Cv. lxxiii. 153; lxxviii. 87; also Cv. *Trs.* ii. 18, n. 3.

Vijita-pura, Vijita-nagara.—A city founded by **Vijita,** minister to **Vijaya.** Near by was **Khandhāvārapiṭṭhi,** where **Duṭṭhagāmaṇī** pitched his camp during his campaign against the **Damiḷas,** and also the village of **Hatthipora** (*q.v.*). The city was a stronghold of the Damiḷas, and was captured by **Duṭṭhagāmaṇī** after a four months' siege.[1]

[1] For details of the siege see Mhv. xxv. 19 ff.

Vijitamitta.—A brahmin, friend of **Bhaddasāla,** and later *aggasāvaka* of **Nārada Buddha.**[1] *v.l.* **Jitamitta.**

[1] Bu. x. 23; BuA. 154.

Vijitasaṅgāma.—A *yavapālaka* who supplied grass to **Tissa Buddha** for his seat.[1]

[1] BuA. 189.

1. **Vijitasena.**—Son of **Koṇḍañña Buddha.** His mother was **Rucidevī.**[1]

[1] Bu. iii. 27; BuA. 107, 111.

2. **Vijitasena.**—Son of **Kassapa Buddha.** His mother was **Sunandā.**[1]

[1] Bu. xxv. 36; DA. ii. 422.

3. **Vijitasena Thera.**—He was born in the family of an elephant-trainer of **Kosala,** and had two maternal uncles, **Sena** and **Upasena,** who were also elephant-trainers and had joined the Order. He saw the Buddha's **Yamakapāṭihāriya** and entered the Order under his uncles, attaining arahantship in due course. In the time of **Atthadassī Buddha** he was a hermit and gave the Buddha some fruit.[1] Several verses uttered by him in self-admonition, in which he displays his knowledge of elephant-craft, are included in the Theragāthā.[2]

He is probably identical with **Bhallātakadāyaka** of the Apadāna.[3]

[1] ThagA. i. 424 f. [2] Thag. vss. 355-9. [3] Ap. ii. 398.

4. **Vijitasena.**—A king of Benares, descendant of **Mahāsammata.** His father was **Vijaya.**[1]

[1] Dpv. iii. 39; MṬ. 130.

1. **Vijitasenā.**—Daughter of the third **Okkāka** and his queen **Hatthā (Bhattā).**[1]

[1] DA. i. 258; SNA. i. 352; MṬ. 131; Mtu. i. 348.

2. **Vijitasenā.**—See **Jitasenā.**

3. **Vijitasenā.**—One of the chief women supporters of **Kassapa Buddha.**[1]

[1] Bu. xxv. 41.

1. **Vijitā.**—One of the five daughters of the third **Okkāka** and his queen **Bhattā (Hatthā).**[1]

[1] DA. i. 258; SNA. i. 352, etc.

2. **Vijitā.**—One of the palaces of **Nārada Buddha,** before his Renunciation.[1]

[1] Bu. x. 19. BuA. (151) calls it **Vijita.**

1. **Vijitāvī.**—A *khattiya* in the time of **Koṇḍañña Buddha.** He lived in the city of **Candavatī,** but, after hearing the Buddha preach, he renounced household life and became a monk.[1]

[1] BuA. 111; Bu. iii. 9; J. i. 30.

2. **Vijitāvī.**—A khattiya of **Arimanda** city. He was the Bodhisatta in the time of **Phussa Buddha.** He later joined the Order and became an eminent monk.[1]

[1] BuA. 194; Bu. xix. 7; J. i. 40.

3. **Vijitāvī.**—One of the palaces occupied by **Nārada Buddha** in his last lay life.[1]

[1] BuA. 151; but see s.v. **Nārada.**

4. **Vijitāvī.**—A Burmese author of **Vijitapura** (Panyā); he wrote a **Kaccāyanavaṇṇanā** on the **Sandhikappa** and the **Vācakopadesa.**[1]

[1] Sās. p. 90; Bode, *op. cit.*, 46.

1. **Vijjā Sutta.**—Ten qualities, the possession of which makes a man's accomplishment complete in every detail.[1]

[1] A. v. 12 f.

2. **Vijjā Sutta.**—Just as ignorance is in the forefront of all evil, so is knowledge (*vijjā*) in the forefront of all good.[1]

[1] A. v. 214.

3. **Vijjā Sutta.**—**Anuruddha** declares that, by cultivating the four *satipaṭṭhānas,* he has been able (1) to remember divers existences in the past; (2) to discern the arising and going of beings according to their merits; and (3) to destroy the *āsavas.*[1]

[1] S. v. 305.

4. **Vijjā Sutta.**—Knowledge is knowledge of *dukkha,* its cause, etc.[1]

[1] S. v. 429.

5. **Vijjā Sutta.**—Preached to the **Vajjians** at **Koṭigāma.** It is through not understanding *dukkha,* its cause, etc., that beings wander on in *saṃsāra.*[1]

[1] S. v. 431.

6. **Vijjā Sutta.**—Those recluses who understand *dukkha,* its cause, etc., as they really are, realize in this very life the reality of their recluseship.[1]

[1] S. v. 432.

7. **Vijjā Sutta.**—See **Bhikkhu Sutta** (4).

Vijjādhara-guhā, -lena.—A cave in **Pulatthipura,** forming part of **Uttarārāma.**[1] The boundary of the **Baddhasīmāpāsāda** grounds passed fifty staves (375 ft.) to the north of this cave.[2]

[1] Cv. lxxviii. 73. [2] *Ibid.*, vs. 66. See Cv. *Trs.* ii. 111, n. 2.

Vijjābhāgiya Sutta.—The six parts of wisdom: the idea of impermanence, of ill in impermanence, of not-self in ill, of renunciation, of dispassion, of ending.[1]

[1] A. iii. 334.

Vijjāmaṇḍapa.—A building in the **Dīpuyyāna.** It was built to demonstrate the various branches of science.[1]

[1] Cv. lxxiii. 115.

Vijjāvimutti Sutta.—The holy life is lived with the realization of the fruits of knowledge for its aim.[1]

[1] S. v. 28.

Vijjha.—A horizontal rock on which the stream, flowing from the eastern mouth of **Anotatta,** divides into five rivers: **Gaṅgā, Yamunā, Aciravatī, Sarabhū** and **Mahī.**[1] *v.l.* **Viñjha.**

[1] UdA. 301 f.; SNA. ii. 439; AA. ii. 760; MA. ii. 586.

1. **Viñjha.**—See **Vijjha.**

2. **Viñjha, Viñjhāṭavi.**—The Vindhyā mountains and the forests surrounding them, through which lay the road from **Tāmalitti** to **Pāṭaliputta.** Along this road **Asoka** travelled bearing the Bodhi-tree.[1] This was also the road leading from Ceylon to Pāṭaliputta.[2] Near the forest was a great monastery from which sixty thousand monks, led by **Uttara,** went to attend the Foundation Ceremony of the **Mahā Thūpa.**[3] At the foot of the mountain was a market town named **Muṇḍa.**[4] The forest was the abode of *petas.*[5]

[1] Mhv. xix. 6; Dpv. xvi. 2.
[2] *Ibid.*, xv. 87. [3] Mhv. xxix. 40.
[4] DhA. iv. 128; elsewhere, however (*e.g.*, Sp. iii. 655), Viñjhāṭavi is described as *agāmakaṃ araññaṃ.*
[5] See, *e.g.*, PvA. 43, 192, 244.

1. **Viññāṇa Sutta.**—In him who contemplates the enjoyment of all that makes for enfettering, there comes descent of consciouness. Name-

and-form is conditioned by consciousness, sense by name-and-form, contact by sense, etc.[1]

[1] S. ii. 91.

2. **Viññāṇa Sutta.**—One of the suttas taught by the Buddha to **Rāhula.** Consciousness is fleeting.[1]

[1] S. ii. 246.

3. **Viññāṇa Sutta.**—Eye-consciousness is impermanent, changeable—likewise ear-consciousness, etc.[1]

[1] S. iii. 226.

4. **Viññāṇa Sutta.**—The arising of eye-consciousness and of the other factors—this is the appearing of decay-and-death. Their ceasing is the end of decay-and-death.[1]

[1] S. iii. 229.

5. **Viññāṇa Sutta.**—The desire-and-lust that is in eye-consciousness is a corruption of the heart; likewise that which is ear-consciousness, etc.[1]

S. iii. 232.

6. **Viññāṇa Sutta.**—**Moggallāna** says that, when he entered into and abode in the realm of infinite consciousness, the Buddha appeared before him and warned him not to be remiss. Then he passed beyond it.[1]

[1] S. iv. 266.

Viññāṇañcāyatanūpagādevā.—A class of devas living in the **Arūpaloka.** Their life lasts for forty thousand *mahākappā*.[1]

[1] M. iii. 103; *Compendium*, p. 143.

Viṭu and **Viṭucca.**—Vassals of the **Cātummahārājikā.** They were present at the preaching of the **Mahāsamaya Sutta.**[1]

[1] D. ii. 258.

Viṭeṇḍu.—One of the vessels of the **Cātummahārājikā** present at the preaching of the **Mahāsamaya Sutta.**[1]

[1] D. ii. 257.

Viṭṭāra.—A Damiḷa chief, ally of **Kulasekhara.**[1]

[1] Cv. lxxvi. 146.

Viḍūḍabha.—Son of **Pasenadi** and **Vāsabhakhattiyā.** On the birth of Viḍūbha, the king, glad at having a son, sent word to his own grandmother asking her to choose a name. The minister who delivered the message was deaf, and when the grandmother spoke of Vāsabhakhattiyā as being dear to the king, mistook "*vallabha*" for "Viḍūḍabha," and, thinking that this was an old family name, bestowed it on the prince. When the boy was quite young, Pasenadi conferred on him the rank of *senāpati*, thinking that this would please the Buddha.[1]

When Viḍūḍabha was seven years old, he wished to visit his maternal grandparents, hoping to be given presents, like his companions by theirs, but Vāsabhakhattiyā persuaded him against this, telling him that they lived too far away. But he continued to express this desire, and when he reached the age of sixteen she consented to his going. Thereupon, accompanied by a large retinue, he set out for **Kapilavatthu.** The Sākyans sent all the younger princes away, there being thus none to pay obeisance to him in answer to his salute, the remaining ones being older than he. He was shown every hospitality and stayed for several days. On the day of his departure, one of his retinue overheard a contemptuous remark passed by a slave woman who was washing, with milk and water, the seat on which Viḍūḍabha had sat. This was reported to him, and, having discovered the deceit which had been practised on his father, he vowed vengeance on the Sākyans. Pasenadi cut off all honours from Vāsabhakhattiyā and her son, but restored them later, at the Buddha's suggestion.

After Pasenadi's death, which was brought about by the treachery of **Dīghakārāyaṇa** in making Viḍūḍabha king,[2] Viḍūḍabha remembered his oath, and set out with a large army for Kapilavatthu. The Buddha, aware of this, stood under a tree, with scanty shade, just within the boundaries of the Sākyan kingdom. On the boundary was a banyan which gave deep shade. Viḍūḍabha, seeing the Buddha, asked him to sit under the banyan. "Be not worried," said the Buddha, "the shade of my kinsmen keeps me cool."[3] Viḍūḍabha understood and returned home with his army. Three times he marched against the Sākyans and three times he saw the Buddha under the same tree and turned back. The fourth time the Buddha knew that the fate of the Sākyans could not be averted and remained away. In a previous existence they had conspired and thrown poison into a river.

[1] It was for the same reason he married Vāsabhakhattiyā; both in the **Piyajātika** (M. ii. 110) and the **Kaṇṇakatthala** (M. ii. 127) Suttas Viḍūḍabha is spoken of as senāpati.

[2] For details see *s.v.* Pasenadi.

[3] This exposure to the sun gave the Buddha a headache which lasted throughout his life (UdA. 265; Ap. i. 300).

The Sākyans went armed into the battle, but not wishing to kill, they shot their arrows into Viḍūḍabha's ranks without killing anyone. On this being brought to Viḍūḍabha's notice, he gave orders that all the Sākyans, with the exception of the followers of the Sākyan **Mahānāma,** should be slain. The Sākyans stood their ground, some with blades of grass and some with reeds. These were spared, and came to be known as **Tiṇasākiyā** and **Naḷasākiyā** respectively.[4] The others were all killed, even down to the infants. Mahānāma was taken prisoner and went back with Viḍūḍabha, who wished him to share his meal. But Mahānāma said he wished to bathe, and plunged into a lake with the idea of dying rather than eating with a slave-woman's child. The Nāgas of the lake, however, saved him and took him to the Nāga-world. That same night Viḍūḍabha pitched his camp on the dry bed of the **Aciravatī.** Some of his men lay on the banks, others on the river-bed. Some of those who lay on the river-bed were not guilty of sin in their past lives, while some who slept on the bank were. Ants appeared on the ground where the sinless ones lay, and they changed their sleeping-places. During the night there was a sudden flood, and Viḍūḍabha and those of his retinue who slept in the river-bed were washed into the sea.[5]

[4] According to Chinese records, Viḍūḍabha took five hundred Sākyan maidens into his harem, but they refused to submit to him and abused him and his family. He ordered them to be killed, their hands and feet to be cut off, and their bodies thrown into a ditch. The Buddha sent a monk to preach to them, and they were reborn after death in heaven. Sakra collected their bones and burnt them (Beal, *op. cit.* ii. 11 f.). The eleventh Pallava of the *Avadānakalpalatā* has a similar story. Viḍūḍabha killed seventy-seven thousand Sākyans and stole eighty thousand boys and girls. The girls were rude to him, and he ordered their death.

[5] This account is taken from DhA. i. 346-9, 357-61; but see also J. i. 133 and iv. 146 f., 151 f.

Viḍoja.—An epithet of **Indra.**[1]

[1] UdA. 75; see also n. 12.

1. **Vitakka Sutta.**—Sense-desire-thinking is got rid of by renunciation, ill-will-thinking and harm-thinking by the cultivation of their opposites.[1]

[1] A. iii. 446.

2. **Vitakka Sutta.**—Concentration accompanied by thought, both directed and sustained, only sustained, neither directed nor sustained, is the path which leads to the " Uncompounded."[1]

[1] S. iv. 360.

3. **Vitakka Sutta.**—Thoughts of lust, hatred, and delusion are unprofitable. Thoughts of ill, its cause, etc., are concerned with profit.[1]

[1] S. v. 417.

Vitakkasanthāna Sutta.—The twentieth sutta of the **Majjhima Nikāya**, preached to the monks at **Sāvatthi.** A monk can, in five ways, get rid of bad thoughts associated with lust, hatred, and delusion: by diverting his mind elsewhere; by scrutiny of their perilous consequence; by ignoring bad and wrong thoughts; by allaying what moulds these thoughts; by subduing them by sheer force of mind. These different methods are illustrated by similes.[1]

[1] M. i. 118-122.

Vitakkita Sutta.—See **Ayoniso Sutta.**

Vitiṇṇa.—One of the chief lay supporters of **Padumuttara Buddha.**[1]

[1] Bu. xi. 26.

Vitta Sutta.—Preached in answer to a deva's questions; the best wealth is faith, right deeds bring happiness, truth has the sweetest taste, a life of wisdom is the best.[1]

[1] S. i. 42.

1. **Vitthata Sutta.**—A detailed account of the four kinds of progress: painful progress with sluggish intuition, the painful mode with swift intuition, the pleasant mode with sluggish intuition, the pleasant mode with swift intuition.[1]

[1] A. ii. 149 f.

2. **Vitthata Sutta.**—A detailed description of the powers of a learner: the power of faith, of conscientiousness, of fear of blame, of energy, of insight.[1]

[1] A. iii. 2 f.

3. **Vitthata Sutta.**—The same as Sutta (2); the powers being of faith, energy, mindfulness, concentration, insight.[1]

[1] A. iii. 10 f.

4. **Vitthata Sutta.**—A detailed description of the advantages of observing the *uposatha* vows.[1]

[1] A. iv. 251.

1. **Vitthāra Sutta.**—The five *indriyas*, if completely cultivated, lead to arahantship; in lesser degree to lower attainments.[1]

[1] S. v. 201 f.

2. **Vitthāra Sutta.**—A detailed account of deeds which are dark with dark result, bright with bright result, dark and bright with mixed results, neither dark nor bright—the last leading to non-doing.[1]

[1] A. ii. 230 f.

Vidadhimukhamaṇḍanaṭīkā.—A Commentary by **Vepullabuddhi.**[1] It was, perhaps, a Commentary to **Vidaghamukhamaṇḍana** (a book of riddles) by **Dhammadāsa.**[2]

[1] Gv. 64, 74. [2] Bode, *op. cit.*, 28, n. 3.

Viditvisesa.—The name under which **Ajātasattu** will become a Pacceka Buddha.[1]

[1] DA. i. 238.

Viduragga.—Senāpati of **Udaya IV.**[1]

[1] Cv. liii. 46; *cf.* **Vajiragga.**

Vidurā.—One of the wives of **Udaya IV.** She fixed a mandorla (*pādajāla*) on an image of the Buddha which was in the **Mahāvihāra.**[1]

[1] Cv. liii. 50.

Vidūra Jātaka.—See **Sucira Jātaka.**

1. **Videha.**—A seṭṭhi in the time of **Padumuttara Buddha.** He was a previous birth of **Mahā Kassapa** (*q.v.*). His wife was **Bhaddā Kāpilānī** in this age.[1]

[1] Ap. ii. 578.

2. **Videha, Videhā.**—A country and its people. At the time of the Buddha, Videha formed one of the two important principalities of the **Vajjian** confederacy. Its capital was **Mithilā** (*q.v.*). The kingdom bordered on the Ganges, on one side of which was **Magadha** and on the other Videha.[1] Adjacent to it were **Kāsi** and **Kosala.** In the **Gandhāra Jātaka**[2] the kingdom of Videha is said to have been three hundred leagues in extent, with sixteen thousand villages, well-filled storehouses and sixteen thousand dancing girls. Videha was a great trade centre, and mention is made[3] of merchants coming from **Sāvatthi** to sell their

[1] See, *e.g.*, M. i. 225; MA. i. 448. [2] J. iii. 365; iv. 316. [3] PvA. 227.

wares in Videha. The **Suruci Jātaka** (*q.v.*) seems to show that a close connection existed between Videha and Benares. In the Buddha's time, one of **Bimbisāra's** queens was probably from Videha (see **Vedehiputta**). Mention is also made[4] of a friendship existing between the kings of **Gandhāra** and Videha. In earlier times Videha was evidently a kingdom, its best-known kings being **Mahājanaka** and **Nimi** (*q.v.*); but in the Buddha's time it was a republic, part of the Vajjian federation. According to the Mahāgovinda Sutta,[5] it was King **Reṇu** who, with the help of **Mahāgovinda Jotipāla,** founded the Videha kingdom. The Commentaries[6] state that Videha was colonized by the inhabitants, who were brought from **Pubbavideha** by King **Mandhātā.**

The Śatapatha Brāhmaṇa (I. iv. 1), however, ascribes the kingdom to Māthava the Videgha, and gives as its boundaries Kausikī in the east, the Ganges to the south, the Sadārūra in the west, and the Himālaya in the north. In the centre of Videha was **Pabbataraṭṭha,** in which was the city **Dhammakoṇḍa,** the residence of **Dhaniya.**[7]

The strainer used by the Buddha was honoured, after his death, by the people of Videha.[8]

Uruvela Kassapa was, in a previous birth, king of Videha.[9]

[4] MA. i. 534.
[5] D. ii. 235.
[6] *E.g.*, DA. ii. 482; MA. i. 184.
[7] SNA. i. 26.
[8] Bu. xxviii. 11.
[9] Ap. ii. 483.

3. **Videha.**—The name of a king of **Videha,** the father of the Bodhisatta in the **Vinīlaka Jātaka** (*q.v.*). *v.l.* **Vedeha.**

4. **Videha.**—A king of **Videha** who later became an ascetic. For his story see the **Gandhāra Jātaka.** He is identified with **Ānanda.**[1] *v.l.* **Vedeha.**

[1] J. iii. 369.

5. **Videha.**—See **Vedeha.**

1. **Videhiputta.**—A name given to **Ajāra** (*q.v.*).[1]

[1] J. v. 166.

2. **Videhiputta.**—See **Vedehiputta.**

Viddumagāma.—A village in Ceylon in which was the **Sirighanānanda-pariveṇa.**[1]

[1] Cv. xc. 98.

Vidhavā.—A river in the inner regions of **Himavā** (*anto-Himavante*).[1]

[1] J. iii. 467.

Vidhā Sutta.—Recluses and brahmins of mighty power and majesty in the past, present or future, all owe their power to the cultivation of the four *satipaṭṭhānas*.[1]

[1] S. v. 274.

Vidhātā.—Given as the name of a god to whom sacrifices should be offered as a means of obtaining happiness.[1]

[1] J. vi. 201.

1. **Vidhura.**—A brahmin, chaplain of the king of Benares. For details see the **Sambhava Jātaka.** He is identified with **Mahā Kassapa.**[1] Vidhura's son was **Bhadrakāra.**[2]

[1] J. v. 67. [2] *Ibid.*, 60.

2. **Vidhura.**—The Bodhisatta born as the minister of **Dhanañjaya-Korabba.** See the **Vidhurapaṇḍita Jātaka.** His father was the brahmin **Canda,**[1] and he owned three palaces: **Koñca, Mayūra** and **Piyaketa.**[2] **Anujjā** was his wife and **Cetā** his daughter-in-law; among his sons was **Dhammapāla.**[3] In one place[4] he is spoken of as having one thousand wives and seven hundred female slaves.

The Vidhurapaṇḍita of the **Dhūmakāri Jātaka** (*q.v.*) is probably identical with the above, as also the minister of the same name in the **Dasabrāhmaṇa Jātaka** (*q.v.*). The latter contains a long discussion between Vidhūra and the Korabba king regarding the qualities of a true brahmin.

[1] J. vi. 262.
[2] *Ibid.*, 289.
[3] *Ibid.*, 290.
[4] *Ibid.*, 301.

3. **Vidhura.**—The Milindapañha[1] refers to a birth of the Bodhisatta in which he was a wise man (*paṇḍita*) named **Vidhura.** At that time **Devaddata,** although a jackal, brought the kings of all **Jambudīpa** under his sway. The reference is evidently to the **Sabbadāṭha Jātaka** (No. 241), but there the Bodhisatta's name is not given.

[1] Mil. p. 202.

4. **Vidhura.**—See also **Vidhūra.**

Vidhurapaṇḍita Jātaka (No. 545). *v.l.* **Vidhūrapaṇḍita.**—Four kings —**Dhanañjaya-Korabba,** king of **Indapatta: Sakka,** the Nāga king

Varuṇa, and **Venateyya** king of the **Supaṇṇas**—having taken the *uposatha*-vows, meet together in a garden and there have a dispute as to which of them is the most virtuous. They cannot decide among themselves and agree, therefore, to refer the matter to Dhanañjaya's minister, **Vidhura-paṇḍita** (the Bodhisatta). The minister listens to the claims of each. and then declares that all are equal; their virtues are like the spokes of a wheel. They are pleased, and Sakka gives the minister a silk robe, Varuṇa a jewel, the Supaṇṇa king a golden garland, and Dhanañjaya one thousand cows.

Vimalā, Varuṇa's wife, hearing from her husband of Vidhura's wisdom, is so enchanted that she yearns to see him, and in order to do so feigns illness, and says that she must have Vidhura's heart. Varuṇa's daughter, **Irandatī,** is offered to anyone who can get possession of Vidhura's heart, and the yakkha **Puṇṇaka,** nephew of **Vessavaṇa,** who sees her and is fascinated by her beauty, accepts the condition. He obtains Vessavaṇa's consent by a ruse and visits Dhanañjaya's court. There he challenges the king to a game of dice, giving his name as **Kaccāyana,** and offers as stake his wonderful steed and all-seeing gem, provided the king will offer Vidhura as his. Dhanañjaya agrees, plays and loses. Vidhura agrees to go with Puṇṇaka; the king asks him questions regarding the householder's life for his own guidance, and Vidhura is given three days' leave to visit his family. Having taken leave of them, he goes with Puṇṇaka. On the way Puṇṇaka tries in vain to kill him by frightening him. When Vidhura discovers Puṇṇaka's intention, he preaches to him as he sits on the top of the **Kāḷapabbata,** and the Yakkha is so moved that he offers to take Vidhura back to Indapatta. But in spite of his protestations, Vidhura insists on going on to the Nāga-world. They arrive in Varuṇa's abode; Vidhura preaches first to Varuṇa and then to Vimalā. They are both delighted, and Puṇṇaka wins the hand of Irandatī. In his great joy Puṇṇaka gives Vidhura his marvellous jewel and takes him back to Indapatta. There Vidhura relates his adventures and gives the jewel to the king. A festival lasting one month is held in honour of Vidhura's return.

The story was related in reference to the Buddha's wisdom. Vidhura's chief wife, **Anujjā,** is identified with **Rāhulamātā;** his eldest son, Dhammapāla, with **Rāhula;** Varuṇa with **Sāriputta;** the Supaṇṇa king with **Moggallāna;** Sakka with **Anuruddha,** and Dhanañjaya with **Ānanda.**[1]

The Jātaka is also referred to as the **Puṇṇaka Jātaka.**[2] Four scenes from the Jātaka are found on the Bharhut Tope.[3]

[1] J. vi. 255-329. [2] *E.g.*, J. iv. 14, 182. [3] Cunningham, *Bharhut*, p. 82.

Vidhūpanadāyaka Thera.—An arahant. He gave a fan to **Padumuttara Buddha** and sang his praises as he fanned him. He became an arahant at the age of seven. He was king sixteen times under the name of **Vijamāna.**[1]

[1] Ap. i. 103 f.

1. **Vidhūra.**—One of the two chief disciples of **Kakusandha Buddha.**[1] He received his name because he was a peerless preacher of the Dhamma.[2]

[1] D. ii. 4; S. ii. 191; Bu. xxiii. 20; J. i. 42. [2] M. i. 333; quoted at PSA. p. 496.

2. **Vidhūra.**—See **Vidhura.**

Vinataka.—One of the seven mountain ranges round **Sineru.**[1]

[1] J. vi. 125; SNA. ii. 443; Sp. i. 119, etc.

Vinatā.—A river, probably in **Himavā.**[1] In a former birth **Vanvaccha** lived there as a tortoise.[2] **Nanda** also lived there.[3]

[1] Ap. i. 295, etc. [2] ThagA. i. 58. [3] *Ibid.*, 276.

Vinaya Vagga.—The eighth chapter of the Sattaka Nipāta of the Aṅguttara Nikāya.[1]

[1] A. iv. 140-44.

Vinayagaṇṭhipada.—A Vinaya treatise ascribed to a thera named **Moggallāna** of Ceylon and written in the time of **Parakkamabāhu I.** This authority was quoted by the **Ekaṃsikas** in support of their views.[1]

[1] Bode, *op. cit.*, 75 f; see also 75, n. 2, where the author is called **Joti**; also P.L.C. 189 f.

Vinayagaṇḍhi, Vinayagandhi.—See **Vajirabuddhiṭīkā.**

Vinayagūḷhatthadīpanī.—A work ascribed to **Chapaṭa.** It explains difficult passages of the Vinayapiṭaka.[1]

[1] Bode, *op. cit.*, 18.

Vinayaṭṭhakathā.—See **Samantapāsādikā.**

Vinayatthamañjūsā.—A ṭīkā on the **Kaṅkhāvitaraṇī,** written by **Buddhanāga.**[1]

[1] Gv. 61; Svd. 1212.

Vinayadhara Suttā.—A group of four suttas on seven qualities which make a monk skilled in the Vinaya.[1]

[1] A. iv. 140 f.

Vinayadharasobhana Sutta.—Seven qualities which make a monk skilled in discipline and illustrious; the qualities are the same as those of the **Vinayadhara Sutta.**[1]

[1] A. iv. 142.

Vinayavinicchaya.—A Vinaya treatise by **Buddhadatta,** written at the request of his pupil **Buddhasīha.** The **Uttaravinicchaya** is a supplement to this work. Two ṭīkās on it are found; one by **Revata** and the other by **Vācissara.**[1]

[1] P.L.C. 108 f.

Vinayasaṅgīti.—A name given to the recital held at **Vesālī** in connection with the **Vajjiputta** heresy.[1]

[1] Sp. i. 34.

Vinayasaṅgaha.—A very important summary of the Vinayapiṭaka, written by **Sāriputta** of **Pulatthipura.** There exist on it two ṭīkās, one ascribed to Sāriputta himself.[1]

[1] P.L.C. 191; Gv. 61; Sās. 33.

Vinayasamuṭṭhānadīpanī.—A Vinaya treatise by **Chapaṭa.**[1]

[1] Gv. 64; Bode, *op. cit.*, 18.

Vinayālaṅkāra-ṭīkā.—A Vinaya compilation by **Tipiṭakālaṅkāra** of **Tiriyapabbata.**[1]

[1] Svd. 1214; Bode, *op. cit.*, 54.

Vinibandha Sutta.—On the five forms of mental bondage: bondage to lusts, to the body, to shapes, to sleep, to the desire to become a deva.[1]

[1] A. iii. 249; iv. 461.

Vinīla.—The son of a golden goose and a crow. He is identified with **Devadatta.** See the **Vinīlaka Jātaka.**

Vinīlaka Jātaka (No. 160).—A golden goose once paired with a crow and they had a son of blue-black hue, whom they called **Vinīlaka.** The goose had two sons, and they, noticing that their father often went to **Mithilā** to see Vinīlaka, offered to go and fetch him. They perched

Vinīlaka on a stick and flew with the ends of the stick in their beaks. As they flew over Mithilā, Vinīlaka saw King **Videha** (the Bodhisatta) riding in his state-chariot and boasted that Videha was no better off than he himself, since he was being carried by a pair of golden geese. The geese, in their anger, wished to drop him, but took him on to their father and told him of his son's words. The goose was very angry on hearing this and sent Vinīlaka home to his mother.

The story was related in reference to an attempt by **Devadatta,** at **Gayāsīsa,** to imitate the Buddha when he was visited by **Sāriputta** and **Moggallāna.**

Vinīlaka is identified with Devadatta.[1]

[1] J. ii. 38 f.

Vinelapupphiya Thera.—An arahant. Thirty-one kappas ago he met **Sikhī Buddha** and offered him a *vinela*-flower. Twenty-nine kappas ago he was a king named **Sumeghaghana.**[1] He is probably identical with **Rāmaṇeyya Thera.**[2] *v.l.* **Minela.**

[1] Ap. i. 203f.

[2] ThagA. i. 121.

Vindaka.—One of the horses of **Candakumāra.**[1]

[1] J. vi. 135.

Vindusāra.—See **Bindusāra.**

Vipakkhasevaka-bhikkhu Vatthu.—The story of a monk who joined **Devadatta's** followers because of the rich offerings which he received, afterwards returning to his companions. He was reported to the Buddha, who related the **Mahilāmukha Jātaka** and identified the elephant of the story with the monk.[1]

[1] DhA. iv. 95-7.

1. **Vipatti Sutta.**—On the three kinds of failure: failure in morals, in mind *(citta)*, and in view.[1]

[1] A. i. 268.

2. **Vipatti Sutta.**—On seven things which lead to a lay disciple's decline: failure to see monks; neglect in hearing the Dhamma; lack of training in higher virtue; having no trust in elders, novices or mid-term monk; listening to the Dhamma in order to criticise; giving gifts first outside the Order.[1]

[1] A. iv. 26 f.

Vipallāsa Sutta.—On four perversions: seeing permanence in impermanence, ill in not-ill, self in not-self, fair in foul.[1]

[1] A. ii. 52.

Vipallāsakathā.—The eighth chapter of the Paññāvagga of the Paṭisambhidāmagga.[1]

[1] PS. ii. 80 f.

Vipassanākathā.—The ninth chapter of the Paññavagga of the Paṭisambhidāmagga.[1]

[1] PS. ii. 263-43.

Vipassanā Sutta.—On insight as to the path which leads to the "Uncompounded."[1]

[1] S. iv. 362.

Vipassī.—The nineteenth of the twenty-four Buddhas. He was born in the **Khema**-park in **Bandhumatī,** his father being **Bandhumā** and his mother **Bandhumatī.** He belonged to the **Koṇḍañña-gotta.** For eight thousand years he lived as a householder in three palaces: **Nanda, Sunanda** and **Sirimā.** His body was eighty cubits in height. His wife was **Sutanā** (*v.l.* **Sudassanā**) and his son **Samavattakkhandha.** He left the household in a chariot and practised austerities for eight months. Just before his enlightenment, the daughter of **Sudassana-seṭṭhi** gave him milk-rice, while a yavapālaka named **Sujāta** gave grass for his seat. His bodhi was a *pāṭali*-tree. He preached his first sermon in **Khemamigadāya** to his step-brother **Khandha** and his purohita's son **Tissa**; these two later became his chief disciples. His constant attendant was **Asoka**; **Candā** and **Candamittā** were his chief women disciples. His chief lay-patrons were **Punabbasummitta** and **Nāga** among men, and **Sirimā** and **Uttarā** among women. He died in **Sumittārāma** at the age of eighty thousand, and his relics were enshrined in a *thūpa* seven leagues in height. The Bodhisatta was a Nāga-king named **Atula.**[1]

Three reasons are given for the name of this Buddha[2]: (1) Because he could see as well by night as by day; (2) because he had broad eyes; (3) because he could see clearly after investigation. Vipassī held the *uposatha* only once in seven years,[3] but on such occasions the whole Saṅgha was present.[4] The construction of a **Gandhakuṭi** for Vipassī brought **Meṇḍaka** great glory in the present age. Meṇḍaka's name at

[1] Bu. xx. 1 ff.; BuA. 195 f.; D. ii. 2 ff.

[2] BuA. 195; *cf.* DA. ii. 454; SA. ii. 15.

[3] DhA. iii. 236.

[4] Sp. i. 186.

the time was **Avaroja.**[5] **Aññākoṇḍañña** was then known as **Cūlakāla,** and nine times he gave Vipassī Buddha the firstfruits of his fields.[6]

[5] DhA. iii. 364 f. [6] *Ibid.*, i. 81 f.

Vipassī Sutta.—On the mental evolution of **Vipassī,** leading to his Enlightenment.[1]

[1] S. ii. 5; *cf.* D. ii. 30 f.

1. **Vipula.**—A *khattiya*, father of **Revata Buddha.**[1]

[1] J. i. 35; Bu. vi. 16.

2. **Vipula.**—One of the five peaks near **Rājagaha,** the highest of them. See **Vepulla.**[1]

[1] S. i. 67; J. vi. 518; Mil. 242.

Vipula Sutta.—Four conditions leading to the growth of insight.[1]

[1] S. v. 412.

Vipulā.—Mother of **Revata Buddha.**[1]

[1] J. i. 35; Bu. vi. 6.

Vipulābhāsa.—Twenty-nine kappas ago there were several kings of this name, previous births of **Belaṭṭhānika** (Campakapupphiya) **Thera.**[1]

[1] ThagA. i. 205; Ap. i. 167.

Vibbhanta-bhikkhu Vatthu.—The story of a monk, living with **Mahā Kassapa,** who returned to lay-life and associated with bad companions. One day Kassapa saw him being led to execution for some crime and asked him to recall the meditation which, in former days, had enabled him to gain the Fourth Jhāna. The man did so and was without fear. The executioners, finding him unconcerned with their punishments of him, took him to the king who, after enquiry, released him. Later he visited the Buddha and became an arahant.[1]

[1] DhA. iv. 52 f.

Vibhaṅga.—The collective name for two closely connected works of the Vinayapiṭaka, which, in manuscripts, are generally called **Pārājikā** and **Pācittiya.** The collection is considered to be an extensive treatise on the **Pāṭimokkha** rules, giving the occasion for the formulating of each rule, with some explanation or illustration of various terms employed in the wording of the rule. The rule is sometimes further illustrated by reference to cases which come within it and to others which form exceptions to it. The collection is also called **Sutta Vibhanga** and is divided into two parts, the **Bhikkhu-vibhaṅga** and the **Bhikkhuṇi-vibhaṅga.**

Vibhaṅga Vagga.—The fourteenth Vagga of the **Majjhima Nikāya**[1] (suttas 131-42).

[1] M. iii. 187-257.

1. **Vibhaṅga Sutta.**—A detailed analysis of the causal law.[1]

[1] S. ii. 2 f.

2. **Vibhaṅga Sutta.**—An analysis of the Ariyan Eightfold Path.[1]

[1] S. v. 12.

3. **Vibhaṅga Sutta.**—An analysis of the four *satipaṭṭhānas.*[1]

[1] S. v. 183.

4. **Vibhaṅga Sutta.**—Two suttas containing an analysis of the five *indriyas.*[1]

[1] S. v. 196 f.

5. **Vibhaṅga Sutta.**—Three suttas containing an analysis of the five indriyas of ease, discomfort, happiness, unhappiness and indifference.[1]

[1] S. v. 209 f.

6. **Vibhaṅga Sutta.**—An analysis of the four bases of psychic power.[1]

[1] S. v. 276 f.

Vibhaṅgappakaraṇa.—One of the seven books of the Abhidhammapiṭaka; it is generally placed second in the list.[1] It deals in a general way with the different categories and formulas given in the **Dhammasaṅganī,** though different methods of treatment are used. The book is divided into eighteen chapters, each of which is called a vibhaṅga. Each chapter has three portions: *Suttantabhājaniya, Abhidhammabhājaniya* and *Paññāpucchaka* or list of questions. The Commentary to the Vibhaṅga is called **Sammohavinodanī.**

[1] *E.g.,* Mil. 12.

Vibhajjavāda.—The name given to the *Dhamma* by the orthodox; the term is identical with **Theravāda** and the Buddha is described as **Vibhajjavādī.**[1]

[1] *E.g.*, Mhv. v. 171; VibhA. 130; *cp.* Kvu. *Trs.* introd. p. 38.

Vibhatti Sutta.—Preached by **Sāriputta** on the four branches of analytical knowledge: meanings (*attha*); conditions (*dhammā*); definitions (*nirutti*); intellect (*paṭibhāna*).[1]

[1] A. ii. 159 f.

Vibhattikathā.—A treatise, probably grammatical, by a Ceylon monk.[1]

[1] Gv. 65, 75.

1. **Vibhattyattha.**—A work on Pāli cases by Kyocva's daughter.[1]

[1] Sās., p. 77.

2. **Vibhattyattha.**—A Pāli grammatical treatise by **Saddhammañāṇa.**[1]

[1] Bode, *op. cit.*, 26.

Vibhāta.—One of the eleven children of **Paṇḍuvāsudeva** and **Bhaddakaccānā.**[1]

[1] Dpv. x. 3; see also xviii. 41, 44.

Vibhītakamiñjiya Thera.—An arahant. He gave a *vibhītaka*-fruit to **Kakusandha Buddha.**[1] He is perhaps identical with **Sopāka Thera.**[2]

[1] Ap. ii. 396. [2] ThagA. i. 95.

Vibhīsana-vihāra.—A monastery built by **Dhātusena.**[1]

[1] Cv. xxxviii. 49.

Vibhūsaka-Brahmadatta.—A king of Benares, so called from his great fondness for ornaments. He developed the habit of sleeping by day and suffered from biliousness. This made him realize his folly, and, developing insight, he became a Pacceka Buddha. His *udānagāthā* is included in the **Khaggavisāṇa Sutta.**[1]

[1] SN. vs. 59; SNA. i. 111.

Vimaticchedanī.—A Commentarial work on the Abhidhamma by an Elder named **Kassapa.**[1]

[1] Gv. 60, 70; P.L.C. 160.

Vimativinodanī.—A Commentary on the Vinaya by **Kassapa Thera.** It was one of the authorities quoted by the **Pārupaṇas** against the **Ekaṃsikas** and it was held in high esteem by King **Dhammaceti.**[1]

[1] Gv. 61; Sās. 69; P.L.C. 179.

1. **Vimala.**—One of the four friends of **Yasa** who, following the latter's example, joined the Order and attained arahantship.[1]

[1] Vin. i. 18 f.

2. **Vimala Thera.**—He belonged to a rich family of **Rājagaha** and received his name because he was born free of all dirt. Much impressed by the majesty of the Buddha when the latter visited Rājagaha, Vimala entered the Order, and lived in a mountain cave in **Kosala.** One day a vast cloud spread over the sky; rain fell, allaying the heat and discomfort, and Vimala, concentrating his mind, attained arahantship.

He belonged to a family of conch-blowers in the time of **Vipassī Buddha,** and one day honoured the Buddha by playing on his conch-shell. He bathed the Bodhi-tree of **Kassapa Buddha** with fragrant water and washed the seats and the clothes of holy monks. Twenty-four kappas ago he was king six times, under the name of **Mahānigghosa.**[1]

[1] ThagA. i. 121 f.; his *udāna* verse is included in Thag. vs. 50.

3. **Vimala Thera.**—He was born in a brahmin family of Benares and entered the Order under **Somamitta Thera,**[1] who encouraged him to attain arahantship. In the days of **Padumuttara Buddha** he was a householder, and, when the Buddha's body was being carried to the pyre for cremation, amidst impressive celebrations, he offered *sumana*-flowers in his honour.[2]

[1] In the story of *Somamitta,* however, Vimala is said to have been his teacher. For details see *s.v.* **Somamitta.**

[2] ThagA. i. 377; three verses ascribed to him occur in Thag. (vs. 264-6).

4. **Vimala.**—A **Pacceka Buddha.**[1]

[1] M. iii. 70; ApA. i. 107.

5. **Vimala.**—One of the palaces of **Piyadassī Buddha** before his renunciation.[1]

[1] Bu. xiv. 16.

6. **Vimala.**—A king of sixty-one kappas ago, a former birth of **Udakadāyaka (Sānu) Thera.**[1]

[1] Ap. i. 205; ThagA. i. 115.

7. **Vimala.**—A king of twenty-one kappas ago who lived in the palace **Suddassana** in **Reṇuvatī.** He was a former birth of **Rāhula.**[1]

[1] Ap. i. 61.

Vimalakoṇḍañña Thera.—The son of **Ambapālī** and **Bimbisāra.** Vimala was his earlier name, but later he came to be called Vimalakoṇḍañña. When the Buddha visited **Vesālī,** Vimala was impressed by his majesty and entered the Order, attaining arahantship soon afterwards.

In the time of **Vipassī Buddha** he was a rich householder, and one day, being present while the Buddha preached to a large number of people, he rejoiced so much that he offered him four golden flowers. The Buddha, by his magic power, caused the golden hue of the flowers to pervade the whole region. Vimala died soon after and was reborn in **Tusita.** Forty-three kappas ago he became king sixteen times under the name of **Nemī.**[1] A sermon preached by Vimala helped Ambapālī to develop insight and win arahantship.[2]

[1] ThagA. i. 145 f.; a verse containing a riddle and ascribed to Vimala is given in Thag. vs. 64.
[2] ThigA. 207.

Vimalatthavilāsinī.—A Commentary by **Dhammapāla** on the **Vimāna Vatthu,**[1] forming part of the **Paramatthadīpanī.**

[1] BuA. p. 236.

1. **Vimaladhammasūriya.**—King of Ceylon (1592-1604 A.C.).[1] He succeeded **Rājasīha I.** and ruled in **Sirivaḍḍhanapura.** He built a temple for the Tooth Relic in the capital[2] and, having sent an embassy to **Rakkhaṅga,** obtained a chapter of monks under **Nandicakka** to re-establish the Order in Ceylon. He built the **Gaṇṭhamba-vihāra** and held there a ceremony of ordination. He was succeeded by his cousin **Senaratna,** whom he persuaded to leave the Order that he might assume the duties of kingship.[3]

[1] For his father, etc., see Cv. *Trs.* ii. 227, n. 1.
[2] He seems to have made a special casket for the Relics, which **Kittisirirājasīha** later overlaid with gold; Cv. c. 21; Cv. *Trs.* ii. 276, n. 1.
[3] Cv. xciv. 6 ff.

2. **Vimaladhammasūriya.**—King of Ceylon (**Vimaladhammasūriya II.,** 1687-1707 A.C.). He was the son of **Rājasīha II.** He held festivals in honour of the Tooth Relic and the Footprint at **Sumanakūṭa,** and, sending an embassy to **Rakkhaṅga,** obtained thirty-three monks, headed by **Santāna Thera,** to reorganize the Order in Ceylon. He was succeeded by his son, **Narindasīha.**[1]

[1] Cv. xcvii. 1 ff.

1. **Vimalabuddhi Thera.**—Author of the **Mukhamattadīpanī** on **Kaccāyana's** grammar and a ṭīkā on the **Abhidhammatthasaṅgaha**. To him is also ascribed the authorship of the Nyāsa of Kaccāyana's grammar.[1] He was probably of Ceylon, but the Sāsanavaṃsa[2] claims him as a thera of Pagan. He is sometimes called **Mahāvimalabuddhi.**

[1] P.L.C. 204; Bode, *op. cit.*, 21; Gv. 63, 72. [2] p. 75.

2. **Vimalabuddhi.**—Called **Cūlavimalabuddhi** or **Navavimalabuddhi.** He wrote a ṭīkā on the **Vuttodaya.**[1]

[1] Gv. 67; he lived either in Pagan or in Panya; Sās. 75.

3. **Vimalabuddhi.**—See **Navavimalabuddhi.**

Vimalavilāsinī.—A Commentary by **Dhammapāla** on the **Vimāna Vatthu**[1]; it forms part of the **Paramatthadīpanī.**

[1] BuA. p. 236.

1. **Vimalā Therī.**—The daughter of a courtesan of **Vesāli.** Having one day seen **Moggallāna** begging in Vesāli for alms, she went to his dwelling and tried to entice him.[1] The Elder rebuked and admonished her, and she became a lay-follower and later entered the Order. There, after great effort, she became an arahant.[2]

[1] Some say, adds the Commentator, that she was influenced by the heretics. The incident is referred to at ThagA. ii. 178, but Vimalā's name is not given.

[2] ThigA. 76 f.; her *udāna* verses are included in Thig. (vs. 72-6).

2. **Vimalā.**—A Nāga-maiden, queen of **Varuṇa.** See the **Vidhurapaṇḍita Jātaka.**

3. **Vimalā.**—Wife of **Piyadassī Buddha** in his last lay life.[1]

[1] Bu. xiv. 17.

4. **Vimalā.**—A Nāga-maiden; **Uppalavaṇṇā** in the time of **Padumuttara Buddha.**[1]

[1] Ap. ii. 553.

Vimāna Vatthu.—The sixth book of the **Khuddaka Nikāya.** It describes the splendour of various celestial abodes belonging to different devas, obtained by them as reward for some meritorious act performed in a previous life. The stories were learnt from the devas themselves, by **Moggallāna, Vaṅgīsa** and others, during their sojourn in the deva-worlds, and reported by them to the Buddha. A Commentary on the work exists by **Dhammapāla,** forming part of the **Paramatthadīpanī,** and sometimes called **Vimalatthavilāsinī** (*q.v.*).

Stories from the Vimāna Vatthu were related by **Mahinda** in Ceylon in his first sermon to **Anulā** and her five hundred companions.[1]

[1] Mhv. xiv. 58.

Vimutti Sutta.—On the five spheres of release experienced when one teaches the Dhamma to another, when yet another listens, when one learns it oneself, when one ponders and reflects on it, and when one has rightly penetrated into it.[1]

[1] A. iii. 21 f.

Vimokkha Sutta.—On eight kinds of deliverance.[1]

[1] A. iv. 306 f.

Vimokkhakathā.—The fifth chapter of the Mahāvagga of the **Paṭisambhidāmagga.**[1]

[1] PS. ii. 35-73.

1. **Viraja.**—One of the three palaces occupied by **Dhammadassī Buddha** before his Renunciation.[1]

[1] Bu. xvi. 14.

2. **Viraja.**—A Pacceka Buddha.[1]

[1] ApA. i. 107; M. iii. 70.

1. **Viraddha Sutta.**—Whoever neglects the Noble Eightfold Path neglects the way leading to the destruction of *dukkha.*[1]

[1] S. v. 23.

2. **Viraddha Sutta.**—He who neglects the four bases of psychic power neglects the way leading to the destruction of Ill.[1]

[1] S. v. 254.

3. **Viraddha** or **Āraddha Sutta.**—Whoever neglects the seven limbs of wisdom neglects the way leading to the destruction of Ill; whoever cultivates them undertakes that way.[1]

[1] S. v. 82.

Viravapupphiya Thera.—An arahant. Ninety-one kappas ago he met **Siddhattha Buddha** and gave him a *virava*-flower.[1]

[1] Ap. i. 223.

1. **Virāga Sutta.**—The Buddha teaches non-attachment and the path thereto.[1]

[1] S. iv. 371.

2. **Virāga Sutta.**—Dispassion is the aim of the holy life as taught by the Buddha, and the way thereto is the Noble Eightfold Path.[1]

[1] S. v. 27.

3. **Virāga Sutta.**—The idea of dispassion, if cultivated, leads to great profit.[1]

[1] S. v. 133.

4. **Virāga Sutta.**—The four *satipaṭṭhānas*, if cultivated, lead to dispassion.[1]

[1] S. v. 179.

Virāgakathā.—The fifth chapter of the Yuganandha Vagga of the **Paṭisambhidāmagga.**[1]

[1] Ps. ii. 140-7.

Viriya.—A pleasaunce in **Vebhāra** where **Siddhattha Buddha** was born.[1]

[1] BuA. p. 185.

1. **Viriya Sutta.**—Energy is necessary in order to see things as they really are.[1]

[1] S. ii. 132.

2. **Viriya Sutta.**—A woman who, among other qualities, has energy is reborn in a happy condition.[1]

[1] S. iv. 244.

1. **Virūpakkha.**—One of the **Cātummahārājano** (Regent Kings). He is Regent of the western quarter and lord of the Nāgas.[1] In the assembly of the devas he sits facing east.[2] **Kālakaṇṇī** is his daughter.[3] All Nāgas visit him regularly as their lord and wait on him, and any question of dispute arising among them would be referred to him for solution.[4]

[1] D. ii. 258; D. iii. 199; Dvy. 126, 148.
[2] D. ii. 207, 221.
[3] J. iii. 257.
[4] *E.g.*, J. vi. 168; *cf.* AA. i. 143.

2. **Virūpakkha.**—The name of a **Nāga** family[1]; they were, perhaps, followers of **Virūpakkha** (*q.v.*).

[1] Vin. ii. 109; A. ii. 72; J. ii. 145.

Virūḷha, Virūḷhaka.—One of the **Cātummahārājāno.** He is the king of the south, and, in the assembly of the devas, sits facing north.[1] He is lord of the **Kumbhaṇḍas.**[2]

[1] D. ii. 207, 221. [2] *Ibid.*, iii. 198; Dvy. 126, 148.

Virocana.—Nine kappas ago there were three kings of this name, all previous births of **Sālapupphadāyaka (Ajjuṇa) Thera.**[1]

[1] Ap. i. 169; ThagA. i. 186.

Virocana Jātaka (No. 143).—The Bodhisatta was once a lion and lived in **Kañcanaguhā.** He granted to a jackal the favour of being allowed to inform him of the presence of prey, the animal being given a portion of the carcase in return for this service. In time the jackal grew strong and begged to be allowed to kill an elephant. The lion reluctantly agreed to this, but the jackal, in his attempts to leap on to the elephant, missed his aim and fell to the ground where he was crushed to death.

The story was related in reference to **Devadatta's** attempt to pose as the Buddha and his failure to do so, wherefore he received a kick on the chest from **Kokālika** (*q.v.*). The jackal is identified with Devadatta.[1]

[1] J. i. 490-3.

Virocamānā.—Wife of **Kakusandha Buddha** before his Renunciation.[1]

[1] Bu. xxiii. 17. BuA. (p. 210) calls her Rocaṇā.

Vilattākhaṇḍa.—The weir of a tank repaired by **Parakkamabāhu I.**[1]

[1] Cv. lxxix. 67.

Vilāta.—A country.[1]

[1] Mil. 327, 331; Rhys Davids identifies it with Tartary (Mil. *Trs.* ii. 204).

Vilāna.—A place near **Āḷisāra,** mentioned in the wars of **Gajabāhu.**[1]

[1] Cv. lxx. 166.

Vilokana.—A king of eighty-one kappas ago, a former birth of **Māṇava (Sammukhāthavika) Thera.**[1]

[1] Ap. i. 159; ThagA. i. 164.

Villavarāyara.—A Damiḷa chief, ally of **Kulasekhara.** He was slain by the soldiers of **Laṅkāpura.**[1]

Cv. lxxvi. 94, 163; but see 173 and 185.

Villikābā.—A district of Ceylon, once the residence of **Vijayabāhu I.**[1]

[1] Cv. lviii. 29.

Vivara Vagga.—The first chapter of the Catukka Nipāta of the **Jātakaṭṭhakathā.**[1]

[1] J. iii. 1-33.

1. **Vivāda Sutta.**—On the six roots of contention: scorn, hypocrisy, envy, deceit, evil-mindedness, prejudice.[1]

[1] A. iii. 334 f.; *cf.* D. iii. 246; M. ii. 245; Vin. ii. 89.

2. **Vivāda Suttā.**—Two suttas, preached in answer to a question by **Upāli,** on ten things which are the causes of contention.[1]

[1] A. v. 77 f.

Vivādamūla Sutta.—Ten causes, different from the above, of contention.[1]

[1] A. v. 78 f.

1. **Viveka Sutta.**—An admonition spoken by a deva on seeing a monk in a forest tract of Kosala indulging in wrong and evil thoughts.[1]

[1] S. i. 197.

2. **Viveka Sutta.**—**Sāriputta** tells **Ānanda,** in answer to his questions, that the clearness of his senses and the agreeable colour of his face are due to the fact that he had passed the siesta in **Andhavana,** aloof from passions and from evil things.[1]

[1] S. iii. 235 f.

Vivekakathā.—The fourth chapter of the Paññāvagga of the **Paṭisambhidāmagga.**[1]

[1] PS. ii. 219-25.

Visama Sutta.—Crooked actions of body, speech and mind lead one to purgatory; their opposites to heaven.[1]

[1] A. i. 293.

Visayha.—The Bodhisatta born as a seṭṭhi of Benares. See the **Visayha Jātaka.**

Visayha Jātaka (No. 340).—The Bodhisatta was once born as **Visayha,** seṭṭhi of Benares, and gave alms daily to six hundred thousand persons in six different parts of the city. Sakka's throne was heated by his great generosity, and, feeling nervous for his safety, Sakka contrived that all Visayha's possessions should disappear. Quite undaunted, Visayha became a grass-cutter, and for six days gave alms from the money so earned, he and his wife fasting. On the seventh day, while cutting grass, he fainted, and Sakka, appearing before him, suggested that he should be moderate in his generosity. Visayha rejected the suggestion as unworthy and declared that his aim was Buddhahood. Thereupon Sakka praised him and made him prosperous.

The story was related to **Anāthapiṇḍika,** as mentioned in the **Khadiraṅgāra Jātaka.** Visayha's wife is identified with **Rāhulamātā.**[1]

The story is given in the **Jātakamālā** (No. 5), where the seṭṭhi is called Aviṣayha.

[1] J. iii. 128-32; see also J. i. 45.

Visavanta Jātaka (No. 69).—The Bodhisatta was once a snake-bite doctor, and, on one occasion, when a countryman had been bitten by a snake, the doctor ordered the snake to be brought and asked it to suck the poison out of the wound. This the snake refused to do even though threatened with death by the doctor.

The story was told in reference to a vow taken by **Sāriputta.** Some villagers once brought some meal-cakes to the monastery, and when the monks present there had eaten, it was suggested that what remained should be saved for those monks who were absent in the village. This was done, but a young colleague of Sāriputta, arriving very late, found that Sāriputta had already eaten his portion, whereat he was very disappointed. Sāriputta immediately vowed never again to touch meal-cakes, and the Buddha said that Sāriputta would never return to anything which he had once renounced. The snake is identified with Sāriputta.[1]

[1] J. i. 310 f.

1. **Visākha.**—Husband of **Dhammadinnā.** He was a rich merchant of **Rājagaha** and accompanied **Bimbisāra** on his visit to the Buddha, who was then at **Rājagaha** for the first time after his Enlightenment. Visākha, on that occasion, became a *sotāpanna,* after hearing the Buddha preach; he later became a *sakadāgāmī* and then an *anāgāmī.* After he became an *anāgāmī* his behaviour to his wife completely changed, and when he explained to her the reason, offering her all his wealth and freedom to do as she wished, she asked his leave to join the Order. Visākha informed Bimbisāra of her wish, and, at his request, the king ordered that the city be decked in her honour on the day of

her renunciation and that she be taken to the nunnery in a golden palanquin.

After Dhammadinnā had joined the Order, she left the city and retired into the country, returning to Rājagaha after she had attained arahantship. Visākha, hearing of her return, visited her at the nunnery and asked her various questions regarding the Buddha's teachings, all of which she answered.[1] Their conversation is recorded in the **Culla-Vedalla Sutta.**[2] Visākha then visited the Buddha and reported their conversation to him, winning the Buddha's praises for Dhammadinnā.

In the time of **Phussa Buddha,** Visākha and Dhammadinnā had been husband and wife.[3] Visākha had been the treasurer, appointed by the three sons of **Jayasena,** in charge of the provisions given by them for the almsgiving held in honour of Phussa Buddha and his monks.

Visākha is mentioned[4] as one of the seven lay disciples in the time of the Buddha who had each five hundred followers.

[1] MA. i. 514 f.; ThigA. 15, 19.
[2] M. i. 299 f.; *cf.* DhA. iv. 229 f.; AA. i. 197.
[3] For details see PvA. 20 ff.; *cf.* KhpA. 202 f.; DhA. i. 86 f. AA. i. 144 f.
[4] SA. iii. 223.

2. **Visākha.**—Called **Pañcāliputta.** He was son of a provincial governor (*maṇḍalikarājā*) of **Magadha,** and was called **Pañcāliputta** because his mother was the daughter of the **Pañcāla** king.[1] He succeeded his father, and, hearing one day that the Buddha had arrived near his village, he visited him, heard him preach and joined the Order. He then accompanied the Buddha to **Sāvatthi,** where he became an arahant. Later, out of compassion, he visited his relations.

One day he was asked how many qualities were necessary to a man in order that he should be considered a skilful preacher of the Dhamma. Visākha's answer is included in the Theragāthā.[2]

Fourteen kappas ago he was a poor householder, and one day, while searching in the forest for fruit, he saw a Pacceka Buddha and offered him a *vallī*-fruit. He is evidently to be identified with **Valliphaladāyaka** of the Apadāna.[3]

Visākha was evidently a clever and arresting preacher, and the books mention that the Buddha heard him preach and praised him.[4]

[1] AA. ii. 511 calls him the son of Pañcālibrāhmaṇī.
[2] Thag. vs. 209-10; ThagA. i. 331 f.
[3] Ap. i. 296.
[4] S. ii. 280; A. ii. 51.

3. **Visākha Thera.**—He was a rich householder of **Pāṭaliputta** who, hearing that there were many shrines in Ceylon, made over his property to his family and left home with one single coin wrapt in the hem of his

garment. He had to spend one month at the port waiting for a ship, and, during that time, made one thousand by his skill in trade. Arrived at the **Mahāvihāra,** he asked to be ordained, and when, at the time of his ordination, the money was discovered, he distributed it among those who were present. After five years he set out travelling, and, with the help of a devatā, found his way to **Cittalapabbata-vihāra,** where he stayed for four months. As he was about to leave, the devatā of the *jambu*-tree which stood at the head of his *caṅkamaṇa* appeared before him weeping, and explained that while the Thera was there the non-humans lived in peace, but that when he had gone they would start quarrelling and talking loudly. Several times he tried to leave but was thus prevented, until, at last, he became an arahant and died there.[1]

[1] Vsm. i. 312 f.; the story is referred to at AA. ii. 865.

4. **Visākha.**—One of the chief lay supporters of **Maṅgala Buddha.**[1]

[1] Bu. v. 25.

5. **Visākha.**—One of the chief lay supporters of **Phussa Buddha.**[1]

[1] Bu. xix. 21.

6. **Visākha.**—A minister of **Duṭṭhagāmaṇi.** He and **Sirideva** were in charge of the arrangements for the Foundation Ceremony of the **Mahā Thūpa.**[1]

[1] MṬ. 517.

7. **Visākha.**—See also **Vesākha.**

Visākha Sutta.—The Buddha listens to a sermon by **Visākha Pañcāliputta** and praises his skill in the assembly of monks. The Sutta also contains a teaching as to how the Dhamma should be preached.[1]

[1] A. ii. 51 f.; S. ii. 280 f.

1. **Visākhā.**—One of the chief lay women supporters of **Piyadassī Buddha.**[1]

[1] Bu. xiv. 22.

2. **Visākhā.**—Mother of **Kakusandha Buddha** and wife of **Aggidatta.**[1]

[1] Bu. xxiii. 58; J. i. 94; D. ii. 7.

3. **Visākhā.**—One of the five queens of the third **Okkāka.**[1]

[1] DA. i. 258; SNA. i. 352; MṬ. 131.

4. **Visākhā Therī.**—She belonged to the harem of the Bodhisatta and left the world with **Mahāpajāpatī.** She received a topic of meditation from the Buddha and in due course won arahantship. A verse uttered by her, admonishing her companions, is included in the Therīgāthā.[1]

[1] Thig. vs. 13; ThigA. 20.

5. **Visākhā.**—The chief among the female lay disciples of the Buddha and declared by him to be foremost among those who ministered to the Order (*dāyikānaṃ aggā*).[1] Her father was **Dhanañjaya,** son of **Meṇḍaka,** and her mother **Sumanā.** She was born in the city of **Bhaddiya** in **Aṅga.** When she was seven years old, the Buddha visited Bhaddiya with a large company of monks, out of compassion for the brahmin **Sela** and others. Meṇḍaka gave Visākhā five hundred companions, five hundred slaves, and five hundred chariots, that she might visit the Buddha. She stopped the chariots some distance away and approached the Buddha on foot. He preached to her and she became a *sotāpanna.* For the next fortnight Meṇḍaka invited the Buddha and his monks daily to his house, where he fed them.

Later, when, at **Pasenadi's** request, **Bimbisāra** sent Dhanañjaya to live in **Kosala,** Visākhā accompanied her parents and lived in **Sāketa.** The messengers, sent by **Migāra** of **Sāvatthi** to find a suitable bride for his son **Paññavaddhana,** saw Visākhā on her way to the lake to bathe on a feast-day. At that moment there was a great shower. Visākhā's companions ran for shelter, but Visākhā herself, walking at her usual pace, came to the place where the messengers, already greatly impressed, were awaiting her. When they asked her why she did not run to seek shelter and so preserve her clothes, she answered that she had plenty of clothes in the house, but that if she ran she might damage a limb which would be a great loss. "Unmarried girls," she said, "are like goods awaiting sale, they must not be disfigured." The messengers offered her a bouquet of flowers (*mālāguḷaṃ*), which she accepted as a proposal of marriage, and then went on to her father's house. The messengers followed and laid Puṇṇavaddhana's suit before Dhanañjaya. The proposal was accepted and confirmed by an exchange of letters.

When Pasenadi heard of it, he offered to accompany Puṇṇavaddhana to Sāketa, as a mark of signal favour. Dhanañjaya welcomed the king and his retinue, Migāra, Puṇṇavaddhana and their followers, with all honour, attending personally to all the details of hospitality. He persuaded the king to stay with him during the rains, providing all that was necessary.[2] Five hundred goldsmiths were engaged to make the

[1] A. i. 26; she is considered the ideal lay woman—*e.g.*, A. iv. 348.

[2] According to the DhA. account (*loc. cit.*) Visākhā superintended all the arrangements.

Mahālatāpasādhana (ornament), *q.v.*, for the bride; three months passed, but it was still unfinished. The supply of firewood ran out, and orders were given that the wood of dilapidated houses should be used. This wood lasted for a fortnight, and then the storehouses containing cloths were opened, the cloths soaked in oil and used for cooking the food. The ornament was finished in four months.[3]

Dhanañjaya gave his daughter, as dowry, five hundred carts full of money, five hundred with vessels of gold, five hundred each of silver, copper, various silks, ghee, rice husked and winnowed; also ploughs, ploughshares, and other farm implements, five hundred carts with three slavewomen in each, everything being provided for them. The cattle given by him filled an enclosure three quarters of a league in length and eight rods across, standing shoulder to shoulder, and in addition to these, sixty thousand bulls and sixty thousand milch cows escaped from their stalls and joined the herd already gifted to her.[4]

When the time came for Visākhā to leave, Dhanañjaya gave her ten admonitions, which Migāra overheard from the next room. These admonitions were: Not to give fire from the house outside; not to take into the house fire from without; to give only to those who give in return; not to give to those who do not give in return; to give to him that gives and to him that gives not; to sit, eat and sleep happily; to tend the fire and to honour household deities.[5]

On the following day Dhanañjaya appointed eight householders to be sponsors to his daughter and to enquire into any charges which might be brought against her. When she left, Dhanañjaya allowed any inhabitants of his fourteen tributary villages to accompany her if they so wished. As a result the villages were left empty; but Migāra, fearing that he should have to feed them, drove most of them back. Visākhā entered Sāvatthi standing in her chariot, so that all might see her glory. The citizens showered gifts on her, but these she distributed among the people.

Migāra was a follower of the **Nigaṇṭhas**, and, soon after Visākhā's arrival in his house, he sent for them and told her to minister to them. But

[3] In the time of **Kassapa Buddha** she gave bowls and robes to twenty thousand monks, also thread and needles and sewing materials; as a result of this, she received her parure in this life (DhA. i. 395).

[4] In her birth as **Saṅghadāsī**, she gave the five products of the cow to twenty thousand monks, begging them to eat; hence the escaping of the cattle for her benefit (DhA. i. 397). Visākhā's relations continued to send her costly gifts even after her marriage. The Udāna (ii. 9) contains a story of a dispute she had with the customs-officers regarding the duty they levied on one of her presents. She visited Pasenadi several times, trying to get the matter settled; but he had no time to give to the matter, and, in the end, she sought consolation from the Buddha.

[5] These riddles were later explained by Visākhā to her father-in-law (DhA. i. 403 f.).

Visākhā, repulsed by their nudity, refused to pay them homage. The Nigaṇṭhas urged that she should be sent away, but Migāra bided his time. One day, as Migāra was eating, while Visākhā stood fanning him, a monk was seen standing outside his house. Visākhā stood aside, that Migāra might see him, but as Migāra continued to eat without noticing the monk, she said to the latter, "Pass on, Sir, my father-in-law eats stale fare." Migāra was angry and threatened to send her away, but, at her request, the matter was referred to her sponsors. They enquired into the several charges brought against her and adjudged her not guilty. Visākhā then gave orders that preparations should be made for her return to her parents. But Migāra begged her forgiveness which she granted, on condition that he would invite to the house the Buddha and his monks. This he did, but, owing to the influence of the Nigaṇṭhas, he left Visākhā to entertain them, and only consented to hear the Buddha's sermon at the end of the meal from behind a curtain. At the conclusion of this sermon, however, he became a *sotāpanna*. His gratitude towards Visākhā was boundless; henceforth she was to be considered as his mother and to receive all the honour due to a mother; from this time onwards she was called **Migāramātā.**[6] Migāra got made for her everyday use an ornament called *ghanamaṭṭhaka*, at a cost of one hundred thousand.[7] On the day of the presentation of this ornament, Migāra held for her a special festival in her honour, and she was made to bathe in sixteen pots of perfumed water.[8]

Visākhā had ten sons and ten daughters, each of whom had a similar number of children, and so on down to the fourth generation. Before her death, at the age of one hundred and twenty, she had eighty-four thousand and twenty direct lineal descendants, all living.[9] She herself kept, all her life, the appearance of a girl of sixteen. She had the strength of five elephants, and it is said that once she took the trunk of an elephant, which was sent to test her, between her two fingers and forced him back on his haunches.[10] Visākhā owned such a great reputation for bringing good fortune that the people of Sāvatthi always invited her to their houses on festivals and holidays.[11]

[6] In DhA. i. 406 we are told that in order to confirm this declaration, Migāra sucked the breast of Visākhā. This account adds that she had also a son named **Migāra**; thus there was a double reason for the name. AA. i. 313 says that Migāra was her eldest son.

[7] Some time after, Visākhā sold the Matālatāpasādhana and built the **Migāramātupāsāda** (*q.v.* for details).

[8] This account of Visākhā is summarized from DhA. i. 384 ff.; AA. i. 219 ff. contains a similar account but with far less detail. The DhA. account contains numerous other particulars, some of which are given below.

[9] But see Ud. viii. 8, which speaks of the death of a grand-daughter and of Visākhā's great grief; this evidently refers to **Dattā** (*q.v.*).

[10] DhA. i. 409.

[11] *Ibid.*

Visākhā fed five hundred monks daily at her house.[12] In the afternoon she visited the Buddha, and, after listening to his sermon, would go round the monastery inquiring into the needs of the monks and nuns.[13] In these rounds she was sometimes accompanied by **Suppiyā**.[14] Visākhā begged for, and was granted, eight boons by the Buddha: that as long as she lived she be allowed to give robes to the members of the Order for the rainy season; food for monks coming into Sāvatthi[15]; food for those going out; food for the sick; food for those who wait on the sick; medicine for the sick; a constant supply of rice-gruel for any needing it; and bathing robes for the nuns.[16]

With the construction of the **Migāramātupāsāda** (*q.v.*) in the **Pubbārāma** Visākhā's ambitions were fulfilled, and it is said[17] that when the monastery was completed and the festival of opening in progress, as the evening drew on she walked round the monastery accompanied by her children, her grandchildren and her great-grandchildren, and in five stanzas sang her joy, saying, "Now is entirely fulfilled the prayer which I prayed in times of yore."[18]

The monks heard her sing and told the Buddha; he related to them how, in the time of **Padumuttara Buddha,** Visākhā had been the friend of the principal women benefactors of that Buddha. In the time of **Kassapa Buddha** she was Saṅghadāsī, youngest of the seven daughters of **Kiki,** and for long after her marriage she gave alms and performed other good works with her sisters.[19]

[12] Thus, *e.g.*, J. iv. 144; two thousand, according to DhA. i. 128; later she appointed her grand-daughter (probably Dattā) to officiate for her.

[13] Because she wished the Saṅgha well she was appointed on the committee set up to enquire into the charge of misbehaviour brought against the mother of **Kumārakassapa** (*q.v.*); Visākhā's experience as the mother of several children stood her in good stead.

[14] For an incident connected with one of these visits, see *s.v.* **Suppiyā.** DhA. (i. 100 f.) says that once five hundred young men of good family entrusted the care of their wives to Visākhā. On one occasion, when accompanying her to the monastery, they became drunk and committed improprieties in the presence of the Buddha. The Buddha frightened them by emitting a dark blue ray of light, thus restoring them to their senses. This was the occasion of the preaching of the **Kumbha Jātaka**; see also J. v. 11 f.

[15] Probably on account of this boon the monks who had been to see **Khadiravanīya Revata** (*q.v.*) visited Visākhā immediately after their return to Sāvatthi; but see the **Piṭha Jātaka.**

[16] This list of boons and Visākhā's reasons for begging them are given at Vin. i. 290 ff. According to the **Suruci Jātaka** (*q.v.*), she obtained the boons owing to her virtue in the past as well—*e.g.*, in her birth as Sumedhā (J. iv. 315 ff.); see also Vin. i. 296, where the Buddha accepts a face-towel as a special gift from Visākhā but would not accept an earthenware foot-scrubber (Vin. ii. 129 f.).

[17] DhA. i. 416 f.

[18] The wishes mentioned in these stanzas as having been fulfilled differ from the eight boons mentioned above.

[19] AA. i. 219.

According to the **Vihāravimānavatthu,**[20] Visākhā was born, after death, among the **Nimmānaratidevā** as the consort of the deva-king **Sunimmita.** Buddhaghosa says[21] that Visākhā, like **Sakka** and **Anāthapiṇḍika,** will enjoy one hundred and thirty-one kappas of happiness in the Brahma-worlds before she finally passes away into nibbāna.

Among Visākhā's relations are also mentioned, in addition to her two sons **Migajāla** and **Migāra,** a sister **Sujātā,** who became Anāthapiṇḍika's daughter-in-law[22]; a grandson, **Saḷha** (*q.v.*); a granddaughter, **Dattā,** who died[23]; and **Uggaha** (*q.v.*), called **Meṇḍakanattā.** Mention is also made of a grandson of hers on whose behalf she interceded with the Buddha when the monks refused to ordain him during the rainy season.[24]

The books contain numerous suttas preached by the Buddha to Visākhā during her frequent visits to him, chief among such suttas being the famous discourse on the keeping of the *uposatha,*[25] the discourse of the eight qualities which win for women power in this world and power and happiness in the next,[26] and eight qualities which win for a woman birth among the **Manāpakāyika-devas.**[27]

[20] Vv. iv. 6; VvA. 189, 191.
[21] DA. iii. 740.
[22] A. iv. 91; AA. ii. 724; J. ii. 347.
[23] DhA. iii. 278.
[24] Vin. i. 153.
[25] A. i. 205 ff.; *cf.* iv. 255; DhA. iii. 58 f.
[26] A. iv. 269.
[27] *Ibid.*, 267.

6. **Visākhā.**—One of the women who will renounce the world at the same time as the future Buddha **Metteyya.** She will be accompanied by eighty-four thousand other women.[1]

[1] Anāgat. vs. 63.

1. **Visākhā Sutta.**—The Buddha tells **Visākhā** (5) of the advantages of keeping the *uposatha* day.[1]

[1] A. iv. 255.

2. **Visākhā Sutta.**—The Buddha tells **Visākhā** (5) of eight qualities in a woman which will secure for her birth among the **Manāpakāyika-devā.**[1]

[1] A. iv. 267.

Visākhā-bhāṇavāra.—The second chapter of the Cīvarakhandhaka of the **Mahāvagga.**[1]

[1] Vin. i. 281-94.

Visāṇā.—The name given to the kingdom (*rājadhāni*) over which **Kuvera** rules; hence his name, **Vessavaṇa.**[1]

[1] D. iii. 201; DA. iii. 967; J. vi. 270; SNA. i. 369.

1. **Visārada Sutta.**—A man who takes life takes what is not given, is given over to lust, lies, and takes spirituous liquors, such a man lives as a layman without confidence. Following the opposite course, he lives with confidence.[1]

[1] A. iii. 203; *cf.* No. 3.

2. **Visārada Sutta.**—Five things that give confidence to a woman: beauty, wealth, kindred, sons and virtue.[1]

[1] S. iv. 246.

3. **Visārada Sutta.**—A woman who abstains from taking life, theft, sensual lusts, lying and intoxicants, lives in confidence.[1]

[1] S. iv. 250; *cf.* No. 1 above.

Visāla.—The capital of Ceylon (then known as **Maṇḍadīpa**) in the time of **Kassapa Buddha.** It was to the west of **Mahāsāgara-uyyāna,** and its king at the time was **Jayanta.**[1]

[1] Mhv. xv. 127; Dpv. xv. 60; xvii. 6; Sp. i. 87.

Visālamutta.—A Damiḷa chief, ally of **Kulasekhara.**[1]

[1] Cv. lxxvii. 81, 91.

Visālakkhi-vimāna Vatthu.—The story of **Sunandā** (*q.v.*), the daughter of a garland-maker of **Rājagaha.** The story was told by **Sakka** to **Vaṅgīsa,** who reported it to the Buddha.[1]

[1] Vv. iii. 9; VvA. 170 f.

Visālā.—See **Vesālī.**

Visirātthala.—A tank in Ceylon.[1]

[1] Cv. lxviii. 49.

Visudatta Thera.—A teacher of the Abhidhamma.[1]

[1] DhSA. p. 32.

Visuddhajanavilāsinī.—The name of the Commentary on the **Apadāna.** Its author is unknown.

Visuddhācariya Thera.—A monk sent by **Dhammika,** ruler of **Ayojjhā,** to Ceylon, at the head of a group of monks, and at the request of **Kitti-**

sirirājasīha, to reinstate the Order in that Island. He remained in Ceylon, admitting many monks into the Order, to whom he taught the doctrine.[1]

[1] Cv. c. 131, 171 f.

Visuddhimagga.—An encyclopædia of the Buddha's teaching, written by **Bhuddhaghosa** at the request of **Saṅghapāla Thera.** It is said[1] that when Buddhaghosa arrived at the **Mahāvihāra** and asked permission to translate the Sinhalese Commentaries into Pāli, the monks, to test him, gave him two stanzas (quoted at the beginning of the book) on which they asked him to write a thesis. As soon as he had finished this, the devas hid the copy, and the same thing happened after it was rewritten. He then rewrote it a third time, and when it was being read in the assembly of monks, the two previous copies suddenly reappeared and were found to agree in every detail with the new one.[2] A Commentary on the work exists, called the **Paramatthamañjūsa,** by **Dhammāpāla,**[3] and a **Visuddhimaggagaṇṭhipadattha** was written by **Sāradassī,** a monk of **Ava.**[4]

[1] Cv. xxxvii. 236.

[2] For a description of the book, see Law, *Hist. of Pāli Lit.*, ii. 399 f.

[3] P.L.C. 113; Svd. 1231.

[4] Sās. 116; Bode, *op. cit.*, 56.

Vissakamma, Vissukamma.—A deva, inhabitant of **Tāvatiṃsa.** He is the chief architect, designer and decorator among the devas, and Sakka asks for his services whenever necessary. Thus he was ordered to build the palace called **Dhamma** for **Mahāsudassana**[1] and another for **Mahāpanāda.**[2] He also built the hermitages for the Bodhisatta in various births—*e.g.*, as **Sumedha,**[3] **Kuddālapaṇḍita,**[4] **Hatthipāla,**[5] **Ayoghara,**[6] **Jotipāla,**[7] **Sutasoma,**[8] **Temiya**[9] and **Vessantara.**[10] Vissakamma also built the hermitage for **Dukūlaka** and **Pārikā.**[11]

On the day that the Buddha renounced the world, Sakka sent Vissakamma in the guise of a shampooer to bathe him and clothe him in his royal ornaments[12]; he also sent him to adorn Temiya on the day he left the kingdom.[13] Vissakamma erected the jewelled pavilion, twelve leagues in compass, under the **Gaṇḍamba,** where the Buddha performed the Twin Miracle and built the three stairways of jewels, silver and gold,

[1] D. ii. 180.

[2] J. iv. 323; DA. iii. 856.

[3] J. i. 7.

[4] *Ibid.*, 314.

[5] J. iv. 489.

[6] *Ibid.*, 499.

[7] J. v. 132.

[8] *Ibid.*, 190.

[9] J. vi. 21, 29.

[10] *Ibid.*, 519 f.

[11] J. vi. 72.

[12] J. i. 60; DhA. i. 70; BuA. 232; he also constructed ponds in which the prince might bathe (AA. i. 379).

[13] J. vi. 12.

used by the Buddha in his descent from **Tāvatiṃsa** to **Saṅkassa.**[14] He built the pavilions in which the Buddha and five hundred arahants travelled to **Uggapura,** at the invitation of **Culla-Subhaddā.**[15] When **Ajātasattu** deposited his share of the Buddha's relics in a thūpa, Sakka ordered Vissakamma to construct around the thūpa a *vālasaṅghātayanta* (revolving wheel ?) to prevent anyone from approaching the relics. Later, when **Dhammāsoka (Piyadassī)** wished to obtain these relics for his vihāra, Vissakamma appeared before him in the guise of a village youth and, by shooting an arrow at the controlling screw of the machine, stopped its revolutions.[16] He constructed the jewelled pavilion in which **Sonuttara** placed the relics he brought from the Nāga-world till the time came for them to be deposited in the **Mahā Thūpa,**[17] and on the day of their enshrinement, Vissakamma, acting on Sakka's orders, decorated the whole of Ceylon.[18] He also provided the bricks used in the construction of the **Mahā Thūpa.**[19] Sometimes he would enter into a workman's body and inspire him with ideas—*e.g.*, in designing the form of the Mahā Thūpa.[20] He was also responsible for the construction of the golden vase in which the branch of the Bodhi-tree was conveyed to Ceylon.[21]

As in the case of **Mātali** and **Sakka,** Vissakamma is evidently the name of an office and not a personal name. Thus, in the **Suruci Jātaka,**[22] Vissakamma is mentioned as a previous birth of **Ānanda,** while, according to the Dhammapada Commentary,[23] the architect who helped **Magha** and his companions in their good works, was reborn as Vissakamma.

See *s.v.* Visvakarma in Hopkins' *Epic Mythology.*

14 J. iv. 265 f.

15 DhA. iii. 470; and again for the journey to **Sunāpuranta** (MA. ii. 1017).

16 DA. ii. 613, 614.

17 Mhv. xxxi. 76.

18 *Ibid.*, 34.

19 *Ibid.*, xxviii. 8.

20 *Ibid.*, xxx. 11.

21 *Ibid.*, xviii. 24.

22 J. iv. 325.

23 DhA. i. 272. The story given regarding Vissakamma in SNA. i. 233, evidently refers to the **Mahākaṇha Jātaka.** The deva who accompanied Sakka in the guise of a dog in that Jātaka was Mātali and *not* Vissakamma.

Vissasena.—A king of Benares. See the **Ārāmadūsa Jātaka.**

Vissāsabhojana Jātaka (No. 93).—The Bodhisatta was once a rich merchant and had a herdsman to guard his cows in a forest shieling. They gave but little milk, through fear of a lion living in the forest. The merchant, knowing that the lion loved a doe, had her caught and her body rubbed with poison. When she returned to the forest, the lion licked her body and died.

The Buddha related this story to the monks to show them the necessity for circumspection in accepting gifts.[1]

1 J. i. 387 f.

Vihatābhā.—A king of twenty-nine kappas ago, a previous birth of **Campakapupphiya** (or **Belaṭṭhānika**) **Thera.**[1]

[1] Ap. i. 167; ThagA. i. 205.

1. **Vihāra Sutta.**—On the nine kinds of abiding (*vihārā*) in the four *jhānas* and in the spheres of infinite space, infinite consciousness, nothingness, neither perception nor non-perception, and in the sphere where feeling and perception have ended.[1]

[1] A. iv. 410.

2. **Vihāra Sutta.**—On the nine attainments of gradual abidings, similar to Sutta 1, the "abidings" being the same.

3. **Vihāra Sutta.**—See the **Padesavihāra Sutta.**

Vihāradevī.—Wife of **Kākavaṇṇatissa** and mother of **Duṭṭhagāmaṇī** and **Saddhātissa.** She was the daughter of **Tissa,** king of **Kalyāṇī,** and was cast adrift in a boat on the ocean in order to appease the sea-gods in their wrath against Tissa for having killed an arahant. Her name was **Devī,** but because she came ashore near the monastery of **Tolaka**[1] (?) she was called **Vihāradevī.**[2] When with her first child, she longed to eat a honeycomb one *usabha* in length and to drink the water in which had been washed the sword used in cutting off the head of **Nandasārathī,** chief of **Eḷāra's** warriors.[3] When she was the second time with child, she wished to lie under a *campaka*-tree in bloom and inhale its fragrance.[4]

When her husband died, Saddhātissa carried her off, hoping thus to win the kingdom, but she was later restored to Duṭṭhagāmaṇī. She was wise and practical and helped in Duṭṭhagāmaṇī's campaigns, especially in the capture of **Ambatittha** and **Anurādhapura.**[5] We know nothing of her later history.

[1] This is probably the correct reading of the name; see MṬ. 432.
[2] Mhv. xxii. 20 ff.
[3] *Ibid.*, 42 ff.; MṬ. 441.
[4] *Ibid.*, 443.
[5] Mhv. xxv. 9, 55.

Vihārabīja.—A village in Ceylon from which five hundred young men entered the Order on the occasion of the enshrinement of the Buddha's collar-bone in the **Thūpārāma.**[1]

[1] Mhv. xvii. 59.

Vihāravejjasālatittha.—A ford in the **Mahāvāḷukagaṅgā.**[1]

[1] Cv. lxxii. 25.

Vihāravāpi.—A village in Ceylon, near **Tulādhārapabbata.** It was the birthplace of **Labhiya-Vasabha.**[1]

[1] Mhv. xxiii. 90.

Vihāsava.—A king of the race of **Makhādeva.** He ruled in Benares and his son was **Vijitasena.**[1]

[1] MṬ. 130; but Dpv. iii. 39 calls him **Vijaya.**

Vijamāna.—Sixty thousand kappas ago there were sixteen kings of this name, all previous births of **Vidhūpanadāyaka Thera.**[1]

[1] Ap. i. 103.

Vitaṃsā.—One of the ten rivers flowing from **Himālaya.**[1]

[1] Mil. 114; see Mil. *Trs.* i. xliv, for a suggested identification with Vitastā, the modern Bihat (or Jhelum).

Vitamāla.—A king of fifty-seven kappas ago, a previous birth of **Koraṇḍapupphiya (Ramaṇiyavihāri) Thera.**[1]

[1] Ap. i. 206; ThagA. i. 116.

Vitarāga.—A Pacceka Buddha.[1]

[1] M. iii. 71; ApA. i. 107.

Vitarāga Sutta.—A monk who is not free from passion, corruption and infatuation, but is full of cant and deceit, cannot become what he should become.[1]

[1] A. iii. 111.

Vitasoka Thera.—A younger brother of **Dhammāsoka** and a lay pupil of **Giridatta Thera.** One day he saw grey hairs on his head as he was being dressed and, seated as he was, he became a *sotāpanna.* Later he entered the Order and became an arahant.

In the time of **Siddhattha Buddha** he was a brahmin, skilled in various branches of learning, and later became an ascetic. On his way to see the Buddha he died, and was reborn in the deva-world.[1] He is probably identical with **Buddhasaññaka Thera** of the Apadāna.[2]

[1] ThagA. i. 295 f.; two verses attributed to him are given in Thag. (169-70).
[2] Ap. ii. 419 f.; *cf.* Dvy. 366 f.

Viṇāthūṇa Jātaka (No. 232).—The Bodhisatta was once a rich merchant, and a marriage was arranged between his son and the daughter of a Benares merchant. In her parents' house, the girl saw honour being offered to a bull, and seeing a hunchback in the street on the day of her marriage, she thought him worthy of great honour (because of his hunch) and went away with him in disguise, carrying her jewellery. The Bodhisatta's friends saw her, and persuading her of her folly, took her back home.

The story was told in reference to a rich girl of **Sāvatthi** who went away with a hunchback in similar circumstances. The girls of both stories were the same.[1]

[1] J. ii. 224 f.

Viṇūpamovāda.—The name given[1] to a discourse preached by the Buddha to **Soṇa Koḷvisa** (*q.v.*) at **Gijjhakūṭa.** It is generally called **Soṇa Sutta.**[2]

[1] *E.g.*, at ThagA. i. 545. [2] See A. iii. 374.

Vīticcha Jātaka (No. 244).—The Bodhisatta was once a wise hermit living in a hut on the bend of a river. A pilgrim, a clever disputant, came to try and defeat him in debate. But, in answer to his question, the hermit asked him another, and the pilgrim was forced to retire discomfited.

The story was related in reference to a **Paribbājaka** who came to **Sāvatthi** to debate with the Buddha, but who was forced to own defeat. The two disputants were identical.[1]

[1] J. ii. 257 f.

Vīthisammajjaka Thera.—An arahant. He once saw the **Buddha Sikhī** in the street with sixty-eight thousand monks, and, after sweeping the road, he set up a flag in honour of the Buddha. Four kappas ago he was a king named **Sudhaja.**[1] He is probably identical with **Vacchagotta Thera.**[2]

[1] Ap. i. 177. [2] ThagA. i. 221.

Vīmaṃsaka Sutta.—The Buddha tells the monks at **Jetavana** that the enquiring monk, who searches the heart of others, should study the Tathāgata. He then proceeds to give details as to how the study should be undertaken.[1]

[1] M. i. 317 ff.

Vīmaṃsana-khaṇḍa.—The section of the **Mūgapakkha Jātaka** which describes the various tests applied to **Temiya** to discover whether his appearance of being deaf and dumb was a pretence.[1]

[1] J. vi. 9.

1. **Vīra Thera.**—He was born in **Sāvatthi** in the family of a minister of **Pasenadi** and became a great warrior. He married, and, on the birth of his son, left the world, attaining arahantship in due course. His former wife tried to win him back to household life, but he showed her in a verse[1] that her efforts were futile.

In the time of **Vipassī Buddha** he swept the Buddha's hermitage and offered him *nigguṇṭhi*-flowers. Later, he was born as King **Mahāpatāpa.** In the time of **Kassapa Buddha** he was a very rich merchant and gave milk-rice to the monks and alms to the poor.[2]

He is probably identical with **Nigguṇḍipupphiya Thera** of the Apadāna.[3]

[1] Thag. vs. 8. [2] ThagA. i. 50. [3] Ap. i. 205.

2. **Vīra.**—A seṭṭhi whose daughter gave milk-rice to **Tissa Buddha** immediately before his Enlightenment.[1]

[1] BuA. 189.

3. **Vīra.**—The village in which **Vīra-seṭṭhi** lived.[1]

[1] BuA. 189.

Vīraka.—The Bodhisatta born as a marsh crow. See the **Vīraka Jātaka.**

Vīraka Jātaka (No. 204).—The Bodhisatta was once born as a marsh crow, named **Vīraka,** and lived near a pool. There was a drought in **Kāsi,** and a crow, named **Saviṭṭhaka,** finding no food, went with his wife to where Vīraka lived, and, becoming his servant, ate of the fishes which Vīraka caught in the pool. Later, Saviṭṭhaka, in spite of Vīraka's warning, tried to catch fish himself and was drowned.

The story was told in reference to **Devadatta's** attempt to imitate the Buddha. Devadatta is identified with the crow Saviṭṭhaka.[1]

[1] J. ii. 148 f.; quoted at DhA. i. 122.

Vīraṅkurārāma.—A monastery in **Abhayagiri-vihāra;** it was built by **Sena I.**[1]

[1] Cv. l. 68.

Vīragaṅga.—Name of several Damiḷa chiefs, allies of **Kulasekhara.**[1]

[1] Cv. lxxvi. 131, 140, 179, 181, 187, 190.

Vīraṇatthambhaka.—A cemetery near Benares where **Somadatta** taught his father, **Aggidatta,** how to behave at court when he visited the king.[1]

[1] DhA. iii. 124.

Vīraṇukkara.—A district in South India, mentioned in the account of the campaigns of **Laṅkāpura.**[1]

[1] Cv. lxxvii. 2.

Vīradeva.—Ruler of **Palandīpa,** who invaded Ceylon in the reign of **Jayabāhu I. Vikkamabāhu** marched against him, but was defeated at **Mannāra** and had to retreat to **Koṭṭhasāra.** Thither he was pursued by **Vīradeva,** who, however, was slain in a battle at **Antaraviṭṭhika.**[1]

[1] Cv. lxi. 36 ff.

Vīrapaṇḍu.—The youngest son of **Parakkama,** king of **Paṇḍu.** When his father was murdered he fled, but **Laṅkāpura** took him under his protection and restored his kingdom. He was crowned at **Madhurā,** the **Lambakaṇṇas** officiating.[1]

[1] Cv. lxxvi. 193 f.; lxxvii. 5, 25, 103; see also Cv. *Trs.* ii. 100, n. 1.

Vīrapperaya.—Name of several Damiḷa chiefs, allies of **Kulasekhara.**[1]

[1] Cv. lxxvi. 138, 316; lxxvii. 6, 7.

1. **Vīrabāhu.**—Younger brother of **Vijayabāhu I.** He was made *uparājā* and put in charge of **Dakkhiṇadesa.** He married **Subhaddā.** He helped the king in the conquest of **Pulatthipura** when the **Velakkāra** troops revolted.[1]

[1] Cv. lix. 11, 43; lx. 40.

2. **Vīrabāhu.** The surname assumed by **Māṇābharaṇa I.** when he became governor of **Dakkhiṇadesa,** with his headquarters at **Puṅkhagāma.** He also bore the title of **Mahādipāda.** This Mānābharaṇa was the father of **Parakkamabāhu I.**[1]

[1] Cv. lxi. 26; lxii. 4, 62.

3. **Vīrabāhu.**—Son of **Kittinissaṅka.** He ruled for only one night.[1]

[1] Cv. lxxx. 27.

4. **Vīrabāhu.**—Sister's son to **Parakkamabāhu I.** He defeated the **Jāvakas** under Candabhānu, and, in celebration of his victory, worshipped **Viṣṇu** at **Devanagara** and erected the **Nandana-pariveṇa.**[1] When **Vijayabāhu IV.** became king, Vīrabāhu lived at court, helped the king in his duties as a devoted friend and was constantly in his company. He was specially commissioned by the king to restore **Pulatthipura** to its original grandeur, and, after its restoration,[2] was appointed to live there as

[1] Cv. lxxxiii. 41 ff. [2] *Ibid.*, lxxxvii. 15; lxxxviii. 5, 27, 55, 67, 90; lxxxix. 11, 48.

governor of the Northern Province. He was in charge of the ordination ceremony at **Sahassatittha** (*q.v.*).

5. **Vīrabāhu.**—Successor to **Bhuvanekabāhu V.**[1]

[1] Cv. xci. 13; see Cv. *Trs.* ii. 214, n. 2.

Vīravamma.—Husband of **Yasodharā,** daughter of **Vijayabāhu I.** They had two daughters, **Līlāvatī** and **Sugalā.** He was given as dowry the province of **Merukandara.**[1]

[1] Cv. lix. 27.

Vīravāpi.—A tank restored by **Parakkamabāhu I.**[1]

[1] Cv. lxxix. 36.

Vīravikkama.—King of Ceylon (*circa* 1542 A.C.). He succeeded **Vijayabāhu VI.** and claimed descent from **Sirisaṅghabodhi.** He lived in **Sirivaḍḍhanapura** (modern Kandy), built eighty-six dwelling-houses for the monks and had the Tipiṭaka copied. He went on a pilgrimage to **Mahiyaṅgaṇa** and **Sumanakūṭa.** He cultivated a rice-field himself, and, from the produce, gave alms.[1]

[1] Cv. xcii. 6 ff.

1. **Vīrā Therī.**—A certain lay-follower gave her a robe, and a Yakkha aware of this, went about praising his piety.[1] *v.l.* **Cīrā.**

[1] S. i. 213.

2. **Vīrā.**—See **Dhīrā.**

1. **Vuṭṭhāna Sutta.**—Among those who practise meditation are those who are skilled in emerging from concentration.[1]

[1] S. iii. 265.

2. **Vuṭṭhāna Sutta.**—Some that are skilled in emerging from concentration are not skilled in the object of concentration, the range, the resolve, in zeal, perseverance and profit.[1]

[1] S. iii. 273 f.

1. **Vuṭṭhi Sutta.**—A conversation between two devas and the Buddha's comments thereon. Of things making for progress, knowledge is the best; ignorance is the greatest worsener; among beings that walk, the Saṅgha is the best; among declarants, the Buddha is the best.[1]

[1] S. i. 42.

2. **Vuṭṭhi Sutta.**—At the end of the rains, **Sāriputta** takes leave of the Buddha to go into the country. As he is about to start, a monk reports to the Buddha that Sāriputta has offended him and has not asked his pardon.[1] Sāriputta is sent for and asked to explain; he declares with a wealth of simile that he is free from hatred and ill-will; he has nothing but loathing for his body; how then would he offend a brother monk and not ask his pardon? The accuser is convinced of his folly and begs forgiveness.[2]

[1] The Commentary (AA. ii. 797) explains that the skirt of Sāriputta's robe brushed the Elder; some say the wind blew it without his knowledge.

[2] A. iv. 373 ff.; *cf.* DhA. ii. 178 ff., where the story recurs.

1. **Vuḍḍhi Sutta.**—The seven *bojjhaṅgas*, if cultivated, conduce to increase and not decrease.[1]

[1] S. v. 94.

2. **Vuḍḍhi Sutta.**—Four conditions which conduce to the growth of insight.[1]

[1] S. v. 411.

Vuttamālāsandesasataka.—A Pāli poem of the fifteenth century, containing one hundred and two stanzas and written by **Upatapassi,** who calls himself *Sarasigāmamūlamahāsāmī*. It contains laudatory verses on the reigning king, contemporary monks and several places of worship. The book is supposed to have aimed at teaching students the right pronunciation of sounds and the proper modulation of voice in reciting verses.[1]

[1] P.L.C. 253 f.

Vuttodaya.—A work on Pāli prosody, in six chapters, partly prose, partly verse, written by **Saṅgharakkhita Thera** of Ceylon. It is based on works dealing with Sanskrit prosody—*e.g.*, of Piṅgala—and has borrowed their terms and method of treatment. There exist several Commentaries on the work, chief of which are the **Vuttodaya-pañcikā** (or **Chandosāratthavikāsinī**) by **Saddhammañāṇa** and *Ṭīkās* by **Vepullabuddhi** of Pagan, and **Navavimalabuddhi** or **Culla-vimalabuddhi** of Panyā.[1]

[1] Gv. 61, 64, 70; Svd. 1210; P.L.C. 198 f.; Bode, *op. cit.*, 26, 27, 28.

Vekhanassa.—A **Paribbājaka,** teacher of **Sakuladāyī.**[1] See **Vekhanassa Sutta.**

MA. ii. 716.

Vekhanassa Sutta.—**Vekhanassa** visits the Buddha at **Jetavana** and argues about perfection. As in the **Cūla-Sakuladāyī Sutta,** the Buddha says that what Vekhanassa defines as perfection is merely a refinement of pleasure, and that only arahants can grasp the real meaning of perfection. Vekhanassa is annoyed, but the Buddha soothes him, and he becomes the Buddha's follower.[1] In the sutta Vekhanassa is called **Kaccāna.** The Commentary[2] says that Vekhanassa visited the Buddha because he wished to discover for himself why his favourite pupil, **Sakuludāyī,** should have been defeated by the Buddha; he, therefore, travelled all the way from **Rājagaha** to **Sāvatthi,** a distance of forty-five leagues, to see the Buddha.

[1] M. ii. 40 ff.

[2] MA. ii. 716.

Vegabbarī.—See **Veṭambharī.**

Veghanasā.—A class of devas present at the preaching of the **Mahāsamaya Sutta.**[1]

[1] D. ii. 261.

Vejanīya Sutta.—See **Saṃvejanīya Sutta.**

1. **Vejayanta.**—A *pāsāda* belonging to **Sakka.** When **Moggallāna** visited Sakka to discover if he had fully understood the Buddha's teaching in the **Cūlataṇhā-saṅkhaya Sutta,** Sakka tried to evade his questions by showing him this palace. It has one hundred towers, each seven storeys high, with seven nymphs in each storey, waited on by seven attendants. The palace appeared in **Tāvatiṃsa** on the day of Sakka's decisive victory over the **Asuras.** Moggallāna allowed himself to be shown round, and then, with his big toe, he made the palace quake and rock.[1] The palace is one thousand leagues high, and is so called because it arose in the hour of victory.[2] It is decked with banners, each three hundred leagues long—banners of gold on jewelled staffs and *vice versâ*; and the whole palace is built of the seven precious substances. It arose as the result of the rest-house built by Sakka, in his birth as **Magha,** for the use of the multitude.[3] When the Buddha visited Tāvatiṃsa with **Nanda,** Sakka was in the palace with his crimson-footed (*kakuṭapādiniyo*) nymphs and came forward with them to greet him. The nymphs had given oil for the massaging of **Kassapa Buddha's** feet, hence the colour of their own feet.[4]

[1] M. i. 252 f.; *cf.* Thag. 1196 f.; ThagA. ii. 184. The palace was also made to rock by the novice **Saṅgharakkhita** (*q.v.*) on the day he joined the Order (DA. ii. 558).

[2] J. i. 203.

[3] DhA. i. 273; *cf.* DA. iii. 698.

[4] SNA. i. 274.

When King **Sādhīna** of **Mithilā** went to Tāvatiṃsa, he lived, according to human computation, seven hundred years in Vejayanta.[5]

The Vejayantapāsāda is illustrated on the Bharhut Tope.[6]

[5] J. iv. 357. [6] Cunningham, *Bharhut Tope*, p. 137.

2. **Vejayanta.**—A chariot owned by **Sakka,** one hundred and fifty leagues in length,[1] and drawn by one thousand horses, with **Mātali** as charioteer.[2] Sakka rode into battle in this chariot,[3] and it was sent to fetch distinguished humans to **Tāvatiṃsa**—*e.g.*, **Nimi, Guttila** and **Sādhīna** (*q.v.*). The **Sudhābhojana Jātaka**[4] contains a description of the chariot with its pole of gold and its framework overlaid with gilt representations of various animals and birds. When the chariot travelled the whole world was filled with the sound of its wheels.

[1] DA. ii. 481; SA. i. 261; J. i. 202.
[2] S. i. 224.
[3] J. i. 202.
[4] J. v. 408 f.

3. **Vejayanta.**—The chief of the eighty-four thousand chariots owned by **Mahāsudassana.**[1] The navel of its wheels was made of sapphire, the spokes of seven kinds of precious things, the rim of coral, the axle of silver, etc.[2]

[1] S. iii. 145; D. ii. 187. [2] SA. ii. 237.

1. **Veṭambarī.**—One of a group of devas who visited the Buddha at **Veḷuvana** and spoke of their beliefs. Veṭambarī spoke two verses, one condemning asceticism, and the other, which followed immediately on the first, in praise of the same.[1] The Commentary says[2] that the second verse was inspired by **Māra.**

[1] S. i. 65, 67. [2] SA. i. 100.

2. **Veṭambarī.**—The name of **Buddhūpaṭṭhāyaka's** father in his birth thirty-one kappas ago.[1]

[1] Ap. i. 242.

Veṭendu.—A vassal of the **Cātummahārājāno,** present at the preaching of the **Mahāsamaya Sutta.**[1]

[1] D. ii. 258.

Veṭṭhapura.—See **Veṭhipura.**

Veṭhadīpa, Veṭhadīpaka.—A brahmin settlement, the chieftain of which claimed a part of the Buddha's relics; having obtained the relics, he built a *thūpa* over them.[1] According to the Dhammapada Commentary,[2] the kings of **Veṭhadīpaka** and **Allakappa** once lived in intimate friendship.

[1] D. ii. 165, 167; Bu. xxviii. 3. [2] DhA. i. 161; see *J.R.A.S.* 1907, p. 1049.

1. **Veṭhadīpaka.**—The brahmin of **Veṭhadīpa,** who claimed an eighth share of the Buddha's relics.[1]

[1] D. ii. 165, 167.

2. **Veṭhadīpaka.**—The king of **Veṭhadīpa** and friend of the king of **Allakappa.** They left the world together and became ascetics in the **Himālaya.** Veṭhadīpaka died and was reborn in the deva-world. He then visited his friend, and, learning that he had been troubled by elephants, taught him a charm to ward off any harm which might come from them. This charm **Udena** later learnt from Allakappa.[1]

[1] DhA. i. 163 f.

Veṭhipura.—A city in India, the birthplace of **Abhibhūta Thera.**[1] *v.l.* **Veṭṭhapura.**

[1] ThagA. i. 372.

Veṇī.—A she-jackal, wife of **Pūtimaṃsa.** See the **Putimaṃsa Jātaka.**

Veṇu.—A river in Ceylon, on the way from **Anurādhapura** to **Dakkhiṇadesa.** It lay between the **Tissavāpi** and **Jajjaranadī.**[1]

[1] VibhA. p. 446.

Veṇudatta Thera.—A monk. **Valliya Thera** heard him preach and questioned him. Pondering on what he had heard, he gained insight.[1]

[1] ThagA. i. 292.

Veṇumatī.—A channel branching off from the **Toyavāpi** on its western side. It was constructed by **Parakkamabāhu I.**[1]

[1] Cv. lxxix. 46.

Veṇḍu.—A devaputta. He visited the Buddha and asked him a question.[1]

[1] S. i. 52; SA. (i. 87) calls him **Veṇhu.**

Veṇḍu Sutta.—The question asked by **Veṇḍu** (*q.v.*) and the Buddha's answer.[1]

[1] S. i. 52.

Veṇhu.—A deva who was present, with his retinue, at the preaching of the **Mahāsamaya Sutta.**[1] See also **Veṇḍu** above. Veṇhu is a Pāli form of Viṣṇu. See also **Andhakaveṇhudāsaputta.**

[1] D. ii. 259.

Vetaraññī.—The waters of the **Vetaraṇī.**[1]

[1] J. vi. 250.

Vetaraṇī.—A river in **Mahā-niraya.**[1] Buddhaghosa explains[2] that this is the name of a *mahatā khāraodikā nadī* (the great "Caustic River") referred to in the **Devadatta Sutta.**[3] Its waters are sharp and bitter (*tiṇhadhārā, khuradhārā*),[4] and the river flows by the **Asipattavana.** When beings enter it to bathe and drink (because it looks like a sheet of water) they are hacked by swords and other sharp weapons which stand concealed along the river bank.[5] Sometimes Vetaraṇī is used in a general way to indicate **Niraya.**[6] Those guilty of abortion are reborn in the Vetaraṇīnadī,[7] as are also oppressors of the weak.[8]

[1] S. i. 21; SN. vs. 674.
[2] SNA. ii. 482.
[3] M. iii. 185.
[4] SN. vs. 674; *cf.* J. v. 269.
[5] SNA. ii. 482; J. v. 275; vi. 105; where a long description is given of the horrors of Vetaraṇī.
[6] As "*desanāsīsa*"—*e.g.*, J. iii. 473; SA. i. 48; *cf.* J. iv. 273.
[7] J. v. 269.
[8] J. vi. 106.

2. **Vetaraṇī.**—A physician of old, famous for curing snake-bites.[1]

[1] J. iv. 496.

Vetullavāda.—A heretical doctrine which was introduced into Ceylon by **Vohārika-Tissa,** but was suppressed by his minister **Kapila.**[1] It appeared again later, and though officially disapproved, it does seem to have pushed its way among the monks of Ceylon, chiefly the **Dhammarucikas** (*q.v.*).[2] **Vetullavāda** is generally identified with the Mahāyāna school of Buddhism.[3] The **Vetulla-piṭaka,** the canon of the **Vetullavādins,** is condemned as *abuddhavacana.*[4]

[1] Mhv. xxxvi. 41; Dpv. xxii. 40.
[2] *E.g.*, in the reigns of Gothabhaya (Mhv. xxxvi. 111), Mahāsena, (xxxvii. 1 ff.), and Aggabodhi I. (Cv. xlii. 35).
[3] See Mhv. *Trs.* 259, n. 2; also Hocart, *Memoirs of the Archæol. Survey of Ceylon*, i. 1922, p. 15 ff.
[4] *E.g.*, SA. ii. 150; *cf.* Sp. iv. 742, where it is called **Vedaḷha-piṭaka.**

1. **Vettavatī.**—A river, probably in the kingdom of **Mejjha.** According to the **Mātaṅga Jātaka,**[1] **Mātaṅga** lived in a hermitage on the upper reaches of the river in order to humble the pride of **Jātimanta,** who lived

[1] J. iv. 388; *cf.* Dvy. 451, 456.

lower down. On the banks of the river was a city, also called **Vettavatī.** In the Milindapañha,[2] the Vettavatī is mentioned as one of the ten chief rivers flowing from the **Himālaya.** It is probably identical with the Vetravatī mentioned in Kālidāsa's Meghadūta, and is identified with the modern Betuva in Bhopal (the ancient Vidīsa).

[2] p. 114.

2. **Vettavatī.**—A channel branching off from the **Parakkamasamudda;** the sluice from which it started bore the same name.[1]

[1] Cv. lxxix. 44.

Vettavāsa-vihāra.—A monastery in **Pācīnakaṇḍakarājī** in Ceylon. It was given by King **Aggabodhi II.** to the minister of the **Kāliṅga** king who came over to Ceylon during his reign and entered the Order under **Jotipāla;** the minister gave it back to the Saṅgha.[1]

[1] Cv. xlii. 48; see also Cv. *Trs.* i. 71, n. 2.

Vedaññā.—See **Vedhaññā.**

Vedanā Saṃyutta.—The thirty-sixth section of the **Saṃyutta Nikāya.**[1]

[1] S. iv. 204-37.

1. **Vedanā Sutta.**—On how diversity of feelings arise because of the diversity in elements.[1]

[1] S. ii. 141.

2. **Vedanā Sutta.**—Diversity of feelings arises because of the diversity in elements and not *vice versâ.*[1]

[1] S. ii. 142.

3. **Vedanā Sutta.**—Feeling that is born of sense-contact is not abiding but fleeting.[1]

[1] S. ii. 247.

4. **Vedanā Sutta.**—The Noble Eightfold Path is the way to the comprehension of the three kinds of feelings.[1]

[1] S. iv. 255.

5. **Vedanā Sutta.**—The cultivation of the Noble Eightfold Path is for the full comprehension of the three kinds of feelings.[1]

[1] S. v. 57.

Vedanāpariggaha Sutta.—See the **Dīghanakha Sutta,** for which this was evidently another name.[1]

[1] *E.g.*, DA. ii. 418; DhA. i. 79; ThagA. ii. 95.

1. " **Vedanāya** " **Sutta.**—Feelings arising from eye-contact are impermanent, likewise from ear-contact, etc.[1]

[1] S. iii. 226.

2. " **Vedanāya** " **Sutta.**—The feeling born of contact by the eye, ear, etc., this is the appearing of decay and death. The ceasing of the former is the coming to end of the latter.[1]

[1] S. iii. 230.

3. " **Vedanāya** " **Sutta.**—The desire-and-lust that is in feeling born of contact of the eye, etc., this is a corruption of the heart.[1]

[1] S. iii. 233.

1. **Vedabbha.**—The name of a charm and of a brahmin who knew it. See the **Vedabbha Jātaka.**

2. **Vedabbha Jātaka** (No. 48).—There was once a brahmin who knew the **Vedabbha** charm which, if repeated at a certain conjunction of the planets, made the seven precious things rain down from the sky. The Bodhisatta was his pupil, and one day, while journeying in the forest, they were attacked by five hundred robbers called " despatchers " (*pesanka-corā*).[1] These robbers kept the brahmin and sent the Bodhisatta for the ransom. The Bodhisatta, knowing that that night the conjunction of the stars would occur, which ensured the efficacy of the charm, warned the brahmin not to make use of it. But when night came the brahmin repeated the charm, and the robbers were so delighted that he was able to persuade them to set him free. They set off with the treasures that had fallen from the sky, the brahmin accompanying them, but on the way they were attacked by another robber-band. These were told that the brahmin could make treasures fall from the sky; they were therefore set free, only the brahmin being kept back. But on being told that they must wait for one year for the necessary conjunction of planets, they were angry, cut the brahmin in two, and pursued the first band of robbers, destroying them entirely. Unable to agree on the division of the spoils which they thus obtained, the second band fought among themselves

[1] They were so called because when they took two prisoners they would keep one, sending the other for ransom.

till only two were left. These took the treasure and hid it in a jungle near the village. One guarded it while the other went to the village for rice. When he returned he cooked the rice, ate his share, and put poison in the rest hoping thus to rid himself of his companion; the latter, however, killed him, then ate the rice and died himself. The Bodhisatta returning with the ransom, found all the dead bodies, in various places, and realized what had happened. He took the treasure to his own house.

The story was told in reference to a self-willed monk who is identified with the Vedabbha brahmin.[2]

[2] J. i. 253-6.

Vedalla.—The last of the nine *aṅgas* or divisions of the Tipiṭaka, according to matter.[1] It includes such suttas as the **Culla-Vedalla, Mahāvedalla, Sammādiṭṭhi, Sakkapañha, Saṅkhārabhājanīya, Mahāpuṇṇama,** and others, which were preached in answer to questions asked through knowledge and joy (*sabbe pi vedañ ca tuṭṭhiñ ca laddhā pucchitasuttantā*).[2]

[1] M. i. 133; Pug. iv. 9; Gv. 27; Vin. iii. 8; Mil. 263.

[2] DA. i. 24.

Vedalla Sutta.—See **Culla-vedalla** and **Mahā-vedalla.**

Vedikāraka Thera.—An arahant. He built a railing round the *thūpa* of **Piyadassī Buddha.** Sixteen kappas ago he was king thirty-two times under the name of **Maṇippabhāsa.**[1] He is evidently identical with **Vijaya Thera.**[2]

[1] Ap. i. 171.

[2] ThagA. i. 192.

Vediya, Vediyaka.—A mountain to the north of **Ambasaṇḍā,** in which was the **Indasālaguhā,** where the Buddha stayed. The mountain was bathed in radiance when **Sakka** visited the Buddha on the occasion of the preaching of the **Sakkapañha Sutta.**[1]

Buddhaghosa says[2] that the mountain was so called because its base was covered with a forest-belt, which looked like a jewel-railing (*maṇivedikā*). On the mountain lived an owl, who would accompany the Buddha half-way to the village when he went for alms, and return with him. One day the owl stood with lowered wings, its claws clasped together. The Buddha smiled when he saw it, and, in reply to **Ānanda's** question, said that the owl, after spending one hundred thousand kappas among gods and men, would become a Pacceka Buddha named **Somanassa.**[3]

[1] D. ii. 263, 264.

[2] DA. iii. 697.

[3] MA. i. 255 f.; *cp.* KhpA. 151, where the mountain is called **Vedisaka.**

Vediyadāyaka Thera.—An arahant. He built a railing round the Bodhi-tree of **Vipassī Buddha.** Eleven kappas ago he was a king named **Sūriyassama.**[1]

[1] Ap. i. 219 f.

Vedisa, Vedisagiri.—A city, the home of **Devī,** mother of **Mahinda.** He and **Saṅghamittā** were born there, and, just before he left for Ceylon, he went there to visit his mother and stayed for one month in the monastery, which was also called **Vedisagiri.**[1] Vedisa was fifty yojanas from **Pāṭaliputta** and was founded by the Sākyans who fled from **Viḍūḍabha's** massacre.[2]

Vedisa is identified with the modern Bhilsa in Gwalior State, twenty-six miles north-east of Bhopal.[3]

[1] Dpv. vi. 15; xii. 14, 35; Sp. i. 70, 71; Mhv. xiii. 6-9, 18.

[2] Mbv., p. 98.

[3] Mhv. *Trs.* 88, n. 4.

Vedisaka.—See **Vediyaka.**

Vedisadevī.—Wife of **Asoka;** she was the daughter of **Deva,** a seṭṭhi of **Vedisagiri,** and her children were **Mahinda** and **Saṅghamittā.**[1]

[1] MṬ. 324.

1. **Vedeha.**—The title of several kings of **Mithilā,** capital of **Videha**—*e.g.*, **Suruci** (J. iv. 319); **Sādhīna** (J. iv. 355, 356); **Somanassa** (J. vi. 47); **Nimi** (J. vi. 102), and **Aṅgati** (J. vi. 222, etc.). *v.l.* **Videha.**

2. **Vedeha.**—See **Videha (2) and (3).**

3. **Vedeha.**—The personal name of the king of **Kāsi,** mentioned in the **Mātuposaka Jātaka.**[1] He is identified with **Ānanda.**[2]

[1] J. iv. 94.

[2] *Ibid.*, 95.

4. **Vedeha.**—The personal name of the king of **Mithilā,** whose minister was **Mahosadha.** For his story see the **Mahāummagga Jātaka.** He is identified with **Lāḷudāyī.**[1]

[1] J. vi. 478.

5. **Vedeha.**—A rich householder of **Haṃsavatī,** in the time of Padumuttara Buddha. He was a former birth of **Mahā Kassapa** (*q.v.*).[1]

[1] AA. i. 93; ThagA. ii. 134; SA. ii. 135; ApA. i. 209.

6. **Vedeha.**—A Thera of Ceylon, who belonged to the **Araññavāsī Nikāya.** He wrote the **Rasavāhinī** and the **Samantakūṭavaṇṇanā,** and also, probably, the Sinhalese grammar known as the *Sidatsaṅgarā*. He lived in the thirteenth century and was a pupil of **Ānanda Vanaratna.**[1]

[1] P.L.C. 222 f.; Svd. 1263.

Vedehaputta.—An epithet of **Sotthisena,** king of **Kāsī.** The scholiast explains that his mother was a **Videha** princess.[1]

[1] J. v. 90.

Vedehamuni.—A name given to **Ānanda.**[1] The Commentary explains[2] Vedeha by *paṇḍita*. (*Vedehamunino ti paṇḍitamunino. Paṇḍito hi ñāṇasaṅkhātena vedena īhati sabbakiccāni karoti, tasmā vedeho ti vuccati. Vedeho ca so muni cāti=Vedehamuni*). The Apadāna Commentary,[3] however, gives another explanation, according to which Ānanda was the son of a Videha lady (*Videharaṭṭhe jātā, tassā deviyā putto*).

[1] S. i. 215, 219; *cf.* Mhv. iii. 36; Ap. i. 7; DhSA., p. 1.

[2] SA. ii. 132; *cf.* MṬ. 149 (*vedena paññāya īhati pavattatīti = vedeho*).

[3] ApA. i. 106.

Vedeharajja, Vedeharaṭṭha.—Name given to the kingdom of **Videha.**[1]

[1] *E.g.*, J. vi. 393, 411.

Vedehā.—The people of **Videha** (*q.v.*).

Vedehikā.—A lady (*gahapatānī*) of **Sāvatthī** who had a reputation for gentleness till her servant-girl, **Kāḷī**, convinced people that it was not deserved.[1] For the story see *s.v.* **Kāḷī** (3).

Buddhaghosa says[2] that she was called Vedehikā either because she came from a **Videha** family or because she was wise.

[1] M. i. 125 f.

[2] MA. i. 318; *cf.* **Vedehiputta, Vedehamuni.**

Vedehiputta.—An epithet constantly used in connection with **Ajātasattu** (*q.v.*). Buddhaghosa[1] explains it by saying that Videhī here means a wise woman and *not* the Videha-lady, because Ajātasattu's mother was the daughter, not of a king of **Videha,** but of a **Kosala** king.[2] According to the Nirayāvalī Sūtra,[3] there was, among the wives of **Bimbisāra,** Callanā, daughter of Ceṭaka, a rājā of Vaiśāli, whose sister Triśālā was

[1] *Vedehiputto ti, vedehīti paṇḍitādhivacanaṃ etaṃ; paṇḍititthiyā putto ti attho* (SA. i. 120); *cf.* DA. i. 139.

[2] *E.g.*, J. iii. 121; iv. 342; she was called Kosaladevī—*e.g.*, J. ii. 403.

[3] Jacobi, *Jaina Sutras*, SBE. xxii. Introd., p. xiii.

the mother of Mahāvīra. She was also called Śrībhadrā. According to the Tibetan Dulvā,[4] Ajatasattu's mother was Vāsavī, daughter of Siṃha of Vaiśāli. It was foretold that Vāsavī's son would kill his father.

Cf. **Vedehikā, Vedehamuni.**

[4] Rockhill: *Life of the Buddha*, 63 f.

Vedhañña, Vedañña.—A family of **Sākyans.** Buddhaghosa says[1] they were skilled in archery (hence their name the "Archers"). They learnt their craft in a technical college (*sippuggahanapāsāda*) built in a mango-grove. It was there that the **Pāsādika Sutta** was preached.[2] From the **Sāmagāma Sutta**[3] it would appear that these Sākyans lived in **Sāmagāma.**

[1] DA. iii. 905. [2] D. iii. 17. [3] M. ii. 244.

Venateyya.—A **Garuḷa,** husband of **Kākātī** (*q.v.*). He is identified with **Kuṇāla.**[1]

[1] J. v. 428.

Venasāra Jātaka.—See the **Dhonasākha Jātaka.**

Venāga Sutta.—Preached at **Venāgapura.** The brahmins of that village visit the Buddha, and their leader **Vacchagotta** expresses his admiration of the Buddha's translucent colour in various similes, suggesting that it may be due to the luxurious beds on which the Buddha is able to sleep. The Buddha, however, answers that the costly beds mentioned by Vacchagotta are not for recluses like himself, but that he has three different "couches," each of which gives him great comfort of body and mind: the broad celestial (*dibba*) couch, the sublime couch, and the Ariyan couch. He explains the nature of these couches and of the four *jhānas.* The Venāgapura brahmins thereupon accept the Buddha as their teacher.[1]

[1] A. i. 180 ff.

Venāgapura.—A brahmin village of **Kosala,** where the Buddha preached the **Venāga Sutta** (*q.v.*).[1]

[1] A. i. 180.

Vepacitti.—An **Asura** chieftain, who was present with **Namuci (Māra)** at the preaching of the **Mahāsamaya Sutta.**[1] It is said[2] that among the

[1] D. ii. 259.

[2] *E.g.*, AA. ii. 758, Vepacitti being the highest (*sabbajeṭṭhaka*, SA. i. 263).

Asuras, **Vepacitti, Rāhu** and **Pahārada** were the chiefs. Vepacitti was the friend of Rāhu, and when Rāhu seized **Candimā** and **Suriya** and these invoked the power of the Buddha, it was to Vepacitti that Rāhu fled for comfort.[3] The Asuras being once defeated in a fight with the Devas, the latter took Vepacitti prisoner, and brought him, bound hand and foot, to **Sakka** in the **Sudhammā**-hall. There Vepacitti reviled and railed at Sakka with scurrilous words, both on entering and on leaving the hall, but Sakka remained silent, and, when questioned by **Mātali**, said it was not proper for him to bandy words with a fool.[4] On another occasion Vepacitti suggested that victory should be given to him or to Sakka, according to their excellence in speech. Sakka agreed to this, and Vepacitti, as the *older god*, was asked to speak a verse. Sakka spoke another, the Devas applauding. Several verses were spoken by each, and both Devas and Asuras decided in favour of Sakka, because Vepacitti's verses belonged, they said, to the sphere of violence, while those of Sakka belonged to one of concord and harmony.[5] Once, when Sakka was revolving in his mind the thought that he should not betray even his enemy, Vepacitti read his thoughts and came up to him. "Stop," said Sakka, "thou art my prisoner"; but Vepacitti reminded him of his thought, and was allowed to go free.[6]

Buddhaghosa says[7] that Vepacitti's original name was **Sambara** (*q.v.*). When Sambara refused to give to the seers, who visited him, a pledge that the Asuras would not harm them, the seers cursed him, and from that time onwards he slept badly and was plagued by nightmares. This so deranged his mind (*cittaṃ vepati*) that he came to be called Vepacitti ("Crazy-nerve"). When Vepacitti lay ill of this disease, Sakka visited him and offered to cure him if he would teach him Sambara's magic art. Vepacitti consulted the Asuras, and, as they were unwilling, he refused Sakka's offer, warning him that Sambara, having practised magic, was suffering in purgatory and that he should avoid a similar fate.[8]

Buddhaghosa explains[9] that, if Vepacitti had taught him the art, it was Sakka's intention to take Vepacitti to the seers and persuade them to forgive him.

[3] S. i. 50, 51.

[4] *Ibid.*, 221 f.; *cf.* S. iv. 201, according to which his bondage caused him no inconvenience so long as he remained with the devas, but the moment he experienced the wish to rejoin the Asuras, he felt himself bound. Vepacitti's capture is referred to in Thag. vs. 749.

[5] S. i. 222 f.

[6] *Ibid.*, 225.

[7] SA. i. 266.

[8] S. i. 238 f.

[9] SA. i. 272. This episode seems to contradict Buddhaghosa's previous statement that Sambara and Vepacitti were identical. Perhaps, as Mrs. Rhys Davids suggests (KS. i. 305, n. 4), Sambara was the name of an office rather than that of a person.

Mention is made[10] of a visit once paid by Sakka and Vepacitti to a company of seers dwelling in a forest-hut. Vepacitti, in his buskins, his sword hanging at his side and his state canopy borne over his head, entered by the main gate, while Sakka, in all humility, used the side gate. Buddhaghosa explains[11] the strange relations of Sakka and Vepacitti by saying that they were father- and son-in-law, and that they were sometimes at war with each other; sometimes, however, they lived in concord. The Dhammapada Commentary[12] gives the story of the romantic marriage of Sakka to Vepacitti's daughter, **Sujā** (*q.v.*).

According to the Kathāvatthu, other members of Vepacitti's family appear to have intermarried with the devas, and the Kathāvatthu Commentary says that a troop of Asuras, belonging to the retinue of Vepacitti, was once freed from the fourfold plane of misery and was taken up among the devas.[13]

The Sanskrit texts call him Vemacitra or Vemacitrī.[14]

[10] S. i. 226.
[11] SA. i. 265.
[12] DhA. i. 278 f.; *cf.* J. i. 205 f.
[13] See *Points of Controversy*, p. 211.
[14] *E.g.*, Dvy., pp. 126, 148; Mtu. iii. 138, 254.

Vepacitti (or **Khanti**) **Sutta.**—**Vepacitti** is led in bonds to **Sakka,** whom he abuses. Sakka remains silent till the departure of Vepacitti. Then, in reply to **Mātali,** Sakka says that the man who, when reviled, does not, in his turn, revile, wins a twofold victory.[1]

[1] S. i. 221 f.; *cf.* S. iv. 201.

Vepulla, Vipula.—The highest of the five mountains surrounding **Rājagaha.**[1] In the time of **Kakusandha Buddha,** the mountain was called **Pācīnavaṃsa;** in the time of **Koṇāgamana, Vaṅkaka;** while in that of **Kassapa Buddha,** it was **Supassa;** and the people living near it were called, respectively, **Tivaras, Rohitassas** and **Suppiyas.** The mountain has diminished in size, for the Tivaras, who lived for forty thousand years, took four days to climb it and four to descend; the Rohitassas lived for thirty thousand years and took three days each way; while the Suppiyas, with a life-span of twenty thousand years, did the journey there and back in four days. In the present age, the **Magadhans,** who lived for about one hundred years, could both climb and descend the mountain in very little time.[2]

Vepulla was the abode of the Yakkha **Kumbhīra** and his one hundred thousand followers.[3] According to the **Dummedha Jātaka**[4] it was possible for an elephant to climb to the top of Vepulla. From Vepulla, the

[1] S. i. 67.
[2] *Ibid.*, ii. 190 f.
[3] D. ii. 257.
[4] J. i. 445.

Cakkavatti gets his *cakkaratana*,[5] and it was this gem which **Puṇṇaka** obtained from the mountain to be offered as stake in his game of dice with **Dhanañjaya Koravya.**[6]

[5] KhpA. p. 173; J. iv. 232.

[6] J. vi. 271, 272, 326.

Vepullatā Sutta.—Four conditions which, if cultivated, lead to the increase of insight.[1]

[1] S. v. 411.

Vepullapabbata Sutta.—It gives the particulars (names, etc.) regarding Mt. **Vepulla** (*q.v.*) in the age of the four last Buddhas.[1]

[1] S. ii. 190 ff.

Vepullabuddhi.—A monk of Pagan of the fourteenth century; author of ṭīkās on the **Vuttodaya,** the **Saddasāratthajālini**, the **Abhidhammatthasaṅgaha,** and the **Vidadhimukhamaṇḍana.** He was author also of the **Paramatthamañjūsa** and the **Vacanatthajotī.**[1]

[1] Gv. 64, 67; Sās. 75; Bode, *op. cit.*, 28.

Vebhaliṅga.—See **Vehaliṅga.**

1. **Vebhāra.**—One of the five hills surrounding **Rājagaha.**[1] At its foot was the **Sattapaṇṇiguhā,** where the first Convocation was held.[2] The river **Tapodā** (*q.v.*) rose in a lake at the foot of Vebhāra.[3]

[1] *E.g.*, M. iii. 68.

[2] Vin. ii. 76; iii. 159; Sp. i. 10, etc.

[3] SA. i. 30 f.

2. **Vebhāra.**—A city in which **Padumuttara Buddha** preached and ordained ninety crores of men.[1]

[1] Bu. xi. 9.

3. **Vebhāra.**—The birthplace of **Siddhattha Buddha,** where, later, he preached the **Buddhavaṃsa,** when ninety crores of beings realized the Truth.[1]

[1] Bu. xvii. 5, 13; BuA. p. 186; J. i. 40.

4. **Vebhāra.**—A city built by **Vissakamma,** where **Valliya Thera (Candanamāliya)** lived in a previous birth.[1]

[1] ThagA. i. 294; Ap. ii. 424.

5. **Vebhāra.**—*v.l.* for **Dvebhāra** (*q.v.*).

Veyyākaraṇa.—A portion of the Tipiṭaka in its arrangement according to matter (*aṅga*). According to Buddhaghosa[1] it includes the whole of the Abhidhammapiṭaka and suttas not composed in verse.

[1] DA. i. 24; Pug. iv. 9, 28.

Veyyāvaccaka Thera.—An arahant. Ninety-one kappas ago he was a servant to **Vipassī Buddha,** and, having nothing to give, worshipped his feet. Eight kappas ago he was a king called **Sucintita.**[1] He is probably identical with **Sañjaya Thera.**[2]

[1] Ap. i. 138. [2] ThagA. i. 120.

1. **Vera Sutta.**—Preached to **Anāthapiṇḍika,** on the five dread hatreds: taking life, theft, fleshly lusts, lying, and indulgence in intoxicants.[1]

[1] A. iii. 204.

2. **Vera Sutta.**—Preached to **Anāthapiṇḍika,** on the advantages of getting rid of the fivefold dreads[1] (given in Sutta 1 above).

[1] A. iv. 405 f.

3. **Vera Sutta.**—The same as Sutta (2); preached to the monks.[1]

[1] A. iv. 407.

4. **Vera Sutta.**—Preached to **Anāthapiṇḍika,** on the advantages of the destruction of the five dread hatreds.[1]

[1] A. v. 182 f.

Verañja.—A brahmin. See **Verañjā.** According to Buddhaghosa,[1] his real name was **Udaya,** but he was called Verañja because he was born and lived at Verañjā.

[1] Sp. i. 111.

Verañja Sutta.—Describes the interview between the Buddha and the brahmin **Verañja.**[1] See **Verañjā.**

[1] A. iv. 172 ff.

Verañjaka Sutta.—Preached to the brahmins of **Verañjā,** who visited the Buddha at **Sāvatthī.**[1] The subject matter is identical with that of the **Sāleyyaka Sutta** (*q.v.*).

[1] M. i. 290.

Verañjakā.—The brahmins of **Verañjā,** to whom the **Verañjaka Sutta** was preached.[1]

[1] M. i. 290.

Verañjabhāṇavāra.—The first section of the **Sutta vibhaṅga.**[1]

[1] Vin. iii. 1-11.

Verañjā.—A town in which the Buddha once spent the rainy season[1] at the invitation of the brahmin **Verañja.** Verañja visits the Buddha at the foot of the **Naḷerupicumanda,** where he is staying, and asks him a series of questions, the first of which is: whether it be true that the Buddha pays no respect to aged brahmins. The Buddha replies that he has not seen a brahmin in the whole world to whom such respect is due from him. If the Tathāgata were so to honour anyone, that person's head would split in pieces. Other questions follow on the Buddha's doctrine and practices. The Buddha concludes by giving an account of his attainment of the threefold knowledge.[2] The interview ends with the conversion of Verañja and his invitation to the Buddha to spend his rainy season there.

At that time there was a famine, and five hundred householders of **Uttarāpatha,** staying at Verañjā, supplied the monks with food. **Moggallāna** proposed to get food by the exercise of his magic power or by going with the monks to **Uttarakuru,** but he was dissuaded by the Buddha. During this stay **Sāriputta** received from the Buddha an explanation as to why the religious systems of the three previous Buddhas lasted so long, while those of the three preceding them—**Vipassī, Sikhī** and **Vesabhū**—did not.

At the conclusion of the *vassa,* the Buddha wished to take leave of Verañja before setting out, as was the custom of Buddhas when they received hospitality. Verañja admitted that, though he had invited the Buddha, he had not kept his promise, and this was due to his having too many duties in the house.[3] He invited the Buddha and the monks to a meal the next day, and, at the end of the meal, presented a set of three robes to the Buddha and a pair to each of the monks.

After leaving Verañjā the Buddha went to Benares, passing through

[1] In the twelfth year, according to Buddhaghosa—*e.g.,* AA. ii. 758; *cf.* BuA. 3.

[2] Here he spoke of the *Vijjāttaya,* says UdA. (p. 183), because all the monks with the Buddha were *chalabhiññā,* and therefore no special mention was needed of *abhiññā.*

[3] The Commentators add that Verañja forgot his invitation because **Māra,** being in a spiteful mood, had taken possession of him and of all the inhabitants of Verañjā (Sp. i. 178 f.; DhA. ii. 153; *cf.* J. iii. 494).

Soreyya, Saṅkassa and **Kaṇṇakujja,** and crossing the Ganges at **Payāgapatiṭṭhāna.** From Benares he proceeded to **Vesāli.**[4]

It is said[5] that the devas put flavour (*ojā*) into every mouthful of food taken by the Buddha at Verañjā. According to the Apadāna,[6] the Bodhisatta was born of a noble house in the time of **Phussa Buddha,** and, once, seeing the monks eating good food, he had reviled them and asked them to eat oats (*yava*). It was for this reason the Buddha was condemned to eat *yava* during three months at Verañjā.

A road led from Verañjā to **Madhurā,** and the Aṅguttara Nikāya[7] contains a sermon preached by the Buddha to a large number of people while he rested by the roadside. There was evidently frequent intercourse between **Sāvatthi** and Verañjā, and the **Verañjaka Sutta** (*q.v.*) was preached to some brahmins who visited the Buddha at Sāvatthi, whither they had gone on business. The books also record[8] a visit paid by the Asura **Pahārāda** to the Buddha at Verañjā. The **Vālodaka Jātaka** (*q.v.*) and the **Cullasuka Jātaka** (*q.v.*) were preached soon after the Buddha's return from Verañjā.

[4] This account, of the Buddha's visit to Verañjā, forms the introduction to the Vinaya and is found at Vin. iii. 1-11. The interview with Verañja is given at A. iv. 172 ff. The road taken by the Buddha from Verañjā to Benares was, according to Buddhaghosa (Sp. i. 201), the shortest, and the Buddha knew the monks were tired after their experiences in Verañjā. Soon after, he appears to have visited **Kapilavatthu.** There he was visited by **Mahānāma,** the Sākyan, who asked permission to entertain him and the monks for four months that they might recover their strength. At the end of the four months he renewed his request, and thus looked after the monks for a whole year. It was this act that won for him the title of *aggo paṇītadāyakānaṃ* (AA. i. 213).

[5] SNA. i. 154; Mil. 232.

[6] Ap. i. 301; ApA. i. 103 f.; *cf.* UdA. 265.

[7] A. ii. 57 f.

[8] *Ibid.*, iv. 198 f.

Verambā, Verambhā.—Probably a name for the monsoon winds. The scholiast says[1] that, according to some, it was the name of a rocky glen (*pabbataguhāpabbhāra*).

[1] ThagA. i. 534.

Verambā Sutta.—A monk whose heart is possessed by gains and flattery, and whose senses are unguarded in the presence of women—he is like a bird caught in a hurricane[1] (*verambavāta*).

[1] S. ii. 231.

Verahaccāni.—The name of a brahmin clan (*gotta*). The Saṃyutta Nikāya mentions a lady of the gotta living in **Kāmaṇḍā,** who was evidently a teacher. A pupil of hers (*antevāsī māṇavaka*) having visited **Udāyi,** then staying in the **Todeyya-ambavana,** told her of his excellences.

He was asked to invite Udāyī to a meal, and, when it was over, the teacher put on her sandals, sat on a high seat, and, with her head veiled, asked Udāyī to preach the doctrine. "A time will come for that, Sister," he said, and went away. Three times this happened, and then she told her pupil. He pointed out to her her mistake in not showing respect for the Doctrine. The next time Udāyī came, she approached him after the meal with all humility and asked him what, according to the arahants, was the cause of weal and woe. "The existence of the senses," answered Udāyī; and she, expressing her satisfaction, declared herself a follower of Udāyī.[1]

[1] S. iv. 121 f.

Verahaccāni Sutta.—Contains an account of the conversion of the brahmin lady of the **Verehaccānigotta**[1] (*q.v.*).

[1] S. iv. 412 f.

Verī Jātaka (No. 103).—The Bodhisatta was once a rich merchant, and one day, while on his way home from a village where he had collected his dues, he noticed that there were robbers about. He, therefore, urged his oxen on to the top of their speed and reached home safely.

The story was told to **Anāthapiṇḍika,** who had a similar experience.[1]

[1] J. i. 412 f.

Veroca.—An **Asura** chieftain. All the hundred sons of **Bali** were named after him.[1] Buddhaghosa says[2] that Veroca was another name for **Rāhu,** and that he was the uncle of Bali's sons. He is probably identical with **Verocana,** lord of the Asuras, who, according to the **Samyutta Nikāya,**[3] went with Sakka to visit the Buddha during his siesta. They waited upon the Buddha, leaning against a doorpost, and each uttered two stanzas on the necessity of striving until one's aim is accomplished.

[1] D. ii. 259. [2] DA. ii. 689. [3] S. i. 225 f.

1. **Verocana.**—See **Veroca.**

2. **Verocana.**—A jewel, given to **Kusa** by **Sakka** when the former went out to fight against the seven kings who claimed **Pabhāvatī's** hand.[1]

[1] J. v. 310, 311.

2. **Verocana.**—A Nāga king, who lived in the Ganges. When **Nārada Buddha** converted the Nāga **Mahādoṇa,** Verocana invited the Buddha to a palace which he had built on the river and entertained him and

the monks with great ceremony. Eighty thousand men entered the Order after having heard the Buddha return thanks on this occasion.[1]

[1] Bu. x. 12; BuA. 154 f.

Verocana Sutta.—Records the visit of **Verocana** and **Sakka** to the Buddha. See **Veroca.**

1. **Velaṅgaviṭṭhika.**—A monastery built by **Saddhatissa.**[1]

[1] Mhv. xxxiii. 8.

2. **Velaṅgaviṭṭhika.**—A tank in Ceylon, built by **Mahāsena.**[1]

[1] Mhv. xxxvii. 48.

Velakkāra.—A troop of mercenary soldiers employed by the mediæval kings of Ceylon. They revolted against **Vijayabāhu I.**, pillaged **Pulatthipura,** burnt down the palace, and took captive the king's sister **Mittā.** Vijayabāhu had to flee to **Vātagiri,** but later he quelled the rebellion and had the ringleaders tortured to death.[1] They revolted against **Gajabāhu**[2] and later against **Parakkamabāhu I.**[3] In both cases the rebellion was crushed and the leaders punished.

[1] Cv. lx. 36 ff.
[2] *Ibid.*, lxiii. 24, 29.
[3] *Ibid.*, lxxiv. 44; for details see Cv. *Trs.* i. 217, n. 5.

Velaṅkuṇḍi.—A village in South India, used as a stronghold in the campaigns of **Laṅkāpura.**[1]

[1] Cv. lxxvii. 89, 93.

Velagāmi-vihāra.—A monastery in Ceylon, restored by **Vijayabāhu I.**[1]

[1] Cv. lx. 62.

Velamikā.—Chief of the eighty-four thousand women who waited on **Mahāsudassana,** king of **Kusāvatī.** She was also called **Khattiyānī.**[1]

[1] S. iii. 146; but at D. ii. 187 the chief queen is called **Subhaddā.**

Velāma.—The Bodhisatta born as the chaplain of Benares. He was son of the preceding chaplain, and went with the crown prince to **Takkasilā** to study. There, in due course, he became a famous teacher, with eighty-four thousand princes among his pupils. Later, he became chaplain to the Benares king. Every year the eighty-four thousand princes came to Benares to pay their respects to the king, causing great suffering to the people. These complained to the king, and he asked Velāma to find a way out of the difficulty. Velāma marked out eighty-four thousand provinces for the princes, and, thereafter, they obtained their supplies from their respective dominions.

Velāma was exceedingly wealthy and wished to give alms. Therefore, turning his water-jar upside down, he wished that if there were holy men in the world, the water should flow downwards. The water, however, remained in the jar. He then discovered by the same means that his gifts would be free from blame. He thereupon held great almsgivings, distributing during seven years the seven precious things and gifts of great value, pouring forth his riches as though " making into one stream the five great rivers."[1]

Velāma's almsgiving became famous in literature as the *Velāmamahāyañña.*[2]

[1] A list of his gifts is found at A. iv. 393 f. Velāma's story is given in AA. ii. 802 ff.; it is referred to in the **Velāma Sutta** and in the introductory story to the **Khadiraṅgāra Jātaka** (*q.v.*).

[2] *E.g.*, MA. ii. 616.

Velāma Sutta.—**Anāthapiṇḍika** loses all his wealth, and laments one day to the Buddha that he can only afford to give to the monks a coarse mixture of broken rice grains and sour gruel. The quality of the food is not important, says the Buddha, but only the heart of the giver, whether the giving is done casually or considerately and with devotion, and whether the recipients are worthy. He then tells of the great gifts made by **Velāma** (*q.v.*). Though the gifts were great, Velāma could find no holy persons as recipients. The Buddha then goes on to say that greater than the giving of alms, or even the building of monasteries, is the taking of the Refuges, the observance of good conduct, the practice of amity, and the thinking of impermanence, each of these being greater than the last.[1]

It was on this occasion that the **Khadiraṅgāra Jātaka** (*q.v.*) was preached.

[1] A. iv. 392 ff.; the sutta is referred to at DhA. iii. 11; KhA. 222; DA. i. 234 VibhA. 414.

Vellināba.—A stronghold in South India.[1]

[1] Cv. lxxvii. 39.

Veḷa, Veḷu.—A friend of **Vasabha** and father of **Veḷusumana,** who was named after his father and his father's friend **Sumana,** governor of **Girijanapada.**[1]

[1] Mhv. xxiii. 69.

Veḷuka.—A viper. See the **Veḷuka Jātaka.**

Veḷuka Jātaka (No. 43).—The Bodhisatta was once at the head of five hundred hermits, one of whom had a pet viper which was called **Veḷuka,** because it was kept in a bamboo. The Bodhisatta warned the ascetic against the snake, but his warning was unheeded. The hermit thus came to be called **Veḷukapitā.** One day the hermits went into the forest and were away for a few days, and when Veḷukapitā touched the viper on his return, the animal, hungry and angry, bit him, and he fell down dead. The story was told in reference to a headstrong monk who is identified with **Veḷukapitā.**[1]

[1] J. i. 245 f.

Veḷukaṇṭakī, Veḷukaṇḍakī, Veḷukaṇṭakiyā.—A lady of **Veḷukaṇṭa (Veḷukaṇḍa).** She is mentioned as an exemplary lay woman.[1] She founded, for the Order headed by **Sāriputta** and **Moggallāna,** an offering which the Buddha praised, because it was endowed with the six requisite qualities.[2]

Once she rose before dawn and sang the **Parāyaṇa. Vessavaṇa** happened to be passing over her house on his way from north to south,[3] and hearing the song, stopped at her window to praise it and to reveal his identity. She greeted him cordially, and in return for her greeting he announced to her that Sāriputta and Moggallāna were on their way to Veḷukaṇṭa. She, delighted with the news, made all preparations and sent word to the monastery, inviting the monks to the house. After the meal, she informed the Elders that Vessavaṇa had told her of their arrival. When they expressed their amazement, she told them of several other virtues possessed by her. Her only son **Nanda** was seized by the king's men and killed before her eyes, but she experienced no disquiet, nor did she when her husband, after his death, having been born as a Yakkha,[4] revealed himself to her. She was guilty of no transgression of the precepts, could enter into the four *jhānas* at will, and had cast off the five lower fetters. The monks expressed their great admiration and Sāriputta preached to her.[5]

Buddhaghosa says[6] that she was an *anāgāmin*, and that, when she promised to share with Vessavaṇa the merits she would gain by entertaining the monks, headed by the two Chief Disciples, Vessavaṇa, to show his gratitude, filled her stores with rice, and these stores remained always full throughout her life. They thus became proverbial.

The Sutta Nipāta Commentary[7] states that she kept a daily fast

[1] A. i. 88; ii. 164.

[2] See **Dāna Sutta** (1).

[3] To see the Buddha, says SNA. i. 369.

[4] *Bhummadevatā* says the Commentary.

[5] A. iv. 63 ff.

[6] AA. ii. 718; *cf.* SNA. i. 370.

[7] SNA. i. 370.

and knew the Piṭakas by heart. It also says that, at the end of her recital of the Parāyaṇa, Vessavaṇa offered her a boon, and she asked that, as her servants were weary of carrying the harvest home from the fields, Vessavaṇa should allow his Yakkhas to do the work for them. To this he agreed, and his followers filled for her one thousand two hundred and fifty store-houses. Vessavaṇa then went to the Buddha and told him of what had happened.

The Dhammapada Commentary[8] mentions **Veḷukaṇṭakī Nandamātā** and **Khujjattarā** as the chief lay-women disciples of the Buddha. But in the Aṅguttara list[9] of eminent lay-women, while Veḷukaṇṭakī Nandamātā's name does not occur, Khujjatarā is mentioned. Mention is made of a **Nandamātā,** eminent in meditation, but she is called **Uttarā.**

[8] DhA. i. 340.

[9] A. i. 26; *cf.* S. ii. 236, where the same two are mentioned; Mrs. Rhys Davids thinks that Velukaṇṭakī Nandamātā is probably identical with Uttarā Nandamātā (*Brethren* 4, n. 1). This identification does not seem to be correct. See **Uttarā Nandamātā**; see also **Nanda-Kumāputta.**

Veḷukaṇḍa, Veḷukaṇṭa.—A city in **Avanti,** birthplace of **Nanda Kumāputta.**[1] **Moggallāna** and **Sāriputta** visited the place in the course of a journey in **Dakkhiṇāgiri** and were entertained by **Nandamātā.**[2] See **Veḷukaṇṭakī.** Buddhaghosa says[3] that the city was so called because bamboos were thickly planted for protection round the walls and fortifications.

[1] ThagA. i. 100. [2] A. iv. 62 f. [3] AA. ii. 717; SNA. i. 370.

Veḷukapitā.—See the **Veḷuka Jātaka.**

Veḷugāma.—A village in **Avanti,** birthplace of **Isidatta Thera.** *v.l.* **Vaḍḍhagāma.**

[1] ThagA. i. 238.

Veḷudanta, Veḷudatta.—Teacher of **Vaḍḍha Thera.**[1]

[1] ThagA. i. 413.

Veḷudvāra.—A brahmin village of the **Kosalans** where the Buddha once stayed and preached the **Veḷudvāreyya Sutta.**[1] Buddhaghosa says[2] that the place was so called owing to the tradition of the presence of a bamboo thicket at the entrance to the village.

[1] S. v. 352. [2] SA. iii. 217.

Veḷudvāra Vagga.—The first chapter of the **Sotāpatti Saṃyutta.**[1]

[1] S. v. 342-60.

Veḷudvāreyya Sutta.—The brahmins and householders of **Veḷudvāra** visit the Buddha when he comes to their village and ask for a teaching which will be profitable to them. The Buddha points out to them the advantages of keeping the five precepts: abstention from taking life, from theft, etc., avoidance of slander, harsh speech and frivolous talk, and of having faith in the Buddha, the Dhamma and the Saṅgha.[1]

[1] S. v. 352 f.

Veḷuppa.—A Damiḷa warrior who helped **Aggabodhi III.** in his war against **Jeṭṭhatissa III.** As Jeṭṭhatissa lay exhausted on his elephant in the thick of the battle, he saw Veḷuppa approach, and, unwilling to be killed by him, cut his own throat.[1]

[1] Cv. xliv. 111 f.

Veḷuriya.—A village and a rock near which are found *veḷuriyā* (sapphires).[1]

[1] VvA. 27.

Veḷuvagāma.—See **Beḷuvagāma.**

1. **Veḷuvana.**—A park near **Rājagaha,** the pleasure garden of **Bimbisāra.** When the Buddha first visited Rājagaha, after his Enlightenment, he stayed at the **Laṭṭhivanuyyāna.**[1] The day after his arrival, he accepted the king's invitation to a meal at the palace, at the end of which the king, seeking a place for the Buddha to live—"not too far from the town, not too near, suitable for coming and going, easily accessible to all people, by day not too crowded, by night not exposed to noise and clamour, clean of the smell of people, hidden from men and well fitted to seclusion"—decided on Veḷuvana, and bestowed it on the Buddha and the fraternity. This was the first *ārāma* accepted by the Buddha, and a rule was passed allowing monks to accept such an *ārāma.*[2] The Buddha at once went to stay there, and it was during this stay that **Sāriputta** and **Moggallāna** joined the Order.[3]

[1] Vin. i. 35.

[2] *Ibid.*, 39 f.; according to BuA. (19; *cf.* ApA. i. 75) the earth trembled when the water—poured over the Buddha's hand by Bimbisāra in dedication of Veḷuvana—fell on the earth. This was the only *ārāma* in **Jambudīpa,** the dedication of which was accompanied by a tremor of the earth. It was the dedication of Veḷuvana which was quoted as precedent by **Mahinda,** when he decided to accept the **Mahāmeghavana,** at **Anurādhapura,** from **Devānampiyatissa** (Mhv. xv. 17).

[3] Vin. i. 42.

Kalandakanivāpa (*q.v.*) is the place nearly always mentioned as the spot where the Buddha stayed in Veḷuvana. There many Vinaya rules were passed—*e.g.*, on the keeping of the vassa,[4] the use of food cooked in the monastery,[5] the picking of edible (*kappiya*) fruit in the absence of any layman from whom permission to do so could be obtained,[6] surgical operations on monks,[7] the eating of sugar,[8] the rubbing of various parts of the body against wood,[9] the use of the kinds of dwelling[10] and the use of gold and silver.[11]

During the Buddha's stay at Veḷuvana, **Dabba Mallaputta,** at his own request, was appointed regulator of lodgings and apportioner of rations,[12] and Sāriputta and Moggallāna brought back the five hundred monks whom **Devadatta** had enticed away to **Gayāsīsa.**[13] The Buddha spent the second, third, and fourth vassas at Veḷuvana.[14] It was a very peaceful place, and monks, who had taken part in the first Convocation, rested there, in **Kalandakanivāpa,** after their exertions. It was there that they met **Purāṇa,** who refused to acknowledge the authenticity of their Recital.[15]

Numerous Jātakas were recited at Veḷuvana[16]—*e.g.*, **Asampadāna, Upahāna, Ubhatobhaṭṭha, Kandagalaka, Kālabāhu, Kukkuṭa, Kumbhila, Kuruṅga, Kuruṅgamiga, Giridanta, Guttila, Culladhammapāla, Cūlahaṃsa, Cūlanandiya, Jambu, Tayodhamma, Thusa, Dummedha, Dūbhiyamakkaṭa, Dhammaddhaja, Nigrodha, Parantapa, Pucimanda, Maṅgala, Maṇicora, Manoja, Mahākapi, Mahāhaṃsa, Mūsika, Romaka, Rohantamiga, Ruru, Lakkhaṇa, Laṭukika, Vānara, Vānarinda, Vinīlaka, Virocana, Saccaṅkura, Sañjīva, Sabbadāṭha, Sarabhaṅga, Sāliya, Sigāla, Sīlavanāga, Suvaṇṇakakkaṭa, Haṃsa** and **Hāritamātā.**

The books mention, in addition, various suttas which were preached there. Among those who visited the Buddha at Veḷuvana were several devaputtas: **Dīghalaṭṭha, Nandana, Candana, Sudatta, Subrahmā, Asama, Sahali, Niṅka, Ākoṭaka, Veṭambarī** and **Māṇavagāmiya;** also the Dhanañjanī brahmin; the **Bhāradvājas: Akkosaka, Asurinda, Bilaṅgika, Aggika, Acela-Kassapa, Susīma;** the thirty monks from **Pāvā**[17]; Theras,

[4] Vin. i. 137.
[5] *Ibid.*, 210 f.
[6] *Ibid.*, 212.
[7] *Ibid.*, 215 f.
[8] *Ibid.*, 226.
[9] *Ibid.*, ii. 105.
[10] *Ibid.*, 146.
[11] *Ibid.*, 196.
[12] *Ibid.*, 74. The Buddha was at Veḷuvana when Dabba also decided to die. He went there to take leave of the Buddha (Ud. viii. 9).
[13] Vin. ii. 200.
[14] BuA. 3; it was while the Buddha was at Veḷuvana that Devadatta attempted to kill him by causing **Nāḷāgiri** to be let loose against him (J. v. 335).
[15] Vin. ii. 289 f.
[16] Most of these refer to Devadatta, some to Ajātasattu, and some to Ānanda's attempt to sacrifice his life for the Buddha.
[17] S. ii. 187.

like **Mahākappina Aññākondañña** (just before his death); **Soṇagahapatiputta, Samiddhi, Moliya-Sīvaka, Tālapuṭa, Maṇicūḷaka, Mahācunda** (during his illness),[18] **Visākha** (after his visit to **Dhammadinnā,** who preached to him the **Culla-Vedalla Sutta), Abhayarājakumāra, Gulissāni, Vacchagotta, Bhūmija, Samiddhi, Aciravata, Sabhiya, Vassaka, Suppabuddha, Pilindavaccha, Jāṇussoni** and the princess **Cundī;** also Bimbisāra's wife, **Khemā,** who went to Veḷuvana because she had heard so much of its beauty. Sāriputta and Ānanda[19] visited the Buddha there on several occasions, sometimes alone, sometimes in the company of others, and Ānanda lived there for some time after the Buddha's death, and during his stay there preached the **Gopakamoggallāna Sutta.**

It is said that **Māra** visited Veḷuvana several times[20] in order to work his will on the Buddha. The Buddha was there when three of the monks committed suicide—**Vakkali, Godhika** and **Channa**—and he had to pronounce them free from blame. News was brought to the Buddha, at Veḷuvana, of the illness of three of his disciples—**Assaji, Moggallāna** and **Dīghāvu**—and he set out to visit them and comfort them with talks on the doctrine. Near Veḷuvana was a **Paribbājakārāma,** where the Buddha sometimes went with some of his disciples in the course of his alms rounds. Two of his discussions there are recorded in the **Cūla-** and **Mahā-Sakuladāyī Suttas.**

During the Buddha's lifetime, two thūpas were erected at the gate of Veḷuvana, one containing the relics of **Aññā-Koṇḍañña,**[21] and the other those of **Moggallāna.**[22]

Veḷuvana was so called because it was surrounded by bamboos (*veḷu*). It was surrounded by a wall, eighteen cubits high, holding a gateway and towers.[23]

After the Buddha's death, **Dāsaka, Upāli's** pupil, lived at Veḷuvana, and there ordained **Soṇaka** with fifty-five companions. From there Soṇaka went to the **Kukkuṭārāma.**[24]

The dedication of Veḷuvana was among the scenes depicted in the Relic Chamber of the **Mahā Thūpa.**[25]

On one side of the main building of the Veḷuvana-vihāra was a building called **Ambalaṭṭhika.**[26] There was also a *senāsana*, built for the use of monks practising austerities.[27]

[18] S. v. 181.

[19] Sāriputta is mentioned as having held discussions there with, among others, **Candikāputta** and **Lāḷudāyī.** A sermon preached by **Mahā Kassapa** to the monks at Veḷuvana is given at A. v. 161 ff.; for other suttas preached by the Buddha, see also S. i. 231; ii. 32, 183, 242, 254; iv. 20; v. 446; Ud. iv. 9.

[20] *E.g.*, S. i. 106 f.

[21] SA. i. 219.

[22] J. v. 127.

[23] SNA. ii. 419; Sp. iii. 576.

[24] Mhv. v. 115 f., 122; Dpv. iv. 39.

[25] Mhv. xxx. 80.

[26] MA. ii. 635.

[27] *Ibid.*, 932.

It is said that, after death, **Vassakāra** was born as a monkey in Veḷuvana and answered to his name. He had been told during his lifetime that this destiny awaited him, and therefore took the precaution of seeing that the place was well supplied with fruit trees.[28]

According to Hiouen Thsang,[29] the Kalandaka-nivāpa (**Karaṇḍaveṇuvana,** as he calls it) lay one *li* to the north of Rājagaha.

[28] MA. ii. 854. [29] Beal, *op. cit.*, ii. 159.

2. **Veḷuvana.**—A bamboo-grove in **Kajaṅgalā,** where the Buddha once stayed. The upāsakas of Kajaṅgalā, having questioned the **Kajaṅgalā-bhikkhuṇī,** went to the Buddha there and asked him to verify her answers.[1]

[1] A. v. 54 f.

3. **Veḷuvana.**—A bamboo-grove in **Kimbilā,** where the Buddha stayed and was visited by **Kimbila.**[1]

[1] A. iii. 247, 339: iv. 84.

4. **Veḷuvana.**—A monastery in Ceylon, built by **Aggabodhi II.** It was given by him to the **Sāgalikas.**[1] It probably lay between **Anurādhapura** and **Maṇihīra,** and **Saṅghatissa** once lay in hiding there disguised as a monk.[2] **Jeṭṭhatissa III.** gave to the vihāra the village of **Kakkalaviṭṭhi.**[3]

[1] Cv. xlii. 43. [2] *Ibid.*, xliv. 29; Cv. *Trs.* i. 77, n. 2. [3] Cv. xliv. 99.

5. **Veḷuvana.**—A monastery erected by **Parakkamabāhu I.** in the suburb of **Vijita** in **Pulatthipura.** It consisted of three image-houses, each three storeys high, a thūpa, a cloister, a two-storeyed *pāsāda*, four gateways, four long pāsādas, eight small ones, one refectory, one sermon-hall, seven fire hoses and twelve privies.[1]

[1] Cv. lxxiii. 152, lxxviii. 87 f.; see also Cv. *Trs.* ii. 113, n. 1.

Veḷusumana.—A general of **Duṭṭhagāmaṇī.** He was the son of **Vasabha,** a householder of **Kuṭumbiyaṅgaṇa** in **Girijanapada.** When the child was born, two friends of Vasabha, **Veḷa** and **Sumana,** came with gifts, and the boy was given their two names. When Veḷusumana grew up, he went to live with Sumana, governor of **Girijanapada,** and broke in a horse with which everyone else had failed. Sumana therefore gave him one hundred thousand and sent him to **Kākavaṇṇatissa's** court.[1]

When **Vihāradevī** wished to drink water in which had been washed the sword which cut off the head of **Nandasārathi, Eḷāra's** chief warrior,

[1] Mhv. xxiii. 68 ff.

Veḷusumana was entrusted with the task of killing Nandasārathi. He therefore went to **Anurādhapura,** where he became friendly with the keeper of the king's state horse, **Vāha.** One day he took the horse to bathe in the **Kadambanadī,** and, after announcing his name, rode away on him. Eḷarā sent Nandasārathi in pursuit. Veḷusumana stood concealed behind a thicket, on a mound called **Nigrodhasāla,** with drawn sword, and as Nandasārathi rode past quickly, he was transfixed by Veḷusumana's sword.[2]

Veḷusumana took a prominent part in the capture of **Vijitapura.**[3]

[2] Mhv. xxii. 51 ff.; MṬ. 440 f.

[3] Mhv. xxv. 25.

Vevaṭiyakapi Jātaka. *v.l.* for **Mahākapi** (*q.v.*).[1]

[1] J. iii. 178.

Vesākha.—The month of April–May. Tradition says that the Buddha's birth, Enlightenment and death, took place on the full-moon day of Vesākha.[1] The **Vesākhapūjā** was always celebrated by the kings of Ceylon.[2] The full-moon day of Vesākha was chosen for very solemn undertakings, such as the crowning of **Devānampiyatissa,**[3] the laying of the Foundation Stone of the **Mahā Thūpa,**[4] etc.

[1] *E.g.*, J. i.; BuA. 248; Mhv. iii. 2.

[2] See, *e.g.*, *ibid.*, xxxii. 35; xxxv. 100; Cv. li. 84.

[3] Mhv. xi. 42.

[4] *Ibid.*, xxix. 1.

Vesāyī.—A name for **Yama.**[1]

[1] J. ii. 317, 318.

Vesārajja Sutta.—The four confidences of a Tāthāgata: he must be perfectly enlightened, have destroyed the *āsavas*, the hindrances declared by him must really be hindrances, the Doctrine preached by him must never fail in its aim.[1]

[1] A. ii. 8.

Vesālā.—The Nāgas of **Vesāli** who were present at the preaching of the **Mahāsamaya Sutta.**[1]

[1] D. ii. 258; DA. ii. 688.

Vesālī.—A city, capital of the **Licchavis.** The Buddha first visited it in the fifth year after the Enlightenment, and spent the *vassa* there.[1] The Commentaries[2] give detailed descriptions of the circumstances of

[1] BuA., p. 3.

[2] KhpA. 160 ff.=SNA. i. 278; DhA. iii. 436 ff.; *cp.* Mtu. i. 253 ff.

this visit. Vesāli was inhabited by seven thousand and seven rājās, each of whom had large retinues, many palaces and pleasure parks. There came a shortage in the food supply owing to drought, and people died in large numbers. The smell of decaying bodies attracted evil spirits, and many inhabitants were attacked by intestinal disease. The people complained to the ruling prince, and he convoked a general assembly, where it was decided, after much discussion, to invite the Buddha to their city. As the Buddha was then at **Veḷuvana** in **Rājagaha,** the Licchavi **Mahāli,** friend of **Bimbisāra** and son of the chaplain of **Vesāli,** was sent to Bimbisāra with a request that he should persuade the Buddha to go to Vesāli. Bimbisāra referred him to the Buddha himself, who, after listening to Mahāli's story, agreed to go. The Buddha started on the journey with five hundred monks. Bimbisāra decorated the route from Rājagaha to the Ganges, a distance of five leagues, and provided all comforts on the way. He accompanied the Buddha, and the Ganges was reached in five days. Boats, decked with great splendour, were ready for the Buddha and his monks, and we are told that Bimbisāra followed the Buddha into the water up to his neck. The Buddha was received on the opposite bank by the Licchavis, with even greater honour than Bimbisāra had shown him. As soon as the Buddha set foot in the **Vajjian** territory, there was a thunderstorm and rain fell in torrents. The distance from the Ganges to Vesāli was three leagues; as the Buddha approached Vesāli, **Sakka** came to greet him, and, at the sight of the devas, all the evil spirits fled in fear. In the evening the Buddha taught **Ānanda** the **Ratana Sutta,** and ordered that it should be recited within the three walls of the city, the round of the city being made with the Licchavi princes. This Ānanda did during the three watches of the night, and all the pestilences of the citizens disappeared. The Buddha himself recited the Ratana Sutta to the assembled people, and eighty-four thousand beings were converted. After repeating this for seven consecutive days, the Buddha left Vesāli.[3] The Licchavis accompanied him to the Ganges with redoubled honours, and, in the river itself, Devas and Nāgas vied with each other in paying him honour. On the farther bank, Bimbisāra awaited his arrival and conducted him back to Rājagaha. On his return there, the Buddha recited the **Saṅkha Jātaka.** (See *s.v.* 2.)

It was probably during this visit of the Buddha to Vesāli that **Suddhodana** died.[4] According to one account,[5] the Buddha went through the

[3] According to the DhA. account the Buddha stayed only seven days in Vesāli; KhA. says two weeks.

[4] See ThigA., p. 141; AA. i. 186.

[5] It was during this visit of the Buddha to Kapilavatthu (*tadā*) that **Mahāpajāpati Gotamī** first asked his permission to join the Order, but her request was refused (AA. i. 186).

air to visit his dying father and to preach to him, thereby enabling him to attain arahantship before his death. It is not possible to know how many visits were paid by the Buddha to Vesāli, but the books would lead us to infer that they were several. Various Vinaya rules are mentioned[6] as having been laid down at Vesāli. It was during a stay in Vesali, whither he had gone from **Kapilavatthu,** that **Mahāpajāpatī Gotamī** followed the Buddha with five hundred other Sākyan women, and, with the help of Ānanda's intervention, obtained permission for women to enter the Order under certain conditions.[7]

The books describe[8] at some length the Buddha's last visit to Vesāli on his way to **Kusinārā.** On the last day of this visit, after his meal, he went with **Ānanda** to **Cāpāla-cetiya** for his siesta, and, in the course of their conversation, he spoke to Ānanda of the beauties of Vesāli: of the **Udena-cetiya,** the **Gotamaka-cetiya,** the **Sattambaka-cetiya,** the **Bahuputta-cetiya,** and the **Sārandada-cetiya.**[9] The Buddha generally stayed at the **Kūṭāgārasālā** (*q.v.*) during his visits to Vesāli, but it appears that he sometimes lived at these different shrines.[10] During his last visit to the Cāpāla-cetiya he decided to die within three months, and informed **Māra** and, later, Ānanda, of his decision. The next day he left Vesāli for **Bhaṇḍagāma,** after taking one last look at the city, " turning his whole body round, like an elephant " (*nāgāpalokitaṃ apaloketvā*).[11] The rainy season which preceded this the Buddha spent at **Beluvagāma,** a suburb of **Vesāli,** while the monks stayed in and around Vesāli. On the day before he entered into the *vassa*, **Ambapāli** invited the Buddha and the monks to a meal, at the conclusion of which she gave her **Ambavana** for the use of the Order.[12]

Vesāli was a stronghold of the **Nigaṇṭhas,** and it is said[13] that of the forty-two rainy seasons of the latter part of **Mahāvīra's** ascetic life, he passed twelve at Vesāli. Thė Buddha's presence in Vesāli was a source

[6] See, *e.g.*, Vin. i. 238, 287 f.; ii. 118, 119-27. The visit mentioned in the last context seems to have been a long one; it was on this occasion that the Buddha ordered the monks to turn their bowls upon the Licchavi **Vaḍḍha** (*q.v.*). For other Vinaya rules laid down at Vesāli, see also Vin. ii. 159 f.; iii. and iv. *passim*.

[7] Vin. ii. 253 ff. ; see *s.v.* **Mahāpajāpatī Gotamī.**

[8] *E.g.*, D. ii. 95 ff.

[9] *Cf.* Mtu. i. 300, where a Kapinayhacetiya is also mentioned. All these were once shrines dedicated to various local deities, but after the Buddha's visit to Vesāli, they were converted into places of Buddhist worship. Other monasteries are also mentioned, in or near Vesāli —*e.g.*, **Pāṭikārāma, Vālikārāma.**

[10] See *s.v.*, also D. ii. 118.

[11] *Ibid.*, 122.

[12] *Ibid.*, 98; but see Dial. ii. 102, n. 1.

[13] Jacobi: *Jaina Sūtras* (S.B.E.) *Kalpa Sūtra*, sect. 122; Vesāli was also the residence of **Kandaramasuka** and **Pāṭikaputta** (*q.v.*). Among eminent followers of the Buddha who lived in Vesāli, special mention is made of **Ugga** (chief of those who gave pleasant gifts), **Piṅgiyāni, Kāraṇapāli, Sīha, Vāseṭṭha** (A. iv. 258), and the various Licchavis (see *s.v.* **Licchavi.**)

of discomfort to the Nigaṇṭhas, and we find mention[14] of various devices resorted to by them to prevent their followers from coming under the influence of the Buddha.

At the time of the Buddha, Vesāli was a very large city, rich and prosperous, crowded with people and with abundant food. There were seven thousand seven hundred and seven pleasure grounds and an equal number of lotus ponds. Its courtezan, **Ambapālī,** was famous for her beauty, and helped in large measure in making the city prosperous.[15] The city had three walls, each one *gāvuta* away from the other, and at three places in the walls were gates with watch-towers.[16] Outside the town, leading uninterruptedly up to the Himālaya, was the **Mahāvana**[17] (*q.v.*), a large, natural forest. Near by were other forests, such as **Gosiṅgalasāla.**[18]

Among important suttas preached at Vesāli are the **Mahāli, Mahāsīhanāda, Cūla-Saccaka, Mahā-Saccaka, Tevijja, Vacchagotta, Sunakkhatta** and **Ratana.**[19] The **Telovāda Jātaka** (No. 246) and the **Sigāla Jātaka** (No. 152) were preached at Vesāli. After the Buddha's death a portion of his relics was enshrined in the city.[20]

One hundred years later Vesāli was again the scene of interest for Buddhists, on account of the "Ten Points" raised by the **Vajjiputtakā,** (*q.v.*), and the second Council held in connection with this dispute at the **Vālikārāma.**

The city was also called **Visālā.**[21] There were Nāgas living in Vesāli; these were called **Vesālā.**[22]

Vesāli is identified with the present village of Basrah in the Muzafferpur district in Tirhut.[23]

[14] See, *e.g.*, *s.v.* **Sīha.**

[15] Vin. i. 268.

[16] J. i. 504; *cf.* i. 389. Perhaps these three walls separated the three districts of Vaiśālī mentioned in the Tibetan Dulva (Rockhill, p. 62); Hoernle (*Uvāsagadasāo Translation* ii., p. 4, n. 8) identifies these three districts with the city proper, Kuṇḍapura and Vāṇiyagāma, respectively mentioned in the Jaina books. Buddhaghosa says (*e.g.*, Sp. ii. 393) that Vesāli was so called because it was extensive (*visālībhūtatā Vesāli ti uccati*); *cf.* UdA. 184 (*tikkhattuṃ visālabhūtattā*); and MA. i. 259.

[17] DA. i. 309.

[18] A. v. 134.

[19] See also A. i. 220, 276; ii. 190, 200; iii. 38, 49 ff., 75, 142, 167, 236, 239; iv. 16, 79, 100, 179, 208, 274 ff., 279 ff., 308 ff.; v. 86, 133, 342; S. i. 29, 112, 230; ii. 267, 280; iii. 68, 116; iv. 109, 210 ff., 380; v. 141 f., 152 f., 258, 301, 320, 389, 453; D. ii. 94 ff.; the subjects of these discourses are mentioned *passim*, in their proper places; see also DhA. i. 263; iii. 267, 279, 460, 480.

[20] D. ii. 167; Bu. xxviii. 2.

[21] *E.g.*, AA. i. 47; Cv. xcix. 98.

[22] D. ii. 258.

[23] See Vincent Smith, *J.R.A.S.* 1907, p. 267 f., and Marshall, *Arch. Survey of India*, 1903-4, p. 74.

1. **Vesāli Sutta.**—See **Vajjiputta Sutta.**

2. **Vesāli Sutta.**—**Ugga** visits the Buddha at the **Kūṭāgārasālā** and asks a question; the Buddha explains to him that it is grasping of objects, etc., which prevents some people from being quite free in this very life.[1]

[1] S. iv. 109.

3. **Vesāli Sutta.**—The Buddha once addressed the monks on the great benefits of meditating on *asubha,* and then retired into solitude in the **Mahāvana** for a fortnight. The monks, filled with the idea of *asubha,* felt loathing for their bodies and many committed suicide. The Buddha hearing of this, summoned the monks to the **Kūṭāgārasālā** and taught them the great merits of concentration on breathing.[1]

[1] S. v. 320 f.

Vessagiri.—A monastery in Ceylon, near **Anurādhapura.** It was built by **Devānampiyatissa** for the five hundred *vessas* (merchants) who were ordained by **Mahinda.**[1] Near the monastery was a forest, where **Vaṭṭagāmaṇī,** in his flight, hid the almsbowl of the Buddha. There he also met the Elder **Kupikkala-Mahātissa.**[2] The almsbowl was discovered and taken by a Damiḷa to India, but was later recovered.[3] To the south of Vessagiri was the **Pabbata-vihāra,** and, near it, the village of **Silāsobbhakaṇḍaka.**[4]

[1] Mhv. xx. 15; Mhv. *Trs.* 137, n. 3.
[2] Mhv. xxxiii. 48 f.
[3] *Ibid.*, 55.
[4] MṬ. 616.

1. **Vessantara.**—An owl, identified with **Sāriputta.**[1] See the **Tesakuṇa Jātaka.**

[1] J. v. 125.

2. **Vessantara.**—The Bodhisatta, born as king of **Sivi.** See the **Vessantara Jātaka.**

Vessantara Jātaka (No. 547).—**Vessantara** (the Bodhisatta) was the son of **Sañjaya,** king of **Sivi,** and queen **Phusatī,** and was so called because his mother started in labour as she passed through the *vessa*-street in the city of **Jetuttara,** and he was born in a house in the same street. He spoke as soon as he was born.[1] On the same day was also born a white elephant named **Paccaya.** At the age of eight, Vessantara wished to make a great gift and the earth trembled. He married **Maddī** at the age of sixteen, and their children were **Jāli** and **Kaṇhajinā.**

At that time there was a great drought in **Kāliṅga,** and eight brahmins came from there to Vessantara to beg his white elephant, which had the

[1] *Cf.* BuA. 228.

power of making rain to fall. He granted their request, and gave the elephant together with its priceless trappings.[2] The citizens of Jetuttara were greatly upset that their elephant should have been given away, and demanded of Sañjaya that Vessantara should be banished to **Vaṅkagiri.** The will of the people prevailed, and Vessantara was asked to take the road along which those travel who have offended. He agreed to go, but before setting out, obtained the king's leave to hold an almsgiving called the " Gift of the Seven Hundreds " (**Sattasataka**), in which he gave away seven hundred of each kind of thing. People came from all over **Jambudīpa** to accept his gifts, and the almsgiving lasted for a whole day.

When Vessantara took leave of his parents and prepared for his journey, Maddī insisted on accompanying him with her two children. They were conveyed in a gorgeous carriage drawn by four horses, but, outside the city, Vessantara met four brahmins who begged his horses. Four devas then drew the chariot, but another brahmin soon appeared and obtained the chariot. Thenceforward they travelled on foot, through **Suvaṇṇagiritāla,** across the river **Kantimārā,** to beyond Mount **Arañjaragiri** and **Dunniviṭṭha,** to his uncle's city, in the kingdom of **Ceta.** The devas shortened the way for them, and the trees lowered their fruit that they might eat. Sixty thousand *khattiyas* came out to welcome Vessantara and offered him their kingdom, which, however, he refused. He would not even enter the city, but remained outside the gates, and, when he left early the next morning, the people of Ceta, led by **Cetaputta,** went with him for fifteen leagues, till they came to the entrance to the forest. Vessantara and his family then proceeded to **Gandhamādana,** northwards, by the foot of Mount **Vipula** to the river **Ketumatī,** where a forester entertained them and gave them to eat. Thence they crossed the river to beyond **Nālika,** along the bank of Lake **Mucalinda,** to its north-eastern corner, then along a narrow footpath into the dense forest, to **Vaṅkagiri.** There **Vissakamma** had already built two hermitages, by order of **Sakka,** one for Vessantara and one for Maddī and the children, and there they took up their residence. By Vessantara's power, the wild animals to a distance of three leagues became gentle. Maddī rose daily at dawn, and, having fetched water to wash, went into the forest for yams and fruit. In the evening she returned, washed the children, and the family sat down to eat. Thus passed four months.

Then from Dunniviṭṭha there came to the hermitage an old brahmin, called **Jūjaka,** who had been sent by his young wife, **Amittatāpanā,** to find slaves for her, because when she went to the well for water the other women had laughed at her, calling her " old man's darling." She told

[2] J. vi. 488 f. gives the details of these.

Jūjaka that he could easily get Vessantara's children as slaves, and so he came to Vaṅkagiri. Asking the way of various people, including the hermit **Accuta,** Jūjaka arrived at Vaṅkagiri late in the evening and spent the night on the hilltop. That night Maddī had a dream, and, being terrified, she sought Vessantara. He knew what the dream presaged, but consoled her and sent her away the next day in search of food. During her absence, Jūjaka came and made his request. He would not await the return of Maddī, and Vessantara willingly gave him the two children. But they ran away and hid in a pond till told by their father to go with Jūjaka. When Vessantara poured water on Jūjaka's hand as a symbol of his gift, the earth trembled with joy. Once more the children escaped and ran back to their father, but he strengthened his resolve with tears in his eyes. Jūjaka led the children away, beating them along the road till their blood flowed.

It was late in the evening when Maddī returned because devas, assuming the form of beasts of prey, delayed her coming, lest she should stand in the way of Vessantara's gift. In answer to her questions, Vessantara spoke no word, and she spent the night searching for the children. In the morning she returned to the hermitage and fell down fainting. Vessantara restored her to consciousness and told her of what had happened, explaining why he had not told her earlier. When she had heard his story she expressed her joy, affirming that he had made a noble gift for the sake of omniscience.

And then, lest some vile creature should come and ask for Maddī, **Sakka,** assuming the form of a brahmin, appeared and asked for her. Vessantara looked at Maddī, and she expressed her consent. So he gave Maddī to the brahmin, and the earth trembled. Sakka revealed his identity, gave Maddī back to Vessantara, and allowed him eight boons. Vessantara asked that (1) he be recalled to his father's city, (2) he should condemn no man to death, (3) he should be a helpmate to all alike, (4) he should not be guilty of adultery, (5) his son should have long life, (6) he should have celestial food, (7) his means of giving should never fail, (8) after death he should be reborn in heaven.

In the meantime, Jūjaka had travelled sixty leagues with the children, whom the devas cared for and protected. Guided by the devas, they arrived in fifteen days at Jetuttara, though Jūjaka had intended to go to **Kāliṅga.** Sañjaya bought the children from Jūjaka, paying a high price, including the gift of a seven-storeyed palace. But Jūjaka died of over-eating, and as no relation of his could be traced, his possessions came back to the king. Sañjaya ordered his army to be prepared and a road to be built from Jetuttara to Vaṅkagiri, eight *usabhas* wide. Seven days later, led by Jāli, Sañjaya and Phusatī started for Vaṅkagiri.

In the army was the white elephant, who had been returned because the people of Kāliṅga could not maintain him. There was great rejoicing at the reunion of the family, and the six royal personages fell in a swoon till they were revived by rain sent by Sakka, the rain only wetting those who so wished it. Vessantara was crowned king of Sivi, with Maddī as his consort. After a month's merry-making in the forest, they returned to Jetuttara. On the day Vessantara entered the city he set free every captive, including even cats. In the evening, as he lay wondering how he would be able to satisfy his suitors the next day, Sakka's throne was heated, and he sent down a shower of the seven kinds of precious things, till the palace grounds were filled waist-high. Vessantara was thus able to practise his generosity to the end of his days. After death he was born in **Tusita.**[3]

The story was related on the occasion of the Buddha's first visit to **Kapilavatthu.** The Buddha's kinsmen escorted him to the **Nigrodhārāma,** but sat round him without doing any obeisance, because of their great pride. The Buddha then performed the Twin Miracle, and the **Sākyans,** led by **Suddhodana,** worshipped him. There was then a shower of rain, refreshing all and falling only on those who so wished. When the people expressed their wonder, the Buddha related this story, showing that in the past, too, rain had fallen on his kinsfolk to revive them.[4]

Devadatta is identified with Jūjaka, **Cincā** with Amittatāpanā, **Channa** with Cetaputta, **Sāriputta** with Accuta, **Anuruddha** with Sakka, **Sañjaya** with Suddhodana, **Mahāmāyā** with Phusatī, **Rāhulamātā** with Maddī, **Rāhula** with Jāli, and **Uppalavaṇṇā** with Kaṇhajinā.[5]

The story also occurs in the Cariyāpiṭaka,[6] and is often referred to[7] as that of a birth in which the Bodhisatta's *dāna-pāramitā* reached its culmination. The earth shook seven times when Vessantara made his gifts, and this forms the subject of a dilemma in the Milindapañha.[8]

The story of the Jātaka was sculptured in the Relic Chamber of the **Mahā Thūpa.**[9]

The story of Vessantara is the first of the Jātakas to disappear from the world.[10] See also **Gūḷha-Vessantara.**

[3] J. i. 47; DhA. i. 69.

[4] According to BuA. 245, the Jātaka was related at the end of the recital of the **Buddhavaṃsa.**

[5] The story is given at J. vi. 479-593.

[6] i. 9.

[7] *E.g.*, Sp. i. 245; VbhA. 414; Cv. xlii. 5; c. 74.

[8] Mil. p. 113; for another question, see *ibid.*, 274 f.

[9] Mhv. xxx. 88.

[10] AA. i. 51.

1. **Vessabhū.**—The twenty-first of the twenty-four Buddhas. He was born in the pleasaunce of **Anoma** (Commentary, **Anūpama**), his father

being the *khattiya* **Suppatita** (**Supatita**) and his mother **Yasavatī.** On the day of his birth he roared "like a bull" a shout of triumph, hence his name (*vasabhanādahetuttā*).[1] For six thousand years he lived in the household in three palaces: **Ruci, Suruci** and **Vaḍḍhana** (**Rativaḍḍhana**); his wife was **Sucittā,** and their son **Suppabuddha.** He left home in a golden palanquin, practised austerities for six months, was given milk-rice by **Sirivaḍḍhanā** of **Sucittanigama,** and grass for his seat by the Nāga king **Narinda,** and attained Enlightenment under a *sāla*-tree. He preached his first sermon at **Anurārāma** to his brothers, **Soṇa** and **Uttara,** who became his chief disciples. Among women his chief disciples were **Dāmā** and **Samālā,** his constant attendant **Upasanta** (**Upasannaka**), his chief lay patrons **Sotthika** and **Rāma** among men, and **Gotamī** (**Kāligotamī**) and **Sirimā** among women. He was sixty cubits in height and lived for sixty thousand years. He died at the **Khemārāma** in **Usabhavatī** and his relics were scattered. The Bodhisatta was King **Sudassana** of **Sarabhavatī.**[2]

Vessabhū Buddha kept the uposatha once in every six years.[3]

[1] But MṬ. 63 gives another explanation: *hīnaṃ janānaṃ abhibhūto maggena abhibhavitakilesahīno ti vā.* Dvy. 333 calls him Viśvabhū.

[2] Bu. xxii. 1 ff.; BuA. 205 ff.; D. ii. 5.; J. i. 41.

[3] DhA. iii. 236.

2. **Vessabhū.**—King of **Avanti** in the time of **Reṇu.** His capital was **Māhissatī.**[1]

[1] D. ii. 236.

Vessara.—A pleasaunce in which **Maṅgala Buddha** died.[1]

[1] Bu. iv. 32.

Vessavaṇa.—One of the names of **Kuvera** (*q.v.*), given to him because his kingdom is called **Visāṇā.**[1] He is one of the **Cātummahārājāno** (*q.v.*) and rules over the **Yakkhas,** his kingdom being in the north.[2] In the **Āṭānātiya Sutta**[3] he is the spokesman, and he recited the Āṭānāṭiya-rune for the protection of the Buddha and his followers from the Yakkas who had no faith in the Buddha. He rides in the **Nārīvāhana,** which is twelve yojanas long, its seat being of coral. His retinue is composed of ten thousand crores of Yakkhas.[4] He is a *sotāpanna* and his life-span is ninety thousand years.[5] The books record a conversation between him

[1] D. iii. 201; SNA. i. 369, etc.

[2] *E.g.,* D. ii. 207.

[3] *Ibid.,* iii. 194; he was spokesman because "he was intimate with the Buddha, expert in conversation, well-trained" (DA. iii. 962).

[4] SNA. i. 379; the preacher's seat in the **Lohapāsāda** at **Anurādhapura** was made in the design of the Nārīvāhaṇa (Mhv. xxvii. 29).

[5] AA. ii. 718.

and **Veḷukaṇṭakī Nandamātā** (*q.v.*), when he heard her sing the **Parāyana Vagga** and stayed to listen. When **Cūlasubhaddā** wished to invite the Buddha and his monks to her house in **Sāketa,** and felt doubtful about it, Vessavaṇa appeared before her and said that the Buddha would come at her invitation.[6]

On another occasion[7] he heard **Uttara Thera** preaching to the monks in **Dhavajālikā** on the **Saṅkheyya** Mountain, near **Mahisavatthu,** and went and told Sakka, who visited Uttara and had a discussion with him.

Once when Vessavaṇa was travelling through the air, he saw **Sambhūta Thera** wrapt in *samādhi.* Vessavaṇa descended from his chariot, worshipped the Thera, and left behind two Yakkhas with orders to wait until the Elder should emerge from his trance. The Yakkhas then greeted the Thera in the name of Vessavaṇa and told him they had been left to protect him. The Elder sent thanks to Vessavaṇa, but informed him, through the Yakkhas, that the Buddha had taught his disciples to protect themselves through mindfulness, and so further protection was not needed. Vessavaṇa visited Sambhūta on his return, and finding that the Elder had become an arahant, went to **Sāvatthi** and carried the news to the Buddha.[8]

Mention is made of Vessavaṇa's **Gadāvudha**[9] and his mango-tree, the **Atulamba.**[10] **Āḷavaka's** abode was near that of Vessavaṇa.[11]

Bimbisāra, after death, was born seven times as one of the ministers (*paricaraka*) of Vessavaṇa, and, while on his way with a message from Vessavaṇa to **Virūḷhaka,** visited the Buddha and gave him an account of a meeting of the devas which Vessavaṇa had attended and during which **Sanaṅkumāra** had spoken in praise of the Buddha and his teachings.[12] Vessavaṇa seems to have been worshipped by those desiring children.[13] There was in **Anurādhapura** a banyan-tree dedicated as a shrine to Vessavaṇa in the time of **Paṇḍukābhaya.**[14] Vessavaṇa is mentioned as having been alive in the time of **Vipassī Buddha.** When **Vipassī** died, there was a great earthquake which terrified the people, but Vessavaṇa appeared and quieted their fears.[15] Vessavaṇa accompanied Sakka when he showed **Moggallāna** round **Vejayanta-pāsāda.**[16]

[6] *Ibid.*, 483.

[7] A. iv. 162; on his way to see the Buddha.

[8] ThagA. i.46 f. Just as he encouraged the good, so he showed his resentment against the wicked; see, *e.g.*, *s.v.* **Revatī.**

[9] SNA. i. 225; the books (*e.g.*, SA. i. 249; Sp. ii. 440) are careful to mention that he used his *Gadāvudha* only while he was yet a *puthujjana.*

[10] J. iv. 324, also called **Abbhantaramba** (see the **Abbharantara Jātaka**).

[11] SNA. i. 240.

[12] D. ii. 206 f.

[13] See, *e.g.*, the story of **Rājadatta** (ThagA. i. 403).

[14] Mhv. x. 89.

[15] ThagA. i. 149.

[16] M. i. 253; because he was Sakka's very intimate friend (MA. i. 476).

As lord of the Yakkhas, it was in the power of Vessavaṇa to grant to any of them special privileges, such as the right of devouring anyone entering a particular pond, etc.[17]

Vessavaṇa, like **Sakka,** was not the name of a particular being, but of the holder of an office. When one Vessavaṇa died, Sakka chose another as his successor. The new king, on his accession, sent word to all the Yakkhas, asking them to choose their special abodes.[18] It was the duty of Yakkhiṇīs to fetch water from **Anotatta** for Vessavaṇa's use. Each Yakkhiṇī served her turn, sometimes for four, sometimes for five months. But sometimes they died from exhaustion before the end of their term.[19]

Vessavaṇa's wife was **Bhuñjatī** (*q.v.*), who, like himself, was a devoted follower of the Buddha.[20] They had five daughters: **Latā, Sajjā, Pavarā, Acchimatī,** and **Sutā.**[21] **Puṇṇaka** was Vessavaṇa's nephew.[22]

The pleasures and luxuries enjoyed by Vessavaṇa have become proverbial.[23]

An ascetic named **Kañcanapatti**[24] is mentioned as having been the favourite of Vessavaṇa. See also *s.v.* **Yakkha.**

[17] See, *e.g.*, DhA. iii. 74; J. i. 128; iii. 325 (**Makhādeva**). Sometimes, *e.g.*, in the case of **Avaruddhaka** (DhA. ii. 237), a Yakkha had to serve Vessavaṇa for twelve years in order to obtain a particular boon (*cf.* J. ii. 16, 17). (Three years at J. iii. 502.) Vessavaṇa sometimes employs the services of uncivilized human beings (*paccantamilakkhavāsika*) DA. iii. 865 f. The Yakkhas fear him greatly. If he is angry and looks but once, one thousand Yakkhas are broken up and scattered "like parched peas hopping about on a hot plate" (J. ii. 399). This was probably before he became a *sotāpanna.*

[18] J. i. 328.

[19] DhA. i. 40; also J. iv. 492; v. 21.

[20] D. ii. 270.

[21] For a story about them, see VvA. 131 f.

[22] J. vi. 265, 326.

[23] See, *e.g.*, Vv. iv. 3, 46 (*bhuñjāmi kāmakāmī rājā Vessavaṇo yathā*); MṬ. 676 (*Vessavaṇassa rājaparihārasadisaṃ*); *cf.* J. vi. 313.

[24] J. ii. 399.

Vessānara.—A name for the God of Fire.[1]

[1] J. vi. 203.

1. **Vessāmitta.**—A celebrated sage of old.[1]

[1] Vin. i. 245; D. i. 104; M. ii. 169, 200; A. iii. 224; iv. 61, etc.

2. **Vessāmitta.**—A king of old who led a good life and was reborn in Sakka's heaven.[1]

[1] J. vi. 251.

3. **Vessāmitta.**—A Yakkha chief who, with five hundred others of the same name, was present at the preaching of the **Mahāsamaya Sutta.**[1]

[1] D. ii. 257.

He is mentioned among the Yakkha chiefs to be invoked in time of need by followers of the Buddha.[2] Buddhaghosa says[3] he was so called because he lived on a mountain called **Vessāmitta.**

[2] *Ibid.*, iii. 205. [3] DA. ii. 686; iii. 970.

Vehapphala.—One of the Brahma-worlds of the Rūpaloka plane. Beings are born there as a result of developing the Fourth Jhāna.[1] Their life-span is five hundred *mahākalpas*,[2] and even *puthujjanas* can be born there.[3] Baka-Brahma was once an inhabitant of Vehapphala.[4] Anāgāmins born there reach Nibbāna without going elsewhere.[5] Buddhaghosa[6] explains the name thus: *vipulā phalā ti=Vehapphalā.* In ages in which the world is destroyed by wind, Vehapphala forms the limit of the destruction.[7]

[1] AbhS. chap. v., sec. 3 (d).
[2] *Ibid.*, sec. 6; A. ii. 128, 129.
[3] VbhA. 376. [4] J. iii. 358; SA. i. 162.
[5] VbhA. 522.
[6] *Ibid.*, 521=MA. i. 29.
[7] CypA. 9.

Vehaliṅga (*v.l.* **Vekaliṅga, Vebhaliṅga**).—A township (*nigama*) where lived **Ghaṭīkāra,** friend of **Jotipāla.**[1] The township was in **Kosala,** and once, during his long stay in Kosala, the Buddha visited the *ārāma* in which **Kassapa Buddha** had preached to Jotipāla, and there he himself preached the **Ghaṭīkāra Sutta.**[2]

[1] S. i. 34, 60. [2] M. ii. 45 ff.

Voyalaggamu.—A village in **Rohaṇa,** mentioned in the account of the campaigns of **Parakkamabāhu I.**[1]

[1] Cv. lxxiv. 122.

1. **Vohāra Suttā.**—Four suttas on modes of speech which are Ariyan and non-Ariyan.[1]

[1] A. iv. 307.

2. **Vohāra Suttā.**—Two suttas, one on the eight un-Ariyan practices and the other on their opposites.[1]

[1] A. iv. 307.

Vohārapatha Suttā.—Two suttas, similar to **Vohāra Sutta.**[1]

[1] A. ii. 227=ii. 229.

Vohārikatissa.—King of Ceylon (269-91 A.C.). He was the son of **Sirināga** and his name was **Tissa.** He was called " Vohārika " because of his knowledge of law and tradition; he repealed the penalty of bodily injury. He patronized **Deva Thera** of **Kappukagāma** and **Mahātissa** of **Anurārāma.** He built the **Sattapaṇṇakapāsāda,** and erected parasols on eight thūpas and walls round six vihāras.[1] On days when the **Ariyavaṃsa** was being read, he held almsgiving throughout Ceylon. He suppressed the **Vetulya** heresy with the help of his minister **Kapila.** He was killed by his brother, **Abhayanāga.**[2]

[1] For details see Mhv. xxxvi. 33 f. [2] *Ibid.*, xxxvi. 27 ff.

Vyaggha Jātaka (No. 272).—The Bodhisatta was once a tree-sprite and lived near another tree-sprite. No one dared to enter the forest, fearing a lion and a tiger who roamed about there. So the people could not collect wood. One day the second tree-sprite assumed an awful shape, in spite of the Bodhisatta's advice, and frightened away the lion and the tiger. The people, finding that they had disappeared, began cutting down the trees. Then the foolish tree-sprite tried in vain to bring the animals back.

The story was told in reference to **Kokālika's** attempt to bring **Sāriputta** and **Moggallāna** back, after having insulted them. Kokālika is identified with the foolish sprite, Sāriputta with the lion, and Moggallāna with the tiger.[1]

[1] J. ii. 356-8; *cf.* the **Takkāriya Jātaka.**

Vyagghapajja.—The name given to the city of the **Koliyans** (*q.v.*), because it was built on a tiger's track. The Koliyans themselves thus came to be called **Vyagghapajjā.**[1]

[1] AA. ii. 558, 778; SNA. i. 356; DA. i. 262; *cf.* Mtu. i. 355.

Vyasana Sutta.—Ten evils which befall a monk who reviles Āriyans and his fellow-celibates.[1]

[1] A. v. 169=317.

1. **Vyākaraṇa Sutta.**—Five qualities, including knowledge of the four kinds of analysis, which enable a monk to attain his aim.[1]

[1] A. iii. 110.

2. **Vyākaraṇa Sutta.**—Preached by **Mahā Moggallāna,** on ten qualities which should be abandoned in order to achieve one's purpose in the *sāsana.*[1]

[1] A. v. 155 f.

S.

Saṃyama.—A king of Benares, mentioned in the **Mahāhaṃsa Jātaka** (*q.v.*). **Khemā** was his chief consort. He is identified with **Sāriputta.**[1]

[1] J. v. 354, 382.

Saṃyutta Nikāya, Saṃyuttāgama.—One of the five divisions of the **Sutta Piṭaka.** It consists of 7,762 suttas,[1] and, at the First Council, was given in charge of **Mahā Kassapa** and his pupillary succession (*nissitaka*).[2] The Nikāya is divided into five main Vaggas and fifty-six sections, called Saṃyuttas, each Saṃyutta being again subdivided into minor Vaggas or chapters. Buddhaghosa wrote a Commentary on the Saṃyutta, called **Sāratthappakāsinī.** The Saṃyutta Nikāya is quoted in the Milindapañha.[3]

Kittisirirājasīha, king of Ceylon, had the Saṃyutta Nikāya copied by scribes.[4] One of the Saṃyuttas, the **Anamatagga,** was preached by **Rakkhita** in **Vanavāsa**[5] and by **Mahinda** in **Ceylon,**[6] soon after their respective arrivals in these countries, at the conclusion of the Third Council. The Nikāya has been translated into Burmese.[7]

[1] DA. i. 17; Gv. 56.

[2] DA. i. 15.

[3] *E.g.*, pp. 137, 242, 377, 379; see also Vin. ii. 306, where Uposatha Saṃyutta is mentioned, but what is evidently meant is the Uposatha Khandhaka.

[4] Cv. xcix. 33.

[5] Mhv. xii. 32.

[6] *Ibid.*, xv. 186.

[7] Bode, *op. cit.*, 92.

Saṃyoga Sutta.—On how men and women forge bonds for themselves by being attached to sex.[1]

[1] A. iv. 57.

Saṃyojana Sutta.—On the ten *saṃyojanas.*[1]

[1] A. v. 17.

Saṃvaṇṇanānayadīpanī.—A grammatical work by **Jambudhaja Thera** of Pagan.[1]

[1] Bode, *op cit.*, 55.

1. **Saṃvara.**—The youngest of the hundred sons of Brahmadatta, king of Benares. See the **Saṃvara Jātaka.**

2. **Saṃvara.**—The Ājīvaka mentioned in the **Paṇḍara Jātaka** (*q.v.*).[1]

[1] J. v. 87; see scholiast, *ibid.*, line 27.

3. **Saṃvara.**—A chieftain of the **Asuras,** skilled in wiles.[1] *Cf.* **Sambara.**

[1] J. v. 452, 454.

Saṃvara Jātaka (No. 462).—The Bodhisatta was the teacher of **Saṃvara** (1), youngest of the hundred sons of the king of Benares. When he had finished his studies, the king offered him a province, but, at the suggestion of his teacher, he preferred to live near his father. There, acting on the Bodhisatta's advice, he won all hearts, and on the death of his father the courtiers made him king. The brothers protested, and Saṃvara, again following his teacher's advice, divided his father's wealth among them. Then his brothers, led by **Uposatha,** acknowledged him king.

The story was told to a monk who had dwelt in the forest and had then given up striving. He is identified with Saṃvara and **Sāriputta** with Uposatha.[1]

[1] J. iv. 130 ff.; see also the **Alīnacitta Jātaka** and **Gāmaṇi Jātaka.**

Saṃvara Sutta.—On the four efforts: to restrain, abandon, make become and watch over.[1]

[1] A. ii. 6.

Saṃvasita.—A king of twenty-eight kappas ago, a former birth of **Gandhodaka Thera.**[1]

[1] Ap. i. 106.

Saṃvāsa Suttā.—Two Suttas—one preached to some householders on the road between **Madhurā** and **Verañjā,** the other to the monks—on four ways of living together: a vile man with a vile woman, a vile man with a *devī*, a *deva* with a vile woman, a *deva* with a *devī*.[1]

[1] A. ii. 57 ff.

Saṃvutta Sutta.—The three spheres—*kāma, rūpa, arūpa*—must be given up and three kinds of training must be developed: greater virtue (*adhisīla*), greater thought, greater insight.[1]

[1] A. iv. 444.

Saṃvejanīya Sutta.—Four spots connected with the Buddha—the scenes of his birth, his Enlightenment, the preaching of his first sermon, and his death—which should be looked upon with emotion by believers.[1] *v.l.* **Vejanīya.**

[1] A. ii. 120; D. ii. 140.

Saṃsaya.—A divine musician or a musical instrument.[1]

[1] VvA. 93, 372.

Saṃsāraphala.—A park in Ceylon, laid out by **Parakkamabāhu I.**[1]

[1] Cv. lxxix. 10.

Saṃsāramocakā.—A class of *micchādiṭṭhikas.*[1]

[1] *E.g.*, PvA. 67.

Sa-ādhāna Vagga.—The sixth chapter of the Aṭṭhaka Nipāta of the **Aṅguttara Nikāya.**[1]

[1] A. iv. 274-93.

Sakacittaniya Thera.—An arahant. Ninety-one kappas ago, in the time of **Sikhī Buddha,** he made a *thūpa* of bamboos in the name of the Buddha and offered flowers to it. Eighty kappas ago he was a king.[1]

[1] Ap. i. 111 f.

Sakaṭa.—A **Yakkha** who, with five thousand others, guarded the fifth door of **Jotiya's** palace.[1] *v.l.* **Kasakaṇḍa.**

[1] DhA. iv. 209.

1. **Sakalikā Sutta.**—Seven hundred devas of the **Satullapa** group visit the Buddha at **Maddakucchi** as he lay grievously hurt by a stone splinter. They express their admiration, in various ways, of the Buddha's mindfulness and self-possession and blame his enemy (**Devadatta**) for trying to injure so marvellous a being.[1]

[1] S. i. 27 f.

2. **Sakalikā Sutta.**—**Māra** approaches the Buddha at **Maddakucchi** as he lay there in great pain, and tries to grieve him by saying that he is idle and full of brooding thoughts. The Buddha denies the charge.[1]

[1] S. i. 110.

Sakā.—A tribe, mentioned in a list.[1] The name probably refers to the Scythians.

[1] Mil. 327, 331.

Sakiṃsammajjaka Thera.—An arahant. He saw the *Pāṭali*-bodhi of **Vipassī Buddha** and swept around it and paid it honour. On the way home he was killed by a python.[1]

[1] Ap. i. 378 f.

Sakuṇa Jātaka (No. 36).—The Bodhisatta was once a bird, leader of a large flock. He lived in a tree, and noticing one day that two of the boughs were grinding one against the other and producing smoke, he warned his flock of the risk of fire and left for elsewhere. The wiser birds followed him, but some remained behind and were burnt to death.

The story was related to a monk whose cell was burnt down. He told the villagers of this, and they continually promised to build him a new one, but failed to do so. As a result the monk lived in discomfort and his meditations were fruitless. When he reported this, the Buddha blamed him for not going elsewhere.[1]

[1] J. i. 215 f.

Sakuṇagghi Jātaka (No. 168).—The Bodhisatta was once a quail and was seized one day by a falcon. The quail lamented, saying that if he had remained in the feeding ground of his own people he would not have suffered thus. The falcon, hearing this, let him go, saying that he could catch him, no matter where he was. The quail flew back and perched on an immense clod, whence he called to the falcon. The falcon swooped down, but the quail just turned over, and the falcon was dashed to pieces against the clod.[1]

The Jātaka was related on the occasion of the preaching of the **Sakuṇovāda Sutta** (*q.v.*).

[1] J. ii. 58 f.

Sakuṇagghi Sutta.—See **Sakuṇovāda Sutta.**

Sakuṇovāda Sutta.—A monk must keep to his own pasture ground, his own native beat (*pettikavisaya*)—viz., the four satipaṭṭhānas. Objects, sounds, etc., are passion-fraught, inciting to lust.[1]

The introduction of the sutta contains the **Sakuṇagghi Jātaka** (*q.v.*). The name given in the *uddāna* of the Saṃyutta is the **Sakuṇagghi Sutta.**

[1] S. v. 146 f.

1. **Sakula.**—A city in **Mahiṃsakaraṭṭha.**[1]

[1] J. v. 337.

2. **Sakula.**—A king of **Sakula.** See the **Cullahaṃsa Jātaka.** He is identified with **Sāriputta.**[1]

[1] J. v. 337, 353.

1. **Sakulā Therī.**—She belonged to a brahmin family of **Sāvatthi** and became a believer on seeing the Buddha accept **Jetavana.** Later,

she heard an arahant monk preach, and, being agitated in mind, joined the Order. Having developed insight, she won arahantship. Afterwards the Buddha declared her foremost among nuns in *dibbacakkhu*.[1]

In the time of **Padumuttara Buddha** she was **Nandā,** daughter of King **Ānanda,** and, therefore, half-sister of the Buddha. One day she heard the Buddha declare a nun chief among possessors of the "heavenly eye" and herself wished for similar honour. In the time of **Kassapa Buddha** she was a brahminee and later became a **Paribbājikā.** One day she offered alms at the Buddha's *thūpa* and kept a lamp burning there all night. She was then reborn in **Tāvatiṃsa.**[2]

[1] *Cf.* A. i. 25. [2] Thig. vss. 98-101; ThigA. 91 f.; Ap. ii. 569 f.; AA. i. 199 f.

2. **Sakulā.**—Sister of **Somā.** They were both wives of **Pasenadi** and followers of the Buddha. Once, when Pasenadi was staying at **Ujjuññā,** he went to see the Buddha, and carried to him the greetings of the two queens.[1]

[1] M. ii. 125 f.; MA. ii. 757.

Sakuludāyī.—A famous **Paribbājaka.** The **Mahā-Sakuladāyī** and the **Culla-Sakuladāyī Suttas** (*q.v.*) record two conversations between him and the Buddha in the **Paribbājakārāma** at **Moranivāpa** in **Rājagaha.** He is also said to have been present when the Buddha visited the Paribbājakārāma on the **Sappinī** River and talked to the Paribbājakas there.[1] In these contexts he is said to have been in the company of **Annabhāra** (**Anugāra**) and **Varadhara,** evidently themselves eminent Paribbājakas. Sakuladāyī's teacher was **Vekhanassa.**[2]

[1] A. ii. 29, 176. [2] MA. ii. 716.

Sakoṭa, or **Koraṇḍadāyaka Thera.**—An arahant. Thirty-one kappas ago he saw the footprint of **Sikhī Buddha** and worshipped it, covering it with *koraṇḍa*-flowers.[1]

[1] Ap. i. 283.

Sakka.—Almost always spoken of as "*devānaṃ indo,*" chief (or king) of the devas. The **Saṃyutta Nikāya**[1] contains a list of his names: he is called **Maghavā,** because as a human being, in a former birth, he was a brahmin named **Magha.**[2] As such he bestowed gifts from time to time, hence his name **Purindada**[3] (generous giver in former births or giver in towns). Because he gives generously and thoroughly (*sakkaccaṃ*) he is known as **Sakka.**[4] Because he gives away dwelling-places (*āvasa*-

[1] S. i. 229; DhA. i. 264.

[2] But see *s.v.* **Magha**; *cf.* Sanskrit Maghavant as an epithet of Indra.

[3] *Cf.* Indra's epithet Purandara (destroyer of cities).

[4] Śakra occurs many times in the Vedas as an adjective, qualifying gods (chiefly Indra), and is explained as meaning "able, capable." It is, however, not found as a name in pre-Buddhistic times.

thaṃ) he is called **Vāsava.**[5] Because in one moment he can think of one thousand matters, he is called **Sahassakkha.**[6] Because he married the Asura maiden **Sujā,** he is called **Sujampati.**[7] Because he governs the devas of **Tāvatiṃsa,** he is called *Devānam Indo.*[8] Elsewhere[9] Sakka is addressed as **Kosiya** (*q.v.*). He is also spoken of as **Yakkha.**[10]

Sakka rules over Tāvatiṃsa *devaloka,* the lowest heaven but one of the lower plane. His palace is **Vejayanta** (*q.v.*) and his chariot bears the same name. Though king of the Tāvatiṃsa devas, he is no absolute monarch. He is imagined rather in the likeness of a chieftain of a **Kosala**-clan. The devas meet and deliberate in the **Sudhammā-sabhā** and Sakka consults with them rather than issues them commands. On such occasions, the Four Regent Devas are present in the assembly with their followers of the **Cātummahārājika**-world.[11] Among the Tāvatiṃsa devas, Sakka is more or less *primus inter pares,* yet he surpasses his companions in ten things: length of life, beauty, happiness, renown, power; and in the degree of his five sense-experiences: sight, hearing, smelling, taste and touch.[12]

In the Saṃyutta Nikāya[13] the Buddha gives seven rules of conduct, which rules Sakka carried out as a human being, thus attaining to his celestial sovereignty. When the devas fight the **Asuras**[14] they do so under the banner and orders of Sakka. **Pajāpati, Varuṇa** and **Isāna** are also mentioned as having been associated with him in supreme command.[15]

In the Saṃyutta Nikāya a whole Saṃyutta—one of the shortest, consisting of twenty-five short suttas—is devoted to Sakka. In the first and second suttas Sakka praises energy (*viriya*); in the third he denounces timidity; in the fourth he shows forbearance to his enemy[16];

[5] But see *s.v.* **Vāsava.**

[6] Also **Sahassanetta.**

[7] For the romantic story of Sakka's marriage, see *s.v.* **Sujā.** Thus Sujā's father, **Vepacitti** (*q.v.*), became Sakka's father-in-law. Several quaint stories are related about father- and son-in-law. The two sometimes quarrelled and at others lived together in peace (SA. i. 265).

[8] See *s.v.* **Inda.**

[9] *E.g.*, D. ii. 270; M. i. 252.

[10] M. i. 252; *cf.* S. i. 206 (Sakkanāmako Yakkho); at S. i. 47 **Māghadevaputta** (Sakka) is called **Vatrabhū,** slayer of Vṛtra (SA. i. 83); Sakka is also, in the Jātakas, called **Gandhabbarāja** (J. vi. 260) and **Mahinda** (J. v. 397, 411).

[11] See, *e.g.*, D. ii. 207 f., 220 f.

[12] A. iv. 242; these are also attributed to the rulers of the other deva-worlds.

[13] S. i. 228, 229, 231; *cf.* Mil. 90; for details of these see **Magha.**

[14] For details of Sakka's conquest of the Asuras see *s.v.* **Asura.** The Asuras called him **Jara-sakka** (J. i. 202).

[15] S. i. 219.

[16] The enemy, in this case, is his father-in-law, **Vepacitta.** Sakka had a reputation for great forbearance. In sutta 22 a Yakkha is said to have come and to have sat on his throne, to anger him. But Sakka showed him great honour and the Yakkha vanished. The Commentary adds (S.A. i. 272) that it was no Yakkha, but a Rūpāvacara Brahmā, named **Kodhabhakkha,** who had come to test Sakka's patience.

in the fifth he advocates the conquest of anger by kindness; in the sixth kindness to animals; in the seventh he denounces trickery, even towards enemies; and in the ninth he preaches courtesy and honour towards the wise. In the eleventh are described the seven life-long habits which raised him to his present eminent position; twelve and thirteen repeat this and explain his titles. In the fourteenth Sakka explains how new gods, who outshine the old ones, do so because they have observed the Buddha's teaching. In the fifteenth he describes as the most beautiful spot that where arahants dwell; in the sixteenth he praises gifts to the Order[17]; in the seventeenth he praises the Buddha, but is told by **Sahampati** that he has selected the wrong attributes for praise. In eighteen to twenty he says that whereas brahmins and nobles on earth and the gods of the Cātummahārājika-world and of Tāvatiṃsa worship him, he himself worships good men and arahants. Numbers twenty-one, twenty-two, twenty-four and twenty-five are against anger, and twenty-three is against deceit.

These and other passages show that Sakka was considered by the early Buddhists as a god of high character, kindly and just, but not perfect, and not very intelligent. His imperfections are numerous: in spite of his very great age,[18] he is still subject to death and rebirth[19]; as an example of this, it is mentioned that **Sunetta** had thirty-five times been reborn as Sakka,[20] a statement confirmed by the Buddha.[21] Sakka is not free from the three deadly evils—lust, ill-will, stupidity[22]; nor is he free from anxiety. He is timid, given to panic, to fright, to running away.[23]

In the **Sakkapañha Sutta** (*q.v.*), Sakka is said to have visited the Buddha at **Vediyagiri** in **Ambasaṇḍā** and to have asked him a series of questions.

[17] The story connected with this sutta is that of Sakka, seeing the people of **Aṅga** and **Magadha** make preparations for a great sacrifice to Mahā Brahmā, feels pity for them and comes among them in the guise of Brahmā, advising them to take their offerings to the Buddha and seek his counsel (SA. i. 270).

[18] At J. ii. 312, Sakka's life is given as lasting thirty million and sixty times one hundred thousand years.

[19] A. i. 144.

[20] *Ibid.*, iv. 105.

[21] *Ibid.*, 89.

[22] *Ibid.*, i. 144. The story of **Rohiṇī** shows that Sakka was very susceptible to the charms of beauty. He evidently liked other people to enjoy life and sent a heavenly dancer to amuse **Mahāpanāda** when nobody on earth could accomplish that feat (SNA. ii. 400). On another occasion, as Sakka was rejoicing in his triumph over the Asuras, he saw a crane on a hill-top who wished to be able to eat fish without going down into the stream. Sakka immediately sent the stream, in full flood, to the hill-top (J. iii. 252).

[23] He is mentioned in the Jātakas as being frightened of ascetics who practised severe penances, lest they should unseat him from his throne, *e.g.*, J. ii. 394; also the stories of **Visayha, Lomasakassapa, Kaṇha, Akitti, Mahā-Kañcana** and **Isisiṅga.**

He sends **Pañcasikha** with his *vīnā*[24] to play and sing to the Buddha and to obtain permission for him (Sakka) to visit him and question him. The Buddha says to himself that Sakka, for a long time past, has led a pure life, and gives him permission to question him on any subject. It is stated in the course of the sutta[25] that it was not the first time that Sakka had approached the Buddha for the same purpose. He had gone to him at the **Saḷalaghara** in **Sāvatthi,** but found him in meditation, with **Bhuñjati,** wife of **Vessavaṇa,** waiting on him. He therefore left with a request to Bhuñjatī to greet the Buddha in his name. He also declares[26] that he has become a *sotāpanna* and has earned for himself the right to be reborn eventually in the **Akaniṭṭhā**-world, whence he will pass entirely away.

The Commentary says[27] that Sakka was constantly seeing the Buddha and was the most zealous of the devas in the discharge of his duties to the *sāsana.* But this visit to the Buddha at Vediyagiri had a special object. Sakka saw signs that his life was drawing to an end and was frightened by this knowledge. He therefore went to the Buddha to seek his help. It adds[28] that, as Sakka sat listening to the Buddha, he died in his old life and was reborn a new and young Sakka; only Sakka himself and the Buddha was aware of what had happened. The Commentary continues[29] that Sakka became an "*uddhaṃ-sota,*" treading the path of *anāgāmins.* As such he will live in **Avihā** for one thousand kappas, in **Atappa** for two thousand, in **Sudassanā** for four thousand, and will end in the Akaniṭṭha-world, after having enjoyed life in the Brahma-worlds for thirty-one thousand kappas.

An account of another interview which Sakka had with the Buddha is given in the **Cūlataṇhāsaṅkhaya Sutta** (*q.v.*). There the question arises regarding the extirpation of cravings. Sakka accepts the Buddha's answer and leaves him. Anxious to discover whether Sakka has understood the Buddha's teaching, **Moggallāna** visits Sakka and questions him. Sakka evades the questions and shows Moggallāna the glories of his Vejayanta palace. Moggallāna then frightens him by a display of *iddhi*-power, and Sakka repeats to him, word for word, the Buddha's answer. Moggallāna departs satisfied, and Sakka tells his handmaidens that Moggallāna is a "fellow of his" in the higher life, meaning, probably,

[24] It was Sakka who had given the **Beluvapaṇḍuvīnā** to Pañcasikha (SNA. ii. 394).

[25] D. ii. 270.

[26] *Ibid.*, 286.

[27] DA. iii. 697. In the sutta Sakka admits (D. ii. 284) that he visited other brahmins and recluses as well. They were pleased to see him, and boasted that they had nothing to teach him; but he had to teach them what he knew.

[28] DA. iii. 732; *cp.* DhA. iii. 270.

[29] DA. iii. 740.

that he himself is a *sotāpanna* and therefore a kinsman of the arahant.[30]

The later books contain a good deal of additional information regarding Sakka. His city extends for one thousand leagues, and its golden streets are sixty leagues long; his palace Vejayanta is one thousand leagues high; the Sudhammā-hall covers five hundred leagues, his throne of yellow marble (**Paṇḍukambalasilāsana**) is sixty leagues in extent, his white umbrella with its golden wreath is five leagues in circumference, and he himself is accompanied by a glorious array of twenty-five million nymphs.[31] Other features of his heaven are the **Pāricchattaka**-tree, the **Nandā-pokkharaṇī** and the **Cittalatāvana.**[32] His body is three gavutas in height[33]; his chief conveyance is the marvellous elephant **Erāvaṇa** (*q.v.*), but he goes to war in the **Vejayanta-ratha** (*q.v.*). Reference is often made to his throne, the Paṇḍukambalasilāsana (*q.v.*), composed of yellow stone. It grows hot when Sakka's life draws towards its end; or his merit is exhausted; or when some mighty being prays; or, again, through the efficacy of virtue in recluses or brahmins or other beings, full of potency.[34]

Sakka's devotion to the Buddha and his religion is proverbial. When the Bodhisatta cut off his hair and threw it into the sky, Sakka took it and deposited it in the **Cūḷāmaṇi-cetiya.**[35] He was present near the Bodhi-tree, blowing his **Vijayuttara-saṅkha** (*q.v.*), when **Māra** arrived to prevent the Buddha from reaching Enlightenment.[36] When the Buddha accepted **Bimbisāra's** invitation to dine in his palace, Sakka, in the guise of a young man, preceded the Buddha and his monks along the street to the palace, singing the Buddha's praises.[37] When the Buddha performed his **Yamaka-pāṭihāriya** at the foot of the **Gaṇḍamba,** it was Sakka who built for him a pavilion, and gave orders to the gods of the Wind and the Sun to uproot the pavilions of the heretics and cause them great discomfort.[38] When the Buddha returned to **Saṅkassa** from Tāvatiṃsa, whither he went after performing the Twin Miracle, Sakka

[30] In a passage in the Saṃyutta (S. i. 201) Sakka is represented as descending from heaven to make an enquiry about Nibbāna, and in another (S. iv. 269 f.), as listening, in heaven, to Moggallāna's exposition of the simplest duties of a good layman. On another occasion, at Vessavaṇa's suggestion, Sakka visited **Uttara Thera** on the **Saṅkheyyaka** Mountain and listened to a sermon by him (A. iv. 163 f.). See also **Sakka Sutta** (2) and (3).

[31] J. v. 386.

[32] DA. iii. 716; see also *s.v.* Tāvatiṃsa.

[33] DhA. iii. 269.

[34] J. iv. 8; when the Buddha, however, sat on it, he was able to conceal it in his robe (DhA. iii. 218).

[35] J. i. 65.

[36] *Ibid.*, 72.

[37] Vin. i. 38.

[38] DhA. iii. 206, 208.

created three ladders—of gold, of silver, and of jewels respectively—for the Buddha and his retinue.[39]

Sakka was present at **Vesāli** when the Buddha visited that city in order to rid it of its plagues. His presence drove away the evil spirits, and the Buddha's task was thus made easier.[40] When the Buddha and his monks wished to journey one hundred leagues, to visit **Culla Subhaddā** at **Uggapura,** Sakka, with the aid of **Vissakamma,** provided them with pavilions (**kūṭāgāra**) in which they might travel by air.[41] Once, when the ponds in Jetavana were quite dry, the Buddha wished to bathe, and Sakka immediately caused rain to fall and the ponds were filled.[42] In Sakka's aspect as **Vajirapāṇi** (*q.v.*) he protected the Buddha from the insults of those who came to question him.[43] During the Buddha's last illness, Sakka ministered to him, performing the most menial tasks, such as carrying the vessel of excrement.[44] He was present at the Buddha's death, and uttered, in verse, a simple lament, very different from the studied verses ascribed to **Brahmā.**[45] At the distribution, by **Doṇa,** of the Buddha's relics, Sakka saw Doṇa hide the Buddha's right tooth in his turban. Realizing that Doṇa was incapable of rendering adequate honour to the relic, Sakka took the relic and deposited it in the Cūḷāmaṇicetiya.[46] And when **Ajātasattu** was making arrangements to deposit his share of the relics, Sakka gave orders to Vissakamma to set up a **vāḷasaṅghāṭayanta** for their protection.[47]

Sakka did all in his power to help followers of the Buddha in their strivings for the attainment of the goal, as in the case of **Paṇḍitasāmaṇera,** when he sent the Four Regent Gods to drive away the birds, made the Moon-deity shroud the moon, and himself stood guard at the door of Paṇḍita's cell, lest he should be disturbed.[48] Often, when a monk achieved

[39] DhA., *ibid.*, 225. [40] *Ibid.*, 441

[41] *Ibid.*, 470. [42] J. i. 330.

[43] See also the story of **Ciñcā-māṇavikā,** when Sakka protected the Buddha from her charges. Sakka also regarded it as his business to protect the Buddha's followers, as is shown by the manner in which he came to the rescue of the four seven-year-old novices—**Saṅkicca, Paṇḍita, Sopāka** and **Revata**—when they were made to go hungry by a brahmin and his wife (DhA. iv. 176 f.).

[44] *Ibid.*, 269 f. He did the same for other holy men—*e.g.*, **Sāriputta.** Sakka also waited on the Buddha when he was in **Gayāsīsa** for the conversion of the **Tebhātikajaṭilas** (Vin. i. 28 f.); see also the story of **Jambuka** (DhA. ii. 59). The Udāna (iii. 7) contains a story of Sakka assuming the guise of a poor weaver and Sujā that of his wife, in order to give alms to **Mahā Kassapa** who had just risen from a trance. They succeeded in their ruse, to the great joy of Sakka (*cp.* DhA. i. 424 f.). On other occasions—*e.g.*, in the case of **Mahāduggata**—Sakka helped poor men to gain merit by providing them with the means for giving alms to the Buddha (DhA. ii. 135 ff.).

[45] D. ii. 157; on the importance of this verse, however, see Dial. ii. 176, n. 1.

[46] DA. ii. 609.

[47] *Ibid.*, 613.

[48] DhA. ii. 143; *cf.* the story of **Sukha** *ibid.*, iii. 96 f.

his ambition, Sakka was there to express his joy and do him honour.[49] He was ready to help, not only monks and nuns, but also eminent laymen, such as **Jotika,** for whom he built a palace of wondrous splendour, and provided it with every luxury.[50] Sakka was always ready to come to the rescue of the good when in distress—*e.g.*, in the case of **Cakkhupāla** when he became blind; Sakka led him by the hand and took him to Sāvatthi.[51] He loved to test the goodness of men, as in the case of the leper **Suppabuddha,**[52] to see if their faith was genuine. The Jātaka contains several stories of his helping holy men by providing them with hermitages, etc.—*e.g.*, **Kuddāla-paṇḍita, Hatthipāla, Ayoghara, Jotipāla** (**Sarabhaṅga**), **Sutasoma, Dukūlaka, Pārikā** and **Vessantara.** Sometimes, when he found that ascetics were not diligently practising their duties, he would frighten them—*e.g.*, in the **Vighāsa** and **Somadatta Jātakas.** The Aṅguttara Nikāya[53] contains a story of Sakka punishing a deva called **Supatiṭṭha,** who lived in a banyan-tree, because he failed to keep the *rukkhadhamma.*

Sakka appears as the guardian of moral law in the world. When wickedness is rampant among men, or kings become unrighteous, he appears among them to frighten them so that they may do good instead of evil. He is on the side of the good against the wicked, and often helps them to realize their goal. Instances of this are seen in the **Ambacora, Ayakūṭa, Udaya, Kaccāni, Kāma, Kāmanīta, Kumbha, Keḷisīla, Kharaputta, Culladhanuggaha, Dhajaviheṭha, Biḷārikosiya, Maṇicora, Mahākaṇha, Vaka, Sarabhaṅga, Sarabhamiga** and **Sudhābhojana Jātakas.** Sakka patronised good men; some of the more eminent he invited to his heaven, sending his charioteer **Matali** to fetch them, and he showed them all honour—*e.g.*, **Guttila, Mandhātā, Sādhīna,** and **Nimi;** others he rewarded suitably—see, *e.g.*, the **Uraga Jātaka.**

The lesser gods consulted Sakka in their difficulties and problems—*e.g.*, in the case of the deity of **Anāthapiṇḍika's** fourth gateway, who incurred the displeasure of Anāthapiṇḍika by advising him to refrain from too much generosity towards the Buddha and his monks.[54] Sakka has also to deal with disputes arising among the devas themselves.[55] On several occasions Sakka helped the Bodhisatta in the practice of his Perfections—*e.g.*, as King **Sivi, Temiya, Nimi** and **Vessantara,** also in

[49] See, *e.g.*, the story of **Mahāphussa** (SNA. i. 55 f.).

[50] DhA. iv. 207 f.

[51] *Ibid.*, i. 14 f. Many instances are found in the Jātaka where Sakka rescued the good in distress—*e.g.*, **Dhammaddhaja, Guttila, Kaccāni,** the Kinnarī **Candā, Sambulā, Kusa, Mahājanaka's** mother, **Candakumāra's** mother, **Candā,** and **Mahosadha.**

[52] DhA. ii. 34 f.; see also the story of the courtezan in the **Kurudhamma Jātaka** (J. ii. 380).

[53] iii. 370 f.

[54] J. i. 229.

[55] DA. iii. 705.

his birth as a hare; in this last story, the **Sasa Jātaka** (*q.v.*), Sakka paints the picture of a hare in the moon to commemorate the Bodhisatta's sacrifice.

Sakka sometimes answers the prayers of good and barren women and gives them sons—*e.g.*, **Sumedhā, Sīlavatī, Candādevī.** Mention is also made of other boons granted by Sakka to various persons. Thus in the **Mahāsuka Jātaka** he visited the parrot who clung to the dead stump of a tree through gratitude, and granted him the boon that the tree should once more become fruitful.[56] He granted four boons to **Kaṇha,** that he might be calm, bear no malice or hatred against his neighbour, feel no greed for others' glory, and no lust towards his neighbour.[57] To **Akitti** he granted several boons, the last of which was that he should have no more visits from Sakka[58]! When Sivi became blind, Sakka gave him two eyes; these were not natural eyes, but the eyes of Truth, Absolute and Perfect (*saccapāramitā-cakkhuṇī*). Sakka confesses that he has not the power of restoring sight; it was the virtue of Sivi himself which had that power.[59] When Sīlavatī wished for a boon, Sakka took her to heaven, where he kept her for seven days; then he granted that she should have two sons, one wise and ugly and the other a fool and handsome. He also presented her with a piece of *kusa*-grass, a heavenly robe, a piece of sandalwood, the flower of the Pāricchattaka-tree and a **Kokanda-lute.** All this passed into the possession of **Kusa,** and, later, Sakka gave him the **Verocana-**jewel.[60] He gave **Phusatī,** mother of Vessantara, ten boons[61] and to Vessantara himself he gave eight.[62]

In the **Sarabhaṅga Jātaka**[63] mention is made of four daughters of Sakka —**Āsā, Saddhā, Hirī** and **Sirī.** His wife, **Sujā,** accompanied him everywhere on his travels,[64] even into the world of men, because that was the boon she had asked for on her marriage to him.[65] **Vessavaṇa** was Sakka's special friend,[66] and when one Vessavana died, it was Sakka's duty to appoint a successor.[67] **Matāli** (*q.v.*) is Sakka's charioteer and constant companion. **Vissakamma** (*q.v.*) is his "handy-man." Sakka has twenty-five million handmaids and five hundred dove-footed nymphs (*kakuṭapādiniyo*), famed for their beauty. It was the sight of these which tempted the Buddha's step-brother, **Nanda,** to give up thoughts of *Janapadakalyāṇī-Nandā.*[68] Sakka's special weapon

56 J. iii. 493.
57 J. iv. 10.
58 *Ibid.*, 240 f.
59 *Ibid.*, 410 f.
60 J. v. 280 f., 310.
61 J. vi. 481 f.
62 *Ibid.*, 572.
63 J. v. 392.
64 *E.g.*, J. iii. 491.
65 DhA. i. 279.
66 MA. i. 476 f.
67 J. i. 328.
68 J. ii. 93.

is the **Vajirāvudha** (*q.v.*), and his special drum the **Āḷambara** (*q.v.*). His voice is sweet, like the tintinabulation of golden bells.[69]

It is Sakka's special duty to protect the religion of the Buddha in Ceylon. As the Buddha lay dying, he enjoined on Sakka the task of looking after **Vijaya** and his successors. This duty Sakka, in turn, entrusted to the god **Uppalavaṇṇa.**[70] Sakka informed **Mahinda** of the right moment for his visit to Ceylon.[71] When **Devānampiyatissa** wished for relics to place in the **Thūpārāma-Thūpa, Sumana-sāmaṇera** visited Sakka and obtained from him the right collar-bone of the Buddha, which Sakka had placed in the **Cuḷāmaṇi-cetiya.**[72] Again, when **Duṭṭhagāmaṇī** was in need of building materials for the **Mahā Thūpa,** it was Sakka who supplied them.[73] On the occasion of the enshrining of the relics in the **Mahā Thūpa,** Sakka gave orders to **Vissakamma** to decorate the whole of Ceylon. He also provided the throne and casket of gold for the relics brought from the Nāgā-world by **Soṇuttara** and was himself present at the festival, blowing his conch-shell.[74]

Other Cakkavāḷas have also their Sakka,[75] and in one place[76] mention is made of many thousands of Sakkas.

It is evident from the foregoing account that, as Rhys Davids suggests,[77] Sakka and Indra are independent conceptions. None of the personal characteristics of Sakka resemble those of Indra. Some epithets are identical but are evidently borrowed, though they are differently explained. The conception of the popular god which appealed to a more barbarous age and to the clans fighting their way into a new country, seems to have been softened and refined in order to meet the ideals of a more cultured and peaceful civilization. The old name no longer fitted the new god, and, as time went on, Sakka came to be regarded as an entirely separate god.

[69] SA. i. 273.
[70] Mhv. vii. 1 ff.
[71] *Ibid.*, xiii. 15.
[72] *Ibid.*, xvii. 9 ff.
[73] *Ibid.*, xxviii. 6 ff.
[74] *Ibid.*, xxxi. 34, 75, 78.
[75] (*aññehi Cakkavāḷehi Sakkā āgacchanti*) J. i. 203.
[76] *Ibid.*, 204.
[77] Dial. ii. 297 f.

2. **Sakka.**—A **Yakkha.** See **Sakka Sutta** (1).

3. **Sakka.**—Another form of **Sākya** (*q.v.*).[1]

[1] *E.g.*, A. iv. 195; v. 334.

Sakka Saṃyutta.—The eleventh section of the **Saṃyutta Nikāya.**[1] It contains twenty-five short discourses connected with **Sakka** (*q.v.*).

[1] S. i. 216-42.

1. **Sakka Sutta.**—A Yakkha visits the Buddha at **Gijjhakūṭa** and tells him that he should not spend his time teaching others. The Buddha answers that he does it out of sympathy and compassion.[1]

The Commentary adds[2] that this Sakka was a Yakkha belonging to **Māra's** faction (*Mārapakkhiko*).

[1] S. i. 206. [2] SA. i. 232.

2. **Sakka Sutta.**—**Sakka,** king of the devas, visits the Buddha at **Gijjhakūṭa** and asks him why only some beings are fully set free in this life. Because of grasping, answers the Buddha.[1]

[1] S. iv. 101.

3. **Sakka Sutta.**—A series of four conversations which **Sakka** and his retinue had with **Moggallāna,** at **Jetavana,** on various simple topics, such as taking refuge in the Buddha, having unwavering faith in him, etc.[1]

[1] S. iv. 269 ff.

Sakkacca Vagga.—The fourth section of the **Sekhiyā** in the **Vinaya Piṭaka.**[1]

[1] Vin. iv. 191-4.

Sakkacca Sutta.—Four qualities, including zeal, desirable in those who practise meditation.[1]

[1] S. iii. 267, 271, 277.

Sakkaṭa.—A Yakkha who, with five hundred others, stood guard over the fifth gates of **Joṭiya's** palace.[1] *v.l.* **Kasakanda.**

[1] DhA. iv. 209.

"Sakkatvā" Sutta.—**Sāriputta,** seated in seclusion and pondering as to whom a monk should respect and rely on, finds, in answer, that a monk should respect and revere the Buddha, the Dhamma and the Saṅgha, and should rely on goodwill. He visits the Buddha and consults him, and the Buddha tells him that his conclusions are correct.[1]

[1] A. iv. 120 f.

Sakkadattiya.—This word, occurring several times in the Jātaka,[1] is evidently not a name but an adjective, meaning "provided by Sakka."

[1] *E.g.,* **J. iii. 463; iv. 489; vi. 21, etc.**

1. **Sakkanamassa Sutta.**—The Buddha tells the monks of how **Sakka** once ordered **Mātali** to fetch his chariot that he might visit his gardens. The chariot was brought, and before entering it, Sakka clasped his hands and did obeisance to the several quarters. On being asked by Mātali as to whom he so honoured, Sakka answered that he worshipped all monks and laymen who led the virtuous life.[1]

[1] S. i. 234.

2. **Sakkanamassa Sutta.**—Similar to (1). The honour was paid to the Buddha.[1]

[1] S. i. 235.

3. **Sakkanamassa Sutta.**—Similar to (1). The honour was paid to the Order of monks.[1]

[1] S. i. 236.

Sakkapañha Sutta.—The twenty-first of the **Dīgha Nikāya.**[1] **Sakka**[2] visits the Buddha at the **Indasālaguhā** in **Vediyagiri,** and, having obtained leave from the Buddha through **Pañcasikha,** asks a series of fourteen questions on the causes of malice and avarice, favour and disfavour, of desire, of mental preoccupation, obsession (*papañca*), happiness (*somanassa*), sorrow (*domanassa*), equanimity, good behaviour of body and speech (as enjoined in the Pāṭimokkha), right pursuit (*pariyesanā*), control of the sense-faculties, the presence of divers persuasions (*anekadhātu*), and failure in attaining the right ideal.[3] The Sutta also contains the story of the Sākyan maiden **Gopikā** (*q.v.*). Sakka is greatly pleased with the Buddha's answers, and, together with eighty thousand devas, becomes a *sotāpanna.*

In order to show his gratitude to **Pañcasikha,** he obtains for him as his wife, **Timbarū's** daughter, **Bhaddā Suriyavaccasā.**

The sutta is quoted by name at S. iii. 13. Buddhaghosa says[4] that the sutta comes under the **Vedalla** division.

[1] D. ii. 263-89.
[2] For details of this visit see *s.v.* **Sakka.**
[3] A summary of the Sutta is given at DA. iii. 738.
[4] DA. i. 24; also Gv. 57.

Sakkapabba.—A section of the **Vessantara Jātaka,** dealing with the story of **Sakka** obtaining from **Vessantara** his queen **Maddī** as handmaiden and his restoration of her to Vessantara.[1]

[1] J. vi. 573.

Sakkasenāpati.—An office granted by **Kassapa V.** to his son, who was entrusted with the care of the **Dhammapotthaka** (?). Kassapa's wife was Devā. The prince was later sent to India to help the **Paṇḍu** king against the king of **Coḷa.** There he died of the *upasagga*-plague.[1]

[1] Cv. lii. 52, 62, 72 ff.

Sakkā.—See **Sakyā.**

1. **Sakkā Sutta.**—**Mahānāma** visits the Buddha at **Nigrodhārāma,** where he was convalescing, and questions him regarding knowledge and concentration. **Ānanda,** wishing to save the Buddha's strength, takes Mahānāma aside and talks to him of *sīla*, *samādhi* and *paññā*, both of the learner (*sekha*) and of the adept (*asekha*).[1]

[1] A. i. 219 f.

2. **Sakkā Sutta.**—A large number of **Sākyans** visit the Buddha at **Nigrodhārāma,** and he impresses on them the very great advantage of keeping the fast day well.[1]

[1] A. v. 83.

1. **Sakkāya Sutta.**—The Buddha teaches the monks about *sakkāya*, its arising, its cessation, and the way thereto.[1]

[1] S. iii. 159.

2. **Sakkāya Sutta.**—It is by the realization of impermanence in all things that *sakkāya-diṭṭhi* can be abandoned.[1]

[1] S. iv. 147.

3. **Sakkāya Sutta.**—**Sāriputta** tells **Jambukhādaka** that *sakkāya* is the five factors of grasping; the Noble Eightfold Path leads to its comprehension.[1]

[1] S. iv. 259.

Sakkāra.—See **Sakkhara.**

Sakkupaṭṭhāna Vatthu.—The story of **Sakka** ministering to the Buddha in his last illness.[1]

[1] DhA. iii. 269 f.

Sakkodana.—A Sākyan, one of the five sons of **Sīhahanu** and **Kaccānā.**[1] He was brother to **Suddhodana,** the Buddha's father.[2]

[1] Mhv. ii. 20; Dpv. iii. 45. [2] MA. i. 289.

Sakkhara. *v.l.* **Sakkara.**—A township of the Sākyans where the Buddha once stayed with **Ānanda.**[1] It was not far from **Rājagaha** and was the residence of **Macchariya-Kosiya.**[2] It was forty-five yojanas from **Jetavana.**[3]

[1] S. v. 2. [2] DhA. i. 367; J. i. 345. [3] *Ibid.*, 348.

Sakkharālayagaṅgā.—A river in Ceylon, mentioned in the account of the campaigns of **Parakkamabāhu I.**[1]

[1] Cv. lxxii. 29; see Cv. *Trs.* i. 322, n. 1.

Sakkharasobbha.—A port in **Rohaṇa** where **Iḷanāga** landed on his return from India to Ceylon.[1]

[1] Mhv. xxxv. 28.

Sakkhi Sutta.—A monk who does not know, for a fact, what things partake of failure, of stability, distinction and penetration, and is not strenuous, zealous, or helpful—such a one is incapable (*abhabba*) of any achievement.[1]

[1] A. iii. 426.

Sakyaputtiyā.—The name given to the monks of the Buddha's Order,[1] as followers of **Sakyamuni.**

[1] *E.g.*, Ud. iv. 8; D. iii. 84.

Sakyamuni.—An epithet of the Buddha.[1]

[1] See Bu. xxvi. 9; Mil. 115.

Sakyā, Sakka, Sākiyā.—A tribe in North India, to which the **Buddha** belonged. Their capital was **Kapilavatthu.** Mention is also made of other Sākyan settlements—*e.g.*, **Cātumā, Khomadussa, Sāmagāma, Devadaha, Silāvatī, Nagaraka, Medatalumpa, Sakkhara** and **Uḷumpa** (*q.v.*). Within the Sākyan tribe there were probably several clans, *gottā*. The Buddha himself belonged to the **Gotamagotta.** It has been suggested[1] that this was a brahmin clan, claiming descent from the ancient *isi* **Gotama.** The evidence for this suggestion is, however, very meagre. Nowhere do we find the Sākyans calling themselves brahmins. On the other hand, we find various clans claiming a share of the Buddha's relics on the ground that they, like the Buddha, were *khattiyas.*[2] It is stated[3] that the Sākyans were a haughty people. When the Buddha first visited them, after his Enlightenment, they refused to honour him on account of his youth. The Buddha then performed a miracle and preached the **Vessantara Jātaka,** and their pride was subdued. They were

[1] *E.g.*, Thomas, *op. cit.*, 22.

[2] D. ii. 165.

[3] Vin. ii. 183; D. i. 90; J. i. 88; DhA. iii. 163. Hiouen Thsang, however, found them obliging and gentle in manners (Beal, *op. cit.*, ii. 14).

evidently fond of sports and mention is made of a special school of archery conducted by a Sākyan family, called **Vedhaññā**.[4] When the prince **Siddhattha Gotama** (later the Buddha) wished to marry, no Sākyan would give him his daughter until he had showed his proficiency in sport.[5]

The Sākyans evidently had no king. Theirs was a republican form of government, probably with a leader, elected from time to time. The administration and judicial affairs of the *gotta* were discussed in their *Santhāgāra*, or Mote-Hall, at Kapilavatthu.[6] **Ambaṭṭha** (*q.v.*) once visited it on business; so did the envoys of **Pasenadi**, when he wished to marry a Sākyan maiden (see below). A new Mote-Hall was built at Kapilavatthu while the Buddha was staying at the **Nigrodhārāma**, and he was asked to inaugurate it. This he did by a series of ethical discourses lasting through the night, delivered by himself, **Ānanda**, and **Moggallāna**.[7]

The Sākyans were very jealous of the purity of their race; they belonged to the **Ādiccagotta**,[8] and claimed descent from **Okkāka** (*q.v.*). Their ancestors were the nine children of Okkāka, whom he banished in order to give the kingdom to **Jantukumāra**, his son by another queen. These nine children went towards **Himavā**, and, having founded **Kapilavatthu** (*q.v.* for details), lived there. To the eldest sister they gave the rank of mother, and the others married among themselves. The eldest sister, **Piyā**, later married **Rāma**, king of Benares, and their descendants became known as the **Koliyans** (see *s.v.* **Koliyā** for details). When Okkāka heard of this, he praised their action, saying, "*Sakyā vata bho kumārā, paramasakyā vata bho rājakumārā*[9]"; hence their name came to be "Sakyā."

[4] D. iii. 117; DA. iii. 905.

[5] J. i. 58.

[6] See, *e.g.*, D. i. 91; the Sākyans had a similar Mote Hall at **Cātumā** (M. i. 457). The **Mallas** of **Kusinārā** also had a *Santhāgāra* (D. ii. 164); so did the **Licchavis** of **Vesāli** (Vin. i. 233; M. i. 228).

[7] M. i. 353 f.; S. iv. 182 f.; the hall is described at SA. iii. 63; *cf.* UdA. 409.

[8] *Ādiccā nāma gottena, Sākiyā nāma jātiyā* (SN. vs. 423).

[9] SNA. i. 352 f.; *cf.* DA. i. 258. Okkāka had a slave girl, **Disā**, her offspring were the **Kaṇhāyanas**, to which *gotta* belonged Ambaṭṭha (*q.v.*). The Mhv. (ii. 12 ff.) gives the history of the direct descent of the Buddha from Okkāka, and this contains a list of the Sākyan chiefs of Kapilavatthu: **Okkāmukha** was Okkāka's eldest son; **Nipuna, Candimā, Candamukha, Sivisañjaya, Vessantara, Jāli, Sīhavāhana** and **Sīhassara** were among his descendants. Sīhassara had eighty-two thousand sons and grandsons, of whom **Jayasena** was the last. Jayasena's son was **Sīhahanu**, and his daughter **Yasodharā**. Sīhahanu's wife was **Kaccāna**, daughter of **Devadahasakka** of **Devadaha**, whose son **Añjana** married Yasodharā. Añjana had two sons, **Daṇḍapāṇi** and **Suppabuddha**, and two daughters, **Māyā** and **Pajāpatī**. Sīhahanu had five sons and two daughters: **Suddhodana, Dhotodana, Sakkodana, Sukkodana, Amitodana, Amitā** and **Pamitā**. Māyā and Pajāpatī were married to Suddhodana, and Māyā's son was the Buddha. Suppabuddha married **Amitā** and they had two children, **Bhaddakaccānā** and **Devadatta**. The consort of the Bodhisatta was Bhaddakaccānā; their son was Rāhula.

From the very first there seems to have been intermarriage between the Sākyans and the Koliyans; but there was evidently a good deal of endogamy among the Sākyans, which earned for them the rebuke of the Koliyans in the quarrel between them—" like dogs, jackals, and such-like beasts, cohabiting with their own sisters."[10]

A quarrel, which broke out in the Buddha's lifetime, between the Sākyans and the Koliyans is several times referred to in the books. The longest account is found in the introductory story of the **Kuṇāla Jātaka.** The cause of the dispute was the use of the water of the River **Rohiṇī** (*q.v.*), which flowed between the two kingdoms. The quarrel waxed fierce, and a bloody battle was imminent, when the Buddha, arriving in the air between the two hosts, asked them, " Which is of more priceless value, water or *khattiya* chiefs ?" He thus convinced them of their folly and made peace between them. On this occasion he preached five Jātaka stories—the **Phandana, Daddabha, Laṭukika, Rukkhadhamma** and **Vaṭṭaka** (Sammodamāna)—and the **Attadaṇḍa Sutta.** To show their gratitude the Sākyans and Koliyans gave each two hundred and fifty young men from their respective families to join the Order of the Buddha.[11] Earlier, during the Buddha's first visit to Kapilavatthu, when he had humbled the pride of his kinsmen by a display of miracles, each Sākyan family had given one representative to enter the Order and to help their famous kinsman. The wives of these, and of other Sākyans who had joined the Order, were the first to become nuns under **Pajāpatī Gotamī** (*q.v.*) when the Buddha gave permission for women to enter the Order. Among the most eminent of the Sākyan young men, who now joined, were **Anuruddha, Ānanda, Bhaddiya, Kimbila, Bhagu** and **Devadatta.** Their barber, **Upāli,** entered the Order at the same time; they arranged that he should be ordained first, so that he might be higher than they in seniority and thus receive their obeisance, and thereby humble their pride.[12]

The Buddha states, in the **Aggañña Sutta,**[13] that the Sākyans were vassals of King **Pasenadi** of **Kosala.** Yet, when Pasenadi wished to establish connection with the Buddha's family by marrying one of the daughters of a Sākyan chief, the Sākyans decided in their Mote-Hall that it would be beneath their dignity to marry one of their daughters to

[10] *E.g.*, SNA. i. 357; J. v. 412 f.; there were eighty-two thousand rājās among the Koliyans and Sākyans (SNA. i. 140).

[11] J. v. 412 f.; for their history see also SNA. i. 358 f.

[12] Vin. ii. 181 f.; according to DhA. i. 133, eighty thousand Sākyan youths had joined the Order.

[13] D. iii. 83 (*Sakyā . . . Pasenadi-Kosalassa anuyuttā bhavanti, karonti Sakyā rañño Pasenadimhi Kosale nipacca-kāraṃ abhivādanaṃ paccupaṭṭhānaṃ añja-likammaṃ sāmīcikammaṃ*); *cf.* SN. vs. 422, where the Buddha describes his country as being " *Kosalesu niketino.*"

the King of Kosala. But as they dared not refuse Pasenadi's request, the Sākyan chieftain, **Mahānāma,** solved the difficulty by giving him **Vāsabhakhattiyā** (*q.v.*), who was his daughter by a slave-girl, **Nāgamuṇḍā.** By her Pasenadi had a son, **Viḍūḍabha.** When Pasenadi discovered the trick, he deprived his wife and her son of all their honours, but restored them on the intervention of the Buddha. Later, when Viḍūḍabha, who had vowed vengeance on the Sākyans for the insult offered to his father, became king, he marched into Kapilavatthu and there massacred the Sākyans, including women and children. The Buddha felt himself powerless to save them from their fate because they had committed sin in a previous life by throwing poison into a river. Only a few escaped, and these came to be called the **Naḷasākiyā** and the **Tiṇasākiyā.**[14] Among the Sākyans who thus escaped was **Paṇḍu,** son of **Amitodana.** He crossed the Ganges, and, on the other side of the river, founded a city. His daughter was **Bhaddakaccānā** (*q.v.*), who later married **Paṇḍuvāsudeva,** king of Ceylon.[15] Thus the kings of Ceylon were connected by birth to the Sākyans.

[14] The Mhv. Ṭīkā (p. 180) adds that, during this massacre, some of the Sākyans escaped to the **Himālaya,** where they built a city, which came to be called **Moriyanagara** because the spot resounded with the cries of peacocks. This was the origin of the Moriya dynasty, to which **Asoka** belonged (189). Thus Asoka and the Buddha were kinsmen.

[15] Mhv. viii. 18 ff. Six of her brothers also came to Ceylon, where they founded settlements: **Rāma, Uruvela, Anurādha Vijita, Dīghāyu** and **Rohaṇa** (Mhv. ix 6 ff.).

1. **Sakhā Sutta.**—Seven qualities which make a man a desirable friend: he gives what is hard to give, does what is hard to do, bears what is hard to bear, confesses his own secrets, keeps others' secrets, does not forsake one in time of need, and does not despise one in time of one's ruin.[1]

[1] A. iv. 31.

2. **Sakhā Sutta.**—Seven things which make a person a desirable friend: he is genial, pleasant, grave, cultured, eloquent, gentle, profound in speech, and urges one on at the proper time.[1]

[1] A. iv. 32.

Sagara.—A mythical king of the line of **Okkāka.** He had sixty thousand sons, who ruled in as many towns in **Jambudīpa.**[1]

[1] Cv. lxxxvii. 34; the legend of Sagara and his sons is given in the *Mahābhārata* (iii. 106 ff.).

Sagaradeva.—A king who dug the ocean.[1] The reference is evidently to **Sagara** (*q.v.*), who, through anger, caused the earth to be excavated, and the earth came thus to have the ocean as her bosom. From this the ocean has come to be called Sāgara.[2]

[1] DA. i. 91; MA. ii. 689. [2] Mahābhārata xii. 29.

1. **Sagātha Vagga.**—The first section of the **Saṃyutta Nikāya.**

2. **Sagātha Vagga.**—The first chapter of the **Vedanā Saṃyutta.**[1]

[1] S. iv. 204-16.

Sagāthapuññābhisanda Vagga.—The fifth chapter of the **Sotāpatti Saṃyutta.**[1]

[1] S. v. 399-404.

Sagga.—A minstrel of **Tamba,** king of Benares. See the **Sussondī Jātaka.**

Saṅkantikā.—A heretical sect, a division of the **Kassapiyā.**[1]

[1] Mhv. v. 9; Dpv. v. 48.

Saṅkappa Jātaka (No. 251).—The Bodhisatta was once born into a very rich family of Benares. When his parents died he gave away his wealth, became an ascetic in the **Himālaya,** and developed *iddhi*-powers. During the rains he returned to Benares, where, at the king's invitation, he lived in the royal park. For twelve years he did this, till, one day, the king had to leave to quell a frontier rebellion, after having instructed the queen to look after the ascetic. One evening the ascetic returned rather late to the palace, and the queen, rising hastily at his arrival, let her garment slip. The ascetic's mind became filled with thoughts of lust, and he lost his powers. On his return to the hermitage, he lay there for seven days without touching food. On his return, the king visited the ascetic, who explained that his heart had been wounded. Asking the king to retire from the hut, he once more developed his trance. He then took leave of the king and returned to Himavā.

The story was told to a monk who was filled with discontent because he had fallen in love with a woman whom he met on his alms rounds. The king is identified with **Ānanda.**[1]

[1] J. ii. 271-77.

Saṅkappa Vagga.—The first chapter of the Tika Nipāta of the **Jātakaṭṭhakathā.**[1]

[1] J. ii. 271-321.

Saṅkassa.—A city, thirty leagues from **Sāvatthi.**[1] It was there that the Buddha returned to earth, after preaching the **Abhidhammapiṭaka** in **Tāvatiṃsa,** following the performance of the Twin Miracle under the **Gaṇḍamba** tree. As the time approached for the Buddha to leave Tāvatiṃsa, **Moggallāna**[2] announced his coming return to the multitude, who had been waiting at Sāvatthi, fed by **Culla-Anāthapiṇḍika,** while Moggallāna expounded the Dhamma. They then made their way to Saṅkassa. The descent of the Buddha took place on the day of the *Mahāpavāraṇa* festival. **Sakka** provided three ladders for the Buddha's descent from **Sineru** to the earth: on the right was a ladder of gold for the gods; on the left a silver ladder for **Mahā Brahmā** and his retinue; and in the middle a ladder of jewels for the Buddha. The assembled people covered the earth for thirty leagues round. There was a clear view of the nine Brahma-worlds above and of **Avīci** below. The Buddha was accompanied by **Pañcasikha, Mātali, Mahā Brahmā** and **Suyāma. Sāriputta** was the first to welcome him,[3] and the Buddha preached the Law, starting with what was within the comprehension even of a *puthujjana*, and ending with what only a Buddha could understand. On this occasion was preached the **Parosahassa Jātaka** (*q.v.*) to proclaim to the multitude the unparalleled wisdom of Sāriputta.[4] It is said[5] that the Buddha's descent to Saṅkassa had provided opportunity for Moggallāna to show his eminence in *iddhi*, **Anuruddha** in *dibbacakkhu*, and **Puṇṇa** in skill in preaching, and the Buddha wished to give Sāriputta a chance of shining in his wisdom. He therefore asked of Sāriputta questions which no one else could answer. The opening words of the **Sāriputta Sutta** (*q.v.*) are supposed to refer to this descent from Tusita (*sic*). The site of the city gate of Saṅkassa is one of the "unchangeable" spots of the world (*avijahitaṭṭhānaṃ*). All Buddhas descend at that spot to the world of men after preaching the Abhidhamma.[6] From Saṅkassa the Buddha went to Jetavana.[7] A shrine was erected on the spot where the Buddha's right foot first touched the ground at Saṅkassa.[8] When the Chinese pilgrims, Hiouen Thsang and Fa Hien, visited the place, they found three ladders, which had been built of brick and stone by the ancients, to commemorate the Buddha's descent, but the ladders were nearly sunk in the earth.[9]

There was, in the Buddha's time, a deer park at Saṅkassa where

[1] DhA. iii. 224.

[2] **Anuruddha,** according to SNA. ii. 570; *cf.* Vsm., p. 391.

[3] Followed by **Uppalavaṇṇā** (SNA. ii. 570).

[4] DhA. iii. 224 ff.; see also SNA. ii. 570.

[5] *Ibid., loc. cit.*; J. iv. 266; see also **Jhānasodhana, Sarabhamiga,** and **Candābha Jātakas.**

[6] BuA. 106, 247; MA. i. 371, etc.

[7] J. i. 193.

[8] DhA. iii. 227.

[9] Beal, *op. cit.*, i. 203; Fa Hien, p. 24.

Suhemanta Thera heard the Buddha preach.[10] During the **Vajjiputta** controversy, **Revata Thera,** on his way from **Soreyya** to **Sahājāti,** went through Saṅkassa. The road he took passed through Saṅkassa, **Kaṇṇakujja, Udumbarā** and **Aggāḷapura.**[11]

Saṅkassa is now identified with Sankissa-Basantapura on the north bank of the Ikkhumatī (Kālīnadī), between Atranji and Kanoj, twenty-three miles west of Fatehgarh and forty-five north of Kanoj.

[10] ThagA. i. 212. [11] Vin. ii. 299 f.

Saṅkāsanā Sutta.—The Buddha says that in the Four Ariyan Truths, as taught by him, there are numberless shades and variations of meaning.[1]

S. v. 430.

1. **Saṅkicca Thera.**—He was born in a very eminent brahmin family of **Sāvatthi.** His mother died just before his birth and was cremated, but he was found unburnt on the funeral pyre.[1] The men who burnt his mother's body, turning the pyre over with sticks, pierced the womb and injured the pupil of the child's eye. Hence his name (*Saṅkunā chinnakkhikoṭitāya = Saṅkicco*). When he was discovered, they consulted soothsayers, who told them that if he lived in the household seven generations would be impoverished, but if he became a monk he would be the leader of five hundred. At the age of seven he came to know of his mother's death and expressed a wish to join the Order. His guardians agreeing to this, he was ordained under **Sāriputta.** He won arahantship in the Tonsure-hall.[2]

At that time, thirty men of Sāvatthi, who had entered the Order and had practised the duties of higher ordination for four years, wished to engage in meditation. The Buddha, foreseeing danger for them, sent them to Sāriputta. Sāriputta advised them to take with them the novice Saṅkicca, and they reluctantly agreed. After a journey of one hundred and twenty leagues, they came to a village of one thousand families, where they stayed at the request of the inhabitants, who provided all their needs. At the beginning of the rains, the monks agreed among themselves not to talk to one another; if any among them fell ill, he was to strike a bell. One day, as the monks were eating their meal on the banks of a neighbouring river, a poor man who had travelled far stood near them and they gave him some food. He then decided to stay with them, but after two months, wishing to see his daughter, he left the monks without a word. He travelled through a forest where lived five hundred robbers, who had vowed to offer a human sacrifice to a spirit of the forest.

[1] *Cf.* the story of **Dabba.** [2] ThagA. i. 533.

As soon as they saw him, they captured him and prepared for the sacrifice. The man then offered to provide them with a victim of far higher status than himself, and led them to the monks. Knowing their habits, he struck the bell and they all assembled. When the robbers made known their design, each one of the monks offered himself as a victim, and in the end Saṅkicca, with great difficulty, persuaded the others to let him go. The thieves took Saṅkicca, and, when all was ready, the leader approached him with drawn sword. Saṅkicca entered into *samādhi*, and when the blow was struck, the sword buckled and bent at the end and split from hilt to top. Marvelling at this, the thieves did obeisance to Saṅkicca, and, after listening to his preaching, asked leave to be ordained. Saṅkicca agreed to this, and, having ordained them, took them to the other monks. There he took leave of them and went with his following to the Buddha. In due course, Saṅkicca received the higher ordination, and ten years later he ordained his sister's son, **Atimuttaka (Adhimuttaka),** who, likewise, ordained five hundred thieves.[3]

The **Nāgapeta Vatthu** (*q.v.*) contains a story of another of Saṅkicca's pupils.[4] The Theragāthā[5] contains a series of stanzas spoken by Saṅkicca in praise of the charms of the forest in reply to a layman who, wishing to wait upon him, wished him to dwell in the village.

Saṅkicca is one of the four novices mentioned in the **Catusāmaṇera Vatthu** (*q.v.*). Saṅkicca's *iddhi* is described[6] as *ñāṇavipphāra-iddhi*. The *iddhi* referred to in this connection is Saṅkicca's escape from death while his mother's body was being burnt.[7]

[3] DhA. ii. 240 ff.; for the story of **Atimuttaka** see *s.v.* Saṅkicca's story is often referred to—*e.g.*, Vsm. 313; J. vi. 14.

[4] PvA. 53 ff. [5] Thag. vs. 597-607.

[6] Ps. ii. 211; BuA. 24.

[7] Vsm., p. 379.

2. **Saṅkicca.**—See **Kisa-Saṅkicca,** where Saṅkicca is given as a *gotta*-name.

3. **Saṅkicca.**—The Bodhisatta, born as an ascetic. See the **Saṅkicca Jātaka.**

Saṅkicca Jātaka (No. 530).—The Bodhisatta was once born in the family of the chaplain of the king of Benares and was educated in **Takkasilā,** with the king's son. They became great friends, and, when the prince became viceroy, they lived together. The prince, having conceived the plan of killing his father in order to become king, confided this idea to Saṅkicca. The latter tried to dissuade him, but finding his efforts in vain, he fled to the Himālaya, where he became an ascetic. The prince killed his father, but was later filled with remorse and could find no peace of mind. He longed to see Saṅkicca, but it was not till fifty years later that Saṅkicca, with five hundred followers, came to the garden of **Dayāpassa** in Benares. The king visited him and questioned him on the results of wickedness. Saṅkicca described the horrors of hell awaiting the wicked, illustrating his story with stories of **Ajjuna** who annoyed the sage **Gotama,** of **Daṇḍaki,** who defied **Kisavaccha,** of the king of **Mejjha,** whose country became a desert, of the **Andhaveṇhudāsaputtā** who assailed **Dīpāyana,** and of **Cecca,** swallowed up by the earth.[1] After describing the terrors awaiting the victims of various hells, Saṅkicca showed the king the *deva*-worlds and ended his discourse, indicating the possibility of making amends.

The king was much comforted and changed his ways. He is identified with **Ajātasattu,** in reference to whose parricide and its consequences the story was related. It was not till Ajātasattu sought the Buddha and listened to his preaching that he found peace of mind.[2]

[1] For details of these stories see *s.v.* [2] J. v. 261-77.

Saṅkita Sutta.—A monk who haunts the house of a widow, an unmarried woman (*thullakumārī*), a eunuch, or the premises of a nun, is suspect.[1]

[1] A. iii. 128.

Saṅkiliṭṭhābhā.—A class of devas. Beings are born in their world when they have absorbed the idea of tarnished brilliance.[1]

[1] M. iii. 147.

Saṅkilesiya Sutta.—See **Kilesiya Sutta.**

Saṅkamanattā Therī.—An arahant. Seeing **Koṇḍañña Buddha** walking along the road, she came out of her house and prostrated herself. The Buddha touched her head with his foot.[1]

[1] Ap. ii. 514.

Saṅketahāla.—A place in Ceylon where the **Damiḷas** captured **Brāhmaṇatissa.**[1] *v.l.* **Guttahāla, Gottahāla.**

[1] MṬ. 613.

1. **Saṅkha.**—The Bodhisatta, born as a brahmin in **Molinīnagara** (Benares). See the **Saṅkha Jātaka.**

2. **Saṅkha.**—The Bodhisatta, born as a seṭṭhi of **Rājagaha.** See the **Asampadāna Jātaka.**

3. **Saṅkha.**—A future king, who will be the Cakkavatti of **Ketumatī** at the time of the appearance of **Metteyya Buddha** in the world. He will raise up again the palace of King **Mahāpanāda** and live there. But later he will give it to the Order and become an arahant.[1]

According to the Commentary,[2] he was one of two cane-workers (*naḷakārā*), father and son, who made a hut for a Pacceka Buddha. After death, both were born in heaven. The son became Mahāpanāda, and, later, **Bhaddaji** (*q.v.*). The father is in the deva-world and will be reborn as Saṅkha. Mahāpanāda's palace still remains undestroyed, ready for his use.

[1] D. iii. 75 f.; Anāgat. p. 42 (vs. 10). [2] DA. iii. 856.

4. **Saṅkha.**—A Nāga-king; a previous birth of **Rāhula.**[1]

[1] SNA. i. 341; but elsewhere (*e.g.*, SA. iii. 26) he is called **Pālita.** See *s.v.* **Pālita.**

5. **Saṅkha.**—One of the treasure troves which arose from the earth for the use of the Bodhisatta in his last lay life. These appeared on the day of his birth.[1]

[1] DA. i. 284.

6. **Saṅkha.**—The Bodhisatta born as a brahmin in **Takkasilā.** He was the father of **Susīma.** See the **Saṅkha Jātaka** (2).

7. **Saṅkha.**—A general of **Kittisirimegha;** he lived in **Badalatthalī.** The king entrusted him with the celebrations in connection with the *upanayana*-ceremony of **Parakkamabāhu** (afterwards **Parakkamabāhu I.**). When Parakkamabāhu returned to Badalatthalī in his tour of preparation, Saṅkha welcomed him and paid him all honour. But Parakkamabāhu proved treacherous and had him slain.[1]

[1] Cv. lxiv. 8 f., 22 f.; lxv. 13 f., 27 f.

8. **Saṅkha.**—A Sinhalese general who maintained a stronghold in **Gaṅgādoṇi** in the **Maṇimekhala** district, while **Māgha** ruled in the capital.[1]

[1] Cv. lxxxi. 7 f.

1. **Saṅkha Jātaka** (No. 442).—The Bodhisatta was once born in **Molini-nagara** (Benares) as a very rich brahmin, named **Saṅkha.** He spent six thousand daily on almsgiving. He had a ship built, equipped and prepared to sail for **Suvaṇṇabhūmi.** A Pacceka Buddha, seeing him with his divine eye, and foreseeing the danger in store for him,

appeared before him on the way to the seaport. Saṅkha paid him all honour and presented him with his shoes and umbrella.

Saṅkha's ship sprang a leak on the seventh day. Taking with him one companion, he dived overboard and swam in the direction of Molinī. He swam thus for seven days, till **Maṇimekhalā,** seeing his plight, came to his rescue and offered him food. But this he refused, as he was keeping the fast. The goddess told him that his purity in worshipping the Pacceka Buddha had been the cause of her coming to his aid and offered him a boon. He chose to be sent back to Molinī. The goddess provided him with a ship full of treasure, and he returned safely to Molinī with his attendant.

The story was related by way of thanks to a pious layman of **Sāvatthi,** who, having entertained the Buddha and his monks for seven days, presented shoes to the Buddha and to the members of his Order.

Ānanda is identified with Saṅkha's attendant and **Uppalavaṇṇā** with Maṇimekhalā.[1] The story is also called the **Saṅkhabrāhmaṇa Jātaka.**[2]

[1] J. iv. 15-22. [2] *E.g., ibid.,* 120.

2. **Saṅkha Jātaka.**—The Bodhisatta was once born as a brahmin in **Takkasilā** and had a son, **Susīma.** When Susīma was about sixteen, he took leave of his father and went to Benares to study the Vedas. His teacher, who was a friend of his father's, taught him all he knew, and then Susīma went to **Isipatana,** where lived some Pacceka Buddhas. He entered the Order under them, attained arahantship, and died while yet young. Having heard no news of his son for some time, Saṅkha was alarmed and went to Benares in search of him. There, after enquiry, he heard of his son's death as a Pacceka Buddha, and was shown the shrine erected in his memory. Saṅkha weeded the grass round the shrine, sprinkled sand, watered it, scattered wild flowers round it, and raised aloft his robe as banner over it. He then planted his parasol over the top and departed.

The Buddha related the story to the monks at **Rājagaha,** after his return from **Vesāli,** to explain the unparalleled honours he had received during the journey. Because he had uprooted the grass round Susīma's shrine, a road of eight leagues was prepared for him to journey comfortably; because he had spread sand, his route was also so spread; because he had scattered flowers, his route was covered with flowers; because he had sprinkled water, there was a shower in Vesāli on his arrival; because he had raised a banner and set up a parasol, the whole *cakkavāḷa* was gay with flags and parasols.[1]

[1] DhA. iii. 445 f.; KhpA. 198 f. The story is not given in the Jātakaṭṭhakathā.

Saṅkha Sutta.—The Buddha, at the **Pāvārika-ambavana,** has a discussion with **Asibandhakaputta** regarding the teachings of **Nigaṇṭha-Nātaputta** and proves to him that Nigaṇṭha's teachings are contradictory and misleading as compared with his own. The Ariyan disciple, by following the Buddha's teaching, cultivates kindliness, compassion and equanimity and suffuses the four quarters with these qualities, as easily as a powerful conchblower fills the four quarters with sound.[1]

[1] S. iv. 317 f.

Saṅkhata Sutta.—There are three condition marks in that which is "conditioned" (*Saṅkhata*). Its genesis is apparent, likewise its passing away and its changeability while it persists.[1]

[1] A. i. 152.

Saṅkhatthali, Saṅkhanāyakatthalī, Saṅkhanāthatthalī.—An important place in the **Dakkhiṇadesa** of Ceylon, where **Kittisirimegha** had his capital. It was near **Badalatthalī,** and is mentioned several times in the account of the campaigns of **Parakkamabāhu I.**[1]

[1] Cv. lxiii. 43; lxiv. 22; lxvi. 9; lxvii. 78, 82; also Cv. *Trs.* i. 241, n. 2.

Saṅkhadhamana Jātaka. (No. 60).—The Bodhisatta was once a conchblower. He went with his father to a public festival, where they earned a great deal of money. On their way through a forest infested with robbers, the son warned his father not to blow on his conch-shell, but his father persisted, and they were plundered by the robbers.

The story was told to a self-willed monk who is identified with the father.[1]

[1] J. i. 284.

Saṅkhadhātu.—One of the **Daṇḍanāyaka-bhātaro**[1] (*q.v.*).

[1] Cv. lxxii. 162.

1. **Saṅkhapāla.**—The Bodhisatta born as a Nāga-king. See the **Saṅkhapāla Jātaka.** Saṅkhapāla is evidently a generic name for the Nāgas of that world.

2. **Saṅkhapāla.**—A king of **Ekabala. Mahosadha** (*q.v.*), hearing that he was collecting arms and assembling an army, sent a parrot to find out about it. The parrot reported that there was no reason to fear Saṅkhapāla.[1]

[1] J. vi. 390.

3. **Saṅkhapāla.**—A lake in the **Mahiṃsakaraṭṭha.** It was the residence of the Nāga king, **Saṅkhapāla.** From the lake rose the river **Kaṇṇapeṇṇā.**[1]

[1] J. v. 162.

4. **Saṅkhapāla Thera.**—A pupil of **Buddhadatta,** to whom he dedicated his **Vinayavinicchaya.**[1]

[1] Gv. 40; P.L.C. 109.

Saṅkhapāla Jātaka (No. 524).—The Bodhisatta born as **Duyyodhana,** son of the king of **Rājagaha.** When he came of age his father handed over the kingdom to him, became an ascetic, and lived in the royal park. There Duyyodhana frequently visited him; finding this inconvenient, the ascetic went to **Mahiṃsakaraṭṭha** and lived in a hut on a bend of the **Kaṇṇapeṇṇā River,** which flows from the **Saṅkhapāla Lake** near Mount **Candaka.** There he was visited by the Nāga-king **Saṅkhapāla,** to whom he preached the Dhamma. Later, Duyyodhana discovered the whereabouts of the ascetic and visited him. There he saw the Nāga-king, and, impressed by his great magnificence, desired to visit the Nāga-world. On his return to the capital, Duyyodhana engaged in works of merit, and was born after death in the Nāga-world and became its king under the name of **Saṅkhapāla.** In course of time, he grew weary of his magnificence, and, leaving the Nāga-world, lived near the Kaṇṇapeṇṇā, on an ant-hill, keeping the holy fast. As he lay there, sixteen men, roaming in the forest, saw him and seized him. They drove stakes into his body, and made holes in the stakes and fastened ropes to them in order to drag him along. But Saṅkhapāla showed no resentment. A landowner of **Mithilā,** called **Aḷāra,** saw him being ill-treated and had him released. Thereupon, Saṅkhapāla invited Aḷāra to the Nāga-world, and Aḷāra lived there for one year. He later became an ascetic, and, in due course, visited Benares, where he told the king the story of his visit to the Nāga-world. After the rains he returned to the Himālaya.

The story was told to some laymen who kept the fast.

The Bodhisatta's father is identified with **Mahā Kassapa,** the king of Benares with **Ānanda,** and Aḷāra with **Sāriputta.**[1]

The story is given in the Cariyāpiṭaka[2] to illustrate *Sīla-pāramitā.*

[1] J. v. 161-71. See also *s.v.* **Aḷāra.**
[2] ii. 10; see also J. i. 45; MA. ii. 617; BuA. 50.

Saṅkhabrāhmaṇa Jātaka.—See the **Saṅkha Jātaka** (1).

Saṅkhavaḍḍhamāna.—A river in Ceylon, which unites with the **Kumbhīlavāṇa.** At the spot where they unite, the **Sūkaranijjhara** was constructed.[1]

[1] Cv. lxviii. 32; see Cv. *Trs.* i. 279, n. 4.

Saṅkhaseṭṭhi.—See **Saṅkha** (1).

Saṅkhāna Sutta.—Four powers that are in the world: of computation, cultivation, innocence and collectedness.[1]

[1] A. ii. 142.

Saṅkhāra Sutta.—Some people accumulate acts of body, speech and mind that are discordant; others those that are harmonious; yet others those that are both discordant and harmonious.[1]

[1] A. i. 122.

Saṅkhāruppatti Sutta.—The 120th sutta of the **Majjhima Nikāya.** A monk who possesses the five *saṅkhāras* (" plastic forces ") of faith, virtue, learning, munificence and wisdom, if he cultivate and develop them, can be reborn in any condition or world he may desire; he can even, thereby, win Nibbāna.[1] The sutta contains a long list of Deva-worlds and Brahma-worlds.

[1] M. iii. 99 ff.

Saṅkhitta Saṃyutta.—Mentioned by Buddhaghosa[1] as an example of a collection of discourses connected with *Suññatā.* The reference is probably to the **Saṭṭhipeyyāla.**[2]

[1] SA. ii. 168.

[2] At Saṃyutta iv. 148 ff.

Saṅkhepaṭṭhakathā.—A compilation quoted by Buddhaghosa[1] as opposed to the **Mahāaṭṭhakathā**.

[1] *E.g.*, at Sp. ii. 494.

Saṅkhepavaṇṇanā.—A *navaṭīkā* by **Saddhammajotipāla**[1] on the **Abhidhammattha-Saṅgaha.**

[1] Gv. 40.

Saṅkheyya-pariveṇa.—A monastery in **Sāgala** where **Āyupāla** and, later, **Nāgasena,** lived. **Milinda** visited this monastery to discuss with these monks.[1]

[1] Mil. 19, 22, etc.

Saṅkhyāpakāsaka.—A grammatical work by **Ñāṇavilāsa** of Laos. **Sirimaṅgala** wrote a *ṭīkā* on it.[1]

[1] Bode, *op. cit.*, 47.

Saṅgagāma.—A village in Ceylon, near the **Kālavāpi.**[1]

[1] Cv. xlviii. 91.

1. **Saṅgayha Sutta.**—On the six spheres of contact—eye, ear, etc.—and the necessity for controlling them in order to get rid of lust and hate.[1]

[1] S. iv. 70 f.

2. **Saṅgayha Sutta.**—**Māluṅkyaputta** visits the Buddha in his old age and asks for a teaching in brief. The Buddha teaches him to guard the six senses.[1]

[1] S. iv. 72 f.

3. **Saṅgayha Sutta.**—The Buddha explains to the monks that they are fortunate to be born as men, and neither in hell, where all things are uninviting, nor in heaven, where all things are attractive.[1]

[1] S. iv. 126.

Saṅgaha Sutta.—The four bases of sympathy (*saṅgahavatthu*) are charity, kind speech, kind action, and like treatment of all men.[1]

[1] A. ii. 31 = *ibid.*, 248.

Saṅgāma.—A king of **Magadha. Buddhaghosa's** father, **Kesī,** was his purohita.[1]

[1] Gv. 66.

Saṅgāmaji Thera.—He was the son of a very rich seṭṭhi of Benares. When he came of age, his parents married him and he had a son. One day he joined a party of people going to **Jetavana,** and, at the conclusion of the Buddha's sermon, asked the Buddha to ordain him. But the Buddha wished him to have his parent's leave. This he obtained only with the greatest difficulty and with the promise to visit them later. After ordination he lived in a forest grove, and soon afterwards attained arahantship.

When he returned to **Sāvatthi,** after having paid homage to the Buddha, he spent the noonday under a tree. His parents, hearing of his arrival, went to see him. Their efforts to persuade him to return to lay life were too insistent, and he would not even speak to them. They returned discomfited and sent his wife and son to him. His wife appealed to him with various arguments, but he refused even to look at her. She then placed the child on his lap and went away. When she discovered that **Saṅgāmaji** would not even talk to his son, she took him away, saying that her husband was a useless man.

The Buddha saw all this with his divine eye and expressed his joy in verse.[1]

Posiya Thera was Saṅgāmaji's younger brother.[2]

[1] Ud. i. 8; UdA. 71 ff.; the verse is quoted at Netti, p. 150. [2] ThagA. i. 97.

Saṅgāmāvacara Jātaka (No. 182).—The Bodhisatta was once a skilled elephant-trainer. The king, in whose service he was, attacked Benares, riding the state elephant; but the elephant was so scared by the missiles and noise that he would not approach the place. Thereupon his trainer encouraged him, telling him that he should feel at home on the battle-field, and the elephant, impressed by his words, broke down all obstacles and achieved victory for his master.

The story was told in reference to the Buddha's step-brother **Nanda** (*q..v*), who, at first, kept the precepts of the Order, because the Buddha had promised to get for him the dove-footed nymphs (*kakuṭapādiniyo*) of Sakka's heaven; but later, moved by **Sāriputta's** words, he put forth effort and attained arahantship. Nanda was the elephant and **Ānanda** the king.[1]

[1] J. ii. 92-5.

Saṅgārava.—A very learned brahmin of **Caṇḍalakappa.** One day he saw **Dhānañjānī** trip up, and heard her exclaim three times, "Glory to the Buddha, the arahant, the all-enlightened." He blamed her for thus extolling a shaveling monk, but when she told him of the Buddha's marvellous qualities, he felt a desire to see him. Some time after, the Buddha went to Caṇḍalakappa and stayed in **Todeyya's** Mango-grove. When Dhānañjānī told Saṅgārava that he was there, Saṅgārava visited him and questioned him on his views on brahmins. The Buddha said he had great regard for brahmins who had here and now won the goal, having discovered unaided a doctrine before unknown. He himself was one of these. He then proceeds to describe how he came to leave the household life and how, in due course, he won Enlightenment.

Saṅgārava asks further whether there are any gods. The Buddha answers that of that there is no doubt; the whole world is in agreement on that point. Saṅgārava is pleased and accepts the Buddha as his teacher.[1] Buddhaghosa says[2] that Saṅgārava was the youngest of the **Bhāradvājas** (*q.v.*), brothers of Dhānañjānī's husband.

[1] M. ii. 209 ff. [2] MA. ii. 808.

The Saṃyutta[3] mentions a Saṅgārava who is perhaps distinct from the above. He lived in **Sāvatthi** and was a "bath-ritualist," believing in purification by water, bathing morning and evening. The Buddha, at **Ānanda's** request, visited his house and preached to him the Doctrine, after which he became the Buddha's follower.

The Commentary[4] explains that Ānanda and Saṅgārava had, as laymen, been friends, and Ānanda was anxious to prevent "this wretch (*varāko*) who, for all our friendship has contracted wrong views, from becoming a hell-filler; moreover he has a circle of friends, and hundreds may follow if he is converted."

Another Saṃyutta passage[5] contains a sutta in which the brahmin Saṅgārava visits the Buddha and asks him why he can remember certain mantras with great ease and others not at all. It may be this same brahmin who is mentioned several times also in the Aṅguttara.[6] The Commentary states[7] that he was an overseer in charge of the repair of the dilapidated buildings in Rājagaha (*Rājagahanagare jiṇṇapaṭisaṅkharaṇakārako āyuttakabrāhmaṇo*).

[3] S. i. 182 f.
[4] SA. i. 207.
[5] S. v. 121 f.; see **Saṅgārava Sutta** (3).
[6] A. i. 168 f.; iii. 230 f.; v. 232, 252. For details see **Saṅgārava Suttā** (4-7).
[7] AA. i. 396.

1. **Saṅgārava Sutta.**—The 100th Sutta of the Majjhima Nikāya. It contains an account of the discussion between the Buddha and **Saṅgārava-brāhmaṇa** of **Caṇḍalakappa.**[1] See **Saṅgārava.**

[1] M. ii. 209 ff.

2. **Saṅgārava Sutta.**—An account of the visit of the Buddha and **Ānanda** to **Saṅgārava-brāhmaṇa** of **Sāvatthi.** Saṅgārava explains to the Buddha that he washes away his faults by bathing morning and evening. The Buddha says that the only true purification is through the Dhamma.[1]

[1] S. i. 182 f.

3. **Saṅgārava Sutta.**—The Buddha explains to **Saṅgārava** that mantras learnt at a time when the heart is possessed by sensual lust, malevolence, sloth and torpor, excitement and flurry, doubt and wavering, are easily forgotten; as is the case of a man who tries to see his reflection in a bowl of water, either mixed with some dye, or heated on the fire, or overspread with mossy grass, or ruffled by the wind, or muddied and set in the dark. The cultivation of the seven *bojjhaṅgas* will remove these disadvantages.[1]

[1] S. v. 121 ff.; *cf.* No. 5 below.

4. **Saṅgārava Sutta.**—**Saṅgārava** visits the Buddha and states that a brahmin is of more use than a **Paribbājaka** because he not only performs sacrifices himself, but makes others do likewise. The Buddha says that the appearance of a Tathāgata in the world is of benefit to many beings. **Ānanda** asks Saṅgārava which of the two practices appears to him the simpler and of greater profit. Saṅgārava evades a straight answer, even though asked three times. The Buddha then tells him of the marvels of *iddhi*, *ādesanā* and *anusāsanā* possessed by monks, and describes them in detail. Saṅgārava admits that the *ādesanā-pāṭihāriya* appeals most to him. The Buddha tells him that numerous monks in the Order possess all three marvels.[1]

[1] A. i. 168 ff.

5. **Saṅgārava Sutta.**—Saṅgārava visits the Buddha and questions him on the power of remembering mantras.[1] Same as No. 3 above.

[1] A. iii. 230 f.

6. **Saṅgārava Sutta.**—The Buddha tells **Saṅgārava,** in answer to a question, that wrong view, wrong thinking, speech, action, living, effort, mindfulness, concentration, knowledge and release, are the "hither shore" and their opposites the "further shore."[1]

[1] A. v. 232 f.

7. **Saṅgārava Sutta.**—The Buddha tells **Saṅgārava** that taking life, theft, wrong sexual conduct, falsehood, spiteful and bitter speech, idle babble, coveting, harmfulness, wrong view, are the "hither shore" and abstention from these is the "further shore."[1]

[1] A. v. 252 f.

Saṅgillagāma.—A village in Ceylon, the residence of **Bhayasiva.**[1]

[1] Cv. xli. 69.

Saṅgīti Sutta.—The thirty-third sutta of the **Dīgha Nikāya,**[1] preached at **Ubbhaṭaka,** the new Mote-Hall of the **Mallas** of **Pāvā.** They had invited the Buddha to consecrate it by preaching there, and this he did until late into the night. Then, seeing that his audience wished for more, he asked **Sāriputta** to continue the preaching while he himself rested. Sāriputta therefore preached the Saṅgīti Sutta, at the end of which the Buddha expressed his great appreciation of Sāriputta's exposition.

This sutta, like the **Dasuttara,** is arranged in a new plan—which is

[1] D. iii. 207 ff.

regularly followed in the Aṅguttara Nikāya—of grouping the points or chief items brought forward, numerically, in arithmetical progression—in this case 1 to 10. This scheme is a kind of thematic index to the doctrines scattered through the Four Nikāyas.

The Sarvāstivādins held this Sutta in high esteem, and included it (under the name of *Saṅgītipariyāya*) among the seven books constituting their Abhidhamma Piṭaka. The Tibetan recensions attribute the Sutta to **Mahā Koṭṭhita.**[2] The sutta treats of the *dasadhammā* (or ten conditions) in much the same way as the Puggalapaññatti deals with the *dasapuggalā* (ten individuals).

[2] See Takākusu's article on the Sarvāstivādins (*J.P.T.S.* 1904-5).

1. **Saṅgha.**—An astrologer (*saṃvaccharikanāyaka*) who predicted the destiny of **Kitti** (afterwards **Vijayabāhu I.**). It was this prediction which made **Buddharāja** support Kitti.[1]

[1] Cv. lvii. 48.

2. **Saṅgha.**—Father of **Sūranimmila;** he was the father of seven sons and lived in **Khaṇḍaviṭṭhika.**[1]

[1] Mhv. xxiii. 19.

3. **Saṅgha.**—An *upāsaka* who will wait on **Metteyya Buddha**[1] and be his chief lay patron.[2]

[1] Anāgat. vs. 61. [2] *Ibid.*, 98.

Saṅgha Sutta.—The Buddha tells **Upāli** of ten things which disunite the Order and their ten opposites which unite it.[1]

[1] A. v. 73.

Saṅghakapiṭṭha.—See **Kapiṭṭha.**

1. **Saṅghatissa.**—A **Lambakaṇṇa** who became king of Ceylon (303-7 A.C.) after slaying **Vijayakumāra.** He set up a parasol on the **Mahā Thūpa** and did other works of merit. Having heard from the **Thera Mahādeva** of **Dāmahālaka** of the merits of giving rice-gruel, he arranged for a regular distribution of it. He used to visit **Pācīnadīpaka** in order to eat *jambu*-fruits there, and the people, annoyed by his visits, poisoned him. He was succeeded by **Saṅghabodhi.**[1]

[1] Mhv. xxxvi. 58 ff.; Dpv. xxii. 48 f.

2. **Saṅghatissa.**—Called **Asiggāha.** He succeeded **Aggabodhi II.** as king of Ceylon (611-13 A.C.). **Moggallāna** (afterwards **Moggallāna III.**)

rose against him, and **Anurādhapura** was deserted by the people. Saṅghatissa was once forced to eat food prepared for the monks at the **Mahāpāli**. His Senāpati proved treacherous, the king was defeated in battle and was forced to flee to **Merumajjara**. From there he went to **Veḷuvana**, where, at the suggestion of the monks, he put on yellow robes and went towards **Rohaṇa** with his son and minister. He was, however, recognized and taken captive at **Maṇihira**, brought to **Sīhagiri**, and beheaded at the command of Moggallāna. His son asked to be beheaded before him, and his request was granted; his minister was also beheaded, because he refused to leave his king. Saṅghatissa had another son, **Jeṭṭhatissa**.[1]

[1] Cv. xliv. 1 ff.; see Cv. *Trs.* i. 74, n. 1.

3. **Saṅghatissa**.—A viceroy (*uparāja*) of **Aggabodhi IV**. He built the **Uparājaka-pariveṇa**.[1]

[1] Cv. xlvi. 24.

Saṅghadāyikā.—See **Saṅghadāsī** (1).

1. **Saṅghadāsī**.—The youngest of the seven daughters of **Kiki**, king of Benares. She was **Visākhā** in the present age.[1] One day, as she was giving the five products of the cow to a company of twenty thousand monks, she persuaded them to accept her gifts even when they covered their bowls, saying: "Enough, enough." For this reason, when, as Visākhā, she was given cattle by her father at the time of her marriage, other herds of cattle joined them, in spite of the efforts of men to prevent them.[2]

The Apadāna,[3] however, gives her name as **Saṅghadāyikā**.

[1] J. vi. 481. [2] DhA. i. 396 f., 418. [3] Ap. ii. 655 (vs. 16).

2. **Saṅghadāsī**.—An eminent nun of **Jambudīpa**.[1]

[1] Dpv. xviii. 10.

1. **Saṅghapāla**.—A *pariveṇa*, residence of **Goṭhābhaya Thera**.[1] The Mahāvaṃsa Commentary[2] calls it *Saṅghapālaṅgaṇa*.

[1] xxxvi. 114. [2] MṬ. 673.

2. **Saṅghapāla**.—A monk of the **Mahāvihāra**, teacher of **Buddhaghosa**.[1] The **Vissuddhimagga** was composed according to the wishes of Saṅghapāla.[2]

[1] Cv. xxxvii. 232. [2] Vsm., p. 711.

Saṅghabodhi.—A **Lambakaṇṇa**, king of Ceylon (307-9 A.C.), generally called **Sirisaṅghabodhi**. He succeeded **Saṅghatissa** and set up a *salākā*-

house in the **Mahāvihāra.** He was a very good king, and made rain fall by virtue of his goodness. He quelled the Yakkha **Rattakkhi,** who devastated his territory. When his treasurer, **Goṭhakābhaya,** rose in revolt, he abdicated in his favour and became an ascetic. Later, he gave his head in gratitude to a poor man who gave him a meal, so that the man could win from the king the price which had been set on his head.[1]

The legend of the king surrendering his head is famous in Ceylon, and forms the theme of a Pāli Chronicle, the **Hatthavanagallavihāravaṃsa.**[2]

[1] Mhv. xxxvi. 73 ff.; Dpv. xxii. 53 f. [2] *q.v.*

Saṅghabhaddā.—A queen of **Aggabodhi II.**[1]

[1] Cv. xlii. 42.

Saṅghabheda Sutta.—The results of bringing about dissension in the Order.[1]

[1] A. v. 74.

Saṅghabedaka Jātaka.[1]—Probably another name for the **Sandhibheda Jātaka.** *Cf.* **Kosambī Jātaka.**

[1] J. iii. 211.

Saṅghabhedaka-Khandhaka.—The seventh chapter of the Culla Vagga of the Vinayapiṭaka.[1]

[1] Vin. ii. 180-206.

Saṅghabhedakagāma.—A village in **Rohaṇa,** mentioned in the account of the campaigns of **Parakkamabāhu I.**[1]

[1] Cv. lxxv. 125, 127.

Saṅghabhedaparisakkana Vatthu.—The story of how **Devadatta** informed **Ānanda** of his intention to bring about schism in the Order.[1]

[1] DhA. iii. 154 f.

Saṅghamāna.—A Malaya king.[1]

[1] Cv. xlvii. 3.

Saṅghamitta.—A **Coḷa** monk, follower of the **Vetullavāda.** At the **Thūpārāma** he defeated in argument the Thera **Goṭhābhaya,** and became a favourite of King **Goṭhābhaya,** being appointed tutor to his sons, **Jeṭṭhatissa** and **Mahāsena.** When Jeṭṭhatissa came to the throne, Saṅghamitta returned to Coḷa, as he was not greatly liked by the king; but on the accession of Mahāsena he returned to Ceylon. Acting on

Saṅghamitta's advice, Mahāsena decreed that no alms should be given to the monks of **Mahāvihāra,** and all the treasures belonging to **Mahāvihāra** were taken to **Abhayagiri** with the help of the minister **Soṇa.** Saṅghamitta had the **Lohapāsāda** destroyed. It was not till his favourite minister, **Meghavaṇṇābhaya,** rose in revolt against him, that Mahāsena saw the error of his ways and cast off Saṅghamitta. While the king was away, Saṅghamitta attempted to destroy the Thūpārāma, and one of the king's wives persuaded a labourer to kill both Saṅghamitta and Soṇa.[1]

[1] Mhv. xxxvi. 113 f.; xxxvii. 2 ff.; Cv. xxxviii. 55, 58.

Saṅghamitta-vihāra.—A monastery in Ceylon, restored by **Aggabodhi V.**[1]

[1] Cv. xlviii. 6.

Saṅghamittā Therī.—Daughter of **Asoka** and sister of **Mahinda.** She was born in **Ujjeni** and was married to **Aggibrahmā**—who later joined the Order—and had by him a son, **Sumana.** She was ordained in her eighteenth year together with **Mahinda,** her preceptor being **Dhammapālā** and her teacher **Āyupālā.**[1] After her ordination and attainment of arahantship she lived in **Pāṭaliputta,** and, when **Anuḷā** and other women of **Devānampiyatissa's** court at **Anurādhapura** wished to enter the Order, Devānampiyatissa, at Mahinda's suggestion, sent an embassy, led by **Ariṭṭha,** to Asoka, asking that Saṅghamittā might be sent to Ceylon, and with her a branch of the Bodhi-tree for Anurādhapura. Asoka granted the request, and sent Saṅghamittā, by sea, with eleven other nuns, carrying a branch of the Bodhi-tree. On the way, when **Nāgas** surrounded the Bodhi-tree, Saṅghamittā frightened them away by assuming the form of a **Garuḍa.** She landed at **Jambukola,** and, after her arrival at Anurādhapura, ordained Anulā and her companions. She lived at the **Upāsikā-vihāra,** and had twelve buildings erected there for the use of the nuns. Later, the king built for her the **Hatthāḷhaka-vihāra** (*q.v.*). She died at the age of fifty-nine, in the ninth year of the reign of King **Uttiya,** and celebrations, lasting one whole week, were held in her honour throughout Ceylon. Her body was cremated to the east of the Thūpārāma near the (later) **Cittasālā,** in sight of the Bodhi-tree, on a spot indicated by the Therī herself before her death. Uttiya had a *thūpa* erected over her ashes.[2]

[1] Mhv. v. 190-208; xiii. 4, 11; Dpv. vi. 17; vii. 18, 19; xv. 77, 90; xvii. 20; xviii. 11, 25; Sp. i. 51.

[2] Mhv. xviii. 13 f.; xix. 5, 20, 53, 65, 68 ff., 83 f.; xx. 48 ff.; Sp. i. 90 f.

1. **Saṅgharakkhita Thera.**—He belonged to a wealthy family of **Sāvatthi,** and, after joining the Order, lived with another monk in a

forest tract, meditating. Near them a doe had given birth in a thicket to a fawn. While she tended it, her love kept her always near it, and she was famished for lack of grass and water. On seeing her, the Thera repeated: "Alas ! this world suffers, bound in bonds of craving," and with this as his incentive, he developed insight and won arahantship. Seeing his companion cherish wrong thoughts, the Thera admonished him in a verse,[1] and he, too, became an arahant.

Ninety-four kappas ago, Saṅgharakkhita saw seven Pacceka Buddhas at the foot of a rock and offered them *kadamba*-flowers. Ninety-two kappas ago he was king seven times, under the name of **Phulla.**[2]

He is evidently identical with **Kadambapupphiya** of the Apadāna.[3]

[1] This is given in Thag. vs. 109. [2] ThagA. i. 216 f. [3] Ap. i. 178.

2. **Saṅgharakkhita.**—A monk, probably of Ceylon. Reference is made[1] to a novice under him who, seeing the king on an elephant's back, developed thoughts of the foulness of the body and became an arahant.

[1] Vsm. 194; DhsA. 200.

3. **Saṅgharakkhita.**—A novice, nephew of **Mahānāga Thera.** He became an arahant in the Tonsure-hall, and, having discovered that no other monk had made the **Vejayanta-pāsāda** tremble, on the very day he became an arahant, the novice, standing on it, tried in vain to shake it. The nymphs within laughed at him. Discomfited, he sought his teacher, who was spending his siesta in a cave on the edge of the ocean, and, having consulted him, he returned to Vejayanta. The nymphs again laughed at him, but he made a resolve that the space on which Vejayanta stood should turn into water. When this happened, he touched the pinnacle of the palace with his toe and it rocked till the nymphs begged for mercy.[1]

[1] DA. ii. 558 f.

4. **Saṅgharakkhita.**—See also **Bhāgineyya Saṅgharakkhita** and **Mahā-Saṅgharakkhita.**

5. **Saṅgharakkhita.**—A Thera of Ceylon. He was a pupil of **Sāriputta** and **Medhaṅkara.** He wrote several books dealing with grammar, rhetoric, and prosody: the **Vuttodaya, Subodhālaṅkāra, Susaddasiddhi, Sambandhacintā, Yogavinicchaya** and **Khuddasikkhā-ṭīkā.**[1]

[1] P.L.C. 197 f.; Gv. 6. 66. 71; Sās. 69. 70; Svd. 1209.

6. **Saṅgharakkhita.**—An Elder, who lived in the time of **Vijayabāhu III.** The king made him head of the Order and entrusted him with the Tooth

Relic and the Alms Bowl; he also gave into his charge the education of the heir to the throne.[1]

[1] Cv. lxxxi. 76 f.

7. **Saṅgharakkhita.**—An eminent monk in the time of **Kittisirirājasīha.** He was entrusted by the king with the restoration of the **Majjhapalli-vihāra.**[1]

[1] Cv. c. 234.

Saṅghasivā.—Wife of **Mahātissa.** She was the daughter of the ruler of **Rohaṇa** and had three sons: **Aggabodhi, Dappula** and **Maṇiakkhika.**[1]

[1] Cv. xlv. 39.

Saṅghasena.—A building in the **Mahāvihāra,** erected by **Sena I.** and his queen, **Saṅghā.**[1]

[1] Cv. l. 70.

Saṅghasenapabbata.—A building in the **Abhayagiri-vihāra,** erected by **Saṅghā,** wife of **Sena II.**[1]

[1] Cv. li. 86.

1. **Saṅghā Therī.**—She belonged to Prince **Siddhattha's** court, and having joined the Order with **Pajāpatī Gotamī,** became an arahant.[1]

[1] Thig. vs. 18; ThigA. 24.

2. **Saṅghā.**—Daughter of **Mahānāma** and step-sister of **Sotthisena.** She killed Sotthisena and gave the kingdom to her husband, who was his umbrella-bearer, but he died within a year.[1]

[1] Cv. xxxviii. 1 f.

3. **Saṅghā.**—Wife of King **Mānavamma.** She was the daughter of the **Malayarāja Saṅghasena.**[1]

[1] Cv. xlvii. 3, 8.

4. **Saṅghā.**—Daughter of **Aggabodhi VI.** and wife of **Aggabodhi VII.** Her husband once struck her in anger, and, when she complained to her father, he sent her to a nunnery. There her maternal cousin, also called **Aggabodhi,** became friendly with her and ran away with her to Rohaṇa. But her husband made war on him and seized both him and Saṅghā. After that husband and wife lived in peace.[1]

[1] Cv. xlviii. 54 ff.

5. **Saṅghā.**—Mahesī of **Sena I.** She and her husband built **the Pubbārāma** and the **Saṅghasenārāma** in the **Mahāvihāra.** Saṅghā also built the **Uttara-vihāra** and the **Mahindasena-pariveṇa.**[1]

[1] Cv. l. 7, 69, 79.

6. **Saṅghā.**—Daughter of **Kittaggabodhi** and **Devā** and wife of **Sena II.** She had a son (**Kassapa V.**). She built the **Saṅghasenapabbatārāma** and placed a sapphire diadem on the stone image of the Buddha.[1]

[1] Cv. l. 58; li. 6, 9, 86; Saṅghā's son (Kassapa V.), is called *dvayābhiseka-sañjāta* (born of the twice-anointed queen). Tradition has it that after the death of Sena II. she became the wife of his successor, who made her his *mahesī*.

7. **Saṅghā.**—Wife of **Kassapa V.** She was a daughter of **Mahinda,** *yuvarāja* of **Sena II.** and of **Tissā.**[1]

[1] Cv. li. 15, 18.

8. **Saṅghā.**—An *upāsikā*, mentioned among those who will wait on **Metteyya Buddha.** She will be his chief patron among lay-women.[1]

[1] Anāgat. vs. 61, 99.

Saṅghāṭagāma.—A village given by **Vijayabāhu I.** to the **Lābhavāsins.**[1]

[1] Cv. lx. 68.

Saṅghāta.—A **Niraya.** It is so called because massive rocks of heated iron meet and crush the victims.[1]

[1] J. v. 256, 270.

Saṅghādisesa.—The second division of the **Pārājikā** of the Vinayapiṭaka. It comprises thirteen rules, violation of which involves temporary separation from the Order.

Saṅghanandi.—A monk to whom is attributed the *Vutti* of **Kaccāyana's** grammar.[1]

[1] P.L.C. 180.

Saṅghupaṭṭhāka Thera.—An arahant. He was a servant in the monastery of **Vessabhū Buddha** and waited on the Saṅgha with great devotion. Seven kappas ago he was king seven times, under the name of **Samotthata.**[1]

[1] Ap. i. 191.

Sacakkhu.—Five kappas ago there were twelve kings of this name, previous births of **Ekadhammasavaṇiya** (or **Maggasaññaka**) **Thera.**[1]

[1] ThagA. i. 152; Ap. i. 151.

Sacitta Vagga.—The sixth chapter of the Dasaka Nipāta of the **Aṅguttara Nikāya.**[1]

[1] A. v. 92-112.

Sacitta Sutta.—Like a man or woman fond of self-adornment, examining the reflection of the face to see if it is clean, even so should a monk examine himself, and, finding evil qualities in himself, should strive to get rid of them as earnestly as though his head were on fire.[1]

[1] A. v. 92 f.

Sacca.—A Pacceka Buddha.[1]

[1] M. iii. 70; ApA. i. 107.

Sacca Saṃyutta.—The last section of the **Saṃyutta Nikāya.**[1] It was preached by **Mahinda** to **Anulā** and her companions, and they became *sotāpannas.*[2]

[1] S. v. 414-78. [2] Mhv. xiv. 58.

1. **Sacca Sutta.**—The Buddha visits the **Paribbājakārāma** on the **Sappinikā,** and tells the Paribbājakas that, in his view, the brahmin truths are as follows: all living things should be inviolate, all sense-delights are impermanent, painful, void of self; so with all becomings, "I have no part in anything anywhere, and herein, for me, there is no attachment to anything."[1]

[1] A. ii. 176 f.

2. **Sacca Sutta.**—The Buddha teaches Truth and the path thereto.[1]

[1] S. iv. 269.

Saccaka.—A **Nigaṇṭha** who had two interviews with the Buddha, as recorded in the **Cūla-Saccaka** and **Mahā-Saccaka Suttas** (*q.v.*). He is addressed as **Aggivessana,** that being his *gotta*-name (the *Agniveṣyāyanas*). Buddhaghosa says[1] that both his parents were Nigaṇṭhas, skilled debaters, who married at the suggestion of the **Licchavis,** because they were unable to defeat each other in argument. The Licchavis provided for their maintenance. Four daughters were born to them: **Saccā, Lolā, Paṭācārā**

[1] MA. i. 450; *cf.* J. iii. 1, where Sivāvatikā is called **Avavādakā.**

and **Sivāvatikā.** These engaged in a discussion with **Sāriputta,** and were defeated by him. Having then entered the Order, they became arahants. Saccaka was their brother and was the youngest of them. He was a teacher of the Licchavis and lived at **Vesāli.**

When Saccaka was defeated by the Buddha, as stated in the Cūla-Saccaka Sutta, one of the Licchavis, **Dummukha,** compared him to a crab in a pool, its claws being smashed one after the other and unable to return to the pool. Saccaka owned defeat, and begged the Buddha to take a meal at his house. The Buddha agreed, and Saccaka became his follower.[2]

It is said[3] that, in a later birth, long after the Buddha's death, Saccaka was born in Ceylon as the **Thera Kāḷa-Buddharakkhita** and attained arahantship. Saccaka is identified with **Senaka** of the **Mahāummagga Jātaka.**[4]

[2] M. i. 234 f. [3] MA. i. 469 f. [4] J. vi. 478.

Saccaka Sutta.—See **Cūla-Saccaka** and **Mahā-Saccaka** Suttas.

Sacca-kathā.—The second chapter of the **Yuganandha Vagga** of the **Paṭisambhidāmagga.**[1]

[1] Ps. ii. 104-15.

Saccakāmā.—See **Sabbakāmā.**

Saccakāli.—A younger brother of **Sumedha Buddha.** The Buddha preached to him his first sermon, and he became an arahant.[1]

[1] BuA. 164.

Saccaṅkira Jātaka (No. 73).—The king of Benares had a son called **Duṭṭhakumāra,** who was hated by everyone. One day, when he was bathing in the river, a storm came on, and he ordered his servants to take him into the middle of the river and there bathe him. The servants thereupon flung him into the water and reported to the king that he was lost. As he was swept along on the stream, he caught hold of a tree-trunk, and on to this tree-trunk there came to cling, also, a snake, a rat, and a parrot, who had all lost their dwelling-places in the storm. The Bodhisatta, who was an ascetic living on the bank of the river, rescued Duṭṭha and his companions and looked after them. When they bade him farewell, the snake said that he had forty crores hidden in a certain spot, and the ascetic had only to ask for these and they were his. The rat had thirty crores, also at the ascetic's disposal; the parrot promised the ascetic waggonloads of rice; and Duṭṭha promised to provide him with the four requisites. In his heart, however, he hated the ascetic for an imaginary slight, and vowed vengeance.

After Duṭṭha became king, the ascetic wished to test the faith of his former guests. He went to the snake and called out his name, and the snake at once appeared, offering his treasure. The rat and the parrot did likewise, but Duṭṭha, riding in a procession and seeing him from afar, gave orders that the ascetic should be beaten and put to death. On his way to the place of execution the ascetic kept on repeating: "They knew the world who framed this proverb true: a log pays better salvage than some men!" When asked what these words meant, he related the whole story.

The enraged citizens, seizing Duṭṭha, put him to death and made the ascetic king. Later, he brought the snake, the rat, and the parrot to the palace and looked after them.

The story was told in reference to **Devadatta's** attempts to kill the Buddha. Devadatta is identified with **Duṭṭha,** the snake with **Sāriputta,** the rat with **Moggallāna,** and the parrot with **Ānanda.**[1]

[1] J. i. 322-7.

Saccatapāvī.—A white-robed nun (*setasamaṇī*) who lived in a hut in a cemetery near Benares and abstained from four out of every five meals. She was held in high esteem. On a certain festival day, some goldsmiths were seated in a tent making merry. One of them, becoming sick through drink, vomited, saying: "Praise be to Saccatapāvī." One of the others called him a fool, saying that all women were alike, and accepted a wager of one thousand that he would seduce Saccatapāvī. The next day he disguised himself as an ascetic and stood near her hut, worshipping the sun. Saccatapāvī saw him and worshipped him, but he neither looked at her nor spoke. On the fourth day he greeted her, and on the sixth day, as she stood near him, they talked of the penances they practised, and the ascetic professed that his were far more severe than hers. But he confessed that he had found no spiritual calm; neither had she, and they agreed that it would be better to return to and enjoy the lay life. He brought her to the city, and having lain with her and made her drunk, he handed her over to his friends.

This story was related by **Kuṇāla** (*q.v.*), who said that he was the goldsmith of the story.[1]

[1] J. iv. 424, 427 f.

Saccanāmā.—One of the two chief women disciples of **Dhammadassī Buddha.**[1] *v.l.* **Sabbanāmā.**

[1] Bu. xvi. 19; J. i. 39.

Saccabaddha, Saccabandha.—A mountain between **Sāvatthi** and **Sunāparanta.** The Buddha stopped there on his way to see **Puṇṇa** in Sunāparanta, and preached to the hermit who lived on the mountain, and who also was called Saccabaddha. At the end of the sermon the hermit became an arahant. From Saccabaddha the Buddha went to Sunāparanta. On the way back to Sāvatthi he stopped at the river **Nammadā,** and from there he proceeded to Saccabaddha, where he left his footprint on the hard stone as clear as on kneaded clay. From Saccabaddha he returned to **Jetavana.**[1]

There is in Siam a sacred mountain called **Saccabandhava,** which holds a footprint of the Buddha, said to have appeared there miraculously. Perhaps it is to be identified with the above. **King Dhammika** of Siam sent a model of this footprint, together with other gifts, to **Kittisirirājasīha,** king of Ceylon.[2]

[1] SA. iii. 17 f.; MA. ii. 1017 f.   [2] Cv. c. 253; Cv. *Trs.* ii. 295, n. 2.

Saccavibhaṅga Sutta.—The Buddha addresses the monks in the Migadāya at **Isipatana** and tells them how he had first preached the Four Noble Truths there. He exhorts them to follow **Sāriputta** and **Moggallāna,** and then retires to his cell. Sāriputta takes up the discourse and gives a detailed explanation of the Truths.[1]

[1] M. iii. 248-52. This sutta is incorporated in the concluding portion of the **Mahāsatipaṭṭhāna Sutta** (*q.v.*).

Saccasaṅkhepa.—A short treatise of five chapters on Abhidhamma topics. It was written by **Culladhammapāla.**[1] The **Saddhammasaṅgaha**[2] attributes it to Dhammapāla's teacher, **Ānanda. Vācissara** and **Sumaṅgala** wrote *ṭīkās* on it, the first being older than the second.[3]

[1] Gv. 60, 71, 75; Sās. 89; Svd. 1220.   [2] p. 64.   [3] P.L.C. 203 f.

Saccasaññaka Thera.—An arahant. Twenty-nine kappas ago he heard **Vessabhū Buddha** preach, and was reborn in the deva-world. Twenty-six kappas ago he was King **Ekaphusita** (*v.l.* **Ekapaññita**).[1]

[1] Ap. i. 209.

Saccasandha.—See **Janasandha.**

Saccā.—A **Licchavi** maiden, daughter of a Nigaṇṭha and a Nigaṇṭhī. She was sister to **Saccaka.** She was a great disputant, and, one day, she and her sisters, **Paṭācarā, Lolā** and **Avavādakā,** engaged in a dispute with

Sāriputta. Having been defeated, she joined the Order and became an arahant.[1]

[1] J. iii. 1 f.

Sacchikātabba Sutta.—One should realize the All as impermanent, woeful, void of self.[1]

[1] S. iv. 29.

Sacchikiriyā Sutta.—The eight releases must be realized by one's own person; former life by recollections; the death and rebirth of beings by sight; and the destruction of the *āsavas* by wisdom.[1]

[1] A. ii. 182.

Sañcetanika Vagga.—The eighteenth chapter of the Catukka Nipāta of the **Aṅguttara Nikāya.**[1]

[1] A. ii. 157-70.

Sajjā.—One of the four daughters of **Vessavaṇa.**[1] See **Latāvimāna.**

[1] VvA. 371.

Sajjanela.—A Koliyan village, the residence of **Suppavāsā Koliyadhītā,** mother of **Sīvalī.** The Buddha is said to have stayed there.[1]

[1] A. ii. 62.

Sajjha.—A **Paribbājaka** who visited the Buddha at **Gijjhakūṭa.** The Buddha told him of the nine standards which an arahant monk cannot possibly transgress.[1]

[1] A. iv. 371.

Sajjha Sutta.—Contains the story of **Sajjha's** visit to the Buddha.[1]

[1] A. iv. 371.

Sajjhadāyaka Thera.—An arahant, evidently identical with **Mudita Thera.**[1] *v.l.* **Pacchidāyaka.**

[1] Ap. i. 284 f.; ThagA. i. 401.

Sajjhāya Sutta.—See **Dhamma Sutta** (4).

1. **Sañjaya.**—A gardener (*uyyānapāla*) of **Brahmadatta,** king of Benares. See the **Vātamiga Jātaka.** He is identified with the slave girl who tried to tempt **Cullapiṇḍapātika-Tissa Thera.**[1]

[1] J. i. 156 f.

2. **Sañjaya.**—A rājā of **Tagara.** He renounced the world with ninety crores of others and became an ascetic. **Dhammadassī Buddha** preached to them and they all attained arahantship.[1]

[1] Bu. xvi. 3; BuA. 183.

3. **Sañjaya.**—Father of **Vessantara.** He was the son of **Sivi,** king of **Jetuttara,** and after his father's death succeeded him as king. His wife was **Phusatī.** He is identified with **Suddhodana** of the present age.[1]

[1] See the **Vessantara Jātaka** for details. He is mentioned in a list of kings at Dpv. iii. 42.

4. **Sañjaya Thera.** He was the son of a wealthy brahmin of **Sāvatthi,** and, following the example of **Brahmāyu, Pokkharasāti,** and other well-known brahmins, found faith in the Buddha and became a *sotāpanna.* He entered the Order and attained arahantship in the Tonsure-hall.

In the time of **Vipassī Buddha** he spent all his wealth in good deeds and was left poor. Even then he continued to wait on the Buddha and his monks and led a good life. Eight kappas ago he was a king named **Sucintita.**[1] He is evidently to be identified with **Veyyāvacaka Thera** of the Apadāna.[2]

[1] Thag. vs. 48; ThagA. i. 119 f. [2] Ap. i. 138.

5. **Sañjaya-Ākāsagotta.**—In the **Kaṇṇakatthala Sutta** (*q.v.*) **Viḍūdabha** tells the Buddha that it was Sañjaya who started the story round the palace to the effect that, according to the Buddha, no recluse or brahmin can ever attain to absolute knowledge and insight. Sañjaya is sent for by **Pasenadi,** but, on being questioned, says that Viḍūdabha was responsible for the statement.[1]

[1] M. ii. 127, 132.

6. **Sañjaya.**—Son of the brahmin **Vidhura** and younger brother of **Bhadrakāra.** See the **Sambhava Jātaka.** He is identified with **Sāriputta.**[1]

[1] J. v. 67.

7. **Sañjaya-Belaṭṭhiputta.**—One of the six famous heretical teachers of the Buddha's day. He was a great sceptic, his teaching being the evasion of problems and the suspension of judgment. His doctrines seem to have been identical with those of the **Amarāvikkhepikas** ("Eel-wrigglers") who, when asked a question, would equivocate and wriggle like an eel.[1]

It is probable that Sañjaya suspended his judgments only with regard to those questions the answers to which must always remain a matter of

[1] Sañjaya's teachings are given at D. i. 58; *cf.* the "Eel-wrigglers" at D. i. 27.

speculation. It may be that he wished to impress on his followers the fact that the final answer to these questions lay beyond the domain of speculation, and that he wished to divert their attention from fruitless enquiry and direct it towards the preservation of mental equanimity. Buddhaghosa gives us no particulars about Sañjaya, beyond the fact that he was the son of **Belaṭṭha.**[2] Sanskrit texts call him Sañjayī-Vairaṭiputra[3] and Sañjayi-Vairaṭṭīputra.[4]

He is evidently identical with Sañjaya the Paribbājaka who was the original teacher of **Sāriputta** and **Moggallāna.**[5] It is said[6] that when these two disciples left Sañjaya to become pupils of the Buddha, they were joined by two hundred and fifty others. Sañjaya then fainted, and hot blood issued from his mouth. The Paribbājaka **Suppiya** (*q.v.*) was also a follower of Sañjaya.[7]

Barua thinks[8] that the **Aviruddhakas** mentioned in the Aṅguttara[9] were also followers of Sañjaya—that they were called Amarāvikkhepakā for their philosophical doctrines, and Aviruddhakā for their moral conduct.

[2] DA. i. 144.
[3] *E.g.*, Mtu. iii. 59 f.
[4] *E.g.*, Dvy. 143, 145.
[5] Vin. i. 39.
[6] *Ibid.*, 42; according to DhA. i. 78, Sāriputta and Moggallāna tried to persuade Sañjaya to accept the Buddha's doctrine, but they failed, and only one half of his disciples joined them.
[7] DA. i. 35.
[8] *Op. cit.*, 326.
[9] A. iii. 276.

Sañjikāputta.—A young brahmin, friend of **Bodhirājakumāra.** He was sent to invite the Buddha to Bodhi's palace, **Kokanada.**[1] When Bodhi formed a plan to kill the architect of Kokanada, lest he should build another similar palace, Sañjikāputta warned the architect of Bodhi's intention.[2]

[1] Vin. ii. 127 f.; M. ii. 91.
[2] DhA. iii. 134.

1. **Sañjīva.**—One of the two chief disciples of **Kakusandha Buddha.**[1] He was expert in *samādhi*, and lived in cells, caves, etc., sustaining himself on *samādhi*. One day, when in a state of trance in a forest, woodmen, thinking him dead, burnt his body, but he, emerging at the proper time from his trance, shook out his robes and entered the village for alms; hence his name, *Sañjīva* (" Quick ").[2] This feat is referred to as an example of *samādhivipphāra-iddhi.*[3]

[1] D. ii. 4; J. i. 42; Bu. xxiii. 20.
[2] M. i. 333; *cf.* DA. ii. 417; MA. i. 522; PSA. 496.
[3] *E.g.*, Vsm. 380, 706; PS. ii. 212; BuA. 24, etc.

2. **Sañjīva.**—A **Niraya.** Beings born there are subjected to numerous tortures, but contrive to survive them; hence the name.[1]

[1] J. v. 266, 270.

3. **Sañjīva.**—A brahmin who could bring the dead to life; see the **Sañjīva Jātaka.** He is identified with **Ajātasattu.**[1]

[1] J. i. 511.

Sañjīva Jātaka (No. 150).—The Bodhisatta was a famous teacher in Benares, and among his pupils was a young brahmin, **Sañjīva,** who was taught a spell for raising the dead, but not the counter spell. One day he went with his companions into the forest, and they came across a dead tiger. He uttered the charm and restored it to life. The tiger instantly killed him and fell down dead again.

The story was told in reference to **Ajātasattu** after his visit to the Buddha. The Buddha said that had it not been for his crime of patricide he would have become a *sotāpanna,* but because of his early association with **Devadatta,** he had committed numerous bad deeds and shut himself out from that possibility.

Sañjīva is identified with Ajātasattu.[1]

[1] J. i. 508-11.

Saññaka Thera.—An arahant. Ninety-two kappas ago he saw the rag robe of **Tissa Buddha** hanging on a tree and worshipped it. Four kappas ago he was a king named **Dumasāra.**[1]

[1] Ap. i. 120.

Saññasāmika Thera.—An arahant. Ninety-four kappas ago he mastered the Vedas when only seven years old. He prepared a great sacrifice about which he consulted **Siddhattha Buddha.** The Buddha taught him that happiness was not to be found that way, and the boy, following his advice, was reborn in **Tusita.**[1]

[1] Ap. i. 261.

Saññā Vagga.—The seventh chapter of the Pañcaka Nipāta of the **Aṅguttara Nikāya.**[1]

[1] A. iii. 79 f.

1. **Saññā Sutta.**—The thought of foulness, death, peril, cloying of food, distaste—these, if cultivated, are of great advantage.[1]

[1] A. iii. 79.

2. **Saññā Sutta.**—The thoughts of impermanence, of not-self, death, the cloying of food, distaste—these, if developed, lead to great profit.[1]

[1] A. iii. 79.

3. **Saññā Sutta.**—To get rid of thoughts of sense-desire, ill-will and harm, their opposites must be cultivated.[1]

[1] A. iii. 446.

4. **Saññā Sutta.**—Thoughts of impermanence, not-self, unlovely things, peril, renunciation, dispassion, ending—these lead to growth and not to decline.[1]

[1] A. iv. 24.

5. **Saññā Sutta.**—Thoughts of the unattractive, death, cloying of food, all-world discontent, impermanence, of all therein, of no-self in ill—are of great advantage.[1]

[1] A. iv. 46.

6. The same as (5), in greater detail.[1]

[1] A. iv. 47.

7. **Saññā Sutta.**—Same as (5), with the addition of thoughts of abandoning, fading, and ending.[1]

[1] A. v. 105.

8. **Saññā Sutta.**—The same as (2), with the addition of thoughts of the skeleton, worms, discoloured corpse, fissured corpse, and swollen corpse.[1]

[1] A. v. 106.

9. **Saññā Sutta.**—If a recluse develops the thoughts that he has come to the state of being an outcast, that his life is dependent on others, that he must now behave differently—that will develop in him the seven conditions.[1]

[1] A. v. 210 f.

10. **Saññā Sutta.**—Diversity of thoughts is due to diversity of elements; hence arises diversity of aims, desires, yearnings, and quests.[1]

[1] S. ii. 143.

11. **Saññā Sutta.**—Perception of a visible object is fleeting.[1]

[1] S. ii. 247.

12. **Saññā Sutta.**—Perception of body is impermanent; likewise sound, scent, etc.[1]

[1] S. iii. 227.

13. **Saññā Sutta.**—See **Aniccatā Sutta.**

1. **Saññāmanasikāra Sutta.**—**Ānanda** asks the Buddha how a monk can so develop concentration that he is quite unaware of all that is seen, heard, sensed, cognized, attained, sought after, or thought of. By the calming of all activities, the ending of craving, by Nibbāna, answers the Buddha.[1]

[1] A. v. 318 f.

2. **Saññāmanasikāra Sutta.**—Ānanda asks the same question as in (1), and the Buddha gives the same answer.[1]

[1] A. v. 319 f.

3. **Saññāmanasikāra Sutta.**—**Ānanda** asks the Buddha how a monk can so develop concentration that he pays no heed to what is seen, heard, etc., and yet does so. The answer is as in (1).[1]

[1] A. v. 321 f.

Saññī Sutta.—**Sāriputta** explains to **Ānanda** how he dwelt in the sphere of " neither perception nor non-perception."[1]

[1] S. iii. 238.

Saññojana Sutta.—The seven fetters—of complying, resisting, of view, uncertainty, conceit, worldly lusts, and ignorance.[1]

[1] A. iv. 7.

Saṭayha Sutta.—See **Ogadha Sutta.**

Saṭṭhikūṭa(sahassa)peta.—There was once a cripple in Benares adept in throwing stones. He lived at the city gate, under a banyan tree, and cut the leaves of the tree into different shapes for children who gave him some of their food. One day, the king discovered his skill and engaged his services to throw a pint-pot of goat's dung into the mouth of a brahmin who never stopped talking. The cripple sat behind a curtain through which he threw the pellets of dung as the brahmin talked. Then the king told the brahmin, and he was cured of his talking and the cripple won great wealth. Desiring gain, a certain man ministered to the cripple and learnt his art, and, when he left, the cripple warned him not to throw stones at anyone who had father or mother or owner. While wandering about, the man came across the Pacceka Buddha **Sunetta,** and, thinking him a fit victim, threw a stone through his ear. The Pacceka Buddha suffered great pain and died. When it was discovered, the man was killed and was reborn in **Avīci.** Later he became a peta on **Gijjhakūṭa,** and **Moggallāna** saw him going through the air, while sixty thousand blazing hammers rose and fell on his head.[1]

[1] Pv. iv. 16; PvA. 282-6; DhA. ii. 68 ff; *cf.* J. i. 418 f.. (**Sālittaka Jātaka**).

Saṭṭhipeyyāla.—A series of short suttas, forming the seventeenth chapter of the **Saḷāyatana Saṃyutta.**[1]

[1] S. iv. 148-57.

Saṇṭhita Thera.—An arahant. Thirty-one kappas ago he saw the *assattha*-bodhi of a Buddha and fixed his mind on him. Thirteen kappas ago he was a king, named **Dhaniṭṭha.**[1]

[1] Ap. i. 210 f.

Saṇhā.—An eminent Therī of Ceylon.[1]

[1] Dpv. xviii. 38.

Satacakkhu.—A king of thirty-four kappas ago, a previous birth of **Pañcadīpaka Thera.**[1]

[1] Ap. i. 108.

Satadhamma, Santadhamma.—A youth of Benares. See the **Satadhamma Jātaka.**

Satadhamma Jātaka (No. 179).—The Bodhisatta was once born in the lowest caste, and one day went on a journey, taking his food in a basket. On the way he met a young man from Benares, Satadhamma, a magnifico. They travelled together, and when the time came for the meal, because Satadhamma had no food, the Bodhisatta offered him some. " I could not possibly take yours," said the magnifico, " because you are the lowest of the low." The Bodhisatta ate some of the food and put the rest away. In the evening they bathed, and the Bodhisatta ate without offering Satadhamma anything. The latter had expected to be asked again and was very hungry. But finding that he was offered nothing, he asked the Bodhisatta for some and ate it. As soon as he had finished he was seized with remorse that he should thus have disgraced his family. So greatly was he upset that he vomited the food, and with it some blood. He plunged into the wood and was never heard of again.

The story was related in reference to monks who earned their living in the twenty-one unlawful ways, as physicians, messengers, etc. The Buddha summoned them and warned that food unlawfully come by was like red-hot iron, a deadly poison. It was like partaking of the leavings of the vilest of mankind.[1]

[1] J. ii. 82-5.

1. **Satapatta.**—A king of seventy-three kappas ago, a previous birth of **Naḷinakesariya Thera.**[1]

[1] Ap. i. 223.

2. **Satapatta.**—A palace, once occupied by **Ukkhittapadumiya Thera.**[1]

[1] Ap. i. 275.

Satapatta Jātaka (No. 279).—A landowner of Benares had given one thousand to some one and had died before recovering it. His wife, lying on her deathbed, asked her son to get it for her while she was yet alive. He went and recovered the money; but while he was away his mother died, and, because of her great love for him, was born as a jackal. She tried to prevent him from entering a wood infested with robbers, headed by the Bodhisatta, but the man did not understand what the jackal said and kept on driving her away. A crane, flying overhead, cried out to the robbers, announcing the lad's approach, but he, taking it to be a bird of good omen, saluted it. The Bodhisatta heard both sounds, and when his band captured the man, he told him that he did not know how to distinguish between friend and foe and sent him off with a warning.

The story was told in reference to two of the **Chabbaggiyā, Paṇḍu** and **Lohitaka.** They questioned the Buddha's teachings on certain points and encouraged others to do the same, the result being quarrel and strife. The Buddha sent for them and told them that this was a foolish policy; they did not know what was good for them.[1]

[1] J. ii. 387-90.

Sataporisa.—A **Niraya,** meant especially for matricides. It is filled with decaying corpses.[1]

[1] J. v. 269, 274.

1. **Sataraṃsi.**—A Pacceka Buddha of ninety-four kappas ago to whom **Ambayāgudāyaka,** in a previous birth, gave a meal of mango-curry (? *ambayāgu*).[1]

[1] Ap. i. 284.

See also under **Sigālapitā** and **Sambulakaccāyana,** who are mentioned as having given him *tāla*-fruits as offerings.

2. **Sataraṃsi.**—Twelve kappas ago there were eight kings of this name, previous births of **Maṇipūjaka Thera.**[1]

[1] Ap. i. 190.

Sataraṃsika Thera.—An arahant. In the past he saw **Padumuttara Buddha** and worshipped him. In this life he joined the Order at the age of seven, and rays constantly issued from his body. Sixty thousand kappas ago he was king four times under the name of **Roma.**[1]

[1] Ap. i. 104 f.

Satarasa.—A kind of food which **Paripuṇṇaka Thera** was in the habit of eating before joining the Order.[1] It was probably made of one hundred essences.

[1] ThagA. i. 190.

Sataruddhā.—A canal flowing eastward from the **Aciravatī** Channel in Ceylon.[1]

[1] Cv. lxxix. 53.

Sati Vagga.—The ninth chapter of the Aṭṭhaka Nipāta of the **Aṅguttara Nikāya.**[1]

[1] A. iv. 336-50.

1. **Sati Sutta.**—Mindfulness is necessary for one who sees not things as they really are.[1]

[1] A. ii. 132.

2. **Sati Sutta.**—When mindfulness and self-possession are lacking, various evil results follow, as in the case of a tree which is devoid of branches and foliage.[1]

[1] A. iv. 336 f.

Satipaṭṭhāna Vagga.—The seventh chapter of the Navaka Nipāta of the **Aṅguttara Nikāya.**[1]

[1] A. iv. 457-61.

Satipaṭṭhāna Saṃyutta.—The forty-seventh section of the **Saṃyutta Nikāya.**[1]

[1] S. v. 141-2.

1. **Satipaṭṭhāna Sutta.**—The tenth sutta of the **Majjhima Nikāya.** It is identical with the **Mahā-Satipaṭṭhāna Sutta** of the Dīgha Nikāya, except that towards the end the Dīgha Sutta interpolates paragraphs explaining in detail the Four Noble Truths. These, in the Majjhima, form a separate sutta, the **Sacca-Vibhaṅga Sutta** (*q.v.*).

2. **Satipaṭṭhāna Sutta.**—A monk who is mindful regarding the rise and fall of things sees nothing attractive in the body, is conscious of the cloying of food, has distaste for the world, and perceives impermanence in the "Compounded"—such a one becomes either an arahant in this life or an *anāgāmī*.[1]

[1] A. iii. 142.

3. **Satipaṭṭhāna Sutta.**—The four *satipaṭṭhānas* form the path that goes to the "Uncompounded."[1]

[1] S. iv. 360.

4. **Satipaṭṭhāna Sutta.**—A monk who abides, contemplating body, etc., follows the path to the "Uncompounded."[1]

[1] S. iv. 363.

Satipaṭṭhānakathā.—The eighth chapter of the **Paññā Vagga** of the **Paṭisambhidāmagga.**[1]

[1] PS. ii. 232-6.

Satulakāyī.—The wife of **Jotika.** She came to him from **Uttarakuru** and brought with her a single pint-pot of rice and three burning-glasses (crystals). Whenever a meal was desired, the pot was placed on the crystals and the crystals blazed up. The food so prepared was never exhausted. When Jotika joined the Order, the divinities took Satulakāyī back to Uttarakuru.[1]

[1] DhA. iv. 209, 223.

Satullapakāyikā.—A class of **Devas.** The Saṃyutta contains[1] a whole group of suttas in which these devas are stated to have visited the Buddha, asking him several questions on different topics.

Buddhaghosa says[2] that, in a previous birth, they were a ship's crew on a trading line. Their vessel was overwhelmed by stormy seas, and sank with all on board. During the storm, the terrified crew saw one of their number seated like a *yogī*, calm and self-possessed. On being asked what he thought of, he said he thought of the good deeds he had done

[1] S. i. 16-22. [2] SA. i. 43 f.

before starting on the voyage. These would ensure him happy rebirth, so why should he worry ? The others then implored his assistance and compassion. He divided them into seven groups of one hundred each, and shouted to them, above the tempest, the Five Precepts, assuring them that their *sīla* would bring them to a happy dawn. They took the precepts as the waters rose, and were reborn in **Sakka's** heaven, in different groups, each with his own *vimāna*. Their teacher had a golden *vimāna* of one hundred leagues in the middle of the others. As soon as born they realized the reason for their happiness, and visited the Buddha in order to praise their wonderful teacher. They were called **Satullapā** because they shouted the precepts while divided in groups of one hundred (*sata-ullapā*).

1. **Sato Sutta.**—The Buddha tells the monks, at **Ambapālivana,** how to be mindful and composed.[1]

[1] S. v. 142.

2. **Sato Sutta.**—The same as (1), but differently treated in detail.[1]

[1] S. v. 180.

3. **Sato Sutta.**—The Buddha instructs the monks how to be mindful.[1]

[1] S. v. 186.

1. **Satta Sutta.**—Seven things which help a monk to destroy the *āsavas*.[1]

[1] A. iv. 85.

2. **Satta Sutta.**—The Buddha explains to **Rādha** what is meant by " *satta* " (being).[1]

[1] S. iii. 189.

3. **Satta Sutta.**—On the nine spheres of being, as regards body, perceptive power, feeling, consciousness, etc.[1]

[1] A. iv. 401 f.

Sattakadambapupphiya Thera.—An arahant. Ninety-four kappas ago he met seven Pacceka Buddhas on **Kadamba** Mountain and offered them seven garlands of *kadamba*-flowers.[1]

[1] Ap. i. 382 f.

Sattakammapatha Sutta.—On seven courses of action.[1]

[1] S. ii. 167.

Sattaṭṭhāna Sutta.—Seven points, skill in which makes a monk who is an investigator in three separate ways claim to accomplish in the Dhammavinaya, one who has reached mastership (*vusitavā*), a superman (*uttamapuriso*).[1]

[1] S. iii. 61 f.

Sattadāraka-pañha.—A section of the **Mahāummagga Jātaka,** dealing with seven riddles solved by **Mahosadha.**[1]

[1] J. vi. 339.

Sattanāsa Sutta.—On the unworthy man and the still more unworthy; the worthy man and the still more worthy.[1]

[1] A. ii. 218.

Sattapaṇṇaka-pāsāda.—A building in **Anurādhapura** for the residence of the monks, evidently built by **Vohārikatissa.**[1] The Mahāvaṃsa Commentary[2] says that it was attached to the palace.

[1] Mhv. xxxvi. 32.
[2] MṬ. 662.

Sattapaṇṇiguhā.—A cave in **Rājagaha,** on the slope of Mount **Vebhāra.** Once, when the Buddha was staying there, he gave to **Ānanda** the opportunity of asking him to live for an æon, but Ānanda, because of his unmindfulness, failed to take it.[1] The cave was sometimes used as a residence for monks coming from afar.[2] According to the Commentaries and the Chronicles[3] the First Council was held in a hall erected by **Ajātasattu** outside the Sattapaṇṇiguhā.

[1] D. ii. 116.
[2] *E.g.*, Vin. ii. 76; iii. 159.
[3] S. i. 9; Sp. i. 10; Mhv. iii. 19; Dpv. iv. 14; v. 5; ThagA. i. 351; the cave is not mentioned in the Vinaya account of the Council, in the eleventh chapter of the Culla Vagga.

Sattapaṇṇiya Thera.—An arahant. One hundred thousand kappas ago he offered a *sattapaṇṇi*-flower to **Sumana Buddha.**[1]

[1] Ap. i. 292.

Sattapaduminiya Thera.—An arahant. Ninety-four kappas ago he was a brahmin, named **Nesāda,** and, seeing **Siddhattha Buddha** in the forest, he swept his hut and offered lotus-flowers. Seven kappas ago he was king four times, under the name of **Pādapāvara.**[1]

[1] Ap. i. 254.

Sattapāṭaliya Thera.—An arahant. Ninety-four kappas ago he saw the Buddha (? **Siddhattha**) and offered him *pāṭali*-flowers.[1]

[1] Ap. i. 227.

Sattaputtakhādakā.—A *petī* who ate seven of her children because of a false oath sworn by her in a previous birth.[1] *Cf.* **Pañcaputtakhādakā.**

[1] Pv. i. 7; PvA. 36 f.

Sattabhariyā Sutta.—Once, when the Buddha visited **Anāthapiṇḍika's** house, he heard a great noise, and when he asked the reason for this, he was told that it was due to Anāthapiṇḍika's daughter-in-law, **Sujātā,** who had come from a wealthy family and would not listen to anyone's advice. The Buddha sent for her and told her of seven kinds of wives in the world—the slayer, the robber, the mistress, the mother, the sister, the companion, the handmaid—and described their qualities. Sujātā, much impressed, said that henceforth she would be a handmaid.[1]

The Commentary says[2] that she was established in the Refuges; but see *s.v.* **Sujātā.**

[1] A. iv. 91 f.

[2] AA. ii. 724.

Sattabhū.—The king of the **Kāliṅgas** in the time of **Reṇu.** His purohita was **Jotipāla,** and his capital, **Dantapura.**[1]

[1] D. ii. 236.

Sattamba, Sattambaka.—A shrine near **Vesāli.**[1] It was so called because, in the past, seven princesses, daughters of **Kiki,** king of Benares, left Rājagaha and fought for attainment at that spot. It was originally dedicated to some deity, but after the Buddha's visit to Vesāli, it became a place of residence for him.[2] It was to the west of Vesāli.[3]

[1] D. ii. 102; Ud. vi. 1; S. v. 259; A. iv. 309, etc.

[2] UdA. 323, etc.

[3] D. iii. 9.

Sattarasavaggiyā.—A group of monks in the Buddha's time, who seem to have incurred the enmity of the **Chabbaggiyas** (*q.v.*). The latter turned them out of a vihāra as soon as they had prepared it, and were violent towards them.[1]

[1] Vin. ii. 166; *cf.* DhA. iii. 48 f.

"Satta vassāni" Sutta.—**Māra** approaches the Buddha under the **Ajapālanigrodha** in **Uruvelā,** and engages him in conversation. He asks the Buddha to go about among men and make friends and be happy, satisfied with having discovered the path of immortality for himself without feeling it necessary to teach others. But the Buddha refuses his request, and Māra confesses that he has no longer any power over him; he is like a crab whose claws have been broken one by one. The sutta adds that Māra had been awaiting an opportunity to find a flaw in the Buddha for seven years.[1] He retires discomfited and sits not far away from the Buddha, brooding, scratching the earth with a stick.[2]

[1] The Commentary adds "six before the Enlightenment and one after."
[2] S. i. 122 ff.

Sattasatikakhandhaka.—The twelfth chapter of the Culla Vagga of the Vinayapiṭaka. It gives an account of the Second Council.[1]

[1] Vin. ii. 294 f.

Sattasirīsaka.—A group of seven *sirīsaka*-trees, near Benares, where the Buddha preached to the Nāga-king **Erakaputta** (*q.v.*).[1]

[1] DhA. iii. 230, 232.

Sattasuriya Sutta.—Mentioned in the scholiast to the **Ayoghara Jātaka.**[1] The reference is evidently to the **Suriya Sutta** of the **Aṅguttara Nikāya.**[2]

[1] J. iv. 498.
[2] A. iv. 100 f.; see **Suriya Sutta** (1).

Sattānisaṃsa Sutta.—Seven advantages resulting from the cultivation of the five *indriyas.*[1]

[1] S. v. 237.

Sattāvāsa Vagga.—The third chapter of the Navaka Nipāta of the **Aṅguttara Nikāya.**[1]

[1] A. iv. 396-409.

Sattāhapabbajita Thera.—An arahant. Ninety-one kappas ago he had a quarrel with his kinsmen and joined the Order under **Vipassī Buddha** for seven days. Sixty-seven kappas ago he was king seven times, under the name of **Sunikkhamma.**[1]

[1] Ap. i. 242.

Satti Vagga.—The third chapter of the **Devatā Saṃyutta.**[1]

[1] S. i. 13-16.

Satti Sutta.—Attempts to overthrow a mind which had developed liberation of the will through love are as futile as the attempt to double up a sharp spear.[1]

[1] S. ii. 265.

Sattigumba.—**Devadatta** born as a parrot. See the **Sattigumba Jātaka.**

Sattigumba Jātaka (No. 503).—Two parrots were once carried away by the wind during the moulting season. One of them fell among the weapons in a robber-village and was called **Sattigumba;** the other fell in a hermitage among flowers and was called **Pupphaka.** He was the Bodhisatta. One day, **Pañcāla,** king of **Uttarapañcāla,** went out hunting. While chasing the deer with his charioteer, he was separated from his bodyguard and found himself in a glen near the robbers' village. There he slept. The robbers were absent, leaving only Sattigumba and a cook, named **Patikolamba.** The parrot, seeing the king, plotted with the cook to kill him. The king overheard the plan and fled with his charioteer. In his flight he came to the hermitage, where he was made welcome by Pupphaka till the return of the sages. The king told his story, and Pupphaka explained that though he and Sattigumba were brothers, their upbringing had been different, which accounted for the difference in their natures. The king decreed immunity to all parrots and provided for the comfort of sages in his park.

The story was told in reference to **Devadatta's** attempt to kill the Buddha by hurling a stone at him. Sattigumba is identified with Devadatta and the king with **Ānanda.**[1]

[1] J. iv. 430-7.

Sattipaṇṇiya Thera.—An arahant. One hundred thousand kappas ago he offered a *satti*-flower to the body of the Buddha (? **Padumuttara**) when it was being taken for cremation.[1] He is evidently identical with **Vimala Thera.**[2]

[1] Ap. ii. 406. [2] ThagA. i. 377.

Sattimāgavī Sutta.—The story of a peta seen by **Moggallāna,** going through the air while javelins kept rising and falling on his body. He had been a deer-hunter in **Rājagaha.**[1]

[1] S. ii. 257.

" Sattiyā " Sutta.—The Buddha tells a deva that *sakkāyadiṭṭhi* should be got rid of by a monk as though he were smitten down by an impending sword.[1]

[1] S. i. 13.

Sattisata Sutta.—A wise householder should be glad if an offer were made to him that he should comprehend the Four Noble Truths after being tormented with one hundred spears three times a day for one hundred years. For incalculable is *saṃsāra*.[1]

[1] S. v. 440.

Sattisūla.—A Niraya. **Ajjuna** was once born there because he tortured **Aṅgirasa Gotama.** His body was three leagues in height. The attendants pierced him with red-hot stakes and made him mount a heated iron mountain. From there a wind threw him down on to a stake.[1]

[1] J. v. 143, 145.

1. **Sattuka.**—A robber. See the **Sulasā Jātaka.**

2. **Sattuka.**—The son of a chaplain of **Rājagaha.** He later turned robber.[1] For the story, see **Bhaddā Kuṇḍalakesā.** *v.l.* **Satthuka.**

[1] ThigA. 99; AA. i. 200; *cf.* DhA. ii. 217 f.

3. **Sattuka.** A sage of old.[1]

[1] Ap. i. 46 (vs. 123).

Sattuttama.—A **Cakkavatti** of nine kappas ago, a previous birth of **Kakkārupupphiya (Jenta) Thera.**[1]

[1] Ap. i. 177; ThagA. i. 220.

Sattuppalamālikā Therī.—An arahant.[1] Evidently identical with **Abhayā Therī** (*q.v.*).[2]

[1] Ap. ii. 517.

[2] ThigA. 42 f.

Sattubhasta Jātaka (No. 402).—The Bodhisatta was once **Senaka,** counsellor to **Janaka,** king of Benares. He preached the Law once a fortnight, on fast days, and large numbers of people, including the king, went to hear him.

An old brahmin, begging for alms, was given one thousand pieces. He gave these to another brahmin to take care of, but the latter spent them, and when the owner came to ask for them, he gave his young daughter as wife, instead of the pieces. This girl had a lover, and, in order to be able to see him, she asked her husband to go begging for a maid to help her in the house. She filled a bag of provisions for the journey. On his way home, having earned seven hundred pieces, the brahmin opened his bag, and after having eaten some of the food, went to a stream to drink, leaving the bag open. A snake crept into the bag and lay there. A tree-sprite, thinking to warn the brahmin, said, "If you stop on the way you will die, if you return home your wife will die," and then disappeared. Much alarmed, the brahmin went towards Benares, weeping along the way, and, as it was the fast day, people going to hear Senaka, directed the brahmin to him. Senaka, hearing the brahmin's story, guessed the truth, and had the bag opened in front of the people. The snake crept out and was seized. To show his gratitude, the brahmin gave Senaka his seven hundred pieces, but Senaka gave them back with another three hundred, warning the brahmin not to take the money home. He buried the money under a tree, but could not keep the secret from his wife. She told her lover, and the money was stolen. The brahmin again sought Senaka, who told him of a plan for discovering the lover, and when he was found, Senaka sent for him and made him confess his guilt.

The story was related in reference to the Buddha's wisdom. **Ānanda** was the brahmin and **Sāriputta** the tree-sprite.[1] The story is often referred to as exemplifying the Buddha's practice of the Perfection of *paññā*.[2]

[1] J. iii. 341-51. [2] *E.g.*, J. i. 46; BuA. 50 f.

Satthavāha.—Son of **Koṇāgamana Buddha** in his last lay life. His mother was **Rucigattā.**[1]

[1] Bu. xxiv. 19; DA. ii. 422.

Satthā.—A Pacceka Buddha.[1]

[1] M. iii. 70; MA. ii. 890.

Satthuka.—See **Sattuka** (2).

Sadāmattā.—A class of **Devas,** present at the preaching of the **Mahāsamaya Sutta.**[1]

[1] D. ii. 260.

Sadinacchedana.—A **Cakkavatti** of eighty-seven kappas ago; a previous birth of **Māṇava (Sammukhāthavika) Thera.**[1] *v.l.* **Saritacchedana.**

[1] Ap. i. 159; ThagA. i. 163.

Saddakārikā.—A Pāli work, probably grammatical, by **Sabbaguṇākara.**[1]

[1] Svd. 1245.

Saddatthacintā, Saddatthabhedacintā.—A grammatical work by **Saddhammasiri.**[1] There are several Commentaries on it, the best known

[1] Gv. 62, 72; Svd. 1246. Bode, *op cit.*, 20, 22.

being the Mahāṭīkā by **Abhaya** of Pagan. There exist also a *nissaya* and a *dīpanī* on the work.

Saddanīti.—A very important grammatical work by **Aggavaṃsa** of Pagan. A few years after its completion in 1154, **Uttarajīva** visited the **Mahāvihāra** in Ceylon, and took with him, as a gift, a copy of the Saddanīti, which was received with enthusiastic admiration.[1]

[1] Gv. 63, 72; Svd. 1238; Bode, 16, 17.

Saddabindu.—A grammatical work by Kyocvā of Pagan. A Commentary on it, called **Līnatthavisodhanī,** is ascribed to **Ñāṇavilāsa** of Pagan. There is also a *ṭīkā* called **Saddabinduvinicchaya** by **Sirisaddhammakitti-Mahāphussadeva.**[1]

[1] Gv. 64, 73; Sās. 76; Bode, 25 and n. 4.

Saddavutti, Saddavuttipakāsaka.—A grammatical treatise by **Saddhammapāla** of Pagan. There is a *ṭīkā* on it by **Sāriputta,** and another, called the **Saddavuttivivaraṇa,** by an unknown author.[1]

[1] Gv. 64, 65, 75; Bode, 29; the Sās. (p. 90) calls the author of the Saddavutti **Saddhammaguru.**

1. **Saddasaññaka Thera.**—An arahant. Ninety-two kappas ago he heard **Phussa Buddha** preach in **Himavā.**[1]

[1] Ap. i. 131.

2. **Saddasaññaka Thera.**—An arahant. Ninety-four kappas ago he saw an eclipse and heard the great tumult which announced the arrival of a Buddha in the world. With devoted heart he thought of the Buddha, though he did not see him.[1]

[1] Ap. i. 245.

3. **Saddasaññaka Thera.**—An arahant. Ninety-four kappas ago he heard **Siddhattha Buddha** preach, and listened to him with wrapt attention.[1]

[1] Ap. i. 256.

4. **Saddasaññaka Thera.**—An arahant. Thirty-one kappas ago he was a hunter, and, while wandering in the forest, listened to a sermon by **Sikhī Buddha.**[1]

[1] Ap. i. 282.

Saddasāratthajālinī.—An important grammar by **Nāgita (Khaṇṭakakhipa)** of Sagu. It was written under the patronage of **Kittisīhasūra,**

There is a Commentary on it, called **Sāramañjūsā**, and a *ṭīkā* by **Vepullabuddhi.**[1]

[1] Bode, 27 and n. 5, 28; Gv. 64, 74; Svd. 1249.

Saddha.—See **Sandha.**

Saddhamma Vagga.—The sixteenth chapter of the Pañcaka Nipāta of the **Aṅguttara Nikāya.**[1]

[1] A. iii. 174-85.

Saddhammakitti Thera.—A pupil of **Ariyavaṃsa.** He lived in **Ketumatī** (Taungo) and wrote the famous **Ekakkharakosa,** and, probably, the **Sirivicittālaṅkāra.**[1]

[1] Bode, 45 and n. 3.

Saddhammaguru.—An author of Pagan. The **Sāsanavaṃsa** calls him the author of the **Saddavutti** (but see *s.v.*).[1]

[1] Sās. p. 90.

Saddhammajotipāla (generally known as **Chapaṭa**).—Pupil of **Uttarajīva** of Pagan. He went to Ceylon with his teacher, received the higher ordination there, and lived in the **Mahāvihāra** for some years. Among his works are the **Kaccāyana-suttaniddesa,** the **Saṅkhepavaṇṇanā,** the **Sīmālaṅkāra,** the **Vinayagūḷhatthadīpanī,** the **Nāmācāradīpanī** (on ethics), the **Gaṇṭhisāra** (an anthology of texts), and the **Mātukatthadīpanī** and **Paṭṭhānagaṇānaya** (both on Abhidhamma topics).

On Chapaṭa's return to Burma, he brought four companions from Ceylon—**Rāhula, Ānanda, Sīvalī** and **Tāmalinda**—and, with their help, he founded the **Sīhalasaṅgha** in Pagan, followers of the Mahāvihāra tradition. King **Narapatisithu** gave them his patronage, but extended it to other sects as well, and the **Sīhalasaṅgha,** therefore, remained only as one sect among several in Burma. Chapaṭa lived in the twelfth century.[1]

[1] Gv. 64, 74; Sās. 65, 74; Svd. 1247 f.; Bode, 17, 18, 19.

Saddhammacakkasāmī.—An eminent monk sent by Bayin Naung of Burma to purify the religion in Laos in 1578 A.C.[1]

[1] Sās. 51; Bode, 47.

Saddhammacārī.—A monk of Ceylon, who was quoted as their authority by the **Ekaṃsikas** of Burma.[1]

[1] Bode, *op. cit.*, 66; Sās. 119.

Saddhammañāṇa.—A scholar of Pagan of the early fourteenth century. He wrote the **Vibhatyattha,** the **Chandosāratthavikāsinī** (or **Vuttodaya-pañcikā**) on the **Vuttodaya,** and translated the Sanskrit grammar Kātantra into Pāli.[1]

[1] Bode, 26.

Saddhammaṭṭhitikā.—A Commentary on the **Niddesa,** written at the request of **Deva Thera** by **Upasena** of Ceylon.[1] The **Sāsanavaṃsa**[2] calls it **Saddhammapajjotikā,** and it is probably known by that name in Ceylon.

[1] Gv. 61; Sās. 69; P.L.C. 117. [2] p. 69.

Saddhammanandī.—A nun of Anurādhapura, expert in the Vinaya.[1]

[1] Dpv. xviii. 14.

Saddhammanāsinī.—A *ṭīkā* on **Kaccāyana's** grammar, by **Siridhamma-vilāsa** of Pagan.[1]

[1] Bode, 26.

Saddhammaniyāma Suttā.—Three suttas on five things which make a man enter the right way, in right things.[1]

[1] A. iii. 174 ff.

Saddhammapajjotikā.—See **Saddhammaṭṭhitikā.**

Saddhammapatirūpaka Sutta.—The Buddha explains to **Mahā Kassapa** how it comes about in the *sāsana* that there are more precepts and less members of the Order becoming arahants. Then a counterfeit doctrine arises and the true doctrine disappears.[1]

[1] S. ii. 223 f.

Saddhammapāla.—An author of Pagan, probably of the fourteenth century. He wrote the **Saddavutti.**[1]

[1] Bode, 29.

Saddhammappakāsinī.—A Commentary on the **Paṭisambhidāmagga** by **Mahānāma** of Ceylon.[1]

[1] Gv. 61.

Saddhammavilāsa.—A monk of Pagan, probably of the twelfth century; he was the author of the **Sammohavināsinī.**[1]

[1] Bode, 27.

Saddhammasaṅgaha.—A Chronicle, in eleven chapters, containing a history of Buddhism, commencing with the three Convocations. It was written by **Dhammakitti,** a monk of Ayodhyā, and probably belonged to the fourteenth century.[1]

[1] P.L.C. 245 f.

Saddhammasammosa Suttā.—Three suttas on three groups of five things which lead to the confounding and the disappearance of the *dhamma.*[1]

[1] A. iii. 176 ff.

Saddhammasiri.—A monk of Pagan, probably of the twelfth century, author of **Saddatthabhedacintā.**[1]

[1] Gv. 63, 73; Bode, 22.

Saddhammālaṅkāra.—An author of **Haṃsavatī,** probably of the sixteenth century. He wrote the **Paṭṭhānasāradīpanī** on the Abhidhamma.[1]

[1] Sās. 48; Bode, 47.

Saddhammika Vagga.—The eighth section of the **Pācittiya.**[1]

[1] Vin. iv. 141-57.

Saddhammopāyana.—A treatise in verse, in nineteen chapters, dealing with various topics, such as the difficulties of being born as a human, etc., by an author named Abhayagiri Kavicakravarti Ānanda, probably of the thirteenth century. A Commentary exists on it, called the **Saddhammopāyanaviggaha.**[1]

[1] P.L.C. 212.

1. **Saddhā.**—An upāsikā of **Sāvatthi.** Thinking that to allow a monk to have intercourse with her would be the highest gift, she accosted a monk and offered herself. The offer was, however, refused.[1]

[1] Vin. iii. 39.

2. **Saddhā.**—One of **Sakka's** daughters. See the **Sudhābhojana Jātaka.**

1. **Saddhā Sutta.**—A group of **Satullapakāyika Devas** visit the Buddha and one of them speaks in praise of *saddhā.*[1]

[1] S. i. 25.

2. **Saddhā Sutta.**—On the five advantages resulting from faith.[1]

[1] A. iii. 42.

3. **Saddhā Sutta.**—The perfect monk is he who has faith, virtue learning, is master of the *dhamma*, enters into the *jhānas*, etc.[1]

[1] A. iv. 314.

4. **Saddhā Sutta.**—Eight qualities which make a monk perfect.[1]

[1] A. iv. 315.

5. **Saddhā Sutta.**—Ten qualities which give perfection to a monk.[1]

[1] A. v. 10 f.

6. **Saddhā** (or **Āpaṇa**) **Sutta.**—The Buddha, staying at **Āpaṇa,** asks **Sāriputta** if a monk who is utterly devoted to the Tathāgata, and has perfect faith in him, can have any doubt or wavering as to the Tathāgata or his teaching. Sāriputta answers in the negative and proceeds to explain.[1]

[1] S. v. 225 f.

Saddhā-Tissa.—King of Ceylon (77-59 B.C.). He was the brother of **Duṭṭhagāmaṇī** and was about a year younger. When he was ten, at the ceremony of initiation, he was forced to make a vow that he would never fight against his brother; but when his father, **Kākavaṇṇatissa,** died, he seized the throne in the absence of Duṭṭhagāmaṇī. Up to that time he had been in charge of the **Dīghavāpi** district. Duṭṭhagāmaṇī now made war upon him, but was defeated at **Cūḷaṅganiyapiṭṭhi.** Later the tide turned, and Tissa had to flee to a monastery. Duṭṭhagāmaṇī surrounded the monastery, but some young monks carried Tissa out on a bed, covered up like a dead body. Gāmaṇī discovered the ruse, but refrained from action. Through the intervention of **Godhagatta-Tissa Thera,** the brothers were reconciled, and, thereafter, seem to have been devoted to one another.

After Gāmaṇī's conquest of **Anurādhapura,** Tissa seems to have returned as governor of Dīghavāpi. When Gāmaṇī lay dying, Tissa was sent for to complete the work of the **Mahā Thūpa,** that the king might see it before his death. This he got done by means of temporary structures, cunningly devised. He was enjoined to retain unimpaired all the services on behalf of the religion inaugurated by his brother, and, when the latter died, he was succeeded by Tissa, who ruled for eighteen years. He rebuilt the **Lohapāsāda** after it was burnt down, and erected many vihāras—**Dakkhiṇāgiri, Kallakālena, Kalambaka, Pettaṅgavālika, Velaṅgaviṭṭhika, Dubbalavāpitissaka, Dūratissaka, Mātuvihāraka** and **Dīghavāpi.** He built a vihāra to every yojana on the road from **Anurādhapura** to **Dīghavāpi.** He had two sons, **Lañjatissa** and **Thūlathana.**

Tissa was reborn after death in **Tusita,** and will be the second Chief Disciple of **Metteyya Buddha.**[1]

He was a very pious king, entirely devoted to the cause of religion. Various stories are mentioned about him in the Commentaries.[2] He once walked five leagues to **Maṅgana** to pay his respects to **Kujjatissa**[3] (*q.v.*). On another occasion, he gave snipe to a novice from **Kanthakasālapariveṇa,** who would, however, accept only very little. Pleased with his moderation, the king paid him great honour.[4] He seems to have been specially fond of the monks of **Cetiyagiri.**[5] He was, apparently, also known as **Dhammika-Tissa. Dhammika-Tissa** once distributed one-hundred cartloads of sugar (*guḷa*) among twelve thousand monks. A seven-year-old novice was sent by a monk who had just come to Cetiyagiri from Anurādhapura to fetch for him some sugar, about the size of a *kapiṭṭha*-fruit. The attendant offered to give him a plateful, but the novice refused to take so much. The king heard the conversation, and, pleased with the novice, sent a further four hundred cartloads of sugar to be given to the Order.[6] See also the story of **Kukkuṭagiri.**

[1] Mhv. xxii. 73, 83; xxiv. 2 ff.; xxxii. 83; xxxiii. 4-17; Dpv. xx. 2, 4 ff.
[2] See, *e.g.*, *s.v.* **Kāḷabuddharakkhita.**
[3] AA. i. 384 f.
[4] *Ibid.*, 264.
[5] See VibhA. 473.
[6] *E.g.*, SA. iii. 48.

1. **Saddhiya Sutta.**—As long as monks are full of faith, conscientious, afraid of blame, great listeners, great in energy, mindful and wise—so long may growth be expected, not decline.[1]

[1] A. iv. 23.

2. **Saddhiya Sutta.**—Seven things—such as faith, conscientiousness, fear of blame, etc.—which cause, not decline, but growth.[1]

[1] A. iv. 23.

Saṇṭhita Thera.—An arahant. Thirty-one kappas ago he saw the *asattha*-bodhi of a Buddha and thought of the Buddha's virtues. Thirteen kappas ago he was a king named **Dhaniṭṭha.**[1]

[1] Ap. i. 210.

Sanaṅkumāra.—A **Mahā-Brahmā.** In the Nikāyas[1] he is mentioned as the author of a famous verse, there quoted:

> "*Khattiyo seṭṭho jane tasmiṃ ye gottapaṭisārino*
> *Vijjācaraṇasampanno so seṭṭho devamānuse.*"

In one place[2] the verse is attributed to the Buddha, thus endowing it with the authoritativeness of a pronouncement by the Buddha himself. Sanaṅkumāra is represented as a very devout follower of the Buddha. In a sutta of the Saṃyutta,[3] he is spoken of as visiting the Buddha on the banks of the **Sappinī**, and it was during this visit that the above verse was spoken. Sanaṅkumāra was present at the preaching of the **Mahāsamaya Sutta.**[4] In the **Janavasabha Sutta, Janavasabha** describes to the Buddha an occasion on which Sanaṅkumāra attended an assembly of the **Devas,** presided over by **Sakka** and the Four Regent Gods. There was suddenly a vast radiance, and the devas knew of the approach of Sanaṅkumāra. As the usual appearance of the Brahmā is not sufficiently materialized for him to be perceived by the Devas of **Tāvatiṃsa,** he is forced to appear as a relatively gross personality which he specially creates. As he arrives, the Devas sit in their places with clasped hands waiting for him to choose his seat. Then Sanaṅkumāra takes on the form of Pañcasikha[5] and sits, above the assembly, cross-legged, in the air. So seated, he expresses his satisfaction that Sakka and all the Tāvatiṃsa Devas should honour and follow the Buddha. His voice has all the eight characteristics of a Brahmā's voice.[6] He then proceeds to create thirty-three shapes of himself, each sitting on the divan of a Tāvatiṃsa Deva, and addresses the Devas, speaking of the advantages of taking refuge in the Buddha, the Dhamma and the Saṅgha. Each deva fancies that only the shape sitting on his own divan has spoken and that the others are silent. Then Sanaṅkumāra goes to the end of the Hall, and, seated on Sakka's throne, addresses the whole assembly on the four ways of *iddhi*; on the three avenues leading to Bliss, as manifested by the Buddha; on the four *satipaṭṭhānas*, and the seven *samādhiparikkhārā*. He declares that more than twenty-four lakhs of **Magadha** disciples, having followed the teachings of the Buddha, have been born in the deva-worlds. When Sanaṅkumāra has finished his address, **Vessavaṇa** wonders if there have been Buddhas in the past and will be in the future. The Brahmā reads his thoughts and says there certainly were and will be.

[1] D. i. 121; M. i. 358; S. i. 153; A. v. 327.

[2] S. ii. 284.

[3] *Ibid.*, i. 153.

[4] D. ii. 261.

[5] Because all devas like Pañcasikha, says the Commentary (DA. ii. 640).

[6] These are given at D. ii. 211.

Sanaṅkumāra means "ever young." Buddhaghosa says[7] that, in his former birth, he practised *jhānas* while yet a boy with his hair tied in five knots (*pañcacūḷakakumārakāle*), and was reborn in the Brahma-world with the *jhāna* intact. He liked the guise of youth and continued in the same, hence the name. Rhys Davids[8] sees in the legend of Sanaṅkumāra the Indian counterpart of the European legend of Galahad. The oldest mention of it is in the *Chāṇḍogya Upaniṣad* (Chap. VII.), where the ideal, yet saintly knight, teaches a typical brahmin the highest truths. In the *Mahābhārata*[9] he expresses a sentiment very similar to that expressed in the stanza quoted above. In mediæval literature he is said to have been one of five or seven mind-born sons of **Brahmā** who remained pure and innocent. A later and debased Jaina version of the legend tells in detail of the love adventures and wives of this knight, with a few words at the end on his conversion to the saintly life.[10]

[7] MA. ii. 584; *cf.* SA. i. 171.
[8] Dial. ii. 292, n. 3; *cf.* i. 121, n. 1.
[9] iii. 185 (Bombay Edition).
[10] See *J.R.A.S.* 1894, p. 344; 1897, p. 585 f.; *Revue de l'Histoire des Religions*, vol. xxxi. pp. 29 ff.

Sanaṅkumāra Sutta.—**Brahmā Sanaṅkumāra** visits the Buddha on the banks of the **Sappinī,** and speaks a verse[1] in praise of learning and good conduct. The Buddha approves of the sentiment contained in the verse.[1]

[1] S. i. 153; for the verse see *s.v.* **Sanaṅkumāra.**

Sanidāna Sutta.—Sense desires, ill-will, renunciation, etc., all arise with casual basis.[1]

[1] S. ii. 151 f.

Sanimaṇḍapa.—A building in the **Dīpuyyāna.** It was decorated with ivory.[1]

[1] Cv. lxxiii. 118.

1. **Santa.**—Aggasāvaka of **Atthadassī Buddha.**[1] He was son of the king of **Sucandaka,** and **Upasanta,** son of the chaplain, was his friend. These two placed four very learned men at the four gates of the city to inform them of the arrival of any wise men. They announced the arrival of Atthadassī Buddha. Santa and Upasanta visited the Buddha and his monks, gave them meals for seven days, and listened to the Buddha's preaching. On the seventh day they became arahants, with ninety thousand others.[2]

[1] J. i. 39; Bu. xv. 19.

[2] BuA. p. 179.

2. **Santa.**—Fifty-seven kappas ago there were four kings of this name, previous births of **Tissa Thera.**[1]

[1] ThagA. i. 200; but see Ap. i. 174, where he is called **Bhavanimmita.**

3. **Santa.**—A general of **Parakkamabāhu I.** He is called **Jitagiri,** and was in charge of the **Vihāravajjasāla** ford.[1]

[1] Cv. lxxv. 25.

Santa Sutta.—On ten qualities which make a monk altogether charming and complete in every attribute.[1]

[1] A. v. 11.

Santaka Sutta.—The Buddha explains to Ānanda how feelings arise and cease to be, what is their " satisfaction " and their " misery."[1]

[1] S. iv. 219.

Santakāya Thera.—He was never guilty of any improper movement of hand or foot, but always carried himself with composure and dignity. This was because his mother was a lioness. For a lioness, when she has eaten prey, goes into her cave where she lies, for seven days, on a bed of red arsenic and yellow orpiment. When she rises on the seventh day, if she finds the bed disturbed by any movement on her part, she again lies down for seven days, saying : " This does not become your birth or lineage." When the monks praised Santakāya to the Buddha, he held up the Elder as an example to be followed.[1]

[1] Dhp. iv. 113 f.

Santacitta.—A Pacceka Buddha.[1]

[1] M. iii. 70.

Santati.—A minister of **Pasenadi.** Because he quelled a frontier disturbance, the king gave over the kingdom to him for seven days, and gave him a woman skilled in song and dance. For seven days Santati enjoyed himself, drinking deeply; on the seventh day he went to the bathing place fully adorned, riding the state elephant. The Buddha met him on the way, and Santati saluted him from the elephant. The Buddha smiled and passed on. When questioned by **Ānanda,** the Buddha answered that on that very day Santati would attain arahantship and die.

Santati spent part of the day amusing himself in the water, and then sat in the drinking hall of the park. The woman came on the stage and sang and danced, but she had fasted for seven days to acquire more grace of body, and, as she danced, she fell down dead. Santati was overwhelmed with a mighty sorrow, and straightway became sober. He then sought the Buddha for consolation in his grief. The Buddha preached a four-line stanza, and Santati attained arahantship and asked the Buddha's permission to pass into nibbāna. The Buddha agreed, on condition that he rose into the air and told to the assembled people the story of his past life. Santati agreed to this, and, rising to a height of seven palm-trees, related the meritorious deed of his past life.

Ninety kappas ago, in the time of **Vipassī Buddha,** he was a householder of **Bandhumatī,** and became a follower of the Buddha and went about proclaiming the virtues of the Three Refuges. King **Bandhumā** met him and gave him a garland of flowers to wear and a horse on which to ride, while proclaiming the Law. He later gave him a chariot, great wealth, beautiful jewels and an elephant. Thus, for eighty-four thousand years, Santati went about preaching the Dhamma, and there was diffused from his body the fragrance of sandalwood, and from his mouth the fragrance of the lotus.

As he related his story, seated cross-legged in the air, he developed the idea of fire and passed into nibbāna. Flames burst from his body and burnt it up. The Buddha had his relics collected and a shrine built for them at the meeting of four highways. Discussion arose as to whether Santati should be called a brahmin or a monk. The Buddha said that both names were equally appropriate.[1]

[1] DhA. iii. 78-84; SN. i. 350; MA. i. 188; *cf.* the story of **Abhayarājakumāra.**

Santāna Thera.—An Elder who came to Ceylon from **Rakkhaṅga,** at the head of thirty-three monks, at the invitation of **Vimaladhamma-suriya II.**[1]

[1] Cv. xcvii. 10.

Santi Sutta.—On four kinds of person: he bent on his own profit, on another's, on that of both, on that of neither.[1]

[1] A. ii. 96 f.

Santike Nidāna.—The portion of the **Jātakaṭṭhakathā** which gives an account of the activities of the Buddha—such as where he lived—from the time of his Enlightenment up to his death.[1] This name is specially given to a portion of the **Nidānakathā.**[2]

[1] BuA. p. 4 f. [2] J. i. 77-94.

1. **Santuṭṭha.**—A disciple of the Buddha at **Ñātikā.** He was born after death in **Akaniṭṭhābhavana,** there to pass entirely away.[1]

[1] D. ii. 92; S. v. 358 f.

2. **Santuṭṭha.**—A palace of **Koṇāgamana Buddha** in his last lay life.[1]

[1] Bu. xxiv. 18.

Santuṭṭha Sutta.—The Buddha speaks in praise of **Mahā Kassapa,** his contentment with whatever he receives in the way of robes, alms, lodgings and medicaments. He is an example worthy of imitation.[1]

[1] S. ii. 194.

Santuṭṭhi Sutta.—Four things are easily available: rag-robes, scraps of food, the root of a tree, and ammonia (*pūtimutta*) from urine. A monk should learn to be content with these.[1]

[1] A. ii. 26.

1. **Santusita.**—Chief of the devas of the **Tusita**-world.[1] It was the name of the Bodhisatta when he was in **Tusita**[2] and also that of his successor.[3] At important festivals, Santusita appears with a yak-tail whisk.[4]

[1] D. i. 218; A. iv. 243; S. iv. 280.
[2] BuA. 45; J. i. 48.
[3] *Ibid.*, 81.
[4] *E.g.*, Mhv. xxxi. 78.

2. **Santusita.**—One of the palaces of **Koṇāgamana Buddha** before his renunciation.[1]

[1] Bu. xxiv. 18.

3. **Santusita.**—A king. See **Samphusita.**

Santhava Jātaka (No. 162).—The Bodhisatta was once a brahmin, and, when he grew up, he lived in a hermitage in the forest, tending his birth-fire (*jātaggi*). One day, having received a present of rice and ghee, he took it home, made his fire blaze up, and put the rice into the fire. The flames rose up and burnt his hut. Deciding that the company of the wicked was dangerous, he put out the fire and went up into the mountains. There he saw a hind licking the faces of a lion, a tiger, and a panther. Nothing is better than good friends thought the Bodhisatta.

The story was related to show the uselessness of tending the sacred fire.[1]

[1] J. ii. 41 f.

Santhava Vagga.—The second chapter of the Duka Nipāta of the **Jātakaṭṭhakathā.**[1]

[1] J. ii. 41-63.

Santhāra Vagga.—The fourteenth chapter of the Duka Nipāta of the **Aṅguttara Nikāya.**[1]

[1] A. i. 93 f.

Sandaka.—A **Paribbājaka.** See the **Sandaka Sutta.**

Sandaka Sutta.—**Ānanda,** staying at the **Ghositārāma** in **Kosambī,** visits the **Pilakkhaguhā** near **Devakaṭa** pool, where the **Paribbājaka Sandaka** is staying with some five hundred followers. Ānanda is asked to give a discourse on the Buddha's teachings, and speaks of the four antitheses to the higher life: there is the teacher who holds that it does not matter whether actions are good or bad; the teacher who holds that no evil is done by him who acts himself or causes others to act; the teacher holding that there is no cause for either depravity or purity; and, lastly, the teacher who holds, among other things, that men make an end of ill only when they have completed their course of transmigrations, like a ball of twine which continues rolling as long as there is string to unwind.[1]

Ānanda then proceeds to explain the four comfortless vocations: the teacher who claims to be all-knowing and all-seeing; the teacher whose doctrine is traditional and scriptural; the rationalist of pure reason and criticism teaching a doctrine of his own reasoning; and, lastly, the teacher who is stupid and deficient. Ānanda then describes the Buddha's own teaching, leading up to the four *Jhānas*. Sandaka and his followers accept the Buddha as their teacher.[2]

[1] On these heresies *cf.* **Sāleyyaka Sutta.** The reference is evidently to the teachings of **Purāṇa Kassapa, Makkhali Gosāla** and others.

[2] M. i. 513-24.

1. **Sandiṭṭhika Sutta.**—A conversation between the Buddha and **Moliya-Sīvaka** on how the *dhamma* is for this life.[1]

[1] A. iii. 356.

2. **Sandiṭṭhika Sutta.**—The same as (1), but the conversation is with a brahmin.[1]

[1] A. iii. 357.

3. **Sandiṭṭhika Sutta.**—**Ānanda** explains to **Udāyī (Kāḷudāyī)** how the Buddha's teaching is to be seen for oneself in this life.[1]

[1] A. iv. 453.

4. **Sandiṭṭhika Sutta.**—The same as (3), on how nibbāna can be realized in this life.[1]

[1] A. iv. 453.

Sandimā.—A king of long ago; a previous birth of **Ramaṇīyakuṭika Thera.**[1]

ThagA. i. 133.

Sandeha, Sandeva.—An Elder in direct pupillary succession in Jambu dīpa, of teachers of the Abhidhamma.[1]

[1] DhSA., p. 32.

Sandha.—A monk who visited the Buddha at **Ñātikā** in the **Giñjakāvasatha,** when the Buddha preached to him the **Sandha Sutta** (*q.v.*).[1] *v.l.* **Saddha** (see GS. v. 204, n. 2; and 216, n. 2). It is, perhaps, the same monk who is mentioned[2] as **Saddho** (*v.l.* **Sandho**) **Kaccāyano.** He asks the Buddha a question on *dhātu*, and the Buddha explains it to him. In neither case does the Commentary say anything about Saddho (or Sandho). The translator of the Saṃyutta regards saddho as an epithet.

[1] A. v. 323 f. [2] S. ii. 153 (Giñjakāvastha Sutta).

Sandhāna.—A householder of **Rājagaha.** He was a follower of the Buddha, and it was his conversation with the **Paribbājaka Nigrodha** that led to the preaching of the **Udumbarika-Sīhanāda Sutta** (*q.v.*).

Buddhaghosa says[1] that he was the leader of five hundred *upāsakas* and was an *anāgāmin.* On one occasion, the Buddha sang his praises in the assembly for six qualities which he possessed. In the Aṅguttara[2] he is mentioned in a list of eminent lay disciples.

[1] DA. iii. 832. [2] A. iii. 451; *cf.* Dvy. 540.

Sandhita Thera.—He belonged to a wealthy family of Kosala. Having listened to a sermon on impermanence, after coming of age, he joined the Order and attained arahantship.

Thirty-one kappas ago, in the time of **Sikhī Buddha,** he was a cowherd. After the death of the Buddha he heard a monk preach on his virtues, and, acquiring discernment of impermanence, he paid great honour to the Buddha's *bodhi*-tree. In his last life he recalled this act with great joy, as having helped him to win the goal.[1]

[1] Thag. vs. 217 f.; ThagA. i. 337 f.

Sandhibheda Jātaka (No. 349).—The Bodhisatta was once king of Benares. One day a cowherd left behind, inadvertently, a cow which was in calf, and a friendship sprang up between her and a lioness. The cow bore a calf and the lioness a cub, and these two young ones became playmates. A forester, seeing them together, reported the matter to the king, who wished to be informed should a third animal appear on the scene. A jackal, seeing the calf and the cub, and hoping for food, became friendly with them, and soon managed to make them quarrel. The king was informed of this, and by the time he arrived on the scene the two animals were dead.

The story was related to the **Chabbaggiyā** as a warning against their habit of back-biting.[1]

This is probably the story referred to[2] as the **Saṅghabheda Jātaka.**

[1] J. iii. 149 ff. [2] *Ibid.*, 211.

Sannaka.—One of the chief lay-supporters of **Piyadassī Buddha.**[1]

[1] Bu. xiv. 22.

Sannidhāpaka Thera.—An arahant. He had been a householder, and later an ascetic in the time of **Padumuttara Buddha.** He gave the Buddha a gourd (*āmaṇḍa*) and water to drink. Forty-one kappas ago he was a king named **Arindama.**[1]

[1] Ap. i. 97.

Sannibbāpaka.—A king of one hundred and seven kappas ago, a previous birth of **Āsanūpaṭṭhāyaka Thera.**[1]

[1] Ap. i. 144.

Sannīratittha.—A vihāra in **Pulatthipura,** established by **Mahinda II.**[1]

[1] Cv. xlviii. 134.

Sannīrasela.—A village in Ceylon given by **Parakkamabāhu IV.** for the maintenance of the *pariveṇa* which he built for **Medhaṅkara Thera.**[1]

[1] Cv. xc. 87.

Sapattaṅgārakokirī Sutta.—The story of a petī seen by **Moggallāna.** She went through the air dried up, sooty, uttering cries of distress. She had been the chief queen of a **Kāliṅga** king. Mad with jealousy, she had scattered a brazier of coals over one of the king's women.[1]

[1] S. ii. 260.

Sapatta. An eminent nun, expert in the Vinaya in Ceylon.[1]

Dpv. xviii. 29.

Sapara.—A province in Ceylon,[1] also called **Saparagamu.**[2] It is said to have derived its name from the inhabitants, the **Saparā** or **Sabarā** (**Savarā**), probably another name for the Veddas.

[1] Cv. lxviii. 8. [2] *Ibid.*, xciv. 12.

Saparivāra.—A king of twenty-seven kappas ago, a previous birth of **Paccuggamaniya Thera.**[1]

[1] Ap. i. 240.

Saparivāracchattadāyaka Thera.—An arahant. He heard **Padumuttara Buddha** preach, and, opening a parasol, threw it up into the air. It stood above the Buddha. The Elder joined the Order at the age of seven, and on the day of his ordination, **Sunanda,** a brahmin, held a parasol over him. **Sāriputta** saw this and expressed his joy.[1]

[1] Ap. i. 265 f.

Saparivāriya Thera.—An arahant. He built a palisade of sandalwood round the *thūpa* of **Padumuttara Buddha.** Fifteen kappas ago he was king eight times under the name of **Pamatta** (*v.l.* **Samagga**).[1]

[1] Ap. i. 172.

Saparivārāsana Thera.—An arahant. He prepared a seat decked with jasmine for **Padumuttara Buddha,** and, when the Buddha was seated, gave him a meal.[1]

[1] Ap. i. 107 f.

1. **Sappa Sutta.**—Once, when the Buddha was staying at the **Kalandakanivāpa** in **Veḷuvana, Māra** appeared before him in the shape of a monstrous cobra and tried to frighten him. But the Buddha, recognizing him, said that Buddhas knew no fear.[1]

[1] S. i. 106 f.

2. **Sappa Sutta.**—The five disadvantages in a black snake, and the same disadvantages in a woman—they are unclean, evil-smelling, timid, fearful and betray friends.[1]

[1] A. iii. 260.

3. **Sappa Sutta.**—Same as (2), the qualities being anger, ill-will, poison (passion in a woman), forked tongue and treachery.[1]

[1] A. iii. 260.

Sappaka.—See **Sabbaka.**

Sappagahana.—See **Sabbagahana.**

Sappañña Vagga.—The sixth chapter of the **Sotāpatti Saṃyutta.**[1]

[1] S. v. 404-14.

Sappadāsa Thera.—He was born in **Kapilavatthu** as the son of **Suddhodana's** chaplain. He received faith on the occasion of the Buddha's visit to his own people, and entered the Order. Overmastered by corrupt habits of mind and character, for twenty-five years he was unable to develop concentration. This so distressed him that he was about to commit suicide, when, inward vision suddenly expanding, he attained arahantship.[1] According to the Dhammapada Commentary,[2] he tried to kill himself by making a snake, caught by the monks, bite him. But the snake refused to bite, in spite of all efforts to provoke him. Sappadāsa then threw it away, thinking it to be non-poisonous. But the other monks declared it was a cobra, because they had seen its hood and heard its hissing.

Sappadāsa acted as barber to the monastery, and, one day, taking a razor, he applied it to his windpipe as he leaned against a tree. And then he thought how blameless his life had been and was filled with joy. Thereupon he developed insight and became an arahant. When the monks reported this to the Buddha, the Buddha said that the snake had been the Elder's slave in his third previous life, and therefore did not dare bite him. This incident gave the monk his name, Sappadāsa.

[1] Thag. vs. 405-10. ThagA. i. 448 f. [2] DhA. ii. 256 f.

Sappanārukokillagāma.—A village in Ceylon in which the Buddha's Alms Bowl and Tooth Relic were once deposited.[1]

[1] Cv. lxxiv. 142.

Sappasoṇḍika-pabbhāra.—A mountain cave in the **Sītavana,** near **Rājagaha.**[1] A conversation which took place there between **Sāriputta** and **Upasena,** just before the latter's death, is recorded in the Saṃyutta Nikāya. Upasena died of snake-bite.[2] The cave was used as a residence by monks who come to Rājagaha from afar.[3] Buddhaghosa says[4] that the cave was so called because it was shaped like a snake's hood. It was here that the Buddha met and preached to **Tissa,** the rājā of **Roruva.**[5]

[1] D. ii. 116. [2] S. iv. 40. [3] *E.g.*, Vin. ii. 76. [4] SA. iii. 10. [5] ThagA. i. 200.

Sappānaka Vagga.—The seventh chapter of the **Pācittiya.**

1. **Sappidāyaka Thera.**—An arahant. Ninety-two kappas ago he gave an offering of ghee to **Phussa Buddha.** Fifty kappas ago he was a king named **Samodaka.**[1]

[1] Ap. i. 184.

2. **Sappidāyaka Thera.**—An arahant. Ninety-four kappas ago he saw **Siddhattha Buddha** lying ill and gave him some ghee. Seventeen kappas ago he was a king named **Jutideva.**[1]

[1] Ap. i. 212.

Sappini, Sappinikā.—A river, which flowed through **Rājagaha.** On its bank was a Paribbājakārāma where famous Paribbājakas lived in the Buddha's time.[1] The river lay between **Andhakavinda** and Rājagaha, and probably rose in **Gijjhakūṭa.**[2] It is identified with the Pañcāna River.[3]

[1] A. i. 185; ii. 29, 176; S. i. 153.
[2] See *Vin. Texts* i. 254, n. 2.
[3] Law, E.G.I., p. 38.

Sappurisa Vagga.—The twenty-first chapter of the Catukka Nipāta of the **Aṅguttara.**[1]

[1] A. ii. 217-25.

1. **Sappurisa Sutta.**—The unworthy man (*asappurisa*) always speaks what is discreditable to another, never what is discreditable to himself, and always sings his own praises. The worthy man is just the reverse.[1]

[1] A. ii. 77.

2. **Sappurisa Sutta.**—The birth of a good man is like a good shower; it brings happiness to all.[1]

[1] A. iii. 46=*ibid.*, iv. 244.

3. **Sappurisa Sutta.**—The gifts of a good man are well chosen, proper, seasonable, given with care, repeatedly and with calm mind; after giving, he is glad.[1]

[1] A. iv. 243.

4. **Sappurisa Sutta.**—The good man's gifts are given in faith, with deference, seasonably, with unrestrained heart, and without hurt to himself or others.[1]

[1] A. iii. 172.

5. **Sappurisa Sutta.**—The 113th sutta of the **Majjhima Nikāya,** preached at **Jetavana.** The good monk does not exalt himself or disparage others

on grounds of family distinction, of eminent wealth, personal fame, gifts and instruction received, capacity for preaching, knowledge of the dhamma, observance of austere practices, etc.; the bad monk does.[1]

[1] M. iii. 37-45.

6. **Sappurisa Sutta.**—See **Asappurisa Sutta.**

Sappurisānisaṃsa Sutta.—Because of a good man, one grows in virtue, concentration, wisdom and emancipation, qualities which are dear to the Ariyans.[1]

[1] A. ii. 239.

Sabara.—See **Sapara.**

Sabala.—A dog of the **Lokantaraniraya.** It has iron teeth which it uses on the victims of that **Niraya.**[1]

[1] J. vi. 247.

Sabalā.—An eminent Therī of **Jambudīpa,** expert in the Vinaya.[1]

[1] Dpv. xviii. 10.

Sabba Vagga.—The third chapter of the **Saḷāyatana Saṃyutta.**[1]

[1] S. iv. 15-26.

1. **Sabba Sutta.**—There is no other "all" except eye-and-object, ear-and-sound, nose-and-scent, tongue-and-savour, body-and-tangible things, mind-and-mindstates.[1]

[1] S. iv. 15.

2. **Sabba Sutta.**—Another name for the **Ambapāli Sutta** 2 (*q.v.*).

Sabbaka (Sappaka).—An arahant Thera. He belonged to a brahmin family of **Sāvatthi,** and, after hearing the Buddha preach, entered the Order. He lived in **Loṇagiri-vihāra** (*v.l.* **Lena-vihāra**), on the banks of the **Ajakaraṇī,** practising meditation, and, in due course, won arahantship. He visited Sāvatthi to worship the Buddha, and stayed there a few days, entertained by his kinsfolk. When he wished to return to his dwelling they begged him to stay and be supported by them, but he refused because he loved retirement.[1]

Thirty-one kappas ago he was a Nāga-king of great power who, having

[1] The verses he spoke on this occasion are given in Thag. (vs. 307-10).

seen the Pacceka Buddha **Sambhavaka,** wrapt in *samādhi,* under the open sky, remained beside him holding a lotus over his head.[2]

He is probably to be identified with **Padumapūjaka** of the Apadāna.[3]

[2] ThagA. i. 399 f.

[3] Ap. i. 279 f.; *cf.* Ap. ii. 453 f. (**Padumudhāriya**).

1. **Sabbakāma.**—One of the chief disciples of **Sumedha Buddha.**[1]

[1] J. i. 38; Bu. xii. 23.

2. **Sabbakāma** (*v.l.* **Sabbakāmī**).—An arahant Thera. He was born in a noble family of **Vesāli,** shortly before the Buddha's death. When he came of age he gave away his possessions to his kinsfolk and joined the Order under **Ānanda.** In the course of his studies, he returned to Vesāli with his teacher and visited his family. His former wife, afflicted, thin, in sad array and in tears, greeted him and stood by. Seeing her thus, he was overwhelmed with love and pity and felt carnal desire. When he realized this, he was filled with anguish and hurried to the charnel-field, there to meditate on foulness. He developed insight and became an arahant. Later, his father-in-law brought his wife to the vihāra, beautifully dressed, and accompanied by a great retinue, hoping to make him return, but the Thera convinced them that he had rid himself of all such desires.[1]

Sabbakāma lived on to one hundred and twenty years of age, and was consulted by **Yasa, Soreyya Revata,** and others, in connection with the **Vajjiputta** heresy. He was, at that time, the oldest Thera in the world. He sat on the committee appointed to examine the points in dispute and decided against the Vajjaputtakas, giving his reasons point by point.[2] The Theragāthā Commentary adds[3] that, before his death, Sabbakāmā requested the **Brahmā Tissa** (afterwards **Moggaliputta Tissa**) to see that the heresies, which were to arise in the time of **Asoka,** were put down. Sabbakāma's resolve to dispel heresy was made in the time of **Padumuttara Buddha.**[4]

[1] See Thag. vss. 453-8.

[2] For details see Vin. ii. 303 ff.; also Dpv. iv. 49; v. 22; Mhv. iv. 48, 576; Sp. i. 34.

[3] ThagA. i. 467.

[4] *Ibid.*, 465 f.

Sabbakāmā.—Wife of **Sikhī Buddha** before his renunciation. Their son was **Atula.**[1]

[1] Bu. xxi. 17; DA. ii. 422.

Sabbakāmī.—See **Sabbakāma** (2).

Sabbakittika Thera.—An arahant.[1] He is evidently identical with **Adhimutta Thera** (*q.v.*).

[1] Ap. i. 224 f.

Sabbagandhiya Thera.—An arahant. Ninety-one kappas ago he offered flowers and incense to **Vipassī Buddha** and gave him a garment of *koseyya*-cloth. Fifteen kappas ago he was a king, named **Sucela.**[1]

[1] Ap. i. 248 f.

Sabbagahana.—A king of one hundred kappas ago, a previous birth of **Anulomadāyaka (Mettaji) Thera.**[1] *v.l.* **Sappagahana, Sabbosana.**

[1] Ap. i. 173: ThagA. i. 195.

Sabbagiri-vihāra.—See **Pipphali-vihāra.**

Sabbattha-abhivassī.—Thirty-eight kappas ago there were sixteen kings of this name, previous births of **Kuṭidāyaka Thera.**[1]

[1] Ap. i. 229.

Sabbatthivādī.—A group of heretical monks (Sarvāstivādins), an offshoot of the **Mahiṃsāsakas.** The **Kassapiyā** were a branch of the same.[1] They held that everything is, exists, is constantly existing, because it is, was, or will be, matter and mind, and these continually exist[2]; that penetration of truth is won little by little.[3] They agreed with the **Uttarāpathakas** that conscious flux may amount to *samādhi*,[4] and with the **Vajjiputtiyas** that an arahant may fall away.[5]

[1] Mhv. v. 8 f.; Dpv. v. 47.
[2] Kvu. i. 6, 7.
[3] *Ibid.*, ii. 9.
[4] *Ibid.*, xi. 6.
[5] *Ibid.*, i. 2; see *J.R.A.S.* 1892, 1 ff., 597; 1894, 534; *J.P.T.S.* 1905, 67 f.

Sabbadatta.—King of **Rammanagara** (Benares). He was the father of the Bodhisatta in his birth as **Yuvañjaya** (*q.v.*), and is identified with **Suddhodana.**[1]

[1] J. iv. 119 f., 123.

Sabbadassī.—One of the two chief disciples of **Piyadassī Buddha.**[1] He was the son of the chaplain of **Sumaṅgalanagara** and the friend of **Pālita**[2] (*q.v.*).

[1] Bu. xiv. 20; J. i. 39.
[2] BuA. 176.

Sabbadāṭha.—**Devadatta** born as a jackal. See the **Sabbadāṭha Jātaka.**

Sabbadāṭha Jātaka (No. 241).—The Bodhisatta was once chaplain to the king of Benares and knew a spell called **Paṭhavījaya** (subduing the world). One day he retired to a lonely place and was reciting the spell. A jackal, hiding in a hole near by, overheard it and learned it by heart. When the Bodhisatta had finished his recital, the jackal appeared before him, and saying: "Ho, brahmin, I have learnt your spell," ran away. The Bodhisatta chased him, but in vain. As a result of learning the spell, the jackal subdued all the creatures of the forest and became their king, under the name of **Sabbadāṭha.** On the back of two elephants stood a lion and on the lion's back sat Sabbadāṭha, with his consort.

Filled with pride, the jackal wished to capture Benares, and went with his army and besieged the city. The king was alarmed, but the Bodhisatta reassured him, and, having learnt from Sabbadāṭha that he proposed to capture the city by making the lions roar, gave orders to the inhabitants to stop their ears with flour. Then he mounted the watch-tower and challenged Sabbadāṭha to carry out his threat. This Sabbadāṭha did, and even the lions on which he rode joined in the roar. The elephants were so terrified that, in their fright, they dropped Sabbadāṭha, who was trampled to death. The carcases of the animals which died in the tumult covered twelve leagues.

The story was related in reference to **Devadatta's** attempts to injure the Buddha, which only resulted in working harm upon himself.

The jackal is identified with Devadatta and the king with **Ānanda.**[1]

The story is referred to in the Milindapañha,[2] and there the Bodhisatta's name is given as **Vidhura.**

[1] J. ii. 242-6. [2] Mil. p. 202.

Sabbadāyaka Thera.—An arahant. He is evidently identical with **Yasa Thera**[1] (*q.v.*).

[1] Ap. i. 333 f.

Sabbadinna.—One of the attendants of **King Milinda.**[1]

[1] Mil. pp. 29, 56.

Sabbananda Thera.—A disciple of **Kassapa Buddha,** who was left behind in Ceylon (then known as **Maṇḍadīpa**) with one thousand monks, when the Buddha had visited the Island.[1]

[1] Mhv. xv. 158; Dpv. xv. 60, 64; xvii. 25; Sp. i. 87.

Sabbanāmā.—See **Saccanāmā.**

Sabbaphaladāyaka Thera.—An arahant.[1] He is evidently identical with **Suppiya Thera** (*q.v.*).

[1] Ap. ii. 452 f.

1. **Sabbamitta Thera.**—He belonged to a brahmin family of **Sāvatthi,** and entered the Order after seeing the Buddha's acceptance of **Jetavana.** He dwelt in the forest, meditating. Once, on his way to Sāvatthi to worship the Buddha, he saw a fawn caught in a trapper's net. The doe, though not in the net, remained near, out of love for her young, yet not daring to approach the snare. The Thera was much moved by the thought of all the suffering which was caused by love. Farther on he saw bandits wrapping in straw a man whom they had caught and were preparing to set on fire. The Thera was filled with anguish, and, developing insight, won arahantship.[1] He preached to the bandits and they joined the Order under him.

In the time of **Tissa Buddha,** he was a hunter who lived on game. One day, the Buddha, out of compassion for him, left three of his footprints outside his hut. The hunter saw them, and, owing to good deeds done in the past, recognized them as the Buddha's, and offered to them *koraṇḍa*-flowers. After death he was born in **Tāvatiṃsa.**[2] His Apadāna verses are given in two places under the name of **Koraṇḍapupphiya** (*q.v.*).[3]

[1] He uttered, in his anguish, the two verses included in Thag. 149-50.

[2] ThagA. i. 269 f.

[3] Ap. ii. 383, 434; *cf.* **Sugandha Thera.**

2. **Sabbamitta.**—An eminent teacher belonging to the *udicca-brāhmaṇa-kula.* He was extremely learned, and was the second teacher employed by **Suddhodana** to teach the Buddha in his youth.[1]

[1] Mil. p. 236.

3. **Sabbamitta.**—The constant attendant of **Kassapa Buddha.**[1]

[1] D. ii. 7; Bu. xxv. 39; J. i. 43.

4. **Sabbamitta.**—A king of **Sāvatthi.** See the **Kumbha Jātaka** (No. 512). He is identified with **Ānanda.**[1]

[1] J. v. 20.

Sabbaratanamālaka.—See **Ratanamālaka.**

"Sabbalahusa" Sutta.—The minimum evil effects of violating each of the Five Precepts (against murder, etc.).[1]

[1] A. iv. 247.

Sabbaloka Sutta.—Another name for the **Anabhirati Sutta** (*q.v.*).

Sabbasaṃhāraka-pañha.—Evidently another name for the *Ganṭhi-pañha* of the **Mahāummagga Jātaka.**[1] It is elsewhere[2] referred to as a special Jātaka (No. 110).

[1] See J. vi. 335 f. [2] J. i. 424.

Sabbābhibhū.—A Pacceka Buddha.[1]

[1] Ap. i. 299.

Sabbāsava Sutta.—The second sutta of the **Majjhima Nikāya.** It was preached at **Jetavana,** and describes how the cankers (*āsavā*) can be destroyed. Extirpation of the *āsavas* comes only to those who know and see things as they really are. *Āsavas* can be got rid of in many ways: by scrutiny, restraint, use, endurance, avoidance, removal and culture. The sutta describes these various ways.[1]

[1] M. i. 6 ff.

Sabbūpasama.—See **Najjūpasama.**

Sabbosadha.—A king of eight kappas ago, a previous birth of **Tikicchaka Thera.**[1]

[1] Ap. i. 190.

Sabbosama.—See **Sabbagahana.**

" **Sabrahmakāni** " **Sutta.**—Families in which parents are honoured and worshipped are like those in which **Brahmā** resides, or kindly teachers, or Devas, or those worthy of offerings.[1]

[1] A. ii. 70.

Sabhattadesabhoga.—A monastic building, erected by **Aggabodhi VI.,** in the **Abhayuttara-vihāra.**[1]

[1] Cv. xlviii. 64.

Sabhāgata Sutta.—The **Devas** delight in talking to those who are possessed of unwavering loyalty to the Buddha, the Dhamma and the Saṅgha, and who possess virtues dear to the Ariyans.[1]

[1] S. v. 394.

Sabhāsammata.—Thirteen kappas ago there were five kings of this name, previous births of **Pañcahatthiya Thera.**[1]

[1] Ap. i. 193.

Sabbhi Sutta.—A conversation between the Buddha and a group of **Satullapakāyika Devas.** The Buddha impresses on them the necessity of making companions of good men.[1]

[1] S. i. 16 f.

1. **Sabhiya (Sambhiya).**—The constant attendant of **Phussa Buddha.**[1]

[1] J. i. 41; Bu. xix. 19.

2. **Sabhiya Thera.**—His mother was a nobleman's daughter whose parents had committed her to the charge of a **Paribbājaka,** that she might learn various doctrines and usages. The Paribbājaka seduced her, and, when she was with child, the fraternity abandoned her. Her child was born in the open (*sabhāyaṃ*), while she was wandering about alone—hence his name. When Sabhiya grew up he, in his turn, became a Paribbājaka and was famous as a dialectician. He had a hermitage by the city gate, where he gave lessons to the sons of noblemen and others. He devised twenty questions, which he put before recluses and brahmins, but none could answer them. These questions had been handed on to him by his mother who had developed insight and had been reborn in a Brahma-world.[1] Then, as related in the **Sabhiya Sutta** 1 (*q.v.*), Sabhiya visited the Buddha in Veḷuvana and, at the end of the discussion, entered the Order, where, developing insight, he won arahantship.

In the time of **Kakusandha Buddha** he was a householder and gave the Buddha a pair of sandals. After Kassapa Buddha's death he, with six others, joined the Order and lived in the forest. Failing to develop *jhāna*, they went to the top of a mountain, determined to reach some attainment or to die of starvation. The eldest became an arahant, the next became an *anāgāmī* and was reborn in the **Suddhāvāsā.** The remaining five died without achieving their aim. These five were, in this age, **Pukkusāti, Sabhiya, Bāhiya, Kumārakassapa** and **Dabbamallaputta.**[2]

Sabhiya is mentioned as an example of a *paṇḍita-paribbājaka.*[3] A series of verses spoken by him, in admonishing monks who sided with **Devadatta,** are given in the **Theragāthā.**[4] **Yasadatta** (*q.v.*) was Sabhiya's companion.

[1] But see **Sabhiya Sutta** (1).

[2] ThagA. i. 381 f.; SNA. ii. 419 ff.; Ap. ii. 473; DhA. ii. 212.

[3] SA. ii. 188.

[4] vs. 275-8; see also Mtu. iii. 389 ff.

3. **Sabhiya.**—A **Paribbājaka,** perhaps identical with **Sabhiya** (2). The Saṃyutta[1] records a discussion which took place at **Ñātikā** between him and **Vacchagotta** on various questions, such as the existence of the Buddha after death, etc. In this sutta, Sabhiya is addressed as **Kaccāna,** and he says that he had then been three years in the Order. It is probably this same Paribbājaka who is mentioned as **Abhiya-Kaccāna** in the **Anuruddha Sutta** (*q.v.*).[2]

[1] S. iv. 401 f.

[2] M. iii. 148 f.

1. **Sabhiya Sutta.**—The sixth sutta of the Mahāvagga of the **Sutta Nipāta.**[1] A *devatā,* who in a previous life had been a relation of **Sabhiya** (see **Sabhiya** 1), asks him a series of questions and exhorts him to join the Order of any recluse who can answer them satisfactorily. Sabhiya wanders about asking his questions of several well-known teachers; failing to find satisfaction, he visits the Buddha in **Veḷuvana** at **Rājagaha** and is given permission to ask anything he wishes, the Buddha promising to solve his difficulties. Then follows a series of questions answered by the Buddha. Sabhiya, in the end, asks permission to join the Buddha's Order. This permission is given, and after the usual probationary period of four months, he becomes an arahant.

According to the Theragāthā Commentary,[2] quoted also in the Sutta Nipāta Commentary, the questions were formulated by Sabhiya's mother, who, feeling revulsion for her womanhood, developed the *jhānas* and was reborn in a Brahma-world. But the Sutta Nipāta Commentary itself[3] says that they were taught to Sabhiya by an *anāgamī* **Brahmā,** who had been a fellow-celibate of Sabhiya in the time of **Kassapa Buddha's** dispensation. The Sutta is also called **Sabhiya-pucchā,** and is given[4] as an example of the Buddha's *sabbaññupavāraṇa,* his willingness to answer any question whatever without restriction.

It is said[5] that **Yasadatta,** Sabhiya's companion, was present at the discussion with the Buddha and listened eagerly hoping for a chance of criticism. But the Buddha read his thoughts and admonished him at the end of the sutta.

The questions contained in the sutta had been asked and answered in the time of Kassapa Buddha, too, but, while the questions remained, the answers disappeared.[6]

[1] SN., pp. 91 f.

[2] ThagA. i. 382.

[3] SNA. ii. 421.

[4] *E.g.,* DA. i. 155.

[5] ThagA. i. 427.

[6] VibhA., p. 432.

2. **Sabhiya Sutta.**—Records the discussion between **Sabhiya Kaccāna** (**Sabhiya** 2) and **Vacchagotta.**[1]

[1] S. iv. 401 f.

1. **Samagga.**—One hundred and fifteen kappas ago there were eight kings of this name, previous births of **Khaṇḍasumana Thera.**[1] *v.l.* **Pamatta**.

[1] ThagA. i. 258.

2. **Samagga.**—A mountain near **Himavā.**[1] *v.l.* **Samaṅga.**

[1] ThagA. i. 258; Ap. ii. 437.

1. **Samaṅga.**—The constant attendant of **Tissa Buddha.**[1]

[1] Bu. xviii. 21; BuA (p. 191) calls him **Samata.**

2. **Samaṅga.**—See **Samagga.**

Samaṅgī.—The wife of **Sobhita Buddha** before his renunciation.[1] The Buddhavaṃsa Commentary[2] calls her **Makhiladevī.**

[1] Bu. vii. 18.

[2] BuA. 137.

Samacitta Vagga.—The fourth chapter of the Duka Nipāta of the **Aṅguttara Nikāya.**[1]

[1] A. i. 61-9.

Samacitta(-pariyāya) Sutta.—A large number of Devas of Tranquil Mind (**Samacittā**) come to the Buddha at **Jetavana** and ask him if he will visit **Sāriputta,** who is preaching at the **Migāramātupāsāda** on the person who is fettered both inwardly and outwardly. The Buddha agrees in silence and appears at the Migāramātupāsāda. Sāriputta greets the Buddha and salutes him. The Buddha relates to him the visit of the Devas and tells him that a large number of them can stand in a space not greater than the point of a gimlet, and that, too, without crowding each other. This is because they have trained themselves to be tranquil in the senses and in the mind. Such tranquillity leads to tranquillity also of body, speech, and thought. Followers of other schools do not know this teaching.[1]

In the discourse of Sāriputta,[2] referred to by the Devas, the Elder explains that the monk who keeps the *pātimokkha* restraints is proficient in the practice of right conduct, seeing danger in the slightest faults—such a one is reborn among the Devas and is therefore a " Returner." Thus he is fettered inwardly to the self. Others there are who are born in Deva-worlds and there become *anāgāmins.* These are fettered outwardly. Yet others are proficient in revulsion, in the ending of sensuality, of any existence and become *anāgāmins.*

[1] A. i. 64 f.

[2] *Ibid.*, 62 f.

It is said[3] that at the conclusion of this sutta, as at the conclusion of the **Mahāsamaya, Maṅgala,** and **Cūḷa-Rāhulovāda Suttas,** one hundred thousand crores attained arahantship.

The sutta was preached by **Mahinda** on the evening of his arrival in Ceylon. After his interview with **Devānampiyatissa,** Mahinda asked **Sumana-sāmaṇera** to announce the preaching of the Dhamma. This announcement was heard throughout the Island, and gradually the news of it spread to Brahmā's heaven. There was then an assembly of Devas, just as on the occasion of Sāriputta's preaching of the sutta.[4]

[3] AA. i.320; *cf.* SNA., p. 174; Mil. p. 20. [4] Mhv. xiv. 34 ff.

Samajīvī Sutta.—The Buddha visits the house of **Nakulapitā,** while staying in the **Bhesakalāvana** on **Suṃsumāragiri.** Both Nakulapitā and his wife declare their faithfulness to each other and their desire to be husband and wife in subsequent births. That, says the Buddha, is possible if they are matched in faith, virtue, generosity and wisdom.[1]

[1] A. ii. 61 f.

Samaṇa.—One of the chief lay supporters of **Kakusandha Buddha.**[1]

[1] Bu. xxiii. 22.

Samaṇa Vagga.—The ninth chapter of the Tika Nipāta[1] of the **Aṅguttara.**

[1] A. i. 229-39.

1. **Samaṇa Sutta.**—A monk has three pursuits: training in the higher morality, higher thought and higher insight. He must follow these pursuits with keenness; otherwise his presence in the Order will be like that of an ass in a herd of cattle.[1]

[1] A. i. 229.

2. **Samaṇa Sutta.** On the four kinds of monk to be found in the Order —*sotāpannas, sakadāgāmins, anāgāmins* and *arahants.* These are not to be found among the followers of contrary teachings.[1]

[1] A. ii. 238.

3. **Samaṇa Sutta.**—On the different names by which a Tathāgata is known.[1]

[1] A. iv. 340.

Samaṇakolañña.—A king of **Kāliṅga.** He was a **Cakkavatti,** but when he was riding his elephant through the air, he could not pass over the spot where the *bodhi*-tree was.[1] The reference is evidently to the story in the **Kāliṅgabodhi Jātaka,**[2] but there the king's name is not given.

[1] Mil. p. 256. [2] J. iv. 232 f.

Samaṇaguttaka.—A bandit, employed by the heretics to kill **Moggallāna Thera.**[1] See the **Sarabhaṅga Jātaka.**

[1] J. v. 126.

Samaṇaguttā.—The second of the seven daughters of **Kikī,** king of Benares. She was **Uppalavaṇṇā** in the present age.[1]

[1] Ap. ii. 546; *cf.* J. vi. 481.

Samaṇabrāhmaṇa Vagga.—The eighth chapter of the **Nidāna Saṃyutta.**[1]

[1] S. ii. 129.

1. **Samaṇabrāhmaṇa Sutta.**—Recluses and brahmins who know decay-and-death, its uprising, its cessation and the way thereto—they are held in honour; not so the others.[1]

[1] S. ii. 14 f.

2. **Samaṇabrāhmaṇa Sutta.**—Similar to (1). They know not only decay-and-death but likewise all the factors of this entire mass of Ill; such realize, in this very life, the goal of recluseship.[1]

[1] S. ii. 45 f.

3. **Samaṇabrāhmaṇa Suttā.**—A group of suttas similar to the above; the good recluses and brahmins know about decay and death, birth, becoming, grasping, craving, feeling, contact, sense, name-and-form, consciousness and activities.[1]

[1] S. ii. 129 f.

4. **Samaṇabrāhmaṇa Sutta.**—Honoured recluses and brahmins are those who know the satisfaction, the danger and the escape regarding gains, favours and flattery.[1]

[1] S. ii. 236 f.

5. **Samaṇabrāhmaṇa Sutta.**—Real recluses and brahmins are those who understand the arising, destruction, satisfaction, danger and escape from the three kinds of feeling.[1]

[1] S. iv. 234 f.

6. **Samaṇabrāhmaṇa Sutta.**—Recluses and brahmins who have understood fully the five controlling powers (*indriyāni*) are worthy of honour.[1]

[1] S. v. 195.

7. Similar to (6), regarding the six sense-faculties.[1]

[1] S. v. 206.

8. **Samaṇabrāhmaṇa Sutta.**—Same as (6), but the controlling powers are different—case, etc.[1]

[1] S. v. 208.

9. **Samaṇabrāhmaṇa Sutta.**—The results of the development of the four *iddhipādas* by recluses and brahmins.[1]

[1] S. v. 273 f.

10. **Samaṇabrāhmaṇa Sutta.**—Recluses and brahmins who have gained, are gaining, and will gain, the highest wisdom, do so through understanding of the Four Noble Truths.[1]

[1] S. v. 416 f.

Samaṇamaṇḍikā Sutta.—**Pañcakaṅga,** on his way to the Buddha, visits the Paribbājaka **Uggāhamāna** at the **Samayappavādaka** in the **Tindukācīra** in the **Mallikārāma.** Uggāhamāna tells him that, in his view, the triumphant recluse is he who does no evil, says and thinks no evil, and earns his living in no evil way. Pañcakaṅga reports this to the Buddha, who says that, according to Uggāhamāna, a tiny babe on its back would be such a recluse! No, says the Buddha, the triumphant recluse is one who is an adept in the Noble Eightfold Path and in utter knowledge and in utter deliverance, and he goes on to describe such a recluse in detail.[1] *v.l.* **Samaṇamuṇḍikā.**

[1] M. ii. 22-9.

Samaṇamaṇḍikāputta.—A name for the **Paribbājaka Uggāhamāna** (*q.v.*).

Samaṇasaññā Vagga.—The eleventh chapter of the Dasaka Nipāta of the **Aṅguttara Nikāya.**[1]

[1] A. v. 210 ff.

Samaṇā, Samaṇī.—The eldest of the seven daughters of King **Kikī.** She was **Khemā** in the present age.[1]

[1] J. vi. 481; Ap. ii. 546; ThigA. 18, etc.

Samaṇupaṭṭhāka.—Twenty-three kappas ago there were four kings of this name, previous births of **Buddhūpaṭṭhāyaka Thera.**[1]

[1] Ap. i. 242.

Samata.—See **Samaṅga.**

1. **Samatta.**—One hundred and fifteen kappas ago there were eight kings of this name, previous births of **Nandiya Thera.**[1]

[1] ThagA. i. 82.

2. **Samatta.**—See **Pamatta.**

1. **Samatta Sutta.**—**Sāriputta** tells **Anuruddha** that it is by cultivating the four *satipaṭṭhānas* that one becomes an adept (*asekha*).[1]

S. v. 175.

2. **Samatta Sutta.**—It is by practising the four *iddhipādas* that recluses and brahmins can perfectly practise *iddhi*-power.[1]

[1] S. v. 256.

Samatha Sutta.—A monk should practise introspection as to whether he has won insight of the higher and insight into the dhamma, and also peace of heart. Then he must put forth special effort to acquire what he has not won, and he must obtain his requisites in such a way that unprofitable states wane in him and profitable states increase.[1]

[1] A. v. 98 ff.

Samathakkhandhaka.—The fourth section of the Cullavagga of the Vinaya.[1]

[1] Vin. ii. 73-104.

Samanupassanā Sutta.—On how thoughts of self lead to ignorance and to varying views.[1]

[1] S. iii. 46.

Samantakūṭa, Samantagiri, Sumanakūṭa, Sumanagiri, Sumanācala.—A mountain peak in Ceylon. It was the residence of the Deva **Mahāsumana,**[1] and when the Buddha visited the Island for the third time, he

[1] Mhv. i. 33.

left on the mountain the mark of his footprint.[2] Owing to this, the mountain became a sacred place of pilgrimage. In later times many kings of Ceylon paid the shrine great honour. **Vijayabāhu I.** gifted the village of **Gilīmalaya** for the feeding of pilgrims, and set up rest-houses for them on the different routes, for the maintenance of which he provided.[3] **Kittinissaṅka** made a special pilgrimage to Sumanakūṭa and mentioned it in his inscriptions.[4] **Parakkamabāhu II.** did likewise, and also gave ten *gāvutas* of rich land for the shrine on the top of the peak.[5] He further gave orders to his pious minister, **Devappatirāja,** to make the roads leading to the mountain easy of access. The minister repaired the roads, and built bridges at **Bodhitala** over the **Khajjotanadī,** at **Ullapanaggāma,** and at **Ambaggāma.** He constructed rest-houses at suitable spots, and placed stepping-stones on the way to the summit. Then the king himself visited the peak and held a great festival there lasting for three days.[6] **Vijayabāhu IV.,** too, made a pilgrimage to the sacred mountain.[7] King **Vīravikkama** also went there and lit a lamp, fifteen cubits in girth and five cubits high.[8] **Rājasīha I.,** in his desire to take revenge on the Buddhist monks, handed the shrine over to Hindu priests,[9] but **Vimaladhammasūriya II.** restored to it all honours and held a great festival, lasting for seven days, at the peak.[10] His son, **Narindasīha,** made two pilgrimages there,[11] while **Vijayarājasīha** had a feast of lamps celebrated there.[12] **Kittisirirājasīha** had a *maṇḍapa* built round the footprint surmounted by a parasol, and assigned the revenues from the village of **Kuṭṭāpiṭi** to the monks who looked after the shrine.[13]

The districts round Samantakūṭa were, in early times, the habitation of the **Pulindas.** It was believed[14] that, when **Vijaya** forsook **Kuveṇī,** her children fled thither and that their descendants were the Pulindas. In later times, too, mention is made[15] of the fact that the people dwelling in the neighbourhood of Samantakūṭa refused to pay taxes to the king. From very early times the mountain was the dwelling of numerous monks. Thus, in the time of **Duṭṭhagāmaṇī,** there were nine hundred monks there, under **Malayamahādeva Thera.**[16] The Damiḷa **Dīghajantu** offered a red robe to the **Ākāsacetiya** in **Samantagiri-vihāra,** and, as a result, won heaven, because he remembered the gift at the moment of his death.[17] The rivers **Mahāvāluka** and **Kalyāṇī** rise in Sumanakūṭa.

[2] *Ibid.*, 77; *cf.* Nammadā and Saccabaddha (*q.v.*).

[3] Cv. lx. 64 f.

[4] *Ibid.*, lxxx. 24; Cv. *Trs.* ii. 128, n. 4.

[5] Cv. lxxxv. 118.

[6] *Ibid.*, lxxxvi. 9, 18 ff.

[7] *Ibid.*, lxxxviii. 48.

[8] *Ibid.*, xcii. 17.

[9] *Ibid.*, xciii. 12.

[10] *Ibid.*, xcvii. 16 f.

[11] *Ibid.*, 31

[12] *Ibid.*, xcviii. 84.

[13] *Ibid.*, c. 221.

[14] Mhv. vii. 67.

[15] *E.g.*, Cv. lxi. 70.

[16] Mhv. xxxii. 49.

[17] AA. i. 375; MA. ii. 955.

Samantakūṭavaṇṇanā.—A Pāli poem, of about eight hundred verses, written in the thirteenth century by **Vedeha Thera,** at the request of **Rāhula,** a monk. It contains a description of **Samantakūṭa** and the stories connected with it.[1]

[1] P.L.C. 223 f.

Samantagandha.—Five kappas ago there were thirteen kings of this name, previous births of **Padapūjaka Thera.**[1] *v.l.* **Samantabhadda.**

[1] Ap. i. 142.

Samantagiri.—See **Samantakūṭa.**

1. **Samantacakkhu.**—A king of seven kappas ago, a previous birth of **Devasabha (Bandhujīvaka) Thera.**[1]

[1] ThagA. i. 204; Ap. i. 176.

2. **Samantacakkhu.**—A king of fifty-five kappas ago, a previous birth of **Araṇadīpaka Thera.**[1]

[1] Ap. i. 231.

Samantacchadana.—A king of fifty-five kappas ago, a previous birth of **Ummāpupphiya Thera.**[1]

[1] Ap. i. 258.

Samantadharaṇa.—A king of eighty-seven kappas ago, a former birth of **Pupphadhāraka Thera.**[1]

[1] Ap. i. 244.

Samantanemi.—Seventy-three kappas ago there were thirteen kings of this name, previous births of **Asanabodhiya Thera.**[1]

[1] Ap. i. 111.

1. **Samantapāsādika.**—Thirty-three kappas ago there were thirteen kings of this name, previous births of **Tipupphiya Thera.**[1]

[1] Ap. i. 136.

2. **Samantapāsādika.**—Seventy-eight kappas ago there were sixteen kings of this name, previous births of **Hatthidāyaka Thera.**[1]

[1] Ap. i. 208.

Samantapāsādikā.—A Commentary on the Vinaya Piṭaka written by **Buddhaghosa Thera.**[1] It was written at the request of **Buddhasiri** and

[1] Gv. 59.

was based on the **Mahāpaccariya** and the **Kurundī Aṭṭhakathā.** See also **Sāratthadīpanī.**[2]

[2] Sp. i. 2.; the reason for the name is given at Sp. i. 201.

Samantabhadda.—Five kappas ago there were thirteen kings of this name, previous births of **Uttiya (Padapūjaka) Thera.**[1] *v.l.* **Samantagandha.**

[1] ThagA. i. 125; Ap. i. 142.

Samantabhadraka.—The name of a book. Probably a wrong reading.[1]

[1] See SNA. i. 21, 25.

Samantamalla.—A Malaya chief in the time of **Parakkamabāhu I.**[1]

[1] Cv. lxx. 26, 28.

Samantavaruṇa.—Twenty-seven kappas ago there were four kings of this name, previous births of **Ādhāradāyaka Thera.**[1]

[1] Ap. i. 207.

Samantāodana.—See **Odana.**

1. **Samaya Sutta.**—On the wrong and right times for striving.[1]

[1] A. iii. 65.

2. **Samaya Sutta.**—On six occasions when one should visit a monk.[1]

[1] A. iii. 317.

3. **Samaya Sutta.**—**Mahā Kaccāna** repeats sutta (2) in order to settle a dispute which arose among the monks.[1]

[1] A. iii. 320.

4. **Samaya Sutta.**—The introductory part of the **Mahāsamaya Sutta** (*q.v.*), included in the **Saṃyutta.**[1]

[1] S. i. 26 f.

Samayappavādaka.—A descriptive epithet of the **Mallikārāma** in **Sāvatthi.** It was so called because teachers of diverse views used to meet there and state their opinions (*attano attano samayaṃ pavadanti*).[1]

[1] MA. ii. 710; DA. ii. 365.

Samayavimutti Sutta.—Five things that lead to the falling away of a monk who is temporarily released.[1]

[1] A. iii. 173.

Samalaṅkata.—A king of seventy kappas ago, a previous birth of **Supāricariya Thera.**[1]

[1] Ap. i. 181.

Samavattakkhandha.—The son of **Vipassī Buddha** in his last lay life. His mother was **Sutanā.**[1]

[1] Bu. xx. 25, etc.

Samasīsakathā.—The seventh chapter of the Paññāvagga of the **Paṭisambhidāmagga.**[1]

[1] Ps. ii. 230-32.

Samādapaka Thera.—An arahant. Ninety-one kappas ago he was leader of a guild in **Bandhumatī,** and he and his colleagues built a courtyard (*mālā*) for **Vipassī Buddha** and his monks. Fifty-nine kappas ago he was a king, named **Āveyya.**[1]

[1] Ap. i. 185.

Samādapetabba Sutta.—The Buddha tells **Ānanda** of three particulars regarding which advice should be given to one's loved ones—on unwavering loyalty to the Buddha, the Dhamma, and the Saṅgha. The results of such loyalty are unchanging.[1]

[1] A. i. 222.

Samādhi Vagga.—The first chapter of the **Sacca Saṃyutta.**[1]

[1] S. v. 414-20.

Samādhi Saṃyutta.—Another name for the **Jhāna Saṃyutta.**[1]

[1] S. iii. 263-79.

1. **Samādhi Sutta.**—One who is concentrated is one who knows as it really is the arising of the body and the passing away thereof; the same with feeling, perception, activities and consciousness.[1]

[1] S. iii. 13; *cf. ibid.*, v. 414; on this sutta see Sylvain Lévi, JA. 1908, xii. 102.

2. **Samādhi Sutta.**—On the six forms of concentration.[1]

[1] S. iv. 362.

3. **Samādhi Sutta.**—On four ways of developing concentration.[1]

[1] A. ii. 44 f.

4. **Samādhi Sutta.**—On four kinds of people in the world: those who gain mental calm but not higher wisdom, those who gain higher wisdom but not mental calm, those who gain neither, those who gain both.[1]

[1] A. ii. 92.

5. **Samādhi Sutta.**—The same as (3), but this sutta adds that those who have gained neither one nor both should strive energetically to obtain them.[1]

[1] A. ii. 93.

6. **Samādhi Sutta.**—The same as (3), but adds a description as to how mental calm and insight can be united.[1]

[1] A. ii. 94.

7. **Samādhi Sutta.**—On the fivefold knowledge which arises in those that are wise and mindful and have developed infinite concentration.[1]

[1] A. iii. 24.

8. **Samādhi Sutta.**—On five qualities that obstruct right concentration —sights, sounds, etc.[1]

[1] A. iii. 137.

9. **Samādhi Sutta.**—The Buddha explains how a monk who has won such concentration as to be unaware of earth, water, etc., yet contrives to have perception.[1]

[1] A. v. 7 f.; *cf. ibid.*, 353 f.

10. **Samādhi Sutta.**—**Ānanda** asks the same question, as in sutta (8), of **Sāriputta,** and the latter explains it from his own experience in **Andhavana.**[1]

[1] A. v. 8 f.

Samādhisamāpatti Sutta.—Of the four persons who practise meditation, he who is skilled both in concentration and in the fruits thereof is the best, just as the strainings of ghee are the best part of milk.[1]

[1] S. iii. 263.

Samānā.—A class of **Devas** present at the preaching of the **Mahāsamaya Sutta.**[1]

[1] D. ii. 260.

Samāpatti Vagga.—The fifteenth chapter of the Duka Nipāta of the **Aṅguttara Nikāya.**[1]

[1] A. i. 94 f.

Samālā.—One of the two chief women disciples of **Vessabhū Buddha.**[1]

[1] Bu. xxii. 24; J. i. 42.

Samita.—A king of fourteen kappas ago, a previous birth of **Buddhasaññaka (Meghiya) Thera.**[1]

[1] Ap. i. 152; ThagA. i. 150.

Samitanandana.—A king of fifty kappas ago, a previous birth of **Yūthikapupphiya Thera.**[1]

[1] Ap. i. 202.

Samitigutta Thera.—He belonged to a brahmin family of **Sāvatthi** and entered the Order after hearing the Buddha preach. He attained to entire purity of conduct, but, because of some action in his former life, was attacked by leprosy, and his limbs gradually decayed. He therefore lived in the infirmary. One day **Sāriputta,** while visiting the sick, saw him and gave him an exercise on contemplation of feeling. Practising this, Samitigutta developed insight and became an arahant. Then he remembered his past action and uttered a verse.[1]

In the past he was a householder and offered jasmine-flowers to **Vipassī Buddha.** In another birth he saw a Pacceka Buddha and insulted him, calling him a "leprous starveling" and spitting in his presence. For this he suffered long in hell, and was reborn on earth in the time of **Kassapa Buddha.** He became a Paribbājaka, and, losing his temper with a follower of the Buddha, cursed him—"May you become a leper." He also soiled the bath-powders placed by people at bathing-places; hence his affliction in the present age.[2]

He is evidently identical with **Jātipūjaka** of the Apadāna.[3]

[1] Included in Thag. (vs. 81). [2] ThagA. i. 175 f. [3] Ap. i. 154.

1. **Samiddha.**—King of Ceylon (**Varadīpa**) in the time of **Koṇāgamana Buddha.** His capital was **Vaḍḍhamāna.**[1]

[1] Mhv. xv. 117; Dpv. xv. 48; xvii. 7; Sp. i. 86.

2. **Samiddha.**—Brother of **Jayanta,** king of Ceylon (**Maṇḍadīpa**). It was war between the brothers that brought **Kassapa Buddha** to Ceylon.[1]

[1] MṬ. 356.

1. **Samiddhi Thera.**—He belonged to a householder's family of **Rājagaha.** From the time of his birth his family prospered, and he himself was happy and good, hence his name. He was present at the

meeting between the Buddha and **Bimbisāra,** and was so impressed thereby that he joined the Order. Once, while he was at the **Tapodārāma** musing on his good fortune as a monk, **Māra** tried to terrify him. Samiddhi told the Buddha of this, but the Buddha asked him to stay on where he was.[1] He obeyed, and soon afterwards won arahantship. He then declared his *aññā* in a verse,[2] and Māra retired discomfited.

In the past he met **Siddhattha Buddha,** to whom he gave some flowers with stalks, which he picked with the help of his bow and arrow. Fifty-one kappas ago he was a king named **Jutindhara.**[3] He is probably identical with **Salaḷamāliya** of the Apadāna.[4]

Once when Samiddhi was drying himself after bathing in the Tapodā, a Deva approached and questioned him on the **Bhaddekaratta Sutta.** Samiddhi confessed ignorance, and the Deva asked him to learn it from the Buddha. This he did from a brief sermon preached to him by the Buddha, which **Mahā Kaccāna** later enlarged into the **Mahā-Kaccāna-Bhaddekaratta Sutta**[5] (*q.v.*). A conversation between **Potaliputta** and **Samiddhi,** three years after the latter had joined the Order, led to the preaching of the **Mahākammavibhaṅga Sutta** (*q.v.*).[6] In the sutta the Buddha speaks of Samiddhi as *moghapurisa,* and Samiddhi is also teased by Potaliputta for pretending to expound the Dhamma after being only three years in the Order. According to the Aṅguttara Commentary,[7] Samiddhi was a pupil (*saddhivihārika*) of **Sāriputta,** and the Aṅguttara[8] contains a record of a lesson given by **Sāriputta** to Samiddhi regarding *saṅkappavitakkas.* See also the **Samiddhi Jātaka** and the **Samiddhi Sutta** (2).

[1] This episode is also given at S. i. 119 f., but the place mentioned is not the Tapodārāma, but **Silāvatī.**
[2] Thag. vs. 46.
[3] ThagA. i. 117 f.
[4] Ap. i. 206.
[5] M. iii. 192 f.
[6] *Ibid.,* 207.
[7] AA. ii. 799.
[8] A. iv. 385 f.

2. **Samiddhi.**—See **Samiddhisumana.**

3. **Samiddhi.**—A brahmin of **Sāvatthi,** father of **Puṇṇamāsa Thera.**[1]

[1] ThagA. i. 53.

4. **Samiddhi.**—A brahmin of **Nāḷaka,** father of **Mahāgavaccha Thera.**[1]

[1] ThagA. i. 57.

Samiddhi Jātaka (No. 167).—The Bodhisatta was once a young ascetic in the **Himālaya,** and on one occasion, after wrestling all night with his spirit, he bathed at sunrise and stood in one garment to dry his body in the sun. A nymph, seeing him, tried in vain to tempt him.

The story was told in reference to **Samiddhi Thera,** who had a similar experience on the banks of the **Tapodā.** Seeing his youth and beauty, a nymph reminded him that he was yet young, asceticism could be practised in old age. Samiddhi replied that no one knew if he would live to see old age. The nymph vanished.[1]

[1] J. ii. 56-8.

1. **Samiddhi Sutta.**—The story of a nymph who tried to tempt **Samiddhi Thera.** The story is similar to the introductory story of the **Samiddhi Jātaka,** but the discussion between Samiddhi and the devatā is given at greater length. When Samiddhi told her of his aim in leading the religious life, she wished to know more of the Buddha's teaching, and asked him to find an opportunity for her to see the Buddha. This Samiddhi did, and the Buddha preached to her.[1]

[1] S. i. 8 ff.

2. **Samiddhi Sutta.**—Describes the unsuccessful attempt of **Māra** to frighten **Samiddhi Thera** (*q.v.*). Māra made a tremendous noise near him, and Samiddhi sought the Buddha's advice. The Buddha explained to him that the noise was made by Māra, and the next time he came Samiddhi challenged him to do his worst.[1]

[1] S. i. 119 f.

3. **Samiddhi Sutta.**—Preached at the **Kalandakanivāpa** in **Veḷuvana,** in answer to **Samiddhi's** question as to what **Māra** is and what are his distinguishing qualities.[1]

[1] S. iv. 38 f.

4. **Samiddhi Sutta.**—Records a lesson given by **Sāriputta** to **Samiddhi** on *saṅkappavitakkā* (purposive thoughts).[1]

[1] A. iv. 385 f.

Samiddhisumana.—A **Deva** who lived in the *rājāyatana*-tree standing at the gate of **Jetavana.** He accompanied the Buddha on his second visit to Ceylon. In his last birth he had been a man in **Nāgadīpa,** and seeing some Pacceka Buddhas eating their meal, had provided them with *rājāyatana*-branches with which to clean their bowls. The *rājāyatana*-tree was held as parasol over the Buddha's head on his journey to Ceylon and was left behind in **Kalyāṇī** for the Nāgas to worship.[1]

[1] Mhv. i. 52 ff.

Samīti.—A waggon-builder of **Sāvatthi.** In the **Aṅgana Sutta** (*q.v.*), **Moggallāna** tells **Sāriputta** how he once saw Samīti shaping a felloe; by his side, **Paṇḍuputta** was watching, wishing that Samīti might shape the felloe without crook, twist, or blemish. When Samīti did this, Paṇḍuputta sang with joy, saying that Samīti had read his thoughts.[1]

[1] M. i. 31 f.

Samīrukkhatittha.—A ford in the **Mahāvālukagaṅgā.**[1]

[1] Cv. lxxii. 9, 33.

Samugga Jātaka (No. 436).—The Bodhisatta was once an ascetic of great *iddhi*-power. Near his hut lived an **Asura** who from time to time listened to his preaching. One day the Asura saw a beautiful woman of **Kāsi** going with an escort to visit her parents. The Asura swooped down on the party and, as soon as the men had fled, took the woman and made her his wife. For her safe protection he put her in a box, which he then swallowed. Some time later the Asura went to bathe, and having taken out the box and let the woman bathe, he allowed her to remain out until he himself had bathed. A son of **Vāyu,** a magician, was travelling through the air, and the woman, seeing him, invited him to her box and there covered him up. The Asura, all unsuspecting, shut up the box and swallowed it. Then he visited the Bodhisatta, who said in greeting, "Welcome to all three of you." The Asura expressed his surprise, and the Bodhisatta explained the matter to him. The box was produced and the truth of his story proved. The magician went his way and the woman was allowed to go hers.

The story was related to a monk who was hankering after a woman.[1] It is also referred to[2] as the **Karaṇḍaka Jātaka.**

[1] J. iii. 527-31. [2] J. v. 455.

Samuggata.—Fifty thousand kappas ago there were seven kings of this name, all previous births of **Sobhita (Rakkhita) Thera.**[1]

[1] Ap. i. 164; ThagA. i. 173.

Samuccaya-khandha.—The third chapter of the Culla Vagga of the Vinaya Piṭaka.[1]

[1] Vin. ii. 38-72.

Samujjavasālā.—A building in **Anurādhapura.** The clay from under the northern steps of the building was used for the construction of utensils used in the coronation festival of the kings of Ceylon.[1]

MṬ. 307.

Samudaya Sutta.—The *puthujjanas* do not know the arising and going out of body, feelings, etc.[1]

[1] S. iii. 82, 174.

1. **Samudayadhamma Sutta.**—Ignorance means ignorance that the nature of the body, feeling, etc., is to come to be and then pass away.[1]

[1] S. iii. 170.

2. **Samudayadhamma Sutta.**—The same as Sutta (1), but the explanation is given by **Sāriputta** to **Mahākoṭṭhita.**[1]

[1] S. iii. 171.

3. **Samudayadhamma Sutta.**—The Buddha teaches the monks about arising and the ending of the four *satipaṭṭhānas.*[1]

[1] S. v. 184.

1. **Samudda.**—See **Sundara-samudda.**

2. **Samudda.**—A sage of long ago.[1]

[1] J. vi. 99.

3. **Samudda.**—One of the chief lay patrons of **Siddhattha Buddha.**[1]

[1] Bu. xvii. 20.

Samudda Jātaka (No. 296).—The Bodhisatta was once a sea-spirit, and heard a water-crow flying about, trying to check shoals of fish and flocks of birds, saying, "Don't drink too much sea water, be careful of emptying the sea." The sea-spirit, seeing his greediness, assumed a terrible shape and frightened him away.

The story was related in reference to the great greediness of **Upananda** the **Sākyan** (*q.v.*). He is identified with the water-crow.[1]

[1] J. ii. 441 f.

Samudda Vagga.—The sixteenth chapter of the **Saḷāyatana Saṃyutta.**[1]

[1] S. iv. 157-72.

1. **Samudda Sutta.**—Two or three drops of water, if taken from the sea, are infinitesimal compared with what is left.[1]

[1] S. ii. 136 f.

2. **Samudda Sutta.**—In the discipline of the Ariyans it is sight, sounds, etc., which constitute the ocean. The world is, for the most part, plunged therein.[1]

[1] S. iv. 157.

3. **Samudda Sutta.**—The same as sutta (1). For the person who has understanding the *dukkha* which he has destroyed is infinitesimal compared with what remains in the world.[1]

[1] S. v. 463.

Samuddakappa.—A king of fourteen kappas ago; a former birth of **Bandhujīvaka Thera.**[1]

[1] Ap. i. 192.

Samuddagiri-vihāra.—A vihāra in **Sunāparanta,** where **Puṇṇa** lived for some time. The cloister (*caṅkamaṇa*) there was surrounded by magnetic rocks, and no one could walk in it.[1]

[1] MA. ii. 1015; SA. iii. 15.

Samuddagiripariveṇa.—A building in the **Mahāvihāra** erected by **Kassapa IV.,** and given over to the **Paṃsukulikas.**[1]

[1] Cv. lii. 21.

Samuddajā.—Mother of **Bhūridatta.** See the **Bhūridatta Jātaka.**

1. **Samuddadatta.**—A monk whom **Devadatta** persuaded to join him in trying to bring about schism in the Order.[1] He was a favourite of **Thullanandā.**[2]

[1] Vin. ii. 196; iii. 171. [2] *Ibid.*, iv. 66.

2. **Samuddadatta.**—A king who traced his descent from **Mahāsammata.** He was the first of a dynasty of twenty-five kings who ruled in **Rājagaha.**[1]

[1] MṬ. 129.

Samuddanavā.—A princess, who later became an eminent Therī in Ceylon.[1]

[1] Dpv. xviii. 34.

Samuddapaṇṇasālā.—A hall, erected on the spot from where **Devānampiyatissa** saw the Bodhi-tree approaching on the ocean.[1] It was on the road from **Anurādhapura** to **Jambukola.**[2]

[1] Mhv. xix. 26 f. [2] MṬ. 403.

Samuddavāṇija Jātaka (No. 466).—Once one thousand carpenters, unable to meet their debts, built a ship, and sailed away till they came to a fertile island. There they found a castaway, from whom they learned that the island was safe and fruitful. So they stayed there, and, as time went on, they grew fat and began to drink toddy made from sugar-cane. The deities, incensed because the island was being fouled with their excrement, decided to send a wave up to drown them. A friendly deity, wishing to save them, gave them warning; but another cruel deity asked them to pay no heed to her words. Five hundred of the families, led by a wise man, built a ship in which they placed all their belongings in case the warning should prove true. No harm would be done should it prove false. The others, led by a fool, laughed at them. At the end of the dark fortnight the sea rose; the five hundred wise families escaped, the others were drowned.

The story was told in reference to five hundred families who were born in Niraya as a result of following **Devadatta.**[1]

[1] J. iv. 158-66.

Samuddavijayā.—Queen of **Bharata,** ruler of **Roruva.** See the **Āditta Jātaka.** She is identified with **Rāhulamātā.**[1]

[1] J. iii. 474.

Samudda-vihāra.—A vihāra built by **Mahādāṭhika-Mahānāga,**[1] but a monk, called **Mahānāga,** is said to have lived in the **Samudda-vihāra** in the time of **Duṭṭhagāmaṇī.**[2] Probably Mahādāthika only restored it.

[1] Mhv. xxxiv. 90. [2] MṬ. 606.

1. **Samuddā.**—One of the two chief women disciples of **Koṇāgamana Buddha.**[1]

[1] J. i. 431; Bu. xxiv. 23.

2. **Samuddā.**—An eminent Therī of Ceylon.[1]

[1] Dpv. xviii. 28.

Samuddhara.—A king of sixty-seven kappas ago, a previous birth of **Yūthikapupphiya Thera.**[1]

[1] Ap. i. 184.

Samogadha.—A king of fifty-five kappas ago, a previous birth of **Taraṇiya Thera.**[1]

[1] Ap. i. 238.

Samotthata.—Seven kappas ago there were seven kings of this name, all previous births of **Saṅghupaṭṭhāka Thera.**[1]

[1] Ap. i. 191.

1. **Sampadā Sutta.**—The three attainments and the three growths —faith, virtue, insight.[1]

[1] A. i. 287.

2. **Sampadā Sutta.**—The five attainments—faith, virtue, learning, charity, insight.[1]

[1] A. iii. 53.

3. **Sampadā Sutta.**—The five attainments—virtue, concentration, insight, emancipation, knowledge and vision of insight.[1]

[1] A. iii. 119.

4. **Sampadā Sutta.**—The five losses—of kin, wealth, health, virtue, right view. Their opposites are five profits.[1]

[1] A. iii. 147.

5. **Sampadā Sutta.**—The eight attainments—alertness, wariness, good company, even life, faith, virtue, charity, wisdom.[1]

[1] A. iv. 322.

Sampasādaka Thera.—An arahant. Ninety-four kappas ago, when in danger of his life, he saw **Siddhattha Buddha** and asked for his protection. The Buddha exhorted him to put his faith in the Order. He died soon afterwards and was reborn in **Tusita.**[1]

[1] Ap. i. 250.

Sampasādanīya Sutta.—The twenty-eighth sutta of the **Dīgha Nikāya.** The Buddha is staying at the **Pāvārika-ambavana** in **Nālandā. Sāriputta** worships him and declares that there has been, is, and will be, no one greater than the Buddha, or wiser, as regards *sambodhi*. He admits, in answer to the Buddha, that he knows nothing either of past Buddhas or of future ones, and that he is unable to comprehend the Buddha's mind with his own. But he knows the lineage of the Norm (*Dhammanvaya*), and is able to deduce therefrom the qualities of past and future Buddhas. He then proceeds to recount the qualities and attainments in which the Buddha is unsurpassed and unsurpassable. The Buddha agrees that Sāriputta's statements are in agreement with the Dhamma. **Mahā Udāyī,** who is present, declares his amazement that the Buddha, though possessed of such marvellous qualities, should yet be so serene and resigned. The sutta ends with an exhortation by the Buddha that Sāriputta should often discourse on this topic to men and women that their doubts may be set at rest.[1]

[1] D. iii. 99-116.

Sampuṇṇamukha.—See **Puṇṇamukha.**

Samphala.—See **Sambala.**

1. **Samphassa Sutta.**—Because of diversity in elements arises diversity of contact.[1]

[1] S. ii. 140.

2. **Samphassa Sutta.**—The Buddha makes **Rāhula** realize that sense contact is fleeting.[1]

[1] S. ii. 246.

Samphusita.—A king of three kappas ago, a previous birth of **Tambapupphiya Thera.**[1]

[1] Ap. i. 176.

Sambandhacintā.—A work of the twelfth century by **Saṅgharakkhita.** It is a grammatical treatise dealing with the Pāli verb and its use in syntax, together with a description of the six *kārakas* used with the verb in the sentence.[1] **Abhaya Thera** of Pagan wrote a *ṭīkā* on it.[2]

[1] P.L.C. 199. [2] Bode, *op. cit.*, 22.

Sambandhamālinī.—A grammatical work by an author of Pagan.[1]

[1] Bode, *op. cit.*, 29.

Sambara.—A chief of the **Asuras.** In the "**Isayo Samuddakā Sutta**"[1] (*q.v.*) we are told that, because Sambara refused the request of the sages for a guarantee of safety, they cursed him, and his mind was deranged. Buddhaghosa adds[2] that, on account of this mental derangement, he came to be called **Vepacitti** (*s.v.*). Elsewhere,[3] however, it is said that once Sakka asked Vepacitti to teach him Sambara's magic art (**Sambarimāyā**). Vepacitti consulted the Asuras and then warned Sakka against learning it because, through his art, Sambara had fallen into purgatory, where he had been suffering for a century. Buddhaghosa, in this

[1] S. i. 227. [2] SA. i. 266. [3] S. i. 239.

context,[4] calls Sambara an *Asurinda*, a juggler (*māyāvī*) who, having practised his *māyā*, has roasted for the past century in purgatory.

Mrs. Rhys Davids[5] thinks there was a rank of Sambara resembling that of Sakka, and that each succeeding Sambara learnt the magic art. See also **Samvara.**

[4] SA. i. 272. [5] KS. i. 306 n.

Sambara Sutta.—See " **Isayo Samuddakā Sutta.**"

1. **Sambala.**—One of the chief disciples of **Siddhattha Buddha.**[1] *v.l.* **Samphala** and **Sambahula.**

[1] J. i. 40; Bu. xvii. 48.

2. **Sambala.**—One of the chief lay patrons of **Tissa Buddha.**[1]

[1] Bu. xviii. 23.

3. **Sambala.**—One of the monks who accompanied **Mahinda** to Ceylon.[1] **Sirimeghavaṇṇa** had an image made of him for purposes of worship.[2]

[1] Mhv. xii. 7; Dpv. xii. 12, 38; Sp. i. 62. [2] Cv. xxxvii. 87.

Sambahula.—A chief of **Amaranagara,** where he and his brother, **Sumitta,** ruled. He heard **Siddhattha Buddha** preach at **Amaruyyāna** and became an arahant.[1] He is probably identical with **Sambala** (1).

[1] BuA. 186.

1. **Sambahula Sutta.**—**Māra,** in the guise of a brahmin, with top-knot and antelope skin, aged and bent, visits a number of monks at **Silāvatī** and asks them to enjoy pleasures because they are yet young. They should not abandon the things of this life in order to run after matters involving time. Natural desires, they reply, are matters involving time, full of sorrow and despair, not the doctrine practised by them which is immediate in its results.

The brahmin retires discomfited, and when the matter is reported to the Buddha, he identifies him with Māra.[1]

[1] S. i. 117 f.

2. **Sambahula Sutta.**—A deity in a Kosalan forest tract laments when the monks, who have been living there, depart on tour. Another deity comforts him saying that monks are free and own no home.[1]

[1] S. i. 199.

3. **Sambahula Sutta.**—A deity in a Kosalan forest tract sees a company of monks vain, noisy, heedless and unintelligent. He draws near and admonishes them.[1]

[1] S. i. 203.

Sambuddha Sutta.—On the difference between the Tathāgata who is a fully-enlightened one and a monk who is freed by insight.[1]

[1] S. iii. 65 f.

Sambula Jātaka (No. 519).—**Sambulā** was the wife of **Sotthisena,** king of Benares, whose father was the Bodhisatta. Sambulā was very beautiful, but when Sotthisena, being seized with leprosy, left his kingdom and went into the forest, she went with him and tended him with great devotion. One day, after fetching food from the forest, she went to bathe, and was drying herself, when she was seized by a Yakkha who threatened to carry her away. By her power **Sakka's** throne was heated, and Sakka, coming with his thunderbolt, frightened the Yakkha and put him in chains. It was late when Sambulā returned home, and Sotthisena, wishing to test her love, refused to believe her story. She then performed an Act of Truth, declaring that she was faithful, and sprinkled water on Sotthisena. He was completely healed, and together they went to Benares, where Sotthisena's father was still king. He made Sotthisena king and became an ascetic. Sotthisena gave himself up to pleasure and neglected Sambulā. The ascetic, returning, found her thin and miserable, and, learning the reason, admonished Sotthisena.

The story was related in reference to **Mallikā's** great devotion to her husband. She is identified with Sambulā and **Pasenadi** with Sotthisena.[1]

[1] J. v. 88-98.

Sambula-Kaccāna Thera.—He belonged to a family of the **Kaccānas** in **Magadha,** and, having entered the Order, lived in a cave, called **Bheravā,** near the **Himālaya,** engaged in meditation. One day there arose a great and unseasonable storm; the clouds massed up in the sky amid thunder and forked lightning. All creatures cried out in fear and trembling. But Sambula, heedless of the noise and cooled by the storm, composed his mind, developed insight and became an arahant. Then, filled with joy, he uttered a pæan.[1]

Ninety-four kappas ago he had seen a Pacceka Buddha, named **Sataraṃsi,** just risen from *samādhi*, and had given him a palm-fruit.[2] He is evidently identical with **Tālaphaliya** of the Apadāna.[3]

[1] This is included in Thag. vss. 189-90. [2] ThagA. i. 313 f. [3] Ap. i. 447.

Sambulā.—Queen of Sotthisena. See the **Sambula Jātaka.**

Sambojjhaṅga Sutta.—A definition of the seven *bojjhaṅgas.*[1]

[1] S. iv. 367.

Sambodha Vagga.—The first chapter of the Navaka Nipāta of the **Aṅguttara Nikāya.**[1]

[1] A. iv. 351-466.

Sambodhi Vagga.—The eleventh chapter of the Tika Nipāta of the **Aṅguttara Nikāya.**[1]

[1] A. i. 258-65.

Sambodhi Sutta.—Conditions that should be developed in order to get awakening—good friends, virtue, helpful talk, strenuous purpose, wisdom.[1]

[1] A. iv. 251 f.

" Sambodhena " Sutta.—The Buddha explains how it was only after his Enlightenment that he could understand the satisfaction and the misery and the way of escape from the eye, ear, etc.[1]

[1] S. iv. 6 f.

1. **Sambhava.**—One of the two chief disciples of **Sikhī Buddha.**[1]

[1] D. ii. 4; J. i. 41; Bu. xxi. 20; S. i. 155.

2. **Sambhava.**—The constant attendant of **Revata Buddha.**[1]

[1] J. i. 35; Bu. vi. 21.

3. **Sambhava.**—The constant attendant of **Tissa Buddha.**[1]

[1] J. i. 40, but see **Samaṅga.**

4. **Sambhava.**—A Pacceka Buddha of thirty-one kappas ago. **Sappaka Thera,** in a previous birth, was a **Nāga** and held a lotus over him.[1]

[1] ThagA. i. 399.

5. **Sambhava.**—The Bodhisatta, born as the son of **Vidhura** and brother of **Sañjaya** and **Bhadrakāra.** See the **Sambhava Jātaka.**

Sambhava Jātaka (No. 515).—**Dhanañjaya Koravya,** king of **Indapatta,** asks a question of his chaplain **Sucīrata** on *dhammayāga* (the Service of

Truth). Sucīrata confesses ignorance, and declares that none but **Vidhura,** chaplain of the king of Benares, could find the answer. At once the king sends him with an escort and a present and a tablet of gold on which the answer may be written. Sucīrata visits other sages on the way, and finally Vidhura, who had been his school-mate. When the question is asked, Vidhura refers it to his son **Bhadrakāra,** who, however, is busy with an intrigue with a woman and cannot give attention to the matter. He sends Sucīrata to his younger brother, **Sañjaya,** but he, too, is occupied, and sends him on to his brother **Sambhava** (the Bodhisatta), a boy of seven. Sucīrata finds him playing in the street, but when he is asked the question, he answers it with all the fluent mastery of a Buddha. All Benares, including the king, hears the answer and stays to listen. Sambhava is paid great honour and receives many presents. Sucīrata notes the answer on the golden tablet and brings it to Dhañanjaya.

The story is related in reference to the Buddha's great wisdom. Dhañjaya is identified with **Ānanda,** Sucīrata with **Anuruddha,** Vidhura with **Kassapa,** Bhadrakāra with **Moggallāna,** and Sañjaya with **Sāriputta.**[1]

[1] J. v. 57-67.

Sambhiya.—See **Sabhiya** (1).

1. **Sambhūta.**—A *caṇḍāla,* brother of **Citta.** He was the Bodhisatta's sister's son. See the **Citta-Sambhūta Jātaka.** Sambhūta is identified with **Ānanda.**[1]

[1] J. iv. 401.

2. **Sambhūta Thera.**—A brahmin of **Rājagaha** who, with his friends, **Bhūmija, Jeyyasena** and **Abirādhana,** entered the Order. Because he stayed continuously in the **Sītavana,** meditating on the nature of the body, he came to be called "**Sītavaniya.**" In due course he won arahantship, and the verses, declaring his *aññā,* are included in the Theragāthā.[1]

It is said[2] that when Sambhūta was meditating, **Vessavaṇa,** passing that way, saw him and worshipped him, and left two Yakkhas to keep guard and to tell Sambhūta of his visit. When the Thera had finished his meditations, the Yakkhas gave him Vessavaṇa's message offering him protection. But he refused their protection saying that the mindfulness taught by the Buddha was sufficient guard. On his return journey, Vessavaṇa again visited him, and, realizing from the appearance of the Elder that he had achieved his goal, went to the Buddha at Sāvatthi and announced to him Sambhūta's attainment.

Sambhūta had been a householder in the time of **Atthadassī Buddha,**

[1] Thag. vs. 6. [2] ThagA. i. 46.

and conveyed the Buddha and a large company across a river. He is probably identical with **Taraṇiya Thera** of the Apadāna.[3]

[3] Ap. i. 204 f.; see also VibhA. 306 and SA. iii. 201, where Sambhūta is given as an example of one who developed *lokuttaradhamma* by developing the heart (*cittaṃ dhuraṃ katvā*).

3. **Sambhūta Thera.**—He belonged to a family of clansmen and joined the Order under **Ānanda,** after the Buddha's death, attaining arahantship in due course. He lived in the bliss of emancipation, till one century after the Buddha's death, and, when the **Vajjiputtaka** heresy arose, his help was sought by **Yasa Kākaṇḍakaputta.** At that time he lived on **Ahogaṅgapabbata** and was called **Sāṇavāsī** because he wore a hempen robe. At the assembly of the arahants held on Ahogaṅgapabbata, Sambhūta suggested that they should seek the support of **Soreyya Revata.** Together they went to **Sabbakāmī,** and Sambhūta questioned him regarding the " Ten Points." Sambhūta was one of the monks appointed to the committee to discuss the points raised, and when they were declared heretical, he joined in the holding of the Second Council.[1]

A series of verses uttered by Sambhūta, moved by righteous emotion at the proposed perversion of the *dhamma* and *vinaya* by the Vajjiputtakas, is included in the Theragāthā.[2]

In the past, during a period when there were no Buddhas in the world, Sambhūta was a *kinnara* on the banks of the **Candabhāgā,** and seeing a Pacceka Buddha, he worshipped him and offered him *ajjuna*-flowers. He is evidently identical with **Ajjunapupphiya** of the Apadāna.[3]

[1] Vin. ii. 298 f., 303 ff.; ThagA. i. 390 f.; Mhv. iv. 18, 57; Dpv. iv. 49; v. 22; Sp. i. 34 f.

[2] Thag. vss. 291-4.

[3] Ap. i. 450.

Sammata.—See **Sammitā.**

Sammappadhāna Vagga.—The eighth chapter of the Navaka Nipāta of the **Aṅguttara Nikāya.**[1]

[1] A. iv. 462 f.

Sammappadhāna Saṃyutta.—The forty-ninth section of the **Saṃyutta Nikāya.**[1]

[1] S. v. 244-8.

1. **Sammappadhāna Sutta.**—The four *sammappadhānas*—this is the path leading to the " Uncompounded."[1]

[1] S. iv. 360.

2. **Sammappadhāna Sutta.**—Details of the four *sammappadhānas.*[1]

[1] S. iv. 364.

Sammasā Sutta.—A detailed description of the " inward handling."[1]

[1] S. ii. 107 f.

Sammādiṭṭhi Sutta.—**Sāriputta** explains to the monks at **Jetavana** what is right view. It is the comprehension of right and wrong and other sources. The monk who has it understands sustenance, its origin and cessation, and the way thereto; also Ill, its origin, etc.; decay and death, birth, existence, attachment, craving, feeling, contact, the six sense spheres, name-and-form, consciousness, the *saṅkhāras*, ignorance, the *āsavas*—the origin of these, their cessation and the way thereto.[1]

[1] M. i. 46-55.

Sammāparibbājaniya Sutta.—Also called **Mahāsamaya Sutta,** because it was preached on the day of the **Mahāsamaya.** The sutta was preached by the Buddha in reply to a question asked at the **Mahāsamaya** concourse, by the created (*nimmita*) Buddha.[1] It was the last of the suttas preached on that occasion, and was intended for those devas who were *rāgacaritas.* At the end of the discourse one thousand crores attained to arahantship.[2]

The sutta is a dissertation on the right path for a *bhikkhu.* He has no belief in omens, dreams, etc., subdues his passion, puts away slander, anger, avarice etc., and is liberated from bonds. He is free from attachments, is not opposed to anyone, has no pride, and longs for nibbāna.[3]

[1] SNA. i. 352. [2] *Ibid.*, 361, 367. [3] SN. vss. 359-75.

Sammāsambuddha Sutta.—It is by knowledge of the Four Ariyan Truths that a Tathāgata becomes a fully Awakened One.[1]

[1] S. v. 433.

Sammiti, Sammatiyā.—A division of the **Vajjiputtakā.**[1] They held that there is no higher life practised among Devas, that the convert gives up corruption piecemeal, and that the *puthujjana* renounces passion and hate.[2] They also held various views in common with other schismatic schools, such as the **Andhakas, Pubbaseliyas,** etc. In Tibetan sources they are called Sammatiyā, and are described as disciples of a teacher named **Sammata.**[3]

[1] Dpv. v. 46; Mhv. v. 7; Mbv. p. 96.
[2] Kvu. i. 1, 3, 4, 5.
[3] Rockhill, *op. cit.*, 184.

Sammillabhāsinī.—The name of **Rāhulamātā** in the **Ananusociya Jātaka** (*q.v.*).

1. **Sammukhāthavika.**—A king of ninety kappas ago, a former birth of **Māṇava Thera.**[1]

[1] ThagA. i. 163.

2. **Sammukhāthavika Thera.**—An arahant. Evidently identical with **Māṇava Thera.** He was king several times, under the name of **Sammukhāthavika, Paṭhavidundubhi, Obhāsamata, Saritacchadana, Agginibbāpana, Vātasama, Gatipacchedana, Ratanapajjala, Padavikkamana** and **Vilokana.**[1]

[1] Ap. i. 158 f.; ThagA. i. 163 f.

Sammuñjanī Thera.—So called because he was always sweeping. One day he saw **Revata** in his cell and thought him an idler. Revata read his thoughts, and, wishing to admonish him, asked him to return after a bath. When Sammuñjanī did so, Revata preached to him on the duties of a monk. Sammuñjanī became an arahant, and all the rooms remained unswept. The monks reported this to the Buddha, who, however, declared him free from blame, since there was no need for him to continue sweeping.[1]

[1] DhA. iii. 168 f.

Sammoda-kumāra.—See **Pakkha.**

Sammodamāna Jātaka (No. 33).—The Bodhisatta was once a quail. There was a fowler who enticed quails by imitating their cry and then throwing a net over them. The Bodhisatta suggested that when the fowler did this, they should all fly away with the net. This they did, and, day after day, the fowler returned empty-handed till his wife grew angry. One day, two of the quails started quarrelling, and the Bodhisatta, hearing their wrangling, decided to go elsewhere with his following. When the fowler came again and spread his net, the two quails started quarrelling, and he was able to capture them.

This was one of the stories related at the time of the quarrel (**Cumbaṭakalaha**) between the **Sākyans** and the **Koliyans.**[1] See also the introductory story of the **Kuṇāla Jātaka.** Elsewhere[2] the story is called the **Vaṭṭaka Jātaka.**

[1] J. i. 208-10.   [2] *E.g.*, J. v. 414.

Sammohavināsinī.—A *ṭikā* on the **Kaccāyanasāra,** by **Saddhamma-vilāsa** of Pagan.[1]

[1] Bode, *op. cit.*, 37.

Sammohavinodanī.—A Commentary on the **Vibhaṅgapakaraṇa** by **Buddhaghosa.**[1]

[1] Sad. p. 58.

"Sayaṃ-kata" Sutta.—When one has right view, one knows that weal and woe are self-wrought, etc.[1]

[1] A. iii. 440.

Sayakhattaka.—A locality in the Malaya district of Ceylon, mentioned in the account of the campaigns of **Parakkamabāhu I.**[1]

[1] Cv. lxx. 15.

Sayana Sutta.—Few are they who abstain from high and low beds.[1]

[1] S. v. 471.

Sayanakalaha.—The name given to a quarrel between **Mallikā** and **Pasenadi.** See the **Sujāta Jātaka** (No. 306).

1. **Sayanadāyaka Thera.**—An arahant. Ninety-four kappas ago he gave a bed to **Siddhattha Buddha.** Fifty-one kappas ago he was a king, named **Varuṇa.**[1]

[1] Ap. i. 98 f.

2. **Sayanadāyaka Thera.**—An arahant. He gave a bed to **Padumuttara Buddha.**[1]

[1] Ap. i. 105.

Sayampaṭibhāniya Thera.—An arahant.[1] He is evidently to be identified with **Khujjasobhita Thera** (*q.v.*).

[1] Ap. ii. 410 f.

Sayampabha.—A king of seventy-two kappas ago, a previous birth of **Pañcaṅguliya Thera.**[1]

[1] Ap. i. 186.

Sayampabhā.—A class of **Devas,** among whom virtuous men, such as those that maintain their parents and engage in harmless trades, are born.[1]

From the Commentary[2] it would appear that Sayampabhā is probably a

[1] SN. vs. 404. [2] SNA. p. 379.

generic name for all Devas (*ye te attano ābhāya andhakāraṃ vidhamitvā ālokakaraṇena Sayampabhāti laddhanāmā cha kāmāvacaradevā*).

1. **Sayha.**—A Pacceka Buddha, mentioned in a nominal list.[1]

[1] M. iii. 70.

2. **Sayha.**—A minister of the king of Benares, identified with **Sāriputta.** See the **Sayha Jātaka.**

3. **Sayha.**—A counsellor of **Brahmadatta,** king of Benares. He is identified with **Sāriputta.** See the **Lomasa Kassapa Jātaka.**

Sayha Jātaka (No. 310).—The Bodhisatta was once the son of the chaplain of **Brahmadatta,** king of Benares. He was brought up with the king's son, and they studied together in **Takkasilā,** becoming great friends. When the prince succeeded to the throne, the Bodhisatta, not desiring to live a householder's life, became an ascetic and lived in the **Himālaya.** As time passed, the king began to think of him, and sent his minister, **Sayha,** to fetch the ascetic, that he might become the royal chaplain. But the Bodhisatta refused to come, saying that he had no need of such honour.

The story was related in reference to a monk who, loving a woman, was discontented. The king is identified with **Ānanda** and Sayha with **Sāriputta.**[1]

[1] J. iii. 30-33.

Sayhaka Sutta.—See **Abhisanda Sutta** (2).

Sarakāṇi (Saraṇāni).—A **Sākyan.** When he died the Buddha declared that he was a *sotāpanna,* bound for enlightenment. But many of the Sākyans spoke scornfully of him, saying that he had failed in the training and had taken to drink. **Mahānāma** reported this to the Buddha, who said that Sarakāṇi had, for a long time, taken refuge in the Buddha, the Dhamma and the Saṅgha, and possessed qualities which secured him from birth in hell among the lowest animals and the *peta*-world.[1]

[1] S. v. 375 f.

1. **Sarakāṇi (Saraṇāni) Sutta.**—**Mahānāma** reports to the Buddha the rumours prevalent among the Sākyans regarding **Sarakāṇi** (*q.v.*). The Buddha says that Sarakāṇi had long since taken the Three Refuges, and he then goes on to describe various qualities, beginning from those which

lead to the destruction of the *āsavas* to those, such as affection for the Buddha, which prevent men from going to the Downfall.[1]

[1] S. v. 375 f.

2. **Sarakāṇi Sutta.**—**Mahānāma** brings to the Buddha's notice that the Sākyans are surprised at the Buddha's statement regarding the attainment of *sotāpatti* by **Sarakāṇi.** The Buddha then describes the virtues which make a man an *anāgāmin*, a *sakadāgāmin*, or a *sotāpanna*. The Buddha's doctrine is like a good field, well stubbed, the seeds sown therein capable of sprouting and happily planted, and the sky-god supplying a constant rain.[1]

[1] S. v. 378 f.

Sarakāṇi (*v.l.* **Saraṇāni**) **Vagga.**—The third chapter of the **Sotāpatti Saṃyutta.**[1]

[1] S. v. 369-91.

Saraggāma.—A village in the district of **Mahātila,** in the **Dakkhiṇadesa** of Ceylon, mentioned in the account of the campaigns of **Parakkamabāhu I.**[1]

[1] Cv. lxvi. 71; lxvii. 59, 79.

Sarañjita.—A class of Devas (the gods of "Passionate Delight"). According to the belief of some, a man who dies fighting is born among them.[1]

[1] S. iv. 308.

1. **Saraṇa.**—One of the two chief disciples[1] and also step-brother[2] of **Sumana Buddha.**

[1] J. i. 34; Bu. v. 26. [2] BuA. 126.

2. **Saraṇa.**—One of the chief lay-supporters of **Sumana Buddha.**[1]

[1] Bu. v. 28.

3. **Saraṇa.**—One of the two chief disciples of **Sumedha Buddha.**[1] He was the Buddha's younger brother.[2]

[1] Bu. xii. 23; J. i. 38. [2] BuA. 164.

4. **Saraṇa.**—The city of birth of **Dhammadassī Buddha.**[1] It was there that he met his two chief disciples, **Paduma** and **Phussadeva.**[2]

[1] J. i. 39; Bu. xvi. 13. [2] BuA. 183.

5. **Saraṇa.**—Father of **Dhammadassī Buddha.**[1]

[1] Bu. xvi. 13.

Saraṇa Sutta.—The Buddha teaches the "refuge" and the path thereto.[1]

[1] S. v. 372.

1. **Saraṇaṅkara.**—The Buddha who appeared in the world immediately before **Dīpaṅkara.**[1]

[1] Bu. xxvii. 1; J. i. 44; MA. i. 188.

2. **Saraṇaṅkara Thera.**—An eminent monk of Ceylon. **Narindasīha,** attracted by his piety and learning, gave him, while yet a *sāmaṇera,* a reliquary studded with seven hundred jewels and numerous books, and also made provision for his maintenance. At the instance of the king, Saraṇaṅkara composed the Sāratthasaṅgraha and Sinhalese Commentaries on the **Mahābodhivaṃsa** and the **Bhessajjamañjūsā.**[1] When **Vijayarājasīha** came to the throne, Saraṇaṅkara lived in the **Uposathārāma** and composed, at the king's request, a Sinhalese Commentary on the **Catubhāṇavāra.**[2] In the reign of **Kittisirirājasīha** he carried out, with the king's help, many reforms among the monks, adopting strong measures against delinquents. He was also instrumental in persuading the king to send an embassy to King **Dhammika** of Siam (**Sāminda**) in order to obtain from there a chapter of monks for the re-establishment of the *upasampadā* in Ceylon. When this had been done, the king invested Saraṇaṅkara with the dignity of Saṅgharāja over Ceylon.[3]

[1] Cv. xcvii. 48 ff. [2] *Ibid.*, xcviii. 23 f. [3] *Ibid.*, c. 49 ff.; 101 ff.

Saraṇattaya.—The first section of the **Khuddakapāṭha.**

Saraṇāgamaniya Thera.—An arahant. Thirty-one kappas ago, while he was travelling by sea with a monk and an **Ājīvaka,** the boat capsized and the monk gave him the Refuges.[1]

[1] Ap. i. 285=ii. 455.

1. **Sarada.**—The name of **Sāriputta** (*q.v.*) in the time of **Anomadassī Buddha.**[1]

[1] DhA. i. 89; but see Ap. i. 21, where he is called **Suruci.**

2. **Sarada.**—An ascetic who, with his large following, was converted by **Padumuttara Buddha.**[1]

[1] BuA. 160.

Sarabha.—A **Paribbājaka** who joined the Order and soon after left it. He then went about proclaiming in **Rājagaha** that he knew the *Dhamma* and *Vinaya* of the **Sākyaputta** monks, and that that was why he had left their Order. The Buddha, being told of this, visited the **Paribbājakārāma,** on the banks of the **Sappinikā,** and challenged Sarabha to repeat his statement. Three times the challenge was uttered, but Sarabha sat silent. The Buddha then declared to the Paribbājakas that no one could say that his claim to Enlightenment was unjustified, or that his *dhamma,* if practised, did not lead to the destruction of Ill. After the Buddha's departure, the Paribbājakas taunted and abused Sarabha.[1]

It is said[2] that Sarabha joined the Order at the request of the Paribbājakas. They had failed to find any fault with the Buddha's life, and thought that his power was due to an "*āvaṭṭanīmāyā,*" which he and his disciples practised once a fortnight behind closed doors. Sarabha agreed to find it out and learn it. He therefore went to **Gijjhakūṭa,** where he showed great humility to all the resident monks. An Elder, taking pity on him, ordained him. In due course he learned the *pātimokkha,* which, he realized, was what the Paribbājakas took to be the Buddha's "*māyā.*" Having learned it, he went back to the Paribbājakas, taught it to them, and with them went about in the city boasting that he knew the Buddha's teaching and had found it worthless.

[1] A. i. 185 ff. [2] AA. i. 412 f.

Sarabha Jātaka.—See the **Sarabhamiga Jātaka.**

Sarabha Sutta.—Relates the story of the Buddha's visit to Sarabha (*q.v.*) at the Paribbājakārāma.[1]

[1] A. i. 185 f.

1. **Sarabhaṅga.**—A Pacceka Buddha.[1]

[1] M. iii. 70. ApA. i. 107.

2. **Sarabhaṅga Thera.**—He belonged to a brahmin family of **Rājagaha,** and was given a name according to the family traditions. When he grew up, he became an ascetic, and made a hut for himself of reed stalks, which he had broken off—hence his name, **Sarabhaṅga** ("Reed-plucker"). The Buddha saw in him the conditions of arahantship, and went to him and taught the Dhamma. He listened and joined the Order, attaining arahantship in due course. He continued to live in his hut till it decayed and crumbled away, and, when asked why he did not repair it, he answered that he had looked after it during his ascetic practices, but that now he

had no time for such things. He then declared his *aññā* in a series of verses.[1]

[1] ThagA. i. 480 f. These verses are found in Thag. (vs. 487-93).

3. **Sarabhaṅga.**—The Bodhisatta born as a great teacher. See the **Sarabhaṅga Jātaka.**

Sarabhaṅga Jātaka (No. 522).—The Bodhisatta was once born as the son of the *purohita* of the king of Benares. He was called **Jotipāla** because, on the day of his birth, there was a blaze of all kinds of arms for a distance of twelve leagues round Benares. This showed that he would be the chief archer of all India.

After having been educated in **Takkasilā,** he returned to Benares and entered the king's service, receiving one thousand a day. When the king's attendants grumbled at this, the king ordered Jotipāla to give an exhibition of his skill. This he did, in the presence of sixty thousand archers. With the bow and arrow he performed twelve unrivalled acts of skill and cleft seven hard substances. Then he drove an arrow through a furlong of water and two furlongs of earth and pierced a hair at a distance of half a furlong. The sun set at the conclusion of this exhibition, and the king promised to appoint him commander-in-chief the next day. But during the night, Jotipāla felt a revulsion for the household life, and, departing unannounced, went into the **Kapiṭṭha-vana** on the **Godhāvarī** and there became an ascetic. On **Sakka's** orders, **Vissakamma** built a hermitage for him, in which he lived, developing great *iddhi*-powers. When his parents and the king with his retinue visited him, he converted them to the ascetic life, and his followers soon numbered many thousands.

He had seven pupils—**Sālissara, Meṇḍissara, Pabbata, Kāḷadevala, Kisavaccha, Anusissa** and **Nārada.** When Kapiṭṭhavana became too crowded, Jotipāla, now known as **Sarabhaṅga,** sent his pupils away to different parts of the country: Sālissara to **Lambacūlaka,** Meṇḍissara to **Sātodikā,** Pabbata to **Añjana Mountain,** Kāḷadevala to **Ghanasela,** Kisavaccha to **Kumbhavatī** and Nārada to **Arañjara,** while Anusissa remained with him. When Kisavaccha,[1] through the folly of a courtezan, was ill-treated by King **Daṇḍakī** of **Kumbhavatī** and his army, Sarabhaṅga heard from the king's commander-in-chief of this outrage and sent two of his pupils to bring Kisavaccha on a palanquin to the hermitage. There he died, and when his funeral was celebrated, for the space of half a league round his pyre there fell a shower of celestial flowers.

Because of the outrage committed on Kisavaccha, sixty leagues of Daṇḍakī's kingdom were destroyed together with the king. When the

[1] For details see *s.v.*

news of this spread abroad, three kings—**Kaliṅga, Aṭṭhaka** and **Bhīmaratha**—recalling stories of other similar punishments that had followed insults to holy men, went to visit Sarabhaṅga in order to get at the truth of the matter. They met on the banks of the Godhāvarī, and there they were joined by Sakka. Sarabhaṅga sent Anusissa to greet them and offer them hospitality, and, when they had rested, gave them permission to put their questions. Sarabhaṅga explained to them how **Daṇḍaka, Nāḷikira, Ajjuna** and **Kalābu,** were all born in hell owing to their ill-treatment of holy men, and went to expound to them the moral law. Even as he spoke the three kings were filled with the desire for renunciation, and at the end of Sarabhaṅga's discourse they became ascetics under him.

The story was told in reference to the death of **Moggallāna** (*q.v.*). It is said that after Moggallāna had been attacked by brigands and left by them for dead, he recovered consciousness, and, flying to the Buddha, obtained his consent to die. The six deva-worlds were filled with great commotion, and, after his death, the devas brought offerings of flowers and incense to his pyre, which was made of sandalwood and ninety-nine precious things. When the body was placed on the pyre flowers rained down for the space of one league round, and for seven days there was a great festival. The Buddha had the relics collected and deposited in a shrine in **Veḷuvana.** The Buddha identified Moggallāna with Kisavaccha and related this Jātaka. Of the others, Sālissara was **Sāriputta,** Meṇḍissara **Kassapa,** Pabbata **Anuruddha,** Devala **Kaccāyana,** and Anusissa **Ānanda.**[2]

[2] J. v. 125-51.

Sarabhamiga Jātaka (No. 483).—The Bodhisatta was once born as a stag. The king of Benares went out hunting with his courtiers, who contrived to drive the stag near the king; he shot, the stag rolled over as if hit, but soon got up and ran away. The courtiers laughed, and the king set off in pursuit of the stag. During the chase he fell into a pit, and the stag, feeling pity for him, drew him out and taught him the Law. On the king's return, he decreed that all his subjects should observe the five virtues. The king told no one of what had befallen him, but the chaplain, hearing him repeat six stanzas, divined what had happened. He questioned the king, who told him the story.

Many men and women, following the king's instructions, were reborn in heaven, and **Sakka,** realizing the reason for this, appeared before the king, who was practising shooting, and contrived that he should proclaim the Bodhisatta's nobility.

The story was told in reference to **Sāriputta's** wisdom. It is said that, when the Buddha descended from **Tāvatiṃsa** after preaching the Abhidhamma, wishing to demonstrate the unique wisdom of Sāriputta, he propounded certain questions before the multitude at **Saṅkassa,** which none but Sāriputta could answer. What the Buddha asked in brief Sāriputta answered in detail.

Ānanda is identified with the king and Sāriputta with the chaplain.[1] The story is also included in the *Jātakamālā* (No. 25) as the *Śarabha Jātaka.*

[1] J. iv. 263-75.

Sarabhavatī.—A city, the capital of King **Sudassana** (the Bodhisatta). It was visited by **Vessabhū Buddha,** who preached to the king.[1]

[1] BuA. 207.

1. **Sarabhū Thera.**—A disciple of **Sāriputta.** When the Buddha died, Sarabhū recovered from the pyre the Buddha's collar-bone, and, bringing it to Ceylon, deposited it in the **Mahiyaṅgana-cetiya,** covering the relic-chamber with *medavaṇṇa* stones in the presence of a large number of monks. He raised the cetiya to a height of twelve cubits.[1]

[1] Mhv. i. 37.

2. **Sarabhū.**—One of the five great rivers of northern India.[1] It formed the boundary between the two divisions of **Kosala, Uttara-** and **Dakkhiṇa-Kosala.** The **Acīravatī** was its tributary. **Sāketa** was situated on the banks of the Sarabhū, which flowed through the **Añjanavana.**[2] The Sanskrit name is Sarayū. The Sarayū itself flows into the Ghaṅghara, which is a tributary of the Ganges. See also **Gavampati (1).**

[1] Vin. ii. 237; Ud. v. 5; S. ii. 135; A. iv. 101; SNA. ii. 439; see also MA. ii. 586.
[2] *E.g.*, ThagA. i. 104.

3. **Sarabhū.**—A channel which branched off to the north from the **Puṇṇavaḍḍhana** tank.[1]

[1] Cv. lxxix. 47.

Sarasigāma.—A village in Ceylon, the centre of a monastic establishment and the headquarters of the Vilgammūla (**Sarasigāmamūla**) fraternity.[1] See below, **Sarogāmatittha.**

[1] P.L.C. 253.

1. **Sarassatī.**—A river in India, rising in the **Himālaya.**[1] It is evidently the Sarasvatī of Sanskrit literature, which, according to the Brāhmaṇas,

[1] Thag. 1104; Mil. 114 and AA. ii. 737; SNA. i. 321.

etc., formed the western boundary of the brahmanical Madhyadeśa. It rises in the hills of Sirmu in the Himalayan range, called the Semalik, and enters the plain at Ād-Badvi in Ambala. It is considered sacred by the Hindus.[2]

[2] Law : *Early Geog.*, p. 39; also CAGI. 382 f.

2. **Sarassati.**—A channel branching off from the **Toyavāpi** to the **Puṇṇavaḍḍhanavāpi.**[1]

[1] Cv. lxxix. 46.

Sarassatimaṇḍapa.—A building, erected by **Parakkamabāhu I.** near his palace at **Pulatthipura.** It was devoted to the arts of the Muses and was adorned with frescoes dealing with the life of the king.[1]

[1] Cv. lxxiii. 83 f.

Sarā Sutta.—Records a conversation between a deva and the Buddha—where the four elements find no further footing, the flood ebbs, and there is no whirlpool.[1]

[1] S. i. 15.

Sāraga Sutta.—Four persons are found in the world: the lustful, the hateful, the deluded, the proud.[1]

[1] A. ii. 71.

Sarājita.—A Niraya in which those who die in battle are born.[1] The Commentary[2] says that it is not a distinctive purgatory, but a part of **Avīci,** where fighters of all sorts fight in imagination. *Cf.* **Sarañjita.**

[1] S. iv. 311. [2] SA. iii. 100.

Saritacchadana.—A king of eighty-seven kappas ago, a previous birth of **Sammukhāthavika Thera.**[1]

[1] Ap. i. 159.

Sarīraṭṭha Sutta.—Ten conditions inherent in the body: cold and heat, hunger and thirst, evacuation and urination, restraint of body, speech, living, and the aggregate that produces becoming (*bhavasaṅkhāra*).[1]

[1] A. v. 88.

Sarīvaggapiṭṭhi.—A village in **Rohaṇa,** mentioned in the account of the campaigns of **Vijayabāhu I.**[1]

[1] Cv. lvii. 53.

Sareheru.—A tank in Ceylon, restored by **Vijayabāhu I.**[1]

[1] Cv. lx. 48.

Sarogāmatittha.—A ford on the **Mahāvālikanadī,** mentioned in the account of the campaigns of **Parakkamabāhu I.**[1] It is probably identical with **Sarasigāma.**

[1] Cv. lxxi. 18; lxxii. 1, 31; see also Cv. *Trs.* i. 316, n. 2.

Salaḷaghara.—See **Salaḷāgāra.**

Salaḷapupphikā Therī.—An arahant.[1] Evidently identical with **Sāmā** (*q.v.*).

[1] Ap. ii. 524.

1. **Salaḷapupphiya Thera.**—An arahant. Ninety-one kappas ago he was a *kinnara* on the **Candabhāgā,** and, seeing **Vipassī Buddha,** offered him a *salaḷa*-flower.[1]

[1] Ap. i. 233.

2. **Salaḷapupphiya Thera.**[1] The story is identical with that in (1).

[1] Ap. i. 289.

Salaḷamaṇḍapiya Thera.—An arahant.[1] Evidently identical with **Kimbila Thera** (*q.v.*).

[1] Ap. i. 333.

Salaḷamāliya Thera.—An arahant.[1] Evidently identical with **Samiddhi Thera** (*q.v.*).

[1] Ap. i. 206.

1. **Salaḷavatī.**—A river, forming the boundary on the south-east side of **Majjhimadesa.**[1]

[1] Vin. i. 197; DA. i. 173; J. i. 49.

2. **Salaḷavatī.**—A canal branching off from the **Kiḷakaruyyāna** sluice of the **Parakkamasamudda.**[1]

[1] Cv. lxxix. 43.

Salaḷāgāra, Salaḷaghara.—A building in **Jetavana.** Once when **Sakka** went to visit the Buddha he found him in the Salaḷāgāra, wrapt in *samādhi*, with **Bhuñjatī** waiting on him. Sakka therefore left a message with her.[1] Buddhaghosa[2] defines it as *salaḷamayagandhakuṭi*. Else-

[1] D. ii. 270.
[2] DA. ii. 705.

where[3] he says it was a hut of *salaḷa*-trees (*salaḷarukkhamaya*) or a hut with a *salaḷa*-tree at its door. In the Commentary to the **Mahāpadāna Sutta**[4] the Salaḷaghara is spoken of as one of the four chief buildings (*mahāgehāni*) of Jetavana. It was built by **Pasenadi** at a cost of one hundred thousand. **Anuruddha** is also mentioned as having stayed there.[5]

[3] SA. iii. 205. [4] DA. ii. 407. [5] S. v. 300.

Salaḷāgāra Sutta.—**Anuruddha,** addressing the monks at the **Salaḷāgāra,** tells them that it is as difficult to make a monk who has developed the four *satipaṭṭhānas* return to the lower life, as to make the Ganges flow westward.[1]

[1] S. v. 300 f.

1. **Salla Sutta.**—The eighth sutta of the Mahāvagga of the **Sutta Nipāta.** Death is inevitable, lamenting is therefore useless.[1] The sutta was preached in order to console a devout patron of the Buddha who, when his son died, starved for seven days.[2] The sutta is described[3] as *pāḷivasena gambhīro.*

[1] SN. vss. 574-93. [2] SNA. ii. 457. [3] *E.g.*, AA. i. 326.

2. **Salla Sutta.**—See **Sālā Sutta.**

" Sallattena " Sutta.—The noble disciple weeps not, nor grieves, when afflicted with pain, because, though hurt physically, mentally he is free. He is like a man pierced with only a single barb.[1] *v.l.* **" Sallena " Sutta.**

[1] S. iv. 207 f.

Sallekha Sutta.—The eighth sutta of the **Majjhima Nikāya. Mahā Cunda** visits the Buddha at **Jetavana** and asks him how to get rid of the various false views current about self and the universe. The Buddha answers that it is by right comprehension of the fact that there is no " mine," " I," or " self." He then goes on to explain how false views can be expunged, how the will may be developed, and how emancipation can be found.[1]

The Sallekha Sutta is given[2] as an example of a discourse where *brahmacariyā* is defined as *methunavirati.* It is also sometimes[3] described as *pāḷivasena gambhīro.*

[1] M. i. 40 ff. [2] DA. i. 178; MA. i. 275. [3] *E.g.*, SA. ii. 168.

" Sallena " Sutta.—See **Sallattena Sutta.**

Saḷa Vagga.—The tenth chapter of the **Saḷāyatana Saṃyutta.**[1]

[1] S. iv. 70-85.

1. **Saḷāyatana Vagga.**—The fifteenth section of the **Majjhima Nikāya.**[1]

[1] M. iii. 258-302.

2. **Saḷāyatana Vagga.**—The fourth section of the **Saṃyutta Nikāya.**[1]

[1] S. iv. 1-403.

Saḷāyatana Vibhaṅga Sutta.—A series of definitions of the six internal senses, six external sense-objects, six groups of consciousness, six groups of contacts, eighteen mental researches, thirty-six tracks for creatures, six satisfactions to the banished, three bases of mindfulness, and the supreme trainer of the human heart.[1]

[1] M. iii. 215-22.

Saḷāyatana Saṃyutta.—The thirty-fifth division of the **Saṃyutta Nikāya.**[1]

[1] S. iv. 1-204.

Sava.—A stronghold in **Rohaṇa.**[1]

[1] Cv. lxxiv. 60.

Savattha.—A sage. **Sāvatthi** (*q.v.*) was founded on the site of his hermitage.[1]

[1] SNA. i. 300; PSA. 367.

Savanaviyala.—A place in **Rohaṇa.**[1]

[1] Cv. lxxv. 2.

Savara.—See **Sapara.** In the Milinda,[1] Savara is mentioned as a place where people are unable to appreciate the value of red sandal-wood. Tradition calls it a city of Caṇḍālas.[2]

[1] pp. 191. [2] See *Milinda Questions*, i. 267, n. 1.

Savāraka.—A village where **Rukkha,** a kinsman of **Kassapa IV.,** built a vihāra, which he handed over to the **Mahāvihāra.**[1]

[1] Cv. lii. 31.

Saviṭṭha Thera.—In the **Aṅguttara**[1] he is represented as saying, in the course of a conversation between him, **Sāriputta** and **Koṭṭhita,** that he preferred the person who obtains relief by faith (*saddhā*), to one who

[1] A. i. 118 f.

testifies to the truth with the body or one who has won view. The Commentary[2] explains that Saviṭṭha himself won arahantship through faith, and that therefore he praises faith. The Saṃyutta[3] contains two conversations of Saviṭṭha, both of which took place at the **Ghositārāma** in **Kosambī.** The first is with **Musīla** and deals with the *paṭiccasamuppāda.* Musīla, in answer to Saviṭṭha's questions, says that he has realized the truth of the paṭiccasamuppāda as his very own. "Then you are an arahant," says Saviṭṭha, and Musīla remains silent. In the other conversation, **Nārada,** present at the discussion, in the company of **Ānanda,** requests that the same questions be put to him. This Saviṭṭha does, and he tells Saviṭṭha that he has realized the truth of the *paṭiccasamuppāda* by right insight and that, yet, he is not an arahant. He is like a man who sees a well containing water, but who has neither rope nor vessel. "*Now*, what will you say of Nārada ?" asks Ānanda. "Nothing that is not lovely and good," answers Saviṭṭha.

[2] AA. i. 353. [3] S. ii. 113 f.

1. **Saviṭṭhaka.**—An example of a low family name.[1]

[1] Vin. iv. 8, 13.

2. **Saviṭṭhaka.**—**Devadatta** born as a crow. See the **Vīraka Jātaka.**

Sasa(-paṇḍita) Jātaka (No. 316).—The Bodhisatta was once born as a Hare. He lived with three friends: a Monkey, a Jackal, and an Otter. The three lived in great friendship, and the Hare was their guide in the good life. One day, the Hare, observing the approach of the full moon, told his friends that the next day would be a fast-day and that they must collect food and give it to any beggar who approached them. The animals all went out very early in the morning, one by one; the Otter found some fish buried in the sand; the Jackal a dead lizard, some meat, and a pot of curds; and the Monkey some fruits; and, finding that nobody appeared to claim them, each took them to his own dwelling. The Hare had only *kusa* grass, which he could not offer to anyone. He therefore decided to give his own body, and, because of this brave decision, **Sakka's** throne was heated. Disguised as a brahmin, he came to test the Hare. He went first to the other animals in turn and they all offered him what they had. He then approached the Hare, whom he asked for food. The Hare asked him to collect faggots from the wood and make a fire. Then, telling the brahmin that he would give him his own body, without the brahmin having the necessity of killing him, he shook out any animals which might lurk in his fur, and then jumped into the fire as into a lotus-bed. By the power of Sakka, the fire remained as cool as snow, and Sakka revealed his identity. Then, so that the Hare's nobility might be known to all the world, he took some essence of the Himālaya and painted the form of a hare in the moon, to remain there during this whole kappa. Having done this, he went to the Hare and talked of the Doctrine, and then, making the Hare lie down on his bed of grass, Sakka went back to his heaven.

The story was related in the course of giving thanks to a landowner of **Sāvatthī** who had entertained the Buddha and his monks for seven days. **Ānanda** is identified with the Otter, **Moggallāna** with the Jackal, and **Sāriputta** with the Monkey.[1]

The story is included in the Cariyāpiṭaka[2] and in the Jātakamālā.[3] It is also referred to in the **Jayaddisa Jātaka.**[4] This Jātaka exemplifies the practice of *dānapāramitā.*[5]

[1] J. iii. 51-6. [2] i. 10. [3] No. 6. [4] J. v. 33. [5] BuA. 50.

Sasaṅkhāra Sutta.—On four kinds of persons—one is set free in this life, but after some effort (*sasaṅkhāraparinibbāyī*); another is set free when body breaks up; a third is set free in this life, without effort; a fourth is set free when body breaks up even without effort.[1]

[1] A. ii. 155 f.

Sahaka Thera.—He was a member of the Order in the time of **Kassapa Buddha,** and, having developed the first jhāna, was born after death, in the **Brahma**-world, where he is known as **Sahampati.**[1]

[1] SA. i. 155; SNA. i. 476.

Sahakapati.—See **Sahampati.**

Sahajāti, Sahajātā.—A township where **Yasa Kākaṇḍakaputta** met **Soreyya Revata,** whom he wished to consult regarding the Ten Points raised by the **Vajjiputtakas.** Revata had gone there from **Soreyya,** and Yasa followed him, passing through **Saṅkassa, Kaṇṇakujja, Udumbara** and **Aggaḷapura.** Sahajāti was on the river (? Ganges), and the Vajjiputtakas went there from **Vesāli** by boat.[1]

In the Aṅguttara Nikāya,[2] Sahajāti is described as a *nigama* of the **Cetis,** and **Mahā-Cunda** is mentioned as having stayed there and preached three sermons. According to the Saṃyutta,[3] **Gavampati** also lived there at one time.

[1] Vin. ii. 299 f., 301; Mhv. iv. 23-8.

[2] A. iii. 355; v. 41, 157.

[3] S. v. 436; the text says **Sahañcanika,** but for a correct reading see KS. v. 369, n. 3.

Sahañcanika.—Evidently a wrong reading for **Sahajāti** (*q.v.*).

1. **Sahadeva Thera.**—An arahant. He accompanied the **Thera Majjhima** to the region of Himavā.[1]

[1] Sp. i. 68; Dpv. viii. 10; MṬ. 317.

2. **Sahadeva.**—Son of the **Paṇḍu** king. He was the youngest of five brothers, all husbands of **Kaṇhā,** the others being **Ajjuna, Nakula, Bhīmasena** and **Yudhiṭṭhira.**[1]

[1] J. v. 424, 426.

Sahadhammā.—A class of Devas, present at the preaching of the **Mahāsamaya Sutta.**[1]

[1] D. ii. 260; DA. ii. 690.

Sahannagara.—A village in Ceylon, given by **Jeṭṭhatissa III.** to the **Mayettikassapavāsa-vihāra.**[1]

[1] Cv. xliv. 100.

Sahabhū.—A class of Devas present at the preaching of the **Mahāsamaya Sutta.**[1]

[1] D. ii. 260; DA. ii. 690.

Sahampati.—A **Mahābrahmā.** When the Buddha was at the **Ajapālanigrodha,** hesitating as to whether or not he should preach the Dhamma, **Sahampati** appeared before him and begged of him to open to the world the doors of Immortality. The Buddha agreed to this urgent request,[1] and accepted from Sahampati the assurance that all the Buddhas of the past had also had no other teacher than the Dhamma discovered by them.[2] Buddhaghosa[3] explains that the Buddha was reluctant to preach, not on account of indolence, but because he wished Sahampati to make him this request. For, thought the Buddha, the world honours Brahmā greatly, and when people realized that Brahmā himself had begged of the Buddha to spread his teaching, they would pay more attention to it. Sahampati was, at this time, the most senior of the Brahmās (*jeṭṭha-Mahābrahmā*).[4]

Sahampati once saw that the brahminee, mother of **Brahmadeva Thera,** habitually made offerings to Brahmā. Out of compassion for

[1] Vin. i. 5 f.; S. i. 137 f.

[2] *Ibid.*, 139; see also S. v. 167 f., 185, 232, where he gives the same assurance to the Buddha regarding the four *satipaṭṭhānas* and the five *indriyas*; A. ii. 10 f.

[3] *E.g.*, SA. i. 155.

[4] DA. ii. 467.

her, Sahampati appeared before her and exhorted her to give her offerings to Brahmadeva instead.[5] On another occasion, when **Kokāliya** died and was born in **Padumaniraya,** Sahampati appeared before the Buddha and announced the fact to him.[6] The Saṃyutta[7] contains a series of verses spoken by Sahampati at **Andhakavinda,** when the Buddha sat out in the open during the night and rain fell drop by drop. The verses are in praise of the life and practices of the monks and of the results thereof. Sahampati again visited the Buddha, simultaneously with **Sakka,** and as they stood leaning against a doorpost of the Buddha's cell, Sakka uttered a verse in praise of the Buddha. Sahampati then added another verse, exhorting the Buddha to preach the Doctrine, as there were those who would understand.[8] A verse spoken by him immediately after the Buddha's death is included in the books.[9]

During the time of **Kassapa Buddha,** Sahampati was a monk, named **Sahaka,** who, having practised the five *indriyas* (*saddhā*, etc.), was reborn in the Brahma-world. Thereafter he was called Sahampati.[10] The Commentaries say[11] that he was an *Anāgāmī-Brahmā* born in the **Suddhāvāsā,** there to pass a whole *kappa*, because he had developed the first *Jhāna* as a monk. The Buddhavaṃsa Commentary[12] says that, strictly speaking, his name should be "**Sahakapati.**" When the Buddha attained Enlightenment, Sahampati held over the Buddha's head a white parasol three yojanas in diameter.[13] Once he offered to the Buddha a chain of jewels (*ratanadāma*) as large as **Sineru.**[14] On the day that **Ālindakavāsi-Mahāphussadeva** attained arahantship, Sahampati came to wait upon him.[15]

It has been suggested[16] that Brahmā Sahampati is very probably connected with Brahmā Svayambhū of brahmanical literature.

5 S. i. 140 f.
6 SN. p. 125; *cp.* S. i. 151; A. v. 172.
7 S. i. 154 f.
8 *Ibid.*, 233.
9 D. ii. 157; S. i. 158.
10 S. v. 233.
11 SNA. ii. 476; SA. i. 155.
12 BuA. p. 11; see also p. 29.
13 *Ibid.*, 239; this incident was sculptured in the Relic Chamber of the **Mahā Thūpa** (Mhv. xxx. 74); *cp.* J. iv. 266.
14 KhA. 171; Sp. i. 115; Vsm. 201.
15 VibhA. 352.
16 VT. i. 86, n. 1.

Sahali.—A devaputta, follower of **Makkhali Gosāla.** He visited the Buddha at **Veḷuvana,** in the company of several other Devas, and spoke a verse in praise of Makkhali.[1]

1 S. i. 65 f.

Sahali.—A class of Devas, present at the preaching of the **Mahāsamaya Sutta.**[1]

1 D. ii. 259; DA. ii. 690.

Sahassa Vagga.—The eighth chapter of the **Dhammapada.**

1. **Sahassa Sutta.**—**Anuruddha** explains to the monks, in answer to their question, how it was by cultivating the *satipaṭṭhānas* that he came to comprehend the thousandfold world-system.[1]

[1] S. v. 203.

2. **Sahassa Sutta.**—One thousand nuns once visited the Buddha in the Royal Park (**Rājakārāma**) at **Sāvatthi.** He taught them that those possessed of unwavering loyalty to the Buddha, the Dhamma, and the Saṅgha, and cultivate the virtues dear to the Ariyans, they are assured of Enlightenment.[1]

[1] J. v. 360.

Sahassaka (Rājakārāma) Vagga.—The second chapter of the **Sotāpatti Saṃyutta.**[1]

[1] S. v. 360 ff.

Sahassakkha.—A name of **Sakka** (*q.v.*).

Sahassatittha.—A ford in the **Mahāvāluka-gaṅgā,** to the south of **Pulatthipura. Vijayabāhu IV.,** at the instigation of his father, **Parakkamabāhu II.,** arranged that the whole community of monks in Ceylon should assemble there and perform the ceremony of admitting new members into the Order.[1] In this he was assisted by his brother, **Vīrabāhu,** and the Chronicles[2] give great details of the preparations for the ceremony, which lasted for a fortnight. At the conclusion, Vijayabāhu conferred various ranks on the most eminent monks.

[1] Cv. lxxxvii. 71; for identification see Cv. *Trs.* ii. 182, n. 4.

[2] *E.g.*, Cv. lxxxix. 47 ff.

Sahassanetta.—A name for **Sakka** (*q.v.*).

Sahassayāga Sutta.—Evidently a name given to one of the **Satullapakāyika Suttas,**[1] in which the Buddha praises the worth of a small but righteous gift as being far greater than large gifts made unrighteously. A stanza from this sutta is quoted in the **Biḷārikosiya Jātaka**[2] and in the **Mahāvaṃsa Ṭīkā.**[3]

[1] S. i. 19.

[2] J. iv. 66.

[3] MṬ. 596.

Sahassaratha.—Fifteen kappas ago there were seven kings of this name, previous births of **Kumudamāliya Thera.**[1]

[1] Ap. i. 187.

1. **Sahassarāja.**—One hundred and sixty-five kappas ago, there were three kings of this name, previous births of **Udakapūjaka (Kuṭivihāriya) Thera.**[1]

[1] Ap. i. 143; ThagA. i. 129.

2. **Sahassarāja.**—Eleven kappas ago there were eight kings of this name, previous births of **Dhammacakkika Thera.**[1]

[1] Ap. i. 90.

Sahassavatthu-aṭṭhakathā, Sahassavatthuppakaraṇa.—A book mentioned in the Mahāvaṃsa Ṭīkā as being one of its sources.[1] It was evidently a collection of legends and folk-tales, and, probably, formed the basis of the **Rasavāhinī** and the Sinhalese *Saddhamālaṅkāraya.*[2]

[1] *E.g.*, p. 451, 452, 607. [2] P.L.C. 224 f.

Sahassāra.—A king of eleven kappas ago, a previous birth of **Sumanāveḷiya Thera.**[1]

[1] Ap. i. 247.

Sahāya Sutta.—The Buddha speaks in praise of two monks, comrades of **Mahā Kappina.** They have achieved the goal for which clansmen leave home.[1]

[1] S. ii. 285.

Sahodaragāma.—A village in **Rohaṇa,** where **Rakkha,** general of **Parakkamabāhu I.,** fought a battle.[1]

[1] Cv. lxxiv. 78.

1. **Sākacchā Sutta.**—Five qualities in a monk which justify his talking to his fellows on the good life.[1]

[1] A. iii. 81.

2. **Sākacchā Sutta.**—The same, mentioned by **Sāriputta.**[1]

[1] A. iii. 190.

Sākavatthu-vihāra.—A monastery in Ceylon, founded by **Dāṭhopatissa I.**[1]

[1] Cv. xliv. 135.

Sākiyavaṃsa-vihāra.—A monastery in Ceylon. **Maliyadeva Thera** once preached there the **Cha Cakka Sutta,** and sixty monks, hearing him, became arahants.[1]

[1] MA. ii. 1024.

Sākiyā.—See **Sakyā.**

Sākulā.—A tribe mentioned in a nominal list.[1]

[1] Ap. ii. 358.

Sāketa.—A town in **Kosala.** It was regarded in the Buddha's time as one of the six great cities of India, the others being **Campā, Rājagaha, Sāvatthi, Kosambi** and **Benares.**[1] It was probably the older capital of **Kosala,** and is mentioned as such in the **Nandiyamiga Jātaka.**[2] The Dhammapada Commentary,[3] however, states that the city was founded in the Buddha's time by **Dhanañjaya,** father of **Visākhā,** when, at the special invitation of **Pasenadi,** he went from Rājagaha to live in Kosala. On the way to Sāvatthi with Pasenadi, Dhañanjaya pitched his camp for the night, and learning from the king that the site of the camp was in Kosalan territory and seven leagues from Sāvatthi, Dhanañjaya obtained the king's permission to found a city there. And because the site was first inhabited in the evening (*sāyaṃ*), the city came to be called Sāketa.[4] The reference is probably to a new settlement established by Dhanañjaya in the old city.

We also learn from the Visuddhimagga[5] that the distance from Sāketa to **Sāvatthi** was seven leagues (*yojanas*), and there we are told that when the Buddha, at the invitation of **Cūla-subhaddā,** went from Sāvatthi to Sāketa, he resolved that the citizens of the two cities should be able to see each other. In the older books,[6] however, the distance is given as six leagues. The town lay on the direct route between Sāvatthi and Patiṭṭhāna, and is mentioned[7] as the first stopping-place out of Sāvatthi. The distance between the two places could be covered in one day, with seven relays of horses,[8] but the books contain several references[9] to the dangers of the journey when undertaken on foot. The road was infested with robbers, and the king had to maintain soldiers to protect travellers.

[1] D. ii. 146.

[2] J. iii. 270; *cf.* Mtu. i. 348, 349, 350, where it is called the capital of King Sujāta of the Sākyan race. See also the **Kumbha Jātaka** (J. ii. 13), where Sāketa is mentioned as one of the places into which alcohol was introduced quite soon after its discovery by **Sura** and **Varuṇa.** According to the **Mahānārada-Kassapa Jātaka** (J. vi. 228), it was the birthplace of **Bījaka,** æons ago. In this context it is called **Sāketā.** According to a tradition, recorded in the Mahāvastu, Sāketa was the city from which Sākyan princes were exiled when they founded **Kapilavatthu.** E. J. Thomas accepts this view (*op. cit.*, 16 f.).

[3] DhA. i. 386.

[4] The Divyāvadāna (211) has another explanation of the name, in connection with the coronation of **Mandhātā** (*Svayam āgatam svayam āgatam Sāketa-Sāketam iti saññā saṃvṛttā*).

[5] p. 390; but see below.

[6] *E.g.*, Vin. i. 253.

[7] SN. vss. 1011-1013.

[8] M. i. 149.

[9] *E.g.*, Vin. i. 88, 89, 270; iii. 212; iv. 63, 120.

Midway between Sāketa and Sāvatthi was **Toraṇavatthu,** and it is said[10] that, when Pasenadi went from the capital to Sāketa, he spent a night in Toraṇavatthu, where he visited **Khemā Therī** who lived there. Between Sāketa and Sāvatthi was a broad river which could be crossed only by boat.[11] Near Sāketa was the **Añjanavana,** where the Buddha sometimes stayed during his visits to Sāketa and where he had several discussions—*e.g.*, with **Kakudha,**[12] **Meṇḍasira** (*q.v.*), and **Kuṇḍaliya.**[13] On other occasions he stayed at the Kāḷakārāma[14] gifted to the Order by **Kāḷaka** (*q.v.*), and the **Tikaṇṭakivana,**[15] both of which were evidently near the city. Mention is also made[16] of **Sāriputta, Moggallāna** and **Anuruddha** staying together in Sāketa; **Bhaddākāpilānī**[17] also stayed there, so did **Ānanda.** Once when Ānanda was staying in the Migadāya in the **Anjanavana,** a nun, described as **Jaṭilagāhikā** (probably a follower of the Jaṭilas), visited him and questioned him regarding concentration.[18] Buddhaghosa says[19] that there lived at Sāketa a brahmin and his wife who, in five hundred lives, had been the parents of the Buddha. When the Buddha visited Sāketa they met him, and, owing to their fondness for him, came to be called **Buddhapitā** and **Buddhamātā,** their family being called **Buddhakula.**

According to some accounts,[20] **Anāthapiṇḍika's** daughter, **Cūla-Subhaddā,** was married to the son of **Kāḷaka,** a seṭṭhi of Sāketa. Kāḷaka was a follower of the Nigaṇṭhas, but he allowed Subhaddā to invite the Buddha to a meal. She did this by scattering eight handfuls of jasmine-flowers into the air from her balcony. The Buddha read her thoughts, and went to Sāketa the next day with five hundred arahants. At **Sakka's** request, **Vessavaṇa** (? **Vissakamma**) provided gabled chambers in which the Buddha and his monks travelled by air to Sāketa. At the end of the meal, the Buddha preached to **Kāḷakaseṭṭhi,** who became a *sotāpanna,* and gave the Kāḷakārāma for the use of the monks.

The Vinaya[21] mentions another seṭṭhi of Sāketa. His wife had suffered for seven years from a disease of the head, and even skilled physicians failed to cure her. **Jīvaka,** on his way to Rājagaha, after finishing his studies in **Takkasilā,** visited Sāketa, heard of her illness, and offered to

[10] S. iv. 374 ff. [11] Vin. iv. 65, 228.

[12] S. i. 54.

[13] S. v. 73; see also **Kāḷaka Sutta** and **Jarā Sutta** and **Sāketa Sutta.**

[14] A. ii. 24.

[15] *Ibid.*, iii. 169.

[16] *E.g.*, S. v. 174, 298 f.; for Sāriputta, see also Vin. i. 289.

[17] *Ibid.*, iv. 292.

[18] A. iv. 427. Among others who lived in Sāketa were **Jambugāmikaputta, Gavampati, Meṇḍasira, Uttara, Madhuvāseṭṭha** and his son **Mahānāga,** and **Visākhā. Bhūta Thera** (*q.v.*) was born in a suburb of Sāketa.

[19] SNA. ii. 532 f.; *cf.* DhA. iii. 317 f. and **Saketa Jātaka.**

[20] *E.g.*, AA. ii. 482; but see *s.v.* **Cūla-Subhaddā.**

[21] Vin. i. 270 f.

cure her. At first the seṭṭhi was sceptic, but in the end allowed Jīvaka to attend on his wife. Jīvaka cured her by the administration of ghee through the nose, and, as reward, received sixteen thousand kahāpaṇas from her and her various kinsmen.

Sāketa is supposed to be identical with Ayojjhā,[22] but as both cities are mentioned in the Buddha's time, they are probably distinct. Rhys Davids thinks[23] that possibly they adjoined each other "like London and Westminster." The site of Sāketa has been identified with the ruins of Sujān Kot, on the Sai River, in the Unao district of the modern province of Oudh. The river referred to is probably the Sarayū, which flows into the Gharghara, a tributary of the Ganges.

[22] CAGI. 405.
[23] *Bud. India*, p. 39. See also **Sāketa Sutta, Sāketa Jātaka, Sāketapañha.**

1. **Sāketa Jātaka** (No. 68).—Once, when the Buddha visited **Sāketa,** an old brahmin met him at the gate and fell at his feet, calling him his son, and took him home to see his "mother"—the brahmin's wife—and his "brothers and sisters"—the brahmin's family. There the Buddha and his monks were entertained to a meal, at the end of which the Buddha preached the **Jarā Sutta.** Both the brahmin and his wife became *Sakadāgāmins.* When the Buddha returned to **Añjanavana,** the monks asked him what the brahmin had meant by calling him his son. The Buddha told them how the brahmin had been his father in five hundred successive past births, his uncle in a like number, and his grandfather in another five hundred. The brahmin's wife had similarly been his mother, his aunt, and his grandmother.[1]

[1] J. i. 308 f.; *cf.* DhA. iii. 317 f.; SNA. ii. 532 f.

2. **Sāketa Jātaka** (No. 237).—The story of the present is the same as in Jātaka (1) above. When the Buddha returned to the monastery he was asked how the brahmin had recognized him. He explained how, in those who have loved in previous lives, love springs afresh, like lotus in the pond.[1]

[1] J. i. 234 f.

Sāketa Sutta.—The Buddha explains to the monks at **Sāketa** how it is possible to reckon the five *indriyas* as the five *balas* and the five *balas* as the five *indriyas.* By developing the five indriyas, release can be attained.[1]

[1] S. v. 219 f.

Sāketaka.—An inhabitant of **Sāketa.**[1]

[1] Mil. p. 331.

Sāketa-Tissa Thera.—He was not fond of learning, saying that he had no time for it. When asked by the others, " Have you time for death ?" he left them and went to **Kaṇikāravālikasamudda-vihāra.** There, during the rainy season, he was very helpful to the monks, both young and old, and at the end of the *vassa*, on the full-moon day, he preached a sermon which greatly agitated his listeners.[1]

[1] AA. i. 44; *cf.* DA. iii. 1061.

Sāketa-pañha.—The **Atthasālinī**[1] mentions that once the Elder **Tipiṭaka-Mahādhammarakkhita,** in talking of consciousness, referred to the " *Saketapañha.*" It is said that in Sāketa the monks raised the query, " When by one volition kamma is put forth, is there one conception only, or different conceptions ?" Unable to decide, they consulted the Abhidhamma Elders, who declared that just as from one mango only one sprout puts forth, so by one volition there is only one conception, and for different volitions, different conceptions.

[1] DhSA. 267.

Sāketabrāhmaṇa Vatthu.—The story of the brahmin of **Sāketa** who called himself the Buddha's father.[1] See the **Sāketa Jātaka.**

[1] DhA. iii. 317 f.

Sākkuṇḍa.—A grove near the **Sakkharālayagaṅgā.** It is mentioned in the account of the campaigns of **Parakkamabāhu I.**[1]

[1] Cv. lxxii. 29.

Sākyā.—See **Sakyā.**

1. **Sākha.**—A deer, a previous birth of **Devadatta.** See the **Nigrodhamiga Jātaka.**[1]

[1] J. i. 149 ff.; *cf.* DhA. i. 148; Mtu. i. 359.

2. **Sākha.**—A seṭṭhiputta of **Rājagaha,** a former birth of **Devadatta.** For his story see the **Nigrodha Jātaka.**[1]

[1] J. iv. 37 ff.; *cf.* Mil. 203.

Sākhāpattagāma.—A village in **Rohaṇa,** mentioned in the account of the campaigns of **Parakkamabāhu I.**[1]

[1] Cv. lxxiv. 166; see Cv. *Trs.* ii. 36, n. 5.

1. **Sāgata Thera.**—He was the personal attendant of the Buddha at the time when **Soṇa Koḷvisa** visited **Bimbisāra,** with overseers of the eighty

thousand townships of Bimbisāra's kingdom. Sāgata was endowed with supernatural power, and the overseers, who went to visit the Buddha at **Gijjhakūṭa,** were very impressed by his *iddhi,* so much so that even while the Buddha was preaching they could not take their eyes off him. The king thereupon asked Sāgata to show them a greater marvel, and Sāgata, having shown in the open sky wonders of various kinds, fell at the Buddha's feet and declared the Buddha his teacher.[1]

Later, when the Buddha went to stay in **Bhaddavatikā,** having heard men warn the Buddha of the proximity of a Nāga of great power in the Jaṭila hermitage at **Ambatittha,** Sāgata went there and lived in the Nāga's abode. The Nāga showed great resentment, but Sāgata overpowered him with his *iddhi* and then returned to Bhaddavatikā. From there he went with the Buddha to **Kosambī,** where the lay disciples, hearing of his wondrous feat, paid him great honour. When they asked what they could do for his comfort, he remained silent, but the **Chabbaggiyā** suggested that they should provide him with white spirits (*kāpotikā*).

The next day, when Sāgata went for alms, he was invited to various houses, where the inmates plied him with intoxicating drinks. So deep were his potations that on his way out of the town he fell prostrate at the gateway. The monks carried him, and at the monastery they laid him down with his head at the Buddha's feet, but he turned round so that his feet lay towards the Buddha. The Buddha pointed out his condition to the monks, using it as an example of the evil effects of liquor; and he made this the occasion for the passing of a rule against the use of alcohol.[2] It is said[3] that on the next day, when Sāgata came to himself and realized the enormity of his offence, he sought the Buddha and, having begged his forgiveness, developed insight, attaining arahantship. The Buddha later declared him foremost among those skilled in the contemplation of the heat-element (*tejodhātukusalānaṃ*).[4]

It is curious that no verses are ascribed to Sāgata in the Theragāthā. The Apadāna[5] contains a set of verses said to have been spoken by him. In the time of **Padumuttara Buddha** he was **Sobhita,** a brahmin. The Buddha came to his hermitage with his disciples, and Sāgata spoke verses in praise of the Buddha, who declared his future destiny. The Commentary adds that he was called Sāgata because he was greatly welcome (*sāgata*) to his parents.

[1] Vin. i. 179 f.

[2] *Ibid.*, iv. 108 f.; the story is also given as the introduction to the **Surāpāna Jātaka** (J. i. 360 ff.) which, too, was preached on this occasion; *cf.* AA. i. 178 f.

[3] AA. i. 179.

[4] A. i. 25.

[5] Ap. i. 83 f.

2. **Sāgata.**—The personal attendant of **Dīpaṅkara Buddha.**[1]

[1] J. i. 29; Bu. ii. 213; BuA. 104; Mhv. 5.

1. **Sāgara.**—The personal attendant of **Sumedha Buddha.**[1]

[1] J. i. 38; Bu. xii. 23.

2. **Sāgara.**—A *khattiya,* father of **Atthadassī Buddha** and husband of **Sudassanā.** He lived in **Sobhana.**[1] The Apadāna[2] mentions a monk, named **Sāgara,** a disciple of Atthadassī Buddha, who continued to live after the Buddha's death. The two may have been identical.

[1] Bu. xv. 14; J. i. 39. [2] Ap. i. 153; *cf.* ThagA. i. 153.

3. **Sāgara.**—See **Guṇasāgara.**

4. **Sāgara.**—A king of long ago, mentioned in a list of persons, who, though they held great almsgivings, could not attain beyond the *Kāmāvacara*-worlds.[1] It is probably the same king that is mentioned in the **Bhūridatta Jātaka**[2] as having become a *mahesakkha-deva* after death.

[1] J. vi. 99. [2] *Ibid.*, 203.

5. **Sāgara.**—Elder son of **Mahāsāgara,** king of **Uttaramadhurā. Upasāgara** was his younger brother. Sāgara was killed by the **Andhakaveṇhuputtā.** The story is given in the **Ghata Jātaka.**[1]

[1] J. iv. 79 f.

6. **Sāgara.**—A king of the line of **Mahāsammata.** He was the son of **Mucalinda** and father of **Sāgaradeva.**[1]

[1] Dpv. iii. 6; Mhv. ii. 3.

7. **Sāgara.**—One of the eminent monks present at the **Foundation** Ceremony of the **Mahā Thūpa.**[1]

[1] Dpv. xix. 8; MṬ. 525.

Sāgaradeva.—A king descended from **Mahāsammata.** His father was **Sāgara** and his son **Bharata.**[1]

[1] Dpv. iii. 6; Mhv. ii. 4.

Sāgara-Brahmadatta.—The son of **Brahmadatta** and a Nāga maiden. For his story see the **Bhūridatta Jātaka.**

Sāgaramatī.—Another name for **Sāriputta Thera** of Ceylon (*q.v.*).

Sāgala, Sāgalā.—A city in India, capital of King **Milinda.**[1] In various Jātakas—*e.g.*, the **Kāliṅgabodhi**[2] and the **Kusa,**[3] and also in the scholiast

[1] Mil. pp. 1, 3, etc. [2] J. iv. 230. [3] J. v. 283.

of the **Mahāummagga**[4]—Sāgala is mentioned as the capital of the **Madda** kings. It was also evidently called **Sākala.**[5] Sāgala was the birthplace of **Khemā Therī,**[6] of **Bhaddā Kāpilānī,**[7] and of Queen **Anojā.**[8] It is said[9] that when **Aritthigandhakumāra** refused to marry any woman unless she resembled a golden image possessed by him, the messengers sent by his parents found a girl in Sāgala who possessed the necessary requirements, but she was delicate, and died on her way from Sāgala to Sāvatthi. It is perhaps the same city which is mentioned in the Vinaya[10] as the residence of **Daḷhika.**

Sāgala is identified with the modern Sialkot in the Panjab.[11]

[4] J. vi. 471, 473.

[5] *E.g., Mahābhārata* 14, 32; (*tataḥ Sākalam abhyetvā Mādrānām puṭabhedanam*).

[6] ThigA. 127; Ap. ii. 546; AA. i. 187.

[7] ThigA. 68; Ap. ii. 583; AA. i. 99.

[8] DhA. ii. 116.

[9] *Ibid.*, iii. 281 f.; *cp.* the story of **Anitthigandha,** a Pacceka Buddha, given in SNA. i. 69.

[10] Vin. iii. 67.

[11] Law, Geog. 53.

Sāgalikā, Sāgaliyā.—One of the heterodox sects which branched off from the **Theravāda** in Ceylon.[1] They formed a part of the **Dhammarucikas,** and separated from that body three hundred and forty-one years after the establishment of Buddhism in Ceylon. They lived at first in the **Dakkhiṇa-vihāra,** but later went to the **Jetavana-vihāra,** built by **Mahāsena.** They made certain alterations in the *Ubhatovibhaṅga.*[2] According to the Sinhalese *Nikāyasaṅgrahaya,*[3] the Sāgalikas took their name from their leader, Sāgala Thera, and their separation took place seven hundred and ninety-five years after the Buddha's death, in the reign of King **Goṭhābhaya.** Moggallāna I. gave the vihāras of **Daḷha** and **Dāṭhākoṇḍañña,** on **Sīhagiri,** to the Dhammarucikas and the Sāgalikas, while he also gave the **Rājinī** nunnery for the use of the nuns of the Sāgalika sect.[4] **Aggabodhi II.** gave the **Veḷuvana-vihāra,** which he had built, to the Sāgalikas.[5] **Kassapa IV.** built for them the **Kassapasena-vihāra.**[6]

[1] Mhv. v. 13.

[2] MṬ. 175, 176; *cf.* Sās, p. 24; see also Mhv. xxxvii. 32 ff., and MṬ. 680.

[3] Quoted in Geiger's *Dīpavaṃsa and Mahāvaṃsa* (p. 90).

[4] Cv. xxxix. 41, 43.

[5] *Ibid.*, xlii. 43.

[6] *Ibid.* lii. 17.

Sājīva Sutta.—Five qualities which make a monk an example to his fellows: the achievement of virtue, concentration, insight, emancipation and the knowledge thereof; also the ability to explain questions on these matters.[1]

[1] A. iii. 81.

Sāṭimattiya Thera.—He belonged to a brahmin family of **Magadha** and, after entering the Order, lived in the forest and developed the sixfold *abhiññā*. Thereupon he instructed monks and preached to large numbers of lay people. One family in particular he converted to the Faith, and in that family he was waited on respectfully by a beautiful girl. **Māra,** wishing to disgrace him, once went to the house disguised as the Elder, and grasped the girl's hand. But she, feeling that the touch was not human, took her hand away. The others, however, saw this and lost faith in the Thera. He, all unconscious, was aware next day of their changed manner. Discerning the work of Māra, he made them tell him what had happened. The father begged his forgiveness, and said that henceforth he himself would wait on the Elder.[1]

The Thera is evidently identical with **Sumanatālavaṇṭiya** of the **Apadāna.**[2] Ninety-four kappas ago he met **Siddhattha Buddha** and offered him a palmyra fan (*tālavaṇṭa*) covered with *sumana* flowers.

[1] ThagA. i. 368 f.; verses ascribed to him are found in Thag. (246-8) [2] Ap. ii. 408.

1. **Sāṇavāsī, Sāṇavāsika.**—An epithet of **Sambhūta Thera** (*q.v.*).

2. **Sāṇavāsī.**—See **Sānuvāsī.**

Sātapabbata.—A mountain in **Majjhimadesa,** the abode of **Sātāgira.**[1] Many other Yakkas also lived there, three thousand of whom were present at the preaching of the **Mahāsamaya Sutta.**[2]

[1] SNA. i. 197. [2] D. ii. 257.

Sātavāhana.—A king. It is said[1] that, when **Anāthapiṇḍika's** family fell into poverty, owing to the alms given by him, a girl of the family, wishing to give alms, went to **Sātavāhana's** kingdom, swept a threshing-floor and gave alms with the money so obtained. A monk told this to the king, who sent for the girl and made her his chief queen. *v.l.* **Setavāhana.**

[1] DA. i. 303; is this Sātavāhana the king of the **Kathāsaritsāgara** i. 32 ?

Sātā.—An eminent Therī of Ceylon.[1]

[1] Dpv. xviii. 16.

Sātāgira.—A Yakkha. He and his friend, **Hemavata,** were two of the twenty-eight leaders of the **Yakkhas.** They had both been monks in the time of **Kassapa Buddha,** but had been guilty of deciding wrongly in the dispute which arose between **Dhammavādī** and **Adhammavādī** (*q.v.*), hence their birth as Yakkhas, Sātāgira in **Sātapabbata,** and Hemavata in **Himavā.** They recognized each other at the Yakkha assembly in the **Bhagalavatī-pabbata,** and promised to inform each other if, in their lives, they came across anything of interest.

When the Buddha was born and when he preached his first sermon, Sātāgira was present in the assembly, but, because he was constantly looking about to see if Hemavata was there, he could not concentrate his mind on the Buddha's teaching. When the sun set and the Buddha was still preaching, he went with five hundred of his followers to fetch Hemavata. At Rājagaha they met Hemavata, who was on the way to invite Sātāgira to Himavā, which was covered with such flowers as had never before been seen. Sātāgira explains that the reason for this miracle is the appearance of the Buddha in the world, and, in answer to Hemavata's questions, declares the greatness of the Buddha. Their conversation is found in the introductory *gāthā* of the **Hemavata Sutta** (*q.v.*). Buddhaghosa says[1] that, according to some, this meeting took place, not on the occasion of the first sermon, but later, when the Buddha was living in the **Gotāmaka-cetiya. Kālī Kuraragharikā** (*q.v.*), as she sat by her window cooling herself, heard the conversation of the two Yakkhas, and her mind being filled with devotion to the Buddha, as she heard his wonderful qualities being enumerated she attained *sotāpatti*.

When Hemavata is satisfied, from Sātāgira's description, that the Buddha is really the Awakened One, he decides to go to him with Sātagira. Together they go with their followers to **Isipatana** in the middle watch of the night, and Hemavata questions the Buddha about his teaching. Hemavata is, by nature, powerful and wise and filled with respect for the good, and the Buddha's marvellous exposition of the dhamma fills him with great joy. He sings the Buddha's praises in five stanzas, and, after taking leave of him and of Sātāgira, returns home with the promise that he will wander from place to place carrying the joyful news of the Buddha and his Dhamma among all beings.[2]

Later, when journeying through the air in various conveyances, on their way to the Yakkha assembly, Sātāgira and Hemavata and their followers were about to pass over **Āḷavaka's** hermitage; but because the Buddha was then inside, the Yakkhas found that their conveyances remained stationary as no one could pass over the head of the Buddha. When they thus discovered his presence, they alighted and made obeisance to the Buddha, and congratulated Āḷavaka on his extreme good fortune in having an opportunity of meeting and listening to the Buddha.[3]

[1] SNA. i. 199.

[2] This story is given in the Commentary to the **Hemavata Sutta;** SNA. i. 194-216; *cf.* **AA.** i. 134 f.

[3] *Ibid.*, 221; a similar story is related (**UdA.** 64) about them when they passed the abode of the **Yakkha Ajakalāpaka.**

Sātāgira is mentioned in the **Āṭānāṭiya Sutta**[4] as one of the Yakkhas to be invoked in time of need by the Buddha's followers. He is identified with the Yakkha of the Bhisa Jātaka.[5]

[4] D. iii. 204. [5] J. iv. 314.

Sātāgira Sutta.—Another name for the Hemavata Sutta (*q.v.*).[1]

[1] SNA. i. 194.

Sāti Thera.—He was a fisherman's son and held the false view that, according to the Buddha's teaching, a man's consciousness runs on and continues without break of identity.

Sāti's colleagues did their best to change his way of thinking, but failing to do so, they reported the matter to the Buddha. He questioned Sāti, who, however, sat silent and glum; then the Buddha preached to him and the assembled monks the **Mahātaṇhāsaṅkhaya Sutta.**[1]

Buddhaghosa explains[2] that Sāti was not a learned man. He knew only the Jātakas, and his views were due to the fact that in the Jātakas various characters were identified with the Buddha.

[1] M. i. 256 ff. [2] MA. i. 477.

Sātodikā.—A river in **Suraṭṭha** (Surat). **Sālissara** lived in a hermitage on its banks after he left the **Kaviṭṭhaka** hermitage.[1]

[1] J. iii. 463; but at J. v. 133 it is **Meṇḍissara** who lived there.

Sādiyaggāmavāpi.—A tank, repaired by **Parakkamabāhu I.**[1]

[1] Cv. lxviii. 44.

Sādhika Suttā.—Three suttas on the advantages of reciting the *Pātimokkha* rules twice a month.[1]

[1] A. i. 231 f.

Sādhinī, Sādhanī.—Mother of **Sodhana** and of **Kapila,** who, in a later birth, became **Kapilamaccha.** She and her daughter, **Tāpanā,** became nuns, but because they followed Kapila's example and abused and reviled good monks, they were born, after death, in **Niraya.**[1]

[1] DhA. iv. 37, 42; SNA. i. 305.

1. **Sādhīna.**—The Bodhisatta, born as king of **Mithilā.** See the **Sādhīna Jātaka.**

2. **Sādhīna.**—The last of the dynasty of king **Purindada.** He reigned in **Vajira (Vajiravutti)** while his descendants, twenty-two in number, ruled in **Madhurā.**[1]

[1] Dpv. iii. 21; MṬ. 128.

Sādhīna Jātaka (No. 494).—The Bodhisatta was once born as **Sādhīna,** king of **Mithilā.** He built six alms-halls and spent daily six hundred thousand pieces on alms. He lived a good life, and his subjects followed his example. In the assembly of the Devas his praises were spoken, and various Devas wished to see him. So **Sakka** sent **Mātali,** with his chariot, to fetch Sādhīna to **Tāvatiṃsa.** When he arrived, Sakka gave him half his kingdom and his luxuries. For seven hundred years, in human reckoning, Sādhīna ruled in heaven, and then he became dissatisfied and returned to his royal park on earth. The park-keeper brought news of his arrival to **Nārada,** the reigning king, seventh in direct descent from Sādhīna. Nārada arrived, paid homage to Sādhīna, and offered him the kingdom. But Sādhīna refused it, saying that all he wished was to distribute alms for seven days. Nārada arranged a vast largesse for distribution. For seven days Sādhīna gave alms, and on the seventh day he died and was born in Tāvatiṃsa. The story was related to lay disciples to show them the importance of keeping the fast-day.

Ānanda is identified with Nārada and **Anuruddha** with Sakka.[1]

Sādhīna was one of the four human beings who went to Tavatiṃsa while in their human body.[2]

[1] J. iv. 355-60. [2] Mil. 115, 271; MA. ii. 738.

Sādhu Vagga.—The fourteenth[1] and eighteenth[2] chapters of the Dasaka Nipāta of the **Aṅguttara Nikāya.**

[1] A. v. 240-4. [2] *Ibid.*, 273-7.

Sādhu Sutta.—Six devas of the **Satullapakāya** visit the Buddha at **Jetavana** and each utters a stanza in praise of generosity. The Buddha then utters a verse, in which he exalts practice of the Dhamma above gifts.[1]

[1] S. i. 20 f.

Sādhuka.—A village in **Kosala** where **Isidatta** and **Purāṇa** once stayed.[1] Buddhaghosa says[2] the village belonged to them.

[1] S. v. 348. [2] SA. iii. 215.

Sādhujanavilāsinī.—A *ṭīkā* on the **Dīgha Nikāya** by **Ñāṇābhivaṃsa** of Burma.[1]

[1] Sās. 134; Bode, *op. cit.*, 78.

Sādhudevī.—A seṭṭhi's daughter, who gave milk-rice to **Revata Buddha** just before his Enlightenment.[1]

[1] BuA. p. 132.

Sādhuvādī.—A celestial musician.[1]

[1] Vv. ii. 1; VvA. 324; but see VvA. 374.

Sādhusīla Jātaka (No. 200).—The Bodhisatta was once a famous brahmin teacher. A certain brahmin had four daughters who were wooed by four suitors—one handsome, another advanced in years, another of noble family, and the last virtuous. Unable to decide between them, the brahmin sought the teacher's advice and gave all his four daughters to the virtuous man.

The story was related to a brahmin of **Sāvatthi** who consulted the Buddha in a similar case. The two brahmins were identical.[1]

[1] J. i. 137 f.

Sānu Thera.—He was born in a family of **Sāvatthi** after his father had left home for the ascetic life. The mother, naming him **Sānu,** took him at the age of seven to the monks for ordination, thinking thus to ensure for him supreme happiness. He was known as Sānu (**Sānu-Sāmaṇera**) the Novice, and became a very learned teacher of the doctrine, practising the meditation of love (*mettā*), and was popular among gods and men. His mother in a previous birth was a Yakkha. Later, Sānu lost his intellectual discernment and grew distraught and longed to go roaming. His former Yakkha-mother seeing this, warned his human mother as described in the **Sānu Sutta** (*q.v.*). The latter was overwhelmed with grief, and, when Sānu visited her, he found her weeping. She told him that he was as good as dead in that he had rejected the Buddha's teaching and turned again to lower things, hence her sorrow. Sānu was filled with anguish, and, strengthening his insight, he soon won arahantship.[1]

He is evidently identical with **Udakadāyaka** of the Apadāna.[2] In the past, he saw **Siddhattha Buddha** having his meal and brought him water for his hands and feet and face and mouth. Sixty-one kappas ago he was a king, named **Vimala.**

The story of Sānu is given also in the Saṃyutta and Dhammapada Commentaries,[3] but the details differ. There, Sānu's human mother is portrayed as encouraging him to return to the lay life. His Yakkha-mother went to his human mother's home, where Sānu was waiting for a meal, took possession of his body, twisted his neck, and felled him to the

[1] ThagA. i. 113 f. [2] Ap. i. 205. [3] SA. i. 235 ff.; DhA. iv. 18 ff.

ground, where he lay foaming at the mouth. Sānu's mother was filled with despair. The Yakkhiṇī then revealed herself and exhorted Sānu not to behave foolishly by disregarding the Buddha's teaching. When he regained his senses, his human mother, too, pointed out the disadvantages of household life. When he declared his intention of not returning to lay life, she fed him with choice food and gave him a set of three robes that he might receive the *upasampadā* ordination. He then sought the Buddha, who urged him to fresh and strenuous effort. Sānu was famous as a mighty teacher throughout **Jambudīpa.** He lived to one hundred and twenty years.

Sānu Sutta.—Contains the conversation between **Sānu's** mothe and the Yakkhiṇī, who possessed Sānu (see **Sānu**) in order to prevent him from "losing his soul." Sānu's mother says she cannot understand how Yakkhas can possess holy men who keep the fasts and lead holy lives. The Yakkhiṇī says she is right; but holiness consists in refraining from evil, both open and secret. Sānu's mother understands, and, when her son regains consciousness and asks her why she weeps as he is not dead, she replies that he is as good as dead in that he wishes to return to the household life, like goods, which having been rescued from the fire, wish to be thrown into it once more.[1]

[1] S. i. 208 f.

Sānupabbata.—A mountain in the region of **Himavā.**[1]

[1] J. v. 415.

Sānumātā.—The name given to the **Yakkhiṇī** who had been the mother of **Sānu** (*q.v.*) in a previous birth. When the Yakkhas assembled to hear Sānu preach the Law, they paid her great respect, owing to her kinship with him.[1]

[1] SA. i. 236; DhA. iv. 19.

Sānuvāsīpabbata.—A hill near the village of **Kuṇḍi,** where lived **Poṭṭhapāda** (or **Kuṇḍinagarīya) Thera.**[1]

[1] Pv. iii. 2; PvA. 179.

Sāntanerī.—A fortress in South India, mentioned in the account of the campaigns of **Laṅkāpura.**[1]

[1] Cv. lxxvii. 44.

Sāpatagāma.—A village in **Rohaṇa; Mañju,** general of **Parakkamabāhu I.,** fought a battle there against **Sūkarabhātu.**[1]

[1] Cv. lxxiv. 131.

Sāpūga.—A village of the **Koliyans**, where **Ānanda** once stayed, and where he preached to the inhabitants. They were called **Sāpūgiyā.**[1]

[1] A. ii. 194.

Sāpūgiyā.—The people of **Sāpūga** (*q.v.*).

Sāpūgiya Sutta.—The inhabitants of **Sāpūga** visit **Ānanda,** who is living there. He tells them of the four factors of exertion (*padhāniyaṅgāni*): for the utter purification of morals, thought, view, and for the utter purity of release.[1]

[1] A. ii. 194 f.

1. **Sāma.**—The king of Benares[1] in the **Giridanta Jātaka** (*q.v.*).

[1] J. ii. 98.

2. **Sāma.**—One of the hounds of the **Lokantaraniraya.**[1]

[1] J. vi. 247.

3. **Sāma.**—The Bodhisatta born as a hunter's son. He was also called **Suvaṇṇasāma.** For his story see the **Sāma Jātaka.** He is given as an example of one who was conceived by umbilical attrition.[1]

[1] *E.g.*, Mil. 123.

4. **Sāma.**—The Milinda refers to a Jātaka story where **Devadatta** was a man named **Sāma,** and the Bodhisatta a king of deer, named **Ruru.** The reference is evidently to the **Rurumiga Jātaka,**[1] but there the man is called **Mahādhanaka.**

[1] J. iv. 255 ff.; but see Cyp. ii. 6.

Sāma Jātaka (No. 540).—Once two hunters, chiefs of villages, made a pact that if their children happened to be of different sexes, they should marry each other. One had a boy called **Dukūlaka,** because he was born in a wrapping of fine cloth; the other had a daughter called **Pārikā,** because she was born beyond the river. When they grew up the parents married them, but, because they had both come from the Brahma-world, they agreed not to consummate the marriage. With their parents' consent they became ascetics, and lived in a hermitage provided for them by **Sakka** on the banks of the **Migasammatā.** Sakka waited on them, and perceiving great danger in store for them, persuaded them to have a son. The conception took place by Dukūlaka touching Pārikā's navel at the proper time. When the son was born they called him **Sāma,** and, because he was of golden colour, he came to be called **Suvaṇṇasāma.** He was the Bodhisatta.

One day, after Sāma was grown up, his parents, returning from collecting roots and fruits in the forest, took shelter under a tree on an anthill. The water which dripped from their bodies angered a snake living in the anthill, and his venomous breath blinded them both. When it grew late Sāma went in search of them and brought them home. From then onwards he looked after them.

Piliyakkha, king of Benares, while out hunting one day, leaving his mother in charge of the kingdom, saw Sāma drawing water, and, lest he should escape, shot at him with his arrow. The king took him for some supernatural being, seeing that the deer, quite fearless, drank of the water while Sāma was filling his jar.

When Piliyakkha heard who Sāma was and of how he was the mainstay of his parents, he was filled with grief. Sāma fell down fainting from the poisoned arrow, and the king thought him dead. A goddess, **Bahusodarī,** who had been Sāma's mother seven births earlier, lived in **Gandhamādana** and kept constant watch over him. This day she had gone to an assembly of the gods and had forgotten him for a while, but she suddenly became aware of the danger into which he had fallen. She stood in the air near Piliyakkha, unseen by him, and ordered him to go and warn Sāma's parents. He did as he was commanded, and, having revealed his identity, gradually informed them of Sāma's fate and his own part in it. But neither Dukūlaka nor Pārikā spoke to him one word of resentment. They merely asked to be taken to where Sāma's body lay. Arrived there, Pārikā made a solemn Act of Truth (*saccakiriyā*), and the poison left Sāma's body, making him well.

Bahusodarī did likewise in Gandhamādana, and Sāma's parents regained their sight. Then Sāma preached to the marvelling king, telling him how even the gods took care of those who cherished their parents.

The story was told in reference to a young man of **Sāvatthi.** Having heard the Buddha preach, he obtained his parents' leave with great difficulty and joined the Order. Five years he lived in the monastery, and, failing to attain insight, he returned to the forest and strove for twelve years more. His parents grew old, and as there was no one to look after them, their retainers robbed them of their goods. Their son, hearing of this from a monk who visited him in the forest, at once left his hermitage and returned to Sāvatthi. There he tended his parents, giving them food and clothing which he acquired by begging, often starving himself that they might eat. Other monks blamed him for supporting lay-folk, and the matter was reported to the Buddha. But the Buddha, hearing his story, praised him and preached to him the **Mātuposaka Sutta** (*q.v.*).

Dukūlaka is identified with **Kassapa,** Pārikā with **Bhaddā Kāpilānī,** Piliyakkha with **Ānanda,** Sakka with **Anuruddha,** and Bahusodarī with **Uppalavaṇṇā.**[1]

The **Sālikedāra Jātaka** (*q.v.*) was preached in reference to the same monk.

[1] J. vi. 68-95; the story is referred to at Mil. 198 f.; J. iv. 90, etc.; see also Mtu. ii. 212 ff.

Sāmagalla.—A village in Ceylon.[1] At the time of the compilation of the **Mahāvaṃsa Ṭīkā,**[2] it was called **Moragalla.** Its full name was **Mātuvelaṅga-Sāmagalla.** It was in the Malaya country, and **Vaṭṭagāmaṇī Abhaya** lived there during a part of his exile in the house of **Tanasīva.**

[1] Mhv. xxxiii. 52 f. [2] MṬ. 616.

Sāmagāma.—A **Sākyan** village where the **Sāmagāma Sutta** was preached.[1] There was a lotus pond in the village.[2] The Vedhaññā (*q.v.*) probably lived there, because, according to the **Pāsādika Sutta,**[3] the Buddha was in the mango-grove of the Vedhañña Sākyans when the news, as given in the **Sāmagāma Sutta,** of **Nigaṇṭha Nātaputta's** death, was brought to him. According to Buddhaghosa[4] the village was called Sāmagāma, *Sāmakānaṃ ussanattā.*

[1] M. ii. 243. [2] A. iii. 309. [3] D. iii. 117. [4] MA. ii. 829.

1. **Sāmagāma Sutta.**—While the Buddha is at **Sāmagāma,** news is brought to **Ānanda** by **Cunda Samaṇuddesa** of the death of **Nigaṇṭha Nātaputta** at **Pāvā,** and of the division of his followers into two factions engaged in fighting each other. Ānanda gives the news to the Buddha, who asks if there be any difference of opinion among monks regarding the Buddha's teaching. "No," answers Ānanda, but adds that such differences may arise after the Buddha's death. The Buddha says that quarrels regarding rigours of regimen or of the Vinaya are of little concern. It is quarrels regarding the Path or the course of training that are really important. He then explains the six causes from which disputes grow, the four adjudications (*adhikaraṇa*) regarding disputes, and the seven settlements of adjudication—by giving a summary verdict in the presence of the parties, a verdict of innocence, of past insanity; confession may be admitted; a chapter'sdecision may be taken; there is also specific wickedness and there is covering up. Then there are six things which lead to conciliations: acts of love, words of love, sharing equally whatever

gifts one receives, strict practice of virtue without flaw or blemish, and the holding of noble views which make for salvation.[1]

Buddhaghosa adds[2] that, while in the **Kosambiya Sutta** the *Sotāpattimagga* is called *sammādiṭṭhi*, in this sutta, *Sotāpattiphala* itself is so called.

[1] M. ii. 243-51; *cf.* the **Pāsādika Sutta.** [2] MA. ii. 840.

2. **Sāmagāma Sutta.**—The Buddha was once staying near the lotus pond at **Sāmagāma** and late at night is visited by a deva. After saluting the Buddha, he states that there are three things which lead to a monk's failure: delight in worldly activity, delight in talk, and delight in sleep. So saying, he departs. The next day the Buddha relates to the monks the Deva's statement and adds three other things which lead to failure: delight in company, evil speaking, and friendship with bad men.[1]

[1] A. iii. 309 f.

Sāmañcakāni.—See **Sāmaṇḍakāni.**

Sāmañña Sutta.—Few are they who reverence recluses, many they who do not.[1]

[1] S. v. 468.

Sāmaññakāni Thera.—He was the son of a **Paribbājaka** and entered the Order after seeing the Buddha perform the Twin Miracle; he later attained arahantship through *jhāna*. There was a Paribbājaka, named **Kātiyāna,** whom he had known as a layman, and Kātiyāna, having become destitute after the Buddha's appearance in the world, asked Sāmaññakāni what he could do to get happiness in this world and the next. His friend answered that he should follow the Noble Eightfold Path.[1] We are told[2] that Kātiyāna later joined the Order and became an arahant.

Sāmaññakāni is evidently identical with **Mañcadāyaka (Pecchadāyaka)** of the Apadāna.[3] Ninety-one kappas ago he gave a bed to **Vipassi Buddha.** Perhaps he is also identical with **Sāmaṇḍakāni** (*q.v.*).

[1] Thag. vs. 35; ThagA. i. 98 f. [2] *Ibid.*, 450. [3] Ap. i. 455.

Sāmaññaphala Sutta.—The second sutta of the **Dīgha Nikāya. Ajātasattu,** accompanied by **Jīvaka,** visits the Buddha at Jīvaka's **Ambavana** and questions him on the fruits of recluseship, wherefor men join the Buddha's Order. The Buddha answers and includes in his answer his justification for the foundation of the Order, for the enunciation of the Vinaya, and the practical rules by which life in the Order is regulated

The sutta also contains a list of ordinary occupations followed by people in the Buddha's day, which forms interesting reading.

In the introductory story, Ajātaputta explains that he has already put the question to the founders of six other Orders: **Pūraṇa Kassapa, Makkhali Gosāla, Ajita Kesakambala, Pakudha Kaccāyana, Nigaṇṭha Nātaputta** and **Sañjaya Belaṭṭhiputta.** But these teachers, instead of answering his questions, give a general statement of their theories.

The summaries given here of their teachings are of great interest, because they form some sort of evidence, at least, as to the speculations favoured by them. By means of a counter-question, the Buddha finds from Ajātasattu that even if a servant of his joined the Order, he would receive the king's honour and respect. Then the Buddha proceeds to show, step by step, the fruits higher and nobler, which await the *samaṇa*, immediate in their effect, culminating in the sixfold *abhiññā* of the arahant. The king is greatly impressed, takes refuge in the Buddha, and expresses his remorse for having killed his father. The Buddha utters no word of blame, but after the departure of the king, he informs the monks that if Ajātasattu had not been guilty of patricide he would have realized the first-fruit of the Path.[1]

The Commentary adds[2] that as a result of hearing this discourse, Ajātasattu would, in the future, become a Pacceka Buddha named **Viditavisesa.** From this moment, Ajātasattu was one of the Buddha's most devoted followers. It is said that, after his father's death, Ajātasattu could never sleep at night until he had heard the Buddha, after which he enjoyed peaceful sleep.

[1] D. i. 47-86. [2] DA. i. 238.

Sāmaṇera Sutta, Sāmaṇeriya Sutta.—On two novices, a man and a woman, who were born as *petas* because of their evil deeds in the time of **Kassapa Buddha. Moggallāna** saw them as he descended **Gijjhakūṭa.**[1]

[1] S. ii. 261.

Sāmaṇḍaka, Sāmaṇḍakāni, Sāmañcakāni.—A **Paribbajjaka,** mentioned[1] as having visited **Sāriputta** at **Ukkācelā (Ukkāvelā)** and questioned him regarding Nibbāna, and again[2] at **Nālakagāma,** where he questioned him regarding weal and woe. He is, perhaps, to be identified with **Sāmaññakāni** (*q.v.*).

[1] S. iv. 261 f. [2] A. v. 121 f.

Sāmaṇḍaka or **Sāmañcakāni Saṃyutta.** The thirty-ninth section of the **Saṃyutta Nikāya.**[1]

[1] S. iv. 261 f.

Sāmadevī.—A favourite of King **Bhātika** of Ceylon. On one occasion a large number of men were charged before the king with having eaten beef. He inflicted a fine, but, as they were unable to pay, he appointed them as scavengers to the palace. One of them had a beautiful daughter, Sāmadevī, whom the king liked and installed in his harem. Owing to her, her kinsmen, too, lived happily.[1]

[1] VibhA. 440.

1. **Sāmā.**—The chief woman disciple of **Kakusandha Buddha.**[1]

[1] Bu. xxiii. 21; J. i. 42.

2. **Sāmā.**—One of the chief lay-women disciples of **Koṇāgamaṇa Buddha.**[1]

[1] Bu. xxiv. 24.

3. **Sāmā.**—A courtezan of Benares; for her story see the **Kaṇavera Jātaka.**[1]

[1] J. iii. 59 ff.

4. **Sāmā Therī.**—She belonged to an eminent family of **Kosambī,** and when her friend **Sāmāvatī** died she left the world in distress of mind. Unable to subdue her grief, she could not grasp the Ariyan way. One day, while listening to **Ānanda's** preaching, she won insight, and, on the seventh day from then became an arahant.[1]

[1] Thig. vs. 37-8; ThigA. 44.

5. **Sāmā Therī.**—She belonged to a family of **Kosambī** and left the world in distress on the loss of her friend, **Sāmāvatī.** For twenty-five years she was unable to gain self-mastery, till, in her old age, she heard a sermon and won arahantship.

Ninety-one kappas ago she was a *kinnarī* on the banks of the **Candabhāgā.** One day, while amusing herself in company of her friends, she saw **Vipassī Buddha** and worshipped him with *saḷala*-flowers.[1] She is evidently identical with **Saḷalapupphikā** of the Apadāna.[2]

[1] Thig. 39-41; ThigA. 45 f.

[2] Ap. ii. 524.

6. **Sāmā.**—The original name of **Sāmāvatī** (*q.v.*).

Sāmāvatī.—One of the three chief consorts of King **Udena.** She was the daughter of the seṭṭhi **Bhaddavatiya** of **Bhaddavatī,** who was a friend of **Ghosaka** of **Kosambī.** When plague broke out in Bhaddavatī, she and her parents fled to Kosambī, and there obtained food from the alms-hall provided by Ghosaka. On the first day Sāmāvatī asked for three portions, on the second two, on the third only one. For her father had died after the meal on the first day, her mother on the second. When, on the third day, she asked for only one portion, **Mitta,** who was distributing alms, teased her, saying: "Today you know the capacity of your belly." She asked what he meant, and when he explained his words, she told him what had happened. Mitta pitied her and adopted her as his daughter.

One day, when she arrived at the refectory, she found a great uproar going on, people rushing everywhere to get alms. She asked to be allowed to bring order into this chaos, and had a fence erected round the refectory with separate doors for entrance and exit. This put an end to the disturbances. Ghosaka, hearing no noise in the refectory as before, inquired the reason, and, finding out what Sāmāvatī had done, adopted her as his own child. Sāmāvatī's original name was **Sāmā,** but after building the fence (*vati*) round the refectory she was called **Sāmāvatī.**

On a festival day Udena saw Sāmāvatī going to the river to bathe, and, falling in love with her, asked Ghosaka to send her to the palace. But Ghosaka refused, and the king turned him and his wife out of doors and sealed up his house. When Sāmāvati discovered this, she made Ghosaka send her to the palace, and Udena made her his chief consort. Some time afterwards Udena took **Māgandiyā** (*q.v.*) also as consort.

When the Buddha visited Kosambī at the request of **Ghosaka, Kukkuṭa** and **Pāvāriya, Khujjutarā,** the servant-woman of Sāmāvatī, heard him preach and became a *sotāpanna*. She had been on her way to the gardener, **Sumana,** to buy flowers for Sāmāvatī, with the eight pieces of money given to her daily by the king for this purpose. On Sumana's invitation, she had gone to hear the Buddha at his house. On other days she had spent only half the money on flowers, appropriating the rest for herself; but this day, having become a *sotāpanna*, she bought flowers with the whole amount and took them to Sāmāvatī, to whom she confessed her story. At Sāmāvatī's request, Khujjuttarā repeated to her and her companions the sermon she had heard from the Buddha. After this, she visited the Buddha daily, repeating his sermon to Sāmāvatī and her friends. Having learnt that the Buddha passed along the street in which the palace stood, Sāmāvatī had holes made in the walls so that she and her friends might see the Buddha and do obeisance to him. Māgandiyā heard of this during a visit to Sāmāvatī's quarters, and, because of her hatred for the Buddha, she determined to have Sāmāvatī punished.[1]

At first her plots miscarried, and Udena, convinced of Sāmāvatī's

[1] For details see *s.v.* **Māgandiyā.**

goodness, gave her a boon, and she chose that the Buddha be invited to visit the palace daily and to preach to her and her friends. But the Buddha sent **Ānanda** instead, and they provided him with food every day and listened to the Law. One day they presented him with five hundred robes given to them by the king, who, at first, was very angry, but on hearing from Ānanda that nothing given to the monks was lost, he gave another five hundred robes himself.

In the end, Māgandiyā's plot succeeded, and Sāmāvatī and her companions were burned to death in their own house. Udena was in his park, and, on his arrival, he found them all dead. When the Buddha was asked, he said that some of the women had attained to the First Fruit of the Path, others to the second, yet others to the third. It is said that in a previous birth Sāmāvatī and her friends had belonged to the harem of the king of Benares. One day they went bathing with the king, and, feeling cold when they came out of the water, they set fire to a tangle of grass near by. When the grass burned down, they found a Pacceka Buddha seated in the tangle, and fearing that they had burnt him to death, they pulled more grass, which they placed round his body, and, after pouring oil on it, set fire to it so that all traces of their crime might be destroyed. The Pacceka Buddha was in *samādhi* and nothing could therefore harm him, but it was this act which brought retribution to Sāmāvatī and her companions.[2]

The two Therī's named **Sāmā** (*q.v.*) were friends of Sāmāvatī, and were so filled with grief over her death that they left home and joined the Order.

Sāmāvatī is reckoned among the most eminent of the lay-women who were followers of the Buddha, and was declared by him foremost among those who lived in kindliness (*aggaṃ mettāvihāriṇaṃ*).[3]

Her *iddhi*, in warding off the arrow shot at her by Udena, is often referred to.[4]

[2] The story of Sāmāvatī is included in the story cycle of Udena. For details see especially DhA. i. 187-91, 205-225; the story also appears, with certain variations in detail, in AA. i. 232-4, 236 ff., and is given very briefly in UdA. 382 f., omitting the account of the reason for Sāmāvatī's death which is given at length in an explanation of an Udāna (Ud. vii. 10) dealing with the incident. *Cf.* Dvy. 575 f. According to the Visuddhimagga (p. 380 f.), Māgandiyā's desire to kill Sāmāvatī arose from her desire to be herself chief queen.

[3] A. i. 26; *cf.* iv. 348.

[4] *E.g.*, BuA. 24; ItA. 23; PSA. 498; AA. ii. 791.

Sāmidatta Thera.—He belonged to a brahmin family of **Sāvatthi,** and used to go to the vihāra to hear the Buddha preach. One day the Buddha preached for his special benefit, and, very much moved, he joined the Order. But because of his immaturity of knowledge, he continued some time without application. Later he was impressed by another sermon of the Buddha, and became devoted and intent, attaining arahantship soon afterwards.[1]

He is evidently identical with **Adhichattiya** (or **Chattādhichattiya**) of the Apadāna.[2] In the past he erected a parasol over the cetiya of **Atthadassī Buddha.**

[1] Thag. vs. 90. ThagA. i. 189. [2] Ap. i. 170.

Sāmindavisaya.—The Pāli name for Siam. There was very close relationship between Ceylon and Siam from the middle ages.[1] When Buddhism fell on evil days in Ceylon, the kings of that Island turned to Siam for help in the restoration of the Faith. **Kittisirirājasīha** obtained copies of the **Mahāvaṃsa** from Siam and completed the chronicle down to his day.[2] With the help of the Olandā (Dutch), he sent an embassy to **Ayojjhā**—capital of **Dhammika,** king of Siam—asking that a chapter of monks might be sent to Ceylon. Ten monks were sent, with **Upāli** and **Ariyamuni** at their head, together with many books and other gifts. The monks took up their residence in the **Pupphārāma** in **Siri-vaḍḍhanapura** (Kandy), and, under the king's patronage, the ceremony of ordination was held on the 2296th year after the Buddha's death, on the full-moon day of Asāḷha.

Some time later, **Dhammika** again sent a chapter led by **Visuddhācariya** and **Varañāṇamuni.** As a token of his gratitude, Kittisirirājasiha sent to Dhammika a model of the Buddha's Tooth Relic in Kandy, together with various other gifts. Dhammika returned his courtesy by sending various books not to be found in Ceylon, a replica of the Buddha's footprint found on the **Saccabaddha** Mountain, etc.[3]

[1] For details see *J.R.A.S.* (Ceylon) xxxii. 190 ff. [2] Cv. xcix. 78 f. [3] *Ibid.*, c. 63 ff., 136 ff.

Sāmisantosuyyāna.—A park laid out by **Parakkamabāhu I.**[1]

[1] Cv. lxxix. 12.

Sāmugāma.—A village gifted by **Aggabodhi III.** to the *padhānaghara*, called **Mahallarāja.**[1]

[1] Cv. xliv. 120.

Sārakappa.—The name given to a *kappa* in which only one Buddha is born.[1]

[1] BuA. 158.

1. **Sārajja Sutta.**—Five qualities which give confidence to a monk: faith, virtue, learning, energy, insight.[1]

[1] A. iii. 127.

2. **Sārajja Sutta.**—The same as Sutta (1).[1]

[1] A. iii. 183.

3. **Sārajja Sutta.**—Abstention from the five sins (taking life, theft, etc.) gives a monk confidence.[1]

[1] A. iii. 203.

Sāratthadīpanī.—A *ṭīkā* on Buddhaghosa's **Samantapāsādikā,** by **Sāriputta Thera** of Ceylon. Many of the illustrative stories are about Ceylon monks. The book contains a valuable account of the eighteen sects into which the Saṅgha was divided at the time of the Third Council.[1]

[1] Gv. 61, 65; SadS. 62; P.L.C. 192 f.; Bode, *op. cit.*, 39.

Sāratthappakāsinī.—**Buddhaghosa's** Commentary on the **Saṃyutta Nikāya,** written at the request of **Jotipāla,** a monk.[1]

[1] Gv. 59; SadS. 58.

Sāratthamañjūsā.—A *ṭīkā* on the **Aṅguttara Nikāya,** attributed to **Sāriputta** of Ceylon.[1]

[1] Gv. 61; SadS. 61; P.L.C. 192.

Sāratthavikāsinī.—A *ṭīkā* on **Kaccāyana's** Pāli grammar by **Ariyālaṅkāra** of Ava.[1]

[1] Bode, *op. cit.*, 37 n. 2; 55.

Sāratthavilāsinī or **Susaddasiddhi.** A *ṭīkā* on the **Moggallāna-pañjikā** by **Saṅgharakkhita** of Ceylon.[1]

[1] P.L.C. 200.

1. **Sāratthasaṅgaha.**—A religious work, ascribed to **Buddhappiya.**[1]

[1] Gv. 60, 71; P.L.C. 222.

2. **Sāratthasaṅgaha.**—A religious work, in sixty sections, by **Siddhattha Thera,** written in the thirteenth century A.C. It deals with various topics of religious interest.[1]

[1] P.L.C. 229 f.

3. **Sāratthasaṅgaha.**—A religious work (*Sārārthasaṅgraha*), written in Sinhalese, by **Saraṇaṅkara Saṅgharāja.**[1]

[1] Cv. xcvii. 57.

Sāratthasamuccaya.—The name given to the **Catubhāṇavāraṭṭhakathā.** It was written by a pupil of **Ānanda** at the request of **Vanaratana Thera** of Ceylon.[1]

[1] Published in Hewavitarne Bequest Series (Colombo), vol. xxvii.

Sāratthasālinī.—A *Nava-ṭīkā* on **Dhammapāla's Saccasaṅkhepa,** by **Sumaṅgala,** pupil of **Sāriputta** of Ceylon.[1]

[1] P.L.C. 200.

1. **Sāradassī Thera.**—He lived in Nayyinyua in Ava, in the seventeenth century. He was the author of the **Gūḷhatthadīpanī** on the Abhidhamma and of the **Visuddhimaggagaṇṭhipada.** He translated the **Nettippakaraṇa** into Burmese. He was blamed for indulging in certain luxuries, such as a head-covering and a fan, but he later renounced them and lived in the forest.[1]

[1] Sās. 116; Bode, *op. cit.*, 56.

2. **Sāradassī.**—A monk of Pagan of the eighteenth century. He wrote the **Dhātukathāyojanā.**[1]

[1] Bode, *op. cit.*, 67.

1. **Sārandada Sutta.**—Once, five hundred **Licchavis** met at the **Sārandada-cetiya** and their discussion turned on the five treasures in the world: elephant, horse, jewel, woman, householder. Unable to decide on these matters, they stationed a man at the road to watch for the approach of the Buddha, who was then living in the **Mahāvana** in **Vesālī.** On being invited to the Sārandada-cetiya, the Buddha went to them, and, having heard of their discussion, told them of five treasures much more rare in the world: the Tathāgata, his Dhamma, a person able to recognize the Dhamma in the world, one who follows it, and one who is grateful.[1]

[1] A. iii. 167 f.

2. **Sārandada Sutta.**—Once, a number of **Licchavis** visited the Buddha at the **Sārandada-cetiya,** and he told them of seven things which would ensure their welfare and prevent them from falling: frequent assemblies, concord, honouring of tradition and convention, respect for elders, courtesy towards women, homage paid to places of worship, and protection of holy men in their midst.[1]

This sutta is often referred to in the books, and the virtues mentioned are famous as the *satta aparihāniyadhammā.* The sutta was also probably called the **Vajji Sutta.**[2]

[1] A. iv. 16 f.; *cf.* D. ii. 72 ff.

[2] See, *e.g.*, DA. ii. 524.

Sārandada-cetiya.—A shrine of pre-Buddhistic worship at **Vesāli.** It was dedicated to the Yakkha **Sārandada,** but, later, a vihāra was erected on the site for the Buddha and his Order.[1]

[1] D. ii. 75, 102; Ud. vi. 1; DA. ii. 521; UdA. 323; AA. ii. 701.

Sāramaṇḍakappa.—The name given to a *kappa* in which four Buddhas are born.[1]

[1] BuA. 159.

Sārambha.—The Bodhisatta, born as an ox. See the **Sārambha Jātaka.**

Sārambha Jātaka (No. 88).—The story is the same as that of the **Nandivisāla Jātaka** (No. 28) (*q.v.*), but with this difference, that the Bodhisatta was an ox named **Sārambha,** and belonged to a learned brahmin of **Takkasilā.**[1]

[1] J. i. 374 f.

Sārāṇīya Vagga.—The second chapter of the Chakka Nipāta of the **Aṅguttara Nikāya.**[1]

[1] A. iii. 288-308.

1. **Sārāṇīya Sutta.**—A king must remember where he was born, where he was anointed, and where he won a battle. A monk must remember where he was ordained, where he realized the four Ariyan Truths, and where he attained arahantship.[1]

[1] A. i. 106 f.

2. **Sārāṇīya Suttā.**—Two suttas on what a monk should bear in mind in order that his conduct shall endear him to others, bring concord, and lead to singleness of heart.[1]

[1] A. iii. 288 f.

1. **Sāriputta Thera.**—The chief disciple (*aggasāvaka*) of **Gotama Buddha.** He is also called **Upatissa,** which was evidently his personal name.[1] The commentators say that Upatissa was the name of his village and that he was the eldest son of the chief family in the village, but other accounts give his village as **Nālaka.** His father was the brahmin, **Vaṅganta,**[2] and his mother, **Rūpasārī.** It was because of his mother's name that he came to be called Sāriputta.[3] The name Upatissa is hardly

[1] M. i. 150.
[2] DhA. ii. 84.
[3] In Sanskrit texts his name occurs as Sāriputra, Śāliputra, Śārisuta, Śāradvatīputra. In the Apadāna (ii. 480) he is also called **Sārisambhava.**

ever mentioned in the books. He had three younger brothers—**Cunda, Upasena,** and **Revata** (afterwards called **Khadiravaniya**)—and three sisters—**Cālā, Upacālā** and **Sisūpacālā;** all of whom joined the Order.[4]

The story of Sāriputta's conversion and the account of his past lives, which prepared him for his eminent position as the Buddha's Chief Disciple, have been given under **Mahā Moggallāna** (*q.v.*). Sāriputta had a very quick intuition, and he became a *sotāpanna* immediately after hearing the first two lines of the stanza spoken by **Assaji.** After his attainment of *sotāpatti*, **Kolita (Moggallāna)** wished to go with him to **Veḷuvana** to see the Buddha, but Sāriputta, always grateful to his teachers, suggested that they should first seek their teacher, **Sañjaya,** to give him the good news and go with him to the Buddha. But Sañjaya refused to fall in with this plan. Moggallāna attained arahantship on the seventh day after his ordination, but it was not till a fortnight later that Sāriputta became an arahant. He was staying, at the time, with the Buddha, in the **Sūkarakhatalena** in **Rājagaha,** and he reached his goal as a result of hearing the Buddha preach the **Vedānapariggaha Sutta** to **Dīghanakha.**[5]

In the assembly of monks and nuns, Sāriputta was declared by the Buddha foremost among those who possessed wisdom (*etadaggaṃ mahāpaññānaṃ*[6]). He was considered by the Buddha as inferior only to himself in wisdom.[7] The Buddha would frequently merely suggest a topic, and Sāriputta would preach a sermon on it in detail, and thereby win the Buddha's approval.[8] The Buddha is recorded[9] as speaking high praise of him: " Wise art thou, Sāriputta, comprehensive and manifold thy wisdom, joyous and swift, sharp and fastidious. Even as the eldest son of a Cakkavatti king turns the Wheel as his father hath turned

[4] DhA. ii. 188; *cf.* Mtu. iii. 50; for details of them see *s.v.*; mention is also made of an uncle of Sāriputta and of a nephew, both of whom he took to the Buddha, thereby rescuing them from false views (DhA. ii. 230-2); **Uparevata** was his nephew (SA. iii. 175).

[5] This account is summarized from DhA. i. 73 ff.; AA. i. 88 ff.; ThagA. ii. 93 ff. Ap. i. 15 ff.; the story of their conversion is given at Vin. i. 38 ff.

[6] A. i. 23.

[7] SA. ii. 45; his greatest exhibition of wisdom followed the Buddha's descent from **Tāvatiṃsa** to the gates of **Saṅkassa,** when the Buddha asked questions of the assembled multitude, which none but Sāriputta could answer. But some questions were outside the range of any but a Buddha (DhA. iii. 228 f.; *cf.* SNA. ii. 570 f.). Similarly knowledge of the thoughts and inclinations of people were beyond Sāriputta; only a Buddha possesses such knowledge (DhA. iii. 426; J. i. 182). Further, only a Buddha could find suitable subjects for meditation for everybody without error (SNA. i. 18), and read their past births without limitation (SNA. ii. 571).

[8] See, *e.g.*, M. i. 13; iii. 46, 55, 249.

[9] S. i. 191; *cf.* SN. vs. 556 f., where the Buddha is asked by **Sela,** who is his general, and the Buddha replies that it is Sāriputta who turns the Wheel of the Law; also M. iii. 29.

it, so dost thou rightly turn the Wheel Supreme of the Dhamma, even as I have turned it." He thus came to be called **Dhammasenāpati,** just as **Ānanda** was called **Dhammabhaṇḍāgārika.** The **Anupada Sutta** is one long eulogy of Sāriputta by the Buddha. He is there held up as the supreme example of the perfect disciple, risen to mastery and perfection in noble virtue, noble concentration, noble perception, noble deliverance.[10] In the **Saccavibhaṅga Sutta**[11] he is compared to a mother-teacher, while **Moggallāna** is like a child's wet nurse; Sāriputta trains in the fruits of conversion, Moggallāna trains in the highest good. In the **Piṇḍapātapārisuddhi Sutta**[12] the Buddha commends Sāriputta for the aloofness of his life and instructs him in the value of reflection. Other instances are given of the Buddha instructing and examining him on various topics—*e.g.*, on *bhūtaṃ* (" what has come to be "),[13] on the five *indriyas,*[14] and on *sotāpatti.*[15]

We also find instances of Sāriputta questioning his colleagues, or being questioned by them, on various topics. Thus he is questioned by **Mahā Koṭṭhita** on *kamma* (S. ii. 112 f.); and on *yonisomanasikāra* (progressive discipline, S. iii. 176 f.); on *avijjā* and *vijjā* (*ibid.*, 172 f.); on the fetters of sense-perception (S. iv. 162 f.); on certain questions pronounced by the Buddha as indeterminate (*ibid.*, 384 f.); on whether anything is left remaining after the passionless ending of the six spheres of contact (A. ii. 161); and on the purpose for which monks lead the *brahmacariyā* under the Buddha (A. iv. 382). The **Mahāvedalla Sutta** (M. i. 292 ff.) records a long discourse preached by Sāriputta to Maha

[10] M. iii. 25 ff. In the **Mahāgosiṅga Sutta** Sāriputta expresses his view that that monk is best who is master of his heart and is not mastered by it. The Buddha explains that Sāriputta was stating his own nature (M. i. 215 f.). The Buddha did not, however, hesitate to blame Sāriputta when necessary—*e.g.*, the occasion when some novices, becoming noisy, were sent away by the Buddha, whose motive Sāriputta misunderstood (M. i. 459). And again, when Sāriputta did not look after Rāhula properly, making it necessary for Rāhula to spend the whole night in the Buddha's jakes (J. i. 161 f.).

[11] M. iii. 248.

[12] *Ibid.*, 294 f.

[13] S. ii. 47 f.

[14] *Ibid.*, v. 220 f., 225 f., 233 f.

[15] *Ibid.*, 347; we find the Buddha also instructing him on the cultivation of tranquillity (A. i. 65); on the destruction of "I" and "mine" (A. i. 133); the reasons for failure and success in enterprises (A. ii. 81 f.); the four ways of acquiring personality (*attabhāva*) (A. ii. 159); the methods of exhortation (A. iii. 198); the acquisition of joy that comes through seclusion (A. iii. 207); the noble training for the layman (211 f.); six things that bring spiritual progress to a monk (424 f.); seven similar things (A. iv. 30); the seven grounds for praising a monk (35); the things and persons a monk should revere (120 f.); the eight attributes of a monk free from the cankers (223 f.); the nine persons who, although they die with an attached remainder for rebirth, are yet free from birth in hell among animals and among petas (379 f.); and the ten powers of a monk who has destroyed the cankers (A. v. 174 f.).

Koṭṭhita. He is mentioned as questioning **Mahā Kassapa** on the terms *ātāpī* and *ottāpī* (S. ii. 195 f.), and **Anuruddha** on *sekha* (S. v. 174 f., 298 f.). On another occasion, Anuruddha tells Sāriputta of his power of seeing the thousandfold world-system, his unshaken energy, and his untroubled mindfulness. Sāriputta tells him that his deva-sight is mere conceit, his claims to energy conceit, and his mindfulness just worrying, and exhorts him to abandon thoughts of them all. Anuruddha follows his advice and becomes an arahant.[16]

Moggallāna asks Sāriputta regarding the " undefiled " (their conversation forms the **Anaṅgana Sutta,** M. i. 25 ff.), and, at the conclusion of the **Gulissāni Sutta,** inquires whether the states of consciousness mentioned in that sutta were incumbent only on monks from the wilds or also on those from the villages (M. i. 472 f.). Sāriputta questions **Upavāna** regarding the *bojjhaṅgā* (S. v. 76), and is questioned by Ānanda regarding *sotāpatti* (S. v. 346, 362) as regards the reason why some beings are set free in this very life while others are not (A. ii. 167), and on the winning of perfect concentration (A. v. 8, 320). Ānanda also questions Sāriputta (A. iii. 201 f.) on the speedy knowledge of aptness in things (*kusaladhammesu khippanisanti*), and, again, on how a monk may learn new doctrines and retain old ones without confusion (A. iii. 361). In both these cases Sāriputta asks Ānanda to answer the questions himself, and, at the end of his discourse, praises him. The **Rathavinīta Sutta** (M. i. 145 ff.) records a conversation between Sāriputta and **Puṇṇa Mantāniputta,** for whom he had the greatest respect, after hearing the Buddha's eulogy of him. Sāriputta had given instructions that he should be told as soon as Puṇṇa came to Sāvatthi and took the first opportunity of seeing him. Among others who held discussions with Sāriputta are mentioned **Samiddhi** (A. iv. 385), **Yamaka** (S. iii. 109 f.), **Candikāputta** (A. iv. 403), and **Laḷudāyi** (A. iv. 414).

Among laymen who had discussions with Sāriputta are **Atula** (DhA. iii. 327), **Nakulapitā** (S. iii. 2 f.) and **Dhānañjāni** (M. ii. 186); **Sīvalī** (immediately after his birth; J. i. 408), also the **Paribbājakas, Jambukhādaka** (S. iv. 251 f.), **Sāmaṇḍaka** (S. iv. 261 f.; A. v. 120), and **Pasūra** (SNA. ii. 538), and the female Paribbājakas **Saccā, Lolā, Avavādakā** and **Paṭācārā** (J. iii. 1), and **Kuṇḍalakesī** (DhA. ii. 223 f.). He is also said to have visited the Paribbājakas in order to hold discussion with them (A. iv. 378); see also S. iii. 238 f., where a Paribbājaka consults him on modes of eating.

The care of the Saṅgha and the protection of its members' integrity was Sāriputta's especial concern by virtue of his position as the Buddha's Chief Disciple. Thus we find him being sent with Moggallāna to bring

[16] A. i. 281 f.

back the monks who had seceded with **Devadatta.**[17] His admonitions to the monks sometimes made him unpopular—*e.g.*, in the case of the **Assaji-Punaabbasukā,** the **Chabbaggiyā** (who singled him out for special venom) and **Kokālika.**[18] When **Channa** declared his intention of committing suicide, Sāriputta attempted to dissuade him, but without success.[19] Monks sought his advice in their difficulties.[20] He was greatly perturbed by the dissensions of the monks of **Kosambī,** and consulted the Buddha, at length, as to what he could do about it.[21] He was meticulous about rules laid down by the Buddha. Thus a rule had been laid down that one monk could ordain only one sāmaṇera, and when a boy was sent to him for ordination from a family which had been of great service to him, Sāriputta refused the request of the parents till the Buddha had rescinded the rule.[22] Another rule forbade monks to eat garlic (*lasuna*), and when Sāriputta lay ill and knew he could be cured by garlic, even then he refused to eat them till permission was given by the Buddha for him to do so.[23] The Dhammapada Commentary[24] describes how, at the monastery in which Sāriputta lived, when the other monks had gone for alms, he made the round of the entire building, sweeping the unswept places, filling empty vessels with water, arranging furniture, etc., lest heretics, coming to the monastery, should say: "Behold the residences of Gotama's pupils." But even then he did not escape censure from his critics. A story is told[25] of how he was once charged with greed, and the Buddha himself had to explain to the monks that Sāriputta was blameless. While Sāriputta was severe in the case of those who failed to follow the Buddha's discipline, he did not hesitate to rejoice with his fellow-monks in their successes. Thus we find him congratulating Moggallāna on the joy he obtained from his *iddhi*-powers, and praising his great attainments (praise which evoked equally generous counter-praise),[26] and eulogising **Anuruddha** on his perfected discipline won through the practice of the four *satipaṭṭhānas.*[27] It was the great encouragement given by Sāriputta to **Samitigutta** (*q.v.*), when the latter lay ill with leprosy in the infirmary, which helped him to become an arahant. It was evidently the custom of Sāriputta to visit sick monks, as did the Buddha himself.[28] So great was Sāriputta's desire to encourage and recognize merit in his colleagues, that he once went about praising

[17] See **Devadatta.**

[18] See *s.v.* for details; also **Channa,** who reviled both Sāriputta and Moggallāna (DhA. ii. 110 f.).

[19] S. iv. 55 ff.; see also the **Channovāda Sutta.**

[20] See, *e.g.*, S. iv. 103, where a monk reports to him that a colleague has returned to the household life, and asks what he is to do about it.

[21] Vin. i. 354.

[22] *Ibid.*, 83.

[23] *Ibid.*, ii. 140.

[24] ii. 140 f.

[25] DhA. iv. 184 f.

[26] S. ii. 275 f.

[27] *Ibid.*, v. 301 f.

[28] See ThagA. i. 176.

Devadatta's *iddhi*-powers, which made it difficult for him when later he had to proclaim, at the bidding of the Saṅgha, Devadatta's evil nature.[29]

Several instances are given[30] of Sāriputta instructing the monks and preaching to them of his own accord on various topics—apart from the preaching of the well-known suttas assigned to him. Sometimes these suttas were supplementary to the Buddha's own discourses.[31] Among the most famous of Sāriputta's discourses are the **Dasuttara** and the **Saṅgīti Suttas** (*q.v.*). Though Sāriputta was friendly with all the eminent monks surrounding the Buddha, there was very special affection between him and **Ānanda** and also Moggallāna. We are told that this was because Ānanda was the Buddha's special attendant, a duty which Sāriputta would have been glad to undertake.[32] Ānanda himself had the highest regard and affection for Sāriputta. It is recorded in the Saṃyutta Nikāya[33] that once, when the Buddha asked Ānanda, "Do you also, Ānanda, approve of our Sāriputta ?" Ānanda replied, " Who, Sir, that is not childish or corrupt or stupid or of perverted mind, will not approve of him ? Wise is he, his wisdom comprehensive and joyous and swift, sharp and fastidious. Small is he in his desires and contented; loving seclusion and detachment, of rampant energy. A preacher is he, accepting advice, a critic, a scourge of evil."

Sāriputta was specially attached, also, to Rāhula, the Buddha's son, who was entrusted to Sāriputta for ordination. Mention is made of a special sutta in the **Majjhima Nikāya,**[34] in which he urges Rāhula to practise the study of breathing. The special regard which Sāriputta had for the Buddha and Rāhula extended also to **Rāhulamātā,** for we find that when she was suffering from flatulence, Rāhula consulted Sāriputta, who obtained for her some mango-juice, a known remedy for the disease.[35] On another occasion[36] he obtained from **Pasenadi** rice mixed with ghee and with red fish for flavouring when Rāhulamātā suffered from some stomach trouble. Among laymen Sāriputta had special regard for **Anāthapiṇḍika;** when the latter lay ill he sent for Sāriputta, who visited him with Ānanda and preached to him the **Anāthapiṇḍikovāda Sutta.** At the end of the discourse Anāthapiṇḍika said he had never before heard such a homily. Sāriputta said they were reserved for monks only, but Anāthapiṇḍika asked that they could

[29] Vin. ii. 189.

[30] *E.g.*, S. ii. 274; v. 70; A. i. 63; ii. 160; iii. 186, 190, 196, 200, 292, 340; iv. 325, 328, 365; v. 94, 102, 123, 315, 356 f.

[31] *E.g.*, M. i. 13, 24, 184, 469.

[32] For details of this see *s.v.* **Mahā Moggallāna, Ānanda.**

[33] S. i. 63.

[34] The **Mahā Rāhulovāda Sutta**; M. i. 421 f.

[35] J. ii. 392 f.

[36] *Ibid.*, 433.

be given to the laity and to young men of undimmed vision. Anāthapiṇḍika died soon after and was reborn in **Tusita.**[37]

Sāriputta also, evidently, had great esteem for the householder **Citta,** for we are told[38] that he once paid a special visit to **Macchikāsaṇḍa** to see him.

Several incidents are related in the books showing the exemplary qualities possessed by Sāriputta—*e.g.*, the stories of **Tambadāṭhika, Puṇṇa** and his wife, the poor woman in the **Kuṇḍakakucchisindhava Jātaka** and **Losaka-Tissa** (*q.v.*). These show his great compassion for the poor and his eagerness to help them. Reference has already been made to his first teacher, **Sañjaya,** whom he tried, but failed, to convert to the Buddha's faith. His second teacher was **Assaji.** It is said[39] that every night on going to bed he would do obeisance to the quarter in which he knew Assaji to be and would sleep with his head in that direction. The stories of the Sāmaṇeras **Sukha** and **Paṇḍita,** and of the monk **Rādhā,** also show his gratitude towards any who had shown him favour.[40] His extreme affection for and gratitude to the Buddha are shown in the **Sampasādanīya Sutta** (*q.v.*). That Sāriputta possessed great patience is shown by the story[41] of the brahmin who, to test his patience, struck him as he entered the city for alms. But when he was wrongly accused and found it necessary to vindicate his good name, he did not hesitate to proclaim his innocence at great length and to declare his pre-eminence in virtue.[42] Another characteristic of Sāriputta was his readiness to take instruction from others, however modest. Thus one story relates how, in absent-mindedness, he let the fold of his robe hang down. A novice said, " Sir, the robe should be draped around you," and Sāriputta agreed, saying, " Good, you have done well to point it out to me," and going a little way, he draped the robe round him.[43] A quaint story is told[44] of a Yakkha who, going through the air at night, saw Sāriputta wrapt in meditation, his head newly shaved. The sight of the shining head was a great temptation to the Yakkha, and, in spite of his companion's warning, he dealt a blow on the Thera's head. The blow was said to have been hard enough to shatter a mountain, but Sāriputta suffered only a slight headache afterwards.

[37] M. iii. 258 ff.; *cf.* S. v. 380, which probably refers to an earlier illness of Anāthapiṇḍika. He recovered immediately after the preaching of Sāriputta's sermon, and served Sāriputta with rice from his own cooking pot.

[38] DhA. ii. 74.

[39] DhA. iv. 150 f.; *cf.* SNA. i. 328. If Assaji were in the same vihāra, Sāriputta would visit him immediately after visiting the Buddha. It was in connection with this that the **Dhamma Sutta** (*q.v.*) was preached.

[40] See also Vin. i. 55 f.

[41] DhA. iv. 146 f.

[42] See, *e.g.*, his " lion's roar " at A. iv. 373 ff.

[43] ThagA. ii. 116.

[44] Ud. iv. 4.

Mention is made of two occasions on which Sāriputta fell ill. Once he had fever and was cured by lotus-stalks which Moggallāna obtained for him from the **Mandākinī** Lake.[45] On the other occasion he had stomach trouble, which was again cured by Moggallāna giving him garlic (*lasuna*), to eat which the rule regarding the use of garlic had to be rescinded by the Buddha.[46]

Sāriputta was fond of meal-cakes (*piṭṭhakhajjaka*), but finding that they tended to make him greedy he made a vow never to eat them.[47]

Sāriputta died some months before the Buddha. It is true that the account of the Buddha's death in the **Mahāparinibbāna Sutta** ignores all reference to Sāriputta, though it does introduce him[48] shortly before as uttering his "lion's roar" (*sīhanāda*), his great confession of faith in the Buddha, which, in the commentarial account, he made when he took leave of the Buddha to die. The Saṃyutta Nikāya[49] records that he died at **Nālagāmaka** (the place of his birth), and gives an eulogy of him pronounced by the Buddha after his death.[50] There is no need to doubt the authenticity of this account. It merely states that when Sāriputta was at Nālagāmaka he was afflicted with a sore disease. His brother, **Cunda-Samaṇuddesa,** was attending on him when he died. His body was cremated, and Cunda took the relics to Sāvatthi with Sāriputta's begging-bowl and outer robe. The relics were wrapped in his water-strainer. Cunda first broke the news to Ānanda, who confessed that when he heard it his mind was confused and his body felt as though drugged.[51] Together they sought the Buddha and told him of the event, and the Buddha pointed out to them the impermanence of all things.

The Commentaries give more details. The Buddha returned to Sāvatthi after his last *vassa* in **Beḷuvagāma.** Sāriputta sought him there, and, realizing that his death would come in seven days, he decided to visit his mother, for she, though the mother of seven arahants, had no faith in the Saṅgha.[52] He therefore asked his brother, Cunda, to prepare for the journey to Nālagāmaka with five hundred others, and then took leave of the Buddha after performing various miracles and declaring his faith in the Buddha and uttering his "lion's roar." A large concourse followed him to the gates of Sāvatthi, and there he addressed them

[45] Vin. i. 214. [46] *Ibid.*, ii. 140.
[47] J. i. 310. [48] D. ii. 81 ff.
[49] S. v. 161. [50] *Ibid.*, 163 f.
[51] *Cf.* Thag. vs. 1034; see also the eulogy of Sāriputta by **Vaṅgīsa** during his lifetime (Thag. 1231-3). Hiouen Thsang saw the *stūpa* erected over the relics of Sāriputta in the town of Kālapināka (Beal, *op. cit.*, ii. 177).

[52] This was because all her children joined the Order and left her desolate in spite of the forty crores of wealth which lay in the house. It is said (DhA. iv. 164 f.) that when Sāriputta had gone home on a previous occasion, she abused both him and his companions roundly. **Rāhula** was also in the company.

and bade them stay behind. In seven days he reached Nālaka, where he was met by his nephew, **Uparevata,** outside the gates. Him he sent on to warn his mother of his arrival with a large number of people. She, thinking that he had once more returned to the lay life, made all preparations to welcome him and his companions. Sāriputta took up his abode in the room in which he was born (*jātovaraka*). There he was afflicted with dysentery. His mother, unaware of this and sulking because she found he was still a monk, remained in her room. The Four Regent Gods and **Sakka** and **Mahā Brahmā** waited upon him. She saw them, and having found out who they were, went to her son's room. There she asked him if he were really greater than all these deities, and, when he replied that it was so, she reflected on the greatness of her son and her whole body was suffused with joy. Sāriputta then preached to her, and she became a *sotāpanna*. Feeling that he had paid his debt to his mother, he sent Cunda to fetch the monks, and, on their arrival, he sat up with Cunda's help and asked if he had offended them in any way during the forty-four years of his life as a monk. On receiving their assurance that he had been entirely blameless, he wiped his lips with his robe and lay down, and, after passing through various trances, died at break of dawn.

His mother made all arrangements for the funeral, and **Vissakamma** assisted in the ceremony. When the cremation was over, **Anuruddha** extinguished the flames with perfumed water, and Cunda gathered together the relics.[53] Among those who came to pay honour to the pyre was the goddess **Revatī** (*q.v.*). Sāriputta died on the full-moon day of **Kattika** (October to November) preceding the Buddha's death, and Moggallāna died a fortnight later.[54]

Sāriputta had many pupils, some of whom have already been mentioned. Among others were **Kosiya, Kaṇḍhadinna, Cullasārī, Vanavāsika-Tissa, Saṅkicca** (*q.v.*), and **Sarabhū,** who brought to Ceylon the Buddha's collar-bone, which he deposited in the **Mahiyaṅgana-cetiya.**[55] Sāriputta's brother, **Upavāna,** predeceased him, and Sāriputta was with him when he died of snake-bite at **Sappasoṇḍikapabbāra.**[56]

Sāriputta's special proficiency was in the Abhidhamma. It is said[57] that when preaching the Abhidhamma to the gods of **Tavātiṃsa,** the

[53] This account is summarized from SA. iii. 172 ff.; similar accounts are found at DA. ii. 549 f., etc. Sāriputta's death is also referred to at J. i. 391.

[54] SA. iii. 181; J. i. 391; both Sāriputta and Moggallāna were older than the Buddha because they were born "*anuppanne yeva hi Buddhe*" (DhA. i. 73).

[55] Mhv. i. 37 f.

[56] S. iv. 40 f.

[57] DhSA. 16 f.; *cf.* DA. i. 15, where it is said that at the end of the First Recital the Abhidhamma was given in charge of five hundred arahants (Sāriputta being already dead).

Buddha would visit **Anotatta** every day, leaving a *nimmita*-Buddha on Sakka's throne to continue the preaching. After having bathed in the lake he would take his midday rest. During this time Sāriputta would visit him and learn from the Buddha all that had been preached of the Abhidhamma during the previous day. Having thus learnt the Abhidhamma, Sāriputta taught it to his five hundred pupils. Their acquirement of the seven books of the Abhidhamma coincided with the conclusion of the Buddha's sermon in Tāvatiṃsa. Thus the textual order of the Abhidhamma originated with Sāriputta, and the numerical series was determined by him.

Sāriputta is identified with various characters in numerous Jātakas. Thus he was **Canda-kumāra** in the **Devadhamma, Lakkhaṇa** in the **Lakkhaṇa,** the knight in the **Bhojājānīya,** the monkey in the **Tittira,** the snake in the **Visavanta** and **Saccaṅkira,** the tree-sprite in the **Sīlavanāga,** the brahmin youth in the **Mahāsupina,** the chief disciple in the **Parosahassa,** the **Jhānasodhana** and the **Candābha,** the king of Benares in the **Dummedha,** the good ascetic in the **Godha** (No. 138) and the **Romaka,** the charioteer of the king of Benares in the **Rājovāda,** the father-elephant in the **Alīnacitta,** the teacher in the **Susīma,** the **Cūḷa-Nandiya,** the **Sīlavīmaṃsana** and the **Mahādhammapāla,** the merchant in the **Gijjha** (No. 164), a goose in the **Catumaṭṭa,** the Nāga-king in the **Jarudapāna** and the **Sīlavimaṃsa,** the woodpecker in the **Kuruṅgamiga,** the thoroughbred in the **Kuṇḍakakucchisindhava,** the lion in the **Vyaggha, Tittira** (No. 438) and **Vaṇṇāroha,** the rich man in the **Kurudhamma,** the ascetic **Jotirasa** in the **Abbhantara, Sumukha** in the **Supatta, Nandisena** in the **Cullakaliṅga, Sayha** in the **Sayha,** the spirit of the Bodhi-tree in the **Pucimanda,** the commander-in-chief in the **Khantivādī,** the hunter in the **Maṃsa,** a deity in the **Kakkāru, Nārada** in the **Kesava,** the brahmin in the **Kāraṇḍiya** and **Nandiyamiga,** the Caṇḍāla in the **Setaketu,** the horse in the **Kharapatta, Pukkusa** in the **Dasaṇṇaka,** the sprite in the **Sattubhasta** and the **Mahāpaduma,** the roc-bird in the **Koṭisimbali,** the pupil in the **Aṭṭhasadda, Sālissara** in the **Indriya** (No. 423) and the **Sarabhaṅga, Āṇi-Maṇḍavya** in the **Kaṇhadīpāyana, Canda** in the **Biḷārikosiya,** the senior pupil in the **Mahāmaṅgala, Vāsudeva** in the **Ghata, Lakkhaṇa** in the **Dasaratha, Uposatha** in the **Saṃvara,** the northern deity in the **Samuddavāṇija,** the second goose in the **Javanahaṃsa,** the chaplain in the **Sarabhamiga** and the **Bhikkhāparampara,** the osprey in the **Mahāukkusa,** one of the brothers in the **Bhisa,** the snake in the **Pañcūposatha,** the Nāga-king in the **Mahāvāṇija,** the king in the **Rohantamiga,** and the **Haṃsa** (No. 502), **Rakkhita** in the **Somanassa, Uggasena** in the **Campeyya, Assapāla** in the **Hatthipāla,** the ascetic in the **Jayadissa, Sañjaya** in the **Sambhava,** the Nāga-king in the **Paṇḍara, Aḷāra** in the **Saṅkhapāla,** the elder son in the **Cullasutosoma, Ahipāraka** in the **Ummadantī, Manoja** in the **Sonananda,** the king in the **Cullahaṃsa** and the **Mahāhaṃsa, Nārada** in the **Sudhābhojana, the Kuṇāla** and the **Mahājanaka, Kāḷahatthi** in the **Mahāsutasoma,** the charioteer in the **Mūgapakkha, Suriyakumāra** in the **Khaṇḍapāla, Sudassana** in the **Bhūridatta, Vijaya** in the **Mahānāradakassapa, Varuṇa** in the **Vidhurapaṇḍita, Cūḷanī** in the **Mahāummagga** and the ascetic **Accuta** in the **Vessantara.**

2. **Sāriputta Thera.**—A monk of Ceylon. He lived in the reign of **Parakkamabāhu I.,** and was called **Sāgaramati**[1] on account of his erudition. The king built for him a special residence attached to the **Jetavanavihāra** in **Pulatthipura.**[2] Among his works are the **Vinayasaṅgaha** or the **Vinayavinicchaya,** a summary of the Vinaya, and the **Sāratthadīpanī** on the **Samantapāsādikā,** the **Sāratthamañjūsā** on the **Atthasālinī** and the **Līnatthappakāsinī** on the **Papañcasūdanī.** Sāriputta had several well-known pupils, among whom were **Saṅgharakkhita, Sumaṅgala, Buddhanāga, Udumbaragiri Medhaṅkara** and **Vācissara.**[3] Sāriputta was also a Sanskrit scholar, and wrote the *Pañjikālaṅkāra* or *Ratnamatipañjikāṭīkā* to Ratnaśrījñāna's Pañjikā to the *Candragomivyākaraṇa.*

1 SadS. 63.
2 Cv. lxxviii. 34.
3 Gv. 67, 71; Svd. 1203; Sās. 69; P.L.C. 189 ff.

3. **Sāriputta.**—A monk of Dala in the **Rāmañña** country. He was born in **Padīpajeyya** in the reign of **Narapatisithu,** and was ordained by **Ānanda** of the **Sīhalasaṅgha.** He became one of the leaders of this group in Rāmañña. Narapati conferred on him the title of "Dhammavilāsa," and he was the author of one of the earliest law codes (*dhammasattha*) of Burma.[1]

1 Sās. 41 f.; Bode, *op. cit.*, 31.

4. **Sāriputta.**—A Choliyan monk, author of the **Padāvatāra.**[1]

1 Gv. 67; Svd. 12, 44.

5. **Sāriputta.**—One of the sons of king **Buddhadāsa.**[1]

1 Cv. xxxvii. 177.

Sāriputta Saṃyutta.—The twenty-eighth division of the **Saṃyutta Nikāya.**[1]

1 S. iii. 235-40.

1. **Sāriputta Sutta.**—The sixteenth sutta of the **Aṭṭhakavagga** of the **Sutta Nipāta.** Sāriputta asks the Buddha how a monk should conduct

himself in order to achieve his goal. The Buddha explains that a monk must avoid the five dangers, endure heat and cold and other discomforts, and must not be guilty of theft, anger, lying or arrogance. He should be guided by wisdom and moderation.[1] The Commentary explains[2] that the sutta is also called the **Therapañha Sutta,** and that it was preached on the occasion of the Buddha's descent from **Tāvatiṃsa** to **Saṅkassa.** The Buddha desired that Sāriputta's wisdom should be adequately recognized, for **Moggallāna's** iddhi, **Anuruddha's** clairvoyance and **Puṇṇa's** eloquence were already famous, but Sāriputta's skill remained unknown. The Buddha therefore related the **Parosahassa Jātaka** in order to show Sāriputta's wisdom in a past life. At the end of the story, Sāriputta questioned the Buddha in eight stanzas, and the rest of the sutta was spoken by the Buddha in answer to these questions.

[1] SN. 955-75. [2] SNA. ii. 569 f.

2. **Sāriputta Sutta.**—The Buddha instructs **Sāriputta** on how to train oneself in order to get rid of notions of "I" and "mine." The sutta contains a quotation from the **Udayapañha.**[1]

[1] A. i. 133.

3. **Sāriputta Sutta.**—**Sāriputta** relates to **Ānanda** how once, when he was in **Andhavana,** he attained to perfect concentration.[1]

[1] A. v. 8.

Sārī.—A brahminee, mother of **Sāriputta** (1) (*q.v.*). Her full name was **Rūpasārī.**

Sāruppa Sutta.—On the proper way of approach to the uprooting of all conceits.[1]

[1] S. iv. 21.

Sāropama Sutta.—See **Cūla-Sāropama** and **Mahā-Sāropama Suttas.**

Sāla.—Brother of **Paduma Buddha** and, later, his Chief Disciple. The people of **Usabhavatī** gave him a special *kaṭhina*-robe, in the making of which the Buddha himself assisted.[1]

[1] Bu. ix. 21; BuA. 147 f.

Sālaka.—A monkey. See the **Sālaka Jātaka.**

Sālaka Jātaka (No. 249).—A snake-charmer had a monkey called **Sālaka,** whom he trained to play with a snake; by this means the man earned his living. During a feast he entrusted the monkey to his friend, the Bodhisatta born as a merchant, and when he returned seven days later he beat the monkey and took him away. When the man was asleep the monkey broke away and refused to be enticed back by the man.

The story was related in reference to an Elder who ill-treated a novice ordained by him. Several times the novice returned to the lay life, but came back at the Elder's request, but in the end he refused to be persuaded. The novice was the monkey.[1]

[1] J. ii. 266 f.

Sālakusumiya Thera.—An arahant. One hundred thousand kappas ago he offered a *sāla*-flower to the *thūpa* of a Buddha.[1]

[1] Ap. ii. 407.

Sālaggāma.—A village in Ceylon given by **Aggabodhi III.** to the **Mayettikassapāvāsa-vihāra.**[1] A river flowed through the village, and over the river **Devappatirāja** built a bridge of forty staves.[2] Later, **Parakkamabāhu IV.** gave the village to **Kāyasatti Thera** of the **Vijayabāhu-pariveṇa.**[3]

[1] Cv. xliv. 121.
[2] *Ibid.*, lxxxvi. 41.
[3] *Ibid.*, xc. 92; see Cv. *Trs.* ii. 209, n. 2.

Sālapādapasobbha.—A swamp over which **Devappatirāja** built a bridge of one hundred and fifty cubits.[1]

[1] Cv. lxxxvi. 42.

Sālapupphadāyaka Thera.—An arahant.[1] He is evidently identical with **Ajjuna Thera**[2] (*q.v.*).

[1] Ap. i. 169.
[2] ThagA. i. 186.

Sālapupphiya Thera.—An arahant. He was a confectioner of **Aruṇavatī** in the time of **Siddhattha** Buddha, to whom he gave a *sāla*-flower. Fourteen kappas ago he was a king named **Amitañjala.**[1]

[1] Ap. i. 218 f.

Sālamaṇḍapiya Thera.—An arahant.[1] He is evidently identical with **Tissa Thera**[2] (see **Tissa** 12).

[1] Ap. i. 431 f.
[2] ThagA. i. 272 f.

Sālavatikā, Sālavatī.—A Kosalan village, given by **Pasenadi** to the brahmin **Lohicca.** There the **Lohicca Sutta** was preached.[1] It was so called because *sāla*-trees grew within its boundary.[2]

[1] D. i. 224. [2] DA. ii. 395.

1. **Sālavatī.**—A city; in it was the **Kesārāma** where **Dhammadassī Buddha** died.[1]

[1] BuA. 185.

2. **Sālavatī.**—A courtezan of **Rājagaha.** She was the mother of **Jīvaka-Komārabhacca**[1] and of his sister **Sirimā**[2] (*q.v.*).

[1] Vin. i. 268 f.
[2] SNA. i. 244; see also AA. i. 216, where **Abhayarājakumāra** is called Jīvaka's father.

1. **Sālavāṇa-vihāra.**—One of the eighteen vihāras built by King **Dhātusena.**[1]

[1] Cv. xxxviii. 49.

2. **Sālavāṇa-vihāra.**—A monastery built by **Aggabodhi,** son of **Mahātissa** and **Saṅghasivā.**[1]

[1] Cv. xlv. 45.

1. **Sālā.**—A brahmin village of **Kosala,** its inhabitants were called **Sāleyyakā.** The **Apaṇṇaka Sutta** and the **Saleyyaka Sutta** were preached there.[1] See also **Sālā Sutta.**

[1] M. i. 285, 400.

2. **Sālā.**—One of the two chief women disciples of **Phussa Buddha.**[1]

[1] BuA. 194; but see *s.v.* **Phussa.**

1. **Sālā Sutta.**—The Buddha, while staying at **Sālā,** addresses the monks, teaching them the necessity of the preaching the four *satipaṭṭhānas* by novices, *sekhas* and arahants.[1]

[1] S. v. 144 f.

2. **Sālā Sutta.**—Preached at **Sālā.** Just as the lion is the chief of animals, so is insight chief of the *bodhipakkhiyā-dhammā* (a list of which is given in the sutta).[1]

[1] S. v. 227; on the title of the sutta see KS. v. 202, n. 3.

Sāli, Sāliya.—Only son of **Duṭṭhagāmaṇī.** He renounced the throne and married **Asokamālā,** a Caṇḍāla-girl.[1] In his previous birth he had

[1] Mhv. xxxiii. 1 f.

been a smith, named **Tissa,** in **Muṇḍagaṅgā,** and his wife was **Nāgā (Sumanā).** The couple gave a meal with pork to eight arahants,[2] led by **Dhammadinna Thera** of **Talaṅgatissapabbata.** It is said that on the day of birth the whole of Ceylon was filled with paddy, hence his name. Sāli was very pious, and all the revenues given to him by his father he gave away in charity. He kept the fast days in the **Issarasamaṇa-vihāra** and built the **Sālipabbata-vihāra.**[3] He will be the son of **Metteyya Buddha** in his next birth.[4]

[2] For their names see MṬ. 606. [3] *Ibid.*, 606. [4] *Ibid.*, xxxii. 83.

Sālikedāra Jātaka (No. 484). Once, when King **Magadha** was reigning in **Rājagaha,** the Bodhisatta was a parrot and looked after his aged parents. When the fields of the brahmin **Kosiyagotta,** of **Sālindiya** in **Magadha,** were ripe, the parrot went there with his flock, and, having fed himself, took some corn for his parents. The watchman of the fields reported this to Kosiyagotta, and, on his instructions, a snare was set and the Bodhisatta caught. When he raised the alarm, the other parrots fled. The Bodhisatta explained to Kosiyagotta why he carried the corn away—to feed his parents, his young ones, and those who were in need, thus, as it were, paying a debt, giving a loan, and setting up a store of merit. The brahmin was very pleased, and gave permission to the Bodhisatta to take the corn of all his thousand acres; but the Bodhisatta accepted only eight.[1]

For the introductory story see the **Sāma Jātaka.** **Channa** is identified with the watchman and **Ānanda** with Kosiyagotta.

[1] J. iv. 276-82.

Sāligāma.—A carpenter's village near the west gate of **Anurādhapura.** It was the birthplace of **Asokamālā.**[1]

[1] MṬ. 606, 607.

Sāligiri.—A village, given by **Parakkamabāhu IV.** for the maintenance of the **Parakkamabāhupāsāda.**[1]

[1] Cv. xc. 97; for identification see Cv. *Trs.* ii. 209, n. 6.

Sālittaka Jātaka (No. 107).—The king of Benares once had a very talkative chaplain. Outside the city gate was a cripple, who lived under a banyan tree, so clever that he could cut the leaves of the tree into various shapes by throwing stones at them. The king, seeing him, engaged his services to cure his chaplain. The cripple obtained a pea-shooter filled with dry goat's dung, and, sitting behind a curtain with a hole in it, he shot pellets of dung into the mouth of the chaplain as he talked away ceaselessly. When half a peck had thus been shot, the king revealed the plot to the chaplain and advised an emetic. The chaplain realized his folly and did not offend again. The cripple was given four villages, bringing in four thousand a year.

The story was told in reference to a novice on the banks of the **Acira-vatī** who, challenged by his companions, shot a pebble through the eye of a swan in flight, the pebble emerging through the other eye.

The novice is identified with the cripple and **Ānanda** with the king. The Bodhisatta was one of the king's courtiers.[1] See also *s.v.* **Sunetta** (3).

[1] J. i. 418 f.; *cf.* DhA. ii. 69 f.; Pv. iv. 16; PvA. 282 f.

Sālindiya.—A brahmin village of **Magadha** to the north-east of Rājagaha. It was the residence of the brahmin **Kosiyagotta.**[1]

[1] J. iv. 276; *cf.* J. iii. 293.

1. **Sālipabbata-vihāra.**—A monastery, built by Prince **Sāli** from the revenues which he obtained when living in the west of **Anurādhapura.**[1]

[1] MṬ. 607.

2. **Sālipabbata-vihāra.**—A monastery built by King **Mahallaka-Nāga** in **Nāgadīpa.**[1]

[1] Mhv. xxxv. 124.

Sālipota.—A park laid out by **Parakkamabāhu I.**[1]

[1] Cv. lxxix. 10.

1. **Sāliya.**—One of the ministers of **Vaṭṭagāmaṇī.**[1] He built the **Sāliyārāma.**[1]

[1] Mhv. xxxiii. 90.

2. **Sāliya.**—An ox. See the **Gandatindu Jātaka.**

3. **Sāliya.**—See **Sāli.**

Sāliya Jātaka (No. 367).—Once a village doctor saw a snake lying in the fork of a tree and asked the Bodhisatta, who was then a village boy, to get it for him, telling him that it was a hedgehog. The boy climbed the tree and seized the animal by its neck, but, on discovering that it was a snake, threw it away. The snake fell on the doctor and bit him so severely that he died.

The story was told in reference to **Devadatta's** attempts to kill the

Buddha.[1] Elsewhere,[2] however, the story is told in reference to the hunter **Koka** (*q.v.*), with whom the doctor is identified.

[1] J. iii. 202 f. [2] DhA. iii. 31 f.

Sāliyā.—One of the chief women supporters of **Dhammadassī Buddha.**[1]

[1] Bu. xvi. 20.

Sālissara.—A sage; the chief disciple of the Bodhisatta in his birth as **Sarabhaṅga.** For his story see the **Sarabhaṅga** and **Indriya** (No. 423) **Jātakas.** He is identified with **Sāriputta.**[1]

[1] J. iii. 469; v. 151.

Sālūka.—A pig. See the **Sālūka Jātaka.**

Sālūka Jātaka (No. 286).—The Bodhisatta was once an ox named **Mahālohita** and his brother was **Cullalohita.** They both belonged to a village family, and when the girl of the family grew up and was married, a pig, called **Sālūka,** was fattened for the feast. Cullalohita saw this and coveted the food which was being given to the pig, but when he complained to his brother, it was explained to him that the pig's lot was an unhappy one.

The introductory story is given in the **Culla Nāradakassapa Jātaka.** Sālūka is identified with the love-sick monk of that story, and Cullalohita with **Ānanda.**[1]

[1] J. ii. 419 f.

Sāleyyaka Sutta.—The inhabitants of **Sālā** ask the Buddha why some are born after death in places of woe and others in places of joy. The Buddha explains that it is due to their deeds, good or bad.[1]

[1] M. i. 285 ff.

Sāleyyakā.—The inhabitants of **Sālā.**[1]

[1] M. i. 285.

1. **Sāḷha,** called **Migāranattā.**—He once visited **Nandaka Thera** with **Pekkhuṇiya's** grandson, **Rohaṇa.** See the **Sāḷha Sutta.**[1] He built a vihāra for the nuns and **Sundarīnandā** was appointed to supervise the work. As a result, Sāḷha and Sundarīnandā saw each other frequently and fell in love. Wishing to seduce her, Sāḷha invited a party of nuns to his house and set apart seats for those nuns who were older than Nandā in one part, and for those younger in another, so that Nandā

[1] A. i. 193 f.

would be alone. But she, guessing the reason for the invitation, did not go, and, instead, sent an attendant nun to Sāḷha's house for her alms, excusing herself on the plea that she was taken ill. Saḷha, hearing of this, set a servant to look after the other nuns and ran off to the monastery. Nandā, on her bed, was waiting for him, and he seduced her.[2] Buddhaghosa explains[3] that Sāḷha was called Migāranattā because he was the grandson of **Migaramātā (Visākhā).**

[2] Vin. iv. 211 f. [3] Sp. iv. 900.

2. **Sāḷha.**—A **Licchavi,** who once visited the Buddha at the **Kūṭāgārasālā.**[1] See **Saḷha Sutta** (2).

[1] A. ii. 200.

3. **Sāḷha.**—A monk of **Ñātikā.** The Buddha declared that he died an arahant.[1]

[1] D. ii. 91; S. v. 356.

4. **Sāḷha.**—An eminent monk who took a prominent part in the Second Council. He lived in **Sahajāti,** and, on hearing of the heresy of the **Vajjiputtakas,** retired into solitude in order to decide whether he thought their contentions right. There an inhabitant of the **Suddhāvāsā** informed him that the Vajjiputtakas were wrong. He was one of the four appointed on behalf of the **Pācīnakas (Vajjiputtakas)** on the committee which discussed the dispute. He was a pupil of **Ānanda.**[1]

[1] Vin. ii. 302 ff.; Mhv. iv. 4 f., 48, 57; Dpv. iv. 49; v. 22; Sp. i. 34.

1. **Sāḷha Sutta.**—Records a conversation between **Nandaka Thera, Sāḷha Migāranattā,** and **Rohaṇa Pekkhuṇiyanattā.**[1]

[1] A. i. 193 f.

2. **Sāḷha Sutta.**—The **Licchavis, Sāḷha** and **Abhaya,** visit the Buddha at the **Kūṭāgārasālā** and question him regarding the way that is made by purity of morals and that made by self-mortification. The Buddha answers the question with many similes. The last part of the sutta describes a fighting man who is a "long-distance shooter," one who shoots by lightning, and a smashei of large objects, and the corresponding classes of the Ariyan disciples.[1]

[1] A. ii. 200 f.

1. **Sāvajja Sutta.**—Blameworthy actions of body, speech and mind, lead to **Niraya;** their opposites to heaven.[1]

[1] A. i. 292.

2. **Sāvajja Sutta.**—On four kinds of persons: the blameworthy, the very blameworthy, the slighty blameworthy, the blameless.[1]

[1] A. ii. 135.

3. **Sāvajja Sutta.**—The four kinds of blameworthy actions—of body, speech, thought, and view—and their opposites.[1]

[1] A. ii. 237.

Sāvatthi.—The capital town of **Kosala** in India and one of the six great Indian cities during the lifetime of the Buddha.[1] It was six leagues from **Sāketa,**[2] forty-five leagues north-west of **Rājagaha,**[3] thirty leagues from **Saṅkassa,**[4] one hundred and forty-seven from **Takkasilā,**[5] one hundred and twenty from **Suppāraka,**[6] and was on the banks of the **Aciravatī.**[7] It was thirty leagues from **Āḷavī,**[8] thirty from **Macchikāsaṇḍa,**[9] one hundred and twenty from **Kukkuṭavatī,**[10] and the same distance from **Uggapura**[11] and from **Kuraraghara.**[12] The road from **Rājagaha** to Sāvatthi passed through **Vesāli,**[13] and the **Parāyaṇavagga**[14] gives the resting-places between the two cities—**Setavyā, Kapilavatthu, Kusinārā, Pāvā** and **Bhoganagara.** Further on, there was a road running southwards from Sāvatthi through **Sāketa** to **Kosambī.** One gāvuta from the city was the **Andhavana** (*q.v.*). Between Sāketa and Sāvatthi was **Toraṇavatthu.**[15]

The city was called Sāvatthi because the sage **Savattha** lived there. Another tradition says there was a caravanserai there, and people meeting there asked each other what they had—"Kiṃ bhandaṃ atthi ?" "Sabbaṃ atthi"—and the name of the city was based on the reply.[16]

The Buddha passed the greater part of his monastic life in Sāvatthi. His first visit there was at the invitation of **Anāthapiṇḍika.**[17] It is said[18] that he spent twenty-five rainy seasons in the city—nineteen of them in **Jetavana** and six in the **Pubbārāma.** Sāvatthi also contained the monastery of **Rājakārāma** (*q.v.*), built by **Pasenadi,** opposite **Jetavana.** Outside the city gate of Sāvatthi was a fisherman's village of five hundred families.[19]

[1] D. ii. 147.
[2] Vin. i. 253; seven according to others (DhA. i. 387).
[3] SA. i. 243.
[4] J. iv. 265.
[5] MA. ii. 987.
[6] DhA. ii. 213.
[7] Vin. i. 191, 293.
[8] SNA. i. 220.
[9] DhA. ii. 79.
[10] *Ibid.*, 118.
[11] *Ibid.*, iii. 469.
[12] *Ibid.*, iv. 106.
[13] Vin. ii. 159 f.
[14] SN. vss. 1011-13.
[15] S. iv. 374.
[16] SNA. i. 300; PSA. 367.
[17] *q.v.* for details.
[18] DhA. i. 4.
[19] *Ibid.*, iv. 40.

Savatthi is the scene of each Buddha's **Yamaka-pāṭihāriya**[20]; Gotama Buddha performed this miracle under the **Gaṇḍamba** (*q.v.*).

The chief patrons of the Buddha in Sāvatthi were **Anāthapiṇḍika, Visākhā, Suppavāsā** and **Pasenadi.**[21] When **Bandhula** (*q.v.*) left **Vesālī** he came to live in Sāvatthi.

Buddhaghosa says[22] that, in the Buddha's day, there were fifty-seven thousand families in Sāvatthi, and that it was the chief city in the country of **Kāsi-Kosala,** which was three hundred leagues in extent and had eighty thousand villages. The population of Sāvatthi was eighteen crores.[23]

Sāvatthi is identified with Sāhet-Māhet on the banks of the Rapti.[24]

Hiouen Thsang found the old city in ruins, but records the sites of various buildings.[25]

Woodward states[26] that, of the four Nikāyas, 871 suttas are said to have been preached in Sāvatthi; 844 of which are in Jetavana, 23 in the Pubbārāma, and 4 in the suburbs. These suttas are made up of 6 in the Dīgha, 75 in the Majjhima, 736 in the Saṃyutta, and 54 in the Aṅguttara. Mrs. Rhys Davids conjectures[27] from this that either the Buddha "mainly resided there or else Sāvatthi was the earliest emporium (library ?) for the collection and preservation (however this was done) of the talks." The first alternative is the more likely, as the Commentaries state that the Buddha spent twenty-five rainy seasons in Sāvatthi (see earlier), this leaving only twenty to be spent elsewhere. The Buddhavaṃsa Commentary[28] gives a list of these places showing that the second, third, fourth, seventeenth and twentieth were spent in Rājagaha, the thirteenth, eighteenth and nineteenth in **Cāliyapabbata,** and the rest in different places.

20 DhA. iii. 205; *cf.* Mtu. iii. 115; J. i. 88.
21 DhA. i. 330.
22 Sp. iii. 614.
23 SNA. i. 371.
24 Cunningham, AGI. 469.
25 Beal, *op. cit.*, ii. 1-13.
26 KS. v. xviii.
27 M. iv., Introd., p. vi.
28 BuA. p. 3.

Sāvitti.—A hymn, mentioned as chief of the Vedas (*chandato mukhaṃ*).[1] It consists of three lines of twenty-four letters (*tipadaṃ catuvīsakkharaṃ*).[2] The Commentary[3] explains that the latter refers to the **Ariya-Sāvitti,** which consists of the formula "*Buddhaṃ saraṇaṃ, gacchāmi, Dhammaṃ—pe—, Saṅghaṃ—pe—* "

1 SN. vs. 568. 2 *Ibid.*, 457. 3 SNA. ii. 403.

Sāsana Sutta.—The Buddha tells **Upāli** in brief as to how various doctrines can be regarded as belonging to the Dhamma or otherwise.[1]

1 A. iv. 143.

Sāsanavaṃsa.—An ecclesiastical chronicle by **Paññasāmi** of Burma, written in 1861 A.C. The first part of the work begins with the birth of the Buddha and brings the history up to the Third Council and the sending of missionaries to nine different countries: **Sīhala, Suvaṇṇabhūmi, Yoṇakaraṭṭha, Vanavāsī, Kasmīra-Gandhāra, Mahiṃsakamaṇḍala, Cīnaraṭṭha, Mahāraṭṭha** (Siam) and **Aparanta.** Then follow accounts of the religions of these countries, a separate chapter being devoted to each. But the accounts of Sīhala (Ceylon) and Suvaṇṇabhūmi (Burma) show more completeness than the others. The second part is entirely devoted to **Aparanta** of Burma proper.[1]

[1] Published by the P.T.S. 1897.

Sāsapa Sutta.—If a man were to take once in one hundred years one seed from a heap of mustard one yojana in length, breadth, and height, he would come to an end of the seeds before one æon is passed. Incalculable is *saṃsāra.*[1]

[1] S. ii. 182.

Sāhasamalla.—A king of Ceylon who belonged to the **Okkāka** dynasty and reigned for only two years, till he was deposed by **Āyasmanta.**[1]

[1] Cv. lxxx. 32; but see Cv. *Trs.* ii. 130, n. 1; the date of his accession (August 23rd, 1200) is said to be the only absolutely certain date in the history of Ceylon.

Siṃsapā Sutta.—The Buddha, while staying in **Siṃsapāvana** in **Kosambī,** takes up a handful of leaves and tells the monks that the things he has discovered and not revealed, compared to those he has revealed, are as the handful of leaves to the leaves in the forest. What he has not revealed does not conduce to tranquillity, Nibbāna. He has revealed Ill, its cause, cessation, and the way thereto; this *does* conduce to Nibbāna.[1]

[1] S. v. 437.

1. **Siṃsapāvana.**—A grove in **Āḷavi,** where the Buddha stayed in the **Gomagga** and was visited by **Hatthaka of Āḷavi.**[1]

[1] A. i. 136.

2. **Siṃsapāvana.**—A grove in **Kosambī,** where the Buddha once stayed. See **Siṃsapā Sutta.**[1]

[1] S. v. 437.

3. **Siṃsapāvana.**—A grove to the north of **Setavyā,** where **Kumāra Kassapa** once stayed. The Buddha also once stayed there during a journey.[1] It was the scene of the preaching of the **Pāyāsi Sutta.**[2]

[1] DhA. i. 59.

[2] D. ii. 316.

Siṃsapāvana Vagga.—The fourth chapter of the **Sacca Saṃyutta.**[1]

[1] S. v. 437 ff.

1. **Sikkhā Sutta.**—The three forms of training in the higher insight.[1]

[1] A. i. 235.

2. **Sikkhā Sutta.**—One must train oneself in the Dhamma.[1]

[1] S. ii. 131.

3. **Sikkhā Sutta.**—A monk who returns to the lower life must blame himself for five things: having no faith in right things, no conscientiousness, no fear of blame, no energy, no insight into right things.[1]

[1] A. iii. 4.

Sikkhānisaṃsa Sutta.—*Brahmacariyā* is lived for the sake of the profit of the training, of further wisdom, of the essence of release, of the mastery of mindfulness.[1]

[1] A. ii. 243 f.

1. **Sikkhāpada Sutta.**—The unworthy man is he who takes life, steals, etc. The worthy man, he who abstains from these things.[1]

[1] A. ii. 217.

2. **Sikkhāpada Sutta.**—The four kinds of deeds: dark with dark result, bright with bright result, neither dark nor bright, both dark and bright.[1]

[1] A. ii. 233.

Sikkhāpadavalañjanī.—A Pāli translation, by **Pañcapariveṇādhipati Thera,** of the Sinhalese work *Sikhavalanda*, on monastic rules.[1]

[1] P.L.C. 216.

Sikhaṇḍī.—A *khattiya* of thirty-one kappas ago, brother of **Sikhī Buddha.** When the Buddha died he erected a *thūpa* over his remains.[1]

[1] Netti, p. 142.

Sikhaddī, Sikhaṇḍī.—A **Gandhabba,** son of **Mātali; Bhaddā Suriyavaccasā** was at first in love with him, but she was won later by **Pañcasikha.**[1]

[1] D. ii. 268; *cf.* Mtu. ii. 190.

Sikhā-Moggallāna.—A brahmin who once visited the Buddha, saying that he had been told by **Soṇakāyana** that the Buddha preached the ineffectiveness of all deeds and asking if this were true.[1]

[1] A. ii. 232.

The Commentary explains[2] that he was a brahmin of the **Moggallāna-gotta** and wore a large tuft (*sikhā*) on the crown of his head, hence his name.

[2] AA. ii. 578; *cf.* **Moliya.**

Sikhānāyaka.—An officer of **Parakkamabāhu I.** He lived in the **Moriya** district and was a **Lambakaṇṇa.**[1]

[1] Cv. lxix. 12.

Sikhī.—The twentieth of the twenty-four Buddhas. He was born in the **Nisabha** pleasaunce in **Aruṇavatī,** his father being the khattiya **Aruṇa (Aruṇavā)** and his mother **Pabhāvatī.** He was so named because his *uṇhīsa* stood up like a flame (*sikhā*). For seven thousand years he lived in the household in three palaces—**Sucanda, Giri, Vahana**[1]—his wife being **Sabbakāmā** and his son **Atula.** He left home on an elephant, practised austerities for eight months, was given milk-rice by the daughter of **Piyadassī-seṭṭhi** of **Sudassananigama,** and grass for his seat by **Anomadassī.** His Bodhi was a *puṇḍarīka.* His first sermon was preached in the **Migācira** pleasaunce near **Aruṇavatī,** and his Twin Miracle was performed near **Suriyavatī** under a *campaka*-tree. The Bodhisatta was **Arindama,** king of **Paribhutta. Abhibhū** and **Sambhava** were his chief disciples among monks, and **Akhilā (Makhilā)** and **Padumā** among nuns. His constant attendant was **Khemaṅkara.** Among his patrons were **Sirivaḍḍha** and **Canda (Nanda)** among men, and **Cittā** and **Suguttā** among women. His body was sixty cubits high, and he lived to the age of seventy thousand years, dying in **Dussārāma (Assārāma)** in **Sīlavatī.** Over his relics was erected a *thūpa* three leagues in height.[2] Sikhī Buddha held the *Pāṭimokkha* ceremony only once in six years.[3]

For a visit paid by him to the Brahma-world see *s.v.* **Abhibhū.** His name also occurs in the **Aruṇavatī Paritta** (*q.v.*).

[1] BuA. (p. 201) calls them **Sucanda-kasiri, Giriyasa** and **Nārivasabha.**

[2] Bu. xxi.; BuA. 201 ff.; *cf.* D. ii. 7; iii. 195 f.; J. i. 41, 94; DhA. i. 69; S. ii. 9; Dvy. 333.

[3] DhA. iii. 236; *cf.* Sp. i. 191.

Sikhī Sutta.—The process by which **Sikhī Buddha,** like the other Buddhas, reached Enlightenment.[1]

[1] S. iii. 9.

Sigāla.—See **Sigālovāda Sutta.**

1. **Sigāla Jātaka** (No. 113).—The people of Benares once held a sacrifice to the Yakkhas, placing meat and liquor in their courtyards. A jackal,

who entered the city through a sewer, regaled himself with food and drink and then went to sleep in some bushes in the city. He did not awake till morning, and then, looking for a way of escape, met a brahmin. Promising to show him a spot where lay hidden two hundred pieces of gold, he persuaded the brahmin to carry him out of the city in his waist-cloth. Arrived at the cemetery, he asked the brahmin to spread his robe and dig under a tree. While the brahmin dug, the jackal fouled the robe and ran away. The Bodhisatta, then a tree-sprite, advised the brahmin to wash his robe and cease being a fool.

The story was told in reference to **Devadatta,** who is identified with the jackal.[1]

[1] J. i. 424-26.

2. **Sigāla Jātaka** (No. 142).—Once, during a festival in Benares, some rogues were drinking and eating till late at night, and when the meat was finished, one of them offered to go to the charnel-field and kill a jackal for food. Taking a club, he lay down as though dead. The Bodhisatta, then king of the jackals, came there with his flock, but in order to make sure that it was a corpse, he pulled at the club. The man tightened his grip, and the Bodhisatta mocked at his silliness. The man then threw the club at the jackals, but they escaped.

The story was told in reference to **Devadatta,** who is identified with the rogue.[1]

[1] J. i. 489 f.

3. **Sigāla Jātaka** (No. 148).—The Bodhisatta was once born as a jackal, and, coming across the dead body of an elephant, ate into it from behind and lived inside it. When the body dried up, he became a prisoner and made frenzied efforts to escape. Then a storm broke, moistening the hide and allowing him to emerge through the head, but not without losing all his hair as he crawled through. He thereupon resolved to renounce greediness.

The story was told in reference to five hundred companions, rich men of **Sāvatthi,** who joined the Order. One night the Buddha perceived that they were filled with thoughts of lust. He therefore sent **Ānanda** to summon all the monks in the monastery, and told this tale to illustrate the evil effects of desire. The five hundred monks became arahants.[1]

[1] J. i. 501 f.

4. **Sigāla Jātaka** (No. 152).—The Bodhisatta was once a lion with six brothers and one sister. When the lions were away after food, a jackal who had fallen in love with the lioness told her of his love. She

was greatly insulted, and resolved to tell her brothers and then die. The jackal slunk away and hid in a cave. One by one the lions came in, and when their sister told them of the insult, they tried to reach the jackal by leaping upwards, but perished in the attempt. At last came the Bodhisatta; being wise, he roared the lion's roar three times and the jackal died. He then consoled his sister.

The story was told to a barber in **Vesāli** who served the king's household. His son used to go with him to the palace, and, having fallen in love with a **Licchavi** girl, died of a broken heart because he could not have her. The barber, who was a pious follower of the Buddha, visited the Buddha some time after and told him of what had happened.

The jackal was the barber's son, the lioness the Licchavi girl, and the six young lions the **Chabbaggiyā.**[1]

[1] J. ii. 5 ff.

Sigāla Vagga.—The tenth section of the Duka Nipāta of the Jātaka Commentary.[1]

[1] J. ii. 242-70.

1. **Sigālaka.**—Son of **Sigālakapitā** (*q.v.*).

2. **Sigālaka.**—Son of **Sigālakamātā** (*q.v.*).

3. **Sigālaka.**—See **Siṅgālaka.**

1. **Sigālaka Sutta.**—An old jackal, afflicted by mange, finds no pleasure in lonely places, or in the woods, or in the open air. Wherever he goes he falls into misfortune and disaster. Even so is a monk whose heart is possessed by gains, favours, or flattery.[1]

[1] S. ii. 230.

2. **Sigālaka Sutta.**—Some old jackals, afflicted with mange, can go wherever they like. There are some **Sākyan** monks who cannot get even so much release.[1]

[1] S. ii. 271; the Commentary (SA. ii. 169) says that the sutta was preached in reference to **Devadatta.**

3. **Sigālaka Sutta.**—Some **Sākyan** monks have not as much gratitude as a jackal.[1] The Commentary adds[2] that the sutta was preached in reference to **Devadatta,** and the story was about a jackal who was released

[1] S. ii. 272. [2] SA. ii. 170.

by a peasant from a snake who had coiled round it. The snake attacked the peasant, and the jackal brought the peasant his axe in its mouth, enabling the man to kill the snake.

Sigālakapitā (Siṅgālaka°) Thera.—He was a householder of **Sāvatthi** and had a son called **Sigālaka.** Later he entered the Order, and the Buddha asked him to meditate on the idea of a skeleton. He lived in the **Bhesakalāvana** in **Suṃsumāragiri,** and there a woodland sprite once encouraged him with a verse.[1] Thus, urged to strive, he developed insight and became an arahant.

Ninety-four kappas ago he had given a *tāla*-fruit to the Pacceka Buddha **Sataraṃsī.** In the time of **Kassapa Buddha** he was a monk and developed meditation on the idea of a skeleton.[2]

[1] Given in Thag. vs. 18. [2] ThagA. i. 70 f.

Sigālakamātā Therī.—She belonged to a seṭṭhi's family in **Rājagaha,** and, after marriage, had a son called **Sigālaka.** She heard the Buddha preach and entered the Order. She was full of faith, and, when she went to hear the Buddha preach, would gaze at his beauty of personality. The Buddha, realizing her nature, preached so that her faith might reach its culmination, and, in due course, she became an arahant. Later she was declared chief of nuns who had attained release by faith (*saddhādhimuttānaṃ*).

In the time of **Padumuttara Buddha** she belonged to a minister's family, and once went with her father to hear the Buddha preach. Full of faith, she entered the Order, and, hearing a nun declared foremost of those who had faith, she wished for similar eminence.[1]

According to the Apadāna,[2] she was the mother of **Sigāla(-ka),** to whom the Buddha preached the sutta regarding the worship of the directions (evidently the **Sigālovāda Sutta).** She heard the sermon and became a *sotāpanna.*

[1] A. i. 25; AA. i. 206 f. [2] Ap. ii. 603 f.

Sigālovāda, Siṅgālovāda Sutta.—**Sigāla (Siṅgāla)**, a young householder of **Rājagaha,** was in the habit of rising early, bathing, and, with wet hair and garments, worshipping the several quarters of the earth and sky. The Buddha saw him once and asked him the reason for this. Sigāla's reply was that his dead father had asked him to do so. The Buddha then taught him that, in his religion, too, there was worship of the six quarters, but that these quarters were different. Urged by Sigāla to explain, the Buddha taught him the six vices in conduct, the four motives for such evil action, the six channels for dissipating wealth, and the different kinds of friends. He then taught him the six quarters to be honoured by performing the duties owing to them—parents are the east, teachers the south, wife and children the west, friends and companions the north, servants and workpeople the nadir, religious teachers and brahmins the zenith. Details are then given of the duties owing to these and of their counter-duties.

The sutta is an exposition of the whole domestic and social duty of a layman, according to the Buddhist point of view, and, as such, it is famous under the name of **Gihivinaya.**[1]

Sigālaka became the Buddha's follower. According to the Apadāna,[2] it was this Sigālaka's mother who was known as **Sigālakamātā** (*q.v.*).

[1] D. iii. 180-93. [2] Ap. ii. 604.

1. **Siggava.**—A king of long ago, who was destroyed by the gods because he insulted holy ascetics. He was a former birth of **Upāli Thera.**[1]

[1] ThagA. i. 368.

2. **Siggava.**—A minister's son of **Pāṭaliputta,** who lived in three palaces in great luxury. When he was eighteen, he visited, with his friend **Caṇḍavajji, Soṇaka Thera** at the **Kukkuṭārāma** and entered the Order with five hundred companions. During seven years, Siggava visited for alms the house in which **Moggaliputta Tissa** (*q.v.*) was born, without so much as receiving a word of welcome, but, in the end, he converted and ordained him, teaching him the Tipiṭaka.[1] Siggava's father was **Sirivaḍḍha.**[2]

[1] Mhv. v. 99, 120-51; Dpv. iv. 40, 57, 89; Sp. i. 32, 235; DhSA. 32. [2] MṬ. 215.

Siṅgatthala.—A village in Ceylon, given by **Kittisirirājasīha** for the **Majjhavela-vihāra.**[1]

[1] Cv. c. 230.

Siṅgāravimāna.—A four-storeyed building, painted with various pictures, in the **Dīpuyyāna.**[1]

[1] Cv. lxxiii. 122.

Siṅgāla.—One of the four leading merchants of **Pupphavatī** (Benares) in the time of **Ekarāja.**[1]

[1] J. vi. 135.

Sitthagāma.—A village which **Sena IV.** converted into a *pariveṇa*, evidently for his retirement.[1] Later, a monk, named **Dhammamitta,** lived there and wrote a Commentary on the Abhidhamma.[2]

[1] Cv. liv. 6. [2] *Ibid.*, 35.

1. **Siddhattha.**—The sixteenth of the twenty-four Buddhas. He was born in the **Viriya** pleasaunce in the city of **Vebhāra,** his father being the *khattiya* **Udena** and his mother **Suphassā.** At the time of his birth all enterprises succeeded, hence his name. He lived as a householder for ten thousand years in three palaces—**Kokā, Suppala** and **Kokanuda (Paduma)**—his wife being **Sumanā (Somanassā)** and his son **Anupama.** He left home in a golden palanquin, practised auterities for ten months, had milk rice given to him by a brahmin maiden, **Sunettā** of **Asadisa,** and grass for his seat by a Yavapāla, **Varuṇa.** His bodhi was a *kaṇikāra,* and his first sermon was preached at **Gayā.** The Bodhisatta was an ascetic named **Maṅgala,** of **Surasena. Samphala** and **Sumitta** were his chief disciples among monks, and **Sīvalā** and **Surāmā** among nuns, while **Revata** was his attendant. Chief among his lay-patrons were **Suppiya** and **Samudda** and **Rammā** and **Surammā.** His body was sixty cubits high. He lived for one hundred thousand years, and died in the **Anomārāma** in the city of **Anoma.** His *thūpa* was four leagues in height.[1]

[1] Bu. xvii.; BuA. 185 ff.; J. i. 49.

2. **Siddhattha.**—The personal name of **Gotama Buddha.**[1]

[1] J. i. 56, 58, etc.; iv. 50, 328; vi. 479; DhA. iii. 195; Dpv. iii. 197; xix. 18; Mhv. ii. 24, 25. In the Mtu. he is called Sarvārthasiddha.

3. **Siddhattha.**—An eminent monk in the time of **Duṭṭhagāmaṇī.** Foreseeing dangers lying ahead, he prevented the king from marking out a very large site for the **Mahā Thūpa.**[1] He was evidently at the head of the monks present at the Foundation Ceremony of the Mahā Thūpa.[2]

[1] Mhv. xxix. 52.

[2] See MṬ. 522, 524.

4. **Siddhattha.**—A son of King **Kassapa IV.** He was appointed governor of the **Malaya** district and came to be called **Malayarājā.** He died young, however, and Kassapa built a hall for the monks in his name and instituted an offering of alms.[1]

[1] Cv. lii. 68 f.

5. **Siddhattha.**—A monk of the **Uposathārāma,** to whom King **Kittisirirājasīha** gave over the **Rajata-vihāra.** The monk had it repaired and had many additions made to it.[1]

[1] Cv. c. 238 ff.

6. **Siddhattha.**—One of the palaces which will be occupied by **Metteyya Buddha** in his last lay life.[1]

[1] Anāgat., p. 46.

7. **Siddhattha.**—A monk of Ceylon of the thirteenth century; he was a pupil of **Buddhappiya** and wrote the **Sāratthasaṅgaha.**[1]

[1] P.L.C. 228 f.

Siddhatthikā.—One of the seven heterodox sects which branched off in the second century after the Buddha's death.[1] They belonged to the **Andhakas** (*q.v.*) and held the same views.[2]

[1] Mhv. v. 12; Dpv. v. 54.
[2] Kvu. 104; Introd. xx.

Sinipura, Sinisura.—A son of the third **Okkāka,** his mother being **Hatthā.** He was an ancestor of the **Sākyans.**[1] *v.l.* **Nipura.**

[1] DA. i. 258; SNA. 352; Mhv. ii. 12; Dpv. iii. 41.

Sineru.—A mountain, forming the centre of the world. It is submerged in the sea to a depth of eighty-four thousand yojanas and rises above the surface to the same height. It is surrounded by seven mountain ranges—**Yugandhara, Īsadhara, Karavīka, Sudassana, Nemindhara, Vinataka** and **Assakaṇṇa.**[1] On the top of Sineru is **Tāvatiṃsa,**[2] while at its foot is the **Asurabhavana**[3] of ten thousand leagues; in the middle are the four **Mahādīpā** with their two thousand smaller *dīpā*.

Sineru is often used in similes, its chief characteristic being its unshakeability (*suṭṭhuṭhapita*).[4] It is also called **Meru** or **Sumeru,**[5] **Hemameru**[6] and **Mahāneru.**[7] Each **Cakkavāla** has its own Sineru,[8] and a time comes when even Sineru is destroyed.[9] When the Buddha went to Tāvatiṃsa, he covered the distance there from the earth in three strides —he set his right foot down on the top of **Yugandhara** and his left on **Sineru,** the next step brought him to Tāvatiṃsa, the whole distance so covered being sixty-eight hundred thousand leagues.[10]

[1] SNA. ii. 443; Sp. i. 119; Vsm. 206; *cp.* Mtu. ii. 300; Dvy. 217; it is eighty thousand leagues broad (A. iv. 100).
[2] SNA. ii. 485 f.
[3] The Asurabhavana was not originally there, but sprang up by the power of the Asuras when they were thrown down from Tāvatiṃsa (DhA. i. 272); see, *e.g.*, SNA. i. 201.
[4] *E.g.*, SN. vs. 683.
[5] *E.g.*, Cv. xlii. 2.
[6] *E.g.*, *ibid.*, xxxii. 79.
[7] M. i. 338; also Neru, J. iii. 247.
[8] A. i. 227; v. 59.
[9] S. iii. 149.
[10] DhA. iii. 216.

Sineru Sutta.—The *dukkha* destroyed by the Noble Disciple (arahant) compared with what is yet left to him until his death, is like seven grains of sand on the top of Sineru.[1]

[1] S. v. 457 f.

Sindhaka.—A servant of **Aṅkura** (*q.v.*).[1]

[1] Pv. ii. 9 (vs. 39, 40); PvA. 127.

Sindhavasandana.—A king of twenty-seven kappas ago, a previous birth of **Khomadāyaka Thera.**[1]

[1] Ap. i. 81.

Sindhavā.—See **Sindhu.**

Sindhu.—A river in India; one of the most important of those that flow from the **Himālaya.**[1] The best horses were born in the country around its banks,[2] hence their name Sindhava.[3] **Serī** (*q.v.*) was king of both Sindhu (**Sindhavaraṭṭha**) and **Sodhika** (? **Sovīra**).[4] Mention is made[5] of merchants from **Aṅga** and **Magadha** going to **Sindhu-Sovīra** and passing through great wildernesses on the way. The **Sindhavā** are mentioned in the Apadāna[6] in a list of tribes.

The Sindhunadī is the modern Indus.

Isidāsī was once born as a goat in **Sindhavārañña.**[7]

[1] Mil. p. 114.
[2] AA. ii. 756; MA. i. 248.
[3] J. v. 260 (22); *cf.* ii. 290.
[4] SA. i. 90.
[5] VvA. 332.
[6] Ap. ii. 359.
[7] Thig. vs. 438.

Sindhūravāna.—A place in Ceylon, between **Hatthiselapura** and **Gaṅgāsiripura,** on the way to **Sumanakūṭa.** There **Vijayabāhu IV.** built the **Vanaggāmapāsāda-vihāra** and the **Abhayarāja-pariveṇa.**[1]

[1] Cv. lxxxviii. 50.

Sippatthala.—A village in **Rohaṇa,** near **Kājaragāma,** mentioned in the account of the campaigns of **Vijayabāhu I.**[1]

[1] Cv. lvii. 70; lviii. 7.

Sibbi.—See **Sivi.**

Simbali.—A **Niraya.**[1]

[1] J. v. 275.

Simbalivana, Simbalidaha.—The abode of **Garuḍas**[1] (*q.v.*).

[1] J. i. 202; DhA. i. 279; MA. ii. 638.

Siyāmahantakuddāla.—A village near **Anurādhapura** and close to **Tissavāpi,** mentioned in the account of the campaigns of **Gajabāhu.**[1]

[1] Cv. lxx. 149, 154, 161.

1. **Siri.**—One of the palaces of **Anomadassī Buddha** in his last lay life.[1]

[1] Bu. viii. 18.

2. **Siri.**—One of the palaces of **Sujāta Buddha** in his last lay life.[1]

[1] Bu. xiii. 21.

3. **Siri.**—One of the patrons of **Tissa Buddha.**[1]

[1] Bu. xviii. 23.

Siri Jātaka (No. 284).—The Bodhisatta was once an ascetic and had, as patron, an elephant-trainer. A stick-gatherer, sleeping at night in a temple, heard two cocks, roosting on a tree near by, abusing each other. In the course of the quarrel one cock boasted that whoever ate his flesh would be king; his exterior, commander-in-chief or chief queen; his bones, royal treasurer or king's chaplain. The man killed the cock and his wife cooked it; then, taking it with them, they went to the river to bathe. They left the meat and the rice on the bank, but, as they bathed, a breeze blew the pot holding the food into the river. It floated down-stream, where it was picked up by the elephant-trainer. The Bodhisatta saw all this with his divine eye and visited the trainer at meal-time. There he was offered the meat and divided it, giving the flesh to the trainer, the exterior to his wife, and keeping the bones for himself. Three days later the city was besieged by enemies. The king asked the trainer to don royal robes and mount the elephant, while he himself fought in the ranks. There he was killed by an arrow, and the trainer, having won the battle, was made king, his wife being queen, and the ascetic his chaplain.

The story was told in reference to a brahmin who tried to steal **Anāthapiṇḍika's** good fortune (*siri*). He perceived that this lay in a white cock, for which he begged. Anāthapiṇḍika gave it to him, but the good fortune left the cock and settled in a jewel. He asked for that also and was given it. But the good fortune went into a club. The club was also asked for, and Anāthapiṇḍika giving it, asked the brahmin to take it and be gone. But the good fortune now settled on Anāthapiṇḍika's wife. The brahmin then owned defeat, and confessed his intentions to Anāthapiṇḍika, who told the story to the Buddha.[1]

[1] J. ii. 409 ff.; *cf.* **Khadiraṅga Jātaka.**

Sirika.—The name of the elephant which **Sunanda** (**Upāli** in this life) was riding when he insulted the Pacceka Buddha **Devala** by driving the elephant at him.[1]

[1] ThagA. i. 368.

Sirikaṇha.—Another name for **Asita.**[1]

[1] SNA. ii. 487; *cf.* SN. vs. 689 (**Kaṇhasiri**).

1. **Sirikāḷakaṇṇi Jātaka** (No. 192).—Another name for the **Sirikāḷakaṇṇipañha** (*q.v.*).

2. **Sirikāḷakaṇṇi Jātaka** (No. 382).—The Bodhisatta was once a merchant of Benares, and, because his household observed the rules of piety, he came to be called **Suciparivāra** ("pure household"). He kept an unused couch and bed for anyone who might come to his house and was purer than himself. One day **Kālakaṇṇī,** daughter of **Virūpakka** and **Sirī, Dhataraṭṭha's** daughter, went to bathe in **Anotatta,** and a quarrel arose as to which should bathe first. As neither the Four Regent Gods nor Sakka were willing to decide, they referred the two goddesses to Suciparivāra. Kālakaṇṇī first appeared before him in blue raiment and jewels, and, on being asked what were her qualities, she told him, and was asked to vanish from his sight. Then came Sirī, diffusing yellow radiance, and the Bodhisatta, discovering her identity and her virtues, welcomed her and offered her his unused couch. Thus was the dispute settled. The bed used by Sirī came to be called **Sirisaya,** hence the origin of *Sirisayana*.

Sirī is identified with **Uppalavaṇṇā.**[1]

[1] J. iii. 257-64.

Sirikāḷakaṇṇipañha.—The name given to that section of the **Mahāummagga Jātaka** which deals with the coming of **Vedeha** to win **Udumbarā,** when she was deserted by **Piṅguttara.** It also tells of how **Mahosadha** once rescued her from the king's wrath.[1]

This was also evidently called a Jātaka by the same name.[2]

[1] J. vi. 349.
[2] *E.g.*, at J. ii. 115.

Sirikuḍḍa, Sirikūṭa.—Evidently another name for **Mahānāma,** king of Ceylon, who was Buddhaghosa's patron. Buddhaghosa says, in the colophon to several of his works,[1] that he composed them in the monastery erected for him by the monarch **Sirikuḍḍa (Sirikūṭa).**

[1] *E.g.*, DhA. iv. 235.

1. **Sirigutta.**—Maternal uncle of **Sirimitta Thera.**[1] He was a *sotāpanna* and a friend of **Garahadinna.**[2] For his story see *s.v.* **Garahadinna.**

[1] ThagA. i. 488.
[2] DhS. i. 434 f.

2. **Sirigutta.**—The name of **Eḷāra's** second horse.[1]

[1] MṬ. 441.

Sirighanānanda.—A pariveṇa in **Viddumagāma,** built by **Parakkamabāhu IV.**[1]

[1] Cv. xc. 98.

Sirighara.—A place in the **Nandārāma** where, at the foot of a *sirīsa*-tree, **Dīpaṅkara Buddha** defeated the *titthiyā*.[1]

[1] Bu. ii. 212.

Sirideva.—A minister of **Duṭṭhagāmaṇī,** who, with **Visākha,** was in charge of the arrangements for the Foundation Ceremony of the **Mahā Thūpa.**[1]

[1] MṬ. 517.

Sirideviṇaga.—A mountain in the **Dakkhiṇadesa** of Ceylon. It was near **Buddhagāma,** and is mentioned in the account of the early campaigns of **Parakkamabāhu I.**[1]

[1] Cv. lxvi. 19.

Siridhara.—A king of twenty-seven kappas ago, a previous birth of **Rahosaññaka (Sunāga) Thera.**[1]

[1] Ap. i. 167; ThagA. i. 182.

Sirinanda.—A palace of **Kassapa Buddha,** before his renunciation.[1]

[1] Bu. xxv. 35.

1. **Sirinandana.**—A pleasaunce in **Upakārī,** where **Sumedha Buddha** preached to a large concourse.[1]

[1] BuA. 165.

2. **Sirinandana.**—A treasurer and his residence. His daughter gave a meal of milk-rice to **Sujāta Buddha.**[1]

[1] BuA. 168.

Sirinandā.—Wife of **Sujāta Buddha,** in his last lay life.[1]

[1] Bu. xiii. 22.

Sirināga I.—King of Ceylon (249-68 A.C.). He was the brother of **Kuñcanāga's** queen and was his commander-in-chief. He rebelled against the king and defeated him; he then reigned in **Anurādhapura.** He erected a parasol over the **Mahā Thūpa,** rebuilt the **Lohapāsāda,** and restored the steps leading to the Bodhi-tree. His son was **Vohārika-Tissa.**[1]

[1] Mhv. xxxvi. 21 ff.; Dpv. xxii. 34 f.

2 **Sirināga II.**—King of Ceylon (300-302 A.C.). He was the son of **Tissa (Vohārika-Tissa)** and brother of **Abhayanāga.** He restored the wall round the Bodhi-tree and built the Haṃsavaṭṭa of the Bodhi-tree temple. His son was **Vijayakumāra.**[1]

[1] Mhv. xxxvi. 54 f.; Dpv. xxii. 46 f.

Sirinivāsa.—Another name for **Mahānāma,** king of Ceylon.[1]

[1] P.L.C. 84, 96.

Siripāsāda.—A building erected by **Mānavamma** in the **Sirisaṅghabodhi-vihāra.**[1]

[1] Cv. xlvii. 64.

Siripiṭṭhika.—A village in Ceylon, mentioned in the account of the wars of **Aggabodhi III.**[1]

[1] Cv. xliv. 88.

1. **Sirimaṅgala.**—A Burmese monk of the fourteenth century, author of several commentaries on **Buddhaghosa's** works.[1] *v.l.* **Sirisumaṅgala.**

[1] Bode, *op. cit.*, 27.

2. **Sirimaṅgala.**—A monk of Laos of the sixteenth century; he wrote the **Maṅgaladīpanī** and a *ṭīkā* on the **Saṅkhyāpakāsaka.**[1]

[1] Bode, *op. cit.*, 47.

Sirimaṇḍa Thera.—He belonged to a brahmin family of **Suṃsumāragiri** and entered the Order, after hearing the Buddha preach in **Bhesakalāvana.** One fast-day, while seated where the *Pāṭimokkha* was being recited, he pondered on the advantages to be gained by the confession of faults, and uttered eagerly, " How utterly pure is the teaching of the Buddha." Thus expanding insight he attained arahantship. Later, reviewing his life, he admonished his colleagues.[1]

[1] Thag. vss. 447-52; ThagA. i. 462 f.

Sirimaṇḍagalla.—One of the villages given by **Vijayabāhu I.** to the **Lābhavāsins.**[1]

[1] Cv. lx. 68.

Sirimanda Jātaka (No. 500).—Evidently another name for the **Sirimandapañha.**[1]

[1] J. iv. 412.

Sirimaṇḍapañha.—A section of the **Mahāummagga Jātaka,** containing a discussion between **Senaka** and **Mahosadha** in the presence of **Vedeha** on the merits of wealth and wisdom.[1] This section evidently also formed a separate Jātaka.[2]

[1] J. vi. 356-63. [2] *E.g.*, J. iv. 412.

1. **Sirimā Thera.**—He was born in the family of a householder of **Sāvatthi** and was called **Sirimā** on account of the unfailing success of his family. His younger brother was **Sirivaḍḍha.** They were both present when the Buddha accepted **Jetavana,** and, struck by his majesty, they entered the Order. Sirivaḍḍha, though possessed of no special attainments, received great honour from the laity and recluses, but Sirimā was little honoured. Nevertheless, exercising calm and insight, he soon won arahantship. Ordinary monks and novices continued to disparage him, and the Thera had to blame them for their faulty judgment. Sirivaḍḍha, agitated by this, himself became an arahant.

In the time of **Padumuttara Buddha,** before the Buddha's appearance in the world, Sirimā was an ascetic, named **Devala,** with a large following, and, having learnt the power of the Buddha through a study of the science of prognostication, he built a sand-*thūpa*, to which he paid homage in the name of past Buddhas. The Buddha was born in the world, his birth being accompanied by various omens. The ascetic showed these to his pupils, and, having made them eager to see the Buddha, died, and was reborn in the Brahma-world. Later, he appeared before them, inspiring them to greater exertions.[1]

He is evidently identical with **Puḷinuppādaka Thera** of the Apadāna.[2]

[1] Thag. vss. 159-60; ThagA. i. 279 f. [2] Ap. ii. 426.

2. **Sirimā.**—Mother of **Sumana Buddha.** Her husband was **Sudatta.**[1]

[1] Bu. v. 21; J. i. 34.

3. **Sirimā.**—Mother of **Phussa Buddha** and wife of **Jayasena.**[1]

[1] Bu. xix. 14; J. i. 41.

4. **Sirimā.**—A lay woman, one of the chief patrons of **Revata Buddha.**[1]

[1] Bu. vi. 23.

5. **Sirimā.**—Wife of **Anomadassī Buddha** before his renunciation.[1]

[1] Bu. viii. 19.

6. **Sirimā.**—One of the chief lay women supporters of **Sumedha Buddha.**[1]

[1] Bu. xii. 25.

7. **Sirimā.**—One of the chief lay women supporters of **Dīpaṅkara Buddha.**[1]

[1] Bu. ii. 215.

8. **Sirimā.**—One of the chief lay women supporters of **Vipassī Buddha.**[1]

[1] Bu. xx. 30.

9. **Sirimā.**—One of the chief lay women supporters of **Vessabhū Buddha.**[1]

[1] Bu. xxii. 25.

10. **Sirimā.**—One of the palaces occupied by **Vipassī Buddha** in his last lay life.[1]

[1] Bu. xx. 24.

11. **Sirimā.**—One of the palaces occupied by **Maṅgala Buddha** in his last lay life.[1]

[1] BuA. 116.

12. **Sirimā.**—A courtezan of **Rājagaha** and younger sister of **Jīvaka.** She was once employed by **Uttarā (Nandamātā)** to take her place with her husband (**Sumana**) while Uttarā herself went away in order to indulge in acts of piety. During this time Sirimā tried to injure Uttarā, on account of a misunderstanding, but on realizing her error, she begged forgiveness both of Uttarā, and, at the latter's suggestion, of the Buddha.[1] At the conclusion of a sermon preached by the Buddha in Uttarā's house, Sirimā became a *sotāpanna.* From that day onwards she gave alms daily to eight monks in her house.

A monk in a monastery, three leagues away, having heard of the excellence of Sirimā's alms and of her extraordinary beauty from a visiting monk, decided to go and see her. Having obtained a ticket for alms, he went to her house, but Sirimā was ill, and her attendants looked after the monks. When the meal had been served she was brought into the dining hall to pay her respects to the monks. The lustful monk at once fell in love with her and was unable to eat. That same day Sirimā died. The Buddha gave instructions that her body should not be burnt, but laid in the charnel-ground, protected from birds and beasts. When putrefaction had set in, the king proclaimed that all citizens, on penalty of a fine, should gaze on Sirimā's body. The Buddha, too, went with the monks, the lustful monk accompanying them. The Buddha made the king proclaim, with beating of the drum, that anyone who would pay a thousand could have Sirimā's body. There was no response. The

[1] The details of this incident are given *s.v.* **Uttarā Nandamātā.**

price was gradually lowered to one-eighth of a penny. Yet no one came forward, even when the body was offered for nothing. The Buddha addressed the monks, pointing out how even those who would have paid one thousand to spend a single night with Sirimā would not now take her as a gift. Such was the passing nature of beauty. The lustful monk became a *sotāpanna*.[2]

Buddhaghosa says[3] that Sirimā was **Sālavatī's** daughter, and succeeded to her mother's position as courtezan. After death, Sirimā was born in the **Yāma**-world as the wife of **Suyāma.** When the Buddha was speaking to the monks at her cremation, she visited the spot with five hundred chariots. **Janapadakalyānī Nandā,** who at that time was also a nun, was present, and when the Buddha preached the **Kāyavicchandanika Sutta** (*q.v.*) she became an arahant, while Sirimā became an *anāgāmī*.

The Vimānavatthu[4] gives the same story, adding that **Vaṅgīsa** was also present at the preaching of the sermon, and, having obtained the Buddha's permission, questioned Sirimā and made her reveal her identity. Here Sirimā is said to have been born in the **Nimmānarati**-world, and no mention is made of her becoming an *anāgāmī*; while the lustful monk is said to have become an arahant. Sirimā is mentioned in a list of eminent *upāsikās*.[5] Eighty-four thousand persons realized the truth after listening to the Buddha's preaching at the cremation of Sirimā.[6]

[2] DhA. iii. 104 f.; VvA. 74 ff.
[3] SNA. i. 244 f., 253 f.
[4] pp. 78 f., 86.
[5] A. iv. 347; AA. ii. 791.
[6] Mil. 350.

Sirimā-vimānavatthu.—The story of **Sirimā's** death and subsequent events.[1]

[1] Vv. i. 16; VvA. 67 ff.

Sirimitta Thera.—He belonged to a rich landowner's family of **Rājagaha** and was the nephew of **Sirigutta.** He saw the Buddha subdue the elephant, **Dhanapāla,** and, much impressed, entered the Order, becoming an arahant in due course. One day, rising from his seat to recite the *Pāṭimokkha*, he took a painted fan[1] and, reseating himself, he spoke eight verses in admonition of the monks and by way of confessing his *aññā*.[2]

[1] *Cf.* Khujjuttarā (DhA. i. 209).
[2] Thag. vss. 502-9; ThagA. i. 488 f.

Sirimeghavaṇṇa.—King of Ceylon (362-409 A.D.). He was the son of **Mahāsena.** He restored the monastic buildings destroyed by **Mahāsena** and held a festival in the **Ambatthala-cetiya** in honour of **Mahinda,** of whom he made a life-size image of gold. He erected the **Sotthiyākara-vihāra** and built a stone terrace round the **Tissavasabha-bodhi.** The

Buddha's Tooth Relic was brought to Ceylon in the ninth year of the king's reign, and the king placed it in the **Dhammacakka-pāsāda.** He held a great festival in honour of the Relic, and decreed that similar festivals should be held yearly in the **Abhayuttara-vihāra.** He is said to have built eighteen vihāras. He was succeeded by **Jeṭṭhatissa.**[1]

[1] Cv. xxxvii. 53 ff.

Siriyavala.—A district in South India.[1]

[1] Cv. lxxvi. 170, etc.

Siriyālagāma.—A village near **Siridevipabbata,** mentioned in the account of the early campaigns of **Parakkamabāhu I.**[1]

[1] Cv. lxvi. 20, 69.

1. **Sirivaḍḍha.**—The name of **Mahā Moggallāna** (*q.v.*) in the time of **Anomadassī Buddha.**[1]

[1] ThagA. ii. 90; see also Bu. viii. 24.

2. **Sirivaḍḍha.**—Chief lay supporter of **Sikhī Buddha.**[1]

[1] Bu. xxi. 22; J. i. 94.

3. **Sirivaḍḍha.**—An **Ājīvaka,** who gave grass for his seat to **Sumedha Buddha.**[1]

[1] BuA. 164.

4. **Sirivaḍḍha.**—A *Yavapāla* who gave grass for his seat to **Dhammadassī Buddha.**[1]

[1] BuA. 182.

5. **Sirivaḍḍha.**—An ascetic who gave grass for his seat to **Phussa Buddha.**

He was originally a rich man and had left the world. The Buddha preached to him and his followers.[1]

[1] BuA. 192, 193.

6. **Sirivaḍḍha.**—A palace occupied by **Anomadassī Buddha** in his last lay life.[1]

[1] BuA. 141; Bu. viii. 18 calls it Vaḍḍha.

7. **Sirivaḍḍha.**—A palace occupied by **Sumedha Buddha** in his last lay life.[1]

[1] Bu. xii. 19.

8. **Sirivaḍḍha.**—A palace that will be occupied by **Metteyya Buddha** before his renunciation.[1]

[1] Anāgat. p. 46.

9. **Sirivaḍḍha Thera.**—The brother of **Sirimā Thera.** For his story see **Sirimā** (1).

10. **Sirivaḍḍha Thera.**—His father was a rich man of **Rājagaha** and he was present when the Buddha visited **Bimbisāra.** Impressed by the Buddha's majesty, **Sirivaḍḍha** joined the Order and lived in a forest near **Vebhāra** and **Paṇḍava** meditating. A great storm arose one day, and the Thera, cooled by the rain, was able to concentrate his mind and win arahantship.[1]

He is probably identical with **Kiṅkhanikapupphiya Thera** of the Apadāna.[2] In the past he offered a *kiṇkhani*-flower to **Vipassī Buddha.** Seventy-seven kappas ago he was a king, named **Bhīmaratha.**

[1] Thag. vs. 41; ThagA. i. 107 f. [2] Ap. i. 204.

11. **Sirivaḍḍha.**—A seṭṭhi of **Mithilā,** father of **Mahosadha.** He is identified with **Suddhodana.**[1]

[1] J. vi. 331, 478.

12. **Sirivaḍḍha.**—A minister of **Pasenadi,** who once sent a message through him to **Ānanda.**[1]

[1] M. ii. 112.

13. **Sirivaḍḍha.**—A householder of **Rājagaha.** When he was ill he sent word to **Ānanda** asking him to visit him. Ānanda went and preached to him on the four *satipaṭṭhānas.* Sirivaḍḍha became an *anāgāmī.*[1]

[1] S. v. 176 f.

14. **Sirivaḍḍha.**—Father of **Siggava Thera**[1] (*q.v.*).

[1] MṬ. 215.

15. **Sirivaḍḍha.**—The name by which **Soṇa Koḷivisa** (*q.v.*) was known in the time of **Padumuttara Buddha.**[1]

[1] AA. i. 130.

Sirivaḍḍha Sutta.—Records the visit of **Ānanda** to **Sirivaḍḍha** of **Rājagaha.** See **Sirivaḍḍha** (13).

Sirivaḍḍhaka.—The name of the architect of the **Mahā Thūpa.**[1]

[1] MṬ. 535.

1. **Sirivaḍḍhanapura.**—A city built by **Parakkamabāhu II.** It was half a yojana from **Jambuddoṇi.**[1]

[1] Cv. lxxxv. 1; Cv. *Trs.* ii. 159, n. 1.

2. **Sirivaḍḍhana.**—See **Senkhaṇḍasela.**

Sirivaḍḍhanā.—A girl of **Sucitta-nigama,** who gave milk-rice to **Vessabhū Buddha.**[1]

[1] BuA. 205.

1. **Sirivaḍḍha-pāsāda.**—One of the chief buildings of the **Upāsikā-vihāra;** it was later called **Ariṭṭhaṭhapitaghara.**[1]

[1] MṬ. 408, 409.

2. **Sirivaḍḍha-pāsāda.**—A building, evidently in **Rohaṇa,** repaired by **Dappula,** son of **Saṅghasivā.**[1]

[1] Cv. xlv. 56.

Sirivaḍḍhamānavāpi.—A tank in the **Dakkhiṇadesa** of Ceylon, built by the Yuvarāja of **Aggabodhi I.**[1]

[1] Cv. xlii. 8.

Sirivaḍḍhā.—A seṭṭhi's daughter who gave milk-rice to **Phussa Buddha.**[1]

[1] BuA. 192.

1. **Sirivallabha.**—Nephew of **Vijayabāhu I.** He was the son of the king's sister **Mittā** and the **Paṇḍu** king. He married **Sugalā** and became governor of **Aṭṭhasahassa,** with his capital in **Uddhanadvāra,** a village built by himself. He had two children—**Mānābharaṇa** and **Līlāvatī.** Later he fought against **Gajabāhu.**[1]

[1] Cv. lix. 42, 45; lxi. 24; lxii. 2; lxiii. 20, 31, 32; lxiv. 18, 19.

2. **Sirivallabha.**—Son of **Mānābharaṇa** (2). He was captured by the forces of **Parakkamabāhu I.,** but escaped and later fought with that king.[1]

[1] Cv. lxxii. 291, 299.

3. **Sirivallabha.**—A Damiḷa chieftain, ally of **Kulasekhara.**[1]

[1] Cv. lxxvii. 6.

Sirivijayarājasīha.—King of Ceylon (1739-47 A.C.). He was **Narinda-sīhā's** brother-in-law and succeeded him. His wives came from **Madhurā**

and he reigned in **Sirivaḍḍhanapura.** He had great regard for **Saraṇaṅkara-Sāmaṇera** (*q.v.*), and invited him to write a commentary on the **Catu-Bhāṇavāra.** He held a great festival in honour of the Tooth Relic, erected images in **Ālokalena,** and with the help of the Olandā (Dutch), he sent an embassy to Siam (**Sāminda**) to fetch monks from **Ayojjhā,** but died before they arrived.[1]

[1] Cv. xcviii. 2 ff.

Sirivijayasundarārāma.—A monastery in **Jambuddoṇi,** erected by **Vijayabāhu III. Parakkamabāhu II.** built round it a wall with gate towers.[1]

[1] Cv. lxxxv. 90 f.

Sirivivāda.—See the **Sujāta Jātaka** (No. 306).

Sirivīraparakkamanarindasīha.—King of Ceylon (1707-39 A.C.). He was the son of **Vimaladhammasūriya II.** He held great festivals in **Mahiyaṅgana, Sumanakūṭa** and **Anurādhapura,** and built a suburb called **Kuṇḍasālā,** where he lived. The temple of the Tooth Relic, built by his father, he adorned with paintings of thirty-two Jātakas. He showed great honour to **Saraṇaṅkara-sāmaṇera** and gave him a golden casket studded with seven hundred jewels. At his request, Saraṇaṅkara wrote the **Sāratthasaṅgaha** and Commentaries on the **Mahābodhivaṃsa** and the **Bhesajjamañjūsā.**[1]

[1] Cv. xcix. 23 ff.

1. **Sirisaṅghabodhi.**—See **Saṅghabodhi.**

2. **Sirisaṅghabodhi.**—The surname of **Aggabodhi III.,**[1] of **Aggabodhi IV.,**[2] and **Vijayabāhu I.**[3]

[1] Cv. xliv. 83. [2] *Ibid.*, xlvi. 1. [3] *Ibid.*, lix. 10.

1. **Sirisaṅghabodhi-vihāra.**—A monastery, built by **Meghavaṇṇābhayā,** to the south of **Issarasamaṇa-vihāra** and on the spot where **Saṅghabodhi's** (*q.v.*) body was cremated.[1]

[1] MṬ. 671.

2. **Sirisaṅghabodhi-vihāra.**—A *pariveṇa* built by **Aggabodhi I.**[1] **Mānavamma** built the **Siripāsāda** there.[2]

[1] Cv. xlii. 11. [2] *Ibid.*, xlvii. 64.

Sirisaddhammavilāsa.—A Burmese author of the fourteenth century. He wrote a *ṭīkā* on **Kaccāyana's** grammar called **Saddhammanāsinī.**[1]

[1] Bode, *op. cit.*, 26.

1. **Sirī.**—The goddess of Luck; she was the daughter of **Dhataraṭṭha.**[1] For a story about her see the **Sirikāḷakaṇṇi Jātaka.** She is identified with **Uppalavaṇṇā.**[2]

[1] J. iii. 257. [2] *Ibid.*, 264.

2. **Sirī.**—One of the four daughters of **Sakka.**[1] See the **Sudhābhojana Jātaka.**

[1] J. v. 392.

3. **Sirī.**—See the **Siri Jātaka.** There Siri is personified as Luck.[1]

[1] See also DA. i. 97; Mil. 191; *cf.* **Lakkhī.**

Sirīsamālaka.—A sacred spot in **Anurādhapura,** where **Kakusandha Buddha** preached during his visit to Ceylon.[1] It was to the south of the **Nāgamalāka**[2] and to the north of the Bodhi-tree, near the **Silāsobbhakaṇḍaka-cetiya.**[3] King **Thūlatthana** built a *thūpa* on the spot.[4]

[1] Mhv. xv. 84. [2] *Ibid.*, 118. [3] MṬ. 351. [4] *Ibid.*, 355.

Sirīsavatthu.—A city of the Yakkhas in Ceylon (**Tambapaṇṇidīpa**).[1] According to the Mahāvaṃsa Ṭīkā,[2] at the time of **Vijaya's** arrival in Ceylon, the chief Yakkha of the city was **Mahākālasena. Jutindhara** was the name of another Yakkha who lived there.[3]

[1] See the **Valāhassa Jātaka**; *cf.* Mhv. vii. 32.
[2] MṬ. 259.
[3] *Ibid.*, 289.

Silākāla.—A **Lambakaṇṇa,** son of **Dāṭhāpabhuti.** He fled to **Jambudīpa,** through fear of **Kassapa I.,** and became a monk in the **Bodhimaṇḍavihāra.** There, because of a mango which he presented to the community, he came to be known as **Ambasāmaṇera.** In the time of **Moggallāna I.,** he brought the Buddha's Hair Relic to Ceylon and was greatly honoured by the king. Silākāla returned to the lay life, and Moggallāna appointed him sword-bearer to the relic—hence his name, **Asiggāhaka-Silākāla.** He married the king's sister and also the daughter of **Upatissa III.** He then returned to the **Malaya** district, where he rebelled against Upatissa. He defeated the king's son, **Kassapa,** who committed suicide, and when Upatissa died of grief, Silākāla became king under the name of **Ambasāmaṇera-Silākāla,** ruling for thirteen years (524-37 A.C.). He had three sons: **Moggallāna, Dāṭhāpabhuti** and **Upatissa.**[1]

[1] Cv. xxxix. 44, 55; xli. 10 ff.

Silācetiya.—A *thūpa* in **Anurādhapura,** probably near the **Thūpārāma.**[1] The spot was sanctified by the Buddha sitting there in meditation.[2]

[1] AA. i. 385. [2] Mhv. i. 82.

Silātissabodhi.—Son of **Dāṭhānāma** and brother of King **Dhātusena.**[1]

[1] Cv. xxxviii. 15.

Silādāṭha.—See **Silāmeghavaṇṇa.**

Silāpaṭṭapokkharaṇī.—A lotus pond in Benares, in which the Pacceka Buddha **Mahāpaduma** was born in a lotus.[1]

[1] SNA. i. 80.

Silāpassayapariveṇa.—A building in the **Tissārāma.** It was there that the Sāmaṇera died who, in this life, became **Duṭṭhagāmaṇī.**[1]

[1] Mhv. xxii. 28.

Silāmayamuninda.—See **Silāsambuddha.**

1. **Silāmegha.**—A nunnery,[1] restored by the queen of Udaya I.[2]

[1] MṬ. 117; Cv. xlviii. 139. [2] *Ibid.*, xlix. 25.

2. **Silāmegha.**—A surname of **Aggabodhi VI.**[1] and of **Sena I.**[2]

[1] Cv. xlviii. 42, 76, 90. [2] *Ibid.*, l. 43.

3. **Silāmegha.**—A Damiḷa chief, also called **Silāmeghara;** he was an ally of **Kulasekhara.**[1]

[1] Cv. lxxvi. 98, 238, etc.

Silāmeghapabbata.—A building erected by **Kassapa V.** in the **Abhayagiri-vihāra.**[1]

[1] Cv. lii. 58; see Cv. *Trs.* i. 168, n. 1.

Silāmeaghavaṇṇa.—King of Ceylon, He was the son of the senāpati of **Moggallāna III.** and held the office of sword-bearer. He rebelled against the king and killed him at **Sīhagiri.** Then he killed **Dalla-Moggallāna** and became king of **Anurādhapura,** reigning for nine years (617-626 A.C.).

Urged by a monk, named **Bodhi,** he proclaimed a regulation act against the undisciplined monks of **Abhayagiri;** but these monks murdered Bodhi and were severely punished by the king. Later he quarrelled with the **Theravāda** monks and retired to **Dakkhiṇadesa,** where he died.[1] **Aggabodhi III.** and **Kassapa II.** were his sons. He was also evidently known as **Silādāṭha.**[2]

[1] Cv. xliv. 43, 53 ff. [2] See *ibid.*, xlv. 51; also Cv. *Trs.* 94, n. 1.

Silāyupa Sutta.—**Sāriputta** tells the monks that when a monk is wholly freed, objects, sounds, scents, etc., that come within the range of his senses, cannot overwhelm his mind. It is like a stone-column ten cubits long, one half of it buried in the ground, which cannot be shaken by the wind.

The sutta was preached as the result of a conversation between **Sāriputta** and **Candikāputta** regarding the teachings of **Devadatta.**[1]

[1] A. iv. 402 f.

Silārāma.—A park in **Candavatī,** where **Sujāta Buddha** died.[1]

[1] Bu. xiii. 36; BuA. 171.

Silāvatī.—A village of the **Sākyans.** Once, when the Buddha was there with a large number of monks, **Māra** tempted them in the guise of a *jaṭaṇḍuva*-brahmin.[1] The village was the birthplace of **Bandhura Thera.**[2] A story is also told of the temptation by Māra of **Samiddhi** when he was with the Buddha.[3]

[1] S. i. 117.
[2] ThagA. i. 208.
[3] S. i. 118, but in ThagA. (i. 117) the incident is located in **Tapodārāma.**

Silāsambuddha.—A famous stone image in **Anurādhapura,** evidently held in great reverence. It was originally in the **Abhayuttara-vihāra,** and **Buddhadāsa** placed a Nāga-gem as one of its eyes[1]; but this was lost, and then **Dhātusena** had a pair of costly eyes made.[2] It was referred to under various names: **Silāsatthā, Silāmayamuninda, Kālaselasatthā,** etc. **Sena II.** found the temple containing the image in ruins and had it repaired,[3] while his queen **Saṅghā** placed on the image a dark blue diadem.[4]

[1] Cv. xxxvii. 123. [2] *Ibid.*, xxxviii. 62. [3] *Ibid.*, li. 77. [4] *Ibid.*, 87.

Silāsobbhakaṇḍaka.—A village in which **Vaṭṭagāmaṇī** lived for some time during the usurpation of his throne by the Damiḷas.[1] The village was to the south of **Vessagiri-vihāra** and near **Pabbata-vihāra.**[2]

[1] Mhv. xxxiii. 51. [2] MṬ. 616.

Silāsobbhakaṇḍaka-cetiya.—A *thūpa* to the north of the **Mahā Thūpa**, built by **Vaṭṭagāmaṇi.**[1] The **Sirisamālaka** lay between it and the **Nāgamālaka.**[2]

[1] Mhv. xxxiii. 88. [2] MṬ. 355.

Silesaloma.—A **Yakkha.** See the **Pañcāvudha Jātaka.** He is identified with **Aṅgulimāla.**[1]

[1] J. i. 275.

1. **Siva.**—The name of a god.[1] A devaputta, named Siva, is mentioned in the Saṃyutta[2] as visiting the Buddha and speaking several verses on the benefit of consorting only with the good. It is interesting that Buddhaghosa makes no particular comment on the name in this context. In the *Samantapāsādikā,*[3] however, he refers to the worship of the *Sivaliṅga.*

[1] Cv. xciii. 9, 10. [2] S. i. 56. [3] Sp. iii. 626; *cf.* UdA. 351, where mention is made of *Khandadeva-Sivādi-paricaraṇaṃ.*

2. **Siva.**—See **Sivi.**

3. **Siva.**—A palace-guard, paramour of **Anulā.** He reigned for fourteen months, at the end of which time he was killed in favour of **Vaṭuka.**[1]

[1] Mhv. xxxiv. 18.

4. **Siva.**—One of the eleven children of **Paṇḍuvāsudeva** and **Kaccānā.**[1]

[1] Dpv. x. 3.

5. **Siva.**—One of the ten sons of **Muṭasiva.**[1] He reigned for ten years and established the **Nagaraṅgana-vihāra.**[2]

[1] Dpv. xi. 7; xvii. 76. [2] *Ibid.*, xviii. 45.

Siva Sutta.—Describes the visit of **Sivadevaputta** to the **Buddha.**[1]

[1] S. i. 56.

1. **Sivi.**—A king of **Ariṭṭhapura,** father of the Bodhisatta.[1] See the **Sivi Jātaka.**

[1] J. iv. 401.

2. **Sivi.**—A king of **Jetuttara** city, father of **Sañjaya.**[1]

[1] J. vi. 480.

3. **Sivi.**—King of **Dvāravatī.** He was the son of **Vāsudeva** and a Caṇḍāla woman named **Jambāvatī.**[1]

[1] J. vi. 421.

4. **Sivi.**—The Bodhisatta. See the Sivi Jātaka.

5. See **Siviraṭṭha.**

Sivi Jātaka (No. 499).—The Bodhisatta was once born as **Sivi,** king of **Ariṭṭhapura,** his father bearing the same name as himself. He ruled well, and daily gave alms to the amount of six hundred thousand. One day the desire came to him to give part of his body to any who might ask for it. **Sakka** read his thoughts, and, appearing before him as a blind brahmin, asked for his eyes. The king agreed to give them, and sent for his surgeon **Sīvaka.** Amid the protests and lamentations of his family and his subjects, Sivi had his eyes removed and given to the brahmin. It is said that the surgeon did his work in several stages, giving Sivi chances of withdrawing his offer. When the sockets healed Sivi wished to become an ascetic, and went into the park with one attendant. Sakka's throne grew hot, and appearing before Sivi, he offered him a boon. The king wished to die, but Sakka insisted on his choosing something else. He then asked that his sight might be restored. Sakka suggested an Act of Truth (*saccakiriyā*), as not even Sakka could restore lost sight. The eyes reappeared, but they were neither natural eyes nor divine, but eyes called "Truth, Absolute and Perfect." Sivi collected all his subjects, and, resting on a throne in a pavilion, taught them the value of gifts.

The story was related in reference to **Pasenadi's Asadisadāna.** On the seventh day of the almsgiving the king gave all kinds of requisites and asked the Buddha to preach a thanksgiving sermon, but the Buddha left without doing so. The next day, on being questioned by the king, he explained his reasons for this.[1] The king, greatly pleased with the Buddha's explanation, gave him an outer robe of *Siveyyaka*-cloth worth one thousand. When the monks started commenting on how tireless the king was in giving, the Buddha related to them the old story, in which **Ānanda** is identified with **Sīvaka,** the physician, and **Anuruddha** with Sakka.[2]

The *Sivirājacariyā* is included in the Cariyāpiṭaka.[3] It forms the topic of one of the dilemmas of the Milindapañha.[4]

[1] For details see *s.v.* **Asadisadāna.**
[2] J. iv. 401-12; *cf.* CypA. 52 f.
[3] Cyp. i. 8; the story is also given with variant details in the *Avadānaśataka* i. 183-6.
[4] Mil. p. 119 f.

Siviputta.—See **Sivirattha.**

Siviraṭṭha.—The country of the **Sivi** people, referred to several times in the Jātakas. In the **Sivi, Ummadantī** and **Mahāummagga Jātakas,**[1] **Ariṭṭhapura** is given as the capital, while in the **Vessantara Jātaka,**[2] **Jetuttara** is the capital. In the last-named Jātaka,[3] **Vessantara** is sometimes spoken of as king of Siviraṭṭha and his children as **Siviputtā.**[4] The family name of the kings of this country seems to have been **Sivi.**[5] The country was evidently famous for its cloth, which was called *Siveyyaka.*[6] **Pajjota** gave a pair of robes of this material to **Jīvaka,** as a present for his cure. These robes Jīvaka gave to the Buddha.[7]

[1] J. iv. 401; v. 210; vi. 419.
[2] *Ibid.*, 480.
[3] *E.g.*, p. 511.
[4] p. 563.
[5] See J. vi. 251, where Sivī is explained by *porāṇakarājā*.
[6] Vin. i. 278.
[7] *Ibid.*, 280.

Sīka.—A general of **Gajabāhu.**[1]

[1] Cv. lxx. 113.

Sīkaviyala.—A place near **Pulatthipura,** mentioned in the account of the wars of **Gajabāhu.**[1]

[1] Cv. lxx. 231.

Sīta Sutta.—Cool weather is produced by the **Sītavalāhakā** devas wishing to regale their bodies.[1]

[1] S. iii. 256.

Sītalaggāmalena.—A cave temple in Ceylon restored by **Vijayabāhu I.**[1]

[1] Cv. lx. 59.

Sītavana.—A grove near **Rājagaha** where **Anāthapiṇḍika** (*q.v.*) first met the Buddha. In the grove was a cemetery described as *bhaya-bherava,*[1] and, when Anāthapiṇḍika approached it, he was filled with fear and trembling. But he was reassured by a friendly Yakkha, **Sīvaka.**[2]

In the Sītavana was the **Sappasoṇḍikapabbhāra,**[3] where **Upasena** was killed by a snake-bite[4] and **Soṇa Koḷivisa** tried, without success, to practise asceticism.[5] **Sambhūta Thera** (*q.v.*) so loved the Sītavana that he came to be called **"Sītavaniya."** In **Asoka's** day his brother **Tissakumāra,**

[1] ThagA. i. 47; *cf.* Dvy. 264, 268.
[2] Vin. ii. 155 f.; when the Buddha was staying there, **Māra** asked him to die (D. ii. 116).
[3] S. i. 210 f.; Vin. ii. 76; iv. 159.
[4] S. iv. 40.
[5] A. iii. 374.

(**Ekavihāriya**) is also mentioned as delighting in the solitude of Sītavana.[6] There were five hundred " walks " (*caṅkamanāni*) in Sītavana.[7]

[6] Thag. vs. 540; or does this Sītavana not refer to any particular place ?

[7] AA. ii. 679.

Sītavaniya.—See **Sambhūta.**

Sītavalāhakā.—A class of devas. When they wish to regale their bodies, the weather becomes cool.[1] They live in the **Cātummahārājika** world.[2]

[1] S. iii. 256.

[2] MNidA. 108.

Sītā.—Daughter of King **Dasaratha** and sister of **Rāmapaṇḍita** and **Lakkhaṇa.** See the **Dasaratha Jātaka.** She is identified with **Rāhulamātā.**[1]

[1] J. iv. 130; her devotion to Rāma is sometimes referred to—*e.g.*, J. vi. 557.

Sītāluka-Brahmadatta.—King of Benares. He left the world and lived in the forest, but there he lacked food and drink and was troubled by heat and cold and insects. He wished to go elsewhere, but mastered the desire and, after living there for seven years, became a Pacceka Buddha. His verse is included in the **Khaggavisāṇa Sutta.**[1]

[1] SN. vs. 52; SNA. i. 101.

Sītāvaka.—A town in Ceylon, the capital of King **Rājasīha I.**[1]

[1] Cv. xciii. 5; see Cv. *Trs.* ii. 224, n. 1.

Sītāharaṇa.—The story of **Sītā's** rape is referred to in the Commentaries as *niratthakakathā*[1] or *pāpakaṃ-sutaṃ.*[2]

[1] DA. i. 76.

[2] MNidA. 148; VibhA. 490.

Sīti Vagga.—The ninth chapter of the Chakka Nipāta of the **Aṅguttara Nikāya.**[1]

[1] A. iii. 435-40.

Sīti Sutta.—Six things which prevent a monk from realizing the " cool "[1] (*nibbāna*).

[1] A. iii. 435.

Sīdantara-samudda.—The sea between every two ranges round **Sineru;** Nāgas live in this sea.[1]

[1] J. vi. 125.

Sidarī.—A Pacceka Buddha.[1]

[1] M. iii. 70.

1. **Sīdā.**—A large river flowing from **Uttarahimavā**; its specific gravity is so slight that nothing can float on it. It flows through the **Kañcanapabbata** and many thousands of ascetics live on its banks.[1]

[1] J. vi. 100, 101.

2. **Sīdā.**—An ocean,[1] probably identical with **Sīdantara.** It is the abode of Nāgas.[1]

[1] J. vi. 125.

3. **Sīdā.**—A canal flowing eastwards from the **Aciravatī**[1] (the channel of the **Mahāvālukanadī**).

[1] Cv. lxxix. 53.

Sīdupabbatagāma.—A village in **Rohaṇa,** where **Mahinda V.** lived for some time.[1]

[1] Cv. lv. 8.

Sīmatālatthalī.—A village in **Rohaṇa,** mentioned in the account of the campaigns of **Parakkamabāhu I.**[1]

[1] Cv. lxxv. 101.

Sīmanadī.—Probably the name of a river which formed one of the boundaries of the **Vijayabāhu-pariveṇa.** On its banks was **Sālaggāma.**[1]

[1] Cv. xc. 92.

Sīmālaṅkārasaṅgaha.—A work on boundaries and sites for religious ceremonies, written by **Vācissara** of Ceylon.[1] **Chapaṭa** wrote a Commentary on it.[2]

[1] Gv. 62; Svd. 1213. [2] Bode, *op. cit.*, 18; Svd. 1247; Gv. 64.

Sīla Vagga.—The second chapter of the Eka Nipāta of the Jātaka Commentary.[1]

[1] J. i. 142-72.

1. **Sīla Sutta.**—The Buddha exhorts the monks to live perfect in virtue; then will they be ardent, scrupulous and resolute.[1]

[1] A. ii. 14.

9. **Sīla Sutta.**—On four persons, as regards their completeness in virtue, concentration and wisdom.[1]

[1] A. ii. 136.

3. **Sīla Sutta.**—On four persons, as regards their respect for virtue, concentration and wisdom.[1]

[1] A. ii. 136.

4. **Sīla Sutta.**—A monk who is virtuous, learned, has a pleasant and smooth speech, is able to develop the four *jhānas* at will, and has attained the destruction of the *āsavas*—such a one has achieved his goal.[1]

[1] A. iii. 113.

5. **Sīla Sutta.**—A monk who has achieved virtue, concentration, insight, emancipation and the vision of emancipation—such a one is worthy of offerings and homage.[1]

[1] A. iii. 134.

6. **Sīla Sutta.**—A man, wanting in morals, loses wealth through neglect; evil rumour spreads about him; he has no confidence in gatherings; he is muddled in thought; and goes, after death, to a place of ill.[1]

[1] A. iii. 252.

7. **Sīla Sutta.**—**Sāriputta** tells **Mahā-Koṭṭhita,** in answer to a question, that the virtuous monk should methodically ponder on the five *upādāna-kkhandhā.*[1]

[1] S. iii. 167.

8. **Sīla Sutta.**—Even as the dawn is the forerunner of the sun, so is virtue the forerunner of the Noble Eightfold Path.[1]

[1] S. v. 30.

9. **Sīla Sutta.**—The benefits which come through monks being possessed of virtue, concentration, insight, release—release by knowledge and insight.[1]

[1] S. v. 67 f.

10. **Sīla Sutta.**—**Ānanda** tells **Bhadda,** in the **Kukkuṭārāma** in **Pāṭali-putta,** that the virtuous habits, spoken of by the Buddha, are those which come by cultivation of the four *satipaṭṭhānas.*[1]

[1] S. v. 171.

Sīlakūṭa.—The summit of the **Missakapabbata** in **Ambatthala.** It was there that **Mahinda** alighted on his arrival in Ceylon.[1] In the time of **Kakusandha Buddha,** it was called **Devakūṭa**; in the time of **Koṇāgamana, Sumanakūṭa**; in the time of **Kassapa, Subhakūṭa.**[2]

[1] Mhv. xiii. 20. [2] Dpv. xvii. 14.

Sīlakkhandha Vagga.—The first division of the **Dīgha Nikāya,** containing suttas 1-13.[1]

[1] D. i. 2-253.

Sīlakhaṇḍa.—A section of the **Bhūridatta Jātaka.**[1]

[1] J. vi. 184.

1. **Sīlava.**—The Bodhisatta, born as king of Benares; see the **Mahāsīlava Jātaka.**

2. **Sīlava.**—The Bodhisatta, born as an elephant. See the **Sīlavanāga Jātaka.**

3. **Sīlava.**—Son of **Maṅgala Buddha,** in his last lay life.[1] *v.l.* **Sīvala.**

[1] BuA. i. 124.

1. **Sīlavaṃsa.**—A monk of Ava, of the fifteenth century. He wrote the **Buddhālaṅkāra,** a poetical version of the **Sumedhakathā,** a poem on his native city, therein called **Pabbatabbhantara.** He also wrote an *atthayojanā* on the **Nettīpakaraṇa** in Burmese, and the **Parāyanavatthu.**[1]

[1] Bode, *op. cit.*, 43.

2. **Sīlavaṃsa.**—A monk of Ceylon, author of the **Kaccāyana-dhātumañjūsa.**[1]

[1] P.L.C. 237.

1. **Sīlavatī.**—The chief queen of **Okkāka,** king of **Kusāvatī,** and mother of **Kusa.** See the **Kusa Jātaka.**

2. **Sīlavatī.**—The city in which **Sikhī Buddha** died, in the **Dussārāma (Assārāma).**[1]

[1] BuA. 204.

Sīlavanāga Jātaka (No. 72).—The Bodhisatta was once an elephant in the **Himālaya,** head of a herd of eighty thousand. His name was **Sīlava.** One day he saw a forester of Benares who had lost his way, and, feeling compassion for him, took him to his own dwelling, fed him with all kinds of fruit, and then, taking him to the edge of the forest, set him on his way to Benares. The wretched man noted all the landmarks, and, on reaching the city, entered into an agreement with ivory workers to supply them with Sīlava's tusks. He then returned to the forest and begged Sīlava for a part of his tusks, pleading poverty and lack of livelihood. Sīlava allowed the ends of his tusks to be sawn off. The man returned again and again, until, at last, Sīlava allowed him to dig out the stumps as well. As the man was on his way back to Benares, the earth opened and swallowed him up into the fires of hell. A tree-sprite, who had witnessed all this, spoke a stanza illustrating the evils of ingratitude.

The story was related in reference to **Devadatta's** wickedness; he is identified with the forester and **Sāriputta** with the tree-sprite.[1]

The birth as Sīlava is mentioned among those in which the Bodhisatta practised *sīla pāramitā* to perfection.[2]

[1] J. i. 319-22; the story is referred to in the Milindapañha, p. 202.

[2] *E.g.*, MA. ii. 617.

Sīlavā Thera.—He was the son of **Bimbisāra.**[1] His brother, **Ajātasattu,** wished to kill him, but failed, owing to Sīlavā's destiny. The Buddha, discerning all this, sent **Moggallāna** to fetch Sīlavā. The prince, seeing the Elder, descended from his elephant and did obeisance to the Buddha.

The Buddha preached to him, and he entered the Order, becoming an arahant. He lived in **Kosala.** Ajātasattu sent men to kill him; but Sīlavā taught them and converted them, and they, too, entered the Order.[2]

[1] Thag. vss. 608-19.

[2] ThagA. i. 536 f.

Sīlavā Sutta.—The inhabitants of a village or suburb in which good hermits dwell for their support earn much merit in deed, word and thought.[1]

[1] A. i. 151.

1. **Sīlavīmaṃsa Jātaka** (No. 330).—The Bodhisatta was once chaplain of the king of Benares, later becoming an ascetic. One day he saw a hawk, attacked by other birds, drop a piece of meat he had stolen. On another day he saw a slave-girl, **Piṅgalā,** waiting for her lover until late into the night, and, when he did not come, she fell asleep. On a third occasion he saw a hermit meditating. Drawing a moral from these incidents, he lived the hermit-life and was reborn in the Brahma-world.[1]

The story was told in reference to a brahmin who was ever proving his virtue.

[1] J. iii. 100-102.

2. **Sīlavīmaṃsa Jātaka** (No. 362).—The Bodhisatta was chaplain to the king of Benares. He was both learned and good; but wishing to test which quality brought him greater honour, he started stealing money from the treasurer. On the third occasion he was arrested and led before the king. He then explained his behaviour to the king, and, having discovered that virtue was the more highly esteemed, he became an ascetic with the king's leave.

The story was told in reference to a brahmin of **Sāvatthi** who carried out the same test.[1]

[1] J. iii. 193-5.

1. **Sīlavīmaṃsana Jātaka** (No. 86).—The Bodhisatta was chaplain to the king of Benares and wished to test the respective powers of virtue and learning (as given above in the **Sīlavīmaṃsa Jātaka** 1). When being led before the king, he saw snake-charmers exhibiting their snake and warned them lest it should bite them. "He is not like you," they replied, "for he is good." The king ordered the chaplain to be executed; but, on hearing of his intentions, he allowed him to become an ascetic.

The story was related in reference to a learned and pious brahmin, in the service of the king of **Kosala,** who carried out a similar test. Then he joined the Order and became an arahant.[1]

[1] J. i. 369-71.

2. **Sīlavīmaṃsana Jātaka** (No. 290).—Very similar to No. 1 above.

3. **Sīlavīmaṃsana Jātaka** (No. 305).—The Bodhisatta was once a brahmin, head of five hundred students under one teacher. The teacher, wishing to test them, told them that he wished to give his daughter in marriage, and asked them to steal things for her ornaments and clothes without letting anyone know. They all did this except the Bodhisatta, who brought nothing. When asked the reason of this behaviour, he said: "You accept nothing unless brought in secrecy; but in wrong-doing there is no secrecy." The teacher then explained his intention, and, very pleased with the Bodhisatta, gave him his daughter in marriage. The names of six pupils who stole were: **Dujjacca, Ajacca, Nanda, Sukha Vacchana, Vajjha** and **Addhuvasīla.**

The story was related, late at night, to a company of monks who went about discussing the pleasures of the senses. The Buddha asked **Ānanda** to collect them and preached to them. At the end of the sermon they became *sotāpannas*. **Sāriputta** is identified with the teacher.[1]

[1] J. iii. 18-20.

Sīlānisaṃsa Jātaka (No. 190).—Once a pious disciple of **Kassapa Buddha** went to sea with a barber who had been placed in his charge. The ship was wrecked, and together they swam by means of a plank to a desert island. There the barber killed some birds and ate them; but the lay-disciple refused a share and meditated on the Three Jewels. The Nāga-king of the island, moved by this, turned his body into a ship, and, with the Spirit of the Sea as helmsman, offered to take the lay-disciple to **Jambudīpa.** The barber also wished to go, but his plea was refused because he was not holy. Thereupon the lay disciple made over to him the merits of his own virtues, and the barber was taken on board. Both were conveyed to Jambudīpa, where wealth was provided for them.

The story was related to a holy believer who, coming one day to **Jetavana,** found there none of the ferry boats which crossed the **Aciravatī;** not wishing to return, he started to walk across the river, his mind full of thoughts of the Buddha. In the middle he lost his train of thought, and was about to sink when he again put forth effort and crossed over. The Buddha, hearing of this, told him this story, and at its conclusion the man became a *sakadāgāmin*. The Nāga-king was **Sāriputta** and the Sea-spirit was the Bodhisatta.[1]

[1] J. ii. 111-113.

Sīluccaya.—Fifteen thousand kappas ago there were eight kings of this name, previous births of **Sīhāsanadāyaka Thera.**[1]

[1] Ap. i. 189.

1. **Sīva Thera.**—A monk of Ceylon, an eminent teacher of the Vinaya.[1]

[1] Vin. v. 3.

2. **Sīva.**—See **Mahāsīva, Cūlasīva, Tanasīva, Bhayasīva,** etc.

3. **Sīva.**—King of Ceylon (522 A.C.). He was the maternal uncle of **Kumāradhātusena,** whom he killed in order to seize the throne. He reigned only twenty-five days, and was killed by **Upatissa.**[1]

[1] Cv. xli. 1-5.

1. **Sīvaka.**—A Yakkha who helped **Anāthapiṇḍika** to find the Buddha at **Sītavana.**[1] He is mentioned among the chief Yakkhas to be invoked by followers of the Buddha in time of need.[2]

[1] Vin. ii. 155 f.; S. i. 211. [2] D. iii. 205.

2. **Sīvaka.**—See **Moliya-Sīvaka.**

3. **Sīvaka.**—The physician of King **Sivi.** See the **Sivi Jātaka.** He is identified with **Ānanda.**[1]

[1] J. iv. 412.

4. **Sīvaka Thera.**—The nephew of **Vanavaccha.** When Vanavaccha's sister heard that he had left the world and was living in the forest, she sent her son Sīvaka to be ordained under the Elder and to wait upon

him. He lived in the forest with his uncle, and one day, while on his way to the village, fell very ill. The Elder, on finding that he did not return, went in search of him, and, finding him ill, tended him; but as dawn drew near, he suggested that they should both return to the forest as he had never before stayed in the village since joining the Order. Sīvaka agreed, and entered the forest leaning on his uncle's arm. There Sīvaka won arahantship.

Thirty-one kappas ago he had seen **Vessabhū Buddha** in the forest and offered him a *kāsumārika*-fruit.[1] He is probably identical with **Kāsumāraphaladāyaka** of the Apadāna.[2]

[1] Thag. vs. 14; ThagA. i. 60 f. [2] Ap. ii. 445.

5. **Sīvaka Thera.**—He belonged to a brahmin family of **Rājagaha,** and, when he had acquired a good education, became a **Paribbājaka.** Then he heard the Buddha preach, entered the Order, and became an arahant.

Ninety-one kappas ago he had given **Vipassī Buddha** a bowl of boiled rice (*kummāsa*).[1] He is evidently identical with **Kummāsadāyaka** of the Apadāna.[2]

[1] Thag. vss. 183-4; ThagA. i. 307 f. [2] Ap. ii. 415.

Sīvaka Sutta.—Gives an account of the visit of **Moliya-Sīvaka** (*q.v.*) to the Buddha.[1]

[1] S. iv. 230.

Sīvala.—Son of **Maṅgala Buddha** in his last lay life.[1]

[1] Bu. iv. 20.

1. **Sīvalā, Sīvalī.**—An *aggasāvikā* of **Siddhattha Buddha.**[1]

[1] Bu. xvii. 19; J. i. 40.

2. **Sīvalā, Sīvalī.**—An *aggasāvikā* of **Maṅgala Buddha.**[1]

[1] Bu. iv. 24; J. i. 34.

3. **Sīvalā.**—One of the chief women patrons of **Koṇāgamana Buddha.**[1]

[1] Bu. xxiv. 24.

4. **Sīvalā.**—A daughter of **Muṭasīva.**[1]

[1] Dpv. xi. 7.

5. **Sīvalā.**—An eminent Therī, teacher of the Vinaya in Ceylon.[1]

[1] Dpv. xviii. 27.

6. **Sivalā.**—An eminent Therī of Jambudīpa who, with **Mahāruhā,** came to Ceylon at the head of twenty thousand nuns at the invitation of King **Abhaya** and taught the Tipiṭaka in **Anurādhapura.**[1]

[1] Dpv. xviii. 31 f.

7. **Sivalā.**—See **Sivalī.**

1. **Sivalī.**—Daughter of **Polajanaka.** See the **Mahājanaka Jātaka.** She is identified with **Rāhulamātā.**[1]

[1] J. vi. 68.

2. **Sīvalī Thera.**—He was the son of **Suppavāsā,** daughter of the king of **Koliya.** For seven years and seven days he lay in her womb, and for seven days she was in labour and was unable to bring forth the child. She said to her husband: " Before I die I will make a gift," and sent a gift by him to the Buddha. He accepted the gift and pronounced a blessing on her. She was immediately delivered of a son. When her husband returned, she asked him to show hospitality to the Buddha and his monks for seven days.

From the time of his birth, Sīvalī could do anything. **Sāriputta** talked with him on the day of his birth and ordained him with Suppavāsā's permission. Sivalī became a *sotāpanna* in the Tonsure-hall when his first lock of hair was cut, and a *sakadāgāmin* with the second. Some say that after his ordination he left home on the same day and lived in a secluded hut, meditating on the delays in his birth, and thus, winning insight, attained arahantship.

In **Padumuttara Buddha's** time he made the resolve to be pre-eminent among recipients of gifts, like **Sudassana** (*q.v.*), disciple of Padumuttara. To this end he gave alms for seven days to the Buddha and his monks. In the time of **Vipassī Buddha** he was a householder near **Bandhumatī.** The people gave alms to the Buddha and the Order in competition with the king, and when they were in need of honey, curds and sugar, Sīvalī gave enough of these for sixty-eight thousand monks. In the time of **Atthadassī Buddha** he was a king, named **Varuṇa,** and when the Buddha died, he made great offerings to the Bodhi-tree, dying under it later. Then he was born in the **Nimmānarati**-world. Thirty-four times he was king of men, under the name of **Subāhu.**[1] According to the Apadāna account,[2] his father in his last birth was the **Licchavi Mahāli.** The

[1] Thag. vs. 60; ThagA. i. 135.

[2] Ap ii. 492 f.

Asātarūpa Jātaka[3] (*q.v.*) gives the reason for the delay in Sīvalī's birth.

Sīvalī was declared by the Buddha[4] pre-eminent among recipients of gifts. It is said[5] that when the Buddha visited **Khadiravaniya-Revata,** he took Sīvalī with him because the road was difficult and provisions scarce. Sīvalī went to the **Himālaya** with five hundred others, to test his good luck. The gods provided them with everything. On **Gandhamādana** a deva, named **Nāgadatta,** entertained them for seven days on milk-rice.

[3] *Cf. ibid.*, 494, vs. 29 f. The story of Sīvalī is given also at Ud. ii. 8; AA. i. 136 f.; DhA. iv. 192 f.; ii. 196; J. i. 408 f. The Ud. follows the DhA. (iv. 192 f.) very closely. Both Ud. and J. say that a lay supporter of **Moggallāna** postponed his entertainment of the Buddha (who requested him to do so) to enable the Buddha to accept Suppavāsā's invitation after the birth of the child. Other accounts omit this. Ud. says nothing about Sīvalī's retirement from the world. The DhA. account of this differs from the others.

[4] A. i. 24.

[5] ThagA. i. 138; Ap. ii. 495; AA. i. 139.

3. **Sīvalī.**—Daughter of **Āmaṇḍagāmaṇi** and sister of **Culābhaya.** She reigned in Ceylon for four months (in 93 A.C.); she was then dethroned by **Iḷanāga.** Her surname was **Revatī.**[1]

[1] Mhv. xxxv. 14; Dpv. xxi. 40 f.

4. **Sīvalī Thera.** An eminent monk present at the Foundation Ceremony of the **Mahā Thūpa.**[1]

[1] Dpv. xix. 8.

5. **Sīvalī.**—See **Sīhasīvalī.**

6. **Sīvalī.**—One of the founders of the **Sīhalasaṅgha** in Burma.[1] He later founded a sect of his own.[2]

[1] Sās., p. 65. [2] *Ibid.*, 67.

Sīvalīputtāru.—A stronghold in South India.[1]

[1] Cv. lxxvii. 41.

Sīveyyaka.—See **Sīviraṭṭha.**

Sīsupacālā Therī.—One of the sisters of **Sāriputta. Māra** once tempted her with thoughts of the pleasures of the *Kāmaloka*, but she sent him away discomfited.[1] Her story resembles that of **Cālā.** She had a son of the same name as herself.[2]

[1] Thig. vss. 196-203; ThigA. 168 f.; S. i. 133 f. [2] ThagA. i. 110.

Sīsupācāla Sutta.—The story of **Māra's** temptation of **Sīsupacālā.**[1]

[1] S. i. 133 f.

1. **Sīha.**—A **Licchavi** general of **Vesāli.** He was a follower of the **Nigaṇṭhas.** When the Buddha visited Vesāli, Sīha, having heard reports of his greatness, wished to see him, but **Nigaṇṭha Nātaputta** dissuaded him, saying that **Gotama** denied the result of actions and was not worth a visit. But in the end Sīha, accompanied by five hundred chariots, went to the Buddha. Having discovered in conversation with the Buddha that he was falsely accused of preaching wrong doctrines, Sīha declared himself the Buddha's follower. The Buddha accepted his adherence on condition that he would continue to give alms to any Nigaṇṭhas who sought them at his house. This generosity made Sīha honour the Buddha even more highly, and he invited him and the monks to a meal on the next day. Meat formed one of the dishes, and the Nigaṇṭhas went about Vesāli crying that Sīha had killed a large ox to provide meat for the Buddha and his monks and that the food had been accepted. This was the occasion for the formulation of the rule that no monk should eat flesh where he has reason to believe that the animal had been specially killed for him.[1]

Sīha was, at one time, one of the most famous patrons of the Nigaṇṭhas, the others being **Upāligahapati** of **Nālandā,** and **Vappa,** the **Sākyan** of **Kapilavatthu.**[2]

The Aṅguttara Nikāya[3] contains two discussions, in more or less identical terms, in which Sīha asks the Buddha if it is possible to show the visible results of giving. The Buddha, by means of a counter question, elicits from Sīha that the giver has his reward in this world itself, and in the end Sīha acknowledges that he has experienced the benefits which the Buddha set forth.

Sīha had a niece, **Sīhā** (*q.v.*).

[1] Vin. i. 233 f.; A. iv. 179 f.; see also the **Telovāda Jātaka.**

[2] AA. ii. 751.

[3] A. iii. 38 f.; iv. 79f.

2. **Sīha Thera.**—He was born in the family of a *rājā* in the **Malla** country and visited the Buddha. The Buddha preached to him a sermon suitable to his temperament, and he entered the Order. He lived in the forest in meditation, but his thoughts were distracted. The Buddha, seeing this, went through the air and spoke to him alone, asking him to persevere. Thus incited, he strove hard and attained arahantship.

He was once a *kinnara* on the banks of the **Candabhāgā,** and seeing **Atthadassī Buddha** journeying through the air, he stood still, gazing at him with clasped hands. The Buddha alighted and sat under a tree, where the *kinnara* offered him flowers and sandalwood. Sīha was three times king, under the name of **Rohiṇī.**[1] He is probably identical with **Candanapūjaka** of the Apadāna.[2]

[1] ThagA. i. 179. [2] Ap. i. 165.

3. **Sīha.**—A novice who entered the Order at the age of seven and was a great favourite among the monks for his charm. He was much liked by the Buddha. He was a student under **Nāgita,** and was with him when the Buddha once stayed in **Vesāli.** Seeing a great number of people coming to visit the Buddha, he informed Nāgita of this, and, with his permission, went to tell the Buddha. This led to the preaching of the **Mahāli Sutta.**[1] Buddhaghosa adds[2] that Nāgita was fat and lazy and that most of his work was done by Sīha, who was his sister's son.

[1] D. i. 151. [2] DA. i. 310.

4. **Sīha.**—Son of **Sobhita Buddha,** in his last lay-life.[1] *v.l.* **Makhilā.**

[1] Bu. vii. 18.

5. **Sīha.**—The constant attendant (*upaṭṭhāka*) of **Metteyya Buddha.**[1]

[1] Anāgat. p. 50, vs. 97.

Sīha Jātaka.—See the **Guṇa Jātaka.**

1. **Sīha Sutta.**—When the lion comes from his lair in the evening and utters his lion's roar all the birds and beasts that hear it quake and tremble. Similarly when a Buddha appears in the world, all those holding wrong beliefs realize their error. The Buddha's teaching has, as its aim, the ending of *sakkāya.*[1]

[1] A. ii. 33 f.

2. **Sīha Sutta.**—**Sīha** (*q.v.*), the general, visits the Buddha at the **Kūṭāgārasālā** in **Vesāli** and questions him on the visible results of giving.[1]

[1] A. iii. 38 f.

3. **Sīha Sutta.**—When a lion hunts he hunts carefully, be it but for a hare or cat, lest his skill should fail him. Similarly, when a Buddha preaches, be it but to a fowler going about with grain, he teaches with care, out of respect for the Dhamma.[1]

[1] A. iii. 121.

4. **Sīha Sutta.**—Very similar to No. 2 above.[1]

[1] A. iv. 79 f.

5. **Sīha Sutta.**—Describes the conversion of **Sīha,** the general[1] (*q.v.*).

[1] A. iv. 180 f.

6. **Sīha Sutta.**—While the Buddha is preaching to a large congregation at **Jetavana, Māra** approaches and asks him how he can be so confident, like to a lion. The Buddha answers that it is because he has won the tenfold power.[1]

[1] S. i. 109.

7. **Sīha Sutta.**—Very similar to No. 1.[1]

[1] S. iii. 84 f.

8. **Sīha Sutta.**—Contains details of the tenfold power of a Tathāgata.[1]

[1] A. v. 32 f.

Sīhakoṭṭhuka Jātaka (No. 188).—The Bodhisatta was once a lion and had a cub by a she-jackal. The cub was like his sire in appearance, but like his dam in voice. One day, after rain, when the lions were gambolling and roaring together, the cub thought to roar too, and yelped like a jackal. Thereupon all the lions at once fell silent. When the Bodhisatta was told of this by another cub he advised the jackal-cub to keep quiet.

The story was related in reference to **Kokālika's** attempt to preach. Kokālika is identified with the jackal-voiced cub and **Rāhula** with his brother.[1]

[1] J. ii. 108 f.

Sīhagiri, Sīhapabbata, Sīhācala.—A rocky fortress in the **Malaya** district of Ceylon.[1] When **Kassapa I.** had slain his father, he took refuge there, clearing the land about the rock, surrounding it with a wall, and building a staircase to it in the form of a lion. Kassapa and his retinue lived in the fortress till he was defeated by his brother **Moggallāna,** and then killed himself.[2] Mention is made of several vihāras on Sīhagiri, among them being **Daḷha** and **Dāṭhākoṇḍañña,** which Moggallāna I. gave to the **Dhammaruci** and **Sāgalika** schools.[3] King **Saṅghatissa,** his son, and his minister, were executed on Sīhagiri,

[1] Now Sigiri, about thirty-eight miles south-east of **Anurādhapura** (Cv. *Trs.* i. 42, n. 1). Perhaps the rock itself resembled the form of a recumbent lion, especially the forepart of his body.

[2] Cv. xxxix. 2 f.

[3] *Ibid.*, 41. Perhaps the fortress was originally a centre of the Dhammarucikas, and Kassapa may have borrowed from them the idea of making use of it.

at the command of **Moggallāna III.**,[4] and later Moggallāna himself was slain there by **Silāmeghavaṇṇa.**[5]

The rock is now famous for its frescoes, which are very similar to those of Ajaṇṭā.

[4] Cv. xliv. 32 f. [5] *Ibid.*, 60.

Sīhaghosa.—An eminent monk in the time of **Padumuttara Buddha.** It was the eminence of this monk which made **Uruvelakassapa** wish for similar honour for himself.[1]

[1] Ap. ii. 481.

Sīhacamma Jātaka (No. 189).—Once a merchant used to go about hawking goods, his pack carried by a donkey. After the day's work he would throw a lion's skin over the donkey and let him loose in the fields. The farmers, taking him for a lion, dared not stop him eating their crops. But one day they summoned up courage and armed themselves, and approached the animal with great uproar. The donkey, frightened to death, heehawed. The farmers cudgelled him to death.

The story was told in reference to **Kokālika,** who is identified with the donkey.[1]

[1] J. ii. 109 f.

Sīhadvāra.—One of the fourteen gates of **Pulatthipura.**[1]

[1] Cv. lxxiii. 160.

1. **Sīhanāda Vagga.**—The second section of the **Majjhima Nikāya,** containing suttas 11-20.[1]

[1] M. i. 63 ff.

2. **Sīhanāda Vagga.**—The second chapter of the Navaka Nipāta on the **Aṅguttara Nikāya.**[1]

[1] A. iv. 373-96.

1. **Sīhanāda Sutta.**—On the six powers of a Tathāgata.[1]

[1] A. iii. 417 f.

2. **Sīhanāda Sutta.**—See **Cūlasīhanāda, Mahāsīhanāda** and **Cakkavatti-sīhanāda.**

3. **Sīhanāda Sutta.**—In the Aṅguttara Commentary[1], the **Abhibhū Sutta**[2] is called the **Sīhanāda Sutta.**

[1] AA. i. 441. [2] A. i. 226 f.

Sīhapapāta.—One of the seven great lakes of **Himavā.**[1] The water in it never grew warm.[2]

[1] A. iv. 107; DA. i. 164; UdA. 390; AA. ii. 759; J. v. 415, etc. [2] SNA. ii. 407.

Sīhapabbata.—See **Sīhagiri.**

1. **Sīhapura.**—A city, built by the third son of King **Upacara** of the **Mahāsammata** dynasty.[1]

[1] J. iii. 460.

2. **Sīhapura.**—A town in **Lāḷa,** from which **Vijaya** and his followers went to Ceylon. It was founded by **Sīhabāhu,** who became its first king.[1] **Tilokasundarī,** consort of **Vijayabāhu I.,** was born in Sīhapura.[2] It was to the north of **Kālinga.** The south-eastern district of Chutiā Nāgpur, to the west of Bengal, is still called Siṅghabhūm.[3]

[1] Mhv. vi. 35; Dpv. ix. 4, 5, 43. [2] Cv. lix. 46. [3] Cv. *Trs.* i. 213, n. 1.

3. **Sīhapura.**—A suburb of **Pulatthipura,** in which was the **Kusinārā-vihāra.**[1]

[1] Cv. lxxviii. 84.

Sīhabāhu.—Father of **Vijaya.** According to legend, his father was a lion and his mother a princess of **Vaṅga** (see **Susīmā).** His hands and feet were like a lion's paws. He had a sister, **Sīhasīvalī.** When he was sixteen he escaped with his mother and sister and arrived in the capital of Vaṅga. Later he killed his father for a reward and was offered the throne of Vaṅga. He refused this and founded a city, **Sīhapura,** in his native country of **Lāḷa,** and there lived with Sīhasīvalī, whom he made his consort. They had thirty-two children, of whom **Vijaya** was the eldest and **Sumitta** the second.[1]

[1] Dpv. ix. 2-6; Mhv. vi. 11 f., 24-38; viii. 2, 6.

Sīhamukha.—One of the mouths of the **Anotatta.** From it flowed a river, on the banks of which lions lived; hence its name.[1]

[1] SNA. ii. 438; UdA. 301.

Sīhala, Sīhalā.—The name given to **Vijaya** and his companions, founders of the Sinhalese race in Ceylon. It is said[1] that *Sīhala* was the name given to **Sīhabāhu** because he had killed the lion (*sīhaṃ adinnavā iti*), and because of their connection with him, Vijaya and his companions were also called **Sīhalā**. The word, thereafter, became the

[1] Mhv. vii. 42; *cf.* Dpv. ix. 1.

name of the inhabitants of Ceylon, as opposed to the **Damiḷas** and others.

The Sīhalā had a *vīṇā* with very fine strings.[2]

[2] KhA. 47.

Sīhalacetikā.—It is said[1] that once sixty monks heard a Sinhalese girl singing in her own language, on birth, old age, and death. They reflected on her words and became arahants.[1]

[1] SNA. ii. 397.

Sīhalaṭṭhakathā.—The old Commentary on the Tipiṭaka which contained the **Mahāvihāra** tradition. It was supposed to have been compiled by, or at least under, **Mahinda.** Buddhaghosa learnt it under **Saṅghapāla** and retranslated it into the Magadha (Pāli) tongue, while living in the **Ganthākara-pariveṇa.**[1] It evidently contained a great deal of historical material as well.[2]

[1] Cv. xxxvii. 228-234. [2] For its nature and contents see MṬ. Introd. lvii ff.

Sīhaladīpa.—The name given to Ceylon (**Tambapaṇṇi**) since it became the country of the **Sīhalā.** It is mentioned as a *patirūpadesa.*[1]

[1] DhSA., p. 103.

Sīhalavatthu.—A Commentary[1]; probably another name for the **Sīhalaṭṭhakathā** (*q.v.*).

[1] Gv. 62, 72.

Sīhalasaṅgha.—A sect founded in Pagan by **Chapaṭa** and his four companions: **Rāhula, Ānanda, Sīvali** and **Tāmalinda.** It first enjoyed the patronage of King **Narapatisithu,** but later the sect split into four sections, each following one of the four theras who had come from Ceylon.[1]

[1] Sās. 65, 66; Bode, *op. cit.,* 19, 23 f.

Sīhavāhana.—A king of long ago, descendant of **Mahāsammata.**[1]

[1] Mhv. ii. 13; Dpv. iii. 42.

Sīhasinānatittha.—A place in **Anurādhapura,** through which the boundary of the **Mahāvihāra** passed.[1]

[1] Mbv. 136.

Sīhasīvalī.—Sister and, later, wife of **Sīhabāhu** and mother of **Vijaya.** Her mother was **Susīmā** and her father a lion.[1]

[1] Mhv. vi. 10, 34, 36; Dpv. ix. 3.

Sīhasūra.—Name of a king.[1]

[1] Gv. 73.

Sīhassara.—A king of long ago.[1]

[1] Mhv. ii. 13 f.; Dpv. iii. 42.

Sīhahanu.—Father of **Suddhodana,** and therefore grandfather of the Buddha. His father was **Jayasena.** Sīhahanu had five sons and two daughters: **Suddhodana, Dhotodana, Sakkodana, Sukkadana** and **Amitodana,** and **Amitā** and **Pamitā.** His wife was **Kaccānā.**[1] Till the time of **Sīhahanu,** great friendship existed between the **Sākyans** and the **Koliyans.**[2] **Asita** (*q.v.*) was his purohita.

[1] Mhv. ii. 15 f.; Dpv. iii. 44 f. [2] SNA. i. 356.

Sīhā Therī.—She was the niece of **Sīhasenāpati** and was born in **Vesālī.** She heard, one day, the Buddha preach to **Sāriputta,** and entered the Order with her parents' consent. For seven years she tried, without success, to concentrate her mind. Then she tied a noose round her neck and fastened the end to a tree, and in this position she compelled her mind to gain insight. Then she loosened the noose.[1]

[1] Thig. vss. 77-81; ThigA. 79.

Sīhācala.—See **Sīhagiri.**

Sīhāsana Vagga.—The second chapter of the **Apadāna.**[1]

[1] Ap. i. 55 ff.

1. **Sīhāsanadāyaka Thera.**—An arahant. He erected a throne in honour of **Padumuttara Buddha** and made offerings to it. He was eight times king under the name of **Silùccaya.**[1]

[1] Ap. i. 188 f.

2. **Sīhāsanadāyaka Thera.**—An arahant. He made a throne in honour of **Siddhattha Buddha** and made offerings to it. He was king three times under the name of **Inda,** three times under that of **Sumana,** and three times under that of **Varuṇa.**[1]

[1] Ap. i. 55.

Sīhāsanavījanīya Thera.—An arahant.[1] He is evidently identical with **Jambuka** (*q.v.*).

[1] Ap. i. 403.

Suṃsumāra Jātaka (No. 208).—The Bodhisatta was once a monkey, living on the banks of the Ganges. The wife of a crocodile living in the river saw him and wished to eat his heart. Her husband, therefore, grew friendly with the monkey, whom he suggested taking across the river on his back, so that he might eat of fresh fruit on the opposite bank. The monkey trusted him and climbed on to his back, but, half-way across the river, the crocodile began to sink and then confessed his intentions. The monkey thereupon laughed and told him that he never took his heart with him when he went climbing trees for food, otherwise it would get torn to pieces; but he, like all the other monkeys, hung it on a tree, and he showed it to the crocodile hanging there on the opposite bank.

The crocodile believed him and took him across, where he hoped to get the heart. But the monkey jumped on the bank and laughed at his stupidity.

The story was related in reference to **Devadatta's** attempts to kill the Buddha. The crocodile is identified with Devadatta and his wife with **Ciñcā.**[1]

[1] J. ii. 159 f.; *cf.* Cyp. iii. 7; Mtu. ii. 208.

Suṃsumāragiri.—A city in the **Bhagga** country, of which it was probably the capital.[1] The Buddha spent the eighth *vassa* there.[2] Near the city was the **Bhesakalāvana** (*q.v.*) where the Buddha stayed. During his visits there he preached the **Anumāna Sutta**[3] and the **Bodhirāja Sutta.**[4] The city was the residence of **Nakulapitā** and his wife,[5] with whom the Buddha had several interviews. It is said that once, when the Buddha was at Suṃsumāragiri, he saw with his divine eye **Moggallāna** at **Kallavālamutta** half asleep, and appeared before him and admonished him.[6] On another occasion, he saw **Anuruddha** in the **Veḷuvana** in the **Ceti** country, pondering over the seven *Mahāpurisavitakkas,* and appeared before him to encourage him.[7] Both incidents show that the Buddha visited Suṃsumāragiri quite early in his career, in the first year after the Enlightenment. Moggallāna also stayed in Suṃsumāragiri, and there **Māra** is said to have entered his stomach and to have given him trouble.[8] Suṃsumāragiri was the birthplace of **Sirimaṇḍa Thera**[9] and the scene of the meditations of **Siṅgālakapitā.**[10]

Several Vinaya rules were passed during the Buddha's stay at Suṃsu-

[1] See, *e.g.*, Sp. iv. 862.
[2] BuA. 3.
[3] M. i. 95 f.
[4] *Ibid.*, ii. 91 f.
[5] *E.g.*, A. ii. 61; iii. 295 f.; iv. 268; S. iii. 1; iv. 116.
[6] A. iv. 85.
[7] *Ibid.*, 228 f.
[8] M. i. 332 f.; *cf.* Thag. vs. 1208.
[9] ThagA. i. 462.
[10] See *s.v.*

māragiri.[11] The **Dhonasākha Jātaka** was preached there.[12] Prince **Bodhi,** the governor of the **Bhagga** country, evidently lived in Suṃsumāragiri, and it was there that he had his famous palace, called **Kokanada.**[13]

It is said[14] that the city was so called because when it was being built a crocodile (*suṃsumāra*) made a noise in a lake near by.

[11] Vin. ii. 127; iv. 115 f.; 198 f.
[12] J. iii. 157 f.
[13] See *s.v.* for details.
[14] MA. i. 292; SA. ii. 181.

Suka Jātaka (No. 255).—The Bodhisatta was once a parrot. When he grew old his eyes became weak and he was looked after by his son. The son once discovered a special kind of mango on an island, and, having eaten of it himself, brought some home to his parents. The Bodhisatta recognized the mango and warned his son that parrots visiting that island were short-lived. But the son took no heed, and one day, while flying back from the island, he fell asleep from weariness and was eaten by a fish.

The story was told in reference to a monk who died of over-eating. The parrot is identified with him.[1]

[1] J. ii. 291-4.

Sukaṭaveliya Thera.—An arahant. In the time of **Sikhī Buddha** he was a garland-maker, named **Asita,** and one day, while on his way with a garland to the king, he met the Buddha and offered it to him. Fifty-two kappas ago he was a king named **Dvebhāra.**[1]

[1] Ap. i. 217.

Sukka Sutta.—In a man whose heart is possessed by gains, favours and flatteries, even the bright conditions (*sukkā*) are extirpated.[1]

[1] S. ii. 240.

Sukkapakkhūposatha.—The name of the festival held in honour of **Mahinda** on the eighth day of the bright half of the month of **Assayuja,** the day of his death.[1]

[1] Mhv. xx. 33; MṬ. 418.

1. **Sukkā Therī.**—She belonged to a householder's family of **Rājagaha,** and, very impressed by the Buddha's majesty when he visited Rājagaha, she became a lay believer. Later she heard **Dhammadinnā** preach, and entered the Order under her, attaining arahantship not long after.

In the time of **Vipassī Buddha** she had been a nun, and, after a sojourn in **Tusita,** a nun again in the time of **Sikhī, Vessabhū, Kakusandha, Koṇāgamana** and **Kassapa Buddhas.**

In her last life she was a great preacher, at the head of five hundred nuns. One particular sermon to the nuns is specially mentioned, and a tree-sprite, living at the end of the nun's *caṅkamana*, went about Rājagaha, singing Sukkā's praises. People, hearing the sprite, flocked to hear Sukkā.[1]

[1] Thig. vss. 54-6; ThigA. 57 f.; Ap. ii. 605 f.; the incident of the tree-sprite's praise is twice mentioned in the Saṃyutta as well. There the sprite is called a Yakkha (S. i. 212); in the second account (*ibid.*, 213) it says that the Yakkha's praise was owing to a meal given to Sukkā by a lay follower of Rājagaha.

Sukkā.—A class of Devas who were present, in the company of the **Veghanasā,** at the preaching of the **Mahāsamaya Sutta.**[1]

[1] D. ii. 261.

Sukkodana, Sukkhodana.—A **Sākyan** prince, son of **Sīhahanu** and paternal uncle of **Gotama Buddha.**[1] **Mahānāma** and **Anuruddha** were his sons.[2]

[1] Mhv. ii. 20; see SNA. i. 357.

[2] MA. i. 289.

1. **Sukha.**—A monk, generally known a **Sukha Sāmaṇera.** In his past life he had been **Bhattabhatika** (*q.v.*). In his last life he was born in the house of a supporter of **Sāriputta.** During her pregnancy, his mother gave alms to five hundred monks, with Sāriputta at their head. When he was seven years old, he entered the Order under Sāriputta, on which occasion his parents held a special almsgiving lasting for seven days.

Once, while going with Sāriputta for alms, he noticed several things, and like the novice **Paṇḍita** (*q.v.*) asked the Elder numerous questions. Then he expressed a wish to return to the monastery. Sāriputta agreed, and Sukha turned back saying, " Sir, when you bring my food, pray bring me food of one hundred flavours. If you cannot obtain it through your own merit, you can obtain it through mine." So saying, he returned to his cell and meditated on the nature of the body. **Sakka's** throne was heated, and he sent the Four Regent Gods to keep away all noise from Sukha's cell. He also bade the Sun and Moon stand still. Sukha, helped by this silence, became an *anāgāmī*.

Meanwhile, Sāriputta had gone to a house where he knew he could get the food desired by Sukha, and, having eaten there, returned with Sukha's portion to the monastery. The Buddha, thinking that Sāriputta's arrival might impede Sukha's attainment of arahantship, appeared near the gate of Sukha's cell and stood guard. As he stood there, the Buddha asked Sāriputta four questions. When the last question was answered, Sukha became an arahant. Thereupon Sāriputta opened the door and gave Sukha his food. Sukha ate it and washed the bowl. The Four Regent God's left their post, Sakka let go the rope of the door of the novice's cell, and the Sun and Moon started once more on their course. Evening at once came on, and the Buddha, on being asked the reason, explained that it was a usual occurrence when they who possess merit engage in meditation.[1]

[1] DhA. iii. 95 ff.; *cp.* the story of **Paṇḍita.**

2. **Sukha.**—A general of **Māṇābharaṇa** (2).[1]

[1] Cv. lxxii. 123 f.

3. **Sukha.**—A *Jīvitapotthakī*, one of the generals of **Parakkamabāhu I.**[1]

[1] Cv. lxx. 174.

1. **Sukha Vagga.**—The fifteenth chapter of the **Dhammapada.**

2. **Sukha Vagga.**—The seventh chapter of the Eka Nipāta of the **Aṅguttara Nikāya.**[1]

[1] A. i. 80 f.

1. **Sukha Sutta.**—A monk who delights in Dhamma, in growth, in renunciation, in solitude, in being free of ill-will, and in non-diffuseness—such a one lives in happiness and contentment and will entirely destroy the *āsavas.*[1]

[1] A. iii. 431.

2. **Sukha Sutta.**—Two discussions between **Sāriputta** and the **Paribbājaka Sāmaṇḍakāni** at **Nālakagāmaka.**[1]

[1] A. v. 120.

Sukhagirigāma.—A village in **Rohaṇa,** mentioned in the account of the campaigns of **Parakkamabāhu I.**[1]

[1] Cv. lxxiv. 164.

Sukhatta Sutta.—A farmer must first plough and harrow his field and then grow his seed at the proper season. He must further let water in and out as required. A monk must carry out the three preliminaries for arahantship: training in the higher morality, higher thought, higher insight.[1]

[1] A. i. 229.

Sukhadukkhī Sutta.—The self is both bliss and suffering, without sickness, after death.[1]

[1] S. iii. 220.

Sukhavihārī Jātaka (No. 10).—The Bodhisatta was once an *Udicca*-brahmin and later became a leader of ascetics. When the ascetics came to Benares for the rainy season, the king invited their leader to stay behind while the others returned at the end of the rains. One day the Bodhisatta's chief disciple visited him and sat down on a mat by his side, exclaiming: " Oh happiness, what happiness !" The king came to pay his respects to the teacher, but was displeased because the disciple still sat there. The Bodhisatta explained that the disciple had also been a king who had renounced his kingship for the ascetic life.

The story was related in reference to **Bhaddiya** who, after he had won arahantship, kept on saying " *aho sukhaṃ, aho sukhaṃ,*" because he realized how full of fear he had been as a layman and how free from fear he was as an arahant. Bhaddiya is identified with the chief disciple of the Bodhisatta.[1]

[1] J. i. 140-2.

" Sukhāya " Sutta.—He who sees the world as ill, false and perishable, frees himself from it.[1]

[1] S. iv. 204.

Sukhita.—See **Surakkhita.**

Sukhita Sutta.—Incalculable is *saṃsāra*; everyone has enjoyed prosperity in the course of his wanderings.[1]

[1] S. ii. 186.

Sukhitta.—See **Sumitta.**

Sukhindriya, or **Uppaṭi Vagga.**—The fourth chapter of the **Indriya Saṃyutta.**[1]

[1] S. v. 207-16.

Sukhuma Sutta.—A monk who can penetrate through the subtility of body, feeling, perception, and of the *Saṅkhāras*, has overcome **Māra.**[1]

[1] A. ii. 17.

" Sukhena " Sutta.—**Moggallāna** explains to the monks how the Buddha helped him to perfect the third *jhāna.*[1]

[1] S. iv. 264.

Sugatavinaya Sutta.—The benefits which accrue to the world through a Tathāgata and his Vinaya and the four things which lead to the confusion of the Saddhamma.[1]

[1] A. ii. 147 f.

1. **Sugandha Thera.**—He belonged to a rich family of **Sāvatthi.** In the past he had smeared the **Gandhakuṭi** of **Kassapa Buddha** with costly sandalwood paste and had desired that he might be reborn with a fragrant body: therefore he, on the day of his birth, and his mother, while she carried him, filled the house with fragrance—hence his name. When he grew up, he heard **Mahāsela Thera** preach and entered the Order, attaining arahantship in seven days.

In the time of **Tissa Buddha** he was a hunter. Tissa Buddha saw him, and, out of compassion for him, left his footprint where the hunter might see it. The hunter recognized the footprint as that of a Great Being and offered to it *karaṇḍaka*-flowers.[1]

He is probably identical with **Karaṇḍapupphiya Thera** of the Apadāna.[2]

[1] Thag. vs. 24; ThagA. i. 80 f.
[2] Ap. ii. 434; the same verses occur at Ap. ii. 383; *cf.* ThagA. i. 270; i. 405, where they are found under **Subhūti.**

2. **Sugandha.**—A *khattiya* of thirty-one kappas ago, a former birth of **Ātuma (Gandhodakiya) Thera.**[1]

[1] ThagA. i. 162; Ap. i. 158.

3. **Sugandha Thera.**—In the past he had been a *seṭṭhiputta* of Benares and had joined the Order under **Kassapa Buddha,** becoming famous as a preacher. After death he was born in **Tusita,** and in this life was born among men, with a fragrant body—hence his name. He entered the Order and became an arahant.[1]

[1] Ap. ii. 459-63.

Sugalā.—Younger daughter of **Vīravamma.** Her mother was the daughter of **Vijayabāhu I.** She married **Sirivallabha** and had two children, **Māṇābharaṇa** and **Līlāvatī.** After the death of Māṇābharaṇa, Sugalā revolted against **Parakkamabāhu I.** On finding her position untenable, she retired to **Uruvelā** with the Tooth Relic and Alms Bowl, which had fallen into her hands. She then carried on her activities in **Aṭṭhasahassaka.** She was captured at **Vanagāma** and sent to the king. After that we hear no more of her.[1]

[1] Cv. lix. 28, 45; lxii. 2; lxxiv. 28, 36, 88; lxxv. 154 f., 171, 195.

Suguttā.—One of the chief lay-women patrons of **Sikhī Buddha.**[1]

[1] Bu. xxi. 22.

1. **Sucanda.**—A palace occupied by **Sikhī Buddha** before his renunciation.[1]

[1] Bu. xxi. 16; BuA. (201) calls it Sucandaka Siri.

2. **Sucanda.**—A palace occupied by **Sumana Buddha** before his renunciation.[1]

[1] Bu. v. 22.

3. **Sucanda.**—A palace occupied by **Sumedha Buddha** before his renunciation.[1]

[1] Bu. xii. 19.

1. **Sucandaka.**—A palace occupied by **Rāmapaṇḍita.**[1]

[1] J. iv. 130.

2. **Sucandaka.**—The city where **Atthadassī Buddha** first met his Chief Disciples.[1]

[1] BuA. 179.

Sucandā.—Mother of **Piyadassī Buddha** and wife of **Sudatta.**[1]

[1] Bu. xiv. 15; BuA. (172) calls her **Candā.**

Sucarita Vagga.—The twenty-third chapter of the Catukka Nipāta of the **Aṅguttara Nikāya.**[1]

[1] A. ii. 228-30.

Sucarita Sutta.—The Buddha says, in answer to a question, that those who practise good conduct are born in the **Gandhabba**-world, because such is their wish.[1]

[1] S. iii. 250.

Sucarūdassana.—Seventeen kappas ago there were eight kings of this name, previous births of **Puṇṇamāsa (Paccāgamanīya) Thera.**[1]

[1] ThagA. i. 54; Ap. i. 113.

Sucitta.—A village—the residence of **Sirivaḍḍhanā,** who gave milk-rice to **Vessabhū Buddha.**[1]

[1] BuA. 205.

Sucimhita.—A celestial musician, or perhaps a musical instrument.[1]

[1] Vv. ii. 10; VvA. 93, 96, 211; but see 372.

Sucittā.—Wife of **Vessabhū Buddha,** before his renunciation.[1]

[1] Bu. xxii. 20.

Sucitti.—An **Asura,** one of the **Dānaveghasas,** present at the preaching of the **Mahāsamaya Sutta.**[1]

[1] D. ii. 259.

1. **Sucintita.**—A Paceka Buddha to whom, when very ill, **Ajina (Ghatamaṇḍadāyaka) Thera,** in a former birth, gave ghee.[1]

[1] ThagA. i. 250; Ap. ii. 436.

2. **Sucintita Thera.**—An arahant. Ninety-two kappas ago he gave a seat to **Tissa Buddha.** Thirty-eight kappas ago he was king three times, under the names of **Ruci, Uparuci** and **Mahāruci** respectively.[1]

[1] Ap. i. 133 f.

3. **Sucintita Thera.**—An arahant. He was a farmer of **Haṃsavatī** in the time of **Padumuttara Buddha** and gave the first-fruits of his fields to the Buddha and his monks.[1]

[1] Ap. ii. 385 f.

4. **Sucintita Thera.**—An arahant. In the time of **Atthadassī Buddha** he was a hunter, and, seeing the Buddha, offered him a meal of flesh. Thirty-eight kappas ago he was king eight times, under the name of **Dīghāyuka,** and one hundred and sixty kappas ago he was king twice, under the name of **Varuṇa.**[1]

[1] Ap. i. 115.

5. **Suncitita.**—A king of eight kappas ago, a previous birth of **Veyyāvaccaka** (or **Sañjaya**) **Thera.**[1]

[1] Ap. i. 138; ThagA. i. 120.

Sucindhara.—A pleasaunce near **Sobhana,** where **Atthadassī Buddha** was born.[1]

[1] BuA. 178.

Sucindhara.—A *mahāsāla* brahmin, father of **Candamāṇava.**[1]

[1] BuA. 110.

Sucindharā.—A Nāgī who gave a meal of milk-rice to **Atthadassī Buddha** just before his Enlightenment.[1]

[1] BuA. 178.

1. **Suciparivāra.**—The Bodhisatta born as seṭṭhi of Benares. See the **Sirikālakaṇṇi Jātaka.**[1]

[1] J. iii. 257 f.

2. **Suciparivāra.**—A very rich merchant of Benares. See the **Gaṅgamāla Jātaka.**[1]

[1] J. iii. 444 f.

Sucimā.—One of the palaces occupied by **Maṅgala Buddha** in his last lay life.[1]

[1] BuA. 116; but see *s.v.* **Maṅgala.**

Sucimukhī.—A **Paribbājikā.** She once saw **Sāriputta** in **Rājagaha** eating his meal, which he had begged from house to house, leaning against a wall. Sucimukhī asked him why he looked downwards while eating. When Sāriputta disclaimed doing so, she asked him, respectively, why he ate looking upwards, towards the four quarters, between the four quarters. He denied the truth of all her statements, and then explained to her his reason for his denial. He lived neither by such low arts as divination, nor by star-gazing, going errands, or palmistry. Sucimukhī understood, and went about Rājagaha praising the blamelessness of Sākyan monks.[1]

[1] S. iii. 238 f.; SA. ii. 253.

Sucira Jātaka.—Another name for the **Āditta Jātaka.**[1]

[1] See J. iv. 360.

Suciloma, Sūciloma.—A Yakkha. Once, when the Buddha was at the **Ṭaṅkitamañca** in **Gayā,** which was the abode of **Suciloma,** Suciloma and his friend, **Khara,** happened to be passing by, and Suciloma, coming up to the Buddha, bent his body against the Buddha's. The Buddha bent his body in the opposite direction, saying that contact with him was an evil thing. Then Suciloma asked him a question regarding the origin of various persuasions, and the Buddha answered him.[1]

It is said[2] that Suciloma was a lay follower of **Kassapa Buddha** and used to visit the vihāra eight times a month to hear the Dhamma. One day, when he heard the gong announcing the preaching, he was working in a field near the vihāra, and thinking he would be late if he stayed to wash, he entered the *uposatha*-hall, where he lay on a very costly rug. As a result of this action, the hairs of his body resembled needles—hence his name. At the end of the Buddha's sermon Suciloma became a *sotāpanna*.

An expressive statue of Suciloma is to be found among the bas-reliefs of the Bhārhūt Stūpa.[3]

[1] S. i. 207 f.; found also at SN. i. 47 f.

[2] SNA. i. 302, 305; in the Saṃyutta Commentary (SA. i. 233) he is said to have been a monk.

[3] Cunningham: Bhārhūt, p. 136.

Suciloma Sutta.—Describes the visit of the Buddha to **Suciloma's** abode.[1]

[1] S. i. 207 f.; SN. p. 47 f.

Sucīmatī.—Mother of **Bhaddā Kāpilānī** (*q.v.*), when she was born in **Sāgala** as the daughter of the brahmin **Kapila.**[1]

[1] ThigA. 73.

Sucīrata.—A brahmin of the **Bhāradvājagotta,** chaplain to **Dhanañjaya-Koravya** of **Indapatta.** See the **Sambhava Jātaka.** He is identified with **Anuruddha.**[1]

[1] J. v. 67; referred to at DA. i. 155.

Sucela.—Seven kappas ago there were eight kings of this name, previous births of **Kapparukkhiya (Kappa) Thera.**[1]

[1] Ap. i. 91.

Succaja Jātaka (No. 320).—The Bodhisatta was once minister to the king of Benares, and the king, fearing his son, the viceroy, gave orders that he should live outside the city. The viceroy therefore left the city with his wife and lived in a hut in a frontier village. When he discovered, by observing the stars, that the king was dead, he returned with his wife to take the throne. On the way they passed a mountain, and his wife asked: "If this mountain were of pure gold, would you give me some of it?" "Not an atom," he replied, and she was deeply hurt. She became queen, but was shown no respect or honour by the king. The Bodhisatta, noticing this, questioned her and made her promise to repeat her story in the king's presence. This she did, and the king, realizing her affection for him, bestowed all honour on her.

The story was told to a landowner of Sāvatthi who went with his wife to collect a debt. They received a cart in satisfaction of the debt, and, leaving it with friends, were on the way home when they saw a mountain, and a conversation, identical with the one above, took place. Arrived at Sāvatthi, they went to Jetavana, and when the Buddha asked the wife if she were happy, she told him what had happened. The Buddha then related the story of the king and queen who were the landowner and his wife. At the end of the story they became *sotāpannas.*[1]

[1] J. iii. 66-70.

Succhavi.—A king of twenty-four kappas ago, a previous birth of **Telamakkhiya Thera.**[1]

[1] Ap. i. 231.

Sujampati.—A name for **Sakka** (*q.v.*).

Sujā.—One of the four wives of **Magha** and his maternal cousin. When Magha's other wives helped him in his good acts, Sujā, claiming kinship with him, spent her time in adorning herself. When Magha was born as **Sakka** and looked for Sujā, he found that she had been born as a crane in a mountain cave. He visited her and carried her to **Tāvatiṃsa** to show her how her companions had been born there, as a result of their good acts. He then exhorted her to keep the five precepts. This she did, eating only such fish as had died a natural death. One day, Sakka, wishing to test her, assumed the form of a fish and pretended to be dead. Just as Sujā was about to swallow the fish, it wriggled its tail and she let it go. A few days later she died, and was born as the daughter of a potter of Benares. Sakka filled a cart with treasures disguised as cucumbers and drove it through the city. When people asked him for cucumbers, he said, "I give them only to a woman who has kept the five precepts." Sujā claimed them, and Sakka, revealing his identity, gave them to her.

Then she was reborn as the daughter of **Vepacitti,** king of the **Asuras,** a bitter enemy of Sakka. Because of her great beauty, Vepacitti granted to Sujā the boon of choosing her own husband, and Sakka, disguised as an aged Asura, came to the assembly where she was to choose. Filled with love for him, owing to their previous association, she threw the garland round the aged Asura, and when the others exclaimed that he was old enough to be her grandfather, Sakka took Sujā up into the air and declared his identity. The Asuras started in pursuit, but **Mātali** drove the **Vejayantaratha,** and Sujā was installed in Tāvatiṃsa as Sakka's chief consort, at the head of twenty-five million apsarases. She asked for and was granted as a boon that she should be allowed to accompany Sakka wherever he went.[1]

[1] DhA. i. 269, 271, 274 ff.; DA. iii. 716 f.; J. i. 201 f.; also J. iii. 491 f., where Sujā accompanies Sakka in his travels; at p. 494 she is called **Sujātā**; *cf.* DA. iii. 716.

1. **Sujāta.**—The twelfth of the twenty-four Buddhas. He was born in the city of **Sumaṅgala,** his father being the *khattiya* **Uggata** and his mother **Pabhāvatī.** He was called Sujāta because his birth brought happiness to all beings. He lived as a householder for nine thousand years in three palaces—**Siri, Upasiri** and **Nanda**—his wife being **Sirinandā** and his son **Upasena.** He left home on a horse, named **Haṃsavaha,** practised austerities for nine months, and attained Enlightenment under a bamboo (*mahāveḷu*) tree, after a meal of milk-rice given by the

daughter of **Sirinandanaseṭṭhi** of **Sirinandana;** grass for his seat was given by an **Ājīvaka** named **Sunanda.** His first sermon was to his younger brother, **Sudassana,** and the chaplain's son, **Deva,** in the **Sumaṅgala Park.** He performed the Twin Miracle at the gate of Sudassana Park. The Bodhisatta was a **Cakkavatti,** and entered the Order under the Buddha. Sujāta's chief disciples were **Sudassana** and **Deva (Sudeva)** among monks and **Nāgā** and **Nāgasamālā** among nuns. **Nārada** was his attendant. **Sudatta** and **Citta** were his chief lay patrons among men and **Subhaddā** and **Padumā** among women. His body was fifty cubits high; he lived for ninety thousand years, and died at **Silārāma** in **Candavatī** city, where a *thūpa*, three *gāvutas* in height, was erected in his honour.[1]

[1] Bu. xiii. 1 ff.; BuA. 168 ff.; J. i. 38; Mhv. i. 8, etc.

2. **Sujāta.**—Cousin of **Padumuttara Buddha** and brother of **Devala.** He later became one of Padumuttara's Chief Disciples.[1] **Heraññakāni (Upaḍḍhadussadāyaka) Thera,** in a previous birth, gave him a piece of cloth for a robe,[2] while **Khemā** gave him three meal-cakes and cut off her hair as an offering to him.[3] **Dhammadinnā** also did obeisance to him and offered him alms.[4]

[1] Bu. xi. 24; BuA. 159; DA. ii. 489.
[2] ThagA. i. 266; Ap. ii. 435.
[3] ThigA. 127; AA. i. 187.
[4] *Ibid.*, 196; MA. i. 516.

3. **Sujāta.**—An **Ājīvaka,** who gave grass for his seat to **Piyadassī Buddha.**[1]

[1] BuA. 172.

4. **Sujāta.**—A king, father of **Nārivāhana** (*q.v.*).

5. **Sujāta.**—A king, who later became a hermit. He was the Bodhisatta in the time of **Tissa Buddha.**[1]

[1] Bu. xviii. 9 f.; J. i. 40.

6. **Sujāta.**—A *yavapālaka*, who gave grass for his seat to **Vipassī Buddha.**[1]

[1] BuA. 195.

7. **Sujāta.**—A king of fifty-seven kappas ago; a former birth of **Raṃsisaññaka Thera.**[1]

[1] Ap. i. 210.

8. **Sujāta.**—The name of **Upāli Thera** (*q.v.*) in the time of **Padumuttara Buddha.**[1]

[1] ThagA. i. 229.

9. **Sujāta Thera.**—He was a brahmin of Benares, father of **Sundarī Therī.** While grieving for the death of his son, he met **Vāsiṭṭhī Therī,** and from her he heard about the Buddha, whom he visited at **Mithilā.** He entered the Order under the Buddha, attaining arahantship on the third day.[1]

It is perhaps this Thera who is mentioned in the Saṃyutta Nikāya[2] as having won the special praise of the Buddha because of his bright expression.

[1] ThigA. 229. [2] S. ii. 278 f.

10. **Sujāta.**—A householder of Benares. He once went to hear the leader of a company of ascetics preach in the royal park and spent the night there. During the night, he saw **Sakka** arrive with his apsarases to pay homage to the ascetics, and he fell in love with one of them. His passion for her was so great that he died of starvation. The story is given in the **Mahāsutasoma Jātaka.**[1]

[1] J. v. 468 f.

11. **Sujāta.**—The Bodhisatta born as a landowner of Benares. See the **Sujāta Jātaka** (3).

12. **Sujāta.**—Son of the **Assaka** king in **Polanagara.** He was expelled from the country at the request of his stepmother and lived in the forest. At that time **Mahā Kaccāna,** following on the holding of the First Council, was living in the **Assaka** country. One of Sujāta's friends, a devaputta in **Tāvatiṃsa,** appeared before Sujāta in the shape of a deer, and, after leading him to Mahā Kassapa, disappeared. Sujāta saw the Thera and talked with him. Mahā Kassapa saw that Sujāta had but five months to live, and, after stirring up his mind, sent him back to his father, urging him to good deeds. When the king heard his story he sent a messenger for Mahā Kaccāna. Sujāta lived another four months and, after death, was reborn in Tāvatiṃsa. Later he visited Mahā Kaccāna to show his gratitude and revealed his identity.[1]

[1] The story is known as the **Cūḷarathavimāna.** Vv. v. 13; VvA. 259-270.

13. **Sujāta.**—Called **Sujāta Pippalāyana** of **Mahātittha.** He married the daughter of the brahmin Kapila, a previous birth of **Bhaddā Kāpilānī.**[1]

[1] ThigA. 73.

1. **Sujāta Jātaka** (No. 269).—The Bodhisatta was once king of Benares. His mother was a passionate woman, harsh and ill-tongued, and the

Bodhisatta waited for an opportunity of admonishing her. One day, as he accompanied her to the park, a blue jay screeched, and the courtiers stopped their ears, saying: " What a scream! Stop it!" On another day they heard a cuckoo singing and stood listening eagerly. The Bodhisatta pointed this out to his mother and left her to draw her own inference. She understood and reformed herself.

The story was related to **Anāthapiṇḍika's** daughter-in-law, **Sujātā,** who was identified with the queen-mother.[1]

[1] J. ii. 347-51.

2. **Sujāta Jātaka** (No. 306).—The Bodhisatta was once chaplain to the king of Benares. One day, the king heard a fruiterer's daughter, **Sujātā,** hawking sweets, and falling in love with her voice he sent for her and made her his queen. Some time later she saw the king eating sweets from a golden dish and asked him what those egg-shaped fruits were. The king was very angry; but the Bodhisatta interceded on her behalf and she was pardoned.

The story was told in reference to a quarrel between **Mallikā** and **Pasenadi,** which became famous under the name of **Sirivivāda** or **Sayanakalaha.** Pasenadi ignored Mallikā completely, and the Buddha, knowing this, went to the palace with five hundred monks. The king invited them to a meal, and as the food was being served, the Buddha covered his bowl and asked for Mallikā. She was sent for, and the Buddha made peace between them. Mallikā is identified with Sujātā and Pasenadi with the king of Benares.[1]

[1] J. iii. 20-22.

3. **Sujāta Jātaka** (No. 352).—The Bodhisatta was once a landowner of Benares, named **Sujāta.** When his grandfather died his father gave himself up to despair and, having erected a mound over the dead man's bones, spent all his time offering flowers there. Wishing to cure him, Sujāta feigned madness, and, seeing a dead ox outside the city, put grass and water near it and kept on trying to make it eat and drink. News of this was carried to his father, who hurried to the spot. In the course of their conversation Sujāta convinced his father of his folly.

The story was told to a lay-follower of the Buddha who, after his father's death, gave himself up to grief. The Buddha visited him and told him this story.[1]

[1] J. iii. 155-7. The story is given in PvA. 39 f., but there it is related to the monks and not to the householder; he, however, became a *sotāpanna.*

Sujāta Sutta.—The Buddha sees **Sujāta Thera** coming towards him, and praises him both for beauty of appearance and beauty of attainment.[1]

[1] S. ii. 278 f.

1. **Sujātā.**—An *aggasāvikā* of **Sobhita Buddha.**[1]

[1] J. i. 35; Bu. vii. 22.

2. **Sujātā.**—An *aggasāvikā* of **Piyadassī Buddha.**[1]

[1] J. i. 39; Bu. xiv. 21.

3. **Sujātā.**—Mother of **Padumuttara Buddha.**[1]

[1] J. i. 37; Bu. xi. 19; MA. ii. 722; DhA. i. 417.

4. **Sujātā.**—Mother of **Koṇḍañña Buddha.**[1]

[1] Bu. iii. 25; J. i. 30.

5. **Sujātā.**—An **Asura** maiden who became the wife of **Sakka.** See **Sujā.**

6. **Sujātā.**—Daughter of **Senānī,** a landowner of the village of **Senānī** near **Uruvelā.** She made a promise to the god of the banyan-tree near by that she would offer a meal of milk-rice to the god if she gave birth to a son. Her wish was fulfilled, the son was born, and she sent her maid, **Puṇṇā,** to prepare the place for the offering. This was on the very day of the Buddha's Enlightenment, and **Puṇṇā,** finding **Gotama** sitting under the banyan, thought that he was the tree-god present in person to receive the offering. She brought the news to Sujātā, who, in great joy, brought the food in a golden bowl and offered it to him. Gotama took the bowl to the river bank, bathed at the **Suppatiṭṭhita** ford and ate the food. This was his only meal for forty-nine days.[1]

Sujātā's meal was considered one of the most important of those offered to the Buddha, and the Devas, therefore, added to it divine flavours.

Yasa (*q.v.*) was Sujātā's son, and when he attained arahantship his father, who had come in search of him, became the Buddha's follower and invited him to a meal. The Buddha accepted the invitation and went with Yasa to the house. The Buddha preached at the end of the meal, and both Sujātā and Yasa's wife became *sotāpannas.* On that day

[1] J. i. 68 f.; DhA. i. 71, etc. In Lal. 334-7 (267 f.) nine girls are mentioned as giving food to the Buddha during his austerities. *Cf.* Dvy. 392, where two are given, Nandā and Nandabalā.

Sujātā took the threefold formula of Refuge. She thus became foremost among lay women who had taken the threefold formula (*aggaṃ upāsikānaṃ paṭhamaṃ saraṇaṃ gacchantīnaṃ*).[2] She had made an earnest resolve to attain this eminence in the time of **Padumuttara Buddha.**[3]

[2] SNA. i. 154; *cf.* D. ii. 135. [3] A. i. 26; AA. i. 217 f.

7. **Sujātā.**—An *upāsikā* of **Ñātikā.** The Buddha said that she had become a *sotāpanna* and had thus assured for herself the attainment of arahantship.[1]

[1] D. ii. 92; S. v. 356 f.

8. **Sujātā.**—Youngest sister of **Visākhā.** She was the daughter of **Dhanañjayaseṭṭhi** and was given in marriage to **Anāthapiṇḍika's** son. She was very haughty and obstinate. One day, when the Buddha visited Anāthapiṇḍika's house, she was scolding the servants. The Buddha stopped what he was saying, and, asking what the noise was, sent for her and described to her the seven kinds of wives that were in the world. She listened to the sermon and altered her ways.[1]

The **Sujāta Jātaka** (No. 269) was preached to her.

[1] A. iv. 91 f.; J. ii. 347 f.

9. **Sūjātā.**—A maiden of Benares. See the **Maṇicora Jātaka.** She is identified with **Rāhulamātā.**[1]

[1] J. ii. 125.

10. **Sujātā Therī.**—She was the daughter of a *seṭṭhi* of **Sāketa** and was given in marriage to a husband of equal rank, with whom she lived happily. One day, while on her way home from a carnival, she saw the Buddha at **Añjanavana** and listened to his preaching. Even as she sat there her insight was completed, and she became an arahant. She went home, obtained her husband's permission, and joined the Order.[1]

[1] Thig. 145-50; ThigA. 136 f.

Suñña Sutta.—The Buddha explains to **Ānanda** that the world is void of "self" and of what belongs to "self."[1]

[1] S. iv. 54.

Suññakathā.—The tenth chapter of the **Yuganandha Vagga** of the **Paṭisambhidāmagga.**[1]

[1] Ps. ii. 177-84.

Suññatā Vagga.—The thirteenth section of the **Majjhima Nikāya,** containing suttas 121-130.[1]

[1] M. iii. 104 ff.

Suññatā Sutta.—See **Cūlasuññatā** and **Mahāsuññatā Suttas.**

Sutana.—The Bodhisatta, born as a poor householder. See the **Sutano Jātaka.**

1. **Sutanā, Sutanī.**—A gazelle, sister of the Bodhisatta. See the **Rohantamiga Jātaka.** She is identified with **Khemā.**[1]

[1] J. iv. 423.

2. **Sutanā.**—An eminent *upāsikā.*[1] *v.l.* **Sudhanā.**

[1] A. iv. 347.

3. **Sutanā.**—One of the *aggasāvikā* of **Maṅgala Buddha.**[1]

[1] Bu. iv. 25.

4. **Sutanā.**—See **Sutanū.**

Sutanu.—A stream at **Sāvatthi. Anuruddha** is mentioned as having stayed near by.[1]

[1] S. v. 297.

Sutanu Sutta.—**Anuruddha** explains to some monks who visit him on the banks of the **Sutanu River** that he gained *iddhi*-power by cultivating the four *satipaṭṭhānas.*[1]

[1] S. v. 297 f.

Sutanū, Sutanā.—Wife of **Vipassī Buddha,** in his last lay life.[1] She was also called **Sudassanā.**[2] *v.l.* **Sudhanā.**

[1] Bu. xx. 25. [2] BuA. 195.

Sutano Jātaka (No. 398).—The Bodhisatta was once a poor householder, named **Sutana,** and supported his parents. One day the king of Benares went hunting, and, after chasing a deer, killed it, and was returning with the carcase when he passed under a tree belonging to the Yakkha **Makhādeva,** who, by the power conferred on him by **Vessavaṇa,** claimed him as his food. The king was set free on condition that he sent one man daily to the Yakkha for food. As time went on, no one could be found to take rice to the Yakkha, because all knew what awaited them. Then the king offered one thousand, and the Bodhisatta, for the sake of his parents and against his mother's wishes, consented to go. Before going he obtained from the king his slippers, his umbrella, his sword, and his golden bowl filled with rice. Sutana then approached the Yakkha's tree, and, with the point of his sword, pushed the bowl of rice to him. The Yakkha then started talking to Sutana and was very pleased with him. Sutana exhorted him to give up his evil ways, and returned to Benares with the Yakkha, who was given a settlement at the city gate and provided with rich food.

For the introductory story see the **Sāma Jātaka.** The Yakkha is identified with **Aṅgulimāla** and the king with **Ānanda.**[1]

[1] J. iii. 324 f.

Suta-Brahmadatta.—A king of Benares, so called because he never tired of learning (*suta*). He was once visited by eight **Pacceka Buddhas** and entertained them. At the end of the meal, they rose and, each speaking only a word or two as thanks, went away. The king was at first disappointed, but realizing the import of their words, he renounced the world and became a Pacceka Buddha. His verse is included in the **Khaggavisāna Sutta** (verse 57).[1]

[1] SNA. i. 109 f.; ApA. i. 157.

1. **Sutavā.**—A king of thirty-three kappas ago, a previous birth of **Dhammasaññaka Thera.**[1]

[1] Ap. i. 249.

2. **Sutavā.**—A Pacceka Buddha mentioned in a nominal list.[1]

[1] M. iii. 69; ApA. i. 106.

3. **Sutavā.**—A **Paribbājaka** who visited the Buddha on **Gijjhakūṭa** and questioned him regarding the description of an arahant.[1]

[1] A. iv. 369 f.

1. **Sutavā Sutta.**—Describes the visit of the **Paribbājaka Sutavā** to the Buddha.[1]

[1] A. iv. 369 f.

2. **Sutavā Sutta.**—A learned monk should ponder carefully on the five groups of grasping (*upādānakkhandhā*).[1]

[1] S. iii. 169.

1. **Sutasoma.**—The Bodhisatta born as king of Benares. See the **Cullasutasoma Jātaka.**

2. **Sutasoma.**—The Bodhisatta, born as king of **Indapatta.** See the **Mahāsutasoma Jātaka.**

Sutasoma Jātaka.—See **Cullasutasoma** and **Mahāsutasoma Jātakas.**

Sutta.—One of the nine divisions of the **Tipiṭaka,** according to matter (*aṅga*).[1]

[1] DA. i. 23; Gv. 57, etc.

Sutta Nipāta.—One of the books, generally the fifth, of the **Khuddaka Nikāya.** It consists of five Vaggas—**Uraga, Cūla, Mahā, Aṭṭhaka** and **Pārāyaṇa**—the first four consisting of fifty-four short lyrics, while the fifth contains sixteen suttas. Of the thirty-eight poems in the first three cantos, six are found in other books of the canon, showing that they had probably existed separately, as popular poems, before being incorporated in the Sutta Nipāta. The fourth canto is referred to in the Saṃyutta Nikāya, the Vinaya Piṭaka and the Udāna, as a separate work, and this canto was probably very closely associated with the last, because the **Niddesa** is obviously an old Commentary on them and takes no notice of the remaining cantos.[1]

The **Dīghabhāṇakas** included the Sutta Nipāta in the Abhidhamma Piṭaka.[2]

A Commentary exists on the Sutta Nipāta, written by **Buddhaghosa,** and called the **Paramatthajotikā** (*q.v.*).

[1] For a detailed account see Law, *Pāli Literature* i. 232 f. [2] DA. i. 15.

Suttaṇḍara.—A Damiḷa chief, ally of **Kulasekhera.**[1]

[1] Cv. lxxvi. 181.

Suttaniddesa, also called **Kaccāyanasuttaniddesa.**—A grammatical treatise, explaining the *suttas* (aphorisms) of **Kaccāyaṇa's** grammar. It is generally ascribed to **Kaccāyana** himself, but sometimes **Chapaṭa** is mentioned as the author and it is said that he wrote it at **Arimaddana** (Pagan) at the request of his pupil, **Dhammacāri.**[1]

[1] Sās. 74; Gv. 64, 74; Svd. vs. 1247 f.

Suttapiṭaka, or **Suttantapiṭaka.**—One of the three divisions of the **Tipiṭaka.** It consists of five **Nikāyas—Dīgha, Majjhima, Saṃyutta,**

Aṅguttara and **Khuddaka.** The first four are homogeneous and cognate in character. A number of suttas appear in two or more of them.

Suttavādā.—A heretical sect, a branch of the **Saṅkantikas.**[1]

[1] Dpv. v. 48; Mhv. v. 9; *Points of Controversy*, pp. 3, 5.

Suttavibhaṅga.—See **Vibhaṅga** (2).

Suttasaṅgaha.—A post-canonical work which, in Burma, is regarded as one of the volumes of the **Khuddaka Nikāya.**[1] It is a miscellaneous collection of suttas and legends and was probably written in **Anurādhapura.**

[1] Bode, *op. cit.*, 5, 73.

1. **Sudatta.**—One of the eight brahmins who was called in to examine the signs at the **Buddha's** birth.[1]

[1] J. i. 56; Mil. 236.

2. **Sudatta.**—A *khattiya* of **Mekhala,** father of **Sumana Buddha.**[1]

[1] Bu. v. 32; J. i. 34.

3. **Sudatta.**—A *khattiya,* father of **Sumedha Buddha.**[1]

[1] Bu. xii. 18; J. i. 38; but BuA. (172) calls him **Sudassana.**

4. **Sudatta.**—One of the chief lay patrons of **Sobhita Buddha.**[1]

[1] Bu. vii. 23.

5. **Sudatta.**—The personal name of **Anāthapiṇḍika** (*q.v.*).

6. **Sudatta.**—A lay disciple of **Nādikā** who had become a *sakadāgāmin.*[1]

[1] D. ii. 92; S. v. 356 f.

7. **Sudatta.**—A devaputta who visited the Buddha at **Jetavana** and spoke two stanzas on the value of earnestness.[1]

[1] S. i. 53.

8. **Sudatta.**—One of the chief lay patrons of **Metteyya Buddha.**[1]

[1] Anāgat. vs. 62.

9. **Sudatta.**—Father of **Piyadassī Buddha.**[1]

[1] Bu. xiv. 15; but see **Sudinna** (1).

10. **Sudatta.**—One of **Sujāta Buddha's** chief lay patrons.[1]

[1] Bu. xiii. 30.

11. **Sudatta Thera** (*v.l.* **Sudanta**).—He belonged to a rich family of **Velukaṇṭaka.** Some give his name as **Vāsula.** He was a close friend of **Kumāputta,** and, on hearing that the latter had left the world, he, too, visited the Buddha with a similar end in view. The Buddha preached to him, and he entered the Order and lived on a hill with **Kumāputta,** engaged in meditation. But they were disturbed by the comings and goings of numerous monks, and, owing to the disturbance, spurred on to greater endeavour, Sudatta put forth effort and became an arahant. Ninety-four kappas ago, in the time of **Siddhattha Buddha,** he was a householder, and going into the forest, he made walking-sticks, which he gave to the monks.[1]

He is evidently identical with **Daṇḍadāyaka** of the Apadāna,[2] and is generally known as **Kumāputtasahāya Thera.**

[1] Thag. vs. 37; ThagA. i. 101 f. [2] Ap. i. 283.

1. **Sudatta Sutta.**—Describes the visit of **Sudatta** the Devaputta to the Buddha.[1]

[1] S. i. 53.

2. **Sudatta Sutta.**—The Buddha tells **Anāthapiṇḍika** that he who gives food gives four things to the receiver thereof: life, beauty, happiness, strength.[1]

[1] A. ii. 63.

1. **Sudattā.**—Mother of **Sumedha Buddha.**[1]

[1] Bu. xii. 18; J. i. 38.

2. **Sudattā.**—An *aggasāvikā* of **Tissa Buddha.**[1]

[1] Bu. xviii. 22; J. i. 40.

Sudanta.—See **Sudatta** (11).

1. **Sudassana.**—The city of birth of **Sumedha Buddha.**[1]

[1] J. i. 37, 38; Bu. xii. 18.

2. **Sudassana.**—A monastery in **Rammanagara** where **Dīpaṅkara Buddha** lived.[1]

[1] J. i. 11; DhA. i. 69.

3. **Sudassana.**—Younger brother and *Aggasāvaka* of **Sujāta Buddha.**[1]

[1] J. i. 38; Bu. xiii. 25; BuA. 169.

4. **Sudassana.**—A park, at the gates of which **Sujāta Buddha** performed his Twin Miracle[1] before going to **Tusita.**

[1] BuA. 168.

5. **Sudassana.**—The horse ridden by **Atthadassī Buddha** when he left the world.[1]

[1] BuA. 178.

6. **Sudassana.**—The city where **Atthadassī Buddha** preached to the Bodhisatta.[1]

[1] BuA. 180.

7. **Sudassana.**—Father of **Piyadassī Buddha**[1]; but see **Sudatta** (9).

[1] BuA. 172.

8. **Sudassana.**—A palace occupied by **Dhammadassī Buddha**[1] in his last lay life; from this palace he left the world.[1]

[1] Bu. xvi. 14; BuA. 182.

9. **Sudassana.**—A pleasaunce in **Subhavatī** where **Anomadassī Buddha** preached his first sermon.[1]

[1] BuA. 143.

10. **Sudassana.**—A city where **Sobhita Buddha** performed his **Yamaka-pāṭihāriya** under the *cittapāṭali*; King **Jayasena** built for him there a vihāra one league in extent.[1]

[1] BuA. 138.

11. **Sudassana.**—The city in which **Nārada Buddha** died.[1]

[1] Bu. x. 33.

12. **Sudassana.**—A palace occupied by **Revata Buddha** before his renunciation.[1]

[1] Bu. vi. 17.

13. **Sudassana.**—A palace in **Reṇuvatī** occupied by **Vimala** (7).[1]

[1] Ap. i. 61.

14. **Sudassana.**—A deva-king of **Sudassana-pabbata** who was a heretic. **Piyadassī Buddha** visited him, refuted his views, and converted him with his ninety crores of followers.[1]

[1] Bu. xiv. 4 f.; BuA. 173.

15. **Sudassana.**—A *seṭṭhi* whose daughter gave a meal of milk-rice to **Vipassī Buddha.**[1]

[1] BuA. 195.

16. **Sudassana.**—A *nigama* where the daughter of **Piyadassī-seṭṭhi** gave milk-rice to **Sikhī Buddha.**[1]

[1] BuA. 201.

17. **Sudassana.**—A king of **Sarabhavatī.** He was the Bodhisatta in the time of **Vessabhū Buddha.** He later renounced his kingdom and became a monk.[1]

[1] Bu. xxii. 11; BuA. 207; J. i. 42.

18. **Sudassana.**—A city near **Isipatana** where **Koṇāgamana Buddha** preached.[1] Sudassana was an old name for Benares.[2]

[1] BuA. 214.

[2] See J. iv. 119; v. 177.

19. **Sudassana.**—A king of seventy-one kappas ago; a previous birth of **Ekasaṅkhiya Thera.**[1]

[1] Ap. ii. 391.

20. **Sudassana.**—One of the disciples of **Padumuttara Buddha.** He was declared eminent among those who possessed Luck. It was his example which inspired **Sīvalī** to wish for similar honour.[1]

[1] Ap. ii. 493.

21. **Sudassana.**—A park-keeper of **Dhaññavatī;** he gave grass to **Nārada Buddha** for his seat.[1]

[1] BuA. 151.

22. **Sudassana.**—Thirty-four kappas ago there were four kings of this name, previous births of **Madhupiṇḍika Thera.**[1]

[1] Ap. i. 137.

23. **Sudassana.**—A garland-maker of **Haṃsavatī.** He gave a jasmine garland to **Padumuttara Buddha.** He was a former birth of **Muṭṭhipupphiya Thera.**[1]

Ap. i. 142; *cf.* ThagA. i. 127.

24. **Sudassana.**—A Pacceka Buddha of thirty-one kappas ago. **Kuṭajapupphiya (Hārita)**[1] and **Candana Thera**[2] met him in **Cāvala-(Vassala-)pabbata** and paid him homage.

[1] Ap. i. 451; ThagA. i. 87 f.; *cf.* M. iii. 69, 87.

[2] ThagA. i. 395.

25. **Sudassana.**—A Nāga-rāja, son of **Dhataraṭṭha.** He was brother to **Bhūridatta.** See the **Bhūridatta Jātaka.** He is identified with **Sāriputta.**[1]

[1] J. vi. 219; see also J. iv. 182.

26. **Sudassana Thera.**[1]—Evidently another name for **Ugga Thera** (*q.v.*).[2]

[1] Ap. i. 164 f. [2] ThagA. i. 174 f.

27. **Sudassana.**—A vihāra built by the rājā of **Sīlavatī** as an offering to **Bandhura Thera.**[1]

[1] ThagA. i. 208 f.

28. **Sudassana.**—Nephew of **Pasenadi.** The Buddha taught him a stanza to recite whenever Pasenadi sat down to a meal, in order that the king might observe moderation in eating. For this service Pasenadi paid him one hundred kahāpaṇas a day.[1]

[1] S. i. 82; DhA. iii. 264 f. This story is also given at *ibid.*, iv. 15 f., but there the nephew is called **Uttara.**

29. **Sudassana,** called **Sudassana-kūṭa, Sudassanagiri, Sudassanasiluccaya.**—The first of the five mountain ranges surrounding **Anotatta.** It is of a golden colour, two hundred leagues in height, and bent inwards like a crow's beak.[1] **Dīpaṅkara Buddha** held an assembly of his monks there.[2]

[1] SNA. ii. 437; *cf.* 443; AA. ii. 759; J. vi. 125. [2] Bu. ii. 200.

30. **Sudassana.**—The personal attendant of **Piyadassī Buddha.**[1]

[1] ThagA. i. 230.

31. **Sudassana.**—A king of the dynasty of **Mahāsammata.**[1]

[1] Mhv. ii. 5; Dpv. iii. 7.

32. **Sudassana.**—The name given to the city of the gods (*devanagara*).[1]

[1] J. ii. 114; BuA. 67, etc.

Sudassana Sutta.—See **Mahāsudassana Sutta.**

Sudassana-khumbha.—A water-pot, set on **Erāvaṇa,** for the use of **Sakka.** It is thirty leagues in circumference, and above it is a canopy twelve leagues wide made of precious stones. Surrounding it are thirty-two other pots.[1]

[1] DhA. i. 273; SNA. i. 369.

Sudassanamāla.—A place in **Anurādhapura,** near the **Ratanamāla. Koṇāgamana** and **Kassapa Buddhas** preached there on their visits to Ceylon.[1]

[1] Mhv. xv. 124, 158.

1. **Sudassanā.**—Mother of **Atthadassī Buddha.**[1]

[1] Bu. xv. 14; J. i. 39.

2. **Sudassanā.**—Wife of **Revata Buddha,** in his last lay life.[1]

[1] Bu. vi. 18.

3. **Sudassanā.**—See **Sutanū.**

Sudassanārāma.—A monastery in which **Dhammadassī Buddha** held an assembly of his monks. There he declared the eminence of his disciple, **Hārita.**[1]

[1] BuA. 183.

Sudassā.—A Brahma-world; one of the **Suddhāvāsā.** Five kinds of *anāgāmins* are born there.[1]

[1] M. i. 289; D. ii. 52; iii. 237; KhA. 183; VibhA. 521; Kvu. 207.

Sudassī.—A Brahma-world, one of the **Suddhāvāsā.** The inhabitants of this world are friendly with those of **Akaniṭṭhā.**[1] Some *anāgāmins* obtain *parinibbāna* in Sudassī.[2]

[1] D. ii. 52; M. i. 259; D. iii. 237; M. iii. 103; KhA. 120; Vsm. 473. [2] PSA. 319.

1. **Sudāṭha.**—A Pacceka Buddha in a nominal list.[1]

[1] M. iii. 70.

2. **Sudāṭha.**—The lion in the **Vaṇṇāroha Jātaka** (*q.v.*). He is identified with **Sāriputta.**[1]

[1] J. iii. 193.

Sudāyaka.—A king of five kappas ago, a previous birth of **Ajinadāyaka Thera.**[1]

[1] Ap. i. 214.

1. **Sudinna.**—Father of **Piyadassī Buddha**[1]; but see **Sudatta** (9).

[1] J. i. 39.

2. **Sudinna Kalandakaputta.**—A monk who, after being ordained, returned to his former wife and had relations with her, thus becoming

guilty of the first *Pārājikā* offence. When there was a famine in the **Vajji** country, Sudinna went to **Vesāli,** hoping to be kept by his rich relations, to the mutual benefit of both parties. They gave him sixty bowls of rice, which he distributed among his colleagues. When he went to his father's house, in **Kalandakagāma,** he saw a servant girl about to throw away some boiled rice and asked her to put it into his bowl. The girl, recognizing his hands and feet and voice, told his mother of his arrival. Both she and his father visited him as he was eating the rice, and his father took him by the hand and led him home. There he was provided with a seat and asked to eat: but he refused, saying he had already eaten. The next day he was again invited; he went, and they tried to tempt him back to the lay life. His former wife joined in the attempt, but on being addressed by him as "Sister," she fell fainting. Then he begged for his meal, saying that if they desired to give it to him they should do so without worrying him. Later his wife visited him, with his mother, at the **Mahāvana,** and begged that he would give her a son, so that the **Licchavis** might not confiscate their wealth for want of an heir. Sudinna agreed, and had intercourse three times with her. She became pregnant, and in due course a son was born, who was called **Bījaka.** When Sudinna realized what he had done he was filled with remorse, and his colleagues, discovering the reason, reported him to the Buddha, who blamed him greatly.[1]

The Buddha's censure of Sudinna forms the topic of one of the dilemmas of the Milindapañha.[2]

[1] Vin. iii. 11-21; see Sp. i. 270, where Sudinna is held not guilty of the *Pārājikā* offence because he was an *ādikammika*. [2] p. 170 f.

3. **Sudinna.**—Evidently a famous commentator. **Buddhaghosa** quotes[1] him as saying that there is no word of the Buddha which is not a sutta (*asuttaṃ nāma kiṃ buddhavacanaṃ atthi* ?) and thus rejecting the **Jātaka, Paṭisambhidā, Niddesa, Sutta Nipāta, Dhammapada, Itivuttaka, Vimānavatthu, Petavatthu, Thera-** and **Therī-gāthā** and **Apadāna.**

[1] DA. ii. 566; AA. ii. 551.

Sudinnabhāṇavāra.—The second chapter of the **Sutta Vibhaṅga** of the Vinaya.[1]

[1] Vin. iii. 11-21.

Sudūra Sutta.—Four pairs of things which are very far from each other: the sky and the earth, the hither and further shores of the ocean, the positions of sunrise and sunset, the Dhammas of good and bad monks.[1]

[1] A. ii. 50.

1. **Sudeva.**—A king of **Dhaññavatī,** father of **Nārada Buddha.**[1]

[1] Bu. x. 18; but J. i. 37 calls him Sumedha.

2. **Sudeva.**—*Aggasāvaka* of **Maṅgala Buddha.**[1]

[1] J. i. 34; Bu. iv. 23.

3. **Sudeva.**—*Aggasāvaka* of **Sujāta Buddha**[1]; but see **Deva.**

[1] Bu. xiii. 25.

1. **Suddhaka Sutta.**—On the benefits of the four *satipaṭṭhānas.*[1]

[1] S. v. 173.

2. **Suddhaka Sutta.**—On the six sense faculties.[1]

[1] S. v. 203.

3. **Suddhaka Sutta.**—If cultivated and made much of, concentration on in-breathing and out-breathing is of great profit and point.[1]

[1] S. v. 313.

4. **Suddhaka Sutta.**—The four qualities which make the Noble Disciple a *sotāpanna.*[1]

[1] S. v. 403.

Suddhaṭṭhaka Sutta.—The fourth of the **Aṭṭhakavagga** of the **Sutta Nipāta.** The sutta was preached in reference to **Candābha** (*q.v.*).[1] Mere knowledge of various systems of philosophy cannot purify a man, for each sponsor of a system claims superiority for his views, and all go from one teacher to another and are never calm and thoughtful. But the wise, who have understood the Dhamma, are never led away by passion. They do not embrace anything in the world as the highest.[2]

[1] SNA. ii. 523 f. [2] SN. vss. 788-95.

1. **Suddhanā.**—One of the chief lay women followers of **Metteyya Buddha.**[1]

[1] Anāgat. vs. 60.

2. **Suddhanā.**—An eminent lay woman disciple of the Buddha.[1]

[1] A. iv. 347.

Suddhavāsa.—A Pacceka Brahmā who, with **Subrahmā,** went to visit the Buddha, but, finding him in meditation during the noonday heat, went to see a certain Brahmā who was infatuated with his own importance.

They told him of the greater power and majesty of the Buddha, whom they persuaded him to visit.[1]

[1] S. i. 146.

Suddhāvāsakāyikā-devā.—A group of devas, inhabitants of the **Suddhāvāsā,** who appeared before the Buddha and recited three verses in praise of the Saṅgha.[1]

[1] S. i. 26; *cf.* D. ii. 253 f.

Suddhāvāsā.—The "Pure Abodes"; a name given to a group of Brahma-worlds—the five highest Rūpa-worlds—consisting of **Avihā, Atappā, Sudassā, Sudassī** and **Akaniṭṭhā.**[1] There *anāgāmins* are born, and there they attain arahantship; such anāgāmins are divided into twenty-four classes.[2] Bodhisattas are never born there.[3] The Suddhavāsā are described as *buddhānaṃ khandhāvāraṭṭhānasadisā.* Sometimes, for asaṅkheyyas of kappas, when no Buddhas are born, these worlds remain empty.[4] The Buddha is mentioned as having visited the Suddhāvāsā.[5] When a Buddha is about to be born, the inhabitants of the Suddhāvāsā insert a knowledge of the signs of a Great Being in the Vedas and teach this among men in the guise of brahmins, calling such knowledge *buddha-manta.* Men learn it and are thus able to recognize a Great Being.[6] The inhabitants of the Suddhāvāsā know how many Buddhas will be born in any particular kappa by observing the number of lotuses which spring up on the site of the **Bodhi-pallaṅka** when the earth gradually emerges after the destruction of the world.[7] It is the Suddhāvāsā Brahmās who provide the four omens which lead to a Bodhisatta's renunciation in his last lay life.[8]

[1] *E.g.*, D. iii. 237; for details of these see *s.v.*

[2] See, *e.g.*, KhA. 182 f.; *cf.* PSA. 319; Vsm. 710.

[3] SNA. i. 50; BuA. 224.

[4] AA. ii. 808; *cf.* MA. i. 30.

[5] *E.g.*, D. ii. 50.

[6] MA. ii. 761; SNA. ii. 448.

[7] DA. ii. 411.

[8] See, *e.g.*, DA. ii. 455 f.

Suddhika.—A householder, one of the chief supporters of **Metteyya Buddha.**[1]

[1] Anāgat. vs. 60.

Suddhika Vagga.—The first chapter of the **Indriya Saṃyutta.**[1]

[1] S. v. 193-99.

1. **Suddhika Sutta.**—Describes the visit of **Suddhika-Bhāradvāja** to the Buddha.[1] See also **Bhikkhu Sutta** (5).

[1] S. i. 265.

2. **Suddhika Sutta.**—The four kinds of **Nāgas** : the egg-born, the womb-born, the sweat-born, those born parentless.[1]

[1] S. iii. 240.

3. **Suddhika Sutta.**—The same as above, regarding *Supaṇṇas.*[1]

[1] S. iii. 246.

4. **Suddhika Sutta.**—The different kinds of **Gandhabbas** : those that dwell in the fragrance of root-wood, heart-wood, pith, bark, sap, leaves, flowers, savours, scents.[1]

[1] S. iii. 249.

5. **Suddhika Sutta.**—On the five *indriyas*: faith, energy, mindfulness, concentration and insight.[1]

[1] S. v. 193.

6. **Suddhika Sutta.**—On the five *indriyas* : ease, discomfort, happiness (*somanassa*), unhappiness, indifference.[1]

[1] S. v. 207.

7. **Suddhika Sutta** or **Samuddaka Sutta.**—Nothing is permanent.[1]

[1] S. iii. 149.

Suddhika or **Nirāmisa Sutta.**—On the zest that is carnal or not carnal, the pleasure that is carnal or not carnal, the indifference that is carnal or not carnal.[1]

[1] S. iv. 235 f.

Suddhika-Bhāradvāja.—A brahmin who visited the Buddha at Jetavana and stated that a man can be purified only by knowledge of the Vedas. The Buddha answered that it is not knowledge of runes, but the purity of heart of a man, which is important, of a man who has put forth effort to win supreme purity of conduct.[1] Buddhaghosa says[2] that the brahmin was called Suddhika to distinguish him from other Bhāradvājas by the nature of his enquiry.

[1] S. i. 165. [2] SA. i. 179.

Suddhodana.—A **Sākyan** Rājā of **Kapilavatthu** and father of **Gotama Buddha.** He was the son of **Sīhahanu** and **Kaccānā.** His brothers were **Dhotodana, Sakkodana, Sukkodana** and **Amitodana,** and his sisters were **Amitā** and **Pamitā. Māyā** was his chief consort, and, after her death, her sister **Pajāpatī** was raised to her position.[1] When soothsayers

[1] Mhv. ii. 15 f.; Dpv. iii. 45; J. i. 15, etc.

predicted that his son Gotama had two destinies awaiting him, either that of universal sovereignty or of Buddhahood, he exerted his utmost power to provide the prince with all kinds of luxuries in order to hold him fast to household life. It is said[2] that when **Asita,** who was his father's chaplain and his own teacher, visited Suddhodana to see the newly born prince, and paid homage to the infant by allowing his feet to rest on his head, Suddhodana was filled with wonder and himself worshipped the child. And when, at the ploughing ceremony, Suddhodana saw how the *jambu*-tree under which the child had been placed kept its shadow immoveable in order to protect him, and that the child was seated cross-legged in the air, he again worshipped him.[3]

Later, when, in spite of all his father's efforts, the prince had left household life and was practising austerities, news was brought to Suddhodana that his son had died owing to the severity of his penances. But he refused to believe it, saying that his son would never die without achieving his goal.[4] When this was afterwards related to the Buddha, he preached the **Mahādhammapāla Jātaka** (*q.v.*) and showed that in the past, too, Suddhodana had refused to believe that his son could have died even when he was shown the heap of his bones.

When news reached Suddhodana that his son had reached Enlightenment, he sent a messenger to **Veḷuvana** in **Rājagaha** with ten thousand others to invite the Buddha to visit Kapilavatthu. But the messenger and his companions heard the Buddha preach, entered the Order, and forgot their mission. Nine times this happened. On the tenth occasion, Suddhodana sent **Kāḷudāyī** with permission for him to enter the Order on the express condition that he gave the king's invitation to the Buddha. Kāḷudāyī kept his promise and the Buddha visited Kapilavatthu, staying in the **Nigrodhārāma.** There, in reference to a shower of rain that fell, he preached the **Vessantara Jātaka** (*q.v.*). The next day, when Suddhodana remonstrated with the Buddha because he was seen begging in the streets of Kapilavatthu, the Buddha told him that begging was the custom of all Buddhas, and Suddhodana hearing this became a *sotāpanna.* He invited the Buddha to his palace, where he entertained him, and at the end of the meal the Buddha preached to the king, who became a *sakadāgāmin.*[5] He became an *anāgāmin* after hearing the **Mahādhammapāla Jātaka,**[6] and when he was about to die, the Buddha came from Vesāli to see him and preach to him, and Suddhodana became an arahant and died as a lay arahant.[7]

Nanda was Suddhodana's son by **Mahā Pajāpatī,** and he had also a

[2] *E.g.*, J. i. 54.
[3] *Ibid.*, 57 f.
[4] *Ibid.*, 67.
[5] *Ibid.*, 90; *cf.* DhA. iii. 164 f.
[6] DhA. i. 99; J. iv. 55.
[7] ThigA. 141.

daughter called **Sundarī Nandā.** When the Buddha ordained both **Rāhula** and Nanda, Suddhodana was greatly distressed lest other parents should be similarly afflicted, and persuaded the Buddha to establish a rule that none should be ordained without the permission of his parents.[8]

Suddhodana was the Bodhisatta's father in numerous births, but he is specially mentioned as such by name in only a few Jātakas—*e.g.*, **Kaṭṭhahāri, Alīnacitta, Susīma, Bandhanāgāra, Kosambī, Mahādhammapāla, Dasaratha, Hatthipāla, Mahāummagga** and **Vessantara.**

[8] Vin. i. 82 f.

Sudhaja.—A king of four kappas ago, a previous birth of **Vacchagotta Thera.**[1]

[1] ThagA. i. 221; *cf.* Ap. i. 177.

1. **Sudhañña.**—A *seṭṭhi*, father of **Dhaññavatī**[1] (*q.v.*).

[1] BuA. 147.

2. **Sudhañña.**—The city of birth of **Piyadassī Buddha**[1]; but see **Anoma** (11).

[1] Bu. xiv. 15.

Sudhaññaka, Sudhaññavatī.—The city of birth of **Revata Buddha.**[1]

[1] Bu. vi. 16; J. i. 35; BuA. 131 calls it **Sudhaññavatī.**

Sudhaññavatī.—See **Sudhaññaka.**

Sudhanā.—See **Sutanū.**

1. **Sudhamma.**—The city of birth of **Sobhita Buddha.**[1]

[1] Bu. vii. 16; J. i. 35.

2. **Sudhamma.**—A king, father of **Sobhita Buddha.**[1]

[1] Bu. vii. 16.

3. **Sudhamma.**—The park in which **Sobhita Buddha** was born and in which he preached his first sermon.[1]

[1] Bu. vii. 16.

4. **Sudhamma.**—A park in **Sudhammavatī** City, where **Sujāta Buddha** held his first assembly of monks.[1]

[1] BuA. 169.

5. **Sudhamma Thera.**—He lived in **Macchikāsaṇḍa,** in a monastery[1] provided by **Citta.** Citta used to invite Sudhamma to his house for meals. One day **Sāriputta,** at the head of several eminent monks, visited Macchikāsaṇḍa and stayed in the monastery. Citta heard Sāriputta preach,[2] and, at the end of the sermon, invited him and the monks to his house the next day. He also invited Sudhamma, but because he had been invited after the others, Sudhamma refused to go. Early the next day he visited Citta's house to see what offerings had been prepared, and after seeing them, remarked that one thing was missing: sesame-cakes (*tilasaṅgulikā*). Then Citta rebuked him, comparing him to a crow, the offspring of a cock and a crow. Sudhamma left the house in anger, and going to **Sāvatthi,** reported the matter to the Buddha. The Buddha blamed Sudhamma and said that the Saṅgha should pass the *paṭisāraṇīyakamma* on him. Sudhamma, thereupon, went to Macchikāsaṇḍa to ask pardon of Citta, but Citta would not forgive him. The Buddha then gave him a companion, and together they went to Citta, and Sudhamma again asked pardon for his fault. Citta pardoned him and asked to be pardoned himself.[3] Later Sudhamma became an arahant.[4]

[1] The **Ambāṭakārāma** (*q.v.*).
[2] And became a *sakadāgāmin,* says DhA.
[3] Vin. i. 15-20; *cf.* DhA. ii. 74 ff.
[4] AA. i. 210.

Sudhammapura.—The Pāli name for the city of Thaton.[1]

[1] Bode, *op. cit.*, 12.

Sudhammavatī.—A city in whose park **Sujāta Buddha** held the first assembly of his monks.[1]

[1] BuA. 169.

Sudhamma-sāmaṇera.—Given[1] as an example of one whose *paṭisambhidā* became clear (*visada*) from listening to the Dhamma.

[1] VibhA. 389.

1. **Sudhammā.**—An *aggasāvikā* of **Atthadassī Buddha.**[1]

[1] Bu. xv. 20; J. i. 39.

2. **Sudhammā.**—The queen consort of **Reṇu,** king of **Uttarapañcāla.** See the **Somanassa Jātaka.** She is identified with **Mahāmāyā.**[1]

[1] J. i. 453.

3. **Sudhammā.**—One of the four wives of **Magha.** When Magha and his companions were building a rest-house for travellers, they did not wish women to have any share in the work. But Sudhammā bribed

the carpenter, who made a pinnacle of seasoned wood for the building and laid it aside with the words: "*Sudhammā nāma ayaṃ sālā.*" When the time for the erection of the pinnacle came, he told Magha and the others that it was impossible to make a pinnacle then, as it must be of well-seasoned wood. A search was started for a seasoned pinnacle. Sudhammā agreed to give hers if she were allowed a share in the building. The men were at first unwilling, but in the end gave their consent.

After death, Sudhammā was born in **Tāvatiṃsa,** and, because of her merit in the past, there came into being for her **Sudhammā,** the Moot Hall of the Devas, nine hundred leagues in extent.[1] There the Devas hold their meetings on the eighth day of each month, or when the Dhamma is preached, and also all their important festivals and gatherings.[2] All Buddhas preach the Abhidhamma in the Sudhammā-hall. It is said[3] that every devaloka has a *Sudhammā-sabhā*; this title is often used in comparisons to denote a fine hall.

1 DhA. i. 269 f., 274 f.; J. i. 201 f.
2 See, *e.g.*, D. ii. 268; M. ii. 79; S. i. 221; J. vi. 97, 126; Thag. vs. 1198.
3 ThagA. ii. 185.

4. **Sudhammā.**—The sixth daughter of **Kiki,** king of Benares. She is identified sometimes with **Mahāmāyā**[1] and sometimes with **Dhammadinnā.**[2]

1 *E.g.*, J. vi. 481. 2 *E.g.*, Ap. ii. 546, 548; ThigA. 104, 114.

5. **Sudhammā Therī.**—An arahant. She lived in the time of **Kassapa Buddha.** At the Buddha's wish, she took a branch of the Bodhi-tree with her and planted it in the **Mahāsāgaruyyāna** in Ceylon.[1]

1 Dpv. xvii. 19 f.; Mhv. xv. 147 f.

6. **Sudhammā.**—A class of Devas belonging to the *Tāvatiṃsa-deva-nikāya.*[1]

1 VvA. 258.

7. **Sudhammā.**—Mother of **Sobhita Buddha.**[1]

1 Bu. vii. 16; J. i. 35.

Sudhammā-sabhā.—See **Sudhammā** (3).

Sudhāpiṇḍiya Thera.—An arahant. Ninety-four kappas ago he gave mortar (*sudhāpiṇḍa*) for the construction of the *cetiya* of **Siddhattha Buddha.** Thirty kappas ago he was king thirteen times under the name of **Paṭisaṅkhāra.**[1]

1 Ap. i. 133.

Sudhābhojana Jātaka (No. 535). There once lived in Benares a wealthy householder, worth eighty crores. He offered his wealth to the king, who, however, had no need for it; so he gave much away in gifts and was born as **Sakka.** Equally generous were his descendants —**Canda, Suriya, Mātali** and **Pañcasikha.** But the next in descent, Pañcasikha's son, **Maccharikosiya,** became a miser. He stopped all giving and lived in abject poverty. One day, seeing his sub-treasurer eating rice-porridge, he wished for some himself, but, owing to his miserliness, he went in disguise to the river with a little rice and there started to cook it with the help of a slave. Sakka saw this, and, accompanied by Canda and the others, appeared before him disguised as a brahmin. Advancing towards him, Sakka asked him the way to Benares, and, pretending to be deaf, approached the place where the porridge was being cooked and asked for some. Maccharikosiya refused to give him any, but Sakka insisted on reciting to him some stanzas on the value of giving, and then Kosiya agreed to give him a little porridge. One by one the others, also disguised as brahmins, approached, and, in spite of all his efforts, Kosiya was forced to invite them to share his meal. He asked them to fetch small leaves, but in their hands small leaves became large. After the porridge had been served, Pañcasikha assumed the form of a dog, then of a horse of changing colours, and started chasing Kosiya, while the others stood motionless in the air. Kosiya asked how beings could gain such powers, and Sakka explained to him and revealed their identity. Maccharikosiya went back to Benares and gave away his wealth in charity. Later he became a hermit and lived in a hut.

At that time the four daughters of Sakka—**Āsā, Saddhā, Sirī** and **Hirī**— went to **Anotatta** to play in the water. There they saw **Nārada** under a *pāricchattaka*-flower, which served him as a sunshade, and each asked him for the flower. Nārada said he would give it to the best of them, and referred them to Sakka. Sakka sent (by **Mātali**) a cup of ambrosia (*sudhābhojana*) to Kosiya, and said that whichever of his daughters succeeded in persuading Kosiya to share with her his drink would be adjudged the best. He listened to all their claims and decided in favour of Hirī. Sakka, wishing to know why he decided thus, sent Mātali in his chariot to ask him. While Mātali was yet speaking to him, Kosiya died and was reborn in Tāvatiṃsa. Sakka gave him Hirī as wife and also a share of the kingdom of Tāvatiṃsa.

The story was told in reference to a monk of **Sāvatthi,** who was so generous that he would give away his own food and drink and so starve. He is identified with **Maccharikosiya, Uppalavaṇṇā** with Hirī, **Anuruddha** with Pañcasikha, **Ānanda** with Mātali, **Kassapa** with Suriya, **Moggallāna** with Canda, **Sāriputta** with Nārada, and Sakka with the Buddha himself.[1]

[1] J. v. 382-412.

Sudhāmuṇḍakavāsī-dahara.—Given as an example of one who came to grief through hearing a woman's voice.[1]

[1] AA. i. 15.

Sunakkhatta.—A **Licchavi** prince of **Vesāli.** He was, at one time, a member of the Order and the personal attendant of the Buddha (*anibaddhaupaṭṭhāka*), but was later converted to the views of **Korakkhattiya** and went about defaming the Buddha, saying that he had nothing superhuman and was not distinguished from other men by preaching a saving faith: that the doctrine preached by him did not lead to the destruction of sorrow, etc. Sāriputta, on his alms rounds in Vesāli, heard all this and reported it to the Buddha, who thereupon preached the **Mahāsīhanāda Sutta**[1] and the **Lomahaṃsa Jātaka.**[2] The **Sunakkhatta Sutta**[3] was evidently preached to Sunakkhatta before he joined the Order, while the **Pāṭika Sutta**[4] gives an account of his dissatisfaction.

His grievance was that the Buddha showed no mystic superhuman wonders, that he had not shown him the beginning of things. The Buddha reminded him that he had not promised to do any of these things, and that, at one time, Sunakkhatta had been loud in his praise of the Buddha and the Dhamma. The Buddha warned him that people would say he had left the Order because its discipline had proved too hard for him. The Buddha had told him that Korakkhattiya, whom he so much admired, would be born after death among the **Kālakañjaka Asuras** within seven days. It happened as the Buddha prophesied, and the dead body of Kora declared that he was right. But even so, Sunakkhatta was not convinced.

Later he transferred his allegiance to **Kandaramasaka,** who died, as the Buddha had prophesied, fallen from grace and fame. The next teacher to win the admiration of Sunakkhatta was **Pāṭikaputta,** and Sunakkhatta wished the Buddha to pay honour to him. But the Buddha quoted to Sunakkhatta the words of **Ajita,** the Licchavi general who had been born in **Tāvatimsa,** to the effect that Pāṭikaputta was "a liar and a cheat," and was later able to prove that these words were true. But Sunakkhatta did not return to the Order. He had probably remained in it for several years before actually leaving it. For we find in the **Mahāli Sutta**[5] the Licchavi **Oṭṭhaddha** relating to the Buddha how Sunakkhatta had come to him *three* years after joining the Order, claiming that he could see divine forms but could not hear heavenly sounds. Buddhaghosa explains[6] that he could not acquire the power

[1] M. i. 68 ff.; the Buddha was, at this time, eighty years old (M. i. 82).

[2] J. i. 389 f.; see also J. iv. 95.

[3] M. ii. 252 ff.

[4] D. iii. 1 ff.

[5] *Ibid.*, i. 152.

[6] DA. i. 311.

of hearing divine sounds because in a previous birth he had ruptured the ear-drum of a holy monk and made him deaf. The Sutta itself gives[7] as the reason that he had only developed one-sided concentration of mind.

Sunakkhatta is identified with **Kāṇāriṭṭha** of the **Bhūridatta Jātaka.**[8]

[7] D. i. 153. [8] J. vi. 219.

Sunakkhatta Sutta.—Preached at **Vesālī** to **Sunakkhatta,** before he joined the Order. He asks the Buddha if the monks have really won all they profess or if some of them are extravagant in their professions. The Buddha explains that some of the monks are worldly, their hearts set on material things; others are free from worldly bondage, their hearts set on permanence; yet others on various *jhānas*; while the last have their hearts set on *nibbāna*; all these will act according to their beliefs. The Buddha then explains further, using the simile of a surgeon: a patient is wounded by a poisoned arrow, even when the surgeon has removed the poison the patient must go slowly till the wound is healed. Craving is the arrow; the wound represents the six sense organs within; ignorance is the poison; mindfulness is the surgeon's probing; Noble Understanding is the surgeon's knife; and the Tathāgata the surgeon.[1]

[1] M. ii. 252-61.

Sunakha.—One of the **Mahānirayas.** Nālikīra was born there.[1]

[1] J. v. 145.

Sunakha Jātaka (No. 242).—There was in Benares a man who owned a dog which had been fattened on rice. A villager saw the dog, and, having bought it from its master, took it away on a lead. Arrived at the edge of the forest, he entered a hut, tied up the dog, and lay down to sleep. The Bodhisatta, seeing the dog, asked him why he did not bite through the lead and escape. " I am going to," answered the dog, " as soon as all are asleep." And he did so.

The story was told in reference to a dog belonging to a water-carrier who used to be fed near the **Ambalakoṭṭhaka** in Jetavana. Once a villager saw it and bought it from the water-carrier and took it away on a chain. The dog followed quietly, and the man, thinking it to be fond of him, let it loose. The dog ran away and returned to its old home. The two dogs were identical.[1]

[1] J. ii. 246-8.

1. **Sunanda.**—Father of **Padumuttara Buddha.**[1] He became an ascetic and the Buddha preached to him. In this life he was **Puṇṇa Mantāniputta.**[2]

[1] DhA. i. 417; but J. i. 37 and Bu. xi. 19 call him Ānanda. [2] ThagA. i. 361 f.

2. **Sunanda Khattiya.**—Father of **Koṇḍañña Buddha.**[1]

[1] J. i. 30; Bu. iii. 25.

3. **Sunanda.**—A village, where **Yasodharā** gave a meal of milk-rice to **Koṇḍañña Buddha.**[1]

[1] BuA. 108.

4. **Sunanda.**—An **Ājīvaka** who gave grass for his seat to **Koṇḍañña Buddha.**[1]

[1] BuA. 108.

5. **Sunanda.**—An **Ājīvaka** who gave grass for his seat to **Sujāta Buddha.**[1]

[1] BuA. 168.

6. **Sunanda.**—An **Ajīvaka** who gave grass for his seat to **Dīpaṅkara Buddha.**[1]

[1] BuA. 68.

7. **Sunanda.**—The park where **Anomadassī Buddha** was born.[1]

[1] BuA. 141.

8. **Sunanda.**—A disciple of **Dhammadassī Buddha.**[1]

[1] Ap. i. 196.

9. **Sunanda.**—A palace of **Vipassī Buddha,** in his last lay life.[1]

[1] Bu. xx. 24.

10. **Sunanda.**—A brahmin in the time of **Padumuttara Buddha;** a former birth of **Nīta (Pupphachadanīya) Thera.**[1]

[1] ThagA. i. 181; Ap. i. 166.

11. **Sunanda.**—A brahmin, who gave an umbrella to **Sāriputta.**[1]

[1] Ap. i. 266.

12. **Sunanda.**—Son of King **Añjasa.** Once, while riding the elephant **Sirika,** he saw the Pacceka Buddha **Devala,** and drove the elephant against him. He was a previous birth of **Upāli.**[1]

[1] ThagA. i. 367 f.

13. **Sunanda.**—A king of thirty-seven kappas ago, a previous birth of **Akkanta-Saññaka.**[1]

[1] Ap. i. 212.

14. **Sunanda.**—A charioteer of the king of **Kāsi,** in the **Mūgapakkha Jātaka.**[1] He is identified with **Sāriputta.**[2]

[1] J. vi. 10 ff. [2] p. 30.

15. **Sunanda.**—A charioteer of King **Sivi** in the **Ummadantī Jātaka** (*q.v.*). He is identified with **Ānanda.**[1]

[1] J. v. 227.

16. **Sunanda.**—A king of **Surabhi** in the time of **Maṅgala Buddha;** the Buddha preached to him.[1]

[1] Bu. iv. 6; BuA. 119 f.

17. **Sunanda.**—A city. See **Naradeva** (2).

Sunandaka.—The residence of an **Ājīvaka** who gave grass for his seat to **KoṇḍaññaBuddha.**[1]

[1] BuA. 108.

Sunandavatī.—A city where **Sumana Buddha** performed the **Yamaka-pāṭihāriya.**[1] King **Uggata** built there, for **Sobhita Buddha,** a vihara named **Surinda.**[2] In this city **Tissa Buddha** died in the **Sunandārāma.**[3]

[1] BuA. 128. [2] *Ibid.*, 139. [3] *Ibid.*, 192.

1. **Sunandā.**—An *aggasāvikā* of **Dīpaṅkara Buddha.**[1]

[1] J. i. 29; Bu. ii. 214.

2. **Sunandā.**—Mother of **Dhammadassī Buddha.**[1]

[1] J. i. 39; Bu. xvi. 13.

3. **Sunandā.**—Wife of **Kassapa Buddha,** in his last lay life.[1] She gave him milk-rice before his Enlightenment.[2]

[1] Bu. xxv. 36. [2] BuA. 218.

4. **Sunandā.**—One of the chief women supporters of **Atthadassī Buddha.**[1]

[1] Bu. xv. 21.

5. **Sunandā.**—One of the chief women supporters of **Kakusandha Buddha.**[1]

[1] Bu. xxiii. 22.

6. **Sunandā.**—Wife of **Ekarājā.**[1] See the **Khaṇḍahāla Jātaka.**

[1] J. vi. 134.

7. **Sunandā.**—A garland-maker's daughter of **Rājagaha.** She was a *sotāpanna* and daily visited the *thūpa* built by **Ajātasattu** in **Rājagaha,** offering to it flowers and garlands sent by her father. On fast days she would go of her own accord. When she died, she was reborn in **Tāvatiṃsa** in the retinue of **Sakka,** and when questioned by him, recounted her actions in the past. Sakka related the story to **Vaṅgīsa,** who, in his turn, told it to the *saṅgītikārakas.*[1]

[1] Vv. iii. 9; VvA. 170 f.

8. **Sunandā.**—A celestial musician or a musical instrument.[1]

[1] VvA. 93, 96, 211, 372.

1. **Sunandārāma.**—A monastery in which **Dīpaṅkara Buddha** died.[1]

[1] BuA. 68.

2. **Sunandārāma.**—A monastery in which **Tissa Buddha** died.[1]

[1] BuA. 192; but Bu. xviii. 28 calls it **Nandārāma.**

Sunāga.—The son of a brahmin of **Nāḷakagāma,** a friend of **Sāriputta** before the latter left the world. Later, Sunāga heard the Buddha preach, entered the Order, and attained arahantship.

In the time of **Sikhī Buddha,** thirty-one kappas ago, he was a brahmin versed in the Vedas, and lived in a forest hut near Mount **Vasabha** as teacher of three thousand pupils. One day he met Sikhī Buddha, and, knowing by the signs on his body that he was a Buddha of infinite wisdom, he was suffused with joy, as a result of which he was born after death in the *deva*-world. Twenty-seven kappas ago he was a king named **Siridhara.**[1]

He is evidently identical with **Rahosaññaka** of the Apadāna.[2]

[1] Thag. vs. 85; ThagA. i. 182. [2] Ap. i. 166 f.

Sunāparanta.—A country in which was the port of **Suppāraka,** birthplace of **Puṇṇa Thera.** From there he went with a caravan to **Sāvatthi,** and, after hearing the Buddha preach, entered the Order. Later, obtaining the Buddha's permission, he returned to Sunāparanta.[1] There he attained arahantship, and five hundred men and five hundred women became lay followers of the religion. Under his direction they built

[1] ThagA. i. 158.

a **Gandhakuti,** called **Candanasālā,** and Puṇṇa, wishing the Buddha to be present at the dedication festival, sent a flower through the air to the Buddha at Savatthi as invitation.

The Buddha accepted this invitation and went to Sunāparanta with four hundred and ninety-nine arahants, including **Kuṇḍadhāna** and **Ānanda,** all in pinnacled palanquins, provided by **Vissakamma,** acting under orders from **Sakka.** On the way the Buddha stopped at **Saccabaddhapabbata,** where he converted the *tāpasa* of the mountain, who became an arahant and travelled on with the party in the five hundredth palanquin. The Buddha spent the day in Sunāparanta, and, on his way back, stopped on the banks of the river **Nammadā.** There the Nāgarājā paid him homage, and the Buddha left his footprint in the Nāga's abode for him to worship.[2]

The people of Sunāparanta were reported as being fierce and violent.[3]

Sunāparanta was also the birthplace of **Culla-Puṇṇa** and **Isidinna (Isidatta)** (*q.v.*).

Sunāparanta is probably identical with **Aparanta;** the Burmese, however, identify it with the country on the right bank of the Irrawaddy River, near Pagan.[4]

[2] MA. ii. 101 f.; SA. iii. 176; according to the latter account the Buddha spent seven days in Sunāparanta, at the **Maṅkulārāma.**

[3] M. iii. 268; S. iv. 61 f.

[4] Sās. Introd., p. ix.

Sunāma.—A minister of Aṅgati, king of **Mithilā.** See the **Mahānāradakassapa Jātaka.** He is identified with **Bhaddaji.**[1]

[1] J. vi. 255.

Sunāri.—A Kāliṅga princess; see **Sundarī.**

Sunikkhamma.—Sixty-seven kappas ago there were seven kings of this name, previous births of **Sattāhapabbajita Thera.**[1]

[1] Ap. i. 242.

Suniddā.—See **Niddā.**

Sunidha.—A minister of **Magadha,** who, with **Vassakāra,** was in charge of the fortifications of **Pāṭaligāma,** built in order to repel the **Vajjis.** These two are always mentioned together. They invited the Buddha to a meal, and, after his departure, named the gate by which he had left the city **Gotamadvāra,** and the ford by which he crossed the Ganges, **Gotamatittha.**[1]

[1] Vin. i. 228 f.; D. ii. 86 f.; Ud. viii. 6.

Sunimmita.—A devaputta, king of the **Nimmānarati**-world.[1] **Visākhā** became his wife, after her birth among the **Nimmānarati**-devā.[2]

[1] J. i. 81; S. iv. 280; A. iv. 243; *cf.* Dvy. 140. [2] VvA. 189.

Sunisāvimānavatthu.—The story of a woman of **Sāvatthi**. She had no family, and one day, seeing an arahant there begging for alms, she gave him a piece of cake (*pūvabhāgaṃ*). After death she was born in **Tāvatiṃsa**, where Moggallāna learnt her story.[1]

[1] Vv. i. 13; VvA. 61.

Sunīta Thera.—He belonged to a family of flower-scavengers in **Rājagaha** and eked out a miserable existence as road-sweeper. One day the Buddha saw that Sunīta was destined for arahantship and visited him at dawn, as he was sweeping the street and collecting the scraps in his basket. Seeing the Buddha, he was filled with awe, and, finding no place to stand, stood stiffly against a wall. The Buddha approached him and asked if he would like to be a monk. He expressed great joy, and the Buddha ordained him with the "*ehi bhikkhu*" *pabbajjā*. Then he took Sunīta to the vihāra and taught him a subject of meditation, by which he won arahantship. Then many men and gods came to pay homage to him, and Sunīta preached to them on his way of attainment.

In the past he had spoken disparagingly of a Pacceka Buddha.[1]

[1] Thag. vss. 620–31; ThagA. i. 540 f.

1. **Sunetta.**—*Aggasāvaka* of **Sobhita Buddha.**[1] He was the Buddha's stepbrother and his first convert.[2]

[1] Bu. vii. 21; J. i. 35. [2] BuA. 137.

2. **Sunetta Thera.**—Attendant of **Dhammadassī Buddha.**[1]

[1] J. i. 39; Bu. xvi. 18.

3. **Sunetta.**—A **Pacceka Buddha.** A man who had learnt the art of pelting stones with great skill, from the cripple of the **Sālittaka Jātaka** (*q.v.*), looking for a target for testing his skill, saw Sunetta entering the city for alms and aimed a pebble at his ear. The pebble went into one ear and out at the other, and the Pacceka Buddha died after suffering great pain. Men, who saw this, killed the stone-thrower, and, after a sojourn in Avici, he became a sledgehammer ghost in **Gijjhakūṭa.**[1]

On another occasion, the son of **Kitavassa,** king of Benares, saw Sunetta begging for alms, and, angered that he did not do him homage, took the begging bowl from Sunetta's hand and dashed it to the ground.[2]

[1] DhA. ii. 71 f.; Pv. iv. 16; PvA. 283 f. [2] Pv. iii. 2; iv. 7; PvA. 177 f., 264.

4. **Sunetta.**—A teacher of old. He had numerous disciples, and those who followed his teachings were reborn in the Brahma-world and in various other worlds. Then Sunetta, seeing that some among his disciples were as good as himself, developed *mettā* to a much greater degree; but even so, he could not free himself from birth, old age, etc. It was because he had not comprehended Noble Conduct, Noble Concentration, Noble Wisdom, Noble Release.[1]

[1] A. iv. 103 f.; he is referred to at A. iii. 371; iv. 135.

Sunetta Sutta.—Contains a list of teachers, including **Sunetta** (*q.v.*), who taught their followers the way to the **Brahma**-world.[1]

[1] A. iv. 135.

Sunettā.—A brahmin maiden of **Asadisagāma,** who gave a meal of milk-rice to **Siddhattha Buddha.**[1]

[1] BuA. 185.

Sunela.—A king of one hundred and twenty-three kappas ago, a former birth of **Muṭṭhipūjaka Thera.**[1]

[1] Ap. i. 201.

1. **Sundara.**—A city where **Kassapa Buddha** performed the **Yamaka-pāṭihāriya** at the foot of an *asana*-tree,[1] and **Koṇāgamana Buddha** under a *mahāsāla*-tree.[2]

[1] BuA. 218. 2. *Ibid.*, 214.

2. **Sundara.**—A monk of **Rājagaha.** One day, as he walked through the street, a woman asked him to stop for a moment that she might worship him, and, raising the end of his robe, took his penis into her mouth. A doubt arose in his mind as to whether any blame attached to him and he consulted the Buddha, who said that as Sundara had not acquiesced in the act, he was blameless.[1]

[1] Vin. iii. 36; *cf.* the story of St. Anthony.

3. **Sundara.**—A monk who, with five hundred others of the same name, was present at the Foundation Ceremony of the **Mahā Thūpa.**[1]

[1] MṬ. 522.

Sundarananda.—See **Nanda.**

Sundarapaṇḍu.—A Damiḷa chief of South India. An ally of **Kula-sekhara.**[1]

[1] Cv. lxxvi. 126, 174.

Sundarapabbata.—See **Subhagiri.**

Sundarasamudda Thera.—He was the son of a wealthy *seṭṭhi* of **Rājagaha** and was called Sundara on account of his beauty. While yet young, he realized the majesty of the Buddha, when he visited Rājagaha, and Samudda entered the Order. He once went to **Sāvatthi,** where he stayed with a friend, learning how to practise insight. On a festival day his mother thought of him and wept, seeing the sons of other families enjoying themselves with their wives. A courtezan offered to entice him back, and the mother promised that should she succeed she would make her Samudda's wife and give her many gifts. The courtezan went, well attended, to Sāvatthi and took lodgings in a house to which Samudda frequently came for alms. She saw that he was well seen to and showed herself to him, decked and adorned and wearing golden slippers. One day, slipping off her sandals at the door, she saluted him with clasped hands as he passed, and invited him in with seductive manner.

Then the thera, realizing that the heart of a worldling is unsteady, made then and there a supreme effort and attained arahantship.[1]

According to the Dhammapada Commentary,[2] Samudda accepted the invitation of the courtezan and went with her to the top floor of her seven-storeyed house. There she provided him with a seat and practised her wiles. Samudda suddenly realized what he was doing and was much distressed.

The Buddha, seated in **Jetavana,** forty-five leagues away, saw what was happening and smiled. On being asked by **Ānanda** why he smiled, he said: "A battle royal is being waged between Sundarasamudda and a courtezan, but Samudda will win." So saying, he sent forth a ray of light to Samudda and preached to him. At the end of the sermon Samudda became an arahant.

[1] Thag. vss. 459-65; ThagA. i. 467 f.

[2] DhA. iv. 194 ff.; *cf.* the story of **Cullapiṇḍapātikatissa.**

Sundarika Sutta.—Describes the meeting between the Buddha and **Sunadarika-Bhāradvāja** (*q.v.*).[1]

[1] S. i. 167 f.

Sundarika-Bhāradvāja.—A brahmin, one of the **Bhāradvājas.** Once, when he was performing Fire-rites on the banks of the **Sundarikā,** he looked round to see if there were anyone to whom he could give what was left over from the oblations. He saw the Buddha seated under a tree,[1] his head covered; he approached him with the oblation and a water pitcher and addressed him. The Buddha uncovered his head. The sight of the shaven head at first made Sundarika draw back, but, realizing that some brahmins too were shaved, he questioned the Buddha about his birth. The Buddha explained to him that the important thing was not birth, but the leading of a good life. The brahmin was pleased and offered him the oblation, but the Buddha refused it, saying that he did not accept presents for chanting verses. He advised Sundarika to throw the food into the water, where there were no creatures, for who could digest food which had once been offered to a Buddha? The brahmin followed this advice and saw the water hiss and seethe with steam and smoke. Alarmed and with hair on end, he worshipped the Buddha, who preached to him. Sundarika entered the Order and became an arahant.[2]

Sundarika-Bhāradvāja was so called from his habit of offering oblations on the banks of the Sundarikā.[3] He is also mentioned[4] as meeting the Buddha on the banks of the **Bāhukā** and asking him whether he bathed in that river, because it had the reputation of cleansing sins. The Buddha answered that purity was not to be won that way and preached to him the **Vatthūpama Sutta** (*q.v.*).

According to the Dhammapada Commentary,[5] Sundarika was the brother of **Akkosaka** and **Bilaṅgika Bhāradvāja.** There he is mentioned as having abused the Buddha in much the same way as **Akkosaka**.

[1] To rouse the brahmin's curiosity and to prevent him from being repelled by the sight of a shaven head, says the Commentary.

[2] S. i. 167 f. The account of the meeting between the Buddha and Sundarika is given in the Sutta Nipāta too (p. 79 f.), but there the details differ greatly, though the topic of discussion is the same. Several additional verses are attributed to the Buddha regarding the true "sacrifice." The Commentary calls the SN. discourse the **Pūraḷāsa Sutta** (SNA. ii. 400).

[3] SA. i. 181 f.

[4] M. i. 39 f.

[5] DhA. iv. 163.

Sundarika-Bhāradvāja Sutta.—Describes the meeting between the Buddha and **Sundarika-Bhāradvāja** (*q.v.*). The Commentary calls it the **Pūraḷāsa Sutta.**[1]

[1] SN. p. 79 f.; SNA. ii. 400.

1. **Sundarikā.**—A river in **Kosala,** reputed to be efficacious in washing away sins.[1] There **Sundarika-Bhāradvāja** held sacrifices in honour of Agni and met the Buddha during such a sacrifice.[2]

[1] M. i. 39.

[2] S. i. 167; SN. p. 79, etc.

2. **Sundarikā.**—See **Sundarī** (3).

1. **Sundarī.**—An *aggasāvikā* of **Anomadassī Buddha.**[1]

[1] J. i. 36; Bu. viii. 23.

2. **Sundarī Therī.**—She was born in Benares as the daughter of the brahmin **Sujāta** (see **Sujāta** 9). When her father joined the Order at **Mithilā** and sent his charioteer home, Sundarī, with her mother's consent, gave all away and joined the Order, attaining arahantship in due course. Then one day, with the leave of her teacher, she left Benares, accompanied by a large number of nuns, and, visiting the Buddha at **Sāvatthi,** uttered her "lion's roar."

Thirty-one kappas ago she was born in a clansman's family, and seeing **Vessabhu Buddha** begging for alms, gave him a ladleful of food.

Fifty times she became the wife of **Cakkavattis.**[1]

[1] Thig. vss. 326-332; ThigA. 228 f.

3. **Sundarī, Sundarikā.**—A **Paribbājikā.** She listened to the persuasions of her colleagues, the heretics, and would be seen in the evenings going towards **Jetavana** with garlands, perfumes, fruits, etc. When asked where she was going, she would reply that she was going to spend the night in the Buddha's cell. She would then spend it in a neighbouring monastery of the Paribbājakas and be seen again early in the morning coming from the direction of Jetavana. After some days, the heretics hired some villains to kill Sundarī and hide her body under a heap of rubbish near Jetavana. Then they raised a hue and cry and reported to the king that Sundarī was missing. A search was made, and her body was found near the **Gandhakuṭi** of the Buddha. Placing the body on a litter, they went about the streets of the city crying: "Behold the deeds of the Sākyan monks!" As a result, the monks were subjected to great insults in the streets. For seven days the Buddha stayed in the Gandhakuṭi, not going to the city for alms, and **Ānanda** even suggested that they should go to another city. But the Buddha pointed out to him the absurdity of running away from a false report, and said that in seven days the truth would be known. The king employed spies, who found the murderers quarrelling among themselves after strong drink. They were seized and brought before the king, where they confessed their crime. The king sent for the heretics and compelled them to retract their accusations against the Buddha and his monks and to confess their own wickedness. They were then punished for murder.[1]

It is said[2] that once the Bodhisatta was a pleasure-seeker named

[1] Ud. iv. 8; UdA. 256 ff.; DhA. iii. 474 f.; SNA. ii. 528 f.; J. ii. 415 f.

[2] Ap. i. 299; UdA. 263.

Munāli. One day he saw **Surabhi,** a Pacceka Buddha, putting on his outer robe just outside the city. Near by a woman was walking, and Munāli said in jest, "Look, this recluse is no celibate, but a rake." It was this utterance of the Bodhisatta that brought to the Buddha, as retribution, the disgrace in connection with Sundarī.

The **Duṭṭhaka Sutta** (*q.v.*) and the **Maṇisūkara Jātaka** (*q.v.*) were preached in this connection.

4. **Sundarī.**—A **Kāliṅga** princess, kinswoman of **Tilokasundarī.** She married **Vikkamabāhu.**[1] *v.l.* **Sūnarī.**

[1] Cv. lix. 49; for the correctness of the name see Cv. *Trs.* i. 213, n. 2.

1. **Sudarī-Nandā.**—Younger sister of **Thullanandā ;** she had two other sisters, **Nandā** and **Nandavatī. Sāḷha Migāranattā** (*q.v.*) seduced her, and she was proclaimed guilty of a *Parājikā* offence.[1] She was also blamed for her greediness as regards food.[2]

[1] Vin. iv. 211 f. [2] *Ibid.*, 232 f., 234.

2. **Sundarī-Nandā.**—A Therī. She was the daughter of **Suddhodana** and **Mahāpajāpatī** and sister of **Nanda Thera.** Seeing that most of her kinsmen had joined the Order, she too became a nun, not from faith, but from love of her kin. Being intoxicated with her own beauty, she did not go to see the Buddha lest he should rebuke her. The rest of her story is very similar to that of **Abhirūpa Nandā** (*q.v.*). The Buddha preached to her and she became a *sotāpanna.* He then gave her a topic of meditation, and she, developing insight, became an arahant. Later she was declared foremost among nuns in power of meditation, an eminence which she had resolved to obtain in the time of **Padumuttara Buddha.**[1]

She seems to have been called **Rūpanandā**[2] too; there seems to have been some confusion in the legends of the different Therīs named **Nandā.**

[1] Thag. vs. 82-6; ThigA. 80 f.; Ap. ii. 572 f.; A. i. 25; AA. i. 198 f. [2] *Ibid.*, 198.

Suṇhāta-pariveṇa.—A *pariveṇa* built by **Devānampiyatissa** on the bank of the bathing-tank of **Mahinda.**[1]

[1] Mhv. xv. 207.

Supajjalita.—Twenty-seven kappas ago there were seven kings of this name, previous births of **Citapūjaka Thera.**[1]

[1] Ap. i. 244.

Supaṇṇa.—See **Garuḍa.**

Supaṇṇa Saṃyutta.—The thirtieth section of the **Saṃyutta Nikāya.**[1]

[1] S. iii. 246-9.

1. **Supatta.**—The Bodhisatta born as a crow; see the **Supatta Jātaka.**

2. **Supatta.**—A king of the vultures and son of the Bodhisatta. See the **Gijjha Jātaka** (No. 427).

3. **Supatta.**—One of the five horses of King **Kappina.** Only the king rode Supatta, while messengers were allowed to ride the others.[1]

[1] DhA. ii. 117.

Supatta Jātaka (No. 292).—The Bodhisatta was once a crow, named **Supatta,** king of eighty-four thousand crows. His chief mate was **Suphassā** and his chief companion **Sumukha.** One day, while Supatta and Suphassā were out looking for food, they noticed that the king's cook had prepared a host of dishes and had left some of them out in the open to cool. Suphassā sniffed at the food but said nothing. The next day, however, she wished to stay behind and taste some of the king's food. Supatta consulted his captain, and they went with a large number of crows, whom they set in groups round the kitchen. As the cook was taking the dishes on a pingo, Sumukha, as arranged, attacked him with beak and claw and made him drop them. Then the crows ate their fill and flew away with food for Supatta and Suphassā. Sumukha was caught and taken before the king, who has seen what had happened. When questioned by the king, he told him the whole story and said that he would gladly lose his life for his king, Supatta. The king sent for Supatta and listened to his preaching, and, thereafter protecting all creatures, practised the good life.

The story was told in reference to **Sāriputta,** who had obtained from **Pasenadi** a meal of red rice and new ghee, flavoured with red fish, because he had been informed by **Rāhula** that **Bimbādevī (Rāhulamātā)** suffered from gastric trouble and would be cured by this food.

The king of Benares is identified with **Ānanda,** Sumukha with **Sāriputta,** and Suphassā with **Rāhulamātā.**[1]

[1] J. ii. 433-6.

Supatiṭṭha-cetiya.—A shrine near the **Laṭṭhivanuyyāna** in **Rājagaha.**[1]

[1] Vin. i. 35.

Supatiṭṭhita.—A **Paccека Buddha,** mentioned in a nominal list.[1]

[1] M. iii. 70.

Supabbā.—An *upāsikā* of **Rājagaha.** She held the view that one who offered herself for sexual intercourse gave the supreme gift.[1]

[1] Vin. iii. 39.

Supassa.—The name of **Mount Vepulla** in the time of **Kassapa Buddha**[1] (*v.l.* **Suphassa.**) The people of **Rājagaha** at that time were called **Suppiyā.**[1]

[1] S. ii. 192.

1. **Supāricariya.**—Three kappas ago there were thirty-four kings of this name, previous births of **Samitigutta** (**Jātipūjaka**) **Thera.**[1]

[1] ThagA. i. 176; Ap. i. 154.

2. **Supāricariya Thera.**—Evidently identical with **Khitaka Thera** (*q.v.*).[1]

[1] Ap. i. 181; ThagA. i. 209.

Supina Sutta.—The five great dreams which the Buddha had on the night before his Enlightenment.[1]

[1] A. iii. 240 f.; they are referred to J. i. 69.

Supuṭakapūjaka Thera.—An arahant. Ninety-one kappas ago he saw **Vipassī Buddha** begging for alms and gave him a packet of salt (? *loṇasupuṭaka*).[1]

[1] Ap. i. 284.

Suppagedha.—A **Yakkha,** to be invoked by followers of the Buddha in time of need.[1]

[1] D. iii. 205.

Suppati Sutta.—Once, in **Veḷuvana,** the Buddha had been walking about for the greater part of the night; then having washed his feet and entered his cell, he lay down to sleep, and **Māra** appeared and asked him why he slept. The Buddha replied that his wishes were the sole arbiter in this matter.[1]

[1] S. i. 107 f.

1. **Suppatiṭṭhita.**—A ford, across the **Nerañjarā,** where the Buddha bathed just before eating the meal given by **Sujātā.**[1]

[1] J. i. 70; BuA. 7.

2. **Suppatiṭṭhita.**—A *nigrodha*-tree belonging to king **Koravya.** The king and his court ate the first portion of the fruit—as big as pipkins

and sweet; the army had the second portion, the town and country people the third, recluses and holy men the fourth, and birds and beasts the last. None guarded its fruit, and none would hurt another in order to obtain its fruit.

One day there came a man who ate his fill of the fruit, broke a branch, and went his way. The deva of the tree was angry, and the tree bore no more fruit. Koravya visited **Sakka** and consulted him. Sakka sent a squall to punish the deva and made the deva appear before him full of repentance. Then Sakka warned him to keep the *Rukkhadhamma*, which was that various people take and make use of various parts of a tree; it is not for the deva of the tree to mope and pine on that account.[1]

[1] A. iii. 369 f.

3. **Suppatiṭṭhita.**—The minister who traced the foundations of the **Mahā Thūpa.** His father was **Nandisena** and his mother **Sumanādevī.**[1]

[1] Dpv. xix. 8; MṬ. 528.

4. **Suppatiṭṭhita.**—A king of sixty-five kappas ago, a previous birth of **Gosīsanikkhepa Thera.**[1]

[1] Ap. i. 245.

Suppatīta.—King of **Anoma** or **Anupama ;** father of **Vessabhū Buddha.**[1]

[1] J. i. 42; Bu. xxxii. 18; D. ii. 7.

1. **Suppabuddha.**—A **Sākyan** prince, son of **Añjana** and **Yasodharā.** He had a brother, **Daṇḍapāni,** and two sisters, **Māyā** and **Pajāpatī.** He married **Amitā** and had two children, **Bhaddakaccānā** and **Devadatta.** Thus he was father-in-law to the Buddha.[1] It is said[2] that he was offended with the Buddha for deserting his daughter and for being hostile to Devadatta. One day he took strong drink and blocked the Buddha's path, refusing to move in spite of the repeated requests of the monks. The Buddha thereupon turned back. **Ānanda** seeing the Buddha smile and enquiring the reason for the smile, was told that, at the end of seven days, Suppabuddha would be swallowed up by the earth at the foot of his stairs. Suppabuddha overheard this, and had all his belongings carried to the seventh storey of his house. He removed the stairway, closed all doors, and set a strong guard. On the seventh day a state charger belonging to Suppabuddha broke loose. None could manage him except Suppabuddha, and he, desiring to seize the animal, moved towards the door. The doors opened of their own

[1] Mhv. ii. 19, 21; but see also **Añjana.** [2] DhA. iii. 44 f.; *cf.* Mil. 301.

accord, the stairway returned to its place, and the strong guard threw him down the stairs. When he landed at the bottom of the stairway the earth opened and swallowed him up in **Avīci.** He was also evidently called **Mahāsuppabuddha.**[3]

[3] *E.g.*, ThigA. 140.

2. **Suppabuddha.**—A poor leper of Rājagaha who, one day seated in the outer circle of people, heard the Buddha preach and became a *sotāpanna*. While waiting the departure of the crowd so that he could pay homage to the Buddha and express his gratitude, **Sakka,** desiring to test him, approached him and offered him untold wealth if he would repudiate the Buddha, his teachings, and the Order. But although Sakka revealed his identity, Suppabuddha rebuked him for a fool and said he had no need of more wealth, because he possessed already the seven stores of *Ariyadhana* (Noble Wealth). Sakka reported this conversation to the Buddha, who said that no power in the world would change Suppabuddha. Soon after, Suppabuddha visited the Buddha, and, having worshipped him, was on his way to the city when he was gored to death by a cow, the cow which killed also **Pukkusāti, Bāhiya Dārucīriya** and **Tambadāṭhika.**

The cow was a Yakkhiṇī, who had once been a courtezan. These four men had then been sons of wealthy merchants, who, having taken her one day to a pleasure garden, took their pleasure with her. In the evening they killed her and took the jewels and money which they themselves had given her. At the moment of her death she had vowed vengeance on them and had killed them in one hundred existences. In a previous birth, Suppabuddha had insulted the Pacceka Buddha **Tagarasikhī** by calling him a "leper" (*kuṭṭhi*)—because he wore a patched robe—and by spitting on him.[1]

[1] Ud. v. 3; UdA. 279 ff.; DhA. ii. 33 f. The Udāna account does not include the interlude of Sakka.

3. **Suppabuddha.**—Son of **Vessabhū Buddha** in his last lay life.[1]

[1] D. ii. 7; Bu. xxii. 20.

4. **Suppabuddha.**—A king of fifty-seven kappas ago, a former birth of **Eraka (Maggadāyaka) Thera.**[1]

[1] ThagA. i. 193; Ap. i. 173.

Supparikā.—The name of a tribe.[1]

[1] Ap. ii. 359 (vs. 19).

Suppala.—One of the palaces of **Siddhattha Buddha** before his renunciation.[1]

[1] Bu. xvii. 14.

Suppavāsā Koliyadhītā.—Mother of **Sīvalī.** Before he was born, she lay for seven days in labour suffering great pain, and it was not till the Buddha blessed her that she was able to bring forth the child.[1] It is said that the child was seven years in her womb, and the reason for this is given in the **Asātarūpa Jātaka** (*q.v.*).[2] Suppavāsā was the daughter of the rājā of **Koliya.**[3] Her husband was the Licchavi **Mahāli,**[4] and she lived in the Koliyan village of **Sajjanela,** where the Buddha visited her and preached to her on the efficacy of giving food.[5] She was described by the Buddha as foremost among those who gave excellent alms (*aggaṃ paṇītadāyikānaṃ*),[6] an eminence which she had earnestly resolved to attain in the time of **Padumuttara Buddha.**[7]

She is included in a list of eminent *upāsikās*,[8] and is mentioned[9] with **Anāthapiṇḍika, Culla Anāthapiṇḍika** and **Visākhā,** as givers of gifts which were gladly accepted by the monks.

[1] For details see *s.v.* **Sīvalī.**

[2] The seven years probably means that she had seven consecutive miscarriages.

[3] J. i. 407.

[4] Ap. ii. 494 (vs. 28); but see AA. i. 244, where her husband is described as a **Sākyan** noble.

[5] A. ii. 62 f.

[6] A. i. 26.

[7] AA. i. 244.

[8] A. iv. 348.

[9] DhA. i. 339; in this context she is spoken of as living in **Sāvatthi**; this was probably after **Mahāli** (*q.v.*) went to live there; *cf.* DhA. iv. 193 f.

Suppavāsā Sutta.—The Buddha visits **Suppavāsā** in **Sajjanela** and is entertained by her. He preaches to her that an Ariyan *upāsikā*, who gives food, gives four things to the receiver of the food—life, beauty, happiness and strength—and is sure of happiness in later lives.[1]

[1] A. ii. 62 f.

Suppasanna.—A king of eight kappas ago, a previous birth of **Rattipupphiya Thera.**[1]

[1] Ap. i. 188.

Suppāra, Suppāraka.—A seaport in India. It was in the **Sunāparanta** country and was the birthplace of **Puṇṇa** (*q.v.*). There was regular trade between **Bhārukaccha, Suppāraka** and **Suvaṇṇabhūmi.**[1] From Suppāra to **Sāvatthi** was one hundred and twenty leagues,[2] Sāvatthi being to the north-east of Suppāra.[3] **Vijaya** and his followers

[1] See, *e.g.*, Ap. ii. 476 (vs. 13 f.); AA. i. 156

[2] DhA. ii. 214; UdA. 85.

[3] *Ibid.*, 84 (*pubbuttaradisābhāgāyaṃ*).

landed there on their way to Ceylon, but had to leave because the people were incensed by their behaviour.[4] **Ubbarī** was once born in Suppāraka as a horse-dealer's daughter.[5] It was also the residence of **Bāhiya Dārucīriya** (*q.v.*).

Suppāraka (Skt. Sūrpāraka) is identified with the modern Sopāra in the Thāna district, to the north of Bombay.[6]

[4] Mhv. vi. 46; Dpv. ix. 15 f.
[5] DhA. iv. 50.
[6] Imperial Gazetteer of India *s.v.*, but see *s.v.* **Sunāparanta.**

Suppāraka.—The Bodhisatta born as a master mariner (*niyyāmaka-jeṭṭha*) of **Bhārukaccha.** See the **Suppāraka Jātaka.**

Suppāraka Jātaka (No. 463).—The Bodhisatta was once a master mariner of **Bhārukaccha.** His eyes were injured by the salt water and he went completely blind. The king appointed him valuer and assessor. One day an elephant was brought before him which was designed to be the state elephant, but, feeling it over with his hands, he condemned it, saying that its dam had dropped it in its youth, injuring its hind feet. He similarly condemned a horse, a chariot, and a blanket for various reasons, all these things having been designed for royal use. All his judgments were verified by the king and found to be correct; but he only gave Suppāraka eight pieces of money each time, and so Suppāraka left his service in disgust.

Some merchants had commissioned a ship, and, while searching for a captain, thought of Suppāraka. When Suppāraka refused, saying that he was blind, they replied that blind he might be, but no ship could founder if he were at the helm. After seven days the ship was caught in a storm and Suppāraka drove her through various oceans—**Khuramāla, Aggimāla, Dadhimāla, Nīlavaṇṇakusamāla, Nalamāla** and **Vaḷabhāmukha.** When he arrived at the last sea he saw that there was no means of rescuing the ship, and so performed an act of Truth. In one day the ship sailed back to Bhārukaccha.

The story was related in reference to the Buddha's perfection of wisdom.[1]

[1] J. iv. 136-47; *cf. Sapāraga Jātaka* in the *Jātakamālā* (No. 14).

1. **Suppiya.**—A **Paribbājaka.** He was the teacher of **Brahmadatta.** It was the discussion between these two, in the **Ambalaṭṭhikā** park, regarding the virtues of the Buddha, his Dhamma and his Order, which led to the preaching of the **Brahmajāla Sutta.**[1] Suppiya was a follower of **Sañjaya Belaṭṭhiputta.**[2]

[1] D. i. 1.
[2] DA. i. 35.

2. **Suppiya.**—One of the chief lay supporters of **Siddhattha Buddha.**[1]

[1] Bu. xvii. 20.

3. **Suppiya Thera.**—He was born in **Sāvatthi** in a family of cemetery-keepers. Converted by the preaching of his friend, the **Thera Sopāka,** he entered the Order and attained arahantship.

In the time of **Padumuttara Buddha** he was a brahmin, named **Varuṇa,** who left his ten children and became an ascetic in the forest. There he met the Buddha and his monks and gave them fruit. He belonged to a *khattiya* family in the time of **Kassapa Buddha,** but through pride of birth and learning used to detract his colleagues—hence his birth in a low caste in his last life.[1]

[1] Thag. vs. 32; ThagA. i. 92 f.; Ap. ii. 452 f.

4. **Suppiya.**—See **Suppiyā** (2).

1. **Suppiyā.**—The name of the inhabitants of **Rājagaha** in the time of **Kassapa Buddha.** At that time **Vepulla** was called **Supassa** (Suphassa).[1]

[1] S. ii. 192.

2. **Suppiyā.**—An *upāsikā* of Benares. Her husband was **Suppiya,** and they were both greatly devoted to the Order. One day, while on a visit to the monastery, Suppiyā saw a sick monk who needed a meat broth. On her return home, she sent an attendant to fetch meat; but there was none to be had in the whole of Benares. She therefore, with a knife, cut a piece of flesh from her thigh and gave it to her servant to make into soup for the monk. She then went to her room and lay on her bed. When Suppiya returned and discovered what had happened he was overjoyed, and, going to the monastery, invited the Buddha to a meal the next day. The Buddha accepted the invitation, and when, on the next day, he arrived with his monks, he asked for Suppiyā. On hearing that she was ill, he desired that she be brought to see him. At the moment when the Buddha saw her the wound was healed, covered with good skin, on which grew fine hairs as on the rest of her body.

It was as a result of this incident that the Buddha lay down a rule forbidding monks to eat human flesh, even when willingly given.[1]

Suppiyā is given as an example of one whose good deeds bore fruit in this very life.[2] She was declared by the Buddha foremost among

[1] Vin. i. 216 f.

[2] Mil. 115; *cf.* 291.

women who waited on the sick,[3] an eminence she had resolved to win in the time of **Padumuttara Buddha.**[4]

[3] A. i. 26.

[4] AA. i. 244 f.; she is mentioned in a list of eminent women lay disciples (A. iv. 348).

3. **Suppiyā.**—One of the five daughters of the third **Okkāka** and **Bhattā (Hatthā).**[1]

[1] DA. i. 258; MṬ. 131; SNA. ii. 352.

Suphassa.—See **Supassa.**

1. **Suphassā.**—A female crow, wife of **Supatta** (*q.v.*). She is identified with **Rāhulamātā.**[1]

[1] J. ii. 436.

2. **Suphassā.**—Mother of **Siddhattha Buddha.**[1]

[1] J. i. 40; Bu. xvii. 13.

3. **Suphassā.**—A celestial musician or a musical instrument.[1]

[1] VvA. 94.

Subandhu (Subuddha).—A brahmin of Benares, father of **Tekicchakāri Thera.** He incurred the wrath of **Cāṇakka** and was thrown into prison by **Candagutta.**[1]

[1] ThagA. i. 440.

1. **Subāhu Thera.**—He was the son of a *seṭṭhi* family of Benares, and was the friend of **Yasa.** When Yasa and his companions joined the Order Subāhu followed his example, and they all became arahants.[1]

[1] Vin. i. 19 f.

2. **Subāhu Thera.**—He was the son of a **Malla** rājā of **Pāvā.** He joined the Order on the occasion of the Buddha's first visit to **Rājagaha** and attained arahantship together with his friends **Godhika, Valliya** and **Uttiya. Bimbisāra** built a hut for them but forgot the roof; there was no rain until this defect had been made good.[1]

Ninety-nine kappas ago Subāhu paid homage to **Siddhattha Buddha.** Thirty-seven kappas ago he was king sixteen times, under the name of **Agada.** He is perhaps identical with **Ñāṇasaññaka** of the *Apadāna.*[2]

[1] Thag. vs. 52; ThagA. i. 123 f.

[2] Ap. i. 140 f.

3. **Subāhu.**—Five hundred kappas ago there were thirty-four kings of this name, previous births of **Ekāsaniya (Sīvalī) Thera.**[1]

[1] Ap. i. 150; ThagA. i. 139.

4. **Subāhu.**—A tiger. See the **Vaṇṇāroha** and **Tittira** (No. 438) **Jātakas.** He is identified with **Moggallāna.**[1]

[1] J. iii. 192, 540.

5. **Subāhu.**—A **Pacceka Buddha.**[1]

[1] M. iii. 70; ApA. i. 107.

1. **Subuddha.**—See **Susuddha.**

2. **Subuddha.**—See **Subandhu.**

Subodhālaṅkāra.—A work on Pāli prosody by **Saṅgharakkhita Thera** of Ceylon.[1]

[1] Gv. 61; P.L.C. 199 f.

Subbata.—A king of long ago, a previous birth of **Kuṭivihāriya (Nalamāliya) Thera.**[1]

[1] ThagA. i. 131; Ap. i. 143.

1. **Subrahmā.**—A Devaputta. He visits the Buddha at **Veḷuvana** and tells him that his heart is full of dismay. The Buddha replies that the only path out of sorrow is by way of wisdom, renunciation and restraint.[1] According to the Commentary,[2] he was a devaputta of **Tāvatiṃsa,** and one day went to the **Nandana** Park with one thousand nymphs. Five hundred of them sat with him under the **Pāricchattaka**-tree, while the others climbed the tree, from which they threw garlands and sang songs. Suddenly all of them vanished and were born in **Avīci.** Subrahmā, discovering their destiny and investigating his own, finds that he has only seven days more to live. Full of grief, he seeks the Buddha for consolation. At the end of the Buddha's discourse he becomes a *sotāpanna.*

[1] S. i. 53. [2] SA. i. 88 f.; DA. iii. 750; MA. i. 190 f.

2. **Subrahmā.**—A **Pacceka Brahmā.** He was a follower of the Buddha, and, after visiting him together with **Suddhavāsa,** he went on to another **Brahmā,** who was infatuated with his own importance. There, by a display of magic power, Subrahmā convinced him that he was far more powerful than the Brahmā, but declared that his own power was as

nothing compared with that of the Buddha.[1] On another occasion, Subrahmā visited the Buddha to declare the folly of **Kokālika** and of **Kaṭamoraka Tissa.**[2] Subrahmā was present at the preaching of the **Mahāsamaya Sutta.**[3]

[1] S. i. 146 f. [2] *Ibid.*, 148. [3] D. ii. 261.

3. **Subrahmā.**—A brahmin who will be the father of **Metteyya Buddha.** His wife will be **Brahmavatī.**[1] He will be the chaplain of King **Saṅkha.**[2] According to the *Mahāvaṃsa*[3] he is identical with **Kākavaṇṇatissa.**

[1] DhSA. 415; Vsm. 434. [2] Anāgat. vs. 96. [3] Mhv. xxxii. 82.

Subrahmā Sutta.—Describes the visit of the devaputta **Subrahmā** to the Buddha.[1]

[1] S. i. 53.

1. **Subha.**—A Pacceka Buddha.[1]

[1] M. iii. 70; ApA. i. 106.

2. **Subha.**—A young man (*māṇava*) called **Todeyyaputta.** He once visited the Buddha in **Sāvatthi,** asking him various questions. The interview is described in the **Subha Sutta** (*q.v.*). At the end of the discourse he declared himself the Buddha's follower. While on his way back from the city, he met **Jāṇussoṇi,** and, on being asked what he thought of the Buddha, spoke of him in terms of the highest praise, saying that none but Gotama's own peer could utter sufficient praise of him.[1] Subha is described[2] as the son of the brahmin **Todeyya** (*q.v.*) of **Tudigāma.**

Elsewhere,[3] however, a different account is given of his conversion. Subha's father was a very rich merchant, chaplain to **Pasenadi,** but a great miser. After death he was born as a dog in the same home. One day, when the Buddha was going his alms round in Tudigāma near Sāvatthi, he arrived at Subha's house. The dog saw the Buddha and barked, and the Buddha addressed it as "Todeyya." The dog thereupon ran into the house and lay on a bed, from which no one could drive it away. When Subha asked the cause of the uproar, he was told the story. Thereupon he was very angry, saying that his father had been born in the Brahmaloka, and, in order to refute the Buddha, he visited the monastery. This was the occasion for the preaching of the **Subha Sutta.** Soon after the Buddha's death, when **Ānanda** was staying in

[1] M.i.196 f., 208 f.; Jāṇussoṇi addresses him as **Bhāradvāja.**

[2] MA. ii. 802; *cf.* M. i. 202.

[3] DA. ii. 384 f.; *cf.* MA. ii. 963 f., which adds that the Buddha proved the identity of the dog by getting it to indicate the place where Todeyya's treasure lay buried.

Sāvatthi, Subha sent a young man to Ānanda with his respects and an invitation to his house. Ānanda, having taken medicine, did not go that day. But he went the next day, accompanied by a monk of **Cetiya (Cetaka).** Their conversation is recorded in the **Subha Sutta** (2).[4] See also **Cūlakammavibhaṅga Sutta,** which too was preached to Subha.

[4] D. i. 204 f.

3. **Subha.**—A palace guard, son of **Datta.** He closely resembled King **Yasalālaka-Tissa** in appearance, and the king used to place him on the throne, decked in royal ornaments, and watch the ministers doing obeisance to him, while he himself took the guard's place. One day, while Subha was on the throne, he reprimanded the king, disguised as a guard, for smiling disrespectfully, and had him led away and executed before the truth was discovered. Subha then became king and ruled for six years (120–6 A.C.). He built the **Subharāja-pariveṇa,** the **Valli-vihāra,** the **Ekadvāra-vihāra** and the **Nandigāmaka-vihāra.** He was deposed by **Vasabha.**[1] His daughter married **Vaṅkanāsika-Tissa.** She had been adopted by a bricklayer, but Vasabha discovered her identity and married her to his son. Her good fortune was owing to a meal she had given to an arahant thera.[2]

[1] Mhv. xxxv. 51 ff.; Dpv. xxi. 45.
[2] For details see Mhv. xxxv. 101 ff.; see also Cv. xxxviii. 13 f.

4. **Subha.**—A palace occupied by **Koṇḍañña Buddha** before his renunciation.[1]

[1] Bu. iii. 26.

5. **Subha.**—A palace occupied by **Gotama Buddha** before his renunciation.[1]

[1] BuA. 230; but Bu. xxvi. 14 calls it Subhata.

6. **Subha.**—A *senāpati* who, during the thirteenth century, built a fortress in **Subhagiri.**[1]

[1] Cv. lxxxi. 4.

1. **Subha Sutta.**—**Subha Todeyyaputta** (*q.v.*) visits the Buddha at **Sāvatthi** and asks him various questions regarding the Dhamma, comparing it with the teachings of the brahmins regarding ultimate salvation. He admits that no one among the brahmins or the early sages had fully discerned and realized the qualities laid down by them for the attainment of merit and the achievement of right. He quotes **Pokkharasāti** as saying that those who, like Gotama, profess to transcend ordinary

human beings and rise to the heights of Ariyan knowledge are idle boasters. The Budda retorts that Pokkharasāti cannot even read the thoughts of his slave-girl, **Puṇṇikā.** The Buddha then convinces Subha that he has discovered the way to union with **Brahmā,** and, at his request, teaches him this way, as being the four *Brahma-vihāras.* Subha acknowledges himself the Buddha's follower.[1]

[1] M. ii. 196-209.

2. **Subha Sutta.**—A conversation between **Subha Todeyyaputta** (*q.v.*) and **Ānanda** at **Sāvatthi** soon after the Buddha's death. Subha asks Ānanda what were the bodies of doctrine which the Buddha was wont to praise, to which he incited others and in which he established them. Ānanda explains to him. The sutta is almost word for word identical with the **Sāmaññāphala Sutta.**[1]

[1] D. i. 204-10.

3. **Subha Sutta.**—According to Buddhaghosa,[1] **Subha Sutta** is the real name for the **Cūla-kammavibhaṅga Sutta** (*q.v.*).

[1] MA. ii. 962, 967.

Subhakiṇṇā, Subhakiṇhā.—A class of Brahmas who occupy the ninth Rūpa-world; a division of the **Subha-devā.**[1] Beings are born in that world as a result of developing the third *jhāna*, and their life span is sixty-four *kappas.*[2] They are filled and pervaded with happiness and are serenely blissful; they experience only sublime happiness, unlike the **Ābhassarā,** who exclaim in their joy.[3] They agree both in body and in perceptive power.[4] They radiate light from their bodies in a steady brightness and not in flashes.[5] When the world is destroyed by water, the world of the Subhakiṇhas forms the limit to which the water rises.[6]

[1] M. iii. 102; D. ii. 69; M. i. 2, etc. *Compendium*, p. 138.

[2] MA. i. 553 and SA. i. 162; but see A. ii. 127, 129, where their life is given as four *kappas.*

[3] D. iii. 219.

[4] A. iv. 401; *cf.* iv. 40.

[5] AA. ii. 713; *cf.* PSA. 80.

[6] *Ibid.*, 256.

Subhakūṭa.—The name of **Missaka** Mountain (**Sīlakūṭa**) in the time of **Kassapa Buddha.** Ceylon was then known as **Maṇḍadīpa.** It was on Subhakūṭa that Kassapa Buddha landed when he arrived in Ceylon.[1]

[1] Mhv. xv. 131 f.; Dpv. xvii. 14.

Subhaga.—A son of the Nāga-king, **Dhataraṭṭha.** See the **Bhūridatta Jātaka.** He is identified with **Moggallāna.**[1]

[1] J. vi. 219.

Subhagavatī.—The pleasaunce in **Khemavatī** where **Kakusandha Buddha** was born.[1]

[1] BuA. 213.

Subhagavana.—A wood in **Ukkaṭṭhā.** Once, when the Buddha was there, he visited the **Avihā** gods[1] and, again, from there he visited **Baka Brahmā,** to whom he preached the **Brahmanimantanika Sutta.**[2] It was under a *sāla*-tree in Subhagavana that the **Mūlapariyāya Sutta** was preached.[3]

The wood was so called because of its beauty. People often went there for pleasure, and, influenced by the romantic nature of the surroundings, would plan pleasant things, which would come to pass.[4]

[1] D. ii. 50.
[2] M. i. 326; but see S. i. 142, where the Buddha is said to have been at **Jetavana.**
[3] M. i. 1; also the Jātaka of the same name (J. ii. 259).
[4] MA. i. 10.

Subhagiri, Subha-pabbata, Sundara-pabbata.—An isolated rock in Ceylon. It was evidently named after the *senāpati* **Subha,** who built a fortress there in the time of **Māgha.**[1] Later, it was occupied by **Bhuvanekabāhu** (brother of **Vijayabāhu IV.**), and formed the centre of the campaign in the battle of Vijayabāhu IV. against **Candabhānu.** Later, Bhuvanekabāhu continued to live there.[2] After Vijayabāhu IV. was killed by his *senāpati* **Mitta,** Bhuvanekabāhu, who had succeeded to the throne at **Jambuddoṇi,** had once more to seek refuge in Subhagiri, and for some time it was the seat of government. A town seems to have grown up there in the same way as at **Sīhagiri.**[3]

Bhuvanekabāhu himself ruled there for eleven years.[4] After his death, **Āriyacakkavatti** laid waste the town,[5] and the capital was later moved to **Hatthigiri(sela)pura.**[6]

Subhagiri is identified with the modern Yāpahu, near Maho.[7]

[1] Cv. lxxxi. 3.
[2] *Ibid.*, lxxxviii. 26, 61, 64 f., 79.
[3] *Ibid.*, xc. 11, 28, 30, 35.
[4] *Ibid.*, 42.
[5] *Ibid.*, 45.
[6] *Ibid.*, 59.
[7] Cv. *Trs.* ii. 135, n. 3.

Subhadeva.—Uncle of **Abhayanāga.** Abhayanāga had Subhadeva's hands and feet cut off and left him behind, that he might bring about division in the kingdom of **Vohārika-Tissa.** When the time was come, he sent word to Abhayanāga, and the latter seized the throne.[1]

[1] Mhv. xxxvi. 45 f.; MṬ. 663.

1. **Subhadda.**—One of the chief lay patrons of **Dhammadassī Buddha.**[1]

[1] Bu. xvi. 20.

2. **Subhadda.**—A youth who joined the Order under **Koṇḍañña Buddha** with ten thousand others, and became an arahant. He was the Buddha's *aggasāvaka*.[1]

[1] Bu. iii. 30; J. i. 30; BuA. 111.

3. **Subhadda.**—A *yavapālaka* who gave grass for his seat to **Kakusandha Buddha.**[1]

[1] BuA. 210.

4. **Subhadda.**—Son of **Upaka** the **Ājīvaka** and **Cāpā.**[1]

[1] ThigA. 221; SNA. i. 260.

5. **Subhadda.**—A barber of **Ātumā.** He entered the Order and resented having to observe various rules, great and small. When the Buddha died and the monks stood weeping, Subhadda asked them to rejoice instead, saying: "We are well rid of the *Mahāsamaṇa*; we shall now do just as we like." **Mahā Kassapa** heard this while he was on his way from **Pāvā** to **Kusinārā,** and it was this remark which made him decide to hold the First Council after the Buddha's death.[1]

Subhadda had been a *sāmaṇera* at the time of the Buddha's visit to Ātumā, and had two sons before he joined the Order. When he heard that the Buddha was coming, he sent for his two sons and gave orders for various foods to be collected to feed the Buddha and the twelve hundred and fifty monks. The Buddha arrived in the evening and took up his residence in Ātumā. All night long Subhadda went about giving instructions regarding the preparation of the food. In the morning of the next day the Buddha went out for alms, and Subaddha approached him and invited him to partake of the food which he had prepared. But the Buddha questioned him, and, discovering what he had done, refused to accept the meal, forbidding the monks to do so too. This angered Subhadda, and he awaited an opportunity of expressing his disapproval of the Buddha. This opportunity came when he heard of the Buddha's death.[2]

[1] Vin. ii. 284 f.; D. ii. 162; Mhv. iii. 6.

[2] DA. ii. 599; *cf.* Vin. i. 249 f.

6. **Subhadda Thera.**—He was a brahmin of high rank (of the *udiccabrāhmaṇamahāsālakula*), and, having become a **Paribbājaka,** was living in **Kusinārā** when the Buddha went there on his last journey. Having heard that the Buddha would die in the third watch of the night, Subhadda went to the *sāla*-grove, where the Buddha lay on his death-bed, and asked **Ānanda** for permission to see him. But three times Ānanda refused the request, saying that the Buddha was weary. The Buddha over-

heard the conversation and asked Subhadda to come in. Subhadda asked the Buddha if there were any truth in the teachings of other religious instructors. The Buddha said he had no time to discuss that, but that any system devoid of the Noble Eightfold Path was useless for salvation, and he taught Subhadda the Doctrine. Subhadda asked to be allowed to join the Order, and the Buddha gave Ānanda special permission to admit him at once without waiting for the usual probationary period. Subhadda dwelt in solitude and in meditation and soon became an arahant. He was the last disciple to be converted by the Buddha.[1]

Buddhaghosa says[2] that when the Buddha gave him permission to ordain Subhadda, Ānanda took him outside, poured water over his head, made him repeat the formula of the impermanence of the body, shaved off his hair and beard, clad him in yellow robes, made him repeat the Three Refuges, and then led him back to the Buddha. The Buddha himself admitted Subhadda to the higher ordination and gave him a subject for meditation. Subhadda took this, and, walking up and down in a quiet part of the grove, attained arahantship and came and sat down beside the Buddha.

In the past, Subhadda and **Aññāta Koṇḍañña** had been brothers. They had a cornfield, and the elder (Aññāta Koṇḍañña) gave the first-fruits of the corn to the monks in nine stages. The younger (Subhadda) found fault with him for damaging the corn. They then divided the field, thus settling the dispute.[3] Subhadda rubbed the dead body of **Padumuttara Buddha** with sandalwood and other fragrant essences and placed a banner on his *thūpa*. In the time of **Kassapa Buddha,** the Buddha's *aggasāvaka*, **Tissa,** was Subhadda's son. Subhadda spoke disparagingly of him, hence his tardiness in meeting the Buddha in his last life. Subhadda died on the day of his ordination and arahantship.[4]

The conversation between the Buddha and Subhadda forms the topic of a dilemma in the *Milindapañha*.[5] Subhadda's ordination was the Buddha's last "official" act.[6]

[1] D. ii. 148 ff.; *cf.* DhA. iii. 376 f.
[2] DA. ii. 590.
[3] DA. ii. 588.
[4] Ap. i. 100 f.
[5] p. 130.
[6] KhA., p. 89.

7. **Subhadda.**—A lay disciple of **Nātikā.** He was an *anāgāmin* and was born in the **Suddhavāsā,** never to be reborn.[1]

[1] D. ii. 92; S. v. 348 f.

Subhaddakaccā.—See **Bhaddakaccā.**

1. **Subhaddā.**—*Aggasāvikā* of **Revata Buddha.**[1]

[1] J. i. 35; Bu. vi. 22.

2. **Subhaddā.**—One of the chief women lay-supporters of **Sujāta Buddha.**[1]

[1] Bu. xiii. 30.

3. **Subhaddā.**—Wife of **Tissa Buddha** before his renunciation.[1]

[1] Bu. xviii. 18.

4. **Subhaddā.**—See **Mahāsubhaddā** and **Cūlasubhaddā.**

5. **Subhaddā.**—Daughter of the **Madda** king and wife of the king of Benares. See the **Chaddanta Jātaka.**

6. **Subhaddā.**—Wife of **Mahāsudassana.** See **Mahāsubhaddā.**

7. **Subhaddā.**—A celestial musician or a musical instrument.[1]

[1] VvA. 94, 211.

8. **Subhaddā.**—One of the five daughters of **Vijayabāhu I.** and **Tilokasundarī.** She married **Vīrabāhu.**[1]

[1] Cv. lix. 31, 43.

Subhaddācetiya.—A cetiya in **Pulatthipura** built by **Parakkamabāhu I.**[1]

[1] Cv. lxxviii. 51.

Subhapabbata, Subhācala.—See **Subhagiri.**

1. **Subhavatī.**—A city in the time of **Piyadassī Buddha.** Near by was **Sudassanapabbata,** where lived the deva-king **Sudassana.**[1]

[1] BuA. 173.

2. **Subhavatī.**—A city in the time of **Anomadassī Buddha.** Near by was the **Sudassanuyyāna,** where the Buddha preached his first sermon.[1]

[1] BuA. 143.

1. **Subhā.**—A group of Brahmās; the group includes the **Parittasubhā,** the **Appamāṇasubhā** and the **Subhakiṇhā.**[1]

[1] M. iii. 102; for details see *s.v.*

2. **Subhā Kammāradhītā.**—She was the daughter of a rich goldsmith of **Rājagaha.** One day she went to pay obeisance to the Buddha and he preached to her. She became a *sotāpanna*, and later she joined the Order under **Mahāpajāpatī.** From time to time her relations tried to persuade her to leave the Order and return to the world. One day she set forth, in twenty-four verses, the dangers of household life and dismissed them, convinced of her rightness. Then, striving for insight, she attained arahantship on the eighth day.[1] The Buddha saw this and praised her in three verses.[2] **Sakka** visited her with the gods of **Tāvatiṃsa** and uttered another verse in her praise.[3]

[1] Thig. vs. 338-61. [2] *Ibid.*, 362-4. [3] *Ibid.*, 365; ThigA. 236 f.

3. **Subhā Jīvakambavanikā.**—She belonged to an eminent brahmin family of **Rājagaha,** and, seeing the bane in the pleasures of sense, became a nun under **Pajāpatī Gotamī.** She was called Subhā because her body was beautiful. One day, in **Jīvakambavana,** a libertine, in the prime of youth, seeing her going to her siesta, stopped her, inviting her to sensual pleasures. She talked to him of the evils of such pleasures, but he persisted. Seeing that he was particularly enamoured of the beauty of her eyes, she pulled out one of them, saying: "Come, here is the offending eye." The man was appalled and asked her forgiveness. Subhā went to the Buddha, and, at sight of him, her eye recovered. Filled with joy, she stood worshipping him, and he taught her and gave her an exercise for meditation. She developed insight and became an arahant.[1]

[1] Thig. vss. 366-399; ThigA. 245 f.

Subhāsita Sutta.—The Buddha tells the monks that good speech is that which is spoken well, righteously, affectionately and truthfully. **Vaṅgīsa,** who is present, renders the Buddha's speech into verse.[1]

[1] S. i. 188; *cf.* SN., p. 78 f.

Subhūta Thera.—He belonged to a clansman's family of **Magadha,** and, because of his predisposition to renunciation, left domestic life and joined sectarian ascetics. Dissatisfied with them and seeing the happiness enjoyed by **Upatissa, Kolita, Sela** and others, after they had joined the Order, he too became a monk under the Buddha, winning the favour of his teachers. He went into solitude with an exercise for meditation, and soon afterwards attained arahantship.

In the time of **Kassapa Buddha** he belonged to a very rich family of Benares, and, after hearing the Buddha preach, rubbed the Buddha's **Gandhakuṭi** eight times a month with the four kinds of perfumes.

As a result of this, he was born, in all his births, with a fragrant body.[1]

He is probably identical with **Cūlasugandha** of the Apadāna.[2]

[1] Thag. vss. 320-4; ThagA. i. 405 f.
[2] Ap. ii. 508 f.; but see ThagA. i. 80 and Ap. ii. 459.

Subhūtacandana.—A Thera of Pagan who wrote the **Liṅgatthavivaraṇa,** a Pāli grammar.[1]

[1] Gv. 63, 72; Bode, *op. cit.*, 22.

Subhūti Thera.—He was the son of **Sumanaseṭṭhi** and the younger brother of **Anāthapiṇḍika.** On the day of the dedication of **Jetavana,** he heard the Buddha preach and left the world. After ordination he mastered the two categories (of Vinaya rules), and, after obtaining a subject for meditation, lived in the forest. There he developed insight, and attained arahantship on the basis of *mettājhāna.* Teaching the Dhamma without distinction or limitation, he was declared chief of those who lived remote and in peace (*araṇavihārinaṃ aggo*), and of those who were worthy of gifts (*dakkhiṇeyyānaṃ*).[1] It is said that when he went begging for alms he would develop *mettājhāna* at each door, hence every gift made to him was of the highest merit. In the course of his travels he came to **Rājagaha,** and **Bimbisāra** promised to build him a dwelling-place. But the king forgot his promise, and Subhūti meditated in the open air. There was no rain, and, discovering the cause, the king had a leaf hut built for him. As soon as Subhūti entered the hut and seated himself cross-legged on the bed of hay, rain began to fall.

In the time of **Padumuttara Buddha** he belonged to a rich family and was called **Nanda.** Later he left the world and lived the hermit's life, at the head of forty-four thousand others. The Buddha visited Nanda's hermitage and accepted from him a gift of fruit and flowers. He asked one of his monks, proficient in *mettā* and eminent in receiving gifts, to preach the *anumodanā.* At the end of the sermon all the other hermits became arahants, but Nanda's attention was fixed on the majesty of the preaching monk, and he did not reach any attainment. Later, discovering the qualities in which the preacher had attained eminence, Nanda resolved that he too would reach similar eminence.[2]

Verses attributed to him are included in the *Theragāthā*[3] and also in the *Milindapañha.*[4] See also **Subhūti Sutta.**

[1] A. i. 24; *cf.* Ud. vi. 7, where the Buddha commends his proficiency in meditation.
[2] AA. i. 124 f.; ThagA. i. 17 ff.; UdA. 348 f.; see also Ap. i. 67 f., where Nanda is called **Kosiya.**
[3] vs. 1.
[4] pp. 356, 391.

Subhūti Sutta.—Subhūti Thera visits the Buddha with a companion, and the Buddha asks him who his companion is. Subhūti answers that he is the son of a believing disciple and has gone forth from a believer's home to homelessness. The Buddha then asks Subhūti if his colleague conforms to the traditional signs of the believer. Subhūti begs of the Buddha to define these signs, and the Buddha explains them at length.[1]

[1] A. v. 337 f. The Commentary says that the monk was the son of **Anāthapiṇḍika** and therefore Subhūti's nephew (AA. ii. 865).

1. **Sumaṅgala.**—*Aggasāvaka* of **Dīpaṅkara Buddha.**[1]

[1] J. i. 29; Bu. ii. 213.

2. **Sumaṅgala.**—One of the chief lay patrons of **Kassapa Buddha.**[1] He spread the ground with bricks of gold for a space of twenty usabhas and spent an equal sum on a monastery for the Buddha. He saw a man sleeping, and thought to himself that the man must be a thief. The man conceived a grudge against Sumaṅgala, and burned his fields seven times, cut the feet off the cattle in his pen seven times, and burned his house seven times. Then knowing that Sumaṅgala loved the Buddha's **Gandhakuṭi,** he also set fire to that. It was burnt down by the time Sumaṅgala could arrive there; seeing it, he clasped his hands, saying that now he could build another in its place. Then the thief went about with a knife concealed on him, waiting to kill Sumaṅgala. One day Sumaṅgala held a great almsgiving, at the conclusion of which he said: "Sir, there is evidently an enemy of mine trying to do me harm. I have no anger against him, and will give over to him the fruits of this offering." The thief heard and was filled with remorse, and begged his forgiveness. The thief was later born as a *peta* on **Gijjhakuṭa.**[2]

[1] Bu. xxv. 41; J. i. 92.
[2] DhA. iii. 61 f.

3. **Sumaṅgala.**—City of birth of **Sujāta Buddha.**[1] He preached his first sermon in the park in the city.[2]

[1] Bu. xiii. 20; J. i. 38.
[2] BuA. 168.

4. **Sumaṅgala.**—The city where **Piyadassī Buddha** preached to **Pālita** and **Sabbadassī,** who later became his chief disciples.[1]

[1] BuA. 176.

5. **Sumaṅgala.**—A king of seven hundred kappas ago, a previous birth of **Susārada (Phaladāyaka) Thera.**[1]

[1] ThagA. i. 167; Ap. i. 161.

6. **Sumaṅgala.**—Nineteen kappas ago there were several kings of this name, previous births of **Khitaka Thera.**[1]

[1] ThagA. i. 209.

7. **Sumaṅgala Thera.**—He was born in a poor family in a hamlet near Sāvatthi. When he grew up, he earned his living in the fields. One day he saw **Pasenadi** hold a great almsgiving to the Order, and, seeing the food served to the monks, desired to enter the Order that he might lead a life of ease and luxury. A Thera to whom he confessed his desire ordained him, and sent him to the forest with an exercise for meditation. In solitude he pined and wavered, and finally returned to his village. As he went along he saw men working in the fields in the hot wind, with soiled garments, covered with dust. And thinking how miserable they were, he put forth fresh effort in his meditations, and, winning insight, attained arahantship.

In the past he saw **Siddhattha Buddha** (? **Atthadassī Buddha**) standing in one robe, after a bath. Pleased with this sight, he clapped his hands. One hundred and sixteen kappas ago he was twice king, under the name of **Ekacintita.**[1]

[1] Thag. vs. 43; ThagA. i. 111 f.; Ap. i. 147 f.

8. **Sumaṅgala Thera.**—An arahant. One hundred and eighteen kappas ago he was a brahmin. One day, having made preparations for a great sacrifice, he saw **Piyadassī Buddha** arriving at his door with one thousand arahants, and placed all the food in his house at the disposal of the Buddha and his monks.[1]

[1] Ap. i. 65 f.

9. **Sumaṅgala.**—A Pacceka Buddha.[1]

[1] M. iii. 70; ApA. i. 107.

10. **Sumaṅgala.**—A park-keeper of the king of Benares. See the **Sumaṅgala Jātaka.** He is identified with **Ānanda.**[1]

[1] J. iii. 444.

11. **Sumaṅgala.**—A monk of Ceylon, pupil of **Sāriputta.** He wrote a *ṭīkā* on the **Abhidhammāvatāra,** called the **Abhidhammatthavibhāvinī.**[1] He also wrote the **Sāratthasālinī,** on the **Saccasaṅkhepa.**[2]

[1] P.L.C. 108, 173.

[2] *Ibid.*, 200; Gv. 62, 72.

12. **Sumaṅgala.**—The tenth future Buddha, the first being **Metteyya.**[1]

[1] Anāgat., p. 40.

Sumaṅgala Jātaka (No. 420).—The Bodhisatta was once king of Benares and had a park-keeper called Sumaṅgala. A Pacceka Buddha came from **Nandamūlapabbhāra** and took up his abode in the park. The king, seeing him as he went begging, invited him to the palace, fed him, and urged him to continue to stay in the park. The Pacceka Buddha agreed to do so, and the king told Sumaṅgala to look after him. One day the Pacceka Buddha went away to a village, and, after an absence of some days, returned in the evening. Putting away his bowl and robe, he sat on a stone seat. Sumaṅgala, looking in the park for some meat in order to feed some relations who had suddenly arrived, saw the Pacceka Buddha, and, taking him for a deer, shot him. The Pacceka Buddha revealed his identity and made Sumaṅgala pull out the arrow. Sumaṅgala was full of remorse, but the Pacceka Buddha died. Feeling sure that the king would never forgive him, Sumaṅgala fled with his wife and children. After a year he asked a friend, a minister at court, to discover how the king felt towards him. The man uttered his praises in the king's presence, but the king remained silent. This was repeated every year, and in the third year, knowing that the king now bore him no ill-will, he returned to the king, who, after hearing from him how the accident had happened, forgave him. When asked why he had remained silent, the king replied that it was wrong for a king to act hastily in his anger.

Sumaṅgala is identified with **Ānanda.** The story was related in connection with the admonition of a king.[1]

[1] J. iii. 439-44

Sumaṅgala-pariveṇa.—A monastery, probably in **Anurādhapura** at the time of **Buddhaghosa. Dāṭhanāga Thera** (*q.v.*) lived there.

Sumaṅgalappasādanī.—A *ṭīkā* on the **Khuddasikkhā,** written by **Vācissara** of Ceylon at the request of **Sumaṅgala.**[1]

[1] Gv. 62, 71; Svd. 1227

Sumaṅgalamātā Therī.—She was born in a poor family of **Sāvatthi** and was married to a rush-plaiter (*naḷakāra*). Her first child was a son, named **Sumaṅgala,** who left the world and became an arahant.[1] She became a nun, and one day, while reflecting on all she had suffered in the lay life, she was much affected, and, her insight quickening, she became an arahant.[2]

[1] See **Sumaṅgala** (7).

[2] Thig. vss. 23-24; ThigA. 28 f.

Sumaṅgalavilāsinī.—**Buddhaghosa's** Commentary of the **Dīgha Nikāya.**[1] It was written at the request of **Dāṭhanāga Thera,** incumbent of the **Sumaṅgala pariveṇa.** It is quoted in the **Manorathapūraṇī.**[2]

[1] Gv. 59. [2] *E.g.*, AA. i. 407.

1. **Sumana.**—The fourth of the twenty-four Buddhas. He was born in **Mekhala,** his father being the *khattiya* **Sudatta** and his mother **Sirimā.** For nine thousand years he lived as a householder in three palaces—**Canda, Sucanda** and **Vataṃsa**[1]—his wife being **Vataṃsikā** and his son **Anupama.** He left the world on an elephant, practised austerities for ten months, and attained enlightenment under a *nāga*-tree, being given a meal of milk-rice by **Anupamā,** daughter of **Anupama-seṭṭhi** of **Anoma,** and grass for his seat by the **Ājīvaka Anupama.** His first sermon was preached in the **Mekhala Park,** and among his first disciples were his step-brother **Saraṇa** and the purohita's son **Bhāvitatta.** His Twin-miracle was performed in **Sunandavatī.** The Bodhisatta was a Nāga-king **Atula.** One of the Buddha's chief assemblies was on the occasion of his solving the questions of King **Arindama** on *Nirodha.*

Saraṇa and **Bhāvitatta** were his chief monks and **Soṇā** and **Upaseṇā** his chief nuns. **Udena** was his personal attendant. **Varuṇa** and **Saraṇa** were his chief lay supporters among men and **Cālā** and **Upacālā** among women. His body was ninety cubits in height, and he died at the age of ninety thousand in **Aṅgārāma,** where a thūpa of four yojanas was erected over his ashes.[2]

[1] BuA. calls them **Nārivaḍḍhana, Somavaḍḍhana** and **Iddhivaḍḍhana** (125).

[2] Bu. v. 1 ff.; BuA. 125 f.; J. i. 30, 34, 35, 40.

2. **Sumana.**—Attendant of **Padumuttara Buddha.**[1] His eminence prompted **Ānanda (Sumana** in that birth) to resolve to be an attendant of some future Buddha.[2]

[1] J. i. 37; Bu. xi. 24. [2] ThagA. ii. 122; see also Ap. i. 195.

3. **Sumana.**—Step-brother of **Padumuttara Buddha.** He obtained, as boon from the king, the privilege of waiting on the Buddha for three months. He built in the park of **Sobhana** a vihāra. The park belonged to the householder **Sobhana,** and he built the vihāra on land for which he gave one hundred thousand. There he entertained the Buddha and his monks. Sunanda is identified with **Ānanda.**[1]

[1] ThagA. ii. 122 f.; AA. i. 160 f.; SA. ii. 68 f.

4. **Sumana.**—A pupil of **Anuruddha.** He represented the monks from **Pāveyyaka** at the Second Council. **Vāsabhagāmi** was his colleague.[1] See also **Sumana** (8).

[1] Mhv. iv. 49, 58; Dpv. iv. 48; v. 24; Vin. ii. 305, etc.

5. **Sumana.**—A garland-maker, given as an example of one whose acts bore fruit in this very life.[1] He was **Bimbisāra's** gardener, and provided the king daily with eight measures of jasmine flowers, for which he received eight pieces of money. One day, while on his way to the palace, he saw the Buddha, and threw two handfuls of flowers into the air, where they formed a canopy over the Buddha's head. Two handfuls thrown on the right, two on the left and two behind, all remained likewise in the air and accompanied the Buddha as he walked through the city, a distance of three leagues, that all might see the miracle.

When Sumana returned home with his empty basket and told his wife what he had done, she was fearful lest the king should punish him. Going to the palace, she confessed what he had done, and asked for forgiveness for herself as she had had no part in the deed. Bimbisāra visited the Buddha and then sent for Sumana. Sumana confessed that when he offered the flowers to the Buddha he was quite prepared to lose his life. The king gave him the eightfold gift: eight female slaves, eight sets of jewels, eight thousand pieces of money, eight women from the royal harem, and eight villages.

In reply to a question by **Ānanda,** the Buddha said that in the future the garland-maker would become a Pacceka Buddha, **Sumana.**[2]

[1] Mil. 115, 291, 350; *cf.* DhSA. 426; PSA. 498.

[2] DhA. ii. 40 f.; KhA. 129. According to KhA., the Pacceka Buddha's name will be **Sumanissara.**

6. **Sumana.**—Chief lay supporter of **Kassapa Buddha.**[1]

[1] DA. ii. 424; but see **Sumaṅgala** (2).

7. **Sumana Thera.**—He belonged to a brahmin family of **Kosala.** His mother's brother was an arahant, and ordained him as soon as he grew up. Sumana soon acquired the four *jhānas* and fivefold *aññā* and, in due course, attained arahantship.

Ninety-five kappas ago he gave a *harītaka*-fruit to a Pacceka Buddha who was ill.[1] He is evidently identical with **Harītakadāyaka** of the *Apadāna.*[2]

[1] Thag. vss. 330-4; ThagA. i. 411 f.

[2] Ap. ii. 394; *cf. Avadānas* ii. 67-70.

8. **Sumana Thera.**—See **Cūla-Sumana** (3). He is probably identical with **Sumana** (4), and may be identical with **Sumana** (7) if the uncle mentioned in connection with the latter is **Anuruddha.**

Thirty-one kappas ago he was a garland-maker and offered jasmine-flowers to **Sikhī Buddha.** Twenty-six kappas ago he was king four times, under the name of **Mahāyasa.**[1]

[1] Thag. vss. 429-34; ThagA. i. 457 f.

9. **Sumana Thera.**—He is mentioned as having lived in **Andhavana** with **Khema.** Together they visited the Buddha, and, when Khema had gone away, Sumana talked with the Buddha about arahants.[1] He is probably identical with **Sumana** (7) or (8).

[1] A. iii. 348 f.

10. **Sumana.**—A *seṭṭhi* in the time of **Padumuttara Buddha.** He was the employer and, later, the friend of **Annabhāra** (*q.v.*).

11. **Sumana.**—A householder in the time of **Duṭṭhagāmaṇī Abhaya,** in the village of **Bhokkanta** in South Ceylon. Later he lived in the village **Mahāmuni,** in the district of **Dīghavāpi. Ubbirī** was born as his daughter and was named **Sumanā.** Sumanā married **Lakuṇṭaka Atimbara.**[1]

[1] DhA. iv. 50 f.

12. **Sumana.**—A seṭṭhi of **Sāvatthi.** He was the father of **Anāthapiṇḍika** and **Subhūti Thera.**[1]

[1] ThagA. i. 23; AA. i. 125, 208.

13. **Sumana.**—A Pacceka Buddha of thirty-one kappas ago, to whom, in a previous birth, **Bhalliya**[1] and **Bhāradvāja Thera**[2] gave *vallikāra*-fruit.

[1] ThagA. i. 49.

[2] *Ibid.*, 303; *cf.* Ap. ii. 416.

14. **Sumana.**—Eldest son of King **Bindusāra.** He was killed by **Asoka. Nigrodha-sāmaṇera** was his son and **Sumanā** his wife.[1]

[1] Mhv. v. 38, 41; Sp. i. 45.

15. **Sumana.**—Son of **Saṅghamittā** and Aggibrahmā.[1] He joined the Order at the age of seven; even as a *sāmaṇera* he was gifted with the sixfold *abhiññā* and accompanied **Mahinda** to Ceylon.[2] Once when he announced that Mahinda was going to preach his voice was heard all over Ceylon.[3] In order to get relics for the cetiyas in Ceylon, he went (by air) to **Pupphapura (Pāṭaliputta),** and from there to **Sakka's** abode, for the Buddha's right collar-bone. He supervised the placing of the relics in the **Thūpārāma-cetiya.**[4]

[1] Mhv. v. 170.

[2] *Ibid.*, xiii. 4, 18.

[3] *Ibid.*, xiv. 33.

[4] *Ibid.*, xvii. 7, 21; xix. 24, 42; see also Dpv. xii. 13, 26, 39; xv. 5 f., 28, 93.

16. **Sumana.**—Governor of **Girijanapada** in the time of **Kākavaṇṇatissa.** He was a friend of **Veḷusumana's** father.[1]

[1] Mhv. xxiii. 69.

17. **Sumana.**—A **Yakkha** chief, to be invoked in time of need by followers of the Buddha.[1]

[1] D. iii. 205.

18. **Sumana.**—One of the chief lay patrons of **Metteyya Buddha.**[1]

[1] Anāgat. vs. 98.

19. **Sumana.**—A Pacceka Buddha of the future. See **Sumana** (5).

20. **Sumana.**—A gardener of **Kosambī.** He worked for three *seṭṭhis*: **Ghosaka, Kukkuṭa** and **Pāvāriya.** With their permission, he entertained the Buddha one day, and it was at his house that **Khujjuttarā** (*q.v.*) met and heard the Buddha.[1]

[1] DhA. i. 208 f.

21. **Sumana.**—A *seṭṭhiputta* of **Rājagaha. Puṇṇa (Puṇṇasīha)** (*q.v.*) was his servant, but, later, Puṇṇa, as the result of giving alms to **Sāriputta,** became rich and Sumana married his daughter, **Uttarā.** Sumana was an unbeliever, and Uttarā, wishing for leisure in which to practise her religion, obtained for him the services of the courtezan **Sirimā,** paying her with the money obtained from her father.[1]

[1] DhA. iii. 104, 302 f.

22. **Sumana.**—A deity who lived in the fortified chamber over the gate in **Jetavana.**[1]

[1] DhA. i. 41.

23. **Sumana.**—See **Samiddhisumana.**

24. **Sumana.**—An eminent monk, who was present at the Foundation Ceremony of the **Mahā Thūpa.**[1]

[1] Dpv. xix. 8; in MṬ. (524) he is called **Mahā Sumana.**

25. **Sumana.**—The guardian deity of **Samantakūṭa** (*q.v.*). See also Cv. lxxxvi. 19.

26. **Sumana.**—The personal name of **Uggahamāna.**[1]

[1] MA. ii. 709.

Sumanakūṭa.—See **Samantakūṭa.**

Sumanagalla.—A district in **Rohaṇa,** mentioned in the account of the campaigns of **Parakkamabāhu I.**[1]

[1] Cv. lxxiv. 123.

Sumanagiri-vihāra.—See **Samantakūṭa.**

Sumanatālavaṇṭiya Thera.—An arahant. Ninety-four kappas ago he gave to **Siddhattha Buddha** a fan (*tālavaṇṭa*) covered with jasmine-flowers.[1] See also **Sāṭimattika.**[2]

[1] Ap. i. 293 = Ap. ii. 408. [2] ThagA. i. 359.

Sumanadāmadāyaka Thera.—An arahant. Ninety-four kappas ago he stood in front of **Siddhattha Buddha,** with a garland of *sumana* flowers in his hand to honour him.[1]

[1] Ap. i. 293.

1. **Sumanadeva.**—A tree-deity whose daughter, **Kāḷī,** was married to **Dīghataphala.** Because **Kāḷaviḷaṅgiya's** (*q.v.*) wife, disguised as a man, brought him the news of the birth of a son to Kāḷī, he gave her the treasures which lay buried within range of the shadow of his tree.[1]

[1] MA. ii. 813.

2. **Sumanadeva.**—An Elder of Ceylon, teacher at the **Lohapāsāda.** He was an eminent expert of the Abhidhamma.[1]

[1] DhSA. 31.

1. **Sumanadevī.**—Mother of **Mahā Kassapa Thera.**[1]

[1] Ap. ii. 583.

2. **Sumanadevī.**—Mother of **Suppatiṭṭhita.**[1]

[1] MṬ. 528.

3. **Sumanadevī.**—Step-sister of **Khallāṭanāga.** She had three sons—**Tissa, Abhaya** and **Uttara**—who conspired against the king. On the failure of their conspiracy, they jumped into the fire on the spot where now stands the **Abhayagiri-cetiya.**[1]

[1] MṬ. 612.

4. **Sumanadevī.**—Youngest daughter of **Anāthapiṇḍika.** When her sisters, **Mahāsubhaddā** and **Cullasubhaddā,** married and went to live

with their husbands, Anāthapiṇḍika appointed her to look after the feeding of the monks in his house. She became a *sakadāgāmī* and remained unmarried. Because of her failure to obtain a husband, she refused to eat, and fell ill. One day, when Anāthapiṇḍika was in the refectory, he received a message from her. He went immediately and asked her what was the matter. She addressed him as "Younger brother," and saying that she had no fear, she died. Anāthapiṇḍika, in great sorrow, sought the Buddha and confessed his grief that she should have died while talking incoherently. The Buddha explained that, inasmuch as she was a *sakadāgāmī* and he but a *sotāpanna*, her addressing him as "Younger brother" was quite in order. After death she was born in **Tusita,** said the Buddha.[1]

[1] DhA. i. 151 f.

5. **Sumanadevī.**—Mother of **Visākhā.** Her husband was **Dhanañjaya,** son of **Meṇḍakaseṭṭhi** of **Bhaddiya-nagara.**[1] She was one of the **Mahāpuññā.**[2]

[1] DhA. i. 384 f.; SA. i. 116, etc. [2] Vsm. 383; PSA. 509, etc.

Sumanapabbata.—A monastic building in **Kelivāta,** erected by **Aggabodhi I.**[1]

[1] Cv. xlii. 19.

Sumanavāpigāma.—A village in Ceylon, four *yojanas* to the south-east of **Anurādhapura.** Precious stones appeared there, when **Duṭṭhagāmaṇī** wished to build the **Mahā Thūpa.**[1]

[1] Mhv. xxviii. 18.

Sumanavījaniya Thera.—An arahant,[1] evidently identical with **Isidinna**[2] (*q.v.*).

[1] Ap. ii. 415. [2] ThagA. i. 313.

1. **Sumanā.**—An *aggasāvikā* of **Anomadassī Buddha.**[1]

[1] J. i. 36; Bu. viii. 23.

2. **Sumanā.**—Wife of **Sirivaḍḍhaka** and mother of **Mahosadha.**[1]

[1] J. vi. 331.

3. **Sumanā.**—A Nāga maiden, wife of the Nāga-king **Campeyya.** See the **Campeyya Jātaka.** She is identified with **Rāhulamātā.**[1]

[1] J. iv. 468.

4. **Sumanā.**—Wife of **Sumana** (14) and mother of **Nigrodha-sāmaṇera.**[1]

[1] Mhv. v. 41.

5. **Sumanā.**—Wife of **Sumedha Buddha** in his last lay life.[1]

[1] Bu. xii. 20.

6. **Sumanā.**—Called **Sumanārājakumārī.** She was the daughter of the king of **Kosala** and sister of **Pasenadi.** She is included among the eminent *upāsikās.*[1] She once visited the Buddha, with five hundred royal maidens in five hundred royal chariots, and questioned him regarding the efficacy of giving.[2]

The Commentary explains[3] that these five hundred companions were born on the same day as herself. She was seven years old when the Buddha paid his first visit to **Sāvatthi,** and she was present at the dedication of **Jetavana** with her five hundred companions, carrying vases, flowers, etc., as offering to the Buddha. After the Buddha's sermon she became a *sotāpanna.*

It is said that, in the time of **Vipassī Buddha,** she belonged to a *seṭṭhi* family, her father being dead. When the people, almost at the point of the sword, obtained the king's permission to entertain the Buddha and his monks, it was the *senāpati's* privilege to invite the Buddha to his house on the first day. When Sumanā came back from playing, she found her mother in tears, and when asked the reason, her mother replied, "If your father had been alive, ours would have been the privilege of entertaining the Buddha today." Sumanā comforted her by saying that that honour should yet be theirs. She filled a golden bowl with richly flavoured milk-rice, covering it with another bowl. She then wrapped both vessels all round with jasmine-flowers and left the house with her slaves. On the way to the *senāpati's* house she was stopped by his men, but she coaxed them to let her pass, and, as the Buddha approached, saying that she wished to offer him a jasmine garland, she put the two vessels into his alms bowl. She then made the resolve that in every subsequent birth she should be named **Sumanā** and that her body should be like a garland of jasmine. When the Buddha arrived in the senāpati's house and was served first with soup, he covered his bowl saying that he had already been given his food. At the end of the meal the senāpati made enquiries, and, full of admiration for Sumanā's courage, invited her to his house and made her his chief consort. Ever after that she was known as Sumanā, and, wherever she was born, a shower of jasmine-flowers fell knee-deep on the day of her birth.

[1] A. iv. 347. [2] See **Sumanārājakumārī Sutta** (A. iii. 32 f.). [3] AA. ii. 593 f.

According to the Therīgathā Commentary,[4] Sumanā joined the Order in her old age. She was present when the Buddha preached to Pasenadi, the discourse[5] beginning with, "There are four young creatures, Sire, who may not be disregarded," and Pasenadi was established in the Refuges and the Precepts. Sumanā wished to leave the world, but put off doing so that she might look after her grandmother as long as she lived.

After the grandmother's death, Sumanā went with Pasenadi to the vihāra, taking such things as rugs and carpets, which she presented to the Order. The Buddha preached to her and to Pasenadi, and she became an *anāgāmī*. She then sought ordination, and, at the conclusion of the stanza[6] preached to her by the Buddha, attained arahantship.

[4] ThigA. 22 f. [5] Given at S. i. 68-70. [6] Thig. vs. 16.

7. **Sumanā Therī.**—She was a **Sākyan** maiden, belonging to the harem of the Bodhisatta before his renunciation. She joined the Order under **Mahāpajāpatī Gotamī,** and, as she sat meditating, the Buddha appeared before her in a ray of glory. She developed insight and became an arahant.[1]

[1] Thig. vs. 14; ThigA. 20.

8. **Sumanā.**—Wife of **Siddhattha Buddha** in his last lay life.[1]

[1] Bu. xvii. 15; BuA. (185, 187) calls her **Somanassā.**

9. **Sumanā.**—See **Sumanadevī.**

10. **Sumanā.**—An *aggasāvikā* of **Metteyya Buddha.**[1]

[1] Anāgat. vs. 98.

11. **Sumanā.**—The name of **Ubbirī,** when she was born in **Bhokkantagāma,** as the daughter of **Sumana.** She married **Lakuṇṭaka Atimbara, Duṭṭhagāmaṇī's** minister. Later she joined the **Pañcabalaka** nuns and became an arahant. See **Ubbirī** (1).

12. **Sumanā.**—An eminent teacher of the Vinaya in Ceylon.[1]

[1] Dpv. xviii. 17.

13. **Sumanā.**—One of four women of **Paṇṇakaṭanagara** in **Esikāraṭṭha.** They saw a monk begging for alms, and one gave him a sheaf of *indīvara*-flowers, another a handful of blue lilies, another of lotuses, and the fourth some jasmine blossoms. They were all reborn in **Tāvatiṃsa,** their *vimānas* adjoining each other. **Moggallāna** saw them and learnt their

story, which is recorded in the *Vimānavatthu* as the story of the **Catu-ritthivimāna.** The last-mentioned of the women, who offered *sumana*-flowers, was called **Sumanā.**[1]

[1] Vv. iv. 7; VvA. 195 f.

Sumanā Vagga.—The fourth chapter of the Pañcaka Nipāta of the **Aṅguttara Nikāya.**[1]

[1] A. iii. 32-44.

Sumanā-rājakumārī Sutta.—**Sumanā,** sister of **Pasenadi,** visits the Buddha at **Jetavana** with five hundred companions in five hundred chariots and asks him whether, in the case of two disciples, alike in faith, virtue and insight, the one being an almsgiver and the other not, there be any distinction. The Buddha replies that whether they be born in the deva-world or in the world of men, the giver would be superior in life-span, beauty, happiness, honour and power. There would still be a difference between them, even when, in later life, they both enter the Order, but the difference would cease to exist on their becoming arahants.[1] The Commentary adds[2] that Sumanā's questions were the result of a conversation between two babies born in the house of the King of **Kosala,** one as the king's son, the other as the son of one of the attendant women. The children were laid side by side on two beds, the prince's bed being higher and better. They had both been monks in their previous life; the prince was a *sārāṇīyadhammapūraka*, the other a *bhattaggapūraka*. The prince saw his past life, and, realizing that the other had not taken his advice and had, therefore, suffered eclipse, addressed him as he lay on the next bed. Sumanā heard their talk, but spoke no word of it to anyone, in case the children should be thought to be possessed of evil spirits.

[1] A. iii. 32 f. [2] AA. ii. 595 f.

Sumanāveḷiya Thera.—An arahant. Thirty-one kappas ago he placed a bunch of *sumana*-flowers in front of the seat of **Vessabhū Buddha.** After death he was born in the **Nimmanaratī**-world; eleven kappas ago he was a king named **Sahassāra.**[1]

[1] Ap. i. 264.

Sumā.—An eminent Therī of India who came over to **Anurādhapura** in the time of **Devānampiyatissa** and taught the Vinaya there.[1]

[1] Dpv. xviii. 24.

Sumāgadhā (Sumāgavā).—A lotus-pond near **Rājagaha.** The *Saṃyutta Nikāya* mentions the Buddha as relating the story of a man who went to Sumāgadhā with the thought, "I will speculate about the world." He saw an army, with its four divisions, enter a lotus-stalk. He then thought he must be mad and told everyone so. The Buddha explained that what the man had seen was real; it was an **Asura** army, fleeing from the devas in panic, through a lotus-stalk.[1] Near the pond was the **Moranivāpa,** and within walking distance was the **Paribbājakārāma** in Queen **Udumbarikā's** park. The Buddha was walking about in the open air near Sumāgadhā just before he preached the **Udumbarikasīhanāda Sutta.**[2]

[1] S. v. 447 f.; *cf.* *Rāmāyaṇa* i. 34. [2] D. iii. 40.

1. **Sumitta.**—An **Ājīvaka** who gave grass for his seat to **Padumuttara Buddha.**[1]

[1] BuA. 158.

2. **Sumitta.**—Son of **Sumedha Buddha** in his last lay life.[1]

[1] Bu. xii. 20; BuA. (160) calls him **Punabbasumitta.**

3. **Sumitta.**—Brother of **Sambahula** and king of **Amaranagara;** he entered the Order and became the *aggasāvaka* of **Siddhattha Buddha.**[1]

[1] Bu. xvii. 18; J. i. 40; BuA. 186.

4. **Sumitta.**—A king of one hundred and thirty kappas ago; a previous birth of **Nāgita (Atthasandassaka) Thera.**[1] *v.l.* **Sukhitta.**

[1] ThagA. i. 184; Ap. i. 168.

5. **Sumitta.**—A sage of **Kāsi,** a former birth of **Mahā Kassapa;** his wife was **Bhaddā Kāpilānī.**[1]

[1] Ap. ii. 582.

6. **Sumitta.**—Younger brother of **Vijaya** and son of **Sīhabāhu.** His wife, **Cittā,** was the daughter of the **Madda** King. He reigned in **Sīhapura,** and was invited by Vijaya to Ceylon to succeed to the throne; but he sent, instead, his son **Paṇḍuvāsudeva.** He had two other sons.[1]

[1] Mhv. vi. 38; viii. 2, 6, 10.

7. **Sumitta Thera.**—He was the younger son of **Kuntikinnarī.** He was ordained, with his brother **Tissa,** by **Mahāvaruṇa** and attained to arahantship. Tissa died from the bite of a venomous insect because it proved impossible to get any ghee, though Sumitta went about seeking for some. Sumitta died, while walking in meditation in the Caṅkama-hall, in the eighth year of **Asoka's** reign.[1]

[1] Mhv. v. 213-27.

1. **Sumittā.**—One of the five daughters of **Vijayabāhu I.** and **Tilokasundarī.** She married **Jayabāhu.**[1]

[1] Cv. lix. 31, 43.

2. **Sumittā.**—**Yasodharā (Rāhulamātā)** in a previous birth.[1]

[1] Ap. ii. 587.

Sumittārāma.—The monastery in which **Vipassī Buddha** died.[1]

[1] Bu. xx. 36.

1. **Sumukha.**—A Yakkha chief, to be invoked in time of need by followers of the Buddha.[1]

[1] D. iii. 205.

2. **Sumukha.**—A crow, general of **Supatta.** See the **Supatta Jātaka.** He is identified with **Sāriputta.**[1]

[1] J. ii. 436.

3. **Sumukha.**—A swan, general of a flock of swans whose king was **Dhataraṭṭha.** See the Haṃsa Jātaka (No. 502) and **Mahāhaṃsa Jātaka** (No. 534). He is identified with **Ānanda.**[1]

[1] J. iv. 430; v. 382.

Sumucalindasara.—A lake,[1] evidently identical with **Mucalinda** (*q.v.*).

[1] J. vi. 582.

Sumekhala.—A king whose country was destroyed because he ill-treated holy men.[1]

[1] ThagA. i. 368.

Sumekhali.—A king of fifty-four kappas ago, a former birth of **Bilālidāyaka Thera.**[1]

[1] ThagA. i. 145.

Sumeghaghana.—A king of twenty-nine kappas ago; a previous birth of **Minela-(Vinela-)pupphiya Thera.**[1]

[1] Ap. i. 204.

1. **Sumedha.**—The Bodhisatta in the time of **Dīpaṅkara Buddha.** He was a very rich brahmin of **Amaravatī,** and, having left the world, became an ascetic of great power in the **Himālaya.** While on a visit to **Ramma-nagara,** he saw people decorating the road for Dīpaṅkara

Buddha, and undertook to do one portion of the road himself. The Buddha arrived before his work was finished, and Sumedha lay down on a rut for the Buddha to walk over him. He resolved that he, too, would become a Buddha, and Dīpaṅkara, looking into the future, saw that his wish would come true. This was the beginning of **Gotama Buddha's** qualification for Enlightenment.[1]

[1] J. i. 2 ff.; DhA. i. 68; Bu. ii. 5 ff.; SNA. i. 49; in Chinese Records he is called Megha. The Dvy. (p. 247) calls him Sumati.

2. **Sumedha.**—A *khattiya*, father of **Dīpaṅkara Buddha.**[1]

[1] J. i. 29; but Bu. iii. 25 calls him **Sunanda.**

3. **Sumedha.**—A *khattiya*, father of **Nārada Buddha.**[1]

[1] J. i. 37; but Bu. ix. 18 calls him **Sudeva.**

4. **Sumedha.**—The eleventh of the twenty-four Buddhas. He was born in **Sudassana,** his father being the *khattiya* **Sudatta** and his mother **Sudattā.** He lived in the household for nine thousand years, in three palaces, **Sucanda, Kañcana (Koñca)** and **Sirivaḍḍha,** his wife being **Sumanā** and his son **Sumitta (Punabbasumitta).** He left home on an elephant, practised austerities for eight months, was given a meal of milk-rice by **Nakulā,** and grass for his seat by the **Ājīvaka Sirivaḍḍha.** He obtained Enlightenment under a *mahānimba*(*mahānīpa*)-tree. His body was eighty-eight cubits in height. His chief disciples were **Saraṇa** and **Sabbakāma** among monks and **Rāmā** and **Surāmā** among women. **Sāgara** was his personal attendant. His chief lay patrons were **Uruvela** and **Yasava** among men, and **Yasodharā** and **Sirimā** among women. He preached his first sermon at **Sudassana,** to his younger brothers. The Bodhisatta was the ascetic, **Uttara.** Sumedha lived for ninety thousand years and died in **Medhārāma.** His relics were scattered.[1]

[1] Bu. xii. 1 ff.; BuA. 163 f.

5. **Sumedha.**—The name of a brahmin family in the time of **Tissa Buddha. Vāraṇa Thera** was born in the family.[1]

[1] ThagA. i. 353.

6. **Sumedha.**—An *upaṭṭhāka* of **Sumedha Buddha,** whom **Pilindavaccha** met at that time.[1]

[1] Ap. i. 59; but see Bu. xii. 23, where Sumedha's *upaṭṭhāka* is called **Sāgara.** Perhaps this refers to another.

7. **Sumedha.**—A king of twenty kappas ago, a previous birth of **Āvopphiya Thera.**[1]

[1] Ap. i. 112.

8. **Sumedha.**—A king of seven kappas ago, a previous birth of **Padasaññaka Thera.**[1]

[1] Ap. i. 119.

9. **Sumedha.**—An Elder of Ceylon, at whose request **Buddhanāga** wrote the **Vinayatthamañjūsā.**[1]

[1] P.L.C. 201.

10. **Sumedha.**—A Thera of **Cūtaggāma,** probably of the fourteenth century; author of the **Sādhucaritodaya** and the **Anāpattidīpanī.**[1]

[1] P.L.C. 247.

Sumedhakathā.—The first section of the Jātaka Commentary, dealing with **Sumedha's** meeting with **Dīpaṅkara Buddha.**[1]

[1] J. i. 2-28.

Sumedhayasa.—A king of twenty-nine kappas ago, a former birth of **Rāmaṇeyya Thera.**[1]

[1] ThagA. i. 121.

1. **Sumedhā Therī.**—She was the daughter of King **Koñca** of **Mantāvatī.** When she came of age, her parents let **Anikadatta,** king of **Vāraṇavatī,** see her. But she had frequent association with nuns, and cut off her hair by herself, and then, concentrating her attention on the idea of the "foul," she attained the first *jhāna*. When her parents entered her room with Anikadatta, she converted them all, and obtained permission to join the Order. Shortly afterwards she attained arahantship.

In the time of **Koṇāgamana Buddha** she and her friends (afterwards **Dhanañjānī** and **Khemā**), clansmen's daughters, agreed together to have a large monastery built, and this they made over to the Buddha and the Order. In the time of **Kassapa Buddha** she belonged to a very rich family and was a friend of the seven daughters of **Kikī.**[1]

[1] Thig. vs. 448-522; ThigA. 272 f.; Ap. ii. 512 f.; *cf.* 545 (vs. 24).

2. **Sumedhā.**—Mother of **Dīpaṅkara Buddha.**[1]

[1] J. i. 29; Bu. ii. 207.

3. **Sumedhā.**—Mother of **Padumuttara Buddha.**[1]

[1] SA. ii. 67; DA. ii. 488; but Bu. xi. 19 calls her **Sujātā.**

4. **Sumedhā.**—Chief queen of King **Suruci** of **Mithilā** and mother of **Mahāpanāda.** See the **Suruci Jātaka.** She is identified with **Visākhā.**[1]

[1] J. iv. 325; DA. iii. 856.

1. **Sumbha.**—A Pacceka Buddha.[1]

[1] M. iii. 70; ApA. i. 106.

2. **Sumbha.**—A country in which was **Desaka** (?), where **Udāyi** visited the Buddha during a stay there, and had a conversation with him.[1]

[1] S. v. 89; *cf.* 168, and J. i. 393; also SA. iii. 181.

Summa Thera.—An incumbent of **Dīpavihāra** in Ceylon. He was evidently an eminent commentator, and is quoted by **Buddhaghosa. Tipiṭaka-Cūḷanāga** was his pupil.[1]

[1] MA. i. 126; AA. ii. 845.

Suyasā.—A palace occupied by **Paduma Buddha** before his renunciation.[1]

[1] Bu. ix. 17; but see BuA. 146.

Suyāna.—Seventy-seven kappas ago there were eight kings of this name, previous births of **Pānadhidāyaka Thera.**[1]

[1] Ap. i. 209.

1. **Suyāma.**—One of the eight brahmins consulted at the birth of the Buddha to predict his future.[1]

[1] J. i. 56; Mil. 236.

2. **Suyāma.**—A devaputta, chief of the **Yāma**-devas.[1] The courtezan, **Sirimā,** was reborn after death, as the wife of Suyāma.[2] When the Buddha descended from the *deva*-world to earth, at **Saṅkassa,** Suyāma accompanied him, holding a yak's-tail fan (*vālavījana*).[3]

[1] A. iv. 242; D. i. 217.
[2] SNA. i. 244.
[3] DhA. iii. 226; Vsm. 392; *cf.* BuA. 239; J. i. 48, 53; Mhv. xxxi. 78.

3. **Suyāma.**—A king of Benares, son of **Puthuvindhara.** His son was **Kikī Brahmadatta.**[1]

[1] ThagA. i. 151.

4. **Suyāma (Suyāmana) Thera.**—He belonged to a brahmin family of **Vesāli** and was expert in the three Vedas. He saw and heard the Buddha at Vesāli, and, having entered the Order, attained arahantship while his head was being shaved.

Ninety-one kappas ago he was a brahmin of **Dhaññavatī**, and, having invited **Vipassī Buddha** to his house, gave him a seat spread with flowers. He was once a king, called **Varadassana**.[1] He is evidently identical with **Kusumāsanīya** of the *Apadāna*.[2]

[1] Thag. 74; ThagA. i. 165 f. [2] Ap. i. 160.

Sura.—A hunter, who discovered fermented liquor. See the **Kumbha Jātaka.**

Surakitti.—A king of Burma in the fifteenth century. He built a four-storeyed vihāra for **Tipiṭakālaṅkāra Thera**.[1]

[1] Bode, *op. cit.*, 53.

Surakkhita.—An *aggasāvaka* of **Phussa Buddha**; he was a prince of **Kaṇṇakujja**.[1]

[1] J. i. 41; BuA. 193; but Bu. xix. calls him **Sukhita.**

Suragiri.—A palace occupied by **Atthadassī Buddha** before his renunciation.[1]

[1] Bu. xv. 15.

Suraṭṭha.—A country[1] in which **Sālissara** lived, on the banks of the **Sātodikā**.[2] Two hundred years after the Buddha's death the king of Suraṭṭha was **Piṅgala**.[3]

The country is identified with modern Kathiawad.

[1] Mil. 331, 359; Pv. iv. 3; Ap. ii. 359.
[2] J. iii. 463; but see v. 133.
[3] PvA. 244.

Surabhi.—A Pacceka Buddha whom the Bodhisatta (in his birth as **Munāli**) insulted.[1]

[1] Ap. i. 299; UdA. 264.

Suramāna.—A tank restored by **Parakkamabāhu I.**[1]

[1] Cv. lxxix. 36.

Suramma.—A seven-storeyed palace, occupied by **Gotama Buddha** before his Renunciation.[1]

[1] BuA. 230; Bu. xxvi. 14 calls it Surāma.

Suramukha.—A noble steed, belonging to **Ekarāja**.[1]

[1] J. vi. 135.

Surammā.—One of the chief lay-women supporters of **Siddhattha Buddha.**[1]

[1] Bu. xvii. 70.

1. **Surasena.**—One of the sixteen **Mahājanapadā** (*q.v.*). It is mentioned with **Maccha,** and was located in the south of the **Kuru** country. Its capital was Mathurā. It is famous in the Epics and the Purāṇas because of its connection with Kṛṣṇa, and the Yādavas.

2. **Surasena.**—A city in the time of **Siddhattha Buddha,** where the Bodhisatta was born as the brahmin **Maṅgala.**[1]

[1] BuA. 187.

Surādha Thera.—The younger brother of **Rādha.** He followed his brother's example, entered the Order, and became an arahant. Thirty-one kappas ago he gave a *mātuluṅga*-fruit to **Sikhī Buddha.**[1] He is probably identical with **Mātuluṅgaphaladāyaka** of the *Apadāna.*[2]

[1] Thag. vss. 135-6; ThagA. i. 254 f. [2] Ap. ii. 446.

Surādha Sutta.—The Buddha teaches **Surādha** (*q.v.*) how to get rid of all idea of " I " and " mine," so that the mind may go beyond the ways of conceit and be utterly liberated.[1]

[1] S. iii. 80 f.

Surādhā.—An aggasāvikā of **Paduma Buddha.**[1]

[1] Bu. ix. 22.

Surāpāna Jātaka (No. 81).—The Bodhisatta was once born in the *Udiccabrāhmaṇakula,* and became a hermit with five hundred pupils. One day his pupils went, with his leave, to Benares, to the haunts of men, for salt and vinegar. The king welcomed them, and invited them to stay in the royal park for four months. During this time a drinking festival was held in the city, and the people, thinking to give the hermits a rare gift, entertained them to the best they had. The hermits became drunk and behaved with undue hilarity. When they emerged from their stupor and realized what they had done, they left the city and hastened back to their teacher.

The story was related in reference to the occasion on which **Sāgata Thera** (*q.v.*) got drunk.[1]

[1] J. i. 360 f.

1. **Surāma.**—A palace occupied by **Koṇḍañña Buddha** before his renunciation.[1]

[1] BuA. 107; but see Bu. iii. 26.

2. **Surāma.**—See **Suramma.**

1. **Surāmā.**—An *aggasāvikā* of **Siddhattha Buddha.**[1]

[1] J. i. 40; Bu. xvii. 19.

2. **Surāmā.**—An *aggasāvikā* of **Sumedha Buddha.**[1]

[1] J. i. 38; Bu. xii. 24.

Surāvinicchaya.—A work by **Mahāparakkama Thera** of Taungu (**Ketumatī**) on the evil effects of intoxicants.[1]

[1] Sās., p. 81; Bode, *op. cit.*, 46.

Surindavatī.—A city in the time of **Koṇāgamana Buddha.** In a park in the city **Koṇāgamana** preached to **Bhīyasa** and **Uttara,** who later became his chief disciples.[1]

[1] BuA. 215.

Surinda-vihāra.—A monastery built in **Sunandavatī** by King **Uggata** for **Sobhita Buddha.**[1]

[1] BuA. 138.

1. **Suriya.**—A Devaputta. Once, when he was seized by **Rāhu,** lord of the **Asuras,** he invoked the power of the Buddha, and the Buddha enjoined on Rāhu to let him go. This Rāhu did, and Suriya is spoken of as seeking **Vepacitti** and standing by his side, trembling and with stiffened hair.[1] Suriya is one of the inhabitants of the **Cātummahārājika**-world.[2] Suriya and **Candimā** are both under the rule of **Sakka,** and we find Sakka asking them to stop their journeyings at his behest.[3] Suriya was present at the preaching of the **Mahāsamaya Sutta.**[4] He is sometimes[5] described as **Ādicca** (Aditi's son). The disk of the sun, which forms Suriya's *vimāna,* is fifty leagues in diameter.[6]

[1] S. i. 51; *cf.* **Candimā.**

[2] MNidA. 108.

[3] *E.g.,* when he wished the Sāmaṇeras **Paṇḍita** and **Sukha** to be able to meditate undisturbed (DhA. ii. 143; iii. 97). See also DhA. iii. 208.

[4] D. ii. 260.

[5] PSA. 253.

[6] *E.g.,* D. iii. 196.

2. **Suriya.**—A son of **Sakka** (*q.v.*).

1. **Suriya Sutta.**—Describes the occasion on which **Suriya** (*q.v.*) was seized by **Rāhu.**[1]

[1] S. i. 51.

2. **Suriya Sutta.**—The Buddha explains to the monks the destruction of the world by the gradual appearance of seven consecutive suns. Details are given of the havoc caused by each subsequent sun. The sutta is intended to show that all things are impermanent; but only those who possess Ariyan knowledge realize this. Even so great a teacher as **Sunetta** (*q.v.*) could not find the way out of sorrow.[1] The sutta was also evidently called **Sattasuriya** or **Sattasuriyuggamana Sutta.**

[1] A. iv. 100 f.

3. **Suriya Sutta.**—Just as, in the autumn when the sky is clear, the sun drives away all darkness, so, of all profitable conditions, earnestness is the chief.[1]

[1] S. v. 44.

1. **Suriyakumāra.**—Brother of **Candakumāra.** See the **Khaṇḍahāla Jātaka.** He is identified with **Sariputta.**[1]

[1] J. vi. 157.

2. **Suriyakumāra.**—A son of **Brahmadatta,** king of Benares, and step-brother of **Mahiṃsāsa.** See the **Devadhamma Jātaka.** He is identified with **Ānanda.**[1]

[1] J. i. 133; *cf.* DhA. iii. 73 f.

Suriyagabbha.—A mountain range on the way to **Gandhamādana.**[1]

[1] SNA. i. 66.

1. **Suriyagutta Thera.**—He was present from the **Kelāsa-vihāra,** with ninety-six thousand others, at the Foundation Ceremony of the **Mahā Thūpa.**[1]

[1] Mhv. xxix. 43; Dpv. xix. 8.

2. **Suriyagutta.**—A Thera belonging to the pupillary succession of **Mahā Kassapa. Candagutta** was his teacher and **Assagutta** his pupil.[1]

[1] SA. iii. 125.

Suriyadeva.—The fourth son of **Devagabbhā;** one of the **Andhaka-veṇhudāsaputtā.**[1]

[1] J. iv. 8.

Suriyapassapabbata.—One of the seven mountain ranges surrounding **Chaddantadaha.**[1]

[1] J. v. 138.

Suriyapeyyāla.—A series of discourses based on the sun.[1]

[1] S. v. 29.

Suriyavaccasā.—A **Gandhabba** maiden, daughter of **Timbaru.** When she went to dance before **Sakka, Pañcasikha** saw her and fell in love with her, but she favoured **Mātali's** son **Sikhaṇḍi.** Later she heard Pañcasikha sing love-songs in her honour, which also contained references to his deep attachment to the Buddha. This influenced her choice, and she became his wife.[1]

Her personal name was **Bhaddā.** She was called Suriyavaccasā because of her bodily beauty (*sarīrasampattiyā*).[2]

[1] D. ii. 258, 268 f. [2] DA. iii. 704.

Suriyavatī.—A city in which, at the foot of a *campaka*-tree, **Sikhī Buddha** performed the **Yamakapāṭihāriya.**[1]

[1] BuA. 202.

1. **Suriyopama Sutta.**—Just as the dawn is the forerunner of the sun, so is right view the forerunner of the four Ariyan truths.[1]

[1] S. v. 442.

2. **Suriyopama Sutta.**—Just as there is darkness in the world till the sun or the moon rises, so is there ignorance of the four Ariyan truths till a Buddha arises.[1]

[1] S. v. 442 f.

1. **Suruci.**—The Bodhisatta born as a brahmin in the time of **Maṅgala Buddha.**[1]

[1] J. i. 32; Bu. iv. 10.

2. **Suruci.**—A king of **Mithilā.** See the **Suruci Jātaka.**[1]

[1] *Cf.* Mhv. ii. 4; Dpv. iii. 7; Mtu. i. 348.

3. **Suruci.**—A king of **Mithilā,** father of **Mahāpanāda.** See the **Suruci Jātaka.**

4. **Suruci.**—A palace, occupied by **Vessabhū Buddha** before his renunciation.[1]

[1] Bu. xxii. 19.

5. **Suruci.**—A palace occupied by **Kakusandha Buddha** before his renunciation.[1]

[1] Bu. xxiii. 16.

6. **Suruci.**—A *tāpasa.* See **Sarada.**

Suruci Jātaka (No. 489).—There once reigned in **Mithilā** a king, named **Suruci.** He had a son also called **Suruci-kumāra,** who studied at **Takkasilā,** where Prince **Brahmadatta** of Benares was his fellow student. They became great friends, and agreed to bring about an alliance between the two royal houses. Suruci came to the throne of Mithilā and had a son called after himself. Brahmadatta became king of Benares and had a daughter, **Sumedhā.** A marriage was arranged between Suruci and Sumedhā, but Brahmadatta agreed to the alliance only on condition that Sumedhā should be Suruci's only wife. Suruci accepted this condition, but, though Sumedhā lived in the palace for ten thousand years, she had no child. The people clamoured for an heir, but Suruci refused to take another queen, though Sumedhā herself obtained for him many thousands of women for his harem, sixteen thousand in all. Forty thousand years thus passed, but no child was born in the palace.

Then Sumedhā vowed an Act of Truth; **Sakka's** throne was heated, and he asked the god **Naḷakāra** (*q.v.*) to be born as Sumedhā's son. Naḷakāra reluctantly agreed. Then Sakka went to the king's park disguised as a sage and offered to give any woman who was virtuous a son. "If thou seek virtue, seek Sumedhā," they said. He then went to the palace, and having made Sumedhā declare to him her virtue, he revealed his identity and promised her a son. In due course a son was born—**Mahāpanāda.** He grew up amid great splendour, and, when he was sixteen, the king built for him a grand palace.

It is said that Sakka sent **Vissakamma** as mason to help with the building. When the palace was completed, three ceremonies were held on the same day: the dedication of the palace, Mahāpanāda's coronation and his marriage. The festival lasted for seven years, and the people began to grumble; but the king would not bring the festival to an end, for all this time Mahāpanāda had not once laughed, and the king said the feast could not end till he was made to laugh. Various people came to amuse him, among them two jugglers, **Bhaṇḍukaṇṇa** and **Paṇḍukaṇṇa;** but it was not till Sakka sent a divine dancer to dance the "Half-body" dance, in which one half of the body danced while the rest stood still, that Mahāpanāda smiled.

The story was related on the occasion on which the Buddha gave **Visākhā** eight boons. One night there was a great storm, and the Buddha asked the monks to drench themselves in the rain as that would be the last great rain-storm in his time. Together with them the Buddha appeared at Visākhā's house, but as soon as they arrived on the threshold they were quite dry.

Bhaddaji is identified with Mahāpanāda, **Visākhā** with Sumedhā, **Ānanda** with Vissakamma, and the Bodhisatta was Sakka.[1]

[1] J. iv. 314-25; *cf.* DA. iii. 856 f.; and J. ii. 334.

Surundhana.—A city in **Kāsī**; an old name for Benares.[1]

[1] J. iv. 104, 119.

Surullagāma.—A village in Ceylon, mentioned in the campaigns of **Parakkamabāhu I.**[1]

[1] Cv. lxxii. 139.

Sulakkhaṇā.—Wife of **Añjanasakka** and mother of **Mahāpajāpatī Gotamī.**[1]

[1] Ap. ii. 538 (vs. 115); but see Mhv. ii. 18, where Añjana's wife is called **Yasodharā.** This may have been another wife.

1. **Sulasā.**—A *nagarasobhiṇī* (courtezan) of Benares. See the **Sulasā Jātaka.**

2. **Sulasā.**—A *nagarasobhiṇī* (courtezan) of **Rājagaha.** One day she saw the son of **Mahādhanaseṭṭhi** being led to execution for his crimes and, feeling compassion for him because she had once enjoyed his patronage, she sent him four cakes and some drink. **Moggallāna** appeared before him as soon as the cakes were given to him, and the condemned man offered them to the Elder. After death he was born as a *devatā* on a *nigrodha*-tree in the park near the city. One day, when Sulasā entered the park, the deity, creating a great darkness, carried her away. Seven days later he took her to **Veḷuvana** and left her there on the edge of the crowd who were listening to the **Dhamma.** When she related her experiences, the people were at first inclined to laugh at her; but her story was verified, and they were amazed. The story was reported to the Buddha, who made it the subject for a sermon.[1]

[1] Pv. i. 1; PvA. 4 f. It is probably this story which is repeated at Milinda, p. 350, as the "assembly of Sulasā."

Sulasā Jātaka (No. 419).—Once in Benares there lived a courtezan, **Sulasā,** whose price was one thousand a night. In Benares also lived a robber, **Sattaka.** One day he was taken by the king's men, and, as he was being led to execution, Sulasā saw him and fell in love with him.

She bribed the chief guard to free him and lived with him. After a few months Sattaka tired of her, and, wishing to kill her, took her to a lonely mountain top, saying that he had made a vow to the deity dwelling there. When Sulasā discovered his real intention, she begged leave to be allowed to pay obeisance to him before her death, and, as she walked round him, she watched her opportunity and pushed him down the precipice, where he was crushed to death.

The story was related in reference to **Puññalakkhaṇā,** a slave-girl of **Anāthapiṇḍika's** wife. The girl borrowed a costly jewel belonging to her mistress and went to the pleasure garden. There a thief became friendly with her and planned to kill her. But she, reading his thoughts, asked him to draw some water for her from a well near by, and as he did so, she pushed him into the well and threw a stone down on to his head. The characters in the two stories were identical.[1]

[1] J. iii. 435-9; *cf.* the story of **Bhaddā Kuṇḍalakesā** and also the **Kaṇavera Jātaka.**

Suleyyā.—A class of devas present at the preaching of the **Mahāsamaya Sutta.**[1]

[1] D. ii. 260.

1. **Suvaca Sutta.**—A deva tells the Buddha of seven things which lead to a monk's growth: reverence for the Buddha, the Dhamma, the Saṅgha, the training, concentration, fair speech, good friendship.[1]

[1] A. iv. 29.

2. **Suvaca Sutta.**—**Sāriputta** explains the foregoing sutta.[1]

[1] A. iv. 30.

Suvaccha.—A brahmin in the time of **Padumuttara Buddha,** a previous birth of **Dhammasava (Nāgapupphiya) Thera.**[1] He became a hermit and lived in a forest hut. One day Padumuttara performed miracles near his hut, and Suvaccha threw *nāga*-flowers on him in token of his honour.[1]

[1] ThagA. i. 214; Ap. i. 179.

Suvaṇṇakakkaṭa Jātaka (No. 389).—The Bodhisatta was a brahmin farmer of **Sālindiya.** On the way to his fields he passed a pond and grew friendly with a golden crab living in the pond. A she-crow longed to eat the farmer's eyes, and persuaded her husband to induce a snake to bite the farmer. This he did, and, overcome with the poison, the farmer fell near the pool. Attracted by the noise, the crab emerged, and, seeing the crow about to peck out the farmer's eyes, caught the crow with his claws. When the snake came to the rescue of the crow, the crab fastened on him too. The crab made the snake suck the poison from the farmer's body, and, when he stood up, the crab crushed the necks of both the snake and the crow and killed them.

The story was told in reference to **Ānanda's** attempt to save the Buddha from the elephant (**Dhanapāla**) sent by **Devadatta** to kill him, by standing between the elephant and the Buddha.

Māra was the serpent, Devadatta the crow, and Ānanda the crab. **Ciñcāmāṇavikā** was the female crow.[1]

[1] J. iii. 293-8.

Suvaṇṇakāra Sutta.—A monk developing the higher consciousness should be like a goldsmith working with sterling gold. The analogous details are given of both processes.[1]

[1] A. i. 257 f.

Suvaṇṇakuṭi.—A building in the **Dakkhiṇagiri-vihāra,** where **Appihāsāmaṇera** lived.[1]

[1] MṬ. 552.

Suvaṇṇakūṭa.—The name of the **Cetiyapabbata** (**Missakapabbata**) in the time of **Koṇāgamana Buddha.**[1]

[1] Sp. i. 87, etc.; but Mhv. xv. 96 calls it Sumanakūṭa.

Suvaṇṇagāma.—A minister of **Kittisirirājasīha.** He built an *uposatha*-hall in the **Sūkara-vihāra.**[1]

[1] Cv. c. 296.

Suvaṇṇagiritāla.—A mountain five *yojanas* from **Jetuttara.** The river **Kontimāra** was five leagues further away.[1]

[1] J. vi. 514.

1. **Suvaṇṇagūha.**—A cave in **Cittakūṭapabbata:** it was the abode of the golden geese.[1]

[1] J. iii. 208; v. 237, 469; vi. 50.

2. **Suvaṇṇagūha.**—One of the three caves in **Nandamūla-Pabbhāra.**[1]

[1] SNA. i. 66.

Suvaṇṇatissa.—A tank restored by **Parakkamabāhu I.**[1]

[1] Cv. lxxix. 32; see Cv. *Trs.* ii. 119, n. 2.

Suvaṇṇatthambha.—A ford—considered dangerous—on the **Mahāvālukagaṅgā.**[1]

[1] Cv. xcvi. 10.

Suvaṇṇadoṇī.—A village in the **Malaya** district of Ceylon.[1]

[1] Cv. lxx. 11.

Suvaṇṇapabbata.—A mountain in **Himavā.**[1]

[1] J. i. 50, 55; SNA. i. 358.

Suvaṇṇapassapabbata.—One of the seven mountain ranges on the way to **Gandhamādana.**[1] It was the seventh range surrounding the **Chaddantadaha.**[2]

[1] SNA. i. 66. [2] J. v. 38, etc.

Suvaṇṇapālī.—Daughter of **Girikaṇḍasiva** and wife of **Paṇḍukābhaya.** Paṇḍukābhaya saw her on her way to her father's field with food and made her entertain him and his followers. Her name was Pālī, and she was given her soubriquet because the banyan leaves, on which she served the meal to Paṇḍukābhaya, turned into gold in her hands. She had five brothers, all of whom were killed by Paṇḍukābhaya's companion, **Canda.**[1]

[1] Mhv. x. 30 ff.

Suvaṇṇapiṇḍatissa.—The name by which **Sūratissa** was known before his accession.[1]

[1] Mhv. xxi. 9.

Suvaṇṇapupphiya Thera.—An arahant, evidently identical with **Vimalakoṇḍañña** (*q.v.*).[1]

[1] Ap. i. 150; ThagA. i. 146.

Suvaṇṇabimbohaniya Thera.—An arahant. Ninety-one kappas ago he gave as gift a bed and a cushion. Sixty-three kappas ago he was a king named **Asama.**[1]

[1] Ap. i. 234.

Suvaṇṇabhūmi.—A country. At the end of the Third Council, the theras **Soṇa** and **Uttara** visited this country in order to convert it to Buddhism. At that time a female deity of the sea was in the habit of eating every heir born to the king. The arrival of the theras coincided with the birth of a prince. At first the people thought that the monks were the friends of the demon, but later the monks, being told the story, drove away the demon by their *iddhi*-power and erected a bulwark round the country by reciting the **Brahmajāla Sutta.** Sixty thousand people embraced the new faith, while three thousand five hundred young men and fifteen hundred girls of noble family entered the Order. Thenceforth all princes born into the royal family were called **Soṇuttara.**[1]

There seems to have been regular trade between **Bharukaccha** and **Suvaṇṇabhūmi,**[2] and also between the latter and Benares **(Moliṇi),**[3] **Mithilā,**[4] **Sāvatthi,**[5] and **Pāṭaliputta.**[6]

The distance between Ceylon and Suvaṇṇabhūmi was seven hundred leagues, and, with a favourable wind, could be covered in seven days and nights.[7]

Suvaṇṇabhūmi is generally identified with Lower Burma, probably the Pagan and Moulmein districts. It probably included the coast from Rangoon to Singapore. The chief place in Suvaṇṇabhūmi was **Sudhammanagara**—*i.e.*, Thaton—at the mouth of the Sittaung River.[8] Fleet suggests,[9] however, that it might be the district in Bengal called by Hiouen Thsang "Ka-lo-na-su-fa-la-na" (Karṇasuvarṇa), or else the country along the river Son in Central India, a tributary of the Ganges, on the right bank of the river which is also called Hiraṇyavāha. The probability is that there were two places of the same name, one originally in India itself and the other in Further India. *cf.* **Sunāparanta.**

1 Mhv. xii. 6, 44 f.; Dpv. viii. 12; Sp. i. 64.
2 See, *e.g.*, J. iii. 188.
3 J. iv. 15.
4 J. vi. 34.
5 PvA. 47.
6 *Ibid.*, 271.
7 AA. i. 265.
8 See Sās. Introd., p. 4, and n. 3.
9 *J.R.A.S.* 1910, p. 428.

Suvaṇṇamalaya.—A place in **Rohaṇa,** mentioned in the account of the campaigns of **Parakkamabāhu I.**[1]

1 Cv. lxxv. 62, 65, 66.

Suvaṇṇamāli.—A name for the **Mahā Thūpa** (*q.v.*).

Suvaṇṇamiga Jātaka (No. 359).—The Bodhisatta was a young stag of golden colour who lived happily with a beautiful doe. The stag was the leader of eight myriads of deer. One day a hunter set a snare and the Bodhisatta's foot got entangled therein. He gave a succession of warning cries and the herd fled. The doe, however, came up to him and encouraged him to try to break the noose. But all his efforts were in vain, and, when the hunter approached, the doe went up to him and asked to be allowed to die in her mate's place. The hunter was so touched and amazed that he set them both free, and the stag gave him a magic jewel which he had found on the feeding-ground.

The story was told in reference to a girl of **Sāvatthi** who belonged to a family devoted to the two Chief Disciples. She married an unbeliever, but was allowed to practise her own religion unmolested. She finally persuaded her husband to listen to a sermon by **Sāriputta,** and both husband and wife became *sotāpannas*. Later, they joined the Order and became arahants.

Channa (the husband) is identified with the hunter, while the woman was the doe.[1]

[1] J. iii. 182-7.

Suvaṇṇa-Vimāna Vatthu.—The story of a man who built for the Buddha a **Gandhakuṭi** on a bare rock (*muṇḍikapabbata*) in **Andhakavinda,** and was reborn, after death, in **Tāvatiṃsa,** where a golden palace appeared for him. **Moggallāna** saw him there and learnt his story.[1]

[1] Vv. vii. 4; VvA. 302 f.

Suvaṇṇavīthi.—A street in **Tāvatiṃsa,** sixty leagues in length.[1]

[1] J. v. 386.

Suvaṇṇasāma.—The Bodhisatta born as the son of **Dukūlaka** and **Pārikā.** See the **Sāma Jātaka.**

Suvaṇṇahaṃsa Jātaka (No. 136).—The Bodhisatta was once a brahmin. He had three daughters: **Nandā, Nandavatī** and **Sundarīnandā.** After death he was born as a golden goose, and, remembering his past birth, he flew to where his wife and daughters lived and gave one of his golden feathers. This happened several times, till at last his wife planned to pull out all his feathers. Now the feathers taken from a golden goose, against his wish, cease to be golden and become like the feathers of a crane. The woman discovered this when she had pulled out all his feathers, so she flung him into a barrel and fed him there. Later white feathers grew on him, and he flew away never to return.

The story was told in reference to **Thulla-Nandā** (*q.v.*). One day she went to a bailiff's house for some garlic, as he was in the habit of giving this to the nuns. But the supply was finished, and she was asked to get some from the field. She went there and took away a large quantity, and the bailiff was very angry.

Thulla-Nandā is identified with the greedy woman and her three sisters with the three daughters.[1]

[1] J. i. 474-7.

Suvaṇṇahāra (Suvaṇṇabhāra).—A palace occupied by **Phussa Buddha** before his renunciation.[1]

[1] Bu. xix. 15.

Suvidehā.—The name of a country and its inhabitants.[1] It is that part of **Videha** which is opposite **Magadha**, on the other side of the **Ganges.**[2]

[1] M. i. 225. [2] MA. ii. 448.

1. **Suvīra.**—A Deva. Once, when the **Asuras** marched against the Devas, Sakka sent for **Suvīra** and asked him to fight the Asuras. Suvīra agreed to do this, but was very lazy about it. This happened three times. Sakka admonished him after the third time on the evils of laziness.

The Buddha related the story to the monks to show them the value of exertion and energy.[1]

[1] S. i. 216 f.

2. **Suvīra Sutta.**—The story of **Suvīra** (*q.v.*).

Susaddasiddhi.—Another name for the **Sāratthavilāsinī** by **Saṅgharakkhita** of Ceylon; it is a *ṭīkā* on the **Moggallānapañjikā.**[1]

[1] P.L.C. 200.

Susuddha.—A king of thirty-two kappas ago, a previous birth of **Pabbhāradāyaka Thera.**[1]

[1] Ap. i. 252.

Susammuṭṭha Sutta.—A deva tells the Buddha that followers of other creeds have their vision fully blurred.[1]

[1] S. i. 4.

Susārada Thera.—He was born in the family of a kinsman of **Sāriputta** and was given his name because he was a dullard. He heard Sāriputta preach, entered the Order, and became an arahant.

In the time of **Padumuttara Buddha** he was a brahmin, who became an ascetic. One day he saw the Buddha begging for alms and filled his bowl with sweet fruits. Seven hundred kappas ago he was a king, named **Sumaṅgala.**[1] He is evidently identical with **Phaladāyaka** of the *Apadāna.*[2]

[1] Thag. vs. 75; ThagA. i. 167. [2] Ap. i. 160. f.

1. **Susīma.**—The Bodhisatta in the time of **Atthadassī Buddha.** He was a *Mahāsāḷa* brahmin of **Campaka** and became an ascetic of great power. He heard the Buddha preach at **Sudassana** and was converted.[1]

[1] J. i. 39; Bu. xv. 9 f.; BuA. 180.

2. **Susīma.**—The Bodhisatta, son of the chaplain of the king of Benares. He later became king himself. See the **Susīma Jātaka** (No. 411).

3. **Susīma.**—A king of Benares. See the **Susīma Jātaka** (No. 163). He is identified with **Ānanda.**[1]

[1] J. ii. 50.

4. **Susīma.**—A Devaputta. Once, when **Ānanda** utters high praise of **Sāriputta, Susīma,** who is present, reflects on it and confirms all that Ānanda has said. The retinue of Susīma listen enraptured, waxing wondrous, in divers colour-tones (" even as a beautiful lustrous beryl-stone of eight facets, well polished, when laid in an orange-coloured cloth, shines, glows and blazes, etc.").[1]

It is said[2] that Susīma had been a fellow-celibate of Sāriputta.

[1] S. 163 f. [2] SA. i. 98.

5. **Susīma.**—One of the thousand sons of **Sakka.** He was one of the *deva*-generals in the fight with the **Asuras,** but he was lazy, and Sakka had to admonish him.[1] He is probably identical with **Susīma** (4).

[1] S. i. 217; SA. i. 262.

6. **Susīma.**—A **Paribbājaka**[1] of **Rājagaha.** When the Buddha's fame spread and his gains increased, Susīma's followers suggested that he should learn the Buddha's doctrine and preach it to the laity so that he and his followers, too, could reap some of the advantages. Susīma agreed, and sought **Ānanda,** who, with the Buddha's sanction, ordained him. In discussion with the monks who declared that they had obtained complete emancipation, etc., Susīma discovered that all of them did not possess supernatural powers, but thought they had gained nibbāna " through insight." He thereupon sought the Buddha to have the matter explained. The Buddha asked him many questions, and made him realize the truth of their statement. Susīma confessed his original purpose in joining the Order and asked for forgiveness.[2] He developed insight and became an arahant.[3]

[1] Skilled in the *Vedaṅgas*, says Buddhaghosa (SA. ii. 93).
[2] S. ii. 119 ff. [3] SA. ii. 96.

7. **Susīma.**—A brahmin of **Takkasilā** and son of **Saṅkha.** He went to Benares and apprenticed himself to a teacher, who was his father's friend and who taught him various things. But he was able to understand only the beginning and the middle, and not the end. He therefore consulted his teacher, who confessed that neither did he understand the end, and advised him to seek the **Pacceka Buddhas** who were living in **Isipatana.** Susīma went there, entered the Order, and became a Pacceka Buddha. Soon afterwards he died, and Saṅkha, coming in search of his

son, was told of what had happened. Saṅkha is identified with the Bodhisatta.[1]

[1] DhA. iii. 445 f.; KhA. 198 f.

1. **Susīma Jātaka** (No. 163).—**Susīma** was king of Benares, and the Bodhisatta was his chaplain's son. The chaplain had been master of ceremonies in the king's elephant-festival, and, as a result, had amassed great wealth. He died when his son was sixteen. Soon after, another elephant-festival came round, and other brahmins obtained the king's consent to be in charge of the ceremonies on the plea that the chaplain's son was too young. When but four days remained before the festival, the Bodhisatta found his mother weeping. She explained that for seven successive generations their family had managed the elephant-festival and that she felt the change deeply. The Bodhisatta discovered that a teacher expert in elephant-lore lived in **Takkasilā,** two thousand *yojanas* away. He comforted his mother and proceeded to Takkasilā, reaching it in a single day. There he paid his fee of one thousand pieces to the teacher and explained the urgency of his mission. In one night the teacher taught him the three Vedas and the elephant-lore, and the pupil could even excel his teacher in knowledge. The next morning he left early for Benares and reached it in one day.

On the day of the festival the Bodhisatta went in all his array before the king and protested against the alienation of his rights. He challenged anyone to show his superiority over him in elephant-lore, and nobody could be found to do so. The king then appointed him to conduct the ceremonies.

The story was related in reference to an attempt on the part of the heretics to prevent the people of **Sāvatthi** from giving alms to the Buddha. All the people of the city made a collection to hold an almsgiving, but they were divided in their allegiance, some wishing to entertain the Buddha, others favouring heretical teachers. A vote was passed, and the majority were found to be in favour of the Buddha. For a whole week alms were given on a lavish scale, and, at the end of the week, the Buddha pronounced a benediction.

Ānanda is identified with Susīma, **Sāriputta** with the teacher, **Mahāmāyā** with the Bodhisatta's mother, and **Suddhodana** with his father.[1]

[1] J. ii. 45-50.

2. **Susīma Jātaka** (No. 411). The Bodhisatta was born as son of the chaplain of the king of Benares and was called **Susīma.** The king's son, born on the same day, was called **Brahmadatta.** Together they grew up, and then studied under the same teacher in **Takkasilā.** Later

Brahmadatta became king and Susīma his chaplain. One day, when Susīma was taking part in a procession with the king, the queen-mother saw him and fell desperately in love with him. The king, discovering this, made Susīma king in his place and the queen-mother Susīma's queen. But Susīma soon tired of royalty, and after establishing Brahmadatta once more on the throne, returned to the **Himālaya** in spite of his wife's protests. There he became an ascetic.

The story was told in reference to the Buddha's Renunciation. **Ānanda** is identified with Brahmadatta and the queen-mother with **Rāhulamātā.**[1]

[1] J. iii. 391-7.

1. **Susīma Sutta.**—Describes the visit of **Susīmadevaputta (Susīma** 4) to the Buddha.[1]

[1] S. i. 63 f.

2. **Susīma Sutta.**—Gives Sakka's admonition to his son, **Susīma** (5).[1]

[1] S. i. 217.

3. **Susīma Sutta.**—Describes the visit of **Susīma Paribbājaka** to the Buddha, and their conversation. See **Susīma** (6).[1]

[1] S. ii. 119 ff.

Susīmadevī.—Wife of **Amitodana.** Her daughter, **Bhaddākaccānā,** became queen of **Paṇḍuvāsudeva.**[1]

[1] MṬ. 275.

Susimā.—Mother of **Sīhabāhu** and **Sīhasīvalī.** She was the daughter of the king of **Vaṅga,** and is said to have consorted with a Lion. The descendants of this union became the **Sīhalā.**[1]

[1] Dpv. ix. 2 f.; *cf.* Mhv. vi. 1 ff.

Susunāga.—King of **Magadha** and father of **Kāḷāsoka.** He reigned for eighteen years.[1] According to the *Mahāvaṃsa Ṭīkā*,[2] he was the son of a **Licchavi** rājā and a courtezan. When he was born he looked like a lump of flesh, and his mother gave orders that he should be put in a vessel and cast on the rubbish heap. The Nāga-king of the city kept guard over the vessel, but when the people crowded round him and said "*Su-sū*," he left it and went away. In the crowd was a minister's son, and, when the vessel was opened and the child was discovered, he decided to

[1] Mhv. iv. 6; but see Dpv. v. 98, where his reign is given as ten years, in the eighth year of which **Dasaka Thera** died. *Cf.* Sp. i. 33.

[2] M.Ṭ. 155 f.

adopt him. In due course the child grew up, and when the infuriated populace deposed the parricide **Nāgadāsaka,** they placed Susunāga on the throne. He was called Susunāga because he was guarded by the Nāga who disappeared when the people said "Su-sū."

Sussondī.—Wife of **Tamba,** king of Benares. See the **Sussondī Jātaka.**

Sussondī Jātaka (No. 360).—**Tamba** was a king of Benares and his wife was the beautiful **Sussondī. Nāgadīpa** was then known as **Seruma,** and the Bodhisatta was a young **Garuḍa** living there. He used to go in disguise to Benares and play at dice with Tamba. The queen heard of his beauty and contrived to see him, and they fell in love with each other. The Garuḍa, by his power, raised a storm in the city and covered it with darkness, under cover of which he carried off Sussondī. The king was filled with grief, not knowing what had happened to his queen, as the Garuḍa continued to play at dice with him. Tamba therefore sent **Sagga,** a minstrel, to search for her. In the course of his wanderings, Sagga came to **Bhārukaccha** and took ship for **Suvaṇṇabhūmi.** In the middle of the ocean the sailors asked Sagga to play for them, but Sagga told them that his music would excite the big fish and trouble would ensue. The sailors, however, insisting, Sagga played, and the fish, maddened by the sound, splashed about, and the ship broke in two under the leap of a sea-monster. Sagga lay on a plank, which drifted to Nāgadīpa. There he saw and was recognized by Sussondī. Sussondī tookhim home, and, keeping him hidden from the Garuḍa, enjoyed herself with him when the Garuḍa was away playing at dice. Six weeks later a ship, with merchants for Benares, touched at Nāgadīpa, and Sagga returned home. He found Tamba playing at dice with the Garuḍa and recounted his adventures in song. The Garuḍa heard the song and understood the references. Filled with remorse that he had not been able to keep his wife, he brought her back to Tamba.

The story was related in reference to a love-sick monk. **Ānanda** is identified with Tamba.[1]

[1] J. iii. 187-90.

Suhanu.—A horse belonging to the king of Benares. See the **Suhanu Jātaka.**

Suhanu Jātaka (No. 158).—The Bodhisatta was minister to the king of Benares. The king had a wild horse called **Mahāsoṇa.** The king was miserly, and one day, when some horse-dealers brought horses for sale, he gave orders, unknown to his minister, that Mahāsoṇa should be let loose among these horses, and that when he had bitten and weakened them, they should be bought at reduced price. The dealers complained to the minister. After inquiring into the matter, he advised them to bring **Suhanu,** a very strong horse they had, the next time they visited Benares. This they did, and when Mahāsoṇa and Suhanu were confronted with each other they showed great affection, and started licking each other. The king saw this, and was told by his minister that the horses recognized each other's virtues. He then warned the king against excessive covetousness.

The story was told in reference to two hot-headed monks, both passionate and cruel. One lived in **Jetavana** and the other in the country. One day the country monk came to Jetavana, and the monks eagerly awaited their quarrel. But when the two monks met they showed great affection. The Buddha explained that this was because of their like nature.[1]

[1] J. ii. 30-32.

Suhemanta Thera.—He belonged to a rich brahmin family of a border kingdom. One day he heard the Buddha preach in the Deer Park in **Saṅkassa,** and, after joining the Order, became a reciter of the Tipiṭaka, attaining arahantship in due course. He then became a teacher and counsellor of the monks, instructing them and solving their difficulties.

In the time of Tissa Buddha he was a forester, and, seeing the Buddha at the foot of a tree, offered him *punnāga*-flowers. Ninety-one kappas ago he was a king, named **Tamonuda.**[1] He is evidently identical with **Punnāgapupphiya** of the *Apadāna.*[2]

[1] Thag. vs. 106; ThagA. i. 212 f. [2] Ap. i. 180.

Suhemā.—Probably the wife of the goose-king **Dhataraṭṭha.**[1]

[1] J. v. 366.

Sūka Sutta.—If a spike-bearded wheat or barley be badly grasped by hand or foot, it does not pierce hand or foot; but it will if firmly grasped. Similarly a mind which is ill-directed will not pierce ignorance or draw knowledge; but it will if well directed.[1]

[1] A. i. 8 f.

Sūkara Jātaka (No. 153).—The Bodhisatta was a lion living in a mountain cave; on the banks of a lake nearby lived many boars, and in the neighbourhood were some hermits. One day the lion, having eaten some game, went to the lake to drink; but after he had drunk, seeing a boar which he did not wish to frighten away, having the idea of eating it when food should be scarce, he slunk away. The boar saw this, and, thinking that the lion was afraid of him, challenged him to a fight. The lion agreed to fight a week later. The boar was overjoyed, and told his relations of this. But they all frightened him and advised him to spend the next seven days rolling in the hermits' dunghill. When the dirt was dry, he was to moisten his body with dew and go to the meeting-place early, standing well to windward. This he did, and when the lion arrived and smelt the filth, the boar was allowed to go away uninjured.

The story was told in reference to an old and foolish monk. One night the Buddha returned to his cell late at night after preaching. Then **Moggallāna** asked **Sāriputta** various questions, which the latter explained. The people stayed on, entranced with Sāriputta's expositions. An old monk, wishing to attract attention to himself, stood up and asked a foolish question. Sāriputta, reading his thoughts, rose from his seat and walked away; so did Moggallāna. The laymen who were present were annoyed with the old monk and chased him away. As he ran he fell into a cesspit and was covered with filth. The laymen then felt remorse and visited the Buddha to ask his forgiveness. The old monk is identified with the boar.[1]

[1] J. ii. 9-12; *cf.* DhA. iii. 344 f.; it is said that the story was told concerning **Lāḷudāyī.**

Sūkarakhata Sutta.—The Buddha questions **Sāriputta** at **Sūkarakhatalena** as to why a monk who has destroyed the *āsavas* should revere the Buddha and his teachings. Sāriputta answers that it is because such a monk has secured freedom from the yoke. "What kind of security is it?" asks the Buddha, and Sāriputta explains that it is security obtained by the cultivation of the five *indriyas* of faith, energy, etc.[1]

[1] S. v. 233 f.

Sūkarakhatalena.—A cave on the side of **Gijjhakūṭa,** where the Buddha stayed. There he preached the **Dīghanakha** (or **Vedanāpariggaha**) **Sutta** to **Dīghanakha. Sāriputta** was also present, and the sutta led to his attainment of arahantship.[1] A conversation which the Buddha had there with Sāriputta is recorded in the **Saṃyutta Nikāya.**[2] The Commentary says[3] that, in the time of **Kassapa Buddha,** this cave was found as a hollow in the ground when the earth was yet growing, during the interval between the two Buddhas. One day a boar dug up the soil in the neighbourhood of the ground which concealed the cave. The sky-god sent rain which washed away the soil, and the cave was disclosed.

[1] M. i. 497, 501; DhA. i. 79; UdA. 189. [2] S. v. 233 f. [3] SA. iii. 197.

A forest-dweller saw it and looked after it, thinking it to be the dwelling of holy men. He removed the earth round it, fenced it in, cleaned it out, and, making it as beautiful as a golden bowl, furnished it with couch and stool and presented it to the Buddha. The cave was deep and could only be reached by climbing.

Sūkaraggāma.—A fortress in the **Dakkhiṇadesa** of Ceylon, mentioned in the account of the wars of **Gajabāhu.**[1]

[1] Cv. lxx. 134.

Sūkaraggāmavāpi.—A tank restored by **Parakkamabāhu I.**[1]

[1] Cv. lxviii. 46.

Sūkaratittha.—A place, probably in the north of Ceylon, where the Damiḷas **Māgha** and **Jayabāhu** set up fortifications.[1]

[1] Cv. lxxxiii. 18.

Sūkaranijjhara.—A dyke constructed by **Parakkamabāhu I.** at the junction of the rivers **Saṅkhavaḍḍhamānaka** and **Kumbhīlavāṇa.** A canal was carried from there to the **Mahāgallaka-tank.**[1]

[1] Cv. lxviii. 33 f.

1. **Sūkarapeta.**—A *peta* who lived on **Gijjhakūṭa.** His body was human, but his head was that of a pig; out of his mouth grew a tail, and from the tail oozed maggots. **Moggallāna** saw him and reported the matter to the Buddha. The Buddha said that he, too, had seen the *peta.* In a previous birth he had been a preacher of the Law, but, wishing to obtain possession of a monastery which he visited, he brought about dissension between the two monks who had lived there on the friendliest terms. After death he suffered in **Avīci** for a whole Buddhantara, and was reborn in the *peta*-world.[1]

[1] DhA. iii. 410 ff.

2. **Sūkarapeta.**—A monk in the time of **Kassapa Buddha,** reborn as a *peta* on **Gijjhakūṭa,** where he was seen by **Nārada.** He had been restrained in his bodily actions, but had an evil tongue. He had the face of a pig.[1]

[1] Pv. i. 3; PvA. 9 f.

Sūkarabhātu.—An officer of **Mānābharaṇa.** He was captured and put in chains by **Parakkamabāhu I.** He escaped, however, and the **Adhikāri Mañju** was sent to seize him. Sūkarabhātu became the commander-in-chief of the rebels and caused great damage to Parakkamabāhu's forces. It was not until **Damiḷādhikāri** and **Laṅkāpura Deva** concentrated all their attention on him that he could be defeated. He died fighting, near **Mahānāgahula.**[1]

[1] Cv. lxxiv. 127 f., 153; lxxv. 126 f.

Sūkarārāma.—A monastery near **Dohalapabbata,** where a minister of **Kittisirirājasīha** built an image-house and **Suvaṇṇagāma** erected an *uposatha*-hall.[1]

[1] Cv. c. 295.

Sūkarālibheripāsāṇa.—A place in **Rohaṇa** mentioned in the account of the campaigns of **Parakkamabāhu I.**[1]

[1] Cv. lxxv. 98, 146; see also Cv. ii. 53, n. 4.

Sūci Jātaka (No. 387).—The Bodhisatta was once a very clever smith of **Kāsi,** but was very poor. The principal royal smith had a beautiful daughter, and the Bodhisatta, wishing to win her, made a delicate needle that could pierce dice and float on water, and for this needle he made seven sheaths. He then went to the village of the head smith, stood outside his house, and sang the praises of his needle. The smith's daughter, who was fanning her father, spoke to the Bodhisatta and asked him to go elsewhere, as no one in that village would want needles. The Bodhisatta answered that his were no ordinary needles, and the head smith asked him to show them. The Bodhisatta suggested that all the smiths be summoned, and in their presence he gave the needle-tube to the head smith. He thought that it was the needle itself, for he could find no end or tip. The tube was handed back to the Bodhisatta, who took out the first sheath. In this way the seven sheaths were removed, and when the needle was at last revealed he made the needle pierce the anvil and lie on the surface of a vessel of water. The whole assembly was filled with envy and admiration, and the head smith gave his daughter to the Bodhisatta.

The story was related in the same circumstances as the **Mahāummagga Jātaka** (*q.v.*). The smith's daughter is identified with **Rāhulamātā.**[1]

[1] J. iii. 281-6.

Sūcidāyaka Thera.—An arahant. In a previous birth he had given a needle to **Sumedha Buddha.** He was king four times, under the name of **Dīpādhipati.**[1]

[1] Ap. i. 122.

Sūciloma.—See **Suciloma.**

Sūtighara-cetiya.—A *thūpa*, one hundred and twenty cubits in height, in **Puṅkhagāma,** erected by **Parakkamabāhu I.** on the site of the house of his birth.[1]

[1] Cv. lxxix. 61.

Sūra.—A messenger of **Kuvera**[1] (*q.v.*).

[1] D. iii. 201.

Sūra-Ambaṭṭha.—An eminent lay disciple, declared by the Buddha foremost among his followers in unwavering loyalty (*aggaṃ aveccappasannānaṃ*).[1] He resolved to acquire this eminence during his birth in the time of **Padumuttara Buddha.** He was born, in this Buddha-age, in a banker's family in **Sāvatthi** and became a follower of the heretics. One day the Buddha, seeing Sūra's fitness for conversion, went to his door for alms. Out of respect for the Buddha, Sūra invited him in, and, giving him a comfortable seat, entertained him to a meal. At the end of the meal, when the Buddha returned thanks, Sūra became a *sotāpanna*. Some time after the Buddha had left, **Māra,** disguised as the Buddha, visited Sūra and, in reply to Sūra's questioning, said that he had returned to contradict a wrong statement which he had made earlier. He had said that all the *saṅkhāras* were impermanent, etc., but, on further reflection, he had come to the conclusion that only some *saṅkhāras* were of that nature. Sūra recognized Māra and drove him away.[2]

[1] A. i. 26; *cf.* iii. 451.
[2] AA. i. 215; *cf.* DA. iii. 864.

Sūra-ambavana.—A place in Ceylon, mentioned in the account of the wars of **Parakkamabāhu I.**[1] It evidently formed part of **Ambavana,** the district round the *Ambaṅgaṅga.*[2]

[1] Cv. lxx. 87.
[2] Cv. *Trs.* i. 294, n. 3.

Sūratissa.—King of Ceylon (187-177 B.C.). He was the younger brother and successor of **Mahāsiva.** He built five hundred vihāras, including the **Nagaraṅgana, Hatthikkhandha, Goṇṇagirika, Pācīnapabbata, Kolambahālaka, Makulaka, Acchagallaka** and **Girinelavāhanaka.** He died at the age of sixty, after being conquered by the Damiḷas **Sena** and **Guttika.** He was called **Suvaṇṇapiṇḍatissa** before his accession.[1]

[1] Mhv. xxi. 3 ff.; Dpv. xviii. 46 f.; see also *s.v.* **Acchagiri.**

Sūradaddara.—A Nāga-king of **Daddarapabbata.** See the **Daddara Jātaka.** He was the father of **Mahādaddara.**

Sūradeva.—A Damiḷa chief, ally of **Kulasekhara.**[1]

[1] Cv. lxxvii. 13.

Sūra-rājā.—A messenger of **Kuvera**[1] (*q.v.*).

[1] DA. iii. 967.

Sūravāmagotta.—A son of Ekarāja and step-brother of Candakumāra. He is identified with Mahā Kassapa.[1] See Khaṇḍahāla Jātaka.

[1] J. vi. 157.

1. **Sūrasena.**—See **Surasena.**

2. **Sūrasena.**—Another name for **Dhanañjaya-Korabba.**[1]

[1] J. vi. 280, 281.

Sekīrapadma.—A Damiḷa chief, ally of **Kulasekhara.**[1]

[1] Cv. lxxvii. 76.

1. **Sekha Sutta.**—A pupil is one who is under training in the higher morality, the higher thought and the higher insight.[1]

[1] A. i. 231.

2. **Sekha Sutta.**—On five things leading to decline in a monk's training: delight in business, in gossip, in sleeping, in company, and want of reflection on the mind as freed.[1]

[1] A. iii. 116.

3. **Sekha Sutta.**—The same as (2) above, but in greater detail under each head.[1]

[1] A. iii. 117 f.

4. **Sekha Sutta.**—On six things which lead to failure in a monk's training: delight in worldly activity, in talk, in sleep, in company, want of restraint in the senses, immoderate eating.[1]

[1] A. iii. 329.

5. **Sekha Sutta.**—On seven things: the six given in sutta (4), to which is added inattention to business of the Order.[1]

[1] A. iv. 24.

6. **Sekha Sutta.**—The learner (*sekha*) is one imperfectly possessed of right view, etc.[1]

[1] S. iv. 14.

7. **Sekha Sutta.**—A detailed explanation of the difference between a learner (*sekha*) and an adept (*asekha*).[1]

[1] S. v. 229 f.

8. **Sekha Sutta.**—Preached by **Ānanda** at **Kapilavatthu,** in the new Mote-hall of the **Licchavis.** The Buddha preached until late into the night and then asked Ānanda to continue, suggesting to him as a topic the training of an adept (*asekha*). Ānanda explained in detail how a monk could be virtuous, watchful over his senses, temperate in eating, vigilant, established in the seven virtuous qualities (faith, etc.), and be able at will to induce the four *jhānas.*[1]

[1] M. i. 353 ff.

Sekhabala Vagga.—The first chapter of the Pañcaka Nipāta of the **Aṅguttara Nikāya.**[1]

[1] A. iii. 1-9.

Sekhiyā.—One of the sub-divisions of the **Pācittiya** of the **Sutta Vibhaṅga** of the Vinaya Piṭaka.[1]

[1] Vin. iv. 185 ff., 349 ff.

Seggu.—A greengrocer's daughter. See the **Seggu Jātaka.**

Seggu Jātaka (No. 217).—The story of a greengrocer who, in order to test his daughter, **Seggu,** took her to the woods and made as if wishing to seduce her. But she begged for his protection, and he, convinced of her virtue, gave her in marriage to a good young man.

The story was told in reference to a greengrocer of **Sāvatthi,** who similarly tested his daughter. The characters in both stories were identical.[1]

[1] J. ii. 179 f.

Seṅkhaṇḍasela-Sirivaḍḍhanapura.—The ancient name of modern Kandy, in Ceylon. It first became the capital under King **Vīravikkama,**[1] and tradition has it that it was founded on a site originally occupied by a hermit named **Seṅkhaṇḍa.** It continued to be the capital of Ceylon until 1815 A.C., when the island was ceded to the British.

[1] Cv. xcii. 7.

Seṅkuṇḍiya.—A Damiḷa chief, ally of Kulasekhara, and later ally of Laṅkapura.[1]

[1] Cv. lxxvi. 138, 221; *ibid.*, lxxvii. 7, 35.

Sejalaka.—A vihāra to the east of **Anurādhapura,** built by **Mahallaka-Nāga.**[1] *v.l.* **Pejalaka.**

[1] Mhv. xxxv. 124.

Seṭṭhināyaka.—A **Lambakaṇṇa** of the **Moriya** district. He, with four other Lambakaṇṇas, took up arms under **Parakkamabāhu I.** and brought to him one thousand warriors.[1]

[1] Cv. lxix. 12.

Seṭṭhiputta-petavatthu.—The story of four *seṭṭhiputtas* of **Sāvatthi.**[1] See the Lohakumbhi Jātaka.

[1] Pv. iv. 15; PvA. 279 f.

1. **Seta.**—The chief peak of the **Himālaya.**[1] It was evidently another name for Kailāsa.

[1] S. i. 67=Mil. 242.

2. **Seta.**—The state elephant of **Pasenadi,** on whose account the Buddha preached a special sermon.[1] He was so called because he was white.[2]

[1] A. iii. 345.

[2] AA. ii. 669; *cf.* ThagA. ii. 7.

Setaka, Sedaka.—See **Desaka.**

Setakaṇṇika.—A village forming the southern boundary of **Majjhima-desa.**[1]

[1] Vin. i. 197; DA. i. 173; J. i. 49; KhA. 133, etc.; AA. i. 55, 265; MA. i. 397.

1. **Setaketu.**—The Bodhisatta, born in **Tusita** in his penultimate birth.[1]

[1] Sp. i. 161; MA. i. 103.

2. **Setaketu.**—A young man, son of an *Udicca-brahmin.* See the **Setaketu Jātaka.**

Setaketu Jātaka (No. 377).—The Bodhisatta was once a far-famed teacher, with five hundred pupils, chief among whom was **Setaketu,** an *Udicca-brahmin,* who prided himself on his high caste. One day, meeting a Caṇḍāla, Setaketu told him to pass on his leeward side, but the Caṇḍāla refused, challenging Setaketu to answer a question. Setaketu accepted the challenge, and he was asked what were the four " quarters." Setaketu gave the usual answer, whereupon the Caṇḍāla forced him between his feet. When this was reported to the teacher, he told Setaketu that the four quarters were parents, teachers, generous householders, and deliverance from misery. Later, Setaketu left for **Takkasilā,** and, after finishing his studies there, went to Benares with five hundred ascetics. There they practised false penances and won the king's approval; the king's chaplain, however, warned him against them, saying that they possessed only false knowledge and had no morality. The chaplain persuaded Setaketu and his followers to become laymen and enter the king's service.

The story was related in the same circumstances as the **Uddāla Jātaka** (*q.v.*). Setaketu is identified with the false priest, the Caṇḍāla with **Sāriputta,** and the king's chaplain with the **Bodhisatta.**[1]

[1] J. iii. 232-7.

Setambangaṇa.—A place in Ceylon. When King **Mahānāga** was fleeing from Ceylon to India, he received help from an Elder living there. Later, when he regained his throne, he made a great gift of medicine to Setambaṅgaṇa for as long as he should live.[1] *v.l.* **Pemambaṅgaṇa.**

[1] DhSA. 399.

Setavyā.—A town in **Kosala,**[1] near which was **Ukkaṭṭha.** The Aṅguttara Nikāya[2] records a conversation between the Buddha and the brahmin **Doṇa,** whom the Buddha met on the road from Ukkaṭṭha to Setavyā. The city was on the road, taken by **Bāvārī's** disciples,[3] from **Sāvatthi** to **Rājagaha,** and was the first halting-place outside Sāvatthi. Beyond it were **Kapilavatthu, Kusinārā, Pāvā,** etc. To the north of Setavyā was the **Siṃsapāvana,** where **Kumāra Kassapa** lived, and where he preached the **Pāyāsi Sutta** to the brahmin **Pāyāsi,** who held a royal fief there.[4] The city was the birthplace of the Theras **Ekadhammasavaṇiya** and **Mahākāḷa** (*q.v.*). Mahākāḷa's brothers **Cūlakāḷa** and **Majjhimakāḷa** also lived there.[5] The Aṅguttara Commentary[6] says that Kassapa Buddha was born in Setavyā, but both the *Buddhavaṃsa* and its Commentary say that he was born in Benares.[7] The Buddhavaṃsa Commentary[8] records further that Kassapa died in the **Setārāma** in Setavyā, but adds that Setavyā was a city in Kāsi.

[1] D. ii. 316.
[2] A. ii. 37.
[3] SN. vs. 1012.
[4] D. ii. 316.
[5] DhA. i. 55.
[6] AA. ii. 504.
[7] Bu. xxv. 33; BuA. 217.
[8] *Ibid.*, 223.

Setārāma.—A park (in **Setavyā**) where **Kassapa Buddha** died.[1]

[1] BuA. 195; Bu. (xix. 52) calls it **Sonārāma.**

Setibhinda.—The Pāli name for King Hsin-hpyu-shin of Pegu.[1]

[1] Bode, *op. cit.*, 37.

Setuccha Thera.—He belonged to the family of a provincial ruler (*maṇḍalikarājā*), but was unable to maintain his country's independence, and lost his throne. While wandering about in misery, he saw and heard the Buddha, entered the Order, and won arahantship.

In the time of **Tissa Buddha** he was a householder, and gave the Buddha a *panasa*-fruit mixed with a curry of cocoanut. Thirteen kappas ago he was a king named **Indasama.**[1] He is evidently identical with **Khajjadāyaka** of the *Apadāna.*[2]

[1] Thag. vs. 102; ThagA. i. 206. [2] Ap. i. 182.

Setudāyaka Thera.—An arahant.[1] He is evidently identical with **Uttarapāla**[2] (*q.v.*).

[1] Ap. ii. 408. [2] ThagA. i. 371.

Sedaka.—See **Desaka.**

1. **Sena.**—King of Ceylon (**Sena I.,** 831-51 A.C.). He was the younger brother and the successor of **Aggabodhi IX.** He had three younger brothers: **Mahinda, Kassapa** and **Udaya.** His queen was **Saṅghā.** During his reign the **Paṇḍu** king invaded Ceylon, and Sena had to retire into the **Malaya** district. After the army of the Paṇḍu king had plundered a great part of the kingdom, Sena made a treaty with him and regained his throne. He adopted the three sons and the three daughters of **Kittaggabodhi: Kassapa, Sena** and **Udaya,** and **Saṅghā, Tissā** and **Kitti.** Among the king's good acts was the construction of a monastery on **Ariṭṭhapabbata** for the **Paṃsukulikas,** and a many-storeyed *pāsāda* in **Jetavana.** He also built the **Vīraṅkurārāma,** the **Pubbārāma, Saṅghasena-pariveṇa, Senaggabodhi-vihāra,** a refectory in the **Mahāmettapabbata-vihāra,** and single cells in the **Kappūra-** and **Uttarāḷha-pariveṇas.** He completed the **Dappulapabbata-** and the **Kassaparājaka-vihāras.** Among Sena's ministers were **Bhadda** (the *senāpati*), **Uttara, Vajira** and **Rakkhasa.** His capital was in **Pulatthinagara.**[1] He was also known as **Silāmegha.**[2]

[1] Cv. l. 1 ff. [2] *Ibid.*, 43.

2. **Sena.**—Son of the **Ādipāda Kassapa,** and therefore nephew of **Sena I.** On the death of his father, Sena became king as **Sena II.** (851-85 A.C.). He married **Saṅghā,** daughter of **Kittaggabodhi,** and had a son, **Kassapa.** Sena sent an expeditionary force against the **Paṇḍu** king, captured

Madhurā, and brought back the treasures which had been pillaged by the Paṇḍus in the time of **Sena I.** The **Paṃsukulika** monks separated from the incumbents of **Abhayagiri** in the twentieth year of Sena's reign. He built the **Maṇimekhala** dam and a dam across the **Kaṇavāpi** at **Kaṭṭhantanagara.** He endowed various monasteries—**Buddhagāma, Mahiyaṅgana, Kūṭatissa, Maṇḍalagiri,** and **Sobbha**—and held a special ceremony in honour of the image of Ānanda. He held a consecration festival at the **Hemavāluka-cetiya (Mahā Thūpa)**, and decreed that this festival should be repeated annually. His *senāpati* was **Kuṭṭhaka.**[1]

[1] Cv. li. 1 ff.

3. **Sena.**—Son of **Kittaggabodhi.**[1]

[1] Cv. l. 56.

4. **Sena.**—Called **Mahālekhaka Sena.** He was a minister of **Kassapa V.** and built the **Mahālekhakapabbata**-house in the **Mahāvihāra.**[1] His mother was **Nālā.**[2]

[1] Cv. lii. 33. [2] Cv. *Trs.* i. 138, n. 3; 165, n. 1.

5. **Sena.**—Upāraja of **Udaya III.**, and later **Sena III.**, king of Ceylon (937-45 A.D.). According to some accounts he was the brother of **Udaya III.** He observed the *uposatha*-day regularly, and among his benefactions was the **Daṇḍissara** offering to mendicant artists. He made the stone paving of **Abhayuttara-cetiya** and endowed the **Nāgasālā-pariveṇa.**[1]

[1] Cv. liii. 13, 28 ff.

6. **Sena.**—Uparāja of **Udaya IV.**, and afterwards king of Ceylon (**Sena IV.** 953-6 A.D.). He was learned, and used to explain the suttantas in the **Lohapāsāda.** Because of his piety, the gods sent timely rain. He made a casket for the Tooth Relic and built the **Sitthagāma-pariveṇa.**[1]

[1] Cv. liii. 39; liv. 1 ff.

7. **Sena.**—Senāpati of **Mahinda IV.** and of **Sena V.** He was sent to **Nāgadīpa,** where he subdued the **Vallabha** king. Once, when he was absent, Sena V. had the *senāpati's* younger brother, **Mahāmalla,** slain for an offence with the queen-mother, and appointed a court official **Udaya** as *senāpati.* When Sena *senāpati* heard of this, he marched against the king, who had to flee to **Rohaṇa.** The queen-mother joined Sena, and he lived in **Pulatthipura.** This king, later, dismissed Senāpati Udaya and made peace with Sena, whose daughter he married.[1]

[1] Cv. liv. 13 f.; lviii. 70.

8. **Sena.**—Son of **Mahinda IV.** and king of Ceylon (**Sena V.** 972-81 A.C.). His mother was a **Kāliṅga** princess. He came to the throne at the age of twelve. His senāpati was also called **Sena** (see **Sena 7**), and for some time the king had to live in Rohaṇa from fear of Sena. But later he made peace, and married Sena's daughter and had a son, **Kassapa.** The king drank much, and died of digestive trouble in the tenth year of his reign.[1]

[1] Cv. liv. 57-72.

9. **Sena.**—Adhikāri of **Kittisirimegha** (2). He was sent to fight against **Parakkamabāhu I.** at **Siriyāla** and **Buddhagāma,** but was defeated.[1]

[1] Cv. lxvi. 66 f.

10. **Sena Ilaṅga.**—Senāpati of **Kassapa IV.** He was of royal lineage. He built a dwelling for the monks to the west of the **Thūpārāma.** He also founded the **Dhammārāma-vihāra** and **Hadayauṇha-vihāra** for the **Dhammarucikas** and **Kassapasena** for the **Sāgalikas.** For forest-dwelling ascetics he built a hut on **Rattamālapabbata.** For the **Paṃsukulikas** he built the **Samuddagiri-pariveṇa** in the **Mahāvihāra,** and for the bhikkhuṇīs the **Tissārāma.** He erected hospitals in **Anurādhapura** and **Pulatthipura,** against the *upasagga* disease.[1]

[1] Cv. lii. 30.

11. **Sena.**—A Damiḷa usurper who, with his companion **Guttika,** both of them horse-dealers, defeated **Sūratissa** and occupied the throne at **Anurādhapura** for twenty-two years (177-55 B.C.). At the end of that time they were overpowered by **Asela.**[1]

[1] Mhv. xxi. 10 f.; Dpv. xviii. 47 f.; Cv. lxxxii. 21.

12. **Sena Thera.**—An arahant. He was the maternal uncle of **Vijitasena Thera.** His brother was **Upasena.**[1]

[1] ThagA. i. 424.

13. **Sena.**—Elder brother of **Jotika,** when the latter was born as **Aparājita.** He entered the Order under **Vipassī Buddha** and became an arahant.[1]

[1] DhA. iv. 201 f.

14. **Sena.**—The name of **Bhūta Thera** in the time of **Siddhattha Buddha.** He was a brahmin, and, having seen the Buddha, uttered his praises in four stanzas.[1]

[1] ThagA. i. 493; Ap. i. 113.

15. **Sena.**—Son of **Atthadassī Buddha.**[1]

[1] Bu. xv. 16; BuA. (178) calls him **Sela.**

1. **Senaka.**—A minister of King **Vedeha.** See the **Mahāummagga Jātaka,** a large portion of which is devoted to the battle of wits between **Senaka** and **Mahosadha.** Senaka once killed a courtezan in order to take her ornaments.[1] He is identified with **Saccaka.**[2]

[1] J. vi. 382. [2] *Ibid.*, 478.

2. **Senaka.**—The Bodhisatta, born as a brahmin; he was the minister of **Janaka,** king of Benares. See the **Sattabhasta Jātaka.**

3. **Senaka.**—The Bodhisatta, born as a brahmin; he was the minister of **Madda,** king of Benares. See the **Dasannaka Jātaka.**

4. **Senaka.**—King of Benares. See the **Kharaputta Jātaka.**

5. **Senaka.**—A monkey, born as the nephew of the Bodhisatta. See the **Tinduka Jātaka.** He is identified with **Mahānāma** the **Sākyan.**[1]

[1] J. ii. 79.

6. **Senaka Thera.**—He was born in a brahmin family as the son of **Uruvela-Kassapa's** sister. Senaka heard the Buddha preach at the **Gayāphagguna** festival, was converted, entered the Order, and attained arahantship.

In the time of **Sikhī Buddha** he gave to the Buddha a handful of peacock feathers.[1] He is evidently identical with **Morahatthiya** of the *Apadāna.*[2]

[1] Thag. vss. 287-90; ThagA. i. 388 f. [2] Ap. ii. 403.

Senaka Vagga.—The second chapter of the Chakka Nipāta of the **Jātakaṭṭhakathā.**[1]

[1] J. iii. 275-316.

Senaguttagāma.—A village in **Rohaṇa,** mentioned in the account of the campaigns of **Parakkamabāhu I.**[1]

[1] Cv. lxxv. 6.

Senaggabodhi.—A shrine built by **Sena I.** on the **Thusavāpi** at **Pulatthipura.**[1]

[1] Cv. l. 73.

Senaggabodhipabbata.—A building erected in **Vāhadīpa** by **Udaya I.**[1]

[1] Cv. xlix. 33.

Senaratana.—King of Ceylon (1604–35 A.D.). He was the cousin and successor of **Vimaladhammasūriya I.** and had his capital at **Sirivaḍḍhanapura.** Because the Paraṅgī (Portuguese) did much damage to Buddhism, he removed the Tooth Relic to **Pañcasata.** He had three sons: **Kumārasīha, Vijayapāla,** and the best known of all, **Rājasīha** (afterwards **Rājasīha II.**). He divided the country among his sons seven years before his death.[1]

[1] Cv. xcv. 1 ff.

Senasenāpati-pariveṇa.—A monastic building erected by **Kuṭṭhaka,** *senāpati* of **Sena II.**[1] See also **Senānātha-pariveṇa.**

[1] Cv. li. 88; see also Cv. *Trs.* i. 156, n. 2.

1. **Senā.**—Queen of **Udaya I.**[1]

[1] Cv. xlix. 2.

2. **Senā.**—Daughter of **Kassapa,** *yuvarāja* of **Udaya II.** She married the king's brother's son.[1]

[1] Cv. li. 93.

Senāgāma.—A village and fortification near the **Kālavāpi.** It is mentioned in the account of the campaigns of **Parakkamabāhu I.** and was once the headquarters of his senāpati, **Deva.**[1]

[1] Cv. lxx. 131 f., 245.

Senānātha-pariveṇa.—Evidently identical with the **Senasenāpati-pariveṇa** (*q.v.*). **Vijayabāhu IV.** appointed the Thera of the *pariveṇa* in charge of the restoration of the **Ratanavāli-cetiya.**[1]

[1] Cv. lxxxviii. 85.

Senāninigama.—The village in which **Senānī** lived. It was the residence also of his daughter **Sujātā,** who gave milk-rice to the Buddha. It was near **Uruvelā** and on the banks of the **Nerañjarā.**[1] The name seems originally to have been **Senānigama.**[2] **Buddhaghosa** himself does not seem to have been sure of the spelling. He says[3] it was so called because it was occupied by soldiers at the beginning of the *kappa* (*paṭhamakappikānaṃ senāya niviṭṭhokāse patiṭṭhitagāmo*) or because it was the village of Sujātā's father Senānī (*Sujātāya vā pitu Senānī nāma nigamo*). The Lalitavistara[4] calls it Senāpatigrāma.

[1] J. i. 68.
[2] *E.g.*, S. i. 106; Vin. i. 21; M. i. 166, 240.
[3] SA. i. 135.
[4] p. 311 (248).

Senāni.—A wealthy landowner of **Senāninigama;** he was the father of **Sujātā.**[1]

[1] J. i. 68; BuA. 238.

Senāpatigumbaka.—The name given to the spot to which the general of **Paṇḍukābhaya's** uncles fled when the latter were defeated.[1]

[1] Mhv. x. 71.

Senāmagāma.—A village given by **Dāṭhopatissa II.** to the **Kassapa-vihāra.**[1]

[1] Cv. xlv. 27.

Senāsana Sutta.—The five factors which make an ideal lodging-place, and the five factors which a monk should possess in order to make good use of such lodgings.[1]

[1] A. v. 15 f.

Senāsanakkhandha.—The sixth chapter of the Culla Vagga of the Vinaya Piṭaka.[1]

[1] Vin. ii. 146 ff.

Senāsandāyaka Thera.—An arahant.[1] He is evidently identical with **Channa Thera**[2] (*q.v.*).

[1] Ap. i. 137 f. [2] ThagA. i. 155.

1. **Seniya.**—A naked ascetic who practised the "Canine-vow," behaving like a dog. After his visit to the Buddha, as recorded in the **Kukkura-vatika Sutta** (*q.v.*), he joined the Order and, in due course, became an arahant.[1]

[1] M. i. 387 ff.

2. **Seniya.**—The personal name, according to Buddhaghosa, of King **Bimbisāra,**[1] who is almost always referred to as **Seniya Bimbisāra.** Dhammapāla says,[2] however, that Bimbisāra was called Seniya either because he had a large army, or because he belonged to the *Seniya*-gotta (*mahatiyā senāya samannāgātatta vā Seniyagottatā vā*).

[1] MA. i. 292; but see SNA. ii. 448 (*mahatiyā senāya samannāgatattā*). [2] UdA. 104.

Sepaṇṇi-pāsāda.—A building erected by **Māṇavamma** in the **Padhāna-rakkha-vihāra.**[1] It is perhaps identical with the **Sepaṇṇipuppha-pāsāda** restored by **Parakkamabāhu I.**[2]

[1] Cv. xlvii. 64. [2] *Ibid.*, lxxviii. 105.

Semponmārī.—A place in South India. There was a fortress there which played a part in the campaigns of **Laṅkāpura.**[1]

[1] Cv. lxxvi. 241 ff.

Seyya.—See **Saṃyama.**

Seyya Jātaka (No. 282).—The Bodhisatta was king of Benares and ruled well. One of his courtiers was found guilty of an intrigue in the harem and was banished. He went to the court of an enemy king and persuaded him to lead an army against Benares. The Bodhisatta offered no resistance, and was captured and cast into the prison in chains. While there he developed the ecstasy of pity towards his enemy, whose body became filled with great pain. Having discovered the reason, he set the prisoner free and restored to him his kingdom.

The story was related in reference to a courtier of the king of **Kosala** who was imprisoned on a false charge. Owing to his virtue he became a *sotāpanna*, and the king, discovering his innocence, set him free.

Ānanda is identified with the marauding king.[1]

[1] J. ii. 400, 403; *cf.* the **Mahāsīlava Jātaka.**

Seyya Sutta.—The Buddha explains how the feelings of superiority, inferiority, or equality are brought about.[1]

[1] S. iv. 88.

Seyyasaka.—A monk of **Sāvatthī** who was found guilty of various Vinaya offences, and was therefore subjected to the *Nissayakamma*. **Udāyī (Lāḷudāyī)** was his friend and his evil genius.[1]

[1] Vin. iii. 110 f.

Seyyā Sutta.—On the four postures: that of *petas*, of the luxurious, of the lion, and of the Tathāgata.[1]

[1] A. ii. 244.

Serinī.—A courtezan of **Hatthinipura** in the **Kuru** kingdom. Once a large number of monks assembled there, and when she was asked to help in entertaining them, she abused the monks, calling them "shavelings." Later she was born as a *peta* in a village far away. She revealed her identity to an *upāsaka*, who had come from Hatthinipura on business. He reported the matter to her mother, who gave alms in her name, and after that the *peta* was happy.[1]

[1] Pv. iii. 6; PvA. 201 ff.

1. **Seriva.**—The name of a country.[1]

[1] J. i. 111.

2. **Seriva, Serivā.**—See the **Serivāṇija Jātaka.**

Serivāṇija Jātaka (No. 3).—The Bodhisatta was a hawker of **Seriva,** and was called **Serivā.** Once, in the company of a greedy merchant of the same name, he crossed the **Telavāha** and entered **Andhapura.** In that city was a family fallen on evil days, the sole survivors being a girl and her grandmother. The greedy merchant went to their house with his wares. The girl begged her grandmother to buy her a trinket, and suggested that they should give the hawker in exchange the bowl from which they ate. This was an heirloom and made of gold; but it had lost its lustre, and the women did not know its value. The hawker was called in and shown the bowl. He scratched it with a needle and knew it was of gold, but, wishing to have it for nothing, said it was not worth one half-farthing. So saying he threw it away and left. Later the Bodhisatta came to the same street and was offered the same bowl. He told them the truth, gave them all the money he had and his stock, leaving only eight pieces of money for himself. These he gave to a boatman, and entered his boat to cross the river. Meanwhile the greedy merchant went again to the old woman's house, hoping to get the bowl in exchange for a few trinkets. When he heard of what had happened he lost command of himself, and, throwing down all he had, ran down to the river, to find the Bodhisatta's boat in mid-stream. He shouted to the boatman to return, but the Bodhisatta urged him on. The merchant, realizing what he had lost through his greed, was so upset that his heart burst, and he fell down dead.

The story was told to a monk who had given up striving. The greedy merchant is identified with **Devadatta,** and this was the beginning of his enmity towards the Bodhisatta.[1]

[1] J. i. 110 ff.

1. **Serissaka.**—A **Yakkha** chieftain to be invoked in time of need by followers of the Buddha.[1]

[1] D. iii. 205.

2. **Serissaka, Serisaka.**—A *vimāna* in the **Cātummahārājika**-world, which was occupied by **Pāyāsi** during his life there. **Gavampati,** who used to go there for his siesta, met him and had a conversation with him, which he reported to the Buddha.[1] The deva of the *vimāna* was also

[1] D. ii. 356 f.

called **Serīsaka,** and is evidently to be identified with the Yakkha **Serissaka.** Pāyāsi was born in the Serīsaka-vimāna, because, though he gave generously, he was careless about the manner of giving. **Vessavaṇa** therefore stationed him in a desert, devoid of shade or water, to protect travellers from the dangers which beset them at the hands of non-humans. He came across some merchants from **Aṅga** and **Magadha** who had lost their way while journeying to **Sindhusovīra.** He revealed to them his identity, and they offered to hold a festival in his honour when they reached safety. But he suggested that gifts be given in his name to a pious man, named **Sambhava,** who was in their company. Later Sambhava joined the Order and became an arahant.[2] It is said[3] that the vimāna was called Serīsaka because there was, at its entrance, a large *serīsa*-tree, which bore fruit once in fifty years. Gavampati had earlier occupied the vimāna when born as a *devaputta.* After his rebirth among humans, the *vimāna* was empty till occupied by **Pāyāsi.** But Gavampati sometimes visited it even after becoming an arahant.

[2] Vv. vii. 10; VvA. 331. [3] DA. iii. 814; *cf.* ThagA. i. 103.

Serī.—A *devaputta* who visited the Buddha at **Jetavana** and held a conversation with him regarding the giving of food. He tells the Buddha that he was formerly a king, a great giver of gifts at the four gates of his capital. Then the women of the court wished also to give, and he allowed them to give at one gate; thus some of his own gifts came back to him. Then the nobles, the army, the brahmins and the householders wished to do the same, and he allowed them to distribute gifts, each class at one gate, and the result was that his gifts were not given at all. He then decreed that out of all his revenues one-half should be given away from the source and only half sent to him.[1] Buddhaghosa adds[2] that **Serī** was king of **Sindhava** and **Sodhika,** and that, at each gate, he gave away one thousand pieces daily.

[1] S. i. 57 f. [2] SA. i. 90.

Serumadīpa.—An old name for **Nāgadīpa.**[1]

[1] J. iii. 187, 189.

Sereyyaka Thera.—An arahant. In the time of **Vipassī Buddha** he was a learned brahmin, and, seeing the Buddha in the forest, offered him *sereyyaka* (*sirīga*) flowers, which formed a canopy over the Buddha's head. Fifteen kappas ago he was king twenty-five times under the name of **Cīnamāla.**[1]

[1] Ap. i. 155; *cf.* Kassapa (ThagA. i. 178).

1. **Sela.**—A king of long ago who, in spite of great sacrifices, could not get beyond the world of the *Petas* (*Pitṛs*).[1]

[1] J. vi. 99.

2. **Sela.**—A brahmin of **Aṅguttarāpa.** He was a great friend of **Keniya,** the **Jaṭila,** and visited him when Keniya was making preparations to entertain the Buddha. Having heard the word " Buddha " from Keniya, Sela was filled with joy and fortitude, and went with his two hundred and fifty pupils to visit the Buddha in the woodland near **Āpana.** There he observed on the person of the Buddha the thirty-two marks of a Great Being all except two—viz., hidden privates and the long tongue. The Buddha read his thoughts and contrived, by his *iddhi*-power, that Sela should be satisfied on these two points as well.[1] Sela then praised the Buddha in a series of verses and asked questions of him. At the end of his talk, Sela entered the Order with his pupils, and, at the end of a week, he attained arahantship.[2]

In the time of **Padumuttara Buddha** Sela had been the leader of the same guild of three hundred men, and, together with them, had built a *pariveṇa* for the Buddha and done many good acts. As a result of these they received the " *ehi bhikkhu-pabbajjā* " in this last life.[3]

Mahāsela, mentioned as the teacher of **Sugandha Thera,**[4] is probably identical with this Sela. Sela lived to the age of one hundred and twenty.[5]

According to the Dhammapada Commentary,[6] the Buddha first met Sela on his way to **Bhaddiya** to convert **Visākhā** and her kinswomen. Visākhā was then seven years old. The Apadāna says[7] that Sela's father was a wealthy brahmin, named **Vāseṭṭha.**

[1] This is referred to at Mil. 167; DA. i. 276, etc.

[2] SN. p. 104 ff.=M. ii. 146 f.

[3] SNA. ii. 455; MA. ii. 782; see also Ap. i. 316; Thag. vs. 818-41; ThagA. ii. 47 f.

[4] *Ibid.*, i. 80 f.

[5] DA. ii. 413.

[6] DhA. i. 384; also AA. i. 219.

[7] Ap. i. 318.

3. **Sela.**—A mountain in **Himavā.**[1]

[1] ApA. i. 96.

4. **Sela.**—Son of **Atthadassī Buddha** in his last lay life.[1]

[1] BuA. 180; but see **Sena** (15).

Sela Sutta.—Records the visit of **Sela** (1) to the Buddha, his conversion, and attainment of arahantship. One part of the sutta deals with the Buddha's interview with **Keniya,** the **Jaṭila.**[1]

[1] SN., p. 102 ff.=M. i. 146 ff.

Selantarasamūha.—The name of a monastic building provided by the king of Ceylon (probably **Māṇavamma**[1]) for **Dāṭhopatissa** after his ordination. Later **Yasodharā,** daughter of **Vijayabāhu I.,** erected there a building called the **Pasādapāsāda.**[2]

[1] Cv. lvii. 37 f.; Cv. *Trs.* i. 196, n. 2. [2] Cv. lx. 84.

Selantarāyatana.—A monastery, evidently in **Rohaṇa. Nanda Thera** was its chief incumbent in the time of **Parakkamabāhu I.**[1]

[1] Cv. lxxviii. 10.

1. **Selā.**—A princess, younger sister of **Candakumāra.**[1] She is identified with **Uppalavaṇṇā.**[2]

[1] J. vi. 143. [2] *Ibid.*, 157.

2. **Selā Therī.**—She was born in **Āḷavī** as daughter of the king: therefore she was also called **Āḷavikā.** When she was still unmarried the Buddha visited **Āḷavī** with **Āḷavaka,** whom he had converted, carrying his begging bowl and robe. On that occasion Selā went with her father to hear the Buddha preach. She became a lay disciple, but later, agitated in mind, she joined the Order and became an arahant. After that she lived in **Sāvatthī.** One day, as she was enjoying her siesta in the **Andhavana** under a tree, **Māra,** in the guise of a stranger, approached her and tried to tempt her. But she refuted his statements regarding the attractions of lay life, and Māra had to retire discomfited.[1]

In the time of **Padumuttara Buddha** Selā was born in the family of a clansman of **Haṃsavatī** and was given in marriage. After her husband's death she devoted herself to the quest of good, and went from *ārāma* to *ārāma* and *vihāra* to *vihāra,* teaching the Dhamma to followers of the religion. One day she came to the Bodhi-tree of the Buddha and sat down there thinking, "If a Buddha be peerless among men, may this tree show the miracle of Enlightenment." Immediately the tree blazed forth, the branches appeared golden, and the sky was all shining. Inspired by the sight, she fell down and worshipped the tree, and sat there for seven days. On the seventh day she performed a great feast of offering and worship to the Buddha.[2] Her Apadāna verses, quoted in the Therīgāthā Commentary, are, in the *Apadāna* itself, attributed to a Therī called **Pañcadīpikā,** and are twice repeated[3]; in these verses, however, she is mentioned as having attained arahantship at the age of seven, and there is no reference to her life as daughter of the king of Āḷavī. See also **Selā (3).**

[1] S. i. 134; Thig. vss. 57-9. [2] ThigA. 61 f. [3] Ap. ii. 519, repeated at 527 f.

3. **Selā Therī.**—An arahant. In the time of **Kassapa Buddha** she belonged to a lay disciple's family in **Sāvatthi.** She heard the Buddha preach and learnt the Doctrine. She was born after death in **Tāvatiṃsa.** In her last life she was the daughter of a *seṭṭhi*, and hearing the Buddha preach, she entered the Order and attained arahantship.[1]

[1] Ap. ii. 614 f.

Selā Sutta.—The story of **Māra's** unsuccessful temptation of **Selā Therī** (2).[1]

[1] S. i. 134.

Selissariya.—See **Poṭiriya.**

Sevitabba-asevitabba Sutta.—The one hundred and fourteenth sutta of the **Majjhima Nikāya,** preached to the monks at **Jetavana** regarding the twofold behaviour in act, speech, and thought—that which should be followed and that which should not. **Sāriputta,** who is present, asks the Buddha at the end of the discourse several questions, in order that certain statements made by the Buddha should be clearer to his hearers.[1]

[1] M. iii. 45 f.

Sehālauparājaka.—A monastic building erected by **Saṅghatissa,** *uparāja* of **Aggabodhi IV.**[1]

[1] Cv. xlvi. 24.

Sokatiṇṇā.—The name of an *apsaras*, or of a divine musical instrument.[1]

[1] VvA. 94; *cf.* 211, 372.

Sogandhika.—A **Niraya,** or, more probably, a period of suffering in **Avīci.**[1]

[1] S. i. 102; SN. 126; SNA. ii. 476.

1. **Soṇa Thera.**—*Aggasāvaka* of **Vessabhū Buddha.** He was the Buddha's younger brother, and the Buddha's first sermon was preached to him.[1]

[1] J. i. 42; Bu. xxii. 23; BuA. 205; D. ii. 4.

2. **Soṇa Thera.**—The enemy and rival of **Piyadassī Buddha,** corresponding to **Devadatta.** He conspired with **Mahāpaduma** to kill the Buddha, but was unsuccessful.[1]

[1] BuA. 174 f.; for details see *s.v.* **Piyadassī.**

3. **Soṇa.**—A fierce horse belonging to the king of Benares; he was also called **Mahāsoṇa.** See the **Suhanu Jātaka.**

4. **Soṇa-Kuṭikaṇṇa, Soṇa-Koṭikaṇṇa.**—A Thera, declared chief of those possessing clear utterance.[1] He was the son of **Kāḷī Kuraragharikā,** and was conceived before the Buddha appeared in the world.[2] A little while before the birth of the child Kāḷī went to her parents' house in **Rājagaha,** and one day, as she was cooling herself, she heard a conversation between two Yakkhas, **Sātāgira** and **Hemavata.** As she listened to their talk, her mind was filled with thoughts of the virtues of the Buddha, and she became a *sotāpanna.* That same night the child was born and was called **Soṇa.** His mother later returned to **Kuraraghara.** At that time **Mahā Kaccāna** lived near by and often visited her home. Soṇa was very attached to him, and was later ordained by him. Three years later he received the *upasampadā,* and, with Mahā Kaccāna's leave, visited the Buddha. Kāḷī gave him a large carpet to spread in the Buddha's **Gandhakuṭi.**

When Soṇa arrived at the Gandhakuṭi, he worshipped the Buddha, who asked **Ānanda** to find him a lodging. Ānanda, reading the Buddha's thoughts, spread a rug in the Buddha's chamber. Late at night Soṇa went to bed, and, very early the next morning, the Buddha woke him and asked him to recite the Dhamma. Soṇa recited the whole of the **Aṭṭhakavagga,** which he had learnt from Mahā Kaccāna. At the end of the recital the Buddha applauded him and gave him a boon. Soṇa asked for the "*vinayadharapañcamagaṇena upasampadā,*"[3] which Kaccāna had asked him to choose. Later he returned to Kuraraghara and visited his mother's house. She had heard of the Buddha's applause from the devas, and wished Soṇa to recite the Dhamma just as he had done before the Buddha, and this he did.

In the time of **Padumuttara Buddha** Soṇa had resolved to win this eminence. In the time of **Vipassī Buddha** he was a member of the Order and sewed a robe for a monk. Later he was a tailor of Benares and mended a Pacceka Buddha's robe.[4]

The Dhammapada Commentary says[5] that, on the day when Soṇa recited the Dhamma in Kuraraghara, Kāḷī went to listen to him, leaving only one female slave in the house. Her house had seven walls and

[1] A. i. 24.

[2] According to ThagA. i. 429, his father was a rich *seṭṭhi*; no mention is made there of his mother.

[3] This means permission to admit a monk into the Order with a chapter of only five monks, one of whom was versed in the Vinaya. For details of Soṇa's visit to the Buddha, see Vin. i. 194 ff.; *cf.* Ud. v. 6.

[4] Thag. vss. 365-9; AA. i. 133 f.; ThagA. i. 429.

[5] DhA. iv. 103 f.

fortified gates and savage dogs on leash. Molten lead flowed round the walls at night, and in the night it proved a slippery surface, difficult to walk on. Nine hundred thieves had been awaiting a chance of breaking into the house, and this day they saw their opportunity. They stationed one of their number to watch Kāḷī going to the monastery, and to kill her if she started homewards after the thieves entered her house. When they came her female servant ran to the monastery to tell her about it. But she would not be disturbed and sent her back. Again the servant went, and again she was sent back. When the thief, stationed near Kāḷī, saw her extraordinary piety, he was filled with remorse, and, at the end of the sermon, begged her forgiveness. All the nine hundred thieves joined the Order under Soṇa Kuṭikaṇṇa, and on the day they became arahants the Buddha appeared before them in a ray of light to encourage them.

According to the Udāna Commentary,[6] Soṇa was called Kuṭikaṇṇa because he wore ear ornaments worth one crore (*koṭi*). It is said that he once went with a caravan to **Ujjeni,** and when the caravan stopped for the night he slept away from the rest of its members. The caravan started very early and nobody waked Soṇa. When he finally awoke, he ran along the road till he came to a large tree. There he saw an ugly man tearing off his own flesh and eating it. On enquiry, Soṇa learnt that he had been a wicked merchant of **Bhārukaccha,** who had been born as a *peta* because he had deceived his patrons. This revelation filled Soṇa with great misgivings, which were increased by the sight of two *peta*-boys with blood pouring out of their lips. They had been youths, also of Bhārukaccha, who had found fault with their mother for feeding an arahant monk. When Soṇa returned from Ujjeni he consulted Mahā Kaccāna about these things, and resolved to enter the Order.

The Vinaya says[7] that when Kaccāna wished to confer the higher ordination on Soṇa, it was three years before he could get together the necessary chapter of ten monks. This was because there were but few monks in **Avanti** and in the Southern Country; hence Soṇa's request to the Buddha that he should allow five monks to officiate in **Avanti.** Other boons asked for by Soṇa and allowed by the Buddha were: (1) Permission to use, in Avanti, shoes with thick linings, because the soil of Avanti was black and always muddy; (2) permission to bath constantly; (3) to use skins for coverlets; (4) to accept robes set apart for absent monks even after the lapse of ten days.

Soṇa is evidently identical with **Pāṭhirasaññaka** of the *Apadāna*.[8] **Gosāla Thera** was a friend of Soṇa Kuṭikaṇṇa.[9]

[6] UdA. 307. [7] Vin. i. 195 f. [8] Ap. ii. 392. [9] ThagA. i. 79.

5. **Soṇa-Koḷivisa Thera,** also called **Sukhumāla Soṇa.**[1]—He was born in **Campā,** his father being **Usabhaseṭṭhi.** From the time of his conception his father's wealth continued to increase, and, on the day of his birth, the whole town kept festival. Because in a previous birth he had given a ring, worth one hundred thousand, to a Pacceka Buddha, his body was like burnished gold—hence his name.[2] His hands and feet were soft like *bandhujīvaka*-flowers, and a fine down grew on them[3] curved "like ear-ornaments." He lived in great luxury in three palaces, each having its own season.

King **Bimbisāra,** hearing of him, sent for him, and Soṇa went with eighty thousand fellow townsmen.[4] In **Rājagaha** he heard the Buddha preach, and, winning faith, entered the Order with his parents' consent. The Buddha gave him a subject for meditation, and he went to **Sītavana,** but many people visited him and he was unable to concentrate. He strove hard, and, through pacing up and down in meditation, painful sores developed on his feet. But he won no attainment and was filled with despair. The Buddha saw this and visited him, and by preaching to him the **Vīṇūpamovāda Sutta** (see **Soṇa Sutta**), taught him how to temper energy with calm. Thus corrected, he put forth fresh effort and attained arahantship.[5]

In the time of **Anomadassī Buddha** he was a very rich *seṭṭhi,* and, having gone with others to the *vihāra* and heard the Buddha preach, he decorated a *caṅkamana* for the Buddha and a long hall (*dīghasālā*) for the monks. On the *caṅkamana* he scattered various flowers, and, above it, he hung canopies. In the time of **Padumuttara Buddha** he was a *seṭṭhi* of **Haṃsavatī** named **Sirivaḍḍha.** It was then that he resolved to win eminence as foremost of those who strove energetically (*aggaṃ āraddhaviriyānaṃ*), and in this he was successful.[6] After the death of **Kassapa Buddha** Soṇa was a householder in Benares, and built a hut by the river for a Pacceka Buddha, whom he looked after during the rainy

[1] AA. ii. 679.

[2] He was evidently called *Koḷivisa* because he was a Koliyan (Ap. i. 95 (21)).

[3] Four inches long on his feet (Ap. i. 298).

[4] The Vinaya (i. 179 ff.) gives details of Soṇa's visit to Bimbisāra. The king, being curious to see Soṇa's feet, sent for him. He and his eighty thousand companions went to see the Buddha, and there they were greatly impressed by the *iddhi*-power of **Sāgata.** Soṇa then sought the Buddha alone and joined the Order. After ordination he walked about meditating, his feet bled, and his *caṅkamana* was covered with blood "like a slaughter-house for oxen." After Soṇa attained arahantship, the Buddha gave him permission to wear shoes with one lining. Soṇa said he had abandoned eighty cartloads of gold and a retinue of seven elephants. He did not wish, as a monk, to have any luxuries which his colleagues did not share. The Buddha then gave permission to all monks to wear shoes with one lining.

[5] Thag. vss. 632-44.

[6] A. i. 24.

season. He was king of the gods for twenty-five kappas, and seventy-seven times king among men under the name of **Yasodhara.**[7]

The *Apadāna* mentions[8] a Thera, called **Soṇa Koṭivīsa,** evidently identical with the above, the reason given for the name being that he gave away wealth equal in value to twenty crores (*vīsa koṭi*). His eminence is ascribed to the fact that, in the time of **Vipassī Buddha,** he made a *leṇa* (cave) for the Buddha and his monks and spread it with rugs. Buddhaghosa[9] gives a variant of his name, calling him **Koṭivessa,** and explains this by saying that he belonged to a *vessa* (merchant) family worth a crore.

The **Soṇa Sutta**[10] (*q.v.*) mentions that Soṇa was a clever player of the *vīnā* before he joined the Order. It was the example of Soṇa Koḷivisa which urged **Nandaka** and his brother, **Bharata,** to leave the world.[11]

[7] ThagA. i. 544 f.; *cf.* Ap. i. 93 f., where he is called **Koḷiyavessa.** The ApA. confused his story with that of **Kuṭikaṇṇa**; see also AA. i. 130 f., where the details are different, especially regarding the honour paid by Soṇa to the Pacceka Buddha. Once, on visiting the Pacceka Buddha's cell, he noticed that the ground outside it was muddy; so he spread on the ground a rug worth one hundred thousand, so that the Pacceka Buddha's feet might not be soiled.

[8] Ap. i. 298.

[9] AA. i. 130.

[10] *Cf. ibid.*, ii. 680, where he is described as "*gandhabbasippe cheko.*"

[11] ThagA. i. 299.

6. **Soṇa.**—An arahant monk who was sent with **Uttara** to convert **Suvaṇṇabhūmi.**[1]

[1] Dpv. viii. 12; Sp. i. 68, 69; Mhv. xii. 6, 44 ff.; for details see *s.v.* **Suvaṇṇabhūmi.**

7. **Soṇa.**—A minister of **Mahāsena** and a follower of the heretic monk, **Saṅghamitta.** He helped Saṅghamitta in the despoliation of the **Lohapāsāda** and other buildings. He was killed in an attempt to destroy the **Thūpārāma.**[1] In the *Dīpavaṃsa*[2] he is called **Pāpasoṇa.**

[1] Mhv. xxxvii. 10, 13, 28.

[2] Dpv. xxii. 70, 71.

8. **Soṇa.**—See **Mahāsoṇa.**

9. **Soṇa-Poṭiriyaputta** (or **Seṭṭhiputta**) **Thera.**—He was born in **Kapilavatthu** as the son of the zemindar **Poṭiriya** (**Selissariya**), and became chief of the forces of the Sākyan **Bhaddiya.** When Bhaddiya left the world, Soṇa followed his example and entered the Order. But he was lazy and not given to meditation. The Buddha saw this from the **Ambavana** at **Anupiyā** and, sending forth a ray of glory, spurred him on. Soṇa became agitated, and putting forth effort became an arahant.

In the time of **Sikhī Buddha** he was a forester and gave the Buddha a *kuruñjiya*-fruit.[1] He is probably identical with **Kuruñjiyaphaladāyaka** of the *Apadāna*.[2]

[1] Thag. vss. 193, 194; ThagA. i. 316 f. [2] Ap. ii. 448 f.

10. **Soṇa.**—A *gahapatiputta* of **Rājagaha.** He is mentioned as having had two conversations with the Buddha at **Veḷuvana:** one on the impermanence of the body, feelings, etc., their origin and their cessation[1]; and, on another occasion, as to why some beings achieve complete cessation in this life and others do not.[2]

[1] S. iii. 48 f. [2] *Ibid.*, iv. 113.

11. **Soṇa.**—A gifted preacher, who lived in the **Pipphali-vihāra** at the foot of **Sonnagiri.** His father was a hunter, and all Soṇa's efforts to lead him away from sin failed, until he was very old, when Soṇa ordained him just before his death. The old man saw the **Niraya** and dogs coming to devour him. He shouted in his fright, and Soṇa took him on his bed to the vihāra and made him worship the *cetiya*, the *bodhi*-tree, etc., and offered various things in his father's name. He then saw the Devaloka before him.[1]

[1] VibhA. 439; *cf.* AA. i. 255, where the vihāra is called **Pañcala-vihāra,** and MA. ii. 887, where it is called **Paceli°.**

12. **Soṇa.**—A Thera of the **Mahāvihāra,** at whose request the **Kaṅkhā-vitaraṇī** was written.[1]

[1] Knv., p. 1.

13. **Soṇa.**—See **Sona** and its **compounds.**

1. **Soṇa Suttā.**—Two suttas, recording conversations between the Buddha and **Soṇa-gahapati** of **Rājagaha.**[1]

[1] S. iii. 48 f.; iv. 113.

2. **Soṇa Sutta.**—**Soṇa Koḷivisa,** living in **Sītavana,** despairs of ever attaining arahantship. The Buddha, on **Gijjhakūṭa,** becomes aware of this and visits him. The Buddha reminds him that when he was a *vīnā* player his *vīnā* sounded neither tuneful nor playable when the strings were either over-strung or over-lax. Even so, energy, when over-strung, ends in flurry, when over-lax, in idleness. Soṇa profits by the lesson and becomes an arahant. He then visits the Buddha and declares to him his new-found vision.[1]

[1] A. iii. 374 f.

1. **Soṇaka Thera.**—He was the son of a leader of a caravan of **Kāsi,** and once, when he was fifteen, he went with his parents to **Rājagaha** and then into the **Veḷuvana-vihāra.** He had with him fifty-five companions. He saw Dāsaka Thera, and, very pleased with him, he entered the Order, after starving for three meals, until his parents gave their consent. He soon became an arahant and leader of one thousand monks. Later, as Soṇaka sat in a trance, he was seen by **Siggava** and **Caṇḍavaggi,** who spoke to him. But he would not answer, and when they heard his explanation, they entered the Order under him.[1]

[1] Mhv. v. 104, 114 ff.; Dpv. iv. 39 f.; v. 79 f.; Sp. i. 32, 235; Vin. v. 2.

2. **Soṇaka.**—See **Sonaka.**

Soṇakāyana.—A youth who, according to **Sikhā Moggallāna,** went about saying that the Buddha proclaimed the ineffectiveness of all deeds, and thereby preached the annihilation of the world. The Buddha said he did not know Soṇakāyana, even by sight.[1]

[1] A. ii. 232.

Soṇakāyana Sutta.—**Sikhā Moggallāna's** conversation with the Buddha regarding **Soṇakāyana** (*q.v.*).

Soṇagiri, Soṇṇagiri.—A mountain district in Ceylon. King **Mahācūli Mahātissa** once worked in a sugar mill there for three years in order to earn money wherewith to give alms.[1] Near Soṇṇagiri was the **Pipphalī-vihāra.**[2]

According to the **Mahāvaṃsaṭīkā,**[3] Soṇṇagiri was part of the **Ambaṭṭha-kola-range.**

[1] Mhv. xxxiv. 4. [2] VibhA. 439. [3] MṬ. 624; see also Mhv. *Trs.* 238, n. 1.

Soṇatthera Vagga.—Also called **Mahā Vagga.** The fifth chapter of the **Udāna.**

Soṇadaṇḍa.—A rich brahmin of **Campā,** very learned in the Vedas; he lived in a royal domain, given to him as royal fief by King **Bimbisāra.** When the Buddha was in Campā, on the banks of the **Gaggarā**-lake, Soṇadaṇḍa visited him in spite of the protests of his friends and colleagues. Their conversation is recorded in the **Soṇadaṇḍa Sutta.** At the end of the discourse, Soṇadaṇḍa expressed his appreciation of the Buddha and his doctrine, and invited him and his monks to a meal. At the conclusion of the meal Soṇadaṇḍa asked the Buddha to forgive him if, in the presence of the brahmins, he did not make humble obeisance to the Buddha, but merely saluted him. Buddhaghosa explains[1] that this was because Soṇadaṇḍa was much older than the Buddha and did not wish people to see him paying homage to one young enough to be his grandson. But, probably, Soṇadaṇḍa's conversion to the faith was only partial.

Aṅgaka (*q.v.*) was Soṇadaṇḍa's sister's son.

[1] D. i. 111 ff.; DA. i. 292 ff.

Soṇadaṇḍa Sutta.—The fourth sutta of the **Dīgha Nikāya.** It records the discussion between the Buddha and **Soṇadaṇḍa.** The Buddha asks him what things enable a man to make a just claim to be a brahmin and Soṇadaṇḍa answers him. The Buddha makes him admit that birth is of no importance, only the good life matters. The Buddha then teaches him what is meant by the good life in the Buddha's own doctrine, in very much the same way as in that of the **Sāmaññaphala Sutta.**[1]

[1] D. i. 111 ff.

Soṇadinna.—A devaputta who had seven mansions in **Tāvatiṃsa.** King **Nimi** saw these on his visit to **Sakka,** and **Mātali** explained to him that **Soṇadinna** had been a householder in a **Kāsi** village in the time of **Kassapa Buddha** and had built hermitages for holy men, providing them with all necessaries.[1]

[1] J. vi. 118 f.

Soṇadinnā.—An *upāsikā* of **Nālandā,** a very good woman. She listened to the Buddha preaching and became a *sotāpanna.* After death she was born in **Tāvatiṃsa,** where **Moggallāna** met her and learnt her story.[1]

[1] Vv. ii. 6; VvA. 114 f.

1. **Soṇā.**—One of the chief women patrons of **Dīpaṅkara Buddha.**[1]

[1] Bu. ii. 215.

2. **Soṇā.**—An *aggasāvikā* of **Sumana Buddha.**[1]

[1] Bu. v. 24; J. i. 34.

3. **Soṇā.**—An eminent lay woman, disciple of the Buddha.[1]

[1] A. iv. 348.

4. **Soṇā.**—An eminent Therī of Ceylon.[1]

[1] Dpv. xviii. 38.

5. **Soṇā.**—A Therī. She was declared foremost among nuns for capacity of effort (*āraddhaviriyānaṃ*). She belonged to the family of a clansman of **Sāvatthi,** and because, after marriage, she had ten sons and daughters, she came to be called **Bahuputtikā.** When her husband renounced the world, she distributed her wealth among her children, keeping nothing for herself.

Her children soon ceased to show her any respect, and she entered the Order in her old age. She waited on the nuns and studied most of the night. Soon her strenuous energy became known to the Buddha, and he, sending forth a ray of glory, spoke to her. Then she attained arahantship. Her resolve to win eminence was made in the time of **Padumuttara Buddha,** when she was the daughter of a rich seṭṭhi.[1]

The Aṅguttara Commentary says[2] that after she became an arahant she wished her colleagues to know this because they had been in the habit of constantly finding fault with her for various things, and she did not wish them to continue doing so and thereby commit a sin. She therefore filled a vessel with water, which she heated by her *iddhi*-power, using no fire. When the nuns came to look for water she told them that if they wanted warm water they could have it from the vessel. They found the water hot, and understood. Then they begged her forgiveness.

[1] A. i. 25; Thig. vss. 102-6; ThigA. 95 f.; Ap. ii. 576; *cf.* the story of **Bahuputtikā** at DhA. ii. 276 f.
[2] AA. i. 199.

6. **Soṇā.**—An eminent teacher of the Vinaya in **Jambudīpa.**[1]

[1] Dpv. xviii. 10.

Soṇāyamātā.—An eminent laywoman, disciple of the Buddha.[1] She was evidently mother of **Soṇā Therī** (**Soṇa** 5).

[1] A. iv. 348.

1. **Soṇuttara Thera.**—An arahant. He lived in the **Pūjā-pariveṇa** in the **Mahāvihāra** and was entrusted by **Duṭṭhagāmaṇī** with the task of finding relics for the **Mahā Thūpa.** In the time of the Buddha he had been the brahmin **Nanduttara,** and had entertained the Buddha on the occasion on which, at **Payāgatittha, Bhaddaji Thera** had raised, from the bed of the Ganges, the palace he had occupied as **Mahāpanāda.** Filled with marvel, Nanduttara wished that he might have the power of procuring relics possessed by others. Soṇuttara visited the **Mañjerika-nāga-bhavana** and asked the Nāga-king, **Mahākāla,** to give him the relics which he had there and which had once been enshrined in **Rāmagāma.** But Mahākāla, unwilling to part with them, told his nephew, **Vāsuladatta,**

to hide them. Soṇuttara knew this, and when Mahākāla told him he might take the relics if he could find them, Soṇuttara, by his magic power, took the relic-casket from Vāsuladatta, unknown to him, and brought it to **Anurādhapura,** where the relics were deposited in the Mahā Thūpa.[1]

[1] Mhv. xxxi. 4-74.

2. **Soṇuttara.**—A brahmin of **Kajaṅgala,** father of **Nāgasena Thera.**[1]

[1] Mil. 8.

3. **Soṇuttara.**—The name given to the princes of **Suvaṇṇabhūmi** (*q.v.*) after the visit of **Soṇa** and **Uttara** to that country.[1]

[1] Mhv. xii. 54.

4. **Soṇuttara.**—The horse on which **Tissa Buddha** left the household life.[1]

[1] BuA. 189.

5. **Soṇuttara.**—See **Sonuttara.**

Soṇṇamāli.—See **Mahā Thūpa.**

Soṇṇābha.—Twenty kappas ago there were eight kings of this name, previous births of **Kaṇikāracchadanīya.**[1]

[1] Ap. i. 183.

1. **Sota Sutta.**—The Ariyan disciple who really knows and understands the five *indriyas* is a stream-winner (*sotāpanna*).[1]

[1] S. v. 193.

2. **Sota** (or **Sotāpanna**) **Sutta.**—The Ariyan disciple who really knows and understands the six sense-faculties is a *sotāpanna.*[1]

[1] S. v. 205.

" Sotarā " Sutta.—The detailed qualities of a state-elephant, as hearer, destroyer, warder, endurer, and goer; and the corresponding qualities of a monk.[1]

[1] A. iii. 161.

Sotānugata Sutta.—A detailed explanation of the four advantages to be looked for from the frequent verbal practice of teachings heard with the ear, from considering them in the mind, and from thoroughly penetrating them by view.[1]

[1] A. ii. 185 ff.

Sotāpanna Saṃyutta.—The fifty-fifth Saṃyutta of the **Saṃyutta Nikāya.**[1]

[1] S. v. 342-60.

1. **Sotāpanna Sutta.**—The Ariyan disciple who really knows and understands the five *upādānakkhandhas* is a stream-winner.[1]

[1] S. iii. 160.

2. **Sotāpanna Sutta.**—The same as sutta (1), but addressed to **Rādha.**[1]

[1] S. iii. 192.

Sotārāma.—A pleasaunce in which **Sobhita Buddha** died.[1]

[1] BuA. 140; but Bu. vii. 30 calls it Sihārāma.

Sotumbarā.—A river on whose banks buffaloes live.[1]

[1] J. vi. 507.

Sotthika.—A *seṭṭhi,* one of the chief lay patrons of **Vessabhū Buddha.**[1]

[1] Bu. xxii. 25; BuA. 208; but J. i. 94 calls him **Sotthiya.**

Sotthija, Sotthiya.—The constant attendant of **Koṇāgamana Buddha.**[1]

[1] Bu. xxiv. 22; J. i. 43; D. ii. 6.

1. **Sotthiya.**—A grass-cutter (*uṇchānaka*) who gave grass for his seat to the Buddha.[1]

[1] J. i. 70; BuA. 238; SNA. ii. 391, etc.

2. **Sotthiya.**—See also **Sotthika** and **Sotthija.**

3. **Sotthiya.**—A brahmin of **Sāvatthi** who entered the Order and became an arahant after a conversation he had with **Anāthapiṇḍika's** slave-girl, **Puṇṇikā (Puṇṇā).**[1]

[1] Ap. ii. 611 (vss. 6-11).

Sotthiyākara.—A monastery erected by King **Sirimeghavaṇṇa** at the eastern gate of **Anurādhapura.** For twelve days the image of **Mahinda,** made by the king, remained there; after which it was installed in the **Mahāvihāra.**[1]

[1] Cv. xxxvii. 82 f.; for identification see Cv. *Trs.* i. 6, n. 1.

Sotthivatī.—A city, the capital of the **Ceti** country, in the time of King **Upacara (Apacara).**[1]

[1] J. iii. 454.

1. **Sotthisena.**—King of Benares and son of **Brahmadatta.** His wife was **Sambulā.** See the **Sambula Jātaka.** He is identified with the king of **Kosala** (? **Pasenadi**).[1]

[1] J. v. 98.

2. **Sotthisena.**—Son of King **Mahānāma** and a Damiḷa queen. He succeeded **Mahānāma** in 431 A.C., and was killed, almost immediately after his accession, by his step-sister, **Saṅghā.**[1]

[1] Cv. xxxviii. 1.

Sodhana.—The elder brother of **Kapila,** who later became **Kapilamaccha** (*q.v.*). His mother was **Sādhinī** and his sister **Tāpanā.** He entered the Order with **Kapila,** in the time of **Kassapa Buddha,** and lived in the forest, engaged in meditation, attaining arahantship soon after.[1]

[1] DhA. iv. 37; SNA. i. 305 f.

Sodhika.—A country over which **Serī** (*q.v.*) reigned as king.[1]

[1] SA. i. 90.

1. **Sona.**—The Bodhisatta born as a brahmin of Benares. See the **Sona-Nanda Jātaka.**

2. **Sona.**—See **Soṇa.**

Sonaka.—Son of a chaplain of **Rājagaha.** He afterwards became a Pacceka Buddha. See the **Sonaka Jātaka.**

Sonaka Jātaka (No. 529).—The story of the Bodhisatta in his birth as **Arindama** and of his friend, **Sonaka,** who became a **Pacceka Buddha.**[1] For the story see *s.v.* **Arindama.** It was related regarding the Buddha's *Nekkhammapāramitā.*

[1] J. v. 247-61; *cf.* Ntu. iii. 450.

Sona-Nanda Jātaka (No. 532).—Once when **Manoja** was king of **Brahmavaddhana** (Benares), the Bodhisatta was born as **Sona,** the son of a rich brahmin. He had a brother **Nanda.** When the boys grew up their parents wanted them to marry, but they refused, and declared their desire to become ascetics after the death of their parents. Then the parents suggested that they should all, at once, become ascetics; this they did, and lived in a pleasant grove in the **Himālaya.** After some time, because Nanda brought unripe fruit for his parents in spite of Sona's warning, Sona dismissed him. Nanda thereupon sought **Manoja,** and, with his magic power, helped him to win various kingdoms in **Jambudīpa**, bringing into subjection one hundred and one kings in seven years, seven months and seven days. All these kings Manoja brought to **Brahmavaddhana,** where he caroused with them. Nanda spent his time in the **Suvaṇṇaguhā** in the **Himālaya,** obtaining his alms from **Uttarakuru.** At the end of the seventh day Manoja looked for Nanda, who, reading his thoughts, appeared before him. Manoja wished to give some token of his gratitude, and Nanda asked that he should intercede for him with Sona and win for him Sona's forgiveness. Together they went to Sona accompanied by a large retinue. Sona explained why he had forbidden Nanda to look after their parents, and Nanda asked his forgiveness for having given his parents unripe fruit in his eagerness to wait on them. Sona forgave him, and they all lived together once more, while the kings returned to their countries, where they ruled wisely.

The occasion for the story is the same as that for the **Sāma Jātaka** (*q.v.*), regarding a monk who supported his mother. Nanda is identified with **Ānanda** and Manoja with **Sāriputta.**[1]

The story is also given in the *Cariyāpiṭaka.*[2]

[1] J. v. 312, p. 332. [2] Cyp. iii. v.

Sonārāma.—The monastery in which **Phussa Buddha** died.[1]

[1] Bu. xix. 25; BuA. (195) calls it **Setārāma.**

Sonuttara.—**Devadatta** born as a hunter. See the **Chaddanta Jātaka.**

Sonemi.—Name of a **Pacceka Buddha.**[1]

[1] ApA. i. 107.

1. **Sopāka Thera.**—He was the son of a very poor woman of **Sāvatthi.** While in labour his mother fell into a long and deep swoon, and her kinsfolk, thinking her dead, took her to the cemetery and prepared for cremation. But a spirit prevented the fire from burning with a storm of wind and rain, and they went away. The child was safely born and the mother died. The spirit, in human shape, took the child and put it in the watchman's hut, feeding it for a time. After that the watchman adopted it, and the child grew up with the watchman's son, **Suppiya** (*q.v.*). He was called Sopāka (the " waif ") because he was born in the cemetery. When he was seven years old he came under the notice of the Buddha, who visited him in the cemetery. Gladdened by the Buddha's teaching, he sought his father's consent and entered the Order. The Buddha gave him, as his subject of meditation, the thought of *mettā*, and Sopāka, developing insight, soon attained arahantship.

In the time of **Kakusandha Buddha,** he was a householder's son and gave the Buddha some *bījapūra*-fruits. He also provided three monks with milk-rice daily to the end of his life. In another birth he gave a meal of milk-rice to a Pacceka Buddha.[1]

He is perhaps identical with **Vibhīṭakamiñjaya** of the *Apadāna*.[2]

[1] Thag. vs. 33; ThagA. i. 94 f. [2] Ap. ii. 396.

2. **Sopāka Thera.**—He was born as the child of a cemetery-keeper and was therefore called Sopāka. Others say that he was born in a trader's family and that Sopāka was merely a name. Four months after birth his father died suddenly and he was adopted by his uncle. When he was only seven years old, his uncle took him to a charnel-field because he quarrelled with his cousin, bound his hands, and tied him fast to a corpse, hoping that the jackals would eat him. At midnight the jackals came and the child started crying. The Buddha, seeing Sopāka's destiny for arahantship, sent a ray of glory, and, by the Buddha's power, the boy broke his bonds and stood before the Buddha's **Gandhakuṭi,** a *sotāpanna*. His mother started seeking for him, and the uncle telling her nothing, she came to the Buddha, thinking "The Buddhas know all, past, present and future." When she came, the Buddha, by his *iddhi*-power, made the boy invisible and taught her the Dhamma, saying that sons are no shelter, blood-bonds no refuge. As she listened she became a *sotāpanna* and the boy an arahant. Then the Buddha revealed the boy's presence to his mother, and she allowed him to enter the Order. Some time later the Buddha, wishing to confer on him the higher ordination, asked him the questions which came to be known as the "**Kumārapañhā.**" Sopāka answered these, and the Buddha, satisfied, gave him the *upasampadā*.

Sopāka had been a brahmin in the time of **Siddhattha Buddha,** expert in the Vedas. He later became an ascetic and lived on a mountain. The Buddha, foreseeing his imminent death, visited him. The brahmin spread for him a seat of flowers. The Buddha preached to him on impermanence and left through the air.[1]

[1] Thag. vss. 480-6; ThagA. i. 477 f.; Ap. i. 64 f.; KhpA. 76; see also DhA. iv. 176 f.

Sobaragāma.—A village mentioned in the account of the campaigns of **Parakkamabāhu I.**[1]

[1] Cv. lxx. 187.

Sobbha-vihāra.—A monastery in which **Sena II.** built an image-house.[1]

[1] Cv. li. 76.

Sobha.—King of **Sobhavatī** in the time of **Koṇāgamana Buddha.**[1] He sent a branch of the Bodhi-tree to Ceylon in the care of **Kanakadattā.**[2]

[1] Bu. xxiv. 16; D. ii. 7. [2] MṬ. 355, where he is called **Sobhana.**

"Sobhati" Sutta.—Monks, nuns and lay disciples, both male and female, who are accomplished in wisdom, disciplined, confident, deeply learned, hearers of the Dhamma, living according to the Dhamma—these illumine the religion.[1]

[1] A. ii. 8.

1. **Sobhana.**—An *ārāma*, given by **Upāli** in a previous birth as **Sumana,** for the use of **Padumuttara Buddha.**[1]

[1] ThagA. i. 362.

2. **Sobhana.**—A householder (*kuṭumbika*). **Ānanda,** born as **Sumana,** bought his park (also called **Sobhana**) for one sum of one hundred thousand and built in it a *vihāra* for **Padumuttara Buddha.**[1]

[1] ThagA. ii. 123; DA. ii. 490; SA. ii. 69 f.; AA. i. 162, etc.

3. **Sobhana.**—The city of birth of **Atthadassī Buddha,** where he later preached to his relations.[1]

[1] Bu. xv. 5, 14; BuA. 179; but J. i. 39 calls it **Sobhita.**

4. **Sobhana.**—A city, built by **Vessakamma** for the use of **Ukkāsatika,** in his birth as a **Cakkavatti,** fifty-five kappas ago.[1]

[1] Ap. ii. 414.

5. **Sobhana.**—*v.l.* for **Sobha.**

Sobhanā.—An eminent Therī of Ceylon.[1]

[1] Dpv. xviii. 15.

Sobhavatī.—The city of birth of **Koṇāgamana Buddha.** Its king was **Sobha (Sobhana).**[1]

[1] Bu. xxiv. 16; J. i. 43; D. ii. 7.

1. **Sobhita.**—The sixth of the twenty-four Buddhas. He was born in the city of **Sudhamma,** his father being the *khattiya* **Sudhamma** and his mother **Sudhammā.** For nine thousand years he lived as a householder in three palaces—**Kumuda, Naḷira** and **Paduma**—his wife being **Samaṅgī (Makhilā** according to the BuA.) and his son **Sīha.** He entered the monastic life in the palace itself and there attained the four *jhānas.*

His wife gave him a meal of milk-rice. After practising austerities for only seven days, he attained Enlightenment at the foot of a *Nāga*-tree in the palace garden, going there through the air with all his retinue. He preached his first sermon to his step-brothers, **Asama** and **Sunetta**—who later became his chief Disciples—in the **Sudhamma** pleasaunce. **Anuma** was his constant attendant. His chief disciples among nuns were **Nakulā** and **Sujātā**. **Ramma** and **Sudatta** were his chief lay patrons among men and **Nakulā** and **Cittā** among women. His height was fifty-eight hands. He lived for ninety thousand years and died in the **Sīhārāma**. The Bodhisatta was a brahmin named **Sujāta**.[1]

[1] Bu. vii. 1 ff.; BuA. 137 ff.; Mhv. i. 7, etc.

2. **Sobhita.**—The constant attendant of **Piyadassī Buddha**.[1]

[1] Bu. xiv. 20; J. i. 34.

3. **Sobhita.**—See **Sobhana** (3).

4. **Sobhita.**—A Pacceka Buddha.[1] Ninety-four kappas ago he lived in **Cittakūṭa**, and **Kaṇhadinna**, in a previous birth, offered him *punnāga*-flowers.[2]

[1] M. iii. 71.

[2] ThagA. i. 304; *cf.* Ap. ii. 416.

5. **Sobhita.**—A mountain near **Himavā**.[1]

[1] Ap. i. 328, 416.

6. **Sobhita.**—A brahmin in the time of **Padumuttara Buddha**; a previous birth of **Sāgata Thera**. He uttered verses in praise of **Padumuttara**.[1]

[1] Ap. i. 83.

7. **Sobhita.**—A *tāpasa* in the time of **Padumuttara Buddha**; he was a previous birth of **Tissametteyya**.[1]

[1] Ap. ii. 339.

8. **Sobhita Thera.**—He belonged to a brahmin family of **Sāvatthī** and, after hearing the Buddha preach, entered the Order, attaining arahantship. Later the Buddha declared him foremost among those who could remember past births (*pubbenivāsānussarantānaṃ*). He had resolved to win this eminence in the time of **Padumuttara Buddha**, when he was a householder in **Haṃsavatī**.

In the time of **Sumedha Buddha** he was a brahmin, expert in the Vedas. Later he left household life and lived in a hermitage near **Himavā**.

Having heard of the appearance of a Buddha in the world, he went to **Bandhumatī** with all possible speed and uttered the Buddha's praises in six stanzas.[1]

He is evidently identical with **Ñaṇatthavika** of the **Apadāna.**[2] He was once accused of claiming to possess *uttarimanussadhamma,* but was exonerated by the Buddha.[3] He was evidently an exponent of the Abhidhamma.[4]

[1] A. i. 25; Thag. vss. 165, 166; AA. i. 172; ThagA. i. 288 f.
[2] Ap. ii. 421 f.
[3] Vin. iii. 109.
[4] See DhSA., p. 32.

9. **Sobhita Thera.**—An arahant.[1] He is evidently identical with **Rakkhita Thera**[2] (*q.v.*).

[1] Ap. i. 163.
[2] ThagA. i. 173.

10 **Sobhita.**—An *ārāma* in **Haṃsavatī,** on the banks of the river, and at the city gate. **Padumuttara Buddha** once lived there.[1]

[1] Ap. ii. 343.

11. **Sobhita.**—See **Khujjasobhita.**

Sobhitā.—An eminent Therī of **Jambudīpa.**[1]

[1] Dpv. xviii. 9.

1. **Soma.**—See **Sutasoma.**

2. **Soma.**—A deva to whom sacrifice is offered; he is generally mentioned with **Varuṇa, Pajāpati** and **Yama.**[1] In the **Āṭānāṭiya Sutta**[2] he is spoken of as a **Yakkha** chief. He is identified with the Moon-god of later literature,[3] the founder of the *Somavaṃsa* (dynasty).

[1] D. i. 244; ii. 259; J. v. 28; vi. 201, 568, 571.
[2] D. iii. 204.
[3] *E.g.,* Cv. lxii. 5; lxiii. 14.

3. **Soma.**—A *Yavapāla* who offered grass for his seat to **Kassapa Buddha.**[1]

[1] BuA. 218; *cf.* Mtu. iii. 105, 106.

1. **Somadatta.**—The Bodhisatta born as the son of the brahmin **Aggidatta** (*q.v.*).

2. **Somadatta.**—The younger brother of **Sutasoma.** He is identified with **Ānanda.**[1]

[1] J. v. 185, 192.

3. **Somadatta.**—A brahmin. For his story see the **Bhūridatta Jātaka.** He is identified with **Ānanda.**[1]

[1] J. vi. 219.

4. **Somadatta.**—An elephant-calf. See the **Somadatta Jātaka** (No. 410).

1. **Somadatta Jātaka** (No. 211).—The story of the Bodhisatta when he was born as the son of **Aggidatta.** For details see *s.v.* **Aggidatta.**[1] The story was related in reference to **Lāḷudāyī,** who is identified with Aggidatta, and is repeated in the *Dhammapada Commentary.*[2]

[1] J. ii. 164-7. [2] DhA. iii. 123 ff.

2. **Somadatta Jātaka** (No. 410).—A wealthy brahmin of Benares once left the world and became an ascetic in the Himālaya, where he adopted an elephant-calf, calling it **Somadatta.** One day the elephant ate too much and fell ill. The brahmin went in search of wild fruit for it, but before he could return, the animal was dead. The ascetic was filled with grief. **Sakka** (the Bodhisatta) saw this and, appearing before him, reminded him that it was not for this that he had left wife, wealth and children.

The story was related in reference to a monk who had ordained a novice, and, when the latter died, he was full of grief. Somadatta is identified with the novice and the brahmin with the monk.[1]

[1] J. iii. 388-91.

1. **Somadeva.**—Nine kappas ago there were eighty-five kings of this name, previous births of **Ummāpupphiya (Cakkhupāla) Thera.**[1] *v.l.* **Hemadeva.**

[1] Ap. i. 172; ThagA. i. 196.

2. **Somadeva.**—One of the chief lay patrons of **Koṇāgamana Buddha.**

[1] Bu. xxiv. 24.

Somadevī.—Second queen of King **Vaṭṭagāmaṇī.** During his flight from the Damiḷas in a chariot, Somadevī, finding the chariot too heavy, descended of her own accord and the king gave her his diadem-jewel. One of the Damiḷa chiefs captured her and took her to India. Later, when Vaṭṭagāmaṇi recovered his kingdom, he sent for Somadevī, and raising her once more to her former rank, built in her name the **Somārāma (Maṇisomārāma).**[1]

[1] Mhv. xxxiii. 46, 54, 84.

Somanadeva.—Father of **Sapattā, Channā** and **Upālī,** who were eminent Therīs, expert in the Vinaya.[1]

[1] Dpv. xviii. 29.

1. **Somanassa.**—A king of **Videha,** who is credited with having founded the city of **Mithilā.**[1]

[1] J. vi. 47, 51.

2. **Somanassa.**—The Bodhisatta born as the son of **Reṇu,** king of **Uttarapañcāla.** See the **Somanassa Jātaka.**

3. **Somanassa.**—A Pacceka Buddha. Once, when the Buddha was staying at **Indasālaguhā** in **Vediyakapabbata,** an owl became fond of him, and even when he went for alms would accompany him half-way, wait for his return, and then go back with him. One day when the Buddha was seated in the assembly of monks, the owl descended from its rock and worshipped him by lowering its wings, putting together its claws and bending its head. The Buddha, seeing this, smiled, and said, in answer to **Ānanda's** question, that one hundred thousand kappas hence the bird would become a Pacceka Buddha, Somanassa by name.[1]

[1] MA. i. 255 f.; KhpA. 151.

Somanassa Jātaka (No. 505).—Once, when **Reṇu** was king of **Uttarapañcāla,** an ascetic, **Mahārakkhita,** visited him with five hundred others from the Himālaya. The king entertained them and told them of his worry because he had no sons. Some time later, when the ascetics were returning, Mahārakkhita saw that the king would have a son and told his companions so. One of the ascetics, a cheat, hoping to get gain thereby, feigned illness, and, returning to the palace, told the king that a son would be born to his queen, **Sudhammā.** The king showed him great honour, and he came to be called **Dibbacakkhuka.** In due course, the Bodhisatta was born as the king's son, and was named **Somanassa.** When the boy was seven years old the king had to leave home to quell a border rising, and Somanassa was left in the charge of the cheating ascetic. The boy soon discovered his real nature and paid him no honour. As soon as the king returned, Dibbacakkhu complained to him that the prince had ill-treated him. Somanassa was ordered to be executed, but he exposed the cheat's knavery, and men, sent to search his hut, found bundles of money in it. Disgusted with life at court, Somanassa obtained the king's leave and became an ascetic in the **Himālaya,** where **Vissakamma,** commanded by **Sakka,** built a hermitage for him. The cheat was stoned to death by the people.

The story was related in reference to **Devadatta's** attempt to kill the Buddha. He is identified with Dibbacakkhu, **Sāriputta** with **Mahārakkhita** and Somanassa's mother with **Mahāmāyā.**[1]

[1] J. iv. 445 ff.

Somanassamāḷaka.—A sacred spot in **Anurādhapura,** where **Kassapa Buddha** preached during his visit to Ceylon.[1] Later, **Uttiya,** brother of **Devānampiyatissa,** built a *cetiya* there.[2]

[1] Mhv. xv. 159.

[2] MṬ. 358.

Somanassā.—Wife of **Siddhattha Buddha** before his renunciation.[1]

[1] BuA. 185; but Bu. xvii. calls her **Sumanā.**

Somanātha.—A park laid out by **Parakkamabāhu I.**[1]

[1] Cv. lxxix. 10.

Somamitta Thera.—He belonged to a brahmin family of Benares and was expert in the Vedas. Later, owing to his association with **Vimala Thera,**[1] he entered the Order and lived with him. But finding **Vimala** given to sloth and laziness, Somamitta left him and joined **Mahā Kassapa,** under whose direction he soon attained arahantship. Later he visited **Vimala** and rebuked him. Vimala then put forth effort and became an arahant.

Somamitta was a householder in the time of **Sikhī Buddha,** and, very pleased with the Buddha, he picked some *kiṃsuka*-flowers from a tree and offered them to him.[2]

He is perhaps identical with **Kiṃsukapupphiya Thera** of the *Apadāna.*[3]

[1] But, according to ThagA. i. 377, Vimala was ordained by Somamitta.

[2] Thag. vs. 147 f.; ThagA. i. 267 f.

[3] Ap. ii. 435; but see ThagA. i. 87.

Somayāga.—One of the seven great sages (*isī*) of great power.[1]

[1] J. vi. 99.

Somara, Somāra.—Evidently the name of a country famous for its silk (*somarapaṭa*).[1]

[1] *E.g.*, VibhA. 159; Vsm. 109, 550.

Somavaḍḍhana.—One of the palaces occupied by **Sumana Buddha** before his renunciation.[1]

[1] BuA. 185; but see *s.v.* **Sumana** (1).

Somavati.—A channel leading from the **Kaddūravaḍḍhamāna** tank to the **Arimaddavijayaggāma** tank.[1]

[1] Cv. lxxix. 56.

1. **Somā Therī.**—She was the daughter of the chaplain of King **Bimbisāra.** When she grew up, she saw the Buddha on his first visit to **Rājagaha** and became a lay disciple. Later she joined the Order, developed insight, and became an arahant.

One day, as she was spending her siesta at the foot of a tree in **Andhavana, Māra,** wishing to interrupt her privacy, approached her, invisible in the air, and teased her, remarking on the "two-finger" consciousness of women.[1] Somā rebuked him, saying that the fact of being a woman was no obstacle to the comprehension of the Dhamma.[2]

In the time of **Sikhī Buddha** Somā was born into the family of an eminent nobleman and became the chief consort of King **Aruṇavā.**[3] The rest of her story is identical with that of **Abhayā Therī** (*q.v.*). She is evidently identical with **Uppaladāyikā** of the *Apadāna.*[4]

[1] The Commentary explains that women, when boiling rice, cannot tell if it is cooked without testing it between two fingers, hence the expression.

[2] This incident is given also at S. i. 129.

[3] Thig. vs. 60-62; ThigA. 66 f.

[4] Ap. ii. 601 f.

2. **Somā.**—Sister of **Sakulā** and queen of **Pasenadi.** She was a devout follower of the Buddha.[1]

[1] M. ii. 125; MA. ii. 757; she is probably the eminent lay-woman referred to at A. iv. 347.

3. **Somā.**—An eminent Therī of Ceylon, expert in the Vinaya.[1]

[1] Vin. xviii. 14.

Somā Sutta.—Describes the temptation of **Somā Therī** (1) by **Māra.**[1]

[1] S. i. 129 f.

Somārāma.—A vihāra built in the name of **Somadevī** by **Vaṭṭagāmaṇi,** on the spot where she had seen, while in hiding, a *samaṇera,* who had used his hand to screen himself while urinating.[1]

[1] Mhv. xxxiii. 84; for identification see Mhv. *Trs.* 235, n. 3.

Sora Laṅkagiri.—A general of **Parakkamabāhu I.,** who took part in his Indian campaign.[1]

[1] Cv. lxxvi. 250.

Soraṭṭhakā.—The inhabitants of **Suraṭṭha** (*q.v.*).[1]

[1] Mil. 331.

Soraṇḍakkoṭṭa.—A stronghold in South India.[1]

[1] Cv. lxxvi. 304.

1. **Sorata.**—A Pacceka Buddha.[1]

[1] M. iii. 70.

2. **Sorata.**—A devout layman in the time of **Kassapa Buddha.**[1] For his story see *s.v.* **Andhavana.**

[1] MA. i. 337; but at SA. i. 148 he is called **Yasodhara.**

1. **Soreyya.**—A town where **Soreyya-Revata** lived.[1] In the time of the Buddha there was a caravan route between Soreyya and **Takkasilā.**[2] There was also a direct route from **Verañjā** to **Payāgatittha,** passing through **Soreyya, Saṅkassa** and **Kaṇṇakuja.**[3]

At one time **Mahā Kaccāyana** lived near Soreyya.[4] It was evidently a very ancient city, for **Anomadassī Buddha** is mentioned as having twice preached there—once to King **Isidatta** and again to the king of Soreyya; and it was there that he held his first assembly of monks.[5] **Vessabhū Buddha** also preached there later to a very large assembly.[6]

[1] Vin. ii. 299.
[2] DhA. i. 326.
[3] Vin. iii. 11; see also *s.v.* **Soreyya-Revata.**
[4] DhA. i. 325.
[5] BuA. 143, 144.
[6] *Ibid.*, 206.

2. **Soreyya.**—A *seṭṭhiputta* of **Soreyya.** Once, when he and a friend with a large retinue were driving out of the city to bathe, he saw **Mahā Kaccāyana** adjusting his robe before entering the city for alms. Soreyya saw the Elder's body, and wished that he could make him his wife or that his wife's body might become in colour like the Elder's. Immediately Soreyya turned into a woman, and, hiding from his companions, went with a caravan bound for **Takkasilā.** Arrived at Takkasilā, he became the wife of the Treasurer of that city and had two sons. He had already two sons in Soreyya, born to him before his transformation. Some time after, he saw his former friend driving in a carriage through Takkasilā, and, sending a slave-woman to him, invited him to the house and entertained him. The friend was unable to recognize him till he revealed the truth. Thereupon they both returned to Soreyya and invited Mahā Kaccāyana to a meal. Soreyya fell at his feet, confessed his fault, and asked for forgiveness. When the Elder pardoned him, he once more became a man. He entered the Order under the Elder and went

with him to **Sāvatthi.** There people having heard his story worried him with questions. He therefore retired into solitude, and, developing insight, became an arahant. Before that, when people asked him which of his children he loved best, he would say: "Those to whom I gave birth while a woman"; but after attaining arahantship he would say: "My affections are set on no one."[1]

[1] DhA. i. 324 ff.

Soreyya-Revata.—See **Revata.**

Sovaṇṇakattarika Thera.—An arahant. In a previous birth he gave an *alābu* to **Padumuttara Buddha.**[1]

[1] Ap. ii. 389.

Sovaṇṇakiṅkhaṇiya Thera.—An arahant. In the time of **Atthadassī Buddha** he was an ascetic, and built a *thūpa* of sand in the name of the Buddha. Because he was too ill to visit the Buddha, he offered it *soṇṇa-kiṅkhanika*-flowers.[1]

[1] Ap. ii. 388.

Sovaṇṇapālī.—See **Suvaṇṇapālī.**

Sovīra.—A country mentioned in the **Mahāgovinda Sutta,**[1] and again in the **Āditta Jātaka.**[2] In the time of King **Reṇu, Bharata** was king of Sovīra, and **Roruka** was its capital. Cunningham[3] identifies Sovīra with Eder, a district in the province of Gujerat, at the head of the gulf of Cambay. The compound **Sindhu-Sovīra**[4] suggests that Sovīra was situated between the Indus and the Jhelum.

[1] D. ii. 235.

[2] J. iii. 470; *cf.* Mil. 359, where it is mentioned as a place to be visited by sea.

[3] *Anct. Geog. of India,* p. 569 f.; he identifies Sauvīra with Sophir or Ophir; *cf.* Hopkins, *Great Epic,* 373, 474.

[4] *E.g.,* VvA. 332.

Sovīra Jātaka.—See the **Āditta Jātaka.**

Sosānika-Mahākumāra Thera.—An Elder who lived in a charnel-field for sixty years. He was unknown to any other monk.[1]

[1] AA. i. 44.

H.

1. **Haṃsa.**—A palace occupied by **Kassapa Buddha** in his last lay life, before his renunciation.[1]

[1] Bu. xxv. 35; BuA. (217) calls it **Haṃsavā.**

2. **Haṃsa.**—A palace occupied by **Phussa Buddha** before his renunciation.[1]

[1] Bu. xix. 15.

1. **Haṃsa Jātaka** (No. 502).—Once **Khemā,** wife of King **Bahuputtaka** of Benares, dreamed of a golden goose preaching the Law and craved for her dream to come true. The king had a lake, called **Khemā,** dug outside the city, and put into it various kinds of food in order to entice the golden geese which lived in **Cittakūṭa.** They came, led by **Dhataraṭṭha** the Bodhisatta, who was caught in the snare laid by the king's hunter. The Bodhisatta gave the alarm, and all the geese fled except **Sumukha,** his captain, who refused to leave him even though told to do so. When the hunter came, Sumukha persuaded him to let Dhataraṭṭha free and to take him instead. The hunter agreed, but when the Bodhisatta heard of the reason for his capture, he, too, insisted on going before the king. Both geese were, therefore, led before the king, who was overjoyed. Dhataraṭṭha preached the Law and the queen's craving was appeased; the geese were then allowed to fly away.

The story was related in reference to **Ānanda's** readiness to give his life for the Buddha. **Channa** is identified with the huntsman, **Sāriputta** with the king, **Khemā Therī** with the queen, and **Ānanda** with Sumukha.[1]

[1] J. iv. 423-30; *cf.* the **Mahāhaṃsa Jātaka.**

2. **Haṃsa Jātaka.**—See the **Culla-haṃsa** and **Mahāhaṃsa Jātakas.**

Haṃsavaṭṭa.—A religious building erected by **Sirināga** to the south of the **Mucela**-tree in **Anurādhapura.**[1]

[1] Mhv. xxxvi. 56; MṬ. 664.

1. **Haṃsavatī.**—The city of birth of **Padumuttara Buddha.**[1] It existed in the time of **Tissa Buddha** also, for he preached to **Brahmadeva** and **Udayana** of **Haṃsavatī.**[2] The river **Bhagīrathī** flowed by the city.[3]

[1] J. i. 37; Bu. xi. 19, etc. [2] BuA. 189. [3] Ap. ii. 343.

2. **Haṃsavatī.**—The Pāli name for the city of Pegu in Burma.[1]

[1] Bode, *op. cit.*, 36.

Haṃsavaha.—The horse on which **Sujāta Buddha** left household life.[1]

[1] BuA. 168.

Hamsā.—A palace occupied by **Dīpaṅkara Buddha** before his renunciation.[1]

[1] Bu. ii. 208.

Haṃsā Vagga.—The twelfth section of the Eka Nipāta of the **Jātakaṭṭhakathā.**[1]

[1] J. i. 424-40.

Haṃsārāma.—A monastery in **Haṃsavatī**, where **Padumuttara Buddha** lived.[1]

[1] Ap. ii. 501.

Haṅkana-vihāra.—A monastery in Ceylon, where lived an old Thera who believed himself to be an arahant. Dhammadinna of **Talaṅgara** (*q.v.*) asked him to create an elephant and make it approach him. This he did, but was so scared at the sight that he knew his mistake regarding his attainment, and asked pardon of Dhammadinna.[1]

[1] MA. i. 150.

Haṅkanaka.—A place, evidently in Ceylon, where lived **Mahādatta Thera.**[1]

[1] VibhA. 489; Vsm. 634.

Haṅkāra.—A village in Ceylon, given by **Aggabodhi III.** for the *Padhānaghara*, called **Mahallarāja.**[1]

[1] Cv. xliv. 120.

Haṅkārapiṭṭhi.—A place in Ceylon outside the gate of **Kapallakkhaṇḍa.** There **Iḷanāga** inflicted a great defeat on the **Lambakaṇṇas**, who had risen against him.[1]

[1] Mhv. xxxv. 34.

Hattanna.—A village near **Nālanda,** in Ceylon, mentioned in the account of the wars of **Parakkamabāhu I.**[1]

[1] Cv. lxx. 215, 296.

1. **Hatthaka,** called **Āḷavaka.**—An eminent lay disciple of the Buddha declared foremost among those who gather a following by means of the four bases of sympathy (*catūhi vatthūhi parisaṃ saṅgaṅhantānaṃ*).[1] He was the son of the king of **Āḷavī** (hence his name **Āḷavaka**), and the Buddha saved him from being eaten by the Yakkha **Āḷavaka** (*q.v.*). He was given the name of Hatthaka because he was handed to the Buddha by the Yakkha, after the latter's conversion, and by the Buddha to the king's messengers. He was thus "handed" from one to another (*hatthato hatthaṃ gatattā*).[2]

When he grew up Hatthaka heard the Buddha preach, and, in due course, became an *Anāgāmin*. He was always accompanied by five hundred lay disciples, and was one of seven laymen who had such a following.[3] The books record several conversations between the Buddha and Hatthaka. He once saw the Buddha at **Gomagga** in **Siṃsapavana**, near **Āḷavi,** and asked him if he were one of those who lived happily. The Buddha said he was always happy in any circumstances.[4] On another occasion the Buddha asked Hatthaka how he could command the allegiance of such a large company. "By the four bases of sympathy," he answered, "by giving gifts, by kindly words, by kindly deeds, by equality of treatment." And when Hatthaka had gone, the Buddha praised him for his eminence, in that he possessed eight marvellous qualities: faith, virtue, conscientiousness, fear of blame, ability to listen well, charity, wisdom, modesty.[5] Together with **Citta-gahapati,** Hatthaka is often held up as an example to be copied by others.[6]

After death, Hatthaka was born in **Avihā,** there to pass away entirely. From there he once visited the Buddha and tried to stand in his presence, but collapsed and could not remain upright. The Buddha then asked him to create a gross body-form, and when he did this he was able to stand. He told the Buddha that he was constantly surrounded by devas wishing to learn the Dhamma from him, and confessed that he had died regretting three things—of not having seen enough of the Buddha, heard enough of the Dhamma, served enough the Saṅgha.[7]

In the *Buddhavaṃsa*,[8] Citta and Hatthakāḷavaka are mentioned as the chief lay patrons (*aggupaṭṭhākā*) of Gotama Buddha.

[1] A. i. 26.
[2] AA. i. 212; SNA. i. 240.
[3] SA. iii. 223.
[4] A. i. 136 f.
[5] *Ibid.*, iv. 218 f.; his modesty is especially mentioned elsewhere also e.g., at A. iv. 216.
[6] *E.g.*, at S. ii. 235; A. i. 88; ii. 164; iii. 451, etc.
[7] *Ibid.*, i. 278 f.
[8] Bu. xxvi. 19.

2. **Hatthaka.**—A monk. He was a **Sākyan** and loved holding discussions with the heretics. When he suffered defeat at their hands,

he would resort to falsehood and evasion, or would ask his opponent to meet him somewhere and then go there before the appointed time and give it out that his opponent had avoided him. This matter was reported to the Buddha, who rebuked Hatthaka for his conduct.[1]

[1] Vin. iv. 1 f.; *cf.* DhA. iii. 390.

1. **Hatthaka Sutta.**—Describes the visit to the Buddha of **Hatthaka Āḷavaka** after his birth as a *devaputta* (*Brahmā*) in **Avihā.**[1]

[1] A. i. 278 f.

2. **Hatthaka Sutta.**—The Buddha praises **Hatthaka Āḷavaka** (*q.v.*) for eight qualities possessed by him.[1]

[1] A. iv. 216 f.

1. **Hatthadāṭha.**—A nephew of **Dāṭhopatissa I.** who fled to **Jambudīpa** when Dāṭhopatissa was defeated by **Kassapa II.** He later returned with a Damiḷa force, defeated **Dappula II.,** who was then on the throne, and became king under the name of **Dāṭhopatissa II.** (650-58 A.C.).[1] His nephew, **Aggabodhi,** became Viceroy and governor of **Dakkhiṇadesa.** Hatthadātha gave **Senāmagāma** to the **Kassapa-vihāra, Mahāgalla** to the **Padhānaghara, Kasagāma** to the **Mora-pariveṇa,** and **Puṇṇeli** to the **Thūpārāma.** He built the **Kappura-pariveṇa** and the **Tiputthulla-pariveṇa** in the **Abhayuttara-vihāra. Mānavamma** of **Rohaṇa** rose in rebellion against him, but was defeated in a battle. Dāṭhopatissa was succeeded by **Aggabodhi VI.**[2]

[1] Cv. xliv. 154. [2] *Ibid.*, xlv. 22, 78 f.; xlvi. 1; xlvii. 4, 36, 39.

2. **Hatthadāṭha.**—A native of **Uṇhanagara.** He was summoned to Ceylon by the Damiḷa **Potthakuṭṭha** and consecrated king (676 A.C.). He built the *Padhānaghara* in **Kāladīghāvika** and died after a reign of only six months, killed by the soldiers of **Mānavamma.**[1]

[1] Cv. xlvi. 45; xlvii. 57; see also Cv. *Trs.* i. 102, n. 3.

Hatthapadūpamā Sutta.—Where there is a hand, there are seen taking up and putting down. Similarly, with a foot are coming and going; with a limb, bending and stretching; with a belly, hunger and thirst. Likewise, where there is eye, arises eye-contact, and consequent personal weal and woe, etc.[1]

[1] S. iv. 171 f.

Hatthavanagalla-vihāra.—A monastery, erected by **Goṭhābhaya** on the spot where **Sirisaṅghabodhi** (*q.v.*) gave his head as a gift to a poor man. It was repaired by **Parakkamabāhu II. Vijayabāhu III.** was cremated near the vihāra, and **Parakkamabāhu II.** built there a cetiya and an octagonal image-house which contained a stone image of the Buddha.[1] It is said that a king, named **Upatissa,** had built in the monastery a five-storeyed *pāsāda* in honour of a monk who made the earth and sky resound with thunder at the moment of his attainment of arahantship. **Parakkamabāhu II.** found it fallen into decay and had it restored in his name. His minister, **Devappatirāja,** erected, in the king's name, a three-storeyed *pāsāda,* gave it to **Anomadassī Thera,** who was chief incumbent of the vihāra at that time, and set up a stone inscription to record the gift.[2]

[1] Cv. lxxxv. 73 f. [2] *Ibid.*, lxxxvi. 12 f., 37 f.

1. **Hatthā** (*v.l.* **Bhattā**).—The chief wife of the third **Okkāka.** She had five sons and four daughters: **Okkāmukha, Karakaṇḍu, Hatthinika, Sinisūra,** and **Piyā ; Suppiyā, Ānandā, Vijitā** and **Vijitasenā.**[1]

[1] DA. i. 258; SNA. ii. 352; MṬ. 131.

2. **Hatthā.**—One of the chief lay-women supporters of **Padumuttara Buddha.**[1]

[1] Bu. xi. 26.

Hatthāroha.—A *gāmaṇi* of **Rājagaha** who visited the Buddha and asked him what destiny awaited him after death. The Buddha replied that he would be born in the **Sārañjita (Sārājita) Niraya.**[1]

[1] S. iv. 310.

Hatthārohaputta Thera.—He was born in the family of an elephant-driver of **Sāvatthi** and became expert in elephant-lore. One day, while training an elephant by the river, he felt that it would be better if he were to train himself. So he went to the Buddha, heard him preach, and, having entered the Order, attained arahantship.[1]

In the time of **Vipassī Buddha** he was a householder. Having seen the Buddha, he offered him flowers and paid him homage. Forty-one kappas ago he was a king, named **Varaṇa.** He is probably identical with **Gaṇṭhipupphiya Thera** of the *Apadāna.*[2]

[1] Thag. vs. 77; ThagA. i. 170 f. [2] Ap. i. 162.

Hatthāḷhaka-vihāra.—A nunnery built by **Devānampiyatissa** for the use of **Saṅghamittā.** It was called Hatthāḷhaka because it was built near the spot where the king's state elephant was fettered. Saṅghamittā's following came to be called **Hatthaḷhakā** from living in the vihāra.

Later, they occupied also all the twelve buildings attached to the **Upāsikā-vihāra,** even when other sects arose.[1] The vihāra was originally within the city wall of **Anurādhapura ;** but later, when **Kuṭikaṇṇa-Tissa** and **Vasabha** raised the boundary-wall, part of the vihāra grounds lay outside. The original boundary included the Kadambanadī.[2]

[1] Mhv. xix. 71, 83; xx. 21 f., 49. [2] MṬ. 611.

Hatthi Sutta.—See **Bhadda Sutta.**

Hatthikucchipabbhāra.—A glen in which was the **Mahindaguhā,** covered by forest, at the entrance to a deep valley.[1]

[1] Vsm. 110.

Hatthikucchi-vihāra.—A monastery in Ceylon where **Aggabodhi I.** built a *pāsāda*, bearing the name of his daughter **Dāṭhā.**[1] **Aggabodhi VI.** built there another *pāsāda*[2] which was restored by **Aggabodhi IX.**[3] It was evidently a famous vihāra.[4]

[1] Cv. xlii. 21. [2] *Ibid.*, xlviii. 65. [3] *Ibid.*, xlix. 76. [4] See, *e.g.*, Vsm. 120.

Hatthikkhandha-vihāra.—A monastery built by **Sūratissa** to the east of **Anurādhapura**[1] and near the village of **Dvāramaṇḍala.**[2]

[1] Mhv. xxi. 4. [2] MṬ. 424.

Hatthigāma.—A village on the road from **Vesāli** to **Bhoganagara.** It was the residence of **Ugga-gahapati** and is described as a village of the **Vajjians.** The Buddha stayed there and was visited by **Ugga.**[1] On his last journey he again rested in the village.[2]

[1] A. iv. 212; AA. i. 214; S. iv. 109. [2] D. ii. 123.

Hatthigiripura, Hatthiselapura.—The Pāli name for the modern town of Kurunegala in Ceylon. It is so called because near by is a mountain shaped like a reclining elephant. It is first mentioned in the time of **Parakkamabāhu II.,** who made his *yuvarāja*, **Bhuvanekabāhu,** build a vihāra there.[1] The king was cremated close to the vihāra, and his son, **Vijayabāhu,** made a pilgrimage to the vihāra and to the place of cremation.[2] Bhuvanekabāhu removed the capital from **Subhagiri** to Hatthigiripura, where it remained till the death of **Parakkamabāhu IV.**[3]

[1] Cv. lxxxv. 62. [2] *Ibid.*, lxxxviii. 53 f. [3] *Ibid.*, xc. 59, 106.

Hatthidāyaka Thera.—An arahant. Ninety-four kappas ago he presented an elephant to **Siddhattha Buddha.** Seventy-eight kappas ago he was king sixteen times, under the name of **Samantapāsādika.**[1]

[1] Ap. i. 208.

Hatthidvāra.—One of the gates of **Pulatthipura.**[1]

[1] Cv. lxxiii. 160.

Hatthināga Vagga.—The second section of the **Cariyāpiṭaka.**

Hatthinika.—One of the four sons of the third **Okkāka,** by his queen **Hatthā** (*q.v.*).[1]

[1] In Mtu. (i. 348) he is called Hastika-Śirṣa.

Hatthinipura.—A city in the kingdom of **Kuru,** the residence of the courtesan **Serinī**[1] (*q.v.*).

[1] PvA. 201 f.

"Hatthino" Sutta.—Few are they who refrain from accepting elephants, cattle, horses and mares, many who do not.[1]

[1] S. v. 472.

Hatthipadopama Sutta.—See **Culla-** and **Mahā-hatthipadopama Suttas.**

1. **Hatthipāla.**—A teacher of old, with a following of many hundred disciples to whom he taught the way to union with **Brahmā.**[1]

He is perhaps identical with **Hatthipāla** (2).

[1] A. iii. 371, 373; iv. 135.

2. **Hatthipāla.**—The Bodhisatta, born as son of the chaplain of **Esukārī,** king of Benares. See the **Hatthipāla Jātaka.**

Hatthipāla Jātaka (No. 509).—**Esukārī,** king of Benares, had no sons. His chaplain, hearing that the deity of a certain banyan tree had the power of giving sons, went to the tree and threatened to cut it down unless Esukārī had a son. The tree deity consulted **Sakka,** who persuaded four devas to be born as the sons, not of Esukārī, but of his chaplain. On the day when the chaplain came to cut down the tree, the deity told him of Sakka's decision, and also warned him that the sons would not live the household life. In due course the sons were born and were named **Hatthipāla, Gopāla, Assapāla** and **Ajapāla.** Various devices were adopted to prevent them from turning to the ascetic life. But when Hatthipāla grew up he insisted on leaving home and becoming an ascetic, heedless of the entreaties both of his father and of Esukārī. His brothers, when their time came, acted in the same way. Later, their parents joined them. The king sent for all their wealth, but the queen, being wise, made him realize by means of a simile the folly of such an act. Together they left the world and joined Hatthipāla and his family. The citizens followed their example till the whole city was empty.

Hatthipāla preached to them and they all became ascetics. His company covered an area of thirty leagues, and with it he went to the **Himālaya,** where **Vissakamma,** acting under Sakka's orders, built for them a hermitage extending over thirty-six leagues, on the banks of the Ganges. Soon after, other kings who, with their followers, had gone, one after another, to take Benares, realizing their folly, joined Hatthipāla and became ascetics.

The story was related in reference to the Buddha's Great Renunciation. Suddhodana was Esukārī, **Mahāmāyā** his queen, **Kassapa** the chaplain, **Bhaddā Kapilānī** his wife, **Anuruddha** Ajapāla, **Moggallāna** Gopāla, **Sāriputta** Assapāla and the Buddha himself Hatthipāla.

The large concourse that followed Hatthipāla is called **Hatthipālasamāgama,** and in it were several who later attained arahantship in Ceylon—**Phussadeva** of **Kaṭakandhakāra, Mahāsaṅgharakkhita** of **Uparimaṇḍalakamalaya, Maliyamahādeva, Mahādeva** of **Bhaggagiri, Mahāsiva** of **Vāmantapabbhāra,** and **Mahānāga** of **Kāḷavallimaṇḍapa.**[1] A Burmese monk of Ava, **Raṭṭhasāra** by name, born in 1468, composed a metrical version of the **Hatthipāla Jātaka.**[2]

[1] J. iv. 473-91; referred to at J. i. 45. [2] Bode, *op. cit.*, 44.

Hatthipura.—A city founded by the eldest son of **Apacara,** king of **Ceti.**[1] Later, thirty-six kings of the dynasty of **Mahāsammata,** sons and grandsons of a king named **Brahmadatta,** reigned in Hatthipura, the last king being **Kambalavasabha.**[2]

[1] J. iii. 460. [2] Dpv. iii. 18; MṬ. 127, 130.

Hatthipora.—A village in Ceylon, built on the spot where **Nandhimitta** forced the elephant **Kaṇḍula** to squat on its haunches.[1]

[1] Mhv. xxv. 23.

Hatthiporikā.—A tribe,[1] probably the people of **Hatthipura.**

[1] Ap. ii. 359.

Hatthibhoga.—The district given for the maintenance of **Iḷanāga's** state elephant, who saved the king from the prison into which he was cast by the **Lambakaṇṇas.**[1] It was in the south of Ceylon and in the village was the **Paṅgura-vihāra.**[2]

[1] Mhv. xxv. 20 f., 44. [2] MA. i. 530.

Hatthimukha.—One of the mouths of the **Anotattadaha.**[1]

[1] SNA. ii. 438.

Hatthisāriputta.—See **Citta Hatthisāriputta.**

Hatthisālā.—A religious building in **Anrādhapura. Mahinda IV.** built for it an alms-hall, and gave to beggars who came there alms and couches.[1]

[1] Cv. liv. 30.

Hatthiselapura.—See **Hatthigiripura.**

Hadayuṇha-pariveṇa.—A monastery on **Cetiyagiri,** built by **Sena Ilaṅga** and given over to the **Dhammarucikas.**[1]

[1] Cv. lii. 18.

Hanumantadvāra.—One of the gates of **Pulatthipura.**[1]

[1] Cv. lxxiii. 161.

Hambaṭṭhī.—A tank built by King **Dhātusena.**[1]

[1] Cv. xxxviii. 50.

Hambugallaka.—A monastery in Ceylon, where a Thera, named **Tissa,** versed in the Nikāyas, brought about reconciliation between **Vaṭṭagāmaṇi** and his disaffected ministers.[1]

[1] Mhv. xxxiii. 71 ff.

Haya Sutta.—See **Assa Sutta.**

"Haranti" Sutta.—On the four kinds of birth as harpies **(Supaṇṇā)** and their ability to carry away the different kinds of **Nāgas.**[1]

[1] S. iii. 247.

Harayo-devā.—A class of devas present at the preaching of the **Mahāsamaya Sutta.**[1] The Commentary explains[2] that they were all named **Hari.**

[1] D. ii. 260. [2] DA. ii. 691.

Hari.—See **Harayo.**

Haritaca Jātaka.—See the **Hārita Jātaka.**

Haritamāta Jātaka (No. 239).—The Bodhisatta was once born as a Green Frog. A water-snake, looking for fish, fell into a wicker cage set by men to catch fish. The fishes, seeing the snake, bit him till he fled, dripping with blood. Exhausted, he lay on the edge of the water. Seeing the Green Frog at the mouth of the cage, the snake asked him if the fish had done right in attacking him. "Why not ?" asked the Frog; "you eat fish which get into your place and they eat you when you get into theirs." The fish, hearing this, fell upon the snake and did him to death.

The story was related in reference to **Ajātasattu's** war with **Pasenadi.** When he was victorious, Ajātasattu showed great delight, but when he lost he was quite downcast. The snake is identified with Ajātasattu.[1]

[1] J. ii. 237-39.

Harittaca.—The Bodhisatta born as a brahmin. See the **Hārita Jātaka.**

Haritakīvāta.—A place in **Rohaṇa,** mentioned in the account of the wars of **Parakkamabāhu I.**[1]

[1] Cv. lxxv. 173.

Haliddavasana.—A township of the **Koliyans.** The Buddha, when staying there, preached the **Kukkuravatika Sutta** to **Puṇṇa-koliyaputta** and **Seniya Kukkuravatika.**[1]

[1] M. i. 387; see also S. v. 115 f., where another Buddha is mentioned as having preached a sermon there.

Haliddirāga Jātaka (No. 435).—The story is very similar to that of the **Culla-Nārada Jātaka** (*q.v.*). The girl tried to seduce the young ascetic when his father was away and take him back with her to the haunts of men, but he told her to go on, saying that he would follow after taking leave of his father. When the latter heard his story and learnt his intention, he exhorted the youth not to be ensnared by thoughts of lust. His son realized his folly and remained in the hermitage.[1]

[1] J. iii. 524-6.

Hāragaja.—A class of devas present at the preaching of the **Mahāsamaya Sutta.**[1]

[1] D. ii. 260.

Hāni Sutta.—On seven things which lead to a lay disciple's decline—failure to see monks, neglect of the Dhamma, etc.[1]

[1] A. iv. 25.

Hārika.—A bandit of **Rājagaha.** After death he was born as a *peta* with a headless trunk, and was seen by **Moggallāna.** His mouth and his eyes were on his chest.[1] *v.l.* **Hārita.**

[1] S. ii. 260.

1. **Hārita.**—The same as **Harittaca.** See the **Hārita Jātaka.**

2. **Hārita.**—A **Mahā Brahmā** who was present at the preaching of the **Mahāsamaya Sutta,** at the head of one hundred thousand other Brahmās.[1] He was one of the chief Brahmās.[2]

[1] D. ii. 261; DA. ii. 693; *cf. ibid.*, i. 40.

[2] See, *e.g.*, DA. ii. 693; MA. ii. 576.

3. **Hārita Thera.**—He was the son of a wealthy brahmin of **Sāvatthi,** and had a beautiful wife. One day, while contemplating her beauty, he realized that it was impermanent. A few days later his wife was bitten by a snake and died. In his anguish he sought the Buddha, and, comforted by him, left the world. For some time he could not concentrate. Then one day, going to the village for alms, he saw a fletcher straightening his arrow. So he turned back and stirred up insight. The Buddha, standing in the air above him, admonished him in a verse, and Hārita attained arahantship.

Thirty-one kappas ago he offered some *kuṭaja*-flowers to a Pacceka Buddha, named **Sumana.**[1] He is evidently identical with **Kuṭajapupphiya Thera** of the *Apadāna.*[2]

[1] Thag. vs. 29; ThagA. i. 87 f.

[2] Ap. ii. 451.

4. **Hārita Thera.**—He was a brahmin of **Sāvatthi,** and, because of pride of birth, used to call others low-born. Later he entered the Order, but even then this habit persisted. One day, after hearing the Buddha preach, he reviewed his mind, and was distressed by his conceit and arrogance. Thereupon, putting forth effort, he conjured up insight and won arahantship.

In the time of **Padumuttara Buddha** he offered perfumes at the Buddha's funeral pyre.[1] He is evidently identical with **Gandhapūjaka Thera** of the *Apadāna.*[2]

[1] Thag. vss. 261-3; ThagA. i. 376 f.

[2] Ap. ii. 406.

5. **Hārita.**—A mountain near **Himavā.**[1]

[1] Ap. i. 278; ThagA. i. 247.

6. **Hārita Thera.**—An arahant. **Dhammadassī Buddha** preached to him in the **Sudassanārāma** and declared him foremost of those who practised austerities.[1]

[1] BuA. 183.

Hārita Jātaka (No. 431).—The Bodhisatta was born in a wealthy brahmin family and was called **Harittaca** because of his golden colour. When his father died, he left the world and became an ascetic, with great supernatural powers. He went to Benares, and was invited by the king to live in the royal park. He accepted the invitation, and lived there for twelve years. The king was then called away to quell a frontier rebellion, and instructed the queen to look after the ascetic. One day, as the Bodhisatta came in late for his meal, the queen rose hastily and her robe of fine cloth fell from her. Harittaca was filled with lust, and, taking her hand and drawing a curtain round them, he lay with her. This then became a daily occurrence and the scandal spread abroad. The ministers wrote to the king, who, however, refused to believe them. When he returned he questioned the queen, who confessed her wrongdoing, but even then the king refused to believe it till Harittaca (or **Hārita** as he is also called) acknowledged his guilt. The king was full of admiration for his truthfulness and forgave him, but Harittaca, after preaching to the king on the misery of sinful desire, once more developed his mystic powers, took leave of the king, and returned to the **Himālaya.**

The story was told in reference to a monk who had grown discontented because of a beautiful woman.[1]

[1] J. iii. 496-501.

Hāritā.—A yakkhiṇī, wife of **Paṇḍaka.** These two and their five hundred children became *sotāpannas* when **Majjhantika Thera** preached to them in the **Himālaya** country.[1]

[1] Mhv. xii. 21.

Hālakola.—A Damiḷa stronghold, captured by **Duṭṭhagāmaṇī. Issariya** was general of the fort.[1]

[1] Mhv. xxv. 11.

Hālavāhanaka.—A Damiḷa general, subdued by **Duṭṭhagāmaṇī.**[1]

[1] Mhv. xxv. 13.

Hāliddakāni, Hāliddikāni.—An eminent lay disciple of **Avanti.** Once when **Mahā Kaccāna** was staying in the **Kuraragharapapāta,** Hāliddakāni visited him and consulted him at length on the subjects treated in **Māgandiyapañha**[1] and again on those of the **Sakkapañha.**[2]

On another occasion[3] he questioned the Elder regarding the diversity of sensations.

[1] S. iii. 9 f. [2] *Ibid.*, 13 f. [3] S. iv. 115 f.

Hāliddakāni Suttā.—Three suttas[1] which describe the interviews which **Hāliddakāni** (*q.v.*) had with **Mahā Kaccāna** at **Kuruaragharapapāta** in **Avanti.**

[1] S. iii. 9 f.; 13 f.. iv. 115 f.; the last is called **Hāliddaka Sutta.** See also MNid. i. 197 f.

Hāsajanaka Thera.—An arahant. Ninety-one kappas ago he saw the rag robe of a Buddha hanging from the branch of a tree. Pleased with the sight, he did obeisance to it.[1]

[1] Ap. i. 259.

Hiṃsaka.—See **Aṅgulimāla.**

Hiṅga.—A Pacceka Buddha.[1]

[1] M. iii. 70.

Hiṅgulapabbata.—A mountain in **Himavā,**[1] where **Nālaka** died.[2]

[1] J. v. 415. [2] SNA. ii. 501; but see J. v. 415 for a variation.

Hiṅgū.—A Pacceka Buddha.[1]

[1] M. iii. 70.

Hintālavanagāma.—A village in **Rohaṇa,** mentioned in the account of the campaigns of **Parakkamabāhu I.**[1]

[1] Cv. lxxiv. 162; lxxv. 7, 11, 17; see Cv. *Trs.* ii. 44, n. 3.

Himavanta Sutta.—See **Pabbatūpama Sutta.**

Himavā, Himācala, Himavanta, etc.—The name given to the **Himālaya.** It is one of the seven mountain ranges surrounding **Gandhamādana.**[1] It is three hundred thousand leagues in extent,[2] with eighty-four thousand peaks, its highest peak being five hundred *yojanas.*[3] In Himavā are seven

[1] SNA. i. 66. [2] *Ibid.*, 224. [3] *Ibid.*, ii. 443.

great lakes, each fifty leagues in length, breadth and depth—**Anotatta, Kaṇṇamuṇḍa, Rathakāra, Chaddanta, Kuṇāla, Mandākinī** and **Sīhappapātaka**; these lakes are never heated by the sun.[4] From Himavā flow five hundred rivers.[5]

In numerous Jātakas Himavā is mentioned as the place to which ascetics retire when they leave household life. It is full of woodlands and groves, suitable for hermits.[6] In Himāva is a peak named **Mahāpapāta** where **Pacceka Buddhas** die.[7] **Nāgas** go to Himavā to give birth to their young.[8] The mountain is often used in similes; it is then referred to as *pabbatarājā*.[9] **Sīvalī Thera** once went there from **Sāvatthi** with five hundred others. The journey took them eight days.[10]

The country round Himavā was converted by **Majjhima Thera.**[11] He was accompanied by four others: **Kassapagotta, Mūladeva (Alakadeva), Sahadeva** and **Dundubhissara.**[12] Majjhima preached the **Dhammacakkappavattana Sutta** and eighty crores attained salvation. These five Theras converted five kingdoms and each ordained one hundred thousand persons.[13]

Devas brought for **Asoka's** use, from the Himālaya, twigs of the *nāgalatā* to clean his teeth, healthful fruits, myrobalan, teminalia and mango-fruit,[14] while, for the foundation of the **Mahā Thūpa,** sāmaṇeras with *iddhi*-power brought sweet-scented *marumba.*[15]

The **Kuṇāla Jātaka** (*q.v.*) was preached in the region of Himavā. The Buddha took the **Sākyan** princes there and showed them the various features, including many mountain peaks, such as: **Maṇipabbata, Hiṅgulapabbata, Añjanapabbata, Sānupabbata,** and **Phalikapabbata.**[16] On fast days the gods assemble in Himavā and hold discourses.[17]

4 A. iv. 101; SNA. ii. 407; *cf.* AA. ii. 759.
5 SNA. ii. 437; but according to Mil. 114, only ten of these are to be reckoned, the others flowing only intermittently. These ten are: **Gaṅgā, Yamunā, Aciravatī, Sarabhū, Mahī, Sindhu, Sarassatī, Vettavatī, Vitaṃsā** and **Candabhāgā.**
6 *E.g.*, SA. i. 265.
7 SNA. i. 129.
8 SA. iii. 120; *cf.* S. v. 63.
9 *E.g.*, S. ii. 137; v. 464; A. iii. 311; M. iii. 166, etc.
10 Details are given at ThagA. ii. 138; PSA. 252.
11 Mhv. xii. 41.
12 Dpv. viii. 10; MṬ. 317.
13 Mhv. xii. 42 f.
14 *Ibid.*, v. 25 f.
15 *Ibid.*, xxix. 9.
16 J. v. 415.
17 Sp. iv. 759.

Himavā Sutta.—Six things, possession of which will enable a monk to cleave Himavā.[1]

1 A. iii. 311.

Himiyānaka.—A Vanni chief in the service of **Bhuvanekabāhu I.**[1]

1 Cv. xc. 33.

Hiraññamalaya.—A locality in **Rohaṇa.**[1]

[1] Cv. lvii. 62.

1. **Hiraññavatī.**—Another name for **Bhagalavatī,** the residence of **Kuvera**[1] (*q.v.*).

[1] J. vi. 269, 270.

2. **Hiraññavatī.**—A river, on the bank of which was the **Upavattana Sālavana** of the **Mallas** of **Kusināra,** where the Buddha died.[1] It is identified with the Little Gandak; it flows through the district of Gorakhpur, about eight miles west of Great Gandak, and falls into the Gogrā (**Sarayū**).[2]

[1] D. ii. 137. [2] Law, *Geography*, 37.

Hiri.—A Yakkha chieftain to be invoked in time of need by followers of the Buddha.[1]

[1] D. iii. 205; DA. iii. 970.

Hiri Jātaka (No. 363).—The story of both the present and the past[1] is the same as those of the **Akataññu Jātaka** (*q.v.*).

[1] J. iii. 196 f.

1. **Hiri Sutta.**—A conversation between the Buddha and a deva regarding *hiri* (conscientiousness).[1]

[1] S. i. 7.

2. **Hiri Sutta.**—The disadvantages of lack of *hiri* (conscientiousness) and fear of blame, and the advantages of their possession.[1]

[1] A. iv. 99.

3. **Hiri Sutta.**—The third sutta of the **Cūla Vagga** of the **Sutta Nipāta.**[1] It was preached in answer to questions asked by an ascetic. He had been a very rich brahmin of **Sāvatthi** before the birth of the Buddha. He gave away all his wealth and became an ascetic in **Himavā.** There, filled with joy on hearing the news of the Buddha's appearance in the world, he went to Sāvatthi and visited him. The Buddha preached to him, and at the end of the sermon he entered the Order, attaining arahantship.[2]

The sutta is a short dissertation on true friendship. A friend is one who helps in time of need, who not only speaks pleasant words, but means them, who encourages and fosters all that is good.

[1] SN. vs. 253-7. [2] SNA. i. 294 f.

Hiri, Hiridevi.—Daughter of **Sakka.** See the **Sudhābhojana Jātaka.** She is identified with **Uppalavaṇṇā.**[1]

[1] J. v. 412; *cf.* Mtu. iii. 309.

Hillapattakakhaṇḍa.—A ford in the **Mahāvālukagaṅgā,** mentioned in the account of the wars of **Parakkamabāhu I.**[1] There was also a tank of the same name.[2]

[1] Cv. lxxii. 41. [2] *Ibid.*, lxxix. 37.

Hihobu.—A place in **Rohaṇa,** mentioned in the account of the campaigns of **Parakkamabāhu I.**[1]

[1] Cv. lxxiv. 94.

Hiyagalla.—A place near **Anurādhapura,** through which passed the *sīmā* of the **Mahāvihāra.**[1]

[1] Mbv. 135, 136.

Hukitti.—A **Laṅkānātha,** chief of **Rerupallika,** in the **Malaya** district; he was defeated by the officers of **Parakkamabāhu I.**[1]

[1] Cv. lxx. 25.

Hundarivāpigāma.—A village in the **Kuḷumbari** district, the birthplace of **Duṭṭhagāmaṇi's** general, **Mahāsoṇa.**[1]

[1] Mhv. xxiii. 45.

Huyalagāma.—A village in **Rohaṇa,** mentioned in the account of the campaigns of **Parakkamabāhu I.**[1]

[1] Cv. lxxv. 18. 149, 150; see Cv. *Trs.* ii. 59, n. 1.

Hulapiṭṭhi-vihāra.—A monastery in Ceylon, built by King **Mahāsena.**[1] *v.l.* **Cūlaviṭṭhi.**

[1] Mhv. xxxvii. 43.

Huvācakaṇṇikā.—A district in Ceylon where **Mahādaṭhika-Mahānāga** built the **Cūlanāgapabbata-vihāra.**[1] The district was in **Rohaṇa.**[2]

[1] Mhv. xxxiv. 90. [2] MṬ. 637.

Huhuṅka.—The descriptive name of a brahmin who visited the Buddha at the **Ajapālanigrodha** seven days after his Enlightenment and asked him questions regarding the true brahmin. The Buddha explained the matter, but made no impression on him.[1] Buddhaghosa explains that

[1] Vin. i. 2; see also Ud. i. 4; UdA. 54; *cf.* Mtu. iii. 325.

the brahmin was a *diṭṭhamaṅgalika*, filled with haughtiness and wrath, and went about uttering the sound "*hu-huṃ*"—hence his name.

Hūvaraṭṭha, Ūvaraṭṭha.—A district in the **Malaya** province in Ceylon.[1]

[1] Cv. lx. 66; xcv. 22.

1. **Hetu Sutta.**—Body, feeling, etc., and their cause, are all impermanent.[1]

[1] S. iii. 23.

2. **Hetu Sutta.**—Suffering and its cause are both impermanent.[1]

[1] S. iii. 23.

3. **Hetu Sutta.**—The body, etc., are void of self, so is their cause.[1]

[1] S. iii. 24.

4. **Hetu Sutta.**—It is not because of beauty, wealth, kin or sons, that a woman is born happy after death, but because of her virtue.[1]

[1] S. iv. 248.

5. **Hetu Sutta.**—See **Pubbā Sutta.**

Hedillakhaṇḍagāma.—A ford in the **Mahāvālukagaṅgā.**[1]

[1] Cv. lxxii. 45.

Hema.—A class of elephants having the strength of one hundred million men.[1]

[1] UdA. 403; AA. ii. 832; BuA. 37, etc.

Hemaka.—One of the **Bāvarī's** disciples. He went to the Buddha, asked questions, and became an arahant.[1]

In the time of **Piyadassī Buddha** he was an ascetic, named **Anoma,** and offered the Buddha a seat of jewels.[2]

[1] SN. vs. 1006, 1084-7. [2] Ap. ii. 352 f.

Hemaka-pucchā.—The questions asked of the Buddha by **Hemaka.**[1]

[1] SN. 1084-7.

Hemamandira.—A building erected in **Pulatthipura** by **Parakkamabāhu I.** for the ceremonies of expiation by the brahmins.[1]

[1] Cv. lxxiii. 71.

Hemamālaka, Hemamālī.—Another name for the **Mahā Thūpa** (*q.v.*)

Hemamālā.—Daughter of **Guhasīva,** king of **Kāliṅga.** She and her husband, **Dantakumāra,** brought the Tooth Relic to Ceylon.[1]

[1] *Dāthāvaṃsa* iv. 9 f.

Hemameru.—See **Meru.**

Hemavata.—A Yakkha chief, to be invoked by followers of the Buddha in time of need.[1] He was present at the preaching of the **Mahāsamaya Sutta.**[2] He was the friend of **Sātāgira** (*q.v.* for his story).

[1] D. iii. 204. [2] *Ibid.*, ii. 256.

Hemavata Sutta.—Contains the conversation between **Hemavata** and **Sātāgira** (*q.v.*) regarding the Buddha, and the details of their visit to the Buddha. It is the ninth sutta of the **Uraga Vagga** of the **Sutta Nipāta.**[1]

[1] SN. 153-80.

1. **Hemavatā.**—A river.[1] See the **Bhallāṭiya Jātaka.**

[1] J. iv. 437, 438.

2. **Hemavatā.**—A heretical sect in **Jambudīpa.**[1] They were so called because they lived on Mount Himavata.[2] They held that a Bodhisatta was not an ordinary mortal, that even a *tīrthaka* could have the five *abhiññā*, that the *puggala* is separate from the *khandhas.*[3]

[1] Mhv. v. 12; Dpv. v. 54. [2] Rockhill, *Life of Buddha*, p. 184. [3] *Ibid.*, 190.

Hemavatī.—A channel branching off from the **Parakkamasamudda** in the direction of the **Mahāmeghavana.**[1]

[1] Cv. lxxix. 41.

Hemavālika-(Mālika)-cetiya.—See **Mahā Thūpa.**

Hemasāli-vihāra.—A monastery in Ceylon. In the time of **Mahinda II.** there was a Thera in the vihāra expert in the Abhidhamma, and the king had the Abhidhamma recited by him, and built a bathing-tank for the Thera's use.[1]

[1] Cv. xlviii. 142.

Hemā.—An eminent Therī who accompanied **Saṅghamittā** to Ceylon.[1]

[1] Dpv. xv. 78; xviii. 11.

Hemāsā.—An eminent Therī, teacher of the Vinaya at **Anurādhapura** in the time of **Devānampiyatissa.**[1]

[1] Dpv. xviii. 24.

Heraññakāni Thera.—He was the son of an official of the king of **Kosala** who turned bandit. On his father's death he succeeded to his place. He was present when the Buddha accepted **Jetavana,** and, filled with wonder, he entered the Order, where he soon attained arahantship. Later he persuaded his brother too, with some difficulty, to become a monk.

In the time of **Padumuttara Buddha** he was a labourer (*bhataka*), and seeing the Buddha's disciple, **Sujāta,** looking for rags for his robe, gave him half a garment.[1]

He is evidently identical with **Upaḍḍhadussadāyaka** of the *Apadāna.*[2]

[1] Thag. vs. 145-6; ThagA. i. 266 f. [2] Ap. ii. 435 f.

1. **Heligāma.**—A village near **Mahāgāma,** gifted by King **Vasabha** to the **Anurārāma-vihāra.**[1]

[1] Mhv. xxxv. 83.

2. **Heligāma.**—A *pāsāda* erected by **Kassapa III.**[1]

[1] Cv. xlviii. 24; see Cv. *Trs.* i. 112, n. 3.

Helloligāma.—A village in Ceylon. King **Buddhadāsa** saved a **Caṇḍāla** woman there from death in childbirth.[1]

[1] Cv. xxxvii. 140.

Hoṇa, Hoṇaka.—See **Goṇaka.**

APPENDIX

ADDENDA AND CORRIGENDA

Aggappasāda Sutta.—*Add :* The Sutta Saṅgaha (No. 25) gives the name Aggappasāda Sutta to the first Sutta of the fifth Vagga of the Itivuttaka, Tika Nipāta.[1] The whole Sutta is found in Aṅguttara (ii. 34 f.), but the *uddāna* of the Aṅguttara calls it **Pasāda Sutta.** See **Pasāda Sutta** (2).

[1] Itv. 89 f.

Aṅgaka.—Nephew (sister's son) of **Soṇadaṇḍa** (*q.v.*).[1]

[1] D. i. 123.

7. **Aṅgīrasa.**—*To refs. add :* J. v. 267.

Acchimatī.—One of the five daughters of **Vessavaṇa.** She was married to **Sakka. Latā** (*q.v.*) was her sister.[1]

[1] VvA. 131.

Ajitajana.—A king of the race of **Mahāsammata.** His descendants reigned in **Kapilapura.**[1]

[1] MṬ. 127; Dpv. iii. 17 calls him **Abhitatta.**

1. **Ajjuna.**—*Add :* He was also once a *cakkavattī,* named **Verocana.**

Ajjhattikaṅga Sutta.—The name given in the Sutta Saṅgaha (No. 77) to a sutta of the Itivuttaka on the virtues of *yonisomanasikāra.*[1]

[1] Itv. 9 f.

Aññāta-Koṇḍañña.—*Add to* p. 44, *last para. :* **Mantānī** was Aññāta-Koṇḍañña's sister.

Aṭṭhakanāgara Sutta.—*Add :* The Sutta is also called **Dasama Sutta.**

Aṭṭhipuñja Sutta.—A name given in the Sutta Saṅgaha (No. 21) for **Puggala Sutta** (4) (*q.v.*).

Atta-piya Sutta.—A name given in the Sutta Saṅgaha (No. 46) for **Piya Sutta** (2) (*q.v.*).

Anāthapiṇḍika.—*On* p. 68, *para.* 2, *the name of* A.'s *brother should be* **Subhūti.** *To para.* 1 *on* p. 69 *add :* Besides Kāḷa, A. had another son, who joined the Order under Subhūti Thera.[1]

[1] AA. ii. 865.

Anurārāma.—*Add :* See also **Mahādevarattakurava.**

1. **Anuruddha.**—*On* p. 86 *add to last para.:* He was one hundred and fifteen years old at the time of his death.[1]

[1] DA. ii. 413.

1. **Anussati Sutta.**—*Add :* In the Visuddhimagga (p. 226) it is called **Gedha S.**

5. **Anoma.**—*v.l.* **Aranemi.**

Antaragaṅga.—A district in Ceylon.[1]

[1] Ras. ii. 10.

Apacāyika Sutta.—See **Pacāyika S.**

3. **Andhakavinda Sutta.**—Evidently another name for the **Yāgudānānumodanā Sutta** of the Vinaya.[1]

[1] Vin. i. 220 f.

Apadāna.—*Add :* According to Gv. (p. 69) the Commentary on the Apadāna was written by Buddhaghosa at the request of five monks.

Aparādiṭṭhi Sutta.—*Add :* See also **Bakabrahma Sutta.**

Apalāla.—*Add :* According to the Vinaya of the Mūlla-Sarvāstivādins, the Buddha converted A. during a visit to Kashmir in the company of the Yakṣa Vajrapāṇī (JA. 1914, vol. iv. 510).

Appaka Sutta.—**Pasenadi** tells the Buddha that in his view few are they that are not intoxicated by great wealth and misconduct themselves when they become rich. The Buddha agrees.[1]

[1] S. 73; the Sutta is also called **Pamāda Sutta.**

9. **Appamāda Sutta.**—The name given in the Sutta Saṅgaha to a sutta quoted from the Itivuttaka on the value of *appamāda.*[1]

[1] Itv. 16.

Abbhuta-Dhamma Sutta.—*Read* **Suttā,** *and add :* Three Suttas on . . .

Abhaya Sutta.—*Add :* See **Gijjhakūṭa Sutta.**

Abhayagirikā.—*Add :* A summary of their heresies is given at MṬ. 676 f.

Abhidhammapaṇṇarasaṭṭhāna.—A treatise by **Nava-Vimalabuddhi.**[1]

[1] Gv. 64, 74.

Abhidhammatthasaṅgaha.—*Add :* According to Gv. (p. 71) the work was written at the request of an *upāsaka* named **Nambha (Nampa).**

Abhidhammāvatāra.—*Add :* Gv. (p. 69) says that Buddhadatta wrote it at the request of his pupil **Sumati.**

Abhītatta.—See **Ajitajana.**

Amaruppala.—The name borne by **Kākavaṇṇatissa** when he was a hunter in a village near **Amaruppala-lena.**[1]

[1] Ras. ii. 56.

Amaruppala-lena.—A cave in the Malaya province of Ceylon. **Kākavaṇṇatissa** was once born in a hunters' village near it.[1]

[1] Ras. ii. 56.

Amitabhogā.—Five seṭṭhīs in **Bimbisāra's** dominions, whose wealth was limitless. They were **Jotiya, Jaṭila, Meṇḍaka, Puṇṇaka,** and **Kākavaliya.**[1]

[1] AA. i. 220; for details see *s.v.*

Ambakhādaka-Mahātissa.—See **Mahātissa** (3).

Ambaviṭṭhi.—A village in the north of Ceylon. It was the birthplace of **Culatissa Thera.**[1]

[1] Ras. ii. 30.

Ambāmacca.—Son of **Venigāma.** He was very rich; but once, during a drought, there being no food, he made ready to go to the mountains with his retinue. Just before starting they found a measure of rice, and, having cooked it, were about to eat it, when Amba saw **Cūlapiṇḍpātika-Nāga Thera** returning from the village with empty bowl. He invited the monk and gave him the food. The Thera retired into the forest and attained arahantship before eating it. Tired and hungry, Amba slept, and, on waking, asked his wife if any scrapings were left. She went into the kitchen and found the pot full of food, which they shared with the whole village.[1]

[1] Ras. ii. 145 f.

3. **Aranemi.**—See **Anoma** (5).

Ariyaka-Vihāra.—A monastery in Ceylon.[1]

[1] Ras. ii. 174.

Ayyamitta.—See **Mahāmitta.**

Ayya-Uttiya.—*For ref.* [1] *read* MṬ. 431. The province was near the sea (*samuddatīrasamipe*).

Ariyagāla-tittha.—A ford, probably on the **Mahāvāluka-nadī.**[1]

[1] Ras. ii. 38.

Ariyagālatissa.—Son of **Mahādhanadeva,** of **Mahāgāma.** When he was a child he was called **Keḷiyatissa,** because he liked to play. Later he joined the Order. Dissatisfied after five years, he gave up his robes and swam down a river. Two women bathing saw him and both claimed him. When they saw he was naked one went to fetch clothes; the other gave him half her garment and took him to her parents and married him. The wife was **Sumanā.** Because he was found in the river he was called **Gaṅga-tissa;** but because he was lazy they called him **Nikkammatissa.** Sumanā's people complained of him and sent them away. Tissa sought work under a headman, **Candasuriya,** a friend of Mahādhanadeva, and reaped and threshed a field of 500 *karīsas* in one day. Candasuriya, marvelling at his strength, gave him all the grain.

Thereafter, Tissa and his wife gave alms daily to eight monks, but as his meals were not tasty, the monks called him **Udakaloṇa-tissa.** Discovering this, he gave them milk-rice and was called **Khīrabhatta-tissa.** Later he gave rice mixed with ghee and his name became **Kalyāṇabhatta-tissa.** In due course he fed 500 monks daily. One day, while looking for yams in **Kumbulapabbata,** he discovered 60 treasure-troves and took them home. Later he fed many thousands of monks in **Cetiyamba-vihāra, Anurādhapura** and **Nāgadīpa** and lived in **Ariyagālatittha** as a ferryman, taking people across, free of charge. **Sakka,** wishing to test him, came as an old brahmin and, having tried his patience, filled his house with valuables and gave him a field of rice.

Once a discussion arose in **Piyaṅgudīpa,** as to where the most devout people were to be found. **Satisambodhi Thera** said they were in Ceylon, while **Yoṇakarājaputta Mahābuddharakkhita** said they were in **Yoṇakaraṭṭha.** To test this, Satisambodhi arrived in Tissa's house. His wife, having fed 12,000 monks, was resting, but having seen the Elder she prepared for him a bowl of *catumadhura.* He asked her to throw the bowl up into the air. It travelled to Piyaṅgudīpa, and Sumanā saw the monks as they ate the contents.

As Tissa lay dying, devas brought him chariots from the six deva-worlds; he chose to be born in **Tusita.** His wife, knowing his wishes, retired into her room and died before him. They were both born in Tusita. In a past birth Tissa had been in **Chagāma** and honoured the Bodhi-tree there.[1]

[1] Ras. ii. 34 f.

Ariyākara Vihāra.—A monastery in Ceylon.[1]

[1] Ras. ii. 189.

Aruṇavatī Paritta.—Same as **Aruṇavatī Sutta** (*q.v.*).

Asiggāhaka-pariveṇa.—A building in the **Thūpārāma.**[1]

[1] Ras. ii. 123.

Asitābhū Jātaka.—The kinnarī's name was **Candā.** See **Candā** (9).

Asura.—*Add :* A story is told by the Buddha (S. 2, v. 446) of a man who once saw a whole army with its four divisions enter a lotus stalk and the man thought he was mad. But the B. says that it was an Asura army in flight. Here the Asuras would seem to be fairies or nature-spirits.

Asekhiya Sutta.—Five things which make a monk worthy of offerings, etc.[1]

[1] A. iii. 134.

Asela.—*For refs.* [3] *and* [4] *read* MṬ. 425 and 358 respectively.

1. **Asoka.**—*Add :* Asoka had three palaces for the three seasons: **Mahāsappika, Moragīva** and **Maṅgala.**[1]

[1] Ras. i. 93.

Asokamālaka.—*For ref.* [2] *read* MṬ. 358.

Asokamālā.—*Add :* Her name was **Devī,** and her father was the chief caṇḍāla in **Hallolagāma.** Her story is given at great length in Ras. ii. 117 f.

2. **Assagutta.**—An arahant Thera of **Vattaniya-senāsana** who ordained **Jarasāṇa** (*q.v.*).

Assamaṇḍala.—A village near **Hallolagāma.**[1]

[1] Ras. ii. 121.

Ahināga.—Dr. A. K. Coomaraswamy suggests that the word "Ahināga," appearing in Vinaya (i. 25), is a proper name, like **Ahicchatta.** For a discussion see JAOS. vol. 55, 391-392 (notes).

Ahinda Sutta.—*Add :* Another name for it is the **Khandhaka Paritta.**

Ākāsagotta.—See **Sañjaya-Ākāsagotta.**

Āṭānāṭiya Sutta.—*Add :* DA. iii. 969 gives a long description of the ritual to be followed when reciting the Āṭānāṭiya Paritta.

1. **Ānanda.**—*To ref.* [69] *add :* Ānanda had been a tailor in a past birth and had given a Pacceka Buddha a piece of cloth, the size of his hand, and a needle. Because of the gift of the needle he was wise, because of the cloth he got 500 robes.[1]

[1] AA. i. 239.

Ābhassara.—*Add :* According to the scholiast of the **Candābha Jātaka** (*q.v.*), beings who meditate on the Sun and Moon are born in this world. The Moon appears at the wish of the Ābhassara Brahmās. See *s.v.* **Candimā.**

Araññaka Sutta.—The name given in the Sutta Saṅgaha (No. 85) to the **Anāgata Sutta** (*q.v.*).

Araññaka-Mahāabhaya.—A monk. For twelve years a devotee gave him his requisites including cloth for his robes; but a thief, **Harantika,** always stole the cloth. Discovering this, the devotee caught the rogue, beat him soundly, and, having tied him to a corpse, warned the villagers that a Yakkha would be prowling about that night, calling himself Harantika. The villagers fastened their doors and gave him no admission, even his wife refusing to recognise his voice. Then Harantika went to Mahāabhaya, and having confessed his guilt, asked for protection. Mahāabhaya bathed him in warm water and rubbed oil on his body, saying it was not his business to take revenge. Harantika later became a monk and attained arahantship.[1]

[1] Ras. ii. 5 f.

15. **Abhaya.**—Called **Ābhidhammika Abhaya.** A monk of **Vālikapiṭṭhi Vihāra** (*q.v.*).

Āraddhaviriya Sutta.—A name given in the Sutta Saṅgaha (No. 80) to a Sutta in the Itivuttaka (p. 115 f.), which is called in the Aṅguttara as **Cara Sutta** (*q.v.*).

2. **Indagutta.**—*Add:* Indagutta originally lived in **Sīhakumbha-vihāra** in **Devaputta,** at the head of a large congregation. **Asoka,** having heard of his fame, imvited him to Pāṭaliputta. He went with 60,000 monks and Asoka received them with great honour. At the sight of the honours paid to him Indagutta was filled with pride. Asoka noticing this, admonished him. Indagutta benefiting by the advice, developed insight even as he stood and became an arahant.[1]

[1] Ras. i. 80 f.

Indasālaguhā.—*Add:* See also **Somanassa** (3).

Indriya Jātaka.—*Add to refs.:* See also **Sarabhaṅga Jātaka.**

Uṭṭhāna Sutta.—*Add:* See also **Pāsādakampana Sutta.**

1. **Uttara.**—*Add to refs.:* Ras. i. 52 f.

38. **Uttara.**—See **Bherapāsāṇa Vihāra.**

Uttaroḷiya.—A village in Ceylon, in **Rājaraṭṭha.** Near it was **Uttaroḷiyavāpī.** The Rasavāhinī has a story of a cowherd boy of the village who gave his rice-cake to a *piṇḍaptāika-thera.* The monk developed arahantship before eating it. In his next birth the boy was born in the same village. By virtue of his merit, a treasure-trove appeared in the lake, which no one could get except his mother. The king heard of it, and, having tested the truth of the story, gave it to the boy.[1]

[1] Ras. ii. 22 f.

Uttaroḷiya Vagga.—The sixth section of the Rasavāhinī.

Udakapūjā.—A celebration held by a Nāga king in honour of **Kañcanadevī** (*q.v.*).

Udakaloṇa-tissa.—See **Ariyagāla-tissa.**

Udāna Sutta.—Preached by the Buddha at **Daṇḍakappa.** The Tathāgata possesses full knowledge of the hearts of men.[1]

[1] A. iii. 402.

1. **Udāyī.**—The incident given in para. 2, p. 375, refers to **Lāḷudāyī** and *not* to **Mahāudāyī.**

Uddalolaka Vihāra.—A monastery in Ceylon; it was the residence of an Elder, named **Mahā-Abhaya.**[1]

[1] Ras. ii. 1; SadS. 82.

5. **Upananda.**—See **Nandopananda.**

2. **Upasena.**—*Add :* See also **Vaka Jātaka.**

Upāsakacaṇḍāla and **Upāsakaratana Suttas.**—The Sutta Saṅgaha divides into two Suttas (Nos. 9 and 10) the Sutta which appears in the Aṅguttara as one Sutta, under the name of **Caṇḍāla Sutta** (*q.v.*).

Uposathāgāra. A building connected with the **Thūpārāma.** It was built by **Bhātikābhaya** and enlarged by **Āmaṇḍagāmaṇi-Abhaya.**[1]

[1] Mhv. xxxiv. 39; xxxv. 3; MṬ. 629, 639.

Ubhaka.—One of the ten sons of **Kālāsoka** (*q.v.*).

Uḷumpa.—*Add :* See also **Medataḷumpa.**

Ekadvāra.—*Add :* The **Ekadvārika-pabbata** was also called **Vaṅganta-pabbata.**[1]

[1] MṬ. 424.

Erakavassa, Erakavassakhaṇḍa.—A locality in Ceylon.[1]

[1] Ras. ii. 181, 185.

Eḷāra.—*For ref.* [4] *read* p. 483.

2. **Kakudha.**—*Add :* According to Tibetan sources (*e.g.*, Rockhill, p. 89), Kakudha was the son of Kauṇḍinya (Koṇḍañña). Which Koṇḍañña is referred to here it is impossible to say.

Kakubandhakandara.—A stream, near **Pāsāṇavāpigāma.**[1]

[1] Ras. i. 103.

Kakubandhagāma.—A village in **Rohaṇa.**[1]

[1] Ras. ii. 188.

Kañcanadevī.—Daughter of the king of **Devaputta.** On the day of her birth jewels fell from the sky and her body was so bright that no lamps were needed when she was by. She entered the Order when she grew up and became an arahant. In her past birth, when she was listening to a sermon at the end of celebrations held at Devaputta in honour of the Bowl Relic, a Nāga-king fell in love with her. When she refused his attentions, the Nāga wrapt her body with his coils, but she continued to listen unmoved. By power of her virtue the Nāga was subdued, and he paid her great honour by means of an **Udakapūjā.**[1]

[1] Ras. i. 34 f.

Kaṇikāravālikasamudda Vihāra.—*Add to refs. :* MA. i. 350; DA. iii. 1061.

Kaṇḍarājika.—A village in **Rājaraṭṭha** in Ceylon. See *s.v.* **Tambasumana.**

Kaṇḍula.—The Rasavāhinī contains a story of how he once looked after the monks of **Mahānijjhara Vihāra.**[1]

[1] Ras. ii. 29.

Kadalisālagāma.—A village in Ceylon, the residence of **Vilasa** (*q.v.*).

Kappakandara.—*Add :* According to the Rasavāhinī[1] the village was near **Cittalapabbata Vihāra.**[1]

[1] Ras. ii. 160.

1. **Kalahavivāda Sutta.**—*Add :* Probably the **Attadaṇḍa Sutta** (*q.v.*) was also called by this name. *See* AA. i. 186, where the story of the 500 Sakyan youths is given. In other accounts the Sutta which led to their joining the Order is called Attadaṇḍa. See *s.v.* **Rohiṇī** (3).

Kalyāṇabhatta-tissa.—See **Ariyagāla-tissa.**

Kākavaṇṇatissa.—*Add :* He was once a *milakkha* in India and looked after a Pacceka Buddha. One day he gave the Pacceka Buddha a meal of ripe jak-fruit. On another occasion, when the Pacceka Buddha visited his house in his absence, his wife tried to tempt him. Having failed, she complained to the husband that the

Pacceka Buddha had assaulted her. The latter sought the P.B. to kill him, but, seeing him in mid-air putting on his robe, he was filled with wonder and asked the P.B.'s forgiveness. Later he was born in a hunters' village near **Amaruppala-lena,** his name being **Amaruppala,** and did various good deeds.

He was called Kākavaṇṇatissa because he knew the speech of crows.[1]

[1] Ras. ii. 53 f.; see also p. 64, where a crow announces various things to him.

Kāraka.—A village in Ceylon, near **Serisara.**[1]

[1] Ras. ii. 183.

Kāladāna Sutta.—The name given in the Sutta Saṅgaha (No. 1) for **Kāla Sutta** (3) (*q.v.*).

Kāḷakagāma.—*Add:* It was evidently the same as Kallagama (*q.v.*).

Kāḷatinduka Vihāra.—A monastery in Ceylon.[1]

[1] Ras. ii. 165.

Kāḷadīghavāpi.—*Add:* There was evidently a vihāra attached to it. The Majjhima Comty. (Ma. i. 353 f.) gives a story of a novice who lived there.

Kāḷāsoka.—*Add:* He had ten sons, whose names were: Bhaddasena, Koraṇḍavaṇṇa, Maṅgura, Sabbañjaha, Jālika, Ubhaka, Sañjaya, Korabya, Nandivaḍḍhana, and Pañcamaka.[1]

[1] Mbv. p. 98.

Kiñcisaṅghā.—Daughter of Kākavaṇṇatissa's minister **Sangha** (*q.v.*).

Kilañjakāsanasālā.—A building in Anurādhapura, mentioned in connection with **Pītamalla Thera** (*q.v.*).

Kukkuṭagiri.—A place in Ceylon. Buddhaghosa says[1] that it was so called because it was there that **Saddhātissa's** attendant, Tissa (see **Tissa** 43), refused to kill some pheasants and set them free at the risk of losing his own life.

[1] SA. iii. 50.

Kuṭumbiya Vihāra.—A monastery in Ceylon. It was once the residence of **Tissamahānāga Thera** (*q.v.*).

2. **Kuṭumbiyaputta-tissa.**—*Add:* See also **Bodhimātu-mahātissa.**

Kuḍḍarajja.—Probably a district in Rohaṇa. See also **Mahāvāpi Vihāva.**

Kuḍḍavāṭakapāsāṇa.—A rock in **Pāsāṇatittha** (*q.v.*).

Kuṇḍalā.—Daughter of the king of **Devaputta.** Once she was a bitch in **Kakubandhakandara** and a sāmaṇera, Tissa, had given her a little food. Later, when Tissa was on his way to the Bodhi-tree (in Gayā) she saw him, and, remembering her past existence, invited him to the palace and entertained him. Later she built a vihāra for him, where he attained arahantship.[1]

[1] Ras. i. 103 f.

Kumāputtasahāya.—See **Sudatta** (11).

Kumārapañha.—*Add :* See also SA. iii. 99, where Buddhaghosa says that **Cittagahapati,** in a discussion with **Nigaṇṭha Nātaputta,** referred to the Kumārapañha.

Kumbalatissa-pabbata.—A mountain in Ceylon.[1]

[1] Ras. ii. 189.

Kumbulapabbata.—A mountain in Ceylon. **Ariyagālatissa** found sixty treasure-troves there.[1]

[1] Ras. ii. 37.

Kumbhaṇḍā.—A class of beings (fairies or gnomes) grouped with Yakkhas, Rakkhasas, Asuras and others. **Virūḷha** is their king. They have large bellies (*kumbhaṇḍa*=gourd), and their genitals are also large like pots (*kumbho viya*), hence their name.[1]

[1] D. iii. 198; DA. iii. 964.

Kumbhīla Vihāra.—A monastery in Ceylon.[1]

[1] Ras. ii. 111.

Kurudeva.—A poor man, who lived in **Vattura Vihāra,** eating large quantities of food and doing no work. Listening to the advice of a monk, he took the five precepts and fed fishes with a part of his meal. He was later born as **Mahānela** (*q.v.*).

Keḷiya-tissa.—See **Ariyagāla-tissa.**

Kevaṭṭa-Nanda.—One of the **Nava-Nandā** (*q.v.*).

Koṭṭapaṭṭana.—A ford in Ceylon.[1]

[1] Ras. ii. 124.

Koṭṭhasāla.—A village in Ceylon,[1] probably the same as **Koṭṭhasāra** (*q.v.*).

[1] Ras. ii. 24.

Kodhabhakkha.—A Rūpāvacara Brahmā, who came to test **Sakka's** patience and sat on his throne.[1]

[1] SA. i. 272.

Kontaraṭṭhapabbata Vihāra.—A monastery in Ceylon, the residence of **Mahānāga Thera.** When **Kākavaṇṇatissa** heard from a crow of the monk's death he went there and held great celebrations.[1]

[1] Ras. ii. 64.

Koraṇḍavaṇṇa.—One of the ten sons of **Kāḷāsoka** (*q.v.*).

Korabya.—One of **Kālāsoṅka's** ten sons.

Kovariyaputta.—See **Lāḷudāyī.**

Khañjadeva.—*Add :* See also Ras. ii. 99 f.

Khīrabhatta-tissa.—See **Ariyagāla-tissa.**

Gaṅgā-tissa.—See **Ariyagāla-tissa.**

Gaṇatissa.—Son of **Paṇḍuvāsudeva** (Mbv. 112). According to the Rājāvaliya, he reigned as king for forty years. See also Cv. *Trs.* ii. Introd. p. ix.

Gāmantā.—See **Mahāsiva** (2), also **Vāmatna.**

Giritimbilatissa.—A mountain and a vihāra in Rohaṇa. Near it was the village **Siva.**[1] See *s.v.* **Dhammā.**

[1] Ras. ii. 42.

Gihipaṭipadā Sutta.—A name given in the Sutta Saṅgaha (No. 65) to the **Gihisāmīci Sutta** (*q.v.*).

Guttavaṅka.—See **Taṅguttavaṅka.**

Guḷapūvatintinī.—A place on the outskirts of **Anurādhapura,** near **Cetiyagiri.**[1]

[1] Ras. ii. 50.

Goṭhagāma.—A village on the south coast of Ceylon.[1]

[1] Ras. ii. 170.

Goṭhayimbara.—*Add :* See also Ras. ii. 87 f., which says that he was so called because he was short, but that according to the **Uttaravihāra** monks he was given the name because, when he went hunting, he killed animals by dashing them on *koṭṭhayimbara*-trees. Once when he was holding a feast in his house, after defeating the Damiḷas, a Yakkha, named **Jayasena** of **Ariṭṭhapabbata,** happened to pass by, and, entering the house, fell in love with G.'s wife. G. challenged him to a fight and defeated him. He celebrated the victory for seven days and went to the palace drunk. Being refused admission, he swam across to **Kāvīrapaṭṭana,** and, having gone as far as the Himālaya in search of holy monks, was about to kill himself in despair when an arahant Thera appeared before him and ordained him. He later attained arahantship.

Goḷa-upāsaka.—A pious man of Goṭhagāma, so called because he was slightly hunched. His story is given at Ras. ii. 170 f.

Govisānaka-Nanda.—One of the **Nava-Nandā** (*q.v.*).

Ghanamaṭṭhaka.—An ornament which **Migāra** presented to **Visākhā** to show her his gratitude.[1]

[1] DhA. i. 407.

1. **Cakka Sutta.**—On the four wheels that lead to prosperity: dwelling in fit places, association with the good, perfect self-adjustment (*attasammāpanidhi*) and merit done aforetime.[1]

[1] A. ii. 32 f.; D. iii. 276; *cf.* **Maṅgala Sutta.**

2. **Cakka Sutta.**—A king who knows the good (*attha*) *dhamma*, the measure (*matta*), the season (*kāla*), and the nature of his assemblies (*parisā*) wields dominion that cannot be wrested from him. A Buddha's dominion is also the same.[1]

[1] A. iii. 147 f.

Cakkavatti.—The special name given in the books to a World-ruler. The world itself means "Turner of the Wheel," the Wheel (*Cakka*) being the well-known Indian symbol of empire. There are certain stock epithets used to describe a Cakkavatti: *dhammiko, dhammarājā, cāturanto* (ruler of the four quarters), *vijitāvī* (conqueror), *janapadatthavāriyappatto* (guardian of the people's good), and *sattaratanasamannāgato* (possessor of the Seven Treasures). More than one thousand sons are his; his dominions extend throughout the earth to its ocean bounds (*sāgarapariyantam*); and is established not by the scourge, nor by the sword, but by righteousness (*adaṇḍena asatthena dhammen'eva abhivijiva*).[1]

From the **Mahāpadāna Sutta** it would appear that the birth of a Cakkavatti is attended by the same miracles as that of the birth of a Buddha. A Cakkavattī's youth is the same as that of Buddha; he, too, possesses on his body the **Mahāpurisalakkhaṇāni** (*q.v.*), and soothsayers are able to predict at the child's birth only that one of two destinies await him.

Of the Seven Treasures of a Cakkavatti, the **Cakkaratana** (*q.v.*) is the chief. When he has traversed the Four Continents—**Pub-**

[1] Particulars are found chiefly in the Mahāsudassana, Mahāpadāna, Cakkavattisīhanāda, Bālapaṇḍita and Ambaṭṭha Suttas. See also S. v. 98.

bavideha, Jambudīpa, Aparagoyāṇa and **Uttarakuru**—accompanied by the Cakkaratana, received the allegiance of all the inhabitants and admonished them to lead the righteous life, he returns to his own native city. After the Wheel, other Treasures make their appearance: first the Elephant, *Hatthiratana*; it is either the youngest of the **Chaddanta-kula** or the oldest of the **Uposatha-kula.** Next the Horse, *Assaratana*, named **Valāhaka,** all-white with crow-black head, and dark mane, able to fly through the air. Then the *Veḷuriya*-gem from **Vepullapabbata,** with eight facets, the finest of its species, shedding light for a league around. This is followed by the Woman, belonging either to the royal family of **Madda** or of **Uttarakuru,** desirable in every way, both because of her physical beauty and her virtuous character. Then the Treasurer (*Gahapati*) possessed of marvellous vision, enabling him to discover treasures, and then the Adviser (*Parināyaka*), who is generally the Cakkavatti's eldest son.[2]

Judging from the story of **Mahāsudassana** (*q.v.*), who is the typical Cakkavatti, the World-emperor has also four other gifts (*iddhī*): a marvellous figure, a life longer than that of other men, good health, and popularity with all classes of his subjects. The perfume of sandalwood issues from his mouth, while his body is like a lily.

When the Cakkavatti is about to die the Wheel slips down from its place and sinks down slightly. When the king sees this he leaves the household life, and retires into homelessness, to taste the joys of contemplation, having handed over the kingdom to his eldest son. At the king's death, the Elephant, the Horse and the Gem return to where they came from, the Woman loses her beauty, the Treasurer his divine vision, and the Adviser his efficiency.[3]

Cakkavattis are rare in the world, and are born in *kappas* in which Buddhas do not arise.[4] The **Cakkavattisīhanāda Sutta** (*q.v.*)., however, gives the names of seven who succeeded one another. In the case of each of them the Wheel disappeared, but, when his successor practised the Ariyan duty of a Cakkavatti, honouring the Dhamma and following it to perfection, the Wheel reappeared. In the case of the seventh his virtues gradually disappeared through forgetfulness; crime spread, among his subjects, and the Wheel vanished for ever.

In the earlier literature the term Cakkavatti seems to have been reserved for a World-ruler; but later three sorts of Cakkavattis are mentioned: *cakkavāḷa*- or *cāturanta-cakkavatti* (ruling over the

[2] For descriptions of these see D. ii. 174 f.; DA. ii. 624 f.; MA. ii. 941 f.

[3] DA. ii. 635.

[4] SA. iii. 131.

four continents), *dīpa-cakkavatti* (ruling over one), and *padesa-cakkavatti* (over part of one).[5]

No woman can become a Cakkavatti.[6] A Cakkavatti is as worthy of a *thūpa* as a Buddha.[7]

[5] DA. i. 249. [6] The reasons for this are given at AA. i. 254. [7] D. ii. 143.

2. **Cakkavatti Sutta.**—*Add:* It was also evidently called **Ratana Sutta.** See DA. i. 250.

Catupaccayasantosabhāvanārāma-Mahāariyavaṃsa. See **Mahāariyavaṃsa Sutta.**

Caturaṅgabala.—An officer of state of Jambudīpa; an author.[1]

[1] Gv. 67.

Caturitthi Vimāna.—See **Sumanā** (13).

Catusāmanera Vatthu.—The story of the four sāmaṇeras: Saṅkicca, Paṇḍita, Sopāka and Revata. See **Pañcacchiddageha. Ñāṇābhivaṃsa** (*q.v.*) wrote a fresh account of the story.

Candamukha.—A cave in **Dhūmarakkhapabbata. Maliyamahādeva Thera** once lived there.[1]

[1] Ras. ii. 126.

Candamukhī.—The wife of **Meghavaṇṇa-devaputta.**[1]

[1] Ras. ii. 126.

Candavaṅkavīthi.—A street in **Anurādhapura.**[1]

[1] Ras. ii. 123.

Candasuriya.—A friend of **Mahādhanadeva.** See **Ariyagāla-tissa.**

Carimālopa Sutta.—A name given in the Sutta Saṅgaha (No. 57) to a Sutta of the Itivuttaka (Itv. p. 18 f.). The Buddha says that if people knew as much as he did of the results of giving they would share even their last morsel of food with others.

Cumbaṭakalaha.—The name given (*e.g.*, J. i. 208) to the quarrel between the Sākyans and the Koliyans about the water of the **Rohiṇī** (*q.v.*).

Cullagalla.—A village and a vihāra near the **Jajjaranadī.** For the story of a pious man who lived in the village see Ras. ii. 152 f.

Cullatavālagāma.—A village probably on the Mahāvālukanadī. See **Tambasumana.**

Cullasaṅgha.—Brother of **Kākavaṇṇatissa's** minister **Sangha** (*q.v.*).

Cūlatissa.—A minister of Duṭṭhagāmaṇī. Once when **Kaṇḍula** was lost, he was sent in search and found him looking after the monks of **Mahānijjhara.** Tissa gave the monks a drink of *kāra*-fruit and sugar, and took the animal back to the king. Later, Tissa was born in **Ambaviṭṭhi** and entered the Order. Afterwards, while on a voyage to the Bodhi-tree in Gayā, his ship ran short of water. Tissa let down his bowl into the sea. The water became fresh and sweet, and he shared it with the others. After death he was born in the deva-world.[1]

[1] Ras. ii. 29 f.

4. **Cūlanāga.**—A monk of **Pidhānagalla** in the time of **Duṭṭhagāmaṇi. Saṅghadattā** (*q.v.*) gave him a robe.

5. **Cūlanāga.**—A monk of **Asiggāhaka-pariveṇa.** One day, after having obtained alms in **Candavaṅkavīthi,** he fed a starving bitch. That same evening he got large quantities of ghee and molasses which he gave to his colleagues. For thirty-two years he gave alms to thousands of monks from food given to him by the people of Candavaṅkavīthi. Later, he became an arahant. Once, 500 monks on pilgrimage to the Bodhi-tree, took him with them to avert danger. In four months they reached Koṭṭapaṭṭana and in seven months the Bodhi-tree, being well entertained everywhere. On the way back Cūlanāga was seized with a colic and died; but before death he advised his colleagues to cremate his body and take his ashes that they might be provided with their wants.[1]

[1] Ras. ii. 122 f.

6. **Cūlanāga.**—A fortress in Rājaraṭṭha (in Ceylon).[1]

[1] Ras. ii. 145.

2. **Cūlapāsāda.** Omit this from p. 900.

Cūlapiṇḍapātika-Nāga.—A monk of Nalakhaṇḍapadhāna. See **Ambāmacca.**

Cūlaraṭṭha.—A district in India, near Benares.[1]

[1] Ras. i. 36.

Cūlaviṭṭhi.—See **Hulaviṭṭhi.**

Cetiyakapabbata.—Probably a *v.l.* for **Vedisagiri** (*q.v.*). See Ras. i. 99.

Cetiyadamiḷa.—The chief warrior of **Eḷāra,** killed by **Veḷusumana.**[1]

[1] Ras. ii. 62; but see *s.v.* **Veḷusumana.**

Chagāma.—A village in Rohaṇa.[1]

[1] Ras. ii. 34.

Chattavimāna.—See **Chatta** (3).

Jarāmaraṇa Sutta.—A name given in the Sutta Saṅgaha (No. 44) for **Rāja Sutta** (4) (*q.v.*).

Jāgaraṇa Sutta.—A sutta of the Itivuttaka (p. 41) quoted in the Sutta Saṅgaha (No. 81) on the value of wakefulness.

Jālika.—One of the ten sons of Kalasoka (*q.v.*).

Jīvitapotthakī.—See **Kitti** (7).

5. **Jutindhara.**—A brother of **Vedisadevī**; he was one of the nobles who escorted the Bodhi-tree to Ceylon.[1]

[1] Mbv. 166.

Takka.—A city in India twelve leagues from **Kāvīrapaṭṭana.** It was the residence of monks.[1]

[1] Ras. ii. 108.

Taṅguttavaṅka.—*Add* : The Pariveṇa was attached to the Mahāvihāra.[1]

[1] Ras. i. 1.

"Tamo-tama" Sutta.—A name given in the Sutta Saṅgaha (No. 49) to the **Puggala Sutta** (3) (*q.v.*). See also **Tamo Sutta.**

Tambasumana.—He was once a minister of **Saddhātissa.** Having gone to **Koṭṭhasāla** on official business he gave to a monk the food prepared by the people for him. He was then born in **Vallavāhagāma** and was called **Sumana.** Later he entered the Order in **Brāhmanārāma** and became an arahant. A deity of a *timbaru*-tree provided him and 500 companions with food during the **Brahmaṇatiya** famine. Later, during their travels near **Kaṇḍarājika,** the monks, about to eat, had doubts regarding the time because the sun was hidden. Tambasumana threw a stone into the sky, and, making it shine like the sun, dispelled their doubts. The spot came to be called **Maṇisūriya.** On another occasion, at **Cullatavālagāma,** he converted a whole river into ghee from the ford of **Vālagāma-vihāra** to **Bhuttakatittha,** a distance of two yojanas.[1]

[1] Ras. ii. 24 f.

Talaṅgarasamuddapabbata.—Mentioned in the Rasavāhinī (ii. 50) as the residence of **Mahādhammadinna.** It is probably the same as Talaṅgara (*q.v.*).

Tindukagāma.—A village near the **Mahāvālukanadī.**[1]

[1] Ras. ii. 157.

Tiṇḍukācira.—See *s.v.* **Mallikārāma.**

45. **Tissa.**—A sāmaṇera of **Tissavihāra** in Mahāgāma. See *s.v.* **Kuṇḍalā.**

46. **Tissa.**—A novice who later became a devaputta on a tree near **Nāga-vihāra.** For details see Ras. ii. 168.

47. **Tissa.**—A monk who, when his brother's wife sent men to kill him, broke his thigh-bones as token he would not run away, and having begged leave for one night, attained arahantship.[1]

[1] MA. i. 188 f.

Tathāgatuppatti.— A Pāli work by **Ñāṇagambhīra.**[1]

[1] Gv. 62, 72.

Tissamahāvihāra.—*Add :* Buddhaghosa says[1] that in his time all monks living in Ceylon, south of the **Mahāvālukanadī,** assembled there twice a year, on the first and last day of the *vassa.*

[1] DA. ii. 581.

Tissambatittha.—A village in Rohaṇa. See **Tissā** (10).

[1] Ras. ii. 31.

Tissamahānāga Thera.—A monk of **Kuṭumbiya Vihāra.** Having heard the **Satipaṭṭhāna Sutta** from **Tissa Thera** of **Ambalena,** he was on his way back when he met a wild elephant. By his virtue the elephant was subdued and Tissamahānāga took shelter from a storm under the elephant's body. There he developed arahantship. He then went to **Viyoḷaka-vihāra** with the elephant, and for thirty years the animal waited on him. After death the monk's remains were cremated at Kuṭumbiya Vihāra, and the elephant participated in the celebrations.[1]

[1] Ras. ii. 185 f.

10. **Tissā.**—Wife of **Muṇḍagutta.** Wishing to give alms, they sold their son and bought a cow, which gave them rich ghee. A minister, displeased with them, had the cow confiscated by the king; but the king discovering that Tissā alone could milk her, asked her her story, and gave them great rewards, making the minister their slave. They lived in **Tissambatittha** in the time of **Saddhātissa.**[1]

[1] Ras. ii. 31 f.

Tissāmacca.—Son of **Venisāla.** Having heard the **Dakkhiṇāvibhaṅga Sutta** in the **Tissamahārāma,** he never ate without giving a share of his food to monks. He was later born as a tree deity near **Kāḷatindukavihāra.**[1]

[1] Ras. ii. 163. f.

Tuṇḍagāma.—A village in the dominions of the Kosala king.[1]

[1] Ras. i. 46.

Tuṇḍila.—A parrot, who had a tiger as friend. For their story see Ras. i. 36.

Telumapāli.—A place through which the *sīmā* of the **Mahāvihāra** passed.[1]

[1] Mbv. 135.

Tālacatukka.—A place included in the *sīmā* of the **Mahāvihāra.**[1]

[1] Mbv. 135.

Tomaṇaratittha.—A ford in Ceylon.[1]

[1] Ras. ii. 184.

Thulū.—See **Bumū.**

Therambalaka Vihāra.—A monastery built by **Sakka. Dāṭhāsena** lived there.[1]

[1] Ras. ii. 109.

Theraputtābhaya.—The Rasavāhinī (ii. 92 f.) contains a story of his youth when he was a novice in **Kappakandara-vihāra. Goṭhayimbara** visited the place and ate the coconuts, throwing the husks about. The novice beat him soundly.

Daṇḍagoṇa.—A village in Ceylon. For a story of a jackal who lived there see Ras. ii. 130 f.

Danta.—A householder of **Nāgakāragāma.** He gave alms for many years to **Maliyamahādeva Thera** and the monks of **Piyaṅgudīpa.** Once, on his way to **Suvaṇṇabhūmi,** he was shipwrecked, but was rescued by **Sīhabāhu Thera** and brought to Piyaṅgudīpa. There he saw **Sakka** and was provided with a ship full of valuables. The king having heard of him gave him **Dantagāma.**[1]

[1] Ras. ii. 191 f.

Dantagāma.—See **Danta.**

Dasadhamma Sutta.—The name given in the Sutta Saṅgaha (No. 84) to the **Dhamma Sutta** (2) (*q.v.*).

Dasasiddhika Nanda.—One of the **Nava-Nandā** (*q.v.*).

Dāṭhāsena.—A warrior. In the time of **Kassapa Buddha** he gave milk-rice to monks for 20,000 years. Later he was born in **Kubukandha** and joined **Duṭṭhagāmaṇi,** taking a prominent part in the capture of **Mahela-nagara.** Then the king's mind was poisoned against him and an elephant was let loose on him. But he killed it and went to Mahājallika, where he defeated a fisherman of immense strength, then swam across to **Coḷa** and was ordained by **Mahāvaruṇa Thera.** He lived for a time in **Therambalaka Vihāra,** sixty leagues away;

but finding it unsuitable, he moved to **Lohakūṭapabbata-vihāra,** fifteen leagues away, and there attained arahantship.[1]

[1] Ras. ii. 104 f.

Dīghavāpi.—For a story connected with the *cetiya* see **Dhajagga Paritta.**

Dīyavāsa.—A locality through which passed the sima of the Mahavihara.[1]

[1] Mbv. 135.

Dubbuṭṭhi.—A king of Ceylon. He held a **Giribhaṇḍamahāpūjā.**[1]

[1] Ras. ii. 183, 185.

Dubbuṭṭhi-Mahātissa.—A rich man of **Mahelanagara.** Once a debtor, hoping to harm him, invited **Tissa Thera** and 500 monks of **Abhayuttara-vihāra** in Dubbuṭṭhi's name on the day D. had a ploughing ceremony. When the monks arrived, D.'s wife prepared food and fed them. When D. discovered this he was full of gratitude to his debtor and tore up the promissory note.[1]

[1] Ras. ii. 166 f.

13. **Deva.**—A minister of **Devagāma.** He once gave food to a starving dog. He was reborn in the same village, and later entered the Order at **Pupphavāsa Vihāra.** During the **Brāhmaṇatiya** famine a tree deity looked after him for twelve years. Once men looking for food wished to kill him, but he was saved by his luck. He became an arahant, and the deity looked after him for twelve years more.[1]

[1] Ras. ii. 13 f.

Devagāma.—A village to the west of Ceylon. Near it was the **Pupphavāsa Vihāra.**[1]

[1] Ras. ii. 13.

Devacavana Sutta.—The name given in the Sutta Saṅgaha (No. 29) to a Sutta of the Itivuttaka (p. 76 f.), describing the signs attendant on a deva's decease and the factors determining his future.

Devadāniya.—A robber. See *s.v.* **Mahālatāpasādhana** and **Bandhula.**

Devaputta.—A city in India, fifteen leagues from **Pāṭaliputta.** In it was the **Sīhakumbha Vihāra.** It was the birthplace of **Rūpadevī** and **Kañcanadevī.** At one time the Buddha's Bowl Relic was there and celebrations were held in its honour. The king of Devaputta, in the time of **Asoka,** was also called Devaputta.[1]

[1] Ras. i. 25, 34, 80.

Devarakkhitalena.—A cave in Ceylon, once the residence of **Mahādhammadinna Thera** of **Talaṅgaratissapabbata.**[1]

[1] SadS. 88.

Devārohaṇa.—The name given to the episode describing the Buddha's ascent to the deva-world to preach the Abhidhamma and his descent at **Saṅkassa** (*q.v.*).

Doḷa.—A minister of **Devānampiyatissa.** Saṅghamittā lived in his house before the **Upāsikārāma** was built, so did **Anulā** till her ordination.[1]

[1] MṬ. 388, 408.

Dhajagga Paritta.—*Add:* It is said that once a sāmaṇera, helping to plaster the **Dīghavāpi-cetiya,** fell from the top. His colleagues shouted to him to recall the Dhajagga Paritta. He did so, and was miraculously saved.[1]

[1] SA. i. 262 f.

Dhanañjaya Jātaka.—The name should be corrected to Dhūmakāri Jātaka and the particulars given should appear on p. 1161 under that name.

2. **Dhammagutta.**—A brother of **Vedisadevī.** He was one of the nobles who escorted the Bodhi-tree. He was made **Moriyaseṭṭhi** and given the **Moriyajanapada** by **Devānampiyatissa.**[1]

[1] Mbv. 166.

3. **Dhammadinna.**—A monk of Tissamahā-vihāra near **Talaṅgarapabbata.** Once, while on pilgrimage to **Nāgadīpa** with 500 others, he stopped at **Sāgiri Vihāra,** and they were looked after by **Bahulamassutissa Thera.** The next day they went for alms to **Puṇṇasālakoṭṭhaka,** where a resident entertained them to a meal with hare's flesh. Dhammadinna later asked why Tissa Thera did not admonish his follower on the evils of killing, seeing that there was a heap of bones outside the house. Tissa asked Dhammadinna to do so the next day. This was done; the devotee confessed that he had never killed a hare, but in his house there was never any want of hare's flesh, and he did not know why. Dhammadinna, with his divine eye, revealed to him that in the time of **Padumuttara Buddha** he had given alms with hare's flesh.[1]

[1] Ras. ii. 128 f.

Dhammaratha Sutta.—A name given in the Sutta Saṅgaha (No. 42) to the **Accharā Sutta** (*q.v.*).

Dhammasīva.—A village in Ceylon. See **Dhammā** (6).

Dhammasoṇḍa.—The Bodhisatta born as king of Benares. He was so called because, at the time of his birth, all beings were filled with a desire for righteousness. The religion of **Kassapa Buddha** had disappeared, and D. was unable to get anyone to preach the Dhamma to him. He therefore left the kingdom and entered the forest. By his virtue **Sakka's** throne was heated, and Sakka, coming down as a Rakkhasa, agreed to preach to D. if he would allow himself to be eaten. D. consented, and, climbing a rock three gāvutas high, threw himself into the Rakkhasa's mouth, listening to his preaching as he fell. Sakka then revealed his identity, took him to the deva-world and taught him a stanza on impermanence, which had been spoken by Kassapa.[1]

[1] Ras. i. 2 f.; the story is very popular in Ceylon.

Dhammasoṇḍaka Vagga.—The first section of the **Rasavāhinī.**

6. **Dhammā.**—A very poor woman of **Sīva** village. Once she gave a garment to the monks of **Giritimbilatissapabbata Vihāra,** and they agreed among themselves that none but an arahant should wear it. One of them became an arahant that very day and wore it; he then passed it on to another, and before the end of the rains they all thus became arahants. On the day of the *pavāraṇa*, King **Lañjitissa** ordered the monastery to be decorated. The monks set up Dhamma's garment as a banner at the entrance. The king, having discovered the reason, gave Dhammā the village of Sīva, which then came to be called **Dhammasīva.**[1]

[1] Ras. ii. 42.

Dhammasīva.—See **Dhammā** (6).

"Na Uññātabba" Sutta.—The name given in the Sutta Saṅgaha (No. 43) to the **Dahara Sutta** (*q.v.*).

5. **Nakula.**—An *upāsaka*. Because of his poverty he borrowed twelve kahāpaṇas, keeping his daughter as security. Having obtained the money later, he was on his way to redeem the debt when he saw **Cūlapiṇḍapātiya Tissa** of **Tissamahāvihāra,** and, as it was meal-time, he bought food from a wayfarer, paying all he had, and gave it to the monk. Tissa developed arahantship before eating. When Nakula told his daughter of this she was glad. That same day Tissa Thera died, and told his colleagues that none but Nakula would be able to remove his body. When **Kākavaṇṇatissa** heard of this he sent for Nakula and gave him a village, which came to be called **Nakulakaṇṇikā.**[1]

[1] Ras. ii. 143 f.

Nakulakaṇṇikā.—See **Nakula** (5).

Nandimitta.—*Add :* See also Ras. ii. 78 f. for a very detailed story.

Nandapañña.—A native of Haṃsaraṭṭha; author of the **Gandhavaṃsa** (*q.v.*).

Nandimitta Vihāra.—A monastery built by **Nandimitta** on the banks of the **Jajjaranadī.**[1]

[1] Ras. ii. 81.

Nandirāja Vagga.—The second section of the Rasavāhinī.

Nandivaddhana.—One of the ten sons of **Kāḷāsoka** (*q.v.*).

Nandivāṇija.—A merchant of **Mahātitthapaṭṭana.** He was away from home for three years, and the king's minister, **Siva,** wishing to possess his wife, paid a necromancer to send a demon to kill Nandi. The demon went to the ship, but on Nandi's advice the crew sought the Three Refuges, and the demon fled. Baulked of his prey, the demon killed both the necromancer and Siva.[1]

[1] Ras. ii. 139 f.

Nandī.—The name of **Mahākassapa** when he was king of Benares. The story is given in Ras. i. 26 f. The name is evidently a variant of Nanda. See **Nanda** (11).

Nalakhaṇḍapadhāna.—A practising hall. It was the residence of Culapindapatiyanaga Thera.[1]

[1] Ras. ii. 145.

Nava Nandā.—See **Nanda** (20).

Navavaṃsa.—Probably another name for the **Cūlavaṃsa.** It is ascribed to **Nava-Mahānāma.**[1]

[1] Gv. 70.

Nāgakāragāma.—A village in the north of Ceylon.[1]

[1] Ras. ii. 191.

Nāgagāma.—A village in **Nāgadīpa.**[1]

[1] Ras. ii. 51.

Nāgadīpa.—*Add :* According to the Rasavāhinī (ii. 19) the place was so called because it was given as gift to the woman named Nagā. See **Nāgā** (7).

7. **Nāgā.**—A woman who lived near the **Rājāyatana-cetiya.** Once, seeing sixty monks return from the village with empty bowls, she, although already pledged to work by day, borrowed some money on promise to work at night as well, and gave them food. The monks retired to **Mucalindavana** and developed arahantship before

eating. The deity of the king's parasol shouted applause, and the king, having heard the story, gave Nāgā the whole Island, which thus came to be called **Nāgādīpa.**[1]

[1] Ras. ii. 16 f.

8. **Nāgā.**—A class of beings classed with **Garuḷas** and **Supaṇṇas** and playing a prominent part in Buddhist folk-lore. They are gifted with miraculous powers and great strength. Generally speaking, they are confused with snakes, chiefly the hooded Cobra, and their bodies are described as being those of snakes, though they can assume human form at will. They are broadly divided into two classes: those that live on land (*thalaja*) and those that live on water (*jalaja*). The *Jalaja-nāgā* live in rivers as well as in the sea, while the *Thalaja-nāgā* are regarded as living beneath the surface of the earth. Several Nāga dwellings are mentioned in the books: *e.g.*, **Mañjerika-bhavana** under **Sineru, Daddara-bhavana** at the foot of Mount **Daddara** in the **Himālaya,** the **Dhataraṭṭha-nāgā** under the river **Yamunā,** the **Nābhāsā** Nāgā in Lake **Nabhasa,** and also the Nāgas of **Vesāli, Tacchaka,** and **Payāga** (D. ii. 258). The Vinaya (ii. 109) contains a list of four royal families of Nāgas (*Ahirājakulāni*): **Virūpakkhā, Erāpathā, Chabyāputtā** and **Kaṇhagotamakā.** Two other Nāga tribes are generally mentioned together: the **Kambalas** and the **Assataras.** It is said (SA. iii. 120) that all Nāgas have their young in the Himālaya.

Stories are given—*e.g.*, in the **Bhūridatta Jataka**—of Nāgas, both male and female, mating with humans; but the offspring of such unions are watery and delicate (J. vi. 160). The Nāgas are easily angered and passionate, their breath is poisonous, and their glance can be deadly (J. vi. 160, 164). They are carnivorous (J. iii. 361), their diet consisting chiefly of frogs (J. vi. 169), and they sleep, when in the world of men, on ant-hills (*ibid.*, 170). The enmity between the Nāgas and the Garuḷas is proverbial (D. ii. 258). At first the Garuḷas did not know how to seize the Nāgas, because the latter swallowed large stones so as to be of great weight, but they learnt how in the **Paṇḍara Jātaka** (*q.v.*). The Nāgas dance when music is played, but it is said (J. vi. 191) that they never dance if any Garuḷa is near (through fear) or in the presence of human dancers (through shame).

The best known of all Nāgas is **Mahākāla,** king of **Mañjerika-bhavana** (*q.v.*). He lives for a whole *kappa*, and is a very pious follower of the Buddha. The Nāgas of his world had the custodianship of a part of the Buddha's relics till they were needed for the **Mahā Thūpa** (Mhv. xxxi. 27 f.), and when the Bodhi-tree was being brought to Ceylon they did it great honour during the voyage (Mbv. p. 153 f.). Other Nāga kings are also mentioned as ruling with great power and majesty and being converted to the Buddha's faith—*e.g.*, **Āravāla, Apalāla, Erapatta, Nandopananda,** and **Paṇṇaka.** (See also **Ahicchatta** and **Ahināga.**) In the **Āṭānāṭiya Sutta** (D. iii. 198 f.), speaking of dwellers of the **Cātummahārājika** world, the Nāgas are mentioned as occupying the Western Quarter, with Virūpakkha as their king.

The Nāgas had two chief settlements in Ceylon, in **Nāgadīpa** (*q.v.*) and at the mouth of the river **Kalyāṇī.** It was to settle a dispute between two Nāga chiefs of Nāgadīpa, Mahodara and Cūlodara, that the Buddha paid his second visit to Ceylon. During that visit he made a promise to another Nāga-king, **Maṇiakkhika** of Kalyāṇī, to pay him a visit, and the Buddha's third visit was in fulfilment of that undertaking (Mhv. i. 48 f.).

The Nāgas form one of the guards set up by **Sakka** in Sineru against the **Asuras** (J. i. 204). The Nāgas were sometimes worshipped by human beings and were offered sacrifices of milk, rice, fish, meat and strong drink (J. i. 497 f.). The jewel of the Nāgas is famous for its beauty and its power of conferring wishes to its possessor (J. vi. 179, 180).

The word Nāga is often used as an epithet of the Buddha and the Arahants, and in this connection the etymology given is *āgum na karotī ti Nāgo* (*e.g.*, MNid. 201). The Bodhisatta was born several times as king of the Nāgas: **Atula, Campeyya, Bhūridatta, Mahādaddara,** and **Saṅkhapāla.**

In the accounts given of the Nāgas, there is undoubtedly great confusion between the Nāgas as supernatural beings, as snakes, and as the name of certain non-Aryan tribes, but the confusion is too difficult to unravel.

3. **Nārivāhana.**—The chariot of **Vessavaṇa** (*q.v.*).

Nikkammatissa.—See **Ariyagālatissa.**

Nigrodhasālakhaṇḍa.—A village in Ceylon.[1]

[1] Ras. ii. 46.

Nirayuppatti Sutta.—A man whose mind is soiled (*paduṭṭha*) is born after death in hell.[1]

[1] Itv. 12 f.

Nilapabbata Vihāra.—A monastery near **Halloligāma.**

Paceli Vihāra.—*Add* : See also **Pipphali Vihāra.**

Pacceka Buddha.—*Add* : See also **Mātaṅga** (2).

Pacchidāyaka.—See **Sajjhadāyaka.**

Pañcamaka.—One of the ten sons of **Kāḷāsoka** (*q.v.*).

Pañcaṭṭhānadāna Sutta.—The name given in the Sutta Saṅgaha (No. 58) to the **Bhojana Sutta** (2) (*q.v.*).

Pañcala Vihāra.—*Add* : See also Pipphali Vihāra.

Paṭipattisaṅgaha.—A Pāli work by an unknown author.[1]

[1] Gv. 62, 72.

Paṭṭhāna Sutta.—Three good results for which the good life should be lived.[1]

[1] Sutta Saṅgaha No. 29; Itv. 67 f. Perhaps the correct name is **Patthanā Sutta.** The *Uddāna* calls it **Sukka Sutta.**

Paṇḍuka Nanda.—One of the **Nava-Nandā** (*q.v.*).

Paṇḍugati Nanda.—One of the **Nava Nandā** (*q.v.*).

2. **Pamada Sutta**—Another name for the **Appaka Sutta** (*q.v.*).

2. **Paramatthadīpanī.**—The name given to the **Pañcappakaraṇaṭṭhakathā.**[1]

[1] SadS. 60.

Paramatthapakāsinī.—The name given to the Mūlaṭikā on the Abhidhammapiṭaka written in Ceylon under **Mahākassapa.**[1]

[1] SadS. 60.

Paramatthavinicchaya.—*Add* : It was written at the request of **Saṅgharakkhita.**[1]

[1] Gv. 71.

Parasamuddavāsī Therā.—Referred to in the Commentaries (*e.g.*, MA. ii. 726); the reference is probably to the monks of India, as opposed to those of Ceylon.

" Pavāsī " Sutta.—A name given in the Sutta Saṅgaha (No. 37) to **Mitta Sutta** (*q.v.*).

Pasādabahula Sutta.—See **Pāsādabahula,** which is a wrong reading.

Pasenadi.—*Add* : The Sutta Vibhanga (Vin. iv. 298) mentions a *Cittāgāra* (? Art Gallery) which belonged to him.

Pācīnatissa Vihāra.—A vihāra probably near **Jambukola.** When the Bodhi-tree arrived in Ceylon, it was taken there on the tenth day.[1]

[1] Mbv. 158.

Pātheyya Sutta.—Spoken in answer to a deva's questions. Faith is the provision for the way (of saṃsāra); desires drag men round and round.[1]

[1] S. i. 44.

Pāsāṇavāpigāma.—A village in **Rohaṇa,** near **Mahāgāma.**[1]

[1] Ras. i. 103.

Picumālaka.—A locality in **Anurādhapura** where the rank of **Jayamahālekhaka** was conferred on **Bodhigutta.**[1]

[1] Mbv. 164.

Piṇḍapātika-tissa.—See **Saddhātissa** (2).

Piṇḍiyālopa Sutta.—A sutta quoted in the Sutta Saṅgaha (No. 79) from the Itivuttaka (p. 89) on the heinousness of a *dussīla* accepting alms from the pious.

Pipphali Vihāra.—*Add :* AA. i. 225 calls it **Pañcala** and MA. ii. 887 **Paceli.**

Pilayakūṭa.—Evidently another name for **Sīlakūṭa.** See Mbv. 126, 128, 129.

Puññavaḍḍhana Sutta.—A name given in the Sutta Saṅgaha (No. 60) to the **Vanaropa Sutta** (1) (*q.v.*).

Puppha Sutta.—See **Vaddha Sutta.**

Pupphavāsa.—A vihāra in the west of Ceylon. Near it was **Devagāma.**[1]

[1] Ras. ii. 13.

Pubbakoṭṭhaka.—*Add :* Details of this are given at MA. i. 370 f. There were four bathing-places: for the king, for the people, for the Buddha, and the Saṅgha.

Pūvagallagāma.—A village on the banks of the **Mahāvālukanadī.** In it was the **Pūvagalla Vihāra.**[1]

[1] Ras. ii. 27; *v.l.* **Pūvapabbata.**

Pūvapabbata.—See **Pūvagalla.**

Pūvapabbatavāsī-Tissa.—A monk of **Pūvagalla Vihāra.** Because in a past birth he had given a meal of peacocks' flesh, he got that flesh wherever he went. For his story see Ras. ii. 27 f.

Phussadeva.—*Add :* See also Ras. ii. 100 f.

Baladāna Sutta.—A name given in the Sutta Saṅgaha (No. 59) to the **Kindada Sutta** (*q.v.*).

Balākapāsāṇa.—A place passed by the sima of the Mahavihara.[1]

[1] Mbv. 135.

Bahulamassu-Tissa.—A monk, incumbent of **Sāgiri Vihāra.**[1]

[1] Ras. ii. 128; see also **Dhammadinna** (3).

Bahula.—A caṇḍāla who was put to death with his seven sons because he refused to give to **Sirināga** the secret of entering the cetiya in **Dakkhiṇamahāvihāra.** As they were impaled devas brought chariots to take them to the deva-worlds.[1]

[1] Ras. ii. 7 f.

Bāhiraṅga Sutta.—A name given in the Sutta Saṅgaha (No. 78) to a Sutta of the Itivuttaka (p. 10) on the virtues of *kalyāṇamittatā.*

Bimbisāra.—*Add to ref.* [21]*:* See also MA. i. 292.

2. **Buddhadāsa.**—A pious man of **Tuṇḍagāma.** He drove away a Yakkha who had taken possession of a friend of his.[1]

[1] Ras. i. 46 f.

Buddhavamma.—A merchant of **Pāṭaliputta.** He once gave the Buddha and the monks grape juice and molasses, and later he got grape juice wherever he was.[1]

[1] For details see Ras. i. 22 f.

2. **Buddhasīha.**—See **Madhuratthavilāsinī.**

Buddhenī.—A pious woman of **Pāṭaliputta.** She got as gift from a merchant a horse that could fly through the air, and she made regular pilgrimages to the Bodhi-tree. One day robbers waylaid her, but the horse helped her to escape.[1]

[1] Ras. i. 11 f.

Bodhirāja-kumārī.—Daughter of **Somadatta** of **Pāṭaliputta.** She had a horse **Suvīraka** that could fly, and her story is similar to that of **Buddhenī.** In her past life she had been born in **Hakureli** in Ceylon.[1]

[1] Ras. i. 100 f.

Brahmacola.—A village in the south of Ceylon.[1]

[1] Ras. i. 11, 40.

Brāhmaṇārāma.—A monastery in Ceylon, where **Tambasumana** was ordained. It was probably near **Vallavāhagāma.**[1]

[1] Ras. ii. 24.

Bhaṇḍārapotthakī.—See **Kitti** (7).

Bhaddavāggiyā.—*Add :* According to the Extended Mahāvaṃsa (i. 298) they were the step-brothers of the king of **Kosala.**

Bhaddasena.—One of the ten sons of **Kāḷāsoka** (*q.v.*).

Bharaṇa.—*Add :* See also Ras. ii. 96 f.

Bhidura Sutta.—A sutta quoted in the Sutta Saṅgaha (No. 83) from the Itivuttaka (p. 69 f.). The body breaks up, consciousness is contemptible; all things change.

Bhuttakatittha.—A ford, probably on the **Mahāvālukanadī.** It was two leagues from **Vālagāma Vihāra.** See **Tambasumana.**

Bhūtapāla Nanda.—One of the **Nava-Nandā** (*q.v.*).

12. **Maṅgala.**—A monk of **Khaṇḍasīmā** and teacher of **Vedeha** (*q.v.*).

13. **Maṅgala.**—A palace occupied by **Asoka.**[1]

[1] Ras. ii. 93.

Maṅgalavīthi.—A street in **Mahāgāma.**[1]

[1] Ras. ii. 34.

Maṅgujanapada.—A district in Ceylon.[1]

[1] Ras. ii. 180.

Maṅgura.—One of the ten sons of **Kāḷāsoka** (*q.v.*).

Macala Vihāra.—A vihara in Mahagama.[1]

[1] Ras. ii. 52.

"**Maccunābbhāhata**" **Sutta.**—A name in the Sutta Saṅgaha (No. 38) to the **Abbhāhata Sutta** (*q.v.*).

Macchera Sutta.—See **Maccharī Sutta.**

Maṇiakkhika.—*Add:* According to the Extended Mahāvaṃsa (i. 700) he was the uncle (*mātula*) of **Mahodara.**

Maṇicetiya.—A *thūpa* in **Rājamahāvihāra** in Mahāgāma.[1]

[1] Ras. ii. 3.

Maṇisūriya.—See **Tambasumana.**

Madhupiṭṭhika.—A village near Mahāgaṅgā in Pācīnapassa. In it was the **Madhupiṭṭhiya-cetiya,** once pillaged by **Sirināga.**[1]

[1] Ras. ii. 8.

Manāpa Sutta.—See **Pāṭali Sutta.**

Marutta.—A brahmin of **Homagāma.** Once he gave food to a mangy dog, which later saved his life.[1]

[1] See Ras. i. 42 f. for details.

3. **Mahāabhaya.**—A monk of **Uddalokaka Vihāra.**[1]

[1] Ras. ii. 1. f.

Mahā-Kassapa.—*Add to ref*[6]*:* The robe which Kassapa exchanged with the Buddha was Puṇṇā's cloak. See **Puṇṇā** (6).

Mahājallika.—A fishing village in Ceylon. In it was a fisherman, also called **Mahājallika,** whom **Dāṭhāsena** overcame.[1]

[1] Ras. ii. 107.

Mahātaḷāka.—A monastery in Ceylon, the residence of **Āraññaka-Mahāabhaya.**[1]

[1] Ras. ii. 5.

Mahātissagāma.—A village at the foot of **Laṅkāpabbata.**[1]

[1] Ras. ii. 159.

Mahādhanadeva.—Father of **Ariyagālatissa** (*q.v.*).

Mahānanda.—*Add : v.l.* **Mahānāma.**

17. **Mahānāga.**—A monk of **Kontaraṭṭhakapabbata Vihāra.** He died seated in mid-air, and **Kākavaṇṇatissa,** having heard of it from a crow, paid him great honour.[1]

[1] Ras. ii. 64.

Mahānijjhara.—A monastery in Ceylon. Once the elephant **Kaṇḍula** looked after the monks there.[1]

[1] Ras. ii. 29.

9. **Mahānāma.**—A lake in **Nāgadīpa.** Near it was the Mucalinda-vana.[1]

[1] Ras. ii. 18; see also **Naga.**

Mahānela.—A servitor of **Kākavaṇṇatissa.** He was very fleet of foot, though he refused to work with his hands. In his past birth he was **Kurudeva** (*q.v.*).[1]

[1] Ras. ii. 111 f.

1. **Mahāpanāda.**—*Add :* See also **Saṅkha** (3).

Mahābuddharakkhita.—A monk of **Piyaṅgudīpa,** described as *Yoṇaka-rājaputta.* See Ariyagālatissa.

Mahā-Mandhātā.—See **Mandhātā.** His story is also given at Ras. i. 20 f.

Mahāmitta.—A monk of **Kassakalena.** A very poor woman provided him with food. When a tree deity pointed out this to him he put forth effort and became an arahant (*v.l.* **Ayyamitta**).[1]

[1] MA. i. 237 f.; DA. iii. 790.

Mahāmeghavana.—*Add :* For a deposition of the various spots of the Mahāmeghavana see Mbv. 137.

Mahārabbhaka-lena.—Once the residence of **Mahādhammadinna** of **Talaṅgatissapabbata.** See Ras. ii. 131 f.

Mahālena Vihāra.—A monastery in Ceylon. See **Saṅghadattā.**

Mahāvattaniya.—A desert in India.[1]

[1] Ras. i. 23.

Mahavāpi Vihāra.—A monastery in **Mahāgāma.** For a story connected with it see Ras. ii. 4 f.

Mahavālukavīthi.—A street in **Anurādhapura.**[1]

[1] Ras. ii. 49.

6. **Mahā-Saṅgharakkhita.**—An arahant thera who preached to **Rūpadevī** (*q.v.*).

Mahā-Saccaka.—See **Saccaka.**

8. **Mahāsiva.**—A monk of **Piyaṅgudīpa.** See **Mahāsena** (5).

4. **Mahāsumana.**—A devaputta of **Ariṭṭhapabbata.**[1]

[1] Ras. ii. 169.

5. **Mahāsena.**—A king of **Pāṭaliputta.** He and his sister worked with their own hands and gave alms to 500 monks from **Piyaṅgudīpa,** among whom was **Mahāsiva** (8). The monk wished that they should see their alms being eaten by the monks in Piyaṅgudīpa.[1]

[1] Ras. i. 72 f.

Mahāsena Vagga. The fourth section of the Rasavāhinī.

2. **Mahāsoṇa.**—*Add :* See also Ras. ii. 86 f.

Mahāsappika.—One of **Asoka's** palaces.[1]

[1] Ras. i. 93.

"**Mā-puñña-bhāyi**" **Sutta.**—A sutta quoted in the Sutta Saṅgaha (No. 30) from the Itivuttaka (p. 14 f.). The Buddha admonishes monks to do good, assuring them that he has always profited by doing good.

Mātula Vihāra.—A monastery in **Roliyajanapada.**[1]

[1] Ras. ii. 51.

Māra.—*Add on* Vol. ii., p. 619 : Kāḷī (Kāḷā) is the mother of Māra of the present age. See **Kāḷī** (4).

Māsapiṭṭhigāma.—A village near **Brahmacola.** It was built near the spot where a spring appeared by the virtue of a girl who gave water to a thirsty monk.[1]

[1] Ras. ii. 42.

Migapotaka Vagga.—The fifth section of the Rasavāhinī.

Muggagāma Vihāra.—A monastery in Ceylon. See **Vilasa.**

Muggāyatana-raṭṭha.—A district in Ceylon.[1]

[1] Ras. ii. 181.

Mucalinda-vana.—A forest tract in **Nāgadīpa;** in it was the **Mahānāma** lake.[1]

[1] Ras. ii. 18; see also **Nāgā** (7).

Muṇḍagutta.—A resident of **Tissambatittha.**[1] His wife was **Tissā** (10).

[1] Ras. ii. 31.

Meghavaṇṇa.—A devaputta of **Udumbarapabbata.** He was once a very poor man of **Hallolagāma** and had given alms at **Nīlapabbata-vihāra.** His wife was **Candamukhī.** He once visited with his wife **Maliyadeva Thera** in **Candamukhalena.**[1]

[1] Ras. ii. 125 f.

Moragīva.—A palace occupied by **Asoka.**[1]

[1] Ras. i. 93.

Moriya.—A very pious brahmin of **Macala.** He and his wife **Senā** gave alms till all their wealth was exhausted, but a deity gave him wealth again.[1]

[1] Ras. i. 86 f.

Moriyajanapada.—See **Dhammagutta** (2).

Yāgudānānumodanā Sutta.—A sutta quoted in the Sutta Saṅgaha (No. 61) from the **Mahāvagga** of the Vinaya Piṭaka (Vin. i. 220 f.) on the virtues of giving congey (*yāgu*). The MṬ. (p. 666) calls it **Andhakavinda Sutta.**

"Yāva-jarā" Sutta.—A name given in the Sutta Saṅgaha (No. 36) to the **Jarā Sutta** (2) (*q.v.*).

Yodha Vagga.—The eighth section of the **Rasavahinī.**

Raṭṭhapāla Nanda.—One of the **Nava-Nandā** (*q.v.*).

Raṇamaddava.—The state horse of **Eḷāra.** It was stolen by **Veḷusumana.**[1] But see **Vaha.**

[1] Ras. ii. 62.

Rathapāsāṇa-vana.—A forest tract near **Villagāma.**[1]

[1] Ras. ii. 147.

Rāsimālaka.—A holy spot on the west of the **Mahāmeghavana.**[1]

[1] Mbv. 137.

Rucakaviṭṭhi.—A village in Ceylon; near it was a large monastery.[1]

[1] Ras. ii. 148, 151.

"Rūpajīrana" Sutta.—A name given in the Sutta Saṅgaha (No, 40) to the **"Na Jīrati" Sutta** (*q.v.*).

Rūpadevī.—A pious woman of **Devaputta.** Because of alms given in the time of **Vipassī Buddha,** she got food whenever she desired. One day **Mahā Sangharakkhita,** who visited her house, revealed to her the reason for this and she became a *sotāpanna.*[1]

[1] Ras. i. 24 f.

Revatī Vimāna.—See **Revatī** (1).

Roliya-janapada.—A district in Ceylon, forty-four leagues from **Mahāgāma.** In it was the **Mātula Vihāra.**[1]

[1] Ras. ii. 51, 52.

Lokānuvicaraṇa Sutta.—A name given in the Sutta Saṅgaha (No. 51) to the **Raja Sutta** (2) (*q.v.*).

Lokappadīpakasāra.—A religious treatise of the fourteenth century by **Medhaaṅkara,** Sangharāja of Burma.[1]

[1] Bode, *op. cit.*, 35 f.

Lohakūṭapabbata Vihāra.—A monastery in a very remote place in India. It could be reached only by hanging on to the branch of a tree when the wind bent it. Dāṭhāsena attained arahantship there.[1]

[1] Ras. ii. 110 f.

Vagguli Vatthu.—The story of 500 bats who were born in heaven by listening to a recital of the Abhidhamma.[1]

[1] SadS. 81 f.

Vajirabuddhi.—*Read :* See **Mahāvajirabuddhi.**

6. **Vaḍḍhamāna.**—A district in Ceylon, given by King **Saddhātissa** to his minister, **Saddhātissa** (2).[1]

[1] Ras. ii. 10.

Vaḍḍhamānaka-tittha.—A ford on the **Mahāvālukanadī**; it was later called **Sahassa-tittha** and **Assamaṇḍala-tittha.**[1]

[1] Ras. ii. 61, 63.

Vattura Vihāra.—A monastery on the banks of the **Kappakandaranadī.**[1]

[1] Ras. ii. 111.

Vatthulapabbata.—A mountain in Ceylon.[1]

[1] Ras. ii. 19 f.

Vallavahagāma.—A village in Ceylon, the birthplace of **Tambasumana.**

[1] Ras. ii. 24.

8. **Vasabha.**—An arahant Thera in the time of **Padumuttara Buddha**, declared foremost for austere practices.[1] The name is evidently a variant of **Nisabha** (*q.v.*).

[1] Ras. i. 27.

Vassakārānumodanā Sutta. A sutta quoted in the Sutta Saṅgaha (No. 62) from the Vinaya Piṭaka (i. 229 f.), where the Buddha gives thanks to Sunīdha and Vassakāra for a meal given to him.

Vālagāma Vihāra.—A monastery near **Cullatavālagāma.** See **Tambasumana.**

1. **Vidhurinda.**—A Nāga king who was given in charge of the Bodhi-tree by Asoka during its travels to Ceylon.[1]

[1] Mbv. 153.

2. **Vidhurinda.**—One of the brothers of **Vedisadevī.** He escorted the Bodhi-tree to Ceylon and was given the rank of *Laṅkāparisuddhanāyaka*.[1]

[1] Mbv. 169.

Vidhola.—A hunter, who later joined the Order at **Tissa Vihāra** in **Mahāgama** and became an arahant.[1]

[1] Ras. i. 132 f.

Vinaya Piṭaka.—One of the three divisions of the Tipiṭaka. It contains rules and regulations for the conduct of monks and nuns in all the details of their lives. The rules are attributed to the Buddha himself, and an old commentary, incorporated into the text, gives accounts of the occasions on which the rules were formulated. A certain amount of historical matter is also found regarding the Order, especially in the last two chapters of the Cullavagga. The Vinaya Piṭaka consists of the Suttavibhanga, the Khandhakas, the Parivāra, and the Pātimokkha. The first is divided into Pārājikā and Pācittiya and the second into Mahāvagga and Cullavagga.

Viyoḷaka Vihāra.—A monastery in Ceylon. **Tissamahānāga** lived there for thirty years.[1]

[1] Ras. ii. 187.

Vilasa.—A very rich man of **Kandalisālagāma.** His wealth was fabulous, and the king, wishing to test its extent, asked him to supply various luxuries. The **Muggagāma Vihāra** was built on the spot where his carts, bringing green peas to the king, stopped outside the city.[1]

[1] Ras. ii. 130 f.

Villagāma.—A village in the south of Ceylon.[1]

[1] Ras. ii. 147.

Visamaloma.—Son of **Dhammāsoka** and his chief queen, so called because of his coarse hair. Once he crossed the **Candabhāgā** in flood, killing with his hands 120 crocodiles that attacked him. Asoka was frightened and had him put in chains, but later made him viceroy. He had given alms to a monk in the time of **Kassapa Buddha.**[1]

[1] Ras. i. 32 f.

Visākhūposatha Sutta.—The name given in the Sutta Saṅgaha (No. 12) to the **Uposatha Sutta** (4) (*q.v.*).

Vihāradānānaumodanā Sutta.—A sutta quoted in the Sutta Saṅgaha (No. 63) from the Vinaya Piṭaka (Vin. 147 f.) on the value of gifting vihāras.

Vedisadevī.—*Add :* She had eight brothers—Bodhigutta, Sumitta, Candagutta, Devagutta, Dhammagutta, Suriyagutta, Gotama and Jutindhara—who escorted the Bodhi-tree to Ceylon and were known as the Bodhi-dhāra princes.[1]

[1] Mbv. 165 f.

Venisāla. Father of **Tissāmacca** (*q.v.*).

Venigāma.—The Chief of **Cūlanāga. Ambāmacca** was his son.[1]

[1] Ras. ii. 145.

Veriya Vihāra.—A monastery, probably near the **Jajjaranadī. Maliyamahādeva** once lived there.[1]

[1] Ras. ii. 153.

Veḷuvanadānānumodanā Sutta.—A sutta quoted in the Sutta Saṅgaha (No. 64) from the introduction to the Buddhavaṃsa Commentary, giving an account of the gift of **Veḷuvana** by **Bimbisāra.**

Veḷusumana.—*Add :* See also Ras. ii. 6 f. and 97 f. where the details differ.

Vessamittā.—Queen of Kosambī. When her husband was killed in battle his conqueror wished to marry her, but she refused. He ordered her to be burnt, but by her piety she was unscathed and received great honour.[1]

[1] Ras. i. 18 f.

Sakkagaṅga.—A river in Ceylon.[1]

[1] Ras. ii. 184.

4. **Saṅgha.**—A minister of **Duṭṭhagāmaṇī.** He gave alms, in circumstances that won applause from the deity of the king's parasol, to **Mahānāga Thera** of **Koṭagallapabbata,** to a monk of **Timbarugāma,** and to another of **Devagirivihāra** and **Cetiyapabbata.** The king

sent for him and made him Treasurer. It is probably this same Saṅgha that is mentioned in the Extended Mahāvaṃsa (xxxii. 246) as destined to become the chief patron of **Matteyya Budda.**[1] His wife was **Saṅghadattā** (*q.v.*).

[1] Ras. ii. 75 f., 180.

5. **Saṅgha.**—A minister of **Kākavaṇṇatissa;** his brother was **Cullasaṅgha** and his daughter **Kiñcisanghā.** When the latter was taught cooking, the first meal she made was given to the monks. Thus she came to be called **Saṅghupaṭṭhāyikā.** Later, she was abandoned by her parents at Nigrodhasālakhaṇḍa, but she was rescued by **Sakka** in the guise of a youth. She gave alms to a monk of **Cittalapabbāta** when she had been starving for seven days, and also gave her only garment, herself wearing leaves. The king heard of this from the deity of his parasol, and, having sent for her, gave her in marriage to one of his sons.[1]

[1] Ras. ii. 45 f.

Saṅghadatta Thera.—He lived in **Mahālena Vihāra** and for twelve years, during the **Brahmaṇatiya** famine, a deity looked after him. In the past he had given a meal to a hungry dog.[1]

[1] Ras. ii. 181 f.

Saṅghadattā.—Wife of the minister Sangha, who married her because she walked instead of running in a shower of rain. She gave a robe to Culanaga Thera of Pidhanagalla, and Sakka provided her with divine robes, which she offered at Dakkhinacetiya and Ratanamalicetiya.[1]

[1] Ras. ii. 177 f.

Saṅghupaṭṭhāyikā.—Another name for **Kiñcisaṅghā** (*q.v.*).

8. **Sañjaya.**—One of the ten sons of **Kāḷāsoka** (*q.v.*).

Satisambodhi Thera.—A monk of **Piyaṅgudīpa.** See **Ariyagālatissa.**

2. **Saddhātissa.**—A minister. He once gave to Pindapatikatissa Thera of Sudassanapadhanasala a bowl of food which he had bought for 8 kahapanas. The monk became an arahant before eating it. The deity of the king's parasol applauded and king Saddhātissa having sent for him gave him the district of Vaddhamanananagara. Later he shared with 30,000 monks water brought to him by the devas during a drought. The king hearing of this gave him Antaraganga. Sometime afterwards he became a sotapanna, gladdened by the sight of 12,000 monks walking round Ambatthala cetiya clad in robes given by him.[1]

[1] Ras. ii. 9 f.

Saddhāsumanā.—See **Sumanā.**

Saddhāsumanatissa.—A monk of Ceylon. He joined the Order after gaining his parents[1] consent with great difficulty. Once, when on pilgrimage to **Nāgadīpa,** he saw an assembly of monks, and, moved by the sight, sat under a tree and developed arahantship.[1]

[1] SadS. 85 f.

"Saddhīdha" Sutta.—A name given in the Sutta Saṅgaha (No. 39) to the **Vitti Sutta** (*q.v.*).

Sabbañjaha.—One of the sons of **Kāḷāsoka** (*q.v.*).

"Sabrahmaka" Sutta.—See **"Sabrahmakāni"** (8). It is given also in the Sutta Saṅgaha (No. 25) and the Itivuttaka (p. 109 f.)

Samaṇagāma.—A village in Ceylon.[1]

[1] Ras. ii. 11.

Saraṇa Thera.—A monk. He was given the name because, when he was in his mother's womb, she was rescued from death by her virtue. She was the daughter of **Sumana** and **Sujampatikā** of Sāvatthi. Saraṇa later became an arahant.[1]

[1] For details see Ras. i. 15 f.

Salla Sutta.—A sutta quoted in the Sutta Saṅgaha (No. 82) from the Itivuttaka (p. 46) on the three varieties of feeling.

Sāgiri.—A monastery near **Puṇṇasālakoṭṭhaka.** It was the residence of **Bahulamassutissa.**[1]

[1] Ras. ii. 128.

Sāratthamañjūsā.—*Add:* All the Mūlaṭīkā on the Sutta Piṭaka seem to have borne this name. See SadS. 59.

Sāliya.—*Add:* See also Ras. ii. 114 f.

3. **Sirināga.**—A brahmin. Wishing to become king of Ceylon, he sought to obtain the treasures from the cetiya in **Dakkhiṇamahāvihāra.** But **Bahula,** who knew the secret passage, refused to help him and was put to death. Sirināga pillaged the **Madhupiṭṭhiya Cetiya,** and, with its wealth, became king of **Anurādhapura.** Later he fell ill of gastric disease and was reborn in hell.[1]

[1] Ras. ii. 7 f.

Silutta Vatthu. The story of a blind rat-snake (*silutta*), near **Devarakkhitalena,** who heard the **Satipaṭṭhāna Sutta** being recited by **Talaṅgapabbatavāsī Mahādhammadinna Thera.** The snake was killed by a *godhā,* and was born as **Tissāmacca,** minister of Duṭṭhagāmaṇi.[1]

[1] SadS. 88 f.; Ras. ii. 131 f.

Siva.—A village near **Giritimbilatissa-pabbata.**[1]

[1] Ras. ii. 42.

Sihabodhi Thera.—A colleague of Yoṇaka-Mahā **Buddharakkhita Thera** and **Maliyamahādeva Thera.**[1]

[1] Ras. ii. 188 f.

Sugatuppatti Sutta.—A man whose mind is pure is born after death in heaven.[1]

[1] Itv. p. 13, quoted in the Sutta Saṅgaha (No. 28).

Sujampatikā.—See **Saraṇa Thera.**

Sudassanapadhanasala.—A building in Talacatukka.[1]

[1] Ras. ii. 9.

Supubbaṇha Sutta.—A name given in the Sutta Saṅgaha (No. 52) to the **Pubbaṇha Sutta** (*q.v.*).

Suppādevī.—Mother of **Sīhabāhu and Sīhasīvalī.**[1]

[1] MṬ. 243 f.

Sumana Sutta.—See **Sumanarajakumari Sutta.**

14. **Sumanā.**—Wife of **Ariyagālatissa** (*q.v.*).

15. **Sumanā.**—A woman of the **Mahāvālukavīthi** in **Anurādhapura.** She spent much time in the monastery and was sent away in anger by her husband. She starved for seven days, and on the way back to her house from Mahāgāma, where she was married, gave some food, which **Sakka** provided for her, to **Mahādhammadinna Thera** of **Talaṅgapabbata,** at **Nigrodhasālakhaṇḍa.** Later, another deity took her in a cart to **Guḷapūvatintinī,** near Anurādhapura. The king, hearing of her, made her his chief queen.[1]

[1] Ras. ii. 49 f.

Sūranimmila.—One of the ten warriors of **Duṭṭhagāmaṇī.** For details see Mhv. xxiii. 19 f. According to the Rasavāhinī (ii. 71) he was so called because he drank a large quantity of toddy before the attack on **Vijitapura.**

Suvaṇṇatilakā.—A caṇḍāla maiden of Uttara Madhurā. She was very beautiful, and was so called because she had a golden mole between her breasts. When the king heard that she wanted to marry a man of high lineage he challenged her to win **Uddāḷa** of **Pañcamadhurā** who hated women. She accepted the challenge and went with her father. On the way seven kings offered to marry her, but she refused them. Uddāḷa fell in love with her at sight and lived with her for four months, neglecting all his duties. His pupils were enraged and killed Suvaṇṇatilakā. He thereupon jumped into her pyre.

In her last life S. had been born in Anurādhapura. One day she went with her mother to **Abhayuttaracetiya,** and, when her mother went to fetch water to wash the altar, S. offered the flowers without waiting. The mother was angry and called her "caṇḍālī." S. retorted, saying, "You are the caṇḍālī, not I." This was why she became a caṇḍālī.[1]

[1] Ras. i. 74 f.

Suvīraka.—The horse of **Bodhirājakumarī** (*q.v.*).

Sūkarapotika Vatthu.—The story of **Ubbarī** (*q.v.*).

Serisara.—A lake in Ceylon; near it was the village of **Kāraka.**[1]

[1] Ras. ii. 183.

4. **Soma.**—Friend of **Somadatta** (5).

5. **Somadatta.**—A brahmin of Sāvatthi. He once played dice with another brahmin, **Soma,** and won the latter's possessions, including his upper garment and signet-ring. When Soma said he could not walk home barefoot, nor face his family without his ring, Somadatta returned his winnings and the two became great friends. Somadatta was later sentenced to death for repeated adultery. When Soma discovered this he offered his life instead and was killed. He was reborn as a deva and took Somadatta to the deva-world for a week, sending him back with a wish-conferring gem. Later Somadatta too was born near Soma.[1]

[1] Ras. i. 46 f.

Hakureli.—A village in Ceylon, where **Bodhirājakumārī** lived in her former life.[1]

[1] Ras. i. 100.

Harantika.—A thief who later became an arahant. *See* **Āraññaka-Mahāabhaya.**

Hallolagāma.—A caṇḍāla village near Anurādhapura, where **Asokamālā** was born.[1] Elsewhere[2] it is described as being near **Mahāgama.**

[1] Ras. ii. 117. [2] *Ibid.*, 125.

Hemā.—A woman who lived in a village near **Anurādhapura.** She married a man near **Mahātitthapaṭṭana.** Once, wishing to see her husband, she went along the sea and was seized by a Nāga. But when he discovered that she knew the **Dhammacakkappavattana Sutta** by heart he paid her great honour.[1]

[1] Ras. ii. 135 f.

Homagāma.—A village on the banks of the **Candabhāgā.** It was the residence of **Marutta** (*q.v.*).